W9-AEJ-927

2011 Writer's Market®

ROBERT LEE BREWER, EDITOR

WRITER'S DIGEST
BOOKS
WritersDigest.com
Cincinnati, Ohio

Complaint Procedure

- If you feel you have not been treated fairly by a listing in *Writer's Market* or *Writer's Market Deluxe Edition*, we advise you to take the following steps:
- First try to contact the listing. Sometimes one phone call or a letter can quickly clear up the matter.
- Document all your correspondence with the listing. When you write to us with a complaint, provide the details of your submission, the date of your first contact with the listing and the nature of your subsequent correspondence
- We will enter your letter into our files and attempt to contact the listing.
- The number and severity of complaints will be considered in our decision whether to delete the listing from the next edition.

Publisher & Editorial Director, Writing Communities: Jane Friedman
Managing Editor, Writer's Digest Market Books: Alice Pope

Writer's Market website: www.writersmarket.com
Writer's Digest website: www.writersdigest.com

Distributed in Canada by Fraser Direct
100 Armstrong Avenue
Georgetown, ON, Canada L7G 5S4
Tel: (905) 877-4411

Distributed in the U.K. and Europe by David & Charles
Brunel House, Newton Abbot, Devon, TQ12 4PU, England
Tel: (Þpl44) 1626 323200, Fax: (Þpl44) 1626 323319
E-mail: mail@davidandcharles.co.uk

Distributed in Australia by Capricorn Link
Loder House, 126 George Street
Windsor, NSW 2756 Australia
Tel: (02) 4577-3555

Library of Congress Catalog Number 31-20772
ISSN: 0084-2729
ISBN-13: 978-1-58297-948-9
ISBN-13: 978-1-58297-949-6 (*Writer's Market Deluxe Edition*)
ISBN-10: 1-58297-948-0
ISBN-10: 1-58297-949-9 (*Writer's Market Deluxe Edition*)

Cover design by Claudean Wheeler
Production coordinated by Greg Nock
Illustrations © Dominique Bruneton/PaintoAlto

Attention Booksellers: This is an annual directory of F + W Media, Inc.
Return deadline for this edition is December 31, 2011.

Contents

TRADE JOURNALS

NEWSPAPERS

SCREENWRITING

PLAYWRITING

GREETING CARDS

CONTESTS & AWARDS

RESOURCES

INDEXES

From the Editor

There is more to Writer's Market than just the listings. Of course, the listings are a very important component of Writer's Market (always have been and always will be), but the articles in the front of the book are just as useful for a freelance writer. In fact, they can even be more useful for some freelancers.

"Query Letter Clinic" (on page 19) and "Feature Article Writing" (on page 29) include sample query letters—both good and bad. "Launching Your Freelance Business" (on page 61) informs freelancers on how to successfully launch their freelance careers, and pieces like "Build a Platform" (on page 78) and "Social Media 101" (on page 85) explain how to create and communicate to your audience. Plus, this edition of Writer's Market includes a fully updated version of the "How Much Should I Charge?" pay rate chart (on page 67), which some freelancers consider worth the price of the book alone.

My advice to any reader of Writer's Market is to read the articles in the front of this book before researching the listings. After all, having the contact information for magazines, book publishers, literary agents, contests, or any other listing section won't do any writers good if they don't know how to submit their writing properly or how to connect with their target audience.

The articles provide the winning strategies that you can then apply to the listings. If you use both together, you'll improve your rate of success significantly.

Until next we meet, keep writing and marketing what you write.

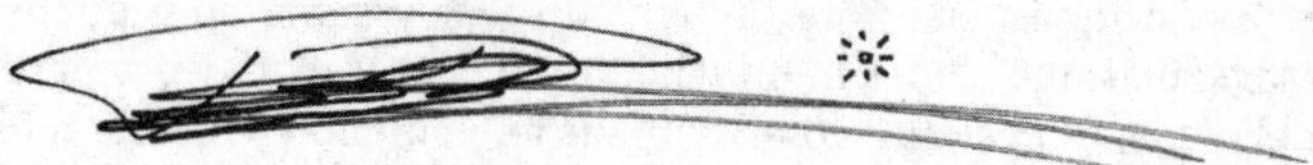

Robert Lee Brewer
Senior Content Editor
Writer's Market & WritersMarket.com
http://blog.writersdigest.com/poeticasides

P.S. If you currently only use the book, check out www.writersmarket.com, where we make daily updates to a searchable online database of listings.

How to Use *Writer's Market*

W*riter's Market* is here to help you decide where and how to submit your writing to appropriate markets. Each listing contains information about the editorial focus of the market, how it prefers material to be submitted, payment information, and other helpful tips.

WHAT'S INSIDE?

Since 1921, *Writer's Market* has been giving you the information you need to knowledgeably approach a market. We've continued to develop improvements to help you access that information more efficiently.

Navigational tools. We've designed the pages of *Writer's Market* with you, the user, in mind. Within the pages you will find **readable market listings** and **accessible charts and graphs**. One such chart can be found in the ever-popular **How Much Should I Charge?** on page **67**. We've taken all of the updated information in this feature and put it into an easy-to-read and navigate chart, making it convenient for you to find the rates that accompany the freelance jobs you're seeking.

Tabs. You will also find user-friendly tabs for each section of *Writer's Market* so you can quickly find the section you need most. Once inside the Consumer Magazines, Trade Journals and Contests & Awards sections, you'll have subject headings at the top of the page to help guide and speed up your search.

Symbols. There are a variety of symbols that appear before each listing. A complete Key to Symbols & Abbreviations appears on the back inside cover and on a removable bookmark. In Book Publishers, note the which quickly sums up a publisher's interests. In Consumer Magazines, the zeroes in on what areas of that market are particularly open to freelancers—helping you break in. Other symbols let you know whether a listing is new to the book (N), a book publisher accepts only agented writers (A), comparative pay rates for a magazine (**$-$$$$**), and more.

Acquisition names, royalty rates and advances. In the Book Publishers section, we identify acquisition editors with the boldface word **Acquisitions** to help you get your manuscript to the right person. Royalty rates and advances are also highlighted in boldface, as is other important information on the percentage of first-time writers and unagented writers the company publishes, the number of books published, and the number of manuscripts received each year.

Editors, pay rates, and percentage of material written by freelance writers. In the Consumer Magazines and Trade Journals sections, we identify to whom you should send your query or article with the boldface word **Contact**. The amount (percentage) of material accepted from freelance writers, and the pay rates for features, columns and departments, and fillers are also highlighted in boldface to help you quickly identify the information you need to know when considering whether to submit your work.

Query formats. We asked editors how they prefer to receive queries and have indicated in the listings whether they prefer them by mail, e-mail, fax or phone. Be sure to check an editor's individual preference before sending your query.

Articles. Most of the articles are new to this edition. Newer, unpublished writers should be sure to read the articles in **The Basics** section, while more experienced writers should focus on those in the **Beyond the Basics** section. In addition, there is a section devoted to **Personal Views** featuring interviews with and articles by industry professionals and other career-oriented professionals, as well as best-selling authors.

Important Listing Information

Important

1. Listings are based on editorial questionnaires and interviews. They are not advertisements; publishers do not pay for their listings. The markets are not endorsed by *Writer's Market* editors. F+W Publications, Inc., Writer's Digest Books, and its employees go to great effort to ascertain the validity of information in this book. However, transactions between users of the information and individuals and/or companies are strictly between those parties.

2. All listings have been verified before publication of this book. If a listing has not changed from last year, then the editor said the market's needs have not changed and the previous listing continues to accurately reflect its policies.

3. Writer's Market reserves the right to exclude any listing.

4. When looking for a specific market, check the index. A market may not be listed for one of these reasons:
   - It doesn't solicit freelance material.
   - It doesn't pay for material.
   - It has gone out of business.
   - It has failed to verify or update its listing for this edition.
   - It hasn't answered *Writer's Market* inquiries satisfactorily. (To the best of our ability, and with our readers' help, we try to screen fraudulent listings.)

5. Individual markets that appeared in last year's edition but are not listed in this edition are included in the General Index, with a notation giving the reason for their exclusion.

2011 WRITER'S MARKET KEYS TO SYMBOLS

market new to this edition

market accepts agented submissions only

market does not accept unsolicited manuscripts

Canadian market

market located outside of the U.S. and Canada

online opportunity

$ market pays 0-9¢/word or $0-$150/article

$$ market pays 10-49¢/word or $151-$750/article

$$$ market pays 50-99¢/word or $751-$1,500/article

$$$$ market pays $1/word or over $1,500/article

• comment offering additional market information from the editor of *Writer's Market*

O━ tips to break into a specific market

ms, mss manuscript(s)

b&w black & white (photo)

SASE self-addressed, stamped envelope

SAE self-addressed envelope

IRC International Reply Coupon, for use in countries other than your own

(For words and expressions relating specifically to writing and publishing, see the Glossary in the back of this book)

Find a handy pull-out bookmark, a quick reference to the icons used in this book, right inside the front cover.

IF WRITER'S MARKET IS NEW TO YOU . . .

A quick look at the **Contents** pages will familiarize you with the arrangement of *Writer's Market*. The three largest sections of the book are the market listings of Book Publishers; Consumer Magazines; and Trade Journals. You will also find other sections of market listings for Literary Agents; Newspapers; Screenwriting Markets; Playwriting Markets; Greeting Card Companies; and Contests & Awards.

Narrowing your search

After you've identified the market categories that interest you, you can begin researching specific markets within each section.

Consumer Magazines and Trade Journals are categorized by subject within their respective sections to make it easier for you to identify markets for your work. If you want to publish an article dealing with retirement, you could look under the Retirement category of Consumer Magazines to find an appropriate market. You would want to keep in mind, however, that magazines in other categories might also be interested in your article. (For example, women's magazines publish such material.)

Interpreting the markets

Once you've identified companies or publications that cover the subjects in which you're interested, you can begin evaluating specific listings to pinpoint the markets most receptive to your work and most beneficial to you.

In evaluating an individual listing, first check the location of the company, the types of material it is interested in seeing, submission requirements, and rights and payment policies. Depending on your personal concerns, any of these items could be a deciding factor as you determine which markets you plan to approach. Many listings also include a reporting time, which lets you know how long it will typically take for the publisher to respond to your initial query or submission. (We suggest that you allow an additional two months for a response, just in case your submission is under further review or the publisher is backlogged.)

Check the Glossary on page 985 for unfamiliar words. Specific symbols and abbreviations are explained in the Key to Symbols & Abbreviations appearing on the inside cover, as well as on a removable bookmark. The most important abbreviation is SASE—self-addressed, stamped envelope. Always enclose a SASE when you send unsolicited queries, proposals or manuscripts.

A careful reading of the listings will reveal that many editors are very specific about their needs. Your chances of success increase if you follow directions to the letter. Often companies do not accept unsolicited manuscripts and return them unread. If a company does not accept unsolicited manuscripts, it is indicated in the listing with a (⊘) symbol. (Note: You may still be able to query a market that does not accept unsolicited manuscripts.)

Whenever possible, obtain writer's guidelines before submitting material. You can usually obtain guidelines by sending a SASE to the address in the listing. Magazines often post their guidelines on their Web sites, and many book publishers do so as well. Most of the listings indicate how writer's guidelines are made available. You should also familiarize yourself with the company's publications. Many of the listings contain instructions on how to obtain sample copies, catalogs or market lists. The more research you do upfront, the better your chances of acceptance, publication and payment.

Guide to listing features

Below is an example of the market listings you'll find in each section of *Writer's Market*. Note the callouts that identify various format features of the listing.

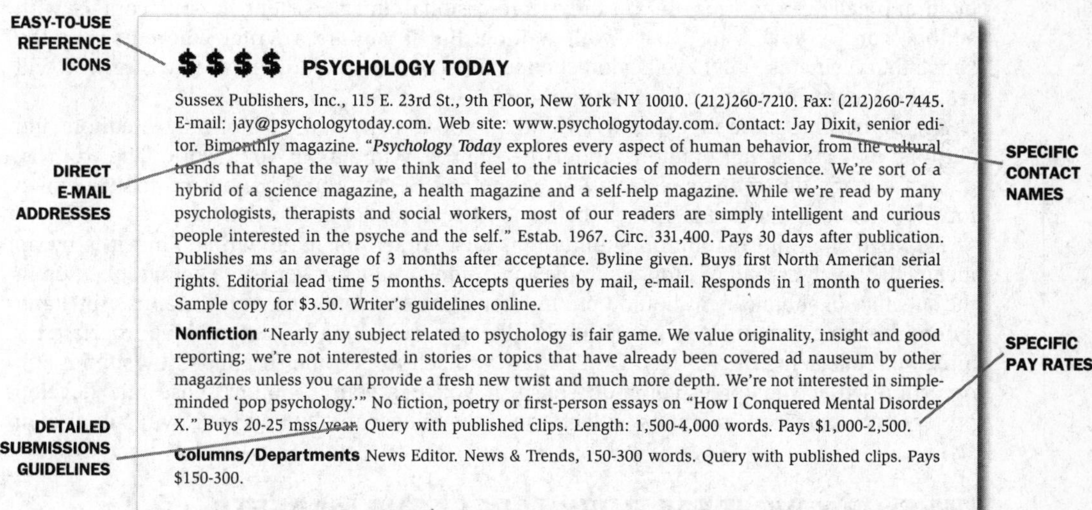

$ $ $ $ PSYCHOLOGY TODAY

Sussex Publishers, Inc., 115 E. 23rd St., 9th Floor, New York NY 10010. (212)260-7210. Fax: (212)260-7445. E-mail: jay@psychologytoday.com. Web site: www.psychologytoday.com. Contact: Jay Dixit, senior editor. Bimonthly magazine. "*Psychology Today* explores every aspect of human behavior, from the cultural trends that shape the way we think and feel to the intricacies of modern neuroscience. We're sort of a hybrid of a science magazine, a health magazine and a self-help magazine. While we're read by many psychologists, therapists and social workers, most of our readers are simply intelligent and curious people interested in the psyche and the self." Estab. 1967. Circ. 331,400. Pays 30 days after publication. Publishes ms an average of 3 months after acceptance. Byline given. Buys first North American serial rights. Editorial lead time 5 months. Accepts queries by mail, e-mail. Responds in 1 month to queries. Sample copy for $3.50. Writer's guidelines online.

Nonfiction "Nearly any subject related to psychology is fair game. We value originality, insight and good reporting; we're not interested in stories or topics that have already been covered ad nauseum by other magazines unless you can provide a fresh new twist and much more depth. We're not interested in simple-minded 'pop psychology.'" No fiction, poetry or first-person essays on "How I Conquered Mental Disorder X." Buys 20-25 mss/year. Query with published clips. Length: 1,500-4,000 words. Pays $1,000-2,500.

Columns/Departments News Editor. News & Trends, 150-300 words. Query with published clips. Pays $150-300.

THE BASICS

Before Your First Sale

Everything in life has to start somewhere and that somewhere is always at the beginning. Stephen King, J.K. Rowling, John Grisham, Nora Roberts—they all had to start at the beginning. It would be great to say becoming a writer is as easy as waving a magic wand over your manuscript and "Poof!'' you're published, but that's not how it happens. While there's no one true "key'' to becoming successful, a long, well-paid writing career *can* happen when you combine four elements:

- Good writing
- Knowledge of writing markets
- Professionalism
- Persistence

Good writing is useless if you don't know which markets will buy your work or how to pitch and sell your writing. If you aren't professional and persistent in your contact with editors, your writing is just that—your writing. But if you are a writer who embraces the above four elements, you have a good chance at becoming a paid, published writer who will reap the benefits of a long and successful career.

As you become more involved with writing, you may read articles or talk to editors and authors with conflicting opinions about the right way to submit your work. The truth is, there are many different routes a writer can follow to get published, but no matter which route you choose, the end is always the same—becoming a published writer.

The following information on submissions has worked for many writers, but it is by no means the be-all-end-all of proper submission guidelines. It's very easy to get wrapped up in the specifics of submitting (Should I put my last name on every page of my manuscript?) and ignore the more important issues (Will this idea on ice fishing in Alaska be appropriate for a regional magazine in Seattle?). Don't allow yourself to become so blinded by submission procedures that you forget common sense. If you use your common sense and develop professional, courteous relations with editors, you will eventually find your own submission style.

DEVELOP YOUR IDEAS, THEN TARGET THE MARKETS

Writers often think of an interesting story, complete the manuscript, and then begin the search for a suitable publisher or magazine. While this approach is common for fiction, poetry and screenwriting, it reduces your chances of success in many nonfiction writing areas. Instead, try choosing categories that interest you and study those sections in *Writer's Market*. Select several listings you consider good prospects for your type of writing. Sometimes the individual listings will even help you generate ideas.

Next, make a list of the potential markets for each idea. Make the initial contact with markets using the method stated in the market listings. If you exhaust your list of possibilities, don't give up. Instead, reevaluate the idea or try another angle. Continue developing ideas and approaching markets. Identify and rank potential markets for an idea and continue the process.

As you submit to the various publications listed in *Writer's Market*, it's important to remember that every magazine is published with a particular audience and slant in mind. Probably the number one complaint we receive from editors is the submissions they receive are completely wrong for their magazines or book line. The first mark of professionalism is to know your market well. Gaining that knowledge starts with *Writer's Market*, but you should also do your own detective work. Search out back issues of the magazines you wish to write for, pick up recent issues at your local newsstand, or visit magazines' Web sites—anything that will help you figure out what subjects specific magazines publish. This research is also helpful in learning what topics have been covered ad nauseum—the topics you should stay away from or approach in a fresh way. Magazines' Web sites are invaluable as most post the current issue of the magazine, as well as back issues, and most offer writer's guidelines.

The same advice is true for submitting to book publishers. Research publisher Web sites for their submission guidelines, recently published titles and their backlist. You can use this information to target your book proposal in a way that fits with a publisher's other titles while not directly competing for sales.

Prepare for rejection and the sometimes lengthy wait. When a submission is returned, check your file folder of potential markets for that idea. Cross off the market that rejected the idea. If the editor has given you suggestions or reasons why the manuscript was not accepted, you might want to incorporate these suggestions when revising your manuscript.

After revising your manuscript mail it to the next market on your list.

Take rejection with a grain of salt

Rejection is a way of life in the publishing world. It's inevitable in a business that deals with such an overwhelming number of applicants for such a limited number of positions. Anyone who has published has lived through many rejections, and writers with thin skin are at a distinct disadvantage. A rejection letter is not a personal attack. It simply indicates your submission is not appropriate for that market. Writers who let rejection dissuade them from pursuing their dream or who react to an editor's "No" with indignation or fury do themselves a disservice. Writers who let rejection stop them do not get published. Resign yourself to facing rejection now. You will live through it, and you'll eventually overcome it.

Reminder

QUERY AND COVER LETTERS

A query letter is a brief, one-page letter used as a tool to hook an editor and get him interested in your idea. When you send a query letter to a magazine, you are trying to get an editor to buy your idea or article. When you query a book publisher, you are attempting to get an editor interested enough in your idea to request your book proposal or your entire manuscript. (Note: Some book editors prefer to receive book proposals on first contact. Check individual listings for which method editors prefer.)

Here are some basic guidelines to help you create one that's polished and well-organized. For more tips see Query Letter Clinic on page 19.

- **Limit it to one page, single-spaced**, and address the editor by name (Mr. or Ms. and the surname). *Note*: Do not assume that a person is a Mr. or Ms. unless it is obvious from the name listed. For example, if you are contacting a D.J. Smith, do not assume that D.J. should be preceded by Mr. or Ms. Instead, address the letter to D.J. Smith.
- **Grab the editor's attention with a strong opening.** Some magazine queries, for example, begin with a paragraph meant to approximate the lead of the intended article.
- **Indicate how you intend to develop the article or book.** Give the editor some idea of the work's structure and content.

- **Let the editor know if you have photos** or illustrations available to accompany your magazine article.
- **Mention any expertise or training that qualifies you** to write the article or book. If you've been published before, mention it; if not, don't.
- **End with a direct request to write the article.** Or, if you're pitching a book, ask for the go-ahead to send in a full proposal or the entire manuscript. Give the editor an idea of the expected length and delivery date of your manuscript.

A common question that arises is: If I don't hear from an editor in the reported response time, how do I know when I can safely send the query to another market? Many writers find it helpful to indicate in their queries that if they don't receive a response from the editor (slightly after the listed reporting time), they will assume the editor is not interested. It's best to take this approach, particularly if your topic is timely.

A brief, single-spaced cover letter is helpful when sending a manuscript as it helps personalize the submission. However, if you have previously queried the editor, use the cover letter to politely and briefly remind the editor of that query—when it was sent, what it contained, etc. "Here is the piece on low-fat cooking that I queried you about on December 12. I look forward to hearing from you at your earliest convenience." Do not use the cover letter as a sales pitch.

If you are submitting to a market that accepts unsolicited manuscripts, a cover letter is useful because it personalizes your submission. You can, and should, include information about the manuscript, yourself, your publishing history, and your qualifications.

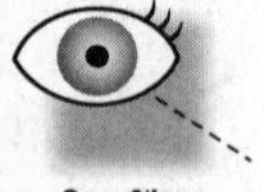
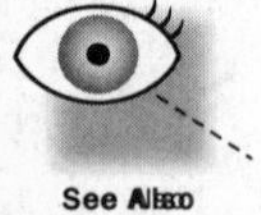
See Also

In addition to tips on writing queries, The Query Letter Clinic on page 19 offers eight example query letters, some that work and some that don't, as well as editors' comments on why the letters were either successful or failed to garner an assignment or contract.

Querying for fiction

Fiction is sometimes queried, but more often editors prefer receiving material. Many fiction editors won't decide on a submission until they have seen the complete manuscript. When submitting a fiction book idea, most editors prefer to see at least a synopsis and sample chapters (usually the first three). For fiction published in magazines, most editors want to see the complete short story manuscript. If an editor does request a query for fiction, it should include a description of the main theme and story line, including the conflict and resolution. Take a look at individual listings to see what editors prefer to receive.

Query Letter Resources

For More Info

The following list of books provide you with more detailed information on writing query letters, cover letters, and book proposals. All titles are published by Writer's Digest Books.

- *Formatting & Submitting Your Manuscript*, 3rd Edition, by Chuck Sambuchino
- *How to Write Attention-Grabbing Query & Cover Letters*, by John Wood
- *How to Write a Book Proposal*, 3rd Edition, by Michael Larsen
- *Writer's Market Companion*, 2nd Edition, by Joe Feiertag and Mary Cupito

THE SYNOPSIS

Most fiction books are sold by a complete manuscript, but most editors and agents don't have the time to read a complete manuscript of every wannabe writer. As a result, publishing decision makers use the synopsis and sample chapters to help the screening process of fiction. The synopsis, on its most base level, communicates what the book is about.

The length and depth of a synopsis can change from agent to agent or publisher to publisher. Some will want a synopsis that is 1-2 single-spaced pages; others will want a synopsis that can run up to 25 double-spaced pages. Checking your listings in *Writer's Market*, as well as double-checking with the listing's website will help guide you in this respect.

The content should cover all the essential points of the novel from beginning to end and in the correct order. The essential points include main characters, main plot points, and, yes, the ending. Of course, your essential points will vary from the editor who wants a 1-page synopsis to the editor who wants a 25-page synopsis.

NONFICTION BOOK PROPOSALS

Most nonfiction books are sold by a book proposal—a package of materials that details what your book is about, who its intended audience is, and how you intend to write the book. It includes some combination of a cover or query letter, an overview, an outline, author's information sheet, and sample chapters. Editors also want to see information about the audience for your book and about titles that compete with your proposed book.

Submitting a nonfiction book proposal

A proposal package should include the following items:

- **A cover or query letter.** This letter should be a short introduction to the material you include in the proposal.
- **An overview.** This is a brief summary of your book. It should detail your book's subject and give an idea of how that subject will be developed.
- **An outline.** The outline covers your book chapter by chapter and should include all major points covered in each chapter. Some outlines are done in traditional outline form, but most are written in paragraph form.
- **An author's information sheet.** This information should acquaint the editor with your writing background and convince him of your qualifications regarding the subject of your book.
- **Sample chapters.** Many editors like to see sample chapters, especially for a first book. Sample chapters show the editor how you write and develop ideas from your outline.
- **Marketing information.** Facts about how and to whom your book can be successfully marketed are now expected to accompany every book proposal. If you can provide information about the audience for your book and suggest ways the book publisher can reach those people, you will increase your chances of acceptance.
- **Competitive title analysis.** Check the *Subject Guide to Books in Print* for other titles on your topic. Write a one-or two-sentence synopsis of each. Point out how your book differs and improves upon existing topics.

For more information on nonfiction book proposals, read Michael Larsen's *How to Write a Book Proposal* (Writer's Digest Books).

A WORD ABOUT AGENTS

An agent represents a writer's work to publishers, negotiates contracts, follows up to see that contracts are fulfilled, and generally handles a writer's business affairs, leaving the writer free to write. Effective agents are valued for their contacts in the publishing industry, their knowledge about who to approach with certain ideas, their ability to guide an author's career, and their business sense.

While most book publishers listed in *Writer's Market* publish books by unagented writers, some of the larger houses are reluctant to consider submissions that have not reached them through a literary agent. Companies with such a policy are noted by an (A) icon at the beginning of the listing, as well as in the submission information within the listing.

Writer's Market includes a list of 85 literary agents who are all members of the Association of Authors' Representatives and who are also actively seeking new and established writers. For a more comprehensive resource on finding and working with an agent, see *2011 Guide to Literary Agents*.

MANUSCRIPT FORMAT

You can increase your chances of publication by following a few standard guidelines regarding the physical format of your manuscript. It should be your goal to make your manuscript readable. Follow these suggestions as you would any other suggestions: Use what works for you and discard what doesn't.

In general, when submitting a manuscript, you should use white, 8½ × 11, 20 lb. paper, and you should also choose a legible, professional looking font (i.e., Times New Roman)—no all-italic or artsy fonts. Your entire manuscript should be double-spaced with a 1½-inch margin on all sides of the page. Once you are ready to print your manuscript, you should print either on a laser printer or an ink-jet printer.

ESTIMATING WORD COUNT

Many computers will provide you with a word count of your manuscript. Your editor will count again after editing the manuscript. Although your computer is counting characters, an editor or production editor is more concerned about the amount of space the text will occupy on a page. Several small headlines or subheads, for instance, will be counted the same by your computer as any other word of text. However, headlines and subheads usually employ a different font size than the body text, so an editor may count them differently to be sure enough space has been estimated for larger type.

For short manuscripts, it's often quickest to count each word on a representative page and multiply by the number of pages. You can get a very rough count by multiplying the number of pages in your manuscript by 250 (the average number of words on a double-spaced typewritten page).

PHOTOGRAPHS AND SLIDES

In some cases, the availability of photographs and slides can be the deciding factor as to whether an editor will accept your submission. This is especially true when querying a publication that relies heavily on photographs, illustrations or artwork to enhance the article (i.e., craft magazines, hobby magazines, etc.). In some instances, the publication may offer additional payment for photographs or illustrations.

Check the individual listings to find out which magazines review photographs and what their submission guidelines are. Most publications prefer you do not send photographs with your submission. However, if photographs or illustrations are available, you should indicate that in your query. As with manuscripts, never send the originals of your photographs or illustrations. Instead, send prints or duplicates of slides and transparencies. Also, more magazines and book publishers are using digital images.

SEND PHOTOCOPIES

If there is one hard-and-fast rule in publishing, it's this: *Never* send the original (or only) copy of your manuscript. Most editors cringe when they find out a writer has sent the only copy of their manuscript. You should always send photocopies of your manuscript.

Some writers choose to send a self-addressed, stamped postcard with a photocopied submission. In their cover letter they suggest if the editor is not interested in their manuscript,

Manuscript Formatting Sample

1 Type your real name (even if you use a pseudonym) and contact information

2 Double-space twice

3 Estimated word count and the rights you are offering

4 Type your title in capital letters, double-space and type "by," double-space again, and type your name (or pseudonym if you're using one)

5 Double-space twice, then indent first paragraph and start text of your manuscript

6 On subsequent pages, type your name, a dash, and the page number in the upper left or right corner

Your name
Your street address
City, State ZIP code
Day and evening phone numbers
E-mail address

50,000 words
World rights

TITLE

by

Your Name

You can increase your chances of publication by following a few standard guidelines regarding the physical format of your article or manuscript. It should be your goal to make your manuscript readable. Use these suggestions as you would any other suggestions: Use what works for you and discard what doesn't.

In general, when submitting a manuscript, you should use white, 8½ x11, 20-lb. bond paper, and you should also choose a legible, professional-looking font (i.e., Times New Roman)—no all-italic or artsy fonts. Your entire manuscript should be double-spaced with a

Your Name - 2

1½ -inch margin on all sides of the page. Once you are ready to print your article or manuscript, you should print either on a laser printer or an ink-jet printer.

Remember, though, articles should either be written after you send a one-page query letter to an editor, and the editor then asks you to write the article. If, however, you are sending an article "on spec" to an editor, you should send both a query letter and the complete article.

Fiction is a little different from nonfiction articles, in that it is only sometimes queried, but more often not. Many fiction editors it may be tossed out and a reply sent on the postcard. This method is particularly helpful when sending your submissions to international markets.

MAILING SUBMISSIONS

No matter what size manuscript you're mailing, always include a self-addressed, stamped envelope (SASE) with sufficient return postage. The website for the U.S. Postal Service (www.usps.com) and the website for the Canadian Post (www.canadapost.ca) both have postage calculators if you are unsure of how much postage you'll need to affix.

A book manuscript should be mailed in a sturdy, well-wrapped box. Enclose a self-addressed mailing label and paper clip your return postage to the label. However, be aware that some book publishers do not return unsolicited manuscripts, so make sure you know the practice of the publisher before sending any unsolicited material.

Types of mail service

There are many different mailing service options available to you whether you are sending a query letter or a complete manuscript. You can work with the U.S. Postal Service, United Parcel Service, Federal Express, or any number of private mailing companies. The following are the five most common types of mailing services offered by the U.S. Postal Service.

- **First Class** is a fairly expensive way to mail a manuscript, but many writers prefer it. First-Class mail generally receives better handling and is delivered more quickly than Standard mail.
- **Priority Mail** reaches its destination within two or three days.
- **Standard Mail** rates are available for packages, but be sure to pack your materials carefully because they will be handled roughly. To make sure your package will be returned to you if it is undeliverable, print "Return Postage Guaranteed" under your address.
- **Certified Mail** must be signed for when it reaches its destination.
- **Registered Mail** is a high-security method of mailing where the contents are insured. The package is signed in and out of every office it passes through, and a receipt is returned to the sender when the package reaches its destination.

Mailing Manuscripts

- Fold manuscripts under five pages into thirds, and send in a #10 SASE.
- Mail manuscripts five pages or more unfolded in a 9 × 12 or 10 × 13 SASE.
- For return envelope, fold the envelope in half, address it to yourself, and add a stamp or, if going to Canada or another international destination, International Reply Coupons (available at most post office branches).
- Don't send by Certified Mail—this is a sign of an amateur.

THE BASICS

Query Letter Clinic

Many great writers ask year after year, "Why is it so hard to get published?'' In many cases, these writers have spent years—and possibly thousands of dollars on books and courses—developing their craft. They submit to the appropriate markets, yet rejection is always the end result. The culprit? A weak query letter.

The query letter is often the most important piece of the publishing puzzle. In many cases, it determines whether an editor or agent will even read your manuscript. A good query letter makes a good first impression; a bad query letter earns a swift rejection.

The elements of a query letter

A query letter should sell editors or agents on your idea or convince him to request your finished manuscript. The most effective query letters get into the specifics from the very first line. It's important to remember that the query is a call to action, not a listing of features and benefits.

In addition to selling your idea or manuscript, a query letter can include information on the availability of photographs or artwork. You can include a working title and projected word count. Depending on the piece, you might also mention whether a sidebar might be appropriate and the type of research you plan to conduct. If appropriate, include a tentative deadline and indicate whether the query is being simultaneously submitted.

Biographical information should be included as well, but don't overdo it unless your background actually helps sell the article or proves that you're the only person who could write your proposed piece.

Things to avoid in a query letter

The query letter is not a place to discuss pay rates. This step comes after an editor has agreed to take on your article or book. Besides making an unprofessional impression on an editor, it can also work to your disadvantage in negotiating your fee. If you ask for too much, an editor may not even contact you to see if a lower rate might work. If you ask for too little, you may start an editorial relationship where you are making far less than the normal rate.

You should also avoid rookie mistakes, such as mentioning that your work is copyrighted or including the copyright symbol on your work. While you want to make it clear that you've researched the market, avoid using flattery as a technique for selling your work. It often has the opposite effect of what you intend. In addition, don't hint that you can re-write the piece, as this only leads the editor to think there will be a lot of work involved in shaping up your writing.

Also, never admit several other editors or agents have rejected the query. Always treat your new audience as if they are the first place on your list of submission possibilities.

How to format your query letter

It's OK to break writing rules in a short story or article, but you should follow the rules when it comes to crafting an effective query. Here are guidelines for query writing.

- Use a normal font and typeface, such as Times New Roman and 10- or 12-point type.
- Include your name, address, phone number, e-mail address and website, if possible.
- Use a one-inch margin on paper queries.
- Address a specific editor or agent. (Note: The listings in *Writer's Market* provide a contact name for most submissions. It's wise to double-check contact names online or by calling.)
- Limit query letter to one single-spaced page.
- Include self-addressed, stamped envelope or postcard for response with post submissions. Use block paragraph format (no indentations). Thank the editor for considering your query.

When and how to follow up

Accidents do happen. Queries may not reach your intended reader. Staff changes or interoffice mail snafus may end up with your query letter thrown away. Or the editor may have set your query off to the side for further consideration and forgotten it. Whatever the case may be, there are some basic guidelines you should use for your follow-up communication.

Most importantly, wait until the reported response time, as indicated in *Writer's Market* or their submission guidelines, has elapsed before contacting an editor or agent. Then, you should send a short and polite e-mail describing the original query sent, the date it was sent, and asking if they received it or made a decision regarding its fate.

The importance of remaining polite and businesslike when following up cannot be stressed enough. Making a bad impression on an editor can often have a ripple effect—as that editor may share his or her bad experience with other editors at the magazine or publishing company.

How the clinic works

As mentioned earlier, the query letter is the most important weapon for getting an assignment or a request for your full manuscript. Published writers know how to craft a well-written, hard-hitting query. What follows are eight queries: four are strong; four are not. Detailed comments show what worked and what did not. As you'll see, there is no cut-and-dried "good" query format; every strong query works on its own merit.

Good Nonfiction Magazine Query

Jimmy Boaz, editor
American Organic Farmer's Digest
8336 Old Dirt Road
Macon, GA 00000

My name is only available on our magazine's Web site and on the masthead. So this writer has done her research.

Dear Mr. Boaz,

There are 87 varieties of organic crops grown in the United States, but there's only one farm producing 12 of these—Morganic Corporation.

Here's a story that hasn't been pitched before. I didn't know Morganic was so unique in the market. I'm interested to know more.

Located in the heart of Arkansas, this company spent the past decade providing great organic crops at a competitive price helping them grow into the ninth leading organic farming operation in the country. Along the way, they developed the most unique organic offering in North America.

As a seasoned writer with access to Richard Banks, the founder and president of Morganic, I propose writing a profile piece on Banks for your Organic Shakers department. After years of reading this riveting column, I believe the time has come to cover Morganic's rise in the organic farming industry.

The author has access to her interview subject, and she displays knowledge of the magazine by pointing out the correct section in which it would run.

The piece would run in the normal 800-1,200 word range with photographs available of Banks and Morganic's operation.

I've been published in *Arkansas Farmer's Deluxe*, *Organic Farming Today* and in several newspapers.

While I probably would've assigned this article based off the idea alone, her past credits do help solidify my decision.

Thank you for your consideration of this article. I hope to hear from you soon.

Sincerely,

Jackie Service
34 Good St.
Little Rock, AR 00000
jackie.service9867@email.com

Bad Nonfiction Magazine Query

This is sexist, and it doesn't address any contact specifically. It shows a complete lack of research on the part of the writer.

An over-the-top, bold claim by a writer who does not impress me with his publishing background.

Insults the magazine, and then reassures me he won't charge too much?

While I do assign material from time-to-time, I prefer writers pitch me on their own ideas after studying the magazine.

I'm sure people aren't going to be knocking down his door anytime soon.

Dear Gentlemen,

I'd like to write the next great article you'll ever publish. My writing credits include exposé pieces I've done for local and community newspapers and for my college English classes. I've been writing for years and years.

Your magazine may not be a big one like *Rolling Stone* or *Sports Illustrated*, but I'm willing to write an interview for you anyway. I know you need material, and I need money (but don't worry I won't charge too much).

Just give me some people to interview, and I'll do the best job you've ever read. It will be amazing, and I can re-write the piece for you if you don't agree. I'm willing to re-write 20 times if needed.

You better hurry up and assign me an article though, because I've sent out letters to lots of other magazines, and I'm sure to be filled up to capacity very soon.

Later gents,

Carl Bighead
76 Bad Query Lane
Big City, NY 00000

Good Fiction Magazine Query

Follows the format we established in our guidelines. Being able to follow directions is more important than many writers realize.

Marcus West
88 Piano Drive
Lexington, KY 00000

August 8, 2008

Jeanette Curic, editor
Wonder Stories
45 Noodle Street
Portland, OR 00000

Story is in our word count, and the description sounds like the type of story we would consider publishing.

Dear Ms. Curic,

Please consider the following 1,200-word story, "Turning to the Melon," a quirky coming of age story with a little magical realism thrown in the mix.

It's flattering to know he reads our magazine. While it won't guarantee publication, it does make me a little more hopeful that the story I'm reading will be a good fit. Also, good to know he's been published before.

After reading *Wonder Stories* for years, I think I've finally written something that would fit with your audience. My previous short story credits include *Stunned Fiction Quarterly* and *Faulty Mindbomb*.

Thank you in advance for considering "Turning to the Melon."

Sincerely,

Marcus West
(123) 456-7890
marcusw87452@email.com

I can figure it out, but it's nice to know what other materials were included in the envelope.

Encl: Manuscript and SASE

This letter is not flashy or gimmicky: It just gives me the basics and puts me in the right frame of mind to read the actual story.

Bad Fiction Magazine Query

We do not accept e-mail queries or submissions.

This is a little too informal.

First off, what did he write? An epic novel or short story? Second, 25,000 words is way over our 1,500-word max.

I'm lost for words.

Money and movie rights? We pay moderate rates and definitely don't get involved in movies.

I'm sure the writer was just trying to be nice, but this is a little bizarre and kind of a scary stalker ending to the letter. I do not so desire any more contact with "Harry."

To: curic@wonderstories808.com
Subject: A Towering Epic Fantasy

Hello there.

I've written a great fantasy epic novel short story of about 25,000 words that may be included in your magazine if you so desire.

More than 20 years, I've spent chained to my desk in a basement writing out the greatest story of our time. And it can be yours if you so desire to have it.

Just say the word, and I'll ship it over to you. We can talk money and movie rights after your acceptance. I have big plans for this story, and you can be part of that success.

Yours forever (if you so desire),

Harold
(or Harry for friends)

Good Nonfiction Book Query

Effective subject line. Lets me know exactly what to expect when I open the e-mail.

Good lead. Six kids and teaches high school. I already believe her.

Nice title that would fit well with others that we currently offer.

Her platform as a speaker definitely gets my attention.

25,000 e-mail subscribers? She must have a very good voice to gather that many readers.

To: corey@bigbookspublishing.com
Subject: Query: Become a Better Parent in 30 Days

Dear Mr. Corey,

As a parent of six and a high school teacher for more than a decade, I know first-hand that being a parent is difficult work. Even harder is being a good parent. My proposed title *Taking Care of Yourself and Your Kids: A 30-day Program to Become a Better Parent While Still Living Your Life* would show how to handle real-life situations and still be a good parent.

This book has been years in the making, as it follows the outline I've used successfully in my summer seminars I give on the topic to thousands of parents every year. It really works, because past participants contact me constantly to let me know what a difference my classes have made in their lives.

In addition to marketing and selling *Taking Care of Yourself and Your Kids* at my summer seminars, I would also be able to sell it through my Web site and promote it through my weekly e-newsletter with over 25,000 subscribers. Of course, it would also make a very nice trade title that I think would sell well in bookstores and possibly retail outlets, such as K-Mart, Wal-Mart and Target.

If you would like to look over my proposal, please just shoot an e-mail back.

Thank you for your consideration.

Sincerely,

Marilyn Parent
8647 Query St.
Norman, OK 00000
mparent8647@email.com
www.marilynsbetterparents.com

I was interested after the first paragraph, but every paragraph after made it impossible to not request her proposal.

Bad Nonfiction Book Query

The subject line is so vague, I almost deleted this e-mail as spam without even opening it.

This almost sounds like a sales pitch for a book. Maybe this is spam after all? The reason we don't publish such a book is easy—we don't do hobby titles.

I'm not going to open an attachment from an unknown sender via e-mail, especially of someone who's not the prettiest person. Also, copyrighting your work is the sign of an amateur.

1,000 possible buyers is a small market, and I'm not going to pay a writer to do research on a book proposal.

Not even a last name? Or contact information? At least, I won't feel guilty for not responding.

To: info@bigbookspublishing.com
Subject: a question for you

I really liked this book by Mega Book Publishers called *Build Better Trains in Your Own Backyard*. It was a great book that covered all the basics of model train building. My father and I would read from it together and assemble all the pieces, and it was magical like Christmas all through the year. Why wouldn't you want to publish such a book?

Well, here it is. I've already copyrighted the material for 1999 and can help you promote it if you want to send me on a worldwide book tour. As you can see from my attached digital photo, I'm not the prettiest person, but I am passionate.

There are at least 1,000 model train builders in the United States alone, and there might be even more than that. I haven't done enough research yet, because I don't know if this is an idea that appeals to you. If you give me maybe $500, I could do that research in a day and get back to you on it.

Anyway, this idea is a good one that brings back lots of memories for me.

Jacob

Good Fiction Book Query

Novel is correct length and has the suspense and supernatural elements we're seeking.

The quick summary sounds like something we would write on the back cover of our paperbacks. That's a good thing, because it identifies the triggers that draw a response out of our readers.

She mentions similar titles we've done and that she's done research on our Web site. She's not afraid to put in a little extra effort.

At the moment, I'm not terribly concerned that this book could become a series, but it is something good to file away in the back of my mind for future use.

Jeremy Mansfield, editor
Novels R Us Publishing
8787 Big Time Street
New York NY 00000

Dear Mr. Mansfield,

My 62,000-word novel, *Love in April*, is a psychologically complex thriller in the same mold as James Patterson, but with a touch of the supernatural á la Anne Rice.

Supernatural genre bending novels have been money in the bank lately with the emergence of the Anita Blake series and the Highlander series. *Love in April* comes from this same tradition, but like all bestselling fiction makes its own path.

Rebecca Frank is at the top of the modeling world, posing for magazines in exotic locales all over the world and living life to its fullest. Despite all her success, she feels something is missing in her life. Then she runs into Marcus Hunt, a wealthy bachelor with cold blue eyes and an ambiguous past.

Within 24 hours of meeting Marcus, Rebecca's understanding of the world turns upside down, and she finds herself fighting for her life and the love of a man who may not have the ability to return her the favor.

Filled with demons, serial killers, trolls, maniacal clowns and more, this novel will put Rebecca through a gauntlet of trouble and turmoil, leading up to a final climatic realization that may lead to her unraveling.

Love in April should fit in well with your other titles, such as *Bone Dead* and *Carry Me Home*, though it is a unique story. Your Web site mentioned supernatural suspense as a current interest, so I hope this is a good match.

My short fiction has appeared in many mystery magazines, including a prize-winning story in *The Mysterious Oregon Quarterly.* This novel is the first in a series that I'm working on (already half-way through the second).

As stated in your guidelines, I've included the first 30 pages. Thank you for considering *Love in April*.

Sincerely,

Merry Plentiful
54 Willow Road
East Lansing MI 00000
merry865423@email.com

Bad Fiction Book Query

Jeremy Mansfield
Novels R Us Publishing
8787 Big Time Street
New York NY 00000

Dear Editor,

My novel has an amazing twist ending that could make it a worldwide phenomenon overnight while you are sleeping. It has spectacular special effects that will probably lead to a multi-million dollar movie deal that will also spawn action figures, lunch boxes, and several other crazy subsidiary rights. I mean, we're talking big-time money here.

While I love to hear enthusiasm from a writer about his or her work, this kind of unchecked excitement is worrisome for an editor.

I'm not going to share the twist until I have a signed contract that authorizes me to a big bank account, because I don't want to have my idea stolen and used to promote whatever new initiative "The Man" has in mind for media nowadays. But let it be known that you will be rewarded handsomely for taking a chance on me.

I need to know the twist to make a decision on whether to accept the manuscript. Plus, I'm troubled by the paranoia and emphasis on making a lot of money.

Did you know that George Lucas once took a chance on an actor named Harrison Ford by casting him as Han Solo in Star Wars? Look at how that's panned out. Ford went on to become a big actor in the Indiana Jones series, *The Fugitive*, *Blade Runner* and more. It's obvious that you taking a risk on me could play out in the same dramatic results.

I'm confused. Does he think he's Harrison Ford?

I realize you've got to make money, and guess what? I want to make money too. So we're on the same page, you and I. We both want to make money, and we'll stop at nothing to do so.

If you want me to start work on this amazing novel with an incredible twist ending, just send a one-page contract agreeing to pay me a lot of money if we hit it big. No other obligations will apply. If it's a bust, I won't sue you for millions.

So that's the twist: He hasn't even written it yet. I can't make a decision without a completed manuscript. There's no way I'm going to offer a contract for a novel that hasn't been written by someone with no experience or idea of how the publishing industry works.

Sincerely,

Kenzel Pain
92 Bad Writer Road
Austin TX 00000

THE BASICS

Feature Article Writing

The Query in 3 Parts

by Chuck Sambuchino

If you want to write freelance articles for editors, the query letter is your best and most effective tool. It's essentially a one-page business plan for your idea—explaining what the idea is, why it will be a good fit for their publication, and why you're a qualified writer for the assignment.

You see, editors for magazines, newspapers and websites have one thing in common: They're all incredibly busy. They have very little time for anything, so they need to consider article ideas quickly, and that's where your query comes in. It's your pitch, and you have one short page to get their attention and convince them to pay you money in exchange for an assignment. Although there is no "perfect" or "surefire" way to structure a query, I have adopted and slowly tried to refine a three-part approach that seems to work well. Read on, and dig deeper into what comprises a successful, eye-catching query letter.

THE FIRST SECTION: THE HOOK

Nothing works better in a query letter than hooking an editor right away with your idea. By the end of the first sentence, they should be intrigued and want to know more. The first paragraph is designed to pique interest and give them a taste of what your article will be about. It's also the best chance you have in a query to show the flavor of your writing—your voice, for lack of a better term. If the article is going to be light and funny, your intro should reflect that. If it's going to be heavy and serious, make sure your query is, too. Keep in mind that if you are contacting a person you know or through a referral, that is always a great way to start—explaining your connection.

If you don't have a connection or referral, here are a few ways to get an editor's attention immediately with your query:

Start with an eye-catching fact

Alaska not only has the country's highest ratio of low birth weight babies, the percentage is actually going up yearly.

Last year's dreaded recession brought countless white wedding plans to a screeching halt. According to David Bridal's recent national survey, 75% of

---

CHUCK SAMBUCHINO is a freelancer as well as the editor of *Guide to Literary Agents* (www.guidetoliteraryagents.com/blog). He also helmed the third edition of *Formatting & Submitting Your Manuscript* (Writer's Digest Books) and is the author of *How to Survive a Garden Gnome Attack* (Sept. 2010, Ten Speed Press). More than 600 of his articles have appeared in print.

> American brides-to-be are searching high and low for a way to still have the wedding of their dreams—without spending a fortune.

With an approach like this, you're aiming to immediately tell the editor that what you have to say is news—and it's important.

Use an interesting tidbit

> There are 87 varieties of organic crops grown in the United States, but there's only one farm producing 12 of these—Morganic Corporation.
>
> If I asked you which sports hobby was the most popular for retirees in South Florida, you may say bowling or shuffleboard. Perhaps some would even throw out softball or darts—but all those guesses would be wrong. The truth is: The mini-golf movement has hit South Florida big time, and it's taking over everywhere.

When you have a story that isn't hard news (perhaps a feature or profile), an interesting fact works well. Think of it like this: You learned about something and were interested enough to research more and pitch an article. Try to get us interested in the subject just like you were.

Start in media res—in the middle of a story

> It was 2:14 a.m. when a drunk driver smashed into the bedroom of Mike Edson's condo and took the life of his wife.
>
> I'm right in the middle of my weeklong quest to find the best cheeseburger in DC when a monstrosity known only as "The Goliath" is dropped in front of me on a plate. It's less of a burger than it is a defining moment in your life. I notice my hands are shaking as I reach to pick it up—all three pounds of it.

When your piece focuses on a front-to-back narrative (that can involve you or others), you can always just show an interesting moment right in the middle. This gets us editors asking questions such as "How did he get to this moment?" "Does he finish the burger?" "What was his final decision as to the best burger in the city?" In other words, I want to know more.

THE SECOND SECTION: THE SPECS

If you've done your job, the editor is still reading your query. You've caught their attention with the first sentence then expounded on your idea by putting more meat on the bones. The second part of the query letter is where you take a step back and start to talk about the specs of the article itself. A safe way is to start this paragraph with "I propose an article on ..."

With a paragraph or two, your goal is to explain more about the size and scope of the piece, what the article will look like on the page, and, finally, prove to the editor that you read their publication and are familiar with the type of content readers like to see.

Mind the Details

Here are things you want to address/include:

- Estimated length (word count).
- Targeted section of the magazine. Where will this article appear in the publication?
- What kind of story is it? Feature? Profile? Column?
- The slant, if it needs explaining. For example, let's say you hear about a local woman who's planting a rose in town for every soldier that dies fighting the war on terror. You could pitch an article about her to a gardening magazine, a military/patriotic magazine, and a local interest magazine. But each one with one, you will have a different focus—a different slant.

- Do you have access to people you will interview? If you are proposing to profile famous screenwriter Charlie Kaufman for Creative Screenwriting, you will need to say that you have access to him somehow. Do you want to sit down with Kevin Garnett? How can you secure an interview?
- Do you have access to images or will you provide art/pictures? If you're writing for Popular Woodworking or Ohio Game and Fish, will you be taking your own photos to provide with the piece? You increase your chances of success if you do so.
- Any sources lined up—or at least the names of whom you would interview. If you are writing a piece on low birth weight, to continue that example, you should quickly list the names of people you will consult and interview for the piece. With luck, you've already spoken with one and have a quote you can include in the query.

THE THIRD SECTION: THE BIO

If an editor is still reading your query by the end, she must love the idea and feel that it has promise for their publication. What a writer must do now is convince her as to why they're the idea person to compose this piece. In other words, she's looking for credentials—a bio.

Elements of a Bio

- Do you have any qualifications of relevance? For example, if you're writing for Men's Fitness, do you hold any degrees or certifications in the health field?
- Have you written about this subject before?
- What publications have you written for, if any?

If you have enclosed or attached clips (previously published samples of your writing), say so. You can attach PDF scans of a piece, or simply paste a link to an online article. Ideally, you want to show them clips that have some comparison to what you want to write about. For instance, if you want to do a profile of gymnast who is considered the most promising eight-

Book Queries

Book queries are slightly different than article queries whether you're submitting to a literary agent or directly to a publisher. Again, there is no surefire format, but they are still one page long and you can still employ a three-part structure—but the three parts will be:

Part 1: The basics. Provide the title, word count and genre/category. Also, why are you contacting this agent/editor? Explain why you picked,this agent/editor out of all your options. Explain why they're a great match for your book. Try to establish a connection. If you are contacting by referral, or because you met them at a writers' conference, say so upfront.

Part 2: The pitch. This is where you explain what your project is about in 3-10 sentences. If you're writing a novel or memoir, go to the nearest Barnes & Noble and start looking at the backs of DVD boxes and the inside covers of novels. This will get you in the mindset of writing a concise and compelling pitch paragraph. You will see how a pitch is composed and how they're designed to pique your interest but not reveal the ending.

Part 3: The bio. Again, list who you are and what credits you have. If you are writing nonfiction, this section—explaining your platform and marketing ability—will be the most important aspect of the letter.

year-old in the world in her field, then do you have any sample profiles for the editor to see? Mentioning that you write about cars for the local paper shows that you're a professional, but doesn't yet convince her that you can tackle a profile on an eight-year-old.

And if You Have No Credits?

Keep in mind that if you have no clips to include, don't embellish or exaggerate. Just skip the clips part. Thank the editor for considering the submission and wrap up with "Sincerely, (Name)."

The higher you aim for an assignment, the more editors will demand credentials and credits. If you query the local parenting magazine that's usually found for free in supermarkets, you don't need a slew of impressive articles in your pocket. You probably just need a good idea and professional-looking query. But if you want to write for a mid-size magazine like The Pastel Journal or Girlfriends Magazine, you will likely need some bylines to your name.

QUERY FAQ

Do queries have a specific font or format? Your best bet is to use a normal font and typeface, such as Times New Roman or Arial. Use 10- or 12-pt font.

Should I discuss payment in a query? No. If you've done your research, you should have a general idea of what a magazine pays. The payment discussion will come up organically as the conversation goes along. Bringing up payment too quickly may show that you're hard to work with.

Who do I address the letter to? Every publication has a submissions editor—meaning, an individual who is charge of reviewing queries and accepting good ideas. With a tiny website or magazine, there is likely a staff of one, and the top editor is reviewing everything. For larger publications, such as our magazines here at our publishing house—Writer's Digest or Watercolor Artist—the top editor is not the contact person for submissions. Seek out a copy of the publication's submission guidelines to get the name of the submissions editor. If it doubt, contact the publication by e-mail or phone and simply ask who to address the letter to and the best e-mail address to use.

Should I mention the work is copyrighted? No. The editors already know this, and mentioning what the editors already know comes off amateurish.

Do editors want to know if it's a simultaneous submission? You don't *have* to mention it, but yes, editors appreciate knowing.

What if the query has been rejected in the past? Don't mention it when contacting editors. Letting them know this just makes the idea sound worse. They get to thinking, "If four other people have rejected it, the idea must not be worth it…"

What if the material's been published before? Let editors know. If what you're pitching is a reprinted article or an excerpt from a book you wrote, that's A-OK—just let them know upfront.

Should writers submit via e-mail vs. snail mail? Once again, check the submission guidelines to see how publications like to get queries. Over the past decade, there has been a gradual yet large shift toward e-queries—and that's a good thing. E-mail queries are quicker and less expensive. If you have the option to submit either way, it makes no real difference.

Can I follow up if I don't hear back? Sure, but check guidelines first. If a magazine says they respond to ideas within six weeks, I'd wait eight before following up. In your follow-up, be polite and humble, simply mentioning that you had not heard back and are afraid the first e-mail got lost in cyberspace, which is why you're resubmitting the original query below (just cut and paste it again).

How do you end a query? A safe bet is always to thank the editor for their time and sign off. If you're querying an agent, ask if you can send some pages of your work (or the full proposal for nonfiction).

Article Query Letter

One of many letterhead styles you can use.

John Q. Writer
johnqwriter@email.com
(323) 555-0000

Jan. 30, 2009

Jane Smith, managing editor
New Mexico Magazine
4200 Magazine Blvd. Santa Fe, NM 87501

Always address the correct editor.

Ms. Smith:

A lead designed to hook and pique interest.

According to the Bible, it took two days for God to create all living creatures. The way New Mexican Regina Gordon sees it, the 48-Hour Film Project involves the same amount of time—with only a slightly less complicated task.

"Every second counts, when you have 48 hours to make a film." That's the motto of the 48-Hour Film Project (www.48hourfilm.com), a nationwide event that challenges local filmmakers to form teams and create four-minute movies—from script to set design to finished product—in 48 hours or less. Albuquerque is no stranger to the fray, and will again participate in the competition in 2009.

Estimated word count.

Targeting a specific section of the magazine shows you're familiar with the publication.

Also returning in 2009 is the city's area producer: Gordon. More than 20 area teams competed in 2008—with all of these guerilla filmmakers reporting to one woman—Gordon—who must substitute passion, adrenaline, and insane amounts of coffee for sleep she certainly won't get. So what drives her and other participants to exhaust themselves like they do? I propose a 800-word short profile on Gordon and, with it, New Mexico's involvement in the project for *New Mexico Magazine*. (I've already touched based with Gordon.) I believe that a Gordon feature would be a great fit for the "Introducing" section of your magazine. To give readers a feel for what a kinetic, exciting, shoot-from-the-hip experience this is, I would interview Langston to hear anecdotes from last year and discover what lies in store for this year—as a sense of community for the project continues to build in the area.

Highlight qualifications quickly and effectively.

In 2003, I covered Philadelphia's involvement in the project for *Artspike* magazine. Thank you for considering this piece. My résumé and clips are enclosed.

Be polite.

Respectfully,

Signature. If you're mailing the letter, leave enough room here to sign your cursive signature.

John Q. Writer

Detail your enclosures,

Encl.: Clips and résumé

Bad Article Query – Mistakes to Avoid

Richard D. Bonehead
123 Mistake Lane
Rejectionville, USA

March 24, 2009

Editors
Atlanta Journal-Constitution

Dear Sir/Ma'am:

I have an idea for newspaper article. I have a feeling that it would be a controversial and explosive story that would sell a whole bunch of copies—its that good. What I want to do is give you some of my early thoughts, and if you're interested, we can talk some specifics over the phone (though bear with me; my cell phone gets bad reception).

This is what I'm thinking. I write an article on how the social networking juggernaut MySpace is affecting the dating scene in the ATL. Cool, huh? I know that I could have pitched this to *Atlanta Magazine* or even *People*, but I figured I would give you a shot. For the article, I would need some ideas for sources, and probably some upfront money to buy a laptop. At this point, I'm thinking the article will run about 5,000 words.

My writing influences are Stephen King, James Patterson and Joe Eszterhas. I've blogged on MySpace plenty of times before and I also regularly comment on Web site forums and message boards, so I think I have the necessary experience to tackle such an article.

I'm offering a seven-day window on this query because I think that's fair. After all, this is a sizzling topic. Please get back to me right quick.

Peace,

Richard D. Bonehead

No e-mail or phone number is included.

Address is missing.

Not targeting a certain editor shows you didn't even do the basic research to find an editor's name.

This simple grammatical error could have been caught with some proofreading.

Every query recipient wants to feel like you've picked this market for a reason, and arrogant talk like this will kill a query

Why does this matter?

An editor doesn't need seven days. He'll just say no now.

There might be something here, but the idea is not fleshed out and there is no indication of how you would hook readers.

Always be humble. Adopting an attitude never works.

This proposed length is way too long for virtually any publication. Suggesting such an outrageous word count will torpedo your chances.

While you want to list credentials, something worse would be to list meaningless accomplishments.

Good Query to Agent: Novel/Memoir

Including full contact information.

A good query letter is a lot like a good cover letter. It should be well structured and grammatically correct with an appropriate salutation. The tone should be polite and professional.

It doesn't take long for Doreen to get the hook, or "elevator pitch," and quickly explain what her memoir is about.

This does a great job conveying both the subject matter and tone of the book. If you're writing a humorous memoir like Doreen, it's OK to inject a bit of humor into your query—just make sure your letter isn't so informal that it's off-putting.

Lastly, Doreen sums up her platform —i.e., why she's the go-to gal to write this book, and how she's going to get media attention for it—nicely. Her writing credits are impressive and she's obviously got the connections in place to spread the word about this book once it comes out.

Dorien Orion
123 Author Lane
Writerville, USA
(323) 555-0000
johnqwriter@email.com

Mollie Glick
Foundry Literary + Media
33 West 17th St. PH
New York, NY 10011

Dear Ms. Glick:

I am a psychiatrist, published author, and expert for the national media seeking representation for my memoir titled, *Queen of the Road: The True Tale of 47 States, 22,000 Miles, 200 Shoes, 2 Cats, 1 Poodle, a Husband, and a Bus with a Will of Its Own.* Because you are interested in unique voices , I thought we might be a good match.

When Tim first announced he wanted to "chuck it all" and travel around the country in a converted bus for a year, I gave this profound and potentially life-altering notion all the thoughtful consideration it deserved. "Why can't you be like a normal husband with a midlife crisis and have an affair or buy a Corvette?" I asked, adding, "I will never, ever, EVER live on a bus."

What do you get when you cram married shrinks — one in a midlife crisis, the other his materialistic, wise-cracking wife — two cats who hate each other and a Standard Poodle who loves licking them all, into a bus for a year? *Queen of the Road* is a memoir of my dysfunctional, multi-species family's travels to and travails in the 49 continental states. (Tim insisted on seeing them all, despite my assurances that there were a few we could skip.)

As a psychiatrist, award-winning author (*I Know You Really Love Me*, Macmillan/Dell) and frequent media expert on psychiatric topics, (including "Larry King" "GMA," "48 Hours," *The New York Times* and *People Magazine*), my life has centered on introspection, analysis and storytelling. Yet, I count among my greatest accomplishments that last year, ou bus was featured as the centerfold of *Bus Conversions Magazine*, thus fulfilling my life-long ambition of becoming a Miss September.

I hope you are interested in seeing sample pages if so, would be most happy to send them to you via e-mail or snail mail.

Best wishes,

Doreen Orion

Note how this is a nonfiction book, but memoirs are treated like novels because they read like novels. Comments provided by Mollie Glick of Foundry Literary + Media.

Bad Query to Agent: Mistakes to Avoid

The author's name, phone number, and e-mail are missing. Be sure to include all pertinent contact information.

123 Author Lane
Writerville, USA
July 24, 2009

Big Time Literary Agency
200 W. Broadway
New York, NY 10125

Always address your query to a specific agent.

Dear Agent:

Don't ask an agent for advice or criticism—that's not the agent's job nor the purpose of the query letter.

I have just completed my first novel and would like to sell it to a publisher. I have never had a book published but I know this novel will be a bestseller. I'm looking for an agent to help me. I would really appreciate it if you could read over the enclosed chapters and give me some advice on whether you think this a good novel and if it needs any extra work to make it a bestseller.

This is vague and tells the agent very little about the book. There is no "hook" to capture the agent's attention.

There is nothing here to indicate how this book will distinguish itself from the thousands of other similar books that have been published. How will this book be different?

The Subject of Susan is about 60,000 words long and is geared toward an adult audience. It is all about a headstrong woman named Susan and her trials and tribulations throughout the 1950s and beyond as she makes her way in the legal world after graduating from law school as the only woman in her graduating class.

Never mention that you're a first-time writer or that you have never been published—it singles you out as an amateur.

Don't draw attention to your lack of experience as a writer, and don't mention anything about yourself that is not pertinent to the novel. Keep all your information focused on the book itself.

This is my first novel and while I am not familiar with the legal world, since I'm not a lawyer, I find the subject fascinating and think readers will too. I've written a lot of short stories dealing with women's lives but they were much more romanticized than the story of Susan. Susan is someone you would know in real life. I have spent the last 20 years of my life raising my children and think I have what it takes to become a successful writer.

Don't mention copyright information or payment expectations. This is a query to assess an agent's interest in your novel.

I own the copyright on this book and would like to discuss possible advances and royalties with you sometime soon.

Thank you very much,

John Q. Writer

THE BASICS

9 Steps to Writing a One-Page Synopsis

by Catherine Gentile

After completing my four hundred-page novel I pegged the challenge of distilling it into a six-page synopsis as the most diabolical exercise ever conceived, but I was mistaken; reducing it to a one-page synopsis was worse. I'd spent five years fleshing out my characters, weaving them into a coherent tale of real people whose driving needs refused to be dismissed. The task of summarizing their lives felt counterintuitive, not to mention disloyal. But my encounter with another group whose needs were equally compelling reminded me that working as an author entailed other dimensions.

Agents interested in my work varied in their submission requirements, including the length of the synopsis. I consulted the requisite how-to books, gleaned the wisdom applicable to my novel, and considered suggestions regarding format, voice, and verb tense.

Those decisions proved easy. But determining which aspects of content to include tossed me headfirst into the thorniest of briar patches. Eventually, I relinquished characters and their dilemmas to the guardianship of broad strokes and universal truths. Countless drafts later, I condensed my four hundred-page novel to ten, double-spaced synopsis pages.

Agents encouraged me with invaluable feedback regarding my manuscript. Thus fortified, I undertook another round of revisions. Armed with the gift of perspective that only time can give, I followed up with a six-page synopsis. Agents responded positively. Despite my burgeoning confidence, when it came to titrating my hard-won manuscript into a one-page synopsis, I balked and secretly relegated anyone requesting a one-pager to my poison pen list.

But desire necessitates invention, and when a tempting opportunity to enter a publication contest presented itself, I had no choice but to harness my egotism. I couldn't do this alone. Help came in the form of an external structure, gentle but firm with potential for simmering my novel's essence down to a flavorful single page. I developed a systematic nine-step approach that provided guidelines for reassembling my multi-page synopsis into a more tightly focused one-pager. Sinfully concrete, my method worked. As an added bonus, my sentiments towards those on my poison pen list gentled.

Should you find yourself in similar straights, try reducing your multi-page synopsis by using this nine-step process. As you work, remember that the generally accepted conventions of a one-page synopsis differ only in quantity from its multi-paged cousin. More specifically, write in the present tense through which you'll address essential characters, their major conflicts and motivations. Use bold print or capital letters to signal the introduction of a new character. Return to standard lettering when referring to that character thereafter.

CATHERINE GENTILE's short fiction has appeared in *The Chaffin Journal*, *Kaleidoscope*, *The Ledge*, and other publications. In addition to her novel, Sunday's Orphan, Gentile has completed a short story collection, *After the Chrysalis*. She regularly writes for *Portland Trails* and *Maine In Print* and welcomes comments at catherinegentile@maine.rr.com.

Your opening hook should be spot-on, grab-your-attention succinct. Follow with the turning points that show growth and plot line as they relate to your essential characters and major theme or themes. And please, don't keep secrets from the agent or contest official who'll be reviewing your synopsis. Be sure to reveal the resolutions to the major conflicts you've introduced. Okay, let's get started:

1. **Working from your multi-page synopsis, choose 40 lines that embody the salient features of your novel.** Why 40? This is the number of single-spaced lines using 12-point Times New Roman font that fill a standard page setup.
2. **Next, highlight, copy and paste these 40 lines onto a new document.** Don't worry if you're a little over, you'll trim to one-page later in the process.
3. **Scrutinize this draft to determine whether you've included the crucial elements of who your characters are, what motivates them and why, along with when and where they live.** Check to insure you've identified each of the five w's. Labeling them in italics within the body of your synopsis will give you a quick visual reference you can delete later. Count them. If anything is missing, return to your multi-page synopsis, locate the needed information and add it to your one-pager. For example:

   Born in 1910 (when), twenty-year-old protagonist PROMISE MEARS CRAWFORD (who) grew up (what) in rural Georgia (where) thinking she was white (why).

4. **To expand on step #3, if you need to add material about a character, embed it within your one-page synopsis.** This way, you'll be able to fold in defining characterizations and basic information while remaining within the forty-line limit. Italics in this example indicate the original sentence:

   Raised by her adoptive uncle, TAYLOR CRAWFORD, a former Harvard University professor dismissed for his unorthodox ideals on ending racial inequality, Promise assumes she is free of prejudice.

5. **Insert transitions and additional supporting information.** Although this synopsis is only one page, you still want to engage your reader in a seamless overview of the characters and the pivotal plot points comprising your novel.
6. **Review word choices.** Where you've used several words to denote one concept, compress them to one or two: e.g., I confess rather than I choose to reveal. In doing so, be sure to remain true to your novel's style.
7. **Remove unnecessary words, phrases, and information that illuminate or develop your story line.** While nuance and subplots are vital to your novel, in this instance they absorb precious space.
8. **Condense scenes that span several paragraphs into one.** Hint: the last sentence in a scene often summarizes the preceding context and strikes an emotional note:

   Instinct tells Promise to send Daffron packing, but she can't; not if he can lead her to her mother.

9. **Print out your one-page synopsis, even if you're over the page limit.** Count the lines in excess of one page, and repeat steps 3-9. Don't be discouraged if it takes several revisions before reaching a coherent one-page synopsis. We all have trouble deleting our darlings.

Writing & Selling Your Greeting Card Ideas

by Sandra Miller-Louden

How many times have you read a greeting card verse and thought: "I could write that!"?

Exactly! And, as a professional greeting card writer since 1986, the author of the best-selling *Write Well & Sell: Greeting Cards* and a greeting card writing teacher online since 1998 (and in a traditional classroom setting since 1991), I am here to tell you, that yes, you could definitely write that!

Getting started

However, there is a cavernous difference between writing greeting card verses and selling them to existing companies. So, precisely how do you go about selling your work? Well, right off the bat, there are three things you do not want to do. Three things that most aspiring greeting card writers tend to do—things that immediately turn off today's greeting card editors.

If you want to sell your greeting card verses, do not...I repeat, do not...

1. Submit rhymed, metered verse in the tradition of Helen Steiner Rice
2. Submit drawings or photographs with your verses
3. Submit verses to Hallmark and American Greetings

In three short phrases, I've just given you the top prevailing myths that stubbornly continue to plague would-be greeting card writers. While writers eventually may be given specific assignments to write rhymed, metered verse, for a freelance (a.k.a. "cold") submission, don't do it. Many small and mid-size companies today don't even published rhymed, metered verse. Their verses may be short phrases, quips or verses that depend on an outside visual—the verse itself may often be fewer than ten words. If you submit flowery Victorian-era poetry, you won't stand a chance.

A second misguided myth is that writers must be able to draw in order to sell their verses. It's ironic that it's just the opposite. Editors don't want "the entire package," since that would constitute a line of cards (more on that later). If your verse depends on a visual to get its meaning across, by all means verbally suggest a visual...but do not submit a drawing or photograph. For the vast majority of mid-size and smaller companies, the visual is entirely separate from the verse as far as the independent contractor (that's you as a freelance writer) relationship goes.

SANDRA MILLER-LOUDEN is a freelance writer and leads workshops on writing greeting cards.

So what's wrong with Hallmark and American Greetings? Absolutely nothing...both fine companies that publish terrific greeting cards! However, let me ask you a question here. Have you heard of companies such as Oatmeal Studios, Palm Press, Avanti, Gallant Greetings, Leanin' Tree, Paper Trail Press, Northern Exposure, NobleWorks, Ronnie Sellers, Comstock, Design Design or Ephermera, among others? I thought not. And here is where so many would-be greeting card writers completely miss the ship. They submit to the top two greeting card companies which receive thousands of submissions weekly instead of submitting to the mid-size and smaller companies where freelance submissions are actually read and often acted upon in the form of future assignments or actual on-the-spot sales.

Finding freelance opportunities

But how do I go about finding cards published by these smaller companies, you ask? Although I cover this aspect of seeking out card companies in my online classes, here is a brief rundown on finding card companies with smaller staffs and a real interest in finding new talent to match their offerings.

Huge chains such as K-Mart, Wal-Mart, Rite-Aid, CVS, etc., are not where you'll find freelancing opportunities. Also, keep in mind that card "names" such as Ambassador, Carlton, Tender Thoughts, Shoebox, Winking Moon Press etc., are really extremely successful lines owned by either Hallmark or American Greetings.

You should begin your search by going to various niche stores. Concrete examples of different card companies found at various stores in an area:

- Papyrus (Marcel Schurman – Owned by Marcel Schurman, who recently changed its card company name to Papyrus)
- Craft Stores (Portal Publication, Laura Leiden Calligraphy)
- Convenience Stores (P.S. Greetings, Majestic Greetings, Gallant Greetings, Fravessi)
- Dollar Stores (Mostly Gallant Greetings, some American Greetings. Also Novo Cards)
- Restaurant Gift Stores, e.g. Cracker Barrel (Leanin' Tree, Attic Salt, etc.)
- Book Stores (Papyrus, Palm Press, Paper Magic Group, Graphique de France)
- Hardware Stores (Leanin' Tree)
- Kitchen/Bath Needs (Portal Publication)
- Pet Stores (Avanti, Portal, Northern Exposure)
- Office Supply Stores/Shipping Companies/Copying Centers (Avanti, Recycled Paper Greetings, Nobleworks, Oatmeal Studios)
- Specialty Card Stores/Party/Stationery Stores (DCI, Palm Press, Paper Trail Press, Oatmeal Studios, Marian Heath, It Takes Two, Recycled Paper Greetings, Caspari, Pictura)
- Christian Stores (Dayspring, Fravessi, It Takes Two, Lang, Marian Heath)
- Small-Town Grocery Stores/Gift Shops (Eclectic Mix including Lovelace Family LTD, Fravessi, Design Design)
- Small, Non-Chain Gift Stores (Attic Salt, Leanin' Tree)

Keep in mind there is nothing like old-fashioned footwork—pounding the pavement, picking up card after card, getting to know the companies first-hand that make up this industry. If you're limited in your traveling due to external factors, there's always the internet—and it's a solid friend in helping you with your greeting card search. Most companies have a website; many post their writing guidelines online. You can often study their entire card offering and when you see that ubiquitous "Contact Us" icon, use it! (Also most sites have a "Store Locator" icon which is invaluable in locating their actual published cards). Having a pre-printed writer's guidelines request letter that you can copy and paste will facilitate the procedure of finding out if the company will e-mail their creative guidelines to you.

Do it yourself?

Now what about starting a greeting card company of your own—another aspect of this

It's So a Laughing Matter!

By Nadia Ali

How would you like to write approximately two sentences and be paid about $50? That's the average pay that freelance greeting card writers get for simply writing short, funny quips that give a knockout punch.

Sounds easy right? Well, when I first dabbled in the greeting card market, it started off as a fun venture that offered some comic relief from the long word-counts of writing feature articles. Then once I got my first acceptance, a world of humor opened its doors and I found myself taking the whole genre quite seriously. As I looked at the process of writing, certain questions arose. Who is my audience? What age group am I writing for? How do I write a card that is genderless? How do I tickle a funny bone without being insulting?

I needed to do some research, so I headed down to my nearest card shop and spent a long time browsing through the rows of everyday greeting cards - much to the dismay of the sales clerk.

Having looked at the cards in the shop, then online cards and finally soliciting present needs lists from greeting card companies, one thing was obvious – humor sells!

But just how do I get that punch into a two line sentiment? The wording has to be very precise, capturing just the right emotion that makes the reader want to buy the card.

Writers are always being told about the 'hook', with regards to greeting cards the outside of the card is the hook and the inside is the punch-line. Think about how comedians deliver jokes to an audience, well you have to deliver your greeting card idea to one person – the creative editor.

Given that the theme is a funny birthday, I began to worry which sparked an idea about the worry birthdays tend to cause.

OUTSIDE: For your birthday, throw out all the digits that are of no use to you
INSIDE: Like those that tell your age, height and weight. Happy Birthday

The creative editor will either laugh and consider buying it or simply say that line that no writer likes to hear, "best of luck placing this elsewhere."

Thankfully, the old format of submissions via index cards sent in an SASE envelope in the post is almost a thing of the past. Email submissions are now widely accepted. The email format for submissions includes a reference number that makes the greeting unique to the writer and is easier to transact business with. Mine is made up of my initials and a four digit number –though it's up to you how many digits you want to have. See the example below:

OUTSIDE: Lots of people are excited about your birthday...
INSIDE: ...historians, archaeologists!

Reference number: NA-1001

One of the most difficult things for me to write was the request for a genderless card, particularly when the greeting card company wanted it for the category of anniversaries. Here's an example of one:

OUTSIDE: Sweetheart, I would give you paradise for our anniversary
INSIDE: But you got that when you married me!

Not a laugh out loud moment but it did tackle the challenge of being genderless.

Writing greeting cards can take so many directions such as double meanings, intentional misinterpretation, an unlikely turn of events, twisted meanings, play on words or the use of an old cliché'. Above all, the card must be positive without being rude or insulting

OUTSIDE: Confucius say, with every passing of a birthday wisdom is gained
INSIDE: Hopefully your wisdom will kick in any day now! Happy Birthday

The choice of words, the slant, and the pun; it makes all the difference between an acceptance or a rejection. Always try to make a play on words, even incorporate a unique spin on a universal truth:

OUTSIDE: Women of our age get to experience summer all year round
INSIDE: They don't call it hot flashes for nothing! Happy Birthday

As writers we are always on the look out for well paid markets and although greeting cards acceptances may be far and few between, the rate per word is one of the highest. After all, when last did you get paid $50 for two sentences?

For those who think that writing greeting cards is a dying niche; the US Greeting Card Organization has some strong evidence to the contrary. Approximately $7.5 billion is spent annually in retail sales in the US alone. Across the ocean in the UK, the Greeting Card Association states that the buying public spent 1.5 billion in greeting cards. It is also interesting to note that almost 90% of cards are bought by women and approximately half of all cards bought are for birthdays.

It is definitely a market that is growing every year and like every other market it is one where you have to keep up with the trends. What possible trends can there be in greeting cards you may well ask? It has expanded into card lines to apply specifically to ethnic markets such as the African/American and Latin cultures where the cards are written in Spanish.

Then with the digital age influence on the card industry we are now seeing the introduction of many innovative products such as DVD greetings that compliment themed cards, digital slideshow greeting cards, mobile greetings, digital scrapbooks, cards with recorded sounds and even just released augmented 3-d cards. This goes to show that despite the instant availability of electronic greetings, the ever popular SMS messaging and the convenience of email, the public still prefer paper greetings.

But one thing that remains the same is that humor is memorable, entertaining and it sells. And with more than 3,000 greeting card publishers in the US alone; there is definitely a market out there who will share your humor. So, get out there with some short, sweet and to the point punch lines and make your mark on the greeting card market while earning top dollars.

industry where I receive substantial e-mails?

Having been in this industry for over 25 years, I've seen many perfectly wonderful, creative, exciting companies...disappear. Why? In a nutshell, the creative side often obliterates the mundane, business side of starting one's own greeting card company—the identification of exactly who's going to buy your greeting card, getting quotes on printing and advertising among other considerations, ferreting out your competition (you may have a terrific angle for dieting or dating, for instance—however, if another card company has established its dominion on these topics, you'll have an uphill struggle) and perhaps most important, finding businesses that will give up cherished retail space to display and sell your product. Just as in the classic 1941 film, *Citizen Kane*, the spirit behind "It would be fun to run a newspaper" often, heartbreakingly prevails in folks wanting to run a greeting card company.

And although there are several successful companies I can offer in this article as hope: www.amorcitos.com; www.cardsbyanne.com; www.scentsational-greetings.com; www.zazzle.com/scarletsfeathers; plus a targeted booklet, *Seven Steps to Take BEFORE Starting A Greeting Card Company*, by Pat Ferdinandi (owner of Scarlet's Feathers), I would like to also offer an alternative that many people don't even consider.

Creating a concept

You don't have to start with an entire greeting card company—you can start with a concept—or line—of cards...which gives creative people the cohesiveness of a centralized theme or look, yet does not break the bank as far as committing yourself to a company before you, perhaps, don't really even understand the industry.

A line of cards is best defined as any group of cards carrying a central theme or hook. The number of cards in a line can vary, although generally it is a number divisible by four. Two common quantities in a line are either 24 cards or 36 cards. Keep in mind that when an established card company commits to a line of cards, it takes an enormous risk. When the companies are in the mid-size or smaller tier range, that risk multiplies. Companies invest much time, energy and cash to get a line of cards up, running, distributed and advertised. Major card companies we all have heard of receive hundreds of line proposals; even when the creative people behind the line are known in the industry, it's an uphill climb to have their line see the light of day. For someone just beginning or unknown in the world of greeting cards, it's even more of a struggle. However—and this is a huge however—it is a miniscule risk compared to starting one's own greeting card company.

Begin by sending creative ideas, unrelated to and not part of your line, to existing card companies. As I stress in my book, *Write Well & Sell: Greeting Cards* and in all my online classes, the mid-size and smaller card companies are where you'll have your greatest opportunity to be published. Continue sending individual ideas to these companies, simultaneously working on your line in the background.

As a professional, working freelancer writing individual verses, you'll learn valuable lessons about meeting deadlines, tackling simultaneous assignments, working under pressure. You'll get to know editors and more importantly, they'll get to know you and your work. After working with various editors, you'll also begin to realize where your potential line could possibly fit—which companies publish the type of writing and/or artwork you're proposing. These would naturally be the companies you would approach—after first working with these companies in a freelance capacity.

What about Copyright?

I'm also asked if it's necessary to copyright one's greeting card work. I am not a copyright attorney and this advice is not meant to replace the advice of a copyright attorney, which I highly recommend your consulting before pitching a line of work to a company. Common sense, however, tells you that you should first give the entire line a name; for example, if it's a line based on zoo animals and what they say and do, you might entitle the line: Zoopers. Under the title Zoopers, you would list the individual verses you intend to place in this line. You would not, of course, separate these verses or send them out in any other form to a card company, except as part of the greeting card line, entitled Zoopers. As you would add new verses to the line, you would update your copyright application to reflect these additions.

If you haven't already—and I certainly hope you have—go to existing card racks and spinners and really study what's out there. Turn the card over; the line name is generally found in the middle, although not always. Examples of lines that, for example, American Greetings have are: Intuitions, Fresh Apple Cards, 78th Street or Pet Tales. Find cards in various lines and read the verses in the line—you'll see how they're connected in many subtle, as well as, overt ways, including the type of artwork, whether the verse is totally inside or divided between outside and inside, certain occasions, certain age groups. This research is a must and should not be side-stepped or skimped on.

If you're considering the development of a line of greeting cards, I applaud you for your creativity and encourage you to continue. If I've given you a dose of reality about pitching a line, it's better to know what you're up against now, rather than several months—and many huge envelopes with corresponding postage—later. New lines of greeting cards come out constantly and your line could very well be one of them in the future. Do the necessary background work first and your chances of having your line published will increase substantially. From a line of greeting cards may come various lines. These, in turn, may well become the next greeting card company...namely, yours.

PERSONAL VIEWS

Gwendolyn Heasley

Confessions of a Literista

by Jude Tulli

When Gwendolyn Heasley finished her masters degree in journalism at the University of Missouri-Columbia, she couldn't see the twists and turns over which she'd soon careen as her career path unfolded. Of necessity she migrated back home to her parents' empty nest, where she embarked in earnest on her debut novel, *Confessions of a Teenage Recessionista* (HarperCollins, 2011).

"After college I had no idea what I was going to do," Heasley says. "I life-guarded. I sold greeting cards. I really liked the creative aspect of the greeting cards. . .[but] I decided to go to journalism school instead." While searching for a job at a magazine, an enterprise that turned out to be more difficult than she had expected, she "took [an online course] to write a YA book in twelve weeks."

Heasley carried the best of her journalist perspective and ability to "feel out people" into fiction-writing and unleashed all the creative license she had been longing to exercise. "As a novelist I got to have a lot more artistic freedom. I think my voice is much more of a fiction voice; a little more sarcastic, a little more snarky."

All she needed was a premise. In the end, it stemmed loosely from her own life circumstances. Heasley says, "I thought I'd just write about [what was] going on. So it's the story of a girl in the recession and her life being turned upside down."

At home, Heasley watched a lot of television with her father. She noticed an unsavory pattern creeping into the crime dramas: ". . .the murderer is always an adult living at home." The media's skewed portrayal of twenty-somethings who fly back to their childhood roosts before soaring the skies once again, "was part of the motivation for the book."

But Heasley is not her main character. "[Corrine] starts off as a total b-i-t-c-h. There's really not much to like about her [at first] except she's funny."

At its heart, "It's a fish out of water story of a Manhattanite teen who's forced to move to Texas to her mother's hometown to live with her formerly estranged grandparents." Corrine becomes more likeable as the as the story progresses: "She's very wealthy, materialistic, and then she gets a job. She learns about drugstore makeup but more than that she learns about what having friends [means, and] who her mother was before she came to Manhattan and shed her Texas identity."

Though Heasley draws generously from her own life experience, she notes the major differences between herself and Corrine: "I'm not nearly as cool as she is. I don't think as highly of myself as she does. It was fun to write."

JUDE TULLI has contributed to several recent editions of the *Writer's Market* and the *Novel and Short Story Writer's Market*. His short fiction has appeared online in Scribblers and Inkspillers' Copper Wire. He resides in the Sonoran Desert with his beloved wife Trish and a small pride of housecats.

Recessionista's representation

Heasley estimates that she sent queries to about ten agents. From that initial wave she received two offers of representation. She identifies the timeliness of her title as a likely catalyst for such an astounding success rate, coupled with having found her voice.

"It's a very trendy title," she says, "the recession was on people's mind[s]. . .I truly believe it was the title that. . .drew people's attention." Ironically, she and her editor have not yet decided whether the title will change before publication.

Besides, a fashionable name can only advance a submission so far. The passion she found for the themes of coming of age and adapting to new and contrasting surroundings certainly must have shone through the story itself.

"I think maybe YA is the best genre for me." Heasley enjoys the freedoms that were denied in her background field of journalism. "I wanted to be able to get my point across as a journalist," yet "the truth was I knew that I would do better in a field where I could be in narrative control. As a journalist, you are bound to the truth as defined by accuracy and ethical reporting. As an author, you can make up stories and lies in order to tell a bigger truth. I love the freedom that being an author gives me."

Ultimately she chose Leigh Feldman of Darhansoff Verrill Feldman to represent her. Without editorial changes, Feldman submitted the manuscript and quickly secured Heasley a two-book deal with HarperCollins.

Heasley credits her agent's talent for a large part of her authorial successes. "She was the first person to truly validate me as a writer and I am forever grateful."

What's up second?

"There's a chance I might write about one of the other characters in the book," Heasley hints. "That's possible, but I'm also working on a completely separate novel." Option number two is a story about a new heroine's adventures at a weight-loss camp. Either way, she's been afforded over half a year to "produce a full manuscript."

Which story is on deck depends in large part upon which idea Heasley's editor "falls in love with, and hopefully I'll love it, too. I think that's the best part of writing. . .falling in love and in hate with your character."

Surprises are all a welcome part of the game for Heasley. "YA is the market where teenagers are trying to figure out who they are. And so they do things that surprise not only their peers and their parents but also. . .themselves."

Though her writing career is off to a quick start, Heasley has no intention of quitting her other part-time jobs: agenting and teaching. Indeed, being a full-time writer is not her long-term goal. "I don't want to exist just in a room by myself all the time. It's important for me to meet other people and see what's going on in the world."

Furthermore, Heasley says, "I think that quitting a job and writing full-time for some people is a good idea, but it also makes writing stressful." She encourages writers to "Try to keep your day job as long as possible. To keep the passion."

From author to Artists and Artisans agent

Heasley had long considered becoming a literary agent as a possible dream job. She worked for a while in book publicity, learning "how books are marketed and how books come to life and everything." She believes that having her own book on a publisher's slate was the qualification that finally tipped the scales in her favor.

Her advice for others who desire to become a literary agent? She figured that, like the wind, the odds would be at her back if she moved to New York, where a preponderance of opportunities knock about. Having arrived with no inside connections, Heasley tells it as she saw it, ". . .you have to be willing, unfortunately to start as an intern. So you're going to have to be willing to have a couple of jobs. Part of this new generation is that we're going to have to juggle a lot of balls to get the dream jobs we really want."

As with writing, perseverance is key. "Keep applying for jobs; eventually someone's going to recognize your talent. And you work your way up."

But the climb itself can be fun. "Book people are always really interesting. You do a lot of reading. You do a lot of talking. You do a lot of lunching." As a side effect, she says she's probably "gained ten pounds for this job, but it's fine." She sees it as a small price to pay for doing something she loves.

New agent

As a part-time agent, Heasley has hand-selected her first five clients and for the moment she is content with that number. "If something fantastic comes through my e-mail I'm not going to push them away but right now I really want to focus on who I've already signed."

Heasley describes her editorial style with clients as decidedly hands-on. "I don't just read it once and send them notes once. I go through several drafts." This remains foremost in her mind when considering new projects. It only makes sense that ". . .if I'm going to work that intensely with a story I want it to be a story that I also love. . .and want to have a fingerprint on. Something that I want to work with for hours and hours and hours."

The goal is clear: "I want to get manuscripts into tip-top shape before [submitting] them. I think as an agent if I'm going to get fifteen percent of your money then I should work hard for the fifteen percent and help you shape your book."

But Heasley is no slave driver; her working style leaves plenty of room for fun. "I am very much a people person. I don't just want to talk to you about your books. I want to know about your life. I want it to be a relationship that goes beyond just the page."

She counts among her assets her colleagues' eagerness to help. "The great thing is [that Artists and Artisans is] a completely open office and we're not competing against each other. . .we do a lot of reading for each other. Most agencies don't do that. . .I am new but I also have all of Adam [Chromy]'s experience plus all of Jamie [Brenner]'s experience behind me as well.

Personal tastes

Heasley is the first to admit that many well-written and thoroughly marketable manuscripts will be overlooked by herself and many of her contemporaries. Though discouraging on the face of it, she sees it as good reason for writers to persevere in their searches for agents and editors whose aesthetics will align with their work. "I look at the market and what's going to sell but I want to work with manuscripts that I love. So a lot of it is. . .personal taste as well. It doesn't say anything about the quality of your work."

She also concedes that, "Agents have strengths and weaknesses." Even if Heasley can appreciate the genius of a work, she may happen to be ill-equipped to sell it at the present time, for example, if it's "the most fantastic story [in a genre] that I don't know enough about."

At about a hundred per day, Heasley finds the rolling avalanche of queries daunting. "With the volume [agents] can't actually read all of them that carefully." She believes that in the electronic age, "writers are going to have to query more people" to find the best match for their work.

Though Heasley hopes to find many clients from unsolicited queries, "I don't feel like everyone gets the attention they deserve." Nevertheless, she enjoys the process and finds it "really fun to see what people send me."

Still sorting out the bitter from the sweet to some extent on her own literary palette, Heasley has noticed a few trends in the work she's accepted so far. "I really love first person. I love being in someone's head. I love hearing someone's thoughts. . .[and] taking a ride with one character. I like stories that are supernatural. . .How about some supernatural girls? Human boys [could] fall under their spell and give up their eternity to be with them." One universal constant for Heasley: "I'm always looking for middle grade," in all genres and flavors.

As for literary influences that have settled in her soul, Heasley extols, "I can't even emphasize how big a part of my life Baby-Sitters Club was. They were like the other people

Querying Confessions

This is the query letter that introduced Gwendolyn Heasley to her agent:

Dear Ms. Feldman,

16-year-old Manhattanite Corrine Corcoran is shopping for her first year at boarding school when her parents call a family meeting. Within an hour, Corrine's life turns upside down. Due to the recession, Corrine is no longer heading to Connecticut's Kent Boarding School with her best friend Waverly and her credit cards. Instead, Corrine, her brother Tripp and her mother Cici are heading back to Cici's hometown, Broken Spoke Texas to live with Cici's long-estranged parents.

Follow Corrine's adventures as she navigates public school, Texan football, a stick truck named Billie Jean the II, an after school job shoveling manure, and a rodeo. With the help of her grandparents and new best friend, Kitsy, Corrine learns that not everything of value requires a charge account. And just as Corrine's finding her footing in the Texan two-step, her old best friend Waverly comes for a visit.

Will Corrine fall back into her materialistic ways? Will she return to New York?

With the recession as the backdrop, *Confessions of A Teenage Recessionista* touches on a cultural vein about learning to live in a new reality and reprioritizing one's life. Although this novel is comical, both young adults and adults alike will hopefully think twice about what defines us as people in these difficult economic times.

I have my Master's in Journalism from University of Missouri where I wrote my thesis on celebrity news. I will present that thesis at the Association of Education of Journalism and Media Studies this August. This is my first novel.

I have attached the first 50 pages of my novel. Thank you for your time and consideration.

Sincerely,

Gwendolyn Heasley

I knew. My other friends were the baby-sitters club. I used to be able to recite all the titles. I'd love to meet Ann Martin because she really inspired my dream."

Hopes for the future

Heasley holds her hopes high all around. In ten years, she says, "I hope to be. . .a writer who's [still] producing books. Even if nobody wants to read my books and I'm just producing manuscripts that only I read, I hope I'm still writing."

She envisions herself continuing to represent all of the authors she takes on between now and then. "I hope to have the same clients. Because that will be amazing to be with the same people in ten years and see what they're producing."

But that's not all; her dreams pervade beyond the printed word. "I'd love to see my clients' work as movies. And my own." She welcomes the advancing e-book technologies, too. "People crave that kind of interactive multimedia. But I also hope they're publishing real books and it's not all gone to Kindle. I hope it becomes a complement versus a replacement."

Advice for writers

Heasley believes authors are well-advised to keep the realities of writing close to heart. "People need to realize how hard it is to make a living off of just writing."

Still, she encourages writers not to underestimate their own ability. "When you read a book, it's been through several editors' hands. Never think, 'Oh, my writing's not good enough,' because it's probably not true."

Craft-wise, Heasley sees some common threads in the works with which she resonates. "I like backstories to naturally unfold." To avoid starting a book too early in the story, she suggests, "If you create another universe. . .write all about all the characters, and tell yourself the story and then write the manuscript after you've told yourself the story."

Another writer's trap ensnared even Heasley when the light shone through tunnel's end of her own book. "I started to summarize when I needed to be expanding." It's important not to gloss over the ending just because you can taste it. Polyurethane is, after all, inedible.

Writers often spend so much time and attention attracting the interest of an agent that they can forget an agent's true role in the publishing world. "If you do get an agent," Heasley says, "[he or she works] for you. You should help [him or her] as much as you can. But [he or she] really should be looking out for your best interests."

PERSONAL VIEWS

Cliff Dorfman

Find Your Voice, Then Write for Everything

by Joanna Masterson

Cliff Dorfman started writing a book when he was 12 years old, documenting his life at home and the normal issues adolescents deal with. As he wrote, he found himself inserting "author's notes" with a sardonic, edgy way of looking at situations.

Cliff Dorfman started writing a book when he was 12 years old, documenting his life at home and the normal issues adolescents deal with. As he wrote, he found himself inserting "author's notes" with a sardonic, edgy way of looking at situations.

"I didn't realize until much later that was my voice," he says, emphasizing how crucial it is for writers to find their own point of view. "Anyone can pick up a book and learn structure; that's rudimentary. You can never learn your voice. If you don't know structure, but you find your voice, then you will be able to get paid to write."

Dorfman has been a working writer in Los Angeles for about 20 years. He first ventured west in 1987, hoping to be an actor. He got "spit back out," returned home to Long Island, New York, and then gave California another try in the early 1990s.

As Dorfman made his way in Hollywood, people encouraged him to trade in acting for writing. He had no formal training, but taught himself the ropes and started working with other writers and getting involved in the development game, quickly learning that most scripts never come to life.

He also endured some grunt work ghostwriting for a writer on the hit HBO series *Entourage*. Though Dorfman didn't receive any credit for his contributions to the first season, he made connections and eventually was hired to write for the show's second season.

"I'd written a lot of scripts and features and was always working with people ... but that was my first big break," Dorfman says.

The *Entourage* gig led to *The Hollywood Reporter* naming him a "writer to watch," as well as a Writers Guild of America award nomination. "I never expected to win and didn't, but it was thrilling," he says, "and then I moved on."

Leaving *Entourage* behind

What kind of writer would leave a wildly successful show after being recognized by the industry? One who wants to create, Dorfman says.

"I didn't want to be an on-staff writer. A lot of people start out and work their way up the ranks [staff writer, executive story writer, producer, etc.] and then go off and do another show. But if you really want to create, staffing is not the way to go."

Under the advice of his agent, Dorfman's next move was to shop an original pilot. Paramount TV bought the pilot under a blind script deal and rolled it over into the next

---

JOANNA MASTERSON writes for and edits a construction trade association magazine in Arlington, Va.

Cliff Dorfman on...

Editors: "I have not had a bad editor. I hear horror stories, but I've gotten very lucky. It's all-consuming to be an editor—they really love what they do."

Differences between writing for TV/film and magazines: "The development process is a lot different and the formatting is different. But at the end of the day, everything is about great characters."

Whether scriptwriters need to live in LA: "You have to be in LA to take advantage of networking. There's an ongoing connective tissue that exists in this town. The assistant you make friends with is the development executive that will buy your show in five years."

Needing an agent: "Currently I just have a manager and a lawyer. An agent is helpful to start, and if you want to staff on a show or do assignments, having an agent is vital. If you want to partner up with people and want to write on your own or buy source material and adopt it, agencies don't offer as much help."

Advice for new writers: "You don't get if you don't ask. You can't be shy. If you see an opportunity, ask. If you think you'd never be able to get a job, ask."

development season. In the meantime, Dorfman wrote for another CBS show that never came to fruition. He's also done some short-term work writing story concepts for Sega and EA video games. ("It's a great job to have while you're working on something else," Dorman says, particularly for a gamer.)

And, after his stint with *Entourage*, DC Comics enlisted him to do a takeoff on *Aquaman*—a comic book superhero and fictional movie in which *Entourage*'s main character stars. Though that project didn't pan out, the relationship snowballed into a collaboration with actor/producer/director David Arquette on a vigilante werewolves comic.

Juggling projects

And so it goes in the writing business, where managing a variety of projects—in a variety of genres—is virtually an art form.

"It's frenetic, but you have some amount of latitude with deadlines," Dorfman says. "Sometimes a project that pays you the most is going to take the front seat. Other people can juggle projects; I can't jump from one world to another world."

Dorfman also follows the advice of a mentor who told him to "sit down every day to write and pray that the movie/TV/writing golds are going to speak to you. When they do, they'll say you need to work on this project right now. Get that project out, and that will make room for the next thing."

These days, Dorfman continues to develop shows with a variety of writing partners. But with fewer pilots getting made and movies not bringing in as much money, he's also making room for magazine writing. He currently churns out 10, 400- 600-word columns a year for *Los Angeles Confidential*, a magazine covering the people, places and styles that define LA. He builds each article around a quote from a great film, song or book—always crediting the screenwriter, songwriter or author.

With magazines, Dorfman says he can escape the long development process that accompanies screenwriting and just be free to write what he wants (thanks to "amazing" editors, he notes). Most screenwriting projects never come to fruition, so magazine writing keeps him "current."

"There's freedom to it," he says. "Even if they're giving me an assignment, there's still a freedom in how you attack that assignment. Obviously everything has a word count, but words on a page that you can write in any order ... no fade in, slug line, action line ... there's a free form in that that's really sexy."

On the horizon

So, what does someone who has written for TV, film, magazines, video games and comic books take on next?

"I'd like to tackle a novel about first love," Dorfman admits, revealing a bit of self-doubt. "I was a mediocre actor—good at best, but never going to be great. I believe the ability for me to be a great writer exists, but I'm not sure it exists in novels."

Dorfman's profound respect for and admittedly purist outlook on novelists seem to be holding him back. "Unless I knew I could really do it justice, I wouldn't want to tread on that snow," he says. Considering Dorfman found his voice writing a book at age 12, a return to fiction may be in the cards after all. And it couldn't hurt to follow the advice he gives to other writers: "Don't feel trapped in one medium. If you can write and have found your voice, then writing for everything. There are no boundaries."

PERSONAL VIEWS

Charlaine Harris

True Blood and Success With Vampires

by Andrea Campbell

What does über success sound like? Well, can you imagine hearing that the Chief Executive Office of Penguin has told Publishers Weekly that your book was "making up" most of the huge sales numbers for the past year—and that, oh, yes, your hardcover had shipped some 540,000 copies? And what if you find out right after that your mass market individual titles, and the 8-paperbacks-to-a-boxed-set variety, are also flying off the shelves? Welcome to the world of Charlaine Harris.

Jodi Rosoff, Director of publicity at Penguin Group, is more than pleased at the Southern Vampire Series' success, "To have the entire series on the New York Time's list simultaneously, no one here can remember it ever happening before… It may be some kind of publishing record!"

Unless you've been living in a cave, you have probably watched the HBO series, *True Blood*. It is a not a tale for the sheepish mind you, because the protagonist, Sookie Stackhouse, has got herself a whole lotta hurt going on in fictional Bon Temps, Louisiana. What with her ability to read people's unpleasant thoughts, the loss of her beloved 'Gran' in a bloody murder—not to mention having to deal with vampires, shape-shifters, and the other unworldly creatures who happen to frequent Merlotte's where she works as a barmaid—life is a test.

Alan Ball, the man who bought into the whole southern vampire opus is the producer behind another HBO hit, *Six Feet Under*. Ball likes to say that *True Blood* is "…popcorn for smart people," mainly for its intriguing plots and unique, addictive world. Accordingly, the fan phenomenon for this quirky, fantastical series has produced Internet sites such as Fangbangers.com and EricNorthman.net, among a cadre Facebook fans, commemorative screensavers, and even a store where you can buy your own "Tru blood" drink set, in authentic bottles. One of the most popular cable shows, right up there with *The Sopranos* and *Sex and the City*, *True Blood* was nominated for two Golden Globes and a number of other awards.

And if you ever get a chance to meet celebrated author Charlaine Harris, you will find that despite the publishing triumphs, she is a charming, unassuming southern lady herself—born in Louisiana—and living a relatively small town life. And Charlaine would be the first to tell you it took two years to sell her paranormal tour de force, finally landing a home for Sookie with Ace Books, a sci-fi and fantasy imprint.

Charlaine, for readers who don't know you, can you tell them what it is like to be an "overnight success"?

ANDREA CAMPBELL is a freelance writer based in Arkansas. Follow her on Twitter at http://twitter.com/andreacampbell.

Of course, it took about twenty-five years for this to happen. I probably appreciate my success more since it came so late in my career.

What was the impetus for writing about vampires, shape shifters, etc., and when did that come about?

I had a hard look at my middle-of-the-road career when I was looking at turning fifty. It was time for a change. I decided to write about something new in a completely different genre. It was a lot of fun.

Sookie Stackhouse, your protagonist, can read minds, was that clear to you when you created her character? And, just as an aside, did "Stackhouse" have anything to do with her figure?

No, "Stackhouse" just sounded good with "Sookie" (it rhymes with "bookie"). I knew from the outset that Sookie had some kind of disability. It took me quite a while to think of what would work best in the books. Telepathy fit the bill. I couldn't wish anything worse on anyone.

How did you find your agent and what did he think about the first book, Dead Until Dark?

My agent asked me if he could represent me about twenty years ago. We had a mutual friend, a writer he represented, and she recommended us to each other. We've been together ever since, through some very thin times. He wasn't crazy about *Dead Until Dark* the first time he read it. But since I believed in it so strongly, he worked hard to sell it. That took two years.

And now that you have tons of success, we want to know how that feels. Are you grateful to your agent, or is he more of a friend? Was he encouraging and helping you get through the leaner times?

My agent and I know each other's lives pretty well after all these years, though we still have a professional relationship. He was my agent before our last child was born, and he stuck with me through the lean times. Believe me, there were plenty of years I was glad to make a few thousand dollars. But he never seemed to lose faith in my work, and though many other writers assumed I'd change agents when my fortunes were on the upswing, I never entertained the idea as a serious possibility. Joshua (Bilmes, of JABberwocky Literary Agency) and I have made a good team over two decades.

Of course I always wanted a wider readership. He couldn't make that happen for me, but he did his best. At least my books kept getting published. I've always thought it was ironic that the book he liked least was the book that ended up making our fame and fortune. I give him great credit for working hard to find a publisher for a book he wasn't that crazy about. The paranormal field was just getting started then, and the term "urban fantasy" hadn't been coined. The Sookie books were a mixture of things that hadn't been categorized—mystery, romance, violence, the supernatural—and booksellers weren't sure where to shelve such novels. Now, of course, they're everywhere.

When did you know that the Sookie Stackhouse books were going to be an ongoing enterprise?

When my then-editor, John Morgan, came back to me very soon after the first book was published to offer me a contract for more. And then more.

What did you think of your publisher and your editor at Ace? Were you on the same page so-to-speak?

My first editor at Ace was John Morgan, who's since gone to DC Comics, where he's had huge success. I still love John, and we swap emails every now and then. When John left Ace, he passed me on to Ginjer Buchanan, who's been at Ace for many years. Ginjer is very well known and respected in the science fiction community, and she gets nominated for awards all the time . . . far more than I do! I think Ginjer and I have a good relationship. I try hard not to be a pain in the butt, and Ginjer is an astute editor with some good ideas. I have always wanted more editing, rather than less. When Ginjer presents me with a different perspective on something I've turned in, I've found that it's a good idea to mull it over. More often than not, I conclude that she's right.

Though publicists seem to have a high turnover, I've had some outstanding ones at Ace. My current publicist, Jodi Rosoff, is amazing. My experience at Ace has been wonderful. What a great bunch of people to work with.

How did it come about that the books got optioned for the HBO series: True Blood?

Alan Ball picked up a copy of *Dead Until Dark* at a bookstore because he was early for a dentist appointment. He went back the next day and bought all the other books. Then his agent called my agent. I had other offers, but his was the best artistically.

What is your impression of the interpretation from book to television screen? Are you happy with the way things are going? Do you like the casting?

I love the casting, and I couldn't be happier with the way the show is going. I knew there would be drastic differences between the books and the show, and that's fine with me. It provides two separate entertainment experiences with the same characters.

I noticed you had a cameo on one of the episodes, did many people catch that? What was it like?

Oh, yes, a lot of people were waiting for that. I announced it on my website, and Alan said something about it, too. It was wonderful being on the set and watching the crew and cast work. Very interesting.

Your books have become New York Times (and other lists) bestsellers, how has that changed your work and your life?

I have less time; that's the main difference. I'm always supposed to be doing something. It's harder to get the writing time I used to have. I try not to let it change my life any more than I can help. Some days that's not much.

Does it feel wonderful to finally get some serious money? (Especially in this economy when everyone talks about the demise of books!)

Money. Yes, it's great to earn so much. Since I got $5,000 for *Dead Until Dark*, my price per book has definitely gone up. My first few years as a writer . . . well, our accountant said, "If it wasn't for your husband's job, you'd qualify for food stamps." I've been lucky to have my husband to back me up, and believe me, I appreciate his willingness to do so. Now that our circumstances have changed, I find that my biggest pleasure lies in buying any book I want. Isn't that fabulous? And I don't have to worry any more about being overdrawn. Luxury!

I'm interested in knowing if other authors are envious. I know I have a touch of envy but I know how many books you've written and you deserve it. You are the kind of storyteller that is, well, accessible and you can build a world and that is powerful. So we want to know more.

Being a more high-profile writer not only means you get more reader attention, it also means you get more critical attention, and a lot of that is unkind. Unsigned reviews are especially vicious, and I no longer read them. I know my work is not perfect, and I know that there are justifiable critical comments that might be leveled at my books; but a few people are simply mean and personal. I am learning to let that roll off my back. Every time I start a new book, I make every effort to make it better than the last one. Sometimes I succeed. Sometimes I don't. I like to think that in twenty-six years of writing, I've learned something. And I'm always hoping to find the absolute best way to write a book, the way that won't involve pain. But that hasn't happened.

I am the most fortunate person in the world. I have a family I'm proud of, a supportive husband, and a great career. I never wanted to be anything but a writer, and I've gotten to live out my dream. I've had plenty of sadness in my life, and some very tough moments—hasn't everyone had those?—but I wouldn't begin to appreciate what I've got now if it had been any other way.

Are fans getting too friendly? Do you love it when you see a long line of people with books to sign? How does that feel?

I used to be delighted when I had fifteen people at a signing. I'm still glad to see fifteen, but now I have so many more that it's almost daunting. I don't have time to visit with everyone. In order to get through my entire signing line, I have to greet the reader, sign the book, say a word or two, and then move to the next person. It's not how I like to do things, but if it's a choice between being brisk and sending people home with unsigned books, I'll take brisk! Big signings are where bookstore organization really pays off.

Can you give us some insight into how you plan out the series? There are a lot of secondary recurring characters and other subplots, how are you plotting it and how far ahead have you gone?

I pretty much fly by the seat of my pants. I have a few arcs planned, but the rest is just whatever I think of while I'm working.

You have other series characters, such as Aurora Teagarden and Lily Bard "Shakespeare," any action there?

The Aurora and Lily series are pretty much at an end. I wrote four books in the Harper Connelly series, and I think I'm through with that. I don't want to outstay my welcome. I have signed a contract for three more Sookie books, and I like to write other stuff, too.

Are you leaving southwestern Arkansas a lot more now?

Oh, yes, I travel a lot. I'm trying to cut back on that, because it reduces my writing time still further.

What are your plans for the future? Do you feel additional pressure that you hadn't felt before?

Yes, I do feel more pressure. I always try to set new goals, but I'm casting around for things to aspire to now. I've been so incredibly fortunate. I'm just going to keep working, and I hope that people continue to enjoy what I write.

Can you give novice writers any advice on how to create their own series; or do you have suggestions to seasoned authors about their contracts?

I'm not big on giving advice. First of all, there comes a time when you have to stop world-building and start writing. Nothing will come to you until you actually write your book. So I usually tell aspiring writers to read, read, read, and then write, write, write. Don't show your work to a lot of people. Don't tell lots of people what you PLAN to write. Do the work.

I am not business-savvy at all. I advise all writers to get agents, reputable agents, as soon as they can.

Is there anything else you would like to tell Writer's Market readers?

This is an incredibly tough business. The bottom line is money, as it is in any business. I do believe that if you write an incredible book it has a good chance of getting published, if you do your research and work hard.

Minding the Details

Writers who've been successful in getting their work published know that publishing requires two different mind-sets. The first is the actual act of writing the manuscript. The second is the business of writing—the marketing and selling of the manuscript. This shift in perspective is necessary if you want to become a successful career writer. You must keep the business side of the industry in mind as you develop your writing.

Each of the following sections and accompanying sidebars discusses a writing business topic that affects anyone selling a manuscript. Our treatment of the business topics that follow is necessarily limited, so look for short blocks of information and resources throughout this section to help you further research the content.

CONTRACTS AND AGREEMENTS

If you've worked as a freelance writer, you know contracts and agreements vary from publisher to publisher. Some magazine editors work only by verbal agreement, as do many agents; others have elaborate documents you must sign in duplicate and return to the editor before you even begin the assignment. It is essential that you consider all of the elements involved in a contract, whether verbal or written, and know what you stand to gain and lose by agreeing to the contract. Maybe you want to repurpose the article and resell it to a market that is different from the first publication to which you sold it. If that's the case, then you need to know what rights to sell.

In contract negotiations, the writer is usually interested in licensing the work for a particular use, but limiting the publisher's ability to make other uses of the work in the future. It's in the publisher's best interest, however, to secure as many rights as possible, both now and later on. Those are the basic positions of both parties. The contract negotiation involves compromising on questions relating to those basic points—and the amount of compensation to be given the writer for his work. If at any time you are unsure about any part of the contract, it is best to consult a lawyer who specializes in media law and contract negotiation.

A contract is rarely a take-it-or-leave-it proposition. If an editor tells you his company will allow no changes to the contract, you will then have to decide how important the assignment is to you. However, most editors are open to negotiations, so you need to learn how to compromise on points that don't matter to you, and stand your ground on those that do matter.

RIGHTS AND THE WRITER

A creative work can be used in many different ways. As the author of the work, you hold all rights to the work in question. When you agree to have your work published, you are granting a publisher the right to use your work in any number of ways. Whether that right is to publish the manuscript for the first time in a publication, or to publish it as many times and in as many different ways as a publisher wishes, is up to you—it all depends on the agreed-upon terms. As a general rule, the more rights you license away, the less control you have over your work and the money you're paid. You should strive to keep as many rights to your work as you can.

Writers and editors sometimes define rights in a number of different ways. Below you will find a classification of terms as they relate to rights.

- **First Serial Rights**—Rights that the writer offers a newspaper or magazine to publish the manuscript for the first time in any periodical. All other rights remain with the writer. Sometimes the qualifier "North American" is added to these rights to specify a geographical limitation to the license. When content is excerpted from a book scheduled to be published, and it appears in a magazine or newspaper prior to book publication, this is also called first serial rights.
- **One-Time Rights**—Nonexclusive rights (rights that can be licensed to more than one market) purchased by a periodical to publish the work once (also known as simultaneous rights). That is, there is nothing to stop the author from selling the work to other publications at the same time.
- **Second Serial (Reprint) Rights**—Nonexclusive rights given to a newspaper or magazine to publish a manuscript after it has already appeared in another newspaper or magazine.
- **All Rights**—This is exactly what it sounds like. "All rights'' means an author is selling every right he has to a work. If you license all rights to your work, you forfeit the right to ever use the work again. If you think you may want to use the article again, you should avoid submitting to such markets or refuse payment and withdraw your material.
- **Electronic Rights**—Rights that cover a broad range of electronic media, from online magazines and databases to CD-ROM magazine anthologies and interactive games. The contract should specify if—and which—electronic rights are included. The presumption is unspecified rights remain with the writer.
- **Subsidiary Rights**—Rights, other than book publication rights, that should be covered in a book contract. These may include various serial rights; movie, TV, audiotape, and other electronic rights; translation rights, etc. The book contract should specify who controls the rights (author or publisher) and what percentage of sales from the licensing of these rights goes to the author.
- **Dramatic, TV, and Motion Picture Rights**—Rights for use of material on the stage, on TV, or in the movies. Often a one-year option to buy such rights is offered (generally for 10 percent of the total price). The party interested in the rights then tries to sell the idea to other people—actors, directors, studios, or TV networks. Some properties are optioned numerous times, but most fail to become full productions. In those cases, the writer can sell the rights again and again.

Sometimes editors don't take the time to specify the rights they are buying. If you sense that an editor is interested in getting stories, but doesn't seem to know what his and the writer's responsibilities are, be wary. In such a case, you'll want to explain what rights you're offering (preferably one-time or first serial rights only) and that you expect additional payment for subsequent use of your work. The Copyright Law that went into effect January

Contracts and Contract Negotiation

For More Info

- **The Authors Guild** (www.authorsguild.org), 31 E. 32nd St., 7th Floor, New York NY 10016. (212)563-5904. Fax: (212)564-5363. E-mail: staff@authorsguild.org.
- **National Writers Union** (www.nwu.org), 113 University Place, 6th Floor, New York NY 10003. (212)254-0279. Fax: (212)254-0673. E-mail: nwu@wu.org.

Filing for Copyright

For More Info

To register your work with the U.S. Copyright Office, you need to complete the following steps.

1. **Fill out an application form** (Form TX), which is available by calling (202)707-9100 or downloading from www.copyright.gov/forms.
2. **Send the application form**, a nonreturnable copy of the work in question, and your application fee to:

   The Library of Congress
   U.S. Copyright Office
   Register of Copyrights
   101 Independence Ave. SE
   Washington DC 20559-6000

1, 1978, states writers are primarily selling one-time rights to their work unless they—and the publisher—agree otherwise in writing. Book rights are covered fully by contract between the writer and the book publisher.

SELLING SUBSIDIARY RIGHTS

The primary right in book publishing is the right to publish the book itself. All other rights (movie rights, audio rights, book club rights, etc.) are considered secondary, or subsidiary, to the right to print publication. In contract negotiations, authors and their agents traditionally try to avoid granting the publisher subsidiary rights they feel comfortable marketing themselves. Publishers, on the other hand, want to obtain as many of the subsidiary rights as they can.

Larger agencies have experience selling subsidiary rights, and many authors represented by such agents prefer to retain those rights and let their agents do the selling. On the other hand, book publishers have subsidiary rights departments whose sole job is to exploit the subsidiary rights the publisher was able to retain during the contract negotiation.

The marketing of electronic rights can be tricky. With the proliferation of electronic and multimedia formats, publishers, agents, and authors are going to great lengths to make sure contracts specify exactly which electronic rights are being conveyed (or retained). Compensation for these rights is a major source of conflict because many book publishers seek control of them, and many magazines routinely include electronic rights in the purchase of all rights, often with no additional payment.

COPYRIGHT

Copyright law exists to protect creators of original works. It is also designed to encourage the production of creative works by ensuring that artists and writers hold the rights by which they can profit from their hard work.

The moment you finish a piece of writing—or in fact, the second you begin to pen the manuscript—the law recognizes only you can decide how the work is used. Copyright protects your writing, recognizes you (its sole creator) as its owner, and grants you all the rights and benefits that accompany ownership. With very few exceptions, anything you write today will enjoy copyright protection for your lifetime, plus 70 years. Copyright protects "original works of authorship" that are fixed in a tangible form of expression. *Copyright law cannot protect titles, ideas, and facts.*

Some writers are under the mistaken impression that a registered copyright with the U.S. Copyright Office (www.copyright.gov) is necessary to protect their work, and that their work is not protected until they "receive" their copyright paperwork from the government. *This is not true.* You don't have to register your work with the U.S. Copyright Office for it to be protected. Registration for your work does, however, offer some additional protection (specifically, the possibility of recovering punitive damages in an infringement suit) as well as legal proof of the date of copyright.

Most magazines are registered with the U.S. Copyright Office as single collective entities themselves; that is, the works that make up the magazine are *not* copyrighted individually in the names of the authors. You'll need to register your article yourself if you wish to have the additional protection of copyright (your name, the year of first publication, and the copyright symbol ©) appended to any published version of your work. You may use the copyright symbol regardless of whether your work has been registered with the U.S. Copyright Office.

One thing you need to pay particular attention to is work-for-hire arrangements. If you sign a work-for-hire agreement, you are agreeing that your writing will be done as a work for hire, and you will not control the copyright of the completed work—the person or organization who hired you will be the copyright owner. These agreements and transfers of exclusive rights must appear in writing to be legal. In fact, it's a good idea to get every publishing agreement you negotiate in writing before the sale.

FINANCES AND TAXES

You will find that as your writing business expands, so will your need to keep track of writing-related expenses and incomes. Keeping a close eye on these details will prove very helpful when it comes time to report your income to the IRS. It will also help you pay as little tax as possible and keep you aware of the state of your freelance writing as a business. This means you need to set up a detailed tracking and organizing system to log all expenses and income. Without such a system, your writing as a business will eventually fold. If you dislike handling finance-related tasks, you can always hire a professional to oversee these duties for you. However, even if you do hire a professional, you still need to keep all original records.

The following tips will help you keep track of the finance-related tasks associated with your freelance business.

- Keep accurate records.
- Separate your writing income and expenses from your personal income and expenses.
- Maintain a separate bank account and credit card for business-related expenses.
- Record every transaction (expenses and earnings) related to your writing.
- Begin keeping records when you make your first writing-related purchase.
- Establish a working, detailed system of tracking expenses and income. Include the date; the source of income (or the vendor of your purchase); a description of what was sold or bought; how the payment was rendered (cash, check, credit card); and the amount of the transaction.
- Keep all check stubs and receipts (cash purchases and credit cards).
- Set up a record-keeping system, such as a file folder system, to store all receipts.

Tax Information

Important

- While we cannot offer you tax advice or interpretations, we can suggest several sources for the most current information.
- Check the IRS website (www.irs.gov)..
- Call your local IRS office.
- Obtain basic IRS publications by phone or by mail; most are available at libraries and some post offices.

BEYOND THE BASICS

Launching Your Freelance Business

by I.J. Schecter

Starting something from scratch takes guts, faith and a healthy dose of stubborn optimism. Some would argue that deciding to launch a freelance writing practice requires a touch of masochism, too. But let's look at this rationally. First, you aren't starting from scratch; you're starting with talent, knowledge, skill, connections, and, probably, the moral support of a good number of people. Second, starting a writing business is no more or less difficult than starting any other type of business, whether a bakery, real estate brokerage or piano-tuning service. Third, you're peddling an extremely valuable product. Most businesses figure out pretty fast that if they don't know how to communicate, they're going to have a hard time winning customers. And in today's world of short attention spans and stimulus overload, the ability to communicate succinctly and powerfully is more valuable than ever.

PRE-WORK

Before putting your name out there, there are a few things you need to take care of. At the top of the list is getting business cards and letterhead printed. When you do start to tell people about your practice, the last thing you want is to be stuck without a card to hand over. And after you do offer it, hopefully prompting a discussion about your potential client's needs, you'll want to send a follow-up letter immediately—but on your own stationery, not some generic one. From the moment you decide to freelance professionally, you must think of yourself as a brand. Most writers feel hesitant about marketing themselves in any specific way because they don't want to cut off other opportunities. But when you're starting out, establishing a firm brand perception—that is, a clear statement about what you do and why it's valuable—is more important than appearing able do it all. Demonstrate expertise in a few specific areas, and others will inevitably find their way into your lap.

SELLING YOURSELF

Almost all writers share an aversion to self-selling—but it's mostly a function of unfair conditioning. That is, they assume they hate marketing themselves before they even try because other writers have convinced them one can't be a good writer and a good salesman at the same time.

The truth is plenty of good writers are natural salesmen, too, but they feel the superficial selling part undermines the authentic writing part. Take a moment to think about it and you'll

---

I.J. SCHECTER (www.ijschecter.com) is an award-winning writer, interviewer and essayist based in Toronto. His bestselling collection, *Slices: Observations from the Wrong Side of the Fairway* (John Wiley & Sons), is available in bookstores and online.

realize all businesspeople have to market themselves just like writers do. A restaurateur needs to do more than just open his doors to generate traffic. An investment broker must go beyond merely getting a license if he hopes to succeed. A psychologist wanting to build a practice ought to take a few steps in addition to simply hanging a shingle. And a writer needs to do more than just write. "This job is about sales as much as it is about writing," says Toronto-based freelancer Ian Harvey. "One of the simple rules guiding my practice is this: Hustle, hustle, hustle."

So how does a writer generate buzz? There are several ways: letters, flyers, brochures, newsletters, blogs, samples, cold calls, and so on. When I launched my practice, the first thing I did (after getting business cards and letterhead printed, of course) was to send out hundreds of introductory letters—to those I knew, to those I didn't know, to people, to businesses . . . to just about everyone whose address I could get. I discriminated little in this initial blitz, though naturally with each letter I dropped into the mailbox I became even more nervous that all the money, time and effort I was expending might lead nowhere.

Then I received a phone call. One of my letters had gone to a high school acquaintance working at a company that manufactured and distributed musical compilations on CD. She had received my letter just as her boss was looking for a writer to help write snappy liner notes. Years later, this company remains one of my biggest corporate clients.

Another of my letters went to an old colleague. He had become the head of an executive degree program at a local university and was preparing to design the program brochure, for which a writer was sorely needed. I won the assignment, which led to another three.

The lesson? You truly never know where work is going to come from. More important, you can't count on finding yourself in the right place at the right time; you have to create the possibility of being there.

GROWING PAINS

There are two parts to selling yourself. First is developing the nerve to do it. Second is developing the right type of skin: rhino. "Rejections are part of the game," says Harvey, "but this is the only game in which rejection doesn't mean no. It means not now, or not for me, or not for me right now. It doesn't mean no forever." While it's fair to spend a little time—very little—getting annoyed or frustrated at rejection, it's best to take that annoyed or frustrated energy and pour it into something productive. Few businesses explode overnight; the ones that end up successful demand lots of grunt work up front, reach a minimum threshold after a few years, and then begin to grow in earnest.

It's imperative you commit to the up-front part. "Most businesses fail because the proprietors underestimate the amount of work required to get the business off the ground and overestimate the revenue in the first year or two," says Paul Lima, a professional writer for over 25 years and author of *The Six-Figure Freelancer*. Adds Vancouver-based freelancer Teresa Murphy, author of more than 1,000 magazine articles, "You need the ability to work

Tax Tip

Sure, self-employment doesn't come with medical and dental, but it does offer plenty of opportunities for tax write-offs. Among the expenses you can potentially deduct are car, phone, restaurant meals, postage, magazine purchases, and, if you work from home, a portion of your monthly mortgage (or rent) and utilities. Have a chat with your accountant about this and hold onto your receipts so calculations are easy come tax season. You'll be glad you did.

Answering the Question

Friends familiar with your long-time desire to write may good-naturedly tease you about the risk of giving up your thankless but stable 9-to-5 grind to tackle something so daunting. Former colleagues may wonder aloud about your decision. Busybody aunts will gossip about how no one makes money writing and what a nice doctor or lawyer you would have made.

Change their perception by embracing and celebrating your decision rather than timidly defending it. When people ask, "So what are you doing now?" answer with pride and conviction. Don't say, "I thought I'd give freelancing a go and see how it works out," or "I'm going to try being a freelance writer, though I'm not really sure what that means."

Have your "elevator speech"—a business term for the 30-second spiel that describes what you do—always at the ready. When people ask me what I do, I respond, "I'm a freelance writer and communications consultant." If they want to know more, I tell them my practice is divided evenly between commercial writing, like magazine features, and corporate writing, which entails everything from marketing brochures to ghostwriting business books. Suddenly they're intrigued. They see writing as a real, viable, honest-to-goodness business—not because I've dropped figures but because I've spoken about it in a clear, confident manner.

Let's stop apologizing for being writers. I love being one, and I bet you do, too. Tell anyone who asks.

15 hours a day and love it, day in and day out. That means holidays, summer weekends and all-nighters when clients have rush projects. I've worked Boxing Day, New Year's Eve, Easter Sunday until midnight."

Of course, if you've decided to take the plunge in the first place, no doubt you've got this much passion and then some, because, like these professionals, you've realized that, despite the challenges of the writing life, nothing in the world makes you feel happier or more fulfilled.

GAINING, AND SUSTAINING, MOMENTUM

Investing the time and energy at the outset will lead to a point of critical mass—that first small group of people interested in your work, the first pebble in your pond. This could include a magazine editor, the president of a company or a friend needing some editing help. To help that first small ripple expand outward, you need to embed two vital behavioral principles.

1. Overdelivery. Whether you're writing an article for your local newspaper, a marketing brochure for a multinational conglomerate or an essay for your best friend's medical school application, do the very best job you can. Your writing is judged every time you put pen to paper or fingers to keys. Force yourself to knock the ball out of the park at every opportunity and you'll develop the kind of reputation that leads to positive word of mouth, constant repeat business and sparkling testimonials.

2. Professionalism. From editors to executives, just about everyone is stretched thin these days—and that's why being known as someone easy to work with can distinguish you from other writers who also deliver solid work. Acting like a professional means a number of things. Dressing a certain way. Acting a certain way. Hitting deadlines. Returning calls and e-mails promptly.

It also means not ever being petty, spiteful or antagonistic. Following the publication of my first short story collection, I lucked into a chance to set up a small table at a prominent outdoor literary festival. Beside me was the editor of an esteemed literary journal—along with her large dog, in a cage a few feet behind us. The dog began barking his head off just as people starting checking out the book tables, and he didn't stop for an hour, scaring off just about anyone who wandered anywhere near me and my book. The woman did nothing. I didn't just want to offer her a few choice words; I wanted to write her a scathing letter several pages long. Friends and family urged me to resist, and, though it was hard, I did. A few years later, when I sent this editor a story for consideration in her journal, she accepted it (though she had no recollection of me from the festival), creating a writing credit that remains one of my most important. The moral? In this business just like any other, people, and circumstances, will irk you—but in almost every case it behooves you to take the high road. Reacting emotionally can only harm you; staying cool can only benefit you.

THE NUMBERS GAME

Writing is dynamic and fluid; it can be endlessly revised, massaged, tweaked, twisted and reversed back over itself. For this reason, it's essential that you get every one of your assignments in writing (no pun intended; OK, slightly intended). Commercial assignments will usually come with a contract; corporate assignments almost never will. To address this, prepare two versions of your own standard agreement. For commercial gigs, this document should include a brief description of the assignment, word count, pay rate, and deadline, along with all the other legal bits you can find by looking up any typical freelance contract. For corporate assignments, it should include a more detailed description of the project (including each piece of work if there are multiple parts), the agreed timeline, the fee (either an overall flat rate or an hourly rate), and, crucially, a definition of completion. For example, in my standard corporate agreement, I have a clause indicating that, for the agreed-upon fee, I will deliver the described work by the noted deadline and then allow two rounds of requested revisions or suggestions from the client, after which I will start charging extra. This creates clear mutual expectations between the client and me and helps avoid awkward conversations toward the end of the project when the senior partner tries to add an arbitrary comma for the third time.

For corporate work, you'll also have to develop the skill of estimating. It's one thing to name an hourly rate when a potential client first asks; it's another to try to come up with a total number of hours based on his incredibly vague description of the assignment. But come up with one you must—only to be met with, in some cases, a response gently questioning why the work ought to take so long. Here we have a quandary: By and large, people vastly underestimate how long good writing actually takes. I've found the best way to deal with this is to be truthful. I tell my clients up front that writing and communications work tends to take quite a bit longer than non-writers imagine, and that, in fact, most projects end up taking 20 percent more hours than I initially estimate because the client themselves didn't realize going in how much would be involved. As long as I deliver good work, this ceases to be an issue.

How much or how little should you charge for your work? It depends—based on your experience, where you live, and a host of other factors. (See page 67 for a range of rates for different types of writing projects.) Make sure, before you enter any negotiation, that you've decided upon the lowest figure you're willing to accept. Or, as freelancer Colette van Haaren puts it, "You need three things in this business: a good nose to sniff out stories, a thick skin for when rejection hits, and a backbone for when you have to negotiate."

SURE I'M WORKING HARD. IN MY HEAD

Only about half my time is spent actually working on assignments. The other half is spent crafting queries, doing research, maintaining correspondence, or, to be honest, just brainstorming. My favorite part of being a writer is that I can work anywhere, since so much of the work is done between my ears. Often someone will ask me a question, and, when I don't answer, my wife will murmur to him or her, "Oh, he's just working." And she's right.

I also believe, however, that the luxury of being able to do mental work represents an important responsibility. During spells when my plate isn't full with deadlines, I don't rest on my laurels. Instead, I record ideas, I query like crazy, I read other writers, I think about

Where Is Your Stapler?

Many writers and other artists claim that their extreme lack of organization is simply an occupational hazard. Others practically boast about it, claiming it as a distinct imprint of creativity. Whether or not creative types are naturally disinclined toward self-organization, the sooner you decide to get organized and stay organized, the more successful you and your practice will become. Why? Two reasons, one physical, the other mental.

Physically speaking, when your work environment is organized, you spend more time writing and less time trying to locate the calculator or paper clips or this file or that folder. Simple odds dictate that using your time more productively will lead to more work.

The mental aspect is just as important. We all know how aggravating it is having to scramble to find that copy of the current contract for that magazine when we've forgotten what the word count was, or trying desperately to remember where we put the CD with the backup copy of that article after the electrical storm has wiped out our operating system with the deadline looming.

It stands to reason that the less energy you need to put into non-writing activities, the more energy you can direct toward your actual work, improving its overall quality and thereby making you a more desirable commodity. Sure, a little anxiety can be healthy for writing, but it should be anxiety borne of the drive to produce stellar work, not anxiety based on wondering where the stamps got to for the umpteenth time.

Organizing yourself is probably a lot easier than you imagine, and you might even be surprised at how good a little structure makes you feel.

Start small: Buy a box of multicolored file folders, some labels, some CDs or a memory stick, and several upright magazine files. Label one of the magazine files Contracts, then place in it different file folders labeled with the subject area for a given contract. For me, these folders include, among others, Bridal, Fitness, Golf, Men's, Gardening, and, of course, Writing and Publishing.

Label another of the magazine files **Current Assignments** and a third **Story Ideas**, and populate them as you did the first. Use consistent colors for specific topics—in other words, gardening always gets a yellow file folder whether it's in the **Story Ideas** or the **Contracts** file. This will make for easy cross-referencing.

And that's just a start. Odds are this small bit of organization will spur you, and soon you'll be creating files for every aspect of your work—character sketches, source notes, dialogue snippets, conferences and retreats, news items.

"Organization is everything," says freelancer Heather Cook, author of Rookie Reiner: Surviving and Thriving in the Show Pen (Trafalgar Square Books). "From maintaining accurate records for tax purposes to structuring a weekly plan to include marketing and administrative tasks, it allows me to stay focused and efficient—and that makes my overall work better."

new marketing angles. In short, given the nature of my profession, I have no excuse for down time. "If you don't care about your business, no one else will," says freelancer Sharon Aschaiek. "Use slow times to indirectly generate more work—develop new pitches, follow up with previous editors and clients, explore new marketing avenues. Even use the time to take care of accounting and administrative issues. Just don't let yourself get complacent."

THE BOTTOM LINE

Is freelancing hard work? Sure—damned hard. But it's no harder than any other profession. Like every job, it requires a combination of skill, thoroughness and dependability. The difference is you don't have anyone defining the parameters of the job for you or providing incentives to succeed. The discipline and drive have to come solely from you. Or, in the words of full-time freelancer and book author Lisa Bendall, "All the talent in the world won't help if you aren't willing to put in the time at your desk and actually work. You've got to crack your own whip."

Now get cracking!

BEYOND THE BASICS

How Much Should I Charge?

by Lynn Wasnak

If you're a beginning freelance writer, or don't know many other freelancers, you may wonder how anyone manages to earn enough to eat and pay the rent by writing or performing a mix of writing-related tasks. Yet, smart full-time freelance writers and editors annually gross $35,000 and up—sometimes up into the $150,000-200,000 range. These top-earning freelancers rarely have names known to the general public. (Celebrity writers earn fees far beyond the rates cited in this survey.) But, year after year, they sustain themselves and their families on a freelance income, while maintaining control of their hours and their lives.

Such freelancers take writing and editing seriously—it's their business.

Periodically, they sit down and think about the earning potential of their work, and how they can make freelancing more profitable and fun. They know their numbers: what it costs to run their business; what hourly rate they require; how long a job will take. Unless there's a real bonus (a special clip, or a chance to try something new) these writers turn down work that doesn't meet the mark and replace it with a better-paying project.

If you don't know your numbers, take a few minutes to figure them out. Begin by choosing your target annual income—whether it's $25,000 or $100,000. Add in fixed expenses: social security, taxes, and office supplies. Don't forget health insurance and something for your retirement. Once you've determined your annual gross target, divide it by 1,000 billable hours—about 21 hours per week—to determine your target hourly rate.

Remember—this rate is flexible. You can continue doing low-paying work you love as long as you make up for the loss with more lucrative jobs. But you must monitor your rate of earning if you want to reach your goal. If you slip, remind yourself you're in charge. As a freelancer, you can raise prices, chase better-paying jobs, work extra hours, or adjust your spending."

"Sounds great," you may say. "But how do I come up with 1,000 billable hours each year? I'm lucky to find a writing-related job every month or two, and these pay a pittance."

That's where business attitude comes in: network, track your time, join professional organizations, and study the markets. Learn how to query, then query like mad. Take chances by reaching for the next level. Learn to negotiate for a fee you can live on—your plumber does! Then get it in writing.

You'll be surprised how far you can go, and how much you can earn, if you believe in your skills and act on your belief. The rates that follow are a guide to steer you in the right direction.

This report is based on input from sales finalized in 2009 and 2010 only. The data is generated from voluntary surveys completed by members of numerous professional writers' and editors' organizations and specialty groups. We thank these responding groups, listed on page 991, and their members for generously sharing information. If you would like to contribute your input, e-mail lwasnak@fuse.net for a survey.

LYNN WASNAK (www.lynnwasnak.com) was directed to the market for her first paid piece of deathless prose ("Fossils in Your Driveway" published by *Journeys* in 1968 for $4) by *Writer's Market*. In the 40 years since, she's made her living as a freelancer and has never looked back.

Beyond the Basics

	PER HOUR			PER PROJECT			OTHER		
	HIGH	LOW	AVG	HIGH	LOW	AVG	HIGH	LOW	AVG
Advertising & Public Relations									
Advertising copywriting	$150	$35	$83	$9,000	$150	$2,752 $400/day	$3/word	25¢/word	$1.56/word
Advertising editing	$125	$20	$64	n/a	n/a	n/a	$1/word	25¢/word	65¢/word
Advertorials	$180	$50	$92	$1,875	$200	$479	$3/word	75¢/word	$1.57/word
Business public relations	$180	$30	$84	n/a	n/a	n/a	$500/day	$200/day	$356/day
Campaign development or product launch	$150	$35	$95	$8,750	$1,500	$4,540	n/a	n/a	n/a
Catalog copywriting	$150	$25	$71	n/a	n/a	n/a	$350/item	$25/item	$116/item
Corporate spokesperson role	$180	$70	$107	n/a	n/a	n/a	$1,200/day	$500/day	$740/day
Direct-mail copywriting	$150	$35	$84	$8,248	$500	$2,839	$4/word $400/page	$1/word $200/page	$2.17/word $314/page
Event promotions/publicity	$125	$30	$75	n/a	n/a	n/a	n/a	n/a	$500/day
Press kits	$180	$30	$82	n/a	n/a	n/a	$2/word	50¢/word	$1.27/word
Press/news release	$180	$30	$78	$1,500	$125	$700	$2/word $750/page	40¢/word $150/page	$1.17/word $348/page
Radio Commercials	$99	$30	$72	n/a	n/a	n/a	$850/60sec	$120/60sec	$456/60sec
Speech writing/editing for individuals or corporations	$167	$35	$90	$10,000	$2,700	$5,036	$350/minute	$100/minute	$204/minute
Book Publishing									
Abstracting and abridging	$125	$30	$74	n/a	n/a	n/a	$2/word	$1/word	$1.48/word
Anthology editing	$80	$23	$51	$7,900	$1,200	$4,588	n/a	n/a	n/a
Book chapter	$100	$35	$60	$2,500	$1,200	$1,758	20¢/word	8¢/word	14¢/word
Book production for clients	$100	$40	$67	n/a	n/a	n/a	$17.50/page	$5/page	$10/page
Book proposal consultation	$125	$25	$66	$1,500	$250	$788	n/a	n/a	n/a
Book proposal writing	$125	$30	$80	$12,000	$500	$4,872	n/a	n/a	n/a

	PER HOUR			PER PROJECT			OTHER		
	HIGH	LOW	AVG	HIGH	LOW	AVG	HIGH	LOW	AVG
Advertising & Public Relations									
Advertising copywriting	$150	$35	$83	$9,000	$150	$2,752 $400/day	$3/word	25¢/word	$1.56/word
Advertising editing	$125	$20	$64	n/a	n/a	n/a	$1/word	25¢/word	65¢/word
Advertorials	$180	$50	$92	$1,875	$200	$479	$3/word	75¢/word	$1.57/word
Business public relations	$180	$30	$84	n/a	n/a	n/a	$500/day	$200/day	$356/day
Campaign development or product launch	$150	$35	$95	$8,750	$1,500	$4,540	n/a	n/a	n/a
Catalog copywriting	$150	$25	$71	n/a	n/a	n/a	$350/item	$25/item	$116/item
Corporate spokesperson role	$180	$70	$107	n/a	n/a	n/a	$1,200/day	$500/day	$740/day
Direct-mail copywriting	$150	$35	$84	$8,248	$500	$2,839	$4/word $400/page	$1/word $200/page	$2.17/word $314/page
Event promotions/publicity	$125	$30	$75	n/a	n/a	n/a	n/a	n/a	$500/day
Press kits	$180	$30	$82	n/a	n/a	n/a	$2/word	50¢/word	$1.27/word
Press/news release	$180	$30	$78	$1,500	$125	$700	$2/word $750/page	40¢/word $150/page	$1.17/word $348/page
Radio Commercials	$99	$30	$72	n/a	n/a	n/a	$850/60sec	$120/60sec	$456/60sec
Speech writing/editing for individuals or corporations	$167	$35	$90	$10,000	$2,700	$5,036	$350/minute	$100/minute	$204/minute
Book Publishing									
Abstracting and abridging	$125	$30	$74	n/a	n/a	n/a	$2/word	$1/word	$1.48/word
Anthology editing	$80	$23	$51	$7,900	$1,200	$4,588	n/a	n/a	n/a
Book chapter	$100	$35	$60	$2,500	$1,200	$1,758	20¢/word	8¢/word	14¢/word
Book production for clients	$100	$40	$67	n/a	n/a	n/a	$17.50/page	$5/page	$10/page
Book proposal consultation	$125	$25	$66	$1,500	$250	$788	n/a	n/a	n/a

Beyond the Basics

	PER HOUR			PER PROJECT			OTHER		
	HIGH	LOW	AVG	HIGH	LOW	AVG	HIGH	LOW	AVG
Book publicity for clients	n/a	n/a	n/a	$10,000	$500	$2,000	n/a	n/a	n/a
Book query critique	$100	$50	$72	$500	$75	$202	n/a	n/a	n/a
Children's book writing [1]	$75	$35	$50	n/a	n/a	n/a	$5/word $5,000/adv	$1/word $450/adv	$2.75/word $2,286/adv
Content editing (scholarly/textbook)	$125	$20	$51	$15,000	$500	$4,477	$20/page	$3/page	$6.89/page
Content editing (trade)	$125	$19	$54	$20,000	$1,000	$6,538	$20/page	$3.75/page	$8/page
Copyediting (trade)	$100	$16	$46	$5,500	$2,000	$3,667	$6/page	$1/page	$4.22/page
Encyclopedia articles	n/a	n/a	n/a	n/a	n/a	n/a	50¢/word $3,000/item	15¢/word $50/item	35¢/word $933/item
Fiction book writing (own)	n/a	n/a	n/a	n/a	n/a	n/a	$40,000/adv	$525/adv	$14,193/adv
Ghostwriting, as told to	$125	$35	$67	$47,000	$5,500	$22,892	$100/page	$50/page	$87/page
Ghostwriting, no credit	$125	$30	$73	n/a	n/a	n/a	$3/word $500/page $100,000/adv	50¢/word $50/page $5,000/adv	$1.79/word $206/page $28,580/adv
Guidebook writing/editing	n/a	n/a	n/a	n/a	n/a	n/a	$14,000/adv	$10,000/adv	$12,000/adv
Indexing	$60	$22	$35	n/a	n/a	n/a	$12/page	$2/page	$4.72/page
Manuscript evaluation and critique	$100	$23	$66	$2,000	$150	$663	n/a	n/a	n/a
Manuscript typing	n/a	n/a	$20	n/a	n/a	n/a	$3/page	95¢/page	$1.67/page
Movie novelizations	n/a	n/a	n/a	$15,000	$5,000	$9,159	n/a	n/a	n/a
Nonfiction book writing (collaborative)	$125	$40	$80	n/a	n/a	n/a	$110/page $75,000/adv	$50/page $1,300/adv	$80/page $22,684/adv $600/day
Nonfiction book writing (own)	$125	$40	$72	n/a	n/a	n/a	$110/page $50,000/adv	$50/page $1,300/adv	$80/page $14,057
Novel synopsis (general)	$60	$30	$45	$450	$150	$292	$100/page	$10/page	$37/page
Personal history writing/editing (for clients)	$125	$30	$60	$40,000	$750	$15,038	n/a	n/a	n/a

[1] Adv=advance.

	PER HOUR			PER PROJECT			OTHER		
	HIGH	LOW	AVG	HIGH	LOW	AVG	HIGH	LOW	AVG
Proofreading	$75	$15	$31	n/a	n/a	n/a	$5/page	$2/page	$3.26/page
Research for writers or book publishers	$150	$15	$52	n/a	n/a	n/a	$600/day	$450/day	$525/day
Rewriting/structural editing	$120	$25	$67	$50,000	$2,500	$13,929	15¢/word	6¢/word	11¢/word
Translation – literary	n/a	n/a	n/a	$10,000	$7,000	$8,500	20¢/target word	6¢/target word	11¢/target word
Translation –nonfiction/technical	n/a	n/a	n/a	n/a	n/a	n/a	35¢/target word	8¢/target word	16¢/target word
Business									
Annual reports	$180	$45	$92	$15,000	$500	$5,708	$600	$100	$349
Brochures, booklets, flyers	$150	$30	$81	$15,000	$300	$4,215	$2.50/word $800/page	35¢/word $50/page	$1.21/word $341/page
Business editing (general)	$150	$25	$70	n/a	n/a	n/a	n/a	n/a	n/a
Business letters	$150	$30	$74	n/a	n/a	n/a	$2/word	$1/word	$1.47/word
Business plan	$150	$30	$82	$15,000	$200	$4,100	n/a	n/a	$1/word
Business writing seminars	$200	$60	$107	$8,600	$550	$2,919	n/a	n/a	n/a
Consultation on communications	$180	$40	$95	n/a	n/a	n/a	$1,200/day	$500/day	$823/day
Copyediting for business	$125	$25	$60	n/a	n/a	n/a	$4/page	$2/page	$3/page
Corporate histories	$180	$35	$86	$160,000	$5,000	$54,500	$2/word	$1/word	$1.50/word $600/day
Corporate periodicals, editing	$125	$35	$69	n/a	n/a	n/a	$2.50/word	$75¢/word	$1.42/word
Corporate periodicals, writing	$135	$35	$78	n/a	n/a	$1,875	$3/word	$1/word	$1.71/word
Corporate profiles	$180	$35	$88	n/a	n/a	$3,000	$2/word	$1/word	$1.50/word
Ghostwriting for business execs	$150	$25	$84	$3,000	$500	$1,393	$2.50/word	50¢/word	$2/word
Grantwriting for businesses	$250	$35	$109	$3,000	$500	$1,756	n/a	n/a	n/a
Newsletters, desktop publishing/ production	$135	$35	$71	$6,600	$1,000	$3,480	$750/page	150/page	$429/page
Newsletters, editing	$125	$25	$67	n/a	n/a	$3,600	$230/page	$150/page	$185/page

	PER HOUR			PER PROJECT			OTHER		
	HIGH	LOW	AVG	HIGH	LOW	AVG	HIGH	LOW	AVG
Newsletters, writing[1]	$125	$25	$77	$6,600	$800	$3,567	$5/word $1,250/page	$1/word $150/page	$2.30/word $514/page
Translation services for business use	$75	$35	$52	n/a	n/a	n/a	$35/target word $1.40/target line $120/1000 words	6¢/target word $1/target line $90/1000 words	18¢/target word $1.20/target line $105/1000 words
Resume writing	$100	$60	$72	$500	$150	$287.20	n/a	n/a	n/a
Computer, Internet & Technical									
Blogging — paid	n/a	n/a	$100	$2,000	$500	$1,240	$500/post	$6/post	$49/post
E-mail copywriting	$125	$35	$85	n/a	n/a	$300	$2/word	30¢/word	91¢/word
Educational webinars	$500	$0[1]	$195	n/a	n/a	n/a	n/a	n/a	n/a
Hardware/Software help screen writing	$95	$60	$81	$6,000	$1,000	$4,000	n/a	n/a	n/a
Hardware/Software manual writing	$165	$30	$80	$23,500	$5,000	$11,500	n/a	n/a	n/a
Internet Research	$95	$25	$55	n/a	n/a	n/a	n/a	n/a	n/a
Keyword Descriptions	n/a	n/a	n/a	n/a	n/a	n/a	$200/page	$135/page	$165/page
Online videos for clients	$95	$60	$76	n/a	n/a	n/a	n/a	n/a	n/a
Social media postings for clients	$95	$30	$62	n/a	n/a	$500	n/a	n/a	$10/word
Technical editing	$150	$25	$65	n/a	n/a	n/a	n/a	n/a	n/a
Technical writing	$160	$30	$80	n/a	n/a	n/a	n/a	n/a	n/a
Web editing	$100	$25	$57	n/a	n/a	n/a	$10/page	$3/page	$5.67/page
Webpage design	$150	$35	$80	$4,000	$200	$1,278	n/a	n/a	n/a
Website or blog promotion	n/a	n/a	n/a	$650	$195	$335	n/a	n/a	n/a
Website reviews	n/a	n/a	n/a	$900	$50	$300	n/a	n/a	n/a
Website search engine optimization	$89	$60	$76	$50,000	$8,000	$12,000	n/a	n/a	n/a

[1] Sometimes offered free for promotion of services.

	PER HOUR			PER PROJECT			OTHER		
	HIGH	LOW	AVG	HIGH	LOW	AVG	HIGH	LOW	AVG
White Papers	$135	$25	$82	$10,000	$2,500	$4,927	n/a	n/a	n/a
Editorial/Design Packages									
Desktop publishing	$150	$25	$67	n/a	n/a	n/a	$750/page	$30/page	$202/page
Photo brochures	$125	$65	$87	$15,000	$400	$3,869	$65/picture	$35/picture	$48/picture
Photography	$100	$50	$71	$10,500	$50	$2,100	$2,500/day	$500/day	$1,340/day
Photo research	$75	$25	$49	n/a	n/a	n/a	n/a	n/a	n/a
Picture editing	$100	$40	$64	n/a	n/a	n/a	$65/picture	$35/picture	$53/picture
Educational & Literary Services									
Author appearances at national events	n/a n/a	n/a n/a	n/a n/a	n/a n/a	n/a n/a	n/a n/a	$500/hour $30,000/event	$100/hour $500/event	$285/hour $5,000/event
Author appearances at regional events	n/a	n/a	n/a	n/a	n/a	n/a	$1,500/event	$50/event	$615/event
Author appearances at local groups	$63	$40	$47	n/a	n/a	n/a	$400/event	$75/event	$219/event
Authors presenting in schools	$125	$25	$78	n/a	n/a	n/a	$350/class	$50/class	$183/class
Educational grant and proposal writing	$100	$35	$67	n/a	n/a	n/a	n/a	n/a	n/a
Manuscript evaluation for theses/ dissertations	$100	$15	$53	$1,550	$200	$783	n/a	n/a	n/a
Poetry manuscript critique	$100	$25	$62	n/a	n/a	n/a	n/a	n/a	n/a
Private writing instruction	$60	$50	$57	n/a	n/a	n/a	n/a	n/a	n/a
Readings by poets, fiction writers	n/a	n/a	n/a	n/a	n/a	n/a	$3,000/event	$50/event	$225/event
Short story manuscript critique	$150	$30	$75	$175	$50	$112	n/a	n/a	n/a
Teaching adult writing classes	$125	$35	$82	n/a	n/a	n/a	$800/class $550/day $5,000/course	$150/class $150/day $500/course	$450/class $356/day $2,667/course

1 Per project figures based on four-page newsletters.

Beyond the Basics

	PER HOUR			PER PROJECT			OTHER		
	HIGH	LOW	AVG	HIGH	LOW	AVG	HIGH	LOW	AVG
Writer's workshop panel or class	$220	$30	$92	n/a	n/a	n/a	$5,000/day	$60/day	$1,186/day
Writing for scholarly journals	$100	$40	$63	$450	$100	$285	n/a	n/a	n/a
Film, Video, TV, Radio, Stage									
Book/novel summaries for film producers	n/a	n/a	n/a	n/a	n/a	n/a	$34/page	$15/page	$23/page $120/book
Business film/video scriptwriting	$150	$50	$97	n/a	n/a	$600	$1,000/run min	$50/run min	$334/run min $500/day
Comedy writing for entertainers	n/a	n/a	n/a	n/a	n/a	n/a	$150/joke $500/group	$5/joke $100/group	$50/joke $283/group
Copyediting audiovisuals	$90	$22	$53	n/a	n/a	n/a	n/a	n/a	n/a
Educational or training film/video scriptwriting	$125	$35	$81	n/a	n/a	n/a	$500/run min	$100/run min	$245/run min
Feature film options [1]	First 18 months, 10% WGA minimum; 10% minimum each 18 month period thereafter.								
TV options [1]	First 180 days, 5% WGA minimum; 10% minimum each 180 day period thereafter.								
Industrial product film/video scriptwriting	$150	$30	$99	n/a	n/a	n/a	$500/run min	$100/run min	$300/run min
Playwriting for the stage	5-10% box office/Broadway, 6%-7% box office/off-Broadway, 10% box office/regional theatre								
Radio documentaries	$1,500	$100	$508	n/a	n/a	n/a	n/a	n/a	n/a
Radio editorials	$70	$50	$60	n/a	n/a	n/a	$200/run min $400/day	$45/run min $250/day	$124/run min $325/day
Radio interviews	n/a	n/a	n/a	$1,500	$150	$683	n/a	n/a	n/a
Screenwriting (original screenplay-incl treatment)[1]	n/a	n/a	n/a	n/a	n/a	n/a	$117,602	$62,642	$90,122
Script synopsis for agent or film [1]	$2,344/30 min, $4,441/60 min, $6,564/90 min								
Script synopsis for business	$75	$45	$62	n/a	n/a	n/a	n/a	n/a	n/a

[1] WGA minimums—contract terms through 5/1/11.

	PER HOUR			PER PROJECT			OTHER		
	HIGH	LOW	AVG	HIGH	LOW	AVG	HIGH	LOW	AVG
TV commercials	$99	$60	$81	n/a	n/a	n/a	$2,500/30 sec	$150/30 sec	$1,204/30 sec
TV news story/feature [1]	$1,455/5 min, $2,903/10 min, $4,105/15 min								
TV scripts (non-theatrical) [1]	Prime Time: $33,681/60 min, $47,388/90 min; Not Prime Time: $12,857/30 min, $23,370/60 min, $35,122/90 min								
TV scripts (Teleplay/MOW) [1]	$68,150/120 min								
Magazines & Trade Journals									
Article manuscript critique	$125	$25	$64	n/a	n/a	n/a	n/a	n/a	n/a
Arts query critique	$100	$50	$75	n/a	n/a	n/a	n/a	n/a	n/a
Arts reviewing	$95	$60	$79	$325	$100	$194	$1.20/word	8¢/word	58¢/word
Book reviews	n/a	n/a	n/a	$900	$25	$338	$1.50/word	15¢/word	68¢/word
City magazine calendar	n/a	n/a	n/a	$250	$50	$140	$1/word	30¢/word	70¢/word
Comic book/strip writing	$200 original story, $500 existing story, $35 short script.								
Consultation on magazine editorial	$150	$30	$81	n/a	n/a	n/a	n/a	n/a	$100/page
Consumer magazine column	n/a	n/a	n/a	$2,500	$75	$898	$2.50/word	37¢/word	$1.13/word
Consumer front-of-book	n/a	n/a	n/a	$850	$350	$600	n/a	n/a	n/a
Content editing	$125	$25	$57	$6,500	$2,000	$3,819	15¢/word	6¢/word	11¢/word
Contributing editor	n/a	n/a	n/a	n/a	n/a	n/a	$156,000/ contract	$20,000/ contract	$51,000 contract
Copyediting magazines	$100	$18	$50	n/a	n/a	n/a	$10/page	$2.90/page	$5.68/page
Fact checking	$125	$15	$46	n/a	n/a	n/a	n/a	n/a	n/a
Gag writing for cartoonists	$35/gag; 25% sale on spec.								
Ghostwriting articles (general)	$200	$30	$102	$3,500	$1,100	$2,229	$10/word	60¢/word	$2.25/word
Magazine research	$100	$15	$47	n/a	n/a	n/a	$500/item	$100/item	$200/item
Proofreading	$75	$15	$35	n/a	n/a	n/a	n/a	n/a	n/a

[1] WGA minimums—contract terms through 5/1/11.

	PER HOUR			PER PROJECT			OTHER		
	HIGH	LOW	AVG	HIGH	LOW	AVG	HIGH	LOW	AVG
Reprint fees	n/a	n/a	n/a	$1,500	$20	$461	$1.50/word	10¢/word	73¢/word
Rewriting	$125	$20	$68	n/a	n/a	n/a	n/a	n/a	$50/page
Trade journal feature article	$122	$40	$80	$4,950	$150	$1,412	$3/word	20¢/word	$1.16/word
Transcribing interviews	$180	$90	$50	n/a	n/a	n/a	$3/min	$1/min	$2/min
Medical/Science									
Medical/scientific conference coverage	$125	$50	$85	n/a	n/a	n/a	$800/day	$300/day	$600/day
Medical/scientific editing	$125	$21	$73	n/a	n/a	n/a	$12.50/page $600/day	$3/page $500/day	$4.40/page $550/day
Medical/scientific writing	$250	$30	$95	$5,000	$1,000	$3,354	$2/word	25¢/word	$1.12/word
Medical/scientific multimedia presentations	$100	$50	$75	n/a	n/a	n/a	$100/slide	$50/slide	$77/slide
Medical/scientific proofreading	$125	$18	$64	n/a	n/a	$500	$3/page	$2.50/page	$2.75/page
Pharmaceutical writing	$125	$90	$105	n/a	n/a	n/a	n/a	n/a	n/a
Newspapers[1]									
Arts reviewing	$69	$30	$53	$200	$15	$101	60¢/word	6¢/word	36¢/word
Book reviews	$69	$45	$58	$350	$15	$140	60¢/word	25¢/word	44¢/word
Column, local	n/a	n/a	n/a	$600	$25	$206	$1/word	38¢/word	65¢/word
Column, self-syndicated	n/a	n/a	n/a	n/a	n/a	n/a	$35/insertion	$4/insertion	$16/insertion
Copyediting	$35	$15	$27	n/a	n/a	n/a	n/a	n/a	n/a
Editing/manuscript evaluation	$75	$25	$35	n/a	n/a	n/a	n/a	n/a	n/a
Feature writing	$79	$40	$63	$1,040	$85	$478	$1.60/word	10¢/word	59¢/word
Investigative reporting	n/a	n/a	n/a	n/a	n/a	n/a	$10,000/grant	$250/grant	$2,250/grant

1 Please note LC for large circulation urban newspapers; SC for small city, or small circ; ALT for alternative pubs, ONL for Online Only.)

	PER HOUR			PER PROJECT			OTHER		
	HIGH	LOW	AVG	HIGH	LOW	AVG	HIGH	LOW	AVG
Obituary copy	n/a	n/a	n/a	$225	$35	$124	n/a	n/a	n/a
Proofreading	$45	$15	$23	n/a	n/a	n/a	n/a	n/a	n/a
Stringing	n/a	n/a	n/a	$2,400	$40	$525	n/a	n/a	n/a
Nonprofit									
Grantwriting for nonprofits	$150	$19	$70	$3,000	$500	$1,852	n/a	n/a	n/a
Nonprofit annual reports	$100	$30	$64	n/a	n/a	n/a	n/a	n/a	n/a
Nonprofit writing	$150	$20	$77	$17,600	$200	$4,706	n/a	n/a	n/a
Nonprofit editing	$125	$25	$54	n/a	n/a	n/a	n/a	n/a	n/a
Nonprofit fundraising literature	$110	$35	$74	$3,500	$300	$1,597	$1,000	$500/day	$767/day $1/word
Nonprofit presentations	$100	$50	$73	n/a	n/a	n/a	n/a	n/a	n/a
Nonprofit public relations	$100	$20	$60	n/a	n/a	n/a	n/a	n/a	n/a
Politics/Government									
Government agency writing/editing	$100	$20	$57	n/a	n/a	n/a	$1.25/word	25¢/word	76¢/word
Government grant writing/editing	$150	$19	$68	n/a	n/a	n/a	n/a	n/a	n/a
Government sponsored research	$100	$35	$66	n/a	n/a	n/a	n/a	n/a	$600/day
Public relations for political campaigns	$150	$40	$86	n/a	n/a	n/a	n/a	n/a	n/a
Speechwriting for government officials	$200	$30	$96	$4,500	$1,000	$2,750	$200/run min	$110/run min	$155/run min
Speechwriting for political campaigns	$150	$60	$101	n/a	n/a	n/a	$200/run min	$100/run min	$162/run min

BEYOND THE BASICS

Build a Platform

Or You'll Miss the Train

by Jeff Yeager

"Jeff, you're a wonderful writer!"

Coming from the seasoned New York literary agent, I just wanted those words to hang there, in suspended celebration, while we enjoyed a leisurely lunch at the trendy Manhattan eatery she'd chosen for our meeting. Even though I'm not a dessert fan, I started thinking that maybe I'd stick around after all for some crème brûlée and an espresso or two.

"But the fact is," she continued, "there are lots of wonderful writers—and even lots of truly great writers—who never get a book published." Darn it, so much for basking in the moment. I hadn't even started my salad. Check please!

"The thing that interests me about you, and frankly the reason I agreed to meet with you today, is your platform. I know you're just starting out, but I think publishers will be impressed with the exposure you're already getting and what that means for your platform going forward." I thoughtfully crunched on a crouton from my salad, hoping to suggest that I was contemplating the wisdom of the agent's words. But I'm too honest to be a good bluffer.

"That's fantastic!" I said, enthusiastically spraying the woman I hoped would be my future agent in a shower of soggy crouton crumbs.

"Look," I continued, trying to divert my gaze from what appeared to be an entire crushed baggett clinging to the front of the poor agent's Ann Taylor dress suit. "I really hope you'll agree to represent me, and I want you to know that I always believe in being honest. So I have to confess: I have absolutely no idea what a *platform* is ... although I'm delighted that you think I have such a good one."

WHAT THE HECK IS A PLATFORM?

With that awkward self-confessional a few short years ago, I began my journey—and more importantly my education—into the über competitive, promotion-driven world of book publishing.

Simply put, a platform is a writer's capacity to help promote and market his own work to potential readers. It's a writer's ability to attract a fan base of his own, outside of the promotional efforts of his publisher. It's a writer's ability to get his message out to the world.

Ideally a platform has more than just one plank. For example, it's more than just a strong website or a weekly column in your local newspaper, although either of those planks would be a terrific start. It's a combination of assets, skills, expertise, activities, and professional

---

JEFF YEAGER is the author of *The Ultimate Cheapskate's Road Map to True Riches* (Broadway).

connections that both strengthen each other and enhance the writer's chances for commercial success

In my case I was lucky enough to inadvertently receive some national television exposure early in my writing career (see 2008 *Writer's Market* Freelance Success Stories), which I then opportunistically parlayed into more press exposure and a growing network of media contacts. By the time I went looking for a literary agent to represent me in a book deal, I'd only had a few articles published and most of those were online. And while the media visibility I'd received prior to that point was not inconsequential, it wasn't nearly enough to carry a book.

But it was a start, and it proved to an agent—and then to a publisher—that I had the wherewithal to build a viable platform; that I was a horse worth betting on. That was two book deals ago, and my platform has since grown to include professional speaking and television reporting gigs, as well as blogging on a number of high traffic websites and authoring articles for a range of national publications.

At first blush my story might seem plucky to the point of being irrelevant to the careers of most writers. After all, how many newbie writers make their media debut on NBC's *Today* show, as I did? But what I've come to appreciate about platform building is this: Even with luck, you need persistence and promotional savvy, and—even without luck—persistence and promotional savvy is probably all you need.

It's also true what they say about making your own luck. Or, as quote-meister H. Jackson Brown, Jr. puts it, "Opportunity dances with those already on the dance floor." The key to building a successful promotional platform is to make sure you're always out there on the dance floor, shakin' what you got.

PRIORITIES AND GETTING STARTED

Given the laundry list of possible tactics for developing a platform (see sidebar), you need to set priorities in order to use your time and resources effectively, while at the same time remaining flexible enough to quickly act on unanticipated opportunities as they come your way. After all, you never know who's going to ask you to dance once you're out there on the floor.

Logically, the first step is to identify the target audience(s) for your writing. The more focused you can be in defining your audience, the more effective you'll be in reaching out to them. For example, if you're writing a book about dieting, you're obviously looking to reach people who would like to lose weight. But can you be even more specific? Maybe your niche is really middle-aged women hoping to lose weight, or parents who want to help their kids lose weight. Or say you write young adult fiction. Does it appeal more to boys or girls, teens or preteens, urban kids or rural kids, or particular YA book discussion groups, etc.?

Now that you know who your audience is, you need to figure out where and how you can best reach them. This is when the brainstorming really starts. What websites or online discussion boards do they frequent? What magazines and other print publications do they read? Are there certain TV or radio shows that appeal to them? Are there any special events they attend, or clubs or associations they join? In short, what are their favorite dance floors?

Identifying publications, media, and other forums through which you can reach your target audience is a never ending process, because they're constantly changing and you're always looking to expand your platform. When you've tapped into one forum, for example a website that caters to middle-aged women hoping to lose weight, always ask the people you meet there what other websites they visit, magazines they read, books they've enjoyed, and so on. I call this a *progressive focus group*, relying on everyone I meet in my target audience to educate me further about themselves and where I can find more folks just like them.

IT'S ALL ABOUT CONTENT

Once you've identified your target audience and started building a list of dance floors where they hang out, it's time to introduce yourself, to get to know them, and to make sure they get

10 Ways to Build Your Platform

1. Create your own website, keep it current with a blog and other updated content, and make it interactive with forums, contests, surveys, newsletters, a guestbook, etc.
2. Write articles, stories, op-eds, and even letters to the editor for magazines, newsletters, and other print publications read your target audience.
3. Contact other high-traffic websites frequented by your target audience, offer to guest blog or contribute content to them (even for free), link your site to theirs, and participate in their networking forums.
4. Position yourself as the go-to source for information regarding your area of expertise by joining related professional organizations, earning certifications, and registering with online and print directories like LinkedIn.com and *Who's Who*, as well as social networking sites like FaceBook and MySpace.
5. Send periodic press releases about yourself, your activities, or some timely aspect of your work/field to targeted print and broadcast media, and offer to sit for an interview—you might be surprised by the response.
6. Hold a publicity event—or dare I say a publicity stunt or gimmick? Challenge your church group to see how much weight they can lose by following the instructions in the diet book you're writing, or hype the mystery novel you're writing by hiding clues around town to the location of the buried treasure—the real treasure might be the media exposure you generate.
7. Give talks, teach classes, offer workshops about your specialty at libraries, schools, churches, and online – but make sure the press knows all about it.
8. Get involved as a volunteer or board member with nonprofit organizations related to your field of interest/expertise; it looks good on your resume and they can be valuable marketing partners for your work.
9. Partner with or co-author a book with a well established, widely recognized expert or celebrity, or try publishing your book through an established franchise like the Dummies or Chicken Soup serials, where your personal platform is less of a factor.
10. Post your own book trailers and other video content on YouTube, create your own podcasts, or publish your own ezine – even amateurish efforts can catch fire.

to know *you*. For most writers, this means providing content; content that helps to establish your reputation, builds name recognition (AKA "brand recognition"), and ideally creates for you a positive notoriety or even celebrity status among members of your target audience.

If you're a nonfiction writer, you typically provide content from the perspective of being an expert in the field (again, a weight loss expert, for example). If you write fiction, the content you provide is hopefully deemed desirable because of your creative and literary prowess. Who wouldn't want to read the words posted on some obscure website by a future J.K. Rowling?

Content, of course, can take many different forms. It's an article or story you get paid handsomely to write for a national magazine, as well as something you write without compensation for an association newsletter read by your target audience. It's the content of your own website and the guest blogs you write for another high-traffic website frequented by your target audience, and it's also every word you type in a chat room where your audience hangs out, even if it's just passing the time of day. It's the talk you give at the local library about what you do for a living. It's the interview you give on radio or national TV.

The content you provide is the basic building block of your platform, so make sure you have plenty of it and that it reflects the quality and style you want to be associated with. Remember, the most valuable words many authors have ever written are the words they most wish they could take back.

A VIRTUAL PLATFORM?

There's no denying that the Internet has had a profound impact on the enterprises of writing and publishing, and also on the ability of an author to develop a platform. Pre-Internet, writers had to rely on traditional print and broadcast media, as well as public appearances and other in-person networking, to gain visibility and establish credibility.

But is it possible to build a promotional platform entirely through online activities—a *virtual platform*, if you will? If you have your own winning website, soft-market yourself through online chat rooms, maybe blog or contribute content to other sites, will that do the trick?

Timothy Ferriss, author of the bestselling book *The 4 Hour Workweek*, attributes much of his success to viral marketing, particularly his efforts to befriend fellow bloggers who then hyped his book. But viral or old school, it all comes back to content. Ferriss said in an interview with Leo Babauta on writetodone.com, "Marketing can get you an initial wave of customers, but you need a good product to go viral ... Focus on making yourself a credible expert vs. pushing a book."

Clearly a strong presence on the Internet can not only be a major plank in an author's platform, but it's also a logical place for many writers to begin building their platforms.

"The barriers (e.g. cost, skill, etc.) for gaining exposure through the Internet are very low," says Kristine Puopolo, Senior Editor with Doubleday Broadway Publishing. "The good news is that almost anyone can publish a blog or create his own website. The bad news is that almost *everyone does* publish a blog and create his own website," she says. Getting noticed on the information superhighway has become increasingly difficult as traffic congestion has increased. "The Internet is a terrific place to create buzz about a book or an author," Puopolo says. "But success is getting that buzz picked up by other media, like TV and print."

So if you were hoping to build your platform solely by sitting at a computer keyboard, Google "try again." Even Ferriss says that his relationships with fellow bloggers were not forged so much over the Internet or even by phone, but by speaking at events they attended and—talk about old school—joining them for some beers afterwards.

COMMON MYTHS ABOUT PLATFORMS

That's not my job, man. Talk to anyone in the publishing business, and the answer is always the same: Gone are the days when authors were just expected to write books and publishers were expected to market them, if those golden days ever existed in the first place. Luke Dempsey knows how it works from both sides of the desk. He's the editor-in-chief of Hudson Street Press, a division of Penguin USA, and he's also author of *A Supremely Bad Idea*, published by Bloomsbury in 2008. "These days book promotion is, at best, a partnership between an author and a publisher. If an author has a strong platform, it's also more likely that the publisher will get excited about the project and put their backs into it as well."

Only nonfiction authors need a platform. It's true that the publishing industry has historically expected most nonfiction authors to have a strong promotional platform of their

5 Top-O-Mind Tips

Keep these things in mind as you build your platform, or you'll kick yourself later:

- **Build relationships, not just a Roladex file.** Do you still see yourself in the writing business five years from now? Nurture the relationships you develop with press contacts, readers, and the other folks you encounter in the publishing industry, rather than just milking them for a one-off interview, etc. Keep in touch, do them favors, and treat them as friends so that they'll be glad to help you out again in the future.
- **No publicity is bad publicity...** or at least that's the way the saying goes. And it's true in a great many cases, particularly when you're just starting out and you're relatively unknown. But also remember that it can be hard to shake an unfavorable reputation once the publicity Gods have saddled you with one, so think twice before jumping at publicity for publicity's sake.
- **Mailing lists are golden.** Capturing the names and contact information for everyone you meet—from readers and potential readers to press contacts and booksellers—is key to building your platform. Distribute sign-up lists at your events, collect business cards religiously, and start building a computerized database of your contacts from day one.
- **Remember the "soft" in "soft-marketing."** Particularly when it comes to promoting yourself online, in social networking forums, chat rooms, etc., tread lightly. First get to know the community and contribute content that's not self-promotional before you ever start talking about yourself and your writing. I've never encountered an online forum that doesn't have an eager Spam Master (or ten) to bounce you out if you come on too strong with self-promotion.
- **Recognize your strengths and weaknesses.** It's a truly rare and talented writer who has the skills, resources, and time to develop a robust platform without outside help. Consider hiring a publicist, getting professional "media training," taking a public speaking class, or securing other professional assistance to compliment your strengths and weaknesses.

own. After all, nonfiction writers are usually considered experts regarding their subject matter, and their expertise should be both in demand and validated by appearing in the media, serving as a source, and writing articles and other content related to their field. But as the book industry has become more competitive, fiction writers are now commonly expected to come to the table with a promotional platform as well.

"It used to be that fiction sold pretty much just as a result of good reviews," Kristine Puopolo says. "But with so many books on the market today and the increased competition for media attention, a fiction author with a compelling personal story, winning personality, or a degree of celebrity definitely has a leg up." Puopolo says that fiction writers can develop their platforms using some of the same techniques as nonfiction writers (e.g. blogs, personal appearances, etc.), and also with things like "virtually hosting" book discussion groups online or by phone, joining local and national literary organizations, and participating in other genre specific forums. Fiction or nonfiction, Puopolo says effective platforms grow out

Creating Effective Press Releases

by Lisa Abeyta

I often hear from other writers who take one of my workshops or online classes that they do not know how to market their own work. Writing the entire novel was an easier task than approaching stores, newspapers, or online venues about carrying their book. But whether a writer landed a coveted spot with a major publisher, chose to go with a small local press or ventured into the world of print on demand and vanity presses, it often falls on the shoulders of the author to market their own book. A few fortunate authors will gain access to a publicist through their publisher, but many will be completely on their own.

Writing a press release does not have to be a daunting task. In fact, for anyone who has already written a query letter, you are well on your way to mastering a press release. The goal is the same: catch the reader's attention right away, build interest in your project, and motivate the reader to act on your request.

Basic press release format

Beyond the basics of not using all caps (nobody wants to be shouted at, even if you excited) and checking your grammar, start your press release with the following headline: For Immediate Release. The next line should be in bold and should contain the headline of your press release. Follow this with a very brief paragraph summarizing the content below and then with the body of the press release. Finish with a short About the Author paragraph and end with your contact information, including your address, phone number, email and website.

Quality content Is a must

One of the best ways to get your press release past the intern who screens the incessant influx of information is to write your release as a completed article. If your text is compelling, interesting, and complete, you have a much better shot of finding that same text in the Sunday Arts section of the paper. Editors are busy people, and the gift if print-ready text is hard to pass up.

Years ago, when I was working as an artist's representative, I sent press packages to media outlets ahead of each performance in a new city. Editors would often print the press release verbatim, although some would call the artist and conduct an interview. But the press release did its job either way by gaining invaluable publicity before a performance.

Study articles about authors and books. Learn the voice and tone of those articles. Mimic it in your own writing, and you'll be far more likely to generate interest in your project.

Where to send your release

A press release can be a stand alone product or as part of a press package. A package should contain a headshot of yourself and art from your book, both printed and on cd in low and high resolution where possible. The more options you provide, the more likely art will accompany any story published from your press release. It should also include a press copy of the book when possible. You can also attach a sheet with upcoming appearances, other titles, and any other pertinent information.

Press releases can be emailed directly to the appropriate editors or reviewers or uploaded to a variety of online PR distribution sites. And while these sites are great for getting the word out on the web, it is still recommended that you take the time to directly contact the editors who will possibly run your story in print or online. And remember to follow up your press releases with a personal phone call. Nothing will set you apart from the pile of press releases like a friendly follow-up call.

There has been a proliferation of online distribution sites focusing on public relations. Someof these include www/PRWeb.com, www.PRLeap.com, and www.24-7pressrelease.com, and www.epressreleases.com. While many of these sites offer free basic online distribution, there are additional fee-based products for you to consider.

of the "authenticity" of the author. "Follow who and what you are. Don't try to be something that you aren't."

Okay, I've built my platform. Now I can get back to writing. As you probably appreciate by now, your platform is not a static set of achievements, but an evolving portfolio of capacities which will hopefully grow and expand along with your writing career. Everything you write, every media appearance you make, every book talk you give, opens a new avenue for extending and strengthening your platform. You need to start building your platform as soon as you start writing—not when you go shopping for a book deal—and the process continues as long as you continue writing. When it comes to your platform as a writer, it's true what they say: "If you're not growing, you're dying."

MORE THAN A MEANS TO AN END

Another common misconception, particularly among new authors, is that platform building is simply a step—perhaps even a necessary evil—in getting your book published.

But here's a bright point to end on: From a business perspective, a robust platform *is* an author's business. In manufacturing terms, it's the sum total of *product lines* that a writer has with which to earn a living. And the payout is that in many cases the non-writing product lines that make up an author's platform may grow to be even more lucrative than writing.

"We're not in the book business. We're in the brand business." That's the prophetic advice Bruce Feiler gave me when I was first starting out. Feiler is a *New York Times* bestselling author of seven books, including *Walking the Bible*, and he has strategically coupled his authorship with television, speaking, and other writing work that has put far more fishes and loaves on his table than writing books alone. In fact Feiler considers the book business to be a "dying industry," which is precisely why he has expanded his product lines.

Stacey Glick, a literary agent with the prestigious firm Dystel and Goderich in New York, wholeheartedly agrees with Feiler. "The thing you need to understand is that most authors can no longer afford to be one dimensional; that is, just authors," she told me. "An author's appeal to a publisher is largely his platform, and his platform in turn benefits from the books he writes. Round and round you go."

And I always value Stacey Glick's advice. After all, she's not only my agent, but she didn't even send me the dry cleaning bill for her Ann Taylor dress suit.

BEYOND THE BASICS

Social Media 101

by Feoshia Henderson

Social media networks such as Facebook and Twitter are opening a new world of opportunity for freelance writers. But like any tool, you have to learn the best, most helpful way to use it as part of your work. Like many things in the online world, social networks change and evolve, and there aren't many hard a fast rules on "Facebooking" or "Tweeting" but freelance writers who've successfully used these sites gave WM a few guidelines on getting the most out of the experience.

So what is social networking? If you're new to it, or just getting started, these web sites give freelancers an online opportunity what they've done offline for years: create personal and professional relationships that can lead to work. They also give writers another outlet to present, or brand, themselves to potential clients as an available writer.

Three of the most popular sites for writers are Facebook, Twitter and LinkedIn. Millions of people, non-profit organizations, businesses and media publications use these sites to varying degrees.

Reach the masses

Allena Tapia, the About.com (freelancewrite.about.com) Guide to Freelance Writing uses all three sites and teaches a social media class at a local community college in Lansing, Mich. "When I'm looking for work I feel Twitter and Facebook reach so many more people. It's a plain old numbers name," explained Tapia, who is a full-time freelancer and former marketing and project editor.

Tapia first started with LinkedIn in 2006, and has been using Twitter and Facebook for the past two years. "I started by connecting with fellow writers. If I'd read their blogs or found them on a message forum, I would connect with them," she said.

Tapia, who specializes in writing about Latino issues, began to join Latino professional organizations on LinkedIn as well. "I ran a search and approached people that way. I knew those were the people who had the work that I wanted," she said.

Usually, though not always, if you "follow" someone on Twitter or "friend" someone on Facebook (reference sidbar), the conversation is expected to be two-way. This offers an opportunity to share your work or expertise with others as well find information from your connection. You can also use your network to find experts to interview for your articles.

"If I'm looking for someone who is in politics and Latino, I can see people's professional affiliation using LinkedIn," Tapia said.

FEOSHIA HENDERSON is a full-time freelance writer and journalist living in Cincinnati, Ohio. She is a former reporter for the Cincinnati Enquirer.

10 Dos and Don'ts in social networking

1. **Do get started.** Social media is a growing part of the freelance writing world. If haven't signed up on at least one site, join one (or two) today and get networking! Start by searching for people online that you know or worked with.

2. **Do fill out your profile.** Add a picture, tell a little about yourself, what you do, where you live, your email address and some of your hobbies. To be cautious, limit very specific information, including street address, birth date or telephone number. People may ignore requests to connect if they don't have some idea of who you are, and why you want to "friend" or "follow" them.

3. **Do jump into the conversation.** When someone asks a question within your realm of experience, answer it. It could be work- or fun-related, like an opinion on a new movie. Don't be afraid to talk to your new friends.

4. **Do update your status, blog etc. regularly.** People join social networking sites because they want to interact, part of that is interaction is letting people know what you're up to. Facing a tight deadline? Broadcast it. Find a fabulous new local restaurant? Talk about it. Read something interesting online (including your own work)? Post a link to it. How often you should update is up to you but strive for at least three times a week. And respond to people who comment on your status or blog updates.

5. **Do be selective in your connections.** There are millions of people who use social networking sites and not all are people you want to associate with. If someone wants to connect, check out their profile first. If you don't want to connect with a person, don't accept their "friend" request. (They won't get a message telling them they were rejected.)

6. **Don't bad mouth others.** Like in the offline world, bad mouthing people (a client, another friend, or a fellow writer) is in bad form. But unlike speaking ill, once you write something online it's out there for your entire network, and others to see. You might be able to delete a message, or you might not (Twitter doesn't let you delete updates). Even if you can delete it, people may have already seen it. So really, you can't take it back.

7. **Don't post questionable material.** Including pictures of yourself or updates that you wouldn't want every person you've worked with, or hope to work with, to see. What's inappropriate for one person may not be for another. Each individual must use their own gauge.

8. **Don't let online conversation completely replace face to face meetings.** People can form strong connections on the Internet, but nothing replaces a face-to-face meeting or phone conversation in landing work or forming long-lasting professional relationships.

9. **Don't just talk about yourself and your work search.** It can come across as boring and overly self-promoting. And don't bombard people over and over with the same messages and links, lest you become labeled a dreaded spammer. You are not just your work, and people are interested in you as a person.

10. **Maybe consider both a personal and professional profile.** Some writers like to keep their personal and professional worlds separate. Consider a private personal profile and a public professional profile. You can direct the appropriate people to each.

How to Blog Successfully

by Fran Johns

Successful blog writing calls for much the same as any other kind of writing: a lot of hard work and a little bit of luck. But some steps can boost your chances in this ever-growing market niche, and keeping up with changing opportunities will guarantee you'll never be bored. The tips offered here are illustrated with my own venture into the blogosphere – I did some things right and some wrong, but wound up with a great job that brings a respectable income.

Create an identity. The best way to do this is with a blog of your own, which gives you an immediate online presence. It should highlight who you are and what writing credentials you possess. Put up your best photo(s) and concise information about your interests and abilities. If you've not already started a blog, sites such as Blogger.com, TypePad or WordPress will walk you through the process, free.

Find a niche. The earlier you home in on an area that fits, the better. Look for something particularly your own: Maybe you're into quilting... or you coach kids' soccer... or you've published short stories in an offbeat genre. Keep the focus narrow enough to showcase your skills and unique perspective. There's no law that says you can't have more than one blog – but keep in mind the limited number of hours there are in a day.

An illustration: My logical niche was end-of-life issues, thanks to one book ("Dying Unafraid") and countless articles on the topic, plus real-time volunteer work with related causes. Not wanting to restrict myself, I named my start-up blog "Fran Johns on Celebrations." That rates an A for creating an identity but about a D-minus for finding a niche. Fortunately, my niche came later.

Build an audience. Once you've got your blog started, work to draw readers interested in your topic(s). Sites such as Digg, Reddit, StumbleUpon and Yahoo Buzz all offer opportunities to share your posts with like-minded readers and writers; these help expand your base. And here's your first chance to bring in money: once you have a following you can build income through ad sales or product links. Say you enjoy going to garage sales and you've built a blog around antiques and collectables. Your next step will be to connect your expertise or information (walnut tables, perhaps) to businesses that sell furniture. Sites such as Smorty.com (pay-per-click advertising or payment for opinion-blogging), ReviewMe.com (pays your blog for reviews or promotions), PayPerPost.com (connects you with advertisers for your blog) or BloggingAds.com (pays for ads on your posts) can point you in these directions.

An illustration: My 'Celebrations' blog built a small audience with potential for ads targeting markets such as assisted living communities. I never capitalized on this... partly because a better route, for me, presented itself:

Pitch to your strength. Having shown you can create an interesting, well-written blog – don't throw up bad grammar or poorly constructed sentences thinking no one will notice – go after a paid blog on an appropriate site. Find an established site (United Furniture Makers of America) to which you can bring a new audience. In the 'Contact us' field of your chosen site, home in on either your readership numbers, your unique perspective on their business, or both – and then link to your blog.

An illustration: I found a new, all-journalist news aggregate site, True/Slant.com, which had plenty of good, young bloggers doing news and opinion writing, and pitched them on a blog targeting over-50 generations. It's a new voice that adds to the T/S readership, but fits the site. Best of all, it pays monthly.

Popular Social Media Web sites

Twitter (www.twitter.com)
A purposely austere "microblogging" Web site where users can send, receive and read short messages (called tweets) restricted to 140 characters. Users have a brief profile with one picture and short description. Subscribers or "followers" can read and respond to your tweets and vice versa. Tweets often link to other websites, videos or articles where followers can read more.

Facebook (www.facebook.com)
A more complex, interactive site, Facebook users create an extensive profile that includes education, workplace and personal information. Facebook allows users to organize and share multiple online photo albums. You can write messages on your profile and your connections or "friends" can read and comment on them. Facebook also has a chat feature. Users to create groups and fan pages where individuals can join to keep up with a business's, entertainer's, publication's or a professional's etc. profile.

LinkedIn (www.linkedin.com)
A business and professional networking site, LinkedIn is more formal in tone than Facebook and Twitter. LinkedIn profiles allow you to connect and find other professionals and interact through status updates and groups. Users can join professional groups on LinkedIn to find people with similar interests, work experience or potential clients. The site allows you to post a basic online resume; and it has a job posting section. LinkedIn requires you have some sort of previous relationship to connect with and send messages to other users. A basic account is free, but you can pay for an upgrade with more advanced features.

Find work and make connections

Bob Medak, a freelance writer from north central Nebraska, maintains blogs for several companies, writes book reviews and ghostwrites. He uses Twitter to look for work by searching for specific phrases included in status updates. These phrases, also called hashtags, can be found by searching for a phase proceeded by the # sign. Popular search terms include #freelancecopywriter, #articlewriter and #freelancejobs.

Medak also uses social media connections to help him grow as a businessperson. "I am hooked up with other writers, connected with people that do social marketing and small business coaches. When I follow them I gather information that helps me. I apply it to my business," he said.

Social networking is far from all business. After all, you are expected to actually be social. That's why it's important to flush out any profile you set up, and to be transparent about who you are and what you are trying to accomplish. Do things like going weeks without participating, or leaving out important information like your name or your picture will turn off other users.

"If someone doesn't have a bio, I don't follow them," Medack said. "Not having a bio is kind of like setting up a Web page and not putting anything on it. I want to know 'Well are you a writer? Are you a reader? Are you a learner? What is your thing besides piling up thousands of people?"

Interacting person-to-person is an important part of successfully using these web sites. People want to get to know about your personality as well as your work expertise. It just makes sense that people who like you are more likely to want to work with you, or give you job tips and recommendations. And each social networking conversation is as unique as the millions users. So just be yourself.

Follow your own path

"You've got to get away from thinking 'there is formula to this;' there isn't a formula. Everything in social media is a conversation. There are crappy conversations and there are ones you want to be part of and enjoy," said George "Loki" Williams, a freelance web content producer and social media consultant from New Orleans who's freelance career was boosted after his extensive online coverage of Hurricane Katrina's aftermath. That led him to work on a Project Katrina: An Unnatural Disaster, funded by the prominent Soros Foundation Network (www.soros.org/resources/multimedia/katrina/projects).

While social media has the potential to bring new work, success in the social media world won't happen overnight.

"The thing to remember is integrity, transparency, authenticity and quality. It's not an easy thing and not an instant thing. It's like other jobs, you have to put in some time and pay your dues. And the quality of your network is important. How many people are interested in what you have to say? I'd rather have 300 hanging on every word than 5,000 who aren't paying attention," Williams said.

Open yourself to serendipity

Cultivating the right relationships can pay off. It did for Tania Katherine, Marketing & Creative Services Director at American Homeowner Preservation, LLC. She's a New York City transplant to Cincinnati. Connecting with a former boss in a Facebook group helped her crack into freelance copywriting.

She explained, "A friend of hers was looking for a copywriter for just a quick batch of work. Since I'd never really written copy, formally, I thought I'd respond just to see what would happen. Since I already had an 'in' with the hirer, they took my content writing experience as a show of my abilities and hired me for the quick gig. I never even talked to them outside of Facebook. I wish I could get more jobs like that. It's easy and gets the job done for everyone."

Big Bucks From Small Markets

Cashing in on Resales

by Cynthia Washam

We all start out with dreams of making the big sale – a $10,000 cover story for *Esquire, The New Yorker*, maybe *Vanity Fair*. Then all too soon, we wake up to the reality that our first sales are more likely to end up as $25, page-three stories in the *Snoozeville Sun*. While that may not be the sale of our dreams, it comes with an opportunity not seen in sales to the biggies. We writers for small publications can resell our work enough to see that measly $25 double, triple, maybe even quadruple.

I discovered the income boost from resales a couple years after I started writing a monthly column for *South Florida Parenting* magazine. I collected a year's worth of previously published columns and sent them to editors of small, regional parenting magazines around the country. Within weeks, the checks started coming in. One was from Pennsylvania. Another, California. The $480 *South Florida Parenting* paid me for 12 columns swelled to more than $1,200. All I had to do was dig up a few e-mail addresses and hit the send button.

Twelve years later, I'm still reselling my It Figures column to parenting publications nationwide. I've also cashed in on the resale market with health articles, humor pieces and a column of statistics related to running. Opportunities for resales, in fact, have never been better. Cash-strapped publishers are looking for bargains. Many don't care if your work appeared already in two, four or 50 publications, as long as their readers haven't seen it and the price is right.

Breaking In: Stick Close to Home

Unless you're already an established freelancer, the easiest way to break into multiple sales is by starting locally. Seek out publications that run the type of stories you enjoy writing. Just about every major city has a dozen or more local specialty publications targeting such groups as parents, seniors, fitness buffs, socialites and young hipsters. Newspapers offer another arena for freelancers with their feature sections devoted to food, home and gardening, travel and books.

"Go visit the paper," advises Will Atkins, editor and publisher of the weekly *Oak Hill Gazette* in Austin, Texas. "Make it easy for me. I like writers who generate ideas for stories."

If you write for a regional publication like the *Gazette*, you'll most likely sell first North American serial rights. In other words, the publisher will be the first to publish the article. You're then free to sell reprint rights to other publishers outside his area. But before querying other editors, discuss your plans with the assigning editor just to be sure you both agree on the rights. Better yet, get a written contract.

CYNTHIA WASHAM is a freelance writer who works hard to make both sales and re-sales of her articles.

Finding Your Niche

The easiest stories to sell multiple times are those with universal appeal. Think how-to features, personal columns, humor, travel, consumer advice. My best-selling reprints have been my It Figures column of family-related statistics. Parents are fascinated by such trivia as the increase in twin births since the 1980s – 60 percent – whether they live in Miami or Milwaukee.

News features with quotes from local sources are tougher to sell outside the area, but not impossible. When I market them, I offer one price for the article as is, and a slightly higher price for the article with additional quotes from a source in the buyer's area. Editors like getting a story with a local feel for little more than the cost of a reprint. Some even make my job a breeze by referring me to their local source.

The key to multiple sales is tapping into different readerships. Geography is only one way to separate readers. Another possibility is by genre. You could sell an article about an Alaskan cruise to a national magazine for lawyers, for example, then resell the same article to a national magazine for doctors, and one for insurance executives. Still another way to separate readers is by time. Some publishers allow resales to competing publications after a set time following first publication, say six months to a year. Be sure to check with your editor on time limits.

Finding New Markets

A good place to start your search for resale markets is *Writer's Market* or WritersMarket.com. Both include lists of regional specialty publications including lifestyle, parenting, sports, alternative, and home and garden, along with local and national trade publications. If you want to dig deeper into a market, try the Internet. Most specialty publishers have their own trade associations, which typically list members on their web sites. I've found the names, phone numbers and e-mail addresses for the editors of more than 100 regional parenting magazines on the Parenting Publications of America site. The Alliance of Area Business Publications lists 70 regional business magazines and the Association of Alternative Newsweeklies lists 130 alternative newspapers.

Querying about a reprint is different, and easier, than querying with a story proposal. I don't waste the editor's time with a lengthy description of the story or my credentials. The attached story can sell itself. I just write a couple sentences I hope will entice her to read it. I also explain the rights I'm offering, and when and where the story was first published. Occasionally, I'll send a list of several stories of a certain type, such as children's health. If a title catches an editor's eye, she can then ask me to e-mail the story.

"Don't worry if you know an editor," says Martha Wegner, a Minnesota-based freelance writer whose columns have appeared in more than 100 parenting magazines. "It's really an anonymous operation. The more you send, the more bites you're going to get."

The Delicate Discussion of Dollars

Payment for reprint rights is as variable as payment for first rights. Some small publications have surprisingly deep pockets. Others pay as little as $5 per article. Quite a few pay nothing at all. Writing for the satisfaction of getting a byline is fine for the neighborhood newsletter, but avoid it when you're writing for money-making periodicals, even if you are still building your portfolio. Writers willing to work for nothing make it harder for those of us who write for a living to earn what we deserve.

When I offer editors reprint rights for It Figures, I state my price of $145 for 12 columns. I feel that naming my own price is fair to the potential buyers. I'd hate to imagine 10 of them meeting and finding each had talked me into a different price. Other writers, though, take a different approach. Wegner is among those who never name a price in her queries.

"Sometimes editors say, 'How much do you want,'" Wegner says. "I say $25 to $60. You decide based on the length."

That may not sound like much, but Wegner has had as many as 20 sales of a single story. Try that with a $10,000 Esquire cover story.

BEYOND THE BASICS

Editor FAQs

by Robert Lee Brewer

The publishing world is filled with so many nooks and crannies that even the most experienced writers have common questions about various topics, such as co-authoring, self-publishing, ghostwriting and more. I know, because writers tend to ask me the same questions whether I'm speaking at a bookstore or a writer's conference, or fielding questions through WritersMarket.com. Here are some of those most frequently asked questions with my most frequently given answers.

What's the trick to getting published?

There really *is* no trick to getting published. There's no tried-and-true gimmick that will build your career for you. Making it as a writer requires a lot of hard work, discipline and perseverance.

The first step is always to work on the craft of writing. You can improve your craft by participating in writer's groups, attending writer's conferences, taking online courses, or going to workshops at local universities. Instructional books on technique (many can be found online at www.WritersDigest.com) can provide exercises, spark ideas, and give advice on plotting, characterization and more.

Once your work is at a publishable level, you should sit down with a pad of paper and outline what your long-term goals are. Then, identify some short-term goals you think will get you there.

It's hard to get somewhere without knowing where you're going, so don't discount this step in the process of becoming a successful writer. Sure, you can change directions if you see a better destination along the way, but it's important that you always have a goal in mind. Your goals will help direct which skills you need to focus on the most and will play an important role in how your writing is crafted.

How does co-authoring work?

In a situation where you wish to co-author a book or article, I suggest defining the roles of each author upfront to avoid ambiguity, hurt feelings, or disputes during the writing process and later on during the submission process. Make sure each author agrees on the goals, responsibilities, rights, compensation and deadlines for the project. Communication throughout the process is key.

When contacting a publisher or agent, it's best to elect one main contact person to avoid

---

ROBERT LEE BREWER is a Senior Content Editor for the Writer's Digest Writing Community. He edits *Writer's Market*, *Poet's Market* and WritersMarket.com, in addition to maintaining his Poetic Asides poetry blog (http://blog.writersdigest.com/poeticasides). Follow him on Twitter at http://twitter.com/robertleebrewer.

confusion. This person should be good at communicating with the publisher or agent and the other co-author or authors.

What about ghostwriting?

Ghostwriting is the process where you take another person's ideas and write an article or book for them, either under their name or "as told to." Authoritative experts with no writing experience use this process, as well as celebrities with stories to tell.

Ghostwriting is not a glamorous job, since you usually don't get credit or recognition, but it does pay the bills for many hard-working and organized writers. As with co-authoring, be sure to get goals, rights, payment, responsibilities, deadlines and other details ironed out before starting any project.

Whether you are looking for a ghostwriter or you wish to become one, the following Websites can help: www.freelancewriting.com; www.craigslist.org; www.writers-editors.com. On these Websites, you can look for job openings or post one.

Should I hire an editor or book doctor?

Some writers hire professional editors to strengthen their manuscripts before submitting to publishers or agents. These editors can check for content, flow, do line-by-line edits, offer general critiques, and more (or less—on a case-by-case basis). However, it is often hard to evaluate how good an editor is until you've already invested a good deal of time and money into the process. A much more affordable and possibly more effective solution is to join a writing group in your area or attend a writing workshop that addresses your type of writing. Writer's conferences also offer critiques by professional writers, editors and agents. If these options are not available, then you could try hiring a graduate student from a local college.

You can hunt down possible editors online at the following Websites: www.writerseditors.com; www.freelancewriting.com; www.absolutewrite.com. Also, check out classified ads in the back of the *Writer's Digest* magazine.

When do I need an agent?

First, you only need an agent if you are writing a book or a screenplay. Second, nonfiction writers need a completed book proposal together before hunting down an agent, and fiction writers need a completed manuscript. Third, agents are most helpful for selling to the larger book publishers, so if you're writing a book that will only appeal to academics or a very small audience, using an agent will not make as much sense.

A good agent will place your work with a publisher; negotiate the best package of subsidiary rights, advance money, and royalty terms possible; help you develop your career as a writer for the short-and long-term; and many also provide guidance in the development of writing projects and promotional opportunities.

For more information on agents, check out *2011 Guide to Literary Agents*, edited by Chuck Sambuchino (Writer's Digest Books). In addition to listing more than 550 agents, this resource is filled with articles explaining how to find and work with an appropriate agent.

Is self-publishing a better option for writers?

Self-publishing is definitely tied up in the whole equation of determining your goals as a writer. Many writers envision publishing a book that will be sold in bookstores, and possibly as a bestseller. If that's your goal, then self-publishing should only be used as a last resort.

Unless you're writing for a very specialized audience or trying to publish a book of poetry, then I suggest trying to get an agent first. If that doesn't work out, try submitting directly to book publishers. If that doesn't work, maybe you need to revise your query letter or manuscript and try again. This is especially true if you keep hearing the same comments and suggestions from agents and editors.

If you've exhausted all these options and you still think you can reach an audience, then self-publishing could be an option for you. However, make sure you research all your self-publishing options to save time, money and headaches. Self-publishing is a very rough road for any writer and often turns into a full-time job with a very low rate of success.

How do I handle a pseudonym?

Many writers working under a pseudonym wonder if they have to deceive their publishers and live a double life. The best policy is to bring your pseudonym up at the beginning of your communication with an agent or editor. In your initial query or cover letter, use your real name, but explain in one sentence somewhere in that letter (and not in the first paragraph) that you write under a pen name. That way payment can be made to your real name, helping you avoid any possible taxation or banking snafus. Also, to avoid confusion, use your pseudonym on the actual manuscript.

Should I copyright my work before submitting?

For all practical and legal purposes, your work is protected by copyright once you put it on paper (or save it electronically). While registering your copyright will add an extra level of protection for your writing against possible manuscript thieves, it is not necessary and can often label you as an amateur. Most cases of plagiarism occur after a work has been published and is under the protection of copyright. Do not write that your work is copyrighted or include a copyright symbol on your manuscript or in your query or cover letter; this will generally get your submission rejected before it is even read.

How do I know a publisher won't steal my work?

As in life, there are no guarantees in publishing. However, it is rare to hear an actual first-person account of an editor or agent stealing someone else's work before it is published. Most people who relay these tall tales of publishing will say "a friend of a friend'' had her work stolen by an editor. While there may be a case or two where this has happened, you probably have better odds of winning the lottery than having your work stolen. Whether that's a good or bad thing is open to interpretation.

In addition, *Writer's Market* strives to list only reputable publishers and viable markets within its pages. From including screening questions in our questionnaires to scanning online writer groups and responding to writer complaints, we work to maintain the highest quality directory available to writers trying to get published and paid for their writing. (If you feel you have not been treated fairly by a listing in the book, please follow the Complaint Procedure found on the copyright page of this book—next to the Table of Contents.)

BEYOND THE BASICS

Publishers & Their Imprints

The publishing world is in constant transition. With all the buying, selling, reorganizing, consolidating, and dissolving, it's hard to keep publishers and their imprints straight. To help make sense of these changes, here's a breakdown of major publishers (and their divisions)—who owns whom and which imprints are under each company umbrella. Keep in mind that this information changes frequently. The website of each publisher is provided to help you keep an eye on this ever-evolving business.

HACHETTE BOOK GROUP USA

www.hachettebookgroupusa.com

Center Street
FaithWords

Grand Central Publishing
Business Plus
5-Spot
Forever
Springboard Press
Twelve
Vision
Wellness Central

Hachette Book Group Digital Media
Hachette Audio

Little, Brown and Company
Back Bay Books
Bulfinch
Reagan Arthur Books

Little, Brown Books for Young Readers
LB Kids
Poppy

Orbit

Yen Press

HARLEQUIN ENTERPRISES

www.eharlequin.com

Harlequin
Harlequin American Romance
Harlequin Bianca
Harlequin Blaze

Harper Festival
HarperTeen
Rayo
Katherine Tegen Books

Harlequin Deseo
Harlequin Historical
Harlequin Intrigue
Harlequin Tiffany
Harlequin Teen
Harlequin Medical Romance
Harlequin NASCAR
Harlequin Presents
Harlequin Romance
Harlequin Superromance
Harlequin eBooks
Harlequin Special Releases
Harlequin Nonfiction
Harlequin Historical Undone

HQN Books
HQN eBooks

LUNA
Luna eBooks

MIRA
Mira eBooks

Kimani Press
Kimani Press Arabesque
Kimani Press Kimani Romance
Kimani Press Kimani TRU
Kimani Press New Spirit
Kimani Press Sepia
Kimani Press Special Releases
Kimani Press eBooks

Red Dress Ink
Red Dress eBooks

Silhouette
Silhouette Desire
Silhouette Nocturne
Silhouette Nocturne Bites
Silhouette Romantic Suspense
Silhouette Special Edition
Silhouette eBooks

SPICE
SPICE Books
SPICE Briefs

Steeple Hill
Steeple Hill Café©
Steeple Hill Love Inspired
Steeple Hill Love Inspired Historical
Steeple Hill Love Inspired Suspense
Steeple Hill Women's Fiction
Steeple Hill eBooks
Worldwide Library

Rogue Angel

Worldwide Mystery
Worldwilde Library eBooks

Harlequin Canada

Harlequin U.K.
Mills & Boon

HARPERCOLLINS

www.harpercollins.com

HarperMorrow
Amistad
Avon
- Avon A
- Avon Inspire
- Avon Red

Collins Design
Ecco
Eos
Harper
- Harper Business
- HarperLuxe
- Harper Paperbacks
- Harper Perennial
- HarperAudio
- HarperBibles

HarperCollins e-Books
- HarperOne
- ItBooks

Rayo
William Morrow

HarperCollins Children's Books
Amistad
Balzer + Bray
Greenwillow Books
HarperCollins
Children's Audio

TOKYOPOP
HarperCollins e-Books

HarperCollins U.K.
Fourth Estate
HarperPress
HarperPerennial
The Friday Project
HarperThorsons/Element
HarperNonFiction
HarperTrue
HarperSport
HarperFiction
  Voyager
  Blue Door
  Angry Robot
  Avon U.K.
HarperCollins Childrens Books
Collins
  Collins Geo
  Collins Education
  Collins Language

HarperCollins Canada
www.harpercollins.ca
HarperCollinsPublishers
Collins Canada
HarperPerennial Canada
HarperTrophyCanada
Phyllis Bruce Books

HarperCollins Australia
HarperCollins
Angus & Robertson
HarperSports
Fourth Estate
Harper Perennial
Collins
Voyager

HarperCollins India

HarperCollins New Zealand
HarperCollins
HarperSports
Flamingo
Voyager
Perennial

Zondervan
Zonderkids
Editorial Vida
Youth Specialties

MACMILLAN US (Holtzbrinck)

http://us.macmillan.com

MacMillan
Farrar, Straus & Giroux
Faber and Faber, Inc
Farrar, Straus
Hill & Wang

Henry Holt & Co.
Henry Holt Books for Young Readers
Holt Paperbacks
Metropolitan
Times

MacMillan Children's
Feiwel & Friends
Farrar, Straus and Giroux Books for Young Readers
Kingfisher
Holt Books for Young Readers
Priddy Books
Roaring Brook Press
First Second
Square Fish

Picador

Palgrave MacMillan

Tor/Forge Books
Tor
Forge
Orb
Tor/Seven Seas

St. Martin's Press
Minotaur Press
Thomas Dunne Books

Bedford, Freeman & Worth Publishing Group

Bedford/St. Martin's

Hayden-McNeil

W.H. Freeman

Worth Publishers

Macmillan Kids

Young Listeners

MacMillan Audio

PENGUIN GROUP (USA), INC.

www.penguingroup.com

Penguin Adult Division
Ace
Alpha
Amy Einhorn Books/Putnam
Avery
Berkley
Current
Dutton
G.P. Putnam's Sons
Gotham
HPBooks
Hudson Street Press
Jeremy P. Tarcher
Jove
NAL
Pamela Dorman Books
Penguin
Penguin Press
Perigree
Plume
Portfolio
Prentice Hall Press

Riverhead
Sentinel
Tarcher
Viking Press
Price Stern Sloan

Young Readers Division
Dial Books for Young Readers
Dutton Children's Books
Firebird
Frederick Warne
Grosset & Dunlap
Philomel

Puffin Books
Razorbill
Speak
Viking Books for Young Readers

RANDOM HOUSE, INC. (Bertelsmann)

www.randomhouse.com

Crown Trade Group
Amphoto Books
Backstage Books
Billboard Books
Broadway Business
Crown
Crown Business
Crown Forum
Clarkson Potter
Doubleday Religion
Harmony
Monacelli Press
Potter Craft
Potter Style
Three Rivers Press
Ten Speed Press
Tricycle Press
Shaye Areheart Books
Waterbrook Multnomah
Watson-Guptill

Knopf Doubleday Publishing Group
Alfred A. Knopf

Anchor Books
Doubleday
Everyman's Library
Nan A. Talese
Pantheon Books
Schocken Books
Vintage/Anchor

Random House Publishing Group
Ballantine Books
Bantam
Dell
Del Rey
Del Rey/Lucas Books
The Dial Press
The Modern Library
One World
Presidio Press
Random House Trade Group
Random House Trade Paperbacks
Spectra
Spiegel and Grau
Villard Books

Random House Audio Publishing Group
Listening Library
Random House Audio

Random House Children's Books
Kids@Random
Golden Books
Bantam Books
David Fickling Books
Delacorte Press Books for Young Readers
Delacorte Press Trade Paperbacks
Disney Books for Young Readers
Doubleday Books for Young Readers
Dragonfly
Laurel-Leaf
Picturebacks
Robin Corey Books
Schwartz and Wade Books
Wendy Lamb Books
Yearling

Random House Information Group
Fodor's Travel
Living Language
Prima Games
Princeton Review
RH Puzzles & Games
RH Reference Publishing
Sylvan Learning

Random House International
Arete
McClelland & Stewart Ltd.
Plaza & Janes
RH Australia
RH of Canada Limited
RH Mondadori
RH South America
RH United Kingdom
Transworld UK
Verlagsgruppe RH

SIMON & SCHUSTER

www.simonandschuster.com

Simon & Schuster Adult Publishing
Atria Books/Beyond Words
Beach Lane Books
Folger Shakespeare Library
Free Press
Gallery Books
Howard Books
Pocket Books
Scribner
Simon & Schuster
Strebor
The Touchstone & Fireside Group
Pimsleur
Simon & Schuster Audioworks

Simon & Schuster Children's Publishing
Aladdin Paperbacks
Atheneum Books for Young Readers
Libros Para Niños
Little Simon®
Margaret K. McElderry Books
Simon & Schuster Books for Young Readers
Simon Pulse
Simon Spotlight®

Simon & Schuster International
Simon & Schuster Australia
Simon & Schuster Canada
Simon & Schuster UK

Literary Agents

The literary agencies listed in this section are open to new clients and are members of the Association of Authors' Representatives (AAR), which means they do not charge for reading, critiquing, or editing. Some agents in this section may charge clients for office expenses such as photocopying, foreign postage, long-distance phone calls, or express mail services. Make sure you have a clear understanding of what these expenses are before signing any agency agreement.

FOR MORE...

The *2011 Guide to Literary Agents* (Writer's Digest Books) offers more than 800 literary agents, as well as information on writers' conferences. It also offers a wealth of information on the author/agent relationship and other related topics.

SUBHEADS

Each listing is broken down into subheads to make locating specific information easier. In the first section, you'll find contact information for each agency. Further information is provided which indicates an agency's size, its willingness to work with a new or previously unpublished writer, and its general areas of interest.

Member Agents Agencies comprised of more than one agent list member agents and their individual specialties to help you determine the most appropriate person for your query letter.

Represents Here agencies specify what nonfiction and fiction subjects they consider.

⊶ Look for the key icon to quickly learn an agent's areas of specialization or specific strengths.

How to Contact In this section agents specify the type of material they want to receive, how they want to receive it, and how long you should wait for their response.

Recent Sales To give a sense of the types of material they represent, agents provide specific titles they've sold.

Terms Provided here are details of an agent's commission, whether a contract is offered, and what additional office expenses you might have to pay if the agent agrees to represent you. Standard commissions range from 10-15 percent for domestic sales, and 15-20 percent for foreign or dramatic sales.

Writers Conferences Here agents list the conferences they attend.

Tips Agents offer advice and additional instructions for writers looking for representation.

WritersMarket.com lists all the publishing opportunities found in *Writer's Market*, plus thousands more. Visit **www.WritersMarket.com** to log in or sign up today.

DOMINICK ABEL LITERARY AGENCY, INC.

146 W. 82nd St., #1A, New York NY 10024. (212)877-0710. Fax: (212)595-3133. E-mail: agency@dalainc.com. Member of AAR. Represents 100 clients. Currently handles: adult fiction and nonfiction.

How to Contact Query via e-mail.

Terms Agent receives 15% commission on domestic sales. Agent receives 20% commission on foreign sales.

ADAMS LITERARY

7845 Colony Road C4, #215, Charlotte NC 28226. (704)542-1440. Fax: (704)542-1450. E-mail: info@adamsliterary.com. Website: www.adamsliterary.com. **Contact:** Tracey Adams, Josh Adams, Quinlan Lee. Member of AAR. Other memberships include SCBWI and WNBA.

Member Agents Tracey Adams; Josh Adams; Quinlan Lee..

- Adams Literary is a full-service literary agency exclusively representing children's book authors and artists.

How to Contact "Guidelines are posted (and frequently updated) on our website."

MIRIAM ALTSHULER LITERARY AGENCY

53 Old Post Road N., Red Hook NY 12571. (845)758-9408. Website: www.miriamaltshulerliteraryagency.com. **Contact:** Miriam Altshuler. Estab. 1994. Member of AAR. Represents 40 clients. Currently handles: nonfiction books 45%, novels 45%, story collections 5%, juvenile books 5%.

- Ms. Altshuler has been an agent since 1982.

Represents Nonfiction books, novels, short story collections, juvenile. **Considers these nonfiction areas:** biography, ethnic, history, language, memoirs, multicultural, music, nature, popular culture, psychology, sociology, film, women's. **Considers these fiction areas:** literary, mainstream, multicultural, some selective children's books.

- Looking for literary commercial fiction and nonfiction. Does not want self-help, mystery, how-to, romance, horror, spiritual, fantasy, poetry, screenplays, science fiction or techno-thriller, western.

How to Contact Send Query; If we want to see your ms we will respond via email (if you do not have an email address, please send an SASE. We will only respond if interested in materials. Submit contact info with e-mail address. Prefers to read materials exclusively. Accepts simultaneous submissions. Responds in 3 weeks to mss. Obtains most new clients through recommendations from others.

Terms Agent receives 15% commission on domestic sales. Agent receives 20% commission on foreign sales. Charges clients for overseas mailing, photocopies, overnight mail when requested by author.

Writers Conferences Bread Loaf Writers' Conference; Washington Independent Writers Conference; North Carolina Writers' Network Conference.

Tips See the website for specific submission details.

BETSY AMSTER LITERARY ENTERPRISES

P.O. Box 27788, Los Angeles CA 90027-0788. **Contact:** Betsy Amster. Estab. 1992. Member of AAR. Represents more than 65 clients. 35% of clients are new/unpublished writers. Currently handles: nonfiction books 65%, novels 35%.

- Prior to opening her agency, Ms. Amster was an editor at Pantheon and Vintage for 10 years, and served as editorial director for the Globe Pequot Press for 2 years.

Represents Nonfiction books, novels. **Considers these nonfiction areas:** art & design, biography, business, child guidance, cooking/nutrition, current affairs, ethnic, gardening, health/medicine, history, memoirs, money, parenting, popular culture, psychology, science/technology, self-help, sociology, travelogues, social issues, women's issues. **Considers these fiction areas:** ethnic, literary, women's, high quality.

- "Actively seeking strong narrative nonfiction, particularly by journalists; outstanding literary fiction (the next Richard Ford or Jhumpa Lahiri); witty, intelligent commercial women's fiction (the next Elinor Lipman or Jennifer Weiner); mysteries that open new worlds to us; and high-profile self-help and psychology, preferably research based." Does not want to receive poetry, children's books, romances, Western, science fiction, action/adventure, screenplays, fantasy, techno thrillers, spy capers, apocalyptic scenarios, or political or religious arguments.

How to Contact For adult titles: b.amster.assistant@gmail.com. See submission requirements online at website. The requirements have changed and only e-mail submissions are accepted. Accepts simultaneous submissions. Responds in 1 month to queries. Responds in 2 months to mss. Obtains most new clients through recommendations from others, solicitations, conferences.

Terms Agent receives 15% commission on domestic sales. Agent receives 20% commission on foreign sales. Offers written contract, binding for 1 year; 3-month notice must be given to terminate contract.

Charges for photocopying, postage, long distance phone calls, messengers, galleys/books used in submissions to foreign and film agents and to magazines for first serial rights.
Writers Conferences USC Masters in Professional Writing; San Diego State University Writers' Conference; UCLA Extension Writers' Program; Los Angeles Times Festival of Books; The Loft Literary Center.

ARCADIA

31 Lake Place N., Danbury CT 06810. E-mail: arcadialit@sbcglobal.net. **Contact:** Victoria Gould Pryor. Member of AAR.
Represents Nonfiction books, literary and commercial fiction. **Considers these nonfiction areas:** biography, business, current affairs, health, history, psychology, science, true crime, women's, investigative journalism; culture; classical music; life transforming self-help.

- "I'm a very hands-on agent, which is necessary in this competitive marketplace. I work with authors on revisions until whatever we present to publishers is as strong as possible. I represent talented, dedicated, intelligent and ambitious writers who are looking for a long-term relationship based on professional success and mutual respect." Does not want to receive science fiction/ fantasy, horror, humor or children's/YA. "We are only able to read fiction submissions from previously published authors."

How to Contact Query with SASE. This agency accepts e-queries (no attachments).

THE AXELROD AGENCY

55 Main St., P.O. Box 357, Chatham NY 12037. (518)392-2100. E-mail: steve@axelrodagency.com. **Contact:** Steven Axelrod. Member of AAR. Represents 15-20 clients. 1% of clients are new/unpublished writers. Currently handles: novels 95%.

- Prior to becoming an agent, Mr. Axelrod was a book club editor.

Represents Novels. **Considers these fiction areas:** mystery, romance, women's.
How to Contact Query with SASE. Accepts simultaneous submissions. Responds in 3 weeks to queries. Responds in 6 weeks to mss. Obtains most new clients through recommendations from others.
Terms Agent receives 15% commission on domestic sales. Agent receives 20% commission on foreign sales. No written contract.
Writers Conferences RWA National Conference.

THE BALKIN AGENCY, INC.

P.O. Box 222, Amherst MA 01004. Phone/Fax: (413)322-8697. E-mail: rick62838@crocker.com. **Contact:** Rick Balkin, president. Member of AAR. Represents 50 clients. 10% of clients are new/unpublished writers. Currently handles: nonfiction books 85%, 5% reference books.

- Prior to opening his agency, Mr. Balkin served as executive editor with Bobbs-Merrill Company.

Represents Nonfiction books. **Considers these nonfiction areas:** animals, anthropology, current affairs, health, history, how-to, nature, popular culture, science, sociology, translation, biography, et alia.

- This agency specializes in adult nonfiction. Does not want to receive fiction, poetry, screenplays, children's books or computer books.

How to Contact Query with SASE. Submit proposal package, outline. Responds in 1 week to queries. Responds in 2 weeks to mss. Obtains most new clients through recommendations from others.
Terms Agent receives 15% commission on domestic sales. Agent receives 20% commission on foreign sales. Offers written contract, binding for 1 year. This agency charges clients for photocopying and express or foreign mail.
Recent Sales Sold 15 titles in the last year. *No Tongue Shall Speak*, by Utpal Sandesara/Tom Wooten (Prometheus Books); *Wrong*, by David H. Freedman (Little, Brown); *The Musical Vision of Gustavo Dudamel*, by Tricia Tunstall, W.W. Norton & Co.
Tips "I do not take on books described as bestsellers or potential bestsellers. Any nonfiction work that is either unique, paradigmatic, a contribution, truly witty, or a labor of love is grist for my mill."

LORETTA BARRETT BOOKS, INC.

fiction and non-fiction, 220 E. 23rd St., 11th Floor, New York NY 10010. (212)242-3420. E-mail: query@lorettabarrettbooks.com. Website: www.lorettabarrettbooks.com. **Contact:** Loretta A. Barrett, Nick Mullendore. Estab. 1990. Member of AAR. Currently handles: nonfiction books 50%, novels 50%.

- Prior to opening her agency, Ms. Barrett was vice president and executive editor at Doubleday and editor-in-chief of Anchor Books.

Member Agents Loretta A. Barrett; Nick Mullendore.
Represents Nonfiction books, novels. **Considers these nonfiction areas:** biography, child guidance, current affairs, ethnic, government, health/nutrition, history, memoirs, money, multicultural, nature, popular culture, psychology, religion, science, self help, sociology, spirituality, sports, women's, young

adult, creative nonfiction. **Considers these fiction areas:** contemporary, psychic, adventure, detective, ethnic, family, fantasy, historical, literary, mainstream, mystery, thriller, young adult.

- "The clients we represent include both fiction and non-fiction authors for the general adult trade market. The works they produce encompass a wide range of contemporary topics and themes including commercial thrillers, mysteries, romantic suspense, popular science, memoirs, narrative fiction and current affairs." No children's, juvenile, cookbooks, gardening, science fiction, fantasy novels, historical romance.

How to Contact See guidelines online. Use email or if by post, query with SASE. Accepts simultaneous submissions. Responds in 3-6 weeks to queries.

Terms Agent receives 15% commission on domestic sales. Agent receives 20% commission on foreign sales. Offers written contract. Charges clients for shipping and photocopying.

MEREDITH BERNSTEIN LITERARY AGENCY

2095 Broadway, Suite 505, New York NY 10023. (212)799-1007. Fax: (212)799-1145. Member of AAR. Represents 85 clients. 20% of clients are new/unpublished writers. Currently handles: nonfiction books 50%, other 50% fiction.

- Prior to opening her agency, Ms. Bernstein served at another agency for 5 years.

Represents Nonfiction books, novels. **Considers these fiction areas:** literary, mystery, romance, thriller, young adult.

- "This agency does not specialize. It is very eclectic."

How to Contact Query with SASE. Accepts simultaneous submissions. Obtains most new clients through recommendations from others, conferences, developing/packaging ideas.

Terms Agent receives 15% commission on domestic sales. Agent receives 20% commission on foreign sales. Charges clients $75 disbursement fee/year.

Recent Sales More of the best-selling New York Times, USA Today, and Wall Street Journal; *House of Nighy* series, by P.C. Cast and Kristin Cast; *The No Cry Separation Anxiety Solution*, by Elizabeth Pantrey, and *Following the Waters*, by David Carroll (a McArthur Genius Award Winner) and nominee for National Book Award in 2009.

Writers Conferences Southwest Writers' Conference; Rocky Mountain Fiction Writers' Colorado Gold; Pacific Northwest Writers' Conference; Willamette Writers' Conference; Surrey International Writers' Conference; San Diego State University Writers' Conference.

BOOKENDS, LLC

136 Long Hill Rd., Gillette NJ 07933. Website: www.bookends-inc.com; bookendslitagency.blogspot.com. **Contact:** Jessica Faust, Kim Lionetti. Member of AAR. RWA, MWA Represents 50+ clients. 10% of clients are new/unpublished writers. Currently handles: nonfiction books 50%, novels 50%.

Member Agents Jessica Faust (fiction: romance, erotica, women's fiction, mysteries and suspense; nonfiction: business, finance, career, parenting, psychology, women's issues, self-help, health, sex); Kim Lionetti (women's fiction, mystery, true crime, pop science, pop culture, and all areas of romance)."

Represents Nonfiction books, novels. **Considers these nonfiction areas:** business, child, ethnic, gay, health, how-to, money, psychology, religion, self help, sex, true crime, women's. **Considers these fiction areas:** detective, cozies, mainstream, mystery, romance, thriller, women's.

- "BookEnds is currently accepting queries from published and unpublished writers in the areas of romance (and all its sub-genres), erotica, mystery, suspense, women's fiction, and literary fiction. We also do a great deal of nonfiction in the areas of self-help, business, finance, health, pop science, psychology, relationships, parenting, pop culture, true crime, and general nonfiction." BookEnds does not want to receive children's books, screenplays, science fiction, poetry, or technical/military thrillers.

How to Contact Review website for guidelines, as they change.

BOOKS & SUCH LITERARY AGENCY

52 Mission Circle, Suite 122, PMB 170, Santa Rosa CA 95409. E-mail: representation@booksandsuch.biz. Website: www.booksandsuch.biz. **Contact:** Janet Kobobel Grant, Wendy Lawton, Etta Wilson, Rachel Zurakowski. Member of AAR. Member of CBA (associate), American Christian Fiction Writers. Represents 150 clients. 5% of clients are new/unpublished writers. Currently handles: nonfiction books 50%, novels 50%.

- Prior to becoming an agent, Ms. Grant was an editor for Zondervan and managing editor for *Focus on the Family*; Ms. Lawton was an author, sculptor and designer of porcelein dolls. Ms. Wilson emphasizes middle grade children's books. Ms. Zurakowski concentrates on material for 20-something or 30-something readers.

Represents Nonfiction books, novels, juvenile books. **Considers these nonfiction areas:** child, humor, religion, self help, women's. **Considers these fiction areas:** contemporary, family, historical, mainstream, religious, romance, African American adult.

- This agency specializes in general and inspirational fiction, romance, and in the Christian booksellers market. Actively seeking well-crafted material that presents Judeo-Christian values, if only subtly.

How to Contact Query via e-mail only, no attachments. Accepts simultaneous submissions. Responds in 1 month to queries. *"If you don't hear from us asking to see more of your writing within 30 days after you have sent your email, please know that we have read and considered your submission but determined that it would not be a good fit for us."* Obtains most new clients through recommendations from others, conferences.

Terms Agent receives 15% commission on domestic sales. Agent receives 20% commission on foreign sales. Offers written contract; 2-month notice must be given to terminate contract. No additional charges.

Recent Sales Sold 125 titles in the last year. *One Simple Act*, by Debbie Macomber (Howard Books); *Victim of Grace*, by Robin Jones Gunn (Zondervan); *Paradise Valley*, by Dale Cramer (Bethany House). Other clients include: Lauraine Snelling, Lori Copeland, Rene Gutteridge, Dale Cramer, BJ Hoff, Diann Mills.

Writers Conferences Mount Hermon Christian Writers' Conference; Society of Childrens' Writers and Illustrators Conference; Writing for the Soul; American Christian Fiction Writers' Conference; San Francisco Writers' Conference.

Tips "The heart of our agency's motivation is to develop relationships with the authors we serve, to do what we can to shine the light of success on them, and to help be a caretaker of their gifts and time."

GEORGES BORCHARDT, INC.

136 E. 57th St., New York NY 10022. Member of AAR.

Member Agents Anne Borchardt; Georges Borchardt; Valerie Borchardt..

- This agency specializes in literary fiction and outstanding nonfiction.

How to Contact *No unsolicited mss.* Obtains most new clients through recommendations from others.

Terms Agent receives 15% commission on domestic sales. Agent receives 20% commission on foreign sales. Offers written contract.

THE HELEN BRANN AGENCY, INC.

94 Curtis Road, Bridgewater CT 06752. Fax: (860)355-2572. Member of AAR.

How to Contact Query with SASE.

CURTIS BROWN, LTD.

10 Astor Place, New York NY 10003-6935. (212)473-5400. Website: www.curtisbrown.com. Alternate address: Peter Ginsberg, president at CBSF, 1750 Montgomery St., San Francisco CA 94111. (415)954-8566. Member of AAR. Signatory of WGA.

Member Agents Ginger Clark; Katherine Fausset; Holly Frederick; Emilie Jacobson, senior vice president; Elizabeth Hardin; Ginger Knowlton, vice president; Timothy Knowlton, CEO; Laura Blake Peterson; Maureen Walters, senior vice president; Mitchell Waters. San Francisco Office: Nathan Bransford, Peter Ginsberg (President).

Represents Nonfiction books, novels, short story collections, juvenile. **Considers these nonfiction areas:** agriculture horticulture, Americana, crafts, interior, juvenile, New Age, young, animals, anthropology, art, biography, business, child, computers, cooking, current affairs, education, ethnic, gardening, gay, government, health, history, how to, humor, language, memoirs, military, money, multicultural, music, nature, philosophy, photography, popular culture, psychology, recreation, regional, religion, science, self help, sex, sociology, software, spirituality, sports, film, translation, travel, true crime, women's, creative nonfiction. **Considers these fiction areas:** contemporary, glitz, new age, psychic, adventure, comic, confession, detective, erotica, ethnic, experimental, family, fantasy, feminist, gay, gothic, hi lo, historical, horror, humor, juvenile, literary, mainstream, military, multicultural, multimedia, mystery, occult, picture books, plays, poetry, regional, religious, romance, science, short, spiritual, sports, thriller, translation, western, young, women's.

How to Contact Prefers to read materials exclusively. *No unsolicited mss.* Responds in 3 weeks to queries. Responds in 5 weeks to mss. Obtains most new clients through recommendations from others, solicitations, conferences.

Terms Offers written contract. Charges for some postage (overseas, etc.)

Recent Sales This agency prefers not to share information on specific sales.

BROWN LITERARY AGENCY

410 Seventh St. NW, Naples FL 34120. Website: www.brownliteraryagency.com. **Contact:** Roberta Brown. Member of AAR. Other memberships include RWA, Author's Guild. Represents 45 clients. 5% of clients are new/unpublished writers.

Represents Novels. **Considers these fiction areas:** erotica, romance, women's, single title and category.

O¬ "This agency is selectively reading material at this time."

How to Contact Query via e-mail only. Send synopsis and two chapters in Word attachment. Response time varies.

Terms Agent receives 15% commission on domestic sales. Agent receives 20% commission on foreign sales. Offers written contract; 30-day notice must be given to terminate contract.

Writers Conferences RWA National Conference.

Tips "Polish your manuscript. Be professional."

SHEREE BYKOFSKY ASSOCIATES, INC.

PO Box 706, Brigantine NJ 08203. E-mail: submitbee@aol.com. Website: www.shereebee.com. **Contact:** Sheree Bykofsky. Member of AAR. Other memberships include ASJA, WNBA. Currently handles: nonfiction books 80%, novels 20%.

- Prior to opening her agency, Ms. Bykofsky served as executive editor of The Stonesong Press and managing editor of Chiron Press. She is also the author or co-author of more than 20 books, including *The Complete Idiot's Guide to Getting Published*. Ms. Bykofsky teaches publishing at NYU and SEAK, Inc.

Member Agents Janet Rosen, associate.

Represents Nonfiction books, novels. **Considers these nonfiction areas:** Americana, crafts, interior, new age, animals, art, biography, business, child, cooking, current affairs, education, ethnic, gardening, gay, government, health, history, how to, humor, language, memoirs, military, money, personal finance, multicultural, music, nature, philosophy, photography, popular culture, psychology, recreation, regional, religion, science, self help, sex, sociology, spirituality, sports, film, translation, travel, true crime, women's, anthropology; creative nonfiction. **Considers these fiction areas:** literary, mainstream, mystery.

O¬ This agency specializes in popular reference nonfiction, commercial fiction with a literary quality, and mysteries. "I have wide-ranging interests, but it really depends on quality of writing, originality, and how a particular project appeals to me (or not). I take on fiction when I completely love it - it doesn't matter what area or genre." Does not want to receive poetry, material for children, screenplays, westerns, horror, science fiction, or fantasy.

How to Contact E-mail short queries to submitbee@aol.com. Please, no attachments, snail mail, or phone calls. Accepts simultaneous submissions. Responds in 3 weeks to queries with SASE. Responds in 1 month to requested mss. Obtains most new clients through recommendations from others.

Terms Agent receives 15% commission on domestic sales. Agent receives 20% commission on foreign sales. Offers written contract, binding for 1 year. Charges for postage, photocopying, fax.

Recent Sales *Red Sheep: The Search for my Inner Latina*, by Michele Carlo (Citadel/Kensington); *Bang the Keys: Four Steps to a Lifelong Writing Practice*, by Jill Dearman (Alpha, Penguin); *Signed, Your Student: Celebrities on the Teachers Who Made Them Who They Are Today*, by Holly Holbert (Kaplan); *The Five Ways We Grieve*, by Susan Berger (Trumpeter/Shambhala).

Writers Conferences ASJA Writers Conference; Asilomar; Florida Suncoast Writers' Conference; Whidbey Island Writers' Conference; Florida First Coast Writers' Festibal; Agents and Editors Conference; Columbus Writers' Conference; Southwest Writers' Conference; Willamette Writers' Conference; Dorothy Canfield Fisher Conference; Maui Writers' Conference; Pacific Northwest Writers' Conference; IWWG.

Tips "Read the agent listing carefully and comply with guidelines."

MARIA CARVAINIS AGENCY, INC.

1270 Avenue of the Americas, Suite 2320, New York NY 10019. (212)245-6365. Fax: (212)245-7196. E-mail: mca@mariacarvainisagency.com. **Contact:** Maria Carvainis, Chelsea Gilmore. Member of AAR. Signatory of WGA. Other memberships include Authors Guild, Women's Media Group, ABA, MWA, RWA. Represents 75 clients. 10%% of clients are new/unpublished writers. Currently handles: nonfiction books 35%, novels 65%.

- Prior to opening her agency, Ms. Carvainis spent more than 10 years in the publishing industry as a senior editor with Macmillan Publishing, Basic Books, Avon Books, and Crown Publishers. Ms. Carvainis has served as a member of the AAR Board of Directors and AAR Treasurer, as well as serving as chair of the AAR Contracts Committee. She presently serves on the AAR Royalty Committee. Ms. Gilmore started her publishing career at Oxford University Press, in the Higher

Education Group. She then worked at Avalon Books as associate editor. She is most interested in women's fiction, literary fiction, young adult, pop culture, and mystery/suspense.

Member Agents Maria Carvainis, president/literary agent; Chelsea Gilmore, literary agent.

Represents Nonfiction books, novels. **Considers these nonfiction areas:** biography, business, history, memoirs, science, pop science, women's. **Considers these fiction areas:** historical, literary, mainstream, mystery, thriller, young, women's, middle grade.

- Does not want to receive science fiction or children's picture books.

How to Contact Query with SASE. Responds in up to 3 months to mss and to queries. Obtains most new clients through recommendations from others, conferences, query letters.

Terms Agent receives 15% commission on domestic sales. Agent receives 20% commission on foreign sales. Offers written contract. Charges clients for foreign postage and bulk copying.

Recent Sales *A Secret Affair*, by Mary Balogh (Delacorte); *Tough Customer*, by Sandra Brown (Simon & Schuster); *A Lady Never Tells*, by Candace Camp (Pocket Books); *The King James Conspiracy*, by Phillip Depoy (St. Martin's Press).

Writers Conferences BookExpo America; Frankfurt Book Fair; London Book Fair; Mystery Writers of America; Thrillerfest; Romance Writers of America.

CASTIGLIA LITERARY AGENCY

1155 Camino Del Mar, Suite 510, Del Mar CA 92014. (858)755-8761. Fax: (858)755-7063. Website: home.earthlink.net/~mwgconference/id22.html. Member of AAR. Other memberships include PEN. Represents 50 clients. Currently handles: nonfiction books 55%, novels 45%.

Member Agents Julie Castiglia; Winifred Golden; Sally Van Haitsma; Deborah Ritchken.

Represents Nonfiction books, novels. **Considers these nonfiction areas:** animals, anthropology, biography, business, child, cooking, current affairs, ethnic, health, history, language, memoir, money, multi-cultural, narrative, nature, politics, psychology, religion, science, self-help, women's issues. **Considers these fiction areas:** commercial, literary, thrillers, young adult.

- Does not want to receive horror, screenplays, poetry or academic nonfiction.

How to Contact Query with SASE. Obtains most new clients through recommendations from others, solicitations, conferences.

Terms Agent receives 15% commission on domestic sales. Agent receives 25% commission on foreign sales. Offers written contract; 6-week notice must be given to terminate contract.

Recent Sales *Germs Gone Wild*, by Kenneth King (Pegasus); *The Insider*, by Reece Hirsch (Berkley/Penguin); *The Leisure Seeker*, by Michael Zadoorian (Morrow/HarperCollins); *Beautiful: The Life of Hedy Lamarr*, by Stephen Shearer (St. Martin's Press); *American Libre*, by Raul Ramos y Sanchez (Grand Central); *The Two Krishnas*, by Ghalib Shiraz Dhalla (Alyson Books).

Writers Conferences Santa Barbara Writers' Conference; Southern California Writers' Conference; Surrey International Writers' Conference; San Diego State University Writers' Conference; Willamette Writers' Conference.

Tips "Be professional with submissions. Attend workshops and conferences before you approach an agent."

FRANCES COLLIN, LITERARY AGENT

P.O. Box 33, Wayne PA 19087-0033. Website: www.francescollin.com. **Contact:** Sarah Yake, Associate Agent. Member of AAR. Represents 90 clients. 1% of clients are new/unpublished writers. Currently handles: nonfiction books 50%, fiction 50%.

Represents Nonfiction books, fiction, young adult.

- Does not want to receive cookbooks, craft books, poetry, screenplays, or books for young children.

How to Contact Query via e-mail describing project (text in the body of the e-mail only, no attachments) to queries@francescollin.com. "Please note that all queries are reviewed by both agents." No phone or fax queries. Accepts simultaneous submissions.

Terms Agent receives 15% commission on domestic sales. Agent receives 20% commission on foreign sales. Offers written contract.

DH LITERARY, INC.

P.O. Box 805, Nyack NY 10960-0990. **Contact:** David Hendin. Member of AAR. Represents 10 clients. Currently handles: nonfiction books 80%, novels 10%, scholarly books 10%.

- Prior to opening his agency, Mr. Hendin served as president and publisher for Pharos Books/World Almanac, as well as senior VP and COO at sister company United Feature Syndicate.
- *Not accepting new clients. Please do not send queries or submissions.*

Terms Agent receives 15% commission on domestic sales. Agent receives 20% commission on foreign sales. Offers written contract, binding for 1 year. Charges for out-of-pocket expenses for overseas postage specifically related to the sale.
Recent Sales *Big Nate, In a Class By Himself* (plus 5 additional titles) and *Zacula* (3 titles), by Lincoln Peirce to Harper Collins; *Miss Manners Guide to a Surprisingly Dignified Wedding*, by Judith and Jacobina Martin (Norton); *Killer Cuts*, by Elaine Viets (NAL/Signet); *The New Time Travelers*, by David Toomey (Norton).

SANDRA DIJKSTRA LITERARY AGENCY

1155 Camino del Mar, PMB 515, Del Mar CA 92014. (858)755-3115. Fax: (858)794-2822. E-mail: elise@dijkstraagency.com. Website: www.dijkstraagency.com. Member of AAR. Other memberships include Authors Guild, PEN West, Poets and Editors, MWA. Represents 100+ clients. 30% of clients are new/unpublished writers. Currently handles: nonfiction books 50%, novels 45%, juvenile books 5%.
Member Agents Sandra Dijkstra; Jill Marsal; Kevan Lyon; Elise Capron; Kelly Sonnack..
Represents Nonfiction books, novels. **Considers these nonfiction areas:** Americana, juvenile, animals, pets, anthropology, business, cooking, ethnic, gay, government, health, history, language, memoirs, military, money, nature, psychology, regional, religion, science, self help, sociology, travel, women's, Asian studies; art; accounting; biography; environmental studies; technology; transportation. **Considers these fiction areas:** erotica, ethnic, fantasy, juvenile, YA, middle grade, literary, mainstream, mystery, science, thriller, graphic novels.

⊶ Does not want to receive Western, screenplays, short story collections or poetry.

How to Contact "Please see guidelines on our website. Due to the large number of unsolicited submissions we receive, we are now ONLY able to respond those submissions in which we are interested. Unsolicited submissions in which we are not interested will receive no response. (Therefore, please do not enclose a self addressed stamped envelope [SASE], and do not send any pages or material you need returned to you. In your materials, please be sure to include all your contact information, including your email address. We accept hard copy submissions only, and will not read or respond to emailed submissions." Responds in 6 weeks to queries. Obtains most new clients through recommendations from others, solicitations, conferences.
Terms Agent receives 15% commission on domestic sales. Agent receives 20% commission on foreign sales. Offers written contract. Charges clients for expenses for foreign postage and copying costs if a client requests a hard copy submission to publishers.
Tips Be professional and learn the standard procedures for submitting your work. Be a regular patron of bookstores, and study what kind of books are being published and will appear on the shelves next to yours. Read! Check out your local library and bookstores—you'll find lots of books on writing and the publishing industry that will help you. At conferences, ask published writers about their agents. Don't believe the myth that an agent has to be in New York to be successful. We've already disproved it!

THE JONATHAN DOLGER AGENCY

49 E. 96th St., Suite 9B, New York NY 10128. Fax: (212)369-7118. Member of AAR.
Represents Nonfiction books, novels. **Considers these nonfiction areas:** biography, history, women's, cultural/social. **Considers these fiction areas:** women's, commercial.
How to Contact Query with SASE. No e-mail queries.
Terms Agent receives 15% commission on domestic sales. Agent receives 25% commission on foreign sales.
Tips "Writers must have been previously published if submitting fiction. We prefer to work with published/established authors, and work with a small number of new/previously unpublished writers."

DONADIO & OLSON, INC.

121 W. 27th St., Suite 704, New York NY 10001. (212)691-8077. Fax: (212)633-2837. E-mail: mail@donadio.com. **Contact:** Neil Olson. Member of AAR.
Member Agents Neil Olson (no queries); Edward Hibbert (no queries); Carrie Howland (query via snail mail or e-mail).
Represents Nonfiction books, novels.

⊶ This agency represents mostly fiction, and is very selective.

How to Contact Query by snail mail is preferred; for e-mail use mail@donadio.com; only send submissions to open agents. Obtains most new clients through recommendations from others.

DUNHAM LITERARY, INC.

156 Fifth Ave., Suite 625, New York NY 10010-7002. (212)929-0994. Website: www.dunhamlit.com. **Contact:** Jennie Dunham. Member of AAR. Represents 50 clients. 15% of clients are new/unpublished writers. Currently handles: nonfiction books 25%, novels 25%, juvenile books 50%.

- Prior to opening her agency, Ms. Dunham worked as a literary agent for Russell & Volkening. The Rhoda Weyr Agency is now a division of Dunham Literary, Inc.

Represents Nonfiction books, novels, short story collections, juvenile. **Considers these nonfiction areas:** anthropology, biography, ethnic, government, health, history, language, nature, popular culture, psychology, science, women's. **Considers these fiction areas:** ethnic, juvenile, literary, mainstream, picture books, young adult.

How to Contact Query with SASE. Responds in 1 week to queries. Responds in 2 months to mss. Obtains most new clients through recommendations from others, solicitations.

Terms Agent receives 15% commission on domestic sales. Agent receives 20% commission on foreign sales.

Recent Sales America the Beautiful, by Robert Sabuda; Dahlia, by Barbara McClintock; Living Dead Girl, by Tod Goldberg; In My Mother's House, by Margaret McMulla; Black Hawk Down, by Mark Bowden; Look Back All the Green Valley, by Fred Chappell; Under a Wing, by Reeve Lindbergh; I Am Madame X, by Gioia Diliberto.

DYSTEL & GODERICH LITERARY MANAGEMENT

1 Union Square W., Suite 904, New York NY 10003. (212)627-9100. Fax: (212)627-9313. E-mail: mbourret@dystel.com. Website: www.dystel.com. **Contact:** Michael Bourret and Jim McCarthy. Member of AAR. SCBWI Represents 617 clients. 50% of clients are new/unpublished writers. Currently handles: nonfiction books 65%, novels 35%.

- Dystel & Goderich Literary Management recently acquired the client list of Bedford Book Works.

Member Agents Jane Dystel; Stacey Glick; Michael Bourret; Jim McCarthy; Jessica Papin; Lauren Abramo; Chasya Milgrom; Rachel Oakley.

Represents Nonfiction books, novels, cookbooks. **Considers these nonfiction areas:** new age, animals, anthrolpology, biography, business, cooking, current affairs, education, ethnic, gay, government, health, history, humor, military, money, popular culture, psychology, religion, science, true crime, women's, child guidance. **Considers these fiction areas:** adventure, detective, ethnic, family, gay, literary, mainstream, mystery, thriller.

O→ "This agency specializes in cookbooks and commercial and literary fiction and nonfiction."

How to Contact Query with SASE. Please include the first 3 chapters in the body of the email. Email queries preferred (Michael Bourret only accepts email queries); will accept mail. See website for full guidelines. Accepts simultaneous submissions. Responds in 6 to 8 weeks to queries. Responds within 8 weeks to mss. Obtains most new clients through recommendations from others, solicitations, conferences.

Terms Agent receives 15% commission on domestic sales. Agent receives 19% commission on foreign sales. Offers written contract.

Writers Conferences Backspace Writers' Conference; Pacific Northwest Writers' Association; Pike's Peak Writers' Conference; Writers League of Texas; Love Is Murder; Surrey International Writers Conference; Society of Children's Book Writers and Illustrators; International Thriller Writers; Willamette Writers Conference; The South Carolina Writers Workshop Conference; Las Vegas Writers Conference; Writer's Digest; Seton Hill Popular Fiction; Romance Writers of America; Geneva Writers Conference.

Tips "DGLM prides itself on being a full-service agency. We're involved in every stage of the publishing process, from offering substantial editing on mss and proposals, to coming up with book ideas for authors looking for their next project, negotiating contractsand col, cting molenies for our clients. We follow a book from its inception through its sale to a publisher, its publication, and beyond. Our commitment to our writers does not, by any means, end when we have collected our commission. This is one of the many things that makes us unique in a very competitive business."

ANNE EDELSTEIN LITERARY AGENCY

20 W. 22nd St., Suite 1603, New York NY 10010. (212)414-4923. Fax: (212)414-2930. E-mail: info@aeliterary.com. Website: www.aeliterary.com. Member of AAR.

Member Agents Anne Edelstein; Krista Ingebretson.

Represents Nonfiction books, fiction. **Considers these nonfiction areas:** narrative history, memoirs, psychology, religion. **Considers these fiction areas:** literary.

O→ This agency specializes in fiction and narrative nonfiction.

How to Contact Query with SASE; submit 25 sample pages.

Recent Sales *Confessions of a Buddhist Atheist*, by Stephen Batchelor (Spiegel & Grau); *April &*

Oliver, by Tess Callahan (Doubleday).

THE LISA EKUS GROUP, LLC

57 North St., Hatfield MA 01038. (413)247-9325. Fax: (413)247-9873. E-mail: LisaEkus@lisaekus.com. Website: www.lisaekus.com. **Contact:** Lisa Ekus-Saffer. Member of AAR.

Represents Nonfiction books. **Considers these nonfiction areas:** cooking, occasionally health/well-being and women's issues.

How to Contact Submit a one-page query via e-mail or submit your complete hard copy proposal with title page, proposal contents, concept, bio, marketing, TOC, etc. Include SASE for the return of materials.

Recent Sales Please see the regularly updated client listing on website.

Tips "Please do not call. No phone queries."

ANN ELMO AGENCY, INC.

305 Seventh Avenue, # 1101, New York NY 10001. (212)661-2880. Fax: (212)661-2883. E-mail: aalitagent@sbcgobal.net. **Contact:** Lettie Lee. Member of AAR. Other memberships include Authors Guild.

Member Agents Lettie Lee; Mari Cronin (plays); A.L. Abecassis (nonfiction).

Represents Nonfiction books, novels. **Considers these nonfiction areas:** biography, current affairs, health, history, how to, popular culture, science. **Considers these fiction areas:** ethnic, family, mainstream, romance, contemporary, gothic, historical, regency, thriller, women's.

How to Contact Only accepts mailed queries with SASE. Do not send full ms unless requested. Responds in 3 months to queries. Obtains most new clients through recommendations from others.

Terms Agent receives 15% commission on domestic sales. Agent receives 20% commission on foreign sales. Offers written contract.

Tips "Query first, and only when asked send a double-spaced, readable manuscript. Include a SASE, of course."

THE ELAINE P. ENGLISH LITERARY AGENCY

4710 41st St. NW Suite D, Washington DC 20016. (202)362-5190. Fax: (202)362-5192. E-mail: elaine@elaineenglish.com; kvn.mcadams@yahoo.com. Website: www.elaineenglish.com. **Contact:** Elaine English.. Kevin McAdams, Executive V.P., 400 East 11th St., # 7, New York, NY 10009 Represents 20 clients. 25% of clients are new/unpublished writers. Currently handles: novels 100%.

- Ms. English has been working in publishing for more than 20 years. She is also an attorney specializing in media and publishing law.

Represents Novels.

THE ELAINE P. ENGLISH LITERARY AGENCY

4710 41st St. NW, Suite D, Washington DC 20016. (202)362-5190. Fax: (202)362-5192. E-mail: elaine@elaineenglish.com; naomi@elaineenglish.com. Website: www.elaineenglish.com. **Contact:** Elaine English or Naomi Hackenberg for YA fiction. Member of AAR. Represents 20 clients. 25% of clients are new/unpublished writers. Currently handles: novels 100%.

- Ms. English has been working in publishing for more than 20 years. She is also an attorney specializing in media and publishing law.

Represents Novels. **Considers these fiction areas:** historical, multicultural, mystery, romance, single title, historical, contemporary, romantic, suspense, chick lit, erotic, thriller, general women's fiction. The agency is slowly but steadily acquiring in all mentioned areas..

- Actively seeking women's fiction, including single-title romances, and young adult fiction. Does not want to receive any science fiction, time travel, or picture books.

How to Contact Generally prefers e-queries sent to queries@elaineenglish.com or YA sent to naomi@elaineenglish.com. If requested, submit synopsis, first 3 chapters, SASE. Please check website for further details. Responds in 4-8 weeks to queries; 3 months to requested submissions Obtains most new clients through recommendations from others, conferences, submissions.

Terms Agent receives 15% commission on domestic sales. Agent receives 20% commission on foreign sales. Offers written contract; 30-day notice must be given to terminate contract. Charges only for shipping expenses; generally taken from proceeds.

Writers Conferences RWA National Conference; Novelists, Inc.; Malice Domestic; Washington Romance Writers Retreat, among others.

FELICIA ETH LITERARY REPRESENTATION

555 Bryant St., Suite 350, Palo Alto CA 94301-1700. (650)375-1276. Fax: (650)401-8892. E-mail: feliciaeth@aol.com. **Contact:** Felicia Eth. Member of AAR. Represents 25-35 clients. Currently handles: nonfiction books 85%, novels 15% adult.

Represents Nonfiction books, novels. **Considers these nonfiction areas:** animals, anthropology, biography, business, child, current affairs, ethnic, government, health, history, nature, popular culture, psychology, science, sociology, true crime, women's. **Considers these fiction areas:** literary, mainstream.

- This agency specializes in high-quality fiction (preferably mainstream/contemporary) and provocative, intelligent, and thoughtful nonfiction on a wide array of commercial subjects.

How to Contact Query with SASE. Accepts simultaneous submissions. Responds in 3 weeks to queries. Responds in 4-6 weeks to mss.

Terms Agent receives 15% commission on domestic sales. Agent receives 20% commission on foreign sales. Agent receives 20% commission on film sales. Charges clients for photocopying and express mail service.

Recent Sales Sold 70-10 titles in the last year. *Bumper Sticker Philosophy*, by Jack Bowen (Random House); *Boys Adrift,* by Leonard Sax (Basic Books); *A War Reporter*, by Barbara Quick (HarperCollins); Pantry, by Anna Badkhen (Free Press/S&S).

Writers Conferences "Wide Array - from Squaw Valley to Mills College."

Tips "For nonfiction, established expertise is certainly a plus—as is magazine publication—though not a prerequisite. I am highly dedicated to those projects I represent, but highly selective in what I choose."

FOLIO LITERARY MANAGEMENT, LLC

505 Eighth Ave., Suite 603, New York NY 10018. Website: www.foliolit.com. Alternate address: 1627 K St. NW, Suite 1200, Washington DC 20006. Member of AAR. Represents 100+ clients.

- Prior to creating Folio Literary Management, Mr. Hoffman worked for several years at another agency; Mr. Kleinman was an agent at Graybill & English; Ms. Wheeler was an agent at Creative Media Agency; Ms. Fine was an agent at Vigliano Associates and Trident Media Group; Ms. Cartwright-Niumata was an editor at Simon & Schuster, HarperCollins, and Avalon Books; Ms. Becker worked as a copywriter, journalist and author.

Member Agents Scott Hoffman; Jeff Kleinman; Paige Wheeler; Celeste Fine; Erin Cartwright-Niumata, Laney K. Becker; Rachel Vater (fantasy, young adult, women's fiction).

Represents Nonfiction books, novels, short story collections. **Considers these nonfiction areas:** animals, equestrian, business, child, history, how to, humor, memoirs, military, nature, popular culture, psychology, religion, science, self help, women's, narrative nonfiction; art; espionage; biography; crime; politics; health/fitness; lifestyle; relationship; culture; cookbooks.. **Considers these fiction areas:** erotica, fantasy, literary, mystery, religious, romance, science, thriller, psychological, young, women's, Southern; legal; edgy crime..

How to Contact Query via e-mail only (no attachments). Read agent bios online for specific submission guidelines. Responds in 1 month to queries.

Tips "Please do not submit simultaneously to more than one agent at Folio. If you're not sure which of us is exactly right for your book, don't worry. We work closely as a team, and if one of our agents gets a query that might be more appropriate for someone else, we'll always pass it along. It's important that you check each agent's bio page for clear directions as to how to submit, as well as when to expect feedback."

GELFMAN SCHNEIDER LITERARY AGENTS, INC.

250 W. 57th St., Suite 2122, New York NY 10107. (212)245-1993. Fax: (212)245-8678. E-mail: mail@gelfmanschneider.com. **Contact:** Jane Gelfman, Deborah Schneider. Member of AAR. Represents 300+ clients. 10% of clients are new/unpublished writers.

Represents Fiction and nonfiction books. **Considers these fiction areas:** literary, mainstream, mystery, women's.

- Does not want to receive romance, science fiction, westerns, or children's books.

How to Contact Query with SASE. Send queries via snail mail only. Responds in 1 month to queries. Responds in 2 months to mss.

Terms Agent receives 15% commission on domestic sales. Agent receives 20% commission on foreign sales. Agent receives 15% commission on film sales. Offers written contract. Charges clients for photocopying and messengers/couriers.

GOODMAN ASSOCIATES

500 West End Ave., New York NY 10024-4317. (212)873-4806. Member of AAR.

- Accepting new clients by recommendation only.

IRENE GOODMAN LITERARY AGENCY

27 W. 24th Street, Suite 700B, New York NY 10010. E-mail: queries@irenegoodman.com. Website: www.irenegoodman.com. **Contact:** Irene Goodman, Miriam Kriss. Member of AAR.

Member Agents Irene Goodman; Miriam Kriss; Barbara Poelle; Jon Sternfeld.

Represents Nonfiction books, novels. **Considers these nonfiction areas:** narrative nonfiction dealing with social, cultural and historical issues; an occasional memoir and current affairs book, parenting, social issues, francophilia, anglophilia, Judaica, lifestyles, cooking, memoir. **Considers these fiction areas:** historical, intelligent literary, modern urban fantasies, mystery, romance, thriller, women's.

- "Specializes in the finest in commercial fiction and nonfiction. We have a strong background in women's voices, including mysteries, romance, women's fiction, thrillers, suspense. Historical fiction is one of Irene's particular passions and Miriam is fanatical about modern urban fantasies. In nonfiction, Irene is looking for topics on narrative history, social issues and trends, education, Judaica, Francophilia, Anglophilia, other cultures, animals, food, crafts, and memoir." Barbara is looking for commercial thrillers with strong female protagonists; Miriam is looking for urban fantasy and edgy sci-fi/young adult.

How to Contact Query. Submit synopsis, first 10 pages. E-mail queries only! See the website submission page. No e-mail attachments. Responds in 2 months to queries.

Recent Sales *The Ark*, by Boyd Morrison; *Isolation*, by C.J. Lyons; *The Sleepwalkers*, by Paul Grossman; *Dead Man's Moon*, by Devon Monk; *Becoming Marie Antoinette*, by Juliet Grey; *What's Up Down There*, by Lissa Rankin; *Beg for Mercy*, by Toni Andrews; *The Devil Inside*, by Jenna Black.

Tips "We are receiving an unprecedented amount of email queries. If you find that the mailbox is full, please try again in two weeks. Email queries to our personal addresses will not be answered. Emails to our personal in-boes will be deleted."

SANFORD J. GREENBURGER ASSOCIATES, INC.

55 Fifth Ave., New York NY 10003. (212)206-5600. Fax: (212)463-8718. E-mail: queryHL@sjga.com. Website: www.greenburger.com. Member of AAR. Represents 500 clients.

Member Agents Heide Lange; Faith Hamlin; Dan Mandel; Matthew Bialer; Courtney Miller-Callihan, Michael Harriot, Brenda Bowen, Lisa Gallagher.[.

Represents Nonfiction books and novels. **Considers these nonfiction areas:** agriculture horticulture, Americana, crafts, interior, juvenile, new age, young adult, animals, anthropology, art, biography, business, child, computers, cooking, current affairs, education, ethnic, gardening, gay, government, health, history, how-to, humor, language, memoirs, military, money, multicultural, music, nature, philosophy, photography, popular culture, psychology, recreation, regional, religion, science, self-help, sex, sociology, software, sports, film, translation, travel, true crime, women's. **Considers these fiction areas:** glitz, psychic, adventure, detective, ethnic, family, feminist, gay, historical, humor, literary, mainstream, mystery, regional, sports, thriller.

- No romances or Westerns.

How to Contact Submit query, first 3 chapters, synopsis, brief bio, SASE. Accepts simultaneous submissions. Responds in 2 months to queries and mss. Responds to mss. Obtains most new clients through recommendations from others.

Terms Agent receives 15% commission on domestic sales. Agent receives 20% commission on foreign sales. Charges for photocopying and books for foreign and subsidiary rights submissions.

THE JOY HARRIS LITERARY AGENCY, INC.

156 Fifth Ave., Suite 617, New York NY 10010. (212)924-6269. Fax: (212)924-6609. Website: joyharrisliterary.com. **Contact:** Joy Harris. Member of AAR. Represents more than 100 clients. Currently handles: nonfiction books 50%, novels 50%.

Represents Nonfiction books, novels, and young adult. **Considers these fiction areas:** glitz, ethnic, experimental, family, feminist, gay, hi lo, historical, humor, literary, mainstream, multicultural, multimedia, mystery, regional, short, spiritual, translation, young adult, women's.

- No screenplays.

How to Contact Visit our website for guidelines. Query with sample chapter, outline/proposal, SASE. Accepts simultaneous submissions. Responds in 2 months to queries. Obtains most new clients through recommendations from clients and editors.

Terms Agent receives 15% commission on domestic sales. Agent receives 20% commission on foreign sales. Charges clients for some office expenses.

JOHN HAWKINS & ASSOCIATES, INC.

71 W. 23rd St., Suite 1600, New York NY 10010. (212)807-7040. Fax: (212)807-9555. E-mail: jha@jhalit.com. Website: www.jhalit.com. **Contact:** Moses Cardona (moses@jhalit.com). Member of AAR. Represents over 100 clients. 5-10% of clients are new/unpublished writers. Currently handles: nonfiction books 40%, novels 40%, juvenile books 20%.

Member Agents Moses Cardona; Anne Hawkins (ahawkins@jhalit.com); Warren Frazier (frazier@jhalit.com); William Reiss (reiss@jhalit.com).

Represents Nonfiction books, novels, young adult. **Considers these nonfiction areas:** agriculture horticulture, Americana, interior, young, anthropology, art, biography, business, current affairs, education, ethnic, gardening, gay, government, health, history, how-to, language, memoirs, money, multicultural, nature, philosophy, popular culture, psychology, recreation, science, self-help, sex, sociology, software, film, travel, true crime, music, creative nonfiction. **Considers these fiction areas:** glitz, psychic, adventure, detective, ethnic, experimental, family, feminist, gay, gothic, hi lo, historical, literary, mainstream, military, multicultural, multimedia, mystery, religious, short, sports, thriller, translation, western, young, women's.

How to Contact Submit query, proposal package, outline, SASE. Accepts simultaneous submissions. Responds in 1 month to queries. Obtains most new clients through recommendations from others.

Terms Agent receives 15% commission on domestic sales. Agent receives 20% commission on foreign sales. Charges clients for photocopying.

Recent Sales *Celebration of Shoes*, by Eileen Spinelli; *Chaos*, by Martin Gross; *The Informationist*, by Taylor Stevens; *The Line*, by Olga Grushin

HEACOCK HILL LITERARY AGENCY, INC.

West Coast Office, 1020 Hollywood Way #439, Burbank CA 91505. (505)585-0111 - NM office.... E-mail: agent@heacockhill.com. Website: www.heacockhill.com. **Contact:** Catt LeBaigue. Member of AAR. Other memberships include SCBWI.

- Prior to becoming an agent, Ms. LeBaigue spent 18 years with Sony Pictures and Warner Bros.

Member Agents Tom Dark (adult fiction, nonfiction); Catt LeBaigue (juvenile fiction, adult nonfiction including arts, crafts, anthropolgy, astronomy, nature studies, ecology, body/mind/spirit, humanities, self-help)..

Represents Nonfiction, fiction. **Considers these nonfiction areas:** hiking.

How to Contact E-mail queries only. No unsolicited manuscripts. No e-mail attachments. Obtains most new clients through recommendations from others, solicitations.

Terms Offers written contract.

Tips "Write an informative original e-query expressing your book idea, your qualifications, and short excerpts of the work. No unfinished work, please."

RICHARD HENSHAW GROUP

22 West 23rd St., Fifth Floor, New York NY 10010. (212)414-1172. Fax: (212)414-1182. E-mail: submissions@henshaw.com. Website: www.rich.henshaw.com. **Contact:** Rich Henshaw. Member of AAR. Other memberships include SinC, MWA, HWA, SFWA, RWA. Represents 35 clients. 20% of clients are new/unpublished writers. Currently handles: nonfiction books 35%, novels 65%.

- Prior to opening his agency, Mr. Henshaw served as an agent with Richard Curtis Associates, Inc.

Represents Nonfiction books, novels. **Considers these nonfiction areas:** animals, biography, business, computers, cooking, current affairs, gay, government, health, humor, military, money, music, nature, New Age, popular culture, psychology, science, sociology, sports, true crime. **Considers these fiction areas:** glitz, psychic, adventure, detective, ethnic, family, fantasy, historical, horror, humor, literary, mainstream, mystery, romance, science, sports, thriller.

O- This agency specializes in thrillers, mysteries, science fiction, fantasy and horror.

How to Contact Query with SASE. Responds in 3 weeks to queries. Responds in 6 weeks to mss. Obtains most new clients through recommendations from others, solicitations, conferences.

Terms Agent receives 15% commission on domestic sales. Agent receives 20% commission on foreign sales. No written contract. Charges clients for photocopying and book orders.

Recent Sales *Kate Shugak* mystery by Dana Stabenow; *Wind River* mystery by Margaret Coel; *Diving Into the Wreck* series by Kristine Kathryn Rusch; *History of the World* series, by Susan Wise Bauer; *Maiden Lane* series by Elizabeth Hoyt.

Tips "While we do not have any reason to believe that our submission guidelines will change in the near future, writers can find up-to-date submission policy information on our website. Always include a SASE with correct return postage."

KIRCHOFF/WOHLBERG, INC., AUTHORS' REPRESENTATION DIVISION

897 Boston Post Road, Madison CT 06443. (203)245-7308. Fax: (203)245-3218. E-mail: trade@kirchoffwohlberg.com. **Contact:** Ronald Zollshan. Member of AAR. Other memberships include SCBWI, AAP, Society of Illustrators, SPAR, Bookbuilders of Boston, New York Bookbinders' Guild, AIGA. 10% of clients are new/unpublished writers. Currently handles: nonfiction books 5%, novels 25%, other 5% young adult.

- Kirchoff/Wohlberg has been in business for over 60 years.

⊶ This agency specializes in juvenile fiction and non-fiction through Young Adult.

How to Contact Submit by mail to address above. Include SASE. Accepts simultaneous submissions.
Terms Offers written contract, binding for at least 1 year. Agent receives standard commission, depending upon whether it is an author only, illustrator only, or an author/illustrator book.

HARVEY KLINGER, INC.

300 W. 55th St., Suite 11V, New York NY 10019. (212)581-7068. E-mail: queries@harveyklinger.com. Website: www.harveyklinger.com. **Contact:** Harvey Klinger. Member of AAR. Represents 100 clients. 25% of clients are new/unpublished writers. Currently handles: nonfiction books 50%, novels 50%.

Member Agents David Dunton (popular culture, music-related books, literary fiction, young adult, fiction, and memoirs); Sara Crowe (children's and young adult authors, adult fiction and nonfiction, foreign rights sales); Andrea Somberg (literary fiction, commercial fiction, romance, sci-fi/fantasy, mysteries/thrillers, young adult, middle grade, quality narrative nonfiction, popular culture, how-to, self-help, humor, interior design, cookbooks, health/fitness).

Represents Nonfiction books, novels. **Considers these nonfiction areas:** biography, cooking, health, psychology, science, self help, spirituality, sports, true crime, women's. **Considers these fiction areas:** glitz, adventure, detective, family, literary, mainstream, mystery, thriller.

⊶ This agency specializes in big, mainstream, contemporary fiction and nonfiction.

How to Contact Query with SASE. No phone or fax queries. Don't send unsolicited manuscripts or e-mail attachments. Responds in 2 months to queries and mss Obtains most new clients through recommendations from others.

Terms Agent receives 15% commission on domestic sales. Agent receives 25% commission on foreign sales. Offers written contract. Charges for photocopying mss and overseas postage for mss.

Recent Sales *Woman of a Thousand Secrets*, by Barbara Wood; *I am Not a Serial Killer*, by Dan Wells; untitled memoir, by Bob Mould; *Children of the Mist*; by Paula Quinn; *Tutored*, by Allison Whittenberg; *Will You Take Me As I Am*, by Michelle Mercer. Other clients include: George Taber, Terry Kay, Scott Mebus, Jacqueline Kolosov, Jonathan Maberry, Tara Altebrando, Alex McAuley, Eva Nagorski, Greg Kot, Justine Musk, Alex McAuley, Nick Tasler, Ashley Kahn, Barbara De Angelis.

LINDA KONNER LITERARY AGENCY

10 W. 15th St., Suite 1918, New York NY 10011-6829. (212)691-3419. E-mail: ldkonner@cs.com. Website: www.lindakonnerliteraryagency.com. **Contact:** Linda Konner. Member of AAR. Signatory of WGA. Other memberships include ASJA. Represents 85 clients. 30-35% of clients are new/unpublished writers. Currently handles: nonfiction books 100%.

Represents Nonfiction books. **Considers these nonfiction areas:** biography (celebrity only), gay, health, diet/nutrition/fitness, how to, money, personal finance, popular culture, psychology, pop psychology, self help, women's issues; African American and Latino issues; business; parenting; relationships.

⊶ This agency specializes in health, self-help, and how-to books. Authors/co-authors must be top experts in their field with a substantial media platform.

How to Contact Query with SASE, synopsis, author bio, sufficient return postage. Prefers to read materials exclusively for 2 weeks. Accepts simultaneous submissions. Obtains most new clients through recommendations from others, occasional solicitation among established authors/journalists.

Terms Agent receives 15% commission on domestic sales. Agent receives 25% commission on foreign sales. Offers written contract. Charges one-time fee for domestic expenses; additional expenses may be incurred for foreign sales.

Recent Sales *Organize Your Mind, Organize Your Life*, by Paul Hammerness, PhD, Margaret Moore and John Hanc, with the editors of Harvard Health Publications; *Southern Plate: Cherished Recipes and Stories From My 13 Grandparents*, by Christy Jordan (Harper Studio); *Second Acts: Finding a*

Passionate New Career, by Kerry Hannon (Chronicle Books); *Who Do You Think You Are?: Tracing Your Family History*, a tie-in to the NBC tv series, by Megan Smolenyak (Viking).
Writers Conferences ASJA Writers Conference, Harvard Medical School's "Publishing Books, Memoirs, and Other Creative Nonfiction" Annual Conference.

BARBARA S. KOUTS, LITERARY AGENT

P.O. Box 560, Bellport NY 11713. (631)286-1278. Fax: (631) 286-1538. **Contact:** Barbara S. Kouts. Member of AAR. Represents 50 clients. 10% of clients are new/unpublished writers.
Represents Juvenile.

- This agency specializes in children's books.

How to Contact Query with SASE. Accepts simultaneous submissions. Responds in 1 week to queries. Responds in 2 months to mss. Obtains most new clients through recommendations from others, solicitations, conferences.
Terms Agent receives 10% commission on domestic sales. Agent receives 20% commission on foreign sales. This agency charges clients for photocopying.
Tips "Write, do not call. Be professional in your writing."

STUART KRICHEVSKY LITERARY AGENCY, INC.

381 Park Ave. S., Suite 914, New York NY 10016. (212)725-5288. Fax: (212)725-5275. E-mail: query@skagency.com. Website: www.skagency.com. Member of AAR.
Member Agents Stuart Krichevsky; Shana Cohen (science fiction, fantasy); Jennifer Puglisi (assistant)..
Represents Nonfiction books, novels.
How to Contact Submit query, synopsis, 1 sample page via e-mail (no attachments). Snail mail queries also acceptable. Obtains most new clients through recommendations from others, solicitations.

MICHAEL LARSEN/ELIZABETH POMADA, LITERARY AGENTS

1029 Jones St., San Francisco CA 94109-5023. (415)673-0939. E-mail: larsenpoma@aol.com. Website: www.larsen-pomada.com. **Contact:** Mike Larsen, Elizabeth Pomada. Member of AAR. Other memberships include Authors Guild, ASJA, PEN, WNBA, California Writers Club, National Speakers Association. Represents 100 clients. 40-45% of clients are new/unpublished writers. Currently handles: nonfiction books 70%, novels 30%.

- Prior to opening their agency, Mr. Larsen and Ms. Pomada were promotion executives for major publishing houses. Mr. Larsen worked for Morrow, Bantam and Pyramid (now part of Berkley); Ms. Pomada worked at Holt, David McKay and The Dial Press. Mr. Larsen is the author of the 4th edition of *How to Write a Book Proposal* and *How to Get a Literary Agent* as well as the coauthor of *Guerilla Marketing for Writers: 100 Weapons for Selling Your Work*, which was republished in September 2009.

Member Agents Michael Larsen (nonfiction); Elizabeth Pomada (fiction & narrative nonfiction)..
Represents Considers these nonfiction areas: anthropology, art, biography, business, current affairs, ethnic, film, foods, gay, health, history, humor, memoirs, money, music, nature, , popular. culture, psychology, science, sociology, sports, travel, futurism. **Considers these fiction areas:** adventure, detective, ethnic, feminist, gay, glitz, historical, humor, literary, mainstream, mystery, romance, paranormal adventure, chick lit.

- We have diverse tastes. We look for fresh voices and new ideas. We handle literary, commercial and genre fiction, and the full range of nonfiction books. Actively seeking commercial, genre and literary fiction. Does not want to receive children's books, plays, short stories, screenplays, pornography, poetry or stories of abuse.

How to Contact Query with SASE. Responds in 8 weeks to pages or submissions.
Terms Agent receives 15% commission on domestic sales. Agent receives 20% (30% for Asia) commission on foreign sales. May charge for printing, postage for multiple submissions, foreign mail, foreign phone calls, galleys, books, legal fees.
Recent Sales Sold at least 15 titles in the last year. *Secrets of the Tudor Court*, by D. Bogden (Kensington); *Zen & the Art of Horse Training*, by Allan Hamilton, M.D. (Storey Pub.); *The Solemn Lantern Maker*, by Merlinda Bobis (Delta); *Bite Marks*, the fifth book in an urban fantasy series by J.D. Rardin (Orbit/Grand Central); *The Iron King*, by Julie Karawa (Harlequin Teen).
Writers Conferences This agency organizes the annual San Francisco Writers' Conference (www.sfwriters.org).
Tips "We love helping writers get the rewards and recognition they deserve. If you can write books that meet the needs of the marketplace and you can promote your books, now is the best time ever to be a writer. We must find new writers to make a living, so we are very eager to hear from new writers

whose work will interest large houses, and nonfiction writers who can promote their books. For a list of recent sales, helpful info, and three ways to make yourself irresistible to any publisher, please visit our website."

SARAH LAZIN BOOKS

126 Fifth Ave., Suite 300, New York NY 10011. (212)989-5757. Fax: (212)989-1393. **Contact:** Sarah Lazin. Member of AAR. Represents 75+ clients. Currently handles: nonfiction books 80%, novels 20%.
Member Agents Sarah Lazin; Rebecca Ferreira.
Represents Nonfiction books, novels. **Considers these nonfiction areas:** biography, ethnic, gay, history, memoirs, music, popular culture, religious, Works with companies who package their books; handles some photography.
How to Contact Query with SASE. No e-mail queries.
Terms Agent receives 15% commission on domestic sales. Agent receives 20% commission on foreign sales.

LESCHER & LESCHER, LTD.

346 E. 84th St., New York NY 10028. (212)396-1999. Fax: (212)396-1991. **Contact:** Robert Larson; Carolyn Larson. Member of AAR. Represents 150 clients. Currently handles: nonfiction books 80%, novels 20%.
Represents Nonfiction books, novels. **Considers these nonfiction areas:** current affairs, history, memoirs, popular culture, biography; cookbooks/wines; law; contemporary issues; narrative nonfiction. **Considers these fiction areas:** literary, mystery, commercial.
- Does not want to receive screenplays, science fiction or romance.

How to Contact Query with SASE. Obtains most new clients through recommendations from others.
Terms Agent receives 15% commission on domestic sales. Agent receives 10% commission on foreign sales.

LITERARY AND CREATIVE ARTISTS, INC.

2123 Paris Metz Rd., Chattanooga TN 37421. E-mail: southernlitagent@aol.com. **Contact:** Muriel Nellis. Member of AAR. Other memberships include Authors Guild, American Bar Association. Currently handles: nonfiction books 50%, novels 50%.
Member Agents Prior to becoming an agent, Mr. Powell was in sales and contract negotiation..
Represents Nonfiction books, novels, art, biography, business, photography, popular culture, religion, self help, literary, regional, religious, satire. **Considers these nonfiction areas:** biography, business, cooking, government, health, how to, memoirs, philosophy, human drama; lifestyle.
- "We focus on authors that live in the Southern United States. We have the ability to translate and explain complexities of publishing for the Southern author. Actively seeking quality projects by authors with a vision of where they want to be in 10 years and a plan of how to get there." Does not want to receive unfinished, unedited projects that do not follow the standard presentation conventions of the trade. No Romance.

How to Contact Query via e-mail first and include a synopsis. Accepts simultaneous submissions. Responds in 2-3 months to queries. Responds in 1 week mss. Through recommendations from others.
Terms Agent receives 15% commission on domestic sales. Agent receives 25% commission on foreign sales. Offers written contract. Charges clients for long-distance phone/fax, photocopying, shipping.
Tips "If you are an unpublished author, join a writers group, even if it is on the Internet. You need good honest feedback. Don't send a manuscript that has not been read by at least five people. Don't send a manuscript cold to any agent without first asking if they want it. Try to meet the agent face to face before signing. Make sure the fit is right."

NANCY LOVE LITERARY AGENCY

250 E. 65th St., New York NY 10065-6614. (212)980-3499. Fax: (212)308-6405. E-mail: nloveag@aol.com. **Contact:** Nancy Love. Member of AAR. Represents 60-80 clients. 25% of clients are new/unpublished writers. Currently handles: nonfiction books 100%.
Member Agents *This agency is not taking on any new fiction writers at this time..*
Represents Nonfiction books. **Considers these nonfiction areas:** biography, cooking, current affairs, ethnic, government, health, history, how-to, nature, popular culture, psychology, science, sociology, women's issues.
- This agency specializes in adult nonfiction. Actively seeking narrative nonfiction.

How to Contact Query with SASE. No fax queries. Accepts simultaneous submissions. Responds in 3 weeks to queries. Responds in 6 weeks to mss. Obtains most new clients through recommendations from others, solicitations.

Terms Agent receives 15% commission on domestic sales. Agent receives 20% commission on foreign sales. Offers written contract.

Recent Sales *Reset: Iran, Turkey, and America's Future*, by Stephen Kinzer (Henry Holt); *The Ten Stupidest Mistakes Men Make When Facing Divorce*, by Joseph E. Cordell, Esq. (Crown); *Brazil on the Rise*, by Larry Rohter (Macmillan).

Tips "Nonfiction authors and/or collaborators must be an authority in their subject area and have a platform. Send an SASE if you want a response."

LYONS LITERARY, LLC

27 West 20th St., Suite 10003, New York NY 10011. (212)255-5472. Fax: (212)851-8405. E-mail: info@lyonsliterary.com. Website: www.lyonsliterary.com. **Contact:** Jonathan Lyons. Member of AAR. Other memberships include The Author's Guild, American Bar Association, New York State Bar Association, New York State Intellectual Property Law Section. Represents 37 clients. 15% of clients are new/unpublished writers. Currently handles: nonfiction books 60%, novels 40%.

Represents Nonfiction books, novels. **Considers these nonfiction areas:** crafts, animals, biography, cooking, current affairs, ethnic, gay, government, health, history, how to, humor, memoirs, military, money, multicultural, nature, popular culture, psychology, science, sociology, sports, translation, travel, true crime, women's. **Considers these fiction areas:** psychic, detective, fantasy, feminist, gay, historical, humor, literary, mainstream, mystery, regional, science, sports, thriller, women's, chick lit.

- "With my legal expertise and experience selling domestic and foreign language book rights, paperback reprint rights, audio rights, film/TV rights and permissions, I am able to provide substantive and personal guidance to my clients in all areas relating to their projects. In addition, with the advent of new publishing technology, Lyons Literary, LLC is situated to address the changing nature of the industry while concurrently handling authors' more traditional needs."

How to Contact Only accepts queries through online submission form. Accepts simultaneous submissions. Responds in 8 weeks to queries. Responds in 12 weeks to mss. Obtains most new clients through recommendations from others.

Terms Agent receives 15% commission on domestic sales. Agent receives 20% commission on foreign sales. Offers written contract.

Writers Conferences Agents and Editors Conference.

Tips "Please submit electronic queries through our website submission form."

CAROL MANN AGENCY

55 Fifth Ave., New York NY 10003. (212)206-5635. Fax: (212)675-4809. E-mail: eliza@carolmannagency.com. Website: www.carolmannagency.com/. **Contact:** Eliza Dreier. Member of AAR. Represents roughly 200 clients. 15% of clients are new/unpublished writers. Currently handles: nonfiction books 90%, novels 10%.

Member Agents Carol Mann (health/medical, religion, spirituality, self-help, parenting, narrative nonfiction); Laura Yorke; Gareth Esersky, Myrsini Stephanides.

Represents Nonfiction books, novels. **Considers these nonfiction areas:** anthropology, art, biography, business, child, current affairs, ethnic, government, health, history, money, popular culture, psychology, self help, sociology, sports, womens, music. **Considers these fiction areas:** literary, commercial.

- This agency specializes in current affairs, self-help, popular culture, psychology, parenting, and history. Does not want to receive genre fiction (romance, mystery, etc.).

How to Contact Keep initial query/contact to no more than two pages. Responds in 4 weeks to queries.

Terms Agent receives 15% commission on domestic sales. Agent receives 20% commission on foreign sales. Offers written contract.

THE DENISE MARCIL LITERARY AGENCY, INC.

156 Fifth Ave., Suite 625, New York NY 10010. (212)337-3402. Fax: (212)727-2688. Website: www.DeniseMarcilAgency.com. **Contact:** Denise Marcil, Anne Marie O'Farrell. Member of AAR.

- Prior to opening her agency, Ms. Marcil served as an editorial assistant with Avon Books and as an assistant editor with Simon & Schuster.

Member Agents Denise Marcil (women's commercial fiction, thrillers, suspense, popular reference, how-to, self-help, health, business, and parenting.

- *This agency is currently not taking on new authors.*

Terms Agent receives 15% commission on domestic sales. Agent receives 20% commission on foreign sales. Offers written contract, binding for 2 years. Charges $100/year for postage, photocopying, long-distance calls, etc.

Recent Sales For Denise Marcil: A Chesapeake Sores Christmas, by Sherryl Woods; Prime Time Health, by William Sears, M.D. and Martha Sears, R.N.; The Autism Book, by Robert W. Sears, M.D.; The Yellow House and The Linen Queen, by Patricia Falvey; The 10-Minute Total Body Breakthrough, by Sean Foy. For Anne Marie O'Farrell: Think Confident, Be Confident, by Leslie Sokol Ph.d and Marci G. Fox, Ph.d; Hell Yes, by Elizabeth Baskin; Breaking Into the Boys Club, by Molly Shepard, Jane K. Stimmler, and Peter Dean.

THE EVAN MARSHALL AGENCY

Six Tristam Place, Pine Brook NJ 07058-9445. (973)882-1122. Fax: (973)882-3099. E-mail: evanmarshall@optonline.net. **Contact:** Evan Marshall. Member of AAR. Other memberships include MWA, Sisters in Crime. Currently handles: novels 100%.

Represents novels. **Considers these fiction areas:** adventure, erotica, ethnic, historical, horror, humor, literary, mainstream, mystery, religious, romance, contemporary, gothic, historical, regency, science, western.

How to Contact Query first with SASE; do not enclose material. No e-mail queries. Responds in 1 week to queries. Responds in 3 months to mss. Obtains most new clients through recommendations from others.

Terms Agent receives 15% commission on domestic sales. Agent receives 20% commission on foreign sales. Offers written contract.

Recent Sales *Blood Vines*, by Erica Spindler (St. Martin's Press); *Breakneck*, by Erica Spindler (St. Martin's Press); *Such a Pretty Face*, by Cathy Lamb (Kensington); *If He's Sinful*, by Hannah Howell (Zebra).

MARTIN LITERARY MANAGEMENT

321 High School Rd., Suite D3 #316, Bainbridge Island WA 98110. E-mail: sharlene@martinliterarymanagement.com. Website: www.MartinLiteraryManagement.com. **Contact:** Sharlene Martin. 75% of clients are new/unpublished writers.

- Prior to becoming an agent, Ms. Martin worked in film/TV production and acquisitions.

Member Agents Sharlene Martin (nonfiction). NEW: Bree Ogden (Children's books and Graphic Novels only) Bree@MartinLiteraryManagement.com.

Represents Considers these nonfiction areas: biography, business, child, current affairs, health, history, how-to, humor, memoirs, popular culture, psychology, religion, self-help, true crime, women's.

- This agency has strong ties to film/TV. Actively seeking nonfiction that is highly commercial and that can be adapted to film. "We are being inundated with queries and submissions that are wrongfully being submitted to us, which only results in more frustrated for the writers."

How to Contact Query via e-mail with MS Word only. No attachments on queries; place letter in body of e-mail. Accepts simultaneous submissions. Responds in 2 weeks to queries. Responds in 3-4 weeks to mss. Obtains most new clients through recommendations from others.

Terms Agent receives 15% commission on domestic sales. Agent receives 25% commission on foreign sales. Offers written contract, binding for 1 year; 1-month notice must be given to terminate contract. Charges author for postage and copying if material is not sent electronically. 99% of materials are sent electronically to minimize charges to author for postage and copying.

Recent Sales *Publish Your Nonfiction Book*, by Keith and Brooke Desserich; *Getting It Through My Thick Skull*, by Mary Jo Buttafuoco; *I Want*, by Jane Velez-Mitchell. Sales are updated weekly on website.

Tips "Have a strong platform for nonfiction. Please don't call. I welcome e-mail. I'm very responsive when I'm interested in a query and work hard to get my clients materials in the best possible shape before submissions. Do your homework prior to submission and only submit your best efforts. Please review our website carefully to make sure we're a good match for your work. If you read my book, *Publish Your Nonfiction Book: Strategies For Learning the Industry, Selling Your Book and Building a Successful Career* (Writer's Digest Books) you'll know exactly how to charm me."

THE MCCARTHY AGENCY, LLC

7 Allen St., Rumson NJ 07660. Phone/Fax: (732)741-3065. E-mail: mccarthylit@aol.com. **Contact:** Shawna McCarthy. Member of AAR. Currently handles: nonfiction books 25%, novels 75%.

Member Agents Shawna McCarthy.

Represents Nonfiction books, novels. **Considers these nonfiction areas:** biography, history, philosophy, science. **Considers these fiction areas:** fantasy, juvenile, mystery, romance, science, womens.

How to Contact Query via e-mail only. Accepts simultaneous submissions.

SALLY HILL MCMILLAN & ASSOCIATES, INC.

429 E. Kingston Ave., Charlotte NC 28203. (704)334-0897. **Contact:** Sally Hill McMillan. Member of AAR.

- "We are not seeking new clients at this time. Agency specializes in Southern fiction, women's fiction, mystery and practical nonfiction."

How to Contact *No unsolicited submissions.*

MENDEL MEDIA GROUP, LLC

115 West 30th St., Suite 800, New York NY 10001. (646)239-9896. Fax: (212)685-4717. E-mail: scott@mendelmedia.com. Website: www.mendelmedia.com. Member of AAR. Represents 40-60 clients.

- Prior to becoming an agent, Mr. Mendel was an academic. "I taught American literature, Yiddish, Jewish studies, and literary theory at the University of Chicago and the University of Illinois at Chicago while working on my PhD in English. I also worked as a freelance technical writer and as the managing editor of a healthcare magazine. In 1998, I began working for the late Jane Jordan Browne, a long-time agent in the book publishing world."

Represents Nonfiction books, novels, scholarly, with potential for broad/popular appeal. **Considers these nonfiction areas:** Americana, animals, anthropology, art, biography, business, child, cooking, current affairs, education, ethnic, gardening, gay, government, health, history, how to, humor, language, memoirs, military, money, multicultural, music, nature, philosophy, popular culture, psychology, recreation, regional, religion, science, self help, sex, sociology, software, spirituality, sports, true crime, women's, Jewish topics; creative nonfiction. **Considers these fiction areas:** contemporary, glitz, adventure, detective,. erotica, ethnic, feminist, gay, historical, humor, juvenile, literary, mainstream, mystery, picture books, religious, romance, sports, thriller, young, Jewish fiction.

- "I am interested in major works of history, current affairs, biography, business, politics, economics, science, major memoirs, narrative nonfiction, and other sorts of general nonfiction." Actively seeking new, major or definitive work on a subject of broad interest, or a controversial, but authoritative, new book on a subject that affects many people's lives." I also represent more light-hearted nonfiction projects, such as gift or novelty books, when they suit the market particularly well." Does not want "queries about projects written years ago that were unsuccessfully shopped to a long list of trade publishers by either the author or another agent. I am specifically not interested in reading short, category romances (regency, time travel, paranormal, etc.), horror novels, supernatural stories, poetry, original plays, or film scripts."

How to Contact Query with SASE. Do not e-mail or fax queries. For nonfiction, include a complete, fully-edited book proposal with sample chapters. For fiction, include a complete synopsis and no more than 20 pages of sample text. Responds in 2 weeks to queries. Responds in 4-6 weeks to mss. Obtains most new clients through recommendations from others.

Terms Agent receives 15% commission on domestic sales. Agent receives 20% commission on foreign sales.

Writers Conferences BookExpo America; Frankfurt Book Fair; London Book Fair; RWA National Conference; Modern Language Association Convention; Jerusalem Book Fair.

Tips "While I am not interested in being flattered by a prospective client, it does matter to me that she knows why she is writing to me in the first place. Is one of my clients a colleague of hers? Has she read a book by one of my clients that led her to believe I might be interested in her work? Authors of descriptive nonfiction should have real credentials and expertise in their subject areas, either as academics, journalists, or policy experts, and authors of prescriptive nonfiction should have legitimate expertise and considerable experience communicating their ideas in seminars and workshops, in a successful business, through the media, etc."

HOWARD MORHAIM LITERARY AGENCY

30 Pierrepont St., Brooklyn NY 11201. (718)222-8400. Fax: (718)222-5056. Website: www.morhaimliterary.com/. Member of AAR.

Member Agents Howard Morhaim, Kate McKean, Katie Menick.

- Actively seeking fiction, nonfiction and young-adult novels.

How to Contact Query via e-mail with cover letter and three sample chapters. See each agent's listing for specifics.

NELSON LITERARY AGENCY

1732 Wazee St., Suite 207, Denver CO 80202. (303)292-2805. E-mail: query@nelsonagency.com. Website: www.nelsonagency.com. **Contact:** Kristin Nelson, president and seniorn literary agent; Sara Megibow, associate literary agent. Member of AAR. RWA, SCBWI, SFWA

- Prior to opening her own agency, Ms. Nelson worked as a literary scout and subrights agent for agent Jody Rein.

Represents Novels, select nonfiction. **Considers these nonfiction areas:** memoirs. **Considers these fiction areas:** literary, romance, includes fantasy with romantic elements, science fiction, fantasy, young adult, women's, chick lit (includes mysteries); commercial/mainstream.

0→ NLA specializes in representing commercial fiction and high caliber literary fiction. Actively seeking Latina writers who tackle contemporary issues in a modern voice (think *Dirty Girls Social Club*). Does not want short story collections, mysteries (except chick lit)', thrillers, Christian, horror, or children's picture books.

How to Contact Query by e-mail only.

Recent Sales New York Times Bestselling author of *I'd Tell You I Love You, But Then I'd Have to Kill You*, Ally Carter's fourth novel in the Gallagher Girls series; *Hester* (historical fiction), by Paula Reed, *Proof by Seduction* (debut romance), by Courtney Milan, *Soulless* (fantasy debut), by Gail Carriger, *The Shifter* (debut children's fantasy), by Janice Hardy, *Real Life & Liars* (debut women's fiction), by Kristina Riggle, *Hotel on the Corner of Bitter and Sweet* (debut literary fiction), by Jamie Ford.

HAROLD OBER ASSOCIATES

425 Madison Ave., New York NY 10017. (212)759-8600. Fax: (212)759-9428. Website: www.haroldober.com. **Contact:** Craig Tenney. Member of AAR. Represents 250 clients. 10% of clients are new/unpublished writers. Currently handles: nonfiction books 35%, novels 50%, juvenile books 15%.

- Mr. Elwell was previously with Elwell & Weiser.

Member Agents Phyllis Westberg; Pamela Malpas; Craig Tenney (few new clients, mostly Ober backlist); Jake Elwell (previously with Elwell & Weiser.

How to Contact Submit concise query letter addressed to a specific agent with the first five pages of the manuscript or proposal and SASE. No fax or e-mail. Does not handle scripts. Responds as promptly as possible. Obtains most new clients through recommendations from others.

Terms Agent receives 15% commission on domestic sales. Agent receives 20% commission on foreign sales. Charges clients for photocopying and express mail/package services.

THE RICHARD PARKS AGENCY

Box 693, Salem NY 12865. (518)854-9466. Fax: (518)854-9466. E-mail: rp@richardparksagency.com. Website: www.richardparksagency.com. **Contact:** Richard Parks. Member of AAR. Currently handles: nonfiction books 55%, novels 40%, story collections 5%.

Represents Nonfiction books, novels. **Considers these nonfiction areas:** crafts, animals, anthropology, art, biography, business, child, cooking, current affairs, ethnic, gardening, gay, government, health, history, how to, humor, language, memoirs, military, money, music, nature, popular culture, psychology, science, self help, sociology, film, travel, women's.

0→ Actively seeking nonfiction. Considers fiction by referral only. Does not want to receive unsolicited material.

How to Contact Query with SASE. Other Responds in 2 weeks to queries. Obtains most new clients through recommendations/referrals.

Terms Agent receives 15% commission on domestic sales. Agent receives 20% commission on foreign sales. Charges clients for photocopying or any unusual expense incurred at the writer's request.

L. PERKINS ASSOCIATES

5800 Arlington Ave., Riverdale NY 10471. (718)543-5344. Fax: (718)543-5354. E-mail: lperkinsagency@yahoo.com. **Contact:** Lori Perkins, Sandy Lu (Sandy@lperkinsagency@com). Member of AAR. Represents 90 clients. 10% of clients are new/unpublished writers.

- Ms. Perkins has been an agent for 20 years. She is also the author of *The Insider's Guide to Getting an Agent* (Writer's Digest Books), as well as three other nonfiction books. She has also edited 12 erotic anthologies, and is also the Editorial Director of Ravenousromance.com, an epublisher.

Represents Nonfiction books, novels. **Considers these nonfiction areas:** popular culture. **Considers these fiction areas:** erotica, fantasy, horror, literary, paranormal romance, dark, science, urban fantasy.

0→ "Most of my clients write both fiction and nonfiction. This combination keeps my clients publishing for years. I am also a published author, so I know what it takes to write a good book." Actively seeking a Latino *Gone With the Wind* and *Waiting to Exhale*, and urban ethnic horror. Does not want to receive anything outside of the above categories (westerns, romance, etc.).

How to Contact E-queries only. Accepts simultaneous submissions. Responds in 12 weeks to queries. Responds in 3-6 months to mss. Obtains most new clients through recommendations from others, solicitations, conferences.
Terms Agent receives 15% commission on domestic sales. Agent receives 20% commission on foreign sales. No written contract. Charges clients for photocopying.
Writers Conferences NECON; Killercon; BookExpo America; World Fantasy Convention, RWA, Romantic Times.
Tips "Research your field and contact professional writers' organizations to see who is looking for what. Finish your novel before querying agents. Read my book, *An Insider's Guide to Getting an Agent*, to get a sense of how agents operate. Read agent blogs - agentinthemiddle.blogspot.com and ravenousromance.blogspot.com."

SUSAN ANN PROTTER, LITERARY AGENT

320 Central Park West, Suite 12E, New York NY 10025. Website: SusanAnnProtter.com. **Contact:** Susan Protter. Member of AAR. Other memberships include Authors Guild.

- Prior to opening her agency, Ms. Protter was associate director of subsidiary rights at Harper & Row Publishers.

How to Contact *"We are currently not accepting new unsolicited submissions."*

JODIE RHODES LITERARY AGENCY

8840 Villa La Jolla Drive, Suite 315, La Jolla CA 92037-1957. Website: jodierhodesliterary.com. **Contact:** Jodie Rhodes, president. Member of AAR. Represents 74 clients. 60% of clients are new/unpublished writers. Currently handles: nonfiction books 45%, novels 35%, juvenile books 20%.

- Prior to opening her agency, Ms. Rhodes was a university-level creative writing teacher, workshop director, published novelist, and vice president/media director at the N.W. Ayer Advertising Agency.

Member Agents Jodie Rhodes; Clark McCutcheon (fiction); Bob McCarter (nonfiction).
Represents Nonfiction books, novels. **Considers these nonfiction areas:** biography, child, ethnic, government, health, history, memoirs, military, science, women's. **Considers these fiction areas:** ethnic, family, historical, literary, mainstream, mystery, thriller, young adult, women's.

- "Actively seeking witty, sophisticated women's books about career ambitions and relationships; edgy/trendy YA and teen books; narrative nonfiction on groundbreaking scientific discoveries, politics, economics, military and important current affairs by prominent scientists and academic professors." Does not want to receive erotica, horror, fantasy, romance, science fiction, religious/inspirational, or children's books (does accept young adult/teen).

How to Contact Query with brief synopsis, first 30-50 pages, SASE. Do not call. Do not send complete ms unless requested. This agency does not return unrequested material weighing a pound or more that requires special postage. Include e-mail address with query. Accepts simultaneous submissions. Responds in 3 weeks to queries. Obtains most new clients through recommendations from others, agent sourcebooks.
Terms Agent receives 15% commission on domestic sales. Agent receives 20% commission on foreign sales. Offers written contract; 1-month notice must be given to terminate contract. Charges clients for fax, photocopying, phone calls, postage. Charges are itemized and approved by writers upfront.
Recent Sales Sold 42 titles in the last year. *The Ring*, by Kavita Daswani (HarperCollins); *Train to Trieste*, by Domnica Radulescu (Knopf); *A Year With Cats and Dogs*, by Margaret Hawkins (Permanent Press); *Silence and Silhouettes*, by Ryan Smithson (HarperCollins); *Internal Affairs*, by Constance Dial (Permanent Press); *How Math Rules the World*, by James Stein (HarperCollins); Diagnosis of Love, by Maggie Martin (Bantam); Lies, Damn Lies, and Science, by Sherry Seethaler (Prentice Hall); Freaked, by Jeanne Dutton (HarperCollins); The Five Second Rule, by Anne Maczulak (Perseus Books); The Intelligence Wars, by Stephen O'Hern (Prometheus); Seducing the Spirits, by Louise Young (The Permanent Press), and more.
Tips "Think your book out before you write it. Do your research, know your subject matter intimately, and write vivid specifics, not bland generalities. Care deeply about your book. Don't imitate other writers. Find your own voice. We never take on a book we don't believe in, and we go the extra mile for our writers. We welcome talented, new writers."

ANGELA RINALDI LITERARY AGENCY

P.O. Box 7877, Beverly Hills CA 90212-7877. (310)842-7665. Fax: (310)837-8143. E-mail: amr@rinaldiliterary.com. Website: www.rinaldiliterary.com. **Contact:** Angela Rinaldi. Member of AAR. Represents 50 clients. Currently handles: nonfiction books 50%, novels 50%.

- Prior to opening her agency, Ms. Rinaldi was an editor at NAL/Signet, Pocket Books and Bantam, and the manager of book development for *The Los Angeles Times*.

Represents Nonfiction books, novels, TV and motion picture rights (for clients only). **Considers these nonfiction areas:** biography, business, health books that address specific issues, career, personal finance, self help, true crime, women's issues/studies, current issues, psychology, popular reference, prescriptive and proactive self help,, books by journalists, academics, doctors and therapists, based on their research, motivational. **Considers these fiction areas:** commercial/literary fiction, upmarket contemporary women's fiction, suspense, literary historical thrillers like Elizabeth Kostova's *The Historian*, gothic suspense like Diane Setterfield's *The Thirteenth Tale* and Matthew Pearl's *The Dante Club*, women's book club fiction—novels where the story lends itself to discussion like Kim Edwards' *The Memory Keeper's Daughter*.

O→ Actively seeking commercial and literary fiction. Does not want to receive humor, techno thrillers, KGB/CIA espionage, drug thrillers, Da Vinci-code thrillers, category romances, science fiction, fantasy, horror, westerns, film scripts, poetry, category romances, magazine articles, religion, occult, supernatural.

How to Contact For fiction, send first 3 chapters, brief synopsis, SASE or brief email inquiry with the first 10 pages pastsed into the email—no attachments unless asked for. For nonfiction, query with detailed letter or outline/proposal, SASE or email—no attachments unless asked for. Do not send certified or metered mail. Other Responds in 6 weeks to queries that are posted; email queries 2-3 weeks.

Terms Agent receives 15% commission on domestic sales. Agent receives 25% commission on foreign sales. Offers written contract.

ANN RITTENBERG LITERARY AGENCY, INC.

30 Bond St., New York NY 10012. (212)684-6936. Fax: (212)684-6929. Website: www.rittlit.com. **Contact:** Ann Rittenberg, President and Penn Whaling, Associate. Member of AAR. Currently handles: fiction 75%, nonfiction 25%.

Represents Considers these fiction areas: Considers these fiction areas: Upmarket women's novels and thrillers, literary.

O→ This agent specializes in literary fiction and literary nonfiction. Does not want to receive screenplays, straight genre fiction, poetry, self-help.

How to Contact Query with SASE. Submit outline, 3 sample chapters, SASE. Query via postal mail *only*. Accepts simultaneous submissions. Responds in 6 weeks to queries. Responds in 2 months to mss. Obtains most new clients through referrals from established writers and editors.

Terms Agent receives 15% commission on domestic sales. Agent receives 20% commission on foreign sales. Offers written contract. This agency charges clients for photocopying only.

Recent Sales *The Given Day*, by Dennis Lehane; *My Cat Hates You*, by Jim Edgar; *Never Wave Goodbye*, by Doug Magee; *House and Home*, by Kathleen McCleary; *Nowhere to Run*, by CJ Box; and *Daughter of Kura*, by Debra Austin.

RLR ASSOCIATES, LTD.

Literary Department, 7 W. 51st St., New York NY 10019. (212)541-8641. Fax: (212)262-7084. E-mail: sgould@rlrassociates.net. Website: www.rlrliterary.net. **Contact:** Scott Gould. Member of AAR. Represents 50 clients. 25% of clients are new/unpublished writers. Currently handles: nonfiction books 70%, novels 25%, story collections 5%.

Represents Nonfiction books, novels, short story collections, scholarly. **Considers these nonfiction areas:** interior, animals, anthropology, art, biography, business, child, cooking, current affairs, education, ethnic, gay, government, health, history, humor, language, memoirs, money, multicultural, music, nature, photography, popular culture, psychology, religion, science, self help, sociology, sports, translation, travel, true crime, women's. **Considers these fiction areas:** adventure, comic, detective, ethnic, experimental, family, feminist, gay, historical, horror, humor, literary, mainstream, multicultural, mystery, sports, thriller.

O→ "We provide a lot of editorial assistance to our clients and have connections." Actively seeking fiction, current affairs, history, art, popular culture, health and business. Does not want to receive screenplays.

How to Contact Query by either e-mail or mail. Accepts simultaneous submissions. Responds in 4-8 weeks to queries. Obtains most new clients through recommendations from others.

Terms Agent receives 15% commission on domestic sales. Agent receives 20% commission on foreign sales. Offers written contract.

Recent Sales Clients include Shelby Foote, The Grief Recovery Institute, Don Wade, Don Zimmer, The Knot.com, David Plowden, PGA of America, Danny Peary, George Kalinsky, Peter Hyman,

Daniel Parker, Lee Miller, Elise Miller, Nina Planck, Karyn Bosnak, Christopher Pike, Gerald Carbone, Jason Lethcoe, Andy Crouch.

Tips "Please check out our website for more details on our agency."

B.J. ROBBINS LITERARY AGENCY

5130 Bellaire Ave., North Hollywood CA 91607-2908. E-mail: Robbinsliterary@gmail.com. **Contact:** (Ms.) B.J. Robbins. Member of AAR. Represents 40 clients. 50% of clients are new/unpublished writers. Currently handles: nonfiction books 50%, novels 50%.

Represents Nonfiction books, novels. **Considers these nonfiction areas:** biography, current affairs, ethnic, health, humor, memoirs, music, popular culture, psychology, self help, sociology, sports, film, travel, true crime, women's. **Considers these fiction areas:** detective, ethnic, literary, mainstream, mystery, sports, thriller.

How to Contact Query with SASE. Submit outline/proposal, 3 sample chapters, SASE. Accepts e-mail queries (no attachments). Accepts simultaneous submissions. Responds in 2-6 weeks to queries. Responds in 6-8 weeks to mss. Obtains most new clients through conferences, referrals.

Terms Agent receives 15% commission on domestic sales. Agent receives 20% commission on foreign sales. Offers written contract; 3-month notice must be given to terminate contract. This agency charges clients for postage and photocopying (only after sale of ms).

Recent Sales Sold 15 titles in the last year. *Getting Stoned With Savages*, by J. Maarten Troost (Broadway); *Hot Water*, by Kathryn Jordan (Berkley); *Between the Bridge and the River*, by Craig Ferguson (Chronicle); *I'm Proud of You*, by Tim Madigan (Gotham); *Man of the House*, by Chris Erskine (Rodale); *Bird of Another heaven*, by James D. Houston (Knopf); *Tomorrow They Will Kiss*, by Eduardo Santiago (Little, Brown); *A Terrible Glory*, by James Donovan (Little, Brown); *The Writing on My Forehead*, by Nafisa Haji (Morrow); *Seen the Glory*, by John Hough Jr. (Simon & Schuster); *Lost on Planet China*, by J. Maarten Troost (Broadway).

Writers Conferences Squaw Valley Writers Workshop; San Diego State University Writers' Conference.

RITA ROSENKRANZ LITERARY AGENCY

440 West End Ave., Suite 15D, New York NY 10024-5358. (212)873-6333. **Contact:** Rita Rosenkranz. Member of AAR. Represents 35 clients. 30% of clients are new/unpublished writers. Currently handles: nonfiction books 99%, novels 1%.

- Prior to opening her agency, Ms. Rosenkranz worked as an editor at major New York publishing houses.

Represents Nonfiction books. **Considers these nonfiction areas:** animals, anthropology, art, autobiography, biography, business, child guidance, computers, cooking, crafts, cultural interests, current affairs, dance, decorating, economics, ethnic, film, gay, government, health, history, hobbies, how-to, humor, inspirational, interior design, language, law, lesbian, literature, medicine, military, money, music, nature, parenting, personal improvement, photography, popular culture, politics, psychology, religious, satire, science, self-help, sports, technology, theater, war, women's issues, women's studies.

- "This agency focuses on adult nonfiction, stresses strong editorial development and refinement before submitting to publishers, and brainstorms ideas with authors." Actively seeks authors who are well paired with their subject, either for professional or personal reasons.

How to Contact Send query letter only (no proposal) via regular mail or e-mail. Submit proposal package with SASE only on request. No fax queries. Accepts simultaneous submissions. Responds in 2 weeks to queries. Obtains most new clients through directory listings, solicitations, conferences, word of mouth.

Terms Agent receives 15% commission on domestic sales. Agent receives 20% commission on foreign sales. Offers written contract, binding for 3 years; 3-month written notice must be given to terminate contract. Charges clients for photocopying. Makes referrals to editing services.

Recent Sales Sold 35 titles in the last year. *29 GIFTS: How a Month of Giving Can Change Your Life*, by Cami Walker (DaCapo Press), *Writers Gone Wild: The Feuds, Frolics and Follies of Literature's Great Adventurers, Drunkards, Lovers, Iconoclasts, and Misanthropes*, by Bill Peschel (Perigee), *Study Your Brains Out!* by Anne Crossman (Ten Speed Press).

Tips "Identify the current competition for your project to make sure the project is valid. A strong cover letter is very important."

HAROLD SCHMIDT LITERARY AGENCY

415 W. 23rd St., #6F, New York NY 10011. (212)727-7473. Fax: (212)807-6025. **Contact:** Harold Schmidt. Member of AAR. Represents 3 clients.

Represents Nonfiction, fiction. **Considers these fiction areas:** contemporary issues, gay, literary, original fiction with unique narrative voices, high quality psychological suspense and thrillers, likes offbeat/quirky.

○→ Seeking novels.

How to Contact Query with SASE; do not send material without being asked. No telephone or e-mail queries.

THE SEYMOUR AGENCY

475 Miner St., Canton NY 13617. (315)386-1831. E-mail: marysue@twcny.rr.com. Website: www.theseymouragency.com. **Contact:** Mary Sue Seymour. Member of AAR. Signatory of WGA. Other memberships include RWA, Authors Guild. Represents 50 clients. 5% of clients are new/unpublished writers. Currently handles: nonfiction books 50%, other 50% fiction.

- Ms. Seymour is a retired New York State certified teacher.

Represents Nonfiction books, novels. **Considers these nonfiction areas:** business, health, how-to, self-help, Christian books; cookbooks; any well-written nonfiction that includes a proposal in standard format and 1 sample chapter. **Considers these fiction areas:** religious, Christian books, romance, any type.

How to Contact Query with SASE, synopsis, first 50 pages for romance. Accepts e-mail queries. Accepts simultaneous submissions. Responds in 1 month to queries. Responds in 3 months to mss.

Terms Agent receives 12-15% commission on domestic sales.

Recent Sales Dinah Bucholz's *The Harry Potter Cookbook* to Adams Media.com; Vannetta Chapman's *A Simple Amish Christmas* to Abingdon Press; Shelley Shepard Gray's current book deal to Harper Collins; Shelley Galloway's Multibook Deal to Zondervan; Beth Wiseman's Christmas Two Novellas and Multibook Deal to Thomas Nelson; Mary Ellis's Multibook Deal to Harvest House, Barbara Cameron's Novellas to Thomas Nelson and Multibook Deal to Abingdon Press.

DENISE SHANNON LITERARY AGENCY, INC.

20 W. 22nd St., Suite 1603, New York NY 10010. (212)414-2911. Fax: (212)414-2930. E-mail: info@deniseshannonagency.com. Website: www.deniseshannonagency.com. **Contact:** Denise Shannon. Estab. 2002. Member of AAR.

- Prior to opening her agency, Ms. Shannon worked for 16 years with Georges Borchardt and International Creative Management.

Represents Nonfiction books, novels. **Considers these nonfiction areas:** biography, business, health, narrative nonfiction; politics; journalism; memoir; social history. **Considers these fiction areas:** literary.

○→ "We are a boutique agency with a distinguished list of fiction and nonfiction authors."

How to Contact Query by email to: submissions@deniseshannonagency.com, or mail with SASE. Submit query with description of project, bio, SASE. See guidelines online.

Tips "Please do not send queries regarding fiction projects until a complete manuscript is available for review. We request that you inform us if you are submitting material simultaneously to other agencies."

WENDY SHERMAN ASSOCIATES, INC.

27 W. 24th St., New York NY 10010. (212)279-9027. Website: www.wsherman.com. **Contact:** Wendy Sherman.. Member of AAR. Represents 50 clients. 30% of clients are new/unpublished writers. Currently handles: nonfiction books 50%, novels 50%.

- Prior to opening the agency, Ms. Sherman served as vice president, executive director, associate publisher, subsidiary rights director, and sales and marketing director for major publishers.

Member Agents Wendy Sherman (board member of AAR).

Represents Nonfiction, fiction. **Considers these nonfiction areas:** memoirs, psychology, narrative; practical. **Considers these fiction areas:** literary, women's, suspense.

○→ "We specialize in developing new writers, as well as working with more established writers. My experience as a publisher has proven to be a great asset to my clients."

How to Contact Query via e-mail to submissions@wsherman.com Accepts simultaneous submissions. Responds in 1 month to queries. Obtains most new clients through recommendations from others.

Terms Agent receives 15% commission on domestic sales. Agent receives 20% commission on foreign and film sales. Offers written contract.

Recent Sales *Daughters of the Witching Hill*, by Mary Sharratt; *The Measure of Brightness*, by Todd Johnson; *Supergirls Speak Out*, by Liz Funk; *Love in 90 Days*, by Diana Kirschner; *A Long Time Ago and Essentially*, by Brigid Pasulka; *Changing Shoes*, by Tina Sloan.

Tips "The bottom line is: Do your homework. Be as well prepared as possible. Read the books that will help you present yourself and your work with polish. You want your submission to stand out."

ROSALIE SIEGEL, INTERNATIONAL LITERARY AGENCY, INC.

1 Abey Dr., Pennington NJ 08543. (609)737-1007. Fax: (609)737-3708. **Contact:** Rosalie Siegel. Member of AAR. Represents 35 clients. 10% of clients are new/unpublished writers. Currently handles: nonfiction books 45%, novels 45%, other 10% young adult books; short story collections for current clients.

How to Contact Obtains most new clients through referrals from writers and friends.

Terms Agent receives 15% commission on domestic sales. Agent receives 20% commission on foreign sales. Offers written contract; 2-month notice must be given to terminate contract. Charges clients for photocopying.

SPENCERHILL ASSOCIATES

P.O. Box 374, Chatham NY 12037. (518)392-9293. Fax: (518)392-9554. E-mail: submissions@spencerhillassociates.com. Website: www.spencerhillassociates.com. **Contact:** Karen Solem or Jennifer Schober (and please refer to our website for the latest information). Member of AAR. Represents 96 clients. 10% of clients are new/unpublished writers.

- Prior to becoming an agent, Ms. Solem was editor-in-chief at HarperCollins and an associate publisher.

Member Agents Karen Solem; Jennifer Schober.

Represents Novels. **Considers these fiction areas:** detective, historical, literary, mainstream, religious, romance, thriller, young adult.

- "We handle mostly commercial women's fiction, historical novels, romance (historical, contemporary, paranormal, urban fantasy), thrillers, and mysteries. We also represent Christian fiction only—no nonfiction." No nonfiction, poetry, science fiction, children's picture books, or scripts.

How to Contact Query submissions@spencerhillassociates.com with synopsis and first three chapters attached as a .doc or .rtf file. Please note we no longer accept queries via the mail. Responds in 6-8 weeks to queries if we are interested in pursuing.

Terms Agent receives 15% commission on domestic sales. Agent receives 20% commission on foreign sales. Offers written contract; 3-month notice must be given to terminate contract.

PHILIP G. SPITZER LITERARY AGENCY, INC

50 Talmage Farm Ln., East Hampton NY 11937. (631)329-3650. Fax: (631)329-3651. E-mail: luc.hunt@spitzeragency.com. Website: www.spitzeragency.com. **Contact:** Luc Hunt. Member of AAR. Represents 60 clients. 10% of clients are new/unpublished writers. Currently handles: nonfiction books 35%, novels 65%.

- Prior to opening his agency, Mr. Spitzer served at New York University Press, McGraw-Hill, and the John Cushman Associates literary agency.

Represents Nonfiction books, novels. **Considers these nonfiction areas:** Biography, History, Travel, Politics, Current Events. **Considers these fiction areas:** general fiction, detective, literary, mainstream, mystery, sports, thriller.

- This agency specializes in mystery/suspense, literary fiction, sports and general nonfiction (no how-to).

How to Contact Query with SASE. Responds in 2 weeks to queries. Responds in 6 weeks to mss. Obtains most new clients through recommendations from others.

Terms Agent receives 15% commission on domestic sales. Agent receives 20% commission on foreign sales. Charges clients for photocopying.

Writers Conferences London Bookfair, Frankfurt, BookExpo America.

STEELE-PERKINS LITERARY AGENCY

26 Island Ln., Canandaigua NY 14424. (585)396-9290. Fax: (585)396-3579. E-mail: pattiesp@aol.com. **Contact:** Pattie Steele-Perkins. Member of AAR. Other memberships include RWA. Currently handles: novels 100%.

Represents Novels. **Considers these fiction areas:** romance, women's, All genres: category romance, romantic suspense, historical, contemporary, multi-cultural, and inspirational.

How to Contact Submit synopsis and one chapter via e-mail (no attachments) or snail mail. Snail mail submissions require SASE. Accepts simultaneous submissions. Responds in 6 weeks to queries. Obtains most new clients through recommendations from others, queries/solicitations.

Terms Agent receives 15% commission on domestic sales. Offers written contract, binding for 1 year; 1-month notice must be given to terminate contract.
Recent Sales Sold 130 titles last year. This agency prefers not to share specific sales information.
Writers Conferences RWA National Conference; BookExpo America; CBA Convention; Romance Slam Jam.
Tips "Be patient. E-mail rather than call. Make sure what you are sending is the best it can be."

STIMOLA LITERARY STUDIO, INC.

306 Chase Court, Edgewater NJ 07020. Phone/Fax: (201)945-9353. E-mail: info@stimolaliterarystudio.com. Website: www.stimolaliterarystudio.com. **Contact:** Rosemary B. Stimola. Member of AAR.
How to Contact Query via e-mail (no unsolicited attachments). Responds in 3 weeks to queries "we wish to pursue further." Responds in 2 months to requested mss. Obtains most new clients through referrals. Unsolicited submissions are still accepted.
Terms Agent receives 15% commission on domestic sales. Agent receives 20% (if subagents are employed) commission on foreign sales.
Recent Sales *The Hunger Games Trilogy*, by Suzanne Collins (Scholastic); *Another Brother, by Matt Cordell (Feiwel & Friends/Macmillan); Don't Stop Now*, by Julie Halpern (Feiwel & Friends/Macmillan); *The Anti-Prom*, by Abby McDonald (Candlewick Press); *Not That Kind of Girl*, by Siobhan Vivian (Scholastic, Push); *Courage Has No Color*, by Tanya Lee Stone (Candlewick); *Crossing Lines*, by Paul Voponi (Viking/Penguin).

THE STROTHMAN AGENCY, LLC

Specializes in narrative nonfiction and literary fiction, young adult and middle grade fiction and nonfiction, Six Beacon St., Suite 810, Boston MA 02108. (617)742-2011. Fax: (617)742-2014. E-mail: info@strothmanagency.com. Website: www.strothmanagency.com. **Contact:** Wendy Strothman, Lauren MacLeod. Member of AAR. Other memberships include Authors' Guild. Represents 50 clients. Currently handles: nonfiction books 70%, novels 10%, scholarly books 20%.

- Prior to becoming an agent, Ms. Strothman was head of Beacon Press (1983-1995) and executive vice president of Houghton Mifflin's Trade & Reference Division (1996-2002).

Member Agents Wendy Strothman; Lauren MacLeod.
Represents Nonfiction books, novels, scholarly, young adult and middle grade. **Considers these nonfiction areas:** current affairs, government, history, language, nature. **Considers these fiction areas:** literary, young adult, middle grade.

"Because we are highly selective in the clients we represent, we increase the value publishers place on our properties. We specialize in narrative nonfiction, memoir, history, science and nature, arts and culture, literary travel, current affairs, and some business. We have a highly selective practice in literary fiction, young adult and middle grade fiction, and nonfiction. We are now opening our doors to more commercial fiction but ONLY from authors who have a platform. If you have a platform, please mention it in your query letter." "The Strothman Agency seeks out scholars, journalists, and other acknowledged and emerging experts in their fields. We are now actively looking for authors of well written young-adult fiction and nonfiction. Browse the Latest News to get an idea of the types of books that we represent. For more about what we're looking for, read Pitching an Agent: The Strothman Agency on the publishing website www.strothmanagency.com." Does not want to receive commercial fiction, romance, science fiction or self-help.

How to Contact Open to email (strothmanagency@gmail.com) and postal submissions. See submission guidelines. Accepts simultaneous submissions. Responds in 4 weeks to queries. Responds in 6 weeks to mss. Obtains most new clients through recommendations from others.
Terms Agent receives 15% commission on domestic sales. Agent receives 20% commission on foreign sales. Offers written contract; 30-day notice must be given to terminate contract.

EMMA SWEENEY AGENCY, LLC

245 East 80th St., Suite 7E, New York NY 10075. E-mail: queries@emmasweeneyagency.com. Website: www.emmasweeneyagency.com. **Contact:** Eva Talmadge. Member of AAR. Other memberships include Women's Media Group. Represents 80 clients. 5% of clients are new/unpublished writers. Currently handles: nonfiction books 50%, novels 50%.

- Prior to becoming an agent, Ms. Sweeney was director of subsidiary rights at Grove Press. Since 1990, she has been a literary agent.

Member Agents Emma Sweeney, president; Eva Talmadge, rights manager and agent (Represents literary fiction, young adult novels, and narrative nonfiction. Considers these nonfiction areas: popular science, pop culture and music history, biography, memoirs, cooking, and anything relating to animals.

Considers these fiction areas: literary (of the highest writing quality possible), young adult. eva@ emmasweeneyagency.com); Justine Wenger, junior agent/assistant (justine@emmasweeneyagency.com)..

Represents Nonfiction books, novels.

- "We specialize in quality fiction and non-fiction. Our primary areas of interest include literary and women's fiction, mysteries and thrillers; science, history, biography, memoir, religious studies and the natural sciences." Does not want to receive romance and westerns or screenplays.

How to Contact Send query letter and first ten pages in body of e-mail (no attachments) to queries@ emmasweeneyagency.com. No snail mail queries.

Terms Agent receives 15% commission on domestic sales. Agent receives 10% commission on foreign sales.

Writers Conferences Nebraska Writers' Conference; Words and Music Festival in New Orleans.

TESSLER LITERARY AGENCY, LLC

27 W. 20th St., Suite 1003, New York NY 10011. (212)242-0466. Fax: (212)242-2366. E-mail: michelle@ tessleragency.com. Website: www.tessleragency.com. **Contact:** Michelle Tessler. Member of AAR.

- Prior to forming her own agency, Ms. Tessler worked at Carlisle & Co. (now a part of Inkwell Management). She has also worked at the William Morris Agency and the Elaine Markson Literary Agency.

Represents Nonfiction books, novels.

- "The Tessler Agency is a full-service boutique agency that represents writers of literary fiction and high quality nonfiction in the following categories: popular science, reportage, memoir, history, biography, psychology, business and travel."

How to Contact Submit query through website only.

RALPH M. VICINANZA LTD.

303 W. 18th St., New York NY 10011. (212)924-7090. Fax: (212)691-9644. Member of AAR.

Member Agents Ralph M. Vicinanza; Chris Lotts; Christopher Schelling, Matthew Mahoney.

How to Contact This agency takes on new clients by professional recommendation only.

Terms Agent receives 15% commission on domestic sales. Agent receives 20% commission on foreign sales.

WALES LITERARY AGENCY, INC.

P.O. Box 9426, Seattle WA 98109-0426. (206)284-7114. E-mail: waleslit@waleslit.com. Website: www.waleslit.com. **Contact:** Elizabeth Wales, Neal Swain. Member of AAR. Other memberships include Book Publishers' Northwest, Pacific Northwest Booksellers Association, PEN. Represents 60 clients. 10% of clients are new/unpublished writers. Currently handles: nonfiction books 60%, novels 40%.

- Prior to becoming an agent, Ms. Wales worked at Oxford University Press and Viking Penguin.

Member Agents Elizabeth Wales; Neal Swain.

- This agency specializes in quality fiction and nonfiction. Does not handle screenplays, children's literature, genre fiction, or most category nonfiction.

How to Contact Accepts queries sent with cover letter and SASE, and email queries with no attachments. No phone or fax queries. Accepts simultaneous submissions. Responds in 2 weeks to queries, 2 months to mss.

Terms Agent receives 15% commission on domestic sales. Agent receives 20% commission on foreign sales.

Recent Sales *The Dirty Doll Diaries,* A novel by Cinthia Ritchie (Grand Central/Hachette, 2011); *Heat: A Natural and Unnatural History*, by Bill Streever (Little, Brown, 2012); *Cheesemonger: A Life on the WedgeI, by Gordon Edgar (Chelsea Green, 2010); Special Exits: My Parents,* A Memoir by Joyce Farmer (Fantagraphics, 2010); *Unterzakhn: A Graphic Novel*, by Leela Corman (Schocken/Pantheon, 2010).

Writers Conferences Pacific Northwest Writers Conference, annually; and others.

Tips "We are especially interested in work that espouses a progressive cultural or political view, projects a new voice, or simply shares an important, compelling story. We also encourage writers living in the Pacific Northwest, West Coast, Alaska, and Pacific Rim countries, and writers from historically underrepresented groups, such as gay and lesbian writers and writers of color, to submit work (but does not discourage writers outside these areas). Most importantly, whether in fiction or nonfiction, the agency is looking for talented storytellers."

TED WEINSTEIN LITERARY MANAGEMENT

307 Seventh Ave., Suite 2407, Dept. GLA, New York NY 10001. Website: www.twliterary.com. **Contact:** Ted Weinstein. Member of AAR. Represents 75 clients. 50% of clients are new/unpublished writers. Currently handles: nonfiction books 100%.

Represents Considers these nonfiction areas: biography, business, current affairs, government, health, history, popular culture, science, self help, travel, true crime, lifestyle, narrative journalism, popular science.

How to Contact Please visit website for detailed guidelines before submitting. E-mail queries only. Other Responds in 3 weeks to queries.

Terms Agent receives 15% commission on domestic sales. Agent receives 20% commission on foreign sales. Agent receives 20% commission on film sales. Offers written contract, binding for 1 year. Charges clients for photocopying and express shipping.

Tips "Accepts email queries ONLY; paper submissions are discarded. See agency's Web site (www.twliterary.com) for full guidelines."

WOLGEMUTH & ASSOCIATES, INC

8600 Crestgate Circle, Orlando FL 32819. (407)909-9445. Fax: (407)909-9446. E-mail: ewolgemuth@wolgemuthandassociates.com. **Contact:** Erik Wolgemuth. Member of AAR. Represents 60 clients. 10% of clients are new/unpublished writers. Currently handles: nonfiction books 90%, novella 2%, juvenile books 5%, multimedia 3%.

- "We have been in the publishing business since 1976, having been a marketing executive at a number of houses, a publisher, an author, and a founder and owner of a publishing company."

Member Agents Robert D. Wolgemuth; Andrew D. Wolgemuth; Erik S. Wolgemuth.

Represents Material used by Christian families.

⊶ "We are not considering any new material at this time."

Terms Agent receives 15% commission on domestic sales. Offers written contract, binding for 2-3 years; 30-day notice must be given to terminate contract.

MARKETS

Book Publishers

The markets in this year's Book Publishers section offer opportunities in nearly every area of publishing. Large, commercial houses are here as are their smaller counterparts.

When you have compiled a list of publishers interested in books in your subject area, read the detailed listings. Pare down your list by cross-referencing two or three subject areas and eliminating the listings only marginally suited to your book. When you have a good list, send for those publishers' catalogs and manuscript guidelines, or check publishers' Web sites, which often contain catalog listings, manuscript preparation guidelines, current contact names, and other information helpful to prospective authors. You want to use this information to make sure your book idea is in line with a publisher's list but is not a duplicate of something already published.

You should also visit bookstores and libraries to see if the publisher's books are well represented. When you find a couple of books the house has published that are similar to yours, write or call the company to find out who edited those books. This extra bit of research could be the key to getting your proposal to precisely the right editor.

Publishers prefer different methods of submission on first contact. Most like to see a one-page query with SASE, especially for nonfiction. Others will accept a brief proposal package that might include an outline and/or a sample chapter. Some publishers will accept submissions from agents only. Each listing in the Book Publishers section includes specific submission methods, if provided by the publisher. Make sure you read each listing carefully to find out exactly what the publisher wants to receive.

When you write your one-page query, give an overview of your book, mention the intended audience, the competition for your book (check local bookstore shelves), and what sets your book apart from the competition. You should also include any previous publishing experience or special training relevant to the subject of your book. For more on queries, read ''Query Letter Clinic'' on page 19.

Personalize your query by addressing the editor individually and mentioning what you know about the company from its catalog or books. Never send a form letter as a query. Envelopes addressed to "Editor'' or "Editorial Department'' end up in the dreaded slush pile. Under the heading **Acquisitions**, we list the names of editors who acquire new books for each company, along with the editors' specific areas of expertise. Try your best to send your query to the appropriate editor. Editors move around all the time, so it's in your best interest to look online or call the publishing house to make sure the editor you are addressing your query to is still employed by that publisher.

Author-subsidy publishers' not included

Writer's Market is a reference tool to help you sell your writing, and we encourage you to work with publishers that pay a royalty. Subsidy publishing involves paying money to a publishing house to publish a book. The source of the money could be a government, foundation or university grant, or it could be the author of the book. If one of the publishers listed in this book offers you an author-subsidy arrangement (sometimes called "cooperative publishing," "co-publishing," or "joint venture"); or asks you to pay for part or all of the cost of any aspect of publishing (editing services, manuscript critiques, printing, advertising, etc.); or asks you to guarantee the purchase of any number of the books yourself, we would like you to inform us of that company's practices immediately.

INFORMATION AT A GLANCE

There are a number of icons at the beginning of each listing to quickly convey certain information. In the Book Publisher sections, these icons identify new listings (N), Canadian markets (✚), publishers that accept agented submissions only (A), and publishers who do not accept unsolicited manuscripts (⊘). Different sections of *Writer's Market* include other symbols; check the back inside cover for an explanation of all the symbols used throughout the book. How much money?

What are my odds?

We've also highlighted important information in boldface, the "quick facts" you won't find in any other market guide but should know before you submit your work. These items include: how many manuscripts a publisher buys per year; how many manuscripts from first-time authors; how many manuscripts from unagented writers; the royalty rate a publisher pays; and how large an advance is offered. Standard royalty rates for paperbacks generally range from 7½ to 12½ percent, and from 10 to 15 percent for hardcovers . Royalty rates for children's books are often lower, generally ranging from 5 to 10 percent; 10 percent for picture books (split between the author and the illustrator).

Publishers, their imprints, and how they are related

In this era of big publishing—and big mergers—the world of publishing has grown even more intertwined. A "family tree" on page 95 lists the imprints and divisions of the largest conglomerate publishers.

Keep in mind that most of the major publishers listed in this family tree do not accept unagented submissions or unsolicited manuscripts. You will find many of these publishers and their imprints listed within the Book Publishers section, and many contain only basic contact information. If you are interested in pursuing any of these publishers, we advise you to see each publisher's website for more information.

ABINGDON PRESS

Imprint of The United Methodist Publishing House 201 Eighth Ave. S., P.O. Box 801, Nashville TN 37202-0801. (615)749-6000. Fax: (615)749-6512. Website: www.abingdonpress.com. **Contact:** Robert Ratcliff, senior editor (professional clergy and academic); Judy Newman St. John (children's); Ron Kidd, senior editor (general interest). Estab. 1789. Publishes hardcover and paperback originals. **Publishes 120 titles/year. 3,000 queries received/year. 250 mss received/year. 85% from unagented writers. Pays 7 ½% royalty on retail price.** Publishes book 2 years after acceptance of ms. Responds in 2 months to queries. Book catalog available free. Guidelines available online.

Imprints Dimensions for Living; Kingswood Books; Abingdon Press.

O⇁ "Abingdon Press, America's oldest theological publisher, provides an ecumenical publishing program dedicated to serving the Christian community—clergy, scholars, church leaders, musicians, and general readers—with quality resources in the areas of Bible study, the practice of ministry, theology, devotion, spirituality, inspiration, prayer, music and worship, reference, Christian education, and church supplies."

Nonfiction Subjects include education, religion, theology. Query with outline and samples only. The author should retain a copy of any unsolicited material submitted.

Recent Title(s) *The First 48 Hours: Spiritual Caregivers as First Responders*, by Jennifer S. Cisney and Kevin L. Ellers; *Jersusalem at the Time of Jesus.*

ABSEY & CO.

23011 Northcrest Dr., Spring TX 77389. (281)257-2340. Fax: (281)251-4676. E-mail: info@absey.biz. Website: www.absey.biz. **Contact:** Edward Wilson, publisher. Publishes hardcover, trade paperback, and mass market paperback originals. **Publishes 6-10 titles/year. 50% of books from first-time authors. 50% from unagented writers. Royalty and advance vary.** Publishes book 1 year after acceptance of ms. Responds in 3 months to queries. Responds in 9 months to manuscripts. Guidelines available online.

O⇁ "Our goal is to publish original, creative works of literary merit. Currently emphasizing educational, young adult literature. De-emphasizing self-help."

Nonfiction Subjects include education, language, literature, language, literature arts, general nonfiction. Query with SASE.

Fiction Subjects include juvenile, mainstream, contemporary, short story collections. "Since we are a small, new press, we are looking for book-length manuscripts with a firm intended audience." Query with SASE.

Poetry "Publishes the Writers and Young Writers Series. Interested in thematic poetry collections of literary merit." Query.

Recent Title(s) *Adrift*, by Greg Raver-Lampman; *Where I'm From*, by George Ella Lyon (poetry); *Stealing a Million Kisses*, by Jennifer Skaggs.

Tips "We work closely and attentively with authors and their work. Does not download mss or accept e-mail submissions."

ACADEMY CHICAGO PUBLISHERS

363 W. Erie St., Suite 4W, Chicago IL 60610-3125. (312)751-7300. Fax: (312)751-7306. E-mail: info@academychicago.com. Website: www.academychicago.com. **Contact:** Anita Miller, editorial director/senior editor. Estab. 1975. Publishes hardcover and some paperback originals and trade paperback reprints. **Publishes 10 titles/year. Pays 7-10% royalty on wholesale price.** Publishes book 18 months after acceptance of ms. Book catalog available online. Guidelines available online.

O⇁ "We publish quality fiction and nonfiction. Our audience is literate and discriminating. No novelized biography, history, or science fiction."

Nonfiction Subjects include history, travel. Submit proposal package, outline, bio, 3 sample chapters.

Fiction Subjects include historical, mainstream, contemporary, military, war, mystery. We look for quality work, but we do not publish experimental, avant garde novels. Submit proposal package, clips, 3 sample chapters.

Tips "At the moment, we are looking for good nonfiction; we certainly want excellent original fiction, but we are swamped. No fax queries, no disks. No electronic submissions. We are always interested in reprinting good out-of-print books."

ACTA PUBLICATIONS

5559 W. Howard St., Skokie IL 60077. (847)676-2282. Fax: (847)676-2287. E-mail: acta@actapublications.com. Website: www.actapublications.com. **Contact:** Andrew Yankech, acquisitions dir. Estab. 1958. Publishes trade paperback originals. **Publishes 12 titles/year. 100 queries received/year. 25 mss received/year. 50% of books from first-time authors. 90% from unagented writers. Pays 10-12%**

royalty on wholesale price. Publishes book 1 year after acceptance of ms. Responds in 2-3 months to proposals. Book catalog and ms guidelines available online or with #10 SASE.

- "While some of ACTA's material is specifically Catholic in nature, most of the company's products are aimed at a broadly ecumenical audience."

O- "ACTA publishes nonacademic, practical books aimed at the mainline religious market."

Nonfiction Subjects include religion, spirituality. Submit outline, 1 sample chapter. No e-mail submissions. Reviews artwork/photos. Send photocopies.

Recent Title(s) *The Geography of God's Mercy*, by Patrick Hannon (spirituality/stories); *Portraits of Grace*, by James Stephen Behrens (spirituality/photography); *God's Word is Alive*, by Alice Camille (lectionary).

Tips "Don't send a submission unless you have examined our catalog, website and several of our books."

ADAMS MEDIA

Division of F+W Media, Inc. 57 Littlefield St., Avon MA 02322. (508)427-7100. Fax: (800)872-5628. E-mail: paula.munier@fwmedia.com. Website: www.adamsmedia.com. **Contact:** Paula Munier. Estab. 1980. Publishes hardcover originals, trade paperback originals and reprints. **Publishes more than 250 titles/year. 5,000 queries received/year. 1,500 mss received/year. 40% of books from first-time authors. 40% from unagented writers. Pays standard royalty or makes outright purchase. Pays variable advance.** Publishes book 12-18 months after acceptance of ms. Accepts simultaneous submissions. Responds in 3 months to queries. Guidelines available online.

O- "Adams Media publishes commercial nonfiction, including self-help, inspiration, women's issues, pop psychology, relationships, business, careers, pets, parenting, New Age, gift books, cookbooks, how-to, reference, and humor. Does not return unsolicited materials. Does not accept electronic submissions."

Recent Title(s) *365 Ways to Live Cheap; WTF?; My Mom Is My Hero; The Maxims of Manhood; Surviving a Layoff.*

AERONAUTICAL PUBLISHERS

1 Oakglade Circle, Hummelstown PA 17036-9525. (717)566-0468. Fax: (717)566-6423. E-mail: info@possibilitypress.com. Website: www.aeronauticalpublishers.com. **Contact:** Mike Markowski, publisher. Estab. 1981. Publishes trade paperback originals. **Pays variable royalty.** Responds in 2 months to queries. Guidelines available online.

Imprints American Aeronautical Archives, Aviation Publishers, Aeronautical Publishers.

O- "Our mission is to help people learn more about aviation and model aviation through the written word."

Nonfiction Subjects include history, aviation, hobbies, recreation, radio control, free flight, indoor models, micro radio control, home-built aircraft, ultralights, and hang gliders. Prefers submission by mail. Include SASE.

Recent Title(s) *Flying Models*, by Don Ross; *Those Magnificent Fast Flying Machines*, by C.B. Hayward.

Tips "Our focus is on books of short to medium length that will serve the emerging needs of the hobby. We also want to help youth get started, while enhancing everyone's enjoyment of the hobby. We are looking for authors who are passionate about the hobby, and will champion their book and the messages of their books, supported by efforts at promoting and selling their books."

ALLWORTH PRESS

10 E. 23rd St., Suite 510, New York NY 10010-4402. (212)777-8395. Fax: (212)777-8261. E-mail: pub@allworth.com. Website: www.allworth.com. **Contact:** Bob Porter, associate publisher. Estab. 1989. Publishes hardcover and trade paperback originals. **Publishes 12-18 titles/year. Pays advance.** Responds in 1 month to queries. Responds in 2 months to proposals. Book catalog and ms guidelines free.

O- "Allworth Press publishes business and self-help information for artists, designers, photographers, authors and film and performing artists, as well as books about business, money and the law for the general public. The press also publishes the best of classic and contemporary writing in art and graphic design. Currently emphasizing photography, graphic & industrial design, performing arts, fine arts and crafts, et al."

Nonfiction Subjects include art, architecture, business, economics, film, cinema, stage, music, dance, photography, film, television, graphic design, performing arts, writing, as well as business and legal guides for the public. "We are currently accepting query letters for practical, legal, and technique books targeted to professionals in the arts, including designers, graphic and fine artists, craftspeople, photographers, and those involved in film and the performing arts." Query.

Recent Title(s) *Designers Don't Read*, by Austin Howe; *How to Start and Run a Commercial Art Gallery*, by Edward Winkleman; *Emotional Branding*, by Marc Gobe; *Selling Your Photography*, by Richard Weisgrau; *Performing Arts Management*, by Tobie Stein and Jessica Bathurst.
Tips We are helping creative people in the arts by giving them practical advice about business and success.

ALPHA WORLD PRESS

530 Oaklawn Avenue, Green Bay WI 54304. (866)855-3720. E-mail: office@alphaworldpress.com. Website: www.alphaworldpress.com. **Contact:** Tracey Vandeveer, owner. Estab. 2006. Publishes trade paperback originals, and mass market paperback originals. **Publishes 12 titles/year. 120 queries received/year. 12 mss received/year. 75% of books from first-time authors. 100% from unagented writers. Pays 10-30% royalty on retail price.** Publishes book 3 months after acceptance of ms. Responds in 1 month to queries. Responds in 1 month to proposals. Responds in 2 months to manuscripts. Book catalog available online. Guidelines available free.

- *Alpha World Press is not accepting new submissions at this time. Please check back later.*

O→ "Our press is dedicated to publishing high-quality work by, for and about lesbians from all walks of life. We publish fiction, non-fiction, and poetry. We welcome all manuscripts from lesbians. We want the voices and perspectives of lesbians from all across the world to be heard through the books that we publish. We work very closely with our authors in all aspects of publishing - from editing, graphic design, to actual production, promotion & marketing."

Nonfiction Subjects include community, contemporary culture, gay, lesbian, history, social sciences, sports. Only submit nonfiction if it is written by or relates to lesbians. Submit proposal package, outline. Reviews artwork/photos. Send via e-mail.
Fiction Subjects include adventure, confession, gay, lesbian, historical, horror, humor, juvenile, literary, mainstream, contemporary, mystery, romance, science fiction, short story collections, spiritual, sports, suspense, western, young adult. We publish only lesbian-themed books for the lesbian market. Submit proposal package, 3 sample chapters, clips. Send it via e-mail in pdf.
Recent Title(s) *Meditative Rose*, by Lynn Gravbelle; *Made For You*, by Geneva St. James; *Marti Brown and the House of Face*, by Teresa R. Allen.
Tips Our audience is lesbians only.

AMACOM BOOKS

American Management Association 1601 Broadway, New York NY 10019-7406. (212)586-8100. Fax: (212)903-8168. Website: www.amacombooks.org. **Contact:** Ellen Kadin, executive editor (marketing, career, personal development); Robert Nirkind, senior editor (sales, customer service, project management, finance); Christina Parisi, executive editor (human resources, leadership, training, management). Estab. 1923. Publishes hardcover and trade paperback originals, professional books.

O→ AMACOM is the publishing arm of the American Management Association, the world's largest training organization for managers and their organizations—advancing the skills of individuals to drive business success. AMACOM's books are intended to enhance readers' personal and professional growth, and to help readers meet the challenges of the future by conveying emerging trends and cutting-edge thinking.

Nonfiction Subjects include all business topics. Publishes books for consumer and professional markets, including general business, management, strategic planning, human resources, manufacturing, project management, training, finance, sales, marketing, customer service, career, technology applications, history, real estate, parenting, communications and biography. Submit proposals including brief book description and rationale, TOC, author bio and platform, intended audience, competing books and sample chapters. Proposals returned with SASE only.
Recent Title(s) *Just Listen*, by Mark Goulston; *The AMA Handbook of Leadership*, by Marshall Goldsmith, John Baldoni, and Sarah McArthur; *Exceptional Service, Exceptional Profit*, by Leonardo Inghilleri and Micah Solomon; *And Chaotics*, by Philip Kotler and John Caslione; *The Power of Charm*, by Brian Tracy.

AMERICAN CORRECTIONAL ASSOCIATION

206 N. Washington St., Suite 200, Alexandria VA 22314. (703)224-0194. Fax: (703)224-0179. E-mail: aliceh@aca.org. Website: www.aca.org. **Contact:** Alice Heiserman, manager of publications and research. Estab. 1870. Publishes trade paperback originals. **Publishes 18 titles/year. 90% of books from first-time authors. 100% from unagented writers.** Publishes book 1 year after acceptance of ms. Responds in 4 months to queries. Book catalog available free. Guidelines available online.

O→ "American Correctional Association provides practical information on jails, prisons, boot camps, probation, parole, community corrections, juvenile facilities and rehabilitation programs, substance abuse programs, and other areas of corrections."

Nonfiction "We are looking for practical, how-to texts or training materials written for the corrections profession. We are especially interested in books on management, development of first-line supervisors, and security-threat group/management in prisons." Query with SASE. Reviews artwork/photos.

Recent Title(s) *TRY: Treatment Readiness for Youth at Risk*; *Changing Criminal Thinking*; *Becoming a Model Warden*.

Tips "Authors are professionals in the field of corrections. Our audience is made up of corrections professionals and criminal justice students. No books by inmates or former inmates. This publisher advises out-of-town freelance editors, indexers, and proofreaders to refrain from requesting work from them."

AMERICAN COUNSELING ASSOCIATION

5999 Stevenson Ave., Alexandria VA 22304. (703)823-9800. Fax: (703)823-4786. E-mail: cbaker@counseling.org. Website: www.counseling.org. **Contact:** Carolyn C. Baker, director of publications. Estab. 1952. Publishes paperback originals. **Publishes 10-12 titles/year. 1% of books from first-time authors. 90% from unagented writers.** Accepts simultaneous submissions. Responds in 1 month to queries. Guidelines available free.

O→ "The American Counseling Association is dedicated to promoting public confidence and trust in the counseling profession. We publish scholarly texts for graduate level students and mental health professionals. We do not publish books for the general public."

Nonfiction Subjects include education, gay, lesbian, health, multicultural, psychology, religion, sociology, spirituality, women's issues. Query with SASE. Submit proposal package, outline, 2 sample chapters, vitae.

Recent Title(s) *Ethics Desk Reference for Counselors; The ACA Encyclopedia of Counseling; The Professional Counselor*, 4e; *Counseling Strategies for Loss and Grief; Career Counseling*, 3e.

Tips "Target your market. Your books will not be appropriate for everyone across all disciplines."

⊘ AMERICAN PRESS

60 State St., Suite 700, Boston MA 02109. (617)247-0022. E-mail: americanpress@flash.net. Website: www.americanpresspublishers.com. **Contact:** Jana Kirk, editor. Estab. 1911. Publishes college textbooks. **Publishes 25 titles/year. 350 queries received/year. 100 mss received/year. 50% of books from first-time authors. 90% from unagented writers. Pays 5-15% royalty on wholesale price.** Publishes book 9 months after acceptance of ms. Responds in 3 months to queries.

• "Mss proposals are welcome in all subjects & disciplines."

Nonfiction Subjects include agriculture, anthropology, archeology, art, architecture, business, economics, education, government, politics, health, medicine, history, horticulture, music, dance, psychology, science, sociology, sports. "We prefer that our authors actually teach courses for which the manuscripts are designed." Query, or submit outline with tentative TOC. *No complete mss.*

Recent Title(s) *Alabama Football: Stallings to Saban*, by Donald Staffo; *Coaching: A Problem-Solving Approach*, by William F. Stier, Jr.; *Coaching: Becoming A Successful Athletic Coach*, by William F. Stier, Jr.

AMERICAN QUILTER'S SOCIETY

Schroeder Publishing P.O. Box 3290, Paducah KY 42002-3290. (270)898-7903. Fax: (270)898-1173. E-mail: editor@aqsquilt.com. Website: www.americanquilter.com. **Contact:** Andi Reynolds, executive book editor (primarily how-to and patterns, but other quilting books sometimes published, including quilt-related fiction). Estab. 1984. Publishes trade paperback originals. **Publishes 20-24 titles/year. 100 queries received/year. Multiple submissions okay. 60% of books from first-time authors. Pays 5% royalty on retail price.** Publishes book 12-18 months. after acceptance of ms. Accepts simultaneous submissions. Responds in 1 week to 2 months to proposals. Proposal guidelines online.

O→ "American Quilter's Society publishes how-to and pattern books for quilters (beginners through intermediate skill level). We are not the publisher for non-quilters writing about quilts."

Nonfiction No queries; proposals only. Note: 1 or 2 completed quilt projects must accompany proposal.

Recent Title(s) *Liberated Quiltmaking II*, by Gwen Marston; *Jelly Roll Quilts & More*, by Kimberly Einmo; *Beautiful Alphabet Applique*, by Zena Thorpe.

AMERICAN WATER WORKS ASSOCIATION

6666 W. Quincy Ave., Denver CO 80235. (303)347-6278. Fax: (303)794-7310. E-mail: mkozyra@awwa.org. Website: www.awwa.org/communications/books. **Contact:** Mary Kay Kozyra, Acquisitions Editor. Estab. 1881. Publishes hardcover and trade paperback originals. Responds in 4 months to queries. Book catalog and ms guidelines free.

O→ "AWWA strives to advance and promote the safety and knowledge of drinking water and related issues to all audiences—from kindergarten through post-doctorate."

Nonfiction Subjects include nature, environment, science, software, drinking water- and wastewater-related topics, operations, treatment, sustainability. Query with SASE. Submit outline, bio, 3 sample chapters. Reviews artwork/photos. Send photocopies.

Recent Title(s) *Climate Change and Water: International Perspectives on Mitigation and Adaptation*, by Joel Smith, Carol Howe, and Jim Henderson, editors.

Tips "See website to download submission instructions."

AMERICA WEST PUBLISHERS

P.O. Box 2208, Carson City NV 89702-2208. (775)885-0700. Fax: (877)726-2632. E-mail: global@nohoax.com. Website: www.nohoax.com. **Contact:** George Green, president. Estab. 1985. Publishes hardcover and trade paperback originals and reprints. **Publishes 20 titles/year. 90% of books from first-time authors. 90% from unagented writers. Pays 10% royalty on wholesale price. Pays $300 average advance.** Publishes book 6 months after acceptance of ms. Accepts simultaneous submissions. Responds in 1 month to queries. Book catalog and ms guidelines free.

Imprints Bridger House Publishers, Inc.

O→ "America West seeks the other side of the picture, political cover-ups, and new health alternatives."

Nonfiction Subjects include business, economics, government, politics, including cover-up, health, medicine, holistic self-help, New Age, UFO-metaphysical. Submit outline, sample chapters. Reviews artwork/photos.

Recent Title(s) *Day of Deception*, by William Thomas.

Tips "We currently have materials in all bookstores that have areas of UFOs; also political and economic nonfiction."

AMHERST MEDIA, INC.

175 Rano St., Suite 200, Buffalo NY 14207. (716)874-4450. Fax: (716)874-4508. E-mail: amherstmed@aol.com. Website: www.AmherstMedia.com. **Contact:** Craig Alesse, publisher. Estab. 1974. Publishes trade paperback originals and reprints. **Publishes 30 titles/year. 60% of books from first-time authors. 90% from unagented writers. Pays 6-8% royalty on retail price. Pays advance.** Publishes book 1 year after acceptance of ms. Accepts simultaneous submissions. Responds in 2 months to queries. Book catalog free and online (catalog@amherstmedia.com). Guidelines free and available online.

O→ Amherst Media publishes how-to photography books.

Nonfiction Subjects include photography. Looking for well-written and illustrated photo books. Query with outline, 2 sample chapters, and SASE. Reviews artwork/photos.

Recent Title(s) *Minimalist Lighting*, by Kirk Tuck; *Portrait Photographer's Handbook*, by Bill Hurter.

Tips "Our audience is made up of beginning to advanced photographers. If I were a writer trying to market a book today, I would fill the need of a specific audience and self-edit in a tight manner."

ARCADIA PUBLISHING

420 Wando Park Blvd., Mt. Pleasant SC 29464. (843)853-2070. Fax: (843)853-0044. Website: www.arcadiapublishing.com. **Contact:** Editorial Director. Estab. 1993. Publishes trade paperback originals. **Publishes 600 titles/year. Pays 8% royalty on retail price.** Publishes book 9 months after acceptance of ms. Accepts simultaneous submissions. Book catalog available online. Guidelines available free.

- The following submissions e-mail addresses are divided by region: publishingnortheast@arcadiapublishing.com; publishingsouth@arcadiapublishing.com; publishingwest@arcadiapublishing.com; publishingmidwest@arcadiapublishing.com.

O→ "Arcadia publishes photographic vintage regional histories. We have more than 3,000 Images of America series in print. We have expanded our California program."

Nonfiction Subjects include history, local, regional. "Arcadia accepts submissions year-round. Our editors seek proposals on local history topics and are able to provide authors with detailed information about our publishing program as well as book proposal submission guidelines. Due to the great demand for titles on local and regional history, we are currently searching for authors to work with us on new photographic history projects. Please contact one of our regional publishing teams if you are interested in submitting a proposal." Specific proposal form to be completed.

Tips "Writers should know that we only publish history titles. The majority of our books are on a city or region, and contain vintage images with limited text."

ARCHEBOOKS PUBLISHING

ArcheBooks Publishing Inc. 6081 Silver King Blvd., Cape Coral FL 33914. (239)542-7595. Fax: (239)542-0080. E-mail: publisher@archebooks.com. Website: www.archebooks.com. **Contact:** Robert E. Gelinas, publisher & editor-in-chief. Estab. 2003. Publishes hardcover originals, electronic originals and trade paperback originals. **Publishes 6-10 titles/year. 100+ queries received/year. 100+ mss received/year. 75% of books from first-time authors. 50% from unagented writers. Pays royalty on retail price. Minimum of $2,500, subject to negotiation and keeping prior history and corporate policy in mind.** Publishes book 2-6 months after acceptance of ms. Accepts simultaneous submissions. Responds in 2-6 months on queries, proposals, and manuscripts. Book catalog & guidelines available online.

Nonfiction Subjects include business, creative nonfiction, history, philosophy, true crime. Submit proposal package. See website for complete proposal guidelines.

Fiction Subjects include adventure, fantasy, historical, horror, humor, literary, mainstream, contemporary, mystery, romance, science fiction, suspense, western, young adult, women's fiction. "Writers should be prepared to participate in very aggressive and orchestrated marketing and promotion campaigns, using all the promotional tools and training that we provide, at no charge. We're expanding in all areas." Submit proposal package. See website for complete proposal guidelines.

Recent Title(s) *One Big Itch*, by Sara Williams; *Choices Meant for Kings*, by Sandy Lender (Book 2 of the Choices Trilogy; *The Don Juan Con*, by Sara Williams

Tips " Learn to write a good proposal. An article on this topic can be found for free on our website in the Author's Corner section of Writer's Resources."

ARKANSAS RESEARCH, INC.

P.O. Box 303, Conway AR 72033. (501)470-1120. E-mail: desmond@arkansasresearch.com. Website: www.arkansasresearch.com. **Contact:** Desmond Walls Allen, owner. Estab. 1985. Publishes trade paperback originals and reprints. **Publishes 10 titles/year. 10% of books from first-time authors. 100% from unagented writers. Pays 5-10% royalty on retail price.** Publishes book 6 months after acceptance of ms. Responds in 1 month to queries. Book catalog for $1. Guidelines available free.

- "Our company opens a world of information to researchers interested in the history of Arkansas."

Nonfiction All Arkansas-related subjects. Subjects include Americana, ethnic, history, hobbies, genealogy, military, war, regional. Query with SASE. Reviews artwork/photos. Send photocopies.

Recent Title(s) *Life & Times from the Clay County Courier Newspaper published at Corning, Arkansas, 1893-1900.*

ASA, AVIATION SUPPLIES & ACADEMICS

7005 132nd Pl. SE, Newcastle WA 98059. (425)235-1500. E-mail: feedback@asa2fly.com. Website: www.asa2fly.com. Book catalog available free.

- "ASA is an industry leader in the development and sales of aviation supplies, publications, and software for pilots, flight instructors, flight engineers and aviation technicians. All ASA products are developed by a team of researchers, authors and editors."

Nonfiction All subjects must be related to aviation education and training. Subjects include education. "We are primarily an aviation publisher. Educational books in this area are our specialty; other aviation books will be considered." Query with outline. Send photocopies.

Recent Title(s) *The Savvy Flight Instructor: Secrets of the Successful CFI*, by Greg Brown.

Tips "Two of our specialty series include ASA's *Focus Series*, and ASA *Aviator's Library*. Books in our *Focus Series* concentrate on single-subject areas of aviation knowledge, curriculum and practice. The *Aviator's Library* is comprised of titles of known and/or classic aviation authors or established instructor/authors in the industry, and other aviation specialty titles."

ASCE PRESS

1801 Alexander Bell Dr., Reston VA 20191-4382. (703)295-6275. Fax: (703)295-6278. E-mail: ascepress@asce.org. Website: pubs.asce.org. Estab. 1989. **Publishes 10-15 titles/year. 20% of books from first-time authors. 100% from unagented writers.** Request ASCE Press book proposal submission guidelines. Guidelines available online.

- "ASCE Press publishes technical volumes that are useful to practicing civil engineers and civil engineering students, as well as allied professionals. We publish books by individual authors and editors to advance the civil engineering profession. Currently emphasizing geotechnical, structural engineering, sustainable engineering and engineering history. De-emphasizing highly specialized areas with narrow scope."

Nonfiction "We are looking for topics that are useful and instructive to the engineering practitioner." Query with proposal, sample chapters, CV, TOC, and target audience.

Recent Title(s) *Circles in the Sky: Life and Times of George Ferris*, by Richard G. Weingardt; *Field Guide to Environmental Engineering for Development Workers*, by James Michelcic, et al.; *Marine Outfall Construction*, by Robert A. Grace.

Tips "As a traditional publisher of scientific and technical materials, ASCE Press applies rigorous standards to the expertise, scholarship, readability and attractiveness of its books."

ATRIAD PRESS, LLC

13820 Methuen Green, Dallas TX 75240. (972)671-0002. Fax: (214)367-4343. E-mail: ginnie@atriadpress.com. Website: www.atriadpress.com. **Contact:** Mitchel Whitington, senior editor. Estab. 2002. trade paperback originals. **Writers selected for this collection of personal ghost tales will receive a copy of the book in which their story appears. Authors can purchase additional copies of the books at discounted prices, and re-sell them at book signings, speaking engagements, etc. for additional revenue. A photo and brief bio of the author will be included at the end of the story.** Accepts simultaneous submissions. Book catalog available online. Guidelines available online. If you have any questions regarding the Writer's Guidelines, please contact us by e-mail at editor@atriadpress.com.

- "We are seeking books on supernatural happenings focused on the State of Texas. The first two titles in this series are: *True Tales of Texas Ghosts: Living in a Haunted House* and *True Tales of Texas Ghosts: Spirits in the Workplace*. A submission should be based on a true, supernatural encounter that you have personally experienced in the State of Texas. Length requirements are somewhat flexible, but stories should be 1000-2000 words. Longer stories will be considered."

Nonfiction "Atriad Press publishes non-fiction Texas genre books only." Query first. We prefer e-mail rather than postal mail.

Recent Title(s) *Texas UFO Tales, From Denison 1868 to Stephenville 2008; Texas Little Trips, Great Getaways Near You; Texas Hysterical Society, the Wild & Wacky Side of the Lone Star State.*

Tips "Manuscripts should be written on an adult level, but please keep in mind that we market to school libraries. Approximate length should be 65,000 words. The market for ghost stories ranges from young to old. Please check your manuscript carefully for errors in spelling and structure."

BALCONY MEDIA, INC.

512 E. Wilson, Suite 213, Glendale CA 91206. (818)956-5313. E-mail: ann@balconypress.com. **Contact:** Ann Gray, publisher. Publishes hardcover and trade paperback originals. **Publishes 6-8 titles/year. 75% of books from first-time authors. 90% from unagented writers. Pays 10% royalty on wholesale price.** Accepts simultaneous submissions. Responds in 1 month to queries and proposals. Responds in 3 months to manuscripts. Book catalog available online.

- "We also now publish *Form: pioneering design magazine, bi-monthly to the architecture and design professions.* Editor: Alelxi Drosu, www.formmag.net."

Nonfiction Subjects include art, architecture, ethnic, gardening, history, relative to design, art, architecture, and regional. "We are interested in the human side of design as opposed to technical or how-to. We like to think our books will be interesting to the general public who might not otherwise select an architecture or design book." Query by e-mail or letter. Submit outline and 2 sample chapters with introduction, if applicable.

Recent Title(s) *Tall Building: Imagining the Skyscraper*, by Scott Johnson; *Water is Key: A Better Future for Africa*, by Gil Garcetti.

Tips "Audience consists of architects, designers, and the general public who enjoy those fields. Our books typically cover California subjects, but that is not a restriction. It's always nice when an author has strong ideas about how the book can be effectively marketed. We are not afraid of small niches if a good sales plan can be devised."

BAREFOOT BOOKS

2067 Massachusettes Ave., Cambridge MA 02140. Website: www.barefootbooks.com. **Contact:** Submissions Editor. Publishes hardcover and trade paperback originals. **Publishes 30 titles/year. 2,000 queries received/year. 3,000 mss received/year. 35% of books from first-time authors. 60% from unagented writers. Pays 2½-5% royalty on retail price. Pays advance.** Publishes book 2 years after acceptance of ms. Accepts simultaneous submissions. Book catalog for 9 × 12 SAE stamped with $1.80 postage. *Barefoot Books are unable to accept submissions at this time. Please check website in 2011 for updated guidelines.*

O→ "We are a small, independent publishing company that publishes high-quality picture books for children of all ages and specializes in the work of artists and writers from many cultures. We focus on themes that support independence of spirit, encourage openness to others, and foster a life-long love of learning. Prefers full manuscript."

Fiction Subjects include juvenile. "Barefoot Books only publishes children's picture books and anthologies of folktales. We do not publish novels. We encourage authors to send their full manuscript. Always include SASE."

Recent Title(s) *We All Went on Safari: A Counting Journey Through Tanzania*, by Laurie Krebs (early learning picture book); *The Fairie's Gift*, by Tanya Robyn Batt (picture book); *The Lady of Ten Thousand Names: Goddess Stories From Many Cultures*, by Burleigh Mutén (illustrated anthology).

Tips "Our audience is made up of children and parents, teachers and students, of many different ages and cultures. Since we are a small publisher, and we definitely publish for a 'niche' market, it is helpful to look at our books and our website before submitting, to see if your book would fit into the type of book we publish."

BARRICADE BOOKS, INC.

185 Bridge Plaza N., Suite 309, Fort Lee NJ 07024. (201)944-7600. Fax: (201)944-6363. Website: www.barricadebooks.com. **Contact:** Carole Stuart, publisher. Estab. 1991. Publishes hardcover and trade paperback originals, trade paperback reprints. **Publishes 12 titles/year. 200 queries received/year. 100 mss received/year. 80% of books from first-time authors. 50% from unagented writers. Pays 10-12% royalty on retail price for hardcover. Pays advance.** Publishes book 18 months after acceptance of ms. Responds in 1 month to queries.

O→ "Barricade Books publishes nonfiction, mostly of the controversial type, and books we can promote with authors who can talk about their topics on radio and television and to the press."

Nonfiction Subjects include business, economics, ethnic, gay, lesbian, government, politics, health, medicine, history, nature, environment, psychology, sociology, true crime. Query with SASE. Submit outline, 1-2 sample chapters. Material will not be returned or responded to without SASE. We do not accept proposals on disk or via e-mail. Reviews artwork/photos. Send photocopies.

Recent Title(s) *Mail for Mikey*, by Orson Bean; *Jailing the Johnstown Gang*, by Bruce Mowday.

Tips "Do your homework. Visit bookshops to find publishers who are doing the kinds of books you want to write. Always submit to a person—not just `Editor.' Always enclose a SASE or you may not get a response."

BARRON'S EDUCATIONAL SERIES, INC.

250 Wireless Blvd., Hauppauge NY 11788. (800)645-3476. Fax: (631)434-3723. Website: www.barronseduc.com. **Contact:** Wayne Barr, Acquisitions Manager. Estab. 1941. Publishes hardcover, paperback and mass market originals and software. **Publishes 400 titles/year. 2,000 queries received/year. 15% of books from first-time authors. 75% from unagented writers. Pays $3,000-4,000 advance.** Publishes book 18 months after acceptance of ms. Accepts simultaneous submissions. Responds in 3 months to queries. Responds in 4 months to manuscripts. Book catalog available free. Guidelines available online.

O→ "Barron's tends to publish series of books, both for adults and children. No adult fiction. We are always on the lookout for creative nonfiction ideas for children and adults."

Nonfiction Subjects include foreign language pet care, business, economics, child guidance, education, health, hobbies, literature, new age, sports, translation, adult education, foreign language, review books. Main business is test prep guides. Query with SASE. Submit outline, 2-3 sample chapters. Reviews artwork/photos.

Recent Title(s) *Math Wizardry For Kids; Barron's American Slang Dictionary; 101 Sci-Fi Movies You Must See Before You Die*, Steven Jay Schneider, ed.; *Night at the Museum: Battle of the Smithsonian; Mathopolis: Parting is Such Sweet Sorrow.*

Tips "Audience is mostly educated self-learners and students. Try to fit into one of our series. Children's books have less chance for acceptance because of the glut of submissions. On children's stories, better to send query e-mail without attachments. SASE must be included for the return of all materials. Please be patient for replies."

BASIC HEALTH PUBLICATIONS, INC.

28812 Top of the World Dr., Laguna Beach CA 92651. (949)715-7327. Fax: (949)715-7328. Website: www.basichealthpub.com. **Contact:** Norman Goldfind, publisher. Estab. 2001. Publishes hardcover trade paperback and mass market paperback originals and reprints. Accepts simultaneous submissions. Book catalog available online. Guidelines for #10 SASE.

Nonfiction Subjects include health, medicine. "We are very highly focused on health, alternative medicine, nutrition, and fitness. Must be well researched and documented with appropriate references. Writing should be aimed at lay audience but also be able to cross over to professional market." Submit proposal package, outline, 2-3 sample chapters, introduction.

Recent Title(s) *The Sinatra Solution: Metabolic Cardiology*, by Stephen Sinatra, MD; *Umbilical Cord Stem Cell Therapy: The Gift of Life From Healthy Newborns*, by David Steenblock, MSDD, and Anthony F. Payne, PhD.

Tips "Our audience is over 30, well educated, middle to upper income. We prefer writers with professional credentials (M.D.s, PhD.s, N.D.s, etc.), or writers with backgrounds in health and medicine."

BAYLOR UNIVERSITY PRESS

One Bear Place 97363, Waco TX 76798. (254)710-3164; 3522. Fax: (254)710-3440. E-mail: carey_newman@baylor.edu. Website: www.baylorpress.com. **Contact:** Dr. Carey C. Newman, Director. Publishes hardcover and trade paperback originals. **Publishes 30 titles/year. Pays 10% royalty on wholesale price.** Publishes book 1 year after acceptance of ms. Accepts simultaneous submissions. Responds in 2 months to proposals. Guidelines available online.

- "We publish contemporary and historical scholarly works about culture, religion, politics, science, and the arts."

Nonfiction Submit outline, 1-3 sample chapters.

Recent Title(s) *Aldersgate and Athens - John Wesley and the Foundations of Christian Belief*, by William J. Abraham; *Inside Out Families - Living the Faith Together*, by Diana R. Garland; *Nonviolence - A Brief History - The Warsaw Lectures*, by John Howard Yoder, Compiled by Sheila Martin; *Encyclopedia of Evangelicalism*, by Randall Balmer; *Not Quite American? The Shaping of Arab and Muslim Identity in the United States*, by Yvonne Yazbeck Haddad.

BEARMANOR MEDIA

P.O. Box 71426, Albany GA 31708. (229)436-4265. Fax: (760)9696. E-mail: books@benohmart.com. Website: www.bearmanormedia.com. Estab. 2001. Publishes trade paperback originals and reprints. **Publishes 70 titles/year. 90% of books from first-time authors. 90% from unagented writers.** Accepts simultaneous submissions. Book catalog for #10 SASE. Guidelines available via e-mail.

Nonfiction Subjects include old-time radio, voice actors, old movies, classic television. Query with SASE. E-mail queries preferred. Submit proposal package, outline, list of credits on the subject.

Recent Title(s) *Son of Harpo Speaks*, by Bill Marx; *Fred MacMurray*, by Charles Tranberg; *John Holmes*, by Jill Nelson.

Tips "My readers love the past. Radio, old movies, old television. My own tastes include voice actors and scripts, especially of radio and television no longer available. I prefer books on subjects that haven't previously been covered as full books. It doesn't matter to me if you're a first-time author or have a track record. Just know your subject!"

N BLACK VELVET SEDUCTIONS PUBLISHING

1350-C W. Southport, Box 249, Indianapolis IN 46217. (888)556-2750. E-mail: lauriesanders@blackvelvetseductions.com. Website: www.blackvelvetseductions.com. **Contact:** Laurie Sanders, acquisitions editor. Estab. 2005. Publishes trade paperback and electronic originals and reprints. **Publishes about 20 titles/year. 500 queries received/year. 1,000 mss received/year. 90% of books from first-time authors. 100% from unagented writers. Pays 10% royalty for paperbacks; 50% royalty for electronic books.** Publishes book 6-12 months after acceptance of ms. Accepts simultaneous submissions. Responds in 6 months to queries. Responds in 8 months to proposals. Responds in 8-12 months to manuscripts. Catalog free or online. Guidelines online (guidelines@blackvelvetseductions.com).

Imprints Forbidden Experiences (erotic romance of all types); Tender Destinations (sweet romance of all types); Sensuous Journeys (sensuous romance of all types); Amorous Adventures (romantic suspense).

- "We only publish romance novels, romantic short story collections, and romantic erotic stories. If the piece is not a romance, we will not accept it. We do not accept mainstream fiction. We look for well-crafted stories with a high degree of emotional impact. We do not accept material written in first person. All material must be in third person point of view."

Fiction Subjects include erotic romance, historical romance, multicultural romance, romance, short story collections romantic stories, romantic suspense, western romance. All books must have a strong romance element. Query with SASE. Submit proposal package, clips, 3 sample chapters. Submit complete ms. Only accepts electronic submissions.

Recent Title(s) *Fool Me Once*, by Jessica Joy; *Night Angel*, by Renee Reeves; *Toy's Story: Acquisition of a Sex Toy*, by Robert Cloud, *His Perfect Submissive*, by Alyssa Aaron.

Tips "We publish romance and erotic romance. We look for books written in very deep point of view."

BOA EDITIONS, LTD.

250 North Goodman St., Suite 306, Rochester NY 14607. (585)546-3410. Fax: (585)546-3913. E-mail: info@boaeditions.org. Website: www.boaeditions.org. Estab. 1976. Publishes hardcover and trade paperback originals. **Publishes 11-13 titles/year. 1,000 queries received/year. 700 mss received/year. 15% of books from first-time authors. 90% from unagented writers. Negotiates royalties. Pays variable advance.** Publishes book 18 months after acceptance of ms. Accepts simultaneous submissions. Responds in 1 week to queries. Responds in 5 months to manuscripts. Book catalog available online. Guidelines available online.

"BOA Editions publishes distinguished collections of poetry, fiction and poetry in translation. Our goal is to publish the finest American contemporary poetry, fiction and poetry in translation."

Fiction Subjects include literary, poetry, poetry in translation, short story collections. "We now publish literary fiction through our American Reader Series. While aesthetic quality is subjective, our fiction will be by authors more concerned with the artfulness of their writing than the twists and turns of plot. Our strongest current interest is in short story collections (and short-short story collections), although we will consider novels. We strongly advise you to read our first published fiction collections."

Poetry "Readers who, like Whitman, expect of the poet to `indicate more than the beauty and dignity which always attach to dumb real objects. They expect him to indicate the path between reality and their souls,' are the audience of BOA's books."

Recent Title(s) *You & Yours*, by Naomi Shihab Nye; *The Rooster's Wife*, by Russell Edson; *The Heaven-Sent Leaf*, by Katy Lederer.

N BOLD STROKES BOOKS, INC.

P.O. Box 249, Valley Falls NY 12185. (518)753-6642. Fax: (518)753-6648. E-mail: publisher@boldstrokesbooks.com. Website: www.boldstrokesbooks.com. **Contact:** Len Barot, acq. director (general/genre gay/lesbian fiction). Trade paperback originals and reprints; electronic originals and reprints. **Publishes 60 + titles/year. 300 queries/year; 300 mss/year. 10-20% of books from first-time authors. 95% from unagented writers.** Publishes book 12-16 months after acceptance of ms. Catalog free on request - PDF. Guidelines online at website.

Imprints BSB Fiction (publishes 48/year), Matinee Books Romances (8/year), Victory Editions Lesbian Fiction (6/year), Liberty Editions Gay Fiction (8/year), Aeros eBooks (12-15/year).

Nonfiction Subjects include gay, lesbian, memoirs, young adult. Submit completed ms with bio, cover letter, and synopsis electronically only. Does not review artwork.

Fiction Subjects include adventure, erotica, fantasy, gay, gothic, historical, horror, lesbian, literary, mainstream, mystery, romance, science fiction, suspense, western, young adult. "Submissions should have a gay, lesbian, transgendered, or bisexual focus and should be positive and life-affirming." Submit completed ms with bio, cover letter, and synopsis—electronically only.

Recent Title(s) *Wall of Silence*, by Gabrielle Goldsby (mystery-2007 Lambda Literary Award winner); *The Lonely Hearts Club*, by Radclyffe (romance-bestseller).

Tips "We are particularly interested in authors who are interested in craft enhancement, technical development, and exploring and expanding traditional genre definitions and boundaries and are looking for a long-term publishing relationship ."

BRENNER INFORMATION GROUP

Imprint of Brenner Microcomputing, Inc. P.O. Box 721000, San Diego CA 92172. (858)538-0093. Fax: (Call first). E-mail: brenner@brennerbooks.com. Website: www.brennerbooks.com. **Contact:** Jenny Hanson, acquisitions manager (pricing & ranges). Estab. 1982. Publishes trade paperback and electronic originals specializing in pricing and performance time standards. **Publishes 4 titles/year. 1 ms and 6 queries received/year. 1% of books from first-time authors. 1% from unagented writers. Pays 5-15% royalty on wholesale price. Pays $0-1,000 advance.** Publishes book 1 year after acceptance of ms. Accepts simultaneous submissions. Responds in 1 month to queries, proposals, and manuscripts.

BURFORD BOOKS

32 Morris Ave., Springfield NJ 07081. (973)258-0960. Fax: (973)258-0113. E-mail: info@burfordbooks.com. Website: www.burfordbooks.com. **Contact:** Burford Books Editorial Departmetn. Estab. 1997.

Publishes hardcover originals, trade paperback originals and reprints. **Publishes 12 titles/year. 300 queries received/year. 200 mss received/year. 30% of books from first-time authors. 60% from unagented writers. Pays royalty on wholesale price.** Publishes book 18 months after acceptance of ms. Accepts simultaneous submissions. Responds in 1 month to queries. Responds in 1 month to proposals. Responds in 2 months to manuscripts. Book catalog and ms guidelines free. See website.

Burford Books publishes books on all aspects of the outdoors, from backpacking to sports, practical and literary.

Nonfiction Subjects include animals, cooking, foods, nutrition, hobbies, military, war, nature, environment, recreation, sports, travel. "Burford Books welcomes proposals on new projects, especially in the subject areas in which we specialize: sports, the outdoors, golf, nature, gardening, food and wine, travel, and military history. We are not currently considering fiction or children's books. In general it's sufficient to send a brief proposal letter that outlines your idea, which can be mailed, faxed, or e-mailed as you prefer. If you would like to send a sample chapter or two, please do so by mail. In all cases where you would like material returned, you must include a SASE." Reviews artwork/photos. Send photocopies.

Recent Title(s) *Saltwater Fishing*, by Jim Freda; *One Hundred Stretches*, by Jim Brown.

CANDLEWICK PRESS

99 Dover St., Somerville MA 02144. (617)661-3330. Fax: (617)661-0565. Website: www.candlewick.com. **Contact:** Deb Wayshak, executive editor (fiction); Joan Powers, editor-at-large (picture books); Liz Bicknell, editorial director/associate publisher (poetry, picture books, fiction); Mary Lee Donovan, executive editor (picture books, nonfiction/fiction); Hilary Van Dusen, senior editor (nonfiction/fiction); Sarah Ketchersid, senior editor (board, toddler). Estab. 1991. Publishes hardcover and trade paperback originals and reprints. **Publishes 200 titles/year. 5% of books from first-time authors.**

"Candlewick Press publishes high-quality, illustrated children's books for ages infant through young adult. We are a truly child-centered publisher."

Nonfiction Good writing is essential; specific topics are less important than strong, clear writing. *No unsolicited mss.*

Fiction Subjects include juvenile, picture books, young adult. *No unsolicited mss.*

Recent Title(s) *Good Masters! Sweet Ladies! Voices from a Medieval Village*, by Amy Schlitz.

Tips *"We no longer accept unsolicited mss*. See our website for further information about us."

CENTERSTREAM PUBLICATIONS

P.O. Box 17878, Anaheim Hills CA 92817. (714)779-9390. Fax: (714)779-9390. E-mail: centerstrm@aol.com. Website: www.centerstream-usa.com. **Contact:** Ron Middlebrook, Cindy Middlebrook, owners. Estab. 1980. Publishes music hardcover and mass market paperback originals, trade paperback and mass market paperback reprints. **Publishes 12 titles/year. 15 queries received/year. 15 mss received/year. 80% of books from first-time authors. 100% from unagented writers. Pays 10-15% royalty on wholesale price. Pays $300-3,000 advance.** Publishes book 8 months after acceptance of ms. Accepts simultaneous submissions. Responds in 3 months to queries. Book catalog and ms guidelines for #10 SASE.

Centerstream publishes music history and instructional books, all instruments plus DVDs.

Nonfiction Query with SASE.

Recent Title(s) *Guitar Chord Shapes of Charlie Christian*.

CHALICE PRESS

1221 Locust St., Suite 670, St. Louis MO 63103. (314)231-8500. Fax: (314)231-8524. E-mail: submissions@cbp21.com. Website: www.chalicepress.com. **Contact:** Cyrus N. White, president and publisher. Publishes hardcover and trade paperback originals. **Publishes 35 titles/year. 300 queries received/year. 250 mss received/year. 10% of books from first-time authors. 100% from unagented writers.** Publishes book 1 year after acceptance of ms. Accepts simultaneous submissions. Responds in 1 month to queries. Responds in 2 months to proposals. Responds in 3 months to manuscripts. Book catalog available online. Guidelines available online.

Nonfiction Subjects include religion, Christian spirituality. Submit proposal package, outline, 1-2 sample chapters.

Recent Title(s) *Preaching and the Other: Studies of Postmodern Insights*, by Ronald J. Allen; *Planning for Christian Education Formation: A Community of Faith Approach*, by Israel Galindo and Marty Canaday; *Oh God, Oh God, Oh God! Young Adults Speak Out about Sexuality and Christian Spirituality*, by Heather Godsey and Lara Blackwood Pickerel; *Passage into Discipleship: Guide to Baptism*, by Christopher Wilson.

Tips "We publish for professors, church ministers, and lay Christian readers."

CHELSEA GREEN PUBLISHING CO.

P.O. Box 428, White River Junction VT 05001-0428. (802)295-6300. Fax: (802)295-6444. E-mail: submissions@chelseagreen.com. Website: www.chelseagreen.com. **Contact:** Joni Praded, editorial director. Estab. 1984. Publishes hardcover and trade paperback originals and reprints. **Publishes 18-25 titles/year. 600-800 queries received/year. 200-300 mss received/year. 30% of books from first-time authors. 80% from unagented writers. Pays royalty on publisher's net. Pays $2,500-10,000 advance.** Publishes book 18 months after acceptance of ms. Responds in 2 weeks to queries. Responds in 1 month to proposals. Responds in 1 month to manuscripts. Book catalog free or online. Guidelines available online.

O→ "Chelsea Green's Science writers series publishes books on cutting-edge topics that advance science and the role it can play in preserving or creating sustainable civilizations and ecosystems."

Nonfiction Subjects include agriculture, alternative lifestyles, ethical & sustainable business, environment, foods, organic gardening, health, green building, progressive politics, science, social justice, simple living, renewable energy; and other sustainability topics. We prefer electronic queries and proposals via e-mail (as a single attachment). If sending via snail mail, submissions will only be returned with SASE. Please review our guidelines carefully before submitting. Reviews artwork/photos.

Fiction We do not publish fiction or children's books.

Recent Title(s) *Obama's Challenge*, by Robert Kutner; *Cheesemonger*, by Gordon Edgar; *The Winter Harvest Handbook*, by Eliot Coleman; *The Raw Milk Revolution*, by David Gumpert; *The Transition Handbook*, by Rob Hopkins; *Wind Energy Basics, 2nd ed.*, by Paul Gipe.

Tips "Our readers and our authors are passionate about finding sustainable and viable solutions to contemporary challenges in the fields of energy, food production, economics, and building. It would be helpful for prospective authors to have a look at several of our current books, as well as our website."

CHICAGO REVIEW PRESS

814 N. Franklin, Chicago IL 60610-3109. (312)337-0747. Fax: (312)337-5110. E-mail: Frontdesk@chicagoreviewpress.com. Website: www.chicagoreviewpress.com. **Contact:** Cynthia Sherry, publisher (general nonfiction, children's nonfiction); Yuval Taylor, senior editor (general nonfiction, especially performing arts-related); Jerome Pohlen, senior editor (popular science, children's nonfiction); Susan Bradanini Betz, senior editor (African-American, Latino-American, progressive politics). Estab. 1973. Publishes hardcover and trade paperback originals, and trade paperback reprints. **Publishes 40-50 titles/year. 400 queries received/year. 800 mss received/year. 50% of books from first-time authors. 50% from unagented writers. Pays 7-12½% royalty. Pays $3,000-10,000 average advance.** Publishes book 18 months after acceptance of ms. Accepts simultaneous submissions. Responds in 3 months to queries. ms guidelines for #10 SASE or online at website.

Imprints Lawrence Hill Books (contact Susan Bradanini Betz); A Cappella Books (contact Yuval Taylor); Zephyr Press (contact Jerome Pohlen).

O→ Chicago Review Press publishes intelligent nonfiction on timely subjects for educated readers with special interests. Does not accept fiction submissions.

Nonfiction Subjects include architecture, art, child guidance, creative nonfiction, education, environment, gardening, health, history, hobbies, memoirs, muticultural, music, nature, recreation, regional, science. Query with outline, TOC, and 1-2 sample chapters.

Recent Title(s) *Harry Truman's Excellent Adventure: The True Story of a Great American Road Trip*, by Matthew Algeo.

Tips "Along with a table of contents and 1-2 sample chapters, also send a cover letter and a list of credentials with your proposal. Also, provide the following information in your cover letter: audience, market, and competition—who is the book written for and what sets it apart from what's already out there."

CHOSEN BOOKS

A division of Baker Publishing Group 3985 Bradwater St., Fairfax VA 22031-3702. (703)764-8250. Fax: (703)764-3995. E-mail: jcampbell@chosenbooks.com. Website: www.chosenbooks.com. **Contact:** Jane Campbell, editorial director. Estab. 1971. Publishes hardcover and trade paperback originals. **Publishes 20 titles/year. 10% of books from first-time authors. 99% from unagented writers. Pays small advance.** Publishes book 12-18 months after acceptance of ms. Accepts simultaneous submissions. Responds in 3 months to queries. Guidelines sent electronically on request.

O→ "We publish well-crafted books that recognize the gifts and ministry of the Holy Spirit, and help the reader live a more empowered and effective life for Jesus Christ."

Nonfiction "We publish books reflecting the current acts of the Holy Spirit in the world, books with a charismatic Christian orientation, or thematic first-person narrative: query briefly by e-mail first."

Submit synopsis, chapter outline, 2 chapters, resume and SASE or e-mail address. No computer disks. E-mail attachments okay.

Recent Title(s) *Lord, Help Me Break This Habit: You Can Be Free From Doing the Things You Hate,* by Quin Sherrer and Ruthanne Garlock; *The Prophetic Intercessor,* by James W. Goll.

Tips "We look for solid, practical advice for the growing and maturing Christian from authors with professional or personal experience platforms. No chronicling of life events, please. Narratives have to be theme-driven. State the topic or theme of your book clearly in your query."

CLEAR LIGHT PUBLISHERS

823 Don Diego, Santa Fe NM 87505-4224. (505)989-9590. E-mail: publish@clearlightbooks.com. **Contact:** Harmon Houghton, publisher. Estab. 1981. Publishes hardcover and trade paperback originals. **Publishes 20-24 titles/year. 100 queries received/year. 10% of books from first-time authors. 50% from unagented writers. Pays 10% royalty on wholesale price. Offers advance, a percent of gross potential.** Publishes book 1 year after acceptance of ms. Accepts simultaneous submissions. Responds in 3 months to queries. Book catalog available free. Guidelines available online.

- "Clear Light publishes books that accurately depict the positive side of human experience and inspire the spirit."

Nonfiction Subjects include Americana, anthropology, archeology, art, architecture, cooking, foods, nutrition, ethnic, history, nature, environment, philosophy, photography, regional, Southwest. Query with SASE. Reviews artwork/photos. Send photocopies.

Recent Title(s) *American Indian History,* by Robert Venables; *Celebrations Cookbook,* by Myra Baucom; *American Indian Love Stories,* by Herman Grey.

CLEIS PRESS

Cleis Press & Viva Editions, 2246 Sixth St., Berkeley CA 94710. (510)845-8000 or (800)780-2279. Fax: (510)845-8001. E-mail: cleis@cleispress.com. Website: www.cleispress.com. **Contact:** Brenda Knight, Associate Publisher. Estab. 1980. Publishes trade paperback originals and reprints. **Publishes 45 titles/ year. 2,000 10% of books from first-time authors. 90% from unagented writers. Pays variable royalty on retail price.** Publishes book 2 years after acceptance of ms. Responds in 1 month to queries.

- Cleis Press publishes provocative, intelligent books in the areas of sexuality, gay and lesbian studies, erotica, fiction, gender studies, and human rights.

Nonfiction Subjects include gay, lesbian, women's issues, women's studies, sexual politics. "We are interested in books on topics of sexuality, human rights and women's and gay and lesbian literature. Please consult our website first to be certain that your book fits our list." Query or submit outline and sample chapters

Fiction Subjects include feminist, gay, lesbian, literary. "We are looking for high quality fiction by women and men." "Submit complete ms. *Writer's Market* recommends sending a query with SASE first."

Recent Title(s) *Afternoon Delight Erotica For Couples,* Edited by Alison Tyler; *Deconstructing Tyrone,* (nonfiction); *Jia,* (fiction); *Whole Lesbian Sex Book,* (nonfiction).

Tips "Be familiar with publishers' catalogs; be absolutely aware of your audience; research potential markets; present fresh new ways of looking at your topic; avoid `PR' language and include publishing history in query letter."

COLLEGE PRESS PUBLISHING CO.

P.O.Box 1132, 223 W. 3rd St., Joplin MO 64801. (800)289-3300. Fax: (417)623-8250. E-mail: books@collegepress.com. Website: www.collegepress.com. **Contact:** Acquisitions Editor. Estab. 1959. Publishes hardcover and trade paperback originals and reprints. Accepts simultaneous submissions. Responds in 3 months to proposals. Responds in 2 months to mss. Book catalog for 9 × 12 envelope and 5 first-class stamps. Guidelines available online.

Imprints HeartSpring Publishing (nonacademic Christian, inspirational, devotional and Christian fiction).

- College Press is a traditional Christian publishing house. Seeks proposals for Bible studies, topical studies (biblically based), apologetic studies, historical biographies of Christians, Sunday/Bible School curriculum (adult electives).

Nonfiction Seeks Bible studies, topical studies, apologetic studies, historical biographies of Christians, and Sunday/Bible school curriculum. Query with SASE. Always send a proposal or query letter first and requested manuscripts to: Acquisitions Editor.

Recent Title(s) *Dinner With Skeptics,* by Jeff Vines.

Tips "Our core market is Christian Churches/Churches of Christ and conservative evangelical Christians. Have your material critically reviewed prior to sending it. Make sure that it is non-Calvinistic and that it leans more amillennial (if it is apocalyptic writing)."

⊘ COPPER CANYON PRESS

P.O. Box 271, Bldg. 313, Port Townsend WA 98368. (360)385-4925. Fax: (360)385-4985. E-mail: poetry@coppercanyonpress.org. Website: www.coppercanyonpress.org. **Contact:** Michael Wiegers, Director/executive editor. Estab. 1972. Publishes trade paperback originals and occasional cloth-bound editions. **Publishes 18 titles/year. 2,000 queries received/year. 1,500 mss received/year. 0% of books from first-time authors. 95% from unagented writers. Pays royalty.** Publishes book 2 years after acceptance of ms. Responds in 4 months to queries. Book catalog & guidelines available online.

Imprints Ausable Press, Chase Twichell (Editor-at-Large, poet)

- The imprint Ausable Press, an independent literary press located in the Adirondack Mountains of northern New York, will join forces with CCR on Jan. 1, 2009. All contracts will be honored. Our offices will be kept open through 2009.

O- "Copper Canyon Press is dedicated to publishing poetry in a wide range of styles and from a full range of the world's cultures."

Poetry We have suspended our Hayden Carruth Award while considering other options for considering the work of new and emerging poets. We strongly encourage poets with first-book mss. to consider submitting to 'The American Poetry Review'/Honickman First Book Award. More information can be found on our website under Opportunities. *No unsolicited mss.*

Recent Title(s) *Steal Away*, by C.D. Wright; *Twigs & Knucklebones*, by Sarah Lindsay; *The Hands of Day*, by Pablo Neruda.

Tips "CCP publishes poetry exclusively and is the largest poetry publisher in the U.S. We will not review queries if guidelines are not followed. We will read queries from poets who have published a book. Please read our query guidelines."

THE COUNTRYMAN PRESS

P.O. Box 748, Woodstock VT 05091-0748. (802)457-4826. Fax: (802)457-1678. E-mail: countrymanpress@wwnorton.com. Website: www.countrymanpress.com. Estab. 1973. Publishes hardcover originals, trade paperback originals and reprints. **Publishes 60 titles/year. 1,000 queries received/year. 30% of books from first-time authors. 70% from unagented writers. Pays 5-15% royalty on retail price. Pays $1,000-5,000 advance.** Publishes book 18 months after acceptance of ms. Accepts simultaneous submissions. Responds in 2 months to proposals. Book catalog available free. Guidelines available online.

Imprints Backcountry Guides, Berkshire House.

O- "Countryman Press publishes books that encourage physical fitness and appreciation for and understanding of the natural world, self-sufficiency, and adventure."

Nonfiction "We publish several series of regional recreation guidebooks—hiking, bicycling, walking, fly-fishing, canoeing, kayaking—and are looking to expand them. We're also looking for books of national interest on travel, gardening, rural living, nature, and fly-fishing." Subjects include cooking, foods, nutrition, gardening, history, nature, environment, recreation, regional, travel, country living. Submit proposal package, outline, bio, 3 sample chapters, market information, SASE. Reviews artwork/photos. Send photocopies.

Recent Title(s) *Eatingwell Comfort Foods Made Easy; San Miguel de Allende: Great Destinations; Old Ghosts of New England; Volunteer Vacations Across America.*

COVENANT COMMUNICATIONS, INC.

920 E. State Rd., American Fork UT 84003. (801)756-9966. Fax: (801)756-1049. E-mail: info@covenant-lds. Website: www.covenant-lds.com. **Contact:** Kathryn Jenkins, managing editor. Estab. 1958. **Publishes 80-100 titles/year. 350 queries, 1,200 mss 60% of books from first-time authors. 99% from unagented writers. Pays 6½-15% royalty on retail price.** Publishes book 6 months to a year after acceptance of ms. Accepts simultaneous submissions. Responds in 1 month on queries & proposals; 4 months on manuscripts. Guidelines available online.

O- "Currently emphasizing inspirational, doctrinal, historical, biography. Our fiction is also expanding, and we are looking for new approaches to LDS literature and storytelling."

Nonfiction Subjects include history, religion, spirituality. "We target an exclusive audience of members of The Church of Jesus Christ of Latter-day Saints. All mss must be written for that audience." Submit complete ms. Reviews artwork. Send photocopies.

Fiction "We publish exclusively to the 'Mormon' (The Church of Jesus Christ of Latter-Day Saints) market. Fiction must feature characters who are members of that church, grappling with issues relevant to that religion." Subjects include adventure, historical, mystery, regional, religious, romance, spiritual, suspense. Submit complete ms.

Recent Title(s) *Exploring the Connection Between Mormons and Masons*, by Matthew B. Brown (nonfiction); *Tribunalk*, by Sandra Grey (historical); *Methods of Madness*, by Stephanie Black (suspense); *The Best of Times*, by Anita Stansfield (romance).

Tips "Our audience is exclusively LDS (Latter-Day Saints, 'Mormon')."

COWLEY PUBLICATIONS

Rowman & Littlefield 4501 Forbes Blvd., Suite 200, Lanham MD 20706. Website: www.rowmanlittlefield.com/imprints/cowley.shtml. **Contact:** Sarah Stanton, acquisitions editor. Estab. 1979. Publishes cloth and paperback originals. **Publishes 5-10 titles/year. 500 queries received/year. 300 mss received/year. 50% of books from first-time authors. 90% from unagented writers. Pays 8-15% royalty on wholesale price. Pays $0-5,000 advance.** Publishes book 12-18 months after acceptance of ms. Accepts simultaneous submissions. Responds in 2 months to queries; 3 months to proposals; 4 months to manuscripts. Book catalog available online. Guidelines available online.

- Purchased by Rowman & Littlefield Publishing Group.

Nonfiction Subjects include religion, spirituality. "We publish books and resources for those seeking spiritual and theological formation. We are committed to developing a new generation of writers and teachers who will encourage people to think and pray in new ways about spirituality, reconciliation, and the future. We are interested in the many ways that faith and spirituality intersect with the world, in arts, social concerns, ethics, and so on." Query with SASE. Submit proposal package, outline, 1 sample chapter, other materials as specified online.

Recent Title(s) *Conversations With Scripture and With Each Other*," by M. Thomas Shaw, SSJE; *Pilgrims of Christ on the Muslim Road*," by Paul-Gordon Chandler.

Tips "We envision an audience of committed Christians and spiritual seekers of various denominations and faiths. Familiarize yourself with our catalog and our outlook on spiritual and theological formation. Prepare proposals/manuscripts that are of professional caliber and demonstrate an understanding of and commitment to your book's reader."

CRAFTSMAN BOOK CO.

6058 Corte Del Cedro, Carlsbad CA 92011. (760)438-7828 or (800)829-8123. Fax: (760)438-0398. Website: www.craftsman-book.com. **Contact:** Laurence D. Jacobs, editorial manager. Estab. 1957. Publishes paperback originals. **Publishes 12 titles/year. 85% of books from first-time authors. 98% from unagented writers. Pays 7½-12½% royalty on wholesale price or retail price.** Publishes book 2 years after acceptance of ms. Accepts simultaneous submissions. Responds in 2 months to queries. Book catalog and ms guidelines free.

O→ Publishes how-to manuals for professional builders. Currently emphasizing construction software.

Nonfiction All titles are related to construction for professional builders. Query with SASE. Reviews artwork/photos.

Recent Title(s) *Steel-Frame House Construction*, by Tim Waite.

Tips "The book submission should be loaded with step-by-step instructions, illustrations, charts, reference data, forms, samples, cost estimates, rules of thumb, and examples that solve actual problems in the builder's office and in the field. It must cover the subject completely, become the owner's primary reference on the subject, have a high utility-to-cost ratio, and help the owner make a better living in his chosen field."

CROSS-CULTURAL COMMUNICATIONS

Cross-Cultural Literary Editions, Ltd.; Express Editions; Ostrich Editions 239 Wynsum Ave., Merrick NY 11566-4725. (516)869-5635. Fax: (516)379-1901. E-mail: cccpoetry@aol.com. Website: www.cross-culturalcommunications.com. **Contact:** Stanley H. Barkan, publisher/editor-in-chief (bilingual poetry); Bebe Barkan, Mia Barkan Clarke, art editors (complementary art to poetry editions). Estab. 1971. Publishes hardcover and trade paperback originals. **Publishes 10 titles/year. 200 queries received/year. 50 mss received/year. 25%% of books from first-time authors. 100%% from unagented writers.** Publishes book 12 months after acceptance of ms. Responds in 1 month to proposals. Responds in 2 months to manuscripts. Book catalog (sample flyers) for #10 SASE.

Imprints Expressive Editions (contact Mia Barkan Clarke).

Nonfiction Subjects include language, literature, memoirs, multicultural. Query first; we basically do not want the focus on nonfiction. Query with SASE. Reviews artwork/photos. Send photocopies.

Fiction Subjects include historical, multicultural, poetry, poetry in translation, translation, Bilingual poetry. Do not query until mid-2010. For bilingual poetry: Submit 3-6 short poems in original language with translation, a brief (3-5 lines) bio of the author and translator(s). Query with SASE.
Poetry Query.
Recent Title(s) *Your Lover's Beloved*, by Hafez, translated by Mahmood Karimi-Hakak & Bill Wolak (bilingual Persian classical poetry); *Tea With Nana*, by Mia Barkan Clarke (poetry & paintings); *Vagabond Dawns*, by Carolyn Mary Kleefeld (poetry); *Paumanok: Poems and Pictures of Long Island*, compiled by Kathleen Donnelley (anthology designed by Tchouki, edited by Stanley H. Barkan); *No! Love*, by Aleksey Dayen (part bilingual Russian poetry); *Rivulets of Light: Poems of Point Lobos and Carmel Bay*, by John Dotson.
Tips "Best chance: poetry from a translation."

DAW BOOKS, INC.

Distributed by Penguin Group (USA) 375 Hudson St., New York NY 10014-3658. (212)366-2096. Fax: (212)366-2090. Website: www.dawbooks.com. **Contact:** Peter Stampfel, submissions editor. Estab. 1971. Publishes hardcover and paperback originals and reprints. **Publishes 50-60 titles/year. Pays in royalties with an advance negotiable on a book-by-book basis.** Responds in 3 months to manuscripts. Guidelines available online.

- Simultaneous submissions not accepted, unless prior arrangements are made by agent.

O→ DAW Books publishes science fiction and fantasy.

Nonfiction We do not want any nonfiction.
Fiction "Currently seeking modern urban fantasy and paranormals. We like character-driven books with appealing protagonists, engaging plots, and well-constructed worlds. We accept both agented and unagented manuscripts." Submit entire ms, cover letter, SASE.
Recent Title(s) *Gwenhwyfar*, by Mercedes Lackey (fantasy); *Shadowrise*, by Tad Williams (fantasy); *Regenesis*, by C.J. Cherryh (science fiction).

DEVORSS & COMPANY

DeVorss Publications P.O. Box 1389, Camarillo CA 93011-1389. E-mail: editorial@devorss.com. Website: www.devorss.com. Publishes hardcover and trade paperback originals and reprints. **700 queries received/year. 300 mss received/year. 95% of books from first-time authors. 100% from unagented writers. 10% maximum royalty on retail price.** Publishes book 6 months after acceptance of ms. Accepts simultaneous submissions. Responds in 1 month to manuscripts. Book catalog online and for #10 SASE. Guidelines available online and for #10 SASE.

O→ "We presently focus on high quality books in the following categories: New Thought, spirituality, self-improvement, alternative health & lifestyle, religion, and positive thinking. Our titles appeal to the mind/body/spirit market. We do not accept poetry."

Nonfiction Subjects include creative nonfiction, philosophy, psychology, spirituality, Body, Mind, and Spirit. We do not accept proposals on disc, over the internet, by e-mail, or by fax. Send copies of your material and keep the original for your records.Query with SASE. Reviews artwork/photos. Send photocopies.
Recent Title(s) *Little Green Apples*, by O.C. Smith and James Shaw.
Tips "Our audience is people using their mind to improve health, finances, relationships, life changes, etc. Ask for guidelines first. Don't submit outlines, proposals, or manuscripts. Don't call. Please send submissions and inquiries by mail only."

DISKUS PUBLISHING

P.O. Box 43, Albany IN 47320. Website: www.diskuspublishing.com. **Contact:** Joyce McLaughlin, inspirational and children's editor; Holly Janey, submissions editor. Estab. 1996. Publishes e-books. **Publishes 50 titles/year. Pays 40% royalty.** Publishes book 6-8 months after acceptance of ms. Accepts simultaneous submissions. Up to 1 year. Book catalog for #10 SASE. Guidelines for #10 SASE or online.

- *At this time DiskUs Publishing is closed for submissions. We will reopen for submissions in the near future. We get thousands of submissions each month and our editors need time to get through the current ones. Keep checking our website for updates on the status of our submissions reopen date.*

Fiction Subjects include adventure, ethnic, general, fantasy, space fantasy, historical, horror, humor, juvenile, literary, mainstream, contemporary, military, war, multicultural, general, mystery, religious, romance, science fiction, short story collections, suspense, western, young adult. Submit publishing history, bio, Estimated Word Count and Genre. Submit complete ms.
Recent Title(s) *The Best Laid Plans*, by Leta Nolan Childers (romance); *Brazen*, by Lori Foster (adventure/romance); *A Change of Destiny*, by Marilyn Mansfield (science fiction/futuristic).

DIVERSION PRESS

P.O. Box 270, Campbell Hall, New York NY 10916. E-mail: diversionpress@yahoo.com. Website: www.diversionpress.com. **Contact:** Attn: Acquisition Editor. Estab. 2008. Publishes hardcover, trade and mass market paperback originals. **Publishes 20-30 titles/year. 75% of books from first-time authors. 95% from unagented writers. Pays -10% royalty on wholesale price.** Publishes book 12-29 months after acceptance of ms. Responds in 2 weeks to queries. Responds in 1 month to proposals. Guidelines available online.

Nonfiction Subjects include Americana, animals, community, contemporary culture, education, ethnic, government, politics, health, medicine, history, hobbies, humanities, language, literature, literary criticism, memoirs, military, war, multicultural, philosophy, psychology, recreation, regional, science, social sciences, sociology, travel, women's issues, women's studies, world affairs. "The editors have doctoral degrees and are interested in a broad range of academic works. We are also interested in how-to, slice of life, and other nonfiction areas." Send query/proposal first. Mss accepted by request only. Reviews artwork/photos. Send photocopies.

Fiction Subjects include adventure, fantasy, gothic, historical, horror, humor, literary, mainstream, contemporary, mystery, poetry, science fiction, short story collections, suspense, young adult. "We will happily consider any children's or young adult books if they are illustrated. If your story has potential to become a series, please address that in your proposal. Fiction short stories and poetry will be considered for our anthology series. See website for details on how to submit your ms."

Poetry "Poetry will be considered for anthology series and for our poetry award." Submit 5 sample poems.

Recent Title(s) *Ellabug*, by Greg Turner-Rahman.

Tips Check out Ellabug, our first children's book, on Diversion Press Blog.

DK PUBLISHING, INC.

Pearson Plc 375 Hudson St., New York NY 10014. (212)213-4800. Website: www.dk.com. **Pays royalty or flat fee.**

- "DK Publishing is world renowned for its distinctive, highly visual books that inform, inspire, and entertain readers of all ages. Publisher of the recent New York Times bestsellers *Real Sex for Real Women* by Dr. Laura Berman, *Do Not Open*, and *Star Wars: The Clone Wars: The Visual Guide* among others, DK also publishes the award-winning Eyewitness series for children and Eyewitness Travel Guides. BradyGames and Rough Guides are also available from DK, a division of Penguin Group (USA)."
- Publishes picture books for middle-grade and older readers. Also, illustrated reference books for adults and children.

Fiction Agented submissions only.

DOWN EAST BOOKS

Imprint of Down East Enterprise, Inc. P.O. Box 679, Camden ME 04843-0679. (207)594-9544, 800-766-1670. Fax: (207)594-7215. E-mail: jviehman@downeast.com. Website: www.downeast.com. **Contact:** Paul Doiron, editor-in-chief. Estab. 1967. Publishes hardcover and trade paperback originals, trade paperback reprints. **Publishes 24-30 titles/year. 50% of books from first-time authors. 90% from unagented writers. Pays $500 average advance.** Publishes book 1 year after acceptance of ms. Accepts simultaneous submissions. Responds in 3 months to queries. Send SASE for ms guidlines. Send 9 × 12 SASE for guidelines, plus recent catalog.

- Down East Books publishes books that capture and illuminate the unique beauty and character of New England's history, culture, and wild places.

Nonfiction Subjects include Americana, history, nature, environment, recreation, regional, sports. Books about the New England region, Maine in particular. All of our regional books must have a Maine or New England emphasis. Query with SASE. Do not send CD, DVD, or disk. Reviews artwork/photos.

Fiction Subjects include juvenile, mainstream, contemporary, regional. We publish 2-4 juvenile titles/year (fiction and nonfiction), and 0-1 adult fiction titles/year. Query with SASE.

Recent Title(s) *Looking Astern: An Artist's View of Maine's Historic Waterfronts*, by Loretta Krupinski; *The Winter Visitors*, by Karel Hayes; *At Home By the Sea*, by Brian Vanden Brink and Bruce Snider; *A Healing Touch*, Richard Russo, Editor.

EDUCATOR'S INTERNATIONAL PRESS, INC.

18 Colleen Rd., Troy NY 12180. (518)271-9886. Fax: (518)266-9422. E-mail: bill@edint.com. Website: www.edint.com. **Contact:** William Clockel, publisher. Estab. 1996. Publishes hardcover and trade

paperback originals and reprints. Accepts simultaneous submissions. Book catalog and ms guidelines free.

O→ "Educator's International publishes books in all aspects of education, broadly conceived, from pre-kindergarten to postgraduate. We specialize in texts, professional books, videos and other materials for students, faculty, practitioners and researchers. We also publish a full list of books in the areas of women's studies, and social and behavioral sciences."

Nonfiction Subjects include education, language, literature, philosophy, psychology, software, women's studies. Submit TOC, outline, 2-3 chapters, resumè with SASE. Reviews artwork/photos.

Recent Title(s) *Journal of Curriculum and Pedagogy*; *Democratic Responses in an Era of Standardization*, (Relationship and the Arts in Teacher Education).

Tips Audience is professors, students, researchers, individuals, libraries.

EDUPRESS, INC.

401 S. Wright Road, Janesville WI 53547. (800)835-7978. E-mail: edupress@highsmith.com. Website: www.edupressinc.com. Estab. 1979. Publishes trade paperback originals. Book catalog and ms guidelines free.

O→ Edupress, Inc., publishes supplemental curriculum resources for PK-6th grade. Currently emphasizing reading and math materials, as well as science and social studies.

Nonfiction Subjects include education, resources for pre-school through middle school.

Tips "Audience is classroom teachers and homeschool parents."

ELLORA'S CAVE PUBLISHING, INC.

1056 Home Ave., Akron OH 44310. E-mail: service@ellorascave.com. Website: www.ellorascave.com. **Contact:** Raelene Gorlinsky, managing editor; Kelli collins, editor-in-chief. Estab. 2000. Publishes electronic originals and reprints; print books. **Pays 37.5% royalty on gross (cover price).** Accepts simultaneous submissions. Responds in 2 months to queries and to proposals. Responds in 2-6 months to manuscripts. Guidelines available online.

Fiction Erotic romance of every subgenre, including gay/lesbian, menage and more, and BDSM. All must be under genre romance. All must have erotic content or author must be willing to add sex during editing. Submit query letter, full synopsis, first three chapters, and last chapter.

Tips "Our audience is romance readers who want explicit sexual detail. They come to us because we offer not erotica, but Romantica™—sex with romance, plot, emotion. In addition to erotic romance with happy-ever-after endings, we also publish pure erotica, detailing sexual adventure, experimentation, and coming of age."

ENTREPRENEUR PRESS

2445 McCabe Way, Suite 400, Irvine CA 92614. (949)261-2325. Fax: (949)261-7729. E-mail: press@entrepreneur.com. Website: www.entrepreneurpress.com. **Contact:** Jere L. Calmes, publisher. Publishes quality hardcover and trade paperbacks. **Publishes 60+ titles/year. 1,200 queries received/year. 600 mss received/year. 40% of books from first-time authors. 60% from unagented writers. Pays competitive net royalty.** Accepts simultaneous submissions. Guidelines available online.

- *Entrepreneur* continues to be the definitive guide to all the diverse challenges of business ownership. *Entrepreneur.com* is the most widely used website by entrepreneurs and emerging businesses worldwide."

O→ "We are an independent publishing company that publishes titles focusing on starting and growing a business, personal finance, real estate and careers.

Nonfiction Subjects include business, economics, start-up, small business management, marketing, finance, real estate, careers, personal finance, accounting, motivation, leadership, legal advise, business travel, and management. When submitting work to us, please send as much of the proposed book as possible. Proposal should include: cover letter, preface, marketing plan, analysis of competition and comparative titles, author bio, TOC, 2 sample chapters. Go to website for more details. Reviews artwork/photos. Send transparencies and all other applicable information.

Recent Title(s) *Masters of Sales*, by Ivan R. Misner and Don Morgan; *Official Get Rich Guide to Information Marketing*, by Dan Kennedy, Robert Skrob and Bill Glazer; *Startup Guide to Guerrilla Marketing*, by Jay Conrad Levinson and Jeannie Levinson.

Tips We are currently seeking proposals covering sales, small business, startup, real estate, online businesses, marketing, etc.

EPICENTER PRESS, INC.

P.O. Box 82368, Kenmore WA 98028. Fax: (425)481-8253. E-mail: info@epicenterpress.com. Website: www.epicenterpress.com. **Contact:** Lael Morgan, 420 Ferry Rd., Saco, ME 04072. Estab. 1987. Publishes hardcover and trade paperback originals. **Publishes 4-8 titles/year. 200 queries received/year. 100 mss received/year. 75% of books from first-time authors. 90% from unagented writers.** Publishes book 12-24 months after acceptance of ms. Responds in 3 months to queries. Book catalog and ms guidelines on website.

O┳ "We are a regional press founded in Alaska whose interests include but are not limited to the arts, history, environment, and diverse cultures and lifestyles of the North Pacific and high latitudes."

Nonfiction Our focus is Alaska and the Pacific Northwest. We do not encourage nonfiction titles from outside this region. Subjects include animals, ethnic, history, nature, environment, recreation, regional, women's issues. Submit outline and 3 sample chapters. Reviews artwork/photos. Send photocopies. We are not interested in any content that does not relate in some way to Alaska.

F+W MEDIA, INC. (BOOK DIVISION)

4700 E. Galbraith Rd., Cincinnati OH 45236. (513)531-2690. Website: www.fwmedia.com. **Contact:** President: Sara Domville, President: David Blansfield; Publisher and Editorial Director, Karen Cooper (Adams Media), Publisher and Editorial Director, Dianne Wheeler (Antiques & Collectibles), Publisher and Editorial Director, Jeff Pozorski (Automotives), Publisher and Editorial Director, Jamie Markle (Art), Publisher and Editorial Director, Stephen Bateman (David & Charles), Publisher and Editorial Director, Gary Lynch (Design), Publisher and Editorial Director, Jim Schlender (Firearms & Knives), Publisher and Editorial Director, Guy LeCharles Gonzalez (Horticulture), Publisher and Editorial Director, Scott Tappa (Numismatics), Publisher and Editorial Director, Brad Rucks (Outdoors), Publisher and Editorial Director, Dean Listle (Sports, Construction Trade), Publisher and Editorial Director, Steve Shanesy (Woodworking), Publisher and Editorial Director, Jane Friedman (Writer's Digest, HOW Books). Estab. 1913. Publishes trade paperback originals and reprints. **Publishes 400 + titles/year.** Guidelines available online.

Imprints Adams Media (general interest series); David & Charles (crafts, equestrian, railroads, soft crafts); HOW Books (graphic design, illustrated, humor, pop culture); IMPACT Books (fantasy art, manga, creative comics and popular culture); Krause Books (antiques and collectibles, automotive, coins and paper money, comics, crafts, games, firearms, militaria, outdoors and hunting, records and CDs, sports, toys); Memory Makers (scrapbooking); North Light Books (crafts, decorative painting, fine art); Popular Woodworking Books (shop skills, woodworking); Warman's (antiques and collectibles, field guides); Writer's Digest Books (writing and reference).

- Please see individual listings for specific submission information about the company's imprints.

O┳ "In October 2008, F + W Media moved from a divisionally structured company to a Community structure, wherein the Publisher and Editorial Director for each community has full responsibility for the books, magazines, online, events, and educational products associated with their community. F + W Media produces more than 400 new books per year, maintains a backlist of more than 2,500 titles, publishes 39 magazines, owns and operates dozens of informational and subscription-based Web sites, and operates a growing number of successful consumer shows annually."

FACTS ON FILE, INC.

Infobase Publishing 132 W. 31st St., 17th Floor, New York NY 10001. (212)967-8800. Fax: (212)339-0326. E-mail: llikoff@factsonfile.com. Website: www.factsonfile.com. **Contact:** Laurie Likoff, Editorial Director (science, fashion, natural history); Frank Darmstadt (science & technology, nature, reference); Owen Lancer, senior editor (American history, women's studies); James Chambers, trade editor (health, pop culture, true crime, sports); Jeff Soloway, acquisitions editor (language/literature). Estab. 1941. Publishes hardcover originals and reprints. **Publishes 135-150 titles/year. 25% from unagented writers. Pays 10% royalty on retail price. Pays $5,000-10,000 advance.** Accepts simultaneous submissions. Responds in 2 months to queries. Book catalog available free. Guidelines available online.

Imprints Checkmark Books.

O┳ Facts on File produces high-quality reference materials on a broad range of subjects for the school library market and the general nonfiction trade.

Nonfiction "We publish serious, informational books for a targeted audience. All our books must have strong library interest, but we also distribute books effectively to the trade. Our library books fit the junior and senior high school curriculum." Subjects include contemporary culture, education, health, medicine, history, language, literature, multicultural, recreation, religion, sports, careers, entertainment, natural history, popular culture. Query or submit outline and sample chapter with SASE. No submissions returned without SASE.

Tips "Our audience is school and public libraries for our more reference-oriented books and libraries, schools and bookstores for our less reference-oriented informational titles."

FAIRLEIGH DICKINSON UNIVERSITY PRESS

285 Madison Ave., M-GH2-01, Madison NJ 07940. (973)443-8564. Fax: (973)443-8364. E-mail: fdupress@fdu.edu. Website: www.fdupress.org. **Contact:** Harry Keyishian, director. Estab. 1967. Publishes hardcover originals and occasional paperbacks. **Publishes 30-40 titles/year. 33% of books from first-time authors. 95% from unagented writers.** Publishes book approximately 1 year after acceptance of ms. Responds in 2 weeks to queries.

- "Contract is arranged through Associated University Presses of Cranbury, New Jersey. We are a selection committee only. Non-author subsidy publishes 2% of books."

O-ᴛ Fairleigh Dickinson publishes scholarly books for the academic market, in the humanities and social sciences.

Nonfiction Subjects include agriculture, art, architecture, business, economics, contemporary culture, ethnic, film, cinema, stage, gay, lesbian, government, politics, history, local, literary criticism, multicultural, music, dance, philosophy, psychology, regional, religion, sociology, translation, women's issues, women's studies, world affairs, Civil War, film, Jewish studies, scholarly editions. "The Press discourages submissions of unrevised dissertations. We do look for scholarly editions of literary works in all fields, in English, or translation. We welcome inquiries about essay collections if the majority of the material is previously unpublished; that the essays have a unifying and consistent theme, and that the editors provide a substantial scholarly introduction." Query with outline, detailed abstract, and sample chapters (if possible). Reviews artwork/photos. Send only copies of illustrations during the evaluation process.

Recent Title(s) *Shakespeare Studies XXXIV*; *Lady in the Labyrinth: Milton's Comus as Initiation*, by William Shullenberger (co-winner of Milton Society Award for best book on Milton for 2008); *The Imagined Immigrant*, by Illaria Serra; *Willa Cather and the Dance*, by Wendy Perriman; *Consuming Politics: Jon Stewart, Branding, and the Youth Vote in America*.

Tips "Press books are reviewed regularly in leading academic circles. Each year between 150,000-200,000 brochures are mailed to announce new works. Research must be up-to-date. Poor reviews result when bibliographies and notes don't reflect current research. We follow Chicago Manual of Style (15th edition) in scholarly citation. We welcome proposals for essay collections, including unpublished conference papers if they relate to a strong central theme and have scholarly merit. For further details, consult our online catalog."

FENCE BOOKS

Science Library 320, Univ. of Albany, 1400 Washington Ave., Albany NY 12222. (518)591-8162. E-mail: fence.fencebooks@gmail.com. Website: www.fenceportal.org. **Contact:** Submissions Manager. Hardcover originals. Guidelines available online.

O-ᴛ "Fence is closed to submissions right now. We'll have another reading period in the Spring. Fence Books offers 2 book contests (in addition to the National Poetry Series) with 2 sets of guidelines and entry forms on our website."

Fiction Subjects include poetry.

Poetry Enter National Poetry Series Contest See Open Competition Guidelines online. Also the annual Fence Books Motherwell Prize 2011 ($5,000) for a first or second book of poetry by a woman. Submit 48-60 pages during the month of November; and Fence Modern Poets Series 2011, for a poet writing in English at any stage in his or her career. $25 entry fee. Submissions may be sent through regular USPS mail, UPS, Fedex-type couriers, or certified mail.

Recent Title(s) *Unspoiled Air*, by Kaisa Ullsvick Miller (poetry); *The Mandarin*, by Aaron Kunin; *Rogue Hemlocks*, by Carl Martin.

Tips "At present Fence Books is a self-selecting publisher; mss come to our attention through our contests and through editors' investigations. We hope to become open to submissions of poetry and fiction mss in the near future."

[A] FOGHORN PUBLISHERS

The Scribes Ink, Inc. P.O. Box 8286, Manchester CT 06040-0286. (860)216-5622. Fax: (860)290-8291. E-mail: foghornpublisher@aol.com. **Contact:** Dr. Aaron D. Lewis, publisher. Publishes hardcover and trade paperback originals. **Publishes 10-20 titles/year. 200 queries received/year. 1,000 mss received/year. 60% of books from first-time authors. Pays 9-15% royalty on wholesale price.** Publishes book

12 months after acceptance of ms. Accepts simultaneous submissions. Responds in 1 month to queries, proposals and manuscripts. Guidelines available free.
Imprints Judah Press, Independicia Press.
Nonfiction Subjects include religion, spirituality, audio; history; money, finance, health/wellness, natural healing. Query with SASE. Submit complete ms. Agented submissions only.
Fiction Subjects include religious, spiritual. Agented submissions only.
Recent Title(s) *The Obama Principle:Creating a Life of Reward through the Power of Perseverance*, by Dr. Aaron D. Lewis; *Alone with a Jihadist:A Biblical Response to Holy War*, by Aaron D. Taylor (Current Events); *Go Into the House*, by Rodney A. Winters (Marriage/Divorce); *The Laws of Thinking*, by E. Bernard Jordan (spiritual/self-help); *What in Hell Is Holding You Back*, by Edward Stephens (Christian living).

FORT ROSS INC. RUSSIAN-AMERICAN PUBLISHING PROJECTS

26 Arthur Place, Yonkers NY 10701. (914)375-6448. E-mail: vkartsev2000@yahoo.com. **Contact:** Dr. Vladimir P. Kartsev, executive director. Estab. 1992. Publishes paperback originals. **Publishes 10 titles/year. 100 queries received/year. 100 mss received/year. 10% of books from first-time authors. 10% from unagented writers. Pays 6-8% royalty on wholesale price or makes outright purchase of $500-1,500. Pays $500-$1,000; negotiable advance.** Publishes book 12 months after acceptance of ms. Accepts simultaneous submissions. Responds in 1 month to queries. Responds in 1 month to proposals. Responds in 3 months to manuscripts.

O┳ "Generally, we publish Russia-related books in English or Russian. Sometimes we publish various fiction and nonfiction books in collaboration with the East European publishers in translation. We are looking mainly for well-established authors."

Fiction Subjects include adventure, fantasy, space fantasy, sword and sorcery, horror, mainstream, contemporary, mystery, amateur sleuth, police procedural, private eye/hardboiled, romance, futuristic/time travel, science fiction, hard science fiction/technological, soft/sociological, suspense. Query with SASE.
Recent Title(s) *Cosack Galloped Far Away*, by Nikolas Feodoroff; *Little Hands: The Theme and Variations*, by Oxana Yablonskaya; *Ageless Memory*, by Lorrain; *The Old Man and the Sea*, by Ernest Hemingway (in Russian).

WALTER FOSTER PUBLISHING, INC.

Suite A, Irvine CA 92618. (800)426-0099. Fax: (949)380-7575. E-mail: info@walterfoster.com. Website: www.walterfoster.com. Estab. 1922. Publishes trade paperback originals.

O┳ "Walter Foster publishes instructional how-to/craft instruction as well as licensed products."

FOX CHAPEL PUBLISHING

1970 Broad St., East Petersburg PA 17520. (717)560-4703. Fax: (717)560-4702. E-mail: editors@foxchapelpublishing.com. Website: www.foxchapelpublishing.com. **Contact:** Peg Couch, acquisitions editor. Publishes hardcover and trade paperback originals and trade paperback reprints. **Publishes 25-40 titles/year. 50% of books from first-time authors. 100% from unagented writers. Pays royalty or makes outright purchase. Pays variable advance.** Publishes book 6-18 months after acceptance of ms. Accepts simultaneous submissions. Responds in 2 months to queries.

O┳ Fox Chapel publishes woodworking, woodcarving, and design titles for professionals and hobbyists.

Nonfiction Submission guidelines on website Reviews artwork/photos. Send photocopies.
Recent Title(s) *Celebrating Birch*; *Pinewood Derby Design Secrets*; *Woodworker's Guide to Veneering and Inlay*.
Tips "We're looking for knowledgeable artists, craftspeople and woodworkers, all experts in their fields, to write books of lasting value."

FREE SPIRIT PUBLISHING, INC.

217 Fifth Ave. N., Suite 200, Minneapolis MN 55401-1299. (612)338-2068. Fax: (612)337-5050. E-mail: acquisitions@freespirit.com. Website: www.freespirit.com. **Contact:** Acquisitions Editor. Estab. 1983. Publishes trade paperback originals and reprints. **Publishes 12-18 titles/year. 5% of books from first-time authors. 75% from unagented writers. Pays advance.** Book catalog and ms guidelines online.

O┳ "We believe passionately in empowering kids to learn to think for themselves and make their own good choices."

Nonfiction Subjects include child guidance, education, pre-K-12, study and social sciences skills, special needs, differentiation but not textbooks or basic skills books like reading, counting, etc., health, medicine, mental/emotional health for/about children, psychology for/about children, sociology for/about children. "Many of our authors are educators, mental health professionals, and youth workers involved in helping kids and teens." Query with cover letter stating qualifications, intent, and intended audience and market analysis (how your book stands out from the field), along with outline, 2 sample chapters, rèsumè, SASE. Do not send original copies of work.

Recent Title(s) *Good-Bye Bully Machine*; *Real Friends vs. The Other Kind*; *Making Differentiation a Habit.*

Tips "Our books are issue-oriented, jargon-free, and solution-focused. Our audience is children, teens, teachers, parents and youth counselors. We are especially concerned with kids' social and emotional well-being and look for books with ready-to-use strategies for coping with today's issues at home or in school—written in every-day language. We are not looking for academic or religious materials, or books that analyze problem's with the nation's school systems. Instead, we want books that offer practical, positive advice so kids can help themselves and parents and teachers can help kids succeed."

GAUTHIER PUBLICATIONS, INC.

Frog Legs Ink P.O. Box 806241, Saint Clair Shores MI 48080. Fax: (586)279-1515. E-mail: info@gauthierpublications.com. Website: www.gauthierpublications.com. **Contact:** Elizabeth Gauthier, Creative Director (Children's/Fiction). Hardcover originals and Trade paperback originals. **Publishes 10 titles/year. 50% of books from first-time authors. 50% from unagented writers. Pays 5-10% royalty on retail price.** Guidelines available for #10 SASE, or online at website http://gauthierpublications.com, or by e-mail at: submissions@gauthierpublications.com.

Imprints Frog Legs Ink, Hungry Goat Press, Dragon-Fish Comics.

Nonfiction Subjects include creative nonfiction, photography, self help. Query with SASE.

Fiction Subjects include adventure, confession, ethnic, experimental, fantasy, feminist, gothic, historical, horror, humor, juvenile, literary, mainstream, contemporary, military, war, multicultural, multimedia, mystery, plays, poetry, poetry in translation, regional, religious, romance. "We are particularly interested in mystery, thriller, graphic novels and Young Adult areas for the upcoming year. We do, however, consider most subjects if they are intriguing and well written." Query with SASE.

Recent Title(s) *Milestones*, Armin (young adult novel); *Island of Betrayal*, by Alan L. Moss (thriller); *The Legacy*, by Andrew McGinn (graphic novel); *Lulu McDunn*, by Kelly Pulley (childrens' picture book), *The Wee Musketeers*, by Robert Bresloff (middle reader); *Out of the Nursery*, by Elizabeth Gauthier (Children's Picture Book).

N GENEALOGICAL PUBLISHING CO., INC.

3600 Clipper Mill Rd., Baltimore MD 21211. (410)837-8271. Fax: (410)752-8492. E-mail: info@genealogical.com. Website: www.genealogical.com. **Contact:** Joe Garonzik, mktg. dir. (history & genealogy). Hardcover and trade paperback originals and reprints. **Publishes 100 titles/year. 100 queries/year; 20 mss/year. 10% of books from first-time authors. 99% from unagented writers.** Publishes book 6 months after acceptance of ms. Accepts simultaneous submissions. Catalog free on request. Guidelines not available.

Nonfiction Subjects include Americana, ethnic, history, hobbies. Submit outline, 1 sample chapter. Reviews artwork/photos as part of the mss package.

Recent Title(s) *Genealogist's Address Book (6th ed.)*, by Elizabeth P. Bentley (directory); *Social Networking for Genealogists*, by Drew Smith (how-to).

Tips "Our audience is genealogy hobbyists."

GENESIS PRESS, INC.

P.O. Box 101, Columbus MS 39701. (888)463-4461. Fax: (662)329-9399. E-mail: books@genesis-press.com. Website: www.genesis-press.com. Estab. 1993. Publishes hardcover and trade paperback originals and reprints. Responds in 2 months to queries. Responds in 4 months to manuscripts. Guidelines available online.

Imprints Indigo (romance); Black Coral (fiction); Indigo Love Spectrum (interracial romance); Indigo After Dark (erotica); Obsidian (thriller/myster); Indigo Glitz (love stories for young adults); Indigo Vibe (for stylish audience under 35 years old); Mount Blue (Christian); Inca Books (teens); Sage (self-help/inspirational).

> Genesis Press is the largest privately owned African-American book publisher in the country. Genesis has steadily increased its reach, and now brings its readers everything from suspense and science fiction to Christian-oriented romance and non-fiction.

Nonfiction Submit outline, 3 sample chapters, SASE. If you would like your ms returned, you must follow all the rules on our website. Please use Priority or First Class mail-no Media Mail, Fed Ex, and no metered mail. We cannot return partials or manuscripts outside the US . No International Reply Coupons, please.

Fiction Subjects include adventure, erotica, ethnic, multicultural, mystery, romance, science fiction, women's. Submit clips, 3 sample chapters, SASE.

Recent Title(s) *Falling*, by Natalie Dunbar; *Hearts Awakening*, by Veronica Parker.

Tips Be professional. Always include a cover letter and SASE. Follow the submission guidelines posted on our website or send SASE for a copy.

DAVID R. GODINE, PUBLISHER, INC.

9 Hamilton Place, Boston MA 02108. (617)451-9600. Fax: (617)350-0250. E-mail: info@godine.com. Website: www.godine.com. Estab. 1970. Publishes hardcover and trade paperback originals and reprints. **Publishes 35 titles/year. Pays royalty on retail price.** Publishes book 3 years after acceptance of ms. Book catalog for 5 × 8 envelope and 3 First-Class stamps.

- "Our particular strengths are books about the history and design of the written word, literary essays, and the best of world fiction in translation. We also have an unusually strong list of children's books, all of them printed in their entirety with no cuts, deletions, or side-stepping to keep the political watchdogs happy."

Nonfiction Subjects include Americana, art, architecture, gardening, literary criticism, nature, environment, photography, book arts, typography. *No unsolicited mss*

Fiction Subjects include historical, literary, translation, literature, novels. *No unsolicited mss*

Tips "Please visit our website for more information about our books and detailed submission policy. No phone calls, please."

GOLDEN PEACH PUBLISHING

1223 Wilshire Blvd., #1510, Santa Monica CA 90403-5400. E-mail: info@goldenpeachbooks.com. Website: www.goldenpeachbooks.com. Trade paperback originals. **Publishes 20 titles/year.** Accepts simultaneous submissions.

- "We publish quality Chinese, English and bilingual books to bridge the gap between the Eastern and Western worlds, with a focus on children's and young adult titles."

Nonfiction Subjects include architecture, art, ethnic, health, history, language, literature, medicine, memoirs, multicultural, young adult. Submit proposal package, including outline, 2 sample chapters. Reviews artwork/photos; send photocopies.

Fiction Subjects include adventure, comic books, ethnic, fantasy, juvenile, mystery, picture books. "See our website." Submit proposal package, including: synopsis, 3 sample chapters, and illustration copies, if any.

Recent Title(s) *Spine-Related Diseases*, by Wei Guihang (professional); *The Dragon Arch*, by Teri Tao (YA); *The Monkey King and the Book of Death*, adapted by Ted Tao (YA); *Legend Of The White Snake*, by Teri Tao (bilingual reader); *The Girl Who Flew to The Moon*, by Teri Tao (bilingual reader), and more.

THE GRADUATE GROUP

P.O. Box 370351, West Hartford CT 06137-0351. (860)233-2330. Fax: (860)233-2330. E-mail: graduategroup@hotmail.com. Website: www.graduategroup.com. **Contact:** Mara Whitman, partner; Robert Whitman, vice president. Estab. 1964. Publishes trade paperback originals. **Publishes 50 titles/year. 100 queries received/year. 70 mss received/year. 60% of books from first-time authors. 85% from unagented writers. Pays 20% - royalty on retail price.** Publishes book 3 months after acceptance of ms. Accepts simultaneous submissions. Responds in 1 month to queries. Book catalog available free. Guidelines available online.

- The Graduate Group helps college and graduate students better prepare themselves for rewarding careers and helps people advance in the workplace. Currently emphasizing test preparation, career advancement, and materials for prisoners, law enforcement, books on unique careers.

Nonfiction Subjects include business, economics, education, government, politics, health, medicine, money, finance, law enforcement. Submit complete ms and SASE with sufficient postage.

Recent Title(s) *Real Life 101: Winning Secrets You Won't Find in Class*, by Debra Yergen; *Getting In: Applicant's Guide to Graduate School Admissions*, by David Burrell.

Tips "We are open to all submissions."

GRAYWOLF PRESS

250 Third Avenue North, Suite 600, Minneapolis MN 55401. Website: www.graywolfpress.org. **Contact:** Katie Dublinski, editorial manager (nonfiction, fiction). Estab. 1974. Publishes trade cloth and paperback originals. **Publishes 23 titles/year. 3,000 queries received/year. 20% of books from first-time authors.**

50% from unagented writers. Pays royalty on retail price. Pays $1,000-25,000 advance. Publishes book 18 months after acceptance of ms. Responds in 3 months to queries. Book catalog available free. Guidelines available online.

"Graywolf Press is an independent, nonprofit publisher dedicated to the creation and promotion of thoughtful and imaginative contemporary literature essential to a vital and diverse culture."

Nonfiction Subjects include contemporary culture, language, literature, culture. Query with SASE.
Fiction Subjects include short story collections, literary novels. "Familiarize yourself with our list first." Query with SASE. Please do not fax or e-mail.
Poetry "We are interested in linguistically challenging work." Query with SASE.
Recent Title(s) *The Long Meadow*, by Vijay Seshaudri; *Wounded*, by Percival Everett; *Dictionary Days*, by Ilan Stavans.

GREENWILLOW BOOKS

HarperCollins Publishers 1350 Avenue of the Americas, New York NY 10019. (212)261-6500. Website: www.harperchildrens.com. Estab. 1974. Publishes hardcover originals and reprints.

Greenwillow Books publishes quality picture books and fiction for young readers of all ages, and nonfiction primarily for children under seven years of age. "We hope that at the heart of each book there is honesty, emotion and depth—conveyed by an author or an artist who has something that is worth saying to children and who says it in a way that is worth reading."

Fiction Juvenile. Subjects include fantasy, humor, literary, mystery, picture books.
Recent Title(s) *The Train of States*, by Peter Sis; *If Not for the Cat*, by Jack Prelutsky, illustrated by Ted Rand; *Happy Haunting, Amelia Bedelia*, by Herman Parish, illustrated by Lynn Sweat.
Tips Currently not accepting unsolicited mail, mss or queries.

GREENWOOD PRESS

ABC-CLIO 130 Cremona Dr., Santa Barbara CA 93117. (805)968-1911. E-mail: ccasey@abc-clio.com. Website: www.abc-clio.com. **Contact:** Vince Burns, vice president of editorial. Publishes hardcover originals. **Publishes 200 titles/year. 1,000 queries received/year. 25% of books from first-time authors. Pays variable royalty on net price. Pays rare advance.** Publishes book 1 year after acceptance of ms. Accepts simultaneous submissions. Responds in 6 months to queries. Book catalog and ms guidelines online.

Greenwood Press publishes reference materials for high school, public and academic libraries in the humanities and the social and hard sciences.

Nonfiction Subjects include humanities, literary criticism, social sciences, humanities and the social and hard sciences. Query with proposal package, including scope, organization, length of project, whether complete ms is available or when it will be, cv or resume and SASE. *No unsolicited mss.*
Recent Title(s) *All Things Shakespeare*, by Kirstin Olsen.

GROUP PUBLISHING, INC.

1515 Cascade Ave., Loveland CO 80538. (970)669-3836. Fax: (970)679-4370. E-mail: kloesche@grouppublishing.com. Website: www.group.com. **Contact:** Kerri Loesche, contract & copyright administrator. Estab. 1974. Publishes trade paperback originals. **Publishes 65 titles/year. 500 queries received/year. 500 mss received/year. 40% of books from first-time authors. 95% from unagented writers. Pays up to 10% royalty on wholesale price or makes outright purchase or work for hire. Pays up to $1,000 advance.** Publishes book 18 months after acceptance of ms. Accepts simultaneous submissions. Responds in 1 month to queries. Responds in 6 months to proposals andmanuscripts. Book catalog for 9 × 12 envelope and 2 First-Class stamps. Guidelines available online at www.grouppublishing.com/submissions.asp.

"Our mission is to equip churches to help children, youth, and adults grow in their relationship with Jesus."

Nonfiction Subjects include education, religion. "We're an interdenominational publisher of resource materials for people who work with adults, youth or children in a Christian church setting. We also publish materials for use directly by youth or children (such as devotional books, workbooks or Bibles stories). Everything we do is based on concepts of active and interactive learning as described in *Why Nobody Learns Much of Anything at Church: And How to Fix It*, by Thom and Joani Schultz. We need new, practical, hands-on, innovative, out-of-the-box ideas—things that no one's doing.. yet." Query with SASE. Submit proposal package, outline, 3 sample chapters, cover letter, introduction to book, and sample activities if appropriate.
Recent Title(s) *Outflow*, by Steve Sjogren and Dave Ping; *Dare to Be Uncommon*, by Tony Dungy and Karl Leuthauser; *Hope Lives*, by Amber Van Schooneveld.

Tips "Our audience consists of pastors, Christian education directors, youth leaders, and Sunday school teachers."

GRYPHON HOUSE, INC.

10770 Columbia Pike, Suite 201, Silver Spring MD 20901. 1-800-638-0928. Fax: (877)638-7576. E-mail: kathyc@ghbooks.com. Website: www.gryphonhouse.com. **Contact:** Kathy Charner, editor-in-chief. Estab. 1981. Publishes trade paperback originals. **Publishes 12-15 titles/year. Pays royalty on wholesale price.** Responds in 3-6 months to queries. Guidelines available online.

O→ "Gryphon House publishes books that teachers and parents of young children (birth-age 8) consider essential to their daily lives."

Nonfiction Subjects include child guidance, education, early childhood. Currently emphasizing reading; de-emphasizing after-school activities. "We prefer to receive a letter of inquiry and/or a proposal, rather than the entire manuscript. Please include: The proposed title The purpose of the book, Table of contents, Introductory material, 20-40 sample pages of the actual book. In addition, please describe the book, including the intended audience, why teachers will want to buy it, how it is different from other similar books already published, and what qualifications you possess that make you the appropriate person to write the book. If you have a writing sample that demonstrates that you write clear, compelling prose, please include it with your letter."

Recent Title(s) *Reading Games*, by Jackie Silberg; *Primary Art*, by Mary Ann Kohl; *Preschool Math*, by Robert Williams, Debra Cunningham and Joy Lubawy.

N GULF PUBLISHING COMPANY

2 Greenway Plaza, Suite 1020, Houston TX 77046. (713)529-4301. Fax: (713)520-4433. E-mail: svb@gulfpub.com. Website: www.gulfpub.com. **Contact:** Katie Hammon, assoc. pub.; Rusty Meador, pub. (energy, engineering, petroleum, natural gas, offshore, refining, petrochemical, environmental, chemistry). Hardcover originals and reprints; electronic originals and reprints. **Publishes 12-15 titles/year. 3-5 queries and mss received in a year. 30% of books from first-time authors. 80% from unagented writers. Pays $1,000-$1,500 advance.** Publishes book 8-9 months after acceptance of ms. Accepts simultaneous submissions. Catalog free on request. Guidelines available by e-mail.

O→ "Gulf Publishing Company is the leading publisher to the oil and gas industry. Our specialized publications reach over 100,000 people involved in energy industries worldwide. Our magazines and catalogs help readers keep current with information important to their field and allow advertisers to reach their customers in all segments of petroleum operations. More than half of Gulf Publishing Company's editorial staff have engineering degrees. The others are thoroughly trained and experienced business journalists and editors."

Nonfiction Engineering. "We don't publish a lot in the year, therefore we are able to focus more on marketing and sales—we are hoping to grow in the future." Submit outline, 1-2 sample chapters, completed ms. Reviews artwork. Send high res. file formats with high dpi in black & white.

Recent Title(s) *Gulf Drilling Series: Managed Pressure Drilling*, by Bill Rehm, Jerome Schubert, Arash Haghshenas, Amir Paknejad, Jim Hughes; *Well Productivity*, by Boyun Guo, Kai Sun, Ali Ghalamabor; *Advanced Piping Design*, Rutger Botermans, Peter Smith.

Tips "Our audience would be engineers, engineering students, academia, professors, well managers, construction engineers. We recommend getting contributors to help with the writing process—this provides a more comprehensive overview for technical and scientific books. Work harder on artwork. It's expensive and time-consuming for a publisher to redraw a lot of the figures."

GUN DIGEST BOOKS

F+W Media 700 East State St., Iola WI 54990. (888)457-2873. E-mail: dan.shideler@fwmedia.com. Website: www.krause.com. **Contact:** Dan Shideler, editor (all aspects of firearms history, scholarship, nonpolitical literature). Hardcover, trade paperback, mass market paperback, and electronic originals (all). **Publishes 25 titles/year. 75 submissions received/year. 30% of books from first-time authors. 80% from unagented writers. $2,800-$5,000** Publishes book 7 months after acceptance of ms. Accepts simultaneous submissions. Catalog online at website http://www.krause.com. Guidelines available by e-mail at: corrina.peterson@fwmedia.com.

Imprints Gun Digest Books, Krause Publications.

Nonfiction Firearms, hunting-related titles only. "Must have mainstream appeal and not be too narrowly focused." Submit proposal package, including outline, 2 sample chapters, and author bio; submit completed manuscript. Review artwork/photos (required); high-res digital only (.jpg, .tif)

Recent Title(s) *2009 Standard Catalog of Firearms, 19th Ed.*, by Dan Shideler; *The Gun Digest® Book of the AK & SKS*, by Patrick Sweeney; *The Gun Digest® Book of Concealed Carry*, by Massad Ayoob. http://www.krausebooks.com/category/firearms_knives.
Tips "Our audience is shooters, collectors, hunters, outdoors enthusiasts. We prefer not to work through agents."

HALF HALT PRESS, INC.

P.O. Box 67, Boonsboro MD 21713. (301)733-7119. Fax: (301)733-7408. E-mail: mail@halfhaltpress.com. Website: www.halfhaltpress.com. **Contact:** Elizabeth Rowland, publisher. Estab. 1986. Publishes 90% hardcover and trade paperback originals and 10% reprints. **Publishes 10 titles/year. 25% of books from first-time authors. 50% from unagented writers. Pays 10-12 ½% royalty on retail price.** Publishes book 1 year after acceptance of ms.

- "We publish high-quality nonfiction on equestrian topics, books that help riders and trainers do something better."

Nonfiction Subjects include animals, horses, sports. "We need serious instructional works by authorities in the field on horse-related topics, broadly defined." Query with SASE. Reviews artwork/photos.
Recent Title(s) *Dressage in Harmony*, by Walter Zettl.
Tips "Writers have the best chance selling us well-written, unique works that teach serious horse people how to do something better. Offer a straightforward presentation, letting the work speak for itself, without hype or hard sell. Allow the publisher to contact the writer, without frequent calling to check status. As the publisher/author relationship becomes close and is based on working well together, early impressions may be important, even to the point of being a consideration in acceptance for publication."

HAMPTON ROADS PUBLISHING CO., INC.

500 Third Street, Suite 230, San Francisco CA 94107. E-mail: submissions@hrpub.com. Website: www.hrpub.com. **Contact:** Chris Nelson, Acquisitions Manager. Estab. 1989. Publishes hardcover and trade paperback originals. Publishes and distributes hardcover and paperback originals on subjects including metaphysics, health, complementary medicine, visionary fiction, and other related topics. **Publishes 35-40 titles/year. 1,000 queries received/year. 1,500 mss received/year. 50% of books from first-time authors. 70% from unagented writers. Pays royalty. Pays $1,000-50,000 advance.** Publishes book 1 year after acceptance of ms. Accepts simultaneous submissions. Responds in 2-4 months to queries. Responds in 1 month to proposals. Responds in 6-12 months to manuscripts. Guidelines available online.

- "Please know that we only publish a handful of books every year, and that we pass on many well written, important works, simply because we cannot publish them all. We review each and every proposal very carefully. However, due to the volume of inquiries, we cannot respond to them all individually. Please give us 30 days to review your proposal. If you do not hear back from us within that time, this means we have decided to pursue other book ideas that we feel fit better within our plan."
- "Our reason for being is to impact, uplift, and contribute to positive change in the world. We publish books that will enrich and empower the evolving consciousness of mankind. Though we are not necessarily limited in scope, we are most interested in manuscripts on the following subjects: Body/Mind/Spirit, Health and Healing, Self-Help. Please be advised that at the moment we are not accepting: Fiction or Novelized material that does not pertain to body/mind/spirit, Channeled writing." "

Nonfiction Subjects include New Age, spirituality. Query with SASE. Submit synopsis, SASE. No longer accepting electronic submissions. Reviews artwork/photos. Send photocopies.
Fiction Subjects include literary, spiritual, Visionary fiction, past-life fiction based on actual memories. Fiction should have 1 or more of the following themes: spiritual, inspirational, metaphysical, i.e., past-life recall, out-of-body experiences, near-death experience, paranormal. Query with SASE. Submit outline, 2 sample chapters, clips. Submit complete ms.
Recent Title(s) *Why I Am a Buddhist*, by Stephen T. Asma, PhD; *The Beethoven Factor*, by Paul Pearsall; *The Natural Way to Heal*, by Walter Last; *Phoenix Lights*, by Lynn D. Kitei, M.D.

HANCOCK HOUSE PUBLISHERS

Hancock Wildlife Foundation 1431 Harrison Ave., Blaine WA 98230-5005. (604)538-1114. Fax: (604)538-2262. E-mail: david@hancockwildlife.org. Website: www.hancockwildlife.org. **Contact:** David Hancock. Estab. 1971. Publishes hardcover and trade paperback originals and reprints. **Publishes 12-20 titles/year. 50% of books from first-time authors. 90% from unagented writers. Pays 10% royalty.** Publishes book up to 1 year after acceptance of ms. Accepts simultaneous submissions. Book catalog available free. Guidelines available online.

- "Hancock House Publishers is the largest North American publisher of wildlife and Native Indian titles. We also cover Pacific Northwest, fishing, history, Canadiana, biographies. We are seeking agriculture, natural history, animal husbandry, conservation, and popular science titles with a regional (Pacific Northwest), national, or international focus. Currently emphasizing nonfiction wildlife, cryptozoology, guide books, native history, biography, fishing."

Nonfiction Centered around Pacific Northwest, local history, nature guide books, international ornithology, and Native Americans. Subjects include agriculture, animals, ethnic, history, horticulture, nature, environment, regional. Submit proposal package, outline, 3 sample chapters, selling points, SASE. Reviews artwork/photos. Send photocopies.

Recent Title(s) *Stagecoaches Across the American West; Wings Over the Wilderness; Bigfoot Encounters.*

HARVARD BUSINESS REVIEW PRESS

Imprint of Harvard Business School Publishing Corp. 60 Harvard Way, Boston MA 02163. (617)783-7400. Fax: (617)783-7489. E-mail: cschink@hbr.org. Website: www.hbr.org. **Contact:** Courtney Schinke, Editorial Coordinator. Estab. 1984. Publishes hardcover originals and several paperback series. **Publishes 40-50 titles/year. Pays escalating royalty on retail price. Advances vary depending on author and market for the book.** Accepts simultaneous submissions. Responds in 1 month to proposals and manuscripts. Book catalog available online. Guidelines available online.

- The Harvard Business Review Press publishes books for senior and general managers and business scholars. Harvard Business Review Press is the source of the most influential ideas and conversations that shape business worldwide.

Nonfiction Submit proposal package, outline, sample chapters.

Recent Title(s) *Blue Ocean Strategy*, by W. Chan Kim and Renee Mauborgne; *Groundswell*, by Charlene Li and Josh Bernoff; *A Sense of Urgency*, by John P. Kotter; *Profit From The Core*, by Chris Zook with James Allen.

Tips "We do not publish books on real estate, personal finance or business parables."

THE HARVARD COMMON PRESS

535 Albany St., 5th Floor, Boston MA 02118-2500. (617)423-5803. Fax: (617)695-9794. E-mail: info@harvardpress.com. Website: www.harvardcommonpress.com. **Contact:** Valerie Cimino, executive editor. Estab. 1976. Publishes hardcover and trade paperback originals and reprints. **Publishes 16 titles/year. 20% of books from first-time authors. 40% from unagented writers. Pays royalty. Pays average $2,500-10,000 advance.** Publishes book 1 year after acceptance of ms. Accepts simultaneous submissions. Responds in 2 months to queries. Book catalog for 9 × 12 envelope and 3 first-class stamps. Guidelines for #10 SASE or online.

Imprints Gambit Books.

- "We want strong, practical books that help people gain control over a particular area of their lives. Currently emphasizing cooking, child care/parenting, health. De-emphasizing general instructional books, travel."

Nonfiction Subjects include child guidance, cooking, foods, nutrition, health, medicine. A large percentage of our list is made up of books about cooking, child care, and parenting; in these areas we are looking for authors who are knowledgeable, if not experts, and who can offer a different approach to the subject. We are open to good nonfiction proposals that show evidence of strong organization and writing, and clearly demonstrate a need in the marketplace. First-time authors are welcome. Submit outline. Potential authors may also submit a query letter or e-mail of no more than 300 words, rather than a full proposal; if interested, we will ask to see a proposal. Queries and questions may be sent via e-mail. We will not consider e-mail attachments containing proposals. No phone calls, please.

Recent Title(s) *Icebox Desserts*, by Lauren Chattman; *Pie*, by Ken Haedrich; *Not Your Mother's Slow Cooker Cookbook*, by Beth Hensperger and Julie Kaufmann.

Tips "We are demanding about the quality of proposals; in addition to strong writing skills and thorough knowledge of the subject matter, we require a detailed analysis of the competition."

HAY HOUSE, INC.

P.O. Box 5100, Carlsbad CA 92018-5100. (760)431-7695. Fax: (760)431-6948. E-mail: editorial@hayhouse.com. Website: www.hayhouse.com. **Contact:** East-coast acquisitions: Patty Gift (pgift@hayhouse.com), West-coast acquisitions: Alex Freemon (afreemon@hayhouse.com). Estab. 1985. Publishes hardcover and trade paperback originals. **Publishes 50 titles/year. Pays standard royalty.** Publishes book 14-16 months after acceptance of ms. Accepts simultaneous submissions. Guidelines available online.

Imprints Hay House Lifestyles; New Beginnings Press; SmileyBooks.

"We publish books, audios, and videos that help heal the planet."

Nonfiction Subjects include cooking, foods, nutrition, education, health, medicine, money, finance, nature, environment, New Age, philosophy, psychology, sociology, women's issues, women's studies, mind/body/spirit. Hay House is interested in a variety of subjects as long as they have a positive self-help slant to them. No poetry, children's books, or negative concepts that are not conducive to helping/healing ourselves or our planet. Accepts submissions from agents only.

Recent Title(s) *Excuses Begone!*, by Dr. Wayne W. Dyer; *The Vortex*, by Esther and Jerry Hicks; *Fractal Times*, by Gregg Braden; *Defy Gravity*, by Caroline Myss; *Living Through the Racket*, by Corina Morariu; *The Core Balance Diet*, by Marcelle Pick, MSN, Ob/Gyn, NP, with Genevieve Morgan.

Tips "Our audience is concerned with our planet, the healing properties of love, and general self-help principles. If I were a writer trying to market a book today, I would research the market thoroughly to make sure there weren't already too many books on the subject I was interested in writing about. Then I would make sure I had a unique slant on my idea. Simultaneous submissions from agents must include SASE's. No e-mail submissions."

WILLIAM S. HEIN & CO., INC.

1285 Main St., Buffalo NY 14209-1987. (716)882-2600. Fax: (716)883-8100. E-mail: sjarrett@wshein.com. Website: www.wshein.com. **Contact:** Sheila Jarrett, publications manager. Estab. 1961. **Publishes 30 titles/year. 80 queries received/year. 40 mss received/year. 30% of books from first-time authors. 100% from unagented writers. Pays 10-20% royalty on net price.** Publishes book 9 months after acceptance of ms. Accepts simultaneous submissions. Responds in 3 months to queries. Book catalog available online. Guidelines: send e-mail for info and mss proposal form.

"William S. Hein & Co. publishes reference books for law librarians, legal researchers, and those interested in legal writing. Currently emphasizing legal research, legal writing, and legal education."

Nonfiction Subjects include education, government, politics, women's issues, world affairs, legislative histories.

Recent Title(s) *A Higher Law*, by Jeffrey A. Brauch; *Reflections of a Lawyer's Soul*, edited by Amy Timmer & Nelson P. Miller; *Acing Your First Year of Law School 2nd ed.*, by Shana Connell Noyes & Henry S. Noyes; *Congress and Sports Agents: A Legislative History of the Sports Agent Responsibility and Trust Act (SPARTA)*, by Edmund P. Edmonds & William H. Manz; *California Legal Research Handbook 2nd ed.*, by Larry D. Dershem; *1000 Days to the Bar*, by Dennis J. Tonsing; *Librarian's Copyright Companion*, by James S. Heller.

HELLGATE PRESS

P.O. Box 3531, Ashland OR 97520. (541)973-5154. E-mail: harley@hellgatepress.com. Website: www.hellgatepress.com. **Contact:** Harley B. Patrick, editor. Estab. 1996. **Publishes 15-20 titles/year. 85% of books from first-time authors. 95% from unagented writers. Pays royalty.** Publishes book 6-9 months after acceptance of ms. Responds in 2 months to queries.

"Hellgate Press specializes in military history, other military topics, and travel adventure."

Nonfiction Subjects include history, memoirs, military, war, travel adventure. Query/proposal only with SASE or by e-mail. *Do not send mss.* Reviews artwork/photos. Send photocopies.

Recent Title(s) *Camera Boy*, by Fred Minnick; *The Ether Zone*, by R.C. Morris; *Canoe Trip: North to Athabasca*, by David Curran.

HENDRICKSON PUBLISHERS, INC.

140 Summit St., P.O. Box 3473, Peabody MA 01961-3473. Fax: (978)573-8276. E-mail: editorial@hendrickson.com. Website: www.hendrickson.com. **Contact:** Shirley Decker-Lucke, editorial director. Estab. 1983. Publishes trade reprints, bibles, and scholarly material in the areas of New Testament; Hebrew Bible; religion and culture; patristics; Judaism; and practical, historical, and Biblical theology. **Publishes 35 titles/year. 800 queries received/year. 10% of books from first-time authors. 90% from unagented writers.** Publishes book an average of 1 year after acceptance of ms. Responds in 3-4 months to queries. Book catalog and ms guidelines for #10 SASE.

"Hendrickson is an academic publisher of books that give insight into Bible understanding (academically) and encourage spiritual growth (popular trade). Currently emphasizing Biblical helps and reference, ministerial helps, and Biblical studies."

Nonfiction Subjects include religion. "No longer accepting unsolicited manuscripts or book proposals. Cannot return material sent or respond to all queries." Submit outline, sample chapters, and CV.

JOSEPH HENRY PRESS

National Academy Press 500 5th St., NW, Lockbox 285, Washington DC 20055. (202)334-3336. Fax: (202)334-2793. E-mail: tsmith@nas.edu. Website: http://www.nap.edu/about.html. **Contact:** Terrell Smith, project editor. Publishes hardcover and trade paperback originals. **Publishes 15-20 titles/year. 200 queries received/year. 60 mss received/year. 30% of books from first-time authors. 50% from unagented writers. Pays standard trade book list-price royalties. Pays occasional, varying royalty advance.** Publishes book 1 year after acceptance of ms. Accepts simultaneous submissions. Responds in 1 month to queries.

> "The Joseph Henry Press seeks manuscripts in general science and technology that will appeal to young scientists and established professionals or to interested lay readers within the overall categories of science, technology and health. We'll be looking at everything from astrophysics to the environment to nutrition."

Nonfiction Subjects include health, medicine, nature, environment, psychology, technology, nutrition, physical sciences. Submit proposal package, bio, TOC, prospectus (via mail or e-mail), SASE.

Recent Title(s) *Prime Obsession: Berhard Riemann and the Greatest Unsolved Problem in Mathematics*, by John Derbyshire; *Einstein Defiant: Genius Versus Genius in the Quantum Revolution*, by Edmund Blair Bolles; *Mendel in the Kitchen: A Scientist's View of Genetically Modified Foods*, by Nina V. Fedoroff and Nancy Marie Brown.

HERITAGE BOOKS, INC.

100 Railroad Ave., #104, Westminster MD 21157. (866)282-2689. E-mail: submissions@heritagebooks.com. Website: www.heritagebooks.com. **Contact:** Editorial Director. Estab. 1978. Publishes hardcover and paperback originals and reprints. **Publishes 200 titles/year. 25% of books from first-time authors. 100% from unagented writers. Pays 10% royalty on list price** Accepts simultaneous submissions. Responds in 3 months to queries. Book catalog and ms guidelines free.

> "Our goal is to celebrate life by exploring all aspects of American life: settlement, development, wars, and other significant events, including family histories, memoirs, etc. Currently emphasizing early American life, early wars and conflicts, ethnic studies."

Nonfiction Subjects include Americana, ethnic, origins and research guides, history, memoirs, military, war, regional, history. Query with SASE. Submit outline via e-mail. Reviews artwork/photos.

Tips "The quality of the book is of prime importance; next is its relevance to our fields of interest."

HIBBARD PUBLISHERS

P.O. Box 73182, Lynnwood Ridge 0040, South Africa. (27)(12)804-3990. Fax: (27)(12)804-1240. E-mail: publisher@hibbard.co.za. Website: www.hibbard.co.za.

Imprints Bard (literature/academic); Thandi Art Press (African language literature); Galactic (math workbooks/poster series); Manx (fiction); Manx Juvenile (children's); GSAT (arts & culture); Five Star Study Guides.

> "Our mission is to take the products of our authors' dreams and efforts, and to transform and shape these into the best possible product for end users, i.e. readers, teachers, learners and their parents."

Recent Title(s) *Everyday Math @ Home and @ School.*

Tips "When the pressure is on, we make use of the services of some of the best free-lancers in various fields."

HISTORY PUBLISHING COMPANY, INC.

P.O. Box 700, Palisades NY 10964. Fax: (845)231-6167. E-mail: historypublish@aol.com. Website: www.historypublishingco.com. **Contact:** Leslie Hayes, editorial director. Estab. 2001. Publishes hardcover and trade paperback originals and reprints; also, electronic reprints. **Publishes 20 titles/year. 50% of books from first-time authors. 75% from unagented writers. Pays 7-10% royalty on wholesale price. Does not pay advances to unpublished authors.** Publishes book 1 year after acceptance of ms. Accepts simultaneous submissions. Responds in 1 month to queries and proposals. Responds in 2 months to manuscripts. Guidelines via e-mail.

Nonfiction Subjects include Americana, business, economics, contemporary culture, creative nonfiction, government, politics, history, military, war, social sciences, sociology, world affairs. Query with SASE. Submit proposal package, outline, 3 sample chapters. Submit complete ms. Reviews artwork/photos. Send photocopies.

Recent Title(s) History Publishing Company: *Homeland Insecurity*; *The Words of War*; *Hunting the American Terrorist*; *A Lovely Little War*; *Legerdemain.* Today's Books imprint: *How To Survive in an*

Organization; Career of Gold; Chronology Books imprint: *Don't Shoot! We're Republicans!; Custer Survivor.*

Tips "We focus on an audience interested in the events that shaped the world we live in and the events of today that continue to shape that world. Focus on interesting and serious events that will appeal to the contemporary reader who likes easy-to-read history that flows from one page to the next."

HOLY CROSS ORTHODOX PRESS

Hellenic College 50 Goddard Ave., Brookline MA 02445. (617)850-1321. Fax: (617)850-1457. E-mail: press@hchc.edu. **Contact:** Dr. Anton C. Vrame. Estab. 1974. Publishes trade paperback originals. **Publishes 8 titles/year. 10-15 queries received/year. 10-15 mss received/year. 85% of books from first-time authors. 100% from unagented writers. Pays 8-12% royalty on retail price.** Publishes book 24 months after acceptance of ms. Accepts simultaneous submissions. Responds in 6 months to manuscripts. Book catalog available online.

Imprints Holy Cross Orthodox Press, Hellenic College Press.

O→ "Holy Cross publishes titles that are rooted in the tradition of the Eastern Orthodox Church."

Nonfiction Subjects include ethnic, religion, Greek Orthodox. Holy Cross Orthodox Press publishes scholarly and popular literature in the areas of Orthodox Christian theology and Greek letters. Submissions are often far too technical usually with a very limited audiences. Submit outline. Submit complete ms. Reviews artwork/photos. Send photocopies.

Recent Title(s) *Remembering and Reclaiming Diakonia*, by John Chryssavgis; *Holistic Healing In Byzantium*, edited by John Chirban.

HOW BOOKS

Imprint of F + W Media, Inc. 4700 E. Galbraith Rd., Cincinnati OH 45236. (513)531-2690. E-mail: megan.patrick@fwmedia.com. Website: www.howdesign.com. **Contact:** Megan Patrick, acquisitions editor. Estab. 1985. Publishes hardcover and trade paperback originals. **Publishes 15 titles/year. 50 queries received/year. 5 mss received/year. 50% of books from first-time authors. 50% from unagented writers. Pays 10% royalty on wholesale price. Pays $2,000-6,000 advance.** Publishes book 18-24 months after acceptance of ms. Accepts simultaneous submissions. Responds in 1 month to queries and proposals. Responds in 3 months to manuscripts. Book catalog available online. Guidelines available online.

Nonfiction Subjects include graphic design, creativity, pop culture. "We look for material that reflects the cutting edge of trends, graphic design, and culture. Nearly all HOW Books are intensely visual, and authors must be able to create or supply art/illustration for their books." Query with SASE. Submit proposal package, outline, 1 sample chapter, sample art or sample design. Reviews artwork/photos. Send photocopies and PDF's (if submitting electronically).

Recent Title(s) *Milk Eggs Vodka*, by Bill Keaggy (humor/pop culture); *Monster Spotter's Guide to North America*, by Scott Francis (humor); *Color Index 2*, by Jim Krause (graphic design).

Tips "Audience comprised of graphic designers. Your art, design, or concept."

IBEX PUBLISHERS

P.O. Box 30087, Bethesda MD 20824. (301)718-8188. Fax: (301)907-8707. E-mail: info@ibexpub.com. Website: www.ibexpublishers.com. Estab. 1979. Publishes hardcover and trade paperback originals and reprints. **Publishes 10-12 titles/year. Payment varies.** Accepts simultaneous submissions. Book catalog available free.

Imprints Iranbooks Press.

O→ "IBEX publishes books about Iran and the Middle East and about Persian culture and literature."

Nonfiction Subjects include cooking, foods, nutrition, language, literature. Query with SASE, or submit proposal package, including outline and 2 sample chapters.

Poetry "Translations of Persian poets will be considered."

ICONOGRAFIX, INC.

1830A Hanley Rd., P.O. Box 446, Hudson WI 54016. (715)381-9755. Fax: (715)381-9756. E-mail: dcfrautschi@iconografixinc.com. Website: www.enthusiastbooks.com. **Contact:** Dylan Frautschi, editorial director. Estab. 1992. Publishes trade paperback originals. **Publishes 24 titles/year. 100 queries received/year. 20 mss received/year. 50% of books from first-time authors. 100% from unagented writers. Pays 8-12% royalty on wholesale price. Pays $1,000-3,000 advance.** Publishes book 1 year after acceptance of ms. Accepts simultaneous submissions. Responds in 1 month to queries. Responds in 3 months to proposals and manuscripts. Book catalog and ms guidelines free.

O⊸ "Iconografix publishes special, historical-interest photographic books for transportation equipment enthusiasts. Currently emphasizing emergency vehicles, buses, trucks, railroads, automobiles, auto racing, construction equipment, snowmobiles."

Nonfiction Interested in photo archives. Subjects include Americana, photos from archives of historic places, objects, people, history, hobbies, military, war, transportation (older photos of specific vehicles). Query with SASE, or submit proposal package, including outline. Reviews artwork/photos. Send photocopies.

Recent Title(s) *Trolley Buses Around the World*, by William A. Luke; *Vintage Snowmobilia*, by Jon D. Bertolinol.

IMPACT BOOKS

Imprint of F+W Media, Inc. 4700 E. Galbraith Rd., Cincinnati OH 45236. Fax: (513)531-2686. E-mail: pam.wissman@fwmedia.com. Website: www.northlightshop.com. **Contact:** Pamela Wissman, Editorial Director (art instruction for fantasy, comics, manga, anime, popular culture, graffiti, cartooning, body art). Estab. 2004. Publishes trade paperback originals and reprints. **Publishes 8-9 titles/year. 50 queries received/year. 10-12 mss received/year. 80% of books from first-time authors. 100% from unagented writers.** Publishes book 11 months after acceptance of ms. Accepts simultaneous submissions. Responds in 4 months to queries. Responds in 4 months to proposals. Responds in 2 months to manuscripts. Book catalog available free. Guidelines available online.

Nonfiction Subjects include art, art instruction, contemporary culture, creative nonfiction, hobbies. Submit proposal package, outline, 1 sample chapter, at least 1 example of sample art. Reviews artwork/photos. Send digital art, hard copies, or anything that represents the art well, preferably in the form the author plans to submit art if contracted.

Recent Title(s) *Dracopedia*, by William O'Connor; *Graff: Draw Furries*, by Lindsay Cibos and Jared Hodges; *The Insider's Guide to Creating Comics and Graphic Novels*, by Andy Schmidt; *GRAFF: the Art and Technique of Graffiti*, by Scape Martinez.

Tips "Audience comprised primarily of 12- to 18-year-old beginners along the lines of comic buyers, in general—mostly teenagers—but also appealing to a broader audience of young adults 19-30 who need basic techniques. Art must appeal to teenagers and be submitted in a form that will reproduce well. Authors need to know how to teach beginners step-by-step. A sample step-by-step is important."

INFORMATION TODAY, INC.

143 Old Marlton Pike, Medford NJ 08055. (609)654-6266. Fax: (609)654-4309. E-mail: jbryans@infotoday.com. Website: www.infotoday.com. **Contact:** John B. Bryans, editor-in-chief/publisher. Publishes hardcover and trade paperback originals. **Publishes 15-20 titles/year. 200 queries received/year. 30 mss received/year. 30% of books from first-time authors. 90% from unagented writers. Pays 10-15% royalty on wholesale price. Pays $500-2,500 advance.** Publishes book 9 months after acceptance of ms. Accepts simultaneous submissions. Responds in 1 month to queries. Responds in 2 months to proposals. Responds in 3 months to manuscripts. Book catalog free or on website. Proposal guidelines free or via e-mail as attachment.

Imprints ITI (academic, scholarly, library science); CyberAge Books (high-end consumer and business technology books-emphasis on Internet/WWW topics including online research).

O⊸ "We look for highly-focused coverage of cutting-edge technology topics, written by established experts and targeted to a tech-savvy readership. Virtually all our titles focus on how information is accessed, used, shared, and transformed into knowledge that can benefit people, business, and society. Currently emphasizing Internet/online technologies, including their social significance; biography, how-to, technical, reference, scholarly. De-emphasizing fiction."

Nonfiction Subjects include business, economics, computers, electronics, education, science, Internet and cyberculture. Query with SASE. Reviews artwork/photos. Send photocopies.

Recent Title(s) *Consider the Source: A Critical Guide to 100 Prominent News and Information Sites on the Web*, by James F. Broderick and Darren W. Miller; *Social Software in Libraries: Building Collaboration, Communication, and Community Online*, by Meredith G. Farkas; *The Extreme Searcher's Internet Handbook: A Guide for the Serious Searcher*, by Randolph Hock.

Tips "Our readers include scholars, academics, indexers, librarians, information professionals (ITI imprint), as well as high-end consumer and business users of Internet/WWW/online technologies, and people interested in the marriage of technology with issues of social significance (i.e., cyberculture)."

INTERLINK PUBLISHING GROUP, INC.

46 Crosby St., Northampton MA 01060. (413)582-7054. Fax: (413)582-7057. E-mail: info@interlinkbooks.com. Website: www.interlinkbooks.com. **Contact:** Michel Moushabeck, publisher. Estab. 1987.

Publishes hardcover and trade paperback originals. **Publishes 90 titles/year. 30% of books from first-time authors. 50% from unagented writers. Pays 6-8% royalty on retail price. Pays small advance.** Publishes book 18 months after acceptance of ms. Accepts simultaneous submissions. Responds in 3-6 months to queries. Book catalog and guidelines available free online.

Imprints Crocodile Books, USA; Codagan Guides, USA; Interlink Books; Olive Branch Press; Clockroot Books.

- Interlinkis a indenpendent publisher of a general trade list of adult fiction and nonfiction with an emphasis on books that have a wide appeal while also meeting high intellectual and literary standards.

Nonfiction Subjects include world travel, world literature, world history and politics, art, world music & dance, international cooking, children's books from around the world. Submit outline and sample chapters.

Fiction Subjects include ethnic, international adult. We are looking for translated works relating to the Middle East, Africa or Latin America. Query with SASE. Submit outline, sample chapters.

Recent Title(s) Capitalism Hits the Fan: *The Global Economic Meltdown and What to Do About It*, by Richard D. Wolff; Ending the US War in Afghanistan: *A Primer*, by David Wildman and Phyllis Bennis; Pure and Simple: *Homemade Indian Vegetarian Cuisine*, by Vidhu Mittal.

Tips "Any submissions that fit well in our publishing program will receive careful attention. A visit to our website, your local bookstore, or library to look at some of our books before you send in your submission is recommended."

INTERNATIONAL PRESS

P.O. Box 43502, Somerville MA 02143. (617)623-3855. Fax: (617)623-3101. Website: www.intlpress.com. **Contact:** Brian Bianchini, general manager (research math and physics). Estab. 1992. Publishes hardcover originals and reprints. **Publishes 12 titles/year. 200 queries received/year. 500 mss received/year. 10% of books from first-time authors. 100% from unagented writers. Pays 3-10% royalty.** Publishes book 6 months after acceptance of ms. Responds in 5 months to queries and proposals. Responds in 1 year to manuscripts. Book catalog available free. Guidelines available online.

- With close ties to the Chinese math community and the community of Chinese American mathematicians, International Press is developing a strong partnership with publishers and distributors of academic books throughout China.
- International Press of Boston, Inc. is an academic publishing company that welcomes book publication inquiries from prospective authors on all topics in Mathematics and Physics. International Press also publishes high-level mathematics and mathematical physics book titles and textbooks.

Nonfiction Subjects include science. All our books will be in research mathematics. Authors need to provide ready to print latex files. Submit complete ms. Reviews artwork/photos. Send EPS files.

Recent Title(s) *Collected Works on Ricci Flow*; *Current Developments in Mathematics*; *Surveys in Differential Geometry*, Vol. XIII; *The Founders of Index Theory*, 2nd Ed.; *Current Developments in Mathematics, 2007.*

Tips "Audience is PhD mathematicians, researchers and students."

INTERVARSITY PRESS

P.O. Box 1400, Downers Grove IL 60515-1426. Website: www.ivpress.com/submissions. **Contact:** David Zimmerman, associate editor (Likewise); Cindy Bunch, Sr. editor (IVP Connect, Formatio); Mike Gibson, associate editor (academic, reference); Gary Deddo, sr. ed. (IVP Academic) or Dan Reid, sr. ed. (reference, academic); Al Hsu, assoc. ed. (IVP Books). Estab. 1947. Publishes hardcover originals, trade paperback and mass market paperback originals. **Publishes 110-130 titles/year. 450 queries received/year. 900 mss received/year. 13% of books from first-time authors. 86% from unagented writers. Pays 14-16% royalty on retail price. Outright purchase is $75-1,500. Pays negotiable advance.** Publishes book 18 months after acceptance of ms. Accepts simultaneous submissions. Responds in 3 months to proposals "from pastors, professors, or previously published authors. We are unable to respond to other proposals or queries." Book catalog for 9 × 12 SAE and 5 first-class stamps, or online at website. Guidelines available online.

Imprints IVP Academic; IVP Connect; IVP Books.

- "We think of ourselves as the leading publisher of thoughtful Christian books, and we envision our audience to be similarly thoughtful about their Christian lives-people who really want to think through what it means to be a Christ-follower and to live biblically, and then take some concrete steps toward living more in that direction."

"InterVarsity Press publishes a full line of books from an evangelical Christian perspective targeted to an open-minded audience. We serve those in the university, the church, and the world, by publishing books from an evangelical Christian perspective."

Nonfiction Subjects include business, child guidance, contemporary culture, economics, ethinic, government, history, memoirs, multicultural, philosophy, psychology, religion, science, social sciences, sociology, spirituality, women's issues, women's studies. "InterVarsity Press publishes a full line of books from an evangelical Christian perspective targeted to an open-minded audience. We serve those in the university, the church, and the world, by publishing books from an evangelical Christian perspective." Query with SASE. Does not review artwork.

Recent Title(s) *Culture-Making*, by Andy Crouch (general book/Christian culture critique); *Justification*, by N. T. Wright (academic book/theology of justification).

Tips "The best way to submit to us is to go to a conference where one of our editors are. Networking is key. We're seeking writers who have good ideas and a presence/platform where they've been testing their ideas out (a church, university, on a prominent blog). We need authors who will bring resources to the table for helping to publicize and sell their books (speaking at seminars and conferences, writing for national magazines or newspapers, etc.)."

IRON GATE PUBLISHING

P.O. Box 999, Niwot CO 80544-0999. (303)530-2551. Fax: (303)530-5273. E-mail: editor@irongate.com. Website: www.irongate.com. **Contact:** Dina C. Carson, publisher (how-to, genealogy, local history). Publishes hardcover and trade paperback originals. **Publishes 6-10 titles/year. 100 queries received/year. 20 mss received/year. 30% of books from first-time authors. 10% from unagented writers. Pays royalty on a case-by-case basis.** Publishes book 1 year after acceptance of ms. Accepts simultaneous submissions. Responds in 2 months to proposals. Book catalog and writer's guidelines free or online.

Imprints Reunion Solutions Press; KinderMed Press.

"Our readers are people who are looking for solid, how-to advice on planning reunions or self-publishing a genealogy."

Nonfiction Subjects include hobbies, genealogy, local history, reunions, party planning. Query with SASE, or submit proposal package, including outline, 2 sample chapters, and marketing summary. Reviews artwork/photos. Send photocopies.

Recent Title(s) *The Genealogy and Local History Researcher's Self-Publishing Guide*; *Reunion Solutions: Everything You Need to Know to Plan a Family, Class, Military, Association or Corporate Reunion*.

Tips "Please look at the other books we publish and tell us in your query letter why your book would fit into our line of books."

JAIN PUBLISHING CO.

P.O. Box 3523, Fremont CA 94539. (510)659-8272. Fax: (510)659-0501. E-mail: mail@jainpub.com. Website: www.jainpub.com. **Contact:** M. Jain, editor-in-chief. Estab. 1989. Publishes hardcover and paperback originals and reprints. **Publishes 12-15 titles/year. 300 queries received/year. 100% from unagented writers. Pays 5-15% royalty on net sales.** Publishes book 12-24 months after acceptance of ms. Responds in 3 months to manuscripts. Book catalog and ms guidelines online.

Jain Publishing Co. publishes college textbooks and supplements, as well as professional and scholarly references, e-books and e-courses.

Nonfiction Subjects include humanities, social sciences, Asian studies, medical, business, scientific/technical. Submit proposal package, publishing history. Reviews artwork/photos. Send photocopies.

Recent Title(s) *A Student Guide to College Composition*, by William Murdiek.

JIST PUBLISHING

7321 Shadeland Station, Suite 200, Indianapolis IN 46256-3923, United States. (317)613-4200. Fax: (317)845-1052. E-mail: spines@jist.com. Website: www.jist.com. **Contact:** Susan Pines, associate publisher (career and education reference and library titles, assessments, videos, e-products); Lori Cates Hand, product line manager, trade and workbooks (Career, job search, and education trade and workbook titles). Estab. 1981. Hardcover and trade paperback originals. **Publishes 60 titles/year. Receives 40 submissions/year 25% of books from first-time authors. 75% from unagented writers. Pays 8-10% royalty on net receipts. Pays advance: 12 months.** Accepts simultaneous submissions. Responds in 6 months to queries, proposals, and mss. Book catalog available online. Guidelines available online.

"Our purpose is to provide quality job search, career development, occupational, and life skills information, products, and services that help people manage and improve their lives and careers-and the lives of others. Publishes practical, self-directed tools and training materials that are used in employment and training, education, and business settings. Whether reference books, trade books, assessment tools, workbooks, or videos, JIST products foster self-directed job-search attitudes and behaviors."

Nonfiction Subjects include business, economics, education. Specializes in job search, career development, occupational information, character education, and domestic abuse topics. We want text/workbook formats that would be useful in a school or other institutional setting. We also publish trade titles for all reading levels. Will consider books for professional staff and educators, appropriate software and videos. Submit proposal package, including outline, 1 sample chapter, and author resume, competitive analysis, marketing ideas. Does not review artwork/photos.

Recent Title(s) *Resumé Magic, The Twitter Job Search Guide, Best College For You, Make Job Loss Work For YOu, Your First Year as a Lawyer Revealed, 100 Fastest-Growing Careers, The Smart New Way to Get Hired, Community College Companion, Step-by-Step Cover Letters.*

Tips "Our audiences are students, job seekers, and career changers of all ages and occupations who want to find good jobs quickly and improve their futures. We sell materials through the trade as well as to institutional markets like schools, colleges, and one-stop career centers."

THE JOHNS HOPKINS UNIVERSITY PRESS

2715 N. Charles St., Baltimore MD 21218. (410)516-6900. Fax: (410)516-6968. E-mail: tcl@press.jhu.edu. Website: www.press.jhu.edu. **Contact:** Trevor Lipscombe, editor-in-chief (physics and mathematics; tcl@press.jhu.edu); Jacqueline C. Wehmueller, executive editor (consumer health and history of medicine; jwehmueller@press.jhu.edu); Henry Y.K. Tom, executive editor (social sciences; htom@press.jhu.edu); Wendy Harris, senior acquisitions editor (clinical medicine, public health, health policy; wharris@press.jhu.edu); Robert J. Brugger, senior acquisitions editor (American history, history of science and technology, regional books; rbrugger@press.jhu.edu); Vincent J. Burke, senior acquisitions editor (biology; vjb@press.jhu.edu); Matthew McAdam, acquisitions editor (humanities, classics, and ancient studies; mlonegro@press.jhu.edu); Ashleigh McKown, assistant acquisitions editor (higher education; amckown@press.jhu.edu). Estab. 1878. Publishes hardcover originals and reprints, and trade paperback reprints. **Publishes 140 titles/year. Pays royalty.** Publishes book 12 months after acceptance of ms.

Nonfiction Subjects include government, politics, health, medicine, history, humanities, literary criticism, regional, religion, science. Submit proposal package, outline, 1 sample chapter, curriculum vita. Reviews artwork/photos. Send photocopies.

Recent Title(s) *A Contract With the Earth*, by Newt Gingrich; *Abraham Lincoln: A Life*, by Michael Burlingame; *The Quantum Frontier: The Large Hadron Collider*, by Don Lincoln.

JOURNEYFORTH

Imprint of BJU Press 1700 Wade Hampton Blvd., Greenville SC 29614. (864)242-5100, ext. 4350. Fax: (864)298-0268. E-mail: jb@bjup.com. Website: www.bjupress.com. **Contact:** Nancy Lohr, youth acquisitions editor; Suzette Jordan, adult acquisitions editor. Estab. 1974. Publishes paperback originals and reprints. **Publishes 25 titles/year. 10% of books from first-time authors. 8% from unagented writers. Pays royalty.** Publishes book 12-18 months after acceptance of ms. Does accept simultaneous submissions. Responds in 1 month to queries. Responds in 3 months to manuscripts. Book catalog available free. Guidelines available online.

O→ "Small independent publisher of trustworthy novels and biographies for readers pre-school through high school from a conservative Christian perspective, Christian living books, and Bible studies for adults."

Nonfiction Nonfiction Christian living, Bible studies, church and ministry, church history. We produce books for the adult Christian market that are from a conservative Christian worldview.

Fiction Subjects include adventure, historical, animal, easy-to-read, series, mystery, sports, children's/juvenile, suspense, young adult, western. Our fiction is all based on a moral and Christian worldview. Submit 5 sample chapters, synopsis, SASE.

Tips "Study the publisher's guidelines. No picture books and no submissions by e-mail."

JOURNEY STONE CREATIONS

3533 Danbury Rd., Fairfield OH 45014. Website: www.jscbooks.com.

O→ "We specialize in children's book publishing. Over the last five years, we have published 57 books and are now focusing on special markets and private label products. We are also creating customized books for numerous national and regional organizations. Anyone who has a message and wants that message delivered to children, are our potential clients. We will write, illustrate and publish a book with your message to kids. Our new clients include grocery chains, hospitals, banks, safety organizations, ecology and animal rights organizations and the entertainment business." "

Tips "Make sure you submit only your best work. For writers, if it is not letter perfect, we don't want to see it. Review our guidelines. We cannot stress the importance of submitting only after you have read our needs. Don't waste your time and money submitting things we do not need. We are only publishing children's fiction/non-fiction, no adult or teen fiction at this time."

JUDSON PRESS

P.O. Box 851, Valley Forge PA 19482-0851. (610)768-2127. Fax: (610)768-2441. E-mail: acquisitions@judsonpress.com. Website: www.judsonpress.com. **Contact:** Rebecca Irwin-Diehl. Estab. 1824. Publishes hardcover and paperback originals. **Publishes 12-15 titles/year. 750 queries received/year. Pays royalty or makes outright purchase.** Publishes book 12 months after acceptance of ms. Accepts simultaneous submissions. Responds in 3-6 months to queries. Book catalog for 9 × 12 SAE with 4 first-class stamps. Guidelines available online.

O→ "Our audience is comprised primarily of pastors, leaders, and Christians who seek a more fulfilling personal spiritual life and want to serve God in their churches, communities, and relationships. We have a large African-American readership. Currently emphasizing small group resources. De-emphasizing biography, children's books, poetry."

Nonfiction Adult religious nonfiction of 30,000-80,000 words. Subjects include multicultural, religion. Query with SASE or by e-mail. Submit annotated outline, sample chapters, CV, competing titles, marketing plan.

Recent Title(s) *Marriage ROCKs for Christian Couples*, by Harold Arnold Jr., PhD.; *Autism & Alleluias*, by Kathleen Deyer Bolduc; *Coming Together in the 21st Century: The Bible's Message in an Age of Diversity*, by Curtiss Paul DeYoung; *I'm a Piece of Work: Sisters Shaped by God*, by Cynthia L. Hale.

Tips "Writers have the best chance selling us practical books assisting clergy or laypersons in their ministry and personal lives. Our audience consists of Protestant church leaders and members. Be informed about the market's needs and related titles. Be clear about your audience, and be practical in your focus. Books on multicultural issues are very welcome. Also seeking books that respond to real (felt) needs of pastors and churches."

KALMBACH PUBLISHING CO.

21027 Crossroads Circle, P.O. Box 1612, Waukesha WI 53187-1612. (262)796-8776. Fax: (262)798-6468. E-mail: books@kalmbach.com. Website: corporate.kalmbach.com. **Contact:** Mark Thompson, editor-in-chief (hobbies). Estab. 1934. Publishes paperback originals and reprints. **Publishes 40-50 titles/year. 50% of books from first-time authors. 99% from unagented writers. Pays 7% royalty on net receipts. Pays $1,500 advance.** Publishes book 18 months after acceptance of ms. Responds in 2 months to queries.

Nonfiction "Kalmbach publishes reference materials and how-to publications for hobbyists, jewelry-makers, and crafters." "Focus on beading, wirework, and one-of-a-kind artisan creations for jewelry-making and crafts and in the railfan, model railroading, plastic modeling and toy train collecting/operating hobbies." Query with 2-3 page detailed outline, sample chapter with photos, drawings, and how-to text. Reviews artwork/photos.

Recent Title(s) *The Model Railroader's Guide to Coal Railroading*, by Tony Koester; *Polymer Pizzazz: 27 Great Polymer Clay Jewelry Projects*.

Tips "Our how-to books are highly visual in their presentation. Any author who wants to publish with us must be able to furnish good photographs and rough drawings before we'll consider his or her book."

KAR-BEN PUBLISHING

A Divison of Lerner Publishing Group 241 First Avenue No., Minneapolis MN 55401, United States. Fax: 612-332-7615. E-mail: editorial@karben.com. Website: www.karben.com. **Contact:** Joni Sussman, publisher (juvenile Judaica). Estab. 1976. Publishes hardcover, trade paperback and electronic originals; hardcover and trade paperback reprints. **Publishes 12-15 titles/year. 800 mss received/year. 70% of books from first-time authors. 70% from unagented writers. Pays 3-5% royalty on wholesale price. Pays $500-2,500 advance.** Publishes book 24 months after acceptance of ms. Accepts simultaneous submissions. Responds in 2 months to queries, proposals, & manuscripts. Book catalog available online; free on request. Guidelines available online.

O→ "Kar-Ben Publishing publishes high-quality materials on Jewish themes for young children and families."

Nonfiction Subjects include Jewish content children's books only. "We seek stories that reflect the rich diversity of the contemporary Jewish community." Submit completed ms. Does not review artwork. Send website info where illustration samples are available for review.
Fiction Subjects include juvenile; Jewish content only. "We seek picture book mss of about 1,000 words on Jewish-themed topics for children." Submit proposal package, including synopsis, 2 sample chapters, and ms if picture book.
Recent Title(s) *Engineer Ari and the Rosh Hoshanah Ride, Jodie's Hannukkah Dig.*
Tips "Do a literature search to make sure similar title doesn't already exist."

KENT STATE UNIVERSITY PRESS

P.O. Box 5190, 1118 University Library, 1125 Risman Drive, Kent OH 44242-0001. (330)672-8099. Fax: (330)672-3104. E-mail: ksupress@kent.edu. Website: www.kentstateuniversitypress.com. **Contact:** Joyce Harrison, acquiring editor. Estab. 1965. Publishes hardcover and paperback originals and some reprints. **Publishes 30-35 titles/year. Non-author subsidy publishes 20% of books. Standard minimum book contract on net sales.** Responds in 4 months to queries. Book catalog available free.

O→ "Kent State publishes primarily scholarly works and titles of regional interest. Currently emphasizing US history, US literary criticism."

Nonfiction Subjects include anthropology, archeology, art, architecture, history, language, literature, literary criticism, regional, true crime, literary criticism, material culture, textile/fashion studies, US foreign relations. "Especially interested in scholarly works in history (US and world) and US literary studies of high quality, any titles of regional interest for Ohio, scholarly biographies and general nonfiction. Send a letter of inquiry before submitting mss. Decisions based on in-house readings and 2 by outside scholars in the field of study." Please, no faxes, phone calls, or e-mail submissions. For your convenience, the Press provides the following downloadable guidelines in PDF format: Electronic Manuscript Guidelines for Authors, Illustration Submission Guidelinesfor Authors, Copyright Guidelines for Authors. Enclose return postage.
Recent Title(s) *Musical Mysteries From Mozart to John Lennon*, by Albert Borowitz; *A Passion for the Land - John F. Seiberling and the Environmental Movement*, by Daniel Nelson.

KOENISHA PUBLICATIONS

3196 53rd St., Hamilton MI 49419-9626. Phone/Fax: (269)751-4100. E-mail: koenisha@macatawa.org. Website: www.koenisha.com. **Contact:** Sharolett Koenig, publisher; Earl Leon, acquisition editor. Publishes trade paperback originals. **Publishes 10-12 titles/year. 500 queries received/year. 500 mss received/year. 95% of books from first-time authors. 100% from unagented writers.** Publishes book 1 year after acceptance of ms. Guidelines available online.
Nonfiction *Not accepting submissions from new authors at this time.*
Fiction Subjects include humor, mainstream, contemporary, mystery, romance, suspense, young adult. Query with SASE. Submit proposal package, clips, 3 sample chapters.
Poetry Submit 3 sample poems.
Recent Title(s) *JimJim Meets Poster Guy*, by Gary Crow and Brock Crow (children's read-along); *Cruisin' For a Bruisin'*, by Gayle Wigglesworth (mystery); *The Bonsai Keeper*, by Sharolett Koenig (nonfiction).
Tips "We're not interested in books written to suit a particular line or house or because it's trendy. Instead write a book from your heart—the inspiration or idea that kept you going through the writing process."

KRAUSE PUBLICATIONS

A Division of F+W Media, Inc. 700 E. State St., Iola WI 54990. (715)445-2214. Fax: (715)445-4087. Website: www.krausebooks.com. **Contact:** Paul Kennedy (antiques and collectibles, music); Corrina Peterson (firearms/outdoors); Candy Wiza (Simple Living); Debbie Bradley (Numismatics). Publishes hardcover and trade paperback originals. **Publishes 80 titles/year. 300 queries received/year. 40 mss received/year. 50% of books from first-time authors. 95% from unagented writers. Pays advance. Photo budget.** Publishes book 18 months after acceptance of ms. Responds in 3 months to proposals. Responds in 2 months to manuscripts. Book catalog for free or on website. Guidelines available free.

O→ "We are the world's largest hobby and collectibles publisher."

Nonfiction Submit proposal package, including outline, table of contents, a sample chapter, and letter explaining your project's unique contributions. Reviews artwork/photos. Accepts digital photography. Send sample photos.
Recent Title(s) *Woodstock: Peace, Music & Memories*, by Brad Littleproud and Joanne Hague; *Standard Catalog of Winchester Firearms*, by Joseph Cornell; *The Heart of Simple Living*, by Wanda Urbanska.

Tips Audience consists of serious hobbyists. "Your work should provide a unique contribution to the special interest."

LARK BOOKS

67 Broadway, Asheville NC 28801. (828)253-0467. Fax: (828)253-7952. Website: www.larkbooks.com. **Contact:** Nicole McConville, acquisitions. Estab. 1976. Publishes hardcover and trade paperback originals and reprints. **Publishes 60-70 titles/year. 300 queries received/year. 100 mss received/year. 75% of books from first-time authors. 80% from unagented writers.** Publishes book 1 year after acceptance of ms. Accepts simultaneous submissions. Responds in 3 months to queries, proposals, and to manuscripts. Book catalog available online. Guidelines available online.

O-ₜ "Lark Books publishes high quality, highly illustrated books, primarily in the crafts/leisure markets celebrating the creative spirit. We work closely with bookclubs. Our books are either how-to, `gallery' or combination books. If you've got an idea that you'd love to see in print, we're happy to consider any book proposals on craft and leisure activity topics. We publish a variety of camera manuals and how-to reference books on photography and digital imaging techniques."

Nonfiction Subjects include nature, environment, photography. We want a humorous take on any nonfiction subject. Query with SASE. Submit proposal package, outline, 1-2 sample chapters. Query first. If asked, submit outline and 1 sample chapter, sample projects, TOC, visuals. Reviews artwork/photos. Send photocopies.

Fiction "We currently do not publish fiction, and we rarely publish non-illustrated books."

Recent Title(s) *Doodle-Stitching*, by Aimee Ray.

Tips "Make sure your humor submissions are edgy and contain a nonfiction element."

LEE & LOW BOOKS

95 Madison Ave., New York NY 10016. E-mail: general@leeandlow.com. Website: www.leeandlow.com. **Contact:** Louise May, editor-in-chief (multicultural children's fiction/nonfiction). Estab. 1991. Publishes hardcover originals and trade paperback reprints of our own titles. **Publishes 12 titles/year. Receives 100 queries/year; 1,200 mss/year. 15-20%% of books from first-time authors. 50% from unagented writers. Pays net royalty. Pays advance (range depends on project, whether author or author/illustrator).** Publishes book 24-36 months after. after acceptance of ms. Responds in 6 months to mss if interested. Book catalog available online. Guidelines available online or by written request with SASE.

O-ₜ "Our goals are to meet a growing need for books that address children of color, and to present literature that all children can identify with. We only consider multicultural children's books. Currently emphasizing material for 5-12 year olds. Sponsors a yearly New Voices Award for first-time picture book authors of color. Contest rules online at website or for SASE."

Nonfiction "We publish only books featuring people of color for children ages 5-10 (illustrated picture books) plus a limited number of middle grade and YA stories." Submit completed ms. Reviews artwork/photos only if writer is also a professional illustrator or photographer. Send photocopies and nonreturnable art samples only.

Fiction Subjects include contemporary and historical fiction featuring people of color. Also accepts thematic or narrative poetry collections with a multicultural focus. Send complete ms.

Poetry Submit complete ms.

Recent Title(s) *Capoeira: Game! Dance! Martial Art!*, by George Ancona (children's photo-essay); *Surfer of the Century*, by Ellie Crowe (illustrated picture book bio); *Bird*, by Zetta Elliott (realistic fiction, illustrated picture book); *Yum! MmMm! Què Rico!*, by Pat Mora (children's illus. picture book).

Tips "Check our website to see the kinds of books we publish. Do not send mss that don't fit our mission."

LILLENAS PUBLISHING CO.

Imprint of Lillenas Drama Resources P.O. Box 419527, Kansas City MO 64109. (816)931-1900. Fax: (816)412-8390. E-mail: drama@lillenas.com. Website: www.lillenasdrama.com. **Contact:** Kim Messer, product manager (Christian drama). Publishes mass market paperback and electronic originals. **Publishes 50+ titles/year. Pays royalty on wholesale price. Makes outright purchase.** Responds in 4-6 months to material. See guidelines online at website.

O-ₜ We purchase only original, previously unpublished materials. Also, we require that all scripts be performed at least once before it is submitted for consideration. We do not accept scripts that are sent via fax or e-mail. Direct all manuscripts to the Drama Resources Editor.

Nonfiction Subjects include religion, life issues. Query with SASE. Submit complete ms.

Fiction Looking for sketch and monologue collections for all ages – adults, children and youth. For these collections, we request 12 to15 scripts to be submitted at one time. Unique treatments of spiritual themes, relevant issues and biblical messages are of interest. Contemporary full-length and one-act plays that have conflict, characterization, and a spiritual context that is neither a sermon nor an apologetic for youth and adults. We also need wholesome so-called secular full-length scripts for dinner theatres and schools.

Tips "We never receive too many manuscripts."

N LILY RUTH PUBLISHING

P.O. Box 2067, Jacksonville TX 75766. Website: www.lilyruthpublishing.com. **Contact:** Acquisitions: Jennifer L. Stone. **Publishes 1.5 titles/year. 75% of books from first-time authors.** Publishes book 6 months to a year after acceptance of ms. Accepts simultaneous submissions. Catalog available on website.

- "We believe that literature for children should be above all, fun. Strong stories from authors with unique voices are what make reading entertaining and exciting, inspiring a love of reading that will last a life time."

Fiction Subjects include Early & Middle Readers: adventure, fantasy, humor. Young Adults/Teens: adventure, fantasy, humor. Average word length: middle readers—25,000; young adults— 50,000. Query with outline/synopsis and 3 sample chapters.

Recent Title(s) My Weird Family Series: *My Vampire Cousin*, by J.K. Hawkins (middle reader, adventure, humor); My Weird Family Series: *My Werewolf Brothers*, by J.K. Hawkins (middle reader, adventure, humor).

LINDEN PUBLISHING, INC.

2006 S. Mary, Fresno CA 93721. (559)233-6633. Fax: (559)233-6933. E-mail: richard@lindenpub.com. Website: www.lindenpub.com. **Contact:** Richard Sorsky, president; Kent Sorsky, vice president. Estab. 1976. Publishes trade paperback originals; hardcover and trade paperback reprints. **Publishes 10-12 titles/year. 30+ queries received/year. 5-15 mss received/year. 40% of books from first-time authors. 50% from unagented writers. Pays 7½ -12% royalty on wholesale price. Pays $500-6,000 advance.** Publishes book 18 months after acceptance of ms. Responds in 1 month to queries and proposals. Book catalog available online. Guidelines available via e-mail.

Nonfiction Subjects include history, regional, hobbies, woodworking, Regional California history. Submit proposal package, outline, 3 sample chapters, bio. Reviews artwork/photos. Send electronic files, if available.

Recent Title(s) *Teen 2.0, Death in California, Civil War Woodworking, How to Choose and Use Bench Planes, PR Therapy, The Complete Geezer Guidebook.*

LISTEN & LIVE AUDIO

P.O. Box 817, Roseland NJ 07068. E-mail: alisa@listenandlive.com. Website: www.listenandlive.com. **Contact:** Alisa Weberman, publisher. **Publishes 30+ titles/year.** Catalog available online.

- Independent audiobook publisher. "We also license audiobooks for the download market. We specialize in the following genres: Fiction, Mystery, Non-Fiction, Self-help, Business, Children's and Teen."

Recent Title(s) *Zingerman's Guide to Giving Great Service*, by Ari Weinzweig (business audio); *The Jane Austin Book Club*, by Karen Joy Fowler (women's audio); *The Perilous Road*, by William O. Steele (classic children's audio).

LOFT PRESS, INC.

P.O. Box 150, Fort Valley VA 22652. (540)933-6210. Website: www.loftpress.com. **Contact:** Ann A. Hunter, editor-in-chief. Publishes hardcover and trade paperback originals and reprints. **Publishes 8-16 titles/year. 850 queries received/year. 300 mss received/year. 75% of books from first-time authors. 100% from unagented writers.** Publishes book 6 months after acceptance of ms. Guidelines available online.

Imprints Punch Press, Eschat Press, Far Muse Press (for all contact Stephen R. Hunter, publisher).

Nonfiction Subjects include Americana, art, architecture, business, economics, computers, electronics, government, politics, history, language, literature, memoirs, philosophy, regional, religion, science. Submit proposal package, outline, 1 sample chapter. Reviews artwork/photos. Send photocopies.

Fiction Subjects include literary, poetry, regional, short story collections. Submit proposal package, 1 sample chapter, clips.

Poetry Submit 5 sample poems.

Recent Title(s) *Essential Self, Your True Identity*, by Joseph Walsh; *Quest for Justice*, by Henry E. Hudson; *Tilly the White-Liver Woman*, by Isaac Chin; *Zula Remembers*, by Zula Dietrich.

LOVING HEALING PRESS INC.

5145 Pontiac Trail, Ann Arbor MI 48105-9627. (888)761-6268. E-mail: info@lovinghealing.com. Website: www.lovinghealing.com. **Contact:** Victor R. Volkman, Sr. Editor (psychology, self-help, personal growth, trauma recovery). Hardcover originals and reprints; Trade paperback originals and reprints. **Publishes 20 titles/year. Receives 200 queries/year; 100 mss/year 50% of books from first-time authors. 80% from unagented writers.** Publishes book 10 months after acceptance of ms. Accepts simultaneous submissions. Catalog available online at website. Guidelines online at website http://lovinghealing.com/aboutus.

Nonfiction Subjects include child guidance, health, memoirs, psychology, social work. We are primarily interested in self-help books which are person-centered and non-judgmental. Submit proposal package, including: outline, 3 sample chapters; submit completed ms. Reviews artwork/photos as part of the ms package; send JPEG files.

Fiction Subjects include multicultural, social change. Submit completed ms.

LRP PUBLICATIONS, INC.

P.O. Box 980, Horsham PA 19044. (215)784-0860. Fax: (215)784-9639. Website: www.lrp.com. **Contact:** See website for contacts by product group. Estab. 1977. Publishes hardcover and trade paperback originals. **Pays royalty.** Book catalog available free. Guidelines available free.

- LRP publishes two industry-leading magazines, *Human Resource Executive®* and *Risk & Insurance®*, as well as hundreds of newsletters, books, videos and case reporters in the fields of: human resources, federal employment, workers' compensation, public employment law, disability, bankruptcy, education administration and law.

Nonfiction Subjects include business, economics, education. Submit proposal package, outline.

THE LYONS PRESS

Imprint of The Globe Pequot Press, Inc. Box 480, 246 Goose Lane, Guilford CT 06437. (203)458-4500. Fax: (203)458-4668. E-mail: info@globepequot.com. Website: www.lyonspress.com. **Contact:** Janice Goldklang, exec. editor (general nonfiction, memoir, bio, cooking, history, current events), Keith Wallman, senior editor (military history, martial arts, narrativenonfiction, sports, current affairs); Mary Norris, senior editor (narrative nonfiction, adventure, women's issues, cooking, bio, memoir, self-help, animals, cooking); Holly Rubino, editor (narrative nonfiction, home). Estab. 1984 (Lyons & Burford), 1997 (The Lyons Press). Publishes hardcover and trade paperback originals and reprints. **Publishes 200 titles/year. 50% of books from first-time authors. 30% from unagented writers. Pays 5-10% royalty on wholesale price. Pays $3,000-25,000 advance.** Publishes book 1 year after acceptance of ms. Accepts simultaneous submissions. Responds in 2 months to queries, proposals and to manuscripts. Book catalog available online. Guidelines available online.

- The Lyons Press has teamed up to develop books with The Explorers Club, Orvis, L.L. Bean, *Field & Stream*, Outward Bound, Buckmasters, and *Golf Magazine*.
- The Lyons Press publishes practical and literary books, chiefly centered on outdoor subjects—natural history, all sports, gardening, horses, fishing, hunting, survival, self-reliant living, plus cooking, memoir, bio, non-fiction.

Nonfiction Subjects include agriculture, Americana, animals, art & reference, cooking, foods & wine, nutrition, history, military, war, nature, environment, recreation, sports, adventure, fitness, the sea, woodworking. Visit our website and note the featured categories. Query with SASE. Submit proposal package, outline, 3 sample chapters. marketing description. Reviews artwork/photos. Send photocopies and nonoriginal prints.

Recent Title(s) *The Dangerous World of Butterflies - The Startling Subculture of Criminals, Collectors, and Conservationists*, by Peter Taufer, Ph.D.; *Believe*, by Buck Brannaman (horses); *The Orvis Ultimate Book of Fly Fishing*, by Tom Rosenbauer (fishing); *Lost in Tibet*, by Richard Starks and Miriam Murcutt (adventure/military history).

MANDALEY PRESS

720 Rio Grande Dr., Suite 100, Alpharetta GA 30022. E-mail: msatt@mindspring.com. **Contact:** Mark Satterfield, president (business books with a particular interest in sales training). Estab. 2001. Publishes hardcover, trade paperback, and mass market paperback originals. **Publishes 10 titles/year. 50 queries received/year. 50 mss received/year. 80% of books from first-time authors. 100% from unagented writers. Pays 10-20% royalty on wholesale price.** Publishes book 6 months after acceptance of ms. Accepts simultaneous submissions. Responds in 1 month to queries. Responds in 2 months to proposals and manuscripts.

Nonfiction Subjects include audio, business, economics. "We are looking for authors in the sales marketing arena with a value-added message. There are many books currently available that focus on 'what' successful sales professionals do. We are interested in 'how' specifically to achieve success." Query with SASE. Reviews artwork/photos.

⊘ MCBOOKS PRESS

ID Booth Building, 520 N. Meadow St., Ithaca NY 14850. (607)272-2114. Fax: (607)273-6068. E-mail: jackie@mcbooks.com. Website: www.mcbooks.com. **Contact:** Jackie Swift, editorial director. Estab. 1979. Publishes trade paperback and hardcover originals and reprints. **Publishes 6 titles/year. Pays 5-10% royalty on retail price. Pays $1,000-5,000 advance.** Accepts simultaneous submissions. Responds in 3 months to queries and proposals. Guidelines available online.

- "In the current tough book market, the author's ability to use the internet for self promotion is extremely important. Show that you're savvy with personal websites, blogs, and social networking; and show you know who your audience is and how to generate word-of-mouth."

Nonfiction Query with SASE. "Give us a general outline of your book. Let us know how your book differs from what is currently on the market and what your qualifications are for writing it. Give us an idea how you would go about promoting/marketing your book."

Fiction Subjects include historical, nautical, naval and military historical, action/adventure historical. "We will consider any type of fiction except sci-fi, fantasy, religious, and children's." E-mail queries prefered. If querying by mail, include SASE. Send excerpt as RTF file attachment.

Recent Title(s) *Night of Flames*, by Douglas W. Jacobson; *Four Kings*, by George Kimball; *Better Than Peanut Butter & Jelly, 2nd Ed.*, by Marty Mattare and Wendy Muldawer.

MCFARLAND & CO., INC., PUBLISHERS

Box 611, Jefferson NC 28640. (336)246-4460. Fax: (336)246-5018. E-mail: info@mcfarlandpub.com. Website: www.mcfarlandpub.com. **Contact:** Steve Wilson, editorial director (automotive, general); David Alff, editor (general); Gary Mitchem, acquisitions editor (general, baseball). Estab. 1979. Publishes hardcover and quality paperback originals; a nontrade publisher. **Publishes 350 titles/year. 50% of books from first-time authors. 95% from unagented writers.** Publishes book 10 months after acceptance of ms. Responds in 1 month to queries. Guidelines available online.

- "McFarland publishes serious nonfiction in a variety of fields, including general reference, performing arts, popular culture, sports (particularly baseball); women's studies, librarianship, literature, Civil War, history and international studies. Currently emphasizing medieval history, automotive history. De-emphasizing memoirs."

Nonfiction Subjects include art, architecture, automotive, health, medicine, history, military, war/war, popular contemporary culture, music, dance, recreation, sociology, world affairs, sports (very strong), African-American studies (very strong). Reference books are particularly wanted—fresh material (i.e., not in head-to-head competition with an established title). We prefer manuscripts of 250 or more double-spaced pages or at least 75,000 words. Query with SASE. Submit outline, sample chapters. Reviews artwork/photos.

Recent Title(s) *American Cars, 1946-1959*, by J. "Kelly" Flory, Jr.; *Classic Home Video Games, 1972-1984*, by Brett Weiss; *African American Mystery Writers*, by Frankie Y. Bailey.

Tips "We want well-organized knowledge of an area in which there is not information coverage at present, plus reliability so we don't feel we have to check absolutely everything. Our market is worldwide and libraries are an important part. McFarland also publishes six journals: the *Journal of Information Ethics, North Korean Review, Base Ball: A Journal of the Early Game, Black Ball: A Negro Leagues Journal, Clues: A Journal of Detection*, and *Minerva Journal of Women and War*."

MEADOWBROOK PRESS

5451 Smetana Dr., Minnetonka MN 55343. (952)930-1100. Fax: (952)930-1940. E-mail: info@meadowbrookpress.com. Website: www.meadowbrookpress.com. **Contact:** Submissions Editor. Estab. 1975. Publishes trade paperback originals and reprints. **Publishes 12 titles/year. 1,500 queries received/year. 10% of books from first-time authors. Pays 7½% royalty. Pays small advance.** Publishes book 18 months-2 years after acceptance of ms. Accepts simultaneous submissions. Responds only if interested to queries. Book catalog for #10 SASE. Guidelines available online.

- "We are not currently accepting unsolicited manuscripts or queries for the following genres: adult fiction, adult poetry, humor, and children's fiction. Also note that we do not currently publish picture books for children, travel titles, scholarly, or literary works. For children's poetry guidelines, please go to our website."

"Meadowbrook is a family-oriented press. We specialize in pregnancy, baby care, child care, humorous poetry for children, party planning, and children's activities. We are also the number one publisher of baby name books in the country, with eight baby-naming books in print."

Nonfiction Subjects include child guidance, cooking, foods, nutrition, pregnancy. "We prefer a query first; then we will request an outline and/or sample material. Send for guidelines." Query or submit outline with sample chapters.

Poetry Children's poetry books.

Recent Title(s) *Tinkle, Tinkle, Little Tot*, by Bruce Lansky, Robert Pottle and friends (childcare); *The Official Lamaze Guide*, by Judith Lothion and Charlotte DeVries (pregnancy).

Tips "Always send for guidelines before submitting material. Always submit nonreturnable copies; we do not respond to queries or submissions unless interested."

MENCS: The National Association for Music Education

1806 Robert Fulton Dr., Reston VA 20191-4348. Fax: (703)860-9443. Website: www.menc.org. **Contact:** Ella Wilcox, editor. Estab. 1907. **Pays royalty on retail price.**

"JOURNALS: See www.menc.org for our guidelines for contributors. Our mission is to advance music education by encouraging the study and making of music by all. *Music Educators Journal* and *Teaching Music* are two of our journal publications. *Music Educators Journal (MEJ)* encourages music education professionals who are MENC members to submit mss about all phases of music education in schools and communities, practical instructional techniques, teaching philosophy, and current issues in music teaching and learning. (See separate listing for Teaching Music.) BOOKS: Publishes hardcover and trade paperback originals. Publishes 10 titles/year. 75 queries received/year. 50 mss received/year. 40% of books from first-time authors. 100% from unagented writers. Pays royalty on retail price. Publishes book 1-2 years after acceptance of ms. Responds in 2 months to queries. Responds in 4 months to proposals. Book catalog available online. Guidelines available online.

Nonfiction Subjects include child guidance, education, multicultural, music, dance, music education. Mss evaluated by professional music educators. Submit proposal package, outline, 1-3 sample chapters, bio, CV, marketing strategy. For journal articles, submit electronically to http://mc.manuscriptcentral.com/mej. Authors will be required to set up an online account on the SAGETRACK system powered by ScholarOne (this can take about 30 minutes). From their account, a new submission can be initiated.

Tips "Look online for book proposal guidelines. No telephone calls. We are committed to music education books that will serve as the very best resources for music educators, students and their parents."

MERIWETHER PUBLISHING, LTD.

P.O. Box 7710, Colorado Springs CO 80903. Fax: (719)594-9916. E-mail: editor@meriwether.com. **Contact:** Theodore Zape, assoc. editor. Estab. 1969. Publishes paperback originals and reprints. **Pays 10% royalty or negotiates purchase.** Accepts simultaneous submissions. Responds in 6 weeks. Book catalog and ms guidelines for $2 postage.

"We are specialists in theater arts books and plays for middle grades, high schools, and colleges. We publish textbooks for drama courses of all types. We also publish for mainline liturgical churches—drama activities for church holidays, youth activities, and fundraising entertainment. These may be plays, musicals, or drama-related books. Query with synopsis or submit complete script."

Nonfiction "Most of the plays we publish are one-acts, 15-45 min. in length. We also publish full-length two-act musicals or three-act plays, 90 min. in length. We prefer comedies. Musical shows should have large cast for 20-25 performers. Comedy sketches, monologues, and plays are welcome. We prefer simple staging appropriate to middle school, high school, college, college, or church performance. We like playwrights who see the world with a sense of humor. Offbeat themes and treatments are accepted if the playwright can sustain a light touch. In documentary or religious plays we look for good research and authenticity. We are publishing many scenebooks for actors (which can be anthologies of great works excerpts), scenebooks on special themes, and speech and theatrical arts textbooks. We also publish many books of monologs for young performers. We are especially interested in authority-books on a variety of theater-related subjects." "Contemporary Drama Service is now looking for play or musical adaptations of classic stories by famous authors and playwrights. Also looking for parodies of famous movies or historical and/or fictional characters (i.e., Robin Hood, Rip Van Winkle, Buffalo Bill, Huckleberry Finn). Obtains either amateur or all rights."

Fiction Plays and musical comedies for middle grades through college only. Subjects include mainstream, contemporary, plays, and musicals, religious, children's plays and religious Christmas and Easter plays, suspense, all in playscript format, comedy. Query with SASE.

Recent Title(s) *Break a leg! An Introductory Guide to Stage Directing*, by Andrea Gibbs; *The Theatre Audition Book 2*, by Gerald Lee Ratliff; *Drama Games and Acting Exercises*, by Rod Martin; *175 Theatre Games*, by Nancy Hurley.

Tips "Contemporary Drama Service is looking for creative books on comedy, monologs, staging amateur theatricals, and Christian youth activities. Our writers are usually highly experienced in theatre as teachers or performers. We welcome books that reflect their experience and special knowledge. Any good comedy writer of monologs and short scenes will find a home with us."

MERRIAM PRESS

133 Elm St., Suite 3R, Bennington VT 05201-2250. (802)447-0313. E-mail: ray@merriam-press.com. Website: www.merriam-press.com. Estab. 1988. Publishes hardcover and softcover trade paperback originals and reprints. **Publishes 12+ titles/year. 70-90% of books from first-time authors. 100% from unagented writers. Pays 10% royalty on actual selling price.** Publishes book 6 months or less after acceptance of ms. Responds quickly (e-mail preferred) to queries. Book catalog available for $2 or visit website to view all available titles and access writer's guidelines and info.

O→ "Merriam Press publishes only military history - particularly World War II history."

Nonfiction Subjects include military, war, World War II. Query with SASE or by e-mail first. Reviews artwork/photos. Send photocopies on disk/flash drive/e-mail attachment.

Recent Title(s) *What Were They Thinking? A Fresh Look at Japan at War, 1941-45*, by John D. Beatty and Lee A. Rochwerger; I'll Be Home for the Christmas Rush: Letters From Europe, 1944-45, by Albert W. Hoffman; *Dead Men Flying: Victory in Viet Nam, The Legend of Dust Off, America's Battlefield Angels*, by Patrick Henry Brady with Meghan Brady Smith; *The Mailman Went UA: A Vietnam Memoir*, by David Mulldune; *Here Rests in Honored Glory: Life Stories of our Country's Medal of Honor Recipients*, by Andrew J. Dekever.

Tips "Our books are geared for military historians, collectors, model kit builders, wargamers, veterans, general enthusiasts. We do not publish any fiction or poetry, only WWII military history, general military history and veteran memoirs."

MICHIGAN STATE UNIVERSITY PRESS

1405 S. Harrison Rd. Manly Miles Bldg., Suite 25, East Lansing MI 48823-5202. (517)355-9543. Fax: (517)432-2611. E-mail: msupress@msu.edu. **Contact:** Martha Bates, acquisitions editor. Estab. 1947. Publishes hardcover and softcover originals. **Pays variable royalty.** Book catalog and ms guidelines for 9 × 12 SASE or online.

- Distributes books for: University of Calgary Press, Penumbra Press, National Museum of Science (UK), African Books Collective, University of Alberta Press, University of Manitoba Press.

O→ Michigan State University publishes scholarly books that further scholarship in their particular field. In addition, they publish nonfiction that addresses, in a more contemporary way, social concerns, such as diversity, civil rights, and the environment. They also publish literary fiction and poetry.

Nonfiction Subjects include Americana, American studies, business, economics, creative nonfiction, ethnic, Afro-American studies, government, politics, history, contemporary civil rights , language, literature, literary criticism, regional, Great Lakes regional, Canadian studies, women's issues, women's studies. Submit proposal/outline and sample chapter. We prefer a hard copy but also accept e-mail proposals. Initial submissions to MSU Press should be in the form of a short letter of inquiry and a sample chapter, as well as our preliminary Marketing Questionnaire. Download our Questionnaire, fill it out, and mail it with your manuscript. We do not accept: e-mail manuscripts, Festschrifts, conference papers, or unrevised dissertations (Festschrift: A complimentary or memorial publication usually in the form of a collection of essays, addresses, or biographical, bibliographic, scientific, or other contributions). Reviews artwork/photos.

Recent Title(s) *5 Years of the 4th Genre*, edited by Martha A. Bates; *Jewish Life in the Industrial Promised Land, 1855-2005*, by Nora Faires and Nancy Hanflik; *My Father on a Bicycle*, by Patricia Clark.

MICROSOFT PRESS

E-mail: 4bkideas@microsoft.com. Website: www.microsoft.com/learning/books. **Contact:** Editor. **Publishes 80 titles/year. 25% of books from first-time authors. 90% from unagented writers.** Book proposal guidelines available online.

Nonfiction "We place a great deal of emphasis on your proposal. A proposal provides us with a basis for evaluating the idea of the book and how fully your book fulfills its purpose." Subjects include software. A book proposal should consist of the following information: a table of contents, a resumè with author biography, a writing sample, and a questionnaire.

MILKWEED EDITIONS

1011 Washington Ave. S., Minneapolis MN 55415. (612)332-3192. E-mail: editor@milkweed.org. Website: www.milkweed.org. Estab. 1979. Publishes hardcover, trade paperback, and electronic originals; trade paperback and electronic reprints. **Publishes 15-20 titles/year. 25% of books from first-time authors. 75% from unagented writers. Pays 7% royalty on retail price. Pays varied advance from $500-10,000.** Publishes book 18 months. after acceptance of ms. Accepts simultaneous submissions. Responds in 6 months to queries, proposals, and mss. Book catalog available online at website. Guidelines available online at website http://www.milkweed.org/content/blogcategory/.

Nonfiction Subjects include agriculture, animals, archaeology, art, contemporary culture, creative nonfiction, environment, gardening, gay, government, history, humanities, language, literature, multicultural, nature, politics, literary, regional, translation, women's issues, world affairs. Please consider our previous publications when considering submissions to Milkweed Editions. Submit complete ms with SASE. Milkweed strongly encourages digital submissions through our website. Does not review artwork.

Fiction Subjects include experimental, short story collections, translation, young adult. Novels for adults and for readers 8-13. High literary quality. For adult readers: literary fiction, nonfiction, poetry, essays. For children (ages 8-13): literary novels. Translations welcome for both audiences. Query with SASE, submit completed ms.

Poetry Query with SASE; submit completed ms

Recent Title(s) *The Wet Collection*, by Joni Tevis (creative nonfiction); *The Future of Nature*, ed. by Barry Lopiz (environmental lit); *The Farther Shore*, by Matthew Eck (literary); *Driftless*, by David Rhodes (literary); *Hallelujah Blackout*, by Alex Lemon (poetry);*The Book of Props*, by Wayne Miller (poetry).

Tips "We are looking for excellent writing with the intent of making a humane impact on society. Please read submission guidelines before submitting and acquaint yourself with our books in terms of style and quality before submitting. Many factors influence our selection process, so don't get discouraged. Nonfiction is focused on literary writing about the natural world, including living well in urban environments."

MONDIAL

203 W. 107th St., Suite 6C, New York NY 10025. (212)851-3252. Fax: (208)361-2863. E-mail: contact@mondialbooks.com. Website: www.mondialbooks.com. **Contact:** Andrew Moore, editor. Estab. 1996. Publishes trade paperback originals and reprints. **Publishes 20 titles/year. 2,000 queries received/year. 500 mss received/year. 20%% of books from first-time authors. Pays 10% royalty on wholesale price.** Publishes book 4 months after acceptance of ms. Accepts simultaneous submissions. Guidelines available online.

Nonfiction Subjects include alternative, ethnic, gay, lesbian, history, language, literature, literary criticism, memoirs, multicultural, philosophy, psychology, sex, sociology, translation. Submit proposal package, outline, 1 sample chapters. Send only electronically by e-mail.

Fiction Subjects include adventure, erotica, ethnic, gay, lesbian, historical, literary, mainstream, contemporary, multicultural, mystery, poetry, romance, short story collections, translation.

Recent Title(s) *Concise Encyclopedia of the Original Literature of Esperanto* (740-page encyclopedia); *Two People,* by Donald Windham (novel/gay classics); *Terminologie und Terminologieplanung in Esperanto*, by Wera Blanke (linguistic); *Winter Ridge. A Love Story*, by Bruce Kellner (mature love story); *Bitterness (An African Novel from Zambia)*, by Malama Katulwende (love story and student revolt in Zambia).

MOREHOUSE PUBLISHING CO.

Church Publishing Incorporated 4475 Linglestown Rd., Harrisburg PA 17112. Fax: (717)541-8136. E-mail: dperkins@cpg.org. Website: www.morehousepublishing.org. **Contact:** Davis Perkins. Estab. 1884. Publishes hardcover and paperback originals. **Publishes 35 titles/year. 50% of books from first-time authors. Pays small advance.** Publishes book 18 months after acceptance of ms. Accepts simultaneous submissions. Responds in 2-3 months to queries. Guidelines available online.

O→ Morehouse Publishing publishes mainline Christian books, primarily Episcopal/Anglican works. Currently emphasizing Christian spiritual direction.

Nonfiction Subjects include religion, Christian, women's issues, women's studies, Christian spirituality, liturgies, congregational resources, issues around Christian life. Submit outline, résumé, 1-2 sample chapters, market analysis.
Recent Title(s) *Welcome to Sunday*, by Christopher Webber; *Knitting Into the Mystery*, by Susan Jorgensen; *A Wing and a Prayer*, by Katharine Jefferts Schori.

MOUNTAIN PRESS PUBLISHING CO.

P.O. Box 2399, Missoula MT 59806-2399. (406)728-1900 or (800)234-5308. Fax: (406)728-1635. E-mail: info@mtnpress.com. Website: www.mountain-press.com. **Contact:** Jennifer Carey, editor. Estab. 1948. Publishes hardcover and trade paperback originals. **Publishes 15 titles/year. 50% of books from first-time authors. 90% from unagented writers. Pays 7-12% royalty on wholesale price.** Publishes book 2 years after acceptance of ms. Responds in 3 months to queries. Book catalog available online.

- Expanding children's/juvenile nonfiction titles.

O➛ "We are expanding our Roadside Geology, Geology Underfoot, and Roadside History series (done on a state-by-state basis). We are interested in well-written regional field guides—plants and flowers—and readable history and natural history."

Nonfiction Subjects include animals, history, Western, nature, environment, regional, science, Earth science. Query with SASE. Submit outline, sample chapters. Reviews artwork/photos.
Recent Title(s) *You Can Be a Nature Detective*, by Peggy Kochanoff; *California Rocks*, by Katherine J. Baylor; *Roadside Geology of Minnesota*, by Richard W. Ojakangas.
Tips "Find out what kind of books a publisher is interested in and tailor your writing to them; research markets and target your audience. Research other books on the same subjects. Make yours different. Don't present your manuscript to a publisher—sell it. Give the information needed to make a decision on a title. Please learn what we publish before sending your proposal. We are a "niche" publisher."

NAVAL INSTITUTE PRESS

US Naval Institute 291 Wood Rd., Annapolis MD 21402-5034. (410)268-6110. Fax: (410)295-1084. E-mail: cparkinson@usni.org; books@usni.org. Website: www.usni.org. **Contact:** Tom Cutler, senior acquisitions editor. Estab. 1873. **Publishes 80-90 titles/year. 50% of books from first-time authors. 90% from unagented writers.** Guidelines available online.

O➛ "The Naval Institute Press publishes trade and scholarly nonfiction. We are interested in national and international security, naval, military, military jointness, intelligence, and special warfare, both current and historical."

Nonfiction Submit proposal package with outline, author bio, TOC, description/synopsis, sample chapter(s), page/word count, number of illustrations, ms completion date, intended market; or submit complete ms. Send SASE with sufficient postage for return of ms. Send by postal mail only. No e-mail submissions, please.

⊘ NAVPRESS, (THE PUBLISHING MINISTRY OF THE NAVIGATORS)

P.O. Box 35001, Colorado Springs CO 80935. Fax: (719)260-7223. E-mail: customerservice@navpress.com. Website: www.navpress.com. Estab. 1975. Publishes hardcover, trade paperback, direct and mass market paperback originals and reprints; electronic books and bible studies. **Pays royalty. Pays low or no advances.** Book catalog available free.
Nonfiction Subjects include child guidance, parenting, sociology, spirituality and contemporary culture, Christian living, marriage.
Recent Title(s) *Trusting in His Goodness, Faithbook of Jesus, Dwelling In His Presence, Becoming a Woman of Simplicity, The Kingdom LIfe, Learning to Soar, Live Like You Mean It.*

NEAL-SCHUMAN PUBLISHERS, INC.

100 William St., Suite 2004, New York NY 10038-4512. (212)925-8650. Fax: (212)219-8916. Website: www.neal-schuman.com. **Contact:** Charles Harman, V.P./ director of publishing. Estab. 1976. Publishes trade paperback originals. **Publishes 36 titles/year. 150 queries. 80% of books from first-time authors. 100% from unagented writers. Pays 10-15% royalty on wholesale price. Pays infrequent advance.** Publishes book 5 months after acceptance of ms. Accepts simultaneous submissions. Responds in 1 month to queries, proposals, & mss. Book catalog free. Mss guidelines not available.

O➛ "Neal-Schuman publishes books about library management, archival science, records management, digital curation, information literary, the Internet and information technology. Especially submitting proposals for undergraduate information studies, archival science, records management, and knowledge management textbooks."

Nonfiction Subjects include computers, electronics, education, software, Internet guides, library and information science, archival studies, records management. Submit proposal package, outline, 1 sample chapter. Reviews artwork. Send photocopies.
Tips "Our audience are professional librarians, archivists, and records managers."

NEW AMERICAN LIBRARY

Penguin Putnam, Inc. 375 Hudson St., New York NY 10014. (212)366-2000. Fax: (212)366-2889. Website: www.penguinputnam.com. Estab. 1948. Publishes mass market and trade paperback originals and reprints. **Pays negotiable royalty. Pays negotiable advance.** Book catalog for SASE.
Imprints Onyx; ROC; Signet; Signet Classic; NAL trade paperback; Signet Eclipse.

NAL publishes commercial fiction and nonfiction for the popular audience.

Nonfiction Subjects include animals, child guidance, ethnic, health, medicine, military, war, psychology, sports, movie tie-in. Agented submissions only.
Fiction Subjects include erotica, ethnic, fantasy, historical, horror, mainstream, contemporary, mystery, romance, science fiction, suspense, western, chicklit. All kinds of commercial fiction. Query with SASE. Agented submissions only. State type of book and past publishing projects.
Recent Title(s) *The Vitamin D Solution: A 3-Step Strategy to Cure Our Most Common Health Problem*, by Michael F. Holick, Ph.D., M.D; *How to Be Famous*, by Alison Bond; *Secret Commandos*, by John Plaster; *Notes From the Underbelly*, by Risa Green.

NEW FORUMS PRESS

New Forums P.O. Box 876, Stillwater OK 74076. (405)372-6158. Fax: (405)377-2237. E-mail: contact@newforums.com. Website: www.newforums.com. **Contact:** Doug Dollar, president (interests: higher education, Oklahoma-Regional). Hardcover & trade paperback originals. **60%% of books from first-time authors. 100%% from unagented writers.** Use Author Guidelines online or call (800)606-3766 with any questions.

"New Forums Press is an independent publisher offering works devoted to various aspects of professional development in higher education, home and office aides, and various titles of a regional interest. We welcome suggestions for thematic series of books and thematic issues of our academic journals—addressing a single issue, problem, or theory."

Nonfiction Subjects include business, finance, history, literature, money, music, politics, regional, sociology, young adult. "We are actively seeking new authors — send for review copies and author guidelines, and visit our website." Manuscripts should be submitted as a Microsoft Word document, or a similar standard word processor document (saved in RTF rich text), as an attachment to an e-mail sent to submissions@newforums.com. Otherwise, submit your manuscript on 8½ × 11 inch white bond paper (one original). The name and complete address, telephone, fax number, and e-mail address of each author should appear on a separate cover page, so it can be removed for the blind review process.
Recent Title(s) *It Works For Me as a Scholar-Teacher: Shared Tips for the Classroom*, by Hal Blythe & Charlie Sweet; *Dollars & Sense: A Guide to Financial Security*, by Sherry Raines & William Austin; *Stillwater: A Cradle of Oklahoma History*, by D. Earl Newsom.

NEW HARBINGER PUBLICATIONS

5674 Shattuck Ave., Oakland CA 94609. (510)652-0215. Fax: (510)652-5472. E-mail: proposals@newharbinger.com. Website: www.newharbinger.com. **Contact:** Catharine Sutker, acquisitions director. Estab. 1973. **Publishes 55 titles/year. 1,000 queries received/year. 300 mss received/year. 60% of books from first-time authors. 75% from unagented writers.** Publishes book 1 year after acceptance of ms. Accepts simultaneous submissions. Responds in 2 weeks to queries. Responds in 1 month to proposals. Responds in 2 months to manuscripts. Book catalog available free. Guidelines available online.

"We look for psychology and health self-help books that teach readers how to master essential life skills. Mental health professionals who want simple, clear explanations or important psychological techniques and health issues also read our books. Thus, our books must be simple ane easy to understand but also complete and authoritative. Most of our authors are therapists or other helping professionals."

Nonfiction Subjects include health, medicine, psychology, women's issues, women's studies, psycho spirituality, anger management, anxiety, coping, mindfulness skills. Authors need to be qualified psychotherapists or health practitioners to publish with us. Submit proposal package, outline, 2 sample chapters, TOC, competing titles, and a compelling, supported reason why the book is unique.
Recent Title(s) *The Gift of ADHD*, by Lara Honos-Webb, PhD; *Get Out of Your Mind and Into Your Life*, by Steven C. Hayes, PhD; *Five Good Minutes*, by Jeffrey Brantley, MD, and Wendy Millstine.

Tips "Audience includes psychotherapists and lay readers wanting step-by-step strategies to solve specific problems. Our definition of a self-help psychology or health book is one that teaches essential life skills. The primary goal is to train the reader so that, after reading the book, he or she can deal more effectively with health and/or psychological challenges."

NEW HOPE PUBLISHERS

Woman's Missionary Union P.O. Box 12065, Birmingham AL 35202-2065. (205)991-4950. Fax: (205)991-4015. E-mail: new_hope@wmu.org. Website: www.newhopepublishers.com. **Contact:** Acquisitions Editor. **Publishes 20-28 titles/year. several hundred queries received/year. 25% of books from first-time authors. small% from unagented writers.** Publishes book 2 years after acceptance of ms. Book catalog for 9 × 12 envelope and 3 first-class stamps.

- "Our vision is to challenge believers to understand and be radically involved in the missions of God. This market does not accept unsolicited mss."

Nonfiction "We publish books dealing with all facets of Christian life for women and families, including health, discipleship, missions, ministry, Bible studies, spiritual development, parenting, and marriage. We currently do not accept adult fiction or children's picture books. We are particularly interested in niche categories and books on lifestyle development and change." Subjects include child guidance, from Christian perspective, education, Christian church, health, medicine, Christian, multicultural, religion, spiritual development, Bible study, life situations from Christian perspective, ministry, women's issues, women's studies, Christian, church leadership. Prefers a query and prospectus.

Recent Title(s) *Life Unhindered,* by Jennifer Kennedy Dean; *Crash Course*, by Dan Darling; *Embraced by the Father*, by Susanne Scheppmann

NEWMARKET PRESS

18 E. 48th St., 15th Floor, New York NY 10017. (212)832-3575. Fax: (212)832-3629. E-mail: mailbox@newmarketpress.com. Website: www.newmarketpress.com. **Contact:** Editorial Department. Publishes hardcover and trade paperback originals and reprints. **Publishes 20-30 titles/year. Pays royalty. Pays varied advance.** Accepts simultaneous submissions. Ms guidelines for #10 SASE or online.

- Currently emphasizing movie tie-in/companion books, health, psychology, child care & parenting, film & performing arts, health & nutrition, biography, history, business & personal finance, and popular self-help & reference. De-emphasizing fiction.

Nonfiction Subjects include child guidance, cooking, foods, nutrition, health, medicine, history, psychology, business/personal finance. Submit proposal package, complete ms, or 1-3 sample chapters, TOC, marketing info, author credentials, SASE.

Recent Title(s) *Condi*, by Antonia Felix; *Hotel Rwanda: Bringing the True Story of an African Hero to Film*, edited by Terry George; *In Good Company*, by Paul Weitz.

Tips Newmarket's list includes such popular and acclaimed books as the 2 million-copy bestselling *What's Happening To My Body?* series of puberty education books for boys and girls by Lynda Madaras; Suze Orman's *You've Earned It, Don't Lose It*; Sam Wyly's business memoir *1,000 Dollars and an Idea*; biographies of Condoleezza Rice and Buster Keaton; Daphne Oz's *The Dorm Room Diet*; Dr Georgia Witkin's *The Female Stress Syndrome and The Male Stress Syndrome*; Gene Hackman & Daniel Lenihan's first novel *Wake of the Perdido Star;* Stuart Avery Gold's international bestseller *Ping: A Frog in Search of a New Pond*; and *Shalom, Friend: The Life and Legacy Of Yitzhak Rabin*, winner of the 1996 National Jewish Book Award in nonfiction.

NEW SEEDS BOOKS

Imprint of Shambhala Publications 300 Massachusetts Ave., Boston MA 02115. Fax: (617)236-1563. E-mail: editors@shambala.com. Website: www.newseedsbooks.com. **Contact:** David O'Neal, senior editor. Estab. 2005. Publishes hardcover and trade paperback originals, as well as hardcover and trade paperback reprints. **Publishes 90-100 (Shambhala); 10 (New Seeds Books) titles/year. Pays 7.5-15% royalty on retail price.** Publishes book 1 year after acceptance of ms. Accepts simultaneous submissions. Responds in 3 months to queries, proposals and manuscripts. Guidelines available via e-mail.

Nonfiction Subjects include religion, spirituality, contemplative Christianity. New Seeds publishes works exemplifying the wisdom of Christianity, with a special emphasis on the traditions of contemplation and prayer. Query with SASE. Submit proposal package, outline, bio, 2 sample chapters. Submit complete ms. Reviews artwork/photos. Send photocopies.

Recent Title(s) *Where God Happens: Discovering Christ in One Another*, by Rowan Williams; *The Unknown Sayings of Jesus*, by Marvin Meyer; *Angelic Mistakes*, by Roger Lipsey.

NEW WORLD LIBRARY

14 Pamaron Way, Novato CA 94949. (415)884-2100. Fax: (415)884-2199. Website: www.newworldlibrary.com. **Contact:** Jonathan Wichmann, submissions editor. Estab. 1979. Publishes hardcover and trade paperback originals and reprints. **Publishes 35-40 titles/year. 10% of books from first-time authors. 40% from unagented writers.** Accepts simultaneous submissions. Responds in 3 months to queries. Book catalog available free. Guidelines available online.

Imprints H.J. Kramer.

- Prefers e-mail submissions. No longer accepting unsolicited children's mss.

O‑‑ "NWL is dedicated to publishing books that inspire and challenge us to improve the quality of our lives and our world."

Nonfiction Submit outline, bio, 2-3 sample chapters, SASE. Reviews artwork/photos. Send photocopies.

Recent Title(s) *Secrets of Great Marriages*, by Charlie and Linda Bloom; *Zen Wrapped in Karma Dipped in Chocolate*, by Brad Warner; *The Secret History of Dreaming*, by Robert Moss.

NORTH LIGHT BOOKS

Imprint of F + W Media, Inc. 4700 E. Galbraith Rd., Cincinnati OH 45236. Website: www.fwmedia.com. Publishes hardcover and trade paperback how-to books. **Publishes 70-75 titles/year. Pays 10% royalty on net receipts and $4,000 advance.** Accepts simultaneous submissions. Responds in 2 months to queries. Book catalog for 9 × 12 envelope and 6 first-class stamps.

O‑‑ "North Light Books publishes art and craft books, including watercolor, drawing, mixed media and decorative painting, knitting, jewelry making, sewing, and needle arts that emphasize illustrated how-to art instruction. Currently emphasizing drawing including traditional, fantasy art, and Japanese-style comics as well as creativity and inspiration."

Nonfiction Art, how-to. Subjects include hobbies, watercolor, realistic drawing, creativity, decorative painting, comics drawing, paper arts, knitting, collage and other craft instruction books. Interested in books on acrylic painting, basic drawing, pen and ink, colored pencil, decorative painting, and beading. Query with SASE. Submit outline.

Recent Title(s) *Rethinking Acrylic*, by Pat Brady; *Dreamscapes*, by Stephanie Pui-Mun Law; *Knitted Wire Jewelry*, by Samantha Lopez; *Creative Awareness*, by Sheri Gaynor.

NURSESBOOKS.ORG

American Nurses Association 8515 Georgia Ave., Suite 400, Silver Spring MD 20901-3492. (301)628-5212. Fax: (301)628-5003. E-mail: camille.walker@ana.org. Website: www.nursesbooks.org. **Contact:** Rosanne Roe, publisher; Eric Wurzbacher, editor/project manager; Camille Walker, business operations coordinator/project manager. Publishes professional paperback originals and reprints. **Publishes 10 titles/year. 50 queries received/year. 8-10 mss received/year. 75% of books from first-time authors. 100% from unagented writers.** Publishes book 4 months after acceptance of ms. Responds in 3 months to proposals and manuscripts. Book catalog available online. Guidelines available free.

O‑‑ "Nursebooks.org publishes books designed to help professional nurses in their work and careers. Through the publishing program, Nursebooks.org provides nurses in all practice settings with publications that address cutting-edge issues and form a basis for debate and exploration of this century's most critical health care trends."

Nonfiction Subjects include advanced practice, computers, continuing education, ethics, health care policy, nursing administration, psychiatric and mental health, quality, nursing history, workplace issues, key clinical topics, such as geriatrics, pain management, public health, spirituality and home health. Submit outline, 1 sample chapter, CV, list of 3 reviewers and paragraph on audience and how to reach them. Reviews artwork/photos. Send photocopies.

Recent Title(s) *Nursing and Health Care Ethics: A Legacy and A Vision; Genetics and Ethics in Health Care: New Questions in the Age of Genomic Health; Teaching IOM: Implications of the IOM Reports for Nursing Education*, 2nd Edition.

OAK KNOLL PRESS

310 Delaware St., New Castle DE 19720. (302)328-7232. Fax: (302)328-7274. E-mail: Laura@oakknoll.com. Website: www.oakknoll.com. **Contact:** Laura R. Williams, publishing director. Estab. 1976. Publishes hardcover and trade paperback originals and reprints. **Publishes 40 titles/year. 250 queries received/year. 100 mss received/year. 50% of books from first-time authors. 100% from unagented writers.** Publishes book 12 months after acceptance of ms. Accepts simultaneous submissions. Guidelines available online.

O‑‑ "Oak Knoll specializes in books about books and manuals on the book arts-preserving the art and lore of the printed word."

Nonfiction Reviews artwork/photos. Send photocopies.
Recent Title(s) *ABC for Book Collectors, 8th Ed.*, by John Carter and Nicolas Barker; *Early Type Specimens*, by John Lane; *The Great Libraries*, by Konstantinos Staikos.

OPEN COURT PUBLISHING CO.

70 E. Lake Street, Ste. 300, Chicago IL 60601. Website: www.opencourtbooks.com. Estab. 1887. Publishes hardcover and trade paperback originals. **Publishes 20 titles/year. Pays 5-15% royalty on wholesale price.** Publishes book 2 years after acceptance of ms. Book catalog available online. Guidelines available online.
Nonfiction Subjects include philosophy, Asian thought, religious studies and popular culture. Query with SASE. Submit proposal package, outline, 1 sample chapter, TOC, author's cover letter, intended audience.
Recent Title(s) *Stephen Colbert and Philosophy*, edited by Aaron Allen Schiller (philosophy); *The Philosophy of Richard Rorty*, edited by Auxier and Hahn (philosophy)
Tips "Audience consists of philosophers and intelligent general readers."

OPEN ROAD PUBLISHING

P.O. Box 284, Cold Spring Harbor NY 11724. (631)692-7172. E-mail: jopenroad@aol.com. Website: openroadguides.com. Estab. 1993. Publishes trade paperback originals. **Publishes 20-22 titles/year. 200 queries received/year. 75 mss received/year. 30% of books from first-time authors. 98% from unagented writers. Pays 5-6% royalty on retail price. Pays $1,000-3,500 advance.** Publishes book 3 months after acceptance of ms. Accepts simultaneous submissions. Responds in 1 month to queries. Responds in 2 months to proposals. Book catalog online. Ms guidelines sent if proposal is accepted.

O━ "Open Road publishes travel guides and has expanded into other areas with its new imprint, Cold Spring Press, particularly sports/fitness, topical, biographies, history, fantasy."

Nonfiction Subjects include travel guides and travelogues. Query with SASE.
Recent Title(s) *Tahiti & French Polynesia Guide*, by Jan Prince; *Paris With Kids*, by Valerie Gwinner; *Open Road's Best of Ireland*, by Dan Quillen; *Quest For the Kasbah*, by Richard Bangs.

ORANGE FRAZER PRESS, INC.

P.O. Box 214, 37½ W. Main St., Wilmington OH 45177. (937)382-3196. Fax: (937)383-3159. Website: www.orangefrazer.com. **Contact:** John Baskin, editor (sports/history). Publishes hardcover and trade paperback originals. **Publishes 25 titles/year. 50 queries received/year. 35 mss received/year. 80% of books from first-time authors. 100% from unagented writers. Pays 10% royalty on wholesale price. 50% of our books are author-subsidy published/year if the author can afford it. Pays advance.** Publishes book 10 months after acceptance of ms. Accepts simultaneous submissions. Responds in 6 months to proposals. Book catalog and guidelines available free.
Imprints Marcy Hawley, Publisher.

O━ "Orange Frazer Press accepts nonfiction only; corporate histories; town celebrations; anniversary books."

Nonfiction Accepts Ohio nonfiction only. Subjects include audio, anthropology, archaeology, art, architecture, business, economics, cooking, foods, nutrition, education, history, nature, environment, photography, regional, sports, travel. Sports and personalities are our main focus. Submit proposal package, outline, 3 sample chapters, and marketing plan. Reviews artwork/photos. Send photocopies.
Recent Title(s) *1968: The Year That Saved Ohio State Football*, by David Hyde (sports); *Catch Every Ball; How to Handle Life's Pitches*, by Johnny Bench (sports).
Tips "For our commercial titles we focus mainly on sports and biographies. Our readers are interested in sports or curious about famous persons/personalities."

OUR SUNDAY VISITOR PUBLISHING

200 Noll Plaza, Huntington IN 46750-4303. (260)356-8400. Fax: (260)359-6453. E-mail: booksed@osv.com. Website: www.osv.com. **Contact:** Acquisitions Editor. Estab. 1912. Publishes paperback and hardbound originals. **Publishes 40-50 titles/year. 8% of books from first-time authors. 100% from unagented writers. Pays variable royalty on net receipts. Pays $2,000 average advance.** Publishes book 1-2 years after acceptance of ms. Accepts simultaneous submissions. Responds in 3 months to queries. Book catalog for 9 × 12 envelope and first-class stamps. Ms guidelines for #10 SASE or online.

O━ "We are a Catholic publishing company seeking to educate and deepen our readers in their faith. Currently emphasizing devotional, inspirational, catholic identity, apologetics, and catechetics."

Nonfiction Catholic viewpoints on family, prayer, and devotional books, and Catholic heritage books. Prefers to see well-developed proposals as first submission with annotated outline and definition of intended market. Reviews artwork/photos.
Recent Title(s) *Doers of the Word*, by Archibishop Timothy Dolan; *The Heavens Proclaim: Astronomy and the Vatican*, edited by Guy Consolmagno, S.J.
Tips "Solid devotional books that are not first person, or lives of the saints and catechetical books have the best chance of selling to our firm. Make it solidly Catholic, unique, without pious platitudes."

THE OVERLOOK PRESS

141 Wooster St., New York NY 10012. (212)673-2210. Fax: (212)673-2296. Website: www.overlookpress.com. Estab. 1971. Publishes hardcover and trade paperback originals and hardcover reprints. **Publishes 100 titles/year.** Book catalog available free.

"Overlook Press publishes fiction, children's books, and nonfiction."

Nonfiction Subjects include art, architecture, film, cinema, stage, history, regional, New York State, current events, design, health/fitness, how-to, lifestyle, martial arts. The Overlook Press is an independent general-interest publisher. The publishing program consists of nearly 100 new books per year, evenly divided between hardcovers and trade paperbacks. The list is eclectic, but areas of strength include interesting fiction, history, biography, drama, and design. Agented submissions only.
Fiction Subjects include literary, some commercial, foreign literature in translation. Agented submissions only.
Recent Title(s) *Dragon's Eye*, by Andy Oakes; *The Brontes*, by Juliet Barker; *Triomf*, translated from the Afrikaans by Leon de Kock.

P & R PUBLISHING CO.

P.O. Box 817, Phillipsburg NJ 08865. Fax: (908)859-2390. Website: www.prpbooks.com. Estab. 1930. Publishes hardcover originals and trade paperback originals and reprints. **Publishes 40 titles/year. 300 queries received/year. 100 mss received/year. 5% of books from first-time authors. 95% from unagented writers. Pays 10-14% royalty on wholesale price.** Accepts simultaneous submissions. Responds in 3 months to proposals. Guidelines available online.
Nonfiction Subjects include history, religion, spirituality, translation. Only accepts electronic submission with completion of online Author Guidelines. Hard copy mss will not be returned.
Recent Title(s) *Tying the Knot Tighter: Because Marriage Lasts a Lifetime*, by Martha Peace and John Crotts (marriage); *The Law Is Not of Faith: Essays on Works and Grace in the Mosaic Covenant*, edited by Bryan D. Estelle, J. V. Fesko, and David Van Drunen (theology/doctrine); *Where Is God in All of This? Finding God's Purpose in Our Suffering*, by Deborah Howard (Christian living); *The Betrayal: A Novel on John Calvin*, by Douglas Bond (historical fiction).
Tips "Our audience is evangelical Christians and seekers. All of our publications are consistent with Biblical teaching, as summarized in the Westminster Standards."

PACIFIC PRESS PUBLISHING ASSOCIATION

Trade Book Division P.O. Box 5353, Nampa ID 83653-5353. (208)465-2500. Fax: (208)465-2531. E-mail: booksubmissions@pacificpress.com. Website: www.pacificpress.com. **Contact:** Scott Cady, acquisitions editor (children's stories, biography, Christian living, spiritual growth); David Jarnes, book editor (theology, doctrine, inspiration). Estab. 1874. Publishes hardcover and trade paperback originals and reprints. **Publishes 35 titles/year. 35% of books from first-time authors. 100% from unagented writers. Pays 8-16% royalty on wholesale price.** Publishes book up to 24 months after acceptance of ms. Responds in 3 months to queries. Guidelines available online.

"We publish books that fit Seventh-day Adventist beliefs only. All titles are Christian and religious. For guidance, see www.adventist.org/beliefs/index.html. Our books fit into the categories of this retail site: www.adventistbookcenter.com."

Nonfiction Subjects include child guidance, cooking, foods, nutrition, vegetarian only, health, history, nature, environment, philosophy, religion, spirituality, women's issues, family living, Christian lifestyle, Bible study, Christian doctrine, prophecy. Query with SASE or e-mail, or submit 3 sample chapters, cover letter with overview of book. Electronic submissions accepted. Reviews artwork/photos.
Fiction Subjects include religious. "Pacific Press rarely publishes fiction, but we're interested in developing a line of Seventh-day Adventist fiction in the future. Only proposals accepted; no full manuscripts."
Recent Title(s) *Grounds for Belief*, by Ed Dickerson (doctrine); *Chosen by Grace*, by Stuart Tyner (doctrine); *Peter: Fisher of Men*, by Noni Beth Gibbs (Biblical fiction); *Shepherd Warrior*, by Bradley Booth (children's).

Tips "Our primary audience is members of the Seventh-day Adventist denomination. Almost all are written by Seventh-day Adventists. Books that do well for us relate the Biblical message to practical human concerns and focus more on the experiential rather than theoretical aspects of Christianity. We are assigning more titles, using less unsolicited material—although we still publish manuscripts from freelance submissions and proposals."

PALADIN PRESS

7077 Winchester Circle, Boulder CO 80301. (303)443-7250. Fax: (303)442-8741. E-mail: editorial@paladin-press.com. Website: www.paladin-press.com. Estab. 1970. Publishes hardcover originals and paperback originals and reprints, videos. **Publishes 50 titles/year. 50% of books from first-time authors. 95% from unagented writers. We pay royalties in full and on time. Pays advance.** Publishes book 1 year after acceptance of ms. Accepts simultaneous submissions. Responds in 2 months to proposals. Book catalog available free.

Imprints Sycamore Island Books; Flying Machines Press; Outer Limits Press; Romance Book Classics.

O— "Paladin Press publishes the action library of nonfiction in military science, police science, weapons, combat, personal freedom, self-defense, survival."

Nonfiction Paladin Press primarily publishes original manuscripts on military science, weaponry, self-defense, personal privacy, financial freedom, espionage, police science, action careers, guerrilla warfare, and fieldcraft. Subjects include government, politics, military, war. If applicable, send sample photographs and line drawings with complete outline and sample chapters. To submit a book proposal to Paladin Press, send an outline or chapter description along with 1-2 sample chapters (or the entire ms) to the address below. If applicable, samples of illustrations or photographs are also useful. Do not send a computer disk at this point, and be sure keep a copy of everything you send us. We are not accepting mss as electronic submissions at this time. Please allow 2-6 weeks for a reply. If you would like your sample material returned, a SASE with proper postage is required. Editorial Department, Paladin Press Gunbarrel Tech Center,7077 Winchester Circle, Boulder, CO 80301, or e-mail us at: editorial@paladin-press.com. Query with SASE. Submitting a proposal for a video project is not much different than a book proposal. See guidelines online and send to: All materials related to video proposals should be addressed directly to: David Dubrow, Video Production Manager.

Recent Title(s) *Surviving Workplace Violence: What to Do Before a Violent Incident; What to Do When the Violence Explodes*, by Loren W. Christensen.

Tips "We need lucid, instructive material aimed at our market and accompanied by sharp, relevant illustrations and photos. As we are primarily a publisher of `how-to' books, a manuscript that has step-by-step instructions, written in a clear and concise manner (but not strictly outline form) is desirable. No fiction, first-person accounts, children's, religious, or joke books. We are also interested in serious, professional videos and video ideas (contact Michael Rigg)."

PARKWAY PUBLISHERS, INC.

Box 3678, Boone NC 28607. (828)265-3993. Fax: (828)265-3993. E-mail: editor@parkwaypublishers.com. Website: www.parkwaypublishers.com. **Contact:** Rao Aluri, president. Publishes hardcover and trade paperback originals. **Publishes 5-6 titles/year. 15-20 queries received/year. 20 mss received/year. 75% of books from first-time authors. 100% from unagented writers.** Publishes book 8 months after acceptance of ms.

O— "Parkway Publishers, Inc. is primarily interested in non-fiction manuscripts about western North Carolina in particular and North Carolina and Appalachia in general. We prefer manuscripts of 150 to 250 pages long - double-spaced, 8.5" × 11" pages. We would like to receive a hardcopy rather than an e-mail submission. We are interested in books about the history of region, biographies, and tourist-oriented books. Will consider fiction if it highlights the region."

Nonfiction Subjects include history, biography, tourism, and natural history. Query with SASE. Submit complete ms.

Recent Title(s) *The Picture Man*, by Julila Taylor Ebel; *A Picture of the Past: A Memoir*, by Taylor Reese; *Jack Tales & Mountain Yarns as Told by Orville Hicks*, by Julia Taylor Ebel.

PASSKEY PUBLICATIONS

P.O. Box 580465, Elk Grove CA 95758. (916)712-7446. Website: www.passkeypublications.com. **Contact:** Christine P. Silva, president. Trade paperback originals. **Publishes 15 titles/year. 375 queries/year; 120 mss/year 15% of books from first-time authors. 90% from unagented writers.** Publishes book 3-6 months after acceptance of ms. Accepts simultaneous submissions. Catalog and guidelines online at website www.pineapplepublications.com.

Imprints Pineapple Study Guides, PassKey EA Review

Nonfiction Subjects include business, economics, finance, money, real estate, accounting, taxation, study guides for professional examinations. "Books on taxation and accounting are generally updated every year to reflect tax law changes, and the turnaround on a ms must be less than 3 months for accounting and tax subject matter. Books generally remain in publication only 11 months and are generally published every year for updates." Submit complete ms. Reviews artwork/photos as part of ms package. Send electronic files on disk, via e-mail, or jump drive.
Fiction Subjects include occult, metaphysical. Submit completed ms.
Recent Title(s) *How to Start a Successful Home-based Freelance Bookkeeping & Tax Preparation Business; EA Exam Review Complete, IRS Enrolled Agent Exam Study Guide.*
Tips "Our audience is professional, technical & scholarly adults with above college or some college education. Authors with a professional designation, such as a CPA, EA, or Ph.D. will have a better chance at publication."

PAULIST PRESS

997 Macarthur Blvd., Mahwah NJ 07430. (201)825-7300. Fax: (201)825-8345. E-mail: info@paulistpress.com. Website: www.paulistpress.com. **Contact:** Lawrence Boadt, editorial director for all fields; Paul McMahon, man. ed. all fields. Estab. 1865. Publishes hardcover and electronic originals and electronic reprints. **Publishes 85 titles/year. 250/year 50% of books from first-time authors. 95% from unagented writers. Pays 6-8%/min, 12%/max royalty on wholesale price; $1,000-2,000 for outright purchase. Pays advance.** Publishes book 12-18 months after acceptance of ms. Accepts simultaneous submissions. Responds in 2 months to queries and proposals; 2-3 months on mss. Book catalog available free on request and online. Guidelines available online and by e-mail.

O→ "Paulist Press publishes "ecumenical theology, Roman Catholic studies, and books on scripture, liturgy, spirituality, church history, and philosophy, as well as works on faith and culture. Our publishing is oriented toward adult-level nonfiction. We do not publish poetry."

Nonfiction Subjects include religion. "It should deal with traditional Catholic spirituality, sacraments, church doctrine or practical aids for ministry and prayer, or be intended as a textbook in religion classes in college or high school. Children's books should have strong religious (not just spiritual) or moral content, or deal with learning to be Catholic." Submit proposal package, including: outline, 1 sample chapter; submit completed ms. Reviews artwork/photos. Writers should send photocopies.
Fiction Subjects include picture books (ages 2-5), chapter books (ages 8-12), Christian and Catholic themes. Submit resume, ms, SASE. Accepts unsolicited mss, but most of our titles have been commissioned.
Recent Title(s) *Ewe*, by Ryan Metlen; *Coming Down the Mountain*, by Thomas Hart, *The Catholic Prayer Bible, Ascend* by Eric Stoltz and Vince Tomkovicz; *Spiritual Masters for All Seasons,* by Michael Ford; *The Life of St. Paul,* by Lawrence Boadt.
Tips "Our typical reader is probably Roman Catholic and wants the content to be educational about Catholic thought and practice, or else the reader is a spiritual seeker who looks for discovery of God and spiritual values which churches offer but without the church connection."

PFLAUM PUBLISHING GROUP

6162 N. 114th, Milwaukee WI 53225. (414)353-5528. Fax: (414)353-5529. E-mail: kcannizzo@pflaum.com. **Contact:** Karen A. Cannizzo, editorial director. **Publishes 20 titles/year. Payment may be outright purchase, royalty, or down payment plus royalty.** Book catalog and ms guidelines free.

O→ "Pflaum Publishing Group, a division of Peter Li, Inc., serves the specialized market of religious education, primarily Roman Catholic. We provide high quality, theologically sound, practical, and affordable resources that assist religious educators of and ministers to children from preschool through senior high school."

Nonfiction Query with SASE.
Recent Title(s) *Absolutely Advent; Totally Lent.*

PLANNERS PRESS

Imprint of the American Planning Association 122 S. Michigan Ave., Ste. 1600, Chicago IL 60603. (312)431-9100. Fax: (312)431-9985. E-mail: plannerspress@planning.org. Website: www.planning.org/plannerspress/index.htm. **Contact:** Timothy Mennel, Ph.D. (planning practice, urban issues, land use, transportation). Estab. 1970. Publishes hardcover, electronic, and trade paperback originals; and trade paperback and electronic reprints. **Publishes 12 titles/year. 50 queries received/year. 35 mss received/year. 25% of books from first-time authors. 100% from unagented writers. Pays 10-15% royalty on wholesale price. Pays advance.** Publishes book 15 months after acceptance of ms. Accepts simultaneous submissions. Responds in 1 month to queries. Responds in 2 months to proposals and manuscripts. Book catalog online at website www.planningbooks.com. Guidelines available by e-mail at plannerspress@planning.org.

"Our books often have a narrow audience of city planners and frequently focus on the tools of city planning."

Nonfiction Subjects include agriculture, business, economics, community, contemporary culture, economics, environment, finance, government, politics, history, horticulture, law, money, finance, nature, environment, politics, real estate, science, social sciences, sociology, transportation, world affairs. Submit proposal package, including: outline, 1 sample chapter and c.v. Submit completed ms. Reviews artwork/photos. Send photocopies.

Fiction We do not publish fiction.

Recent Title(s) *Foreclosing the Dream,* by William H. Lucy; *Delta Urbanism New Orleans,* by Richard Campanella; *The High Cost of Free Parking,* by Donald Shoup; *Making Places Special: The Citizen's Guide to Planning,* by Gene Bunnell.

Tips "Our audience is professional planners but also anyone interested in community development, urban affairs, sustainability, and related fields."

POPULAR WOODWORKING BOOKS

Imprint of F+W Media, Inc. 4700 Galbraith Rd., Cincinnati OH 45236. (513)531-2690. Website: popularwoodworking.com/booksandmore/. **Contact:** David Thiel, executive editor. Publishes trade paperback and hardcover originals and reprints. **Publishes 6-8 titles/year. 30 queries received/ year. 10 mss received/year. 20% of books from first-time authors. 95% from unagented writers.** Publishes book 1 year after acceptance of ms. Accepts simultaneous submissions. Responds in 1 month to queries.

"Popular Woodworking Books is one of the largest publishers of woodworking books in the world. From perfecting a furniture design to putting on the final coat of finish, our books provide step-by-step instructions and trusted advice from the pros that make them valuable tools for both beginning and advanced woodworkers. Currently emphasizing woodworking jigs and fixtures, furniture and cabinet projects, smaller finely crafted boxes, all styles of furniture. De-emphasizing woodturning, woodcarving, scroll saw projects."

Nonfiction "We publish heavily illustrated how-to woodworking books that show, rather than tell, our readers how to accomplish their woodworking goals." Subjects include hobbies, woodworking/wood crafts. Query with SASE, or electronic query. Proposal package should include an outline and digital photos.

Recent Title(s) *Puzzle Boxes,* by Jeff Vollmer; *Grove Park Inn, Arts & Crafts Furniture,* by Bruce E. Johnson; *The Perfect Edge,* by Ron Hock.

Tips "Our books are for beginning to advanced woodworking enthusiasts."

PPI (PROFESSIONAL PUBLICATIONS, INC.)

1250 Fifth Ave., Belmont CA 94002-3863. (650)593-9119. Fax: (650)592-4519. E-mail: acquisitions@ppi2pass.com. Website: www.ppi2pass.com. Estab. 1975. Publishes hardcover, paperback, and electronic products, CD-ROMs and DVDs. **Publishes 10 titles/year. 5% of books from first-time authors. 100% from unagented writers.** Publishes book 4-18 months after acceptance of ms. Accepts simultaneous submissions. Responds in 1 month to queries. Book catalog and ms guidelines free.

"PPI publishes professional, reference, and licensing preparation materials. PPI wants submissions from both professionals practicing in the field and from experienced instructors. Currently emphasizing engineering, interior design, architecture, landscape architecture and LEED exam review."

Nonfiction Subjects include architecture, science, landscape architecture, engineering mathematics, engineering, surveying, interior design, greenbuilding, sustainable development, and other professional licensure subjects. Especially needs review and reference books for all professional licensing examinations. Please submit ms and proposal outlining market potential, etc. Proposal template available upon request. Reviews artwork/photos.

Recent Title(s) *LEED Prep GA: What You Really Need to Know to Pass the Green Associate Exam; Core Engineering Concepts for Students and Professional.*

Tips "We specialize in books for those people who want to become licensed and/or accredited professionals: engineers, architects, surveyors, interior designers, LEED APs, etc. Exam Prep Lines generally include online and print products such as review manuals, practice problems, sample exams, E-Learning Modules, IPhone Apps, and more. Demonstrating your understanding of the market, competition, appropriate delivery methods, and marketing ideas will help sell us on your proposal."

PRUETT PUBLISHING

P.O. Box 2140, Boulder CO 80306. (303)449-4919. Fax: (303)443-9019. Website: www.pruettpublishing.com. **Contact:** Jim Pruett, publisher. Estab. 1959. Publishes hardcover and trade paperback originals, trade paperback reprints. **75-80 mss received/year. 90%% of books from first-time authors. 90%% from unagented writers. Pays $1,000-1,500 advance.** Publishes book 12-18 months after acceptance of ms. Accepts simultaneous submissions. Responds in 1 month to queries. Responds in 3 months to proposals and manuscripts.

- "We are focused on the mountain West. Our trade books cover topics that range from fly fishing to hiking and biking, history, nature, and the environment. We also publish textbooks for grade-school students about the history of Colorado."

Nonfiction Subjects include alternative, Americana, education, history, nature, environment, sports, travel. Query with SASE. Submit outline, 2 sample chapters. Reviews artwork/photos. Send photocopies.
Recent Title(s) *Hike Around Ft. Collins*, by Melody Edwards (hiking); *Telluride Trails*, by Don Scarmuzzi; *OBIT*, by Jim Sheeler (obituaries); *Discover Colorado, Its People, Places, and Times*, (social studies textbook for third and fourth graders) by Matthew Downey and Ty Bliss; *Preparation for Childbirth*, by Donna and Roger Ewy.
Tips "We focus on outdoor recreationalists—hikers, fly-fishers, travelers. There has been a movement away from large publisher's mass market books toward small publisher's regional interest books, and in turn distributors and retail outlets are more interested in small publishers. Authors don't need to have a big name to have a good publisher. Look for similar books that you feel are well-produced—consider design, editing, overall quality, and contact those publishers. Get to know several publishers, and find the one that feels right—trust your instincts."

PRUFROCK PRESS, INC.

5926 Balcones Dr., Ste. 220, Austin TX 78731. (512)300-2220. Fax: (512)300-2221. E-mail: info@prufrock.com. Website: www.prufrock.com. **Contact:** Lacy Elwood, Jennifer Robins, Lacy Compton. Publishes trade paperback originals and reprints. Book catalog and ms guidelines free.

- "Prufrock Press publishes exciting, innovative and current resources supporting the education of gifted and talented learners."

Nonfiction Subjects include child guidance, education. We publish for the education market. Our readers are typically teachers or parents of gifted and talented children. Our product line is built around professional development books for teachers and activity books for gifted children. Our products support innovative ways of making learning more fun and exciting for gifted and talented children. Submit book prospectus (download form on website).
Recent Title(s) *Take Control of Asperger's Syndrome*, by Janet Price and Jennifer Engel Fisher; *Science Sleuths*, by Howard Schindler and Dennis Mucenski; *Free College resource book*, by Doug Hewitt and Robin Hewitt.
Tips "We are looking for practical, classroom-ready materials that encourage children to creatively learn and think."

PURDUE UNIVERSITY PRESS

Stewart Center 370, 504 West State St., West Lafayette IN 47907-2058. (765)494-2038. E-mail: pupress@purdue.edu. Website: www.thepress.purdue.edu. **Contact:** Acquisitions Editor. Estab. 1960. Publishes hardcover and trade paperback originals and trade paperback reprints. **Publishes 20-25 titles/year.** Book catalog and ms guidelines for 9 × 12 SASE.
Imprints PuP Books.

- "We look for books that look at the world as a whole and offer new thoughts and insights into the standard debate. Currently emphasizing technology, human-animal issues, business. De-emphasizing literary studies."

Nonfiction "We publish work of quality scholarship and titles with regional (Midwest) flair. Especially interested in innovative contributions to the social sciences and humanities that break new barriers and provide unique views on current topics. Expanding into veterinary medicine, technology, and business topics." Subjects include agriculture, Americana, business,government, politics, health, history, language, literary criticism, philosophy, regional, science, social sciences, sociology. Always looking for new authors who show creativity and thoroughness of research. Print and electronic projects accepted. Query before submitting.
Recent Title(s) *Blowing the Whistle on Genocide*, by Rafael Medoff; *New York's Poop Scoop Law*, by Michael Brandow; *What's Buggin' You Now?* by Tom Turpin; *Words at War*, by David B. Sachsman, S. Kittrell Rushing, and Roy Morris Jr.

G.P. PUTNAM'S SONS HARDCOVER

Imprint of Penguin Group (USA), Inc., 375 Hudson, New York NY 10014. (212)366-2000. Fax: (212)366-2664. Website: www.penguinputnam.com. Publishes hardcover originals. **Pays variable royalties on retail price. Pays varies advance.** Accepts simultaneous submissions. Request book catalog through mail order department.

Nonfiction Subjects include animals, business, economics, child guidance, contemporary culture, cooking, foods, nutrition, health, medicine, military, war, nature, environment, religion, science, sports, travel, women's issues, women's studies, celebrity-related topics. Agented submissions only. *No unsolicited mss.*

Fiction Subjects include adventure, literary, mainstream, STET, mystery, suspense, women's. Agented submissions only. *No unsolicited mss.*

Recent Title(s) *A Voice for the Dead*, by James Starrs and Katherine Ramsland; *Prince of Fire*, by Daniel Silva.

QUEST BOOKS

Imprint of Theosophical Publishing House 306 W. Geneva Rd., P.O. Box 270, Wheaton IL 60187. E-mail: submissions@questbooks.net. Website: www.questbooks.net. **Contact:** Richard Smoley, editor. Estab. 1965. Publishes hardcover and trade paperback originals and reprints. **Publishes 10 titles/year. 150 ms; 350 queries received/year. 20% of books from first-time authors. 80% from unagented writers. Pays royalty on retail price. Pays varying advance.** Publishes book 12 months after acceptance of ms. Accepts simultaneous submissions. Responds in 2 months to queries, proposals, & mss. Book catalog available free. Guidelines available online at: www. questbooks.net/aboutquest.cfm#submission.

Imprints Quest Books.

- "Quest Books is the imprint of the Theosophical Publishing House, the publishing arm of the Theosophical Society in America. Since 1965, Quest books has sold millions of books by leading cultural thinkers on such increasingly popular subjects as transpersonal psychology, comparative religion, deep ecology, spiritual growth, the development of creativity, and alternative health practices."

Nonfiction Subjects include philosophy, psychology, religion, spirituality, New Age, astrology/psychic. Our speciality is high-quality spiritual nonfiction with a self-help aspect. Great writing is a must. We seldom publish `personal spiritual awakening' stories. No submissions accepted that do not fit the needs outlined above. No fiction, poetry, children's books, or any literature based on channeling or personal psychic impressions. Submit proposal package, including outline, 1 sample chapter. Prefer online submissions; attachments must be sent as a single file in Microsoft Word, Rich Text, or PDF formats. Reviews artwork/photos. Hard copies of mss. and artwork will not be returned. Reviews artwork/photos. Writers should send photocopies or transparencies, but note that none will be returned.

Recent Title(s) *The Cynical Idealist: A Spiritual Biography of John Lennon*, by Gary Tillery; *A New Science of the Paranormal* by Lawrence LeShan, Ph.D. *Politics and the Occult: The Left, The Right, and the Radically Unseen*, by Gary Lachman (religion & politics); *The Golden Thread: Ageless Wisdom of the Western Mystery Traditions*, by Joscelyn Godwin (religion/spirituality); *War and the Soul: Healing the Nation's Veterans From Post-traumatic Stress Disorder*, by Edward Tick (psychology).

Tips "Our audience includes readers interested in spirituality, particularly the world's mystical traditions. Read a few recent Quest titles and submission guidelines before submitting. Know our books and our company goals. Explain how your book or proposal relates to other Quest titles. Quest gives preference to writers with established reputations/successful publications. Please be advised that proposals or manuscripts WILL NOT BE ACCEPTED if they fall into any of the following categories: Works intended for or about children, teenagers, or adolescents; Fiction or literary works (novels, short stories, essays, or poetry); Autobiographical material (memoirs, personal experiences, or family stories; Works received through mediumship, trance, or channeling; Works related to UFOs or extraterrestrials; Works related to self-aggrandizement (e.g., "how to make a fortune") or "how to" books."

RADCLIFFE PUBLISHING LTD

18 Marcham Road, Abingdon OX14-1AA, United Kingdom. (44)(123)552-8820. Fax: (44)(123)552-8830. E-mail: contact.us@racliffemed.com. Website: www.radcliffe-oxford.com. **Contact:** Andrew Box, managing editor; Gillian Nineham, editorial director. Estab. 1987. **Publishes 90 or fewer titles/year. Pays royalty.** Guidelines available via e-mail.

- "Send proposal to Gillian Nineham. Unsolicited manuscripts, synopses and ideas welcome. We are not interested in non-medical or medical books aimed at lay people. Every proposal we receive is discussed at length in-house, and most are sent out for external review (usually by experts in the field who also fit the intended market profile). The reviewers' comments are passed back to you anonymously for your reference. Often reviewer feedback will elicit further development of the proposal."

Nonfiction Subjects include health, medicine, sociology, nursing, midwifery, health services management and policy. Submit proposal package, outline, resume, publishing history, bio.

Recent Title(s) *Integrated Contraceptive and Sexual Healthcare*, Sarah Bekart and Alison White (Health); *Counselling For Death and Dying*, Richard Bryant-Jeffries (Self-help).

Tips Receive book proposal guidelines by e-mail and study them.

RAVENHAWK™ BOOKS

The 6DOF Group 7739 Broadway Blvd., #95, Tucson AZ 85710. E-mail: ravenhawk6dof@yahoo.com. Website: www.ravenhawk.biz. Estab. 1998. Publishes hardcover and paperback originals. **Pays 45-60% royalty.** Publishes book 18 months after acceptance of ms. Responds in weeks to queries. Responds in months to manuscripts. Book catalog available online.

Fiction Subjects include fantasy, space fantasy, sword and sorcery, horror, dark fantasy, futuristic, psychological, supernatural, humor, literary, mainstream, contemporary, mystery, amateur sleuth, cozy, police procedural, private eye/hardboiled, religious, religious mystery/suspense, religious thriller, romance, contemporary, romantic suspense, science fiction, hard science fiction/technological, soft/sociological, short story collections, young adult, adventure, easy-to-read, fantasy/science fiction fiction, horror, mystery/suspense, problem novels, series. Query by invitation only.

RAVEN TREE PRESS

A Division of Delta Publishing Company 1400 Miller Pkwy., McHenry IL 60050. (800)323-8270. Fax: (800)909-9901. E-mail: raven@raventreepress.com. Website: www.raventreepress.com. **Contact:** Check website for most current submission guidelines (children's picture books). Estab. 2000. Publishes hardcover and trade paperback originals. **Publishes 10 titles/year. 1,500 mss received/year. 75% of books from first-time authors. 90% from unagented writers. Pays royalty. Pays variable advance.** Publishes book 2 years after acceptance of ms. Accepts simultaneous submissions. Responds in 2 months to manuscripts. Book catalog available online. Guidelines available online.

Nonfiction "Submission guidelines available online. Do not query or send mss without first checking submission guidelines on our website for most current information."

⊘ RED HEN PRESS

P.O. Box 3537, Granada Hills CA 91394. (818)831-0649. Fax: (818)831-6659. E-mail: redhenpressbooks.com. Website: www.redhen.org. **Contact:** Mark E. Cull, publisher/editor (fiction). Estab. 1993. Publishes trade paperback originals. **Publishes 10 titles/year. 2,000 queries received/year. 500 mss received/year. 10% of books from first-time authors. 90% from unagented writers.** Publishes book 1 year after acceptance of ms. Accepts simultaneous submissions. Responds in 1 month to queries. Responds in 2 months to proposals. Responds in 3 months to manuscripts. Book catalog available free. Guidelines available online.

- The mission of Red Hen Press is to discover, publish, and promote works of literary excellence that have been overlooked by mainstream presses, and to build audiences for literature in two ways: by fostering the literacy of youth and by bringing distinguished and emerging writers to the public stage.

O━ "*Red Hen Press is not currently accepting unsolicited material.* At this time, the best opportunity to be published by Red Hen is by entering one of our contests. Please find more information in our award submission guidelines."

Nonfiction Subjects include ethnic, gay, lesbian, language, literature, memoirs, women's issues, women's studies, political/social interest. Query with SASE. Reviews artwork/photos. Send photocopies.

Fiction Subjects include ethnic, experimental, feminist, gay, lesbian, historical, literary, mainstream, contemporary, poetry, poetry in translation, short story collections. We prefer high-quality literary fiction. Query with SASE.

Poetry Query and submit 5 sample poems.

Recent Title(s) *The Misread City: New Literary Los Angeles*, edited by Dana Gioia and Scott Timberg; *Rebel*, by Tom Hayden.

Tips "Audience reads poetry, literary fiction, intelligent nonfiction. If you have an agent, we may be too small since we don't pay advances. Write well. Send queries first. Be willing to help promote your own book."

REFERENCE SERVICE PRESS

5000 Windplay Dr., Suite 4, El Dorado Hills CA 95762. (916)939-9620. Fax: (916)939-9626. E-mail: info@rspfunding.com. Website: www.rspfunding.com. **Contact:** Stuart Hauser, acquisitions editor. Estab.

1977. Publishes hardcover originals. **Publishes 10-20 titles/year. 100% from unagented writers. Pays 10% royalty. Pays advance.** Publishes book 6 months after acceptance of ms. Accepts simultaneous submissions. Responds in 2 months to queries. Book catalog for #10 SASE.

"Reference Service Press focuses on the development and publication of financial aid resources in any format (print, electronic, e-book, etc.). We are interested in financial aid publications aimed at specific groups (e.g., minorities, women, veterans, the disabled, undergraduates majoring in specific subject areas, specific types of financial aid, etc.)."

Nonfiction Subjects include agriculture, art, architecture, business, economics, education, ethnic, health, medicine, history, religion, science, sociology, women's issues, women's studies, disabled. Submit outline, sample chapters.

Recent Title(s) *Financial Aid for Veterans, Military Personnel, and Their Dependents, 2008-2010*; *Directory of Financial Aids for Women, 2007-2009*; *How to Pay for Your Degree in Journalism, 2008-2010.*

Tips "Our audience consists of librarians, counselors, researchers, students, re-entry women, scholars, and other fundseekers."

REPUBLIC OF TEXAS PRESS

Imprint of Taylor Trade Publishing, and part of Rowman and Littlefield Publishing Group 5360 Manhattan Circle, #101, Boulder CO 80303. (303)543-7835, ext. 318. E-mail: tradeeditorial@rowman.com. Website: www.rlpgtrade.com. **Contact:** Acquisitions Director. Publishes trade and paperback originals. **Publishes 10-15 titles/year. 95% from unagented writers. Pays industry-standard royalty on net receipts. Pays small advance.** Publishes book 9 months to 1 year after acceptance of ms. Accepts simultaneous submissions. Responds in 1 month to queries.

Nonfiction "Republic of Texas Press specializes in Texas history and general Texana nonfiction, including ethnic, history, nature/environment, regional, sports, travel, women's issues/studies, Old West, Texas military, and ghost accounts." Proposals should be limited to a query letter; an e-mail will generate the quickest response. If querying by e-mail, please note in the memo box "book proposal." Send no attachments unless requested. What we look for at this stage is suitability of the proposed book to our publishing program (see categories) as well as the author's unique qualifications for writing his or her book.

Recent Title(s) *Texas Bandits: From Real to Reel*, by Mona Sizer; *Texas Women in World War II*, by Cindy Wiegand; *Alamo Traces: New Evidence and New Conclusions*, by Thomas Ricks Lindley.

Tips "Do not submit any original materials, as they will not be returned. Our market is adult."

RIO NUEVO PUBLISHERS

Imprint of Treasure Chest Books P.O. Box 5250, Tucson AZ 85703. Fax: (520)624-5888. E-mail: info@rionuevo.com. Website: www.rionuevo.com. **Contact:** Acquisitions Department. Estab. 1975. Publishes hardcover and trade paperback originals and reprints. **Publishes 12-20 titles/year. 20 queries received/year. 10 mss received/year. 30% of books from first-time authors. 100% from unagented writers. Pays $1,000-4,000 advance.** Publishes book 1 year after acceptance of ms. Accepts simultaneous submissions. Responds in 6 months to queries, proposals and manuscripts. Book catalog available online. Guidelines available via e-mail.

Nonfiction Subjects include animals, cooking, foods, nutrition, gardening, history, nature, environment, regional, religion, spirituality, travel. "We cover the Southwest but prefer titles that are not too narrow in their focus. We want our books to be of broad enough interest that people from other places will also want to read them." Query with SASE. Submit proposal package, outline, 2 sample chapters. Reviews artwork/photos. Send photocopies.

Recent Title(s) *Yard Full of Sun: The Story of a Gardener's Obsession That Got a Little Out of Hand*; *The Prickley Pear Cookbook*; *Clouds for Dessert: Sweet Treats From the Wild West.*

Tips "We have a general audience of intelligent people interested in the Southwest-nature, history, culture. Many of our books are sold in gift shops throughout the region; we are also distributed nationally by W.W. Norton."

ROWMAN & LITTLEFIELD PUBLISHING GROUP

4501 Forbes Blvd., Suite 200, Lanham MD 20706. (301)459-3366. Fax: (301)429-5748. E-mail: mboggs@rowman.com; jbraunstein@rowman.com. Website: www.rowmanlittlefield.com. **Contact:** See website for a detailed list of editors and addresses by subject area at: http://www.rowmanlittlefield.com/contact/. Estab. 1949. Publishes hardcover and trade paperback originals and reprints. **Pays advance.** Book catalog online. Guidelines available online.

Imprints Lexington Books; Rowman & Littlefield Publishers; Madison Books; Scarecrow Press; Cooper Square.

O→ "We are an independent press devoted to publishing scholarly books in the best tradition of university presses; innovative, thought-provoking texts for college courses; and crossover trade books intended to convey scholarly trends to an educated readership. Our approach emphasizes substance and quality of thought over ephemeral trends. We offer a forum for responsible voices representing the diversity of opinion on college campuses, and take special pride in several series designed to provide students with the pros and cons of hotly contested issues."

Nonfiction "Rowman & Littlefield is seeking proposals in the serious non-fiction areas of history, politics, current events, religion, sociology, philosophy, communication and education. All proposal inquiries can be e-mailed or mailed to the respective acquisitions editor listed on the contacts page on our website."

Recent Title(s) *Crime, Punishment, and Policing in China*, by Børge Bakken; *The Making of Arab News*, by Noha Mellor; *African Americans in the U.S. Economy*, edited by Cecilia A. Conrad, John Whitehead, Patrick Mason, and James Stewart.

N RUKA PRESS

P.O. Box 1409, Washington DC 20013. E-mail: contact@rukapress.com. Website: www.rukapress.com. **Contact:** Daniel Kohan, owner. Publishes in trade paperback originals, electronic. **Publishes 2-4/year titles/year. Pays no advance. Royalties are 10-25% on wholesale price.** Publishes book Time between acceptance and publication is 9 months after acceptance of ms. Accepts simultaneous submissions. Book catalogue available online. Guidelines available online.

O→ "We publish nonfiction books with a strong information-design component for a general audience. We are looking for books that explain things, that make an argument, that demystify. We are interested in economics, science, the arts, climate change and sustainability, but we're open to other areas, too—surprise us. We like building charts and graphs, tables and timelines. Our politics are progressive, but our books need not be political."

Nonfiction Subjects include business, contemporary culture, economics, finance, government, health, medicine, money, politics, psychology, science, social sciences, sociology, transportation. Submit proposal package, including outline, resume, bio, or CV, and one sample chapter.

Tips "We appeal to an audience of intelligent, educated readers with broad interests. Be sure to tell us why your proposal is unique, and why you are especially qualified to write this book. We are looking for originality and expertise."

SAE INTERNATIONAL

400 Commonwealth Dr., Warrendale PA 15096-0001. (724)776-4841. E-mail: writeabook@sae.org. Website: www.sae.org/writeabook. **Contact:** Martha Swiss, intellectual property manager; Kevin Jost, editorial director. Estab. 1905. Publishes hardcover and trade paperback originals, eBooks. **Publishes approximately 10 titles/year. 50 queries received/year. 20 mss received/year. 70% of books from first-time authors. 100% from unagented writers. Pays royalty. Pays possible advance.** Publishes book 9-10 months after acceptance of ms. Accepts simultaneous submissions. Responds in 4 months to queries. Book catalog free. Guidelines available online.

O→ Automotive means anything self-propelled. We are a professional society serving engineers, scientists, and researchers in the automobile, aerospace, and off-highway industries.

Nonfiction Query with proposal—see www.sae.org/writeabook for details on submitting a proposal.

Recent Title(s) *Opposed Piston Engines: Evolution, Use, and Future Applications; We Were the Ramchargers—Inside Drag Racing's Legendary Team; An Introduction to Engine Testing and Development.*

Tips "Audience is automotive and aerospace engineers and managers, automotive safety and biomechanics professionals, students, educators, enthusiasts, and historians."

SAFARI PRESS, INC.

15621 Chemical Lane, Bldg. B, Huntington Beach CA 92649-1506. (714)894-9080. Fax: (714)894-4949. E-mail: info@safaripress.com. Website: www.safaripress.com. **Contact:** Jacqueline Neufeld, editor. Estab. 1985. Publishes hardcover originals and reprints, and trade paperback reprints. **Publishes 25-30 titles/year. 70% of books from first-time authors. 80% from unagented writers. Pays 8-15% royalty on wholesale price.** Book catalog for $1. Guidelines available online.

- The editor notes that she receives many mss outside the areas of big-game hunting, wingshooting, and sporting firearms, and these are always rejected.

O→ Safari Press publishes books only on big-game hunting, sporting, firearms, and wingshooting; this includes African, North American, European, Asian, and South American hunting and wingshooting. Does not want books on 'outdoors' topics (hiking, camping, canoeing, etc.).

Nonfiction "We discourage autobiographies, unless the life of the hunter or firearms maker has been exceptional. We routinely reject manuscripts along the lines of 'Me and my buddies went hunting for.. and a good time was had by all!" Query with SASE. Submit outline.
Recent Title(s) *Royal Quest: The Hunting Saga of H.I.H. Prince Abdorreza of Iran;; The Best of Holland & Holland: England's Premier Gunmaker;; Safari Guide 2007-2008.*

SAINT MARY'S PRESS

702 Terrace Heights, Winona MN 55987-1318. (800)533-8095. Fax: (800)344-9225. E-mail: submissions@smp.org. Website: www.smp.org. **Contact:** Submissions Editor. Ms guidelines online or by e-mail.
Nonfiction Subjects include religion, prayers, spirituality. Titles for Catholic youth and their parents, teachers, and youth ministers. Query with SASE. Submit proposal package, outline, 1 sample chapter, SASE. Brief author biography.
Recent Title(s) *The Catholic Faith Handbook for Youth; The Catholic Youth Bible, Catholic Connections Handbook for Middle Schoolers, The Essential Guide to Biblical Life and Times, Everyday Justice: 365 Reflections.*
Tips "Request product catalog and/or do research online of Saint Mary Press book lists before submitting proposal."

🄰 SCRIBNER

Imprint of Simon & Schuster Adult Publishing Group 1230 Avenue of the Americas, 12th Floor, New York NY 10020. (212)698-7000. Website: www.simonsays.com. **Contact:** Nan Graham (literary fiction, nonfiction); Beth Wareham (fiction); Alexis Gargagliano (literary fiction, nonfiction); Brant Rumble (nonfiction); Colin Harrison (fiction, nonfiction); Samantha Martin (fiction, nonfiction); Whitney Frick (fiction, nonfiction); Kara Watson (fiction, nonfiction); Paul Whitlatch (fiction, nonfiction). Publishes hardcover originals. **Publishes 70-75 titles/year. Thousands queries received/year. 20% of books from first-time authors. 0% from unagented writers. Pays 7½-15% royalty. Pays variable advance.** Publishes book 9 months after acceptance of ms. Accepts simultaneous submissions. Responds in 3 months to queries.
Imprints Lisa Drew Books; Scribner Classics (reprints only); Scribner Poetry (by invitation only).
Nonfiction Subjects include education, ethnic, gay, lesbian, health, medicine, history, language, literature, nature, environment, philosophy, psychology, religion, science, criticism. Agented submissions only.
Fiction Subjects include literary, mystery, suspense. Agented submissions only.
Recent Title(s) *Under the Dome*, by Stephen King; *The Ultramind Solution*, by Mark Hyman; *Raymond Carver*, by Carol Sklenicka.

SEEDLING PUBLICATIONS, INC.

Continental Press, Inc. 520 E. Bainbridge St., Elizabethtown PA 17022. (800)233-0759. E-mail: lsalem@jinl.com. Website: www.continentalpress.com. **Contact:** Megan Bergonzi, managing editor]. Estab. 1937. Publishes Seedling books in an 8-, 12-, or 16-page format for beginning readers. **Publishes 10-20 titles/year. 450 mss received/year. 50% of books from first-time authors. 100% from unagented writers. Makes outright purchase.** Publishes book 1 year after acceptance of ms. Accepts simultaneous submissions. Responds in 9-12 months to queries. Guidelines for #10 SASE. All submissions must be accompanied by a self-addressed stamped envelope of appropriate size with sufficient postage.

- Does not accept mss via fax. Does not accept queries at all.

O━ "We are an education niche publisher, producing books for beginning readers. Stories must include language that is natural to young children and story lines that are interesting to 5-7-year-olds and written at their beginning reading level. Continental Press's Seedling product line focuses on fiction and nonfiction leveled readers and other materials that support early literacy in prekindergarten through second grade. Familiarity with reading recovery, guided reading, and other reading intervention programs will give you a sense of the kinds of materials needed for Seedling products.]"

Nonfiction Science, math, or social studies concepts are considered. Reviews artwork/photos. Send photocopies.
Fiction Subjects include juvenile. Submit complete ms.
Recent Title(s) *Sherman in the Talent Show*, by Betty Erickson; *Moth or Butterfly?*, by Ryan Durney; *The Miller, His Son, and the Donkey*, by Lynn Salem and Josie Stewart. *Sherman's Shenanigans, Ben's Zoo Collection, Little Duck and Little Goose, Jamie the Lifeguard, Our Family Reunion.*
Tips "Follow our guidelines. Do not submit full-length picture books or chapter books. We are an education niche publisher. Our books are for children, ages 5-7, who are just beginning to read independently. We do not accept stories that rhyme or poetry at this time. Try your manuscript with young readers.

Listen for text that doesn't flow when the child reads the story. Rewrite until the text sounds natural to beginning readers. Visit our website to be sure your manuscript fits our market."

SENTIENT PUBLICATIONS

1113 Spruce St., Boulder CO 80302. E-mail: contact@sentientpublications.com. Website: www.sentientpublications.com. **Contact:** Connie Shaw, acq. editor. Estab. 2001. Publishes hardcover and trade paperback originals; trade paperback reprints. **Publishes 12 titles/year. 200 queries received/year. 100 mss received/year. 70% of books from first-time authors. 50% from unagented writers. Pays royalty on wholesale price. Pays advance.** Publishes book 6 months after acceptance of ms. Accepts simultaneous submissions. Responds in 1 month to queries. Responds in 2 months to proposals and manuscripts. Book catalog available online.

Nonfiction Subjects include audio, alternative, art, architecture, child guidance, contemporary culture, cooking, foods, nutrition, creative nonfiction, education, gardening, health, medicine, history, language, literature, memoirs, nature, environment, New Age, philosophy, photography, psychology, science, sex, social sciences, sociology, spirituality, travel, women's issues, women's studies. "We're especially looking for holistic health books that have something new to say." Submit proposal package, See our website. Submit complete ms. Does not review artwork/photos.

Fiction Subjects include experimental, literary. The quality of the writing is the most important factor. Submit complete ms.

Recent Title(s) *Changing the Course of Autism*, by Bryan Jepson and Jane Johnson (holistic health); *If Holden Caulfield Were in My Classroom*, by Bernie Schein (alternative education); *God Is an Atheist*, by N. Nosirrah (novella).

SHEED & WARD BOOK PUBLISHING

Imprint of Rowman & Littlefield Publishing Group 4501 Forbes Blvd., Suite 200, Lanham MD 20706. (301)459-3366. Fax: (301)429-5747. Website: www.sheedandward.com. **Contact:** Sarah Stanton, acquisitions. Publishes hardcover and paperback originals. Book catalog free or on website. Guidelines available online.

- "We are looking for books that help our readers, most of whom are college educated, gain access to the riches of the Catholic/Christian tradition. We publish in the areas of history, biography, spirituality, prayer, ethics, ministry, justice, liturgy."

Nonfiction Subjects include religion, spirituality, family life, theology, ethics. Submit proposal package to the appropriate acquistions editor, including outline, 2 sample chapters, strong cover letter indicating why the project is unique and compelling. Please do not send your entire manuscript. If an acquisitions editor would like to see the complete manuscript, he or she will let you know. Reviews artwork/photos. Send photocopies.

Recent Title(s) *Becoming Fully Human*, by Joan Chittister, OSB; *Exploring Catholic Literature*, by Mary R. Reichardt.

Tips "We prefer that writers get our author guidelines either from our website or via mail before submitting proposals."

N SLACK, INC.

6900 Grove Rd., Thorofare NJ 08086. (856)848-1000. Fax: (856)853-5991. E-mail: bookspublishing@slackinc.com. Website: www.slackbooks.com. **Contact:** John Bond, publisher. Estab. 1960. Publishes hardcover and softcover originals. **Publishes 35 titles/year. 80 queries received/year. 23 mss received/year. 75% of books from first-time authors. 100% from unagented writers. Pays 10% royalty. Pays advance.** Publishes book 8 months after acceptance of ms. Accepts simultaneous submissions. Responds in 1 month to queries and proposals. Responds in 3 months to manuscripts. Book catalog and ms guidelines free. Guidelines available online.

- SLACK INC. publishes academic textbooks and professional reference books on various medical topics in an expedient manner.

Nonfiction Subjects include health, medicine, ophthalmology. Submit proposal package, outline, 2 sample chapters, market profile and cv. Reviews artwork/photos. Send photocopies.

Recent Title(s) *Handbook of Ophthalmology*, by Amar Agarural; *Patient Practitionor Interaction*, by Carol Davis.

SOHO PRESS, INC.

853 Broadway, New York NY 10003. E-mail: soho@sohopress.com. Website: www.sohopress.com. **Contact:** Bronwen Hruska, Publisher; Katie Herman, editor. Estab. 1986. Publishes hardcover and trade paperback originals; trade paperback reprints. **Publishes 60-70 titles/year. 15-25% of books from first-**

time authors. 10% from unagented writers. 7.5-15% royalty on retail price (varies under certain circumstances) Publishes book 18 months after acceptance of ms. Accepts simultaneous submissions. 3 months on queries and mss. Guidelines available online.

- Soho Press publishes primarily fiction, as well as some narrative literary nonfiction and mysteries set abroad. No electronic submissions, only queries by e-mail.

Nonfiction Subjects include creative nonfiction, ethnic, memoirs. "We do not buy books on proposal. We always need to see a complete ms before we buy a book, though we prefer an initial submission of 3 sample chapters. We do not publish books with color art or photographs or a lot of graphical material." Submit 3 sample chapters and a cover letter with a synopsis and author bio; SASE. Send photocopies.
Fiction Subjects include ethnic, historical, humor, literary, mystery, In mysteries, we only publish series with foreign or exotic settings, usually procedurals. Submit 3 sample chapters and cover letter with synopsis, author bio, SASE.
Recent Title(s) *Murder in the Latin Quarter*, by Cara Black (mystery); *Chose By a Horse*, by Susan Richards (memoir); *Light Fell*, by Evan Fallenberg (literary fiction).
Tips "Soho Press publishes discerning authors for discriminating readers, finding the strongest possible writers and publishing them. Before submitting, look at our website for an idea of the types of books we publish, and read our submission guidelines."

SOLAS HOUSE/TRAVELERS' TALES

853 Alma St., Palo Alto CA 94301. (650)462-2110. Fax: (650)462-2114. E-mail: submit@travelerstales.com. Website: www.travelerstales.com. **Contact:** James O'Reilly and Larry Habegger, series editors; Sean O'Reilly, editor-at-large (sales/publicity). Publishes inspirational travel books, mostly anthologies and travel advice books. Solas House publishes self-help and general nonfiction. **Publishes 8-10 titles/year. Pays $100 honorarium for anthology pieces.** Accepts simultaneous submissions. Guidelines available online.

Imprints Travelers' Tales Guides; Footsteps; Travelers' Tales Classics.

- "Due to the volume of submissions, we do not respond unless the material submitted meets our immediate editorial needs. All stories are read and filed for future use contingent upon meeting editorial guidelines."

Nonfiction Subjects include all aspects of travel.
Recent Title(s) *The Best Travelers' Tales 2010; You Unstuck; Mousejunkies; 100 Best Places in Italy for Women; More Sand in My Bra; Cruise Confidential.*
Tips "We publish personal nonfiction stories and anecdotes—funny, illuminating, adventurous, frightening, or grim. Stories should reflect that unique alchemy that occurs when you enter unfamiliar territory and begin to see the world differently as a result. Stories that have already been published, including book excerpts, are welcome as long as the authors retain the copyright or can obtain permission from the copyright holder to reprint the material. We do not publish fiction."

STACKPOLE BOOKS

5067 Ritter Rd., Mechanicsburg PA 17055. Fax: (717)796-0412. E-mail: jschnell@stackpolebooks.com. Website: www.stackpolebooks.com. **Contact:** Judith Schnell, editorial director (outdoor sports and fishing); Chris Evans, editor (history); Mark Allison, editor (nature); Dave Reisch, editor (military); Kyle Weaver, editor (regional/Pennsylvania, travel, true crime and paranormal titles/submissions). Estab. 1935. Publishes hardcover and paperback originals and reprints. **Publishes 130 titles/year. Pays industry standard advance.** Publishes book 1 year after acceptance of ms. Responds in 1 month to queries. See catalog and guidelines online.

- "Stackpole maintains a growing and vital publishing program by featuring authors who are experts in their fields."

Nonfiction Subjects include history, military reference, war, nature, outdoor sports, crafts and hobbies, Pennsylvania. "First of all, send your query to an individual editor. The more information you can supply, the better." Reviews artwork/photos.
Recent Title(s) *Band of Sisters; Fishing Knots; True Crime New Jersey.*
Tips "Stackpole seeks well-written, authoritative manuscripts for specialized and general trade markets. Proposals should include chapter outline, sample chapter, illustrations, and author's credentials."

STANDARD PUBLISHING

Standex International Corp. 8805 Governor's Hill Dr., Suite 400, Cincinnati OH 45249. (513)931-4050. Website: www.standardpub.com. **Contact:** Acquisitions Editor. Estab. 1866. Guidelines and current publishing objectives available online.

- Publishes resources that meet church and family needs in the area of children's ministry.

Recent Title(s) *Second Guessing God*, by Brian Jones; *Devotions by Dead People*, by Lynn Lusby Pratt; *My Little Good Night Storybook*, by Susan Lingo.

STANFORD UNIVERSITY PRESS

1450 Page Mill Rd., Palo Alto CA 94304-1124. (650)723-9434. Fax: (650)725-3457. E-mail: info@www.sup.org. Website: www.sup.org. **Contact:** Stacy Wagner (Asian studies, US foreign policy, Asian-American studies); Kate Wahl (law, political science, public policy); Margo Beth Crouppen (economics, finance, business). Estab. 1925. **Pays variable royalty (sometimes none) Pays occasional advance.** Guidelines available online.

O⸺ "Stanford University Press publishes scholarly books in the humanities and social sciences, along with professional books in business, economics and management science; also high-level textbooks and some books for a more general audience."

Nonfiction Subjects include anthropology, archeology, business, economics, ethnic, studies, gay, lesbian, government, politics, history, humanities, language, literature, literary criticism, and literary theory, nature, environment, philosophy, psychology, religion, science, social sciences, sociology, political science, law, education, history and culture of China, Japan and Latin America, European history, linguistics, geology, medieval and classical studies. Query with prospectus and an outline. Reviews artwork/photos.

Recent Title(s) *Culture and Public Action*; *The Sovereignty Revolution*; *Maps, Myths, and Men*.

Tips "The writer's best chance is a work of original scholarship with an argument of some importance."

ST. AUGUSTINE'S PRESS

P.O. Box 2285, South Bend IN 46680-2285. (574)-291-3500. Fax: (574)291-3700. E-mail: bruce@staugustine.net. Website: www.staugustine.net. **Contact:** Bruce Fingerhut, president (philosophy). Publishes hardcover originals and trade paperback originals and reprints. **Publishes 20 titles/year. 350 queries received/year. 100 mss received/year. 2% of books from first-time authors. 95% from unagented writers. Pays 6-15% royalty. Pays $500-5,000 advance.** Publishes book 8 months after acceptance of ms. Accepts simultaneous submissions. Responds in 2-6 months to queries. Responds in 3-8 months to proposals. Responds in 4-8 months to manuscripts. Book catalog available free.

Imprints Carthage Reprints.

O⸺ "Our market is scholarly in the humanities. We publish in philosophy, religion, cultural history, and history of ideas only."

Nonfiction Query with SASE. Reviews artwork/photos. Send photocopies.

Recent Title(s) *The Last Superstition: A Refutation of the New Atheism*, by Edward Feser; *Socrates in the Underworld: On Plato's Gorgias*, by Nalin Ranasinghe; *What Catholics Believe*, by Josef Pieper.

Tips "Scholarly and college student audience."

STERLING PUBLISHING

387 Park Ave. S., 11th Floor, New York NY 10016-8810. (212)532-7160. Fax: (212)213-2495. Website: www.sterlingpub.com. **Contact:** Category Editor (i.e., Children's Editor). Estab. 1949. Publishes hardcover and paperback originals and reprints. **Pays royalty. Pays advance.** Guidelines available online.

Imprints Sterling/Books; Sterling/Ethos; Lark; Sterling/Children's; Sterling/Epicure; Ecosystem; Puzzlewright Press; Union Square Press; Ecosystem; Sandy Creek; Sterling/Innovation; Fall River Press; Metro Books; Flashkids; Quamut; Silver Lining Calendars; Hearst Books.

- Our mission is to publish high-quality books that educate, entertain, and enrich the lives of our readers."

O⸺ "Sterling publishes highly illustrated, accessible, hands-on, practical books for adults and children.

Nonfiction Publishes nonfiction only. Subjects include alternative, animals, art, architecture, ethnic, gardening, health, medicine, hobbies, New Age, recreation, science, sports, fiber arts, games and puzzles, children's humor, children's science, nature and activities, pets, wine, home decorating, dolls and puppets, ghosts, UFOs, woodworking, crafts, medieval, Celtic subjects, alternative health and healing, new consciousness. Proposals on subjects such as crafting, decorating, outdoor living, and photography should be sent directly to Lark Books at their Asheville, North Carolina offices. Complete guidelines can be found on the Lark site: www.larkbooks.com/submissions. Submit outline, publishing history, 1 sample chapter (typed and double-spaced), SASE. Explain your idea. Send sample illustrations where applicable. For Children's books, please submit full manuscripts. We do not accept electronic (e-mail) submissions. Be sure to include information about yourself with particular regard to your skills and qualifications in the subject area of your submission. It is helpful for us to know your publishing history—whether or not you've written other books and, if so, the name of the publisher and whether those books are currently in print. Reviews artwork/photos. Send photocopies.

Fiction "At present we do not publish fiction."

Recent Title(s) *AARP Crash Course in Estate Planning*, by Michael Palermo and Ric Edelman.

STIPES PUBLISHING LLC

P.O. Box 526, Champaign IL 61824-9933. (217)356-8391. Fax: (217)356-5753. E-mail: stipes01@sbcglobal.net. Website: www.stipes.com. **Contact:** Benjamin H. Watts, (engineering, science, business); Robert Watts (agriculture, music, and physical education). Estab. 1925. Publishes hardcover and paperback originals. **Publishes 15-30 titles/year. 50% of books from first-time authors. 95% from unagented writers. Pays 15% maximum royalty on retail price.** Publishes book 4 months after acceptance of ms. Responds in 2 months to queries. Guidelines available online.

"Stipes Publishing is oriented towards the education market and educational books with some emphasis in the trade market."

Nonfiction Subjects include agriculture, business, economics, music, dance, nature, environment, recreation, science. "All of our books in the trade area are books that also have a college text market. No books unrelated to educational fields taught at the college level." Submit outline, 1 sample chapter.

Recent Title(s) *Keyboard Musicianship: Piano For Adults, Book One, 9th edition*, by James Lyke, *et. al; Manual Of Woody Landscape Plants, 6th edition*, by Michael Dirr; *Health Ethics*, by John M. Charles.

STOREY PUBLISHING, LLC

210 MASS MoCA Way, North Adams MA 01247. (413)346-2100. Fax: (413)346-2196. Website: www.storey.com. **Contact:** Deborah Balmuth, editorial director (building, sewing, gift). Estab. 1983. Publishes hardcover and trade paperback originals and reprints. **Publishes 40 titles/year. 600 queries received/year. 150 mss received/year. 25% of books from first-time authors. 60% from unagented writers. We offer both work-for-hire and standard royalty contracts. Pays advance.** Publishes book within 2 years after acceptance of ms. Accepts simultaneous submissions. Responds in 1 month to queries. Responds in 3 months to proposals andmanuscripts. Book catalog available free. Guidelines available online.

"We publish practical information that encourages personal independence in harmony with the environment."

Nonfiction Subjects include animals, gardening, nature, environment, home, mind/body/spirit, birds, beer and wine, crafts, building, cooking. Reviews artwork/photos.

Recent Title(s) *The Veggie Gardener's Answer Book*, by Barbara W. Ellis; *The Home Creamery*, by Kathy Farrell-Kingsley; *Happy Dog, Happy You*, by Arden Moore.

ST PAULS/ALBA HOUSE

Society of St. Paul 2187 Victory Blvd., Staten Island NY 10314-6603. (718)761-0047. Fax: (718)761-0057. E-mail: edmund_lane@juno.com. Website: www.stpauls.us. **Contact:** Edmund C. Lane, SSP, acquisitions editor. Estab. 1957. Publishes trade paperback and mass market paperback originals and reprints. **Publishes 22 titles/year. 250 queries received/year. 150 mss received/year. 10% of books from first-time authors. 100% from unagented writers. Pays 5-10% royalty.** Publishes book 10 months after acceptance of ms. Responds in 1 month to queries and proposals. Responds in 2 months to manuscripts. Book catalog and ms guidelines free.

Nonfiction Subjects include philosophy, religion, spirituality. Alba House is the North American publishing division of St. Paul, an International Roman Catholic Missionary Religious Congregation dedicated to spreading the Gospel message via the media of communications. Submit complete ms. Reviews artwork/photos. Send photocopies.

Recent Title(s) *Those Mysterious Priests*, by Fulton J. Sheen (spirituality); *Captured Fire*, by S. Joseph Krempa (homiletics).

Tips "Our audience is educated Roman Catholic readers interested in matters related to the Church, spirituality, Biblical and theological topics, moral concerns, lives of the saints, etc."

SUN BOOKS / SUN PUBLISHING

P.O. Box 5588, Santa Fe NM 87502-5588. (505)471-5177. E-mail: info@sunbooks.com. Website: www.sunbooks.com. **Contact:** Skip Whitson, director. Estab. 1973. Publishes trade paperback originals and reprints. **Publishes 10-15 titles/year. 5% of books from first-time authors. 90% from unagented writers. Pays 5% royalty on retail price. Occasionally makes outright purchase.** Publishes book 16 to 18 months after acceptance of ms. Will respond within 2 mos, via e-mail, to queries if interested. Book catalog available online at www.sunbooks.com or www.abooksource.com. Queries via e-mail only, please.

Nonfiction Subjects include self-help, leadership, motivational, recovery, inspirational.
Recent Title(s) *Eight Pillars of Prosperity*, by James Allen; *Ambition and Success*, by Orson Swett Marden; *Cheerfulness as a Life Power*, by Orson Swett Marden.

SYLVAN DELL PUBLISHING

976 Houston Northcutt Blvd., Suite 3, Mt. Pleasant SC 29464. Website: www.sylvandellpublishing.com. **Contact:** Donna German, editor. Estab. 2004. Publishes hardcover, trade paperback, and electronic originals. **Publishes 10 titles/year. 2,000 mss received/year. 50%% of books from first-time authors. 100%% from unagented writers. Pays 6-8% royalty on wholesale price. Pays small advance.** Publishes book 12-18 months. May hold onto mss of interest for 12 months until acceptance. after acceptance of ms. Accepts simultaneous submissions. Acknowledges receipt of ms submission within one week. Book catalog and guidelines available online.

O→ "The picture books we publish are usually, but not always, fictional stories that relate to animals, nature, the environment, and science. All books should subtly convey an educational theme through a warm story that is fun to read and that will grab a child's attention. Each book has a 3-5 page *For Creative Minds*' section to reinforce the educational component. This section will have a craft and/or game as well as 'fun facts' to be shared by the parent, teacher, or other adult. Authors do not need to supply this information. Mss. should be <1,500 words and meet all of the following 4 criteria: Fun to read—mostly fiction with nonfiction facts woven into the story; National or regional in scope; Must tie into early elementary school curriculum; must be marketable through a niche market such as a zoo, aquarium, or museum gift shop."

Nonfiction Subjects include science, math. We only accept e-submissions. Reviews artwork/photos. Send 1-2 JPEGS.
Fiction Subjects include picture books, subjects related to math and science (think *historical fiction*).
Recent Title(s) *Sort It Out!* by Barbara Mariconda; *Ocean Hide and Seek*, by Jennifer Krammer; *Henry the Impatient Heron*, by Donna Love; *One Wolf Howls*, by Scotti Cohn.
Tips "We want the children excited about the books. We envision the books being used at home and in the classroom."

SYNERGEBOOKS

P.O. Box 185, Haines City FL 33844. (863)956-3010. E-mail: synergebooks@aol.com. Website: www.synergebooks.com. **Contact:** Debra Staples, publisher/acquisitions editor. Estab. 1999. Publishes trade paperback and electronic originals. **Publishes 40-60 titles/year. 250 queries received/year. 250 mss received/year. 95% of books from first-time authors. 99.9% from unagented writers. Pays 15-40% royalty; makes outright purchase.** Accepts simultaneous submissions. Book catalog available online at www.synergebooks.com/paperbacks.html. Guidelines available online at www.synergebooks.com/subguide.html.

Nonfiction Subjects include New Age, philosophy, spirituality, travel, young adult. Submit proposal package, 1-3 sample chapters. Reviews artwork/photos. Send jpg via attached mail.
Fiction Subjects include fantasy, historical, horror, humor, mainstream, contemporary, military, magic, mystery, philosophy, poetry, religious, romance, science fiction, short story collections, spiritual, suspense, western, young adult, and audio books. SynergEbooks published at least 40 new titles a year, and only 1-5 of those are put into print in any given year. "SynergEbooks is first and foremost a digital publisher, so most of our marketing budget goes to those formats. Authors are required to direct-sell a minimum of 100 digital copies of a title before it's accepted for print." Submit proposal package, including synopsis, 1-3 sample chapters, and marketing plans.
Poetry Anthologies must be a unique topic or theme. Query and submit 1-5 sample poems.
Recent Title(s) *A Talent to Deceive*, by William Norris (True Crime); *LOBO: The Strange Life of William Jameson*, by John H. Manhold (Historical Fiction); *Lucky Dog: The True Story of a Little Mexico Street Dog Who Goes Internationa*l (Travel/Humor).
Tips "At SynergEbooks, we work with the author to promote their work."

SYRACUSE UNIVERSITY PRESS

621 Skytop Road, Suite 110, Syracuse NY 13244-5290. (315)443-5534. Fax: (315)443-5545. Website: syracuseuniversitypress.syr.edu. **Contact:** Alice R. Pfeiffer, director. Estab. 1943. **Publishes 50 titles/year. 25% of books from first-time authors. 95% from unagented writers.** Publishes book an average of 15 months after acceptance of ms. Book catalog on our website. Guidelines available online.

O→ "Currently emphasizing Middle East studies, Jewish studies, Irish studies, peace studies, dissability studies, television and popular culture, Native American studies, gender and ethnic studies, New York State."

Nonfiction Subjects include regional. "Special opportunity in our nonfiction program for freelance writers of books on New York state, sports history, Jewish studies, the Middle East, religious studies, television, and popular culture. Provide precise descriptions of subjects, along with background description of project. The author must make a case for the importance of his or her subject." Submit query with SASE or online, or submit outline and 2 sample chapters. Reviews artwork/photos.
Recent Title(s) *Besa: Muslims Who Saved Jews in World War II*, by Norman Gershman; *Eminent Persians: The Men and Women Who Made Modern Iran 1941-1979*, by Abbas Milani; *Get Off Your Knees: A Story of Faith, Courage and Determination*, by John Robinson; *Moonfixer: The Basketball Journal of Earl Lloyd*, by Earl Lloyd and Sean Kirst; *The Pistachio Seller*, by Reem Bassiouney; *Seven Generations of Iroquois Leadership: The Six Nations Since 1800*, by Lawrence Hauptman; *God and the Editor: My Search for Meaning at the New York Times*, by Robert Phelps.
Tips "We're seeking well-written and well-researched books that will make a significant contribution to the subject areas listed above and will be well-received in the marketplace."

TAYLOR TRADE PUBLISHING

5360 Manhattan Circle, #101, Boulder CO 80303. (303)543-7835. E-mail: rrinehart@rowman.com. Website: www.rlpgtrade.com. **Contact:** Acquisitions Editor. Publishes hardcover originals, trade paperback originals and reprints. **Publishes 70 titles/year. 15% of books from first-time authors. 65% from unagented writers.** Publishes book 1 year after acceptance of ms. Responds in 2 months to queries. See catalog online at website. Submission guidelines available on website under "Editorial."
Nonfiction Subjects include child guidance, cooking, foods, nutrition, gardening, health, medicine, history, Texas/Western, nature, environment, sports, contemporary affairs, music, film, theater, art, nature writing, exploration, women's studies, African-American studies, literary studies. All proposals may be sent via e-mail. Proposals should be limited to a query letter; an e-mail will generate the quickest response. If querying by e-mail, please note in the memo box "book proposal." Send no attachments unless requested. If using postal mail, query with SASE. What we look for at this stage is suitability of the proposed book to our publishing program (see categories) as well as the author's unique qualifications for writing his or her book.

N TEACHER IDEAS PRESS

Libraries Unlimited ABC-CLIO, P.O. Box 1911, Santa Barbara CA 93116-1911. Website: www.teacherideaspress.com. **Contact:** Cynthia Anderson, editor. Contact customer service by phone or e-mail for free updated catalog. Guidelines and catalog available online.

> "Teacher Ideas Press offers books written by teachers for teachers. Our books offer a clear and strong focus on literary and 21st century learning skills. We publish the best in innovative, practical, hands-on lessons and classroom-tested activities, all designed to help you teach 21st century literacy skills and improve student achievement. We are proud to be your partner in promoting excellence in the K-12 classroom. Whether you're a classroom, subject, or special area teacher or a library media specialist, you'll find instructional value in these resources. They include research-based strategies and materials for helping you differentiate for students who are gifted, are at risk, have special needs, or are English language learners. Send us proposals for books to teach reading comprehension, fluency, vocabulary, writing, and information literacy skills in collaboration with the school librarian."

Recent Title(s) *Nine Thousand Straws*, by Jeanne Knodt; *War Stories for Readers Theatre: World War II*, by Suzanne Barchers; *Fairy Tales Readers Theatre*, by Anthony D. Fredericks; *Fun with Finance*, by Carol Peterson.

N TEMPLE UNIVERSITY PRESS

2450 West Hunting Park Ave., Philadelphia PA 19129. (215)926-2143. Fax: (215)204-2141. E-mail: tempress@temple.edu. Website: www.temple.edu/tempress/. **Contact:** Alex Holzman, director; Janet Francendese, editor-in-chief; Micah Kleit, executive editor; Mick Gusinde-Duffy, senior acquisitions editor. Estab. 1969. **Publishes 60 titles/year. Pays advance.** Publishes book 10 months after acceptance of ms. Responds in 2 months to queries. Book catalog available free. Guidelines available online.

> "Temple University Press has been publishing path-breaking books on Asian-Americans, law, gender issues, film, women's studies and other interesting areas for nearly 40 years."

Nonfiction Subjects include ethnic, government, politics, health, medicine, history, photography, regional, Philadelphia, sociology, labor studies, urban studies, Latin American/Latino, Asian American, African American studies, public policy, women's studies. Query with SASE. Reviews artwork/photos.
Recent Title(s) *From Black Power to Hip Hop*, by Patricia Hill Collins; *Pictures From A Drawer: Prison and the Art of Portraiture*, by Bruce Jackson.

TEXAS A&M UNIVERSITY PRESS

College Station TX 77843-4354. (979)845-1436. Fax: (979)847-8752. E-mail: d-vance@tamu.edu. Website: www.tamupress.com. **Contact:** Mary Lenn Dixon, editor-in-chief (presidential studies, anthropology, borderlands, western history); Shannon Davies, senior editor (natural history, agriculture). Estab. 1974. **Publishes 60 titles/year. Pays royalty.** Publishes book 1 year after acceptance of ms. Responds in 1 month to queries. Book catalog available free. Guidelines available online.

"Texas A&M University Press publishes a wide range of nonfiction, scholarly trade, and crossover books of regional and national interest, reflecting the interests of the university, the broader scholarly community, and the people of our state and region."

Nonfiction Subjects include agriculture, anthropology, archeology, art, architecture, history, American and Western, language, literature, Texas and western, military, war, nature, environment, regional, Texas and the Southwest, Mexican-US borderlands studies, nautical archaeology, ethnic studies, presidential studies. Nonreturnable queries; e-mail preferred.

Recent Title(s) *Finding Birds on the Great Texas Coastal Birding Trail*, by Ted Lee Eubanks, et al; *The History of Texas Music*, by Gary Hartman.

Tips "Proposal requirements are posted on the website."

THIRD WORLD PRESS

P.O. Box 19730, Chicago IL 60619. (773)651-0700. Fax: (773)651-7286. E-mail: twpress3@aol.com. **Contact:** Bennett J. Johnson. Estab. 1967. Publishes hardcover and trade paperback originals and reprints. **Publishes 20 titles/year. 200-300 queries received/year. 200 mss received/year. 20% of books from first-time authors. 80% from unagented writers. Compensation based upon royalties. Individual arrangement with author depending on the book, etc.** Publishes book 18 months after acceptance of ms. Accepts simultaneous submissions. Responds in 6 months to queries. Responds in 5 months to manuscripts. Book catalog available free. Guidelines for #10 SASE.

- Third World Press is open to submissions in July only.

Nonfiction Subjects include anthropology, archeology, education, ethnic, government, politics, health, medicine, history, language, literature, literary criticism, philosophy, psychology, regional, religion, sociology, women's issues, women's studies, Black studies. Query with SASE. Submit outline, 5 sample chapters. Reviews artwork/photos. Send photocopies.

Fiction Subjects include ethnic, feminist, historical, juvenile, animal, easy-to-read, fantasy, historical, contemporary, literary, mainstream, contemporary, picture books, plays, short story collections, young adult, easy-to-read/teen, folktales, historical, African-centered, African-American materials, preschool/picture book. "We primarily publish nonfiction, but will consider fiction by and about Blacks." Query with SASE. Submit outline, clips, 5 sample chapters.

Poetry Ethnic/African-centered and African-American materials. Submit complete ms.

Recent Title(s) *Yellowblack*, by Haki Madhubuti; *1996*, by Gloria Naylor.

TIGHTROPE BOOKS

602 Markham St., Toronto ON M6G 2L8. Website: http://tightropebooks.com. **Contact:** Shirarose Wilensky, editor (fiction, poetry, nonfiction). Hardcover and trade paperback originals. **Publishes 12 titles/year. 70% of books from first-time authors. 100% from unagented writers. $200-750** Publishes book 12 months after acceptance of ms. Catalog and guidelines free on request and online at website.

Imprints Zurita, Latino-Canadian imprint, Halli Villegas, Publisher.

Nonfiction Subjects include alternative lifestyles, architecture, art, contemporary culture, creative nonfiction, ethnic, gay, language, lesbian, literary criticism, literature, multicultural, womens issues. Query with SASE. Submit proposal package, including outline, 1 sample chapter and complete ms. Reviews artwork. Send photocopies.

Fiction Subjects include contemporary, ethnic, experimental, fantasy, feminist, gay, horror, juvenile, lesbian, literary, mainstream, multicultural, poetry, poetry in translation, short story collections, translation, young adult. Query with SASE. Submit proposal package, including: synopsis, 1 sample chapter and completed ms.

Poetry Query. Submit 10 sample poems. Submit complete ms.

Recent Title(s) *The Best Canadian Essays 2009*, edited by Alex Boyd and Carmine Starnino (anthology); *She's Shameless: Women write about growing up, rocking out and fighting back*, editing by Stacey May Fowles and Megan Griffith-Greene (anthology); *Wrong Bar*, by Nathaniel G. Moore (experimental, post-modern novel); *The Best Canadian·Poetry in English 2009*, ed. by Molly Peacock and A.F. Moritz (anthology); *Contents of a Mermaid's Purse*, by Phoebe Tsang (lyric poetry; debut collection).

Tips "Audience is young, urban, literary, educated, unconventional."

TILBURY HOUSE, PUBLISHERS

Imprint of Harpswell Press, Inc. 103 Brunswick Ave., Gardiner ME 04345. (207)582-1899. Fax: (207)582-8227. E-mail: tilbury@tilburyhouse.com. Website: www.tilburyhouse.com. **Contact:** Karen Fisk, children's book editor. Estab. 1990. Publishes hardcover originals, trade paperback originals. **Publishes 10 titles/year. Pays royalty.** Book catalog available free. Guidelines available online.

Nonfiction Regional adult biography/history/maritime/nature, and children's picture books that deal with issues, such as bullying, multiculturalism, etc. Submit complete ms. Reviews artwork/photos. Send photocopies.

Recent Title(s) *Remember Me*, by Donald Soctomah and Jean Flahive; *Bear-ly There*, by Rebekah Raye, *Always My Brother*, by Jean Reagan

🅰 MEGAN TINGLEY BOOKS

Imprint of Little, Brown & Co. 1271 Avenue of the Americas, New York NY 10020. (212)522-8700. Fax: (212)522-7997. Website: www.lb-kids.com. **Contact:** Megan Tingley, editor-in-chief; Nancy Consescu, assistant editor. Publishes hardcover and trade paperback originals and reprints. **Publishes 80-100 titles/year. 500-1,000 queries received/year. 500-1,000 mss received/year. 2% of books from first-time authors. 5% from unagented writers. Pays 0-15% royalty on retail price. Makes outright purchase.** Publishes book 1-2 years after acceptance of ms. Accepts simultaneous submissions. Responds in 1 month to queries. Responds in 6-8 weeks to proposals. Responds in 6-8 weeks to manuscripts.

- Note the Stand Up For Something Contest. Must be legal US resident (residents of Hawaii are excluded from Contest) between the ages of 6 and 12 as of December 21, 2009 to enter. Parent or legal guardian signature is required. Contest begins December 21, 2009 and ends April 30, 2010 (if entry is postmarked by April 30, 2010 and received no later than May 7, 2010). Visit http://www.sitinbook.com for Official Rules and details. Prize is trip for 3 to Washington, D.C.

O→ Megan Tingley Books is an imprint of the children's book department of Little, Brown and Company. Currently looking for all formats with special interest in humor, music, multicultural, supernatural, narrative nonfiction, poetry, and unusual art styles. No fairy tales.

Nonfiction Subjects include animals, art, architecture, cooking, foods, nutrition, creative nonfiction, ethnic, gay, lesbian, history, language, literature, memoirs, multicultural, music, dance, photography. *Agented submissions and queries only*. Ideally, books should be about a subject that hasn't been dealt with for children before. Reviews artwork/photos. Send Send photocopies. No original pieces.

Fiction Picture books, middle grade, young adult. Subjects include adventure, fantasy, gay, lesbian, historical, humor, multicultural, suspense, political, chick lit. *Agented submissions only*.

Recent Title(s) *Luna*, by Julie Ann Peters; *Harlem Stomp!*, by Laban Carrick Hill; *You Read to Me, I'll Read to You*, by Mary Ann Hoberman; illustrated by Michael Emberley.

Tips Do your research. Know our submission policy. Do not fax or call.

THE TOBY PRESS, LTD.

P.O. Box 8531, New Milford CT 06776-8531. Fax: (203)830-8512. Website: www.tobypress.com. **Contact:** Editorial Director (fiction, biography). Publishes hardcover originals and paperbacks. **Publishes 20-25 titles/year. over 2,000 queries received/year. 20% of books from first-time authors. 10% from unagented writers. Pays advance.** Publishes book up to 2 year after acceptance of ms. Accepts simultaneous submissions.

- *The Toby Press is booked through Autumn 2011 and is not accepting submissions at this time.*

O→ "The Toby Press publishes literary fiction."

Fiction Subjects include literary.

Recent Title(s) *Foiglman*, by Aharon Megged; *With*, by Donald Harington.

TODD PUBLICATIONS

P.O. Box 1752, Boca Raton FL 33429. (561)910-0440. E-mail: toddpub@aol.com. Website: www.toddpub.info. **Contact:** Barry Klein, president. Estab. 1973. Publishes reference books and trade paperback originals. **Publishes 10 titles/year. 10% of books from first-time authors. 100% from unagented writers.** Publishes book 3 months after acceptance of ms. Accepts simultaneous submissions. Responds in 1 month to proposals. Book listing available via e-mail.

O→ "Todd Publications publishes/distributes reference books and directories of all types."

Nonfiction Subjects include ethnic, health, medicine & fitness. Submit outline and 2 sample chapters.

Recent Title(s) *Aging: Quotations, Poetry, Resources & Bibliography; Wellness & Fitness: Quotations, Hints & Tips, Resources & Bibliography; Mail Order Business Directory*, 28th ed.; *Guide to American & International Directories*, 20th ed.; *Reference Encyclopedia of the American Indian*, 15th ed.; *Directory of MasterCard & VISA Credit Card Sources*, 8th Ed.

TORAH AURA PRODUCTIONS

4423 Fruitland Ave., Los Angeles CA 90058. (800)238-6724. Fax: (323)585-0327. E-mail: misrad@torahaura.com. Website: www.torahaura.com. **Contact:** Jane Golub. Estab. 1982. Publishes hardcover and trade paperback originals. **Publishes 25 titles/year. 5 queries received/year. 10 mss received/year. 2% of books from first-time authors. 100% from unagented writers. Pays 10% royalty on wholesale price.** Publishes book 2-3 years after acceptance of ms. Accepts simultaneous submissions. Responds in 6 months to manuscripts. Book catalog available free.

O━ Torah Aura publishes educational materials for Jewish classrooms only.

Nonfiction Subjects include language, literature, Hebrew, religion, Jewish. Query with SASE. Reviews artwork/photos. Send photocopies.

Fiction Subjects include juvenile, religious, young adult. All fiction must have Jewish interest. Query with SASE. Reviews artwork/photos as part.

Recent Title(s) *Artzeinu*, by Joel Lurie Grishaver, Josh Mason-Barkin and Ethan Bair; *Apples and Oranges*, by Rabbi David Lieb; *Yisrael Sheli*, by David Singer; *Eizehu Gibor*, by Joel Lurie Grishaver; *Morah, Morah, Teach Me Torah*, by Nechama Retting and Tobey Greenberg; *V'Khol Banayikh—Jewish Education for All: A Jewish Special Needs Resource Guide*, by Sara Rubinow Simon, Linda Forrest and Ellen Fishman.

TORQUERE PRESS

P.O. Box 2545, Round Rock TX 78680. (512)586-6921. Fax: (866)287-4860. E-mail: submissions@torquerepress.com. Website: www.torquerepress.com. **Contact:** Shawn Clements, submissions editor (homoerotica, suspense, gay/lesbian); Lorna Hinson, senior editor (gay/lesbian romance, historicals). Estab. 2003. Publishes trade paperback originals and electronic originals and reprints. **Publishes 140 titles/year. 500 queries received/year. 200 mss received/year. 25% of books from first-time authors. 100% from unagented writers. Pays 8-40% royalty. Pays $35-75 for anthology stories.** Publishes book 6 months after acceptance of ms. Responds in 1 month to queries and proposals. Responds in 2-4 months to manuscripts. Book catalog available online. Guidelines available online.

Imprints Top Shelf (Shawn Clements, editor); Single Shots (Kil Kenny, editor); Screwdrivers (M. Rode, editor); High Balls (Vincent Diamond, editor).

Fiction Subjects include adventure, erotica, gay, lesbian, historical, horror, mainstream, contemporary, multicultural, mystery, occult, romance, science fiction, short story collections, suspense, western. "We are a gay and lesbian press focusing on romance and genres of romance. We particularly like paranormal and western romance." Submit proposal package, 3 sample chapters, clips.

Recent Title(s) *Filet Gumbo*, by B.A. Tortuga (contemporary romance); *X-Factor*, by Sean Michael (contemporary romance).

Tips "Our audience is primarily people looking for a familiar romance setting featuring gay or lesbian protagonists. Please read guidelines carefully and familiarize yourself with our lines."

TRAFALGAR SQUARE BOOKS

P.O. Box 257, N. Pomfret VT 05053-0257. (802)457-1911. Website: www.horseandriderbooks.com. **Contact:** Martha Cook, managing director; Rebecca Didier, senior editor. Estab. 1985. Publishes hardcover and trade paperback originals. **Publishes 12 titles/year. 50% of books from first-time authors. 80% from unagented writers. Pays royalty. Pays advance.** Publishes book 18 months after acceptance of ms. Responds in 1 month to queries, 2 months to proposals, 2-3 months to mss. Catalog free on request and by e-mail.

Imprints Trafalgar Square Books.

O━ "We publish high quality instructional books for horsemen and horsewomen, always with the horse's welfare in mind."

Nonfiction Subjects include animals, horses/dogs. Query with SASE. Submit proposal package including outline, 1-3 sample chapters, letter of introduction including qualifications for writing on the subject and why the proposed book is an essential addition to existing publications. Reviews artwork/photos as part of the ms package. We prefer color laser thumbnail sheets or duplicate prints (do not send original photos or art!).

Recent Title(s) *The Rider's Pain-Free Back*, by James Warson; *The Ultimate Horse Behavior and Training Book*, by Linda Tellington-Jones.

Tips "Our audience is horse lovers and riders interested in doing what is best in the interest of horses."

TRUMAN STATE UNIVERSITY PRESS

100 E. Normal St., Kirksville MO 63501-4221. (660)785-7336. Fax: (660)785-4480. E-mail: tsup@truman.edu. Website: tsup.truman.edu. **Contact:** Barbara Smith-Mandell (American studies, poetry); Michael Wolfe (early modern studies). **Publishes 13 titles/year.** Guidelines available online.

Nonfiction Early modern, American studies, poetry.

Recent Title(s) *Deaths on Pleasant Street; What Lurks Beyond, Passion for History.*

N 23 HOUSE PUBLISHING

405 Moseley St., Jefferson TX 75657. Fax: (214)367-4343. E-mail: editor@23house.com. Website: www.23house.com. **Contact:** Editor. Publishes trade paperback originals and electronic book format. Accepts simultaneous submissions. Book catalog and ms guidelines online.

- "We are looking for regional titles around the U.S., specifically in the folklore and supernatural genre. An idea of the market for the book should be included as part of the proposal."

O→ "We have produced books in almost every genre."

Nonfiction Haunted locations, interesting history, etc. "We are looking for regional nonfiction titles that can build an audience in specific locations in the U.S." Submit proposal via e-mail, and we'll go from there.

Fiction Subjects include horror, mostly, but it is a small part of our catalog.

Recent Title(s) *Dead Set: A Zombie Anthology; Florida Frights: Ghosts of the Keys; Spirits of Gettysburg: Tales of a Ghost Tour Guide.*

Tips "Please check our current needs on the guidelines section of our website. If you're pitching a book to us, we're as interested in the market for it as we are the work itself."

UNIVERSITY OF NEBRASKA PRESS

1111 Lincoln Mall, Lincoln NE 68588-0630. (800)755-1105. Fax: (402)472-6214. E-mail: pressmail@unl.edu. Website: nebraskapress.unl.edu. **Contact:** Heather Lundine, managing editor. Publishes hardcover and trade paperback originals and trade paperback reprints. Book catalog available free. Guidelines available online.

Imprints Bison Books (paperback reprints of classic books).

O→ "We primarily publish nonfiction books and scholarly journals, along with a few titles per season in contemporary and regional prose and poetry. On occasion, we reprint previously published fiction of established reputation, and we have several programs to publish literary works in translation."

Nonfiction Subjects include agriculture, animals, anthropology, archeology, creative nonfiction, history, memoirs, military, war, multicultural, nature, environment, religion, sports, translation, women's issues, women's studies, Native American studies, American Lives series, experimental fiction by American-Indian writers. Submit book proposal with overview, audience, format, detailed chapter outline, sample chapters, sample bibliography, timetable, CV.

Fiction Series and translation only. Occasionally reprints fiction of established reputation.

Poetry Contemporary, regional.

Recent Title(s) *Lights on a Ground of Darkness*, by Ted Kooser; *The Blue Tattoo*, by Margot Mifflin; *In the United States of Africa*, by Abdourahman A. Waberi; *We Will Dance our Truth*, by David Delgado Shorter; *New Perspectives on Native North America*, by Sergei A. Kan and Pauline Turner Strong.

UNIVERSITY OF NEW MEXICO PRESS

1 University of New Mexico, MSC05 3185, Albuquerque NM 87131-0001. (505)277-3324 or (800)249-7737. Fax: (505)277-3343. E-mail: unmpress@unm.edu. Website: www.unmpress.com. **Contact:** W. Clark Whitehorn, senior acquisitions editor. Estab. 1929. Publishes hardcover originals and trade paperback originals and reprints. **Pays variable royalty. Pays advance.** Book catalog available free. Please read and follow the submission query guidelines on the Author Information page online. Do not send your entire manuscript or additional materials until requested. If your book is accepted for publication, you will be notified.

O→ "The Press is well known as a publisher in the fields of anthropology, archeology, Latin American studies, art and photography, architecture and the history and culture of the American West, fiction, some poetry, Chicano/a studies and works by and about American Indians. We focus on American West, Southwest and Latin American regions."

Nonfiction Subjects include Americana, anthropology, archeology, art, architecture, biography, creative nonfiction, ethnic, gardening, gay, lesbian, government, politics, history, language, literature, memoirs, military, war, multicultural, music, dance, nature, environment, photography, regional, religion, science, translation, travel, women's issues, women's studies, contemporary culture, cinema/stage, true crime, general nonfiction. Query with SASE. Reviews artwork/photos. Send photocopies.

Recent Title(s) *Constructing Lives at Mission San Francisco: Native Californians and Hispanic Colonists, 1776-1821,* by Quincy Newell; *The American Military Frontiers: The United States Army in the West, 1783-1900,* by Robert Wooster; *Country of Bullets, Chronicles of War*, by Juanita León, Translated by Guillermo Bleichmar.

UNIVERSITY OF NORTH TEXAS PRESS

1155 Union Circle, #311336, Denton TX 76203-5017. (940)565-2142. E-mail: Ronald.Chrisman@unt.edu; Karen.DeVinney@unt.edu. **Contact:** Ronald Chrisman, director; Karen DeVinney, managing editor. Estab. 1987. Publishes hardcover and trade paperback originals and reprints. **Publishes 14-16 titles/year. 500 queries received/year. 50% of books from first-time authors. 95% from unagented writers.** Publishes book 1-2 years after acceptance of ms. Responds in 1 month to queries. Book catalog for 8½ × 11 SASE. Guidelines available online.

> "We are dedicated to producing the highest quality scholarly, academic, and general interest books. We are committed to serving all peoples by publishing stories of their cultures and experiences that have been overlooked. Currently emphasizing military history, Texas history and literature, music, Mexican-American studies."

Nonfiction Subjects include Americana, ethnic, government, politics, history, music, dance, biography, military, war, nature, regional, women's issues/studies. Query with SASE. Reviews artwork/photos. Send photocopies.

Fiction The only fiction we publish is the winner of the Katherine Anne Porter Prize in Short Fiction, an annual, national competition with a $1,000 prize, and publication of the winning manuscript each Fall.

Poetry "The only poetry we publish is the winner of the Vassar Miller Prize in Poetry, an annual, national competition with a $1,000 prize and publication of the winning manuscript each Spring." Query.

Tips "We publish series called War and the Southwest; Texas Folklore Society Publications; the Western Life Series; Practical Guide Series; Al-Filo: Mexican-American studies; North Texas Crime and Criminal Justice; Katherine Anne Porter Prize in Short Fiction; and the North Texas Lives of Musicians Series."

UNIVERSITY OF PENNSYLVANIA PRESS

3905 Spruce St., Philadelphia PA 19104. (215)898-6261. Fax: (215)898-0404. Website: www.pennpress.org. **Contact:** Jerome Singerman, humanities editor; Peter Agree, editor-in-chief and social sciences editor; Jo Joslyn, art and architecture editor; Robert Lockhart, history editor; Bill Finan, politics, international relations. Estab. 1890. Publishes hardcover and paperback originals, and reprints. **Publishes 100 + titles/year. 20-30% of books from first-time authors. 95% from unagented writers. Royalty determined on book-by-book basis. Pays advance.** Publishes book 10 months after delivery of ms after acceptance of ms. Responds in 3 months to queries. Book catalog available online. Guidelines available online.

> "Manuscript submissions are welcome in fields appropriate for Penn Press's editorial program. The Press's acquiring editors, and their fields of responsibility, are listed in the Contact Us section of our Web site. Although we have no formal policies regarding manuscript proposals and submissions, what we need minimally, in order to gauge our degree of interest, is a brief statement describing the manuscript, a copy of the contents page, and a reasonably current vita. Initial inquiries are best sent by letter, in paper form, to the appropriate acquiring editor."

Nonfiction "Serious books that serve the scholar and the professional, student and general reader." Subjects include Americana, art, architecture, history, American, art, architecture, literary criticism, sociology, anthropology, literary criticism, cultural studies, ancient studies, medieval studies, urban studies, human rights. Follow the *Chicago Manual of Style*. Query with SASE. Submit outline, resume. Reviews artwork/photos. Send photocopies.

UNIVERSITY PRESS OF KANSAS

2502 Westbrooke Circle, Lawrence KS 66045-4444. (785)864-4154. Fax: (785)864-4586. E-mail: upress@ku.edu. Website: www.kansaspress.ku.edu. **Contact:** Michael J. Briggs, editor-in-chief (military history, political science, law); Ranjit Arab, acquisitions editor (western history, American studies, environmental studies, women's studies); Fred M. Woodward, director, (political science, presidency, regional). Estab. 1946. Publishes hardcover originals, trade paperback originals and reprints. **Publishes 55 titles/year. 600 queries received/year. 20% of books from first-time authors. 98% from unagented writers. Pays selective advance.** Publishes book 10 months after acceptance of ms. Responds in 1 month to proposals. Book catalog and ms guidelines free.

O— "The University Press of Kansas publishes scholarly books that advance knowledge and regional books that contribute to the understanding of Kansas, the Great Plains, and the Midwest."

Nonfiction Subjects include Americana, anthropology, archeology, government, politics, history, military, war, nature, environment, regional, sociology, women's issues, women's studies. "We are looking for books on topics of wide interest based on solid scholarship and written for both specialists and informed general readers. Do not send unsolicited, complete manuscripts." Submit outline, sample chapters, cover letter, cv, prospectus. Reviews artwork/photos. Send photocopies.

Recent Title(s) *Armageddon in Stalingrad*, by David M. Glantz with Jonathan M. House; *The Discretionary President*, by Benjamin A. Kleinerman; *Guantanamo, USA*, by Stephen Irving May Schwab.

UNIVERSITY PRESS OF MISSISSIPPI

3825 Ridgewood Rd., Jackson MS 39211-6492. (601)432-6205. Fax: (601)432-6217. E-mail: press@mississippi.edu. Website: www.upress.state.ms.us. **Contact:** Craig Gill, editor-in-chief (regional studies, art, folklore, music). Estab. 1970. Publishes hardcover and paperback originals and reprints. **Publishes 60 titles/year. 20% of books from first-time authors. 90% from unagented writers. Competitive royalties and terms. Pays advance.** Publishes book 1 year after acceptance of ms. Responds in 3 months to queries.

O— "University Press of Mississippi publishes scholarly and trade titles, as well as special series, including: American Made Music; Conversations with Comic Artists; Conversations with Filmmakers; Faulkner and Yoknapatawpha; Literary Conversations; Studies in Popular Culture; Hollywood Legends; Caribbean Studies."

Nonfiction Subjects include Americana, art, architecture, ethnic, minority studies, government, politics, health, medicine, history, language, literature, literary criticism, music, dance, photography, regional, Southern, folklife, literary criticism, popular culture with scholarly emphasis, literary studies. "We prefer a proposal that describes the significance of the work and a chapter outline." Submit outline, sample chapters, cv.

Recent Title(s) *Lost Plantations of the South*, by Marc R. Matrana; *Dictionary of Louisiana French as Spoken in Cajun, Creole, and American Indian Communities*, Senior Editor Albert Valdman.

UNLIMITED PUBLISHING LLC

P.O. Box 3007, Bloomington IN 47402. Website: www.unlimitedpublishing.com. **Contact:** Acquisitions Manager (short nonfiction with a clear audience). **Publishes 25-50 titles/year. Receives 1,000 queries/year; 500 manuscripts/year. 20% of books from first-time authors. 40% from unagented writers.** Publishes book 3 months after acceptance of ms. Catalog online at website http://unlimitedpublishing.com/sitemap.htm.

Imprints Harvardwood Books.

O— "We prefer short nonfiction and fiction with a clear audience, and expect authors to be actively involved in publicity. A detailed marketing plan is required with all submissions. Moderate to good computer skills are necessary."

Nonfiction Subjects include agriculture, alternative lifestyles, Americana, animals, anthropology, archaeology, architecture, art, business, career guidance, child guidance, communications, community, computers, contemporary culture, counseling, crafts, creative nonfiction, economics, education, electronics, environment, ethnic, finance, gardening, gay, government, health, history, hobbies, horticulture, humanities, labor, language, law, lesbian, literary criticism, literature, marine subjects, medicine, memoirs, military, money, multicultural, music, nature, parenting, philosophy, politics, psychology, real estate, recreation, regional, religion, science, sex, social sciences, sociology, software, sports, translation, transportation, travel, women's issues, women's studies, world affairs, young adult. Submit proposal package , including: outline and 10-page excerpt in rich text format, a standard 'save-as option with Microsoft Word', author bio and detailed marketing plan.

Fiction Subjects include adventure, ethnic, experimental, fantasy, feminist, historical, horror, humor, juvenile, literary, mainstream, contemporary, military, war, multicultural, mystery, occult, regional, religious, science fiction fiction, short story collections, spiritual, sports, suspense, translation, war, western, young adult. Submit proposal package, including: outline and 10-page excerpt in rich text format, author bio and detailed marketing plan.

Recent Title(s) *Anything But a Dog! The perfect pet for a girl with congenital CMV (cytomegalovirus)*, by Lisa Saunders (biography-memoir, inspirational, health); *Beijing Journal: A Live, Day-by-Day Account from Backstage at the 2008 Olympics*, by Mark Butler (sports, travel, bio); *The Site*, by Andrew Dawber (adventure, thriller, men's fiction).

Tips "The growth of online bookselling allows authors and publishers to jointly cultivate a tightly targeted grassroots audience in specialty or niche markets before expanding to mainstream book industry channels based on proven public demand."

N UNTREED READS PUBLISHING

506 Kansas St., San Francisco CA 94107. (415)621-0465. Fax: (415)621-0465. E-mail: general@untreedreads.com. Website: www.untreedreads.com. **Contact:** Jay A. Hartman, editor-in-chief (fiction-all genres). Format publishes in electronic originals and reprints. **Publishes 35 titles/year. Receives 50 submissions/year. 80% of books from first-time authors. 75% from unagented writers.** Publishes book 3 months after acceptance of ms. Accepts simultaneous submissions. Catalog and guidelines available online at website.

Imprints Untreed Reads, Jay Hartman, editor-in-chief.

Nonfiction Subjects include agriculture, alternative lifestyles, Americana, animals, anthropology, archeology, architecture, art, astrology, automotive, beauty, business, career guidance, child guidance, cinema, communications, community, computers, contemporary culture, cooking, counseling, crafts, creative nonfiction, dance, economics, education, electronics, entertainment, environment, ethnic, fashion, film, finance, foods, games, gardening, gay, government, health, history, hobbies, horticulture, house and home, humanities, labor, language, law, lesbian, literary criticism, literature, marine subjects, memoirs, military/war, money/finance, multicultural, music/dance, nature/environment/new age, philosophy, photography, psychology, real estate, recreation, regional, religion, science, sex, social sciences, sociology, software, spirituality, sports, translation, transportation, travel, women's issues/studies, world affairs, young adult. "We are very interested in developing our textbook market. Ereaders don't currently support graphs, tables, images, etc. as well as print books; however, we plan to be trendsetters in this as the technology in the ereaders improves. Also we are eager to increase our number of business books. We always look for series or works that could develop into a series." Submit proposal package, including 3 sample chapters. Submit completed mss. Reviews artwork/photos. Send photocopies. Author must provide signed release of permission to use the photographs.

Fiction Subjects include multiple subjects. "We look forward to long-terms relationships with our authors. We encourage works that are either already a series or could develop into a series. We are one of the few publishiers publishing short stories and are happy to be a resource for these good works. We welcome short story collections. Also, we look forward to publishing children's books, cookbooks, and other works that have been known for illustrations in print as the technology in the multiple ereaders improves. We hope to be a large platform for diverse content and authors. We seek mainstream content, but if you're an author or have content that doesn't seem to always 'fit' into traditional market we'd like to hear from you." Submit porposal package with 3 sample chapters. Submit completed ms.

Poetry "We are not accepting individual poems currently, but will accept proposals for poetry collections."

Recent Title(s) *How to Eat Fruit*, by Anne Brooke (short story); *Dancing With Lions*, by Anne Brooke (short story).

Tips "For our fiction titles we lean toward a literary audience. For nonfiction titles, we want to be a platform for business people, entrepreneurs, and speakers to become well known in their fields of expertise. However, for both fiction and nonfiction we want to appeal to many audiences."

UPSTART BOOKS

Highsmith Press P.O. Box 5207, 401 S. Wright Rd., Janesville WI 53547-5207. (608)743-8000. Fax: (608)743-8009 (8 pp. or less). Website: www.highsmith.com. **Contact:** Matt Mulder, publications manager. Estab. 1990. Publishes hardcover and paperback originals. **Publishes 12 titles/year. 500-600 queries received/year. 400-500 mss received/year. 30% of books from first-time authors. 100% from unagented writers. Pays $250-1,000 advance.** Publishes book 6 months after acceptance of ms. Accepts simultaneous submissions. Responds in 1 month to queries. Responds in 2 months to proposals and mss. Book catalog available online. Guidelines available online.

Imprints Alleyside Press, Upstart Books (creative supplemental reading, library and critical thinking skills materials designed to expand the learning environment).

- Upstart Books publishes educational resources to meet the practical needs of librarians, educators, readers, library users, media specialists, schools and related institutions, and to help them fulfill their valuable functions.

Nonfiction Subjects include education, language, literature, multicultural. "We are primarily interested in manuscripts that stimulate or strengthen reading, library and information-seeking skills and foster critical thinking." Query with outline and 1-2 sample chapters. Reviews artwork/photos. Send transparencies.

Fiction Our current emphasis is on storytelling collections for preschool-grade 6. We prefer stories that can be easily used by teachers and children's librarians, multicultural topics, and manuscripts that feature fold and cut, flannelboard, tangram, or similar simple patterns that can be reproduced.
Recent Title(s) *Finger Tales*, by Joan Hilyer Phelps; *Characters with Character*, by Diane Findlay.

VANDERBILT UNIVERSITY PRESS

VU Station B 351813, Nashville TN 37235. (615)322-3585. Fax: (615)343-8823. E-mail: vupress@vanderbilt.edu. Website: www.vanderbiltuniversitypress.com. **Contact:** Michael Ames, director. Publishes hardcover originals and trade paperback originals and reprints. **Publishes 20-25 titles/year. 500 queries received/year. 25% of books from first-time authors. 90% from unagented writers. Pays rare advance.** Publishes book 10 months after acceptance of ms. Accepts simultaneous submissions. Responds in 2 weeks to proposals. Book catalog available free online. Guidelines available online.

- Also distributes for and co-publishes with Country Music Foundation.

O→ "Vanderbilt University Press publishes books on healthcare, social sciences, education, and regional studies, for both academic and general audiences that are intellectually significant, socially relevant, and of practical importance."

Nonfiction Subjects include Americana, anthropology, archeology, education, ethnic, government, politics, health, medicine, history, language, literature, multicultural, music, dance, nature, environment, philosophy, women's issues, women's studies. Submit prospectus, sample chapter, cv. Does not accept electronic submissions. Reviews artwork/photos. Send photocopies.
Recent Title(s) *Lost Delta Found*, edited by Robert Gordon and Bruce Nemerov.
Tips "Our audience consists of scholars and educated, general readers."

VIVISPHERE PUBLISHING

675 Dutchess Turnpike, Poughkeepsie NY 12603. (845)463-1100, ext. 314. Fax: (845)463-0018. Website: www.vivisphere.com. **Contact:** Lisa Mays. Estab. 1995. Publishes paperback originals and paperback reprints. **Pays royalty.** Publishes book 3-12 months after acceptance of ms. Accepts simultaneous submissions. Responds in 3 months to queries. Book catalog free; ms guidelines free or online.

O→ "Cookbooks should have a particular slant or appeal to a certain niche. Also publish out-of-print books."

Nonfiction Subjects include history, military, war, New Age, game of bridge. Vivisphere Publishing is now considering new submissions from any genre. Please see our News & Events board online for more information. Query with SASE. Please submit a *hardcopy* (printed paper copy) of the first 20 pages, or first chapter of your work, along with your contact information to: Attn: New Submissions, at our address.
Fiction Subjects include feminist, gay, lesbian, historical, horror, literary, mainstream, contemporary, military, war, science fiction, western. Query with SASE.

VOYAGEUR PRESS

400 First Ave., Suite 300, Minneapolis MN 55401. (651)430-2210. Fax: (651)430-2211. E-mail: mdregni@voyageurpress.com; jleventhal@voyageurpress.com; dprnu@mbipublishing.com; kcornell@voyageurpress.com. **Contact:** Michael Dregni, publisher; Kari Cornell, acquistions editor crafts and cookbooks; Dennis Pernu, senior editor music titles; Josh Leventhal, publisher sports books. Estab. 1972. Publishes hardcover and trade paperback originals. **Publishes 80 titles/year. 1,200 queries received/year. 500 mss received/year. 10% of books from first-time authors. 90% from unagented writers. Pays royalty. Pays advance.** Publishes book 1 year after acceptance of ms. Accepts simultaneous submissions. Responds in 3 months to queries.
Imprints MVP Books.

O→ "Voyageur Press (and its sports imprint MVP Books) is internationally known as a leading publisher of quality music, sports, country living, crafts, natural history, and regional books. No children's or poetry books."

Nonfiction Subjects include Americana, cooking, environment, history, hobbies, music, nature, regional, sports, collectibles, country living, knitting and quilting, outdoor recreation. Query with SASE. Submit outline. Send sample digital images or transparencies (duplicates and tearsheets only).
Recent Title(s) *The Snowflake* (popular science and microphotography look at snow crystals); *The Replacements* (oral history of post-punk rock'n'roll band); *The Surfboard* (history of surfboards); *How to Raise Chickens.*
Tips "We publish books for an audience interested in regional, natural, and cultural history on a wide variety of subjects. We seek authors strongly committed to helping us promote and sell their books. Please present as focused an idea as possible in a brief submission (1-page cover letter; 2-page outline

or proposal). Note your credentials for writing the book. Tell all you know about the market niche and marketing possibilities for proposed book."

🄽 W&A PUBLISHING

One Peregrine Way, P.O. Box 849, Cedar Falls IA 50613. (319)266-0441. E-mail: kgolden@w-apublishing.com. Website: www.w-apublishing.com. **Contact:** Karris Golden, executive editor. Hardcover and electronic originals; hardcover reprints. **Publishes 10-12/year titles/year. 90%% of books from first-time authors. 100%% from unagented writers.** Publishes book 3-6 months after acceptance of ms. Accepts simultaneous submissions. Catalog available online at website. Guidelines available online at website and by e-mail at editorial@w-apublishing.com.

Nonfiction Subjects include business, economics, finance, money, Investing/trading; investment/trading strategies, systems, and techniques; hot trends; trading/investment psychology; trading guidelines and how-to; new, tested trading/investment methods; anthologies of articles related to the above. "We are always interested in great ideas, fresh voices, and new methods, strategies, and approaches that will educate readers interested in improving their skills as traders and investors." Submit proposal packages, including: outline/synopsis, 1-3 sample chapters(s), table of contents and author's biographical information; prefer e-mailed submissions Writers should send photocopies; scans; computer-generated graphics.

Recent Title(s) *We're All Screwed: How Toxic Regulation Will Crush the Free Market System*, by Stephen A. Boyko (analysis of capital market regulation); *Trade the Patters: The Revolutionary Way of Trading the CCI*, by Ken "Woodie" Wood (trading how-to); *Dow Theory Unplugged: Charles Dow's Original Editorials*, by Dow, Richard Russell, Charles Carlson, Papul Shread (reference, trading); *Rookie's Guide to Options: The Beginner's Handbook of Trading Equity Options*, by Mark Wolfinger (options trading how-to).

Tips "Our readers have increased knowledge and awareness of discrete investment products and tools. They are interested in an education and want to learn from practicing financial professionals. Our goal is to offer readers materials highlighting new techniques, in-depth analysis, and solid information that helps them hone their skills and make informed decisions. We are interested in providing accompanying workbook materials in print and electronic form to augment the published book. (We prefer workbook/training materials that are supplemental rather than incorporated into the book.)"

WESLEYAN PUBLISHING HOUSE

P.O. Box 50434, Indianapolis IN 46250. Website: www.wesleyan.org/wph. Hardcover and trade paperback originals. **Publishes 25 titles/year. 150-175 submissions received. 50% of books from first-time authors. 90% from unagented writers.** Publishes book 11 months after acceptance of ms. Accepts simultaneous submissions. Catalog available online at website www.wesleyan.org/wph. Guidelines available online at website www.wesleyan.org/wg and by e-mail.

Nonfiction Subjects include Christianity/religion. Submit proposal package, including outline, 3-5 sample chapters, bio. See writer's guidelines. Does not review artwork.

Fiction Does not publish fiction.

Recent Title(s) *Rethink Your Life*, by Stan Toler (Christian living); *Common Ground*, by Keith Drury (Christian living).

Tips "Our books help evangelical Christians learn about the faith or grow in their relationship with God."

WESTMINSTER JOHN KNOX PRESS

Division of Presbyterian Publishing Corp. 100 Witherspoon St., Louisville KY 40202-1396. Fax: (502)569-5113. Website: www.wjkbooks.com. **Contact:** Jana Riess, acquisitions editor. Publishes hardcover and paperback originals and reprints. **Publishes 70 titles/year. 2,500 queries received/year. 750 mss received/year. 10% of books from first-time authors. Pays royalty on net price.** Responds in 8-10 weeks or longer. Proposal guidelines online.

> 🔑 "All WJK books have a religious/spiritual angle, but are written for various markets-scholarly, professional, and the general reader. Westminster John Knox is affiliated with the Presbyterian Church USA. No phone queries. We do not publish fiction, poetry, memoir, or children's books, and we generally do not publish dissertations. We will not return submissions without an accompanying self-addressed, stamped envelope with sufficient postage."

Nonfiction Subjects include religion, spirituality. Submit proposal package according to the WJK book proposal guidelines found online.

⊘ WHITAKER HOUSE

1030 Hunt Valley Circle, New Kensington PA 15068. E-mail: publisher@whitakerhouse.com. Website: www.whitakerhouse.com. **Contact:** Tom Cox, managing editor. Estab. 1970. Publishes hardcover, trade paperback, and mass market originals. **Publishes 50 titles/year. 600 queries received/year. 200 mss received/year. 15% of books from first-time authors. 60% from unagented writers. Pays 5-15% royalty on wholesale price.** Publishes book 7 months after acceptance of ms. Accepts simultaneous submissions. Responds in 3 months to queries, proposals and manuscripts. Book catalog available online. Guidelines available online and by e-mail.

Nonfiction Accepts submissions on any topic as long as they have a Christian perspective. Subjects include religion, Christian. Accepts submissions on topics with a Christian perspective. Subjects include Christian living, prayer, spiritual warfare, healing, gifts of the spirit, etc. Query with SASE. Does not review artwork/photos.

Fiction All fiction must have a Christian perspective. Subjects include religious, Christian, historial romance, African American romance and Amish fiction. Query with SASE.

Recent Title(s) *Principles and Benefits of Change*, by Dr. Myles Munroe (Christian living); *Abbie Anne*, by Sharlene MacLaren (historical romance); *10 Hours To Live*, by Brian Wills.

Tips "Audience includes those seeking uplifting and inspirational fiction and nonfiction."

N WHITE PINE PRESS

P.O. Box 236, Buffalo NY 14201. (716)627-4665. Fax: (716)627-4665. E-mail: wpine@whitepine.org. Website: www.whitepine.org. **Contact:** Dennis Maloney, editor (poetry & translation). Trade paperback originals. **Publishes 10-12 titles/year. 500 queries/yearly 1% of books from first-time authors. 100% from unagented writers.** Publishes book 18 months after acceptance of ms. Accepts simultaneous submissions. Catalog available online at website; for #10 SASE. Guidelines available online at website.

Nonfiction Subjects include language, literature, multicultural, translation, poetry. We are currently not considering nonfiction mss. We do not review artwork/photos,

Fiction Subjects include poetry, poetry in translation, translation. "We are currently not reading U.S. fiction. We are currently reading unsolicited poetry only as part of our Annual Poetry Contest. The reading period is July 1 - November 30 for fiction and poetry in translation only." For fiction & poetry in translation ONLY-query with SASE; submit proposal package, including synopsis & 2 sample chapters."

Poetry See above re: poetry contest

WILSHIRE BOOK CO.

9731 Variel Ave., Chatsworth CA 91311-4315. (818)700-1522. Fax: (818)700-1527. E-mail: mpowers@mpowers.com. Website: www.mpowers.com. **Contact:** Rights Department. Estab. 1947. Publishes trade paperback originals and reprints. **Publishes 25 titles/year. 1,200 queries received/year. 70% of books from first-time authors. 90% from unagented writers. Pays standard royalty. Pays advance.** Publishes book 6-9 months after acceptance of ms. Accepts simultaneous submissions. Responds in 2 months.

Nonfiction Subjects include psychology, personal success. Minimum 30,000 words Submit 3 sample chapters. Submit complete ms. Include outline, author bio, analysis of book's competition and SASE. No e-mail or fax submissions. Reviews artwork/photos. Send photocopies.

Fiction Adult allegories that teach principles of psychological growth or offer guidance in living. Minimum 30,000 words. Submit 3 sample chapters. Submit complete ms. Include outline, author bio, analysis of book's, competition and SASE.

Recent Title(s) *The Dragon Slayer with a Heavy Heart*, by Marcia Powers; *The Secret of Overcoming Verbal Abuse*, by Albert Ellis, PhD, and Marcia Grad Powers; *The Princess Who Believed in Fairy Tales*, by Marcia Grad.

Tips "We are vitally interested in all new material we receive. Just as you are hopeful when submitting your manuscript for publication, we are hopeful as we read each one submitted, searching for those we believe could be successful in the marketplace. Writing and publishing must be a team effort. We need you to write what we can sell. We suggest you read the successful books similar to the one you want to write. Analyze them to discover what elements make them winners. Duplicate those elements in your own style, using a creative new approach and fresh material, and you will have written a book we can catapult onto the bestseller list. You are welcome to telephone or e-mail us for immediate feedback on any book concept you may have. To learn more about us and what we publish—and for complete manuscript guidelines-visit our website."

WINDRIVER PUBLISHING, INC.

72 N. WindRiver Rd., Silverton ID 83867-0446. (208)752-1836. Fax: (208)752-1876. E-mail: info@windriverpublishing.com. Website: www.windriverpublishing.com. **Contact:** E. Keith Howick, Jr., president; Gail Howick, vice president/editor-in-chief. Estab. 2003. Publishes hardcover originals and reprints, trade paperback originals, and mass market originals. **Publishes 8 titles/year. 1,000 queries received/year. 300 mss received/year. 95% of books from first-time authors. 90% from unagented**

writers. Publishes book 12 months after acceptance of ms. Accepts simultaneous submissions. Responds in 1-2 months to queries. Responds in 4-6 months to proposals and manuscripts. Book catalog available online. Guidelines available online.

"Authors who wish to submit book proposals for review must do so according to our Submissions Guidelines, which can be found on our website, along with an on-line submission form, which is our preferred submission method. We do not accept submissions of any kind by e-mail."

Nonfiction Subjects include business, computers, education, environment, gardening, government, health, history, hobbies, language, literature, medicine, nature, philosophy, religion, science, spirituality, sports, true crime, antiques/collectibles. Follow online instructions for submitting proposal, including synopsis and 3 sample chapters. *Ms submissions by invitation only*. Reviews artwork/photos.

Fiction Subjects include adventure, fantasy, historical, horror, humor, juvenile, literary, military, war, mystery, occult, religious, romance, science fiction, short story collections, spiritual, sports, suspense, western, young adult, drama; espionage; political; psychological; fairy tales/folklore; graphic novels. Follow online instructions.

Recent Title(s) *Blow Us Away! Publishers' Secrets for Successful Manuscripts*, by JB Howick; *A Study in Valor: Faith of a Bataan Death March Survivor*, by William Garner.

Tips "We do not accept manuscripts containing graphic or gratuitous profanity, sex, or violence. See online instructions for details."

WISCONSIN HISTORICAL SOCIETY PRESS

816 State St., Madison WI 53706. (608)264-6465. Fax: (608)264-6486. E-mail: whspress@wisconsinhistory.org. Website: www.wisconsinhistory.org/whspress/. **Contact:** Kate Thompson, editor. Estab. 1855. Publishes hardcover and trade paperback originals. Trade paperback reprints. **Publishes 12-14 titles/year. 60-75 queries received/year. 20%% of books from first-time authors. 90%% from unagented writers. Pays royalty on wholesale price.** Publishes book 18-24 months after acceptance of ms. Book catalog available free. Guidelines available online.

Imprints Wisconsin Magazine of History.

Nonfiction Subjects include Wisconsin history and culture: archaeology, architecture, cooking, foods, ethnic, history (Wisconsin), memoirs, regional, sports. Submit proposal package, form from website. Reviews artwork/photos. Send photocopies.

Tips "Our audience reads about Wisconsin. Carefully review the book."

WRITER'S DIGEST BOOKS

Imprint of F+W Media, Inc. 4700 E. Galbraith Rd., Cincinnati OH 45236. E-mail: writersdigest@fwmedia.com. Website: www.writersdigest.com. **Contact:** Kelly Messerly, Acquisitions Editor. Estab. 1920. Publishes hardcover originals and trade paperbacks. **Publishes 18-20 titles/year. 300 queries received/year. 50 mss received/year. 30% from unagented writers. Pays average $3,000 advance.** Publishes book 6-12 months after acceptance of ms. Accepts simultaneous submissions. Responds in 3 months to queries. Our catalog of titles is available to view online at www.WritersDigestShop.com.

- Writer's Digest Books accepts query letters and complete proposals via e-mail at writersdigest@fwmedia.com.

"Writer's Digest Books is the premiere source for instructional books on writing and publishing for an audience of aspirational writers. Typical mss are 80,000 words. E-mail queries strongly preferred; no phone calls please."

Nonfiction "Our instruction books stress results and how specifically to achieve them. Should be well-researched, yet lively and readable. We do not want to see books telling readers how to crack specific nonfiction markets: *Writing for the Computer Market* or *Writing for Trade Publications*, for instance. We are most in need of fiction-technique books written by published authors. Be prepared to explain how the proposed book differs from existing books on the subject." Query with SASE. Submit outline, sample chapters, SASE.

Recent Title(s) *The Constant Art of Being a Writer*, by N.M. Kelby; *Write Like the Masters*, by William Cane; *The Daily Writer*, by Fred White; *The Fire in Fiction*, by Donald Maass; *Novel Shortcuts*, by Lauren Whitcomb.

Tips "Most queries we receive are either too broad (how to write fiction) or too niche (how to write erotic horror), and don't reflect a knowledge of our large backlist of 150 titles. We rarely publish new books on journalism, freelancing, magazine article writing or marketing/promotion. We are actively seeking fiction and nonfiction writing technique books with fresh perspectives, interactive and visual writing instruction books, similar to *Pocket Muse*, by Monica Wood; and general reference works that appeal to an audience beyond writers."

🅽 YBK PUBLISHERS, INC.

39 Crosby St., New York NY 10013. E-mail: info@ybkpublishers.com. Website: www.ybkpublishers.com. **Contact:** George Ernsberger, editor-in-chief. Estab. 2000. Publishes hardcover and trade paperback originals. **Publishes 12 titles/year. 90%% of books from first-time authors. 100%% from unagented writers. Pays -15% royalty on retail price.** Publishes book 3 months after acceptance of ms. Accepts simultaneous submissions. Responds in 1 month to queries, proposals and manuscripts. Book catalog available online. Guidelines available online.

Nonfiction We seek highly directed niche subjects directed at a market that is narrow, identifiable, and economically reachable. Reviews artwork/photos.

Tips "Our audience wants academic and special interest topics."

🌐 YOGI IMPRESSIONS BOOKS PVT. LTD.

1711, Centre 1, World Trade Centre, Cuffe Parade Mumbai 400 005, India. E-mail: yogi@yogiimpressions.com. Website: www.yogiimpressions.com. **Contact:** Submissions Editor. Estab. 2000. Guidelines available online.

- 🔑 "Yogi Impressions are Self-help, Personal Growth and Spiritual book publishers based in Mumbai, India. Established at the turn of the millennium, at Mumbai, Yogi Impressions publishes books which seek to revive interest in spirituality, enhance the quality of life and, thereby, create the legacy of a better world for future generations."

Nonfiction Subjects include audio, child guidance, multicultural, religion, spirituality, alternative health, enlightened business, self-improvement/personal growth. Submit outline/proposal, bio, 2-3 sample chapters, market assessment, SASE.

Recent Title(s) *Forever Ours*, by Janis Amatuzio, MD; *Surrender*, by A.A. Khan.

ZONDERVAN

Division of HarperCollins Publishers 5300 Patterson Ave. SE, Grand Rapids MI 49530-0002. (616)698-6900. Fax: (616)698-3454. Website: www.zondervan.com. **Contact:** Manuscript Review Editor. Estab. 1931. Publishes hardcover and trade paperback originals and reprints. **Publishes 200 titles/year. 10% of books from first-time authors. 60% from unagented writers. Pays 14% royalty on net amount received on sales of cloth and softcover trade editions; 12% royalty on net amount received on sales of mass market paperbacks. Pays variable advance.** Responds in 2 months to queries. Responds in 3 months to proposals. Responds in 4 months to manuscripts. Guidelines available online.

Imprints Zondervan, Zonderkidz, Youth Specialties, Editorial Vida.

- We're currently accepting unsolicited book proposals only for the following categories: Academic (only college and seminary textbooks in the areas of theology, biblical studies, church history, etc.) Reference (commentaries, handbooks, encyclopedias, etc.) Ministry Resources (books and resources for pastors and ministry professionals). A proposal for one of these categories should be saved as a Microsoft Word document (unless it contains Hebrew, Greek, or language other than English, in which case it should be saved as an Adobe PDF document) and sent electronically as an attachment to submissions@zondervan.com, putting the appropriate category in the subject line. Your proposal should include the book title a table of contents, including a 2 or 3-sentence description of each chapter, a brief description of the proposed book, including the unique contribution of the book and why you feel it must be published, your intended reader and your vita, including your qualifications to write the book. The proposal should be no more than 5 pages. If we're interested in reviewing more material from you, we'll respond within 6 weeks. All unsolicited proposals or manuscripts received outside of the above instructions, either hard copy or electronically, will be discarded. No longer accepts unsolicited mailed submissions. Instead, submissions may be submitted electronically to (ChristianManuscriptSubmissions.com).
- 🔑 "Our mission is to be the leading Christian communications company meeting the needs of people with resources that glorify Jesus Christ and promote biblical principles."

Nonfiction All religious perspective (evangelical). Subjects include history, humanities, memoirs, religion, Christian living, devotional, bible study resources, preaching, counseling, college and seminary textbooks, discipleship, worship, church renewal for pastors, professionals and lay leaders in ministry, theological, and biblical reference books. Submit TOC, chapter outline, intended audience, curriculum vitae.

Fiction Refer to nonfiction. Inklings-style fiction of high literary quality. Christian relevance in all cases. Will not consider collections of short stories or poetry. Submit TOC, curriculum vitae, chapter outline, intended audience.

Recent Title(s) *The Purpose Driven Life*, by Rick Warren (Christian living); *Ever After*, by Karen Kingsbury (fiction).

ZUMAYA PUBLICATIONS, LLC

3209 S. Interstate 35, #1086, Austin TX 78741. E-mail: acquisitions@zumayapublications.com. Website: www.zumayapublications.com. **Contact:** Elizabeth Burton, executive editor. Estab. 1999. Publishes trade paperback and electronic originals and reprints. **Publishes 20-25 titles/year. 1,000 queries received/ year. 100 mss received/year. 75% of books from first-time authors. 98% from unagented writers.** Publishes book 6-24 months after acceptance of ms. Accepts simultaneous submissions. Responds in 6 months to queries and proposals. Responds in 6-9 months to manuscripts. Guidelines available online.

Imprints Zumaya Arcane (New Age, inspirational fiction & nonfiction), Zumaya Boundless (GLBT); Zumaya Embraces (romance/women's fiction); Zumaya Enigma (mystery/suspense/thriller); Zumaya Thresholds (YA/middle grade); Zumaya Otherworlds (SF/F/H), Zumaya Yesterdays (memoirs, historical fiction, fiction, western fiction).

- "We are currently closed to submissions until further notice while we endeavor to catch up on our publishing queue. We will begin accepting queries for some imprints in July of 2010. Please review the guidelines page near that time for information on which imprints will be opened when."

Nonfiction Subjects include creative nonfiction, memoirs, New Age, spirituality, true ghost stories. "The easiest way to figure out what I'm looking for is to look at what we've already done. Our main nonfiction interests are in collections of true ghost stories, ones that have been investigated or thoroughly documented, memoirs that address specific regions and eras and books on the craft of writing. That doesn't mean we won't consider something else." Electronic query only. Reviews artwork/photos. Send digital format.

Fiction Subjects include adventure, fantasy, bisexual, gay, lesbian, historical, horror, humor, juvenile, literary, mainstream, contemporary, multicultural, mystery, occult, romance, science fiction, short story collections, spiritual, suspense, transgender, western, young adult. "We are currently oversupplied with speculative fiction and are reviewing submissions in SF, fantasy and paranormal suspense by invitation only. We are much in need of GLBT and YA/middle grade, historical and western, New Age/inspirational (no overtly Christian materials, please), non-category romance, thrillers. As with nonfiction, we encourage people to review what we've already published so as to avoid sending us more of the same, at least, insofar as the plot is concerned. While we're always looking for good specific mysteries, we want original concepts rather than slightly altered versions of what we've already published." Electronic query only.

Recent Title(s) *The Obsidian Seed*, by R. J. Leahy (sf); *Memory's Desire*, by Gale Storm (contemporary romance); *The Emerald City (A Spencer The Adventurer Book)*, by Stephen L. Keeney (middle grade); *Busting Loose: Cancer Survivors Tell You What Your Doctor Won't*, by Cheryl Swanson (health/self-help).

Tips "We're catering to readers who may have loved last year's best seller but not enough to want to read 10 more just like it. Have something different. If it does not fit standard pigeonholes, that's a plus. On the other hand, it has to have an audience. And if you're not prepared to work with us on promotion and marketing, it would be better to look elsewhere."

MARKETS

Canadian & International Book Publishers

Canadian and international book publishers share the same mission as their U.S. counterparts—publishing timely books on subjects of concern and interest to a targetable audience. Most of the publishers listed in this section, however, differ from U.S. publishers in that their needs tend toward subjects specific to Canada or intended for an international audience. Some are interested in submissions from Canadian writers only. There are many regional publishers that concentrate on region-specific subjects.

U.S. writers hoping to do business with Canadian and international publishers should follow specific paths of research to find out as much about their intended markets as possible. The listings will inform you about what kinds of books the Canadian and international companies publish and tell you whether they are open to receiving submissions from writers in the U.S. To further target your markets and see specific examples of the books these houses are publishing, send for catalogs from publishers, or check their websites.

Once you have determined which publishers will accept your work, it is important to understand the differences that exist between U.S. mail and Canadian and international mail. U.S. postage stamps are useless on mailings originating outside of the U.S. When enclosing a SASE for return of your query or manuscript from a Canadian or international publisher, you must include International Reply Coupons (IRCs).

THE ALTHOUSE PRESS

University of Western Ontario, Faculty of Education, 1137 Western Rd., London ON N6G 1G7, Canada. (519)661-2096. Fax: (519)661-3714. E-mail: press@uwo.ca. Website: www.edu.uwo.ca/althousepress. **Contact:** Katherine Butson, editorial assistant. Publishes trade paperback originals and reprints. **Publishes 1-5 titles/year. 60 queries received/year. 14 mss received/year. 50% of books from first-time authors. 100% from unagented writers. Pays 10% royalty. Pays $300 advance.** Publishes book 8-18 months after acceptance of ms. Accepts simultaneous submissions. Responds in 1-2 months to queries. Responds in 4 months to manuscripts. Book catalog available free. Guidelines available online.

"The Althouse Press publishes both scholarly research monographs in education and professional books and materials for educators in elementary schools, secondary schools, and faculties of education. De-emphasizing curricular or instructional materials intended for use by elementary or secondary school students."

Nonfiction Subjects include education, scholarly. "Do not send incomplete manuscripts that are only marginally appropriate to our market and limited mandate." Reviews artwork/photos. Send photocopies.

Recent Title(s) *Critical Thinking Education and Assessment: CanHigher Order Thinking Be Tested?* Edited by Jan Sobocan and Leo Groarke with Ralph H. Johnson and Frederick S. Ellett, Jr.; *Creating Safe SchoolEnvironments: From Small Steps to Sustainable Change*, by Peter G. Jaffe, Claire V. Crooks, C. Lynn Watson.

Tips "Audience is practising teachers and graduate education students."

ANNICK PRESS, LTD.

15 Patricia Ave., Toronto ON M2M 1H9, Canada. (416)221-4802. Fax: (416)221-8400. E-mail: annickpress@annickpress.com. Website: www.annickpress.com. **Contact:** Rick Wilks, director; Colleen MacMillan, associate publisher. Publishes picture books, juvenile and YA fiction and nonfiction; specializes in trade books. **Publishes 25 titles/year. 5,000 queries received/year. 3,000 mss received/year. 20% of books from first-time authors. 80-85% from unagented writers.** Publishes book 2 years after acceptance of ms. Book catalog and guidelines available online.

- *Does not accept unsolicited mss.*

"Annick Press maintains a commitment to high quality books that entertain and challenge. Our publications share fantasy and stimulate imagination, while encouraging children to trust their judgment and abilities."

Recent Title(s) *Adventures on the Ancient Silk Road,* by Priscilla Galloway with Dawn Hunter; *and Pharaohs and Foot Soldiers: One Hundred Ancient Egyptian Jobs You Might Have Desired or Dreaded*, by Kristin Butcher, illustrated by Martha Newbigging.

AWARENESS PUBLISHING GROUP

P.O. Box 1955, Gallo Manor 2052, South Africa. (27)(11)802-7810. E-mail: awareness@mweb.co.za. Website: www.awarenesspublishing.co.za. Estab. 2001.

"Publishes educational books for school children that focus on life skills."

Nonfiction Subjects include education, ethnic, health, medicine, history, religion, social sciences.

BETWEEN THE LINES

720 Bathurst St., Suite 404, Toronto ON M5S 2R4, Canada. (416)535-9914. Fax: (416)535-1484. E-mail: btlbooks@web.ca. Website: www.btlbooks.com. **Contact:** Amanda Crocker, editorial coordinator. Publishes trade paperback originals. **Publishes 8 titles/year. 350 queries received/year. 50 mss received/year. 80% of books from first-time authors. 95% from unagented writers. Pays 8% royalty.** Publishes book 1 year after acceptance of ms. Accepts simultaneous submissions. Responds in 2 months to queries and proposals. Responds in 4 months to manuscripts. Book catalog and ms guidelines for 8½ × 11 SAE and IRCs. Guidelines available online.

"Between the Lines publishes non-fiction books in the following subject areas: politics and public policy issues, social issues, development studies, history, education, the environment, health, gender and sexuality, labour, technology, media, and culture. Please note that we do not publish fiction or poetry. We prefer to receive proposals rather than entire manuscripts for consideration."

Nonfiction Subjects include education, gay, lesbian, government, politics, health, medicine, history, nature, environment, social sciences, sociology, development studies, labor, technology, media, culture. Submit proposal package, outline, resume, 2-3 sample chapters, cover letter, SASE. No email or fax submissions at this time.

Recent Title(s) *Not Paved With Gold*, by Vincenzo Pietropaolo; *Empire's Law*, edited by Amy Bartholomew; *Beyond the Promised Land*, by David F. Noble.

BRICK BOOKS

Box 20081, 431 Boler Rd., London ON N6K 4G6, Canada. (519)657-8579. E-mail: brick.books@sympatico.ca. Website: www.brickbooks.ca. **Contact:** Don McKay, editor (poetry); Stan Dragland, editor (poetry); Barry Dempster, editor (poetry). Estab. 1975. Publishes trade paperback originals. **Publishes 7 titles/year. 30 queries received/year. 100 mss received/year 30% of books from first-time authors. 100% from unagented writers.** Publishes book 2 years after acceptance of ms. Responds in 3-4 months to queries. Book catalog free or online. Guidelines available online.

- Brick Books has a reading period of January 1-April 30. Mss received outside that period will be returned. No multiple submissions. Pays 10% royalty in book copies only.

Fiction Subjects include poetry.

Recent Title(s) *All Our Wonder Unavenged*, by Don Domanski; *Night Work: The Sawchuk Poems*, by Randall Maggs.

Tips "Writers without previous publications in literary journals or magazines are rarely considered by Brick Books for publication."

BROADVIEW PRESS, INC.

P.O. Box 1243, Peterborough ON K9J 7H5, Canada. (705)743-8990. Fax: (705)743-8353. E-mail: customerservice@broadviewpress.com. Website: www.broadviewpress.com. **Contact:** See Editorial Guidelines online. Estab. 1985. **Publishes over 40 titles/year. 500 queries received/year. 200 mss received/year. 10% of books from first-time authors. 99% from unagented writers. Pays royalty.** Publishes book 12 months after acceptance of ms. Accepts simultaneous submissions. Responds in 1 month to queries. Responds in 2 months to proposals. Responds in 4 months to manuscripts. Book catalog available free. Guidelines available online.

O→ "We publish in a broad variety of subject areas in the arts and social sciences. We are open to a broad range of political and philosophical viewpoints, from liberal and conservative to libertarian and Marxist, and including a wide range of feminist viewpoints."

Nonfiction Subjects include language, literature, philosophy, religion, politics. Our focus is very much on English studies and Philosophy, but within those two core subject areas we are open to a broad range of academic approaches and political viewpoints. We welcome feminist perspectives, and we have a particular interest in addressing environmental issues. Our publishing program is internationally-oriented, and we publish for a broad range of geographical markets-but as a Canadian company we also publish a broad range of titles with a Canadian emphasis. Query with SASE. Submit proposal package. Reviews artwork/photos. Send photocopies.

Recent Title(s) *More Precisely*, by Eric Steinhart; *Folk and Fairy Tales*, 4th ed., by Martin Hallet and Barbara Karasek; *Diary of a Nobody*, by George and Weedon Grossmith, ed. by Peter Morton.

Tips "Our titles often appeal to a broad readership; we have many books that are as much of interest to the general reader as they are to academics and students."

BROKEN JAW PRESS

Box 596, STN A, Fredericton NB E3B 5A6, Canada. (506)454-5127. Fax: (506)454-5134. E-mail: editors@brokenjaw.com. Website: www.brokenjaw.com. **Contact:** Editorial Board. "Publishes almost exclusively Canadian-authored literary trade paperback originals and reprints". **Publishes 3-6 titles/year. 20% of books from first-time authors. 100% from unagented writers. Pays 10% royalty on retail price. Pays $0-500 advance.** Publishes book 18 months after acceptance of ms. Responds in 1 year to manuscripts. Book catalog for 6 × 9 SAE with 2 first-class Canadian stamps in Canada or download PDF from website. Guidelines available online.

Imprints Book Rat; Broken Jaw Press; SpareTime Editions; Dead Sea Physh Products; Maritimes Arts Projects Productions.

O→ "We publish poetry, fiction, drama and literary nonfiction, including translations and multilingual books."

Nonfiction Subjects include gay, lesbian, history, language, literature, literary criticism, regional, women's issues, women's studies, contemporary culture. Reviews artwork/photos.

Fiction Subjects include literary novels and short story collections stories.

Recent Title(s) *Aquella luz, que estremece/The Light that Makes Us Tremble*, poetry by Nela Rio; Hugh Hazelton, translator; *The York County Jail: A Brief Illustrated History*, George MacBeath and Emelie Hubert.

Tips "Unsolicited queries and manuscripts are not welcome at this time."

COACH HOUSE BOOKS

401 Huron St. on bpNichol Lane, Toronto ON M5S 2G5, Canada. (416)979-2217. Fax: (416)977-1158. Website: www.chbooks.com. **Contact:** Alana Wilcox, editor. Publishes trade paperback originals by Canadian authors. **Publishes 16 titles/year. 80% of books from first-time authors. 100% from unagented writers. Pays 10% royalty on retail price.** Publishes book 1 year after acceptance of ms. Responds in 6 months to queries. Guidelines available online.

Nonfiction Query with SASE.

Fiction Subjects include experimental, literary, plays. "Electronic submissions of **Fiction** and drama are welcome. (The spacing often gets garbled in poetry, so we prefer hard copies of poetry submissions.) If submitting electronically, please email a Word file – no PDFs please – to editor@chbooks.com. You can include the cover letter and CV as a separate file or as a part of the MS. Be patient. We try to respond promptly, but we do receive hundreds of submissions, so it may take us months to get back to you." Consult website for submissions policy.

Recent Title(s) *Portable Altamount*, by Brian Joseph Davis (poetry); *Your Secrets Sleep With Me*, by Darren O'Donnell (fiction); *Goodness*, by Michael Redhill (drama).

Tips "We are not a general publisher, and publish only Canadian poetry, fiction, artist books and drama. We are interested primarily in innovative or experimental writing."

COTEAU BOOKS

Thunder Creek Publishing Co-operative Ltd. 2517 Victoria Ave., Regina SK S4P 0T2, Canada. (306)777-0170. Fax: (306)522-5152. E-mail: coteau@coteaubooks.com. Website: www.coteaubooks.com. **Contact:** Geoffrey Ursell, publisher. Estab. 1975. Publishes trade paperback originals and reprints. **Publishes 16 titles/year. 200 queries received/year. 200 mss received/year. 25% of books from first-time authors. 90% from unagented writers. Pays 10% royalty on retail price. 12 months** Responds in 3 months to queries and manuscripts. Book catalog available free. Guidelines available online.

> "Our mission is to publish the finest in Canadian fiction, nonfiction, poetry, drama, and children's literature, with an emphasis on Saskatchewan and prairie writers. De-emphasizing science fiction, picture books."

Nonfiction Subjects include creative nonfiction, ethnic, history, language, literature, memoirs, regional, sports, travel. *Canadian authors only.* Submit bio, 3-4 sample chapters, SASE.

Fiction Subjects include ethnic, fantasy, feminist, gay, lesbian, historical, humor, juvenile, literary, mainstream, contemporary, multicultural, multimedia, mystery, plays, poetry, regional, short story collections, spiritual, sports, teen/young adult, novels/short fiction, adult/middle years. *Canadian authors only*. Submit bio, complete ms, SASE.

Recent Title(s) *The Tales of Three Lands Trilogy* (juvenile fantasy series for ages 9 and up); *Mud Girl*, by Alison Acheson (teen fiction); *The Book of Beasts*, by Bernice Friesen (novel); *The Hour of Bad Decisions*, by Russell Wangersky (short stories).

Tips "Look at past publications to get an idea of our editorial program. We do not publish romance, horror, or picture books but are interested in juvenile and teen fiction from Canadian authors. Submissions, even queries, must be made in hard copy only. We do not accept simultaneous/multiple submissions. Check our website for new submission timing guidelines."

CRESCENT MOON PUBLISHING

P.O. Box 393, Maidstone Kent ME14 5 × U, United Kingdom. (44)(162)272-9593. E-mail: cresmopub@yahoo.co.uk. Website: www.crescentmoon.org.uk. **Contact:** Jeremy Robinson, director (arts, media, cinema, literature); Cassidy Hushes (visual arts). Estab. 1988. Publishes hardcover and trade paperback originals. **Publishes 25 titles/year. 300 queries received/year. 400 mss received/year. 1% of books from first-time authors. 1% from unagented writers. Pays royalty. Pays negotiable advance.** Publishes book 18 months after acceptance of ms. Accepts simultaneous submissions. Responds in 2 months to queries. Responds in 4 months to proposals and mss. Book catalog and ms guidelines free.

Imprints Joe's Press, *Pagan America Magazine, Passion Magazine*.

> "Our mission is to publish the best in contemporary work, in poetry, fiction, and critical studies, and selections from the great writers. Currently emphasizing nonfiction (media, film, music, painting). De-emphasizing children's books."

Nonfiction Subjects include Americana, art, architecture, gardening, government, politics, language, literature, music, dance, philosophy, religion, travel, women's issues, women's studies, cinema, the media, cultural studies. Query with SASE. Submit outline, 2 sample chapters, bio. Reviews artwork/photos. Send photocopies.

Fiction Subjects include erotica, experimental, feminist, gay, lesbian, literary, short story collections, translation. "We do not publish much **Fiction** at present but will consider high quality new work." Query with SASE. Submit outline, clips, 2 sample chapters, bio.
Recent Title(s) *J.R.R. Tolkien*, by Jeremy Robinson; *Media Hell: Global Media Warning*, by Oliver Whitehorne; *Colourfield Painting*, by Stuart Morris.
Tips "Our audience is interested in new contemporary writing."

DAYA PUBLISHING HOUSE

1123/74, Deva Ram Park, Tri Nagar Delhi 110 035, India. (91)(011)27383999. Fax: (91)(011)2326-0116. Website: www.dayabooks.com. **Publishes 100 titles/year.**

"Publishes wide range of disciplines and subject areas; specialist books at the professional level."

Nonfiction Subjects include agriculture, animals, anthropology, archeology, art, architecture, business, economics, child guidance, education, history, language, literature, nature, environment, philosophy, religion, science, social sciences, sociology, women's issues, women's studies, engineering, geography, library science, political science, public administration, rural development. Download online questionnaire form and submit it via e-mail, mail or fax.
Recent Title(s) *Swine Flu: Diagnosis and Treatment*, by Sameer Prakash; *Technological Applications in Wastewater Engineering*, by Drs. S.N. Kaul, Lidia Szpyrkowicz, Ashutosh Gautam; *Advanced Organic Chemistry*, by Akhilesh K. Verma; *Agriculture and Food Security*, by Ram Niwas Sharma; *The Aryan Path of the Buddha*, by K. Manohar Gupta.
Tips "If you have recently written or are considering writing within a subject which covers our areas of interest and would like to discuss the various commercial and developmental aspects of your project with a view to possible future publication, then we would like to hear from you - please do get in touch."

DUNEDIN ACADEMIC PRESS LTD

Hudson House, 8 Albany St., Edinburgh EH1 3QB, United Kingdom. (44)(131)473-2397. E-mail: mail@dunedinacademicpress.co.uk. Website: www.dunedinacademicpress.co.uk. **Contact:** Anthony Kinahan, managing director. Estab. 2001. **Publishes 15-20 titles/year. 20% of books from first-time authors. 90% from unagented writers. Pays royalty.** Book catalog and proposal guidelines available online.

"Ask for and look over our author proposal guidelines before submitting. Synopses and ideas welcome. Approach first in writing, outlining proposal and identifying the market."

Nonfiction Subjects include education, health policy, vocal music, philosophy, religion, earth science. "Look over our author proposal guidelines before submitting. Synopses and ideas welcome. Approach us first in writing, outlining proposal and identifying the market." Reviews artwork/photos.
Recent Title(s) *Mathematical Methods for Earth Scientists*; *Faith Schools in the Twenty-first Century*; *Dementia and Well-being.*
Tips "Although located in Scotland, Dunedin's list contains authors and subjects from the wider academic world and DAP's horizons are far broader than our immediate Scottish environment. One of the strengths of Dunedin is that we are able to offer our authors that individual support that comes from dealing with a small independent publisher committed to growth through careful treatment of its authors."

FINDHORN PRESS

305A The Park, Findhorn, Forres Scotland IV36 3TE, United Kingdom. (44)(1309) 690-582. Fax: (44)(131) 777-2711. Website: www.findhornpress.com. **Contact:** Thierry Bogliolo, publisher. Estab. 1971. Publishes trade paperback originals. **Publishes 20 titles/year. 1,000 queries received/year. 50% of books from first-time authors. 80% from unagented writers. Pays 10-15% royalty on wholesale price.** Publishes book 12 months after acceptance of ms. Responds in 2-3 months to proposals, due to the large number of submissions. Book catalog and ms guidelines online.
Nonfiction Subjects include health, nature, spirituality. No fiction, short stories, or poetry.
Recent Title(s) *2012 and Beyond*, by Diana Cooper; *Gems of Wisdom*, by Eileen Caddy; *Fully Fertile*, by Quinn, Heller & Bussell; *The Confident Creative*, by Cat Bennett.

HERITAGE HOUSE PUBLISHING CO., LTD.

#340-1105 Pandora Ave., Victoria BC V8V 3P9, Canada. 250-360-0829. E-mail: editorial@heritagehouse.ca. Website: www.heritagehouse.ca. **Contact:** Rodger Touchie, publisher/president. Publishes trade paperback and hardcovers. **Publishes 10-12 titles/year. 200 queries received/year. 60 mss received/year. 50% of books from first-time authors. 90% from unagented writers. Pays 12-15% royalty on net proceeds. Advances are rarely paid.** Publishes book Usually 1-2 years after acceptance of ms. Responds in 6 months to queries. Catalogue and guidelines available online.

"Heritage House is primarily a regional publisher of books that celebrate the historical and cultural heritage of Western Canada and, to an extent, the Pacific Northwest; we also publish some titles of national interest and a series of books aimed at young and casual readers, called *Amazing Stories*."

Nonfiction Subjects include regional history, nature, environment, recreation, true crime, First Nations, adventure. Writers should include a sample of their writing, an overview sample of photos or illustrations to support the text, and a brief letter describing who they are writing for. Query with SASE. Include synopsis, outline, marketing strategy, 2-3 sample chapters, indicate supporting illustrative material available. No fiction.

Recent Title(s) *The Green Chain: Nothing Is Ever Clear Cut*, by Mark Leiren-Young; *Walking Vancouver: 36 Strolls to Dynamic Neighbourhoods, Hip Hangouts, and Spectacular Waterfronts*, by John Lee; *The Chilcotin War: A Tale of Death and Reprisal*, by Rich Mole; *Wild Beauty: A Visual Exploration of BC*, by Al Harvey; *The Mad Trapper: Unearthing a Mystery*, by Barbara Smith; *Medicine Paint: The Art of Dale Auger*.

Tips "Our books appeal to residents of and visitors to the northwest quadrant of the continent. We're looking for good stories and good storytellers. We focus on work by Canadian authors."

HIPPOPOTAMUS PRESS

22 Whitewell Rd., Frome, Frome Somerset BA11 4EL, UK. (44)(173)466-6653. E-mail: rjhippopress@aol.com. **Contact:** R. John, editor; M. Pargitter (poetry); Anna Martin (translation). Estab. 1974. Publishes hardcover and trade paperback originals. **Publishes 6-12 titles/year. 90% of books from first-time authors. 90% from unagented writers. Pays 7 ½-10% royalty on retail price. Pays advance.** Publishes book 10 months after acceptance of ms. Accepts simultaneous submissions. Responds in 1 month to queries. Book catalog available free.

"Hippopotamus Press publishes first, full collections of verse by those well represented in the mainstream poetry magazines of the English-speaking world."

Nonfiction Subjects include language, literature, translation. Query with SASE. Submit complete ms.

Recent Title(s) *Touching on Love*, by David Clarke; *Mystic Bridge*, by Edward Lowbury.

Tips "We publish books for a literate audience. We have a strong link to the Modernist tradition. Read what we publish."

IRISH ACADEMIC PRESS

2 Brookside, Dundrum Road, Dundrum Dublin 14, Ireland. (353)(1)2989937. Fax: (353)(1)2982783. E-mail: info@iap.ie. Website: www.iap.ie. **Contact:** Lisa Hyde, editor. Estab. 1974. **Publishes 15 titles/year. Pays royalty.** Accepts simultaneous submissions. Guidelines available free.

Imprints Vallentine-Mitchell Publishers.

- Request submission guidelines before submitting.

Nonfiction Subjects include art, architecture, government, politics, history, literary criticism, military, war, womens issues, womens studies, genealogy, Irish history. Query with SASE. Submit proposal package, outline, resume, publishing history, bio, target audience, competing books, SASE.

Recent Title(s) *Other Edens, The Life and Work of Brian Coffey*, by Keating and Woods, *Between the Shadows: Modern Irish Writing and Culture*, by Foster.

KEY PORTER BOOKS

6 Adelaide St. E., 10th Floor, Toronto ON M5C 1H6, Canada. (416)862-7777. Fax: (416)862-2304. E-mail: info@keyporter.com. Website: www.keyporter.com. **Contact:** Jordan Fenn, publisher. Estab. 1979. Publishes hardcover and trade paperback originals and reprints. **Publishes 100 titles/year. Pays royalty.**

Imprints Key Porter Kids; L&OD.

- No unsolicited mss.

"Key Porter specializes in autobiography, biography, children's, cookbook, gift book, how-to, humor, illustrated book, self-help, young adult. Subjects include art, architecture, business, economics, parenting, food, creative nonfiction, gardening, general nonfiction, politics, health, history, humanities, memoirs, military, personal finance, nature, environment, photography, psychology, science, social sciences, sociology, sports, translation, travel, women's issues, world affairs, and literary fiction."

KINDRED PRODUCTIONS

1310 Taylor Ave., Winnipeg MB R3M 3Z6, Canada. (204)669-6575. Fax: (204)654-1865. E-mail: kindred@mbconf.ca. Website: www.kindredproductions.com. **Contact:** Ashley Thiessen, Customer Service.

Publishes trade paperback originals and reprints. **Publishes 3 titles/year. 1% of books from first-time authors. 100% from unagented writers.** Publishes book 18 months after acceptance of ms. Accepts simultaneous submissions. Responds in 3 months to queries. Responds in 5 months to manuscripts. Guidelines available by email request.

- Kindred Productions publishes, promotes, and markets print and nonprint resources that will shape our Christian faith and discipleship from a Mennonite Brethren perspective. Currently emphasizing Mennonite Brethren Resources. De-emphasizing personal experience, biographical. No children's books or fiction.

Nonfiction Subjects include religion, historical. "Our books cater primarily to our Mennonite Brethren denomination readers." Query with SASE. Submit outline, 2-3 sample chapters.

Recent Title(s) *Just One More Day*, by Beverlee Buller Keck; *Being With Jesus*, by Carol Baergen; *Turning the World Upside Down*, by Edmund Janzen; *Out of the Strange Silence*, by Brad Thiessen.

Tips "Most of our books are sold to churches, religious bookstores, and schools. We are concentrating on inspirational books. We do not accept children's manuscripts."

LOON IN BALLOON INC.

133 Weber St. N., Suite #3-513, Waterloo ON N2J 3G9, Canada. E-mail: info@looninballoon.com. Website: www.looninballoon.com. Estab. 2003. Publishes trade paperback originals. **Publishes 5-10 titles/year. 100 mss received/year. 50% of books from first-time authors. 75% from unagented writers. Pays 8-10% royalty on retail price.** Publishes book 6 months after acceptance of ms. Accepts simultaneous submissions. Responds in 3-6 months to queries, proposals and manuscripts. See Guidelines online.

Fiction Looking for stories that could translate into film. Please only **Fiction** novels. E-mail proposal package: author bio, short summary, first 2 chapters.

Recent Title(s) *Hawkmoon*, by Nancy Williams; *The Kremlin in Betrayal*, by Leon Berger.

Tips "We publish adult popular fiction. We are small, but aggressive."

MAVERICK MUSICALS AND PLAYS

89 Bergann Rd., Maleny QLD 4552, Australia. Phone/Fax: (61)(7)5494-4007. E-mail: helen@mavmuse.com. Website: www.mavmuse.com. **Contact:** The Editor. Estab. 1978. Guidelines available online.

Fiction Subjects include plays. "Looking for two-act musicals and one- and two-act plays. See website for more details."

Recent Title(s) *Outside the Window* (1 Act Play/Adult); *That's That Then* (1 Act Play/Comedy); *The Golden Touch* (1 Act Play) adapted by award-winning children's writer Cynthia Medley-England.

MELBOURNE UNIVERSITY PUBLISHING, LTD.

Subsidiary of University of Melbourne 187 Grattan St., Carlton VIC 3053, Australia. (61)(3)934-20300. Fax: (61)(3)9342-0399. E-mail: mup-info@unimelb.edu.au. Website: www.mup.com.au. **Contact:** The Executive Assistant. Estab. 1922. **Publishes 80 titles/year.** Responds to queries in 4 months if interested. Guidelines available online.

Imprints Melbourne University Press; The Miegunyah Press (strong Australian content); Victory Books

Nonfiction Subjects include art, politics, philosophy, science, social sciences, Aboriginal studies, cultural studies, gender studies, natural history. Submit using MUP Book Proposal Form available online.

Recent Title(s) *The Costello Memoirs*, by Peter Costello & Peter Coleman; *Infiltration*, by Colin McLaren; *The March of Patriots*, by Paul Kelly; *Shannon Bennett's Paris*, by Shannon Bennett; *I, Mick Gatto*, by Mick Gatto with Tom Noble.

MUSSIO VENTURES PUBLISHING LTD.

5811 Beresford St., Burnaby BC V5J1K1, Canada. (604)438-3474. Fax: (604)438-3470. Website: www.backroadmapbooks.com. Estab. 1993. **Publishes 5 titles/year. 5 queries received/year. 2 mss received/year. 25% of books from first-time authors. 0% from unagented writers. Makes outright purchase of $2,000-4,800. Pays $1,000 advance.** Publishes book 12 months after acceptance of ms. Accepts simultaneous submissions. Responds in 1 month to queries, proposals and manuscripts. Book catalog available free.

- "Backroad Mapbooks Introduces new contests all the time. Check our website to see which one suits you. Email us at updates@backroadmapbooks.com"
- "We are in the business of producing, publishing, distributing and marketing Outdoor Recreation guidebooks and maps. We are also actively looking to advance our digital side of the business including making our products Google Earth, cell phone or iPhone and GPS compatible."

Nonfiction Subjects include nature, environment, maps and guides. Submit proposal package, outline/proposal, 1 sample chapter. Reviews artwork/photos. Send photocopies and digital files.

Recent Title(s) *Nova Scotia Backroad Mapbook*, by Linda Akosmitis; *Northern BC Backroad Mapbook*, by Trent Ernst.
Tips "Audience includes outdoor recreation enthusiasts and travellers. Provide a proposal including an outline and samples."

NAPOLEON & COMPANY

235-1173 Dundas Street East, Toronto ON M4M 3P1, Canada. (416)465-9961. Fax: (416)465-3241. E-mail: napoleon@napoleonandcompany.com. Website: www.napoleonandcompany.com. **Contact:** A. Thompson, editor. Estab. 1990. Publishes hardcover and trade paperback originals and reprints. **Publishes 15 titles/year. 200 queries received/year. 100 mss received/year. 50% of books from first-time authors. 75% from unagented writers.** Publishes book 18 months after acceptance of ms. Accepts simultaneous submissions. Responds in 1 month to queries. Responds in 3 months to proposals. Responds in 6 months to manuscripts. Book catalog and guidelines available online.

- "Napoleon is not accepting children's picture books at this time. Rendezvous Crime is not accepting mysteries. Check website for updates. We are accepting general adult fiction only for RendezVous Press and Darkstar Fiction."

Rendezvous publishes adult fiction. Napoleon publishes children's books.
Nonfiction Query with SASE. Submit outline, 1 sample chapter.
Recent Title(s) *Law and Disorder*, by Mary Jane Maffini; *The Space Between*, by JP Rodriguez; *Arctic Blue Death*, by R.J. Harlick; *Betrayed*, by Chris Dinsdale.
Tips Canadian resident authors only.

NEW AFRICA BOOKS

New Africa Books (Pty) Ltd P.O. Box 46962, Glosderry 7702, South Africa. (27)(21)674-4136. Fax: (27)(21)674-3358. E-mail: info@newafricabooks.co.za. Website: www.newafricabooks.co.za. **Contact:** David Philip, publisher. **Publishes 8-10 titles/year. 40% of books from first-time authors. 80% from unagented writers. Pays royalty.**
Imprints New Africa Education; David Phillip Publishers; Spearhead Press (business, self-improvement, health, natural history, travel, fiction, cookery, and newsworthy books).

"New Africa Books strives to be the leading African publisher – the world's definitive gateway to African content and information."
Nonfiction Subjects include art, architecture, education, history, memoirs, politics, science, lifestyle.
Fiction Subjects include juvenile, literary.
Recent Title(s) *Quite Footsteps*, by Dr Mongane Wally Serote; *In the Manure*, by Ronnie Govender; *Soliloquy*, by Stephen Finn; *Soldier Blue*, by Paul Williams.

ONEWORLD PUBLICATIONS

185 Banbury Rd., Oxford OX2 7AR, United Kingdom. (44)(1865)310597. Fax: (44)(1865)310598. E-mail: submissions@oneworld-publications.com. Website: www.oneworld-publications.com. Estab. 1986. Publishes hardcover and trade paperback originals and trade paperback reprints. **Publishes 50 titles/year. 200 queries received/year. 50 mss received/year. 20% of books from first-time authors. 50% from unagented writers. Pays 10% royalty on wholesale price. Pays $1,000-20,000 advance.** Publishes book 15 months after acceptance of ms. Book catalog available online. Guidelines available online.

"We publish accessible but authoritative books, mainly by academics or experts for a general readership and cross-over student market. Authors must be well qualified. Currently emphasizing current affairs, popular science, history, and psychology; de-emphasizing self-help."
Nonfiction Subjects include politics, history, multicultural, philosophy, psychology, religion, science, sociology, women's issues, women's studies. Submit through online proposal form.
Fiction Focusing on well-written literary and commercial **Fiction** from a variety of cultures and periods, many exploring interesting issues and global problems.
Recent Title(s) *Strange Fruit*, by Keenan Malik; *Oilopoly*, by Marshall Goldman; *What's the Point of School*, by Guy Claxton.
Tips "We don't require agents—just good proposals with enough hard information."

ORCA BOOK PUBLISHERS

P.O. Box 5626, Stn. B, Victoria BC V8R 6S4, Canada. Fax: (877)408-1551. E-mail: orca@orcabook.com. Website: www.orcabook.com. **Contact:** Christi Howes, editor (picture books); Sarah Harvey, editor (young readers); Andrew Wooldridge, editor (juvenile and teen fiction); Bob Tyrrell, publisher (YA, teen). Estab. 1984. Publishes hardcover and trade paperback originals, and mass market paperback originals and reprints. **Publishes 30 titles/year. 2,500 queries received/year. 1,000 mss received/year.**

20% of books from first-time authors. 75% from unagented writers. Pays 10% royalty. Publishes book 12-18 months after acceptance of ms. Responds in 1 month to queries. Responds in 2 month to proposals andmanuscripts. Book catalog for 8½x11 SASE. Guidelines available online.

- Only publishes Canadian authors.

Nonfiction Subjects include multicultural, picture books. Only publishes Canadian authors. Query with SASE.

Fiction Subjects include hi-lo, juvenile (5-9), literary, mainstream, contemporary, young adult (10-18). Ask for guidelines, find out what we publish. Looking for children's fiction. Query with SASE. Submit proposal package, outline, clips, 2-5 sample chapters, SASE.

Recent Title(s) *Sister Wife*, by Shelley Hrdlitschka (teen fiction); *Buttercup's Lovely Day*, by Carolyn Beck (picture book)

Tips "Our audience is for students in grades K-12. Know our books, and know the market."

PEMMICAN PUBLICATIONS, INC.

150 Henry Ave., Winnipeg MB R3B 0J7, Canada. (204)589-6346. Fax: (204)589-2063. E-mail: pemmican@pemmican.mb.ca. Website: www.pemmican.mb.ca. **Contact:** Randal McILroy, managing editor (Metis culture & heritage). Estab. 1980. Publishes trade paperback originals and reprints. **Publishes 5-6 titles/year. 120 queries received/year. 120 mss received/year. 50% of books from first-time authors. 100% from unagented writers. Pays 10% royalty on retail price** Publishes book 1-2 years after acceptance of ms. Accepts simultaneous submissions. Responds in 3 months to queries, proposals & manuscripts. Book catalog available free with SASE. Guidelines available online.

"Pemmican Publications is a Metis publishing house, with a mandate to publish books by Metis authors and illustrators and with an emphasis on culturally relevant stories. We encourage writers to learn a little about Pemmican before sending samples. Pemmican publishes titles in the following genres: Adult Fiction, which includes novels, story collections and anthologies; Non-Fiction, with an emphasis on social history and biography reflecting Metis experience; Children's and Young Adult titles; Aboriginal languages, including Michif and Cree."

Nonfiction Subjects include alternative, creative nonfiction, education, ethnic, history, language, literature, military, war, nature, environment. All mss must be Metis culture and heritage related. Submit proposal package including outline and 3 sample chapters. Reviews artwork/photos. Send photocopies.

Fiction Subjects include adventure, ethnic, historical, juvenile, literary, mystery, picture books, short story collections, sports, suspense, young adult. All manuscripts must be Metis culture and heritage related. Submit proposal package including outline and 3 sample chapters.

Recent Title(s) *River of Tears*, by Linda Ducharme (fiction); *Flight of the Wild Geese*, by T.D. Thompson (young adult); *Kawlija's Blueberry Promise*, by Audrey Guiboche (children's fiction).

Tips "Our mandate is to promote Metis authors, illustrators and stories. No agent is necessary."

PETER OWEN PUBLISHERS

73 Kenway Road, London SW5 0RE, United Kingdom. (44)(207)373-5628. Fax: (44)(207)373-6760. E-mail: aowen@peterowen.com. Website: www.peterowen.com. **Contact:** Antonia Owen, editorial director. Publishes hardcover originals and trade paperback originals and reprints. **Publishes 20-30 titles/year. 3,000 queries received/year. 800 mss received/year. 70% from unagented writers. Pays 7½-10% royalty. Pays negotiable advance.** Publishes book 1 year after acceptance of ms. Responds in 2 months to queries. Responds in 3 months to proposals and manuscripts. Book catalog for SASE, SAE with IRC or on website.

"We are far more interested in proposals for nonfiction than fiction at the moment. No poetry or short stories."

Nonfiction Subjects include history, literature, memoirs, translation, travel, art, drama, literary, biography. Query with SASE. Submit outline, 1-3 sample chapters. Submit complete ms with return postage or e-mail with attachments including synopsis.

Fiction Subjects include literary and translation. "No first novels-Authors should be aware that we publish very little new **Fiction** these days. Will consider excerpts from novels of normal length from established authors if they submit sample chapters and synopses." Query with SASE or by e-mail.

Recent Title(s) *The Life of a Long-Distance Writer: The Biography of Alan Sillitoe* by Richard Bradford; *The Idle Years* by Orhan Kemal.

PIPERS' ASH, LTD.

Pipers' Ash, Church Road, Christian Malford, Chippenham, Wiltshire SN15 4BW, United Kingdom. (44)(124)972-0563. Fax: (44)(870)056-8916. E-mail: pipersash@supamasu.com. Website: www.supamasu.com. **Contact:** Manuscript Evaluation Desk. Estab. 1976. Publishes hardcover and paperback editions.

Publishes 12 titles/year. 1,000 queries received/year. 400 mss received/year. 90% of books from first-time authors. 99% from unagented writers. Pays 10% royalty on wholesale price, and 5 author's copies. Publishes book 6 months after acceptance of ms. Responds in 1 month to queries. Responds in 1 month to proposals. Responds in 3 months to manuscripts. Book catalog for A5 SASE and on website. Guidelines available online.

Imprints Salisbury; Canterbury; Lincoln; Gloucester; Durham; Ely.

Nonfiction Subjects include creative nonfiction, ethnic, history, humanities, language, literature, military, war, philosophy, recreation, religion, translation. Query with SASE.

Fiction Subjects include adventure, confession, feminist, historical, juvenile, literary, mainstream, contemporary, military, war, plays, poetry, poetry in translation, regional, religious, romance, science fiction, short story collections, sports, suspense, translation. We publish 30,000-word novels and short story collections. Query with SASE. Submit sample chapters, 25-word synopsis (that sorts out the writers from the wafflers).

Recent Title(s) *Blue Moon*, by Richard Norcross; *Girls From the Children's Home*, by Jasmine Maria Hill; *Cubs With a Difference*, by Stephen Andrews.

PRESSES DE L'UNIVERSITÉ DE MONTREAL

Case postale 6128, Succursale Centre-ville, Montreal QC H3C 3J7, Canada. (514)343-6933. Fax: (514)343-2232. E-mail: pum@umontreal.ca. Website: www.pum.umontreal.ca. **Contact:** Elise Bachant-Lagace, rights and sales. Publishes hardcover and trade paperback originals. **Publishes 40 titles/year.** Publishes book 6 months after acceptance of ms. Responds in 1 month to queries and proposals. Responds in 3 months to manuscripts. Book catalog and ms guidelines free.

Nonfiction Subjects include education, health, medicine, history, language, literature, philosophy, psychology, sociology, translation. Submit outline, 2 sample chapters.

PURICH PUBLISHING

Box 23032, Market Mall Post Office, Saskatoon SK S7J 5H3, Canada. (306)373-5311. Fax: (306)373-5315. E-mail: purich@sasktel.net. Website: www.purichpublishing.com. **Contact:** Donald Purich, publisher; Karen Bolstad, publisher. Estab. 1992. Publishes trade paperback originals. **Publishes 3-5 titles/year. 20% of books from first-time authors. 100% from unagented writers. Pays 8-12% royalty on retail price.** Publishes book within 4 months of completion of editorial work, after acceptance of ms. after acceptance of ms. Responds in 1 month to queries. Responds in 3 months to manuscripts. Book catalog available free.

"Purich publishes books on law, Aboriginal/Native American issues, and Western Canadian history for the academic and professional trade reference market."

Nonfiction Subjects include Aboriginal and social justice issues, Western Canadian history. "We are a specialized publisher and only consider work in our subject areas." Query with SASE.

Recent Title(s) *The Duty to Consult: New Relationships With Aboriginal Peoples*, by Dwight G. Newman; *Negotiating the Numbered Treaties: An Intellectual and Political Biography of Alexander Morris*, by Robert J. Talbot; *Indigenous Diplomacy and the Rights of Peoples*, by James Sa'ke'j. Youngblood Henderson.

REALITY STREET

63 All Saints St., Hastings, E. Sussex TN34 3BN, UK. +44(0)1424 431271. E-mail: info@realitystreet.co.uk. Website: freespace.virgin.net/reality.street. **Contact:** Ken Edwards, editor/publisher. Estab. 1993. Trade paperback originals. **Publishes 3-4 titles/year.** Book catalog available online.

Reality Street is based in Hastings, UK, publishing new and innovative writing in English and in translation from other languages. Some established writers whose books they have published are Nicole Brossard, Allen Fisher, Barbara Guest, Fanny Howe, Denise Riley, Peter Riley, and Maurice Scully.

Fiction Subjects include poetry, poetry in translation, translation, experimental fiction, anthologies.

Recent Title(s) *Rapid Eye Movement*, by Peter Jaeger (dream narrative collaged from multiple sources); *Let Me Tell You*, by Paul Griffiths (a short novel in the Oulipo tradition); *Botsotso*, edited by Allan Kolski Horwitz & Ken Edwards (anthology of contemporary multi-lingual, multi-ethnic poetry from post-apartheid So. Africa).

Tips "Unsolicited Submissions discouraged-please acquaint yourself with the output of the press, preferably by buying our books, before sending us any proposals."

ROCKY MOUNTAIN BOOKS

406-13th Ave. NE, Calgary AB T2E 1C2, Canada. (403)249-9490. Fax: (403)249-2968. E-mail: rmb@heritagehouse.ca. Website: www.rmbooks.com. **Contact:** Fraser Seely, publisher. Publishes trade paperback originals. **Publishes 15 titles/year. 30 queries received/year. 75% of books from first-time**

authors. 100% from unagented writers. Rarely offers advance. Publishes book 1 year after acceptance of ms. Accepts simultaneous submissions. Responds in 2 months to queries. Book catalog and ms guidelines available online at website.

"Rocky Mountain Books publishes books on outdoor recreation, mountains, and mountaineering in Western Canada."

Nonfiction Subjects include nature, environment, recreation, regional, travel. Our main area of publishing is outdoor recreation guides to Western and Northern Canada. Query with SASE.

Recent Title(s) *Caves of the Canadian Rockies and Columbia Mountains*, by Jon Rollins; *Exploring Prince George*, by Mike Nash.

RONSDALE PRESS

3350 W. 21st Ave., Vancouver BC V6S 1G7, Canada. (604)738-4688. Fax: (604)731-4548. Website: http://ronsdalepress.com. **Contact:** Ronald B. Hatch, director (fiction, poetry, social commentary); Veronica Hatch, managing director (children's literature). Estab. 1988. Publishes trade paperback originals. **Publishes 10 titles/year. 300 queries received/year. 800 mss received/year. 60% of books from first-time authors. 95% from unagented writers. Pays 10% royalty on retail price.** Publishes book 6 months after acceptance of ms. Accepts simultaneous submissions. Responds in 2 weeks to queries. Responds in 1 month to proposals. Responds in 3 months to manuscripts. Book catalog for #10 SASE. Guidelines available online.

Canadian authors only. Ronsdale publishes fiction, poetry, regional history, biography and autobiography, books of ideas about Canada, as well as young adult historical fiction.

Nonfiction Subjects include history, Canadian, language, literature, nature, environment, regional.

Fiction Subjects include literary, short story collections, novels. *Canadian authors only*. Query with at least the first 80 pages. Short stories must have some previous magazines publication.

Recent Title(s) *Red Goodwin*, by John Wilson (YA historical fiction); *When Eagles Call*, by Susan Dobbie (novel).

Tips "Ronsdale Press is a literary publishing house, based in Vancouver, and dedicated to publishing books from across Canada, books that give Canadians new insights into themselves and their country. We aim to publish the best Canadian writers."

SCRIBE PUBLICATIONS

595 Drummond St., Carlton North VIC 3054, Australia. (61)(3)9349-5955. Fax: (61)(3)9348-2752. E-mail: info@scribepub.com.au. Website: www.scribepub.com.au. Estab. 1976. **Publishes 70 titles/year. 10-25% of books from first-time authors. 10-20% from unagented writers.** Submission guidelines available on website under Contact Scribe.

Nonfiction Subjects include environment, government, politics, history, memoirs, nature, environment, psychology, current affairs, social issues. "We strongly recommend you call first to discuss your proposal." "Please refer first to our website before contacting us or submitting anything, because we explain there who we will accept proposals from."

Recent Title(s) *Mindsight: Change Your Brain and Your Life*, by Daniel J. Siegel, MD; Tokyo Vice, by Jake Adelstein; *The Good Soldiers*, by David Finkel; *The Song Is You: A Novel*, by Arthur Phillips.

SHEARSMAN PRESS

58 Velwell Rd., Exeter England EX4 4LD, UK. Website: www.shearsman.com. **Contact:** Tony Frazer, editor. Estab. 1982. Trade paperback originals. **Publishes 45-58 titles/year. Pays 10% royalty on retail price after 150 copies have sold; authors also receive 10 free copies of their books.** Responds in 2-3 months to manuscripts. Book catalog available online. Guidelines available online.

Nonfiction Subjects include memoirs, translation, essays.

Recent Title(s) *The Look of Goodbye*, by Peter Robinson (poetry collection); *The Council of Heresy-A primer of poetry in a balkanised terrain*, by Andrew Duncan (a study of contemporary poetry); *New and Selected Poems*, by Jennifer Clement.

Tips "Book ms submission: most of the ms must have already appeared in the UK or USA magazines of some repute, and it has to fill 70-72 pages of half letter or A5 pages. You must have sufficient return postage. Submissions can also be made by email. It is unlikely that a poet with no track record will be accepted for publication as there is no obvious audience for the work. Try to develop some exposure to the UK and US magazines and try to assemble a ms only later."

J. GORDON SHILLINGFORD PUBLISHING INC.

P.O. Box 86, RPO Corydon Ave., Winnipeg MB R3M 3S3, Canada. Phone/Fax: (204)779-6967. E-mail: jgshill@allstream.net. Website: www.jgshillingford.com. **Contact:** Clarice Foster, poetry editor; Glenda

MacFarlane, drama editor, Gordon Shillingford, nonfiction editor. Estab. 1993. Publishes trade paperback originals. **Publishes 14 titles/year. 100 queries received/year. 50 mss received/year. 15% of books from first-time authors. 60% from unagented writers. Pays 10% royalty on retail price.** Accepts simultaneous submissions. Responds in 3-6 months to queries. Book catalog available online. Guidelines available online.

Imprints True

Publishes nonfiction and poetry. Does not publish fiction, self-help or children's material. Only publishes Canadian citizens.

Nonfiction Subjects include government, politics, religion, true crime, social history. Query with CV, 2-page sample, SASE.

Recent Title(s) *Innocence Lost*, by Beverley Cooper; *The Selkie Wife*, by Kelley Jo Burke; *They Call Me Chief: Warriors On Ice*, by Don Marks.

STELLER PRESS LTD.

13, 4335 W. 10th Ave., Vancouver BC V6R 2H6, Canada. (604)222-2955. Fax: (604)222-2965. E-mail: info@stellerpress.com. Website: www.stellerpress.com. **Contact:** Steve Paton (regional interest, outdoors, gardening, history, travel). Publishes and distributes trade paperback originals. **75% of books from first-time authors. 100% from unagented writers. Pays royalty on retail price. Pays $500-2,000 advance.**

"Most titles are specific to the Pacific Northwest, local interest, or by Canadian authors. Currently emphasizing regional interest, gardening, history, outdoors and travel and some fiction. De-emphasizing poetry."

Nonfiction Subjects include gardening, history, nature, environment, regional, travel.

Recent Title(s) *Vancouver Walks*, by Michael Kluckner and John Atkin; *Skytrain Explorer*, by John Atkin.

TRENTHAM BOOKS, LTD.

Westview House, 734 London Rd., Stoke on Trent ST4 5NP, United Kingdom. (44)(178)274-5567. E-mail: tb@trentham-books.co.uk. Website: www.trentham-books.co.uk. **Contact:** Gillian Klein, commissioning editor (education, race). Publishes hardcover and trade paperback originals. **Publishes 32 titles/year. 1,000 queries received/year. 600 mss received/year. 60% of books from first-time authors. 70% from unagented writers. Pays 7½% royalty on wholesale price.** Publishes book 4 months after acceptance of ms. Responds in 1 month to queries. Book catalog for #10 SASE. Guidelines available online.

"Our mission is to enhance the work of professionals in education, law, and social work. Currently emphasizing curriculum, professional behavior. De-emphasizing theoretical issues."

Nonfiction Subjects include education, ethnic, multicultural, language/literacy, psychology, women's issues. Query with SASE.

Recent Title(s) *Get Global: A Practical Guide to Integrating the Global Dimension into the Primary Curriculum*, by Tony Pickford, ed.; *Multilingual Europe: Diversity and Learning*, by Charmian Kenner and Tina Hickey, ed.

UNIVERSITY OF OTTAWA PRESS

542 King Edward, Ottawa ON K1N 6N5, Canada. (613)562-5246. Fax: (613)562-5247. E-mail: puo-uop@uottawa.ca. Website: www.press.uottawa.ca. **Contact:** Eric Nelson, acquisitions editor. Estab. 1936. **Publishes 25-50 titles/year. 20% of books from first-time authors. 95% from unagented writers.** Publishes book 16-18 months after acceptance of ms. Responds in 1 month to queries. Responds in 6 months to manuscripts. Book catalog and ms guidelines free.

"Publishes books for scholarly and serious nonfiction audiences. This is the only bilingual university press in Canada. Currently emphasizing French in North America, translation studies, philosophy, Canadian studies, criminology, international development, governance."

Nonfiction Subjects include education, government, politics, philosophy, sociology, translation, Canadian literature. Send proposals or first chapters to the attention of the acquisitions editor. Replies are not guaranteed. Check website to see if your project fits the scholarly disciplines of the University of Ottawa Press. Submit outline, sample chapters, CV.

Recent Title(s) *Revolution or Renaissance: Making the Transition From an Economic Age to a Cultural Age*, by D. Paul Schafer; *Histories of Kanatha: Seen and Told*, by Georges Sioui; *Multicultural Dynamics and the Ends of History: Exploring Kant, Hegel and Marx*, by Rèal Fillion.

Tips "No unrevised theses! Envision audience of academic specialists and readers of serious nonfiction."

WALL & EMERSON, INC.

21 Dale Ave., Suite 533, Toronto ON M4W 1K3, Canada. (416)901-3855. Fax: (416)352-5368. E-mail: wall@wallbooks.com. Website: www.wallbooks.com. **Contact:** Byron E. Wall, Senior Lecturer, Department of Mathematics and Statistics. Estab. 1987. Publishes hardcover originals and reprints. **Publishes 3 titles/year. 10 queries received/year. 8 mss received/year. 50% of books from first-time authors. 100% from unagented writers. Pays 5-12% royalty on wholesale price.** Publishes book 12 months after acceptance of ms. Accepts simultaneous submissions. Responds in 1 month to queries and proposals. Responds in 3 months to manuscripts. Book catalog and ms guidelines free or online.

- "We are 'client publishers' of the University of Toronto Press."
- "Currently emphasizing history of science and adult education."

Nonfiction Subjects include education, health, philosophy, science. "At the moment we are publishing no new titles, only new editions of existing works. However this may change within the next two years and we may return to normal operations, which is looking for any undergraduate text that meets the needs of a well-defined course in colleges in the U.S. and Canada." Submit proposal package, outline, 2 sample chapters.

Recent Title(s) *Delivering Instruction to Adult Learners*, 3rd ed.; *Glimpses of Reality: Episodes in the History of Science*; *The Price of Prosperity: Civilization and the Natural World.*

Tips "Our audience consists of college undergraduate students and college libraries. Our ideal writer is a college professor writing a text for a course he or she teaches regularly. If I were a writer trying to market a book today, I would identify the audience for the book and write directly to the audience throughout the book. I would then approach a publisher that publishes books specifically for that audience."

WHITECAP BOOKS, LTD.

351 Lynn Ave., North Vancouver BC V7J 2C4, Canada. (640)980-9852. Fax: (604)980-8197. Website: www.whitecap.ca. Publishes hardcover and trade paperback originals. **Publishes 40 titles/year. 500 queries received/year. 1,000 mss received/year. 20% of books from first-time authors. 90% from unagented writers. Pays royalty. Pays negotiated advance.** Publishes book 12 months after acceptance of ms. Accepts simultaneous submissions. Responds in 2-3 months to proposals. Catalog and guidelines available online at website.

- "Whitecap Books is a general trade publisher with a focus on food and wine titles. Although we are interested in reviewing unsolicited manuscript submissions, please note that we only accept submissions that meet the needs of our current publishing program. Please see some of most recent releases to get an idea of the kinds of titles we are interested in."

Nonfiction Subjects include animals, cooking, foods, nutrition, gardening, history, nature, environment, recreation, regional, travel. "Writers should take the time to research our list and read the submission guidelines on our website. This is especially important for children's writers and cookbook authors. We will only consider submissions that fall into these categories: Cookbooks, Wine and spirits, Regional travel, Home and garden, Canadian history, North American natural history, Juvenile series-based fiction." Submit cover letter, synopsis, SASE via ground mail. See guidelines online at website. Reviews artwork/photos. Send photocopies.

Fiction See guidelines.

Recent Title(s) *Wild Sweets: Chocolate*, by Dominique and Cindy Duby; *Texas: A Visual Journey*, **by** Claire Philipson; *Saddle Island Series No. 3: Race to the Rescue*, by Sharon Siamon.

Tips "We want well-written, well-researched material that presents a fresh approach to a particular topic."

Small Presses

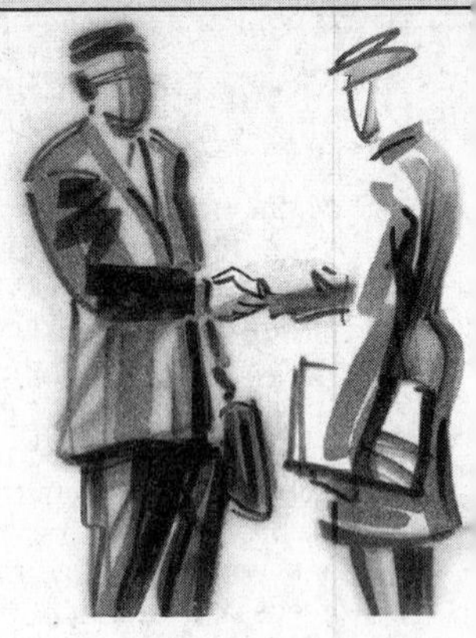

Small press is a relative term. Compared to the dozen or so conglomerates, the rest of the book publishing world may seem to be comprised of small presses. A number of the publishers listed in the Book Publishers section consider themselves small presses and cultivate the image. For our classification, small presses are those that publish, on average, less than 10 books per year.

The publishing opportunities are slightly more limited with the companies listed here than with those in the Book Publishers section. Not only are they publishing fewer books, but small presses are usually not able to market their books as effectively as larger publishers, and their print runs and royalty arrangements are usually smaller.

However, realistic small press publishers don't try to compete with Penguin Group (USA), Inc., or Random House. Most small press publishers get into book publishing for the love of it, not solely for the profit. Of course, every publisher, small or large, wants successful books, but small press publishers often measure success in different ways.

Many writers actually prefer to work with small presses. Since small publishing houses are usually based on the publisher's commitment to the subject matter, and since they work with far fewer authors than the conglomerates, small press authors and their books usually receive more personal attention than the larger publishers can afford to give them. Promotional dollars at the big houses tend to be siphoned toward a few books each season that they have decided are likely to succeed, leaving hundreds of "midlist'' books underpromoted. Since small presses only commit to a very small number of books every year, they are vitally interested in the promotion and distribution of each book.

Just because they publish fewer titles than large publishing houses does not mean small press editors have the time to look at complete manuscripts. In fact, the editors with smaller staffs often have even less time for submissions. The procedure for contacting a small press with your book idea is exactly the same as it is for a larger publisher. Send a one-page query with SASE first. If the press is interested in your proposal, be ready to send an outline or synopsis, and/or a sample chapter or two.For more information on small presses, see *Novel & Short Story Writer's Market* and *Poet's Market* (Writer's Digest Books).

ADAMS-BLAKE PUBLISHING

8041 Sierra St., Fair Oaks CA 95628. (916)962-9296. Website: www.adams-blake.com. **Contact:** Monica Blane, acquisitions editor. Estab. 1992. Publishes trade paperback originals. **Publishes 5 titles/year. 50 queries received/year. 15 mss received/year. 80% of books from first-time authors. 99% from unagented writers. Pays 10% royalty on wholesale price.** Publishes book 9 months after acceptance of ms. Accepts simultaneous submissions. Responds in 3 months on queries, proposals and mss. Catalog not available. Guidelines not available.

- "We look for an audience of business and technical readers. We like to look at 'oddball' titles that might appeal to people in specific industries, especially financial services (insurance, brokerage, etc.) A big part of our publishing is in the 'special markets' or what might be called 'premium' or 'give away' sales to large companies where we can print for a dollar, sell for three dollars in quantities of many thousands—No returns."

Nonfiction Subjects include business, economics, computers, electronics, counseling, career guidance, labor, money, finance. "We like titles in sales and marketing, but which are targeted to a specific industry. We don't always look for retail trade titles but more to special markets where we sell 10,000 copies to a company to give to their employees." Query with SASE. Submit proposal package, including outline, 1 sample chapter and marketing information—Demographics of readership, pricing, etc. Does not review artwork/photos.

Tips "If you have a book that a large company might buy and give away at sales meetings, send us a query. We like books on sales, especially in specific industries—Like 'How to Sell Annuities' or 'How to Sell High-Tech.' We look for the title that a company will buy several thousand copies of at a time. 'We often personalize' for the company."

ADAMS-HALL PUBLISHING

P.O. Box 491002, Los Angeles CA 90049. (800)888-4452. E-mail: adamshallpublish@aol.com. Website: www.adams-hall.com. **Contact:** Sue Ann Bacon, editorial director. Publishes hardcover and trade paperback originals and reprints. **Publishes 3-4 titles/year. Pays negotiable advance.** Responds in 1 month to queries.

Nonfiction Subjects include money, finance, business. Small successful house that aggressively promotes select titles. Only interested in business or personal finance titles with broad appeal. Submit query, title, synopsis, your qualifications, a list of three competitive books and how it's widely different from other books. Do not send ms or sample chapters.

Recent Title(s) *Fail Proof Your Business.*

AHSAHTA PRESS

1910 University Dr., MS 1525, Boise ID 83725-1525. (208)426-4210. E-mail: ahsahta@boisestate.edu. Website: ahsahtapress.boisestate.edu. **Contact:** Director/Editor-in-Chief: Janet Holmes. Estab. 1974. Publishes trade paperback originals. **Publishes 7 titles/year. 800 mss received/year. 15% of books from first-time authors. 100% from unagented writers. Pays 8% royalty on retail price.** Publishes book 6-36 months after acceptance of ms. Accepts simultaneous submissions. Responds in 3 months to manuscripts. Book catalog available online.

- "Our usual reading period is March 1-May 1, but because of a backlog of accepted manuscripts, *Ahsahta* cannot read unsolicited work until further notice. Please check our site periodically for announcements if you are interested. Ahsahta Press publishes chapbooks only occasionally and by invitation only. Please include in your submission: a cover letter containing relevant autobiographical information and a brief description of the manuscript; a list of published works, if applicable; a book-length manuscript (48-100 pages), and a SASE for reply. Manuscripts will not be returned. For notification of receipt of manuscript, please enclose a self-addressed stamped postcard. Handwritten manuscripts are not accepted. We cannot take submissions of any kind by phone, fax, or e-mail. During the Sawtooth Poetry Prize Competition (January 1 through March 1) we are not able to consider manuscripts unless they are contest entries. We have a small editorial staff, which sometimes makes the reading slower than we or our poets would like. However, we try to respond to submissions within 3 months. The press will continue to read manuscripts for the $1500 Sawtooth Poetry Prize Competition each year between January 1 and March 1. Please see the competition guidelines for more information."

Recent Title(s) *100 Notes on Violence*, by Julie Carr; *The Last 4 Things*, by Kate Greenstreet; *Dick of the Dead*, by Rachel Loden; *FAQ*, by Ben Doller.

Tips "Ahsahta's motto is that poetry is art, so our readers tend to come to us for the unexpected—poetry that makes them think, reflect, and even do something they haven't done before."

ALONDRA PRESS, LLC

10122 Shadow Wood Dr., #19, Houston TX 77043. E-mail: lark@alondrapress.com. Website: www.alondrapress.com. **Contact:** Kathleen Palmer, chief editor; Solomon Tager, nonfiction editor. Estab. 2007. Publishes trade paperback originals and reprints. **Publishes 4 titles/year. 75% of books from first-time authors. 75% from unagented writers.** Publishes book 8 months after acceptance of ms. Accepts simultaneous submissions. Responds in 1 month to queries and proposals. Responds in 3 month to manuscripts. Guidelines available online.

Nonfiction Subjects include anthropology, archaeology, history, philosophy, psychology, translation. Submit complete ms.

Fiction Subjects include literary, all fiction genres. "Just send us a few pages, or the entire manuscript in an e-mail attachment. We will look at it quickly and tell you if it interests us."

Recent Title(s) *Nessus the Centaur*, by Henry Hollenbaugh (literary, adventure); *Canyon Chronicles*, by K. Gray Jones (historical fiction); *Spinoza's God*, by Franklin L. Dixon (philosophy).

Tips "We will be looking for unusual stories, similar to The Wind Thief. Send your submissions in an e-mail attachment only."

ALPINE PUBLICATIONS

38262 Linman Road, Crawford CO 81415. (970)921-5005. Fax: (970)921-5081. E-mail: alpinepubl@aol.com. Website: alpinepub.com. **Contact:** Ms. B.J. McKinney, publisher. Estab. 1975. Publishes hardcover and trade paperback originals and reprints. **Publishes 6-10 titles/year. 40% of books from first-time authors. 95% from unagented writers. Pays 8-15% royalty on wholesale price. Pays advance.** Publishes book 18 months after acceptance of ms. Accepts simultaneous submissions. Responds in 1-3 weeks to queries. Responds in 1 month to proposals and manuscripts. Book catalog available free. Guidelines available online.

Imprints Blue Ribbon Books.

Nonfiction Subjects include animals. Alpine specializes in books that promote the enjoyment of and responsibility for companion animals with emphasis on dogs and horses. Reviews artwork/photos. Send photocopies. No fiction.

Recent Title(s) *Agility Start to Finish*, by Diane Bauman; *Successful Show Dog Handling*, by Peter Green and Mario Migliorini; *Dictionary of Veterinary Terms*, by Jennifer Coates; *Dog Driver*, by Miki and Julie Collins.

Tips "Our audience is pet owners, breeders, exhibitors, veterinarians, animal trainers, animal care specialists, and judges. Our books are in-depth and most are heavily illustrated. Look up some of our titles before you submit. See what is unique about our books. Write your proposal to suit our guidelines."

N AMERICAN CARRIAGE HOUSE PUBLISHING

PO Box 1778, Penn Valley CA 95946. (530)432-8860. Fax: (530)432-7379. E-mail: editor@americancarriagehousepublishing.com. Website: www.americancarriagehousepublishing.com. **Contact:** Lynn Taylor, editor (parenting, reference, child, women). Format publishes in trade paperback and electronic originals. **Publishes 10 titles/year. 10% of books from first-time authors. 100% from unagented writers.** Publishes book 12 months after acceptance of ms. Accepts simultaneous submissions. Catalog free on request. Guidelines not available.

Nonfiction Subjects include child guidance, education, parenting, women's issues, women's studies, young adult. Query with SASE. Reviews artwork/photos. Send photocopies.

Fiction Subjects include religious, spiritual, young adult. Query with SASE.

Recent Title(s) *So I Was Thinking About Adoption...*, by Mardie Caldwell (reference, women's issue, pregnancy); *Is Your Child Autistic?*, by Mardie Caldwell (rerence, health, children).

AMERICAN CATHOLIC PRESS

16565 S. State St., South Holland IL 60473. (312)331-5845. Fax: (708)331-5484. E-mail: acp@acpress.org. Website: www.acpress.org. **Contact:** Rev. Michael Gilligan, PhD, editorial director. Estab. 1967. Publishes hardcover originals and hardcover and paperback reprints. **Publishes 4 titles/year. Makes outright purchase of $25-100.** Guidelines available online.

Nonfiction Subjects include education, music, dance, religion, spirituality. "We publish books on the Roman Catholic liturgy—for the most part, books on religious music and educational books and pamphlets. We also publish religious songs for church use, including Psalms, as well as choral and instrumental arrangements. We are interested in new music, meant for use in church services. Books, or even pamphlets, on the Roman Catholic Mass are especially welcome. We have no interest in secular topics and are not interested in religious poetry of any kind."

Tips "Most of our sales are by direct mail, although we do work through retail outlets."

AMIGADGET PUBLISHING CO.

P.O. Box 1696, Lexington SC 29071. (803)794-6018. E-mail: amigadget@fotoartista.com. Website: www.fotoartista.com/amigadget. **Contact:** Jay Gross, editor-in-chief. Publishes trade paperback originals. **Publishes 1 titles/year.**

Nonfiction Query via e-mail only. *All unsolicited mss returned unopened.*

Recent Title(s) *The Coffee Experience*, by J. Gross (travel).

Tips "We are not currently seeking new paper publishing projects."

ANHINGA PRESS

P.O. Box 10595, Tallahassee FL 32302. (850)422-1408. Fax: (850)442-6323. E-mail: info@anhinga.org. Website: www.anhinga.org. **Contact:** Rick Campbell, editor. Publishes hardcover and trade paperback originals. **Publishes 5 titles/year. Pays 10% royalty on retail price. Offers Anhinga Prize of $2,000.** Accepts simultaneous submissions. Responds in 3 months to queries, proposals, and manuscripts. Book catalog for #10 SASE or online. Guidelines available online.

"Publishes only full-length collections of poetry (60-80 pages). No individual poems or chapbooks."

Recent Title(s) *Blood Almanac*, by Sandy Langhorn; *Morning of the Red Admirals*, by Robert Dana; *Dubious Angels*, by Keith Ratzlaff.

ARCHIMEDES PRESS, INC.

6 Berkley Rd., Glenville NY 12302. (518)265-3269. Fax: (518)384-1313. E-mail: archimedespress@verizon.net. Website: www.archimedespress.com. **Contact:** Richard DiMaggio, chief editor. Estab. 2002. Publishes broad-based hardcover, trade paperback, and mass market paperback originals. **Publishes 3-6 titles/year. Pays 5-15% royalty.** Publishes book 6 months after acceptance of ms. Responds in 2 months to queries.

"Right now we are doing web magazine publishing only, and our website is www.didyouweekend.com."

Nonfiction Subjects include alternative, business, economics, child guidance, community, cooking, foods, nutrition, creative nonfiction, education, government, politics, history, humanities, language, literature, money, finance, photography, sex, social sciences, travel, and weekend getaways. E-mail submissions acceptable. Please snail mail complete manuscripts. If a consumer wants it, so do we. Query with SASE. Submit sample chapters, marketing plan, SASE. Submit complete ms. Reviews artwork/photos. Send photocopies.

Recent Title(s) *Real Estate Professionals Liability Review*; *Financial Empowerment Infomercials*.

Tips "Our audience is the consumer, plain and simple. That means everyone. We are a small press and try hard to avoid the limitations of the industry. While agented submissions are preferred, they are not necessary with professional submissions. We want fresh, creative ideas and will accept unsolicited manuscripts. These, however, will not be returned without a SASE. E-mails are OK. No phone calls, please."

ARIEL STARR PRODUCTIONS, LTD.

P.O. Box 17, Demarest NJ 07627. E-mail: arielstarrprod@aol.com. **Contact:** Attn: Acquisitions Editor. Trade and mass market paperback originals; electronic originals. **Publishes 5 titles/year. Receives 40 queries/year, 4 mss/year. 80% of books from first-time authors. 80% from unagented writers.** Publishes book 12 months after acceptance of ms. Accepts simultaneous submissions. Catalog not available. Guidelines available by e-mail.

Nonfiction Subjects include environment, nature, New Age, religion, spirituality. "We are open to other areas but we ask the person to submit a query letter, one-page outline, and a SASE first; nothing more unless we ask for it." Query with SASE. Reviews artwork/photos; send photocopies.

Fiction Subjects include adventure, fantasy, poetry, religious, science fiction, spiritual. Query with SASE and one-page proposal.

Recent Title(s) *Focused or Dead*, by George E. Soroka (self-help); *The Dark Chronicles Series*, by Cynthia Soroka (dark fantasy).

Tips "We want books that stimulate the brain and inspire the mind. Be honest and decent in your queries."

ASHLAND POETRY PRESS

401 College Avenue, Ashland OH 44805. (419)289-5957. Fax: (419)289-5255. E-mail: app@ashland.edu. Website: www.ashland.edu/aupoetry. **Contact:** Stephen Haven, director. Estab. 1969. Publishes trade paperback originals. **Publishes 2-3 titles/year. 360 mss received/year. 50% of books from first-time**

authors. 100% from unagented writers. Makes outright purchase of $500-1,000. Publishes book 10 months after acceptance of ms. Accepts simultaneous submissions. Responds in 1 month to queries. Responds in 6 months to manuscripts. Book catalog available online. Guidelines available online.
Tips "We rarely publish a title submitted off the transom outside of our Snyder Prize competition."

ASIAN HUMANITIES PRESS

Jain Publishing Co. P.O. Box 3523, Fremont CA 94539. (510)659-8272. Fax: (510)659-0501. E-mail: mail@jainpub.com. Website: www.jainpub.com. **Contact:** M. Jain, editor-in-chief. Estab. 1989. Publishes hardcover and trade paperback originals and reprints. **Publishes 6 titles/year. 100% from unagented writers.** Publishes book 12-24 months after acceptance of ms. Responds in 3 months to manuscripts. Book catalog available online. Guidelines available online.

"Asian Humanities Press publishes in the areas of humanities and social sciences pertaining to Asia, commonly categorized as Asian Studies. Currently emphasizing undergraduate-level textbooks."

Nonfiction Subjects include language, literature, philosophy, psychology, religion, spirituality, Asian classics, social sciences, art/culture. Submit proposal package, vita, list of prior publications. Reviews artwork/photos. Send photocopies.
Recent Title(s) *A Handbook for Analyzing Chinese Characters*, by Zhifang Ren.

ASPICOMM MEDIA

Aspicomm Books P.O. Box 1212, Baldwin NY 11510. (516)642-5976. Fax: (516)489-8916. E-mail: rdlagler@aspicomm.com. Website: www.aspicomm.com. **Contact:** Valerie Daniel. Publishes mass market paperback originals. **25 queries received/year. 5 mss received/year. 90% of books from first-time authors. 50% from unagented writers.** Publishes book 6-8 months after acceptance of ms. Responds in 2-3 months to queries. Guidelines available online.
Fiction Subjects include mainstream, contemporary. Query with SASE. Unsolicited mss returned unopened.
Recent Title(s) *Mountain High, Valley Low*, by Renee Flagler; *Miss Guided*, by Renee Flagler; *In Her Mind*, by Renee Flagler.
Tips If you are an author interested in submitting a manuscript, please send a query letter, synopsis, and three chapters from your book along with a SASE to Author Submissions.

A.T. PUBLISHING

23 Lily Lake Rd., Highland NY 12528. (845)691-2021. **Contact:** Anthony Prizzia, publisher (education); John Prizzia, publisher. Estab. 2001. Publishes trade paperback originals. **Publishes 1-3 titles/year. 5-10 queries received/year. 100% of books from first-time authors. 100% from unagented writers. Pays 15-25% royalty on retail price. Makes outright purchase of $500-2,500. Pays $500-1,000 advance.** Accepts simultaneous submissions. Responds in 1 month to queries. Responds in 2 months to proposals. Responds in 4 months to manuscripts.
Nonfiction Subjects include cooking, foods, nutrition, education, recreation, science, sports. Query with SASE. Submit complete ms. Reviews artwork/photos. Send photocopies.
Recent Title(s) *The Portion Principle*, by Kaitlin Louie; *The Waiter and Waitress's Guide to a Bigger Income*, by Anthony Thomas; *Why is the Teacher's Butt so Big?* by Debra Craig.
Tips "Audience is people interested in a variety of topics, general. Submit typed manuscript for consideration, including a SASE for return of manuscript."

AUTUMN HOUSE PRESS

87½ Westwood St., Pittsburgh PA 15211. (412)381-261. E-mail: msimms@autumnhouse.org. Website: www.autumnhouse.org. **Contact:** Michael Simms, editor-in-chief (fiction). Hardcover, trade paperback, and electronic originals. **Publishes 8 titles/year. 1,000 mss/year 10% of books from first-time authors. 100% from unagented writers. Pays $0-2,500 advance.** Publishes book 9 months after acceptance of ms. Accepts simultaneous submissions. Catalog free on request. Guidelines online at website; free on request; or for #10 SASE.
Fiction Subjects include literary. "We consider all fiction mss. Submit only through our annual contest. See guidelines online. Submit completed ms."
Recent Title(s) *Drift and Swerve*, by Samuel Ligon; *New World Order*, by Derek Green; *She Heads into the Wilderness*, by Anne Marie Macari; *The Son of the Horse*, by Samuel Hazo; *House Where a Woman*, by Lori Wilson.
Tips "The competition to publish with Autumn House is very tough. Submit only your best work."

BALL PUBLISHING

P.O. Box 1660, West Chicago IL 60186. (630)231-3675. Fax: (630)231-5254. E-mail: cbeytes@ballpublishing.com. Website: www.ballpublishing.com. **Contact:** Chris Beytes. Publishes hardcover and trade paperback originals. **Publishes 4-6 titles/year.** Accepts simultaneous submissions. Book catalog for 8 ½ × 11 envelope and 3 first-class stamps.

O→ "We publish for the book trade and the horticulture trade. Books on both home gardening/landscaping and commercial production are considered."

Nonfiction Subjects include agriculture, gardening, floriculture. Query with SASE. Submit proposal package, outline, 2 sample chapters. Reviews artwork/photos. Send photocopies.

Recent Title(s) *Great Flowering Landscape Shrubs*, by Vincent A. Simeone; *Kids' Container Gardening*, by Cindy Krezel; *Biocontrol in Protected Culture*, by Kevin M. Heinz et al.

Tips "We are expanding our book line to home gardeners, while still publishing for green industry professionals. Gardening books should be well thought out and unique in the market. Actively looking for photo books on specific genera and families of flowers and trees."

BANCROFT PRESS

P.O. Box 65360, Baltimore MD 21209-9945. (410)358-0658. Fax: (410)764-1967. E-mail: bruceb@bancroftpress.com; HDemchick@bancroftpress.com (if Bancroft account is down). Website: www.bancroftpress.com. **Contact:** Bruce Bortz, editor and publisher (health, investments, politics, history, humor, literary novels, mystery/thrillers, chick lit, young adult). Publishes hardcover and trade paperback originals. **Publishes 4-6 titles/year. Pays 6-8% royalty. Pays various royalties on retail price. Pays $750 advance.** Publishes book up to 3 years after acceptance of ms. Accepts simultaneous submissions. Responds in 6-12 months to queries, proposals and manuscripts. Guidelines available online.

O→ "Bancroft Press is a general trade publisher. We publish young adult fiction and adult fiction, as well as occasional nonfiction. Our only mandate is 'books that enlighten.'"

Nonfiction All quality books on any subject of interest to the publisher. Subjects include business, economics, government, politics, health, medicine, money, finance, regional, sports, women's issues, women's studies, popular culture. "We advise writers to visit the website." Submit proposal package, outline, 2 sample chapters, competition/market survey.

Fiction Subjects include ethnic, general, feminist, gay, lesbian, historical, humor, literary, mainstream, contemporary, military, war, mystery, amateur sleuth, cozy, police procedural, private eye/hardboiled, regional, science fiction, hard science fiction/technological, soft/sociological, translation, frontier sage, traditional, young adult, historical, problem novels, series, thrillers.

Recent Title(s) *The Sinful Life of Lucy Burns*, by Elizabeth Leiknes; Thanksgiving at the Inn, by Tim Whitney; *Dracula is Dead: How Romania Survived Communism, Ended It, and Emerged Since 1989 as the New Italy*, by Sheilah Kast and Jim Rosapepe.

BANTER PRESS

561 Hudson St., Suite 57, New York NY 10014. (718)864-5080. Fax: (718)965-3603. E-mail: info@banterpress.com. Website: www.banterpress.com. **Contact:** David McClintock, president. Estab. 2002. Publishes trade paperback and electronic originals and reprints. **Publishes 1-3 titles/year. 25 queries received/year. 12 mss received/year. 80% of books from first-time authors. 90% from unagented writers. Pays 15% royalty on wholesale price, negotiable.** Publishes book 6-18 months after acceptance of ms. Accepts simultaneous submissions. Responds in 4-12 weeks to queries. Book catalog available online. Guidelines available online.

Nonfiction Subjects include audio, health, written for patients, entrepreneurship, consumer protection, consulting, public speaking, publishing, communication-oriented and teamwork-oriented topics, business communication, online marketing, and social media. "We seek authors who are active speakers within their industry, especially those who do seminars or consulting. We're small but very experienced and selective. We are relaunching with an emphasis on business communication, online marketing, and social media." Submit proposal package, outline, maximum sample chapters, bio, analysis of competing books, author's plan for promoting the book. Reviews artwork/photos. Send photocopies; never send originals.

Tips "Our readers are curious, technologically savvy professionals who need inspiring, up-to-date business information. Please don't mail us manuscripts! E-mail them as PDFs, or as plain text files (.txt). Best yet, paste text into a giant e-mail."

BENDALL BOOKS

145 Tyee Dr., PMB 361, Point Roberts WA 98281. (250)743-2946. Fax: (250)743-2910. E-mail: admin@bendallbooks.com. Website: www.bendallbooks.com. **Contact:** Mary Moore, publisher. Publishes trade

paperback originals. **Publishes 1 title/year. 30 queries received/year. 5 mss received/year. 50% of books from first-time authors. 100% from unagented writers. Pays 5-15% royalty on wholesale price.** Publishes book 1 year after acceptance of ms. Accepts simultaneous submissions. Book catalog available free. Guidelines available online.
Nonfiction Subjects include education. Query with SASE.
Recent Title(s) *Daily Meaning*, edited by Allan Neilsen; *Fiction Workshop Companion*, by Jon Volkmer.

BETTERWAY HOME BOOKS

Imprint of F + W Media, Inc. 4700 E. Galbraith Rd., Cincinnati OH 45236. (513)531-2690, ext. 11467. E-mail: jacqueline@fwmedia.com. Website: www.fwmedia.com. **Contact:** Jacqueline Musser, acquisitions editor. Publishes trade paperback and hardcover originals. **Publishes 6-8 titles/year. 6 queries received/year. 6 mss received/year. 60% of books from first-time authors. 95% from unagented writers. Pays 8-10% royalty on wholesale price. Pays $3,000-5,000 advance.** Publishes book 18 months after acceptance of ms. Accepts simultaneous submissions. Responds in 1 month to queries and proposals. Responds in 3 months to manuscripts.
Nonfiction Subjects include house and home, basic home repair and home improvement, home organization, homemaking. Query with SASE. Submit proposal package, outline, 1 sample chapter. Reviews artwork/photos. Send photocopies and PDFs (if submitting electronically).
Recent Title(s) *Fix it in a Flash*, by Jodi Marks; *Go Organize!*, by Marilyn Bohn; *No-Hassle Housecleaning*, by Christina Spence.
Tips Audience comprised of new and first time homeowners, those who take the 'weekend warrior' approach to home improvement/nesting. "We're looking for authors who bring a fresh, unique approach to home skills. We prefer authors who already have established marketing platforms for their work."

BICK PUBLISHING HOUSE

307 Neck Rd., Madison CT 06443. (203)245-0073. Fax: (203)245-5990. E-mail: bickpubhse@aol.com. Website: www.bickpubhouse.com. **Contact:** Dale Carlson, president (psychology); Hannah Carlson (special needs, disabilities); Irene Ruth (wildlife). Estab. 1994. Publishes trade paperback originals. **Publishes 4 titles/year. 100 queries received/year. 100 mss received/year. 55% of books from first-time authors. 55% from unagented writers. Pays $500-1,000 advance.** Publishes book 12 months after acceptance of ms. Responds in 1 month to queries. Responds in 2 months to proposals. Responds in 3 months to manuscripts. Book catalog available free. Guidelines for #10 SASE.

"Bick Publishing House publishes step-by-step, easy-to-read professional information for the general adult public about physical, psychological, and emotional disabilities or special needs. Currently emphasizing science, psychology for teens."

Nonfiction Subjects include health, medicine, disability/special needs, psychology, young adult or teen science, psychology, wildlife rehabilitation. Query with SASE. Submit proposal package, outline, resume, 3 sample chapters.
Recent Title(s) *The Courage to Lead Support Groups: Mental Illnesses and Addictions*, by Hannah Carlson; *In and Out of Your Mind Teen Science*, by Dale Carlson; *Who Said What, Philosophy Quotes for Teens: What Are You Doing With Your Life?*, by J. Krishnamurti.

BIOGRAPHICAL PUBLISHING COMPANY

95 Sycamore Dr.,, Prospect CT 06712-1493. (203)758-3661. Fax: (253)793-2618. E-mail: biopub@aol.com. Website: www.biopub.co.cc. **Contact:** John R. Guevin, ed. Hardcover originals & reprints; trade paperback originals & reprints. **Publishes 6 titles/year. Receives 25 queries/year; 12 mss/year. 50% of books from first-time authors. 90% from unagented writers.** Publishes book 4 months after acceptance of ms. Catalog & guidelines free on request.
Nonfiction Subjects include animals, career guidance, child guidance, community, cooking, counseling, education, environment, ethnic, finance, foods, games, gardening, government, health, history, hobbies, house and home, humanities, language, literature, medicine, memoirs, military, money, multicultural, nature, nutrition, politics, psychology, public affairs, recreation, regional, science, social sciences, spirituality. Query with SASE; submit completed ms. Reviews artwork/photos. Send photocopies.
Fiction Subjects include adventure, contemporary, ethnic, historical, humor, juvenile, literary, mainstream, military, multicultural, mystery, picture books, poetry, regional, religious, romance, science fiction, short story collections, spiritual, sports, suspense, war, western, young adult. Query with SASE; submit completed ms.
Recent Title(s) *Interlude in Ravenna*, by Wolf Arnold (fiction); *Sensory Integration Strategies for Parents*, by Jeanne Ganz (nonficition); *Loving Michael Jackson!!*, by Selena Millman (poetry).

BIRCH BROOK PRESS

P.O. Box 81, Delhi NY 13753. Fax: (607)764-7453. E-mail: birchbrook@copper.net. Website: www.birchbrookpress.info. **Contact:** Editor/publisher: Tom Tolnay; Associate Editor: Barbara dela Cuesta. Estab. 1982. Publishes trade paperback originals; "letterpress editions are printed in our own shop." **Publishes 4 titles/year. 200+ queries received/year. 200+ mss received/year. 95% from unagented writers. Pays modest royalty.** Publishes book 10-18 months after acceptance of ms. Accepts simultaneous submissions. Responds in 3-6 months to manuscripts. Book catalog available online.

Imprints Birch Brook Press; Birch Brook Impressions.

Nonfiction Subjects include film, music, (rare) nonfiction of cultural interest, including stage, opera, including outdoors.

Fiction Publishes fiction, mostly anthologies with a theme established in-house. Subjects include mainstream, contemporary, poetry, poetry in translation, short fiction (occasionally), sports (outdoors/fly fishing/baseball). Query with SASE.

Recent Title(s) *Sea-Crossing of St. Brendan*, by Matthew Brennan; *The Bells of Moses Henry*, by Peter Skinner; *Seasons of Defiance*, by Lance Lee; *Tony's World*, by Barry Wallenstein; *And This is What Happens Next*, by Marcus Rome; *North of Easie*, by Robert J. Romano Jr.

Tips "Our audience is college educated."

BKMK PRESS

University of Missouri-Kansas City 5101 Rockhill Rd., Kansas City MO 64110-2499. (816)235-2558. Fax: (816)235-2611. E-mail: bkmk@umkc.edu. Website: www.umkc.edu/bkmk. **Contact:** Ben Furnish, managing editor. Estab. 1971. Publishes trade paperback originals. Accepts simultaneous submissions. Responds in 4-6 months to queries. Guidelines available online.

O━ "BkMk Press publishes fine literature. Reading period January-June."

Nonfiction Creative nonfiction essays. Submit 25-50 pp. sample and SASE.

Fiction Subjects include literary, short story collections. Query with SASE.

Recent Title(s) *Cleaning a Rainbow*, by Gary Gildner; *Love Letters from a Fat Man*, by Naomi Benarons; *Dream Lives of Butterflies*, by Jaimee Wriston Colbert.

Tips "We skew toward readers of literature, particularly contemporary writing. Because of our limited number of titles published per year, we discourage apprentice writers or `scattershot' submissions."

BLACK DOME PRESS CORP.

1011 Route 296, Hensonville NY 12439. (518)734-6357. Fax: (518)734-5802. E-mail: blackdomep@aol.com. Website: www.blackdomepress.com. Estab. 1990. Publishes cloth and trade paperback originals and reprints. Accepts simultaneous submissions. Book catalog and guidelines available online.

- Do not send the entire work. Mail a cover letter, table of contents, introduction, sample chapter (or two), and your C.V. or brief biography to the Editor. Please do not send computer disks or submit your proposal via e-mail. If your book will include illustrations, please send us copies of sample illustrations. Do not send originals.

Nonfiction Subjects include history, nature, environment, photography, regional, New York state, Native Americans, grand hotels, genealogy, colonial life, quilting, architecture, railroads. New York state regional material only. Submit proposal package, outline, bio.

Recent Title(s) *American Wilderness*, by Barbara Babcock; *Berkshire & Taconic Trails*, by Edward G. Henry.

Tips "Our audience is comprised of New York state residents, tourists, and visitors."

N BLACK OCEAN

P.O. Box 52030, Boston MA 02205. (617)304-9011. Fax: (617)849-5678. E-mail: carrie@blackocean.org. Website: www.blackocean.org. **Contact:** Carrie Olivia Adams, poetry editor. **Publishes 3 titles/year.**

Recent Title(s) Zachary Schomburg, Joshua Harmon, Paula Cisewski, Rauan Klassnik, Aase Berg, Johannes Goransson.

BLUEBRIDGE

Imprint of United Tribes Media, Inc. 240 W. 35th St., Suite 500, New York NY 10001. (212)244-4166. Fax: (212)279-0927. E-mail: janguerth@aol.com. Website: www.bluebridgebooks.com. **Contact:** Jan-Erik Guerth, publisher (general nonfiction). Estab. 2004. Publishes hardcover and trade paperback originals. **Publishes 6-8 titles/year. 1,000 queries received/year. 5% of books from first-time authors. Pays variable royalty on wholesale price. Pays variable advance.** Publishes book 12-24 months after acceptance of ms. Accepts simultaneous submissions. Responds in 1 month to queries and proposals. Book catalog for #10 SASE.

Nonfiction Subjects include Americana, anthropology, archaeology, art, architecture, business, economics, child guidance, contemporary culture, creative nonfiction, ethnic, gardening, gay, lesbian, government, politics, health, medicine, history, humanities, language, literature, literary criticism, multicultural, music, dance, nature, environment, philosophy, psychology, religion, science, social sciences, sociology, spirituality, travel, women's issues, world affairs. BlueBridge is an independent publisher of international nonfiction based in New York City. The BlueBridge mission: Thoughtful Books for Mind and Spirit. Query with SASE or preferably by e-mail.

Recent Title(s) *Revolutionary Spirits*, by Gary Kowalski; *The Gift of Years*, by Joan Chittister; *Horse*, by J. Edward Chamberlin; *The Door of No Return*, by William St. Clair; *Mr. Langshaw's Square Piano*, by Madeline Goold.

Tips "We target a broad general audience."

N BOBO STRATEGY

2506 N. Clark, #287, Chicago IL 60614. E-mail: info@bobostrategy.com. Website: www.bobostrategy.com. **Contact:** Chris Cunliffe, editor-in-chief. Trade paperback originals. **Publishes 1-5 titles/year.** Publishes book 6 months after acceptance of ms. Accepts simultaneous submissions. Catalog online at website. Guidelines available by e-mail.

> "We seek writing that brings clarity and simplicity to the complex. If your idea is good, we're willing to take a chance on you."

Nonfiction Subjects include architecture, art, chess, creative nonfiction, government, humanities, memoirs, politics, regional, travel, world affairs. Query with SASE; submit proposal package, including: outline, 1 sample chapter. Reviews artwork; send photocopies. E-mail okay.

Fiction Subjects include poetry, regional, short story collections. Query; submit proposal package, including: synopsis, 1 sample chapter. E-mail okay.

Recent Title(s) *A Dream in the Clouds*, a politically-neutral collection of poetry, prose, and art inspired by the 2008 United States Presidential Election; *Let Nothing You Dismay*, by Benjamin Shultz.

BREWERS PUBLICATIONS

Imprint of Brewers Association 736 Pearl St., Boulder CO 80302. (303)447-0816. Fax: (303)447-2825. E-mail: kristi@brewersassociation.org. Website: beertown.org. **Contact:** Kristi Switzer, publisher. Estab. 1986. Publishes hardcover and trade paperback originals. **Publishes 2 titles/year. 50% of books from first-time authors. 100% from unagented writers. Pays small advance.** Publishes book 9 months after acceptance of ms. Accepts simultaneous submissions. Responds in 3 months to relevant queries. Only those submissions relevant to our needs will receive a response to queries. Guidelines available online.

> "Brewers Publications is the largest publisher of books on beer-related subjects."

Nonfiction "We only publish nonfiction books of interest to amateur and professional brewers. Our authors have many years of brewing experience and in-depth practical knowledge of their subject. We are not interested in fiction, drinking games or beer/bar reviews. If your book is not about how to make beer, then do not waste your time or ours by sending it. Those determined to fit our needs will subscribe to and read *Zymurgy* and *The New Brewer*." Query first with proposal and sample chapter.

Recent Title(s) *Brewing with Wheat: The 'Wit' and 'Weizen' of World Wheat Beer Styles*; by Stan Hieronymus; *Great Beers of Belgium*, by Michael Jackson.

BRIGHT MOUNTAIN BOOKS, INC.

206 Riva Ridge Dr., Fairview NC 28730. (828)628-1768. Fax: (828)628-1755. E-mail: bmbmarthafullington@charter.net. Website: www.brightmountainbooks.com. **Contact:** Cynthia F. Bright, Senior Editor. Estab. 1983. Publishes trade paperback originals and reprints. **Publishes 3 titles/year. 50% of books from first-time authors. 100% from unagented writers. Pays royalty.** Responds in 1 month to queries. Responds in 3 months to manuscripts.

Imprints Historical Images, Ridgetop Books.

> Currently, Bright Mountain Books has nearly forty titles in print, all written by local authors or having subject matter relevant to the region of the Southern Appalachian Mountains.

Nonfiction Subjects include history, regional. "Our current emphasis is on regional titles set in the Southern Appalachians and Carolinas, which can include nonfiction by local writers." Query with SASE.

Recent Title(s) *Mountain Fever*, by Tom Alexander; *Cabins & Castles*, by Douglas Swain; Asheville: Mountain Majesty, by Lou Harshaw; *John Henry Moss*, by Bob Terrell; *The Carolina Mountains*, by Margaret W. Marley.

BRONZE MAN BOOKS

Bronze Man Books, Millikin Univ., 1184 W. Main, Decatur IL 62522, U.S. (217)424-6264. Website: www.bronzemanbooks.com. **Contact:** Dr. Randy Brooks, editorial board (Area of interest: children's books, fiction, poetry, nonfiction); Edwin Walker, editorial board (art, exhibits, graphic design). Hardcover, trade paperback, & mass market paperback originals. **Publishes 3-4 titles/year. Receives 45 queries; 25 mss. 80% of books from first-time authors. 100% from unagented writers.** Publishes book 6 months after acceptance of ms. Catalog free on request. Guidelines not available.

Nonfiction "We do not publish author subsidy books." Subjects include art, architecture, children's, graphic design, exhibits. Query with SASE; submit proposal package, including outline and 3 sample chapters. Reviews artwork/photos. Send photocopies.

Fiction Subjects include art, exhibits, graphic design, general. Submit completed ms.

Recent Title(s) *Robert Marshall Root: Something More Than Praise*, by Edwin Walker (68 pages, nonfiction); *Ants in the Band Room*, by Laura Podeschi (children's trade paperback with audio CD); *Commas & Ampersands*, by Steve Moore (short dramas chapbook); *Millikin University Haiku Anthology* (poetry); *Simple Universal*, by Jeffrey Allen (chapbook, 32 pages); *Mathematics of Fire*, by Josh Wild (chapbook, 24 pages, hand sewn).

Tips "The art books are intended for serious collectors and scholars of contemporary art, especially of artists from the Midwestern U.S. These books are published in conjunction with art exhibitions at Millikin University or the Decatur Area Arts Council. The children's books have our broadest audience, and the literary chapbooks are intended for readers of contemporary fiction, drama, and poetry."

BROOKS BOOKS

3720 N. Woodridge Dr., Decatur IL 62526. E-mail: brooksbooks@sbcglobal.net. Website: www.brooksbookshaiku.com. **Contact:** Randy Brooks, editor (haiku poetry, tanka poetry). Publishes hardcover, trade paperback, & electronic originals. **Publishes 2-3 titles/year. 100 queries received/year. 25 mss received/year. 10% of books from first-time authors. 100% from unagented writers. Outright purchase based on wholesale value of 10% of a press run.** Publishes book 6-12 months after acceptance of ms. Responds in 2 months to queries. Responds in 3 months to proposals and manuscripts. Book catalog free on request or online at website. Guidelines free on request, for #10 SASE.

Imprints Brooks Books.

O→ "Brooks Books, formerly High/Coo Press, publishes English-language haiku books, chapbooks, magazines, and bibliographies."

Recent Title(s) *HAIKU: the Art of the Short Poem, by Tazuo Yamaguchi; Sky In my Teacup: haiku & photographs, by Anne LB Davidson, online edition. See website; Lull Before Dark: Haiku, by Caroline Gourlay; To Hear the Rain: Selected Haiku*, by Peggy Lyles.

Tips "The best haiku capture human perception—moments of being alive conveyed through sensory images. They do not explain nor describe nor provide philosophical or political commentary. Haiku are gifts of the here and now, deliberately incomplete so that the reader can enter into the haiku moment to open the gift and experience the feelings and insights of that moment for his or her self. Our readership includes the haiku community, readers of contemporary poetry, teachers and students of Japanese literature and contemporary Japanese poetics."

CAVE HOLLOW PRESS

P.O. Drawer J, Warrensburg MO 64093. E-mail: gbcrump@cavehollowpress.com. Website: www.cavehollowpress.com. **Contact:** G.B. Crump, editor. Estab. 2001. Publishes trade paperback originals. **Publishes 1 title/year. 70 queries received/year. 6 mss received/year. 80% of books from first-time authors. 100% from unagented writers. Pays 7-12% royalty on wholesale price. Pays negotiable amount in advance.** Publishes book 1 year after acceptance of ms. Accepts simultaneous submissions. Responds in 1-2 months to queries and proposals. Responds in 3-6 months to manuscripts. Book catalog for #10 SASE. Guidelines available free.

Fiction Subjects include mainstream, contemporary. "Our website is updated frequently to reflect the current type of fiction Cave Hollow Press is seeking." Query with SASE.

Recent Title(s) *Up From Thunder*, by Suzan K. Salzer; *The Feedsack Dress*, by Carolyn Mulford (young adult); *A Horse Named Kat*, by Lucy Lauer (middle reader); *Triskaideka: Murder, Mystery, Magic, Madness and Mayhem II*, by various (anthology).

Tips "Our audience varies based on the type of book we are publishing. We specialize in Missouri and Midwest regional fiction. We are interested in talented writers from Missouri and the surrounding Midwest. Check our submission guidelines on the website for what type of fiction we are interested in currently."

CELLAR DOOR PUBLISHING, LLC

3439 NE Sandy Blvd., Suite 309, Portland OR 97232-1959. E-mail: info@cellardoorpublishing.com. Website: www.cellardoorpublishing.com. Estab. 2004. Publishes hardcover originals, trade paperback originals and electronic originals. **Publishes 3-4 titles/year. Pays a percentage of sales on royalty.** Accepts simultaneous submissions. Guidelines available via e-mail.

"Cellar Door Publishing specializes in the publication of high-quality illustrated literature and graphic novels. We are looking for all genres and age groups. We encourage creators to experiment with format and content, though it is not required. We do accept a limited number of submissions for books without illustrations. This is generally reserved for books that are either unique in content or controversial in nature, or literary projects that can be released in a serialized format."

Nonfiction Nonfiction submissions will also be considered if they fall into one of our categories. Submit online. Reviews artwork/photos. Send photocopies.

Fiction Subjects include adventure, comic books, erotica, experimental, fantasy, gothic, historical, horror, humor, juvenile, literary, mainstream, contemporary, multimedia, mystery, occult, picture books, romance, science fiction, suspense, western, young adult, translation. "We currently accept unsolicited submissions via online submission form and comic book conventions only. We no longer accept unsolicited submissions through traditional mail. To submit book proposals for consideration, please use the online submission form."

CHANNEL LAKE, INC.

P.O. Box 1771, New York NY 10156-1771. (800)592-1566. Fax: (866)794-5507. E-mail: info@channellake.com. Website: www.touristtown.com. **Contact:** Dirk Vanderwilt, publisher (travel guide books). Trade paperback originals. **Publishes 8-10 titles/year. 75% of books from first-time authors. 75% from unagented writers.** Publishes book 3 months after acceptance of ms. Accepts simultaneous submissions. Catalog available online at www.touristtown.com. Guidelines free on request.

Imprints Tourist Town Guides (Dirk Vanderbilt, Publisher).

Nonfiction Subjects include travel guide books. "We strongly suggest that you query us before sending a completed manuscript. Our editorial team has very strict content and formatting requirements. Contact us for details." Query. Does not review artwork/photos.

Recent Title(s) *Key West*, by Sarah Goodwin-Nguyen (travel guide); *Myrtle Beach*, by Liz and Charlie Mitchell (travel guide).

Tips "Our books are 'local interest' and 'travel books' that are marketed and sold near or in the destination city. Our audience is primarily tourists and vacationers to the destination city. Query first for ms guidelines. The query should include the destination city (U.S. only) that you are interested in writing about."

CLARITY PRESS, INC.

3277 Roswell Rd. NE, #469, Atlanta GA 30305. (877)613-1495. Fax: (404)231-3899 and (877)613-7868. E-mail: claritypress@usa.net. Website: www.claritypress.com. **Contact:** Diana G. Collier, editorial director (contemporary social justice issues). Estab. 1984. Publishes hardcover and trade paperback originals. **Publishes 4 titles/year.** Accepts simultaneous submissions. Responds to queries if interested.

Nonfiction Publishes books on contemporary issues in US, Middle East and Africa. Subjects include ethnic, world affairs, human rights/socioeconomic and minority issues. Query by e-mail only with synopsis, TOC, résumé, publishing history.

Recent Title(s) *The Power of Israel in the United States*, by James Petras; *Biowarfare and Terrorism*, by Francis A. Boyle.

Tips "Check our titles on the website."

CLOVER PARK PRESS

P.O. Box 5067, Santa Monica CA 90409-5067. (310)452-7657. E-mail: cloverparkpress@verizon.net. Website: www.cloverparkpress.com. **Contact:** Martha Grant, acquisitions editor. Estab. 1991. Publishes hardcover and trade paperback originals. **Publishes 1-3 titles/year. 800 queries received/year. 500 mss received/year. 90% of books from first-time authors. 80% from unagented writers. Pays royalty. Makes outright purchase. Pays modest advance.** Publishes book less than 12 months after acceptance of ms. Accepts simultaneous submissions. Responds in 2-4 months to queries, proposals, and to manuscripts. Book catalog available online. Guidelines for #10 SASE. Current list and guidelines available on website.

Nonfiction Subjects include creative nonfiction, multicultural, nature, environment, regional, science, travel, women's issues, women's studies, world affairs. Query with SASE. Proposal package should contain outline, bio, 30-50 pages (including the first chapter), SASE.

Small Presses

Recent Title(s) *Last Moon Dancing: A Memoir of Love and Real Life in Africa*, by Monique Maria Schmidt.

Tips "Our audience is primarily women, high school, and college students, readers with curiosity about the world. Initial contact by e-mail or query letter. We welcome good writing. Have patience, we will respond."

N CONIFER BOOKS, LLC

9599 S. Turkey Creek Rd., Morrison CO 80465. Website: www.sleuthguides.com. **Contact:** David Peterka, editor. Firm publishes trade paperback and electronic originals. **Publishes 3-7 titles/year. Receives 100 queries/year; receives 10 mss/year. 50% of books from first-time authors. 50% from unagented writers. Pays $500-1,000 advance.** Publishes book 6 months after acceptance of ms. Accepts simultaneous submissions. Catalog not available. Guidelines are online at website: http://www.sleuthguides.com/sleuthauthor.htm, and are available by e-mail.

"We publish reference and how-to books for the 55+ reader. This includes a large range of readers—from working Baby Boomers, retired Seniors, and the active Elderly."

Nonfiction Subjects include alternative lifestyles, animals, art/architecture, astrology/psychic, automotive, business/economics, child guidance/parenting, communications, community/public affairs, computers/electronics, contemporary culture, cooking/foods/nutrition, crafts, education, entertainment/games, gardening, government/politics, health/medicine, hobbies, house & home, language/literature, money/finance, music/dance, nature/environment, photography, real estate, recreation, regional, religion, science, sex, spirituality, sports, travel, aging, baby boomers, reference for senior citizens. "We publish reference and how-to books for the 55+ market. We are interested in educating seniors on modern topics and promoting active lifestyles. We are looking for informative, easy-to-read, nonfiction books written for the curious senior citizen. Our goal is to provide a trusted resource for investigations into a variety of senior topics including technology, travel, family, fitness, health, finances, and many more." Submit proposal package, including: outline, 1 sample chapter, brief list of competing titles, and author bio. Reviews artwork/photos as part of the ms package. Send appropriate electronic files.

Recent Title(s) *The Senior Sleuth's Guide to Technology for Seniors*, by David Peterka (how-to/reference).

Tips "Visit our website for an up-to-date list of current titles and our topic wish-list. Your book should address topics specifically relevant to the 55+ reader. Our books are positive, funny, and inspire an active lifestyle. Your submission should reflect this tone."

CONSUMER PRESS

13326 SW 28 St., Suite 102, Ft. Lauderdale FL 33330. (954)370-9153. E-mail: info@consumerpress.com. **Contact:** Joseph Pappas, editorial director. Estab. 1989. Publishes trade paperback originals. **Publishes 2-5 titles/year. Pays royalty on wholesale price or on retail price, as per agreement.** Book catalog available free.

Imprints Women's Publications.

Nonfiction Subjects include child guidance, health, medicine, money, finance, women's issues, women's studies, homeowner guides, building/remodeling, food/nutrition. Query with SASE.

Recent Title(s) *The Ritalin Free Child*, by Diana Hunter; *Before You Hire a Contractor, 2nd Ed.*, by Steve Gonzalez, CRC; *Food Smart: Understanding Nutrition in the 21st Century*, by Diana Hunter.

CORNELL MARITIME PRESS, INC.

Schiffer Publishing P.O. Box 456, Centreville MD 21617-0456. (410)758-1075. Fax: (410)758-6849. Website: www.cmptp.com. **Contact:** Jonna Jones, managing editor. Estab. 1938. Publishes hardcover originals and quality paperbacks. **Publishes 7-9 titles/year. 80% of books from first-time authors. 99% from unagented writers.** Publishes book 1 year after acceptance of ms. Responds in 2 months to queries, 3 months to mss.

Imprints *Tidewater* Publishers (regional history, outdoor sports, and wildlife of the Chesapeake Bay and the Delmarva Peninsula).

"Cornell Maritime Press publishes books for the merchant marine and a few recreational boating books for professional mariners and yachtsmen. We are expanding our outdoor and leathercraft lines, and are particularly interested in books on fishing, hunting, cooking, knots, and leatherwork. Any submissions outside of this focus will not be reviewed or returned."

Nonfiction Look online for current acquisition needs and submission guidelines. No phone calls or e-mails concerning unsolicited submissions are accepted. Please allow at least three months to review submissions.

Recent Title(s) *Osprey Adventure*, by Jennifer Keats Curtis; *Beetle Boddiker*, by Priscilla Cummings.

COTTONWOOD PRESS, INC.

109-B Cameron Dr., Fort Collins CO 80525. (800)864-4297. Fax: (970)204-0761. E-mail: cottonwood@cottonwoodpress.com. Website: www.cottonwoodpress.com. **Contact:** Cheryl Thurston, editor. Estab. 1986. Publishes trade paperback originals. **Publishes 2-8 titles/year. 50 queries received/year. 40 mss received/year. 50% of books from first-time authors. 100% from unagented writers.** Publishes book 1 year after acceptance of ms. Accepts simultaneous submissions. Responds in 1 month to queries and proposals. Responds in 3 months to manuscripts. Book catalog for 10 × 12 envelope and 2 first-class stamps. Guidelines available online.

- accepts simultaneous submissions, but must be notified about it.

O‑ᴛ "Cottonwood Press publishes creative and practical materials for English and language arts teachers, grades 5-12. We believe English should be everyone's favorite subject."

Nonfiction Subjects include education, language, literature. "We are always looking for truly original, creative materials for teachers." Query with SASE. Submit outline, 1-3 sample chapters.

Recent Title(s) *Sentence CPR—Breathing Life Into Sentences That Might as Well Be Pushing Up Daisies*! by Phyllis Beveridge Nissila; Phunny *Stuph-Proofreading Exercises With a Sense of Humor*, by M.S. Samston; *Twisting Arms-Teaching Students to Write to Persuade*, by Dawn DiPrince; *Rock & Rap in Middle School*, by Sheree Sevilla and Suzanne Stansbury.

Tips "We publish only supplemental textbooks for English/language arts teachers, grades 5-12, with an emphasis upon middle school and junior high materials. Please don't assume we publish educational materials for all subject areas. We do not. Never submit anything to us before looking at our catalog. We have a very narrow focus and a distinctive style. Writers who don't understand that are wasting their time. On the plus side, we are eager to work with new authors who show a sense of humor and a familiarity with young adolescents."

COUNCIL ON SOCIAL WORK EDUCATION

1701 Duke St., Suite 200, Alexandria VA 22314-4703. (703519-2076. Fax: (703)683-8493. E-mail: publications@cswe.org. Website: www.cswe.org. **Contact:** Elizabeth Simon, publications manager. Estab. 1952. Publishes trade paperback originals. **Publishes 4 titles/year. 12 queries received/year. 8 mss received/year. 25% of books from first-time authors. 100% from unagented writers. Pays sliding royalty scale, starting at 10%** Publishes book 1 year after acceptance of ms. Responds in 2 months to queries. Responds in 3 months to proposals and manuscripts. Book catalog and ms guidelines free via website or with SASE.

O‑ᴛ "Council on Social Work Education produces books and resources for social work educators, students and practitioners."

Nonfiction Subjects include education, sociology, social work. Books for social work and other educators. Query via e-mail only with proposal package, including CV, outline, expected audience, and 2 sample chapters.

Recent Title(s) *Clinical Social Work: A Narrative Approach*, by Gary Paquin; *Integrating Technology Into the Social Work Curriculum*, by Joanne Coe Regan and Paul Freddolino; *Group Work Education in the Field*, by Julianne Wayne and Carol S. Cohen; *Ethics Education in Social Work*, by Frederic G. Reamer.

Tips "Audience is Social work educators and students and others in the helping professions. Check areas of publication interest on website."

⊘ CROSSQUARTER PUBLISHING GROUP

PO BOX 23749, Santa Fe NM 87502. E-mail: info@crossquarter.com. Website: www.crossquarter.com. **Contact:** Anthony Ravenscroft. Publishes trade paperback originals and reprints. **Publishes 5-10 titles/year. 1,200 queries received/year. 90% of books from first-time authors. Pays 8-10% royalty on wholesale or retail price.** Publishes book 1-2 years after acceptance of ms. Accepts simultaneous submissions. Responds in 3 months to queries. Book catalog for $1.75. Guidelines available online.

- Query letters are required. *No unsolicited mss.*

O‑ᴛ "We emphasize personal sovereignty, self responsibility and growth with pagan or pagan-friendly emphasis for young adults and adults."

Nonfiction Subjects include health, medicine, nature, environment, New Age, philosophy, psychology, religion, pagan only, spirituality, autobiography. Query with SASE. Reviews artwork/photos. Send photocopies.

Fiction Subjects include science fiction, visionary fiction. Query with SASE.

Recent Title(s) *Parasitic People and Other Daily Hazards*, by Norm Dubeski; *The Mirrors of Castaway Time*, by Douglas Arvidson; *Polyamory*, by Anthony Ravenscroft; *Extinction*, by John Lee Schneider.

Tips "Our audience is earth-conscious people looking to grow into balance of body, mind, heart and spirit."

DANIEL & DANIEL PUBLISHERS, INC.

P.O. Box 2790, McKinleyville CA 95519. (707)839-3495. Fax: (707)839-3242. E-mail: dandd@danielpublishing.com. Website: www.danielpublishing.com. **Contact:** John Daniel, publisher. Estab. 1980. Publishes hardcover originals and trade paperback originals. Publishes poetry, fiction and nonfiction. **Publishes 4 or fewer titles/year. 50% of books from first-time authors. 90% from unagented writers. Pays 10% royalty on wholesale price. Pays $0-500 advance.** Publishes book 12 months after acceptance of ms. Accepts simultaneous submissions. Responds in 1 month to queries and proposals. Responds in 2 months to manuscripts. Book catalog and guidelines available online.

Imprints John Daniel & Company; Fithian Press (belle lettres: fiction, poetry, memoir, essay); Perseverance Press (literary mysteries).

Nonfiction Subjects include creative nonfiction, memoirs. "We seldom publish books over 70,000 words. Other than that, we're looking for books that are important and well-written." Query with SASE. Submit proposal package, outline, 5 pages.

Fiction Subjects include literary, short story collections. Query with SASE. Submit proposal package, clips, 5 pages.

Recent Title(s) *Leaving Bayberry House*, by Ann L. McLaughlin (novel); *The Lapp King's Daughter*, by Stina Katchadourian (memoir); *Wolf Tones*, by Irving Weinman (novel); *Devora in Exile*, by Barbara Cherne (stories).

Tips "Audience includes literate, intelligent general readers. We are very small and very cautious, and we publish fewer books each year, so any submission to us is a long shot. But we welcome your submissions, by mail or e-mail only, please. We don't want submissions by phone, fax or disk."

DANTE UNIVERSITY OF AMERICA PRESS, INC.

P.O. Box 812158, Wellesley MA 02482. Fax: (781)790-1056. E-mail: danteu@danteuniversity.org. Website: www.danteuniversity.org/dpress.html. **Contact:** Josephine Tanner, president. Estab. 1975. Publishes hardcover and trade paperback originals and reprints. **Publishes 5 titles/year. 50% of books from first-time authors. 50% from unagented writers. Pays royalty. Pays negotiable advance.** Publishes book 10 months after acceptance of ms. Responds in 2 months to queries.

- "The Dante University Press exists to bring quality, educational books pertaining to our Italian heritage as well as the historical and political studies of America. Profits from the sale of these publications benefit the Foundation, bringing Dante University closer to a reality."

Nonfiction Subjects include history, Italian-American, humanities, translation, from Italian and Latin, general scholarly nonfiction, Renaissance thought and letter, Italian language and linguistics, Italian-American culture, bilingual education. Query with SASE. Reviews artwork/photos.

Fiction Translations from Italian and Latin. Query with SASE.

Recent Title(s) *Italian Poetry*, by Gayle Ridinger; *Marconi My Beloved*, by Maria/Elettra Marconi; *Romeo and Juliet*, by Adolph Caso.

MAY DAVENPORT, PUBLISHERS

26313 Purissima Rd., Los Altos Hills CA 94022. (650)947-1275. Fax: (650)947-1373. E-mail: mdbooks@earthlink.net. Website: www.maydavenportpublishers.com. **Contact:** May Davenport, editor/publisher. Estab. 1976. Publishes hardcover and paperback originals. **Publishes 4 titles/year. 95% of books from first-time authors. 100% from unagented writers. Pays 15% royalty on retail price (if book sells). Pays no advance.** Publishes book 12 months after acceptance of ms. Responds in 1 month to queries. Book catalog and ms guidelines for #10 SASE.

Imprints md Books (nonfiction and fiction).

- "May Davenport publishes literature for teenagers (before they graduate from high school) as supplementary literary material in English courses nationwide. Looking particularly for authors able to write for the teen Internet generation who don't like to read in-depth. Currently emphasizing more upper-level subjects for teens."

Nonfiction Subjects include Americana, language, literature, humorous memoirs for children/young adults. "For children ages 6-8: stories to read with pictures to color in 500 words. For preteens and young adults: Exhibit your writing skills and entertain them with your literary tools." Query with SASE.

Fiction Subjects include humor, literary. "We want to focus on novels junior and senior high school teachers can read aloud, share with their reluctant readers in their classrooms." Query with SASE.

Recent Title(s) *Comic Tales Easy Reader* (series of books of poems, articles, short stories including authors in anthologies published in the U.S. in 1979); *Comic Tales Anthology #3* and *#4* (#4 will include new writers), Editor, May Davenport (poems, articles & short storiers); *Summer of Suspense, a teenage girl's unexpected adventure*, by Frances Drummond Waines (mystery); *Comic Tales Easy Reader, Anthology #3*, Editor, May Davenport, by 33 professional journalists/teachers and young writers. The Sections of

Poems, Articles, and Short Stories begin on a simple reading-level then progresses to a higher-reading level of aesthetics and satire. The writers reflect a sense of humor. Useful book for students in schools, or young/old at home. (Printed words with illustrations not animated is a challenge for high-tech youth (our focus) to enjoy such books); *Surviving Sarah, the Sequel: Brown Bug and China Doll,* by Dinah Leigh (nonfiction).

Tips "Just write your fictional novel humorously. If you can't write that way, create youthful characters so teachers, as well as 15-18-year-old high school readers, will laugh at your descriptive passages and contemporary dialogue. Avoid 1-sentence paragraphs. The audience we want to reach is today's high-tech teens who are talented with digital cameras hooked up to computers. Show them what you can do 'in print' for them and their equipment."

DAWN PUBLICATIONS

12402 Bitney Springs Rd., Nevada City CA 95959. (530)274-7775. Fax: (530)274-7778. Website: www.dawnpub.com. **Contact:** Glenn Hovemann, editor. Estab. 1979. Publishes hardcover and trade paperback originals. **Publishes 6 titles/year. 2,500 queries or mss received/year. 15% of books from first-time authors. 90% from unagented writers. Pays advance.** Publishes book 1 to 2 years after acceptance of ms. Accepts simultaneous submissions. Responds in 2 months to queries. Book catalog available online. Guidelines available online.

- Dawn accepts mss submissions by e-mail; follow instructions posted on website. Submissions by mail still OK.

O‒ "Dawn Publications is dedicated to inspiring in children a sense of appreciation for all life on earth. Dawn looks for nature awareness and appreciation titles that promote a relationship with the natural world and specific habitats, usually through inspiring treatment and nonfiction."

Nonfiction Subjects include animals, nature, environment.

Recent Title(s) *The Web at Dragonfly Pond,* by Brian Fox Ellis; *City Beats,* by S. Kelly Rammell; *If You Were My Baby,* by Fran Hodgkins.

Tips "Publishes mostly creative nonfiction with lightness and inspiration."

DEMONTREVILLE PRESS, INC.

P.O. Box 835, Lake Elmo MN 55042-0835. E-mail: publisher@demontrevillepress.com. Website: www.demontrevillepress.com. **Contact:** Kevin Clemens, publisher (automotive fiction and nonfiction). Estab. 2006. Publishes trade paperback originals and reprints. **Publishes 4 titles/year. 150 queries received/year. 100 mss received/year. 90% of books from first-time authors. 90% from unagented writers. Pays 20% royalty on sale price.** Publishes book 18 months after acceptance of ms. Accepts simultaneous submissions. Responds in 3 months to queries. Responds in 4 months to proposals. Responds in 6 months to manuscripts. Book catalog available online. Guidelines available online.

Nonfiction Subjects include current events, automotive, environment, motorcycle. "We want novel length automotive or motorcycle historicals and/or adventures. Environmental energy and infrastructure books wanted." Submit proposal package online, outline, 3 sample chapters, bio. Reviews artwork/photos. Do not send photos until requested.

Fiction Subjects include current events, environment, adventure, mystery, sports, young adult, automotive, motorcycle. "We want novel length automotive or motorcycle historicals and/or adventures." Submit proposal package, 3 sample chapters, clips, bio.

Tips "Environmental, energy and transportation nonfiction works are now being accepted. Automotive and motorcycle enthusiasts, adventurers, environmentalists and history buffs make up our audience."

DOWN THE SHORE PUBLISHING

Box 100, West Creek NJ 08092. Fax: (609)597-0422. E-mail: dtsbooks@comcast.net. Website: www.down-the-shore.com. Publishes hardcover and trade paperback originals and reprints. **Publishes 4-10 titles/year. Pays royalty on wholesale or retail price, or makes outright purchase.** Accepts simultaneous submissions. Responds in 3 months to queries. Book catalog for 8 × 10 SAE with 2 first-class stamps or on website. Guidelines available online.

O‒ "Bear in mind that our market is regional-New Jersey, the Jersey Shore, the mid-Atlantic, and seashore and coastal subjects."

Nonfiction Subjects include Americana, art, architecture, history, nature, environment, regional. Query with SASE. Submit proposal package, 1-2 sample chapters, synopsis. Reviews artwork/photos. Send photocopies.

Fiction Subjects include regional. Query with SASE. Submit proposal package, clips, 1-2 sample chapters.

Recent Title(s) *Steel Pier, Atlantic City*, by Steve Liebowitz (history, coffee-table book); *Fisherman's Wife*, by Josephine Lehman Thomas (essay); *Cold Rolled Dead*, by Paul D'Ambrosio (fiction).
Tips "Carefully consider whether your proposal is a good fit for our established market."

DRAM TREE BOOKS

Whittler's Bench Press P.O. Box 7183, Wilmington NC 28406. Website: www.dramtreebooks.com. **Contact:** Jack E. Fryar, Jr., publisher (nonfiction/fiction). Estab. 2000. Publishes trade paperback originals and reprints. **Publishes 8-12 titles/year. 90% of books from first-time authors. 100% from unagented writers. Pays 10-15% royalty on retail price. Pays $50-100 advance.** Publishes book 1 year after acceptance of ms. Responds in 2 months to queries and proposals. Responds in 4 months to manuscripts. Book catalog for #10 SASE. Guidelines available via e-mail.
Imprints Whittler's Bench Press.
Nonfiction Subjects include Americana, art, architecture, creative nonfiction, education, history, hobbies, military, war, regional, travel. Query with SASE. Submit proposal package, outline, 3 sample chapters, bio. Reviews artwork/photos. Send photocopies and JPEGs on CD-ROM.
Recent Title(s) *Redcoats on the River: Southeastern North Carolina in the Revolutionary War*, by Robert M. Dunkerly; *Wild, Wicked, Wartime Wilmington*, by Robert J. Cooke; *Potter's Raid: The Union Cavalry's Boldest Expedition in Eastern North Carolina*, by David A, Norris; *Cecilia's Harvest*, by Blonnie Bunn Wyche; *The Lost Rocks: The Dare Stones and the Unsolved Mystery of Sir Walter Raleigh's Lost Colony*, by David La Vere.
Tips "Our readers are native North Carolinians, recent transplants to the state or tourists visiting our state. We also enjoy a healthy audience among former residents of the Tar Heel State that now reside elsewhere. All of our books have a central theme: North Carolina history (particularly that of the Cape Fear region and North Carolina coast). Don't give us dry names and dates. Tell us a story! Just make sure it's a true one."

EAGLE'S VIEW PUBLISHING

6756 North Fork Rd., Liberty UT 84310. (801)745-0905. Fax: (801)745-0903. Website: www.eaglesviewpub.com. **Contact:** Denise Knight, editor-in-chief. Estab. 1982. Publishes trade paperback originals. **Publishes 2-4 titles/year. 40 queries received/year. 20 mss received/year. 90% of books from first-time authors. 100% from unagented writers. Pays 8-10% royalty on net selling price.** Publishes book 12 months or more after acceptance of ms. Accepts simultaneous submissions. Responds in 1 year to proposals. Book catalog and ms guidelines for $4.00.

> "Eagle's View primarily publishes how-to craft books with a subject related to historical or contemporary Native American/Mountain Man/frontier crafts/bead crafts. Currently emphasizing bead-related craft books. De-emphasizing history except for historical Indian crafts."

Nonfiction Subjects include anthropology, archaeology, Native American crafts, ethnic, Native American, history, American frontier historical patterns and books, hobbies, crafts, especially beadwork. Submit outline, 1-2 sample chapters. Reviews artwork/photos. Send photocopies and sample illustrations.
Recent Title(s) *Treasury of Beaded Jewelry*, by Mary Ellen Harte; *Beads and Beadwork of the American Indian*, by William C. Orchard; *Hemp Masters: Getting Knotty*, by Max Lunger.
Tips "We will not be publishing any new beaded earrings books for the foreseeable future. We are interested in other craft projects using seed beads, especially books that feature a variety of items, not just different designs for 1 item."

EASTLAND PRESS

P.O. Box 99749, Seattle WA 98139. (206)217-0204. Fax: (206)217-0205. E-mail: info@eastlandpress.com. Website: www.eastlandpress.com. **Contact:** John O'Connor, managing editor. Estab. 1981. Publishes hardcover and trade paperback originals. **Publishes 4-6 titles/year. 25 queries received/year. 30% of books from first-time authors. 90% from unagented writers. Pays 12-15% royalty on receipts.** Publishes book 12 to 24 months after acceptance of ms. Accepts simultaneous submissions. Responds in 1 month to queries. Book catalog available free.

> "Eastland Press is interested in textbooks for practitioners of alternative medical therapies, primarily Chinese and physical therapies, and related bodywork."

Nonfiction Subjects include health, medicine. "We prefer that a manuscript be completed or close to completion before we will consider publication. Proposals are rarely considered, unless submitted by a published author or teaching institution." Submit outline and 2-3 sample chapters. Reviews artwork/photos. Send photocopies.
Recent Title(s) *Anatomy of Breathing*, by Blandine Calais-Germain; *The Fasciae: Anatomy, Dysfunction & Treatment*, by Serge Paoletti; *Chinese Herbal Medicine*, by Dan Bensky.

ENC PRESS

P.O. Box 833, Hoboken NJ 07030. E-mail: publisher@encpress.com. Website: www.encpress.com. **Contact:** Olga Gardner Galvin, publisher; Heather Chapman, editorial director. Estab. 2003. Publishes trade paperback originals. **Publishes 2-4 titles/year. 90% of books from first-time authors. 100% from unagented writers. Pays 50% royalty on retail price.** Publishes book 12 months after acceptance of ms. Responds in 8-12 weeks to queries. Responds in 4-6 months to manuscripts. Book catalog available online. Guidelines available online.

Fiction Subjects include geopolitical, political satire, utopias/dystopias, social satire, picaresque, full-length novels only. Query through e-mail.

Recent Title(s) *Mean Martin Manning,* by Scott Stein (social satire); *$everance,* by Richard Kaempfer (social satire); *Monkey See,* by Walt Maguire (social satire); Dear Mr. Unabomber, by Ray Cavanaugh (social satire).

Tips "Please submit queries only after reading our submissions guidelines."

⊘ ERIE CANAL PRODUCTIONS

4 Farmdale St., Clinton NY 13323. E-mail: eriecanal@juno.com. Website: www.eriecanalproductions.com. **Contact:** Scott Fiesthumel, president. Estab. 2001. Publishes trade paperback originals. **Publishes 1-2 titles/year. 50% of books from first-time authors. 100% from unagented writers. Pays negotiable royalty on net profits.** Responds in 1 month to queries. Book catalog available free.

Nonfiction Subjects include Americana, history, sports. Query with SASE. *All unsolicited mss returned unopened.*

Recent Title(s) *The Legend of Wild Bill Setley,* by Tony Kissel; *S. Fiesthumel,* (biography); *Diamond Dynasty,* by Billy Mills; *The Bank With the Gold Dome,* by Scott Fiesthumel.

Tips "We publish nonfiction books that look at historical places, events, and people along the traditional route of the Erie Canal through New York State."

EXCALIBUR PUBLICATIONS

P.O. Box 89667, Tucson AZ 85752-9667. (520)575-9057. E-mail: excalibureditor@earthlink.net. **Contact:** Alan M. Petrillo, editor. Estab. 1990. Publishes trade paperback originals. **Publishes 4 titles/year. Pays royalty** Responds in 1 month to queries and manuscripts.

- "Excalibur Publications publishes nonfiction historical and military works from all time periods. We do not publish fiction."

Nonfiction Subjects include history, military, war, strategy and tactics, as well as the history of battles, firearms, arms, and armor, historical personalities. "We are seeking well-researched and documented works. Unpublished writers are welcome." Query with synopsis, first chapter, SASE. Include notes on photos, illustrations, and maps. Accepts e-mail pitches.

Recent Title(s) *Present Sabers: A History of the U.S. Horse Cavalry,* by Allan Heninger; *Japanese Rifles of World War II,* by Duncan O. McCollum; *Famous Faces of World War II,* by Robert Van Osdol.

Tips "New writers are welcome, especially those who have a fresh approach to a subject. In addition to a synopsis or proposal, we also like to see a brief bio that indicates any related experience you have, as well as information on particular marketing strategies for your work."

FAIRVIEW PRESS

2450 Riverside Ave., Minneapolis MN 55454. (612)672-4774. Fax: (612)672-4980. E-mail: press@fairview.org. Website: www.fairviewpress.org. **Contact:** Steve Deger, acquisitions and marketing. Estab. 1988. Publishes hardcover and trade paperback originals and reprints. **Publishes 8-12 titles/year. 3,000 queries received/year. 1,500 mss received/year. 40% of books from first-time authors. 65% from unagented writers. Advance and royalties negotiable.** Publishes book 1 year after acceptance of ms. Accepts simultaneous submissions. Responds in 6 months to proposals. Book catalog available free. Guidelines available online.

- "Fairview Press publishes books dedicated to the physical, emotional, and spiritual health of children, adults, and seniors — specializing in books on: Aging and Eldercare, Grief and Bereavement, Health and Wellness, Inspiration, Parenting, and Childcare."

Nonfiction "At this time we are particularly interested in acquiring mss on the following topics: pregnancy and childbirth, health issues for young adults, complementary/holistic/integrative medicine, diet & exercise, and inspiration & mindfulness. We are de-emphasizing our former focus on end-of-life issues, but will consider proposals on any topic pertaining to physical, emotional, or spiritual wellness." Submit proposal package with cover letter, outline, sample chapter(s), marketing plan, SASE. Please take the time to study our catalog and the guidelines before submitting a proposal. We prefer that you mail your proposal rather than submitting it by phone, fax, or e-mail. Reviews artwork/photos. Send photocopies.

Recent Title(s) *The Little Book of Positive Quotations-Gift Edition*, by Steve Deger and Leslie Ann Gibson.

Tips "We publish practical books written for a lay audience, often by educated professionals who are active within their disciplines. We are not interested in fiction, poetry, children's picture books, or personal memoirs about coping with illness."

FATHER'S PRESS

2424 SE 6th St., Lee's Summit MO 64063. Website: www.fatherspress.com. **Contact:** Mike Smitley, owner (fiction, nonfiction). Estab. 2006. Publishes hardcover, trade paperback, and mass market paperback originals and reprints. **Publishes 6-10 titles/year. Pays 10-15% royalty on wholesale price.** Publishes book 6 months after acceptance of ms. Responds in 1 month to queries and proposals. Responds in 3 months to manuscripts. Guidelines available online.

Nonfiction Subjects include animals, cooking, foods, nutrition, creative nonfiction, history, military, war, nature, regional, religion, travel, women's issues, world affairs. Query with SASE. Unsolicited mss returned unopened. Call or e-mail first. Reviews artwork/photos. Send photocopies.

Fiction Subjects include adventure, historical, juvenile, literary, mainstream, contemporary, military, war, mystery, regional, religious, suspense, western, young adult. Query with SASE. Unsolicited mss returned unopened. Call or e-mail first.

Recent Title(s) *The Christian and the Struggle With Truth*, by Charles Scheele (Christian); *Six Years' Worth*, by Daniel Lance Wright (fiction); *Spending God's Money*, by Mary Kinney Branson (Christian); *Faith vs. Science*, by Dr. Jerome Goddard (Christian Science); *Disturbing Questions*, by Ron Bourque (social history); *Pressing Matters*, by Larry Tobin (fiction); *All That You Can't Leave Behind*, by Ryan Murphy (Christian); *America Unraveling*, by Dr. L. Scott Smith (social history).

FIELDSTONE ALLIANCE, INC.

P.O. Box 8009, St. Paul MN 55108. (651)556-4505. E-mail: mpiotrowski@fieldstonealliance.org. Website: www.fieldstonealliance.org. Publishes professional trade paperback originals. **Publishes 6 titles/year. 30 queries received/year. 15 mss received/year. 75% of books from first-time authors. 100% from unagented writers. Pays advance.** Publishes book 18 months after acceptance of ms. Accepts simultaneous submissions. Responds in 6 weeks to queries and proposals. Responds in 3 months to manuscripts. Book catalog and ms guidelines online.

O➛ "Fieldstone Alliance emphasizes community development, nonprofit organization management, and books for foundations and grant makers. Actively seeking authors and editorial outside vendors of color."

Nonfiction "We are seeking manuscripts that report `best practice' methods using handbook or workbook formats for nonprofit and community development managers." Submit 3 sample chapters, complete topical outline, and full proposal based on online guidelines. Phone query OK before submitting proposal with detailed chapter outline, SASE, statement of the goals of the book, statement of unique selling points, identification of audience, author qualification, competing publications, marketing potential.

Recent Title(s) *The Accidental Techie*; *A Funder's Guide to Evaluation*; *Benchmarking for Nonprofits*.

Tips "Writers must be practitioners with a passion for their work in nonprofit management or community building and experience presenting their techniques at conferences. Writers receive preference if they can demonstrate the capacity to help sell their books via trainings, a large established e-mail or client list, or other direct connections with customers, who are largely nonprofit leaders, managers and consultants. We seek practical, not academic books. Our books identify professional challenges faced by our audiences and offer practical, step-by-step solutions. Never send us a manuscript without first checking our online guidelines. Queries showing evidence that the author has not reviewed our guidelines will be ignored."

FINNEY COMPANY, INC.

8075 215th St. W., Lakeville MN 55044. (952)469-6699. Fax: (952)469-1968. E-mail: feedback@finneyco.com. Website: www.finneyco.com. **Contact:** Alan E. Krysan, president. Publishes trade paperback originals. **Publishes 2 titles/year. Pays 10% royalty on wholesale price. Pays advance.** Publishes book 1 year after acceptance of ms. Responds in 10-12 weeks to queries.

Nonfiction Subjects include business, economics, education, career exploration/development. Finney publishes career development educational materials. Query with SASE. Reviews artwork/photos.

Recent Title(s) *Planning My Career*, by Capozziello; *On the Job*, edited by Laurie Diethelm, et. al.

FLASHLIGHT PRESS

527 Empire Blvd., Brooklyn NY 11225. E-mail: editor@flashlightpress.com. Website: www.flashlightpress.com. **Contact:** Shari Dash Greenspan, editor. Estab. 2004. Publishes hardcover and trade paperback originals. **Publishes 2 titles/year. 1,200 queries received/year. 120 mss received/year. 40% of books from first-time authors. 90% from unagented writers. Pays 8-10% royalty on wholesale price.** Publishes book 36 months after acceptance of ms. Accepts simultaneous submissions. Responds in 1 month to queries. Responds in 3 months to manuscripts. Book catalog available online. Guidelines available online.

Fiction Subjects include picture books. "We only publish fiction-2 picture books a year, so we're extremely selective. Looking for gems."

Recent Title(s) *That Cat Can't Stay*, by Thad Krasnesky, illustrated by David Parkins (ages 4-8, picture book); *I Always, ALWAYS Get My Way,* by Thad Krasnesky, illustrated by David Parkins (ages 4-8, picture book); *I Need my Monster,* by Amanda Noll, illustrated by Howard McWilliam (ages 4-8, picture book); *I'm Really Not Tired,* by Lori Sunshine, illustrated by Jeffrey Ebbeler (ages 4-8, picture book); *Grandfather's Wrinkles,* by Kathryn England, illustrated by Richard McFarland (ages 4-8, picture book); *Grandpa for Sale,* by Dotti Enderle and Vicki Sansum, illustrated by T. Kyle Gentry (ages 4-8, picture book); *Getting to Know Ruben Plotnick,* by Roz Rosenbluth, illustrated by Maurie J. Manning (ages 5-9, picture book).

Tips "Our audience is 4-8 years old. Follow our online submissions guide."

FLORICANTO PRESS

Inter American Development 650 Castro St., Suite 120-331, Mountain View CA 94041-2055. (415)552-1879. Fax: (702)995-1410. E-mail: editor@floricantopress.com. Website: www.floricantopress.com. **Contact:** Roberto Cabello-Argandona. Estab. 1982. Publishes hardcover and trade paperback originals and reprints. Book catalog for #10 SASE. Guidelines available online.

"Floricanto Press is dedicated to promoting Latino thought and culture."

Nonfiction Subjects include anthropology, archeology, cooking, foods, nutrition, ethnic, Hispanic, health, medicine, history, language, literature, psychology, women's issues, women's studies. "We are looking primarily for nonfiction popular (but serious) titles that appeal to the general public on Hispanic subjects." Submit ms with word count, author bio, SASE.

Recent Title(s) *Between Borders: Essays on Chicana/Mexicana History*, by Adelaida del Castillo; *Bring me more Stories: Tales of the Sephardim*, by Sally Benforado; *Borrowing Time: A Latino Sexual Odyssey*, by Carlos T. Mock, M.D.

Tips "Audience is general public interested in Hispanic culture. We need authors that are willing to promote their work heavily."

FLORIDA ACADEMIC PRESS

P.O. Box 540, Gainesville FL 32602. (352)332-5104. Fax: (352)331-6003. E-mail: fapress@gmail.com. Website: www.floridaacademicpress.com. Estab. 1997. Hardcover and trade paperback originals. **Publishes 4-8 titles/year. 2,000 queries received/year. 1,200 mss received/year. 90% of books from first-time authors. 100% from unagented writers. 5-8% royalty on retail price and higher on sales of 2,500+ copies a year.** Publishes book 3 months after acceptance of ms. Responds in 2 months on mss if rejected; 3-4 months if sent for external review. Catalog available online.

Nonfiction SASE returns. Subjects include government/politics, philosophy, psychology, social sciences, world affairs. We only assess complete mss that do not require extensive copy-editing. Submit completed ms only and CV. Query letters or works in progress of little interest—submit only final ms. Reviews artwork/photos. Send photocopies.

Fiction Subjects include historical, literary. Submit completed ms.

Recent Title(s) *Lucette Desvigness*, by Jerry Curtis (Bio-literary criticism of France's greatest living authoress); *Out of Eden*, by L. F. Baggett (The inter-war period in the Deep South); *Sweet Prince: The Passion of Hamlet*, by Doug Brode.

Tips "Match our needs—do not send blindly. Books we accept for publication must be submitted in camera-ready format. The Press covers all publication/promotional expenditures."

FLYING PEN PRESS LLC

20000 Mitchell Pl., Suite 25, Denver CO 80249. (303)375-0499. Fax: (303)375-0499. E-mail: publisher@flyingpenpress.com. Website: www.flyingpenpress.com. **Contact:** David A. Rozansky, publisher. Trade paperback and electronic originals. **Publishes 5 titles/year. 120 queries/year; 360 mss/year. 55% of books from first-time authors. 88% from unagented writers. No advances.** Publishes book 6 months after acceptance of ms. Accepts simultaneous submissions. Catalog free on request; available online at website http://www.flyingpenpress.com/catalog. Guidelines free on request and available online.

Nonfiction Subjects include alternative lifestyles, Americana, animals, anthropology, archaeology, business, career guidance, child guidance, communications, community, computers, contemporary culture, counseling, creative nonfiction, economics, electronics, entertainment, environment, ethnic, finance, games, government, health, history, hobbies, humanities, labor, language, literature, medicine, memoirs, military, money, multicultural, nature, parenting, philosophy, politics, public affairs, recreation, regional (CO, S.W. U.S., Nat'l Parks, Rocky Mountains), science, social sciences, sociology, software, translation, transportation, travel, war, world affairs, aviation, aerospace, game books, travel guides, puzzle books. Submit book proposals and completed ms by e-mail only. No unsolicited mss. Reviews artwork/photos. Send JPG, TIF, or PDF files.

Fiction Subjects include adventure, comic books, contemporary, ethnic, experimental, fantasy, gothic, historical, horror, humor, literary, mainstream, military, multicultural, mystery, regional, romance, science fiction, short story collections, sports, suspense, translation, western. "We have changed our focus to be platform centric. We seek ideas for series, and we invite trademark holders and blogging personalities to submit ideas for a line of books." Submit completed ms by e-mail only.

Recent Title(s) *The Game Day Poker Almanac Official Rules of Poker*, by Kelli Mix (poker rulebook); *Looking Glass*, by James R. Strickland (cyberpunk science fiction); *She Murdered Me With Science*, by David Boop (sci-fi hard boiled detective fusion); Feral World Series (*Migration of the Kamishi, Trials of the Warmland)*, by Gaddy Bergmann (post-apocalyptic lit); *Seventh Daughter*, by Ronnie Seagren (action, adventure).

Tips "Create a series concept that will attract readers, which we can then assign to writers for several books in the line. Trademarked characters, movie and TV tie-ins, and popular blogs are suitable platforms."

FRONT ROW EXPERIENCE

540 Discovery Bay Blvd., Discovery Bay CA 94505. (925)634-5710. E-mail: service@frontrowexperience.com. Website: www.frontrowexperience.com. **Contact:** Frank Alexander, editor. Estab. 1974. Publishes trade paperback originals and reprints. **Publishes 1-2 titles/year.** Accepts simultaneous submissions. Responds in 1 month to queries.

Imprints Kokono.

O‒ "Front Row publishes books on movement education and coordination activities for pre-K to 6th grade."

Nonfiction Subjects include movement education, perceptual-motor development, sensory motor development, hand-eye coordination activities. Query.

Recent Title(s) *Perceptual-Motor Lesson Plans, Level 2.*

Tips "Be on target—find out what we want, and only submit queries. If you want to send documents, send as a pdf file to our e-mail."

GEM GUIDES BOOK CO.

345 Cloverleaf Dr., Suite C, Baldwin Park CA 91706-6510. (626)855-1611. Fax: (626)855-1610. E-mail: gembooks@aol.com. Website: www.gemguidesbooks.com. **Contact:** Greg Warner, editor. Estab. 1965. **Publishes 6-8 titles/year. 60% of books from first-time authors. 100% from unagented writers. Pays 6-10% royalty on retail price.** Publishes book 1 year after acceptance of ms. Accepts simultaneous submissions. Responds in 5 months to queries.

Imprints Gembooks.

O‒ "Gem Guides prefers nonfiction books for the hobbyist in rocks and minerals; lapidary and jewelry-making; crystals and crystal healing; travel and recreation guide books for the West and Southwest; and other regional local interest. Currently emphasizing how-to, field guides, West/Southwest regional interest. De-emphasizing stories, history, poetry."

Nonfiction Subjects include history, Western, hobbies, rockhounding, prospecting, lapidary, jewelry craft, nature, recreation, regional, Western US, science, earth, travel. Query with outline/synopsis and sample chapters with SASE. Reviews artwork/photos.

Recent Title(s) *Fee Mining and Mineral Adventures in the Eastern U.S.*, by James Martin Monaco and Jeannette Hathaway Monaco; *Baby's Day Out in Southern California: Fun Places to Go With Babies and Toddlers*, by JoBea Holt; *The Rockhound's Handbook*, by James R. Mitchell; *Crystal & Gemstone Divination*, by Gail Butler.

Tips "We have a general audience of people interested in recreational activities. Publishers plan and have specific book lines in which they specialize. Learn about the publisher and submit materials compatible with that publisher's product line."

GIFTED EDUCATION PRESS

10201 Yuma Court, Manassas VA 20109. (703)369-5017. E-mail: mfisher345@comcast.net. Website: www.giftedpress.com. **Contact:** Maurice Fisher, publisher. Estab. 1981. Publishes trade paperback originals. **Publishes 5 titles/year. 20 queries received/year. 10 mss received/year. 90% of books from first-time authors. 100% from unagented writers. Pays 10% royalty on retail price.** Publishes book 4 months after acceptance of ms. Accepts simultaneous submissions. Responds in 1 month to queries, proposals and manuscripts. Book catalog available online. Guidelines available online.

"Searching for rigorous texts on teaching science, math and humanities to gifted students."

Nonfiction Subjects include child guidance, computers, electronics, education, history, humanities, philosophy, science, teaching, math, biology, Shakespeare, chemistry, physics, creativity. Query with SASE. *All unsolicited mss returned unopened.* Reviews artwork/photos.

Recent Title(s) *Snibbles*, by Judy Micheletti; *Laboratory Physics Experiments for the Gifted*, by Raja Almukahhal; *Why Don't Birds Get Lost?*, by Franklin H. Bronson.

Tips "Audience includes teachers, parents, gift program supervisors, professors. Be knowledgeable about your subject. Write clearly and don't use educational jargon."

GIVAL PRESS

Gival Press, LLC P.O. Box 3812, Arlington VA 22203. (703)351-0079. E-mail: givalpress@yahoo.com. Website: www.givalpress.com. **Contact:** Robert L. Giron, editor-in-chief (Area of interest: literary). Estab. 1998. Publishes trade paperback, electronic originals, and reprints. **Publishes 5-6 titles/year. over 200 queries received/year. 60 mss received/year. 50% of books from first-time authors. 70% from unagented writers. Royalties (% varies).** Publishes book 12 months after acceptance of ms. Accepts simultaneous submissions. Responds in 1 month to queries, 3 months to proposals & mss. Book catalog available online, free on request/for #10 SASE. Guidelines available online, by e-mail, free on request/for #10 SASE.

Imprints Gival Press.

Nonfiction Subjects include gay, lesbian, memoirs, multicultural, translation, women's issues, women's studies, scholarly. Submit between October-December only. Always query first via e-mail; provide plan/ms content, bio, and supportive material. Reviews artwork/photos; query first.

Fiction Subjects include gay, lesbian, literary, multicultural, poetry, translation. Always query first via e-mail; provide description, author's bio, and supportive material.

Recent Title(s) *That Demon Life*, by Lowell Mick White (fiction); *A Tomb on the Periphery*, by John Domini (crime/literary fiction); *Voyeur*, by Rich Murphy (poetry).

Tips "Our audience is those who read literary works with depth to the work. Visit our website-there is much to be read/learned from the numerous pages."

GLB PUBLISHERS

1028 Howard St., #503, San Francisco CA 94103. (415)621-8307. Website: www.glbpubs.com. Hardcover, trade paperback, and electronic originals; trade paperback and electronic reprints. **Publishes 4-5 titles/year. Receives 50 queries/year; 40 mss/year 20% of books from first-time authors. 90% from unagented writers.** Publishes book 2-3 months after acceptance of ms. Catalog and guidelines free on request and online at website.

Imprints GLB.

Nonfiction Subjects include alternative lifestyles, child guidance, contemporary culture, creative nonfiction, entertainment, ethnic, gay, government, health, history, humanities, lesbian, medicine, memoirs, multicultural, New Age, photography, politics, social sciences, travel, women's issues. Must apply to and be appropriate for gays, lesbians, bisexuals, transgenders. Reviews artwork/photos. Send originals or scanned files.

Fiction Subjects include adventure, erotica, fantasy, feminist, gay, gothic, historical, humor, literary, multicultural, mystery, plays, poetry, romance, science fiction, short story collections, suspense, western, young adult. "Must be gay, lesbian, bisexual, or transgender subjects." Submit completed ms.

Recent Title(s) *Crossing Borders*, by Will Carr; *Man In Shadow*, by Russell Thomas; *Basic Butch* Collection of Short Stories, by R. P. Andrews; *Homo Erectus*, by Edward Proffitt.

Tips "Our audience consists of 'adults of all ages.'".

GOLLEHON PRESS, INC.

6157 28th St. SE, Grand Rapids MI 49546. (616)949-3515. Fax: (616)949-8674. E-mail: john@gollehonbooks.com. Website: www.gollehonbooks.com. **Contact:** Lori Adams, editor. Publishes hardcover, trade paperback, and mass market paperback originals. **Publishes 6-8 titles/year. 100 queries received/year. 30 mss received/year. 85% of books from first-time authors. 90% from unagented writers. Pays 7%**

royalty on retail price. Pays $500-1,000 advance. Publishes book usually 6 months after acceptance of ms. Accepts simultaneous submissions. Responds in 1 month (if interested) to proposals. Responds in 2 months to manuscripts. Book catalog and ms guidelines online.

O→ "Currently emphasizing theology (life of Christ), political, current events, pets (dogs only, rescue/heroic), self-help, and gardening. *No unsolicited mss*; brief proposals only with first 5 pages of Chapter 1. Writer must have strong credentials to author work."

Nonfiction Submit brief proposal package only with bio and first 5 pages of Chapter 1. "We do not return materials unless we specifically request the full manuscript." Reviews artwork/photos. Send Writer must be sure he/she owns all rights to photos, artwork, illustrations, etc., submitted for consideration (all submissions must be free of any third-party claims).. Never send original photos or art.

Tips "Mail brief book proposal, bio, and a few sample pages only. We will request a full manuscript if interested. We cannot respond to all queries. Full manuscript will be returned if we requested it, and if writer provides SASE. We do not return proposals. Simultaneous submissions are encouraged."

N GOODMAN BECK PUBLISHING

P.O. Box 253, Norwood NJ 07648-2428. (201)403-3097. E-mail: info@goodmanbeck.com. Website: www.goodmanbeck.com. **Contact:** David Michael, editor. trade paperback originals and reprints; mass market paperback originals and reprints. **Publishes 5-6 titles/year. 65% of books from first-time authors. 90% from unagented writers. NA.** Publishes book 6-9 months after acceptance of ms. Accepts simultaneous submissions. Catalog or guidelines are not available.

- "Our audience is adults trying to cope with this 'upside down world.' With our self-help books, we are trying to improve the world one book at a time."

O→ "Our primary interest at this time is mental health, personal growth, aging well, positive psychology, accessible spirituality, and self-help."

Nonfiction Subjects include creative nonfiction, health, medicine, philosophy, psychology, spirituality. Query with SASE. Reviews artwork/photos. Send photocopies.

Fiction Subjects include contemporary, mainstream, mystery, poetry, short story collections, suspense. "Fiction books should be able to generate a passionate response from our adult readers." Query with SASE.

Recent Title(s) *The Happiness Solution*, by Alan Gettis, Ph.D. (self-help); *Seven Times Down Eight Times Up: Landing On Your Feet in an Upside Down World, 2nd Edition, Revised & expanded* (self-help); *In the Beak of a Duck*, by Kyle Wade & Alan Gettis (children's poetry).

Tips "Your book should be enlightening and marketable. Be prepared to have a comprehensive marketing plan. You will be very involved."

GRAND CANYON ASSOCIATION

1824 S. Thompson St., Suite 205, Flagstaff AZ 86001. (928)863-3878. Fax: (928)779-7279. E-mail: tberger@grandcanyon.org. Website: www.grandcanyon.org. **Contact:** Todd R. Berger, Director of Publishing. (Grand Canyon-related geology, natural history, outdoor activities, human history, photography, ecology, etc., posters, postcards and other non-book products). Estab. 1932. Publishes hardcover originals and reprints, and trade paperback originals and reprints. **Publishes 6 titles/year. 100 queries received/year. 70% of books from first-time authors. 99% from unagented writers. Pays royalty on wholesale price. Makes outright purchase.** Publishes book 1 month-2 years after acceptance of ms. Accepts simultaneous submissions. Responds in 2 months to queries, proposals and manuscripts. Book catalog available online. Ms guidelines available by e-mail.

Nonfiction Subjects include Grand Canyon-related animals, anthropology, archaeology, art, architecture, children's books, creative nonfiction, history, nature, environment, photography, recreation, regional, science, sports, travel, geology. Grand Canyon Association (GCA) is a nonprofit organization established to support education, research, and other programs for the benefit of Grand Canyon National Park and its visitors. GCA operates bookstores throughout the park, publishes books and other materials related to the Grand Canyon region, supports wildlife surveys and other research, funds acquisitions for the park's research library, and produces a wide variety of free publications and exhibits for park visitors. Since 1932, GCA has provided Grand Canyon National Park with over $23 million in financial support. Query with SASE. Submit proposal package, outline, 3-4 sample chapters, list of publication credits, and samples of previous work. Submit complete ms. Reviews artwork/photos. Send transparencies, color or b&w prints, or digital samples of images.

Recent Title(s) *Grand Canyon: Views Beyond the Beauty* (nature/photography); *Ancient Landscapes of the Colorado Plateau* (nature); *The Adventures of Salt and Soap at Grand Canyon* (children's).

Tips "Do not send any proposals that are not directly related to the Grand Canyon or do not have educational value about the Grand Canyon."

GREAT NORTHWEST PUBLISHING & DIST. CO., INC.

P.O. Box 212383, Anchorage AK 99521-2383. E-mail: aob-billing@alaskaoutdoorbooks.com. Website: www.alaskaoutdoorbooks.com. **Contact:** Marvin Clark. Estab. 1979. Publishes hardcover originals, trade paperback originals, hardcover reprints and trade paperback reprints. **Publishes 2 titles/year. 75 queries received/year. 20 mss received/year. 80% of books from first-time authors. 100% from unagented writers. Pays 10% royalty on wholesale price.** Publishes book 18 months after acceptance of ms. Accepts simultaneous submissions. Responds in 2 weeks to queries. Book catalog available online. Guidelines available free.

O━ "Great Northwest Publishing now is able to offer hunters and outdoorsmen its "Alaska Outdoor Books" library. Each volume is a carefully selected work, written by an authentic Alaska Big game hunting and outdoor authority."

Nonfiction Subjects include hunting and Alaska. "We are interested only in works from authors with personal knowledge or experience in the matters written about." Query with SASE. Submit complete ms. Reviews artwork/photos. Send photocopies.

Recent Title(s) *Kodiak Island and Its Bears*, by Harry B. Dodge III; *Alaska Safari*, by Harold Schetzle.

Tips Audience includes upscale outdoorsmen and others interested in the Alaska outdoors.

GREAT POTENTIAL PRESS

P.O. Box 5057, Scottsdale AZ 85261. (602)954-4200. Fax: (602)954-0185. E-mail: info@giftedbooks.com. Website: www.giftedbooks.com. **Contact:** Janet Gore, editor, or James T. Webb, Ph.D., president. Estab. 1986. Publishes trade paperback originals. **Publishes 6-10 titles/year. 75 queries received/year. 20-30 mss received/year. 50% of books from first-time authors. 100% from unagented writers. Pays 10% royalty on retail price.** Publishes book 6-12 months after acceptance of ms. Accepts simultaneous submissions. Responds in 2 months to queries. Responds in 3 months to proposals. Responds in 4 months to manuscripts. Book catalog free or on website. Guidelines available online.

O━ "Specializes in non-fiction books that address academic, social and emotional issues of gifted and talented children and adults."

Nonfiction Subjects include child guidance, education, multicultural, psychology, translation, travel, women's issues, gifted/talented children and adults, misdiagnosis of gifted, parenting gifted, teaching gifted, meeting the social and emotional needs of gifted and talented, and strategies for working with gifted children and adults. Submit proposal package, including preface or introduction, TOC, chapter outline, 2-3 sample chapters and an explanation of how work differs from similar published books.

Recent Title(s) *Inspiring Middle School Minds: Gifted, Creative, & Challenging*, by Judy Willis, M.D., M.Ed., *Living with Intensity*, edited by Susan Daniels, Ph.D. and Michael Piechowski, Ph.D., *Boosting Your Baby's Brain Power*, by Holly Engel-Smothers and Susan Heim, and *Academic Advocacy for Gifted Children: A Parent's Complete Guide*, by Barbara Gilman, M.S.

Tips "Manuscripts should be clear, cogent, and well-written and should pertain to gifted, talented, and creative persons and/or issues."

N HARBOR HOUSE

111 10th St., Augusta GA 30901. (706)738-0354. Fax: (706)823-5999. E-mail: harborhouse@harborhousebooks.com. Website: www.harborhousebooks.com. **Contact:** E. Randall Floyd, publisher/owner. Estab. 1997. Publishes hardcover and trade paperback originals. **Publishes 8-10 titles/year. 200 queries received/year. 100 mss received/year. 90% of books from first-time authors. 95% from unagented writers. Pays 7-10% royalty on retail price.** Publishes book 24 months after acceptance of ms. Accepts simultaneous submissions. Responds in 3-6 months to queries and proposals. Responds in 6-9 months to manuscripts. Guidelines available online.

O━ *No longer accepting submissions.*

Nonfiction Subjects include business, economics, community, contemporary culture, creative nonfiction, government, politics, history, memoirs, military, war, money, finance, nature, environment, philosophy, regional, religion, social sciences, sociology, spirituality, sports, world affairs, the unexplained. Submit proposal package, outline, 3 sample chapters, bio, marketing plan, SASE. Reviews artwork/photos. Send photocopies.

Fiction Subjects include adventure, fantasy, horror, humor, literary, mainstream, contemporary, military, war, mystery, regional, suspense, Thrillers. Submit proposal package, 3 sample chapters, clips, bio, marketing plan, SASE.

Recent Title(s) *A Few Flowers for my Soul*, by Robbie Williams (relationship book); *In the Realm of Miracles & Visions*, by E. Randall Floyd (explanatory); *Jacob's Daughter*, by Naomi Williams (contemporary fiction).

Tips "General adult readership. We would like paper submissions."

HEALTH PROFESSIONS PRESS

P.O. Box 10624, Baltimore MD 21285-0624. (410)337-9585. Fax: (410)337-8539. E-mail: mmagnus@healthpropress.com. Website: www.healthpropress.com. **Contact:** Mary Magnus, director of publications (aging, long-term care, health administration). Publishes hardcover and trade paperback originals. **Publishes 6-8 titles/year. 70 queries received/year. 12 mss received/year. 50% of books from first-time authors. 100% from unagented writers. Pays 8-18% royalty on wholesale price.** Publishes book 10 months after acceptance of ms. Accepts simultaneous submissions. Responds in 1 month to queries. Responds in 3 months to proposals. Responds in 4 months to manuscripts. Book catalog free or online. Guidelines available online.

O━ "We are a specialty publisher. Our primary audiences are professionals, students, and educated consumers interested in topics related to aging and eldercare."

Nonfiction Subjects include health, medicine, psychology. Query with SASE. Submit proposal package, outline, resume, 1-2 sample chapters, cover letter.

Recent Title(s) *Falls in Older People; Cases in Health Services Management; Strengthen Your Mind Program; Dementia Beyond Drugs; Facing Drugs; Facing Death; Managing & Treating Urinary Incontinence.*

HENSLEY PUBLISHING

6116 E. 32nd St., Tulsa OK 74135-5494. (918)664-8520. E-mail: editorial@hensleypublishing.com. Website: www.hensleypublishing.com. **Contact:** Acquisitions Department. Publishes trade paperback originals. **Publishes 5 titles/year. 200 queries received/year. 50% of books from first-time authors. 50% from unagented writers.** Publishes book 18 months after acceptance of ms. Responds in 4 months to queries. Guidelines available online.

O━ "Hensley Publishing publishes Bible studies that offer the reader a wide range of topics. Currently emphasizing 192-page (8.5 × 11) workbook studies and Bible studies of varying sizes and lengths, both workbook and non-workbook style."

Nonfiction Subjects include child guidance, money, finance, religion, women's issues, marriage/family, various Bible study topics such as topical, general, issue oriented. Query with synopsis and sample chapters.

Recent Title(s) *Fear Is Never Our Friend*, by Gary L. Richardson; *So You're a Christian! Now What?*, by Catherine Painter; *Walking With God*, by Mindy Ferguson.

Tips "Submit something that crosses denominational lines directed toward the large Christian market, not small specialized groups. We serve an interdenominational market—all Christian persuasions. Our goal is to get readers back into studying the Bible instead of studying about the Bible."

HIGHLAND PRESS PUBLISHING

P.O. Box 2292, High Springs FL 32655. (386) 454-3927. Fax: (386) 454-3927. E-mail: The.Highland.Press@gmail.com. Website: http://www.highlandpress.org. **Contact:** Leanne Burroughs, CEO (fiction); she will forward all mss to appropriate editor. Paperback originals. **Publishes 30/year titles/year. 90% from unagented writers.** Publishes book within 18 months after acceptance of ms. Accepts simultaneous submissions. Catalog and guidelines available online.

- *Highland Wishes* was a 2006 Winner, Reviewers International Award of Excellence. *Blue Moon Enchantment* won the 2007 P.E.A.R.L. Award (two separate stories). *Christmas Wishes* received the 2007 Linda Howard Award of Excellence. *Her Highland Rogue* received the 2006 Reviewer's International Award, the 2006 National Readers Choice Award. *Cat O'Nine Tales* had several stories as finalists or won the 2007 P.E.A.R.L. Award, 2007 Linda Howard Award of Excellence, and the 2007 Reviewers International Organization Award of Excellence.

O━ "With our focus on historical romances, Highland Press Publishing is known as your 'Passport to Romance.' We focus on historical romances and our award-winning anthologies. Our short stories/novellas are heart warming. As for our historicals, we publish historical novels like many of us grew up with and loved. History is a big part of the story and is tactfully woven throughout the romance." We have recently opened our submissions up to all genres, with the exception of erotica. Our newest lines are inspirational, regency, and young adult.

Fiction Send query letter. Query with outline/synopsis and sample chapters. Accepts queries by snail mail, e-mail. Include estimated word count, target market.

Recent Title(s) *Abendlied*, by Jennifer Linforth; *In the Lion's Mouth*, by Jean Harrington; *Eternal Hearts*, by Jean Adams, *On a Cold Winter's Night* anthology; *Second Time Around* anthology; *A Piece of My Heart*, by Kemberlee Shortland; *Operation: L.O.V.E* anthology; *The Mosquito Tapes*, by Chris Holmes; *Romance on Route 66*, by Judith Leigh and Cheryl Norman, *On the Wild Side*, by Gerri Bowen.

Tips Special interests: Children's ms must come with illustrator. "We will always be looking for good historical manuscripts. In addition, we are actively seeking inspirational romances and Regency period romances." Numerous romance anthologies are planned. Topics and word count are posted on the Website. Writers should query with their proposal. After the submission deadline has passed, editors select the stories.

HIGH TIDE PRESS

2081 Calistoga Dr., Suite 2N, New Lenox IL 60451. (815)717-3780. Website: www.hightidepress.com. **Contact:** Monica Regan, managing editor. Estab. 1995. Publishes hardcover and trade paperback originals. **Publishes 2-3 titles/year. 20 queries received/year. 3 mss received/year. 50% of books from first-time authors. 100% from unagented writers. Pays royalty. Percentages vary.** Publishes book Publishes book up to 12 months after acceptance. after acceptance of ms. Accepts simultaneous submissions. Responds in 0-6 months to queries and proposals. Catalog available online. Guidelines available at http://www.hightidepress.com/main/submissions.php.

O→ "High Tide Press is a leading provider of resources for disability and nonprofit professionals - publications and training materials on intellectual/developmental disabilities, behavioral health, and nonprofit management."

Nonfiction Subjects include business, economics, education, health, medicine, how-to, human services, nonprofit management, psychology, reference, All of these topics as they relate to developmental, learning and intellectual disabilities, behavioral health, and human services management. "We do not publish personal stories. We produce materials for direct support staff, managers and professionals in the fields of disabilities and human services, as well as educators." Query via e-mail.

Recent Title(s) *Creating a Meaningful Day: An Innovative Curriculum for People with Significant Intellectual Disabilities*, by Linda Cofield-Van Dyke (professional manual); *Intellectual Disabilities at Your Fingertips: A Health Care Resource*, by Dr. Carl V. Tyler, MD (medical reference).

Tips "Our readers are leaders and managers, mostly in the field of human services, and especially those who serve persons with intellectual disabilities or behavioral health needs."

HOST PUBLICATIONS

277 Broadway, Suite 210, New York NY 10007. (212)905-2365. Fax: (212)905-2369. E-mail: tracey@hostpublications.com. Website: www.hostpublications.com. **Contact:** Joe W. Bratcher III and Elzbieta Szoka, co-editors. Estab. 1987. Hardcover and trade paperback originals. Book catalog available online.

O→ Genres are Anthologies, Drama, Novels, Poetry, & Short Stories.

Nonfiction Subjects include memoirs.

Fiction Subjects include ethnic, historical, literary, multicultural, poetry, short story collections.

Recent Title(s) *Homenagem a Alexandrino Severino*, edited by Margo Milleret & Marshall C. Eakin; *The Young Man from Savoy*, by C-F Ramuz (a novel from Switzerland); *Cage*, by Astrid Cabral (poetry from Brazil).

IDYLL ARBOR, INC.

39129 264th Ave. SE, Enumclaw WA 98022. (360)825-7797. Fax: (360)825-5670. E-mail: editors@idyllarbor.com. Website: www.idyllarbor.com. **Contact:** Tom Blaschko. Estab. 1984. Publishes hardcover and trade paperback originals, and trade paperback reprints. **Publishes 6 titles/year. 50% of books from first-time authors. 100% from unagented writers. Pays 8-15% royalty on wholesale price or retail price.** Publishes book 1 year after acceptance of ms. Accepts simultaneous submissions. Responds in 1 month to queries. Responds in 2 months to proposals. Responds in 6 months to manuscripts. Book catalog and ms guidelines free.

Imprints Issues Press; Pine Winds Press.

O→ "Idyll Arbor publishes practical information on the current state and art of healthcare practice. Currently emphasizing therapies (recreational, aquatic, occupational, music, horticultural), and activity directors in long-term care facilities. Issues Press looks at problems in society from video games to returning veterans and their problems reintegrating into the civilian world."

Nonfiction Subjects include health, medicine, for therapists, activity directors, psychology, recreation as therapy, horticulture (used in long-term care activities or health care therapy). "Idyll Arbor is currently developing a line of books under the imprint Issues Press, which treats emotional issues in a clear-headed manner. The latest books are *Female Sex Offenders: What Therapists, Law Enforcement and Child Protective Services Need to Know* and *Situational Mediation: Sensible Conflict Resolution*. Another series of *Personal Health* books explains a condition or a closely related set of medical or psychological conditions. The target audience is the person or the family of the person with the condition. We want to publish a book that explains a condition at the level of detail expected of the average primary care physician so that our readers can address the situation intelligently with specialists. We look for manuscripts from authors with recent clinical experience. Good grounding in theory is required, but practical experience is more important." Query preferred with outline and 1 sample chapter. Reviews artwork/photos. Send photocopies.

Recent Title(s) *Faces of Combat, PTSD and TBI*, by Eric Newhouse; *Video Games and Your Kids: How Parents Stay in Control*, by Hilarie Cash and Kim McDaniel.

Tips "The books must be useful for the health practitioner who meets face to face with patients or the books must be useful for teaching undergraduate and graduate level classes. We are especially looking for therapists with a solid clinical background to write on their area of expertise."

IMMEDIUM

P.O. Box 31846, San Francisco CA 94131. Website: www.immedium.com. **Contact:** Amy Ma, acquisitions editor. Estab. 2005. Publishes hardcover and trade paperback originals. **Publishes 4 titles/year. 50 queries received/year. 25 mss received/year. 50% of books from first-time authors. 90% from unagented writers. Pays 5% royalty on wholesale price.** Publishes book 24 months after acceptance of ms. Accepts simultaneous submissions. Responds in 1 month to queries. Responds in 2 months to proposals. Responds in 3 months to mss. Book catalog for 9 × 12 envelope and 5 first-class stamps. Guidelines available online.

O→ "*Immedium* focuses on publishing eye-catching children's picture books, Asian American topics, and contemporary arts, popular culture, and multicultural issues."

Nonfiction Subjects include art, architecture, multicultural. Query with SASE. Submit proposal package, outline, 2 sample chapters. Submit complete ms. Reviews artwork/photos. Send photocopies.

Fiction Subjects include comic books, picture books. Submit complete ms.

Recent Title(s) *The Year of the Tiger: Tales From the Chinese Zodiac*, by Oliver Chin and Justin Roth (children's picture book); *Baltazar and the Flying Pirates*, by Oliver Chin and Justin Roth (children's picture book); *Chaff N'Skaffs: Mai and the Lost Moskivvy*, by Skaffs (children's picture book); *The Octonauts & the Great Ghost Reef*, by Meomi (children's picture book).

Tips "Our audience is children, parents. Please visit our site."

INTERNATIONAL PUBLISHERS CO., INC.

235 W. 23 St., Floor 8, New York NY 10011. (212)366-9816. Fax: (212)366-9820. E-mail: service@intpubnyc.com. Website: www.intpubnyc.com. **Contact:** Betty Smith, president. Estab. 1924. Publishes hardcover originals, trade paperback originals and reprints. **Publishes 5-6 titles/year. 50-100 mss received/year. 10% of books from first-time authors. Pays 5-7½% royalty on paperbacks; 10% royalty on cloth.** Publishes book 6 months after acceptance of ms. Accepts simultaneous submissions. Responds in 1 month to queries; 6 months to manuscripts. Book catalog online at website. Guidelines online at website.

O→ "International Publishers Co., Inc. emphasizes books based on Marxist science."

Nonfiction Subjects include art, architecture, economics, government, politics, history, philosophy. Books on labor, black studies, and women's studies based on Marxist science have high priority. Query, or submit outline, sample chapters, and SASE. Reviews artwork/photos.

Recent Title(s) *Blows Against the Empire*, by Gerald Horne; *Can Capitalism Last? A Marxist Update*, by Daniel Rubin; *John Brown-The Cost of Freedom*, by Louis A DeCaro, Jr.

Tips "No fiction or poetry."

ITALICA PRESS

595 Main St., Suite 605, New York NY 10044-0047. (212)935-4230. Fax: (212)838-7812. E-mail: inquiries@italicapress.com. Website: www.italicapress.com. **Contact:** Ronald G. Musto and Eileen Gardiner, publishers. Estab. 1985. Publishes trade paperback originals. **Publishes 6 titles/year. 600 queries received/year. 60 mss received/year. 5% of books from first-time authors. 100% from unagented writers. Pays 7-15% royalty on wholesale price; author's copies.** Publishes book 1 year after acceptance of ms. Accepts simultaneous submissions. Responds in 1 month to queries. Responds in 4 months to manuscripts. Book catalog and guidelines available online.

O→ "Italica Press publishes English translations of modern Italian fiction and medieval and Renaissance nonfiction."

Nonfiction Subjects include translation. "We publish English translations of medieval and Renaissance source materials and English translations of modern Italian fiction." Query with SASE. Reviews artwork/photos. Send photocopies.

Fiction Query with SASE.

Tips "We are interested in considering a wide variety of medieval and Renaissance topics (not historical fiction), and for modern works we are only interested in translations from Italian fiction by well-known Italian authors."

ALICE JAMES BOOKS

238 Main St., Farmington ME 04938. Phone/Fax: (207)778-7071. E-mail: ajb@umf.maine.edu. Website: www.alicejamesbooks.org. Estab. 1973. Publishes trade paperback originals. **Publishes 6 titles/year. 1,000 mss received/year. 50% of books from first-time authors. 100% from unagented writers. Pays through competition awards.** Publishes book 1 to 1½ years after acceptance of ms. Accepts simultaneous submissions. Responds promptly to queries. Responds in 4 months to manuscripts. Book catalog for free or on website. Guidelines for #10 SASE or on website.

- "Alice James Books is a nonprofit cooperative poetry press. The founders' objectives were to give women access to publishing and to involve authors in the publishing process. The cooperative selects mss for publication through both regional and national competitions."

Recent Title(s) *Shelter*, by Carey Salerno; *Slamming Open the Door,* by Kathleen Sheeder Bonanno; *The Bitter Withy*, by Donald Revell; *Winter Tenor*, by Kevin Goodan; *Rough Cradle*, by Betsy Sholl; *Pageant*, by Joanna Fuhrman.

Tips "Send SASE for contest guidelines or check website. Do not send work without consulting current guidelines."

KAEDEN BOOKS

P.O. Box 16190, Rocky River OH 44116. Website: www.kaeden.com. **Contact:** Lisa Stenger, editor. Estab. 1986. Publishes paperback originals. **Publishes 12-20 titles/year. 1,000 mss received/year. 30% of books from first-time authors. 95% from unagented writers. Pays royalty. Makes outright purchase. Pays flat fee or royalty by individual arrangement with author depending on book.** Publishes book 6-9 months after acceptance of ms. Accepts simultaneous submissions. Responds in 12 months to manuscripts. Book catalog and guidelines available online.

- "Children's book publisher for education K-2 market: reading stories, fiction/nonfiction, chapter books, science, and social studies materials."

Nonfiction Subjects include animals, creative nonfiction, science, social sciences. Submit complete ms. Reviews artwork/photos. Send photocopies.

Fiction Grades K-3 only. Subjects include adventure, fantasy, historical, humor, mystery, short story collections, sports, suspense. Send a disposable copy of ms and SASE.

Recent Title(s) *Sammy Gets A Bath*, by Karen Evans (early reader); *Carla's Talent Show*, by Kimberly Beikly (early reader); *Adventures of Sophie Bean Red Flyer*, by Kathryn Yeuchak (early chapter book).

Tips "Our audience ranges from Kindergarten-2nd grade school children. We are an educational publisher."

KITSUNE BOOKS

P.O. Box 1154, Crawfordville FL 32326-1154. E-mail: contact@kitsunebooks.com. Website: www.kitsunebooks.com. **Contact:** Lynn Holschuh, Assistant Editor. Estab. 2006. Publishes trade paperback originals and reprints. **Publishes 4-5 titles/year. 600+ queries received/year. 70 mss received/year. 30% of books from first-time authors. 50% from unagented writers. Pays 10% royalty on retail price. Pays $300-600 advance.** Publishes book 12-18 months after acceptance of ms. Accepts simultaneous submissions. Responds in 2-4 weeks to queries. Responds in 1-3 months to proposals. Responds in 6-9 months to manuscripts. Book catalog and guidelines available online.

Nonfiction Subjects include memoirs, New Age, spirituality, literary commentary, yoga/fitness. Write for the general reader, but demonstrate a thorough, authoritative knowledge of your subject. Query via e-mail only. If you insist on sending a postal letter, you must include SASE. No hardcopy submissions unless requested. Reviews artwork/photos.

Fiction Subjects include literary, mainstream, contemporary, dark fantasy, short story collections, poetry, speculative, noir, magical realism. "We are looking for carefully written fiction that's slightly off the beaten path-interesting novels that don't fit easily into any one category. Graceful command of the language is a plus; technical command of grammar/language mechanics a must. Our latest short story collection is in the Raymond Carver tradition. Looking for authors with a unique voice and style." Query via e-mail. No hardcopy submissions, no previously published material.

Recent Title(s) *Jesus Swept*, by James Protzman (novel); *Living by the Dead*, by Ellen Ashdown (memoir); *You Can't Get There from Here and Other Stories*, by Leonard Nash (literary fiction - 2007 Silver Medal Winner, Florida Book Awards); *The Moving Waters*, by Mary Jane Ryals (poetry collection - 2008-2010 Florida Big Bend Poet Laureate).

Tips "Our readership is eclectic, with a taste for the unusual, the artistic and the unexpected. Kitsune Books caters to lovers of literature, poetry, and well-designed and researched nonfiction. We prefer to deal with mss electronically rather than receiving printouts (saves trees). Please read our category guidelines carefully. Although we do accept some genre fiction, please look carefully at what we don't accept before you submit. Interesting novels that don't fit easily into any one category are considered. No self-published material."

KOMENAR PUBLISHING

1756 Lacassie Ave., Suite 202, Walnut Creek CA 94596-7002. (510)444-2261. Fax: (510)834-2141. Website: www.komenarpublishing.com. **Contact:** Charlotte Cook, president (fiction: mainstream, literary, mystery, historical, science fiction). Estab. 2005. Publishes hardcover originals. **Publishes 2-4 titles/year. 2,000+ mss received/year. 100% of books from first-time authors. Pays 20% royalties after the first 7,500 books have sold.** Publishes book 1 year after acceptance of ms. Accepts simultaneous submissions. Responds in 1-3 months to manuscripts. Book catalog available onlin. Guidelines available online.

- KOMENAR Publishing is not accepting new submissions at this time. Please do not send any submissions, ms pages, or other materials. Questions about previous submissions may be sent to info@komenarpublishing.com. Please allow at least three weeks for a response.

Fiction Subjects include adventure, ethnic, experimental, historical, humor, literary, mainstream, contemporary, multicultural, mystery, suspense. KOMENAR Publishing believes a novel should be a compelling read. Readers are entitled to stories with strong forward momentum, engaging and dynamic characters, and evocative settings. The story must begin in the first chapter. Submit proposal package, bio, cover letter, first 1 pages of ms. See Website for additional details.

Recent Title(s) *Outside Child*, by Alice Wilson-Fried (mystery); *Heroes Arise*, by Laurel Anne Hill (literary parable); *My Half of the Sky*, by Jana McBurney-Lin (literary mainstream).

Tips "Our audience is comprised of habitual readers. Any experimental craft choices should be applied to the story, not to font, margins or punctuation. Chapters of our books are online. Read a couple. Charlotte Cook is likely to call promising authors. It's a good idea to have some familiarity with our books."

LADYBUGPRESS

NewVoices, Inc. 16964 Columbia River Dr., Sonora CA 95370-9111. (209)694-8340. E-mail: georgia@ladybugbooks.com. Website: www.ladybugbooks.com. **Contact:** Georgia Jones, editor-in-chief (new authors). Trade paperback and electronic originals. **Publishes 4-6 trade titles/year. 50 queries/year; 30 mss/year 90% of books from first-time authors. 100% from unagented writers.** Publishes book 2 months after acceptance of ms. Accepts simultaneous submissions. Catalog and guidelines available online or by CD.

Imprints LadybugPress, NewVoices, Ladybug Productions, Partners in Publishing.

Nonfiction Subjects include alternative lifestyles, contemporary culture, creative nonfiction, dance, music, social sciences, women's issues, world affairs. Our primary interest is in women's issues and peace. Query with SASE; We prefer e-mail submissions. Reviews artwork/photos; send electronic files.

Fiction Subjects include contemporary, feminist, historical, literary, mainstream, poetry. "Our tastes are eclectic." Submit proposal package, including synopsis. We prefer electronic submissions, georgia@ladbugbooks.com.

Recent Title(s) *From Deep Within*, by Danielle Joy Linhart (young adult); *Peace Train*, translated by Therese Lynn (women's activism); *Chsin Bridge to the Golden Gate*, by Peter A. Karpaty (memoir); *Lives in Process (audio version)*, by Dottie Moore (spiritual); *Kanai's Journal*, by Kanai Callow (memoir); *Fireflies in Baldwin*, by Lane Willey (suspense).

Tips "We have a lot of information on our website, and have several related sites that give an overview of who we are and what we like to see. Take advantage of this and it will help you make good decisions about submissions."

LAKE CLAREMONT PRESS

P.O. Box 711, Chicago IL 60690. (312)226-8400. Fax: (312)226-8420. E-mail: sharon@lakeclaremont.com. Website: www.lakeclaremont.com. **Contact:** Sharon Woodhouse, publisher. Estab. 1994. Publishes trade paperback originals. **Publishes 6-10 titles/year. 500 queries received/year. 100 mss received/year. 50% of books from first-time authors. 100% from unagented writers. Pays 10-15% royalty on net sales. Pays $500-1,000 advance.** Publishes book 6-12 months after acceptance of ms. Accepts simultaneous submissions. Responds in 1 month to queries. Responds in 2 months to proposals. Responds in 2-6 months to manuscripts. Book catalog available online.

- "We specialize in nonfiction books on the Chicago area and its history, particularly by authors with a passion or organizations with a mission."

Nonfiction Subjects include Americana, ethnic, history, nature, environment, regional, travel, women's issues, film/cinema/stage (regional). Query with SASE, or submit proposal package, including outline and 2 sample chapters, or submit complete ms (e-mail queries and proposals preferred).

Recent Title(s) *Today's Chicago Blues*, by Karen Hanson; *Chicago TV Horror Movie Shows: From Shock Theatre to Svengoolie*, by Ted Okuda and Mark Yurkiw.

Tips "Please include a market analysis in proposals (who would buy this book and where) and an analysis of similar books available for different regions. Please know what else is out there."

LANGMARC PUBLISHING

P.O. Box 90488, Austin TX 78709-0488. (512)394-0989. Fax: (512)394-0829. E-mail: langmarc@booksails.com. Website: www.langmarc.com. **Contact:** Lois Qualben, president (inspirational). Publishes trade paperback originals. **Publishes 3-5 titles/year. 150 queries received/year. 80 mss received/year. 60% of books from first-time authors. 80% from unagented writers. Pays 14% royalty on sales price.** Publishes book 8-14 months after acceptance of ms. Accepts simultaneous submissions. Responds in 3 months to queries. Book catalog available free. Guidelines available online.

Imprints North Sea Press; Harbor Lights Series.

Nonfiction Subjects include child guidance, education. Query with SASE. Reviews artwork/photos. Send photocopies.

Recent Title(s) *I Choose to be Happy: A School Shooting Survivor's Triumph Over Tragedy; The Hard Work of Hope; Journeys of Heartache and Grace; Hairball Diaries: The Courage to Speak Up*; *On the Wings of the Wind: A Journey to Faith*; *Don't Call Me Shy*.

LARSON PUBLICATIONS

4936 Rt. 414, Burdett NY 14818-9729. (607)546-9342. Fax: (607)546-9344. Website: www.larsonpublications.com. **Contact:** Paul Cash, director. Estab. 1982. Publishes hardcover and trade paperback originals. **Publishes 4-5 titles/year. 5% of books from first-time authors. Pays variable royalty. Seldom offers advance.** Publishes book 1-2 years after acceptance of ms. Accepts simultaneous submissions. Responds in 8 weeks to queries. Visit website for book catalog. Guidelines available online at website.

- "What we want most isn't out there yet. We hope we'll recognize it when we see it. You can improve our chances of seeing it in your material by being as clear as you can about: your subject, audience, qualifications, connections. In what other ways can you help bring attention to your book? Answer these questions as well as you can briefly, in 3 pages at the most. Then send your query letter, with SASE, to Acquisitions."

Nonfiction Subjects include philosophy, psychology, religion, spirituality. Query with SASE and outline. Use snail mail.

Recent Title(s) *Astronoesis*, by Anthony Damiani.

Tips "We look for original studies of comparative spiritual philosophy or personal fruits of independent (transsectarian viewpoint) spiritual research/practice."

LEUCROTA PRESS

40485 Murrieta Hot Springs Rd., Suite B-4 #131, Murrieta CA 92562. (619)534-8169. E-mail: submissions@leucrotapress.com. Website: www.leucrotapress.com. **Contact:** Jessica Dall, acquisitions editor. Estab. 2007. Publishes hardcover, trade paperback and electronic originals. **Publishes 6-10 titles/year. 400 queries received/year. 450-600 mss received/year. 80% of books from first-time authors. 90% from unagented writers. Pays up to $2,000 advance.** Publishes book 9-12 months after acceptance of ms. Accepts simultaneous submissions. Responds in 1 month to queries. Responds in 2 months to proposals. Responds in 3 months to manuscripts. Book catalog available online. Guidelines available online.

- Leucrota publishes in two seasons: Spring and Fall. Their submission reading periods are Spring (January 1 - April 30) and Fall (August 1 - December 31). If accepted for publication, your book will be slotted for the following season in which it was read (if you submit in Spring and are accepted, your book will be released the following Spring season).

Fiction Subjects include fantasy, horror, science fiction, graphic novels. Also publishes a yearly short story anthology. "Characterization should be your number one goal. We are looking for character-driven plots, unique settings, established worlds and histories, believable dialogue and new twists on old scenarios. Wow us with something different, something far out of the ordinary." Submit proposal package, three sample chapters, publishing history, cover letter and SASE. Do not submit complete ms unless requested.

Recent Title(s) *Deadfall; Rise of the Dark Son; Malagon Rising; Low Man*, by T. J. Vargo (horror); *The Kult*, by Shaun Jeffrey (horror); *Blood Sin*, by Toni V. Sweeney (science fiction); *One If By Heaven Two If By Hell*, by Rick Maydak (fantasy).
Tips "Visit our Website to get a feel for our editors, our needs, and overall style and attitude."

LIGHTHOUSE POINT PRESS

100 First Ave., Suite 525, Pittsburgh PA 15222-1517. (412)323-9320. Fax: (412)323-9334. **Contact:** Ralph W. Yearick, publisher (business/career/general nonfiction). Estab. 1993. Publishes hardcover and trade paperback originals and trade paperback reprints. **Publishes 1-2 titles/year. Pays 5-10% royalty on retail price.** Responds in 6 months to queries. Queries by e-mail: info@yearick-millea.com.

- "Lighthouse Point Press specializes in business/career nonfiction titles, and books that help readers improve their quality of life. We do not re-publish self-published books."

Nonfiction Subjects include business, economics. "We are open to all types of submissions related to general nonfiction, but most interested in business/career manuscripts." Submit proposal package, outline, 1-2 sample chapters and bio. Complete manuscripts preferred.
Recent Title(s) *The Heart and Craft of Lifestory Writing: How to Transform Memories into Meaningful Stories*, by Sharon M. Lippincott (writing/reference); *On Track to Quality*, by Dr. James K. Todd (business).
Tips "When submitting a manuscript or proposal, please tell us what you see as the target market/audience for the book. Also, be very specific about what you are willing to do to promote the book."

LOST HORSE PRESS

105 Lost Horse Lane, Sandpoint ID 83864. (208)255-4410. Fax: (208)255-1560. E-mail: losthorsepress@mindspring.com. Website: www.losthorsepress.org. **Contact:** Christine Holbert, editor. Estab. 1998. Publishes hardcover and paperback originals. **Publishes 4 titles/year.** Publishes book 1-2 years after acceptance of ms.

- "Does not accept unsolicited mss. However, we welcome submissions for The Idaho Prize for Poetry, a national competition offering $1000 prize money plus publication for a book-length manuscript. Please check the submission guidelines for The Idaho Prize for Poetry online."

Fiction Subjects include literary, poetry, regional, Pacific Northwest, short story collections.
Recent Title(s) *Lucifer*, by Philip Memmer (poetry); *Thistle*, by Melissa Kwasny; *A Change of Maps*, by Carolyne Wright, and *Feeding Strays*, by Stephanie Freele (short stories).

LUCKY PRESS, LLC

Lucky Press, LLC, P.O. Box 754, Athens OH 45701-0754. Website: www.luckypress.com. **Contact:** Janice Phelps Williams, editor-in-chief. trade paperback originals. **Publishes 4 titles/year. 100 queries/year; 25 mss/year. 95% of books from first-time authors. 100% from unagented writers.** Publishes book 8 months after acceptance of ms. Accepts simultaneous submissions. Catalog and guidelines available online at website.

- "We offer personal attention, hope, and encouragement to writers we publish. In return, we ask authors to know their competition, understand what we can provide, and be committed to marketing their book."
- "Lucky Press is a small, independent publisher and a good option for hard-working, talented writers. Our books are sold primarily online and authors must be comfortable maintaining a blog, and creating social networks to promote their book."

Nonfiction Subjects include pets, women's fiction, young adult fiction, autism, regional (OH/WV) women's self-help. "We are interested in the following subjects: pets (i.e., relationship with one's pet; memoirs of a vet; pet rescue stories; parrot stories), inspiration (small books that encourage readers to live positively and consciously; not religious), living with or parenting children with special needs, nonfiction of interest to women over 50. Also stories about people who took their lives in a completely different direction and what they learned along the way." Submit proposal package, including outline, 2 sample chapters, author bio, 1-page synopsis, list of comparative/competitive titles. Does not review artwork.
Fiction Subjects include historical, literary, mainstream/contemporary, mystery, poetry, regional Ohio or Appalachia, romance, short story collections, young adult. "We'll consider any well-written ms. We are looking for literary fiction, particularly by Ohio authors. Mss should be 30,000-95,000 words; but query with only the first 3 chapters." Submit query letter, synopsis, and bio via e-mail to submissions@luckypress.com.
Recent Title(s) *There Are No Words*, by Mary Calhoun Brown; *Rosie Red Bottom*, by Donna Mann; *For the Love of Greys: The Complete Guide to a Healthy and Happy African Grey*, by Bobbi Brinker (nonfiction/

pets); *I Didn't Order This Pink Ribbon*, by Alice Krumm (nonfiction/cancer); *The Life and Times of Mister*, by JRM (YA fiction/cats); *Turner's Defense*, by Chris Davey (historical fiction); *The Killing of Strangers*, by Jerry Holt (fiction: Ohio).
Tips "The author is the biggest key to success in our book sales and our best-selling books are by authors with a strong web presence."

MAGNUS PRESS

P.O. Box 2666, Carlsbad CA 92018. (760)806-3743. Fax: (760)806-3689. E-mail: magnuspres@aol.com. Website: www.magnuspress.com. **Contact:** Warren Angel, editorial director. Estab. 1997. Publishes trade paperback originals and reprints. **Publishes 1-3 titles/year. 200 queries received/year. 220 mss received/year. 44% of books from first-time authors. 89% from unagented writers. Pays 6-15% royalty on retail price.** Publishes book 12 months after acceptance of ms. Accepts simultaneous submissions. Responds in 1 month to queries, proposals and manuscripts. Book catalog and ms guidelines for #10 SASE.
Imprints Canticle Books.
Nonfiction Subjects include religion, from a Christian perspective. "Writers must be well-grounded in Biblical knowledge and must be able to communicate effectively with the lay person." Submit proposal package, outline, sample chapters, bio.
Recent Title(s) *God's Love in the End Times* (biblical studies); *Adventures of an Alaskan Preacher* (inspirational); *Sports Stories and the Bible*, by Stan Nix (inspirational).
Tips "Magnus Press's audience is mainly Christian lay persons, but also includes anyone interested in spirituality and/or Biblical studies and the church. Study our listings and catalog; learn to write effectively for an average reader; read any one of our published books."

N MANAGEMENT ADVISORY PUBLICATIONS

P.O. Box 81151, Wellesley Hills MA 02481-0001. (781)345-3895. Fax: (781)235-5445. Website: www.masp.com. **Contact:** Jay Kuong, editor (corporate governance, compliance, security, audit, IT, business continuity). Mass market paperback originals. **Publishes 2-10 titles/year. 25 queries/year; 10 mss/year. 5% of books from first-time authors.** Publishes book 3-6 months after acceptance of ms. Catalog not available. Guidelines not available.
Nonfiction Subjects include business, computers, economics, electronics. Submit proposal package.
Recent Title(s) *Achieve a Green Enterprise and a Greene IT Infrastructure.*
Tips "Our audience is primarily business and IT professionals and University and Company libraries."

MARINE TECHNIQUES PUBLISHING

126 Western Ave., Suite 266, Augusta ME 04330-7249. (207)622-7984. Fax: (207)621-0821. E-mail: info@marinetechpublishing.com. Website: www.marinetechpublishing.com. **Contact:** James L. Pelletier, president/owner(commercial maritime); Maritime Associates Globally (commercial maritime). Estab. 1983. Trade paperback originals and reprints. **Publishes 2-5 titles/year. 100+ queries received/year. 40+ mss received/year. 50% of books from first-time authors. 75% from unagented writers. Pays 25-55% royalty on wholesale or retail price. Makes outright purchase.** Publishes book 6-12 months after acceptance of ms. Accepts simultaneous submissions. Responds in 2 months to queries, proposals, and manuscripts. Book catalog available online, by e-mail, and for #10 SASE for $5. Guidelines available by e-mail, and for #10 SASE for $5.

O→ "Publishes only books related to the commercial marine/maritime industry."

Nonfiction Subjects include maritime education, marine subjects, counseling, career guidance, maritime labor, marine engineering, global water transportation, marine subjects, water transportation. "We are concerned with 'maritime related works' and not recreational boating, but rather commercial maritime industries, such as deep-sea water transportation, offshore oil & gas, inland towing, coastal tug boat, 'water transportation industries.'" Submit proposal package, including all sample chapters; submit completed ms. Reviews artwork/photos as part of the ms package; send photocopies.
Fiction Subjects include adventure, military, war, maritime. Must be commercial maritime/marine related. Submit proposal package, including all sample chapters. Submit complete ms.
Recent Title(s) *Tugging On A Heartstring: The Sequel*, by E.V. Lambert (bio); *An Officer..Not a Gentleman*, by L.J. Lester (bio); *Mariner's Employment Guide*, by J.L. Pelletier (commercial marine employment reference)
Tips "Audience consists of commercial marine/maritime firms, persons employed in all aspects of the marine/maritime commercial water-transportation-related industries and recreational fresh and salt water fields, persons interested in seeking employment in the commercial marine industry; firms seeking to sell their products and services to vessel owners, operators, and managers; shipyards, vessel repair

yards, recreational and yacht boat building and national and international ports and terminals involved with the commercial marine industry globally worldwide, etc."

⊘ MARLOR PRESS, INC.

4304 Brigadoon Dr., St. Paul MN 55126. (651)484-4600. E-mail: marlin.marlor@minn.net. **Contact:** Marlin Bree, publisher. Estab. 1981. Publishes trade paperback originals. **Publishes 2 titles/year. 100 queries received/year. 25 mss received/year. 100% of books from first-time authors. Pays 8-10% royalty on wholesale price.** Publishes book 1 year after acceptance of ms. Responds in 3-6 weeks to queries.

"Currently emphasizing general interest nonfiction children's books and nonfiction boating books."

Nonfiction Subjects include travel, boating. Primarily how-to stuff. Query first; submit outline with sample chapters only when requested. Do not send full ms. Reviews artwork/photos.

Recent Title(s) *Notable New York*, by Stephen W. Plumb; *The Dangerous Book For Boaters*, by Marlin Bree.

MAUPIN HOUSE PUBLISHING, INC.

2416 NW 71st Place, Gainesville FL 32653. (800)524-0634. Fax: (352)373-5546. E-mail: info@maupinhouse.com. Website: www.maupinhouse.com. **Contact:** Julie Graddy, publisher (areas of interest: education, professional development). Publishes trade paperback originals and reprints. **Publishes 6-8 titles/year. 60% of books from first-time authors. 100% from unagented writers. Pays 10% royalty on retail price.** Publishes book 6-18 months after acceptance of ms. Accepts simultaneous submissions. Responds in less than 1 month to queries, proposals, and mss. Catalog and guidelines free on request and available online at website and by e-mail at: publisher@maupinhouse.com.

"Maupin House publishes professional resource books for language arts teachers K-12."

Nonfiction Subjects include education, language arts, literacy and the arts, reading comprehension, writing workshop. "Study the website to understand our publishing preferences. Successful authors are all teachers or former teachers." Query with SASE or via e-mail. Submit proposal package, including outline, 1-2 sample chapters, and TOC/marketing ideas. Reviews artwork/photos as part of the mss package. Writers should send photocopies, digital files.

Recent Title(s) *That's a Great Answer!* by Nancy Boyles (education/professional); *Purposeful Writing Assessment*, by Susan Koehler (education/professional).

Tips "Our audience is K-12 educators, teachers. Be familiar with our publishing areas and tell us why your book idea is better/different than what is out there. How do you plan to promote it? Successful authors help promote books via speaking engagements, conferences, etc."

N MAYHAVEN PUBLISHING, INC.

P.O. Box 557, Mahomet IL 61853. (217)586-4493. Fax: (217)586-6330. E-mail: mayhavenpublishing@mchsi.com. Website: www.mayhavenpublishing.com/pages/about/mayhave%20html. **Contact:** Doris Replogle Wenzel. **Publishes 9 (6 audios) titles/year.**

Imprints Wild Rose.

"Mayhaven publishes books and audio books for adults and children by established and first-time authors. In 2009, we reprinted two of our titles, published 9 new titles, and produced six new audios. From 1997 to 2007 we also offered Mayhaven's Awards for Fiction. We are temporarily suspending the awards, but all other publishing will continue."

Tips "We publish both fiction and nonfiction books and audio books."

THE MCDONALD & WOODWARD PUBLISHING CO.

431-B E. College St., Granville OH 43023. (740)321-1140. Fax: (740)321-1141. E-mail: mwpubco@mwpubco.com. Website: www.mwpubco.com. **Contact:** Jerry N. McDonald, publisher. Estab. 1986. Publishes hardcover and trade paperback originals. **Publishes 5 titles/year. 25 queries received/year. 20 mss received/year. Pays 10% Royalty** Accepts simultaneous submissions. Responds in less than 1 month to queries, proposals & mss. Book catalog available online. Guidelines free on request; by e-mail.

McDonald & Woodward publishes books in natural history, cultural history, and natural resources. Currently emphasizing travel, natural and cultural history, and natural resource conservation.

Nonfiction Subjects include animals, architecture, environment, nature, travel. Query with SASE. Reviews artwork/photos. Photos are not required.

Fiction Subjects include historical. Query with SASE.

Recent Title(s) *Yellowstone Wolves: A Chronicle of the Animal, the People, and the Politics*, by Cat Urbigkit (conservation); *Chaining Oregon: Surveying the Public Lands of the Pacific NW. 1851-1855*, by Kay Atwood (historical); *Mr. Lincoln's Chair: The Shakers and their Quest for Peace*, by Anita Sanchez.
Tips Our books are meant for the curious and educated elements of the general population.

MEMORY MAKERS BOOKS

Imprint of F+W Media, Inc. 4700 E. Galbraith Rd., Cincinnati OH 45236. Website: www.memorymakersmagazine.com. **Contact:** Christine Doyle, editorial director. Estab. 1998. Publishes trade paperback originals. **Publishes 3 titles/year. 70% of books from first-time authors. 95% from unagented writers. Pays royalty. Pays advance.** Publishes book 12-15 months after acceptance of ms. Accepts simultaneous submissions. Responds in 2 months to queries.

O‑ "Memory Makers Books exclusively publishes titles for the consumer scrapbooking industry in the form of fresh and innovative scrapbooking books. Authors who submit proposal packages must be outstanding scrapbook artists, as well as apt photographers and writers. Authors must possess a well-rounded knowledge of the industry in order to present their special book idea in a concise and complete proposal package to ensure proper evaluation."

Nonfiction Submit a proposal package that includes 40-word synopsis of the book; detailed outline (front and back matter, chapters, sidebars) for a 128-page book; no less than 10 pieces of sample art (jpgs) that illustrate the subject/techniques to be covered in the book; a brief biography and published clips." Subjects include crafts/scrapbooking.
Recent Title(s) *Scrapbook Page Maps* by Becky Fleck; *Scrapbook Secrets* by Kimber McGray; *The Scrapbook Embellishment Handbook* by Sherry Steveson.
Tips "Our readers are savvy scrapbook and paper artists—from beginning to advanced—who are on the lookout for cutting-edge scrapbooking techniques with photo illustration that they can re-create in their own albums with their own photos and journaling. Study our books to see how we present material, then pitch us something fresh, innovative and unlike anything other consumer scrapbooking publishers are producing."

MIDDLE ATLANTIC PRESS

10 Twosome Dr., P.O. BOX 345, Morestown NJ 08057. (856)235-273-9062. Fax: (856)273-7526. E-mail: blake@middleatlanticpress.com. Website: www.middleatlanticpress.com. **Contact:** Blake Koen, publisher. Publishes trade paperback originals and reprints, mass market paperback originals. **Publishes 2-3 titles/year. Pays 6-10% royalty on wholesale price. Pays $500-5,000 advance.** Responds in 3 weeks to queries. Book catalog for 9 × 6 SAE with 2 first-class stamps or online.

O‑ "Middle Atlantic Press is a regional publisher of nonfiction focusing on New York, New Jersey, Pennsylvania, Delaware, Maryland, and the east coast. Currently emphasizing books of information (i.e., guides, travel). De-emphasizing juvenile titles."

Nonfiction Subjects include Americana, cooking, foods, nutrition, history, memoirs, recreation, regional, sports, travel. "MAP is a regional publisher specializing in nonfiction on varied subject matter. Most everything we publish, however, to a large degree, deals with some aspect of the states of the mid-Atlantic region." Query with general description and SASE.
Recent Title(s) *The Great Philadelphia Fan Book*; *Animal Patients: 50 Years in the Life of an Animal Doctor*, by Ed Scanlon VMD; *George Washington's New Jersey*; *Pelle Lindbergh: Behind the White Mask*; *Who's Better: Rangers, Devils, Islanders or Flyers*; *Back Again: The Story of the 2009 Phillies*.

MOMENTUM BOOKS, LLC

117 W. Third St., Royal Oak MI 48067. (248)691-1800. Fax: (248)691-4531. E-mail: info@momentumbooks.com. Website: www.momentumbooks.com. **Contact:** Franklin Foxx, editor. Estab. 1987. **Publishes 6 titles/year. 100 queries received/year; 30 mss received/year. 95% of books from first-time authors. 100% from unagented writers. Pays 10-15% royalty.** Guidelines available online.

O‑ Momentum Books publishes Midwest regional nonfiction.

Nonfiction Subjects include history, sports, travel, automotive, current events, biography, entertainment. Submit proposal package, outline, 3 sample chapters, marketing outline.
Recent Title(s) *Turning White*, by Lee Thomas; *Sirens of Chrome*, by Margery Krevsky; *Eight Dogs Named Jack*, by Joe Borri; *Michigan's Columbus*, by Steve Lehto.
Tips (Also, custom publishing services are available for authors who are considering self-publishing.)

MOUNTAINLAND PUBLISHING, INC.

P.O. Box 150891, Ogden UT 84415. E-mail: editor@mountainlandpublishing.com. **Contact:** Michael Combe, managing editor (Fiction, Non-Fiction). Hardcover, Mass market paperback, and electronic originals. **Publishes 10-12 titles/year. Submissions are accepted by e-mail only as of January 2010. 90% of books from first-time authors. 100% from unagented writers.** Publishes book 6 months after acceptance of ms. Accepts simultaneous submissions. Catalog and guidelines available online at website.

Nonfiction Subjects include Americana, creative nonfiction, education, history, humanities, literary criticism, memoirs, military, philosophy, regional, religion, science, spirituality, war, world affairs. "Nonfiction should read like Fiction. It should be captivating to the audience and on an intriguing subject." Query via e-mail. Submit proposal package, including outline, 3 sample chapters. Reviews artwork/photos. Send photocopies.

Fiction Subjects include adventure, contemporary, fantasy, historical, horror, humor, juvenile, literary, mainstream, military, multicultural, mystery, regional, religious, romance, science fiction, short story collections, spiritual, sports, suspense, war, western, young adult. "Fiction should be able to grab readers and hold their attention with dynamic writing, interesting characters, and compelling plot." Submit synopsis, 1 sample chapter via e-mail.

Recent Title(s) *Trust with a Razor and Other Tales from Two-Bit Street; 500 Things That Make Dogs Happy; Langata Rules: Pirates at Lat 10; The Bone Yard; Moghab Canyon Tips.*

Tips "Our audience is a new generation of readers who enjoy well told storiers and who want to be entertained. They want characters they can feel close to and/or love to hate. Make sure your ms is ready for print. Publishing companies will not wait for you to finish editing your story. Be confident that the work you are submitting is your best work. Please submit all ms electronically. Submissions received by mail may be returned unopened."

MYSTIC RIDGE BOOKS

Subsidiary of Mystic Ridge Productions, Inc. 222 Main St., Suite 142, Farmington CT 06032. Website: www.mysticridgebooks.com. **Contact:** Acquisitions Editor. Estab. "Mystic Ridge Books (and its new children's line, MRB Kidz) is a rapidly growing publishing company - nationally known and respected - whose books are sold at fine booksellers. Our aim is to publish 'can't-put-me-down' books on a variety of interests for adults & children. For adults, we're offering books on personal betterment and happiness, including but not limited to books on: relationships, intimacy, love, and a range of human interests. Look for self-help books, too, in the future. For children, MRB Kidz offers books that delight, entertain, educate, inspire and instill positive values. This line, though new, has drawn rave reviews from the press, teachers, librarians, parents and kids. Its authors have appeared on TV shows throughout the nation." Publishes hardcover, trade paperback, & mass market paperback originals; trade paperback & mass market paperback reprints. **Publishes 6+ titles/year. 500+ queries received/year. 200+ mss received/year. 50% of books from first-time authors. 90% from unagented writers. Pays 10% royalty on wholesale price.** Publishes book 9 months after acceptance of ms. Accepts simultaneous submissions. Responds in 3 months to queries, proposals, and mss. Book catalog and guidelines available online.

Nonfiction Subjects include audio, Americana, animals, anthropology, archeology, business, economics, child guidance, contemporary culture, cooking, foods, nutrition, creative nonfiction, government, politics, health, medicine, history, hobbies, language, literature, memoirs, money, finance, philosophy, psychology, recreation, science, sex, social sciences, spirituality, translation, women's issues, women's studies. "The writer should have a unique angle on a subject (it would be a plus if they are an expert in their field). The target readership should be fairly large. The writer must also be a good self-promoter, willing to be proactive in getting publicity." Query with SASE. Reviews artwork/photos. Send photocopies.

Fiction Subjects include young adult. "We are only looking for juvenile fiction at this time." Query with SASE.

Recent Title(s) *Baring It All*, edited by Layla Shilkret (nonfiction—women's erotica); *Cutting Edge Blackjack*, by Richard Harvey (nonfiction—games/gaming)); *The Fuzzy Escape Artists*, by Michael Isaacs (children's picture book).

Tips "An agent is not necessary. Quality is key. It is helpful if the author has a dynamic, charismatic personality, who is intent on developing a high, public profile. No inquiries by phone, and no queries by certified mail or e-mail."

NAR ASSOCIATES

P.O. Box 233, Barryville NY 12719. (845)557-8713. Website: www.aodceus.com. **Contact:** Nick Roes, Acq. Ed. Estab. 1977. Publishes trade paperback originals. **Publishes 6 titles/year. 10 queries received/year. 10 mss received/year. 80% of books from first-time authors. 100% from unagented writers. Makes outright purchase of $500.** Publishes book 1 month after acceptance of ms. Accepts simultaneous submissions. Responds in 1 month to queries, proposals and manuscripts. Book catalog available online. Guidelines available via e-mail.

Nonfiction Subjects include education, psychology, counseling techniques, professional ethics. "We publish home study courses for addiction and social work professionals." Query with SASE. Reviews artwork/photos. Send photocopies.

Recent Title(s) *Cognitive Behavioral Therapy*, by Sara Pascoe, PhD. (home study course); *Teaching Self Advocacy*, by Edward Guild (home study course).

Tips "Our audience consists of addiction counselors, social workers, and other counseling professionals. Use same format as existing coursework currently in publication."

NATUREGRAPH PUBLISHERS, INC.

P.O. Box 1047, Happy Camp CA 96039. Fax: (530)493-5240. E-mail: nature@sisqtel.net. Website: www.naturegraph.com. **Contact:** Barbara Brown, owner. Estab. 1946. Publishes trade paperback originals. **Publishes 2 titles/year. 300 queries received/year. 12 mss received/year. 80% of books from first-time authors.** Publishes book 24 months after acceptance of ms. Accepts simultaneous submissions. Responds in 1 month to queries. Responds in 2 months to manuscripts. Book catalog for #10 SASE.

Nonfiction Subjects include anthropology, archaeology, multicultural, nature, environment, science, natural history: biology, geology, ecology, astronomy, crafts.

Recent Title(s) *Springer's Quest, Life of a Pacific Chinook Salmon; Where the Wild Things Live; Wildlife Watching Techniques.*

Tips "Please-always send a stamped reply envelope. Publishers get hundreds of manuscripts yearly."

THE NAUTICAL & AVIATION PUBLISHING COMPANY OF AMERICA

2055 Middleburg Ln., Mt. Pleasant SC 29464, United States. (843)856-0561. Fax: (843)856-3164. E-mail: nauticalaviationpublishing@att.net. Website: www.nauticalaviation.bizland.com. **Contact:** Melissa Pluta, Assoc. Ed. (Area of interest: military fiction/nonfiction). Hardcover & trade paperback originals & reprints. **Publishes 6 titles/year.** Accepts simultaneous submissions. Book catalog free on request. Guidelines free on request.

O┳ Publishes military history and fiction.

Nonfiction Subjects include military, war, war history. Query with SASE; submit proposal package, outline. Does not review artwork.

Fiction Subjects include military, war fiction.

Recent Title(s) *A Story of Charleston in the Revolution*, 2nd Printing, by Celia Garth; *A Dictionary of King Arthur's Knights,* by Gwen Bristow; *Cool Deliberate Courage*, by John Eager; *Howard in the American Revolution*, by Jim Piecuch & John Beakes (military bio).

[N] NEW ISSUES POETRY & PROSE

Western Michigan Univ., 1903 W. Michigan Ave., Kalamazoo MI 49008-5463, United States. (269)387-8185. Fax: (269)387-2562. E-mail: new-issues@wmich.edu. Website: www.wmich.edu/newissues. **Contact:** Managing Editor. Hardcover and trade paperback originals. **Publishes 8 titles/year. 50% of books from first-time authors. 95% from unagented writers.** Publishes book 18 months after acceptance of ms. Accepts simultaneous submissions. Online & free on request. Online, by e-mail, free on request for #10 SASE.

Fiction Subjects include literary, poetry, poetry in translation. All unsolicited mss returned unopened.

Recent Title(s) *The Truth*, by Geoff Rips; *One Tribe*, by M. Evelinn Galang; *Tall If*, by Mark Irwin; *Please*, by Jericho Brown.

NEXT DECADE, INC.

39 Old Farmstead Rd., Chester NJ 07930. (908)879-6625. Fax: (908)879-2920. E-mail: barbara@nextdecade.com. Website: www.nextdecade.com. **Contact:** Barbara Kimmel, president (reference); Carol Rose, editor. Publishes trade paperback originals. **Publishes 2-4 titles/year. Pays 8-15% royalty on wholesale price.** Responds in 1 month to queries. Book catalog available online. Guidelines available online.

Nonfiction Subjects include health, medicine, women's, money, finance, multicultural, senior/retirement issues, real estate.

Recent Title(s) *Retire in Style*, by Warren Bland, PhD; *The Hysterectomy Hoax*, by Stanley West, MD.

Tips "We publish books that simplify complex subjects. We are a small, award-winning press that successfully publishes a handful of books each year."

NICOLAS-HAYS, INC AND IBIS PRESS

P.O. Box 540206, Lake Worth FL 33454-0206. (561)798-1040. Fax: (561)798-1042. E-mail: info@nicolashays.com. Website: www.nicolaspress.com. **Contact:** Y. Paglia, acquisitions editor. Publishes hardcover originals and trade paperback originals and reprints. **Publishes 2-4 titles/year. Pays 15% royalty on wholesale price. Pays $200-500 advance.** Responds in 2 months to queries.

Nonfiction Subjects include philosophy, Eastern, psychology, Jungian, religion, alternative, spirituality, women's issues, women's studies. Query with SASE. Submit outline, resume, 3 sample chapters. No submissions via e-mail attachment.

Recent Title(s) *Astrology of the Authentic Self*, by Demetra George; *Healing From Depression*, by Douglas Bloch; *Real Alchemy*, by Robert Bartlett et al.; *A Call to Compassion: Bringing Buddhist Practices of the Heart Into the Soul of Psychology*, by Aura Glaser; *Alchemy of the Soul: The Eros & Psyche Myth as a Guide to Transformation*, by Martin Lowenthal.

Tips "We publish only books that are the lifework of authors—our editorial plans change based on what the author writes."

NOVA PRESS

11659 Mayfield Ave., Suite 1, Los Angeles CA 90049. (310)207-4078. Fax: (310)571-0908. E-mail: novapress@aol.com. Website: www.novapress.net. **Contact:** Jeff Kolby, president. Estab. 1993. Publishes trade paperback originals. **Publishes 4 titles/year.** Publishes book 6 months after acceptance of ms. Book catalog available free.

- "Nova Press publishes only test prep books for college entrance exams (SAT, GRE, GMAT, LSAT, etc.), and closely related reference books, such as college guides and vocabulary books."

Nonfiction Subjects include education, software.

Recent Title(s) *The MCAT Chemistry Book*, by Ajikumar Aryangat.

N OAK TREE PRESS

140 E. Palmer, Taylorville IL 62568. (217)824-6500. E-mail: oaktreepub@aol.com. Website: www.oaktreebooks.com. **Contact:** Acquisitions Editor (prefers e-mail contact). trade paperback and hardcover books. Publishes book 6-9 months (contract says 18 months after signing on) after acceptance of ms. Catalog and guidelines available online.

- "I am always on the lookout for good mysteries, ones that engage quickly. I definitely want to add to our Timeless Love list. I am also looking at a lot of nonfiction, especially in the "how-to" category. We are one of a few publishers who will consider memoirs, especially memoirs of folks who are not famous, and this is because I enjoy reading them myself. In addition, plans are in progress to launch a political/current affairs imprint, and I am actively looking for titles to build this list. Then, of course, there is always that "special something" book that you can't quite describe, but you know it when you see it. "
- "Oak Tree Press is an independent publisher that celebrates writers, and is dedicated to the many great unknowns who are just waiting for the opportunity to break into print. We're looking for mainstream, genre fiction, narrative nonfiction, how-to. Sponsors 3 contests annually: Dark Oak Mystery, Timeless Love Romance and CopTales for true crime and other stories of law enforcement professionals."

Tips "Perhaps my most extreme pet peeve is receiving queries on projects which we've clearly advertised we don't want: science fiction, fantasy, epic tomes, bigoted diatribes and so on. Second to that is a practice I call "over-taping," or the use of yards and yards of tape, or worse yet, the filament tape so that it takes forever to open the package. Finding story pitches on my voice mail is also annoying."

OBERLIN COLLEGE PRESS

50 N. Professor St., Oberlin College, Oberlin OH 44074. (440)775-8408. Fax: (440)775-8124. E-mail: oc.press@oberlin.edu. Website: www.oberlin.edu/ocpress. **Contact:** Linda Slocum, manuscript editor. Estab. 1969. Publishes hardcover and trade paperback originals. **Publishes 2-3 titles/year. Pays 7½-10% royalty.** Responds promptly to queries. Responds in 1 & 1/2 months to manuscripts.

Imprints *FIELD: Contemporary Poetry & Poetics*, a magazine published twice annually, FIELD Translation Series, FIELD Poetry Series, FIELD Editions.

Recent Title(s) *Meaning a Cloud*, by John Marshall; *The Extremities*, by Timothy Kelly; *High Lonesome: On the Poetry of Charles Wright*, (poetry).

Tips "Queries for the FIELD Translation Series: send sample poems and letter describing project. Winner of the annual FIELD poetry prize determines publication. Do not send unsolicited manuscripts."

Small Presses

OOLIGAN PRESS

P.O. Box 751, Portland OR 97207-0751. (503)725-9410. E-mail: ooligan@pdx.edu. Website: www.ooliganpress.pdx.edu. **Contact:** Acquisitions Committee. Estab. 2001. Publishes trade paperback, and electronic originals and reprints. **Publishes 4-6 titles/year. 250-500 queries received/year. 100 mss received/year. 90% of books from first-time authors. 90% from unagented writers. Pays negotiable royalty on retail price.** Book catalog available online. Guidelines available online.

Nonfiction Subjects include agriculture, alternative, anthropology, archeology, art, architecture, community, contemporary culture, cooking, foods, nutrition, creative nonfiction, education, ethnic, film, cinema, stage, gay, lesbian, government, politics, history, humanities, language, literature, literary criticism, memoirs, multicultural, music, dance, nature, environment, philosophy, regional, religion, social sciences, sociology, spirituality, translation, travel, women's issues, women's studies, world affairs. Query with SASE. Submit proposal package, outline, 4 sample chapters, projected page count, audience, marketing ideas and a list of similar titles. Reviews artwork/photos.

Fiction Subjects include adventure, ethnic, experimental, fantasy, feminist, gay, lesbian, historical, horror, humor, literary, mainstream, contemporary, multicultural, mystery, plays, poetry, poetry in translation, regional, science fiction, short story collections, spiritual, suspense, translation, and middle grade. Query with SASE by traditional mail.

Recent Title(s) *Classroom Publishing, A Practical Guide For Teachers* (instructional, nonfiction), *Cataclysms on the Columbia*, by Marjorie and Scott Burns (nonfiction), *Dot-To-Dot, Oregon*, by Sid Miller (poetry), *Killing George Washington, by Anne Jennings Paris (historical fiction, narrative poetry), Rethinking Paper and Ink: The Sustainable Publishing Revolution* (nonfiction).

Tips "For children's books, our audience will be middle grades and young adult, with marketing to general trade, libraries, and schools. Good marketing ideas increase the chances of a manuscript succeeding."

⊘ ORCHISES PRESS

P.O. Box 320533, Alexandria VA 22320-4533. (703)683-1243. E-mail: lathbury@gmu.edu. Website: mason.gmu.edu/~lathbury. **Contact:** Roger Lathbury, editor-in-chief. Estab. 1983. Publishes hardcover and trade paperback originals and reprints. **Publishes 2-3 titles/year. 1% of books from first-time authors. 95% from unagented writers. Pays 36% of receipts after Orchises has recouped its costs.** Publishes book 1 year after acceptance of ms. Accepts simultaneous submissions. Responds in 3 months to queries. Guidelines available online.

- *Orchises Press no longer reads unsolicited mss.*
- Orchises Press is a general literary publisher specializing in poetry with selected reprints and textbooks. No new fiction or children's books.

Nonfiction Query with SASE. Reviews artwork/photos. Send photocopies.

Recent Title(s) *Library*, by Stephen Akey (nonfiction); *Deniability*, by George Witte (poetry).

OZARK MOUNTAIN PUBLISHING, INC.

P.O. Box 754, Huntsville AR 72740-0754, U.S. (479)738-2348. Fax: (479)738-2448. E-mail: info@ozarkmt.com. Website: www.ozarkmt.com. **Contact:** Julie Degan, office mgr. (Areas of interest: New age/metaphysics/spiritual). Estab. 1991. Publishes trade paperback originals. **Publishes 8-10 titles/year. 50-75 queries; 150-200 mss 50% of books from first-time authors. 95% from unagented writers. Pays 10-15% royalty on retail or wholesale price. Pays $250-500 advance.** Publishes book 6-9 months after acceptance of ms. Accepts simultaneous submissions. Responds in 6 months to queries, 7 months on mss. Book catalog free on request. Guidelines available online at website http://www.ozarkmt.com/submissions.htm.

Nonfiction Subjects include new age/metaphysical/body-mind-spirit, philosophy, spirituality. Query with SASE. Submit 4-5 sample chapters.

Recent Title(s) *The Convoluted Universe-Book 3*, by Dolores Cannon (metaphysics); *Beyond Limitations*, by Stuart Wilson & Joann Prentis (spiritual); *Legacy of the Elder Gods*, by M. Don Schorn (ancient history).

Tips "We envision our audience to be open minded, spiritually expanding. Please do not call to check on submissions. Do not submit electronically. Send hard copy only."

PALARI PUBLISHING

P.O. Box 9288, Richmond VA 23227-0288. (866)570-6724. Fax: (866)570-6724. E-mail: dave@palaribooks.com. Website: www.palaribooks.com. **Contact:** David Smitherman, publisher/editor. Estab. 1998. Publishes hardcover and trade paperback originals. **Pays royalty.** Publishes book 1 year after acceptance of ms. Responds in 1 month to queries. Responds in 2-3 months to manuscripts. Guidelines available online.

Small Presses

- Member of Publishers Marketing Association..

O→ Palari provides authoritative, well-written nonfiction that addresses topical consumer needs and fiction with an emphasis on intelligence and quality. We accept solicited and unsolicited manuscripts, however we prefer a query letter and SASE, describing the project briefly and concisely. This letter should include a complete address and telephone number. Palari Publishing accepts queries or any other submissions by e-mail, but prefers queries submitted by US mail. All queries must be submitted by mail according to our guidelines. Promotes titles through book signings, direct mail and the Internet.

Nonfiction Subjects include business, economics, memoirs.

Fiction Subjects include adventure, ethnic, gay, lesbian, historical, literary, mainstream, contemporary, multicultural. Tell why your idea is unique or interesting. Make sure we are interested in your genre before submitting. Query with SASE. Submit bio, estimated word count, list of publishing credits. Accepts queries via e-mail (prefer US Mail), fax.

Recent Title(s) *Poor Man's Philanthropist: The Thomas Cannon Story*, (inspirational); *The 7 Most Powerful Selling Secrets*, (business); *The Guessing Game*, (mystery).

Tips "Send a good bio. I'm interested in a writer's experience and unique outlook on life."

PAPYRUS/LETTERBOX OF LONDON, USA

Yes You Can 10501 Broom Hill Dr., Suite H, Las Vegas NV 89134-7339. **Contact:** Jessie Rose, editor. Estab. 1946. Publishes hardcover and trade paperback originals, health pamphlets. **Publishes 6-8 titles/year. 80 mss received/year. 1% of books from first-time authors. 1% from unagented writers. Pays -10% royalty on wholesale price.** Publishes book 12 months after acceptance of ms. Accepts simultaneous submissions. Responds in 1 month to queries, proposals, and mss. Book catalog for #10 SASE.

Imprints Difficult Subjects Made Easy.

Nonfiction Subjects include health, women's issues, senior singles, speed-dating, proven tips for employment in the hospitality/hotel/restaurant fields. Query with SASE. Submit outline. Reviews artwork/photos. Send photocopies.

Fiction Subjects include mainstream, contemporary, plays, and musicals. "Require creative novels with strong, magnetizing content. No weak romances." Query with SASE.

Recent Title(s) *Yes You Can Control Bladder Incontinence; Out in the Cold*, by Sydney Dawson (adventures in Alaska); *The English Cat Artist*, Louis Wain 1860-1939 (true lifestory plus 65 LW cat pictures); *Is Forever Too Long?* (novel); *How To Be a Whizz at Dating Dozens*.

Tips "We publish for educated adults."

PARADISE CAY PUBLICATIONS

P.O. Box 29, Arcata CA 95518-0029. (800)736-4509. Fax: (707)822-9163. E-mail: info@paracay.com. Website: www.paracay.com. **Contact:** Matt Morehouse, publisher. Publishes hardcover and trade paperback originals and reprints. **Publishes 5 titles/year. 360-480 queries received/year. 240-360 mss received/year. 10% of books from first-time authors. 100% from unagented writers. Pays 10-15% royalty on wholesale price. Makes outright purchase of $1,000-10,000. Does not normally pay advances to first-time or little-known authors.** Publishes book 4 months after acceptance of ms. Responds in 1 month to queries and to proposals. Responds in 2 months to manuscripts. Book catalog and ms guidelines free on request or online.

Imprints Pardey Books.

O→ "Paradise Cay Publications, Inc. is a small independent publisher specializing in nautical books, videos, and art prints. Our primary interest is in manuscripts that deal with the instructional and technical aspects of ocean sailing. We also publish and will consider fiction if it has a strong nautical theme."

Nonfiction Must have strong nautical theme. Subjects include cooking, foods, nutrition, recreation, sports, travel. Include a cover letter containing a story synopsis and a short bio, including any plans to promote their work. The cover letter should describe the book's subject matter, approach, distinguishing characteristics, intended audience, author's qualifications, and why the author thinks this book is appropriate for Paradise Cay. Call first. Reviews artwork/photos. Send photocopies.

Fiction Subjects include adventure, nautical, sailing. All fiction must have a nautical theme. Query with SASE. Submit proposal package, clips, 2-3 sample chapters.

Recent Title(s) *American Practical Navigator*, by Nathaniel Bowditch; *Voyage Toward Vengeance*, (fiction); *Rescue at the Top of the World*.

Tips Audience is recreational sailors. Call Matt Morehouse (publisher).

PASSPORT PRESS

Website: www.paulglassman.com. **Contact:** Paul Glassman. Estab. 1975. Publishes trade paperback originals. **Publishes 4 titles/year. 25% of books from first-time authors. 100% from unagented writers. Pays 6% royalty on retail price. Pays advance.** Publishes book 9 months after acceptance of ms.
Imprints Travel Line Press.

- "Passport Press publishes practical travel guides on specific countries. Currently emphasizing offbeat countries."

Nonfiction Subjects include travel. "Especially looking for mss on practical travel subjects and travel guides on specific countries." Send 1-page query only. Reviews artwork/photos.
Recent Title(s) *Costa Rica Guide: New Authorized Edition*, by Paul Glassman.

PICCADILLY BOOKS, LTD.

P.O. Box 25203, Colorado Springs CO 80936-5203. (719)550-9887. Website: www.piccadillybooks.com. **Contact:** Submissions Department. Estab. 1985. Publishes hardcover originals and trade paperback originals and reprints. **Publishes 5-8 titles/year. 70% of books from first-time authors. 95% from unagented writers. Pays 6-10% royalty on retail price.** Publishes book 1 year after acceptance of ms. Accepts simultaneous submissions. Responds only if interested, unless accompanied by a SASE to queries.

- "Picadilly publishes nonfiction, diet, nutrition, and health-related books with a focus on alternative and natural medicine."

Nonfiction Subjects include cooking, foods, nutrition, health, medicine, performing arts. "Do your research. Let us know why there is a need for your book, how it differs from other books on the market, and how you will promote the book. No phone calls. We prefer to see the entire ms, but will accept a minimum of 3 sample chapters on your first inquiry. A cover letter is also required; please provide a brief overview of the book, information about similar books already in print and explain why yours is different or better. Tell us the prime market for your book and what you can do to help market it. Also, provide us with background information on yourself and explain what qualifies you to write this book."
Recent Title(s) *Cocnut Water for Health and Healing*, by Bruce Fife, ND.
Tips "We publish nonfiction, general interest, self-help books currently emphasizing alternative health."

PLEXUS PUBLISHING, INC.

143 Old Marlton Pike, Medford NJ 08055-8750. (609)654-6500. Fax: (609)654-4309. E-mail: jbryans@plexuspublishing.com. Website: www.plexuspublishing.com. **Contact:** John B. Bryans, editor-in-chief/publisher. Estab. 1977. Publishes hardcover and paperback originals. **Publishes 4-5 titles/year. 70% of books from first-time authors. 90% from unagented writers. Pays $500-1,000 advance.** Accepts simultaneous submissions. Responds in 3 months to proposals. Book catalog and book proposal guidelines for 10 × 13 SAE with 4 first-class stamps.

- Plexus publishes regional-interest (southern New Jersey and the greater Philadelphia area) fiction and nonfiction including mysteries, field guides, nature, travel and history. Also a limited number of titles in health/medicine, biology, ecology, botany, astronomy.

Nonfiction Query with SASE.
Fiction Mysteries and literary novels with a strong regional (southern New Jersey) angle. Query with SASE.
Recent Title(s) *The Philadelphian*, by Richard Powell; *Boardwalk Empire*, by Nelson Johnson.

POCOL PRESS

6023 Pocol Dr., P.O. Box 411, Clifton VA 20124-1333. (703)830-5862. E-mail: chrisandtom@erols.com. Website: www.pocolpress.com. **Contact:** J. Thomas Hetrick, editor. Estab. 1999. Publishes trade paperback originals. **Publishes 6 titles/year. 90 queries received/year. 20 mss received/year. 90% of books from first-time authors. 100% from unagented writers. Pays 10-12% royalty on wholesale price.** Publishes book less than 12 months after acceptance of ms. Responds in 1 month to queries. Responds in 2 months to manuscripts. Book catalog and guidelines available online.

- "Our authors are comprised of veteran writers and emerging talents."

Fiction Subjects include historical, horror, literary, mainstream, contemporary, military, war, mystery, short story collections, thematic, spiritual, sports, western, baseball fiction. "We specialize in thematic short fiction collections by a single author and baseball fiction. Expert storytellers welcome." Query with SASE.

Small Presses

Recent Title(s) *The Last One*, by Stephan Solberg (fiction); *Gulf*, by Brock Adams (short stories); *A Good Death*, by David Lawrence (fiction); *A Whole New Ballgame: The 1969 Washington Senators*, by Stephen Walker (baseball/biography); *Episode*, by Robert Garner McBrearty (short stories).
Tips "Our audience is aged 18 and over."

POSSIBILITY PRESS

One Oakglade Circle, Hummelstown PA 17036-9525. (717)566-0468. Fax: (717)566-6423. E-mail: info@possibilitypress.com. Website: www.possibilitypress.com. **Contact:** Mike Markowski, publisher. Estab. 1981. Publishes trade paperback originals. **Publishes 2-3 titles/year. 90% of books from first-time authors. 100% from unagented writers. Royalties vary.** Responds in 1 month to queries. Guidelines available online.
Imprints Aeronautical Publishers; Possibility Press; Markowski International Publishers.

O⊸ Our mission is to help the people of the world grow and become the best they can be, through the written and spoken word.

Nonfiction Subjects include psychology, pop psychology, self-help, leadership, relationships, attitude, business, success/motivation, inspiration, entrepreneurship, sales marketing, MLM and home-based business topics, and human interest success stories. Prefers submissions to be mailed. Include SASE.
Fiction Parables that teach lessons about life and success.
Recent Title(s) *Yes!*, by John Fuhrman; *The Superhero Factor*, by Tom "Terrific" Schenck.
Tips "Our focus is on co-authoring and publishing short (15,000-30,000 words) bestsellers. We're looking for kind and compassionate authors who are passionate about making a difference in the world, and will champion their mission to do so, especially by public speaking. Our dream author writes well, knows how to promote, will champion their mission, speaks for a living, has a following and a platform, is cooperative and understanding, humbly handles critique and direction, is grateful, intelligent, and has a good sense of humor."

PRICE WORLD PUBLISHING, LLC

1300 W. Belmont Ave., 20g, Chicago IL 60657. Fax: (216)803-0350. E-mail: rprice@priceworldpublishing.com. Website: www.priceworldpublishing.com. **Contact:** Robert Price, President & Executive Editor. Trade and mass market paperback originals. **Publishes 2-5 titles/year titles/year. 35 queries received/year; 20 mss/year. 50% of books from first-time authors. 50% from unagented writers.**
Nonfiction Subjects include sports, fitness. Submit proposal package, including outline, completed ms; visit www.priceworldpublishing.com for proposal submission information. Reviews artwork/photos; send PDF or MS Word docs.
Recent Title(s) *The Ultimate Guide to Weight Training for Fencing; The Ultimate Guide to Weight Training for Skiing; The Ultimate Guide to Weight Training for Bowling; Hardcore Circuit Training for Men; Celebrity Body on a Budget; Pure Physique.*
Tips "The focus of our editorial scope is sports and fitness, with emphasis on instruction for training and performance. We now welcome all nonfiction proposals—visit our website for more information."

PURITAN PRESS, INC.

95 Runnells Bridge Rd., Hollis NH 03049. (603)889-4500. Fax: (603)889-6551. E-mail: books@hollispublishing.com. Website: www.puritanpress.com. **Contact:** Frederick Lyford, editor. Publishes hardcover and trade paperback originals. **Publishes 5 titles/year. 25 queries received/year. 15 mss received/year. 50% of books from first-time authors. 100% from unagented writers. Pays 5-10% royalty on retail price.** Publishes book 6 months after acceptance of ms. Responds in 1 month to queries. Responds in 2 months to manuscripts. Book catalog available free. Guidelines for #10 SASE.

O⊸ "Hollis publishes books on social policy, government, politics, and current and recent events intended for use by professors and their students, college and university libraries, and the general reader. Currently emphasizing works about education, the Internet, government, history-in-the-making, social values and politics."

Nonfiction Subjects include Americana, anthropology, archeology, education, ethnic, government, politics, health, medicine, history, memoirs, nature, environment, regional, sociology, travel. Query with SASE. Submit outline, 2 sample chapters.
Recent Title(s) *Basic Lymphoedema Management: Treatment and Prevention of Problems Associated With Lymphatic Filariasis*, by Gerusa Dreyer, MD, et. al.

RED EYE PRESS, INC.

P.O. Box 65751, Los Angeles CA 90065. Website: www.redeyepress.com. **Contact:** James Goodwin, president. Publishes trade paperback originals. **Publishes 2 titles/year. Pays 8-12% royalty on retail price. Pays $1-2,000 advance.**

- *Currently renovating their website. Come back soon.*

O→ *No unsolicited submissions.*

Nonfiction Subjects include gardening.

Recent Title(s) *Great Labor Quotations—Sourcebook and Reader*, Peter Bollen.

Tips We publish how-to and reference works that are the standard for their genre, authoritative, and able to remain in print for many years.

RED SAGE PUBLISHING, INC.

P.O. Box 4844, Seminole FL 33775. (727)391-3847. Website: www.redsagepub.com. **Contact:** Alexandria Kendall, publisher; Theresa Stevens, managing editor. Estab. 1995. **Publishes 4 titles/year. 50% of books from first-time authors. Pays advance.** Guidelines available online.

- Red Sage publishes erotic romance and ultra-sensual romance in both print and digital formats. These include: Secrets Anthologies and Red Sage Presents (Digital Short Stories, Novellas, and Novels).We start almost all of our new authors in the Red Sage Presents line of e-books. Length can run from 10,000 to 120,000 words, though exceptions can be made. Because of the overwhelming number of submissions we receive for digital short stories, acceptance rates at this length are very low. Our greatest need is for digital novels over 45,000 words in length.

O→ Publishes books of romance fiction, written for the adventurous woman.

Fiction Submit a one-page synopsis showing conflict, plot resolution, and sensuality; the first 10 pages of the completed manuscript (double-spaced); Submit samples in a digital Rich Text Format (RTF) or inline text. Please include writing credentials, if you have any. See more guidelines online.

Recent Title(s) *Treasure of Devils Isle*, by Fiona Jayde; *Secrets, Volume 28*, (an anthology); *Forever Kissed*, (sexy paranormal featuring vampires).

Tips "We define romantic erotica. Sensuous, bold, spicy, untamed, hot, and sometimes politically incorrect, *Secrets* stories concentrate on the sophisticated, highly intense adult relationship. We look for character-driven stories that concentrate on the love and sexual relationship between a hero and the heroine. Red Sage expanded into single-title books in 2004. Author voice, excellent writing, and strong emotions are all important ingredients to the fiction we publish."

SANDLAPPER PUBLISHING CO., INC.

1281 Amelia Street, Orangeburg SC 29115. (803)531-1658. Fax: (803)534-5223. E-mail: agallman@sandlapperpublishing.com. Website: www.sandlapperpublishing.com. **Contact:** Amanda Gallman, managing editor. Estab. 1982. Publishes hardcover and trade paperback originals and reprints. **Publishes 6 titles/year. 80% of books from first-time authors. 95% from unagented writers. Pays 15% maximum royalty on net receipts.** Publishes book 20 months after acceptance of ms. Responds in 3 months to queries. Book catalog and ms guidelines for 9 × 12 SAE with 5 first-class stamps.

O→ We are an independent, regional book publisher specializing in educational nonfiction relating to South Carolina. Emphasizing history and travel.

Nonfiction Subjects include cooking, foods, nutrition, history, humor, regional, culture and cuisine of the Southeast especially South Carolina. We are looking for manuscripts that reveal under-appreciated or undiscovered facets of the rich heritage of our region. If a manuscript doesn't deal with South Carolina or the Southeast, the work is probably not appropriate for us. We don't do self-help books, children's books about divorce, kidnapping, etc., and absolutely no religious manuscripts. Query us by mail with SASE before submitting mss. Submit outline, sample chapters. No phone calls. Do not fax a query or manuscript. Reviews artwork/photos.

Recent Title(s) *Lowcountry Scenes*, by Jon Wongrey.

Tips "Our readers are South Carolinians, visitors to the region's tourist spots, and friends and family that live out-of-state. We are striving to be a leading regional publisher for South Carolina. We will be looking for more history, travel and biography."

N SCARLETTA PRESS

10 S. 5th St., Suite 1105, Minneapolis MN 55402. (612)455-0252. Website: www.scarlettapress.com. **Publishes 3-6 titles/year. 50% of books from first-time authors. 85% from unagented writers.** Accepts simultaneous submissions.

- *Not accepting new submissions at this time.* Please check our website in the future for postings.

Small Presses

Nonfiction Subjects include art, architecture, business, economics, career guidance, counseling, history, humanities, language, literature, memoirs, military, war, photography, sociology, translation, world affairs, creative nonfiction. Submit recommendation from industry professional (agent, professor, writer, etc.) and completed ms. Reviews artwork. E-mail scans (or send CD).
Fiction Subjects include experimental, historical, literary, mainstream, contemporary, multicultural, translation, young adult. All genre fiction should have literary aspirations. Submit recommendation from industry professional (agent, professor, author, etc.) and completed ms.
Recent Title(s) *Tragedy in South Lebanon*, by Cathy Sultan (political science); *The New Writer's Handbook, Vol. 2*, by Philip Martin, ed. (writing how-to); *Greater Trouble in the Lesser Antilles*, by Charles Locks (literary mystery); *Yankee Invasion*, by Ignacio Solares, trans. Timothy Compton (translated historical novel).
Tips "Our audience is thoughtful readers looking to expand their horizons. Know your audience, competition, and marketplace. Be prepared to name possible media outlets and contacts you have."

SEAWORTHY PUBLICATIONS, INC.

626 W. Pierre Lane, Port Washington WI 53074. (262)268-9250. Fax: (262)268-9208. E-mail: queries@seaworthy.com. Website: www.seaworthy.com. **Contact:** Joseph F. Janson, publisher. Publishes trade paperback originals, hardcover originals, and reprints. **Publishes 8 titles/year. 150 queries received/year. 40 mss received/year. 60% of books from first-time authors. 100% from unagented writers. Pays 15% royalty on wholesale price. Pays $1,000 advance.** Publishes book 6 months after acceptance of ms. Responds in 1 month to queries. Book catalog and guidelines available online.

O━ "Seaworthy Publications is a nautical book publisher that primarily publishes books of interest to recreational boaters and bluewater cruisers, including cruising guides, how-to books about boating. Currently emphasizing cruising guides."

Nonfiction Subjects include regional, sailing, boating, regional, boating guide books. Regional guide books, first-person adventure, reference, technical—all dealing with boating. Query with SASE. Submit 3 sample chapters, TOC. Prefers electronic query via e-mail. Reviews artwork/photos. Send photocopies or color prints.
Recent Title(s) *Add a Cruising Guide to Puerto Rico*, by Stephen J. Pavlidis.
Tips "Our audience consists of sailors, boaters, and those interested in the sea, sailing, or long-distance cruising."

N SOTO PUBLISHING COMPANY

P.O. Box 10, Dade City FL 33526, U.S. Website: www.sotopublishingcompany.com. **Contact:** Pedro Soto, publisher (Areas of interest: All genres, fiction and nonfiction, children through adult). Hardcover, trade paperback, & electronic originals. **Publishes 3-5 titles/year. 60% of books from first-time authors. 100% from unagented writers. $250-2,500** Publishes book approximately 6-18 months after acceptance of ms. after acceptance of ms. Accepts simultaneous submissions. Online catalog. Guidelines on website and by e-mail at info@sotopublishingcompany.com.
Nonfiction Subjects include alternative, animals, art, architecture, bio, business/economics, child guidance, children's/juvenile, coffee table book, contemporary, cookbook, cooking, foods, nutrition, crafts, creative nonfiction, education, ethnic, gay, lesbian, government, politics, health, medicine, illustrated, history, hobbies, house, home, scholarly, memoirs, military, war, money, finance, multicultural, nature, environment, new age, photography, real estate, recreation, science, sex education,spirituality, sports, translation, travel, women's issues, women's studies, young adult. Query with SASE. For 1st submission, writer should provide a completed, double-spaced, minimum 12pt font size ms, preferably in digital form (hard copy is acceptable). All figures, images, tables..should be submitted as a separate file from ms (text). Partial mss are acceptable. Provide details concerning how you would best go about promoting your work. Reviews artwork. Writers should send photocopies; digital copies preferred.
Fiction Subjects include adventure, ethnic, experimental, fantasy, gay/lesbian, gothic, horror, humor, juvenile, literary, mainstream/contemporary, military/war, multicultural, mystery, occult, picture books, regional, romance, spiritual, sports, suspense, science fiction, short story collections, young adult. See Nonfiction Overview. Query with SASE. Submit completed ms.
Recent Title(s) *Wormy, the Hairy Caterpillar*, and the Rainbow (children's picture book); *Pumps* (children's picture book); *Mr. Flea's Not So Small Adventure* (children's picture book); *Owen and the Dragon* (chapter book); *Behind Green Glass*, (young adult fantasy novel); *Riddle at the Rodeo* (middle grade mystery).
Tips "Tell us how you will: market your book, get people to talk about it, blog, blog, blog about your book without pushing the sale. You need to let us know what makes your story stand out; what makes it

exceptional. How passionate are you in regards to promoting & marketing your book? If nonfiction, what is your area of expertise? What are your credentials?"

SOUTHERN METHODIST UNIVERSITY PRESS

P.O. Box 750415, Dallas TX 75275-0415. (214)768-1436. Fax: (214)768-1428. Website: www.tamupress.com. **Contact:** Diana Vance. Estab. 1937. Publishes hardcover and trade paperback originals and reprints. **Publishes 10-12 titles/year. 500 queries received/year. 500 mss received/year. 50% of books from first-time authors. 75% from unagented writers. Pays 10% royalty on wholesale price, 10 author's copies. Pays $500 advance.** Publishes book 1 year after acceptance of ms. Accepts simultaneous submissions. Responds in 2 weeks to queries. Responds in 1 month to proposals. Responds in up to 1 year to mss. Book catalog available free. Guidelines available online.

- Known nationally as a publisher of the highest quality scholarly works and books for the "educated general reader," SMU Press publishes in the areas of ethics and human values, literary fiction, medical humanities, performing arts, Southwestern studies, and sport.

Nonfiction Subjects include creative nonfiction, medical ethics/human values. Proposals may be submitted in hard copy or as attachments to e-mails addressed to the appropriate acquisitions editor. To determine who that is, send a brief description of your ms to the acquisitions assistant, Diana Vance. Query with SASE. Submit outline, bio, 3 sample chapters, TOC. Reviews artwork/photos. Send photocopies.

Fiction Subjects include literary, short story collections, novels. We are willing to look at 'serious' or 'literary' fiction. No mass market, science fiction, formula, thriller, romance. Query with SASE.

Recent Title(s) *The Trespasser*, by Edra Ziesk; *The Gateway: Stories*, by T.M. McNally; *Silence Kills: Speaking Out and Saving Lives*, by Lee Gutkind.

STEMMER HOUSE PUBLISHERS

4 White Brook Rd., Gilsum NH 03448. (800)345-6665. Fax: (603)357-2073. E-mail: pbs@pathwaybook.com. Estab. 1975. **Pays advance.** Publishes book 1-2 years after acceptance of ms. Accepts simultaneous submissions. Book catalog for 5½ × 8½ envelope and 2 first-class stamps. Guidelines for #10 SASE.

Imprints The International Design Library®; The NatureEncyclopedia Series.

Nonfiction Subjects include animals, arts, multicultural, nature, environment. Query with SASE.

STRIDER NOLAN PUBLISHING, INC.

1990 Heritage Rd., Huntingdon Valley PA 19006. (215)887-3821. Fax: (215)340-3926. E-mail: infostridernolan@yahoo.com. Website: www.stridernolanmedia.com. Publishes hardcover, trade paperback. **Publishes 5-10 titles/year. 1,000-2,000 queries received/year. 500-1,000 mss received/year. 50% of books from first-time authors. 50% from unagented writers. Pays royalty on retail price.** Accepts simultaneous submissions. Book catalog available online. Guidelines available online.

- "At this time, Strider Nolan is only seeking stories or art for our Visions anthology. Feel free to contact us via e-mail. If you would like to submit a novel to us, we have plenty of material in the pipeline but are always willing to listen. We cannot guarantee anything, so your project would really have to be something special to get us to look at it. We do accept unagented material, although a prior history of published work (even self-published) is preferable. Favored genres include science fiction, horror, and historical fiction (especially westerns or Civil War)."

Recent Title(s) *40 Years*, by Bernd Struben; *The Adelsverein Trilogy*, by Celia B. Hayes.

SWEETGUM PRESS

P.O. Drawer J, 304 Grover, Warrensburg MO 64093. (660)429-5773. Fax: (660)429-3487. E-mail: editors@sweetgumpress.com. Website: www.sweetgumpress.com. **Contact:** R.M. Kinder or Baird Brock, Editors. Estab. 2001. Publishes trade paperback originals. **Publishes 1-2 titles/year. 200 queries received/year. 50 mss received/year. 100% of books from first-time authors. 100% from unagented writers. Pays 10-15% royalty on retail price.** Publishes book 1 year after acceptance of ms. Accepts simultaneous submissions. Responds in 1month to queries. Responds in 3-6 months to manuscripts. Book catalog for #10 SASE. Guidelines available online.

- Sweetgum accepts work only by Midwestern writers. Especially interested in work by Missouri writers.
- "Beginning in January 2009, we will accept only work from Midwestern writers."

Nonfiction Subjects include creative nonfiction, history, memoirs, regional, religion. Check website for current calls for manuscript. Then query, following guidelines. Query with SASE and first 3 pages of manuscript.

Fiction Subjects include experimental, historical, literary, mainstream, contemporary, mystery, regional, short story collections, suspense. Query with SASE and first 3 pages.

Recent Title(s) *Delta Pearls*, by Judith Bader Jones (short fiction); *At the Masthead: Fond Memories of Publishing a Weekly*, by Jim Boan (memoir); *Everyday Wonder*, by James Henry Taylor (short fiction).
Tips "Right now we are only interested in regional writers. Be straightforward about your goals and experience. Good writing is the most persuasive part of a submission, but make reading easy by sending your work in a professional format."

SWITCHGRASS BOOKS

Northern Illinois University Press Switchgrass Books, 2280 Bethany Rd., DeKalb IL 60115. Website: www.switchpress.niu.edu. **Publishes 4 titles/year.** Guidelines are free and available online.
Fiction "We publish only full-length novels set in or about the Midwest. Switchgrass authors must be from the Midwest, current residents of the region, or have significant ties to it. Briefly tell us in your cover letter why yours is an authentic Midwestern voice." Send your complete ms via U.S. mail. E-mail submissions will not be considered. No queries, calls, or e-mails, please. Please include a resume or CV.

N TECHNICAL ANALYSIS OF STOCKS & COMMODITIES

Technical Analysis, Inc. 4757 California Ave. SW, Seattle WA 98116-4499. (206)938-0570. E-mail: editor@traders.com. Website: www.traders.com. **Contact:** Jayanthi Gopalakrishnan, editor. Estab. 1982. Publishes trade paperback originals and reprints. **Makes outright purchase.** Responds in 6 months to queries.
Nonfiction Publishes business and economics books and software about using charts and computers to trade stocks, options, mutual funds or commodity futures. Know the industry and the markets using technical analysis. Query with SASE.
Recent Title(s) *Charting the Stock Market*, by Hutson, Weis, Schroeder (technical analysis).
Tips "Only traders and technical analysts really understand the industry. First consideration for publication will be given to material, regardless of topic, that presents the subject in terms that are easily understandable by the novice trader. One of our prime considerations is to instruct, and we must do so in a manner that the lay person can comprehend. This by no means bars material of a complex nature, but the author must first establish the groundwork."

TEXAS WESTERN PRESS

The University of Texas at El Paso, 500 W. University Ave., El Paso TX 79968-0633. (915)747-5688. Fax: (915)747-7515. E-mail: twp@utep.edu. Website: www.utep.edu/twp. **Contact:** Robert L. Stakes, director. Estab. 1952. Publishes hardcover and paperback originals. **Publishes 1 title/year. Pays standard 10% royalty. Pays advance.** Responds in 2 months to queries. Book catalog available free. Guidelines available online.
Imprints Southwestern Studies.

- "Texas Western Press publishes books on the history and cultures of the American Southwest, particularly historical and biographical works about West Texas, New Mexico, northern Mexico, and the U.S. borderlands. The Press also publishes selected books in the areas of regional art, photography, Native American studies, geography, demographics, border issues, politics, and natural history."

Nonfiction Subjects include education, health, medicine, history, language, literature, nature, environment, regional, science, social sciences. "Historic and cultural accounts of the Southwest (West Texas, New Mexico, northern Mexico). Also art, photographic books, Native American and limited regional fiction reprints. Occasional technical titles. Our *Southwestern Studies* use manuscripts of up to 30,000 words. Our hardback books range from 30,000 words and up. The writer should use good exposition in his work. Most of our work requires documentation. We favor a scholarly, but not overly pedantic, style. We specialize in superior book design." Query with SASE, or submit résumé, 2-3 sample chapters, cover letter, description of ms and special features, TOC, list of competing titles.
Recent Title(s) *Jose Cisneros Immigrant Artist*, by John O. West; *Showtime! From Opera Houses to Picture Palaces in El Paso*, by Cynthia Farah Haines.
Tips "Texas Western Press is interested in books relating to the history of Hispanics in the US. Will experiment with photo-documentary books, and is interested in seeing more contemporary books on border issues. We try to treat our authors professionally, produce handsome, long-lived books and aim for quality, rather than quantity of titles carrying our imprint."

N TO BE READ ALOUD PUBLISHING, INC.

1357 Broadway, Suite 112, New York New York 10018. E-mail: michael@tobereadaloud.org. Website: www.tobereadaloud.org. **Contact:** Michael Powell, president (short stories); Stephen Powell, editor (poetry). Estab. 2006. Publishes trade paperback originals and reprints. **Publishes 4 titles/year. 250**

queries received/year. 200 mss received/year. 90% of books from first-time authors. 90% from unagented writers. Makes outright purchase. Publishes book 4 months after acceptance of ms. Accepts simultaneous submissions. Responds in 3 months to queries. Responds in 3 months to proposals. Responds in 3 months to manuscripts. Guidelines available via e-mail.

Nonfiction Subjects include community, contemporary culture, creative nonfiction, education, ethnic, military, war, multicultural, philosophy, sociology. "Submissions are for the purpose of supporting high school drama coaches and their oral interpretation competitors. Selections should be written to be read aloud. Selections should be less than 3,000 words." Submit complete ms.

Fiction Subjects include adventure, confession, ethnic, gothic, historical, horror, humor, juvenile, literary, multicultural, mystery, poetry, poetry in translation, science fiction, short story collections, sports, suspense, western. Submit complete ms.

Tips "Our audience is high school drama students. Read your selection aloud before submitting."

⊘ TOLLING BELL BOOKS

5555 Oakbrook Parkway, Bldg. 300, Suite 330, Norcross GA 30093. E-mail: info@tollingbellbooks.com. Website: www.tollingbellbooks.com. **Contact:** Lea Thomas, owner (science fiction, mystery, children's). Estab. 2003. Publishes trade paperback originals. **Publishes 2-3 titles/year. 400 queries received/year. 50-100 mss received/year. 50% of books from first-time authors. 90% from unagented writers. Pays royalty. Makes outright purchase.** Publishes book 12-18 months after acceptance of ms. Accepts simultaneous submissions. Responds in 3 months to queries. Responds in 5 months to proposals. Responds in 5 months to manuscripts. Book catalog for $2 (seasonal). Guidelines available online.

Imprints Red Herring Press (mystery); Lil' Bit Books (children's); Andromeda (science fiction).

O→ We specialize in science fiction, mystery, and children's books.

Fiction Subjects include fantasy, juvenile, mystery, picture books, science fiction, young adult. We try to balance our publishing: 1-2 mystery books, 1-2 children's books, and 1 science fiction book. Check our website for what we need and don't need. First query by regular mail.

Recent Title(s) *Obsidian*, (sci-fi); *Runner's High*, (mystery); *Long Lost Teddy*, (children's).

Tips Be sure your work has been proofread (not just spellchecked) for grammar, punctuation, and spelling. It is hard to see the value in a piece of writing if it is full of errors.

TOP PUBLICATIONS, LTD.

3100 Independence Parkway, Suite 311-349, Plano TX 75075. (972)490-9686. Fax: (972)233-0713. E-mail: info@toppub.com. Website: www.toppub.com. **Contact:** Sara Mendoza, Editor. Estab. 1999. Publishes hardcover and paperback originals. **Publishes 4 titles/year. 200 queries received/year. 20 mss received/year. 90% of books from first-time authors. 95% from unagented writers. Pays 15-20% royalty on wholesale price. Pays $250-2,500 advance.** Publishes book 8 months after acceptance of ms. Accepts simultaneous submissions. Acknowledges receipt of queries but only responds if interested in seeing manuscript. Responds in 6 months to manuscripts. Tear sheets available on new titles. Guidelines available online.

Nonfiction "We are primarily a fiction publisher and do not solicit submissions of non-fiction works."

Fiction Subjects include adventure, historical, horror, juvenile, mainstream, contemporary, military, war, mystery, regional, romance, science fiction, short story collections, suspense, young adult. "It is imperative that our authors realize they will be required to promote their book extensively for it to be a success. Unless they are willing to make this commitment, they shouldn't submit to TOP."

Recent Title(s) *Tarizon: The Liberator*, by William Manchee; *Par for the Course*, by Jennifer Vido; *Murder in LA-LA Land*, by the LA Chapter of Sisters in Crime, and *Final Cut*, by Kay Finch.

Tips "Because of the intense competition in this industry, we recommend that our authors write books that appeal to a large mainstream audience to make marketing easier and increase the chances of success. Be patient and don't get your hopes up. We only publish a few titles a year so the odds at getting published at TOP are slim. If we reject your work, don't give it a second thought. It probably doesn't have any reflection on your work. We have to pass on a lot of good material each year simply by the limitations of our time and budget."

TRANSPERSONAL PUBLISHING

P.O. Box 7220, Kill Devil Hills NC 27948. (540)997-0325. E-mail: allenchips@holistictree.com. Website: www.transpersonalpublishing.com. **Contact:** Dr. Allen Chips, acquisitions/publishing director (holistic health texts and metaphysical/near death research). Estab. 1999. Publishes hardcover originals and reprints, trade paperback originals and reprints, electronic originals and reprints, and mass market paperback reprints. **Publishes 3-7 titles/year. 35 queries received/year. 50% of books from first-time authors. 95% from unagented writers. Pays 10-15% royalty.** Publishes book 9-12 months after acceptance of ms. Accepts simultaneous submissions. Responds in 1 month to queries. Responds in 2 months to proposals. Responds in 3 months to manuscripts. Book catalog available online. Guidelines available online.

Nonfiction Subjects include education, health, holistic, alternative medicine, transpersonal psychology, metaphysical research. "We are looking for textbooks, and self-help, how-to books with a holistic health or transpersonal therapy orientation." Query, then submit TOC with 2 sample chapters.

Tips "Audience is people desiring to learn about mind-body-spirit oriented therapies/practices that lead to healing and/or enlightenment. The best authors are engaged in regular travel and seminars/workshops, demonstrating dedication, self-motivation, and a people orientation. Do not phone the company with book ideas; if interested, the publisher will e-mail, then phone you."

⊘ UMI (URBAN MINISTRIES, INC.)

1551 Regency Court, Calumet City IL 60409. Fax: (708)868-6759. Website: www.urbanministries.com. Estab. 1970. Publishes trade paperback originals and reprints. **Publishes 2-3 titles/year.**

- *We no longer accept unsolicited manuscripts.*

Nonfiction Subjects include education, religious/Christian, religion, Christian, spirituality, Christian, Christian living, Christian doctrine, theology. The books we publish are generally those we have a specific need for (i.e., Vacation Bible School curriculum topics); to complement an existing resource or product line; or those with a potential to develop into a curriculum. Query with SASE. Submit proposal package, outline, 2-3 sample chapters, letter why UMI should publish the book and why the book will sell.

Recent Title(s) *Family Ties: Restoring Unity in the African American Family*; *Strategies for Educating African American Children*; *Strategies for Educating African American Adults*.

Tips Our audience is comprised of Christians, mostly African Americans.

N THE UNIVERSITY OF AKRON PRESS

Bierce Library 374B, Akron OH 44325-1703. (330)972-5342. Fax: (330)972-8364. E-mail: uapress@uakron.edu. Website: www.uakron.edu/uapress. **Contact:** Thomas Bacher, Director and Acquisitions. Estab. 1988. Publishes hardcover and paperback originals and reissues. **Publishes 10-12 titles/year. 200-300 queries received/year. 50-75 mss received/year. 40% of books from first-time authors. 80% from unagented writers. Pays 7-15% royalty.** Publishes book 9-12 months after acceptance of ms. Accepts simultaneous submissions. Responds in 2 weeks to queries and proposals. Responds in 3-4 months to solicited manuscripts. Query prior to submitting. Book catalog available free. Guidelines available online.

O⊸ "The University of Akron Press is the publishing arm of The University of Akron and is dedicated to the dissemination of scholarly, professional, and regional books and other content."

Nonfiction Subjects include Applied politics, early American literature, emerging technologies, history of psychology, history of technology, interdisciplinary studies, Northeast Ohio history and culture, Ohio politics, poetics. Query by e-mail. Mss cannot be returned unless SASE is included.

Recent Title(s) *Sketches at Home and Abroad: A Critical Edition of Selections from the Writings of Nathaniel Parker Willis*, edited by Jon Miller; *Columnist's View of Capitol Square: Ohio Politics and Government, 1969-2005*, by Lee Leonard; *Rubber Mirror: Reflections of the Rubber Division's First 100 Years*, by Henry Inman; *Requiem for the Orchard*, by Oliver De La Paz.

UNTAPPED TALENT LLC

P.O. Box 396, Hershey PA 17033-0396. (717)707-0720. E-mail: rena@unt2.com. Website: www.unt2.com. **Contact:** Rena Wilson Fox, (Areas of interest: nonfiction, children's lit, fiction, middle grade). hardcover, trade & mass market paperbacks, & electronic originals. **Publishes 2-10 titles/year. 2,000 queries, 400 mss 80% of books from first-time authors. 80% from unagented writers.** Publishes book 6-12 months, depending on the choice for timing the release. after acceptance of ms. Accepts simultaneous submissions. Catalog and guidelines available online.

O⊸ As a new publishing company, we only have published four titles, not enough for a catalog. Please feel free to view the books at our website.

Nonfiction Subjects include Americana, art, architecture, child guidance, parenting, computers, contemporary culture, cooking, foods, health, medicine, history, memoirs, music, dance, photography, psychology, religion, travel, women's issues/studies, world affairs, young adult. Submit by e-mail: proposal package, outline (if appropriate), 4 sample chapters, & synopsis. Reviews artwork/photos. Send photocopies, computer file.

Fiction Subjects include historical, humor, juvenile, literary, mainstream, contemporary, military, war, multicultural, mystery, regional, religious, romance, suspense, young adult. "We have a strong interest in historical fiction. We are looking for books that are current and fully formulated, modern interpretations—even if the story takes place in the past." Submit proposal package with synopsis, 4 sample chapters, and any background information pertinent to the story.

Recent Title(s) *The Ghost at Old Oak Way*, by Laurie Cameron and Laura Meagher; *Study Tpsi 101: 101 Tips for Studying Success*, by Joshua Shifrin; *The Pro-Child Way: Parenting With an Ex*, by Ellen Kellner.

Tips Follow website instruction, make query brief; if 4 chapters are not many pages, add more; submit to acquisitions editor only.

UPPER ACCESS, INC.

87 Upper Access Rd., Hinesburg VT 05461. (802)482-2988. Fax: (802)304-1005. E-mail: info@upperaccess.com. Website: www.upperaccess.com. **Contact:** Steve Carlson, Publisher. Estab. 1986. Publishes hardcover and trade paperback originals; hardcover and trade paperback reprints. **Publishes 2-3 titles/year. 200 queries received/year. 40 mss received/year. 50% of books from first-time authors. 80% from unagented writers. Pays 10-20% royalty on wholesale price. $200-500 (Advances are tokens of our good faith; author earnings are from royalties a book sells.)** Publishes book 8 months after acceptance of ms. Accepts simultaneous submissions. Responds in 1 month to queries/manuscripts. Catalog online at website. Guidelines available online.

O━ Publishes nonfiction to improve the quality of life.

Nonfiction Subjects include alternative lifestyles, child guidance, community/public affairs, contemporary culture, cooking, foods, nutrition, creative nonfiction, education, ethnic, gardening, government, politics/politics, health, medicine, history, humor, humanities, language, literature, multicultural, nature, environment, philosophy, psychology, science, sex, social sciences, sociology, women's issues, women's studies, world affairs, (gay, lesbian possible). "We are open to considering almost any nonfiction topic that has some potential for national general trade sales." Query with SASE. "We strongly prefer an initial e-mail describing your proposed title. No attachments please. We will look at paper mail if there is no other way, but e-mail will be reviewed much more quickly and thoroughly." Will request artwork, etc. if and when appropriate. "Discuss this with us in your initial e-mail query."

Fiction "Note: Please do not submit fiction, even if it relates to nonfiction subjects. We cannot take novels or poetry of any kind at this time."

Recent Title(s) *True North: Journeys Into the Great Northern Ocean*, by Myron Arms (environment); *About the House with Henri de Marne*, by Henri de Marne (how-to); *Why the Wind Blows: A history of weather and global warming*, by Matthys Levy (environment, science); *Servants of the Fish*, by Myron Arms (environment, history).

Tips "We target intelligent adults willing to challenge the status quo, who are interested in more self-sufficiency with respect for the environment. Most of our books are either unique subjects or unique or different ways of looking at major issues or basic education on subjects that are not well understood by most of the general public. We make a long-term commitment to each book that we publish, trying to find its market as long as possible."

N VANHOOK HOUSE

925 Orchard St., Charleston WV 25302. E-mail: editor@vanhookhouse.com. Website: www.vanhookhouse.com. **Contact:** Jim Whyte, acquisitions, all fiction/true crime/military/war. hardcover and trade paperback originals; trade paperback reprints. **Publishes 6 titles/year. Receives 20 mss/year. 100% of books from first-time authors. 100% from unagented writers. Advance negotiable.** Publishes book 6 months after acceptance of ms. Book catalog and guidelines free on request and available online at website.

- "We employ the expertise of individuals qualified to review works falling within their field of study. Be sure of all sources and facts, as VanHook House *will* confirm any and all information. All editing is done in a way to ensure the author's voice remains unchanged."

O━ "VanHook House is a small press focused on the talents of new, unpublished authors. We are looking for works of fiction and non-fiction to add to our catalog. No erotica or sci-fi, please. Query via e-mail. Queries accepted ONLY during submissions periods."

Nonfiction Subjects include agriculture, Americana, animals, anthropology, architecture, art, automotive, business, career guidance, child guidance, communications, community, computers, contemporary culture, cooking, counseling, crafts, creative nonfiction, dance, education, electronics, entertainment, environment, ethnic, foods, games, gardening, government, health, history, house and home, humanities, labor, language, law, literature, marine subjects, medicine, memoirs, military, multicultural, music, nature, New Age, nutrition, philosophy, photography, politics, psychology, public affairs, real estate, recreation, regional, religion, science, sex, social sciences, sociology, software, spirituality, sports, transportation, travel, women's issues/studies, war, world affairs. Reviews artwork.

Recent Title(s) *Under a Pirate's Flag*, by J. Taylor Anderson (trade paperback fiction); *Heart of the City: A Collection of Raw Verses*, by George M. Gentry (paperback poetry).

Tips "Visit our website."

VITESSE PRESS

PMB 367, 45 State St., Montpelier VT 05601-2100. (802)229-4243. Fax: (802)229-6939. E-mail: dick@vitessepress.com. Website: www.vitessepress.com. **Contact:** Richard H. Mansfield, editor. Estab. 1985. Publishes trade paperback originals. **Publishes 2 titles/year.** Responds in 1 month to queries.

Nonfiction Subjects include health, medicine, regional, mountain biking guides, sports. "We are looking for new projects, particularly regional health/fitness/recreation projects." Query by e-mail.

Recent Title(s) *Cycling Along the Canals of New York*, by Louis Rossi; *Fit Family; Fit & Pregnant.*

WASHINGTON STATE UNIVERSITY PRESS

P.O. Box 645910, Pullman WA 99164-5910. (800)354-7360. Fax: (509)335-8568. E-mail: wsupress@wsu.edu. Website: www.wsupress.wsu.edu. **Contact:** Glen Lindeman, editor-in-chief. Estab. 1928. Publishes hardcover originals, trade paperback originals and reprints. **Publishes 4-6 titles/year. 40% of books from first-time authors. 95% from unagented writers. Pays 5% royalty graduated according to sales** Publishes book 18 months after acceptance of ms. Responds in 4 months to queries. Guidelines available online.

- WSU Press publishes books on the history, pre-history, culture, and politics of the West, particularly the Pacific Northwest.

Nonfiction Subjects include cooking, foods, nutrition, (regional), government, politics, history, nature, environment, regional, (cultural studies), essays. "We seek manuscripts that focus on the Pacific Northwest as a region. No poetry, novels, literary criticism, how-to books. We welcome innovative and thought-provoking titles in a wide diversity of genres, from cultural studies to history, archaeology, and political science." Submit outline, sample chapters. Reviews artwork/photos.

Recent Title(s) *Finding Chief Kamiakin: The Life and Legacy of a Northwest Patriot*; *Crossroads and Connections: Central Washington University Art Alumni Exhibition; Making the Grade: Plucky Schoolmarms of Kittitas Country.*

Tips "We have developed our marketing in the direction of regional and local history and have attempted to use this as the base upon which to expand our publishing program. In regional history, the secret is to write a good narrative—a good story—that is substantiated factually. It should be told in an imaginative, clever way. Have visuals (photos, maps, etc.) available to help the reader envision what has happened. Tell the regional history story in a way that ties it to larger, national, and even international events. Weave it into the large pattern of history."

WAYFINDER PRESS

P.O. Box 217, Ridgway CO 81432-0217. (970)626-5452. Fax: (970)626-4233. E-mail: wayfinderpress@ouraynet.com. Website: http://wayfinderpress.us. **Contact:** Marcus E. Wilson, publisher. Estab. 1990. Publishes trade paperback originals. **Publishes 2 titles/year. Pays 8-10% royalty on retail price.** Responds in 1 month to queries. Catalog online at website.

- Wayfinder Press prints, designs, and publishes books reflecting Southwestern Colorado, featuring: history, biking, hiking, touring, fly fishing, and cross-country skiing in the mountain towns of Telluride, Ouray, Ridgway, Silverton, Durango, Crested Butte, Gunnison and Grand Junction.

Nonfiction Subjects include Americana, government, politics, history, nature, environment, photography, recreation, regional, travel. We are looking for books on southwestern Colorado: history, nature, recreation, photo, and travel. No books on subjects outside our geographical area of specialization. Query with SASE. Submit outline, sample chapters. Reviews artwork/photos.

Recent Title(s) *Ouray Chief of the Utes,* by P. David Smith; *Telluride Story, A Tale of Two Towns,* by David Lavender; *30 Things to Do in Durango, Colorado; 30 Things to Do in Telluride, Colorado,* by Mark D. Williams, Amy Becker Williams.

Tips "Writers have the best chance selling us tourist-oriented books. Our audience is the local population and tourists."

WESTERN PSYCHOLOGICAL SERVICES

12031 Wilshire Blvd., Los Angeles CA 90025. (310)478-2061. Fax: (310)478-7838. E-mail: bthomas@wpspublish.com. Website: www.wpspublish.com. **Contact:** Brian Thomas, marketing manager. Estab. 1948. Publishes psychological and educational assessments and some trade paperback originals.

Publishes 2 titles/year. 60 queries received/year. 30 mss received/year. 90% of books from first-time authors. 95% from unagented writers. Pays 5-10% royalty on wholesale price. Accepts simultaneous submissions. Responds in 2 months to queries. Book catalog available free. Guidelines available online.

O→ "Western Psychological Services publishes psychological and educational assessments that practitioners trust. Our products allow helping professionals to accurately screen, diagnose, and treat people in need. WPS publishes practical books and games used by therapists, counselors, social workers, and others in the helping professionals who work with children and adults."

Nonfiction Subjects include child guidance, psychology, autism, sensory processing disorders. "We publish children's books dealing with feelings, anger, social skills, autism, family problems." Submit complete ms. Reviews artwork/photos. Send photocopies.

Fiction Children's books dealing with feelings, anger, social skills, autism, family problems, etc. Submit complete ms.

Recent Title(s) *Sensory Integration and the Child*, by A. Jean Ayres, PhD; *To Be Me*, by Rebecca Etlinger.

WINDSWEPT HOUSE PUBLISHERS

P.O. Box 159, Mount Desert ME 04660-0159. (207)244-5027. Fax: (207)244-3369. E-mail: windswt@acadia.net. Website: http://www.musarts.net/windswept/. **Contact:** Mavis Weinberger, owner. Publishes hardcover and trade paperback originals. **Publishes 4 titles/year. Pays up to 10% royalty.** Book catalog available online. Guidelines for #10 SASE.

Nonfiction Subjects include animals, history, memoirs, nature, environment, regional. Unsolicited mss returned unopened. Reviews artwork/photos. Send photocopies.

Recent Title(s) *In the Company of Trees, Orbiting the Heart of the Sacred*, by Shamms Mortier; *Canned Plums and Other Vicissitudes of Life*, by Jane Weinberger; *Interview with Mrs. Berlinski*, by Lauren Walden Rabb.

WOLF DEN BOOKS

5794 S.W. 40th St., #221, Miami FL 33155. (877)667-9737. E-mail: info@wolfdenbooks.com. Website: www.wolfdenbooks.com. **Contact:** Gail Shivel. Estab. 2000. Publishes hardcover, trade paperback and electronic originals and reprints. **Publishes 2 titles/year. 40 queries received/year. 10 mss received/year. 0% of books from first-time authors. 100% from unagented writers. Pays 7½% royalty on retail price.** Publishes book 12 months after acceptance of ms. Accepts simultaneous submissions. Responds in 3 months/queries, 6 months/proposals, 8 months/mss. Book catalog available online. Guidelines available via e-mail.

- Do not send postage; mss are not returned.

Nonfiction Subjects include history, humanities, language, literature, literary criticism, philosophy. Query with SASE; submit proposal package, including outline; submit complete ms. Does not review artwork.

Recent Title(s) *Robert Benchley's Wayward Press*, by Robert Benchley (press criticism); *The Columbiad*, by Joel Barlow (American poetry); *Lives of the Most Eminent English Poets*, by Samuel Johnson.

WOODBINE HOUSE

6510 Bells Mill Rd., Bethesda MD 20817. (301)897-3570. Fax: (301)897-5838. E-mail: ngpaul@woodbinehouse.com. Website: www.woodbinehouse.com. **Contact:** Nancy Gray Paul, acquisitions editor. Estab. 1985. Publishes trade paperback originals. **Publishes 10 titles/year. 15% of books from first-time authors. 90% from unagented writers. Pays 10-12% royalty.** Publishes book 18 months after acceptance of ms. Accepts simultaneous submissions. Responds in 3 months to queries. Book catalog for 6x9 SAE with 3 first-class stamps. Guidelines available online.

O→ Woodbine House publishes books for or about individuals with disabilities to help those individuals and their families live fulfilling and satisfying lives in their homes, schools, and communities.

Nonfiction Publishes books for and about children with disabilities. Subjects include specific issues related to a given disability (e.g., communication skills, social sciences skills, feeding issues) and practical guides to issues of concern to parents of children with disabilities (e.g., special education, sibling issues). Submit outline, 3 sample chapters. Reviews artwork/photos.

Fiction Subjects include picture books, children's. Receptive to stories re: developmental and intellectual disabilities, e.g., autism and cerebral palsy. Submit complete ms with SASE.

Recent Title(s) *Self-Help Skills for People With Autism: A Systematic Teaching Approach*, by Stephen R. Anderson, et al.; *Teaching Children With Down Syndrome About Their Bodies, Boundaries, and Sexuality*, by Terri Couwenhoven.

Tips "Do not send us a proposal on the basis of this description. Examine our catalog or website and a couple of our books to make sure you are on the right track. Put some thought into how your book could be marketed (aside from in bookstores). Keep cover letters concise and to the point; if it's a subject that interests us, we'll ask to see more."

WORLD LEISURE

P.O. Box 160, Hampstead NH 03841. (617)569-1966. E-mail: leocha@worldleisure.com. Website: www.worldleisure.com. **Contact:** Charles Leocha, president. Estab. 1977. Publishes trade paperback originals. **Publishes 2-3 titles/year. Pays royalty. Makes outright purchase.** Accepts simultaneous submissions. Responds in 2 months to queries. Book catalog and ms guidelines online.

O→ World Leisure specializes in sports travel books, activity guidebooks, and self-help titles.

Nonfiction Subjects include recreation, sports, skiing/snowboarding, travel. "We will be publishing annual updates to *Ski Snowboard Europe* and *Ski Snowboard America & Canada*. Writers planning any winter resort stories should contact us for possible add-on assignments at areas not covered by our staff." Submit outline, intro sample chapters, annotated TOC, SASE.

Recent Title(s) *Ski Snowboard America*, by Charles Leocha; *Ski Snowboard Europe*, by Charles Leocha.

N YOUR CULTURE GIFTS

P.O. Box 1245, Ellicott City MD 21041, U.S. E-mail: info@yourculturegifts.com. Website: www.yourculturegifts.com. **Contact:** Frank Sauri, Manager. Trade paperback originals. **Publishes 5 titles/year.** Publishes book 18 months after acceptance of ms. Accepts simultaneous submissions. Catalog and guidelines available online.

O→ Limited to cultural, realistic, historical, creative nonfiction, with language and food components.

Nonfiction Subjects include children's/juvenile, cooking, foods, nutrition, creative nonfiction, history, multicultural, social sciences sciences, young adult. Query with SASE. Reviews artwork/photos. E-mail samples after request for ms.

Fiction Subjects include ethnic, historical, juvenile, multicultural, young adult. Query with SASE.

Recent Title(s) *Gift of Yucatan: A Short History* (middle grade history) and *Gift of Yucatan: Maria's Rebellion* (middle grade historical fiction), by Trudy Sauri

Tips "Our audience is middle grade students, ESL students, unmotivated young adult readers, families. Be committed to a long-term project to share cultural information."

MARKETS

Consumer Magazines

Selling your writing to consumer magazines is as much an exercise of your marketing skills as it is of your writing abilities. Editors of consumer magazines are looking not only for good writing, but for good writing which communicates pertinent information to a specific audience—their readers.

Approaching the consumer magazine market

Marketing skills will help you successfully discern a magazine's editorial slant, and write queries and articles that prove your knowledge of the magazine's readership. You can gather clues about a magazine's readership—and establish your credibility with the magazine's editor—in a number of ways:

- **Read** the magazine's listing in *Writer's Market*.
- **Study** a magazine's writer's guidelines.
- **Check** a magazine's website.
- **Read** several current issues of the target magazine.
- **Talk** to an editor by phone.

Writers who can correctly and consistently discern a publication's audience and deliver stories that speak to that target readership will win out every time over writers who submit haphazardly.

What editors want

In nonfiction, editors continue to look for short feature articles covering specialized topics. Editors want crisp writing and expertise. If you are not an expert in the area about which you are writing, make yourself one through research. Always query before sending your manuscript. Don't e-mail or fax a query to an editor unless the listing mentions it is acceptable to do so.

Fiction editors prefer to receive complete manuscripts. Writers must keep in mind that marketing fiction is competitive, and editors receive far more material than they can publish. For this reason, they often do not respond to submissions unless they are interested in using the story. More comprehensive information on fiction markets can be found in *Novel & Short Story Writer's Market* (Writer's Digest Books).

Payment

Most magazines listed here have indicated pay rates; some give very specific payment-per-word rates, while others state a range. **(Note: All of the magazines listed in the Consumer Magazines section are paying markets. However, some of the magazines are not identified by payment icons ($-$$$$) because the magazines preferred not to disclose specific payment information.)** Any agreement you come to with a magazine, whether verbal or written, should specify the payment you are to receive and when you are to receive it. Some magazines pay writers only after the piece in question has been published (on publication). Others pay as soon as they have accepted a piece and are sure they are going to use it (on acceptance).

So what is a good pay rate? There are no standards; the principle of supply and demand operates at full throttle in the business of writing and publishing. As long as there are more writers than opportunities for publication, wages for freelancers will never skyrocket. Rates vary widely from one market to the next. Smaller circulation magazines and some departments of the larger magazines will pay a lower rate.

Editors know the listings in *Writer's Market* are read and used by writers with a wide range of experience, from those unpublished writers just starting out, to those with a successful, profitable freelance career. As a result, many magazines publicly report pay rates in the lower end of their actual pay ranges. Experienced writers will be able to successfully negotiate higher pay rates for their material. Newer writers should be encouraged that as their reputation grows (along with their clip file), they will be able to command higher rates. The article "How Much Should I Charge?" on page 67, gives you an idea of pay ranges for different freelance jobs, including those directly associated with magazines.

INFORMATION AT-A-GLANCE

In the Consumer Magazines section, icons identify comparative payment rates (**$-$$$$**); new listings (**N**); and magazines that do not accept unsolicited manuscripts (⊘). Different sections of *Writer's Market* include other symbols; check the inside back cover for an explanation of all the symbols used throughout the book.

Important information is highlighted in boldface—the "quick facts" you won't find in any other market book, but should know before you submit your work. The word **Contact** identifies the appropriate person to query at each magazine. We also highlight what percentage of the magazine is freelance written; how many manuscripts a magazine buys per year of nonfiction, fiction, poetry, and fillers; and respective pay rates in each category.

Animal

$$ AKC GAZETTE

American Kennel Club, Website: www.akc.org/pubs/index.cfm. **85% freelance written**. Monthly magazine. Geared to interests of fanciers of purebred dogs as opposed to commercial interests or pet owners. We require solid expertise from our contributors—we are *not* a pet magazine. Estab. 1889. Circ. 60,000. Byline given. Pays on publication. Offers 10% kill fee. Publishes ms an average of 6 months after acceptance. Buys first North American serial rights, electronic rights, international rights. Submit seasonal material 6 months in advance. Accepts queries by mail. Responds in 2 months to queries. Guidelines for #10 SASE.

Nonfiction Needs general interest, how-to, humor, interview, photo feature, travel, dog art, training and canine performance sports. No poetry, tributes to individual dogs, or fiction. **Buys 30-40 mss/year.** Length: 1,000-3,000 words. **Pays $300-500.**

Photos Photo contest guidelines for #10 SASE. State availability. Captions, identification of subjects, model releases required. Reviews color transparencies, prints. Pays $50-200/photo Buys one time rights.

Fiction Annual short fiction contest only. Guidelines for #10 SASE.

Tips Contributors should be involved in the dog fancy or be an expert in the area they write about (veterinary, showing, field trialing, obedience training, dogs in legislation, dog art or history or literature). All submissions are welcome but author must be a credible expert or be able to interview and quote the experts. Veterinary articles must be written by or with veterinarians. Humorous features or personal experiences relative to purebred dogs should have broader applications. For features, know the subject thoroughly and be conversant with jargon peculiar to the sport of dogs.

$$ THE AMERICAN QUARTER HORSE JOURNAL

AQHA, 1600 Quarter Horse Dr., Amarillo TX 79104. (806)358-3702. Fax: (806)349-6400. E-mail: jbcampbell@aqha.org. Website: www.aqha.com. Editor-in-Chief: Jim Jennings. **Contact:** Jim Bret Campbell, editor. **30% freelance written. Prefers to work with published/established writers**. Monthly publication covering American Quarter Horses/horse activities/western lifestyle. "Covers the American Quarter Horse breed and more than 30 disciplines in which Quarter Horses compete. Business stories, lifestyles stories, how-to stories and others related to the breed and horse activities." Estab. 1948. Circ. 60,000. Byline given. Pays on acceptance. Offers 60% kill fee. Publishes ms an average of 3 months after acceptance. Buys first North American serial rights, buys electronic rights. Editorial lead time 3 months. Submit seasonal material 3 months in advance. Accepts queries by mail, e-mail. Accepts previously published material. Accepts simultaneous submissions. Responds in 1 week to queries. Responds in 1 month to mss. Sample copy free. Guidelines free.

Nonfiction Needs book excerpts, essays, general interest, historical, how-to, fitting, grooming, showing, or anything that relates to owning, showing, or breeding, humor, inspirational, interview, feature-type stories, travel., "Must be about established horses or people who have made a contribution to the business, new prod, opinion, personal exp, photo, technical, equine updates, new surgery procedures, etc." Annual stallion issue dedicated to the breeding of horses. **Buys 10 mss/year.** Query with published clips. Length: 700-3,000 words. **Pays $250-1,500 for assigned articles. Pays $250-1,500 for unsolicited articles.**

Photos State availability. Captions, identification of subjects required. Reviews GIF/JPEG files. Buys all rights.

Columns/Departments Quarter's Worth (Industry news); Horse Health (health items), 750 words. 6 mss/yr. Query with published clips. **Pays $100-$400.**

Tips "Writers must have a knowledge of the horse business."

$$ APPALOOSA JOURNAL

Appaloosa Horse Club, 2720 West Pullman Rd., Moscow ID 83843. (208)882-5578. Fax: (208)882-8150. E-mail: drice@appaloosajournal.com. Website: www.appaloosajournal.com. **40% freelance written**. Monthly magazine covering Appaloosa horses. Estab. 1946. Circ. 25,000. Byline given. Pays on publication. Publishes ms an average of 3 months after acceptance. Buys first North American serial rights, electronic rights. Responds in 1 month to queries. Responds in 2 months to mss. Sample copy free. Guidelines available online.

- *Appaloosa Journal* no longer accepts material for columns.

Nonfiction Needs historical, interview, photo feature. **Buys 15-20 mss/year.** Send complete ms. Length: 800-1,800 words. **Pays $200-400.**

Photos Send photos. Captions, identification of subjects required. Payment varies.

Tips Articles by writers with horse knowledge, news sense, and photography skills are in great demand. If it's a strong article about an Appaloosa, the writer has a pretty good chance of publication. A good understanding of the breed and the industry, breeders, and owners is helpful. Make sure there's some substance and a unique twist.

$ $ AQUARIUM FISH INTERNATIONAL

Fishkeeping—the Art and the Science, Bowtie, Inc., P.O. Box 6050, Mission Viejo CA 92690. Fax: (949)855-3045. E-mail: aquariumfish@bowtieinc.com. Website: www.aquariumfish.com. **Contact:** Patricia Knight, managing editor. **90% freelance written**. Monthly magazine covering fish and other aquatic pets. "Our focus is on beginning and intermediate fish keeping; we also run one advanced saltwater article per issue. Most of our articles concentrate on general fish and aquarium care, but we will also consider other types of articles that may be helpful to those in the fishkeeping hobby. Freshwater and saltwater tanks, and ponds are covered." Estab. 1988. Byline given. Pays on publication. Buys first North American serial rights, buys electronic rights. Accepts queries by mail, e-mail, fax. Responds in 1 month to queries. Responds in 6 months to mss. Guidelines for #10 SASE.

Nonfiction Needs general interest, species profiles, natural history with home care info, new product, press releases only for Product Showcase section, photo feature, caring for fish in aquariums. "We do have 1 annual; freelancers should query. No fiction, anthropomorphism, articles on sport fishing, or animals that cannot be kept as pets (i.e., whales, dolphins, manatees, etc.)." **Buys 60 mss/year.** Send complete ms. Length: 1,500-2,000 words. **Pays 15¢/word.**

Photos Send for digital image requirements. State availability. Identification of subjects required. Reviews 35mm transparencies, 4 × 5 prints. Offers $15-200/photo. Buys first North American serial rights.

Tips "Take a look at our guidelines before submitting. Writers are not required to provide photos for submitted articles, but we do encourage it, if possible. It helps if writers are involved in fish keeping themselves. Our writers tend to be experienced fish keepers, detailed researchers, and some scientists."

ARABIAN STUDS & STALLIONS ANNUAL

Vink Publishing, Arabian Studs & Stallions Annual, P.O. Box 8369, Woolloongabba QLD 4102 Australia. (61)(7)3334-8000. Fax: (61)(7)3391-5118. E-mail: sharon@vinkpub.com; montbrae@bigpond.net.au. Website: www.vinkpub.com.au. "Annual magazine covering International Arabian horses and people connected with the Arabian horse from Australia and around the world."

- Query before submitting.

THE AUSTRALIAN ARABIAN HORSE NEWS

Vink Publishing, P.O. Box 8369, Woolloongabba QLD 4102 Australia. (61)(7)3334-8000. Fax: (61)(7)3391-5118. E-mail: sharon@vinkpub.com. Website: www.arabianhorse.com.au. **Contact:** Sharon Meyers, ed. Quarterly magazine covering Australian Arabian horses.

- Query before submitting.

$ BIRDING WORLD

Sea Lawn, Coast Road, Cley next the Sea, Holt Norfolk NR25 7RZ United Kingdom. (44)(126)374-0913. E-mail: steve@birdingworld.co.uk. Website: www.birdingworld.co.uk. "Monthly magazine publishing notes about birds and birdwatching. The emphasis is on rarer British and Western Palearctic birds with topical interest." Estab. 1988. No kill fee. Accepts queries by mail, e-mail. Sample copy for £4.50. Guidelines by e-mail.

Nonfiction Pays £2-4/100 words for unsolicited articles.

Photos Reviews digital images, drawings, maps, graphs, paintings. Pays £10-30/color photos; £5-25/b&w photos.

$ $ CAT FANCY

Cat Fancy Query, P.O. Box 6050, Mission Viejo CA 92690. E-mail: query@catfancy.com. Website: www.catfancy.com. **90% freelance written**. Monthly magazine covering all aspects of responsible cat ownership. Estab. 1965. Pays on publication. Buys first North American serial rights. Editorial lead time 6 months. Responds in 3 months to queries. Guidelines available online.

- "*Cat Fancy* does not accept unsolicited mss and only accepts queries from January-May. Queries sent after May will be returned or discarded. Show us how you can contribute something new and unique. No phone queries."

Nonfiction Engaging presentation of expert, up-to-date information. Must be cat oriented. Writing should not be gender specific. Needs how-to, humor, photo feature, travel, behavior, health, lifestyle, cat culture, entertainment. We no longer publish any fiction or poetry. **Buys 70 mss/year.** Query with published clips. Length: 300-1,000 words. **Pays $50-450.**

Photos "Seeking photos of happy, healthy, well-groomed cats and kittens in indoor settings." Captions, identification of subjects, model releases required. Negotiates payment individually. Buys one-time rights.

Tips "Please read recent issues to become acquainted with our style and content."

$$ THE CHRONICLE OF THE HORSE

P.O. Box 46, Middleburg VA 20118-0046. (540)687-6341. Fax: (540)687-3937. E-mail: staff@chronofhorse.com. Website: www.chronofhorse.com. **80% freelance written**. Weekly magazine covering horses. "We cover English riding sports, including horse showing, grand prix jumping competitions, steeplechase racing, foxhunting, dressage, endurance riding, handicapped riding, and combined training. We are the official publication for the national governing bodies of many of the above sports. We feature news, how-to articles on equitation and horse care and interviews with leaders in the various fields." Estab. 1937. Circ. 18,000. Byline given. Pays for features on acceptance; news and other items on publication. Publishes ms an average of 4 months after acceptance. Buys first North American serial rights. Makes work-for-hire assignments. Submit seasonal material 3 months in advance. Accepts queries by mail, e-mail. Responds in 5-6 weeks to queries. Sample copy for $2 and 9 × 12 SAE. Guidelines available online.

Nonfiction Needs general interest, historical, history of breeds, use of horses in other countries and times, art, etc., how-to, trailer, train, design a course, save money, etc., humor, centered on living with horses or horse people, interview, of nationally known horsemen or the very unusual, technical, horse care, articles on feeding, injuries, care of foals, shoeing, etc. Special issues: Steeplechase Racing (January); American Horse in Sport and Grand Prix Jumping (February); Horse Show (March); Intercollegiate (April); Kentucky 4-Star Preview (April); Junior and Pony (April); Dressage (June); Horse Care (July); Combined Training (August); Hunt Roster (September); Amateur (November); Stallion (December). No poetry, Q&A interviews, clinic reports, Western riding articles, personal experience or wild horses. **Buys 300 mss/year.** Send complete ms. 6-7 pages. **Pays $150-250.**

Photos State availability. Identification of subjects required. Reviews e-mailed image, prints or color slides; accepts color for color reproduction. Pays $25-50. Buys one time rights.

Columns/Departments Dressage, Combined Training, Horse Show, Horse Care, Racing over Fences, Young Entry (about young riders, geared for youth), Horses and Humanities, Hunting, Vaulting, Handicapped Riding, Trail Riding, 1,000-1,225 words; News of major competitions (clear assignment with us first), 1,500 words. Query with or without published clips or send complete ms. **Pays $25-200.**

Tips Get our guidelines. Our readers are sophisticated, competitive horsemen. Articles need to go beyond common knowledge. Freelancers often attempt too broad or too basic a subject. We welcome well-written news stories on major events, but clear the assignment with us.

$ COONHOUND BLOODLINES

The Complete Magazine for the Houndsman and Coon Hunter, United Kennel Club, Inc., 100 E. Kilgore Rd., Kalamazoo MI 49002-5584. (269)343-9020. Fax: (269)343-7037. Website: www.ukcdogs.com. **40% freelance written**. Monthly magazine covering all aspects of the 6 Coonhound dog breeds. Writers must retain the 'slang' particular to dog people and to our readers—many of whom are from the South. Estab. 1925. Circ. 16,000. Byline given. Pays on publication. No kill fee. Publishes ms an average of 6 months after acceptance. Buys first North American serial rights. Makes work-for-hire assignments. Editorial lead time 6 months. Submit seasonal material 6 months in advance. Accepts queries by mail, e-mail, fax, phone. Accepts simultaneous submissions. Responds in 6 weeks to queries. Sample copy for $4.50.

Nonfiction Needs general interest, historical, humor, interview, new product, personal experience, photo feature, breed-specific. Six of our 12 issues are each devoted to a specific breed of Coonhound. Special Issues: Treeing Walker (February); English (July); Black & Tan (April); Bluetick (May); Redbone (June); Plott Hound (August), 1,000-3,000 words and photos. **Buys 12-36 mss/year.** Query. Length: 1,000-5,000 words. **Pays variable amount.**

Photos State availability. Captions, identification of subjects required. Reviews contact sheets. Negotiates payment individually. Buys one time rights.

Fiction Must be about the Coonhound breeds or hunting with hounds. Needs adventure, historical, humorous, mystery. **Buys 3-6 mss/year.** Query. Length: 1,000-3,000 words. **Pay varies.**

Tips Hunting with hounds is a two-century old American tradition and an important part of the American heritage, especially east of the Mississippi. It covers a lifestyle as well as a wonderful segment of the American population, many of whom still live by honest, friendly values.

$$ DOG FANCY

P.O. Box 6050, Mission Viejo CA 92690-6050. E-mail: barkback@dogfancy.com. Website: www.dogfancy.com. **95% freelance written**. Monthly magazine for men and women of all ages interested in all phases of dog ownership. Estab. 1970. Circ. 250,000. Byline given. Pays on publication. Offers kill fee. Publishes ms an average of 6 months after acceptance. Buys first North American serial rights, buys nonexclusive electronic and other rights. Accepts queries by e-mail. Responds in 2 months to queries. Guidelines available online.

- Reading period from January through April.

Nonfiction Needs general interest, how-to, humor, inspirational, interview, photo feature, travel. "No stories written from a dog's point of view." **Buys 10 or fewer from new writers; 80 mss/year.** Query. Length: 800-1,200 words. **Pays 40¢/word.**

Photos State availability. of photos. Reviews transparencies, slides. Offers no additional payment for photos accepted with ms.

Columns/Departments News hound, fun dog. Query by e-mail. **Pays 40¢/word.**

Tips "We're looking for the unique experience that enhances the dog/owner relationship. Medical articles are assigned to veterinarians. Note that we write for a lay audience (nontechnical), but we do assume a certain level of intelligence. Read the magazine before making a pitch. Make sure your query is clear, concise, and relevant."

$ DOGS IN CANADA

Apex Publishing, Ltd., 200 Ronson Dr., Suite 401, Etobicoke ON M9W 5Z9 Canada. (416)798-9778. Fax: (416)798-9671. E-mail: editor@dogsincanada.com. Website: www.dogsincanada.com. **90% freelance written**. Monthly magazine covering dogs. "*Dogs in Canada* is considered a reliable and authoritative source of information about dogs. The mix of content must satisfy a diverse readership, including knowledgeable dog owners and fanciers as well as those who simply love dogs." Estab. 1889. Circ. 41,769. Byline given. Pays on publication. Offers 50% kill fee. Publishes ms 3-6 months after acceptance. Buys first North American serial rights, first rights, non-exclusive electronic rights. Editorial lead time 4 months. Submit seasonal material 6 months in advance. Accepts queries by mail, e-mail. Accepts previously published material. Responds in 8 weeks to queries. Responds in 2 months to mss. Guidelines for #10 SASE or via e-mail.

Nonfiction Needs book excerpts, historical, humor, interview. Does not want articles written from the dog's point of view. **Buys 10 mss/year.** Send complete ms. Length: 500-1,800 words. **Pays $100 and above.**

Photos Contact: Kelly Caldwell, art director. State availability of or send photos. Identification of subjects, model releases required. Reviews contact sheets, negatives, transparencies, 5 × 7 prints, GIF/JPEG files. Negotiates payment individually. Rights negotiated individually.

Fillers Accepts less than 10 fillers/year. Length: 150-500 words.

Tips "If high quality photos are available to complement the piece, that helps us considerably. Short features written for web are a good entry point into the magazine. Please familiarize yourself with our magazine before querying. We have covered virtually all of the basics of dog health, nutrition, behavior, etc. Queries with new ideas or a fresh approach will catch our attention."

DOGS LIFE

For People Who Love Their Dogs, Universal Magazines, Ltd., Unit 5, 6-8 Byfield St., North Ryde NSW 2113 Australia. (61)(2)9887-0360. Fax: (61)(2)9805-0714. E-mail: dogslife@universalmagazines.com.au. Website: www.dogslife.com.au. Bimonthly magazine dedicated to dogs. *Dogs Life* isn't afraid to tackle the hard hitting issues that affect dog owners worldwide.

Nonfiction Needs general interest, how-to, inspirational, interview, new product. Query.

$ DOG SPORTS MAGAZINE

4215 S. Lowell Rd., St. Johns MI 48879. (989)224-7225. Fax: (989)224-6033. Website: www.dogsports.com. **5% freelance written**. Monthly tabloid covering working dogs. Estab. 1979. Circ. 2,000. Byline given. Pays on publication. Publishes ms an average of 1 month after acceptance. Buys first North American serial rights, buys second serial (reprint) rights. Editorial lead time 1 month. Submit seasonal material 1 month in advance. Accepts queries by mail, e-mail. Accepts previously published material. Accepts simultaneous submissions. Sample copy free or online.

Nonfiction Needs essays, general interest, how-to, working dogs, humor, interview, technical. **Buys 5 mss/year.** Send complete ms. **Pays $50.**

Photos State availability. of photos. Captions, identification of subjects required. Reviews prints. Offers no additional payment for photos accepted with ms. Buys all rights.

$ $ EQUESTRIAN MAGAZINE

The Official Magazine of Equestrian Sport Since 1937, United States Equestrian Federation (USEF), 4047 Iron Works Parkway, Lexington KY 40511. (859)225-6934. Fax: (859)231-6662. E-mail: bsosby@usef.org. Website: www.usef.org. **10-30% freelance written**. Magazine published 10 times/year covering the equestrian sport. Estab. 1937. Circ. 77,000. Byline given. Pays on publication. Offers 50% kill fee. Buys first North American serial rights, first rights. Editorial lead time 1-5 months. Accepts queries by mail, e-mail, fax, phone. Sample copy and writer's guidelines free.

Nonfiction Needs interview, technical, all equestrian-related. **Buys 20-30 mss/year.** Query with published clips. Length: 500-3,500 words. **Pays $200-500.**

Photos State availability of photos. Captions, identification of subjects, model releases required. Reviews contact sheets. Offers $50-200/photo. Buys one time rights.

Columns/Departments Horses of the Past (famous equines); Horse People (famous horsemen/women), both 500-1,000 words. Buys 20-30 columns/year. Query with published clips. **Pays $100.**

Tips Write via e-mail in first instance with samples, résumé, then mail original clips.

$ EQUINE JOURNAL

103 Roxbury St., Keene NH 03431. (603)357-4271. Fax: (603)357-7851. E-mail: editorial@equinejournal.com. Website: www.equinejournal.com. **Contact:** Kelly Ballou, editor. **90% freelance written**. Monthly tabloid covering horses—all breeds, all disciplines. "The Equine Journal is a monthly, all-breed/discipline regional publication for horse enthusiasts. The purpose of our editorial is to educate, entertain and enable amateurs and professionals alike to stay on top of new developments in the field. Every month, the Equine Journal presents feature articles and columns spanning the length and breadth of horse-related activities and interests from all corners of the country." Estab. 1988. Circ. 26,000. Byline given. Pays on publication. Buys first North American serial rights, electronic rights. Editorial lead time 4 months. Accepts queries by mail, e-mail, fax, phone. Responds in 2 months to queries. Guidelines available online.

Nonfiction Needs general interest, how-to, interview. **Buys 100 mss/year.** Send complete ms. Length: 1,500-2,200 words.

Photos Send photos. Reviews prints. Pays $10.

Columns/Departments Horse Health (health-related topics), 1,200-1,500 words. Query.

EQUUS

656 Quince Orchard Rd., Suite 600, Gaithersburg MD 20878-1409. Fax: (301)990-9015. E-mail: EEQEletters@equinetwork.com. Website: www.equisearch.com. Monthly magazine covering equine behavior. Provides the latest information from the world's top veterinarians, equine researchers, riders, and trainers. Circ. 149,482. No kill fee. Accepts queries by mail. Guidelines available online.

Nonfiction Features on healthcare, behavior, training techniques, veterinary breakthroughs, exercise physiology, etc. Send complete ms. Length: 1,600-3,000 words. **Payment depends on quality, length, and complexity of the story.**

Columns/Departments The Medical Front (research/technology/treatments), 200-400 words; Hands On (everyday horse care), 100-400 words; Roundup (industry news stories), 100-400 words; True Tales (experiences/relationships with horses), 700-2,000 words; Case Report (equine illness/injury), 1,000-2,500 words. Send complete ms. **Payment depends on quality, length, and complexity of the story.**

$ $ FIDO FRIENDLY MAGAZINE

Fido Friendly, Inc., P.O. Box 160, Marsing ID 83639. E-mail: susan@fidofriendly.com. Website: www.fidofriendly.com. **95% freelance written**. Bimonthly magazine covering travel with your dog. "We want articles about all things travel related with your dog". Estab. 2,000. Circ. 44,000. Byline given. Pays on publication. No kill fee. Publishes ms an average of 2 months after acceptance. Buys first North American serial rights, buys electronic rights. Editorial lead time 1-3 months. Submit seasonal material 3 months in advance. Accepts queries by e-mail. Accepts simultaneous submissions. Responds in 2 weeks to queries. Responds in 1 month to mss. Sample copy for $7. Guidelines free.

Nonfiction Contact: Susan Sims, publisher. Needs essays, general interest, how-to, travel with your dog, humor, inspirational, interview, personal experience, travel. No articles about dog's point of view - dog's voice. **Buys 24 mss/year.** Query with published clips. Length: 600-1,200 words. **Pays 10-20¢/word.**

Photos Contact: Susan Sims. Send photos. Captions, identification of subjects, model releases required. Reviews GIF/JPEG files. Offers no additional payment for photos accepted with ms. Buys one time rights.
Columns/Departments Fido Friendly City (City where dogs have lots of options to enjoy restaurants, dog retail stores, dog parks, sports activity.) Buys 6 mss/year. Query with published clips. **Pays 10-20¢/word.**
Fiction Contact: Susan Sims. Needs adventure, (dog). Nothing from dog's point of view. Query. Length: 600-1,200 words. **Pays 10-20¢/word.**
Tips "Accept copies in lieu of payment. Our readers treat their pets as part of the family. Writing should reflect that."

$$ FIELD TRIAL MAGAZINE

Androscoggin Publishing, Inc., P.O. Box 298, Milan NH 03588. (603)449-6767. Fax: (603)449-2462. E-mail: birddog@wildblue.net. Website: www.fielddog.com/ftm. **75% freelance written**. Quarterly magazine covering field trials for pointing dogs. "Our readers are knowledgeable sports men and women who want interesting and informative articles about their sport." Estab. 1997. Circ. 6,000. Byline given. Pays on publication. Publishes ms an average of 6 months after acceptance. Buys first North American serial rights. Editorial lead time 3 months. Submit seasonal material 6 months in advance. Accepts queries by mail, e-mail, fax. Accepts simultaneous submissions. Responds in 2 weeks to queries. Responds in 2 months to mss. Sample copy free. Guidelines available online.
Nonfiction Needs book excerpts, essays, general interest, historical, how-to, interview, opinion, personal experience. No hunting articles. **Buys 12-16 mss/year.** Query. Length: 1,000-3,000 words. **Pays $100-300.**
Photos Send photos. Captions, identification of subjects required. Offers no additional payment for photos accepted with ms. Buys one time rights.
Fiction "Fiction that deals with bird dogs and field trials." **Buys 4 mss/year.** Send complete ms. Length: 1,000-2,500 words. **Pays $100-250.**
Tips "Make sure you have correct and accurate information—we'll work with a writer who has good solid info even if the writing needs work."

$$ FRESHWATER AND MARINE AQUARIUM

Bowtie, Inc., 3 Burroughs, Irvine CA 92618-2804. (949)855-8822. E-mail: emizer@bowtieinc.com. Website: www.fishchannel.com. Clay Jackson. **Contact:** Ethan Mizer, assoc. ed. **95% freelance written**. The freshwater and marine aquarium hobby. "Our audience tends to be more advanced fish-and coral-keepers as well as planted tank fans. Writers should have aquarium keeping experience themselves. FAMA covers all aspects of fish and coral husbandry." Estab. 1978. Circ. 14,000. Byline given. Pays on publication. Pays $50 kill fee. Publishes ms 6-8 months after acceptance. First North American serial rights purchased. 3½ months editorial lead time. Accepts queries by mail, e-mail. Accepts simultaneous submissions. Responds in 3 weeks on queries, 2 months on mss. "If we are interested in a query or ms, we'll e-mail an assignment with guidelines included."
Nonfiction Needs general interest, how-to, interview, new product, personal experience, technical, aquarium-related articles. Three special issues every year. Past issues have included aquarium lighting, invertebrates, planted tanks, food, etc. "No beginner articles, such as keeping guppies and goldfish. If mid-level to advanced aquarists wouldn't get anything new by reading it, don't send it." Writer should query. Length: 1,500-2,000 words. **Pays $300-400; 20¢/word.**
Photos State availability. of photos with submission; Send photos. Captions are required. GIF/JPEG files, RAW files, transparencies (35 mm). Digitals must be 300 dpi. If article is on keeping unusual fish, photos should be included. One-time rights.
Columns/Departments "All of our columns are assigned and written by established columnists." **Pays $250.**
Tips "Check out our website to read about the different topics we cover in our magazine."

$ THE GREYHOUND REVIEW

P.O. Box 543, Abilene KS 67410. (785)263-4660. E-mail: review@ngagreyhounds.com. Website: www.ngagreyhounds.com. **20% freelance written**. Monthly magazine covering greyhound breeding, training, and racing. Estab. 1911. Circ. 3,500. Byline given. Pays on acceptance. No kill fee. Buys first rights. Submit seasonal material 2 months in advance. Responds in 2 weeks to queries. Responds in 1 month to mss. Sample copy for $3. Guidelines free.

Nonfiction "Articles must be targeted at the greyhound industry: from hard news, to special events at racetracks, to the latest medical discoveries." Needs how-to, interview, personal experience. Do not submit gambling systems. **Buys 24 mss/year.** Query. Length: 1,000-10,000 words. **Pays $85-150.**
Reprints Send photocopy. Pays 100% of amount paid for original article.
Photos State availability. Identification of subjects required. Reviews digital images. Pays $10-50 photo. Buys one time rights.

$$$ HORSE&RIDER

The magazine of western riding, 2000 S. Stemmons Freeway, Ste. 101, Lake Dallas TX 75065. E-mail: horseandrider@equinetwork.com. Website: www.horseandrider.com. **Contact:** Erin Sullivan, Editorial Coordinator. **10% freelance written**. Monthly magazine covering Western horse industry, competition, recreation. "*Horse&Rider*'s mission is to enhance the enjoyment and satisfaction readers derive from horse involvement. We strive to do this by providing the insights, knowledge, and horsemanship skills they need to safely and effectively handle, ride, and appreciate their horses, in and out of the competition arena. We also help them find the time, resources, and energy they need to enjoy their horse to the fullest." Estab. 1961. Circ. 164,000. Byline given. Pays on acceptance. Publishes ms an average of 1 year after acceptance. Buys first North American serial rights. Editorial lead time 2 months. Submit seasonal material 6 months in advance. Accepts queries by mail, e-mail. Responds in 3 months to queries. Responds in 3 months to mss. Sample copy and writer's guidelines online.

- Online magazine carries original content not found in the print edition.

Nonfiction Needs book excerpts, general interest, how-to, horse training, horsemanship, humor, interview, new product, personal experience, photo feature, travel, horse health care, trail riding. **Buys 5-10 mss/year.** Send complete ms. Length: 1,000-3,000 words. **Pays $150-1,000.**
Photos State availability of or send photos. Captions, identification of subjects, model releases required. Negotiates payment individually. Buys rights on assignment or stock.
Tips "Writers should have patience, ability to accept critical editing, and extensive knowledge of the Western horse industry and our publication."

$$$ THE HORSE

Your Guide To Equine Health Care, P.O. Box 919003, Lexington KY 40591-9003. (859)278-2361. Fax: (859)276-4450. E-mail: kbrown@thehorse.com. Website: www.thehorse.com. **85% freelance written**. Monthly magazine covering equine health, care, management and welfare. *The Horse* is an educational/news magazine geared toward the hands-on horse owner. Estab. 1983. Circ. 55,000. Byline given. Pays on acceptance. Publishes ms an average of 6 months after acceptance. Buys first world and electronic rights Accepts queries by mail, e-mail. Responds in 3 months to queries. Sample copy for $3.95 or online. Guidelines available online.
Nonfiction Needs how-to, technical, topical interviews. No first-person experiences not from professionals; this is a technical magazine to inform horse owners. **Buys 90 mss/year.** Query with published clips. Length: 250-4,000 words. **Pays $60-850.**
Photos Send photos. Captions, identification of subjects required. Reviews transparencies. Offers $35-350
Columns/Departments News Front (news on horse health), 100-500 words; Equinomics (economics of horse ownership); Step by Step (feet and leg care); Nutrition; Reproduction; Back to Basics, all 1,500-2,200 words. Buys 50 mss/year. Query with published clips. **Pays $50-450.**
Tips We publish reliable horse health care and management information from top industry professionals and researchers around the world. Manuscript must be submitted electronically or on disk.

HORSE-CANADA

Horse Publications Group, Box 670, Aurora ON L4G 4J9 Canada. (905)727-0107. Fax: (905)841-1530. E-mail: info@horse-canada.com. Website: www.horse-canada.com. **80% freelance written**. National magazine for horse lovers of all ages. Readers are committed horse owners with many different breeds involved in a variety of disciplines—from beginner riders to industry professionals. *Horsepower* is for horse-crazy kids and is inserted into *Horse Canada* to entertain and educate future equestrians. Circ. 20,000. No kill fee. Buys all rights. Editorial lead time 2 months. Accepts queries by e-mail. Guidelines available online.
Nonfiction Health and management topics, training tips, rural living, and hot industry issues. Query. Length: 750-1,500 words. **Payment varies.**
Photos State availability of or send photos.
Columns/Departments The Tail End (humor). **Payment varies.**

$ HORSE CONNECTION

Horse Connection, LLC, 1263 Park St., Suite A, Castle Rock CO 80109. (303)663-1300. Fax: (303)663-1331. Website: www.horseconnection.com. **90% freelance written**. Magazine published 12 times/year covering horse owners and riders. Our readers are horse owners and riders. They specialize in English riding. We primarily focus on show jumping and hunters, dressage, and three-day events, with additional coverage of driving, polo, and endurance. Estab. 1995. Circ. 25,000. Byline given. Pays on publication. No kill fee. Publishes ms an average of 1 month after acceptance. Buys first rights, buys second serial (reprint) rights. Editorial lead time 3 months. Submit seasonal material 3 months in advance. Accepts queries by e-mail. Responds in 1 month to queries. Sample copy for $3.50 or online. Guidelines for #10 SASE or online.

Nonfiction Needs humor, interview, personal experience, event reports. No general interest stories about horses. Nothing negative. No western, racing, or breed specific articles. No my first pony stories. **Buys 30-50 mss/year.** Query with published clips. Length: 500-1,000 words. **Pays $25 for assigned articles. Pays $75 for unsolicited articles.**

Photos State availability. Negotiates payment individually Buys one time rights.

Tips Please read the magazine. We are currently focused on the western states and we like stories about English riders from these states.

$$ HORSE ILLUSTRATED

The Magazine for Hands-On Owners & Riders, BowTie, Inc., P.O. Box 8237, Lexington KY 40533. (859)260-9800. Fax: (859)260-1154. Website: www.horseillustrated.com. **Contact:** Elizabeth Moyer. **90% freelance written. Prefers to work with published/established writers but will work with new/unpublished writers**. Monthly magazine covering all aspects of horse ownership. "Our readers are adults, mostly women, between the ages of 18 and 40; stories should be geared to that age group and reflect responsible horse care." Estab. 1976. Circ. 171,000. Byline given. Pays on publication. Publishes ms an average of 8 months after acceptance. Buys one-time rights, requires first North American rights among equine publications. Submit seasonal material 6 months in advance. Accepts queries by mail. Responds in 3 months to queries. Guidelines for #10 SASE and are available online at www.horsechannel.com/horse-magazines/horse-illustrated/submission-guidelines.aspx.

Nonfiction We are looking for authoritative, in-depth features on trends and issues in the horse industry. Such articles must be queried first with a detailed outline of the article and clips. We rarely have a need for fiction. Needs general interest, how-to, horse care, training, veterinary care, inspirational, photo feature. "No little girl horse stories, cowboy and Indian stories or anything not *directly* relating to horses." **Buys 20 mss/year.** Query or send complete ms. Length: 1,000-2,000 words. **Pays $200-400.**

Photos Send high-resolution digital images on a CD with thumbnails.

Tips "Freelancers can break in at this publication with feature articles on Western and English training methods; veterinary and general care how-to articles; and horse sports articles. We rarely use personal experience articles. Submit photos with training and how-to articles whenever possible. We have a very good record of developing new freelancers into regular contributors/columnists. We are always looking for fresh talent, but certainly enjoy working with established writers who `know the ropes' as well. We are accepting less unsolicited freelance work—much is now assigned and contracted."

$ I LOVE CATS

I Love Cats Publishing, 1040 First Ave., Suite 323, New York NY 10022. E-mail: ilovecatseditor@sbcglobal.net. Website: www.iluvcats.com. **100% freelance written**. Bimonthly magazine. "*I Love Cats* is a general interest cat magazine for the entire family. It caters to cat lovers of all ages. The stories in the magazine include fiction, nonfiction, how-to, humorous, and columns for the cat lover." Estab. 1989. Circ. 25,000. Byline given. Pays on publication. No kill fee. Publishes ms an average of 2 years after acceptance. Buys all rights. Editorial lead time 6 months. Submit seasonal material 9 months in advance. Accepts queries by mail, e-mail. Responds in 3 months to queries. Sample copy for $5. Guidelines available online.

Nonfiction Needs essays, general interest, how-to, humor, inspirational, interview, new product, opinion, personal experience, photo feature. No poetry. **Buys 50 mss/year.** Send complete ms. Length: 500-1,000 words. **Pays $50-100, or contributor copies or other premiums if requested.**

Photos Please send copies; art will no longer be returned. Send photos. Identification of subjects required. Offers no additional payment for photos accepted with ms. Buys all rights.

Fiction Needs adventure, fantasy, historical, humorous, mainstream, mystery, novel concepts, slice-of-life vignettes, suspense. "This is a family magazine. No graphic violence, pornography, or other inappropriate material. *I Love Cats* is strictly 'G-rated.'" **Buys 50 mss/year.** Send complete ms. Length: 500-1,000 words. **Pays $50 and offers contributor copies.**

Fillers Needs anecdotes, facts, short humor. Buys 25 fillers. **Pays $25.**

Tips "Please keep stories short and concise. Send complete manuscript with photos, if possible. I buy lots of work from first-time authors. Nonfiction pieces with color photos are always in short supply. With the exception of the standing columns, the rest of the magazine is open to freelancers. Be witty, humorous, or offer a different approach to writing."

$$ JUST LABS

A Celebration of the Labrador Retriever, Village Press, 2779 Aero Park Dr., Traverse City MI 49686. Website: www.justlabsmagazine.com. **50% freelance written**. Bimonthly magazine. "*Just Labs* is targeted toward the family Labrador Retriever, and all of our articles help people learn about, live with, train, take care of, and enjoy their dogs. We do not look for articles that pull at the heart strings (those are usually staff-written), but rather we look for articles that teach, inform, and entertain." Estab. 2001. Circ. 20,000. Byline given. Pays on publication. Offers 40% kill fee. Publishes ms an average of 6 months after acceptance. Buys first North American serial rights. Editorial lead time 6 months. Submit seasonal material 6-8 months in advance. Accepts queries by mail. Responds in 4-6 weeks to queries. Responds in 2 months to mss. Guidelines for #10 SASE.

Nonfiction Needs essays, how-to, (train, health, lifestyle), humor, inspirational, interview, photo feature, technical, travel. We don't want tributes to dogs that have passed on. This is a privilege we reserve for our subscribers. **Buys 30 mss/year.** Query. Length: 1,000-1,800 words. **Pays $250-400.**

Photos Send photos. Captions required. Reviews contact sheets, transparencies, prints, GIF/JPEG files. Offers no additional payment for photos accepted with ms. Buys one time rights.

Tips "Be professional, courteous and understanding of my time. Please be aware that we have been around for several years and have probably published an article on almost every 'dog topic' out there. Those queries providing fresh, unique and interesting angles on common topics will catch our eye."

$ MINIATURE DONKEY TALK

Miniature Donkey Talk, Inc., 1338 Hughes Shop Rd., Westminster MD 21158. (410)875-0118. E-mail: minidonk@qis.net. Website: www.miniaturedonkey.net. **65% freelance written**. Quarterly magazine covering donkeys, with articles on healthcare, promotion, and management of donkeys for owners, breeders, or donkey lovers. Estab. 1987. Circ. 4,925. Byline given. Pays on acceptance. Publishes ms an average of 4 months after acceptance. Buys first rights, buys second serial (reprint) rights. Editorial lead time 2 months. Submit seasonal material 3 months in advance. Accepts queries by mail, e-mail, fax. Accepts previously published material. Responds in 2 weeks to queries. Responds in 1 month to mss. Sample copy for $5. Guidelines free.

Nonfiction We accept breeder profiles—either of yourself or another breeder. We cover nonshow events such as fairs, donkey gatherings, holiday events, etc. We want relevant, informative equine health pieces. We much prefer they deal specifically with donkeys, but will consider articles geared toward horses. If at all possible, substitute the word 'horse' for 'donkey.' We reserve the right to edit, change, delete, or add to health articles. Please be careful with the accuracy of advice or training material, as well as farm management articles and fictional stories on donkeys. Needs book excerpts, humor, interview, personal experience. **Buys 6 mss/year.** Query with published clips. Length: 700-5,000 words. **Pays $25-150.**

Photos State availability. Identification of subjects required. Reviews 3 × 5 prints. Offers no additional payment for photos accepted with ms. Buys one time rights.

Columns/Departments Humor, 2,000 words; Healthcare, 2,000-5,000 words; Management, 2,000 words. Buys 50 mss/year. Query. **Pays $25-100.**

Tips Simply send your manuscript. If on topic and appropriate, good possibility it will be published. No fiction or poetry.

$$ MUSHING

P.O. Box 1195, Willow AK 99688. (907)495-2468. E-mail: editor@mushing.com. Website: www.mushing.com. Bimonthly magazine covering "all aspects of the growing sports of dogsledding, skijoring, carting, dog packing, and weight pulling. *Mushing* promotes responsible dog care through feature articles and updates on working animal health care, safety, nutrition, and training." Estab. 1987. Circ. 6,000. Byline given. Pays within 3 months of publication. No kill fee. Publishes ms an average of 4 months after acceptance. Buys first rights, buys second serial (reprint) rights. Submit seasonal material 4 months in advance. Accepts queries by mail, e-mail, fax, phone. Responds in 8 months to queries. Sample copy for $5 ($6 US to Canada). Guidelines available online.

Nonfiction "We consider articles on canine health and nutrition, sled dog behavior and training, musher profiles and interviews, equipment how-to's, trail tips, expedition and race accounts, innovations, sled dog history, current issues, personal experiences, and humor." Needs historical, how-to. Iditarod and

Long-Distance Racing (January/February); Ski or Sprint Racing (March/April); Health and Nutrition (May/June); Musher and Dog Profiles, Summer Activities (July/August); Equipment, Fall Training (September/October); Races and Places (November/December). Query with or without published clips. Considers complete ms with SASE. Length: 1,000-2,500 words. **Pays $50-250.**

Photos "We look for good quality color for covers and specials." Send photos. Captions, identification of subjects. Reviews digital images only. Pays $20-165/photo Buys one-time and second reprint rights.

Columns/Departments Query with or without published clips or send complete ms.

Fillers Needs anecdotes, facts, newsbreaks, short humor, cartoons, puzzles. Length: 100-250 words. **Pays $20-35.**

Tips "Read our magazine. Know something about dog-driven, dog-powered sports."

$ $ PAINT HORSE JOURNAL

American Paint Horse Association, P.O. Box 961023, Fort Worth TX 76161-0023. (817)834-2742. Website: www.painthorsejournal.com. **10% freelance written. Works with a small number of new/unpublished writers each year**. Monthly magazine for people who raise, breed and show Paint Horses. Estab. 1966. Circ. 20,000. Byline given. Pays on acceptance. Offers negotiable kill fee. Buys first North American serial rights. Submit seasonal material 3 months in advance. Accepts queries by mail, e-mail, fax. Sample copy for $4.50. Guidelines available online.

Nonfiction Needs general interest, personality pieces on well-known owners of Paints, historical, Paint Horses in the past—particular horses and the breed in general, how-to, train and show horses, photo feature, Paint Horses. **Buys 4-5 mss/year.** Query. Length: 1,000-2,000 words. **Pays $100-500.**

Photos Photos must illustrate article and must include registered Paint Horses. Send photos. Captions required. Reviews 35mm or larger transparencies, 3 × 5 or larger color glossy prints, digital images on CD or DVD. Offers no additional payment for photos accepted with accompanying ms.

Tips "Well-written first person articles are welcomed. Submit items that show a definite understanding of the horse business. Be sure you understand precisely what a Paint Horse is as defined by the American Paint Horse Association. Use proper equine terminology. Photos with copy are almost always essential."

🌐 PET NEW ZEALAND

The Fusion Group, LTD, P.O. Box 37 356, Parnell Auckland New Zealand. (64)(9)336-1188. Fax: (64)(9)373-5647. E-mail: editorial@petmag.co.nz. Website: www.petmag.co.nz. Quarterly magazine covering topics for pet owners and animal lovers. "*Pet New Zealand* promotes public awareness of pet issues, educates through practical advice, features heart-warming stories and pet products, and provides expert advice." No kill fee.

- Query before submitting.

$ $ REPTILES

The World's Leading Reptile Magazine, BowTie, Inc., P.O. Box 6050, Mission Viejo CA 92690. (949)855-8822. E-mail: reptiles@bowtieinc.com. Website: www.reptilesmagazine.com. **20% freelance written**. Monthly magazine covering reptiles and amphibians. *Reptiles* covers "a wide range of topics relating to reptiles and amphibians, including breeding, captive care, field herping, etc." Estab. 1992. Byline given. Pays on publication. Offers 20% kill fee. Publishes ms an average of 6-8 months after acceptance. Buys first North American serial rights, buys electronic rights. Accepts queries by mail, e-mail. Responds in 1 month to queries. Responds in 1-2 months to mss. Sample copy available online. Guidelines available online.

Nonfiction Needs general interest, historical, how-to, interview, personal experience, photo feature, travel. **Buys 10 mss/year.** Query. Length: 1,000-2,000 words. **Pays $250-500.**

Tips "Keep in mind that *Reptiles* has a very knowledgeable readership when it comes to herps. While we accept freelance articles, the bulk of what we publish comes from 'herp people.' Do your research, interview experts, etc., for the best results."

$ ROCKY MOUNTAIN RIDER MAGAZINE

Regional All-Breed Horse Monthly, P.O. Box 995, Hamilton MT 59840. (406)363-4085. E-mail: editor@rockymountainrider.com. Website: www.rockymountainrider.com. **90% freelance written**. Monthly magazine for horse owners and enthusiasts. Estab. 1993. Circ. 16,500. Byline given. Pays on publication. No kill fee. Publishes ms an average of 6 months after acceptance. Buys one-time rights. Submit seasonal material 6 months in advance. Accepts simultaneous submissions. Responds in 2 months to queries. Responds in 3 months to mss. Sample copy for $3. Guidelines for #10 SASE.

Nonfiction Needs articles on horse care, horse health issues, anecdotes, historical, humor, personal experience. **Buys 100 mss/year.** Send complete ms. Length: 500-2,000 words. **Pays $15-100.**
Photos Send photos. Captions, identification of subjects required. Reviews 3 × 5 prints, e-mail digital photos. Pays $5/photo. Buys one time rights.
Poetry Needs light verse, traditional. Buys 25 poems/year. Submit maximum 10 poems. Length: 6-36 lines. **Pays $10.**
Fillers Needs anecdotes, facts, gags, short humor. Length: 200-750 words. **Pays $15-30.**
Tips *RMR* is looking for positive, human interest stories that appeal to an audience of horse owners and horse enthusiasts. We accept profiles of unusual people or animals, history, humor, anecdotes, and coverage of regional events. We aren't looking for 'how-to' or training articles, and are not currently looking at any fiction. Our geographical regions of interest is the U.S. West, especially the Rocky Mountain states.

$$ TROPICAL FISH HOBBYIST MAGAZINE

TFH Publications, Inc., One TFH Plaza, Neptune City NJ 07753. E-mail: AssociateEditor@tfh.com. Website: www.tfhmagazine.com. **90% freelance written**. Monthly magazine covering tropical fish. Estab. 1952. Circ. 35,000. Byline given. Pays on acceptance. No kill fee. Buys all rights. Editorial lead time 3 months. Submit seasonal material 6 months in advance. Accepts queries by e-mail. Responds immediately on electronic queries. Guidelines available online.
Nonfiction We cover any aspect of aquarium science, aquaculture, and the tropical fish hobby. Our readership is diverse—from neophytes to mini reef specialists. We require well-researched, well-written, and factually accurate copy, preferably with photos. **Buys 100-150 mss/year. Pays $100-250.**
Photos State availability. Identification of subjects, model releases required. Reviews prints, slides, high-resolution digital images. Negotiates payment individually. Buys multiple nonexclusive rights.
Tips With few exceptions, all communication and submission must be electronic. We want factual, interesting, and relevant articles about the aquarium hobby written by people who are obviously knowledgeable. We publish an enormous variety of article types. Review several past issues to get an idea of the scope.

$$ USDF CONNECTION

United States Dressage Federation, 4051 Iron Works Parkway, Lexington KY 40511. Website: www.usdf.org. **40% freelance written**. Monthly magazine covering dressage (an equestrian sport). All material must relate to the sport of dressage in the US. Estab. 2000. Circ. 35,000. Byline given. Pays on acceptance. Offers 50% kill fee. Publishes ms an average of 3 months after acceptance. Buys first North American serial rights, buys second serial (reprint) rights. Editorial lead time 3 months. Submit seasonal material 6 months in advance. Accepts queries by mail, e-mail. Accepts previously published material. Responds in 1 month to queries. Responds in 1-2 months to mss. Sample copy for $5. Guidelines available online.
Nonfiction Needs book excerpts, essays, how-to, interview, opinion, personal experience. Does not want general interest equine material or stories that lack a US dressage angle. **Buys 40 mss/year.** Query. Length: 650-3,000 words. **Pays $100-500 for assigned articles. Pays $100-300 for unsolicited articles.**
Photos State availability. Captions, identification of subjects required. Reviews prints, GIF/JPEG files. Negotiates payment individually. Buys one time rights.
Columns/Departments Amateur Hour (profiles of adult amateur USDF members), 1,200-1,500 words; Under 21 (profiles of young USDF members), 1,200-1,500 words; Veterinary Connection (dressage-related horse health), 1,500-2,500 words; Mind-Body-Spirit Connection (rider health/fitness, sport psychology), 1,500-2,500 words. Buys 24 mss/year. Query with published clips. **Pays $150-400.**
Tips Know the organization and the sport. Most successful contributors are active in the horse industry and bring valuable perspectives and insights to their stories and images.

Art & Architecture

$$ AMERICAN ARTIST

29 W. 46th St., 3rd Floor, New York NY 10036. (646)841-0050. E-mail: mail@myamericanartist.com. Website: www.myamericanartist.com. Monthly magazine covering art. "Written to provide information on outstanding representational artists living in the US." Estab. 1937. Circ. 116,526. No kill fee. Editorial lead time 18 weeks. Accepts queries by mail. Responds in 6-8 weeks to queries. Guidelines by e-mail.
Nonfiction Needs essays, expose, interview, personal experience, technical. Query with published clips and résumé Length: 1,500-2,000 words.

$$ AMERICAN INDIAN ART MAGAZINE

American Indian Art, Inc., 7314 E. Osborn Dr., Scottsdale AZ 85251. (480)994-5445. Fax: (480)945-9533. E-mail: info@aiamagazine.com. Website: www.aiamagazine.com. **97% freelance written. Works with many new/unpublished writers/year.** Quarterly magazine covering Native American art, historic and contemporary, including new research on any aspect of Native American art north of the US-Mexico border. Estab. 1975. Circ. 22,000. Byline given. Pays on publication. No kill fee. Publishes ms an average of 6 months after acceptance. Buys first rights, buys one-time rights. Responds in 6 weeks to queries. Responds in 3 months to mss. Guidelines for #10 SASE or online.

Nonfiction New research on any aspect of Native American art. No previously published work or personal interviews with artists. **Buys 12-18 mss/year.** Query. Length: 6,000-7,000 words. **Pays $150-300.**

Photos An article usually requires 8-15 photographs. Fee schedules and reimbursable expenses are decided upon by the magazine and the author. Buys one time rights.

Tips The magazine is devoted to all aspects of Native American art. Some of our readers are knowledgeable about the field and some know very little. We seek articles that offer something to both groups. Articles reflecting original research are preferred to those summarizing previously published information.

$$$ AMERICANSTYLE MAGAZINE

The Rosen Group, 3000 Chestnut Ave., Suite 304, Baltimore MD 21211. (410)889-3093. Fax: (410)243-7089. E-mail: hoped@rosengrp.com. Website: www.americanstyle.com. **80% freelance written.** Bimonthly magazine covering arts, crafts, travel, and interior design. "*AmericanStyle* is a full-color lifestyle publication for people who love art. Our mandate is to nurture collectors with information that will increase their passion for contemporary art and craft and the artists who create it. *AmericanStyle*'s primary audience is contemporary craft collectors and enthusiasts. Readers are college-educated, age 35+, high-income earners with the financial means to collect art and craft, and to travel to national art and craft events in pursuit of their passions." Estab. 1994. Circ. 60,000. Pays on publication. Publishes ms an average of 9-12 months after acceptance. Buys first North American serial rights. Editorial lead time 9-12 months. Submit seasonal material at least 1 year in advance. Accepts queries by mail, e-mail. Sample copy for $3. Guidelines available online.

Nonfiction Length: 600-800 words. **Pays $400-800.**

Photos Send photos. Captions required. Reviews oversized transparencies, 35mm slides, low resolution e-images. Negotiates payment individually.

Columns/Departments Portfolio (profiles of emerging and established artists); Arts Tour; Arts Walk; Origins; One on One, all approximately 600 words. Query with published clips. **Pays $400-600.**

Tips " This is not a hobby-crafter magazine. Country crafts or home crafting is not our market. We focus on contemporary American craft art, such as ceramics, wood, fiber, glass, metal. Produced by established working artists, most of whom have gallery and/or museum representation."

ARCHITECTURAL DIGEST

The International Magazine of Interior Design, Conde Nast Publications, Inc., 6300 Wilshire Blvd., Los Angeles CA 90048. (323)965-3700. Fax: (323)965-4975. Website: www.architecturaldigest.com. Monthly magazine covering architecture. A global magazine that offers a look at the homes of the rich and famous. Other topics include travel, shopping, automobiles, and technology. Estab. 1920. Circ. 821,992. No kill fee. Accepts queries by mail. Sample copy for $5 on newsstands.

Nonfiction Send 3 samples of your work with a brief cover letter. Include a paragraph on who else you've written for and a paragraph on any story ideas you have for *Architectural Digest*. Query with published clips.

$$ THE ARTIST'S MAGAZINE

F+W Media, Inc., 4700 E. Galbraith Rd., Cincinnati OH 45236. (513)531-2690, ext. 1489. Fax: (513)891-7153. Website: www.artistsmagazine.com. **Contact:** Maureen Bloomfield, Editor-In-Chief. **80% freelance written**. Magazine published 10 times/year covering primarily two-dimensional art for working artists. "Ours is a highly visual approach to teaching serious amateur and professional artists techniques that will help them improve their skills and market their work. The style should be crisp and immediately engaging, written in a voice that speaks directly to artists. Circ. 150,000. Bionote given for feature material. Pays on publication. Offers 8% kill fee. Publishes ms an average of 6 months-1 year after acceptance. Responds in 6 months to queries Sample copy for $5.99 Guidelines available online

Nonfiction No unillustrated articles. **Buys 60 mss/year.** Length: 500-1,200 words. **Pays $300-500 and up.**

Photos Images of artwork must be in the form of 35mm slides, larger transparencies, or high-quality digital files. Full captions must accompany these. Buys all rights.
Tips "Look at several current issues and read the author's guidelines carefully. Remember that our readers are professional artists. Pitch an article; send clips. Do not send a finished article."

ARTIST'S PALETTE

Express Publications, Ltd., Locked Bag 111, Silverwater NSW 1811 Australia. (61)(2)9741-3899. Fax: (61)(2)9737-8017. Website: www.expresspublications.com.au. *"Artist's Palette* provides insights on, as well as step-by-step demonstrations from, Australian and international artists. Features the latests in news, review, and products from the art world as well as exhibition previews and reviews."
Nonfiction Needs general interest, how-to, interview, new product. Query.

$$ ARTLINK

Australia's Leading Contemporary Art Quarterly, Artlink Australia, P.O. Box 8141, Station Arcade, Adelaide SA Australia. (61)(8)8212-8711. Fax: (61)(8)8212-8911. E-mail: info@artlink.com.au. Website: www.artlink.com.au. Quarterly magazine covering contemporary art in Australia. Estab. 1981. Guidelines available online.
Nonfiction Needs general interest. Write or e-mail the editor with your CV and 2-3 examples of previously published writing. **Pays $300/1,000 words.**
Tips Because *Artlink* is a themed magazine which tries to make art relevant across society, we often need to find contributors who have expert knowledge of subjects outside of the art area who can put the work of artists in a broader context.

ARTNEWS

ABC, 48 W. 38th St., New York NY 10018. (212)398-1690. Fax: (212)819-0394. E-mail: info@artnews.com. Website: www.artnews.com. Monthly magazine. *ARTnews* reports on art, personalities, issues, trends and events that shape the international art world. Investigative features focus on art ranging from old masters to contemporary, including painting, sculpture, prints, and photography. Regular columns offer exhibition and book reviews, travel destinations, investment and appreciation advice, design insights, and updates on major art world figures. Estab. 1902. Circ. 84,012. No kill fee. Accepts queries by mail, e-mail, fax, phone.

$$ ART PAPERS

Atlanta Art Papers, Inc., P.O. Box 5748, Atlanta GA 31107. (404)588-1837. Fax: (404)588-1836. E-mail: editor@artpapers.org. Website: www.artpapers.org. **95% freelance written**. Bimonthly magazine covering contemporary art and artists. *Art Papers*, about regional and national contemporary art and artists, features a variety of perspectives on current art concerns. Each issue presents topical articles, interviews, reviews from across the US, and an extensive and informative artists' classified listings section. Our writers and the artists they cover represent the scope and diversity of the country's art scene. Estab. 1977. Circ. 12,000. Byline given. Pays on publication. No kill fee. Publishes ms an average of 3 months after acceptance. Buys all rights. Editorial lead time 2 months. Submit seasonal material 2 months in advance.
Nonfiction Buys 240 mss/year. Pays $60-325 on spec for unsolicited articles.
Photos Send photos. Identification of subjects required. Reviews color slides, b&w prints. Offers no additional payment for photos accepted with ms.
Columns/Departments Current art concerns and news. Buys 8-10 mss/year. Query. **Pays $100-175.**

$ ART TIMES

Commentary and Resource for the Fine and Performing Arts, P.O. Box 730, Mount Marion NY 12456-0730. (845)246-6944. Fax: (845)246-6944. E-mail: info@arttimesjournal.com. Website: www.arttimesjournal.com. **Contact:** Raymond J. Steiner. **10% freelance written**. Monthly tabloid covering the arts (visual, theater, dance, music, literary, etc.). *"Art Times* covers the art fields and is distributed in locations most frequented by those enjoying the arts. Our copies are distributed throughout the lower part of the northeast as well as metropolitan New York area; locations include theaters, galleries, museums, schools, art clubs, cultural centers and the like. Our readers are mostly over 40, affluent, art-conscious and sophisticated. Subscribers are located across US and abroad (Italy, France, Germany, Greece, Russia, etc.)." Estab. 1984. Circ. 28,000. Byline given. Pays on publication. No kill fee. Publishes ms an average of 3 years after acceptance. Buys first North American serial rights, buys first rights. Submit seasonal material 8 months in advance. Accepts simultaneous submissions. Responds in 6 months to queries. Responds in 6 months to mss. Sample copy for SAE with 9 × 12 envelope and 6 first-class stamps.

Writer's guidelines for #10 SASE or online.

Fiction "We're looking for short fiction that aspires to be literary." Needs adventure, ethnic, fantasy, historical, humorous, mainstream, science fiction, contemporary. "We seek quality literary pieces. Nothing violent, sexist, erotic, juvenile, racist, romantic, political, off-beat, or related to sports or juvenile fiction." **Buys 8-10 mss/year.** Send complete ms. Length: 1,500 words maximum.

Poetry Needs avant-garde, free verse, haiku, light verse, traditional. "We prefer well-crafted 'literary' poems. No excessively sentimental poetry." Buys 30-35 poems/year. Submit maximum 6 poems. Length: 20 lines maximum. **Offers contributor copies and 1 year's free subscription.**

Tips "Be advised that we are presently on an approximate 3-year lead for short stories, 2-year lead for poetry. We are now receiving 300-400 poems and 40-50 short stories per month. We only publish 2-3 poems and 1 story each issue. Be familiar with *Art Times* and its special audience. *Art Times* has literary leanings with articles written by a staff of scholars knowledgeable in their respective fields. Although an 'arts' publication, we observe no restrictions (other than noted) in accepting fiction/poetry other than a concern for quality writing—subjects can cover anything and not specifically arts."

AUSTRALIAN ART COLLECTOR

Gadfly Media, Level 1, 645 Harris St., Ultimo, Sydney NSW 2007 Australia. (61)(2)9281-7523. Fax: (61)(2)9281-7529. E-mail: susan@gadfly.net.au. Website: www.artcollector.net.au. Quarterly magazine covering Australian art collecting. *Australian Art Collector* is the only Australian publication targeted specifically at people who buy art.

Nonfiction Needs expose, general interest, interview. Query.

$$$$ AZURE DESIGN, ARCHITECTURE AND ART

460 Richmond St. W., Suite 601, Toronto ON M5V 1Y1 Canada. (416)203-9674. Fax: (416)203-9842. E-mail: azure@azureonline.com. Website: www.azuremagazine.com. **75% freelance written**. Magazine covering design and architecture. Estab. 1985. Circ. 20,000. Pays on publication. Offers variable kill fee. Publishes ms an average of 1 month after acceptance. Buys first rights. Editorial lead time up to 45 days. Responds in 6 weeks to queries.

Nonfiction Buys 25-30 mss/year. Length: 350-2,000 words. **Pays $1/word (Canadian).**

Columns/Departments Trailer (essay/photo on something from the built environment); and Forms & Functions (coming exhibitions, happenings in world of design), both 300-350 words. Buys 30 mss/year. Query. **Pays $1/word (Canadian).**

Tips Try to understand what the magazine is about. Writers must be well versed in the field of architecture and design. It's very unusual to get something from someone I haven't worked quite closely with and gotten a sense of who the writer is. The best way to introduce yourself is by sending clips or writing samples and describing what your background is in the field.

BELLE

ACP Magazines, Ltd., 54-58 Park St., Sydney NSW 2000 Australia. (61)(2)9282-8000. Fax: (61)(2)9267-4361. Website: www.acp.com.au. **Contact:** Neale Whitaker, editor. Bimonthly magazine committed to great design and architecture and to portraying the best of Australia and overseas. "*belle* seeks to create a seamless expression of taste at the intersection of design, décor, architecture, knowledge and fashionable living." Circ. 30,000.

Nonfiction Needs general interest, how-to, interview, new product, photo feature. Query.

$ BOMB MAGAZINE

New Arts Publications, 80 Hanson Place, Suite 703, Brooklyn NY 11217. (718)636-9100. Fax: (718)636-9200. E-mail: generalinquiries@bombsite.com. Website: www.bombsite.com. Quarterly magazine providing interviews between artists, writers, musicians, directors and actors. Written, edited and produced by industry professionals and funded by those interested in the arts. Publishes work which is unconventional and contains an edge, whether it be in style or subject matter. Estab. 1981. Circ. 36,000. Pays on publication. No kill fee. Publishes ms an average of 3-6 months after acceptance. Buys first rights, buys one-time rights. Editorial lead time 3-4 months. Accepts queries by mail. Responds in 3-5 months to mss. Sample copy for $7, plus $1.59 postage and handling. Guidelines by e-mail.

Fiction Send completed ms with SASE. Needs experimental, novel concepts, contemporary. No genre: romance, science fiction, horror, western. less than 25 pages **Pays $100, and contributor's copies.**

Poetry Send completed ms with SASE. Submit maximum 4-6 poems.

Fillers No more than 25 pages in length.

Tips Mss should be typed, double-spaced, proofread and should be final drafts. Purchase a sample issue before submitting work.

$$ C

international contemporary art, C The Visual Arts Foundation, P.O. Box 5, Station B, Toronto ON M5T 2T2 Canada. (416)539-9495. Fax: (416)539-9903. E-mail: editor@cmagazine.com. Website: www.cmagazine.com. **80% freelance written**. Quarterly magazine covering international contemporary art. *C* provides a vital and vibrant forum for the presentation of contemporary art and the discussion of issues surrounding art in our culture, including feature articles, reviews and reports, as well as original artists' projects. Estab. 1983. Circ. 7,000. Byline given. Pays on publication. Offers kill fee. Offers kill fee Publishes ms an average of 4 months after acceptance. Editorial lead time 3 months. Accepts queries by mail, e-mail, fax. Accepts simultaneous submissions. Responds in 6 weeks to queries. Responds in 4 months to mss. Sample copy for $10 (US). Guidelines for #10 SASE.

Nonfiction Needs essays, general interest, opinion, personal experience. **Buys 50 mss/year.** Length: 1,000-3,000 words. **Pays $150-500 (Canadian), $105-350 (US).**

Photos State availability of or send photos. Captions required. Reviews 35mm transparencies or 8 × 10 prints. Offers no additional payment for photos accepted with ms Buys one-time rights; shared copyright on reprints.

Columns/Departments Reviews (review of art exhibitions), 500 words. Buys 30 mss/year. Query. **Pays $125 (Canadian).**

$$ DIRECT ART MAGAZINE

Slow Art Productions, 123 Warren St., Hudson NY 12534. E-mail: directartmag@aol.com. Website: www.slowart.com. **75% freelance written**. Semiannual fine art magazine covering alternative, anti-establishment, left-leaning fine art. Estab. 1998. Circ. 10,000. Byline sometimes given. Pays on acceptance. No kill fee. Buys one-time rights, buys electronic rights. Editorial lead time 2 months. Submit seasonal material 3 months in advance. Accepts queries by mail, e-mail. Accepts simultaneous submissions. Responds in 2 weeks to queries. Responds in 1 month to mss. Sample copy for sae with 9 × 12 envelope and 10 First-Class stamps. Guidelines for #10 SASE.

Nonfiction Needs essays, expose, historical, how-to, humor, inspirational, interview, opinion, personal experience, photo feature, technical. **Buys 4-6 mss/year.** Query with published clips. Length: 1,000-3,000 words. **Pays $100-500.**

Photos State availability of or send photos. Reviews 35mm slide transparencies, digital files on CD (TIF format). Negotiates payment individually Buys one time rights.

Columns/Departments Query with published clips. **Pays $100-500.**

EASTERN ART REPORT

EAPGROUP International Media, P.O. Box 13666, London England SW14 8WF United Kingdom. E-mail: info@eapgroup.com. Website: www.eapgroup.com. *EAR* has a worldwide readership—from scholars to connoisseurs—with varying knowledge of or interest in the historical, philosophical, practical, or theoretical aspects of Eastern art. Estab. 1989. No kill fee. Accepts queries by mail, e-mail, fax. Guidelines available online.

Nonfiction International Diary (art-related news, previews, reviews); Art market reports written from an individual perspective; books previews and reviews. Query.

Photos Reviews illustrations, electronic images of at least 300 dpi.

$ ESPACE

SCULPTURE, Le Centre de Diffusion 3D, 4888 rue Saint-Denis, Montreal QC H2J 2L6 Canada. (514)844-9858. Fax: (514)844-3661. E-mail: espace@espace-sculpture.com. Website: www.espace-sculpture.com. **95% freelance written**. Quarterly magazine covering sculpture events. Canada's only sculpture publication, *Espace* represents a critical tool for the understanding of contemporary sculpture. Published 4 times a year, in English and French, *Espace* features interviews, in-depth articles, and special issues related to various aspects of three dimensionality. Foreign contributors guarantee an international perspective and diffusion. Estab. 1987. Circ. 1,400. Byline given. Pays on publication. No kill fee. Publishes ms an average of 3 months after acceptance. Buys all rights. Editorial lead time 5 months. Submit seasonal material 3 months in advance. Accepts queries by mail. Accepts simultaneous submissions. Sample copy free.

Nonfiction Needs essays, expose. **Buys 60 mss/year.** Query. Length: 1,000-1,400 words. **Pays $60/page.**

Photos Send photos. Reviews transparencies, prints. Offers no additional payment for photos accepted with ms

LA ARCHITECT

The Magazine of Design in Southern California, Balcony Media, Inc., 512 E. Wilson, Suite 213, Glendale CA 91206. E-mail: Jonathan@formmag.net. Website: www.formmag.net. **80% freelance written**. Bimonthly magazine covering architecture, interiors, landscape, and other design disciplines. *L.A. Architect* is interested in architecture, interiors, product, graphics, and landscape design as well as news about the arts. We encourage designers to keep us informed on projects, techniques, and products that are innovative, new, or nationally newsworthy. We are especially interested in new and renovated projects that illustrate a high degree of design integrity and unique answers to typical problems in the urban cultural and physical environment. Estab. 1999. Circ. 20,000. Byline given. Pays on publication. No kill fee. Publishes ms an average of 3 months after acceptance. Makes work-for-hire assignments. Editorial lead time 4 months. Submit seasonal material 4 months in advance. Accepts queries by mail, e-mail, fax. Responds in 1 month to queries. Responds in 1 month to mss. Sample copy for $5.95. Guidelines available online.

Nonfiction Needs book excerpts, essays, historical, interview, new product. **Buys 20 mss/year.** Length: 500-2,000 words. **Payment negotiable.**

Photos State availability. Captions, identification of subjects, model releases required. Offers no additional payment for photos accepted with ms. Buys one time rights.

Tips Our magazine focuses on contemporary and cutting-edge work either happening in Southern California or designed by a Southern California designer. We like to find little-known talent that has not been widely published. We are not like *Architectural Digest* in flavor so avoid highly decorative subjects. Each project, product, or event should be accompanied by a story proposal or brief description and select images. Do not send original art without our written request; we make every effort to return materials we are unable to use, but this is sometimes difficult and we must make advance arrangements for original art.

$$ THE MAGAZINE ANTIQUES

Brant Publications, 575 Broadway, New York NY 10012. (212)941-2800. Fax: (212)941-2819. E-mail: cdrayton@brantpub.com. Website: www.themagazineantiques.com. **75% freelance written**. Monthly magazine. Articles should present new information in a scholarly format (with footnotes) on the fine and decorative arts, architecture, historic preservation, and landscape architecture. Estab. 1922. Circ. 61,754. Byline given. Pays on publication. No kill fee. Publishes ms an average of 6 months after acceptance. Buys all rights. Editorial lead time 6 months. Submit seasonal material 6 months in advance. Responds in 3 weeks to queries. Responds in 6 months to mss. Sample copy for $10.50 for back issue; $5 for current issue.

Nonfiction Needs historical, scholarly. **Buys 50 mss/year.** Length: 2,850-3,500 words. **Pays $250-500.**

Photos State availability. Captions, identification of subjects required. Reviews contact sheets, negatives, transparencies, prints. Buys one time rights.

$$$$ METROPOLIS

The Magazine of Architecture and Design, Bellerophon Publications, 61 W. 23rd St., 4th Floor, New York NY 10010. (212)627-9977. Fax: (212)627-9988. E-mail: edit@metropolismag.com. Website: www.metropolismag.com. **Contact:** Belinda Lanks, managing editor. **80% freelance written**. Monthly magazine (combined issue July/August) for consumers interested in architecture and design. "*Metropolis* examines contemporary life through design—architecture, interior design, product design, graphic design, crafts, planning, and preservation. Subjects range from the sprawling urban environment to intimate living spaces to small objects of everyday use. In looking for why design happens in a certain way, Metropolis explores the economic, environmental, social, cultural, political, and technological context. With its innovative graphic presentation and its provocative voice, *Metropolis* shows how richly designed our world can be." Estab. 1981. Circ. 45,000. Byline given. Pays 60-90 days after acceptance. No kill fee. Publishes ms an average of 3 months after acceptance. Makes work-for-hire assignments. Submit seasonal material 3 months in advance. Accepts queries by mail, e-mail, fax. Responds in 8 months to queries. Sample copy for $7. Guidelines available online.

Nonfiction Contact: Martin Pedersen, executive editor. Needs essays, design, architecture, urban planning issues and ideas, interview, of multi-disciplinary designers/architects. No profiles on individual architectural practices, information from public relations firms, or fine arts. **Buys 30 mss/year.** Length: 1,500-4,000 words. **Pays $1,500-4,000.**

Photos Captions required. Reviews contact sheets, 35mm or 4 × 5 transparencies, 8 × 10 b&w prints. Payment offered for certain photos. Buys one time rights.

Columns/Departments The Metropolis Observed (architecture, design, and city planning news features), 100-1,200 words, **pays $100-1,200**; Perspective (opinion or personal observation of architecture and design), 1,200 words, **pays $1,200**; Enterprise (the business/development of architecture and design), 1,500 words, **pays $1,500**; In Review (architecture and book review essays), 1,500 words, **pays $1,500**. Direct queries to Belinda Lanks, managing editor. Buys 40 mss/year. Query with published clips.
Tips *Metropolis* strives to tell the story of design to a lay person with an interest in the built environment, while keeping the professional designer engaged. The magazine examines the various design disciplines (architecture, interior design, product design, graphic design, planning, and preservation) and their social/cultural context. We're looking for the new, the obscure, or the wonderful. Also, be patient and don't expect an immediate answer after submission of query.

$$ ☐ MIX

IA Declaration of Creative Independence, Parallelogramme Artist-Run Culture and Publishing, Inc., 401 Richmond St. West, Suite 446, Toronto ON M5V 3A8 Canada. (416)506-1012. E-mail: editor@mixmagazine.com. Website: www.mixmagazine.com. **95% freelance written**. Quarterly magazine covering Artist-Run gallery activities. *Mix* represents and investigates contemporary artistic practices and issues, especially in the progressive Canadian artist-run scene. Estab. 1975. Circ. 3,500. Byline given. Pays on publication. Offers 40% kill fee. Publishes ms an average of 6 months after acceptance. Buys first North American serial rights. Editorial lead time 6 months. Submit seasonal material 4 months in advance. Accepts queries by mail, e-mail, fax. Responds in 2 months to queries. Responds in 3 months to mss. Sample copy for $6.95, 8½ × 101/4 SAE and 6 first-class stamps. Guidelines available online.
Nonfiction Needs essays, interview. **Buys 12-20 mss/year.** Query with published clips. Length: 750-3,500 words. **Pays $100-450.**
Reprints Send photocopy of article and information about when and where the article previously appeared.
Photos State availability. Captions, identification of subjects required. Buys one time rights.
Columns/Departments Features, 1,000-3,000 words; Art Reviews, 500 words. Query with published clips. **Pays $100-450.**
Tips Read the magazine and other contemporary art magazines. Understand the idea 'artist-run.' We're not interested in 'artsy-phartsy' editorial, but rather pieces that are critical, dynamic, and would be of interest to nonartists too.

$$ MODERNISM MAGAZINE

199 George St., Lambertville NJ 08530. (609)397-4104. Fax: (609)397-4409. E-mail: andrea@modernismmagazine.com. Website: www.modernismmagazine.com. **Contact:** Andrea Truppin, editor-in-chief. **70% freelance written**. Quarterly magazine covering 20th century design, architecture and decorative arts. "We are interested in design, architecture and decorative arts and the people who created them. Our coverage begins in the 1920s with Art Deco and related movements, and ends with 1980s Post-Modernism, leaving contemporary design to other magazines." Estab. 1998. Circ. 35,000. Byline given. Pays on publication. Offers 25% kill fee. Publishes ms an average of 4 months after acceptance. Buys all rights. We do sometimes buy one-time rights, but most articles are "work for hire." Editorial lead time 6 months. Submit seasonal material 6 months in advance. Accepts queries by mail, e-mail. Accepts previously published material. Accepts simultaneous submissions. Responds in 1 month to queries. Sample copy for $6.95. Guidelines free.
Nonfiction Needs book excerpts, essays, historical, interview, new product, photo feature. No first-person. **Buys 20 mss/year.** Query with published clips. Length: 1,000-2,500 words. **Pays $300-600.**
Reprints Accepts previously published submissions.
Photos State availability of or send photos. Captions, identification of subjects required. Reviews contact sheets, transparencies, prints. Negotiates payment individually.
Tips "Articles should be well researched, carefully reported, and directed at a popular audience with a special interest in the Modernist movement. Please don't assume readers have prior familiarity with your subject; be sure to tell us the who, what, why, when, and how of whatever you're discussing."

N SOUTHWEST ART

101 Spruce St., Boulder CO 80302. (303)442-0427. Fax: (303)449-0279. E-mail: southwestart@southwestart.com. Website: www.southwestart.com. **60% freelance written**. Monthly magazine directed to art collectors interested in artists, market trends, and art history of the American West. Estab. 1971. Circ. 60,000. Byline given. Pays on acceptance. Publishes ms an average of 1 year after acceptance. Submit seasonal material 8 months in advance. Accepts queries by mail, fax. Responds in 6 months to mss.

Nonfiction Needs book excerpts, interview. No fiction or poetry. **Buys 70 mss/year**. Query with published clips. Length: 1,400-1,600 words.
Photos Photographs, color print-outs, and videotapes will not be considered. Captions, identification of subjects required. Reviews 35mm, 2¼x2¼, 4 × 5 transparencies. Negotiates rights.
Tips "Research the Southwest art market, send slides or transparencies with queries, and send writing samples demonstrating knowledge of the art world."

$$ WATERCOLOR

Interweave Press, 29 W. 46th St., 3rd Floor, New York NY 10036. (646)841-0500. E-mail: mail@myamericanartist.com. Website: www.myamericanartist.com. Quarterly magazine devoted to watermedia artists. Circ. 50,000. No kill fee. Editorial lead time 4 months.
Nonfiction Needs essays, interview, personal experience, technical. Query with published clips. Length: 1,500-2,000 words. **Pays $500.**

$$ WILDLIFE ART

The Art Journal of the Natural World, Pothole Publications, Inc., P.O. Box 219, Ramona CA 92065. Fax: (760)788-9454. E-mail: rmscott-blair@wildlifeartmag.com. Website: www.wildlifeartmag.com. **60% freelance written**. Bimonthly magazine. *Wildlife Art* is the world's foremost magazine of the natural world, featuring wildlife, landscape, and western art. Features living artists as well as wildlife art masters, illustrators, and conservation organizations. Special emphasis on landscape and plein-air paintings. Audience is collectors, galleries, museums, show promoters worldwide. Estab. 1982. Circ. 30,000. Byline given. Pays on publication. Offers negotiable kill fee. Publishes ms an average of 6 months after acceptance. Buys second serial (reprint) rights. Accepts queries by mail, e-mail. Responds in 6 months to queries. Sample copy for sae with 9 × 12 envelope and 10 First-Class stamps. Guidelines available online.
Nonfiction Needs general interest, historical, interview. **Buys 40 mss/year.** Query with published clips, include artwork samples. Length: 800-1,500 words. **Pays $150-500.**
Tips Best way to break in is to offer concrete story ideas, new talent, a new unique twist of artistic excellence.

Associations

$$$$ AAA LIVING

Pace Communications, 1301 Carolina St., Greensboro NC 27401. Fax: (336)383-8272. **70% freelance written**. Published 4 times a year. "AAA Living magazine, published for the Auto Club Group of Dearborn, Michigan, is for members of AAA clubs in 8 Midwest states (IL, N. IN, IA, MI, MN, NE, ND, & WI). Our magazine features lifestyle & travel articles about each state and the region, written by knowledgeable resident writers, as well as coverage of affordable, accessible travel getaways nationally & internationally & information about exclusive AAA products & services." Estab. 1917. Circ. 2.5 million. Byline given. Pays on acceptance. Offers 10% kill fee. Publishes ms an average of 3 months after acceptance. Buys first North American serial rights, buys electronic rights. Editorial lead time 6 months. Submit seasonal material 6 months in advance. Accepts queries by mail, e-mail. Responds in 6 months to mss. Sample copy available online. Guidelines available online.
Nonfiction Needs travel. Query with published clips. Length: 150-1,600 words. **Pays $150-1,800 for assigned articles.**
Photos Send photos. Captions, identification of subjects required. Reviews GIF/JPEG files. Negotiates payment individually. Buys one time rights.
Tips "Articles should have a strong hook, tell an entertaining story, be unique & should avoid merely listing everything there is to do at a location. Take the readers to places the locals love & visitors would never forget. Color & details are essential. Share a sense of experience that goes beyond 'go here, do this.' Touch the readers' senses. You might find yourself in a quaint downtown surrounded by restored historic buildings, but many towns in the Midwest can claim this. What does that downtown sound like? What's going on in the square behind you? What kinds of smells emanate from nearby restaurants? Your stories should show the readers the destination, not simply tell them about it."

$$ ACTION

United Spinal Association, 75-20 Astoria Blvd., Jackson Heights NY 11370-1177. (718)803-3782, ext. 279. E-mail: action@unitedspinal.org. Website: www.unitedspinal.org/publications/action. **75% freelance written**. Bimonthly magazine covering living with spinal cord injury. The monthly news magazine of the United Spinal Association is a benefit to members of the organization: people with spinal cord injury or dysfunction, as well as caregivers, parents and some spinal cord injury/dysfunction professionals. All articles should reflect this common interest of the audience. Assume that your audience is better educated in the subject of spinal cord medicine than average, but be careful not to be too technical. Within these seemingly narrow confines, however, a wide variety of subjects are possible. Articles that feature members or programs of United Spinal are preferred, but any article that deals with issues of living with SCI will be considered. Estab. 1946. Circ. 12,000. Byline given. Pays on publication. No kill fee. Publishes ms an average of 2-3 months after acceptance. Buys all rights. Accepts queries by e-mail. Sample copy for sae. Guidelines for sae.

Nonfiction Needs essays, general interest, how-to, humor, interview, new product, personal experience, photo feature, travel, medical research. Does not want articles that treat disabilities as an affliction or cause for pity, or that show the writer does not get that people with disabilities are people like anyone else. **Buys 36 mss/year.** Query. Length: 1,000-1,800 words. **Pays $400.**

Photos Send photos. Identification of subjects required. Reviews GIF/JPEG files. Offers no additional payment for photos accepted with ms.

Columns/Departments The Observatory (personal essays on subjects related to disability), 750 words. Buys 60 mss/year. Query with published clips. **Pays $200.**

Tips It helps (though is not necessary) if you have a disability, or if you can be comfortable with people with disabilities; they are the subjects of most of our articles as well as the bulk of our readership. Our readers are looking for tips on how to live well with mobility impairment. They're concerned with access to jobs, travel, recreation, education, etc. They like to read about how others deal with like situations. They are sophisticated about spinal cord disabilities and don't need to be 'inspired' by the typical stories about people with disabilities that appear in the human interest section of most newspapers.

$$$$ AMERICAN EDUCATOR

American Federation of Teachers, 555 New Jersey Ave. N.W., Washington DC 20001. E-mail: amered@aft.org. Website: www.aft.org/american_educator/index.html. **50% freelance written**. Quarterly magazine covering education, condition of children, and labor issues. *American Educator*, the quarterly magazine of the American Federation of Teachers, reaches over 800,000 public school teachers, higher education faculty, and education researchers and policymakers. The magazine concentrates on significant ideas and practices in education, civics, and the condition of children in America and around the world. Estab. 1977. Circ. 850,000. Byline given. Pays on publication. Offers 50% kill fee. Publishes ms an average of 2-6 months after acceptance. Buys one-time rights, buys electronic rights. Editorial lead time 1 year. Submit seasonal material 6 months in advance. Accepts queries by mail, e-mail, fax. Accepts previously published material. Accepts simultaneous submissions. Responds in 2 months to queries. Responds in 6 months to mss. Sample copy available online. Guidelines available online.

Nonfiction Needs book excerpts, essays, historical, interview, discussions of educational research. No pieces that are not supportive of the public schools. **Buys 8 mss/year.** Query with published clips. Length: 1,000-7,000 words. **Pays $750-3,000 for assigned articles. Pays $300-1,000 for unsolicited articles.**

Photos State availability. Captions, identification of subjects, model releases required. Reviews contact sheets, negatives, transparencies, 8 × 10 prints, GIF/JPEG files. Negotiates payment individually. Buys one time rights.

CHRISTIAN MANAGEMENT REPORT

The Latest Leadership and Management Trends and Tools for Members of Christian Management Association, Christian Management Association, P.O. Box 4090, San Clemente CA 92674. (949)487-0900. Fax: (949)487-0927. Website: www.cmaonline.org. **50% freelance written**. Bimonthly magazine covering management and leadership issues for Christian nonprofit organizations and churches. Estab. 1976. Circ. 4,000. Byline given. No kill fee. Publishes ms an average of 4-6 weeks after acceptance. Editorial lead time 3 months. Accepts queries by e-mail, phone. Accepts simultaneous submissions. Responds in 2-4 weeks to queries. Responds in 2-4 weeks to mss. Guidelines by e-mail.

Nonfiction Needs book excerpts, how-to, interview, technical. Query.

$$ DAC NEWS

Official Publication of the Detroit Athletic Club, Detroit Athletic Club, 241 Madison Ave., Detroit MI 48226. (313)442-1034. Fax: (313)442-1047. E-mail: kenv@thedac.com. **20% freelance written**. Magazine published 10 times/year. *DAC News* is the magazine for Detroit Athletic Club members. It covers club news and events, plus general interest features. Estab. 1916. Circ. 5,000. Byline given. Pays on publication. No kill fee. Publishes ms an average of 3 months after acceptance. Buys one-time rights. Makes work-for-

hire assignments. Editorial lead time 3 months. Submit seasonal material 3 months in advance. Accepts queries by mail, phone. Responds in 1 month to queries. Sample copy free.
Nonfiction Needs general interest, historical, photo feature. No politics or social issues—this is an entertainment magazine. We do not accept unsolicited manuscripts or queries for travel articles. **Buys 2-3 mss/year.** Length: 1,000-2,000 words. **Pays $100-500.**
Photos Illustrations only. State availability. Captions, identification of subjects, model releases required. Reviews transparencies, 4x6 prints. Negotiates payment individually. Buys one time rights.
Tips Review our editorial calendar. It tends to repeat from year to year, so a freelancer with a fresh approach to one of these topics will get our attention quickly. It helps if articles have some connection with the DAC, but this is not absolutely necessary. We also welcome articles on Detroit history, Michigan history, or automotive history.

$$$ DCM

Data Center Management: Bringing Insight and Ideas to the Data Center Community, AFCOM, 742 E. Chapman Ave., Orange CA 92866. Fax: (714)997-9743. E-mail: afcom@afcom.com. Website: www.afcom.com. **50% freelance written**. Bimonthly magazine covering data center management. *DCM* is the slick, 4-color, bimonthly publication for members of AFCOM, the leading association for data center management. Estab. 1988. Circ. 4,000 worldwide. Byline given. Pays on acceptance for assigned articles and on publication for unsolicited articles. Offers 0-10% kill fee. Publishes ms an average of 3 months after acceptance. Buys all rights. Editorial lead time 6-12 months. Submit seasonal material 6 months in advance. Responds in 1-3 weeks to queries. Responds in 1-3 months to mss. Guidelines available online.

- Prefers queries by e-mail.

Nonfiction Needs how-to, technical, management as it relates to and includes examples of data centers and data center managers. The January/February issue is the annual 'Emerging Technologies' issue. Articles for this issue are visionary and product neutral. No product reviews or general tech articles. **Buys 15+ mss/year**. Query with published clips. 2,000 word maximum **Pays 50¢/word and up, based on writer's expertise.**
Photos We rarely consider freelance photos. State availability. Identification of subjects, model releases required. Reviews TIFF/PDF/GIF/JPEG files. Offers no additional payment for photos accepted with ms. Buys one time rights.
Tips See 'Top 10 Reasons for Rejection' and editorial guidelines online.

$$ THE ELKS MAGAZINE

The Elks Magazine, 425 W. Diversey Pkwy., Chicago IL 60614-6196. (773)755-4740. E-mail: annai@elks.org. Website: www.elks.org/elksmag. **25% freelance written**. Magazine covers nonfiction only; published 10 times/year with basic mission of being the voice of the Elks. All material concerning the news of the Elks is written in-house. Estab. 1922. Circ. 1,037,000. Pays on acceptance. No kill fee. Buys first North American serial rights. Responds in 1 month with a yes/no on ms purchase Guidelines available online

- Accepts queries by mail, but purchase decision is based on final mss only.

Nonfiction "We're really interested in seeing manuscripts on Americana, history, technology, science, sports, health, or just intriguing topics." No fiction, religion, controversial issues, first-person, fillers, or verse. **Buys 20-30 mss/year.** Send complete ms. Length: 1,500-2,000 words. **Pays 25¢/word.**
Photos "If possible, please advise where photographs may be found. Photographs taken and submitted by the writer are paid for separately at $25 each. Send transparencies, slides. Pays $475 for one-time cover rights."
Columns/Departments "The invited columnists are already selected."
Tips "Please try us first. We'll get back to you soon."

$$ HUMANITIES

National Endowment for the Humanities, 1100 Pennsylvania Ave. NW, Washington DC 20506. (202)606-8435. Fax: (202)606-8451. E-mail: dskinner@neh.gov. Website: www.neh.gov. **50% freelance written**. Bimonthly magazine covering news in the humanities focused on projects that receive financial support from the agency. Estab. 1980. Circ. 6,000. Byline given. Pays on publication. Publishes ms an average of 2 months after acceptance. Buys all rights. Makes work-for-hire assignments. Editorial lead time 3 months. Submit seasonal material 4 months in advance. Accepts queries by mail, e-mail, fax, phone. Accepts previously published material. Sample copy available online.
Nonfiction Needs book excerpts, historical, interview, photo feature. **Buys 25 mss/year.** Query with published clips. Length: 400-2,500 words. **Pays $300-600.**

Photos Contact: Contact mbiernik@neh.gov. Identification of subjects, model releases required. Offers no additional payment for photos accepted with ms; negotiates payment individually. Buys one time rights.
Columns/Departments In Focus (directors of state humanities councils), 700 words; Breakout (special activities of state humanities councils), 750 words. Buys 12 mss/year. Query with published clips. **Pays $300.**

$$ ⊘ KIWANIS

3636 Woodview Trace, Indianapolis IN 46268-3196. (317)875-8755. Fax: (317)879-0204. Website: www.kiwanis.org. **10% freelance written**. Magazine published 6 times/year for business and professional persons and their families. Estab. 1917. Circ. 240,000. Byline given. Pays on acceptance. Offers 40% kill fee. Publishes ms an average of 6 months after acceptance. Buys first rights. Accepts queries by mail, e-mail, fax. Responds in 1 month to queries. Sample copy and writer's guidelines for 9 × 12 SAE with 5 first class stamps. Guidelines available online.

- No unsolicited mss.

Nonfiction Articles about social and civic betterment, small-business concerns, children, science, education, religion, family, health, recreation, etc. Emphasis on objectivity, intelligent analysis, and thorough research of contemporary issues. Positive tone preferred. Concise, lively writing, absence of clichés, and impartial presentation of controversy required. Articles must include information and quotations from international sources. We have a continuing need for articles that concern helping youth, particularly prenatal through age 5: day care, developmentally appropriate education, early intervention for at-risk children, parent education, safety and health. No fiction, personal essays, profiles, travel pieces, fillers, or verse of any kind. A light or humorous approach is welcomed where the subject is appropriate and all other requirements are observed. **Buys 20 mss/year.** Length: 500-1,200 words. **Pays $300-600.**
Photos We accept photos submitted with manuscripts. Our rate for a manuscript with good photos is higher than for one without. Identification of subjects, model releases required. Buys one time rights.
Tips We will work with any writer who presents a strong feature article idea applicable to our magazine's audience and who will prove he or she knows the craft of writing. First, obtain writer's guidelines and a sample copy. Study for general style and content. When querying, present detailed outline of proposed manuscript's focus and editorial intent. Indicate expert sources to be used, as well as possible Kiwanis sources for quotations and anecdotes. Present a well-researched, smoothly written manuscript that contains a `human quality' with the use of anecdotes, practical examples, quotations, etc.

$$ THE LION

300 W. 22nd St., Oak Brook IL 60523-8842. E-mail: rkleinfe@lionsclubs.org. Website: www.lionsclubs.org. **35% freelance written. Works with a small number of new/unpublished writers each year.** Monthly magazine covering service club organization for Lions Club members and their families. Estab. 1918. Circ. 490,000. Byline given. Pays on acceptance. No kill fee. Publishes ms an average of 5 months after acceptance. Buys all rights. Accepts queries by mail, e-mail, fax, phone. Responds in 1 month to queries. Sample copy and writer's guidelines free
Nonfiction Welcomes humor, if sophisticated but clean; no sensationalism. Prefers anecdotes in articles. Needs photo feature, must be of a Lions Club service project, informational (issues of interest to civic-minded individuals). No travel, biography, or personal experiences. **Buys 40 mss/year.** Length: 500-1,500 words. **Pays $100-750.**
Photos Purchased with accompanying ms. Photos should be at least 5 × 7 glossies; color prints or slides are preferred. We also accept digital photos by e-mail. Be sure photos are clear and as candid as possible. Captions required. Total purchase price for ms includes payment for photos accepted with ms.
Tips Send detailed description of proposed article. Query first and request writer's guidelines and sample copy. Incomplete details on how the Lions involved actually carried out a project and poor quality photos are the most frequent mistakes made by writers in completing an article assignment for us. No gags, fillers, quizzes, or poems are accepted. We are geared increasingly to an international audience. Writers who travel internationally could query for possible assignments, although only locally related expenses could be paid.

$$$ THE MEETING PROFESSIONAL MAGAZINE

Meeting Professionals International, 3030 LBJ Freeway, Suite 1700, Dallas TX 75234. E-mail: bpotter@mpiweb.org. Website: www.themeetingprofessional.org. **60% freelance written**. Monthly magazine covering the global meeting idustry. *The Meeting Professional* delivers strategic editorial content on meeting industry trends, opportunities and items of importance in the hope of fostering professional development and career enhancement. The magazine is mailed monthly to 20,000 MPI members and 10,000 qualified nonmember subscribers and meeting industry planners. It is also distributed at major industry shows, such as IT&ME and EIBTM, at MPI conferences, and upon individual request. Circ. 30,000. Byline given. Pays on acceptance. Offers kill fee. Offers a negotiable kill fee. Publishes ms an average of 2-3 months after acceptance. Buys all rights. Editorial lead time 2 months. Submit seasonal material 3 months in advance. Accepts queries by e-mail. Sample copy free. Guidelines by e-mail.

Nonfiction Needs general interest, how-to, interview, travel, industry-related. No duplications from other industry publications. **Buys 60 mss/year.** Query with published clips. Length: 1,000-2,500 words. **Pays 50-75¢/word for assigned articles.**

Tips Understand and have experience within the industry. Writers who are familiar with our magazine and our competitors are better able to get our attention, send better queries, and get assignments.

$ $ PENN LINES

Pennsylvania Rural Electric Association, 212 Locust St., Harrisburg PA 17108-1266. E-mail: peter_fitzgerald@prea.com. Website: www.prea.com/pennlines/plonline.htm. Monthly magazine covering rural life in Pennsylvania. News magazine of Pennsylvania electric cooperatives. Features should be balanced, and they should have a rural focus. Electric cooperative sources (such as consumers) should be used. Estab. 1966. Circ. 140,000. Byline given. Pays on publication. No kill fee. Publishes ms an average of 3 months after acceptance. Buys first rights. Editorial lead time 4 months. Submit seasonal material 4 months in advance. Accepts queries by mail, e-mail. Sample copy available online. Guidelines available online.

Nonfiction Needs general interest, historical, how-to, interview, travel, rural PA only. **Buys 6 mss/year.** Query or send complete ms. Length: 500-2,000 words. **Pays $300-650.**

Photos Captions required. Reviews transparencies, prints, GIF/JPEG files. Negotiates payment individually. Buys one-time rights and right to publish online.

Tips Find topics of statewide interest to rural residents. Detailed information on *Penn Lines'* readers, gleaned from a reader survey, is available online.

THE ROTARIAN

Rotary International, One Rotary Center, 1560 Sherman Ave., Evanston IL 60201. (847)866-3000. Fax: (847)866-8554. Website: www.rotary.org. **40% freelance written**. Monthly magazine for Rotarian business and professional men and women and their families, schools, libraries, hospitals, etc. "Articles should appeal to an international audience and in some way help Rotarians help other people. The organization's rationale is one of hope, encouragement, and belief in the power of individuals talking and working together." Estab. 1911. Circ. 510,000. Byline sometimes given. Pays on acceptance. Offers kill fee. Kill fee negotiable Buys one-time rights, buys all rights. Editorial lead time 4-8 months. Accepts queries by mail, e-mail. Accepts previously published material. Sample copy for $1 (e-mail edbrookc@rotaryintl.org). Guidelines available online.

Nonfiction Needs general interest, humor, inspirational, photo feature, technical, science, travel, lifestyle, sports, business/finance, environmental, health/medicine, social issues. No fiction, religious, or political articles. Query with published clips. Length: 1,500-2,500 words. **Pays negotiable rate.**

Reprints "Send tearsheet, photocopy or typed ms with rights for sale noted and information about when and where the material previously appeared." Negotiates payment.

Photos State availability. Reviews contact sheets, transparencies. Buys one time rights.

Columns/Departments Health; Management; Finance; Travel, all 550-900 words. Query.

Tips "The chief aim of *The Rotarian* is to report Rotary International news. Most of this information comes through Rotary channels and is staff written or edited. The best field for freelance articles is in the general interest category. We prefer queries with a Rotary angle. These stories run the gamut from humor pieces and how-to stories to articles about such significant concerns as business management, technology, world health, and the environment."

⊞ SCOTTISH HOME & COUNTRY MAGAZINE

Scottish Women's Rural Institutes, 42 Heriot Row, Edinburgh Scotland EH3 6ES United Kingdom. (44)(131)225-1724. Fax: (44)(131)225-8129. E-mail: swri@swri.demon.co.uk. Website: www.swri.org.uk/magazine.html. Monthly publication that keeps readers in touch with SWRI news and rural events throughout Scotland. No kill fee. Editorial lead time 1 month. Sample copy for £1.35. Guidelines by e-mail.

- SWRI members are not normally paid for submissions.

Nonfiction Crafts, personal histories, social history, health, travel, cookery, general women's interests. Does not want articles on religion or party politics. Send complete ms. Length: 500-1,000 words.

$$ THE TOASTMASTER

Toastmasters International, P.O. Box 9052, Mission Viejo CA 92690-9052. (949)858-8255. E-mail: submissions@toastmasters.org. Website: www.toastmasters.org. **50% freelance written**. Monthly magazine on public speaking, leadership, and club concerns. "This magazine is sent to members of Toastmasters International, a nonprofit educational association of men and women throughout the world who are interested in developing their communication and leadership skills. Members range from novice to professional speakers and from a wide variety of ethnic and cultural backgrounds, as Toastmasters is an international organization." Estab. 1933. Circ. 235,000 in 11,700 clubs worldwide. Byline given. Pays on acceptance. No kill fee. Publishes ms an average of 1 year after acceptance. Buys first rights, buys second serial (reprint) rights, buys all rights. Submit seasonal material 3-4 months in advance. Accepts queries by mail, e-mail. Accepts previously published material. Accepts simultaneous submissions. Responds in 6-8 weeks to queries. Sample copy for 9 × 12 SASE with 4 first-class stamps. Guidelines available online.

- "Our readers are knowledgeable and experienced public speakers; therefore we accept only authentic, well-researched and well-crafted stories. Show, don't tell! Use sources, quotes from experts and other research to back up your views. The best articles have style, depth, emotional impact and take-away value to the reader. A potential feature article needs an unusual hook, compelling story or unique angle. Profiles of colorful, controversial, historically significant, amusing, unusual or unique people are welcome, but keep in mind that our readers live in 92 different countries, so stay away from profiles of American presidents or sports figures. All submissions must be in English, however. Please query first, or send a draft of your proposed article. We recommend you carefully study several issues of the magazine before submitting a query. We are not responsible for unsolicited articles, artwork or photographs, so please don't send anything you can't afford to lose."

Nonfiction Toastmasters members are requested to view their submissions as contributions to the organization. Sometimes asks for book excerpts and reprints without payment, but original contribution from individuals outside Toastmasters will be paid for at stated rates. Needs how-to, humor, interview, well-known speakers and leaders, communications, leadership, language use. **Buys 50 mss/year.** "Please read our guidelines first, then when you are ready, submit through e-mail. Query with published clips by mail or e-mail (preferred)." Length: 700-2,000 words. **"Compensation for accepted articles depends on whether our submission guidelines are followed, the amount of research involved and the article's general value to us."**

Reprints Send typed ms with rights for sale noted and information about when and where the material previously appeared. Pays 50-70% of amount paid for an original article.

Tips "We are looking primarily for how-to articles on subjects from the broad fields of communications and leadership which can be directly applied by our readers in their self-improvement and club programming efforts. Concrete examples are useful. Avoid sexist or nationalist language. Articles with obvious political or religious slants will not be accepted."

$ TRAIL & TIMBERLINE

The Colorado Mountain Club, 710 10th St., Suite 200, Golden CO 80401. (303)996-2745. Fax: (303)279-3080. E-mail: editor@cmc.org. Website: www.cmc.org. **80% freelance written**. Official quarterly publication for the Colorado Mountain Club. "Articles in *Trail & Timberline* conform to the mission statement of the Colorado Mountain Club to unite the energy, interest, and knowledge of lovers of the Colorado mountains, to collect and disseminate information, to stimulate public interest, and to encourage preservation of the mountains of Colorado and the Rocky Mountain region." Estab. 1918. Circ. 10,500. Byline given. Pays on publication. No kill fee. Publishes ms an average of 2 months after acceptance. Buys all rights. Editorial lead time 6 months. Submit seasonal material 6 months in advance. Accepts queries by mail, e-mail. Accepts previously published material. Responds in 1 week to queries. Responds in 1 month to mss. Sample copy for $5. Guidelines available online.

Nonfiction Needs essays, humor, opinion, Switchbacks, personal experience, photo feature, travel, trip reports. **Buys 10-15** mss/year. Send complete ms. Length: 500-2,000 words. **Pays $50.**

Photos Send photos. Captions, identification of subjects, model releases required. Reviews contact sheets, 35mm transparencies, 3 × 5 or larger prints, GIF/JPEG files. Offers no additional payment for photos accepted with ms Buys one time rights.

Poetry Contact: Jared Smith, poetry editor. Needs avant-garde, free verse, traditional. Buys 6-12 poems/year. **Pays $50.**

Tips Writers should be familiar with the purposes and ethos of the Colorado Mountain Club before querying. Writer's guidelines are available and should be consulted—particularly for poetry submissions. All submissions must conform to the mission statement of the Colorado Mountain Club.

$$$ VFW MAGAZINE

Veterans of Foreign Wars of the United States, 406 W. 34th St., Suite 523, Kansas City MO 64111. (816)756-3390. Fax: (816)968-1169. E-mail: magazine@vfw.org. Website: www.vfw.org. Tim Dyhouse, managing ed. **Contact:** Rich Kolb, editor-in-chief. **40% freelance written**. Monthly magazine on veterans' affairs, military history, patriotism, defense, and current events. "*VFW Magazine* goes to its members worldwide, all having served honorably in the armed forces overseas from World War II through the Iraq and Afghanistan Wars." Estab. 1904. Circ. 1.6 million. Byline given. Pays on acceptance. Offers 50% kill fee. Publishes ms 3-6 months after acceptance. Buys first rights. Editorial lead time is 6 months. Submit seasonal material 6 months in advance. Accepts queries by mail, e-mail, fax. Responds in 2 months to queries. Sample copy for 9 × 12 SAE with 5 first-class stamps. Guidelines available by e-mail.

Nonfiction Contact: Richard Kolb. "Veterans' and defense affairs, recognition of veterans and military service, current foreign policy, American armed forces abroad, and international events affecting US national security are in demand." Needs general interest, historical, inspirational. **Buys 25-30 mss/year.** Query with 1-page outline, résumé, and published clips. Length: 1,000-1,500 words. **Pays up to $500-1,000 max. for assigned articles; $500-750 max. for unsolicited articles.**

Photos Send photos. Reviews contact sheets, negatives, GIF/JPEG files, 5 × 7 or 8 × 10 b&w prints. Buys first North American rights.

Tips "Absolute accuracy and quotes from relevant individuals are a must. Bibliographies useful if subject required extensive research and/or is open to dispute. Consult *The Associated Press Stylebook* for correct grammar and punctuation. Please enclose a 3-sentence biography describing your military service and your military experience in the field in which you are writing. No phone queries."

VINTAGE SNOWMOBILE MAGAZINE

Meagher, Inc., P.O. Box 130, Grey Eagle MN 56336. (320)285-7066. E-mail: vsca@vsca.com. Website: www.vsca.com. **75% freelance written**. Quarterly magazine covering vintage snowmobiles and collectors. *Vintage Snowmobile Magazine* is sent to members of the Vintage Snowmobile Club of America. Estab. 1987. Circ. 2,400. Byline sometimes given. Pays on acceptance. No kill fee. Publishes ms an average of 3 months after acceptance. Buys first North American serial rights. Editorial lead time 2 months. Submit seasonal material 3 months in advance. Accepts queries by mail, e-mail, fax, phone.

Nonfiction Needs general interest, historical, humor, photo feature, coverage of shows. Query with published clips. Length: 200-2,000 words.

Photos Send photos. Reviews 3 × 5 prints, GIF/JPEG files. Negotiates payment individually. Buys all rights.

Columns/Departments Featured Sleds Stories, 500 words. Query with published clips.

▣ WALK MAGAZINE

The Ramblers' Association, 2nd Floor, Camelford House, 87-90 Albert Embankment, London England SE1 7TW United Kingdom. +44 020 7339 8500. Fax: +44 020 7339 8501. E-mail: ramblers@ramblers.org.uk. Website: www.ramblers.org.uk. "Quarterly magazine that encourages people to participate in walking, educates people about the countryside, and promotes wider access to—and protection of—the countryside. The magazine is distributed to Ramblers' Association members, organizations, and individuals who want to stay informed on the group's policies." Circ. 140,000. Pays on publication. No kill fee. Editorial lead time 6 weeks. Accepts queries by mail. Sample copy online or for a SASE (A4 and 73 pence). Guidelines by e-mail.

- Book reviews, news stories, and articles on policy issues are normally written in-house.

Nonfiction Feature articles should promote an interest in walking, but should not just profile a location. Articles should describe why a particular walk is special to the writer. It helps if the walk can be accessed by public transportation. Query with synopsis/outline, published clips, SASE. Length: 500-800 words. **Payment is negotiable.**

Photos Send photos. Captions required. Reviews 300 dpi digital images. Payment is negotiated.

Astrology, Metaphysical & New Age

$$$$ BODY & SOUL

Martha Stewart Living Omnimedia, 42 Pleasant St., Watertown MA 02472. (617)926-0200. **60% freelance written**. Magazine published 10 times/year emphasizing personal fulfillment and healthier lifestyles. The audience we reach is primarily female, college-educated, 25-55 years of age, concerned about personal growth, health, earth-friendly living and balance in personal life. Estab. 1974. Circ. 550,000. Byline given. Offers 25% kill fee. Publishes ms an average of 6 months after acceptance. Buys first North

American serial rights, buys electronic rights. Editorial lead time 6-8 months. Submit seasonal material 1 year in advance. Accepts queries by mail. Accepts simultaneous submissions. Responds in 2 months to queries. Sample copy for $5 and 9 × 12 SAE.

Nonfiction Needs how-to, inner growth, spiritual, health news, environmental issues, fitness, natural beauty. **Buys 50 mss/year.** Query with published clips. Length: 100-2,500 words. **Pays 75¢-$1.25/word.**

Columns/Departments Health, beauty, fitness, home, green living, healthy eating, personal growth, and spirituality, 600-1,300 words. Buys 50 mss/year. Query with published clips. **Pays 75¢-$1.25/word**

Tips Read the magazine and get a sense of the type of writing run in column. In particular, we are looking for new or interesting approaches to subjects such as mind-body fitness, earth-friendly products, Eastern and herbal medicine, self-help, community, healthy eating, etc. No e-mail or phone queries, please. Begin with a query, résumé and published clips—we will contact you for the manuscript. A query is 1-2 paragraphs—if you need more space than that to present the idea, then you don't have a clear grip on it.

$$ FATE MAGAZINE

Fate Magazine, Inc., P.O. Box 460, Lakeville MN 55044 U.S. (952)431-2050. Fax: (952)891-6091. E-mail: submissions@fatemag.com. Website: www.fatemag.com. Phyllis Galde, ed.; David Godwin, managing ed. **Contact:** Phyllis Galde. **75% freelance written**. Covering the paranormal, ghosts, ufos, strange science. "*Fate* prefers first-person accounts and investigations of the topics we cover. We do not publish fiction or opinion pieces." Estab. 1948. Circ. 15,000. Byline given. Pays after publication. 3-6 months Buys all rights. 3-6 months Accepts queries by mail, e-mail, fax. Accepts simultaneous submissions. Responds in 4-6 months to queries.

Nonfiction "Personal psychic and mystical experiences, 350-500 words. **Pays $25.** Articles on parapsychology, Fortean phenomena, cryptozoology, spiritual healing, flying saucers, new frontiers of science, and mystical aspects of ancient civilizations, 500-3,000 words. Must include complete authenticating details. Prefers interesting accounts of single events rather than roundups. We very frequently accept manuscripts from new writers; the majority are people's first-person accounts of their own psychic/mystical/spiritual experiences. We do need to have all details, where, when, why, who and what, included for complete documentation. We ask for a notarized statement attesting to truth of the article." Needs general interest, historical, how-to, personal experience, photo feature, technical. We do not publish poetry, fiction, editorial/opinion pieces, or book-length mss. **Buys 100 mss/year.** Query. Length: 500-4,000 words. **Pays 5¢/word.** Pays with merchandise or ad space if requested.

Photos Buys slides, prints, or digital photos/illustrations with ms. Send photos with submission. Reviews GIF/JPEG files; prints (4 × 6). Pays $10. Buys one-time rights.

Columns/Departments True Mystic Experiences: Short reader-submitted stories of strange experiences; My Proof of Survival: Short, reader-submitted stories of proof of life after death, 300-1,000 words. Writer should query. **Pays $25.**

Fillers Fillers are especially welcomed and must be be fully authenticated also, and on similar topics. Length: 100-1,000 words. **Pays 5¢/word.**

Tips "*Fate* is looking for exciting, first-hand accounts of ufo and paranormal experiences and investigations."

$ NEWWITCH

BBI Media, Inc., P.O. Box 687, Forest Grove OR 97116. (888)724-3966. E-mail: editor@newwitch.com. Website: www.newwitch.com. Quarterly magazine covering paganism, wicca and earth religions. *newWitch* is dedicated to witches, wiccans, neo-pagans, and various other earth-based, pre-Christian, shamanic, and magical practitioners. We hope to reach not only those already involved in what we cover, but the curious and completely new as well. Estab. 2002. Circ. 15,000. Byline given. Pays on publication. Offers 100% kill fee. Buys first world wide periodical and nonexclusive electronic rights. Editorial lead time 3-4 months. Submit seasonal material 6 months in advance. Accepts queries by mail, e-mail, fax, phone. Accepts previously published material. Responds in 1-2 weeks to queries. Responds in 1 month to mss. Sample copy for $6. Guidelines available online.

Nonfiction Particularly interested in how-to spellcrafting and material for solitary pagans and wiccans. Needs book excerpts, essays, historical, how-to, humor, inspirational, interview, new product, opinion, personal experience, photo feature, religious, travel. Send complete ms. Length: 1,000-4,000 words. **Pays 2¢/word minimum.**

Photos State availability. Identification of subjects, model releases required. Reviews GIF/JPEG files. Negotiates payment individually; offers no additional payment for photos accepted with ms. Buys first world wide periodical and nonexclusive electronic rights.
Fiction Needs adventure, erotica, ethnic, fantasy, historical, horror, humorous, mainstream, mystery, novel concepts, religious, romance, suspense. Does not want faction (fictionalized retellings of real events). Avoid gratuitous sex, violence, sentimentality and pagan moralizing. Don't beat our readers with the Rede or the Threefold Law. **Buys 3-4 mss/year.** Send complete ms. Length: 1,000-5,000 words. **Pays 2¢/word minimum.**
Poetry Needs avant-garde, free verse, haiku, light verse, traditional. Submit maximum 3-5 poems. **Pays $15.**
Tips Read the magazine, do your research, write the piece, send it in. That's really the only way to get started as a writer: everything else is window dressing.

$ NEW YORK SPIRIT MAGAZINE

107 Sterling Place, Brooklyn NY 11217. (718)638-3733. Fax: (718)230-3459. E-mail: office@nyspirit.com. Website: www.nyspirit.com. Bimonthly tabloid covering spirituality and personal growth and transformation. We are a magazine that caters to the holistic health community in New York City. Circ. 50,000. Byline given. Pays on acceptance. Publishes ms an average of 3 months after acceptance. Buys first rights. Editorial lead time 1 month. Accepts previously published material. Accepts simultaneous submissions. Responds in 1 month to queries. Sample copy for sae with 8 × 10 envelope and 10 First-Class stamps. Guidelines available online.
Nonfiction Needs essays, how-to, humor, inspirational, interview, photo feature. **Buys 30 mss/year.** Query. Length: 1,000-3,500 words. **Pays $150 maximum.**
Photos State availability. Model releases required.
Columns/Departments Fitness (new ideas in staying fit), 1,500 words. **Pays $150.**
Fiction Needs humorous, mainstream, inspirational. **Buys 5 mss/year.** Query with published clips. Length: 1,000-3,500 words. **Pays $150.**
Tips Be vivid and descriptive. We are very interested in hearing from new writers.

PREDICTION MAGAZINE

IPC Focus Network, Leon House, 233 High St., Croydon CR9 1HZ United Kingdom. E-mail: predictionfeatures@ipcmedia.com. Website: www.predictionmagazine.co.uk. Monthly magazine aimed at women of all ages who are interested in mystical—but practical—solutions to love, family, money, and career issues. Readers are fascinated by life's mysteries and the supernatural, and are looking for upbeat ways to predict their future, understand themselves more, and make their lives happier through positive change. Pays on publication. No kill fee. Editorial lead time 4 months. Accepts queries by mail, e-mail. Responds in 6 weeks (if interested). Guidelines available online.
Nonfiction Astrology, divination, psychic phenomena, self-help/personality quizzes, spirituality, ghosts/spirits, angels, crystals, pets, real-life stories. Doesn't accept short stories or poetry. Already has dedicated contributors for horoscopes, tarot, numerology, and dreams. Send complete ms. Length: 800-1,600 words.

$ SHAMAN'S DRUM

A Journal of Experiential Shamanism, Cross-Cultural Shamanism Network, P.O. Box 270, Williams OR 97544. (541)846-1313. Fax: (541)846-1204. **Contact:** Timothy White, editor. **75% freelance written.** Quarterly educational magazine of cross-cultural shamanism. "*Shaman's Drum* seeks contributions directed toward a general but well-informed audience. Our intent is to expand, challenge, and refine our readers' and our understanding of shamanism in practice. Topics include indigenous medicineway practices, contemporary shamanic healing practices, ecstatic spiritual practices, and contemporary shamanic psychotherapies. Our overall focus is cross-cultural, but our editorial approach is culture-specific—we prefer that authors focus on specific ethnic traditions or personal practices about which they have significant firsthand experience. We are looking for examples of not only how shamanism has transformed individual lives but also practical ways it can help ensure survival of life on the planet. We want material that captures the heart and feeling of shamanism and that can inspire people to direct action and participation, and to explore shamanism in greater depth." Estab. 1985. Circ. 6,000. Byline given. Publishes ms an average of 6 months after acceptance. Buys first North American serial rights, buys first rights. Editorial lead time 1 year. Accepts previously published material. Responds in 3 months to queries. Sample copy for $7. Guidelines for #10 SASE.

Nonfiction Needs book excerpts, essays, interview, please query, opinion, personal experience, photo feature. No fiction, poetry, or fillers. **Buys 16 mss/year.** Send complete ms. Length: 5,000-8,000 words. **Pays 5¢/word, depending on how much we have to edit.**
Reprints Send typed manuscript with rights for sale noted and information about when and where the material previously appeared. Pays 50% of amount paid for an original article.
Photos Send photos. Identification of subjects required. Reviews contact sheets, transparencies, All size prints. Offers $40-50/photo. Buys one time rights.
Columns/Departments Contact: Judy Wells, Earth Circles. Timothy White, Reviews. Earth Circles (news format, concerned with issues, events, organizations related to shamanism, indigenous peoples, and caretaking Earth); Reviews (in-depth reviews of books about shamanism or closely related subjects such as indigenous lifestyles, ethnobotany, transpersonal healing, and ecstatic spirituality), 500-1,500 words. Buys 8 mss/year. Query. **Pays 5¢/word.**
Tips "All articles must have a clear relationship to shamanism, but may be on topics which have not traditionally been defined as shamanic. We prefer original material that is based on, or illustrated with, first-hand knowledge and personal experience. Articles should be well documented with descriptive examples and pertinent background information. Photographs and illustrations of high quality are always welcome and can help sell articles."

$ WHOLE LIFE TIMES

1200 S. Hope St., Ste. 300, Los Angeles CA 90015. E-mail: jessica@wholelifetimes.com. Website: www.wholelifetimes.com. Monthly tabloid for cultural creatives. Estab. 1979. Circ. 58,000. Byline given. Pays within 1-2 months after publication. Buys first North American serial rights. Accepts queries by mail, e-mail. Sample copy for $3. Guidelines for #10 SASE.
Nonfiction Healing Arts, Food and Nutrition, Spirituality, New Beginnings, Relationships, Longevity, Arts/Cultures Travel, Vitamins and Supplements, Women's Issues, Sexuality, Science and Metaphysics, Environment/Simple Living. **Buys 60 mss/year.** Send complete ms. **Payment varies.**
Reprints Send typed manuscript with rights for sale noted and information about when and where the material previously appeared. Pays 50% of amount paid for an original article.
Columns/Departments Healing; Parenting; Finance; Food; Personal Growth; Relationships; Humor; Travel; Politics; Sexuality; Spirituality; and Psychology. Length: 750-1,200 words.
Tips Queries should be professionally written and show an awareness of current topics of interest in our subject area. We welcome investigative reporting and are happy to see queries that address topics in a political context. We are especially looking for articles on health and nutrition. No monthly columns sought.

Automotive & Motorcycle

$ AMERICAN MOTORCYCLIST

American Motorcyclist Association, 13515 Yarmouth Dr., Pickerington OH 43147. Fax: (614)856-1920. Website: www.ama-cycle.org. **10% freelance written**. Monthly magazine for enthusiastic motorcyclists investing considerable time and money in the sport. We emphasize the motorcyclist, not the vehicle. Estab. 1947. Circ. 260,000. Byline given. Pays on publication. No kill fee. Buys first North American serial rights. Editorial lead time 3 months. Submit seasonal material 4 months in advance. Accepts queries by mail, e-mail. Responds in 5 weeks to queries. Responds in 6 weeks to mss. Sample copy for $1.25. Guidelines free.
Nonfiction Needs interview, with interesting personalities in the world of motorcycling, personal experience, travel. **Buys 8 mss/year.** Send complete ms. Length: 1,000-2,500 words. **Pays minimum $8/published column inch.**
Photos Send photos. Captions, identification of subjects required. Reviews transparencies, prints. Pays $50/photo minimum. Buys one time rights.
Tips Our major category of freelance stories concerns motorcycling trips to interesting North American destinations. Prefers stories of a timeless nature.

AUSTRALIAN MOTORCYCLE NEWS

ACP Magazines, Ltd., 54-58 Park St., Sydney NSW 2000 Australia. (61)(2)9282-8000. Fax: (61)(2)9267-4361. Website: www.acp.com.au. **Contact:** Matt Shields, editor. Biweekly magazine providing the latest news on sport racing and bike tests. Estab. 1951. Circ. 21,796.

Readers who own & buy bikes/accessories.

Nonfiction Needs general interest, how-to, new product. Query.

$ $ AUTOMOBILE QUARTERLY

The Connoisseur's Magazine of Motoring Today, Yesterday, and Tomorrow, Automobile Heritage Publishing & Communications LLC, 800 E. 8th St., New Albany IN 47150. Fax: (812)948-2816. E-mail: tpowell@autoquartly.com. Website: www.autoquarterly.com. **Contact:** Tracy Powell, managing editor. **85% freelance written**. Quarterly magazine covering "automotive history, with excellent photography." Estab. 1962. Circ. 8,000. Byline given. Pays on acceptance. Publishes ms an average of 1 year after acceptance. Buys first international serial rights. Editorial lead time 9 months. Responds in 1 month to queries. Responds in 2 months to mss. Sample copy for $19.95.

Nonfiction Needs historical, photo feature, technical, biographies. **Buys 25 mss/year.** Query. Length: 2,500-5,000 words. **Pays approximately 35¢/word or more.**

Photos State availability. Reviews 4 × 5 Buys perpetual rights of published photography per work-for-hire freelance agreement.

Tips "Please query, with clips, via snail mail. No phone calls, please. Study *Automobile Quarterly*'s unique treatment of automotive history first."

$ $ AUTO RESTORER

BowTie, Inc., 3 Burroughs, Irvine CA 92618. (949)855-8822. Fax: (949)855-3045. E-mail: tkade@fancypubs.com. Website: www.autorestorermagazine.com. **85% freelance written**. Monthly magazine covering auto restoration. Our readers own old cars and they work on them. We help our readers by providing as much practical, how-to information as we can about restoration and old cars. Estab. 1989. Pays on publication. Publishes ms an average of 3 months after acceptance. Buys first North American serial rights, buys one-time rights. Submit seasonal material 4 months in advance. Accepts queries by mail, e-mail, fax. Responds in 2 months to queries. Sample copy for $7. Guidelines free.

Nonfiction Needs how-to, auto restoration, new product, photo feature, technical, product evaluation. **Buys 60 mss/year.** Query. Length: 200-2,500 words. **Pays $150/published page, including photos and illustrations.**

Photos Technical drawings that illustrate articles in black ink are welcome. Send photos. Reviews contact sheets, transparencies, 5 × 7 prints. Offers no additional payment for photos accepted with ms.

Tips Query first. Interview the owner of a restored car. Present advice to others on how to do a similar restoration. Seek advice from experts. Go light on history and nonspecific details. Make it something that the magazine regularly uses. Do automotive how-tos.

$ $ $ $ AUTOWEEK

Crain Communications, Inc., 1155 Gratiot Ave., Detroit MI 48207. (313)446-6000. Fax: (313)446-1027. Website: www.autoweek.com. **Contact:** Roger Hart, Executive Editor. **5% freelance written, most by regular contributors**. Biweekly magazine. *AutoWeek* is a biweekly magazine for auto enthusiasts. Estab. 1958. Circ. 300,000. Byline given. Pays on publication. Publishes ms an average of 1 month after acceptance. Buys all rights. Accepts queries by e-mail.

Nonfiction Needs historical, interview. **Buys 5 mss/year.** Query. Length: 100-400 words. **Pays $1/word.**

$ $ BACKROADS

Motorcycles, Travel & Adventure, Backroads, Inc., P.O. Box 317, Branchville NJ 07826. (973)948-4176. Fax: (973)948-0823. E-mail: editor@backroadsusa.com. Website: www.backroadsusa.com. **50% freelance written**. Monthly tabloid covering motorcycle touring. "*Backroads* is a motorcycle tour magazine geared toward getting motorcyclists on the road and traveling. We provide interesting destinations, unique roadside attractions and eateries, plus Rip & Ride Route Sheets. We cater to all brands. If you really ride, you need *Backroads*." Estab. 1995. Circ. 50,000. Byline given. Pays on publication. Buys one-time rights. Editorial lead time 1 month. Submit seasonal material 3 months in advance. Accepts queries by mail, e-mail, fax. Sample copy for $4. Guidelines available online.

Nonfiction Contact: Shira Kamil, editor/publisher. Needs essays, motorcycle/touring, new product, opinion, personal experience, travel. No long diatribes on 'How I got into motorcycles.' Query. Length: 500-2,500 words. **Pays 10¢/word minimum for assigned articles. Pays 5¢/word minimum for unsolicited articles.**

Photos Send photos. Offers no additional payment for photos accepted with ms.

Columns/Departments We're Outta Here (weekend destinations), 500-750 words; Great All-American Diner Run (good eateries with great location), 300-800 words; Thoughts from the Road (personal opinion/insights), 250-500 words; Mysterious America (unique and obscure sights), 300-800 words; Big City Getaway (day trips), 500-750 words. Buys 20-24 mss/year. Query. **Pays $75/article.**

Fillers Needs facts, newsbreaks. Length: 100-250 words.
Tips "We prefer destination-oriented articles in a light, layman's format, with photos (digital images on CD). Stay away from any name-dropping and first-person references."

$$$ CANADIAN BIKER MAGAZINE

735 Market St., Victoria BC V8T 2E2 Canada. (250)384-0333. Fax: (250)384-1832. E-mail: edit@canadianbiker.com. Website: www.canadianbiker.com. **65% freelance written**. Magazine covering motorcycling. A family-oriented motorcycle magazine whose purpose is to unite Canadian motorcyclists from coast to coast through the dissemination of information in a non-biased, open forum. The magazine reports on new product, events, touring, racing, vintage and custom motorcycling as well as new industry information. Estab. 1980. Circ. 20,000. Byline given. Publishes ms an average of 1 year after acceptance. Buys first rights. Editorial lead time 3 months. Accepts queries by mail, e-mail, fax, phone. Responds in 6 weeks to queries. Responds in 6 months to mss. Sample copy for $5 or online. Guidelines free.
Nonfiction All nonfiction must include photos and/or illustrations. Needs general interest, historical, how-to, interview, Canadian personalities preferred, new product, technical, travel. **Buys 12 mss/year.** Send complete ms. Length: 500-1,500 words. **Pays $100-200 for assigned articles; $80-150 for unsolicited articles.**
Photos State availability of or send photos. Captions, identification of subjects, model releases required. Reviews 4 × 4 transparencies, 3 × 5 prints. Negotiates payment individually. Buys one time rights.
Tips We're looking for more racing features, rider profiles, custom sport bikes, quality touring stories, `extreme' riding articles. Contact editor first before writing anything. Have original ideas, an ability to write from an authoritative point of view, and an ability to supply quality photos to accompany text. Writers should be involved in the motorcycle industry and be intimately familiar with some aspect of the industry which would be of interest to readers. Observations of the industry should be current, timely, and informative.

$$$$ CAR AND DRIVER

Hachette Filipacchi Magazines, Inc., 1585 Eisenhower Place, Ann Arbor MI 48108. (734)971-3600. Fax: (734)971-9188. E-mail: editors@caranddriver.com. Website: www.caranddriver.com. **Contact:** Mark Gillies, executive editor. Monthly magazine for auto enthusiasts; college-educated, professional, median 24-35 years of age. Estab. 1956. Circ. 1,300,000. Byline given. Pays on acceptance. Offers 25% kill fee. Buys first North American serial rights. Accepts queries by mail, e-mail, fax. Responds in 2 months to queries.
Nonfiction "Seek stories about people and trends, including racing. Two recent freelance purchases include news-feature on cities across America banning cruising and feature on how car companies create new car smells. All road tests are staff-written. Unsolicited manuscripts are not accepted. Query letters must be addressed to the Managing Editor. Rates are generous, but few manuscripts are purchased from outside." **Buys 1 ms/year. Pays max $3,000/feature; $750-1,500/short piece.**
Photos Color slides and b&w photos sometimes purchased with accompanying ms.
Tips "It is best to start off with an interesting query and to stay away from nuts-and-bolts ideas because that will be handled in-house or by an acknowledged expert. Our goal is to be absolutely without flaw in our presentation of automotive facts, but we strive to be every bit as entertaining as we are informative. We do not print this sort of story: `My Dad's Wacky, Lovable Beetle.'"

$$ CAR AUDIO AND ELECTRONICS

Source Interlink, 2400 E. Katella Ave., 11th Floor, Anaheim CA 92806. (714)939-2400. E-mail: featurecar@primedia.com. Website: www.caraudiomag.com. **30% freelance written**. Monthly magazine covering mobile electronics. Circ. 40,000. Byline given. Pays on publication. No kill fee. Publishes ms an average of 5 months after acceptance. Buys first rights, buys electronic rights. Editorial lead time 4 months. Submit seasonal material 5 months in advance. Accepts queries by mail, e-mail. Accepts simultaneous submissions. Responds in 1 week to queries. Responds in 1 month to mss. Sample copy available online. Guidelines available online.
Nonfiction Needs how-to, photo feature, technical. Does not want personal essays, humor, and so on. **Buys 30 mss/year.** Query. Length: 750-1,200 words. **Pays $150-300.**
Photos State availability of or send photos. Model releases required. Reviews GIF/JPEG files. Negotiates payment individually.
Columns/Departments Choices (vehicle feature), 400-500 words. Buys 5 mss/year. Query. **Pays $100-150.**

Tips Most of our freelancers write on assignment. To get in our pool of freelancers, contact us, preferably with published clips. If you are car audio savvy but don't have published clips or don't have published clips that relate to car audio, we may ask you to write a test piece before assigning you a paying article. Another way is to send a query or manuscript on a vehicle you think we'd be interested in featuring. The vehicle should not have run in another magazine, and it should be available for photos.

CAR CRAFT

Primedia Enthusiast Group, 6420 Wilshire Blvd., Los Angeles CA 90048-5515. Website: www.carcraft.com. Monthly magazine. Created to appeal to drag racing and high performance auto owners. Circ. 383,334. No kill fee. Editorial lead time 3 months.

CUSTOM CLASSIC TRUCKS

Source Interlink Media, 774 So. Placentia Ave., Placentia CA 92870. E-mail: john.gilbert@sorc.com. Website: www.customclassictrucks.com. Monthly magazine. Contains a compilation of technical articles, historical reviews, coverage of top vintage truck events and features dedicated to the fast growing segment of the truck market that includes vintage pickups and sedan deliveries. Circ. 104,376. No kill fee.

4X4 AUSTRALIA

ACP Magazines, Ltd., 54-58 Park St., Sydney NSW 2000 Australia. (61)(2)9282-8000. Fax: (61)(2)9267-4361. Website: www.acp.com.au. **Contact:** Dean Mellor, editor. Monthly magazine covering exciting and remote destinations all over Australia. "*4X4 Australia* includes travel planning info on each place, every month. We also test your favorite camping and 4X4 equipment and all the vehicles while we're traveling in Australia's toughest 4X4 locations." Circ. 18,580.

Nonfiction Needs general interest, how-to, new product, travel. Query.

$$$ FOUR WHEELER MAGAZINE

2400 E. Katella Ave., 11th Floor, Anaheim CA 92806. Website: www.fourwheeler.com. **20% freelance written. Works with a small number of new/unpublished writers each year.** Monthly magazine covering four-wheel-drive vehicles, back-country driving, competition, and travel adventure. Estab. 1963. Circ. 355,466. Pays on publication. No kill fee. Publishes ms an average of 4 months after acceptance. Buys all rights. Submit seasonal material 4 months in advance. Accepts queries by mail.

Nonfiction 4WD competition and travel/adventure articles, technical, how-tos, and vehicle features about unique four-wheel drives. We like the adventure stories that bring four wheeling to life in word and photo: mud-running deserted logging roads, exploring remote, isolated trails or hunting/fishing where the 4x4 is a necessity for success. Query with photos. 1,200-2,000 words; average 4-5 pages when published. **Pays $200-300/feature vehicles; $350-600/travel and adventure; $100-800/technical articles.**

Photos Requires professional quality color slides and b&w prints for every article. Prefers Kodachrome 64 or Fujichrome 50 in 35mm or 2¼ formats. Action shots a must for all vehicle features and travel articles. Captions required.

Tips Show us you know how to use a camera as well as the written word. The easiest way for a new writer/photographer to break into our magazine is to read several issues of the magazine, then query with a short vehicle feature that will show his or her potential as a creative writer/photographer.

$$ FRICTION ZONE

Motorcycle Travel and Information, (877)713-9500. E-mail: editor@friction-zone.com. Website: www.friction-zone.com. **60% freelance written**. Monthly magazine covering motorcycles. Estab. 1999. Circ. 26,000. Byline given. Pays on publication. No kill fee. Publishes ms an average of 1 month after acceptance. Buys first North American serial rights. Editorial lead time 6 weeks. Submit seasonal material 2 months in advance. Responds in to queries. Sample copy for $4.50 or on website.

Nonfiction Needs general interest, historical, how-to, humor, inspirational, interview, new product, opinion, photo feature, technical, travel, medical (relating to motorcyclists), book reviews (relating to motorcyclists). Does not accept first-person writing. **Buys 1 ms/year.** Query. Length: 1,000-3,000 words. **Pays 20¢/word.**

Photos Send photos. Captions, identification of subjects, model releases required. Reviews negatives, slides. Offers $15/published photo. Buys one time rights.

Columns/Departments Health Zone (health issues relating to motorcyclists); Motorcycle Engines 101 (basic motorcycle mechanics); Road Trip (California destination review including hotel, road, restaurant), all 2,000 words. Buys 60 mss/year. Query. **Pays 20¢/word**

Fiction We want stories concerning motorcycling or motorcyclists. No 'first-person' fiction. Query. Length: 1,000-2,000 words. **Pays 20¢/word**.

Fillers Needs anecdotes, facts, gags, newsbreaks, short humor. Length: 2,000-3,000 words. **Pays 20¢/word**

Tips Query via e-mail with sample writing. Visit our website for more detailed guidelines.

HOT 4'S & PERFORMANCE CARS

Express Publications, Ltd., 50 Silverwater Road, Silverwater NSW 2128 Australia. (61)(2)9741-3899. Fax: (61)(2)9737-8017. E-mail: rides@hot4s.com.au. Website: www.hot4s.com.au. Monthly magazine dedicated to the modified 4 cylinder and rotary owner. "*Hot 4's* offers a smooth blend of the latest industry trends, news and products, high-performance contemporary road and racecars, technical information and 'old school' 4s and rotaries."

Nonfiction Needs general interest, new product, technical. Query.

HOT ROD MAGAZINE

Source Interlink Media, Inc., 6420 Wilshire Bvld., Los Angeles CA 90048-5515. E-mail: inquiries@automotive.com. Website: www.hotrod.com. Monthly magazine covering hot rods. Focuses on 50s and 60s cars outfitted with current drive trains and the nostalgia associated with them. Circ. 700,000. No kill fee. Editorial lead time 3 months.

- Query before submitting.

$$ IN THE WIND

Paisano Publications, LLC, P.O. Box 3000, Agoura Hills CA 91376-3000. (818)889-8740. Fax: (818)889-1252. E-mail: photos@easyriders.net. Website: www.easyriders.com. **50% % freelance written**. Quarterly magazine. "Geared toward the custom (primarily Harley-Davidson) motorcycle rider and enthusiast, *In the Wind* is driven by candid pictorial-action photos of bikes being ridden, and events." Estab. 1978. Circ. 90,000. Byline given. Pays on publication. No kill fee. Publishes ms an average of 9 months after acceptance. Buys all rights. Editorial lead time 6 months. Accepts queries by mail, e-mail. Responds in 2 weeks to queries. Responds in 2 months to mss.

Nonfiction Needs photo feature, event coverage. No long-winded tech articles **Buys 6 mss/year.** Length: 750-1,000 words. **Pays $250-600.**

Photos Send SASE for return. Send photos. Identification of subjects, model releases required. Reviews transparencies, digital images, b&w, color prints. Buys all rights.

Tips "Know the subject. Looking for submissions from people who ride their own bikes."

KEYSTONE MOTORCYCLE PRESS

Blue Moon Publications, P.O. Box 296, Ambridge PA 15003-0296. (724)774-6542. E-mail: kmppress@aol.com. **65% freelance written**. Monthly tabloid covering motorcycling. "Our publication is geared toward all motorcyclists & primarily focuses on people & events in the great PA region; hence it is named after the Keystone State. The KMP features product reviews, motorcycle tests, industry news, motorcycling personalities, book reviews, and coverage of major national events." Estab. 1988. Circ. 15,000, plus 2,000 samples and free copies per month. Byline given. Pays on publication. Offers kill fee. varies Publishes ms an average of 2 months after acceptance. Buys first rights. Makes work-for-hire assignments. Editorial lead time 1-2 months. Submit seasonal material 3 months in advance. Accepts queries by mail, e-mail. Responds in 2 weeks to queries. Responds in 1 month to mss. Sample copy free. Guidelines by e-mail.

Nonfiction Needs book excerpts, general interest, historical, how-to, humor, inspirational, interview, new product, (Technical), opinion, (Does not mean letters to the editor), religious, travel., (All must relate to motorcycling.). "We do not want personal diatribes. Witty, okay; pointless is not." **Buys 8 mss/year.** Query with published clips. Length: 250-1,500 words.

Photos Contact: Marilyn Shields. Send photos. Captions, identification of subjects required. Reviews GIF/JPEG files. Negotiates payment individually. Photo rights negotiable.

Columns/Departments Contact: Dan Faingnaert. All Things Considered (Various news clips), 70 words; New Products (Short summaries of new products available), 120 words. Buys 18 mss/year. Query with published clips. **Pays $20-200.**

Fiction Buys 2 mss/year. Query with published clips. Length: 500-2,500 words. **Payment negotiable.**

Poetry Needs free verse, haiku, light verse, traditional.

Fillers Needs anecdotes, facts, gags, newsbreaks, short humor. Buys 18 mss/year. Word length variable. **Payment variable.**

Tips "Unique items or news relevant to motorcycling. It is a vast multi-spectrum culture of all types of individuals involved for many different reasons. If one lives in the great PA area, contributing would be very easy. There is much going on in the world of motorcycling now, particularly in light of the current gasoline situation. If one needs some help, try talking to motorcyclists, read a copy or 2 of of *Motorcyclist, Cycle World Rider*, or *American Motorcyclist* magazines or surf the Web for reference materials. If submitting something, do so via e-mail and use the KISS approach: keep it simple, don't embed graphics, photos or illustrations in copy and at least use spell check. Mac users are preferred, but all are welcome."

⊘ LATINOS ON WHEELS

On Wheels, Inc., 645 Griswold St., Suite 1209, Detroit MI 48226. (313)237-6883. Fax: (313)237-6886. E-mail: vmenard@onwheelsinc.com. Website: www.onwheelsinc.com/lowmagazine. English-language Quarterly magazine. "Supplement to leading Latino newspapers in the US. Provides Latino car buyers and car enthusiasts with the most relevant automotive trends." Circ. 500,000. No kill fee.

- Query before submitting.

N ⊕ LIVE TO RIDE

News Magazines, Locked Bag 5030, Alexandria NSW 2015 Australia. (61)(02)8062-2612. Fax: (61)(02)8062-2613. E-mail: pugs@livetoride.com.au. Website: www.livetoride.com.au. Monthly magazine covering Harley-Davidsons. "*Live to Ride* is jam-packed full of parties, personalities, bike features, jokes, technical rundown on Harleys, together with motorcycle and product updates." Circ. 24,000.
Nonfiction Needs general interest, interview, new product, technical. Query.

⊕ MOTOR

ACP Magazines, Ltd., 54-58 Park St., Sydney NSW 2000 Australia. (61)(2)9282-8000. Fax: (61)(2)9267-4361. Website: www.acp.com.au/motor.htm. **Contact:** Andrew MacLean, editor. Monthly magazine covering the world of automotive news, especially in the area of performance and prestige. Circ. 40,103.

O━ Targets men aged 18-55.

Nonfiction Needs general interest, how-to, new product, technical. Query.

MOTOR TREND

Primedia, 6420 Wilshire Blvd., 7th Floor, Los Angeles CA 90048. Website: www.motortrend.com. **5-10% freelance written. Only works with published/established writers.** Monthly magazine for automotive enthusiasts and general interest consumers. Estab. 1949. Circ. 1,250,000. No kill fee. Publishes ms an average of 3 months after acceptance. Buys all rights. Accepts queries by mail. Responds in 1 month to queries.
Nonfiction Automotive and related subjects that have national appeal. Emphasis on domestic and imported cars, road tests, driving impressions, auto classics, auto, travel, racing, and high-performance features for the enthusiast. Packed with facts. Freelancers should confine queries to photo-illustrated exotic drives and other feature material; road tests and related activity are handled in house. A fact-filled query is suggested for all freelancers.
Photos Buys photos of prototype cars and assorted automotive matter.

⊕ NEW ZEALAND 4WD

Adrenalin Publishing Ltd., P.O. Box 65-092, Mairangi Bay Auckland New Zealand. (64)(9)478-4771. Fax: (64)(9)478-4779. E-mail: editor@nz4wd.co.nz. Website: www.nz4wd.co.nz. Magazine published 11 times/year covering topics of interest to 4WD vehicle buyers and drivers, including vehicle selection, accessories/upgrading, 4WD clubs/sports, lifestyle activities associated with 4WD, adventure and track stories, and technical articles. Estab. 1996. No kill fee.

- Query before submitting.

OUTLAW BIKER

Art & Ink Publications, 820 Hamilton St., Charlotte NC 28206-2991. (704)333-3331. Fax: (704)333-3433. E-mail: inked@skinartmag.com. Website: www.outlawbiker.com. **50% freelance written**. Magazine published 4 times/year covering bikers and their lifestyle. All writers must be insiders of biker lifestyle. Features include coverage of biker events, profiles, and humor. Estab. 1983. Circ. 150,000. Byline given. Pays on publication. Publishes ms an average of 3 months after acceptance. Buys first rights. Editorial lead time 3 months. Submit seasonal material 5 months in advance. Accepts queries by mail, e-mail, fax. Accepts previously published material. Accepts simultaneous submissions. Responds in 2 weeks to queries. Responds in 2 months to mss. Sample copy for $5.98. Guidelines for #10 SASE.

Nonfiction Needs historical, humor, new product, personal experience, photo feature, travel. Daytona Special, Sturgis Special (annual bike runs). No first time experiences—our readers already know. **Buys 10-12 mss/year.** Send complete ms. Length: 100-1,000 words.
Photos Send photos. Captions, identification of subjects, model releases required. Reviews transparencies, prints. Offers $0-10/photo. Buys one time rights.
Columns/Departments Buys 10-12 mss/year. Send complete ms.
Fiction Needs adventure, erotica, fantasy, historical, humorous, romance, science fiction, slice-of-life vignettes, suspense. No racism. **Buys 10-12 mss/year.** Send complete ms. Length: 500-2,500 words.
Poetry Needs avant-garde, free verse, haiku, light verse, traditional. Buys 10-12 poems/year. Submit maximum 12 poems. Length: 2-1,000 lines.
Fillers Needs anecdotes, facts, gags, newsbreaks, short humor. Buys 10-12 mss/year. Length: 500-2,000 words.
Tips Writers must be insiders of the biker lifestyle. Manuscripts with accompanying photographs as art are given higher priority.

⊘ POPULAR HOT RODDING

Source Interlink Media, Inc., 774 S. Placentia Ave., Placentia CA 92870. Website: www.popularhotrodding.com. Monthly magazine for the automotive enthusiast; highlights features that emphasize performance, bolt-on accessories, replacement parts, safety, and the sport of drag racing. Circ. 182,000. No kill fee.

- Query before submitting.

$$ RIDER MAGAZINE

Ehlert Publishing Group, 2575 Vista Del Mar Dr., Ventura CA 93001. E-mail: editor@ridermagazine.com. Website: www.ridermagazine.com. **60% freelance written**. Monthly magazine covering motorcycling. *Rider* serves the all-brand motorcycle lifestyle/enthusiast with a slant toward travel and touring. Estab. 1974. Circ. 127,000. Byline given. Pays on publication. Offers 25% kill fee. Publishes ms an average of 6-12 months after acceptance. Buys first North American serial rights, buys electronic rights. Editorial lead time 3 months. Submit seasonal material 6 months in advance. Accepts queries by mail. Responds in 2 months to queries. Sample copy for $2.95. Guidelines by e-mail.
Nonfiction Needs general interest, historical, how-to, humor, interview, personal experience, travel. Does not want to see fiction or articles on `How I Began Motorcycling.' **Buys 40-50 mss/year.** Query. Length: 750-1,800 words. **Pays $150-750.**
Photos Send photos. Captions required. Reviews contact sheets, transparencies, high quality prints, high resolution (4MP+) digital images. Offers no additional payment for photos accepted with ms. Buys one-time and electronic rights.
Columns/Departments Favorite Rides (short trip), 850-1,100 words. Buys 12 mss/year. Query. **Pays $150-750.**
Tips "We rarely accept manuscripts without photos (slides or b&w prints). Query first. Follow guidelines available on request. We are most open to favorite rides, feature stories (must include excellent photography) and material for `Rides, Rallies and Clubs.' Include a map, information on routes, local attractions, restaurants, and scenery in favorite ride submissions."

$$ ROAD KING

Parthenon Publishing, 28 White Bridge Rd., Suite 209, Nashville TN 37205. Website: www.roadking.com. **25% freelance written**. Bimonthly magazine covering the trucking industry. Byline given. Pays 3 weeks from acceptance. Offers 30% kill fee. Publishes ms an average of 3 months after acceptance. Buys first North American serial rights, buys all electronic rights. Editorial lead time 3-4 months. Submit seasonal material 4 months in advance. Accepts queries by mail. Accepts simultaneous submissions. Responds in 3-4 weeks to queries. Sample copy for #10 SASE. Guidelines free.
Nonfiction No essays, no humor, no cartoons. **Buys 12 mss/year.** Query with published clips. Length: 100-1,000 words. **Pays $50-500.**

⊘ SPORT COMPACT CAR

Source Interlink Media, Inc., 2400 E. Katella Ave., 11th Floor, Anaheim CA 92806. (714)939-2400. Fax: (714)978-6390. Website: www.sportcompactcarweb.com. Monthly magazine for owners and potential buyers of new compacts who seek inside information regarding performance, personalization, and cosmetic enhancement of the vehicles. Circ. 117,000. No kill fee. Editorial lead time 4 months.

- Query before submitting.

SPORT RIDER

Source Interlink Media, Inc., 6420 Wilshire Blvd., Los Angeles CA 90048-5515. E-mail: srmail@primedia.com. Website: www.sportrider.com. Bimonthly magazine for enthusiast of sport/street motercycles and emphasizes performance, both in the motorcycle and the rider. Circ. 108,365. No kill fee.

- Query before submitting.

STREET COMMODORES

Express Publications, Ltd., Locked Bag 111, Silverwater NSW 1811 Australia. (61)(2)9741-3899. Fax: (61)(2)9737-8017. E-mail: ben@streetcommodores.com. Website: www.streetcommodores.com.au. **Contact:** Ben Hosking, editor-in-chief. Monthly magazine covering the best Commodores from around the country along with the latest news, reviews, tips and products available for this Aussie automotive legend. "Street Commodores is the market-leading monthly magazine dedicated strictly to Australia's most popular car - the Commodore."

Nonfiction Needs general interest, historical, how-to, new product, technical. Query.

SUPER CHEVY

Source Interlink Media, Inc., 365 W. Passaic St., Rochelle Park NJ 07662. Website: www.superchevy-web.com. "Monthly magazine covering various forms of motorsports where Cheverolet cars and engines are in competition." Circ. 198,995. No kill fee.

- "Query before submitting. Ms must be typed on white paper and accompanied by SASE."

Photos Captions, model releases, original material.

$ TRUCKIN' MAGAZINE

World's Leading Truck Publication, Source Interlink Media, Inc., 2400 E. Katella Ave., Suite 700, Anaheim CA 92806. Website: www.truckinweb.com. Monthly magazine. Written for pickup drivers and enthusiasts. Circ. 186,606. No kill fee. Editorial lead time 3 months.

WHEELS

ACP Magazines, Ltd., 54-58 Park St., Sydney NSW 2000 Australia. (61)(2)9282-8000. Fax: (61)(2)9267-4361. Website: http://wheelsmag.com.au. **Contact:** Ged Bulmer, editor. Monthly magazine covering all aspects of motoring. Estab. 1953. Circ. 63,200.

Nonfiction Needs general interest, new product, technical. Query.

ZOOM

The Magazine That Puts Go Before Show, Express Publications, Ltd., Locked Bag 111, Silverwater NSW 1811 Australia. (61)(2)9741-3899. Fax: (61)(2)9737-8017. E-mail: gconway@expresspublications.com.au. Website: www.zoommagazine.com.au. **Contact:** Greg Conway, ed. Monthly magazine for those in search of brute horsepower. "*Zoom* is packed with technical articles, mechanical theory, engine conversions, DIY performance tips, supercharger and turbocharger installations, bolt on upgrades and product reviews." See guideilnes online at website.

Nonfiction Needs general interest, how-to, new product, technical. Query.

Aviation

AFRICAN PILOT

Serious About Flying, Published by Wavelengths 10 (Pty) Ltd., 303 Spur Rd., Beaulieu, Kyalami, Midrand Johannesburg South Africa. (27)(11)702-2342. Fax: (27)(11)468-2637. E-mail: editor@africanpilot.co.za. Website: www.africanpilot.co.za. **50% freelance written**. Monthly magazine covering all aspects of general aviation, airline, commercial, and military aviation for consumer value in the sub-continent of Africa. (General aviation hardly exists in the remainder of Africa.) Estab. 2002. Circ. 10,000. Byline given. No kill fee. Editorial lead time 2-3 months. Accepts queries by e-mail. Accepts previously published material. Accepts simultaneous submissions. Sample copy available online. Writer's guidelines online or via e-mail.

Nonfiction Needs general interest, historical, interview, new product, personal experience, photo feature, technical. No articles on aircraft accidents. **Buys up to 60 mss/year.** Send complete ms. Length: 1,200-2,800 words.

Photos Send photos. Captions required. Negotiates payment individually. Buys one time rights.

Tips The website is update monthly and all articles are fully published online.

$$$$ AIR & SPACE MAGAZINE

Smithsonian Institution, P.O. Box 37012, MRC 951, Washington DC 20013-7012. (202)275-1230. Fax: (202)275-1886. E-mail: editors@si.edu. Website: www.airspacemag.com. **80% freelance written**. Bimonthly magazine covering aviation and aerospace for a nontechnical audience. 'Emphasizes the human rather than the technological, on the ideas behind the events. Features are slanted to a technically curious, but not necessarily technically knowledgeable, audience. We are looking for unique angles to aviation/aerospace stories, history, events, personalities, current and future technologies, that emphasize the human-interest aspect." Estab. 1985. Circ. 225,000. Byline given. Pays on acceptance. Offers kill fee. Buys first North American serial rights. Accepts queries by mail, e-mail, fax. Responds in 3 months to queries. Sample copy for $7. Guidelines available online.

Nonfiction "We are actively seeking stories covering space and general or business aviation." Needs book excerpts, essays, general interest, on aviation/aerospace, historical, humor, photo feature, technical. **Buys 50 mss/year.** Query with published clips. Length: 1,500-3,000 words. **Pays $1,500-3,000.**

Photos Refuses unsolicited material. State availability. Reviews 35 mm transparencies, digital files.

Columns/Departments Above and Beyond (first person), 1,500-2,000 words; Flights and Fancy (whimsy), approximately 800 words. Soundings (brief items, timely but not breaking news), 500-700 words. Buys 25 mss/year. Query with published clips. **Pays $150-300.**

Tips "We continue to be interested in stories about space exploration. Also, writing should be clear, accurate, and engaging. It should be free of technical and insider jargon, and generous with explanation and background. The first step every aspiring contributor should take is to study recent issues of the magazine."

$ AUTOPILOT MAGAZINE

The AutoPilot Franchise Systems, 1954 Airport Rd., Suite 250, Atlanta GA 30341. (770)255-1014. Fax: (770)274-2375. Website: www.autopilotmagazine.com. **70% freelance written**. Bimonthly magazine covering aviation. *AutoPilot Magazine* is a lifestyle magazine for the aviation enthusiast. We currently have four editions circulating, including Alabama, Georgia, Florida and the Mid-Atlantic region. This magazine differs from other aviation publications, because its focus is specifically on the pilot. Estab. 2000. Circ. 90,000 for all four editions. Byline given. Pays on acceptance. Buys second serial (reprint) rights. Editorial lead time 2-3 weeks. Accepts queries by mail, e-mail, fax, phone. Sample copy free. Guidelines free.

Nonfiction Needs book excerpts, essays, historical, personal experience, photo feature, travel. Query. Length: 500-900 words. **Pays $100.**

Columns/Departments Airport Spotlight (general aviation airports), 500-800 words; Pilot Profiles, 500-800 words; Notable Aviation Organizations, 900 words; Aviation Museums, 900 words; Aviation Memorials, 600 words. **Pays $100.**

Tips Please e-mail with a current résumé and 2 writing samples.

AVIATION BUSINESS ASIA PACIFIC

Yaffa Publishing, 17-21 Bellevue St., Surry Hills NSW 2010 Australia. (61)(2)9281-2333. Fax: (61)(2)9281-2750. E-mail: yaffa@yaffa.com.au. Website: www.yaffa.com.au. Magazine published 6 times/year covering the issues, politics and business of aviation. "*Aviation Business Asia Pacific* is the second oldest aviation magazine in the world."

Nonfiction Needs general interest, interview, new product, technical. Query.

$$ AVIATION HISTORY

Weider History Group, 19300 Promenade Dr., Leesburg VA 20176. E-mail: aviationhistory@weiderhistorygroup.com. Website: www.thehistorynet.com. **95% freelance written**. Bimonthly magazine covering military and civilian aviation from first flight to the jet age. "It aims to make aeronautical history not only factually accurate and complete, but also enjoyable to a varied subscriber and newsstand audience." Estab. 1990. Circ. 45,000. Byline given. Pays on publication. No kill fee. Publishes ms an average of 2 years after acceptance. Buys all rights. Editorial lead time 6 months. Submit seasonal material 1 year in advance. Accepts queries by mail, e-mail, fax. Accepts simultaneous submissions. Responds in 2 months to queries. Responds in 3 months to mss. Sample copy for $5. Guidelines for #10 SASE or online.

Nonfiction Needs historical, interview, personal experience. **Buys 24 mss/year.** Query. Feature articles should be 3,000-3,500 words, each with a 500-word sidebar where appropriate, author's biography, and book suggestions for further reading. **Pays $300.**

Photos State availability. of art and photos with submissions, cite sources. We'll order. Identification of subjects required. Reviews contact sheets, negatives, transparencies. Buys one time rights.
Columns/Departments Aviators, Restored, Extremes all 1,500 words or less. Pays $150 and up. Book reviews, 250-500 words, pays minimum $50.
Tips "Choose stories with strong art possibilities. Include a hard copy as well as an IBM- or Macintosh-compatible CD. Write an entertaining, informative, and unusual story that grabs the reader's attention and holds it. All stories must be true. We do not publish fiction or poetry."

$ BALLOON LIFE

9 Madeline Ave., Westport CT 06880. (203)629-1241. E-mail: bill_armstrong@balloonlife.com. Website: www.balloonlife.com. **75% freelance written**. Monthly magazine covering sport of hot air ballooning. Readers participate as pilots, crew, and official observers at events and spectators. Estab. 1986. Circ. 7,000. Byline given. Pays on publication. Offers 50-100% kill fee. Publishes ms an average of 3-4 months after acceptance. Buys first North American serial rights. Submit seasonal material 4 months in advance. Accepts queries by mail, e-mail. Accepts simultaneous submissions. Responds in 2 weeks to queries. Sample copy for 9 × 12 SAE with $2 postage. Guidelines available online.
Nonfiction Needs book excerpts, general interest, how-to, flying hot air balloons, equipment techniques, interview, new product, technical, events/rallies, safety seminars, balloon clubs/organizations, letters to the editor. **Buys 150 mss/year.** Send complete ms. Length: 1,000-1,500 words. **Pays $50-200.**
Photos Send photos. Captions, identification of subjects required. Reviews transparencies, prints, high-resolution digital images. Offers $15/inside photos, $50/cover. Buys nonexclusive, all rights.
Columns/Departments Crew Quarters (devoted to some aspect of crewing), 900 words; Preflight (a news and information column), 300-500 words; **pays $50**. Logbook (balloon events that have taken place in last 3-4 months), 300-500 words; **pays $20**. Buys 60 mss/year. Send complete ms.
Tips This magazine slants toward the technical side of ballooning. We are interested in articles that help to educate and provide safety information. Also stories with manufacturers, important individuals, and/or historic events and technological advances important to ballooning. The magazine attempts to present how-to articles on flying, business opportunities, weather, equipment, etc. Both our feature stories and Logbook sections are where most manuscripts are purchased.

$ $ FLYING ADVENTURES MAGAZINE

Aviation Publishing Corporation, P.O. Box 93613, Pasadena CA 91109-3613. (626)618-4000. E-mail: editor@flyingadventures.com. Website: www.flyingadventures.com. **20% freelance written**. Bimonthly magazine covering lifestyle travel for owners and passengers of private aircraft. "Our articles cover upscale travelers." Estab. 1994. Circ. 135,858. features, no departments Pays on acceptance. No kill fee. Buys all rights. Editorial lead time 2 weeks to 2 months. Accepts queries by e-mail. Accepts previously published material. Accepts simultaneous submissions. Responds immediately. Sample copy and guidelines free.
Nonfiction Needs travel, Lifestyle. Nothing non-relevant, not our style. See magazine. Query with published clips. Length: 500-1,500 words. **Pays $150-300 for assigned and unsolicited articles.**
Photos Contact: Photographer Director. State availability. Captions, identification of subjects, model releases required. Reviews GIF/JPEG files. Negotiates payment individually. Buys all rights.
Columns/Departments Contact: Editor. Numerous Departments, see magazine. Buys 100+ mss/year. Query with published clips. **Pays $150.**
Tips "Send clip that fits our content and style. Must fit our style!"

FLYING MAGAZINE

Hachette Filipacchi Media U.S., Inc., 1633 Broadway, 45th Floor, New York NY 10019. (212)767-4936. Fax: (212)767-4932. E-mail: flyedit@hfmus.com. Website: www.flyingmag.com. Monthly magazine covering aviation. Edited for active pilots through coverage of new product development and application in the general aviation market. Estab. 1927. Circ. 277,875. No kill fee. Editorial lead time 3 months. Accepts queries by mail, e-mail, fax. Sample copy for $4.99.

- *Flying* is almost entirely staff written; use of freelance material is limited.

Nonfiction We are looking for the most unusual and best-written material that suits *Flying*. Most subjects in aviation have already been done so fresher ideas and approaches to stories are particularly valued. We buy 'I Learned About Flying From That' articles, as well as an occasional feature with and without photographs supplied. Send complete ms.
Photos State availability.

$ $ ⊘ GENERAL AVIATION NEWS

Flyer Media, Inc., 11120 Gravelly Lake Dr., SW #7, Lakewood WA 98499. (800)426-8538. Fax: (253)471-

9911. E-mail: janice@generalaviationnews.com. Website: www.generalaviationnews.com. **20% freelance written. Prefers to work with published/established writers who are pilots**. Monthly magazine covering general aviation across the U.S. Estab. 1949. Circ. 50,000. Byline given. Buys first North American serial rights. Editorial lead time 3-5 months. Accepts queries by e-mail. Accepts simultaneous submissions. Guidelines free.

Nonfiction Needs general interest, how-to, interview, technical, travel. Query. Length: 700-1,000 words. **Pays $75-250.**

Photos Send photos. jpeg/eps/tiff files (300 dpi). Payment negotiable.

$ $ PLANE AND PILOT

Werner Publishing Corp., 12121 Wilshire Blvd., 12th Floor, Los Angeles CA 90025-1176. (310)820-1500. Fax: (310)826-5008. E-mail: editor@planeandpilotmag.com. Website: www.planeandpilotmag.com. **80% freelance written**. Monthly magazine covering general aviation. We think a spirited, conversational writing style is most entertaining for our readers. We are read by private and corporate pilots, instructors, students, mechanics and technicians—everyone involved or interested in general aviation. Estab. 1964. Circ. 150,000. Byline given. Pays on publication. Offers kill fee. Publishes ms an average of 4 months after acceptance. Buys all rights. Submit seasonal material 4 months in advance. Accepts previously published material. Responds in 4 months to queries. Sample copy for $5.50. Guidelines available online.

Nonfiction Needs how-to, new product, personal experience, technical, travel, pilot efficiency, pilot reports on aircraft. **Buys 75 mss/year.** Query. Length: 1,200 words. **Pays $200-500.**

Reprints Send tearsheet, photocopy or typed ms with rights for sale noted and information about when and where the material previously appeared. Pays 50% of amount paid for original article.

Photos Submit suggested heads, decks and captions for all photos with each story. Submit b&w photos, 8 × 10 prints with glossy finish. Submit color photos in the form of 2¼ × 2¼, 4 × 5 or 35mm transparencies in plastic sleeves. Offers $50-300/photo. Buys all rights.

Columns/Departments Readback (any newsworthy items on aircraft and/or people in aviation), 1,200 words; Jobs & Schools (a feature or an interesting school or program in aviation), 900-1,000 words. Buys 30 mss/year. Send complete ms. **Pays $200-500.**

Tips Pilot proficiency articles are our bread and butter. Manuscripts should be kept under 1,800 words—1,200 words is ideal.

Business & Finance

Business National

$ $ $ $ CORPORATE BOARD MEMBER

Board Member Inc., 475 Park Ave. S., 19th Floor, New York NY 10016. Fax: (212)686-3041. E-mail: cleinster@boardmember.com. Website: www.boardmember.com. **100% freelance written**. Bimonthly magazine covering corporate governance. Our readers are the directors and top executives of publicly-held US corporations. We look for detailed and preferably narrative stories about how individual boards have dealt with the challenges that face them on a daily basis: reforms, shareholder suits, CEO pay, firing and hiring CEOs, setting up new boards, firing useless directors. We're happy to light fires under the feet of boards that are asleep at the switch. We also do service-type pieces, written in the second person, advising directors about new wrinkles in disclosure laws, for example. Estab. 1999. Circ. 60,000. Byline given. Pays on acceptance. Offers 25% kill fee. Publishes ms an average of 3 months after acceptance. Buys all rights. Editorial lead time 4-5 months. Submit seasonal material 4-5 months in advance. Accepts queries by e-mail. Responds in 1 week to queries. Responds in 1 week to mss. Sample copy available online. Guidelines by e-mail.

Nonfiction Best Law Firms in America (July/August); What Directors Think (November/December). Does not want views from 35,000 feet, pontification, opinion, humor, anything devoid of reporting. **Buys 100 mss/year.** Query. Length: 650-2,500 words. **Pays $1,200-5,000.**

Tips Don't suggest stories you can't deliver.

$ $ DOLLARS AND SENSE: THE MAGAZINE OF ECONOMIC JUSTICE

Economic Affairs Bureau, 29 Winter St., Boston MA 02108. (617)447-2177. Fax: (617)477-2179. E-mail: dollars@dollarsandsense.org. Website: www.dollarsandsense.org. **10% freelance written**. Bimonthly magazine covering economic, environmental, and social justice. "We explain the workings of the US and international economics, and provide left perspectives on current economic affairs. Our audience is a mix of activists, organizers, academics, unionists, and other socially concerned people." Estab.

1974. Circ. 8,000. Byline given. Pays on publication. No kill fee. Publishes ms an average of 4 months after acceptance. Editorial lead time 3 months. Submit seasonal material 2 months in advance. Accepts queries by mail, e-mail, fax, phone. Sample copy for $5 or on website. Guidelines available online.

Nonfiction Needs exposè, political economics. **Buys 6 mss/year.** Query with published clips. Length: 700-2,500 words. **Pays $0-200.**

Photos State availability. Captions, identification of subjects required. Negotiates payment individually. Buys one time rights.

Tips "Be familiar with our magazine and the types of communities interested in reading us. *Dollars and Sense* is a progressive economics magazine that explains in a popular way both the workings of the economy and struggles to change it. Articles may be on the environment, the World Bank, community organizing, urban conflict, inflation, unemployment, union reform, welfare, changes in government regulation—a broad range of topics that have an economic theme. Find samples of our latest issue on our homepage."

$ $ ELLIOTT WAVE INTERNATIONAL PUBLICATIONS

Elliott Wave International, P.O. Box 1618, Gainesville GA 30503. E-mail: customerservice@elliottwave.com. Website: www.elliottwave.com. **10% freelance written**. Our publications are weekly to monthly in print and online formats covering investment markets. An understanding of technical market analysis is indispensible, knowledge of Elliott wave analysis even better. Clear, conversational prose is mandatory. Estab. 1979. Circ. 80,000. Byline sometimes given. Pays on publication. Publishes ms an average of 1 month after acceptance. Buys all rights. Editorial lead time 1 month. Accepts queries by e-mail.

Nonfiction Needs essays, how-to, technical. **Buys 12 mss/year.** Query with published clips. Length: 500-800 words. **Pays $100-200.**

Columns/Departments Pop culture and the stock market, 500-800 words. Buys 12 mss/year. Query with published clips. **Pays $100-200.**

⊘ FORTUNE

Time, Inc., 1271 Avenue of the Americas, New York NY 10020. (212)522-1212. Fax: (212)522-0810. E-mail: fortune-mail_letters@fortune-mail.com. Website: www.fortune.com. Biweekly magazine. Edited primarily for high-demographic business people. Specializes in big stories about companies, business personalities, technology, managing, Wall Street, media, marketing, personal finance, politics and policy. Circ. 1,066,000. No kill fee. Editorial lead time 6 weeks.

- Does not accept freelance submissions.

$ $ $ $ HISPANIC BUSINESS

Hispanic Business, Inc., 425 Pine Ave., Santa Barbara CA 93117-3709. (805)964-5539. Fax: (805)964-6139. Website: www.hispanicbusiness.com. **40-50% freelance written**. Monthly magazine covering Hispanic business. For more than 2 decades, *Hispanic Business* magazine has documented the growing affluence and power of the Hispanic community. Our magazine reaches the most educated, affluent Hispanic business and community leaders. Stories should have relevance for the Hispanic business community. Estab. 1979. Circ. 220,000 (rate base); 990,000 (readership base). Byline given. Pays on publication. Offers 50% kill fee. Publishes ms an average of 1 month after acceptance. Buys all rights. Editorial lead time 1-3 months. Submit seasonal material 2 months in advance. Accepts queries by mail. Accepts simultaneous submissions. Responds in 3 weeks to queries. Responds in 1 month to mss. Sample copy free.

Nonfiction Needs interview, travel. **Buys 120 mss/year.** Query résumé and published clips. Length: 650-2,000 words. **Pays $50-1,500.**

Photos State availability. Captions required. Reviews GIF/JPEG files. Negotiates payment individually. Buys all rights.

Columns/Departments Tech Pulse (technology); Money Matters (financial), both 800 words. Buys 40 mss/year. Query with résumé and published clips. **Pays $50-450.**

Tips E-mail or snail mail queries with résumé and published clips are the most effective.

⊘ MONEY

Time, Inc., 1271 Avenue of the Americas, 17th Floor, New York NY 10020. (212)522-1212. Fax: (212)522-0189. E-mail: managing_editor@moneymail.com. Website: money.cnn.com. Monthly magazine covering finance. *Money* magazine offers sophisticated coverage in all aspects of personal finance for individuals, business executives, and personal investors. Estab. 1972. Circ. 1,967,420. No kill fee.

- *Money* magazine does not accept unsolicited manuscripts and almost never uses freelance writers.

$ $ $ MYBUSINESS MAGAZINE

Hammock Publishing, 3322 W. End Ave., Suite 700, Nashville TN 37203. (615)690-3419. Website: www.mybusinessmag.com. **75% freelance written**. Bimonthly magazine for small businesses. "We are a guide to small business success, however that is defined in the new small business economy. We explore the methods and minds behind the trends and celebrate the men and women leading the creation of the new small business economy." Estab. 1999. Circ. 600,000. Byline given. Pays on acceptance. Offers 30% kill fee. Publishes ms an average of 4 months after acceptance. Buys first North American serial rights, buys electronic rights. Editorial lead time 4 months. Submit seasonal material 5 months in advance. Accepts queries by mail. Accepts simultaneous submissions. Responds in 3 weeks to queries. Sample copy free. Guidelines available online.

Nonfiction Needs book excerpts, how-to, small business topics, new product. **Buys 8 mss/year.** Query with published clips. Length: 200-1,800 words. **Pays $75-1,000.**

Tips *MyBusiness* is sent bimonthly to the 600,000 members of the National Federation of Independent Business. We're here to help small business owners by giving them a range of how-to pieces that evaluate, analyze, and lead to solutions.

$ $ THE NETWORK JOURNAL

Black Professionals and Small Business Magazine, The Network Journal Communication, 39 Broadway, Suite 2120, New York NY 10006. (212)962-3791. Fax: (212)962-3537. E-mail: editors@tnj.com. Website: www.tnj.com. **25% freelance written**. Monthly magazine covering business and career articles. *The Network Journal* caters to black professionals and small-business owners, providing quality coverage on business, financial, technology and career news germane to the black community. Estab. 1993. Circ. 25,000. Byline given. Pays on publication. Buys all rights. Editorial lead time 2 months. Submit seasonal material 3 months in advance. Accepts queries by mail, e-mail, fax, phone. Accepts previously published material. Accepts simultaneous submissions. Sample copy for $1 or online. Writer's guidelines for SASE or online.

Nonfiction Needs how-to, interview. Send complete ms. Length: 1,200-1,500 words. **Pays $150-200.**

Photos Send photos. Identification of subjects required. Offers $25/photo. Buys one time rights.

Columns/Departments Book reviews, 700-800 words; career management and small business development, 800 words. **Pays $100.**

Tips We are looking for vigorous writing and reporting for our cover stories and feature articles. Pieces should have gripping leads, quotes that actually say something and that come from several sources. Unless it is a column, please do not submit a 1-source story. Always remember that your article must contain a nutgraph—that's usually the third paragraph telling the reader what the story is about and why you are telling it now. Editorializing should be kept to a minimum. If you're writing a column, make sure your opinions are well-supported.

PERDIDO

Leadership with a Conscience, High Tide Press, 3650 W. 183rd St., Homewood IL 60430. (708)206-2054. E-mail: editor@hightidepress.com. Website: www.perdidomagazine.com. Monica Regan, mng. ed. **Contact:** Mary Rundell-Holmes, editor. **60% freelance written**. Quarterly magazine covering leadership and management. We are concerned with what's happening in organizations that are mission-oriented—as opposed to merely profit-oriented. *Perdido* is focused on helping conscientious leaders put innovative ideas into practice. We seek pragmatic articles on management techniques as well as essays on social issues relating to the workplace (not politics or religion). The readership of *Perdido* is comprised mainly of CEOs, executive directors, vice presidents, and program directors of nonprofit and for-profit organizations. We try to make the content of *Perdido* accessible to all decision-makers, whether in the nonprofit or for-profit world, government, or academia. *Perdido* actively pursues diverse opinions and authors from many different fields. Estab. 1994. Circ. 1,300. Byline given. Pays on publication. No kill fee. Publishes ms an average of 3 months after acceptance. Buys first North American serial rights, buys second serial (reprint) rights. 2-3 months Submit seasonal material 2-3 months in advance. Accepts queries by mail, e-mail. Accepts previously published material. Accepts simultaneous submissions. Responds in 2-3 weeks to queries Sample copy online. Guidelines online.

- Especially interesting to *Perdido* readers are new management trends, concepts, practices, philosophies, business leaders and authors. And, the most effective articles are those that back up new ideas with practical applications, and those that use stories or anecdotes to provide the reader with a useful context.

Nonfiction Needs book excerpts, how-to, interview, personal experience (leadership experience only). We do not want anything about new products or specific business, or about any leader in whom you have a personal vested interest. **Buys 4 mss/year.** Query. Length: 900-2,800 words. **Pays 5-7¢/word for assigned and unsolicited articles. Pays $75 for book reviews. Pays in contributor copies.**

Photos State availability. of photos. Send photos. with submission. Captions, identification of subjects, model releases required. Reviews 5 × 7 prints. Negotiates payment individually. Buys one time rights.

Columns/Departments Book Review (new books on management/leadership), 750-900 words; Feature articles, 900-2,800 words. **Pays 5-7¢/word; $75 for book reviews.**

Tips Potential writers for *Perdido* should rely on the magazine's motto—Leadership with a Conscience—as starting point. We're looking for thoughtful reflections on management that help people succeed. While instructive articles are good, we avoid step-by-step recipes. Data and real life examples are very important.

$$$$ PROFIT

Your Guide to Business Success, Rogers Media, 1 Mt. Pleasant Rd., 11th Floor, Toronto ON M4Y 2Y5 Canada. (416)764-1402. Fax: (416)764-1404. Website: www.profitguide.com. **80% freelance written**. Magazine published 6 times/year covering small and medium businesses. We specialize in specific, useful information that helps our readers manage their businesses better. We want Canadian stories only. Estab. 1982. Circ. 110,000. Byline given. Pays on acceptance. Offers variable kill fee. Publishes ms an average of 2 months after acceptance. Buys first North American serial rights, buys electronic rights. Submit seasonal material 6 months in advance. Accepts queries by mail, fax, phone. Responds in 1 month to queries. Responds in 6 weeks to mss. Sample copy for 9 × 12 SAE with 84¢ postage. Guidelines free.

Nonfiction Needs how-to, business management tips, strategies and Canadian business profiles. **Buys 50 mss/year.** Query with published clips. Length: 800-2,000 words. **Pays $500-2,000.**

Columns/Departments Finance (info on raising capital in Canada), 700 words; Marketing (marketing strategies for independent business), 700 words. Buys 80 mss/year. Query with published clips. **Pays $150-600.**

Tips We're wide open to freelancers with good ideas and some knowledge of business. Read the magazine and understand it before submitting your ideas—which should have a Canadian focus.

SMARTMONEY MAGAZINE

1755 Broadway, 2nd Floor, New York NY 10019. E-mail: editors@smartmoney.com. Website: www.smartmoney.com.

- Query before submitting.

$$ TECHNICAL ANALYSIS OF STOCKS & COMMODITIES

The Traders' Magazine, Technical Analysis, Inc., 4757 California Ave. SW, Seattle WA 98116. (206)938-0570. E-mail: editor@traders.com. Website: www.traders.com. **95% freelance written**. "Magazine covers methods of investing and trading stocks, bonds and commodities (futures), options, mutual funds, and precious metals using technical analysis." Estab. 1982. Circ. 65,000. Byline given. Pays on publication. No kill fee. Publishes ms an average of 6 months after acceptance. Buys all rights. Responds in 3 months to queries. Sample copy for $8. Guidelines available online.

- "Eager to work with new/unpublished writers."

Nonfiction Needs how-to, trade, technical, cartoons, trading and software aids to trading, reviews, utilities, real world trading (actual case studies of trades and their results). No newsletter-type, buy-sell recommendations. The article subject must relate to technical analysis, charting or a numerical technique used to trade securities or futures. Almost universally requires graphics with every article. **Buys 150 mss/year.** Send complete ms. Length: 1,000-4,000 words. **Pays $100-500.**

Reprints Send tearsheet with rights for sale noted and information about when and where the material previously appeared.

Photos Contact: Christine M. Morrison, art director. State availability. Captions, identification of subjects, model releases required. Pays $60-350 for b&w or color negatives with prints or positive slides. Buys one-time and reprint rights.

Columns/Departments Length: 800-1,600 words. Buys 100 columns/year. Query. **Pays $50-300**

Fillers Contact: Karen Wasserman, fillers editor. "Must relate to trading stocks, bonds, options, mutual funds, commodities, or precious metals." Buys 20 fillers/year. Length: 500 words. **Pays $20-50.**

Tips "Describe how to use technical analysis, charting, or computer work in day-to-day trading of stocks, bonds, commodities, options, mutual funds, or precious metals. A blow-by-blow account of how a trade was made, including the trader's thought processes, is the very best-received story by our subscribers.

One of our primary considerations is to instruct in a manner that the layperson can comprehend. We are not hypercritical of writing style."

Business Regional

$$ ALASKA BUSINESS MONTHLY

Alaska Business Publishing, 501 W. Northern Lights Blvd., Suite 100, Anchorage AK 99503-2577. (907)276-4373. Fax: (907)279-2900. E-mail: editor@akbizmag.com. Website: www.akbizmag.com. **Contact:** Debbie Cutler, managing editor. **90% freelance written**. "Our audience is Alaska businessmen and women who rely on us for timely features and up-to-date information about doing business in Alaska." Estab. 1985. Circ. 12,000-14,000. Byline given. Pays on publication. Offers $50 kill fee. Publishes ms an average of 4 months after acceptance. Buys all rights. Editorial lead time 5 months. Submit seasonal material 5 months in advance. Accepts queries by mail, e-mail. Accepts previously published material. Responds in 1 month to queries. Sample copy for 9 × 12 SAE and 4 first-class stamps. Guidelines free.

Nonfiction Needs general interest, how-to, interview, new product, Alaska, opinion. No fiction, poetry, or anything not pertinent to Alaska. **Buys approximately 130 mss/year.** Send complete ms. Length: 500-2,000 words. **Pays $150-300.**

Photos State availability.

Tips "Send a well-written manuscript on a subject of importance to Alaska businesses. We seek informative, entertaining articles on everything from entrepreneurs to heavy industry. We cover all Alaska industry to include mining, tourism, timber, transportation, oil and gas, fisheries, finance, insurance, real estate, communications, medical services, technology, and construction. We also cover Native and environmental issues, and occasionally feature Seattle and other communities in the Pacific Northwest."

$$$$ ☐ ALBERTA VENTURE

Venture Publishing Inc., 10259 - 105 St., Edmonton AB T5J 1E3 Canada. (780)990-0839. E-mail: mmccullough@albertaventure.com. Website: www.albertaventure.com. **70% freelance written**. Monthly magazine covering business in Alberta. "Our readers are mostly business owners and managers in Alberta who read the magazine to keep up with trends and run their businesses better." Estab. 1997. Circ. 35,000. Byline given. Pays on publication. Offers 30% kill fee. Publishes ms an average of 2 months after acceptance. Buys first North American serial rights, buys electronic rights. Editorial lead time 3 months. Submit seasonal material 3 months in advance. Accepts queries by e-mail. Responds in 2 weeks to queries. Sample copy available online. Guidelines by e-mail.

Nonfiction Needs how-to, business narrative related to Alberta. Does not want company or product profiles. **Buys 75 mss/year.** Query. Length: 1,000-3,000 words. **Pays $300-2,000 (Canadian).**

Photos Contact: Kim Larson, art director. State availability. Identification of subjects required. Reviews GIF/JPEG files. Negotiates payment individually. Buys one-time rights.

$$ ☐ ATLANTIC BUSINESS MAGAZINE

Communications Ten, Ltd., P.O. Box 2356, Station C, St. John's NL A1C 6E7 Canada. (709)726-9300. Fax: (709)726-3013. Website: www.atlanticbusinessmagazine.com. **80% freelance written**. Bimonthly magazine covering business in Atlantic Canada. We discuss positive business developments, emphasizing that the 4 Atlantic provinces are a great place to do business. Estab. 1989. Circ. 30,000. Byline given. Pays within 30 days of publication. No kill fee. Publishes ms an average of 2 months after acceptance. Buys one-time rights. Editorial lead time 6 months. Accepts queries by mail, e-mail, fax. Sample copy and writer's guidelines free

Nonfiction Needs expose, general interest, interview, new product. We don't want religious, technical, or scholarly material. We are not an academic magazine. We are interested only in stories concerning business topics specific to the 4 Canadian provinces of Nova Scotia, New Brunswick, Prince Edward Island, and Newfoundland and Labrador. **Buys 36 mss/year.** Query with published clips. Length: 1,200-2,500 words. **Pays $300-750.**

Photos Send photos. Captions, identification of subjects required. Reviews contact sheets, transparencies, prints. Negotiates payment individually. Buys one time rights.

Columns/Departments Query with published clips.

Tips Writers should submit their areas of interest as well as samples of their work and, if possible, suggested story ideas.

BCBUSINESS

Canada Wide Magazines & Communications, Ltd., 4180 Lougheed Hwy., 4th Floor, Burnaby BC V5C 6A7 Canada. (604)299-7311. Fax: (604)299-9188. E-mail: mogrady@canadawide.com. Website: www.bcbusinessmagazine.com. **80% freelance written**. Monthly magazine covering significant issues and trends shaping the province's business environment. Stories are lively, topical and extensively researched. Circ. 30,000. Byline given. Pays 2 weeks prior to being published. Offers kill fee. Publishes ms an average of 2 months after acceptance. Buys first rights. Editorial lead time 4 months. Submit seasonal material 4 months in advance. Accepts queries by e-mail. Accepts simultaneous submissions. Responds in 6 weeks to queries. Guidelines free.

Nonfiction Query with published clips. Length: 1,500-2,000 words.

Photos State availability.

$ BLUE RIDGE BUSINESS JOURNAL

Landmark, Inc., 302 Second St., 4th Floor, Roanoke VA 24011. (540)777-6460. Fax: (540)777-6471. E-mail: dansmith@bizjournal.com. Website: www.bizjournal.com. **75% freelance written**. Monthly. We take a regional slant on national business trends, products, methods, etc. Interested in localized features and news stories highlighting business activity. Estab. 1989. Circ. 15,000. Byline given. Pays on acceptance. No kill fee. Publishes ms an average of 1 month after acceptance. Buys all rights. Editorial lead time 10 days. Accepts queries by mail, e-mail, fax. Accepts previously published material. Responds immediately. Call the editor for sample copies and/or writer's guidelines. Writers must live in our region.

Nonfiction Health Care and Hospitals; Telecommunications; Building and Construction; Investments; Personal Finance and Retirement Planning; Guide to Architectural; Engineering and Construction Services; and Manufacturing and Industry. No columns or stories that are not pre-approved. **Buys 120-150 mss/year.** Query. Length: 500-2,000 words.

Photos State availability. Captions, identification of subjects required. Offers $10/photo. Buys all rights.

Tips Talk to the editor. Offer knowledgeable ideas (if accepted they will be assigned to that writer). We need fast turnaround, accurate reporting, neat dress, non-smokers. More interested in writing samples than educational background.

BUSINESS LONDON

P.O. Box 7400, London ON N5Y 4X3 Canada. (519)472-7601. Fax: (519)473-7859. E-mail: editorial@businesslondon.ca. Website: www.businesslondon.ca. **70% freelance written**. Monthly magazine covering London business. Our audience is primarily small and medium businesses and entrepreneurs. Focus is on success stories and how to better operate your business. Estab. 1987. Circ. 14,000. Byline given. Pays on publication. Offers 50% kill fee. Publishes ms an average of 3 months after acceptance. Buys first rights. Editorial lead time 3 months. Accepts queries by e-mail. Responds in 3 months to mss. Sample copy for #10 SASE. Guidelines free.

Nonfiction Needs how-to, business topics, humor, interview, new product, local only, personal experience, must have a London connection. **Buys 30 mss/year.** Query with published clips. Length: 250-1,500 words.

Photos Send photos. Identification of subjects required. Reviews contact sheets, transparencies. Negotiates payment individually. Buys one time rights.

Tips Phone with a great idea. The most valuable things a writer owns are ideas. We'll take a chance on an unknown if the idea is good enough.

BUSINESS NH MAGAZINE

55 S. Commercial St., Manchester NH 03101. (603)626-6354. Fax: (603)626-6359. E-mail: msaturley@millyardcommunications.com. Website: www.millyardcommunications.com. **Contact:** Michelle Saturley, managing editor. **25% freelance written**. Monthly magazine covering business, politics, and people of New Hampshire. Our audience consists of the owners and top managers of New Hampshire businesses. Estab. 1983. Circ. 15,000. Byline given. Pays on publication. No kill fee. Publishes ms an average of 2 months after acceptance. Accepts queries by e-mail, fax.

Nonfiction Needs how-to, interview. No unsolicited manuscripts; interested in New Hampshire writers only. **Buys 24 mss/year.** Query with published clips and résumé Length: 750-2,500 words. **Payment varies.**

Photos Both b&w and color photos are used. Payment varies. Buys one time rights.

Tips I always want clips and résumés with queries. Freelance stories are almost always assigned. Stories must be local to New Hampshire.

$$ CINCY MAGAZINE

The Magazine for Business Professionals, Great Lakes Publishing Co., Cincinnati Club Building, 30 Garfield Place, Suite 440, Cincinnati OH 45202. (513)421-2533. Fax: (513)421-2542. E-mail: news@cincymagazine .com. Website: www.cincymagazine.com. **80% freelance written**. Glossy bimonthly color magazine written for business professionals in Greater Cincinnati, published 10 times annually. *Cincy* is written and designed for the interests of business professionals and executives both at work and away from work, with features, trend stories, news and opinions related to business, along with lifestyle articles on home, dining, shopping, travel, health and more. Estab. 2003. Circ. 15,300. Byline given. Pays on publication. Offers 100% kill fee. Publishes ms an average of 3 months after acceptance. Buys all rights. Editorial lead time 1-3 months. Submit seasonal material 4 months in advance. Accepts queries by mail, e-mail.

Nonfiction Needs general interest, interview. Does not want stock advice. Length: 200-2,000 words. **Pays $75-600.**

Tips Read Cincy online, understand what we want, pitch concisely in e-mail, deliver good writing promptly.

$$ CORPORATE CONNECTICUT MAGAZINE

The Corporate World at Eye Level, Corporate World LLC, P.O. Box 290726, Wethersfield CT 06129. Fax: (860)257-1924. E-mail: editor@corpct.com. Website: www.corpct.com. **50% freelance written**. Quarterly magazine covering regional reporting, global coverage of corporate/business leaders, entreprenuers. *Corporate Connecticut* is devoted to people who make business happen in the private sector and who create innovative change across public arenas. Centered in the Northeast between New York and Boston, Connecticut is positioned in a coastal corridor with a dense affluent population who are highly mobile, accomplished and educated. Estab. 2001. Byline given. Pays on publication. Offers 25% kill fee. Publishes ms an average of 2-3 months after acceptance. Buys first North American serial rights, buys electronic rights, buys all rights, buys negotiable rights. Editorial lead time 3-6 months. Submit seasonal material 10-12 months in advance. Accepts queries by mail, e-mail. Responds in 2 weeks to queries. Sample copy for #10 SASE.

Nonfiction Interested in pieces on hedge funds, venture capital, high-end travel. Query with published clips. **Pays 35¢/word minimum with varying fees for excellence.**

Photos State availability.

Tips Review our online content to get a general feel for the publication. Aim high with content, do research, pitch a unique angle with a global perspective on business and people.

$ CRAIN'S DETROIT BUSINESS

Crain Communications, Inc., 1155 Gratiot, Detroit MI 48207. (313)446-0419. Fax: (313)446-1687. E-mail: achapelle@crain.com. Website: www.crainsdetroit.com. **10% freelance written**. Weekly tabloid covering business in the Detroit metropolitan area—specifically Wayne, Oakland, Macomb, Washtenaw, and Livingston counties. Estab. 1985. Circ. 150,000. Byline given. Pays on publication. No kill fee. Publishes ms an average of 1 month after acceptance. Buys all rights. Accepts queries by mail, e-mail. Sample copy for $1.50. Guidelines available online.

- *Crain's Detroit Business* uses only area writers and local topics.

Nonfiction Needs new product, technical, business. **Buys 20 mss/year.** Query with published clips. 30-40 words/column inch. **Pays $10-15/column inch.**

Photos State availability.

Tips Contact special sections editor in writing with background and, if possible, specific story ideas relating to our type of coverage and coverage area.

$ ⊡ IN BUSINESS WINDSOR

Cornerstone Publications, Inc., 1775 Sprucewood Ave., LaSalle ON N9J 1X7 Canada. (519)250-2880. Fax: (519)250-2881. E-mail: gbaxter@inbusinesswindsor.com. Website: www.inbusinesswindsor.com. **70% freelance written**. Monthly magazine covering business. We focus on issues/ideas which are of interest to businesses in and around Windsor and Essex County (Ontario). Most stories deal with business and finance; occasionally we will cover health and sports issues that affect our readers. Estab. 1988. Circ. 10,000. Byline given. Pays on acceptance. No kill fee. Buys first rights. Editorial lead time 3 months. Submit seasonal material 3 months in advance. Accepts queries by mail, e-mail, fax. Responds in 2 weeks to queries. Responds in 1 month to mss. Sample copy for $3.50.

Nonfiction Needs general interest, how-to, interview. **Buys 25 mss/year.** Query with published clips. Length: 800-1,500 words. **Pays $70-150.**

$$ INGRAM'S

Show-Me Publishing, Inc., P.O. Box 411356, Kansas City MO 64141-1356. (816)842-9994. Fax: (816)474-1111. E-mail: editorial@ingramsonline.com. Website: www.ingramsonline.com. **Contact:** Joe Sweeney, editor in chief. **10% freelance written**. Monthly magazine covering Kansas City business and economic development. *"Ingram's* readers are top-level corporate executives and community leaders, officials and decision makers. Our editorial content must provide such readers with timely, relevant information and insights." Estab. 1975. Circ. 105,000. Byline given. Pays on publication. No kill fee. Publishes ms an average of 1 month after acceptance. Buys all rights. Editorial lead time 1 month. Submit seasonal material 5 months in advance. Accepts queries by e-mail. Sample copy free.

- Only accepts local writers; guest columnist are not paid articles.

Nonfiction All articles must have a Kansas City angle. Needs interview, technical. Does not want humor, inspirational, or anything not related to Kansas City business. **Buys 4-6 mss/year.** Query. Length: 500-1,500 words. **Pays $75-200 depending on research/feature length.**

Columns/Departments Say So (opinion), 1,500 words. Buys 12 mss/year. **Pays $75-100 max.**

Tips "Demonstrate familiarity with the magazine and its purpose and audience in an e-mail query."

$$ THE LANE REPORT

Lane Communications Group, 210 E. Main St., 14th Floor, Lexington KY 40507. (859)244-3500. Fax: (859)244-3555. E-mail: aolsen@lanereport.com. Website: www.kybiz.com. **70% freelance written.** Monthly magazine covering statewide business. Estab. 1986. Circ. 15,000. Byline given. Pays on publication. No kill fee. Buys one-time rights. Editorial lead time 6 weeks. Submit seasonal material 3 months in advance. Accepts queries by mail, e-mail, fax. Accepts previously published material. Accepts simultaneous submissions. Responds in 1 month to queries. Sample copy and writer's guidelines free.

Nonfiction Needs essays, interview, new product, photo feature. No fiction. **Buys 30-40 mss/year.** Query with published clips. Length: 500-2,000 words. **Pays $150-375.**

Photos State availability. Identification of subjects required. Reviews contact sheets, negatives, transparencies, prints, digital images. Negotiates payment individually. Buys one time rights.

Columns/Departments Technology and Business in Kentucky; Advertising; Exploring Kentucky; Perspective; Spotlight on the Arts, all less than 1,000 words.

Tips "As Kentucky's only statewide business and economics publication, we look for stories that incorporate perspectives from the Commonwealth's various regions and prominent industries—tying it into the national picture when appropriate. We also look for insightful profiles and interviews of Kentucky's entrepreneurs and business leaders."

$ MERCER BUSINESS MAGAZINE

White Eagle Publishing Company, 2550 Kuser Rd., Trenton State NJ 08691. (609)586-2056. Fax: (609)586-8052. E-mail: maggih@mercerbusiness.com. Website: www.mercerchamber.org. **100% freelance written.** Monthly magazine covering national and local business-related, theme-based topics. *Mercer Business* is a Chamber of Commerce publication, so the slant is pro-business primarily. Also covers nonprofits, education and other related issues. Estab. 1924. Circ. 8,500. Byline given. Pays on publication. Publishes ms an average of 1 month after acceptance. Makes work-for-hire assignments. Editorial lead time 6 weeks. Submit seasonal material 6 weeks in advance. Accepts queries by e-mail. Accepts simultaneous submissions. Responds in 1 week to queries. Sample copy for #10 SASE. Guidelines by e-mail.

Nonfiction Needs humor. Query with published clips. Length: 1,000-1,800 words. **Pays $150 for assigned articles.**

Photos State availability of or send photos. Captions, identification of subjects, model releases required. Offers no additional payment for photos accepted with ms.

Fillers Needs gags. Buys 24 mss/year. Length: 300-500 words.

Tips Query with cover letter preferred after perusal of editorial calendar.

$$$$ ☒ OREGON BUSINESS

MEDIAmerica, Inc., 610 SW Broadway, Suite 200, Portalnd OR 97205. (503)223-0304. Fax: (503)221-6544. E-mail: editor@oregonbusiness.com. Website: www.oregonbusiness.com. **15-25% freelance written.** Monthly magazine covering business in Oregon. Our subscribers inlcude owners of small and medium-sized businesses, government agencies, professional staffs of banks, insurance companies, ad agencies, attorneys and other service providers. We accept *only* stories about Oregon businesses, issues and trends. Estab. 1981. Circ. 50,000. Byline given. Pays on publication. No kill fee. Buys first North American serial rights, buys electronic rights. Editorial lead time 2 months. Accepts queries by mail, e-mail. Sample copy for $4. Guidelines available online.

Nonfiction Features should focus on major trends shaping the state; noteworthy businesses, practices, and leaders; stories with sweeping implications across industry sectors. Query with résumé and 2-3 published clips. Length: 1,200-3,000 words.

Columns/Departments First Person (opinion piece on an issue related to business), 750 words; Around the State (recent news and trends, and how they might shape the future), 100-600 words; Business Tools (practical, how-to suggestions for business managers and owners), 400-600 words; In Character (profile of interesting or quirky member of the business community), 850 words. Query with résumé and 2-3 published clips.

Tips An *Oregon Business* story must meet at least 2 of the following criteria: Size and location: The topic must be relevant to Northwest businesses. Featured companies (including franchises) must be based in Oregon or Southwest Washington. Service: Our sections (1,200 words) are reserved largely for service pieces focusing on finance, marketing, management or other general business topics. These stories are meant to be instructional, emphasizing problem-solving by example. Trends: These are sometimes covered in a section piece, or perhaps a feature story. We aim to be the state's leading business publication so we want to be the first to spot trends that affect Oregon companies. Exclusivity or strategy: of an event, whether it's a corporate merger, a dramatic turnaround, a marketing triumph or a PR disaster.

$ $ PRAIRIE BUSINESS

Grand Forks (ND) Herald, Forum Communications Company, 808 Third Ave., #400, Fargo ND 58103. Fax: (701)280-9092. E-mail: rschuster@prairiebizmag.com. Website: www.prairiebizmag.com. **Contact:** Ryan Schuster, submissions editor. **30% freelance written**. Monthly magazine covering business on the Northern Plains (North Dakota, South Dakota, Minnesota). "We attempt to be a resource for business owners/managers, policymakers, educators, and nonprofit administrators, acting as a catalyst for growth in the region by reaching out to an audience of decision makers within the region and also venture capitalists, site selectors, and angel visitors from outside the region." Estab. 2000. Circ. 20,000. Byline given. Pays within 2 weeks of mailing date. No kill fee. Publishes ms an average of 1-2 months after acceptance. Buys all rights. Editorial lead time 2 months. Submit seasonal material 2 months in advance. Accepts queries by e-mail. Accepts previously published material. Accepts simultaneous submissions. Responds in 2 weeks to queries. Sample copy free. Guidelines free.

Nonfiction Needs interview, technical, basic online research. "Does not want articles that are blatant self-promotion for any interest without providing value for readers." **Buys 36 mss/year.** Query. Length: 800-1,500 words. **Pays 15¢/word.**

Photos E-mail photos Captions, identification of subjects required. Reviews GIF/JPEG files (hi-res). Offers $30-250/photo. Buys one time rights.

PROVIDENCE BUSINESS NEWS

220 W. Exchange St., Suite 210, Providence RI 02903. (401)273-2201, ext. 215. Fax: (401)274-0670. E-mail: murphy@pbn.com. Website: www.pbn.com. Business magazine covering news of importance to the Providence area.

- Query before submitting.

$ ROCHESTER BUSINESS JOURNAL

Rochester Business Journal, Inc., 45 E. Ave., Suite 500, Rochester NY 14604. (585)546-8303. Fax: (585)546-3398. Website: www.rbjdaily.com. **10% freelance written**. Weekly tabloid covering local business. The *Rochester Business Journal* is geared toward corporate executives and owners of small businesses, bringing them leading-edge business coverage and analysis first in the market. Estab. 1984. Circ. 10,000. Byline given. Pays on publication. No kill fee. Publishes ms an average of 1 month after acceptance. Buys first rights, buys second serial (reprint) rights, buys electronic rights. Editorial lead time 6 weeks. Accepts queries by mail, fax. Responds in 1 week to queries. Sample copy for free or by e-mail. Guidelines available online.

Nonfiction Needs how-to, business topics, news features, trend stories with local examples. Do not query about any topics that do not include several local examples—local companies, organizations, universities, etc. **Buys 110 mss/year.** Query with published clips. Length: 1,000-2,000 words. **Pays $150.**

Tips The *Rochester Business Journal* prefers queries from local published writers who can demonstrate the ability to write for a sophisticated audience of business readers. Story ideas should be about business trends illustrated with numerous examples of local companies participating in the change or movement.

$ $ SMARTCEO MAGAZINE

SmartCEO, 2700 Lighthouse Point E., Suite 220A, Baltimore MD 21224. (410)342-9510. Fax: (410)675-

5280. Website: www.smartceo.com. **Contact:** Jeanine Gajewski. **25% freelance written**. Monthly magazine covering regional business in the Baltimore, MD and Washington, DC areas. "*SmartCEO* is a regional 'growing company' publication. We are not news; we are a resource full of smart ideas to help educate and inspire decision-makers in the Baltimore and DC areas. Each issue contains features, interviews, case studies, columns and other departments designed to help this region's CEOs face the daily challenges of running a business." Estab. 2001. Circ. 34,000. Byline given. Pays on publication. No kill fee. Publishes ms an average of 2 months after acceptance. Buys all rights. Editorial lead time 5 months. Submit seasonal material 5 months in advance. Accepts queries by e-mail, phone. Responds in 4 weeks to queries. Responds in 2 months to mss. Sample copy available online. Guidelines by e-mail.

Nonfiction Needs essays, interview, Business features or tips. "We do not want pitches on CEOs or companies outside the Baltimore, MD or Washington, DC areas; no product reviews, lifestyle content or book reviews, please." **Buys 20 mss/year.** Query. Length: 2,000-5,000 words. **Pays $300-600.**

Photos Contact: Erica Fromherz, art director. State availability. Identification of subjects required. Reviews GIF/JPEG files.

Columns/Departments Project to Watch (overview of a local development project in progress and why it is of interest to the business community), 600 words; Q&A and tip-focused coverage of business issues and challenges (each article includes the opinions of 10-20 CEOs), 500-1,000 words. Buys 0-5 mss/year. Query.

Tips "When pitching a local CEO, tell us why his/her accomplishments tell an inspiring story with appicable lessons for other CEOs. *SmartCEO* is not news; we are a resource full of smart ideas to help educate and inspire decision-makers in the Baltimore and DC areas. Send your pitch via e-mail and follow up with a phone call."

$ SOMERSET BUSINESS MAGAZINE

White Eagle Printing Company, 2550 Kuser Rd., Trenton State NJ 08691. (609)586-2056. Fax: (609)586-8052. E-mail: maggih@sombusmag.com. Website: www.scbp.org. **100% freelance written**. Monthly magazine covering national and local business-related, theme-based topics. *Somerset Business Magazine* is a Chamber of Commerce publication, so the slant is pro-business primarily. Also covers nonprofits, education and other related issues. Estab. 1924. Circ. 6,500. Pays on publication. Publishes ms an average of 1 month after acceptance. Makes work-for-hire assignments. Editorial lead time 6 weeks. Submit seasonal material 6 weeks in advance. Accepts queries by e-mail. Accepts simultaneous submissions. Responds in 1 week to queries. Sample copy for #10 SASE. Guidelines by e-mail.

Nonfiction Needs humor. Query with published clips. Length: 1,000-1,800 words. **Pays $150 for assigned articles.**

Photos State availability of or send photos. Captions, identification of subjects, model releases required. Offers no additional payment for photos accepted with ms.

Tips Query with cover letter preferred after perusal of editorial calendar.

$ $ VERMONT BUSINESS MAGAZINE

2 Church St., Burlington VT 05401. (802)863-8038. Fax: (802)863-8069. E-mail: mcq@vermontbiz.com. Website: www.vermontbiz.com. **80% freelance written**. Monthly tabloid covering business in Vermont. Circ. 8,000. Byline given. Pays on publication. No kill fee. Publishes ms an average of 1 month after acceptance. Buys one-time rights. Responds in 2 months to queries. Sample copy for sae with 11 × 14 envelope and 7 First-Class stamps.

Nonfiction Buys 200 mss/year. Query with published clips. Length: 800-1,800 words. **Pays $100-200.**

Reprints Send tearsheet and information about when and where the material previously appeared.

Photos Send photos. Identification of subjects required. Reviews contact sheets. Offers $10-35/photo

Tips Read daily papers and look for business angles for a follow-up article. We look for issue and trend articles rather than company or businessman profiles. Note: Magazine accepts Vermont-specific material only. The articles must be about Vermont.

Career, College & Alumni

$ $ AFRICAN-AMERICAN CAREER WORLD

Equal Opportunity Publications, Inc., 445 Broad Hollow Rd., Suite 425, Melville NY 11747. (631)421-9421. Fax: (631)421-1352. E-mail: info@eop.com. Website: www.eop.com. **60% freelance written**. Semiannual magazine focused on African-American students and professionals in all disciplines. Estab. 1969. Byline given. Pays on publication. No kill fee. Publishes ms an average of 3 months after acceptance. Buys first North American serial rights. Editorial lead time 3 months. Accepts queries by mail, e-mail, fax, phone.

Accepts simultaneous submissions. Sample copy free. Guidelines free.
Nonfiction Needs how-to, get jobs, interview, personal experience. We do not want articles that are too general. Query. Length: 1,500-2,500 words. **Pays $350 for assigned articles.**
Tips Gear articles to our audience.

$$ AMERICAN CAREERS

Career Communications, Inc., 6701 W. 64th St., Overland Park KS 66202. (800)669-7795. Fax: (913)362-7788. Website: www.carcom.com. **10% freelance written**. Student publication covering careers, career statistics, skills needed to get jobs. *American Careers* provides career, salary, and education information to middle school and high school students. Self-tests help them relate their interests and abilities to future careers. Estab. 1989. Circ. 500,000. Byline given. Pays 1 month after acceptance. No kill fee. Buys all rights. Makes work-for-hire assignments. Accepts queries by mail. Accepts simultaneous submissions. Sample copy for $4. Guidelines for #10 SASE.
Nonfiction Career and education features related to career paths, including arts and communication, business, law, government, finance, construction, technology, health services, human services, manufacturing, engineering, and natural resources and agriculture. No preachy advice to teens or articles that talk down to students. **Buys 5 mss/year.** Query by mail only with published clips Length: 300-1,000 words. **Pays $100-450.**
Photos State availability. Captions, identification of subjects, model releases required. Negotiates payment individually. Buys all rights.
Tips Letters of introduction or query letters with samples and résumés are ways we get to know writers. Samples should include how-to articles and career-related articles. Articles written for teenagers also would make good samples. Short feature articles on careers, career-related how-to articles, and self-assessment tools (10-20 point quizzes with scoring information) are primarily what we publish.

$$ THE BLACK COLLEGIAN

The Career & Self Development Magazine for African-American Students, IMDiversity, Inc., 140 Carondelet St., New Orleans LA 70130. (504)523-0154. Website: www.black-collegian.com. **25% freelance written**. Semiannual magazine for African-American college students and recent graduates with an interest in career and job information, African-American cultural awareness, personalities, history, trends, and current events. Estab. 1970. Circ. 122,000. Byline given. Pays 1 month after publication. Buys one-time rights. Submit seasonal material 2 months in advance. Accepts queries by mail. Responds in 6 months to queries. Sample copy for $5 (includes postage) and 9 × 12 SAE. Guidelines for #10 SASE.
Nonfiction Material on careers, sports, black history, news analysis. Articles on problems and opportunities confronting African-American college students and recent graduates. Needs book excerpts, expose, general interest, historical, how-to, develop employability, inspirational, interview, opinion, personal experience. Query. Length: 900-1,900 words. **Pays $100-500 for assigned articles.**
Photos State availability of or send photos. Captions, identification of subjects, model releases required. Reviews 8 × 10 prints.
Tips Articles are published under primarily 5 broad categories: job hunting information, overviews of career opportunities and industry reports, self-development information, analyses and investigations of conditions and problems that affect African-Americans, and celebrations of African-American success.

BROWN ALUMNI MAGAZINE

Brown University, P.O. Box 1854, 71 George St., Providence RI 02912. (401)863-2873. Fax: (401)863-9599. E-mail: alumni_magazine@brown.edu. Website: www.brownalumnimagazine.com. Bimonthly magazine covering the world of Brown University and its alumni. We are an editorially independent, general interest magazine covering the on-campus world of Brown University and the off-campus world of its alumni. Estab. 1900. Circ. 80,000. Byline given. Pays on acceptance. Publishes ms an average of 3 months after acceptance. Buys North American serial and Web rights. Editorial lead time 3 months. Submit seasonal material 4 months in advance. Accepts queries by mail, e-mail, fax. Responds in several weeks to queries. Sample copy free. Guidelines available online.
Nonfiction Needs book excerpts, essays, expose, general interest, historical, humor, interview, opinion, personal experience, photo feature, travel, profiles. No articles unconnected to Brown or its alumni. **Buys 50 mss/year.** Query with published clips. Length: 150-4,000 words.
Photos State availability. Captions, identification of subjects required. Reviews contact sheets, transparencies, prints. Negotiates payment individually Buys one time rights.
Columns/Departments P.O.V. (essays by Brown alumni), 750 words. Send complete ms.

Tips Be imaginative and be specific. A Brown connection is required for all stories in the magazine, but a Brown connection alone does not guarantee our interest. Ask yourself: Why should readers care about your proposed story? Also, we look for depth and objective reporting, not boosterism.

$$ CIRCLE K MAGAZINE

Kiwanis, 3636 Woodview Trace, Indianapolis IN 46268-3196. Fax: (317)879-0204. E-mail: circlek@kiwanis.org. Website: www.circlek.org. Kasey Jackson. **30% freelance written**. Magazine published once a year. "Our readership consists almost entirely of above-average college students interested in voluntary community service and leadership development. They are politically and socially aware and have a wide range of interests." Circ. 12,000. Byline given. Pays on acceptance. Buys first North American serial rights. Accepts queries by mail, e-mail, fax. Responds in 4 weeks to queries. Sample copy for large SAE with 3 first-class stamps or on website. Guidelines available online.

Nonfiction "Articles published in *CKI* are of 2 types—serious and light nonfiction. We are interested in general interest articles on topics concerning college students and their lifestyles, as well as articles dealing with careers, community concerns, and leadership development. No first-person confessions, family histories, or travel pieces." Query. Length: 300-1,500 words. **Pays $100-400.**

Photos Captions required. Purchased with accompanying ms; total price includes both photos and ms.

Tips "Query should indicate author's familiarity with the field and sources. Subject treatment must be objective and in-depth, and articles should include illustrative examples and quotes from persons involved in the subject or qualified to speak on it. We are open to working with new writers who present a good article idea and demonstrate that they've done their homework concerning the article subject itself, as well as concerning our magazine's style. We're interested in college-oriented trends, for example: entrepreneur schooling, high-tech classrooms, music, leisure, and health issues."

$$ CONCORDIA UNIVERSITY MAGAZINE

Advancement and Alumni Relations, Concordia University Magazine, Concordia University, 1455 De Maisonneuve Blvd. W., Montreal QC H3G 1M8 Canada. (514)848-2424, ext. 3826. Fax: (514)848-4510. E-mail: howard.bokser@concordia.ca. Website: magazine.concordia.ca. **60% freelance written**. Quarterly magazine covering matters relating to Concordia University and its alumni. We only cover topics related to research and teaching at Concordia, and student or administrator news, and we profile university alumni. Estab. 1977. Circ. 85,000. Byline given. Pays on acceptance. Offers 50% kill fee. Publishes ms an average of 1 month after acceptance. Buys first rights. Editorial lead time 2 months. Submit seasonal material 2 months in advance. Accepts queries by mail, e-mail. Accepts previously published material. Accepts simultaneous submissions. Responds in 1 month to queries. Responds in 1 month to mss. Sample copy available online. Guidelines free.

Nonfiction Needs book excerpts, general interest, historical, humor, interview, opinion, personal experience, photo feature. **Buys 10 mss/year.** Query with published clips. Length: 1,500-2,000 words. **Pays $350-450.**

Photos State availability. Identification of subjects required. Reviews contact sheets, 2x2 transparencies, 4x6 prints, GIF/JPEG files. Negotiates payment individually. Buys one time rights.

Columns/Departments End Piece (opinion or essay), 650 words. Buys 4 mss/year. Query with published clips. **Pays $275.**

$$$$ HARVARD MAGAZINE

7 Ware St., Cambridge MA 02138-4037. (617)495-5746. Fax: (617)495-0324. Website: www.harvardmagazine.com. **35-50% freelance written**. Bimonthly magazine for Harvard University faculty, alumni, and students. Estab. 1898. Circ. 245,000. Byline given. Pays on publication. No kill fee. Publishes ms an average of 4 months after acceptance. Buys one-time print and website rights. Editorial lead time 1 year. Accepts queries by mail, fax. Responds in 1 month to queries. Responds in 1 month to mss. Sample copy available online.

Nonfiction Needs book excerpts, essays, interview, journalism on Harvard-related intellectual subjects. **Buys 20-30 mss/year.** Query with published clips. Length: 800-10,000 words. **Pays $400-3,000.**

$$ HISPANIC CAREER WORLD

Equal Opportunity Publications, Inc., 445 Broad Hollow Rd., Suite 425, Melville NY 11747. (631)421-9421. Fax: (631)421-1352. E-mail: info@eop.com. Website: www.eop.com. **60% freelance written**. Semiannual magazine aimed at Hispanic students and professionals in all disciplines. Estab. 1969. Byline given. Pays on publication. No kill fee. Publishes ms an average of 3 months after acceptance. Buys first North American serial rights. Editorial lead time 3 months. Accepts queries by mail, e-mail, fax, phone. Accepts simultaneous submissions. Responds in 2 weeks to queries. Responds in 2 months to mss.

Sample copy free. Guidelines free.
Nonfiction Needs how-to, find jobs, interview, personal experience. Query. Length: 1,500-2,500 words. **Pays $350 for assigned articles.**
Tips Gear articles to our audience.

$ NEXT STEP MAGAZINE

Next Step Publishing, Inc., 2 W. Main St., Suite 200, Victor NY 14564. (585)742-1260. E-mail: editor@nextstepmag.com. Website: www.nextstepmag.com. **75% freelance written**. Bimonthly magazine covering LINK Newsletter, Transfer Guide. "Our magazine is a 5-times-a-school-year objective publication for high school juniors & seniors preparing for college. Articles cover college, careers, life & financial aid." Estab. 1995. Circ. distributed in 20,500+ high schools. No kill fee. Publishes ms an average of 6 months after acceptance. Buys all rights. Editorial lead time 6 months. Submit seasonal material 6 months in advance. Accepts queries by e-mail. Sample copy available online. Guidelines by e-mail.
Nonfiction Needs book excerpts, general interest, how-to, interview, personal experience, travel. *Link* is a newsletter published 5 times a year for high school counselors. Articles run 800-1,500 words & should be focused on helping counselors do their jobs better. Past articles have included counseling students with AD/HD, sports scholarships & motivation tactics. **Buys mss/year.** Query. Length: 500-1,000 words. **Pays $75 for assigned articles.**
Columns/Departments Contact: Laura Jeanne Hammond. College Planning (college types, making a decision, admissions); Financial Air (scholarships, financial aid options); SAT/ACT (preparing for the SAT/ACT, study tips), 400-1,000 words; Career Profiles (profile at least 3 professionals in different aspects of a specific industry), 800-1,000 words; Military (careers in the military, different branches, how to join), 400-600 words. Buys 5-10 mss/year. Query with or without published clips. **Pay varies, averages $75 per article.**
Tips "The best queries are specific, concise & entertaining. Readers should be referred to as 'you', and interviews with expert sources, college faculty, workers in the field or students are required in articles."

$$$$ NOTRE DAME MAGAZINE

University of Notre Dame, 538 Grace Hall, Notre Dame IN 46556-5612. (574)631-5335. Fax: (574)631-6767. E-mail: ndmag@nd.edu. Website: www.nd.edu/~ndmag. http://magazine.nd.edu/. **50% freelance written**. Quarterly magazine covering news of Notre Dame and education and issues affecting contemporary society. "We are a university magazine with a scope as broad as that found at a university, but we place our discussion in a moral, ethical, and spiritual context reflecting our Catholic heritage." Estab. 1972. Circ. 150,000. Byline given. Pays on acceptance. No kill fee. Publishes ms an average of 1 year after acceptance. Buys first rights, buys electronic rights. Accepts queries by mail, e-mail, fax. Responds in 2 months to queries. Sample copy online Guidelines available online.
Nonfiction Needs opinion, personal experience, religious. **Buys 35 mss/year.** Query with published clips. Length: 600-3,000 words. **Pays $250-3,000.**
Photos State availability. Identification of subjects, model releases required. Buys one-time and electronic rights.
Columns/Departments CrossCurrents (essays, deal with a wide array of issues—some topical, some personal, some serious, some light). Query with or without published clips or send complete ms.
Tips "The editors are always looking for new writers and fresh ideas. However, the caliber of the magazine and frequency of its publication dictate that the writing meet very high standards. The editors value articles strong in storytelling quality, journalistic technique, and substance. They do not encourage promotional or nostalgia pieces, stories on sports, or essays that are sentimentally religious."

$$ OREGON QUARTERLY

The Northwest Perspective from the University of Oregon, 5228 University of Oregon, Eugene OR 97403-5228. (541)346-5048. Fax: (541)346-5571. E-mail: quarterly@uoregon.edu. Website: www.uoregon.edu/~oq. **85% freelance written**. Quarterly magazine covering people and ideas at the University of Oregon and the Northwest. Estab. 1919. Circ. 100,000. Byline given. Pays on acceptance. Offers 20% kill fee. Publishes ms an average of 3 months after acceptance. Buys first North American serial rights and online archiving rights. Accepts queries by mail (preferred), e-mail (very rarely). Responds in 2 months to queries Sample copy for 9 × 12 SAE with 4 first-class stamps. Guidelines available online.
Nonfiction "Northwest issues and culture from the perspective of UO alumni and faculty." **Buys 30 mss/year.** Query with published clips. Length: 500-3,000 words. **Payment varies—30-50¢/per word for departments; features more.**
Reprints Only be UO-related authors. See Upfront/Excerpts section for examples. Send photocopy and information about when and where the material previously appeared.

Photos State availability. of story-related images. Identification of subjects required. Reviews 8 × 10 prints. Prefers hi-res digital. Buys one time rights.
Fiction Rarely publishes novel excerpts by UO professors or grads.
Tips "Query with strong, colorful writing on clear display; clips. And please, demonstrate you have a familiarity with our publication."

$ $ ☐ QUEEN'S ALUMNI REVIEW

Queen's University, 99 University Ave., Kingston ON K7L 3N6 Canada. Fax: (613)533-2060. E-mail: cuthberk@post.queensu.ca. Website: alumnireview.queensu.ca. **25% freelance written**. Quarterly magazine. Estab. 1927. Circ. 106,000. Byline given. Pays on publication. Publishes ms an average of 3 months after acceptance. Buys electronic rights, buys first world serial rights. Editorial lead time 3 months. Submit seasonal material 9 months in advance. Accepts queries by mail, e-mail. Responds in 2 weeks to queries. Responds in 2 weeks to mss. Sample copy and writer's guidelines online.
Nonfiction "We publish feature articles, columns, and articles about alumni, faculty, and staff who are doing unusual or worthwhile things." "Does not want religious or political rants, travel articles, how-to, or general interest pieces that do not refer to or make some reference to our core audience." **Buys 10 mss/year.** Send complete ms. Length: 200-2,500 words. **Pays 50¢/word (Canadian) plus 10% e-rights fee for assigned articles.**
Photos Send photos. Identification of subjects required. Reviews transparencies, prints, GIF/JPEG files. Offers $25 minimum or negotiates payment individually.
Columns/Departments Potential freelancers should study our magazine before submitting a query for a column. Buys 10 mss/year. Query with published clips or send complete ms. **Pays 50¢/word (Canadian).**
Tips "We buy freelance material, but our budget is limited, and so we choose carefully. All articles should have a Queen's angle—one that shows how Queen's alumni, faculty, staff, or friends of the university are involved and engaged in the world. We also look for topical articles that start Queen's specific and go on from there to look at issues of a wide topical interest. The writing should be professional, snappy, informative, and engaging. We always have far more editorial material in hand than we can ever publish. Study our magazine before you submit a query. Our circulation is primarily in Canada, but we also have readers in the US, UK, Hong Kong, Australia, and in more than 100 countries. Our readers are young and old, male and female, well educated, well-travelled, and sophisticated. We look for material that will appeal to a broad constituency."

$ $ RIPON COLLEGE MAGAZINE

P.O. Box 248, 300 Seward St., Ripon WI 54971-0248. (920)748-8322. Fax: (920)748-9262. Website: www.ripon.edu. **15% freelance written**. Quarterly magazine that contains information relating to Ripon College and is mailed to alumni and friends of the college. Estab. 1851. Circ. 14,000. Byline given. Pays on publication. Publishes ms an average of 3 months after acceptance. Makes work-for-hire assignments. Accepts queries by mail, e-mail, fax, phone. Responds in 2 weeks to queries.
Nonfiction Needs historical, interview. **Buys 4 mss/year.** Send complete ms. Length: 250-1,000 words. **Pays $25-350.**
Photos State availability. Captions, model releases required. Reviews contact sheets. Offers additional payment for photos accepted with ms. Buys one time rights.
Tips Story ideas must have a direct connection to Ripon College.

SCHOLASTIC ADMINISTR@TOR MAGAZINE

Scholastic, Inc., 557 Broadway, 5th Floor, New York NY 10012. (212)965-7429. Fax: (212)965-7497. E-mail: lrenwick@scholastic.com. Website: www.scholastic.com/administrator. Magazine published 8 times/year. Focuses on helping today's school administrators and education technology leaders in their efforts to improve the management of schools. Circ. 100,000. No kill fee. Editorial lead time 1 month. Sample copy free.

TRANSFORMATIONS

A Journal of People and Change, Worcester Polytechnic Institute, 100 Institute Rd., Worcester MA 01609-2280. Website: www.wpi.edu/+transformations. **60% freelance written**. Quarterly alumni magazine covering "science and engineering/education/business personalities and related technologies and issues for 34,000 alumni, primarily engineers, scientists, entrepreneurs, managers, media." Estab. 1897. Circ. 40,000. Byline given. Pays on publication. Publishes ms an average of 6 months after acceptance. Buys one-time rights. Accepts queries by mail, e-mail. Accepts previously published material. Accepts simultaneous submissions. Responds in 1 month to queries. Sample copy available online.

Nonfiction Needs interview, alumni in engineering, science, etc., photo feature, features on people and programs at WPI. Query with published clips. Length: 300-2,000 words. **Pays negotiable rate.**
Photos State availability. Captions required. Reviews contact sheets. Pays negotiable rate.
Tips "Submit outline of story, story idea, or published work. Features are most open to freelancers with excellent narrative skills, and an ability to understand and convey complex technologies in an engaging way. Keep in mind that this is an alumni magazine, so most articles focus on the college and its graduates."

$$$ UAB MAGAZINE

UAB Publications and Periodicals (University of Alabama at Birmingham), AB 340, 1530 3rd Ave. S., Birmingham AL 35294-0103. (205)934-9420. Fax: (205)975-4416. E-mail: mwindsor@uab.edu. Website: www.uab.edu/uabmagazine. **70% freelance written**. University magazine published 3 times/year covering University of Alabama at Birmingham. *UAB Magazine* informs readers about the innovation and creative energy that drives UAB's renowned research, educational, and health care programs. The magazine reaches active alumni, faculty, friends and donors, patients, corporate and community leaders, media and the public. Estab. 1980. Circ. 33,000. Byline given. Pays on acceptance. Offers 50% kill fee. Publishes ms an average of 3-4 months after acceptance. Buys first North American serial rights, buys electronic rights. Editorial lead time 3 months. Accepts queries by mail, e-mail. Sample copy available online. Guidelines free.
Nonfiction Needs general interest, interview. **Buys 40-50 mss/year.** Query with published clips. Length: 500-5,000 words. **Pays $100-1,200.**

$$ WOMAN ENGINEER

Equal Opportunity Publications, Inc., 445 Broad Hollow Rd., Suite 425, Melville NY 11747. (631)421-9421. Fax: (631)421-1352. E-mail: info@eop.com. Website: www.eop.com. **Contact:** James Schneider, editor. **60% freelance written**. Triannual magazine focusing on advancing careers of women engineering students and professional engineers. Job information for members of minority groups. Estab. 1969. Byline given. Pays on publication. No kill fee. Publishes ms an average of 3 months after acceptance. Buys first North American serial rights. Editorial lead time 3 months. Accepts queries by mail, e-mail, fax, phone. Accepts simultaneous submissions. Responds in 2 weeks to queries. Responds in 2 months to mss. Sample copy free. Guidelines free.
Nonfiction Needs how-to, find jobs, interview, personal experience. "We do not want anything too general." Query. Length: 1,500-2,500 words. **Pays $350 for assigned articles.**
Tips "Gear articles to our audience."

$$ WORKFORCE DIVERSITY FOR ENGINEERING & IT PROFESSIONALS

Equal Opportunity Publications, Inc., 445 Broad Hollow Rd., Suite 425, Melville NY 11747. (631)421-9421. Fax: (631)421-1352. E-mail: info@eop.com. Website: www.eop.com. **60% freelance written**. Quarterly magazine addressing workplace issues affecting technical professional women, members of minority groups, and people with disabilities. Estab. 1969. Byline given. Pays on publication. No kill fee. Publishes ms an average of 3 months after acceptance. Buys first North American serial rights. Editorial lead time 3 months. Accepts queries by mail, e-mail, fax, phone. Accepts simultaneous submissions. Responds in 2 weeks to queries. Responds in 2 months to mss. Sample copy free. Guidelines free.
Nonfiction Needs how-to, find jobs, interview, personal experience. We do not want articles that are too general. Query. Length: 1,500-2,500 words. **Pays $350 for assigned articles.**
Tips Gear articles to our audience.

Child Care & Parental Guidance

$ ATLANTA PARENT/ATLANTA BABY

2346 Perimeter Park Dr., Suite 100, Atlanta GA 30341. (770)454-7599. Website: www.atlantaparent.com. **50% freelance written**. Byline given. Pays on publication. Publishes ms an average of 3 months after acceptance. Buys one-time rights. Submit seasonal material 6 months in advance. Accepts queries by mail, e-mail. Accepts previously published material. Responds in 4 months to queries. Sample copy for $3.
Nonfiction Needs general interest, how-to, humor, interview, travel. Private School (January); Camp (February); Birthday Parties (March and September); Maternity and Mothering (May and October); Childcare (July); Back-to-School (August); Teens (September); Holidays (November/December) No

religious or philosophical discussions. **Buys 60 mss/year.** Send complete ms. Length: 800-1,500 words. **Pays $5-50.**

Reprints Send tearsheet or photocopy with rights for sale noted and information about when and where the material previously appeared. **Pays $30-50.**

Photos State availability of or send photos. Reviews 3 × 5 photos. Offers $10/photo. Buys one time rights.

Tips Articles should be geared to problems or situations of families and parents. Should include down-to-earth tips and be clearly written. No philosophical discussions. We're also looking for well-written humor.

$$$$ BABY TALK

Time, Inc., 530 Fifth Ave., 4th Floor, New York NY 10036. (212)522-4327. Fax: (212)522-8699. E-mail: letters@babytalk.com. Website: www.babytalk.com. Magazine published 10 times/year. *Baby Talk* is written primarily for women who are considering pregnancy or who are expecting a child, and parents of children from birth through 18 months, with the emphasis on pregnancy through first 6 months of life. Estab. 1935. Circ. 2,000,000. Byline given. Accepts queries by mail. Responds in 2 months to queries.

Nonfiction Features cover pregnancy, the basics of baby care, infant/toddler health, growth and development, juvenile equipment and toys, work and day care, marriage and sex—approached from a how-to, service perspective. The message—Here's what you need to know and why—is delivered with smart, crisp style. The tone is confident and reassuring (and, when appropriate, humorous and playful), with the backing of experts. In essence, *Baby Talk* is a training manual of parents facing the day-to-day dilemmas of new parenthood. No phone calls. Query with SASE Length: 1,000-2,000 words. **Pays $500-2,000 depending on length, degree of difficulty, and the writer's experience.**

Columns/Departments Several departments are written by regular contributors. Length: 100-1,250 words. Query with SASE **Pays $100-1,000.**

Tips Please familiarize yourself with the magazine before submitting a query. Take the time to focus your story idea; scattershot queries are a waste of everyone's time. WE do not accept poetry.

BIG APPLE PARENT/QUEENS PARENT/WESTCHESTER PARENT/BROOKLYN PARENT/ROCKLAND PARENT

Davler Media Group, 1040 Avenue of the Americas, New York NY 10018. (212)315-0800. E-mail: hellonwheels@parentsknow.com. Website: www.parentsknow.com. **20% freelance written**. Monthly tabloid covering New York City family life. *BAP* readers live in high-rise Manhattan apartments; it is an educated, upscale audience. Often both parents are working full time in professional occupations. Child-care help tends to be one on one, in the home. Kids attend private schools for the most part. While not quite a suburban approach, some of our *QP* and *BK* readers do have backyards (though most live in high-rise apartments). It is a more middle-class audience in Queens and Brooklyn. More kids are in day care centers; majority of kids are in public schools. Our Westchester county edition is for suburban parents. Estab. 1985. Circ. 80,000, *Big Apple*; 70,000, *Queens Parent*; 70,000, *Westchester Parent*; 45,000, *Brooklyn Parent*. Byline given. No longer pays for freelance articles. Offers 50% kill fee. Buys first New York area rights. Submit seasonal material 3 months in advance. Accepts queries by mail, e-mail, fax. Accepts simultaneous submissions. Responds immediately. Sample copy free. Guidelines available online.

Nonfiction Needs book excerpts, expose, general interest, how-to, inspirational, interview, opinion, personal experience, family health, education. We're always looking for news and coverage of controversial issues. Send complete ms. Length: 600-1,000 words.

Reprints Send tearsheet or typed ms with rights for sale noted and information about when and where the material previously appeared.

Columns/Departments Dads; Education; Family Finance. Send complete ms.

Tips We have a very local focus; our aim is to present articles our readers cannot find in national publications. To that end, news stories and human interest pieces must focus on New York and New Yorkers. We are always looking for news and newsy pieces; we keep on top of current events, frequently giving issues that may relate to parenting a local focus so that the idea will work for us as well. We are not currently looking for essays, humor, general child raising, or travel.

$$ BIRMINGHAM PARENT

Evans Publishing LLC, 115-C Hilltop Business Dr., Pelham AL 35124. (205)739-0090. Fax: (205)739-0073. E-mail: editor@birminghamparent.com. Website: www.birminghamparent.com. **Contact:** Carol Muse Evans. **75% freelance written**. Monthly magazine covering family issues, parenting, education, babies to teens, health care, anything involving parents raising children. "We are a free, local parenting publication in central Alabama. All of our stories carry some type of local slant. Parenting magazines abound: we are the source for the local market." Estab. 2004. Circ. 40,000. Byline given. Pays within 30 days of publication. Offers 20% kill fee. Publishes ms an average of 3-4 months after acceptance. Buys first North American serial rights, buys second serial (reprint) rights, buys electronic rights. Editorial lead time 3-4 months. Submit seasonal material 4 months in advance. Accepts queries by e-mail. Accepts previously published material. Accepts simultaneous submissions. Responds in 2-3 weeks to queries. Responds in 2-3 months to mss. Sample copy for $3. Guidelines available online.

Nonfiction Needs book excerpts, general interest, how-to, interview, parenting. Does not want first person pieces. Our pieces educate and inform: we don't take stories without sources. **Buys 24 mss/year.** Send complete ms. Length: 350-2,500 words. **Pays $50-350 for assigned articles. Pays $35-200 for unsolicited articles.**

Photos State availability. Captions, identification of subjects, model releases required. Reviews GIF/JPEG files. Negotiates payment individually; offers no additional payment for photos accepted with ms. Buys one time rights.

Columns/Departments Parenting Solo (single parenting), 650 words; Baby & Me (dealing with newborns or pregnancy), 650 words; Teens (raising teenagers), 650-1,500 words. Buys 36 mss/year. Query with published clips or send complete ms. **Pays $35-200.**

Tips "Present your story so that you can add local slant to it, or suggest to us how to do so. Please no first person opinion pieces—no '10 great gifts for teachers,' for example, without sources. We expect some sources for our informative stories."

$ CHESAPEAKE FAMILY

Jefferson Communications, 929 West St., Suite 307, Annapolis MD 21401. (410)263-1641. Fax: (410)280-0255. E-mail: editor@chesapeakefamily.com. Website: www.chesapeakefamily.com. **80% freelance written**. Monthly magazine covering parenting. *Chesapeake Family* is a free, regional parenting publication serving readers in the Anne Arundel, Calvert, Prince George's, and Queen Anne's counties of Maryland. Our goal is to identify tips, resources, and products that will make our readers' lives easier. We answer the questions they don't have time to ask, doing the research for them so they have the information they need to make better decisions for their families' health, education, and well-being. Articles must have local angle and resources. Estab. 1990. Circ. 40,000. Byline given. Publishes ms an average of 2 months after acceptance. Buys first rights, buys one-time rights, buys second serial (reprint) rights, buys electronic rights. Makes work-for-hire assignments. Editorial lead time 3-6 months. Submit seasonal material 4 months in advance. Accepts queries by mail, e-mail, fax. Accepts previously published material. Accepts simultaneous submissions. Guidelines available online.

Nonfiction Needs how-to, parenting topics: sign your kids up for sports, find out if your child needs braces, etc., interview, local personalities, travel, family-fun destinations. No general, personal essays (however, personal anecdotes leading into a story with general applicability is fine). **Buys 25 mss/year.** Send complete ms. Length: 800-1,200 words. **Pays $75-125. Pays $35-50 for unsolicited articles.**

Photos State availability. Model releases required. Reviews prints, GIF/JPEG files. Offers no additional payment for photos accepted with ms, unless original, assigned photo is selected for the cover.

Columns/Departments Buys 25 mss/year. **Pays $35-50.**

Tips A writer's best chance is to know the issues specific to our local readers. Know how to research the issues well, answer the questions our readers need to know, and give them information they can act on—and present it in a friendly, conversational tone.

$$ CHICAGO PARENT

141 S. Oak Park Ave., Oak Park IL 60302. (708)386-5555. Fax: (708)524-8360. E-mail: chiparent@chicagoparent.com. Website: www.chicagoparent.com. **60% freelance written**. Monthly tabloid. "*Chicago Parent* has a distinctly local approach. We offer information, inspiration, perspective and empathy to Chicago-area parents. Our lively editorial mix has a `we're all in this together' spirit, and articles are thoroughly researched and well written." Estab. 1988. Circ. 125,000 in 3 zones covering the 6-county Chicago metropolitan area. Byline given. Pays on publication. Offers 10-50% kill fee. Publishes ms an average of 2 months after acceptance. Buys first rights, buys electronic rights. Editorial lead time 4 months. Submit seasonal material 4 months in advance. Accepts queries by mail. Responds in 6 weeks to queries. Sample copy for $3.95 and 11 × 17 SAE with $1.65 postage. Guidelines for #10 SASE.

Nonfiction Needs essays, expose, how-to, parent-related, humor, interview, travel, local interest. include Chicago Baby and Healthy Child. No pot-boiler parenting pieces, simultaneous submissions, previously published pieces or non-local writers (from outside the 6-county Chicago metropolitan area). **Buys 40-**

50 mss/year. Query with published clips. Length: 200-2,500 words. **Pays $25-300 for assigned articles. Pays $25-100 for unsolicited articles.**

Photos State availability. Captions, identification of subjects required. Reviews contact sheets, negatives, prints. Offers $0-40/photo; negotiates payment individually. Buys one time rights.

Columns/Departments Healthy Child (kids' health issues), 850 words; Getaway (travel pieces), up to 1,200 words; other columns not open to freelancers. Buys 30 mss/year. Query with published clips or send complete ms. **Pays $100.**

Tips We don't like pot-boiler parenting topics and don't accept many personal essays unless they are truly compelling.

CHOOSING A SCHOOL FOR YOUR CHILD

Universal Magazines, Ltd., Unit 5, 6-8 Byfield St., North Ryde NSW 2113 Australia. (61)(2)9887-0399. Fax: (61)(2)9805-0714. Website: www.schoolchoice.com.au. Beth Anderson (VIC). **Contact:** Penny Alexopolous (NSW). Annual magazine covering high school education issues. "Choosing A School For Your Child offers detailed profiles of all subjects and activities at the school, complete with details of the school's philosophy and fee structure, plus information parents need on examination methods and education policy. An online resource that complements the magazine, Schoolchoice.com.au, provides parents with the best possible information and advice regarding their child's education. It features articles about choosing the right secondary school for your child, as well as other important issues in education, including the welfare and health of your child, curricular and learning opportunities, exchange programs, comprehensive listings of every secondary school in the State, and much more."

- Versions of magazine for VIC and NSW.

Nonfiction Needs general interest, how-to, interview. Query.

Tips "Choosing a School For Your Child provides information to parents whose children are entering high school in NSW, ACT, VIC, and QLD. Our readership is keen to see their children succeed, they are passionate about education and are ready to invest in their children's future. As *Choosing a School* has a high overseas readership, a section is devoted to the challenges for overseas students in Australia and what options are available."

$ $ COLUMBUS PARENT MAGAZINE

Consumer News Service, 5300 Crosswind Dr., Columbus OH 43216. Fax: (614)461-7527. E-mail: columbusparent@thisweeknews.com. Website: www.columbusparent.com. **50% freelance written.** Monthly magazine covering parenting. A hip, reliable resource for Central Ohio parents who are raising children from birth to 18. Estab. 1988. Circ. 60,000. Byline given. Pays on publication. Offers 10% kill fee. Publishes ms an average of 2 months after acceptance. Buys all rights. Editorial lead time 3 months. Submit seasonal material 5 months in advance. Accepts queries by mail, e-mail, fax. Sample copy available online. Guidelines available online.

Nonfiction Needs general interest, how-to, interview, new product. Does not want personal essays. **Buys 80 mss/year.** Send complete ms. Length: 500-900 words. **Pays 10¢/word.**

Photos State availability. Identification of subjects required. Offers no additional payment for photos accepted with ms. Buys one time rights.

Tips Your best bet for breaking in is to be an Ohio resident.

$ $ N FAMILY

Union County, Morris County, Essex County, Essex County, Central Jersey, Kids Monthly Publications, 1122 Route 22 W., Mountainside NJ 07092. (908)232-2913, ext. 103. Fax: (908)317-9518. E-mail: editor@njfamily.com. Website: www.njfamily.com. **75% freelance written.** Monthly magazine covering parenting and family. Estab. 1991. Circ. 126,000. Byline given. Pays on publication. No kill fee. Publishes ms an average of 2 months after acceptance. Buys first North American serial rights. Editorial lead time 3-6 months. Submit seasonal material 4 months in advance. Accepts queries by e-mail. Accepts previously published material. Accepts simultaneous submissions. Sample copy available online.

- "Our mission is to help New Jersey parents be the best parents they can be. Articles should focus on the facts and what you can do for your child to prevent/promote/help/teach, etc. in any given situation."

Nonfiction Needs book excerpts, new product, personal experience. Raising teens. We do not want self-promotion articles. **Buys 60 mss/year.** Send complete ms. Length: 450-1,200 words. **Pays $50-200.**

Columns/Departments Contact: Farn Dupre. School solutions (elementary education in New Jersey), 350-400 words. 12 mss/year. Query with published clips. **Pays $35-100.**

Fillers Contact: Lucy Banta, Farn Dupre. Needs facts. Buys 4 mss/year. Length: 150-400 words. **Pays $10-25.**

Tips "Know our audience—parents in New Jersey."

$ THE FAMILY DIGEST

P.O. Box 40137, Fort Wayne IN 46804. **95% freelance written.** Quarterly magazine. "*The Family Digest* is dedicated to the joy and fulfilment of the Catholic family and its relationship to the Catholic parish. Estab. 1945. Circ. 150,000. Byline given. Pays within 2 months of acceptance. Buys first North American rights. Submit seasonal material 7 months in advance. Accepts previously published material. Responds in 1-2 months to queries. Sample copy and writer's guidelines are available for 6 × 9 SAE with 2 first-class stamps.

Nonfiction Family life, parish life, prayer life, Catholic traditions, spiritual life, . Needs how-to, inspirational, lives of the saints., lives of the saints. **Buys 45 unsolicited mss/year.** Send complete ms. Length: 750-1,200 words. **Pays $45-60 for accepted articles.**

Reprints "Send typed manuscript with rights for sale noted and information about when and where the material previously appeared."

Fillers Needs anecdotes, tasteful humor based on personal experience. Buys 12 mss/year. Length: 25-100 words. **Pays $25.**

Tips "Prospective freelance contributors should be familiar with the publication and the types of articles we accept and publish. We are especially looking for upbeat articles which affirm the simple ways in which the Catholic faith is expressed in daily life. Articles on family and parish life, including seasonal articles, how-to pieces, inspirational, prayer, spiritual life, and Church traditions, will be gladly reviewed for possible acceptance and publication."

$$$$ FAMILYFUN

Disney Publishing, Inc., 47 Pleasant St., Northampton MA 01060. (413)585-0444. Fax: (413)586-5724. E-mail: queries.familyfun@disney.com. Website: www.familyfun.com. Magazine covering activities for families with kids ages 3-12. "*FamilyFun* is about all the great things families can do together. Our writers are either parents or authorities in a covered field." Estab. 1991. Circ. 2,100,000. Byline sometimes given. Pays on acceptance. Offers 25% kill fee. Makes work-for-hire assignments. Editorial lead time 6 months. Submit seasonal material 6 months in advance. Accepts simultaneous submissions. Responds in 3 months to queries. Sample copy for $5. Guidelines available online.

Nonfiction Needs book excerpts, essays, general interest, how-to, crafts, cooking, educational activities, humor, interview, personal experience, photo feature, travel. **Buys dozens of mss/year.** Query with published clips. Length: 850-3,000 words. **Pays $1.25/word.**

Photos State availability. Identification of subjects, model releases required. Reviews contact sheets, negatives, transparencies. Offers $75-500/photo. Buys all rights.

Columns/Departments "Everyday Fun, Debbie Way, senior editor (simple, quick, practical, inexpensive ideas and projects—outings, crafts, games, nature activities, learning projects, and cooking with children), 200-400 words; query or send ms; **pays per word or $200 for ideas.** Family Getaways, Becky Karush, associate editor (brief, newsy items about family travel, what's new, what's great, and especially, what's a good deal), 100-125 words; send ms; **pays per word or $50 for ideas.** Creative Solutions, Debra Immergut, senior editor (explains fun and inventive ideas that have worked for writer's own family), 1,000 words; query or send ms; **pays $1,250 on acceptance.** Also publishes best letters from writers and readers following column, send to My Great Idea: From Our Readers Editor, 100-150 words, **pays $100 on publication**." Buys 60-80 letters/year; 10-12 columns/year.

Tips "Many of our writers break into *FF* by writing for Everyday Fun or Family Getaways (front-of-the-book departments)."

$ GRAND RAPIDS FAMILY MAGAZINE

Gemini Publications, 549 Ottawa Ave., NW, Suite 201, Grand Rapids MI 49503-1444. (616)459-4545. Fax: (616)459-4800. E-mail: cvalade@geminipub.com. Website: www.grfamily.com. Monthly magazine covering local parenting issues. *Grand Rapids Family* seeks to inform, instruct, amuse, and entertain its readers and their families. Circ. 30,000. Byline given. Pays on publication. Offers $25 kill fee. Buys first North American serial rights, buys simultaneous rights, buys all rights. Makes work-for-hire assignments. Editorial lead time 3 months. Submit seasonal material 4 months in advance. Accepts simultaneous submissions. Responds in 2 months to queries. Responds in 6 months to mss. Guidelines for #10 SASE.

Nonfiction The publication recognizes that parenting is a process that begins before conception/adoption and continues for a lifetime. The issues are diverse and ever changing. *Grand Rapids Family* seeks to identify these issues and give them a local perspective, using local sources and resources. Query. **Pays $25-50.**

Photos State availability. Captions, identification of subjects, model releases required. Reviews contact sheets. Offers $25/photo. Buys one-time or all rights.

Columns/Departments All local: law, finance, humor, opinion, mental health. **Pays $25**

$ GWINNETT PARENTS MAGAZINE

3651 Peachtree Pkwy., Suite 325, Suwanee GA 30024. 888-769-0040. Fax: (678)681-1313. E-mail: editor@localparentmagazine.com. Website: www.gwinnettparents.com. **Contact:** Terrie Carter, editor. "Our mission is to provide the most comprehensive source of parenting information and local resources for families living in and around Gwinnett County, Georgia." Pays on publication. No kill fee. Publishes ms an average of 1-4 weeks after acceptance. Buys nonexclusive online archival rights rights. Editorial lead time 2 months. Accepts queries by e-mail. Responds in 3-4 weeks to queries. Sample copy by e-mail (paul@localparentmagazine.com).

Nonfiction Send queries with a brief bio via e-mail with Editorial Submission in the subject line. Length: 500-1,500 words. **Pays $35 for department articles; $50 for features.**

Photos Accepts color or b&w high resolution images. No images from the Internet. Identification of subjects.

$ HOME EDUCATION MAGAZINE

P.O. Box 1083, Tonasket WA 98855. (509)486-1351. Website: www.homeedmag.com. **80% freelance written**. Bimonthly magazine covering home-based education. "We feature articles which address the concerns of parents who want to take a direct involvement in the education of their children—concerns such as socialization, how to find curriculums and materials, testing and evaluation, how to tell when your child is ready to begin reading, what to do when homeschooling is difficult, teaching advanced subjects, etc." Estab. 1983. Circ. 32,000. Byline given. Pays on publication. Publishes ms an average of 6 months after acceptance. Buys first North American serial rights, buys first rights, buys one-time rights, buys electronic rights. Submit seasonal material 6 months in advance. Accepts queries by mail. Responds in 2 months to queries. Sample copy for $6.50. Writer's guidelines for #10 SASE, via e-mail, or on website.

Nonfiction Needs essays, how-to, related to homeschooling, humor, interview, personal experience, photo feature, technical. **Buys 40-50 mss/year.** Send complete ms. Length: 750-2,500 words. **Pays $50-100.**

Photos Send photos. Identification of subjects required. Reviews enlargements, 35mm prints, CD-ROMs. Pays $100/cover; $12/inside photos. Buys one time rights.

Tips "We would like to see how-to articles (that don't preach, just present options); articles on testing, accountability, working with the public schools, socialization, learning disabilities, resources, support groups, legislation, and humor. We need answers to the questions that homeschoolers ask. Please, no teachers telling parents how to teach. Personal experience with homeschooling is the preferred approach."

$ HOMESCHOOLING TODAY

P.O. Box 244, Abingdon VA 24212. (276)628-7730. E-mail: management@homeschooltoday.com. Website: www.homeschooltoday.com. **75% freelance written**. Bimonthly magazine covering homeschooling. "We are a practical magazine for homeschoolers with a broadly Christian perspective." Estab. 1992. Circ. 13,000. Byline given. Pays on publication. Offers 25% kill fee. Publishes ms an average of 1 year after acceptance. Buys first rights. Editorial lead time 6 months. Submit seasonal material 1 year in advance. Accepts simultaneous submissions. Responds in 4 months to mss. Sample copy and writer's guidelines free

Nonfiction Needs book excerpts, how-to, interview, new product. No fiction. **Buys 30 mss/year.** Send complete ms. Length: 500-2,000 words. **Pays 10¢/word.**

Photos State availability. Captions, identification of subjects required. Offers no additional payment for photos accepted with ms. Buys one time rights.

$ ✪ ISLAND PARENT MAGAZINE

The Resource Publication for Vancouver Island Parents, Island Parent Group, 830 Pembroke St., Suite A-10, Victoria BC V8T 1H9 Canada. (250)388-6905. Fax: (250)388-6920. E-mail: editor@islandparent.ca. Website: www.islandparent.ca. **Contact:** Sue Fast, Editor. **98% freelance written**. Monthly magazine covering parenting. Estab. 1988. Circ. 20,000. Byline given. honorium. No kill fee. Publishes ms an average of 3 months after acceptance. Buys one-time rights, buys electronic rights. Editorial lead time

3 months. Submit seasonal material 3 months in advance. Accepts queries by e-mail. Responds in 4-6 weeks to queries. Sample copy available online. Guidelines available online.

- "Our editorial philosophy is based on the belief that parents need encouragement and useful information. We encourage writers to cover topics of interest to them or that reflect their own experience—we're looking for a variety of perspectives, experiences and beliefs. Our aim is to help readers feel valued, supported and respected. Ideally, we can raise the profile of parenting and help families enjoy each other."

Nonfiction Contact: Sue Fast. Needs book excerpts, essays, general interest, how-to, humor, inspirational, interview, opinion, (does not mean letters to the editor), personal experience, travel. **Buys 80 mss/year.** Query. Length: 400-1,800 words. **Pays $35 for assigned articles. Pays $35 for unsolicited articles.**
Photos Send photos. Reviews GIF/JPEG files. Offers no additional payment for photos accepted with ms. Buys one time rights.
Fillers Needs anecdotes, facts, gags, newsbreaks, short humor. Buys 10 mss/year. Length: 400-650 words. **Pays $35.**

$ KIDS LIFE MAGAZINE

Kids Life Publishing of Tuscaloosa, LLC, 1426 22nd Ave., Tuscaloosa AL 35401. Fax: (205)345-1632. E-mail: kidslife@comcast.net. Website: www.kidslifemagazine.com. **50% freelance written**. Bimonthly magazine covering family and child. *Kids Life Magazine* is a one-stop place for families containing everything the Tuscaloosa area offers our children. Estab. 1996. Circ. 30,000. Byline given. Pays on publication. Buys simultaneous rights. Editorial lead time 2 months. Submit seasonal material 4 months in advance. Accepts queries by e-mail. Accepts previously published material. Accepts simultaneous submissions. Sample copy free. Guidelines available online.
Nonfiction We want anything child and family related. Needs personal experience. **Buys 12 mss/year. Pays up to $25.**
Photos Send photos. Reviews GIF/JPEG files. Offers no additional payment for photos accepted with ms.
Columns/Departments Reel Life with Jane (movie reviews), 1,000 words; Single Parenting, 750 words; Spiritual, 725 words. Buys 3 mss/year. **Pays $0-20.**
Fillers Needs facts, gags, short humor. Length: 500 words.
Tips E-mail submissions. We welcome anyone wanting to be published.

$ LIVING

Living for the Whole Family, Shalom Foundation, 1251 Virginia Ave., Harrisonburg VA 22802. E-mail: tgether@aol.com. Website: www.churchoutreach.com. **90% freelance written**. Quarterly tabloid covering family living. Articles focus on giving general encouragement for families of all ages and stages. Estab. 1985. Circ. 250,000. Byline given. Pays on publication. No kill fee. Publishes ms an average of 6-12 months after acceptance. Buys one-time rights, buys electronic rights. Editorial lead time 4-6 months. Submit seasonal material 6 months in advance. Accepts queries by mail, e-mail. Accepts previously published material. Accepts simultaneous submissions. Responds in 2 months to queries. Responds in 2-4 months to mss. Sample copy for sae with 9 × 12 envelope and 4 First-Class stamps. Guidelines free.

- "Our bias is to use articles 'showing' rather than telling readers how to raise families (stories rather than how-to). We aim for articles that are well written, understandable, challenging (not the same old thing you've read elsewhere); they should stimulate readers to dig a little deeper, but not too deep with academic or technical language; that are interesting and fit our theological perspective (Christian), but are not preachy or overly patriotic. No favorable mentions of smoking, drinking, cursing, etc."

  O‐ "We want our stories and articles to be very practical and upbeat. Since we go to every home, we do not assume a Christian audience. Writers need to take this into account. Personal experience stories are welcome, but are not the only approach.Our audience? Children, teenagers, singles, married couples, right on through to retired persons. We cover the wide variety of subjects that people face in the home and workplace. (See theme list in our guidelines online.)"

Nonfiction Needs general interest, how-to, humor, inspirational, personal experience. We do not use devotional materials intended for Christian audiences. We seldom use pet stories and receive way too many grief/death/dealing with serious illness stories to use. We encourage stories from non-white writers (excuse the phrase). We publish in March, June, September, and December so holidays that occur in other months are not usually the subject of articles. **Buys 48-52 mss/year.** Query. Length: 500-1,200 words. **Pays $35-60.**

Photos Contact: Dorothy Hartman. State availability. Captions, identification of subjects, model releases required. Reviews 4X6 prints, GIF/JPEG files. Offers $15-25/photo. Buys one time rights.

Tips "We prefer 'good news' stories that are uplifting and non-controversial in nature. We want articles that tell stories of people solving problems and dealing with personal issues rather than essays or 'preaching.' If you submit electronically, it is very helpful if you put the specific title of the submission in the subject line and please include your e-mail address in the body of the e-mail or on your manuscript. Also, always please include your address and phone number."

$ METROFAMILY MAGAZINE

Inprint Publishing, 306 S. Bryant C-152, Edmond OK 73034. (405)340-1404. E-mail: editor@metrofamilymagazine.com. Website: www.metrofamilymagazine.com. **20% freelance written**. Monthly tabloid covering parenting. *MetroFamily Magazine* provides local parenting and family fun information for our Central Oklahoma readers. Circ. 35,000. Byline given. Pays on publication. No kill fee; assignments given to local writers only. Publishes ms an average of 2-3 months after acceptance. Buys first North American serial rights, buys second serial (reprint) rights, buys simultaneous rights, buys electronic rights. Editorial lead time 2-3 months. Accepts queries by e-mail. Accepts previously published material. Accepts simultaneous submissions. Responds in 3 weeks to queries. Responds in 1 month to mss. Sample copy for sae with 10 × 13 envelope and 3 First-Class stamps. via e-mail or return with #10 SASE

Nonfiction Needs Family or mom-specific articles; see website for themes. No poetry, fiction (except for humor column), or anything that doesn't support good, solid family values. Send complete ms. Length: 800-1200 words. **Pays $40-60, plus 1 contributor copy.**

Columns/Departments You've Just Gotta Laugh, humor (600 words). Buys 12 mss/year. Send complete ms. **Pays $35.**

$ METROKIDS

Resource Publications for Delaware Valley Families, Kidstuff Publications, Inc., 1412-1414 Pine St., Philadelphia PA 19102. (215)291-5560, ext. 102. Fax: (215)291-5563. E-mail: editor@metrokids.com. Website: www.metrokids.com. **25% freelance written**. "Monthly tabloid providing information for parents and kids in Philadelphia and surrounding counties, South Jersey, and Delaware." Estab. 1990. Circ. 115,000. Byline given. Pays on publication. Buys one-time rights. Submit seasonal material 4 months in advance. Accepts queries by e-mail. Accepts previously published material. Guidelines by e-mail.

- Responds only if interested.

Nonfiction Needs general interest, how-to, new product, travel, parenting, health. Educator's Edition—field trips, school enrichment, teacher, professional development (March & September); Camps (December & June); Special Kids—children with special needs (August); Vacations and Theme Parks (May & June); What's Happening—guide to events and activities (January); Kids 'N Care—guide to childcare (July). **Buys 40 mss/year.** Query with published clips. Length: 800-1,500 words. **Pays $50.**

Reprints E-mail summary or complete article and information about when and where the material previously appeared. Pays $35, or $50 if localized after discussion.

Columns/Departments Techno Family (CD-ROM and website reviews); Body Wise (health); Style File (fashion and trends); Woman First (motherhood); Practical Parenting (financial parenting advice); Kids 'N Care (toddlers and daycare); Special Kids (disabilities), all 650-850 words. Buys 25 mss/year. Query. **Pays $25-50.**

Tips "We prefer e-mail queries or submissions. Because they're so numerous, we don't reply unless interested. We are interested in feature articles (on specified topics) or material for our regular departments (with a regional/seasonal base). Articles should cite expert sources and the most up-to-date theories and facts. We are looking for a journalistic style of writing. We are also interested in finding local writers for assignments."

$$ METRO PARENT MAGAZINE

Metro Parent Publishing Group, 22041 Woodward Ave., Ferndale MI 48220-2520. (248)398-3400. Fax: (248)3399-3970. E-mail: jelliott@metroparent.com. Website: www.metroparent.com. **75% freelance written**. Monthly magazine covering parenting, women's health, education. We are a local magazine on parenting topics and issues of interest to Detroit-area parents. Related issues: *Ann Arbor Parent; African/American Parent; Metro Baby Magazine.* Circ. 85,000. Byline given. Pays on publication. Publishes ms an average of 3 months after acceptance. Buys first rights. Editorial lead time 3 months. Submit seasonal material 3 months in advance. Accepts queries by mail, e-mail. Accepts previously published material. Accepts simultaneous submissions. Responds in 2 weeks to queries. Responds in 3 months to mss. Sample copy for $2.50.

Nonfiction Needs essays, humor, inspirational, personal experience. **Buys 100 mss/year.** Send complete ms. Length: 1,500-2,500 words. **Pays $50-300 for assigned articles.**
Photos State availability. Captions required. Offers $100-200/photo or negotiates payment individually. Buys one time rights.
Columns/Departments Women's Health (latest issues of 20-40 year olds), 750-900 words; Solo Parenting (advice for single parents); Family Finance (making sense of money and legal issues); Tweens 'N Teens (handling teen issues), 750-800 words. Buys 50 mss/year. Send complete ms. **Pays $75-150.**

$ $ PARENT:WISE AUSTIN

Pleticha Publishing Inc., 5501-A Balcones Dr., Suite 102, Austin TX 78731. (512)699-5327. Fax: (512)532-6885. Website: www.parentwiseaustin.com. **25% freelance written**. Monthly magazine covering parenting news, features and issues; mothering issues; maternal feminism; feminism as it pertains to motherhood and work/life balance; serious/thoughtful essays about the parenting experience; humor articles pertaining to the parenting experience. "*Parent:Wise Austin* targets educated, thoughtful readers who want solid information about the parenting experience. We seek to create a warm, nurturing community by providing excellent, well researched articles, thoughtful essays, humor articles, and other articles appealing to parents. Our readers demand in-depth, well written articles; we do not accept, nor will we print, 're-worked' articles on boiler plate topics." Estab. 2004. Circ. 32,000. Byline given. Pays on publication. No kill fee. Publishes ms an average of 2 months after acceptance. Buys first North American serial rights, buys electronic rights. Editorial lead time 6 months. Submit seasonal material 6 months in advance. Accepts queries by e-mail. Responds in 1 week to queries. Responds in 1 month to mss. Sample copy for $41.17 postage. "However, sample copies can be viewed online." Guidelines available online.
Nonfiction Needs essays, humor, opinion, personal experience, travel, hard news, features on parenting issues. Mother's Day issue (May); Father's Day issue (June). "Does not want boiler plate articles or generic articles that have been customized for our market." **Buys 12-20 mss/year.** Query with published clips. Length: 500-2,500 words. **Pays $50-200.**
Photos Contact: Contact Nisa Sharma, art director. State availability. Captions, identification of subjects, model releases required. Reviews JPEG files. Offers no additional payment for photos accepted with ms. Buys one-time and electronic rights.
Columns/Departments My Life as a Parent (humor), 500-700 words; Essay (first-person narrative), 500-1,000 words. Buys 24-50 mss/year. Send complete ms. **Pays $50.**
Poetry Needs avant-garde, free verse, haiku, light verse, traditional. "Does not want poetry that does not pertain to parenting or the parenting experience." Buys 3-5 poems/year. Submit maximum 3 poems. Length: 25 lines.
Tips "We are much more likely to accept an Essay or a My Life as a Parent (humor) article than a cover article. Cover articles generally are assigned months in advance to seasoned journalists who know our market; humor and essay articles are accepted without a query and generally publish within a couple of months of acceptance. For cover articles, we prefer detailed queries (e.g., the theme of the article; who you plan to interview; what you hope to 'discover' or how you plan to educate readers) and clips of previous work. Please e-mail queries, clips and questions to the editor. No phone calls."

PARENTGUIDE

PG Media, 419 Park Ave. S., Floor 13, New York NY 10016. (212)213-8840. Fax: (212)447-7734. E-mail: jenna@parentguidenews.com. Website: www.parentguidenews.com. **80% freelance written**. Monthly magazine covering parenting and family issues. "We are a tabloid-sized publication catering to the needs and interests of parents who have children under the age of 12. Our print publication is distributed in New York City, New Jersey, Long Island, Westchester (County, Rockland County), and Queens. Our website (one of the most popular online parenting sites) is read by parents, psychologists, teachers, caretakers, and others concerned about family matters worldwide. Our columns and feature articles cover health, education, child-rearing, current events, parenting issues, recreational activities and social events. We also run a complete calendar of local events. We welcome articles from professional authors as well as never-before-published writers." Estab. 1982. Circ. 285,000. Byline given. Does not offer financial compensation. No kill fee. Publishes ms an average of 5 months after acceptance. Buys first rights. Editorial lead time 5 months. Submit seasonal material 6 months in advance. Accepts queries by e-mail. Accepts simultaneous submissions. Sample copy available online. Guidelines free.
Nonfiction Needs how-to, (family-related service pieces), inspirational, interview, personal experience, travel, (education, health, fitness, special needs, parenting).
Fiction Needs confession, humorous, slice-of-life vignettes. Query. Length: 800-1,000 words.

$$$$ PARENTING MAGAZINE (Early Years and School Years editions)

Bonnier Corporation, 2 Park Ave., New York NY 10016. (212)779-5000. Website: www.parenting.com. Magazine published 10 times/year for mothers of children from birth to 12, and covering both the emotional and practical aspects of parenting. Estab. 1987. Circ. 2,100,000. Byline given. Pays on acceptance. Offers 25% kill fee. Buys a variety of rights, including electronic rights. Guidelines for #10 SASE.

Nonfiction Contact: Articles Editor. Needs book excerpts, personal experience, child development/behavior/health. **Buys 20-30 mss/year.** Query. Length: 1,000-2,500 words. **Pays $1,000-3,000.**

Columns/Departments Contact: Query to the specific departmental editor. Buys 50-60 mss/year. Query. **Pays $50-400.**

Tips "The best guide for writers is the magazine itself. Please familiarize yourself with it before submitting a query."

PARENTS

Meredith Corp., 375 Lexington Ave., 10th Floor, New York NY 10017. (212)499-2000. Fax: (212)499-2077. Website: www.parents.com. **Contact:** Mary Hickey. Monthly magazine. Estab. 1926. Circ. 1,700,000. Pays on acceptance. Offers 25% kill fee. Submit seasonal material 6-8 months in advance. Accepts queries by mail, e-mail. Responds in 6 weeks to queries. Guidelines available online.

Nonfiction "Before you query us, please take a close look at our magazine at the library or newsstand. This will give you a good idea of the different kinds of stories we publish, as well as their tempo and tone. In addition, please take the time to look at the masthead to make sure you are directing your query to the correct department." Query with published clips.

Columns/Departments As They Grow (issues on different stages of development), 1,000 words.

Tips "We're a national publication, so we're mainly interested in stories that will appeal to a wide variety of parents. We're always looking for compelling human-interest stories, so you may want to check your local newspaper for ideas. Keep in mind that we can't pursue stories that have appeared in competing national publications."

$ PEDIATRICS FOR PARENTS

Pediatrics for Parents, Inc., 35 Starknaught Heights, Gloucester MA 01930. (215)253-4543. Fax: (973)302-4543. E-mail: richsagall@pedsforparents.com. **50% freelance written**. Monthly newsletter covering children's health. "*Pediatrics For Parents* emphasizes an informed, common-sense approach to childhood health care. We stress preventative action, accident prevention, when to call the doctor and when and how to handle a situation at home. We are also looking for articles that describe general, medical and pediatric problems, advances, new treatments, etc. All articles must be medically accurate and useful to parents with children—prenatal to adolescence." Estab. 1981. Circ. 120,000. Byline given. Pays on publication. Publishes ms an average of 4 months after acceptance. Buys first North American serial rights, buys electronic rights. Accepts queries by mail, e-mail, fax. Accepts previously published material. Accepts simultaneous submissions. Responds in 1 month to queries. Sample copy available online. Guidelines available online.

Nonfiction No first person or experience. **Buys 25 mss/year.** Send complete ms. Length: 1,000-1,500 words. **Pays $10-25.**

$ PIKES PEAK PARENT

The Gazette/Freedom Communications, 30 S. Prospect St., Colorado Springs CO 80903. Fax: (719)476-1625. E-mail: parent@gazette.com. Website: www.pikespeakparent.com. **10% freelance written**. Monthly tabloid covering parenting, family and grandparenting. We prefer stories with local angle and local stories. We do not accept unsolicited manuscripts. Estab. 1994. Circ. 35,000. Byline given. Pays on publication. No kill fee. Buys first North American serial rights, buys electronic rights. Editorial lead time 3 months. Submit seasonal material 4 months in advance. Accepts queries by e-mail. Accepts previously published material. Accepts simultaneous submissions. Responds in 1 month to queries. Sample copy available online.

Nonfiction Needs essays, general interest, how-to, medical related to parenting. **Buys 10 mss/year.** Query with published clips. Length: 800-1,000 words. **Pays $20-120.**

Tips Local, local, local—with a fresh slant.

$$$ PLUM MAGAZINE

Groundbreak Publishing, 276 Fifth Ave., Suite 302, New York NY 10001. (212)725-9201. Fax: (212)725-9203. E-mail: editor@plummagazine.com. Website: www.plummagazine.com. **90% freelance written**. Annual magazine covering health and lifestyle for pregnant women over age 35. *Plum* is a patient

education tool meant to be an adjunct to obstetrics care. It presents information on preconception, prenatal medical care, nutrition, fitness, beauty, fashion, decorating, and travel. It also covers newborn health with articles on baby wellness, nursery necessities, postpartum care, and more. Estab. 2004. Circ. 450,000. Byline sometimes given. Pays on publication. Offers 20% kill fee. Publishes ms an average of 3-6 months after acceptance. Buys all rights. Editorial lead time 6 months. Submit seasonal material 8 months in advance. Accepts queries by e-mail. Responds in 6 weeks to queries. Sample copy for $7.95. Guidelines by e-mail.
Nonfiction Needs essays, how-to, interview. Query with published clips. Length: 300-3,500 words. **Pays 75¢-$1/word.**

$ SACRAMENTO PARENT

Reaching Greater Sacramento & the Sierra Foothills, Family Publishing Inc., 457 Grass Valley Hwy., Suite 5, Auburn CA 95603. (530)888-0573. Fax: (530)888-1536. E-mail: amy@sacramentoparent.com. Website: www.sacramentoparent.com. **50% freelance written**. Monthly magazine covering parenting in the Sacramento region. We look for articles that promote a developmentally appropriate, healthy and peaceful environment for children. Estab. 1992. Circ. 50,000. Byline given. Pays on publication. Offers 10% kill fee. Publishes ms an average of 2 months after acceptance. Buys first North American serial rights, buys electronic rights. Editorial lead time 3 months. Submit seasonal material 4 months in advance. Accepts queries by e-mail. Sample copy free. Guidelines by e-mail.
Nonfiction All articles should be related to parenting. Needs book excerpts, general interest, how-to, humor, interview, opinion, personal experience. **Buys 36 mss/year.** Query. Length: 300-1,000 words. **Pays $30-100.**
Columns/Departments Let's Go! (Sacramento regional family-friendly day trips/excursions/activities), 600 words. **Pays $25-45.**

$ SAN DIEGO FAMILY MAGAZINE

1475 Sixth Ave., 5th Floor, San Diego CA 92101-3200. (619)685-6970. Fax: (619)685-6978. E-mail: Kirsten@sandiegofamily.com. Website: www.sandiegofamily.com. **100% freelance written**. Monthly magazine for parenting and family issues. "*SDFM* is a regional family publication. We focus on providing current, informative and interesting editorial about parenting and family life that educates and entertains." Estab. 1982. Circ. 300,000. Byline given. Pays on publication. No kill fee. Publishes ms an average of 1-6 months after acceptance. Buys first rights, buys second serial (reprint) rights, buys electronic rights. Editorial lead time 4 months. Submit seasonal material 6 months in advance. Accepts queries by mail, e-mail. Accepts previously published material. Accepts simultaneous submissions. Responds in 1 month to queries. Responds in 2 months to mss. Sample copy for $4.50 to P.O. Box 23960, San Diego CA 92193. Guidelines available online.
Nonfiction Needs essays, general interest, how-to, interview, technical, travel, informational articles. Does not want humorous personal essays, opinion pieces, religious or spiritual. **Buys 350-500 mss/year.** Query. Length: 600-1,250 words. **Pays $22-90.**
Reprints Send typed manuscript with rights for sale, ted and information about when and where the material previously appeared. Will respond only if SASE is included.
Fiction "No adult fiction. We only want to see short fiction written for children: 'read aloud' stories, stories for beginning readers (400-500 words)." Send complete ms.
Tips "We publish short, informational articles. We give preference to stories about San Diego County personalities/events/etc., and stories that include regional resources for our readers. This is a local publication; don't address a national audience."

$ SCHOLASTIC PARENT & CHILD

Scholastic, Inc., 557 Broadway, New York NY 10012. (212)343-6100. Fax: (212)343-4801. E-mail: parentandchild@scholastic.com. Website: parentandchildonline.com. Bimonthly magazine. Published to keep active parents up-to-date on children's learning and development while in pre-school or child-care enviroment. Circ. 1,224,098. No kill fee. Editorial lead time 10 weeks.

$$ SOUTH FLORIDA PARENTING

1701 Green Rd., Suite B, Deerfield Beach FL 33441. (954)596-5607. Fax: (954)429-1207. E-mail: krlomer@tribune.com. Website: www.sfparenting.com. **Contact:** Kyara Lomer, ed. **90% freelance written**. Monthly magazine covering parenting, family. "*South Florida Parenting* provides news, information, and a calendar of events for readers in Southeast Florida (Palm Beach, Broward and Miami-Dade counties). The focus is on parenting issues, things to do, information about raising children in South Florida." Estab. 1990. Circ. 110,000. Byline given. Pays on publication. No kill fee. Buys one-time rights, buys second serial (reprint) rights. Makes work-for-hire assignments. Editorial lead time 4 months. Submit seasonal material 4 months in advance. Accepts queries by e-mail, fax. Accepts previously published material. Responds in 3 months to queries.

- Preference given to writers based in South Florida.

Nonfiction Needs how-to (parenting issues), interview/profile, family, parenting and children's issues. family fitness, education, spring party guide, fall party guide, kids and the environment, toddler/ preschool, preteen Length: 500-1,000 words. **Pays $40-165.**
Reprints Pays $25-50.
Columns/Departments Dad's Perspective, Family Deals, Products for Families, Health/Safety, Nutrition, Baby Basics, Travel, Toddler/Preschool, Preteen, South Florida News.
Tips "We want information targeted to the South Florida market. Multicultural and well-sourced is preferred. A unique approach to a universal parenting concern will be considered. Profiles or interviews of courageous parents. Opinion pieces on child rearing should be supported by experts and research should be listed. First-person stories should be fresh and insightful. Only accepts stories in e-mail attachment (nothing that has to be retyped)."

$ $ SOUTHWEST FLORIDA PARENT & CHILD

The News-Press, 2442 Dr. Martin Luther King, Jr. Blvd., Fort Myers FL 33901. (239)335-4698. Fax: (239)344-4690. E-mail: pamela@swflparentchild.com. Website: www.gulfcoastmoms.com. **75% freelance written**. Monthly magazine covering parenting. *Southwest Florida Parent & Child* is a regional parenting magazine with an audience of mostly moms but some dads, too. With every article, we strive to give readers information they can use. We aim to be an indispensable resource for our local parents. Estab. 2000. Circ. 25,000. Byline given. Pays on publication. Publishes ms an average of 2-3 months after acceptance. Buys all rights. Editorial lead time 2-3 months. Submit seasonal material 3+ months in advance. Accepts queries by mail, e-mail, fax. Accepts previously published material. Accepts simultaneous submissions.
Nonfiction Needs book excerpts, general interest, how-to, humor, interview, new product, personal experience, photo feature, religious, travel. Does not want personal experience or opinion pieces. **Buys 96-120 mss/year.** Send complete ms. Length: 500-700 words. **Pays $25-200.**
Photos State availability of or send photos. Captions, identification of subjects required. Reviews GIF/ JPEG files. Negotiates payment individually. Buys all rights.

TIDEWATER PARENT

258 Granby St., Norfolk VA 23510. (757)222-3900. Fax: (757)363-1767. E-mail: jenny.odonnell@ portfolioweekly.com. Website: www.tidewaterparent.com. **85% freelance written**. Monthly tabloid targeting families in the Hampton Roads area. All our readers are parents of children ages 0-11. Our readers demand stories that will help them tackle the challenges and demands they face daily as parents. Estab. 1980. Byline given. Pays on publication. Buys first North American serial rights. Editorial lead time 2 months. Submit seasonal material 3 months in advance. Accepts queries by mail, e-mail, fax. Accepts previously published material. Accepts simultaneous submissions. Responds in 1 month to queries. Responds in 4 months to mss. Sample copy free. Guidelines free.
Nonfiction Needs essays, general interest, historical, how-to, humor, interview, personal experience, religious, travel. No poetry or fiction. **Buys 60 mss/year.** Send complete ms. Length: 500-3,000 words.
Photos State availability of or send photos. Captions required. Negotiates payment individually. Buys one time rights.
Columns/Departments Music and Video Software (reviews), both 600-800 words; also Where to Go, What to Do, Calendar Spotlight and Voices. Buys 36 mss/year. Send complete ms.
Tips Articles for *Tidewater Parent* should be informative and relative to parenting. An informal, familiar tone is preferable to a more formal style. Avoid difficult vocabulary and complicated sentence structure. A conversational tone works best. Gain your reader's interest by using real-life situations, people or examples to support what you're saying.

$ $ $ $ TODAY'S PARENT

Rogers Media, Inc., One Mt. Pleasant Rd., 8th Floor, Toronto ON M4Y 2Y5 Canada. Fax: (416)764-2801. E-mail: queries@tpg.rogers.com. Website: www.todaysparent.com. Monthly magazine for parents with children up to the age of 12. Circ. 175,000. No kill fee. Editorial lead time 5 months.
Nonfiction Runs features with a balance between the practical and the philosophical, the light-hearted and the investigative. All articles should be grounded in the reality of Canadian family life. Length: 1,800-2,500 words. **Pays $1,500-2,200.**

Columns/Departments Profile (Canadian who has accomplished something remarkable for the benefit of children), 250 words; **pays $250.** Your Turn (parents share their experiences), 800 words; **pays $200.** Beyond Motherhood (deals with topics not directly related to parenting), 700 words; **pays $800.** Education (tackles straightforward topics and controversial or complex topics), 1,200 words; **pays $1,200-1,500.** Health Behavior (child development and discipline), 1,200 words; **pays $1,200-1,500.** Slice of Life (explores lighter side of parenting), 750 words; **pays $650.**
Tips Because we promote ourselves as a Canadian magazine, we use only Canadian writers.

$$$$ ⊡ TODAY'S PARENT PREGNANCY & BIRTH

Rogers Media, Inc., One Mt. Pleasant Rd., 8th Floor, Toronto ON M4Y 2Y5 Canada. E-mail: queries@tpg.rogers.com. Website: www.todaysparent.com. **Contact:** The Editor. **100% freelance written**. Magazine published 3 times/year. "*P&B* helps, supports and encourages expectant and new parents with news and features related to pregnancy, birth, human sexuality and parenting." Estab. 1973. Circ. 190,000. Pays on acceptance. Publishes ms an average of 8 months after acceptance. Buys first North American serial rights. Editorial lead time 6 months. Accepts queries by mail. Responds in 6 weeks to queries. Guidelines for SASE.
Nonfiction Features about pregnancy, labor and delivery, post partum issues. **Buys 12 mss/year.** Query with published clips; send detailed proposal. Length: 1,000-2,500 words. **Pays up to $1/word.**
Photos State availability. Pay negotiated individually. Rights negotiated individually.
Tips "Our writers are professional freelance writers with specific knowledge in the childbirth field. *P&B* is written for a Canadian audience using Canadian research and sources."

$$ TOLEDO AREA PARENT NEWS

Adams Street Publishing, Co., 1120 Adams St., Toledo OH 43604. (419)244-9859. Fax: (419)244-9871. E-mail: gsares@toledocitypaper.com. Website: www.toledoparent.com. **Contact:** Gina Sares, assignment editor. Monthly tabloid for Northwest Ohio/Southeast Michigan parents. Estab. 1992. Circ. 40,000. Byline given. Pays on publication. No kill fee. Publishes ms an average of 1 month after acceptance. Editorial lead time 3 months. Accepts queries by mail, e-mail, fax. Responds in 1 month to queries. Sample copy for $1.50.
Nonfiction We use only local writers by assignment. We accept queries and opinion pieces only. Send cover letter to be considered for assignments. Needs general interest, interview, opinion. **Buys 10 mss/year.** Length: 1,000-2,500 words. **Pays $75-125.**
Photos State availability. Identification of subjects required. Negotiates payment individually. Buys all rights.
Tips "We love humorous stories that deal with common parenting issues or features on cutting-edge issues."

TREASURE VALLEY FAMILY MAGAZINE

Family Magazine & Media, Inc., 13191 W. Scotfield St., Boise ID 83713. (208)938-2119. Fax: (208)938-2117. E-mail: magazine@tresurevalleyfamily.com. Website: www.treasurevalleyfamily.com. **90% freelance written**. Monthly magazine covering parenting, education, child development. Geared to parents with children 12 years and younger. Focus on education, interest, activities for children. Positive parenting and healthy families. Estab. 1993. Circ. 20,000. Byline given. Pays on publication. Offers 50% kill fee. Publishes ms an average of 3 months after acceptance. Buys first North American serial rights. Editorial lead time 3 months. Submit seasonal material 3 months in advance. Accepts queries by mail, e-mail. Accepts simultaneous submissions. Responds in 2 months to queries. Sample copy for $2. Guidelines available online.
Nonfiction Family Health and Wellness (January); Early Childhood Education (February); Secondary and Higher Education (March); Summer Camps (April); Youth Sports Guide (May); Family Recreation and Fairs & Festivals (June/July); Back-to-School and extra-curricular Activities (August/September); Teens and College Planning (October); Birthday Party Fun (November); Youth in the Arts and Holiday Traditions (December) Query with published clips. Length: 1,000-1,300 words.
Photos State availability. Captions required. Negotiates payment individually Buys one time rights.
Columns/Departments Crafts, travel, finance, parenting. Length: 700-1,000 words. Query with published clips.

$$ TWINS™ MAGAZINE

The Magazine for Parents of Multiples, P.O. Box 271924, Fort Collins CO 80527-1924. E-mail: twinseditor@twinsmagazine.com. Website: www.twinsmagazine.com. **50% freelance written**. "We now publish eight (8) issues per year—4 print/4 digital covering all aspects of parenting twins/multiples. *Twins* is a national/international publication that provides informational and educational articles regarding the parenting of twins, triplets, and more. All articles must be multiple specific and have an upbeat, hopeful, and/or positive ending." Estab. 1984. Circ. 35,000. Byline given. Pays on publication. Buys first North American serial rights. Editorial lead time 4 months. Submit seasonal material 6 months in advance. Accepts queries by U.S. mail, e-mail only. Response time varies. Sample copy for $5 or on website. Guidelines available online.

Nonfiction "We are only interested in articles that are specific to our readers parenting twins/multiples. All pitches need to have something relating to twins. Needs to have either personal experience or professional experience as it relates to multiples." Needs personal experience, first-person parenting experience, professional experience as it relates to multiples. Nothing on cloning, pregnancy reduction, or fertility issues. **Buys 12 mss/year.** Send complete ms. Length: 650-1,200 words. **Pays $25-250 for assigned articles. Pays $25-125 for unsolicited articles.**

Photos State availability. Identification of subjects required. Offers no additional payment for photos accepted with ms.

Columns/Departments A Word From Dad; Mom-2-Mom; LOL: Laugh Out Loud; Family Health; Resource Round Up; Tales From Twins; & Research. Pays $25-75. Buys 8-10 mss/year. Query with or without published clips or send complete ms. **Pays $40-75.**

Tips "All department articles must have helpful information for parents of multiples."

WHAT'S UP KIDS? FAMILY MAGAZINE

496 Metler Rd., Ridgeville ON L0S 1M0 Canada. E-mail: paul@whatsupkids.com. Website: www.whatsupkids.com. **95% freelance written**. Bimonthly magazine covering topics of interest to young families. Editorial is aimed at parents of kids birth-age 14. Kids Fun Section offers a section just for kids. We're committed to providing top-notch content. Estab. 1995. Circ. 200,000. Byline given. Pays 30 days after publication. Publishes ms an average of 4-6 months after acceptance. Buys first North American serial rights. Editorial lead time 6 months. Submit seasonal material 6 months in advance. Accepts queries by e-mail. Responds in 2 weeks if interested, by e-mail. Writer's guidelines online.

Nonfiction Service articles for families. No religious (one sided), personal experience, ADHD, bullying or anything that's all the talk. **Buys 50 mss/year.** Query with published clips. Length: 300-900 words. **Pays variable amount for assigned articles.**

Columns/Departments Understanding Families; Learning Curves; Family Finances; Baby Steps, all 400-600 words. Buys variable number of mss. Query with published clips. **Payment varies.**

Tips We only accept submissions from Canadian writers. Writers should send cover letter, clips, and query. Please do not call, and include e-mail address on all queries.

Comic Books

$ THE COMICS JOURNAL

Fantagraphics Books, 7563 Lake City Way NE, Seattle WA 98115. (206)524-1967. Fax: (206)524-2104. E-mail: dean@tcj.com. Website: www.tcj.com. Magazine covering the comics medium from an arts-first perspective on a six-week schedule. "*The Comics Journal* is one of the nation's most respected single-arts magazines, providing its readers with an eclectic mix of industry news, professional interviews, and reviews of current work. Due to its reputation as the American magazine with an interest in comics as an art form, the *Journal* has subscribers worldwide, and in this country serves as an important window into the world of comics for several general arts and news magazines." Byline given. Buys exclusive rights to articles that run in print or online versions for 6 months after initial publication. Rights then revert back to the writer. Accepts queries by mail, e-mail. Guidelines available online.

Nonfiction "We're not the magazine for the discussion of comic 'universes,' character re-boots, and Spider-Man's new costume—beyond, perhaps, the business or cultural implications of such events." Needs essays, interview, opinion, reviews. Send complete ms. Length: 2,000-3,000 words. **Pays 4¢/word, and 1 contributor's copy.**

Columns/Departments On Theory, Art and Craft (2,000-3,000 words); Firing Line (reviews 1,000-5,000 words); Bullets (reviews 400 words or less). Send inquiries, samples. **Pays 4¢/word, and 1 contributor's copy.**

Tips "Like most magazines, the best writers guideline is to look at the material within the magazine and give something that approximates that material in terms of approach and sophistication. Anything else is a waste of time."

Consumer Service & Business Opportunity

CONSUMER REPORTS

Consumers Union of U.S., Inc., 101 Truman Ave., Yonkers NY 10703-1057. (914)378-2000. Fax: (914)378-2904. Website: www.consumerreports.org. **5% freelance written**. Monthly magazine. *Consumer Reports* is the leading product-testing and consumer-service magazine in the US. We buy very little freelance material, mostly from proven writers we have used before for finance and health stories. Estab. 1936. Circ. 14,000,000. No byline given. Pays on acceptance. Offers negotiable kill fee. Publishes ms an average of 2 months after acceptance. Buys all rights. Editorial lead time 4 months. Submit seasonal material 6 months in advance. Accepts queries by mail.

Nonfiction Needs technical, personal finance, personal health. **Buys 12 mss/year.** Query. Length: 1,000 words. **Pays variable rate.**

KIPLINGER'S PERSONAL FINANCE

1729 H St. NW, Washington DC 20006. (202)887-6400. Fax: (202)331-1206. Website: www.kiplinger.com. **Contact:** Janet Bodnar, editor. **10% freelance written. Prefers to work with published/established writers**. Monthly magazine for general, adult audience interested in personal finance and consumer information. "*Kiplinger's* is a highly trustworthy source of information on saving and investing, taxes, credit, home ownership, paying for college, retirement planning, automobile buying, and many other personal finance topics." Estab. 1947. Circ. 800,000. Pays on acceptance. No kill fee. Publishes ms an average of 2 months after acceptance. Buys all rights. Responds in 1 month to queries.

Nonfiction "Most material is staff-written, but we accept some freelance. Thorough documentation is required for fact-checking." Query with published clips.

Tips "We are looking for a heavy emphasis on personal finance topics. Currently most work is provided by in-house writers."

Contemporary Culture

$$ A&U

America's AIDS Magazine, Art & Understanding, Inc., 25 Monroe St., Suite 205, Albany NY 12210-2729. (888)245-4333. Fax: (888)790-1790. E-mail: chaelneedle@mac.com. Website: www.aumag.org. **50% freelance written**. Monthly magazine covering cultural, political, and medical responses to HIV/AIDS. Estab. 1991. Circ. 205,000. Byline given. Pays 3 months after publication. Publishes ms an average of 3 months after acceptance. Buys first North American serial rights, buys electronic rights. Editorial lead time 6 months. Accepts queries by mail, e-mail. Accepts simultaneous submissions. Responds in 1 month to queries. Responds in 2 months to mss. Sample copy for $5. Guidelines available online.

Nonfiction Needs AIDS-related book excerpts, essays, general interest, how-to, humor, interview, new product, opinion, personal experience, photo feature, travel, reviews (film, theater, art exhibits, video, music, other media), medical news, artist profiles. **Buys 6 mss/year.** Query with published clips. Length: 800-1,200 words. **Pays $150-300 for assigned articles.**

Photos State availability. Captions, identification of subjects, model releases required.

Columns/Departments The Culture of AIDS (reviews of books, music, film), 300 words; Viewpoint (personal opinion), 750 words. Buys 6 mss/year. Send complete ms. **Pays $50-150.**

Fiction Drama. Send complete ms. Length: less than 1,500 words. **Pays $100.**

Poetry Any length/style (shorter works preferred). **Pays $25.**

Tips "We're looking for more articles on youth and HIV/AIDS; more international coverage; celebrity interviews; more coverage of how the pandemic is affecting historically underrepresented communities."

$$$ ADBUSTERS

Adbusters Media Foundation, 1243 W. 7th Ave., Vancouver BC V6H 1B7 Canada. (604)736-9401. Fax: (604)737-6021. E-mail: editor@adbusters.org. Website: www.adbusters.org. **50% freelance written**. Bimonthly magazine. We are an activist journal of the mental environment. Estab. 1989. Circ. 90,000. Byline given. Pays 1 month after publication. Buys first rights. Accepts queries by mail, e-mail, fax. Accepts simultaneous submissions. Guidelines available online.

Nonfiction Needs essays, expose, interview, opinion. **Buys variable mss/year.** Query. Length: 250-3,000 words. **Pays $100/page for unsolicited articles; 50¢/word for solicited articles.**

Fiction Inquire about themes.

Poetry Inquire about themes.

$$ THE AMERICAN SCHOLAR

Phi Beta Kappa, 1606 New Hampshire Ave. NW, Washington DC 20009. (202)265-3808. Fax: (202)265-0083. E-mail: scholar@pbk.org. **100% freelance written**. Quarterly journal. Our intent is to have articles written by scholars and experts but written in nontechnical language for an intelligent audience. Material covers a wide range in the arts, sciences, current affairs, history, and literature. Estab. 1932. Circ. 30,000. Byline given. Pays on publication. Offers 50% kill fee. Publishes ms an average of 1 year after acceptance. Buys first rights. Editorial lead time 6 months. Submit seasonal material 6 months in advance. Accepts queries by mail, e-mail, fax. Responds in 2 weeks to queries. Responds in 2 months to mss. Sample copy for $9. Guidelines for #10 SASE or via e-mail.

Nonfiction Needs essays, historical, humor. **Buys 40 mss/year.** Query. Length: 3,000-5,000 words. **Pays $500 maximum.**

Poetry Contact: Sandra Costich. "We're not considering any unsolicited poetry."

$ BOSTON REVIEW

35 Medford St., Suite 302, Somerville MA 02143. (617)591-0505. Fax: (617)591-0440. E-mail: review@bostonreview.net. Website: www.bostonreview.net. **90% freelance written**. Bimonthly magazine of cultural and political analysis, reviews, fiction, and poetry. "The editors are committed to a society and culture that foster human diversity and a democracy in which we seek common grounds of principle amidst our many differences. In the hope of advancing these ideals, the *Review* acts as a forum that seeks to enrich the language of public debate." Estab. 1975. Circ. 20,000. Byline given. Publishes ms an average of 4 months after acceptance. Buys first North American serial rights, buys first rights. Accepts simultaneous submissions. Responds in 4 months to queries. Sample copy for $5 or online. Guidelines available online.

Nonfiction "We do not accept unsolicited book reviews. If you would like to be considered for review assignments, please send your résumé along with several published clips." **Buys 50 mss/year.** Query with published clips.

Fiction Contact: Junot Diaz, fiction editor. "I'm looking for stories that are emotionally and intellectually substantive and also interesting on the level of language. Things that are shocking, dark, lewd, comic, or even insane are fine so long as the fiction is *controlled* and purposeful in a masterly way. Subtlety, delicacy, and lyricism are attractive too." Needs ethnic, experimental, contemporary, prose poem. No romance, erotica, genre fiction. **Buys 5 mss/year.** Send complete ms. Length: 1,200-5,000 words. **Pays $25-300, and 5 contributor's copies.**

Poetry Contact: Benjamin Paloff and Timothy Donnelly, poetry editors. Reads poetry between September 15 and May 15 each year.

BRIARPATCH MAGAZINE

Briarpatch, Inc., 2138 McIntyre St., Regina SK S4P 2R7 Canada. (306)525-2949. E-mail: editor@briarpatchmagazine.com. Website: www.briarpatchmagazine.com. **90% freelance written**. Magazine published 6 times per year covering social justice, environment, and peace. "Briarpatch publishes six thought-provoking, fire-breathing, riot-inciting issues a year. Fiercely independent and frequently irreverent, Briarpatch delves into today's most pressing challenges from a radical, grassroots perspective, aiming always to challenge, inspire and empower its readers." Estab. 1973. Circ. 2,000. Byline given. No kill fee. Buys first rights. Editorial lead time 3 months. Submit seasonal material 3 months in advance. Accepts queries by e-mail. Accepts previously published material. Accepts simultaneous submissions. Responds in 1 week to queries. Responds in 1 month to mss. Sample copy available online. Guidelines available online.

Nonfiction Needs expose, historical, interview, opinion, personal experience, photo feature, political analysis. Women's issue (March); Labor issue (November). **Buys 1-2 mss/year.** Send complete ms. Length: 600-2,500 words.

Photos State availability. Reviews 4x6 prints, TIF/JPEG files. Pays $20 per photo.

Columns/Departments Parting Shots: Provocative back-page opinion essay, 700 words Send complete ms.

Tips "We welcome queries from unpublished writers, seasoned freelancers, front-line activists, and anyone else with a story to tell and a desire to tell it compellingly."

$$ BROKEN PENCIL

The Magazine of Zine Culture and the Independent Arts, P.O. Box 203, Station P, Toronto ON M5S 2S7 Canada. E-mail: editor@brokenpencil.com. Website: www.brokenpencil.com. **80% freelance written**.

Quarterly magazine covering arts and culture. *Broken Pencil* is one of the few magazines in the world devoted exclusively to underground culture and the independent arts. We are a great resource and a lively read! *Broken Pencil* reviews the best zines, books, Web sites, videos and artworks from the underground and reprints the best articles from the alternative press. From the hilarious to the perverse, *Broken Pencil* challenges conformity and demands attention. Estab. 1995. Circ. 5,000. Byline given. Pays on publication. Publishes ms an average of 2-3 months after acceptance. Buys first rights. Accepts queries by mail, e-mail. Guidelines available online.

Nonfiction Needs essays, general interest, historical, humor, interview, opinion, personal experience, photo feature, travel, reviews. Does not want anything about mainstream art and culture. **Buys 8 mss/year.** Query with published clips. Length: 400-2,500 words. **Pays $100-400.**

Photos Send photos. Identification of subjects required. Reviews prints, GIF/JPEG files. Negotiates payment individually. Buys one time rights.

Columns/Departments Contact: Erin Kobayashi, books editor; James King, ezines editor; Terence Dick, music editor; Lindsay Gibb, film editor. Books (book reviews and feature articles); Ezines (ezine reviews and feature articles); Music (music reviews and feature articles); Film (film reviews and feature articles), all 200-300 words for reviews and 1,000 words for features. Buys 8 mss/year. Query with published clips. **Pays $100-400.**

Fiction Contact: Hal Niedzviecki, fiction editor. We're particularly interested in work from emerging writers. Needs adventure, cond novels, confession, erotica, ethnic, experimental, fantasy, historical, horror, humorous, mystery, novel concepts, romance, science fiction, slice-of-life vignettes. **Buys 8 mss/year.** Send complete ms. Length: 500-3,000 words.

Tips Write in to receive a list of upcoming themes and then pitch us stories based around those themes. If you keep your ear to the ground in the alternative and underground arts communities, you will be able to find content appropriate for *Broken Pencil*.

$$ N BUST MAGAZINE

For Women With Something to Get Off Their Chests, Bust, Inc., 78 5th Ave., 5th Floor, New York NY 10011. E-mail: submissions@bust.com. Website: www.bust.com. **60% freelance written**. Bimonthly magazine covering pop culture for young women. "*Bust* is the groundbreaking, original women's lifestyle magazine & website that is unique in its ability to connect with bright, cutting-edge, influential young women." Estab. 1993. Circ. 100,000. Byline given. Pays on publication. No kill fee. Publishes ms an average of 4 months after acceptance. Buys all rights. Editorial lead time 3-4 months. Submit seasonal material 6 months in advance. Accepts queries by mail, e-mail. Accepts simultaneous submissions.

Nonfiction Needs book excerpts, expose, general interest, historical, how-to, humor, inspirational, interview, new product, personal experience, photo feature, travel. No dates are currently set, but we usually have a fashion issue, a music issue and a *Men We Love* issue periodically. We do not want poetry; no stories not relating to women. **Buys 60+ mss/year.** Query with published clips. Length: 350-3,000 words. **Pays 0-$250 max.**

Photos Contact: Laurie Henzel, Art Director. State availability. Identification of subjects, model releases required. Reviews GIF/JPEG files. Negotiates payment individually.

Columns/Departments Contact: Emily Rems, Managing Ed. Books (Reviews of books by women) assigned by us, Music (Reviews of music by/about women), Movies (Reviews of movies by/about women), 300 words; One-Handed-Read (Erotic Fiction for Women), 1,200 words. Query with published clips. **Pays 0-$100.**

Fiction Contact: Lisa Butterworth, Assoc. Ed. Needs erotica. We only publish erotic fiction. All other content is nonfiction. **Buys 6 mss/year.** Query with published clips. Length: 1,000-1,500 words. **Pays 0-$100.**

Tips "We are always looking for stories that are surprising, and that 'Bust' stereotypes about women."

$ CANADIAN DIMENSION

Dimension Publications, Inc., 91 Albert St., Room 2-E, Winnipeg MB R3B 1G5 Canada. (204)957-1519. Fax: (204)943-4617. E-mail: info@canadiandimension.com. Website: www.canadiandimension.com. **80% freelance written**. Bimonthly magazine covering socialist perspective. We bring a socialist perspective to bear on events across Canada and around the world. Our contributors provide in-depth coverage on popular movements, peace, labour, women, aboriginal justice, environment, third world and eastern Europe. Estab. 1963. Circ. 3,000. Pays on publication. Publishes ms an average of 6 months after acceptance. Accepts previously published material. Accepts simultaneous submissions. Responds in 6 weeks to queries. Sample copy for $2. Guidelines available online.

Nonfiction Needs interview, opinion, reviews. **Buys 8 mss/year.** Length: 500-2,000 words. **Pays $25-100.**
Reprints Send typed manuscript with rights for sale noted and information about when and where the material previously appeared.

$$$ COMMENTARY

165 E. 56th St., New York NY 10022. (212)891-1400. Fax: (212)891-6700. Website: www.commentarymagazine.com. Monthly magazine. Estab. 1945. Byline given. Pays on publication. No kill fee. Publishes ms an average of 2 months after acceptance. Buys all rights. Accepts queries by mail.
Nonfiction Needs essays, opinion. **Buys 4 mss/year.** Query. Length: 2,000-8,000 words. **Pays $400-1,200.**
Tips Unsolicited manuscripts must be accompanied by a self-addressed, stamped envelope.

$$ COMMON GROUND

Common Ground Publishing, 204-4381 Fraser St., Vancouver BC V5V 4G4 Canada. (604)733-2215. Fax: (604)733-4415. E-mail: editor@commonground.ca. Website: www.commonground.ca. **90% freelance written**. Monthly tabloid covering health, environment, spirit, creativity, and wellness. We serve the cultural creative community. Estab. 1982. Circ. 70,000. Byline given. Pays on publication. No kill fee. Publishes ms an average of 1 month after acceptance. Buys one-time rights, buys second serial (reprint) rights. Editorial lead time 2 months. Submit seasonal material 3 months in advance. Accepts queries by e-mail. Accepts simultaneous submissions. Responds in 6 weeks to queries. Responds in 3 months to mss. Sample copy for $5. Guidelines available online.
Nonfiction Topics include health, personal growth, creativity, spirituality, ecology, or short inspiring stories on environment themes. Needs book excerpts, how-to, inspirational, interview, opinion, personal experience, travel, call to action. Send complete ms. Length: 500-2,500 words. **Pays 10¢/word (Canadian).**
Photos State availability. Captions required. Buys one time rights.

$$$ FIRST THINGS

Institute on Religion & Public Life, 156 Fifth Ave., Suite 400, New York NY 10010. (212)627-1985. Fax: (212)627-2184. E-mail: ft@firstthings.com. Website: www.firstthings.com. **70% freelance written**. social and intellectual commentary. "Intellectual journal published 10 times/year containing social and ethical commentary in a broad sense, religious and ethical perspectives on society, culture, law, medicine, church and state, morality and mores." Estab. 1990. Circ. 32,000. Byline given. Pays on publication. Publishes ms an average of 4 months after acceptance. Buys all rights. Editorial lead time 2 months. Submit seasonal material 5 months in advance. Responds in 3 weeks to mss. Sample copy and writer's guidelines for #10 SASE
Nonfiction Needs essays, opinion. **Buys 60 mss/year.** Send complete ms. Length: 1,500-6,000 words. **Pays $400-1,000.**
Poetry Contact: Joseph Bettum, poetry editor. Needs traditional. Buys 25-30 poems/year. Length: 4-40 lines. **Pays $50.**
Tips "We prefer complete manuscripts (hard copy, double-spaced) to queries, but will reply if unsure."

$$$ FLAUNT MAGAZINE

1422 N. Highland Ave., Los Angeles CA 90028. (323)836-1000. E-mail: info@flauntmagazine.com. Website: www.flaunt.com. **40% freelance written**. Monthly magazine covering culture, arts, entertainment, music, fashion and film. *Flaunt* features the bold work of emerging photographers, writers, artists and musicians. The quality of the content is mirrored in the sophisticated, interactive format of the magazine, using advanced printing techniques, fold-out articles, beautiful papers and inserts to create a visually stimulating, surprisingly readable, and intelligent book that pushes the magazine into the realm of art-object. *Flaunt* magazine has for the last 11 years made it a point to break new ground, earning itself a reputation as an engine of the avant-garde and an outlet for the culture of the cutting edge. *Flaunt* takes pride in reinventing itself each month, while consistently representing a hybrid of all that is interesting in entertaiment, fashion, music, design, film, art and literature. Estab. 1998. Circ. 100,000. Byline given. No kill fee. Publishes ms an average of 3 months after acceptance. Buys one-time rights. Editorial lead time 3 months. Submit seasonal material 3 months in advance. Accepts queries by mail, e-mail. Accepts simultaneous submissions. Responds in 2 weeks to queries. Responds in 1 month to mss. Guidelines by e-mail.
Nonfiction Needs book excerpts, essays, expose, general interest, historical, humor, interview, new product, opinion, personal experience, photo feature, travel. September and March (fashion issues);

February (men's issue); May (music issue). **Buys 20 mss/year.** Query with published clips. Length: 500-5,000 words. **Pays $0-500.**

Photos Contact: Contact Lee Corbin, art director. State availability. Identification of subjects, model releases required. Reviews contact sheets, transparencies, prints, GIF/JPEG files. Buys one-time rights.

Fiction Contact: Contact Andrew Pogany, senior editor. **Buys 4 mss/year.** Length: 500-5,000 words. **Pays $0-500.**

THE FUTURIST

Trends, Forecasts, and Ideas About the Future, The World Future, 7910 Woodmont Ave., Suite 450, Bethesda MD 20814. (301)656-8274. Fax: (301)951-0394. E-mail: info@wfs.org. Website: www.wfs.org. **50% freelance written**. Bimonthly magazine covering technological, social, environmental, economic, and public policy trends related to the future. "Articles should have something new & significant to say about the future. For example, an article noting that increasing air pollution may damage human health is something everyone has already heard. Writers should remember that the publication focuses on the future, especially the period 5 to 50 years ahead. We cover a wide range of subject areas—virtually everything that will affect our future or will be affected by the changes the future will bring. Past articles have focused on technology, planning, resources, economics, religion, the arts, values, and health. For quality of writing, make points clearly and in a way that holds the reader's interest. A reader should not have to struggle to guess an author's meaning. Use concrete examples and anecdotes to illustrate your points; keep sentences short, mostly under 25 words. Avoid the jargon of a particular profession; when technical terms are necessary, explain them." Estab. 1966. Circ. 10,000. Byline given. "We pay only in contributors copies." No kill fee. Publishes ms an average of 4 months after acceptance. Buys all rights. Editorial lead time 2 months. Submit seasonal material 3 months in advance. Accepts queries by mail, e-mail. Accepts previously published material. Accepts simultaneous submissions. Responds in 4 weeks to queries. Guidelines available.

Nonfiction Needs book excerpts, essays, expose, general interest, how-to, interview, photo feature, technical. "We don't want articles by authors who aren't experts on what they're writing about, or who can't find expert opinion on the subjects they're covering. Articles we avoid include: (A) overly technical articles that would be of little interest to the general reader; (B) opinion pieces on current government issues; (C) articles by authors with only a casual knowledge of the subject being discussed. *The Futurist* does not publish fiction or poetry. An exception is occasionally made for scenarios presenting fictionalized people in future situations. These scenarios are kept brief." **Buys 5 articles/issue, 30 articles/year.** Send complete ms.

GOOD MAGAZINE

915 N. Citrus Ave., Los Angeles CA 90038. (310)691-1020. Fax: (310)691-1033. E-mail: submissions@goodinc.com. Website: www.goodmagazine.com. *GOOD* is the integrated media platform for people who want to live well and do good. Estab. 2006.

- Has themed issues.

$$ KARMA MAGAZINE

2880 Zanker Rd., Suite 203, San Jose CA 95134. E-mail: editorial@karmamagazine.com. Website: www.karmamagazine.com. **75% freelance written**. Quarterly magazine covering nightlife culture. *Karma* is the premier nightlife resource for those who choose to live it up, while remaining on the periphery of cultural insights. It highlights the lifestyles and interests of dedicated nightlife-revelers through comprehensive reviews of clubs, bars, and restaurants around the world. It also includes thought-provoking celebrity profiles and intelligent editorals of art, culture and news accented by quality, stylized photography. *Karma* engages readers with full access to nightlife culture from around the globe, providing a sure grasp on what makes urbanites tick. Estab. 2003. Circ. 50,000. Byline given. Pays on publication. No kill fee. Publishes ms an average of 3 months after acceptance. Buys first North American serial rights, buys first rights, buys one-time rights, buys electronic rights, buys all rights. Editorial lead time 3 months. Submit seasonal material 3 months in advance. Accepts queries by e-mail. Accepts simultaneous submissions. Responds in 1 month to queries. Sample copy available online.

Nonfiction Needs essays, general interest, how-to, interview, new product, opinion, photo feature, technical, travel. No self-congratulatory or self-obsessed personal experiences about the nightclub scene; no story ideas without original angles. Query with published clips. Length: 100-2,500 words. **Pays 25¢/word.**

Photos State availability. Captions, identification of subjects required. Reviews contact sheets, prints, GIF/JPEG/PDF files. Negotiates payment individually. Buys one-time rights or all rights.

Columns/Departments Features (celebrity interviews and profiles/news in the club industry), 1,500-2,500 words; Zen (nightlife and pop culture trends—art/music/film/product reviews), 50-500 words; Locus (hot-spot reviews of clubs/bars/restaurants), 500-1,000 words. Each issue, *Karma* also features an off-the-beaten path international destination.

$ THE LIST

The List, Ltd., 14 High St., Edinburgh EH1 1TE Scotland. (44)(131)550-3050. Fax: (44)(131)557-8500. Website: www.list.co.uk. **25% freelance written**. Biweekly general interest magazine covering Glasgow and Edinburgh arts, events, listings, and lifestyle. "*The List* is pitched at educated 18-35 year olds in Scotland. All events listings are published free of charge and are accompanied by informative, independent critical comment offering a guide to readers as to what is worth seeing and why. Articles and features are also included previewing forthcoming events in greater detail." Estab. 1985. Circ. 500,000. Byline given. Pays on publication. Offers 100% kill fee. Publishes ms an average of 2 weeks after acceptance. Buys first rights, buys second serial (reprint) rights. Editorial lead time 1 month. Submit seasonal material 1 month in advance. Accepts queries by mail, e-mail. Accepts simultaneous submissions.

Nonfiction Needs interview, opinion, travel. Query with published clips. Length: 300 words. **Pays £60-80.**

Columns/Departments Reviews, 50-650 words, **pays £16-35**; Book Reviews, 150 words; **pays £14**. Comic Reviews, 100 words; **pays £10**. TV/Video Reviews, 100 words; **pays £10**. Record Reviews, 100 words; **pays £10**. Query with published clips.

$$$$ MOTHER JONES

Foundation for National Progress, 222 Sutter St., Suite 600, San Francisco CA 94108. (415)321-1700. E-mail: query@motherjones.com. Website: www.motherjones.com. **80% freelance written**. Bimonthly magazine covering politics, investigative reporting, social issues, and pop culture. "*Mother Jones* is a 'progressive' magazine—but the core of its editorial well is reporting (i.e., fact-based). No slant required. MotherJones.com is an online sister publication." Estab. 1976. Circ. 235,000. Byline given. Pays on publication. Offers 33% kill fee. Publishes ms an average of 4 months after acceptance. Buys first North American serial rights, buys first rights, buys one-time rights, buys electronic rights. Editorial lead time 4 months. Submit seasonal material 6 months in advance. Responds in 2 months to queries. Sample copy for $6 and 9 × 12 SAE. Guidelines available online.

Nonfiction Needs expose, interview, photo feature, current issues, policy, investigative reporting. **Buys 70-100 mss/year.** Query with published clips. Length: 2,000-5,000 words. **Pays $1/word.**

Columns/Departments Outfront (short, newsy and/or outrageous and/or humorous items), 200-800 words; Profiles of Hellraisers, 500 words. **Pays $1/word.**

Tips We're looking for hard-hitting, investigative reports exposing government cover-ups, corporate malfeasance, scientific myopia, institutional fraud or hypocrisy; thoughtful, provocative articles which challenge the conventional wisdom (on the right or the left) concerning issues of national importance; and timely, people-oriented stories on issues such as the environment, labor, the media, healthcare, consumer protection, and cultural trends. Send a great, short query and establish your credibility as a reporter. Explain what you plan to cover and how you will proceed with the reporting. The query should convey your approach, tone and style, and should answer the following: What are your specific qualifications to write on this topic? What 'ins' do you have with your sources? Can you provide full documentation so that your story can be fact-checked?

$$ NATURALLY

Nude Living and Recreation, Internaturally, Inc., P.O. Box 317, Newfoundland NJ 07435. (973)697-3552. Fax: (973)697-8313. E-mail: naturally@internaturally.com. Website: www.internaturally.com. **80% freelance written**. Quarterly magazine covering nudism and naturism. Write about nudists and naturists. More people stories than travel. Estab. 1980. Circ. 30,000. Byline given. Pays on publication. No kill fee. Publishes ms an average of 3 months after acceptance. Buys first North American serial rights, buys first rights, buys one-time rights, buys second serial (reprint) rights, buys simultaneous rights, buys electronic rights, buys all rights, buys rights. Makes work-for-hire assignments. Editorial lead time 3-6 months. Submit seasonal material 6 months in advance. Accepts queries by mail, phone. Accepts previously published material. Accepts simultaneous submissions. Responds in 2 weeks to queries. Responds in 3 months to mss. Sample copy available online. Guidelines available online.

Nonfiction Needs book excerpts, essays, expose, general interest, historical, how-to, for first-time visitors to nudist park., humor, inspirational, interview, new product, personal experience, photo feature, travel. Free-beach activities, public nude events. We don't want opinion pieces and religious slants. **Buys 50**

mss/year. Send complete ms. Length: 500-2,000 words. **Pays $80 per page, text or photos min.; $300 max. for assigned articles.**
Photos Send photos. Model releases required. $80 per page min.; $200 front cover max. promotional.
Columns/Departments Health (nudism/naturism), Travel (nudism/naturism), Celebrities (nudism/naturism). Buys 8 mss/year. Send complete ms.
Fiction Needs humorous. Science fiction. **Buys 6-8 mss/year.** Send complete ms. Length: 800-2,000 words. **Pays $80/page.**
Poetry Needs avant-garde, free verse, haiku, light verse, traditional. Buys 3-6 poems/year. Submit maximum 3 poems.
Fillers Needs anecdotes, facts, gags, newsbreaks, short humor. Buys 4 mss/year.
Tips Become a nudist/naturist. Appreciate human beings in their natural state.

$ NEW HAVEN ADVOCATE

News & Arts Weekly, New Mass Media, Inc., 900 Chapel St., Suite 1100, New Haven CT 06510. (203)789-0010. Fax: (203)787-1418. E-mail: abromage@newhavenadvocate.com. Website: www.newhavenadvocate.com. **10% freelance written.** Weekly tabloid. Alternative, investigative, cultural reporting with a strong voice. We like to shake things up. Estab. 1975. Circ. 55,000. Byline given. Pays on publication. No kill fee. Buys one-time rights. Buys on speculation. Editorial lead time 1 month. Submit seasonal material 2 months in advance. Accepts simultaneous submissions. Responds in 1 month to queries.
Nonfiction Needs book excerpts, essays, expose, general interest, humor, interview. **Buys 15-20 mss/year.** Query with published clips. Length: 750-2,000 words. **Pays $50-150.**
Photos State availability. Captions, identification of subjects, model releases required. Buys one time rights.
Tips Strong local focus; strong literary voice, controversial, easy-reading, contemporary, etc.

THE NEXT AMERICAN CITY

The Next American City, Inc., 1315 Walnut St., Suite 902, Philadelphia PA 19107. E-mail: matt@americancity.org. Website: www.americancity.org. **80% freelance written.** Quarterly magazine covering urban affairs. Estab. 2002. Circ. 3,000. Byline given. No kill fee. Publishes ms an average of 2-3 months after acceptance. Buys all rights. Editorial lead time 3 months. Submit seasonal material 2-3 months in advance. Accepts queries by mail, e-mail. Accepts previously published material. Accepts simultaneous submissions. Responds in 2 weeks to queries. Sample copy available online. Guidelines available online.
Nonfiction Needs book excerpts, essays, expose, historical, humor, interview, personal experience, photo feature, religious, travel. Does not accept pure opinion pieces. Send complete ms. Length: 500-2,800 words.
Photos State availability of or send photos. Captions required. Reviews TIFF files. Offers no additional payment for photos accepted with ms. Buys one time rights.
Columns/Departments Architecture; Book Reviews; Planning; Technology; Business; Education; Environment; Labor; Law; Housing & Last Exit. Query with or without published clips or send complete ms.
Tips We encourage authors to make challenging, even controversial points with implications about the future of American metropolitan areas for more specific information on what kinds of articles we accept. Please review our submission guidelines.

THE OLDIE MAGAZINE

Oldie Publications Ltd, 65 Newman St., London England W1T 3EG United Kingdom. (44)(207)436-8801. Fax: (44)(207)436-8804. E-mail: jeremylewis@theoldie.co.uk. Website: www.theoldie.co.uk. No kill fee. Accepts queries by mail. Responds in 2-3 weeks to mss. Sample copy by e-mail. Guidelines available online.
Nonfiction Send complete ms. Length: 600-1,000 words.
Photos Send photocopies of photographs, cartoons, and illustrations.
Columns/Departments Modern Life (puzzling aspects of today's world); Anorak (owning up to an obsession); The Old Un's Diary (oldun@theoldie.co.uk).
Fiction Buys up to 3 short stories/year. Send complete ms.

$ POETRY CANADA MAGAZINE

Innersurf Publishing, Website: www.poetrycanada.com. **90% freelance written.** "Biannual magazine promoting culture and diversity through art, photography, poetry, and articles. Despite its Canadian root, writers from around the world can submit poetry, book reviews, and articles that will help to advance and inspire the reader to learn more about their craft, society, and environment." Estab. 2003. Circ. 500. Byline given. Pays on publication. No kill fee. Publishes ms an average of 3-12 months after acceptance. Buys one-time rights, buys electronic rights. Editorial lead time 3-12 months. Submit seasonal material 6 months in advance. Accepts queries by e-mail. Responds in 3 days to queries. Sample copy and writer's guidelines online.

Nonfiction Needs general interest, historical, how-to, humor, inspirational, photo feature, art feature. **Buys 60-100 mss/year.** Length: 25-800 words. **Pays $5-100 and a contributor copy.**

Columns/Departments Book Reviews; Top Ways To; Dead Poets Society; Poets Practice; Interviews. Buys 12-15 mss/year. **Pays $5-100.**

Poetry All types and styles; no line limit.

$$ SHEPHERD EXPRESS

Alternative Publications, Inc., 207 E. Buffalo St., Suite 410, Milwaukee WI 53202. (414)276-2222. Fax: (414)276-3312. E-mail: editor@shepherd-express.com. Website: www.shepherd-express.com. **50% freelance written**. Weekly tabloid covering news and arts with a progressive news edge and a hip entertainment perspective. Estab. 1982. Circ. 58,000. Pays 1 month after publication. No kill fee. Publishes ms an average of 1 month after acceptance. Submit seasonal material 2 months in advance. Accepts simultaneous submissions. Sample copy for $3.

Nonfiction Needs book excerpts, essays, expose, opinion. **Buys 200 mss/year.** Send complete ms. Length: 900-2,500 words. **Pays $35-300 for assigned articles. Pays $10-200 for unsolicited articles.**

Photos State availability. Captions, identification of subjects, model releases required. Reviews prints. Negotiates payment individually Buys one time rights.

Columns/Departments Opinions (social trends, politics, from progressive slant), 800-1,200 words; Books Reviewed (new books only: Social trends, environment, politics), 600-1,200 words. Buys 10 mss/year. Send complete ms.

Tips Include solid analysis with point of view in tight but lively writing. Nothing cute. Do not tell us that something is important, tell us why.

$$$ THE SUN

The Sun Publishing Co., 107 N. Roberson St., Chapel Hill NC 27516. Fax: (919)932-3101. Website: www.thesunmagazine.org. **90% freelance written**. Monthly magazine. We are open to all kinds of writing, though we favor work of a personal nature. Estab. 1974. Circ. 72,000. Byline given. Pays on publication. Publishes ms an average of 6-12 months after acceptance. Buys first rights, buys one-time rights. Accepts previously published material. Responds in 3-6 months to queries. Responds in 3-6 months to mss. Sample copy for $5. Guidelines available online.

Nonfiction Needs essays, personal experience, spiritual, interview. **Buys 50 mss/year.** Send complete ms. Length: 7,000 words maximum. **Pays $300-3,000.**

Reprints Send photocopy and information about when and where the material previously appeared.

Photos Send photos. Model releases required. Reviews b&w prints. Offers $100-500/photo. Buys one time rights.

Fiction Contact: Sy Safransky, editor. We avoid stereotypical genre pieces like science fiction, romance, western, and horror. Read an issue before submitting. **Buys 20 mss/year.** Send complete ms. Length: 7,000 words maximum. **Pays $300-2,000.**

Poetry Needs free verse. Rarely publishes poems that rhyme. Buys 24 poems/year. Submit maximum 6 poems. **Pays $100-500.**

Tips Do not send queries except for interviews.

UTNE READER

12 N. 12th St., Ste. 400, Minneapolis MN 55403. (612)338-5040. E-mail: editor@utne.com. Website: www.utne.com. Accepts queries by mail, e-mail. Guidelines available online.

Reprints Send tearsheet or photocopy with rights for sale noted and information about when and where the material previously appeared.

Tips "State the theme(s) clearly, let the narrative flow, and build the story around strong characters and a vivid sense of place. Give us rounded episodes, logically arranged. We do not publish fiction or poetry."

⊘ VANITY FAIR

Conde Nast Publications, Inc., 1166 Avenue of the Americas, 15th Floor, New York NY 10036. (212)790-5100. Fax: (212)790-1822. Website: www.condenet.com. Monthly magazine. *Vanity Fair* is edited for readers with an interest in contemporary society. Circ. 1,131,144. No kill fee.

- Does not buy freelance material or use freelance writers.

Disabilities

$$ ABILITIES

Canada's Lifestyle Magazine for People with Disabilities, Canadian Abilities Foundation, 401-340 College St., Toronto ON M5T 3A9 Canada. (416)923-1885. Fax: (416)923-9829. E-mail: able@abilities.ca. Website: www.abilities.ca. **50% freelance written**. Quarterly magazine covering disability issues. *Abilities* provides information, inspiration, and opportunity to its readers with articles and resources covering health, travel, sports, products, technology, profiles, employment, recreation, and more. Estab. 1987. Circ. 20,000. Byline given. Pays on publication. Offers 50% kill fee. Publishes ms an average of 3 months after acceptance. Buys first rights. Editorial lead time 3 months. Submit seasonal material 4 months in advance. Accepts queries by mail, e-mail, fax. Responds in 3 months to queries. Sample copy free. Writer's guidelines for #10 SASE, online, or by e-mail.

Nonfiction Needs general interest, how-to, humor, inspirational, interview, new product, personal experience, photo feature, travel. Does not want articles that 'preach to the converted'—this means info that people with disabilities likely already know, such as what it's like to have a disability. **Buys 30-40 mss/year.** Query or send complete ms. Length: 500-2,500 words. **Pays $50-400 (Canadian) for assigned articles. Pays $50-350 (Canadian) for unsolicited articles.**

Reprints Sometimes accepts previously published submissions (if stated as such).

Photos State availability.

Columns/Departments The Lighter Side (humor), 700 words; Profile, 1,200 words.

Tips Strongly prefer e-mail queries. When developing story ideas, keep in mind that our readers are in Canada.

$$ DIABETES HEALTH

P.O. Box 395, Woodacre CA 94973-0395. (415)488-1141. Fax: (415)488-1922. Website: www.diabetesinterview.com. **40% freelance written**. Monthly tabloid covering diabetes care. *Diabetes Interview* covers the latest in diabetes care, medications, and patient advocacy. Personal accounts are welcome as well as medical-oriented articles by MDs, RNs, and CDEs (certified diabetes educators). Estab. 1991. Circ. 40,000. Byline given. Pays on publication. No kill fee. Publishes ms an average of 2 months after acceptance. Buys all rights. Editorial lead time 2 months. Submit seasonal material 2 months in advance. Accepts queries by mail, e-mail, fax, phone. Sample copy available online. Guidelines free.

Nonfiction Needs essays, how-to, humor, inspirational, interview, new product, opinion, personal experience. **Buys 25 mss/year.** Send complete ms. Length: 500-1,500 words. **Pays 20¢/word.**

Photos State availability of or send photos. Negotiates payment individually.

Tips Be actively involved in the diabetes community or have diabetes. However, writers need not have diabetes to write an article, but it must be diabetes-related.

$$ DIABETES SELF-MANAGEMENT

R.A. Rapaport Publishing, Inc., 150 W. 22nd St., Suite 800, New York NY 10011-2421. (212)989-0200. Fax: (212)989-4786. E-mail: editor@rapaportpublishing.com. Website: www.diabetesselfmanagement.com. **Contact:** Editor. **20% freelance written**. Bimonthly magazine. "We publish how-to health care articles for motivated, intelligent readers who have diabetes and who are actively involved in their own health care management. All articles must have immediate application to their daily living." Estab. 1983. Circ. 380,000. Byline given. Pays on publication. Offers 20% kill fee. Buys all rights. Submit seasonal material 6 months in advance. Accepts queries by mail, e-mail, fax. Responds in 6 weeks to queries. Sample copy for $4 and 9 × 12 SAE with 6 first-class stamps or online. Guidelines for #10 SASE.

Nonfiction Needs how-to, exercise, nutrition, diabetes self-care, product surveys, technical, reviews of products available, foods sold by brand name, pharmacology, travel, considerations and prep for people with diabetes. No personal experiences, personality profiles, exposès, or research breakthroughs. **Buys 10-12 mss/year.** Query with published clips. Length: 2,000-2,500 words. **Pays $400-700 for assigned articles. Pays $200-700 for unsolicited articles.**

Tips "The rule of thumb for any article we publish is that it must be clear, concise, useful, and instructive, and it must have immediate application to the lives of our readers. If your query is accepted, expect heavy editorial supervision."

$ DIALOGUE

Blindskills, Inc., P.O. Box 5181, Salem OR 97304-0181. E-mail: magazine@blindskills.com. Website: www.blindskills.com. **60% freelance written**. Bimonthly journal covering visually impaired people. Estab. 1962. Circ. 1,100. Byline given. Pays on publication. Publishes ms an average of 6 months after

acceptance. Buys first rights. Editorial lead time 3 months. Accepts queries by e-mail. One free sample on request. Available in large print, Braille, 4-track audio cassette, and e-mail. Guidelines available online.
Nonfiction Mostly features material written by visually impaired writers. Needs essays, general interest, historical, how-to, life skills methods used by visually impaired people, humor, interview, personal experience, sports, recreation, hobbies. No controversial, explicit sex, religious, or political topics. **Buys 80 mss/year.** Send complete ms. Length: 200-1,000/words. **Pays $15-35 for assigned articles. Pays $15-25 for unsolicited articles.**
Columns/Departments All material should be relative to blind and visually impaired readers. Living with Low Vision, 1,000 words; Hear's How (dealing with sight loss), 1,000 words. Technology Answer Book, 800 words. Buys 80 mss/year. Send complete ms. **Pays $10-25.**

HEARING HEALTH

Deafness Research Foundation, 641 Lexington Ave., 15th Floor, New York NY 10022. E-mail: info@drf.org. Website: www.drf.org/hearing_health. Magazine covering issues and concerns pertaining to hearing and hearing loss. Byline given. Pays with contributor copies. Buys exclusive print and online rights. Accepts queries by mail, e-mail. Accepts previously published material. Accepts simultaneous submissions. Guidelines available online.
Nonfiction Topic areas include access, hearing aid technology, cochlear implants, assistive listening devices, telecommunications, success stories, research involving the auditory system, education, coping, tinnitus, balance disorders, disability rights and advocacy. Send complete ms.
Reprints Please do not submit a previously published article unless permission has been obtained in writing that allows the article's use in *Hearing Health*.
Photos State availability. Captions required. Reviews high-resolution digital images.
Columns/Departments Features (800-1,500 words); First-person stories (500-1,500 words); Humor (500-750 words); Viewpoints/Op-Ed (350-500 words). Send complete ms.

$ KALEIDOSCOPE

Exploring the Experience of Disability Through Literature and the Fine Arts, Kaleidoscope Press, 701 S. Main St., Akron OH 44311-1019. (330)762-9755. Fax: (330)762-0912. E-mail: mshiplett@udsakron.org. Website: www.udsakron.org/kaleidoscope.htm. **Contact:** Mildred Shiplett. **75% freelance written. Eager to work with new/unpublished writers.** Semiannual magazine. "Subscribers include individuals, agencies, and organizations that assist people with disabilities and many university and public libraries. Appreciates work by established writers as well. Especially interested in work by writers with a disability, but features writers both with and without disabilities. Writers without a disability must limit themselves to our focus, while those with a disability may explore any topic (although we prefer original perspectives about experiences with disability)." Estab. 1979. Circ. 1,000. Byline given. Pays on publication. No kill fee. Buys first rights. Rights return to author upon publication. Accepts queries by mail, fax. Accepts previously published material. Accepts simultaneous submissions. Responds in 3 weeks to queries. Responds in 6 months to mss. Sample copy for $6 prepaid. Double-space your work, number the pages, & include name. Guidelines available online.
Nonfiction Articles related to disability. Needs book excerpts, essays, humor, interview, personal experience, book reviews, articles related to disability. **Buys 8-15 mss/year.** Length: 5,000 words maximum. **Pays $25-125, plus 2 copies.**
Reprints Send double-spaced typed manuscript with rights for sale noted and information about when and where the material previously appeared. Reprints permitted with credit given to original publication.
Photos Send photos.
Fiction Short stories, novel excerpts. Traditional and experimental styles. Works should explore experiences with disability. Use people-first language. Needs Well-developed plots, engaging characters, and realistic dialogue. We lean toward fiction that emphasizes character and emotions rather than action-oriented narratives. No fiction that is stereotypical, patronizing, sentimental, erotic, or maudlin. No romance, religious or dogmatic fiction; no children's literature. Length: 5,000 words maximum. **Pays $10-125, and 2 contributor's copies.**
Poetry Do not get caught up in rhyme scheme. High quality with strong imagery and evocative language. Reviews any style. Buys 12-20 poems/year. Submit maximum 5 poems.
Tips "Articles and personal experiences should be creative rather than journalistic and with some depth. Writers should use more than just the simple facts and chronology of an experience with disability. Inquire about future themes of upcoming issues. Sample copy very helpful. Works should not use stereotyping, patronizing, or offending language about disability. We seek fresh imagery and thought-provoking language. Please double-space work, number pages & include full name and address."

$ $ PN

Paralyzed Veterans of America, 2111 E. Highland Ave., Suite 180, Phoenix AZ 85016. Fax: (602)224-0507. E-mail: info@pnnews.com. Website: www.pn-magazine.com. Monthly magazine covering news and information for wheelchair users. Writing must pertain to people with disabilities—specifically mobility impairments. Estab. 1946. Circ. 40,000. Byline given. Pays on publication. Publishes ms an average of 2-4 months after acceptance. Buys one-time rights. Editorial lead time 3 months. Submit seasonal material 3 months in advance. Accepts queries by mail, e-mail, fax. Sample copy free. Guidelines free.
Nonfiction Needs how-to, interview, new product, opinion. **Buys 10-12 mss/year.** Send complete ms. Length: 1,200-2,500 words. **Pays $25-250.**

$ $ SPECIALIVING

P.O. Box 1000, Bloomington IL 61702. (309)962-2003. E-mail: gareeb@aol.com. Website: www.specialiving.com. **90% freelance written**. Quarterly online magazine covering the physically disabled/mobility impaired. "We are now an online magazine @ www.specialiving.com. The phone # should be 309-962-2003 There is no subscription fee but can be read free. Subject matter is the same. Payment is still the same, (max 800 words). Need photos with ms." Estab. 2001. Circ. 12,000. Byline given. Pays on publication. Buys one-time rights. Editorial lead time 3 months. Submit seasonal material 6 months in advance. Accepts queries by mail, e-mail, fax, phone. Accepts simultaneous submissions. Responds in 3 weeks to queries.
Nonfiction Needs how-to, humor, inspirational, interview, new product, personal experience, technical, travel. **Buys 40 mss/year.** Query. Length: 800 words. **Pays 10¢/word.**
Photos State availability. Captions, identification of subjects required. Reviews GIF/JPEG files. Offers $10/photo; $50/cover photo. Buys one time rights.
Columns/Departments Shopping Guide; Items. Buys 30 mss/year. Query.

$ $ SPORTS N SPOKES

Paralyzed Veterans of America, 2111 E. Highland Ave., Suite 180, Phoenix AZ 85016. (602)224-0500. Fax: (602)224-0507. E-mail: brenda@pnnews.com. Website: www.sportsnspokes.com. **Contact:** Brenda Martin. Bimonthly magazine covering wheelchair sports and recreation. Writing must pertain to wheelchair sports and recreation. Estab. 1974. Circ. 25,000. Byline given. Pays on publication. Publishes ms an average of 2-3 months after acceptance. Buys first rights. Editorial lead time 2-3 months. Submit seasonal material 2-3 months in advance. Accepts queries by mail, e-mail, fax. Sample copy free. Guidelines free.
Nonfiction Needs general interest, interview, new product. **Buys 5-6 mss/year.** Send complete ms. Length: 1,200-2,500 words. **Pays $20-250.**

Entertainment

$ CINEASTE

America's Leading Magazine on the Art and Politics of the Cinema, Cineaste Publishers, Inc., 243 Fifth Ave., #706, New York NY 10016. (212)366-5720. E-mail: cineaste@cineaste.com. Website: www.cineaste.com. **30% freelance written**. Quarterly magazine covering motion pictures with an emphasis on social and political perspective on cinema. Estab. 1967. Circ. 11,000. Byline given. Pays on publication. Offers 50% kill fee. Publishes ms an average of 4 months after acceptance. Buys first North American serial rights. Editorial lead time 3 months. Submit seasonal material 4 months in advance. Accepts queries by mail, e-mail, fax. Responds in 1 month to queries. Sample copy for $5. Writer's guidelines on website.
Nonfiction Needs book excerpts, essays, expose, historical, humor, interview, opinion. **Buys 20-30 mss/year.** Query with published clips. Length: 2,000-5,000 words. **Pays $30-100.**
Photos State availability. Identification of subjects required. Reviews transparencies, 8 × 10 prints. Offers no additional payment for photos accepted with ms. Buys one-time rights.
Columns/Departments Homevideo (topics of general interest or a related group of films); A Second Look (new interpretation of a film classic or a reevaluation of an unjustly neglected release of more recent vintage); Lost and Found (film that may or may not be released or otherwise seen in the US but which is important enough to be brought to the attention of our readers), all 1,000-1,500 words. Query with published clips. **Pays $50 minimum.**
Tips "We dislike academic jargon, obtuse Marxist terminology, film buff trivia, trendy `buzz' phrases, and show biz references. We do not want our writers to speak of how they have `read' or `decoded' a film, but to view, analyze, and interpret. Warning the reader of problems with specific films is more important to us than artificially `puffing' a film because its producers or politics are agreeable. One article format

we encourage is an omnibus review of several current films, preferably those not reviewed in a previous issue. Such an article would focus on films that perhaps share a certain political perspective, subject matter, or generic concerns (i.e., films on suburban life, or urban violence, or revisionist Westerns). Like individual film reviews, these articles should incorporate a very brief synopsis of plots for those who haven't seen the films. The main focus, however, should be on the social issues manifested in each film, and how it may reflect something about the current political/social/esthetic climate."

$ DANCE INTERNATIONAL

Scotiabant Dance Centre, Level 6 677 Davie St., Vancouver BC V6B 2G6 Canada. (604)681-1525. Fax: (604)681-7732. E-mail: danceint@direct.ca. Website: www.danceinternational.org. **100% freelance written**. Quarterly magazine covering dance arts. Articles and reviews on current activities in world dance, with occasional historical essays; reviews of dance films, video, and books. Estab. 1973. Circ. 4,500. Byline given. Pays on publication. Offers 50% kill fee. Publishes ms an average of 3 months after acceptance. Buys one-time rights. Editorial lead time 3 months. Submit seasonal material 6 weeks in advance. Accepts queries by mail, e-mail, fax, phone. Responds in 2 weeks to queries. Responds in 1 month to mss. Sample copy for $7. Guidelines for #10 SASE.

Nonfiction Needs book excerpts, essays, historical, interview, personal experience, photo feature. **Buys 100 mss/year.** Query. Length: 1,200-2,200 words. **Pays $40-150.**

Photos Send photos. Identification of subjects required. Reviews prints. Offers no additional payment for photos accepted with ms.

Columns/Departments Dance Bookshelf (recent books reviewed), 700-800 words; Regional Reports (events in each region), 1,200 words. Buys 100 mss/year. Query. **Pays $80.**

Tips Send résumé and samples of recent writings.

$$ DIRECTED BY

The Cinema Quarterly, Visionary Media, P.O. Box 1722, Glendora CA 91740-1722. Fax: (626)608-0309. E-mail: visionarycinema@yahoo.com. Website: www.directed-by.com. **10% freelance written**. Quarterly magazine covering the craft of directing a motion picture. "Our articles are for readers particularly knowledgeable about the art and history of movies from the director's point of view. Our purpose is to communicate our enthusiasm and interest in the craft of cinema." Estab. 1998. Circ. 42,000. Byline given. Pays on publication. Offers 25% kill fee. Publishes ms an average of 3 months after acceptance. Buys all rights. Editorial lead time 3 months. Submit seasonal material 3 months in advance. Accepts queries by mail, e-mail. Accepts simultaneous submissions. Responds in 6 weeks to queries. Sample copy for $5. Writer's guidelines free or by e-mail.

Nonfiction Needs interview, photo feature, on-set reports. No gossip, celebrity-oriented material, or movie reviews. **Buys 5 mss/year.** Query. Length: 500-7,500 words. **Pays $50-750.**

Photos State availability. Captions, identification of subjects required. Reviews contact sheets. Offers no additional payment for photos accepted with ms. Buys all rights.

Columns/Departments Trends (overview/analysis of specific moviemaking movements/genres/subjects), 1,500-2,000 words; Focus (innovative take on the vision of a contemporary director), 1,500-2,000 words; Appreciation (overview of deceased/foreign director), 1,000-1,500 words; Final Cut (spotlight interview with contemporary director), 3,000 words; Perspectives (interviews/articles about film craftspeople who work with a featured director), 1,500-2,000 words. Buys 5 mss/year. Query. **Pays $50-750.**

Tips "We have been inundated with 'shelf-life' article queries and cannot publish even a small fraction of them. As such, we have restricted our interest in freelancers to writers who have direct access to a notable director of a current film which has not been significantly covered in previous issues of magazines; said director must be willing to grant an exclusive personal interview to *DIRECTED BY*. This is a tough task for a writer, but if you are a serious freelancer and have access to important filmmakers, we are interested in you."

EAST END LIGHTS

The Quarterly Magazine for Elton John Fans, 114040 Creditview Rd., P.O. Box 188, Mississauga ON L5C 3Y8 Canada. (416)760-3426. Fax: (905)566-7369. E-mail: eastendlights@sympatico.ca. Website: www.eastendlights.com. **90% freelance written**. Quarterly magazine covering Elton John. In one way or another, a story must relate to Elton John, his activities or associates (past and present). We appeal to discriminating Elton fans. No gushing fanzine material. No current concert reviews. Estab. 1990. Circ. 1,700. Byline given. Pays 3 weeks after publication. Publishes ms an average of 3 months after acceptance. Buys first rights, buys second serial (reprint) rights. Submit seasonal material 6 months in advance. Accepts queries by mail, e-mail, fax. Accepts previously published material. Responds in 2 months to queries. Sample copy for $5.

Nonfiction Needs book excerpts, essays, expose, general interest, historical, humor, interview. **Buys 20 mss/year.** Send complete ms. Length: 400-1,000 words.
Reprints Send tearsheet or photocopy with rights for sale noted and information about when and where the material previously appeared.
Photos State availability. Reviews negatives, 5 × 7 prints, high-resolution digital files. Buys one-time and all rights.
Columns/Departments Clippings (nonwire references to Elton John in other publications), maximum 200 words. Buys 12 mss/year. Send complete ms.
Tips Approach us with a well-thought-out story idea. We prefer interviews with Elton-related personalities—past or present. Try to land an interview we haven't done. We are particularly interested in music/memorabilia collecting of Elton material.

EMPIRE

ACP Magazines, Ltd., 54-58 Park St., Sydney NSW 2000 Australia. (02)9282 8000. E-mail: empire@acpmagazines.com.au/magazine. Website: www.acpmagazines.com.au. **Contact:** Rod Yates, editor. Monthly magazine covering movies. *Empire Magazine* is the definitive read for people who love movies. Circ. 24,149.
Nonfiction Needs general interest, interview, new product. Query.

ENTERTAINMENT WEEKLY

Time, Inc., 1675 Broadway, 30th Floor, New York NY 10019. (212)522-5600. Fax: (212)522-0074. Website: www.ew.com. Weekly magazine. Written for readers who want the latest reviews, previews and updates of the entertainment world. Circ. 1,600,000. No kill fee. Editorial lead time 4 weeks.

- Does not buy freelance material or use freelance writers.

$ $ FANGORIA

Horror in Entertainment, The Brooklyn Company, 250 West 49th St., Suite 304, New York NY 10019-7454. Website: www.fangoria.com. **95% freelance written. Works with a small number of new/unpublished writers each year**. Magazine published 10 times/year covering horror films, TV projects, comics, videos, and literature, and those who create them. "We provide an assignment sheet (deadlines, info) to writers, thus authorizing queried stories that we're buying." Estab. 1979. Byline given. Pays 1-3 months after publication. Publishes ms an average of 3 months after acceptance. Buys all rights. Submit seasonal material 4 months in advance. Accepts queries by mail. Responds in 6 weeks to queries. Sample copy for $9 and 10 × 13 SAE with 4 first-class stamps. Guidelines for #10 SASE.
Nonfiction "Book excerpts, interview/profile of movie directors, makeup FX artists, screenwriters, producers, actors, noted horror/thriller novelists and others—with genre credits; special FX and special makeup FX how-it-was-done (on filmmaking only). Occasional think pieces, opinion pieces, reviews, or sub-theme overviews by industry professionals." Needs interviews with technicians and filmmakers in the field. Avoids most articles on science-fiction films. **Buys 120 mss/year.** Query with published clips. Length: 1,000-3,500 words. **Pays $100-250.**
Photos State availability. Captions, identification of subjects required. Reviews transparencies, prints (b&w, color) electronically.
Columns/Departments Monster Invasion (exclusive, early information about new film productions; also mini-interviews with filmmakers and novelists). Query with published clips. **Pays $45-75.**
Tips "Other than recommending that you study one or several copies of *Fangoria*, we can only describe it as a horror film magazine consisting primarily of interviews with technicians and filmmakers in the field. Be sure to stress the interview subjects' words—not your own opinions as much. We're very interested in small, independent filmmakers working outside of Hollywood. These people are usually more accessible to writers, and more cooperative. *Fangoria* is also sort of a de facto bible for youngsters interested in movie makeup careers and for young filmmakers. We are devoted only to reel horrors—the fakery of films, the imagery of the horror fiction of a Stephen King or a Clive Barker—we do not want nor would we ever publish articles on real-life horrors, murders, etc. A writer must enjoy horror films and horror fiction to work for us. If the photos in *Fangoria* disgust you, if the sight of (stage) blood repels you, if you feel `superior' to horror (and its fans), you aren't a writer for us and we certainly aren't the market for you. We love giving new writers their first chance to break into print in a national magazine. We are currently looking for Louisiana- (New Orleans), New Mexico-, Arizona- and Las Vegas-based correspondents, as well as writers stationed in Spain (especially Barcelona), southern US cities, and Eastern Europe."

FILM COMMENT

Film Society of Lincoln Center, 70 Lincoln Center Plaza, New York NY 10023. (212)875-5610. E-mail: editor@filmlinc.com. Website: www.filmlinc.com. **100% freelance written**. Bimonthly magazine covering film criticism and film history. Estab. 1962. Circ. 30,000. Byline given. Pays on publication. Editorial lead time 6 weeks. Accepts queries by mail, e-mail, fax, phone. Accepts simultaneous submissions.

Nonfiction Needs essays, historical, interview, opinion. **Buys 100 mss/year.** Send complete ms. We respond to queries, but rarely assign a writer we don't know. Length: 800-8,000 words.

Photos State availability. No additional payment for photos accepted with ms. Buys one time rights.

Tips We are more or less impervious to `hooks,' don't worry a whole lot about `who's hot who's not,' or tying in with next fall's surefire big hit. (We think people should write about films they've seen, not films that haven't even been finished.) We appreciate good writing (writing, not journalism) on subjects in which the writer has some personal investment and about which he or she has something noteworthy to say. Demonstrate ability and inclination to write *FC*-worthy articles. We read and consider everything we get, and we do print unknowns and first-timers. Probably the writer with a shorter submission (1,000-2,000 words) has a better chance than with an epic article that would fill half the issue.

$$ FLICK MAGAZINE

Decipher, Inc., 259 Granby St., Norfolk VA 23510. (757)623-3600. Fax: (757)623-8368. E-mail: julie.matthews@decipher.com. Website: www.flickmagazine.com. **30-40% freelance written**. Mini-magazine distributed in movie theaters that comes out in conjunction with selected movies covering one specific movie per issue. *Flick*'s mission is to match the passion and personality of fans, taking readers inside Hollywood and increasing their connection to the film they are about to view. Estab. 2005. Circ. 2.5 million. Pays on acceptance. No kill fee. Publishes ms an average of 4 months after acceptance. Makes work-for-hire assignments. Editorial lead time 4-5 months. Accepts queries by mail, e-mail.

Nonfiction Needs essays, humor, interview, opinion, personal experience. Query. Length: 500-1,000 words. **Pays $200-500.**

Photos Contact: Art Director (jeff.hellerman@decipher.com).

Columns/Departments Pays $200-500.

Tips Writing for *Flick* is about research, story angles, subject knowledge, and access to movie cast and crew.

FOXTEL MAGAZINE

ACP Magazines, Ltd., 54-58 Park St., Sydney NSW 2000 Australia. (61)(2)9282-8000. Fax: (61)(2)9267-4361. Website: www.acp.com.au/publication.aspx. Monthly magazine. "Entertainment magazine promoting exciting TV listings guide. The magazine incorporates: Expanded upfront editorial sections, based on genre, providing more diverse editorial environments; A wide format to improve magazine design and appeal. FOXTEL magazine readers are passionate consumers with items such as home entertainment equipment, financial services, cars and travel." Circ. 815,000.

Nonfiction Needs general interest, interview. Query.

GLOBE

American Media, Inc., 1000 American Media Way, Boca Raton FL 33464. (561)997-7733. Fax: (561)989-1004. E-mail: newstips@globefl.com. Website: www.globemagazine.com. Weekly tabloid. *Globe* is edited for an audience interested in a wide range of human-interest stories, with particular emphasis on celebrities. Circ. 631,705. No kill fee.

- Does not buy freelance material or use freelance writers.

INTERVIEW

Brant Publications, Inc., 575 Broadway, 5th Floor, New York NY 10012. (212)941-2900. Fax: (212)941-2934. E-mail: brantinter@aol.com. Website: www.interviewmagazine.com. Monthly magazine. Explores the inside world of music, film, fashion, art, TV, photography, sports, contemporary life and politics through celebrity interviews. Circ. 200,000. No kill fee. Editorial lead time 2 months.

$ IN TOUCH WEEKLY

Bauer Magazine Limited Partnership, 270 Sylvan Ave., Englewood Cliffs NJ 07632. (201)569-6699. E-mail: contactintouch@intouchweekly.com. Website: www.intouchweekly.com. **10% freelance written**. Weekly magazine covering celebrity news and entertainment. Estab. 2002. Circ. 1,300,000. No byline given. Pays on publication. Buys all rights. Editorial lead time 1 week. Accepts queries by mail, e-mail, phone.

Nonfiction Needs interview, gossip. **Buys 1,300 mss/year.** Query. Length: 100-1,000 words. **Pays $50.**

$$ MOVIEMAKER MAGAZINE

MovieMaker Media LLC, 174 Fifth Ave., Suite 300, New York NY 10010. (212)766-4100. Fax: (212)766-4102. E-mail: submissions@moviemaker.com. Website: www.moviemaker.com. **75% freelance written**. Bimonthly magazine covering film, independent cinema, and Hollywood. "*MovieMaker*'s editorial is a progressive mix of in-depth interviews and criticism, combined with practical techniques and advice on financing, distribution, and production strategies. Behind-the-scenes discussions with Hollywood's top moviemakers, as well as independents from around the globe, are routinely found in *MovieMaker*'s pages. E-mail is preferred submission method, but will accept via mail as well. Please, no telephone pitches. We want to read the idea with clips." Estab. 1993. Circ. 55,000. Byline given. Pays 30 days after newsstand publication. Offers kill fee. Offers variable kill fee. Publishes ms an average of 2 months after acceptance. Buys all rights. Editorial lead time 3 months. Submit seasonal material 4 months in advance. Accepts queries by mail, e-mail. Accepts simultaneous submissions. Responds in 2-4 weeks to queries. Responds in 4-6 weeks to mss. Sample copy available online. Guidelines by e-mail.

Nonfiction Needs expose, general interest, historical, how-to, interview, new product, technical. **Buys 20 mss/year.** Query with published clips. Length: 800-3,000 words. **Pays $75-500 for assigned articles.**

Photos State availability. Identification of subjects required. Payment varies for photos accepted with ms. Rights purchased negotiable.

Columns/Departments Documentary; Home Cinema (home video/DVD reviews); How They Did It (first-person filmmaking experiences); Festival Beat (film festival reviews); World Cinema (current state of cinema from a particular country). Query with published clips **Pays $75-300.**

Tips "The best way to begin working with *MovieMaker* is to send a list of 'pitches' along with your résumé and clips. As we receive a number of résumés each week, we want to get an early sense of not just your style of writing, but the kinds of subjects that interest you most as they relate to film. We also want to know that you undersand the magazine and our audience. The fastest way to have your story rejected (besides a typo in the pitch) is to clearly have never read a copy of the magazine. E-mail is the preferred method of correspondence, and please allow 1 month before following up on a query or résumé. All queries must be submitted in writing. No phone calls, please."

$$$ OK! MAGAZINE

Northern & Shell North America Limited, 475 Fifth Ave., New York NY 10017. E-mail: editor@ok-magazine.com. Website: www.ok-magazine.com. **10% freelance written**. Weekly magazine covering entertainment news. We are a celebrity friendly magazine. We strive not to show celebrities in a negative light. We consider ourselves a cross between *People* and *In Style*. Estab. 2005. Circ. 1,000,000. Byline sometimes given. Pays after publication. Publishes ms an average of 1 month after acceptance. Buys first North American serial rights, buys first rights, buys one-time rights. Editorial lead time 2 weeks. Accepts queries by mail, e-mail, fax.

Nonfiction Needs interview, photo feature. **Buys 50 mss/year.** Query with published clips. Length: 500-2,000 words. **Pays $100-1,000.**

Photos Contact: Contact Maria Collazo, photography director.

⊘ PREMIERE MAGAZINE

Hachette Filipacchi Magazines, 1633 Broadway, 41st Floor, New York NY 10019. (212)767-6000. Fax: (212)767-5450. Website: www.premiere.com. Magazine published 10 times/year.

- Does not buy freelance material or use freelance writers.

$$ RUE MORGUE

Horror in Culture & Entertainment, Marrs Media, Inc., 2926 Dundas St. West, Toronto ON M6P 1Y8 Canada. E-mail: jovanka@rue-morgue.com. Website: www.rue-morgue.com. **Contact:** Dave Alexander, editor-in-chief. **50% freelance written**. Monthly magazine covering horror entertainment. "A knowledge of horror entertainment (films, books, games, toys, etc.)." Estab. 1997. Byline given. Pays on publication. No kill fee. Publishes ms an average of 2-4 months after acceptance. Editorial lead time 2 months. Submit seasonal material 4 months in advance. Accepts queries by e-mail. Responds in 6 weeks to queries. Responds in 2 months to mss. Guidelines available by e-mail.

Nonfiction Needs essays, exposè, historical, interview, travel, new product. No reviews. Query with published clips or send complete ms. Length: 500-3,500 words.

Columns/Departments Classic Cut (historical essays on classic horror films, books, games, comic books, music), 500-700 words. Query with published clips.

Tips "The editors are most responsive to special interest articles and analytical essays on cultural/historical topics relating to the horror genre—published examples: Leon Theremin, Soren Kierkegaard, Horror in Fine Art, Murderbilia, The History of the Werewolf."

$ $ $ $ SOUND & VISION

Hachette Filipacchi Media U.S., Inc., 1633 Broadway, New York NY 10019. (212)767-6000. Fax: (212)767-5615. E-mail: soundandvision@hfmus.com. Website: www.soundandvisionmag.com. **Contact:** Mike Mettler, editor-in-chief. **40% freelance written**. Published 8 times/year. "Provides readers with authoritative information on the home entertainment technologies and products that will impact their lives." Estab. 1958. Circ. 400,000. Byline given. Pays on acceptance. Publishes ms an average of 4 months after acceptance. Buys first North American serial rights, buys electronic rights. Accepts queries by mail, e-mail, fax. Sample copy for sae with 9 × 12 envelope and 11 First-Class stamps.

Nonfiction "Home theater, audio, video and multimedia equipment plus movie, music, and video game reviews, how-to-buy and how-to-use A/V gear, interview/profile." **Buys 25 mss/year.** Query with published clips. Length: 1,500-3,000 words. **Pays $1,000-1,500.**

Tips "Send proposals or outlines, rather than complete articles, along with published clips to establish writing ability. Publisher assumes no responsibility for return or safety of unsolicited art, photos, or manuscripts."

⊘ STAR MAGAZINE

American Media, Inc., 1000 American Media Way, Boca Raton FL 33464-1000. E-mail: letters@starmagazine.com. Website: www.starmagazine.com.

- Query before submitting.

⊘ TV GUIDE

Gemstar-TV Guide Ineternational, Inc., 1211 Avenue of the Americas, 4th Floor, New York NY 10036. (212)852-7500. Fax: (212)852-7470. Website: www.tvguide.com. Weekly magazine. Focuses on all aspects of network, cable, and pay television programming and how it affects and reflects audiences. Circ. 9,097,762. No kill fee.

- Does not buy freelance material or use freelance writers.

XXL MAGAZINE

Harris Publications, 1115 Broadway, New York NY 10010. E-mail: xxlmagedit@harris-pub.com. Website: www.xxlmag.com. **Contact:** Vanessa Satten. **50% freelance written**. Monthly magazine. *XXL* is hip-hop on a higher level, an upscale urban lifestyle magazine. Estab. 1997. Circ. 350,000. Byline given. Pays on publication. Buys all rights. Editorial lead time 2 months. Submit seasonal material 3 months in advance. Accepts queries by mail.

Nonfiction Needs interview, music, entertainment, luxury materialism. Query with published clips. Length: 200-5,000 words.

Photos State availability. Captions, model releases required. Reviews contact sheets, transparencies, prints.

Tips Please send clips, query, and cover letter by mail.

Ethnic & Minority

$ $ $ $ AARP SEGUNDA JUVENTUD

AARP, 601 E St. NW, Washington DC 20049. E-mail: segundajuventud@aarp.org. Website: www.aarpsegundajuventud.org. **75% freelance written**. Bimonthly magazine geared toward 50+ Hispanics. With fresh and relevant editorial content and a mission of inclusiveness and empowerment, *AARP Segunda Juventud* serves more than 800,000 Hispanic AARP members and their families in all 50 states, the District of Columbia, Puerto Rico, and the US Virgin Islands. Estab. 2002. Circ. 800,000. Byline given. Pays on acceptance. Offers 33.33% kill fee. Publishes ms an average of 4 months after acceptance. Buys exclusive first worldwide rights. Editorial lead time 2-12 months. Submit seasonal material 4-12 months in advance. Accepts queries by mail, e-mail. Accepts simultaneous submissions. Responds in 4 months to queries. Responds in 4 months to mss. Sample copy available online.

Nonfiction Must have a Hispanic angle targeting the 50+ audience. Needs general interest, interview, new product, travel, reviews (book, film, music). **Buys 36 mss/year.** Query with published clips. Length: 200-1,500 words. **Pays $1-2/word.**

Photos Send photos. Captions, identification of subjects, model releases required. Reviews contact sheets, negatives, transparencies, prints, GIF/JPEG files. Negotiates payment individually.
Columns/Departments Health; Finance; Travel; Celebrity profile; Encore (Hispanic 50+ individuals reinventing themselves). Buys 24 mss/year. Query with published clips. **Pays $1-2/word.**
Fillers Needs facts. Buys 6 mss/year. Length: 200-250 words. **Pays $1-2/word.**
Tips "Look closely at the last 6 issues to get familiar with the magazine topics. Don't submit queries for topics already covered. Write lively but succinct queries that demonstrate you have done your research into our magazine and our demographic, the 50+ Hispanic."

$$ AFRIQUE NEWSMAGAZINE

Afrique Publishing, Inc., 3525 W. Peterson Ave., Suite 200, Chicago IL 60659. (773)463-7200. Fax: (773)463-7264. E-mail: cli@afriquenewsmagazine.com. Website: www.afriquenewsmagazine.com. **50% freelance written**. Monthly tabloid covering African diaspora. The mission of our publication is to connect and empower people of African descent (Africans, African Americans, West Indians, etc.). Writer must be knowledgeable or willing to learn about these communities. Estab. 1991. Circ. 75,000. Byline given. Pays on publication. Publishes ms an average of 1 month after acceptance. Buys all rights. Editorial lead time 2 months. Submit seasonal material 2 months in advance. Accepts queries by mail, e-mail, fax, phone. Accepts previously published material. Accepts simultaneous submissions. Sample copy available online. Guidelines by e-mail.
Nonfiction Needs book excerpts, essays, expose, general interest, historical, how-to, humor, inspirational, interview, new product, opinion, personal experience, photo feature, religious, technical, travel. **Buys 10 mss/year.** Send complete ms. Length: 200+ words. **Pays 10-30¢/word for assigned articles. Pays 10-20¢/word for unsolicited articles.**
Photos State availability. Identification of subjects required. Reviews GIF/JPEG files. Offers no additional payment for photos accepted with ms. Buys all rights.
Columns/Departments West/Central Africa; The Americas; East/Southern Africa; Business, all 500 words. Query. **Pays 10-30¢/word.**
Fiction Needs ethnic, humorous, mainstream. **Buys 10 mss/year.** Query.
Poetry Needs avant-garde, free verse, haiku, light verse, traditional. Buys 10 poems/year.

$$ AMBASSADOR MAGAZINE

National Italian American Foundation, 1860 19th St. NW, Washington DC 20009. (202)387-0600. Fax: (202)387-0800. E-mail: monica@niaf.org. Website: www.niaf.org. **50% freelance written**. Quarterly magazine for Italian-Americans covering Italian-American history and culture. We publish nonfiction articles on little-known events in Italian-American history and articles on Italian-American culture, traditions, and personalities living and dead. Estab. 1989. Circ. 25,000. Byline given. Pays on approval of final draft..Offers $50 kill fee. Buys second serial (reprint) rights. Editorial lead time 3 months. Accepts queries by mail, e-mail, fax. Accepts previously published material. Accepts simultaneous submissions. Responds in 2 months to queries. Sample copy and writer's guidelines free.
Nonfiction Needs historical, interview, photo feature. **Buys 12 mss/year.** Send complete ms. Length: 800-1,500 words. **Pays $250 for photos and article.**
Photos Send photos. Captions, identification of subjects required. Reviews contact sheets, prints. Offers no additional payment for photos accepted with ms. Buys one time rights.
Tips Good photos, clear prose, and a good storytelling ability are all prerequisites.

$$$ B'NAI B'RITH MAGAZINE

2020 K St. NW, Washington DC 20006. (202)857-2701. E-mail: bbm@bnaibrith.org. Website: bnaibrith.org. **90% freelance written**. Quarterly magazine specializing in social, political, historical, religious, cultural, `lifestyle,' and service articles relating chiefly to the Jewish communities of North America and Israel. Write for the American Jewish audience, i.e., write about topics from a Jewish perspective, highlighting creativity and innovation in Jewish life. Estab. 1886. Circ. 110,000. Byline given. Pays on publication. Publishes ms an average of 6 months after acceptance. Buys first rights. Editorial lead time 3 months. Submit seasonal material 5 months in advance. Accepts queries by mail, e-mail, fax. Accepts simultaneous submissions. Responds in 1 month to queries. Responds in 6 weeks to mss. Sample copy for $2. Writer's guidelines for #10 SASE or by e-mail.
Nonfiction General interest pieces of relevance to the Jewish community of US and abroad. Needs interview, photo feature, religious, travel. No Holocaust memoirs, first-person essays/memoirs, fiction, or poetry. **Buys 14-20 mss/year.** Query with published clips. Length: 1,000-2,500 words. **Pays $300-800 for assigned articles. Pays $300-700 for unsolicited articles.**

Photos Rarely assigned. Buys one time rights.
Tips Know what's going on in the Jewish world. Look at other Jewish publications also. Writers should submit clips with their queries. Read our guidelines carefully and present a good idea expressed well. Proofread your query letter.

$ ☐ CELTICLIFE MAGAZINE

Clansman Publishing, Ltd., 1454 Dresden Row, Suite 204, Halifax NS B3J 3T5 Canada. (902)425-5716. Fax: (902)835-0080. E-mail: editorial@celticlife.ca. Website: www.celticlife.ca. **Contact:** Alexa Thompson, editor-in-chief. **95% freelance written**. Quarterly magazine covering culture of North Americans of Celtic descent. "The magazine chronicles the stories of Celtic people who have settled in North America, with a focus on the stories of those who are not mentioned in history books. We also feature Gaelic language articles, history of Celtic people, traditions, music, and folklore. We profile Celtic musicians and include reviews of Celtic books, music, and videos." Estab. 1987. Circ. 5,000 (per issue). Byline given. Pays 2 months after publication. No kill fee. Publishes ms an average of 2 months after acceptance. Buys all rights with electronic negotiable rights. Editorial lead time 2 months. Submit seasonal material 3 months in advance. Accepts queries by mail, e-mail, fax, phone. Accepts previously published material. Responds in 1 week to queries. Responds in 1 month to mss Sample copy available online Digital sample and guidelines available online.

- 80% of content must originate from Canadian citizens or Canadian landed immigrants.

Nonfiction Needs essays, general interest, historical, interview, opinion, personal experience, travel, Gaelic language, Celtic music reviews, profiles of Celtic musicians, Celtic history, traditions, and folklore. No fiction, poetry, historical stories already well publicized. **Buys 100 mss/year.** Query or send complete ms Length: 800-2,500 words. **Pays $50-75 (Canadian). All writers receive a complimentary subscription.**
Photos State availability. Captions, identification of subjects, model releases required. Reviews 35mm transparencies, 5 × 7 prints, JPEG files (300 dpi). We do not pay for photographs.
Columns/Departments Query. **Pays $50-75 (Canadian).**
Tips "The only way to get my attention is to submit a query by e-mail. We are so short staffed that we do not have much time to start a correspondence by regular post."

$ FILIPINAS

A Magazine for All Filipinos, Filipinas Publishing, Inc., GBM Bldg., 1580 Bryant St., Daly City CA 94015. (650)985-2530. Website: www.filipinasmag.com. Monthly magazine focused on Filipino-American affairs. *Filipinas* answers the lack of mainstream media coverage of Filipinos in America. It targets both Filipino immigrants and American-born Filipinos, gives in-depth coverage of political, social, and cultural events in the Philippines and in the Filipino-American community. Features role models, history, travel, food and leisure, issues, and controversies. Estab. 1992. Circ. 40,000. Byline given. Pays on publication. Offers $10 kill fee. Publishes ms an average of 5 months after acceptance. Buys first rights, buys all rights. Editorial lead time 2 months. Submit seasonal material 4 months in advance. Accepts queries by mail, e-mail, fax. Responds in 3 weeks to queries. Responds in 5 months to mss. Writer's guidelines for 9½x4 SASE or on website.

- *Unsolicited mss will not be paid.*

Nonfiction Interested in seeing more issue-oriented pieces, unusual topics regarding Filipino-Americans, and stories from the Midwest and other parts of the country other than the coasts. Needs expose, general interest, historical, inspirational, interview, opinion, personal experience, travel. No academic papers. **Buys 80-100 mss/year.** Query with published clips. Length: 800-1,500 words. **Pays $50-75.**
Photos State availability. Captions, identification of subjects required. Reviews 21/4x21/4 and 4 × 5 transparencies. Offers $15-25/photo.
Columns/Departments Cultural Currents (Filipino traditions and beliefs), 1,000 words; New Voices (first-person essays by Filipino Americans ages 10-25), 800 words; First Person (open to all Filipinos), 800 words. Query with published clips. **Pays $50-75.**

$$ GERMAN LIFE

Zeitgeist Publishing, Inc., 1068 National Hwy., LaVale MD 21502. (301)729-6190. Fax: (301)729-1720. E-mail: mslider@germanlife.com. Website: www.germanlife.com. **50% freelance written**. Bimonthly magazine covering German-speaking Europe. "*German Life* is for all interested in the diversity of German-speaking culture—past and present—and in the various ways that the US (and North America in general) has been shaped by its German immigrants. The magazine is dedicated to solid reporting on cultural, historical, social, and political events." Estab. 1994. Circ. 40,000. Byline given. Pays on publication. Buys first North American serial rights. Editorial lead time 4 months. Submit seasonal material 6 months in advance. Accepts queries by mail, e-mail. Responds in 2 months to queries. Responds in 3 months to mss. Sample copy for $4.95 and SAE with 4 first-class stamps. Guidelines available online.

Nonfiction Needs general interest, historical, interview, photo feature, travel. Oktoberfest-related (October); Seasonal Relative to Germany, Switzerland, or Austria (December); Travel to German-speaking Europe (April). **Buys 50 mss/year.** Query with published clips. Length: 800-1,500 words. **Pays $200-500 for assigned articles. Pays $200-350 for unsolicited articles.**

Photos State availability. Identification of subjects required. Reviews color transparencies, 5 × 7 color or b&w prints. Offers no additional payment for photos accepted with ms. Buys one-time rights.

Columns/Departments German-Americana (regards specific German-American communities, organizations, and/or events past or present), 1,200 words; Profile (portrays prominent Germans, Americans, or German-Americans), 1,000 words; At Home (cuisine, etc. relating to German-speaking Europe), 800 words; Library (reviews of books, videos, CDs, etc.), 300 words. Query with published clips. **Pays $50-150.**

Fillers Length: 100-300 words. **Pays $50-150.**

Tips "The best queries include several informative proposals. Writers should avoid overemphasizing autobiographical experiences/stories."

$ HERITAGE FLORIDA JEWISH NEWS

207 O'Brien Rd., Suite 101, Fern Park FL 32730. (407)834-8787. E-mail: news@orlandoheritage.com. Website: www.heritagefl.com. **20% freelance written**. Weekly tabloid on Jewish subjects of local, national and international scope, except for special issues. Covers news of local, national and international scope of interest to Jewish readers and not likely to be found in other publications. Estab. 1976. Circ. 3,500. Byline given. Pays on publication. No kill fee. Buys first North American serial rights, buys first rights, buys one-time rights, buys second serial (reprint) rights, buys simultaneous rights. Submit seasonal material 3 months in advance. Accepts queries by e-mail. Accepts previously published material. Responds in 1 month to queries. Sample copy for $1 and 9 × 12 SASE.

Nonfiction Especially needs articles for these annual issues: Rosh Hashanah, Financial, Chanukah, Celebration (wedding and bar mitzvah), Passover, Health and Fitness, House and Home, Back to School, Travel and Savvy Seniors. No fiction, poems, first-person experiences. Needs general interest, interview, opinion, photo feature, religious, travel. **Buys 50 mss/year.** Send query only. Length: 500-1,000 words. **Pays 75¢/column inch.**

Reprints Send typed manuscript with rights for sale noted.

Photos State availability. Captions, identification of subjects required. Reviews 8 × 10 prints. Offers $5/photo. Buys one time rights.

$ HORIZONS - THE JEWISH FAMILY MONTHLY

Targum Press, 22700 W. Eleven Mile Rd., Southfield MI 48034. E-mail: horizons@targum.com. Website: www.targum.com. **100% freelance written**. Monthly magazine covering the Orthodox Jewish family. "We include fiction and nonfiction, memoirs, essays, historical, and informational articles—all of interest to the Orthodox Jew." Estab. 1994. Circ. 7,000. Byline given. Pays 4-6 weeks after publication. No kill fee. Publishes ms an average of 6 months after acceptance. Buys one-time rights. Editorial lead time 6 months. Submit seasonal material 8 months in advance. Accepts queries by mail, e-mail, fax. Responds in 1 week to queries. Responds in 2 months to mss. Writer's guidelines available.

Nonfiction Needs essays, historical, humor, inspirational, interview, opinion, personal experience, photo feature, travel. **Buys 150 mss/year.** Send complete ms. Length: 350-3,000 words. **Pays 8¢/word.**

Photos State availability. Offers no additional payment for photos accepted with ms. Buys one time rights.

Fiction Contact: Suri Brand, chief ed. Needs historical, humorous, mainstream, slice-of-life vignettes. Nothing not suitable to Orthodox Jewish values. **Buys 10-15 mss/year.** Send complete ms. Length: 300-3,000 words. **Pays $20-100.**

Poetry Needs free verse, haiku, light verse, traditional. Buys 5-10 poems/year. Submit maximum 3 poems. Length: 3-20 lines. **Pays $15.**

Fillers Length: 50-120 words. **Pays $15.**

Tips "*Horizons* publishes for the Orthodox Jewish market and therefore only accepts articles that are suitable for our readership. We do not accept submissions dealing with political issues or Jewish legal issues. The tone is light and friendly and we therefore do not accept submissions that are of a scholarly nature. Our writers must be very familiar with our market."

$ INTERNATIONAL EXAMINER

622 S. Washington, Seattle WA 98104. (206)624-3925. Fax: (206)624-3046. E-mail: editor@iexaminer.org. Website: www.iexaminer.org. **75% freelance written**. Biweekly journal of Asian-American news, politics, and arts. We write about Asian-American issues and things of interest to Asian-Americans. We do not want stuff about Asian things (stories on your trip to China, Japanese Tea Ceremony, etc. will be rejected). Yes, we are in English. Estab. 1974. Circ. 12,000. Pays on publication. No kill fee. Publishes ms an average of 1 month after acceptance. Buys one-time rights. Editorial lead time 1 month. Submit seasonal material 2 months in advance. Accepts simultaneous submissions. Guidelines for #10 SASE.

Nonfiction Needs essays, expose, general interest, historical, humor, interview, opinion, personal experience, photo feature. **Buys 100 mss/year.** Query by mail, fax, or e-mail with published clips 750-5,000 words depending on subject. **Pays $25-100.**

Reprints Accepts previously published submissions (as long as t published in same area). Send typed ms with rights for sale noted and information about when and where the material previously appeared. Payment negotiable.

Photos State availability. Captions, identification of subjects required. Reviews contact sheets. Negotiates payment individually Buys one time rights.

Fiction Asian-American authored fiction by or about Asian-Americans. Needs novel concepts. **Buys 1-2 mss/year.** Query.

Tips Write decent, suitable material on a subject of interest to the Asian-American community. All submissions are reviewed; all good ones are contacted. It helps to call and run an idea by the editor before or after sending submissions.

$$ ITALIAN AMERICA

Official Publication of the Order Sons of Italy in America, 219 E St. NE, Washington DC 20002. (202)547-2900. E-mail: ddesanctis@osia.org. Website: www.osia.org. **20% freelance written**. Quarterly magazine. *Italian America* provides timely information about OSIA, while reporting on individuals, institutions, issues, and events of current or historical significance in the Italian-American community. Estab. 1996. Circ. 65,000. Byline given. Pays on publication. Offers 50% kill fee. Publishes ms an average of 3 months after acceptance. Buys worldwide nonexclusive rights. Editorial lead time 3 months. Accepts queries by mail, e-mail, fax. Accepts simultaneous submissions. Sample copy free. Guidelines available online.

Nonfiction Needs historical, little known historical facts that must relate to Italian Americans, interview, opinion, current events. **Buys 8 mss/year.** Query with published clips. Length: 750-1,000 words. **Pays $50-250.**

Tips "We pay particular attention to the quality of graphics that accompany the stories. We are interested in little known facts about historical/cultural Italian America."

$$ JEWISH ACTION

Union of Orthodox Jewish Congregations of America, 11 Broadway, New York NY 10004. (212)613-8146. Fax: (212)613-0646. E-mail: ja@ou.org. Website: www.ou.org/publications/ja/. **80% freelance written**. Quarterly magazine covering a vibrant approach to Jewish issues, Orthodox lifestyle, and values. Circ. 40,000. Byline given. Pays 2 months after publication. Submit seasonal material 4 months in advance. Responds in 3 months to queries. Sample copy available online. Guidelines for #10 SASE or by e-mail.

- Prefers queries by e-mail. Mail and fax OK.

Nonfiction Current Jewish issues, history, biography, art, inspirational, humor, music, book reviews. "We are not looking for Holocaust accounts. We welcome essays about responses to personal or societal challenges." **Buys 30-40 mss/year.** Query with published clips. Length: 1,000-3,000 words. **Pays $100-400 for assigned articles. Pays $75-150 for unsolicited articles.**

Photos Send photos. Identification of subjects required.

Columns/Departments Just Between Us (personal opinion on current Jewish life and issues), 1,000 words.

Fiction Must have relevance to Orthodox reader. Length: 1,000-2,000 words.

Poetry Buys limited number of poems/year. **Pays $25-75.**

Tips "Remember that your reader is well educated and has a strong commitment to Orthodox Judaism. Articles on the holidays, Israel, and other common topics should offer a fresh insight. Because the magazine is a quarterly, we do not generally publish articles which concern specific timely events."

$ JULUKA

P.O. Box 4675, Palo Verdes Peninsula CA 90274. (866)458-5852. Fax: (310)707-2255. E-mail: info@julukanews.com. Website: www.julukanews.com. Published in the US for those interested in South Africa. Helps South Africans adapt to life in a new country and provides a forum for networking and exchanging ideas, opinions, and resources. No kill fee. Editorial lead time 1 month. Accepts queries by e-mail.

Nonfiction Needs humor, interview, opinion, personal experience, travel, news, book reviews. **Pays 5¢/word**

Photos Send photos.

Columns/Departments Travel, 520 words; Art & Culture (artist profiles/gallery events), 200-400 words; Culture Shock (personal stories about life in North American/stories about emigrating), 500 words; Sports 200-400 words; Human Interest (personal experiences), 300-1,000 words; Guest Editorial, 150-350 words; Reader Profiles, 400-800 words; Money Matters (financial news), 150-300 words; News You Can Use (law/insurance/financial planning), 250-350 words.

$ KHABAR

The Community Magazine, Khabar, Inc., 3790 Holcomb Bridge Rd., Suite 101, Norcross GA 30092. (770)451-7666, ext. 115. E-mail: parthiv@khabar.com. Website: www.khabar.com. **50% freelance written**. "Monthly magazine covering the Asian Indian community in and around Georgia." Content relating to Indian-American and/or immigrant experience. Estab. 1992. Circ. 27,000. Pays on publication. Offers 25% kill fee. Publishes ms an average of 2 months after acceptance. Buys one-time rights, buys second serial (reprint) rights, buys simultaneous rights, buys electronic rights. Editorial lead time 2 months. Submit seasonal material 2 months in advance. Accepts queries by e-mail. Accepts previously published material. Accepts simultaneous submissions. Sample copy free. Guidelines by e-mail.

Nonfiction Needs essays, interview, opinion, personal experience, travel. **Buys 5 mss/year.** Send complete ms. Length: 750-4,000 words. **Pays $100-300 for assigned articles. Pays $75 for unsolicited articles.**

Photos State availability of or send photos. Captions, identification of subjects required. Negotiates payment individually.

Columns/Departments Book Review, 1,200 words; Music Review, 800 words; Spotlight (profiles), 1,200-3,000 words. Query with or without published clips or send complete ms. **Pays $75+.**

Fiction Needs ethnic, Indian American/Asian immigrant. **Buys 5 mss/year.** Query or send complete ms. **Pays $50-100.**

Tips "Ask for our 'editorial guidelines' document by e-mail."

$$$$ LATINA MAGAZINE

Latina Media Ventures, LLC, 1500 Broadway, Suite 700, New York NY 10036. (212)642-0200. E-mail: editor@latina.com. Website: www.latina.com. **40-50% freelance written**. Monthly magazine covering Latina lifestyle. *Latina Magazine* is the leading bilingual lifestyle publication for Hispanic women in the US today. Covering the best of Latino fashion, beauty, culture, and food, the magazine also features celebrity profiles and interviews. Estab. 1996. Circ. 250,000. Byline given. Pays on publication. Offers 25% kill fee. Publishes ms an average of 2-3 months after acceptance. Buys first rights, buys second serial (reprint) rights, buys electronic rights. Editorial lead time 3 months. Submit seasonal material 4-5 months in advance. Accepts queries by e-mail. Responds in 1 month to queries. Responds in 1-2 months to mss. Sample copy available online.

- Editors are in charge of their individual sections and pitches should be made directly to them. Do not make pitches directly to the editor-in-chief or the editorial director as they will only be routed to the relevant section editor.

Nonfiction Needs essays, how-to, humor, inspirational, interview, new product, personal experience. The 10 Latinas Who Changed the World (December). We do not feature an extensive amount of celebrity content or entertainment content, and freelancers should be sensitive to this. The magazine does not contain book or album reviews, and we do not write stories covering an artist's new project. We do not attend press junkets and do not cover press conferences. Please note that we are a lifestyle magazine, not an entertainment magazine. **Buys 15-20 mss/year.** Query with published clips. Length: 300-2,200 words. **Pays $1/word.**

Photos State availability. Identification of subjects required. Reviews contact sheets, transparencies, GIF/JPEG files. Negotiates payment individually. Buys one time rights.

Tips *Latina*'s features cover a wide gamut of topics, including fashion, beauty, wellness, and personal essays. The magazine runs a wide variety of features on news and service topics (from the issues affecting Latina adoles¢ to stories dealing with anger). If you are going to make a pitch, please keep the following things in mind. All pitches should include statistics or some background reporting that demonstrates why a developing trend is important. Also, give examples of women who can provide a personal perspective. Profiles and essays need to have a strong personal journey angle. We will not cover someone just because they are Hispanic. When pitching stories about a particular person, please let us know the following: timeliness (Is this someone who is somehow tied to breaking news events? Has their story been heard?); the 'wow' factor (Why is this person remarkable? What elements make this story a standout? What sets your subject apart from other women?); target our audience (please note that the magazine targets acculturated, English-dominant Latina women between the ages of 18-39).

$$$ MOMENT

The Magazine of Jewish Culture, Politics and Religion, 4115 Wisconsin Ave. NW, Suite 102, Washington DC 20016. (202)364-3300. Fax: (202)364-2636. E-mail: editor@momentmag.com. Website: www.momentmag.com. **90% freelance written**. Bimonthly magazine. *Moment* is an independent Jewish bimonthly general interest magazine that specializes in cultural, political, historical, religious, and lifestyle articles relating chiefly to the North American Jewish community and Israel. Estab. 1975. Circ. 65,000. Byline given. Pays on publication. Publishes ms an average of 6 months after acceptance. Buys first North American serial rights. Editorial lead time 3 months. Submit seasonal material 6 months in advance. Accepts queries by mail, e-mail, fax. Accepts simultaneous submissions. Responds in 1 month to queries. Responds in 3 months to mss. Sample copy for $4.50 and SAE. Guidelines available online.

Nonfiction We look for meaty, colorful, thought-provoking features and essays on Jewish trends and Israel. We occasionally publish book excerpts, memoirs, and profiles. **Buys 25-30 mss/year.** Query with published clips. Length: 2,500-7,000 words. **Pays $200-1,200 for assigned articles. Pays $40-500 for unsolicited articles.**

Photos State availability. Identification of subjects required. Negotiates payment individually. Buys one time rights.

Columns/Departments 5765 (snappy pieces about quirky events in Jewish communities, news and ideas to improve Jewish living), 250 words maximum; Olam (first-person pieces, humor, and colorful reportage), 600-1,500 words; Book reviews (fiction and nonfiction) are accepted but generally assigned, 400-800 words. Query with published clips. **Pays $50-250.**

Tips Stories for *Moment* are usually assigned, but unsolicited manuscripts are often selected for publication. Successful features offer readers an in-depth journalistic treatment of an issue, phenomenon, institution, or individual. The more the writer can follow the principle of `show, don't tell,' the better. The majority of the submissions we receive are about The Holocaust and Israel. A writer has a better chance of having an idea accepted if it is not on these subjects.

$$ NATIVE PEOPLES MAGAZINE

5333 N. 7th St., Suite C-224, Phoenix AZ 85014. (602)265-4855. Fax: (602)265-3113. E-mail: dgibson@nativepeoples.com. Website: www.nativepeoples.com. Bimonthly magazine covering Native Americans. High-quality reproduction with full color throughout. The primary purpose of this magazine is to offer a sensitive portrayal of the arts and lifeways of Native peoples of the Americas. Estab. 1987. Circ. 50,000. Byline given. Pays on publication. Buys one-time rights, buys nonexclusive Web and reprint rights rights. Accepts queries by mail, e-mail, fax. Responds in 2 months to queries. Guidelines available online.

Nonfiction All features by freelancers. Of the departments, Pathways (travel section), History and Viewpoint most open to freelancers. Needs interview, of interesting and leading Natives from all walks of life, with an emphasis on arts, personal experience. **Buys 35 mss/year.** Length: 1,000-2,500 words. **Pays 25¢/word.**

Photos State availability. Identification of subjects required. Reviews transparencies, prefers high res digital images and 35mm slides. Inquire for details. Offers $45-150/page rates, $250/cover photos. Buys one-time rights and nonexclusive Web and reprint rights.

Tips We are focused upon authenticity and a positive portrayal of present-day Native American life and cultural practices. Our stories portray role models of Native people, young and old, with a sense of pride in their heritage and culture. Therefore, it is important that the Native American point of view be incorporated in each story.

$$ RUSSIAN LIFE

RIS Publications, P.O. Box 567, Montpelier VT 05601. Website: www.russianlife.net. **75% freelance written**. Bimonthly magazine covering Russian culture, history, travel, and business. "Our readers are informed Russophiles with an avid interest in all things Russian. But we do not publish personal travel journals or the like." Estab. 1956. Circ. 15,000. Byline given. Pays on publication. Publishes ms an average of 3-6 months after acceptance. Buys first rights. Editorial lead time 2 months. Submit seasonal material 3 months in advance. Accepts queries by mail. Accepts previously published material. Responds in 1 month to queries. Sample copy for sae with 9 × 12 envelope and 6 First-Class stamps. Guidelines available online.

Nonfiction Needs general interest, photo feature, travel. No personal stories, i.e., How I came to love Russia. **Buys 15-20 mss/year.** Query. Length: 1,000-6,000 words. **Pays $100-300.**
Reprints Accepts previously published submissions rarely.
Photos Send photos. Captions required. Reviews contact sheets. Negotiates payment individually. Buys one time rights.
Tips "A straightforward query letter with writing sample or manuscript (not returnable) enclosed."

$ $ SCANDINAVIAN REVIEW

The American-Scandinavian Foundation, 58 Park Ave., New York NY 10016. (212)879-9779. E-mail: editor@amscan.org. Website: www.amscan.org. **75% freelance written**. Triannual magazine for contemporary Scandinavia. Audience: Members, embassies, consulates, libraries. Slant: Popular coverage of contemporary affairs in Scandinavia. Estab. 1913. Circ. 4,000. Byline given. Pays on publication. No kill fee. Publishes ms an average of 2 months after acceptance. Buys first North American serial rights, buys second serial (reprint) rights. Editorial lead time 3 months. Submit seasonal material 3 months in advance. Accepts previously published material. Responds in 6 weeks to queries. Sample copy available online. Guidelines free.
Nonfiction Needs general interest, interview, photo feature, travel, must have Scandinavia as topic focus. Scandinavian travel No pornography. **Buys 30 mss/year.** Query with published clips. Length: 1,500-2,000 words. **Pays $300 maximum.**
Photos Captions required. Reviews 3 × 5 transparencies, prints. Pays $25-50/photo; negotiates payment individually. Buys one time rights.

SKIPPING STONES

An Award-Winning Multicultural Magazine, P.O. Box 3939, Eugene OR 97403-0939. (541)342-4956. E-mail: editor@skippingstones.org. Website: www.skippingstones.org. **80% freelance written**. "We promote multicultural awareness, international understanding, nature appreciation, and social responsibility. We suggest authors not make stereotypical generalizations in their articles. We like when authors include their own experiences, or base their articles on their personal immersion experiences in a culture or country." Estab. 1988. Circ. 2,000. Byline given. No kill fee. Publishes ms an average of 4-8 months after acceptance. Buys first North American serial rights, non-exclusive reprint, and electronic rights. Editorial lead time 3-4 months. Submit seasonal material 4 months in advance. Accepts queries by mail, e-mail. Accepts simultaneous submissions. Responds in 2-4 weeks to queries. Responds in 4 months to mss. Sample copy for $6. Writer's guidelines online or for business-sized envelope.
Nonfiction Needs essays, general interest, humor, inspirational, interview, opinion, personal experience, photo feature, travel. No 'preachy' or 'screetchy' articles. **Buys 20-30 mss/year.** Send complete ms. Length: 400-800 words.
Photos Send photos. Captions required. Reviews 4X6 prints, low-resolution JPEG files. Offers no additional payment for photos. Buys one time and nonexclusive reprint rights.
Fiction Needs adventure, ethnic, historical, humorous, multicultural, international, social issues. **Buys 20 mss/year.** Send complete ms. Length: 300-800 words. **Pays with contributor copies.**
Poetry Only accepts poetry from youth under age 18. Buys 100-150 poems/year. Submit maximum 4 poems. Length: 30 lines maximum.
Tips "Be original and innovative. Use multicultural, nature, or cross-cultural themes. Multilingual submissions are welcome."

UPSCALE MAGAZINE

Bronner Brothers, 600 Bronner Brothers Way SW, Atlanta GA 30310. (404)758-7467. E-mail: features@upscalemag.com. Website: www.upscalemagazine.com. Monthly magazine covering topics for upscale African-American/black interests. *Upscale* offers to take the reader to the 'next level' of life's experience. Written for the black reader and consumer, *Upscale* provides information in the realms of business, news, lifestyle, fashion and beauty, and arts and entertainment. Estab. 1989. Circ. 250,000. Byline given. Pays on publication. Offers 25% kill fee. Publishes ms an average of 4 months after acceptance. Buys first North American serial rights. Editorial lead time 3-4 months. Accepts queries by mail. Accepts simultaneous submissions. Responds in 1 month to queries. Sample copy available online. Guidelines available online.
Photos State availability. Captions, identification of subjects, model releases required. Negotiates payment individually.
Columns/Departments News & Business (factual, current); Lifestyle (travel, home, wellness, etc.); Beauty & Fashion (tips, trends, upscale fashion, hair); and Arts & Entertainment (artwork, black celebrities, entertainment). 6-10 Query with published clips. **Payment different for each department.**

Tips Make queries informative and exciting. Include entertaining clips. Be familiar with issues affecting black readers. Be able to write about them with ease and intelligence.

$ ☐ WINDSPEAKER

Aboriginal Multi-Media Society of Alberta, 13245-146 St., Edmonton AB T5L 4S8 Canada. (780)455-2700. Fax: (780)455-7639. E-mail: edwind@ammsa.com. Website: www.ammsa.com/windspeaker. **25% freelance written**. Monthly tabloid covering native issues. Focus on events and issues that affect and interest native peoples, national or local. Estab. 1983. Circ. 27,000. Byline given. Pays on publication. Offers kill fee. Publishes ms an average of 1 month after acceptance. Buys first rights. Editorial lead time 1 month. Submit seasonal material 2 months in advance. Accepts queries by mail, e-mail, phone. Accepts simultaneous submissions. Sample copy free. Guidelines available online.

Nonfiction Needs opinion, photo feature, travel, news interview/profile, reviews: books, music, movies. Powwow (June); Travel supplement (May) **Buys 200 mss/year.** Query with published clips and SASE or by phone. Length: 500-800 words. **Pays $3-3.60/published inch.**

Photos Send photos. Identification of subjects required. Offers $25-100/photo. Will pay for film and processing. Buys one time rights.

Tips Knowledge of Aboriginal culture and political issues is a great asset.

Food & Drink

BON APPETIT

Conde Nast Publications, Inc., 6300 wilshire Blvd., Los Angeles CA 90048. Website: www.bonappetit.com. **50% freelance written**. Monthly magazine covering fine food, restaurants, and home entertaining. "*Bon Appetit* readers are upscale food enthusiasts and sophisticated travelers. They eat out often and entertain 4-6 times a month." Estab. 1956. Circ. 1,300,000. Byline given. Pays on acceptance. Buys all rights. Submit seasonal material 1 year in advance. Accepts queries by mail. Responds in 6 weeks to queries. Guidelines for #10 SASE.

Nonfiction Needs travel, food-related, food feature, personal essays. No cartoons, quizzes, poetry, historic food features, or obscure food subjects. **Buys 50 mss/year.** Query with résumé and published clips. No phone calls or e-mails. Length: 150-2,000 words. **Pays $100 and up.**

Photos Never Send photos.

Tips "Writers must have a good knowledge of *Bon Appetit* and the related topics of food, travel, and entertaining (as shown in accompanying clips). A light, lively style is a plus."

$$ CHILE PEPPER

250 W. 57th St., Suite 728, New York NY 10107. (212)262-2247. E-mail: editor@chilepepper.com. **70% freelance written**. Bimonthly magazine on spicy foods. "The magazine is devoted to spicy foods, and most articles include recipes. We have a very devoted readership who love their food hot!" Estab. 1986. Circ. 85,000. Pays on publication. Buys first rights, buys electronic rights. Submit seasonal material 6 months in advance. Guidelines for #10 SASE.

Nonfiction Needs how-to, cooking and gardening with spicy foods, humor having to do with spicy foods, interview, chefs & business people, travel having to do with spicy foods. **Buys 50 mss/year.** Query by e-mail only. Length: 1,000-3,000 words. **Pays $600 minimum for feature article.**

Reprints Send tearsheet or photocopy and information about when and where the material previously appeared.

Photos State availability. Captions, identification of subjects required. Reviews contact sheets, negatives, transparencies, prints. Offers $25/photo minimum Buys one-time rights.

Tips "We're always interested in queries from *food* writers. Articles about spicy foods with 6-8 recipes are just right. No fillers. No unsolicited manuscripts; queries only. E-mail queries preferred."

☐ CLEAN EATING

Improving your life one meal at a time., Robert Kennedy Publishing, Inc., 400 Matheson Blvd. West, Mississauga ON L5R 3M1 Canada. (905)507-3545/(888)254-0767. E-mail: editorial@cleaneatingmag.com. Website: www.cleaneatingmag.com. Bi-monthly magazine covering nutrition. *Clean Eating* encourages eating well. Estab. 2007. Circ. 325,000. Kill fee. Buys all rights.

Nonfiction Send with SAE and $5 for return postage.

Tips Editors seek recipes and stories straight from Mother Nature.

$$$ DRAFT

Draft Publishing, 4350 E. Camelback Rd., Suite A125, Phoenix AZ 85018. (888)806-4677. E-mail: jessica.

daynor@draftmag.com. Website: www.draftmag.com. **60% freelance written**. Bimonthly magazine covering beer and men's lifestyle (including food, travel, sports and leisure). "*DRAFT* is a national men's magazine devoted to beer, breweries and the lifestyle and culture that surrounds it. Read by nearly 300,000 men aged 21-45, *DRAFT* offers formal beer reviews, plus coverage of food, travel, sports and leisure. Writers need not have formal beer knowledge (though that's a plus!), but they should be experienced journalists who can appreciate beer and beer culture." Estab. 2006. Circ. 275,000. Byline given. Pays on publication. Offers 20% kill fee. Publishes ms an average of 2 months after acceptance. Buys first rights, buys electronic rights, buys all rights. All rights for 1 year. Editorial lead time 4 months. Submit seasonal material 6 months in advance. Accepts queries by e-mail. Accepts simultaneous submissions. Responds in 3 weeks to queries. Sample copy for $3 (magazine can also be found on most newsstands for $4.99). Guidelines available at www.draftmag.com/submissions.

Nonfiction Needs features, short front-of-book pieces, how-to's, interviews, travel, food, restaurant and bar pieces, sports and adventure; anything guy-related. The editorial calendar is as follows: November/December: Holiday issue; Jan/Feb: Best of issue; May/June: Food issue; Mar/Apr: Travel issue; July/Aug: All-American issue; Sept/Oct Anniversary issue. Do not want unsolicited mss., beer reviews, brewery profiles. **Buys 80/year. mss/year.** Query with published clips. Length: 250-2,500 words. **50-90¢ for assigned articles.**

Photos Reviews GIF/JPEG files. Offers no additional payment for photos accepted with ms. varies (either one-time rights or no rights).

Columns/Departments Contact: Chris Staten, associate editor, (chris.staten@draftmag.com) for OnTap and OnTap llife, Jessica Daynor, managing editor, for all other departments. 'On Tap' (short FOB pieces on beer-related subjects, 350 words; 'On Tap Life' (short FOB pieces on NON -beer-related subjects (travel, food, sports, home, leisure), 350 words; 'Trek' (travel pieces [need not relate to beer, but it's a plus]), 950 words; 'Taste' (beer-and food-related incident or unique perspective on beer), 750 words. Query with published clips. **Pays 50-80¢.**

Tips "Please see 'What to pitch' and 'what not to pitch' in writer's guidelines."

⊘ FOOD & WINE

American Express Publishing Corp., 1120 Avenue of the Americas, 9th Floor, New York NY 10036. (212)382-5600. Fax: (212)764-2177. Website: www.foodandwine.com. Monthly magazine for the reader who enjoys the finer things in life. Editorial focuses on upscale dining, covering resturants, entertaining at home, and travel destinations. Circ. 964,000. No kill fee. Editorial lead time 6 months.

- Does not buy freelance material or use freelance writers.

GOURMET TRAVELLER WINE

ACP Magazines, Ltd., 54-58 Park St., GPO Box 4088, Sydney NSW 2000 Australia. (61)(2)9282-8000. Fax: (61)(2)9267-4361. Website: www.acp.com.au. **Contact:** Judy Sarris, editor. Bimonthly magazine for the world of wine, celebrating both local and overseas industries. "*Gourmet Traveller WINE* is for wine lovers: It's for those who love to travel, to eat out and to entertain at home, and for those who want to know more about the wine in their glass." Circ. 22,088.

O→ Target men 25-54, professionals & managers.

Nonfiction Needs general interest, how-to, interview, new product, travel. Query.

$$ KASHRUS MAGAZINE

The Bimonthly for the Kosher Consumer and the Trade, The Kashrus Institute, P.O. Box 204, Brooklyn NY 11204. (718)336-8544. E-mail: letters@kashrusmagazine.com. Website: www.kashrusmagazine.com. **25% freelance written. Prefers to work with published/established writers, but will work with new/unpublished writers.** Bimonthly magazine covering the kosher food industry and food production as well as Jewish life in all parts of the world. Estab. 1980. Circ. 10,000. Byline given. Pays on publication. Offers 50% kill fee. Publishes ms an average of 2 months after acceptance. Buys first rights, buys second serial (reprint) rights. Submit seasonal material 2 months in advance. Accepts queries by mail, phone. Accepts previously published material. Accepts simultaneous submissions. Responds in 1 week to queries. Responds in 2 weeks to mss. Sample copy for $2.

Nonfiction Needs general interest, interview, new product, personal experience, photo feature, religious, technical, travel. International Kosher Travel (October); Passover Shopping Guide (March); Domestic Kosher Travel Guide (June). **Buys 8-12 mss/year.** Query with published clips. Length: 1,000-1,500 words. **Pays $100-250 for assigned articles. Pays up to $100 for unsolicited articles.**

Reprints Send tearsheet or photocopy and information about when and where the material previously appeared. Pays 25-50% of amount paid for an original article.

Photos No guidelines; send samples or call. State availability. Offers no additional payment for photos accepted with ms. Buys one time rights.
Columns/Departments Book Review (cookbooks, food technology, kosher food), 250-500 words; People In the News (interviews with kosher personalities), 1,000-1,500 words; Regional Kosher Supervision (report on kosher supervision in a city or community), 1,000-1,500 words; Food Technology (new technology or current technology with accompanying pictures), 1,000-1,500 words; Travel (international, national—must include Kosher information and Jewish communities), 1,000-1,500 words; Regional Kosher Cooking, 1,000-1,500 words. Query with published clips. **Pays $50-250.**
Tips "*Kashrus Magazine* will do more writing on general food technology, production, and merchandising as well as human interest travelogs and regional writing in 2009 than we have done in the past. Areas most open to freelancers are interviews, food technology, cooking and food preparation, dining, regional reporting, and travel, but we also feature healthy eating and lifestyles, redecorating, catering, and hospitals and health care. We welcome stories on the availability and quality of kosher foods and services in communities across the US and throughout the world. Some of our best stories have been by non-Jewish writers about kosher observance in their region. We also enjoy humorous articles. Just send a query with clips and we'll try to find a storyline that's right for you, or better yet, call us to discuss a storyline."

SAVEUR MAGAZINE

Bonnier Publications, 15 East 32nd St., 12th Floor, New York NY 10016. (212)219-7400. Website: www.saveur.com. **Contact:** James Oseland, editor-in-chief. Magazine published 9 times/year. "Saveur seeks out stories from around the globe that weave together culture, tradition, and people through the language of food. On every page the magazine honors a fundamental truth: cooking is one of the most universal - and beautiful - means of human expression. It is written for sophisticated, upscale lovers of food, wine, travel, and adventure." Estab. 1994. Circ. 365,000. No kill fee. Accepts queries by mail, e-mail. Sample copy for $5 at newsstands. Guidelines by e-mail.
Nonfiction Query with published clips.
Columns/Departments Query with published clips.
Tips "Queries and stories should be detailed and specific, and personal ties to the subject matter are important—let us know why you should be the one to write the story. Familiarize yourself with our departments, and the magazine style as a whole, and pitch your stories accordingly. Also, we rarely assign restaurant-based pieces."

⊘ TASTE OF HOME

Reader's Digest Association, Inc., 5400 S. 60th St., Greendale WI 53129. (414)423-0100. Fax: (414)423-8463. E-mail: editors@tasteofhome.com. Website: www.tasteofhome.com. Bimonthly magazine. *Taste of Home* is dedicated to home cooks, from beginners to the very experienced. Editorial includes recipes and serving suggestions, interviews and ideas from the publication's readers and field editors based around the country, and reviews of new cooking tools and gadgets. Circ. 3.5 million. No kill fee.

- Does not buy freelance material or use freelance writers.

TEA A MAGAZINE

Olde English Tea Company, Inc., 3 Devotion Rd., P.O. Box 348, Scotland CT 06264. (860)456-1145. Fax: (860)456-1023. E-mail: teamag@teamag.com. Website: www.teamag.com. **75% freelance written.** Quarterly magazine covering anything tea related. "*Tea, A Magazine* is an exciting magazine all about tea, both as a drink and for its cultural significance in art, music, literature, history and society." Estab. 1994. Circ. 9,500. Byline given. Pays on publication. Publishes ms an average of 1 year after acceptance. Buys all rights. Editorial lead time 9 months. Submit seasonal material 6 months in advance. Responds in 6 months to mss. Guidelines by e-mail.
Nonfiction Needs book excerpts, essays, general interest, historical, how-to, humor, interview, personal experience, photo feature, travel. Send complete ms. **Pays negotiable amount.**
Photos Send photos. Captions, identification of subjects required. Reviews prints, GIF/JPEG files (300 dpi). Negotiates payment individually. Buys all rights.
Columns/Departments Readers' Stories (personal experience involving tea); Book Reviews (review on tea books). Send complete ms. **Pays negotiable amount**
Fiction Does not want anything that is not tea related. Send complete ms. **Pays negotiable amount.**
Poetry Needs avant-garde, free verse, haiku, light verse, traditional. Does not want anything that is not tea related.
Tips "Please submit full manuscripts with photos and make sure it is tea related."

$$$$ WINE ENTHUSIAST MAGAZINE

Wine Enthusiast Companies, 333 North Bedford Rd., Mt. Kisco NY 10549. E-mail: tmoriarty@wineenthusiast.net. Website: winemag.com. **40% freelance written**. Monthly magazine covering the lifestyle of wine. Our readers are upscale and educated, but not necessarily super-sophisticated about wine itself. Our informal, irreverent approach appeals to savvy enophiles and newbies alike. Estab. 1988. Circ. 80,000. Byline given. Pays on acceptance. Offers 25% kill fee. Makes work-for-hire assignments. Editorial lead time 4 months. Submit seasonal material 5 months in advance. Accepts queries by e-mail. Responds in 2 weeks to queries. Responds in 2 months to mss.

Nonfiction Needs essays, humor, interview, new product, personal experience. **Buys 5 mss/year. Pays $750-2,500 for assigned articles. Pays $750-2,000 for unsolicited articles. Pays 50¢/word for website.**

Photos Send photos. Reviews GIF/JPEG files. Offers $135-400/photo.

$$ WINE PRESS NORTHWEST

P.O. Box 2608, Tri-Cities WA 99302. (509)582-1564. Fax: (509)585-7221. E-mail: edegerman@winepressnw.com. Website: www.winepressnw.com. **Contact:** Eric Degerman, managing editor. **50% freelance written**. Quarterly magazine covering Pacific Northwest wine (Washington, Oregon, British Columbia, Idaho). "We focus narrowly on Pacific Northwest wine. If we write about travel, it's where to go to drink NW wine. If we write about food, it's what goes with NW wine. No beer, no spirits." Estab. 1998. Circ. 12,000. Byline given. Pays on publication. Offers 20% kill fee. Publishes ms an average of 3 months after acceptance. Buys first North American serial rights, buys electronic rights. Editorial lead time 3 months. Submit seasonal material 3 months in advance. Accepts queries by mail, e-mail, fax. Accepts simultaneous submissions. Responds in 1 month to queries. Sample copy free or online Guidelines free.

Nonfiction Needs general interest, historical, interview, new product, photo feature, travel. No beer, spirits, non-NW (California wine, etc.) **Buys 30 mss/year.** Query with published clips. Length: 1,500-2,500 words. **Pays $300.**

Photos State availability. Identification of subjects required. Reviews contact sheets. Negotiates payment individually Buys one time rights.

Tips "Writers must be familiar with *Wine Press Northwest* and should have a passion for the region, its wines, and cuisine."

$$$ WINE SPECTATOR

M. Shanken Communications, Inc., 387 Park Ave. S., 8th Floor, New York NY 10016. Fax: (212)684-5424. E-mail: winespec@mshanken.com. Website: www.winespectator.com. **20% freelance written. Prefers to work with published/established writers**. Monthly news magazine. Estab. 1976. Circ. 350,000. Byline given. Pays within 30 days of publication. No kill fee. Publishes ms an average of 2 months after acceptance. Buys all rights. Makes work-for-hire assignments. Submit seasonal material 4 months in advance. Accepts queries by mail, fax. Responds in 3 months to queries. Guidelines for #10 SASE.

Nonfiction Needs general interest, news about wine or wine events, interview, of wine, vintners, wineries, opinion, photo feature, travel, dining and other lifestyle pieces. No winery promotional pieces or articles by writers who lack sufficient knowledge to write below just surface data. Query. Length: 100-2,000 words. **Pays $100-1,000.**

Photos Send photos. Captions, identification of subjects, model releases required. Pays $75 minimum for color transparencies. Buys all rights.

Tips "A solid knowledge of wine is a must. Query letters essential, detailing the story idea. New, refreshing ideas which have not been covered before stand a good chance of acceptance. *Wine Spectator* is a consumer-oriented news magazine, but we are interested in some trade stories; brevity is essential."

Games & Puzzles

$ THE BRIDGE BULLETIN

American Contract Bridge League, 6575 Windchase Dr., Horn Lake MS 38637-1523. (901)332-5586, ext. 1291. Fax: (901)398-7754. E-mail: editor@acbl.org. Website: www.acbl.org. **20% freelance written**. Monthly magazine covering duplicate (tournament) bridge. Estab. 1938. Circ. 155,000. Byline given. Pays on publication. Publishes ms an average of 3 months after acceptance. Buys first rights, buys second serial (reprint) rights. Editorial lead time 2 months. Accepts queries by mail, e-mail. Accepts previously published material. Accepts simultaneous submissions.

Nonfiction Needs book excerpts, essays, how-to, play better bridge, humor, interview, new product, personal experience, photo feature, technical, travel. **Buys 6 mss/year.** Query. Length: 500-2,000 words. **Pays $100/page.**
Photos Color required. State availability. Identification of subjects required. Negotiates payment individually. Buys all rights.
Tips "Articles must relate to contract bridge in some way. Cartoons on bridge welcome."

$ $ CHESS LIFE

United States Chess Federation, P.O. Box 3967, Crossville TN 38557-3967. (931)787-1234. Fax: (931)787-1200. E-mail: dlūcas@uschess.org. Website: www.uschess.org. **15% freelance written. Works with a small number of new/unpublished writers/year.** Monthly magazine. "*Chess Life* is the official publication of the United States Chess Federation, covering news of most major chess events, both here and abroad, with special emphasis on the triumphs and exploits of American players." Estab. 1939. Circ. 85,000. Byline given. No kill fee. Publishes ms an average of 6 months after acceptance. Buys first rights. Submit seasonal material 6 months in advance. Accepts queries by mail, e-mail, fax, phone. Accepts simultaneous submissions. Responds in 3 months to mss. Sample copy and writer's guidelines for 9 × 11 SAE with 5 first-class stamps
Nonfiction All must have some relation to chess. Needs general interest, historical, humor, interview, of a famous chess player or organizer, photo feature, chess centered, technical. No stories about personal experiences with chess. **Buys 30-40 mss/year.** Query with samples if new to publication 3,000 words maximum. **Pays $100/page (800-1,000 words).**
Reprints "Send tearsheet, photocopy or typed ms with rights for sale noted and information about when and where the material previously appeared."
Photos Captions, identification of subjects, model releases required. Reviews b&w contact sheets and prints, and color prints and slides. Pays $25-100 inside; covers negotiable. Buys all or negotiable rights.
Fillers Submit with samples and clips. Buys first or negotiable rights to cartoons and puzzles. **Pays $25 upon acceptance.**
Tips "Articles must be written from an informed point of view. Freelancers in major population areas (except NY and LA) who are interested in short personality profiles and perhaps news reporting have the best opportunities. We're looking for more personality pieces on chess players around the country; not just the stars, but local masters, talented youths, and dedicated volunteers. Freelancers interested in such pieces might let us know of their interest and their range. Could be we know of an interesting story in their territory that needs covering. Examples of published articles include a locally produced chess television program, a meeting of chess set collectors from around the world, chess in our prisons, and chess in the works of several famous writers."

GAMEPRO

IDG Entertainment/GamePro, 555 12th St., Suite 1000, Oakland CA 94607-73635. (510)768-2700. Fax: (510)768-2701. Website: www.gamepro.com. Bob Huseby, sr. v.p. & publisher. **Contact:** Mike Weigand, man. ed. Monthly magazine. "*GamePro* is the industry leader among independent multiplatform video gaming magazines." Estab. 1989. Circ. 2,700,000. Byline given. No kill fee.

- "Our audience delights in reading cover to cover each and every month. Our approachable editorial voice continues to celebrate the fun in gaming while helping our readers find the best games for their playing habits. Contact specific editor. Mostly staff written."

Nonfiction Needs new product. Query.
Tips "GamePro readers are the past, present and future of the video games industry. Reach them today and drive brand awareness and product adoption for years to come."

$ $ POKER AND POOL MAGAZINE

Jester Media, Raleigh NC 27604. E-mail: pokerandpoolmag@aol.com. Website: www.pokerandpoolmagazine.com. **90% freelance written**. Quarterly magazine covering poker and pool. *PPM* is for the player. Informative articles, event calendars, and more. *PPM* is the only magazine of its kind. Estab. 2007. Circ. 25,000. Byline given. Pays on acceptance. Publishes ms an average of 3 months after acceptance. Buys first rights, buys electronic rights. Editorial lead time 2 months. Submit seasonal material 2 months in advance. Accepts queries by mail, e-mail. Responds in 2 weeks to queries. Sample copy available online. Guidelines available online.
Nonfiction Needs book excerpts, essays, expose, general interest, historical, how-to, humor, inspirational, interview, new product, opinion, personal experience, photo feature, technical, travel. Does not want

complaints, gripes, bad beat stories, etc. **Buys 50 mss/year.** Query. Length: 100-10,000 words. **Pays $0-200.**
Photos State availability. Reviews GIF/JPEG files. Offers $0-50/photo. Buys one time rights.
Fiction Needs adventure, fantasy, historical, horror, humorous, mainstream, mystery, romance, science fiction, slice-of-life vignettes, suspense, western. **Buys 10 mss/year.** Query. Length: 500-10,000 words. **Pays $0-200.**
Poetry Needs avant-garde, free verse, haiku, light verse, traditional. Buys 10 poems/year. Submit maximum 5 poems. Length: 3-25 lines.
Fillers Length: 10-200 words. **Pays $0-25.**
Tips Know poker or pool. Get your facts right. Don't waste our time if you don't consider yourself a player.

$$ POKER PRO MAGAZINE

Poker Pro Media, 4733 W. Atlantic Ave., C-18, Delray Beach FL 33445. E-mail: jwenzel@pokerpromedia.com. Website: www. pokerpromagazine.com. **75% freelance written**. Monthly magazine covering poker, gambling, nightlife. "We want articles about poker and gambling-related articles only; also nightlife in gaming cities and articles on gaming destinations." Estab. 2005. Circ. 150,000. Byline given. Pays on publication. No kill fee. Publishes ms an average of 1 month after acceptance. Buys all rights. Editorial lead time 1½ months. Submit seasonal material 2 months in advance. Accepts queries by e-mail. Responds in 1 week to queries. Responds in 1 month to mss. Sample copy by e-mail. Guidelines by e-mail.
Nonfiction Needs book excerpts, essays, expose, general interest, historical, how-to, humor, interview, new product, opinion, personal experience, photo feature, travel. **Buys 125 mss/year.** Query. Length: 800-2,500 words. **Pays $100-$200 for assigned articles. Pays $100-$200 for unsolicited articles.**
Photos State availability. Captions, identification of subjects, model releases required. Reviews GIF/JPEG files. Negotiates payment individually. It varies.

⊘ 🌐 TAKE 5

ACP Magazines, Ltd., 54-58 Park St., Sydney NSW 2000 Australia. (61)(2)9282-8000. Fax: (61)(2)9267-4361. Website: www.acp.com.au. **Contact:** Belinda Wallis, editor. Weekly magazine combining the intrigue of real life stories derived from readers contributions with the opportunity to win prizes through a 24-page pull-out puzzle book. Estab. 255,261.
- Query before submitting.

⊘ 🌐 THAT'S LIFE!

Pacific Magazines, 35-51 Mitchell St., McMahons Point NSW 2060 Australia. (61)(2)9464-3300. Fax: (61)(2)9464-3483. E-mail: thatslife@pacificmags.com.au. Website: www.thatslife.co.au. **Contact:** Linda Smith, editor. Weekly magazine providing hours of fun and the chance to win great games.
- Query before submitting.

WOMAN POKER PLAYER MAGAZINE

915 Chester St., New Westminster BC V3L 4N4 Canada. (604)628-2358. Fax: (516)977-9409. E-mail: editorial@womanpokerplayer.com. Website: www.womanpokerplayer.com. **80% freelance written**. Bimonthly magazine covering poker. *Woman Poker Player* is for the woman who enjoys poker. We are a lifestyle publication that also covers fashion and wellness. Estab. 2005. Circ. 35,000. Byline sometimes given. Pays on publication. No kill fee. Publishes ms an average of 2 months after acceptance. Buys all rights. Editorial lead time 1 month. Submit seasonal material 1 month in advance. Accepts queries by e-mail. Accepts simultaneous submissions. Sample copy free.
Nonfiction Needs book excerpts, humor, interview, poker. Query. Length: 1,100-2,000 words. **Pays variable amount.**
Photos State availability. Captions, model releases required. Reviews contact sheets, GIF/JPEG files. Negotiates payment individually. Buys one time rights.
Fiction Needs cond novels, poker. Query. Length: 1,000-2,000 words.
Tips Send pitch via e-mail stating writing experience.

Gay & Lesbian Interest

$$ THE ADVOCATE

Liberation Publications, Inc., 6380 Wilshire Blvd., Suite 1400, Los Angeles CA 90048. (323)852-7200. Fax:

(323)852-7272. E-mail: newsroom@advocate.com. Website: www.advocate.com. Biweekly magazine covering national news events with a gay and lesbian perspective on the issues. Estab. 1967. Circ. 120,000. Byline given. Pays on publication. Buys first North American serial rights. Responds in 1 month to queries. Sample copy for $3.95. Guidelines by e-mail.

Nonfiction "Here are elements we look for in all articles: *Angling*: An angle is the one editorial tool we have to attract a reader's attention. An *Advocate* editor won't make an assignment unless he or she has worked out a very specific angle with you. Once you've worked out the angle with an editor, don't deviate from it without letting the editor know. Some of the elements we look for in angles are: a news hook; an open question or controversy; a `why' or `how' element or novel twist; national appeal; and tight focus. *Content*: Lesbian and gay news stories in all areas of life: arts, sciences, financial, medical, cyberspace, etc. *Tone*: Tone is the element that makes an emotional connection. Some characteristics we look for: toughness; edginess; fairness and evenhandedness; multiple perspectives." Needs expose, interview, news reporting and investigating. gays on campus, coming out interviews with celebrities, HIV and health Query. Length: 1,200 words. **Pays $550.**

Columns/Departments Arts & Media (news and profiles of well-known gay or lesbians in entertainment) is most open to freelancers, 750 words. Query. **Pays $100-500.**

Tips "*The Advocate* is a unique newsmagazine. While we report on gay and lesbian issues and are published by one of the country's oldest and most established gay-owned companies, we also play by the rules of mainstream-not-gay-community-journalism."

$ BENT MAGAZINE

Top Down Productions LLC, E-mail: query@bent-magazine.com. Website: www.bent-magazine.com. **100% freelance written**. Quarterly magazine covering homoerotic romantic literature. "*BENT Magazine* seeks to provide quality romantic fiction and articles of interest to fans of yaoi and slash. All fiction works must focus on a homosexual male main character and/or male/male romance." Estab. 2006. Circ. 40. Byline given. Pays on publication. Publishes ms an average of 1 month after acceptance. Buys first North American serial rights, buys first rights, buys one-time rights, buys second serial (reprint) rights, buys electronic rights. Editorial lead time 4-6 months. Submit seasonal material 4 months in advance. Accepts queries by e-mail. Accepts previously published material. Accepts simultaneous submissions. Responds in 1 week to queries. Responds in 2-4 months to mss. Sample copy available online. Guidelines available online.

Nonfiction Needs book excerpts, essays, general interest, historical, new product, opinion, reviews. Does not want personal experience testimonials. **Buys 36 mss/year.** Send complete ms. Length: 1,000-5,000 words. **Pays $5.**

Columns/Departments Manga Reviews; Book/Movie/Anime Reviews, 1,000 words. Query with or without published clips or send complete ms. **Pays $5.**

Fiction Needs adventure, erotica, fantasy, historical, horror, humorous, mainstream, mystery, novel concepts, romance, science fiction, serialized, slice-of-life vignettes, suspense, western. Does not want stories that contain heterosexual sex. We are not interested in just-the-sex stories with no development of plot or characters. **Buys 48 mss/year.** Query or send complete ms. Length: 1,000-50,000 words. **Pays $5-30.**

Tips "Stories in the sample issue provide a good generalization of what we are looking for. If unsure whether a submission meets the needs of the magazine, please query first with a brief summary/description of the intended work."

$$ CLOUT MAGAZINE

The Standard for Gays and Lesbians in Southern California, Los Angeles News Group, 300 Oceangate, Suite 150, Long Beach CA 90844. (562)499-1419. Fax: (562)499-1450. E-mail: zamna.avila@presstelegram.com. **99% freelance written**. Bimonthly magazine covering home, travel and entertainment. *Clout* is a new and sophisticated magazine geared toward the more affluent gays and lesbians in the community. Estab. 2008. Circ. 225,000. Byline given. Pays on publication. Offers $50 kill fee. Buys first rights, buys electronic rights. Accepts queries by e-mail.

Nonfiction Needs general interest, historical, how-to, humor, inspirational, interview, opinion, personal experience, photo feature, travel. **Buys 80-100 mss/year.** Query with published clips. Length: 500-2,500 words. **Pays $100-200.**

Photos Send photos. Captions, identification of subjects required. Reviews GIF/JPEG files. Offers $125-200/photo. Buys one time rights.

Columns/Departments She Speaks You Listen (lawyer gives the gay/lesbian perspective on issue); Ask a Hairdresser (advice column for gays and lesbians), both 500 words. Query with published clips. **Pays $125-200.**

Fillers Length: 100-500 words. **Pays $100-150.**

Tips I appreciate people who are local to Southern California, especially Long Beach and have story ideas to contribute. Freelancers must have great work ethics, skillful writing/photo/illustration techniques and flexibility.

$ $ CURVE MAGAZINE

1550 Bryant St., Suite 510, San Francisco CA 94103. E-mail: editor@curvemag.com. Website: www.curvemag.com. **60% freelance written.** Magazine published 10 times/year covering lesbian entertainment, culture, and general interest categories. We want dynamic and provocative articles that deal with issues, ideas, or cultural moments that are of interest or relevance to gay women. Estab. 1990. Circ. 80,000. Byline given. Pays on publication. Offers 25% kill fee. Buys first North American serial rights. Editorial lead time 6 months. Submit seasonal material 6 months in advance. Accepts queries by mail, e-mail, fax. Sample copy for $3.95 with $2 postage. Guidelines available online.

Nonfiction Needs general interest, photo feature, travel, celebrity interview/profile. Sex (February); Travel (March); Fashion + Design (April); Weddings (May); Pride (June); Music (August); School (September); Travel (October); Money/Careers (November); Gift Guide (December). No fiction or poetry. **Buys 100 mss/year.** Query. Length: 200-2,000 words. **Pays 15¢/word.**

Photos Send hi-res photos with submission. Captions, identification of subjects, model releases required. Offers $25-100/photo; negotiates payment individually. Buys one time rights.

Tips Feature articles generally fit into 1 of the following categories: Celebrity profiles (lesbian, bisexual, or straight women who are icons for the lesbian community or actively involved in coalition-building with the lesbian community); community segment profiles—i.e., lesbian firefighters, drag kings, sports teams (multiple interviews with a variety of women in different parts of the country representing a diversity of backgrounds); noncelebrity profiles (activities of unknown or low-profile lesbian and bisexual activists/political leaders, athletes, filmmakers, dancers, writers, musicians, etc.); controversial issues (spark a dialogue about issues that divide us as a community, and the ways in which lesbians of different backgrounds fail to understand and support one another). We are not interested in inflammatory articles that incite or enrage readers without offering a channel for action, but we do look for challenging, thought-provoking work. The easiest way to get published in *Curve* is with a front-of-the-book piece for our Curvatures section, topical/fun/newsy pop culture articles that are 100-350 words.

$ ECHO MAGAZINE

ACE Publishing, Inc., P.O. Box 16630, Phoenix AZ 85011-6630. (602)266-0550. Fax: (602)266-0773. E-mail: editor@echomag.com. Website: www.echomag.com. **30-40% freelance written.** Biweekly magazine covering gay and lesbian issues. *Echo Magazine* is a newsmagazine for gay, lesbian, bisexual, and transgendered persons in the Phoenix metro area and throughout the state of Arizona. Editorial content needs to be pro-gay, that is, supportive of GLBT equality in all areas of American life. Estab. 1989. Circ. 15,000-18,000. Byline given. Pays on publication. No kill fee. Publishes ms an average of less than 1 month after acceptance. Buys all rights. Editorial lead time 1-2 months. Submit seasonal material 1-2 months in advance. Accepts queries by e-mail. Responds in 2 weeks to queries. Responds in 1 month to mss. Sample copy available online. Guidelines by e-mail.

Nonfiction Needs book excerpts, essays, historical, humor, interview, opinion, personal experience, photo feature, travel. Pride Festival (April); Arts issue (August); Holiday Gift/Decor (December). No articles on topics unrelated to our GLBT readers, or anything that is not pro-gay. **Buys 10-20 mss/year.** Query. Length: 500-2,000 words. **Pays $30-40.**

Photos State availability. Captions, identification of subjects, model releases required. Reviews contact sheets, GIF/JPEG files. Negotiates payment individually. Buys all rights.

Columns/Departments Guest Commentary (opinion on GLBT issues), 500-1,000 words; Arts/Entertainment (profiles of GLBT or relevant celebrities, or arts issues), 800-1,500 words. Query. **Pays $30-40.**

Tips Know Phoenix (or other areas of Arizona) and its GLBT community. Please don't send nongay-related or nonpro-gay material. Research your topics thoroughly and write professionally. Our print content and online contenty are very similar.

$ THE GAY & LESBIAN REVIEW

Gay & Lesbian Review, Inc., P.O. Box 180300, Boston MA 02118. (617)421-0082. E-mail: HGLR@glreview.

com. Website: www.glreview.com. **100% freelance written**. Bimonthly magazine covers gay and lesbian history, culture, and politics. In-depth essays on GLBT history, biography, the arts, political issues, written in clear, lively prose targeted to the 'literate nonspecialist.' Estab. 1994. Circ. 12,000. Byline given. Pays on publication. No kill fee. Buys first rights. Editorial lead time 2 months. Accepts queries by mail, e-mail, phone. Accepts simultaneous submissions. Sample copy free. Guidelines free.

Nonfiction Needs essays, historical, humor, interview, opinion, book reviews. Does not want fiction, memoirs, personal reflections. Query. Length: 1,500-5,000 words. **Pays $100.**

Poetry Needs avant-garde, free verse, traditional. **No payment for poems.**

Tips We prefer that a proposal be e-mailed before a completed draft is sent.

$$$$ GENRE

Genre Publishing, 213 W. 35th St., Suite 402, New York NY 10001. (212)594-8181. Fax: (212)594-8263. E-mail: genre@genremagazine.com. Website: www.genremagazine.com. **60% freelance written.** Monthly magazine. *Genre*, America's best-selling gay men's lifestyle magazine, covers entertainment, fashion, travel, and relationships in a hip, upbeat, upscale voice. Estab. 1991. Circ. 50,000. Byline given. Pays on publication. Offers 25% kill fee. Publishes ms an average of 3 months after acceptance. Buys first North American serial rights, buys electronic rights. Editorial lead time 10 weeks. Submit seasonal material 10 weeks in advance. Accepts queries by mail, e-mail, fax. May only respond if interested. Sample copy for $6.95 ($5 plus $1.95 postage).

Nonfiction Needs essays, expose, general interest, historical, how-to, humor, inspirational, interview, new product, opinion, personal experience, photo feature, religious, travel, relationships, fashion. Not interested in articles on 2 males negotiating a sexual situation or coming out stories. **Buys variable number mss/year.** Query with published clips. Length: 500-1,500 words. **Pays $150-1,600.**

Photos State availability. Model releases required. Reviews contact sheets, 3 × 5 or 5 × 7 prints. Negotiates payment individually Buys one time rights.

Columns/Departments Body (how to better the body); Mind (how to better the mind); Spirit (how to better the spirit), all 700 words; Reviews (books, movies, music, travel, etc.), 500 words. variable number of Query with published clips or send complete ms. **Pays $200 maximum**

Fiction Needs adventure, experimental, horror, humorous, mainstream, mystery, novel concepts, religious, romance, science fiction, slice-of-life vignettes, suspense. **Buys 10 mss/year.** Send complete ms. Length: 2,000-4,000 words.

Tips Like you, we take our journalistic responsibilities and ethics very seriously, and we subscribe to the highest standards of the profession. We expect our writers to represent original work that is not libelous and does not infringe upon the copyright or violate the right of privacy of any other person, firm or corporation.

$$ GIRLFRIENDS MAGAZINE

Lesbian Culture, Politics, and Entertainment, H.A.F. Publishing, 3181 Mission St., PMB 30, San Francisco CA 94110. E-mail: staff@girlfriendsmag.com. Website: www.girlfriendsmag.com. Monthly lesbian magazine. *Girlfriends* provides its readers with intelligent, entertaining and visually pleasing coverage of culture, politics, and entertainment—all from an informed and critical lesbian perspective. Estab. 1994. Circ. 75,000. Byline given. Pays on publication. Offers 50% kill fee. Publishes ms an average of 6 months after acceptance. Buys first rights and use for advertising/promoting *Girlfriends*. Editorial lead time 3 months. Submit seasonal material 6 months in advance. Accepts queries by mail, e-mail. Accepts simultaneous submissions. Responds in 3 weeks to queries. Responds in 2 months to mss. Sample copy for $4.95 plus $1.50 postage or online. Guidelines available online.

- *Girlfriends* is not accepting fiction, poetry or fillers.

Nonfiction Needs book excerpts, essays, expose, historical, humor, interview, new product, opinion, personal experience, photo feature, religious, technical, travel, investigative features. Sex, music, bridal, sports and Hollywood issues, breast cancer issue. Special features: Best lesbian restaurants in the US; best places to live. **Buys 20-25 mss/year.** Query with published clips. Length: 1,000-3,500 words. **Pays 15¢/word.**

Reprints Send photocopy or typed ms with rights for sale ted and information about when and where the material previously appeared. Negotiable payment.

Photos Send photos. Captions, identification of subjects, model releases required. Reviews contact sheets, 4 × 5 or 21/4 × 21/4 transparencies, prints. Offers $30-50/photo Buys one time rights.

Columns/Departments Book reviews, 900 words; Music reviews, 600 words; Travel, 600 words; Opinion pieces, 1,000 words; Humor, 600 words. Query with published clips. **Pays 15¢/word.**

Tips Be unafraid of controversy—articles should focus on problems and debates raised in lesbian culture, politics, and sexuality. Avoid being `politically correct.' We don't just want to know what's happening in the lesbian world, we want to know how what's happening in the world affects lesbians.

$$$$ THE GUIDE

P.O. Box 905, Old Chelsea Station, New York NY 10113. (646)448-4223. Fax: (646)448-4223. E-mail: letters@guidemag.com. Website: www.guidemag.com. **Contact:** Mark Sullivan, man. ed. **75% freelance written**. Monthly magazine on the gay and lesbian news, features, and travel. Estab. 1981. Circ. 45,000. Pays on publication. Offers negotiable kill fee. Publishes ms an average of 2 months after acceptance. Buys first rights. Submit seasonal material 4 months in advance. Accepts queries by mail, e-mail. Accepts previously published material. Accepts simultaneous submissions. Responds in 3 months to queries.

Nonfiction Needs book excerpts, if yet unpublished, essays, expose, general interest, historical, humor, interview, opinion, personal experience, photo feature, religious. **Buys 48 mss/year.** Send complete ms. Length: 500-2,500 words. **Pays $100-1,750.**

Reprints Occasionally buys previously published submissions. Pays 100% of amount paid for an original article.

Photos Send photos. Captions, identification of subjects, model releases required. Reviews contact sheets. Pays $15/image used. Buys one-time rights.

Tips "Brevity, humor, and strong point of view appreciated. Writing on sex and politics are particularly appreciated. We purchase very few freelance travel pieces; those that we do buy are usually on less commercial destinations."

$ HX MAGAZINE

Two Queens, Inc., 230 W. 17th St., 8th Floor, New York NY 10011. (212)352-3535. E-mail: info@hx.com. Website: www.hx.com. **25% freelance written**. Weekly magazine covering gay New York City nightlife and entertainment. Estab. 1991. Circ. 39,000. Byline given. Pays on publication. No kill fee. Publishes ms an average of 1 month after acceptance. Buys first North American serial rights, buys second serial (reprint) rights, buys electronic rights. Editorial lead time 2 months. Submit seasonal material 2 months in advance.

Nonfiction Needs general interest, arts and entertainment, celebrity profiles, reviews. **Buys 50 mss/year.** Query with published clips. Length: 500-2,000 words. **Pays $50-150. Pays $25-100 for unsolicited articles.**

Reprints Send tearsheet or photocopy with rights for sale noted and information about when and where the material previously appeared. Pays 50% of amount paid for an original article.

Photos State availability. Captions, identification of subjects, model releases required. Reviews contact sheets, negatives, 8 × 10 prints. Buys one-time, reprint and electronic reprint rights.

Columns/Departments Query with published clips. **Pays $25-125.**

$$ N INSTINCT MAGAZINE

Instinct Publishing, 303 N. Glenoaks Blvd., Suite L-120, Burbank CA 91502. E-mail: editor@instinctmag.com. Website: www.instinctmag.com. **40% freelance written**. Gay men's monthly lifestyle and entertainment magazine. "*Instinct* is a blend of *Cosmo* and *Maxim* for gay men. We're smart, sexy, irreverent, and we always have a sense of humor—a unique style that has made us the #1 gay men's magazine in the US." Estab. 1997. Circ. 115,000. Byline given. Pays on publication. Offers 20% kill fee. Buys all rights. Editorial lead time 2-3 months. Accepts queries by mail, e-mail. Accepts simultaneous submissions. Sample copy available online. Guidelines available online.

Nonfiction Be inventive and specific—an article on 'dating' isn't saying much unless there is a really great hook. Needs expose, general interest, humor, interview, celebrity and non-celebrity, travel, basically anything of interest to gay men will be considered. Does not want first-person accounts or articles. Send complete ms. Length: 850-2,000 words. **Pays $50-300.**

Photos Captions, identification of subjects, model releases required. Negotiates payment individually. Buys all rights.

Columns/Departments Health (gay, off-kilter), 800 words; Fitness (irreverent), 500 words; Movies, Books (edgy, sardonic), 800 words; Music, Video Games (indie, underground), 800 words. **Pays $150-250.**

Tips "While *Instinct* publishes a wide variety of features and columns having to do with gay men's issues, we maintain our signature irreverent, edgy tone throughout. When pitching stories (e-mail is preferred), be as specific as possible, and try to think beyond the normal scope of 'gay relationship' features. An article on 'Dating Tips,' for example, will not be considered, while an article on 'Tips on

Dating Two Guys At Once' is more our slant. We rarely accept finished articles. We keep a special eye out for pitches on investigational/expose-type stories geared toward our audience."

MANDATE

225 Broadway, Suite 2801, New York NY 10007-3079. E-mail: mandatemag@aol.com. Website: www.mandatemag.com. Monthly magazine covering gay male erotica & lifestyle. Male photography, freelance erotic fiction, assigned columns & reviews. Estab. 1974. Circ. 100,000. Byline given. Pays on publication. No kill fee. Publishes ms an average of 5 months after acceptance. Buys first North American serial rights. Second Serial (reprint) Rights very rare Editorial lead time 3 months. Accepts queries by mail, e-mail. immediately. Responds in 1 month to mss. Sample copy available online. Guidelines by e-mail.
Nonfiction Nonfiction columns & reviews are staff written or assigned.
Fiction Contact: Managing editor. Needs erotica. No romance, softcore erotica. **Buys 24 mss/year.** Send complete ms. Length: 2,000-3,500+ words. **Pays $150.**

$$ N MENSBOOK JOURNAL

47 West Communications, LLC, P.O. Box 148, Sturbridge MA 01566. Fax: (508)347-8150. E-mail: editorial@mensbook.com. Website: www.mensbook.com. **Contact:** P.C. Carr, editor/pub. **75% freelance written.** Quarterly paperback book-serial covering gay men's journal. "We target bright, inquisitive, discerning gay men who share our criticism of the gay culture of pride and want more from gay media. We seek primarily first-person autobiographical pieces—then: biographies, political and social analysis, cartoons, short fiction, commentary, travel, humor." Estab. 2008. Circ. start up. Byline given. Pays on publication. Offers $10 kill fee. Buys first rights. Editorial lead time 4 months. Submit seasonal material 6 months in advance. Accepts queries by e-mail. Responds in 4 weeks to queries. Sample copy sent free by pdf. www.mensbook.com/writersguidelines.htm
Nonfiction Contact: P.C. Carr, publisher. Needs first-person pieces; essays; think-pieces; expose; humor; inspirational profiles of courage and triumph over adversity; interview/profile; religion/philosophy vis-a-vis the gay experience; opinion; travel. "We do not want celebrity profiles/commentary, chatty, campy gossip; sexual conjecture about famous people; film reviews." **Buys 25 mss/year.** Query by e-mail. Length: 1,000-2,500 words. **Pays $20-100 for assigned articles and for unsolicited articles.**
Fiction Contact: Payson Fitch, managing editor. Needs adventure, erotica, fantasy, mystery/suspense, slice-of-life vignettes-of-life vignettes. Nothing poorly written. **Buys 10-12 mss/year.** Send complete ms. Length: 750-3,000 words.
Poetry Contact: J. K. Small, poetry editor. Needs avant-garde, free verse, haiku, light verse, traditional. Buys 8 poems/year.
Tips "Be a tight writer, with a cogent, potent message. Structure your work with well-organized progressive sequencing, edit everything down before you send it over so we know it is the best you can do and we'll work together from there."

$$ METROSOURCE MAGAZINE

MetroSource Publishing, Inc., 137 W. 19th St., 2nd Floor, New York NY 10011. E-mail: letters@metrosource.com. Website: www.metrosource.com. **Contact:** Editor. **75% freelance written.** Magazine published 6 times/year. "*MetroSource* is an upscale, glossy, 4-color lifestyle magazine targeted to an urban, professional gay and lesbian readership." Estab. 1990. Circ. 145,000. Byline given. Pays on publication. Publishes ms an average of 2 months after acceptance. Editorial lead time 4 months. Submit seasonal material 4 months in advance. Accepts queries by mail, e-mail, fax, phone. Accepts simultaneous submissions. Sample copy for $5.
Nonfiction Needs exposè, interview, opinion, photo feature, travel. **Buys 20 mss/year.** Query with published clips. Length: 1,000-1,800 words. **Pays $100-400.**
Photos State availability. Captions, model releases required. Negotiates payment individually.
Columns/Departments Book, film, television, and stage reviews; health columns; and personal diary and opinion pieces. Word lengths vary. Query with published clips. **Pays $200.**

OUT

Box 1253, Old Chelsea Station, New York NY 10013. (212)242-8100. Fax: (212)242-8338. E-mail: letters@out.com. Website: www.out.com. **70% freelance written.** Monthly national magazine covering gay and lesbian general-interest topics. Our subjects range from current affairs to culture, from fitness to finance. Estab. 1992. Circ. 165,000. Byline given. Pays on publication. Offers 25% kill fee. Publishes ms an average of 3 months after acceptance. Buys first North American serial rights. second serial (reprint) rights for anthologies (additional fee paid) and 30-day reprint rights (additional fee paid if applicable) Editorial lead time 3 months. Submit seasonal material 5 months in advance. Accepts queries by mail.

Accepts simultaneous submissions. Responds in 6 weeks to queries. Responds in 2 months to mss.

Nonfiction Needs book excerpts, essays, expose, general interest, historical, humor, interview, new product, opinion, personal experience, photo feature, fashion/lifestyle. **Buys 200 mss/year.** Query with published clips and SASE Length: 50-2,500 words. **Pays variable rate.**

Photos State availability. Captions, identification of subjects, model releases required. Reviews contact sheets, transparencies, prints. Negotiates payment individually Buys one time rights.

Tips *Out*'s contributors include editors and writers from the country's top consumer titles: skilled reporters, columnists, and writers with distinctive voices and specific expertise in the fields they cover. But while published clips and relevant experience are a must, the magazine also seeks out fresh, young voices. The best guide to the kind of stories we publish is to review our recent issues. Is there a place for the story you have in mind? Be aware of our long lead time. No phone queries, please.

$ ☐ OUTLOOKS

Outlooks Publication Inc., 303 - 1235 17th Ave SW, Calgary Alberta T2C 0C2 Canada. (403)228-1157. Fax: (403)228-7735. E-mail: main@outlooks.ca. Website: www.outlooks.ca. **100% freelance written**. Monthly national lifestyle publication for Canada's LGBT community. Estab. 1997. Circ. 31,500. Byline given. Pays on publication. Offers 50% kill fee. Publishes ms an average of 2 months after acceptance. Buys first rights. Editorial lead time 2 months. Submit seasonal material 3 months in advance. Accepts queries by e-mail. Accepts simultaneous submissions. Responds in 2 weeks to queries. Sample copy available online. Guidelines free.

Nonfiction Needs essays, general interest, humor, interview, photo feature, travel. Query with published clips. Length: 500-1,500 words. **Pays $100-120.**

Photos State availability. Captions required. Reviews contact sheets. Negotiates payment individually. Buys one time rights.

Columns/Departments Book, movie, and music reviews (600-700 words). Query with published clips.

Fiction Needs adventure, erotica, humorous. **Buys 10 mss/year.** Query with published clips. Length: 1,200-1,600 words. **Pays $120-160**.

OUTSMART

Up & Out Communications, 3406 Audubon Place, Houston TX 77006. (713)520-7237. Fax: (713)522-3275. Website: www.outsmartmagazine.com. **50% freelance written**. Monthly magazine concerned with gay, lesbian, bisexual, and transgender issues. *OutSmart* offers vibrant and thoughtful coverage of the stories that appeal most to an educated gay audience. Estab. 1994. Circ. 60,000. Byline given. Pays on publication. No kill fee. Buys one-time rights, buys simultaneous rights. Permission to publish on website. Editorial lead time 3 months. Submit seasonal material 4 months in advance. Accepts queries by mail, e-mail, fax. Responds in 6 weeks to queries. Responds in 2 months to mss. Sample copy and writer's guidelines online

Nonfiction Needs historical, interview, opinion, personal experience, photo feature, travel, health/wellness. **Buys 24 mss/year.** Send complete ms. Length: 450-2,000 words. **Negotiates payment individually.**

Reprints Send photocopy.

Photos State availability. Identification of subjects required. Reviews 4x6 prints. Negotiates payment individually. Buys one time rights.

Tips *OutSmart* is a mainstream publication that covers culture, politics, personalities, and entertainment as well as local and national news and events. We work to address the diversity of the lesbian, gay, bisexual, and transgender community, fostering understanding among all our readers.

$$ ☐ XTRA

Toronto's Lesbian & Gay Biweekly, Pink Triangle Press, 491 Church St., Suite 200, Toronto ON M4Y 2C6 Canada. (416)925-6665. Fax: (416)925-6674. E-mail: info@xtra.ca. Website: www.xtra.ca. **80% freelance written**. Biweekly tabloid covering gay, lesbian, bisexual and transgender issues, news, arts and events of interest in Toronto. *Xtra* is dedicated to lesbian and gay sexual liberation. We publish material that advocates this end, according to the mission statement of the not-for-profit organization Pink Triange Press, which operates the paper. Estab. 1984. Circ. 45,000. Byline given. Pays on publication. No kill fee. Buys first North American serial rights, buys electronic rights. Editorial lead time 1 month. Accepts queries by e-mail. Accepts previously published material. Accepts simultaneous submissions. Responds in 2 weeks to queries. Sample copy available online. Guidelines by e-mail.

Nonfiction Needs book excerpts, essays, interview, opinion, personal experience, travel. US-based stories or profiles of straight people who do not have a direct connection to the LGBT community. Query with published clips. Length: 200-1,600 words. Limit agreed upon in advance

Photos Send photos. Captions, identification of subjects, model releases required. Offers $60 minimum. Buys Internet rights.
Columns/Departments *Xtra* rarely publishes unsolicited columns. Query with published clips.

General Interest

$ $ THE AMERICAN LEGION MAGAZINE

P.O. Box 1055, Indianapolis IN 46206-1055. (317)630-1200. Fax: (317)630-1280. E-mail: magazine@legion.org. Website: www.legion.org. **70% freelance written. Prefers to work with published/established writers, but works with a small number of new/unpublished writers each year.** Monthly magazine. Working through 15,000 community-level posts, the honorably discharged wartime veterans of The American Legion dedicate themselves to God, country and traditional American values. They believe in a strong defense; adequate and compassionate care for veterans and their families; community service; and the wholesome development of our nation's youth. We publish articles that reflect these values. We inform our readers and their families of significant trends and issues affecting our nation, the world and the way we live. Our major features focus on the American flag, national security, foreign affairs, business trends, social issues, health, education, ethics and the arts. We also publish selected general feature articles, articles of special interest to veterans, and question-and-answer interviews with prominent national and world figures. Estab. 1919. Circ. 2,550,000. Byline given. Pays on acceptance. No kill fee. Publishes ms an average of 6 months after acceptance. Buys first North American serial rights. Accepts queries by mail, e-mail, fax. Responds in 2 months to queries. Sample copy for $3.50 and 9 × 12 SAE with 6 first-class stamps. Guidelines for #10 SASE.
Nonfiction Well-reported articles or expert commentaries cover issues/trends in world/national affairs, contemporary problems, general interest, sharply-focused feature subjects. Monthly Q&A with national figures/experts. Needs general interest, interview. No regional topics or promotion of partisan political agendas. No personal experiences or war stories. **Buys 50-60 mss/year.** Query with SASE should explain the subject or issue, article's angle and organization, writer's qualifications, and experts to be interviewed. Length: 300-2,000 words. **Pays 40¢/word and up.**
Photos On assignment.
Tips Queries by new writers should include clips/background/expertise; no longer than 1½ pages. Submit suitable material showing you have read several issues. *The American Legion Magazine* considers itself '*the* magazine for a strong America.' Reflect this theme (which includes economy, educational system, moral fiber, social issues, infrastructure, technology and national defense/security). We are a general interest, national magazine, not a strictly military magazine. We are widely read by members of the Washington establishment and other policy makers.

AMERICAN PROFILE

Publishing Group of America, 341 Cool Springs Blvd., 4th Fl., Franklin TN 37067. Website: www.americanprofile.com. **90% freelance written**. Weekly magazine with national and regional editorial celebrating the people, places, and experiences of hometowns across America. The 4-color magazine is distributed through small to medium-size community newspapers. Estab. 2000. Circ. 10,000,000. Byline given. Pays on acceptance. No kill fee. Buys first rights, buys electronic rights, buys 6-month exclusive rights rights. Editorial lead time 6 months. Submit seasonal material 1 year in advance. Accepts queries by mail; include SASE. Responds in 1 month to queries. Responds in 1 month to mss. Guidelines available online.
Nonfiction Needs general interest, how-to, interview. No fiction, nostalgia, poetry, essays. **Buys 250 mss/year.** Query with published clips. Length: 350-1,000 words.
Photos State availability. Captions, identification of subjects, model releases required. Reviews transparencies. Negotiates payment individually. Buys one-time rights, nonexclusive after 6 months.
Columns/Departments Health; Family; Finances; Home; Gardening.
Tips "Please visit the website to see our content and writing style."

$ $ $ $ THE ATLANTIC MONTHLY

600 New Hampshire Ave. NW, Washington, DC 20037. (202)266-6000. Website: www.theatlantic.com. Monthly magazine. General magazine for an educated readership with broad cultural and public-affairs interests. Estab. 1857. Circ. 400,000. Byline given. Pays on acceptance. No kill fee. Buys first North American serial rights. Accepts queries by mail. Guidelines available online.

Nonfiction Reportage preferred. Needs book excerpts, essays, general interest, humor, travel. Query with or without published clips or send complete ms to 'Editorial Department' at address above. All unsolicited mss must be accompanied by SASE. Length: 1,000-6,000 words. **Payment varies.**
Fiction Contact: C. Michael Curtis, fiction editor. Seeks fiction that is clear, tightly written with strong sense of 'story' and well-defined characters. No longer publishes fiction in the regular magazine. Instead, it will appear in a special newsstand-only fiction issue. Send complete ms. preferred length: 2,000-6,000 words.
Poetry Contact: David Barber, poetry editor. Buys 30-40 poems/year.
Tips Writers should be aware that this is not a market for beginner's work (nonfiction and fiction), nor is it truly for intermediate work. Study this magazine before sending only your best, most professional work. When making first contact, cover letters are sometimes helpful, particularly if they cite prior publications or involvement in writing programs. Common mistakes: melodrama, inconclusiveness, lack of development, unpersuasive characters and/or dialogue.

$$ AVENTURA MAGAZINE

Discover Magazine, Inc., 18781 Biscayne Blvd., Miami FL 33180. (305)932-2400. E-mail: editorial@aventuramagazine.com. Website: www.aventuramagazine.com. **70% freelance written**. Magazine published 7 times/year covering affluent consumer markets. *AVENTURA Magazine*'s readership identify us as 'the intelligent source to luxury living.' As a horizontally positioned magazine with distribution over 50,000 and readership beyond 125,000, *AVENTURA* is distinguished as the magazine choice for readers pursuing a sophisticated lifestyle and luxury brand. Our typical reader has a household income over $200,000, are well traveled and well-educated. Articles are written for an audience with heightened expectations in all areas of life. Estab. 1998. Circ. 50,000. Byline given. Pays on acceptance. Buys all rights. Editorial lead time 3 months. Submit seasonal material 6 months in advance. Accepts queries by e-mail. Responds in 3 weeks to queries. Sample copy free. Guidelines by e-mail.
Nonfiction Needs expose, interview, travel, luxury living. Does not want to see opinions, essays, religious or how-to pieces. **Buys 1-3 mss/year.** Query. Length: words. **Pays $250+.**
Photos State availability. Captions, identification of subjects, model releases required. Reviews GIF/JPEG files. Negotiates payment individually. Buys all rights.

$ ⊘ BIBLIOPHILOS

A Journal of History, Literature, and the Liberal Arts, The Bibliophile Publishing Co., Inc., 200 Security Building, Fairmont WV 26554. (304)366-8107. **65-70% freelance written**. Quarterly literary magazine concentrating on 19th century American and European history and literature. We see ourself as a forum for new and unpublished writers, historians, philosophers, literary critics and reviewers, and those who love animals. Audience is academic-oriented, college graduate, who believes in traditional Aristotelian-Thomistic thought and education, and has a fair streak of the Luddite in him/her. Our ideal reader owns no television, has never sent nor received e-mail, and avoids shopping malls at any cost. He loves books. Estab. 1981. Circ. 400. Byline given. Pays on publication. Publishes ms an average of 1 year after acceptance. Buys first North American serial rights. Editorial lead time 6 months. Submit seasonal material 6 months in advance. Accepts queries by mail. Responds in 2 weeks to queries. Responds in 1 month to mss. Sample copy for $5.25. Guidelines for sae with 9½x4 envelope and 2 First-Class stamps.

- Query first only, unaccompanied by any ms.

Nonfiction Needs book excerpts, essays, general interest, historical, humor, interview, opinion, personal experience, photo feature, travel, book review-essay, literary criticism. Upcoming theme issues include an annual all book-review issue, containing 10-15 reviews and review-essays, or poetry about books and reading. Does not want to see anything that Oprah would recommend, or that Erma Bombeck or Ann Landers would think humorous or interesting. No `I found Jesus and it changed my life' material. **Buys 25-30 mss/year.** Query by mail only first, not with any ms included. Length: 1,500-3,000 words. **Pays $5-35.**
Photos State availability. Identification of subjects required. Reviews b&w 4x6 prints. Negotiates payment individually. Buys one time rights.
Columns/Departments Features (fiction and nonfiction, short stories), 1,500-3,000 words; Poetry (batches of 5, preferably thematically related), 3-150 lines; Reviews (book reviews or review essays on new books or individual authors, current and past), 1,000-1,500 words; Opinion (man triumphing over technology and technocrats, the facade of modern education, computer fetishism), 1,000-1,500 words. Query by mail only. **Pays $25-40.**
Fiction Contact: Gerald J. Bobango, editor. Needs adventure, ethnic, historical, general, US, Eastern Europe, horror, psychological, supernatural, humorous, mainstream, mystery, police procedural, private

eye/hardboiled, courtroom, novel concepts, romance, gothic, historical, regency period, slice-of-life vignettes, suspense, western, frontier saga, traditional, utopian, Orwellian. No 'I remember Mama, who was a saint and I miss her terribly'; no gay or lesbian topics; no drug culture material; nothing harping on political correctness; nothing to do with healthy living, HMOs, medical programs, or the welfare state, unless it is against statism in these areas. **Buys 25-30 mss/year.** Length: 1,500-3,000 words. **Pays $25-40.**

Poetry Needs free verse, light verse, traditional. Formal and rhymed verse gets read first.

Tips Query first. Do not send material unsolicited. We shall not respond if you do.

$$$$ DIVERSION

300 W. 57th St., New York NY 10019-5238. (212)969-7500. Fax: (212)969-7563. E-mail: shartford@hearst.com. Website: www.diversion.com. Monthly magazine covering travel and lifestyle, edited for physicians. *Diversion* offers an eclectic mix of interests beyond medicine. Regular features include stories on domestic and foreign travel destinations, food and wine, cars, gardening, photography, books, electronic gear, and the arts. Although *Diversion* doesn't cover health subjects, it does feature profiles of doctors who excel at nonmedical pursuits or who engage in medical volunteer work. Estab. 1973. Circ. 190,000. Byline given. Pays 3 months after acceptance. Offers 25% kill fee. Editorial lead time 6 months. Responds in 1 month to queries. Sample copy for $4.50. Guidelines available

Nonfiction We get so many travel and food queries that we're hard pressed to even read them all. Far better to query us on culture, the arts, sports, technology, etc. Query with proposal, published clips, and author's credentials. Length: 1,800-2,000 words. **Pays 50¢-$1/word.**

Columns/Departments Travel, food & wine, photography, gardening, cars, technology. Length: 1,200 words.

⊘ EBONY

Johnson Publishing Co., Inc., 820 S. Michigan Ave., Chicago IL 60605. E-mail: editors@ebony.com. Website: www.ebonyjet.com. Monthly magazine covering topics ranging from education and history to entertainment, art, government, health, travel, sports and social events. African-American oriented consumer interest magazine. Circ. 1,728,986. No kill fee. Editorial lead time 3 months.

- Query before submitting.

$$ FASHION FORUM

The Substance of Style, Business Journals, Inc., 1384 Broadway, 11th Floor, New York NY 10018. (212)710-7442. E-mail: jillians@busjour.com. Website: www.busjour.com. Karen Alberg Grossman, Lisa Montemorra, project manager. **Contact:** Jillian Sprague, managing editor. **80% freelance written.** Semiannual magazine covering luxury fashion (men's 70%, women's 30%), luxury lifestyle. "*Forum* directly targets a very upscale reader interested in profiles and service pieces on upscale designers, new fashion trends and traditional suiting. Lifestyle articles—including wine and spirits, travel, cars, boating, sports, collecting, etc.—are upscale top of the line (i.e., don't write how expensive taxis are)." Circ. 150,000. Byline given. Pays on publication. Offers 50% kill fee. Publishes ms an average of 3-4 months after acceptance. Buys all rights. Editorial lead time 6 months. Submit seasonal material 6 months in advance. Accepts queries by mail, e-mail. Responds in 2-3 weeks to queries. Guidelines by e-mail.

Nonfiction Readers of Forum magazine are frequent shoppers at the member stores of the Forum Group, America's most exclusive independent clothing retailers. Twice a year, the best customers of each retailer in the group get their own edition of Forum, completely customized by the individual merchant to focus on both their apparel and their lifestyle. In addition to great fashion visuals and clothing-related stories, each issue might include features on travel, food, culture and art, plus interviews with leading figures from corporate America, sports, entertainment or fashion. Needs general interest, interview, travel, luxury lifestyle trends, fashion service pieces. Does not want personal essays. We run a few but commission them. No fiction or single product articles. In other words, an article should be on whats new in Italian wines, not about one superspecial brand. **Buys 20-25 mss/year.** Query. Length: 600-1,500 words. **Pays $300-500.**

Photos State availability. Reviews GIF/JPEG files. Offers no additional payment for photos accepted with ms. Buys one time rights.

Columns/Departments Travel, 1,000-1,500 words; Wine + Spirits, 600-1,200 words; Gourmet, 600-1,200 words; Wheels, 600 words. Query. **Pays $300-500.**

Tips "Be prepared to write like you know the upscale lifestyle. Even if you only own one jacket, or stay in hostels, remember our readers, for the most part, don't even know about hostels! Experience in a specific category, or direct access to designers for profiles is a huge in!"

50 SOMETHING

National Seniors, Level 7, 243 Edward St., Brisbane QLD 4000 Australia. (61)(7)3233-9105. E-mail: 50something@nationalseniors.com.au. Website: www.nationalseniors.com.au. **Contact:** Sarah Saunders, editor. Bimonthly magazine covering celebrity profiles, health, the arts, finance, and national and international news, to inform, empower and entertain older Australians. Editorial lead time 2 months.
Nonfiction Needs general interest, interview. Query.

$$ GRIT

American Life and Traditions, Ogden Publications, 1503 SW 42nd St., Topeka KS 66609-1265. (785)274-4300. Fax: (785)274-4305. E-mail: grit@grit.com. Website: www.grit.com. **Contact:** Oscar "Hank" Will, editor. **90% freelance written. Open to new writers.** Bimonthly magazine. "*Grit* focuses on rural lifestyles, country living and small-scale farming. We are looking for useful, practical information on livestock, gardening, farm equipment, home-and-yard improvement and related topics. We also offer one nostalgia article in each issue—what it was like living on the farm in the Great Depression, how the family kept the peace during holidays, etc. What we expect from anyone who wawnts to write for us is that they know what the magazine is about." Estab. 1882. Circ. 230,000. Byline given. Pays on publication. No kill fee. Buys shared rights. Submit seasonal material 6 months in advance. Accepts queries by mail, e-mail. Sample copy and writer's guidelines for $4 and 9 × 12 SASE with at least $2 in postage. Sample articles are posted on website. Guidelines online at www.grit.com/guidelines.aspx.
Nonfiction "No unsolicited manuscripts—assignments only. The best way to sell work is by reading each issue cover to cover." Query by e-mail to Jean Teller, jteller@grit.com. Assignments are made from queries approximately a year in advance. Send queries for 2010 by May 1, 2009. Main features run 1,000-1,200 words. Department features average 800-1,000 words. **Varies: $75 for a short, newsy article for Grit Gazette to $750 or more for long feature articles. We negotiate individually with writers rather than paying a per-word fee.**
Fiction We do not accept fiction or poetry submissions.
Tips "Buys shared rights. We work 6 months or more in advance, so no last-minute queries/submissions, please. No unsolicited mss, assignments only."

$$$$ HARPER'S MAGAZINE

666 Broadway, 11th Floor, New York NY 10012. (212)420-5720. Fax: (212)228-5889. Website: www.harpers.org. **90% freelance written**. Monthly magazine for well-educated, socially concerned, widely read men and women who value ideas and good writing. *Harper's Magazine* encourages national discussion on current and significant issues in a format that offers arresting facts and intelligent opinions. By means of its several shorter journalistic forms—Harper's Index, Readings, Forum, and Annotation—as well as with its acclaimed essays, fiction, and reporting, *Harper's* continues the tradition begun with its first issue in 1850: to inform readers across the whole spectrum of political, literary, cultural, and scientific affairs. Estab. 1850. Circ. 230,000. Pays on acceptance. Offers negotiable kill fee. Publishes ms an average of 3 months after acceptance. Rights purchased vary with author and material. Accepts previously published material. Responds in 6 weeks to queries. Sample copy for $5.95.
Nonfiction For writers working with agents or who will query first only, our requirements are: public affairs, literary, international and local reporting, and humor. Publishes 1 major report/issue. Length: 4,000-6,000 words. Publishes 1 major essay/issue. Length: 4,000-6,000 words. These should be construed as topical essays on all manner of subjects (politics, the arts, crime, business, etc.) to which the author can bring the force of passionate and informed statement. Needs humor. No interviews; no profiles. **Buys 2 mss/year.** Query. Length: 4,000-6,000 words.
Reprints Accepted for Readings section. Send typed ms with rights for sale ted and information about when and where the article previously appeared.
Photos Contact: Stacey Clarkson, art director. Occasionally purchased with ms; others by assignment. State availability. Pays $50-500.
Fiction Will consider unsolicited fiction. Needs humorous. **Buys 12 mss/year.** Query. Length: 3,000-5,000 words. **Generally pays 50¢-$1/word.**
Tips Some readers expect their magazines to clothe them with opinions in the way that Bloomingdale's dresses them for the opera. The readers of *Harper's Magazine* belong to a different crowd. They strike me as the kind of people who would rather think in their own voices and come to their own conclusions.

$$$$ NATIONAL GEOGRAPHIC MAGAZINE

1145 17th St. NW, Washington DC 20036. (202)857-7000. Fax: (202)492-5767. Website: www.nationalgeographic.com. **60% freelance written. Prefers to work with published/established writers.**

Monthly magazine for members of the National Geographic Society. Timely articles written in a compelling, 'eyewitness' style. Arresting photographs that speak to us of the beauty, mystery, and harsh realities of life on earth. Maps of unprecedented detail and accuracy. These are the hallmarks of *National Geographic* magazine. Since 1888, the *Geographic* has been educating readers about the world. Estab. 1888. Circ. 6,800,000.

Nonfiction *National Geographic* publishes general interest, illustrated articles on science, natural history, exploration, cultures and geographical regions. Of the freelance writers assigned, a few are experts in their fields; the remainder are established professionals. Fewer than 1% of unsolicited queries result in assignments. Query (500 words with clips of published articles by mail to Senior Assitant Editor Oliver Payne. Do not send mss. Length: 2,000-8,000 words.

Photos Query in care of the Photographic Division.

Tips State the theme(s) clearly, let the narrative flow, and build the story around strong characters and a vivid sense of place. Give us rounded episodes, logically arranged.

$$$ NEWSWEEK

251 W. 57th St., New York NY 10019. E-mail: editors@newsweek.com. Website: www.newsweek.com. *Newsweek* is edited to report the week's developments on the newsfront of the world and the nation through news, commentary and analysis. Circ. 3,180,000. No kill fee. Buys non-exclusive world-wide rights.

Columns/Departments Contact: myturn@newsweek.com. "We are no longer accepting submissions for the print edition. To submit an essay to our website, please e-mail it to: myturn@newsweek.com. The My Turn essay should be: A) an original piece, B) 850-900 words, C) generally personal in tone, and D) about any topic, but not framed as a response to a Newsweek story or another My Turn essay. Submissions must not have been published elsewhere. Please include your full name, phone number and address with your entry. The competition is very stiff-we get 600 entries per month-and we can only print one a week. **Due to the number of submissions we receive, we cannot respond unless we plan to publish your essay**; if your story is tied to current events, it may not be appropriate. We are fully aware of the time and effort involved in preparing an essay, and each manuscript is given careful consideration. For an automated message with further details about My Turn, you may call: (212) 445-4547. **Pays $1,000 on publication.**

$$$ THE NEW YORK TIMES MAGAZINE

620 Eighth Ave., New York NY 10018. (212)556-1234. Fax: (212)556-3830. E-mail: magazine@nytimes.com. Website: www.nytimes.com/pages/magazine. **Contact:** Gerald Marzorati, editor. *The New York Times Magazine* appears in *The New York Times* on Sunday. The *Arts and Leisure* section appears during the week. The *Op Ed* page appears daily. No kill fee.

- "Because of the volume of submissions for the Lives column, the magazine cannot return or respond to unsolicited manuscripts. If you have a query about about the "Lives" page, please write to lives@nytimes.com. For Randy Cohen/The Ethicist, please write to ethicist@nytimes.com."

Nonfiction *Arts & Leisure*: Wants to encourage imaginativeness in terms of form and approach—stressing ideas, issues, trends, investigations, symbolic reporting and stories delving deeply into the creative achievements and processes of artists and entertainers—and seeks to break away from old-fashioned gushy, fan magazine stuff. Length: 1,500-2,000 words. **Pays $100-350**, depending on length. Address unsolicited articles with SASE to the Arts & Leisure Articles Editor. *Op Ed* page: The Op Ed page is always looking for new material and publishes many people who have never been published before. We want material of universal relevance which people can talk about in a personal way. When writing for the Op Ed page, there is no formula, but the writing itself should have some polish. Don't make the mistake of pontificating on the news. We're not looking for more political columnists. Length: 750 words. **Pays $150.**

$$$ THE OLD FARMER'S ALMANAC

Yankee Publishing, Inc., P.O. Box 520, Dublin NH 03444. (603)563-8111. Website: www.Almanac.com. **95% freelance written**. Annual magazine covering weather, gardening, history, oddities, lore. *"The Old Farmer's Almanac* is the oldest continuously published periodical in North America. Since 1792, it has provided useful information for people in all walks of life: tide tables for those who live near the ocean; sunrise tables and planting charts for those who live on the farm or simply enjoy gardening; recipes for those who like to cook; and forecasts for those who don't like the question of weather left up in the air. The words of the *Almanac*'s founder, Robert B. Thomas, guide us still: 'Our main endeavor is to be useful, but with a pleasant degree of humour.'" Estab. 1792. Circ. 3,750,000. Byline given. Pays on acceptance. Offers 25% kill fee. Publishes ms an average of 9 months after acceptance. Buys electronic rights, buys all rights. Editorial lead time 6 months. Submit seasonal material 1 year in advance. Accepts queries by mail. Responds in 3 weeks to queries. Responds in 2 months to mss. Sample copy for $6 at bookstores or online. Guidelines available online.

Nonfiction Needs general interest, historical, how-to, garden, cook, save money, humor, weather, natural remedies, obscure facts, history, popular culture. No personal recollections/accounts, personal/family histories. Query with published clips. Length: 800-2,500 words. **Pays 65¢/word.**

Fillers Length: 100-200 words. **Pays $25.**

Tips "*The Old Farmer's Almanac* is a reference book. Our readers appreciate obscure facts and stories. Read it. Think differently. Read writer's guidelines online."

$$$ OPEN SPACES

Open Spaces Publications, Inc., PMB 134, 6327-C SW Capitol Hwy., Portland OR 97239-1937. (503)313-4361. Fax: (503)227-3401. E-mail: info@open-spaces.com. Website: www.open-spaces.com. **95% freelance written**. Quarterly general interest magazine. *Open Spaces* is a forum for informed writing and intelligent thought. Articles are written by experts in various fields. Audience is varied (CEOs and rock climbers, politicos and university presidents, etc.) but is highly educated and loves to read good writing. Estab. 1997. Byline given. Pays on publication. Offers 20% kill fee. Publishes ms an average of 6 months after acceptance. Rights purchased vary with author and material. Editorial lead time 9 months. Accepts queries by mail, fax. Accepts simultaneous submissions. Sample copy for $10. Guidelines available online.

Nonfiction Needs essays, general interest, historical, how-to, if clever, humor, interview, personal experience, travel. **Buys 35 mss/year.** Send complete ms. 1,500-2,500 words; major articles up to 6,000 words. **Pays variable amount.**

Photos State availability. Captions, identification of subjects required. Buys one time rights.

Columns/Departments Contact: David Williams, departments editor. Books (substantial topics such as the Booker Prize, The Newbery, etc.); Travel (must reveal insight); Sports (past subjects include rowing, and swing dancing); Unintended Consequences, 1,500-2,500 words. Send complete ms. **Payment varies.**

Fiction Contact: Ellen Teicher, fiction editor. Quality is far more important than type. Read the magazine. Excellence is the issue—not subject matter. **Buys 8 mss/year.** Length: 2,000-6,000 words. **Payment varies.**

Poetry Contact: Susan Juve-Hu Bucharest, poetry editor. Again, quality is far more important than type.

Tips *Open Spaces* reviews all manuscripts submitted in hopes of finding writing of the highest quality. We present a Northwest perspective as well as a national and international one. Best advice is read the magazine.

$$$$ PARADE

ParadeNet, Inc., 711 Third Ave., New York NY 10017-4014. Website: www.parade.com. **Contact:** Megan Brown, articles editor. **95% freelance written**. Weekly magazine for a general interest audience. Estab. 1941. Circ. 81,000,000. Pays on acceptance. Offers kill fee. Kill fee varies in amount Publishes ms an average of 5 months after acceptance. Buys worldwide exclusive rights for 7 days, plus nonexclusive electronic and other rights in perpetuity. Editorial lead time 1 month. Accepts queries by mail. Accepts simultaneous submissions. Sample copy available online. Guidelines available online.

Nonfiction Publishes general interest (on health, trends, social issues or anything of interest to a broad general audience), interview/profile (of news figures, celebrities and people of national significance), and provocative topical pieces of news value. Spot news events are not accepted, as *Parade* has a 2-month lead time. No fiction, fashion, travel, poetry, cartoons, nostalgia, regular columns, personal essays, quizzes, or fillers. Unsolicited queries concerning celebrities, politicians or sports figures are rarely assigned. **Buys 150 mss/year.** Query with published clips. Length: 1,200-1,500 words. **Pays very competitive amount.**

Tips If the writer has a specific expertise in the proposed topic, it increases the chances of breaking in. Send a well-researched, well-written 1-page proposal and enclose a SASE. Do not submit completed manuscripts.

⊘ PEOPLE

Time, Inc., 1271 Avenue of the Americas, New York NY 10020. (212)522-1212. Fax: (212)522-1359. E-mail: editor@people.com. Website: www.people.com. Weekly magazine. Designed as a forum for personality journalism through the use of short articles on contemporary news events and people. Circ. 3,617,127. No kill fee. Editorial lead time 3 months.

- Does not buy freelance materials or use freelance writers.

$ THE POLISHING STONE

Refining the Life You Live Into the Life You Love, 20104 87th St. SE, Snohomish WA 98290-7267. E-mail: submissions@polishingstone.com. Website: www.polishingstone.org. **50% freelance written**. Magazine published 5 times/year. *The Polishing Stone* takes an optimistic and realistic look at the environment and quality of life: whole foods, alternative health, earth-friendly and handcrafted products, mindful parenting, relationships, and social and environmental issues. We focus on healthy lifestyles that are close to the earth, sustainable, and in balance. The issues we cover are serious, but we seek a tone of ease because our personal beliefs lean toward hopefulness about possibilities and opportunities for healing. Facts are encouraged as an accurate assessment of a situation, but should not overshadow the offering of solutions and inspiration. In a world where reporting has become synonymous with shock tactics, speaking from the heart is an effective alternative. Estab. 2004. Byline given. Pays on publication. No kill fee. Publishes ms an average of 4 months after acceptance. Buys first North American serial rights. Editorial lead time 4 months. Submit seasonal material 4 months in advance. Accepts queries by mail. Accepts simultaneous submissions. Responds in 1 month to queries. Responds in 2 months to mss. Sample copy available online. Guidelines available online.

Nonfiction Needs book excerpts, essays, general interest, how-to, accepted for the following columns: Whole Foods, From the Ground Up, Everything Herbal, With our Hands and Treading Lightly, humor, inspirational, interview, new product, personal experience. The Polishing Stone is published in February, April, July, September and December. Articles often relate to the season in which they appear. We do not accept travel, religious or technical articles, or any article that focuses on problems without offering solutions. We do not publish reprints. **Buys 75 mss/year.** Query with published clips. Length: 200-1,600 words.

Columns/Departments Whole Foods (preparation of primarily vegetarian foods); From the Ground Up (earth-friendly gardening); Everything Herbal (information about the healing power of herbs); A Balance of Health (practical alternatives for returning to balanced health); Treading Lightly (sustainable products, processes and services); With our Hands (artisans share design for simple hand-made products); Life out Loud (an honest look at how children shape us); Looking Within (spiritual and psychological insights); In Community (the people responsible for healing/changing communities); This Spinning Earth (information and inspiration to heal the earth); In Print & On Screen (reviews of books and movies that explain and encourage). Query with published clips or send complete ms. **Pays $25-100.**

Poetry Needs free verse, haiku, light verse. Buys 5-10 poems/year. Submit maximum 4 poems. Length: 5-25 lines.

Fillers Length: 50-175 words. **Pays $10.**

Tips If previously published, send query letter and clips. Otherwise, send a completed ms of no more than 1,600 words. Send both queries and completed mss by mail only. We want to give new writers a chance, especially those who are willing to do the work. For queries, this means providing a clear description of your topic, angle, sources, lead, and reason why the article is a good fit for *The Polishing Stone*. Completed manuscripts should be carefully edited and fact-checked prior to submission. As always, read our magazine as a guide to our content and writing style. Draw on your own experiences and expertise and share from the heart.

PORTLAND MAGAZINE

Maine's City Magazine, 165 State, Portland ME 04101. (207)775-4339. E-mail: staff@portlandmonthly.com. Website: www.portlandmagazine.com. **Contact:** Colin Sargent. Monthly city lifestyle magazine—fiction, style, business, real estate, controversy, fashion, cuisine, interviews and art relating to the Maine area. Estab. 1985. Circ. 100,000. Pays on publication. No kill fee. Buys first North American serial rights. Accepts queries by mail, e-mail.

Nonfiction Query first. "Clips and a bio note are appreciated, but we take no responsibility for returning unsolicited materials."

Fiction Contact: Colin Sargent, editor. Send complete ms.

$$ READER'S DIGEST

The Reader's Digest Association, Inc., Box 100, Pleasantville NY 10572-0100. Website: www.rd.com. Monthly magazine. No kill fee.

Columns/Departments Life; @Work; Off Base, **pays $300**. Laugh; Quotes, **pays $100**. Address your submission to the appropriate humor category.

Tips "Full-length, original articles are usually assigned to regular contributors to the magazine. We do not accept or return unpublished manuscripts. We do, however, accept 1-page queries that clearly detail the article idea—with special emphasis on the arc of the story, your interview access to the main characters, your access to special documents, etc. We look for dramatic narratives, articles about everyday heroes, crime dramas, adventure stories. Do include a separate page of your writing credits. We are not interested in poetry, fiction, or opinion pieces. Please submit article proposals on the website."

$$$$ ☐ READER'S DIGEST (CANADA)

1100 Rene Le vesque Blvd. W., Montreal QC H3B 5H5 Canada. E-mail: originals@rd.com. Website: www.readersdigest.ca. **30-50% freelance written**. Monthly magazine of general interest articles and subjects. Estab. 1948. Circ. 1,000,000. Byline given. **Pays on acceptance for original works.** Pays on publication for pickups. Offers $500 (Canadian) kill fee. Buys one-time rights (for reprints), all rights (for original articles). Submit seasonal material 5 months in advance. Accepts queries by mail, e-mail. Accepts previously published material. Guidelines available online.

- Only responds to queries if interested. Prefers Canadian subjects.

Nonfiction We're looking for true stories that depend on emotion and reveal the power of our relationships to help us overcome adversity; also for true first-person accounts of an event that changed a life for the better or led to new insight. No fiction, poetry or articles too specialized, technical or esoteric—read *Reader's Digest* to see what kind of articles we want. Needs general interest, how-to, general interest, humor, jokes, inspirational, personal experience, travel, adventure, crime, health. Query with published clips. Length: 2,000-2,500 words. **Pays $1.50-2.50/word (CDN) depending on story type.**

Reprints Query. Payment is negotiable.

Photos State availability.

Tips *Reader's Digest* usually finds its freelance writers through other well-known publications in which they have previously been published. There are guidelines available and writers should read *Reader's Digest* to see what kind of stories we look for and how they are written. We do not accept unsolicited manuscripts.

$$$$ ROBB REPORT

The Magazine for the Luxury Lifestyle, Curtco Media Labs, 1 Acton Place, Acton MA 01720. (978)264-7500. Fax: (212)264-7501. E-mail: editorial@robbreport.com. Website: www.robbreport.com. **60% freelance written**. Monthly magazine. We are a lifestyle magazine geared toward active, affluent readers. Addresses upscale autos, luxury travel, boating, technology, lifestyles, watches, fashion, sports, investments, collectibles. Estab. 1976. Circ. 111,000. Byline given. Pays on publication. Offers 25% kill fee. Buys first North American serial rights, buys all rights. Submit seasonal material 5 months in advance. Accepts queries by mail, fax. Responds in 2 months to queries. Responds in 1 month to mss. Sample copy for $10.95, plus shipping and handling. Guidelines for #10 SASE.

Nonfiction Needs new product, autos, boats, aircraft, watches, consumer electronics, travel, international and domestic, dining. Special Issues: Home (October); Recreation (March). **Buys 60 mss/year.** Query with published clips. Length: 500-2,000 words. **Pays $1/word.**

Photos State availability. Payment depends on article Buys one time rights.

Tips Show zest in your writing, immaculate research, and strong thematic structure, and you can handle most any assignment. We want to put the reader there, whether the article is about test driving a car, fishing for marlin, or touring a luxury home. The best articles will be those that tell compelling stories. Anecdotes should be used liberally, especially for leads, and the fun should show in your writing.

$$ THE SATURDAY EVENING POST

The Saturday Evening Post Society, 1100 Waterway Blvd., Indianapolis IN 46202. (317)634-1100. Website: www.satevepost.org. **30% freelance written**. Bimonthly general interest, family-oriented magazine focusing on lifestyle, physical fitness, preventive medicine. Ask almost any American if he or she has heard of *The Saturday Evening Post*, and you will find that many have fond recollections of the magazine from their childhood days. Many readers recall sitting with their families on Saturdays awaiting delivery of their *Post* subscription in the mail. *The Saturday Evening Post* has forged a tradition of 'forefront journalism.' *The Saturday Evening Post* continues to stand at the journalistic forefront with its coverage of health, nutrition, and preventive medicine. Estab. 1728. Circ. 350,000. Byline given. Pays on publication. Publishes ms an average of 3 months after acceptance. Buys all rights. Submit seasonal material 4 months in advance. Accepts queries by mail, fax. Accepts simultaneous submissions. Responds in 3 weeks to queries. Responds in 6 weeks to mss.

Nonfiction Needs how-to, gardening, home improvement, humor, interview, medical, health, fitness. No political articles or articles containing sexual innuendo or hypersophistication. **Buys 25 mss/year.** Send complete ms. (Buys very few outside mss) Length: 1,000-2,500 words. **Pays $25-400.**

Photos State availability. Identification of subjects, model releases required. Reviews negatives, transparencies. Offers $50 minimum, negotiable maximum per photo. Buys one-time or all rights.
Columns/Departments Travel (destinations); Post Scripts (well-known humorists); Post People (activities of celebrities). Length 750-1,500. Query with published clips or send complete ms. **Pays $150 minimum, negotiable maximum.**
Poetry Needs light verse.
Tips "Areas most open to freelancers are Health, Fitness, Research Breakthroughs, Nutrition, Post Scripts, and Travel. For travel we like text-photo packages, pragmatic tips, side bars, and safe rather than exotic destinations. Query by mail, not phone. Send clips."

$ SENIOR LIVING

Vancouver & Lower Mainland/Vancouver Island, Stratis Publishing Ltd, 153, 1581-H Hillside Ave., Victoria BC V8T 2CI Canada. (250)479-4705. Fax: (250)479-4808. E-mail: editor@seniorlivingmag.com. Website: www.seniorlivingmag.com. **Contact:** Bobbie Jo Reid, managing editor. **100% freelance written**. 12 times per yr. magazine covering active 50+ living. "Inspiring editorial profiling 'seniors' (50+) who are active & lead interesting lives. Include articles on health, housing, accessibility, sports, travel, recipes, etc." Estab. 2004. Circ. 41,000. Byline given. Pays quarterly. No kill fee. Publishes an average of 2-3 months after acceptance. Buys all rights. Editorial lead time 3 months. Submit seasonal material 6 months in advance. Accepts queries by e-mail. Accepts simultaneous submissions. Sample copy available online. Guidelines available.
Nonfiction Needs historical, how-to, humor, inspirational, interview, personal experience, travel, active living for 50+. Do not want politics, religion, promotion of business, service or products, humor that demeans 50+ demographic or aging process. **Buys 150 mss/year.** Query. Length: 500-1,200 words. **Pays $35-150 for assigned articles. Pays $35-150 for unsolicited articles.**
Photos Send photos. Identification of subjects, model releases required. Reviews GIF/JPEG files. Offers $10-75 per photo. Buys all rights.
Columns/Departments Query with published clips. **Pays $25-$50.**
Tips "Articles need to reflect region in which publication is distributed if about people/profiles/organizations."

$$$$ SMITHSONIAN MAGAZINE

Capital Gallery, Suite 6001, MRC 513, P.O. Box 37012, Washington DC 20013-7012. (202)275-2000. Website: www.smithsonianmag.com. **90% freelance written**. Monthly magazine for associate members of the Smithsonian Institution; 85% with college education. "*Smithsonian Magazine's* mission is to inspire fascination with all the world has to offer by featuring unexpected and entertaining editorial that explores different lifestyles, cultures and peoples, the arts, the wonders of nature and technology, and much more. The highly educated, innovative readers of *Smithsonian* share a unique desire to celebrate life, seeking out the timely as well as timeless, the artistic as well as the academic, and the thought-provoking as well as the humorous." Circ. 2,300,000. Pays on acceptance. Offers 33% kill fee. Publishes ms an average of 6 months after acceptance. Buys first North American serial rights. Editorial lead time 2 months. Submit seasonal material 3 months in advance. Accepts queries by online submission form only. Responds in 3 weeks to queries. Sample copy for $5. Guidelines available online.
Nonfiction "Our mandate from the Smithsonian Institution says we are to be interested in the same things which now interest or should interest the institution: Cultural and fine arts, history, natural sciences, hard sciences, etc." **Buys 120-130 feature (up to 5,000 words) and 12 short (500-650 words) mss/year.** Use online submission form. **Pays various rates per feature, $1,500 per short piece.**
Photos Purchased with or without ms and on assignment. Illustrations are not the responsibility of authors, but if you do have photographs or illustration materials, please include a selection of them with your submission. In general, 35mm color transparencies or black-and-white prints are perfectly acceptable. Photographs published in the magazine are usually obtained through assignment, stock agencies, or specialized sources. No photo library is maintained and photographs should be submitted only to accompany a specific article proposal. Send photos. Captions required. Pays $400/full color page.
Columns/Departments **Buys 12-15 department articles/year.** Length: 1,000-2,000 words. Last Page humor, 550-700 words. Use online submission form. **Pays $1,000-1,500.**
Tips "Send proposals through online submission form only. No e-mail or mail queries, please."

$ SOFA INK QUARTERLY

Sofa Ink, P.O. Box 625, American Fork UT 84003. E-mail: acquisitions@sofaink.com. Website: www.sofaink.com. **95% freelance written**. Quarterly magazine. "The magazine is distributed primarily to waiting rooms and lobbies of medical facilities. All of our stories and poetry have positive endings. We like to publish a variety of genres with a focus on good storytelling and word-mastery that does not include swearing, profaning deity, gore, excessive violence or gratuitous sex." Estab. 2005. Circ. 650. Byline given. Pays on acceptance. Publishes ms an average of 3 months after acceptance. Buys first North American serial rights. Submit seasonal material 4 months in advance. Accepts queries by mail, e-mail. Accepts simultaneous submissions. Responds in 1-3 months to queries. Responds in 1-3 months to mss. Sample copy for $6. Guidelines available online.

Nonfiction Needs essays, general interest, historical, humor, inspirational, interview, personal experience. Send complete ms. Length: 7,500 words. **Pays $5, plus 3 contributor copies.**

Photos Identification of subjects, model releases required. Offers no additional payment for photos accepted with ms. Buys one time rights.

Fiction Needs adventure, ethnic, experimental, fantasy, historical, humorous, mainstream, mystery, romance, science fiction, slice-of-life vignettes, suspense, western. Does not want erotic, religious. **Buys 24-30 mss/year.** Send complete ms. Length: 7,500 words. **Pays $5.**

Poetry Needs avant-garde, free verse, haiku, light verse, traditional. Buys 9-15 poems/year. Submit maximum 5 poems.

Tips Follow the content guidelines. Electronic submissions should be in a Word attachment rather than in the body of the message.

$ SOMA

SOMA Magazine, Inc., 888 O'Farrell St., Suite 103, San Francisco CA 94109. E-mail: arqt@somamagazine.com. Website: www.somamagazine.com. **5% freelance written**. Monthly magazine covering the arts, music, film, fashion, design, architecture, nightlife, etc. *SOMA* explores the contemporary landscape through insightful writing. Estab. 1986. Circ. 115,000. Byline given. Pays on publication. Offers $30 kill fee. Publishes ms an average of 1-3 months after acceptance. Buys first North American serial rights. Editorial lead time 3 months. Submit seasonal material 3 months in advance. Accepts queries by e-mail. Accepts simultaneous submissions. Responds in 3 months to queries. Sample copy for $3.50. Guidelines free.

$$ THRIVE NYC

For New York's Boomers and Beyond, Community Media, LLC, 145 6th Ave., New York NY 10013. (212)229-1890. Fax: (212)229-2790. E-mail: jbladow@aol.com. Website: www.nycplus.com. **Contact:** Janel Bladow, editor in chief. **100% freelance written**. Monthly magazine. "We are looking for well-written stories of substance that relate in some way to our 50+ theme. All genres." Estab. 2005. Circ. 50,000. Byline given. Pays on publication. Publishes ms an average of 3-6 months after acceptance. Buys first rights. Editorial lead time 2-3 months. Submit seasonal material 4-5 months in advance. Accepts queries by e-mail. Accepts simultaneous submissions. Responds in 2 months to queries. Responds in 2 months to mss. Sample copy available online. Guidelines by e-mail.

Nonfiction Needs essays, general interest, historical, humor, inspirational, interview, opinion, personal experience. **Buys 110 mss/year.** Query. Length: 900-4,000 words. **Pays $100-300.**

Columns/Departments Memory (personal experience/nostalgia), 800-1,100 words; Mind/Body (50+), 1,000-1,200 words; Food (old and new), 1,000-1,200 words; Work (2nd career/nonretirement), 1,200-1,600 words.

Fiction Needs humorous, mainstream, slice-of-life vignettes.

Tips Go to our website and read as much content as you can.

⊘ TIME

Time Inc. Magazine, Time & Life Bldg., 1271 Avenue of the Americas, New York NY 10020. (212)522-1212. Fax: (212)522-0323. E-mail: letters@time.com. Website: www.time.com. Weekly magazine. *Time* covers the full range of information that is important to people today—breaking news, national and world affairs, business news, societal and lifestyle issues, culture and entertainment news and reviews. Estab. 1923. Circ. 4,150,000. No kill fee.

- *Time* does not accept unsolicited material for publication. The magazine is entirely staff written and produced.

$$$$ TOWN & COUNTRY

The Hearst Corp., 300 W. 57th St., New York NY 10019-3794. Website: www.townandcountrymag.com. **40% freelance written**. Monthly lifestyle magazine. "*Town & Country* is a lifestyle magazine for the affluent market. Features focus on fashion, beauty, travel, interior design, and the arts, as well as individuals' accomplishments and contributions to society.' Estab. 1846. Circ. 488,000. Byline given.

Pays on acceptance. Offers 25% kill fee. Buys first North American serial rights, buys electronic rights. Accepts queries by mail. Responds in 2 months to queries.

Nonfiction "We're looking for engaging service articles for a high income, well-educated audience, in numerous categories: travel, personalities, interior design, fashion, beauty, jewelry, health, city news, the arts, philanthropy." Needs general interest, interview, travel. "Rarely publishes work not commissioned by the magazine. Does not publish poetry, short stories, or fiction." **Buys 25 mss/year.** Query by mail only with relevant clips before submitting Column items, 100-300 words; feature stories, 800-2,000 words. **Pays $2/word.**

Tips "We have served the affluent market for over 150 years, and our writers need to be expert in the needs and interests of that market. Most of our freelance writers start by doing short pieces for our front-of-book columns, then progress from there."

$$$ YES! MAGAZINE

284 Madrona Way NE, Suite 116, Bainbridge Island WA 98110. E-mail: editorial@yesmagazine.org. Website: www.yesmagazine.org. **70% freelance written.** Quarterly magazine covering politics and world affairs; contemporary culture; nature, conservation and ecology. "*YES! Magazine* documents how people are creating a more just, sustainable and compassionate world. Each issue includes articles focused on a theme—about solutions to a significant challenge facing our world—and a number of timely, non-theme articles. Our non-theme section provides ongoing coverage of issues like health, climate change, globalization, media reform, faith, democracy, economy and labor, social and racial justice and peace building. To inquire about upcoming themes, send an e-mail to submissions@yesmagazine.org; please be sure to type 'themes' as the subject line." Estab. 1997. Circ. 55,000. Byline given. Pays on publication. Offers kill fee. varies Publishes ms an average of 1-6 months after acceptance. Buys Creative Commons License. Editorial lead time 3-6 months. Submit seasonal material 2-6 months in advance. Accepts queries by mail, e-mail. Sample copy and writer's guidelines online.

Nonfiction Please check website for a detailed call for submission before each issue. Needs book excerpts, essays, general interest, how-to, interview, opinion, (does not mean letters to the editor), photo feature. "We don't want stories that are negative or too politically partisan." **Buys 60 mss/year.** Query with published clips. Length: 100-2,500 words. **Pays $50-1,250 for assigned articles. Pays $50-600 for unsolicited articles.**

Reprints Send photocopy or typed ms with rights for sale noted and information about when and where the material previously appeared.

Photos Buys one time rights.

Columns/Departments Signs of Life (positive news briefs), 100-250 words; Commentary (opinion from thinkers and experts), 500 words; Book and film reviews, 500-800 words. **Pays $20-$300.**

Tips "We're interested in articles that: 'change the story' about what is possible; tell specific success stories of individuals, communities, movements, nations or regions that are addressing society's challenges and problems; offer visions of a better world. We're less interested in articles that: only describe or update a problem (unless there are dramatic new developments, reframings or insights); primarily reinforce a sense of being a victim (and therefore powerless); are written in styles or about topics relevant or accessible only to narrow groups; lack grounding in research or reporting (except for occasional essays); have a partisan or polarizing tone."

Health & Fitness

$$ AMERICAN FITNESS

15250 Ventura Blvd., Suite 200, Sherman Oaks CA 91403. Fax: (818)817-0803. E-mail: americanfitness@afaa.com. Website: www.afaa.com. **75% freelance written.** Bimonthly magazine covering exercise and fitness, health, and nutrition. We need timely, in-depth, informative articles on health, fitness, aerobic exercise, sports nutrition, age-specific fitness, and outdoor activity. Absolutely no first-person accounts. Need well-reserched articles for professional readers. Circ. 42,000. Byline given. Pays 30 days after publication. No kill fee. Publishes ms an average of 6 months after acceptance. Submit seasonal material 4 months in advance. Accepts queries by mail, fax. Accepts previously published material. Accepts simultaneous submissions. Responds in 2 months to queries. Sample copy for $4.50 and SAE with 6 first-class stamps.

Nonfiction Needs include health and fitness, including women's issues (pregnancy, family, pre- and post-natal, menopause, and eating disorders); new research findings on exercise techniques and equipment; aerobic exercise; sports nutrition; sports medicine; innovations and trends in aerobic sports; tips on teaching exercise and humorous accounts of fitness motivation; physiology; youth and senior fitness.

Needs historical, history of various athletic events, inspirational, sport's leaders motivational pieces, interview, fitness figures, new product, plus equipment review, personal experience, successful fitness story, photo feature, on exercise, fitness, new sport, travel, activity adventures. No articles on unsound nutritional practices, popular trends, or unsafe exercise gimmicks. **Buys 18-25 mss/year.** Send complete ms. Length: 800-1,200 words. **Pays $200 for features, $80 for news.**

Photos Sports, action, fitness, aquatic aerobics competitions, and exercise class. We are especially interested in photos of high-adrenalin sports like rock climbing and mountain biking. Captions, identification of subjects, model releases required. Reviews transparencies, prints. Pays $35 for transparencies Usually buys all rights; other rights purchased depend on use of photo

Columns/Departments Research (latest exercise and fitness findings); Alternative paths (nonmainstream approaches to health, wellness, and fitness); Strength (latest breakthroughs in weight training); Clubscene (profiles and highlights of fitness club industry); Adventure (treks, trails, and global challenges); Food (low-fat/nonfat, high-flavor dishes); Homescene (home-workout alternatives); Clip 'n' Post (concise exercise research to post in health clubs, offices or on refrigerators). Length: 800-1,000 words. Query with published clips or send complete ms. **Pays $100-200.**

Tips Make sure to quote scientific literature or good research studies and several experts with good credentials to validate exercise trend, technique, or issue. Cover a unique aerobics or fitness angle, provide accurate and interesting findings, and write in a lively, intelligent manner. Please, no first-person accouts of 'how I lost weight or discovered running.' *AF* is a good place for first-time authors or regularly published authors who want to sell spin-offs or reprints.

AUSTRALIAN GOOD TASTE

FPC Magazines, Locked Bag 5030 NSW 2015 Australia. (61)(2)9353-6666. Fax: (61)(2)9353-6699. E-mail: goodtaste@newsmagazines.com. Website: www.australiangoodtaste.com.au. **Contact:** Rebecca Cox, editor. Monthly magazine. "*Australian Good Taste* offers innovative and useful ideas, information on health and nutrition, plus features about real people and the issues that affect them. There are book reviews, beauty ideas and great stories to read." Circ. 178,800.

- *"Australian Good Taste is truly in tune with today's busy lifestyle. Our recipes are easy, delicious and family-friendly, with an emphasis on fresh ingredients. Readers love our added extras like tip boxes, chef's secrets, nutritional panels and information on cost per serving and preparation times. Australian Good Taste is a compelling mix of food and ideas for everyday living."*

Nonfiction Needs general interest, how-to, interview. Query.

$$$ BETTER NUTRITION

Active Interest Media, 300 N. Contintental Blvd., Suite 650, El Segundo CA 90245. (310)356-4100. Fax: (310)356-4110. E-mail: editorial@betternutrition.com. Website: www.betternutrition.com. **Contact:** Tracy Rubert, man. ed. **57% freelance written**. Monthly magazine covering nutritional news and approaches to optimal health. "The new *Better Nutrition* helps people (men, women, families, old and young) integrate nutritious food, the latest and most effective dietary supplements, and exercise/personal care into healthy lifestyles." Estab. 1938. Circ. 460,000. Byline given. Pays on publication. No kill fee. Publishes ms an average of 2 months after acceptance. Rights purchased varies according to article rights. Editorial lead time 3 months. Accepts queries by mail, e-mail. Sample copy free.

Nonfiction Each issue has multiple features, clinical research crystallized into accessible articles on nutrition, health, alternative medicine, disease prevention. **Buys 120-180 mss/year.** Query. Length: 400-1,200 words. **Pays $400-1,000.**

Photos State availability. of photos. Captions, identification of subjects, model releases required. Reviews 4 × 5 transparencies, 3 × 5 prints. Negotiates payment individually. Buys one time rights or non-exclusive reprint rights.

Tips "Be on top of what's newsbreaking in nutrition and supplementation. Interview experts. Fact-check, fact-check, fact-check. Send in a résumé (including Social Security/IRS number), a couple of clips, and a list of article possibilities."

$$ CLIMBING

Primedia Enthusiast Group, Box 420034, Palm Coast FL 32142-0235. (970)963-9449. Fax: (970)963-9442. Website: www.climbing.com. Magazine published 9 times/year covering climbing and mountaineering. Provides features on rock climbing and mountaineering worldwide. Estab. 1970. Circ. 51,000. Pays on publication. No kill fee. Editorial lead time 6 weeks. Accepts queries by e-mail. Sample copy for $4.99. Guidelines available online.

Nonfiction SASE returns Needs interview, interesting climbers, personal experience, climbing adventures, surveys of different areas. Query. Length: 1,500-3,500 words. **Pays 35¢/word.**

Photos State availability. Reviews negatives, 35mm transparencies, prints, digital submissions on CD. Pays $25-800
Columns/Departments Query. **Payment varies**

$ $ DELICIOUS LIVING

New Hope Natural Media, 1401 Pearl St., Boulder CO 80302. (303)939-8440. Fax: (303)939-9886. E-mail: deliciousliving@newhope.com. Website: www.deliciouslivingmag.com. **85% freelance written.** Monthly magazine covering natural products, nutrition, alternative medicines, herbal medicines. "*Delicious Living* magazine empowers natural products shoppers to make health-conscious choices in their lives. Our goal is to improve consumers' perception of the value of natural methods in achieving health. To do this, we educate consumers on nutrition, disease prevention, botanical medicines and natural personal care products." Estab. 1985. Circ. 405,000. Byline given. Pays on publication. Offers 20% kill fee. Editorial lead time 6 months. Submit seasonal material 8 months in advance. Accepts simultaneous submissions. Responds in 3 months to queries. Writer's guidelines free.

O→ Does not accept unsolicited manuscripts.

Nonfiction Needs book excerpts, how-to, interview, green living, health nutrition, herbal medicines, alternative medicine, environmental. Query with published clips. Length: 100-1,200 words.
Photos Does not accept submissions
Columns/Departments Fresh Research, How-Tos, Natural-Industry Trends, 75-200/words; Wellness (natural therapies for specific health conditions), 800-1,000/words; Family (issues and topics relevant to raising a natural family), 600-800/words; Beauty (natural personal care). Query with published clips.
Tips "Highlight any previous health/nutrition/medical writing experience. Demonstrate a knowledge of natural medicine, nutrition, or natural products. Health practitioners who demonstrate writing ability are ideal freelancers."

FIT PREGNANCY

Weider Publications, Inc., 21100 Erwin St., Woodland Hills CA 91367. (818)884-6800. Fax: (818)992-6895. Website: www.fitpregnancy.com. Bimonthly magazine. Circ. 505,000. No kill fee.

- Does not buy freelance material.

GOOD HEALTH

ACP Magazines, Ltd., 54-58 Park St., Sydney NSW 2000 Australia. (61)(2)9282-8000. Fax: (61)(2)9267-4361. Website: goodmedicine.ninemsn.com.au/goodmedicine. **Contact:** Catherine Marshall, editor. Monthly magazine for people with a healthy attitude to life. Our aim is to make *Good Health* informative, up-to-date, relevant to women's lives and entertaining. Circ. 60,123.
Nonfiction Needs general interest, how-to. Query.

$ $ HEALING LIFESTYLES & SPAS

P.O. Box 271207, Louisville CO 80027. (202)441-9557. Fax: (303)926-4099. E-mail: editorial@healinglifestyles.com. Website: www.healinglifestyles.com. **90% freelance written.** *Healing Lifestyles & Spas* is a bimonthly magazine committed to healing, health, and living a well-rounded, more natural life. In each issue we cover retreats, spas, organic living, natural food, herbs, beauty, yoga, alternative medicine, bodywork, spirituality, and features on living a healthy lifestyle. Estab. 1996. Circ. 45,000. Pays on publication. No kill fee. Publishes ms an average of 2-10 months after acceptance. Editorial lead time 6 months. Submit seasonal material 6-9 months in advance. Accepts queries by mail, e-mail. Responds in 6 weeks to queries.
Nonfiction We will consider all in-depth features relating to spas, retreats, lifestyle issues, mind/body well being, yoga, enlightening profiles, and women's health issues. Needs travel, domestic and international. No fiction or poetry. Query. Length: 1,000-2,000 words. **Pays $150-500, depending on length, research, experience, and availability and quality of images.**
Photos If you will be providing your own photography, you must use slide film or provide a Mac-formatted CD with image resolution of at least 300 dpi. Send photos. Captions required.
Columns/Departments All Things New & Natural (short pieces outlining new health trends, alternative medicine updates, and other interesting tidbits of information), 50-200 words; Urban Retreats (focuses on a single city and explores its spas and organic living features), 1,200-1,600 words; Health (features on relevant topics ranging from nutrition to health news and updates), 900-1,200 words; Food (nutrition or spa-focused food articles and recipes), 1,000-1,200 words; Ritual (highlights a specific at-home ritual), 500 words; Seasonal Spa (focuses on a seasonal ingredient on the spa menu), 500-700 words; Spa Origins (focuses on particular modalities and healing beliefs from around the world, 1,000-1,200 words; Yoga, 400-800 words; Retreat (highlights a spa or yoga retreat), 500 words; Spa a la carte (explores a new

treatment or modality on the spa menu), 600-1,000 words; Insight (focuses on profiles, theme-related articles, and new therapies, healing practices, and newsworthy items), 1,000-2,000 words. Query.

$$$$ HEALTH

Time, Inc., Southern Progress Corp., 2100 Lakeshore Dr., Birmingham AL 35209. (205)445-6000. Fax: (205)445-5123. E-mail: health@timeinc.com. Website: www.health.com. Magazine published 10 times/year covering health, fitness, and nutrition. Our readers are predominantly college-educated women in their 30s, 40s, and 50s. Edited to focus not on illness, but on wellness news, events, ideas, and people. Estab. 1987. Circ. 1,360,000. Byline given. Pays on acceptance. Offers 33% kill fee. Buys first publication and online rights. Accepts queries by mail, fax. Accepts simultaneous submissions. Responds in 2 months to queries. Sample copy for $5 to Back Issues. Guidelines for #10 SASE or via e-mail.
Nonfiction No unsolicited mss. **Buys 25 mss/year.** Query with published clips and SASE. **Pays $1.50-2/word.**
Columns/Departments Body, Mind, Fitness, Beauty, Food.
Tips We look for well-articulated ideas with a narrow focus and broad appeal. A query that starts with an unusual local event and hooks it legitimately to some national trend or concern is bound to get our attention. Use quotes, examples and statistics to show why the topic is important and why the approach is workable. We need to see clear evidence of credible research findings pointing to meaningful options for our readers. Stories should offer practical advice and give clear explanations.

$$ LIVER HEALTH TODAY

Management and Treatment—A Practical Guide for Patients, Families, and Friends, Quality Publishing, Inc., 523 N. Sam Houston Tollway E., Suite 300, Houston TX 77060. (281)272-2744. Fax: (713)520-1463. E-mail: gdrushel@liverhealthtoday.com. Website: www.liverhealthtoday.org. **70-80% freelance written**. Quarterly magazine covering Hepatitis health news. Estab. 1999. Circ. 25,000. Byline given. Pays on publication. No kill fee. Publishes ms an average of 2 months after acceptance. Buys first North American serial rights, buys electronic rights. Editorial lead time 6 months. Submit seasonal material 4 months in advance. Accepts queries by mail, e-mail. Accepts simultaneous submissions. Responds in 6 weeks to queries. Sample copy and writer's guidelines free.
Nonfiction Needs inspirational, interview, new product, personal experience. We do not want any one-source or no-source articles. **Buys 42-48 mss/year.** Query. Length: 1,500-2,500 words.
Photos Send photos. Identification of subjects required. Reviews transparencies, prints, GIF/JPEG files. Offers no additional payment for photos accepted with ms. Rights negotiated, usually purchases one-time rights.
Columns/Departments General news or advice on Hepatitis written by a doctor or healthcare professional, 1,500-2,000 words. Query. **Pays $375-500.**
Tips Be specific in your query. Show me that you know the topic you want to write about, and show me that you can write a solid, well-rounded story.

$$$$ MAMM MAGAZINE

Courage, Respect & Survival, MAMM, LLC, 54 W. 22nd St., 4th Floor, New York NY 10010. (646)365-1355. Fax: (646)365-1369. E-mail: editorial@mamm.com. Website: www.mamm.com. **80% freelance written**. Magazine published 10 times/year covering cancer prevention, treatment, and survival for women. *MAMM* gives its readers the essential tools and emotional support they need before, during and after diagnosis of breast, ovarian and other gynecologic cancers. We offer a mix of survivor profiles, conventional and alternative treatment information, investigative features, essays, and cutting-edge news. Estab. 1997. Circ. 100,000. Byline given. Pays within 30 days of publication. Offers 50% kill fee. Publishes ms an average of 3 months after acceptance. Buys exclusive rights up to 3 months after publishing. Submit seasonal material 3-4 months in advance. Accepts simultaneous submissions. Sample copy and writer's guidelines free
Nonfiction Needs book excerpts, essays, expose, how-to, humor, inspirational, interview, opinion, personal experience, photo feature, historic/nostalgic. **Buys 90 mss/year.** Query with published clips. Length: 200-3,000 words. **Pays $100-3,000.** Negotiates coverage of expenses of writers on assignment.
Photos Send photos. Identification of subjects required. Reviews contact sheets, negatives. Negotiates payment individually Buys first rights
Columns/Departments Opinion (cultural/political); International Dispatch (experience); Q and A (interview format), all 600 words. Query with published clips. **Pays $400-800.**

$$ ✪ MAXIMUM FITNESS

For Men, Robert Kennedy Publishing, CANUSA Publishing, 400 Matheson Blvd. West, Mississauga

ON L5R 3MI Canada. E-mail: editorial@maxfitmag.com. Website: www.maxfitmag.com. Bimonthly magazine. *American Health & Fitness* is designed to help male fitness enthusiasts (18-39) stay fit, strong, virile, and healthy through sensible diet and exercise. Estab. 2006. Circ. 310,000. Byline given. Pays on acceptance. No kill fee. Publishes ms an average of 6 months after acceptance. Buys all rights. Editorial lead time 4 months. Submit seasonal material 6 months in advance. Accepts queries by mail, e-mail, fax. Responds in 4 months to queries. Responds in 4 months to mss. Sample copy for $5.

Nonfiction Needs photo feature, bodybuilding and weight training, health & fitness tips, diet, medical advice, workouts, nutrition. **Buys 80-100 mss/year.** Query or send complete ms. Length: 800-1,500 words. **Pays 25-45¢/word for assigned articles.**

Photos Send photos. Captions, identification of subjects required. Reviews 35mm transparencies, 8 × 10 prints. Offers $35 and up/photo Buys all rights.

Columns/Departments Personal Training; Strength & Conditioning; Fitness; Longevity; Natural Health; Sex. Query or send complete ms.

Fillers Length: 100-200 words.

$$$$ MEN'S HEALTH

Rodale, 33 E. Minor St., Emmaus PA 18098. (610)967-5171. Fax: (610)967-7725. E-mail: online@rodale.com. Website: www.menshealth.com. **50% freelance written**. Magazine published 10 times/year covering men's health and fitness. *Men's Health* is a lifestyle magazine showing men the practical and positive actions that make their lives better, with articles covering fitness, nutrition, relationships, travel, careers, grooming, and health issues. Estab. 1986. Circ. 1,600,000. Pays on acceptance. Offers 25% kill fee. Buys all rights. Accepts queries by mail, fax. Responds in 3 weeks to queries. Guidelines for #10 SASE.

Nonfiction Authoritative information on all aspects of men's physical and emotional health. We rely on writers to seek out the right experts and to either tell a story from a first-person vantage or get good anecdotes. **Buys 30 features/year; 360 short mss/year.** Query with published clips. 1,200-4,000 words for features, 100-300 words for short pieces **Pays $1,000-5,000 for features; $100-500 for short pieces.**

Columns/Departments Length: 750-1,500 words. **Pays $ 750- 2,000.**

Tips We have a wide definition of health. We believe that being successful in every area of your life is being healthy. The magazine focuses on all aspects of health, from stress issues and nutrition, to exercise and sex. It is 50% staff written, 50% from freelancers. The best way to break in is not by covering a particular subject, but by covering it within the magazine's style. There is a very particular tone and voice to the magazine. A writer has to be a good humor writer as well as a good service writer. Prefers mail queries. No phone calls, please.

$$$ MUSCLE & FITNESS

Weider Health & Fitness, 21100 Erwin St., Woodland Hills, CA 91367. (818)884-6800. Fax: (818)595-0463. Website: www.muscle-fitness.com. **50% freelance written**. Monthly magazine covering bodybuilding and fitness for healthy, active men and women. It contains a wide range of features and monthly departments devoted to all areas of bodybuilding, health, fitness, sport, injury prevention and treatment, and nutrition. Editorial fulfills 2 functions: information and entertainment. Special attention is devoted to how-to advice and accuracy. Estab. 1950. Circ. 500,000. Pays on publication. No kill fee. Publishes ms an average of 2 months after acceptance. Editorial lead time 5 months. Submit seasonal material 6 months in advance. Accepts queries by mail. Accepts previously published material. Responds in 1 month to queries.

Nonfiction All features and departments are written on assignment. Needs book excerpts, how-to, training, humor, interview, photo feature. **Buys 120 mss/year.** Query with published clips. Length: 800-1,800 words. **Pays $400-1,000.**

Reprints Send photocopy with rights for sale noted and information about when and where the material previously appeared. Payment varies.

Photos State availability.

Tips Know bodybuilders and bodybuilding. Read our magazine regularly (or at least several issues), come up with new information or a new angle on our subject matter (bodybuilding training, psychology, nutrition, diets, fitness, sports, etc.), then pitch us in terms of providing useful, unique, how-to information for our readers. Send a 1-page query letter (as described in *Writer's Market*) to sell us on your idea and on you as the best writer for that article. Send a sample of your published work.

MUSCLEMAG

MuscleMag International-Building Health, Fitness, Physique, Canusa Products, Inc., 400 Matheson Blvd.

W., Mississauga ON L5R 3M1. (905)507-3545. Fax: (905)507-2372. E-mail: editorial@emusclemag.com. Website: www.emusclemag.com. **80% freelance written**. Monthly magazine building health, fitness and physique. Byline given. Pays on acceptance. No kill fee. Publishes ms an average of 6 months after acceptance. Buys all rights. Accepts queries by mail, e-mail. Responds in 4 months to queries. Responds in 4 months to mss. Guidelines available.

Nonfiction Needs how-to, interview, new product, personal experience, photo feature, bodybuilding, strenth training, health, nutrition & fitness. **Pays $80-400 for assigned articles.**

Photos Contact: Rich Baker, photo editor. Send photos. Captions, identification of subjects required. Reviews 35 mm transparencies, 8 × 10 prints and hi-res digital images.

Fillers Length: 100-200 words.

Tips Send in unedited sample articles on training or nutrition to be assessed. Those writers accepted may be added to our roster of freelance writers for future article assignments.

NATURE & HEALTH

Yaffa Publishing, 17-21 Bellevue St., Surry Hills NSW 2010 Australia. (61)(2)9281-2333. Fax: (61)(2)9281-2750. E-mail: yaffa@yaffa.com.au. Website: www.yaffa.com.au. Bimonthly magazine for people interested in maintaining a naturally healthy lifestyle.

Nonfiction "Nature & Health Magazine is a trusted resource for people who are passionate about their health, and it is the first place they turn to for ideas, information, and advice on complementary medicine and natural therapies. Our articles cover a wide spectrum of relevant topics — self-help and preventive health care, healthy food and cookery, diet and nutrition, anti-aging, herbal medicine, vitamins, drug updates, environmental health issues, exercise, beauty and fitness tips, women's health, relationships, mental and spiritual health, natural pet care, yoga, traditional chinese medicine, ayurveda, psychic healing, eco-travel, sustainability, and personal growth. As a premium quality publication, we require a high standard of contributions. Accuracy, in-depth and 'breaking new ground' are features we look for." Query.

$$$ OXYGEN

Serious Fitness for Serious Women, Canusa Products/St. Ives, Inc., 5775 McLaughlin Rd., Mississauga ON L5R 3P7 Canada. (905)507-3545/(888)254-0767. Fax: (905)507-2372. E-mail: editorial@oxygenmag.com. Website: www.oxygenmag.com. **70% freelance written**. Monthly magazine covering women's health and fitness. *Oxygen* encourages various exercise, good nutrition to shape and condition the body. Estab. 1997. Circ. 340,000. Byline given. Pays on acceptance. Offers 25% kill fee. Publishes ms an average of 4 months after acceptance. Buys all rights. Editorial lead time 3 months. Submit seasonal material 6 months in advance. Accepts queries by mail, fax. Responds in 5 weeks to queries. Responds in 2 months to mss. Sample copy for $5.

Nonfiction Needs expose, how-to, training and nutrition, humor, inspirational, interview, new product, personal experience, photo feature. No poorly researched articles that do not genuinely help the readers towards physical fitness, health and physique. **Buys 100 mss/year.** Send complete ms. with SAE and $5 for return postage. Length: 1,400-1,800 words. **Pays $250-1,000.**

Photos State availability of or send photos. Identification of subjects required. Reviews contact sheets, 35mm transparencies, prints. Offers $35-500. Buys all rights.

Columns/Departments Nutrition (low-fat recipes), 1,700 words; Weight Training (routines and techniques), 1,800 words; Aerobics (how-tos), 1,700 words. Send complete ms. **Pays $150-500.**

Tips Every editor of every magazine is looking, waiting, hoping and praying for the magic article. The beauty of the writing has to spring from the page; the edge imparted has to excite the reader because of its unbelievable information.

$$$$ POZ

CDM Publishing, LLC, 500 Fifth Ave., Suite 320, New York NY 10110. (212)242-2163. Fax: (212)675-8505. E-mail: editor-in-chief@poz.com. Website: www.poz.com. **25% freelance written**. Monthly national magazine for people impacted by HIV and AIDS. *POZ* is a trusted source of conventional and alternative treatment information, investigative features, survivor profiles, essays and cutting-edge news for people living with AIDS and their caregivers. *POZ* is a lifestyle magazine with both health and cultural content. Estab. 1994. Circ. 125,000. Byline given. Pays 30 days after publication. Offers 25% kill fee. Publishes ms an average of 3 months after acceptance. Buys first rights. Editorial lead time 4 months. Submit seasonal material 4 months in advance. Accepts simultaneous submissions. Sample copy and writer's guidelines free

Nonfiction Needs book excerpts, essays, exposè, historical, how-to, humor, inspirational, interview, opinion, personal experience, photo feature. Query with published clips. We take unsolicited mss on speculation only. Length: 200-3,000 words. **Pays $1/word.**
Photos Send photos. Identification of subjects required. Reviews contact sheets, negatives. Negotiates payment individually. Buys first rights.

⊘ PREVENTION

Rodale, Inc., 33 E. Minor St., Emmaus PA 18098-0099. E-mail: prevention@rodale.com. Website: www.prevention.com. Monthly magazine covering health and fitness. Written to motivate, inspire and enable male and female readers ages 35 and over to take charge of their health, to become healthier and happier, and to improve the lives of family and friends. Estab. 1950. Circ. 3,150,000. No kill fee.

- *Prevention* does not accept, nor do they acknowledge, unsolicited submissions.

REPS! MAGAZINE

The Science of Building Muscle, Canusa Products, Inc., 400 Matheson Blvd. W., Mississauga ON L5R 3M1 Canada. (905)507-3545. Fax: (905)507-2372. E-mail: editorial@repsmag.com. Website: www.repsmag.com. Quarterly magazine covering bodybuilding. "*Reps! Magazine* brings the best weight-training advice, nutritional news and fat-burning information to help you build the best possible physique." Kill fee for assigned articles. Guidelines available.
Nonfiction Needs how-to, interview, new product, opinion, personal experience, photo feature. Length: 1,500-2,000 words. **Pays 50-80¢/word for assigned articles.**
Photos Send photos. Captions, identification of subjects required. Reviews 35 mm transparencies, 8 × 10 prints. Offers $35 and over. Buys all rights.
Columns/Departments Query and/or send complete ms.
Fillers Length: 100-200 words.

$$$$ SHAPE MAGAZINE

Weider Publications, Inc., 21100 Erwin St., Woodland Hills CA 91367. (818)595-0593. Fax: (818)704-7620. Website: www.shapemag.com. **70% freelance written. Prefers to work with published/established writers.** Monthly magazine covering health, fitness, nutrition, and beauty for women ages 18-34. *Shape* reaches women who are committed to healthful, active lifestyles. Our readers are participating in a variety of fitness-related activities, in the gym, at home and outdoors, and they are also proactive about their health and are nutrition conscious. Estab. 1981. Circ. 1,600,000. Pays on acceptance. Offers 33% kill fee. Buys second serial (reprint) rights, buys all rights. Submit seasonal material 8 months in advance. Accepts queries by mail. Responds in 2 months to queries. Sample copy for sae with 9 × 12 envelope and 4 First-Class stamps. Guidelines available online.
Nonfiction We use some health and fitness articles written by professionals in their specific fields. Needs book excerpts, expose, health, fitness, nutrition related, how-to, get fit, health/fitness, recipes. We rarely publish celebrity question and answer stories, celebrity profiles, or menopausal/hormone replacement therapy stories. **Buys 27 features/year; 36-54 short mss/year.** Query with published clips. 2,500 words/features; 1,000 words/shorter pieces **Pays $1.50/word (on average).**
Tips Review a recent issue of the magazine. Not responsible for unsolicited material. We reserve the right to edit any article.

$$$ SPIRITUALITY & HEALTH MAGAZINE

The Soul Body Connection, Spirituality & Health Publishing, Inc., 129½ E. Front St., Traverse City MI 49684. E-mail: editors@spiritualityhealth.com. Website: www.spiritualityhealth.com. **Contact:** Heather Shaw, man. ed. Bimonthly magazine covering research-based spirituality and health. "We look for formally credentialed writers in their fields. We are nondenominational and non-proselytizing. We are not New Age. We appreciate well-written work that offers spiritual seekers from all different traditions help in their unique journeys." Estab. 1998. Circ. 95,000. Byline given. Pays on acceptance. Offers 50% kill fee. Buys electronic rights, buys worldwide rights. Editorial lead time 4 months. Submit seasonal material 6 months in advance. Accepts queries by e-mail. Accepts simultaneous submissions. Responds in 3-4 months to queries. Responds in 2-4 months to mss. Sample copy and writer's guidelines online.

- The most open department is Updates & Observations. Read it to see what we use. (All back issues are on the website.) News must be current with a four-month lead time.

Nonfiction Needs book excerpts, how-to, news shorts. Does not want proselytizing, New Age cures with no scientific basis, "how I recovered from a disease personal essays," psychics, advice columns, profiles of individual healers or practitioners, pieces promoting one way or guru, reviews, poetry or columns. Send complete ms.

Tips "Start by pitching really interesting, well-researched news shorts for Updates & Observations. Before you pitch, do a search of our website to see if we've already covered it."

$$ ⊘ VIBRANT LIFE

A Magazine for Healthful Living, Review and Herald Publishing Association, 55 W. Oak Ridge Dr., Hagerstown MD 21740-7390. (301)393-4019. Fax: (301)393-4055. E-mail: vibrantlife@rhpa.org. Website: www.vibrantlife.com. **80% freelance written. Enjoys working with published/established writers; works with a small number of new/unpublished writers each year.** Bimonthly magazine covering health articles (especially from a prevention angle and with a Christian slant). The average length of time between acceptance of a freelance-written manuscript and publication of the material depends upon the topics: some immediately used; others up to 2 years. Estab. 1885. Circ. 30,000. Byline given. Pays on acceptance. Offers 50% kill fee. Buys first serial, first world serial, or sometimes second serial (reprint) rights. Submit seasonal material 9 months in advance. Accepts queries by mail, e-mail, fax. Accepts previously published material. Responds in 1 month to queries. Sample copy for $1. Guidelines available online.

- Currently closed to submissions.

Nonfiction We seek practical articles promoting better health and a more fulfilled life. We especially like features on breakthroughs in medicine, and most aspects of health. We need articles on how to integrate a person's spiritual life with their health. We'd like more in the areas of exercise, nutrition, water, avoiding addictions of all types, and rest—all done from a wellness perspective. Needs interview, with personalities on health. **Buys 50-60 feature articles/year and 6-12 short mss/year.** Send complete ms. Length: 500-1,500 words for features, 25-250 words for short pieces. **Pays $75-300 for features, $50-75 for short pieces.**

Reprints Send tearsheet and information about when and where the material previously appeared. Pays 50% of amount paid for an original article.

Photos Not interested in b&w photos. Send photos. Reviews 35mm transparencies.

Columns/Departments Buys 12-18 department articles/year. Length: 500-650 words. **Pays $75-175.**

Tips *Vibrant Life* is published for baby boomers, particularly young professionals, age 40-55. Articles must be written in an interesting, easy-to-read style. Information must be reliable; no faddism. We are more conservative than other magazines in our field. Request a sample copy, and study the magazine and writer's guidelines.

$$$$ VIM & VIGOR

America's Family Health Magazine, 1010 E. Missouri Ave., Phoenix AZ 85014-2601. (602)395-5850. Fax: (602)395-5853. E-mail: stephaniec@mcmurry.com. **90% freelance written**. Quarterly magazine covering health and healthcare. Estab. 1985. Circ. 800,000. Byline given. Pays on acceptance. Publishes ms an average of 6 months after acceptance. Buys all rights. Sample copy for 9 × 12 SAE with 8 first-class stamps. Guidelines for #10 SASE.

Nonfiction Absolutely no complete manuscripts will be accepted/returned. All articles are assigned. Send published samples for assignment consideration. Any queries regarding story ideas will be placed on the following year's conference agenda and will be addressed on a topic-by-topic basis. Send published clips and résumé by mail or e-mail. Length: 500-1,200 words. **Pays 90¢-$1/word.**

Tips Writers must have consumer healthcare experience.

WEBMD THE MAGAZINE

WebMD, 111 8th Ave, 7th Floor, New York NY 10011. (212)624-3700. E-mail: newstip@webmd.net; news@medscape.net. Website: www.webmd.net. www.webmd.net/magazine. **80% freelance written**. Bimonthly magazine covering health, lifestyle health and well-being, some medical. Published by WebMD Health, *WebMD the Magazine* is the print sibling of the website WebMD.com. It aims to broaden our company-wide mandate: 'Better information, better health.' It is a health magazine—with a difference. It is specifically designed and written for people who are about to have what may be the most important conversation of the year with their physician or other medical professional. The magazine's content is therefore developed to be most useful at this critical 'point of care,' to improve and enhance the dialogue between patient and doctor. Our readers are adults (65% women, 35% men) in their 30s, 40s, and 50s (median age is 41) who care about their health, take an active role in their own and their family's wellness, and want the best information possible to make informed healthcare decisions. Estab. 2005. Circ. 1,000,000. Byline given. Pays on acceptance. Offers 30% kill fee. Publishes ms an average of 3 months after acceptance. Buys all rights. Editorial lead time 3-4 months. Submit seasonal material 3-4 months in advance. Accepts queries by e-mail. Accepts previously published material. Sample copy available online.

Tips We only want experienced magazine writers, in the topic areas of consumer health. Writers with experience writing for national women's health magazines preferred. Relevant clips required. Fresh, witty, smart, well-written style, with solid background in health. This is not a publication for writers breaking into the field.

$$ WHJ/HRHJ

Williamsburg Health Journal/Hampton Roads Health Journal, Rian Enterprises, LLC, 4808 Courthouse St., Suite 204, Williamsburg VA 23188. Fax: (757)645-4473. E-mail: info@thehealthjournals.com. Website: www.williamsburghealth.com; www.hamptonroadshealth.com. **70% freelance written**. Monthly tabloid covering consumer/family health and wellness in the Hampton Roads area. "Articles accepted of local and national interest. Health-savvy, college educated audience of all gender, ages, and backgrounds. " Estab. 2005. Circ. 81,000. Byline given. Pays on publication. Publishes ms an average of 1-2 months after acceptance. Buys first rights, buys second serial (reprint) rights. Editorial lead time 4-6 months. Submit seasonal material 4 months in advance. Accepts queries by mail, e-mail, fax. Accepts previously published material. Accepts simultaneous submissions. Only responds to mss of interest. Sample copy available online. Guidelines available online.

Nonfiction Needs book excerpts, essays, expose, general interest, historical, how-to, humor, inspirational, interview, new product, opinion, personal experience, photo feature, technical, travel. Does not want promotion of products, religious material, anything over 2,000 words. **Buys 100 mss/year.** Query with published clips. Length: 400-1,000 words. **Pays 15¢/word, $50/reprint.**

Tips "Write for the consumer. Remain objective. Entertain. Inform. Surprise us! If you are not a health expert on the topic, consult one. Or two. Or three. Writer's point of view is not sufficient unless submitting a personal essay."

WOMEN'S HEALTH & FITNESS

Blitz Publications, P.O. Box 4075, Mulgrave VIC 3170 Australia. (61)(3)9574-8999. Fax: (61)(3)9574-8899. E-mail: angela@blitzmag.com.au. Website: www.sportzblitz.net. Monthly magazine covering health and fitness for today's woman. *Women's Health & Fitness Magazine* is a holistic guide to a happier and healthier lifestyle, offering information on weight training, nutrition, mental well-being, health, beauty, fat loss, life coaching, home workouts, low fat recipes, fitness fashion, fitness tips, diet, supplementation, natural remedies, pregnancy and body shaping.

Nonfiction Needs general interest, how-to, new product. Query.

$$$$ YOGA JOURNAL

475 Sasome St., Suite 850, San Francisco CA 94111. (415)591-0555. Fax: (415)591-0733. E-mail: queries@yogajournal.com. Website: www.yogajournal.com. **Contact:** Kaitlin Quistgaard, editor-in-chief. **75% freelance written**. Magazine published 9 times a year covering the practice and philosophy of yoga. "With comprehensive features on the practice, fitness, well-being and everyday balance, we deliver the yoga tradition suited to today's lifestyle. We welcome professional queries for these departments: **Om**: Covers myriad aspects of the yoga lifestyle (150-400 words). This department includes Yoga Diary, a 250-word story about a pivotal moment in your yoga practice. **Eating Wisely.** A popular, 1,400-word department about relationship to food. Most stories focus on vegetarian and whole-foods cooking, nutritional healing, and contemplative pieces about the relationship between yoga and food. **Well Being.** This 1,500-word department presents reported pieces about holistic health practices." Estab. 1975. Circ. 300,000. Byline given. Pays within 90 days of acceptance. Offers kill fee. Offers kill fee on assigned articles. Publishes ms an average of 10 months after acceptance. Buys first North American serial rights. Submit seasonal material 7 months in advance. Accepts queries by e-mail. Accepts previously published material. Responds in 6 weeks to queries if interested. Sample copy for $4.99. Guidelines available online.

Nonfiction "Yoga is a main concern, but we also highlight other conscious living/New Age personalities and endeavors. In particular we welcome articles on the following themes: 1) Leaders, spokespersons, and visionaries in the yoga community; 2) The practice of hatha yoga; 3) Applications of yoga to everyday life; 4) Hatha yoga anatomy and kinesiology, and therapeutic yoga; 5) Nutrition and diet, cooking, and natural skin and body care. Pays about $1/word." Needs book excerpts, how-to, yoga, exercise, etc., inspirational, yoga or related, interview, opinion, photo feature, travel, yoga-related. Does not want unsolicited poetry or cartoons. Please avoid New Age jargon and in-house buzz words as much as possible. **Buys 50-60 mss/year.** Query with SASE. Length: 3,000-5,000 words. **Pays $800-2,000.**

Reprints Send tearsheet or photocopy with rights for sale noted and information about when and where the material previously appeared.

Columns/Departments Health (self-care; well-being); Body-Mind (hatha Yoga, other body-mind modalities, meditation, yoga philosophy, Western mysticism); Community (service, profiles, organizations, events), all 1,500-2,000 words. **Pays $400-800.** Living (books, video, arts, music), 800 words. **Pays $200-250.** World of Yoga, Spectrum (brief yoga and healthy living news/events/fillers), 150-600 words. **Pays $50-150.**

Tips "Please read several issues of Yoga Journal before submitting a query. Pitch your article idea to the appropriate department with the projected word count, and what sources you'd use. In your query letter, please indicate your writing credentials. If we are interested in your idea, we will require writing samples. Please note that we do not accept unsolicited manuscripts for any departments except Yoga Diary. Please read our writer's guidelines before submission. Do not e-mail or fax unsolicited manuscripts."

History

⊘ AMERICAN HISTORY

Weider History Group, 741 Miller Dr., Suite D-2, Leesburg VA 20175-8994. (703)771-9400. Fax: (703)779-8345. Website: www.historynet.com. **60% freelance written.** Bimonthly magazine of cultural, social, military, and political history published for a general audience. Estab. 1966. Circ. 95,000. Byline given. Pays on acceptance. No kill fee. Buys first rights. Responds in 10 weeks to queries. Sample copy and guidelines for $5 (includes 3rd class postage) or $4 and 9 × 12 SAE with 4 first-class stamps. Guidelines for #10 SASE.

Nonfiction Features events in the lives of noteworthy historical figures and accounts of important events in American history. Also includes pictorial features on artists, photographers, and graphic subjects. Material is presented on a popular rather than a scholarly level. **Buys 20 mss/year.** Query by mail only with published clips and SASE. Length: 2,000-4,000 words depending on type of article.

Photos Welcomes suggestions for illustrations.

Tips Key prerequisites for publication are thorough research and accurate presentation, precise English usage, and sound organization, a lively style, and a high level of human interest. *Unsolicited manuscripts not considered.* Inappropriate materials include: fiction, book reviews, travelogues, personal/family narratives not of national significance, articles about collectibles/antiques, living artists, local/individual historic buildings/landmarks, and articles of a current editorial nature. Currently seeking articles on significant Civil War subjects. No phone, fax, or e-mail queries, please.

N ⊘ AMERICAN LEGACY

Forbes, Inc., 28 W. 23rd St., 10th Floor, New York NY 10010-5254. (212)367-3100. Fax: (212)367-3151. E-mail: apeterson@americanlegacymag.com. Website: www.americanlegacymagazine.net. Quarterly magazine spotlighting the historical and cultural achievements of African American men and women throughout history. No kill fee. Editorial lead time 6 months.

- Query before submitting.

$$ AMERICA'S CIVIL WAR

Weider History Group, 741 Miller Dr., Suite D-2, Leesburg VA 20175-8994. (703)771-9400. Fax: (703)779-8345. Website: www.historynet.com. **95% freelance written.** Bimonthly magazine covering popular history and straight historical narrative for both the general reader and the Civil War buff covering strategy, tactics, personalities, arms and equipment. Estab. 1988. Circ. 78,000. Byline given. Pays on publication. No kill fee. Buys all rights. Accepts queries by mail, e-mail, fax. Sample copy for $5. Writer's guidelines for #10 SASE.

Nonfiction Needs historical, book notices, preservation news. **Buys 24 mss/year.** Query. 3,500-4,000 words and a 500-word sidebar. **Pays $300 and up.**

Photos Send photos. with submission or cite sources. Captions, identification of subjects required.

Columns/Departments Personality (profiles of Civil War personalities); Men & Material (about weapons used); Commands (about units); Eyewitness to War (historical letters and diary excerpts). Length: 2,000 words. Query. **Pays $150 and up.**

Tips All stories must be true. We do not publish fiction or poetry. Write an entertaining, well-researched, informative and unusual story that grabs the reader's attention and holds it. Include suggested readings in a standard format at the end of your piece. Manuscript must be typed, double-spaced on one side of standard white 8½ × 11, 16 to 30 pound paper—no onion skin paper or dot matrix printouts. All submissions are on speculation. Prefer subjects to be on disk (IBM- or Macintosh-compatible floppy disk) as well as a hard copy. Choose stories with strong art possibilities.

$ THE ARTILLERYMAN

Historical Publications, Inc., 234 Monarch Hill Rd., Tunbridge VT 05077. (802)889-3500. Fax: (802)889-5627. E-mail: mail@civilwarnews.com. Website: www.artillerymanmagazine.com. **60% freelance written**. Quarterly magazine covering antique artillery, fortifications, and crew-served weapons 1750-1900 for competition shooters, collectors, and living history reenactors using artillery. Emphasis on Revolutionary War and Civil War but includes everyone interested in pre-1900 artillery and fortifications, preservation, construction of replicas, etc. Estab. 1979. Circ. 1,500. Byline given. Pays on publication. Publishes ms an average of 6 months after acceptance. Buys one-time rights. Accepts queries by mail, e-mail, fax. Accepts previously published material. Accepts simultaneous submissions. Responds in 3 weeks to queries. Sample copy and writer's guidelines for 9 × 12 SAE with 4 first-class stamps

Nonfiction Interested in artillery only, for sophisticated readers. Not interested in other weapons, battles in general. Needs historical, how-to, reproduce ordnance equipment/sights/implements/tools/accessories, etc., interview, new product, opinion, must be accompanied by detailed background of writer and include references, personal experience, photo feature, technical, must have footnotes, travel, where to find interesting antique cannon. **Buys 24-30 mss/year.** Send complete ms. **Pays $20-60.**

Reprints Send tearsheet or photocopy and information about when and where the material previously appeared.

Photos Send photos. Captions, identification of subjects required. Pays $5 for 5 × 7 and larger b&w prints

Tips We regularly use freelance contributions for Places-to-Visit, Cannon Safety, The Workshop, and Unit Profiles departments. Also need pieces on unusual cannon or cannon with a known and unique history. To judge whether writing style and/or expertise will suit our needs, writers should ask themselves if they could knowledgeably talk artillery with an expert. Subject matter is of more concern than writer's background.

BRITISH HERITAGE

Weider History Group, 19300 Promenade Dr., Leesburg VA 20176. (703)771-9400. Fax: (703)779-8345. E-mail: dana.huntley@weiderhistorygroup.com. Website: www.thehistorynet.com. Bimonthly magazine covering British travel and culture. Stories of British life and history with a sense of place in England, Scotland and Wales. Circ. 77,485. Pays on acceptance. Pays kill fee though never had to. Buys all rights. Editorial lead time 6 months. Accepts queries by e-mail.

Nonfiction Buys 50 mss/year. Query by e-mail. Length: 1,000-2,500 words.

Tips "The first rule still stands: Know thy market."

$$$ CIVIL WAR TIMES

Weider History Group, 19300 Promenade Drive, Leesburg VA 20176-6500. (703)779-8371. Fax: (703)779-8345. E-mail: cwt@weiderhistorygroup.com. Website: www.historynet.com. **90% freelance written. Works with a small number of new/unpublished writers each year.** Magazine published 6 times/year. "*Civil War Times* is the full-spectrum magazine of the Civil War. Specifically, we look for nonpartisan coverage of battles, prominent military and civilian figures, the home front, politics, military technology, common soldier life, prisoners and escapes, period art and photography, the naval war, blockade-running, specific regiments, and much more." Estab. 1962. Circ. 108,000. Pays on acceptance and on publication. Publishes ms an average of 18 months after acceptance. Buys unlimited usage rights. Submit seasonal material 1 year in advance. Responds in 3-6 months to queries. Sample copy for $6. Guidelines for #10 SASE.

Nonfiction Needs interview, photo feature, Civil War historical material. "Don't send us a comprehensive article on a well-known major battle. Instead, focus on some part or aspect of such a battle, or some group of soldiers in the battle. Similar advice applies to major historical figures like Lincoln and Lee. Positively no fiction or poetry." **Buys 20 freelance mss/year.** Query with clips and SASE. **Pays $75-800.**

Tips "We're very open to new submissions. Send query after examining writer's guidelines and several recent issues. Include photocopies of photos that could feasibly accompany the article. Confederate soldiers' diaries and letters are especially welcome."

COMMON PATRIOT

The American Revolutionary War Magazine, Two If By Sea Publishing, LLC, 12995 S. Cleveland Ave., Suite 141 #1776, Fort Myers FL 33907. (239)464-9730. E-mail: editor@commonpatriot.com. Website: www.commonpatriot.com. **100% freelance written**. Quarterly magazine covering the American revolutionary war. Estab. 2005. Byline given. Pays on publication. Publishes ms an average of 4-6 months after acceptance. Buys one-time rights. Submit seasonal material 6 months in advance. Accepts queries by mail, e-mail. Accepts previously published material. Accepts simultaneous submissions. Responds in 1 month to queries. Responds in 2-3 months to mss. Sample copy for $6. Guidelines available online.

Nonfiction Needs book excerpts, general interest, historical, inspirational, interview, personal experience, travel. **Buys 20 mss/year.** Query. Length: 2,500 words.

Photos Send photos. Captions, identification of subjects required. Reviews 4x6 prints. Buys one time rights.

Columns/Departments Patriot Profile (biography, history), 500-1,000 words; My Ancestor (genealogy), 500-1,000 words; Am Rev War Today (re-enactments, personal experience, historical), 750-2,000 words; How It Was in Rev War Time (life of being a soldier), 800-1,000 words. Send complete ms.

Tips A well-written article on their 'unknown' common patriot who fought in the American revolutionary war. Check our website for more information.

$$ GATEWAY

(formerly *Gateway Heritage*), Missouri History Museum, P.O. Box 11940, St. Louis MO 63112-0040. (314)746-4558. Fax: (314)746-4548. E-mail: vwmonks@mohistory.org. Website: www.mohistory.org. **75% freelance written**. Annual magazine covering Missouri history and culture. *Gateway* is a popular cultural history magazine that is primarily a member benefit of the Missouri History Museum. Thus, we have a general audience with an interest in the history and culture of Missouri, and St. Louis in particular. Estab. 1980. Circ. 11,000. Byline given. Pays on publication. Offers $100 kill fee. Publishes ms an average of 6 months to 1 year after acceptance. Buys first North American serial rights. Editorial lead time 6 months. Accepts queries by mail, e-mail, fax. Responds in 1 month to queries. Responds in 2 months to mss. Sample copy for $10. online or send #10 SASE

Nonfiction Needs book excerpts, interview, photo feature, historical, scholarly essays, Missouri biographies, viewpoints on events, first-hand historical accounts, regional architectural history, literary history. No genealogies. **Buys 4-6 mss/year.** Query with writing samples. Length: 4,000-5,000 words. **Pays $300-400 (average).**

Photos State availability.

Columns/Departments Origins (essays on the beginnings of organizations, movements, and immigrant communities in St. Louis and Missouri), 1,500-2,500 words; Missouri Biographies (biographical sketches of famous and interesting Missourians), 1,500-2,500 words; Gateway Conversations (interviews); Letters Home (excerpts from letters, diaries, and journals), 1,500-2,500 words. **Pays $250-300**

Tips "You'll get our attention with queries reflecting new perspectives on historical and cultural topics."

$ GOOD OLD DAYS/LOOKING BACK

America's Premier Nostalgia Magazine, Dynamic Resource Group, 306 E. Parr Rd., Berne IN 46711. Fax: (260)589-8093. E-mail: editor@goodolddaysonline.com. Website: www.goodolddaysonline.com. **Contact:** Ken Tate, editor. **75% freelance written**. Monthly magazine of first person nostalgia, 1935-1965. "We look for strong narratives showing life as it was in the middle decades of the 20th century. Our readership is comprised of nostalgia buffs, history enthusiasts, and the people who actually lived and grew up in this era." Byline given. Pays on contract. No kill fee. Publishes ms an average of 8 months after acceptance. Prefers all rights, but will negotiate for First North American serial and one-time rights. Submit seasonal material 10 months in advance. Accepts queries by fax, online submission form. Responds in 2 months to queries. Sample copy for $2. Guidelines available online.

- Queries accepted, but are not necessary.

Nonfiction Regular features: Good Old Days on Wheels (auto, plane, horse-drawn, tram, bicycle, trolley, etc.); Good Old Days In the Kitchen (favorite foods, appliances, ways of cooking, recipes); Home Remedies (herbs and poultices, hometown doctors, harrowing kitchen table operations). Needs historical, humor, personal experience, photo feature, favorite food/recipes, year-round seasonal material, biography, memorable events, fads, fashion, sports, music, literature, entertainment. No fiction accepted. **Buys 350 mss/year.** Query or send complete ms. Length: 500-1,500 words. **Pays $20-100, depending on quality and photos.**

Photos Do not send original photos until we ask for them. You may send photocopies or duplicates. Do not submit laser-copied prints. Send photos. Identification of subjects required.

Tips "Most of our writers are not professionals. We prefer the author's individual voice, warmth, humor, and honesty over technical ability."

$$ ✪ HISTORY MAGAZINE

Moorshead Magazines, 500-505 Consumers Rd., Toronto ON M2J 4V8 Canada. E-mail: magazine@

history-magazine.com. Website: www.history-magazine.com. **90% freelance written**. Bimonthly magazine covering social history. A general interest history magazine, focusing on social history up to the outbreak of World War II. Estab. 1999. Byline given. Pays on publication. Publishes ms an average of 6 months after acceptance. Buys electronic rights, buys world serial rights rights. Editorial lead time 6 months. Submit seasonal material 6 months in advance. Accepts queries by mail, e-mail. Responds in 1 month to queries. Responds in 1 month to mss. Sample copy available online. Guidelines available online.

Nonfiction Needs book excerpts, historical. Does not want first-person narratives or revisionist history. **Buys 50 mss/year.** Query. Length: 400-2,500 words. **Pays $50-250.**

Photos State availability. Captions required. Reviews GIF/JPEG files. Negotiates payment individually. Buys one time rights.

Tips A love of history helps a lot and a willingness to work with us to present interesting articles on the past to our readers.

$$ KANSAS JOURNAL OF MILITARY HISTORY

P.O. Box 828, Topeka KS 66601. (785)357-0510. Fax: (785)357-0579. E-mail: karen@ksjournal.com. Website: www.ksjournal.com. **20% freelance written**. Quarterly magazine that celebrates and explores the military history of Kansas and its territories and the Kansans who have served here and abroad, and promotes tourism by showcasing historic sites and landmarks. Estab. 2004. Circ. 4,000. Byline given. Pays on publication. No kill fee. Publishes ms an average of 6 months after acceptance. Buys first North American serial rights. Editorial lead time 6 months. Submit seasonal material 1 year in advance. Accepts queries by mail, e-mail. Accepts previously published material. Accepts simultaneous submissions. Responds in 2 weeks to queries. Responds in 2 months to mss. Sample copy available online. Guidelines available online.

Nonfiction Needs book excerpts, essays, historical, humor, interview, opinion, personal experience, photo feature. Lights, Camera, Kansas: movie stills, posters, etc. relating to film in Kansas. Does not want to receive fiction or poetry. **Buys 10 mss/year.** Query with published clips. Length: 500-1,500 words. **Pays $50-200.**

Photos Send photos. Captions, identification of subjects, model releases required. Reviews contact sheets, GIF/JPEG files. Offers no additional payment for photos accepted with ms. Buys one time rights.

Columns/Departments Hand to Hand (opinion, pro/con, historic figures), 800-1,000 words. **Pays $50-200.**

Fillers Length: 200-300 words. **Pays $25-50.**

Tips We are interested in history that is fun, compelling, and interesting—not academic. The audience is made up of military members, veterans, tourists, and history buffs (novice and knowledgeable).

$ N LIGHTHOUSE DIGEST

Lighthouse Digest, P.O. Box 250, East Machias ME 04630. (207)259-2121. Fax: (207)259-3323. E-mail: timh@lhdigest.com. Website: www.lighthousedigest.com. **Contact:** Tim Harrison, editor. **15% freelance written**. Monthly magazine covering historical, fiction and news events about lighthouses and similar maritime stories. Estab. 1989. Circ. 24,000. Byline given. Pays on publication. No kill fee. Publishes ms an average of 4 months after acceptance. Buys one-time rights, buys electronic rights. Editorial lead time 3 months. Submit seasonal material 3 months in advance. Accepts queries by e-mail. Accepts simultaneous submissions. Responds in 6 weeks to queries. Sample copy free.

Nonfiction Needs expose, general interest, historical, humor, inspirational, personal experience, photo feature, religious, technical, travel. No historical data taken from books. **Buys 30 mss/year.** Send complete ms. **Pays $75.**

Photos Send photos. Captions, identification of subjects required. Reviews prints. Offers no additional payment for photos accepted with ms. Buys all rights.

Fiction Needs adventure, historical, humorous, mystery, religious, romance, suspense. **Buys 2 mss/year.** Send complete ms. **Pays $75-150.**

Tips "Read our publication and visit the website."

MHQ

MHQ: The Quarterly Journal of Military History, Weider History Group, 19300 Promenade Dr., Leesburg VA 20176-6500. (703)779-8373. Fax: (703)779-8359. Website: www.historynet.com. **100% freelance written**. Quarterly journal covering military history. "*MHQ* offers readers in-depth articles on the history of warfare from ancient times into the 21st century. Authoritative features and departments cover military strategies, philosophies, campaigns, battles, personalities, weaponry, espionage and perspectives, all written in a lively and readable style. Articles are accompanied by classic works of art, photographs and maps. Readers include serious students of military tactics, strategy, leaders and campaigns, as well as general world history enthusiasts. Many readers are currently in the military or retired officers." Estab. 1988. Circ. 22,000. Byline given. Pays on publication. No kill fee. Buys all rights. Editorial lead time 1 year. Submit seasonal material 1 year in advance. Accepts queries by mail, e-mail, fax. Accepts simultaneous submissions. Sample copy for $23 (hardcover), $13 (softcover); some articles on website. Writer's guidelines for #10 SASE or via e-mail.

- With this first quarter issue, there will be no more hardcover editions.

Nonfiction Needs historical, personal experience, photo feature. No fiction or stories pertaining to collectibles or reenactments. **Buys 36 mss/year.** Query preferred; also accepts complete ms. Length: 1,500-6,000 words.

Photos Send photos./art with submission. Identification of subjects required. Reviews transparencies, prints. Negotiates payment individually. Buys all rights.

Columns/Departments Artists on War (description of artwork of a military nature); Experience of War (first-person accounts of military incidents); Strategic View (discussion of military theory, strategy); Arms & Men (description of military hardware or unit), all up to 2,500 words. Send complete ms.

Tips "Less common topic areas—medieval, Asian, or South American military history, for example—are more likely to attract our attention. The likelihood that articles can be effectively illustrated often determines the ultimate fate of manuscripts. Many otherwise excellent articles have been rejected due to a lack of suitable art or photographs. Regular departments—columns on strategy, tactics, and weaponry—average 1,500 words. While the information we publish is scholarly and substantive, we prefer writing that is anecdotal, and above all, engaging, rather than didactic."

MILITARY HISTORY

The Quarterly Journal of Military History, Weider History Group, 19300 Promenade Dr., Leesburg VA 20176. (703)771-9400. Fax: (703)779-8345. Website: www.historynet.com. **70% freelance written**. Magazine published six times/year covering world military history of all ages. We strive to give the general reader accurate, highly readable, often narrative popular history, richly accompanied by period photography or illustration. "We strive to give the general reader accurate, highly readable, often narrative popular history, richly accompanied by period art." Circ. 100,000. Byline given. Pays upon publication. No kill fee. Buys all rights. Submit seasonal material 1 year in advance. Accepts queries by mail, e-mail, fax. Sample copy for $5. Guidelines for #10 SASE.

Nonfiction The best way to break into our magazine is to write an entertaining, informative, and unusual story that grabs the reader's attention and holds it. Needs historical, interview, military figures of commanding interest, personal experience, only occasionally. **Buys 20-30 mss/year.** "Submit a short, self-explanatory query summarizing the story proposed, its highlights and/or significance. State also your own expertise, access to sources or proposed means of developing the pertinent information. Read the magazine, discover our style, and avoid subjects already covered. Avoid sweeping historical overview; focus on specific events/personalities within appropriate context. Provide list of sources, author biography/photo and the authors/titles of two or three books for further reading. Pick stories with strong art possibilities and suggest sources. We accept queries primarily by e-mail, also by mail or fax." Features: 2,000 to 3,000 words with a 200- to 500-word sidebar.

Columns/Departments Interview, What We Learned (lessons from history), Valor (those who have earned medals/awards), Hallowed Ground (battlegrounds of significance) and Reviews (books, video, games, all relating to military history). Length: 700-1,300 words.

Tips "We seek professional submissions that are thoroughly researched and fact-checked and adhere to the Associated Press Stylebook."

NOSTALGIA MAGAZINE

Enriching Today with the Stories of Yesterday, King's Publishing Group, Inc., P.O. Box 203, Spokane WA 99210. (509)299-4041. E-mail: editor@nostalgiamagazine.net. Website: www.nostalgiamagazine.net. **90% freelance written**. Bi-monthly magazine covering "stories and photos of personal, historical, nostalgic experiences: I remember when. *Nostalgia Magazine* is a journal that gathers photos, personal remembrance stories, diaries, and researched stories of well-known—and more often little-known—people, places, and events, and puts them into 1 bi-monthly volume. We glean the best of the past to share and enrich life now." Byline given. No kill fee. Publishes ms an average of 1 year after acceptance. "Uses simultaneous rights and rights to reprint in our regional editions and affiliated media rights." Editorial lead time 6 months. Submit seasonal material 6 months in advance. Accepts queries by mail, e-mail. Accepts previously published material. Accepts simultaneous submissions. Responds in 6 months to queries and mss. Sample copy for $5. Writer's guidelines available via e-mail or mail.

Nonfiction Needs book excerpts, expose, general interest, historical, how-to, humor, inspirational, interview, personal experience, photo feature, religious, travel. Does not want genealogies, current events/news, divisive politics (in historical setting sometimes OK), or glorification of immorality. **Buys 120 mss/year.** Send complete ms. Length: 400-2,000 words.

Photos "Photos are as important as the story. We need 1 candid photo per 400 words of fiction." Send photos. Captions, identification of subjects required. Reviews negatives, transparencies, prints, JPEG files. Offers no payment for photos accepted with ms. Acquires right to use in all publications and affiliated media only.

Poetry Needs free verse, light verse, traditional. "Does not want avant-garde, contemporary/modern experiences, simple junk." Buys 3 poems/year. Submit maximum 1 poems. **Pays in copies.**

Fillers Length: 50-200 words. **Pays with copies of the magazine.**

Tips "Start with an interesting photograph from your past. Good photos are the key to people reading an interesting story in our magazine. Write the who, what, when, where, why, and how."

$$ PERSIMMON HILL

National Cowboy & Western Heritage Museum, 1700 NE 63rd St., Oklahoma City OK 73111. (405)478-2250. Fax: (405)478-4714. E-mail: editor@nationalcowboymuseum.org. Website: www.nationalcowboymuseum.org. **Contact:** Judy Hilovsky. **70% freelance written. Prefers to work with published/established writers; works with a small number of new/unpublished writers each year.** Quarterly magazine for an audience interested in Western art, Western history, ranching, and rodeo, including historians, artists, ranchers, art galleries, schools, and libraries. Estab. 1970. Circ. 7,500. Byline given. Pays on publication. No kill fee. Publishes ms an average of 18 months after acceptance. Buys first rights. Responds in 3 months to queries. Sample copy for $10.50, including postage. Writer's guidelines available on website.

Nonfiction "Historical and contemporary articles on famous Western figures connected with pioneering the American West, Western art, rodeo, cowboys, etc. (or biographies of such people), stories of Western flora and animal life and environmental subjects. We want thoroughly researched and historically authentic material written in a popular style. May have a humorous approach to subject. No broad, sweeping, superficial pieces; i.e., the California Gold Rush or rehashed pieces on Billy the Kid, etc." **Buys 50-75 mss/year.** Query by mail with clips. Word length: 1,500 words. **Pays $150-300**

Photos Purchased with ms or on assignment. Captions required. Reviews digital images and b&w prints. Pays according to quality and importance for b&w and color photos.

Tips "Send us a story that captures the spirit of adventure and indvidualism that typifies the Old West or reveals a facet of the Western lifestyle in comtemporary society. Excellent illustrations for articles are essential! We lean towards scholarly, historical, well-researched articles. We're less focused on Western celebrities than some of the other contemporary Western magazines."

$$$ TIMELINE

Ohio Historical Society, 1982 Velma Ave., Columbus OH 43211-2497. (614)297-2360. Fax: (614)297-2367. E-mail: timeline@ohiohistory.org. **90% freelance written. Works with a small number of new/unpublished writers each year.** Quarterly magazine covering history, prehistory, and the natural sciences, directed toward readers in the Midwest. Estab. 1984. Circ. 7,000. Byline given. Pays on acceptance. Offers $75 minimum kill fee. Publishes ms an average of 1 year after acceptance. Buys first North American serial rights, buys all rights. Submit seasonal material 6 months in advance. Accepts queries by mail, e-mail, fax. Responds in 3 weeks to queries. Responds in 6 weeks to mss. Sample copy for $12 and 9 × 12 SAE. Guidelines for #10 SASE.

Nonfiction Topics include the traditional fields of political, economic, military, and social history; biography; the history of science and technology; archaeology and anthropology; architecture; the fine and decorative arts; and the natural sciences including botany, geology, zoology, ecology, and paleontology. Needs book excerpts, essays, historical, interview, of individuals, photo feature. **Buys 22 mss/year.** Query. 1,500-6,000 words. Also vignettes of 500-1,000 words. **Pays $100-800.**

Photos Submissions should include ideas for illustration. Send photos. Captions, identification of subjects, model releases required. Reviews contact sheets, transparencies, 8 × 10 prints. Buys one-time rights.

Tips "We want crisply written, authoritative narratives for the intelligent lay reader. An Ohio slant may strengthen a submission, but it is not indispensable. Contributors must know enough about their subject to explain it clearly and in an interesting fashion. We use high-quality illustration with all features. If appropriate illustration is unavailable, we can't use the feature. The writer who sends illustration ideas with a manuscript has an advantage, but an often-published illustration won't attract us."

$ THE TOMBSTONE EPITAPH

National Edition, Tombstone Epitaph, Inc., P.O. BOX, 1880, Tombstone AZ 85638. (520)457-2211. E-mail: info@tombstoneepitaph.com. Website: www.tombstoneepitaph.com. **60% freelance written**. Monthly tabloid covering American west to 1900 (-1935, if there's an Old West connection). "We seek lively, well-written, sourced articles that examine the history and culture of the Old West." Estab. 1880. Byline given. End of calendar year. No kill fee. Publishes ms an average of 3 months after acceptance. Buys first North American serial rights. Editorial lead time 3 months. Submit seasonal material 6 months in advance. Accepts queries by e-mail. Accepts previously published material. Responds in 2 weeks to queries. Responds in 1 month to mss. Sample copy for $3. Guidelines by e-mail.

Nonfiction Needs essays, historical, humor, personal experience, (if historically grounded), travel, Past events as interpreted in film, books, magazines, etc. "We do not want poorly sourced stories, contemporary West pieces, fiction, poetry, big 'tell-all' stories." **Buys 25-40 mss/year.** Query. Length: 1,000-5,000 words. **Pays $30-50 for assigned articles. Pays $30 max. for unsolicited articles.**

Photos Send photos./ Captions, identification of subjects required. Reviews GIF/JPEG files. Offers no additional payment for photos accepted with ms. Buys one-time rights.

Tips "Writers desiring to break into the Western historical genre are especially encouraged to query. Editor is very willing to work with new talent committed to bright, accurate and polished stories on the history of the Old West. Read a sample copy first, then query."

$$ TRACES OF INDIANA AND MIDWESTERN HISTORY

Indiana Historical Society, 450 W. Ohio St., Indianapolis IN 46202-3269. (317)232-1877. Fax: (317)233-0857. E-mail: rboomhower@indianahistory.org. Website: www.indianahistory.org. **Contact:** Ray E. Boomhower, Senior editor. **80% freelance written**. Quarterly magazine on Indiana history. "Conceived as a vehicle to bring to the public good narrative and analytical history about Indiana in its broader contexts of region and nation, *Traces* explores the lives of artists, writers, performers, soldiers, politicians, entrepreneurs, homemakers, reformers, and naturalists. It has traced the impact of Hoosiers on the nation and the world. In this vein, the editors seek nonfiction articles that are solidly researched, attractively written, and amenable to illustration, and they encourage scholars, journalists, and freelance writers to contribute to the magazine." Estab. 1989. Circ. 6,000. Byline given. No kill fee. Publishes ms an average of 6 months after acceptance. Buys one-time rights. Submit seasonal material 1 year in advance. Responds in 3 months to mss. Guidelines available online.

Nonfiction Book excerpts, historical essays, historical photographic features on topics of biography, literature, folklore, music, visual arts, politics, economics, industry, transportation, and sports. **Buys 20 mss/year.** Send complete ms. Length: 2,000-4,000 words. **Pays $100-500.**

Photos Send photos. Captions, identification of subjects, True required. Reviews contact sheets, transparencies, photocopies, prints. Pays reasonable photographic expenses. Buys one-time rights.

Tips "Freelancers should be aware of prerequisites for writing history for a broad audience. Writers should have some awareness of this magazine and other magazines of this type published by Midwestern historical societies. Preference is given to subjects with an Indiana connection and authors who are familiar with *Traces*. Quality of potential illustration is also important."

TRAINS

Kalmbach Publishing Co., P.O. Box 1612, Waukesha WI 53187-1612. (262)796-8776. Fax: (262)796-1142. E-mail: editor@trainsmag.com. Website: www.trainsmag.com. Monthly magazine. "that appeals to consumers interested in learning about the function and history of the railroad industry." Circ. 100,000. No kill fee. Editorial lead time 2 months.

- Query before submitting.

$$$ ⊘ TRUE WEST

True West Publishing, Inc., P.O. Box 8008, Cave Creek AZ 85327. (888)687-1881. Fax: (480)575-1903. E-mail: editor@twmag.com. Website: twmag.com. Executive Editor: Bob Boze Bell. **Contact:** Managing Editor. **45% freelance written. Works with a small number of new/unpublished writers each year.** Magazine published 10 times/year covering Western American history from prehistory 1800 to 1930. "We want reliable research on significant historical topics written in lively prose for an informed general audience. More recent topics may be used if they have a historical angle or retain the Old West flavor of trail dust and saddle leather. True West magazine's features and departments tie the history of the American West (between 1800-1930) to the modern western lifestyle through enticing narrative and intelligent analyses." Estab. 1953. Byline given. Pays on publication. Kill fee applicable only to material assigned by the editor, not for stories submitted on spec based on query written to the editor. 50% of original fee should the story have run in the publication. Buys first North American serial rights and archival rights. Editorial lead time 6 months. Accepts queries by mail, e-mail. Sample copy for $3. Guidelines available online

- No unsolicited mss.

Nonfiction No fiction, poetry, or unsupported, undocumented tales. **Buys 30 mss/year.** Send query to Meghan Saar at editor@twmag.com Length: no more than 1,500 words. **Pays $50-800. "Features pay $150-500 with a $20 payment for each photo the author provides that is published with the article and not already part of True West archives."**

Photos State availability. Captions, identification of subjects, model releases required and verification of permission granted for publication by original owner. Reviews contact sheets, negatives, 4 × 5 transparencies, 4 × 5 prints. Offers $20/photo. Buys one-time rights.

Fillers Length: 50-300 words.

Tips "Read our magazines and follow our guidelines. A freelancer is most likely to break in with us by submitting thoroughly researched, lively prose on relatively obscure topics or by being assigned to write for one of our departments. First-person accounts rarely fill our needs. Historical accuracy and strict adherence to the facts are essential. We much prefer material based on primary sources (archives, court records, documents) and should not be based mainly on secondary sources (published books, magazines, and journals). Art is also a huge selling point for us."

VIETNAM

Weider History Group, 741 Miller Dr., Suite D-2, Leesburg VA 20175-8994. (703)771-9400. Fax: (703)779-8345. Website: www.historynet.com. **90% freelance written**. Bimonthly magazine providing in-depth and authoritative accounts of the many complexities that made the war in Vietnam unique, including the people, battles, strategies, perspectives, analysis, and weaponry. Estab. 1988. Circ. 46,000. Byline given. Pays on publication. No kill fee. Buys all rights. Accepts queries by mail, fax. Sample copy for $5. Guidelines for #10 SASE.

Nonfiction Needs historical, military, interview, personal experience. Absolutely no fiction or poetry; we want straight history, as much personal narrative as possible, but not the gung-ho, shoot-'em-up variety, either. **Buys 24 mss/year.** Query.

Photos Send photos. with submission or State availability. and cite sources. Identification of subjects required.

Columns/Departments Arsenal (about weapons used, all sides); Personality (profiles of the players, all sides); Fighting Forces (various units or types of units: air, sea, rescue); Perspectives. Length: 2,000 words. Query.

Tips Choose stories with strong art possibilities. Send hard copy plus an IBM- or Macintosh-compatible floppy disk. All stories must be true. We do not publish fiction or poetry. All stories should be carefully researched third-person articles or firsthand accounts that give the reader a sense of experiencing historical events.

$$ WILD WEST

Weider History Group, 19300 Promenade Dr., Leesburg VA 20176-6500. (703)771-9400. Fax: (703)779-8345. E-mail: wildwest@weiderhistorygroup.com. Website: www.historynet.com. **Contact:** Eric Weider, publisher. **95% freelance written**. Bimonthly magazine covering the history of the American frontier, from its eastern beginnings to its western terminus. "*Wild West* covers the popular (narrative) history of the American West—events, trends, personalities, anything of general interest." Estab. 1988. Circ. 83,500. Byline given. Pays on publication. No kill fee. Publishes ms an average of 2 years after acceptance. Buys all rights. Editorial lead time 10 months. Submit seasonal material 1 year in advance. Accepts queries by mail, e-mail. Accepts simultaneous submissions. Responds in 3 months to queries. Responds in 6 months to mss. Sample copy for $6. Writer's guidelines for #10 SASE or online.

Nonfiction Needs historical, Old West. No excerpts, travel, etc. Articles can be adapted from book. No fiction or poetry—nothing current. **Buys 36 mss/year.** Query. **Pays $300.**

Photos State availability. Captions, identification of subjects required. Reviews negatives, transparencies. Offers no additional payment for photos accepted with ms. Buys one time rights.

Columns/Departments Gunfighters & Lawmen, 2,000 words; Westerners, 2,000 words; Warriors & Chiefs, 2,000 words; Western Lore, 2,000 words; Guns of the West, 1,500 words; Artists West, 1,500 words; Books Reviews, 250 words. Query. **Pays $150 for departments; book reviews paid by the word, minimum $40.**

Tips Always query the editor with your story idea. Successful queries include a description of sources of information and suggestions for color and b&w photography or artwork. The best way to break into our magazine is to write an entertaining, informative, and unusual story that grabs the reader's attention and holds it. We favor carefully researched, third-person articles that give the reader a sense of experiencing historical events. Include a hard copy as well as an IBM- or Macintosh-compatible floppy disk.

$$ WORLD WAR II

Weider History Group, 19300 Promenade Dr., Leesburg VA 20176. (703)771-9400. Fax: (703)779-8345. E-mail: worldwar2@weiderhistorygroup.com. Website: www.historynet.com. **Contact:** Eric Weider, publisher. **95%. Most of our stories are assigned by our staff to professional writers. However, we do accept written proposals for features and for our Time Travel department.** Bimonthly magazine covering military operations in World War II—events, personalities, strategy, national policy, etc. Estab. 1986. Circ. 146,000. Byline given. Pays on publication. No kill fee. Buys all rights. Accepts queries by mail, e-mail, fax. Sample copy for $5. Writer's guidelines for #10 SASE.

Nonfiction World War II military history. Submit anniversary-related material 1 year in advance. No fiction. **Buys 24 mss/year.** Query. Outline the subject and your approach to it, and why you believe this would be an important article. It would also be helpful if you would summarize briefly your prior writing experience in a cover note. List your sources and suggest further readings in standard format at the end of your piece—as a bibliography for our files in case of factual challenge or dispute. 4,000 words with a 500-word sidebar. **Pays $300 and up.**

Photos For photos and other art, send photocopies and cite sources. We'll order. State availability. Captions, identification of subjects required.

Columns/Departments Undercover (espionage, resistance, sabotage, intelligence gathering, behind the lines, etc.); Personality (WWII personalities of interest); Armament (weapons, their use and development); Commands (unit histories); One Man's War (personal profiles), all 2,000 words. Book reviews, 300-750 words. Query. **Pays $150 and up**

Tips "We no longer consider full manuscripts submitted on spec, as all of the articles are now written by freelance writers. All assigned articles are based on queries and prior discussion. All submissions are on speculation. Include a hard copy as well as an IBM- or Macintosh-compatible floppy disk. All stories must be true. Stories should be carefully researched."

Hobby & Craft

$$$$ AMERICAN CRAFT

American Craft Council, 72 Spring St., 6th Floor, New York NY 10012. (212)274-0630. Fax: (212)274-0650. E-mail: letters@craftcouncil.org. Website: www.americancraftmag.org. **75% freelance written.** Bimonthly magazine covering art/craft/design. Estab. 1943. Circ. 40,000. Byline given. Pays 30 days after acceptance. Offers 25% kill fee. Publishes ms an average of 2 months after acceptance. Buys first North American serial rights, buys electronic rights. Editorial lead time 3 months. Submit seasonal material 3 months in advance. Accepts queries by mail, e-mail. Accepts simultaneous submissions. Responds in 1 month to queries. Responds in 2 months to mss. Sample copy free. Guidelines by e-mail.

Nonfiction Needs essays, general interest, interview, new product, opinion, photo feature, travel. Query with published clips. Length: 1,200-3,000 words.

Columns/Departments Critics's Corner (critical essays), 200-2,500 words; Wide World of Craft (travel), 800-1,000 words; Material Culture (material studies), 600-800 words; outskirts (a look at peripheral disciplines), 600-800 words. Query with published clips. **Pays $1-1.50/word.**

Tips Keep pitches short and sweet, a paragraph or two at most. Please include visuals with any pitches.

$$ ☐ ANTIQUE & COLLECTIBLES SHOWCASE

Trajan Publishing Corporation, P.O. Box 1626, Holland Landing ON L9N 1P2 Canada. E-mail: acseditor@rogers.com. Website: www.antiqueandcollectiblesshowcase.ca. **75% freelance written.** Bimonthly magazine covering antiques and contemporary collectibles. Preference is given to Canadian writers, but US writers will be considered if they have a unique angle on a story of interest to Canadian readers. Estab. 2003. Circ. 5,500. Byline given. Pays on publication. Publishes ms an average of 2-3 months after acceptance. Buys first North American serial rights, buys electronic rights. Makes work-for-hire assignments. Editorial lead time 1-3 months. Submit seasonal material 6 months in advance. Accepts queries by mail, e-mail. Responds in 1 month to queries. Sample copy for $5 (Canadian). Guidelines available online.

Nonfiction Needs general interest, how-to, interview, opinion. Does not want poetry, book reports or self-promotion. **Buys 30 mss/year.** Query. Length: 500-1,500 words. **Pays $50-225.**
Photos Send photos. Reviews GIF/JPEG files. Offers no additional payment for photos accepted with ms.
Columns/Departments Antiquing in the 21st Century (modern perspective from knowledgeable sources), 750 words; Decorating With Antiques (how to use Great Aunt Gerdie's bookcase), 750 words. Query. **Pays $50-150.**
Tips Antiques are old, but your ideas and your writing shouldn't be. We want to entertain the reader. Form pitches based on the guidelines. Show e-mail subject as Freelance Query.

$$ ANTIQUE TRADER

F+W Media, Inc., 700 E. State St., Iola WI 54990-0001. (715)445-2214. Fax: (715)445-4087. Website: www.antiquetrader.com. **Contact:** Eric Bradley, editor. **60% freelance written**. Weekly tabloid covering antiques. "We publish quote-heavy stories of timely interest in the antiques field. We cover antiques shows, auctions, and news events." Estab. 1957. Circ. 30,000. Byline given. Pays on publication. No kill fee. Publishes ms an average of 1-3 months after acceptance. Buys exclusive rights. Editorial lead time 2 months. Accepts queries by mail, e-mail, fax. Responds in 1 week to queries. Responds in 2 months to mss Sample copy for cover price, plus postage. Guidelines available online.
Nonfiction Needs book excerpts, general interest, interview, personal experience, show and auction coverage. Does not want the same, dry textbook, historical stories on antiques that appear elsewhere. Our readers want personality and timeliness. **Buys 1,000+ mss/year.** Send complete ms. Length: 750-1,200 words. **Pays $50-150, plus contributor copy.**
Photos State availability. Identification of subjects required. Reviews transparencies, prints, GIF/JPEG files. Offers no additional payment for photos accepted with ms. Buys one-time rights.
Columns/Departments Dealer Profile (interviews with interesting antiques dealers), 750-1,200 words; Collector Profile (interviews with interesting collectors), 750-1,000 words. Query with or without published clips or send complete ms.

$$ BEAD & BUTTON

Kalmbach Publishing, P.O. Box 1612, Waukesha WI 53187. E-mail: editor@beadandbutton.com. Website: www.beadandbutton.com. **50% freelance written**. "*Bead & Button* is a bimonthly magazine devoted to techniques, projects, designs and materials relating to making beaded jewelry. Our readership includes both professional and amateur bead and button makers, hobbyists, and enthusiasts who find satisfaction in making beautiful things." Estab. 1994. Circ. 100,000. Byline given. Pays on acceptance. Offers $75 kill fee. Publishes ms an average of 4-12 months after acceptance. Buys all rights. Accepts queries by mail, e-mail, fax. Guidelines available online.
Nonfiction Needs historical, on beaded jewelry history, how-to, make beaded jewelry and accessories, humor, inspirational, interview. **Buys 20-25 mss/year.** Send complete ms. Length: 750-1,500 words. **Pays $100-400.**
Photos Send photos. Identification of subjects required. Offers no additional payment for photos accepted with ms

$$ BLADE MAGAZINE

The World's #1 Knife Publication, F+W Media, Inc., 700 E. State St., Iola WI 54990-0001. (715)445-2214. Fax: (715)445-4087. E-mail: joe.kertzman@fwmedia.com. Website: www.blademag.com. **Contact:** Joe Kertzman, Managing Editor. **5% freelance written**. Monthly magazine covering working and using collectible, popular knives. *Blade* prefers in-depth articles focusing on groups of knives, whether military, collectible, high-tech, pocket knives or hunting knives, and how they perform. Estab. 1973. Circ. 39,000. Byline given. Pays on publication. No kill fee. Publishes ms an average of 9 months after acceptance. Buys all rights. Editorial lead time 9 months. Submit seasonal material 9 months in advance. Accepts queries by mail, e-mail, fax. Responds in 3 months to queries. Responds in 6 months to mss. Sample copy for $4.99. Guidelines for sae with 8 × 11 envelope and 3 first-class stamps.
Nonfiction "We need stories that are brand new in scope and content. Knives being used for unusual purposes, in adventure settings, etc. New, state-of-the-art knife designs, steels and other knife materials and how they are made are good. The knife collections of celebrities are good. Stories on how to collect knives, what to collect and why, etc., are good." Needs general interest, historical, how-to, interview, new product, photo feature, technical. "We assign profiles, show stories, hammer-in stories, etc. We don't need those. If you've seen the story on the Internet or in another knife or knife/gun magazine, we don't need it. We don't do stories on knives used for self-defense." Send complete ms. Length: 700-1,400 words. **Pays $150-300.**

Photos Send photos. Captions, identification of subjects required. Reviews transparencies, prints, digital images (300 dpi at 1200x1200 pixels). Offers no additional payment for photos accepted with ms. Buys all rights.

Tips "We are always willing to read submissions from anyone who has read a few copies and studied the market. The ideal article for us is a piece bringing out the romance, legend, and love of man's oldest tool—the knife. We like articles that place knives in peoples' hands—in life saving situations, adventure modes, etc. (Nothing gory or with the knife as the villain.) People and knives are good copy. We are getting more well-written articles from writers who are reading the publication beforehand. That makes for a harder sell for the quickie writer not willing to do his homework. Go to knife shows and talk to the makers and collectors. Visit knifemakers' shops and knife factories. Read anything and everything you can find on knives and knifemaking."

$ BREW YOUR OWN

The How-to Homebrew Beer Magazine, Battenkill Communications, 5515 Main St., Manchester Center VT 05255. (802)362-3981. Fax: (802)362-2377. E-mail: edit@byo.com. Website: www.byo.com. www.byo.com/about/guidelines. **85% freelance written**. Monthly magazine covering home brewing. Our mission is to provide practical information in an entertaining format. We try to capture the spirit and challenge of brewing while helping our readers brew the best beer they can. Estab. 1995. Circ. 40,000. Byline given. Pays on acceptance. Offers 25% kill fee. Publishes ms an average of 4 months after acceptance. Buys all rights. Editorial lead time 3 months. Submit seasonal material 3 months in advance. Accepts queries by mail, e-mail, fax. Responds in 2 months to queries. Guidelines available online.

Nonfiction Informational pieces on equipment, ingredients, and brewing methods. Needs historical, how-to, home brewing, humor, related to home brewing, interview, of professional brewers who can offer useful tips to home hobbyists, personal experience, trends. **Buys 75 mss/year.** Query with published clips or description of brewing expertise Length: 800-3,000 words. **Pays $50-350, depending on length, complexity of article, and experience of writer.**

Photos State availability. Captions required. Reviews contact sheets, transparencies, 5 × 7 prints, slides, and electronic images. Negotiates payment individually. Buys all rights.

Columns/Departments News (humorous, unusual news about homebrewing), 50-250 words; Last Call (humorous stories about homebrewing), 700 words. Query with or without published clips. **Pays $75**

Tips "*Brew Your Own* is for anyone who is interested in brewing beer, from beginners to advanced all-grain brewers. We seek articles that are straightforward and factual, not full of esoteric theories or complex calculations. Our readers tend to be intelligent, upscale, and literate."

$$ CANADIAN WOODWORKING AND HOME IMPROVEMENT

Develop Your Skills-Tool Your Shop-Build Your Dreams, Sawdust Media, Inc., 51 Maple Ave. N., RR #3, Burford ON N0E 1A0 Canada. (519)449-2444. Fax: (519)449-2445. E-mail: letters@canadianwoodworking.com. Website: www.canadianwoodworking.com. **20% freelance written**. Bimonthly magazine covering woodworking. Estab. 1999. Byline given. Pays on publication. Offers 50% kill fee. Buys all rights. Accepts queries by e-mail. Sample copy available online. Guidelines by e-mail.

Nonfiction Needs how-to, humor, inspirational, new product, personal experience, photo feature, technical. Does not want profile on a woodworker. Query. Length: 500-4,000 words. **Pays $100-600 for assigned articles. Pays $50-400 for unsolicited articles.**

Photos State availability. Negotiates payment individually. Buys all rights.

CARDMAKING, STAMPING & PAPERCRAFT

Express Publications, Ltd., Locked Bag 111, Silverwater NSW 1811 Australia. (61)(2)9741-3899. Fax: (61)(2)9737-8017. E-mail: emcqueen@expresspublications.com.au. Website: www.scrapbookingmemories.com.au/spc.php. **Contact:** The Editor. "Cardmaking, Stamping & Papercraft has got everything you need to craft gorgeous handmade cards including fabulous projects, techniques, product showcases, the latest trends, tips and special features." Accepts queries by e-mail or mail.

- "Successful contributors will be notified by telephone or e-mail and will be required to supply written instructions for the work."

Nonfiction Needs general interest, how-to, new product, Techniques of all kinds: including ways with rubber stamps, backgrounds, faux looks, interactive cards, papercraft and more! Due Date: July 6th. Artist Trading Cards: Fresh ideas for clear, stamped, printed or coloured acetate. Due Date: July 31st Cardmaking on a Budget: 3-4 cards using a small amount of supplies to your advantage. Studio Steps: create 3 versions of a single card - they should become progressively more difficult to suit a beginner, intermediate and advanced crafter. Due Date: July 31st . Query.

$$ CERAMICS MONTHLY

600 N. Cleveland Ave., Suite 210, Westerville OH 43082. (614)895-4213. Fax: (614)891-8960. E-mail: editorial@ceramicsmonthly.org. Website: www.ceramicsmonthly.org. **Contact:** Jessica Knapp, assistant editor. **70% freelance written**. Monthly magazine (except July and August) covering the ceramic art and craft field. "Each issue includes articles on potters and ceramics artists from throughout the world, exhibitions, and production processes, as well as critical commentary, book and video reviews, clay and glaze recipes, kiln designs and firing techniques, advice from experts in the field, and ads for available materials and equipment. While principally covering contemporary work, the magazine also looks back at influential artists and events from the past." Estab. 1953. Circ. 39,000. Byline given. Pays on publication. Editorial lead time 3 months. Submit seasonal material 6 months in advance. Accepts queries by mail, e-mail, fax, phone. Responds in 2 months to mss. Guidelines available online.

Nonfiction Needs essays, how-to, interview, opinion, personal experience, technical. **Buys 100 mss/year.** Send complete ms. Length: 500-3,000 words. **Pays 10¢/word.**

Photos Send photos. Captions required. Reviews digital images, original slides or 2¼ or 4 × 5 transparencies.

Columns/Departments Upfront (workshop/exhibition review), 500-1,000 words. Send complete ms.

$$ CLASSIC TOY TRAINS

Kalmbach Publishing Co., P.O. Box 1612, 21027 Crossroads Cir., Waukesha WI 53187-1612. (262)796-8776, ext. 524. Fax: (262)796-1142. E-mail: cswanson@classictoytrains.com. Website: www.classictoytrains.com. **Contact:** Carl Swanson, editor. **80% freelance written**. Magazine published 9 times/year covering collectible toy trains (O, S, Standard) like Lionel and American Flyer, etc. "For the collector and operator of toy trains, *CTT* offers full-color photos of layouts and collections of toy trains, restoration tips, operating information, new product reviews and information, and insights into the history of toy trains." Estab. 1987. Circ. 50,000. Byline given. Pays on acceptance. Publishes ms an average of 1 year after acceptance. Buys all rights. Editorial lead time 3 months. Submit seasonal material 6 months in advance. Accepts queries by mail, e-mail. Responds in 3 weeks to queries. Responds in 1 month to mss. Sample copy for $5.95, plus postage. Guidelines available online.

Nonfiction Needs general interest, historical, how-to, restore toy trains; design a layout; build accessories; fix broken toy trains, interview, personal experience, photo feature, technical. **Buys 90 mss/year.** Query. Length: 500-5,000 words. **Pays $75-500.**

Photos Send photos. Captions required. Reviews 4 × 5 transparencies, 5 × 7 prints or 35mm slides preferred. Also accepts hi-res digital photos. Offers no additional payment for photos accepted with ms or $15-75/photo. Buys all rights.

Tips "It's important to have a thorough understanding of the toy train hobby; most of our freelancers are hobbyists themselves. One-half to two-thirds of *CTT*'s editorial space is devoted to photographs; superior photography is critical."

$ COLLECTORS NEWS

P.O. Box 306, Grundy Center IA 50638. (319)824-6981. Fax: (319)824-3414. E-mail: lkruger@pioneermagazines.com. Website: collectors-news.com. **20% freelance written. Works with a small number of new/unpublished writers each year.** Monthly magazine-size publication on offset, glossy cover, covering antiques, collectibles, and nostalgic memorabilia. Estab. 1959. Circ. 9,000. Byline given. Pays on publication. Publishes ms an average of 1 year after acceptance. Buys first rights. Makes work-for-hire assignments. Submit seasonal material 3 months in advance. Accepts queries by mail, e-mail, fax, phone. Responds in 2 weeks to queries. Responds in 6 weeks to mss. Sample copy for $4 and 9 × 12 SAE. Guidelines free.

Nonfiction Needs general interest, collectibles, antique to modern, historical, relating to collections or collectors, how-to, display your collection, care for, restore, appraise, locate, add to, etc., interview, covering individual collectors and their hobbies, unique or extensive; celebrity collectors, and limited edition artists, technical, in-depth analysis of a particular antique, collectible, or collecting field, travel, hot antiquing places in the US. 12-month listing of antique and collectible shows, flea markets, and conventions (January includes events January-December; June includes events June-May); Care & Display of Collectibles (September); holidays (October-December) **Buys 36 mss/year.** Query with sample of writing. Length: 800-1,000 words. **Pays $1.10/column inch.**

Photos Articles must be accompanied by photographs for illustration. A selection of 2-8 images is suggested. Articles are eligible for full-color front page consideration when accompanied by high resolution electronic images. Only 1 article is highlighted on the cover/month. Any article providing a

color photo selected for front page use receives an additional $25. Captions required. Reviews color or b&w digital images. Payment for photos included in payment for ms. Buys first rights.
Tips "Present a professionally written article with quality illustrations—well-researched and documented information."

$ CQ AMATEUR RADIO

The Radio Amateur's Journal, CQ Communications, Inc., 25 Newbridge Rd., Hicksville NY 11801. (516)681-2922. Fax: (516)681-2926. E-mail: cq@cq-amateur-radio.com. Website: www.cq-amateur-radio.com. **Contact:** Gail Sheehan, managing editor or Richard Moseson, editor. **40% freelance written.** Monthly magazine covering amateur (ham) radio. "*CQ* is published for active ham radio operators and is read by radio amateurs in over 100 countries. All articles must deal with amateur radio. Our focus is on operating and on practical projects. A thorough knowledge of amateur radio is required." Estab. 1945. Circ. 60,000. Byline given. Pays on publication. No kill fee. Publishes ms an average of 6 months after acceptance. Buys first North American serial rights. Editorial lead time 4 months. Submit seasonal material 4 months in advance. Accepts queries by mail, e-mail, fax. Responds in 3 weeks to queries. Responds in 3 months to mss. Sample copy free. Guidelines available online.
Nonfiction Needs historical, how-to, interview, personal experience, technical, all related to amateur radio. **Buys 50-60 mss/year.** Query. Length: 2,000-4,000 words. **Pays $40/published page.**
Photos State availability. Captions, identification of subjects, model releases required. Reviews contact sheets, 4x6 prints, TIFF or JPEG files with 300 dpi resolution. Offers no additional payment for photos accepted with ms Buys one time rights.
Tips "You must know and understand ham radio and ham radio operators. Most of our writers (95%) are licensed hams. Because our readers span a wide area of interests within amateur radio, don't assume they are already familiar with your topic. Explain. At the same time, don't write down to the readers. They are intelligent, well-educated people who will understand what you're saying when written and explained in plain English."

$$ CREATING KEEPSAKES

Scrapbook Magazine, Primedia Enthusiast Group, 14850 Pony Express Rd., Bluffdale UT 84065. (801)984-2070. E-mail: marianne.madsen@primedia.com. Website: www.creatingkeepsakes.com. Monthly magazine covering scrapbooks. Written for scrapbook lovers and those with a box of photos high in the closet. Circ. 100,000. No kill fee. Editorial lead time 6 weeks. Accepts queries by mail, e-mail. Guidelines available online.
Nonfiction Accepts articles on a variety of scrapbook and keepsake topics. Query with 2 visuals to illustrate your suggested topic. Length: 800-1,200 words.
Tips Should we opt to pursue the article you've proposed, we will ask you to supply the complete article on disk in WordPerfect, Word or ASCII format. Please supply a paper copy as well. The article should be lively and easy to read, contain solid content, and be broken up with subheads or sidebars as appropriate. We will provide additional guidelines to follow upon acceptance of your query.

$$ DESIGNS IN MACHINE EMBROIDERY

Great Notions News Corp., 2517 Manana Dr., Dallas TX 75220. (888)739-0555. Fax: (413)723-2027. E-mail: www.designsmagazine@dzgns.com. Website: www.dzgns.com. **75% freelance written.** Bimonthly magazine covering machine embroidery. Projects in *Designs in Machine Embroidery* must feature machine embroidery and teach readers new techniques. Estab. 1998. Circ. 50,000. Byline given. Pays on publication. Publishes ms an average of 2 months after acceptance. Buys all rights. Editorial lead time 4 months. Submit seasonal material 4 months in advance. Accepts queries by mail, e-mail. Responds in 2-3 weeks to queries. Guidelines available online.
Nonfiction Needs how-to, interview, new product, technical. Does not want previously published items. **Buys 60 mss/year.** Query. Length: 250-1,000 words. **Pays $250-500.**
Photos Send photos. Captions, identification of subjects, model releases required. Reviews GIF/JPEG files (300 dpi, 4x6 min.). Offers no additional payment for photos accepted with ms.
Tips Projects should be original and fall under one of the following categories: Quilts, Crafts, Clothing, Home Decor. Item or project should be tasteful and mainstream. Since we are an embroidery magazine, the quality of workmanship is critical.

$$ DOLLS

Jones Publishing, Inc., P.O. Box 5000, Iola WI 54945. (715)445-5000. Fax: (715)445-4053. E-mail: editor@dollsmagazine.com. Website: www.dollsmagazine.com. **75% freelance written.** "Magazine published 10 times/year covering dolls, doll artists, and related topics of interest to doll collectors and enthusiasts."

"*Dolls* enhances the joy of collecting by introducing readers to the best new dolls from around the world, along with the artists and designers who create them. It keeps readers up-to-date on shows, sales and special events in the doll world. With beautiful color photography, *Dolls* offers an array of easy-to-read, informative articles that help our collectors select the best buys." Estab. 1982. Circ. 100,000. Byline given. Pays on publication. No kill fee. Buys all rights. Accepts queries by mail, e-mail. Responds in 1 month to queries.

Nonfiction Needs historical, how-to, interview, new product, photo feature. **Buys 55 mss/year.** Send complete ms. Length: 750-1,200 words. **Pays $75-300.**

Photos Send photos. Captions, identification of subjects, model releases required. Reviews transparencies. Offers no additional payment for photos accepted with ms. Buys all rights.

Tips "Know the subject matter and artists. Having quality artwork and access to doll artists for interviews are big pluses. We need original ideas of interest to doll lovers."

F+W MEDIA, INC. (MAGAZINE DIVISION)

(formerly F + W Publications, Inc.), 4700 E. Galbraith Rd., Cincinnati OH 45236. (513)531-2690. E-mail: dave.pulvermacher@fwmedia.com. Website: www.fwmedia.com. "Each month, millions of enthusiasts turn to the magazines from F + W for inspiration, instruction, and encouragement. Readers are as varied as our categories, but all are assured of getting the best possible coverage of their favorite hobby." Publishes magazines in the following categories: **antiques and collectibles** (*Antique Trader*); **automotive** (*Military Vehicles, Old Cars Report Price Guide, Old Cars Weekly*); **coins and paper money** (*Bank Note Reporter, Coins Magazine, Coin Prices, Numismatic News, World Coin News*); **comics** (*Comics Buyer's Guide*); **construction** (*Frame Building News, Metal Roofing, Rural Builder*); **fine art** (*Collector's Guide, Pastel Journal, Southwest Art, The Artist's Magazine, Watercolor Artist*); **firearms and knives** (*Blade, Gun Digest—The Magazine, Gun-Knife Show Calendar*); **genealogy** (*Family Tree Magazine*); **graphic design** (*HOW Magazine, PRINT*); **horticulture** (*Horticulture*); **militaria** (*Military Trader*); **outdoors and hunting** (*Deer & Deer Hunting, Trapper & Predator Caller, Turkey & Turkey Hunting*); **records and CDs** (*Goldmine*); **sports** (*Sports Collectors Digest, Tuff Stuff's Sports Collectors Monthly*); **woodworking** (*Popular Woodworking Magazine); **writing** (*Writer's Digest*). No kill fee.

- "Please see individual listings in the Consumer Magazines and Trade Journals sections for specific submission information about each magazine."

$$$ FAMILY TREE MAGAZINE

F + W Media, Inc., 4700 E. Galbraith Rd., Cincinnati OH 45236. (513)531-2690. Fax: (513)891-7153. Website: www.familytreemagazine.com. **75% freelance written**. Magazine covering family history, heritage, and genealogy research. "*Family Tree Magazine* is a general-interest consumer magazine that helps readers discover, preserve, and celebrate their family's history. We cover genealogy, ethnic heritage, genealogy websites and software, photography and photo preservation, and other ways that families connect with their past." Estab. 1999. Circ. 75,000. Byline given. Pays on acceptance. Offers 25% kill fee. Publishes ms an average of 6 months after acceptance. Buys first rights, electronic rights, all rights. Editorial lead time 8 months. Submit seasonal material 8 months in advance. Accepts queries by mail, e-mail. Responds in 1 month to queries. Sample copy for $8 from website. Guidelines available online.

Nonfiction "Articles are geared to beginners but must provide in-depth instruction for intermediate and veteran genealogists. We emphasize sidebars, tips, and other reader-friendly 'packaging,' and each article aims to give the reader the resources necessary to take the next step in his or her quest for the past." Needs book excerpts, historical, how-to, genealogy, new product, photography, computer, technical, genealogy software, photography equipment. **Buys 60 mss/year.** Query with published clips. Length: 250-4,500 words. **Pays $25-800.**

Photos State availability. Captions required. Reviews color transparencies. Negotiates payment individually. Buys all rights.

Tips "Always query with a specific story idea. Look at sample issues before querying to get a feel for appropriate topics and angles. We see too many broad, general stories on genealogy or records, and personal accounts of `How I found great-aunt Sally' without how-to value."

$$ FIBERARTS

Contemporary Textile Art and Craft, Interweave Press, 201 E. Fourth St., Loveland CO 80537. (970)613-4679. Fax: (970)669-6117. E-mail: lizg@fiberarts.com. Website: www.fiberarts.com. **85% freelance written**. "Magazine published 5 times/year covering textiles as art and craft (contemporary trends in fiber sculpture, weaving, quilting, surface design, stitchery, papermaking, basketry, felting, wearable art, knitting, fashion, crochet, mixed textile techniques, ethnic dying, eccentric tidbits, etc.) for textile artists, craftspeople, collectors, teachers, museum and gallery staffs, and enthusiasts." Estab. 1975. Circ.

27,000. Byline given. Pays on publication. Publishes ms an average of 4 months after acceptance. Buys first rights. Accepts queries by mail. Sample copy for $7.99. Guidelines available online.

Nonfiction "Please be very specific about your proposal. Also, an important consideration in accepting an article is the kind of photos that you can provide as illustration. We like to see photos in advance." Needs essays, interview, artist, opinion, personal experience, photo feature, technical, education, trends, exhibition reviews, textile news, book reviews, ethnic. Query with brief synopsis, SASE, and visuals. No phone queries. Length: 250-2,000 words. **Pays $70-550.**

Photos Color slides, large-format transparencies, or 300 dpi (5-inch-high) TIFF images must accompany every query. "Please include caption information. The names and addresses of those mentioned in the article or to whom the visuals are to be returned are necessary."

Columns/Departments Commentary (thoughtful opinion on a topic of interest to our readers), 400 words; News and Notes; Profiles; The Creative Process; Travel and Traditions; Collecting; Reviews (exhibits and shows; summarize quality, significance, focus and atmosphere, then evaluate selected pieces for aesthetic quality, content and technique. "Because we have an international readership, brief biographical notes or quotes might be pertinent for locally or regionally known artists). (Do not cite works for which visuals are unavailable; you are not eligible to review a show in which you have participated as an artist, organizer, curator or juror.")

Tips "Our writers are usually familiar with textile techniques and textile-art history, but expertise in historical textiles, art, or design can also qualify a new writer. The writer should also be familiar with *Fiberarts* magazine. The professional is essential to the editorial depth of *Fiberarts* and must find timely information in the pages of the magazine, but our editorial philosophy is that the magazine must provide the non-professional textile enthusiast with the inspiration, support, useful information, and direction to keep him or her excited, interested, and committed. Although we address serious issues relating to the fiber arts as well as light, we're looking for an accessible rather than overly scholarly tone."

$ FIBRE FOCUS

Magazine of the Ontario Handweavers and Spinners, 3212 S. Service Rd. W., Oakville ON L6L 6T1 Canada. Website: www.ohs.on.ca. **90% freelance written**. Quarterly magazine covering handweaving, spinning, basketry, beading, and other fibre arts. "Our readers are weavers and spinners who also do dyeing, knitting, basketry, feltmaking, papermaking, sheep raising, and craft supply. All articles deal with some aspect of these crafts." Estab. 1957. Circ. 1,000. Byline given. Pays within 30 days after publication. Buys one-time rights. Editorial lead time 6 months. Submit seasonal material 6 months in advance. Accepts previously published material. Responds in 1 month to queries. Sample copy for $8 Canadian. Guidelines available online.

Nonfiction Needs how-to, interview, new product, opinion, personal experience, technical, travel, book reviews. **Buys 40-60 mss/year.** Word length varies. **Pays $30 Canadian/published page.**

Photos Send photos. Captions, identification of subjects required. Offers additional payment for photos accepted with ms. Buys one time rights.

Tips "Visit the OHS website for current information."

$$ FINE BOOKS & COLLECTIONS

OP Media, LLC, P.O. Box 106, Eureka CA 95502. (707)443-9562. Fax: (707)443-9572. E-mail: scott@finebooksmagazine.com. Website: www.finebooksmagazine.com. **90% freelance written**. Bimonthly magazine covering used and antiquarian bookselling and book collecting. We cover all aspects of selling and collecting out-of-print books. We emphasize good writing, interesting people, and unexpected view points. Estab. 2002. Circ. 5,000. Byline given. Pays on publication. Offers negotiable kill fee. Publishes ms an average of 4 months after acceptance. Buys first North American serial rights, buys second serial (reprint) rights, buys electronic rights. Makes work-for-hire assignments. Editorial lead time 4 months. Submit seasonal material 4 months in advance. Accepts queries by mail, e-mail. Accepts previously published material. Accepts simultaneous submissions. Responds in 1 month to queries. Responds in 2 months to mss. Sample copy for $6.50. Guidelines available online.

Nonfiction Needs book excerpts, essays, expose, general interest, historical, how-to, humor, opinion, personal experience, photo feature, travel. Does not want tales of the gold in my attic vein; stories emphasizing books as an investment. **Buys 40 mss/year.** Query with published clips. Length: 1,000-5,000 words. **Pays $100-400.**

Photos State availability. Captions, identification of subjects required. Reviews GIF/JPEG files. Negotiates payment individually. Buys one-time, plus nonexclusive electronic rights

Columns/Departments Digest (news about collectors, booksellers, and bookselling), 350 words; Book Reviews (reviews of books about books, writers, publishers, collecting), 400-800 words.

Tips Tell compelling stories about people and the passion for book collecting. We aim to make academic writing on books accessible to a broad audience and to enliven the writing of aficionados with solid editing and story development.

$ FINESCALE MODELER

Kalmbach Publishing Co., P.O. Box 1612, Waukesha WI 53187. Website: www.finescale.com. **80% freelance written. Eager to work with new/unpublished writers.** "Magazine published 10 times/year devoted to how-to-do-it modeling information for scale model builders who build non-operating aircraft, tanks, boats, automobiles, figures, dioramas, and science fiction and fantasy models." Circ. 60,000. Byline given. Pays on acceptance. No kill fee. Publishes ms an average of 14 months after acceptance. Buys all rights. Responds in 6 weeks to queries. Responds in 3 months to mss. Sample copy for sae with 9 × 12 envelope and 3 First-Class stamps.

O-→ "Finescale Modeler is especially looking for how-to articles for armor and aircraft modelers.

Nonfiction Needs how-to, build scale models, technical, research information for building models. Query or send complete ms. Length: 750-3,000 words. **Pays $60/published page minimum.**

Photos "Send original high-res digital images, slides, or prints with submission. You can submit digital images at www.contribute.kalmbach.com." Captions, identification of subjects required. Reviews transparencies, color prints. Pays $7.50 minimum for transparencies and $5 minimum for color prints Buys one time rights.

Columns/Departments *FSM* Showcase (photos plus description of model); *FSM* Tips and Techniques (model building hints and tips). Send complete ms. **Pays $25-50.**

Tips "A freelancer can best break in first through hints and tips, then through feature articles. Most people who write for *FSM* are modelers first, writers second. This is a specialty magazine for a special, quite expert audience. Essentially, 99% of our writers will come from that audience."

$$ FINE TOOL JOURNAL

Antique & Collectible Tools, Inc., 27 Fickett Rd., Pownal ME 04069. (207)688-4962. Fax: (207)688-4831. E-mail: ceb@finetoolj.com. Website: www.finetoolj.com. **90% freelance written**. "Quarterly magazine specializing in older or antique hand tools from all traditional trades. Readers are primarily interested in woodworking tools, but some subscribers have interests in such areas as leatherworking, wrenches, kitchen, and machinist tools. Readers range from beginners just getting into the hobby to advanced collectors and organizations." Estab. 1970. Circ. 2,500. Byline given. Pays on publication. Offers $50 kill fee. Publishes ms an average of 6 months after acceptance. Buys first rights, buys second serial (reprint) rights. Editorial lead time 9 months. Submit seasonal material 6 months in advance. Accepts queries by mail. Accepts previously published material. Responds in 2 months to queries. Responds in 3 months to mss. Sample copy for $5. Guidelines for #10 SASE.

Nonfiction "We're looking for articles about tools from all trades. Interests include collecting, preservation, history, values and price trends, traditional methods and uses, interviews with collectors/users/makers, etc. Most articles published will deal with vintage, pre-1950, hand tools. Also seeking articles on how to use specific tools or how a specific trade was carried out. However, how-to articles must be detailed and not just of general interest. We do on occasion run articles on modern toolmakers who produce traditional hand tools." Needs general interest, historical, how-to, make, use, fix and tune tools, interview, personal experience, photo feature, technical. **Buys 24 mss/year.** Send complete ms. Length: 400-2,000 words. **Pays $50-200.**

Photos Send photos. Identification of subjects, model releases required. Reviews 4 × 5 prints. Negotiates payment individually Buys all rights.

Columns/Departments Stanley Tools (new finds and odd types), 300-400 words; Tips of the Trade (how to use tools), 100-200 words. Send complete ms. **Pays $30-60.**

Tips "The easiest way to get published in the *Journal* is to have personal experience or know someone who can supply the detailed information. We are seeking articles that go deeper than general interest and that knowledge requires experience and/or research. Short of personal experience, find a subject that fits our needs and that interests you. Spend some time learning the ins and outs of the subject and with hard work and a little luck you will earn the right to write about it."

$$ FINE WOODWORKING

The Taunton Press, P.O. Box 5506, Newtown CT 06470-5506. (203)426-8171. Fax: (203)426-3434. E-mail: fw@taunton.com. Website: www.taunton.com. **Contact:** Betsy Engel. Bimonthly magazine on woodworking in the small shop. "All writers are also skilled woodworkers. It's more important that a contributor be a woodworker than a writer. Our editors (also woodworkers) will provide assistance and travel to shops to shoot all photography needed." Estab. 1975. Circ. 270,000. Byline given. Pays on acceptance. Offers variable kill fee. Buys first rights and rights to republish in other forms and media, as well as use in promo pieces. Submit seasonal material 6 months in advance. Accepts simultaneous submissions. Responds in 1 month to queries. Writer's guidelines free and online

> O━ "We're looking for good articles on almost all aspects of woodworking from the basics of tool use, stock preparation and joinery, to specialized techniques and finishing. We're especially keen on articles about shop-built tools, jigs and fixtures, or any stage of design, construction, finishing and installation of cabinetry and furniture. Whether the subject involves fundamental methods or advanced techniques, we look for high-quality workmanship, thoughtful designs, and safe and proper procedures."

Nonfiction Needs how-to, woodworking. **Buys 120 mss/year.** Send article outline, any helpful drawings or photos, and proposal letter. **Pays $150/magazine page.**
Columns/Departments Fundamentals (basic how-to and concepts for beginning woodworkers); Master Class (advanced techniques); Finish Line (finishing techniques); Question & Answer (woodworking Q&A); Methods of Work (shop tips); Tools & Materials (short reviews of new tools). **Pays $10-150/ published page**
Tips "Look for authors guidelines and follow them. Stories about woodworking reported by non-woodworkers are *not* used. Our magazine is essentially reader-written by woodworkers."

$$ THE HOME SHOP MACHINIST

P.O. Box 629, Traverse City MI 49685. (231)946-3712. Fax: (231)946-6180. E-mail: nknopf@villagepress.com. Website: www.homeshopmachinist.net. Craig Foster, managing editor. **Contact:** George Bulliss, editor. **95% freelance written**. Bimonthly magazine covering machining and metalworking for the hobbyist. Circ. 34,000. Byline given. Pays on publication. Publishes ms an average of 2 years after acceptance. Buys first North American serial rights. Responds in 2 months to queries. Sample copy free. Guidelines for 9 × 12 SASE.
Nonfiction Needs how-to, projects designed to upgrade present shop equipment or hobby model projects that require machining, technical, should pertain to metalworking, machining, drafting, layout, welding or foundry work for the hobbyist. No fiction or people features. **Buys 40 mss/year.** Send complete ms. open—whatever it takes to do a thorough job. **Pays $40/published page, plus $9/published photo.**
Photos Send photos. Captions, identification of subjects required. Pays $9-40 for 5 × 7 b&w prints; $70/ page for camera-ready art; $40 for b&w cover photo
Columns/Departments Become familiar with our magazine before submitting. Book Reviews; New Product Reviews; Micro-Machining; Foundry. Length: 600-1,500 words. Query. **Pays $40-70.**
Fillers 12-15 Length: 100-300 words. **Pays $30-48.**
Tips The writer should be experienced in the area of metalworking and machining; should be extremely thorough in explanations of methods, processes—always with an eye to safety; and should provide good quality b&w photos and/or clear dimensioned drawings to aid in description. Visuals are of increasing importance to our readers. Carefully planned photos, drawings and charts will carry a submission to our magazine much farther along the path to publication.

$$ KITPLANES

For Designers, Builders, and Pilots of Experimental Aircraft, A Primedia Publication, Kitplanes, 302 Argonne Ave., Suite B105, Long Beach CA 90803. E-mail: editorial@kitplanes.com. Website: www.kitplanes.com. **50% freelance written. Eager to work with new/unpublished writers.** Monthly magazine covering self-construction of private aircraft for pilots and builders. Estab. 1984. Circ. 72,000. Byline given. Pays on publication. Publishes ms an average of 3 months after acceptance. Buys complete rights, except book rights. Submit seasonal material 6 months in advance. Accepts queries by mail, e-mail. Responds in 4 weeks to queries. Responds in 6 weeks to mss Sample copy for $6 Guidelines available online
Nonfiction "We are looking for articles on specific construction techniques, the use of tools—both hand and power—in aircraft building, the relative merits of various materials, conversions of engines from automobiles for aviation use, and installation of instruments and electronics." Needs general interest, how-to, interview, new product, personal experience, photo feature, technical. No general-interest aviation articles, or My First Solo type of articles. **Buys 80 mss/year.** Query. Length: 500-3,000 words. **Pays $150-500 including story photos.**
Photos State availability of or send photos. Captions, identification of subjects required. Pays $300 for cover photos Buys one time rights.
Tips "*Kitplanes* contains very specific information—a writer must be extremely knowledgeable in the field. Major features are entrusted only to known writers. I cannot emphasize enough that articles must

be directed at the individual aircraft builder. We need more 'how-to' photo features in all areas of home-built aircraft."

$ $ KNIVES ILLUSTRATED

The Premier Cutlery Magazine, 265 S. Anita Dr., Suite 120, Orange CA 92868. (714)939-9991. Fax: (714)939-9909. E-mail: editorial@knivesillustrated.com. Website: www.knivesillustrated.com. **40-50% freelance written**. Bimonthly magazine covering high-quality factory and custom knives. We publish articles on different types of factory and custom knives, how-to make knives, technical articles, shop tours, articles on knife makers and artists. Must have knowledge about knives and the people who use and make them. We feature the full range of custom and high tech production knives, from miniatures to swords, leaving nothing untouched. We're also known for our outstanding how-to articles and technical features on equipment, materials and knife making supplies. We do not feature knife maker profiles as such, although we do spotlight some makers by featuring a variety of their knives and insight into their background and philosophy. Estab. 1987. Circ. 35,000. Byline given. Pays on publication. No kill fee. Editorial lead time 3 months. Accepts queries by mail, e-mail, fax. Responds in 2 weeks to queries. Sample copy available Guidelines for #10 SASE.

Nonfiction Needs general interest, historical, how-to, interview, new product, photo feature, technical. **Buys 35-40 mss/year.** Query. Length: 400-2,000 words. **Pays $100-500.**

Photos Send photos. Captions, identification of subjects, model releases required. Reviews 35mm, 2¼ × 2¼ , 4 × 5 transparencies, 5 × 7 prints, electronic images in TIFF, GIF or JPEG Mac format. Negotiates payment individually

Tips Most of our contributors are involved with knives, either as collectors, makers, engravers, etc. To write about this subject requires knowledge. Writers can do OK if they study some recent issues. If you are interested in submitting work to *Knives Illustrated* magazine, it is suggested you analyze at least 2 or 3 different editions to get a feel for the magazine. It is also recommended that you call or mail in your query to determine if we are interested in the topic you have in mind. While verbal or written approval may be given, all articles are still received on a speculation basis. We cannot approve any article until we have it in hand, whereupon we will make a final decision as to its suitability for our use. Bear in mind we do not suggest you go to the trouble to write an article if there is doubt we can use it promptly.

$ $ THE LEATHER CRAFTERS & SADDLERS JOURNAL

222 Blackburn St., Rhinelander WI 54501-3777. (715)362-5393. Fax: (715)362-5391. E-mail: tworjournal@newnorth.net. David Reis. **100% freelance written**. Bimonthly magazine. "A leather-working publication with how-to, step-by-step instructional articles using patterns for leathercraft, leather art, custom saddle, boot and harness making, etc. A complete resource for leather, tools, machinery, and allied materials, plus leather industry news." Estab. 1990. Circ. 8,000. Byline given. Pays on publication. Publishes ms an average of 4 months after acceptance. Buys first North American serial rights, buys second serial (reprint) rights. Submit seasonal material 6 months in advance. Accepts queries by mail, e-mail, fax, phone. Accepts previously published material. Accepts simultaneous submissions. Responds in 1 month to mss. Sample copy for $6. Guidelines for #10 SASE.

Nonfiction "We want only articles that include hands-on, step-by-step, how-to information." **Buys 75 mss/year.** Send complete ms. Length: 500-2,500 words. **Pays $20-250 for assigned articles. Pays $20-150 for unsolicited articles.**

Reprints Send tearsheet or photocopy. Pays 50% of amount paid for an original article.

Photos Send good contrast color print photos and full-size patterns and/or full-size photo-carve patterns with submission. Lack of these reduces payment amount. Captions required.

Columns/Departments Beginners; Intermediate; Artists; Western Design; Saddlemakers; International Design; and Letters (the open exchange of information between all peoples). Length: 500-2,500 words on all.

Tips "We want to work with people who understand and know leathercraft and are interested in passing on their knowledge to others. We would prefer to interview people who have achieved a high level in leathercraft skill."

$ LINN'S STAMP NEWS

Amos Press, P.O. Box 29, Sidney OH 45365. (937)498-0801. Fax: (937)498-0886. Website: www.linns.com. **50% freelance written**. Weekly tabloid on the stamp collecting hobby. "All articles must be about philatelic collectibles. Our goal at *Linn's* is to create a weekly publication that is indispensable to stamp collectors." Estab. 1928. Circ. 33,000. Byline given. Pays within 1 month of publication. Publishes ms an average of 3 months after acceptance. Buys first print and electronic rights. Submit seasonal material 2 months in advance. Responds in 6 weeks to queries. Sample copy online. Guidelines available online.

Nonfiction Needs general interest, historical, how-to, interview, technical, club and show news, current issues, auction realization and recent discoveries. "No articles merely giving information on background of stamp subject. Must have philatelic information included." **Buys 50 mss/year.** Send complete ms. 500 words maximum **Pays $40-75.**

Photos Good illustrations a must. Send scans with submission. Captions required. Reviews digital color at twice actual size (300 dpi). Offers no additional payment for photos accepted with ms. Buys all rights.

Tips "Check and double check all facts. Footnotes and bibliographies are not appropriate to newspaper style. Work citation into the text. Even though your subject might be specialized, write understandably. Explain terms. *Linn's* features are aimed at a broad audience of novice and intermediate collectors. Keep this audience in mind. Provide information in such a way to make stamp collecting more interesting to more people."

$ LOST TREASURE, INC.

P.O. Box 451589, Grove OK 74345. (866)469-6224. Fax: (918)786-2192. E-mail: managingeditor@losttreasure.com. Website: www.losttreasure.com. **75% freelance written**. Monthly and annual magazines covering lost treasure. Estab. 1966. Circ. 55,000. Byline given. Pays on publication. Buys all rights. Accepts queries by mail, e-mail, fax. Responds in 1 month to queries. Responds in 2 months to mss. Sample copy for #10 SASE. Guidelines for 10 × 13 SAE with $1.52 postage or online.

Nonfiction *Lost Treasure* is composed of lost treasure stories, legends, how-to articles, treasure hunting club news, who's who in treasure hunting, tips. Length: 500-1,200 words. *Treasure Cache*, an annual, contains stories about documented treasure caches with a sidebar from the author telling the reader how to search for the cache highlighted in the story. **Buys 225 mss/year.** Query on *Treasure Cache* only. Length: 1,000-2,000 words. **Pays 4¢/word.**

Photos Color or b&w prints, hand-drawn or copied maps, art with source credit with mss will help sell your story.We are always looking for cover photos with or without accompanying ms. Pays $100/published cover photo. Must be vertical. Captions required. Pays $5/published photo.

Tips Queries welcome but not required. If you write about famous treasures and lost mines, be sure we haven't used your selected topic recently—the story must have a new slant or new information. Source documentation required. How-tos should cover some aspect of treasure hunting and how-to steps should be clearly defined. If you have a *Treasure Cache* story we will, if necessary, help the author with the sidebar telling how to search for the cache in the story. *Lost Treasure* articles should coordinate with theme issues when possible.

🌐 MACHINE EMBROIDERY & TEXTILE ART

Express Publications, Ltd., Locked Bag 111, Silverwater NSW 1811 Australia. (61)(2)9741-3899. Fax: (61)(2)9737-8017. E-mail: subs@magstore.com.au. Website: www.expresspublications.com.au. "*Machine Embroidery & Textile Art* is inspirational, creative and informative."

Nonfiction Needs general interest, how-to, new product. Query.

$$ MILITARY TRADER

F+W Media, Inc., 700 E. State St., Iola WI 54990-0001. (715)445-4612. E-mail: tom.polzer@fwmedia.com. Website: www.militarytrader.com. **50% freelance written**. Magazine covering military collectibles. Dedicated to serving people who collect, preserve, and display military relics. Estab. 1994. Circ. 6,500. Byline given. Pays on publication. No kill fee. Publishes ms an average of 1 month after acceptance. Buys first North American serial rights. Accepts queries by mail, e-mail. Accepts simultaneous submissions. Responds in 1 week to queries. Responds in 1 month to mss. Sample copy for $5.

Nonfiction Needs historical, collection comparisons, artifact identification, reproduction alert. **Buys 40 mss/year.** Send complete ms. Length: 1,300-2,600 words. **Pays $0-200.**

Photos Send photos. True required. Reviews contact sheets. Negotiates payment individually. Buys all rights.

Columns/Departments Pays $0-50.

Tips Be knowledgeable on military collectibles and/or military history. Plenty of good photos will make it easier to be published in our publication. Write for the collector: Assume that they already know the basics of historical context. Provide tips on where and how to collect specific items. Articles that teach the reader how to recognize fakes or forgeries are given the highest priority.

$$ MILITARY VEHICLES

F+W Media, Inc., 700 E. State St., Iola WI 54990-0001. (715)445-4612. Website: www.militaryvehiclesmagazine.com. **50% freelance written**. Bimonthly magazine covering historic military vehicles. Dedicated to serving people who collect, restore, and drive historic military vehicles. Circ. 18,500. Byline given. Pays on publication. No kill fee. Publishes ms an average of 1 month after acceptance. Buys first North American serial rights. Accepts queries by mail, e-mail. Accepts simultaneous submissions. Responds in 1 week to queries. Responds in 1 month to mss. Sample copy for $5.

Nonfiction Needs historical, how-to, technical. **Buys 20 mss/year.** Send complete ms. Length: 1,300-2,600 words. **Pays $0-200.**

Photos True required. Buys all rights.

Columns/Departments Pays $0-75.

Tips Be knowledgeable about military vehicles. This magazine is for a very specialized audience. General automotive journalists will probably not be able to write for this group. The bulk of our content addresses US-manufactured and used vehicles. Plenty of good photos will make it easier to be published in our publication. Write for the collector/restorer: Assume that they already know the basics of historical context. Articles that show how to restore or repair military vehicles are given the highest priority.

$ MODEL CARS MAGAZINE

Golden Bell Press, 2403 Champa St., Denver CO 80205. (303)296-1600. Fax: (303)295-2159. E-mail: gregg@modelcarsmag.com. Website: www.modelcarsmag.com. **25% freelance written**. Magazine published 9 times year covering model cars, trucks, and other automotive models. "*Model Cars Magazine* is the hobby's how-to authority for the automotive modeling hobbiest. We are on the forefront of the hobby, our editorial staff are model car builders, and every single one of our writers have a passion for the hobby that is evident in the articles and stories that we publish. We are the model car magazine written by and for model car builders." Estab. 1999. Circ. 8,500. Byline given. Pays on publication. Publishes ms an average of 2-3 months after acceptance. Buys first North American serial rights. Editorial lead time 2-3 months. Accepts queries by mail, e-mail. Sample copy for $5.50.

Nonfiction "We want model car-related articles, features and stories." Needs how-to. Length: 600-3,000 words. **Pays $50/page. Pays $25/page for unsolicited articles.**

$ MODEL RAILROADER

Kalmbach Publishing Co., P.O. Box 1612, Waukesha WI 53187. Fax: (262)796-1142. E-mail: mrmag@mrmag.com. Website: www.trains.com. **Contact:** Neil Besougloff, editor. Monthly magazine for hobbyists in scale model railroading. Byline given. Buys exclusive rights. Accepts queries by mail, e-mail, fax. Responds in 2 months to queries.

Nonfiction Wants construction articles on specific model railroad projects (structures, cars, locomotives, scenery, benchwork, etc.). Also photo stories showing model railroads. Query. **Pays base rate of $90/page.**

Photos Buys photos with detailed descriptive captions only. Pays $15 and up, depending on size and use.

Tips "Before you prepare and submit any article, you should write us a short letter of inquiry describing what you want to do. We can then tell you if it fits our needs and save you from working on something we don't want."

$ MONITORING TIMES

Grove Enterprises, Inc., 7546 Hwy. 64 W., Brasstown NC 28902-0098. (828)837-9200. Fax: (828)837-2216. E-mail: editor@monitoringtimes.com. Website: www.monitoringtimes.com. **15% freelance written**. Monthly magazine for radio hobbyists. Estab. 1982. Circ. 15,000. Byline given. Pays on publication. Publishes ms an average of 4 months after acceptance. Buys first North American serial rights, buys second serial (reprint) rights. Submit seasonal material 4 months in advance. Accepts queries by mail, e-mail. Accepts previously published material. Responds in 1 month to queries. Sample copy for 9 × 12 SAE and 9 first-class stamps Guidelines available online.

Nonfiction Needs general interest, how-to, humor, interview, personal experience, photo feature, technical. **Buys 50 mss/year.** Query. Length: 1,500-3,000 words. **Pays average of $50/published page.**

Reprints Send photocopy and information about when and where the material previously appeared. Pays 50% of amount paid for an original article

Photos Send photos. Captions required. Buys one time rights.

Columns/Departments Query managing editor.

Tips Need articles on radio communications systems and shortwave broadcasters. We are accepting more technical projects.

$ NATIONAL COMMUNICATIONS MAGAZINE

Norm Schrein, Inc., P.O. Box 291918, Kettering OH 45429. (937)299-7226. Fax: (937)299-1323. E-mail:

norm@bearcat1.com. Website: www.nat-com.org. **100% freelance written**. Bimonthly magazine covering radio as a hobby. Estab. 1990. Circ. 5,000. Byline given. Pays on publication. No kill fee. Publishes ms an average of 2 months after acceptance. Buys all rights. Editorial lead time 2 months. Submit seasonal material 2 months in advance. Accepts queries by phone. Accepts previously published material. Accepts simultaneous submissions. Sample copy for $4.

Nonfiction Needs how-to, interview, new product, personal experience, photo feature, technical. Does not want articles off topic of the publication's audience (radio hobbyists). **Buys 2-3 mss/year.** Query. Length: 300 words. **Pays $75 +.**

Photos Send photos. Captions, identification of subjects required. Reviews GIF/JPEG files. Offers no additional payment for photos accepted with ms. Buys all rights.

N ⊕ NEW ZEALAND GENEALOGIST

New Zealand Society of Genealogists, P.O. Box 5523, Moray Place Dunedin New Zealand. (64)(3)467-2036. E-mail: farthing@deepsouth.co.nz. Website: www.genealogy.org.nz. Bimonthly magazine covering articles of interest to NZSG members. No kill fee.

Nonfiction Needs how-to, family reunion notices, information wanted, contact sought, information offered. Query.

Photos Send photos. Reviews copies. Do not send originals.

$$ PAPER CRAFTS MAGAZINE

Primedia Magazines, 14850 Pony Express Rd., Bluffdale UT 84065. (800)815-3538. Fax: (801)816-8301. E-mail: editor@papercraftsmag.com. Website: www.papercraftsmag.com. Magazine published 10 times/year designed to help readers make creative and rewarding handmade crafts. The main focus is fresh, craft-related projects our reader can make and display in her home or give as gifts. Estab. 1978. Circ. 300,000. Byline given. Pays on acceptance. Buys all rights. Editorial lead time 6 months. Accepts queries by mail, e-mail. Responds in 1 month to queries. Guidelines for #10 SASE.

Nonfiction Needs how-to. **Buys 300 mss/year.** Query with photo or sketch of how-to project. Do not send the actual project until request. **Pays $100-500.**

Tips We are looking for projects that are fresh, innovative, and in sync with today's trends. We accept projects made with a variety of techniques and media. Projects can fall in several categories, ranging from home decor to gifts, garden accessories to jewelry, and other seasonal craft projects. Submitted projects must be original, never-before-published, copyright-free work that use readily available materials.

$ PIECEWORK MAGAZINE

Interweave Press, Inc., 201 E. 4th St., Loveland CO 80537-5655. (970)669-7672. Fax: (970)667-8317. E-mail: piecework@interweave.com. Website: www.interweave.com. **90% freelance written**. Bimonthly magazine covering needlework history. *PieceWork* celebrates the rich tradition of needlework and the history of the people behind it. Stories and projects on embroidery, cross-stitch, knitting, crocheting, and quilting, along with other textile arts, are featured in each issue. Estab. 1993. Circ. 30,000. Byline given. Pays on publication. Offers 25% kill fee. Buys first time exclusive rights. Editorial lead time 6 months. Submit seasonal material 6 months in advance. Accepts queries by mail, e-mail, fax, phone. Responds in 6 months to queries. Sample copy and writer's guidelines free.

Nonfiction Needs book excerpts, historical, how-to, interview, new product. No contemporary needlework articles. **Buys 25-30 mss/year.** Send complete ms. Length: 1,000-5,000 words. **Pays $100/printed page.**

Photos State availability of or send photos. Captions, identification of subjects, model releases required. Reviews transparencies, prints. Buys one time rights.

Tips Submit a well-researched article on a historical aspect of needlework complete with information on visuals and suggestion for accompanying project.

$ POPULAR COMMUNICATIONS

CQ Communications, Inc., 25 Newbridge Rd., Hicksville NY 11801. (516)681-2922. Fax: (516)681-2926. E-mail: popularcom@aol.com. Website: www.popular-communications.com. **25% freelance written**. Monthly magazine covering the radio communications hobby. Estab. 1982. Circ. 40,000. Byline given. Pays on publication. Publishes ms an average of 6 months after acceptance. Buys first North American serial rights. Editorial lead time 3 months. Submit seasonal material 6 months in advance. Accepts queries by mail, e-mail. Responds in 1 month to queries. Responds in 2 months to mss. Sample copy free. Guidelines for #10 SASE.

Nonfiction Needs general interest, how-to, antenna construction, humor, new product, photo feature, technical. **Buys 6-10 mss/year.** Query. Length: 1,800-3,000 words. **Pays $135/printed page.**

Photos State availability. Captions, identification of subjects, model releases required. Negotiates payment individually

Tips Either be a radio enthusiast or know one who can help you before sending us an article.

$$$$ POPULAR MECHANICS

Hearst Corp., 300 W. 57th St., New York NY 10019. (212)649-2000. E-mail: popularmechanics@hearst.com. Website: www.popularmechanics.com. **Up to 50% freelance written**. Monthly magazine on technology, science, automotive, home, outdoors. We are a men's service magazine that addresses the diverse interests of today's male, providing him with information to improve the way he lives. We cover stories from do-it-yourself projects to technological advances in aerospace, military, automotive and so on. Estab. 1902. Circ. 1,200,000. Offers 25% kill fee. Publishes ms an average of 6 months after acceptance. Submit seasonal material 6 months in advance.

- **Pays $1/word and up**.

$$ POPULAR WOODWORKING MAGAZINE

F+W Media, Inc., 4700 E. Galbraith Rd., Cincinnati OH 45236. (513)531-2690, ext. 11348. E-mail: megan.fitzpatrick@fwmedia.com. Website: www.popularwoodworking.com. **45% freelance written**. Magazine published 7 times/year. "*Popular Woodworking Magazine* invites woodworkers of all skill levels into a community of professionals who share their hard-won shop experience through in-depth projects and technique articles, which help the readers hone their existing skills and develop new ones for both hand and power tools. Related stories increase the readers' understanding and enjoyment of their craft. Any project submitted must be aesthetically pleasing, of sound construction, and offer a challenge to readers. On the average, we use 2 freelance features per issue. Our primary needs are 'how-to' articles on woodworking. Our secondary need is for articles that will inspire discussion concerning woodworking. Tone of articles should be conversational and informal but knowledgeable, as if the writer is speaking directly to the reader. Our readers are the woodworking hobbyist and small woodshop owner. Writers should have an extensive knowledge of woodworking and excellent woodworking techniques and skills." Estab. 1981. Circ. 180,000. Byline given. Pays on acceptance. No kill fee. Publishes ms an average of 10 months after acceptance. Buys all world rights. Submit seasonal material 6 months in advance. Accepts queries by mail, e-mail, fax, phone. Accepts previously published material. Responds in 2 months to queries. Sample copy for $5.99 and 9 × 12 SAE with 6 first-class stamps or online. Guidelines available online.

Nonfiction Needs how-to (on woodworking projects, with plans), humor (woodworking anecdotes), technical (woodworking techniques). No tool reviews. **Buys 10 mss/year.** Send complete ms. **Pay starts at $250/published page.**

Reprints Send photocopy with rights for sale noted and information about when and where the material previously appeared. Pays 25% of amount paid for an original article

Photos Photographic quality affects acceptance. Need professional quality, high-resolution digital images of step-by-step construction process. Send photos. Captions, identification of subjects required.

Columns/Departments Tricks of the Trade (helpful techniques), End Grain (thoughts on woodworking as a profession or hobby, can be humorous or serious), 500-600 words. Buys 20 mss/year. Query.

Tips "Write an 'End Grain' column for us and then follow up with photos of your projects. Submissions should include materials list, complete diagrams (blueprints not necessary), and discussion of the step-by-step process. We select attractive, practical projects with quality construction for which the authors can supply quality digital photography."

$ QST

American Radio Relay League, 225 Main St., Newington CT 06111. (860)594-0200. Fax: (860)594-0259. E-mail: qst@arrl.org. Website: www.arrl.org. **90% freelance written**. Monthly magazine covering amateur radio. "*QST* is an ARRL membership journal covering subjects of interest to amateur ('ham') radio operators." Estab. 1915. Circ. 150,000. Byline given. Pays on publication. No kill fee. Publishes ms an average of 6 months after acceptance. Buys all rights. Editorial lead time 6 months. Submit seasonal material 6 months in advance. Accepts queries by mail, e-mail, fax, phone. Responds in 1 week to queries. Responds in 1 month to mss Guidelines available online at: www.arrl.org/qst/aguide

Nonfiction Needs general interest, how-to, technical. Query. Length: 900-3,000 words. **Pays $65-125.**

Photos Send photos. Captions, identification of subjects required. Reviews GIF/JPEG files. Offers no additional payment for photos accepted with ms. Buys all rights.

Tips "Submissions must relate to amateur 'ham' radio."

$ $ THE QUILTER

All American Crafts, Inc., 7 Waterloo Rd., Stanhope NJ 07874. (973)347-6900. E-mail: editors@thequiltermag.com. Website: www.thequiltermag.com. **45% freelance written**. Bimonthly magazine on quilting. Estab. 1988. Byline given. Pays on publication. Publishes ms an average of 6 months after acceptance. Submit seasonal material 6 months in advance. Accepts queries by mail, phone. Responds in 6 weeks to queries. Sample copy for sae with 9 × 12 envelope and 4 First-Class stamps. Guidelines available online.

Nonfiction Quilts and quilt patterns with instructions, quilt-related projects, interview/profile, photo feature—all quilt related. Query with published clips. Length: 350-1,000 words. **Pays $150-250/article for original, unpublished mss. Project payments are a flat rate of $175-$375/project.**

Photos Send photos. Captions, identification of subjects required. Reviews transparencies, prints. Offers $10-15/photo Buys one-time or all rights.

Columns/Departments Feature Teacher (qualified quilt teachers with teaching involved—with slides); Profile (award-winning and interesting quilters). Length: 1,000 words maximum. **Pays 10¢/word, $15/photo.**

QUILTER'S COMPANION

Universal Magazines, Ltd., Unit 5, 6-8 Byfield St., North Ryde NSW 2113 Australia. (61)(2)9887-0399. Fax: (61)(2)9805-0714. E-mail: clare_qc@bigpond.net.au. Website: www.universalmagazines.com.au. Quarterly magazine offering the highest quality reading on unique patchwork and quilting.

Nonfiction Needs general interest, how-to, interview, photo feature. Query.

QUILTER'S NEWSLETTER MAGAZINE

OK Media, 741 Corporate Circle, Suite A, Golden CO 80401. (303)215-5600. Fax: (303)215-5601. Website: www.quiltersnewsletter.com. **Contact:** Jan Magee, Editor-in-Chief. Magazine published 6 times/year covering quilt making. "*Quilters Newsletter* is a specialized publication for quilt lovers and quiltmakers." Estab. 1969. Circ. 185,000. Pays 60 days after publication. No kill fee. Does not accept previously published submissions.Sample copy available online. Guidelines available online.

Nonfiction SASE Returns Needs historical, how-to, design techniques, presentation of a single technique or concept with step-by-step approach, interview, new product, reviews (quilt books and videos). Send complete ms.

Photos Color only, no b&w. Captions required. Reviews 2 × 2, 4 × 5 or larger transparencies, 35mm slides, digital hi-res photos (300 dpi or higher). Negotiates payment individually

Tips "Our decision will be based on the freshness of the material, the interest of the material to our readers, whether we have recently published similar material or already have something similar in our inventory, how well it fits into the balance of the material we have on hand, how much rewriting or editing we think it will require, and the quality of the slides, photos or illustrations you include."

$ $ QUILTER'S WORLD

185 Sweet Rd., Lincoln ME 04457. (207)794-3290. E-mail: sandra_hatch@drgnetwork.com. Website: www.quilters-world.com. **100% freelance written. Works with a small number of new/unpublished writers each year**. Bimonthly magazine covering quilting. "*Quilter's World* is a general quilting publication. We accept articles about special quilters, techniques, coverage of unusual quilts at quilt shows, special interest quilts, human interest articles and patterns. We include 2 articles and 12-15 patterns in every issue. Reader is 30-70 years old, midwestern." Circ. 130,000. Byline given. Pays 45 days after acceptance. No kill fee. Buys all rights. Submit seasonal material 10 months in advance. Accepts queries by mail, e-mail. Responds in 3 months to queries. Guidelines available online.

Nonfiction Needs how-to, interview, new product, photo feature feature, technical, quilters, quilt products. Query or send complete ms **Pays $100-$200 for articles; $50-550 for quilt designs.**

Photos State availability. Captions required. Reviews Color slides.

Tips "Read several recent issues for style and content."

$ RENAISSANCE MAGAZINE

One Controls Dr., Shelton CT 06484. (800)232-2224. Fax: (800)775-2729. E-mail: editortom@renaissancemagazine.com. Website: www.renaissancemagazine.com. **90% freelance written**. Bimonthly magazine covering the history of the Middle Ages and the Renaissance. Our readers include historians, reenactors, roleplayers, medievalists, and Renaissance Faire enthusiasts. Estab. 1996. Circ. 33,000. Byline given. Pays on publication. Publishes ms an average of 1 year after acceptance. Buys first North American serial rights. Editorial lead time 6 months. Submit seasonal material 4 months in advance. Accepts queries by mail, e-mail, fax, phone. Accepts previously published material. Responds in 3 weeks to queries. Responds in 2 months to mss. Sample copy for $9. Guidelines available online.

- The editor reports an interest in seeing costuming how-to articles; and Renaissance Festival insider articles.

Nonfiction Needs essays, expose, historical, how-to, interview, new product, opinion, photo feature, religious, travel. **Buys 25 mss/year.** Query or send ms Length: 1,000-5,000 words. **Pays 8¢/word.**
Photos State availability. Captions, identification of subjects, model releases required. Reviews contact sheets, negatives, transparencies, prints. Pays $7.50/photo. Buys all rights.
Tips Send in all articles in the standard manuscript format with photos/slides or illustrations for suggested use. Writers *must* be open to critique, and all historical articles should also include a recommended reading list. A SASE must be included to receive a response to any submission.

$ $ ROCK & GEM

The Earth's Treasures, Minerals and Jewelry, Miller Magazines, Inc., 290 Maple Court, Suite 232, Ventura CA 93003-7783. (805)644-3824, ext. 29. Fax: (805)644-3875. E-mail: editor@rockngem.com. Website: www.rockngem.com. **99% freelance written**. Monthly magazine covering rockhounding field trips, how-to lapidiary projects, minerals, fossils, gold prospecting, mining, etc. This is not a scientific journal. Its articles appeal to amateurs, beginners, and experts, but its tone is conversational and casual, not stuffy. It's for hobbyists. Estab. 1971. Circ. 55,000. Byline given. Pays on publication. No kill fee. Buys first worldwide serial and electronic reprint rights. Editorial lead time 4 months. Submit seasonal material 6 months in advance. Accepts queries by mail. Guidelines available online.

- Contributor agreement required.

Nonfiction Needs general interest, how-to, personal experience, photo feature, travel. Does not want to see The 25th Anniversary of the Pet Rock, or anything so scientific that it could be a thesis. **Buys 156-200 mss/year.** Send complete ms. Length: 2,000-4,000 words. **Pays $100-250.**
Photos Accepts prints, slides or digital art on disk or CD only (provide thumbnails). Send photos. Captions required. Offers no additional payment for photos accepted with ms.
Tips We're looking for more how-to articles and field trips with maps. Read writers guidelines very carefully and follow all instructions in them. Then be patient. Your manuscript may be published within a month or even a year from date of submission.

$ SCALE AUTO

Kalmbach Publishing Co., 21027 Crossroads Circle, P.O. Box 1612, Waukesha WI 53187-1612. (262)796-8776. Fax: (262)796-1383. E-mail: jhaught@kalmbach.com. Website: www.scaleautomag.com. **70% freelance written**. Bimonthly magazine covering model car building. We are looking for model builders, collectors, and enthusiasts who feel their models and/or modeling techniques and experiences would be of interest and benefit to our readership. Estab. 1979. Circ. 35,000. Byline given. Pays on publication. Publishes ms an average of 1 year after acceptance. Buys all rights. Editorial lead time 4 months. Submit seasonal material 4 months in advance. Accepts queries by mail, e-mail, fax, phone. Responds in 3 months to queries. Responds in 3 months to mss. Sample copy and writer's guidelines online.
Nonfiction Needs book excerpts, historical, how-to, build models, do different techniques, interview, personal experience, photo feature, technical. Query or send complete ms Length: 750-3,000 words. **Pays $60/published page.**
Photos When writing how-to articles be sure to take photos during the project. Send photos. Captions, identification of subjects, model releases required. Reviews negatives, 35mm color transparencies, color glossy. Negotiates payment individually. Buys all rights.
Columns/Departments Query. **Pays $60/page.**
Tips First and foremost, our readers like how-to material: how-to paint, how-to scratchbuild, how-to chop a roof, etc. Basically, our readers want to know how to make their own models better. Therefore, any help or advice you can offer is what modelers want to read. Also, the more photos you send, taken from a variety of views, the better choice we have in putting together an outstanding article layout. Send us more photos than you would ever possibly imagine we could use. This permits us to pick and choose the best of the bunch.

$ SCOTT STAMP MONTHLY

Amos Press Inc., P.O. Box 926, 911 S. Vandemark Rd., Sidney OH 45365. (800)448-7293. Fax: (937)498-0807. E-mail: mbaadke@amospress.com. Website: www.scottonline.com. **70% freelance written**. Monthly magazine covering stamp collecting. "Our goal at *Scott Stamp Monthly* is to create a monthly publication that serves every stamp collector, from beginner to advanced with informative and entertaining feature articles covering all aspects of the stamp hobby." Estab. 1868. Circ. 20,000. Byline given. Pays on publication. No kill fee. Publishes ms an average of 6 months after acceptance. Buys first rights, buys electronic rights. Editorial lead time 2 months. Submit seasonal material 6 months in advance. Accepts queries by mail, e-mail, fax, phone. Responds in 6 weeks to queries. Responds in 6 weeks to mss Sample copy for free

Nonfiction Needs general interest, historical, interview, nostalgic, opinion, technical, travel. Does not want non-philatelic articles. **Buys 50 mss/year.** Send complete ms. Length: 2,000 words. **Pays $40-75/ feature.**

Photos Quality illustrations a must. Send images or photos. Send scans with ms. Captions, identification of subjects required. Reviews digital color at twice actual size (300 dpi). Offers no additional payment for photos accepted with ms. Buys all rights.

Tips "Check and double check all facts. Footnotes and bibliographies are not appropriate to magazine style. Work citation into the text. Even though story subject might be specialized, write understandably. Explain stamp terms. *Scott Stamp Monthly* features are aimed at a broad audience that includes relatively novice collectors. Keep this audience in mind. Provide information in such a way to make stamp collecting more interesting to more people."

⊕ SCRAPBOOKING MEMORIES

Express Publications, Ltd., Locked Bag 111, Silverwater NSW 1811 Australia. (61)(2)9741-3899. Fax: (61)(2)9737-8017. E-mail: kevans@expresspublications.com.au. Website: www.scrapbookingmemories.com.au/. Cassie Bellemore, asst. ed. (cbellemore@expresspublications.com.au). **Contact:** Kristy Evans, editor. "*Scrapbooking Memories* incorporates technique and advice from the beginner to the expert with new features like Step-By-Step and Galleries." Accepts queries by e-mail or mail. 2-8 weeks. See submissions guidelines regularly for an update on themes and deadlines.

Nonfiction Needs general interest, how-to, inspirational, new product, photo feature. E-mail a digital photo or scan to Technical Editor, Sharryn Thomson at sthomson@expresspublications.com.au. Please send a jpeg file that is no bigger than 1MB. You will then be notified by e-mail whether you have been successful and informed of the process involved in publishing your layout. If by post, send original work or colour photocopies to Editorial, Scrapbooking Memories, 50 Silverwater Road, Silverwater NSW 2128. Please include full contact details with your submission and please ensure they are packaged in a page protector and braced on either side with thick, sturdy cardboard. The layout should then be packed either in a box (clean pizza boxes are great for 12in × 12in pages) or a tough, padded Postpak bag.

$$ SEW NEWS

Creating for You and Your Home, Primedia Enthusiast Group, 741 Corporate Circle, Suite A, Golden CO 80401. (303)215-5600. Fax: (303)215-5601. E-mail: sewnews@sewnews.com. Website: www.sewnews.com. **70% freelance written. Works with a small number of new/unpublished writers each year.** Monthly magazine covering fashion, gift, and home-dec sewing. "Our magazine is for the beginning home sewer to the professional dressmaker. It expresses the fun, creativity, and excitement of sewing." Estab. 1980. Circ. 185,000. Byline given. Pays on publication. No kill fee. Publishes ms an average of 6 months after acceptance. Buys all rights. Submit seasonal material 6 months in advance. Accepts queries by mail, e-mail, fax. Responds in 2 months to mss. Sample copy for $5.99. Guidelines for #10 SAE with 2 first-class stamps or online.

- All stories submitted to *Sew News* must be on disk or by e-mail.

Nonfiction Needs how-to, sewing techniques, interview, interesting personalities in home-sewing field. **Buys 200-240 mss/year.** Query with published clips if available Length: 500-2,000 words. **Pays $25-500.**

Photos Prefers digital images, color photos, or slides. Send photos. Identification of subjects required. Payment included in ms price. Buys all rights.

Tips "Query first with writing sample and outline of proposed story. Areas most open to freelancers are how-to and sewing techniques; give explicit, step-by-step instructions, plus rough art. We're using more home decorating and soft craft content."

$ SHUTTLE SPINDLE & DYEPOT

Handweavers Guild of America, Inc., 1255 Buford Hwy., Suite 211, Suwanee GA 30024. (678)730-0010. Fax: (678)730-0836. E-mail: hga@weavespindye.org. Website: www.weavespindye.org. **60% freelance written**. Quarterly magazine. "Quarterly membership publication of the Handweavers Guild of America, Inc., *Shuttle Spindle & Dyepot* magazine seeks to encourage excellence in contemporary fiber arts and to support the preservation of techniques and traditions in fiber arts. It also provides inspiration for fiber artists of all levels and develops public awareness and appreciation of the fiber arts. *Shuttle Spindle & Dyepot* appeals to a highly educated, creative, and very knowledgeable audience of fiber artists and craftsmen, weavers, spinners, dyers, and basket makers." Estab. 1969. Circ. 30,000. Byline given. Pays on publication. Publishes ms an average of 6 months after acceptance. Buys first North American serial rights, buys second serial (reprint) rights, buys electronic rights. Editorial lead time 8 months. Submit seasonal material 8 months in advance. Accepts queries by mail, e-mail, fax, phone. Sample copy for $8.00 plus shipping. Guidelines available online.

Nonfiction Needs inspirational, interview, new product, personal experience, photo feature, technical, travel. No self-promotional and no articles from those without knowledge of area/art/artists. **Buys 40 mss/year.** Query with published clips. Length: 1,000-2,000 words. **Pays $75-150.**

Photos State availability. Captions, identification of subjects, model releases required. Offers no additional payment for photos accepted with ms.

Columns/Departments Books and Videos, News and Information, Calendar and Conference, Travel and Workshop (all fiber/art related).

Tips "Become knowledgeable about the fiber arts and artists. The writer should provide an article of importance to the weaving, spinning, dyeing and basket making community. Query by telephone (once familiar with publication) by appointment helps editor and writer."

$ SUNSHINE ARTIST

America's Premier Show & Festival Publication, Palm House Publishing Inc., 4075 L.B. McLeod Rd., Suite E, Orlando FL 32811. (800)597-2573. Fax: (407)228-9862. E-mail: editor@sunshineartist.com. Website: www.sunshineartist.com. Monthly magazine covering art shows in the US. We are the premiere marketing/reference magazine for artists and crafts professionals who earn their living through art shows nationwide. We list more than 2,000 shows monthly, critique many of them, and publish articles on marketing, selling and other issues of concern to professional show circuit artists. Estab. 1972. Circ. 12,000. Byline given. Pays on publication. Publishes ms an average of 3 months after acceptance. Buys first North American serial rights. Responds in 2 months to queries. Sample copy for $5.

Nonfiction We publish articles of interest to artists and crafts professionals who travel the art show circuit. Current topics include marketing, computers, and RV living. No how-to. **Buys 5-10 freelance mss/year.** Send complete ms. Length: 1,000-2,000 words. **Pays $50-150.**

Reprints Send photocopy and information about when and where the material previously appeared.

Photos Send photos. Captions, identification of subjects, model releases required. Offers no additional payment for photos accepted with ms.

$$ TATTOO REVUE

Art & Ink Enterprises, Inc., c/o Art & Ink Enterprises, 820 Hamilton St., Ste. C6, Charlotte NC 28206-2991. (704)333-3331. Fax: (704)333-3433. E-mail: inked@skinartmag.com. Website: www.skinart.com. **25% freelance written**. Interview and profile magazine published 4 times/year covering tattoo artists, their art and lifestyle. All writers must have knowledge of tattoos. Features include interviews with tattoo artists and collectors. Estab. 1990. Circ. 100,000. Byline given. Pays on publication. Publishes ms an average of 3 months after acceptance. Buys one-time rights. Editorial lead time 3 months. Submit seasonal material 5 months in advance. Accepts queries by mail, e-mail, fax. Responds in 2 weeks to queries. Sample copy for $5.98. Guidelines for #10 SASE.

Nonfiction Needs book excerpts, historical, humor, interview, photo feature. Publishes special convention issues—dates and locations provided upon request. No first-time experiences—our readers already know. **Buys 10-30 mss/year.** Send complete ms. Length: 500-2,500 words. **Pays $25-200.**

Photos Send photos. Captions, identification of subjects, model releases required. Reviews transparencies, prints. Offers $0-10/photo Buys one time rights.

Columns/Departments Query with or without published clips or send complete ms. **Pays $25-50.**

Tips All writers must have knowledge of tattoos! Either giving or receiving.

$$ TEDDY BEAR REVIEW

Jones Publishing, Inc., N7450 Aanstad Rd., P.O. Box 5000, Iola WI 54945-5000. (715)445-5000. E-mail: editor@teddybearreview.com. Website: www.teddybearreview.com. **65% freelance written. Works with a small number of new/unpublished writers each year.** Bimonthly magazine on teddy bears for collectors, enthusiasts and bearmakers. Estab. 1985. Byline given. Payment upon publication on the last day of the month the issue is mailed. Contact editor for copy of freelance contributor agreement. Submit seasonal material 6 months in advance. Sample copy and writer's guidelines for $2 and 9 × 12 SAE

Nonfiction Needs historical, how-to, interview. No articles from the bear's point of view. **Buys 30-40 mss/year.** Query with published clips. Length: 900-1,500 words. **Pays $100-350.**

Photos Send photos. Captions required. Reviews transparencies, prints. Offers no additional payment for photos accepted with ms Buys one time rights.

Tips We are interested in good, professional writers around the country with a strong knowledge of teddy bears. Historical profile of bear companies, profiles of contemporary artists, and knowledgeable reports on museum collections are of interest.

$$ THREADS

Taunton Press, 63 S. Main St., P.O. Box 5506, Newtown CT 06470. (203)426-8171. Fax: (203)426-3434. E-mail: th@taunton.com. Website: www.threadsmagazine.com. Bimonthly magazine covering garment sewing, garment design, and embellishments (including quilting and embroidery). "We're seeking proposals from hands-on authors who first and foremost have a skill. Being an experienced writer is of secondary consideration." Estab. 1985. Circ. 129,000. Byline given. Offers $150 kill fee. Buys one-time rights, buys second serial (reprint) rights. Editorial lead time 4 months. Responds in 1-2 months to queries. Guidelines available online.

Nonfiction We prefer first-person experience. **Pays $150/page.**

Columns/Departments Product reviews; Book reviews; Tips; Closures (stories of a humorous nature). Query. **Closures pays $150/page. Each sewing tip printed pays $25.**

Tips Article proposal recommendation: "Send us a proposal (outline) with photos of your own work (garments, samples, etc.)."

$$ TOY FARMER

Toy Farmer Publications, 7496 106 Ave. SE, LaMoure ND 58458-9404. (701)883-5206. Fax: (701)883-5209. E-mail: chegvik@toyfarmer.com. Website: www.toyfarmer.com. **70% freelance written**. Monthly magazine covering farm toys. Estab. 1978. Circ. 27,000. Byline given. Pays on publication. Buys first North American serial rights. Editorial lead time 2 months. Submit seasonal material 3 months in advance. Accepts queries by mail, e-mail, fax, phone. Accepts previously published material. Responds in 1 month to queries. Responds in 2 months to mss. Writer's guidelines available upon request.

- Youth involvement is strongly encouraged.

Nonfiction Needs general interest, historical, interview, new product, personal experience, technical, book introductions. **Buys 100 mss/year.** Query with published clips. Length: 800-1,500 words. **Pays 10¢/word.**

Photos Must be 35mm originals or very high resolution digital images. State availability. Buys one time rights.

$$ TOY TRUCKER & CONTRACTOR

Toy Farmer Publications, 7496 106th Ave. SE, LaMoure ND 58458-9404. (701)883-5206. Fax: (701)883-5209. E-mail: chegvik@toyfarmer.com. Website: www.toytrucker.com. **40% freelance written**. Monthly magazine covering collectible toys. "We are a magazine on hobby and collectible toy trucks and construction pieces." Estab. 1990. Circ. 6,500. Byline given. Pays on publication. No kill fee. Buys first North American serial rights. Editorial lead time 2 months. Submit seasonal material 3 months in advance. Accepts queries by mail, e-mail, fax, phone. Accepts previously published material. Responds in 1 month to queries. Responds in 2 months to mss. Writer's guidelines available on request.

Nonfiction Needs historical, interview, new product, personal experience, technical. **Buys 35 mss/year.** Query. Length: 800-1,400 words. **Pays 10¢/word.**

Photos Must be 35mm originals or very high resolution digital images. Send photos. Captions, identification of subjects, model releases required.

Tips "Send sample work that would apply to our magazine. Also, we need more articles on collectors, builders, model kit enthusiasts and small company information. We have regular columns, so a feature should not repeat what our columns do."

TUFF STUFF'S SPORTS COLLECTORS MONTHLY

a Division of F + W Media, Inc., 700 E. State St., Iola WI 54990-0001. (715)445-2214. Fax: (715)445-4087. E-mail: scott.fragale@fwmedia.com. Website: www.tuffstuff.com. Monthly magazine covering sports collectibles and pricing for sports memorabilia and sports cards. Collectibles expertise is necessary. Estab. 1984. Circ. 140,000. Byline given. Pays on publication. Offers negotiable kill fee. Publishes ms an average of 2 months after acceptance. Makes work-for-hire assignments. Editorial lead time 3 months. Submit seasonal material 3 months in advance. Accepts queries by e-mail. Sample copy free.

Photos State availability. Reviews GIF/JPEG files. Negotiates payment individually. Buys one-time rights.

Tips No general interest sports submissions. Collectibles writers only.

⊘ VOGUE KNITTING

Soho Publishing Co., Inc., 161 Avenue of the Americas, Suite 1301, New York NY 10013. (212)937-2555. Fax: (646)336-3960. E-mail: editors@vogueknitting.com. Website: www.vogueknitting.com. Quarterly magazine created for participants in and enthusiasts of high fashion knitting. Circ. 175,000. No kill fee.

- Query before submitting. Include "editorial submission" in the subject line.

$ WESTERN & EASTERN TREASURES

People's Publishing Co., Inc., P.O. Box 219, San Anselmo CA 94979. Website: www.treasurenet.com. **100% freelance written**. Monthly magazine covering hobby/sport of metal detecting/treasure hunting. *"Western & Eastern Treasures* provides concise, yet comprehensive coverage of every aspect of the sport/hobby of metal detecting and treasure hunting with a strong emphasis on current, accurate information; innovative, field-proven advice and instruction; and entertaining, effective presentation." Estab. 1966. Circ. 50,000. Byline given. Pays on publication. No kill fee. Publishes ms an average of 4+ months after acceptance. Buys all rights. Editorial lead time 4 months. Submit seasonal material 3-4 months in advance. Responds in 3 months to mss. Sample copy for sae with 9 × 12 envelope and 5 First-Class stamps. Guidelines for #10 SASE.

Nonfiction Needs how-to, tips and finds for metal detectorists, interview, only people in metal detecting, personal experience, positive metal detector experiences, technical, only metal detecting hobby-related, helping in local community with metal detecting skills (i.e., helping local police locate evidence at crime scenes—all volunteer basis). *Silver & Gold Annual* (editorial deadline February each year)—looking for articles 1,500+ words, plus photos on the subject of locating silver and/or gold using a metal detector. No fiction, poetry, or puzzles. **Buys 150+ mss/year.** Send complete ms. Length: 1,000-1,500 words. **Pays 3¢/word for articles.**

Photos Send photos. Captions, identification of subjects required. Reviews 35mm transparencies, prints, digital scans (minimum 300 dpi). Offers $5 minimum/photo. Buys all rights.

$$ WOODSHOP NEWS

Soundings Publications, Inc., 10 Bokum Rd., Essex CT 06426-1185. (860)767-8227. Fax: (860)767-1048. E-mail: editorial@woodshopnews.com. Website: www.woodshopnews.com. **20% freelance written.** Monthly tabloid covering woodworking for professionals. Solid business news and features about woodworking companies. Feature stories about interesting professional woodworkers. Some how-to articles. Estab. 1986. Circ. 60,000. Byline given. Pays on publication. Publishes ms an average of 3 months after acceptance. Buys first North American serial rights. Submit seasonal material 4 months in advance. Accepts queries by mail, e-mail, fax. Responds in 1 month to queries. Sample copy available online. Guidelines free.

- *Woodshop News* needs writers in major cities in all regions except the Northeast. Also looking for more editorial opinion pieces.

Nonfiction Needs how-to, query first, interview, new product, opinion, personal experience, photo feature. Key word is newsworthy. No general interest profiles of folksy woodworkers. **Buys 15-25 mss/year.** Send complete ms. Length: 100-1,200 words. **Pays $50-500 for assigned articles. Pays $40-250 for unsolicited articles.**

Photos Send photos. Captions, identification of subjects required. Reviews contact sheets, prints. Buys one time rights.

Columns/Departments Pro Shop (business advice, marketing, employee relations, taxes, etc., for the professional written by an established professional in the field); Finishing (how-to and techniques, materials, spraybooths, staining; written by experienced finishers), both 1,200-1,500 words. Query. **Pays $200-300.**

Tips The best way to start is a profile of a professional woodworker in your area. Find a unique angle about the person or business and stress this as the theme of your article. Avoid a broad, general-interest theme that would be more appropriate to a daily newspaper. Our readers are professional woodworkers who want more depth and more specifics than would a general readership. If you are profiling a business, we need standard business information such as gross annual earnings/sales, customer base, product line and prices, marketing strategy, etc. Color 35mm or high-res digital photos are a must.

Home & Garden

$ THE ALMANAC FOR FARMERS & CITY FOLK

Greentree Publishing, Inc., 840 S. Rancho Dr., Suite 4-319, Las Vegas NV 89106. (702)387-6777. Fax: (702)385-1370. Website: www.thealmanac.com. **30-40% freelance written**. Annual almanac of "downhome, folksy material pertaining to farming, gardening, homemaking, animals, etc." Estab. 1983. Circ. 300,000. Byline given. Pays on publication. No kill fee. Publishes ms an average of 6 months after acceptance. Buys first North American serial rights. Sample copy for $4.99.

- Deadline: March 31.

Nonfiction Needs essays, general interest, historical, how-to, any home or garden project, humor. "No fiction or controversial topics. Please, no first-person pieces!" **Buys 30-40 mss/year.** No queries please. Editorial decisions made from ms only. Send complete ms by mail. Length: 350-1,400 words. **Pays $45/ page.**

Poetry Buys 1-6 poems/year. **Pays $45 for full pages or $15 for short poems.**

Tips "Typed submissions essential as we scan manuscript. Short, succinct material is preferred. Material should appeal to a wide range of people and should be on the 'folksy' side, preferably with a thread of humor woven in. No first-person pieces (using 'I' or 'my')."

$$ THE AMERICAN GARDENER

A Publication of the American Horticultural Society, 7931 E. Boulevard Dr., Alexandria VA 22308-1300. (703)768-5700. Fax: (703)768-7533. E-mail: editor@ahs.org. Website: www.ahs.org. **60% freelance written**. Bimonthly magazine covering gardening and horticulture. "This is the official publication of the American Horticultural Society (AHS), a national, nonprofit, membership organization for gardeners, founded in 1922. The AHS mission is 'to open the eyes of all Americans to the vital connection between people and plants, and to inspire all Americans to become responsible caretakers of the earth, to celebrate America's diversity through the art and science of horticulture, and to lead this effort by sharing the society's unique national resources with all Americans.' All articles are also published on members-only website." Estab. 1922. Circ. 25,000. Byline given. Pays on publication. Offers 25% kill fee. Publishes ms an average of 6 months after acceptance. Buys first North American serial rights. Editorial lead time 6 months. Submit seasonal material at least 1 year in advance. Accepts queries by mail. Responds in 3 months to queries. Sample copy for $5. Writer's guidelines by e-mail and online.

Nonfiction "Feature-length articles include in-depth profiles of individual plant groups; profiles of prominent American horticulturists and gardeners (living and dead); profiles of unusual public or private gardens; descriptions of historical developments in American gardening; descriptions of innovative landscape design projects (especially relating to use of regionally native plants or naturalistic gardening); and descriptions of important plant breeding and research programs tailored to a lay audience. We run a few how-to articles; these should address relatively complex or unusual topics that most other gardening magazines won't tackle—photography must be provided." **Buys 20 mss/year.** Query with published clips. Length: 1,500-2,500 words. **Pays $300-500, depending on complexity and author's experience.**

Reprints Rarely purchases second rights. Send photocopy of article with information about when and where the material previously appeared. Payment varies.

Photos E-mail or check website for guidelines before submitting. Identification of subjects required. Offers $80-350/photo Buys one-time print rights, plus limited rights to run article on members-only website.

Columns/Departments Natural Connections (explains a natural phenomenon—plant and pollinator relationships, plant and fungus relationships, parasites—that may be observed in nature or in the garden), 750-1,200 words. Homegrown Harvest (articles on edible plants delivered in a personal, reassuring voice. Each issue focuses on a single crop, such as carrots, blueberries, or parsley), 800-900 words; Plant in the Spotlight (profiles of a single plant species or cultivar, including a personal perspective on why it's a favored plant), 600 words. Query with published clips. **Pays $100-250.**

Tips "The majority of our readers are advanced, passionate amateur gardeners; about 20 percent are horticultural professionals. Most prefer not to use synthetic chemical pesticides. Our articles are intended to bring this knowledgeable group new information, ranging from the latest scientific findings that affect plants, to in-depth profiles of specific plant groups and leading horticulturalists, and the history of gardening and gardens in America."

$$ ARIZONA HOME & DESIGN

Arizona Business, 1301 N. Central Ave., #1070, Phoenix AZ 85012. (602)277-6045. Fax: (602)650-0827. E-mail: esunna@azbusinessmagazine.com. Website: www.azhomeanddesign.com. **39% freelance written**. Bimonthly magazine covering residential interior design and architecture and products in Arizona. Stories are geared toward an affluent audience living in Arizona who are looking to be inspired by design, rather than learn about how-to projects. Estab. 2000. Circ. 30,000. Byline given. Offers 100% kill fee. Publishes ms an average of 2 months after acceptance. Buys one-time rights. Editorial lead time 3 months. Submit seasonal material 3 months in advance. Accepts queries by mail, e-mail. Accepts simultaneous submissions. Sample copy free. Guidelines free.

Nonfiction Needs general interest, historical, humor, interview, new product, photo feature. Does not want stories without an angle, stories not geared to an affluent reader with a high-end home. Query. Length: 150-2,000 words. **Pays $100-350.**

Photos State availability. Identification of subjects required. Reviews negatives, transparencies, prints, GIF/JPEG files. Negotiates payment individually. Buys one time rights.

Columns/Departments Launch (new companies and products); Style Savvy (miscellaneous product showcase); Artery (noteworthy art for the home); Drab2Fab (before and after photos/copy of remodel projects); Inspiration (top 10 picks of home-related products); Social Life (entertaining at home). Home Away from Home department that features second-home properties in and outside of Arizona. Query. **Pays $100-350.**

Tips E-mail managing editor to introduce yourself. Include an organized list of story ideas.

$$ ATLANTA HOMES AND LIFESTYLES

Network Communications, Inc., 1100 Johnson Ferry Rd., Suite 595, Atlanta GA 30342. (404)252-6670. Fax: (404)252-6673. Website: www.atlantahomesmag.com. **65% freelance written**. Magazine published 12 times/year. *Atlanta Homes and Lifestyles* is designed for the action-oriented, well-educated reader who enjoys his/her shelter, its design and construction, its environment, and living and entertaining in it. Estab. 1983. Circ. 33,091. Byline given. Pays on publication. Publishes ms an average of 6 months after acceptance. Buys all rights. Accepts queries by mail, fax. Responds in 3 months to queries. Sample copy for $3.95. Guidelines available online.

Nonfiction Needs interview, new product, photo feature, well-designed homes, gardens, local art, remodeling, food, preservation, entertaining. We do not want articles outside respective market area, not written for magazine format, or that are excessively controversial, investigative or that cannot be appropriately illustrated with attractive photography. **Buys 35 mss/year.** Query with published clips. Length: 500-1,200 words. **Pays $100-500.** Sometimes pays expenses of writer on assignment

Photos Most photography is assigned. State availability. Captions, identification of subjects, model releases required. Reviews transparencies. Pays $40-50/photo Buys one time rights.

Columns/Departments Pays $50-200.

Tips Query with specific new story ideas rather than previously published material.

AUSTRALIAN COUNTRY COLLECTIONS

Universal Magazines, Ltd., Unit 5, 6-8 Byfield St., North Ryde NSW 2113 Australia. (61)(2)9887-0399. Fax: (61)(2)9805-0714. E-mail: lochdou@iprimus.com.au. Website: www.universalmagazines.com.au. Bimonthly magazine featuring a variety of stunning Australian country homes in every issue, creating a sense of country style for our readers' world.

Nonfiction Needs general interest, inspirational, photo feature. Query.

AUSTRALIAN HOME BEAUTIFUL

Pacific Magazines, Media City, 8 Central Ave., Eveleigh NSW 2015 Australia. (61)(2)9394 2000. Fax: (61)(2)9394 2406. E-mail: homebeautiful@pacificmags.com.au. Website: www.homebeautiful.com.au. Monthly magazine filled with loads of practical information, shopping details and aspirational images.

Nonfiction Needs general interest, how-to, new product, photo feature. Query.

$ BACKHOME

Your Hands-On Guide to Sustainable Living, Wordsworth Communications, Inc., P.O. Box 70, Hendersonville NC 28793. (828)696-3838. Fax: (828)696-0700. E-mail: backhome@ioa.com. Website: www.backhomemagazine.com. **80% freelance written**. Bimonthly magazine. "*BackHome* encourages readers to take more control over their lives by doing more for themselves: productive organic gardening; building and repairing their homes; utilizing renewable energy systems; raising crops and livestock; building furniture; toys and games and other projects; creative cooking. *BackHome* promotes respect for family activities, community programs, and the environment." Estab. 1990. Circ. 42,000. Byline given. Pays on publication. Offers $25 kill fee at publisher's discretion. Publishes ms an average of 1 year after acceptance. Buys first North American serial rights. Editorial lead time 3 months. Submit seasonal material 6 months in advance. Accepts queries by mail, e-mail, fax, phone. Accepts previously published material. Responds in 6 weeks to queries. Responds in 2 months to mss. Sample copy $5 or online. Guidelines available online.

- The editor reports an interest in seeing more renewable energy experiences, *good* small houses, workshop projects (for handy persons, not experts), and community action others can copy.

Nonfiction Needs how-to, gardening, construction, energy, homebusiness, interview, personal experience, technical, self-sufficiency. No essays or old-timey reminiscences. **Buys 80 mss/year.** Query. Length: 750-5,000 words. **Pays $35 (approximately)/printed page.**
Reprints Send photocopy and information about when and where the material previously appeared. Pays $35/printed page.
Photos Send photos. Identification of subjects required. Reviews color prints, 35mm slides, JPEG photo attachments of 300 dpi. Offers additional payment for photos published. Buys one-time rights.
Tips Very specific in relating personal experiences in the areas of gardening, energy, and homebuilding how-to. Third-person approaches to others' experiences are also acceptable but somewhat less desirable. Clear color photo prints, especially those in which people are prominent, help immensely when deciding upon what is accepted.

BATHROOM YEARBOOK

Universal Magazines, Ltd., Unit 5, 6-8 Byfield St., North Ryde NSW 2113 Australia. (61)(2)9887-0367. Fax: (61)9805-0714. E-mail: mgardener@universalmagazines.com.au. Website: www.completehome.com.au. Annual magazine covering all the latest bathroom products and designs.
Nonfiction Needs general interest, new product, photo feature. Query.

$$$$ BETTER HOMES AND GARDENS

1716 Locust St., Des Moines IA 50309-3023. (515)284-3044. Fax: (515)284-3763. Website: www.bhg.com. **Contact:** Gayle Butler, Editor-In-Chief. **10-15% freelance written**. Magazine "providing home service information for people who have a serious interest in their homes." "We read all freelance articles, but much prefer to see a letter of query rather than a finished manuscript." Estab. 1922. Circ. 7,605,000. Pays on acceptance. Buys all rights.
Nonfiction Needs travel, education, gardening, health, cars, home, entertainment. "We do not deal with political subjects or with areas not connected with the home, community, and family. No poetry or fiction." **Pay rates vary.**
Tips "Most stories published by this magazine go through a lengthy process of development involving both editor and writer. Some editors will consider only query letters, not unsolicited manuscripts. Direct queries to the department that best suits your storyline."

$$ BIRDS & BLOOMS

Reiman Publications, 5400 S. 60th St., Greendale WI 53129-1404. (414)423-0100. E-mail: editors@birdsandblooms.com. Website: www.birdsandblooms.com. **15% freelance written**. "Bimonthly magazine focusing on the beauty in your own backyard. *Birds & Blooms* is a sharing magazine that lets backyard enthusiasts chat with each other by exchanging personal experiences. This makes *Birds & Blooms* more like a conversation than a magazine, as readers share tips and tricks on producing beautiful blooms and attracting feathered friends to their backyards." "See contributor's guidelines at: www.birdsandblooms.com/submit-story/contributor-s-guidelines/detail.aspx. Estab. 1995. Circ. 1,900,000. Byline given. Pays on publication. No kill fee. Publishes ms an average of 7 months after acceptance. Buys all rights. Editorial lead time 2 months. Submit seasonal material 4 months in advance. Accepts queries by mail, e-mail. Accepts simultaneous submissions. Responds in 2 months to queries & mss. Sample copy for $2, 9 × 12 SAE and $1.95 postage. Guidelines for #10 SASE.
Nonfiction Needs essays, how-to, humor, inspirational, personal experience, photo feature, natural crafting and plan items for building backyard ac¢. No bird rescue or captive bird pieces. **Buys 12-20 mss/year.** Send complete ms. Length: 250-1,000 words. **Pays $100-400.**
Photos Send photos. Identification of subjects required. Reviews transparencies, prints. Buys one time rights.
Columns/Departments Backyard Banter (odds, ends & unique things); Bird Tales (backyard bird stories); Local Lookouts (community backyard happenings), all 200 words. 12-20 Send complete ms. **Pays $50-75.**
Tips "Focus on conversational writing—like you're chatting with a neighbor over your fence. Manuscripts full of tips and ideas that people can use in backyards across the country have the best chance of being used. Photos that illustrate these points also increase chances of being used."

BUILD HOME

Universal Magazines, Ltd., Unit 5, 6-8 Byfield St., North Ryde NSW 2113 Australia. (61)(2)9887-0366. Fax: (61)(2)9805-0350. E-mail: kmay@universalmagazines.com.au. Website: www.completehome.com.au. Quarterly magazine featuring kit homes, display homes, split-level homes, manufactured homes and special design projects.

- Query before submitting. Versions of magazine for VIC, NSW and QLD.

BURKE'S BACKYARD

ACP Magazines, Ltd., Locked Bag 1000, Artarmon NSW 1570 Australia. (61)(2)9282-8000. Fax: (61)(2)9267-4361. E-mail: magazine@burkesbackyard.com.au. Website: www.burkesbackyard.com.au. Monthly magazine providing trusted, informative ideas and information for Australian homes & gardens. "Our founder is Don Burke. As well as being an expert gardener he's nuts about animals and pets, too. And healthy food, the environment, science, DIY projects and good design anywhere it can be found." Circ. 118,000.

Nonfiction Needs general interest, how-to, new product. Query.

Photos Contact: photos@burkesbackyard.com.au. The ideal format is 300dpi (high-resolution) or a jpeg saved to "best quality".

$$ CALIFORNIA HOMES

The Magazine of Architecture, the Arts and Distinctive Design, McFadden-Bray Publishing Corp., P.O. Box 8655, Newport Beach CA 92658. (949)640-1484. Fax: (949)640-1665. E-mail: edit@calhomesmagazine.com. Website: www.calhomesmagazine.com. **80% freelance written**. Bimonthly magazine covering California interiors, architecture, some food, travel, history, and current events in the field. Estab. 1997. Circ. 80,000. Byline given. Pays on publication. Offers 50% kill fee. Publishes ms an average of 3 months after acceptance. Buys first North American serial rights. Editorial lead time 3 months. Submit seasonal material 6 months in advance. Accepts queries by mail, e-mail, fax. Responds in 1 month to queries. Responds in 2 months to mss. Sample copy for $7.50. Guidelines for #10 SASE.

Nonfiction Query. Length: 500-1,000 words. **Pays $250-750.**

Photos State availability. Captions required. Negotiates payment individually Buys one time rights.

CANADIAN GARDENING MAGAZINE

Transcontinental Media G.P., 25 Sheppard Ave. W., Suite 100, Toronto ON M2N 6S7 Canada. E-mail: editor@canadiangardening.com. Website: www.canadiangardening.com. **Mostly freelance written by assignment.** Magazine published 8 times/year covering Canadian gardening. *Canadian Gardening* is a national magazine aimed at the avid home gardener. Our readers are city gardeners with tiny lots, country gardeners with rolling acreage, indoor gardeners, rooftop gardeners, and enthusiastic beginners and experienced veterans. Estab. 1990. Circ. 152,000. Byline given. Pays on acceptance. Offers 25-50% kill fee. Buys electronic rights. Editorial lead time 4 months. Accepts queries by mail, fax. Accepts simultaneous submissions. Responds in 4 months to queries. Guidelines available online.

Nonfiction Needs how-to, planting and gardening projects, humor, personal experience, technical, plant and garden profiles, practical advice. **Buys 100 mss/year.** Query. Length: 200-1,500 words. **Pays variable amount.**

Photos Send image samples with submission. Reviews color photocopies and PDFs. Negotiates payment individually.

$$ CANADIAN HOMES & COTTAGES

The In-Home Show, Ltd., 2650 Meadowvale Blvd., Unit 4, Mississauga ON L5N 6M5 Canada. (905)567-1440. Fax: (905)567-1442. E-mail: jnaisby@homesandcottages.com. Website: www.homesandcottages.com. **75% freelance written**. Magazine published 6 times/year covering building and renovating; technically comprehensive articles. Estab. 1987. Circ. 89,500. Byline given. Pays on publication. Offers 10% kill fee. Publishes ms an average of 2 months after acceptance. Buys first North American serial rights. Editorial lead time 3 months. Submit seasonal material 3 months in advance. Accepts queries by mail. Sample copy for SAE. Guidelines for #10 SASE.

Nonfiction Looking for how-to projects and simple home improvement ideas. Needs humor, building and renovation related, new product, technical. **Buys 32 mss/year.** Query. Length: 1,000-2,000 words. **Pays $300-750.**

Photos Send photos. Captions, identification of subjects required. Reviews transparencies, prints. Negotiates payment individually Buys one time rights.

Tips Read our magazine before sending in a query. Remember that you are writing to a Canadian audience.

$$ THE CANADIAN ORGANIC GROWER

1205 Rte 915, New Horton NB E4H 1W1 Canada. E-mail: janet@cog.ca. Website: www.cog.ca/magazine.htm. **100% freelance written**. Quarterly magazine covering organic gardening and farming. "We publish articles that are of interest to organic gardeners, farmers and consumers in Canada. We're always looking for practical how-to articles, as well as farmer profiles. At times, we include news about the organic community, recipes and stories about successful marketing strategies." Estab. 1975. Circ. 4,000. Byline given. Pays on publication. Publishes ms an average of 2-3 months after acceptance. Buys first North American serial rights. Editorial lead time 6 months. Submit seasonal material 6 months in advance. Accepts queries by mail, e-mail. Accepts previously published material. Responds in 3 weeks to queries. Responds in 1 month to mss. Sample copy available online. Guidelines available online.

Nonfiction Needs essays, general interest, how-to, garden, farm, market, process organic food, interview, new product, opinion, technical. Does not want rants. **Buys 25 mss/year.** Query. Length: 500-2,500 words. **Pays $150-350 for assigned articles. Pays $150-350 for unsolicited articles.**

Photos State availability. Captions, identification of subjects required. Reviews prints, GIF/JPEG files. Negotiates payment individually. Buys one-time rights.

$ CAROLINA HOMES & INTERIORS

MediaServices, Inc., P.O. Box 22617, Charleston SC 29413. (843)881-1481. Fax: (843)849-6717. E-mail: edit@mediaservices1.com. Website: www.carolinahomes.net. **80% freelance written**. 6 issues per year magazine covering coastal Carolina homes and lifestyles. We feature the finest in coastal living. Highlighting builders, designers, communities, vendors and the many recreational alternatives in the Carolinas, coastal Georgia and Florida, *CH&I* is the region's premiere home and lifestyle guide. Estab. 1983. Circ. 65,000. Byline given. Pays 30 days after publication. Offers 50% kill fee. Publishes ms an average of 2 months after acceptance. Buys one-time rights. Editorial lead time 2 months. Submit seasonal material 4 months in advance. Accepts queries by mail, e-mail. Accepts previously published material. Accepts simultaneous submissions. Responds in 2 weeks to queries. Responds in 1-2 months to mss. Sample copy free. Guidelines by e-mail.

Nonfiction Needs general interest, historical, how-to, inspirational, interview, new product, personal experience, technical, travel. **Buys 50 mss/year.** Query with published clips. Length: 300-2,000 words. **Pays 15 ¢ per word.** Limit agreed upon in advance

Columns/Departments Inner Beauty, 300 words; Outer Beauty, 300 words; Coastal Custom Builders, 430 words; Hot Retirement Towns, 400 words; Things to Do, 500 words; Four!, 500 words; Day Trips, 750 words. Query with published clips. **Pays 15 ¢ per word**

Tips Be creative. Story ideas should reflect the beauty of the region. All writers are welcome, but local writers are preferred. New writers are encouraged to query.

$$$$ COASTAL LIVING

Southern Progress Corp., 2100 Lakeshore Dr., Birmingham AL 35209. (205)445-6007. Fax: (205)445-8655. E-mail: mamie_walling@timeinc.com. Website: www.coastalliving.com. **Contact:** Mamie Walling. "Bimonthly magazine for those who live or vacation along our nation's coasts. The magazine emphasizes home design and travel, but also covers a wide variety of other lifestyle topics and coastal concerns." Estab. 1997. Circ. 660,000. Pays on acceptance. Offers 25% kill fee. Responds in 2 months to queries. Sample copy available online. Guidelines available online.

Nonfiction "The magazine is roughly divided into 5 areas, with regular features, columns and departments for each area. **Currents** offers short, newsy features of 25-200 words written mostly by staff members on new products, seaside events, beach fashions, etc. **Travel** includes outdoor activities, nature experiences, and lodging and dining stories. **Homes** places the accent on casual living, with warm, welcoming houses and rooms designed for living. **Food & Entertainment** is divided into *In the Coastal Kitchen* (recipes and tips) and *Seafood Primer* (basics of buying and preparing seafood). The **Lifestyle** section is a catch all of subjects to help readers live better and more comfortably: *The Good Life* (profiles of people who have moved to the coast), *Coastal Character* (profile of someone connected to a coastal environment), *Collectibles* (treasured items/accessories with a marine connection), *So You Want to Live In.* (profiles of coastal communities), etc." Query with clips and SASE. **Pays $1/word.**

Photos State availability.

Tips Query us with ideas that are very specifically targeted to the columns that are currently in the magazine.

$$ COLORADO HOMES & LIFESTYLES

Wiesner Publishing, LLC, 7009 S. Potomac St., Centennial CO 80112-4029. (303)397-7600. Fax: (303)397-7619. E-mail: mdakotah@coloradohomesmag.com. Website: www.coloradohomesmag.com. **75% freelance written**. Upscale shelter magazine published 9 times/year containing beautiful homes, landscapes, architecture, calendar, antiques, etc. All of Colorado is included. Geared toward home-related and lifestyle areas, personality profiles, etc. Estab. 1981. Circ. 36,000. Byline given. Pays on acceptance. Offers 15% kill fee. Publishes ms an average of 3 months after acceptance. Buys first North American serial rights. Editorial lead time 3 months. Submit seasonal material 1 year in advance. Accepts queries by mail, e-mail. Accepts simultaneous submissions. Responds in 2 months to queries. Sample copy for #10 SASE.

Nonfiction Fine homes and furnishings, regional interior design trends, shopping information, interesting personalities and lifestyles—all with a Colorado slant. No personal essays, religious, humor, technical **Buys 50-75 mss/year.** Query with published clips. Length: 900-1,500 words. **Pays $200-400.** Provide sources with phone numbers

Photos Send photos. Identification of subjects required. Reviews transparencies, b&w glossy prints, CDs, digital images, slides.

Tips Send query, lead paragraph, clips. Send ideas for story or stories. Include some photos, if applicable. The more interesting and unique the subject, the better. A frequent mistake made by writers is failure to provide material with a style and slant appropriate for the magazine, due to poor understanding of the focus of the magazine.

$$ CONCRETE HOMES

Publications and Communications, Inc. (PCI), 13581 Pond Springs Rd., Suite 450, Austin TX 78729. Fax: (512)331-3950. E-mail: homes@pcinews.com. Website: concretehomesmagazine.com. **85% freelance written**. Bimonthly magazine covering homes built with concrete. *Concrete Homes* is a publication designed to be informative to consumers, builders, contractors, architects, etc., who are interested in concrete homes. The magazine profiles concrete home projects (they must be complete) and offers how-to and industry news articles. Estab. 1999. Circ. 25,000. Byline given. Pays on publication. Offers 100% kill fee. Publishes ms an average of 2 months after acceptance. Buys all rights. Editorial lead time 2 months. Submit seasonal material 3-4 months in advance. Accepts queries by mail, e-mail. Accepts simultaneous submissions. Responds in 1 month to queries. Responds in 1 month to mss. Sample copy available online. Guidelines available online.

Nonfiction Needs how-to, interview, new product, technical. **Buys 30-40 mss/year.** Query or query with published clips Length: 800-2,000 words. **Pays $200-250.**

Photos State availability. Captions required. Reviews 8 × 10 transparencies, prints, GIF/JPEG files. Offers no additional payment for photos accepted with ms. Buys all rights.

Tips Demonstrate awareness of concrete homes and some knowledge of the construction/building industry.

$$$$ ☐ COTTAGE LIFE

Quarto Communications, 54 St. Patrick St., Toronto ON M5T 1V1 Canada. (416)599-2000. Fax: (416)599-4070. E-mail: editorial@cottagelife.com. Website: www.cottagelife.com. **80% freelance written**. Bimonthly magazine. "*Cottage Life* is written and designed for the people who own and spend time at waterfront cottages throughout Canada and bordering US states, with a strong focus on Ontario. The magazine has a strong service slant, combining useful `how-to' journalism with coverage of the people, trends, and issues in cottage country. Regular columns are devoted to boating, fishing, watersports, projects, real estate, cooking, design and decor, nature, personal cottage experience, and environmental, political, and financial issues of concern to cottagers." Estab. 1988. Circ. 70,000. Byline given. Pays on acceptance. Offers 50-100% kill fee. Publishes ms an average of 2 months after acceptance. Buys first North American serial rights. Guidelines available online.

Nonfiction Needs book excerpts, expose, historical, how-to, humor, interview, personal experience, photo feature, technical. **Buys 90 mss/year.** Query with published clips and SAE with Canadian postage or IRCs. Length: 150-3,500 words. **Pays $100-3,000.**

Columns/Departments On the Waterfront (front department featuring short news, humor, human interest, and service items), 400 words maximum. **Pays $50-400.** Cooking, Real Estate, Fishing, Nature, Watersports, Decor, Personal Experience, and Issues, all 150-1,200 words. **Pays $100-1,200**. Query with published clips and SAE with Canadian postage or IRCs, or by e-mail.

Tips "If you have not previously written for the magazine, the `On the Waterfront' section is an excellent place to break in."

▦ COUNTRY HOME IDEAS

Express Publications, Ltd., 50 Silverwater Rd., Silverwater NSW 2128 Australia. (61)(2)9741-3899. Fax: (61)(2)9737-8017. E-mail: chi@expresspublications.com.au; locations@expresspublications.com.au. Website: www.countryhomeideas.com.au. **Contact:** Margaret Megard, editor. "We inspire and enthuse the decorator in all of us with a contemporary country flair." Accepts queries by mail, e-mail.

Nonfiction Needs general interest, how-to, new product. Please send a brief query accompanied by clips of your previous work. Include a SASE if you wish to have them returned. If you wish to submit a house for consideration, please send photographic documentation of each room. Please send all queries to locations@expresspublications.com.au, or by post to Editor.

COUNTRY LIVING

The Hearst Corp., 300 W. 57th St., New York NY 10019. (212)649-3500. Monthly magazine covering home design and interior decorating with an emphasis on country style. A lifestyle magazine for readers who appreciate the warmth and traditions associated with American home and family life. Each monthly issue embraces American country decorating and includes features on furniture, antiques, gardening, home building, real estate, cooking, entertaining and travel. Estab. 1978. Circ. 1,600,000. No kill fee.

Nonfiction Subjects covered include decorating, collecting, cooking, entertaining, gardening/landscaping, home building/remodeling/restoring, travel, and leisure activities. **Buys 20-30 mss/year.** Send complete ms and SASE **Payment varies**

Columns/Departments Query first.

Tips Know the magazine, know the market, and know how to write a good story that will interest *our* readers.

$$$$ D HOME AND GARDEN MAGAZINE

D Magazine Partners, 4311 Oak Lawn Ave., Dallas TX 75219. (214)939-3636. Fax: (214)748-4153. Website: www.dhomeandgarden.com. **50% freelance written**. Magazine published 7 times/year covering Dallas home and garden. Estab. 1999. Circ. 25,000. Byline given. Pays on acceptance. Offers 25% kill fee. Publishes ms an average of 2-3 months after acceptance. Buys all rights. Editorial lead time 2-3 months. Submit seasonal material 2-3 months in advance. Accepts queries by mail, e-mail, fax, phone. Sample copy available online. Guidelines free.

Nonfiction Green issue (January/February). Does not want anything not specific to Dallas. **Buys 3-5 mss/year.** Query. Length: 800-2,000 words. **Pays $400-1,500.**

Photos Contact: Contact Andrea Tomek, art director. State availability. Identification of subjects required. Reviews contact sheets, GIF/JPEG files. Negotiates payment individually. Buys one time rights.

$$ ✿ DREAM HOUSE MAGAZINE

Western Canada's Premier fine home and lifestyle publication, Dream House Publications Inc., 106-873 Beatty St., Vancouver BC V6B 2M6 Canada. (604)681-3463. Fax: (604)681-3494. E-mail: tracey@dreamhousemag.com. Website: www.dreamhousemag.com. **50% freelance written**. Magazine published 8 times/year covering fine homes, luxury lifestyle. *Dream House Magazine* serves its readers the best of the best in fine homes and luxury lifestyles. Estab. 2001. Circ. 28,000. Byline given. Pays within 30 days of publication. Offers 50% kill fee. Publishes ms an average of 1 month after acceptance. Buys first North American serial rights. Editorial lead time 3 months. Submit seasonal material 1 month in advance. Accepts queries by mail, e-mail. Guidelines free.

Nonfiction Needs general interest, historical, humor, interview, new product, photo feature, travel. Does not want memoirs. Query with published clips. Length: 500-800 words. **Pays 25-50¢/word.**

Photos Send photos. Reviews TIFF files only (300 dpi at 8 × 10). Offers no additional payment for photos accepted with ms. Buys one time rights.

Columns/Departments Finance; Real Estate; Insurance, all 500-800 words. Query with published clips.

Tips Read magazine. Study our audience. Be well connected in the luxury marketplace.

$$ EARLY AMERICAN LIFE

Firelands Media Group LLC, P.O. Box 221228, Shaker Heights OH 44122-0996. E-mail: queries@firelandsmedia.com. Website: www.ealonline.com. **60% freelance written**. Bimonthly magazine for people who are interested in capturing the warmth and beauty of the 1600-1840 period and using it in their homes and lives today. They are interested in antiques, traditional crafts, architecture, restoration, and collecting. Estab. 1970. Circ. 90,000. Byline given. Pays on acceptance. 25% kill fee. Publishes ms an average of 1 year after acceptance. Buys worldwide rights. Accepts queries by mail, e-mail. Responds in 3 months to queries. Sample copy and writer's guidelines for 9 × 12 SAE with $2.50 postage.

Nonfiction "Social history (the story of the people, not epic heroes and battles), travel to historic sites, antiques and reproductions, restoration, architecture, and decorating. We try to entertain as we inform. We're always on the lookout for good pieces on any of our subjects. Would like to see more on how real people did something great to their homes." **Buys 40 mss/year.** Query us first before sending ms. Length: 750-3,000 words. **Pays $250-700, additionally for photos.**

Tips "Our readers are eager for ideas on how to bring early America into their lives. Conceive a new approach to satisfy their related interests in arts, crafts, travel to historic sites, and especially in houses decorated in the Early American style. Write to entertain and inform at the same time. We are visually oriented, so writers are asked to supply images or suggest sources for illustrations."

$$$$ ECOHOME DESIGNS

Your source for sustainable house plans, Hanley Wood, 1 Thomas Cir., #600, Washington DC 20005-5811. (202)729-3525. E-mail: shyoun@hanleywood.com. Website: www.hanleywood.com. **Contact:** Hillary Gottemoeller, hgottemoeller@hanleywood.com. **75% freelance written**. Semiannual magazine covering sustainable building, green design, predrawn blueprints. "Whether your definition of green building is about the use of sustainable materials or about high performance and energy savings, *Eco-Home Designs* is the perfect place to find the latest editorial about the green building phenomenon as well as predrawn house plans that feature comfortable green designs. Readers will find a wealth of insights about the newest building materials and construction methods, as well as tried-and-true tips on building an energy-efficient custom home." Estab. 2009. Byline given. Pays on acceptance. Offers 50% kill fee. Publishes ms an average of 2 months after acceptance. Makes work-for-hire assignments. Editorial lead time 6 months. Submit seasonal material 3 months in advance. Accepts queries by e-mail. Accepts previously published material. Accepts simultaneous submissions. Responds in 1 week to queries. Responds in 1 month to mss. Guidelines available.

Nonfiction Contact: Simon Hyoun, editor. Needs how-to, choose green building materials; practice green building concepts, new product, photo feature, technical. We do not want personal stories of home building experiences. **Buys 12 mss/year.** Query with published clips. Length: 500-1,000 words. **Pays $.80-$1/word for assigned articles. Pays $.80-$1/word for unsolicited articles.**

Tips "Submissions should demonstrate knowledge of current trends in green building and residential design, as well as the custom home building market."

$$$ FINE GARDENING

Taunton Press, 63 S. Main St., P.O. Box 5506, Newtown CT 06470-5506. (203)426-8171. Fax: (203)426-3434. E-mail: fg@taunton.com. Website: www.finegardening.com. Bimonthly magazine. High-value magazine on landscape and ornamental gardening. Articles written by avid gardeners—first person, hands-on gardening experiences. Estab. 1988. Circ. 200,000. Byline given. Pays on acceptance. No kill fee. Publishes ms an average of 6 months after acceptance. Buys all rights. Editorial lead time 1 year. Submit seasonal material 1 year in advance. Accepts queries by mail, e-mail, fax. Guidelines free.

Nonfiction Needs how-to, personal experience, photo feature, book reviews. **Buys 60 mss/year.** Query. Length: 1,000-3,000 words. **Pays $300-1,200.**

Photos Send photos. Reviews digital images. Buys serial rights

Columns/Departments Book, video and software reviews (on gardening); Last Word (essays/serious, humorous, fact or fiction). Length: 250-500 words. 30 Query. **Pays $ 50- 200.**

Tips It's most important to have solid first-hand experience as a gardener. Tell us what you've done with your own landscape and plants.

$$ FINE HOMEBUILDING

The Taunton Press, 63 S. Main St., P.O. Box 5506, Newtown CT 06470-5506. (203)426-8171. Fax: (203)426-3434. E-mail: fh@taunton.com. Website: www.taunton.com. Bimonthly magazine for builders, architects, contractors, owner/builders and others who are seriously involved in building new houses or reviving old ones. Estab. 1981. Circ. 300,000. Byline given. Pays half on acceptance, half on publication. Offers kill fee. Offers on acceptance payment as kill fee. Publishes ms an average of 1 year after acceptance. Buys first rights. Reprint rights Responds in 1 month to queries. Writer's guidelines for SASE and on website.

Nonfiction We're interested in almost all aspects of home building, from laying out foundations to capping cupolas. Query with outline, description, photographs, sketches and SASE. **Pays $150/published page.**

Photos Take lots of work-in-progress photos. Color print film, ASA 400, from either Kodak or Fuji works best. If you prefer to use slide film, use ASA 100. Keep track of the negatives; we will need them for publication. If you're not sure what to use or how to go about it, feel free to call for advice.

Columns/Departments Tools & Materials, Reviews, Questions & Answers, Tips & Techniques, Cross Section, What's the Difference?, Finishing Touches, Great Moments, Breaktime, Drawing Board (design column). Query with outline, description, photographs, sketches and SASE. **Payment varies**

Tips Our chief contributors are home builders, architects and other professionals. We're more interested in your point of view and technical expertise than your prose style. Adopt an easy, conversational style and define any obscure terms for non-specialists. We try to visit all our contributors and rarely publish building projects we haven't seen, or authors we haven't met.

$$$$ HORTICULTURE

F + W Media, Inc., 4700 E. Galbraith Rd., Cincinnati OH 45236. (513)531-2690. Fax: (513)891-7153. E-mail: edit@hortmag.com. Website: www.hortmag.com. Bimonthly magazine. *Horticulture*, the country's oldest gardening magazine, is designed for active home gardeners. Our goal is to offer a blend of text, photographs and illustrations that will both instruct and inspire readers. Circ. 160,000. Byline given. Offers kill fee. Buys all rights. Submit seasonal material 10 months in advance. Accepts queries by mail, e-mail, fax. Responds in 3 months to queries. Guidelines for SASE or by e-mail.

Nonfiction "Articles should be grounded in fact and serve the purpose of helping readers become better gardeners. However, we appreciate good writing and unique voices, and personal experience, anecdote and opinion play a part in our best articles." **Buys 70 mss/year.** Query with published clips, subject background material and SASE. Length: 800-1,000 words. **Pays $500.**

Columns/Departments Length: 200-600 words. Query with published clips, subject background material and SASE. Include disk where possible. **Pays $250.**

Tips "We believe every article must offer ideas or illustrate principles that our readers might apply on their own gardens. Our readers want to become better, more creative gardeners."

$$$$ HOUSE BEAUTIFUL

The Hearst Corp., 300 W. 57th St., New York NY 10019. (212)903-5000. Website: www.housebeautiful.com. Monthly magazine. Targeted toward affluent, educated readers ages 30-40. Covers home design and decoration, gardening and entertaining, interior design, architecture and travel. Circ. 865,352. No kill fee. Editorial lead time 3 months.

- Query first.

KITCHENS & BATHROOMS QUARTERLY

Universal Magazines, Ltd., Unit 5, 6-8 Byfield St., North Ryde NSW 2113 Australia. (61)(2)9887-0367. Fax: (61)(2)9887-0350. E-mail: mgardener@universalmagazines.com.au. Website: www.completehome.com.au. "Quarterly magazine for planning, designing, building or renovating your kitchen or bathroom."

Nonfiction Needs general interest, how-to, new product, photo feature. Query.

KITCHEN YEARBOOK

Universal Magazines, Ltd., Unit 5, 6-8 Byfield St., North Ryde NSW 2113 Australia. (61)(2)9887-0367. Fax: (61)(2)9887-0350. E-mail: mgardener@universalmagazines.com.au. Website: www.completehome.com.au. Annual magazine covering the year's most innovative and inspiring kitchen designs.

Nonfiction Needs general interest, how-to, inspirational, new product, photo feature. Query.

$$$ LAKESTYLE

Celebrating Life on the Water, Bayside Publications, Inc., P.O. Box 170, Excelsior MN 55331. (952)470-1380. Fax: (952)470-1389. E-mail: editor@lakestyle.com. Website: www.lakestyle.com. **50% freelance written**. Quarterly magazine. *Lakestyle* is committed to celebrating the lifestyle chosen by lake home and cabin owners. Estab. 2000. Circ. 40,000. Byline given. Pays on publication. Offers 10% kill fee. Publishes ms an average of 3 months after acceptance. Buys all rights. Editorial lead time 2 months. Submit seasonal material 3 months in advance. Accepts queries by mail, e-mail, fax, phone. Accepts previously published material. Responds in 3 weeks to queries. Responds in 1 month to mss. Sample copy for $5. Guidelines available online.

Nonfiction Needs essays, historical, how-to, humor, inspirational, interview, new product, photo feature. No direct promotion of product. **Buys 15 mss/year.** Send complete ms. Length: 500-2,500 words. **Pays 25-50¢/word for assigned articles. Pays 10-25¢/word for unsolicited articles.**

Photos State availability of or send photos. Captions, identification of subjects, model releases required. Offers no additional payment for photos accepted with ms Rights purchased vary

Columns/Departments Lakestyle Entertaining (entertaining ideas); Lakestyle Gardening (gardening ideas); On the Water (boating/playing on the lake); Hidden Treasures (little known events); At the Cabin (cabin owner's information); all approximately 1,000 words. Query with or without published clips or send complete ms. **Pays 10-25¢/word**

Tips *Lakestyle* is interested in enhancing the lifestyle chosen by our readers, a thorough knowledge of cabin/lake home issues helps writers fulfill this goal.

N LIFESTYLE POOLS

News Limited, 2 Holt St., Surry Hills NSW 2010 Australia. 02 9288 3000. Fax: 02 9288 8488. Website: www.newsspace.com.au/lifestyle_pools. www.newslimited.com.au. **Contact:** Veda Dante, editor. Bi-annual magazine covering the finest pools from across the country. "*Lifestyle Pools* editorial encompasses

the latest news and products, with informative features, offering helpful advice and inspirational ways to make the most of your outdoor area, delicious recipes for entertaining around the pool or backyard, smart tips for water conservation in your pool and garden."
Nonfiction Needs general interest, photo feature. Query.

LOG HOME LIVING

Home Buyer Publications, Inc., 4125 Lafayette Center Dr., Suite 100, Chantilly VA 20151. (703)222-9411. Fax: (703)222-3209. E-mail: editor@loghomeliving.com. Website: www.loghomeliving.com. **90% freelance written**. Monthly magazine for enthusiasts who are dreaming of, planning for, or actively building a log home. Estab. 1989. Circ. 132,000. Byline given. Pays on acceptance. Offers $100 kill fee. Publishes ms an average of 6 months after acceptance. Buys first North American serial rights, buys second serial (reprint) rights. Editorial lead time 6 months. Submit seasonal material 6 months in advance. Accepts queries by mail, e-mail. Accepts previously published material. Responds in 6 weeks to queries. Sample copy for $4. Guidelines available online.
Nonfiction Needs how-to, build or maintain log home, interview, log home owners, personal experience, photo feature, log homes, technical, design/decor topics, travel. **Buys 60 mss/year.** Query with SASE. Length: 1,000-2,000 words. **Payment depends on length, nature of the work and writer's expertise.**
Reprints Send tearsheet, photocopy or typed ms and information about when and where the material previously appeared.
Photos State availability. Reviews contact sheets, 4 × 5 transparencies, 4x6 prints. Negotiates payment individually Buys one time rights.
Tips *Log Home Living* is devoted almost exclusively to modern manufactured and handcrafted kit log homes. Our interest in historical or nostalgic stories of very old log cabins, reconstructed log homes, or one-of-a-kind owner-built homes is secondary and should be queried first.

🌐 LUXURY HOME DESIGN

Universal Magazines, Ltd., Unit 5, 6-8 Byfield St., North Ryde NSW 2113 Australia. (61)(2)9887-0399. Fax: (61)(2)9805-0714. E-mail: kstjames@universalmagazines.com.au. Website: www.luxuryhome.com.au. Quarterly magazine dedicated to providing readers with a comprehensive overview of design directions in the upper end of the residential market.
Nonfiction Needs general interest, how-to, new product, photo feature. Query.

🌐 LUXURY KITCHENS & BATHROOMS

Universal Magazines, Ltd., Unit 5, 6-8 Byfield St., North Ryde NSW 2113 Australia. (61)(2)9887-0367. Fax: (61)(2)9887-0350. E-mail: mgardener@universalmagazines.com.au. Website: www.completehome.com.au. Annual magazine covering luxury kitchen and bathroom projects and products.
Nonfiction Needs new product. Query.

MIDWEST HOME AND GARDEN

U.S. Trust Bldg., 730 S. Second Ave., Suite 600, Minneapolis MN 55402. Fax: (612)371-5801. E-mail: clee@midwesthomemag.com. Website: www.midwesthomemag.com. **Contact:** Chris Lee, editor. **50% freelance written**. "*Midwest Home and Garden* is an upscale shelter magazine showcasing innovative architecture, interesting interior design, and beautiful gardens of the Midwest. Must have a strong Minnesota connection." Estab. 1997. Circ. 80,000. Byline given. Pays on acceptance. No kill fee. Accepts queries by mail, e-mail, fax. Guidelines available online.
Nonfiction Profiles of regional designers, architects, craftspeople related to home and garden. Photo-driven articles on home decor and design, and gardens. Needs book excerpts, essays, how-to, garden and design, interview, brief, new product, photo feature. Query with résumé, published clips, and SASE. Length: 300-1,000 words. **Payment negotiable.**
Columns/Departments Back Home (essay on home/garden topics), 800 words; Design Directions (people and trends in home and garden), 300 words.
Tips We are always looking for great new interior design, architecture, and gardens—in Minnesota and in the Midwest.

$ $ MILWAUKEE HOME & FINE LIVING

Journal Sentinel Specialty Media Division, 4101 W. Burnham St., West Milwaukee WI 53215. (414)647-4748. Fax: (414)647-4745. E-mail: rbundy@journalsentinel.com. Website: www.milwaukee-home.com. **80% freelance written**. Monthly magazine covering homes, gardens, art, furnishings, food, fashion. Estab. 2004. Circ. 17,500. Byline given. Pays on publication. Offers 25% kill fee. Publishes ms an average of 6 months after acceptance. Buys first North American serial rights, electronic rights. Editorial lead time 6 months. Submit seasonal material 1 year in advance. Accepts queries by mail, e-mail. Responds in 6 weeks to queries. Sample copy for sae with 10 × 13 envelope and 2 First-Class stamps. Guidelines available online.

Nonfiction Needs general interest, historical, interview, nostalgic, photo feature feature, profile. **Buys 80 mss/year.** Query with published clips. Length: 100-1,200 words. **Pays $25-360.**

Columns/Departments Insights (home furnishings, interior design trends, new products); Fine Living (travel, entertaining, food and wine, performing arts); Artisan (local craftspeople); In the Garden (landscaping tips and advice, plant recommendations). **Pays $25-360.**

Tips "Please submit queries on local topics relating to specific homes and gardens, and products that can be obtained in the Milwaukee, Wisconsin, 7-county area. Read the magazine for style and content."

$ $ $ MOUNTAIN HOUSE AND HOME

Planning, Building and Remodeling Your Colorado Home, Colorado Resort Publishing, P.O. Box 8, Vail CO 81658. (970)748-2970. E-mail: knicoletti@coloradoresortpub.com. Website: www.mountainhouseandhome.com. **80% freelance written**. Quarterly magazine covering building, remodeling Colorado homes. "We cater to an affluent population of homeowners (including primary, second and third homeowners) who are planning to build or remodel their Colorado home in the mountains or on the western slope. While we feature luxury homes, we also have a slant toward green building." Estab. 2005. Circ. 35,000. Byline given. Pays on publication. No kill fee. Publishes ms an average of 2-3 months after acceptance. Buys all rights. Editorial lead time 12 months. Submit seasonal material 6 months in advance. Accepts queries by e-mail. Responds in 2-4 weeks to queries. Responds in month to mss. Sample copy available online.

Nonfiction Needs interview, new product, profiles of Colorado homes and features related to them. We do not want do-it-yourself projects. Query with published clips. **Pays $200-650 for assigned articles. We do not buy articles; we only assign articles.**

Photos Send photos. Captions required. Reviews GIF/JPEG files. We negotiate payment individually. Buys all rights.

Columns/Departments Your Green Home (tips for environmentally-conscious building, remodeling and living), 300 words. 4 mss/year. Query.

Tips "Writers should be very familiar with, and preferably live in, the area they are writing about. We set our editorial budget in late spring/early summer for the entire following year, but sometimes we have openings for story ideas; or, more often, we are open to suggestions for featuring a specific, unique home in the area we cover."

$ $ MOUNTAIN LIVING

Network Communications, Inc., 1777 S. Harrison St., Suite 1200, Denver CO 80210. (303)248-2062. Fax: (303)248-2064. E-mail: irawlings@mountainliving.com. Website: www.mountainliving.com. **50% freelance written**. Magazine published 10 times/year covering architecture, interior design and lifestyle issues for people who live in, visit, or hope to live in the mountains. Estab. 1994. Circ. 48,000. Byline given. Pays on acceptance. Offers 15% kill fee. Publishes ms an average of 4 months after acceptance. Buys one-time magazine rights, plus right to archive piece online. Editorial lead time 6 months. Submit seasonal material 8-12 months in advance. Accepts queries by mail, e-mail. Responds in 6 weeks to queries. Responds in 2 months to mss. Sample copy for $7. Guidelines by e-mail.

Nonfiction Needs photo feature, travel, home features. **Buys 30 mss/year.** Query with published clips. Length: 500-1,000 words. **Pays $250-600.**

Photos Provide photos (slides, transparencies, or on disk, saved as TIFF and at least 300 dpi). State availability. All features photography is assigned to photographers who specialize in interior photography. Negotiates payment individually Buys one-time rights plus rights to run photo on website.

Columns/Departments ML Recommends; Short Travel Tips; New Product Information; Art; Insider's Guide; Entertaining. Length: 300-800 words. 35 Query with published clips. **Pays $50-500.**

Tips A deep understanding of and respect for the mountain environment is essential. Think out of the box. We love to be surprised. Write a brilliant, short query, and always send clips. Before you query, please read the magazine to get a sense of who we are and what we like.

▣ 101 LANDSCAPING IDEAS

Express Publications, Ltd., Locked Bag 111, Silverwater NSW 1811 Australia. (61)(2)9741-3899. Fax: (61)(2)9737-8017. Website: www.expresspublications.com.au. "We provide readers with the ideas, inspiration and how-to-do's of turning their backyard into a landscaper's dream. No matter how big or small we provide you with a comprehensive approach to landscaping. An easy read, this magazine has something for everyone, from the beginner to the experienced."

Nonfiction Needs general interest, how-to, inspirational. Query.

$$$$ ORGANIC GARDENING

Rodale, 33 E. Minor St., Emmaus PA 18098. (610)967-8363. Fax: (610)967-7722. E-mail: og@rodale.com. Website: www.organicgardening.com. **75% freelance written**. Bimonthly magazine. "*Organic Gardening* is for gardeners who enjoy gardening as an integral part of a healthy lifestyle. Editorial shows readers how to grow flowers, edibles, and herbs, as well as information on ecological landscaping. Also covers organic topics including soil building and pest control." Estab. 1942. Circ. 300,000. Byline given. Pays between acceptance and publication. No kill fee. Buys all rights. Accepts queries by mail, fax. Responds in 3 months to queries.

Nonfiction Query with published clips and outline **Pays up to $1/word for experienced writers.**

Tips If you have devised a specific technique that's worked in your garden, have insight into the needs and uses of a particular plant or small group of plants, or have designed whole gardens that integrate well with their environment, and, if you have the capacity to clearly describe what you've learned to other gardeners in a simple but engaging manner, please send us your article ideas. Read a recent issue of the magazine thoroughly before you submit your ideas. If you have an idea that you believe fits with our content, send us a 1-page description of it that will grab our attention in the same manner you intend to entice readers into your article. Be sure to briefly explain why your idea is uniquely suited to our magazine. (We will not publish an article that has already appeared elsewhere. Also, please tell us if you are simultaneously submitting your idea to another magazine.) Tell us about the visual content of your idea—that is, what photographs or illustrations would you suggest be included with your article to get the ideas and information across to readers? If you have photographs, let us know. If you have never been published before, consider whether your idea fits into our Gardener to Gardener department. The shorter, narrowly focused articles in the department and its conversational tone make for a more accessible avenue into the magazine for inexperienced writers.

$$ ROMANTIC HOMES

Y-Visionary Publishing, 265 Anita Dr., Suite 120, Orange CA 92868. E-mail: editorial@romantichomes.com. Website: www.romantichomesmag.com. **70% freelance written**. Monthly magazine covering home decor. *Romantic Homes* is the magazine for women who want to create a warm, intimate, and casually elegant home—a haven that is both a gathering place for family and friends and a private refuge from the pressures of the outside world. The *Romantic Homes* reader is personally involved in the decor of her home. Features offer unique ideas and how-to advice on decorating, home furnishings, and gardening. Departments focus on floor and wall coverings, paint, textiles, refinishing, architectural elements, artwork, travel, and entertaining. Every article responds to the reader's need to create a beautiful, attainable environment, providing her with the style ideas and resources to achieve her own romantic home. Estab. 1994. Circ. 200,000. Byline given. Pays 30-60 days upon receipt of invoice. No kill fee. Publishes ms an average of 4 months after acceptance. Buys all rights. Editorial lead time 5 months. Submit seasonal material 6 months in advance. Accepts queries by mail, fax. Accepts simultaneous submissions. Responds in 2 weeks to queries. Responds in 2 months to mss. Guidelines for #10 SASE.

Nonfiction Not just for dreaming, *Romantic Homes* combines unique ideas and inspirations with practical how-to advice on decorating, home furnishings, remodeling, and gardening for readers who are actively involved in improving their homes. Every article responds to the reader's need to know how to do it and where to find it. Needs essays, how-to, new product, personal experience, travel. **Buys 150 mss/year.** Query with published clips. Length: 1,000-1,200 words. **Pays $500.**

Photos State availability of or send photos. Captions, identification of subjects, model releases required. Reviews transparencies. Buys all rights.

Columns/Departments Departments cover antiques, collectibles, artwork, shopping, travel, refinishing, architectural elements, flower arranging, entertaining, and decorating. Length: 400-600 words. **Pays $250.**

Tips Submit great ideas with photos.

$$ SAN DIEGO HOME/GARDEN LIFESTYLES

McKinnon Enterprises, Box 719001, San Diego CA 92171-9001. (858)571-1818. Fax: (858)571-6379. E-mail: carlson@sdhg.net; ditler@sdhg.net. **30% freelance written**. Monthly magazine covering homes, gardens, food, intriguing people, real estate, art and culture for residents of San Diego city and county. Estab. 1979. Circ. 50,000. Byline given. Pays on publication. No kill fee. Publishes ms an average of 3 months after acceptance. Buys first North American serial rights. Submit seasonal material 3 months in advance. Accepts queries by mail. Responds in 3 months to queries. Sample copy for $5.

Nonfiction "Residential architecture and interior design (San Diego-area homes only), remodeling (must be well-designed—little do-it-yourself), residential landscape design, furniture, other features oriented toward upscale readers interested in living the cultured good life in San Diego. Articles must have a local angle." Query with published clips. Length: 500-1,000 words. **Pays $50-375.**
Tips "No out-of-town, out-of-state subject material. Most freelance work is accepted from local writers. Gear stories to the unique quality of San Diego. We try to offer only information unique to San Diego—people, places, shops, resources, etc."

$$ SEATTLE HOMES & LIFESTYLES

Network Communications, Inc., 1221 E. Pike St., Suite 305, Seattle WA 98122-3930. (206)322-6699. Fax: (206)322-2799. E-mail: gsmith@seattlehomesmag.com. Website: www.seattlehomesmag.com. **60% freelance written**. Magazine published 6 times/year covering home design and lifestyles. "*Seattle Homes & Lifestyles* showcases the finest homes and gardens in the Northwest, and the personalities and lifestyles that make this region special. We try to help our readers take full advantage of the resources the region has to offer with in-depth coverage of events, entertaining, shopping, food, and wine. And we write about it with a warm, personal approach that underscores our local perspective." Estab. 1996. Circ. 30,000. Byline given. Pays on acceptance. Offers 25% kill fee. Publishes ms an average of 2 months after acceptance. Buys first rights, buys electronic rights. Editorial lead time 3 months. Submit seasonal material 4 months in advance. Accepts previously published material. Accepts simultaneous submissions. Responds in 4 months to queries.
Nonfiction Needs general interest, how-to, decorating, cooking, interview, photo feature. No essays, travel stories, sports coverage. **Buys 95 mss/year.** Query with published clips via mail. Length: 300-1,500 words. **Pays $150-400.**
Photos State availability. Captions, identification of subjects, model releases required. Reviews contact sheets, transparencies, prints. Negotiates payment individually. Buys one-time rights.
Tips "We're always looking for experienced journalists with clips that demonstrate a knack for writing engaging, informative features. We're also looking for writers knowledgeable about architecture and decorating who can communicate a home's flavor and spirit through the written word. Since all stories are assigned by the editor, please do not submit manuscripts. Send a résumé and 3 published samples of your work. Story pitches are not encouraged. Please mail all submissions—do not e-mail or fax. Please don't call—we'll call you if we have an assignment. Writers from the Seattle area only."

$$$ STYLE AT HOME

Transcontinental Media, G.P., 25 Sheppard Ave. W., Suite 100, Toronto ON M2N 6S7 Canada. (416)733-7600. Fax: (416)218-3632. E-mail: letters@styleathome.com. Website: www.styleathome.com. **Contact:** Gail Johnston Habs, editor-in-chief. **85% freelance written**. Magazine published 12 times/year. "The number one magazine choice of Canadian women aged 25 to 54 who have a serious interest in decorating. Provides an authoritative, stylish collection of inspiring and accessible Canadian interiors, decor projects; reports on style design trends." Estab. 1997. Circ. 235,000. Byline given. Pays on acceptance. Offers 50% kill fee. Buys first rights, buys electronic rights. Editorial lead time 4 months. Submit seasonal material 6 months in advance. Accepts queries by e-mail. Responds in 1 month to queries. Responds in 2 weeks to mss. Guidelines by e-mail.
Nonfiction Needs interview, new product. No how-to; these are planned in-house. **Buys 80 mss/year.** Query with published clips; include scouting shots with interior story queries. Length: 300-700 words. **Pays $300-1,000.**
Tips "Break in by familiarizing yourself with the type of interiors we show. Be very up-to-date with the design and home decor market in Canada. Provide a lead to a fabulous home or garden."

$$$ SU CASA

At Home in the Southwest, Hacienda Press, 4100 Wolcott Ave. NE, Suite B, Albuquerque NM 87109. (505)344-1783. Fax: (505)345-3295. E-mail: cpoling@sucasamagazine.com. Website: www.sucasamagazine.com. **80% freelance written**. Magazine published 5 times/year covering southwestern homes, building, design, architecture for the reader comtemplating building, remodeling, or decorating a Santa Fe style home. Su Casa is tightly focused on Southwestern home building, architecture and design. In particular, we feature New Mexico homes. We also cover alternative construction, far-out homes and contemporary design. Estab. 1995. Circ. 40,000. Byline given. Pays on acceptance. Offers 50% kill fee. Publishes ms an average of 6 months after acceptance. Buys one-time rights, buys second serial (reprint) rights. Editorial lead time 6-9 months. Submit seasonal material 9 months in advance. Accepts queries by mail, e-mail, fax, phone. Responds in 1 week to queries. Responds in 1 month to mss. Sample copy free. Guidelines free.

- All the departments are assigned long term. We encourage writers to pitch feature story ideas. We don't cover trends or concepts, but rather homes that express them.

Nonfiction Needs book excerpts, essays, interview, personal experience, photo feature. The summer issue covers kitchen and bath topics. Does not want how-to articles, product reviews or features, no trends in southwest homes. **Buys 30 mss/year.** Query with published clips. Length: 1,000-2,500 words. **Pays $250-1,000.** Limit agreed upon in advance

Photos State availability of or send photos. Captions, identification of subjects, model releases, True required. Reviews GIF/JPEG files. Offers $25-150/photo. Buys one time rights.

$ $ TEXAS GARDENER

The Magazine for Texas Gardeners, by Texas Gardeners, Suntex Communications, Inc., P.O. Box 9005, Waco TX 76714-9005. (254)848-9393. Fax: (254)848-9779. E-mail: info@texasgardener.com. Website: www.texasgardener.com. **80% freelance written. Works with a small number of new/unpublished writers each year**. Bimonthly magazine covering vegetable and fruit production, ornamentals, and home landscape information for home gardeners in Texas. Estab. 1981. Circ. 20,000. Byline given. Pays on publication. No kill fee. Publishes ms an average of 4 months after acceptance. Buys first North American serial rights, buys all rights. Submit seasonal material 6 months in advance. Accepts queries by mail, e-mail, fax. Responds in 2 months to queries. Sample copy for $4.25 and SAE with 5 first-class stamps. Writers' guidelines available online at website.

Nonfiction "We use articles that relate to Texas gardeners. We also like personality profiles on hobby gardeners and professional horticulturists who are doing somehting unique." Needs how-to, humor, interview, photo feature. **Buys 50-60 mss/year.** Query with published clips. Length: 800-2,400 words. **Pays $50-200.**

Photos "We prefer superb color and b&w photos; 90% of photos used are color." Send photos. Identification of subjects, model releases required. Reviews contact sheets, 2¼ × 2¼ or 35mm color transparencies, 8 × 10 b&w prints. Pays negotiable rates.

Columns/Departments Between Neighbors. **Pays $25.**

Tips First, be a Texan. Then come up with a good idea of interest to home gardeners in this state. Be specific. Stick to feature topics like `How Alley Gardening Became a Texas Tradition.' Leave topics like `How to Control Fire Blight' to the experts. High quality photos could make the difference. We would like to add several writers to our group of regular contributors and would make assignments on a regular basis. Fillers are easy to come up with in-house. We want good writers who can produce accurate and interesting copy. Frequent mistakes made by writers in completing an article assignment for us are that articles are not slanted toward Texas gardening, show inaccurate or too little gardening information, or lack good writing style.

$ $ TEXAS HOME & LIVING

Publications & Communications, Inc., 13581 Pond Springs Rd., Suite 450, Austin TX 78729. (512)381-0576. Fax: (512)331-3950. E-mail: bronas@pcinews.com. Website: www.texasHomeandLiving.com. **75% freelance written**. Bimonthly magazine. "*Texas Home & Living*.the magazine of design, architecture and Texas lifestyle." Estab. 1994. Circ. 50,000. Byline given. Pays on publication. Offers 100% kill fee. Publishes ms an average of 4 months after acceptance. Buys all rights. Editorial lead time 4 months. Submit seasonal material 6 months in advance. Accepts queries by mail, e-mail, fax. Responds in 1 month to queries. Responds in 2 months to mss. Sample copy free. Guidelines available online.

Nonfiction Needs how-to, interview, new product, travel. **Buys 18 mss/year.** Query with published clips. Length: 500-2,000 words. **Pays $200 for assigned articles.**

Photos State availability of or send photos. Captions required. Reviews negatives, transparencies, prints. Offers no additional payment for photos accepted with ms. Buys all rights.

$ $ $ $ THIS OLD HOUSE MAGAZINE

Time Inc., 135 W. 50th St., 10th Floor, New York NY 10020. (212)522-9465. Fax: (212)522-9435. E-mail: toh_letters@thisoldhouse.com. Website: www.thisoldhouse.com. **40% freelance written**. Magazine published 10 times/year covering home design, renovation, and maintenance. "*This Old House* is the ultimate resource for readers whose homes are their passions. The magazine's mission is threefold: to inform with lively service journalism and reporting on innovative new products and materials, to inspire with beautiful examples of fine craftsmanship and elegant architectural design, and to instruct with clear step-by-step projects that will enhance a home or help a homeowner maintain one. The voice of the magazine is not that of a rarefied design maven or a linear Mr. Fix It, but rather that of an eyes-wide-open, in-the-trenches homeowner who's eager for advice, tools, and techniques that'll help him realize his dream of a home." Estab. 1995. Circ. 960,000. Byline given. Pays on acceptance. Publishes ms an average of 3-6 months after acceptance. Buys all rights. Editorial lead time 3-12 months. Submit seasonal material 1 year in advance. Accepts queries by mail, e-mail.

Nonfiction Needs essays, how-to, new product, technical, must be house-related. **Buys 70 mss/year.** Query with published clips. Length: 250-2,500 words. **Pays $1/word.**

Columns/Departments Around the House (news, new products), 250 words. **Pays $1/word.**

$$ UNIQUE HOMES

Network Communications, Inc., 327 Wall St., Princeton NJ 08540. (609)688-1110. Fax: (609)688-0201. E-mail: lkim@uniquehomes.com. Website: www.uniquehomes.com. **30% freelance written**. Bimonthly magazine covering luxury real estate for consumers and the high-end real estate industry. Our focus is the luxury real estate market, i.e., the business of buying and selling luxury homes, as well as regional real estate market trends. Byline given. Pays on publication. No kill fee. Publishes ms an average of 3 months after acceptance. Buys all rights. Editorial lead time 4 months. Submit seasonal material 4 months in advance. Accepts queries by mail, e-mail, fax. Responds in 1 month to queries. Responds in 4 months to mss. Sample copy available online.

Nonfiction Looking for high-end luxury real estate profiles on cities and geographical regions. Golf Course Living; Resort Living; Ski Real Estate; Farms, Ranches and Country Estates; Waterfront Homes; International Homes. **Buys 36 mss/year.** Query with published clips and résumé Length: 500-1,500 words. **Pays $150-500.**

Photos State availability. Captions required. Reviews transparencies, prints. Offers no additional payment for photos accepted with ms. Buys all rights.

Tips For profiles on specific geographical areas, seeking writers with an in-depth personal knowledge of the luxury real estate trends in those locations. Writers with in-depth knowledge of the high-end residential market (both domestic and abroad) are especially needed.

⊘ VERANDA

The Hearst Corp., 455 E. Paces Ferry Rd. NE, Suite 216, Atlanta GA 30305-3319. (404)261-3603. Fax: (404)364-9772. Website: www.veranda.com. **Contact:** Lisa Newsom (residential submissions); Deborah Sanders (product submissions); Meg Evans (miscellaneous submissions). Bimonthly magazine. "Written as an interior design magazine featuring creative design across the country and around the world." Circ. 380,890. No kill fee. Editorial lead time 5 months. Accepts queries by mail. Guidelines on website.

- Does not buy freelance materials or use freelance writers.

$$ VICTORIAN HOMES

Y-Visionary Publishing, LP, 265 S. Anita Dr., Suite 120, Orange CA 92868-3310. (714)939-9991. Fax: (714)939-9909. E-mail: editorial@victorianhomes.com. Website: www.victorianhomesmag.com. **90% freelance written**. Bimonthly magazine covering Victorian home restoration and decoration. *Victorian Homes* is read by Victorian home owners, restorers, house museum management, and others interested in the Victorian revival. Feature articles cover home architecture, interior design, furnishings, and the home's history. Photography is very important to the feature. Estab. 1981. Circ. 100,000. Byline given. Pays on acceptance. Offers $50 kill fee. Publishes ms an average of 1 year after acceptance. Buys first North American serial rights, buys one-time rights. Editorial lead time 4 months. Submit seasonal material 1 year in advance. Accepts queries by mail, e-mail, fax. Accepts simultaneous submissions. Responds in 6 weeks to queries. Responds in 2 months to mss. Sample copy and writer's guidelines for SAE.

Nonfiction Article must deal with structures—no historical articles on Victorian people or lifestyles. Needs how-to, create period style curtains, wall treatments, bathrooms, kitchens, etc., photo feature. **Buys 30-35 mss/year.** Query. Length: 800-1,800 words. **Pays $300-500.**

Photos State availability. Captions required. Reviews 21/4x21/4 transparencies. Negotiates payment individually Buys one time rights.

$$ WATER GARDENING

The Magazine for Pondkeepers, The Water Gardeners, Inc., P.O. Box 607, St. John IN 46373. (219)374-9419. Fax: (219)374-9052. E-mail: wgmag@watergardening.com. Website: www.watergardening.com. **50% freelance written**. Bimonthly magazine. *Water Gardening* is for hobby water gardeners. We prefer articles from a first-person perspective. Estab. 1996. Circ. 25,000. Byline given. Pays on publication. Offers 50% kill fee. Publishes ms an average of 6 months after acceptance. Buys first North American serial rights. Editorial lead time 6 months. Submit seasonal material 6-12 months in advance. Accepts queries by mail, e-mail, fax. Responds in 1 month to queries. Responds in 3 months to mss. Sample copy for $3. Guidelines for #10 SASE.

Nonfiction Needs how-to, construct, maintain, improve ponds, water features, interview, new product, personal experience, photo feature. **Buys 18-20 mss/year.** Query. Length: 600-1,500 words.
Photos State availability. Captions, identification of subjects, model releases required. Reviews contact sheets, 3 × 5 transparencies, 3 × 5 prints. Negotiates payment individually. Buys one time rights.

N ⊕ YOUR GARDEN

Pacific Magazines, 8 Central Ave., Eveleigh NSW 2015 Australia. (61)(2)9464-2381. Fax: (61)(2)9464-3483. Website: www.yourgarden.com.au. **Contact:** Paul Urquhart, editor. Quarterly magazine dedicated to gardeners who seek the inspiration to create a garden of their dreams. "From sophisticated design schemes to simple but effective container gardens for the porch or balcony, we explain design in plain English, banishing the baffling technical jargon usually associated with design issues." Estab. 1949. Circ. 56,118.
Nonfiction Needs general interest, how-to, new product. Query.

Humor

$ FUNNY TIMES

A Monthly Humor Review, Funny Times, Inc., P.O. Box 18530, Cleveland Heights OH 44118. (216)371-8600. Fax: (216)371-8696. E-mail: ft@funnytimes.com. Website: www.funnytimes.com. **50% freelance written**. Monthly tabloid for humor. *Funny Times* is a monthly review of America's funniest cartoonists and writers. We are the *Reader's Digest* of modern American humor with a progressive/peace-oriented/environmental/politically activist slant. Estab. 1985. Circ. 70,000. Byline given. Pays on publication. Publishes ms an average of 3 months after acceptance. Buys one-time rights, buys second serial (reprint) rights. Editorial lead time 2 months. Accepts previously published material. Accepts simultaneous submissions. Responds in 3 months to mss. Sample copy for $3 or 9 × 12 SAE with 3 first-class stamps ($1.14 postage). Guidelines available online.
Nonfiction We only publish humor or interviews with funny people (comedians, comic actors, cartoonists, etc.). Everything we publish is very funny. If your piece isn't extremely funny then don't bother to send it. Don't send us anything that's not outrageously funny. Don't send anything that other people haven't already read and told you they laughed so hard they peed their pants. Needs essays, funny, humor, interview, opinion, humorous, personal experience, absolutely funny. **Buys 60 mss/year.** Send complete ms. Length: 500-700 words. **Pays $60 minimum.**
Columns/Departments Query with published clips.
Fiction Contact: Ray Lesser and Susan Wolpert, editors. Anything funny. **Buys 6 mss/year.** Query with published clips. Length: 500-700 words. **Pays $50-150.**
Tips Send us a small packet (1-3 items) of only your very funniest stuff. If this makes us laugh we'll be glad to ask for more. We particularly welcome previously published material that has been well-received elsewhere.

$$ MAD MAGAZINE

1700 Broadway, New York NY 10019. (212)506-4850. E-mail: submissions@madmagazine.com. Website: www.madmag.com. **100% freelance written**. Monthly magazine always on the lookout for new ways to spoof and to poke fun at hot trends. Estab. 1952. Byline given. Pays on acceptance. Publishes ms an average of 6 months after acceptance. Buys all rights. Submit seasonal material 6 months in advance. Responds in 10 weeks to queries. Sample copy available online. Guidelines available online.
Nonfiction Submit a premise with 3 or 4 examples of how you intend to carry it through, describing the action and visual content. Rough sketches desired but not necessary. One-page gags: 2- to 8-panel cartoon continuities as minimum very funny, maximum hilarious! We're not interested in formats we're already doing or have done to death like 'what they say and what they really mean.' Don't send previously published submissions, riddles, advice columns, TV or movie satires, book manuscripts, top 10 lists, articles about Alfred E. Neuman, poetry, essays, short stories or other text pieces. **Buys 400 mss/year. Pays minimum of $500/page.**
Tips Have fun! Remember to think visually! Surprise us! Freelancers can best break in with satirical nontopical material. Include SASE with each submission. Originality is prized. We like outrageous, silly and/or satirical humor.

Inflight

$$$ GO MAGAZINE

INK Publishing, 68 Jay St., Suite 315, Brooklyn NY 11201. (347)294-1220. Fax: (917)591-6247. E-mail: editorial@airtranmagazine.com. Website: www.airtranmagazine.com. **80% freelance written**. Monthly magazine covering travel. "*Go Magazine* is an inflight magazine covering travel, general interest and light business." Estab. 2003. Circ. 100,000. Byline given. net 45 days upon receipt of invoice. Offers 50% kill fee. Publishes ms an average of 3 months after acceptance. Buys first North American serial rights. Editorial lead time 4 months. Submit seasonal material 5 months in advance. Accepts queries by e-mail. Sample copy available online. Guidelines by e-mail.

Nonfiction Needs general interest, interview, photo feature, travel, light business. Does not want first-person travelogues. **Buys 200 mss/year.** Query with published clips. Length: 400-2,000 words. **Pay is negotiable.**

Photos Contact: Shane Luitjens, art director. State availability. Reviews GIF/JPEG files. Offers no additional payment for photos accepted with ms. Buys one time rights.

Tips "Review past issues online and study the guidelines to get a true sense of the types of features we are looking for."

$$$ HEMISPHERES

Pace Communications for United Airlines, Pace Communications, 1301 Carolina St., Greensboro NC 27401. (336)383-5690. E-mail: Hemiedit@hemispheresmagazine.com. Website: www.hemispheresmagazine.com. **95% freelance written**. Monthly magazine for the educated, sophisticated business and recreational frequent traveler on an airline that spans the globe. *Hemispheres* is an inflight magazine that interprets 'inflight' to be a mode of delivery rather than an editorial genre. As such, Hemispheres' task is to engage, intrigue and entertain its primary readers—an international, culturally diverse group of affluent, educated professionals and executives who frequently travel for business and pleasure on United Airlines. The magazine offers a global perspective and a focus on topics that cross borders as often as the people reading the magazine. That places our emphasis on ideas, concepts, and culture rather than products. We present that perspective in a fresh, artful and sophisticated graphic environment. Estab. 1992. Circ. 500,000. Byline given. Pays on acceptance. Offers 20% kill fee. Publishes ms an average of 4-6 months after acceptance. Buys first worldwide rights. Editorial lead time 8 months. Submit seasonal material 8 months in advance. Accepts queries by mail. Responds in 2 months to queries. Responds in 4 months to mss. Sample copy for $7.50. Guidelines for #10 SASE.

Nonfiction Keeping 'global' in mind, we look for topics that reflect a modern appreciation of the world's cultures and environment. No 'What I did (or am going to do) on a trip.' Needs general interest, humor, personal experience. Query with published clips. Length: 500-3,000 words. **Pays 50¢/word and up.**

Photos Reviews photos only when we request them. State availability. Captions, identification of subjects, model releases required. Negotiates payment individually Buys one time rights.

Columns/Departments Making a Difference (Q&A format interview with world leaders, movers, and shakers. A 500-600 word introduction anchors the interview. We want to profile an international mix of men and women representing a variety of topics or issues, but all must truly be making a difference. No puffy celebrity profiles.); 15 Fascinating Facts (a snappy selection of 1- or 2-sentence obscure, intriguing, or travel-service-oriented items that the reader never knew about a city, state, country, or destination.); Executive Secrets (things that top executives know); Case Study (Business strategies of international companies or organizations. No lionizations of CEOs. Strategies should be the emphasis. We want international candidates.); Weekend Breakway (Takes us just outside a major city after a week of business for several activities for a physically active, action-packed weekend. This isn't a sedentary getaway at a property.); Roving Gourmet (Insider's guide to interesting eating in major city, resort area, or region. The slant can be anything from ethnic to expensive; not just best. The 4 featured eateries span a spectrum from hole in the wall, to expense account lunch, and on to big deal dining.); Collecting (occasional 800-word story on collections and collecting that can emphasize travel); Eye on Sports (global look at anything of interest in sports); Vintage Traveler (options for mature, experienced travelers); Savvy Shopper (Insider's tour of best places in the world to shop. Savvy Shopper steps beyond all those stories that just mention the great shopping at a particular destination. A shop-by-shop, gallery-by-gallery tour of the best places in the world.); Science and Technology (Substantive, insightful stories on how technology is changing our lives and the business world. Not just another column on audio components or software. No gift guides!); Aviation Journal (For those fascinated with aviation. Topics range widely.); Terminal Bliss (a great airports guide series); Grape And Grain (wine and spirits with emphasis on education, not one-upmanship); Show Business (films, music, and entertainment);

Musings (humor or just curious musings); Quick Quiz (tests to amuse and educate); Travel Trends (brief, practical, invaluable, global, trend-oriented); Book Beat (Tackles topics like the Wodehouse Society, the birth of a book, the competition between local bookshops and national chains. Please, no review proposals.); What the World's Reading (residents explore how current bestsellers tell us what their country is thinking). Length: 1,400 words. Query with published clips. **Pays 50¢/word and up**

Fiction Needs adventure, ethnic, historical, humorous, mainstream, mystery, explorations of those issues common to all people but within the context of a particular culture. **Buys 14 mss/year.** Send complete ms. Length: 1,000-4,000 words. **Pays 50¢/word and up**.

Tips We increasingly require writers of 'destination' pieces or departments to 'live whereof they write.' Increasingly want to hear from US, UK, or other English-speaking/writing journalists (business & travel) who reside outside the US in Europe, South America, Central America, and the Pacific Rim—all areas that United flies. We're not looking for writers who aim at the inflight market. *Hemispheres* broke the fluffy mold of that tired domestic genre. Our monthly readers are a global mix on the cutting edge of the global economy and culture. They don't need to have the world filtered by US writers. We want a Hong Kong restaurant writer to speak for that city's eateries, so we need English-speaking writers around the globe. That's the 'insider' story our readers respect. We use resident writers for departments such as Roving Gourmet, Savvy Shopper, On Location, 3 Perfect Days, and Weekend Breakaway, but authoritative writers can roam in features. Sure we cover the US, but with a global view: No 'in this country' phraseology. 'Too American' is a frequent complaint for queries. We use UK English spellings in articles that speak from that tradition and we specify costs in local currency first before US dollars. Basically, all of above serves the realization that today, 'global' begins with respect for 'local.' That approach permits a wealth of ways to present culture, travel, and business for a wide readership. We anchor that with a reader-service mission that grounds everything in 'how to do it.'

$$ HORIZON AIR MAGAZINE

Paradigm Communications Group, 2701 First Ave., Suite 250, Seattle WA 98121. Fax: (206)448-6939. **Contact:** Michele Andrus Dill, Editor. **90% freelance written**. Monthly inflight magazine covering travel, business, and leisure in the Pacific Northwest. *"Horizon Air Magazine* serves a sophisticated audience of business and leisure travelers. Stories must have a Northwest slant." Estab. 1990. Circ. 600,000/ month. Byline given. Pays on publication. Offers 33% kill fee. Publishes ms an average of 1 year after acceptance. Buys first North American serial rights, buys electronic rights. Editorial lead time 6 months. Submit seasonal material 5 months in advance. Accepts queries by mail, fax. Sample copy for 10 × 12 SASE. Guidelines for #10 SASE.

- "Responds only if interested, so include e-mail and phone number but no need to include SASE for queries."

Nonfiction Needs essays, personal, general interest, historical, how-to, humor, interview, personal experience, photo feature, travel, business. Meeting planners' guide, golf, gift guide. No material unrelated to the Pacific Northwest. **Buys approximately 36 mss/year.** Send complete ms. Length: 1,500-3,000 words. **Pays $300-700. Occasionally pays expenses.**

Photos State availability. Captions, identification of subjects, model releases required. Reviews transparencies, prints. Negotiates payment individually. Buys one time rights.

Columns/Departments Region (Northwest news/profiles), 200-400 words; Air Time (personal essays), 700 words. 15 mss/year. Query with published clips. **Pays $100 (Region), $250 (Air Time).**

$$$ MY MIDWEST

INK Publishing, 68 Jay St., Suite 315, Brooklyn NY 11201. (917)254-4865. Fax: (917)591-6247. E-mail: editorial@mymidwest.com. Website: www.mymidwest.com. **80% freelance written**. Quarterly magazine covering travel. *My Midwest* is an inflight magazine covering travel, general interest and light business. Estab. 2006. Circ. 60,000. Byline given. net 45 upon receipt of invoice. Offers 50% kill fee. Publishes ms an average of 3 months after acceptance. Buys first North American serial rights. Editorial lead time 6 months. Submit seasonal material 7 months in advance. Accepts queries by e-mail. Sample copy available online. Guidelines by e-mail.

Nonfiction Needs general interest, photo feature, travel, light business. Does not want first-person travelogues. **Buys 50 mss/year.** Query with published clips. Length: 700-2,000 words. **Pays $315-900.**

Photos Contact: Shane Luitjens, art director. State availability. Reviews GIF/JPEG files. Offers no additional payment for photos accepted with ms. Buys one time rights.

Tips Review past issues online and study the guidelines to get a true sense of the types of features we are looking for.

QANTAS THE AUSTRALIAN WAY

ACP Magazines, Ltd., 54-58 Park St., Sydney NSW 2000 Australia. (61)(2)9282-8000. Fax: (61)(2)9267-4361. Website: www.acp.com.au. **Contact:** Susan Skelly, editor. Monthly inflight magazine on Quantas International & domestic flights delivering a sophisticated yet accessible mix of news, business, people, travel, sport, leisure, arts, fitness and music.

Nonfiction Needs general interest, how-to, interview, new product, photo feature, travel. Query.

$$$ SIGHTS

INK Publishing, 68 Jay St., Suite 315, Brooklyn NY 11201. (917)254-4865. Fax: (917)591-6247. E-mail: editorial@atasights.com. Website: www.atasights.com. **80% freelance written**. Quarterly magazine covering airline destinations. Estab. 2006. Circ. 55,000. Byline given. net 45 days upon receipt of invoice. Offers 50% kill fee. Publishes ms an average of 3 months after acceptance. Buys first North American serial rights. Editorial lead time 6 months. Submit seasonal material 7 months in advance. Accepts queries by e-mail. Sample copy available online. Guidelines by e-mail.

Nonfiction Needs general interest, photo feature, travel. Does not want travelogues, completed manuscripts. **Buys 50 mss/year.** Query with published clips. Length: 700-2,000 words. **Pays $315-900.**

Photos Contact: Shane Luitjens, art director. State availability. Reviews GIF/JPEG files. Offers no additional payment for photos accepted with ms. Buys one time rights.

Tips Review past issues online and study the guidelines to get a true sense of the types of features we are looking for.

$$ SKYLIGHTS

The Inflight Magazine of Spirit Airlines, Worth International Media Group, Inc., 5979 NW 151 St., Suite 120, Miami Lakes FL 33014. (305)828-0123. Fax: (305)828-0799. Website: www.worthit.com. Bimonthly magazine. Like Spirit Airlines, *Skylights* will be known for its practical and friendly sensibility. This publication is a clean, stylish, user-friendly product. This is not an old-school airline, and *Skylights* is not an old-school inflight. Circ. 5.5 million. Byline sometimes given. Pays on publication. No kill fee. Buys first North American serial rights. Editorial lead time 3-6 months. Submit seasonal material 4 months in advance. Accepts queries by mail. Responds in 4-6 weeks to queries. Writer's guidelines via e-mail at millie@worthit.com.

Nonfiction Needs general interest, humor, interview, new product, travel. No first-person accounts or weighty topics. Stories should be practical and useful, but not something-for-everyone-type articles. **Buys 18 mss/year.** Query with published clips. Length: 350-1,200 words. **Pays 25-40¢/word.**

Photos State availability. Captions, identification of subjects, model releases required. Reviews GIF/JPEG files. Negotiaties payment individually Buys one time rights.

Columns/Departments Events calendar (based on Spirit destinations), 1,200 words; Gizmos (latest and greatest gadgets), 250-word descriptions; Biz (bizz buzz), 650-800 words; Fast Reads (quick finds, books, movies, music, food, wine); Skybuys (hot buys and smart shopping options), 150-word descriptions; Beauty and Health Story (specific aspects of staying well), 800 words. Query with published clips. **Pays 25-40¢/word**

Fillers Length: 250-400 words. **Pays 25-40¢/word**

$$$$ SPIRIT MAGAZINE

Pace Communications, Inc., Suite 360, 2811 McKinney Ave., Dallas TX 75204. (214)580-8070. Fax: (214)580-2491. E-mail: ideas@spiritmag.com. Website: www.spiritmag.com. Monthly magazine for passengers on Southwest Airlines. Estab. 1992. Circ. 380,000. Byline given. Pays on acceptance. Buys first North American serial rights, buys electronic rights. Responds in 1 month to queries. Guidelines available online.

Nonfiction Seeking lively, accessible, entertaining, relevant, and trendy travel, business, lifestyle, sports, celebrity, food, tech-product stories on newsworthy/noteworthy topics in destinations served by Southwest Airlines; well-researched and reported; multiple source only. Experienced magazine professionals only. **Buys about 40 mss/year.** Query by mail only with published clips. 3,000-6,000 words (features). **Pays $1/word.**

Columns/Departments Length: 800-900 words. about 21 Query by mail only with published clips.

Tips *Southwest Airlines Spirit* magazine reaches more than 2.8 million readers every month aboard Southwest Airlines. Our median reader is a college-educated, 32- to 40-year-old traveler with a household income around $90,000. Writers must have proven magazine capabilities, a sense of fun, excellent reporting skills, a smart, hip style, and the ability to provide take-away value to the reader in sidebars, charts, and/or lists.

$$ SPIRIT OF ALOHA

The Inflight Magazine of Aloha Airlines, Honolulu Publishing Co., Ltd., 707 Richards St., Suite 525, Honolulu HI 96813. (808)524-7400. Fax: (808)531-2306. E-mail: tchapman@honpub.com. Website: www.spiritofaloha.com. **80% freelance written**. Bimonthly magazine covering Hawaii. Estab. 1978. Circ. 100,000. Byline given. Pays on acceptance. Publishes ms an average of 2 months after acceptance. Buys first rights. Editorial lead time 2 months. Submit seasonal material 4 months in advance. Accepts queries by mail, e-mail. Responds in up to 1 month to queries. Guidelines by e-mail.

Nonfiction Should be related to Hawaii. **Buys 40 mss/year.** Query with published clips. Length: 1,500-2,500 words. **Pays $600 and up.**

Photos State availability. Captions, identification of subjects, model releases required. Reviews transparencies. Negotiates payment individually Buys one time rights.

$$$ STRATOS

Journey Beyond First Class, STRATOS Publishing, 1430 I-85 Parkway, Montgomery AL 36106. E-mail: mnothaft@stratosmag.com. Website: www.stratosmag.com. **90% freelance written**. Magazine published 10 times/year covering luxury lifestyle and travel. Our readers are well-heeled and need exceptional travel experiences that are high end and have an outdoor twist. Estab. 2000. Circ. 65,000. Byline given. Pays on acceptance. Offers 25% kill fee. Publishes ms an average of 3-4 months after acceptance. Buys first North American serial rights. Editorial lead time 3-4 months. Submit seasonal material 6 months in advance. Accepts queries by e-mail. Responds in 1 week to queries.

Nonfiction Needs how-to, interview. Query with published clips. Length: 900-1,500 words. **Pays $600-1,200.**

Photos State availability. Identification of subjects required. Reviews GIF/JPEG files. Negotiates payment individually. Buys one time rights.

Tips Pitch to the magazine format and think high end experiences.

$$$$ US AIRWAYS MAGAZINE

Pace Communications, 1301 Carolina St., Greensboro NC 27401. E-mail: edit@usairwaysmag.com. Website: www.usairwaysmag.com. Monthly magazine for travelers on US Airways. We focus on travel, lifestyle and pop culture. Estab. 2006. Circ. 441,000. Byline given. Pays on acceptance. Publishes ms an average of 4 months after acceptance. Buys exclusive worldwide rights for all media for 120 days rights. Editorial lead time 3 months. Accepts queries by mail, e-mail. Responds in 6 weeks to queries. Responds in 1 month to mss. Sample copy for $7.50 or online. Guidelines available online.

Nonfiction Features are highly visual, focusing on some ususual or unique angle of travel, food, business, or other topic approved by a US Airways editor. Needs general interest, personal experience, travel, food, lifestyle, sports. **Buys 200-350 mss/year.** Query with published clips. Length: 100-1,500 words. **Pays $100-1,500.**

Photos State availability. Identification of subjects, model releases required. Reviews contact sheets, negatives, transparencies. Negotiates payment individually. Buys one time rights.

Columns/Departments Several columns are authored by a single writer under long-term contract with US Airways Magazine. Departments open to freelance pitches include: All Over the Map; Alter Ego; Straight Talk; Hands On; Shelf Life; In Gear; Get Personal; and Get Away. All of these departments may be viewed on the magazine's website.

Tips We look for smart, pithy writing that addresses travel, lifestyle and pop culture. Study the magazine for content, style and tone. Queries for story ideas should be to the point and presented clearly. Any written correspondence should include a SASE.

$$$ WASHINGTON FLYER MAGAZINE

1707 L St., NW, Suite 800, Washington DC 20036. (202)331-9393. Fax: (202)331-2043. E-mail: lauren@themagazinegroup.com. Website: www.fly2dc.com. **60% freelance written**. Bimonthly magazine for business and pleasure travelers at Washington National and Washington Dulles International airports INSI. Primarily affluent, well-educated audience that flies frequently in and out of Washington, DC. Estab. 1989. Circ. 182,000. Byline given. Pays on acceptance. Offers 25% kill fee. Buys first North American serial rights. Submit seasonal material 4 months in advance. Accepts queries by mail, e-mail, fax. Responds in 10 weeks to queries. Sample copy for 9 × 12 SAE with $2 postage. Guidelines available online.

Nonfiction One international destination feature per issue, determined 6 months in advance. One feature per issue on aspect of life in Washington. Needs general interest, interview, travel, business. No personal experiences, poetry, opinion or inspirational. **Buys 20-30 mss/year.** Query with published clips. Length: 800-1,200 words. **Pays $500-900.**

Photos State availability. Identification of subjects required. Reviews negatives, almost always color transparencies. Considers additional payment for top-quality photos accepted with ms. Buys one time rights.

Columns/Departments Washington Insider; Travel; Hospitality; Airports and Airlines; Restaurants; Shopping, all 800-1,200 words. Query. **Pays $500-900.**

Tips Know the Washington market and issues relating to frequent business/pleasure travelers as we move toward a global economy. With a bimonthly publication schedule it's important that stories remain viable as possible during the magazine's 2-month 'shelf life.' No telephone calls, please and understand that most assignments are made several months in advance. Queries are best sent via e-mail.

WILD BLUE YONDER

900 South Broadway, Suite 300, Denver CO 80209. (303)296-0039. Fax: (303)296-3410. E-mail: editorial@Gowildblueyonder.com. Website: www.Gowildblueyonder.com. **60% freelance written**. "Prefers queries via e-mail. Don't waste the editor's time. Know the route and the publication before you query." Pays 10 days after publication. Offers $25 kill fee. Sample copy for $5. Guidelines available online.

Fiction Send complete ms.

Juvenile

$ ADVENTURES

2923 Troost Ave., Kansas City MO 64109. (816)931-1900. Fax: (816)412-8306. E-mail: djbroadbooks@wordaction.com. **25% freelance written**. "Published by Adventures for children ages 6-8. Correlates to the weekly Sunday school lesson." Pays on publication. No kill fee. Publishes ms an average of 1 year after acceptance. Buys all rights. Accepts queries by mail, fax. Responds in 2 months to queries. Sample copy for #10 SASE. Guidelines for #10 SASE.

Columns/Departments Recipes & Crafts, **Pays $15**; Activities, **Pays $15**. Send complete ms.

Fiction "Accepts life application stories that show early elementary children dealing with the issues related to the Bible story, Bible Truth, or lesson goals. Children may interact with friends, family, or other individuals in the stories. Make characters and events realistic. Avoid placing characters in a perfect world or depicting spiritually precocious children." Length: 250 words. **Pays $15.**

Poetry "Short, fun, easy-to-understand, age-appropriate poetry that correlates with the Bible story, Bible Truth, or lesson goals is welcome. We prefer rhythmic, pattern poems, but will accept free verse if reads smoothly out loud." Length: 4-8 lines. **Pays $15**.

$ 🌐 AQUILA MAGAZINE

New Leaf Publishing Ltd, Studio 2, Willowfield Studios, 67a Willowfield Rd., Eastbourne, East Sussex England BN22 8AP United Kingdom. (44)(132)343-1313. Fax: (44)(132)373-1136. E-mail: info@aquila.co.uk. Website: www.aquila.co.uk. Magazine for children 8-12 years old. Circ. 40,000. No kill fee. Sample copy for £5.

Nonfiction "Contact the editor to discuss ideas. Features are only likely to be of interest if they are highly original in presentation and content and use specialist/inside knowledge." Query. Length: 600-800 words. **Pays £50-75.**

Fiction Submit either 1 short story or a 2-4 instalments of a story. Each instalment must be satisfying to read in its own right, but also include an ending that tempts the reader to return for the next part. Length: 1,000-1,500 words. **£90/short story; £80/episode for a serial**.

$ 🆕 BABYBUG

Carus Publishing Co., Cricket Magazine Group, 30 Grove St., Suite C, Peterborough NH 03458. (312)701-1720. Website: www.cricketmag.com. Suzanne Beck, art dir. **Contact:** Marianne Carus, editor-in-chief. **50% freelance written**. "Board-book magazine published monthly except for combined May/June and July/August issues. *Babybug* is `the listening and looking magazine for infants and toddlers,' intended to be read aloud to young children ages 6 months-3 years." Estab. 1994. Circ. 45,000. Byline given. Pays on publication. Accepts simultaneous submissions. Responds in 6 months to mss. Guidelines available online.

Nonfiction Basic words and concepts. **Buys 10-20 mss/year.** Do not query first. Submit complete ms, SASE. 10 words maximum **Pays $25 minimum.**

Photos Artists should submit review samples (tearsheets/photocopies) of artwork to be kept in our illustrator files. Author-illustrators may submit a complete ms with art samples. The ms will be evaluated for quality of concept and text before the art is considered. Responds in 3 months for art samples. Send art to: Carus Publishing, 70 E. Lake St., Chicago IL 60601. Pays $500/spread; $250/page. Buys all rights; the physical artwork remains the property of the illustrator and may be used for self promotion.
Fiction Stories must be simple and concrete. **Buys 10-20 mss/year.**
Poetry Rhythmic, rhyming.
Tips "Imagine having to read your story or poem—out loud—50 times or more! That's what parents will have to do. Babies and toddlers demand, 'Read it again!' Your material must hold up under repetition. And humor is much appreciated by all."

$$$$ BOYS' LIFE

Boy Scouts of America, P.O. Box 152079, Irving TX 75015-2079. (972)580-2366. Fax: (972)580-2079. Website: www.boyslife.org. **Contact:** Michael Goldman, managing editor. **75% freelance written. Prefers to work with published/established writers; works with small number of new/unpublished writers each year.** Monthly magazine covering activities of interest to all boys ages 6-18. Most readers are Boy Scouts or Cub Scouts. *Boys' Life* covers Boy Scout activities and general interest subjects for ages 6-18, Boy Scouts, Cub Scouts and others of that age group. Estab. 1911. Circ. 1,300,000. Pays on acceptance. Publishes ms an average of 1 year after acceptance. Buys one-time rights. Accepts queries by mail. Responds in 2 months to queries. Sample copy for $3.95 and 9 × 12 SAE. Guidelines for #10 SASE or online.
Nonfiction "Subject matter is broad, everything from professional sports to American history to how to pack a canoe. Look at a current list of the BSA's more than 100 merit badge pamphlets for an idea of the wide range of subjects possible. Uses strong photo features with about 500 words of text. Separate payment or assignment for photos." Needs how-to, photo feature, hobby and craft ideas. **Buys 60 mss/year.** Query with SASE. No phone queries Major articles run 500-1,500 words; preferred length is about 1,000 words, including sidebars and boxes. **Pays $400-1,500.**
Columns/Departments "Science, nature, earth, health, sports, space and aviation, cars, computers, entertainment, pets, history, and music are some of the columns for which we use 300-750 words of text. This is a good place to show us what you can do." Query Brad Riddell, Associate Editor. **Pays $100-500.**
Fiction Needs adventure, humorous, mystery, young adult, science fiction, western, young adult, sports. **Buys 12-15 mss/year.** Send complete ms. to Paula Murphey, Senior Editor. Length: 1,000-1,500 words. **Pays $750 minimum.**
Tips "We strongly recommend reading at least 12 issues of the magazine before you submit queries. We are a good market for any writer willing to do the necessary homework."

$ BREAD FOR GOD'S CHILDREN

Bread Ministries, Inc., P.O. Box 1017, Arcadia FL 34265. (863)494-6214. Fax: (863)993-0154. E-mail: bread@sunline.net. **10% freelance written**. Published 6-8 times/year. An interdenominational Christian teaching publication published 6-8 times/year written to aid children and youth in leading a Christian life. Estab. 1972. Circ. 10,000. Byline given. Pays on publication. No kill fee. Publishes ms an average of 6 months after acceptance. Buys first rights. Accepts queries by mail. Accepts simultaneous submissions. Responds in 6 months to mss. Three sample copies for 9 × 12 SAE and 5 first-class stamps. Guidelines for #10 SASE.
Reprints Send tearsheet and information about when and where the material previously appeared.
Columns/Departments Let's Chat (children's Christian values), 500-700 words; Teen Page (youth Christian values), 600-800 words; Idea Page (games, crafts, Bible drills). 5-8 Send complete ms. **Pays $30.**
Fiction We are looking for writers who have a solid knowledge of Biblical principles and are concerned for the youth of today living by those principles. Our stories must be well written, with the story itself getting the message across—no preaching, moralizing, or tag endings. No fantasy, science fiction, or nonChristian themes. **Buys 15-20 mss/year.** Send complete ms. 600-800 words (young children), 900-1,500 words (older children). **Pays $40-50.**
Tips We're looking for more submissions on healing miracles and reconciliation/restoration. Follow usual guidelines for careful writing, editing, and proofreading. We get many manuscripts with misspellings, poor grammar, careless typing. Know your subject—writer should know the Lord to write about the Christian life. Study the publication and our guidelines.

$ CADET QUEST MAGAZINE

P.O. Box 7259, Grand Rapids MI 49510-7259. (616)241-5616. Fax: (616)241-5558. E-mail: submissions@calvinistcadets.org. Website: www.calvinistcadets.org. **Contact:** G. Richard Broene, editor. **40% freelance written. Works with a small number of new/unpublished writers each year.** Magazine published 7 times/year. "*Cadet Quest Magazine* shows boys 9-14 how God is at work in their lives and in the world around them." Estab. 1958. Circ. 7,500. Byline given. Pays on acceptance. No kill fee. Publishes ms an average of 4-11 months after acceptance. Buys first North American serial rights, buys one-time rights, buys second serial (reprint) rights, buys simultaneous rights. Rights purchased vary with author and material. Accepts previously published material. Accepts simultaneous submissions. Responds in 2 months to submissions: Sample copy for 9 × 12 SASE. Guidelines for #10 SASE.

- Accepts submissions by mail, or by e-mail (must include ms in text of e-mail). Will not open attachments.

Nonfiction Articles about young boys' interests: sports (articles about athletes and developing Christian character through sports; photos appreciated), outdoor activities (camping skills, nature study, survival exercises; practical 'how to do it' approach works best. 'God in nature' themes appreciated), science, crafts, and problems. Emphasis is on a Christian perspective. Needs how-to, humor, inspirational, interview, personal experience, informational. Write for new themes list in February. **Buys 20-25 mss/year.** Send complete ms. Length: 500-1,500 words. **Pays 2-5¢/word.**

Reprints Send typed manuscript with rights for sale noted. Payment varies.

Photos Pays $20-30 for photos purchased with ms

Columns/Departments Project Page (uses simple projects boys 9-14 can do on their own made with easily accessible materials; must provide clear, accurate instructions).

Fiction Considerable fiction is used. Fast-moving stories that appeal to a boy's sense of adventure or sense of humor are welcome. Needs adventure, religious, spiritual, sports, comics. Avoid preachiness. Avoid simplistic answers to complicated problems. Avoid long dialogue and little action. No fantasy, science fiction, fashion, horror or erotica. Send complete ms. Length: 900-1,500 words. **Pays 4-6¢/word, and 1 contributor's copy.**

Tips "Best time to submit stories/articles is early in the year (February-April). Also remember readers are boys ages 9-14. Stories must reflect or add to the theme of the issue and be from a Christian perspective."

$$ CALLIOPE

Exploring World History, Cobblestone Publishing Co., 30 Grove St., Suite C, Peterborough NH 03458-1454. (603)924-7209. Fax: (603)924-7380. E-mail: cfbakeriii@meganet.net. Website: www.cobblestonepub.com. **Contact:** Rosalie Baker, editor. **50% freelance written**. Magazine published 9 times/year covering world history (East and West) through 1800 AD for 8 to 14-year-old kids. Articles must relate to the issue's theme. Lively, original approaches to the subject are the primary concerns of the editors in choosing material. Estab. 1990. Circ. 13,000. Byline given. Pays on publication. No kill fee. Buys all rights. Accepts queries by mail. If interested, responds 5 months before publication date. Sample copy for $5.95, $2 shipping and handling, and 10 × 13 SASE. Guidelines available online.

Nonfiction Plays, biographies, in-depth nonfiction. Needs essays, general interest, historical, how-to, crafts/woodworking, humor, interview, personal experience, photo feature, technical, travel, recipes. No religious, pornographic, biased, or sophisticated submissions. **Buys 30-40 mss/year.** Query with writing sample, 1-page outline, bibliography, SASE. 700-800/feature articles; 300-600 words/supplemental nonfiction. **Pays 20-25¢/word.**

Photos If you have photographs pertaining to any upcoming theme, please contact the editor by mail or fax, or send them with your query. You may also send images on speculation. Reviews b&w prints, color slides. Pays $15-100/b&w; $25-100/color; cover fees are negotiated. Buys one-time rights.

Fiction Needs adventure, historical, biographical, retold legends. **Buys 10 mss/year.** 800 words maximum **Pays 20-25¢/word.**

Fillers Crossword and other word puzzles (no word finds), mazes, and picture puzzles that use the vocabulary of the issue's theme or otherwise relate to the theme. **Pays on an individual basis.**

Tips "Authors are urged to use primary resources and up-to-date scholarly resources in their bibliography. In all correspondence, please include your complete address and a telephone number where you can be reached."

$$ ⊘ CHILDREN'S PLAYMATE MAGAZINE

Children's Better Health Institute, 1100 Waterway Blvd., Indianapolis IN 46202. (317)634-1100. Fax: (317)684-8094. Website: www.childrensplaymatemag.org. **40% freelance written. Eager to work with**

new/unpublished writers. Magazine published 8 times/year for children ages 6-8. We are looking for articles, poems, and activities with a health, fitness, or nutrition theme. We try to present our material in a positive light, and we try to incorporate humor and a light approach wherever possible without minimizing the seriousness of what we are saying. Estab. 1929. Circ. 114,907. Byline given. Pays on publication. No kill fee. Buys all rights. Submit seasonal material 8 months in advance. Responds in 3 months to queries. Sample copy for $1.75. Guidelines for SASE or online.

- Closed to submissions until further notice.

Nonfiction We are especially interested in material concerning sports and fitness, including profiles of famous amateur and professional athleters; 'average' atheletes (especially children) who have overcome obstacles to excel in their areas; and new or unusual sports, particularly those in which children can participate. Nonfiction articles dealing with health subjects should be fresh and creative. Avoid encyclopedic or 'preachy' approach. We try to present our health material in a positive manner, incorporate humor and a light approach wherever possible without minimizing the seriousness of the message. Needs interview, famous amateurs and professional athletes, photo feature, recipes (ingredients should be healthful). **Buys 25 mss/year.** Send complete ms. Length: 300-700 words. **Pays up to 17¢/word.**

Photos State availability. Captions, model releases required. $15 minimum Buys one time rights.

Fiction Contact: Terry Harshman, editor. Not buying much fiction right now except for rebus stories of 100-300 words and occasional poems. Vocabulary suitable for ages 6-8. Include word count. No adult or adolescent fiction. Send complete ms. Length: 300-700 words. **Pays minimum of 17¢/word and 10 contributor's copies.**

Fillers Recipes, puzzles, dot-to-dots, color-ins, hidden pictures, mazes. Prefers camara-ready activities. Activity guidelines for #10 SASE.

Tips We would especially like to see more holiday stories, articles, and activities. Please send seasonal material at least 8 months in advance.

$$ CLUBHOUSE MAGAZINE

Focus on the Family, 8605 Explorer Dr., Colorado Springs CO 80920. (719)531-3400. Website: www.clubhousemagazine.com. **25% freelance written**. Monthly magazine. *Clubhouse* readers are 8-12 year old boys and girls who desire to know more about God and the Bible. Their parents (who typically pay for the membership) want wholesome, educational material with Scriptural or moral insight. The kids want excitement, adventure, action, humor, or mystery. Your job as a writer is to please both the parent and child with each article. Estab. 1987. Circ. 85,000. Byline given. Pays on acceptance. No kill fee. Publishes ms an average of 12-18 months after acceptance. Buys the nonexclusive right to publish in print or electronic form worldwide. Editorial lead time 5 months. Submit seasonal material 9 months in advance. Responds in 2 months to mss. Sample copy for $1.50 with 9 × 12 SASE. Guidelines for #10 SASE.

Nonfiction Contact: Jesse Florea, editor. Needs essays, how-to, humor, inspirational, interview, personal experience, photo feature, religious. Avoid Bible stories. Avoid informational-only, science, or educational articles. Avoid biographies told encyclopedia or textbook style. **Buys 6 mss/year.** Send complete ms. Length: 800-1,200 words. **Pays $25-450 for assigned articles. Pays 15-25¢/word for unsolicited articles.**

Fiction Contact: Jesse Florea, editor. Needs adventure, humorous, mystery, religious, suspense, holiday. Avoid contemporary, middle-class family settings (existing authors meet this need), poems (rarely printed), stories dealing with boy-girl relationships. **Buys 10 mss/year.** Send complete ms. Length: 400-1,500 words. **Pays $200 and up for first time contributor and 5 contributor's copies; additional copies available.**

$$ COBBLESTONE

An Introduction to American History, Cobblestone Publishing, 70 E. Lake St., Suite 300, Chicago IL 60601. Fax: (603)924-7380. Website: www.cobblestonepub.com. **50% freelance**. Covers material for ages 9-14. "No unsolicited mss. Query first. Prefers to work with published/established writers. Each issue presents a particular theme, making it exciting as well as informative. Half of all subscriptions are for schools. All material must relate to monthly theme." Circ. 15,000. Byline given. Pays on publication. Offers 50% kill fee. Buys all rights. Accepts queries by mail. Accepts simultaneous submissions. Guidelines available on website or for SASE; sample copy for $6.95, $2 shipping/handling, 10 × 13 SASE

- "Cobblestone stands apart from other children's magazines by offering a solid look at one subject and stressing strong editorial content, color photographs throughout, and original illustrations."

Nonfiction Needs historical, humor, interview, personal experience, photo feature, travel, crafts, recipes, activities. No material that editorializes rather than reports. **Buys 45-50 mss/year.** Query with writing sample, 1-page outline, bibliography, SASE. 800 words/feature articles; 300-600 words/supplemental nonfiction; up to 700 words maximum/activities. **Pays 20-25¢/word.**
Photos Contact: Editor, by mail or fax, or Send photos. with your query. Captions, identification of subjects required. Reviews contact sheets, transparencies, prints. $15-100/b&w Buys one time rights.
Fiction Needs adventure, historical, biographical, retold legends. **Buys 5 mss/year.** 800 words maximum. **Pays 20-25¢/word.**
Poetry Needs free verse, light verse, traditional. Serious and light verse considered. Must have clear, objective imagery. Buys 3 poems/year. 50 lines maximum **Pays on an individual basis.**
Fillers "Crossword and other word puzzles (no word finds), mazes, and picture puzzles that use the vocabulary of the issue's theme or otherwise relate to the theme." **Pays on an individual basis.**
Tips "Review theme lists and past issues to see what we're looking for."

$$ Ⓝ CRICKET

Carus Publishing Co., 700 E. Lake St., Suite 300, Chicago IL 60601. (312)701-1720, ext. 10. Website: www.cricketmag.com. Alice Letvin. **Contact:** Submissions Editor. Monthly magazine for children ages 9-14. "*Cricket* is looking for more fiction and nonfiction for the older end of its 9-14 age range, as well as contemporary stories set in other countries. It also seeks humorous stories and mysteries (not detective spoofs), fantasy and original fairy tales, stand-alone excerpts from unpublished novels, and well-written/researched science articles." Estab. 1973. Circ. 73,000. Byline given. Pays on publication. Accepts queries by mail. Accepts previously published material. Responds in 4-6 months to mss. Guidelines available online.
Nonfiction Adventure, biography, architecture, geography, history, natural history, foreign culture, travel, science, archaeology, sports, technology. A bibliography is required for all nonfiction articles. Submit complete ms, SASE. Length: 200-1,500 words. **Pays 25¢/word maximum.**
Reprints with rights for sale noted and information about when and where the material previously appeared.
Photos Commissions all art separately from the text. Tearsheets/photocopies of both color and b&w work are considered. Accepts artwork done in pencil, pen and ink, watercolor, acrylic, oil, pastels, scratchboard, and woodcut. Does not want work that is overly caricatured or cartoony. It is especially helpful to see pieces showing young people, animals, action scenes, and several scenes from a narrative showing a character in different situations and emotional states.
Fiction Needs fantasy, historical, humorous, mystery, science fiction, realistic, contemporary, folk tales, fairy tales, legends, myths. No didactic, sex, religious, or horror stories. **Buys 75-100 mss/year.** Length: 200-2,000 words. **Pays 25¢/word maximum, and 6 contributor's copies; $2.50 charge for extras.**
Poetry Serious, humorous, nonsense rhymes. Buys 20-30 poems/year. 50 lines maximum **Pays $3/line maximum.**
Fillers Crossword puzzles, logic puzzles, math puzzles, crafts, recipes, science experiments, games and activities from other countries, plays, music, art.

$$ DIG MAGAZINE

Cobblestone Publishing, 30 Grove St., Suite C, Peterborough NH 03458-1454. (603)924-7209. Fax: (603)924-7380. E-mail: cfbakeriii@meganet.net. Website: www.digonsite.com. **Contact:** Rosalie Baker, editor. **75% freelance written.** Magazine published 9 times/year covering archaeology for kids ages 9-14. Estab. 1999. Circ. 20,000. Byline given. Pays on publication. No kill fee. Publishes ms an average of 1 year after acceptance. Buys all rights. Editorial lead time 1 year. Accepts queries by mail. Responds in several months. Sample copy for $5.95 with 8 × 11 SASE or $10 without SASE. Guidelines available online.
Nonfiction Needs personal experience, photo feature, travel, archaeological excavation reports. No fiction. Occasional paleontology stories accepted. **Buys 30-40 mss/year.** Query with published clips. Length: 100-1,000 words. **Pays 20-25¢/word.**
Photos State availability. Identification of subjects required. Negotiates payment individually. Buys one-time rights.
Tips "Please remember that this is a children's magazine for kids ages 9-14 so the tone is as kid-friendly as possible given the scholarship involved in researching and describing a site or a find."

$ ⊘ DISCOVERIES

Word Action Publishing Co., 6401 The Paseo, Kansas City MO 64131. (816)333-7000 ext. 2728. Fax: (816)333-4439. E-mail: JJSmith@nazarene.org. **80% freelance written**. Weekly sunday school take-home paper. Our audience is third and fourth graders. We require that the stories relate to the Sunday school lesson for that week. Circ. 18,000. Byline given. Pays on acceptance. No kill fee. Publishes ms an average of 1-2 year after acceptance. Buys multi-use rights. Accepts queries by mail, e-mail, fax. Accepts previously published material. Accepts simultaneous submissions. Responds in 6 weeks to queries. Sample copy for SASE. Guidelines for SASE.

Fiction Submit contemporary, true-to-life portrayals of 8-10 year olds, written for a third- to fourth-grade reading level. Religious themes. Must relate to our theme list. No fantasy, science fiction, abnormally mature or precocious children, personification of animals. Nothing preachy. No unrealistic dialogue. **Buys 25 mss/year.** Send complete ms. Length: words. **Pays $25.**

Fillers Spot cartoons, puzzles (related to the theme), trivia (any miscellaneous area of interest to 8-10 year olds). Length: 50-100 words. **Pays $15 for trivia, puzzles, and cartoons.**

Tips Follow our theme list and read the Bible verses that relate to the theme.

⊘ 🌐 DISNEY ADVENTURES

ACP Magazines, Ltd., 54-58 Park St., Sydney NSW 2000 Australia. (61)(2)9282-8000. Fax: (61)(2)9267-4361. Website: www.acp.com.au. **Contact:** Fiona Wright, editor. Monthly magazine for 6-15 year-old kids. Circ. 35,647.

- Query before submitting.

⊘ 🌐 DISNEY GIRL

ACP Magazines, Ltd., 54-58 Park St., Sydney NSW 2000 Australia. (61)(2)9282-8000. Fax: (61)(2)9267-4361. Website: www.acp.com.au. home.disney.com.au/errormsg/404.html. **Contact:** Fiona Wright, editor. Monthly magazine for girls 6-13, by girls. "*DisneyGiRL* is packed with reader-driven content, such as poems, short stories and opinion forums. DisneyGiRL engages, inspires and influences today's tweens by delivering a fun mix of celebrity gossip, fashion and beauty, advice, real-life stories, puzzles and competitions. Celebrating the stage they are at, DisneyGiRL prides itself on providing the life skills our readers need now and in the future, like making friends, dealing with puberty and coping with bullies." Circ. 33,477.

- Query before submitting.

$ $ FACES

People, Places and Cultures, Cobblestone Publishing, 30 Grove St., Suite C, Peterborough NH 03458. (603)924-7209. Fax: (603)924-7380. E-mail: facesmag@yahoo.com. Website: www.cobblestonepub.com. **90-100% freelance written.** "Publishes monthly throughout the year, *Faces* covers world culture for ages 9-14. It stands apart from other children's magazines by offering a solid look at one subject and stressing strong editorial content, color photographs throughout, and original illustrations. *Faces* offers an equal balance of feature articles and activities, as well as folktales and legends." Estab. 1984. Circ. 15,000. Byline given. Pays on publication. Offers 50% kill fee. Buys all rights. Accepts queries by mail, e-mail. Accepts simultaneous submissions.

Nonfiction "Interviews, personal accounts, in-depth nonfiction highlighting an aspect of the featured culture." Needs historical, humor, interview, personal experience, photo feature, travel, recipes, activities, crafts. **Buys 45-50 mss/year.** Query with writing sample, 1-page outline, bibliography, SASE. 800 words/ feature articles; 300-600/supplemental nonfiction; up to 700 words/activities. **Pays 20-25¢/word.**

Photos "Contact the editor by mail or fax, or Send photos. with your query. You may also send images on speculation." Captions, identification of subjects, model releases required. Reviews contact sheets, transparencies, prints. Pays $15-100/b&w; $25-100/color; cover fees are negotiated. Buys one time rights.

Fiction Needs ethnic, historical, retold legends/folktales, original plays. 800 words maximum. **Pays 20-25¢/word.**

Poetry Serious and light verse considered. Must have clear, objective imagery. 100 lines maximum. **Pays on an individual basis.**

Fillers "Crossword and other word puzzles (no word finds), mazes, and picture puzzles that use the vocabulary of the issue's theme or otherwise relate to the theme." **Pays on an individual basis.**

$ FUN FOR KIDZ

Bluffton News Printing & Publishing, 101 N. Main St., Bluffton OH 45817. Website: www.funforkidzmagazines.com. **60% freelance written**. Bimonthly magazine. We feature children involved in wholesome activities. Byline given. Pays on publication. No kill fee. Publishes ms an average of up to 4 years after acceptance. Buys first rights, buys one-time rights, buys second serial (reprint) rights, buys electronic rights. Accepts queries by mail. Accepts simultaneous submissions. Responds in 4-6 weeks to queries. Responds in 2 months to mss. Sample copy for $6. Writer's guidelines for #10 SASE or online.

Nonfiction Follow our theme list for article needs. We are always looking for creative activities to go with our themes. **Buys about 18 mss/year.** Send complete ms. **Pays 5¢/word for unsolicited articles.**

Photos Send photos. Offers $5 maximum/photo Buys one time rights.

Fiction Follow our theme list for fiction needs. No fantasy (magic, wizards, etc.), horror (haunted houses, ghosts, etc.), or Halloween-related stories. **Buys about 10 mss/year.** Send complete ms. Maxiumum 600 words. **Pays 5¢/word.**

Poetry Needs free verse, haiku, light verse, traditional. Poetry must follow our pre-set themes. Buys about 12 poems/year. **Pays $10 minimum.**

Tips Read our guidelines to learn about the kind of material we look for. Always include a SASE when sending in manuscripts for consideration.

$ $ GIRLS' LIFE

Monarch Publishing, 4529 Harford Rd., Baltimore MD 21214. E-mail: katiea@girlslife.com. Website: www.girlslife.com. **Contact:** Katie Abbondanza, senior editor. Bimonthly magazine covering girls ages 9-15. Estab. 1994. Circ. 2,000,000. Byline given. Pays on publication. Publishes ms an average of 3 months after acceptance. Buys all rights. Editorial lead time 4 months. Submit seasonal material 5 months in advance. Accepts queries by mail. Responds in 1 month to queries. Sample copy for $5 or online Guidelines available online.

Nonfiction Needs book excerpts, essays, general interest, how-to, humor, inspirational, interview, new product, travel, beauty, relationship, sports. Back to School (August/September); Fall, Halloween (October/November); Holidays, Winter (December/January); Valentine's Day, Crushes (February/March); Spring, Mother's Day (April/May); and Summer, Father's Day (June/July) **Buys 40 mss/year.** Query by mail with published clips. Submit complete mss on spec only. Length: 700-2,000 words. **Pays $350/regular column; $500/feature.**

Photos State availability. Captions, identification of subjects, model releases required. Reviews contact sheets, negatives, transparencies. Negotiates payment individually

Columns/Departments 20 Query with published clips. **Pays $150-450.**

Tips Send queries with published writing samples and detailed résumé. Have new ideas, a voice that speaks to our audience—not *down* to our audience—and supply artwork source.

$ GUIDE

True Stories Pointing to Jesus, Review and Herald Publishing Association, 55 W. Oak Ridge Dr., Hagerstown MD 21740. (301)393-4037. Fax: (301)393-4055. E-mail: guide@rhpa.org. Website: www.guidemagazine.org. **90% freelance written**. Weekly magazine featuring all-true stories showing God's involvement in 10- to 14-year-olds' lives. Estab. 1953. Circ. 32,000. Byline given. Pays on acceptance. No kill fee. Publishes ms an average of 8 months after acceptance. Buys second serial (reprint) rights. first world Editorial lead time 8 months. Submit seasonal material 8 months in advance. Accepts queries by mail, e-mail, fax. Responds in 1 month to queries. Sample copy for 6x9 SAE and 2 first-class stamps Guidelines available online.

- Prefers electronic ms submissions.

Nonfiction Needs religious. No fiction. Nonfiction should set forth a clearly evident spiritual application. **Buys 300 mss/year.** Send complete ms. Length: 500-1,200 words. **Pays $25-140.**

Reprints Send photocopy. Pays 50% of usual rates

Tips The majority of `misses' are due to the lack of a clearly evident (not `preachy') spiritual application.

$ HIGHLIGHTS FOR CHILDREN

803 Church St., Honesdale PA 18431-1824. (570)253-1080. Fax: (570)251-7847. Website: www.Highlights.com. **Contact:** Christine French Clark, editor-in-chief. **80% freelance written**. Monthly magazine for children up to age 12. "This book of wholesome fun is dedicated to helping children grow in basic skills and knowledge, in creativeness, in ability to think and reason, in sensitivity to others, in high ideals, and worthy ways of living—for children are the world's most important people. We publish stories for

beginning and advanced readers. Up to 500 words for beginners (ages 3-7), up to 800 words for advanced (ages 8-12)." Estab. 1946. Pays on acceptance. Buys all rights. Responds in 2 months to queries. Sample copy free. Guidelines on website in "About Us" area.

Nonfiction "We need articles on science, technology, and nature written by persons with strong backgrounds in those fields. Contributions always welcomed from new writers, especially engineers, scientists, historians, teachers, etc., who can make useful, interesting facts accessible to children. Also writers who have lived abroad and can interpret the ways of life, especially of children, in other countries in ways that will foster world brotherhood. Sports material, arts features, biographies, first-person accounts of fieldwork, photo essays, ancient history, high-interest animal articles, world culture, and articles of general interest to children. Direct, original approach, simple style, interesting content, not rewritten from encyclopedias. State background and qualifications for writing factual articles submitted. Include references or sources of information. Articles geared toward our younger readers (3-7) especially welcome, up to 500 words. Also, novel but tested craft ideas with clear directions. Include samples. Projects must require only free or inexpensive, easy-to-obtain materials. Especially desirable if easy enough for early primary grades. Also, fingerplays and action rhymes, easy for young children to grasp and to dramatize. Avoid wordiness. We need creative-thinking puzzles that can be illustrated, optical illusions, brain teasers, games of physical agility, and other `fun' activities of up to 300 words." Accepts queries by mail 800 words maximum **Pays $25 for craft ideas and puzzles; $25 for fingerplays; $150 and up for articles.**

Photos Reviews color 35mm slides, photos, or electronic files.

Fiction "Meaningful stories appealing to both girls and boys, up to age 12. Vivid, full of action. Engaging plot, strong characterization, lively language. Prefers stories in which a child protagonist solves a dilemma through his or her own resources. Seeks stories that the child ages 8-12 will eagerly read, and the child ages 2-7 will like to hear when read aloud (500-800 words). Stories require interesting plots and a number of illustration possiblities. Also need rebuses (picture stories 120 words or under), stories with urban settings, stories for beginning readers (100-500 words), sports and humorous stories, adventures, holiday stories, and mysteries. We also would like to see more material of 1-page length (300 words), both fiction and factual. Needs adventure, fantasy, historical, humorous, animal, contemporary, folktales, multi-cultural, problem-solving, sports. No war, crime or violence. Send complete ms. Length: words. **Pays $150 minimum.**

Tips "We are pleased that many authors of children's literature report that their first published work was in the pages of *Highlights*. It is not our policy to consider fiction on the strength of the reputation of the author. We judge each submission on its own merits. With factual material, however, we do prefer that writers be authorities in their field or people with first-hand experience. In this manner we can avoid the encyclopedic article that merely restates information readily available elsewhere. We don't make assignments. Query with simple letter to establish whether the nonfiction subject is likely to be of interest. A beginning writer should first become familiar with the type of material that *Highlights* publishes. Include special qualifications, if any, of author. Write for the child, not the editor. Write in a voice that children understand and relate to. Speak to today's kids, avoiding didactic, overt messages. Even though our general principles haven't changed over the years, we are contemporary in our approach to issues. Avoid worn themes."

$$ ⊘ HUMPTY DUMPTY'S MAGAZINE

Children's Better Health Institute, P.O. Box 567, Indianapolis IN 46206-0567. (317)636-8881. Fax: (317)684-8094. E-mail: plybarger@cbhi.org. Website: www.humptydumptymag.org. **25% freelance written.** Magazine published 8 times/year covering health, nutrition, hygiene, fitness, and safety for children ages 4-6. "Our publication is designed to entertain and to educate young readers in healthy lifestyle habits. Fiction, poetry, pencil activities should have an element of good nutrition or fitness." Estab. 1948. Circ. 350,000. Byline given. Pays on publication. Publishes ms an average of 8 months after acceptance. Buys all rights. Editorial lead time 8 months. Submit seasonal material 10 months in advance. Accepts simultaneous submissions. Sample copy for $2.95. Guidelines for SASE or on website.

- All work is on speculation only; queries are not accepted nor are stories assigned.

Nonfiction "Material must have a health theme—nutrition, safety, exercise, hygiene. We're looking for articles that encourage readers to develop better health habits without preaching. Very simple factual articles that creatively teach readers about their bodies. We use several puzzles and activities in each issue—dot-to-dot, hidden pictures, and other activities that promote following instructions, developing finger dexterity, and working with numbers and letters. Include word count." **Buys 3-4 mss/year.** Send complete ms. 300 words maximum **Pays 22¢/word.**

Photos Send photos. Offers no additional payment for photos accepted with ms Buys all rights.

Columns/Departments Mix & Fix (no-cook recipes), 100 words. All ingredients must be nutritious—low fat, no sugar, etc.—and tasty. 8 Send complete ms. **Payment varies**

Fiction Contact: Phyllis Lybarger, editor. "We use some stories in rhyme and a few easy-to-read stories for the beginning reader. All stories should work well as read-alouds. Currently we need health/sports/fitness stories. We try to present our health material in a positive light, incorporating humor and a light approach wherever possible. Avoid stereotyping. Characters in contemporary stories should be realistic and reflect good, wholesome values. Include word count." No inanimate talking objects, animal stories, or science fiction. **Buys 4-6 mss/year.** Send complete ms. 350 words maximum **Pays 22¢/word for stories, plus 10 contributor's copies.**

Tips "We would like to see more holiday stories, articles, and activities. Please send seasonal material at least eight months in advance."

$$ JACK AND JILL

Children's Better Health Institute, P.O. Box 567, Indianapolis IN 46206-0567. (317)636-8881. Fax: (317)684-8094. E-mail: j.goodman@cbhi.org. Website: www.jackandjillmag.org. **Contact:** Julia Goodman, editor. **50% freelance written.** Bimonthly magazine published 6 times/year for children ages 8-12. "Material will not be returned unless accompanied by SASE with sufficient postage. No queries. May hold material being seriously considered for up to 1 year." Estab. 1938. Circ. 200,000. Byline given. Pays on publication. Publishes ms an average of 8 months after acceptance. Buys all rights. Submit seasonal material 8 months in advance. Responds in 12 weeks to mss. Sample copy for $2.95. Guidelines available online.

Fiction Pays 15¢/word minimum.

Tips "We are constantly looking for new writers who can tell good stories with interesting slants—stories that are not full of out-dated and time-worn expressions. We like to see stories about kids who are smart and capable, but not sarcastic or smug. Problem-solving skills, personal responsibility, and integrity are good topics for us. Obtain current issues of the magazine and study them to determine our present needs and editorial style."

$$$ JUNIOR SCHOLASTIC

Scholastic, Inc., 557 Broadway, New York NY 10012-3902. (212)343-6100. Fax: (212)343-6945. E-mail: junior@scholastic.com. Website: www.juniorscholastic.com. Magazine published 18 times/year. Edited for students ages 11-14. Circ. 535,000. No kill fee. Editorial lead time 6 weeks.

K-ZONE

Media City, 8 Central Ave., Eveleigh NSW 2015T 2015 Australia. (61)(2)9394 2767. Fax: (61)(2)9394 2788. E-mail: kzone@pacificmags.com.au. Website: www.pacificmagazines.com.au. Monthly magazine arming kids with the latest gossip on new music, movies, TV shows and games.

Nonfiction Needs general interest, how-to, inspirational, interview, new product. Query.

$$ LADYBUG

The Magazine for Young Children, Carus Publishing Co., 700 E. Lake St., Suite 300, Chicago IL 60601. (312)701-1720. Website: www.cricketmag.com. Suzanne Beck, man. art dir. **Contact:** Marianne Carus, editor-in-chief. Monthly magazine for children ages 2-6. We look for quality literature and nonfiction. Estab. 1990. Circ. 125,000. Byline given. Pays on publication. Accepts previously published material. Responds in 6 months to mss. Guidelines available online.

Nonfiction "Concepts, vocabulary, simple explanations of things in a young child's world." **Buys 35 mss/year.** Send complete ms, SASE. Length: 400-700 words. **Pays 25¢/word ($25 minimum).**

Photos Artists should submit tearsheets/photocopies of artwork to be kept in our illustrator files. $500/spread; $250/page Buys all rights; physical art remains the property of the illustrator and may be used for artist's self promotion.

Fiction Read-aloud stories, picture stories, original retellings of folk and fairy tales, multicultural stories. **Buys 30 mss/year.** 800 words maximum. **Pays 25¢/word ($25 minimum).**

Poetry Needs light verse, traditional. Buys 40 poems/year. Submit maximum 5 poems. 20 lines maximum. **Pays $3/line ($25 minimum).**

Fillers Learning activities, games, crafts, songs, finger games. See back issues for types, formats, and length.

Tips "Reread ms before sending. Keep within specified word limits. Study back issues before submitting to learn about the types of material we're looking for. Writing style is paramount. We look for rich, evocative language and a sense of joy or wonder. Remember that you're writing for preschoolers—be age-appropriate, but not condescending or preachy. A story must hold enjoyment for both parent and child through repeated read-aloud sessions. Remember that people come in all colors, sizes, physical conditions, and have special needs. Be inclusive!"

MAGIC DRAGON

Association for Encouragement of Children's Creativity, P.O. Box 687, Webster NY 14580. E-mail: magicdragon@rochester.rr.com. Website: www.magicdragonmagazine.com. Quarterly magazine covering children's writing and art. " All work is created by children up to age 12 (elementary school grades). We consider stories, poems, and artwork. Queries, writing and art accepted by USPS mail and by e-mail." Estab. 2005. Circ. 3,500. Byline given. Pays 1 contributor copy on publication No kill fee. Editorial lead time 3-6 month. Submit seasonal material 6 months in advance. Accepts queries by mail, e-mail`. Responds in 2 weeks to queries. Sample copy for $4. Guidelines available online.
Nonfiction Needs essays, humor, inspirational, personal experience. Send complete ms. 250 words maximum.
Photos Include a SASE with all original artwork. If it's a copy, make sure the colors and copy are the same and the lines are clear. Include an explanation of how you created the art (crayon, watercolor, paper sculpture, etc).
Fiction Needs adventure, fantasy, historical, humorous.
Poetry Needs free verse, haiku, light verse, traditional. 30 lines maximum.

$ $ $ $ NATIONAL GEOGRAPHIC KIDS

Dare to Explore, National Geographic Society, 1145 17th St. NW, Washington DC 20036. Website: www.kidsnationalgeographic.com. **70% freelance written**. Magazine published 10 times/year. It's our mission to excite kids about their world. We are the children's magazine that makes learning fun. Estab. 1975. Byline given. Pays on acceptance. Offers 10% kill fee. $100 Publishes ms an average of 6 months after acceptance. Buys all rights. Makes work-for-hire assignments. Editorial lead time 6+ months. Submit seasonal material 6+ months in advance. Accepts queries by mail. Accepts simultaneous submissions. Sample copy for #10 SAE. Guidelines free.
Nonfiction Needs general interest, humor, interview, technical, travel, animals, human interest, science, technology, entertainment, archaeology, pets. "We do not release our editorial calendar. We do not want poetry, sports, fiction, or story ideas that are too young—our audience is between ages 8-14." Query with published clips and résumé. Length: 100-1,000 words. **Pays $1/word for assigned articles.**
Photos Contact: Jay Sumner, photo director. State availability. Captions, identification of subjects, model releases required. Reviews contact sheets, negatives, transparencies, prints. Negotiates payment individually.
Columns/Departments Amazing Animals (animal heroes, stories about animal rescues, interesting/funny animal tales), 100 words; Inside Scoop (fun, kid-friendly news items), 50-70 words. Query with published clips. **Pays $1/word.**
Tips "Submit relevant clips. Writers must have demonstrated experience writing for kids. Read the magazine before submitting. Send query and clips via snail mail—materials will not be returned. No SASE required unless sample copy is requested."

$ NATURE FRIEND

4253 Woodcock Lane, Dayton VA 22821. (540)867-0764. Website: www.dogwoodridgeoutdoors.com. **Contact:** Kevin Shank. **80% freelance written**. Monthly magazine covering nature. "*Nature Friend* includes stories, puzzles, science experiments, nature experiments—all submissions need to honor God as creator." Estab. 1983. Circ. 13,000. Byline given. Pays on publication. No kill fee. Buys first rights, buys one-time rights. Editorial lead time 4 months. Submit seasonal material 6 months in advance. Accepts simultaneous submissions. Responds in 6 months to mss. Sample copy and writer's guidelines for $10 postage paid.
Nonfiction Needs how-to, nature, science experiments, photo feature, articles about interesting/unusual animals. No poetry, evolution, animals depicted in captivity. **Buys 50 mss/year.** Send complete ms. Length: 250-900 words. **Pays 5¢/word.**
Photos Send photos. Captions, identification of subjects required. Reviews prints. Offers $20-75/photo Buys one time rights.
Columns/Departments Learning By Doing, 500-900 words. Send complete ms.
Tips "We want to bring joy and knowledge to children by opening the world of God's creation to them. We endeavor to create a sense of awe about nature's creator and a respect for His creation. I'd like to see more submissions on hands-on things to do with a nature theme (not collecting rocks or leaves—real stuff). Also looking for good stories that are accompanied by good photography."

$ $ NEW MOON

The Magazine for Girls & Their Dreams, New Moon Publishing, Inc., P.O. Box 161287, Duluth MN 55816. (218)728-5507. Fax: (218)728-0314. E-mail: girl@newmoon.org. Website: www.newmoon.org. **25% freelance written.** Bimonthly magazine covering girls ages 8-14, edited by girls aged 8-14. "In general, all material should be pro-girl and feature girls and women as the primary focus. *New Moon* is for every girl who wants her voice heard and her dreams taken seriously. *New Moon* celebrates girls, explores the passage from girl to woman, and builds healthy resistance to gender inequities. The *New Moon* girl is true to herself and *New Moon* helps her as she pursues her unique path in life, moving confidently into the world." Estab. 1992. Circ. 30,000. Byline given. Pays on publication. Publishes ms an average of 6 months after acceptance. Buys all rights. Editorial lead time 6 months. Submit seasonal material 8 months in advance. Accepts queries by mail, e-mail, fax. Accepts simultaneous submissions. Responds in 2 months to mss. Sample copy for $7 or online. Guidelines for SASE or online.

Nonfiction Needs essays, general interest, humor, inspirational, interview, opinion, personal experience, written by girls, photo feature, religious, travel, multicultural/girls from other countries. No fashion, beauty, or dating. **Buys 20 mss/year.** Send complete ms. Length: 600 words. **Pays 6-12¢/word.**

Photos State availability. Captions, identification of subjects required. Negotiates payment individually Buys one time rights.

Columns/Departments Women's Work (profile of a woman and her job relating the the theme), 600 words; Herstory (historical woman relating to theme), 600 words. 10 Query. **Pays 6-12¢/word**

Fiction Prefers girl-written material. All girl-centered. Needs adventure, fantasy, historical, humorous, slice-of-life vignettes. **Buys 6 mss/year.** Send complete ms. Length: 1,200-1,400 words. **Pays 6-12¢/word.**

Poetry No poetry by adults.

Tips "We'd like to see more girl-written feature articles that relate to a theme. These can be about anything the girl has done personally, or she can write about something she's studied. Please read *New Moon* before submitting to get a sense of our style. Writers and artists who comprehend our goals have the best chance of publication. We love creative articles—both nonfiction and fiction—that are not condescending to our readers. Keep articles to suggested word lengths; avoid stereotypes. Refer to our guidelines and upcoming themes."

$ $ POCKETS

The Upper Room, P.O. Box 340004, Nashville TN 37203-0004. (615)340-7333. Fax: (615)340-7267. E-mail: pockets@upperroom.org. Website: www.pockets.org. **60% freelance written.** Monthly (except February) magazine covering children's and families' spiritual formation. "We are a Christian, inter-denominational publication for children 6-12 years old, focused primarily on the 9-12 age group. Each issue reflects a specific theme." Estab. 1981. Byline given. Pays on acceptance. No kill fee. Publishes ms an average of 1 year after acceptance. Buys first North American serial rights. Submit seasonal material 1 year in advance. Responds in 8 weeks to mss. Each issue reflects a specific theme. Sample copy available with a 9 × 12 SASE with 4 First-Class stamps attached to envelope. Guidelines on website.

Nonfiction "Seek brief biographical sketches, famous or unknown persons, whose lives reflect their Christian commitment and are of particular interest to children. Write in a way that appeals to children. Fictional characters and some elaboration may be included in scripture stories, but the writer must remain faithful to the story." **Buys 10 mss/year.** Length: 400-600 words. **Pays 14¢/word.**

Reprints Accepts one-time previously published submissions. Send ms with rights for sale noted and information about when and where the material previously appeared.

Photos Send 4-6 close-up photos of children actively involved in peacemakers at work activities. Send photos., contact sheets, prints, or digital images. Must be 300 dpi. Pays $25/photo Buys one time rights.

Columns/Departments Poetry and Prayer (related to themes), maximum 24 lines; Family Time, 200-300 words; Peacemakers at Work (profiles of children working for peace, justice, and ecological concerns), 400-600 words. **Pays 14¢/word**. Activities/Games (related to themes). **Pays $25 and up**. Kids Cook (simple recipes children can make alone or with minimal help from an adult). **Pays $25.**

Fiction "Submissions add should contain lots of action, use believable dialogue, be simply written, and be relevant to the problems faced by this age group in every day life. Children need to be able to see themselves in the pages of the magazine. It is important that the tone not be 'preachy' or didactic. Use short sentences and paragraphs. When possible, use concrete words instead of abstractions." Needs adventure, ethnic, historical, general, religious. No violence, science fiction, romance, fantasy, or talking animal stories. **Buys 25-30 mss/year.** Send complete ms. Length: 600-900 words. **Pays 14¢/word, plus 2-5 contributor's copies.**

Poetry Buys 14 poems/year. Length: 4-24 lines. **Pays $2/line, $25 minimum.**
Tips "Theme stories, role models, and retold scripture stories are most open to freelancers. Poetry is also open. It is very helpful if writers read our writers' guidelines and themes on our website."

$ SHINE BRIGHTLY

GEMS Girls' Clubs, P.O. Box 7259, Grand Rapids MI 49510. (616)241-5616. Fax: (616)241-5558. E-mail: christina@gemsgc.org. Website: www.gemsgc.org. **80% freelance written. Works with new and published/established writers.** Monthly magazine. Our purpose is to lead girls into a living relationship with Jesus Christ and to help them see how God is at work in their lives and the world around them. Puzzles, crafts, stories, and articles for girls ages 9-14. Estab. 1971. Circ. 16,000. Byline given. Pays on publication. No kill fee. Publishes ms an average of 1 year after acceptance. Buys first North American serial rights, buys second serial (reprint) rights, buys simultaneous rights. Submit seasonal material 1 year in advance. Accepts previously published material. Accepts simultaneous submissions. Responds in 2 months to queries. Sample copy for 9 × 12 SAE with 3 first class stamps and $1. Guidelines available online.
Nonfiction We do not want easy solutions or quick character changes from good to bad. No pietistic characters. No 'new girl at school starting over after parents' divorce' stories. Constant mention of God is not necessary if the moral tone of the story is positive. We do not want stories that always have a happy ending. Needs include: biographies and autobiographies of heroes of the faith, informational (write for issue themes), multicultural materials. Needs humor, inspirational, seasonal and holiday, interview, personal experience, avoid the testimony approach, photo feature, query first, religious, travel, adventure, mystery. **Buys 35 unsolicited mss/year.** Send complete ms. Length: 100-900 words. **Pays 3¢/word, plus 2 copies.**
Reprints Send typed manuscript with rights for sale noted and information about when and where the material previously appeared.
Photos Purchased with or without ms. Appreciate multicultural subjects. Reviews 5 × 7 or 8 × 10 clear color glossy prints. Pays $25-50 on publication
Columns/Departments How-to (crafts); puzzles and jokes; quizzes. Length: 200-400 words. Send complete ms. **Pay varies**
Fiction Needs adventure, that girls could experience in their hometowns or places they might realistically visit, ethnic, historical, humorous, mystery, believable only, religious, nothing too preachy, romance, stories that deal with awakening awareness of boys are appreciated, slice-of-life vignettes, suspense, can be serialized. **Buys 20 mss/year.** Send complete ms. Length: 400-900 words. **Pays up to $35.**
Poetry Needs free verse, haiku, light verse, traditional. **Pays $5-15.**
Tips Prefers not to see anything on the adult level, secular material, or violence. Writers frequently oversimplify the articles and often write with a Pollyanna attitude. An author should be able to see his/her writing style as exciting and appealing to girls ages 9-14. The style can be fun, but also teach a truth. Subjects should be current and important to *SHINE brightly* readers. Use our theme update as a guide. We would like to receive material with a multicultural slant.

$ SPARKLE

GEMS Girls' Clubs, P.O. Box 7259, Grand Rapids MI 49510. (616)241-5616. Fax: (616)241-5558. E-mail: sarahv@gemsgc.org. Website: www.gemsgc.org. **80% freelance written.** Magazine published 6 times/year that helps girls in first through third grades grow in a stronger relationship with Jesus Christ. *Sparkle*'s mission is to prepare girls for a life of living out their faith. Our mission is to prepare girls to become world changers. We aspire for girls to passionately shadow Jesus, seeking to live, act and talk so that others are drawn toward the savior. Estab. 2002. Circ. 5,000. Byline given. Pays on publication. Offers $20 kill fee. Buys first North American serial rights, buys first rights, buys one-time rights, buys second serial (reprint) rights, buys simultaneous rights. Editorial lead time 3 months. Submit seasonal material 1 year in advance. Accepts queries by mail. Accepts previously published material. Accepts simultaneous submissions. Responds in 3 weeks to queries. Responds in 3 months to mss. Sample copy for 9x13 SAE, 3 first-class stamps, and $1 for coverage/publication cost. Writer's guidelines for #10 SASE or online.
Nonfiction Needs how-to, crafts/recipes, humor, inspirational, personal experience, photo feature, religious, travel. Constant mention of God is not necessary if the moral tone of the story is positive. **Buys 15 mss/year.** Send complete ms. Length: 100-400 words. **Pays $20/article.**
Photos Send photos. Identification of subjects required. Reviews at least 5 × 7 clear color glossy prints, GIF/JPEG files on CD. Offers $25-50/photo. Buys one time rights.

Columns/Departments Crafts; puzzles and jokes; quizzes, all 200-400 words. Send complete ms. **Payment varies.**

Fiction Needs adventure, ethnic, fantasy, humorous, mystery, religious, slice-of-life vignettes. **Buys 10 mss/year.** Send complete ms. Length: 100-400 words. **Pays $20/story.**

Poetry Needs free verse, haiku, light verse, traditional. We do not wish to see anything that is too difficult for a first grader to read. We wish it to remain light. The style can be fun, but also teach a truth. No violence or secular material. Buys 4 poems/year. Submit maximum 4 poems.

Tips Writers should keep stories simple but not write with a 'Pollyanna' attitude. Authors should see their writing style as exciting and appealing to girls ages 6-9. Subjects should be current and important to *Sparkle* readers. Use our theme as a guide. We would like to receive material with a multicultural slant.

$$ SPIDER

The Magazine for Children, Cricket Magazine Group, 70 East Lake St., Suite 300, Chicago IL 60601. (312)701-1720. Fax: (312)701-1728. Website: www.cricketmag.com. **85% freelance written**. Monthly reading and activity magazine for children ages 6 to 9. *Spider* introduces children to the highest quality stories, poems, illustrations, articles, and activities. It was created to foster in beginning readers a love of reading and discovery that will last a lifetime. We're looking for writers who respect children's intelligence. Estab. 1994. Circ. 70,000. Byline given. Pays on publication. Accepts previously published material. Accepts simultaneous submissions. Responds in 6 months to mss. Guidelines available online.

Nonfiction Nature, animals, science, foreign culture, history, fine arts and music, humanities topics. Submit complete ms, bibliography, SASE. Length: 300-800 words. **Pays up to 25¢/word.**

Reprints Send photocopy with rights for sale noted and information about when and where the material previously appeared.

Photos For art samples, it is especially helpful to see pieces showing children, animals, action scenes, and several scenes from a narrative showing a character in different situations. Send photocopies/tearsheets. Also considers photo essays (prefers color, but b&w is also accepted). Captions, identification of subjects, model releases required. Reviews contact sheets, transparencies, 8 × 10 prints.

Fiction Stories should be easy to read. Needs fantasy, humorous, science fiction, folk tales, fairy tales, fables, myths. Length: 300-1,000 words. **Pays up to 25¢/word**.

Poetry Needs free verse, traditional. Submit maximum 5 poems. **Pays $3/line maximum**.

Tips We'd like to see more of the following: engaging nonfiction, fillers, and 'takeout page' activities; folktales, fairy tales, science fiction, and humorous stories. Most importantly, do not write down to children.

$ STONE SOUP

The Magazine by Young Writers and Artists, Children's Art Foundation, P.O. Box 83, Santa Cruz CA 95063-0083. (831)426-5557. Fax: (831)426-1161. E-mail: editor@stonesoup.com. Website: www.stonesoup.com. **Contact:** Ms. Gerry Mandel, editor. **100% freelance written**. Bimonthly magazine of writing and art by children, including fiction, poetry, book reviews, and art by children through age 13. "Audience is children, teachers, parents, writers, artists. We have a preference for writing and art based on real-life experiences; no formula stories or poems." Estab. 1973. Circ. 15,000. Pays on publication. Publishes ms an average of 4 months after acceptance. Buys all rights. Submit seasonal material 6 months in advance. Sample copy for $5 or online. Guidelines available online.

Nonfiction Needs historical, personal experience, book reviews. **Buys 12 mss/year. Pays $40.**

Fiction Contact: Ms. Gerry Mandel, editor. Needs adventure, ethnic, experimental, fantasy, historical, humorous, mystery, science fiction, slice-of-life vignettes, suspense. We do not like assignments or formula stories of any kind. **Buys 60 mss/year.** Send complete ms. Length: 150-2,500 words. **Pays $40 for stories. Authors also receive 2 copies, a certificate, and discounts on additional copies and on subscriptions.**

Poetry Needs avant-garde, free verse. Buys 12 poems/year. **Pays $40/poem**.

Tips "All writing we publish is by young people ages 13 and under. We do not publish any writing by adults. We can't emphasize enough how important it is to read a couple of issues of the magazine. We have a strong preference for writing on subjects that mean a lot to the author. If you feel strongly about something that happened to you or something you observed, use that feeling as the basis for your story or poem. Stories should have good descriptions, realistic dialogue, and a point to make. In a poem, each word must be chosen carefully. Your poem should present a view of your subject, and a way of using words that are special and all your own."

$$ ⊘ U.S. KIDS

A Weekly Reader Magazine, Children's Better Health Institute, P.O. Box 567, Indianapolis IN 46206-

0567. (317)636-8881. Fax: (317)684-8094. Website: www.cbhi.org/magazines/uskids/index.shtml. **50% freelance written**. Magazine published 8 times/year featuring kids doing extraordinary things, especially activities related to health, sports, the arts, interesting hobbies, the environment, computers, etc. Estab. 1987. Circ. 230,000. Byline given. Pays on publication. Publishes ms an average of 4 months after acceptance. Buys all rights. Editorial lead time 6 months. Submit seasonal material 6 months in advance. Responds in 4 months to mss. Sample copy for $2.95 or online. Guidelines for #10 SASE.

- *U.S. Kids* is being retargeted to a younger audience. Closed to submissions until further notice.

Nonfiction Especially interested in articles with a health/fitness angle. Needs general interest, how-to, interview, science, kids using computers, multicultural. **Buys 16-24 mss/year.** Send complete ms. 400 words maximum **Pays up to 25¢/word.**

Photos State availability. Captions, identification of subjects, model releases required. Reviews contact sheets, negatives, transparencies, color photocopies, or prints. Negotiates payment individually Buys one time rights.

Columns/Departments Real Kids (kids doing interesting things); Fit Kids (sports, healthy activities); Computer Zone. Length: 300-400 words. Send complete ms. **Pays up to 25¢/word**

Fiction Buys very little fictional material. **Buys 1-2 mss/year.** Send complete ms. 400 words **Pays up to 25¢/word.**

Poetry Needs light verse, traditional. Buys 6-8 poems/year. Submit maximum 6 poems. Length: 8-24 lines. **Pays $25-50.**

Tips We are retargeting the magazine for first-, second-, and third-graders, and looking for fun and informative articles on activities and hobbies of interest to younger kids. Special emphasis on fitness, sports, and health. Availability of good photos a plus.

Literary & Little

THE ABSENT WILLOW REVIEW

Tales of Horror, Fantasy & Science Fiction, Absent Willow Publishing, LLC, PO Box 66, Rochester NH 03866. E-mail: editor@absentwillowreview.com and rick@absentwillowreview.com. Website: www.absentwillowreview.com. **100% freelance written**. Monthly webzine covering Horror, Fantasy, and Science Fiction. "We are looking for authors who can show us that they know and understand their craft. That sense of wonder we feel when a story transports us to another time or place is what fuels our passion and keeps us reading. Strong characters are a key to capturing our attention." Estab. 2008. Author to share in proceeds if included in an Anthology. No kill fee. Buys electronic rights, buys Anthology rights. Accepts queries by e-mail. Accepts simultaneous submissions. Online at http://absentwillowreview.com/submissions

Fiction Contact: Rick DeCost. "Stories should fall between 2,000 - 8,000 words in length. Stories above 8,000 words may be considered if deemed exceptional by our editorial staff and must not exceed 10,000 words." Needs fantasy, horror, science fiction. "We do not want to see erotica or excessive gore for the sake of gore. We will not publish stories that may be seen as promoting discrimination against other persons based on gender, age, sexual orientation, religion or race. Violence and profanity are not prohibited but should be used with discretion." Send complete ms. Length: 2,000-8,000 words.

Poetry Contact: Rick DeCost, editor. Needs free verse, light verse, traditional.

Tips "Please visit our website to view our submission guidelines. We are looking for quality works of fiction. The best way to break into our magazine and to be considered for our print anthology is to write a compelling story with memorable characters. If your first submission isn't accepted, keep trying. We love new authors and are always eager to read their work."

ACORN

A Journal of Contemporary Haiku, OutOfPocket Press, 22 Calistoga Rd.ALISTOGA RD #135, SANTA ROSA CA 95409, #135, Santa Rose CA 95409. E-mail: acornhaiku@mac.com. Website: www.acornhaiku.com. **Contact:** Carolyn Hall, editor. Biannual magazine dedicated to publishing the best of contemporary English language haiku, and in particular to showcasing individual poems that reveal the extraordinary moments found in everyday life. Estab. 1998. Publishes ms an average of 1-3 months after acceptance. Reads submissions in January-February and July-August only. Buys first rights, buys one-time rights. Accepts queries by mail or e-mail. Responds in 3 weeks to mss. Guidelines and sample poems available online.

Poetry Needs HAIKU. "Decisions made by editor on a rolling basis. Poems judged purely on merit." Sometimes acceptance conditional on minor edits. Often comments on rejected poems. "Does NOT want epigrams, musings, and overt emotion poured into 17 syllables; surreal, science fiction, or political

commentary 'ku;' strong puns or raunchy humor. a 5-7-5 syllable count is not necessary or encouraged." Length: 1-5 lines; 17 or fewer syllables.
Tips "This is primarily a journal for those with a focused interest in HAIKU, rather than an outlet for the occasional short jottings of longer-form poets. It is a much richer genre than one might surmise from many of the recreational websites that claim to promote 'HAIKU.'"

$ AFRICAN AMERICAN REVIEW

Saint Louis University, 317 Adorjan Hall, 3800 Lindell Blvd., St. Louis MO 63108. (314)977-3688. Fax: (314)977-1514. E-mail: keenanam@slu.edu. Website: aar.slu.edu. **65% freelance written**. Quarterly journal covering African-American literature and culture. Essays on African-American literature, theater, film, art and culture generally; interviews; poetry and fiction by African-American authors; book reviews. Estab. 1967. Circ. 2,000. Byline given. Pays on publication. Publishes ms an average of 1 year after acceptance. Buys First North American serial rights. Editorial lead time 1 year. Responds in 1 week to queries. Responds in 3-6 months to mss. Sample copy for $12. Guidelines available online.
Nonfiction Needs essays, interview. **Buys Publishes 30 mss/year.** Query. Length: 6,000-8,500 words.
Photos State availability. Captions required. Pays $100 for covers.
Fiction Contact: Nathan Grant, editor. Needs ethnic, experimental, mainstream. No children's/juvenile/young adult/teen. **Buys 5 mss/year.** Length: No more than 1,500 words. **1 contributor's copy and 5 offprints.**

$ AGNI

Creative Writing Program, Boston University, 236 Bay State Rd., Boston MA 02215. (617)353-7135. Fax: (617)353-7134. E-mail: agni@bu.edu. Website: www.agnimagazine.org. **Contact:** Sven Birkerts, editor. Biannual magazine. "Eclectic literary magazine publishing first-rate poems, essays, translations, and stories." Estab. 1972. Circ. 4,000. Byline given. Pays on publication. Publishes ms an average of 6 months after acceptance. Buys first North American serial rights. Rights to reprint in *AGNI* anthology (with author's consent). Editorial lead time 1 year. Accepts queries by mail. Accepts simultaneous submissions. Responds in 2 weeks to queries. Responds in 4 months to mss. Sample copy for $10 or online. Guidelines available online.

- Reading period September 1-May 31 only. "Online magazine carries original content not found in print edition. All submissions are considered for both." Founding editor Askold Melnyczuk won the 2001 Nora Magid Award for Magazine Editing. Work from *AGNI* has been included and cited regularly in the *Pushcart Prize* and *Best American* anthologies.

Fiction Buys stories, prose poems. "No science fiction or romance." **Buys more than 20 mss/year. Pays $10/page up to $150, 2 contributor's copies, 1-year subscription, and 4 gift copies.**
Poetry Buys more than 120 poems/year poems/year. Submit maximum 5 poems. **Pays $20-150.**
Tips "We're also looking for extraordinary translations from little-translated languages. It is important to look at a copy of *AGNI* before submitting, to see if your work might be compatible. Please write for guidelines or a sample."

$ $ ALASKA QUARTERLY REVIEW

ESB 208, University of Alaska-Anchorage, 3211 Providence Dr., Anchorage AK 99508. (907)786-6916. E-mail: aqr@uaa.alaska.edu. Website: www.uaa.alaska.edu/aqr. **95% freelance written**. Semiannual magazine publishing fiction, poetry, literary nonfiction, and short plays in traditional and experimental styles. "*AQR* publishes fiction, poetry, literary nonfiction and short plays in traditional and experimental styles." Estab. 1982. Circ. 2,700. Byline given. Honorariums on publication when funding permits. Publishes ms an average of 6 months after acceptance. Buys first North American serial rights. Upon request, rights will be transferred back to author after publication. Accepts queries by mail. Responds in 1 month to queries. Responds in 6 months to mss. Sample copy for $6. Guidelines available online.

- *Alaska Quarterly* reports they are always looking for freelance material and new writers.

Nonfiction Literary nonfiction: essays and memoirs. **Buys 0-5 mss/year.** Query. Length: 1,000-20,000 words. **Pays $50-200 subject to funding.**
Fiction Contact: Ronald Spatz, fiction editor. "Works in AQR have certain characteristics: freshness, honesty, and a compelling subject. The voice of the piece must be strong—idiosyncratic enough to create a unique persona. We look for craft, putting it in a form where it becomes emotionally and intellectually complex. Many pieces in AQR concern everyday life. We're not asking our writers to go outside themselves and their experiences to the absolute exotic to catch our interest. We look for the experiential and revelatory qualities of the work. We will champion a piece that may be less polished or stylistically sophisticated, if it engages me, surprises me, and resonates for me. The joy in reading such a work is in discovering something true. Moreover, in keeping with our mission to publish new writers, we

are looking for voices our readers do not know, voices that may not always be reflected in the dominant culture and that, in all instances, have something important to convey." Needs experimental and traditional literary forms., contemporary, prose poem, novel excerpts, drama: experimental & traditional one-acts. No romance, children's, or inspirational/religious. **Buys 20-26 mss/year; 0-2 mss/year drama. mss/year.** not exceeding 100 pages **Pays $50-200 subject to funding; pays in contributor's copies and subscriptions when funding is limited.**

Poetry Needs avant-garde, free verse, traditional. No light verse. Buys 10-30 poems/year. Submit maximum 10 poems. **Pays $10-50 subject to availability of funds; pays in contributor's copies and subscriptions when funding is limited.**

Tips "All sections are open to freelancers. We rely almost exclusively on unsolicited manuscripts. *AQR* is a nonprofit literary magazine and does not always have funds to pay authors."

ALEHOUSE PRESS

P.O. Box 31655, San Francisco CA 94131. E-mail: query@alehousepress.com. Website: www.alehousepress.com. Annual magazine. "In general, unsolicited poetry is considered through the Alehouse Happy Hour Poetry Awards." Estab. 2006. Byline given. No kill fee. Guidelines by e-mail.

Poetry Needs avant-garde, free verse, haiku, light verse, traditional. Length: 1-40 lines.

ALIMENTUM

the literature of food, P.O. Box 210028, Nashville TN 37221. E-mail: submissions@alimentumjournal.com. Website: www.alimentumjournal.com. Biannual magazine covering food in literature. "We're seeking fiction, creative nonfiction, and poetry all around the subject of food or drink. We do not read year-round. Check website for reading periods." Byline given. No kill fee. Accepts queries by mail. Accepts simultaneous submissions. Responds in 1-3 months to mss.

Nonfiction Send complete ms.

Fiction Send complete ms.

Poetry Contact: Cortney Davis, poetry editor. Needs avant-garde, free verse, haiku, light verse, traditional. Buys 5 poem limit/submission poems/year.

Tips "No e-mail submissions, only snail mail. Mark outside envelope to the attention of Poetry, Fiction, or Nonfiction Editor."

$ AMERICAN BOOK REVIEW

The Writer's Review, Inc., School of Arts & Sciences, Univ. of Houston-Victoria, 3000 N. Ben Wilson, Victoria TX 77901. (361)570-4848. E-mail: americanbookreview@llstu.edu. Website: www.americanbookreview.org. Bimonthly magazine covering book reviews. We specialize in reviewing books published by independent presses. Estab. 1977. Circ. 15,000. Byline given. Pays on publication. Offers $50 kill fee. Publishes ms an average of 2-4 months after acceptance. Buys one-time rights. Editorial lead time 1 month. Accepts queries by mail, e-mail, fax, phone. Responds in 2 weeks to queries. Responds in 1-2 months to mss. Sample copy for $4. Guidelines available online.

Nonfiction Book reviews. Does not want fiction, poetry, or interviews. Query with published clips. Length: 750-1,250 words. **Pays $50.**

Tips Most of our reviews are assigned, but we occasionally accept unsolicited reviews. Send query and samples of published reviews.

AMERICAN LETTERS AND COMMENTARY

Dept. of English, Univ. of Texas at San Antonio, One UTSA Circle, San Antonio TX 78249. E-mail: amerletters@satx.rr.com. Website: www.amletters.org. Annual magazine covering innovative and challenging poetry, fiction, and nonfiction essays. "Only previously unpublished work is considered. We publish creative nonfiction essays and critical essays with experimental slant/subject matter." No kill fee. Publishes ms an average of 1 year after acceptance. Accepts simultaneous submissions. Guidelines available.

Nonfiction "No résumés, reviews of your work, or lengthy lists of previous publications. Do not send an SASE for response. Submissions will not be returned."

Fiction Needs experimental. 10 pages or less

Poetry Submit maximum 3-5 poems. Length: 10 lines.

Tips "Our reading period is Oct. 1st - Mar. 1st. A brief cover letter is always welcome. Read a recent issue before submitting—75% of submissions are rejected because they don't fit the journal's aesthetic or don't comply with our guidelines. No e-mailed submissions. We will make contact via e-mail by Sept. 1st for forthcoming issue inclusions. Include an e-mail address in your contact info. All rights are returned to author upon publication."

AMERICAN POETRY REVIEW

American Poetry Review, 1700 Sansom St., Suite 800, Philadelphia PA 19103. (215)496-0439. E-mail: sberg@aprweb.org. Website: www.aprweb.org. Bimonthly pubication covering the very best contemporary poetry and prose from a diverse array of authors. "*American Poetry Review* has helped to make poetry a more public art form without compromising the art of poetry. We publish a broad range of material and bring the diverse international poetry community together." Estab. 1972. Circ. 9,000-12,000. $1,000 prize awarded to 2 poets whose work appeared in *APR* the previous year. No kill fee. Buys first North American serial rights. Accepts queries by mail. Responds in 3 months to mss. Sample copy for $4.25. Online at www.aprweb.org/guidelines.shtml

Nonfiction Needs essays, interview, Review, Translations, Literary Criticism, Social Commentary.

Tips "Do not send mss. by fax or e-mail. Mss. should be typewritten or computer-printed on white 8½ × 11 paper. Prose should be double-spaced. Don't send multiple submissions."

$ $ AMERICAN SHORT FICTION

Badgerdog Literary Publishing, P.O. Box 301209, Austin TX 78703. (512)538-1305. Fax: (512)538-1306. E-mail: editors@americanshortfiction.org. Website: www.americanshortfiction.org. **Contact:** Stacey Swann, Editor. Quarterly magazine publishing new fiction in which transformations of language, narrative, and character occur swiftly, deftly, and unexpectedly. "We are drawn to evocative language, unique subject matter, and an overall sense of immediacy. We target readers who love literary fiction, are drawn to independent publishing, and enjoy short fiction. *ASF* is one of the few journals that focuses solely on fiction." Estab. 1991. Circ. 2,500. Byline given. Pays on publication. Publishes ms an average of 3 months after acceptance. Buys first North American serial rights, buys electronic rights. Accepts queries by online submission form. Accepts simultaneous submissions. Responds in 2 weeks to queries. Responds in 5 months to mss. Sample copies are available for sale through our publisher's online store. Guidelines available online.

Fiction Needs experimental, literary, translations. Does not want young adult or genre fiction. "However, we are open to publishing mystery or speculative fiction if we feel it has literary value." **Buys 20-25 mss/year.** Regular submissions are open. "We have recently switched to online submissions. **To help defray the administrative costs of this new system, we ask that our submitters pay a submission fee of $2 per story.** Submitters should visit our publisher's online store to pay the submission fee. When the transaction is complete, submitters will be directed to our Submission Manager, where they can upload their stories. Our **Submission Manager requires that uploaded files be less than 500 KB**. Send complete ms." Length: 2,000-15,000 words. **Pays $250-500.**

Tips "Anyone wishing to send a story to *American Short Fiction* should first become familiar with the work previously published by the magazine. Our standards for acceptance are extremely high."

THE AMERICAS

A Quarterly Review of Inter-American Cultural History, 3250-60 Chestnut St., MacAlister 3025, Philadelphia PA 19104. E-mail: americas@drexel.edu. Website: www.drexel.edu/academics/coas/theamericas/. Quarterly magazine One of the principal English-language journals of Latin American history. Publishes articles and reviews in history and ethnohistory about all geographical regions of the Americas and their Iberian background. "Our review provides a bridge between scholars of all the Americas and on presenting a range of subjects and perspectives. Articles on the cultural, social, religious, and intellectual history of Latin America and the Borderlands are particularly encouraged, as is research which places these themes in a comparative framework with any region of the world. We take a special interest in the history of the Franciscan presence in the Americas." Estab. 1944. No kill fee. Accepts queries by mail, e-mail. Online at www.drexel.edu/academics/coas/theamericas/style.htm.

Nonfiction Needs essays, expose, historical, opinion, religious, Translations. The Inter-American Notes section is an important part of *The Americas*. It includes short reports on archives, research projects, conferences, scholarly competitions and awards, and cultural news. Other features include publication of translations of documents that may be of use in classroom teaching. We do not accept unsolicited book reviews

Tips "We prefer MS Word or .rtf file submissions. Mss should be double-spaced. Use American spelling rather than British. When in doubt, consult The American Heritage Dictionary of the English Language, 3d ed. Use as few capitals as possible. Use endnotes rather than footnotes. Send your electronic ms as an e-mail attachment. Or, mail two copies."

$ THE ANTIGONISH REVIEW

St. Francis Xavier University, P.O. Box 5000, Antigonish NS B2G 2W5 Canada. (902)867-3962. Fax:

(902)867-5563. E-mail: tar@stfx.ca. Website: www.antigonishreview.com. **Contact:** Bonnie McIsaac, office manager. **100% freelance written**. Quarterly magazine. Literary magazine for educated and creative readers. Estab. 1970. Circ. 850. Byline given. Pays on publication. Offers variable kill fee. Publishes ms an average of 8 months after acceptance. Rights retained by author. Editorial lead time 4 months. Submit seasonal material 4 months in advance. Accepts queries by mail, fax. Responds in 1 month to queries. Responds in 6 months to mss. Sample copy for $7 or online Writer's guidelines for #10 SASE or online

Nonfiction Needs essays, interview, book reviews/articles. No academic pieces. **Buys 15-20 mss/year.** Query. Length: 1,500-5,000 words **Pays $50-150.**

Fiction Literary. No erotica. **Buys 35-40 mss/year.** Send complete ms. Length: 500-5,000 words. **Pays $100 for stories.**

Poetry Buys 100-125 poems/year. Submit maximum 5 poems. **Pays $30/full page**.

Tips "Send for guidelines and/or sample copy. Send ms with cover letter and SASE with submission."

$ ANTIOCH REVIEW

P.O. Box 148, Yellow Springs OH 45387-0148. E-mail: mkeyes@antiochreview.org. Website: http://review.antioch.edu. Quarterly magazine for general, literary, and academic audience. Literary and cultural review of contemporary issues, and literature for general readership. Estab. 1941. Circ. 5,000. Byline given. Pays on publication. Publishes ms an average of 10 months after acceptance. Responds in 3-6 months to mss. Sample copy for $7. Guidelines available online.

Nonfiction Contemporary articles in the humanities and social sciences, politics, economics, literature, and all areas of broad intellectual concern. Somewhat scholarly, but never pedantic in style, eschewing all professional jargon. Lively, distinctive prose insisted upon. We *do not* read simultaneous submissions. Length: 2,000-8,000 words. **Pays $15/printed page.**

Fiction Contact: Fiction editor. Quality fiction only, distinctive in style with fresh insights into the human condition. Needs experimental, contemporary. No science fiction, fantasy, or confessions. generally under 8,000 **Pays $15/printed page.**

Poetry No light or inspirational verse. **Pays $15/printed page.**

$ ☐ ARC

Canada's National Poetry Magazine, Arc Poetry Society, P.O. Box 81060, Ottawa ON K1P 1B1 Canada. E-mail: arc@arcpoetry.ca. Website: www.arcpoetry.ca. Semiannual magazine featuring poetry, poetry-related articles, and criticism. Our focus is poetry, and Canadian poetry in general, although we do publish writers from elsewhere. We are looking for the best poetry from new and established writers. We often have special issues. Send a SASE for upcoming special issues and contests. Estab. 1978. Circ. 1,500. Byline given. Pays on publication. Publishes ms an average of 6 months after acceptance. Buys one-time rights. Responds in 4 months. Guidelines for #10 SASE.

Nonfiction Needs essays, interview, book reviews. Query first. Length: 500-4,000 words. **Pays $40/printed page (Canadian), and 2 copies.**

Photos Query first. Pays $300 for 10 photos Buys one time rights.

Poetry Needs avant-garde, free verse. E-mail submissions not accepted. Buys 60 poems/year. Submit maximum 5 poems. **Pays $40/printed page (Canadian).**

Tips Please include brief biographical note with submission.

ARKANSAS REVIEW

A Journal of Delta Studies, P.O. Box 1890, State University AR 72467. (870)972-3674. Fax: (870)972-3045. E-mail: delta@astate.edu. Website: www.clt.astate.edu/arkreview. **90% freelance written**. Triannual magazine covering the 7-state Mississippi River Delta region. All material, creative and scholarly, published in the *Arkansas Review*, must evoke or respond to the natural and/or cultural experience of the Mississippi River Delta region. Estab. 1998. Circ. 700. Byline given. No kill fee. Buys first North American serial rights. Editorial lead time 4 months. Submit seasonal material 8 months in advance. Accepts queries by mail, fax. Accepts simultaneous submissions. Responds in 2 weeks to queries. Responds in 4 months to mss. Sample copy for $7.50. Guidelines available online.

Nonfiction Needs book excerpts, essays, general interest, historical, interview, personal experience, photo feature. **Buys 2-3 mss/year.** Send complete ms. Length: 500-10,000 words.

Photos Contact: Kim Vickrey, art editor. State availability. Reviews contact sheets, GIF/JPEG files. Offers no additional payment for photos accepted with ms. Buys one time rights.

Fiction Needs ethnic, experimental, historical, humorous, mainstream, mystery, novel concepts. **Buys 6-8 mss/year.** Send complete ms. 10,000 words maximum

Poetry Needs avant-garde, free verse, traditional. Buys 20-24 poems/year. Submit maximum 6 poems. Length: 1-100 lines.

Tips Submit via mail. E-mails are more likely to be overlooked or lost. Submit a cover letter, but don't try to impress us with credentials or explanations of the submission. Immerse yourself in the literature of the Delta, but provide us with a fresh and original take on its land, its people, its culture. Surprise us. Amuse us. Recognize what makes this region particular as well as universal, and take risks. Help us shape a new Delta literature.

ARSENIC LOBSTER

E-mail: lobster@magere.com. Website: http://arseniclobster.magere.com. (Anthology: annual) (Online: Apr., Aug., Dec.) journal & book covering poetry. "Poems should be timeless, rich in imagery and edgy; seeking elegant emotion, articulate experiment. Be compelled to write." No kill fee. Accepts queries by e-mail, online submission form. Accepts simultaneous submissions. Online at: http://arseniclobster.magere.com/submission.html

Photos Reviews PDF or JPG.

Poetry Contact: Lissa Kiernan, poetry editor. Needs free verse. "We do not want political rants or Hallmark poetry." Submit maximum 3-5 poems.

Tips "All works must be previously unpublished. Include a lively, short biography. Poetry topics, reviews and criticism, and art/photographs (pdf or jpg attachment only) are also welcome."

$ ARTS & LETTERS

Journal of Contemporary Culture, Georgia College & State University, Campus Box 89, Milledgeville GA 31061. E-mail: al@gcsu.edu. Website: al.gcsu.edu. Semiannual magazine covering poetry, fiction, creative nonfiction, and commentary on contemporary culture. The journal features the mentors interview series and the world poetry translation series. Also, it is the only journal nationwide to feature authors and artists that represent such an eclectic range of creative work. Estab. 1999. Circ. 1,500. Pays on publication. No kill fee. Publishes ms an average of 6-12 months after acceptance. Rights revert to author after publication. Responds in 2 months to mss. Sample copy for $5, plus $1 for postage. Guidelines available online.

Nonfiction Contact: Karen Salyer McElmurray, creative nonfiction editor. Looking for creative nonfiction.

Fiction Contact: Allen Gee, fiction editor. No genre fiction. **Buys 6 mss/year.** Length: 3,000-7,500 words. **Pays $50 minimum or $10/published page.**

Poetry Contact: Alice Friman, poetry editor.

Tips An obvious, but not gimmicky, attention to fresh usage of language. A solid grasp of the craft of story writing. Fully realized work.

BABEL FRUIT

E-mail: editors@babelfruit.org. Website: www.babelfruit.com. Biannual online poetry journal. "We publish literature of exile, expatriation, repatriation, integration and exploration. We want to read poetry under the influence of 'the other.' Travel, look around or reach within. Wherever you see the other." Accepts previously published material.

Nonfiction Needs book excerpts, essays, interview, Translations, Book Reviews, MP3 Recording of Readings (Please send propaganda.) Don't Share your recreational drug stories (unless you're very good). "Do not send us writing with political intentions. Don't share your recreational drug stories (unless you're very good). We don't accept work that has a primary focus on portraying the other as a victim or oppressor."

Fiction Needs experimental.

Poetry Submit maximum 3-6 poems.

Tips "If you use an attachment to submit, use: babelfruit.submission.doc and put your name in the subject line. We invite new and established writers."

N THE BALTIMORE REVIEW

A National Journal of Poetry, Fiction, and Creative Nonfiction, P.O. Box 36418, Towson MD 21286. Website: www.baltimorereview.org. **100% freelance written**. Semiannual journal. "The Baltimore Review publishes poetry, fiction, and creative nonfiction from Baltimore and beyond." Estab. 1996. Circ. 1,200. Byline given. Contributor paid in copies. No kill fee. Publishes ms an average of 6 months after acceptance. Buys first North American serial rights. Accepts queries by mail. Accepts simultaneous submissions. Responds in 6 weeks to queries. Responds in 4 months to mss. Sample copy for $10. Guidelines available online.

- "We publish work of high literary quality from established and new writers. No specific preferences regarding theme or style, and all are considered."

Nonfiction Needs essays, interview, personal experience, travel. **Buys 4/year mss/year.** Send complete ms. Length: 1,000-6,000 words. Limit agreed upon in advance.
Photos Send photos. Identification of subjects required. Reviews contact sheets. Negotiates payment individually
Fiction Needs ethnic, experimental, novel concepts. No genre fiction. **Buys 25/year mss/year.** Send complete ms. Length: 100-6,000 words.
Poetry Needs avant-garde, free verse, haiku, light verse, traditional. Buys 25/year poems/year. Submit maximum 4 poems. 4 pages
Tips "Please read what is being published in other literary journals, including our own. As in any other profession, writers must know what the trends and the major issues are in the field."

N THE BAREFOOT MUSE

A Journal of Formal Metrical Verse, P.O. Box 115, Hainesport NJ 08036. E-mail: editor@barefootmuse.com. Website: www.barefootmuse.com. **Contact:** Anna Evans, ed. Semiannual magazine covering formal poetry and metrical verse. "Publishes essays on aspects of formal/metrical poetry, and reviews of books with a noticeable proportion of formal poetry. You may submit your book or chapbook for review. Copies will not be returned. Provides balanced, respectful reviews which shrink neither from praise nor criticism, as tools to inform a prospective buyer/reader. Bios requested along with acceptance notices." Estab. 2005. No kill fee. Accepts queries by mail, e-mail. Accepts previously published material. Accepts simultaneous submissions. Responds in 2 months to mss.
Poetry No free verse; only poems in received forms, or which use meter (rhyme is optional). Submit maximum 3-6 poems.
Tips "Submissions are welcome all year. Editorial deadlines are: May 15th for the June issue, and Nov. 15th for the Dec. issue. Include SASE and e-mail address for reply. I will not open attachments without prior arrangement."

N BARRELHOUSE

E-mail: yobarrelhouse@barrelhousemag.com. Website: www.barrelhousemag.com. Biannual magazine featuring fiction, poetry, interviews and essays about music, art and the detritus of popular culture. "Not accepting poetry and fiction at this time. Wants nonfiction & online stuff." Byline given. No kill fee. Does not accept previously published work.Accepts simultaneous submissions. Responds in 2-3 months to mss.
Nonfiction Needs "We're looking specifically for essays that touch on pop culture in some way." Send complete ms; Word or .rft files only. **Pays 2 contributor copies.**
Fiction Needs experimental, humorous, mainstream. Send complete ms. **Pays 2 contributor copies.**
Poetry Submit maximum 3-5 poems.
Tips "We only take submissions through our online submission center now. No snail mail."

BELLINGHAM REVIEW

Mail Stop 9053, Western Washington University, Bellingham WA 98225. (360)650-4863. E-mail: bhreview@wwu.edu. Website: www.wwu.edu/bhreview. **Contact:** Chas Hoppe, managing editor. **100% freelance written**. Annual nonprofit magazine. "*Bellingham Review* seeks literature of palpable quality; stories, essays, and poems that nudge the limits of form or execute traditional forms exquisitely." Estab. 1977. Circ. 1,600. Byline given. Pays on publication when funding allows No kill fee. Publishes ms an average of 6 months after acceptance. Buys first North American serial rights. Editorial lead time 6 months. Accepts simultaneous submissions. Responds in 1-6 months to mss. Sample copy for $7. Guidelines available online.
Nonfiction Contact: Nonfiction Editor. Needs essays, personal experience. Does not want anything nonliterary. **Buys 4-6 mss/year.** Send complete ms. 9,000 words maximum. **Pays as funds allow, plus contributor copies.**
Fiction Contact: Fiction Editor. Literary short fiction. Needs experimental, humorous. Does not want anything nonliterary. **Buys 4-6 mss/year.** Send complete ms. 9,000 words maximum. **Pays as funds allow**.
Poetry Contact: Poetry Editor. Needs avant-garde, free verse, traditional. Will not use light verse. Buys 10-30 poems/year. Submit maximum 3 poems. Indicate approximate word count on prose pieces. **Pays as funds allow**.
Tips "Open submission period is from Sept. 15-Dec. 15. Manuscripts arriving between December 16 and September 14 will be returned unread. The *Bellingham Review* holds 3 annual contests: the 49th Parallel Poetry Award, the Annie Dillard Award in Nonfiction, and the Tobias Wolff Award in Fiction.

Submissions: December 1 and March 15. See the individual listings for these contests under Contests & Awards for full details."

BELOIT POETRY JOURNAL

Beloit Poetry Journal, P.O. Box 151, Farmington ME 04938. (207)778-0020. E-mail: bpj@bpj.org. Website: www.bpj.org. Quarterly magazine covering contemporary poetry. "The *BPJ* is open to a wide range of forms and styles. We are always watching for new poets, quickened language and poems that offer a new purchase on the political or social landscape. The Chad Walsh Poetry Prize ($3,500 in 2009) is awarded to the author of the poem or group of poems the editorial board judges to be outstanding among those we published during the previous year." Estab. 1950. No kill fee. Responds in 1-16 weeks to queries. Sample copy for $5.

Poetry Limit submissions to 5 pages or a single long poem. **We pay in contributor's copies**.

Tips "We seek only unpublished poems or translations of poems not already available in English. Poems may be submitted electronically on our website or by postal mail. Before submitting, please buy a sample issue or browse our website archive."

BIG BRIDGE

Big Bridge Press, P.O. Box 870, Guerniville CA 95446. E-mail: walterblue@bigbridge.org. Website: www.bigbridge.org. Website covering poetry, fiction, nonfiction, essays, journalism and art. "*Big Bridge* is a webzine of poetry and everything else. If we like it, we'll publish it. We're interested in poetry, fiction, nonfiction essays, journalism and art (photos, line drawings, performance, installations, siteworks, comix, graphics)." No kill fee. Accepts previously published material. Guidelines available.

Nonfiction Needs essays, interview, Reviews.

Photos Contact: Terri Carrion, editor. Reviews negatives, prints, GIF/JPEG files. original work.

Fiction Contact: Vernon Frazer, editor.

Poetry Needs avant-garde, free verse, haiku, light verse, traditional.

Tips "Send electronic art and text to: walterblue@bigbridge.org, or mail disks and hard copy (SASE). We are guided by whimsy and passion and urgency. Each issue will feature an online chapbook."

THE BIG UGLY REVIEW

490 Second St., Suite 200, San Francisco CA 94107. E-mail: info@biguglyreview.com. Website: www.biguglyreview.com. **100% freelance written**. Literary magazine published twice a year. *The Big Ugly Review* showcases emerging and established writers, photographers, filmmakers and musicians. Each issue includes fiction (short stories and flash fiction), creative nonfiction, poetry, photo-essays, short films of 5 minutes or less, and original, downloadable songs, all related to that issue's theme. There is also a contest in each issue called And So It Begins. in which writers create a flash fiction story of up to 500 words that begins with a first sentence given on our website. Estab. 2004. Circ. 10,000. Byline given. Publishes ms an average of 1 month after acceptance. Editorial lead time 1-2 months. Accepts queries by mail, e-mail. Accepts previously published material. Accepts simultaneous submissions. Responds in 1 week to queries. Reports 1 month after deadline on mss. Sample copy available online. Guidelines available online.

Nonfiction Needs book excerpts, essays, humor, personal experience, photo feature, creative nonfiction, personal essay, or standalone memoir excerpt inspired by the issue's theme. Please see website for upcoming issue themes. **Accepts 15-20 mss/year.** Send complete ms. Length: 3,000 words maximum.

Photos Contact: photo@biguglyreview.com. Send photos. Captions required. Reviews GIF/JPEG files. Offers no additional payment for photos accepted with ms.

Fiction Contact: Elizabeth Bernstein, fiction editor. "We accept short stories up to 3,000 words on the theme; flash fiction up to 1,000 words on the theme, and submissions to our And So It Begins. contest, in which contributors write a flash fiction story up to 500 words that begins with a sentence we provide on our website." Needs experimental, mainstream, novel concepts, slice-of-life vignettes, literary. Does not want work that is unrelated to the issue's theme. Please check website for theme. **Accepts 30-35 mss/year.** Send complete ms.

Poetry Contact: Miriam Pirone, poetry editor. Needs avant-garde, free verse, traditional. Accepts 15-25 poems/year.

Tips "E-mail submissions are preferred over hard copy. Send submissions to the appropriate editor. *The Big Ugly Review* is a nonpaying market at this time. See website for complete guidelines."

THE BINNACLE

University of Maine at Machias, 9 O'Brien Ave., Machias ME 04654. E-mail: ummbinnacle@maine.edu. Website: www.umm.maine.edu/binnacle. **100% freelance written**. Semiannual alternative paper format covering general arts. We publish an alternative format journal of literary and visual art. We are restless about the ossification of literature and what to do about it. Estab. 1957. Circ. 300. No kill fee. Publishes ms an average of 3 months after acceptance. Buys one-time rights. Editorial lead time 2-3 months. Submit seasonal material 3 months in advance. Accepts queries by mail, e-mail. Accepts simultaneous submissions. Responds in 1 month to queries. Responds in 3 months to mss. Sample copy for $5. Writer's guidelines online at website or by e-mail.

Nonfiction Needs humor, personal experience. **Buys 1-2 mss/year.** Send complete ms. Length: 100-750 words.

Photos Send photos. Reviews prints, GIF/JPEG files. Offers no additional payment for photos accepted with ms. Buys one time rights.

Fiction Needs ethnic, experimental, humorous, mainstream, slice-of-life vignettes. No extreme erotica, fantasy, horror, or religious, but any genre attuned to a general audience can work. **Buys 10-15 mss/year.** Send complete ms. 1,500 words maximum.

Poetry Needs avant-garde, free verse, haiku, light verse, traditional. No greeting card poetry. Buys 10-15 poems/year. Submit maximum 5 poems. 100 lines maximum.

Tips We want fiction, poetry, and images that speak to real people, people who have lives, people who have troubles, people who laugh too.

THE BITTER OLEANDER

The Bitter Oleander Press, 4983 Tall Oaks Dr., Fayetteville NY 13066-9776. Fax: (315)637-5056. E-mail: info@bitteroleander.com. Website: www.bitteroleander.com. **100% freelance written**. Semiannual magazine covering poetry and short fiction, and translations of contemporary poetry and short fiction. "Our intent is to upgrade a language that's been ruined by repetition." Estab. 1974. Circ. 1,200. Byline given. No kill fee. Publishes ms an average of 1-6 months after acceptance. Buys one-time rights, buys rights revert back to author upon publication rights. Editorial lead time 6 months. Accepts queries by mail, e-mail. Accepts simultaneous submissions. Responds in 1 week to submissions Sample copy for $10. Guidelines available online.

Fiction Needs experimental. Does not want family stories with moralistic plots, and no fantasy that involves hyper-reality of any sort. **Buys 8 mss/year.** Query. Length: 300-2,500 words. **Pays in copies.**

Poetry Needs avant-garde, free verse, haiku. Does not want rhyme and meter or most traditional forms. Submit maximum 8 poems. Length: 1-60 lines. **Pays in copies.**

Tips "If you are writing poems or short fiction in the tradition of 95% of all journals publishing in this country, then your work will usually not fit for us."

$ BLACK WARRIOR REVIEW

P.O. Box 862936, Tuscaloosa AL 35486-0027. (205)348-4518. Website: www.bwr.ua.edu. **Contact:** Jenny Gropp Hess, editor. **90% freelance written**. Semiannual magazine of fiction, poetry, essays, art, comics and reviews. "We publish contemporary fiction, poetry, reviews, essays, and art for a literary audience. We publish the freshest work we can find." Estab. 1974. Circ. 2,000. Byline given. Pays on publication. Publishes ms an average of 6 months after acceptance. Buys first rights. Accepts simultaneous submissions. Responds in 4 months to mss. Sample copy for $10. Guidelines available online.

Nonfiction Contact: Katie Jean Shinkle, nonfiction editor. Needs interview, Seeks creative nonfiction that experiments with form and content and offers up new perspectives. **Buys 5 mss/year.** No queries; send complete ms. **Pays up to $100, copies, and a 1-year subscription.**

Fiction Contact: Stephen Gropp Hess, fiction editor. Publishes novel excerpts if under contract to be published. One story/chapter per envelope, please. Want work that is conscious of form and well-crafted. We are open to good experimental writing and short-short fiction. No genre fiction please. **Buys 10 mss/year. Pays up to $150, copies, and a 1-year subscription.**

Poetry Contact: Daniela Olszewska, poetry editor. Buys 35 poems/year. Submit maximum 7 poems. **Pays up to $75, copies, and a 1-year subscription.**

Tips "Read *BWR* before submitting. Send us only your best work. Address all submissions to the appropriate genre editor."

⊘ BOOKLIST

American Library Association, 50 E. Huron St., Chicago IL 60611. (312)280-5715. Fax: (312)337-6787. E-mail: booklist@ala.org. Website: www.ala.org/booklist. **Contact:** Mary Frances Wilkens. **30% freelance written**. Biweekly magazine covering library selection, book publishing. Estab. 1905. Circ. 26,000. Byline given. Pays on publication. No kill fee. Publishes ms an average of 6 weeks after acceptance. Buys all rights. Editorial lead time 3 months. Submit seasonal material 6 months in advance. Accepts queries by mail, fax. Sample copy free. Guidelines available online.

- *Booklist* does not accept unsolicited mss.

Nonfiction No unsolicited mss. Reviews must be assigned by editors. Query with published clips. Length: 140-200 words. **Payment varies for assigned articles.**

Columns/Departments Writers & Readers (established writers talk about writing for the library audience), 1,000 words. 4 Query with published clips. **Payment varies.**

Tips Already-published reviewers are the best prospects. Must demonstrate an understanding of the subject matter and of the public and/or school library markets. Unsolicited reviews or articles are not welcome.

BOOK/MARK QUARTERLY REVIEW

P.O. Box 516, Miller Place NY 11764. (631)331-4118. E-mail: cyberpoet@optonline.net. **Contact:** Mindy Kronenberg, editor. **90% freelance written**. Quarterly newsletter. "*Book/Mark* is dedicated to publishing reviews of books and magazines by small and independent presses. We are eclectic and cover a wide variety of genres and topics, including literary subjects, the arts, popular culture, politics, history, and the sciences." Estab. 1994. Circ. 800. Byline given. No kill fee. Publishes ms an average of 3-6 months after acceptance. Buys first North American serial rights. Editorial lead time 3 months. Submit seasonal material 3-6 months in advance. Accepts queries by mail, e-mail, phone. Accepts previously published material. Accepts simultaneous submissions. Responds in 1 week to queries. Responds in 1 month to mss. Sample copy for $3 and SASE with 1 first-class stamp. Guidelines for #10 SASE.

Nonfiction We only publish book reviews and essays about books. Does not want fiction or poetry. Query. Length: 600-950 words.

Tips "We like reviews that zero in on the virtues and interesting aspects of books. Writers should be empathetic to the topics or close to the genre of each reviewed work."

$$ BOULEVARD

Opojaz, Inc., 6614 Clayton Rd., Box 325, Richmond Heights MO 63117. (314)862-2643. Fax: (314)862-2982. E-mail: richardburgin@att.net. Website: www.boulevardmagazine.org. **Contact:** Richard Burgin, editor. **100% freelance written**. Triannual magazine covering fiction, poetry, and essays. "*Boulevard* is a diverse literary magazine presenting original creative work by well-known authors, as well as by writers of exciting promise." Estab. 1985. Circ. 11,000. Byline given. Pays on publication. Offers no kill fee. Publishes ms an average of 9 months after acceptance. Buys first North American serial rights. Rights revert to author upon publication. Accepts queries by mail. Accepts simultaneous submissions. Responds in 2 weeks to queries. Responds in 3 months to mss. Sample copy for $10 Guidelines available online.

O━ "Break in with a touching, intelligent, and original story, poem, or essay."

Nonfiction Needs book excerpts, essays, interview, opinion, photo feature. No pornography, science fiction, children's stories, or westerns. **Buys 10 mss/year.** Send complete ms. 10,000 words maximum. **Pays $20/page, minimum $150.**

Fiction Contact: Richard Burgin, editor. Needs confession, experimental, mainstream, novel excerpts. "We do not want erotica, science fiction, romance, western, horror, or children's stories." **Buys 20 mss/year.** Send complete ms. 8,000 words maximum. **$20/page; minimum $150**.

Poetry Needs avant-garde, free verse, haiku, traditional. "Do not send us light verse." Buys 80 poems/year. Submit maximum 5 poems. Length: 200 lines. **$25-250 (sometimes higher)**.

Tips "Read the magazine first. The work *Boulevard* publishes is generally recognized as among the finest in the country. We continue to seek more good literary or cultural essays. Send only your best work."

BRAIN, CHILD

The Magazine for Thinking Mothers, March Press, P.O. Box 714, Lexington VA 24450. E-mail: editor@brainchildmag.com. Website: www.brainchildmag.com. **90% freelance written**. Quarterly magazine covering the experience of motherhood. *Brain, Child* reflects modern motherhood—the way it really is. We like to think of *Brain, Child* as a community, for and by mothers who like to think about what raising kids does for (and to) the mind and soul. *Brain, Child* isn't your typical parenting magazine. We couldn't cupcake-decorate our way out of a paper bag. We are more 'literary' than 'how-to,' more *New Yorker* than *Parents*. We shy away from expert advice on childrearing in favor of first-hand reflections by great writers (Jane Smiley, Barbara Ehrenreich, Anne Tyler) on life as a mother. Each quarterly issue is full of essays, features, humor, reviews, fiction, art, cartoons, and our readers' own stories. Our philosophy is pretty simple: Motherhood is worthy of literature. And there are a lot of ways to mother, all of them interesting. We're proud to be publishing articles and essays that are smart, down to earth, sometimes funny, and sometimes poignant. Estab. 2000. Circ. 36,000. Byline given. Pays on publication. No kill fee. Publishes ms an average of 6 months after acceptance. Buys first North American serial rights, buys electronic rights, buys and *Brain, Child* anthology rights. Editorial lead time 3 months. Submit seasonal material 6 months in advance. Accepts queries by mail, e-mail. Accepts simultaneous submissions. Responds in 1 month to queries. Responds in 1-3 months to mss. Sample copy available online. Guidelines available online.

Nonfiction Needs essays, including debate, humor, in-depth features. No how-to articles, advice, or tips. **Buys 40-50 mss/year.** Query with published clips for features and debate essays; send complete ms for essays. Length: 800-5,000 words. **Payment varies.**

Photos State availability. Model releases required. Reviews contact sheets, prints, GIF/JPEG files.

Fiction We publish fiction that has a strong motherhood theme. Needs mainstream, literary. No genre fiction. **Buys 4 mss/year.** Send complete ms. Length: 800-5,000 words. **Payment varies.**

$ $ ☐ BRICK

Brick, P.O. Box 609, Station P, Toronto ON M5S 2Y4 Canada. Website: www.brickmag.com. **90% freelance written**. Semiannual magazine covering literature and the arts. "We publish literary nonfiction of a very high quality on a range of arts and culture subjects." Estab. 1978. Circ. 4,000. Byline given. Pays on publication. No kill fee. Publishes ms an average of 3 months after acceptance. Buys first world, first serial, one-time English language rights. Editorial lead time 5 months. Responds in 6 months to mss Sample copy for $15, plus $3 shipping Guidelines available online

Nonfiction Needs essays, historical, interview, opinion, travel. No fiction, poetry, personal real-life experience, or book reviews. **Buys 30-40 mss/year.** Send complete ms. Length: 250-2,500 words. **Pays $75-500 (Canadian).**

Photos State availability. Reviews transparencies, prints, TIFF/JPEG files. Offers $25-50/photo Buys one time rights.

Tips "*Brick* is interested in polished work by writers who are widely read and in touch with contemporary culture. The magazine is serious, but not fusty. We like to feel the writer's personality in the piece, too."

BUFFALO CARP

Quad City Arts, 1715 2nd Ave., Rock Island IL 61201. (309)793-1213. Fax: (309)793-1265. E-mail: rcollins@quadcityarts.com. Website: www.quadcityarts.com. **100% freelance written**. Annual magazine. "*Buffalo Carp* is an eclectic mix of poetry, fiction, and narrative nonfiction. Our goal is to provide our readers with the best in previously unpublished, contemporary writing." Estab. 1998. Byline given. Pays on publication. Publishes ms an average of 2-4 months after acceptance. Buys first North American serial rights. Editorial lead time 6-8 months. Accepts queries by e-mail. Accepts simultaneous submissions. Responds in 2-4 weeks to queries. Responds in 6-8 months to mss. Sample copy for $5. Guidelines available online.

Nonfiction Needs personal experience, narrative nonfiction (any style). **Buys publishes 1-2 a year mss/year.** Send complete ms. Length: 2,000-3,000 words. **Pays 2 contributor copies.**

Fiction Any style; less interested in genre fiction. Needs adventure, confession, ethnic, experimental, fantasy, humorous, mainstream, mystery, science fiction, slice-of-life vignettes, suspense. Does not want sexually explicit, racist material. **Buys 2-5 mss/year.** Send complete ms. Length: 2,000-3,000 words. **Pays 2 contributor copies.**

Poetry Needs Avant-garde, free verse, light verse, traditional. Any style; no greeting card verse. Buys 15-25 poems/year. Submit maximum 5 poems. **Pays 2 contributor copies.**

Tips "Send us your best, most interesting work. Worry less about how you would classify the work and more about it being high-quality and stand-out. We are looking to go in new directions with upcoming issues, so send us what you think best represents you and not who your influences are. *Buffalo Carp* is not interested in blending in, and has no interest in homogenized work. Blow us away!"

BURNSIDE REVIEW

P.O. Box 1782, Portland OR 97207. E-mail: sid@burnsidereview.org. Website: www.burnsidereview.org. **Contact:** Sid Miller, ed. Semiannual magazine. "This is a non-profit independent poetry journal hailing from Portland, Oregon." Estab. 2004. Byline given. No kill fee. Accepts queries by e-mail. Accepts simultaneous submissions. Responds in 2-4 months to mss. Guidelines available.

Poetry Needs avant-garde, free verse, traditional. Submit maximum 3-5 poems. **Pays contributor copy.**

Tips Sponsors Annual Burnside Review Poetry Chapbook Competition.

$ BUTTON

New England's Tiniest Magazine of Poetry, Fiction and Gracious Living, P.O. Box 77, Westminster MA 01473. E-mail: sally@moonsigns.net. Website: www.moonsigns.net. **10% freelance written**. Annual literary magazine. "*Button* is New England's tiniest magazine of poetry, fiction, and gracious living, published once a year. As 'gracious living' is on the cover, we like wit, brevity, cleverly-conceived essay/recipe, poetry that isn't sentimental or song lyrics. I started *Button* so that a century from now, when people read it in landfils or, preferably, libraries, they'll say, 'Gee, what a great time to have lived. I wish I lived back then.' Submit only between April 1 and September 30 please." Estab. 1993. Circ. 1,500. Byline given. Pays on publication. No kill fee. Publishes ms an average of 3-9 months after acceptance. Buys first North American serial rights. Editorial lead time 6 months. Responds in 1 month to queries. Responds in 2 months to mss. Sample copy for $2.50. Guidelines available online.

Nonfiction Needs personal experience, cooking stories. Does not want "the tired, the trite, the sexist, the multiply-folded, the single-spaced, the sentimental, the self-pitying, the swaggering, the infantile (i.e., coruscated whimsy and self-conscious quaint), poems about Why You Can't Be Together and stories about How Complicated Am I. Before you send us anything, sit down and read a poem by Stanley Kunitz or a story by Evelyn Waugh, Louisa May Alcott, or anyone who's visited the poles, and if you still think you've written a damn fine thing, have at it. A word-count on the top of the page is fine—a copyright or 'all rights reserved' reminder makes you look like a beginner." **Buys 1-2 mss/year.** Length: 300-2,000 words. **Pays small honorarium and copies.**

Fiction Contact: W.M. Davies, fiction editor. Seeking quality fiction. No genre fiction, science fiction, techno-thriller. "Wants more of anything Herman Melville, Henry James, or Betty MacDonald would like to read." **Buys 1-2 mss/year.** Send complete ms. Length: 300-2,000 words. **Pays honorarium and subscriptions.**

Poetry Needs free verse, traditional. Seeking quality poetry. Buys 2-4 poems/year. Submit maximum 3 poems. **Pays $10-25.**

Tips "*Button* writers have been widely published elsewhere, in virtually all the major national magazines. They include, Ralph Lombreglia, Lawrence Millman, They Might Be Giants, Combustible Edison, Sven Birkerts, Stephen McCauley, Amanda Powell, Wayne Wilson, David Barber, Romayne Dawnay, Brendan Galvin, and Diana DerHovanessian. It's $2.50 for a sample, which seems reasonable. Follow the guidelines, make sure you read your work aloud, and don't inflate or deflate your publications and experience. We've published plenty of new folks, but on the merits of the work."

CALYX

A Journal of Art & Literature by Women, Calyx, Inc., P.O. Box B, Corvallis OR 97339. (541)753-9384. Fax: (541)753-0515. E-mail: editor@calyxpress.org. Website: www.calyxpress.org. Biannual journal publishes prose, poetry, art, essays, interviews and critical and book reviews. "*Calyx* exists to publish fine literature and art by women and is committed to publishing the work of all women, including women of color, older women, working class women and other voices that need to be heard. We are committed to discovering and nurturing developing writers." Estab. 1976. Circ. 6,000. No kill fee. Publishes ms an average of 6-12 months after acceptance. Accepts simultaneous submissions. Responds in 4-8 months to mss. Sample copy for $10 plus $4 postage and handling.

- "Annual open submission period is October 1-December 31. Mss received when not open will be returned. Electronic submissions are accepted only from overseas. E-mail for guidelines only."

Fiction Length: 5,000 words. **Payment dependent upon grant support. Also receive free issues and 1 volume subscription.**

Tips "Most mss are rejected because the writers are not familiar with *Calyx*—writers should read *Calyx* and be familar with the publication. We look for good writing, imagination and important/interesting subject matter."

$$ THE CAPILANO REVIEW

2055 Purcell Way, North Vancouver BC V7J 3H5 Canada. (604)984-1712. E-mail: contact@thecapilanoreview.ca. Website: www.thecapilanoreview.ca. **100% freelance written**. Triannual visual and literary arts magazine that "publishes only what the editors consider to be the very best fiction, poetry, drama, or visual art being produced. *TCR* editors are interested in fresh, original work that stimulates and challenges readers. Over the years, the magazine has developed a reputation for pushing beyond the boundaries of traditional art and writing. We are interested in work that is new in concept and in execution." Estab. 1972. Circ. 900. Byline given. Pays on publication. Publishes ms an average of within 1 year after acceptance. Buys first North American serial rights. Accepts queries by mail. Responds in 4 months to mss. Sample copy for $10 (outside of Canada, USD). Guidelines for #10 SASE with IRC or Canadian stamps or online.

Fiction Send complete ms with SASE and Canadian postage or IRCs. Needs experimental, novel concepts, previously unpublished only, literary. No traditional, conventional fiction. Want to see more innovative,

genre-blurring work. **Buys 10-15 mss/year.** 8,000 words **Pays $50-200.**
Poetry Needs avant-garde, free verse. Submit maximum 6-8 poems (with SASE and Canadian postage or IRCs). Buys 40 poems/year. **Pays $50-200.**

CAVE WALL

Cave Wall Press, LLC, P.O. Box 29546, Greensboro NC 27429-9546. E-mail: editor@cavewallpress.com. Website: www.cavewallpress.com. Biannual magazine dedicated to publishing the best in contemporary poetry. Byline given. No kill fee. Buys first North American serial rights. Accepts simultaneous submissions. Responds in 1-5 months to mss.
Poetry Needs avant-garde, free verse, haiku, light verse, traditional. Submit maximum 3-6 poems.
Tips "We encourage you to read an issue of *Cave Wall* before you submit. Find out what kind of poetry we like. Please note that we read blind. Your name should not appear on your poems."

CHA

An Asian Literary Journal, E-mail: editors@asiancha.com. Website: www.asiancha.com. Quarterly website and in the future we'll have a print anthology; covering poetry, short stories, creative nonfiction, drama and reviews from and about Asia. "Strong focus on Asian-themed creative work or work done by Asian writers and artists." Estab. 2007. No kill fee. Accepts previously published material. Accepts simultaneous submissions. Responds in 3 months to mss. by e-mail at: submissions@asiancha.com
Photos Reviews GIF/JPEG files.
Poetry Submit maximum 1-4/year poems.
Tips "Do not send attachments in your e-mail. Include all writing in the body of e-mail. Include a brief biography (100 words). Any submissions received after July 1, 2009 will be considered for Nov. 2009 issue."

$ 🌐 CHAPMAN

Chapman Publishing, 4 Broughton Place, Edinburgh EH1 3RX Scotland. (44)(131)557-2207. E-mail: chapman-pub@blueyounder.co.uk. Website: www.chapman-pub.co.uk. **Contact:** Joy Hendry. **100% freelance written**. Magazine published 3 times/year covering poetry, fiction, articles, and reviews. *Chapman*, Scotland's quality literary magazine, is a dynamic force in Scotland, publishing poetry, fiction, criticism, reviews, and articles on theatre, politics, language, and the arts. Our philosophy is to publish new work, from known and unknown writers—mainly Scottish, but also worldwide. Estab. 1970. Circ. 2,000. Pays on publication. No kill fee. Publishes ms an average of 3 months after acceptance. Buys first rights. Accepts queries by mail only. Guidelines by e-mail.
Nonfiction Needs essays, exposè, general interest, historical, humor, inspirational, interview, personal experience. **Buys 15 mss/year.** Send complete ms. **Pays £8/page (can vary).**
Fiction Any length considered – the criterion is quality. Please do not send more than one item at a time. - Prose: Ideally no longer than 3,000 words. Critical articles are usually commissioned, but not exclusively. Suggestions are always welcome. Please write with outline of idea first. Needs experimental, historical, humorous, Scottish/ international. No horror or science fiction. "Submissions should be presented as double-line-spaced typescript, with indented paragraphs. Use double quotes for dialogue and quotations, indicate italics with underscore. Avoid using footnotes – we are not an academic journal." Length: 1,000-5,000 words. **Negotiates payment individually.**
Poetry Needs avant-garde, free verse, haiku, light verse, traditional. Poetry: Broadly speaking, submissions should normally contain between four and ten poems. We do not publish single poems, exceptional circumstances apart. Poems should be one to a page. Submit maximum 10 poems.
Tips "We have no plans at present to publish longer fiction or novels. - Plays: We do not publish plays that have not been performed. If you would like to get a better impression of Chapman, individual copies of the magazine are available from us. Sample issue costs £3.45 inc p&p."

THE CHARITON REVIEW

Truman State University Press, The Chariton Review, Truman State Univ., 100 E Normal Ave, Kirksville MO 63501. (800)916-6802. E-mail: chariton@truman.edu. Website: tsup.truman.edu. Semiannual magazine covering the best in short fiction, poetry, translations, and essays. Estab. 1975. No kill fee. Guidelines available on website

$ THE CHATTAHOOCHEE REVIEW

Georgia Perimeter College, 2101 Womack Rd., Dunwoody GA 30338-4497. (770)274-5147. Website: www.chattahoochee-review.org. Quarterly magazine. We publish a number of Southern writers, but *Chattahoochee Review* is not by design a regional magazine. All themes, forms, and styles are considered as long as they impact the whole person: heart, mind, intuition, and imagination. Estab. 1980. Circ. 1,350. Byline given. Pays on publication. No kill fee. Publishes ms an average of 3 months after acceptance. Buys first rights. Accepts queries by mail. Responds in 2 weeks to queries. Responds in 4 months to mss. Sample copy for $6. Guidelines available online.

Nonfiction We look for distinctive, honest personal essays and creative nonfiction of any kind, including the currently popular memoiristic narrative. We publish interviews with writers of all kinds: literary, academic, journalistic, and popular. We also review selected current offerings in fiction, poetry, and nonfiction, including works on photography and the visual arts. We do not often, if ever, publish technical, critical, theoretical, or scholarly work about literature, although we are interested in essays written for general readers about writers, their careers, and their work. Needs essays, interviews with authors, reviews. **Buys 10 mss/year.** Send complete ms. 5,000 words maximum

Photos State availability. Identification of subjects required. Negotiates payment individually. Buys one time rights.

Fiction Accepts all subject matter except juvenile, science fiction, and romance. **Buys 12 mss/year.** Send complete ms. 6,000 words maximum **Pays $20/page, $250 max and 2 contributor's copies.**

Poetry Needs avant-garde, free verse, haiku, light verse, traditional. Buys 60 poems/year. Submit maximum 5 poems. **Pays $50/poem.**

Tips Become familiar with our journal and the type of work we regularly publish.

$ $ CHICKEN SOUP FOR THE SOUL

101 Stories to Open the Heart and Rekindle the Spirit, Chicken Soup for the Soul - Enterprises, Inc., Fax: (805)563-2945. E-mail: webmaster@chickensoupforthesoul.com. Website: www.chickensoup.com. **95% freelance written**. Paperback with 8-12 publications/year featuring inspirational, heartwarming, uplifting short stories. Estab. 1993. Circ. Over 200 titles; 100 million books in print. Byline given. Pays on publication. No kill fee. Publishes ms an average of 8 months after acceptance. Buys one-time rights. Accepts queries by mail, e-mail, fax. Accepts previously published material. Responds upon consideration. Guidelines available online.

- "Stories must be written in the first person."

Nonfiction No sermon, essay, eulogy, term paper, journal entry, political, or controversial issues. **Buys 1,000 mss/year.** Send complete ms. Length: 300-1,200 words. **Pays $200.**

Poetry Needs traditional. No controversial poetry.

Tips "We prefer submissions to be sent via our website. We no longer accept submissions by mail or fax. Stories and poems can only be submitted on our website."

$ $ CHRYSALIS READER

1745 Gravel Hill Rd., Dillwyn VA 23936. (434)983-3021. E-mail: chrysalis@hovac.com. Website: www.swedenborq.com/chrysalis. **90% freelance written**. Annual magazine. Each issue focuses on a theme: Bridges: Paths Between Worlds (2010), The Marketplace: Exchange (2011). It is very important to send for writer's guidelines and sample copies before submitting. Content of fiction, articles, poetry, etc. should be focused on that issue's theme and directed to the intellectual reader. Estab. 1985. Circ. 2,000. Byline given. Pays on publication. Publishes ms an average of 15 months after acceptance. Buys first North American serial rights. Accepts queries by mail or e-mail. Accepts simultaneous submissions. Responds in 4 weeks to queries. Responds in 6 months to mss. Sample copy for $10. Guidelines and themes by e-mail and online at website.

Nonfiction Needs essays, interviews, personal experiences. Upcoming special issues will explore contemporary questions on spiruality; include: bridges: paths between worlds; the marketplace: exchange. "We do not want inspirational or religious articles." Length: 1,500-3,000 words. **Pays $75 for assigned articles.**

Photos Send suggestions for illustrations with submission. Buys original artwork for cover and inside copy; b&w illustrations related to theme; **pays $25-150**. Captions, identification of subjects required. Offers no additional payment for photos accepted with ms. Buys one-time rights.

Fiction Contact: Robert Tucker, fiction editor. Needs adventure, fantasy, historical, science fiction: none of an overtly religious nature. Length: 1,500-3,000 words.

Poetry Contact: Rob Lawson, series editor. "We are interested in all forms of poetry, but none of an overtly religious nature." Buys 20 poems/year. Submit maximum of 6 poems. **Pays $75 for prose and $25 for poetry**.

CIMARRON REVIEW

English Dept., Oklahoma State Univ., 205 Morrill Hall, Stillwater OK 74078. E-mail: cimarronreview@okstate.edu. Website: www.cimarronreview.okstate.edu. Quarterly magazine covering fiction, poetry,

essays, and art. "We want strong literary writing. We are partial to fiction in the modern realist tradition and distinctive poetry—lyrical, narrative, etc." Estab. 1967. No kill fee. Buys first North American serial rights. Accepts simultaneous submissions. Responds in 3-6 months to mss. Guidelines available.
Tips "All work must come with SASE. A cover letter is encouraged. No e-mail submissions from authors living in North America. Query first and follow guidelines."

$ THE CINCINNATI REVIEW

P.O. Box 210069, Cincinnati OH 45221-0069. (513)556-3954. E-mail: editors@cincinnatireview.com. Website: www.cincinnatireview.com. **100% freelance written**. Semiannual magazine. A journal devoted to publishing the best new literary fiction, creative nonfiction, and poetry as well as book reviews, essays, and interviews. Estab. 2003. Byline given. Pays on publication. No kill fee. Publishes ms an average of 6 months after acceptance. Buys first North American serial rights, buys electronic rights. Responds in 6-8 weeks to mss. Sample copy for $7 (back issue) or $9 (current issue), subscription for $15. Considers submissions by mail. No e-mail submissions

- Reads submissions September 1-May 31.

Nonfiction Needs essays, interview, poetry reviews. Query. Length: 1,000-5,000 words. **Pays $25/page.**
Columns/Departments Book Reviews; Fine Art; Literary Fiction; Nonfiction; Poetry. 1,500 words. 10 Query. **Pays $25/page**
Fiction Contact: Michael Griffith, fiction editor. "Does not want genre fiction." **Buys 13 mss/year.** Query. Length: 125-10,000 words. **Pays $25/page.**
Poetry Contact: Don Bogen, poetry editor. Needs avant-garde, free verse, traditional. Buys 120 poems/year. Submit maximum 10 poems. **Pays $30/page.**

N CIPHER JOURNAL

Lucas Klein, New Haven CT E-mail: lklein@cipherjournal.com. Published on a continuing basis. Website covering broad literary translation. "Crack open this often neglected field by melding the invisibility of the translator with the identity of the artist. We also include reviews of translated literature. For a better understanding of our aesthetic, look at our Precedents page. We will post new material as it arrives and will follow no periodical schedule. Please keep posted for changes, updates and new literature." No kill fee. Accepts simultaneous submissions.
Nonfiction Needs essays, translation reviews & non-academic essays.
Tips "We welcome all submissions of works of literary translation and of creative variants along similar themes. This includes poetry, fiction, nonfiction, translation reviews and non-academic essays that are either translations themselves or are in some way relevant to a broader understanding of translation as a concept. We welcome new and original translations."

$ COLORADO REVIEW

Center for Literary Publishing, Colorado State Univ. - English Dept., 9105 Campus Delivery, Fort Collins CO 80523. (970)491-5449. E-mail: creview@colostate.edu. Website: coloradoreview.colostate.edu. Literary magazine published 3 times/year. Estab. 1956. Circ. 1,100. Byline given. Pays on publication. No kill fee. Publishes ms an average of 6 months after acceptance. Buys first North American serial rights. Rights revert to author upon publication. Editorial lead time 1 year. Responds in 2 months to mss. Sample copy for $10. Guidelines available online.

- Mss are read from August 1 to April 30. Mss received between May 1 and July 31 will be returned unread. Send no more than 1 story at a time.

Nonfiction Buys 6-9 mss/year. Send complete ms. **Pays $5/page.**
Fiction Contact: Stephanie G'Schwind, editor. Short fiction. No genre fiction. Needs ethnic, experimental, mainstream, contemporary. **Buys 15-20 mss/year.** Send complete ms. Length: under 30 ms pages **Pays $5/page.**
Poetry Contact: Don Revell, Sasha Steensen, and Matthew Cooperman , poetry editors. Considers poetry of any style. Send no more than 5 poems at one time. Buys 60-100 poems/year. **Pays $5/page.**

COMBAT

The Literary Expression of Battlefield Touchstones, P.O. Box 3, Circleville WV 26804-0003. E-mail: majordomo@combat.ws. Website: www.combat.ws. **90% freelance written**. Quarterly magazine covering the revelation and exploration of the ramifications of war upon combatants, noncombatants, and their families. Estab. 2003. Byline given. No kill fee. Buys first North American serial rights, buys first rights, buys electronic rights. Editorial lead time 3 months. Submit seasonal material 3 months in advance. Accepts queries by mail, e-mail. Responds in 3 weeks to queries. Responds in 1 month to mss. Sample copy available online. Guidelines available online.

Nonfiction Needs book excerpts, essays, expose, general interest, historical, humor, inspirational, interview, opinion, personal experience, photo feature, religious, technical, travel. Send complete ms. 8,000 words maximum.
Photos Send photos. Captions, identification of subjects required. Reviews GIF/JPEG files. Offers no additional payment for photos accepted with ms. Buys one time rights.
Fiction Needs adventure, condensed novels, experimental, fantasy, historical, horror, humorous, mystery, religious, science fiction, slice-of-life vignettes, suspense, western. Send complete ms. 8,000 words maximum.
Poetry Needs free verse, haiku, light verse, traditional. Submit maximum 5 poems. 800 words.

COMMON GROUND REVIEW

Publishing Poets Around the World, Western New England College, 40 Prospect St., Unit C1, Westfield MA 01085. E-mail: editors@cgreview.org. Website: http://cgreview.org. Magazine covering poetry from unpublished poets. "We want poems with a fresh message, that instill a sense of wonder. This is the official poetry journal of Western New England College." Estab. 1999. Accepts simultaneous submissions. Guidelines available on website.
Poetry Submit maximum 3 poems. Length: 60 lines.
Tips "For poems, use a few good images. Run-on, convoluted imagery may derail the reader. Poems should be condensed and concise, free from words that do not contribute. The subject matter should be worthy of the reader's time and appeal to a wide range of readers. Sometimes the editors may suggest possible revisions."

$$ CONFRONTATION MAGAZINE

Long Island University's Literary Magazine, Confrontation Press, English Dept., C. W. Post Campus Long Island University, 720 Northern Blvd., Brookville NY 11548-1300. (516)299-2720. Fax: (516)299-2735. E-mail: confrontation@liu.edu. Website: www.liu.edu/confrontation. **75% freelance written**. Semiannual magazine covering all forms and genres of stories, poems, essays, memoirs, and plays. A special section contains book reviews and cultural commentary. We are eclectic in our taste. Excellence of style is our dominant concern. We bring new talent to light. We are open to all submissions, each issue contains original work by famous and lesser-known writers and also contains a thematic supplement that 'confront' a topic; the ensuing confrontation is an attempt to see the many sides of an issue rather than a formed conclusion. Estab. 1968. Circ. 2,000. Byline given. Pays on publication. Offers kill fee. Publishes ms an average of 1 year after acceptance. Buys first North American serial rights, buys first rights, buys one-time rights, buys all rights. Accepts queries by mail, e-mail, phone. Accepts simultaneous submissions. Responds in 3 weeks to queries. Responds in 2 months to mss. Sample copy for $3.

- *Confrontation* does not read mss during June, July, or August and will be returned unread unless commissioned or requested.

Nonfiction Needs essays, personal experience. **Buys 15 mss/year.** Send complete ms. Length: 1,500-5,000 words. **Pays $100-300 for assigned articles. Pays $15-300 for unsolicited articles.**
Photos State availability. Offers no additional payment for photos accepted with ms. Buys one time rights.
Fiction We judge on quality, so genre is open. Needs experimental, mainstream, novel concepts, if they are self -contained stories, slice-of-life vignettes, contemporary, prose poem. No 'proselytizing' literature or genre fiction. **Buys 60-75 mss/year.** Send complete ms. 6,000 words **Pays $25-250.**
Poetry Needs avant-garde, free verse, haiku, light verse, traditional. Buys 60-75 poems/year. Submit maximum 6 poems. Open **Pays $10-100.**
Tips Most open to fiction and poetry. Prizes are offered for The Sarah Tucker Award for fiction, The H. R. Hays Poetry Award, The Sarah Russo Award (for an essay on the subject of exile), and The John V. Gurry Drama Award.

CONJUNCTIONS

Bard College, 21 East 10th St., New York NY 10003. E-mail: webmaster@conjunctions.com. Website: www.conjunctions.com. Website covering innotive fiction, poetry, drama, criticism, interviews, art and other work by some of the leading literary lights of our time, both established and emerging. We provide a forum for writers & artists whose work challenges acccepted forms and modes of expression, experiments with language and thought, and is fully realized art. Estab. 1988. No kill fee. Accepts queries by mail.

- Unsolicited mss cannot be returned unless accompanied by SASE. Electronic and simultaneous submissions will not be considered.

Nonfiction Needs essays, criticism, Interviews, Art.

Tips Final selection of the material is made based on the literary excellence, originality, and vision of the writing. We have maintained a consistently high editorial and production quality with the intention of attracting a large and varied audience.

N CONNECTICUT REVIEW

Connecticut State University, 39 Woodland St., Hartford CT 06105-2337. **Contact:** Lisa Siedlarz, man. ed. **98% freelance written**. Semiannual magazine. "*Connecticut Review* is a high-quality literary magazine. We take both traditional literary pieces and those on the cutting edge of their genres. We are looking for poetry, fiction, short-shorts, creative essays, and scholarly articles accessible to a general audience. Each issue features an 8-page color fine art section with statements from the painters or photographers featured." Estab. 1967. Circ. 2,000. Byline given. No kill fee. Publishes ms an average of 18 months after acceptance. Buys first rights, buys first electronic rights rights. Accepts queries by mail. Accepts simultaneous submissions. Responds in 6 weeks to queries. Responds in 4 months to mss Sample copy for $12 and 3 first-class stamps Guidelines for #10 SASE

- This market pays in contributor copies only. The submission period is September 1-May 15.

Nonfiction "We are looking for creative and literary essays only. They may be scholarly or personal. They should be both accessible and intellectual." Virtuality (2007); Parable and Culture (2008) Send complete ms. Length: 500-4,000 words.

Photos Send photos. Captions, identification of subjects, model releases required. Reviews contact sheets, transparencies, 8 × 10 prints. Offers no additional payment for photos accepted with ms. Buys one-time and electronic rights.

Fiction Needs experimental, literary. "No 'entertainment' fiction, though we don't mind if you entertain us while you plumb for the truth." **Buys 14 mss/year.** Send complete ms. Length: 50-4,000 words.

Poetry Needs avant-garde, free verse, haiku, traditional. No doggerel poetry. Buys 80 poems/year. Submit maximum 5 poems.

Tips "We read manuscripts blind—stripping off the cover letter—but the biographical information should be there. Be patient. Our editors are spread over 4 campuses and it takes a while to move the manuscripts around."

CRAB CREEK REVIEW

7315 34th Ave. NW, Seattle WA 98117. E-mail: crabcreekreview@gmail.com. Website: www.crabcreekreview.org. Byline given. No kill fee. Buys first North American rights. Accepts queries by mail. Accepts simultaneous submissions. Responds in 3-5 months to mss. Guidelines available online.

- "Nominates for the Pushcart Prize and offers annual Crab Creek Review editors' prize of $100 for the best poem, essay, or short story published in the previous year."

Nonfiction Contact: Jennifer Culkin, nonfiction editor. Submit up to 6,000 words. "No academic or critical essays. "

Fiction Contact: Jen Betterley, fiction editor. Accepts only the strongest fiction. Prefers shorter work. Needs confession, experimental, humorous, mainstream. Send complete ms. Length: 6,000 words. **Pays in 2 copies.**

Poetry Contact: Lana Ayers, poetry ed. Needs avant-garde, free verse, traditional. Submit maximum 5 poems. **Pays 1 copy.**

Tips "We currently welcome submissions of poetry, short fiction, and creative nonfiction."

$ CRAB ORCHARD REVIEW

A Journal of Creative Works, Southern Illinois University at Carbondale, English Department, Faner Hall, Carbondale IL 62901-4503. (618)453-6833. Fax: (618)453-8224. Website: www.siu.edu/ ~ crborchd. We are a general interest literary journal published twice/year. We strive to be a journal that writers admire and readers enjoy. We publish fiction, poetry, creative nonfiction, fiction translations, interviews and reviews. Estab. 1995. Circ. 2,200. No kill fee. Publishes ms an average of 9-12 months after acceptance. Buys first North American serial rights. Accepts simultaneous submissions. Responds in 3 weeks to queries. Responds in 9 months to mss. Sample copy for $8. Guidelines for #10 SASE.

Fiction Contact: Jon Tribble, managing editor. Needs ethnic, excerpted novel. No science fiction, romance, western, horror, gothic or children's. Wants more novel excerpts that also stand alone as pieces. Length: 1,000-6,500 words. **Pays $100 minimum; $20/page maximum, 2 contributor's copies and a year subscription.**

Tips We publish two issues per volume—one has a theme (we read from May to November for the theme issue), the other doesn't (we read from January through April for the nonthematic issue). Consult our website for information about our upcoming themes.

CRAZYHORSE

College of Charleston, Dept. of English, 66 George St., Charleston SC 29424. (843)953-7740. E-mail: crazyhorse@cofc.edu. Website: www.crazyhorsejournal.org. Semiannual magazine. We like to print a mix of writing regardless of its form, genre, school, or politics. We're especially on the lookout for original writing that doesn't fit the categories and that engages in the work of honest communication. Estab. 2,000. Circ. 1,500. No kill fee. Publishes ms an average of 6-12 months after acceptance. Buys first North American serial rights. Accepts simultaneous submissions. Responds in 1 week to queries. Responds in 3-5 months to mss. Sample copy for $5. Writer's guidelines for SASE or by e-mail.

Fiction Accepts all fiction of fine quality, including short shorts and literary essays. **Buys 12-15 mss/year. Pays 2 contributor's copies and $20 per page.**

Poetry No previously published poems. No fax, e-mail or disk submissions. Cover letter is preferred. Reads submissions year round, but slows down during the summer. Buys 80 poems/year. Submit maximum 5 poems. **Pays 2 contributor's copies, plus 1-year subscription (2 issues).**

Tips Write to explore subjects you care about. The subject should be one in which something is at stake. Before sending, ask 'What's reckoned with that's important for other people to read?'

$ CREATIVE NONFICTION

Creative Nonfiction Foundation, 5501 Walnut St., Suite 202, Pittsburgh PA 15232. (412)688-0304. Fax: (412)688-0262. E-mail: information@creativenonfiction.org. Website: www.creativenonfiction.org. **100% freelance written**. Magazine published 3 times/year covering nonfiction—personal essay, memoir, literary journalism. "*Creative Nonfiction* is the voice of the genre. It publishes personal essay, memoir, and literary journalism on a broad range of subjects. Interviews with prominent writers, reviews, and commentary about the genre also appear in its pages." Estab. 1993. Circ. 4,000. Byline given. Pays on publication. No kill fee. Publishes ms an average of 1 year after acceptance. Buys all rights. Editorial lead time 6 months. Accepts simultaneous submissions. Responds in 6 months to mss. Sample copy for $10. Guidelines online.

Nonfiction Needs essays, interview, personal experience, narrative journalism. No poetry, fiction. **Buys 30 mss/year.** Send complete ms. 5,000 words maximum. **Pays $10/page—sometimes more for theme issues.**

Tips "Points to remember when submitting to *Creative Nonfiction:* strong reportage; well-written prose, attentive to language, rich with detail and distinctive voice; an informational quality or 'teaching element'; a compelling, focused, sustained narrative that's well-structured and conveys meaning. Manuscripts will not be accepted via fax or e-mail."

THE DEL SOL REVIEW

The Literary Arts Magazine, Web del Sol, 2020 Pennsylvania Ave., NW, Suite 443, Washington DC 20006. E-mail: editor@webdelsol.com. Website: delsolreview.webdelsol.com/. **Contact:** Michael Neff. Website covering unsolicited poetry, prose poetry, creative nonfiction, short stories, and flash fiction. All forms and styles are considered. "The goal of *Del Sol Review* is to publish the best work available. Please note the editors prefer fiction and creative nonfiction containing unique and interesting subject matter." Estab. 1998. No kill fee. Buys one-time rights. Accepts queries by e-mail. *Not accepting submissions at this time.* Guidelines available online.

- "Political motives do not compromise, and we do not publish inferior work simply because a 'name' tag comes attached."

Nonfiction Contact: Lorena Knight, managing editor. "**Fiction, creative nonfiction, and flash submissions** are not being accepted at this time. **Poetry and prose poetry** is not being accepted at this time. Future submissions should be addressed to **Diana Adams**, poetry-dsr@webdelsol.com with the subject line **DSR SUBMISSION**."

Fiction Contact: Lorena Knight.

Poetry Contact: Diana Adams.

Tips "All works should reside in the body of the mail, or attached as an .rtf file. If necessary, italics may be indicated by use of the following characters: [i].[/i]."

$ ◘ DESCANT

Descant Arts & Letters Foundation, P.O. Box 314, Station P, Toronto ON M5S 2S8 Canada. (416)593-2557. Fax: (416)593-9362. E-mail: info@descant.ca. Website: descant.ca. Quarterly journal. Estab. 1970. Circ. 1,200. Pays on publication. No kill fee. Publishes ms an average of 16 months after acceptance. Editorial lead time 1 year. Accepts queries by mail, e-mail, phone. Sample copy for $8.50 plus postage. Guidelines available online.

- Pays $100 honorarium, plus 1-year's subscription for accepted submissions of any kind.

Nonfiction Needs book excerpts, essays, interview, personal experience, historical.
Photos State availability. Reviews contact sheets, prints. Offers no additional payment for photos accepted with ms. Buys one time rights.
Fiction Contact: Karen Mulhallen, editor. Short stories or book excerpts. Maximum length 6,000 words; 3,000 words or less preferred. Needs ethnic, experimental, historical, humorous. No gothic, religious, beat. Send complete ms. **Pays $100 (Canadian); additional copies $8.**
Poetry Needs free verse, light verse, traditional. Submit maximum 6 poems. **Pays $100.**
Tips Familiarize yourself with our magazine before submitting.

DIAGRAM

Dept. of English, Univ. of Arizona, P.O. Box 210067, Tucson AZ 85721-0067. E-mail: editor@thediagram.com. Website: www.thediagram.com. Online journal covers poetry, fiction and nonfiction. We sponsor a yearly chapbook competition. "*Diagram* is an electronic journal of text and art, found and created. We're interested in representations, naming, indicating, schematics, labelling and taxonomy of things; in poems that masquerade as stories; in stories that disguise themselves as indices or obituaries." No kill fee. Buys first North American serial rights. Accepts queries by e-mail. Responds in 1 month to mss

- "We sponsor yearly contests for unpublished hybrid essays and innovative fiction. Guidelines on website."

Nonfiction Contact: Nicole Walker, nonfiction editor.
Photos Reviews prints, slides, zip disks, magnetic tapes, DCs, punch cards.
Tips "Submit interesting text, images, sound and new media. We value the insides of things, vivisection, urgency, risk, elegance, flamboyance, work that moves us, language that does something new, or does something old - well. We like iteration and reiteration. Ruins and ghosts. Mechanical, moving parts, balloons, and frenzy. We want art and writing that demonstrates/interaction; the processes of things; how functions are accomplished; how things become or expire, move or stand. We'll consider anything. We do not consider e-mail submissions, but encourage electronic submissions via our submissions manager software. Look at the journal and submissions guidelines before submitting."

$ DOWNSTATE STORY

1825 Maple Ridge, Peoria IL 61614. (309)688-1409. E-mail: ehopkins@prairienet.org. Website: www.wiu.edu/users/mfgeh/dss. Annual magazine covering short fiction with some connection with Illinois or the Midwest. Estab. 1992. Circ. 500. Pays on acceptance. Publishes ms an average of 1 year after acceptance. Buys first rights. Accepts simultaneous submissions. Responds ASAP. Sample copy for $8. Guidelines available online.
Fiction Contact: Elaine Hopkins, editor. Needs adventure, ethnic, experimental, historical, horror, humorous, mainstream, mystery, romance, science fiction, suspense, western. No porn. **Buys 10 mss/year.** Length: 300-2,000 words. **Pays $50.**
Tips Wants more political fiction. Publishes short shorts and literary essays.

DRUNKEN BOAT

119 Main St., Chester CT 06412. E-mail: editor@drunkenboat.com. Website: www.drunkenboat.com. Covers poetry,prose, photography, video, web art, sound, fiction, nonfiction. No kill fee. Accepts queries by online submission form. Accepts simultaneous submissions. Responds in 3 months to mss. Guidelines available online.
Nonfiction "We are actively looking to publish more nonfiction. Our aesthetic is very broad. Well-written nonfiction of any length & style from the lyric to the journalistic is welcome. Please submit no more than 2 pieces." Needs book excerpts, essays, interview, personal experience, photo feature, Reviews, translation. **Buys 2 mss/year.** See online submissions manager
Fiction "Please submit one story or piece of longer work. We welcome the well-written in every style, from micro-fiction to hypertext to pieces of novels, original and in translation (with the writer's permission), American & from around the globe."
Poetry Needs avant-garde, traditional. "Submit no more than 3 poems, in a single document. Our aesthetic is very broad. We welcome work ranging from received form to the cutting edge avant-garde, from one line to the multi-page, from collaborations to hybridizations & cut-ups as well as works that use other media in their composition, originality & in translation (with the writer's permission), American, & from around the globe." Submit maximum 3 poems. Length: 1 lines.
Tips "Submissions should be submitted in Word & rtf format only. (This does not apply to audio, visual & web work.) Accepts chapbooks. See our submissions manager system."

ECLECTICA

No public address available, E-mail: editors@eclectica.com. Website: www.eclectica.org. Quarterly website covering finest poetry, fiction, reviews, art, essays and more!. "A sterling quality literary magazine on the World Wide Web. Not bound by formula or genre, harnessing technology to further the reading experience and dynamic and interesting in content." Estab. 1996. No kill fee. Buys first North American serial rights, buys one-time, nonexclusive use of electronic rights rights. Accepts simultaneous submissions. Guidelines available.

Nonfiction Contact: Colleen Mondor, review editor; Elizabeth Glixman, interview editor. Needs humor, interview, opinion, travel, satire.

Poetry Contact: Jennifer Finstrom.

Tips "Works which cross genres—or create new ones—are encouraged. This includes prose poems, 'heavy' opinion, works combining visual art and writing, electronic multimedia, hypertext/html, and types we have yet to imagine. No length restrictions. We will consider long stories and novel excerpts, and serialization of long pieces. Include short cover letter."

ECOTONE

Creative Writing Dept., Univ. of No. Carolina Wilmington, 601 S. College Rd., Wilmington NC 28403. (910)962-2547. Fax: (910)962-7461. E-mail: info@ecotonejournal.com. Website: www.ecotonejournal.com. Biannual magazine featuring fiction, poetry and nonfiction. "*Ecotone* is a literary journal of place that seeks to publish creative works about the environment and the natural world while avoiding the hushed tones and cliches of much of so-called nature writing. Reading period is Aug. 15 - Apr. 15." Byline given. No kill fee. Accepts simultaneous submissions. Responds in 3-6 months to mss.

Nonfiction Needs personal experience. Send complete ms.

Fiction Needs experimental, mainstream. Send complete ms.

Poetry Needs avant-garde, free verse, haiku, light verse, traditional. Submit maximum 6 poems.

Tips "www.ecotonejournal.com/submissions.html."

$ ELLIPSIS MAGAZINE

Westminster College of Salt Lake City, 1840 S. 1300 E., Salt Lake City UT 84105. (801)832-2321. E-mail: ellipsis@westminstercollege.edu. Website: www.westminstercollege.edu/ellipsis. Annual magazine. *Ellipsis Magazine* needs good literary poetry, fiction, essays, plays and visual art. Estab. 1967. Circ. 2,500. Byline given. Pays on publication. No kill fee. Publishes ms an average of 3 months after acceptance. Buys first North American serial rights. Accepts queries by mail. Accepts simultaneous submissions. Responds in 6 months to mss. Sample copy for $7.50. Guidelines available online.

- Reads submissions August 1 to November 1.

Nonfiction Needs essays.

Fiction Needs good literary fiction and plays. Send complete ms. Length: 6,000 words. **Pays $50 per story and 1 contributor's copy; additional copies $3.50.**

Poetry All accepted poems are eligible for the *Ellipsis* Award which includes a $100 prize. Past judges have included Jorie Graham, Sandra Cisneros, and Stanley Plumly. Submit maximum 3-5 poems. **Pays $10/poem, plus 1 copy.**

$ EPOCH

Cornell University, 251 Goldwin Smith Hall, Cornell University, Ithaca NY 14853. (607)255-3385. Fax: (607)255-6661. **100% freelance written**. Magazine published 3 times/year. "Well-written literary fiction, poetry, personal essays. Newcomers always welcome. Open to mainstream and avant-garde writing." Estab. 1947. Circ. 1,000. Byline given. Pays on publication. Offers 100% kill fee. Publishes ms an average of 6 months after acceptance. Buys first North American serial rights. Editorial lead time 6 months. Submit seasonal material 8 months in advance. Accepts queries by mail. Responds in 2 weeks to queries. Responds in 6 weeks to mss. Sample copy for $5. Guidelines for #10 SASE.

Nonfiction Send complete ms. Needs essays, interview. No inspirational. **Buys 6-8 mss/year.** Send complete ms. **Pays $5-10/printed page.**

Photos Send photos. Reviews contact sheets, transparencies, any size prints. Negotiates payment individually. Buys one time rights.

Fiction Contact: Joseph Martin, senior editor. Needs ethnic, experimental, mainstream, novel concepts, literary short stories. No genre fiction. Would like to see more Southern fiction (Southern US). **Buys 25-30 mss/year.** Send complete ms. **Pays $5 and up/printed page.**

Poetry Contact: Nancy Vieira Couto. Needs avant-garde, free verse, haiku, light verse, traditional. Buys 30-75 poems/year. Submit maximum 7 poems. **Pays $5 up/printed page.**

Tips "Tell your story, speak your poem, straight from the heart. We are attracted to language and to good writing, but we are most interested in what the good writing leads us to, or where."

$ $ EVENT

Douglas College, P.O. Box 2503, New Westminster BC V3L 5B2 Canada. (604)527-5293. Fax: (604)527-5095. Website: event.douglas.bc.ca. **100% freelance written**. Magazine published 3 times/year containing fiction, poetry, creative nonfiction, notes on writing, and reviews. We are eclectic and always open to content that invites involvement. Generally, we like strong narrative. Estab. 1971. Circ. 1,250. Byline given. Pays on publication. Publishes ms an average of 8 months after acceptance. Buys first North American serial rights. Accepts queries by mail, fax. Accepts simultaneous submissions. Responds in 1 month to queries. Responds in 6 months to mss. Sample copy for $5. Guidelines available online.

- *Event* does not read mss in July, August, December, and January. No e-mail submissions. All submissions must include SASE (Canadian postage or IRCs only).

Fiction We look for readability, style, and writing that invites involvement. Submit maximum 2 stories. Needs humorous, contemporary. No technically poor or unoriginal pieces. **Buys 12-15 mss/year.** Send complete ms. 5,000 words maximum **Pays $22/page up to $500.**

Poetry Needs free verse. We tend to appreciate the narrative and sometimes the confessional modes. No light verse. Buys 30-40 poems/year. Submit maximum 10 poems. **Pays $25-500.**

Tips Write well and read some past issues of *Event*.

THE EXQUISITE CORPSE

A Journal of Letters and Life, LSU English Dept., P.O. Box 25051, Baton Rouge LA 70803. E-mail: submissions@corpse.org. Website: www.corpse.org. Website covering poetry, letters, fiction, news, drama, mixed genre media. "We will read anything—stories, broken language of the heart and loins (poetry, letters, travel reports, news and gossip, mixed genre media with collage, music, sound and web-wide effects." No kill fee. Accepts queries by e-mail. Guidelines available online.

- "We prefer works of language genius, provocation, malignant brilliance, practical utopianism, profound terror, sexual delirium, and resolute enmity against commonplace, cliché, and convention."

Nonfiction Needs essays, general interest, travel.

Fiction No more than 15 double-spaced pages for prose. We will occasionally make exceptions for long essays. Submit less than 1,000 words for flash fiction.

Poetry No more than 10 pages for poetry.

Tips "We will not accept submissions until May 1, 2009. Would-be contributors should look up previous issues for an idea of how we cause damage and promote health. Only submit by e-mail either in the body or as an attachment with .rtf extension. Name your document after your last name. See our guidelines."

FAULTLINE

Journal of Art & Literature, Dept. of English and Comparative Literature, University of California at Irvine, Irvine CA 92697-2650. E-mail: faultline@uci.edu. Website: www.humanities.uci.edu/faultline. **100% freelance written**. Annual magazine covering poetry, fiction, essays, interviews, translations, and art. Estab. 1992. Circ. 1,000. Byline given. Pays on publication. No kill fee. Publishes ms an average of 5 months after acceptance. Buys first North American serial rights. Editorial lead time 4 months. Accepts queries by mail. Accepts simultaneous submissions. Responds in 4 weeks to queries. Responds in 4 months to mss. Sample copy for $5 or online. Writer's guidelines for #10 SASE or online.

- Reading period is September 15-February 15. Submissions sent at any other time will not be read.

Nonfiction Needs book excerpts, essays, humor, interview, personal experience, photo feature, travel. **Buys up to 2 mss/year.** Send complete ms. Maximum 5,000 words.

Photos Send photos. Identification of subjects required. Reviews contact sheets, transparencies, prints. Does not pay for photos. Buys one time rights.

Fiction Needs ethnic, experimental, humorous, slice-of-life vignettes. **Buys 6-9 mss/year.** Send complete ms. "While simultaneous submissions are accepted, multiple submissions are not accepted. Please restrict your submissions to one story at a time, regardless of length." Maximum 5,000 words. **Pays in contributor copies.**

Poetry Needs avant-garde, free verse, haiku, light verse, traditional. Buys 8-15 poems/year. Submit maximum 5 poems. **Pays in contributor copies.**

$ FICTION

c/o Department of English, City College, 138th St. & Covenant Ave., New York NY 10031. Website: www.

fictioninc.com. Semiannual magazine. "As the name implies, we publish only fiction; we are looking for the best new writing available, leaning toward the unconventional. *Fiction* has traditionally attempted to make accessible the inaccessible, to bring the experimental to a broader audience." Estab. 1972. Circ. 4,000. No kill fee. Publishes ms an average of 1 year after acceptance. Buys first rights. Accepts simultaneous submissions. Responds in 3 months to mss. Sample copy for $7. Guidelines available online.

- Reading period for unsolicited mss is September 15-May 15.

Fiction Needs experimental, humorous, satire, contemporary, literary. translations. No romance, science fiction, etc. **Buys 24-40 mss/year.** Length: 5,000 words. **Pays $114.**

Tips "The guiding principle of *Fiction* has always been to go to terra incognita in the writing of the imagination and to ask that modern fiction set itself serious questions, if often in absurd and comedic voices, interrogating the nature of the real and the fantastic. It represents no particular school of fiction, except the innovative. Its pages have often been a harbor for writers at odds with each other. As a result of its willingness to publish the difficult, experimental, and unusual, while not excluding the well known, *Fiction* has a unique reputation in the US and abroad as a journal of future directions."

$ FIELD: CONTEMPORARY POETRY & POETICS

Oberlin College Press, 50 N. Professor St., Oberlin OH 44074-1091. (440)775-8408. Fax: (440)775-8124. E-mail: oc.press@oberlin.edu. Website: www.oberlin.edu/ocpress. **Contact:** Linda Slocum, man. editor. **60% freelance written**. Biannual magazine of poetry, poetry in translation, and essays on contemporary poetry by poets. Estab. 1969. Circ. 1,500. Byline given. Pays on publication. Buys first rights. Editorial lead time 4 months. Accepts queries by mail, e-mail, fax, phone. Responds in 4-6 weeks to mss. Sample copy for $8. Guidelines available online and for #10 SASE.

- "No electronic submissions yet, but are planning for it. Check website after August 1 for new electronic submission guidelines."

Nonfiction Needs , poetry, poetry in translation.

Poetry Contact: Linda Slocum, man. ed. Buys 120 poems/year. Submit maximum 5 with sase poems. **Pays $15/page**.

Tips "Submit 3-5 of your best poems with a cover letter and SASE. No simultaneous submissions. Keep trying! Submissions are read year-round."

$ FIVE POINTS

A Journal of Literature and Art, Georgia State University, P.O. Box 3999, Atlanta GA 30302-3999. Fax: (404)651-3167. Website: www.webdelsol.com/Five_Points. Triannual. *Five Points* is committed to publishing work that compels the imagination through the use of fresh and convincing language. Estab. 1996. Circ. 2,000. No kill fee. Publishes ms an average of 6 months after acceptance. Buys first North American serial rights. Sample copy for $7.

Fiction Contact: Megan Sexton, executive editor. **Pays $15/page minimum; $250 maximum, free subscription to magazine and 2 contributor's copies; additional copies $4.**

THE FLORIDA REVIEW

English Dept., University of Central Florida, P.O. Box 161346, Orlando FL 32816. E-mail: flreview@mail.ucf.edu. Website: http://floridareview.cah.ucf.edu/. "For Summer 2010, The Florida Review will publish a special issue focusing on new American Indian writing. The Florida Review welcomes submissions of poetry, flash fiction, short fiction, creative nonfiction, graphic narrative, and art from Native or Indigenous writers and artists. Deadline: December 5, 2009. The Florida Review is excited to announce the 2nd Annual Young Voices Contest. Visit the contest page for submission guidelines. Deadline: January 15, 2010. 2010. The guidelines for our 2010 Editors' Award are online. Deadline is Feb. 26, 2010."

- Ranked as one of the best markets for fiction writers in *Writer's Digest* magazine's Fiction 50, June 2001.

FOLIATE OAK

University of Arkansas-Monticello, Arts & Humanities, 562 University Dr., Monticello AR 71656. (870)460-1247. E-mail: foliateoak@uamont.edu. Website: www.foliateoak.uamont.edu. **100% freelance written**. Monthly magazine covering fiction, creative nonfiction, poetry, and art. "We are a general literary magazine for adults." Estab. 1973. Circ. 500. Byline given. No kill fee. Publishes ms an average of 1 month after acceptance. Editorial lead time 1 month. Submit seasonal material 1 month in advance. Accepts queries by e-mail. Accepts simultaneous submissions. Responds in 1 week to queries. Responds in 1 month to mss. Sample copy for #10 SASE. Guidelines available online.

Nonfiction Needs essays, exposè, general interest, historical, humor, personal experience, creative nonfiction. Send complete ms. Length: 200-2,500 words.
Photos Reviews GIF/JPEG files. Offers no additional information for photos accepted with ms.
Fiction Needs adventure, ethnic, experimental, mainstream, slice-of-life vignettes. Does not want horror or confession, or pornographic, racist, or homophobic content. Length: 200-2,500 words.
Poetry Needs avant-garde, free verse, haiku, traditional. Submit maximum 5 poems.
Tips "Please submit all material via our online submission manager." http://www.foliateoak.uamont.edu

FOURTH GENRE

Explorations in Nonfiction, Michigan State Univ. Press, Dept. of English, 201 Morrill Hall, MSU, East Lansing MI 48824-1036. Website: www.msupress.msw.edu/journals/fg/. Semiannual website covering notable, innovative nonfiction ranging from personal essays and memoirs to literary journalism and personal criticism. "*Fourth Genre* gives writers a showcase for their work and readers a place to find the liveliest and most creative works in the form. Features interviews with prominent nonfiction writers, round table discussions of topical genre issues, mini-essays by selected photographers and visual artists, book reviews." No kill fee.

- Submissions for 2009 Editor's Prize Contest considered beginning Jan. 15, 2009.

Nonfiction Needs essays, reviews and capsule summaries of current books., interview, with prominent nonfiction writers, letters from readers, mini-essays by selected photographs and visual artists.
Tips "Editors invite works that are lyrical, self-interragative, meditative and reflective, as well as expository, analytical, exploratory, or whimsical. The journal encourages a writer-to-reader conversation."

THE FOURTH RIVER

Chatham College, Woodland Rd., Pittsburgh PA 15232. E-mail: fourthriver@chatham.edu. Website: fourthriver.chatham.edu. **100% freelance written**. "Biannual magazine interested in literature that engages and explores the relationship between humans and their environments through writing that is thoughtful, daring, and richly situated at the confluence of place,.space, and identity." Estab. 2005. Byline given. Pays with contributor copies only. No kill fee. Buys first North American serial rights. Accepts queries by mail. Accepts simultaneous submissions. Responds in 3 months to mss. Sample copy for $10. Guidelines available online.
Nonfiction Needs book excerpts, essays, expose, general interest, historical, humor, opinion, personal experience, travel. Send complete ms. Maximum 25 pages (double-spaced).
Fiction Needs adventure, cond novels, confession, ethnic, experimental, fantasy, historical, horror, humorous, mainstream, mystery, novel concepts, romance, science fiction, slice-of-life vignettes, suspense, western, literary. Send complete ms. Maximum 25 pages (double-spaced).
Poetry Needs avant-garde, free verse, haiku, light verse, traditional. Submit maximum 3 poems. Maximum 10 pages (double-spaced).

$ 🌐 FRANK

An International Journal of Contemporary Writing & Art, Association Frank, 32 rue Edouard Vaillant, Montreuil 93100 France. (33)(1)48596658. Fax: (33)(1)4859-6668. E-mail: submissions@readfrank.com. Website: www.readfrank.com; www.frank.ly. **80% freelance written**. Magazine published twice/year covering contemporary writing of all genres. Bilingual. Writing that takes risks and isn't ethnocentric is looked upon favorably. Estab. 1983. Circ. 4,000. Byline given. Pays on publication. Publishes ms an average of 1 year after acceptance. Buys one-time rights. Editorial lead time 6 months. Responds in 1 month to queries. Responds in 2 months to mss. Sample copy for $10. Guidelines available online.
Nonfiction Needs interview, travel. **Buys 2 mss/year.** Query. **Pays $100.**
Photos State availability. Negotiates payment individually. Buys one time rights.
Fiction Needs experimental, novel concepts, international. At *Frank*, we publish fiction, poetry, literary and art interviews, and translations. We like work that falls between existing genres and has social or political consciousness. **Buys 8 mss/year.** Send complete ms. Length: 1,000-3,000 words. **Pays $10/ printed page.**
Poetry Needs avant-garde. Buys 20 poems/year. Submit maximum 10 poems. **Pays $20.**
Tips Suggest what you do or know best. Avoid query form letters—we won't read the manuscript. Looking for excellent literary/cultural interviews with leading American writers or cultural figures. Very receptive to new Foreign Dossiers of writing from a particular country.

GARGOYLE MAGAZINE

Paycock Press, 3819 North 13th St., Arlington VA 22201. (703)525-9296. E-mail: gargoyle@

gargoylemagazine.com. Annual magazine covering eclectic poetry, fiction, photography, art, essays and interviews. We tend to publish works that are bent or edgy—experimental, magic realism/surrealism. Our next reading period will begin on June 1, 2010. Estab. 1976. No kill fee.

- Electronic submissions preferred.

Nonfiction Needs essays, humor, interview, photo feature.
Fiction Needs experimental, fantasy, horror, Surrealism. Length: 1,000-4,500 words.
Tips Recently published: Sherman Alexie, Kate Braverman, Moira Egan, Susan Gubernat, Myronn Hardy, Dallas Hudgens, Steve Kowit, Susan Smith Nash, Susan Perabo, Deborah Pintonelli, Ronald Wallace, Ian Williams, and many more.

$ THE GEORGIA REVIEW

The University of Georgia, University of Georgia, Athens GA 30602-9009. (706)542-3481. Fax: (706)542-0047. E-mail: garev@uga.edu. Website: www.uga.edu/garev. **99% freelance written**. Quarterly journal. Our readers are educated, inquisitive people who read a lot of work in the areas we feature, so they expect only the best in our pages. All work submitted should show evidence that the writer is at least as well-educated and well-read as our readers. Essays should be authoritative but accessible to a range of readers. Estab. 1947. Circ. 3,500. Byline given. Pays on publication. No kill fee. Publishes ms an average of 6 months after acceptance. Buys first North American serial rights. Accepts queries by mail. Responds in 2 weeks to queries. Responds in 2-3 months to mss. Sample copy for $10 Guidelines available online.

- No simultaneous or electronic submissions.

Nonfiction Needs essays. For the most part we are not interested in scholarly articles that are narrow in focus and/or overly burdened with footnotes. The ideal essay for *The Georgia Review* is a provocative, thesis-oriented work that can engage both the intelligent general reader and the specialist. **Buys 12-20 mss/year.** Send complete ms. **Pays $40/published page.**
Photos Send photos. Reviews 5 × 7 prints or larger. Offers no additional payment for photos accepted with ms. Buys one time rights.
Fiction We seek original, excellent writing not bound by type. Ordinarily we do not publish novel excerpts or works translated into English, and we strongly discourage authors from submitting these. **Buys 12-20 mss/year.** Send complete ms. Open **Pays $40/published page.**
Poetry We seek original, excellent poetry. Buys 60-75 poems/year. Submit maximum 5 poems. **Pays $3/line.**
Tips "Unsolicited manuscripts will not be considered from May 1-August 15 (annually); all such submissions received during that period will be returned unread. Check website for submission guidelines."

$ THE GETTYSBURG REVIEW

Gettysburg College, Gettysburg PA 17325. (717)337-6770. Fax: (717)337-6775. Website: www.gettysburgreview.com. Quarterly magazine. "Our concern is quality. Manuscripts submitted here should be extremely well written. Reading period September-May." Estab. 1988. Circ. 3,000. Byline given. Pays on publication. Publishes ms an average of 6 months after acceptance. Buys first North American serial rights. Editorial lead time 1 year. Submit seasonal material 9 months in advance. Accepts queries by mail, fax. Accepts simultaneous submissions. Responds in 1 month to queries. Responds in 3-6 months to mss. Sample copy for $11. Guidelines available online.
Nonfiction Needs essays. **Buys 20 mss/year.** Send complete ms. Length: 3,000-7,000 words. **Pays $30/page.**
Fiction Contact: Mark Drew, assisant editor. High quality, literary. Needs experimental, historical, humorous, mainstream, novel concepts, serialized, contemporary. "We require that fiction be intelligent and esthetically written." **Buys 20 mss/year.** Send complete ms. Length: 2,000-7,000 words. **Pays $30/page.**
Poetry Buys 50 poems/year. Submit maximum 5 poems. **Pays $2.50/line.**

GINOSKO

P.O. Box 246, Fairfax CA 94978. E-mail: ginoskoeditor@aol.com. Website: www.ginoskoliteraryjournal.com. **Contact:** Robert Paul Cesaretti, editor. "Ginosko: to perceive, understand, realize, come to know; knowledge that has an inception, a progress, an attainment. The recognition of truth by experience." Accepts short fiction and poetry, spoken word recordings, creating nonfiction, interviews, social justice concerns. Published semi-annually in winter and summer. Member CLMP. Circ. 4,500 eZine; website receives 750-1,000 hits/month. No byline given. No kill fee. Rights revert to author upon publication Editorial lead time 3 months. Accepts queries by mail, e-mail. Accepts previously published material. Accepts simultaneous submissions. Prefers e-mail submissions as attachments in works word processor or rich text format; cannot open .doc files

Nonfiction Send complete ms. **Pays in contributor's copies.**

Fiction Short stories and excerpts. Send complete ms. Length: 50-10,000 words. **Pays in contributor's copies.**

Poetry Poetry and prose poetry. 50-10,000 words. **Pays in contributor's copies.**

GLASS: A JOURNAL OF POETRY

No public address available, E-mail: glasspoetry@yahoo.com. Website: www.glass-poetry.com. Triannual website covering high quality poetry of all styles, forms and schools. "We are not bound by any specific aesthetic; our mission is to present high quality writing. Easy rhyme and 'light' verse are less likely to inspire us. We want to see poetry that enacts the artistic and creative purity of glass." No kill fee. Buys first North American serial rights. Accepts queries by e-mail. Accepts simultaneous submissions. Responds in 4 months to queries.

- Submissions must follow our guidelines.

Poetry Submit maximum 4 poems.

Tips "Accepts submissions from Sept. - May. We like poems that show a careful understanding of language, sound, passion and creativity and poems that surprise us. Include brief cover letter and biography. Include your e-mail address."

$ $ GLIMMER TRAIN STORIES

Glimmer Train Press, Inc., 1211 NW Glisan St., Suite 207, Portland OR 97209. Fax: (503)221-0837. E-mail: eds@glimmertrain.org. Website: www.glimmertrain.org. **90% freelance written**. Quarterly magazine of literary short fiction. "We are interested in literary short stories, particularly by new and lightly published writers." Estab. 1991. Circ. 12,000. Byline given. Pays on acceptance. Publishes ms an average of 18 months after acceptance. Buys first rights. Accepts simultaneous submissions. Responds in 2 months to mss. Sample copy for $12 on website. Guidelines available online.

Fiction Buys 40 mss/year. Submit via the website. In a pinch, send paper. up to 12,000 **Pays $700**.

Tips "Make submissions using the online submission procedure on website. Saves paper, time, and allows you to track your submissions. See our contest listings in contest and awards section."

GRIST

The Journal for Writers, English Dept., 301 McClung Tower, Univ. of Tennessee, Knoxville TN 37996-0430. Website: www.gristjournal.com. Annual magazine featuring world class fiction, poetry and creative nonfiction, along with interviews with renowned writers and essayists about craft. *Grist* is distinguished from other journals by a commitment to exploring the nuances of the writer's occupation. Byline given. No kill fee. Accepts simultaneous submissions.

Nonfiction Needs essays, how-to. Send complete ms. **Pays 2 contributor copies.**

Fiction Contact: Brad Tice, fiction editor. Needs experimental, mainstream. Send complete ms. Length: 20,000 words.

Poetry Contact: Josh Robbins, poetry editor. Needs avant-garde, free verse, traditional. Submit maximum 3-6 poems. **Pays 2 contributor copies.**

Tips "*Grist* is seeking work from both emerging and established writers, whose work is of high literary quality and value."

$ $ GUD MAGAZINE

Greatest Uncommon Denominator Magazine, Greatest Uncommon Denominator Publishing, P.O. Box 1537, Laconia NH 03247. E-mail: editor@gudmagazine.com. Website: www.gudmagazine.com. **99% freelance written**. Semiannual magazine covering literary content and art. "*GUD Magazine* transcends and encompasses the audiences of both genre and literary fiction by featuring fiction, art, poetry, essays and reports, comics, and short drama." Estab. 2006. Byline given. Pays on publication. Publishes ms an average of 6-12 months after acceptance. Buys print and world wide electronic rights from the date of first publication until agreement is terminated in writing, by snail mail, by either party. Editorial lead time 6 months. Submit seasonal material 6 months in advance. Accepts queries by online submission form. Accepts previously published material. Accepts simultaneous submissions. Responds in 6 months to mss. Guidelines available online.

Nonfiction Needs book excerpts, essays, historical, humor, interview, personal experience, photo feature, travel, interesting event. **Buys 2-4 mss/year.** submit complete ms using online form Length: 1-15,000 words. **Pays $.03/word for first rights.**

Photos Send photos. and artwork in electronic format. Model releases required for human images. Reviews GIF/JPEG files. Pays $12. Buys all rights.

Fiction Needs adventure, erotica, ethnic, experimental, fantasy, horror, humorous, science fiction, suspense. **Buys 40 mss/year.** Length: 1-15,000 words. **Pays $450.**
Poetry Needs avant-garde, free verse, haiku, light verse, traditional. Does not want anything that rhymes 'love' with 'above.' Buys 12-20 poems/year. **Pays $.03/word for first rights.**
Fillers Buys comics. Reviews GIF/JPEG files. **Pays $12.**
Tips "We publish work in any genre, plus artwork, factual articles, and interviews. We'll publish something as short as 20 words or as long as 15,000, as long as it grabs us. Be warned: We read a lot. We've seen it all before. We are not easy to impress. Is your work original? Does it have something to say? Read it again. If you genuinely believe it to be so, send it. We do accept simultaneous sumbissions, as well as multiple submissions but read the guidelines first."

$ GULF COAST: A JOURNAL OF LITERATURE AND FINE ARTS

University of Houston, Dept. of English, University of Houston, Houston TX 77204-3013. (713)743-3223. E-mail: editors@gulfcoastmag.org. Website: www.gulfcoastmag.org. "Biannual magazine covering innovative fiction, nonfiction, and poetry for the literary-minded." Estab. 1986. No kill fee. Accepts queries by mail, phone. Responds in 3-5 months to mss. Guidelines available online.
Nonfiction Contact: Nonfiction editor.
Fiction Contact: Fiction editor. Buys 5-10 ms/year. **Pays $-$100.**
Poetry Contact: Poetry editor. Submit maximum 1-5 poems.
Tips "Submit only previously unpublished works. Include a cover letter. Online submissions are strongly preferred. Stories or essays should be typed, double-spaced, and paginated with your name, address, and phone number on the 1st page, title on subsequent pages. Poems should have your name, address, and phone number on the 1st page of each."

HARPUR PALATE

A Literary Journal at Binghamton University, English Department, P.O. Box 6000, Binghamton University, Binghamton NY 13902-6000. Website: harpurpalate.binghamton.edu. **Contact:** Barrett Bowlin, Editor-in-Chief. **100% freelance written**. Semiannual literary magazine. "We have no restrictions on subject matter or form. Quite simply, send us your highest-quality fiction and poetry." Estab. 2000. Circ. 700. Byline given. No kill fee. Publishes ms an average of 1-2 months after acceptance. Buys first North American serial rights, buys electronic rights. Accepts simultaneous submissions. Responds in 8 months to mss. Sample copy for $8. Guidelines available online.
Fiction No more than 1 submission per envelope. Length: 250-8,000 words. **Pays 2 contributor copies.**
Poetry No more than 10 pages total. No response without SASE. Submit maximum 3-5 poems. **Pays 2 contributor copies.**
Tips "*Harpur Palate* now accepts submissions all year; deadline for Winter issue is November 15, for Summer issue is April 15. We also sponsor a fiction contest for the Summer issue and a poetry contest for the Winter issue. We do not accept submissions via e-mail. We are interested in high quality writing of all genres, but especially literary poetry and fiction."

N HARVARD REVIEW

Houghton Library of the Harvard College Library, Lamont Library, Harvard University, Cambridge MA 02138. (617)495-9775. Fax: (617)496-3692. E-mail: harvard_review@harvard.edu. Website: www.hcl.harvard.edu/harvardreview/. Semiannual magazine covering poetry, fiction, essays, drama, graphics, and reviews in the spring and fall by an eclectic range of international writers. "Previous contributors include John Updike, Alice Hoffman, Joyce Carol Oates, Miranda July, Jim Crace. We also publish the work of emerging and previously unpublished writers." Estab. 1992. No kill fee. Accepts simultaneous submissions. Responds in 6 months to mss.
Nonfiction Needs essays, reviews. If you are interested in reviewing for the *Harvard Review*, write to the editor and enclose 2 or more recent clips. No unsolicited book reviews or genre fiction (romance, horror, detective, etc.).
Photos Contact: Judith Larsen, visual arts editor.
Fiction Contact: Nam Le, fiction editor. Length: 7,000 words.
Poetry Contact: Major Jackson, poetry editor. Submit maximum 5 poems.
Tips "There is no reading period. Include a cover letter citing recent publications or awards and SASE. Mss must be paginated and labeled with author's name on every page. Do not submit more than 2X/yr. We accept e-mail submissions through http://www.tellitslant.com."

HAWAII REVIEW

University of Hawaii Board of Publications, 1733 Donaghho Rd., Honolulu HI 96822. (808)956-3030.

Fax: (808)956-3083. E-mail: hireview@hawaii.edu. Website: www.hawaii-review.org. **100% freelance written**. Semiannual magazine covering fiction, poetry, reviews, and art. Estab. 1973. Circ. 2000. Byline given. Publishes ms an average of 3 months after acceptance. Buys first North American serial rights, buys electronic rights. Accepts queries by e-mail, fax, phone. Accepts simultaneous submissions. Responds in 3 months to mss. Sample copy for $10. Guidelines available online.

Nonfiction Needs essays, interview. Send complete ms. Length: 0-10,000 words.

Fiction Needs confession, experimental, humorous, novel concepts, short fiction, short stories. "Does not want science fiction/fantasy, erotica, Christian evangelica, horror, cowboy." **Buys 1 ms/year.** Send complete ms.

Poetry Needs avant-garde, free verse, haiku, traditional. Does not want light verse, rhymed poetry, inspirational. Buys 1 poems/year. Submit maximum 8 poems.

Tips "Make it new. Offers $500 prize in poetry, nonfiction, and fiction."

$ HAYDEN'S FERRY REVIEW

Arizona State University, Virginia G. Piper Center for Creative Writing College of Liberal Arts & Sciences, Box 875002, Tempe AZ 85287-5002. (480)965-1337. Fax: (480)727-0820. E-mail: hfr@asu.edu. Website: www.haydensferryreview.org. Fiction, Poetry, or Art Editor. **85% freelance written**. Semiannual magazine. "*Hayden's Ferry Review* publishes the best quality fiction, poetry, and creative nonfiction from new, emerging, and established writers." Estab. 1986. Circ. 1,300. Byline given. Pays on publication. No kill fee. Publishes ms an average of 6 months after acceptance. Buys first North American serial rights. Editorial lead time 5 months. Does not accept previously published work.Accepts simultaneous submissions. Responds in 1 week or less to e-mail queries. Responds in 3-4 months to mss. Sample copy for $7.50. Guidelines available online.

- *Accepts electronic submissions only. Tell us promptly if your work has been accepted elsewhere if you submit simultaneously.*

Nonfiction Needs essays, interview, personal experience. **Buys 2 mss/year.** Send complete ms. Word length open. **Pays $50.**

Photos Send photos. Reviews slides. Offers $50 Honorarium, pays $100 for cover art. Buys one-time rights.

Fiction Contact: Editors change every 1-2 years. Needs ethnic, experimental, humorous, slice-of-life vignettes, contemporary, prose poem. **Buys 10 mss/year.** Send complete ms. Word length open. **True.**

Poetry Needs avant-garde, free verse, haiku, light verse, traditional. Buys 60 poems/year. Submit maximum 6 poems. Word length open. **Pays $50.**

$ THE HOLLINS CRITIC

P.O. Box 9538, Hollins University, Roanoke VA 24020-1538. E-mail: acockrell@hollins.edu. Website: www.hollins.edu/academics/critic. **Contact:** Cathryn Hankla. **100% freelance written**. Magazine published 5 times/year. Estab. 1964. Circ. 400. Byline given. Pays on publication. No kill fee. Publishes ms an average of 1 year after acceptance. Buys first North American serial rights. Accepts queries by online submission form Submit at www.hollinscriticssubmissions.com. Accepts simultaneous submissions. Responds in 2 months to mss. Sample copy for $3. Guidelines for #10 SASE.

- No e-mail submissions.

Poetry Needs avant-garde, free verse, traditional. We read poetry only from September 1-December 15. Buys 16-20 poems/year. Submit maximum 5 poems. **Pays $25.**

Tips We accept unsolicited poetry submissions; all other content is by prearrangement.

$ THE HUDSON REVIEW

A magazine of literature and the arts, The Hudson Review, Inc., 684 Park Ave., New York NY 10065. Website: www.hudsonreview.com. **Contact:** Paula Deitz. **100% freelance written**. Quarterly magazine publishing fiction, poetry, essays, book reviews; criticism of literature, art, theatre, dance, film and music; and articles on contemporary cultural developments. Estab. 1948. Circ. 2,000. Byline given. Pays on publication. No kill fee. Publishes ms an average of 6 months after acceptance. Editorial lead time 3 months. Accepts queries by mail. Responds in 6 months. Sample copy for $10. Guidelines for #10 SASE or online

- Send with SASE. Mss. sent outside accepted reading period will be returned unread if SASE contains sufficient postage.

Nonfiction Contact: Paula Deitz. Needs essays, general interest, historical, opinion, personal experience, travel. **Buys 4-6 mss/year.** Send complete ms between January 1 and March 31 only 3,500 words maximum **Pays 2½¢/word.**

Fiction Reads between September 1 and November 30 only. **Buys 4 mss/year.** 10,000 words maximum.

Pays 2½¢/word.
Poetry Reads poems only between April 1 and June 30. Buys 12-20 poems/year. Submit maximum 7 poems. **Pays 50¢/line.**
Tips "We do not specialize in publishing any particular 'type' of writing; our sole criterion for accepting unsolicited work is literary quality. The best way for you to get an idea of the range of work we publish is to read a current issue. We do not consider simultaneous submissions. Unsolicited manuscripts submitted outside of specified reading times will be returned unread. Do not send submissions via e-mail."

$ HUNGER MOUNTAIN

The Vermont College Journal of Arts & Letters, Vermont College of Fine Arts, 36 College St., Montpelier VT 05602. Fax: (802)828-8649. E-mail: hungermtn@tui.edu. Website: www.hungermtn.org. **30% freelance written**. Semiannual perfect-bound journal covering high quality fiction, poetry, creative nonfiction, interviews, photography, and artwork reproductions. Accepts high quality work from unknown, emerging, or successful writers and artists. No genre fiction, drama, or academic articles, please. Estab. 2002. Byline given. Pays on publication. No kill fee. Publishes ms an average of 1 year after acceptance. Buys first North American serial rights. Submit seasonal material 6 months in advance. Accepts queries by mail. Responds in 1 month to queries. Responds in 3 months to mss. Sample copy for $10. Writer's guidelines for free, online, or by e-mail
Nonfiction Creative nonfiction only. All book reviews and interviews will be solicited. No informative or instructive articles, please. Prose for young adults is acceptable. Query with published clips. **Pays $5/page (minimum $30).**
Photos Send photos. Reviews contact sheets, transparencies, prints, GIF/JPEG files. Slides preferred. Negotiates payment individually. Buys one time rights.
Fiction Needs adventure, ethnic, experimental, novel concepts, high quality short stories and short shorts. No genre fiction, meaning science fiction, fantasy, horror, erotic, etc. Query with published clips. **Pays $25-100.**
Poetry Needs avant-garde, free verse, haiku, traditional. No light verse, humor/quirky/catchy verse, greeting card verse. Buys 10 poems/year.
Tips We want high quality work! Submit in duplicate. Manuscripts must be typed, prose double-spaced. Poets submit at least 3 poems. No multiple genre submissions. We need more b&w photography and short shorts. Fresh viewpoints and human interest are very important, as is originality. We are committed to publishing an outstanding journal of arts & letters. Do not send entire novels, manuscripts, or short story collections. Do not send previously published work. See website for *Hunger Mountain*-sponsored literary prizes.

$ THE ICONOCLAST

1675 Amazon Rd., Mohegan Lake NY 10547-1804. **90% freelance written**. Quarterly literary magazine. "Aimed for a literate general audience with interests in fine (but accessible) fiction and poetry." Estab. 1992. Circ. 900. Byline given. Pays on publication. No kill fee. Publishes ms an average of 9-12 months after acceptance. Buys first North American serial rights. Editorial lead time 1-2 months. Accepts queries by mail. Responds in 2 weeks to queries. Responds in 1 month to mss. Sample copy for $5. Guidelines for #10 SASE.
Nonfiction Needs essays, humor, reviews, literary/cultural matters. "Does not want anything that would be found in the magazines on the racks of supermarkets or convenience stores." **Buys 6-10 mss/year.** Query. Length: 250-2,500 words. **Pays 1¢/word.**
Photos Line drawings preferred. State availability. Reviews 4x6, b&w prints. Negotiates payment individually. Buys one time rights.
Columns/Departments Book reviews (fiction/poetry), 250-500 words. 6 Query. **Pays 1¢/word**
Fiction Contact: Phil Wagner, editor. Buys more fiction and poetry than anything else. Needs adventure, ethnic, experimental, fantasy, humorous, mainstream, novel concepts, science fiction, literary. No character studies, slice-of-life, pieces strong on attitude/weak on plot. **Buys 25 mss/year.** Send complete ms. Length: 250-3,000 words. **Pays 1¢/word.**
Poetry Needs avant-garde, free verse, haiku, light verse, traditional. No religious, greeting card, beginner rhyming. Buys 75 poems/year. Submit maximum 4 poems. Length: 2-50 lines. **Pays $2-5.**
Tips "Professional conduct and sincerity help. Know it's the best you can do on a work before sending it out. Skill is the luck of the prepared. Everything counts. We love what we do, and are serious about it—and expect you to share that attitude. Remember: You're writing for paying subscribers. Ask Yourself: Would I pay money to read what I'm sending? We don't reply to submissions without a SASE, nor do we e-mail replies."

$ ILLUMEN

Sam's Dot Publishing, P.O. Box 782, Cedar Rapids IA 52406-0782. E-mail: illumensdp@yahoo.com. Website: www.samsdotpublishing.com/aoife/cover.htm. **Contact:** Karen L. Newman, ed. **100% freelance written**. Semiannual magazine. "*Illumen* publishes speculative poetry and articles about speculative poetry, and reviews of poetry and collections." Estab. 2004. Circ. 40. Byline given. Offers 100% kill fee. Buys first North American serial rights, buys one-time rights, buys second serial (reprint) rights. Editorial lead time 2 months. Submit seasonal material 6 months in advance. Accepts queries by e-mail. Responds in 2 weeks to queries. Responds in 3-4 months to mss. Sample copy for $8. Guidelines available online.

Nonfiction "*Illumen* buys/publishes reviews of poetry and poetry collections, and interviews with poets, writers, and teachers, so long as the interviews are related to the magazine's specialty." **Buys 5-8 mss/year.** Send complete ms. Length: 2,000 words. **Pays $10 for unsolicited articles.**

Poetry Needs avant-garde, free verse, haiku, light verse, traditional. "Scifaiku is a difficult sell with us because we also publish a specialty magazine—*Scifaikuest*—for scifaiku and related forms." Buys 40-50 poems/year. Submit maximum 5 poems. Length: 200 lines. **Pays 1-2¢/word.**

Tips "*Illumen* publishes beginning writers, as well as seasoned veterans. Be sure to read and follow the guidelines before submitting your work. The best advice for beginning writers is to send your best effort, not your first draft."

$$ IMAGE

3307 Third Ave. W., Seattle WA 98119. (206)281-2988. E-mail: image@imagejournal.org. Website: www.imagejournal.org. **50% freelance written**. Quarterly magazine covering the intersection between art and faith. "*Image* is a unique forum for the best writing and artwork that is informed by—or grapples with—religious faith. We have never been interested in art that merely regurgitates dogma or falls back on easy answers or didacticism. Instead, our focus has been on writing and visual artwork that embody a spiritual struggle, that seek to strike a balance between tradition and a profound openness to the world. Each issue explores this relationship through outstanding fiction, poetry, painting, sculpture, architecture, film, music, interviews, and dance. *Image* also features 4-color reproductions of visual art." Estab. 1989. Circ. 4,500. Byline given. Pays on publication. No kill fee. Publishes ms an average of 8 months after acceptance. Buys first North American serial rights. Accepts queries by mail, e-mail, phone. Responds in 1 month to queries. Responds in 2 months to mss. Sample copy for $16 or online. Guidelines for #10 SASE or online.

Nonfiction Needs essays. No sentimental, preachy, moralistic, or obvious essays. **Buys 10 mss/year.** Send complete ms. Length: 4,000-6,000 words. **Pays $10/page; $150 maximum for all prose articles.**

Fiction "No sentimental, preachy, moralistic, obvious stories, or genre stories (unless they manage to transcend their genre)." **Buys 8 mss/year.** Send complete ms. Length: 4,000-6,000 words. **Pays $10/page; $150 maximum.**

Poetry Buys 24 poems/year. Submit maximum 5 poems. **Pays $2/line; $150 maximum.**

Tips "Read the publication."

$ INDIANA REVIEW

Ballantine Hall 465, Indiana University, Bloomington IN 47405-7103. (812)855-3439. E-mail: inreview@indiana.edu. Website: www.indiana.edu/~inreview. **100% freelance written**. Biannual magazine. "*Indiana Review*, a nonprofit organization run by IU graduate students, is a journal of previously unpublished poetry and fiction. Literary interviews and essays are also considered. We publish innovative fiction, nonfiction, and poetry. We're interested in energy, originality, and careful attention to craft. While we publish many well-known writers, we also welcome new and emerging poets and fiction writers." Estab. 1976. Circ. 5,000. Byline given. Pays on publication. Publishes ms an average of 3-6 months after acceptance. Buys first North American serial rights. Accepts queries by mail, e-mail. Accepts simultaneous submissions. Responds in 2 or more weeks to queries. Responds in 4 or more months to mss. Sample copy for $9. Guidelines available online.

- Break in with 500-1,000 word book reviews of fiction, poetry, nonfiction, and literary criticism published within the last 2 years.

Nonfiction Needs essays, interview, creative nonfiction, reviews. No coming of age/slice of life pieces. **Buys 5-7 mss/year.** Send complete ms. 9,000 words maximum. **Pays $5/page ($10 minimum), plus 2 contributor's copies.**

Fiction Contact: Danny Nguyen, fiction editor. "We look for daring stories which integrate theme, language, character, and form. We like polished writing, humor, and fiction which has consequence beyond the world of its narrator." Needs ethnic, experimental, mainstream, novel concepts, literary, short fictions, translations. No genre fiction. **Buys 14-18 mss/year.** Send complete ms. Length: 250-

10,000 words. **Pays $5/page ($10 minimum), plus 2 contributor's copies.**

Poetry Contact: Hannah Faith Notess, poetry editor. "We look for poems that are skillful and bold, exhibiting an inventiveness of language with attention to voice and sonics. Experimental, free verse, prose poem, traditional form, lyrical, narrative." Buys 80 poems/year. Submit maximum 6 poems. 5 lines minimum **Pays $5/page ($10 minimum), plus 2 contributor's copies.**

Tips "We're always looking for nonfiction essays that go beyond merely autobiographical revelation and utilize sophisticated organization and slightly radical narrative strategies. We want essays that are both lyrical and analytical where confession does not mean nostalgia. Read us before you submit. Often reading is slower in summer and holiday months. Only submit work to journals you would proudly subscribe to, then subscribe to a few. Take care to read the latest 2 issues and specifically mention work you identify with and why. Submit work that `stacks up' with the work we've published. Offers annual poetry, fiction, short-short/prose-poem prizes. See website for full guidelines."

$$ INKWELL

Manhattanville College, 2900 Purchase St., Purchase NY 10577. (914)323-7239. Fax: (914)323-3122. E-mail: inkwell@mville.edu. Website: www.inkwelljournal.org. **100% freelance written.** Semiannual magazine covering poetry, fiction, essays, artwork, and photography. Estab. 1995. Byline given. Pays on publication. No kill fee. Publishes ms an average of 4 months after acceptance. Buys first North American serial rights. Editorial lead time 4 months. Accepts simultaneous submissions. Responds in 1 month to queries. Responds in 4-6 months to mss. Sample copy for $6. Guidelines free.

Nonfiction Needs book excerpts, essays, literary essays, memoirs. Does not want children's literature, erotica, pulp adventure, or science fiction. **Buys 3-4 mss/year.** Send complete ms. 5,000 words maximum **Pays $100-350.**

Photos Send photos./artwork with submission. Reviews 5 × 7 prints, GIF/JPEG files on diskette/cd. Negotiates payment individually. Buys one time rights.

Fiction Needs mainstream, novel concepts, literary. Does not want children's literature, erotica, pulp adventure, or science fiction. **Buys 20 mss/year.** Send complete ms. 5,000 words maximum **Pays $75-150.**

Poetry Needs avant-garde, free verse, traditional. Does not want doggerel, funny poetry, etc. Buys 40 poems/year. Submit maximum 5 poems. **Pays $5-10/page.**

Tips "We cannot accept electronic submissions."

INNISFREE POETRY JOURNAL

Cook Communication, E-mail: editor@innisfreepoetry.org. Website: www.innisfreepoetry.org. **Contact:** Greg McBride. Semiannual online journal publishing contemporary poetry. "Our journal continues the series of Closer Looks at the poetry of a leading contemporary poet (Marianne Boruch)." Estab. 2005. No kill fee. Buys first North American serial rights. Accepts simultaneous submissions. Guidelines available.

Poetry Needs free verse, traditional.

Tips "Welcomes original previously unpublished poems year round. We accept poems only via e-mail from both established and new writers whose work is excellent. We publish well-crafted poems, poems grounded in the specific which speak in fresh language and telling images. And we admire musicality. We welcome those who, like the late Lorenzo Thomas, 'write poems because I can't sing.'"

INTERNATIONAL POETRY REVIEW

Dept. of Romance Languages, Univ. of North Carolina, 2336 MHRA, Greensboro NC 27402-6170. E-mail: mismiths@uncg.edu. Website: www.uncg.edu/rom. **6-10% freelance written.** Semiannual magazine covering poems from contemporary writers in all languages, with facing English translations. "Contemporary translation is our primary focus, appearing in bilingual format, along with a limited section, in every issue, of poetry originally written in English. We do not adhere to any one school of translation theory." Estab. 1975. Circ. < 1,000. No kill fee. Accepts simultaneous submissions. Responds in 3-6 months to mss. Guidelines available.

Poetry Submit maximum 3-5 poems.

Tips "Please indicate clearly if SASE is for notification only. E-mail submissions accepted only from abroad. Be responsible for securing translation and publication rights as necessary."

$ THE IOWA REVIEW

308 EPB, The University of Iowa, Iowa City IA 52242. Website: iowareview.org. Triannual magazine. Stories, essays, and poems for a general readership interested in contemporary literature. Estab. 1970. Circ. 3,500. Pays on publication. Publishes ms an average of 8-12 months after acceptance. Buys first

North American serial rights, buys nonexclusive anthology, classroom, and online serial rights. Responds in 3 months to mss. Sample copy for $9 and online Guidelines available online.

- "This magazine uses the help of colleagues and graduate assistants. Its reading period for unsolicited work is September 1-December 1. From January through April, we read entries to our annual Iowa Awards competition. Check our website for further information."

Fiction "We are open to a range of styles and voices and always hope to be surprised by work we then feel we need." **Pays $25 for the first page and $15 for each additional page, plus 2 contributor's copies and a year-long subscription; additional copies 30% off cover price.**

Tips "We publish essays, reviews, novel excerpts, stories, and poems, and would like for our essays not always to be works of academic criticism. We have no set guidelines as to content or length, but strongly recommend that writers read a sample issue before submitting. **Buys 65-80 unsolicited ms/year**. Submit complete ms with SASE. **Pays $25 for the first page and $15 for each subsequent page of poetry or prose.**"

$ IRREANTUM

A Review of Mormon Literature and Film, The Association for Mormon Letters, P.O. Box 1315, Salt Lake City UT 84110-1315. E-mail: editor@amlpubs.org. Website: www.irreantum.org. Literary journal published 2 times/year. While focused on Mormonism, *Irreantum* is a cultural, humanities-oriented magazine, not a religious magazine. Our guiding principle is that Mormonism is grounded in a sufficiently unusual, cohesive, and extended historical and cultural experience that it has become like a nation, an ethnic culture. We can speak of Mormon literature at least as surely as we can of a Jewish or Southern literature. *Irreantum* publishes stories, one-act dramas, stand-alone novel and drama excerpts, and poetry by, for, or about Mormons (as well as author interviews, essays, and reviews). The journal's audience includes readers of any or no religious faith who are interested in literary exploration of the Mormon culture, mindset, and worldview through Mormon themes and characters either directly or by implication. *Irreantum* is currently the only magazine devoted to Mormon literature. Estab. 1999. Circ. 500. Pays on publication. Publishes ms an average of 3-12 months after acceptance. Buys one-time rights, buys electronic rights. Accepts queries by e-mail. Accepts previously published material. Accepts simultaneous submissions. Responds in 2 weeks to queries. Responds in 2 months to mss. Sample copy for $6. Guidelines by e-mail.

- Also publishes short shorts, literary essays, literary criticism, and poetry.

Fiction Needs adventure, ethnic, Mormon, experimental, fantasy, historical, horror, humorous, mainstream, mystery, religious, romance, science fiction, suspense. **Buys 12 mss/year.** Length: 1,000-5,000 words. **Pays $0-100.**

Tips *Irreantum* is not interested in didactic or polemnical fiction that primarily attempts to prove or disprove Mormon doctrine, history, or corporate policy. We encourage beginning writers to focus on human elements first, with Mormon elements introduced only as natural and organic to the story. Readers can tell if you are honestly trying to explore human experience or if you are writing with a propagandistic agenda either for or against Mormonism. For conservative, orthodox Mormon writers, beware of sentimentalism, simplistic resolutions, and foregone conclusions.

$ ISLAND

P.O. Box 210, Sandy Bay Tasmania 7006 Australia. (61)(3)6226-2325. E-mail: island.magazine@utas.edu.au. Website: www.islandmag.com. Quarterly magazine. "*Island* seeks quality fiction, poetry, essays, and articles. A literary magazine with an environmental heart." Circ. 1,500. Buys one-time rights. Accepts queries by mail. Sample copy for $8.95 (Australian). Guidelines available online.

Nonfiction Articles and reviews. **Pays $100 (Australian)/1,000 words**

Fiction Length: up to 2,500 words. **Pays $100 (Australian).**

Poetry Pays $60.

JACKET

Australian Literary Management, 2-A Booth St., Balmain NSW 2041 Australia. E-mail: p.brown62@gmail.com. Website: http://jacketmagazine.com. John Tranter, ed. Weekly website covering literature distributed over the internet. "Jacket was founded by John Tranter to showcase lively contemporary poetry and prose. Most of the material is original to this magazine, but some is excerpted from or co-produced with hard-to-get books and magazines. I cannot accept unsolicited poetry yet. If you'd like to submit a review, article or interview, send a half-page synopsis with your return e-mail address." Estab. 1997. No kill fee. Buys one-time rights, buys electronic rights. Accepts queries by e-mail. Guidelines available online.

- "Jacket's pages are constantly being polished and refined. Make sure you're looking at the latest

version of each page by choosing your browser's Reload button to refresh each page you visit."
Nonfiction Needs essays, historical, interview, religious, Book reviews.
Poetry Cannot accept unsolicited poetry.

$ THE JOURNAL

The Ohio State University, 164 W. 17th Ave., Columbus OH 43210. (614)292-4076. Fax: (614)292-7816. E-mail: thejournal@osu.edu. Website: english.osu.edu/research/journals/thejournal/. **100% freelance written**. Semiannual magazine. "We're open to all forms; we tend to favor work that gives evidence of a mature and sophisticated sense of the language." Estab. 1972. Circ. 1,500. Byline given. Pays on publication. Publishes ms an average of 1 year after acceptance. Buys first North American serial rights. Accepts queries by mail. Accepts simultaneous submissions. Responds in 2 weeks to queries. Responds in 2 months to mss. Sample copy for $7 or online. Guidelines available online.
Nonfiction Needs essays, interview. **Buys 2 mss/year.** Query. Length: 2,000-4,000 words. **Pays $20 maximum.**
Columns/Departments Reviews of contemporary poetry, 1,500 words maximum 2 Query. **Pays $20.**
Fiction Needs novel concepts, literary short stories. No romance, science fiction or religious/devotional. Open **Pays $20.**
Poetry Needs avant-garde, free verse, traditional. Buys 100 poems/year. Submit maximum 5 poems. **Pays $20.**

THE JOURNAL

once 'of Contemporary Anglo-Scandinavian Poetry', Original Plus, 17 High St., Maryport Cumbria CA15 6BQ UK. 01900 812194. E-mail: smithsssj@aol.com. Website: members.aol.com/smithsssj/index.html. **100% freelance written**. Triannual magazine covering poetry. Estab. 1994. Circ. 150. Byline given. Pays on publication. No kill fee. Publishes ms an average of 6 months after acceptance. Buys all rights. Editorial lead time 6 months. Accepts queries by mail, e-mail. Accepts previously published material. Responds in 4 weeks to queries. Guidelines free.
Tips "Send 6 poems; I'll soon let you know if it's not Journal material."

$ KANSAS CITY VOICES

Whispering Prairie Press, P.O. Box 8342, Kansas City KS 66208-0342. E-mail: kcvoices@yahoo.com. Website: kansascityvoices.tripod.com. **100% freelance written**. Annual magazine. *Kansas City Voices* magazine publishes an eclectic mix of fiction, poetry, personal essays, articles and images of artwork. Though we like works that relate to Kansas City and the surrounding area, quality is our primary concern. Estab. 2003. Circ. 1,000. Byline given. Pays on publication. Publishes ms an average of 6 months after acceptance. Buys first North American serial rights. Accepts queries by mail. Accepts simultaneous submissions. Sample copy for $11.45. Guidelines available online.
Nonfiction Needs book excerpts, essays, general interest, historical, how-to, humor, inspirational, interview, personal experience, photo feature, religious, travel. **Buys 10-15 mss/year.** Send complete ms. Length: 800-2,500 words. **Pays $20-100.**
Photos Send photos. Offers no additional payment for photos accepted with ms.
Fiction Needs adventure, confession, ethnic, experimental, fantasy, historical, horror, humorous, mainstream, mystery, novel concepts, religious, romance, science fiction, slice-of-life vignettes, suspense, western. Send complete ms. Length: 2,500 words. **Pays $20-100.**
Poetry Needs avant-garde, free verse, light verse, traditional. Does not want haiku. Submit maximum 3 poems. 35 lines maximum **Pays $20-100.**
Tips Familiarize yourself with the magazine, check the website and read the guidelines. We have a blind submissions policy, because we want quality work, whether or not it is by writers with long résumés. For fiction, we look for strong stories with active voices. Show, don't tell. Sending us your best work in a proofed, professionally formatted manuscript makes a great first impression.

$ THE KENYON REVIEW

Walton House, 104 College Dr., Gambier OH 43022. (740)427-5208. Fax: (740)427-5417. E-mail: kenyonreview@kenyon.edu. Website: www.kenyonreview.org. **100% freelance written**. Quarterly magazine covering contemporary literature and criticism. "An international journal of literature, culture, and the arts dedicated to an inclusive representation of the best in new writing (fiction, poetry, essays, interviews, criticism) from established and emerging writers." Estab. 1939. Circ. 6,000. Byline given. Pays on publication. No kill fee. Publishes ms an average of 1 year after acceptance. Buys first rights. Editorial lead time 1 year. Submit seasonal material 1 year in advance. Responds in 4 months to mss. Sample copy $12, includes postage and handling. Please call or e-mail to order. Guidelines available online.

Fiction Needs condensed novels, ethnic, experimental, historical, humorous, mainstream, contemporary. 3-15 typeset pages preferred **Pays $30-40/page.**
Tips "We no longer accept mailed or e-mailed submissions. Work will only be read if it is submitted through our online program on our website. Reading period is September 15-January 15."

$ THE KIT-CAT REVIEW

244 Halstead Ave., Harrison NY 10528. (914)835-4833. E-mail: kitcatreview@gmail.com. **Contact:** Claudia Fletcher, ed. **100% freelance written**. Quarterly magazine. "*The Kit-Cat Review* is named after the 18th Century Kit-Cat Club, whose members included Addison, Steele, Congreve, Vanbrugh, and Garth. It is part of the collections of the Univ. of Wisconsin, Madison, and the State Univ. of New York, Buffalo. Its purpose is to promote/discover excellence and originality." Estab. 1998. Circ. 500. Byline given. Pays on publication. Publishes ms an average of 6-12 months after acceptance. Buys first rights. Accepts queries by mail, phone. Accepts simultaneous submissions. Responds in 1 week to queries. Responds in 2 months to mss. Sample copy for $7 (payable to Claudia Fletcher) Guidelines for SASE.
Nonfiction "Shorter pieces stand a better chance of publication." Needs book excerpts, essays, general interest, historical, humor, interview, personal experience, travel. **Buys 6 mss/year.** Send complete ms with brief bio and SASE 5,000 words maximum **Pays $25-100.**
Fiction Needs ethnic, experimental, novel concepts, slice-of-life vignettes. No stories with O. Henry-type formula endings. Shorter pieces stand a better chance of publication. No science fiction, fantasy, romance, horror, or new age. **Buys 20 mss/year.** Send complete ms. 5,000 words maximum **Pays $25-100 and 2 contributor's copies; additional copies $5.**
Poetry Needs free verse, traditional. No excessively obscure poetry. Buys 100 poems/year. **Pays $20-100.**
Tips "Obtaining a sample copy is strongly suggested. Include a short bio, SASE, and word count for fiction and nonfiction submissions."

LITERARY MAMA

SC 29843. E-mail: lminfo@literarymama.com. Website: www.literarymama.com. Website offering writing about the complexities and many faces of motherhood in a variety of genres. Departments include columns, creative nonfiction, fiction, Literary Reflections, poetry, Profiles & Reviews. We are interested in reading pieces that are long, complex, ambiguous, deep, raw, irreverent, ironic, body conscious. Circ. 40,000. Accepts queries by e-mail. Accepts simultaneous submissions. Responds in 3 wks - 3 months to mss. We correspond via e-mail only. Guidelines available at http://www.literarymama.com/submissions/.
Nonfiction Contact: Kate Haas and Susan Ito. "We don't want pieces that read like columns or intellectual reflections on personal experiences; work that would be accepted by the glossy parenting magazines." Length: 500-7,000 words.
Columns/Departments Contact: Alissa McElreath and Delia Scarpitti at lmcolumns@literarymama.com.
Fiction Contact: Suzanne Kamata, Kristina Riggle. E-mail: lmfiction@literarymama.com.
Poetry Contact: Sharon Kraus. E-mail: lmpoetry@literarymama.com. Submit maximum 4 poems.
Tips "We seek top-notch creative writing. We also look for quality literary criticism about mother-centric literature and profiles of mother writers. We publish writing with fresh voices, superior craft, vivid imagery. Please send submission (copied into e-mail) to appropriate departmental editors. Include a brief cover letter. We tend to like stark revelation (pathos, humor & joy), clarity, concrete details, strong narrative development; ambiguity, thoughtfulness, delicacy, irreverence, lyricism, sincerity; the elegant. We need the submissions 3 mos. before Oct.: Desiring Motherhood; May: Mother's Day Month; June: Father's Day Month."

$ 🌐 THE LONDON MAGAZINE

Review of Literature and the Arts, The London Magazine, 32 Addison Grove, London W4 1ER United Kingdom. (44)(208)400-5882. Fax: (44)(208)994-1713. E-mail: editorial@thelondonmagazine.net. Website: www.thelondonmagazine.net. **100% freelance written**. Bimonthly magazine covering literature and the arts. Estab. 1732. Circ. 5,000. Byline given. Pays on publication. Offers kill fee. Kill fee negotiable Publishes ms an average of 4 months after acceptance. Buys first rights. Editorial lead time 3 months. Submit seasonal material 6 months in advance. Accepts queries by mail. Responds in 1 month to queries. Responds in 3 months to mss. Sample copy for £7.50. Guidelines available online.
Nonfiction Needs book excerpts, essays, interview, memoirs. No journalism, reportage, or quasi-marketing. **Buys 16 mss/year.** Send complete ms. 6,000 words maximum. **Pays minimum £20; average £30-50; maximum £150 for a major contribution.**

Fiction Needs adventure, confession, erotica, ethnic, experimental, fantasy, historical, horror, humorous, mainstream, mystery, novel concepts, religious, romance, science fiction, slice-of-life vignettes, suspense. **Buys 32 mss/year.** Send complete ms. 6,000 words maximum. **Pays minimum £20; average £30-50; maximum £150 for a major contribution.**
Poetry Needs avant-garde, free verse, haiku, light verse, traditional. Buys 60 poems/year. Submit maximum 6 poems. 1,000 words maximum (negotiable) **Pays minimum £15; maximum rate is negotiable.**

LULLWATER REVIEW

Emory University, P.O. Box 22036, Atlanta GA 30322. (404)727-6184. E-mail: lullwaterreview@yahoo.com. **100% freelance written**. Semiannual magazine. "*Lullwater Review* reads submissions from September 1st through May 1st. We seek submissions that are strong and original. We require no specific genre or subject." Estab. 1990. Circ. 2,000. Byline given. Pays on publication. No kill fee. Publishes ms an average of 1-2 months after acceptance. Buys first North American serial rights. Accepts queries by mail, e-mail, phone. Accepts simultaneous submissions. Responds in 1-3 months to queries. Responds in 3-6 months to mss. Sample copy for $5. Guidelines for #10 SASE.
Nonfiction Needs book excerpts, essays, general interest, historical, humor, inspirational, personal experience, photo feature, travel. **Buys 1-2 mss/year.** Send complete ms. 5,000 words maximum.
Photos Send photos. Reviews 8 × 11 or smaller prints, GIF/JPEG files. Offers no additional payment for photos accepted with ms. Buys first North American serial rights.
Fiction Needs adventure, condensed novels, ethnic, experimental, fantasy, historical, humorous, mainstream, mystery, novel concepts, religious, science fiction, slice-of-life vignettes, suspense, western. No romance or science fiction, please. **Buys 5-7 mss/year.** Send complete ms. 5,000 words maximum. **Pays 3 contributor copies.**
Poetry Needs avant-garde, free verse, light verse, traditional. Buys 30-40 poems/year. Submit maximum 6 poems. **Pays 3 contributor copies.**
Tips "Be original, honest, and of course, keep trying."

N LUNA PARK

On Literary Magazines, 901 Midland Ave, York PA 17403. E-mail: lunaparkreview@gmail.com. Website: www.lunaparkreview.com. Covering fiction, poetry, occasional reviews of literary magazines—any and all forms of literature and art. "Founded on the idea that literary magazines are credible, important and interesting venues for artistic work—at the same time reminiscent of a fine art gallery and a burlesque carnival." Estab. 2008. No kill fee. Guidelines available.
Nonfiction Needs book excerpts, essays, book reviews, interview.
Poetry Contact: Julia Johnson, poetry editor.
Tips "Writers: send your work by e-mail as .doc or .rtf file attachments. We are most interested in intelligent, exciting engagements with the subjects of art and/or publishing. We publish occasionally and quarterly. Feel free to query. Letters to the editor are to be sent by e-mail or to our mailing address. Literary Magazine Publishers: send issue copies to our mailing address. Galleys or final issues are fine."

$ LYRICAL BALLADS MAGAZINE

Classical Publishing, Ltd., E-mail: submissions@lyricalballads.net. Website: www.lyricalballads.net. **75% freelance written**. Monthly newsletter covering literature. "We are looking for either poetry or short fiction. It should be emotional, meaning that its primary aim should be to make the reader feel something—anything at all. Poetry, if not rhyming, should have some standardized form." Estab. 2007. Circ. 1,000. Byline given. Pays on publication. No kill fee. Publishes ms an average of 1-2 months after acceptance. Buys one-time rights. Editorial lead time 2 months. Submit seasonal material 3 months in advance. Accepts queries by e-mail, online submission form. Accepts simultaneous submissions. Responds in 3 months to queries. Responds in 1 month to mss Sample copy available online Guidelines available online
Nonfiction Needs essays. Send complete ms. Length: 300-3,000 words. **Pays $1-10 for assigned articles. Pays $1-10 for unsolicited articles.**
Fiction We accept only literary short fiction and poetry. **Buys 50-60 mss/year.** Send complete ms. Length: 500-3,000 words.
Poetry Needs traditional. We do not publish free verse of any kind. Buys 20-30/year poems/year. Submit maximum 10 poems. Length: 5-150 lines.

THE MACGUFFIN

Schoolcraft College, 18600 Haggerty Rd., Livonia MI 48152-2696. (734)462-4400, ext. 5327. E-mail: macguffin@schoolcraft.edu. Website: schoolcraft.edu/macguffin. **Contact:** Stephen A. Dolgin. Magazine covering the best new work in contemporary poetry, prose and visual art. "Our purpose is to encourage, support and enhance the literary arts in the Schoolcraft College community, the region, the state, and the nation. We also sponsor annual literary events and give voice to deserving new writers as well as established writers." One-year subscription First rights. Once published, all rights revert back to author. Accepts queries by e-mail. Responds in 2-4 months to mss. Guidelines available.

Nonfiction Translations are welcome and should be accompanied by a copy of the original text. Translators are responsible for author's permission.

Fiction Contact: Elizabeth Kircos. Does not want "obvious pornographic material." Submit 2 stories, maximum. Prose should be typed and double-spaced. Include word count. One submission/envelope/e-mail. Length: 5,000 words.

Poetry Needs avant-garde, free verse, light verse, traditional. Poetry should be typed, single-spaced, only one poem per page. There are no subject biases. Submit maximum 5 poems.

Tips "Also sponsors the National Poet Hunt Contest. See contest rules online. For mail submissions: do not staple work. Include name, e-mail, address, and the page no. on each page. Include SASE for reply only. Submit each work (single story or five-poem submission) as a Word .doc attachment."

$$ MAISONNEUVE

Maisonneuve Magazine Association, 400 de Maisonneuve Blvd. W., Suite 655, Montreal QC H3A 1L4 Canada. (514)482-5089. Fax: (514)482-6734. E-mail: submissions@maisonneuve.org. Website: www.maisonneuve.org. **90% freelance written**. Quarterly magazine covering eclectic curiousity. What does *Maisonneuve* publish? The sky's the limit—hell, what's in a sky? Poems about nothing? Love 'em. Got a cousin who writes long diatribes against houseflies? How about a really good vignette on the way people walk? Photocopies of your childhood collection of gum-wrappers. Audiofiles of people talking at the Jackson Pollock retrospective. Sonnets to your beloved—they better be good. This is a young magazine, and we're still discovering our limits. You are invited to join in. Estab. 2002. Circ. under 10,000. Byline given. Pays on publication. Offers 25% kill fee. Publishes ms an average of 4-6 months after acceptance. Buys first North American serial rights, buys electronic rights. Editorial lead time 4 months. Submit seasonal material 8 months in advance. Accepts simultaneous submissions. Responds in 2 weeks to queries. Responds in 2 months to mss. Sample copy available online. Guidelines available online.

Nonfiction Needs essays, general interest, historical, humor, interview, personal experience, photo feature. **Buys 20 mss/year.** Query with published clips. Length: 50-5,000 words. **Pays 10¢/word.**

Photos Contact: Contact Jenn McIntyre, art director. State availability. Captions, identification of subjects, model releases required. Reviews GIF/JPEG files. Negotiates payment individually. Buys one time rights.

Columns/Departments Open House (witty & whimsical), 800-1,200 words; Profiles + Interviews (character insights), 2,000 words; Studio (spotlight on visual artists/trends), 500 words; Manifesto (passionate calls for change), 800 words. 40-50 Query with published clips. **Pays 10¢/word.**

Fiction Needs adventure, confession, ethnic, experimental, humorous, science fiction, slice-of-life vignettes. **Buys 4 mss/year.** Send complete ms. Length: 1,000-4,000 words. **Pays 10¢/word.**

Poetry Needs avant-garde, free verse, haiku, light verse, traditional. Buys 16-32 poems/year. Submit maximum unlimited poems. **Payment varies.**

Tips *Maisonneuve* has been described as a new *New Yorker* for a younger generation, or as *Harper's* meets *Vice*, or as *Vanity Fair* without the vanity—but *Maisonneuve* is its own creature. *Maisonneuve*'s purpose is to keep its readers informed, alert, and entertained, and to dissolve artistic borders between regions, countries, languages and genres. It does this by providing a diverse range of commentary across the arts, sciences, daily and social life. The magazine has a balanced perspective, and 'brings the news' in a wide variety of ways. At its core, *Maisonneuve* asks questions about our lives and provides answers free of cant and cool.

$$ MANOA

A Pacific Journal of International Writing, English Dept., University of Hawaii, Honolulu HI 96822. (808)956-3070. Fax: (808)956-3083. E-mail: mjournal-l@listserv.hawaii.edu. Website: manoajournal.hawaii.edu. Semiannual magazine. "High quality literary fiction, poetry, essays, personal narrative. In general, each issue is devoted to new work from Pacific and Asian nations. Our audience is international. US writing need not be confined to Pacific settings or subjects. Please note that we seldom publish unsolicited work." Estab. 1989. Circ. 2,500 and large online distribution through Project Muse and JSTOR. Byline given. Pays on publication. Buys first North American serial rights, buys non-exclusive, one-time print rights. Editorial lead time 9 months. Accepts simultaneous submissions. Responds in 3 weeks to queries; 1 month to poetry mss; 6 months to fiction. Sample copy for $15 (US). Guidelines available online.

Nonfiction No Pacific exotica. Query first. Length: 1,000-5,000 words. **Pays $25/printed page.**
Fiction Query first and/or see website. Needs mainstream, contemporary, excerpted novel. No Pacific exotica. **Buys 1-2 in the US (excluding translation) mss/year.** Send complete ms. Length: 1,000-7,500 words. **Pays $100-500 normally ($25/printed page).**
Poetry No light verse. Buys 10-20 poems/year. Submit maximum 5-6 poems. **Pays $25/poem.**
Tips "Not accepting unsolicited manuscripts at this time because of commitments to special projects. See website for more information."

MANY MOUNTAINS MOVING

a literary journal of diverse, contemporary voices, 1705 Lombart St., Philadelphia PA 19146. E-mail: jeffreyethan@att.net. Website: www.mmminc.org. Annual covering unpublished poetry, fiction, nonfiction, and art from writers and artists of all walks of life. Open to all forms of poetry, welcoming outstanding, exciting works which reflect the diversity of our many cultures—writing with intelligence, emotion, wit, and craft. Has published Allen Ginsberg, Robert Bly, Isabel Allende, Amiri Baraka, mary Crow, Adrienne Rich. Poetry published in *MMM* has appeared in 'The Best American Poetry' and Pushcart Prize Anthologies. Estab. 1994. contest winnings. No kill fee. Accepts simultaneous submissions. Responds in 3 mos. - 1 year to mss. Guidelines available online.

- Submissions temporary closed due to overwhelming response; check back periodically on website.

Nonfiction Needs essays, Bok Reviews, Translations.
Columns/Departments Many Mountains Moving Poetry & Flash Fiction Contests - Prize: $200 and publication in *MMM* print annual. Finalists also will be considered for publication. Open to all poets and writers whose work is in English. Deadline: Nov. 1, '08. Guidelines and entry fees are online. Poetry Book Contests - Prize: $1,000 and publications in Spring '09. Past deadline.
Fiction Contact: Thaddeus Rutkowski, fiction editor. Length: 1,000-4,000 words.
Poetry Contact: Jeffrey Ethan Lee, Sr. Poetry Editor. Needs avant-garde, free verse, haiku, light verse, traditional.
Tips Invite readers into a truly multicultural exchange.to look through another's eyes at the world, as only literature and art can do, without being too simplistic. Poetry and Flash Fiction Contests' deadline is Nov. 1, 2008. Guidelines and enry fees are online. Prize money from $200, plus publication in our print annual.

MARGIE

The American Journal of Poetry, Intuit House Press, P.O. Box 250, Chesterfield MO 63006-0250. E-mail: margieonl@aol.com. Website: www.margiereview.com. Annual magazine covering superlative poetry without restriction to form, school or subject matter. A distinctive voice is prized. No kill fee. Accepts queries by mail. Accepts simultaneous submissions. Responds in 1-2 months to mss.
Poetry Submit maximum 3-5 poems. **contest awards $1,000.**
Tips "Open reading period: June 1st-July 15th. Published in the fall. Open to publishing newer and established poets equally. Subscribers only may submit poetry at any time of the year."

$ THE MASSACHUSETTS REVIEW

South College, University of Massachusetts, Amherst MA 01003-9934. (413)545-2689. Fax: (413)577-0740. E-mail: massrev@external.umass.edu. Website: www.massreview.org. Quarterly magazine. Estab. 1959. Circ. 1,200. Pays on publication. Publishes ms an average of 18 months after acceptance. Buys first North American serial rights. Accepts queries by mail. Accepts simultaneous submissions. Responds in 3 months to mss. Sample copy for $8. Guidelines available online.

- Does not respond to mss without SASE.

Nonfiction Articles on all subjects. No reviews of single books. Send complete ms or query with SASE 6,500 words maximum. **Pays $50.**
Fiction Short stories. Wants more prose less than 30 pages. **Buys 10 mss/year.** Send complete ms. 25-30 pages maximum.
Poetry Submit maximum 6 poems. **Pays 50¢/line to $25 maximum.**
Tips "No manuscripts are considered May-September. Electronic submission process on website. No fax or e-mail submissions. No simultaneous submissions."

MEMOIR (AND)

Memoir Journal, P.O. Box 1398, Sausalito CA 94966-1398. (415)339-4142; (415)339-3142. E-mail: submissions@memoirjournal.com. Website: www.memoirjournal.com. **100% freelance written.** Semiannual magazine covering memoirs. "*Memoir (and)* publishes memoirs in many forms, from the traditional to the experimental. The editors strive with each issue to include a selection of prose, poetry, graphic memoirs, narrative photography, lies and more from both emerging and established authors." Estab. 2006. (Contributors Notes in each issue) No kill fee. Publishes ms an average of 3 months after acceptance. Buys one-time rights, buys electronic rights, buys rights to publish in future anthologies rights. Accepts queries by mail, e-mail. Accepts simultaneous submissions. Sample copy available online. Guidelines available online.

- "We have two reading periods per year, with 4 prizes awarded in each: the *Memoir (and)* Prizes for Prose and Poetry ($100, $250, $500 & publication in publication in print and online, plus 3-6 copies of the journal) and the *Memoir (and)* Prize for Graphic Memoir ($100 & publication in print & online, 6 copies). Deadline: Aug. 15, 2009."

Nonfiction Contact: Joan E. Chapman. Needs essays, personal experience, Graphic Memoir. Does not publish themed issues. **Buys 40-80 mss/year.** Send complete ms. Length: 50-10,000 words. **Pays 0 for assigned or unsolicited articles.**

Photos Send photos. Reviews GIF/JPEG files. Offers no additional payment for photos accepted with ms. Buys one time rights.

Poetry Needs avant garde, free verse, haiku, light verse, traditional. Buys 20-40 poems/year poems/year. Submit maximum 5 poems.

Tips "The editors particularly invite submissions that push the traditional boundaries of form and content in the exploration of the representation of self. They also just love a well-told memoir."

METAL SCRATCHES

P.O. Box 685, Forest Lake MN 55025. E-mail: metalscratches@metalscratches.com. Website: www.metalscratches.com. **100% freelance written**. "Semiannual publication looking for stories written about the darker side of humanity—fiction with an edge, a metal scratch." Estab. 2003. Circ. 200. Byline given. No kill fee. Publishes ms an average of 6-12 months after acceptance. Buys one-time rights. Accepts queries by mail, e-mail. Accepts simultaneous submissions. Responds in 1 month to mss. Sample copy for $5 (check made out to Kim Mark). Guidelines by e-mail.

Fiction Needs experimental, literary. Does not want horror, science fiction, children's, religion, or poetry. **Buys 12 mss/year.** Send complete ms. 3,500 words maximum

Tips "We are looking for strong character development, and fiction with an edge, a bite. Nothing 'cute' or 'sweet.' Follow our writer's guidelines."

$ MICHIGAN QUARTERLY REVIEW

0576 Rackham Bldg., 915 E. Washington, University of Michigan, Ann Arbor MI 48109-1070. (734)764-9265. E-mail: mqr@umich.edu. Website: www.umich.edu/~mqr. **75% freelance written**. Quarterly magazine. "An interdisciplinary journal which publishes mainly essays and reviews, with some high-quality fiction and poetry, for an intellectual, widely read audience." Estab. 1962. Circ. 1,000. Byline given. Pays on publication. No kill fee. Publishes ms an average of 1 year after acceptance. Buys first serial rights. Accepts queries by mail. Responds in 2 months to queries. Responds in 2 months to mss. Sample copy for $4. Guidelines available online.

- "The Laurence Goldstein Award is a $1,000 annual award to the best poem published in the *Michigan Quarterly Review* during the previous year. The Lawrence Foundation Award is a $1,000 annual award to the best short story published in the *Michigan Quarterly Review* during the previous year."

Nonfiction "*MQR* is open to general articles directed at an intellectual audience. Essays ought to have a personal voice and engage a significant subject. Scholarship must be present as a foundation, but we are not interested in specialized essays directed only at professionals in the field. We prefer ruminative essays, written in a fresh style and which reach interesting conclusions. We also like memoirs and interviews with significant historical or cultural resonance." **Buys 35 mss/year.** Query. Length: 2,000-5,000 words. **Pays $10/published page.**

Fiction Contact: Fiction Editor. "No restrictions on subject matter or language. We are very selective. We like stories which are unusual in tone and structure, and innovative in language. No genre fiction written for a market. Would like to see more fiction about social, political, cultural matters, not just centered on a love relationship or dysfunctional family." **Buys 10 mss/year.** Send complete ms. Length: 1,500-7,000 words. **Pays $10/published page.**

Poetry Pays $10/published page.

Tips "Read the journal and assess the range of contents and the level of writing. We have no guidelines to offer or set expectations; every manuscript is judged on its unique qualities. On essays—query with a very thorough description of the argument and a copy of the first page. Watch for announcements of special issues which are usually expanded issues and draw upon a lot of freelance writing. Be aware that this is a university quarterly that publishes a limited amount of fiction and poetry and that it is directed at an educated audience, one that has done a great deal of reading in all types of literature."

$ MID-AMERICAN REVIEW

Department of English, Box W, Bowling Green State University, Bowling Green OH 43403. (419)372-2725. E-mail: mikeczy@bgsu.edu. Website: www.bgsu.edu/midamericanreview. **Contact:** Michael Czyzniejewski. **Willing to work with new/unpublished writers.** Biannual magazine of the highest quality fiction, poetry, and translations of contemporary poetry and fiction. Also publishes critical articles and book reviews of contemporary literature. "We try to put the best possible work in front of the biggest possible audience. We publish serious fiction and poetry, as well as critical studies in contemporary literature, translations and book reviews." Estab. 1981. Byline given. Pays on publication when funding is available. No kill fee. Publishes ms an average of 6 months after acceptance. Buys first North American serial rights, buys one-time rights. Accepts queries by online submission form. Responds in 5 months to mss. Sample copy for $7 (current issue); $5 (back issue); $10 (rare back issues). Guidelines available online.

Nonfiction Needs essays, articles focusing on contemporary authors and topics of current literary interest, short book reviews (500-1,000 words). **Pays $10/page up to $50, pending funding.**

Columns/Departments , .

Fiction Contact: Michael Czyzniejewski, fiction editor. Character-oriented, literary, experimental, short short. Needs experimental, Memoir, prose poem, traditional. No genre fiction. Would like to see more short shorts. **Buys 12 mss/year.** 6,000 words **Pays $10/page up to $50, pending funding.**

Poetry Contact: Poetry Editor: Brad Modlin; Assistant Poetry Editors: Angela Gentry, David D. Williams. Buys 60 poems/year. **Pays $10/page up to $50, pending funding.**

Tips "We are seeking translations of contemporary authors from all languages into English; submissions must include the original and proof of permission to translate. We would also like to see more creative nonfiction."

THE MIDWEST QUARTERLY

A Journal of Contemporary Thought, 406b Russ Hall, Pittsburg State University, Pittsburg KS 66762. (620)235-4317. Fax: (620)235-4080. E-mail: midwestq@pittstate.edu. Website: www2.pittstate.edu/engl/mwq/mqindex.html. **Contact:** James B. M. Schick. Quarterly magazine covering scholarly articles for the academic audience dealing with a broad range of subjects of current interest, and poetry. "We seek discussions of an analytical and speculative nature and well-crafted poems. Poems of interest to us use intense, vivid, concrete and/or surrealistic images to explore the mysterious and surprising interactions of the nature and inner human worlds." Estab. 1959. contest winnings. No kill fee. Accepts queries by mail, e-mail, fax, phone. Guidelines available online.

- "For publication in MQ and eligibility for the annual Emmett Memorial Prize competition, the Editors invite submission of articles on any literary topic, but preferably on Victorian or Modern British Literature, Literary Criticism, or the Teaching of Literature. The winner receives an honorarium and invitation to deliver the annual Emmett Memorial Lecture. Contact Dr. Meats, Chairman, English Dept."

Nonfiction Contact: Tim Bailey, book reviews editor. Needs essays, book of poetry reviews. No heavily documented research studies.

Columns/Departments Book Reviews, Book of Poetry Reviews.

Poetry Contact: Dr. Stephen Meats, poetry editor. Needs avant-garde, traditional.

Tips "The quality and format of book reviews are of special importance to us. Their purpose is to evaluate the significance of new scholarly work: identify its contribution to knowledge and its deficiencies. See Guidelines before submitting."

MISSISSIPPI REVIEW

Univ. of Southern Mississippi, 118 College Dr., #5144, Hattiesburg MS 39406-0001. (601)266-4321. Fax: (601)266-5757. Website: www.mississippireview.com. Semiannual. "Literary publication for those interested in contemporary literature—writers, editors who read to be in touch with current modes." Estab. 1972. Circ. 1,500. No kill fee. Buys first North American serial rights. Sample copy for $10.

- "We do not accept unsolicited manuscripts except under the rules and guidelines of the *Mississippi Review* Prize Competition. See website for guidelines."

Fiction Contact: Rie Fortenberry, managing editor. Needs experimental, fantasy, humorous, contemporary, avant-garde and art fiction. No juvenile or genre fiction. 30 pages maximum.

$$$ THE MISSOURI REVIEW

357 McReynolds Hall, University of Missouri, Columbia MO 65211. (573)882-4474. Fax: (573)884-4671. E-mail: tmr@missourireview.com. Website: www.missourireview.com. **90% freelance written.** Quarterly magazine. We publish contemporary fiction, poetry, interviews, personal essays, cartoons, special features—such as History as Literature series and Found Text series—for the literary and the general reader interested in a wide range of subjects. Estab. 1978. Circ. 6,500. Byline given. Offers signed contract. Editorial lead time 6 months. Accepts queries by mail. Responds in 2 weeks to queries. Responds in 10 weeks to mss. Sample copy for $8.95 or online Guidelines available online.

Nonfiction Contact: Evelyn Somers, associate editor. Needs book excerpts, essays. No literary criticism. **Buys 10 mss/year.** Send complete ms. **Pays $1,000.**

Fiction Contact: Speer Morgan, editor. Needs ethnic, humorous, mainstream, novel concepts, literary. No genre or flash fiction. **Buys 25 mss/year.** Send complete ms. no preference. **Pays $30/printed page.**

Poetry Contact: Jason Koo, poetry editor. Publishes 3-5 poetry features of 6-12 pages per issue. Please familiarize yourself with the magazine before submitting poetry. Buys 50 poems/year. **Pays $30/printed page.**

Tips Send your best work.

$ MODERN HAIKU

An Independent Journal of Haiku and Haiku Studies, P.O. Box 33077, Santa Fe NM 87594-9998. E-mail: trumbullc@comcast.net. Website: www.modernhaiku.org. **85% freelance written.** Magazine published 3 times/year. "*Modern Haiku* publishes high quality material only. Haiku and related genres, articles on haiku, haiku book reviews, and translations comprise its contents. It has an international circulation; subscribers include many university, school, and public libraries." Estab. 1969. Circ. 650. Byline given. Pays on acceptance. No kill fee. Publishes ms an average of 6 months after acceptance. Buys first North American serial rights. Editorial lead time 4 months. Accepts queries by mail, e-mail. Responds in 1 week to queries. Responds in 6-8 weeks to mss. Sample copy for $11 in North America, $13 in Canada, $14 in Mexico, $17 overseas. Guidelines available online.

Nonfiction Needs essays, anything related to haiku. Send complete ms. **Pays $5/page.**

Columns/Departments Haiku & Senryu; Haibun; Essays (on haiku and related genres); Reviews (books of haiku or related genres). 40 essay & review mss/year (most are commissioned). Send complete ms. **Pays $5/page.**

Poetry Needs haiku, senryu, haibun, haiga. Does not want "general poetry, tanka, linked verse forms." Buys 750 poems/year. Submit maximum 24 poems. **Pays $1 per haiku.**

Tips "Study the history of haiku, read books about haiku, learn the aesthetics of haiku and methods of composition. Write about your sense perceptions of the suchness of entities; avoid ego-centered interpretations."

MORPHEUS TALES

Morpheus Tales, 116 Muriel St., London N1 9QU— UK. E-mail: morpheustales@blueyonder.co.uk. **100% freelance written.** Quarterly magazine covering horror, science fiction, fantasy. "We publish the best in horror, science fiction and fantasy, both fiction and nonfiction." Estab. 2008. Circ. 1,000. No kill fee. Publishes ms an average of 18 months after acceptance. Buys First British Serial Rights rights. Editorial lead time 3 months. Submit seasonal material 6 months in advance. Accepts queries by e-mail. Responds in 1 week to queries. Responds in 1 month to mss. Sample copy for $7. Guidelines available online.

Nonfiction Needs book excerpts, essays, general interest, how-to, inspirational, interview, new product, opinion, photo feature, Letters to the editor. "We're currently putting together a new Special issue of Morpheus Tales Magazine: The Morpheus Tales Dark Sorcery Special Issue Dark fiction featuring sorcery in all forms, whether of this world, or another. Black magic, mystical rites, wizardry conjured from your nightmares and entities summoned from the netherworld of your imagination: the sky (or the abyss) is the limit. Up to 3,000 words in length, and one submission at a time. Attach submissions as a Word or RTF file, and include "Dark Sorcery Submission" in the title of the e-mail. Please send submissions to: morpheustales@blueyonder.co.uk. We are looking for first world serial rights and first world online rights. The Morpheus Tales Dark Sorcery Special Issue will be published via print-on-demand services, and be available for download. The deadline is June 1st 2010!" All material must be based on horror, science fiction or fantasy genre. **Buys 6 mss/year.** Query. Length: 1,000-3,000 words.

Fiction Needs experimental, fantasy, horror, mystery, novel concepts, science fiction, serialized, suspense. **Buys 20 mss/year.** Send complete ms. Length: 800-3,000 words.

N+1

The Editors, 68 Jay St., #405, Brooklyn NY 11201. E-mail: queries@nplusonemag.com; fiction@nplusonemag.com. Website: www.nplusonemag.com. "Seminannual (print); weekly (web-only) magazine covering politics, literature, and culture for our print magazine. N-1 posts new, web-only material, once or twice a week." "The website will be running *n + 1*-type content that because of its timeliness or its genre, cannot appear in the print issue. Check the Archive for an indication of the sorts of pieces we run; lengths might range from 500-2,500 words. Articles about global warming and other ecological consequences of contemporary capitalism will be considered first, followed by articles about sports. Book reviews will be read grudgingly, but with something resembling an open mind." No kill fee. Sample copy and guidelines available online.

- "No unsolicited poetry at this time."

Nonfiction "Query with outline of your argument or, better yet, the first 500-1,000 words of your proposed piece. Please attach 2 or 3 samples of your work. If you don't hear back from us within 6 weeks, assume the worst." Needs essays, expose, general interest, interview, opinion, Sports.
Photos Contact: Sabine Rogers.
Fiction Contact: fiction@nplusonemag.com. "In an e-mail, please attach 3 short stories or the ms of a story collection or novels, noting which portions of the submitted work, if any, have been published or accepted for publication elsewhere."
Tips "Most of the slots available for a given issue will have been filled many months before publication. If you would like to brave the odds, the best submission guidelines are those implied by the magazine itself. Read an issue or 2 through to get a sense of whether your piece might fit into n + 1."

THE NATIONAL POETRY REVIEW

The National Poetry Review Press, C. J. Sage, Editor, The National Poetry Review, P.O. Box 640625, San Jose CA 95164-0625. Website: www.nationalpoetryreview.com. Semiannual magazine covering well-crafted poetry in both formal and free verse. Artwork submissions are also considered for *The National Poetry Review*'s cover. Editor is fond of fresh, formal verse, rich sound, play within form, lyricality, image, metaphor, especially extended metaphor, unique diction and syntax. Contests: *The National Poetry Review* Book Prize Series, The Finch Prize for Poetry. Estab. 2003. No kill fee. Buys first rights. Accepts queries by mail. Accepts simultaneous submissions.

- No unsolicited e-mail submissions. A few editor favorites are S. D. Lishan's 'Eurydice and Loverboy,' John Brehm's 'Songbird,' Kimberly Johnson's 'Sonnet,' Mary Oliver's 'Poppies,' and Margot Schilpp's 'Manifesto.

Poetry No prose poems, simple confessional work, or vulgarity. Submit maximum 3-5 poems. **Payment is 1 copy of the issue in which your work appears and a small honorarium.**
Tips Memorability, innovation, and joie de vivre are important to TNPR. We agree with Frost about delight and wisdom. We believe in the value of rich sound. Send your best, most memorable poems. We tend to prefer I-less poems—poems that do not reference the self—but will consider all excellent, memorable work. Outside the reading period, we only accept submissions from subscribers. Poetry is temporarily closed to submissions. Will be open again from June 1, 2009 to Aug. 31, 2009.

NEON MAGAZINE

A Literary Magazine, UK. E-mail: neonmagazine@ymail.com. Website: www.neonmagazine.co.uk. **Contact:** Krishan Coupland. Quarterly website covering alternative work of any form of poetry and prose, short stories, flash fiction, photographs, artwork and reviews. "Genre work is welcome. Experimentation is encouraged. We like stark poetry and weird prose. We seek work that is beautiful, shocking, intense and memorable. Darker pieces are generally favored over humorous ones. We are not completely averse to more innocent or whimsical creations, but they should be a good fit for the aesthetic of the magazine. We are concerned with themes of isolation, post-modernism, technology, dislocation, apathy, the apocalypse, memory, Kirk Cameron and urban decay." No kill fee. Buys one-time rights. "After publication all rights revert back to you." Accepts queries by e-mail. Reports in 1 month. Query if you have received no reply after 6 weeks. Guidelines available online.

- "We have now finished reading for the print edition of *Neon*. All submissions from now onwards will be considered for the new, online-only edition. Note: *Neon* was previously published as *FourVolts Magazine*."

Nonfiction "Query by e-mail if you would like to have a book, chapbook or magazine reviewed in a future issue. Query with a sample of your work if you would like to write reviews—this is unpaid but you can keep what you review." Needs essays, Reviews. No word limit.
Photos £5 for 1-4 images.

Fiction Needs experimental, horror, humorous, science fiction, suspense. "No nonsensical prose; we are not appreciative of sentimentality." **Buys 8-12 mss/year.** No word limit. **For 1 short story, or 1-2 flash fictions.**
Poetry "No nonsensical poetry; we are not appreciative of sentimentality. Rhyming poetry is discouraged." Buys 24-30 poems/year. No word limit.
Tips "Send several poems, one or 2 pieces of prose or several images, pasted in the body of an e-mail. Include the word 'submission' in your subject line. Include a short biographical note (up to 100 words). Read submission guidelines before submitting your work."

NERVE COWBOY

Liquid Paper Press, P.O. Box 4973, Austin TX 78765. Website: www.jwhagins.com/nervecowboy.html. Semiannual. "*Nerve Cowboy* publishes adventurous, comical, disturbing, thought-provoking, accessible poetry and fiction. We like to see work sensitive enough to make the hardest hard-ass cry, funny enough to make the most hopeless brooder laugh and disturbing enough to make us all glad we're not the author of the piece." Estab. 1996. Circ. 350. No kill fee. Publishes ms an average of 6-12 months after acceptance. Buys one-time rights. Accepts previously published material. Responds in 3 weeks to queries. Responds in 3 months to mss. Sample copy for $6. Guidelines available online.
Fiction Contact: Joseph Shields or Jerry Hagins, editors. "No racist, sexist or overly offensive work. Wants more unusual stories with rich description and enough twists and turns that leave the reader thinking." Length: 1,500 words. **Pays 1 contributor's copy.**

$ NEW ENGLAND REVIEW

Middlebury College, Middlebury VT 05753. (802)443-5075. E-mail: nereview@middlebury.edu. Website: go.middlebury.edu/nereview. Quarterly magazine. Literary only. Reads September 1-May 31 (postmarked dates). Estab. 1978. Circ. 2,000. Byline given. Pays on publication. No kill fee. Publishes ms an average of 6 months after acceptance. Buys first North American serial rights, buys first rights, buys second serial (reprint) rights. Accepts simultaneous submissions. Responds in 2 weeks to queries. Responds in 3 months to mss. Sample copy for $10 (add $5 for overseas). Guidelines available online.

- No e-mail submissions.

Nonfiction Serious literary only. Rarely accepts previously published submissions (out of print or previously published abroad only.) **Buys 20-25 mss/year.** Send complete ms. 7,500 words maximum, though exceptions may be made. **Pays $10/page ($20 minimum), and 2 copies.**
Fiction Send 1 story at a time, unless it is very short. Serious literary only, novel excerpts. **Buys 25 mss/year.** Send complete ms. Prose length: not strict on word count **Pays $10/page ($20 minimum), and 2 copies.**
Poetry Buys 75-90 poems/year. Submit maximum 6 poems. **Pays $10/page ($20 minimum), and 2 copies.**
Tips "We consider short fiction, including short-shorts, novellas, and self-contained extracts from novels in both traditional and experimental forms. In nonfiction, we consider a variety of general and literary, but not narrowly scholarly essays; we also publish long and short poems; ccreenplays; graphics; translations; critical reassessments; statements by artists working in various media; testimonies; and letters from abroad. We are committed to exploration of all forms of contemporary cultural expression in the US and abroad. With few exceptions, we print only work not published previously elsewhere."

$ NEW LETTERS

University of Missouri-Kansas City, University House, 5101 Rockhill Rd., Kansas City MO 64110-2499. (816)235-1168. Fax: (816)235-2611. E-mail: newletters@umkc.edu. Website: www.newletters.org. **100% freelance written**. Quarterly magazine. "*New Letters* is intended for the general literary reader. We publish literary fiction, nonfiction, essays, poetry. We also publish art." Estab. 1934. Circ. 5,000. Byline given. Pays on publication. No kill fee. Publishes ms an average of 6 months after acceptance. Buys first North American serial rights. Editorial lead time 6 months. Submit seasonal material 6 months in advance. Accepts queries by mail. Responds in 1 month to queries. Responds in 3 months to mss. Sample copy for $10 or sample articles on website. Guidelines available online.

- Submissions are not read between May 1 and October 1.

Nonfiction Needs essays. No self-help, how-to, or nonliterary work. **Buys 8-10 mss/year.** Send complete ms. 5,000 words maximum. **Pays $40-100.**
Photos Send photos. Reviews contact sheets, 2x4 transparencies, prints. Pays $10-40/photo Buys one time rights.
Fiction Contact: Robert Stewart, editor. Needs ethnic, experimental, humorous, mainstream, contemporary. No genre fiction. **Buys 15-20 mss/year.** Send complete ms. 5,000 words maximum. **Pays**

$30-75.

Poetry Needs avant-garde, free verse, haiku, traditional. No light verse. Buys 40-50 poems/year. Submit maximum 6 poems. Open **Pays $10-25.**

Tips "We aren't interested in essays that are footnoted, or essays usually described as scholarly or critical. Our preference is for creative nonfiction or personal essays. We prefer shorter stories and essays to longer ones (an average length is 3,500-4,000 words). We have no rigid preferences as to subject, style, or genre, although commercial efforts tend to put us off. Even so, our only fixed requirement is on good writing."

NEW OHIO REVIEW

English Dept., Ohio University, 360 Ellis Hall, Athens OH 45701. (740)597-1360. E-mail: noreditors@ohio.edu. Website: www.ohiou.edu/nor/. **Contact:** Jill Allyn Rosser. Magazine. Byline given. No kill fee. Accepts queries by mail. Accepts simultaneous submissions. Guidelines available online.

Nonfiction Needs essays, humor. Send complete ms.

Fiction Needs confession, experimental, humorous, mainstream. Send complete ms. **$10/page, $30 minimum honorarium**.

Poetry Needs avant-garde, free verse, haiku, light verse, traditional. Submit maximum 6 poems. **Pays $15/page for poetry, $30 minimum, in addition to two copies of the issue and a one-year subscription.**

Tips "We accept literary submissions in any genre."

$$ THE NEW QUARTERLY

Canadian Writers & Writing, St. Jerome's University, 290 Westmount Rd. N., Waterloo ON N2L 3G3 Canada. (519)884-8111, ext. 28290. E-mail: editor@tnq.ca. Website: www.tnq.ca. **95% freelance written**. Quarterly book covering Canadian fiction and poetry. "Emphasis on emerging writers and genres, but we publish more traditional work as well if the language and narrative structure are fresh." Estab. 1981. Circ. 1,000. Byline given. Pays on publication. No kill fee. Publishes ms an average of 4 months after acceptance. Buys first Canadian rights. Editorial lead time 6 months. Accepts queries by mail. Accepts simultaneous submissions. Responds in 2 weeks to queries. Responds in 4 months to mss. Sample copy for $16.50 (cover price, plus mailing). Guidelines for #10 SASE or online.

- Open to Canadian writers only.

Fiction "*Canadian work only*. We are not interested in genre fiction. We are looking for innovative, beautifully crafted, deeply felt literary fiction." **Buys 20-25 mss/year.** Send complete ms. 20 pages maximum **Pays $200/story**.

Poetry Needs avant-garde, free verse, traditional. *Canadian work only*. Buys 40 poems/year. Submit maximum 3 poems. **Pays $40/poem.**

Tips "Reading us is the best way to get our measure. We don't have preconceived ideas about what we're looking for other than that it must be Canadian work (Canadian writers, not necessarily Canadian content). We want something that's fresh, something that will repay a second reading, something in which the language soars and the feeling is complexly rendered."

$ THE NEW WRITER

P.O. Box 60, Cranbrook Kent TN17 2ZR United Kingdom. (44)(158)021-2626. E-mail: editor@thenewwriter.com. Website: www.thenewwriter.com. Publishes 6 issues per annum. "Contemporary writing magazine which publishes the best in fact, fiction and poetry." Estab. 1996. Circ. 1,500. Pays on publication. No kill fee. Publishes ms an average of 1 year after acceptance. Buys one-time rights. Accepts queries by e-mail, fax. Accepts simultaneous submissions. Responds in 2 months to queries. Responds in 4 months to mss. Sample copy for SASE and A4 SAE with IRCs only. Guidelines for SASE.

Nonfiction "Content should relate to writing." Query. Length: 1,000-2,000 words. **Pays £20-40.**

Fiction *No unsolicited mss.* Accepts fiction from subscribers only. "We will consider most categories apart from stories written for children. No horror, erotic, or cosy fiction." Query with published clips. Length: 2,000-5,000 words. **Pays £10 per story by credit voucher; additional copies for £1.50.**

Poetry Buys 50 poems/year. Submit maximum 3 poems. 40 lines maximum **Pays £3/poem**.

NOON: JOURNAL OF THE SHORT POEM

Minami Motomachi 4-49-506, Shinjuku-ku, Tokyo 160-0012 Japan. E-mail: noonpress@mac.com. Website: nc-haiku.blogspot.com/2008/03/noon-journal-of-short-poem.html. Quarterly magazine covering original, unpublished short poems. Philip Rowland asks taht extra time be spent over these short-short poems and sequences so that subtleties of nuance can be teased out. No kill fee.

Poetry Needs haiku. **Pays with contributor copies.**

Consumer Magazines

Tips Please contact Philip Rowland for further details. Selections for 2008 Summer Issue were already made.

$ THE NORTH AMERICAN REVIEW

University of Northern Iowa, 1222 W. 27th St., Cedar Falls IA 50614-0516. (319)273-6455. Fax: (319)273-4326. E-mail: nar@uni.edu. Website: www.webdelsol.com/northamreview/nar/. **90% freelance written**. Bimonthly magazine. "The *NAR* is the oldest literary magazine in America and one of the most respected; though we have no prejudices about the subject matter of material sent to us, our first concern is quality." Estab. 1815. Circ. under 5,000. Byline given. Pays on publication. No kill fee. Publishes ms an average of 1 year after acceptance. Buys first North American serial rights, buys first rights. Accepts queries by mail. Responds in 4 months to mss. Sample copy for $5. Guidelines available online.

- "This is the oldest literary magazine in the country and one of the most prestigious. Also one of the most entertaining—and a tough market for the young writer."

Nonfiction Contact: Ron Sandvik, nonfiction editor. No restrictions; highest quality only. Open **Pays $5/350 words; $20 minimum, $100 maximum.**
Fiction Contact: Grant Tracey, fiction editor. No restrictions; highest quality only. Needs , Wants more well-crafted literary stories that emphasize family concerns. No flat narrative stories where the inferiority of the character is the paramount concern. Open **Pays $5/350 words; $20 minimum, $100 maximum**.
Poetry No restrictions; highest quality only. Open. **Pays $1/line; $20 minimum, $100 maximum**.
Tips "We like stories that start quickly and have a strong narrative arc. Poems that are passionate about subject, language, and image are welcome, whether they are traditional or experimental, whether in formal or free verse (closed or open form). Nonfiction should combine art and fact with the finest writing. We do not accept simultaneous submissions; these will be returned unread. We read poetry, fiction, and nonfiction year-round."

$ NORTH CAROLINA LITERARY REVIEW

A Magazine of North Carolina Literature, Culture, and History, English Dept., East Carolina University, Greenville NC 27858-4353. (252)328-1537. Fax: (252)328-4889. E-mail: bauerm@mail.ecu.edu. Website: www.ecu.edu/nclr. Annual magazine published in summer covering North Carolina writers, literature, culture, history. "Articles should have a North Carolina slant. First consideration is always for quality of work. Although we treat academic and scholarly subjects, we do not wish to see jargon-laden prose; our readers, we hope, are found as often in bookstores and libraries as in academia. We seek to combine the best elements of magazine for serious readers with best of scholarly journal." Estab. 1992. Circ. 750. Byline given. Pays on publication. No kill fee. Publishes ms an average of 1 year after acceptance. Buys first North American serial rights. Rights returned to writer on request. Editorial lead time 6 months. Accepts queries by mail, e-mail. Responds in 1 month to queries. Responds in 6 months to mss. Sample copy for $10-25. Guidelines available online.
Nonfiction North Carolina-related material only. Needs book excerpts, essays, expose, general interest, historical, humor, interview, opinion, personal experience, photo feature, travel, reviews, short narratives, surveys of archives. No jargon-laden academic articles. **Buys 25-35 mss/year.** Query with published clips. Length: 500-5,000 words. **Pays $50-100 honorarium, extra copies, back issues or subscription (negotiable).**
Photos State availability. True required. Reviews 5 × 7 or 8 × 10 prints; snapshot size or photocopy OK. Pays $25-250. Buys one time rights.
Columns/Departments NC Writers (interviews, biographical/bibliographic essays); Reviews (essay reviews of North Carolina-related fiction, creative nonfiction, or poetry). Query with published clips. **Pays $50-100 honorarium, extra copies, back issues or subscription (negotiable).**
Fiction "Fiction submissions accepted during Doris Betts Prize Competition; see our Submission Guidelines for detail." **Buys 3-4 mss/year.** Query. 5,000 words maximum. **$50-100 honorarium, extra copies, back issues or subscription (negotiable)**.
Poetry *North Carolina poets only*. Buys 5-10 poems/year. Length: 30-150 lines. **$50-100 honorarium, extra copies, back issues or subscription (negotiable)**.
Tips "By far the easiest way to break in is with special issue sections. We are especially interested in reports on conferences, readings, meetings that involve North Carolina writers, and personal essays or short narratives with a strong sense of place. See back issues for other departments. Interviews are probably the other easiest place to break in; no discussions of poetics/theory, etc., except in reader-friendly (accessible) language; interviews should be personal, more like conversations, that explore connections between a writer's life and his/her work."

$ NOTRE DAME REVIEW

University of Notre Dame, 840 Flanner Hall, Notre Dame IN 46556. (574)631-6952. Fax: (574)631-4795. E-mail: english.ndreview.1@nd.edu. Website: www.nd.edu/~ndr/review.htm. Semiannual magazine. The *Notre Dame Review* is an indepenent, noncommercial magazine of contemporary American and international fiction, poetry, criticism, and art. We are especially interested in work that takes on big issues by making the invisible seen, that gives voice to the voiceless. In addition to showcasing celebrated authors like Seamus Heaney and Czelaw Milosz, the *Notre Dame Review* introduces readers to authors they may have never encountered before, but who are doing innovative and important work. In conjunction with the *Notre Dame Review*, the online companion to the printed magazine, the *Notre Dame Re-view* engages readers as a community centered in literary rather than commercial concerns, a community we reach out to through critique and commentary as well as aesthetic experience. Estab. 1995. Circ. 2,000. Pays on publication. Publishes ms an average of 6 months after acceptance. Buys first North American serial rights. Accepts simultaneous submissions. Responds in 4 or more months to mss. Sample copy for $6. Guidelines available online.

Fiction Contact: William O'Rourke, fiction editor. "We're eclectic. Upcoming theme issues planned. List of upcoming themes or editorial calendar available for SASE. Does not read mss May-August." No genre fiction. **Buys 100 (90 poems, 10 stories) mss/year.** Length: 3,000 words. **Pays $5-25.**

Tips "We're looking for high quality work that takes on big issues in a literary way. Please read our back issues before submitting."

NTH POSITION

No public address available, E-mail: val@nthposition.com. Website: www.editred.com/links/submissions/173-nth-position. www.nthposition.com. **5% freelance written**. Website covering all kinds of poetry—from post-modern to mainstream; showcases fresh, urgent voices in poetry and fiction today. Free ezine with politics and opinion, travel writing, fiction and poetry, art reviews and interviews, and some high weirdness. No kill fee. Accepts previously published material. Guidelines available online.

- We can only notify people whose work we accept.

Nonfiction Needs essays, Reviews, opinion, travel.

Photos Art work reviews.

Poetry Contact: Todd Swift. No racisim, nastiness, silkworm farming or diabetes articles. Submit maximum 2-6 poems.

Tips Submit as text in the body of an e-mail, along with a brief bio note (2-3 sentences). If your work is accepted it will be archived into the British Library's permanent collection.

$ ONCE UPON A TIME ONLINE E-ZINE

Once Upon a Time Online, 905 West Franklin St., Monroe NC 28112. E-mail: submissions@onceuponatimeonline.net. Website: www.onceuponatimeonline.net. twice a month website 'zine featuring original, short romantic fiction, as well as author interview and publisher profiles. Estab. 2004. Circ. 200. No kill fee. Buys 1 year exclusive electronic rights rights. Accepts queries by e-mail. Responds in 4-6 weeks to mss. Sample copy free.

Nonfiction Needs interview.

Fiction Pay is based on the author's previous track-record and name recognition. We also compensate with free book cover ads, banners and advertising on various sites in conjunction with our 'zine. Needs erotica, romance, *spicy*, short stories. Length: 3,000-5,000 words. **Pays $30.**

Tips Please send submissions as an attachment to submissions@onceuponatimeonline.net. Please read our guidelines. If you have a question, don't hesitate to ask. Please send an e-mail to customerservice@onceupnatimeonline.net. Indicate your interest in submitting to our publication, and we'll send you a free back-issue of the 'zine.

$ 🄽 ONE-STORY

One-Story, LLC, 232 3rd St., #A111, Brooklyn NY 11215. Website: www.one-story.com. **Contact:** Maribeth Batcha, pub. **100% freelance written**. Literary magazine covering 1 short story. "*One-Story* is a literary magazine that contains, simply, 1 story. It is a subscription-only magazine. Every 3 weeks subscribers are sent *One-Story* in the mail. *One-Story* is artfully designed, lightweight, easy to carry, and ready to entertain on buses, in bed, in subways, in cars, in the park, in the bath, in the waiting rooms of doctor's offices, on the couch, or in line at the supermarket. Subscribers also have access to a website, where they can learn more about *One-Story* authors, and hear about *One-Story* readings and events. There is always time to read *One-Story*." Estab. 2002. Circ. 3,500. Byline given. Pays on publication. Publishes ms an average of 3-6 months after acceptance. Buys first North American serial rights. Buys the rights to publish excerpts on website and in promotional materials. Editorial lead time 3-4 months. Accepts simultaneous submissions. Responds in 2-6 months to mss. Sample copy for $5. Guidelines available online.

- "Accepts submissions via website only (.rtf files). Receives 100 submissions a week. Submit between June & Sept. Publishes each writer one time only."

Fiction *One-Story* only accepts short stories. Do not send excerpts. Do not send more than 1 story at a time. **Buys 18 mss/year.** Send complete ms. Length: 3,000-8,000 words. **Pays $100.**

Tips *"One-Story* is looking for stories that are strong enough to stand alone. Therefore they must be very good. We want the best you can give."

ORBIS

Quarterly International Literary Journal, 17 Greenhow Ave., West Kirby Wirral CH48 5EL UK. E-mail: carolebaldock@hotmail.com. Website: www.kudoswritingcompetitions.com. **Contact:** Carole Baldock, editor. *Orbis* covers 84 pages of news, reviews, views, letters, features, prose and a lot of poetry, and cover artwork. Each writer is eligible for the Readers Award: 50 (plus 50 divided between the runners-up). Poems are also submitted to the Forward Prize (UK) and the Pushcart Prize (USA). "*Orbis has long been considered one of the top 20 Small Press magazines in the UK. We are interested in social inclusion projects and encouraging access to the Arts, young people, Under 20s and 20somethings. Subjects for discussion: 'day in the life,' technical, topical.*" Estab. 1969. No kill fee. Subscribers usually receive an answer re submissions in 3 mos. with the following issue of the magazine.

- Please see guidelines at website before submitting.

Nonfiction Contact: Nessa O'Mahony, reviews editor. Needs essays, Reviews, letters, technical, Features. **Writer receives £50.**

Photos Artwork for cover.

Fiction Buys 12/year. mss/year. Length: 500-1,000 words.

Poetry Readers Award - £50 for piece receiving the most votes in each issue. Four winners selected for submissions to Forward Poetry Prize, Single Poem category. Plus £50 split between 4, or more, runners-up. Feature Writer receives £50. NB, work commissioned: 3-4 poems or 1,500 words. Buys 160/year poems/year.

Tips "Any publication should be read cover to cover because it's the best way to improve your chances of getting published. Enclose SAE with all correspondence. Overseas: 2 IRCs, 3 if work is to be returned. Via e-mail, Overseas only: 2 poems or 1 piece of prose in body. No attachments."

OYEZ REVIEW

Roosevelt University, Dept. of Literature & Languages, 430 S. Michigan Ave., Chicago IL 60605. E-mail: oyezreview@roosevelt.edu. Website: www.roosevelt.edu/oyezreview. **100% freelance written**. Annual magazine publishing fiction, creative nonfiction, poetry, and art. There are no restrictions on style, theme, or subject matter. Estab. 1965. Circ. 600. Byline given. Pays 2 contributor's copies. Publishes ms an average of 2 months after acceptance. Buys first North American serial rights. Accepts queries by mail. Sample copy for $5. Guidelines available online.

- Reading period is August 1-October 1. Responds by mid-December.

Nonfiction We publish creative nonfiction only. Articles must have a distinctly literary flair. Needs essays, personal experience, memoir, literary journalism. **Buys 1-5 mss/year.** Send complete ms. 5,500 words maximum

Photos Accepts b&w artwork. Do not send originals. Reviews prints, slides, GIF/JPEG files. Offers no additional payment for photos accepted with ms.

Fiction We publish short stories and flash fiction on their merit as contemporary literature rather than the category within the genre. **Buys 1-8 mss/year.** Send complete ms. 5,500 words maximum

Poetry Needs avant-garde, free verse, traditional. Buys 10-20 poems/year. Submit maximum 5 poems. 10 pages maximum

Tips Writers should familiarize themselves with a variety of literary magazines in addition to ours in order to understand this niche and find out the scope of what contemporary literary magazines do and do not publish. Note that e-mail submissions, simultaneous submissions, work received without a SASE, and manuscripts received before or after the August 1-October 1 reading period will not be read. We read complete manuscripts rather than queries.

$ PALABRA

A Magazine of Chicano & Latino Literary Art, P.O. Box 86146, Los Angeles CA 90086-0146. E-mail: info@palabralitmag.com. Website: www.palabralitmag.com. Annual magazine featuring poetry, fiction, short plays, and more. *"PALABRA* is about exploration, risk and ganas—the myriad intersections of thought, language, story and art—*el mas alla of letters*, symbols and spaces into meaning." Byline given. No kill fee. Responds in 3-4 months to mss

Nonfiction Pays $25-35.

Fiction Needs experimental/hybrid, mainstream, novel excerpts, flash fiction, short plays. Does not want genre work (mystery, romance, science fiction, etc.). Send complete ms, unpublished work only. Length: 4,000 words. **Pays $25-$35.**

Poetry Needs avant garde, free verse, traditional. Submit maximum 5 poems.

PALO ALTO REVIEW

A Journal of Ideas, Palo Alto College, 1400 W. Villaret Blvd., San Antonio TX 78224. (210)486-3249. E-mail: professor78224-par@yahoo.com. Website: www.accd.edu/pac/english/pareview/index.htm. **80% freelance written**. Annual magazine of 80+ pages covering all subjects that can be considered educational—which means almost anything. "We invite original, unpublished writing on a variety of subjects. As a 'journal of ideas,' we look for wide-ranging investigations that have to do with living and learning. Articles, poems, and stories about interesting people, places, and events, are what we are after. Also humor. Our readers want to be stimulated, entertained, and enlightened." Estab. 1992. Circ. 500. Byline given. No kill fee. Publishes ms an average of 3-15 months after acceptance. Buys first North American serial rights. Editorial lead time 3-6 months. Accepts queries by mail. Accepts simultaneous submissions. Responds in 1-2 weeks to queries. Responds in 1-3 months to mss. Sample copy for $5. Guidelines by e-mail

Nonfiction Needs essays, expose, general interest, historical, how-to, humor, interview, opinion, personal experience, photo feature, travel, book reviews. **Buys 20-25 mss/year.** Send complete ms. 5,000-6,000 words max. **Pays in copies.**

Photos State availability. Identification of subjects required. Reviews prints, GIF/JPEG files. Offers no additional payment for photos accepted with ms. Buys one-time rights.

Fiction Needs adventure, ethnic, historical, humorous, mainstream, mystery, novel concepts, suspense. **Buys 4-6/year mss/year.** Send complete ms. 5,000 words maximum **Pays in copies.**

Poetry Needs avant-garde, free verse, traditional. Buys 12-16 poems/year. Submit maximum 5 poems.

Tips "Send for guidelines. Purchase a sample copy. We are willing to work with writers, and we publish many first-time writers. Guidelines inside front cover."

$$$ THE PARIS REVIEW

62 White Street, New York NY 10013. (212)343-1333. E-mail: queries@theparisreview.org. Website: www.theparisreview.org. Quarterly magazine. "Fiction and poetry of superlative quality, whatever the genre, style or mode. Our contributors include prominent, as well as less well-known and previously unpublished writers. Writers at Work interview series includes important contemporary writers discussing their own work and the craft of writing." Pays on publication. No kill fee. Buys all rights, buys first English-language rights. Accepts queries by mail. Accepts simultaneous submissions. Responds in 4 months to mss. Sample copy for $15 (includes postage). Guidelines available online.

- Address submissions to proper department. Do not make submissions via e-mail.

Fiction Study the publication. Annual Aga Khan Fiction Contest award of $1,000. Send complete ms. no limit **Pays $500-1,000.**

Poetry Contact: Richard Howard, poetry editor. **Pays $35 minimum varies according to length. Awards $1,000 in Bernard F. Conners Poetry Prize contest**.

$$ PARNASSUS: POETRY IN REVIEW

Poetry in Review Foundation, 205 W. 89th St., #8F, New York NY 10024. (212)362-3492. Fax: (212)875-0148. E-mail: parnew@aol.com. Website: www.parnassuspoetry.com. **Contact:** Herbert Leibowitz, editor & publisher. Annual magazine covering poetry and criticism. "We now publish one double issue a year." Estab. 1972. Circ. 1,800. Byline given. Pays on publication. No kill fee. Publishes ms an average of12-14 months after acceptance. Buys one-time rights. Accepts queries by mail. Responds in 2 months to mss. Sample copy for $15.

Nonfiction Needs essays. **Buys 30 mss/year.** Query with published clips. Length: 1,500-7,500 words. **Pays $200-750.**

Poetry Needs avant garde, free verse, traditional. Accepts most types of poetry. Buys Buys 3-4 unsolicited poems/year poems/year.

Tips "Be certain you have read the magazine and are aware of the editor's taste. Blind submissions are a waste of everybody's time. We'd like to see more poems that display intellectual acumen and curiosity about history, science, music, etc., and fewer trivial lyrical poems about the self, or critical prose that's academic and dull. Prose should sing."

PEARL

A Literary Magazine, 3030 E. Second St., Long Beach CA 90803. Website: www.pearlmag.com. Biannual magazine featuring poetry, short fiction, and black and white artwork. We also sponsor the Pearl Poetry Prize, an annual contest for a full length book, as well as the Pearl Short Story Prize. "*Pearl* is an eclectic publication, a place for lively, readable poetry and prose that speaks to real people about real life in direct, living language, profane or sublime." Estab. 1974. Pays with contributor's copy. No kill fee. Publishes ms an average of 6-12 months after acceptance. Accepts queries by mail. Accepts simultaneous submissions. Sample copy for $8. Guidelines available online.

- Submissions are accepted from Jan. - June only. Mss. received between July and Dec. will be returned unread. No e-mail submissions, except from countries outside the U.S. See guidelines.

Photos No photographs. "We only consider camera-ready, black and white spot-art (no shades of gray) that can be reduced without loss of definition or detail. Send clean, high-quality photocopies or original with SASE. Accepted artwork is kept on file and is used as needed."

Fiction "Our annual fiction issue features the winner of our Pearl Short Story Prize contest as well as 'short-shorts,' and some of the longer stories in our contest. Length: 1,200 words. No obscure, experimental fiction. The winner of the Pearl Short Story Prize receives 4250 and 10 copies of the issue the story appears in . A $10 entry fee includes a copy of the magazine; all entries are considered for publication." Nothing sentimental, obscure, predictable, abstract or cliché-ridden poetry or fiction. Length: 1,200 words. **Short Story Prize of $250, 100 copies of the issue the story appears in.**

Poetry "Our poetry issue contains a 12-15 page section featuring the work of a single poet. Entry fee for the Pearl Poetry Prize is $20, which includes a copy of the winning book." No sentimental, obscure, predictable, abstract or cliché-ridden poetry. Submit maximum 3-5 poems. 40 lines max. Send with cover letter and SASE.

Tips "Pays 5 writers with contributor copies. Additional copies may be purchased at a 50% discount."

PEBBLE LAKE REVIEW

15318 Pebble Lake Dr., Houston TX 77095. E-mail: submissions@pebblelakereview.com. Website: www.pebblelakereview.com. **98% freelance written**. Quarterly magazine covering poetry, fiction, creative nonfiction and reviews. *Pebble Lake Review* publishes high quality literary prose and poetry. We strive to publish work by writers whose interest, craft, and usage of words and language reflect in their work. Previous contributors have included Kim Addonizio, Paul Guest, Bob Hicok, Alex Lemon, Timothy Liu, Aimee Nezhukumatathil, Marge Piercy and Eric Shade. We welcome submissions from newer writers if the work exhibits quality. The best indicator of what type of material we accept is to visit our website or order a copy of the publication. Estab. 2003. Circ. 500 (print); 6,000/month (online). Byline given. No kill fee. Publishes ms an average of 3 months after acceptance. Buys one-time rights, buys electronic rights. Editorial lead time 3-6 months. Submit seasonal material 6 months in advance. Accepts queries by mail, e-mail. Accepts simultaneous submissions. Responds in 1 month to queries. Responds in 1-3 months to mss. Sample copy for $10. Guidelines available online.

Nonfiction Needs interview, personal narrative, book reviews. Annual Awards issue, see website for details. Send complete ms. 1,000 maximum for reviews; 3,000 for creative nonfiction

Photos Send photos. Identification of subjects required. Reviews GIF/JPEG files. Offers no additional payment for photos accepted with ms. Buys one time rights.

Fiction Needs mainstream, literary. No genre fiction or anything that uses gratuitous violence, language, or sex. Wants more flash/graphic fiction. **Buys 10-12 mss/year.** Send complete ms. 3,000 words maximum

Poetry Needs avant-garde, free verse. No rhyming poetry, greeting-card verse, haiku, light verse, or vampyre (or similar themed) poems. Buys 75-100 poems/year. Submit maximum 2-5 poems.

Tips Always be professional, and include a cover letter and SASE for reply. Follow guidelines carefully and study the magazine before submitting. Support independent presses by purchasing a copy or subscription to the publication.

THE PEDESTAL MAGAZINE

6815 Honors Court, Charlotte NC 28210. E-mail: pedmagazine@carolina.rr.com. Website: www.thepedestalmagazine.com. Bimonthly website currently accepting submissions of poetry, fiction, and nonfiction. "We are committed to promoting diversity and celebrating the voice of the individual." No kill fee. Buys first rights. All rights reverse back to the author/artist at publication time. We retain the right to publish the piece in any subsequent issue or anthology without additional payment. Accepts queries by e-mail. Accepts simultaneous submissions. Responds in 4-6 weeks to mss. Guidelines available online.

- *Pedestal 56* is now online.

Nonfiction "We accept reviews of poetry and short story collections, novels, and nonfiction books. We are currently accepting freelance interviews. Please query prior to submitting the above.' Needs essays, Reviews, interview. **Pays 2¢/word. Pays for unsolicited articles.**
Photos Reviews JPEG, GIF files.
Fiction "We are receptive to all sorts of high-quality literary fiction. Genre fiction is encouraged as long as it crosses or comments upon its genre and is both character-driven and psychologically acute. We encourage submissions of short fiction, no more than 3 flash fiction pieces at a time. There is no need to query prior to submitting; please submit via the submission form—no e-mail to the editor." Needs traditional literary, experimental, horror, mainstream, mystery, romance, science fiction, Works that don't fit into a specific category. **Buys 10-25 mss/year.** Length: 4,000 words. **Pays $2¢:/word-5¢/word.**
Poetry Needs The poetry section in the April 2010 issue will be dedicated completely to a feature of visual poetry. Please see our guidelines regarding all poetry being submitted from February 28-April 14. "We are open to a wide variety of poetry, ranging from the highly experimental to the traditionally formal. Submit all poems in one form. No need to query before submitting." Submit maximum 6 poems. No length restriction. Pays $40/poem.
Tips "If you send us your work, please wait for a response to your first submission before you submit again."

PEMBROKE MAGAZINE

The University of North Carolina at Pembroke and The North Carolina Arts Council, UNCP Box 1510, Pembroke NC 28372-1510. (910)521-6433. E-mail: shelby.stephenson@uncp.edu. Website: www.uncp.edu/pembrokemagazine. Annual magazine covering poetry, fiction, nonfiction, interviews, and visual arts (painting, graphics, sculpture). Prestigious, nationally known *Pembroke Magazine* with international scope has been at the forefront of innovation. Finds overlooked topics and authors. Offers readers a rare opportunity to move through time, across cultures, such as Native American Literature, and into contemporary literature and art. It feeds the desire for understanding. Themes range from immigration, assimilation, exile, alienation, and fragmented identities to romance and metaphysics. We want to tantalize readers to further explorations or, more importantly, self-reflection. Estab. 1969. No kill fee. Responds in 4-7 weeks to mss. Guidelines available online.
Nonfiction Needs essays, interview, photo feature.
Tips Accepts submissions year round though response time will be slower in the summer. Please enclose SASE if you would like your work returned. No electronic submissions.

PILGRIMAGE MAGAZINE

P.O. Box 9110, Pueblo CO 81001. E-mail: info@pilgrimagepress.org. Website: www.pilgrimagepress.org. Biannual magazine welcoming creative prose and poetry. We favor personal writing on themes of place, spirit, peace and social justice in and beyond the Greater Southwest. Serves an eclectic fellowship of readers, writers, artists, naturalists, contemplatives, activists, seekers, adventurers, and other kindred spirits. Estab. 1976. No kill fee. Guidelines available online.
Poetry Fit poetry on one page.
Tips "Our interests include wildness in all its forms; inward and outward explorations; home ground, the open road, service, witness, peace and justice; symbols, story and myth in contemporary culture; struggle and resilience; insight and transformation; wisdom wherever it is found; and the great mystery of it all. We like good storytellers and a good sense of humor. Must be typed (double-spaced) and submitted along with SASE. No e-mail submissions, please."

$ 🌐 PLANET-THE WELSH INTERNATIONALIST

P.O. Box 44, Aberystwyth Ceredigion SY23 3ZZ United Kingdom. (44)(197)061-1255. Fax: (44)(197)061-1197. E-mail: planet.enquiries@planetmagazine.org.uk. Website: www.planetmagazine.org.uk. Bimonthly journal. A literary/cultural/political journal centered on Welsh affairs but with a strong interest in minority cultures in Europe and elsewhere. Circ. 1,400. Sample copy for £4. Guidelines available online.
Fiction Would like to see more inventive, imaginative fiction that pays attention to language and experiments with form. No magical realism, horror, science fiction. Length: 1,500-4,000 words. **Pays £50/1,000 words.**
Tips We do not look for fiction which necessarily has a 'Welsh' connection, which some writers assume from our title. We try to publish a broad range of fiction and our main criterion is quality. Try to read copies of any magazine you submit to. Don't write out of the blue to a magazine which might be

completely inappropriate for your work. Recognize that you are likely to have a high rejection rate, as magazines tend to favor writers from their own countries.

$ PLEIADES

A Journal of New Writing, Pleiades Press, Department of English, University of Central Missouri, Warrensburg MO 64093. (660)543-4425. Fax: (660)543-8544. E-mail: pleiades@ucmo.edu. Website: www.ucmo.edu/englphil/pleiades. **100% freelance written**. Semiannual journal (5½ × 8½ perfect bound). "We publish contemporary fiction, poetry, interviews, literary essays, special-interest personal essays, reviews for a general and literary audience from authors from around the world." Estab. 1991. Circ. 3,000. Byline given. Pays on publication. No kill fee. Publishes ms an average of 9 months after acceptance. Buys first North American serial rights, buys second serial (reprint) rights. Occasionally requests rights for TV, radio reading, website. Editorial lead time 9 months. Accepts queries by mail. Accepts simultaneous submissions. Responds in 2 months to queries. Responds in 1-4 months to mss. Sample copy for $5 (back issue); $6 (current issue) Guidelines available online.

- "Also sponsors the Lena-Miles Wever Todd Poetry Series competition, a contest for the best book ms by an American poet. The winner receives $1,000, publication by Pleiades Press, and distribution by Louisiana State University Press. Deadline September 30. Send SASE for guidelines."

Nonfiction Contact: Phong Nguyen and Matthew Eck, nonfiction editor. "We accept queries for book reviews. Please send queries and clips of previously published reviews to Kevin Prufer. No unsolicited reviews will be accepted." Needs book excerpts, essays, interview, reviews. Nothing pedantic, slick, or shallow. Do not send submissions after May 31. We résumé reading nonfiction Sept. 1. **Buys 4-6 mss/year.** Send complete ms. Length: 2,000-4,000 words. **Pays $10.**

Fiction Contact: Matthew Eck and Phong Nguyen. We read fiction year-round. Needs ethnic, experimental, humorous, mainstream, novel concepts, magic realism. No science fiction, fantasy, confession, erotica. **Buys 16-20 mss/year.** Send complete ms. Length: 2,000-6,000 words. **Pays $10.**

Poetry Contact: Kevin Prufer and Wayne Miller. Needs avant-garde, free verse, haiku, light verse, traditional. "Nothing didactic, pretentious, or overly sentimental. Do not send poetry after May 31. We résumé reading poetry on Sept. 1." Buys 40-50 poems/year. Submit maximum 6 poems. **Pays $3/poem, and contributor copies.**

Tips Submit only 1 genre at a time to appropriate editors. Show care for your material and your readers—submit quality work in a professional format. Include cover letter with brief bio and list of publications. Include SASE. Cover art is solicited directly from artists. We accept queries for book reviews. For summer submissions, the Poetry and Nonfiction Editors will no longer accept mss sent between June 1 & August 31. Any sent after May 31 will be held until the end of summer. Please do not send your only copy of anything.

$ $ PLOUGHSHARES

Emerson College, Department M, 120 Boylston St., Boston MA 02116. Website: www.pshares.org. **Contact:** Ladette Randolph, editor. Triquarterly magazine for readers of serious contemporary literature. "Our mission is to present dynamic, contrasting views on what is valid and important in contemporary literature, and to discover and advance significant literary talent. Each issue is guest-edited by a different writer. We no longer structure issues around preconceived themes." Estab. 1971. Circ. 6,000. Pays on publication. Offers 50% kill fee for assigned ms not published. kill fee. Publishes ms an average of 6 months after acceptance. Buys first North American serial rights. Accepts simultaneous submissions. Responds in 5 months to mss. Sample copy for $8.50 (back issue). Guidelines available online.

- "A competitive and highly prestigious market. Rotating and guest editors make cracking the line-up even tougher, since it's difficult to know what is appropriate to send. The reading period is August 1-March 31."

Nonfiction Needs essays, personal and literary; accepted only occasionally. 6,000 words maximum **Pays $25/printed page, $50-250.**

Fiction Needs mainstream, literary. No genre (science fiction, detective, gothic, adventure, etc.), popular formula, or commerical fiction whose purpose is to entertain rather than to illuminate. **Buys 25-35 mss/year.** Length: 300-6,000 words. **Pays $25/printed page, $50-250.**

Poetry Needs avant-garde, free verse, traditional. Open **Pays $25/printed page, $50-250.**

Tips "We no longer structure issues around preconceived themes. If you believe your work is in keeping with our general standards of literary quality and value, submit at any time during our reading period."

PMS

poemmemoirstory, University of Alabama at Birmingham, HB 217, 1530 3rd Ave. South, Birmingham AL 35294-1260. (205)934-8578. E-mail: kmadden@uab.edu. Website: www.pms-journal.org/submissions-guidelines. Annual magazine covering poetry, memoirs and short fiction; contains the best work of the best women writers in the world. "This is an all women's literary journal. The subject field is wide open." No kill fee. Sample copy for $7.

- Reading period runs from Jan. 1 - Mar. 31. Submissions received at other times of the year will be returned unread. Best way to make contact is through e-mail.

Nonfiction Needs personal experience. Each issue includes a memoir written by a woman who is not necessary a writer but who has experienced something of historic import. Emily Lyons, the nurse who survived the 1998 New Woman All Women Birgmingham clinic bombing by Eric Rudolph; women who experienced the World Trade Center on 9/11; the Civil Rights Movement in Birmingham, the war in Iraq, Hurricane Katrina, and teaching Milton's *Paradise Lost* to inmates at an Alabama state prison have lent us their stories. Length: 4,300 words.
Fiction Length: 4,300 words.
Poetry Submit maximum 5 poems.
Tips "We seek unpublished original work that we can recycle. Include cover letter, brief bio with SASE. All mss should be typed on 1-side of 8 × 11 white paper with author's name, address, phone no. and e-mail address on front of each submission."

POETIC MONTHLY MAGAZINE

AG Press/Living the Simple Life, 4101 Hearthside Dr., Apt. 104, Wilmington NC 28412. (910)409-5867. E-mail: martin@livingthesimplelife.com. Website: www.poeticmonthly.com. **100% freelance written**. Monthly magazine covering poetry, writing, self-publishing. Follow general theme, relaxed content. Estab. 2006. Byline sometimes given. N/A-Cross Publicity, no pay. No kill fee. Buys Rights. Retain with Author rights. Editorial lead time 1 month. Submit seasonal material 1 month in advance. Accepts queries by mail, e-mail, phone. Accepts simultaneous submissions. Responds in 4 weeks to queries. Responds in 1 month to mss. Sample copy available online. Guidelines free.

- Free PDF, POD printing.

Nonfiction Needs book excerpts, essays, general interest, how-to, humor, interview, new product, personal experience, photo feature, General theme. Poetry itself, unknowns submitted to Top 20. Query.
Photos Contact: Martin White. State availability of or send photos.. Identification of subjects required. Reviews GIF/JPEG files. Offers no additional payment for photos accepted with ms. Buys one-time rights.
Fiction Contact: Martin White. Needs adventure, cond novels, confession, erotica, experimental, fantasy, historical, horror, humorous, mainstream, mystery, novel concepts, romance, serialized, slice-of-life vignettes, suspense. We don't want to to see non-general themes. Query.
Poetry Contact: Martin White. Needs avant-garde, free verse, haiku, light verse, traditional. No cursing words.
Tips "Open to guest writers."

$ POETRY

The Poetry Foundation, 444 N. Michigan Ave., Suite 1850, Chicago IL 60611-4034. (312)787-7070. Fax: (312)787-6650. E-mail: editors@poetrymagazine.org. Website: www.poetrymagazine.org. **Contact:** Helen Klaviter. **100% freelance written**. Monthly magazine. Estab. 1912. Circ. 31,000. Byline given. Pays on publication. No kill fee. Publishes ms an average of 9 months after acceptance. Buys first serial rights. Accepts queries by mail. Responds in 1 month to queries and to mss. Sample copy for $3.75 or online at website. Guidelines available online.
Nonfiction Buys 14 mss/year. Query. Length: 1,000-2,000 words. **Pays $150/page.**
Poetry Accepts all styles and subject matter. Buys 180-250 poems/year. Submit maximum 4 poems. Open **Pays $10/line ($150 minimum payment).**

POETRY EAST

Dept. of English, DePaul University, 802 W. Belden Ave., Chicago IL 60614. (773)325-7487. Fax: (773)325-7328. E-mail: editor@poetryeast.org. Website: www.poetryeast.org. Semiannual magazine covering poetry, translations, criticism, interviews, and art. An award-winning journal dedicated to publishing poetry that is immediate, accessible, and universal. An independent magazine affiliated with DePaul Univeristy and based in Chicago, IL. No kill fee. Accepts queries by mail. Responds in 4 months to mss.
Nonfiction Needs essays, Literary Criticism, interview.
Photos Art.

Tips *Poetry East* has an open submission policy. Please submit typed mss. and include your name, address, and contact info (phone no. and/or e-mail). Use a #10 envelope. Mss. will not be returned unless accompanied by SASE with sufficient postage.

POETRY INTERNATIONAL

San Diego State University, 5500 Campanile Dr., San Diego CA 92182-6020. (619)594-1522. Fax: (619)594-4998. E-mail: poetryinternational@yahoo.com. Website: www.poetryinternational.sdsu.edu. Annual journal covering new poems from emerging and well-established poets, offering commentary on poetry anthologies, books by individual poets, and poetic criticism, art from around the world. "We intend to continue to publish poetry that makes a difference in people's lives, and startles us anew with the endless capacity of language to awaken our senses and expand our awareness." Estab. 1997. No kill fee Accepts queries by mail. Accepts simultaneous submissions. Responds in 6-8 months to mss. Guidelines available on web site

- Features the Poetry International Prize ($1,000) for best original poem. (Deadline April 15 for 2009.) Submit up to 3 poems with a $10 entry fee.

Nonfiction Needs , Translations, query first for book reviews. Reprints photos.
Fiction Query.
Poetry Features the poetry of a different nation of the world as a special section in each issue. Submit maximum 5 poems.
Tips "Seeks a wide range of styles and subject matter. We read unsolicited mss. only between Sept. 1st and Dec. 31st of each year. Mss. received any other time will be returned unread."

POETRY IRELAND REVIEW

Poetry Ireland, 2 Proud's Lane, Off St. Stephen's Green, Dublin 2 Ireland. 01-4789974. Fax: 01-4780205. E-mail: publications@poetryireland.ie. Website: www.poetryireland.ie. Quarterly literary magazine in book form. Estab. 1978. Circ. 2,000. Pays on publication. No kill fee. Accepts queries by mail, e-mail, fax, phone. Responds in 1 week to queries. Responds in 6 months to mss.
Poetry Needs avant-garde, free verse, haiku, traditional. Buys 150 poems/year. Submit maximum 6 poems. **Pays $32/submission.**

POETRY LONDON

London Public Library, Fred Landon Branch, 167 Wortley Rd., London ON Canada. (519)439-6240. E-mail: poetrylondon@yahoo.ca. Website: www.poetrylondon.ca/. Website covering accomplished local poets and emerging poets, and provides national poets a multi-stop Ontario tour. The Oxford Bookshop provides a book sale following each reading. "Everyone who enjoys discussing poetry, or learning more about the art form, is welcome to attend the Poetry Workshops." No kill fee. Guidelines available.
Poetry Send 1-3 poems, along with a cover letter with your full name, contact information, e-mail address, and a brief 50 word bio to: Poetry London Eldon House Project, c/o Christine Walde, 16 The Ridgeway, London Ontario N6C 1A1. Length: 60 lines.

$ POETRY NEW ZEALAND

34B Methuen Rd., Avondale Auckland New Zealand. E-mail: alstair@ihug.co.nz. Website: www.poetrynz.net. "Each issue has 15-20 pages of poetry from a developing or established poet. The rest of the issue is devoted to a selection of poetry from New Zealand and abroad, plus essays, reviews, and general criticism to a total of 112 pages." Estab. 1951. No kill fee. Accepts queries by mail. Responds in 3 months to mss. Guidelines available online.
Nonfiction Essays (related to poetry), 3,000 words. Contributors receive a copy of the magazine. Submit a copy of the magazine. **Featured poets and essayists receive 1 copy of the magazine and a fee.**
Poetry Accepts any theme/style of poetry. Send complete ms, bio, and SASE.

THE PORTLAND REVIEW

Portland State University, Box 347, Portland OR 97207-0347. (503)7254533. E-mail: theportlandreview@gmail.com. Website: www.portlandreview.org. **Contact:** Jacqueline Marie Treiber. **98% freelance written**. Triannual magazine covering short prose, poetry, photography, and art. Estab. 1956. Circ. 1,500. Byline given. No kill fee. Publishes ms an average of 3-6 months after acceptance. Buys first North American serial rights. Accepts simultaneous submissions. Responds in 2-4 months to mss. Sample copy for $9. Guidelines available online. "Automatic rejection of mss not following guidelines."
Photos Black & white only. State availability of or send photos. Reviews prints, GIF/JPEG files. Offers no additional payment for photos accepted with ms. Buys one time rights.
Fiction Needs , Flash, vignette, and reviews of small-press publications or emergent authors. No fantasy,

detective, or western. **Buys 40 mss/year.** Send complete ms. 5,000 words maximum. **Pays contributor's copies.**

Poetry Needs Avant garde, free verse, haiku, light verse, traditional. Buys 50 poems/year. Submit maximum 5 poems.

Tips "View website for current samples and guidelines."

$ THE PRAIRIE JOURNAL

Journal of Canadian Literature, Prairie Journal Trust, P.O. Box 68073, 28 Crowfoot Terrace NW, Calgary AB Y3G 3N8 Canada. E-mail: editor@prairiejournal.org (queries only). Website: prairiejournal.org. **100% freelance written**. Semiannual magazine publishing quality poetry, short fiction, drama, literary criticism, reviews, bibliography, interviews, profiles, and artwork. "The audience is literary, university, library, scholarly, and creative readers/writers." Estab. 1983. Circ. 600. Byline given. Pays on publication. No kill fee. Publishes ms an average of 4-6 months after acceptance. Buys first North American serial rights, buys electronic rights. In Canada author retains copyright with acknowledgement appreciated. Editorial lead time 4-6 months. Accepts queries by mail, e-mail. Responds in 2 weeks to queries. Responds in 6 months to mss. Sample copy for $5. Guidelines available online.

- "Use our mailing address for submissions and queries with samples sor clippings."

Nonfiction Needs essays, humor, interview, literary. No inspirational, news, religious, or travel. **Buys 25-40 mss/year.** Query with published clips. Length: 100-3,000 words. **Pays $50-100, plus contributor's copy.**

Photos State availability. Offers additional payment for photos accepted with ms. Rights purchased is negotiable.

Columns/Departments Reviews (books from small presses publishing poetry, short fiction, essays, and criticism), 200-1,000 words. 5 Query with published clips. **Pays $10-50.**

Fiction No genre (romance, horror, western—sagebrush or cowboys), erotic, science fiction, or mystery. **Buys 6 mss/year.** Send complete ms. Length: 100-3,000 words. **Pays $10-75.**

Poetry Needs avant-garde, free verse, haiku. No heroic couplets or greeting card verse. Buys 25-35 poems/year. Submit maximum 6-8 poems. Length: 3-50 lines. **Pays $5-50.**

Tips "We publish many, many new writers and are always open to unsolicited submissions because we are 100% freelance. Do not send US stamps, always use IRCs."

PRAIRIE SCHOONER

The University of Nebraska Press, Prairie Schooner, 201 Andrews Hall, University of Nebraska, Lincoln NE 68588-0334. (402)472-0911. E-mail: jengelhardt2@unl.edu. Website: prairieschooner.unl.edu. **100% freelance written**. Quarterly magazine. "We look for the best fiction, poetry, and nonfiction available to publish, and our readers expect to read stories, poems, and essays of extremely high quality. We try to publish a variety of styles, topics, themes, points of view, and writers with a variety of backgrounds in all stages of their careers. We like work that is compelling—intellectually or emotionally—either in form, language, or content." Estab. 1926. Circ. 2,500. Byline given. Pays on publication. Publishes ms an average of 1 year after acceptance. Buys all rights, which are returned to the author upon request after publication. Editorial lead time 6 months. Accepts queries by mail, e-mail. Responds in 1 week to queries. Responds in 3-4 months to mss. Sample copy for $6. Guidelines for #10 SASE.

- Submissions must be received between September 1 and May 1.

Nonfiction Needs essays, literary/personal, literary or creative nonfiction, memoir, or essays on literature. No scholarly papers that require footnotes. No pieces written only to express a moral lesson or to inspire. There must be depth and literary quality as well. **Buys 6-8 mss/year.** Send complete ms. Length: 250-20,000 words. **Pays 3 copies of the issue in which the writer's work is published.**

Fiction "We try to remain open to a variety of styles, themes, and subject matter. We look for high-quality writing, 3-D characters, well-wrought plots, setting, etc. We are open to realistic and/or experimental fiction." Needs ethnic, experimental, mainstream, novel concepts, literary. **Buys 15-25 mss/year.** Send complete ms. **Pays 3 copies of the issue in which the writer's work is published.**

Poetry Needs avant garde, free verse, haiku, light verse, traditional. Buys 100-120 poems/year. Submit maximum 7 poems. **Pays 3 copies of the issue in which the writer's work is published.**

Tips "Send us your best, most carefully crafted work and be persistent. Submit again and again. Constantly work on improving your writing. Read widely in literary fiction, nonfiction, and poetry. Read *Prairie Schooner* to know what we publish."

$ PRISM INTERNATIONAL

Department of Creative Writing, Buch E462 Main Mall, University of British Columbia, Vancouver BC V6T 1Z1 Canada. (604)822-2514. Fax: (604)822-3616. E-mail: prism@interchange.ubc.ca. Website:

prismmagazine.ca. **100% freelance written. Works with new/unpublished writers.** A quarterly international journal of contemporary writing—fiction, poetry, drama, creative nonfiction and translation. Readership: public and university libraries, individual subscriptions, bookstores—a world-wide audience concerned with the contemporary in literature. Estab. 1959. Circ. 1,200. Pays on publication. No kill fee. Publishes ms an average of 4 months after acceptance. Buys first North American serial rights. Selected authors are paid an additional $10/page for digital rights. Accepts queries by mail. Responds in 4 months to queries. Responds in 3-6 months to mss. Sample copy for $11, more info online. Guidelines available online.

Nonfiction "Creative nonfiction that reads like fiction. Nonfiction pieces should be creative, exploratory, or experimental in tone rather than rhetorical, academic, or journalistic." No reviews, tracts, or scholarly essays. **Pays $20/printed page, and 1-year subscription.**

Fiction For Drama: one-acts/excerpts of no more than 1500 words preferred. Also interested in seeing dramatic monologues. Needs experimental, novel concepts, traditional. "New writing that is contemporary and literary. Short stories and self-contained novel excerpts. Works of translation are eagerly sought and should be accompanied by a copy of the original. Would like to see more translations. No gothic, confession, religious, romance, pornography, or science fiction." **Buys 12-16 mss/year.** Send complete ms. 25 pages maximum **Pays $20/printed page, and 1-year subscription.**

Poetry Needs avant-garde, traditional. **Buys 10 poems/issue.** Submit maximum 6 poems. **Pays $40/ printed page, and 1-year subscription.**

Tips "We are looking for new and exciting fiction. Excellence is still our No. 1 criterion. As well as poetry, imaginative nonfiction and fiction, we are especially open to translations of all kinds, very short fiction pieces and drama which work well on the page. Translations must come with a copy of the original language work. We pay an additional $10/printed page to selected authors whose work we place on our online version of *Prism*."

PUERTO DEL SOL

a journal of new literature, New Mexico State University, English Department, New Mexico State Univ., Box 30001, MSC 3E, Las Cruces NM 88003. E-mail: contact@puertodelsol.org. Website: puertodelsol.org. Semiannual magazine literary fiction, nonfiction and poetry. Estab. 1964. Circ. 1,000. Byline given. We pay in issues. No kill fee. Buys first North American serial rights. Accepts queries by online submission form. Accepts simultaneous submissions. Sample copy online. Guidelines available.

Nonfiction Needs essays, Lyric Essay. **Buys 0 mss/year.** Send complete ms.

Fiction Needs experimental. Send complete ms.

Poetry Needs avant-garde, free verse.

$ $$ QUARTERLY WEST

University of Utah, 255 S. Central Campus Dr., Room 3500, Salt Lake City UT 84112. E-mail: quarterlywest@yahoo.com. Website: www.utah.edu/quarterlywest. Semiannual magazine. We publish fiction, poetry, and nonfiction in long and short formats, and will consider experimental as well as traditional works. Estab. 1976. Circ. 1,900. Pays on publication. Publishes ms an average of 6 months after acceptance. Buys first North American serial rights, buys all rights. Accepts queries by mail. Accepts simultaneous submissions. Responds in 6 months to mss. Sample copy for $7.50 or online Guidelines available online.

Nonfiction Needs essays, interview, personal experience, travel, book reviews. **Buys 6-8 mss/year.** Send complete ms. 10,000 words maximum **Pays $20-100.**

Fiction No preferred lengths; interested in longer, fuller short stories and short shorts. Needs ethnic, experimental, humorous, mainstream, novel concepts, slice-of-life vignettes, short shorts, translations. No detective, science fiction or romance. **Buys 6-10 mss/year.** Send complete ms. **Pays $15-100, and 2 contributor's copies.**

Poetry Needs avant-garde, free verse, traditional. Buys 40-50 poems/year. Submit maximum 5 poems. **Pays $15-100.**

Tips We publish a special section of short shorts every issue, and we also sponsor a biennial novella contest. We are open to experimental work—potential contributors should read the magazine! Don't send more than 1 story/submission. Biennial novella competition guidelines available upon request with SASE. We prefer work with interesting language and detail—plot or narrative are less important. We don't do Western themes or religious work.

$$ QUEEN'S QUARTERLY

A Canadian Review, 144 Barrie St., Queen's University, Kingston ON K7L 3N6 Canada. (613)533-2667. Fax: (613)533-6822. E-mail: queens.quarterly@queensu.ca. Website: www.queensu.ca/quarterly.

95% freelance written. Quarterly magazine covering a wide variety of subjects, including science, humanities, arts and letters, politics, and history for the educated reader. "A general interest intellectual review, featuring articles, book reviews, poetry, and fiction." Estab. 1893. Circ. 3,000. Byline given. Pays on publication. Publishes ms an average of 6-12 months after acceptance. Buys first North American serial rights. Responds in 2-3 months to queries. Sample copy and guidelines available online.
Fiction Contact: Boris Castel, editor. Needs historical, mainstream, novel concepts, short stories, women's. Length: 2,500-3,000 words. **Pays $100-300, 2 contributor's copies and 1-year subscription; additional copies $5.**
Poetry Buys 25 poems/year. Submit maximum 6 poems.

QUICK FICTION

P.O. Box 4445, Salem MA 01970. Website: www.quickfiction.org. Semiannual print and website magazine covering contemporary microfiction stories and narrative prose of 500 words or less for both the print and website journal. This is a New England literary magazine. Open to most themes. Recent issues include Arielle Greenberg, Steve Almond, Stephen Dixon, and James Tates. Estab. 2001. No kill fee. Buys first North American serial rights, buys electronic rights. Actual rights obtained are specific to individual agreement with each author. Accepts previously published material. Accepts simultaneous submissions.
Nonfiction Needs essays, Critical essays, reviews, articles, Oddities.
Fiction Submit a story online in Submission Guidelines. Length: 25-500 words.
Tips Prefers online submissions. Deadline for issue 15 is Feb. 1st. We seek concept pitches for material published exclusively on our website.

N QUIDDITY INTERNATIONAL LITERARY JOURNAL AND PUBLIC-RADIO PROGRAM

Benedictine University at Springfield, 1500 N. 5th St., Springfield IL 62702. Semiannual magazine publishing exemplary poetry and prose from emerging and established writers around the world. "Each work selected is considered for public-radio program feature offered by NPR-member station (WUIS (PRI affiliate)." Byline and contributor note given. Accepts simultaneous submissions.

- "International submissions are encouraged."

Nonfiction Needs Creative nonfiction. Send complete ms. Length: 5,000 word-maximum
Fiction Needs experimental, mainstream, novel excerpts. Send complete ms. Length: 5,000 word-max.
Poetry Needs avant-garde, free verse, traditional. Query first. Submit maximum 5/max. poems.

QWF (QUALITY WOMEN'S FICTION)

AllWriters' Workplace & Workshop, 234 Brook St., Unit 2, Waukesha WI 53188. (262)446-0284. E-mail: qwfsubmissionsusa@yahoo.com. Website: www.allwriters.org. Semiannual magazine published in January and July. Women throughout history have forged a path of strength, creativity and endurance. *QWF* reflects those values and that admiration of women. Estab. 1994. Circ. 1,000. Pays on publication. Buys first North American serial rights. Responds in 3 months to mss. Guidelines available online.
Fiction Reading periods: January issue (September 1-November 30); July issue (March 1-May 31). All fiction genres accepted, as long as the protagonist is a woman, the story evokes emotion, and the story is written by a woman. **Buys 40 mss/year.** Length: up to 5,000 words. **Pays one copy of the magazine.**
Tips Evoke emotion. Present yourself professionally with a clean manuscript and a cover letter.

RAIN TAXI

Review of Books, Rain Taxi, Inc., P.O. Box 3840, Minneapolis MN 55403-0840. (612)825-1528. Fax: (612)825-1528. E-mail: info@raintaxi.com. Website: www.raintaxi.com. **40% freelance written**. Quarterly magazine covering books. "*Rain Taxi* Review of Books, a nonprofit quarterly, is dedicated to covering literature & the arts, including poetry, graphic novels, cultural critique, & quality fiction in all genres. Winner of an Independent Press Award, *Rain Taxi* is a great vehicle for books & authors that may otherwise get lost in the mainstream media." Estab. 1996. Circ. 18,000. Byline given. Payment in Issues. No kill fee. Publishes ms an average of 2 months after acceptance. Buys first North American serial rights. Editorial lead time 2 months. Submit seasonal material 3 months in advance. Accepts queries by mail, e-mail. Responds in 2 weeks to queries. Responds in 1 month to mss. Sample copy for $5. Guidelines by e-mail.
Nonfiction Contact: Eric Lorberer, editor. Needs essays, interview, Reviews. **Buys 0 mss/year.** Query. Length: 500-2,000 words. **Pays 0 for assigned or unsolicited articles.**

RARITAN

A Quarterly Review, 31 Mine St., New Brunswick NJ 08903. (732)932-7887. Fax: (732)932-7855. Quarterly magazine covering literature, history, fiction, and general culture. Estab. 1981. Circ. 3,500. Byline given. Pays on publication. No kill fee. Publishes ms an average of 1 year after acceptance. Buys first North American serial rights. Editorial lead time 5 months. Accepts queries by mail.

- *Raritan* no longer accepts previously published or simultaneous submissions.

Nonfiction Needs book excerpts, essays. **Buys 50 mss/year.** Send 2 copies of complete ms. 15-30 pages

$ RATTAPALLAX

Rattapallax Press, 217 Thompson St., Suite 353, New York NY 10012. (212)560-7459. E-mail: info@rattapallax.com. Website: www.rattapallax.com. **10% freelance written**. Annual magazine covering international fiction and poetry. *Rattapallax* is a literary magazine that focuses on issues dealing with globalization. Estab. 1999. Circ. 3,000. Byline given. Pays on publication. No kill fee. Publishes ms an average of 6 months after acceptance. Buys first North American serial rights, buys South American rights. Editorial lead time 6 months. Submit seasonal material 6 months in advance. Accepts queries by e-mail. Responds in 2 weeks to queries. Responds in 6 months to mss. Sample copy available online. Guidelines available online.

Poetry Needs avant-garde, free verse, traditional. Submit maximum 5 poems. Length: 5-200 lines.

REDACTIONS: POETRY & POETICS

58 So. Main St., 3rd Floor, Brockport NY 14420. E-mail: redactionspoetry@yahoo.com. Website: www.redactions.com. Every 9 months covering poems, reviews of new books of poems, translations, manifestos, interviews, essays concerning poetry, poetics, poetry movements, or concerning a specific poet or a group of poets; and anything dealing with poetry. No kill fee. All rights revert back to the author. Accepts queries by e-mail. Accepts simultaneous submissions.

Nonfiction Needs essays, Reviews of new books of poems, interview, Art, Translation.

Reprints "Please mention first publication in *Redactions*."

Poetry "Anything dealing with poetry."

Tips "We only accept submissions by e-mail. We read submissions throughout the year. E-mail us and attach submission into one Word, Wordpad, Notepad, .rtf, or .txt document, or, place in the body of an e-mail. Include brief bio and your snail mail address. Query after 90 days if you haven't heard from us."

RED MOUNTAIN REVIEW

1800 8th Ave. N., Birmingham AL 35203. E-mail: rmrsubmissions@gmail.com. Website: www.redmountainreview.net. Magazine covering poetry, short fiction, nonfiction, chapbooks, interviews, reviews. Features Red Mountain Reading Series and Chapbook Contest ($500 prize plus copies) and trip to a joint reading. Seeks writers who do hard work, who tell the hard truths and who do so expecting little more in return than to be heard. *RMR* gravitates toward work that—for reasons of form, length, subject or project—tends to have a difficult time finding the light of day in mainstream commercial venues. No kill fee. Accepts queries by mail. Accepts simultaneous submissions. Responds in 3 months to queries.

Nonfiction Needs essays, Reviews, interview.

Fiction Length: 1,000-7,500 words.

Poetry Submit maximum 5-7 poems. any length or style

Tips Open to poetry and short fiction submissions from Oct. 1, 2008 to Apr. 30, 2009. Simple goal: to produce fine mags and chapbooks that get noticed, with Birmingham's roots in mind.

RED ROCK REVIEW

College of Southern Nevada, Red Rock Review, Dept. of English w20E, College of Southern Nevada, 6375 W. Charleston Blvd., Las Vegas NV 89146. (702)651-. E-mail: redrockreview@csn.edu; richard.logsdon@csn.edu. Website: http://sites.csn.edu/english/redrockreview/. **Contact:** Rich Logsdon. Semiannual magazine covering poetry, fiction and creative nonfiction as well as book reviews. "We are dedicated to the publication of fine contemporary literature." No kill fee. Buys first North American serial rights. All other rights revert to the authors & artists upon publication. Accepts queries by e-mail. No longer accepting snail mail submissions. Send all submissions as MS. Word, RTF, or PDF file attachment to redrockreview@csn.edu. Guidelines available online. Occasionally comments on rejections.

Nonfiction Needs essays. No literary criticism. Length: 5,000 words.

Fiction Contact: John Ziebell (john.zeibell@csn.edu). Length: 7,500 words.

Poetry Contact: Jean French (jean.french@csn.edu). Length: 80 lines.

Tips "Open to short fiction and poetry submissions from Sept. 1-May 31. Include SASE and include brief bio. No general submissions between June 1st and August 31st. See guidelines online."

RHINO

The Poetry Forum, Inc., P.O. Box 591, Evanston IL 60204. E-mail: rhinobiz@hotmail.com. Website: www.rhinopoetry.org. **Contact:** Marcia L. Zuckerman, associate editor. Annual magazine covering high-quality, diverse poetry, short/shorts and translations by new and established writers. "This eclectic annual journal of more than 30 years accepts poetry, flash fiction (1,000 words or less), and poetry-in-translation that experiments, provokes, compels and/or sings. More than 80 poets are showcased. The regular call for poetry as well as the Founder's Contest submission period is from April 1 to October 1." No kill fee. Buys first North American serial rights. Accepts queries by mail. Accepts simultaneous submissions. Response time may exceed 6 weeks. Sample copy for $6. Guidelines available online.

Nonfiction Needs essays, on poetry, humor, Translation.

Fiction Needs humorous, short shorts (1,000 words or less), or translations. Submit by mail. Always include a #10 SASE and "let us know whether we should return your poems or just our response to your work."

Poetry Needs avant-garde, free verse, light verse, traditional. "Please label each poem with your name, address, telephone number, and e-mail address for ease in contacting you." Include SASE. Submit maximum 3-5 poems.

Tips "Please visit our website for further examples that will indicate the quality of poetry we look for, plus additional submission information, including updates on the Rhino Founders Contest."

$ RIVER STYX

Big River Association, 3547 Olive St., Suite 107, St. Louis MO 63103. (314)533-4541. Website: www.riverstyx.org. Triannual magazine. "*River Styx* publishes the highest quality fiction, poetry, interviews, essays, and visual art. We are an internationally distributed multicultural literary magazine. Mss read May-November." Estab. 1975. Byline given. Pays on publication. No kill fee. Publishes ms an average of 1 year after acceptance. Buys first North American serial rights, buys one-time rights. Accepts queries by mail. Accepts simultaneous submissions. Responds in 4 months to mss. Sample copy for $7. Guidelines available online.

Nonfiction Needs essays, interview. **Buys 2-5 mss/year.** Send complete ms. **Pays 2 contributor copies, plus 1 year subscription; pays $8/page if funds are available.**

Photos Send photos. Reviews 5 × 7 or 8 × 10 b&w and color prints and slides. Pays 2 contributor copies, plus 1-year subscription; $8/page if funds are available Buys one time rights.

Fiction Contact: Richard Newman, editor. Needs ethnic, experimental, mainstream, novel concepts, short stories, literary. No genre fiction, less thinly veiled autobiography. **Buys 6-9 mss/year.** Send complete ms. no more than 23-30 manuscript pages. **Pays 2 contributor copies, plus 1-year subscription; $8/page if funds are available.**

Poetry Needs avant-garde, free verse. No religious. Buys 40-50 poems/year. Submit maximum 3-5 poems. **Pays 2 contributor copies, plus a 1-year subscription; $8/page if funds are available.**

$$ THE SAINT ANN'S REVIEW

A Journal of Contemporary Arts and Letters, Saint Ann's School, 129 Pierrepont St., Brooklyn NY 11201. (718)522-1660. Fax: (718)522-2599. E-mail: sareview@saintannsny.org. Website: www.saintannsreview.com. **100% freelance written.** Semiannual literary magazine. We seek honed work that gives the reader a sense of its necessity. Estab. 2000. Circ. 2,000. Byline given. Pays on publication. No kill fee. Publishes ms an average of 4 months after acceptance. Buys first North American serial rights. Submit seasonal material 4 months in advance. Accepts queries by mail. Responds in 1 month to queries. Responds in 4 months to mss. Sample copy for $8. Guidelines available online.

Nonfiction Needs book excerpts, occasionally, essays, humor, interview, personal experience, photo feature. **Buys 10 mss/year.** Send complete ms. 7,500 words maximum **Pays $40/published page, $250/maximum.**

Photos Send photos. Reviews transparencies, prints, GIF/JPEG files, b&w art. Offers $50/photo page or art page, $100 maximum. Buys one time rights.

Columns/Departments Book reviews, 1,500 words. 10 Send complete ms by mail only. **Pays $40/published page, $200 maximum.**

Fiction Needs ethnic, experimental, fantasy, historical, humorous, mainstream, slice-of-life vignettes, translations. **Buys 40 mss/year.** 7,500 words maximum. **Pays $40/published page, $100 maximum.**

Poetry Needs avant-garde, free verse, haiku, light verse, traditional. Buys 30 poems/year. Submit maximum 5 poems. **Pays $50/page, $100 maximum.**

SALT HILL

Creative Writing Program, Syracuse University, English Dept., Syracuse University, Syracuse NY

13244. E-mail: salthilljournal@gmail.com. Website: www.salthilljournal.com. **Contact:** "Please contact appropriate genre editor." *Salt Hill* is a semiannual journal publishing outstanding new poetry, fiction, nonfiction, interviews, and artwork. "Our eclectic taste ranges from traditional to experimental. All we ask is that it's good. Open to most themes." No kill fee. Accepts queries by mail. yesAccepts simultaneous submissions. Guidelines available online

Nonfiction Contact: Mikael Awake, nonfiction editor. Needs essays, interview, reviews, translation, off-beat travelogues.

Photos Contact: Naxielo Mannello, Art Ed.

Fiction Contact: Kayla Blatchley, Aaron Chambers, Alice Holbrook, fiction editors.

Poetry Contact: Carroll Beauvais, Eric Darby, poetry editors. Needs Needs prose and verse poems. Translations accepted. Submit maximum 3-7 poems. No known line limits.

Tips "*Salt Hill* seeks to publish writing that is exciting and necessary, regardless of aesthetic. Rather than trying to fit any subscribed style, send your best work. We recommend reading recent issues or samples on our website prior to submitting. Open submissions from Aug. 1-Apr. 1. Enclose SASE for reply. We recycle mss, and encourage you to use a 'Forever' stamp on your SASE. Clearly mark envelope to the appropriate genre editor's attention."

SANTA CLARA REVIEW

Santa Clara Review, Santa Clara University, P.O. Box 3212, 500 El Camino Real, Santa Clara CA 95053-3212. (408)554-4484. Fax: (408)554-4454. E-mail: info@santaclarareview.com. Website: www.santaclarareview.com. "SCR is one of the oldest literary publications in the West. Entirely student-run by undergraduates at Santa Clara University the magazine draws upon submissions from SCU affiliates as well as contributors from around the globe. The magazine is published in Feb. and May each year. In addition to publishing the magazine the review staff organizes a writing practicum, open mic nights, writers and artist retreats and hosts guest readers. Printed magazine also available to view free online. No kill fee. For contact info, queries and general info visit santaclarareview.com. SCR accepts submissions year round. Estab. 1869. No kill fee. Publishes ms an average of 2 months after acceptance. Accepts queries by online submission form. Please visit website to submit your work electronically.

Nonfiction Length: 5000 words or less. Excerpts from larger works accepted.

Fiction Length: 5,000 words or less. Excerpts from larger works accepted.

Poetry Submit maximum 3 poems. Do not exceed 10 pages in length.

Tips Visual Art: Submit 2 works and provide us with a link to your online portfolio.**Graphic Novels:** 20 page max. Excerpts from larger works accepted. PDF format. **Book or Album Reviews:** 500 - 1,500 words.

$ ⊠ THE SAVAGE KICK LITERARY MAGAZINE

Murder Slim Press, 129 Trafalgar Road West, Gt. Yarmouth Norfolk NR31 8AD United Kingdom. E-mail: moonshine@murderslim.com. Website: www.murderslim.com/savagekick.html. **100% freelance written**. Semiannual magazine. "*Savage Kick* primarily deals with viewpoints outside the mainstream. honest emotions told in a raw, simplistic way. It is recommended that you are very familiar with the *SK* style before submitting. We have only accepted 8 new writers in 4 years of the magazine. Ensure you have a distinctive voice and story to tell." Estab. 2005. Circ. 500+. Byline given. Pays on acceptance. Publishes ms an average of up to 2 months after acceptance. Buys all electronic rights for 3 months. Accepts queries by mail, e-mail. Accepts simultaneous submissions. Responds in 7-10 days to queries. Guidelines free.

Nonfiction "We only accept articles in relation to the authors featured on our reading list." Needs interview, personal experience. **Buys 10-20 mss/year.** Send complete ms. Length: 500-3,000 words. **Pays $25-35.**

Columns/Departments up to 4 Query. **Pays $25-35.**

Fiction Needs mystery, slice-of-life vignettes, crime. "Real-life stories are preferred, unless the work is distinctively extreme within the crime genre. No Poetry of any kind, no mainstream fiction, Oprah-style fiction, Internet/chat language, teen issues, excessive Shakespearean language, surrealism, overworked irony, or genre fiction (horror, fantasy, science fiction, western, erotica, etc.)." **Buys 10-25 mss/year.** Send complete ms. Length: 500-6,000 words. **Pays $35.**

$ THE SEATTLE REVIEW

Box 354330, University of Washington, Seattle WA 98195. (206)543-2302. E-mail: seaview@u.washington.edu. Website: www.seattlereview.org. Semiannual magazine. Includes general fiction, poetry, craft essays on writing, and one interview per issue with a Northwest writer. Estab. 1978. Circ. 1,000. Pays on publication. Buys first North American serial rights. Responds in 8 months to mss. Sample copy for $6.

Guidelines available online.

- Editors accept submissions only from October 1 through May 31.

Fiction Wants more creative nonfiction. "We also publish a series called Writers and their Craft, which deals with aspects of writing fiction (also poetry)—point of view, characterization, etc, rather than literary criticism, each issue." Needs ethnic, experimental, fantasy, historical, horror, humorous, mainstream, mystery, novel concepts, suspense, western, contemporary, feminist, gay, lesbian, literary, psychic/supernatural/occult, regional, translations. "Nothing in bad taste (porn, racist, etc.). No genre fiction or science fiction." **Buys 4-10 mss/year.** Send complete ms. Length: 500-10,000 words. **Pays $0-100.**
Tips "Beginners do well in our magazine if they send clean, well-written manuscripts. We've published a lot of 'first stories' from all over the country and take pleasure in discovery."

N SENECA REVIEW

Hobart and William Smith Colleges, Geneva NY 14456. (315)781-3392. E-mail: senecareview@hws.edu. Website: www.hws.edu/academics/senecareview/index.aspx. Semiannual magazine *Seneca Review* reads manuscripts of poetry, translations, essays on contemporary poetry, and lyric essays (creative nonfiction that borders on poetry). "The editors have special interest in translations of contemporary poetry from around the world. Publisher of numerous laureates and award-winning poets, we also publish emerging writers and are always open to new, innovative work. Poems from *SR* are regularly honored by inclusion in *The Best American Poetry* and *Pushcart Prize* anthologies. Distributed internationally." No kill fee. Accepts queries by mail. Responds in 3 months to mss. Guidelines available online.
Nonfiction Needs essays, (up to 20 pages), Translation. Past special features include Irish women's poetry and Irish prison poetry; Israeli women's poetry; Polish, Catalan, and Albanian poetry; excerpts from the notebooks of 32 contemporary American poets, an issue of essays devoted to Hayden Carruth; an issue of essays devoted to Hayden Carruth, current issue, The Lyric Body, Anthology of Poets, Essayists and Artists to Intimately Address Difference and Disability.
Poetry Submit maximum 3-5 poems.
Tips "One submission per reading period. Mss received during summer are returned."

THE SEWANEE REVIEW

University of the South, 735 University Ave., Sewanee TN 37383-1000. (931)598-1246. E-mail: lcouch@sewanee.edu. Website: www.sewanee.edu/sewanee_review. "A literary quarterly, publishing original fiction, poetry, essays on literary and related subjects, and book reviews for well-educated readers who appreciate good American and English literature." Estab. 1892. Circ. 2,200. Pays on publication. Buys first North American serial rights, buys second serial (reprint) rights. Responds in 6-8 weeks to mss. Sample copy for $8.50 ($9.50 outside US). Guidelines available online.

- Does not read mss June 1 - August 31.

Fiction Send query letter for reviews. Send complete ms for fiction. No erotica, science fiction, fantasy or excessively violent or profane material. **Buys 10-15 mss/year.** Length: 3,500-7,500 words.
Poetry Send complete ms. Submit maximum 6 poems. Length: 40 lines.

SHEARSMAN

the magazine, Shearsman Books Ltd, Shearsman, 58 Velwell Rd., Exeter England EX4 4LD UK. E-mail: editor@shearsman.com. Website: www.shearsman.com/pages/magazine/home.html. Semiannual magazine and website covering contemporary poetry. "We are inclined toward the more exploratory end of the current spectrum. Notwithstanding this, however, quality work of a more conservative kind will always be considered seriously, provided that the work is well written. I always look for some rigour in the work, though I will be more forgiving of failure in this regard if the writer is trying to push out the boundaries." Estab. 1981. No kill fee. Accepts queries by mail, e-mail. Guidelines available online.

- "Our website consists of vastly more material than just the print magazine and is regularly updated. I tend to like mixing work from both ends of the spectrum, and firmly believe that good writing can and should cohabit with other forms of good writing, regardless of the aesthetic that drives it."

Poetry No sloppy writing of any kind.
Tips "We no longer read through the year. Our reading window for magazines is from 1 Mar.-31 Mar., for the Oct. issue, and from 1 Sept. to 30 Sept. for the April issue. Books may be submitted anytime. See guidelines online. Avoid sending attachments with your e-mails unless they are in PDF format. Include SASE; no IRCs."

$ SHENANDOAH

The Washington and Lee University Review, Washington and Lee University, Mattingly House, 2 Lee Ave., Lexington VA 24450-2116. (540)458-8765. Fax: (540)458-8461. E-mail: shenandoah@wlu.edu.

Website: shenandoah.wlu.edu/faq.html. **Contact:** R. T. Smith, editor. Triannual magazine. "Unsolicited manuscripts will not be read between January 1 and October 1, 2010. All manuscripts received during this period will be recycled unread." Estab. 1950. Circ. 2,000. Byline given. Pays on publication. No kill fee. Publishes ms an average of 10 months after acceptance. Buys first North American serial rights, buys one-time rights. Responds in 3 months to mss. Sample copy for $12. Guidelines available online.
Nonfiction Needs essays, Book reviews. **Buys 6 mss/year.** Send complete ms. **Pays $25/page ($250 max).**
Fiction Needs mainstream, short stories. No sloppy, hasty, slight fiction. **Buys 15 mss/year.** Send complete ms. **Pays $25/page ($250 max).**
Poetry "No inspirational, confessional poetry." Buys 70 poems/year. Submit maximum 5 poems. **Pays $2.50/line ($200 max).**

⊘ SHORT STUFF

Bowman Publications, Short Stuff Magazine, Bowman Publications, 301 E. Harmony Rd., Suite 204, Fort Collins CO 80525. (970)232-9066. E-mail: shortstf89@aol.com. **98% freelance written.** Bimonthly magazine. "We are perhaps an enigma in that we publish only clean stories in any genre. We'll tackle any subject, but don't allow obscene language or pornographic description. Our magazine is for grown-ups, not X-rated `adult' fare." Estab. 1989. Circ. 10,400. Byline given. Payment and contract upon publication. Buys first North American serial rights. Editorial lead time 3 months. Submit seasonal material 3 months in advance. Responds in 6 months to mss. Sample copy - send 9 × 12 SAE with 5 first-class (44¢) stamps. Guidelines for #10 SASE.

- "We are now open to submissions."

Nonfiction Most nonfiction is staff written. Needs humor. "We are holiday oriented and each issue reflects the appropriate holidays." **Buys 30 mss/year.** Send complete ms. Include cover letter about the author and synopsis of the story. Length: 500-1,500 words. **Payment varies.**
Photos Send photos. Identification of subjects required. Offers no additional payment for photos accepted with ms Buys one-time rights.
Fiction Needs adventure, historical, humorous, mainstream, mystery, romance, science fiction, (seldom), suspense, western. "We want to see more humor—not essay format—real stories with humor; 1,000-word mysteries, modern lifestyles. The 1,000-word pieces have the best chance of publication. No erotica; nothing morbid or pornographic. **Buys 144 mss/year.** Send complete ms. Length: 500-1,500 words. **Payment varies.**
Tips "Don't send floppy disks or cartridges. We are holiday oriented; mark on outside of envelope if story is for Easter, Mother's Day, etc. We receive 500 manuscripts each month. This is up about 200%. Because of this, I implore writers to send 1 manuscript at a time. I would not use stories from the same author more than once an issue and this means I might keep the others too long. Please don't e-mail your stories! If you have an e-mail address, please include that with cover letter so we can contact you. If no SASE, we destroy the manuscript."

SLIPSTREAM

Dept. W-1, Box 2071, Niagara Falls NY 14301. E-mail: editors@slipstream.org. Website: www.slipstreampress.org/index.html. Annual magazine covering poetry only, black & white photos, drawings and illustrations; A yearly anthology of some of the best poetry and fiction you'll find today in the American small press. "We prefer contemporary urban themes—writing from the grit that is not afraid to bark or bite. We shy away from pastoral, religious, and rhyming verse." Estab. 1980. Chapbook Contest prize is $1,000 plus 50 professionally printed copies of your chapbook. No kill fee. Accepts queries by mail. Accepts previously published material. Accepts simultaneous submissions. Guidelines available online.

- If you're unsure, the editors strongly recommend that you sample a current or back issue of *Slipstream*.

Photos It's better to send scans or photocopies of artwork rather than originals.
Poetry No pastoral, religious, and rhyming verse.
Tips "Slipstream is now accepting poetry submissions for its first theme issue in several years. We seek work exploring SEX-FOOD-DEATH. Your interpretation may include one, two, or all three of the subjects. No previous published work. All submissions must include a SASE for response. Originally examined back in Issue 14, the theme was so popular we have decided to revisit it. Deadline for submissions is: MARCH 1, 2011. Send copies of your poems, not originals. See Submission guidelines online."

$ ⊕ SMITHS KNOLL

Goldings, Golding Lane, Leiston, Suffolk England IP16 4EB UK. Website: www.michael-laskey.co.uk/

smiths_knoll.php. **Contact:** Michael Laskey and Joanna Cutt, co-editors. Magazine covering contemporary poetry. "We are open to new voices. We like to work with poets too on poems that appeal to us but that we think aren't quite there yet, asking questions, maybe making suggestions if it seems helpful. Then we care a lot about the look of the poems: we print them on good quality paper; and give them space, don't cram them in." Estab. 1991. Circ. 500. Pays on publication. No kill fee. Publishes ms an average of 2 weeks after acceptance. Accepts queries by mail. Responds in 1 week to mss. Free if you live in the UK. Guidelines available online.

- "We receive about 6,000 poetry submissions a year."

Poetry Submit maximum 4-6 poems.
Tips We're neurotic about proofreading.

SNOW MONKEY

An Eclectic Journal, Ravenna Press, No known public address, E-mail: snowmonkey.editor@comcast.net. Website: www.ravennapress.com/snowmonkey/. Ten times/year website covering original unpublished poems and micro-prose. Seeks writing "that's like footprints of the Langur monkeys left at 11,000 feet on Poon Hill, Nepal. Open to most themes." No kill fee. Accepts queries by e-mail. Accepts simultaneous submissions. Responds in 2 months to mss. Guidelines available.
Fiction Up to 10 writers are featured in monthly posting from Sept. through June. Length: 500 words.
Tips "Send submissions as text-only in the body of your e-mail. Include your last name in the subject line. We do not currently use bios, but we love to read them."

$ SOLEADO

Revista de Literatura y Cultura, Dept. of International Language and Culture Studies, IPFW, CM 267, 2101 E. Coliseum Blvd., Fort Wayne IN 46805. (260)481-6630. Fax: (260)481-6985. E-mail: summersj@ipfw.edu. Website: www.soleado.org. **100% freelance written**. Annual magazine covering Spanish-language literary, cultural, and creative writing. Our readers are interested in literature and culture, from creative writing to personal essays and beyond. Spanish is of an ever-growing importance in the US and the world, and our readers and writers are people using that language. *Soleado* is a literary magazine, so academic treatises are not on the list of texts we would be excited to see. The focus of the magazine is on Spanish-language writing, although the national origin of the writer does not matter. The subject matter doesn't have to be Hispanic, either. The one exception to the Spanish-language requirement is that certain texts deal with the difficulties of being bilingual and/or bicultural are welcome to be written in 'Spanglish' when that usage is essential to the text. Please don't send anything written only in English. We publish a very limited selection of work in 'Spanglish'—don't send us anything without having read what we have already published. Estab. 2004. Byline given. Pays on publication. No kill fee. Publishes ms an average of 8 months after acceptance. Buys first North American serial rights, buys first rights, buys one-time rights, buys second serial (reprint) rights, buys simultaneous rights, buys electronic rights, buys anthology rights. Editorial lead time 6 months. Submit seasonal material 1 year in advance. Accepts queries by mail, e-mail. Accepts previously published material. Responds in 1 week to queries. Responds in 3 months to mss. Sample copy and writer's guidelines online.
Nonfiction Needs book excerpts, essays, humor, interview, opinion, personal experience, travel, translations, memoir, creative nonfiction. No how-to, general travel, inspirational, religious or anything written in English. All nonfiction must have a literary or cultural slant. **Buys up to 3 mss/year.** Query. **Pays maximum $50.**
Fiction We are looking for good literary writing in Spanish, from Magical Realism a la García Márquez, to McOndo-esque writing similar to that of Edmundo Paz-Soldán and Alberto Fuguet, to Spanish pulp realism like that of Arturo Pérez-Reverte. Testimonials, experimental works like those of Diamela Eltit, and women's voices like Marcela Serrano and Zoé Valdés are also encouraged. We are not against any particular genre writing, but such stories do have to maintain their hold on the literary, as well as the genre, which is often a difficult task. Needs adventure, ethnic, experimental, fantasy, historical, humorous, mainstream, mystery, novel concepts, science fiction, slice-of-life vignettes, suspense, translations, magical realism. **Buys 2-6 mss/year.** Query or send complete ms. up to 8,000 words **Pays $-50.**
Poetry Needs avant-garde, free verse, light verse, traditional. Avoid poetry that takes us to places we have already seen. The best kind of poetry takes readers somewhere unexpected or via an unexpected path, departing from the familiar just when they thought they had things figured out. Buys 10-15 poems/year. Submit maximum 4 poems. 400 words
Tips Whether you are or are not a native speaker of Spanish, have someone read over your manuscript for obvious grammatical errors, flow, and continuity of ideas. We are interested in literary translations into Spanish, as well as original writing. Query before sending submission as an e-mail attachment.

We publish annually, and the reading period runs from September 1 to March 31 of the following year. Anything that comes between April and August won't get a reply until the new reading period begins.

SONORA REVIEW

University of Arizona's Creative Writing MFA Program, University of Arizona, Dept. of English, Tucson AZ 85721. E-mail: sonora@e-mail.arizona.edu. Website: www.coh.arizona.edu/sonora/. **90% freelance written**. Semiannual magazine. We look for the highest quality poetry, fiction, and nonfiction, with an emphasis on emerging writers. Our magazine has a long-standing tradition of publishing the best new literature and writers. Check out our website for a sample of what we publish and our submission guidelines, or send $6 for a sample back issue. Estab. 1980. Circ. 500. Byline given. No kill fee. Publishes ms an average of 3-4 months after acceptance. Buys first North American serial rights, buys one-time rights, buys electronic rights. Accepts queries by mail. Accepts simultaneous submissions. Responds in 2-5 weeks to queries. Responds in 3 months to mss. Sample copy for $6. Guidelines available online.

Nonfiction Needs book excerpts, essays, interview, personal experience. **Buys 2-4 mss/year.** Send complete ms.

Fiction Needs ethnic, experimental, mainstream, novel concepts. **Buys 6-10 mss/year.** Send complete ms. Length: 1,000-8,000 words. **Pays 2 contributor's copies; additional copies for $4.**

Poetry All poetry welcome. Buys 20-40 poems/year. Submit maximum 7 poems.

Tips We have no length requirements, but we usually do not consider poems, stories, or essays that are over 20 pages in length because of space. We publish mostly poems, short stories, and literary nonfiction. We do not read during June or July.

SOUTHERN HUMANITIES REVIEW

Auburn University, 9088 Haley Center, Auburn University AL 36849. (334)844-9088. E-mail: shrengl@auburn.edu. Website: www.auburn.edu/english/shr/home.htm. **Contact:** Karen Beckwith. **99% freelance written**. Quarterly perfect-bound journal covering general humanities. *Southern Humanities Review* publishes fiction, poetry, and critical essays on the arts, literature, philosophy, religion, and history for a well-read, scholarly audience. Estab. 1967. Circ. approximately 700. Byline given. No kill fee. "We contract for all rights until publication. Then copyright reverts to author." Accepts queries by mail, e-mail. Responds in 1-2 weeks to queries. Sample copy for $5 in U.S.; $7 everywhere else. Guidelines for #10 SASE or at www.auburn.edu/shr

Fiction Buys 4-8 mss/year. Send complete ms. Length: 15,000 words. **Pays 2 contributor copies.**

Poetry Any kind; short poems preferred. Buys 10-25 poems/year. Submit maximum 5 poems. **Pays 2 contributor copies.**

$ THE SOUTHERN REVIEW

Louisiana State University, Old President's House, Baton Rouge LA 70803-5001. (225)578-5108. Fax: (225)578-5098. E-mail: southernreview@lsu.edu. Website: www.lsu.edu/tsr. **Contact:** Jeanne Leiby, Editor. **100% freelance written. Works with a moderate number of new/unpublished writers each year; reads unsolicited mss.** Quarterly magazine with emphasis on contemporary literature in the US and abroad. Reading period: September1-June 1. All mss. submitted during summer months will be recycled. Estab. 1935. Circ. 2,900. Byline given. Pays on publication. No kill fee. Publishes ms an average of 6 months after acceptance. Buys first North American serial rights. Accepts queries by mail. Does not accept previously published work.Responds in 2 months. Sample copy for $8. Guidelines available online.

Nonfiction Wants "essays with careful attention to craftsmanship, technique, and seriousness of subject matter. Willing to publish experimental writing if it has a valid artistic purpose. Avoid extremism and sensationalism. Essays should exhibit thoughtful and sometimes severe awareness of the necessity of literary standards in our time. Emphasis on contemporary literature. No footnotes." **Buys 25 mss/year.** Length: 4,000-10,000 words. **Pays $30/page.**

Fiction Contact: Jessica Faust-Spitzfaden, assistant editor. Short stories of lasting literary merit, with emphasis on style and technique; novel excerpts. "We emphasize style and substantial content. No mystery, fantasy or religious mss." Submit one ms. in any genre at a time. "We rarely publish work that is longer than 8,000 words. We consider novel excerpts if they stand alone." Length: 4,000-8,000 words. **Pays $30/page.**

Poetry Submit maximum 5/time poems. 1-4 pages **Pays $30/page.**

THE SOW'S EAR POETRY REVIEW

217 Brookneill Dr., Winchester VA 22602. E-mail: sowsearpoetry@yahoo.com. Website: www.sows-ear.kitenet.net. **Contact:** Kristin Camitta Zimet. **100% freelance written**. Quarterly magazine. "The Sow's

Ear prints fine poetry of all styles and lengths, complemented by black and white art. We also welcome reviews, interviews, and essays related to poetry. We are open to group submissions. Our 'Crossover' section features poetry married to any other art form, including prose, music, and visual media." Estab. 1988. Circ. 700. Publishes ms an average of 1-6 months after acceptance. Buys first North American serial rights. Editorial lead time 1-6 months. Submit seasonal material 3 months in advance. Accepts queries by mail, e-mail. Accepts simultaneous submissions. Responds in 2 weeks to queries. Responds in 3 months to mss. Sample copy for $8. Guidelines by e-mail.

Nonfiction Needs essays, related to poetry, interview, of poets, reviews of poetry books. **Buys 6 mss/year.** Query. Length: 1,000-3,000 words.

Photos Model releases required. Reviews prints, GIF/JPEG files. Offers no additional payment for photos accepted with ms. Buys one-time rights.

Columns/Departments Review of poetry book published within a year (1,000-3,000 words); Interview with a poet; essay related to poetry. Query.

Poetry Needs avant-garde, free verse, haiku, light verse, traditional. Open to any style or length. Buys 100 poems/year. Submit maximum 5 poems. No limits on line length.

Tips "We like work that is carefully crafted, keenly felt, and freshly perceived. We respond to poems with voice, a sense of place, delight in language, and a meaning that unfolds. We look for prose that opens new dimensions to appreciating poetry."

SPOON RIVER POETRY REVIEW

Spoon River Poetry Association, 4241/Publications Unit, Illinois State University, Normal IL 61790-4241. E-mail: lcqetsi@ilstu.edu. Website: litline.org/spoon. **Contact:** Kirstin Hotelling Zona, editor. Semiannual magazine covering contemporary poetry in English from the U.S. and around the world in English translation. The Spoon River Poetry Review, published 2x/year is one of the nation's oldest continuously published poetry journals. We seek to publish the best of all poetic genres, and are proud of our commitment to regional as well as international poets and readers. Spoon River includes black and white photography alongside poems from emergine and established poets, and reviews solicited from poet-critics and translators. Additionally, each issue contains a SRPR Illinois poet feature (12-18 pages of previously unpublished poetry, an interview, and a bio). The Summer/Fall issue also spotlights the winner and runners-up of our annual editor's prize contest. No kill fee. Guidelines available online.

- *Poet's Market* has named the *SRPR* one of the best reads in the poetry publishing world.

Nonfiction Needs interview.

Columns/Departments Teaching Poetry.

Poetry Submit maximum Submit 3-5 poems. Reads submissions between September 15-April 15. Include name, address, and e-mail on every poem. poems.

Tips "Read widely, across styles and time periods. We are looking for poems that are as intellectually and emotionally ambitious as they are attentive to technique. We seek your very best work in any form, and are especially interested in publishing a dynamic variety of poems in every issue."

$ 🌐 STAND MAGAZINE

School of English, University of Leeds, Leeds LS2 9JT United Kingdom. (44)(113)343-4794. E-mail: stand@leeds.ac.uk. Website: www.standmagazine.org. "Quarterly literary magazine." Estab. 1952. Pays on publication. No kill fee. Accepts queries by mail. Guidelines available online at website.

- "U.S. submissions can be made through the Virginia office (see separate listing)."

$$ THE STRAND MAGAZINE

P.O. Box 1418, Birmingham MI 48012-1418. (248)788-5948. Fax: (248)874-1046. E-mail: strandmag@strandmag.com. Website: www.strandmag.com. Quarterly magazine covering mysteries, short stories, essays, book reviews. After an absence of nearly half a century, the magazine known to millions for bringing Sir Arthur Conan Doyle's ingenious detective, Sherlock Holmes, to the world has once again appeared on the literary scene. First launched in 1891, *The Strand*,included in its pages the works of some of the greatest writers of the 20th century: Agatha Christie, Dorothy Sayers, Margery Allingham, W. Somerset Maugham, Graham Greene, P.G. Wodehouse, H.G. Wells, Aldous Huxley and many others. In 1950, economic difficulties in England caused a drop in circulation which forced the magazine to cease publication. Estab. 1998. Circ. 50,000. Byline given. Pays on acceptance. No kill fee. Publishes ms an average of 4 months after acceptance. Buys first North American serial rights. Accepts queries by e-mail. Responds in 1 month to queries. Guidelines for #10 SASE.

Fiction Contact: A.F. Gulli, editor. Needs horror, humorous, mystery, detective stories, suspense, tales of the unexpected, tales of terror and the supernatural written in the classic tradition of this century's great authors. We are not interested in submissions with any sexual content. Length: 2,000-6,000 words.

Pays $50-175.

Tips No gratuitous violence, sexual content, or explicit language, please.

STUDIO

A Journal of Christians Writing, 727 Peel St., Albury NSW 2640 Australia. (61)(2)6021-1135. Fax: (61)(2)6021-1135. E-mail: studio00@bigpond.net.au. **Contact:** Paul Grover, man. editor. **80% freelance written**. Quarterly magazine. "*Studio* publishes poetry and prose of literary merit, offers a venue for previously published, new, and aspiring writers, and seeks to create a sense of community among christians who write." Estab. 1980. Circ. 300. Byline given. No kill fee. Publishes ms an average of 6 months after acceptance. Editorial lead time 3 months. Accepts queries by mail, e-mail. Accepts previously published material. Accepts simultaneous submissions. Responds in 1 week to queries and to mss. Sample copy for $10 (AUD). Guidelines by e-mail.

Poetry Needs free verse, haiku, light verse. Submit maximum 2 poems. Length: 10-40 lines. **contributor copy.**

$$$ SUBTROPICS

University of Florida, P.O. Box 112075, 4008 Turlington Hall, Gainesville FL 32611-2075. E-mail: dleavitt@ufl.edu. Website: www.english.ufl.edu/subtropics. **Contact:** David Leavitt. **100% freelance written.** "Magazine published 3 times/year through the University of Florida's English department. *Subtropics* seeks to publish the best literary fiction, essays, and poetry being written today, both by established and emerging authors. We will consider works of fiction of any length, from short shorts to novellas and self-contained novel excerpts. We give the same latitude to essays. We appreciate work in translation and, from time to time, republish important and compelling stories, essays, and poems that have lapsed out of print by writers no longer living." Estab. 2005. Byline given. Pays on acceptance. Publishes ms an average of 6 months after acceptance. Buys first North American serial rights, buys one-time rights. Responds in 1 month to queries and mss. Guidelines available online

Nonfiction Needs essays, literary nonfiction. No book reviews. **Buys 15 mss/year.** Send complete ms. **Pays $1,000.**

Fiction Literary fiction only, including short-shorts. No genre fiction. **Buys 20 mss/year.** Send complete ms. **Pays $500 for short-shorts; $1,000 for full stories.**

Poetry Buys 50 poems/year. Submit maximum 5 poems. **Pays $100.**

Tips "We publish longer works of fiction, including novellas and excerpts from forthcoming novels. Each issue will include a short-short story of about 250 words on the back cover. We are also interested in publishing works in translation for the magazine's English-speaking audience."

SYCAMORE REVIEW

Purdue University Dept. of English, 500 Oval Dr., West Lafayette IN 47907. E-mail: sycamore@purdue.edu. Website: sycamorereview.com. Semiannual magazine publishing poetry, fiction and nonfiction, books reviews and art. "Strives to publish the best writing by new and established writers. Looks for well crafted and engaging work, works that illuminate our lives in the collective human search for meaning. We would like to publish more work that takes a reflective look at our national identity and how we are perceived by the world. We look for diversity of voice, pluralistic worldviews, and political and social context." No kill fee. Buys first North American serial rights. Accepts queries by mail.

- *Sycamore Review* is Purdue University's internationally acclaimed literary journal, affiliated with Purdue's College of Liberal Arts and the Dept. of English. Art should present politics in a language that can be felt.

Nonfiction Contact: Jess Mehr. Needs essays, Personal, humor, Literary Memoir, Translation. No outside interviews, previously published work (except translations) or genre pieces (conventional sci fi, romance, horror, etc.) No scholarly articles or journalistic pieces. Please query for book reviews, brief critical essays as well as all art.

Poetry Submissions should be typed, double-spaced,with numbered pages and the author's name and the title easily visible on each page. Does not publish creative work by any student currently attending Purdue University. Former students should wait one year before submitting. Submit maximum Submit 4-5 poems in one envelope. "Wait until you have received a response to submit again." poems.

Tips "We look for originality, brevity, significance, strong dialogue, and vivid detail. We sponsor the Wabash Prize for Poetry (deadline: mid-October) and Fiction (deadline: March 1). $1,000 award for each. All contest submissions will be considered for regular inclusion in the *Sycamore Review*. No e-mail submissions-no exception. Include SASE.

$ TAMPA REVIEW

University of Tampa Press, 401 W. Kennedy Blvd., Tampa FL 33606. (813)253-6266. Fax: (813)258-7593. Website: tampareview.ut.edu. Semiannual magazine published in hardback format. An international literary journal publishing art and literature from Florida and Tampa Bay as well as new work and translations from throughout the world. Estab. 1988. Circ. 500. Byline given. Pays on publication. No kill fee. Publishes ms an average of 10 months after acceptance. Buys first North American serial rights. Editorial lead time 18 months. Accepts queries by mail. Responds in 5 months to mss. Sample copy for $7. Guidelines available online.

Nonfiction Contact: Elizabeth Winston, nonfiction editor. Needs general interest, interview, personal experience, creative nonfiction. No how-to articles, fads, journalistic reprise, etc. **Buys 6 mss/year.** Send complete ms. Length: 250-7,500 words. **Pays $10/printed page.**

Photos State availability. Captions, identification of subjects required. Reviews contact sheets, negatives, transparencies, prints, digital files. Offers $10/photo. Buys one time rights.

Fiction Contact: Lisa Birnbaum and Kathleen Ochshorn, fiction editors. Needs ethnic, experimental, fantasy, historical, mainstream, literary. "We are far more interested in quality than in genre. Nothing sentimental as opposed to genuinely moving, nor self-conscious style at the expense of human truth." **Buys 6 mss/year.** Send complete ms. Length: 200-5,000 words. **Pays $10/printed page.**

Poetry Contact: Don Morrill and Martha Serpas, poetry editors. Needs avant-garde, free verse, haiku, light verse, traditional. No greeting card verse, hackneyed, sing-song, rhyme-for-the-sake-of-rhyme. Buys 45 poems/year. Submit maximum 10 poems. Length: 2-225 lines.

Tips "Send a clear cover letter stating previous experience or background. Our editorial staff considers submissions between September and December for publication in the following year."

THIN AIR

Department of English, LA Room 133, P.O. Box 6032, Flagstaff AZ 86011. Website: www.thinairmagazine.com. Publishes contemporary voices for a literary-minded audience. Estab. 1995. Circ. 500. No kill fee. Publishes ms an average of 6-9 months after acceptance. Buys first North American serial rights. Accepts queries by mail, e-mail. Accepts simultaneous submissions. Guidelines available online.

Nonfiction Creative nonfiction. Needs *Not currently accepting submissions.* . Submit cover letter, bio, and up to 25 pages of your ms.

Photos "We accept both b&w and color art and photography. We accept 8 × 10 photographs of your art. Please do not send slides or negatives."

Fiction Needs cond novels, ethnic, experimental, mainstream. No children's/juvenile, horror, romance, erotica. We would like to see more intelligent comedy.

Poetry Submit maximum 6 poems.

THINK JOURNAL

Reason Publishing LLC, P.O. Box 454, Downingtown PA 19335. E-mail: thinkjournal@yahoo.com. Website: http://web.me.com/christineyurick/think_journal/home_page.html. **Contact:** Christine Yurick, Editor. **100% freelance written**. Quarterly magazine. "*Think Journal* focuses on words that have meaning, that are presented in a clear way, and that exhibit the skills demanded by craft. The Journal prints work that achieves a balance between form and content. The most important traits that will be considered are form, structure, clarity, content, imagination, and style." Estab. 2008. Byline given. Publication is payment, along with 1 free contributor's copy. No kill fee. Publishes ms an average of 3-6 months after acceptance. Buys one-time rights. Editorial lead time 3 months. Submit seasonal material 3 months in advance. Accepts queries by mail. Responds in 2-4 weeks to queries. Responds in 1-2 months to mss. Single copy: $7; subscription: $20/year. Sample $6. International please add $3 for single issue, $10 for subscription. Guidelines for SASE or on website.

Nonfiction Needs essays, letter to editor. Especially interested in topics whose focus is literature and/or literary criticism. "We do not want ranting, profanity; would only like well thought-out essays that shed light on an intellectual or philosophical topic." Send complete ms. Length: under 2,500 words.

Fiction Needs novel excerpts, short stories, "Craft and content are important. There should be some discernible conflict and resolution, well-defined characters, depth, meaning to what is happening, something beyond a scene or moment in time, a structured plot and the portrayal of some type of value." Send complete ms. Novel excerpts: please query first, 3,000+ words with summary. Length: 2,000-3,000 words.

Poetry Needs free verse, traditional, "Think Journal is inclined to publish formal work, i.e. work that exhibits knowledge of the traditional characteristics of poetic craft, including but not limited to, form, meter, rhyme, and other poetic techniques." Submit maximum 3-6 poems at a time. poems. No restrictions in length.

Tips "Please visit the website to view samples of previously published work, or purchase a sample issue. Also looking for graphic design artwork for the cover."

THIRD COAST

Western Michigan University Dept. of English, Western Michigan University, Dept. of English, Kalamazoo MI 49008-5331. Website: www.wmich.edu/thirdcoast. **Contact:** Laura Donnelly, editor. **95% freelance written**. Twice-yearly magazine. "*Third Coast* publishes poetry, fiction (including traditional and experimental fiction, shorts, and novel excerpts, but not genre fiction), creative nonfiction (including reportage, essay, memoir, and fragments), drama, and translations." Estab. 1995. Circ. 3,000. Byline given. No kill fee. Publishes ms an average of 6 months after acceptance. Buys first rights. Accepts simultaneous submissions. Responds in 4 months to queries. Responds in 4 months to mss. Sample copy for $6. Guidelines available online at http://www.thirdcoastmagazine.com/submit/.

- Do not query unless prose exceeds 9,000 words.

Nonfiction Contact: Creative Nonfiction Editor. **Buys 2-6 mss/year.** Send complete ms. Length: 600-9,000 words.

Fiction Contact: Fiction Editors, Drama Editors. Fiction and drama needs are in the same paragraph below. Needs experimental stand alone novella and novel excerpts, short-shorts, strong voice, strong narrative, stories of ethnicity, stories of place (especially Great Lakes/Upper Midwest). Drama Editor needs one-act plays of no more than 20 pages; strongly encourages 10-minute plays that have had readings or productions, but have not been published. Submit in standard play format. No genre fiction. **Buys 8-12 mss/year.** Send complete ms. Length: 600-9,000 words.

Poetry Contact: Poetry Editors. No simple narratives or any simplistic poetry. Buys 60 poems/year. Submit maximum 5 poems.

THORNY LOCUST

TL Press, P.O. Box 32631, Kansas City MO 64171. (816)501-4178. "*Thorny Locust* is a literary journal produced quarterly in a dusty corner of the publisher's hermitage. We are interested in poetry, fiction, and artwork with some bite (e.g., satire, epigrams, well-structured tirades, black humor, and bleeding heart cynicism.) Absolutely no natural or artificial sweeteners, unless they're the sugar-coating on a strychnine tablet. We are not interested in polemics, gratuitous grotesques, somber surrealism, weeping melancholy, or hate-mongering. To rewrite Jack Conroy, 'We prefer polished vigor to crude banality.'" Estab. 1993. Circ. 200. Pays with contributor copies. No kill fee. Publishes ms an average of 3-4 months after acceptance. Buys one-time rights. Accepts simultaneous submissions.

Photos Black and white line drawings, cartoons, and photographs.

Fiction No restrictions on style; maximum 1,500 words.

Poetry "Formal and casual, conventional and experimental verse are equally welcome. No hard restrictions on length, but we're unlikely to take anything over 2 manuscript pages."

Tips "We publish more poetry than fiction."

$ $ THE THREEPENNY REVIEW

P.O. Box 9131, Berkeley CA 94709. (510)849-4545. Website: www.threepennyreview.com. **100% freelance written. Works with small number of new/unpublished writers each year.** Quarterly tabloid. We are a general interest, national literary magazine with coverage of politics, the visual arts, and the performing arts as well. Estab. 1980. Circ. 9,000. Byline given. Pays on acceptance. Publishes ms an average of 1 year after acceptance. Buys first North American serial rights. Responds in 1 month to queries. Responds in 2 months to mss. Sample copy for $12 or online Guidelines available online.

- Does not read mss from September to December.

Nonfiction Needs essays, expose, historical, personal experience, book, film, theater, dance, music, and art reviews. **Buys 40 mss/year.** Send complete ms. Length: 1,500-4,000 words. **Pays $400.**

Fiction Contact: Wendy Lesser, editor. No fragmentary, sentimental fiction. **Buys 10 mss/year.** Send complete ms. Length: 800-4,000 words. **Pays $400 per poem or Table Talk piece**.

Poetry Needs free verse, traditional. No poems without capital letters or poems without a discernible subject. Buys 30 poems/year. Submit maximum 5 poems. **Pays $200.**

Tips Nonfiction (political articles, memoirs, reviews) is most open to freelancers.

TIME OF SINGING

A Magazine of Christian Poetry, P.O. Box 149, Conneaut Lake PA 16316. E-mail: timesing@zoominternet.net. Website: www.timeofsinging.com. **100% freelance written**. Quarterly booklet. "*Time of Singing*

publishes 'Christian' poetry in the widest sense, but prefers 'literary' type. Welcome forms, fresh rhyme, well-crafted free verse. Like writers who take chances, who don't feel the need to tie everything up neatly." Estab. 1958. Circ. 250. Byline given. Publishes ms an average of within 1 year after acceptance. Buys first North American serial rights, buys first rights, buys one-time rights, buys second serial (reprint) rights. Editorial lead time 6 months. Submit seasonal material 6 months in advance. Accepts previously published material. Accepts simultaneous submissions. Responds in 3 months to mss. Sample copy for $4/each or 2 for $7. Guidelines for SASE or on website.
Poetry Needs free verse, haiku, light verse, traditional. Does not want sermons that rhyme or greeting card type poetry. Buys 200 poems/year. Submit maximum 5 poems. Length: 3-60 lines.
Tips "Read widely, dead white males and contemporary, 'Christian' and otherwise, and study the craft. Helpful to get honest critique of your work. Cover letter not necessary. Your poems speak for themselves."

$$$ TIN HOUSE

McCormack Communications, P.O. Box 10500, Portland OR 97210. (503)274-4393. Fax: (503)222-1154. E-mail: info@tinhouse.com; submissions@tinhouse.com. Website: www.tinhouse.com. **Contact:** Cheston Knapp; Holly Macarthur. **90% freelance written**. "We are a general interest literary quarterly. Our watchword is quality. Our audience includes people interested in literature in all its aspects, from the mundane to the exalted." Estab. 1998. Circ. 11,000. Byline given. Pays on publication. No kill fee. Publishes ms an average of 6 months after acceptance. Buys first North American serial rights, buys anthology rights. Editorial lead time 6 months. Submit seasonal material 6 months in advance. Accepts queries by mail, online submission form. Accepts simultaneous submissions. Responds in 6 weeks to queries. Responds in 3 months to mss. Sample copy for $15. Guidelines available online.
Nonfiction Needs book excerpts, essays, interview, personal experience. Send complete ms. 5,000 words maximum **Pays $50-800 for assigned articles. Pays $50-500 for unsolicited articles.**
Columns/Departments Lost and Found (mini-reviews of forgotten or underappreciated books), up to 500 words; Readable Feasts (fiction or nonfiction literature with recipes), 2,000-3,000 words; Pilgrimage (journey to a personally significant place, especially literary), 2,000-3,000 words. 15-20 Send complete ms. **Pays $50-500.**
Fiction Contact: Rob Spillman, fiction editor. Needs experimental, mainstream, novel concepts, literary. **Buys 15-20 mss/year.** Send complete ms. 5,000 words maximum **Pays $200-800.**
Poetry Contact: Brenda Shaunessy, poetry editor. Needs avant-garde, free verse, traditional. "No prose masquerading as poetry." Buys 40 poems/year. Submit maximum 5 poems. **Pays $50-150.**
Tips "Remember to send a SASE with your submission."

TRIQUARTERLY

Northwestern University Press, Northwestern University, 629 Noyes St., Evanston IL 60208-4302. (847)491-7614. Fax: (847)467-2096. E-mail: triquarterly@northwestern.edu. Website: www.triquarterly.org. Triannual magazine covering unsolicited fiction, poetry, and occasionally literary essays and graphic art. "We are committed to presenting the finest works of literature and graphic art for discerning readers. By publishing a combination of general issues and occasional special issues such as *for Vladimir Nabokev on his seventieth birthday*, *TriQuarterly* quickly became one of the most widely admired and important literary journals." Estab. 1958. No kill fee. Responds in 3 months to mss. Guidelines available online.
Nonfiction Needs essays, Translation. We do not usually publish philosophical essays.
Tips Work may be submitted without query during our reading period, Oct. 1 to Feb. 28. Mss. submitted between April 1 and Sept. 30 will be returned unreader. All work submitted must be unpublished anywhere. This also applies to translations for which translators must get permission from the author to publish. All mss. should be typed, doubled (poetry may be singled-spaced). Mail to Editors, include SASE.

UPSTREET

Ledgetop Publishing, P.O. Box 105, Richmond MA 01254-0105. (413)441-9702. E-mail: submissions@upstreet-mag.org. Website: www.upstreet-mag.org. **99% freelance written**. Annual magazine covering literary fiction, nonfiction and poetry. Estab. 2005. Circ. 4,000. Byline given. Pays on publication. Publishes ms an average of 6 months after acceptance. Buys first North American serial rights. Editorial lead time 6 months. Accepts queries by e-mail. Accepts simultaneous submissions. Responds in 2 weeks to queries. Responds in 6 months to mss. Sample copy for $12.50. Guidelines by e-mail.
Nonfiction Needs book excerpts, essays, personal experience, literary, personal essay/memoir, lyric essay. Does not want journalism, religious, technical, anything but literary nonfiction. **Buys 8 mss/year.** Send complete ms. Length: 5,000 words.

Fiction Needs experimental, mainstream, novel concepts, quality literary fiction. Does not want run-of-the-mill genre, children's, anything but literary. **Buys 12 mss/year.** Send complete ms. Length: 5,000 words.
Poetry Needs avant-garde, free verse, traditional. Quality is only criterion. Buys 20 poems/year. Submit maximum 3 poems.
Tips Get sample copy, submit electronically, and follow guidelines.

U.S. 1 WORKSHEETS

U.S. 1 Poets' Cooperative, U.S. 1 Worksheets, P.O. Box 127, Kingston NJ 08528. Website: www.us1poets.com. Annual journal covering works from U.S. 1 Poets' Cooperative, along with the best works of poetry we receive. "We are looking for well-crafted poetry with a focused point of view. Representative authors: Baron Wormser, Alicia Ostriker, Richard Jones, Bj Ward, Lois Harrod." Estab. 1972. Circ. 500. Accepts simultaneous submissions. Responds in 3-6 months to mss. Guidelines available online.
Fiction "We no longer consider fiction, with the exception of prose poems."
Poetry Submit maximum 5 poems. Submit no more than 7 pages.
Tips "Mss are accepted from April 15-June 30 and are read by rotating editors from the cooperative. Send us something unusual, something we haven't seen before, but make sure it's poetry. Proofread carefully."

$ $ VERBATIM

The Language Quarterly, Word, Inc., P.O. BOX 1774, Burlingame ILCA 94011. (800)897-3006. E-mail: editor@verbatimmag.com. Website: www.verbatimmag.com. **75-80% freelance written**. Quarterly magazine covering language and linguistics. "*Verbatim* is the only magazine of language and linguistics for the lay person." Estab. 1974. Circ. 1,600. Byline given. Pays on publication. No kill fee. Publishes ms an average of 6-9 months after acceptance. Buys all rights. Editorial lead time 3 months. Submit seasonal material 6 months in advance. Accepts queries by e-mail (only). Responds in 3 weeks to queries. Responds in 2 months to mss. Sample copy for sae with 9 × 12 envelope and 6 first-class stamps. Guidelines available online.
Nonfiction Needs essays, humor, personal experience. Does not want puns or overly cranky prescriptivism. **Buys 24-28 mss/year.** Query. Submissions only accepted online. **Pays $25-400 for assigned articles. Pays $25-300 for unsolicited articles.**
Poetry "We only publish poems explicitly about language. Poems written in language not enough." Buys 4-6 poems/year. Submit maximum 3 poems. Length: 3-75 lines. **Pays $25-50.**
Tips "Humorously write about an interesting language, language topic, or jargon. Also, when querying, include 3-4 lines of biographical information about yourself."

VERBSAP

Concise Prose. Enough Said, No public address known., E-mail: editor@verbsap.com. Website covering the best in minimalist prose writing. We accept short stories, flash fiction, creative nonfiction and novel excerpts that stand along. We look for stark, elegant, concise prose. Good: Stories with strong plots and vivid characters; clarity; research; originality; focus; stories that make us weep or laugh; depictions of human frailty or resilience; absurdity. No kill fee. Buys one-time rights, buys Electronic Rights (60 days) rights. All material published online will be archived. Responds in 2 months to mss. Guidelines available online.
Nonfiction Needs interview, Creative. Length: 3,000 words.
Fiction Needs novel concepts, (that stand alone). No fictionalized violence or depictions of drug use; thinly-veiled rewrites of CSI or Law & Order episodes; stories comprised mainly of dialogue or internal monologues; fables; the torturing of small animals; strong odors; bodily fluids; surprise endings.
Tips We accept submissions during posted reading periods. The next dates will be available shortly. Paste your work in the body of an e-mail. Write 'Submission,' the genre and your name in the subject line. Include your name, e-mail address, and a brief bio. Note that *VerbSap* accepts only original, unpublished work. See Submission guidelines. Query if you haven't heard back in 2 months.

VERSAL

The literary journal of Amsterdam, wordsinhere, Postbus 3865, Amsterdam 1001AR The Netherlands. E-mail: versaljournal@wordsinhere.com. Website: www.wordsinhere.com. **Contact:** Megan M. Garr, editor. Annual print magazine. "We look for the urgent, involved, and unexpected, and are particularly interested in innovative forms and translocal writing." Estab. 2002. Circ. 750. Pays on publication. No kill fee. Publishes ms an average of 3-4 months after acceptance. Buys first rights. Accepts queries by e-mail. Accepts simultaneous submissions. Responds in < 1 week to queries. Responds in < 2 months to mss.

Sample copy available online. Guidelines available.
Nonfiction Query.
Fiction Contact: Robert Glick, editor. Needs experimental, mainstream, novel concepts, Flash fiction, prose poetry. **Buys 10 mss/year. pays in copies.**
Poetry Contact: Megan M. Garr, editor. Needs avant-garde, free verse. Buys 35 poems/year. Submit maximum 5 poems. **Pays in copies.**
Tips "We ask that all writers interested in submitting work first purchase a copy (available from our website) to get an idea of *Versal*'s personality. All unsolicited submissions must be submitted through our online submission system. The link to this system is live during the submission period, which is Sept. 15-Jan. 15 each year."

$ $ VESTAL REVIEW

A flash fiction magazine, 2609 Dartmouth Dr., Vestal NY 13850. E-mail: submissions@vestalreview.net. Website: www.vestalreview.net. Semi-annual print magazine specializing in flash fiction. "We accept only e-mail submissions." Circ. 1,500. Pays on publication. No kill fee. Publishes ms an average of 3-4 months after acceptance. Buys first North American serial rights, buys electronic rights. Accepts queries by e-mail. Accepts simultaneous submissions. Responds in 1 week to queries. Responds in 3 months to mss. Guidelines available online.

- *Vestal Review's* stories have been reprinted in the *Mammoth Book of Miniscule fiction, Flash Writing, E2Ink anthologies*, and in the *WW Norton Anthology Flash Fiction Forward*.

Fiction Needs ethnic, horror, mainstream, speculative fiction. Does not read new submissions in January, June, July, and December. All submissions received during these months will be returned unopened. Length: 50-500 words. **Pays 3-10¢/word and 1 contributor's copy; additional copies $10 (plus postage).**
Tips "We like literary fiction, with a plot, that doesn't waste words. Don't send jokes masked as stories."

$ VIRGINIA QUARTERLY REVIEW

University of Virginia, One West Range, P.O. Box 400223, Charlottesville VA 22904-4223. (434)924-3124. Fax: (434)924-1397. E-mail: editors@vqronline.org (questions only). Website: www.vqronline.org. Quarterly magazine. A national journal of literature and thought. A lay, intellectual audience; people who are not out-and-out scholars but who are interested in ideas and literature. Estab. 1925. Circ. 7,000. Byline given. Pays on publication. No kill fee. Publishes ms an average of 4 months after acceptance. Buys first rights. Editorial lead time 6 months. Submit seasonal material 6 months in advance. Accepts queries by online submission form. Responds in 4 months to mss. Sample copy for $14. Guidelines available online.
Nonfiction Needs book excerpts, essays, general interest, historical, reportage, travel. Send complete ms. Length: 2,000-7,000 words. **Pays $.20/word**
Fiction Needs ethnic, mainstream, mystery, novel excerpts, serialized novels. Send complete ms. Length: 3,000-7,000 words. **Pays $100/page maximum.**
Poetry Submit maximum 5 poems. **Pays $5/line, minimum of $200.**
Tips "Submissions only accepted online."

$ VIRTUE IN THE ARTS

P.O. Box 11081, Glendale CA 91226. E-mail: info@virtueinthearts.com. Website: www.virtueinthearts.com. **50% freelance written.** Semiannual magazine covering virtues. Each publication features short stories, articles, poetry and artwork relating to a different virtue each time (such as honesty, compassion, trustworthiness, etc.). Estab. 2006. Byline given. Pays on publication. Publishes ms an average of 6 months after acceptance. Buys one-time rights. Editorial lead time 6 months. Submit seasonal material 1 month in advance. Accepts queries by mail, e-mail. Accepts previously published material. Accepts simultaneous submissions. Responds in 6 months to mss. Guidelines by e-mail.
Nonfiction Needs essays. Each issue has a theme. See writer's guidelines for the current theme. Does not want articles that show the virtue in a negative light. **Buys 2 mss/year.** Send complete ms. Length: 100-400 words. **Pays $7.**
Photos Send photos. Reviews digital images. Offers $7/photo. Buys one time rights.
Fiction Fiction shedding a positive light on the current theme (a virtue) in an entertaining way. **Buys 2 mss/year.** Send complete ms. Length: 300-1,500 words. **Pays $7.**
Poetry Needs avant-garde, free verse, haiku, light verse, traditional. Poetry needs to reflect the current theme (virtue). Submit maximum 5 poems. Length: 4-32 lines. **Pays $7.**

Tips We're looking for material that promotes virtue. If you promote virtue, you get virtue. Find out the current deadline and the current virtue, then send us your submission.

$ VISIONS-INTERNATIONAL

Black Buzzard Press, 3503 Ferguson Lane, Austin TX 78754. (512)674-3977. **95% freelance written**. Magazine published 2 times/year featuring poetry, essays and reviews. Estab. 1979. Circ. 750. Byline given. Pays on publication. No kill fee. Publishes ms an average of 6 months after acceptance. Buys first North American serial rights. Editorial lead time 1 month. Accepts queries by mail. Responds in 3 weeks to queries. Responds in 2 months to mss. Sample copy for $4.95. Guidelines for #10 SASE.

Nonfiction Needs essays, by assignment after query reviews. Query. 1 page maximum. **Pays $10 and complimentary copies.**

Columns/Departments , .

Poetry Needs avant-garde, free verse, traditional. "No sentimental, religious, scurrilous, sexist, racist, amateurish, or over 3 pages." Buys 110 poems/year. Length: 2-120 lines.

Tips "Know your craft. We are not a magazine for amateurs. We also are interested in translation from modern poets writing in any language into English. No e-mail submissions please."

$$ WEBER STUDIES

Voices and Viewpoints of the Contemporary West, Weber State University, 1214 University Circle, Ogden UT 84408-1214. (801)626-6616 or (801)626-6473. E-mail: weberjournal@weber.edu. Website: weberstudies.weber.edu. **70% freelance written**. Magazine and online text archive published 3 times/year covering preservation of and access to wilderness, environmental cooperation, insight derived from living in the West, cultural diversity, changing federal involvement in the region, women and the West, implications of population growth, the contributions of individuals (scholars, artists and community leaders), a sense of place. We seek works that provide insight into the environment and culture (both broadly defined) of the contemporary western US. We look for good writing that reveals human nature, as well as natural environment. Estab. 1981. Circ. 800-1,000. Byline given. Pays on publication. No kill fee. Publishes ms an average of 6-12 months after acceptance. Buys one-time rights, buys electronic rights. (copyrights revert to authors after publication) Editorial lead time 6 months. Submit seasonal material 6 months in advance. Accepts queries by mail, e-mail, phone. Accepts simultaneous submissions. Responds in 1 month to queries. Responds in 6-9 months to mss. Sample copy for $8. Guidelines for #10 SASE, on website or by e-mail.

Nonfiction Needs essays, historical, interview, opinion, personal experience, photo feature. **Buys 20-25 mss/year.** Send complete ms. Length: 5,000 words. **Pays $150-300, plus 1 contributor copy and 1-year subscription.**

Photos State availability. Captions, identification of subjects, model releases required. Reviews 4X6 prints, 4X6 GIF/JPEG files at 300 dpi. Negotiates pay individually. Buys one time rights.

Columns/Departments Send complete ms. **Pays $100-200.**

Fiction Needs adventure, ethnic, historical, humorous, mainstream, novel concepts, religious, slice-of-life vignettes, western. Send complete ms. Length: 5,000 words. **Pays $150-300.**

Poetry Buys 15-20 sets of poems/year. Submit maximum 6 poems. **Pays $100-150.**

$ WEST BRANCH

Stadler Center for Poetry, Bucknell University, Lewisburg PA 17837-2029. (570)577-1853. Fax: (570)577-1885. E-mail: westbranch@bucknell.edu. Website: www.bucknell.edu/westbranch. Semiannual literary magazine. *West Branch* publishes poetry, fiction, and nonfiction in both traditional and innovative styles. Byline given. Pays on publication. No kill fee. Buys first North American serial rights. Accepts queries by online submission form. Sample copy for $3. Guidelines available online.

Nonfiction Needs essays, general interest, literary. **Buys 4-5 mss/year.** Send complete ms. **Pays $20-100 ($10/page).**

Fiction Needs novel excerpts, short stories,. No genre fiction. **Buys 10-12 mss/year.** Send complete ms. **Pays $20-100 ($10/page).**

Poetry Needs free and formal verse. Buys 30-40 poems/year. Submit maximum 6 poems. **Pays $20-100 ($10/page).**

Tips "All submissions must be sent via our online submission manager. Please see website for guidelines. We recommend that you acquaint yourself with the magazine before submitting."

$ WEST COAST LINE

A Journal of Contemporary Writing & Criticism, West Coast Review Publishing Society, 2027 E. Annex, 8888 University Dr., Simon Fraser University, Burnaby BC V5A 1S6 Canada. (604)291-4287. Fax: (604)291-

4622. E-mail: wcl@sfu.ca. Website: www.sfu.ca/west-coast-line. Triannual magazine of contemporary literature and criticism. Estab. 1990. Circ. 500. Pays on publication. No kill fee. Buys one-time rights. Editorial lead time 4 months. Accepts queries by mail, e-mail. Responds in up to 6 months to queries. Responds in up to 6 months to mss. Sample copy for $10. Guidelines for SASE (US must include IRC).
Nonfiction Needs essays, literary/scholarly/critical, experimental prose. No journalistic articles or articles dealing with nonliterary material. **Buys 8-10 mss/year.** Send complete ms. Length: 1,000-5,000 words. **Pays $8/page, 2 contributor's copies and a 1-year subscription.**
Fiction Needs experimental, novel concepts. **Buys 3-6 mss/year.** Send complete ms. Length: 1,000-7,000 words. **Pays $8/page**.
Poetry Needs avant-garde. No light verse, traditional. Buys 10-15 poems/year. Submit maximum maximum 5-6 poems. **Pays $8/page**.
Tips Submissions must be either scholarly or formally innovative. Contributors should be familiar with current literary trends in Canada and the US. Scholars should be aware of current schools of theory. All submissions should be accompanied by a brief cover letter; essays should be formatted according to the MLA guide. The publication is not divided into departments. We accept innovative poetry, fiction, experimental prose, and scholarly essays.

$ WESTERN HUMANITIES REVIEW

University of Utah, English Department, 255 S. Central Campus Dr., Room 3500, Salt Lake City UT 84112-0494. (801)581-6070. Fax: (801)585-5167. E-mail: whr@mail.hum.utah.edu. Website: www.hum.utah.edu/whr. **Contact:** Dawn Lonsinger, Managing Editor. A tri-annual magazine for educated readers. Estab. 1947. Circ. 1,000. Pays in contributor copies. Publishes ms an average of 1 year after acceptance. Buys one-time rights. Accepts simultaneous submissions. Sample copy for $10. Guidelines available online.

- Reads mss September 1-April 1. Mss sent outside these dates will be returned unread.

Nonfiction Contact: Barry Weller, editor-in-chief. Authoritative, readable articles on literature, art, philosophy, current events, history, religion, and anything in the humanities. Interdisciplinary articles encouraged. Departments on films and books. **Buys 6-8unsolicited/year mss/year.** Send complete ms. **Pays $5/published page.**
Fiction Contact: Lance Olsen, Fiction Editor. Needs experimental, and innovative voices. Does not want genre (romance, sci-fi, etc.). **Buys 5-8 mss/year.** Send complete ms. Length: 5,000 words. **Pays $5/published page (when funds available).**
Poetry Contact: Richard Howard, poetry editor.
Tips "Because of changes in our editorial staff, we urge familiarity with recent issues of the magazine. We do not publish writer's guidelines because we think that the magazine itself conveys an accurate picture of our requirements. Please, no e-mail submissions."

WHISKEY ISLAND MAGAZINE

English Dept., Cleveland State University, Cleveland OH 44115. E-mail: whiskeyisland@papmail.csuohio.edu. Website: http://www.csuohio.edu/class/english/whiskeyisland/. Semiannual magazine covering creative writing, original poetry, fiction, nonfiction, and art submissions year round. "This is a nonprofit literary magazine that has been published (in one form or another) by students of Cleveland State University for over 30 years. Also features the Annual Student Creative Writing Contest ($5000-$400-$250)." No kill fee. Accepts queries by mail, e-mail. Accepts simultaneous submissions. Responds in 6 months to mss.
Tips "See submissions page. Include SASE. Wait at least a year before submitting again."

WILLOW REVIEW

College of Lake County Publications, College of Lake County, 19351 W. Washington St., Grayslake IL 60030-1198. (847)543-2956. E-mail: com426@clcillinois.edu. Website: www.clcillinois.edu/community/willowreview.asp. Magazine covering poems, short fiction, creative nonfiction, reviews of books written by Midwestern writers or published by Midwestern presses. The editors award prizes for best poetry and prose in the issue. Prize awards vary contingent on the current year's budget but normally ranges from $100-400. There is no reading fee or separate application for these prizes. All accepted mss. are eligible. No kill fee. Accepts queries by mail. Guidelines available.
Nonfiction Needs essays, Book Reviews by Midwestern writers or presses. Length: 7,000 words.
Fiction Accepts short fiction.
Tips Include SASE. No e-mail submissions, please.

$ WINDSOR REVIEW

A Journal of the Arts, Dept. of English, University of Windsor, Windsor ON N9B 3P4 Canada. (519)253-

3000. Fax: (519)971-3676. E-mail: uwrevu@uwindsor.ca. Website: www.uwindsor.ca. Semiannual magazine. "We try to offer a balance of fiction and poetry distinguished by excellence." Estab. 1965. Circ. 250. Pays on publication. Publishes ms an average of 6 months after acceptance. Buys one-time rights. Accepts queries by e-mail. Responds in 1 month to queries. Responds in 6 weeks to mss. Sample copy for $7 (US). Guidelines available online.

Fiction Contact: Alistair MacLeod, fiction editor. No genre fiction (science fiction, romance), but would consider if writing is good enough. Send complete ms. Length: 1,000-5,000 words. **Pays $25, 1 contributor's copy and a free subscription.**

Poetry Submit maximum 6 poems.

Tips "Good writing, strong characters, and experimental fiction is appreciated."

WORLD LITERATURE TODAY

Literature, Culture, Politics, 630 Parrington Oval, Suite 110, Norman OK 73019-4033. (405)325-4531. E-mail: dsimon@ou.edu or mfjohnson@ou.edu. Website: www.worldliteraturetoday.com. Bimonthly website covering contemporary literature, culture, topics addressing any geographic region or language area. We prefer essays in the tradition of clear and lively discussion intended for a broad audience, with a minimum of scholarly apparatus. We offer a window to world culture for enlightened readers everywhere. To get an idea of the range of our coverage, see recent issues from our home page. Sponsors The Neustadt International Prize for Literature. Estab. 1927. No kill fee. Responds in 6 weeks to mss. Writer's Guidelines and Style Guide on website.

Nonfiction Please inquire about books you would like to review, including author, title, publisher, publication date, price and ISBN. Length: 350-400 words. Reviews of books published the previous year must be received by Sept. 1st of the current year. Needs essays.

Photos Captions required. Reviews 4X6 or 5 × 7 b&w glossies. prints, GIF/JPEG files (300-600 dpi); PDF or TIF files.

Tips We do not generally accept unsolicited poetry or fiction for publication. In terms of creative writing our general interest, with some exceptions, is in contributions by writers who are born outside the U.S. and with poetry in particular, in poetry translation by writers wo write in languages other than English. Send as fully formatted e-mail attachment.

$$ THE YALE REVIEW

Yale University, P.O. Box 208243, New Haven CT 06520-8243. (203)432-0499. Fax: (203)432-0510. Website: www.yale.edu/yalereview. **20% freelance written**. Quarterly magazine. Estab. 1911. Circ. 7,000. Pays prior to publication. No kill fee. Publishes ms an average of 6 months after acceptance. Buys one-time rights. Responds in 2 months to queries. Responds in 2 months to mss Sample copy for $9, plus postage Guidelines available online

Nonfiction Authoritative discussions of politics, literature and the arts. No previously published submissions. Send complete ms with cover letter and SASE Length: 3,000-5,000 words. **Pays $400-500.**

Fiction Buys quality fiction. Length: 3,000-5,000 words. **Pays $400-500.**

Poetry Pays $100-250.

$ THE YALOBUSHA REVIEW

The Literary Journal of the University of Mississippi, University of Mississippi, P.O. Box 1848, Dept. of English, University MS 38677. (662)915-3175. E-mail: yreditor@yahoo.com. Website: www.olemiss.edu/yalobusha. Annual literary journal seeking quality submissions from around the globe. Reading period is July 15-November 15. Estab. 1995. Circ. 500. Acquires first North American serial rights. Accepts queries by mail. Does not accept previously published workAccepts simultaneous submissions. Responds in 2-4 months to mss. Sample copy for $5. Guidelines for #10 SASE.

Nonfiction Contact: Nonfiction Editor. Interested in both micro nonfiction and longer pieces. Needs essays, memoir, travel, experimental pieces. Does not want sappy confessional or insights into parenthood. Send complete ms with cover letter and SASE. Length: 10,000 words. **Pays honorarium when funding available.**

Fiction Contact: Fiction Editor. Needs experimental, historical, humorous, mainstream, novel excerpts, short shorts. **Buys 3-6 mss/year.** Send complete ms with cover letter and SASE. Length: 10,000 words. **Pays honorarium when funding available.**

Poetry Contact: Poetry Editor. Needs avant-garde, free verse, traditional. Interested in publishing a variety of voices, both new and established. Submit maximum up to 5 poems. **Send cover letter and SASE. Pays 2 contributor's copies.**

YEMASSEE

University of South Carolina, Department of English, Columbia SC 29208. (803)777-2085. E-mail: editor@yemasseejournal.org. Website: www.yemasseejournal.org. **90% freelance written.** Semiannual magazine covering fiction, poetry, interviews, creative nonfiction, reviews, one-act plays. *Yemassee* is the University of South Carolina's literary journal. Our readers are interested in high quality fiction, poetry, drama, and creative nonfiction. We have no editorial slant; quality of work is our only concern. Estab. 1993. Circ. 750. Byline given. Publishes ms an average of 4-6 months after acceptance. Buys first North American serial rights, buys electronic rights. Editorial lead time 3 months. Submit seasonal material 2-3 months in advance. Accepts queries by mail, e-mail. Accepts simultaneous submissions. Responds in 2-4 months to queries. Responds in 2-4 months to mss. Sample copy for $5. Guidelines available online.

Nonfiction Needs book excerpts, essays, expose, general interest, historical, humor, interview, opinion, personal experience, lyric pieces. Does not want inspirational, epiphanic pieces and soapbox diatribes. **Buys 0-1 mss/year.** Send complete ms. Length: 500-5,000 words. **Pays in contributor copies.**

Fiction Contact: Contact: Darien Cavanaugh, co-editor. Needs adventure, experimental, historical, mainstream, novel concepts, romance. **Buys 10 mss/year.** Send complete ms. Length: 250-7,500 words. **Pays in contributor copies.**

Poetry Contact: Contact: Jonathan Maricle, co-editor. Needs avant-garde, free verse, haiku, light verse, traditional. Does not want workshop poems, unpolished drafts, generic/unoriginal themes, bad Hemingway. Buys 20 poems/year. Submit maximum 5 poems. Length: 1-120 lines. **Pays in contributor copies.**

$ ZAHIR

A Journal of Speculative Fiction, Zahir Publishing, 315 South Coast Hwy. 101, Suite U8, Encinitas CA 92024. E-mail: zahirtales@gmail.com. Website: www.zahirtales.com. **100% freelance written.** Quarterly online magazine. "We publish literary speculative fiction." Estab. 2003. Byline given. Pays on publication. No kill fee. Publishes ms an average of 2-12 months after acceptance. Buys first rights, buys second serial (reprint) rights. Accepts queries by online submission form. Accepts previously published material. Responds in 1-2 weeks to queries. Responds in 1-3 months to mss. Writer's guidelines for #10 SASE, by e-mail, or online.

Fiction Needs fantasy, surrealism, magical realism, science fiction, surrealism, magical realism. No children's stories or stories that deal with excessive violence or anything pornographic. **Buys 18-25 mss/year.** Send complete ms. 6,000 words maximum. **Pays $10 and 2 contributor's copies.**

Tips We look for great storytelling and fresh ideas. Let your imagination run wild and capture it in concise, evocative prose.

$ $ $ ZOETROPE: ALL-STORY

Zoetrop: All-Story, The Sentinel Bldg., 916 Kearny St., San Francisco CA 94133. (415)788-7500. Website: www.all-story.com. Quarterly magazine specializing in the best of contemporary short fiction. *Zoetrope: All Story* presents a new generation of classic stories. Estab. 1997. Circ. 20,000. Byline given. No kill fee. Publishes ms an average of 5 months after acceptance. Buys first serial rights. Accepts queries by mail. Responds in 8 months (if SASE included). Sample copy for $8.00. Guidelines available online.

- Does not accept submissions September 1 - December 31.

Fiction Buys 25-35 mss/year. Send complete ms. **Pays $1,000.**

$ ZYZZYVA

The Last Word: West Coast Writers & Artists, P.O. Box 590069, San Francisco CA 94159-0069. (415)752-4393. E-mail: editor@zyzzyva.org. Website: www.zyzzyva.org. **Contact:** Howard Junker. **100% freelance written. Works with a small number of new/unpublished writers each year.** Magazine published in March, August, and November. "We feature work by writers currently living on the West Coast or in Alaska and Hawaii only. We are essentially a literary magazine, but of wide-ranging interests and a strong commitment to nonfiction." Estab. 1985. Circ. 2,500. Byline given. Pays on acceptance. No kill fee. Publishes ms an average of 3 months after acceptance. Buys first North American serial and one-time anthology rights. Accepts queries by mail, e-mail. Responds in 1 week to queries. Responds in 1 month to mss. Sample copy for $7 or online. Guidelines available online.

Nonfiction Needs book excerpts, general interest, historical, humor, personal experience. **Buys 50 mss/year.** Query by mail or e-mail. Open **Pays $50.**

Photos Reviews scans only at 300 dpi, 5½.

Fiction Needs ethnic, experimental, humorous, mainstream. **Buys 60 mss/year.** Send complete ms. Length: 100-7,500 words. **Pays $50.**

Poetry Buys 20 poems/year. Submit maximum 5 poems. Length: 3 200 lines. **Pays $50.**

Tips "West Coast writers means those currently living in California, Alaska, Washington, Oregon, or Hawaii."

Men's

$$$$ CIGAR AFICIONADO

M. Shanken Communications, Inc., 387 Park Ave. S., 8th Floor, New York NY 10016. (212)684-4224. Fax: (212)684-5424. E-mail: gmott@mshanken.com. Website: www.cigaraficionado.com. **75% freelance written**. Bimonthly magazine for affluent men. Estab. 1992. Circ. 275,000. Byline given. Pays on acceptance. Offers 25% kill fee. Publishes ms an average of 3-6 months after acceptance. Buys all rights. Editorial lead time 6 months. Submit seasonal material 6 months in advance. Accepts queries by e-mail. Responds in 1 month to queries. Responds in 2 months to mss. Sample copy free.
Nonfiction Needs general interest. Query. Length: 1,500-4,000 words. **Pays variable amount.**
Photos Contact: Contact Sarina Finkelstein, photo editor.

$$$$ ESQUIRE

Hearst Corp., 300 W. 57th St., 21st. Floor, New York NY 10019. (212)649-4020. E-mail: esquire@hearst.com. Website: www.esquire.com. Monthly magazine covering the ever-changing trends in American culture. Geared toward smart, well-off men. General readership is college educated and sophisticated, between ages 30 and 45. Written mostly by contributing editors on contract. Rarely accepts unsolicited mss. Estab. 1933. Circ. 720,000. Publishes ms an average of 2-6 months after acceptance. Retains first worldwide periodical publication rights for 90 days from cover date. Editorial lead time at least 2 months. Accepts simultaneous submissions. Guidelines for SASE.
Nonfiction Focus is the ever-changing trends in American culture. Topics include current events and politics, social criticism, sports, celebrity profiles, the media, art and music, men's fashion. Queries must be sent by letter. **Buys 4 features and 12 shorter mss/year.** Columns average 1,500 words; features average 5,000 words; short front of book pieces average 200-400 words **Payment varies.**
Photos Uses mostly commissioned photography Payment depends on size and number of photos
Fiction Literary excellence is our only criterion. Needs novel concepts, short stories, memoirs, plays. No pornography, science fiction or 'true romance' stories. Send complete ms.
Tips A writer has the best chance of breaking in at *Esquire* by querying with a specific idea that requires special contacts and expertise. Ideas must be timely and national in scope.

$ GC MAGAZINE

Handel Publishing, P.O. Box 331775, Fort Worth TX 76163. (817)640-1306. Fax: (817)633-9045. E-mail: rosa.gc@sbcglobal.net. **80% freelance written**. Monthly magazine. *GC Magazine* is a general entertainment magazine for men. We include entertainment celebrity interviews (movies, music, books) along with general interest articles for adult males. Estab. 1994. Circ. 53,000. No byline given. Pays on publication. No kill fee. Publishes ms an average of 3 months after acceptance. Buys one-time rights. Editorial lead time 3 months. Submit seasonal material 6 months in advance. Accepts queries by mail, e-mail. Accepts previously published material. Accepts simultaneous submissions. Responds in 3 months to queries. Sample copy for $1.50. Guidelines for #10 SASE.
Nonfiction Needs book excerpts, essays, expose, general interest, historical, how-to, humor, interview, technical, travel, dating tips. **Buys 100 mss/year.** Query. Length: 1,000-2,000 words. **Pays 2¢/word.**
Photos State availability. Model releases required. Reviews 3 × 5 prints, GIF/JPEG files. Offers no additional payment for photos accepted with ms Buys one time rights.
Columns/Departments Actress feature (film actress interviews), 2,500 words; Author feature (book author interviews), 1,500 words; Music feature (singer or band interviews), 1,500 words. 50 Query. **Pays 2¢/word**
Tips Submit material typed and free of errors. Writers should think of magazines like *Maxim* and *Details* when determining article ideas for our magazine. Our primary readership is adult males and we are seeking original and unique articles.

$$$ INDY MEN'S MAGAZINE

The Guy's Guide to the Good Life, Table Moose Media, 8500 Keystone Crossing, Suite 100, Indianapolis IN 46240. (317)255-3850. Fax: (317)254-5944. E-mail: lou@indymensmagazine.com. Website: www.indymensmagazine.com. **50% freelance written**. Monthly magazine. Estab. 2002. Circ. 50,000. Byline given. Pays on publication. Offers 10% kill fee. Buys first North American serial rights. Editorial lead time 3 months. Submit seasonal material 1 year in advance. Accepts queries by mail. Accepts simultaneous submissions. Responds in 3 weeks to queries. Responds in 2 months to mss. Sample copy for $5. Guidelines by e-mail.

Nonfiction Needs essays, travel. No generic pieces that could run anywhere. No advocacy pieces. **Buys 50 mss/year.** Query. Length: 100-2,000 words. **Pays $75-500 for assigned articles. Pays $50-400 for unsolicited articles.**

Photos State availability. Identification of subjects required. Reviews contact sheets, transparencies, prints, GIF/JPEG files. Negotiates payment individually. Buys one time rights.

Columns/Departments Balls (opinionated sports pieces), 1,400 words; Dad Files (introspective parenting essays), 1,400 words; Men At Work (Indianapolis men and their jobs), 100-600 words; Trippin' (experiential travel), 1,500 words. 30 Query with published clips. **Pays $75-400.**

Fiction The piece needs to hold our attention from the first paragraph. Needs adventure, fantasy, historical, horror, humorous, mainstream, mystery, science fiction, suspense. **Buys 12 mss/year.** Send complete ms. Length: 1,000-4,000 words. **Pays $50-250.**

Tips We don't believe in wasting our reader's time, whether it's in a 50-word item or a 6,000-word Q&A. Our readers are smart, and they appreciate our sense of humor. Write to entertain and engage.

$$$$ KING

Harris Publications, Inc., 1115 Broadway, 8th Floor, New York NY 10010. (212)467-9675. Fax: (212)807-0216. E-mail: laura@harris-pub.com. Website: www.king-mag.com. **75% freelance written**. Men's lifestyle magazine published 80 times/year. *King* is a general interest men's magazine with a strong editorial voice. Topics include lifestyle, entertainment, news, women, cars, music, fashion, investigative reporting. Estab. 2001. Circ. 270,000. Byline given. Pays on publication. Offers 25% kill fee. Buys all rights. Editorial lead time 2-3 months. Submit seasonal material 4 months in advance. Accepts queries by e-mail. Responds in 1 month to queries. Guidelines free.

Nonfiction Needs essays, expose, general interest. Does not want completed articles. Pitches only. Query with published clips. Length: 2,000-5,000 words. **Pays $1-1.50/word.**

$$$$ SMOKE MAGAZINE

Cigars & Life's Burning Desires, Lockwood Publications, 26 Broadway, Floor 9M, New York NY 10004. (212)391-2060. Fax: (212)827-0945. E-mail: editor@smokemag.com. Website: www.smokemag.com. **50% freelance written**. Quarterly magazine covering cigars and men's lifestyle issues. A large majority of *Smoke's* readers are affluent men, ages 28-50; active, educated and adventurous. Estab. 1995. Circ. 95,000. Byline given. Pays 1 month after publication. Offers 25% kill fee. Publishes ms an average of 3 (average) months after acceptance. Buys first rights. Editorial lead time 2 months. Submit seasonal material 6 months in advance. Accepts queries by mail, e-mail. Accepts simultaneous submissions. Responds in 6 weeks to queries. Responds in 3 months to mss. Sample copy for $4.99.

Nonfiction Needs essays, expose, general interest, historical, how-to, humor, interview, opinion, personal experience, photo feature, technical, travel, true crime. **Buys 8 mss/year.** Query with published clips. Length: 1,500-3,000 words. **Pays $500-1,200.** Sometimes pays expenses of writers on assignment

Photos State availability. Identification of subjects required. Reviews 21/4x21/4 transparencies. Negotiates payment individually

Columns/Departments Smoke Undercover (investigative journalism, personal experience); Smoke Screen (TV/film/entertainment issues); Smoke City (cigar-related travel), all 1,500 words. 8 Query with published clips. **Pays $500-1,000.**

Tips Send a short, clear query with clips. Go with your field of expertise: cigars, sports, music, true crime, etc.

$$ UMM (URBAN MALE MAGAZINE)

Canada's Only Lifestyle and Fashion Magazine for Men, UMM Publishing Inc., 300-131 Bank St., Ottawa ON K1P 5N7 Canada. (613)723-6216. Fax: (613)723-1702. E-mail: editor@umm.ca. Website: www.umm.ca. **100% freelance written**. Bimonthly magazine covering men's interests. Our audience is young men, aged 18-24. We focus on Canadian activities, interests, and lifestyle issues. Our magazine is fresh and energetic and we look for original ideas carried out with a spark of intelligence and/or humour (and you'd better spell humour with a `u'). Estab. 1998. Circ. 90,000. Byline given. Pays 1 month after publication. No kill fee. Publishes ms an average of 3 months after acceptance. Buys first North American serial rights. Editorial lead time 3 months. Submit seasonal material 4 months in advance. Accepts queries by e-mail. Accepts simultaneous submissions. Responds in 6 weeks to queries. Responds in 6 weeks to mss.

Nonfiction Needs book excerpts, expose, general interest, historical, how-to, humor, interview, new product, personal experience, travel, adventure, cultural, sports, music. **Buys 80 mss/year.** Query with published clips. Length: 1,200-3,500 words. **Pays $100-400.**
Photos State availability. Reviews contact sheets, prints. Negotiates payment individually Buys one time rights.
Tips Be familiar with our magazine before querying. We deal with all subjects of interest to young men, especially those with Canadian themes. We are very open-minded. Original ideas and catchy writing are key.

Military

$$ ☐ AIRFORCE

Air Force Association of Canada, P.O Box 2460, Stn D, Ottawa ON K1P 5W6 Canada. (613)232-2303. Fax: (613)232-2156. E-mail: vjohnson@airforce.ca. Website: www.airforce.ca. **5% freelance written**. Quarterly magazine covering Canada's air force heritage. Stories center on Canadian military aviation—past, present and future. Estab. 1977. Circ. 16,000. Byline given. Pays on publication. Publishes ms an average of 6 months after acceptance. Buys all rights. Editorial lead time 3 months. Submit seasonal material 3 months in advance. Accepts queries by mail, e-mail, fax, phone. Accepts previously published material. Accepts simultaneous submissions. Responds in 2 weeks to queries. Responds in 1 month to mss. Sample copy free. Guidelines by e-mail.
Nonfiction Needs historical, interview, personal experience, photo feature. **Buys 2 mss/year.** Query with published clips. Length: 1,500-3,500 words. Limit agreed upon in advance.
Photos Send photos. Captions, identification of subjects required. Reviews prints, GIF/JPEG files. Buys one time rights.
Tips "Writers should have a good background in Canadian military history."

$$ AIR FORCE TIMES

Army Times Publishing Co., 6883 Commercial Dr., Springfield VA 22159. (703)750-8646. Fax: (703)750-8601. E-mail: kmiller@militarytimes.com; airlet@airforcetimes.com. Website: www.airforcetimes.com. "Weeklies edited separately for Army, Navy, Marine Corps, and Air Force military personnel and their families. They contain career information such as pay raises, promotions, news of legislation affecting the military, housing, base activities and features of interest to military people." Estab. 1940. Byline given. Pays on acceptance. Offers kill fee. Buys first rights. Accepts queries by mail, e-mail, phone. Accepts simultaneous submissions. Responds in 1 month to queries. Sample copy for #10 SASE. Guidelines for #10 SASE.
Nonfiction Features of interest to career military personnel and their families. No advice pieces. **Buys 150-175 mss/year.** Query. Length: 750-2,000 words. **Pays $100-500.**
Columns/Departments Length: 500-900. 75 **Pays $75-125.**
Tips "Looking for stories on active duty, reserve and retired military personnel; stories on military matters and localized military issues; stories on successful civilian careers after military service."

$$ ARMY MAGAZINE

2425 Wilson Blvd., Arlington VA 22201-3385. (703)841-4300. Fax: (703)841-3505. E-mail: armymag@ausa.org. Website: www.ausa.org. **70% freelance written. Prefers to work with published/established writers.** Monthly magazine emphasizing military interests. Estab. 1904. Circ. 90,000. Byline given. Pays on publication. Publishes ms an average of 5 months after acceptance. Buys all rights. Submit seasonal material 3 months in advance. Accepts queries by mail. Sample copy for 9 × 12 SAE with $1 postage or online Writer's guidelines for 9 × 12 SAE with $1 postage or online

- *ARMY Magazine* looks for shorter articles.

Nonfiction We would like to see more pieces about little-known episodes involving interesting military personalities. We especially want material lending itself to heavy, contributor-supplied photographic treatment. The first thing a contributor should recognize is that our readership is very savvy militarily. 'Gee-whiz' personal reminiscences get short shrift, unless they hold their own in a company in which long military service, heroism and unusual experiences are commonplace. At the same time, *ARMY* readers like a well-written story with a fresh slant, whether it is about an experience in a foxhole or the fortunes of a corps in battle. Needs historical, military and original, humor, military feature-length articles and anecdotes, interview, photo feature. No rehashed history. No unsolicited book reviews. **Buys 40 mss/year.** Submit complete ms (hard copy and disk) Length: 1,000-1,500 words. **Pays 12-18¢/word.**

Photos Send photos. Captions required. Reviews prints, slides, high resolution digital photos. Pays $50-100 for 8 × 10 b&w glossy prints; $50-350 for 8 × 10 color glossy prints and 35mm and high resolution digital photos. Buys all rights.

$$ ARMY TIMES

Army Times Publishing Co., 6883 Commercial Dr., Springfield VA 22159. (703)750-9000. Fax: (703)750-8622. E-mail: aneill@militarytimes.com. Website: www.armytimes.com. Weekly for Army military personnel and their families containing career information such as pay raises, promotions, news of legislation affecting the military, housing, base activities and features of interest to military people. Estab. 1940. Circ. 230,000. Byline given. Pays on acceptance. Offers kill fee. Makes work-for-hire assignments. Accepts queries by mail, e-mail. Accepts simultaneous submissions. Responds in 1 month to queries. Sample copy and writer's guidelines for #10 SASE.

Nonfiction Features of interest to career military personnel and their families: food, relationships, parenting, education, retirement, shelter, health, and fitness, sports, personal appearance, community, recreation, personal finance, entertainment. No advice please. **Buys 150-175 mss/year.** Query. Length: 750-2,000 words. **Pays $100-500.**

Columns/Departments Length: 500-900 words. **Pays $75-125.**

Tips Looking for stories on active duty, reserve and retired military personnel; stories on military matters and localized military issues; stories on successful civilian careers after military service.

$ COMBAT HANDGUNS

Harris Tactical Group, 1115 Broadway, New York NY 10010. (212)807-7100. Fax: (212)807-1479. E-mail: comments@harris-pub.com. Website: www.combathandguns.com. Magazine published 8 times/year covering combat handguns. Written for handgun owners and collectors. Circ. 126,498. No kill fee. Editorial lead time 2 months. Accepts queries by mail, e-mail.

Nonfiction Query.

Photos Send photos. Captions required. Reviews GIF/JPEG files.

$$ MARINE CORPS TIMES

Army Times Publishing Co., 6883 Commercial Dr., Springfield VA 22159. (703)750-9000. Fax: (703)750-8767. E-mail: cmark@militarytimes.com. Website: www.marinecorpstimes.com. Weeklies edited separately for Army, Navy, Marine Corps, and Air Force military personnel and their families. They contain career information such as pay raises, promotions, news of legislation affecting the military, housing, base activities and features of interest to military people. Estab. 1940. Circ. 230,000 (combined). Byline given. Pays on publication. Offers kill fee. Buys first rights. Accepts queries by mail, e-mail, phone. Accepts simultaneous submissions. Responds in 1 month to queries. Sample copy for #10 sase. Guidelines for #10 SASE.

Nonfiction Features of interest to career military personnel and their families, including stories on current military operations and exercises. No advice pieces. **Buys 150-175 mss/year.** Query. Length: 750-2,000 words. **Pays $100-500.**

Columns/Departments Length: 500-900 words. 75 **Pays $75-125.**

Tips Looking for stories on active duty, reserve and retired military personnel; stories on military matters and localized military issues; stories on successful civilian careers after military service.

$$$ MILITARY OFFICER

201 N. Washington St., Alexandria VA 22314-2539. (800)234-6622. Fax: (703)838-8179. E-mail: editor@moaa.org. Website: www.moaa.org. **60% freelance written. Prefers to work with published/established writers.** Monthly magazine for officers of the 7 uniformed services and their families. Estab. 1945. Circ. 389,000. Byline given. Pays on acceptance. Publishes ms an average of 1 year after acceptance. Buys first North American serial rights. Accepts queries by e-mail. Responds in 3 months to queries. Sample copy available online. Guidelines available online.

Nonfiction Current military/political affairs, finance, health and wellness, recent military history, travel, military family life-style. Emphasis now on current military and defense issues. "We rarely accept unsolicited manuscripts." **Buys 50 mss/year.** Query with résumé, sample clips Length: 800-2,000 words. **Pays 80¢/word.**

Photos Query with list of stock photo subjects. Images should be 300 dpi or higher. Pays $75-250 for inside color; $300 for cover.

$ PARAMETERS

U.S. Army War College Quarterly, U.S. Army War College, 122 Forbes Ave., Carlisle PA 17013-5238.

(717)245-4943. E-mail: carl_parameters@conus.army.mil. Website: www.carlisle.army.mil/usawc/parameters. **100% freelance written. Prefers to work with published/established writers or experts in the field.** Readership consists of senior leaders of US defense establishment, both uniformed and civilian, plus members of the media, government, industry and academia. Subjects include national and international security affairs, military strategy, military leadership and management, art and science of warfare, and military history with contemporary relevance. Estab. 1971. Circ. 13,500. Byline given. Pays on publication. No kill fee. Publishes ms an average of 6 months after acceptance. Accepts queries by mail, e-mail, phone. Responds in 6 weeks to queries. Sample copy free or online Guidelines available online.

Nonfiction Prefers articles that deal with current security issues, employ critical analysis, and provide solutions or recommendations. Liveliness and verve, consistent with scholarly integrity, appreciated. Theses, studies, and academic course papers should be adapted to article form prior to submission. Documentation in complete endnotes. Send complete ms. 4,500 words average **Pays $200-300 average.**

Tips Make it short; keep it interesting; get criticism and revise accordingly. Write on a contemporary topic. Tackle a subject only if you are an authority. No fax submissions. Encourage e-mail submissions.

$$ PROCEEDINGS

U.S. Naval Institute, 291 Wood Rd., Annapolis MD 21402-5034. (410)268-6110. Fax: (410)295-7940. E-mail: articlesubmissions@usni.org. Website: www.usni.org. **80% freelance written**. Monthly magazine covering Navy, Marine Corps, Coast Guard issues. Estab. 1873. Circ. 60,000. Byline given. Pays on publication. Publishes ms an average of 9 months after acceptance. Buys all rights. Editorial lead time 3 months. Responds in 2 months to queries. Sample copy for $3.95. Guidelines available online.

Nonfiction Needs essays, historical, interview, photo feature, technical. **Buys 100-125 mss/year.** Send complete ms. 3,000 words **Pays $60-150/printed page for unsolicited articles.**

Photos State availability of or send photos.. Reviews transparencies, prints. Offers $25/photo maximum Buys one-time rights.

Columns/Departments Comment & Discussion (letters to editor), 500 words; Commentary (opinion), 700 words; Nobody Asked Me, But. (opinion), less than 700 words. 150-200 mss/year. Query or send complete ms. **Pays $34-150.**

$$$$ SOLDIER OF FORTUNE

The Journal of Professional Adventurers, 5735 Arapahoe Ave., Suite A-5, Boulder CO 80303-1340. (303)449-3750. E-mail: editorsof@aol.com. Website: www.sofmag.com. Lt. Col. Robert A. Brown. **Contact:** Lt. Col. Robert A. Brown, editor/publisher. **50% freelance written**. Monthly magazine covering military, paramilitary, police, combat subjects, and action/adventure. "We are an action-oriented magazine; we cover combat hot spots around the world. We also provide timely features on state-of-the-art weapons and equipment; elite military and police units; and historical military operations. Readership is primarily active-duty military, veterans, and law enforcement." Estab. 1975. Circ. 60,000. Byline given. Offers 25% kill fee. Buys first rights. Responds in 3 weeks to queries. Responds in 1 month to mss. Sample copy for $5. Guidelines for #10 SASE.

Nonfiction Needs expose, general interest, historical, how-to, on weapons and their skilled use, humor, interview, new product, personal experience, photo feature, No. 1 on our list, technical, travel, combat reports, military unit reports, and solid Vietnam and Operation Iraqi Freedom articles. No `How I won the war' pieces; no op-ed pieces unless they are fully and factually backgrounded; no knife articles (staff assignments only). All submitted articles should have good art; art will sell us on an article. **Buys 75 mss/year.** Query with or without published clips or send complete ms. Send mss to articles editor; queries to managing editor Length: 2,000-3,000 words. **Pays $150-250/page.**

Reprints Send disk copy, photocopy of article and information about when and where the material previously appeared. Pays 25% of amount paid for an original article

Photos Send photos. Captions, identification of subjects required. Reviews contact sheets, transparencies. Pays $500 for cover photo Buys one-time rights.

Tips Submit a professionally prepared, complete package. All artwork with cutlines, double-spaced typed manuscript with 5.25 or 3.5 IBM-compatible disk, if available, cover letter including synopsis of article, supporting documentation where applicable, etc. Manuscript must be factual; writers have to do their homework and get all their facts straight. One error means rejection. Vietnam features, if carefully researched and art heavy, will always get a careful look. Combat reports, again, with good art, are No. 1 in our book and stand the best chance of being accepted. Military unit reports from around the world are well received, as are law-enforcement articles (units, police in action). If you write for us, be complete and factual; pros read *Soldier of Fortune*, and are very quick to let us know if we (and the author) err.

Music

$ AMERICAN SONGWRITER MAGAZINE

1303 16th Ave. S., Nashville TN 37212. (615)321-6096. Fax: (615)321-6097. E-mail: info@americansongwriter.com. Website: www.americansongwriter.com. **90% freelance written**. Bimonthly magazine about songwriters and the craft of songwriting for many types of music, including pop, country, rock, metal, jazz, gospel, and r&b. Estab. 1984. Circ. 5,000. Pays on publication. Offers 25% kill fee. Publishes ms an average of 2 months after acceptance. Buys first North American serial rights. Accepts previously published material. Responds in 2 months to queries. Sample copy for $4. Guidelines for #10 SASE or by e-mail.

Nonfiction Needs general interest, interview, new product, technical, home demo studios, movie and TV scores, performance rights organizations. **Buys 20 mss/year.** Query with published clips. Length: 300-1,200 words. **Pays $25-60.**

Reprints Send tearsheet or photocopy and information about when and where the material previously appeared. Pays same amount as paid for an original article

Photos Send photos. Identification of subjects required. Reviews 3 × 5 prints. Offers no additional payment for photos accepeted with ms. Buys one time rights.

Tips *American Songwriter* strives to present articles which can be read a year or 2 after they were written and still be pertinent to the songwriter reading them.

$ $ BLUEGRASS UNLIMITED

Bluegrass Unlimited, Inc., P.O. Box 771, Warrenton VA 20188-0771. (540)349-8181 or (800)BLU-GRAS. Fax: (540)341-0011. E-mail: editor@bluegrassmusic.com. Website: www.bluegrassmusic.com. **10% freelance written. Prefers to work with published/established writers**. Monthly magazine covering bluegrass, acoustic, and old-time country music. Estab. 1966. Circ. 27,000. Byline given. Pays on publication. Offers negotiated kill fee. Publishes ms an average of 4 months after acceptance. Buys first North American serial rights, buys one-time rights, buys second serial (reprint) rights, buys all rights. Submit seasonal material 4 months in advance. Accepts queries by mail, e-mail, fax. Responds in 2 weeks to queries. Responds in 2 months to mss. Sample copy free. Guidelines for #10 SASE.

Nonfiction Needs general interest, historical, how-to, interview, personal experience, photo feature, travel. No fan-style articles. **Buys 30-40 mss/year.** Query. Open **Pays 10-13¢/word.**

Reprints Send photocopy with rights for sale noted and information about when and where the material previously appeared. Payment is negotiable.

Photos State availability of or send photos.. Identification of subjects required. Reviews 35mm transparencies and 3 × 5, 5 × 7 and 8 × 10 b&w and color prints. Also, reviews/prefers digital 300 dpi or better jpg, tif files, index, contact sheet with digital submissions Pays $50-175 for color; $25-60 for b&w prints; $50-250 for color prints Buys all rights.

Fiction Needs ethnic, humorous. **Buys 3-5 mss/year.** Query. Negotiable **Pays 10-13¢/word**.

Tips "We would prefer that articles be informational, based on personal experience or an interview with lots of quotes from subject, profile, humor, etc. We print less than 10% freelance at this time."

BLUNT

New Media, 78 Renwick St., Redfern NSW 2016 Australia. (61)(2)9699-0333. Fax: (61)(2)9310-1315. E-mail: lmarks@next.com.au. Website: www.nextmedia.com.au. Amy Simmons, deputy editor. **Contact:** Adrian Kelly, editor. Monthly magazine covering the very best alternative music from Australia and the world. *Blunt* lives by the motto that music is more than a passion, it's a way of life.

Nonfiction Needs general interest, interview, new product. Query.

$ $ CHAMBER MUSIC

Chamber Music America, 305 Seventh Ave., 5th Floor, New York NY 10001-6008. (212)242-2022. Fax: (212)242-7955. E-mail: egoldensohn@chamber-music.org. Website: www.chamber-music.org. Bimonthly magazine covering chamber music. Estab. 1977. Circ. 13,000. Byline given. Pays on publication. Offers kill fee. Publishes ms an average of 5 months after acceptance. Buys first rights. Editorial lead time 4 months. Accepts queries by mail, phone.

Nonfiction Needs book excerpts, essays, humor, opinion, personal experience, issue-oriented stories of relevance to the chamber music fields written by top music journalists and critics, or music practitioners. No artist profiles, no stories about opera or symphonic work. **Buys 35 mss/year.** Query with published clips. Length: 2,500-3,500 words. **Pays $500 minimum.**

Photos State availability. Offers no payment for photos accepted with ms

$ CHART MAGAZINE

Canada's Music Magazine, Chart Communications, Inc., 41 Britain St., Suite 200, Toronto ON M5A 1R7 Canada. (416)363-3101. Fax: (416)363-3109. E-mail: chart@chartattack.com. Website: www.chartattack.com. **90% freelance written**. Monthly magazine. *Chart Magazine* has a cutting edge attitude toward music and pop culture to fit with youth readership. Estab. 1990. Circ. 40,000 (paid). Byline given. Pays on publication. No kill fee. Publishes ms an average of 3-6 months after acceptance. Buys first North American serial rights, buys electronic rights. Editorial lead time 2 months. Submit seasonal material 3 months in advance. Accepts queries by mail, e-mail, fax, phone. Responds in 4-6 weeks to queries. Responds in 2-3 months to mss. Sample copy for $6 US (via mail order). Guidelines free.

Nonfiction All articles must relate to popular music and/or pop culture. Needs book excerpts, essays, expose, humor, interview, personal experience, photo feature. Nothing that isn't related to popular music and pop culture (i.e., film, books, video games, fashion, etc., that would appeal to a hip youth demographic). Query with published clips and send complete ms. varies. **Payment varies.**

Photos Contact: Steven Balaban, art director. Send photos. Negotiates payment individually. Buys all rights.

CHURCH MUSIC QUARTERLY

The Royal School of Church Music, 19 The Close, Salisbury SP1 2EB United Kingdom. (44)(1722)424848. Fax: (44)(172)242-4849. E-mail: cmq@rscm.com. Website: www.rscm.com. Quarterly publication that offers advice, information, and inspiration to church music enthusiasts around the world. Each issue offers a variety of articles and interviews by distinguished musicians, theologians, and scholars. Circ. 13,500. No kill fee. Accepts queries by e-mail. Guidelines by e-mail.

- Does not pay for unsolcited articles. Pays £60/page upon publication for commissioned articles.

Nonfiction All articles must relate to church music and most have an educational element and fall into one of these categories: church music history, composer profiles, theology of music/liturgy, practical advice for church musicians/clergy, arts/education news, reports on developments in church music around the world. Submit ms, bio. Length: 1,200-1,400 words

Photos Reviews prints, 300 dpi digital images.

$$$ GUITAR ONE

The Magazine You Can Play, 149 5th St., 9th Floor, New York NY 10010. (212)768-2966. Fax: (212)944-9279. E-mail: soundingboard@guitarworld.com. Website: www.guitaronemag.com. **75% freelance written**. Monthly magazine covering guitar news, artists, music, gear. Estab. 1996. Circ. 140,000. Byline given. Pays on publication. Offers 50% kill fee. Publishes ms an average of 1 month after acceptance. Buys one-time rights. Editorial lead time 3 months. Accepts queries by mail, e-mail, fax. Accepts simultaneous submissions. Sample copy available online.

Nonfiction Needs interview, with guitarists. **Buys 15 mss/year.** Query with published clips. Length: 2,000-5,000 words. **Pays $300-1,200 for assigned articles. Pays $150-800 for unsolicited articles.**

Photos State availability. Reviews negatives, transparencies, prints. Negotiates payment individually Buys one time rights.

Columns/Departments Opening Axe (newsy items on artists), 450 words; Soundcheck (records review), 200 words; Gear Box (equipment reviews), 800 words.

Tips Find an interesting feature with a nice angle that pertains to guitar enthusiasts. Submit a well-written draft or samples of work.

$$ GUITAR PLAYER MAGAZINE

New Bay Media, LLC, 1111 Bayhill Dr., Suite 125, San Bruno CA 94403. (650)238-0300. Fax: (650)238-0261. E-mail: mmolenda@musicplayer.com. Website: www.guitarplayer.com. **50% freelance written**. Monthly magazine for persons interested in guitars, guitarists, manufacturers, guitar builders, equipment, careers, etc. Circ. 150,000. Byline given. Pays on acceptance. No kill fee. Publishes ms an average of 3 months after acceptance. Buys first serial and all reprint rights. Accepts queries by e-mail. Responds in 6 weeks to queries. Guidelines for #10 SASE.

Nonfiction Publishes wide variety of articles pertaining to guitars and guitarists: interviews, guitar craftsmen profiles, how-to features—anything amateur and professional guitarists would find fascinating and/or helpful. In interviews with `name' performers, be as technical as possible regarding strings, guitars, techniques, etc. We're not a pop culture magazine, but a magazine for musicians. The essential question: What can the reader take away from a story to become a better player? **Buys 30-40 mss/year.** Query. Open **Pays $250-450.**

Photos Reviews 35 mm color transparencies, b&w glossy prints. Payment varies Buys one time rights.

$ MUSIC FOR THE LOVE OF IT

67 Parkside Dr., Berkeley CA 94705. (510)654-9134. Fax: (510)654-4656. E-mail: tedrust@musicfortheloveofit.com. Website: www.musicfortheloveofit.com. **20% freelance written**. Bimonthly newsletter covering amateur musicianship. A lively, intelligent source of ideas and enthusiasm for a musically literate audience of adult amateur musicians. Estab. 1988. Circ. 600. Byline given. Pays on publication. No kill fee. Publishes ms an average of 2 months after acceptance. Buys one-time rights. Editorial lead time 1 month. Submit seasonal material 1 month in advance. Accepts queries by mail, e-mail, fax, phone. Responds in 1 week to queries. Responds in 1 month to mss. Sample copy for $5. Guidelines available online.

Nonfiction Needs essays, historical, how-to, personal experience, photo feature. No concert reviews, star interviews, CD reviews. **Buys 6 mss/year.** Query. Length: 500-1,500 words. **Pays $50, or gift subscriptions.**

Photos State availability. Identification of subjects required. Reviews 4x6 prints or larger. Offers no additional payment for photos accepted with ms Buys one time rights.

Tips We're looking for more good how-to articles on musical styles. Love making music. Know something about it.

⊘ ROLLING STONE

Wenner Media, 1290 Avenue of the Americas, New York NY 10104. (212)484-1616. Fax: (212)484-1664. E-mail: letters@rollingstone.com. Website: www.rollingstone.com. **Contact:** Jann S. Wenner. Biweekly magazine geared towards young adults interested in news of popular music, entertainment and the arts, current news events, politics and American culture. Circ. 1,254,200. No kill fee. Editorial lead time 1 month.

- Query before submitting.

$$$ SYMPHONY

American Symphony Orchestra League, 33 W. 60th St., Fifth Floor, New York NY 10023. (212)262-5161. Fax: (212)262-5198. E-mail: clane@americanorchestras.org; jmelick@americanorchestras.org. Website: www.symphony.org. **Contact:** Chester Lane, senior editor, or Jennifer Melick, managing editor. **50% freelance written**. Bimonthly magazine for the orchestra industry and classical music enthusiasts covering classical music, orchestra industry, musicians. "Writers should be knowledgeable about classical music and have critical or journalistic/repertorial approach." Circ. 18,000. Byline given. Pays on acceptance. No kill fee. Publishes ms an average of 10 weeks after acceptance. Buys first rights, buys one-time rights. Editorial lead time 6 months. Submit seasonal material 8 months in advance. Accepts queries by mail, e-mail. Accepts simultaneous submissions. Guidelines available online.

Nonfiction Needs book excerpts, essays, inspirational, interview, opinion, personal experience, rare, photo feature, rare, issue features, trend pieces (by assignment only; pitches welcome). Does not want to see reviews, interviews. **Buys 30 mss/year.** Query with published clips. Length: 1,500-3,500 words. **Pays $500-900.**

Photos Rarely commissions photos or illustrations. State availability of or send photos. Captions, identification of subjects required. Reviews contact sheets, negatives, prints, electronic photos (preferred). Offers no additional payment for photos accepted with ms Buys one time rights.

Columns/Departments Repertoire (orchestral music—essays); Comment (personal views and opinions); Currents (electronic media developments); In Print (books); On Record (CD, DVD, video), all 1,000-2,500 words. 12 Query with published clips.

Tips We need writing samples before assigning pieces. We prefer to craft the angle with the writer, rather than adapt an existing piece. Pitches and queries should demonstrate a clear relevance to the American orchestra industry and should be timely.

Mystery

$ HARDBOILED

Gryphon Publications, P.O. Box 209, Brooklyn NY 11228. Website: www.gryphonbooks.com. **100% freelance written**. Semiannual book covering crime/mystery fiction and nonfiction. "Hard-hitting crime fiction and private-eye stories—the newest and most cutting-edge work and classic reprints." Estab. 1988. Circ. 1,000. Byline given. Pays on publication. Offers 100% kill fee. Publishes ms an average of 18 months after acceptance. Buys first North American serial rights, buys one-time rights. Editorial lead time 1 year. Submit seasonal material 9 months in advance. Accepts queries by mail, fax. Accepts previously published material. Accepts simultaneous submissions. Responds in 2 weeks to queries. Responds in 1 month to mss. Sample copy for $10. Guidelines for #10 SASE.

Nonfiction Needs book excerpts, essays, expose. **Buys 4-6 mss/year.** Query. Length: 500-3,000 words. **Pays 1 copy.**

Reprints Query first.

Photos State availability.

Columns/Departments Occasional review columns/articles on hardboiled writers. Query.

Fiction Contact: Gary Lovisi, editor. Needs mystery, private eye, police procedural, noir, hardboiled crime, and private-eye stories, all on the cutting edge. "No pastiches, violence for the sake of violence." **Buys 40 mss/year.** Query or send complete ms. Length: 500-3,000 words. **Pays $5-50.**

Tips "Your best bet for breaking in is short hard crime fiction filled with authenticity and brevity. Try a subscription to *Hardboiled* to get the perfect idea of what we are after."

ALFRED HITCHCOCK'S MYSTERY MAGAZINE

Dell Magazines, 475 Park Ave. S., 11th Floor, New York NY 10016. (212)686-7188. Website: www.themysteryplace.com. **100% freelance written**. Monthly magazine featuring new mystery short stories. Estab. 1956. Circ. 90,000 readers. Byline given. No kill fee. Buys first rights, buys foreign rights. Submit seasonal material 7 months in advance. Responds in 4 months to mss. Sample copy for $6.49 Guidelines for SASE or on website.

Fiction Contact: Linda Landrigan, editor. "Original and well-written mystery and crime fiction. Because this is a mystery magazine, the stories we buy must fall into that genre in some sense or another. We are interested in nearly every kind of mystery: stories of detection of the classic kind, police procedurals, private eye tales, suspense, courtroom dramas, stories of espionage, and so on. We ask only that the story be about crime (or the threat or fear of one). We sometimes accept ghost stories or supernatural tales, but those also should involve a crime." No sensationalism. Send complete ms. Up to 12,000 words **Payment varies**.

Tips "No simultaneous submissions, please. Submissions sent to *Alfred Hitchcock's Mystery Magazine* are not considered for or read by *Ellery Queen's Mystery Magazine*, and vice versa."

$ ELLERY QUEEN'S MYSTERY MAGAZINE

Dell Magazines Fiction Group, 267 Broadway, 4th Floor, New York NY 10017. (212)686-7188. Fax: (212)686-7414. E-mail: elleryqueenmm@dellmagazines.com. Website: www.themysteryplace.com/eqmm. **100% freelance written**. Featuring mystery fiction. "*Ellery Queen's Mystery Magazine* welcomes submissions from both new and established writers. We publish every kind of mystery short story: the psychological suspense tale, the deductive puzzle, the private eye case—the gamut of crime and detection from the realistic (including the policeman's lot and stories of police procedure) to the more imaginative (including 'locked rooms' and 'impossible crimes'). *EQMM* has been in continuous publication since 1941. From the beginning, 3 general criteria have been employed in evaluating submissions: We look for strong writing, an original and exciting plot, and professional craftsmanship. We encourage writers whose work meets these general criteria to read an issue of *EQMM* before making a submission." Estab. 1941. Circ. 100,000. Byline given. Pays on acceptance. No kill fee. Publishes ms an average of 6-12 months after acceptance. Buys first North American serial rights. Accepts simultaneous submissions. Responds in 3 months to mss. Sample copy for $5.50. Guidelines for SASE or online.

Fiction Contact: Janet Hutchings, editor. We always need detective stories. Special consideration given to anything timely and original. Needs mystery. No explicit sex or violence, no gore or horror. Seldom publishes parodies or pastiches. **Buys up to 120 mss/year.** Send complete ms. Most stories 2,500-8,000 words. Accepts longer and shorter submissions—including minute mysteries of 250 words, and novellas of up to 20,000 words from established authors **Pays 5-8¢/word; occasionally higher for established authors**.

Poetry Short mystery verses, limericks. Length: 1 page, double spaced maximum.

Tips "We have a Department of First Stories to encourage writers whose fiction has never before been in print. We publish an average of 10 first stories every year. Mark mss Attn: Dept. of First Stories."

Nature, Conservation & Ecology

$$$ AMERICAN FORESTS

American Forests, P.O. Box 2000, Washington DC 20013. E-mail: mrobbins@amfor.org. Website: www.americanforests.org. **75% freelance written**. Quarterly magazine of trees and forests published by a nonprofit citizens' organization that strives to help people plant and care for trees for ecosystem restoration and healthier communities. Estab. 1895. Circ. 25,000. Byline given. Pays on acceptance. No kill fee. Publishes ms an average of 8 months after acceptance. Buys one-time rights. Submit seasonal material 5 months in advance. Accepts queries by mail, e-mail. Accepts previously published material. Responds in 2 months to queries. Sample copy for $2. Guidelines available online.

Nonfiction All articles should emphasize trees, forests, forestry and related issues. Needs general interest, historical, how-to, humor, inspirational. **Buys 8-12 mss/year.** Query. Length: 1,200-2,000 words. **Pays $250-1,000.**

Reprints Send tearsheet or typed ms with rights for sale noted and information about when and where the material previously appeared. Pays 50% of amount paid for original article

Photos Originals only Send photos. Captions required. Reviews 35mm or larger transparencies, glossy color prints. Offers no additional payment for photos accompanying ms. Buys one time rights.

Tips We're looking for more good urban forestry stories, and stories that show cooperation among disparate elements to protect/restore an ecosystem. Query should have honesty and information on photo support. We *do not* accept fiction or poetry at this time.

$$ APPALACHIAN TRAILWAY NEWS

Appalachian Trail Conservancy, P.O. Box 807, Harpers Ferry WV 25425-0807. (304)535-6331. Fax: (304)535-2667. Website: www.appalachiantrail.org. **40% freelance written**. Bimonthly magazine. Estab. 1925. Circ. 32,000. Byline given. Pays on publication. No kill fee. Buys first North American serial rights, buys second serial (reprint) rights, buys web reprint rights. Responds in 2 months to queries. Sample copy and writer's guidelines online.

- Articles must relate to Appalachian Trail.

Nonfiction Publishes but does not pay for hiking reflections. Needs essays, general interest, historical, how-to, humor, inspirational, interview, photo feature, technical, travel. **Buys 5-10 mss/year.** Query with or without published clips, or send complete ms. Prefers e-mail queries. Length: 250-3,000 words. **Pays $25-300.**

Reprints Send photocopy with rights for sale noted and information about when and where the material previously appeared.

Photos State availability. Identification of subjects required. Reviews contact sheets, 5 × 7 prints, slides, digital images. Offers $25-125/photo; $250/cover

Tips Contributors should display a knowledge of or interest in the Appalachian Trail. Those who live in the vicinity of the Trail may opt for an assigned story and should present credentials and subject of interest to the editor.

$$$ THE ATLANTIC SALMON JOURNAL

The Atlantic Salmon Federation, P.O. Box 5200, St. Andrews NB E5B 3S8 Canada. (506)529-1033. Fax: (506)529-4438. E-mail: martinsilverstone@videotron.ca. Website: www.asf.ca. **Contact:** Martin Silverstone. **50-68% freelance written**. Quarterly magazine covering conservation efforts for the Atlantic salmon, catering to the dedicated angler and conservationist. Circ. 11,000. Byline given. Pays on publication. No kill fee. Publishes ms an average of 6 months after acceptance. Buys first North American serial rights. Buys one-time rights to photos. Submit seasonal material 3 months in advance. Accepts simultaneous submissions. Responds in 2 months to queries. Sample copy for 9 × 12 SAE with $1 (Canadian), or IRC. Guidelines free.

Nonfiction "We are seeking articles that are pertinent to the focus and purpose of our magazine, which is to inform and entertain our membership on all aspects of the Atlantic salmon and its environment, and conservation." Needs exposè, historical, how-to, humor, interview, new product, opinion, personal experience, photo feature, technical, travel, conservation. **Buys 15-20 mss/year.** Query with published clips. Length: 2,000 words. **Pays $400-800 for articles with photos.**

Photos State availability. Captions, identification of subjects required. Pays $50 minimum; $350-500 for covers; $300 for 2-page spread; $175 for full page photo; $100 for 1/2-page photo.

Columns/Departments Fit To Be Tied (Conservation issues and salmon research; the design, construction and success of specific flies); interesting characters in the sport and opinion pieces by knowledgeable writers, 900 words; Casting Around (short, informative, entertaining reports, book reviews and quotes from the world of Atlantic salmon angling and conservation). Query. **Pays $50-300.**

Tips "Articles must reflect informed and up-to-date knowledge of Atlantic salmon. Writers need not be authorities, but research must be impeccable. Clear, concise writing is essential, and submissions must be typed."

$$ THE BEAR DELUXE MAGAZINE

Orlo, P.O. Box 10342, Portland OR 97296. (503)242-1047. E-mail: bear@orlo.org. Website: www.orlo.org. **80% freelance written**. Quarterly magazine. *The Bear Deluxe Magazine* is a national independent environmental magazine publishing significant works of reporting, creative nonfiction, literature, visual art and design. Based in the Pacific Northwest, *The Bear Deluxe* reaches across cultural and political divides to engage readers on vital issues effecting the environment. Estab. 1993. Circ. 19,000. Byline given. Pays on publication. Offers 25% kill fee. Publishes ms an average of 6 months after acceptance. Buys first rights, buys one-time rights. Editorial lead time 6 months. Submit seasonal material 9 months in advance. Accepts queries by mail, e-mail. Accepts previously published material. Accepts simultaneous submissions. Responds in 3-6 months to mail queries. Only responds to e-mail queries if interested. Sample copy for $3. Guidelines for #10 SASE or on website.

Nonfiction Needs book excerpts, essays, expose, general interest, interview, new product, opinion, personal experience, photo feature, travel, artist profiles. Publishes 1 theme/2 years **Buys 40 mss/year.** Query with published clips. Length: 250-4,500 words. **Pays $25-400, depending on piece.**

Photos State availability. Identification of subjects, model releases required. Reviews contact sheets, transparencies, 8 × 10 prints. Offers $30/photo Buys one time rights.

Columns/Departments Reviews (almost anything), 300 words; Front of the Book (mix of short news bits, found writing, quirky tidbits), 300-500 words; Portrait of an Artist (artist profiles), 1,200 words; Back of the Book (creative opinion pieces), 650 words. 16 Query with published clips. **Pays $25-400, depending on piece.**

Fiction Stories must have some environmental context, but we view that in a broad sense. Needs adventure, cond novels, historical, horror, humorous, mystery, novel concepts, western. No detective, children's or horror. **Buys 8 mss/year.** Query or send complete ms. Length: 750-4,500 words. **Pays free subscription to the magazine, contributor's copies and $25-400, depending on piece; additional copies for postage.**

Poetry Needs avant-garde, free verse, haiku, light verse, traditional. Buys 16-20 poems/year. Submit maximum 5 poems. 50 lines maximum **Pays $20, subscription, and copies.**

Tips Offer to be a stringer for future ideas. Get a copy of the magazine and guidelines, and query us with specific nonfiction ideas and clips. We're looking for original, magazine-style stories, not fluff or PR. Fiction, essay, and poetry writers should know we have an open and blind review policy and should keep sending their best work even if rejected once. Be as specific as possible in queries.

$ $ BIRDER'S WORLD

Kalmbach Publishing Co., P.O. Box 1612, Waukesha WI 53187-1612. Fax: (262)798-6468. E-mail: mail@birdersworld.com. Website: www.birdersworld.com. Bimonthly magazine for birdwatchers who actively look for wild birds in the field. "*Birder's World* concentrates on where to find, how to attract, and how to identify wild birds, and on how to understand what they do." Estab. 1987. Circ. 40,000. Byline given. Pays on acceptance. Buys one-time rights. Accepts queries by mail. Guidelines available online.

Nonfiction Needs essays, how-to, attracting birds, interview, personal experience, photo feature, bird photography, travel, birding hotspots in North America and beyond, product reviews/comparisons, bird biology, endangered or threatened birds. No poetry, fiction, or puzzles. **Buys 60 mss/year.** Query with published clips. Length: 500-2,400 words. **Pays $200-450.**

Photos See photo guidelines online. State availability. Identification of subjects required. Buys one time rights.

$ BIRD WATCHER'S DIGEST

Pardson Corp., P.O. Box 110, Marietta OH 45750. (740)373-5285. Fax: (740)373-8443. E-mail: editor@birdwatchersdigest.com. Website: www.birdwatchersdigest.com. **60% freelance written. Works with a small number of new/unpublished writers each year.** Bimonthly magazine covering natural history—birds and bird watching. *BWD* is a nontechnical magazine interpreting ornithological material for amateur observers, including the knowledgeable birder, the serious novice and the backyard bird watcher; we strive to provide good reading and good ornithology. Estab. 1978. Circ. 90,000. Byline given. Pays on publication. Publishes ms an average of 2 years after acceptance. Buys one-time rights, buys second serial (reprint) rights. Submit seasonal material 6 months in advance. Accepts previously published material. Responds in 2 months to queries. Sample copy for $3.99 or online. Guidelines available online.

Nonfiction We are especially interested in fresh, lively accounts of closely observed bird behavior and displays and of bird-watching experiences and expeditions. We often need material on backyard subjects such as bird feeding, housing, gardenening on less common species or on unusual or previously unreported behavior of common species. Needs book excerpts, how-to, relating to birds, feeding and attracting, etc., humor, personal experience, travel, limited, we get many. No articles on pet or caged birds; none on raising a baby bird. **Buys 45-60 mss/year.** Send complete ms. Length: 600-3,500 words. **Pays from $100.**

Photos Send photos. Reviews transparencies, prints. Pays $75 minimum for transparencies Buys one time rights.

Tips We are aimed at an audience ranging from the backyard bird watcher to the very knowledgeable birder; we include in each issue material that will appeal at various levels. We always strive for a good geographical spread, with material from every section of the country. We leave very technical matters to others, but we want facts and accuracy, depth and quality, directed at the veteran bird watcher and at the enthusiastic novice. We stress the joys and pleasures of bird watching, its environmental contribution, and its value for the individual and society.

$ $ $ CANADIAN WILDLIFE

350 Michael Cowpland Dr., Kanata ON K2M 2W1 Canada. (613)599-9594. Fax: (613)271-9591. E-mail: wild@cwf-fcf.org. **60% freelance written**. Magazine published 6 times/year. Only articles about Canadian subjects by Canadian writers will be considered. covering wildlife conservation. Includes topics pertaining to wildlife, endangered species, conservation, and natural history. Estab. 1995. Circ. 15,000. Byline given. Pays on acceptance. Publishes ms an average of 3 months after acceptance. Buys first North American serial rights, buys All material translated for publication in French-language edition, biosphere rights. Editorial lead time 3 months. Submit seasonal material 4 months in advance. Accepts queries by mail, e-mail. Responds in 6 weeks to queries. Responds in 2 months to mss. Guidelines free.

Nonfiction Needs book excerpts, interview, photo feature, science/nature. No standard travel stories. **Buys 20-25 mss/year.** Query with published clips. Length: 800-2,500 words. **Pays an average of 50 ¢ Cdn per word for assigned articles. Pays $300-1,000 for unsolicited articles.**

Photos Send photos. Captions, identification of subjects, model releases required. Reviews transparencies. Negotiates payment individually Buys one time rights.

Tips *Canadian Wildlife* is a benefit of membership in the Canadian Wildlife Federation. Nearly 15,000 people currently receive the magazine. The majority of these men and women are already well versed in topics concerning the environment and natural science; writers, however, should not make assumptions about the extent of a reader's knowledge of topics.

$ $ $ CONSCIOUS CHOICE

The Journal of Ecology & Natural Living, Conscious Enlightenment, LLC, 920 N. Franklin St., Suite 202, Chicago IL 60610-3179. Fax: (312)751-3973. E-mail: editor@consciouschoice.com. Website: www.consciouschoice.com. **95% freelance written**. Monthly tabloid covering the environment, renewable energy, yoga, natural health and medicine, and personal growth and spirituality. Estab. 1988. Circ. 55,000. Byline given. Pays on publication. Offers 50% kill fee. Publishes ms an average of 6 months after acceptance. Buys first North American serial rights, buys electronic rights. Editorial lead time 6 months. Submit seasonal material 6 months in advance. Accepts queries by mail. Accepts simultaneous submissions. Responds in 6 weeks to queries. Responds in 1 month to mss. Sample copy available online. Writer's guidelines free or by e-mail

Nonfiction Needs general interest, to cultural creatives, interview, emphasis on narrative, story telling, environment. **Buys 24 mss/year.** Query with 2-3 published clips. 1,800 words **Pays $150-1,000.**

$ $ E THE ENVIRONMENTAL MAGAZINE

Earth Action Network, P.O. Box 5098, Westport CT 06881-5098. (203)854-5559. Fax: (203)866-0602. E-mail: info@emagazine.com. Website: www.emagazine.com. **60% freelance written**. Bimonthly magazine. *E Magazine* was formed for the purpose of acting as a clearinghouse of information, news, and commentary on environmental issues. Estab. 1990. Circ. 50,000. Byline given. Pays on publication. No kill fee. Buys first North American serial rights. Editorial lead time 3 months. Submit seasonal material 6 months in advance. Accepts queries by mail, e-mail, fax. Accepts simultaneous submissions. Sample copy for $5 or online. Guidelines available online.

- The editor reports an interest in seeing more investigative reporting.

Nonfiction On spec or free contributions welcome. Needs expose, environmental, how-to, new product, book review, feature (in-depth articles on key natural environmental issues). **Buys 100 mss/year.** Query with published clips. Length: 100-4,000 words. **Pays 30¢/word.**

Photos State availability. Identification of subjects required. Reviews printed samples, e.g., magazine tearsheets, postcards, etc., to be kept on file. Negotiates payment individually Buys one time rights.

Columns/Departments On spec or free contributions welcome. In Brief/Currents (environmental news stories/trends), 400-1,000 words; Conversations (Q&As with environmental movers and shakers),

2,000 words; Tools for Green Living; Your Health; Eco-Travel; Eco-Home; Eating Right; Green Business; Consumer News (each 700-1,200 words). Query with published clips.

Tips Contact us to obtain writer's guidelines and back issues of our magazine. Tailor your query according to the department/section you feel it would be best suited for. Articles must be lively, well researched, balanced, and relevant to a mainstream, national readership. On spec or free contributions welcome.

$$ HIGH COUNTRY NEWS

P.O. Box 1090, Paonia CO 81428. (970)527-4898. E-mail: editor@hcn.org. Website: www.hcn.org. **70% freelance written.** Biweekly nonprofit magazine covering environment, rural communities, and natural resource issues in 11 western states for environmentalists, politicians, companies, college classes, government agencies, grass roots activists, public land managers, etc. Estab. 1970. Circ. 25,000. Byline given. Pays on publication. Kill fee of 1/3 of agreed rate. Publishes ms an average of 2 months after acceptance. Buys all rights. Accepts queries by e-mail. Responds in 2 weeks to queries. Sample copy available online. Guidelines available online at: hcn.org/about/submissions.

Nonfiction "Magazine-style stories with strong storytelling, compelling characters, a clear, jargon-free style, and a dedication to intellectual honesty." **Buys 100 mss/year.** Query. up to 3,000 words **Pay negotiable.**

Photos Send photos. Captions, identification of subjects required. Reviews b&w or color prints.

Columns/Departments See guidelines at: hcn.org/about/submissions.

Tips "We use a lot of freelance material. Familiarity with the newsmagazine is a must. Start by writing a query letter. We define 'resources' broadly to include people, culture, and aesthetic values, not just coal, oil, and timber."

$$$ MINNESOTA CONSERVATION VOLUNTEER

Minnesota Department of Natural Resources, 500 Lafeyette Rd., St. Paul MN 55155-4046. Website: www.dnr.state.mn.us/magazine. **50% freelance written.** Bimonthly magazine covering Minnesota natural resources, wildlife, natural history, outdoor recreation, and land use. "*Minnesota Conservation Volunteer* is a donor-supported magazine advocating conservation and wise use of Minnesota's natural resources. Material must reflect an appreciation of nature and an ethic of care for the environment. We rely on a variety of sources in our reporting. More than 140,000 Minnesota households, businesses, schools, and other groups subscribe to this conservation magazine." Estab. 1940. Circ. 164,200. Byline given. Pays on acceptance. Offers 30% kill fee. Publishes ms an average of 2 months after acceptance. Buys first North American serial rights, buys Rights to post to website, and archive rights. Editorial lead time 9 months. Submit seasonal material 9 months in advance. Accepts queries by mail, e-mail. Accepts previously published material. Responds in 1 month to queries. Responds in 2 months to mss. Sample copy free or on website Guidelines available online.

Nonfiction Needs book excerpts, essays, expose, general interest, historical, humor, interview, opinion, personal experience, photo feature, travel, Young Naturalist for children. Rarely publishes poetry or uncritical advocacy. **Buys 10 mss/year.** Query with published clips. Length: up to 1,500 words. **Pays 50¢/word for full-length feature articles.** up to $300

Photos $100/photo

Columns/Departments Close Encounters (unusual, exciting, or humorous personal wildlife experience in Minnesota), up to 1,500 words; Sense of Place (first- or third-person essay developing character of a Minnesota place), up to 1,500 words; Viewpoint (well-researched and well-reasoned opinion piece), up to 1,500 words; Minnesota Profile (concise description of emblematic state species or geographic feature), 400 words. 10 Query with published clips. **Pays 50¢/word**

Tips "In submitting queries, look beyond topics to *stories:* What is someone doing and why? How does the story end? In submitting a query addressing a particular issue, think of the human impacts and the sources you might consult. Summarize your idea, the story line, and sources in 2 or 3 short paragraphs. While topics must have relevance to Minnesota and give a Minnesota character to the magazine, feel free to round out your research with out-of-state sources."

$$$ NATIONAL PARKS

1300 19th St. NW, Suite 300, Washington DC 20036. (202)223-6722. Fax: (202)659-0650. E-mail: npmag@npca.org. Website: www.npca.org/magazine/. **60% freelance written. Prefers to work with published/established writers.** Quarterly magazine for a largely unscientific but highly educated audience interested in preservation of National Park System units, natural areas, and protection of wildlife habitat. Estab. 1919. Circ. 340,000. Pays on acceptance. Offers 33% kill fee. Publishes ms an average of 2 months after acceptance. Responds in 3-4 months to queries. Sample copy for $3 and 9 × 12 SASE or online. Guidelines available online.

Nonfiction All material must relate to US national parks. Needs expose, on threats, wildlife problems in national parks, descriptive articles about new or proposed national parks and wilderness parks. No poetry, philosophical essays, or first-person narratives. No unsolicited mss. Length: 1,500 words. **Pays $1,300 for 1,500-word features and travel articles.**
Photos Not looking for new photographers. Send photos.
Tips Articles should have an original slant or news hook and cover a limited subject, rather than attempt to treat a broad subject superficially. Specific examples, descriptive details, and quotes are always preferable to generalized information. The writer must be able to document factual claims, and statements should be clearly substantiated with evidence within the article. *National Parks* does not publish fiction, poetry, personal essays, or 'My trip to.' stories.

$$$$ NATURAL HISTORY

Natural History, Inc., 36 W. 25th St., 5th Floor, New York NY 10010. E-mail: nhmag@naturalhistorymag.com. Website: www.naturalhistorymag.com. **15% freelance written**. Magazine published 10 times/year for well-educated audience: professional people, scientists, and scholars. Circ. 225,000. Byline given. Pays on acceptance. No kill fee. Publishes ms an average of 3 months after acceptance. Buys first North American serial rights. Becomes an agent for second serial (reprint) rights Submit seasonal material 6 months in advance.
Nonfiction We are seeking new research on mammals, birds, invertebrates, reptiles, ocean life, anthropology, astronomy, preferably written by principal investigators in these fields. Our slant is toward unraveling problems in behavior, ecology, and evolution. **Buys 60 mss/year.** Query by mail or send complete ms Length: 1,500-3,000 words. **Pays $500-2,500.**
Photos Rarely uses 8 × 10 b&w glossy prints; pays $125/page maximum. Much color is used; pays $300 for inside, and up to $600 for cover. Buys one time rights.
Columns/Departments Journal (reporting from the field); Findings (summary of new or ongoing research); Naturalist At Large; The Living Museum (relates to the American Museum of Natural History); Discovery (natural or cultural history of a specific place).
Tips We expect high standards of writing and research. We do not lobby for causes, environmental, or other. The writer should have a deep knowledge of his subject, then submit original ideas either in query or by manuscript.

$$$ NATURE CANADA

75 Albert St., Suite 300, Ottawa ON K1P 5E7 Canada. (613)562-3447. Fax: (613)562-3371. E-mail: info@naturecanada.ca. Website: www.naturecanada.ca. Quarterly magazine covering conservation, natural history and environmental/naturalist community. "Editorial content reflects the goals and priorities of Nature Canada as a conservation organization with a focus on our program areas: federally protected areas (national parks, national wildlife areas, etc.), endangered species, and bird conservation through Canada's important bird areas. Nature Canada is written for an audience interested in nature conservation. Nature Canada celebrates, preserves, and protects Canadian nature. We promote the awareness and understanding of the connection between humans and nature and how natural systems support life on Earth. We strive to instill a sense of ownership and belief that these natural systems should be protected." Estab. 1971. Circ. 27,000. Byline given. Pays on publication. Offers $100 kill fee. Publishes ms an average of 3 months after acceptance. Buys all Nature Canada rights (including electronic). Author retains resale rights elsewhere. Editorial lead time 4 months. Submit seasonal material 6 months in advance. Responds in 4 months to mss. Sample copy for $5. Guidelines available online.
Nonfiction Subjects include: Canadian conservation issues; nature education; reconnecting with nature; enviro-friendly lifestyles, products and consumer reports; federal protected areas; endangered species; birds; sustainable development; company and individual profiles; urban nature; how-to; natural history **Buys 12 mss/year.** Query with published clips. Length: 650-2,000 words. **Pays up to 50¢/word (Canadian).**
Photos State availability. Identification of subjects required. Offers $50-200/photo (Canadian) Buys one time rights.
Tips "Our readers are well-educated and knowledgeable about nature and the environment so contributors should have a good understanding of the subject. We also deal exclusively with Canadian issues and species, except for those relating directly to our international program. E-mail queries preferred. Do not send unsolicited manuscripts. We receive many BC-related queries but need more for the rest of Canada, particularly SK, MB, QC and the Maritimes. Articles must focus on the positive and be supported by science when applicable. We are looking for strong, well-researched writing that is lively, entertaining, enlightening, provocative and, when appropriate, amusing."

$$ NORTHERN WOODLANDS MAGAZINE

Center for Woodlands Education, Inc., 1776 Center Rd., P.O. Box 471, Corinth VT 05039-0471. (802)439-6292. Fax: (802)439-6296. E-mail: dave@northernwoodlands.org. Website: www.northernwoodlands.org. **40-60% freelance written**. Quarterly magazine covering natural history, conservation, and forest management in the Northeast. "*Northern Woodlands* strives to inspire landowners' sense of stewardship by increasing their awareness of the natural history and the principles of conservation and forestry that are directly related to their land. We also hope to increase the public's awareness of the social, economic, and environmental benefits of a working forest." Estab. 1994. Circ. 15,000. Byline given. Pays 1 month prior to publication Publishes ms an average of 6 months after acceptance. Buys one-time rights. Editorial lead time 6 months. Submit seasonal material 6 months in advance. Accepts queries by mail, e-mail. Accepts previously published material. Accepts simultaneous submissions. Responds in 1 month to queries. Responds in 1-2 months to mss Sample copy available online. Guidelines available online

Nonfiction No product reviews, first-person travelogues, cute animal stories, opinion, or advocacy pieces. **Buys 15-20 mss/year.** Query with published clips. Length: 500-3,000 words. **Pay varies per piece.**

Photos State availability. Identification of subjects required. Reviews transparencies, prints, high res digital photos. Offers $35-75/photo Buys one-time rights.

Tips "We will work with subject-matter experts to make their work suitable for our audience."

$$ OCEAN MAGAZINE

to Celebrate and Protect, P.O. Box 84, Rodanthe NC 27968-0084. (252)256-2296. E-mail: diane@oceanmagazine.org. Website: www.oceanmag.org. **100% freelance written**. Quarterly magazine covering the ocean, its ecosystem, its creatures, recreation, pollution, energy sources, the love of it. "*OCEAN Magazine* serves to celebrate and protect the greatest, most comprehensive resource for life on earth, our world's ocean. *OCEAN* publishes articles, stories, poems, essays, and photography about the ocean—observations, experiences, scientific and environmental discussions—written with fact and feeling, illustrated with images from nature." Estab. 2003. Circ. 10,000. Byline given. Pays on publication. Publishes ms an average of 2-4 months after acceptance. Buys one-time rights. Editorial lead time 3-6 months. Submit seasonal material 3-6 months in advance. Accepts queries by mail, e-mail (preferable), phone. Accepts previously published material. .Accepts simultaneous submissions. Responds in 1 day to 4 weeks to queries and mss. Sample copy available online. Guidelines available online.

Nonfiction Needs book excerpts, essays, general interest, historical, inspirational, interview, opinion, personal experience, photo feature, technical, travel, spiritual. Does not want poor writing. **Buys 24-36 mss/year.** Query. Length: 75-5,000 words. **Pays $75-250.**

Photos State availability. Identification of subjects, model releases required. Reviews 3 × 5, 4x6, 5 × 7, 8 × 10, 10 × 12 prints, JPEG files. Negotiates payment individually. Buys one-time rights.

Fiction Needs adventure, fantasy, historical, novel concepts, romance, slice-of-life vignettes. **Buys 1-2 mss/year.** Query. Length: 100-2,000 words. **Pays $75-400.**

Poetry Needs avant-garde, free verse, haiku, light verse, traditional. Buys 12 poems/year. Submit maximum 6 poems. **Pays $75-150.**

Tips "Submit with a genuine love and concern for the ocean and its creatures."

$$$$ ORION

The Orion Society, 187 Main St., Great Barrington MA 01230. E-mail: orion@orionsociety.org. Website: www.oriononline.org. **90% freelance written**. Bimonthly magazine covering nature and culture. *Orion* is a magazine about the issues of our time: how we live, what we value, what sustains us. *Orion* explores an emerging alternative worldview through essays, literary journalism, short stories, interviews, and reviews, as well as photo essays and portfolios of art. Estab. 1982. Circ. 22,000. Byline given. Pays on publication. No kill fee. Publishes ms an average of 3-12 months after acceptance. Buys first North American serial rights. Editorial lead time 3-9 months. Submit seasonal material 9 months in advance. Accepts queries by mail, e-mail. Accepts simultaneous submissions. Responds in 1-2 months to queries. Responds in 4-6 months to mss. Sample copy available online. Guidelines available online.

Nonfiction Needs essays, expose, historical, humor, personal experience, photo feature, reported feature. No What I learned during my walk in the woods; personal hiking/adventure/travel anecdotes; unsolicited poetry; writing that deals with the natural world in only superficial ways. **Buys 40-50 mss/year.** Send complete ms. Length: 2,000-4,500 words. **Pays $300-2,000.**

Photos State availability. Reviews contact sheets, prints. Negotiates payment individually. Buys one time rights.

Columns/Departments Point of View (opinion essay by a noted authority), 625 words; Sacred & Mundane (funny, ironic or awe-inspiring ways nature exists within or is created by contemporary culture), 200-600 words; Health & the Environment (emphasizes and explores relationship between human health and a healthy natural world, or forces that threaten both simultaneously), 1,300 words; Reviews (new books, films and recordings related to *Orion's* mission), 250-600 words; Coda (an endpaper), 650 words. 85 Send complete ms. **Pays $25-300.**

Fiction Needs ethnic, historical, humorous, mainstream, slice-of-life vignettes. No manuscripts that don't carry an environmental message or involve the landscape/nature as a major character. Buys up to 1 ms/year. Send complete ms. Length: 1,200-4,000 words. **Pays 10-20¢/word.**

Tips We are most impressed by and most likely to work with writers whose submissions show they know our magazine. If you are proposing a story, your query must: 1. Be detailed in its approach and reflect the care you will give the story itself; 2. Define where in the magazine you believe the story would be appropriate; 3. Include three tear sheets of previously published work. If you are submitting a manuscript, it must be double-spaced, typed or printed in black ink. Please be sure your name and a page number appear on each page of your submission, and that we have your phone number and SASE.

$$$ OUTDOOR AMERICA

Izaak Walton League of America, 707 Conservation Ln., Gaithersburg MD 20878-2983. (301)548-0150. Fax: (301)548-9409. E-mail: oa@iwla.org. Website: www.iwla.org. Quarterly magazine covering national conservation efforts/issues related to and involving members of the Izaak Walton League. A 4-color publication, *Outdoor America* is received by League members, as well as representatives of Congress and the media. Our audience, located predominantly in the midwestern and mid-Atlantic states, enjoys traditional recreational pursuits, such as fishing, hiking, hunting, and boating. All have a keen interest in protecting the future of our natural resources and outdoor recreation heritage. Estab. 1922. Circ. 40,000. Pays on acceptance. Offers 1/3 original rate kill fee. Publishes ms an average of 2 months after acceptance. Buys first North American serial rights. Accepts queries by mail, e-mail. Responds in 2 months to queries. Sample copy for $2.50. Guidelines available online.

Nonfiction Conservation and natural resources issue stories with a direct connection to the work and members of the Izaak Walton League. Features should be 2,000-3,000 words. Essays on outdoor ethics and conservation (1,500-2,000 words). No fiction, poetry, or unsubstantiated opinion pieces. Query or send ms for short columns/news pieces (500 words or less). Features are planned 6-12 months in advance. **Pays $1,000-1,500 for features.**

Photos Send tearsheets or nonreturnable samples. Pays $100-500.

$$$$ SIERRA

85 Second St., 2nd Floor, San Francisco CA 94105. E-mail: sierra.letters@sierraclub.org. Website: www.sierraclub.org. **Works with a small number of new/unpublished writers each year.** Bimonthly magazine emphasizing conservation and environmental politics for people who are well educated, activist, outdoor-oriented, and politically well informed with a dedication to conservation. Estab. 1893. Circ. 695,000. Byline given. Pays on acceptance. Offers negotiable kill fee. Publishes ms an average of 4 months after acceptance. Buys first North American serial rights. Accepts queries by mail, fax. Accepts previously published material. Responds in 2 months to queries. Sample copy for $3 and SASE, or online. Guidelines available online.

- The editor reports an interest in seeing pieces on environmental heroes, thoughtful features on new developments in solving environmental problems, and outdoor adventure stories with a strong environmental element.

Nonfiction Needs expose, well-documented articles on environmental issues of national importance such as energy, wilderness, forests, etc., general interest, well-researched nontechnical pieces on areas of particular environmental concern, interview, photo feature, photo feature essays on threatened or scenic areas, journalistic treatments of semitechnical topic (energy sources, wildlife management, land use, waste management, etc.). No My trip to . or Why we must save wildlife/nature articles; no poetry or general superficial essays on environmentalism; no reporting on purely local environmental issues. **Buys 30-36 mss/year.** Query with published clips. Length: 1,000-3,000 words. **Pays $800-3,000.**

Reprints Send photocopy with rights for sale noted and information about when and where the material previously appeared. Payment negotiable

Photos Send photos. Pays maximum $300 for transparencies; more for cover photos Buys one time rights.

Columns/Departments Food for Thought (food's connection to environment); Good Going (adventure journey); Hearth & Home (advice for environmentally sound living); Body Politics (health and the environment); Profiles (biographical look at environmentalists); Hidden Life (exposure of hidden environmental problems in everyday objects); Lay of the Land (national/international concerns), 500-700 words; Mixed Media (essays on environment in the media; book reviews), 200-300 words. **Pays $50-500.**

Tips Queries should include an outline of how the topic would be covered and a mention of the political appropriateness and timeliness of the article. Statements of the writer's qualifications should be included.

$$ WHISPER IN THE WOODS

Nature Journal, Turning Leaf Productions, LLC, P.O. Box 1014, Traverse City MI 49685-1014. (231)943-0153. E-mail: editor@whisperinthewoods.com. Website: www.whisperinthewoods.com. **100% freelance written**. Quarterly literary art journal covering nature, art and photography. We focus on the appreciation of the beauty of nature. Estab. 2002. Circ. 10,000. Byline sometimes given. Pays on publication. Offers 20% kill fee. Publishes ms an average of 9 months after acceptance. Buys first North American serial rights. Editorial lead time 1 year. Submit seasonal material 1 year in advance. Accepts queries by mail. Accepts previously published material. Accepts simultaneous submissions. Sample copy for $8. Guidelines available online.

Nonfiction Needs essays, inspirational, personal experience, photo feature, travel. Query with published clips. Length: 600-1,500 words. **Pays $20-300.**

Photos State availability. Captions required. Reviews contact sheets, GIF/JPEG files. Buys one time rights.

Poetry Contact: Denise Baker, managing editor. Needs avant-garde, free verse, haiku, light verse, traditional. Buys 4 poems/year. Submit maximum 5 poems. **Pays $25-40.**

Tips Carefully follow submission guidelines.

$$$$ WILDLIFE CONSERVATION

2300 Southern Blvd., Bronx NY 10460. (718)220-5100. E-mail: nsimmons@wcs.org; membership@wcs.org. Website: www.wcs.org. Bimonthly magazine for environmentally aware readers. Offers 25% kill fee. Buys first North American serial rights. Accepts simultaneous submissions. Responds in 1 month to queries. Sample copy for $4.95 (plus $1 postage). Writer's guidelines available for SASE or via e-mail.

Nonfiction We want well-reported articles on conservation issues, conservation successes, and straight natural history based on author's research. **Buys 30 mss/year.** Query with published clips. Length: 300-2,000 words. **Pays $1/word for features and department articles, and $150 for short pieces**

Personal Computers

⊘ BASELINE

Ziff Davis Media, Inc., 28 E. 28th St., New York NY 10016. (212)503-5900. Fax: (212)503-5454. E-mail: baseline@ziffdavis.com; eileen.feretic@ziffdavisenterprise.com. Website: www.baselinemag.com. "Baseline - the Fusion of Business and Technology - is a handbook for the IT and business leaders who put technology to work for their enterprise. The magazine is dedicated to helping these executives, managers and professionals effectively execute technology initiatives in order to achieve a solid return on those investments. Baseline offers lessons learned in the form of real-world business case studies from a variety of organizations across a wide array of industries." Circ. 125,000. No kill fee. Editorial lead time 3 months.

- Most of the reporting and writing is done by staff writers and editors.

$$$ LAPTOP

Bedford Communications, 1410 Broadway, 21st Floor, New York NY 10018. (212)807-8220. Fax: (212)807-1098. Website: www.laptopmag.com. **60%% freelance written**. Monthly magazine covering mobile computing, such as laptop computers, PDAs, software, and peripherals; industry trends. Publication is geared toward the mobile technology laptop computer buyer, with an emphasis on the small office. Estab. 1991. Byline given. Pays on publication. Offers 20% kill fee. Publishes ms an average of 3 months after acceptance. Buys all rights. Editorial lead time 4 months. Accepts queries by e-mail. Responds in 4 months to queries. Sample copy available online.

Nonfiction Needs how-to, e.g., how-to install a CD-ROM drive, technical, hands-on reviews, features. **Buys 80-100 mss/year.** Length: 300-3,500 words. **Pays $150-1,250.**

Columns/Departments , .

Tips Send résumé with feature-length clips (technology-related, if possible) to editorial offices. Unsolicited manuscripts are not accepted or returned.

$ $ $ $ MACLIFE

4000 Shoreline Ct., Suite 400, South San Francisco CA 94080. (650)872-1642. Fax: (650)872-1643. E-mail: editor@maclife.com. Website: www.maclife.com. **20% freelance written**. Monthly magazine covering Macintosh computers. "*MacLife* is a magazine for Macintosh computer enthusiasts of all levels. Writers must know, love and own Macintosh computers and/or iPhone, depending on the nature of the query/article." Estab. 1996. Circ. 160,000. Byline given. Pays on publication. No kill fee. Publishes ms an average of 3 months after acceptance. Buys all rights. Editorial lead time 3 months. Submit seasonal material 2 months in advance. Accepts queries by mail, e-mail. Responds in 1 month to queries

Nonfiction "Looking for helpful, entertaining, pop culture-savvy articles and pitches." Needs how-to, new product, technical. No humor, case studies, personal experience, essays. **Buys 10-30 mss/year.** Query. Length: 250-7,500 words. **Pays an average of 35¢/word, depending on the nature & length of assignment.**

Columns/Departments Reviews (always assigned), 300-750 words; How-to's (detailed, step-by-step), 500-2,500 words; features, 1,000-3,500 words. 20 Query with or without published clips. **Pays an average of 35¢/word, depending on the nature & length of assignment.**

Tips "Send us an idea for a short one to two page how-to and/or send us a letter outlining your publishing experience and areas of Mac expertise so we can assign a review to you (reviews editor is Roman Loyola). Your submission should have great practical hands-on benefit to a reader, be fun to read in the author's natural voice, and include lots of screenshot graphics. We require electronic submissions. Impress our reviews editor with well-written reviews of Mac products and then move up to bigger articles from there."

$ $ $ SMART COMPUTING

Sandhills Publishing, 131 W. Grand Dr., Lincoln NE 68521. (800)544-1264. Fax: (402)479-2104. E-mail: editor@smartcomputing.com. Website: www.smartcomputing.com. **45% freelance written**. Monthly magazine. "We focus on plain-English computing articles with an emphasis on tutorials that improve productivity without the purchase of new hardware." Estab. 1990. Circ. 200,000. Byline given. Pays on acceptance. Offers 25% kill fee. Publishes ms an average of 2 months after acceptance. Buys all rights. Editorial lead time 4 months. Submit seasonal material 4 months in advance. Accepts queries by mail, e-mail. Accepts simultaneous submissions. Responds in 1 month to queries. Sample copy for $7.99. Guidelines for #10 SASE.

Nonfiction Needs how-to, new product, technical. No humor, opinion, personal experience. **Buys 250 mss/year.** Query with published clips. Length: 800-3,200 words. **Pays $240-960.** Pays expenses of writers on assignment up to $75

Photos Send photos. Captions required. Offers no additional payment for photos accepted with ms. Buys all rights.

Tips "Focus on practical, how-to computing articles. Our readers are intensely productivity-driven. Carefully review recent issues. We receive many ideas for stories printed in the last 6 months."

WIRED MAGAZINE

Condé Nast Publications, 520 Third St., 3rd Floor, San Francisco CA 94107-1815. (415)276-5000. Fax: (415)276-5150. E-mail: submit@wiredmag.com. Website: www.wired.com/wired. **95% freelance written**. Monthly magazine covering technology and digital culture. We cover the digital revolution and related advances in computers, communications and lifestyles. Estab. 1993. Circ. 500,000. Byline given. Pays on publication. Offers 25% kill fee. Publishes ms an average of 3 months after acceptance. Buys all rights for items less than 1,000 words, first North American serial rights for pieces over 1,000 words. Editorial lead time 3 months. Accepts queries by e-mail. Responds in 3 weeks to queries. Sample copy for $4.95. Guidelines by e-mail.

Nonfiction Needs essays, interview, opinion. No poetry or trade articles. **Buys 85 features, 130 short pieces, 200 reviews, 36 essays, and 50 other mss/year.** Query.

Tips Read the magazine. We get too many inappropriate queries. We need quality writers who understand our audience, and who understand how to query.

Photography

$ NATURE PHOTOGRAPHER

Nature Photographer Publishing Co., Inc., P.O. Box 220, Lubec ME 04652. (207)733-4201. Fax: (207)733-4202. E-mail: nature_photographer@yahoo.com. Website: www.naturephotographermag.com. Quarterly magazine written by field contributors and editors; write to above address to become a Field Contributor.

Nature Photographer emphasizes nature photography that uses low-impact and local less-known locations, techniques and ethics. Articles include how-to, travel to world-wide wilderness locations, and how nature photography can be used to benefit the environment and environmental education of the public. Estab. 1990. Circ. 35,000. Pays on publication. Buys one-time rights. Submit seasonal material 8 months in advance. Accepts queries by e-mail. Accepts simultaneous submissions. Responds in 2 months to queries. Sample copy for sae with 9 × 12 envelope and 6 First-Class stamps. Guidelines by e-mail.
Nonfiction Needs how-to, exposure, creative techniques, techniques to make photography easier, low-impact techniques, macro photography, wildlife, scenics, flowers, photo feature, technical, travel. No articles about photographing in zoos or on game farms. **Buys 56-72 mss/year.** Length: 750-2,500 words. **Pays $75-150.**
Photos Send photos. upon request. Do not send with submission. Identification of subjects required. Reviews 35mm and digital images on CD (both scanned and digitally captured images) transparencies. Offers no additional payment for photos accepted with ms. Buys one time rights.
Tips Must have good, solid research and knowledge of subject. Be sure to obtain guidelines before submitting query. If you have not requested guidelines within the last year, request an updated version because *Nature Photographer* is now written by editors and field contributors, and guidelines will outline how you can become a field contributor.

$$ PC PHOTO

Werner Publishing Corp., 12121 Wilshire Blvd., 12th Floor, Los Angeles CA 90025. (310)820-1500. Fax: (310)826-5008. E-mail: editor@pcphotomag.com. Website: www.pcphotomag.com. **60% freelance written**. Bimonthly magazine covering digital photography. Our magazine is designed to help photographers better use digital technologies to improve their photography. Estab. 1997. Circ. 175,000. Byline given. Pays on publication. No kill fee. Publishes ms an average of 4 months after acceptance. Buys one-time rights. Editorial lead time 6 months. Submit seasonal material 6 months in advance. Accepts queries by mail. Responds in 1 month to queries. Sample copy for #10 SASE or online. Guidelines available online.
Nonfiction Needs how-to, personal experience, photo feature. **Buys 30 mss/year.** Query. 1,200 words **Pays $500 for assigned articles. Pays approximately $400 for unsolicited articles.**
Photos Do not send original transparencies or negatives. Send photos. Offers $100-200/photo Buys one time rights.
Tips Since *PCPHOTO* is a photography magazine, we must see photos before any decision can be made on an article, so phone queries are not appropriate. Ultimately, whether we can use a particular piece or not will depend greatly on the photographs and how they fit in with material already in our files. We take a fresh look at the modern photographic world by encouraging photography and the use of new technologies. Editorial is intended to demystify the use of modern equipment by emphasizing practical use of the camera and the computer, highlighting the technique rather than the technical.

$$ PHOTO TECHNIQUES

Preston Publications, Inc., 6600 W. Touhy Ave., Niles IL 60714. (847)647-2900. Fax: (847)647-1155. E-mail: slewis@prestonpub.com. Website: www.phototechmag.com. **50% freelance written. Prefers to work with experienced photographer-writers; happy to work with excellent photographers whose writing skills are lacking.** Bimonthly publication covering photochemistry, lighting, optics, processing, and printing, Zone System, digital imaging/scanning/printing, special effects, sensitometry, etc. Aimed at serious amateurs. Article conclusions should be able to be duplicated by readers. Estab. 1979. Circ. 20,000. Byline given. Pays within 3 weeks of publication. No kill fee. Publishes ms an average of 6 months after acceptance. Buys one-time rights. Sample copy for $6. Guidelines by e-mail.
Nonfiction Needs how-to, photo feature, technical, product review, special interest articles within the above listed topics. Query or send complete ms Open, but most features run approximately 2,500 words or 3-4 magazine pages **Pays $100-450 for well-researched technical articles.**
Photos Photographers have a much better chance of having their photos published if the photos accompany a written article. Prefers JPEGs scanned at 300 dpi and sent via e-mail or CD-ROM, or prints, slides, and transparencies. Captions, True required. Ms payment includes payment for photos. Buys one time rights.
Tips Study the magazine! Virtually all writers we publish are readers of the magazine. We are now more receptive than ever to articles about photographers, history, aesthetics, and informative backgrounders about specific areas of the photo industry or specific techniques. Successful writers for our magazine are doing what they write about.

$ PICTURE MAGAZINE

319 Lafayette St., No. 135, New York NY 10012. (212)352-2700. Fax: (212)352-2155. E-mail: editorial@picturemagazine.com. Website: www.picturemagazine.com. **100% freelance written**. Bimonthly magazine covering professional photography topics. Estab. 1995. Circ. 16,000. Byline given. Pays on publication. No kill fee. Publishes ms an average of 2 months after acceptance. Buys one-time rights. Editorial lead time 3 months. Submit seasonal material 3 months in advance. Accepts queries by e-mail. Accepts previously published material. Accepts simultaneous submissions. Sample copy free. Guidelines free.

Nonfiction Needs general interest, how-to, interview, new product, photo feature, technical. **Buys 5 mss/year.** Send complete ms. Length: 1,500-2,500 words. **Pays $150.**

Photos State availability. Captions required. Offers no additional payment for photos accepted with ms. Buys one time rights.

$ $ VIDEOMAKER

Videomaker, Inc., P.O. Box 4591, Chico CA 95927-4591. (530)891-8410. Fax: (530)891-8443. E-mail: editor@videomaker.com. Website: www.videomaker.com. Monthly magazine covering audio and video production, camcorders, editing, computer video, DVDs. Estab. 1985. Circ. 57,814. Byline given. Pays on publication. No kill fee. Publishes ms an average of 4 months after acceptance. Buys electronic rights, buys all rights. Editorial lead time 5 months. Submit seasonal material 5 months in advance. Accepts queries by mail, e-mail. Responds in 3 weeks to queries. Sample copy and writer's guidelines online.

- The magazine's voice is friendly, encouraging; never condescending to the audience.

Nonfiction Needs how-to, technical. Annual Buyer's Guide in October (13th issue of the year) **Buys 34 mss/year.** Query. Length: 800-1,500 words. **Pays $100-300.** Limit agreed upon in advance

Photos Contact: Melissa Hageman, art director. Model releases required. Negotiates payment individually

Fiction Buys 3 mss/year. Query. Length: 400-600 words. **Pays $150-200.**

Politics & World Affairs

THE AMERICAN SPECTATOR

1611 N. Kent St., Suite 901, Arlington VA 22209. (703)807-2011. Fax: (703)807-2013. E-mail: editor@spectator.org. Website: www.spectator.org. Monthly magazine. "For many years, one ideological viewpoint dominated American print and broadcast journalism. Today, that viewpoint still controls the entertainment and news divisions of the television networks, the mass-circulation news magazines, and the daily newspapers. *American Spectator* has attempted to balance the Left's domination of the media by debunking its perceived wisdom and advancing alternative ideas through spirited writing, insightful essays, humor and, most recently, through well-researched investigative articles that have themselves become news." Estab. 1967. Circ. 50,000. Pays on other. No kill fee. Accepts queries by mail. Responds only if interested in 3-4 weeks.

Nonfiction "Topics include politics, the press, foreign relations, the economy, culture. Stories most suited for publication are timely articles on previously unreported topics with national appeal. Articles should be thoroughly researched with a heavy emphasis on interviewing and reporting, and the facts of the article should be verifiable. We prefer articles in which the facts speak for themselves and shy away from editorial and first person commentary." No unsolicited poetry, fiction, satire, or crossword puzzles. Query with résumé, clips and SASE.

Columns/Departments The Continuing Crisis and Current Wisdom (humor); On the Prowl (Washington insider news). Query with résumé, clips and SASE.

⊘ 🌐 ARENA MAGAZINE

P.O. Box 18, North Carlton VIC 3054 Australia. (61)(3) 9416 0232. E-mail: magazine@arena.org.au. Website: www.arena.org.au. Bimonthly magazine. "Australia's leading magazine of left political, social and cultural commentary."

- Query before submitting.

Nonfiction Needs essays, letters, political commentary.

$ $ CHURCH & STATE

Americans United for Separation of Church and State, 518 C St. NE, Washington DC 20002. (202)466-3234. Fax: (202)466-2587. E-mail: americansunited@au.org. Website: www.au.org. **10% freelance written**. Monthly magazine emphasizing religious liberty and church/state relations matters. "Strongly advocates separation of church and state. Readership is well-educated." Estab. 1947. Circ. 40,000. Pays on acceptance. No kill fee. Publishes ms an average of 2 months after acceptance. Buys all rights. Accepts queries by mail. Accepts simultaneous submissions. Responds in 2 months to queries. Sample copy and writer's guidelines for 9 × 12 SAE with 3 first-class stamps

Nonfiction Needs expose, general interest, historical, interview. **Buys 11 mss/year.** Query. Length: 800-1,600 words. **Pays $150-300.**

Reprints Send tearsheet, photocopy or typed ms with rights for sale noted and information about when and where the material previously appeared.

Photos Send photos. Captions required. Pays negotiable fee for b&w prints Buys one time rights.

Tips "We're looking for feature articles on underreported local church-state controversies. We also consider 'viewpoint' essays that offer a unique or personal take on church-state issues. We are not a religious magazine. You need to see our magazine before you try to write for it."

$ COMMONWEAL

A Review of Public Affairs, Religion, Literature and the Arts, Commonweal Foundation, 475 Riverside Dr., Room 405, New York NY 10115. (212)662-4200. Fax: (212)662-4183. E-mail: editors@commonwealmagazine.org. Website: www.commonwealmagazine.org. Biweekly journal of opinion edited by Catholic lay people, dealing with topical issues of the day on public affairs, religion, literature, and the arts. Estab. 1924. Circ. 20,000. Byline given. Pays on publication. No kill fee. Buys all rights. Submit seasonal material 2 months in advance. Responds in 2 months to queries. Sample copy free. Guidelines available online.

Nonfiction Needs essays, general interest, interview, personal experience, religious. **Buys 30 mss/year.** Query with published clips. Length: 2,000-2,500 words. **Pays $200-300 for longer manuscripts; $100-200 for shorter pieces.**

Columns/Departments Upfronts (brief, newsy reportorials, giving facts, information and some interpretation behind the headlines of the day), 750-1,000 words; Last Word (usually of a personal nature, on some aspect of the human condition: spiritual, individual, political, or social), 800 words.

Poetry Contact: Rosemary Deen, editor. Needs free verse, traditional. Buys 20 poems/year. **Pays 75¢/line.**

Tips "Articles should be written for a general but well-educated audience. While religious articles are always topical, we are less interested in devotional and churchy pieces than in articles which examine the links between `worldly' concerns and religious beliefs."

$$ THE FREEMAN: IDEAS ON LIBERTY

30 S. Broadway, Irvington-on-Hudson NY 10533. (914)591-7230. Fax: (914)591-8910. E-mail: freeman@fee.org. Website: www.fee.org. **85% freelance written**. Monthly publication for the layman and fairly advanced students of liberty. Estab. 1946. Byline given. Pays on publication. No kill fee. Publishes ms an average of 5 months after acceptance. all rights, including reprint rights. Sample copy for 7½ × 10½ SASE with 4 first-class stamps.

- Eager to work with new/unpublished writers.

Nonfiction "We want nonfiction clearly analyzing and explaining various aspects of the free market, private property, limited-government philosophy. Though a necessary part of the literature of freedom is the exposure of collectivistic cliches and fallacies, our aim is to emphasize and explain the positive case for individual responsibility and choice in a free-market economy. We avoid name-calling and personality clashes. Ours is an intelligent analysis of the principles underlying a free-market economy. No political strategies or tactics." **Buys 100 mss/year.** Query with SASE. Length: 3,500 words. **Pays 10¢/word.**

Tips "It's most rewarding to find freelancers with new insights, fresh points of view. Facts, figures and quotations cited should be fully documented, to their original source, if possible."

$$ THE NATION

33 Irving Place, New York NY 10003. (212)209-5400. Fax: (212)982-9000. Website: www.thenation.com. **75% freelance written. Works with a small number of new/unpublished writers each year.** "Weekly magazine firmly committed to reporting on the issues of labor, national politics, business, consumer affairs, environmental politics, civil liberties, foreign affairs and the role and future of the Democratic Party." Estab. 1865. Pays on other. No kill fee. Buys first rights. Accepts queries by mail, e-mail, fax. Sample copy free. Guidelines available online.

Nonfiction "We welcome all articles dealing with the social scene, from an independent perspective. Queries encouraged." **Buys 100 mss/year. Pays $350-500.**

Columns/Departments Editorial, 500-700 words. **Pays $-150.**

Poetry "*The Nation* publishes poetry of outstanding aesthetic quality. Send poems with SASE. See the Contests & Awards section for the Discovery—*The Nation* poetry contest." **Payment negotiable.**

Tips "We are a journal of left/liberal political opinion covering national and international affairs. We are looking both for reporting and for fresh analysis. On the domestic front, we are particularly interested in civil liberties; civil rights; labor, economics, environmental and feminist issues and the role and future of the Democratic Party. Because we have readers all over the country, it's important that stories with a local focus have real national significance. In our foreign affairs coverage we prefer pieces on international political, economic and social developments. As the magazine which published Ralph Nader's first piece (and there is a long list of *Nation* firsts), we are seeking new writers."

⊘ THE NATIONAL VOTER

League of Women Voters, 1730 M St. NW, Suite 1000, Washington DC 20036. (202)429-1965. Fax: (202)429-0854. E-mail: nationalvoter@lwv.org. Website: www.lwv.org. Magazine published 3 times/year. *The National Voter* provides background, perspective and commentary on public policy issues confronting citizens and their leaders at all levels of government. And it empowers people to make a difference in their communities by offering guidance, maturation and models for action. Estab. 1951. Circ. 90,000. Byline given. Pays on publication. No kill fee. Makes work-for-hire assignments. Editorial lead time 2 months. Accepts queries by mail, e-mail. Sample copy free.

- No unsolicited mss.

Photos State availability. Captions, identification of subjects required. Offers no additional payment for photos accepted with ms.

$ $ THE PROGRESSIVE

409 E. Main St., Madison WI 53703. (608)257-4626. Fax: (608)257-3373. E-mail: editorial@progressive.org. Website: www.progressive.org. **75% freelance written**. Monthly. Estab. 1909. Byline given. Pays on publication. No kill fee. Publishes ms an average of 6 weeks after acceptance. Accepts queries by mail. Responds in 1 month to queries. Sample copy for 9 × 12 SAE with 4 first-class stamps or sample articles online. Guidelines available online.

Nonfiction Investigative reporting (exposé of corporate malfeasance and governmental wrongdoing); electoral coverage (a current electoral development that has national implications); social movement pieces (important or interesting event or trend in the labor movement, or the GLBT movement, or in the area of racial justice, disability rights, the environment, women's liberation); foreign policy pieces (a development of huge moral importance where the US role may not be paramount); interviews (a long Q&A with a writer, activist, political figure, or musician who is widely known or doing especially worthwhile work); activism (highlights the work of activists and activist groups; increasingly, we are looking for good photographs of a dynamic or creative action, and we accompany the photos with a caption); book reviews (cover two or three current titles on a major issue of concern). Primarily interested in articles that interpret, from a progressive point of view, domestic and world affairs. Occasional lighter features. *The Progressive* is a *political* publication. General interest is inappropriate. We do not want editorials, satire, historical pieces, philosophical peices or columns. Query. Length: 500-4,000 words. **Pays $500-1,300.**

Poetry Publishes 1 original poem a month. We prefer poems that connect up—in one fashion or another, however obliquely—with political concerns. **Pays $150.**

Tips Sought-after topics include electoral coverage, social movement, foreign policy, activism and book reviews.

$ PROGRESSIVE POPULIST

Journal from America's Heartland, P.O. Box 819, Manchaca TX 78652. (512)828-7245. E-mail: populist@usa.net. Website: www.populist.com. **90% freelance written**. Biweekly tabloid covering politics and economics. "We cover issues of interest to workers, small businesses, and family farmers and ranchers." Estab. 1995. Circ. 15,000. Byline given. Pays quarterly. No kill fee. Publishes ms an average of 1 month after acceptance. Buys first North American serial rights, buys second serial (reprint) rights. Editorial lead time 3 weeks. Submit seasonal material 1 month in advance. Accepts queries by mail, e-mail, fax, phone. Accepts previously published material. Accepts simultaneous submissions. Sample copy and writer's guidelines free

Nonfiction "We cover politics and economics. We are interested not so much in the dry reporting of campaigns and elections, or the stock markets and GNP, but in how big business is exerting more control over both the government and ordinary people's lives, and what people can do about it." Needs essays, expose, general interest, historical, humor, interview, opinion. "We are not much interested in `sound-off' articles about state or national politics, although we accept letters to the editor. We prefer to see more `journalistic' pieces, in which the writer does enough footwork to advance a story beyond the easy realm of opinion." **Buys 400 mss/year.** Query. Length: 600-1,000 words. **Pays $15-50.** Pays writers with contributor copies or other premiums if preferred by writer

Reprints Send photocopy with rights for sale noted and information about when and where the material previously appeared.

Photos State availability. Identification of subjects required. Negotiates payment individually. Buys one-time rights.

Tips "We do prefer submissions by e-mail. I find it's easier to work with e-mail and for the writer it probably increases the chances of getting a response."

$$$$ REASON

Free Minds and Free Markets, Reason Foundation, 3415 S. Sepulveda Blvd., Suite 400, Los Angeles CA 90034. (310)391-2245. Fax: (310)390-8986. E-mail: gillespie@reason.com. Website: www.reason.com. **30% freelance written**. Monthly magazine covering politics, current events, culture, ideas. *Reason* covers politics, culture and ideas from a dynamic libertarian perspective. It features reported works, opinion pieces, and book reviews. Estab. 1968. Circ. 55,000. Byline given. Pays on acceptance. Offers kill fee. Buys first North American serial rights, buys first rights, buys all rights. Editorial lead time 2 months. Submit seasonal material 3 months in advance. Accepts queries by mail, e-mail. Responds in 6 weeks to queries. Responds in 2 months to mss. Sample copy for $4. Guidelines available online.

Nonfiction Needs book excerpts, essays, expose, general interest, humor, interview, opinion. No products, personal experience, how-to, travel. **Buys 50-60 mss/year.** Query with published clips. Length: 850-5,000 words. **Pays $300-2,000.**

Tips We prefer queries of no more than one or two pages with specifically developed ideas about a given topic rather than more general areas of interest. Enclosing a few published clips also helps.

THEORIA

A Journal of Social and Political Theory, Berghahn Books, University of KwaZulu-Natal, Private Bag X17, Belville Western Cape 7535 South Africa. (27)(21)959-2404. E-mail: sherranclarence@gmail.com. Website: www.theoria.ukzn.ac.za. **Contact:** Ms. Sherran Clarence, managing editor. **100% freelance written**. "Academic journal published 4 times/year. *Theoria* is an engaged, multidisciplinary peer-reviewed journal of social and political theory. Its purpose is to address—through scholarly debate—the many challenges posed to intellectual life by the major social, political, and economic forces that shape the contemporary world. Thus, it is principally concerned with questions such as how modern systems of power, processes of globalization, and capitalist economic organization bear on matters such as justice, democracy, and truth." Estab. 1947. Circ. 300. Byline sometimes given. No kill fee. Publishes ms an average of 6 months after acceptance. Buys first rights, buys electronic rights. Editorial lead time 3 months. Submit seasonal material 3 months in advance. Accepts queries by mail, e-mail, fax, phone. Responds in 1 week to queries. Responds in 4-5 months to mss. Sample copy for $18. Writer's guidelines online or via e-mail.

Nonfiction Needs book excerpts, essays, expose, general interest, historical, interview, review articles, book reviews, theoretical, philosophical, political, articles. **Buys 1 ms/year.** Send complete ms. Length: 4,000-8,000 words. **No pay.**

Photos State availability. Identification of subjects required. Reviews GIF/JPEG files. Negotiates payment individually. Buys one-time rights.

Columns/Departments Book Reviews, 1,000 words; Review Articles, 5,000 words. 1 column. Send complete ms.

TRANSFORMATION

Critical Perspectives on Southern Africa, Programme of Economic History, University of KwaZulu-Natal, Durban 4041 South Africa. E-mail: transform@ukzn.ac.za. Website: www.transformation.und.ac.za. "Journal published 3 times/year that draws in academic contributors from South African and international universities. *Transformation* focuses on contemporary society and serves as a forum for analysis and debate about South African society in transition, and the global context that affects southern African developments." Estab. 1987. No kill fee. Accepts queries by mail. Guidelines available online.

Nonfiction "*Transformation* wish contributors to submit copies of their paper, with author details removed. Author details should be supplied on a separate page (with postal, e-mail addresses and telephone numbers). Please include additional information such position, department/programme, university/institution information on this separate sheet. In general follow the style format in the most recent issue of the journal, especially for references." Length: 3,000-8,000 words.

☒ U.S. NEWS & WORLD REPORT

U.S. News & World Report, Inc., 1050 Thomas Jefferson St. NW, Washington DC 20007. (202)955-2000. Website: www.usnews.com. "Weekly magazine devoted largely to reporting and analyzing national and international affairs, politics, business, health, science, technology and social trends." Circ. 2,018,621. No kill fee. Editorial lead time 10 days.

- Query before submitting.

$ $ WASHINGTON MONTHLY

The Washington Monthly Co., 1319 F St. NW, Suite 810, Washington DC 20004. (202)393-5155. Fax: (202)393-2444. E-mail: editors@washingtonmonthly.com. Website: www.washingtonmonthly.com. **50% freelance written**. Monthly magazine covering politics, policy, media. We are a neo-liberal publication with a long history and specific views—please read our magazine before submitting. Estab. 1969. Circ. 28,000. Byline given. Pays on publication. No kill fee. Publishes ms an average of 2 months after acceptance. Buys all rights. Editorial lead time 2 months. Submit seasonal material 4 months in advance. Accepts queries by mail, e-mail, fax, phone. Responds in 3 weeks to queries. Responds in 2 months to mss. Sample copy for 11 × 17 SAE with 5 first-class stamps or by e-mail. Guidelines available online.

Nonfiction Needs book excerpts, essays, expose, general interest, historical, interview, opinion, personal experience, technical, first-person political. No humor, how-to, or generalized articles. **Buys 20 mss/year.** Send complete ms. Length: 1,500-5,000 words. **Pays 10¢/word.**

Photos State availability. Reviews contact sheets, prints. Negotiates payment individually Buys one time rights.

Columns/Departments 10 Miles Square (about DC); On Political Books, Booknotes (both reviews of current political books), 1,500-3,000 words. 10 Query with published clips or send complete ms. **Pays 10¢/word**

Tips Call our editors to talk about ideas. Always pitch articles showing background research. We're particularly looking for first-hand accounts of working in government. We also like original work showing that the government is or is not doing something important. We have writer's guidelines, but do your research first.

$ $ $ YES! MAGAZINE

Positive Futures Network, P.O. Box 10818, Bainbridge Island WA 98110. E-mail: submissions@yesmagazine.org. Website: www.yesmagazine.org. **70% freelance written**. Quarterly magazine covering politics & world affairs; contemporary culture; nature, conservation, & ecology. "*YES! Magazine* documents how people are creating a more just, sustainable, and compassionate world. Each issue of *YES!* includes a series of articles focused on a theme—about solutions to a significant challenge facing our world—and a number of timely, non-theme articles. Our non-theme section provides ongoing coverage of issues like health, climate change, globalization, media reform, faith, democracy, economy and labor, social and racial justice, and peace building. To inquire about upcoming themes, send an e-mail to submissions@yesmagazine.org; please be sure to type 'themes' as the subject line." Estab. 1997. Circ. 55,000. Byline given. Pays on publication. Offers kill fee. varies Publishes ms an average of 1-6 months after acceptance. Buys Creative Commons License, see http://www.yesmagazine.org/default.asp?ID = 14 rights. Editorial lead time 3-6 months. Submit seasonal material 2-6 months in advance. Accepts queries by mail, e-mail. www.yesmagazine.org/default.asp?ID = 15

Nonfiction Needs book excerpts, essays, general interest, how-to, interview, opinion, (does not mean letters to the editor), photo feature. "No stories that are negative or too politically partisan stories." **Buys 60 mss/yr. mss/year.** Query with published clips. Length: 100-2,500 words. **Pays $50-1,250 for assigned articles. Pays $50-600 for unsolicited articles.**

Columns/Departments Signs of Life, positive news briefs, 100-250 words; Commentary, opinion from thinkers and experts, 500 words; Book and film reviews, 500-800 words. **Pays $20-$300.**

Tips "We're interested in articles that: 'Change the story' about what is possible; tell specific success stories of individuals, communities, movements, nations, or regions that are addressing society's challenges and problems; offer visions of a better world.We're less interested in articles that:Only describe or update a problem (unless there are dramatically new developments, reframings, or insights); primarily reinforce a sense of being a victim (and therefore powerless); are written in styles or about topics relevant or accessible only to narrow groups; lack grounding in research or reporting (except for occasional essays)."

Psychology & Self-Improvement

$ $ $ $ PSYCHOLOGY TODAY

Sussex Publishers, Inc., 115 E. 23rd St., 9th Floor, New York NY 10010. (212)260-7210. Fax: (212)260-7445. E-mail: jay@psychologytoday.com. Website: www.psychologytoday.com. Bimonthly magazine. *Psychology Today* explores every aspect of human behavior, from the cultural trends that shape the way we think and feel to the intricacies of modern neuroscience. We're sort of a hybrid of a science magazine, a health magazine and a self-help magazine. While we're read by many psychologists, therapists and social workers, most of our readers are simply intelligent and curious people interested in the psyche and the self. Estab. 1967. Circ. 331,400. Byline given. 30 days after publication. No kill fee. Publishes ms an average of 3 months after acceptance. Buys first North American serial rights. Editorial lead time 5 months. Accepts queries by mail, e-mail. Responds in 1 month to queries. Sample copy for $3.50. Guidelines available online.

Nonfiction Nearly any subject related to psychology is fair game. We value originality, insight and good reporting; we're not interested in stories or topics that have already been covered *ad nauseum* by other magazines unless you can provide a fresh new twist and much more depth. We're not interested in simple-minded `pop psychology.' No fiction, poetry or first-person essays on How I Conquered Mental Disorder X. **Buys 20-25 mss/year.** Query with published clips. Length: 1,500-4,000 words. **Pays $1,000-2,500.**

Columns/Departments Contact: News Editor. News & Trends, 150-300 words. Query with published clips. **Pays $150-300.**

$ ROSICRUCIAN DIGEST

Rosicrucian Order, AMORC, 1342 Naglee Ave., San Jose CA 95191-0001. (408)947-3600. Website: www.rosicrucian.org. "Quarterly magazine (international) emphasizing mysticism, science, philosophy, and the arts for educated men and women of all ages seeking alternative answers to life's questions." Byline given. Pays on acceptance. No kill fee. Publishes ms an average of 6 months after acceptance. Buys first rights, buys second serial (reprint) rights. Accepts queries by mail, phone. Responds in 3 months to queries. Guidelines for #10 SASE.

Nonfiction "How to deal with life—and all it brings us—in a positive and constructive way. Informational articles—new ideas and developments in science, the arts, philosophy, and thought. Historical sketches, biographies, human interest, psychology, philosophical, and inspirational articles. We are always looking for good articles on the contributions of ancient civilizations to today's civilizations, the environment, ecology, inspirational (nonreligious) subjects. Know your subject well and be able to capture the reader's interest in the first paragraph. Be willing to work with the editor to make changes in the manuscript. No religious, astrological, or political material, or articles promoting a particular group or system of thought. Most articles are written by members or donated, but we're always open to freelance submissions. No book-length mss." Query. Length: 1,500-2,000 words. **Pays 6¢/word.**

Reprints Prefers typed ms with rights for sale noted and information about when and where the article previously appeared, but tearsheet or photcopy acceptable. Pays 50% of amount paid for an original article.

Tips "We're looking for more pieces on these subjects: our connection with the past—the important contributions of ancient civilizations to today's world and culture and the relevance of this wisdom to now; how to channel teenage energy/angst into positive, creative, constructive results (preferably written by teachers or others who work with young people—written for frustrated parents); and the vital necessity of raising our environmental consciousness if we are going to survive as a species on this planet."

SCIENCE OF MIND MAGAZINE

2600 W. Magnolia Blvd., Burbank CA 91505. (818)526-7757. E-mail: edit@scienceofmind.com. Website: www.scienceofmind.com. **30% freelance written**. Monthly magazine featuring articles on spirituality, self-help, and inspiration. Our publication centers on oneness of all life and spiritual empowerment through the application of *Science of Mind* principles. Byline given. Pays on acceptance. No kill fee. Publishes ms an average of 5 months after acceptance. Buys first North American serial rights. Submit seasonal material 6 months in advance. Guidelines available online.

Nonfiction Needs book excerpts, essays, inspirational, interview, personal experience, of Science of Mind, spiritual. **Buys 35-45 mss/year.** Length: 750-2,000 words. **Payment varies. Pays in copies for some features written by readers.**

Tips We are interested in how to use spiritual principles in worldly situations or other experiences of a spiritual nature having to do with *Science of Mind* principles.

SHARED VISION

Raven Eagle Partners Co., 873 Beatty St., Suite 301, Vancouver BC V6B 2H6 Canada. (604)733-5062. Fax: (604)731-1050. E-mail: editor@shared-vision.com. Website: www.shared-vision.com. **75% freelance written**. Monthly magazine covering health and wellness, environment, and personal growth. Estab. 1988. Circ. 42,000. Byline given. No kill fee. Editorial lead time 3 months. Submit seasonal material 3 months in advance. Accepts queries by mail, e-mail, fax. Accepts previously published material. Sample copy for $3 Canadian, postage paid. Guidelines available online.
Nonfiction Needs book excerpts, general interest, inspirational, personal experience, travel, health, environment. Query with published clips.
Columns/Departments Footnotes (first-person inspirational). Query with published clips.
Tips Reading the magazine is the optimum method. See website for writer's guidelines.

$ SPOTLIGHT ON RECOVERY MAGAZINE

R. Graham Publishing Company, 9602 Glenwood Rd., #140, Brooklyn NY 11236. (347)831-9373. E-mail: rgraham_100@msn.com. Website: www.spotlightonrecovery.com. **85% freelance written**. Quarterly magazine covering self-help, recovery, and empowerment. "This is the premiere outreach and resource magazine in New York. Its goal is to be the catalyst for which the human spirit could heal. Everybody knows somebody who has mental illness, substance abuse issues, parenting problems, educational issues, or someone who is homeless, unemployed, physically ill, or the victim of a crime. Many people suffer in silence. *Spotlight on Recovery* will provide a voice to those who suffer in silence and begin the dialogue of recovery." Estab. 2001. Circ. 1,500-2,500. Byline sometimes given. Pays on publication. No kill fee. Publishes ms an average of 2 months after acceptance. Buys second serial (reprint) rights, buys electronic rights. Editorial lead time 1 month. Submit seasonal material 1 month in advance. Accepts queries by mail, e-mail. Accepts simultaneous submissions. Responds in 2 weeks to queries. Responds in 1 month to mss. Sample copy and writer's guidelines free.
Nonfiction Needs book excerpts, interview, opinion, personal experience. **Buys 30-50 mss/year.** Query with published clips. Length: 150-1,500 words. **Pays 5¢/word or $75-80/article.**
Photos State availability. Identification of subjects required. Reviews GIF/JPEG files. Pays $5-10/photo. Buys one-time rights.
Columns/Departments 4 mss/year. Query with published clips. **Pays 5¢/word or $75-80/column.**
Fiction Needs ethnic, mainstream, slice-of-life vignettes.
Tips "Send a query and give a reason why you would choose the subject posted to write about."

Regional

General Regional

$ $ BLUE RIDGE COUNTRY

Leisure Publishing, 3424 Brambleton Ave., Roanoke VA 24018. (540)989-6138. Fax: (540)989-7603. E-mail: cmodisett@leisurepublishing.com. Website: www.leisurepublishing.com. **90% freelance written**. Bimonthly magazine. "The magazine is designed to celebrate the history, heritage and beauty of the Blue Ridge region. It is aimed at adult, upscale readers who enjoy living or traveling in the mountain regions of Virginia, North Carolina, West Virginia, Maryland, Kentucky, Tennessee, South Carolina, Alabama, and Georgia." Estab. 1988. Circ. 425,000. Byline given. Pays on publication. Offers kill fee. Offers $50 kill fee for commissioned pieces only. Publishes ms an average of 8 months after acceptance. Buys first North American serial rights. Submit seasonal material 6 months in advance. Accepts queries by mail, e-mail, fax; prefer e-mail. Responds in 3-4 months to queries. Responds in 2 months to mss. Sample copy for 9 × 12 SAE with 6 first-class stamps. Guidelines available online.
Nonfiction Looking for more backroads travel, first person outdoor recreation pieces, environmental news, baby boomer era stories, regional history and well-researched regional legend/lore pieces. Needs general interest, historical, personal experience, photo feature, travel. **Buys 25-30 mss/year.** Send complete ms. Length: 200-1,500 words. **Pays $150-250.**
Photos Photos must be shot in region. Outline of region can be found online. Send photos. Identification of subjects required. Reviews transparencies. Pays $40-150/photo. Buys one-time rights.
Columns/Departments Inns and Getaways (reviews of inns); Mountain Delicacies (cookbooks and recipes); Country Roads (shorts on regional news, people, destinations, events, history, antiques, books);

Inns and Getaways (reviews of inns); On the Mountainside (first-person outdoor recreation pieces excluding hikes). 30-42 Query. **Pays $25-125.**
Fiction Publishes occasional previews and book excerpts of regional relevance.
Poetry Publishes occasional poetry by regional writers and/or on regional topics in conjunction with photo essays.
Tips "Would like to see more pieces dealing with contemporary history (1940s-70s). Freelancers needed for regional departmental shorts and `macro' issues affecting whole region. Need field reporters from all areas of Blue Ridge region, especially more from Kentucky, Maryland, South Carolina and Alabama. We are also looking for updates on the Blue Ridge Parkway, Appalachian Trail, national forests, ecological issues, preservation movements, affordable travel, and interesting short profiles of regional people."

$$$$ COWBOYS & INDIANS MAGAZINE

The Premier Magazine of the West, USFR Media Group, 6688 N. Central Expressway, Suite 650, Dallas TX 75206. E-mail: queries@cowboysindians.com. Website: www.cowboysindians.com. **60% freelance written**. Magazine published 8 times/year covering people and places of the American West. The Premier Magazine of the West, *Cowboys & Indians* captures the romance, drama, and grandeur of the American frontier—both past and present—like no other publication. Undeniably exclusive, the magazine covers a broad range of lifestyle topics: art, home interiors, travel, fashion, Western film, and Southwestern cuisine. Estab. 1993. Circ. 101,000. Byline given. Pays on publication. Offers 20% kill fee. Publishes ms an average of 2 months after acceptance. Buys first North American serial rights, buys electronic rights. Editorial lead time 4 months. Submit seasonal material 6 months in advance. Accepts queries by mail, e-mail, fax. Sample copy for $5. Guidelines by e-mail.
Nonfiction Needs book excerpts, expose, general interest, historical, interview, photo feature, travel, art. No essays, humor, poetry, or opinion. **Buys 40-50 mss/year.** Query. Length: 500-3,000 words. **Pays $250-5,000 for assigned articles. Pays $250-1,000 for unsolicited articles.**
Photos State availability. Captions, identification of subjects required. Reviews contact sheets, 21/4x21/4 transparencies. Negotiates payment individually Buys one time rights.
Columns/Departments Art; Travel; Music; Home Interiors; all 200-1,000 words. 50 Query. **Pays $200-1,500.**
Tips Our readers are educated, intelligent, and well-read Western enthusiasts, many of whom collect Western Americana, read other Western publications, attend shows and have discerning tastes. Therefore, articles should assume a certain level of prior knowledge of Western subjects on the part of the reader. Articles should be readable and interesting to the novice and general interest reader as well. Please keep your style lively, above all things, and fast-moving, with snappy beginnings and endings. Wit and humor are always welcome.

$$$ ESTATES WEST MAGAZINE

Media That Deelivers, Inc., 8132 N. 87th Place, Scottsdale AZ 85258. (480)460-5203. Fax: (480)443-1517. E-mail: editorial@estateswest.com; cringer@estateswest.com. Website: www.estateswest.com. **30% freelance written**. Bimonthly magazine affluent living, real estate, architecture, design, and travel throughout the West. Estab. 2000. Circ. 60,000. Byline given. Pays on publication. No kill fee. Publishes ms an average of 6 months after acceptance. Editorial lead time 3-4 months. Submit seasonal material 4 months in advance. Accepts queries by mail, e-mail. Responds in 1 month to queries. Sample copy and writer's guidelines for #10 SASE.
Nonfiction Needs interview, designers, builders, realtors, architects, new product, travel, decor, real estate. **Buys 10-15 mss/year.** Query with published clips. Length: 900-2,000 words. **Pays 50-60¢/word for assigned articles.**
Photos Send photos. with submission per discussion with editor. Photos must be high resolution. Negotiates payment individually. Buys one time rights.

$$ GUESTLIFE

Monterey Bay/New Mexico/El Paso/Houston/Vancouver, Desert Publications, Inc., 303 N. Indian Canyon Dr., Palm Springs CA 92262. (760)325-2333. Fax: (760)325-7008. Website: www.guestlife.com. **95% freelance written**. Annual prestige hotel room magazine covering history, highlights, and activities of the area named (i.e., *Monterey Bay GuestLife*). *GuestLife* focuses on its respective area and is placed in hotel rooms in that area for the affluent vacationer. Estab. 1979. Byline given. Pays on publication. Offers negotiable kill fee. Publishes ms an average of 9 months after acceptance. Buys electronic rights, buys all rights. Editorial lead time 6 months. Submit seasonal material 8 months in advance. Accepts queries by e-mail. Responds in 1 month to queries. Responds in 1 month to mss. Sample copy for $10.

Nonfiction Needs general interest, regional, historical, photo feature, travel. **Buys 3 mss/year.** Query with published clips. Length: 300-1,500 words. **Pays $100-500.**
Photos State availability. Identification of subjects required. Reviews contact sheets. Negotiates payment individually Buys all rights.

$$ LAKE

713 State St., La Porte IN 46350. E-mail: info@lakemagazine.com. Website: www.lakemagazine.com. **80% freelance written**. Magazine published 10 times/year covering Lake Michigan, in particular the resort communities of Southeast Michigan and Northwest Indiana. Estab. 2000. Circ. 35,000. Byline given. Pays on acceptance. Offers 15% kill fee. Publishes ms an average of 2 months after acceptance. Buys first North American serial rights. Editorial lead time 2 months. Submit seasonal material 4-5 months in advance. Accepts queries by e-mail. Accepts previously published material. Accepts simultaneous submissions. Sample copy available online.
Nonfiction Needs book excerpts, essays, general interest, historical, humor, interview, new product, personal experience, photo feature, travel. Travel (May and September issues); Kids (June issue). Does not want fiction, poetry. **Buys 100 mss/year.** Send complete ms. Length: 250-2,000 words. **Pays 30-50¢/word.**
Columns/Departments Lake's Grapes (wine), 550 words; Field to Table (regional food); My Lake (well-known Harbor Country residents), 1,000 words; Postcard (profile of Harbor County community), 1,000 words. 40-50 Query with published clips or send complete ms. **Pays 30-50¢/word.**
Tips Pitch shorter stories for our front-of-book section. Send well thought out, in-depth queries explaining what angle you'd use and why it's a good or important story for *Lake* to run.

$ MIDWEST LIVING

Meredith Corp., 1716 Locust St., Des Moines IA 50309-3038. (515)284-3000. Fax: (515)284-3836. E-mail: midwestliving@meredith.com. Website: www.midwestliving.com. Bimonthly magazine covering Midwestern families. Regional service magazine that celebrates the interest, values, and lifestyles of Midwestern families. Estab. 1987. Circ. 915,000. Pays on acceptance. No kill fee. Buys all rights. Editorial lead time 6 months. Accepts queries by mail, e-mail. Sample copy for $3.95. Guidelines by e-mail.
Nonfiction Needs general interest, good eating, festivals and fairs, historical, interesting slices of Midwestern history, customs, traditions and the people who preserve them, interview, towns, neighborhoods, families,people whose stories exemplify the Midwest spirit an values, travel, Midwestern destinations with emphasis on the fun and affordable. Query.
Photos State availability.
Tips "As general rule of thumb, we're looking for stories that are useful to the reader with information of ideas they can act on in their own lives. Most important, we want stories that have direct relevance to our Midwest audience."

$$ MOUNTAIN HOMES/SOUTHERN STYLE

P.O. Box 21535, Roanoke VA 24018. E-mail: mountainhomessouthernstyle.com. Bimonthly magazine celebrating the best of upscale living in the Southern mountains—the homes, the events, the art, the style, the food, and the cities and towns that people today are increasingly seeking out for retirement or as an escape from big city living. "Our territory extends from the Shenandoah Valley of Virginia down into northern Georgia and includes all territory in the mountain regions of Virginia, North Carolina, South Carolina, West Virginia, Tennessee, Maryland and Georgia." Pays on publication. Buys first North American serial rights. Accepts queries by mail. Sample copy for $3 and magazine-sized envelope.
Nonfiction Needs general interest, interview, travel. Query. **Pays $150-300.**
Photos We assign photography according to story needs. Buys one time rights with web and collateral reuse.
Columns/Departments "Destinations (everything there is to tell about a great Southern mountain town, city or locale); Food and Wine (covering Southern vinters, chefs and restaurants); Mountain Style (new trends and sources for unique products); Homes and Gardens (spotlight on homes and gardens—often of those who have chosen to relocate to the mountains), 750-2,000 words." Query. **Pays $100-250.**
Tips "Anything that is well-researched, well-written and tied to the Southern mountains, the second-home and retirement demographic trends, and the area's upscale lifestyle would get strong consideration."

THE OXFORD AMERICAN

201 Donaghey Ave., Main 107, Conway AR 72035. (501)450-5376. Fax: (501)450-3490. E-mail: editors@oxfordamerican.org. Website: www.oxfordamerican.org. **Contact:** Carol Ann Fitzgerald, man. editor. Quarterly literary magazine from the South with a national audience. Circ. 20,000. Pays on publication.

Accepts queries by mail. Responds in 2-3 months or sooner to mss. Guidelines available online at http://www.oxfordamerican.org/pages/submission-guidelines

- "*The Oxford American* will consider only unpublished mss that are from and/or about the South. Especially interested in nonfiction from diverse perspectives. Considers excerpts from forthcoming books."

Nonfiction Needs short and long essays (500 to 3,000 words), general interest, how-to, humor, personal experience, travel, reporting, business. Query with SASE or send complete ms.
Photos Uses photos for the cover and throughout issue. Also uses illustration, original art, and comics. Send photos. Reviews contact sheets, GIF/JPEG files, slides.
Columns/Departments Odes, Travel, Politics, Business, Writing on Writing, Southerner Abroad, Reports, Literature.
Fiction Stories should be from or about the South. Send complete ms.
Poetry Poems should be from or about the South. Submit maximum 3-5 poems.

⊘ SOUTHCOMM PUBLISHING COMPANY, INC.

310 Paper Trail Way, Suite 108, Canton GA 30115. (678)624-1075. Fax: (678)623-9979. E-mail: cwwalker@southcomm.com. Website: www.southcomm.com. "Our magazines primarily are used as marketing and economic development pieces, but they are also used as tourism guides and a source of information for newcomers. As such, our editorial supplies entertaining and informative reading for those visiting the communities for the first time, as well as those who have lived in the area for any period of time. We are looking for writers who are interested in writing dynamic copy about Georgia, Tennessee, South Carolina, North Carolina, Alabama, Virginia, Florida, Pennsylvania, Texas, and many other states." Estab. 1985. Byline given. Pays 30 days after acceptance. No kill fee. Publishes ms an average of 1-2 months after acceptance. Buys all rights. Accepts queries by mail, e-mail, fax. Sample copy and writer's guidelines free.
Nonfiction "Our articles are informative pieces about the communities we're covering. Our magazines provide snapshots of community life through articles with a lifestyle publication slant (require interviews and quotes). Departments include: Report Card (education stories); Vital Signs (movers an shakers in healthcare); Business Portfolio (what makes the economy work); Claim to Fame (who's who in the community). "We are not looking for article submissions. We will assign stories to writers in which we're interested. Queries should include samples of published works and biographical information." **Buys 50 + mss/year.** Quer or send complete ms. Length: 100-1,000 words. **Pays $25-200.**
Tips "It is not necessary for writers to live in the areas about which they are writing, but it does sometimes help to be familiar with them. We are not looking for writers to submit articles. We solely are interested in contacting writers for articles that we generate with our clients."

SOUTHERN LIVING

Southern Progress Corp., 2100 Lakeshore Dr., Birmingham AL 35209. (205)445-6000. Fax: (205)445-6700. E-mail: sara_askew_jones@timeinc.com. Website: www.southernliving.com. Monthly magazine covering the southern lifestyle. Publication addressing the tastes and interest of contemporary southerners. Estab. 1966. Circ. 2,526,799. No kill fee. Buys all rights. Editorial lead time 3 months. Accepts queries by mail. Sample copy for $4.99 at newsstands. Guidelines by e-mail.
Columns/Departments Southern Journal: Above all, it must be Southern. We need comments on life in this region—written from the standpoint of a person who is intimately familiar with this part of the world. It's personal, almost always involving something that happened to the writer or someone he or she knows very well. We take special note of stories that are contemporary in their point of view. Length: 500-600 words.

$$$$ SUNSET MAGAZINE

Sunset Publishing Corp., 80 Willow Rd., Menlo Park CA 94025-3691. (650)321-3600. Fax: (650)327-7537. Website: www.sunset.com. Monthly magazine covering the lifestyle of the Western states. *Sunset* is a Western lifestyle publication for educated, active consumers. Editorial provides localized information on gardening and travel, food and entertainment, home building and remodeling. Freelance articles should be timely and only about the 13 Western states. Garden section accepts queries by mail. Travel section prefers queries by e-mail. Byline given. Pays on acceptance. No kill fee. Guidelines available online.
Nonfiction Travel items account for the vast majority of *Sunset's* freelance assignments, although we also contract out some short garden items. However *Sunset* is largely staff-written. Needs travel, in the West. **Buys 50-75 mss/year.** Query. Length: 550-750 words. **Pays $1/word.**
Columns/Departments Building & Crafts, Food, Garden, Travel. Travel Guide length: 300-350 words. Direct queries to specific editorial department.

Tips Here are some subjects regularly treated in *Sunset*'s stories and Travel Guide items: Outdoor recreation (i.e., bike tours, bird-watching spots, walking or driving tours of historic districts); indoor adventures (i.e., new museums and displays, hands-on science programs at aquariums or planetariums, specialty shopping); special events (i.e., festivals that celebrate a region's unique social, cultural, or agricultural heritage). Also looking for great weekend getaways, backroad drives, urban adventures and culinary discoveries such as ethnic dining enclaves. Planning and assigning begins a year before publication date.

Alabama

$$ ALABAMA HERITAGE

University of Alabama, Box 870342, Tuscaloosa AL 35487-0342. (205)348-7467. Fax: (205)348-7473. Website: www.alabamaheritage.com. **90% freelance written**. *Alabama Heritage* is a nonprofit historical quarterly published by the University of Alabama and the Alabama Department of Archives and History for the intelligent lay reader. We are interested in lively, well-written, and thoroughly researched articles on Alabama/Southern history and culture. Readability and accuracy are essential. Estab. 1986. Byline given. Pays on publication. No kill fee. Buys all rights. Accepts queries by mail, e-mail. Sample copy for $6, plus $2.50 for shipping. Guidelines for #10 SASE or online.

Nonfiction Buys 12-16 feature mss/year and 10-14 short pieces. We do not publish fiction, poetry, articles on current events or living artists, and personal/family reminiscences. Query. Length: 750-4,000 words. **Pays $50-350.**

Photos Identification of subjects required. Reviews contact sheets. Buys one time rights.

Tips Authors need to remember that we regard history as a fascinating subject, not as a dry recounting of dates and facts. Articles that are lively and engaging, in addition to being well researched, will find interested readers among our editors. No term papers, please. All areas are open to freelance writers. Best approach is a written query.

$$ ALABAMA LIVING

Alabama Rural Electric Assn., P.O. Box 244014, Montgomery AL 36124. (334)215-2732. Fax: (334)215-2733. E-mail: dgates@areapower.com. Website: www.alabamaliving.com. **80% freelance written**. Monthly magazine covering topics of interest to rural and suburban Alabamians. "Our magazine is an editorially balanced, informational and educational service to members of rural electric cooperatives. Our mix regularly includes Alabama history, Alabama features, gardening, outdoor, and consumer pieces." Estab. 1948. Circ. 0,000. Byline given. Pays on acceptance. No kill fee. Editorial lead time 4 months. Submit seasonal material 4 months in advance. Accepts queries by mail, e-mail. Accepts simultaneous submissions. Responds in 1 month to queries. Sample copy free.

Nonfiction Needs historical, rural-oriented, Alabama slant, Alabama. Gardening (March); Travel (April); Home Improvement (May); Holiday Recipes (December). **Buys 20 mss/year.** Send complete ms. Length: 500-750 words. **Pays $250 minimum for assigned articles. Pays $150 minimum for unsolicited articles.**

Reprints Send typed manuscript with rights for sale noted. Pays $100.

Tips "Preference given to submissions with accompanying art."

Alaska

$$$ ALASKA

Exploring Life on the Last Frontier, 301 Arctic Slope Ave., Suite 300, Anchorage AK 99518. (907)272-6070. E-mail: tim.woody@alaskamagazine.com. Website: www.alaskamagazine.com. **70% freelance written. Eager to work with new/unpublished writers.** Magazine published 10 times/year covering topics uniquely Alaskan. Estab. 1935. Circ. 180,000. Byline given. Pays on publication. No kill fee. Publishes ms an average of 6 months after acceptance. Buys first rights, buys one-time rights. Submit seasonal material 1 year in advance. Accepts queries by mail. Responds in 2 months to queries. Responds in 2 months to mss. Sample copy for $3 and 9 × 12 SAE with 7 first-class stamps. Guidelines available online.

Nonfiction Needs historical, humor, interview, personal experience, photo feature, travel, adventure, outdoor recreation (including hunting, fishing), Alaska destination stories. No fiction or poetry. **Buys 40 mss/year.** Query. Length: 100-2,500 words. **Pays $100-1,250.**

Photos Send photos. Captions, identification of subjects required. Reviews 35mm or larger transparencies, slides labeled with your name.

Tips We're looking for top-notch writing—original, well researched, lively. Subjects must be distinctly Alaskan. A story on a mall in Alaska, for example, won't work for us; every state has malls. If you've got a story about a Juneau mall run by someone who is also a bush pilot and part-time trapper, maybe we'd be interested. The point is *Alaska* stories need to be vivid, focused and unique. Alaska is like nowhere else—we need our stories to be the same way.

Arizona

$$ ARIZONA FOOTHILLS MAGAZINE

Media That Deelivers, Inc., 8132 N. 87th Place, Scottsdale AZ 85258. (480)460-5203. Fax: (480)443-1517. E-mail: editorial@azfoothillsmag.com; editorial@mediathatdeelivers.com. Website: www.azfoothillsmag.com. **10% freelance written**. Monthly magazine covering Arizona lifesyle. Estab. 1996. Circ. 60,000. Byline given. Pays on publication. No kill fee. Publishes ms an average of 6 months after acceptance. Editorial lead time 6 months. Submit seasonal material at least 4 months in advance. Accepts queries by mail, e-mail. Responds in 1 month to queries. Sample copy for #10 SASE.

Nonfiction Needs general interest, photo feature, travel, fashion, decor, arts, interview. **Buys 10 mss/year.** Query with published clips. Length: 900-2,000 words. **Pays 35-40¢/word for assigned articles.**

Photos Photos may be requested. Captions, identification of subjects, model releases required. Reviews contact sheets, transparencies. Negotiates payment individually Occasionally buys one-time rights.

Columns/Departments Travel, dining, fashion, home decor, design, architecture, wine, shopping, golf, performance & visual arts.

Tips We prefer stories that appeal to our affluent audience written with an upbeat, contemporary approach and reader service in mind.

$$$$ ARIZONA HIGHWAYS

2039 W. Lewis Ave., Phoenix AZ 85009-9988. (602)712-2024. Fax: (602)254-4505. Website: www.arizonahighways.com. **100% freelance written**. Magazine that is state-owned, designed to help attract tourists into and through Arizona. Estab. 1925. Circ. 425,000. Pays on acceptance. No kill fee. Buys first North American serial rights. Accepts queries by mail, e-mail, fax. Responds in 1 month to queries. Responds in 1 month to mss. Guidelines available online.

Nonfiction Feature subjects include narratives and exposition dealing with history, anthropology, nature, wildlife, armchair travel, out of the way places, small towns, Old West history, Indian arts and crafts, travel, etc. Travel articles are experience-based. All must be oriented toward Arizona. We deal with professionals only, so include a list of current credits. **Buys 50 mss/year.** Query with a lead paragraph and brief outline of story Length: 600-1,800 words. **Pays up to $1/word.**

Photos Contact: Peter Ensenberger, director of photography. We use transparencies of medium format, 4 × 5, and 35mm when appropriate to the subject matter, or they display exceptional quality or content. If submitting 35mm, we prefer 100 ISO or slower. Each transparency must be accompanied by information attached to each photograph: where, when, what. No photography will be reviewed by the editors unless the photographer's name appears on each and every transparency. For digital requirements, contact the photography department. Pays $125-600 Buys one time rights.

Columns/Departments Focus on Nature (short feature in first or third person dealing with the unique aspects of a single species of wildlife), 800 words; Along the Way (short essay dealing with life in Arizona, or a personal experience keyed to Arizona), 750 words; Back Road Adventure (personal back-road trips, preferably off the beaten path and outside major metro areas), 1,000 words; Hike of the Month (personal experiences on trails anywhere in Arizona), 500 words. **Pays $50-1,000, depending on department**

Tips Writing must be of professional quality, warm, sincere, in-depth, well peopled, and accurate. Avoid themes that describe first trips to Arizona, the Grand Canyon, the desert, Colorado River running, etc. Emphasis is to be on Arizona adventure and romance as well as flora and fauna, when appropriate, and themes that can be photographed. Double check your manuscript for accuracy. Our typical reader is a 50-something person with the time, the inclination, and the means to travel.

$$ DESERT LIVING

2525 E. Camelback Rd., Suite 120, Phoenix AZ 85016. (602)667-9798. Fax: (602)508-9454. E-mail: david@desertlivingmag.com. Website: www.desertlivingmag.com. **75% freelance written**. Lifestyle and culture magazine published 8 times/year with an emphasis on modern design, culinary trends, cultural trends, fashion, great thinkers of our time and entertainment. Estab. 1997. Circ. 50,000. Byline given. Pays 1 month after publication. Offers 50% kill fee. Buys first rights, buys electronic rights. Editorial lead time 3

months. Submit seasonal material 3 months in advance. Accepts queries by mail, e-mail, fax. Responds in 3 weeks to queries. Responds in 2 months to mss. Sample copy for e-mail request Guidelines free.
Nonfiction Needs general interest, interview, new product, photo feature, travel, architecture. Query with published clips. Length: 300-1,500 words. **Pays $25-600.**
Photos State availability. Identification of subjects, model releases required. Reviews contact sheets, negatives, transparencies, prints. Negotiates payment individually Buys one-time or electronic rights
Columns/Departments See website.

$ PHOENIX MAGAZINE

Cities West Publishing, Inc., 15169 N. Scottsdale Road, Ste. C-310, Scottsdale AZ 85254. (866)481-6970. Fax: (602)604-0169. E-mail: aklawonn@citieswestpub.com. Website: www.phoenixmag.com. **Contact:** Adam Klawonn, managing editor. **70% freelance written**. Monthly magazine covering regional issues, personalities, events, neighborhoods, customs, and history of metro Phoenix. Estab. 1966. Circ. 60,000. Byline given. Pays on publication. No kill fee. Publishes ms an average of 3 months after acceptance. Buys first North American serial rights. Submit seasonal material 1 year in advance. Accepts queries by mail, e-mail. Responds in 2 months to queries. Responds in 2 months to mss. Sample copy for $3.95 and 9 × 12 SASE with 5 first-class stamps. Guidelines for #10 sase.
Nonfiction Needs general interest, interview, investigative, historical, service pieces (where to go and what to do around town). "We do not publish fiction, poetry, personal essays, book reviews, music reviews, or product reviews, and our travel stories are staff written. With the exception of our travel stories, all of the content in *Phoenix* magazine is geographically specific to the Phoenix-metro region. We do not publish any non-travel news or feature stories that are outside the Phoenix area, and we prefer that our freelancers are located in the Phoenix metro area." **Buys 50 mss/year.** Query with published clips via e-mail. "Include a short summary, a list of sources, and an explanation of why you think your idea is right for the magazine and why you're qualified to write it." Length: 150-2,000 words.
Tips "Stories must appeal to an educated Phoenix audience. We want solidly reported and diligently researched stories on key issues of public concern and the key players involved."

$$ TUCSON LIFESTYLE

Conley Publishing Group, Ltd., Suite 12, 7000 E. Tanque Verde Rd., Tucson AZ 85715-5318. (520)721-2929. Fax: (520)721-8665. E-mail: scott@tucsonlifestyle.com. **Contact:** Scott Barker, executive editor. **90% freelance written. Prefers to work with published/established writers.** Monthly magazine covering Southern Arizona-related events and topics. Estab. 1982. Circ. 32,000. Byline given. Pays on acceptance. No kill fee. Publishes ms an average of 6 months after acceptance. Buys one-time rights, buys second serial (reprint) rights, buys electronic rights. Submit seasonal material 1 year in advance. Accepts queries by mail, e-mail. Responds in 2 months to queries. Responds in 3 months to mss. Sample copy for $3.99, plus $3 postage. Guidelines free.

O— No fiction, poetry, cartoons, or syndicated columns.

Nonfiction All stories need a Southern Arizona angle. "Avoid obvious tourist attractions and information that most residents of the Southwest are likely to know. No anecdotes masquerading as articles. Not interested in fish-out-of-water, Easterner-visiting-the-Old-West pieces." **Buys 20 mss/year. Pays $50-500.**
Photos Query about photos before submitting anything.
Tips "Read the magazine before submitting anything."

California

$$ BRENTWOOD MAGAZINE

PTL Productions, 2118 Wilshire Blvd., #590, Santa Monica CA 90403. (310)390-5209. Fax: (310)390-0261. E-mail: jenny@brentwoodmagazine.com. Website: www.brentwoodmagazine.com. **100% freelance written**. Bimonthly magazine covering entertainment, business, lifestyles, reviews. Wanting in-depth interviews with top entertainers, politicians, and similar individuals. Also travel, sports, adventure. Estab. 1995. Circ. 50,000. Byline given. Pays on publication. Editorial lead time 3 months. Submit seasonal material 3 months in advance. Accepts queries by mail, e-mail, phone. Accepts simultaneous submissions. Sample copy for $5. Writer's guidelines available.
Nonfiction Needs book excerpts, expose, general interest, historical, humor, interview, new product, opinion, personal experience, photo feature, travel. **Buys 80 mss/year.** Query with published clips. Length: 1,000-2,500 words. **Pays 20¢/word.**

Photos State availability. Captions, identification of subjects required. Reviews contact sheets, negatives, prints. Offers no additional payment for photos accepted with ms
Columns/Departments Reviews (film/books/theater/museum), 100-500 words; Sports (Southern California angle), 200-600 words. 20 Query with or without published clips or send complete ms. **Pays 15¢/word.**
Tips Los Angeles-based writers preferred for most articles.

$$ CARLSBAD MAGAZINE

Wheelhouse Media, 2917 State St., Suite 210, Carlsbad CA 92008. (760)729-9099. Fax: (760)729-9011. E-mail: tim@wheelhousemedia.com. Website: www.clickoncarlsbad.com. **Contact:** Tim Wrisley. **80% freelance written**. Bimonthly magazine covering people, places, events, arts in Carlsbad, California. "We are a regional magazine highlighting all things pertaining specifically to Carlsbad. We focus on history, events, people and places that make Carlsbad interesting and unique. Our audience is both Carlsbad residents and visitors or anyone interested in learning more about Carlsbad. We favor a conversational tone that still adheres to standard rules of writing." Estab. 2004. Circ. 35,000. Byline given. Pays on publication. Publishes ms an average of 6 months after acceptance. Buys first North American serial rights. Editorial lead time 4 months. Submit seasonal material 6-12 months in advance. Accepts queries by mail, e-mail. Accepts simultaneous submissions. Responds in 2 months to queries and to mss. Sample copy for $2.31. Guidelines by e-mail.
Nonfiction Needs historical, interview, photo feature, home, garden, arts, events. Does not want self-promoting articles for individuals or businesses, real estate how-to's, advertorials. **Buys 3 mss/year.** Query with published clips. Length: 300-2,700 words. **Pays 20-30¢/word for assigned articles. Pays 20¢/word for unsolicited articles.**
Photos State availability. Reviews GIF/JPEG files. Offers $15-400/photo. Buys one time rights.
Columns/Departments Carlsbad Arts (people, places or things related to cultural arts in Carlsbad); Happenings (events that take place in Carlsbad); Carlsbad Character (unique Carlsbad residents who have contributed to Carlsbad's character); Commerce (Carlsbad business profiles); Surf Scene (subjects pertaining to the beach/surf in Carlsbad), all 500-700 words. Garden (Carlsbad garden feature); Home (Carlsbad home feature), both 700-1,200 words. 60 columns. Query with published clips. **Pays $50 flat fee or 20¢/word.**
Tips "The main thing to remember is that any pitches need to be subjects directly related to Carlsbad. If the subjects focus on surrounding towns, they aren't going to make the cut. We are looking for well-written feature magazine-style articles. E-mail is the preferred method for queries; you will get a response."

$$$$ DIABLO MAGAZINE

The Magazine of the San Francosco East Bay, Diablo Publications, 2520 Camino Diablo, Walnut Creek CA 94597. Fax: (925)943-1045. E-mail: d-mail@maildiablo.com. Website: www.diablomag.com. **50% freelance written**. Monthly magazine covering regional travel, food, homestyle, and profiles in Contra Costa and southern Alameda counties and selected areas of Oakland and Berkeley. Estab. 1979. Circ. 45,000. Byline given. Pays on acceptance. Offers 25% kill fee. Publishes ms an average of 3 months after acceptance. Buys first rights. Editorial lead time 3 months. Submit seasonal material 5 months in advance. Accepts queries by mail, e-mail, fax. Sample copy available online. Guidelines available online.
Nonfiction Needs general interest, interview, new product, photo feature, technical, travel. No restaurant profiles, out of country travel, nonlocal topics. **Buys 60 mss/year.** Query with published clips. Length: 600-3,000 words. **Pays $300-2,000.**
Photos State availability. Negotiates payment individually Buys one time rights.
Columns/Departments Education; Parenting; Homestyle; Food; Books; Health; Profiles; Regional Politics. Query with published clips.
Tips We prefer San Francisco Bay area writers who are familiar with the area.

$ LOS ANGELES TIMES MAGAZINE

Los Angeles Times, 202 W. First St., Los Angeles CA 90012. (213)237-7811. Fax: (213)237-7386. Website: www.latimes.com. **50% freelance written**. Monthly magazine of regional general interest. Circ. 1,384,688. Byline given. Payment schedule varies. No kill fee. Publishes ms an average of 2 months after acceptance. Buys first North American serial rights. Submit seasonal material 3 months in advance. Accepts simultaneous submissions. Responds in 2 months to queries. Responds in 2 months to mss. Sample copy and writer's guidelines free

Nonfiction Covers California and the West. Needs essays, reported, general interest, interview, investigative and narrative journalism. Query with published clips. Length: 2,500-4,500 words.
Photos Query first; prefers to assign photos. Captions, identification of subjects, model releases required. Reviews color transparencies, b&w prints. Payment varies. Buys one time rights.
Tips Previous national magazine writing experience preferred.

$ NOB HILL GAZETTE

An Attitude: Not an Address, Nob Hill Gazette, Inc., 5 Third St., Suite 222, San Francisco CA 94103. (415)227-0190. Fax: (415)974-5103. E-mail: cherie@nobhillgazette.com. Website: www.nobhillgazette.com. **95% freelance written**. Monthly magazine covering upscale lifestyles in the Bay Area. *Nob Hill Gazette* is for an upscale readership. Estab. 1978. Circ. 82,000. Byline given. Pays on 15th of month following publication. Offers $50 kill fee. Publishes ms an average of 2-3 months after acceptance. Buys all rights. Editorial lead time 1-2 months. Submit seasonal material 1-2 months in advance. Accepts queries by e-mail. Accepts previously published material. Responds in 2 weeks to queries. Responds in 2 months to mss. Sample copy available online. Guidelines free.
Nonfiction Needs general interest, historical, interview, opinion, photo feature, trends, lifestyles, fashion, health, fitness, entertaining, decor, real estate, charity and philanthropy, culture and the arts. Does not want first person articles, anything commercial (from a business or with a product to sell), profiles of people not active in the community, anything technical, anything on people or events not in the Bay Area. **Buys 75 mss/year.** Query with published clips. Length: 1,200-2,000 words. **Pays $100.**
Photos Contact: Contact Shara Hall, photo coordinator. State availability. Captions, identification of subjects required. Reviews GIF/JPEG files. Offers no additional payment for photos accepted with ms. Buys one time rights.
Columns/Departments Contact: Contact Lois Lehrman, publisher. All our columnists are freelancers, but they write for us regularly, so we don't take other submissions.
Tips Before submission, a writer should look at our publication and read the articles to get some idea of our style and range of subjects.

$$$$ OCEAN MAGAZINE

Shoreline Publications, 3334 E. Coast Hwy. #125, Corona del Mar CA 92625. E-mail: editor@oceanmagonline.com. Website: www.oceanmagazine.com. **Contact:** Molly Chizzick, editor-in-chief. **90% freelance written**. Bimonthly magazine covering beauty, fashion, health, decor. A perfect blend of the hippest trends and freshest ideas, *Ocean* stands apart as the first women's beauty, lifestyle and fashion-forward resource for Southern California. Capturing the essence of one of the most stylish, affluent and globally sought after destinations, *Ocean* appeals to all style-seeking women in search of the inside scoop on West Coast style, shopping, beauty and travel. Estab. 2005. Circ. 45,000. No byline given. Pays on publication. Offers 25% kill fee. Publishes ms an average of 1 month after acceptance. Buys all rights. Editorial lead time 3 months. Submit seasonal material 3 months in advance. Accepts queries by e-mail. Guidelines by e-mail.
Nonfiction Needs general interest, interview, new product. Query with published clips. Length: 800-1,000 words. **Pays 45¢-$1/word.**
Photos Send photos. Model releases required. Reviews GIF/JPEG files. Negotiates payment individually. Buys one time rights.

$$ ORANGE COAST MAGAZINE

The Magazine of Orange County, Orange Coast Kommunications, Inc., 3701 Birch St., Suite 100, Newport Beach CA 92660. (949)862-1133. Fax: (949)862-0133. Website: www.orangecoastmagazine.com. **90% freelance written**. Monthly magazine designed to inform and enlighten the educated, upscale residents of Orange County, California; highly graphic and well researched. Estab. 1974. Circ. 52,000. Byline given. Pays on publication. Offers 20% kill fee. Publishes ms an average of 4 months after acceptance. Buys first North American serial rights. Editorial lead time 5 months. Submit seasonal material 6 months in advance. Accepts queries by mail, e-mail. Accepts simultaneous submissions. Responds in 3 months to queries. Responds in 3 months to mss. Sample copy for #10 SASE and 6 first-class stamps. Guidelines for #10 SASE.
Nonfiction Absolutely no phone queries. Needs general interest, with Orange County focus, inspirational, interview, prominent Orange County citizens, personal experience, celebrity profiles, guides to activities and services. Health, Beauty, and Fitness (January); Dining (March and August); International Travel (April); Home Design (June); Arts (September); Local Travel (October). We do not accept stories that do not have specific Orange County angles. We want profiles on local people, stories on issues going on in our community, informational stories using Orange County-based sources. We cannot emphasize the

local angle enough. **Buys up to 65 mss/year.** Query with published clips. Length: 1,000-2,000 words. **Negotiates payment individually.**

Photos State availability. Captions, identification of subjects required. Negotiates payment individually. Buys one time rights.

Columns/Departments Short Cuts (stories for the front of the book that focus on Orange County issues, people, and places), 150-250 words. up to 25 Query with published clips. **Negotiates payment individually.**

Tips We're looking for more local personality profiles, analysis of current local issues, local takes on national issues. Most features are assigned to writers we've worked with before. Don't try to sell us `generic' journalism. *Orange Coast* prefers articles with specific and unusual angles focused on Orange County. A lot of freelance writers ignore our Orange County focus. We get far too many generalized manuscripts.

$$ PALM SPRINGS LIFE

The California Prestige Magazine, Desert Publications, Inc., 303 N. Indian Canyon, Palm Springs CA 92262. (760)325-2333. Fax: (760)325-7008. Website: www.palmspringslife.com. **80% freelance written.** Monthly magazine covering affluent Palm Springs-area desert resort communities. *Palm Springs Life* celebrates the good life. Estab. 1958. Circ. 20,000. Byline given. Pays on publication. Offers negotiable kill fee. Publishes ms an average of 3 months after acceptance. Buys one-time rights (negotiable). Submit seasonal material 6 months in advance. Responds in 4-6 weeks to queries. Sample copy for $3.95. Guidelines available online.

- Increased focus on desert style, home, fashion, art, culture, personalities, celebrities.

Nonfiction Needs book excerpts, essays, interview, feature stories, celebrity, fashion, spa, epicurean. Query with published clips. Length: 500-2,500 words. **Pays $100-500.**

Photos State availability. Captions, identification of subjects, model releases required. Reviews contact sheets. Pays $75-350/photo Buys one time rights.

Columns/Departments The Good Life (art, fashion, fine dining, philanthropy, entertainment, luxury living, luxury auto, architecture), 250-750 words. 12 Query with or without published clips. **Pays $200-350.**

$$$ SACRAMENTO MAGAZINE

Sacramento Magazines Corp., 706 56th St., Suite 210, Sacramento CA 95819. (916)452-6200. Fax: (916)452-6061. E-mail: krista@sacmag.com. Website: www.sacmag.com. **80% freelance written. Works with a small number of new/unpublished writers each year.** Monthly magazine with a strictly local angle on local issues, human interest and consumer items for readers in the middle to high income brackets. Prefers to work with writers local to Sacramento area. Estab. 1975. Circ. 50,000. Pays on publication. No kill fee. Publishes ms an average of 3 months after acceptance. Generally buys shared North American serial rights and electronic rights. Accepts queries by mail. Responds in 3 months to queries. Responds in 3 months to mss. Sample copy for $4.50. Guidelines for #10 SASE.

Nonfiction Local isues vital to Sacramento quality of life. No e-mail, fax or phone queries will be answered. **Buys 5 unsolicited feature mss/year.** Query. 1,500-3,000 words, depending on author, subject matter and treatment. **Pays $400 and up.**

Photos Send photos. Captions, identification of subjects, True required. Payment varies depending on photographer, subject matter and treatment Buys one time rights.

Columns/Departments Business, home and garden, first person essays, regional travel, gourmet, profile, sports, city arts, health, home and garden, profiles of local people (1,000-1,800 words); UpFront (250-300 words). **Pays $600-800.**

$$ SACRAMENTO NEWS & REVIEW

Chico Community Publishing, 1124 Del Paso Blvd., Sacramento CA 95815-3607. (916)498-1234. Fax: (916)498-7920. E-mail: melindaw@newsreview.com; kelm@newsreview.com. Website: www.newsreview.com. **Contact:** Melinda Welsh, editor. **25% freelance written.** Alternative news and entertainment weekly magazine. We maintain a high literary standard for submissions; unique or alternative slant. Publication aimed at a young, intellectual audience; submissions should have an edge and strong voice. We have a decided preference for stories with a strong local slant. "Our mission: To publish great newspapers that are successful and enduring. To create a quality work environment that encourages employees to grow professionally while respecting personal welfare. To have a positive impact on our communities and make them better places to live. " Estab. 1989. Circ. 87,000. Byline given. Pays on publication. Offers 10% kill fee. Publishes ms an average of 2 months after acceptance. Buys first rights, buys electronic rights. Editorial lead time 2 months. Submit seasonal material 2 months in advance. Accepts queries by mail, e-mail. Accepts simultaneous submissions. Responds in 1 month to queries. Responds in 2 months to mss. Sample copy for 50¢. Guidelines available online.

- Prefers to work with Sacramento-area writers.

Nonfiction Needs essays, expose, general interest, humor, interview, personal experience. Does not want to see travel, product stories, business profile. **Buys 20-30 mss/year.** Query with published clips. Length: 750-5,000 words. **Pays $40-500.**

Photos State availability. Identification of subjects required. Reviews 8 × 10 prints. Negotiates payment individually. Buys one-time rights.

$$ SAN DIEGO MAGAZINE

San Diego Magazine Publishing Co., 1450 Front St., San Diego CA 92101. (619)230-9292. Fax: (619)230-0490. E-mail: tblair@sandiegomagazine.com. Website: www.sandiegomag.com. **30% freelance written**. Monthly magazine. We produce informative and entertaining features and investigative reports about politics; community and neighborhood issues; lifestyle; sports; design; dining; arts; and other facets of life in San Diego. Estab. 1948. Circ. 55,000. Byline given. Pays on publication. Offers 25% kill fee. Publishes ms an average of 2 months after acceptance. Buys first North American serial rights, buys second serial (reprint) rights. Editorial lead time 2 months. Submit seasonal material 4 months in advance. Accepts simultaneous submissions.

Nonfiction Needs expose, general interest, historical, how-to, interview, travel, lifestyle. **Buys 12-24 mss/year.** Send complete ms. Length: 1,000-3,000 words. **Pays $250-750.**

Photos State availability. Offers no additional payment for photos accepted with ms Buys one time rights.

$$$$ SAN FRANCISCO

243 Vallejo St., San Francisco CA 94111. (415)398-2800. Fax: (415)398-6777. Website: sanfranmag.com. **50% freelance written. Prefers to work with published/established writers.** Monthly city/regional magazine. Estab. 1968. Circ. 180,000. Byline given. Pays on publication. Offers 25% kill fee. Publishes ms an average of 2 months after acceptance. Submit seasonal material 5 months in advance. Responds in 2 months to queries. Responds in 2 months to mss. Sample copy for $3.95.

Nonfiction All stories should relate in some way to the San Francisco Bay Area (travel excepted). Needs expose, interview, travel, arts. Query with published clips. Length: 200-4,000 words. **Pays $100-2,000 and some expenses.**

$$$ SAN JOSE

The Magazine for Silicon Valley, Renaissance Publications, Inc., 25 Metro Dr., Suite 550, San Jose CA 95110. (408)975-9300. Fax: (408)975-9900. E-mail: jodi@sanjosemagazine.com. Website: www.sanjosemagazine.com. **10% freelance written**. Monthly magazine. As the lifestyle magazine for those living at center of the technological revolution, we cover the people and places that make Silicon Valley the place to be for the new millennium. All stories must have a local angle, though they should be of national relevance. Estab. 1997. Circ. 60,000. Byline given. Pays on publication. Offers 10% kill fee. Publishes ms an average of 3 months after acceptance. Buys first North American serial rights. pays a flat $25 electronic rights fee. Editorial lead time 18 weeks. Submit seasonal material 6 months in advance. Accepts queries by mail, e-mail, fax. Accepts simultaneous submissions. Responds in 1 month to queries. Sample copy for $5. Guidelines for #10 SASE.

Nonfiction Needs general interest, interview, photo feature, travel. No technical, trade or articles without a tie-in to Silicon Valley. **Buys 12 mss/year.** Query with published clips. Length: 1,000-2,000 words. **Pays 35¢/word.**

Photos State availability. Captions, identification of subjects, model releases required. Offers no additional payment for photos accepted with ms

Columns/Departments Fast Forward (a roundup of trends and personalities and news that has Silicon Valley buzzing; topics include health, history, politics, nonprofits, education, Q&As, business, technology, dining, wine and fashion). 5 Query. **Pays 35¢/word.**

Tips Study our magazine for style and content. Nothing is as exciting as reading a tightly written query and discovering a new writer.

$ SAN LUIS OBISPO COUNTY JOURNAL

654 Osos Street, Suite 10, San Luis Obispo CA 93401. (805)546-0609 or (805)544-8711. Fax: (805)546-8827. E-mail: slojournal@fix.net. **Contact:** Erin Mott. "*The Journal* is strictly local to the Central Coast of California, and the writers are local as well."

Nonfiction Needs general interest. Query.

7x7
Hartle Media, 59 Grant Ave., 4th Floor, San Francisco CA 94108. E-mail: chris@7x7mag.com. Website: www.7x7sf.com. **15% freelance written**. Monthly magazine covering the city of San Francisco. Estab. 2001. Circ. 45,000. Byline given. Pays 60 days following publication. Offers 25% kill fee. Buys first North American serial rights, buys electronic rights, buys nonexclusive reprint rights rights. Editorial lead time 3 months. Submit seasonal material 3-6 months in advance. Accepts queries by mail. Sample copy for $4. Guidelines free.

Nonfiction Although the majority of the magazine is written inhouse, *7x7* accepts freelance queries for both its features section and various departments in the magazine. **Buys 6-10 mss/year.** Query with published clips. **Pays negotiable amount.**

Photos Contact: Contact Stefanie Michejda, photo editor.

Tips Please read the magazine. Stories must appeal to an educated, San Francisco-based audience and, ideally, provide a first-person perspective. Most articles are 500-1,000 words in length.

Colorado

$ SOUTHWEST COLORADO ARTS PERSPECTIVE MAGAZINE
Shared Vision Publishing, P.O. Box 3042, Durango CO 81302. (970)739-3200. E-mail: director@artsperspective.com. Website: www.artsperspective.com. **100% freelance written**. Quarterly tabloid covering art. *"Arts Perspective Magazine* offers a venue for all of the arts. Artists, writers, musicians, dancers, performers and galleries are encourage to showcase their work. A resource for supporters of the arts to share a common thread in the continuum of creative expression." Estab. 2004. Circ. 30,000+. Byline given. Pays on publication. Publishes ms an average of 2 months after acceptance. Buys first North American serial rights, buys first rights, buys one-time rights, buys electronic rights. Editorial lead time 2-5 months. Submit seasonal material 2-5 months in advance. Accepts queries by mail, e-mail, phone. Responds in 2 weeks to queries. Responds in 1 month to mss. Sample copy free. www.artsperspective.com/submissions.php.

Photos Send photos. Identification of subjects, model releases required. Reviews GIF/JPEG files. Offers $15-25 per photo. printed online.

Poetry Needs avant-garde, free verse, haiku, light verse, traditional. Buys 4 poems/year. Submit maximum 3 poems. Length: 4-45 lines.

Tips "Take me to lunch; sense of humor, please."

$$ STEAMBOAT MAGAZINE
100 Park Ave., Suite 209, Steamboat Springs CO 80487. (970)871-9413. Fax: (970)871-1922. E-mail: info@steamboatmagazine.com. Website: www.steamboatmagazine.com. **Contact:** Deborah Olsen. **80% freelance written**. Quarterly magazine showcasing the history, people, lifestyles, and interests of Northwest Colorado. Our readers are generally well-educated, well-traveled, upscale, active people visiting our region to ski in winter and recreate in summer. They come from all 50 states and many foreign countries. Writing should be fresh, entertaining, and informative. Estab. 1978. Circ. 20,000. Byline given. Pays 50% on acceptance, 50% on publication. No kill fee. Buys exclusive rights. Submit seasonal material 1 year in advance. Accepts queries by mail, e-mail, fax, phone. Responds in 3 months to queries. Sample copy for $5.95 and SAE with 10 first-class stamps. Guidelines free.

Nonfiction Needs book excerpts, essays, general interest, historical, humor, interview, photo feature, travel. **Buys 10-15 mss/year.** Query with published clips. Length: 150-1,500 words. **Pays $50-300 for assigned articles.**

Photos Contact: Corey Copischke. Prefers to review viewing platforms, JPEGs, and dupes. Will request original transparencies when needed. State availability. Captions, identification of subjects required. Pays $50-250/photo Buys one time rights.

Tips Stories must be about Steamboat Springs and the Yampa Valley to be considered. We're looking for new angles on ski/snowboard stories in the winter and activity-related stories, all year round. Please query first with ideas to make sure subjects are fresh and appropriate. We try to make subjects and treatments `timeless' in nature because our magazine is a `keeper' with a multi-year shelf life.

N TELLURIDE MAGAZINE
Big Earth Publishing, Inc., P.O. Box 964, Telluride CO 81435-0964. (970)728-4245. Fax: (970)728-4302. E-mail: duffy@telluridemagazine.com. Website: www.telluridemagazine.com. **Contact:** Mary Duffy, editor-in-chief. **75**. Telluride: community, events, recreation, ski resort, surrounding region, San Juan Mountains, history, tourism, mountain living. "*Telluride Magazine* speaks specifically to Telluride and

the surrounding mountain environment. Telluride is a resort town supported by the ski industry in winter, festivals in summer, outdoor recreation year round and the unique lifestyle all of that affords. As a National Historic Landmark District with a colorful mining history, it weaves a tale that readers seek out. The local/visitor interaction is key to Telluride's success in making profiles an important part of the content. Telluriders are an environmentally minded and progressive bunch who appreciate efforts toward sustainability and protecting the natural landscape and wilderness that are the region's number one draw." Estab. 1982. Circ. 70,000. Byline given. Pays 60 days from publication. $50 Buys first rights, first print and electronic rights. Editorial lead time and advance on seasonal subs is 6 months. Accepts queries by e-mail. Responds in 2 weeks on queries; 2 months on mss. Sample copy online at website. Guidelines by e-mail.

Nonfiction Needs historical, humor, nostalgic, personal experience, photo feature, travel, recreation, lifestyle. No articles about places or adventures other than Telluride. **Buys 10 mss/year.** Query with published clips. 1,000-2,000 words. **$200-700 for assigned articles; $100-700 for unsolicited articles. Does not pay expenses.**

Photos Send no more than 20 jpeg comps (low-ers) via e-mail or send CD/DVD with submission. Reviews JPEG/TIFF files. Offers $35-300 per photo; negotiates payment individually. Buys one-time rights; includes print and web (electronic).

Columns/Departments Telluride Turns (news and current topics); Mountain Health (health issues related to mountain sports, and living at altitude); Nature Notes (explores the flora, fauna, geology and climate of San Juan Mountains); Green Bytes (sustainable & environmentally sound ideas and products for home building), all 500 words. Buys 40/year Query. **Pays $50-200.**

Fiction "Please contact us; we are very specific about what we will accept." Needs adventure, historical, humorous, slice-of-life vignettes, western, recreation in the mountains. **Buys 2 mss/year.** Query with published clips. 800-1,200 words.

Poetry Needs any poetry; must reflect mountains or mountain living. Buys 1/year poems/year. 3 lines/min. Open/max. **Pays up to to $100.**

$$ VAIL-BEAVER CREEK MAGAZINE

Rocky Mountain Media, LLC, P.O. Box 1397, Avon CO 81620. (970)476-6600. Fax: (970)845-0069. E-mail: bergerd@vail.net. Website: www.vailbeavercreekmag.com. **80% freelance written.** Semiannual magazine showcasing the lifestyles and history of the Vail Valley. We are particularly interested in personality profiles, home and design features, the arts, winter and summer recreation/adventure stories, and environmental articles. Estab. 1975. Circ. 30,000. Byline given. Pays on acceptance. Offers 100% kill fee. Publishes ms an average of 6 months after acceptance. Buys one-time rights. Editorial lead time 1 year. Submit seasonal material 1 year in advance. Accepts queries by mail, e-mail. Accepts simultaneous submissions. Responds in 1 month to queries. Responds in 2 months to mss. Sample copy for $5.95 and SAE with 10 first-class stamps. Guidelines free.

Nonfiction Needs essays, general interest, historical, humor, interview, personal experience, photo feature. **Buys 20-25 mss/year.** Query with published clips. Length: 500-3,000 words. **Pays 20-30¢/word.**

Reprints Send typed manuscript with rights for sale noted and information about when and where the material previously appeared.

Photos State availability. Captions, identification of subjects, model releases required. Reviews transparencies. Offers $50-250/photo. Buys one time rights.

Tips Be familiar with the Vail Valley and its personality. Approach a story that will be relevant for several years to come. We produce a magazine that is a `keeper.'

Connecticut

$$$ N CONNECTICUT MAGAZINE

Journal Register Co., 35 Nutmeg Dr., Trumbull CT 06611. (203)380-6600. Fax: (203)380-6610. E-mail: cmonagan@connecticutmag.com. Website: www.connecticutmag.com. **Contact:** Dale Salm. **75% freelance written. "Prefers to work with published/established writers who know the state and live/have lived here.** Monthly magazine for an affluent, sophisticated, suburban audience. We want only articles that pertain to living in Connecticut." Estab. 1971. Circ. 93,000. Byline given. Pays on publication. Offers 20% kill fee. Publishes ms an average of 4 months after acceptance. Buys first North American serial rights. Submit seasonal material 4 months in advance. Accepts queries by mail, e-mail, fax. Responds in 6 weeks to queries. Guidelines for #10 SASE.

Nonfiction "Interested in seeing hard-hitting investigative pieces and strong business pieces (not advertorial)." Needs book excerpts, expose, general interest, interview, topics of service to Connecticut readers. Dining/entertainment, northeast/travel, home/garden and Connecticut bride twice/year. Also, business (January) and healthcare 4-6x/year. No personal essays. **Buys 50 mss/year.** Query with published clips. 3,000 words maximum. **Pays $600-1,200.**

Photos Send photos. Identification of subjects, model releases required. Reviews contact sheets, transparencies. Pays $50 minimum/photo Buys one time rights.

Columns/Departments Business, Health, Politics, Connecticut Calendar, Arts, Dining Out, Gardening, Environment, Education, People, Sports, Media, From the Field (quirky, interesting regional stories with broad appeal). Length: 1,500-2,500 words. 50 Query with published clips. **Pays $400-700.**

Fillers Short pieces about Connecticut trends, curiosities, interesting short subjects, etc. Length: 150-400 words. **Pays $75-150.**

Tips "Make certain your idea has not been covered to death by the local press and can withstand a time lag of a few months. Again, we don't want something that has already received a lot of press.".

Delaware

$$ DELAWARE TODAY

3301 Lancaster Pike, Suite 5C, Wilmington DE 19805. (302)656-1809. Fax: (302)656-5843. E-mail: editors@delawaretoday.com. Website: www.delawaretoday.com. **50% freelance written**. Monthly magazine geared toward Delaware people, places and issues. All stories must have Delaware slant. No pitches such as Delawareans will be interested in a national topic. Estab. 1962. Circ. 25,000. Byline given. Pays on publication. Offers 50% kill fee. Publishes ms an average of 4 months after acceptance. all rights for 1 year. Editorial lead time 3 months. Submit seasonal material 6 months in advance. Responds in 2 months to queries. Sample copy for $2.95.

Nonfiction Needs historical, interview, photo feature, lifestyles, issues. Newcomer's Guide to Delaware **Buys 40 mss/year.** Query with published clips. Length: 100-3,000 words. **Pays $50-750.**

Photos State availability. Identification of subjects required. Negotiates payment individually. Buys one time rights.

Columns/Departments Business, Health, History, People, all 1,500 words. 24 Query with published clips. **Pays $150-250.**

Tips "No story ideas that we would know about, i.e., a profile of the governor. Best bets are profiles of quirky/unique Delawareans that we'd never know about or think of."

District of Columbia

$$ WASHINGTON CITY PAPER

2390 Champlain St. NW, Washington DC 20009. (202)332-2100. Fax: (202)332-8500. Website: www.washingtoncitypaper.com. **50% freelance written**. Relentlessly local alternative weekly in nation's capital covering city and regional politics, media and arts. No national stories. Estab. 1981. Circ. 93,000. Byline given. Pays on publication. Offers kill fee. Offers 10% kill fee for assigned stories. Publishes ms an average of 6 weeks after acceptance. Buys first rights. Editorial lead time 7-10 days. Responds in 1 month to queries. Guidelines available online.

Nonfiction Our biggest need for freelancers is in the District Line section of the newspaper: short, well-reported and local stories. These range from carefully-drawn profiles to sharp, hooky approaches to reporting on local institutions. We don't want op-ed articles, fiction, poetry, service journalism or play by play accounts of news conferences or events. We also purchase, but more infrequently, longer `cover-length' stories that fit the criteria stated above. Full guide to freelance submissions can be found on website. **Buys 100 mss/year.** District Line: 800-1,500 words; Covers: 2,500-10,000 words **Pays 10-40¢/word.**

Photos Make appointment to show portfolio to art director. Pays minimum of $75.

Columns/Departments Music Writing (eclectic). 100 Query with published clips or send complete ms. **Pays 10-40¢/word.**

Tips Think local. Great ideas are a plus. We are willing to work with anyone who has a strong idea, regardless of vita.

Florida

$$$$ BOCA RATON MAGAZINE

JES Publishing, 6413 Congress Ave., Suite 100, Boca Raton FL 33487. (561)997-8683. Fax: (561)997-

8909. Website: www.bocamag.com. **70% freelance written**. Bimonthly lifestyle magazine devoted to the residents of South Florida, featuring fashion, interior design, food, people, places, and issues that shape the affluent South Florida market. Estab. 1981. Circ. 20,000. Byline given. Pays on acceptance. No kill fee. Publishes ms an average of 3 months after acceptance. Buys second serial (reprint) rights. Submit seasonal material 7 months in advance. Accepts simultaneous submissions. Responds in 1 month to queries. Sample copy for $4.95 and 10 × 13 SAE with 10 first-class stamps. Guidelines for #10 SASE.
Nonfiction Needs general interest, historical, humor, interview, photo feature, travel. Interior Design (September-October); Real Estate (March-April); Best of Boca (July-August). Send complete ms. Length: 800-2,500 words. **Pays $350-1,500.**
Reprints Send tearsheet. Payment varies.
Photos Send photos.
Columns/Departments Body & Soul (health, fitness and beauty column, general interest); Hitting Home (family and social interactions); History or Arts (relevant to South Florida), all 1,000 words. Query with published clips or send complete ms. **Pays $350-400.**
Tips We prefer shorter manuscripts, highly localized articles, excellent art/photography.

COASTLINES

Marine Industries Association of Palm Beach County, Inc., P.O. Box 7597, West Palm Beach FL 33405. (561)832-8444. Fax: (561)659-1824. E-mail: alison@marinepbc.org. Website: www.marinepbc.org. **Contact:** Alison Pruitt, publisher. biannual magazine. Circ. 25,000+. Byline given. No kill fee. Editorial lead time 3 months. Submit seasonal material 3 months in advance. Guidelines available.

$$ EMERALD COAST MAGAZINE

Rowland Publishing, Inc., 1932 Miccosukee Rd., Tallahassee FL 32308. (850)878-0554. Fax: (850)656-1871. Website: www.emeraldcoastmagazine.com. **25% freelance written**. Bimonthly magazine. Lifestyle publication celebrating life on Florida's Emerald Coast. All content has an Emerald Coast (Northwest Florida) connection. This includes Sandestin, Destin, Fort Walton Beach. Estab. 2000. Circ. 18,000. Byline given. Pays on acceptance. No kill fee. Publishes ms an average of 3 months after acceptance. Buys first North American serial rights. Editorial lead time 4 months. Submit seasonal material 6 months in advance. Accepts queries by mail, e-mail. Accepts previously published material. Accepts simultaneous submissions. Responds in 3 months to queries. Responds in 3 months to mss. Sample copy for $4. Guidelines by e-mail.
Nonfiction All must have an Emerald Coast slant. Needs essays, historical, inspirational, interview, new product, personal experience, photo feature. No fiction, poetry, or travel. No general interest—we are Northwest Florida specific. **Buys 5 mss/year.** Query with published clips. Length: 1,800-2,000 words. **Pays $100-250.**
Photos Send photos. Captions, identification of subjects, model releases required. Reviews prints, GIF/JPEG files. Negotiates payment individually. Buys one-time rights.
Tips "We're looking for fresh ideas and new slants that are related to Florida's Emerald Coast. Because we work so far in advance, it is difficult to be timely, so be sure to give us ideas that aren't too time specific."

$$$$ FLORIDA INSIDE OUT

404 Washington Ave., Suite 650, Miami Beach FL 33139. (305)532-2544. Website: www.floridainsideout.com. **60% freelance written**. Bimonthly magazine covering architecture and interior design. *Florida Inside Out* is a smart publication for those interested in design, architecture and interiors. It is product-heavy, but also includes many newsy features on the fields we cover. No press releases or pre-packaged features will be published. We accept original material only. Estab. 2004. Circ. 55,000. Byline given. Pays on publication. Offers 20% kill fee. Publishes ms an average of 1-2 months after acceptance. Buys one-time rights. Editorial lead time 2-3 months. Submit seasonal material 3 months in advance. Accepts queries by mail, e-mail, phone. Accepts simultaneous submissions.
Nonfiction Needs book excerpts, essays, general interest, historical, interview, new product, travel. Does not want pre-packaged material. Query with published clips. Length: 150-1,400 words. **Pays $1/word.**
Photos Contact: Contact Reynaldo Martin, associate art director. Send photos. Identification of subjects required. Reviews GIF/JPEG files. Negotiates payment individually. Buys one time rights.
Columns/Departments Green Matters (landscape, agriculture), 1,000-1,200 words; Fin, Feather, Hoof & Paw (pets and pet-related), 850-1,000 words; History Books (Florida-related history), 850-1,000 words. 18-20 Query. **Pays $1/word.**
Tips Do not approach with anything that has already been published. We assign all of our features, departments, etc. But we do always look for new contributors with fresh ideas.

$$ FLORIDA MONTHLY MAGAZINE

Florida Media, Inc., 999 Douglas Ave., Suite 3301, Altamonte Springs FL 32714-2063. (407)816-9596. Fax: (407)816-9373. E-mail: exec-editor@floridamagazine.com. Website: www.floridamagazine.com. Monthly lifestyle magazine covering Florida travel, food and dining, heritage, homes and gardens, and all aspects of Florida lifestyle. Full calendar of events each month. Estab. 1981. Circ. 225,235. Byline given. Pays on publication. No kill fee. Publishes ms an average of 5 months after acceptance. Buys first rights. Editorial lead time 3 months. Submit seasonal material 6 months in advance. Accepts queries by mail, e-mail, fax. Responds in 9 months to queries. Sample copy for $5. Guidelines by e-mail.

- Interested in material on areas outside of the larger cities.

Nonfiction Needs historical, interview, travel, general Florida interest, out-of-the-way Florida places, dining, attractions, festivals, shopping, resorts, bed & breakfast reviews, retirement, real estate, business, finance, health, recreation, sports. **Buys 50-60 mss/year.** Query with published clips. Length: 500-2,500 words. **Pays $100-400 for assigned articles. Pays $50-250 for unsolicited articles.**

Photos Send photos. Captions required. Reviews 3 × 5 color prints and slides. Offers $6/photo.

Columns/Departments Golf; Homes & Gardenings; Heritage (all Florida-related); 750 words. 24 Query with published clips. **Pays $75-250.**

$ FT. MYERS MAGAZINE

And Pat, LLC, 15880 Summerlin Rd., Suite 189, Fort Myers FL 33908. E-mail: ftmyers@optonline.net. Website: www.ftmyersmagazine.com. **90% freelance written**. Bimonthly magazine covering regional arts and living for educated, active, successful and creative residents of Lee & Collier Counties, Florida and guests at resorts and hotels in Lee County. "Content: Arts, entertainment, media, travel, sports, health, home, garden, environmental issues." Estab. 2001. Circ. 20,000. Byline given. 30 days after publication. No kill fee. Publishes ms an average of 2-6 months after acceptance. Buys one-time rights, buys second serial (reprint) rights. Editorial lead time 2-4 months. Submit seasonal material 2-4 months in advance. Accepts queries by e-mail. Accepts simultaneous submissions. Responds in 3 months to queries and to mss. Guidelines available online.

Nonfiction Needs essays, general interest, historical, how-to, humor, interview, personal experience, reviews, previews, news, informational. **Buys 10-25 mss/year.** Send complete ms. Length: 750-1,500 words. **Pays $50-150 or approximately 10¢/word.**

Photos State availability of or send photos. Captions, identification of subjects required. Negotiates payment individually; generally offers $25-100/photo or art. Buys one-time rights.

Columns/Departments Media: books, music, video, film, theater, Internet, software (news, previews, reviews, interviews, profiles), 750-1,500 words. Lifestyles: art & design, science & technology, house & garden, health & wellness, sports & recreation, travel & leisure, food & drink (news, interviews, previews, reviews, profiles, advice), 750-1,500 words. 60 mss/year. Query with or without published clips or send complete ms. **Pays $50-150.**

$$$ GULFSHORE LIFE

9051 N. Tamiami Trail, Suite 202, Naples FL 34108. (239)449-4111. Fax: (239)594-9986. E-mail: denises@gulfshorelifemag.com. Website: www.gulfshorelifemag.com. **75% freelance written**. Magazine published 10 times/year for southwest Florida, the workings of its natural systems, its history, personalities, culture and lifestyle. Estab. 1970. Circ. 35,000. Byline given. Pays on publication. Publishes ms an average of 4 months after acceptance. Submit seasonal material 8 months in advance. Accepts queries by mail, e-mail, fax. Accepts simultaneous submissions. Sample copy for sae with 9 × 12 envelope and 10 First-Class stamps.

Nonfiction All articles must be related to southwest Florida. Needs historical, interview, issue/trend. **Buys 100 mss/year.** Query with published clips. Length: 500-3,000 words. **Pays $100-1,000.**

Photos Send photos. Identification of subjects, model releases required. Reviews 35mm transparencies, 5 × 7 prints. Pays $50-100. Buys one time rights.

Tips We buy superbly written stories that illuminate southwest Florida personalities, places and issues. Surprise us!

$$ JACKSONVILLE

White Publishing Co., 1261 King St., Jacksonville FL 32204. (904)389-3622. Fax: (904)389-3628. Website: www.jacksonvillemag.com. **50% freelance written**. Monthly magazine covering life and business in northeast Florida for upwardly mobile residents of Jacksonville and the Beaches, Orange Park, St. Augustine and Amelia Island, Florida. Estab. 1985. Circ. 25,000. Byline given. Pays on publication. Offers kill fee. Offers 25-33% kill fee to writers on assignment. Buys first North American serial rights, buys second serial (reprint) rights. Editorial lead time 3 months. Submit seasonal material 4 months in advance. Responds in 6 weeks to queries. Responds in 1 month to mss. Sample copy for $5 (includes postage).

Nonfiction All articles *must* have relevance to Jacksonville and Florida's First Coast (Duval, Clay, St. John's, Nassau, Baker counties). Needs book excerpts, expose, general interest, historical, how-to, service articles, humor, interview, personal experience, photo feature, travel, commentary. **Buys 50 mss/year.** Query with published clips. Length: 1,200-3,000 words. **Pays $50-500 for feature length pieces.**

Reprints Send photocopy. Payment varies.

Photos State availability. Captions, model releases required. Reviews contact sheets, transparencies. Negotiates payment individually. Buys one time rights.

Columns/Departments Business (trends, success stories, personalities), 1,000-1,200 words; Health (trends, emphasis on people, hopeful outlooks), 1,000-1,200 words; Money (practical personal financial advice using local people, anecdotes and examples), 1,000-1,200 words; Real Estate/Home (service, trends, home photo features), 1,000-1,200 words; Travel (weekends; daytrips; excursions locally and regionally), 1,000-1,200 words; occasional departments and columns covering local history, sports, family issues, etc. 40 **Pays $150-250.**

Tips We are a writer's magazine and demand writing that tells a story with flair.

$$ PENSACOLA MAGAZINE

Ballinger Publishing, 41 N. Jefferson St., Suite 402, Pensacola FL 32502. E-mail: kelly@ballingerpublishing.com. Website: www.ballingerpublishing.com. **75% freelance written**. Monthly magazine. *Pensacola Magazine*'s articles are written in a casual, conversational tone. We cover a broad range of topics that citizens of Pensacola relate to. Most of our freelance work is assigned, so it is best to send a résumé, cover letter and 3 clips to the above e-mail address. Estab. 1987. Circ. 10,000. Byline given. Pays at end of shelf life. Offers 20% kill fee. Buys first rights. Makes work-for-hire assignments. Editorial lead time 1 month. Submit seasonal material 6 months in advance. Accepts queries by e-mail. Accepts previously published material. Accepts simultaneous submissions. Responds in 2 weeks to queries. Sample copy for $1, SASE and 1 First-Class stamp. Guidelines available online.

Nonfiction Wedding (February); Home & Garden (May). Query with published clips. Length: 700-2,100 words. **Pays 10-15¢/word.**

Photos State availability of or send photos. Captions, identification of subjects, model releases required. Reviews GIF/JPEG files. Offers $7/photo. Buys one time rights.

Tips We accept submissions for *Pensacola Magazine, Northwest Florida's Business Climate*, and *Coming of Age*. Please query by topic via e-mail to shannon@ballingerpublishing.com. If you do not have a specific query topic, please send a résumé and three clips via e-mail, and you will be given story assignments if your writing style is appropriate. You do not have to be locally or regionally located to write for us.

$$ TALLAHASSEE MAGAZINE

Rowland Publishing, Inc., 1932 Miccosukee Rd., Tallahassee FL 32308. E-mail: editorial@rowlandpublishing.com. Website: www.rowlandpublishing.com. **20% freelance written**. Bimonthly magazine covering life in Florida's Capital Region. All content has a Tallahassee, Florida connection. Estab. 1978. Circ. 18,000. Byline given. Pays on acceptance. No kill fee. Publishes ms an average of 2 months after acceptance. Buys first North American serial rights. Editorial lead time 4 months. Submit seasonal material 6 months in advance. Accepts queries by mail, e-mail. Accepts simultaneous submissions. Responds in 3 months to queries & mss. Sample copy for $4. Guidelines by e-mail.

Nonfiction All must have a Tallahassee slant. Needs book excerpts, essays, historical, inspirational, interview, new product, personal experience, photo feature, travel, sports, business, Calendar items. No fiction, poetry, or travel. No general interest. **Buys 15 mss/year.** Query with published clips. Length: 500-2,500 words. **Pays $100-350.**

Photos Send photos. Captions, identification of subjects, model releases required. Reviews prints, GIF/JPEG files. Negotiates payment individually. Buys one time rights.

Tips "We're looking for fresh ideas and new slants that are related to Florida's Capital Region. Because we work so far in advance, it is difficult to be timely, so be sure to give us ideas that aren't too time specific."

THE THIRTY-A REVIEW

A review of 30-A's finest people, places, things, P.O. Box 12047, Atlanta GA 30355. E-mail: miles@thirtyareview.com. Website: thirtyareview.com. Monthly magazine focusing on 30-A and the surrounding areas. "We tell the human interest stories that make 30-A's entrepreneurs, developers and artists tick, making the magazine appealing to both tourists and locals alike." Accepts queries by e-mail.

Nonfiction Needs general interest, interview. Query with published clips.

$$ TIMES OF THE ISLANDS

Southwest Florida's Island Coast Magazine, Times of the Islands Inc., P.O. Box 1227, Sanibel FL 33957. (239)472-0205. Fax: (239)395-2125. E-mail: editor@toti.com. Website: www.toti.com. **98% freelance written**. Bimonthly magazine. *Times of the Islands* is a magazine that captures the true essence of island living. It is a high-quality, intriguing publication that captures the beauty, style and spirit of island life; a magazine with vision and substance that appeals not only to residents of Sanibel, Captiva and the barrier islands of Southwest Florida, but to vacationers and mainlanders as wellÃ³anyone who shares a passion for the island mystique and lifestyle. Estab. 1997. Circ. 25,000. Byline given. Pays on publication. No kill fee. Publishes ms an average of 4 months after acceptance. Buys one-time rights, buys electronic rights. Editorial lead time 4 months. Submit seasonal material 4 months in advance. Accepts queries by e-mail. Accepts simultaneous submissions. Responds in 1 week to queries. Responds in 1 month to mss. Sample copy free. Guidelines available online.

Nonfiction Needs general interest, humor, interview, photo feature, travel, cuisine. Query with published clips. Length: 1,000-2,000 words. **Pays $250-400.**

Photos Send photos. Captions, identification of subjects required. Reviews contact sheets. Offers $25-50/published photo. Buys one time rights.

Columns/Departments Habitats (homes and living spaces); Arts; Profile (profile of notable person); Coastal Commerce (profile of local business person); Explorer (fun weekend exploration trip); Getaways (traveling trip); Outdoors (outdoor activity); To Your Health (informative health and medical), all 1,000 words. Plus, Making Waves (notable SW Floridians), 300 words. Query with published clips. **Pays $150-250.**

Tips We are looking for exciting, fresh material on subjects that cover anything pertaining to Southwest Florida living.

$$ N WHERE MAGAZINE (WHERE GUESTBOOK, WHERE MAP, WHERE NEWSLETTER)

Morris Visitor Publications, 7300 Corporate Center Dr., Suite 303, Miami FL 33126. Fax: (305)892-1005. E-mail: irene.moore@wheremagazine.com. Website: www.wheretraveler.com. **40% freelance written**. Monthly magazine covering Miami tourism. We cover Miami only. We are a tourism guide, so features are only about where to go and what to do in Miami. Writers must be very familiar with Miami. Estab. 1936. Circ. 30,000. Byline for features only, but all writers listed on masthead. Pays on publication. Buys all rights. Editorial lead time 3 months. Submit seasonal material 3 months in advance. Accepts queries by mail, e-mail. Responds in 1 week to queries Sample copy available online Guidelines by e-mail

Nonfiction Needs new product, photo feature, travel, (in Miami). **Buys 0 mss/year.** Query. Length: 500 words.

Photos Send photos. Captions, identification of subjects, model releases required. Reviews GIF/JPEG files. Negotiates payment individually. Buys all rights.

Columns/Departments Dining; Entertainment; Museums & Attractions; Art Galleries; Shops & Services; Navigating around Miami, 50 words. Queries for writer clips only per page of 1 blurbs per page.

Tips "We look for a new slant on a 'where to go' or 'what to do' in Miami."

Georgia

$$$ ATLANTA LIFE MAGAZINE

2500 Hospital Blvd., Suite 370, Roswell GA 30076. (770)664-6466. Fax: (770)664-6465. E-mail: tboc@atlantalifemag.com. Website: www.atlantalifemag.com. **Contact:** Thomas Boc, editor-in-chief. **50% freelance written**. Bi-monthly magazine. "We are an upscale lifestyle bi-monthly magazine that covers north metro Atlanta. We cover a variety of topics, including sports, fashion, travel, health, finances, home design, etc." Estab. 2006. Byline given. Pays on acceptance. Editorial lead time 2 months. Submit seasonal material 4 months in advance. Accepts queries by e-mail. Past 12 issues may be viewed online. Guidelines free.

Nonfiction Needs essays, expose, general interest, historical, how-to, humor, inspirational, interview, new product, personal experience, travel. **Buys 35 mss/year.** Query with published clips. Length: 750-2,000 words. **Pays 25-75¢/word.**

Photos Contact: Contact Natalie Zieky, Creative Director. State availability of or send photos. Captions, identification of subjects, model releases required. Reviews GIF/JPEG files. Negotiates payment individually. Buys one time rights.

Columns/Departments Travel; Health/Medical; Sports; Fashion, all 750-1,100 words. Also, Mountain & Beach Life, 750-1,200 words. Query with published clips.

Tips "Submit previously published samples. Have high resolution photo support for your article if possible."

$$$$ ATLANTA MAGAZINE

260 Peachtree St., Suite 300, Atlanta GA 30303. (404)527-5500. Fax: (404)527-5575. Website: www.atlantamagazine.com. The magazine's mission is to engage our community through provacative writing, authoritative reporting, superlative design that illuminates the people, trends, and events that define our city. Circ. 69,000. Byline given. Pays on acceptance. Buys first North American serial rights. Accepts queries by mail. Responds in 3 months to queries. Sample copy available online.

- Almost all content staff written except fiction.

Nonfiction *Atlanta* magazine articulates the special nature of Atlanta and appeals to an audience that wants to understand and celebrate the uniqueness of the city. Needs general interest, interview, travel. **Buys 15-20 mss/year.** Query with published clips. Length: 250-5,000 words. **Pays $200-2,000.**

Fiction Need short stories for annual reading issue (Summer). We prefer all fiction to be by Georgia writers and/or have a Georgia/Southern theme. Length: 1,500-5,000 words.

Tips It's *Atlanta* magazine. If your idea isn't about Atlanta, we're not interested.

$$ ATLANTA TRIBUNE: THE MAGAZINE

875 Old Roswell Rd, Suite C-100, Roswell GA 30076. (770)587-0501. Fax: (770)642-6501. Website: www.atlantatribune.com. **30% freelance written**. Monthly magazine covering African-American business, careers, technology, wealth-building, politics, and education. The *Atlanta Tribune* is written for Atlanta's black executives, professionals and entrepreneurs with a primary focus of business, careers, technology, wealth-building, politics, and education. Our publication serves as an advisor that offers helpful information and direction to the black entrepreneur. Estab. 1987. Circ. 30,000. Byline given. Pays on publication. Offers 10% kill fee. Buys electronic rights, buys all rights. Editorial lead time 3 months. Submit seasonal material 4 months in advance. Accepts queries by e-mail. Responds in 6 weeks to queries. Sample copy online or mail a request. Guidelines available online.

Nonfiction Our special sections include Black History; Real Estate; Scholarship Roundup. Needs book excerpts, how-to, business, careers, technology, interview, new product, opinion, technical. **Buys 100 mss/year.** Query with published clips. Length: 1,400-2,500 words. **Pays $250-600.**

Photos State availability. Identification of subjects, model releases required. Reviews 21/4x21/4 transparencies. Negotiates payment individually. Buys one time rights.

Columns/Departments Business; Careers; Technology; Wealth-Building; Politics and Education; all 400-600 words. 100 Query with published clips. **Pays $100-200.**

Tips Send a well-written, convincing query by e-mail that demonstrates that you have thoroughly read previous issues and reviewed our online writer's guidelines.

$ FLAGPOLE MAGAZINE

P.O. Box 1027, Athens GA 30603. (706)549-9523. Fax: (706)548-8981. E-mail: editor@flagpole.com. Website: www.flagpole.com. **75% freelance written**. Local alternative weekly with a special emphasis on popular (and unpopular) music. Will consider stories on national, international musicians, authors, politicians, etc., even if they don't have a local or regional news peg. However, those stories should be original and irreverent enough to justify inclusion. Of course, local/Southern news/feature stories are best. We like reporting and storytelling more than opinion pieces. Estab. 1987. Circ. 16,000. Byline given. Pays on publication. No kill fee. Publishes ms an average of 1 month after acceptance. Makes work-for-hire assignments. Editorial lead time 2 months. Submit seasonal material 2 months in advance. Responds in 2 weeks to queries. Responds in 1 month to mss. Sample copy online.

Nonfiction Needs book excerpts, essays, expose, interview, new product, personal experience. **Buys 50 mss/year.** Query by e-mail Length: 600-2,000 words.

Reprints Send tearsheet, photocopy or typed ms with rights for sale noted and information about when and where the material previously appeared.

Photos State availability. Captions required. Reviews prints. Negotiates payment individually Buys one time rights.

Tips Read our publication online before querying, but don't feel limited by what you see. We can't afford to pay much, so we're open to young/inexperienced writer-journalists looking for clips. Fresh, funny/insightful voices make us happiest, as does reportage over opinion. If you've ever succumbed to the temptation to call a pop record `ethereal' we probably won't bother with your music journalism. No faxed submissions, please.

$$ GEORGIA BACKROADS

Legacy Communications, Inc., P.O. Box 585, Armuchee GA 30105. E-mail: info@georgiabackroads.com. Website: www.georgiahistory.ws. **70% freelance written**. Quarterly magazine for readers interested in travel, history, and lifestyles in Georgia. Estab. 1984. Circ. 18,861. Byline given. Pays on publication. Offers 25% kill fee. Publishes ms an average of 5 months after acceptance. Buys Usually buys all rights. Rights negotiable. rights. Editorial lead time 3 months. Submit seasonal material 6 months in advance. Accepts queries by mail, e-mail, fax. Sample copy for 9 × 12 SAE and 8 first-class stamps, or online. Guidelines for #10 SASE.

Nonfiction Needs historical, how-to, survival techniques; mountain living; do-it-yourself home construction and repairs, etc., interview, celebrity, personal experience, anything unique or unusual pertaining to Georgia history, photo feature, any subject of a historic nature which can be photographed in a seasonal context, i.e., old mill with brilliant yellow jonquils in foreground, travel, subjects highlighting travel opportunities in north Georgia. Query with published clips. **Pays $75-350.**

Photos Send photos. Captions, identification of subjects, model releases required. Reviews contact sheets, transparencies. Negotiates payment individually. Rights negotiable.

Fiction Needs novel concepts.

Tips Good photography is crucial to acceptance of all articles. Send written queries then *wait* for a response. *No telephone calls, please.* The most useful material involves a first-person experience of an individual who has explored a historic site or scenic locale and *interviewed* a person or persons who were involved with or have first-hand knowledge of a historic site/event. Interviews and quotations are crucial. Articles should be told in writer's own words.

$$ GEORGIA MAGAZINE

Georgia Electric Membership Corp., P.O. Box 1707, Tucker GA 30085. (770)270-6951. E-mail: aorowski@georgiaemc.com. Website: www.georgiamagazine.org. **50% freelance written.** We are a monthly magazine for and about Georgians, with a friendly, conversational tone and human interest topics. Estab. 1945. Circ. 460,000. Byline given. Pays on publication. No kill fee. Publishes ms an average of 4 months after acceptance. Buys first North American serial rights, buys electronic rights. Editorial lead time 2 months. Submit seasonal material 6 months in advance. Accepts simultaneous submissions. Responds in 1 month to subjects of interest. Sample copy for $2. Guidelines for #10 SASE.

Nonfiction Needs general interest, Georgia-focused, historical, how-to, in the home and garden, humor, inspirational, interview, photo feature, travel. **Buys 24 mss/year.** Query with published clips. 800-1,000 words; 500 words for smaller features and departments. **Pays $150-500.**

Photos State availability. Identification of subjects, model releases required. Reviews contact sheets, transparencies, prints. Negotiates payment individually. Buys one time rights.

$$ KNOW ATLANTA MAGAZINE

New South Publishing, 450 Northride Pkwy., Suite 202, Atlanta GA 30350. (770)650-1102. Fax: (770)650-2848. E-mail: editor1@knowatlanta.com. Website: www.knowatlanta.com. **80% freelance written.** Quarterly magazine covering the Atlanta area. "Our articles offer information on Atlanta that would be useful to newcomers—homes, schools, hospitals, fun things to do, anything that makes their move more comfortable." Estab. 1986. Circ. 192,000. Byline given. Pays on publication. Offers 100% kill fee. Buys first North American serial rights. Editorial lead time 2 months. Submit seasonal material 2 months in advance. Accepts queries by mail, e-mail, fax. Accepts previously published material. Sample copy free.

Nonfiction Needs general interest, how-to, relocate, interview, personal experience, photo feature. No fiction. **Buys 20 mss/year.** Query with clips. Length: 800-1,500 words. **Pays $100-500 for assigned articles. Pays $100-300 for unsolicited articles.**

Photos Send photos. with submission, if available. Captions, identification of subjects required. Reviews contact sheets. Negotiates payment individually. Buys one time rights.

THE PIEDMONT REVIEW

A review of Atlanta's finest people, places, things, P.O. Box 12047, Atlanta GA 30355. E-mail: mneiman@piedmontreview.com. Website: piedmontreview.com. Monthly magazine covering local business, dining, cultural and charity events, fashion, home and garden features, art reviews, travel and various personal success stories. *The Piedmont Review* is one of Atlanta's most popular lifestyle magazines. Accepts queries by e-mail.

Nonfiction Needs general interest, interview, new product, opinion, personal experience. Query with published clips.

$$ POINTS NORTH MAGAZINE

Serving Atlanta's Stylish Northside, All Points Interactive Media Corp., 568 Peachtree Pkwy., Cumming GA 30041-6820. (770)844-0969. Fax: (770)844-0968. E-mail: julie@ptsnorth.com. Website: www.ptsnorth.com. **15% freelance written**. Monthly magazine covering lifestyle (regional). *Points North* is a first-class lifestyle magazine for affluent residents of suburban communities in north metro Atlanta. Estab. 2000. Circ. 81,000. Byline given. Pays on publication. Offers negotiable (for assigned articles only) kill fee. Publishes ms an average of 3 months after acceptance. Buys electronic rights, buys first serial (in the Southeast with a 6 month moratorium) rights. Editorial lead time 3 months. Submit seasonal material 6 months in advance. Accepts queries by e-mail only. Accepts previously published material. Responds in 6-8 weeks to queries. Responds in 6-8 months to mss. Sample copy for $3.

Nonfiction Contact: Managing Editor. Needs general interest, only topics pertaining to Atlanta area, historical, interview, travel. **Buys 50-60 mss/year.** Query with published clips. Length: 1,200-2,500 words. **Pays $250-500.**

Photos "We do not accept photos until article acceptance. Do not Send photos. with query." State availability. Captions, identification of subjects, model releases required. Reviews slide transparencies, 4x6 prints, GIF/JPEG files. Offers no additional payment for photos accepted with ms.

Tips "The best way for a freelancer, who is interested in being published, is to get a sense of the types of articles we're looking for by reading the magazine."

$$ SAVANNAH MAGAZINE

Morris Publishing Group, P.O. Box 1088, Savannah GA 31402-1088. Fax: (912)525-0611. E-mail: linda.wittish@savannahnow.com. Website: www.savannahmagazine.com. **95% freelance written**. Bimonthly magazine focusing on homes and entertaining covering coastal lifestyle of Savannah and South Carolina area. "*Savannah Magazine* publishes articles about people, places and events of interest to the residents of the greater Savannah areas, as well as coastal Georgia and the South Carolina low country. We strive to provide our readers with information that is both useful and entertaining—written in a lively, readable style." Estab. 1990. Circ. 16,000. Byline given. Pays on publication. Offers 20% kill fee. Publishes ms an average of 2 months after acceptance. Buys first North American serial rights, buys second serial (reprint) rights. Editorial lead time 2 months. Submit seasonal material 4 months in advance. Accepts queries by mail, e-mail, fax. Accepts simultaneous submissions. Responds in 4 weeks to queries. Responds in 6 weeks to mss. Sample copy free. Guidelines by e-mail.

Nonfiction Needs general interest, historical, humor, interview, travel. Does not want fiction or poetry. Query with published clips. Length: 500-750 words. **Pays $250-450.**

Photos Contact: Contact Michelle Karner, art director. State availability. Reviews GIF/JPEG files. Negotiates payment individually. Offers no additional payment for photos accepted with ms. Buys one-time rights.

ST. MARYS MAGAZINE

LowCountry Publishing, 711 Mildred St., St. Marys GA 31558. (912)729-1103. Fax: (912)576-3867. E-mail: info@stmarysmagazine.com. Website: www.stmarysmagazine.com. **50% freelance written**. Semiannual magazine covering coastal Georgia. "We want all positive articles." Estab. 2004. Circ. 20,000. Byline given. Pays on acceptance. Offers kill fee. negotiable Publishes ms an average of 2 months after acceptance. Buys first North American serial rights. Editorial lead time 2 months. Submit seasonal material 2 months in advance. Accepts queries by mail, e-mail. Accepts previously published material. Accepts simultaneous submissions. Responds in 2 weeks to queries. Responds in 1 month to mss. Sample copy free. Guidelines free.

Nonfiction Needs general interest, interview, personal experience, travel, history. Query with published clips. Length: 500-2,000 words. **negotiable for assigned articles.**

Photos Send photos. Captions, identification of subjects, model releases required. Reviews GIF/JPEG fifles. Negotiates payment individually.

Columns/Departments Grape Expectations (wine review), 500 words; Real people (people of coastal Georgia), 1,000 words. 4 mss/year Query with published clips. **TBD**

Fiction Needs historical, slice-of-life vignettes. **Buys 2 mss/year.** Query with published clips. Length: 500-2,000 words. **TBD.**

Tips "Review editorial at website."

Hawaii

$$$ HONOLULU MAGAZINE

PacificBasin Communications, 1000 Bishop St., Suite 405, Honolulu HI 96813. (808)537-9500. Fax: (808)537-6455. E-mail: akamn@honolulumagazine.com; kathrynw@honolulumagazine.com. Website: www.honolulumagazine.com. **Contact:** A. Kam Napier, editor; Kathryn Drury Wagner, executive editor. **Prefers to work with published/established writers.** Monthly magazine covering general interest topics relating to Hawaii residents. Estab. 1888. Circ. 30,000. Byline given. Pays about 30 days after publication. Where appropriate, kill fee of half of assignment fee. Makes work-for-hire assignments. Accepts queries by mail, e-mail. Guidelines available online.

Nonfiction Needs historical, interview, sports, politics, lifestyle trends, all Hawaii-related. "We write for Hawaii residents, so travel articles about Hawaii are not appropriate." Send complete ms. determined when assignments discussed. **Pays $250-1,200.**

Photos Contact: Kristin Lipman, art director. State availability. Captions, identification of subjects, model releases required. Pays $100 for stock, $200 for assigned shot. Package rates also negotiated.

Columns/Departments Length determined when assignments discussed. Query with published clips or send complete ms. **Pays $100-300.**

Idaho

$$ SUN VALLEY MAGAZINE

Valley Publishing, LLC, 111 1st Ave. N. #1M, Meriwether Building, Hailey ID 83333. (208)788-0770. Fax: (208)788-3881. E-mail: edit@sunvalleymag.com. Website: www.sunvalleymag.com. **95% freelance written**. Quarterly magazine covering the lifestyle of the Sun Valley area. *Sun Valley Magazine* presents the lifestyle of the Sun Valley area and the Wood River Valley, including recreation, culture, profiles, history and the arts. Estab. 1973. Circ. 17,000. Byline given. Pays on publication. No kill fee. Publishes ms an average of 5 months after acceptance. Buys first North American serial rights, buys electronic rights. Editorial lead time 1 year. Submit seasonal material 14 months in advance. Accepts queries by mail. Accepts previously published material. Accepts simultaneous submissions. Responds in 5 weeks to queries. Responds in 2 months to mss. Sample copy for $4.95 and $3 postage. Guidelines for #10 SASE.

Nonfiction All articles are focused specifically on Sun Valley, the Wood River Valley and immediate surrounding areas. Needs historical, interview, photo feature, travel. Sun Valley home design and architecture, Spring; Sun Valley weddings/wedding planner, summer. Query with published clips. **Pays $40-500.**

Reprints Only occasionally purchases reprints.

Photos State availability. Identification of subjects, model releases required. Reviews transparencies. Offers $60-275/photo. Buys one-time rights and some electronic rights.

Columns/Departments Conservation issues, winter/summer sports, health & wellness, mountain-related activities and subjects, home (interior design), garden. All columns must have a local slant. Query with published clips. **Pays $40-300.**

Tips Most of our writers are locally based. Also, we rarely take submissions that are not specifically assigned, with the exception of fiction. However, we always appreciate queries.

Illinois

$$$$ CHICAGO MAGAZINE

435 N. Michigan Ave., Suite 1100, Chicago IL 60611. (312)222-8999. E-mail: stritsch@chicagomag.com. Website: www.chicagomag.com. Richard Babcock, ed. **Contact:** Shane Tritsch, man. ed. **50% freelance written. Prefers to work with published/established writers.** Monthly magazine for an audience which is 95% from Chicago area; 90% college educated; upper income, overriding interests in the arts, politics, dining, good life in the city and suburbs. Most are in 25-50 age bracket, well-read and articulate. "Produced by the city's best magazine editors and writers, Chicago Magazine is the definitive voice on top dining, entertainment, shopping and real estate in the region. It also offers provocative narrative stories and topical features that have won numerous awards. Chicago Magazine reaches 1.5 million readers and is published by Tribune Company." Estab. 1968. Circ. 182,000. Pays on acceptance. No kill fee. Publishes ms an average of 3 months after acceptance. Buys first rights. Submit seasonal material 4 months in advance. Accepts queries by mail, e-mail. Responds in 1 month to queries. For sample copy, send $3 to Circulation Dept. Guidelines for #10 SASE.

Nonfiction On themes relating to the quality of life in Chicago: Past, present, and future. Writers should have a general awareness that the readers will be concerned, influential, longtime Chicagoans. We generally publish material too comprehensive for daily newspapers. Needs expose, humor, personal experience, think pieces, profiles, spot news, historical articles. Does not want anything about events outside the city or profiles on people who no longer live in the city. **Buys 100 mss/year.** Query; indicate specifics, knowledge of city and market, and demonstrable access to sources. Length: 200-6,000 words. **Pays $100-3,000 and up.**
Photos Usually assigned separately, not acquired from writers. Reviews 35mm transparencies, color and b&w glossy prints.
Tips Submit detailed queries, be business-like, and avoid cliché ideas.

$$$$ CHICAGO READER

Chicago's Free Weekly, Chicago Reader, Inc., 11 E. Illinois St., Chicago IL 60611. (312)828-0350. Fax: (312)828-9926. E-mail: mail@chicagoreader.com. Website: www.chicagoreader.com. **50% freelance written**. Weekly Alternative tabloid for Chicago. Estab. 1971. Circ. 120,000. Byline given. Pays on publication. Occasional kill fee. Publishes ms an average of 2 weeks after acceptance. Buys one-time rights. Editorial lead time up to 6 months. Accepts queries by mail, e-mail, fax. Accepts simultaneous submissions. Responds if interested. Sample copy free. Writer's guidelines free or online
Nonfiction Magazine-style features; also book excerpts, essays, humor, interview/profile, opinion, personal experience, photo feature. **Buys 500 mss/year.** Send complete ms. Length: 500-50,000 words. **Pays $100-3,000.**
Reprints Occasionally accepts previously published submissions.
Columns/Departments Local color, 500-2,500 words; arts and entertainment reviews, up to 1,200 words.
Tips Our greatest need is for full-length magazine-style feature stories on Chicago topics. We're *not* looking for: hard news (What the Mayor Said About the Schools Yesterday); commentary and opinion (What I Think About What the Mayor Said About the Schools Yesterday); poetry. We are not particularly interested in stories of national (as opposed to local) scope, or in celebrity for celebrity's sake (â ¡ la *Rolling Stone, Interview*, etc.). More than half the articles published in the *Reader* each week come from freelancers, and once or twice a month we publish one that's come in `over the transom'—from a writer we've never heard of and may never hear from again. We think that keeping the *Reader* open to the greatest possible number of contributors makes a fresher, less predictable, more interesting paper. We not only publish unsolicited freelance writing, we depend on it. Our last issue in December is dedicated to original fiction.

$$ CHICAGO SCENE MAGAZINE

233 E. Erie, Suite 603, Chicago IL 60611. Fax: (312)587-7397. E-mail: e-mail@chicago-scene.com. Website: www.chicago-scene.com. **95% freelance written**. Monthly magazine covering dining, nightlife, travel, beauty, entertainment, fitness, style, drinks. *Chicago Scene Magazine* is the premier news and entertainment publication for Chicago's young professional. Estab. 2001. Byline given. Pays on publication. No kill fee. Publishes ms an average of 2 months after acceptance. Buys first North American serial rights. Submit seasonal material 3 months in advance. Accepts queries by e-mail. Sample copy available online. Guidelines free.
Nonfiction Needs how-to, interview, new product, travel. Does not want personal experiences, essays, technical. Query with published clips. Length: 600-2,400 words. **Pays $25-250.**
Columns/Departments Beauty, 840 words; Dining, 1,260-1,680 words; Drinks, 1,260-1,680 words; Fitness, 420-630 words; Travel, 1,260-1,680 words; Nightlife, 1,050-1,680 words; Personal Style, 420 words. Query with published clips. **Pays $25-250.**

$ ILLINOIS ENTERTAINER

4223 W. Lake Street, Suite 420, Chicago IL 60624. (773)533-9333. Fax: (312)922-9341. E-mail: ieeditors@aol.com. Website: www.illinoisentertainer.com. **80% freelance written**. Monthly free magazine covering popular and alternative music, as well as other entertainment: film, media. Estab. 1974. Circ. 55,000. Byline given. Pays on publication. Offers 50% kill fee. Publishes ms an average of 2 months after acceptance. Buys first North American serial rights. Editorial lead time 2 months. Submit seasonal material 2 months in advance. Accepts queries by mail. Accepts simultaneous submissions. Responds in 2 months to queries. Sample copy for $5.
Nonfiction Needs expose, how-to, humor, interview, new product, reviews. No personal, confessional, inspirational articles. **Buys 75 mss/year.** Query with published clips. Length: 600-2,600 words. **Pays $15-160.**

Reprints Send typed manuscript with rights for sale noted and information about when and where the material previously appeared. Pays 100% of amount paid for an original article.
Photos Send photos. Captions, identification of subjects, model releases required. Reviews contact sheets, transparencies, 5 × 7 prints. Offers $20-200/photo. Buys one time rights.
Columns/Departments Spins (LP reviews), 100-400 words. 200-300 Query with published clips. **Pays $8-25.**
Tips Send clips, résumé, etc. and be patient. Also, sending queries that show you've seen our magazine and have a feel for it greatly increases your publication chances. Don't send unsolicited material. No e-mail solicitations or queries of any kind.

$ $ NEWCITY

Chicago's News and Arts Weekly, New City Communications, Inc., 770 N. Halsted, Chicago IL 60622. (312)243-8786. Fax: (312)243-8802. Website: www.newcitychicago.com. **50% freelance written**. Weekly magazine. Estab. 1986. Circ. 50,000. Byline given. Pays 2-12 months after publication. Offers kill fee. Offers 20% kill fee in certain cases. Publishes ms an average of 1 month after acceptance. Buys first rights and non-exclusive electronic rights. Editorial lead time 2 months. Submit seasonal material 2 months in advance. Responds in 1 month to mss. Sample copy for $3. For contact and guidelines, see: http://newcitynetwork.com/editorialart/contributing-to-newcity-guidelines-for-writers-artists-and-photographers/
Nonfiction Needs essays, exposè, general interest, interview, personal experience, travel, related to traveling from Chicago and other issues particularly affecting travelers from this area, service. **Buys 100 mss/year.** Query by e-mail only Length: 100-4,000 words. **Pays $10-200.** Rarely
Photos State availability. Captions, identification of subjects, model releases required. Reviews contact sheets. Buys one-time rights.
Columns/Departments Lit (literary supplement), 300-2,000 words; Music, Film, Arts (arts criticism), 150-800 words; Chow (food writing), 300-2,000 words. 50 Query by e-mail **Pays $15-300.**
Tips "E-mail a solid, sharply written query that has something to do with what our magazine publishes."

$ $ NORTHWEST QUARTERLY MAGAZINE

Old Northwest Territory, Hughes Media Inc., 728 N. Prospect St., Rockford IL 61101. Fax: (815)316-2301. E-mail: janine@northwestquarterly.com. Website: www.northwestquarterly.com. **80% freelance written**. Quarterly magazine covering regional lifestyle of Northern Illinois and Southern Wisconsin, and also Kane and McHenry counties (Chicago collar counties), highlighting strengths of living and doing business in the area. Estab. 2004. Circ. 42,000. Byline given. Pays on publication. Publishes ms an average of 4-6 months after acceptance. Makes work-for-hire assignments. Editorial lead time 6 months. Submit seasonal material 6 months in advance. Accepts queries by mail, e-mail. Responds in 2 weeks to queries. Responds in 2 months to mss. Sample copy and guidelines by e-mail.
Nonfiction Needs historical, interview, photo feature, regional features. Does not want opinion, fiction, anything unrelated to our geographic region. **Buys 150 mss/year.** Query. Length: 700-2,500 words. **Pays $25-500.**
Photos State availability. Captions required. Reviews GIF/JPEG files. Negotiates payment individually. Buys one-time rights.
Columns/Departments Health & Fitness, 1,000-2,000 words; Home & Garden, 1,500 words; Destinations & Recreation, 1,000-2,000 words; Environment & Nature, 2,000-3,000 words. 120 Query. **Pays $100-500.**
Tips "Any interesting, well-documented feature relating to the 15-county area we cover may be considered. Nature, history, geography, culture and destinations are favorite themes."

$ $ OUTDOOR ILLINOIS

Illinois Department of Natural Resources, P.O. Box 19225, Dept. NL, Springfield IL 62794-9225. (217)785-4193. E-mail: dnr.editor@illinois.gov. Website: www.dnr.state.il.us/oi. **25% freelance written**. Monthly magazine covering Illinois cultural and natural resources. *Outdoor Illinois* promotes outdoor activities, Illinois State parks, Illinois natural and cultural resources. Estab. 1973. Circ. 30,000. Byline given. Pays on acceptance. Buys one-time rights. Editorial lead time 4 months. Submit seasonal material 1 year in advance. Accepts queries by mail, e-mail. Responds in 2 weeks to queries. Sample copy free. Guidelines by e-mail.
Nonfiction Needs historical, how-to, humor, interview, photo feature, travel. Does not want first person unless truly has something to say. Query with published clips. Length: 350-1,500 words. **Pays $100-250.**

Photos Contact: Contact Adele Hodde, photography manager. Captions, identification of subjects, model releases required. Reviews contact sheets, GIF/JPEG files. Negotiates payment individually. Buys one time rights.
Tips "Write with an Illinois slant to encourage participation in outdoor activities/events."

$$ WEST SUBURBAN LIVING

C2 Publishing, Inc., P.O. Box 111, Elmhurst IL 60126. (630)834-4995. Fax: (630)834-4996. Website: www.westsuburbanliving.net. **Contact:** Chuck Cozette, Editor. **80% freelance written**. Bimonthly magazine focusing on the western suburbs of Chicago. Estab. 1996. Circ. 25,000. Byline given. Pays on publication. Publishes ms an average of 2-4 months after acceptance. Buys first rights, buys electronic rights. Accepts queries by mail, e-mail, fax. Sample copy available online.
Nonfiction Needs general interest, how-to, travel. "Does not want anything that does not have an angle or tie-in to the area we cover—Chicago's western suburbs." **Buys 15 mss/year. Pays $100-500.**
Photos State availability. Model releases required. Offers $50-700/photo; negotiates payment individually.

Indiana

$$ EVANSVILLE LIVING

Tucker Publishing Group, 100 NW Second St., Suite 220, Evansville IN 47708. (812)426-2115. Fax: (812)426-2134. Website: www.evansvilleliving.com. **80-100% freelance written**. Bimonthly magazine covering Evansville, Indiana, and the greater area. *Evansville Living* is the only full-color, glossy, 100+ page city magazine for the Evansville, Indiana, area. Regular departments include: Home Style, Garden Style, Day Tripping, Sporting Life, and Local Flavor (menus). Estab. 2000. Circ. 50,000. Byline given. Pays on acceptance. No kill fee. Publishes ms an average of 3 months after acceptance. Buys all rights. Editorial lead time 6 months. Submit seasonal material 6 months in advance. Accepts queries by mail, e-mail, fax. Accepts previously published material. Sample copy for $5 or online. Guidelines for free or by e-mail.
Nonfiction Needs essays, general interest, historical, photo feature, travel. **Buys 60-80 mss/year.** Query with published clips. Length: 200-2,000 words. **Pays $100-300.**
Photos State availability. Captions, identification of subjects required. Reviews contact sheets, negatives, transparencies, prints. Negotiates payment individually Buys all rights.
Columns/Departments Home Style (home); Garden Style (garden); Sporting Life (sports); Local Flavor (menus), all 1,500 words. Query with published clips. **Pays $100-300.**

$$$ INDIANAPOLIS MONTHLY

Emmis Publishing Corp., 1 Emmis Plaza, 40 Monument Circle, Suite 100, Indianapolis IN 46204. (317)237-9288. Website: www.indianapolismonthly.com. **30% freelance written. Prefers to work with published/established writers.** "*Indianapolis Monthly* attracts and enlightens its upscale, well-educated readership with bright, lively editorial on subjects ranging from personalities to social issues, fashion to food. Its diverse content and attention to service make it the ultimate source by which the Indianapolis area lives." Estab. 1977. Circ. 45,000. Byline given. Pays on publication. Offers kill fee. Offers negotiable kill fee. Publishes ms an average of 2 months after acceptance. Buys first North American serial rights, buys one-time rights. Editorial lead time 3 months. Submit seasonal material 3 months in advance. Accepts queries by mail, e-mail. Responds in 6 weeks to queries. Sample copy for $6.10.

- "This magazine is using more first-person essays, but they must have a strong Indianapolis or Indiana tie. It will consider nonfiction book excerpts of material relevant to its readers."

Nonfiction Must have a strong Indianapolis or Indiana angle. Needs book excerpts, by Indiana authors or with strong Indiana ties, essays, expose, general interest, interview, photo feature. No poetry, fiction, or domestic humor; no How Indy Has Changed Since I Left Town, An Outsider's View of the 500, or generic material with no or little tie to Indianapolis/Indiana. **Buys 35 mss/year.** Query by mail with published clips Length: 200-3,000 words. **Pays $50-1,000.**
Photos State availability. Captions, identification of subjects, model releases required. Negotiates payment individually. Buys one time rights.
Tips "Our standards are simultaneously broad and narrow: Broad in that we're a general interest magazine spanning a wide spectrum of topics, narrow in that we buy only stories with a heavy emphasis on Indianapolis (and, to a lesser extent, Indiana). Simply inserting an Indy-oriented paragraph into a generic national article won't get it: All stories must pertain primarily to things Hoosier. Once you've cleared that hurdle, however, it's a wide-open field. We've done features on national celebrities—Indianapolis

native David Letterman and *Mir* astronaut David Wolf of Indianapolis, to name 2—and we've published 2-paragraph items on such quirky topics as an Indiana gardening supply house that sells insects by mail. Query with clips showing lively writing and solid reporting. No phone queries, please."

$$ NORTHERN INDIANA LAKES MAGAZINE

1415 W. Coliseum Blvd., Fort Wayne IN 46808. (260)484-0546. Fax: (260)469-0454. E-mail: editor@nilakes.com. Website: www.nilakes.com. **Contact:** Sue Rawlinson, publisher/editor-in-chief. Bimonthly magazine that defines lake living at its best. "*Northern Indiana LAKES Magazine* is the official publication for the good life in northern Indiana. The LAKES country market area is essentially defined as 20 northern Indiana counties: Adams, Allen, DeKalb, Elkhart, Huntington, Jasper, Kosciusko, LaGrange, Lake, LaPorte, Marshall, Newton, Noble, Porter, Pulaski, St. Joseph, Starke, Steuben, Wells and Whitley." Byline given. Pays 2-3 weeks after accepting completed article. Buys one-time rights. Accepts queries by mail. Guidelines by e-mail.

Nonfiction "Our articles take a positive, practical approach to helping readers enjoy and enhance their lifestyle, whether as weekend, seasonal or year-round lake residents. We are not a 'city' magazine that happens to include lake articles; rather, we strive to present articles on issues and subjects unique to the northern Indiana lakes area that cannot be found in any other publication. Our writers help us achieve that goal." Needs general interest, humor, interview, travel. Does not want "personal essays, stories about your vacation, celebrity profiles (with rare exceptions), routine pieces on familiar destinations, completed manuscripts, previously published works." Query with published clips. **Pays 10-50¢/word.**

Tips "Freelance articles are written on assignment, so sending clips and a cover letter explaining your qualifications as a potential writer for *Northern Indiana LAKES* is the best approach. This is not a publication for beginners; please send your best works."

Iowa

$$ THE IOWAN

Pioneer Communications, Inc., 218 6th Ave., Suite 610, Des Moines IA 50309. Fax: (515)282-0125. E-mail: editor@iowan.com. Website: www.iowan.com. **75% freelance written**. Bimonthly magazine covering the state of Iowa. Our mission statement is: To celebrate the people and communities, the history and traditions, and the culture and events of Iowa that make our readers proud of our state. Estab. 1952. Circ. 25,000. Byline given. Pays on acceptance. Offers $100 kill fee. Publishes ms an average of 3 months after acceptance. Buys first rights. Editorial lead time 8-12 months. Submit seasonal material 6 months in advance. Accepts queries by mail, e-mail. Responds to queries received twice/year. Sample copy for $4.50 + s&h.

Nonfiction Needs book excerpts, essays, general interest, historical, interview, photo feature, travel. **Buys 30 mss/year.** Query with published clips. Length: 1,000-2,000 words. **Pays $250-450.**

Photos Send photos. Captions, identification of subjects, model releases required. Reviews contact sheets, GIF/JPEG files (8 × 10 at 300 dpi min). Negotiates payment individually, according to space rates. Buys one time rights.

Columns/Departments Last Word (essay), 800 words. 6 Query with published clips. **Pays $100.**

Tips Must have submissions in writing, either via e-mail or snail mail. Submitting published clips is preferred.

Kansas

$$ KANSAS!

Kansas Department of Commerce, 1000 SW Jackson St., Suite 100, Topeka KS 66612-1354. (785)296-3479. Fax: (785)296-6988. Website: www.kansmag.com. **90% freelance written**. Quarterly magazine emphasizing Kansas travel attractions and events. Estab. 1945. Circ. 38,000. Byline given. Pays on acceptance. No kill fee. Publishes ms an average of 1 year after acceptance. Buys one-time rights. Submit seasonal material 8 months in advance. Accepts queries by mail. Responds in 2 months to queries. Guidelines available online.

Nonfiction Material must be Kansas-oriented and have good potential for color photographs. The focus is on travel with articles about places and events that can be enjoyed by the general public and experimental travel. In other words, events must be open to the public, places also. Query letter should clearly outline story. We are especially interested in Kansas freelancers who can supply their own quality photos. Needs general interest, photo feature, travel. Query by mail. Length: 750-1,250 words. **Pays $200-350.** Pays mileage only for writers on assignment within the State of Kansas.

Photos We are a full-color photo/manuscript publication. Send photos. (original transparencies only or CD with images available in high resolution) with query. Captions required. Pays $50-75 (generally included in ms rate) for 35mm or larger format transparencies.

Tips History and nostalgia or essay stories do not fit into our format because they can't be illustrated well with color photos. Submit a query letter describing 1 appropriate idea with outline for possible article and suggestions for photos. Do not send unsolicited manuscripts.

Kentucky

$ BACK HOME IN KENTUCKY

Back Home In Kentucky, Inc., P.O. Box 1555, Shelbyville KY 40066. (502)633-7766. E-mail: bilmatt@aol.com. **Contact:** Bill Mitchell, publisher. **50% freelance written**. Bimonthly magazine covering Kentucky heritage, people, places, events. We reach Kentuckians and `displaced' Kentuckians living outside the state. Estab. 1977. Circ. 8,000. Byline given. Pays on publication. No kill fee. Publishes ms an average of 4-6 months after acceptance. Buys first North American serial rights. Submit seasonal material 6 months in advance. Responds in 2 months to queries. Sample copy for $3 and 9 × 12 SAE with $1.23 postage affixed. Guidelines for #10 SASE.

- Interested in profiles of Kentucky people and places, especially historic interest.

Nonfiction Needs historical, Kentucky-related eras or profiles, interview, Kentucky residents or natives, photo feature, Kentucky places and events, travel, unusual/little-known Kentucky places, profiles (Kentucky cooks, gardeners, and craftspersons), memories (Kentucky related). No inspirational or religion. No how-to articles. **Buys 20-25 mss/year.** Send complete ms. Length: 500-2,000 words. **Pays $50-200 for assigned articles. Pays $50-100 for unsolicited articles.**

Photos Looking for digital (high resolution) of Kentucky places of interet. Pays $25-$100 per photo. Photo credits given. For inside photos, Send photos. with submission. Identification of subjects, model releases required. Reviews transparencies, 4x6 prints. Occasionally offers additional payment for photos accepted with ms. Rights purchased depends on situation.

Columns/Departments Travel, history, profile, and cookbooks (all Kentucky related), 500-2000 words. 10-12 Query with published clips. **Pays $25-50.**

Tips "We work mostly with unpublished or emerging writers who have a feel for Kentucky's people, places, and events. Areas most open are little known places in Kentucky, unusual history, and profiles of interesting Kentuckians, and Kentuckians with unusual hobbies or crafts."

FORT MITCHELL LIVING

Community Publications, Inc., 179 Fairfield Ave., Bellevue KY 41073. (859)291-1412. Fax: (859)291-1417. E-mail: fortmitchell@livingmagazines.com. Website: www.livingmagazines.com. **Contact:** Editor. Monthly magazine covering Fort Mitchell community. Estab. 1983. Circ. 4,700. Byline given. Pays on publication. Buys all rights. Editorial lead time 2 months. Submit seasonal material 3 months in advance. Guidelines by e-mail.

Nonfiction News and feature stories cover the communities in the Fort Mitchell reading area. For information regarding articles in the magazine contact the editor. Needs book excerpts, essays, expose, general interest, historical, humor, inspirational, interview, new product, personal experience, photo feature, travel. Does not want anything unrelated to Fort Mitchell. Query.

Photos State availability. Captions, identification of subjects, model releases required. Reviews contact sheets, negatives, transparencies, prints, GIF/JPEG files. Negotiates payment individually. Buys all rights.

Columns/Departments Financial; Artistic (reviews, etc.); Historic; Food. Query.

Fiction Needs adventure, historical, humorous, mainstream, slice-of-life vignettes of life. Query.

Poetry Needs free verse, light verse, traditional. Please query.

FORT THOMAS LIVING

Community Publications, Inc., 179 Fairfield Ave., Bellevue KY 41073. (859)291-1412. Fax: (859)291-1417. E-mail: fortthomas@livingmagazines.com. Website: www.livingmagazines.com. **Contact:** Linda Johnson, ed. Monthly magazine covering Fort Thomas community. "Magazine focuses upon people living and working in Fort Thomas and promoting acitvities of interest to this community." Estab. 1977. Circ. 4,400. Byline given. Pays on publication. Buys all rights. Editorial lead time 2 months. Submit seasonal material 3 months in advance. Accepts queries by mail, e-mail, fax. Guidelines by e-mail.

Nonfiction Needs book excerpts, essays, expose, general interest, historical, humor, inspirational, interview, new product, personal experience, photo feature, travel. Does not want any material unrelated to Fort Thomas, Kentucky. Query.
Photos State availability. Captions, identification of subjects, model releases required. Reviews contact sheets, negatives, transparencies, prints, GIF/JPEG files. Negotiates payment individually. Buys all rights.
Columns/Departments Financial; Artistic (reviews, etc.); Historic; Food. Query.
Fiction Needs adventure, historical, humorous, mainstream, slice-of-life vignettes. Query.
Poetry Needs free verse, light verse, traditional. Please query.

$ $ KENTUCKY LIVING

Kentucky Association of Electric Co-Ops, P.O. Box 32170, Louisville KY 40232. (502)451-2430. Fax: (502)459-1611. E-mail: e-mail@kentuckyliving.com. Website: www.kentuckyliving.com. **Mostly freelance written. Prefers to work with published/established writers**. Monthly Feature magazine primarily for Kentucky residents. Estab. 1948. Circ. 500,000. Byline given. Pays on acceptance. No kill fee. Publishes ms an average of 12 months after acceptance. Full rights for Kentucky. Submit seasonal material at least 6 months in advance. Accepts previously published material. Accepts simultaneous submissions. Responds in 1 month to queries. Sample copy for sae with 9 × 12 envelope and 4 first-class stamps.
Nonfiction Kentucky-related profiles (people, places or events), recreation, travel, leisure, lifestyle articles, book excerpts. Needs , Emphasis on electric industry and ties to Kentucky's electric co-op areas of readership. **Buys 18-24 mss/year.** Send complete ms. **Pays $75-850.**
Photos State availability of or send photos.. Identification of subjects required. Reviews photo efiles at online link or sent on CD. Payment for photos included in payment for ms.
Tips "The quality of writing and reporting (factual, objective, thorough) is considered in setting payment price. We prefer general interest pieces filled with quotes and anecdotes. Avoid boosterism. Well-researched, well-written feature articles are preferred. All articles must have a strong Kentucky connection."

$ $ KENTUCKY MONTHLY

P.O.Box 559, Frankfort KY 40602. (502)227-0053. Fax: (502)227-5009. E-mail: amanda@kentuckymonthly.com or steve@kentuckymonthly.com. Website: www.kentuckymonthly.com. **75% freelance written**. Monthly magazine. "We publish stories about Kentucky and by Kentuckians, including those who live elsewhere." Estab. 1998. Circ. 40,000. Byline given. Pays within 3 months of publication. No kill fee. Publishes ms an average of 3 months after acceptance. Buys first North American serial rights. Editorial lead time 3 months. Submit seasonal material 4 months in advance. Accepts queries by mail, e-mail, fax. Accepts simultaneous submissions. Responds in 1 month to queries. Responds in 1 month to mss. Sample copy and writer's guidelines online.
Nonfiction Needs book excerpts, general interest, historical, how-to, humor, interview, photo feature, religious, travel, all with a Kentucky angle. **Buys 60 mss/year.** Query. Length: 300-2,000 words. **Pays $25-350 for assigned articles. Pays $20-100 for unsolicited articles.**
Photos State availability. Captions required. Reviews negatives. Buys all rights.
Fiction Needs adventure, historical, mainstream, novel concepts, all Kentucky-related stories. **Buys 10 mss/year.** Query with published clips. Length: 1,000-5,000 words. **Pays $50-100.**
Tips "Please read the magazine to get the flavor of what we're publishing each month. We accept articles via e-mail, fax, and mail."

Louisiana

$ $ N PRESERVATION IN PRINT

Preservation Resource Center of New Orleans, 923 Tchoupitoulos St., New Orleans LA 70130. (504)581-7032. Fax: (504)636-3073. E-mail: prc@prcno.org. Website: www.prcno.org. **30% freelance written**. Monthly magazine covering preservation. We want articles about interest in the historic architecture of New Orleans. Estab. 1974. Circ. 10,000. Byline given. Pays on acceptance. No kill fee. Publishes ms an average of 1 month after acceptance. Buys all rights. Editorial lead time 1 month. Submit seasonal material 1-2 months in advance. Accepts queries by mail, e-mail, fax, phone. Accepts simultaneous submissions. Sample copy available online Guidelines free
Nonfiction Needs essays, historical, interview, photo feature, technical. **Buys 30 mss/year.** Query. Length: 700-1,000 words. **Pays $100-200 for assigned articles.**

Maine

$ DISCOVER MAINE MAGAZINE

10 Exhcange St., Suite 208, Portland ME 04101. (207)874-7720. Fax: (207)874-7721. E-mail: info@discovermainemagazine.com. **100% freelance written**. Monthly magazine covering Maine history and nostalgia. Sports and hunting/fishing topics are also included. Estab. 1992. Circ. 12,000. Byline given. Pays on publication. No kill fee. Publishes ms an average of 2-3 months after acceptance. Buys one-time rights. Editorial lead time 3 months. Submit seasonal material 3 months in advance. Accepts queries by mail, fax, phone. Accepts previously published material. Accepts simultaneous submissions. Responds in 2 weeks to queries. Responds in 1 month to mss.

Nonfiction Needs historical. Does not want to receive poetry. **Buys 200 mss/year.** Send complete ms. Length: 500-2,000 words. **Pays $20-30**

Photos Send photos. Negotiates payment individually. Buys one time rights.

Tips Call first and talk with the publisher.

Maryland

$ $ BALTIMORE MAGAZINE

Inner Harbor E. 1000 Lancaster St., Suite 400, Baltimore MD 21202. (410)752-4200. Fax: (410)625-0280. Website: www.baltimoremagazine.net. **Contact:** Department Editor. **50-60% freelance written**. Monthly. "Pieces must address an educated, active, affluent reader and must have a very strong Baltimore angle." Estab. 1907. Circ. 70,000. Byline given. Pays within 1 month of publication. Offers kill fee in some cases first rights in all media Submit seasonal material 4 months in advance. Accepts queries by mail, e-mail. Sample copy for $4.45. Guidelines available online.

Nonfiction Needs book excerpts, Baltimore subject or author, essays, expose, general interest, historical, humor, interview, with a Baltimorean, new product, personal experience, photo feature, travel, local and regional to Maryland. "Nothing that lacks a strong Baltimore focus or angle." Query by mail with published clips or send complete ms. Length: 1,600-2,500 words. **Pays 30-40¢/word.**

Columns/Departments "The shorter pieces are the best places to break into the magazine." Hot Shot, Health, Education, Sports, Parenting, Politics. Length: 1,000-2,500 words. Query with published clips.

Tips "Writers who live in the Baltimore area can send résumé and published clips to be considered for first assignment. Must show an understanding of writing that is suitable to an educated magazine reader and show ability to write with authority, describe scenes, help reader experience the subject. Too many writers send us newspaper-style articles. We are seeking: 1) *Human interest features*—strong, even dramatic profiles of Baltimoreans of interest to our readers. 2) *First-person accounts* of experience in Baltimore, or experiences of a Baltimore resident. 3) *Consumer*—according to our editorial needs, and with Baltimore sources. Writers should read/familiarize themselves with style of *Baltimore Magazine* before submitting."

Massachusetts

BOSTON GLOBE MAGAZINE

P.O. Box 55819, Boston MA 02205-5819. (617)929-2000. Website: www.boston.com/magazine. **75% freelance written**. Weekly magazine. Pays on publication. No kill fee. Publishes ms an average of 2 months after acceptance. Buys non exclusive electronic rights. Editorial lead time 2 months. Submit seasonal material 3 months in advance. Sample copy for sae with 9 × 12 envelope and 2 First-Class stamps.

Nonfiction Needs book excerpts, first serial rights only, Q&A, narratives, trend pieces, profiles. Especially interested in medicine, education, sports, relationships, parenting, and the arts. No travelogs or poetry. **Buys up to 100 mss/year.** Query; SASE must be included with ms or queries for return. Length: 1,000-4,000 words.

Photos Purchased with accompanying ms or on assignment. Captions required. Reviews contact sheets. Pays standard rates according to size used.

$ $ CAPE COD LIFE

Cape Cod Life, Inc., 270 Communication Way, Building #6, Hyannis MA 02601. (508)775-9800. Fax: (508)775-9801. Website: www.capecodlife.com. **80% freelance written**. Magazine published 7 times/year focusing on area lifestyle, history and culture, people and places, business and industry, and issues and answers for year-round and summer residents of Cape Cod, Nantucket, and Martha's Vineyard as

well as nonresidents who spend their leisure time here. Circ. 45,000. Byline given. Pays 90 days after acceptance. Offers 20% kill fee. Buys first North American serial rights. Makes work-for-hire assignments. Submit seasonal material 6 months in advance. Accepts queries by mail. Responds in 3 months to queries. Responds in 3 months to mss. Sample copy for $5. Guidelines for #10 SASE.
Nonfiction Needs book excerpts, general interest, historical, interview, photo feature, travel, outdoors, gardening, nautical, nature, arts, antiques. **Buys 20 mss/year.** Query. Length: 800-1,500 words. **Pays $200-400.**
Photos Photo guidelines for #10 SASE. Captions, identification of subjects required. Pays $25-225 Buys first rights with right to reprint
Tips Freelancers submitting *quality* spec articles with a Cape Cod and Islands angle have a good chance at publication. We like to see a wide selection of writer's clips before giving assignments. We also publish *Cape Cod & Islands Home* covering architecture, landscape design, and interior design with a Cape and Islands focus.

$$ CAPE COD MAGAZINE

Rabideau Publishing, P.O. Box 208, Yarmouth Port MA 02765. (508)771-6549. Fax: (508)771-3769. E-mail: editor@capecodmagazine.com. Website: www.capecodmagazine.com. **80% freelance written.** Magazine published 9 times/year covering Cape Cod lifestyle. Estab. 1996. Circ. 16,000. Byline given. Pays 30 days after publication. Offers 25% kill fee. Publishes ms an average of 3 months after acceptance. Buys first North American serial rights, buys electronic rights. Editorial lead time 6 months. Submit seasonal material 1 year in advance. Accepts queries by mail, e-mail. Responds in 3 weeks to queries. Responds in 2 months to mss. Sample copy for $5. Guidelines by e-mail.
Nonfiction Needs book excerpts, essays, general interest, historical, humor, interview, personal experience. Does not want cliched pieces, interviews, and puff features. **Buys 3 mss/year.** Send complete ms. Length: 800-2,500 words. **Pays $300-500 for assigned articles. Pays $100-300 for unsolicited articles.**
Photos State availability of or send photos. Reviews GIF/JPEG files. Negotiates payment individually. Buys one time rights.
Columns/Departments Last Word (personal observations in typical back page format), 700 words. 4 Query with or without published clips or send complete ms. **Pays $150-300.**
Tips Read good magazines. We strive to offer readers the quality they find in good national magazines, so the more informed they are of what good writing is, the better the chance they'll get published in our magazine. Think of art opportunities. Ideas that do not have good art potential are harder to sell than those that do.

$$ CHATHAM MAGAZINE

Rabideau Publishing, 396 Main St., Suite 8, Hyannis MA 02601. (508)771-6549. Fax: (508)771-3769. E-mail: editor@capecodmagazine.com. Website: www.chathammag.com. **80% freelance written.** Annual magazine covering Chatham lifestyle. Estab. 2006. Byline given. Pays 30 days after publication. Offers 25% kill fee. Publishes ms an average of 3 months after acceptance. Buys first North American serial rights, buys electronic rights. Editorial lead time 6 months. Submit seasonal material 1 year in advance. Accepts queries by mail, e-mail. Responds in 3 weeks to queries. Responds in 2 months to mss. Sample copy for $5. Guidelines by e-mail.
Nonfiction Needs book excerpts, essays, general interest, historical, humor, interview, personal experience. Send complete ms. Length: 800-2,500 words. **Pays $300-500 for assigned articles. Pays $100-300 for unsolicited articles.**
Photos State availability of or send photos. Reviews GIF/JPEG files. Negotiates payment individually. Buys one time rights.
Columns/Departments Hooked (fishing issues), 700 words. 4 Query with or without published clips or send complete ms. **Pays $150-300.**
Tips Read good magazines. We strive to offer readers the quality they find in good national magazines, so the more informed they are of what good writing is, the better the chance they'll get published in our magazine. Think of art opportunities. Ideas that do not have good art potential are harder to sell than those that do.

$$ PROVINCETOWN ARTS

Provincetown Arts, Inc., 650 Commercial St., P.O. Box 35, Provincetown MA 02657. (508)487-3167. E-mail: cbusa@comcast.net. Website: www.provincetownarts.org. **90% freelance written.** Annual magazine covering contemporary art and writing. "*Provincetown Arts* focuses broadly on the artists and writers who inhabit or visit the Lower Cape, and seeks to stimulate creative activity and enhance public awareness of the cultural life of the nation's oldest continuous art colony. Drawing upon a 75-year tradition rich in visual art, literature, and theater, *Provincetown Arts* offers a unique blend of interviews, fiction, visual features, reviews, reporting, and poetry." Estab. 1985. Circ. 8,000. Pays on publication. Offers 50% kill fee. Publishes ms an average of 4 months after acceptance. Buys first rights, buys one-time rights, buys second serial (reprint) rights. Editorial lead time 6 months. Submit seasonal material 6 months in advance. Accepts simultaneous submissions. Responds in 3 weeks to queries. Responds in 2 months to mss Sample copy for $10 Guidelines for #10 sase

- "2010 is our 25th anniversary."

Nonfiction Needs book excerpts, essays, humor, interview. **Buys 40 mss/year.** Send complete ms. Length: 1,500-4,000 words. **Pays $150 minimum for assigned articles. Pays $125 minimum for unsolicited articles.**
Photos Send photos. Identification of subjects required. Reviews 8 × 10 prints. Offers $20-$100/photo Buys one time rights.
Fiction Contact: Christopher Busa, editor. Needs mainstream, novel concepts. **Buys 7 mss/year.** Send complete ms. Length: 500-5,000 words. **Pays $75-300.**
Poetry Buys 25 poems/year. Submit maximum 3 poems. **Pays $25-150.**

$$ WORCESTER MAGAZINE

101 Water St., Worcester MA 01604. (508)749-3166. Fax: (508)749-3165. E-mail: mwarshaw@worcestermag.com. Website: www.worcestermag.com. **10% freelance written**. Weekly tabloid emphasizing the central Massachusetts region, especially the city of Worcester. Estab. 1976. Circ. 40,000. Byline given. Pays on publication. No kill fee. Publishes ms an average of 3 weeks after acceptance. Buys all rights. Submit seasonal material 2 months in advance. Accepts queries by mail, e-mail, fax.

- Does not respond to unsolicited material.

Nonfiction We are interested in any piece with a local angle. Needs essays, expose, area government, corporate, general interest, historical, humor, opinion, local, personal experience, photo feature, religious, interview (local). **Buys less than 75 mss/year.** Length: 500-1,500 words. **Pays 10¢/word.**

Michigan

$$$ ANN ARBOR OBSERVER

Ann Arbor Observer Co., 201 E. Catherine, Ann Arbor MI 48104. Fax: (734)769-3375. E-mail: hilton@aaobserver.com. Website: www.arborweb.com. **50% freelance written**. Monthly magazine. "We depend heavily on freelancers and we're always glad to talk to new ones. We look for the intelligence and judgment to fully explore complex people and situations, and the ability to convey what makes them interesting." Estab. 1976. Circ. 60,000. Byline given. Pays on publication. No kill fee. Publishes ms an average of 2 months after acceptance. Accepts queries by mail, e-mail, fax, phone. Responds in 3 weeks to queries. Responds in several months to mss. Sample copy for 12½ × 15 SAE with $3 postage. Guidelines for #10 SASE.
Nonfiction Historical, investigative features, profiles, brief vignettes. Must pertain to Ann Arbor. **Buys 75 mss/year.** Length: 100-2,500 words. **Pays up to $1,000.**
Columns/Departments Up Front (short, interesting tidbits), 150 words. **Pays $100.** Inside Ann Arbor (concise stories), 300-500 words. **Pays $200.** Around Town (unusual, compelling ancedotes), 750-1,500 words. **Pays $150-200.**
Tips "If you have an idea for a story, write a 100-200-word description telling us why the story is interesting. We are open most to intelligent, insightful features about interesting aspects of life in Ann Arbor."

$$ GRAND RAPIDS MAGAZINE

Gemini Publications, 549 Ottawa Ave. NW, Suite 201, Grand Rapids MI 49503-1444. (616)459-4545. Fax: (616)459-4800. E-mail: cvalade@geminipub.com. Website: www.grmag.com. *Grand Rapids* is a general interest life and style magazine designed for those who live in the Grand Rapids metropolitan area or desire to maintain contact with the community. Estab. 1964. Byline given. Pays on publication. No kill fee. Editorial lead time 2 months. Submit seasonal material 2 months in advance. Sample copy for $2 and an SASE with $1.50 postage. Guidelines for #10 SASE.
Nonfiction *Grand Rapids Magazine* is approximately 60 percent service articles—dining guide, calendar, travel, personal finance, humor and reader service sections—and 40 percent topical and issue-oriented editorial that centers on people, politics, problems and trends in the region. In 2003, the editors added a section called 'Design,' which provides a focus on every aspect of the local design community—from

Maya Lin's urban park installation and the new 125-acre sculpture park to architecture and the world's Big Three office furniture manufacturers headquartered here. Query. **Pays $25-500.**

HOUR DETROIT

Hour Media, LLC, 117 W. Third St., Royal Oak MI 48067. (248)691-1800. Website: www.hourdetroit.com. **50% freelance written**. Monthly magazine. "General interest/lifestyle magazine aimed at a middle- to upper-income readership aged 17-70." Estab. 1996. Circ. 45,000. Byline given. Pays on acceptance. Offers 30% kill fee. Publishes ms an average of 2 months after acceptance. Buys first North American serial rights. Editorial lead time 2 months. Submit seasonal material 1 year in advance. Accepts queries by mail. Sample copy for $6.

- "Hour Detroit magazine is metro Detroit's city magazine committed to providing readers with relevant, informative, useful and entertaining coverage of the region and its people."

Nonfiction Needs expose, general interest, historical, interview, new product, photo feature, technical. **Buys 150 mss/year.** Query with published clips. Length: 300-2,500 words.
Photos State availability.

$$ MICHIGAN HISTORY

Michigan Historical Center, Michigan Dept. of History, Arts & Libraries, 702 W. Kalamazoo, Box 30741, Lansing MI 48909-8241. (800)366-3703. Fax: (517)241-4909. E-mail: editor@michigan.gov. Website: www.michiganhistorymagazine.com. **75% freelance written**. Bimonthly magazine We cover Michigan's history, including a wide range of subtopics, such as aviation, agriculture, African Americans, archaeology, business, disasters, economy, engineering marvels, education, geography, government, war, labor, laws, literature, mritime, music, museums, Native Americans, personal profiles, recreation, politics, religion, sports, science and historic travel ideas. Estab. 1917. Circ. 30,000. Byline given. Pays on publication. Publishes ms an average of 6 months after acceptance. Buys one-time rights, buys electronic rights. Editorial lead time 1 year. Submit seasonal material 1 year in advance. Accepts queries by mail, e-mail, phone. Responds in 3 months to queries. Responds in 6 months to mss. Sample copy free. Guidelines free.

Nonfiction Contact: Christine Schwerin, assistant editor. Needs book excerpts, general interest, historical, interview, personal experience, photo feature. Nothing already published, fictional. **Buys 20-24 mss/year.** Send complete ms. Length: 800-3,500 words. **Pays $100-500.**
Photos Contact: Christine Schwerin, assistant editor. Send photos. Identification of subjects, model releases required. Reviews contact sheets, negatives, transparencies, prints, digital photos must be 300 dpi as JPEG or TIFF. Negotiates payment individually. Buys one-time and electronic use rights.
Columns/Departments Columns open to freelancers: Remember the Time (first-person, factual stories, personal experiences that happened in Michigan or to Michiganians-900 words), On This Spot (locations in Michigan where specific, significant historic events have occurred-1,300 words), Back to Basics (simple, basic stories about Michigan's notable personalities, industries or well known events-900 words), History in Your Hometown (accurate, interesting town histories beginning with settlement through modern day, including social, economic, political and religious aspects-1,600 words), The Primary Source (focus on one artifact and its significance to Michigan's history-250 words), Books (send us a review copy of your non-fiction book, must have Michigan or Great Lakes focus). 5 Send complete ms. **Pays $100-400.**
Tips All stories must be well researched, well written, interesting and accurate. Many of our authors are seasoned journalists, graduate students, Ph.D.'s or published book authors. You have a better chance of getting published with us if you skip the query and send us a manuscript. If you do query, be sure to include specific details about your ideas and published clips. Stories about the Upper Peninsula are especially welcome. If your article focuses on history but also has a modern tie-in, your chances of publication are greatly increased. We do not publish any fiction.

$$ TRAVERSE

Northern Michigan's Magazine, Prism Publications, 148 E. Front St., Traverse City MI 49684. (231)941-8174. Fax: (231)941-8391. Website: www.mynorth.com. **20% freelance written**. Monthly magazine covering northern Michigan life. *Traverse* is a celebration of the life and environment of northern Michigan. Estab. 1981. Circ. 30,000. Byline given. Pays on acceptance. Offers 10% kill fee. Buys first North American serial rights. Editorial lead time 1 year. Submit seasonal material 1 year in advance. Accepts queries by mail, fax, phone. Accepts simultaneous submissions. Responds in 2 months to queries. Sample copy for $3. Guidelines for #10 SASE.

Nonfiction Needs book excerpts, essays, general interest, historical, humor, interview, personal experience, photo feature, travel. No fiction or poetry. **Buys 24 mss/year.** Send complete ms. Length: 1,000-3,200 words. **Pays $150-500.**

Photos State availability. Negotiates payment individually. Buys one time rights.
Columns/Departments Up in Michigan Reflection (essays about northern Michigan); Reflection on Home (essays about northern homes), both 700 words. 18 Query with published clips or send complete ms. **Pays $100-200.**
Tips When shaping an article for us, consider first that it must be strongly rooted in our region. The lack of this foundation element is one of the biggest reasons for our rejecting material. If you send us a piece about peaches, even if it does an admirable job of relaying the history of peaches, their medicinal qualities, their nutritional magnificence, and so on, we are likely to reject if it doesn't include local farms as a reference point. We want sidebars and extended captions designed to bring in a reader not enticed by the main subject. We cover the northern portion of the Lower Peninsula and to a lesser degree the Upper Peninsula. General categories of interest include nature and the environment, regional culture, personalities, the arts (visual, performing, literary), crafts, food & dining, homes, history, and outdoor activities (e.g., fishing, golf, skiing, boating, biking, hiking, birding, gardening). We are keenly interested in environmental and land-use issues but seldom use material dealing with such issues as health care, education, social services, criminal justice, and local politics. We use service pieces and a small number of how-to pieces, mostly focused on small projects for the home or yard. Also, we value research. We need articles built with information. Many of the pieces we reject use writing style to fill in for information voids. Style and voice are strongest when used as vehicles for sound research.

Minnesota

$ $ LAKE COUNTRY JOURNAL MAGAZINE

P.O. Box 978, Brainerd MN 56401. (218)828-6424, ext. 14. Fax: (218)825-7816. E-mail: jodi@lakecountryjournal.com. Website: www.lakecountryjournal.com. **Contact:** Jodi Schwen, editor or Tenlee Lund, assistant editor. **90% freelance written**. Bimonthly magazine covering central Minnesota's lake country. "We target a specific geographical niche in central Minnesota. The writer must be familiar with our area. We promote positive family values, foster a sense of community, increase appreciation for our natural and cultural environments, and provide ideas for enhancing the quality of our lives." Estab. 1996. Circ. 14,500. Byline given. Pays on publication. Offers 25% kill fee. Publishes ms an average of 6 months after acceptance. Buys first North American serial rights, buys second serial (reprint) rights, buys electronic rights. Submit seasonal material 1 year in advance. Accepts queries by mail, e-mail. Responds in 2 months to queries. Responds in 3 months to mss. Sample copy for $6. Guidelines available online.

O→ Break in by "submitting department length first—they are not scheduled as far in advance as features. Always in need of original fillers."

Nonfiction Needs essays, general interest, how-to, humor, interview, personal experience, photo feature. "No articles that come from writers who are not familiar with our target geographical location." **Buys 30 mss/year.** Query with or without published clips Length: 1,000-1,500 words. **Pays $100-200.**
Photos State availability. Identification of subjects, model releases required. Reviews transparencies. Negotiates payment individually. Buys one-time rights.
Columns/Departments Profile-People from Lake Country, 800 words; Essay, 800 words; Health (topics pertinent to central Minnesota living), 500 words. 40 mss/year Query with published clips **Pays $50-75.**
Fiction Needs adventure, humorous, mainstream, slice-of-life vignettes, literary, also family fiction appropriate to Lake Country and seasonal fiction. **Buys 6 mss/year.** Length: 1,500 words. **Pays $100-200.**
Poetry Needs free verse. "Never use rhyming verse, avant-garde, experimental, etc." Buys 6 poems/year. Submit maximum 4 poems. Length: 8-32 lines. **Pays $25**.
Tips "Most of the people who will read your articles live in the north central Minnesota lakes area. All have some significant attachment to the area. We have readers of various ages, backgrounds, and lifestyles. After reading your article, we hope to have a deeper understanding of some aspect of our community, our environment, ourselves, or humanity in general."

$ $ LAKE SUPERIOR MAGAZINE

Lake Superior Port Cities, Inc., P.O. Box 16417, Duluth MN 55816-0417. (218)722-5002. Fax: (218)722-4096. E-mail: edit@lakesuperior.com. Website: www.lakesuperior.com. **40% freelance written. Works with a small number of new/unpublished writers each year. Please include phone number and address with e-mail queries.** Bimonthly magazine covering contemporary and historic people, places and current events around Lake Superior. Estab. 1979. Circ. 20,000. Byline given. Pays on publication. No kill fee. Publishes ms an average of 10 months after acceptance. Buys first North American serial rights, buys second serial (reprint) rights. Submit seasonal material 1 year in advance. Accepts queries by mail, e-mail. Responds in 3 months to queries. Sample copy for $4.95 and 6 first-class stamps. Guidelines available online.

Nonfiction Needs book excerpts, general interest, historical, humor, interview, local, personal experience, photo feature, local, travel, local, city profiles, regional business, some investigative. **Buys 15 mss/year.** Query with published clips. Length: 300-1,800 words. **Pays $60-400.**

Photos Quality photography is our hallmark. Send photos. Captions, identification of subjects, model releases required. Reviews contact sheets, 2x2 and larger transparencies, 4 × 5 prints. Offers $50/image; $150 for covers.

Columns/Departments Current events and things to do (for Events Calendar section), less than 300 words; Around The Circle (media reviews; short pieces on Lake Superior; Great Lakes environmental issues; themes, letters and short pieces on events and highlights of the Lake Superior Region); Essay (nostalgic lake-specific pieces), up to 1,100 words; Profile (single personality profile with photography), up to 900 words. Other headings include Destinations, Wild Superior, Lake Superior Living, Heritage, Recipe Box. 20 Query with published clips. **Pays $60-90.**

Fiction Ethnic, historic, humorous, mainstream, novel excerpts, slice-of-life vignettes, ghost stories. Must be targeted regionally. Wants stories that are Lake Superior related. **Buys 2-3 mss/year.** Query with published clips. Length: 300-2,500 words. **Pays $50-125.**

Tips Well-researched queries are attended to. We actively seek queries from writers in Lake Superior communities. We prefer manuscripts to queries. Provide enough information on why the subject is important to the region and our readers, or why and how something is unique. We want details. The writer must have a thorough knowledge of the subject and how it relates to our region. We prefer a fresh, unused approach to the subject which provides the reader with an emotional involvement. Almost all of our articles feature quality photography, color or black and white. It is a prerequisite of all nonfiction. All submissions should include a *short* biography of author/photographer; mug shot sometimes used. Blanket submissions need not apply.

$ $ $ MPLS. ST. PAUL MAGAZINE

MSP Communications, 220 S. 6th St., Suite 500, Minneapolis MN 55402. (612)339-7571. Fax: (612)339-5806. E-mail: edit@mspmag.com. Website: www.mspmag.com. Monthly magazine. *Mpls. St. Paul Magazine* is a city magazine serving upscale readers in the Minneapolis-St. Paul metro area. Circ. 80,000. Pays on publication. Buys all rights. Editorial lead time 3 months. Accepts queries by mail, e-mail, fax. Sample copy for $10. Guidelines available online.

Nonfiction Needs book excerpts, essays, general interest, historical, interview, personal experience, photo feature, travel. **Buys 150 mss/year.** Query with published clips. Length: 500-4,000 words. **Pays 50-75¢/word for assigned articles.**

Mississippi

$ $ MISSISSIPPI MAGAZINE

Downhome Publications, 5 Lakeland Circle, Jackson MS 39216. (601)982-8418. Fax: (601)982-8447. E-mail: editor@mismag.com. Website: www.mississippimagazine.com. **Contact:** Melanie Ward, editor. **90% freelance written.** Bimonthly magazine covering Mississippi—the state and its lifestyles. "We are interested in positive stories reflecting Mississippi's rich traditions and heritage and focusing on the contributions the state and its natives have made to the arts, literature, and culture. In each issue we showcase homes and gardens, in-state travel, food, design, art, and more." Estab. 1982. Circ. 40,000. Byline given. Pays on publication. Offers 25% kill fee. Publishes ms an average of 6 months after acceptance. Buys first North American serial rights. Editorial lead time 6 months. Submit seasonal material 1 year in advance. Accepts queries by mail, fax. Responds in 2 months to queries. Guidelines for #10 SASE or online.

Nonfiction Needs general interest, historical, how-to, home decor, interview, personal experience, travel, in-state. No opinion, political, sports, expose. **Buys 15 mss/year.** Query. Length: 900-1,500 words. **Pays $150-350.**

Photos Send photos. with query. Captions, identification of subjects, model releases required. Reviews transparencies, prints, digital images on CD. Negotiates payment individually Buys one time rights.

Columns/Departments Gardening (short informative article on a specific plant or gardening technique), 750-1,000 words; Culture Center (story about an event or person relating to Mississippi's art, music, theatre, or literature), 750-1,000 words; Made in Mississippi (short article about a nationally or internationally known Mississippian or Mississippi company in any field), 600-700 words; On Being

Southern (personal essay about life in Mississippi; only ms submissions accepted), 750 words. 6 Query. **Pays $150-225.**

Missouri

$$ 417 MAGAZINE

Southwest Missouri's Life-Improvement Magazine, Whitaker Publishing, 2111 S. Eastgate Ave., Springfield MO 65809. (417)883-7417. Fax: (417)889-7417. E-mail: editor@417mag.com. Website: www.417mag.com. **50% freelance written**. Monthly magazine. *417 Magazine* is a regional title serving southwest Missouri. Our editorial mix includes service journalism and lifestyle content on home, fashion and the arts; as well as narrative and issues pieces. The audience is affluent, educated, mostly female. Estab. 1998. Circ. 20,000. Byline given. Pays on acceptance. Publishes ms an average of 2-3 months after acceptance. Buys first rights, buys second serial (reprint) rights, buys simultaneous rights, buys electronic rights. Editorial lead time 6 months. Accepts queries by e-mail. Responds in 1-2 months to queries. Sample copy by e-mail. Guidelines available online.

Nonfiction Needs essays, expose, general interest, how-to, humor, inspirational, interview, new product, personal experience, photo feature, travel, local book reviews. We are a local magazine, so anything not reflecting our local focus is something we have to pass on. **Buys 175 mss/year.** Query with published clips. Length: 300-3,500 words. **Pays $30-500, sometimes more.**

Tips Read the magazine before contacting us. Send specific ideas with your queries. Submit story ideas of local interest. Send published clips. Be a curious reporter, and ask probing questions.

$$ KANSAS CITY HOMES & GARDENS

Network Communications, Inc., 4121 W. 83rd St., Suite 110, Prairie Village KS 66208. (913)648-5757. Fax: (913)648-5783. E-mail: adarr@kc-hg.com. Website: kchandg.com. Magazine published 8 times annually. *KCH&G* creates inspirational, credible and compelling content about trends and events in local home and design for affluent homeowners, with beautiful photography, engaging features and expert insight. We help our readers get smarter about where to find and how to buy the best solutions for enhancing their homes. Estab. 1986. Circ. 18,000. Byline given. Pays on publication. No kill fee. Buys one-time rights, buys electronic rights. Editorial lead time 4 months. Submit seasonal material 4 months in advance. Accepts queries by mail, e-mail, fax. Accepts previously published material. Accepts simultaneous submissions. Responds in 1 month to queries. Responds in 1 month to mss. Sample copy for $5.

Nonfiction Buys 8 mss/year. Query with published clips. Length: 600-1,000 words. **Pays $100-350.**

Photos State availability of or send photos. Identification of subjects required. Reviews transparencies. Offers no additional payment for photos accepted with ms Buys continual rights.

Tips Focus on local home and garden content for the affluent homeowner.

KANSAS CITY MAGAZINE

7101 College Blvd., Suite 400, Overland Park KS 66210. E-mail: eswanson@studioatamq.com. Website: www.kcmag.com. **Contact:** Leigh Elmore, ed. **75% freelance written**. Monthly magazine. "Our mission is to celebrate living in Kansas City. We are a consumer lifestyle/general interest magazine focused on Kansas City, its people and places." Estab. 1994. Circ. 31,000. Byline given. Pays on acceptance. Offers 10% kill fee. Publishes ms an average of 3 months after acceptance. Buys first North American serial rights. Editorial lead time 4 months. Submit seasonal material 6 months in advance. Accepts queries by mail, e-mail, fax. Accepts simultaneous submissions. Sample copy for 8½ × 11 SAE or online.

Nonfiction Needs expose, general interest, interview, photo feature. **Buys 15-20 mss/year.** Query with published clips. Length: 250-3,000 words.

Photos Negotiates payment individually. Buys one time rights.

Columns/Departments Entertainment (Kansas City only), 1,000 words; Food (Kansas City food and restaurants only), 1,000 words. 12 Query with published clips.

$$ MISSOURI LIFE

Missouri Life, Inc., 515 E. Morgan St., Boonville MO 65233. (660)882-9898. Fax: (660)882-9899. E-mail: info@missourilife.com. Website: www.missourilife.com. **85% freelance written**. Bimonthly magazine covering the state of Missouri. *Missouri Life*'s readers are mostly college-educated people with a wide range of travel and lifestyle interests. Our magazine discovers the people, places, and events—both past and present—that make Missouri a great place to live and/or visit. Estab. 1973. Circ. 20,000. Byline given. Pays on publication. Buys all rights, buys nonexclusive rights. Editorial lead time 3 months. Submit seasonal material 6 months in advance. Accepts queries by mail, e-mail, fax. Responds in 2 months to queries. Guidelines available online.

Nonfiction Needs general interest, historical, travel, all Missouri related. Length: 300-2,000 words. **Pays $50-600; 20¢/word.**

Photos State availability. in query; buys all rights nonexclusive. Captions, identification of subjects, model releases required. Offers $50-150/photo

Columns/Departments "All Around Missouri (people and places, past and present, written in an almanac style), 300 words; Missouri Artist (features a Missouri artist), 500 words; Made in Missouri (products and businesses native to Missouri), 500 words.

$ RIVER HILLS TRAVELER

Traveler Publishing Co.,, P.O. Box 220, Valley Park MO 63088-0220. (800)874-8423. Fax: (800)874-8423. E-mail: stories@rhtrav.com. Website: www.riverhillstraveler.com. **80% freelance written**. Monthly tabloid covering outdoor sports and nature in the southeast quarter of Missouri, the east and central Ozarks. Topics like those in *Field & Stream* and *National Geographic*. Estab. 1973. Circ. 5,000. Byline given. Pays on publication. No kill fee. Publishes ms an average of 2 months after acceptance. Buys one-time rights. Editorial lead time 2 months. Submit seasonal material 1 year in advance. Accepts queries by e-mail. Accepts simultaneous submissions. Responds in 2 months to queries. Sample copy for SAE or online Guidelines available online.

Nonfiction Needs historical, how-to, humor, opinion, personal experience, photo feature, technical, travel. No stories about other geographic areas. **Buys 80 mss/year.** Query with writing samples. 1,500 word maximum **Pays $15-50.**

Reprints E-mail manuscript with rights for sale noted and information about when and where the material previously appeared.

Photos Send photos. Reviews JPEG/TIFF files. Negotiates payment individually. Pays $35 for covers. Buys one time rights.

Tips "We are a `poor man's' *Field & Stream* and *National Geographic*—about the eastern Missouri Ozarks. We prefer stories that relate an adventure that causes a reader to relive an adventure of his own or consider embarking on a similar adventure. Think of an adventure in camping or cooking, not just fishing and hunting. How-to is great, but not simple instructions. We encourage good first-person reporting. We like to get stories as part of an e-mail, not an attached document."

$ RURAL MISSOURI MAGAZINE

Association of Missouri Electric Cooperatives, P.O. Box 1645, Jefferson City MO 65102. E-mail: hberry@ruralmissouri.coop. Website: www.ruralmissouri.coop. **5% freelance written**. Monthly magazine covering rural interests in Missouri; people, places and sights in Missouri. "Our audience is comprised of rural electric cooperative members in Missouri. We describe our magazine as 'being devoted to the rural way of life.'" Estab. 1948. Circ. 535,000. Byline given. Pays on acceptance. Publishes ms an average of 6 months after acceptance. Buys one-time rights. Editorial lead time 6 months. Submit seasonal material 6 months in advance. Accepts queries by mail, e-mail. Responds in 6-8 weeks to queries and to mss. Sample copy available online. Guidelines available online.

Nonfiction Needs general interest, historical. Does not want personal experiences or nostalgia pieces. Send complete ms. Length: 1,000-1,100 words. **Pays variable amount for each piece.**

Tips "We look for tight, well-written history pieces. Remember: History doesn't mean boring. Bring it to life for us—attribute quotes. Make us feel what you're describing to us."

Montana

$$ MONTANA MAGAZINE

Lee Enterprises, P.O. Box 5630, Helena MT 59604-5630. Fax: (406)443-5480. E-mail: editor@montanamagazine.com. Website: www.montanamagazine.com. **90% freelance written**. Bimonthly magazine. Strictly Montana-oriented magazine that features community profiles, contemporary issues, wildlife and natural history, travel pieces. Estab. 1970. Circ. 40,000. Byline given. No kill fee. Publishes ms an average of 1 year after acceptance. Buys one-time rights. Submit seasonal material 1 year in advance. Accepts simultaneous submissions. Responds in 6 months to queries. Sample copy for $5 or online. Guidelines available online.

- Accepts queries by e-mail. No phone calls.

Nonfiction Query by September for summer material; March for winter material. Needs essays, general interest, interview, photo feature, travel. Special features on summer and winter destination points. No `me and Joe' hiking and hunting tales; no blood-and-guts hunting stories; no poetry; no fiction; no sentimental essays. **Buys 30 mss/year.** Query with samples and SASE. Length: 300-3,000 words. **Pays 20¢/word.**

Reprints Send photocopy of article with rights for sale and information about when and where the material previously appeared. Pays 50% of amount paid for an original article.

Photos Send photos. Captions, identification of subjects, model releases required. Reviews contact sheets, 35mm or larger format transparencies, 5 × 7 prints. Offers additional payment for photos accepted with ms. Buys one-time rights.

Columns/Departments Memories (reminisces of early-day Montana life), 800-1,000 words; Outdoor Recreation, 1,500-2,000 words; Community Festivals, 500 words, plus b&w or color photo; Montana-Specific Humor, 800-1,000 words. Query with samples and SASE.

Tips "We avoid commonly known topics so Montanans won't ho-hum through more of what they already know. If it's time to revisit a topic, we look for a unique slant."

Nevada

$ NEVADA HOME MAGAZINE

House and Garden Design, Nevada Home LLC, 500 Double Eagle Ct., Reno NV 89521. (775)850-2155. Fax: (775)825-4644. E-mail: lericson@nvhome.biz. Website: www.nvhome.biz. **80% freelance written**. Monthly magazine covering do-it-yourself home improvement, gardening and landscaping specific to the Washoe County, Nevada region. "Stories are all specific to the Reno and Sparks areas. All use local sources as experts. In gardening, the stories must present an understanding of the microclimates here in this area. In home improvement, they must reflect needs and timing based on the local climate and aesthetics." Estab. 2005. Circ. 25,000. Byline given. Pays on publication. No kill fee. Publishes ms an average of 2 months after acceptance. Buys first rights plus usage in all media thereafter, though ownership reverts to writer. Editorial lead time 3 months. Submit seasonal material 4 months in advance. Accepts queries by mail, e-mail. Responds in 3 weeks to queries. Sample copy available online. Guidelines by e-mail.

Nonfiction Needs how-to. Does not want personal experience. **Buys 100 mss/year.** Query. Length: 600-900 words. **Pays $75-125 for assigned articles. Pays $50-100 for unsolicited articles.**

Photos State availability. Captions, identification of subjects, model releases required. Reviews GIF/JPEG files. Negotiates payment individually. Buys first rights plus usage in all media thereafter, though ownership reverts to photographer.

Tips "If you have expertise in either home improvement (construction-related work) or gardening, let me know. Depth of related experience counts. Also, all stories are local to the Washoe County, Nevada area. Include your knowledge of, and time spent in, this area."

$$ NEVADA MAGAZINE

401 N. Carson St., Carson City NV 89701-4291. (775)687-5416. Fax: (775)687-6159. E-mail: editor@nevadamagazine.com. Website: www.nevadamagazine.com. **Contact:** Editor. **50% freelance written. Works with a small number of new/unpublished writers each year**. Bimonthly magazine published by the state of Nevada to promote tourism. Estab. 1936. Circ. 30,000. Byline given. Pays on publication. No kill fee. Publishes ms an average of 6 months after acceptance. Buys first North American serial rights. Submit seasonal material 6 months in advance. Accepts queries by e-mail (preferred). Responds in 1 month to queries.

Nonfiction "We use stories and photos on speculation. Nevada travel topics only." Length: 700-1,000 words. **Pays $50-500.**

Photos Contact: Query art director Tony deRonnebeck (tony@nevadamagazine.com). Reviews digital images. Pays $35-175; cover, $250. Buys one-time rights.

Tips "Keep in mind the magazine's purpose is to promote Nevada tourism. We look for a light, enthusiastic tone of voice without being too cute."

New Hampshire

$$ NEW HAMPSHIRE MAGAZINE

McLean Communications, Inc., 150 Dow St., Manchester NH 03101. (603)624-1442. E-mail: editor@nhmagazine.com. Website: www.nhmagazine.com. **50% freelance written**. Monthly magazine devoted to New Hampshire. "We want stories written for, by, and about the people of New Hampshire with emphasis on qualities that set us apart from other states. We feature lifestyle, adventure, and home-related stories with a unique local angle.' Estab. 1986. Circ. 32,000. Byline given. Pays on publication. Offers 25% kill fee. Buys all rights. Editorial lead time 3 months. Submit seasonal material 3 months in advance. Accepts queries by mail, e-mail, fax. Accepts simultaneous submissions. Responds in 2 months to queries. Responds in 3 months to mss. Guidelines available online.

Nonfiction Needs essays, general interest, historical, photo feature, business. **Buys 30 mss/year.** Query with published clips. Length: 800-2,000 words. **Pays $50-500.**

Photos State availability. Captions, identification of subjects, model releases required. Possible additional payment for photos accepted with ms. Rights purchased vary.

Fillers Length: 200-400 words.

Tips "McLean Communications also publishes a specialty publication called *Destination New Hampshire.* In general, our articles deal with the people of New Hampshire—their lifestyles and interests. We also present localized stories about national and international issues, ideas, and trends. We will only use stories that show our readers how these issues have an impact on their daily lives. We cover a wide range of topics, including healthcare, politics, law, real-life dramas, regional history, medical issues, business, careers, environmental issues, the arts, the outdoors, education, food, recreation, etc. Many of our readers are what we call `The New Traditionalists'—aging Baby Boomers who have embraced solid American values and contemporary New Hampshire lifestyles."

New Jersey

$$$$ NEW JERSEY MONTHLY

The Magazine of the Garden State, New Jersey Monthly, LLC, P.O. Box 920, Morristown NJ 07963-0920. (973)539-8230. Fax: (973)538-2953. Website: www.njmonthly.com. **75-80% freelance written.** Monthly magazine covering just about anything to do with New Jersey, from news, politics, and sports to decorating trends and lifestyle issues. Our readership is well-educated, affluent, and on average our readers have lived in New Jersey 20 years or more. Estab. 1976. Circ. 95,000. Byline given. Pays on completion of fact-checking. Offers 20% kill fee. Publishes ms an average of 3 months after acceptance. Buys first North American serial rights. Editorial lead time 3 months. Submit seasonal material 6 months in advance. Accepts queries by mail, e-mail, fax, phone. Accepts simultaneous submissions. Responds in 2 months to queries.

- This magazine continues to look for strong investigative reporters with novelistic style and solid knowledge of New Jersey issues.

Nonfiction Needs book excerpts, essays, expose, general interest, historical, humor, interview, personal experience, photo feature, travel, within New Jersey, arts, sports, politics. No experience pieces from people who used to live in New Jersey or general pieces that have no New Jersey angle. **Buys 90-100 mss/year.** Query with published magazine clips and SASE. Length: 800-3,000 words. **Pays $750-2,500.** Pays reasonable expenses of writers on assignment with prior approval.

Photos Contact: Donna Panagakos, art director. State availability. Identification of subjects, model releases required. Reviews transparencies, prints. Payment negotiated. Buys one time rights.

Columns/Departments Exit Ramp (back page essay usually originating from personal experience but written in a way that tells a broader story of statewide interest), 1,200 words. 12 Query with published clips. **Pays $400.**

Tips The best approach: Do your homework! Read the past year's issues to get an understanding of our well-written, well-researched articles that tell a tale from a well-established point of view.

$$ NEW JERSEY SAVVY LIVING

CTB, LLC, 30B Vreeland Rd., Florham Park NJ 07932. (973)966-0997. Fax: (973)966-0210. E-mail: njsavvyliving@ctbintl.com. Website: www.njsavvyliving.com. **90% freelance written.** Bimonthly magazine covering New Jersey residents with affluent lifestyles. *Savvy Living* is a regional magazine for an upscale audience, ages 35-65. We focus on lifestyle topics such as home design, fashion, the arts, travel, personal finance, and health and well being. Estab. 1997. Circ. 50,000. Byline given. Pays on publication. Offers $50 kill fee. Publishes ms an average of 3 months after acceptance. variable rights. Editorial lead time 3 months. Accepts queries by mail. Accepts simultaneous submissions. Response time varies. Sample copy for sae with 9 × 12 envelope.

Nonfiction Needs interview, people of national and regional importance, photo feature, travel, home/decorating, finance, health, fashion, beauty. No investigative, fiction, personal experience, and non-New Jersey topics (excluding travel). **Buys 50 mss/year.** Query with published clips. Length: 900-2,000 words. **Pays $250-500.**

Photos State availability. Captions, identification of subjects, model releases required. Offers no additional payment for photos accepted with ms. Buys one time rights.

Columns/Departments Savvy Shoppers (inside scoop on buying); Dining Out (restaurant review); Home Gourmet (gourmet cooking and entertaining). 25 Query with published clips. **Pays $300.**
Tips Offer ideas of interest to a savvy, upscale New Jersey readership. We love articles that utilize local sources and are well focused and keep our readers informed about trends affecting their lives. We work with experienced and stylish writers. Please provide clips.

$$ THE SANDPAPER

Newsmagazine of the Jersey Shore, The SandPaper, Inc., 1816 Long Beach Blvd., Surf City NJ 08008-5461. (609)494-5900. Fax: (609)494-1437. E-mail: letters@thesandpaper.net. Weekly tabloid covering subjects of interest to Long Island Beach area residents and visitors. Each issue includes a mix of news, human interest features, opinion columns, and entertainment/calendar listings. Estab. 1976. Circ. 30,000. Byline given. Pays on publication. Offers 100% kill fee. Publishes ms an average of 1 month after acceptance. Buys first rights, buys all rights. Submit seasonal material 3 months in advance. Accepts queries by mail, e-mail, fax, phone. Accepts simultaneous submissions. Responds in 1 month to queries.
Columns/Departments Speakeasy (opinion and slice-of-life, often humorous); Commentary (forum for social science perspectives); both 1,000-1,500 words, preferably with local or Jersey Shore angle. 50 Send complete ms. **Pays $40**

New Mexico

$$ NEW MEXICO MAGAZINE

Lew Wallace Bldg., 495 Old Santa Fe Trail, Santa Fe NM 87501. (505)827-7447. E-mail: queries@nmmagazine.com. Website: www.nmmagazine.com. **Contact:** any editor. **70**. Covers areas throughout the state. "We want to publish a lively editorial mix, covering both the down-home (like a diner in Tucumcari) and the upscale (a new bistro in world-class Santa Fe)." Explore the gamut of the Old West and the New Age. "Our magazine is about the power of place—in particular more than 120,000 sq. miles of mountains, desert, grasslands, and forest inhabited by a culturally rich mix of individuals. It is an enterprise of the New Mexico Tourism Dept., which strives to make potential visitors aware of our state's multicultural heritage, climate, environment, & uniqueness." Estab. 1923. Circ. 100,000. Pays on acceptance. 20% kill fee. Publishes ms an average of 3 months after acceptance. Buys first North American serial rights, first publication rights exclusive worldwide. Submit seasonal material 1 year in advance. Accepts queries by mail, e-mail (preferred). Does not accept previously published submissions. Responds to queries if interested. Sample copy for $5. Guidelines for SASE.

- No unsolicited mss. Does not return unsolicited material.

Nonfiction "We look for story ideas about New Mexico experiences, with opinionated storytelling and a first-person point of view when appropriate. Inspire readers to follow in your footsteps. We look for writers—both in New Mexico and elsewhere—who are adept at establishing a theme, then sustaining a story with fresh eyes and true insight. We place a premium on good storytelling, tight composition, and factual accuracy. We expect original work." "Submit your story idea along with a working head and subhead and a paragraph synopsis. Include published clips and a short sum-up about your strengths as a writer. We will consider your proposal as well as your potential to write stories we've conceptualized."
Reprints Rarely publishes reprints but sometimes publishes excerpts from novels and nonfiction books.
Photos "Purchased as portfolio or on assignment. Photographers interested in photo assignments should reference submission guidelines on the contributors' page of our website."
Tips "Does not return unsolicited material."

$ NEW MEXICO WOMAN

New Mexico Woman, Inc., P.O. Box 12955, Albuquerque NM 87195. (505)247-9195. Fax: (505)842-5129. E-mail: heygals@nmwoman.com. Website: www.nmwoman.com. **90% freelance written**. Monthly magazine covering women in business and professional women. Estab. 1983. Circ. 15,000. Pays on publication. Publishes ms an average of 3 months after acceptance. Buys one-time rights. Editorial lead time 2 months. Submit seasonal material 2-3 months in advance. Accepts queries by mail, e-mail, fax. Accepts previously published material. Accepts simultaneous submissions. Guidelines available online.
Nonfiction We are interested primarily in education, opportunities, career options, self improvement, women's health issues, and occasionally articles about home, hobby, travel, lifestyle, or nonprofit programs that serve women in the community. Needs general interest, historical, how-to, humor, inspirational, new product, personal experience. **Buys 5-10 mss/year.** Query. Length: 800-1,600 words. **Pays 5¢/word.**

Photos State availability. Captions required. Reviews GIF/JPEG files. Offers no additional payment for photos accepted with ms. Buys one time rights.
Columns/Departments From My Perspective (personal experience); The Inner You (self-improvement); Young Women to Watch (talented young women), all 600 words; and The Seasons of Fitness (fitness advice), 400 words. 12 Query with published clips. **Pays 5¢/word.**

TRADICION REVISTA

LPD Press, 925 Salamanca N.W., Los Ranchos NM 87107-5647. (505)344-9382. Fax: (505)345-5129. E-mail: LPD_Press@msn.com. Website: www.nmsantos.com. **75% freelance written**. Quarterly magazine covering Southwest history and culture. "We publish Southwest art and history, especially the art of New Mexico." Estab. 1995. Circ. 5,000. Byline given. does not pay for articles. No kill fee. Buys Author retains rights. rights. Editorial lead time 6 months. Submit seasonal material 4 months in advance. Accepts queries by e-mail, phone. Accepts simultaneous submissions. Responds in 1 week to queries. Responds in 1 month to mss. Sample copy free.
Nonfiction Needs essays, general interest, historical, interview, photo feature, travel. **Buys 20 (no pay) mss/year.** Query. Length: 500-2,000 words.
Photos Send photos. Captions required. Reviews GIF/JPEG/PDF files. Offers no additional payment for photos accepted with ms. Buys one time rights.
Columns/Departments Query. **no pay.**

New York

$ $ ADIRONDACK LIFE

P.O. Box 410, Jay NY 12941-0410. (518)946-2191. Fax: (518)946-7461. E-mail: astoltie@adirondacklife.com. Website: www.adirondacklife.com. **Contact:** Annie Stoltie, editor. **70% freelance written. Prefers to work with published/established writers.** "Magazine published 8 issues/year, including special Annual Outdoor Guide, emphasizes the Adirondack region and the North Country of New York State in articles covering outdoor activities, history, and natural history directly related to the Adirondacks." Estab. 1970. Circ. 50,000. Byline given. Pays 30 days after publication. No kill fee. Publishes ms an average of 10 months after acceptance. Buys first North American serial rights, buys Web rights. Submit seasonal material 1 year in advance. Accepts queries by mail, e-mail. Does not accept previously published work. Sample copy for $3 and 9 × 12 SAE. Guidelines available online.
Nonfiction *"Adirondack Life* attempts to capture the unique flavor and ethos of the Adirondack mountains and North Country region through feature articles directly pertaining to the qualities of the area." Outdoors (May); Single-topic Collector's issue (September) **Buys 20-25 unsolicited mss/year.** Query with published clips. Accepts queries, but not unsolicited mss., via e-mail. Length: 1,000-4,000 words. **Pays 30¢/word.**
Photos "All photos must have been taken in the Adirondacks. Each issue contains a photo feature. Purchased with or without ms on assignment. All photos must be individually identified as to the subject or locale and must bear the photographer's name." Send photos. Reviews color transparencies, b&w prints. Pays $150 for full page, b&w, or color; $400 for cover (color only,vertical in format). Credit line given.
Columns/Departments Special Places (unique spots in the Adirondack Park); Watercraft; Barkeater (personal to political essays); Wilderness (environmental issues); Working (careers in the Adirondacks); Home; Yesteryears; Kitchen; Profile; Historic Preservation; Sporting Scene. Length: 1,200-2,400 words. Query with published clips. **Pays 30¢/word.**
Fiction Considers first-serial novel excerpts in its subject matter and region.
Tips "Do not send a personal essay about your meaningful moment in the mountains. We need factual pieces about regional history, sports, culture, and business. We are looking for clear, concise, well-organized manuscripts that are strictly Adirondack in subject. Check back issues to be sure we haven't already covered your topic. Please do not send unsolicited manuscripts via e-mail. Check out our guidelines online."

$ $ BUFFALO SPREE MAGAZINE

David Laurence Publications, Inc., 6215 Sheridan Dr., Buffalo NY 14221. (716)634-0820. Fax: (716)810-0075. E-mail: elicata@buffalospree.com. Website: www.buffalospree.com. **90% freelance written**. City regional magazine published 8 times/year. Estab. 1967. Circ. 25,000. Byline given. Pays on publication. No kill fee. Publishes ms an average of 1 month after acceptance. Buys first North American serial rights. Accepts queries by mail, e-mail, fax. Responds in 6 months to queries. Sample copy for $3.95 and 9 × 12 SAE with 9 first-class stamps.

Nonfiction Most articles are assigned not unsolicited. Needs interview, travel, issue-oriented features, arts, living, food, regional. Query with résumé and published clips Length: 1,000-2,000 words. **Pays $125-250.**
Tips Send a well-written, compelling query or an interesting topic, and *great* clips. We no longer regularly publish fiction or poetry. Prefers material that is Western New York related.

$$$$ CITY LIMITS

New York's Urban Affairs News Magazine, City Limits Community Information Service, 120 Wall St., 20th Floor, New York NY 10005. (212)479-3344. Fax: (212)344-6457. E-mail: editor@citylimits.org. Website: www.citylimits.org. **50% freelance written**. Monthly magazine covering urban politics and policy. *City Limits* is a 29-year-old nonprofit magazine focusing on issues facing New York City and its neighborhoods, particularly low-income communities. The magazine is strongly committed to investigative journalism, in-depth policy analysis and hard-hitting profiles. Estab. 1976. Circ. 4,000. Byline given. Pays on publication. Offers 50% kill fee. Publishes ms an average of 3 months after acceptance. Buys first North American serial rights, buys second serial (reprint) rights. Editorial lead time 2 months. Accepts queries by mail, e-mail, fax. Accepts simultaneous submissions. Sample copy for $2.95. Guidelines free.
Nonfiction Needs book excerpts, expose, humor, interview, opinion, photo feature. No essays, polemics. **Buys 25 mss/year.** Query with published clips. Length: 400-3,500 words. **Pays $150-2,000 for assigned articles. Pays $100-800 for unsolicited articles.**
Photos State availability. Reviews contact sheets, negatives, transparencies. Offers $50-100/photo
Columns/Departments Making Change (nonprofit business); Big Idea (policy news); Book Review, all 800 words; Urban Legend (profile); First Hand (Q&A), both 350 words. 15 Query with published clips.
Tips *City Limits'* specialty is covering low-income communities. We want to report untold stories about news affecting neighborhoods at the grassroots. We're looking for stories about housing, health care, criminal justice, child welfare, education, economic development, welfare reform, politics and government.

IN NEW YORK

A Morris Visitor Publication, MVPNY.net, 79 Madison Ave., 8th Floor, New York NY 10016. (212)716-8562. E-mail: trisha.mcmahon@morris.com. Website: www.in-newyork.com. **Contact:** Tricia S. McMahon, editor in chief. Monthly full-color magazine covering shopping, dining, attractions, museums, tours, galleries, nightlife, theater, and special events, created exclusively for sophisticated travelers to the New York Metropolitan area and distributed at most hotels, tourist centers, VIP lounges of Amtrak Acela, airlines, and popular sights. Circ. 146,000. Kill fee 20% Sample copy for free in upscale hotels at concierge desk.
Tips "No unsolicited manuscripts, please. All queries should be snail mail only."

$$$$ NEW YORK MAGAZINE

New York Media Holdings, LLC, 75 Varick Street, New York NY 10013. Website: www.newyorkmag.com. **Contact:** Editorial Submissions. **25% freelance written**. Weekly magazine focusing on current events in the New York metropolitan area. Circ. 433,813. Pays on acceptance. Offers 25% kill fee. Buys electronic rights, buys first world serial rights rights. Submit seasonal material 2 months in advance. Responds in 1 month to queries. Sample copy for $3.50 or on website.
Nonfiction New York-related journalism that covers lifestyle, politics and business. Query by mail. No unsolicited mss. **Pays $1/word.**

NEW YORK SPACES

Wainscot Media, 110 Summit Ave., Montvale NJ 07645. (201)571-7003. Fax: (201)782-5319. Website: www.nyspacesmagazine.com. **Contact:** Jason Kontos, editor in chief. Bimonthly magazine celebrating the best of New York area design. "*New York Spaces* is dedicated to helping affluent, acquisitive users enhance their private worlds, making it a remarkable showcase for the design community and advertisers alike." No kill fee.
Nonfiction Needs general interest, how-to. Query.
Photos "Submit scouting shots (color prints, copies or low-res .jpg files on CD) for consideration. These images are used solely for the purpose of reviewing and selecting which projects we will publish. We'll be in touch to let you know if your project has been selected." State availability of or send photos. Captions, identification of subjects required. Reviews 2¼, 4 × 5, etc. or 35mm slides transparencies, high-resolution digital photos on CD.

$$ SYRACUSE NEW TIMES

A. Zimmer, Ltd., 1415 W. Genesee St., Syracuse NY 13204. Fax: (315)422-1721. E-mail: editorial@syracusenewtimes.com. Website: www.syracusenewtimes.com. **50% freelance written**. Weekly tabloid covering news, sports, arts, and entertainment. *"Syracuse New Times* is an alternative weekly that is topical, provocative, irreverent, and intensely local." Estab. 1969. Circ. 40,000. Byline given. Pays on publication. No kill fee. Publishes ms an average of 1 month after acceptance. Buys one-time rights. Editorial lead time 3 months. Submit seasonal material 3 months in advance. Accepts simultaneous submissions. Responds in 2 weeks to queries. Responds in 1 month to mss. Sample copy for sae with 9 × 12 envelope and 2 first-class stamps. Guidelines for #10 SASE.

Nonfiction Needs essays, general interest. **Buys 100 mss/year.** Query by mail with published clips. Length: 250-2,500 words. **Pays $25-200.**

Photos State availability of or send photos.. Identification of subjects required. Reviews 8 × 10 prints, color slides. Offers $10-25/photo or negotiates payment individually Buys one-time rights.

Tips "Move to Syracuse and query with strong idea."

$ WESTCHESTER ARTSNEWS

Westchester Arts Council, 31 Mamaroneck Ave., White Plains NY 10601. Fax: (914)428-4306. E-mail: jormond@westarts.com. Website: www.westarts.com. **20% freelance written**. Monthly tabloid covering arts and entertainment in Westchester County, New York. We profile artists, arts organizations and write teasers about upcoming exhibitions, concerts, events, theatrical performances, etc. Estab. 1975. Circ. 20,000. Byline given. Pays on publication. Buys all rights. Editorial lead time 1 month. Submit seasonal material 2 months in advance. Accepts queries by mail, e-mail. Sample copy free.

Nonfiction There must be some hook to Westchester County, New York. Query with published clips. Length: 400-500 words. **Pays $75-100.**

Tips Please e-mail cover letter, résumé, 2 clips. No phone calls please.

North Carolina

$$ AAA CAROLINAS GO MAGAZINE

6600 AAA Dr., Charlotte NC 28212. Fax: (704)569-7815. Website: www.aaacarolinas.com. **Contact:** Tom Crosby, Managing Editor. **20% freelance written**. Member publication for the Carolina affiliate of American Automobile Association covering travel, auto-related issues. "We prefer stories that focus on travel and auto safety in North and South Carolina and surrounding states." Estab. 1922. Circ. 1.1 million. Byline given. Pays on publication. No kill fee. Buys all rights. Editorial lead time 2 months. Accepts queries by mail. Sample copy and writer's guidelines for #10 SASE.

- "The online magazine carries original content not found in the print edition. Contact Brendan Byrnes at btbyrnes@mailaaa.com."

Nonfiction Needs travel, auto safety. Length: 750 words. **Pays $150.**

Photos Send photos. Identification of subjects required. Reviews slides. Offers no additional payment for photos accepted with ms. Buys all rights.

Tips "Submit regional stories relating to Carolinas travel."

ALAMANCE MAGAZINE

CCMag Inc., P.O. Box 517, Burlington NC 27216. (336)226-8436. Fax: (336)226-8437. E-mail: alamagkc@bellsouth.net. Website: www.alamancemagazine.com. **90% freelance written**. Monthly magazine. *Alamance Magazine* provides general interest articles for our readers here in Alamance County, North Carolina. Estab. 1986. Circ. 20,000. Byline given. Editorial lead time 3 months. Submit seasonal material 4 months in advance. Accepts queries by mail, e-mail, fax, phone. Accepts simultaneous submissions.

Nonfiction Needs general interest. Query.

$$ CARY MAGAZINE

SA Cherokee, Westview at Weston, 301 Cascade Pointe Lane, #101, Cary NC 27513. (919)674-6020. Fax: (919)674-6027. E-mail: editor@carymagazine.com. Website: www.carymagazine.com. **40% freelance written**. Bimonthly magazine. "Lifestyle publication for the affluent communities of Cary, Apex, Morrisville, Holly Springs, Fuquay-Varina and RTP. Our editorial objective is to entertain, enlighten and inform our readers with unique and engaging editorial and vivid photography." Estab. 2004. Circ. 23,000. Byline given. Negotiated Buys first North American serial rights. Editorial lead time 3 months. Submit seasonal material 3 months in advance. Accepts queries by mail, e-mail. Responds in 2-4 weeks to queries. Responds in 1 month to mss. Sample copy for $4.95. Guidelines free.

Nonfiction Needs historical, specific to Western Wake County, North Carolina, inspirational, interview, human interest, personal experience. Don't submit articles with no local connection. **Buys 2 mss/year.** Query with published clips.
Photos Freelancers should state the availability of photos with their submission or send the photos with their submission. Identification of subjects required. Reviews GIF/JPEG files. Negotiates payment individually Buys one time rights.
Tips "Prefer experienced feature writers with exceptional interviewing skills who can take a fresh perspective on a topic; writes with a unique flare, but clearly with a good hook to engage the reader and evoke emotion; adheres to AP Style and follows basic journalism conventions; and takes deadlines seriously. E-mail inquiries preferred."

$$ CHARLOTTE MAGAZINE

Abarta Media, 127 W. Worthington Ave., Suite 208, Charlotte NC 28203. (704)335-7181. Fax: (704)335-3739. E-mail: richard.thurmond@charlottemagazine.com. Website: www.charlottemagazine.com. **75% freelance written**. Monthly magazine covering Charlotte life. This magazine tells its readers things they didn't know about Charlotte, in an interesting, entertaining, and sometimes provocative style. Circ. 40,000. Byline given. Pays within 30 days of acceptance. Offers 25% kill fee. Publishes ms an average of 3 months after acceptance. Buys first North American serial rights. Editorial lead time 3 months. Submit seasonal material 6 months in advance. Accepts queries by mail, e-mail. Accepts simultaneous submissions. Responds in 6 months to mss. Sample copy for 81/2â—Š11 SAE and $5.
Nonfiction Needs book excerpts, expose, general interest, interview, photo feature, travel. **Buys 35-50 mss/year.** Query with published clips. Length: 200-3,000 words. **Pays 20-40¢/word.**
Photos State availability. Identification of subjects required. Negotiates payment individually. Buys one time rights.
Columns/Departments 35-50 **Pays 20-40¢/word**
Tips A story for *Charlotte* magazine could only appear in *Charlotte* magazine. That is, the story and its treatment are particularly germane to this area. Because of this, we rarely work with writers who live outside the Charlotte area.

$$ FIFTEEN 501

Connecting Life in Durham, Orange and Chatham Counties, Weiss and Hughes Publishing, 189 Wind Chime Ct., Raleigh NC 27615. (919)870-1722. Fax: (919)719-5260. E-mail: dthurber@fifteen501.com. Website: www.fifteen501.com. **50% freelance written**. Quarterly magazine covering lifestyle issues relevant to residents in the US 15/501 corridor of Durham, Orange and Chatham counties. We cover issues important to residents of Durham, Orange and Chatham counties. We're committed to improving our readers' overall quality of life and keeping them informed of the lifestyle amenities there. Estab. 2006. Circ. 30,000. Byline given. within 30 days of publication. Offers 25% kill fee. Publishes ms an average of 2 months after acceptance. Buys all rights. Editorial lead time 2-3 months. Submit seasonal material 6 months in advance. Accepts queries by mail, e-mail. Accepts simultaneous submissions. Responds in 2-4 weeks to queries. Sample copy available online. Guidelines by e-mail.
Nonfiction Needs general interest, historical, how-to, home interiors, landscaping, gardening, technology, inspirational, interview, personal experience, photo feature, technical, travel. Does not want opinion pieces, political or religious topics. Query. Length: 600-1,200 words. **Pays 35¢/word.**
Photos State availability. Captions, identification of subjects required. Reviews transparencies, GIF/JPEG files. Offers no additional payment for photos accepted with ms. Rights are negotiable.
Columns/Departments Around Town (local lifestyle topics), 1,000 words; Hometown Stories, 600 words; Travel (around North Carolina), 1,000 words; Home Interiors/Landscaping (varies), 1,000 words; Restaurants (local, fine dining), 600-1,000 words. 20-25 Query. **Pays 35¢/word.**
Tips All queries must be focused on the issues that make Durham, Chapel Hill, Carrboro, Hillsborough and Pittsboro unique and wonderful places to live.

$$ OUR STATE

Down Home in North Carolina, Mann Media, P.O. Box 4552, Greensboro NC 27404. (336)286-0600. Fax: (336)286-0100. E-mail: editorial@ourstate.com. Website: www.ourstate.com. **95% freelance written**. Monthly magazine covering North Carolina. *Our State* is dedicated to providing editorial about the history, destinations, out-of-the-way places, and culture of North Carolina. Estab. 1933. Circ. 130,000. Byline given. Pays on publication. No kill fee. Publishes ms an average of 6-24 months after acceptance. Buys first North American serial rights. Editorial lead time 4-6 months. Submit seasonal material 4 months in advance. Accepts queries by mail, e-mail, fax. Responds in 6 weeks to queries. Responds in 2 months to mss. Sample copy for $6. Guidelines for #10 SASE.

Nonfiction Needs historical, travel, North Carolina culture, folklore. **Buys 250 mss/year.** Send complete ms. Length: 1,400-1,600 words. **Pays $300-500.**
Photos State availability. Reviews 35mm or 4x6 transparencies, digital. Negotiates payment individually. Buys one time rights.
Columns/Departments Tar Heel Memories (remembering something specific about North Carolina), 1,000 words; Tar Heel Profile (profile of interesting North Carolinian), 1,500 words; Tar Heel Literature (review of books by North Carolina writers and about North Carolina), 300 words.
Tips We are developing a style for travel stories that is distinctly *Our State*. That style starts with outstanding photographs, which not only depict an area, but interpret it and thus become an integral part of the presentation. Our stories need not dwell on listings of what can be seen. Concentrate instead on the experience of being there, whether the destination is a hiking trail, a bed and breakfast, a forest, or an urban area. What thoughts and feelings did the experience evoke? We want to know why you went there, what you experienced, and what impressions you came away with. With at least 1 travel story an issue, we run a short sidebar called, 'If You're Going.' It explains how to get to the destination; rates or admission costs if there are any; a schedule of when the attraction is open or list of relevant dates; and an address and phone number for readers to write or call for more information. This sidebar eliminates the need for general-service information in the story.

$ $ WAKE LIVING

Wake County's Premier Lifestyle Publication, Weiss and Hughes Publishing, 189 Wind Chime Ct., Raleigh NC 27615. (919)870-1722. Fax: (919)719-5260. E-mail: dhughes@wakeliving.com. Website: www.wakeliving.com. **50% freelance written**. Quarterly magazine covering lifestyle issues in Wake County, North Carolina. We cover issues important to residents of Wake County. We are committed to improving our readers' overall quality of life and keeping them informed of the lifestyle amenities here. Estab. 2003. Circ. 40,000. Byline given. Pays within 30 days of publication. Offers 25% kill fee. Publishes ms an average of 2 months after acceptance. Buys all rights. Editorial lead time 2-3 months. Submit seasonal material 6 months in advance. Accepts queries by mail, e-mail. Accepts simultaneous submissions. Responds in 2-4 weeks to queries. Sample copy available online. Guidelines available online.
Nonfiction Needs general interest, historical, how-to, home interiors, technology, landscaping, gardening, inspirational, interview, personal experience, photo feature, technical, travel. Does not want opinion pieces, political topics, religious articles. Query. Length: 600-1,200 words. **Pays 35¢/word.**
Photos State availability. Captions, identification of subjects required. Reviews transparencies, GIF/JPEG files. Offers no additional payment for photos accepted with ms.
Columns/Departments Around Town (local lifestyle topics); Hometown Stories, 600 words; Travel (around North Carolina); Home Interiors/Landscaping, all 1,000 words. Restaurants (local restaurants, fine dining), 600-1,000 words. 20-25 Query. **Pays 35¢/word.**
Tips Articles must be specifically focused on Wake County/Raleigh metro issues. We like unusual angles about what makes living here unique from other areas.

North Dakota

$ $ NORTH DAKOTA LIVING MAGAZINE

North Dakota Association of Rural Electric Cooperatives, 3201 Nygren Dr. NW, P.O. Box 727, Mandan ND 58554-0727. (701)663-6501. Fax: (701)663-3745. E-mail: kbrick@ndarec.com. Website: www.ndarec.com. **20% freelance written**. Monthly magazine covering information of interest to memberships of electric cooperatives and telephone cooperatives. We publish a general interest magazine for North Dakotans. We treat subjects pertaining to living and working in the northern Great Plains. We provide progress reporting on electric cooperatives and telephone cooperatives. Estab. 1954. Circ. 70,000. Byline given. Pays on acceptance. No kill fee. Publishes ms an average of 6 months after acceptance. Buys one-time rights. Makes work-for-hire assignments. Editorial lead time 6 months. Submit seasonal material 6 months in advance. Accepts queries by mail, e-mail. Accepts previously published material. Accepts simultaneous submissions. Sample copy and writer's guidelines not available.
Nonfiction Needs general interest, historical, how-to, humor, interview, new product, travel. **Buys 20 mss/year.** Query with published clips. Length: 1,500-2,000 words. **Pays $100-500 minimum for assigned articles. Pays $300-600 for unsolicited articles.**
Photos State availability. Identification of subjects required. Reviews contact sheets. Negotiates payment individually Buys one time rights.
Columns/Departments Energy Use and Financial Planning, both 750 words. 6 Query with published clips. **Pays $100-300.**

Fiction Needs historical, humorous, slice-of-life vignettes, western. **Buys 1 ms/year.** Query with published clips. Length: 1,000-2,500 words. **Pays $100-400.**

Tips Deal with what's real: real data, real people, real experiences, real history, etc.

Ohio

$$ AKRON LIFE & LEISURE

The Magazine of Greater Akron, Baker Media Group, 90 S. Maple St., Akron OH 44302. Fax: (330)253-5868. E-mail: klindsey@bakermediagroup.com. Website: www.akronlife.com. **10% freelance written.** Monthly regional magazine covering Summit, Stark, Portage and Medina counties. Estab. 2002. Circ. 15,000. Byline given. Pays on publication. Offers 50% kill fee. Publishes ms an average of 4-6 months after acceptance. Buys all rights. Editorial lead time 2+ months. Submit seasonal material 6 months in advance. Accepts queries by mail, e-mail, fax. Sample copy free. Guidelines free.

Nonfiction Needs essays, general interest, historical, how-to, humor, interview, photo feature, travel. Query with published clips. Length: 300-2,000 words. **Pays $0.10 max/word for assigned and unsolicited articles.**

Photos Contact: Kathy Moorehouse, Creative Director. State availability. Captions, identification of subjects, model releases required. Reviews GIF/JPEG files. Negotiates payment individually Buys all rights.

Tips "It's best to submit a detailed query along with samples of previously published works. Include why you think the story is of interest to our readers, and be sure to have a fresh approach."

$ BEND OF THE RIVER MAGAZINE

P.O. Box 859, Maumee OH 43537. (419)893-0022. **98% freelance written. This magazine reports that it is eager to work with all writers. "We buy material that we like whether it is by an experienced writer or not."** Monthly magazine for readers interested in northwestern Ohio history and nostalgia. Estab. 1972. Circ. 6,500. Byline given. Pays on publication. No kill fee. Publishes ms an average of 1 month after acceptance. Buys one-time rights. Submit seasonal material 2 months in advance. Responds in 1 week to queries. Sample copy for $1.25.

Nonfiction "We are looking for Toledo area articles about famous people and events of Ohio, Michigan and Indiana." Needs historical. **Buys 75 unsolicited mss/year.** Send complete ms. 1,500 words **Pays $50 on average.**

Tips "Our stockpile is low. Send us something!"

$$$ CINCINNATI MAGAZINE

Emmis Publishing Corp., 441 Vine St., Suite 200, Cincinnati OH 45202-2039. (513)421-4300. Fax: (513)562-2746. Website: www.cincinnatimagazine.com. **Contact:** "See website for appropriate editor." Monthly magazine emphasizing Cincinnati living. Circ. 38,000. Byline given. Pays on publication. No kill fee. Buys all periodical rights. Accepts queries by mail, e-mail. Send SASE for writer's guidelines; view content on magazine website."

Nonfiction Articles on personalities, business, sports, lifestyle relating to Cincinnati and Northern Kentucky. **Buys 12 mss/year.** Query. Length: 2,500-3,500 words. **Pays $500-1,000.**

Columns/Departments Topics are Cincinnati media, arts and entertainment, people, politics, sports, business, regional. Length: 1,000-1,500 words. 10-15 Query. **Pays $200-400.**

Tips "It's most helpful on us if you query in writing, with clips. All articles have a local focus. No generics, please. Also: No movie, book, theater reviews, poetry, or fiction. For special advertising sections, query special sections editor Marnie Hayutin; for Cincinnati Wedding, query custom publishing editor Steve Smith."

$$$ CLEVELAND MAGAZINE

City Magazines, Inc., 1422 Euclid Ave., Suite 730, Cleveland OH 44115. (216)771-2833. Fax: (216)781-6318. E-mail: gleydura@clevelandmagazine.com. Website: www.clevelandmagazine.com. **60% freelance written. Mostly by assignment.** Monthly magazine with a strong Cleveland/Northeast Ohio angle. Estab. 1972. Circ. 50,000. Byline given. Pays on publication. No kill fee. Publishes ms an average of 3 months after acceptance. Buys first rights, buys second serial (reprint) rights, buys electronic rights. Editorial lead time 6 months. Submit seasonal material 8 months in advance. Accepts queries by mail, e-mail, fax. Accepts simultaneous submissions. Responds in 2 months to queries.

Nonfiction Needs general interest, historical, humor, interview, travel, home and garden. Query with published clips. Length: 800-4,000 words. **Pays $250-1,200.**

Columns/Departments My Town (Cleveland first-person stories), 1,100-1,500 words. Query with published clips. **Pays $300**

$$$ COLUMBUS MONTHLY

P.O. Box 29913, Columbus OH 43229-7513. (614)888-4567. Fax: (614)848-3838. **40-60% freelance written. Prefers to work with published/established writers.** Monthly magazine emphasizing subjects specifically related to Columbus and Central Ohio. Circ. 35,000. Byline given. Pays on publication. No kill fee. Publishes ms an average of 2 months after acceptance. Buys all rights. Responds in 1 month to queries. Sample copy for $6.50.

Nonfiction "We like query letters that are well written, indicate the author has some familiarity with *Columbus Monthly,* give us enough detail to make a decision and include at least a basic résumé of the writer and clips." **Buys 2-3 unsolicited mss/year.** Query. Length: 250-4,000 words. **Pays $85-900.**

Tips "It makes sense to start small—something for our City Journal section, perhaps. Stories for that section run between 250-500 words."

HYDE PARK LIVING

Community Publications, Inc., 179 Fairfield Ave., Bellevue KY 41073. (859)291-1412. Fax: (859)291-1417. E-mail: hydepark@livingmagazines.com. Website: www.livingmagazines.com. Monthly magazine covering Hyde Park community. Estab. 1983. Circ. 6,800. Byline given. Pays on publication. Buys all rights. Editorial lead time 2 months. Submit seasonal material 3 months in advance. Accepts queries by mail, e-mail, fax. Guidelines by e-mail.

Nonfiction Needs essays, general interest, historical, humor, inspirational, interview, new product, personal experience, photo feature feature, travel. "Does not want anything unrelated to Hyde Park, Ohio." Query.

Photos State availability. Captions, identification of subjects, model releases required. Reviews contact sheets, negatives, transparencies, prints, GIF/JPEG files. Negotiates payment individually. Buys all rights.

Columns/Departments Financial; Artistic (reviews, etc.); Historic; Food. Query.

Poetry Needs free verse, light verse, traditional. Please query.

INDIAN HILL LIVING

Community Publications, Inc., 179 Fairfield Ave., Bellevue KY 41074. (859)291-1412. Fax: (859)291-1417. E-mail: indianhill@livingmagazines.com. Website: www.livingmagazines.com. Monthly magazine covering Indian Hill community. Estab. 1983. Circ. 3,000. Byline given. Pays on publication. Buys all rights. Editorial lead time 2 months. Submit seasonal material 3 months in advance. Accepts queries by mail, e-mail, fax. Guidelines by e-mail.

Nonfiction Needs book excerpts, essays, expose, general interest, historical, humor, inspirational, interview, new product, personal experience, photo feature, travel. Does not want anything unrelated to Indian Hill, Ohio. Query.

Photos State availability. Captions, identification of subjects, model releases required. Reviews contact sheets, negatives, transparencies, prints, GIF/JPEG files. Negotiates payment individually. Buys all rights.

Columns/Departments Financial; Artistic (reviews, etc.); Historic; Food. Query.

Fiction Needs adventure, historical, humorous, mainstream, slice-of-life vignettes. Query.

Poetry Needs free verse, light verse, traditional. Please query.

$$$ OHIO MAGAZINE

Great Lakes Publishing Co., 1422 Euclid Ave., Suite 730, Cleveland OH 44115. (216)771-2833. E-mail: editorial@ohiomagazine.com. Website: www.ohiomagazine.com. **50% freelance written**. Monthly magazine emphasizing Ohio-based travel, news and feature material that highlights what's special and unique about the state. Estab. 1978. Circ. 80,000. Byline given. Pays on publication. 20% kill fee. Publishes ms an average of 6 months after acceptance. Buys first North American serial rights, buys one-time rights, buys second serial (reprint) rights, buys all rights. First serial rights Submit seasonal material 6 months in advance. Accepts queries by mail, e-mail, fax. Responds in 3 months to queries. Responds in 3 months to mss. Sample copy for $3.95 and 9 × 12 SAE or online. Guidelines available online.

Nonfiction Length: 1,000-3,000 words. **Pays $300-1,200.**

Reprints Contact Emily Vanuch, advertising coordinator Pays 50% of amount paid for an original article

Photos Contact: Lesley Blake, art director. Rate negotiable

Columns/Departments minimum 5 unsolicited **Pays $100-600.**

Tips "Freelancers should send all queries in writing (either by mail or e-mail), not by telephone. Successful queries demonstrate an intimate knowledge of the publication. We are looking to increase our circle of writers who can write about the state in an informative and upbeat style. Strong reporting skills are highly valued."

$$ OVER THE BACK FENCE

Southern Ohio's Own Magazine, Long Point Media, P.O. Box 756, Chillicothe OH 45601. (800)718-5727. Fax: (330)220-3083. E-mail: sarahw@longpointmedia.com. Website: www.backfencemagazine.com. Bimonthly magazine. "We are a regional magazine serving Southern Ohio. *Over The Back Fence* has a wholesome, neighborly style. It appeals to readers from young adults to seniors, showcasing art and travel opportunities in the area." Estab. 1994. Circ. 15,000. Byline given. Pays on publication. No kill fee. Publishes ms an average of 1 year after acceptance. Buys one-time North American serial rights. Makes work-for-hire assignments. Editorial lead time 1 year. Submit seasonal material 1 year in advance. Accepts queries by mail. Accepts simultaneous submissions. Responds in 3 months to queries. Sample copy for $4 or on website. Guidelines available online.

Nonfiction Needs general interest, historical, humor, inspirational, interview, personal experience, photo feature, travel. **Buys 9-12 mss/year.** Send complete ms. Length: 750-1,000 words. **Pays 10¢/word minimum, negotiable depending on experience.**

Reprints Send photocopy of article or short story and typed ms with rights for sale ted, and information about when and where the material previously appeared. Payment negotiable

Photos If sending photos as part of a text/photo package, please request our photo guidelines and submit samples. Captions, identification of subjects, model releases required. $25-100/photo Buys one time rights.

Columns/Departments The Arts, 750-1,000 words; History (relevant to a designated county), 750-1,000 words; 600-850 words; Profiles From Our Past, 300-600 words; Sport & Hobby, 750-1,000 words; Our Neighbors (i.e., people helping others), 750-1,000 words. All must be relevant to Southern Ohio. 24 Query with or without published clips or send complete ms. **Pays 10¢/word minimum, negotiable depending on experience.**

Fiction Needs humorous. **Buys 4 mss/year.** Query with published clips. Length: 600-800 words. **Pays 10¢/word minimum, negotiable depending on experience.**

Tips "Our approach can be equated to a friendly and informative conversation with a neighbor about interesting people, places, and events in Southern Ohio (counties: Adams, Athens, Brown, Clark, Clermont, Clinton, Coshocton, Fayette, Fairfield, Franklin, Gallia, Greene, Guernsey, Highland, Hocking, Holmes, Jackson, Lawrence, Licking, Madison, Meigs, Miami, Morgan, Muskingum, Noble, Perry, Pickaway, Pike, Ross, Scioto, Vinton, Warren, Washington, and Wayne)."

SYCAMORE LIVING

Community Publications, Inc., 179 Fairfield Ave., Bellevue KY 41073. (859)291-1412. Fax: (859)291-1417. E-mail: sycamore@livingmagazines.com. Website: www.livingmagazines.com. Monthly magazine covering Sycamore community. Estab. 1983. Circ. 6,600. Byline given. Pays on publication. Buys all rights. Editorial lead time 2 months. Submit seasonal material 3 months in advance. Accepts queries by mail, e-mail, fax. Guidelines by e-mail.

Nonfiction Needs book excerpts, essays, expose, general interest, historical, humor, inspirational, interview, new product, personal experience, photo feature, travel. Does not want anything unrelated to Sycamore, Ohio. Query.

Photos State availability. Captions, identification of subjects, model releases required. Reviews contact sheets, negatives, transparencies, prints, GIF/JPEG files. Negotiates payment individually. Buys all rights.

Columns/Departments Financial; Artistic (reviews, etc.); Historic; Food. Query.

Fiction Needs adventure, historical, humorous, mainstream, slice-of-life vignettes. Query.

Poetry Needs free verse, light verse, traditional. Please query.

WYOMING LIVING

Community Publications, Inc., 179 Fairfield Ave., Bellevue KY 41073. (859)291-1412. Fax: (859)291-1417. E-mail: wyoming@livingmagazines.com. Website: www.livingmagazines.com. Monthly magazine covering Wyoming community. Estab. 1983. Circ. 3,400. Byline given. Pays on publication. Buys all rights. Editorial lead time 2 months. Submit seasonal material 3 months in advance. Accepts queries by mail, e-mail, fax. Guidelines by e-mail.

Nonfiction Needs book excerpts, essays, expose, general interest, historical, humor, inspirational, interview, new product, personal experience, photo feature, travel. Does not want anything unrelated to Wyoming, Ohio. Query.
Photos State availability. Captions, identification of subjects, model releases required. Reviews contact sheets, negatives, transparencies, prints, GIF/JPEG files. Negotiates payment individually. Buys all rights.
Columns/Departments Financial; Artistic (reviews, etc.); Historic; Food. Query.
Fiction Needs adventure, historical, humorous, mainstream, slice-of-life vignettes. Query.
Poetry Needs free verse, light verse, traditional. Please query.

Oklahoma

$$ N INTERMISSION

Langdon Publishing, 110 E. 2nd St., Tulsa OK 74103-3212. (918)596-2368. Fax: (918)596-7144. E-mail: nhermann@ci.tulsa.ok.us. Website: www.tulsapac.com. **Contact:** Nancy Hermann. **30% freelance written**. Monthly magazine covering entertainment. "We feature profiles of entertainers appearing at our center, Q&As, stories on the events and entertainers slated for the Tulsa PAC." Byline given. Pays on publication. Offers 50% kill fee. Publishes ms an average of 1 month after acceptance. Buys one-time rights. Editorial lead time 2 months. Submit seasonal material 2 months in advance. Accepts queries by mail, e-mail. Accepts simultaneous submissions. Responds in 2 weeks to queries. Sample copy available online. Guidelines by e-mail.
Nonfiction Needs general interest, interview. Does not want personal experience. **Buys 35 mss/year.** Query with published clips. Length: 600-1,400 words. **Pays $100-200.**
Columns/Departments Q&A (personalities and artists tied into the events at the Tulsa PAC), 1,100 words. 12 Query with published clips. **Pays $100-150.**
Tips "Look ahead at our upcoming events, find an interesting slant on an event. Interview someone who would be of general interest."

$$ OKLAHOMA TODAY

P.O. Box 1468, Oklahoma City OK 73101. (405)521-2496. Fax: (405)522-4588. E-mail: mccune@oklahomatoday.com. Website: www.oklahomatoday.com. **80% freelance written. Works with approximately 25 new/unpublished writers each year.** Bimonthly magazine covering people, places, and things Oklahoman. We are interested in showing off the best Oklahoma has to offer; we're pretty serious about our travel slant but regularly run history, nature, and personality profiles. Estab. 1956. Circ. 45,000. Byline given. Pays on publication. No kill fee. Publishes ms an average of 6 months after acceptance. Buys first worldwide serial rights. Submit seasonal material 1 year in advance. Accepts queries by mail, e-mail. Responds in 4 months to queries. Sample copy for $3.95 and 9 × 12 SASE or online. Guidelines available online.
Nonfiction Needs book excerpts, on Oklahoma topics, historical, Oklahoma only, interview, Oklahomans only, photo feature, in Oklahoma, travel, in Oklahoma. No phone queries. **Buys 20-40 mss/year.** Query with published clips. Length: 250-3,000 words. **Pays $25-750.**
Photos We are especially interested in developing contacts with photographers who live in Oklahoma or have shot here. Send samples. Photo guidelines for SASE. Captions, identification of subjects required. Reviews 4 × 5, 2¼:x2¼, and 35mm color transparencies, high-quality transparencies, slides, and b&w prints. Pays $50-750 for color Buys one-time rights to use photos for promotional purposes.
Fiction Needs novel concepts, occasionally short fiction.
Tips The best way to become a regular contributor to *Oklahoma Today* is to query us with 1 or more story ideas, each developed to give us an idea of your proposed slant. We're looking for lively, concise, well-researched and reported stories, stories that don't need to be heavily edited and are not newspaper style. We have a 3-person full-time editorial staff, and freelancers who can write and have done their homework get called again and again.

Oregon

$$ OREGON COAST

4969 Highway 101 N. #2, Florence OR 97439. E-mail: Rosemary@nwmags.com. Website: www.northwestmagazines.com. **Contact:** Rosemary Camozzi. **65% freelance written**. Bimonthly magazine covering the Oregon Coast. Estab. 1982. Circ. 50,000. Byline given. Pays after publication. Offers 33% (on assigned stories only, not on stories accepted on spec) kill fee. Publishes ms an average of up to

1 year after acceptance. Buys first North American serial rights. Submit seasonal material 6 months in advance. Accepts queries by mail, e-mail. Responds in 3 months to queries. Sample copy for $4.50. Guidelines available on website.

- This company also publishes *Northwest Travel*.

Nonfiction "A true regional with general interest, historical/nostalgic, humor, interview/profile, personal experience, photo feature, travel, and nature as pertains to Oregon Coast." **Buys 55 mss/year.** Query with published clips. Length: 500-1,500 words. **Pays $75-350, plus 2 contributor copies.**
Reprints Send tearsheet or photocopy and information about when and where the material previously appeared. Pays an average of 60% of the amount paid for an original article.
Photos Photo submissions with no ms or stand alone or cover photos. Send photos. Captions, identification of subjects, True required. Slides or high-resolution digital. Buys one time rights.
Tips "Slant article for readers who do not live at the Oregon Coast. At least 1 historical article is used in each issue. Manuscript/photo packages are preferred over manuscripts with no photos. List photo credits and captions for each photo. Check all facts, proper names, and numbers carefully in photo/manuscript packages. Must pertain to Oregon Coast somehow.

Pennsylvania

$ $ BERKS COUNTY LIVING

201 Washington St., Suite 525, GoggleWorks Center for the Arts, Reading PA 19601. (610)898-1928. Fax: (610)898-1933. E-mail: fscoboria@berkscountyliving.com. Website: www.berkscountyliving.com. **Contact:** Francine Scoboria. **90% freelance written**. Bimonthly magazine covering topics of interest to people living in Berks County, Pennsylvania. Estab. 2000. Circ. 36,000. Byline given. Pays on publication. Offers 25% kill fee. Publishes ms an average of 4 months after acceptance. Buys first North American serial rights. Editorial lead time 3 months. Submit seasonal material 4 months in advance. Accepts queries by mail, e-mail. Accepts previously published material. Accepts simultaneous submissions. Responds in 1 week to queries. Responds in 1 month to mss. Sample copy for sae with 9 × 12 envelope and 2 First-Class stamps. Guidelines available online.
Nonfiction Articles must be associated with Berks County, Pennsylvania. Needs expose, general interest, historical, how-to, humor, inspirational, interview, new product, photo feature, travel, food, health. **Buys 25 mss/year.** Query. Length: 750-2,000 words. **Pays $150-400.**
Photos State availability. Captions, identification of subjects, model releases required. Reviews 35mm or greater transparencies, any size prints. Negotiates payment individually Buys one time rights.

$ $ MAIN LINE TODAY

Today Media, Inc., 4699 West Chester Pike, Newtown Square PA 19073. (610)848-6037. Fax: (610)325-5215. Website: www.mainlinetoday.com. **60% freelance written**. Monthly magazine serving Philadelphia's main line and western suburbs. Estab. 1996. Circ. 20,000. Byline given. Pays on publication. Offers 25% kill fee. Publishes ms an average of 3 months after acceptance. Buys first North American serial rights. Editorial lead time 5 months. Submit seasonal material 5 months in advance. Accepts queries by fax. Accepts simultaneous submissions. Responds in 2 weeks to queries. Responds in 1 month to mss. Sample copy free. Guidelines free.
Nonfiction Needs book excerpts, historical, how-to, humor, interview, opinion, photo feature, travel. Health & Wellness Guide (September and March). Query with published clips. Length: 400-3,000 words. **Pays $125-650.**
Photos State availability. Identification of subjects, model releases required. Reviews GIF/JPEG files. Negotiates payment individually. Buys one time rights.
Columns/Departments Profile (local personality); Neighborhood (local people/issues); End of the Line (essay/humor); Living Well (health/wellness), all 1,600 words. 50 Query with published clips. **Pays $125-350.**

$ $ MILFORD MAGAZINE

Navigating the Delware River Highlands, Pike Media Partners, P.O. Box 486, 201 W. Harford St., Milford PA 18337. E-mail: editor@milfordmagazine.com. Website: www.milfordmagazine.com. **100% freelance written**. Monthly magazine covering community, culture & nature specific to the Upper Delaware Highlands Regions. We seek to contribute to the best definition of community that is defined not just by demographic charactertistics but by shared values. We value quality of life, diversity,protection of the environemnt, cultivation of the arts, & smart growth. We welcome those new to the area. Mostly, we value integrity & service to those we share this planet with, this continent, & especially those with whom we share the majesty & magnificence of the Delaware River. Estab. 2001. Circ. 20,000. Byline given. Pays on publication. Offers 10% kill fee. Publishes ms an average of 21 months after acceptance. Buys one-time rights. Editorial lead time 2 months. Submit seasonal material 6 months in advance. Accepts queries by mail, e-mail, fax. Accepts previously published material. Accepts simultaneous submissions. Responds in 2 weeks to queries. No mss. please. Sample copy available online. Guidelines for #10 SASE.

- Ours is a free publication.

Nonfiction Needs essays, general interest, historical, how-to, interview, opinion, personal experience, photo feature, travel, Nature. No fiction. No articles unrelated to our geographic area. **Buys 36 mss/year.** Query. Length: 750-2,000 words. **Pays $100-400 for assigned articles. Pays $100-400 for unsolicited articles.**

Photos Contact: James Sheehan, art director. State availability. Captions, model releases required. Reviews GIF/JPEG files. Offers no additional payment for photos accepted with ms. Offers $25-175 per photo.

Columns/Departments Look Back (Nostalgia-History related to the area-must include photos(s)), 750 words. 10 mss/yr. Query with or without published clips. **Pay $150**

Tips Be sure you write to our target audience & area. The magazine is a free publication for residents & visitors to the Upper Delaware Highlands Region (NY, NJ & PA).

$$ PENNSYLVANIA

Pennsylvania Magazine Co., P.O. Box 755, Camp Hill PA 17001-0755. (717)697-4660. E-mail: pamag@aol.com. Website: www.pa-mag.com. **90% freelance written**. Bimonthly magazine covering people, places, events, and history in Pennsylvania. Estab. 1981. Circ. 33,000. Byline given. Pays on acceptance except for articles (by authors unknown to us) sent on speculation. Offers kill fee. 25% kill fee for assigned articles. Publishes ms an average of 9 months after acceptance. Buys first North American serial rights, buys one-time rights. Submit seasonal material 9 months in advance. Accepts queries by mail, e-mail. Responds in 4-6 weeks to queries. Sample copy free. Guidelines for #10 SASE or by e-mail.

Nonfiction Features include general interest, historical, photo feature, vacations and travel, people/family success stories—all dealing with or related to Pennsylvania. Send photocopies of possible illustrations with query or ms. Include SASE. Nothing on Amish topics, hunting, or skiing. **Buys 75-120 mss/year.** Query. Length: 750-2,500 words. **Pays 15¢/word.**

Reprints Send photocopy with rights for sale noted and information about when and where the material previously appeared. Pays 5¢/word.

Photos No original slides or transparencies. Photography Essay (highlights annual photo essay contest entries and showcases individual photographers). Captions, True required. Reviews 35mm 2¼ × 2¼ color transparencies, 5 × 7 to 8 × 10 color prints, digital photos (send printouts and CD OR DVD or contact eitodro uplo tad to FTP site. Pays $35-45 . Pays $25-35 for inside photos; $150 for covers Buys one-time rights.

Columns/Departments Round Up (short items about people, unusual events, museums, historical topics/events, family and individually owned consumer-related businesses), 250-1,300 words; Town and Country (items about people or events illustrated with commissioned art), 500 words. Include SASE. Query. **Pays 15¢/word.**

Tips "Our publication depends upon freelance work—send queries. Remember that a subject isn't an idea. Send the topic and your approach to the topic when you query. Answer the question: Would this be interesting to someone across the state?"

$$ PENNSYLVANIA HERITAGE

Pennsylvania Historical and Museum Commission and the Pennsylvania Heritage Society, Commonwealth Keystone Bldg., Plaza Level, 400 North St., Harrisburg PA 17120-0053. (717)787-7522. Fax: (717)787-8312. E-mail: miomalley@state.pa.us. Website: www.paheritage.org. **75% freelance written. Prefers to work with published/established writers.** Quarterly magazine. *Pennsylvania Heritage* introduces readers to Pennsylvania's rich culture and historic legacy; educates and sensitizes them to the value of preserving that heritage; and entertains and involves them in such a way as to ensure that Pennsylvania's past has a future. The magazine is intended for intelligent lay readers. Estab. 1974. Circ. 10,000. Byline given. Pays on publication. Publishes ms an average of 1 year after acceptance. Buys all print and electronic rights for the web. Accepts queries by mail, e-mail. Responds in 10 weeks to queries. Responds in 8 months to mss Sample copy for $5 and 9 × 12 SAE or online Guidelines for #10 SASE or online

- *Pennsylvania Heritage* is now considering freelance submissions that are shorter in length (2,000-3,000 words); pictorial/photographic essays; biographies of famous (and not-so-famous) Pennsylvanians; and interviews with individuals who have helped shape, make, and preserve the Keystone State's history and heritage.

Nonfiction "Our format requires feature-length articles. Manuscripts with illustrations are especially sought for publication. We are now looking for shorter (2,000 words) manuscripts that are heavily illustrated with publication-quality photographs or artwork. We are eager to work with experienced travel writers for destination pieces on historical sites and museums that make up `The Pennsylvania Trail of History.' Art, science, biographies, industry, business, politics, transportation, military, historic preservation, archaeology, photography, etc." No articles which do not relate to Pennsylvania history or culture. **Buys 20-24 mss/year.** Prefers to see mss with suggested illustrations. Length: 2,000-3,500 words. **Pays $100-500.**

Photos State availability of or send photos. Captions, identification of subjects required. $25-200 for transparencies; $5-75 for b&w photos Buys one time rights.

Tips "We are looking for well-written, interesting material that pertains to any aspect of Pennsylvania history or culture. Potential contributors should realize that, although our articles are popularly styled, they are not light, puffy, or breezy; in fact they demand strident documentation and substantiation (sans footnotes). The most frequent mistake made by writers in completing articles for us is making them either too scholarly or too sentimental or nostalgic. We want material which educates, but also entertains. Authors should make history readable and enjoyable. Our goal is to make the Keystone State's history come to life in a meaningful, memorable way."

$$ PHILADELPHIA STYLE

Philadelphia's Premier Magazine for Lifestyle & Fashion, Philadelphia Style Magazine, LLC, 141 League St., Philadelphia PA 19147. (215)468-6670. Fax: (215)223-3095. E-mail: info@phillystylemag.com. Website: www.phillystylemag.com. **Contact:** Sarah Schaffer, editor in chief. **50% freelance written**. "Bimonthly magazine covering upscale living in the Philadelphia region. Topics include: celebrity interviews, fashion (men's and women's), food, home and design, real estate, dining, beauty, travel, arts and entertainment, and more. Our magazine is a positive look at the best ways to live in the Philadelphia region. Submitted articles should speak to an upscale, educated audience of professionals that live in the Delaware Valley." Estab. 1999. Circ. 60,000. Byline given. Pays on publication. Offers 25% kill fee. Publishes ms an average of 3 months after acceptance. Buys first rights. Editorial lead time 2-4 months. Submit seasonal material 6 months in advance. Accepts queries by mail, e-mail, fax.

Nonfiction Needs general interest, interview, travel, region-specific articles. "We are not looking for articles that do not have a regional spin." **Buys 100+ mss/year.** Send complete ms. Length: 300-2,500 words. **Pays $50-500.**

Columns/Departments Declarations (celebrity interviews and celebrity contributors); Currents (fashion news); Manor (home and design news); Liberties (beauty and travel news); Dish (dining news); Life in the City (fresh, quirky, regional reporting on books, real estate, art, retail, dining, events, and little-known stories/facts about the region), 100-500 words; Vanguard (people on the forefront of Philadelphia's arts, media, fashion, business, and social scene), 500-700 words; In the Neighborhood (reader-friendly reporting on up-and-coming areas of the region including dining, shopping, attractions, and recreation), 2,000-2,500 words. Query with published clips or send complete ms. **Pays $50-500.**

Tips "Mail queries with clips or manuscripts. Articles should speak to a stylish, educated audience."

$$$$ PITTSBURGH MAGAZINE

WQED Pittsburgh, 4802 Fifth Ave., Pittsburgh PA 15213. (412)622-1360. E-mail: lriley@wged.org. Website: www.pittsburghmag.com. **70% freelance written**. Monthly magazine. *Pittsburgh* presents issues, analyzes problems, and strives to encourage a better understanding of the community. Our region is Western Pennsylvania, Eastern Ohio, Northern West Virginia, and Western Maryland. Estab. 1970. Circ. 75,000. Byline given. Pays on publication. Offers kill fee. Offers kill fee. Publishes ms an average of 2 months after acceptance. Buys first North American serial rights, buys second serial (reprint) rights. Submit seasonal material 6 months in advance. Accepts queries by mail. Responds in 2 months to queries. Sample copy for $2 (old back issues). Writer's guidelines online or via SASE

- The editor reports a need for more hard news and stories targeting readers in their 30s and 40s, especially those with young families. Prefers to work with published/established writers. The monthly magazine is purchased on newsstands and by subscription, and is given to those who contribute $40 or more/year to public TV in western Pennsylvania.

Nonfiction Without exception—whether the topic is business, travel, the arts, or lifestyle—each story is clearly oriented to Pittsburghers of today and to the greater Pittsburgh region of today. Must have greater Pittsburgh angle. No fax, phone, or e-mail queries. No complete mss. Needs expose, lifestyle, sports, informational, service, business, medical, profile. We have minimal interest in historical articles and we do not publish fiction, poetry, advocacy, or personal reminiscence pieces. Query in writing with outline and clips. Length: 1,200-4,000 words. **Pays $300-1,500+.**

Photos Query. Model releases required. Pays prenegotiated expenses of writer on assignment
Columns/Departments The Front (short, front-of-the-book items). Length: 300 words maximum. **Pays $50-150.**
Tips Best bet to break in is through hard news with a region-wide impact or service pieces or profiles with a regional interest. The point is that we want more stories that reflect our region, not just a tiny part. And we *never* consider any story without a strong regional focus. We do not respond to fax and e-mail queries.

$ SUSQUEHANNA LIFE

Central Pennsylvania's Lifestyle Magazine, ELS & Associates, 637 Market St., Lewisburg PA 17837. Fax: (570)524-7796. E-mail: info@susquehannalife.com. Website: www.susquehannalife.com. **80% freelance written**. Quarterly magazine covering Central Pennsylvania lifestyle. Estab. 1993. Circ. 45,000. Byline given. Pays on publication. Offers 50% kill fee. Publishes ms an average of 6-9 months after acceptance. Buys first North American serial rights, buys electronic rights. Editorial lead time 3-6 months. Submit seasonal material 4-6 months in advance. Accepts queries by e-mail. Responds in 4-6 weeks to queries. Responds in 1-3 months to mss. Sample copy for $4.95, plus 5 first-class stamps. Guidelines for #10 SASE.
Nonfiction Needs book excerpts, general interest, historical, how-to, inspirational, related to the region, interview, photo feature, travel. Does not want fiction. **Buys 30-40 mss/year.** Query or send complete ms. Length: 800-1,200 words. **Pays $75-125.**
Photos Send photos. Captions, identification of subjects, model releases required. Reviews contact sheets, prints, GIF/JPEG files. Offers $20-25/photo. Buys one time rights.
Poetry Must have a Central PA angle.
Tips When you query, do not address letter to 'Dear Sir'—address the letter to the name of the publisher/ editor. Demonstrate your ability to write. You need to be familiar with the type of articles we use and the particular flavor of the region. Only accepts submissions with a Central PA angle.

Rhode Island

$$$ RHODE ISLAND MONTHLY

The Providence Journal Co., 717 Allens Ave., Suite 105, Providence RI 02905. (401)649-4800. Website: www.rimonthly.com. **50% freelance written**. Monthly magazine. *Rhode Island Monthly* is a general interest consumer magazine with a strict Rhode Island focus. Estab. 1988. Circ. 41,000. Byline given. Pays on acceptance. Offers 25% kill fee. Publishes ms an average of 3 months after acceptance. Buys all rights for 90 days from date of publication. Editorial lead time 3 months. Submit seasonal material 6 months in advance. Accepts queries by mail, e-mail, fax. Responds in 6 weeks to queries. Guidelines free.
Nonfiction Needs expose, general interest, interview, photo feature. **Buys 40 mss/year.** Query with published clips. Length: 1,800-3,000 words. **Pays $600-1,200.**

South Carolina

$$ HILTON HEAD MONTHLY

P.O. Box 5926, Hilton Head Island SC 29938. Fax: (843)842-5743. E-mail: editor@hiltonheadmonthly.com. Website: www.hiltonheadmonthly.com. **Contact:** Sally Mahan. **75% freelance written**. Monthly magazine covering the business, people, and lifestyle of Hilton Head, South Carolina. "Our mission is to provide fresh, upbeat reading about the residents, lifestyle and community affairs of Hilton Head Island, an upscale, intensely pro-active resort community on the East Coast. We are not even remotely `trendy,' but we like to see how national trends/issues play out on a local level. Especially interested in: home design and maintenance, entrepreneurship, health issues, nature, area history, golf/tennis/ boating, volunteerism." Circ. 28,000. Byline given. Pays on publication. Offers 50% kill fee. Publishes ms an average of 6 months after acceptance. Buys first North American serial rights. Makes work-for-hire assignments. Editorial lead time 3 months. Submit seasonal material 4 months in advance. Accepts queries by mail, e-mail, fax. Accepts previously published material. Accepts simultaneous submissions. Responds in 1 week to queries. Responds in 4 months to mss. Sample copy for $3.
Nonfiction Needs general interest, historical, history only, how-to, home related, humor, interview, Hilton Head residents only, opinion, general humor or Hilton Head Island community affairs, personal experience, travel. No exposé interviews with people who are not Hilton Head residents; profiles of people,

events, or businesses in Beaufort, South Carolina; Savannah, Georgia; Charleston; or other surrounding cities, unless it's within a travel piece. **Buys 225-250 mss/year.** Query with published clips.
Photos State availability. Reviews contact sheets, prints, slides; any size. Negotiates payment individually Buys one time rights.
Columns/Departments News; Business; Lifestyles (hobbies, health, sports, etc.); Home; Around Town (local events, charities and personalities); People (profiles, weddings, etc.). Query with synopsis. **Pays 15¢/word.**
Tips Give us concise, bullet-style descriptions of what the article covers (in the query letter); choose upbeat, pro-active topics; delight us with your fresh (not trendy) description and word choice.

$ SANDLAPPER

The Magazine of South Carolina, The Sandlapper Society, Inc., 3007 Millwood Ave., Columbia SC 29205. (803)779-8763. Fax: (803)359-254-4833. E-mail: aida@sandlapper.org. Website: www.sandlapper.org. **60% freelance written**. Quarterly magazine focusing on the positive aspects of South Carolina. "*Sandlapper* is intended to be read at those times when people want to relax with an attractive, high-quality magazine that entertains and informs them about their state." Estab. 1989. Circ. 18,000 with a readership of 60,000. Byline given. Pays during the dateline period. No kill fee. Publishes ms an average of 1 year after acceptance. Buys first North American serial rights and the right to reprint. Submit seasonal material 6 months in advance. Accepts queries by mail, e-mail, fax. Sample copy available online. Guidelines for #10 SASE.
Nonfiction Feature articles and photo essays about South Carolina's interesting people, places, cuisine, history and culture, things to do. Needs essays, general interest, humor, interview, photo feature. Query with clips and SASE. Length: 500-2,500 words. **Pays $100/published page. Doesn't pay expenses of writers and photographers on assignment.**
Photos *Sandlapper* buys b&w prints and art. Photographers should submit working cutlines for each photograph. We accept prints and digital images. Pays $25-75, $100 for cover or centerspread photo
Tips "We're not interested in articles about topical issues, politics, crime, or commercial ventures. Avoid first-person nostalgia and remembrances of places that no longer exist. We look for top-quality literature. Humor is encouraged. Good taste is a standard. Unique angles are critical for acceptance. Dare to be bold, but not too bold."

Tennessee

$$ AT HOME TENNESSEE

Pinpoint Publishing Group, 671 N. Ericson Rd., Suite 200, Cordova TN 38018. (901)684-4155. Fax: (901)684-4156. Website: www.athometn.com. **50% freelance written**. Monthly magazine. Estab. 2002. Circ. 37,000. Byline given. Pays on publication. Offers 50% kill fee. Makes work-for-hire assignments. Editorial lead time 2 months. Submit seasonal material 2-3 months in advance. Accepts queries by e-mail. Responds in 1-2 months to queries. Sample copy for $4.99. Guidelines free.
Nonfiction Needs general interest, how-to, interview, travel, landscaping, arts, design. Does not want opinion. Query with published clips. Length: 400-900 words. **Pays $50-200.**
Photos Contact: Contact Elizabeth Chapman, art director. Send photos. Reviews GIF/JPEG files.

$$ MEMPHIS DOWNTOWNER MAGAZINE

Downtown Productions, Inc., 408 S. Front St., Suite 109, Memphis TN 38103. Fax: (901)525-7128. E-mail: editor@memphisdowntowner.com. Website: www.memphisdowntowner.com. **50% freelance written**. Monthly magazine covering features on positive aspects with a Memphis tie-in, especially to downtown. "We feature people, companies, nonprofits and other issues that the general Memphis public would find interesting, entertaining, and informative. All editorial focuses on the positives Memphis has. No negative commentary or personal judgements. Controversial subjects should be treated fairly and balanced without bias." Estab. 1991. Circ. 30,000. Byline given. Pays on 15th of month in which assignment is published. Offers 25% kill fee. Publishes ms an average of 2-6 months after acceptance. Buys all rights for 90 days, with re-licensing rights thereafter. Editorial lead time 3-6 months. Submit seasonal material 3-6 months in advance. Accepts queries by mail, e-mail. Responds in 2 weeks to queries. Sample copy free. Guidelines by e-mail.
Nonfiction Needs general interest, historical, how-to, humor, interview, personal experience, photo feature. **Buys 40-50 mss/year.** Query with published clips. Length: 600-2,000 words. **Pays scales vary depending on scope of assignment, but typically runs 15¢/word.**

Photos State availability. Identification of subjects required. Reviews GIF/JPEG files (300 dpi). Negotiates payment individually.
Columns/Departments So It Goes (G-rated humor), 600-800 words; Discovery 901 (Memphis one-of-a-kinds), 1,000-1,200 words. 6 Query with published clips. **Pays $100-150.**
Fillers Unusual, interesting, or how-to or what to look for appealing to a large, general audience.
Tips "Always pitch an actual story idea. E-mails that simply let us know you're a freelance writer mysteriously disappear from our inboxes. Actually read the magazine before you pitch. Get to know the regular columns and departments. In your pitch, explain where in the magazine you think your story idea would best fit. See website for magazine samples and past issues."

Texas

$ HILL COUNTRY SUN

T.D. Austin Lane, Inc., 100 Commons Rd., Suite 7, #319, Dripping Springs TX 78620. (512)484-9715. Fax: (512)847-5162. E-mail: melissa@hillcountrysun.com. Website: www.hillcountrysun.com. **75% freelance written**. Monthly tabloid covering traveling in the Central Texas Hill Country. "We publish stories of interesting people, places and events in the Central Texas Hill Country." Estab. 1990. Circ. 34,000. Byline given. Pays on acceptance. No kill fee. Publishes ms an average of 2 months after acceptance. Buys one-time rights. Editorial lead time 1 month. Submit seasonal material 2 months in advance. Accepts queries by mail and e-mail. Responds in 1 week to queries. Responds in 1 month to mss. Sample copy free. Guidelines available online.
Nonfiction Needs interview, travel. No first person articles. **Buys 50 mss/year.** Query. Length: 600-800 words. **Pays $50-60.**
Photos State availability of or send photos.. Identification of subjects required. No additional payment for photos accepted with ms. Buys one-time rights.
Tips "Writers must be familiar with both the magazine's style and the Texas Hill Country."

$$$ HOUSTON PRESS

New Times, Inc., 1621 Milam, Suite 100, Houston TX 77002. (713)280-2400. Fax: (713)280-2444. E-mail: julia.youssefnia@houstonpress.com. Website: www.houstonpress.com. **40% freelance written**. Weekly tabloid covering news and arts stories of interest to a Houston audience. If the same story could run in Seattle, then it's not for us. Estab. 1989. Byline given. Pays on publication. No kill fee. Publishes ms an average of 2 weeks after acceptance. Buys first North American serial rights, buys website rights. Editorial lead time 2 months. Submit seasonal material 3 months in advance. Sample copy for $3.
Nonfiction Needs expose, general interest, interview, arts reviews. Query with published clips. Length: 300-4,500 words. **Pays $10-1,000.**
Photos State availability. Identification of subjects required. Negotiates payment individually Buys all rights.

$$$ TEXAS HIGHWAYS

The Travel Magazine of Texas, Box 141009, Austin TX 78714-1009. (512)486-5858. Fax: (512)486-5879. Website: www.texashighways.com. **70% freelance written**. Monthly magazine encourages travel within the state and tells the Texas story to readers around the world. Estab. 1974. Circ. 250,000. Pays on acceptance. No kill fee. Publishes ms an average of 1 year after acceptance. Buys first North American serial rights, buys electronic rights. Accepts queries by mail. Responds in 2 months to queries. Guidelines available online.
Nonfiction Subjects should focus on things to do or places to see in Texas. Include historical, cultural, and geographical aspects if appropriate. Text should be meticulously researched. Include anecdotes, historical references, quotations and, where relevant, geologic, botanical, and zoological information. Query with description, published clips, additional background materials (charts, maps, etc.) and SASE. Length: 1,200-1,500 words. **Pays 40-50¢/word.**
Tips We like strong leads that draw in the reader immediately and clear, concise writing. Be specific and avoid superlatives. Avoid overused words. Don't forget the basics—who, what, where, when, why, and how.

$$$$ TEXAS MONTHLY

Emmis Publishing LP, P.O. Box 1569, Austin TX 78767. (512)320-6900. Fax: (512)476-9007. Website: www.texasmonthly.com. **Contact:** Jake Silverstein, editor. **10% freelance written**. Monthly magazine covering Texas. Estab. 1973. Circ. 300,000. Byline given. Pays on acceptance. Publishes ms an average of 1-3 months after acceptance. Buys first North American serial rights, buys first rights, buys one-time rights, buys electronic rights. Editorial lead time 2 months. Submit seasonal material 3 months in advance. Accepts queries by mail, e-mail, fax. Responds in 6-8 weeks to queries. Responds in 6-8 weeks to mss. Sample copy for $7. Guidelines available online.

Nonfiction Contact: Contact John Broders, associate editor. Needs book excerpts, essays, expose, general interest, interview, personal experience, photo feature, travel. Does not want articles without a Texas connection. **Buys 15 mss/year.** Query. Length: 2,000-5,000 words. **Pays $1/word.**

Photos Contact: Contact Leslie Baldwin, photography editor (lbaldwin@texasmonthly.com).

Tips "Stories must appeal to an educated Texas audience. We like solidly researched reporting that uncovers issues of public concern, reveals offbeat and previously unreported topics, or uses a novel approach to familiar topics. Any issue of the magazine would be a helpful guide. We do not use fiction, poetry, or cartoons."

$$ TEXAS PARKS & WILDLIFE

4200 Smith School Rd, Austin TX 78744. (512)389-8793. Fax: (512)707-1913. E-mail: robert.macias@tpwd.state.tx.us. Website: www.tpwmagazine.com. **80% freelance written**. Monthly magazine featuring articles about "Texas hunting, fishing, birding, outdoor recreation, game and nongame wildlife, state parks, environmental issues. All articles must be about Texas. Estab. 1942. Circ. 150,000. Byline given. Pays on acceptance. Offers kill fee. Kill fee determined by contract, usually $200-250 Publishes ms an average of 4 months after acceptance. Buys first rights. Accepts queries by mail. Responds in 1 month to queries. Responds in 3 months to mss. Sample copy available online. Guidelines available online.

- *Texas Parks & Wildlife* needs more short items for front-of-the-book scout section and wildlife articles written from a natural history perspective (not for hunters)."

Nonfiction Needs general interest, Texas only, how-to, outdoor activities, photo feature, travel, state parks and small towns. **Buys 60 mss/year.** Query with published clips; follow up by e-mail 1 month after submitting query. Length: 500-2,500 words. **Pays 50¢/word.**

Photos Send photos. to photo editor Captions, identification of subjects required. Reviews transparencies. Offers $65-500/photo Buys one time rights.

Tips "Queries with a strong seasonal peg are preferred. Our planning progress begins 7 months before the date of publication. That means you have to think ahead. What will Texas outdoor enthusiasts want to read about 7 months from today?"

Vermont

$$ VERMONT LIFE MAGAZINE

6 Baldwin St., Montpelier VT 05602-2109. (802)828-3241. Fax: (802)828-3366. E-mail: editors@vtlife.com. Website: www.vermontlife.com. **90% freelance written. Prefers to work with published/established writers.** Quarterly magazine. "*Vermont Life* is interested in any article, query, story idea, photograph or photo essay that have to do with Vermont. As the state magazine, we are most favorably impressed with pieces that present positive aspects of life within the state's borders. We have no rules, however, about avoiding controversy when the presentation of the controversial subject can illustrate some aspect of Vermont's unique character." Estab. 1946. Circ. 52,000. Byline given. Offers kill fee. Publishes ms an average of 9 months after acceptance. Buys first North American serial rights. Submit seasonal material 1 year in advance. Accepts queries by mail, e-mail. Responds in 1 month to queries. Guidelines available online.

Nonfiction "Wants articles on today's Vermont, those which portray a typical or, if possible, unique aspect of the state or its people. Style should be literate, clear, and concise. No Vermont clichés, and please do not send first-person accounts of your vacation trip to Vermont." **Buys 60 mss/year.** 1,500 words average **Pays $100-900 depending on scope of article**

Photos Buys seasonal photographs. Gives assignments but only with experienced photographers. Query in writing. Digital photos (preferred) from cameras of at least 6 megapixels. Original color transparencies (35-mm slides and medium or larger format transparencies) and black-and-white prints are acceptable. "*Vermont Life* is moving toward using only digital photography. Color prints or transparencies made from prints or negatives not accepted. Photographs should be current—taken within the last five years." Captions, identification of subjects, model releases required. Pays $75-200 inside color; $500 for cover. Buys one time rights.

Tips "Writers who read our magazine are given more consideration because they understand that we want authentic articles about Vermont. If a writer has a genuine working knowledge of Vermont, his or her work usually shows it. Please review the most recent issues of *Vermont Life* to understand the editorial direction, keeping in mind the various departments: Downtowns; Getaways; Ingenuity; Outdoor Recreation; The Working Landscape. *Vermont Life*'s scope is more toward solid journalism than personal or anecdotal essays. Vermont is changing and there is much concern here about what this state will be like in years ahead. It is a beautiful, environmentally sound place now and the vast majority of residents want to keep it so. Articles reflecting such concerns in an intelligent, authoritative, non-hysterical way will be given very careful consideration. The growth of tourism makes us interested in intelligent articles about specific places in Vermont, their history and attractions to the traveling public."

Virginia

$$ ALBEMARLE

Living in Jefferson's Virginia, Carden Jennings Publishing, 375 Greenbrier Dr., Suite 100, Charlottesville VA 22901. (434)817-2000. Fax: (434)817-2020. Website: www.cjp.com. **80% freelance written.** Bimonthly magazine. Lifestyle magazine for central Virginia. Estab. 1987. Circ. 10,000. Byline given. Pays on publication. Offers 30% kill fee. Publishes ms an average of 4 months after acceptance. Buys first North American serial rights. Editorial lead time 6-8 months. Submit seasonal material 6 months in advance. Accepts queries by mail, e-mail, fax. Accepts simultaneous submissions. Responds in 1 month to queries. Responds in 2 months to mss. Sample copy for sae with 10 × 12 envelope and 5 first-class stamps. Guidelines for #10 SASE.

Nonfiction Needs essays, historical, interview, photo feature, travel. No fiction, poetry or anything without a direct tie to central Virginia. **Buys 30-35 mss/year.** Query with published clips. Length: 900-3,500 words. **Pays $75-225 for assigned articles. Pays $75-175 for unsolicited articles.**

Photos State availability. Captions, identification of subjects, model releases required. Reviews transparencies. Negotiates payment individually. Buys one-time rights.

Columns/Departments Etcetera (personal essay), 900-1,200 words; no food; Leisure (travel, sports), 3,000 words. 20 Query with published clips. **Pays $75-150.**

Tips "Be familiar with the central Virginia area and lifestyle. We prefer a regional slant, which should include a focus on someone or something located in the region, or a focus on someone or something from the region making an impact in other parts of the world. Quality writing is a must. Story ideas that lend themselves to multiple sources will give you a leg up on the competition."

$$ THE ROANOKER

Leisure Publishing Co., 3424 Brambleton Ave., Roanoke VA 24018. (540)989-6138. Fax: (540)989-7603. E-mail: jwood@leisurepublishing.com. Website: www.theroanoker.com. **75% freelance written. Works with a small number of new/unpublished writers each year.** Magazine published 6 times/year. "*The Roanoker* is a general interest city magazine for the people of Roanoke, Virginia and the surrounding area. Our readers are primarily upper-income, well-educated professionals between the ages of 35 and 60. Coverage ranges from hard news and consumer information to restaurant reviews and local history." Estab. 1974. Circ. 12,000. Byline given. Pays on publication. No kill fee. Publishes ms an average of 4 months after acceptance. Buys all rights. Makes work-for-hire assignments. Submit seasonal material 4 months in advance. Accepts queries by mail, e-mail, fax. Responds in 2 months to queries. Sample copy for $2 and 9 × 12 SAE with 5 first-class stamps or online.

Nonfiction "We're looking for more photo feature stories based in western Virginia. We place special emphasis on investigative and exposè articles." Needs exposè, historical, how-to, live better in western Virginia, interview, of well-known area personalities, photo feature, travel, Virginia and surrounding states, periodic special sections on fashion, real estate, media, banking, investing. **Buys 30 mss/year.** Send complete ms. 1,400 words maximum **Pays $35-200.**

Photos Send photos. Captions, model releases required. Reviews color transparencies, digital submissions. Pays $25-50/published photograph. Rights purchased vary.

Columns/Departments Skinny (shorts on people, Roanoke-related books, local issues, events, arts and culture).

Tips "We're looking for more pieces on contemporary history (1930s-70s). It helps if freelancer lives in the area. The most frequent mistake made by writers in completing an article for us is not having enough Roanoke-area focus: use of area experts, sources, slants, etc."

$$ VIRGINIA LIVING

Cape Fear Publishing, 109 E. Cary St., Richmond VA 23219. (804)343-7539. Fax: (804)649-0306. E-mail: RichardErnsberger@capefear.com. Website: www.virginialiving.com. **Contact:** Richard Ernsberger, Jr. **80% freelance written**. Bimonthly magazine covering life and lifestyle in Virginia. "We are a large-format (10 × 13) glossy magazine covering life in Virginia, from food, architecture, and gardening, to issues, profiles, and travel." Estab. 2002. Circ. 70,000. Byline given. Pays on publication. Publishes ms an average of 4-6 months after acceptance. Buys first North American serial rights. Editorial lead time 2-6 months. Submit seasonal material 1 year in advance. Accepts queries by mail. Accepts simultaneous submissions. Responds in 1 month to queries. Responds in 1 month to mss. Sample copy for $5.

Nonfiction Needs book excerpts, essays, expose, general interest, historical, interview, new product, personal experience, photo feature, travel, architecture, design. No fiction, poetry, previously published articles, or stories with a firm grasp of the obvious. **Buys 180 mss/year.** Query with published clips or send complete ms. Length: 300-3,000 words. **Pays 50¢/word.**

Photos Contact: Tyler Darden, art director. Captions, identification of subjects, model releases required. Reviews contact sheets, 6x7 transparencies, 8 × 10 prints, GIF/JPEG files. Negotiates payment individually. Buys one time rights.

Columns/Departments Beauty; Travel; Books; Events; Sports (all with a unique Virginia slant), all 1,000-1,500 words. 50 Send complete ms. **Pays $120-200.**

Tips I can then sit down with them and read them. In addition, queries should be about fresh subjects in Virginia. Avoid stories about Williamsburg, Chincoteague ponies, Monticello, the Civil War, and other press release-type topics. We prefer to introduce new subjects, faces, and ideas, and get beyond the many clichés of Virginia. Freelancers would also do well to think about what time of the year they are pitching stories for, as well as art possibilities. We are a large-format magazine close to the size of the old-look magazine, so photography is a key component to our stories.

Washington

$ $ N PUGET SOUND MAGAZINE

2115 Renee Place, Port Townsend WA 98368. (206)414-1589. Fax: (206)932-2574. E-mail: kat@pugetsoundmagazine.com. Website: www.pugetsoundmagazine.com. **50% freelance written.** Online magazine covering regional focus on adventure, travel, recreation, art, food, wine, culture, wildlife, plants, and healthy living on the shoreline communities of Puget Sound and the Salish Sea. Olympia WA to Campbell River, BC. Writing from a personal experience, human interest perspective. We do profiles, historic pieces, how to—mostly features on water-centric lifestyles. Estab. 2008. Circ. 30,000 when go to print in 2011 as a quarterly. Byline given. No kill fee. Publishes ms an average of 2 months after acceptance. Buys contractual rights sometimes. Editorial lead time 2 months. Accepts queries by mail, e-mail. Accepts previously published material. Accepts simultaneous submissions. Responds in 4 weeks to queries. Sample copy free. Guidelines available online.

Nonfiction Contact: Kathleen McKelvey. Needs book excerpts, essays, general interest, historical, how-to, humor, inspirational, interview, personal experience, photo feature, travel. No special issues at this time. Nothing negative, political, pornographic, religious. Send complete ms. Length: 800-2,000 words. **Pays 10¢ for assigned articles and for unsolicited articles.**

Photos Contact: Dave Petrich, graphics/creative. State availability of or send photos.. Photos require captions, identification of subjects. Reviews contact sheets. Negotiates payment individually. Buys all rights.

Fiction Contact: Katherine McKelvey. Needs adventure, historical, humorous, mainstream, mystery, western. **Buys 6 mss/year.** Query with published clips. Word length: 800-1,000 words. **Pays 10¢.word.**

Poetry Contact: Terry Persun, editor. Needs free verse, traditional. Buys 6/yr. poems/year. Submit maximum 3 poems. Length: 25 lines.

Tips "Pay attention to what we ask for. Read the magazine to get the feel of what we do."

$ $ SEATTLE MAGAZINE

Tiger Oak Publications Inc., 1505 Western Ave., Suite 500, Seattle WA 98101. (206)284-1750. Fax: (206)284-2550. E-mail: rachel.hart@tigeroak.com. Website: www.seattlemagazine.com. Monthly magazine serving the Seattle metropolitan area. Articles should be written with our readers in mind. They are interested in social issues, the arts, politics, homes and gardens, travel and maintaining the region's high quality of life. Estab. 1992. Circ. 45,000. Byline given. Pays on or about 30 days after publication. Offers 25% kill fee. Publishes ms an average of 3 months after acceptance. Buys first rights. Editorial lead time 6 months. Submit seasonal material 6 months in advance. Accepts queries by mail, e-mail, fax. Responds in 2 months to queries. Sample copy for #10 SASE. Guidelines available online.

Nonfiction Needs book excerpts, local, essays, expose, general interest, humor, interview, photo feature, travel, local/regional interest. No longer accepting queries by mail. Query with published clips. Length: 100-2,000 words. **Pays $50 minimum.**

Photos State availability. Negotiates payment individually Buys one time rights.
Columns/Departments Scoop, Urban Safari, Voice, Trips, People, Environment, Hot Button, Fitness, Fashion, Eat and Drink Query with published clips. **Pays $225-400.**
Tips The best queries include some idea of a lead and sources of information, plus compelling reasons why the article belongs specifically in *Seattle Magazine*. In addition, queries should demonstrate the writer's familiarity with the magazine. New writers are often assigned front- or back-of-the-book contents, rather than features. However, the editors do not discourage writers from querying for longer articles and are especially interested in receiving trend pieces, in-depth stories with a news hook and cultural criticism with a local angle.

$$$ SEATTLE WEEKLY

Village Voice, 1008 Western Ave., Suite 300, Seattle WA 98104. (206)623-0500. Fax: (206)467-4377. Website: seattleweekly.com. **20% freelance written**. Weekly tabloid covering arts, politics, food, business and books with local and regional emphasis. Estab. 1976. Circ. 105,000. Byline given. Pays on publication. Offers variable kill fee. Publishes ms an average of 1 month after acceptance. Buys first North American serial rights. Submit seasonal material 2 months in advance. Responds in 1 month to queries. Sample copy for $3. Guidelines available online.
Nonfiction Needs book excerpts, expose, general interest, historical, Northwest, humor, interview, opinion. **Buys 6-8 mss/year.** Query with cover letter, résumé, published clips and SASE Length: 300-4,000 words. **Pays $50-800.**
Reprints Send tearsheet. Payment varies
Tips The *Seattle Weekly* publishes stories on Northwest politics and art, usually written by regional and local writers, for a mostly upscale, urban audience; writing is high-quality magazine style.

Wisconsin

LABOR PAPER EXTRA!!

Serving Southern Wisconsin, Union-Cooperative Publishing, 3030 39th Ave., Suite 110, Kenosha WI 53144. (262)657-6116. Fax: (262)657-6153. **30% freelance written**. Monthly tabloid covering union/labor news. Estab. 2002. Circ. 12,000. Byline given. Pays on publication. Publishes ms an average of 2 months after acceptance. Buys all rights. Editorial lead time 1 month. Submit seasonal material 1 month in advance. Accepts queries by mail, fax. Accepts simultaneous submissions. Sample copy and writer's guidelines free.
Nonfiction Needs expose, general interest, historical, humor, inspirational. **Buys 4 mss/year.** Query with published clips. Length: 300-1,000 words.
Photos State availability. Captions required. Negotiates payment individually.

$$ MADISON MAGAZINE

Morgan Murphy Media, 7025 Raymond Rd., Madison WI 53719. (608)270-3600. Fax: (608)270-3636. E-mail: bnardi@madisonmagazine.com. Website: www.madisonmagazine.com. **Contact:** Brennan Nardi. **75% freelance written**. Monthly magazine. Estab. 1978. Byline given. Pays on publication. Offers 33% kill fee. Publishes ms an average of 2 months after acceptance. Editorial lead time 3 months. Submit seasonal material 3-4 months in advance. Accepts queries by mail, e-mail. Accepts simultaneous submissions. Responds in 3 weeks to queries. Responds in 3 weeks to mss. Sample copy free. Guidelines available online.
Nonfiction "Monthly lifestyle and business magazine that informs and entertains our readers, to affect positive change in our community, reaching 107,000 readers." Needs book excerpts, essays, expose, general interest, historical, how-to, humor, inspirational, interview, new product, opinion, personal experience, photo feature, religious, technical, travel.
Photos State availability. Reviews contact sheets. Negotiates payment individually. Buys one time rights.
Columns/Departments Your Town (local events) and OverTones (local arts/entertainment), both 300 words; Habitat (local house/garden) and Business (local business), both 800 words. 120 Query with published clips. **Pays variable amount.**
Tips "Our magazine is local so only articles pertaining to Madison are considered. Specific queries are heavily appreciated. We like fresh, new content taken in a local perspective. Show us what you're like to write for us."

$$$$ MILWAUKEE MAGAZINE

417 E. Chicago St., Milwaukee WI 53202. (414)273-1101. Fax: (414)273-0016. E-mail: milmag@qg.com. Website: www.milwaukeemagazine.com. **40% freelance written**. Monthly magazine. "We publish stories about Milwaukee, of service to Milwaukee-area residents and exploring the area's changing lifestyle, business, arts, politics, and dining." Circ. 40,000. Byline given. Pays on publication. Offers 20% kill fee. Publishes ms an average of 2 months after acceptance. Buys first rights. Submit seasonal material 6 months in advance. Accepts queries by mail, e-mail. Responds in 6 weeks to queries. Sample copy for $4.

Nonfiction Needs essays, expose, general interest, historical, interview, photo feature, travel, food and dining, and other services. "No articles without a strong Milwaukee or Wisconsin angle. Length: 2,500-6,000 words for full-length features; 800 words for 2-page breaker features (short on copy, long on visuals)." **Buys 30-50 mss/year.** Query with published clips. **Pays $800-2,300 for full-length, $250-400 for breaker.**

Columns/Departments Insider (inside information on Milwaukee, exposé, slice-of-life, unconventional angles on current scene), up to 500 words; Mini Reviews for Insider, 125 words. Query with published clips.

Tips "Pitch something for the Insider, or suggest a compelling profile we haven't already done. Submit clips that prove you can do the job. The department most open is Insider. Think short, lively, offbeat, fresh, people-oriented. We are actively seeking freelance writers who can deliver lively, readable copy that helps our readers make the most out of the Milwaukee area. Because we're only human, we'd like writers who can deliver copy on deadline that fits the specifications of our assignment. If you fit this description, we'd love to work with you."

WISCONSIN NATURAL RESOURCES

Wisconsin Department of Natural Resources, P.O. Box 7921, Madison WI 53707-7921. (608)266-1510. Fax: (608)264-6293. E-mail: david.sperling@wi.gov. Website: www.wnrmag.com. **30% freelance written**. Bimonthly magazine covering environment, natural resource management, and outdoor skills. "We cover current issues in Wisconsin aimed to educate and advocate for resource conservation, outdoor recreation, and wise land use." Estab. 1931. Circ. 90,000. Byline given. Publishes ms an average of 8 months after acceptance. Editorial lead time 6 months. Submit seasonal material 1 year in advance. Accepts queries by mail, e-mail. Accepts previously published material. Accepts simultaneous submissions. Responds in 3 weeks to queries. Responds in 6 months to mss. Sample copy free. Guidelines available online.

Nonfiction Needs essays, how-to, photo feature, features on current outdoor issues and environmental issues. Does not want animal rights pieces, poetry or fiction. Query. Length: 1,500-2,700 words.

Photos Also seeks photos of pets at state properties like wildlife areas, campsites, and trails. Send photos. Identification of subjects required. Reviews transparencies, JPEG files. Offers no additional payment for photos accepted with ms.

Tips "Provide images that match the copy."

$$ WISCONSIN TRAILS

P.O. Box 317, Black Earth WI 53515-0317. (608)767-8000. E-mail: hbrown@wistrails.com. Website: wisconsintrails.com. **40% freelance written**. Bimonthly magazine for readers interested in Wisconsin and its contemporary issues, personalities, recreation, history, natural beauty, and arts. Estab. 1960. Circ. 55,000. Byline given. Pays 1 month from publication. No kill fee. Publishes ms an average of 6 months after acceptance. Buys first North American serial rights, buys one-time rights. Submit seasonal material 1 year in advance. Accepts queries by mail, e-mail, fax. Responds in 4 months to queries. Sample copy for $4.95. Guidelines for #10 SASE or online.

Nonfiction Our articles focus on some aspect of Wisconsin life: an interesting town or event, a person or industry, history or the arts, and especially outdoor recreation. No fiction. No articles that are too local for our regional audience, or articles about obvious places to visit in Wisconsin. We need more articles about the new and little-known. **Buys 3 unsolicited mss/year.** Query or send outline Length: 1,000-3,000 words. **Pays 25¢/word.**

Photos Photographs purchased with or without mss, or on assignment. Color photos usually illustrate an activity, event, region, or striking scenery. Prefer photos with people in scenery. Captions, True required. Reviews 35mm or larger transparencies. Pays $45-175 for inside color; $250 for covers.

Tips When querying, submit well-thought-out ideas about stories specific to people, places, events, arts, outdoor adventures, etc., in Wisconsin. Include published clips with queries. Do some research—many queries we receive are pitching ideas for stories we recently have published. Know the tone, content, and audience of the magazine. Refer to our writer's guidelines, or request them, if necessary.

Wyoming

$ WYOMING RURAL ELECTRIC NEWS (WREN)

P.O. Box 549, Gillette WY 82717. (307)682-7527. Fax: (307)682-7528. E-mail: wren@vcn.com. **20% freelance written**. Monthly magazine for audience of small town residents, vacation-home owners, farmers, and ranchers. Estab. 1954. Circ. 41,000. Byline given. Pays on acceptance. No kill fee. Publishes ms an average of 2 months after acceptance. Buys one-time rights. Submit seasonal material 2 months in advance. Accepts queries by mail, e-mail, fax, phone. Responds in 3 months to queries. Sample copy for $2.50 and 9 × 12 SASE. Guidelines for #10 SASE.

Nonfiction "We print science, ag, how-to, and human interest but not fiction. Topics of interest in general include: hunting, cooking, gardening, commodities, sugar beets, wheat, oil, coal, hard rock mining, beef cattle, electric technologies such as lawn mowers, car heaters, air cleaners and assorted gadgets, surge protectors, pesticators, etc. Wants science articles with question/answer quiz at end—test your knowledge. Buys electrical appliance articles. Articles welcome that put present and/or future in positive light." No nostalgia, sarcasm, or tongue-in-cheek. **Buys 4-10 mss/year.** Send complete ms. Length: 500-800 words. **Pays up to $140, plus 4 copies.**

Reprints Send tearsheet or photocopy and information about when and where the material previously appeared.

Photos Color only.

Tips "Always looking for fresh, new writers. Submit entire manuscript. Don't submit a regionally set story from some other part of the country. Photos and illustrations (if appropriate) are always welcomed. We want factual articles that are blunt, to the point, accurate."

Canada/International

$$ ABACO LIFE

Caribe Communications, P.O. Box 37487, Raleigh NC 27627. (919)859-6782. Fax: (919)859-6769. E-mail: jimkerr@mindspring.com. Website: www.abacolife.com. **50% freelance written**. Quarterly magazine covering Abaco, an island group in the Northeast Bahamas. "*Abaco Life* editorial focuses entirely on activities, history, wildlife, resorts, people and other subjects pertaining to the Abacos. Readers include locals, vacationers, second-home owners, and other visitors whose interests range from real estate and resorts to scuba, sailing, fishing, and beaches. The tone is upbeat, adventurous, humorous. No fluff writing for an audience already familiar with the area." Estab. 1979. Circ. 10,000. Byline given. Pays on publication. Offers 40% kill fee. Publishes ms an average of 2 months after acceptance. Buys one-time rights. Editorial lead time 2 months. Submit seasonal material 4 months in advance. Accepts queries by mail, e-mail. Accepts simultaneous submissions. Responds in 2 weeks to queries. Responds in 2 months to mss. Sample copy for $2. Guidelines free.

Nonfiction Needs general interest, historical, how-to, interview, personal experience, photo feature, travel. No general first-time impressions. Articles must be specific, show knowledge and research of the subject and area—`Abaco's Sponge Industry'; `Diving Abaco's Wrecks'; `The Hurricane of '36.' **Buys 8-10 mss/year.** Query or send complete ms Length: 700-2,000 words. **Pays $400-1,000.**

Photos State availability of or send photos.. Captions, identification of subjects, model releases required. Reviews transparencies, prints. Offers $25-100/photo. Negotiates payment individually. Buys one-time rights.

Tips "Travel writers must look deeper than a usual destination piece, and the only real way to do that is spend time in Abaco. Beyond good writing, which is a must, we like submissions on Microsoft Word. We prefer digital photos saved to a disc at 300 dpi minimum JPEG format. Read the magazine to learn its style."

$$$$ ⊡ ALBERTAVIEWS

AlbertaViews, Ltd., Suite 208-320 23rd Ave. SW, Calgary AB T2S 0J2 Canada. (403)243-5334. Fax: (403)243-8599. E-mail: editor@albertaviews.ab.ca. Website: www.albertaviews.ab.ca. **50% freelance written**. Bimonthly magazine covering Alberta culture: politics, economy, social issues, and art. We are a regional magazine providing thoughtful commentary and background information on issues of concern to Albertans. Most of our writers are Albertans. Estab. 1997. Circ. 30,000. Byline given. Pays on publication. Offers 50% kill fee. Publishes ms an average of 3 months after acceptance. Buys first North American serial rights, buys electronic rights. Editorial lead time 4 months. Submit seasonal material 3 months in advance. Accepts queries by e-mail. Responds in 6 weeks to queries. Responds in 2 months to mss. Sample copy free. Guidelines available online.

- No phone queries.

Nonfiction Does not want anything not directly related to Alberta Needs essays. **Buys 18 mss/year.** Query with published clips. Length: 3,000-5,000 words. **Pays $1,000-1,500 for assigned articles. Pays $350-750 for unsolicited articles.**
Photos State availability. Negotiates payment individually Buys one-time rights, Web rights
Fiction Only fiction by Alberta writers. **Buys 6 mss/year.** Send complete ms. Length: 2,500-4,000 words. **Pays $1,000 maximum.**

$$ THE ATLANTIC CO-OPERATOR

Promoting Community Ownership, Atlantic Co-operative Publishers, 123 Halifax St., Moncton, New Brunswick E1C 8N5 Canada. Fax: (506)858-6615. E-mail: editor@theatlanticco-operator.coop. Website: www.theatlanticco-operator.coop. **Contact:** Rayanne Brennan, editor-in-chief. **95% freelance written**. Bimonthly tabloid covering co-operatives. "We publish articles of interest to the general public, with a special focus on community ownership and community economic development in Atlantic Canada." Estab. 1933. Byline given. Pays on publication. No kill fee. Publishes ms an average of 2 months after acceptance. Editorial lead time 2 months. Submit seasonal material 2 months in advance. Accepts queries by mail, e-mail, fax. Accepts simultaneous submissions. Responds in 3 weeks to queries.
Nonfiction Needs expose, general interest, historical, interview. No political stories, economical stories, sports. **Buys 90 mss/year.** Query with published clips. Length: 500-2,000 words. **Pays 22¢/word.**
Photos State availability. Identification of subjects required. Reviews prints, GIF/JPEG files. Offers $25/photo Buys one time rights.
Columns/Departments Health and Lifestyle (anything from recipes to travel), 800 words; International Page (co-operatives in developing countries, good ideas from around the world). 10 Query with published clips.

$$$ THE BEAVER

Canada's History Magazine, Canada's National History Society, 56060 Portage Place RPO, Winnipeg MB R3B 0G9 Canada. (204)988-9300. Fax: (204)988-9309. E-mail: editors@historysociety.ca. Website: www.thebeaver.ca. **50% freelance written**. Bimonthly magazine covering Canadian history. Estab. 1920. Circ. 46,000. Byline given. Pays on acceptance. Offers $200 kill fee. Buys first North American serial rights, buys electronic rights. Editorial lead time 4 months. Submit seasonal material 8 months in advance. Accepts queries by e-mail. Accepts simultaneous submissions. Responds in 6 weeks to queries. Responds in 2 months to mss. Sample copy for sae with 9 × 12 envelope and 2 First-Class stamps. Guidelines available online.
Nonfiction Needs Canadian focus., Subject matter covers the whole range of Canadian history, with emphasis on social history, politics, exploration, discovery and settlement, aboriginal peoples, business & trade, war, culture and sport. Does not want anything unrelated to Canadian history. **Buys 30 mss/year.** Query with published clips, sase. Length: 600-3,500 words. **Pays 50¢/word for major features.**
Photos State availability. Identification of subjects, model releases required. Offers no additional payment for photos accepted with ms Buys one time rights.
Columns/Departments Book and other media reviews and Canadian history subjects, 600 words (These are assigned to freelancers with particular areas of expertise, i.e., women's history, labour history, French regime, etc.) 15 columns. **Pays $125**
Tips "*The Beaver* is directed toward a general audience of educated readers, as well as to historians and scholars. We are in the market for lively, well-written, well-researched, and informative articles about Canadian history that focus on all parts of the country and all areas of human activity. Articles are obtained through direct commission and by submission. *The Beaver* publishes articles of various lengths, including long features (from 1,500-3,500 words) that provide an in-depth look at an event, person or era; short, more narrowly focused features (from 600-1,500 words). Longer articles may be considered if their importance warrants publication. Articles should be written in an expository or interpretive style and present the principal themes of Canadian history in an original, interesting and informative way."

$$$ CANADIAN GEOGRAPHIC

39 McArthur Ave., Ottawa ON K1L 8L7 Canada. (613)745-4629. Fax: (613)744-0947. Website: www.canadiangeographic.ca. **90% freelance written. Works with a small number of new/unpublished writers each year.** Bimonthly magazine. *Canadian Geographic*'s colorful portraits of our ever-changing population show readers just how important the relationship between the people and the land really is. Estab. 1930. Circ. 240,000. Pays on acceptance. Publishes ms an average of 3 months after acceptance. Buys first Canadian rights. Accepts queries by mail, e-mail, fax. Responds in 1 month to queries. Sample copy for $5.95 (Canadian) and 9 × 12 SAE or online.

• *Canadian Geographic* reports a need for more articles on earth sciences. Canadian writers only.
Nonfiction Buys authoritative geographical articles, in the broad geographical sense, written for the average person, not for a scientific audience. Predominantly Canadian subjects by Canadian authors. **Buys 30-45 mss/year.** Query. Length: 1,500-3,000 words. **Pays 80¢/word minimum.** .
Photos Pays $75-400 for color photos, depending on published size

$$ COTTAGE

Recreational Living in Western Canada, OP Publishing, Ltd., Suite 500-200, West Esplanade, North Vancouver BC V7M 1A4 Canada. (604)606-4644. Fax: (604)998-3320. E-mail: editor@cottagemagazine.com. Website: www.cottagemagazine.com. **80% freelance written**. "Bimonthly magazine covering do-it-yourself projects, profiles of people and their innovative solutions to building and maintaining their country homes, issues that affect rural individuals and communities, and the R&R aspect of country living." "Our readers want solid, practical information about living in the country—including alternative energy and sustainable living. The also like to have fun in a wide range of recreational pursuits, from canoeing, fishing, and sailing to water skiing, snowmobiling, and entertaining." Estab. 1992. Circ. 20,000. Byline given. Pays within 1 month of publication. Offers 25% kill fee. Publishes ms an average of 6 months after acceptance. Buys first North American serial rights. Accepts queries by e-mail. Accepts simultaneous submissions. Responds in 1 month to queries.
Nonfiction Buys 18-24 mss/year. Query. Up to 1,500 words. **Pays $100-450 (including visuals).**
Photos Send photos. Reviews with negatives prints, slides, digital.
Columns/Departments Utilities (solar and/or wind power), 800 words; Weekend Project (a how-to most homeowners can do themselves), 800 words; Government (new regulations, processes, problems), 800 words; Diversions (advisories, ideas, and how-tos about the fun things that people do), 800 words; InRoads (product reviews), 50-600 words; This Land (personal essays or news-based story with a broader context), 800 words; Last Word or Cabin Life (personal essays and experiences), 800 words; Elements (short articles focusing on a single feature of a cottage), 600 words; Alternatives (applied alternative energy), 600 words. Query. **Pays $75-250.**
Tips "We serve all of Western Canada, so while it's OK to have a main focus on one region, reference should be made to similarities/differences in other provinces. Even technical articles should have some anecdotal content. Some of our best articles come from readers themselves or from writers who can relay that 'personal' feeling. Cottaging is about whimsy and fun as well as maintenance and chores. Images, images, images: We require sharp, quality photos, and the more, the better."

$ DEVON LIFE

Archant Life Ltd, Archant House, Babbage Road, Totnes Devon TQ9 5JA United Kingdom. (44)(180)386-0910. Fax: (44)(180)386-0922. E-mail: devonlife@archant.co.uk. Website: www.devonlife.co.uk. No kill fee. Accepts queries by mail, e-mail. Sample copy available online. Guidelines by e-mail.
Nonfiction 500-750/single-page articles; 1,000-1,200/2-page articles **Pays Â£60-75/up to 1,200 words; Â£40-50/up to 750 words**
Photos Send photos. Captions required. Reviews transparencies, prints, 300 dpi digital images.

$$$$ HAMILTON MAGAZINE

Town Media, 1074 Cooke Blvd., Burlington ON L7T 4A8 Canada. E-mail: david@townmedia.ca. Website: www.hamiltonmagazine.com. **50% freelance written**. Quarterly magazine devoted to the Greater Hamilton and Golden Horseshoe area. "Mandate: to entertain and inform by spotlighting the best of what our city and region has to offer. We invite readers to take part in a vibrant community by supplying them with authoritative and dynamic coverage of local culture, food, fashion and design. Each story strives to expand your view of the area, every issue an essential resource for exploring, understanding and unlocking the region. Packed with insight, intrigue and suspense, *Hamilton Magazine* delivers the city to your doorstep." Estab. 1978. Byline given. Pays on publication. Offers 50% kill fee. Buys first North American serial rights, buys second serial (reprint) rights. Makes work-for-hire assignments. Editorial lead time 2-3 months. Submit seasonal material 2-3 months in advance. Accepts queries by e-mail. Responds in 1 week to queries and to mss. Sample copy for #10 SASE. Guidelines by e-mail.
Nonfiction Needs book excerpts, essays, expose, historical, how-to, humor, inspirational, interview, personal experience, photo feature, religious, travel. Does not want generic articles that could appear in any mass-market publication. Send complete ms. Length: 800-2,000 words. **Pays $200-1,600 for assigned articles. Pays $100-800 for unsolicited articles.**
Photos Contact: Contact Kate Sharrow, art director. State availability of or send photos. Identification of subjects required. Reviews 8 × 10 prints, JPEG files (8 × 10 at 300 dpi). Negotiates payment individually. Buys one time rights.

Columns/Departments A&E Art, 1,200-2,000 words; A&E Music, 1,200-2,000 words; A&E Books, 1,200-1,400 words. 12 columns. Send complete ms. **Pays $200-400.**

Tips "Unique local voices are key and a thorough knowledge of the area's history, politics and culture is invaluable."

$$ MONDAY MAGAZINE

Black Press Ltd., 818 Broughton St., Victoria BC V8W 1E4 Canada. E-mail: editor@mondaymag.com. Website: www.mondaymag.com. **10% freelance written**. Weekly tabloid covering local news. "*Monday Magazine* is Victoria's only alternative newsweekly. For more than 35 years, we have published fresh, informative and alternative perspectives on local events. We prefer lively, concise writing with a sense of humor and insight." Estab. 1975. Circ. 40,000. Byline given. Pays 1 month after publication. No kill fee. Publishes ms an average of 1 month after acceptance. Buys first North American serial rights, buys second serial (reprint) rights, buys electronic rights. Makes work-for-hire assignments. Editorial lead time 1-2 months. Submit seasonal material 2 months in advance. Accepts queries by Prefers e-mail. Responds in 6-8 weeks to queries. Responds in up to 3 months to mss See Writer's Guidelines on our website.

Nonfiction Needs expose, general interest, humor, interview, opinion, personal experience, technical, travel. Body, Mind, Spirit (October); Student Survival Guide (August). Does not want fiction, poetry, or conspiracy theories. Send complete ms. Length: 300-2,000 words. **Pays 10¢/word**

Photos photos Captions, identification of subjects required. Reviews GIF/JPEG files (300 dpi at 4x6). Offers no additional payment for photos accepted with ms. Buys one-time rights.

Tips "Local writers tend to have an advantage, as they are familiar with the issues and concerns of interest to a Victoria audience. However, we are interested in perspectives from elsewhere as well, especially on universal topics."

$$ OUTDOOR CANADA MAGAZINE

25 Sheppard Ave. W., Suite 100, Toronto ON M2N 6S7 Canada. (416)733-7600. Fax: (416)227-8296. E-mail: editorial@outdoorcanada.ca. Website: www.outdoorcanada.ca. **90% freelance written. Works with a small number of new/unpublished writers each year.** "Magazine published 8 times/year emphasizing hunting, fishing, and related pursuits in Canada *only*." Estab. 1972. Circ. 90,000. Byline given. Pays on publication. No kill fee. Publishes ms an average of 8 months after acceptance. Buys first rights. Submit seasonal material 1 year in advance. Accepts queries by mail, e-mail. Responds in 1 month to queries. Guidelines available online.

Nonfiction Needs how-to, fishing, hunting, outdoor issues, outdoor destinations in Canada. **Buys 35-40 mss/year.** Does not accept unsolicited mss. 2,500 words **Pays $500 and up.**

Reprints Send information about when and where the article previously appeared. Payment varies

Photos Emphasize people in the Canadian outdoors. Captions, model releases required. Pays $100-250 for 35mm transparencies and $400/cover

Fillers Length: 100-500 words. **Pays $50 and up**

$$$$ TORONTO LIFE

111 Queen St. E., Suite 320, Toronto ON M5C 1S2 Canada. (416)364-3333. Fax: (416)861-1169. E-mail: editorial@torontolife.com. Website: www.torontolife.com. **95% freelance written. Prefers to work with published/established writers.** Monthly magazine emphasizing local issues and social trends, short humor/satire, and service features for upper income, well-educated and, for the most part, young Torontonians. Circ. 92,039. Byline given. Pays on acceptance. Offers kill fee. Pays 50% kill fee for commissioned articles only. Publishes ms an average of 4 months after acceptance. Buys first North American serial rights. Responds in 3 weeks to queries. Sample copy for $4.95 with SAE and IRCs.

Nonfiction Uses most types of articles. **Buys 17 mss/issue.** Query with published clips and SASE. Length: 1,000-6,000 words. **Pays $500-5,000.**

Columns/Departments We run about 5 columns an issue. They are all freelanced, though most are from regular contributors. They are mostly local in concern and cover politics, business, performing arts, media, design, and food. Length: 2,000 words. Query with published clips and SASE. **Pays $2,000**

Tips Submissions should have strong Toronto orientation.

$$ THE UKRAINIAN OBSERVER

The Willard Group, 41 Bodgana Khmelnitskoho St., Kiev 01030 Ukraine. (380)(44)502 3005. Fax: (380)(44)501 2342. E-mail: glen.willard@twg.com.ua. Website: www.ukraine-observer.com. **75% freelance written**. Monthly magazine covering Ukrainian news, culture, travel, and history. Our English-language e-zine content is entirely Ukraine-centered. A writer unfamiliar with the country, its politics, or its culture is unlikely to be successful with us. Estab. 2000. Circ. 15,000. Byline given. Pays on publication. Offers 50% kill fee. Publishes ms an average of 2 months after acceptance. Buys all rights. Editorial lead time 1 month. Submit seasonal material 2 months in advance. Accepts queries by mail, e-mail. Responds in 2 weeks to queries. Responds in 1 month to mss. Sample copy free by post to Ukraine addresses only; $3 USD to foreign addresses. Guidelines by e-mail.

Nonfiction Needs general interest, Ukrainian life, history, culture and travel, and significant Ukrainians abroad, historical, Ukrainian history, particular little-known events with significant impact, interview, prominent Ukrainians or foreign expatriates living in Ukraine, photo feature, current or historical photo feature essays on Ukrainian life, history, culture, and travel, travel, within Ukraine. Does not want poetry, nostalgic family stories, personal experiences or recollections. **Buys 30-40 mss/year.** Send complete ms. Length: 800-1,500 words. **Pays $25-250 for assigned articles. Pays $25-50 for unsolicited articles.**

Photos Send photos. Captions, identification of subjects, model releases required. Reviews negatives, GIF/JPEG files. Pays $10/photo. Buys one time rights.

Fiction All fiction should have a Ukrainian setting and/or theme. Needs adventure, ethnic, historical, humorous, mainstream, slice-of-life vignettes. Does not want erotica. **Buys 12 mss/year.** Query or send complete ms. Length: 3,500-4,500 words. **Pays $25-150.**

Tips Obtain, read, and follow our writer's guidelines. We follow Western journalism rules. We are not interested in the writer's opinion—our readers want information to be attributed to experts interviewed for the story. An interesting story that has credible sources and lots of good, direct quotes will be a hit with us. Stories covering political or controversial issues should be balanced and fair.

UP HERE

Explore Canada's Far North, Up Here Publishing, Ltd., 4920 52nd St., Yellowknife NT X1A 3T1 Canada. (867)766-6710. Fax: (867)873-9876. E-mail: aaron@uphere.ca. Website: www.uphere.ca. **Contact:** Aaron Spitzer, editor. **50% freelance written**. Magazine published 8 times/year covering general interest about Canada's Far North. We publish features, columns, and shorts about people, wildlife, native cultures, travel, and adventure in Yukon, Northwest Territories, and Nunavut. Be informative, but entertaining. Estab. 1984. Circ. 22,000. Byline given. Pays on publication. Offers 50% kill fee. Buys first North American serial rights. Editorial lead time 6 months. Accepts queries by e-mail. Sample copy for $4.95 (Canadian) and 9 × 12 SASE.

Nonfiction Needs essays, general interest, how-to, humor, interview, personal experience, photo feature, technical, travel, lifestyle/culture, historical. **Buys 25-30 mss/year.** Query. Length: 1,500-3,000 words. **Fees are negotiable.**

Photos *Please* do not send unsolicited original photos, slides. Send photos. Captions, identification of subjects required. Reviews transparencies, prints. Buys one time rights.

Columns/Departments Write for updated guidelines, visit website, or e-mail. 25-30 Query with published clips.

$$$ VANCOUVER MAGAZINE

Transcontinental Publications, Inc., Suite 560, 2608 Granville St., Vancouver BC V6H 3V3 Canada. E-mail: mail@vancouvermagazine.com. Website: www.vancouvermagazine.com. **70% freelance written**. Monthly magazine covering the city of Vancouver. Estab. 1967. Circ. 65,000. Byline given. Pays on acceptance. Offers negotiable kill fee. Buys first North American serial rights. Editorial lead time 2 months. Submit seasonal material 6 months in advance. Accepts queries by mail, e-mail, fax, phone. Accepts simultaneous submissions. Responds in 2 weeks to queries. Responds in 1 month to mss. Sample copy for $5. Guidelines for #10 SASE or by e-mail.

Nonfiction We prefer to work with writers from a conceptual stage and have a 6-week lead time. Most stories are under 1,500 words. Please be aware that we don't publish poetry and rarely publish fiction. Needs book excerpts, essays, historical, humor, interview, new product, personal experience, photo feature, travel. **Buys 200 mss/year.** Query. Length: 200-3,000 words. **Pays 50¢/word.**

Photos State availability. Captions, identification of subjects, model releases required. Reviews contact sheets, negatives, transparencies, prints, GIF/JPEG files. Negotiates payment individually Buys negotiable rights

Columns/Departments Sport; Media; Business; City Issues, all 1,500 words. Query. **Pays 50¢/word**

Tips Read back issues of the magazine, or visit our website. Almost all of our stories have a strong Vancouver angle. Submit queries by e-mail. Do not send complete stories.

VICTORIA POSTCARDS

Travel, Dining and Lifestyle, Blitz Publications, P.O. Box 4075, Mulgrave VIC 3170 Australia. (61)(3)9574-8999. Fax: (61)(3)9574-8899. E-mail: liat@blitzmag.com.au. Website: www.sportzblitz.net. *PostCards*

magazine is Victoria's most comprehensive guide to travel, dining and lifestyle.
Nonfiction Needs general interest, travel. Query.

Religious

ALIVE NOW

1908 Grand Ave., P.O. Box 340004, Nashville TN 37203-0004. E-mail: alivenow@upperroom.org. Website: alivenow.upperroom.org. **Contact:** Gina Manskar. Bimonthly thematic magazine for a general Christian audience interested in reflection and meditation. Circ. 40,000. No kill fee. Guidelines available online.
Nonfiction Length: 250-400 words. **Pays $35 and up.**
Fiction Length: 250-400 words. **Pays $35 and up**.
Poetry Needs "Can be avant-garde, free verse — we accept any style." Length: 10-45 lines.
Tips "We only accept submissions according to our themes."

$$ AMERICA

106 W. 56th St., New York NY 10019. (212)581-4640. Fax: (212)399-3596. E-mail: articles@americamagazine.org. Website: www.americamagazine.org. Published weekly for adult, educated, largely Roman Catholic audience. Estab. 1909. Byline given. Pays on acceptance. No kill fee. Buys all rights. Responds in 3 weeks to queries. Guidelines available online.
Nonfiction We publish a wide variety of material on religion, politics, economics, ecology, and so forth. We are not a parochial publication, but almost all pieces make some moral or religious point. We are not interested in purely informational pieces or personal narratives which are self-contained and have no larger moral interest. Length: 1,500-2,000 words. **Pays $50-300.**
Poetry Contact: Contact: Rev. James S. Torrens, poetry editor. Only 10-12 poems published a year, thousands turned down. Buys 10-12 poems/year. Length: 15-30 lines.

AUSTRALIAN CATHOLICS

Australian Catholics, Ltd., P.O. Box 553, Richmond VIC 3121 Australia. (61)(3)9421-9666. Fax: (61)(3)9421-9600. E-mail: auscaths@jespub.jesuit.org.au. Website: www.australiancatholics.com.au. Magazine published 5 times/year covering the faith and life of Australians. *Australian Catholics* is aimed at all members of the Catholic community, especially young people and the families of students in Catholic schools. Guidelines available online.
Nonfiction Needs religious. Send complete ms. Length: 1,000 words. **Pays negotiable amount.**
Tips "We are looking for 'good news' stories."

$ BIBLE ADVOCATE

Bible Advocate, Church of God (Seventh Day), P.O. Box 33677, Denver CO 80233. (303)452-7973. E-mail: bibleadvocate@cog7.org. Website: www.cog7.org/publications/ba/. **25% freelance written**. Religious magazine published 6 times/year. "Our purpose is to advocate the Bible and represent the Church of God (Seventh Day) to a Christian audience." Estab. 1863. Circ. 13,500. Byline given. Pays on publication. Offers 50% kill fee. Publishes ms an average of 9 months after acceptance. Buys first rights, buys second serial (reprint) rights, buys electronic rights. Editorial lead time 3 months. Submit seasonal material 6 months in advance. Accepts queries by mail, e-mail; prefers e-mail; attachments ok. Accepts simultaneous submissions. Responds in 2 months to queries. Sample copy for sae with 9 × 12 envelope and 3 first-class stamps. Guidelines available online.
Nonfiction Needs inspirational, personal experience, religious, Biblical studies. No articles on Christmas or Easter. **Buys 15-20 mss/year.** Send complete ms and SASE. Length: 1,000-1,200 words. **Pays $25-55.**
Reprints E-mail manuscript with rights for sale noted.
Photos Send photos. Identification of subjects required. Reviews prints. We no longer buy photos.
Poetry Needs free verse, traditional. No avant-garde. Buys 10-12 poems/year. Submit maximum 5/ poems. poems. Length: 5-20 lines. **Pays $20**.
Tips "Be fresh, not preachy! We're trying to reach a younger audience now, so think how you can cover contemporary and biblical topics with this audience in mind. Articles must be in keeping with the doctrinal understanding of the Church of God (Seventh Day). Therefore, the writer should become familiar with what the Church generally accepts as truth as set forth in its doctrinal beliefs. We reserve the right to edit manuscripts to fit our space requirements, doctrinal stands and church terminology. Significant changes are referred to writers for approval. No fax or handwritten submissions, please."

$$ CATHOLIC DIGEST

P.O. Box 6015, 1 Montauk Ave., Suite 200, New London CT 06320. (800)321-0411. Fax: (860)457-3013.

E-mail: cdsubmissions@bayard-inc.com. Website: www.catholicdigest.com. **12% freelance written**. Monthly magazine. Publishes features and advice on topics ranging from health, psychology, humor, adventure, and family, to ethics, spirituality, and Catholics, from modern-day heroes to saints through the ages. Helpful and relevant reading culled from secular and religious periodicals. Estab. 1936. Circ. 275,000. Byline given. Pays on publication. No kill fee. Buys first rights, buys one-time rights, buys second serial (reprint) rights. Editorial lead time 3 months. Submit seasonal material 5 months in advance. Accepts queries by mail, e-mail. Responds in 2 months to mss. Sample copy free

Nonfiction Most articles we use are reprinted. Needs book excerpts, essays, general interest, historical, how-to, humor, inspirational, interview, personal experience, religious, travel. Send complete ms. Length: 750-2,000 words. **Pays $200-400.**

Reprints Send tearsheet or typed ms with rights for sale noted and information about when and where the material previously appeared. Pays $100.

Photos State availability. Captions, identification of subjects, model releases required. Reviews contact sheets, transparencies, prints. Negotiates payment individually.

Tips Spiritual, self-help, and all wellness is a good bet for us. We would also like to see material with an innovative approach to daily living, articles that show new ways of looking at old ideas, problems. You've got to dig beneath the surface.

$$ CATHOLIC FORESTER

Catholic Order of Foresters, 355 Shuman Blvd., P.O. Box 3012, Naperville IL 60566-7012. Fax: (630)983-3384. E-mail: magazine@catholicforester.com. Website: www.catholicforester.org. **20% freelance written**. Quarterly magazine for members of the Catholic Order of Foresters, a fraternal insurance benefit society. "*Catholic Forester* articles cover varied topics to create a balanced issue for the purpose of informing, educating, and entertaining our readers." Circ. 100,000. Pays on acceptance. Buys first North American serial rights. Editorial lead time 6 months. Submit seasonal material 6 months in advance. Responds in 3 months to mss. Sample copy for sae with 9 × 12 envelope and 4 First-Class stamps. Guidelines available online.

Nonfiction Needs inspirational, religious, travel, health, parenting, financial, money management, humor. **Buys 12-16 mss/year.** Send complete ms by mail, fax, or e-mail. Rejected material will not be returned without accompanying SASE Length: 500-1,500 words. **Pays 50¢/word.**

Photos State availability. Negotiates payment individually. Buys one time rights.

Fiction Needs humorous, religious. **Buys 12-16 mss/year.** Length: 500-1,500 words. **Pays 50¢/word.**

Poetry Needs light verse, traditional. Buys 3 poems/year. 15 lines maximum **Pays 30¢/word.**

Tips "Our audience includes a broad age spectrum, ranging from youth to seniors. Nonfiction topics that appeal to our members include health and wellness, money management and budgeting, parenting and family life, interesting travels, insurance, nostalgia, and humor. A good children's story with a positive lesson or message would rate high on our list."

$$ CELEBRATE LIFE

American Life League, P.O. Box 1350, Stafford VA 22555. (540)659-4171. Fax: (540)659-2586. E-mail: clmag@all.org. Website: www.clmagazine.org. **Contact:** Editor. **50% freelance written**. Bimonthly educational magazine covering "pro-life education and human interest". "We are a religious-based publication specializing in pro-life education through human-interest stories and investigative exposés. Our purpose is to inspire, encourage, motivate, and educate pro-life individuals and activists." Estab. 1979. Circ. 70,000. Byline given. Pays on publication. Buys first serial rights only. Submit seasonal material 4 months in advance. Accepts queries by mail, e-mail. .Accepts simultaneous submissions. Responds in 6 months to mss. Sample copy for sae with 9 × 12 SAE envelope and 4 first-class stamps. Guidelines free.

Nonfiction "No fiction, book reviews, poetry, allegory, devotionals." Query with published clips or send complete ms. Length: 400-1,500 words.

Photos Identification of subjects required. Buys one-time rights.

Tips "All articles must have agreement with the principles expressed in Pope John Paul II's encyclical *Evangelium Vitae*. Our common themes include: abortion, post-abortion healing, sidewalk counseling, adoption, contraception, chastity, euthanasia, eugenics, marriage, opposition to exceptions, organ donation, parenting, political integrity, pro-life/anti-life activities and legislation, pro-life heroes, sanctity of life/personahood, sex education, special needs children/parenting/adoption, and young people in pro-life action."

$$$ CHARISMA & CHRISTIAN LIFE

The Magazine About Spirit-Led Living, Strang Communications Co., 600 Rinehart Rd., Lake Mary FL

32746. (407)333-0600. Fax: (407)333-7133. E-mail: charisma@strang.com. Website: www.charismamag.com. **80% freelance written**. Monthly magazine covering items of interest to the Pentecostal or independent charismatic reader. Now also online. More than half of our readers are Christians who belong to Pentecostal or independent charismatic churches, and numerous others participate in the charismatic renewal in mainline denominations. Estab. 1975. Circ. 250,000. Byline given. Pays on publication. Offers $50 kill fee. Publishes ms an average of 3 months after acceptance. Buys all rights. Editorial lead time 4 months. Submit seasonal material 5 months in advance. Accepts queries by mail, e-mail. Sample copy free. Guidelines by e-mail.

Nonfiction Needs book excerpts, expose, general interest, interview, religious. No fiction, poetry, columns/departments, or sermons. **Buys 40 mss/year.** Query. Length: 2,000-3,000 words. **Pays $1,000 (maximum) for assigned articles.**

Photos State availability. Model releases required. Reviews contact sheets, 2¼ × 2¼ transparencies, 3 × 5 or larger prints, TIF/JPEG files. Negotiates payment individually. Buys one time rights.

Tips Be especially on the lookout for news stories, trend articles, or interesting personality profiles that relate specifically to the Christian reader.

$ $ THE CHRISTIAN CENTURY

104 S. Michigan Ave., Suite 700, Chicago IL 60603-5901. (312)263-7510. Fax: (312)263-7540. E-mail: main@christiancentury.org. Website: www.christiancentury.org. **90% freelance written. Works with new/unpublished writers.** Biweekly magazine for ecumenically-minded, progressive Protestants, both clergy and lay. Authors must have a critical and analytical perspective on the church and be familiar with contemporary theological discussion. Estab. 1884. Circ. 37,000. Byline given. Pays on publication. No kill fee. Buys all rights. Editorial lead time 1 month. Submit seasonal material 4 months in advance. Accepts queries by mail, e-mail. Responds in 2-4 week to queries. Responds in 2 months to mss. Sample copy for $3.50. Guidelines available online.

Nonfiction We use articles dealing with social problems, ethical dilemmas, political issues, international affairs, and the arts, as well as with theological and ecclesiastical matters. We focus on issues of church and society, and church and culture. Needs essays, humor, interview, opinion, religious. No inspirational. **Buys 150 mss/year.** Send complete ms; query appreciated, but not essential. Length: 1,000-3,000 words. **Pays variable amount for assigned articles. Pays $100-300 for unsolicited articles.**

Photos State availability. Reviews any size prints. Buys one time rights.

Poetry Contact: Jill Pelàez Baumgaertner, poetry editor. Needs avant-garde, free verse, haiku, traditional. No sentimental or didactic poetry. Buys 50 poems/year. Length: 20 lines. **Pays $50.**

Tips We seek manuscripts that articulate the public meaning of faith, bringing the resources of Christian tradition to bear on such topics as poverty, human rights, economic justice, international relations, national priorities, and popular culture. We are equally interested in articles that probe classical theological themes. We welcome articles that find fresh meaning in old traditions and which adapt or apply religious traditions to new circumstances. Authors should assume that readers are familiar with main themes in Christian history and theology; are not threatened by the historical-critical study of the Bible; and are already engaged in relating faith to social and political issues. Many of our readers are ministers or teachers of religion at the college level.

$ $ CHRISTIAN HOME & SCHOOL

Christian Schools International, 3350 E. Paris Ave. SE, Grand Rapids MI 49512. (616)957-1070, ext. 239. Fax: (616)957-5022. E-mail: abross@csionline.org. **30% freelance written. Works with a small number of new/unpublished writers each year.** Magazine published 4 times/year during the school year covering family life and Christian education. *Christian Home & School* is designed for parents in the United States and Canada who send their children to Christian schools and are concerned about the challenges facing Christian families today. These readers expect a mature, Biblical perspective in the articles, not just a Bible verse tacked onto the end. Estab. 1922. Circ. 67,000. Byline given. Pays on publication. No kill fee. Publishes ms an average of 4 months after acceptance. Buys first North American serial rights. Submit seasonal material 4 months in advance. Accepts queries by mail, e-mail. Responds in 1 month to queries. Sample copy and writer's guidelines for 9 × 12 SAE with 4 first-class stamps. Writer's guidelines only for #10 SASE or online

- The editor reports an interest in seeing articles on how to experience and express forgiveness in your home, make summer interesting and fun for your kids, help your child make good choices, and raise kids who are opposites, and promote good educational practices in Christian schools.

Nonfiction We publish features on issues that affect the home and school. Needs book excerpts, interview, opinion, personal experience, articles on parenting and school life. **Buys 30 mss/year.** Send complete ms. Length: 1,000-2,000 words. **Pays $175-250.**

Tips Features are the area most open to freelancers. We are publishing articles that deal with contemporary issues that affect parents. Use an informal easy-to-read style rather than a philosophical, academic tone. Try to incorporate vivid imagery and concrete, practical examples from real life. We look for manuscripts with a mature Christian perspective.

COLUMBIA

1 Columbus Plaza, New Haven CT 06510. (203)752-4398. Fax: (203)752-4109. E-mail: columbia@kofc.org. Website: www.kofc.org/columbia. **Contact:** Patrick Scalisi, associate editor. Monthly magazine for Catholic families. Caters primarily to members of the Knights of Columbus. Estab. 1921. Circ. 1,500,000. Pays on acceptance. No kill fee. Buys first worlwide serial rights. Accepts queries by mail, e-mail. Sample copy and writer's guidelines free.

Nonfiction Fact articles directed to the Catholic layman and his family dealing with current events, social problems, Catholic apostolic activities, education, ecumenism, rearing a family, literature, science, arts, sports, and leisure. No reprints, poetry, cartoons, short stories/fiction. Query with SASE or by e-mail. Length: 750-1,500 words.

$$ CONSCIENCE

The Newsjournal of Catholic Opinion, Catholics for Choice, 1436 U St. NW, Suite 301, Washington DC 20009-3997. (202)986-6093. E-mail: conscience@catholicsforchoice.org. Website: www.catholicsforchoice.org. **Contact:** Kate Childs Graham. **80% written by nonstaff writers. Publishes 40 freelance submissions yearly; 10% by unpublished writers, 50% by authors who are new to the magazine, 70% by experts.** "Conscience offers in-depth coverage of a range of topics, including contemporary politics, Catholicism, women's rights in society and in religions, US politics, reproductive rights, sexuality and gender, ethics and bioethics, feminist theology, social justice, church and state issues, and the role of religion in formulating public policy." Estab. 1980. Circ. 12,000. Byline given. Pays on publication. No kill fee. Publishes ms an average of 2 months after acceptance. Buys first North American serial rights. Makes work-for-hire assignments. Accepts queries by mail, e-mail. Responds in 4 months to queries. Sample copy free with 9 × 12 envelope and $1.85 postage. Guidelines for #10 SASE.

Nonfiction "Topics include church-state issues, Catholicism, abortion, contraception, HIV/AIDS, reproductive technologies, sex and sexuality. Informational articles; profiles; interviews; and personal experience and opinion pieces." Needs book excerpts, interview, opinion, personal experience, a small amount, issue analysis. **Buys 4-8 mss/year.** Send complete ms. Length: 1,500-3,500 words. **Pays $200 negotiable.**

Reprints Send typed manuscript with rights for sale noted and information about when and where the material previously appeared. Pays 20-30% of amount paid for an original article.

Columns/Departments Book Reviews, 600-1,200 words. 4-8 **Pays $75.**

Tips "Our readership includes national and international opinion leaders and policymakers, librarians, members of the clergy and the press, and leaders in the fields of theology, ethics, and women's studies. Articles should be written for a diverse and educated audience."

$$ DECISION

Billy Graham Evangelistic Association, 1 Billy Graham Parkway, Charlotte NC 28201. (704)401-2432. Fax: (704)401-3009. E-mail: submissions@bgea.org. Website: www.decisionmag.org. **5% freelance written. Works each year with small number of new/unpublished writers.** "Magazine published 11 times/year with a mission to extend the ministry of Billy Graham Evangelistic Association; to communicate the Good News of Jesus Christ in such a way that readers will be drawn to make a commitment to Christ; and to encourage, strengthen and equip Christians in evangelism and discipleship." Estab. 1960. Circ. 400,000. Byline given. Pays on publication. Publishes ms an average of up to 18 months after acceptance. Buys first rights. Assigns work-for-hire mss, articles, projects. Editorial lead time 6 months. Submit seasonal material 6 months in advance. Sample copy for sae with 9 × 12 envelope and 4 First-Class stamps. Guidelines available online.

- Include telephone number with submission.

Nonfiction Needs personal experience, testimony. **Buys approximately 8 mss/year.** Send complete ms. Length: 400-1,500 words. **Pays $200-400.**

Photos State availability. Captions, identification of subjects, model releases required. Reviews prints. Buys one time rights.

Columns/Departments Finding Jesus (people who have become Christians through Billy Graham Ministries), 500-600 words. 11 Send complete ms. **Pays $200.**

Tips "Articles should have some connection to the ministry of Billy Graham or Franklin Graham. For example, you may have volunteered in one of these ministries or been touched by them. The article does not need to be entirely about that connection, but it should at least mention the connection. Testimonies and personal experience articles should show how God intervened in your life and how you have been transformed by God. SASE required with submissions."

$ DOVETAIL

A Journal By and For Jewish/Christian Families, Dovetail Institute for Interfaith Family Resources, 45 Lilac Ave., Hamden CT 06517. E-mail: Debit4RLS@aol.com. Website: www.dovetailinstitute.org. **75% freelance written**. Quarterly newsletter for interfaith families. "All articles must pertain to life in an interfaith (primarily Jewish/Christian) family. We are broadening our scope to include other sorts of interfaith mixes. We accept all kinds of opinions related to this topic." Estab. 1992. Circ. 1,500. Byline given. Pays on publication. No kill fee. Publishes ms an average of 9 months after acceptance. Buys first rights, buys one-time rights, buys second serial (reprint) rights. Editorial lead time 6 months. Submit seasonal material 6 months in advance. Accepts queries by mail, e-mail, fax, phone. Accepts previously published material. Accepts simultaneous submissions. Responds in 3 months to queries. Sample copy available online. Guidelines available online.

Nonfiction Book reviews, 500 words. **Pays $15, plus 2 copies**. Needs book excerpts, interview, opinion, personal experience. No fiction. **Buys 5-8 mss/year.** Send complete ms. Length: 800-1,000 words. **Pays $25, plus online subscription for 800-1,000 words**

Photos Send photos. Identification of subjects, model releases required. Reviews 5 × 7 prints. Offers no additional payment for photos accepted with ms. Buys one time rights.

Tips Write on concrete, specific topics related to Jewish/Christian or other dual-faith intermarriage: no proselytizing, sermonizing, or general religious commentary. Successful freelancers are part of an interfaith family themselves, or have done solid research/interviews with members of interfaith families. We look for honest, reflective personal experience. We're looking for more on alternative or nontraditional families, e.g., interfaith gay/lesbian, single parent raising child in departed partner's faith.

$$ EFCA TODAY

Evangelical Free Church of America, 418 Fourth St., NE, Charlottesville VA 22902. E-mail: dianemc@journeygroup.com. Website: www.efca.org/today. **30% freelance written**. Quarterly magazine. "*EFCA Today*'s purpose is to unify church leaders around the overall mission of the EFCA by bringing its stories and vision to life, and to sharpen those leaders by generating conversations over topics pertinent to faith and life in this 21st century." Estab. 1931. Circ. 44,000. Byline given. Pays on acceptance. Offers 50% kill fee. Publishes ms an average of 3 months after acceptance. Makes work-for-hire assignments. Editorial lead time 5 months. Submit seasonal material 6 months in advance. Accepts queries by mail, e-mail. Rarely accepts previously published material.Responds in 6 weeks. Sample copy for $1 with SAE and 5 first-class stamps. Guidelines by e-mail.

Nonfiction Needs interview, of EFCA-related subjects, feature articles of EFCA interest, highlighting EFCA subjects. No general-interest inspirational articles. Send complete ms. Length: 200-1,100 words and related/approved expenses for assigned articles. **Pays 23¢/word for first rights, including limited subsidiary rights (free use within an EFCA context).**

Reprints varies.

Columns/Departments On the Radar (significant trends/news of EFCA); Engage (out of the church and into the world); Leader to Leader (what leaders are saying, doing, learning); Catalyst (the passion of EFCA's young leaders; Face to Face (our global family), all between 200 and 600/words. Send complete ms. **Pays 23¢/word and related/approved expenses for assigned articles.**

Tips "One portion of each *EFCA Today* is devoted to a topic designed to stimulate thoughtful dialog and leadership growth, and to highlight how EFCA leaders are already involved in living out that theme. Examples of themes are: new paradigms for 'doing church,' church planting and the 'emerging' church. These articles differ from those in the above sections, in that their primary focus in on the issue rather than the person; the person serves to illustrate the issue. These articles should run between 400 and 800 words. Include contacts for verification of article."

$$ ENRICHMENT

The General Council of the Assemblies of God, 1445 N. Boonville Ave., Springfield MO 65802. (417)862-2781. Fax: (417)862-0416. E-mail: enrichmentjournal@ag.org. Website: www.enrichmentjournal.ag.org. **Contact:** Rick Knoth, managing editor. **15% freelance written**. Quarterly journal covering church

leadership and ministry. "*Enrichment* offers enriching and encouraging information to equip and empower spirit-filled leaders." Circ. 33,000. Byline given. Pays on publication. 50% kill fee. Publishes ms an average of 1 year after acceptance. Buys first rights. Editorial lead time 18 months. Submit seasonal material 18 months in advance. Accepts queries by mail, e-mail. Sample copy for $7. Guidelines free.
Nonfiction Needs religious. Send complete ms. Length: 1,000-3,000 words. **Pays up to 15¢/word.**

$ ☐ THE EVANGELICAL BAPTIST

Fellowship of Evangelical Baptist Churches in Canada, P.O. Box 457, Guelph ON N1H 6K9 Canada. 519-821-4830. Fax: 519-821-9829. E-mail: eb@fellowship.ca. Website: www.fellowship.ca. **10% freelance written**. Magazine published 4 times/year covering religious, spiritual, Christian living, denominational, and missionary news. We exist to enhance the life and ministry of the church leaders and members in Fellowship Congregations. Estab. 1953. Circ. 3,000. Byline given. Pays on publication. No kill fee. Publishes ms an average of 6 months after acceptance. Buys one-time rights, buys second serial (reprint) rights. Editorial lead time 4 months. Accepts queries by e-mail. Accepts previously published material. Accepts simultaneous submissions. Sample copy available online. Guidelines available online.
Nonfiction Needs religious. No poetry, fiction, puzzles. **Buys 4-6 mss/year.** Send complete ms. Length: 500-900 words. **Pays $50.**

$ EVANGELICAL MISSIONS QUARTERLY

A Professional Journal Serving the Missions Community, Billy Graham Center/Wheaton College, P.O. Box 794, Wheaton IL 60189. (630)752-7158. Fax: (630)752-7155. E-mail: emq@wheaton.edu. Website: www.billygrahamcenter.org. **Contact:** Managing Editor. **67% freelance written**. Quarterly magazine covering evangelical missions. This is a professional journal for evangelical missionaries, agency executives, and church members who support global missions ministries. Estab. 1964. Circ. 7,000. Byline given. Pays on publication. Offers negotiable kill fee. Publishes ms an average of 18 months after acceptance. Buys electronic rights, buys all rights. Editorial lead time 1 year. Accepts queries by e-mail. Responds in 2 weeks to queries. Sample copy free Guidelines available online.
Nonfiction Needs essays, interview, opinion, personal experience, religious, book reviews. No sermons, poetry, straight news. **Buys 24 mss/year.** Query. Length: 800-3,000 words. **Pays $25-100.**
Photos Send photos. Identification of subjects required. Offers no additional payment for photos accepted with ms. Buys first rights
Columns/Departments In the Workshop (practical how to's), 800-2,000 words; Perspectives (opinion), 800 words. 8 Query. **Pays $50-100.**
Tips "We prefer articles about deeds done, showing the why and the how, claiming not only success but also admitting failure. Principles drawn from one example must be applicable to missions more generally. EMQ does not include articles which have been previously published in journals, books, websites, etc."

$$ ☐ FAITH & FRIENDS

Inspiration for Living, The Salvation Army, 2 Overlea Blvd., Toronto ON M4H 1P4 Canada. (416)422-6226. Fax: (416)422-6120. E-mail: faithandfriends@can.salvationarmy.org. Website: www.faithandfriends.ca. **25% freelance written**. Monthly magazine covering Christian living and religion. "Our mission statement: to show Jesus Christ at work in the lives of real people, and to provide spiritual resources for those who are new to the Christian faith." Estab. 1996. Circ. 50,000. Byline given. Pays on acceptance. Offers $50 kill fee. Publishes ms an average of 3 months after acceptance. Buys first rights, buys electronic rights. Editorial lead time 3 months. Submit seasonal material 6 months in advance. Accepts queries by mail, e-mail. Accepts previously published material. .Responds in 1 week to queries and to mss. Sample copy available online Guidelines by e-mail
Nonfiction Needs book excerpts, humor, inspirational, interview, personal experience, photo feature, religious, travel. Does not want sermons, devotionals, or Christian-ese. **Buys 12-24 mss/year.** Query. Length: 500-1,250 words. **Pays $50-200.**
Photos Send photos. Captions required. Reviews prints, GIF/JPEG files. Negotiates payment individually. Buys one-time rights.
Columns/Departments God in My Life (how life changed by accepting Jesus); Someone Cares (how life changed through someone's intervention), 750 words. 12-18 mss/year. Query. **Pays $50.**

$$ ☐ FAITH TODAY

To Connect, Equip and Inform Evangelical Christians in Canada, Evangelical Fellowship of Canada, MIP Box 3745, Markham ON L3R 0Y4 Canada. (905)479-5885. Fax: (905)479-4742. Website: www.faithtoday.ca. Bimonthly magazine. "*FT* is the magazine of an association of more than 40 evangelical denominations, but serves evangelicals in all denominations. It focuses on church issues, social issues and personal faith as they are tied to the Canadian context. Writing should explicitly acknowledge that Canadian evangelical context." Estab. 1983. Circ. 18,000. Byline given. Pays on publication. Offers 30-50% kill fee. Publishes ms an average of 4 months after acceptance. Buys first rights. Editorial lead time 4 months. Accepts queries by mail, e-mail, fax. Responds in 6 weeks to queries. Sample copy for SASE in Canadian postage. Guidelines available online at www.faithtoday.ca/writers.

Nonfiction Needs book excerpts, Canadian authors only, essays, Canadian authors only, interview, Canadian subjects only, opinion, religious, news feature. **Buys 75 mss/year.** Query. Length: 400-2,000 words. **Pays $100-500 Canadian.**

Reprints Send photocopy. Rarely used. Pays 50% of amount paid for an original article.

Photos State availability. True required. Reviews contact sheets. Buys one-time rights.

Tips "Query should include brief outline and names of the sources you plan to interview in your research. Use Canadian postage on SASE."

$ FORWARD IN CHRIST

The Word from the WELS, WELS Communication Services, 2929 N. Mayfair Rd., Milwaukee WI 53222-4398. (414)256-3210. Fax: (414)256-3862. E-mail: fic@sab.wels.net. Website: www.wels.net. John A. Braun, exec. ed. **Contact:** Julie K. Wietzke, managing editor. **5% freelance written**. official monthly magazine covering Wisconsin Evangelical Lutheran Synod (WELS) news, topics, issues. The material usually must be written by or about WELS members. Estab. 1913. Circ. 55,000. Byline given. Pays on publication. No kill fee. Publishes ms an average of 6 months after acceptance. Buys one-time rights. Editorial lead time 3 months. Submit seasonal material 4 months in advance. Accepts queries by mail, e-mail, fax. Responds in 2 months to queries. Sample copy and writer's guidelines free Guidelines available on website.

Nonfiction Needs personal experience, religious. Query. Length: 550-1,200 words. **Pays $75/page, $125/2 pages.**

Photos State availability. Captions, identification of subjects, model releases required. Reviews contact sheets. Negotiates payment individually. Buys one-time rights, plus 1 month on Web and in archive

Tips "Topics should be of interest to the majority of the members of the synod—the people in the pews. Articles should have a Christian viewpoint, but we don't want sermons. We suggest you carefully read at least 5 or 6 issues with close attention to the length, content, and style of the features."

$$ GROUP MAGAZINE

Group Publishing, Inc., P.O. Box 481, Loveland CO 80539-0481. Fax: (970)292-4373. E-mail: greditor@youthministry.com. Website: www.groupmag.com. **60% freelance written**. Bimonthly magazine covering youth ministry. "Writers must be actively involved in youth ministry. Articles we accept are practical, not theoretical, and focused for local church youth workers." Estab. 1974. Circ. 57,000. Byline given. Pays on acceptance. Offers $20 kill fee. Publishes ms an average of 6 months after acceptance. Buys all rights. Submit seasonal material 7 months in advance. Responds in 8-10 weeks to queries. Sample copy for $2 and 9 × 12 SAE. Guidelines available online.

Nonfiction "GROUP needs articles on successful youth ministry strategies, including youth-led ministry ideas, understanding kids and youth culture, recruiting/training/keeping adult leaders, family ministry, staff issues, serving and training parents, professionalism, and self-nurture. How-to articles on personal spiritual growth, time management, issues vital to working with young people, leadership skills (listening, discussion-leading), worship ideas, handling specific group problems, fun and experiential programming ideas, and active-learning meeting plans and retreats." Needs how-to, youth ministry issues. No personal testimony, theological or lecture-style articles. **Buys 50-60 mss/year.** Query. Length: 250-2,200 words. **Pays $50-250.**

Tips "Submit a youth ministry idea to one of our mini-article sections—we look for tried-and-true ideas youth ministers have used with kids."

HIGHWAY NEWS

Transport For Christ, P.O. Box 117, 1525 River Rd., Marietta PA 17547. (717)426-9977. Fax: (717)426-9980. E-mail: tfcio@transportforchrist.org. Website: www.transportforchrist.org. **Contact:** Inge Koenig. **50% freelance written**. Monthly magazine covering trucking and Christianity. "We publish human interest stories, testimonials, and teachings that have a foundation in Biblical/Christian values. Since truck drivers and their families are our primary readers, we publish works that they will find edifying and helpful." Estab. 1957. Circ. 39,000. Byline given. No kill fee. Publishes ms an average of 1 year after acceptance. Buys We do not buy any rights. rights. Submit seasonal material 1 year in advance. Accepts queries by mail, e-mail, fax. Accepts previously published material. Accepts simultaneous submissions.

Responds in 1 month to queries. Responds in 2 months to mss. Sample copy free. Writer's guidelines by e-mail (editor@transportforchrist.org).

- Does not pay writers.

Nonfiction Needs essays, general interest, humor, inspirational, interview, personal experience, photo feature, religious, trucking. No sermons full of personal opinions. **Accepts 20-25 mss/year.** Send complete ms. Length: 600-1,200 words.
Photos Send photos. Captions, identification of subjects, model releases required. Reviews prints, GIF/JPEG files. Does not pay for photos. We don't buy anything.
Columns/Departments From the Road (stories by truckers on the road); Devotionals with Trucking theme, both 600 words. Send complete ms.
Fiction Needs humorous, religious, slice-of-life vignettes. No romance or fantasy. We use very little fiction. **Accepts 1 or fewer mss/year.** Send complete ms. Length: 600-1,200 words.
Poetry Needs traditional. Don't send anything unrelated to the trucking industry. Accepts 2 poems/year. Submit maximum 10 poems. Length: 4-20 lines.
Tips "We are especially interested in human interest stories about truck drivers. Find a trucker doing something unusual or good and write a story about him or her. Be sure to send pictures."

$ HORIZONS

The Magazine for Presbyterian Women, 100 Witherspoon St., Louisville KY 40202-1396. (502)569-5897. Fax: (502)569-8085. Website: www.pcusa.org/horizons/. Bimonthly. "Magazine owned and operated by Presbyterian women offering information and inspiration for Presbyterian women by addressing current issues facing the church and the world." Estab. 1988. Circ. 25,000. Pays on publication. No kill fee. Publishes ms an average of 4 months after acceptance. Buys all rights. Sample copy for $4 and 9 × 12 SAE. Guidelines for #10 SASE.
Fiction Send complete ms. Length: 800-1,200 words. **Pays $50/600 words and 2 contributor's copies.**

$$ LEADERS IN ACTION

CSB Ministries, P.O. Box 150, Wheaton IL 60189. (630)582-0630. Fax: (630)582-0623. Website: csbministries.org. Magazine published 3 times/year covering leadership issues for CSB Ministries leaders. "*Leaders in Action* is distributed to leaders with CSB Ministries across North America. CSB is a nonprofit, nondenominational agency dedicated to winning and training boys and girls to serve Jesus Christ. Hundreds of churches throughout the U.S. and Canada make use of our wide range of services." Estab. 1960. Circ. 6,000. Byline given. Pays on acceptance. Offers $35 kill fee. Publishes ms an average of 3 months after acceptance. Buys first rights, buys second serial (reprint) rights. Editorial lead time 3 months. Responds in 1 week to queries. Sample copy for $1.50 and 10 × 13 SAE with 4 first-class stamps. Guidelines for #10 sase.
Nonfiction Buys 8 mss/year. Query. Length: 500-1,500 words. **Pays 5-10¢/word.**
Reprints Send typed manuscript with rights for sale noted. Pays 50% of amount paid for an original article.
Tips "We're looking for writers who can encourage and inspire leaders of children and youth, and work within a tight deadline. We work by assignment only. Send writing samples so we can determine how you might fit with our editorial goals."

$$ LIGHT & LIFE MAGAZINE

Free Methodist Church of North America, P.O. Box 535002, Indianapolis IN 46253-5002. (317)244-3660. Fax: (317)248-9055. E-mail: llmauthors@fmcna.org. Website: www.freemethodistchurch.org. **Contact:** Doug Newton, editor. **20%**. "Bimonthly magazine for maturing Christians emphasizing a holiness lifestyle, contemporary issues, and a Christ-centered worldview. Includes pull-out discipleship and evangelism tools and encouragement cards, denominational news." Estab. 1868. Circ. 38,000. Byline given. Pays on acceptance. No kill fee. Buys one-time rights. Accepts queries by mail, e-mail. Responds in 12 weeks. Sample copy for $4. Guidelines available online.
Nonfiction Query. 800-1,500 words (LifeNotes 1,000 words) **Pays 15¢/word, 3 complimentary copies.**

$$ LIGUORIAN

One Liguori Dr., Liguori MO 63057-9999. (636)464-2500. Fax: (636)464-8449. E-mail: liguorianeditor@liguori.org. Website: www.liguorian.org. **Contact:** Cheryl Plass, Managing Editor. **25% freelance written. Prefers to work with published/established writers**. Magazine published 10 times/year for Catholics. "Our purpose is to lead our readers to a fuller Christian life by helping them better understand the teachings of the gospel and the church and by illustrating how these teachings apply to life and the problems confronting them as members of families, the church, and society." Estab. 1913. Circ. 100,000.

Pays on acceptance. Buys first rights. Submit seasonal material 8 months in advance. Accepts queries by mail, e-mail, fax, phone. Responds in 3 months to mss. Sample copy for 9 × 12 SAE with 3 first-class stamps or online Guidelines for #10 SASE and on website.

Nonfiction Pastoral, practical, and personal approach to the problems and challenges of people today. "No travelogue approach or un-researched ventures into controversial areas. Also, no material found in secular publications—fad subjects that already get enough press, pop psychology, negative or put-down articles. *Liguorian* does not consider retold Bible stories." **Buys 30-40 unsolicited mss/year.** Length: 400-2,000 words. **Pays 10-15¢/word and 5 contributor's copies.**

Photos Photographs on assignment only unless submitted with and specific to article.

Fiction Needs religious, senior citizen/retirement. Send complete ms. 1,500-2,000 words preferred **Pays 10-15¢/word and 5 contributor's copies.**

Tips Authors are advised to read and study several issues of *Liguorian* before submitting articles. Read our guidelines.

$$ LIVE

A Weekly Journal of Practical Christian Living, Gospel Publishing House, 1445 N. Boonville Ave., Springfield MO 65802-1894. (417)862-1447. Fax: (417)862-6059. E-mail: rl-live@gph.org. Website: www.gospelpublishing.com. **100% freelance written**. Weekly magazine for weekly distribution covering practical Christian living. "LIVE is a take-home paper distributed weekly in young adult and adult Sunday school classes. We seek to encourage Christians in living for God through fiction and true stories which apply Biblical principles to everyday problems." We seek to encourage Christians in living for God through fiction and true stories which apply Biblical principles to everyday problems." Estab. 1928. Circ. 35,000. Byline given. Pays on acceptance. No kill fee. Publishes ms an average of 18 months after acceptance. Buys first rights, buys second serial (reprint) rights. Editorial lead time 12 months. Submit seasonal material 18 months in advance. Accepts queries by mail, e-mail. Accepts simultaneous submissions. Responds in 2 weeks to queries. Responds in 6 weeks to mss. Sample copy for #10 SASE. Guidelines for #10 SASE or on website: http://www.gospelpublishing.com/store/startcat.cfm?cat=tWRITGUID

Nonfiction Needs inspirational, religious. No preachy articles or stories that refer to religious myths (e.g., Santa Claus, Easter Bunny, etc.) **Buys 50-100 mss/year.** Send complete ms. Length: 400-1,100 words. **Pays 7-10¢/word.**

Reprints Send tearsheet, photocopy or typed ms with rights for sale noted and information about when and where the material previously appeared. Pays 7¢/word.

Photos Send photos. Identification of subjects required. Reviews 35mm transparencies and 3 × 4 prints or larger. Higher resolution digital files also accepted. Offers $35-60/photo. Buys one-time rights.

Fiction Contact: Richard Bennett, editor. Needs religious, inspirational, prose poem. No preachy fiction, fiction about Bible characters, or stories that refer to religious myths (e.g., Santa Claus, Easter Bunny, etc.). No science or Bible fiction. No controversial stories about such subjects as feminism, war or capital punishment. **Buys 20-50 mss/year.** Send complete ms. Length: 800-1,200 words. **Pays 7-10¢/word.**

Poetry Needs free verse, haiku, light verse, traditional. Buys 15-24 poems/year. Submit maximum 3 poems. Length: 12-25 lines. **Pays $35-60.**

Tips "Don't moralize or be preachy. Provide human interest articles with Biblical life application. Stories should consist of action, not just thought-life; interaction, not just insight. Heroes and heroines should rise above failures, take risks for God, prove that scriptural principles meet their needs. Conflict and suspense should increase to a climax! Avoid pious conclusions. Characters should be interesting, believable, and realistic. Avoid stereotypes. Characters should be active, not just pawns to move the plot along. They should confront conflict and change in believable ways. Describe the character's looks and reveal his personality through his actions to such an extent that the reader feels he has met that person. Readers should care about the character enough to finish the story. Feature racial, ethnic, and regional characters in rural and urban settings."

$ N THE LIVING CHURCH

Living Church Foundation, 816 E. Juneau Ave., P.O. Box 514036, Milwaukee WI 53202-2793. (414)276-5420. Fax: (414)276-7483. E-mail: tlc@livingchurch.org. Website: www.livingchurch.org. **Contact:** David Kalvelage, editor. **50% freelance written**. covering news or articles of interest to members of the Episcopal Church. "Weekly magazine that presents news and views of the Episcopal Church and the wider Anglican Communion, along with articles on spirituality, Anglican heritage, and the application of Christianity in daily life. There are commentaries on scripture, book reviews, editorials, letters to the editor, and special thematic issues." Estab. 1878. Circ. 9,500. Byline given. Does not pay unless article is requested. No kill fee. Publishes ms an average of 3 months after acceptance. Buys one-time rights. Editorial lead time 3 weeks. Submit seasonal material 2 months in advance. Accepts queries by mail, e-mail, fax. Responds in 2 weeks to queries. Responds in 1 month to mss. Sample copy free.

Nonfiction Needs opinion, personal experience, photo feature, religious. **Buys 10 mss/year.** Send complete ms. Length: 1,000 words. **Pays $25-100.**

Photos Send photos. Reviews any size prints. Offers $15-50/photo. Buys one time rights.

Columns/Departments Benediction (devotional), 250 words; Viewpoint (opinion), under 1,000 words. Send complete ms. **Pays $50 maximum.**

Poetry Needs light verse, traditional.

$$ THE LOOKOUT

The Growing Christian's Weekly Resource, Standard Publishing, 8805 Governor's Hill Dr., Suite 400, Cincinnati OH 45249. (513)931-4050. Fax: (513)931-0950. E-mail: lookout@standardpub.com. Website: www.lookoutmag.com. **50% freelance written**. Weekly magazine for Christian adults, with emphasis on spiritual growth, family life, and topical issues. "Our purpose is to provide Christian adults with practical, Biblical teaching and current information that will help them mature as believers." Estab. 1894. Circ. 60,000. Byline given. Pays on acceptance. Offers 33% kill fee. Publishes ms an average of 1 year after acceptance. Buys first rights. Editorial lead time 9 months. Submit seasonal material 1 year in advance. Accepts queries by mail, e-mail. previously published material.Accepts simultaneous submissions. Responds in 10 weeks to queries. Responds in 10 weeks to mss. Sample copy for $1. Guidelines by e-mail.

- Audience is mainly conservative Christians. Manuscripts only accepted by mail.

Nonfiction "We publish strictly according to a theme list. All major articles we will address one of the 52 themes we have scheduled for the year. We no longer purchase non-theme articles for occasional features (salt & light), Faith Around the World, AMD Outlook)." Needs inspirational, interview, opinion, personal experience, religious. No fiction or poetry. **Buys 100 mss/year.** Send complete ms. Check guidelines. **Pays 11-17¢/word.**

Photos State availability. Identification of subjects required. Offers no additional payment for photos accepted with ms.

Tips "*The Lookout* publishes from a theologically conservative, nondenominational, and noncharismatic perspective. We aim primarily for those aged 30-55. Most readers are married and have elementary to young adult children. Our emphasis is on the needs of ordinary Christians who want to grow in their faith. We value well-informed articles that offer lively and clear writing as well as strong application. We often address tough issues and seek to explore fresh ideas or recent developments affecting today's Christians."

$ THE LUTHERAN DIGEST

The Lutheran Digest, Inc., P.O. Box 4250, Hopkins MN 55343. (952)933-2820. Fax: (952)933-5708. E-mail: editor@lutherandigest.com. Website: www.lutherandigest.com. **Contact:** Nicholas A. Skapyak, editor. **95% freelance written**. Quarterly magazine covering Christianity from a Lutheran perspective. "Articles frequently reflect a Lutheran Christian perspective, but are not intended to be sermonettes. Popular stories show how God has intervened in a person's life to help solve a problem." Estab. 1953. Circ. 70,000. Byline given. Pays on acceptance. No kill fee. Publishes ms an average of 6 months after acceptance. Buys first rights, buys second serial (reprint) rights. Editorial lead time 9 months. Submit seasonal material 9 months in advance. Accepts queries by e-mail mss only at microsoft word or pdf attachments. Accepts previously published material. Accepts simultaneous submissions. Responds in 1 month to queries. Responds in 4 months to mss. No response to e-mailed manuscripts unless selected for publication. Sample copy for $3.50. Guidelines available online.

Nonfiction Needs general interest, historical, how-to, personal or spiritual growth, humor, inspirational, personal experience, religious, nature, God's unique creatures. Does not want "to see personal tributes to deceased relatives or friends. They are seldom used unless the subject of the article is well known. We also avoid articles about the moment a person finds Christ as his or her personal savior." **Buys 50-60 mss/year.** Send complete ms. Length: 1,500 words. **Pays $35-50.**

Reprints Accepts previously published submissions. "We prefer this as we are a digest and 70-80% of our articles are reprints."

Photos "We seldom print photos from outside sources." State availability. Buys one time rights.

Tips "Reading our writers' guidelines and sample articles online is encouraged and is the best way to get a 'feel' of the type of material we publish."

$$ MESSAGE MAGAZINE

Review and Herald Publishing Association, 55 West Oak Ridge Dr., Hagerstown MD 21740. (301)393-4099. Fax: (301)393-4103. E-mail: wjohnson@rhpa.org. Website: www.messagemagazine.org. **10-20% freelance written**. Bimonthly magazine. "*Message* is the oldest religious journal addressing ethnic issues in the country. Our audience is predominantly Black and Seventh-day Adventist; however, *Message* is an outreach magazine for the churched and un-churched across cultural lines." Estab. 1898. Circ. 110,000. Byline given. Pays on acceptance. No kill fee. Publishes ms an average of 12 months after acceptance. first North American serial rights Editorial lead time 6 months. Submit seasonal material 6 months in advance. Responds in 9 months to queries. Sample copy by e-mail. Guidelines by e-mail.

Nonfiction Needs general interest; how-to (overcome depression, overcome defeat, get closer to God, learn from failure, deal with the economic crises, etc.). **Buys variable number of mss/year.** Send complete ms. Length: 800-1,200 words. **Payment varies. Payment upon acceptance.**

Photos State availability. Identification of subjects required. Buys one time rights.

Tips "Please look at the magazine before submitting manuscripts. *Message* publishes a variety of writing styles as long as the writing style is easy to read and flows—please avoid highly technical writing styles."

MESSAGE OF THE OPEN BIBLE

Open Bible Churches, 2020 Bell Ave., Des Moines IA 50315-1096. (515)288-6761. Fax: (515)288-2510. E-mail: andrea@openbible.org. Website: www.openbible.org. **5% freelance written**. "*The Message of the Open Bible* is the official bimonthly publication of Open Bible Churches. Its readership consists mostly of people affiliated with Open Bible." Estab. 1932. Circ. 2,700. Byline given. No kill fee. Publishes ms an average of 4-6 months after acceptance. Editorial lead time 6 months. Submit seasonal material 6 months in advance. Accepts queries by mail. Responds in 1 month to queries. Responds in 2 months to mss. Sample copy for sae with 9 × 12 envelope and 3 first-class stamps. Writer's guidelines for #10 SASE or by e-mail (message@openbible.org).

- Does not pay for articles.

Nonfiction Needs inspirational, teachings or challenges, interview, personal experience, religious, testimonies, news. No sermons. Send complete ms. Maximum 650 words.

Photos State availability. Reviews 5 × 7 prints, GIF/JPEG files. Doesn't pay for photos.

$ THE MESSENGER OF THE SACRED HEART

Apostleship of Prayer, 661 Greenwood Ave., Toronto ON M4J 4B3 Canada. (416)466-1195. **20% freelance written**. Monthly magazine for Canadian and U.S. Catholics interested in developing a life of prayer and spirituality; stresses the great value of our ordinary actions and lives. Estab. 1891. Circ. 11,000. Byline given. Pays on acceptance. No kill fee. Buys first North American serial rights, buys first rights. Submit seasonal material 5 months in advance. Responds in 1 month to queries. Sample copy for $1 and 7½ × 10½ SAE. Guidelines for #10 SASE.

Fiction Contact: Rev. F.J. Power, S.J. and Alfred DeManche, editors. Needs religious, stories about people, adventure, heroism, humor, drama. No poetry. **Buys 12 mss/year.** Send complete ms. Length: 750-1,500 words. **Pays 8¢/word, and 3 contributor's copies.**

Tips Develop a story that sustains interest to the end. Do not preach, but use plot and characters to convey the message or theme. Aim to move the heart as well as the mind. Before sending, cut out unnecessary or unrelated words or sentences. If you can, add a light touch or a sense of humor to the story. Your ending should have impact, leaving a moral or faith message for the reader.

$ MONTGOMERY'S JOURNEY

Sharing Hope, Buidling Community, Keep Sharing, 555 Farmington Rd., Montgomery AL 36109. E-mail: deanne@montgomerysjourney.com. **50% freelance written**. Monthly magazine covering Christian living. Includes Protestant Christian writing, topical articles on Christian living, and Christian living articles with helpful information for walking with Christ daily. Estab. 1999. Circ. 8,000. Byline given. Pays on publication. Offers 25% kill fee. Publishes ms an average of 6-12 months after acceptance. Buys one-time rights, buys second serial (reprint) rights. Editorial lead time 1 year. Submit seasonal material 1 year in advance. Accepts queries by e-mail. Accepts previously published material. Accepts simultaneous submissions. Sample copy for $1.75 and self-addressed magazine-size envelope. Guidelines by e-mail.

Nonfiction Needs inspirational, religious. No fiction, poetry, or autobiography. Submit query or complete ms. Length: 1,300-2,200 words. **Pays $25-50 for assigned articles. Pays $25 for unsolicited articles.**

$$ MY DAILY VISITOR

Our Sunday Visitor, Inc., 200 Noll Plaza, Huntington IN 46750. (260)356-8400. Fax: (260)356-8472.

E-mail: mdvisitor@osv.com. Website: www.osv.com. **99% freelance written**. Bimonthly magazine of Scripture meditations based on the day's Catholic Mass readings. Circ. 33,000. Byline given. Pays on acceptance. No kill fee. Publishes ms an average of 6 months after acceptance. Buys one-time rights. Accepts queries by mail, e-mail. Responds in 2 months to queries. Sample copy and writer's guidelines for #10 SAE with 3 first-class stamps.

- Sample meditations and guidelines online. Each writer does 1 full month of meditations on assignment basis only.

Nonfiction Needs inspirational, personal experience, religious. **Buys 12 mss/year.** Query with published clips. 130-140 words times the number of days in month. **Pays $500 for 1 month (28-31) of meditations and 5 free copies.**

Tips Previous experience in writing Scripture-based Catholic meditations or essays is helpful.

A NEW HEART

Encouraging Christians in Healthcare, Hospital Christian Fellowship, Inc., P.O. Box 4004, San Clemente CA 92674. (949)496-7655. Fax: (949)496-8465. E-mail: hcfusa@gmail.com. Website: www.hcfusa.com. **50% freelance written**. Quarterly magazine covering articles and true stories that are health-related, with a Christian message, to encourage healthcare workers, patients, and volunteers to meet specific needs. Estab. 1978. Circ. 5,000. Byline given. No kill fee. Publishes ms an average of 4-6 months after acceptance. Buys simultaneous rights. Editorial lead time 6 months. Submit seasonal material 6 months in advance. Accepts queries by mail, e-mail, fax, phone. Accepts previously published material. Accepts simultaneous submissions. Responds in 2 weeks to queries. Sample copy free. Guidelines free.

Nonfiction Needs humor, inspirational, personal experience, religious. No fiction. **Buys 10-20 mss/year.** Query. Length: 500-1,500 words.

Photos State availability of or send photos.. Captions, identification of subjects required. Offers no additional payment for photos accepted with ms. Buys one-time rights.

Columns/Departments Book Review (medical/Christian), 200 words; Events (medical/Christian), 100-200 words; Chaplains (medical/Christian/inspirational), 200-250 words; On the Lighter Side (medical/clean fun), 100-200 words. 4-6 Send complete ms. **Pays in copies.**

$$ ONE

Catholic Near East Welfare Association, 1011 First Ave., New York NY 10022-4195. (212)826-1480. Fax: (212)826-8979. E-mail: cnewa@cnewa.org. Website: www.cnewa.org. **75% freelance written**. Bimonthly magazine for a Catholic audience with interest in the Near East, particularly its current religious, cultural and political aspects. Estab. 1974. Circ. 100,000. Byline given. Pays on publication. No kill fee. Publishes ms an average of 6 months after acceptance. Buys all rights. Accepts queries by mail, fax. Responds in 1 month to queries. Sample copy and writer's guidelines for 7½ × 10½ SAE with 2 first-class stamps.

Nonfiction Cultural, devotional, political, historical material on the Near East, with an emphasis on the Eastern Christian churches. Style should be simple, factual, concise. Articles must stem from personal acquaintance with subject matter, or thorough up-to-date research. Length: 1,200-1,800 words. **Pays 20¢/edited word.**

Photos Photographs to accompany manuscript are welcome; they should illustrate the people, places, ceremonies, etc. which are described in the article. We prefer color transparencies but occasionally use b&w. Pay varies depending on use—scale from $50-300.

Tips We are interested in current events in the Near East as they affect the cultural, political and religious lives of the people.

$$ ON MISSION

North American Mission Board, SBC, 4200 North Point Pkwy., Alpharetta GA 30022-4176. E-mail: onmission@namb.net. Website: www.onmission.com. **25% freelance written**. Quarterly lifestyle magazine that popularizes evangelism, church planting and missions. "*On Mission*'s primary purpose is to tell the story of southern baptist missionaries in North America and to help readers and churches become more intentional about personal evangelism, church planting, and missions in North America. *On Mission* equips Christians for leading people to Christ and encourages churches to reach people through new congregations." Estab. 1998. Circ. 100,000. Byline given. Pays on acceptance. Publishes ms an average of 6 months after acceptance. Buys first rights, buys electronic rights, buys first North American rights. Editorial lead time 9 months. Submit seasonal material 9 months in advance. Accepts queries by mail, e-mail (prefers e-mail). Responds in 6 weeks to queries. Responds in 4 months to mss. Sample copy free or online Guidelines available online.

Nonfiction Needs how-to, humor, personal experience, stories of sharing your faith in Christ with a non-Christian. **Buys 30 mss/year.** Query with published clips. Length: 350-1,200 words. **Pays 25¢/word, more for cover stories.**
Photos Most are shot on assignment. Captions, identification of subjects required. Buys all rights.
Columns/Departments 2 Query. **Pays 25¢/word.**
Tips "Readers might be intimidated if those featured appear to be `super Christians' who seem to live on a higher spiritual plane. Try to introduce subjects as three-dimensional, real people. Include anecdotes or examples of their fears and failures, including ways they overcame obstacles. In other words, take the reader inside the heart of the missionary or on mission Christian and reveal the inevitable humanness that makes that person not only believable, but also approachable. We want the reader to feel encouraged to become on mission by identifying with people like them who are featured in the magazine."

$$ OUR SUNDAY VISITOR

Our Sunday Visitor, Inc., 200 Noll Plaza, Huntington IN 46750. (260)356-8400. Fax: (260)356-8472. E-mail: jnorton@osv.com. Website: www.osv.com. **70% freelance written. (Mostly assigned)**. Weekly tabloid covering world events and culture from a Catholic perspective. Estab. 1912. Circ. 60,000. Byline given. Pays on acceptance. No kill fee. Publishes ms an average of 2-3 weeks after acceptance. Buys first rights. Accepts queries by mail, e-mail.

$$ OUTREACH MAGAZINE

Outreach, Inc., 2230 Oak Ridge Way, Vista CA 92081-8314. (760)940-0600. Fax: (760)597-2314. E-mail: llowry@outreach.com. Website: www.outreachmagazine.com. **Contact:** Lindy Lowry, editor. **80% freelance written**. Bimonthly magazine covering outreach. "*Outreach* is designed to inspire, challenge, and equip churches and church leaders to reach out to their communities with the love of Jesus Christ." Circ. 30,000, plus newsstand. Byline given. Pays on publication. Offers 10% kill fee. Publishes ms an average of 2-4 months after acceptance. Buys first North American serial rights. Editorial lead time 6 months. Submit seasonal material 6 months in advance. Accepts queries by mail, e-mail, fax. Mail submissions to Editor. Mark Query or Unsolicited manuscript on your envelope. E-mail submissions to editor@outreach.com. No phone calls, please. Accepts previously published material. Accepts simultaneous submissions. Responds in 2 months to queries. Responds in 8 months to mss. Sample copy free. Guidelines free and online.
Nonfiction Needs book excerpts, how-to, humor, inspirational, interview, personal experience, photo feature, religious. Vacation Bible School (January); Church Growth—America's Fastest-Growing Churches (Special Issue). Does not want fiction, poetry, non-outreach-related articles. **Buys 30 mss/year.** Query with published clips. Length: 1,500-2,500 words. **Pays $375-600 for assigned articles. Pays $375-500 for unsolicited articles.**
Photos Contact: Tim Downs, art director. Send photos. Identification of subjects required. Reviews GIF/JPEG files. Negotiates payment individually. Buys all rights.
Columns/Departments Contact: Lindy Lowry, editor. Pulse (short stories about outreach-oriented churches and ministries), 250-350 words; Soulfires (an as-told-to interview with a person about the stories and people that have fueled their passion for outreach), 900 words; Ideas (a profile of a church that is using a transferable idea or concept for outreach), 300 words, plus sidebar; Soulfires (short interviews with known voices about the stories and people that have informed their worldview and faith perspective), 600 words. Buys 6 mss/year. Query with published clips. **Pays $100-375.**
Tips "Study our magazine and writer's guidelines. Send published clips that showcase tight, bright writing as well as your ability to interview; research; and organize numerous sources into an article; and write a 100-word piece as well as a 1,600-word piece."

$$ PENTECOSTAL EVANGEL

The General Council of the Assemblies of God, 1445 N. Boonville, Springfield MO 65802-1894. (417)862-2781. Fax: (417)862-0416. E-mail: pe@ag.org. Website: pe.ag.org. **5-10% freelance written**. Weekly magazine emphasizing news of the Assemblies of God for members of the Assemblies and other Pentecostal and charismatic Christians. "Articles should be inspirational without being preachy. Any devotional writing should take a literal approach to the Bible. A variety of general topics and personal experience accepted with inspirational tie-in." Estab. 1913. Circ. 200,000. Byline given. Pays on acceptance. Offers 100% kill fee. Publishes ms an average of 6 months after acceptance. Buys first North American serial rights, buys one-time rights. Editorial lead time 3 months. Submit seasonal material 6 months in advance. Accepts queries by e-mail. Accepts previously published material. Responds in 2 weeks to queries. Responds in 2 months to mss. Sample copy free. Guidelines available online.

Nonfiction Needs book excerpts, general interest, inspirational, personal experience, religious. Does not want poetry, fiction, self-promotional. **Buys 10-15 mss/year.** Send complete ms. Length: 700-1,200 words. **Pays $25-200.**

Tips "We publish first-person articles concerning spiritual experiences; that is, answers to prayer for help in a particular situation, of unusual conversions or healings through faith in Christ. All articles submitted to us should be related to religious life. We are Protestant, evangelical, Pentecostal, and any doctrines or practices portrayed should be in harmony with the official position of our denomination (Assemblies of God)."

$ THE PENTECOSTAL MESSENGER

Messenger Publishing House/Pentecostal Church of God, P.O. Box 850, Joplin MO 64802-0850. (417)624-7050. Fax: (417)624-7102. E-mail: charlotteb@pcg.org. Website: www.pcg.org. Monthly magazine covering Christian, inspirational, religious, leadership news. "Our organization is Pentecostal in nature. Our publication goes out to our ministers and laypeople to educate, inspire and inform them of topics around the world and in our organization that will help them in their daily walk." Estab. 1919. Circ. 5,000. Byline given. Pays on publication. Buys simultaneous rights. Editorial lead time 6 months. Submit themed material 6 months in advance. Accepts queries by mail. Accepts previously published material. Accepts simultaneous submissions. May contact the *Pentecostal Messenger* for a list of monthly themes.

Nonfiction Needs book excerpts, essays, expose, general interest, inspirational, interview, new product, personal experience, religious. **Buys 12-24 mss/year.** Send complete ms. Length: 750-2,000 words. **Pays $15-40.**

Photos Send photos. Identification of subjects required. Reviews prints. Offers no additional payment for photos accepted with ms. Buys one time rights.

$$ ⊘ THE PLAIN TRUTH

Christianity Without the Religion, Plain Truth Ministries, 300 W. Green St., Pasadena CA 91129. Fax: (626)304-8172. E-mail: managing.editor@ptm.org. Website: www.ptm.org. **90% freelance written.** Bimonthly magazine. We seek to reignite the flame of shattered lives by illustrating the joy of a new life in Christ. Estab. 1935. Circ. 70,000. Byline given. Pays on publication. Offers $50 kill fee. Publishes ms an average of 8 months after acceptance. Buys all-language rights for *The Plain Truth* and its affiliated publications. Editorial lead time 6 months. Submit seasonal material 6 months in advance. Accepts queries by mail, e-mail. Accepts simultaneous submissions. Sample copy for sae with 9 × 12 envelope and 5 First-Class stamps. Guidelines available online.

Nonfiction Needs inspirational, interview, personal experience, religious. **Buys 48-50 mss/year.** Query with published clips and SASE. *No unsolicited mss* Length: 750-2,500 words. **Pays 25¢/word.**

Reprints Send tearsheet or photocopy of article or typed ms with rights for sale ted and information about when and where the article previously appeared with SASE for response. Pays 15¢/word.

Photos State availability. Captions required. Reviews transparencies, prints. Negotiates payment individually. Buys one time rights.

Tips Material should offer Biblical solutions to real-life problems. Both first-person and third-person illustrations are encouraged. Articles should take a unique twist on a subject. Material must be insightful and practical for the Christain reader. All articles must be well researched and Biblically accurate without becoming overly scholastic. Use convincing arguments to support your Christian platform. Use vivid word pictures, simple and compelling language, and avoid stuffy academic jargon. Captivating anecdotes are vital.

$$ POINT

Magazine of Converge Worldwide, Baptist General Conference, 2002 S. Arlington Heights Rd., Arlington Heights IL 60005. Fax: (847)228-5376. E-mail: bputman@baptistgeneral.org. Website: www.bgcworld.org. **5% freelance written.** Nonprofit, religious, evangelical Christian magazine published 6 times/year covering Converge Worldwide. "*Point* is the official magazine of Converge Worldwide (BCG). Almost exclusively uses articles related to Converge, our churches, or by/about Converge people." Circ. 46,000. Byline given. Pays on publication. Offers 50% kill fee. Buys first rights. Editorial lead time 6 months. Submit seasonal material 6 months in advance. Accepts queries by e-mail. Responds in 1 month to queries. Responds in 3 months to mss. Sample copy for #10 SASE. Writer's guidelines, theme list free.

Nonfiction photo, religious, profile, info-graphics, sidebars related to theme Articles about our people, churches, missions. View online at: www.convergeww.org before sending anything. **Buys 20-30 mss/year.** Query with published clips. Length: 300-1,500 words. **Pays $60-280.**

Photos State availability. Captions, identification of subjects, model releases required. Reviews prints, some high-resolution digital. Offers $15-60/photo. Buys one-time rights.

Columns/Departments Converge Connection (blurbs of news happening in Converge Worldwide), 50-150 words. Send complete ms. **Pays $30.**

Tips "Please study the magazine and the denomination. We will send sample copies to interested freelancers and give further information about our publication needs upon request. Freelancers from our churches who are interested in working on assignment are especially welcome."

$ PRAIRIE MESSENGER

Catholic Journal, Benedictine Monks of St. Peter's Abbey, P.O. Box 190, Muenster SK S0K 2Y0 Canada. (306)682-1772. Fax: (306)682-5285. E-mail: pm.canadian@stpeterspress.ca. Website: www.prairiemessenger.ca. **10% freelance written**. "Weekly Catholic journal with strong emphasis on social justice, Third World, and ecumenism." Estab. 1904. Circ. 6,000. Byline given. Pays on publication. No kill fee. Publishes ms an average of 4 months after acceptance. Buys first North American serial rights, buys first rights, buys one-time rights, buys second serial (reprint) rights, buys simultaneous rights. Submit seasonal material 3 months in advance. Accepts queries by mail, e-mail, fax, phone. Responds in 2 months to queries. Sample copy for 9 × 12 SAE with $1 Canadian postage or IRCs. Guidelines available online. "Because of government subsidy regulations, we are no longer able to accept non-Canadian freelance material."

Nonfiction Needs interview, opinion, religious. "No articles on abortion." **Buys 15 mss/year.** Send complete ms. Length: 500-800 words. **Pays $55**

Photos Send photos. Captions required. Reviews 3 × 5 prints. Offers $22.50/photo. Buys all rights.

$$ PRESBYTERIANS TODAY

Presbyterian Church (U.S.A.), 100 Witherspoon St., Louisville KY 40202-1396. (502)569-5637. Fax: (502)569-8632. E-mail: today@pcusa.org. Website: www.pcusa.org/today. **25% freelance written. Prefers to work with published/established writers**. Denominational magazine published 10 times/year covering religion, denominational activities, and public issues for members of the Presbyterian Church (U.S.A.). "The magazine's purpose is to increase understanding and appreciation of what the church and its members are doing to live out their Christian faith." Estab. 1867. Circ. 40,000. Byline given. Pays on acceptance. Offers 50% kill fee. Publishes ms an average of 6 months after acceptance. Buys first North American serial rights, buys all rights. Editorial lead time 3 months. Submit seasonal material 3 months in advance. Accepts queries by mail, e-mail, fax, phone. Responds in 2 weeks to queries. Sample copy free Guidelines available online

Nonfiction "Most articles have some direct relevance to a Presbyterian audience; however, *Presbyterians Today* also seeks well-informed articles written for a general audience that help readers deal with the stresses of daily living from a Christian perspective." Needs how-to, everyday Christian living, inspirational, Presbyterian programs, issues, people. **Buys 20 mss/year.** Send complete ms. Length: 1,000-1,800 words. **Pays $300 maximum for assigned articles. Pays $75-300 for unsolicited articles.**

Photos State availability. Identification of subjects required. Reviews contact sheets, transparencies, color prints, digital images. Negotiates payment individually. Buys one-time rights.

$$ PRISM MAGAZINE

America's Alternative Evangelical Voice, Evangelicals for Social Action, 6 E. Lancaster Ave., Wynnewood PA 19096. (484)384-2990. E-mail: kristyn@esa-online.org. Website: www.esa-online.org. **50% freelance written**. Bimonthly magazine covering Christianity and social justice. "For holistic, Biblical, socially-concerned, progressive Christians." Estab. 1993. Circ. 2,500. Byline given. Pays on publication. Publishes ms an average of 4-6 months after acceptance. Buys first North American serial rights. Editorial lead time 4 months. Submit seasonal material 4 months in advance. Accepts queries by mail, e-mail. Responds in 1 month to queries. Responds in 3 months to mss. Sample copy for $3. Guidelines free.

- "We're a nonprofit, some writers are pro bono. Occasionally accepts previously published material."

Nonfiction Needs essays on culture/faith, interviews, ministry profiles, reviews, etc. **Buys 10-12/year mss/year.** Send complete ms. Length: 500-3,000 words. **Pays $75 per printed page - about 75¢/word. Pays $25-200 for unsolicited articles.**

Photos Send photos. Reviews prints, JPEG files. Pays $25/photo published; $200 if photo used on cover. Buys one time rights.

Tips "We look closely at stories of holistic ministry. It's best to request a sample copy to get to know *PRISM*'s focus/style before submitting—we receive many submissions that are not appropriate."

$ PURPOSE

616 Walnut Ave., Scottdale PA 15683-1999. (724)887-8500. Fax: (724)887-3111. E-mail: horsch@mpn.

net. Website: www.mpn.net. **75% freelance written**. Monthly magazine for adults, young and old, general audience with varied interests. Magazine focuses on Christian discipleship—how to be a faithful Christian in the midst of everyday life situations. Uses personal story form to present models and examples to encourage Christians in living a life of faithful discipleship. Estab. 1968. Circ. 8,500. Pays on acceptance. No kill fee. Publishes ms an average of 18 months after acceptance. Buys one-time rights. Submit seasonal material 1 year in advance. Accepts queries by e-mail. Accepts previously published material. Accepts simultaneous submissions. Responds in 3 months to queries. Sample copy and writer's guidelines for 6x9 SAE and $2

Nonfiction Inspirational stories from a Christian perspective. I want upbeat stories that deal with issues faced by believers in family, business, politics, religion, gender, and any other areas—and show how the Christian faith resolves them. *Purpose* conveys truth through quality fiction or true life stories. Our magazine ac¢ Christian discipleship. Christianity affects all of life, and we expect our material to demonstrate this. I would like story-type articles about individuals, groups, and organizations who are intelligently and effectively working at such problems as hunger, poverty, international understanding, peace, justice, etc., because of their faith. Essays, fiction, and how-to-do-it pieces must include a lot of anecdotal, life exposure examples. **Buys 140 mss/year.** E-mail submissions preferred.

Reprints Send tearsheet, photocopy or typed ms with rights for sale noted and information about when and where the material previously appeared.

Photos Photos purchased with ms must be sharp enough for reproduction; requires prints in all cases. Captions required.

Fiction Contact: James E. Horsch, editor. Produce the story with specificity so that it appears to take place somewhere and with real people. Needs historical, related to discipleship theme, humorous, religious. No militaristic/narrow patriotism or racism. Send complete ms. Length: 600 words. **Pays up to 7¢ for stories, and 2 contributor's copies.**

Poetry Needs free verse, light verse, traditional. Buys 140 poems/year. Length: 12 lines. **Pays $7.50-20/ poem depending on length and quality. Buys one-time rights only.**

QUAKER LIFE

Friends United Meeting, 101 Quaker Hill Dr., Richmond IN 47374. (765)962-7573. Fax: (765)966-1293. E-mail: quakerlife@fum.org. Website: www.fum.org. **Contact:** Katie Wonsik. **50% freelance written**. A Christian Quaker magazine published 6 times/year that covers news, inspirational, devotional, peace, equality, and justice issues. Estab. 1960. Circ. 3,000. Byline given. No kill fee. Publishes ms an average of 3-6 months after acceptance. Buys first North American serial rights. Editorial lead time 2-3 months. Submit seasonal material 4-6 months in advance. Accepts queries by mail, e-mail. Accepts simultaneous submissions. Responds in 1 week to queries. Responds in 1-3 months to mss. Sample copy and writer's guidelines free.

Nonfiction Needs book excerpts, general interest, humor, inspirational, interview, personal experience, photo feature, religious, travel, bible study. No poetry or fiction. Query. Length: 400-1,500 words. **Pays 3 contributor's copies**

Photos Reviews b&w or color prints and JPEG files. Occasionally, line drawings and b&w cartoons are used. Send photos. Does not pay for photos. Buys one-time rights.

Columns/Departments News Brief (newsworthy events among Quakers), 75-200 words; Devotional/ Inspirational (personal insights or spiritual turning points), 750 words; Ideas That Work (ideas from meetings that could be used by others), 750 words; Book/Media Reviews, 75-300 words.

RADIX MAGAZINE

Where Christian Faith Meets Contemporary Culture, Radix Magazine, Inc., P.O. Box 4307, Berkeley CA 94704. (510)548-5329. E-mail: radixmag@aol.com. Website: www.radixmagazine.com. **Contact:** Sharon Gallagher, editor. **10% freelance written**. Quarterly magazine. *"Radix* is for thoughtful Christians who are interested in engaging the world around them." Estab. 1979. Circ. 3,000. Byline given. No kill fee. Publishes ms an average of 6 months after acceptance. interested in first North American serial rights. Editorial lead time 6 months. Submit seasonal material 6 months in advance. Accepts queries by e-mail. Responds in 2 weeks to queries and to mss. Sample copy for $5. Guidelines by e-mail.

- "Needs poetry and book reviews. E-mail submissions only."

Nonfiction Contact: Sharon Gallagher, editor. Needs essays, religious. Query. Length: 500-2,000 words.

Poetry Needs avant-garde, free verse, haiku. "Needs poetry." Buys 8 poems/year. Submit maximum 4 poems. Length: 4-20 lines. **Pays 2 contributor copies**.

Tips "We accept very few unsolicited manuscripts. We do not accept fiction. All articles and poems should be based on a Christian world view. Freelancers should have some sense of the magazine's tone and purpose."

RAILROAD EVANGELIST

Railroad Evangelist Association, Inc., P.O. Box 5026, Vancouver WA 98668. (360)699-7208. E-mail: rrjoe@comcast.net. Website: www.railroadevangelist.com. **80% freelance written**. Magazine published 3 times/year covering the railroad industry. "The *Railroad Evangelist*'s purpose and intent is to reach people everywhere with the life-changing gospel of Jesus Christ. The railroad industry is our primary target, along with model railroad and rail fans." Estab. 1938. Circ. 3,000/issue. Byline sometimes given. No kill fee. Editorial lead time 6 weeks. Submit seasonal material 6 weeks in advance. Accepts queries by mail, e-mail. Accepts previously published material. Sample copy for sae with 10 × 12 envelope and 3 first-class stamps. Guidelines for #10 SASE.

- All content must be railroad related.

Nonfiction Needs inspirational, interview, personal experience, religious. Query. Length: 300-800 words.

Photos State availability. Captions required. Reviews 3 × 5, 8 × 10 prints, GIF/JPEG files. Offers no additional payment for photos accepted with ms.

Columns/Departments Right Track (personal testimony), 300-800 words; Ladies Line (personal testimony), 300-500 words; Kids Corner (geared toward children), 50-100 words. Query. **Pays in contributor copies.**

Fiction Needs historical, religious. Query. Length: 300-800 words. **Pays in contributor copies.**

Poetry Needs traditional. Length: 10-100 lines. **Pays in contributor copies**.

$ $ REFORM JUDAISM

Union for Reform Judaism, 633 Third Ave. 7th Floor, New York NY 10017-6778. (212)650-4240. Fax: (212)650-4249. E-mail: rjmagazine@urj.org. Website: www.reformjudaismmag.org. **30% freelance written**. Quarterly magazine of Jewish issues for contemporary Jews. "*Reform Judaism* is the official voice of the Union for Reform Judaism, linking the institutions and affiliates of Reform Judaism with every Reform Jew. *RJ* covers developments within the Movement while interpreting events and Jewish tradition from a Reform perspective." Estab. 1972. Circ. 310,000. Byline given. Pays on publication. Offers kill fee for commissioned articles. Publishes ms an average of 3 months after acceptance. Buys first North American serial rights. Submit seasonal material 6 months in advance. Accepts previously published material. Accepts simultaneous submissions. Responds in 2 months to queries and to mss Sample copy for $3.50 Guidelines available online

Nonfiction Buys 30 mss/year. Submit complete ms with SASE. Cover stories: 2,500-3,500 words; major feature: 1,800-2,500 words; secondary feature: 1,200-1,500 words; department (e.g., Travel): 1,200 words. **Pays 30¢/published word.**

Reprints Send tearsheet, photocopy or typed ms with rights for sale and information about when and where the material previously appeared. Usually doesn't publish reprints.

Photos Send photos. Identification of subjects required. Reviews 8 × 10/color or slides, b&w prints, and printouts of electronic images. Payment varies. Buys one time rights.

Fiction Needs humorous, religious, sophisticated, cutting-edge, superb writing. **Buys 4 mss/year.** Send complete ms. Length: 600-2,500 words. **Pays 30¢/published word.**

Tips "We prefer a stamped postcard including the following information/checklist: __Yes, we are interested in publishing; __No, unfortunately the submission doesn't meet our needs; __Maybe, we'd like to hold on to the article for now. Submissions sent this way will receive a faster response."

$ $ RELEVANT

Relevant Media Group, 1220 Alden Rd., Orlando FL 32803. (407)660-1411. Fax: (407)660-8555. E-mail: roxanne@relevantmediagroup.com for print queries. ryan@relevantmediagroup.com for online queries. Website: www.relevantmagazine.com. **80% freelance written**. Bimonthly magazine covering God, life, and progressive culture. *Relevant* is a lifestyle magazine for Christians in their 20s and 30s. Estab. 2002. Circ. 83,000. Byline given. Pays 45 days after publication. Offers 50% kill fee. Publishes ms an average of 6 months after acceptance. Buys first North American serial rights. Editorial lead time 4 months. Submit seasonal material 5 months in advance. Accepts queries by e-mail. Accepts simultaneous submissions. Responds in 6 weeks to queries. Responds in 3 months to mss. Sample copy available online. Guidelines available online.

Nonfiction Needs general interest, how-to, inspirational, interview, new product, personal experience, religious. Don't submit anything that doesn't target ages 18-34. Query with published clips. Length: 1,000-1,500 words. **Pays 10-15¢/word for assigned articles. Pays 10¢/word for unsolicited articles.**

Tips The easiest way to get noticed by our editors is to first submit (donate) stories for online publication.

$ $ THE REPORTER

Women's American ORT, Inc., 75 Maiden Lane, 10th Floor, New York NY 10038. (212)505-7700. Fax: (212)674-3057. E-mail: dasher@waort.org. Website: www.waort.org. **85% freelance written**. Semiannual nonprofit journal published by Jewish women's organization covering Jewish women celebrities, issues of contemporary Jewish culture, Israel, anti-Semitism, women's rights, Jewish travel and the international Jewish community. Estab. 1966. Circ. 50,000. Byline given. Pays on acceptance. No kill fee. Publishes ms an average of 1 year after acceptance. Buys first North American serial rights. Submit seasonal material 6 months in advance. Accepts queries by mail, e-mail. Responds in 3 months to queries. Sample copy for sae with 9 × 12 envelope and 3 First-Class stamps. Guidelines for #10 SASE.

Nonfiction Cover feature profiles a dynamic Jewish woman making a difference in Judaism, women's issues, education, entertainment, profiles, business, journalism, arts. Needs essays, expose, humor, inspirational, opinion, personal experience, photo feature, religious, travel. Query. 1,800 words maximum **Pays $200 and up.**

Photos Send photos. Identification of subjects required.

Columns/Departments Education Horizon; Destination (Jewish sites/travel); Inside Out (Advocacy); Women's Business; Art Scene (interviews, books, films); Lasting Impression (uplifting/inspirational).

Fiction Length: 800 words. **Pays $150-300.**

Tips Send query only by e-mail or postal mail. Show us a fresh look, not a rehash. Particularly interested in stories of interest to younger readers.

$ REVIEW FOR RELIGIOUS

3601 Lindell Blvd., Room 428, St. Louis MO 63108-3393. (314)633-4610. Fax: (314)633-4611. E-mail: reviewrfr@gmail.com. Website: www.reviewforreligious.org. **100% freelance written**. Quarterly magazine for Roman Catholic priests, brothers, and sisters. Estab. 1942. Byline given. Pays on publication. No kill fee. Publishes ms an average of 9 months after acceptance. Buys first North American serial rights. Rarely buys second serial (reprint) rights. Accepts queries by mail, fax. Responds in 2 months to queries. Guidelines available online.

Nonfiction Not for general audience. Length: 1,500-5,000 words. **Pays $6/page.**

Tips "The writer must know about religious life in the Catholic Church and be familiar with prayer, vows, community life, and ministry."

SACRED JOURNEY

The Journal of Fellowship in Prayer, Fellowship in Prayer, Inc., 291 Witherspoon St., Princeton NJ 08542. (609)924-6863. Fax: (609)924-6910. E-mail: editorial@sacredjourney.org. Website: www.sacredjourney.org. **70% freelance written**. *Sacred Journey*: The Journal of Fellowship in Prayer is a quarterly multi-faith journal published Winter, Spring, Summer and Autumn. Estab. 1950. Circ. 5,000. No kill fee. Retains one-time rights and then the copyright is returned to the author. Submissions may be selected for publication or on our fellowship in prayer website under "web exclusives." Your agreement for publication grants Fellowship in Prayer non-exclusive publication rights including the right to use and edit the work for publication in the print or electronic version of the journal *Sacred Journal*, display on the world-wide web and to retain the work indefinitly in an online archive. Editorial lead time 3 months. Submit seasonal material 4 months in advance. Accepts queries by e-mail (preferably). Accepts previously published material. Accepts simultaneous submissions. Responds within 4 months of receipt. Submission is considered permission for publication. We reserve the right to edit. We will make every effort to contact the author with content revisions. Please include or be prepared to provide a bio of 50-words or less and/or a headshot phot to accompany your work, should it be selected for the print journal. Sample copy free. Guidelines available online.

- "We publish articles, poems, and photographs which convey a spiritual orientation to life, promote prayer, meditation, and service to others and present topics that will foster a deeper spirit of unity among humankind. The spiritual insights, practices, and beliefs of women and men from a broad spectrum of religious traditions are welcomed."

Nonfiction "Articles should communicate an inspirational message of universal appeal and may be told through an individual's experience. Articles may be written from a particular religious context; however, the language and message should convey inclusiveness. **Buys 30 mss/year.** Send complete ms. Length: Approx. 750-1,500 words, double-spaced. **"You receive a complimentary one-year subscription to Sacred Journey if you work is selected for publication in the journal or on our website. For publication in the print journal you will also receive 5 copies of the issue in which your work appears."**

Photos "We accept Hi-Res digital photographs and illlustrations for possible publication. Cover photos are typically in color while interior photos are usually in black & white. We favor vertical images, but consider horizontal ones."
Poetry Does not want poetry highly specific to a certain faith tradition. Nothing laden with specific faith terminology, nor a lot of Bibe quotes or other quotes. Submit maximum 5 per submission poems. Limited to 35 lines (occasionally longer).
Tips "We are always seeking original prayers to share the richness of the world's religious traditions."

$ N THE SECRET PLACE

National Ministries, ABC/USA, P.O. Box 851, Valley Forge PA 19482-0851. (610)768-2240. E-mail: thesecretplace@abc-usa.org. **100% freelance written**. Quarterly devotional covering Christian daily devotions. Estab. 1937. Circ. 100,000. Byline given. Pays on acceptance. No kill fee. Buys first rights. Editorial lead time 1 year. Submit seasonal material 9 months in advance. For free sample and guidelines, send 6x9 SASE.
Nonfiction Needs inspirational. **Buys about 400 mss/year.** Send complete ms. Length: 100-200 words. **Pays $20.**
Poetry Needs avant-garde, free verse, light verse, traditional. Buys 12-15/year poems/year. Submit maximum 6 poems. Length: 4-30 lines. **Pays $20.**
Tips "Prefers submissions via e-mail."

$$ SHARING THE VICTORY

Fellowship of Christian Athletes, 8701 Leeds Rd., Kansas City MO 64129. (816)921-0909. Fax: (816)921-8755. E-mail: stv@fca.org. Website: www.fca.org. **50% freelance written. Prefers to work with published/established writers, but works with a growing number of new/unpublished writers each year**. Published 9 times/year. "We seek to serve as a ministry tool of the Fellowship of Christian Athletes by informing, inspiring and involving coaches, athletes and all whom they influence, that they may make an impact for Jesus Christ." Estab. 1959. Circ. 80,000. Byline given. Pays on publication. No kill fee. Publishes ms an average of 4 months after acceptance. Buys first rights. Submit seasonal material 6 months in advance. Responds in 3 months to queries. Responds in 3 months to mss. Sample copy for $1 and 9 × 12 SAE with 3 first-class stamps. Guidelines available online.
Nonfiction Must have FCA connection. Needs inspirational, interview, with name athletes and coaches solid in their faith, personal experience, photo feature. **Buys 5-20 mss/year.** Query. Length: 500-1,000 words.
Photos State availability. Reviews contact sheets. Pay based on size of photo. Buys one-time rights.
Tips "Profiles and interviews of particular interest to coed athlete, primarily high school and college age. Our graphics and editorial content appeal to youth. The area most open to freelancers is profiles on or interviews with well-known athletes or coaches (male, female, minorities) who have been or are involved in some capacity with FCA."

$ SOCIAL JUSTICE REVIEW

3835 Westminster Place, St. Louis MO 63108-3472. (314)371-1653. Fax: (314)371-0889. E-mail: centbur@juno.com. Website: www.socialjusticereview.org. **25% freelance written. Works with a small number of new/unpublished writers each year.** Bimonthly magazine. Estab. 1908. No kill fee. Publishes ms an average of 1 year after acceptance. Buys first North American serial rights. Accepts queries by mail. Sample copy for sae with 9 × 12 envelope and 3 First-Class stamps.
Nonfiction Query by mail only with SASE. Length: 2,500-3,000 words. **Pays about 2¢/word.**
Reprints Send typed manuscript with rights for sale noted and information about when and where the material previously appeared. Pays about 2¢/word.
Tips Write moderate essays completely compatible with papal teaching and readable to the average person.

$ SPIRITUAL LIFE

2131 Lincoln Rd. NE, Washington DC 20002-1199. (202)832-5505. Fax: (202)832-8967. E-mail: edodonnell@aol.com. Website: www.spiritual-life.org. **80% freelance written. Prefers to work with published/established writers.** Quarterly magazine for largely Christian, well-educated, serious readers. Circ. 12,000. Pays on acceptance. No kill fee. Publishes ms an average of 1 year after acceptance. Buys first North American serial rights. Responds in 2 months to queries. Sample copy and writer's guidelines for 7x10 or larger SAE with 5 first-class stamps.
Nonfiction Serious articles of contemporary spirituality and its pastoral application to everday life. High quality articles about our encounter with God in the present day world. Language of articles should be

college level. Technical terminology, if used, should be clearly explained. Material should be presented in a postive manner. Buys inspirational and think pieces. Brief autobiographical information (present occupation, past occupations, books and articles published, etc.) should accompany article. Sentimental articles or those dealing with specific devotional practices not accepted.No fiction or poetry. **Buys 20 mss/year.** Length: 3,000-5,000 words. **Pays $50 minimum, and 2 contributor's copies.**

$$ ST. ANTHONY MESSENGER

28 W. Liberty St., Cincinnati OH 45202-6498. (513)241-5615. Fax: (513)241-0399. E-mail: stanthony@americancatholic.org. Website: www.americancatholic.org. **55% freelance written**. Monthly general interest magazine for a national readership of Catholic families, most of which have children or grandchildren in grade school, high school, or college. *St. Anthony Messenger* is a Catholic family magazine which aims to help its readers lead more fully human and Christian lives. We publish articles which report on a changing church and world, opinion pieces written from the perspective of Christian faith and values, personality profiles, and fiction which entertains and informs. Estab. 1893. Circ. 305,000. Byline given. Pays on acceptance. No kill fee. Publishes ms an average of 1 year after acceptance. Buys first North American serial rights, buys electronic rights. first worldwide serial rights. Submit seasonal material 6 months in advance. Accepts queries by mail, e-mail, fax. Responds in 3 weeks to queries. Responds in 2 months to mss. Sample copy for 9 × 12 SAE with 4 first-class stamps. Guidelines available online.

Nonfiction Needs how-to, on psychological and spiritual growth, problems of parenting/better parenting, marriage problems/marriage enrichment, humor, inspirational, interview, opinion, limited use; writer must have special qualifications for topic, personal experience, if pertinent to our purpose, photo feature, informational, social issues. **Buys 35-50 mss/year.** Query with published clips. Length: 1,500-2,500 words. **Pays 20¢/word.**

Fiction Contact: Father Pat McCloskey, O.F.M., editor. Needs mainstream, religious, senior citizen/retirement. We do not want mawkishly sentimental or preachy fiction. Stories are most often rejected for poor plotting and characterization; bad dialogue—listen to how people talk; inadequate motivation. Many stories say nothing, are 'happenings' rather than stories. No fetal journals, no rewritten Bible stories. **Buys 12 mss/year.** Send complete ms. Length: 2,000-3,000 words. **Pays 16¢/word maximum and 2 contributor's copies; $1 charge for extras.**

Poetry Our poetry needs are very limited. Submit maximum 4-5 poems. Up to 20-25 lines; the shorter, the better. **Pays $2/line; $20 minimum.**

Tips The freelancer should consider why his or her proposed article would be appropriate for us, rather than for *Redbook* or *Saturday Review.* We treat human problems of all kinds, but from a religious perspective. Articles should reflect Catholic theology, spirituality, and employ a Catholic terminology and vocabulary. We need more articles on prayer, scripture, Catholic worship. Get authoritative information (not merely library research); we want interviews with experts. Write in popular style; use lots of examples, stories, and personal quotes. Word length is an important consideration.

SUCCESS STORIES

Franklin Publishing Company, 2723 Steamboat Circle, Arlington TX 76006. (817)548-1124. E-mail: ludwigotto@sbcglobal.net. Website: www.franklinpublishing.net. www.londonpress.us. **Contact:** Dr. Ludwig Otto. **59% freelance written**. Monthly journal covering positive responses to the problems in life. Estab. 1983. Circ. 1,000. Byline given. Does not pay, but offers 15% discount on issues purchased and 1-year free membership in the International Association of Professionals No kill fee. Publishes ms an average of 1 month after acceptance. Buys one-time rights. Editorial lead time 1 month. Submit seasonal material 3 months in advance. Accepts queries by mail, e-mail. Accepts previously published material. Accepts simultaneous submissions. Responds in 1 week to queries and to mss. Guidelines available online.

Nonfiction Needs book excerpts, essays, general interest, historical, how-to, humor, inspirational, interview, new product, opinion, personal experience, religious, technical, travel. Send complete ms. Length: 750-6,000 words.

Fiction Needs adventure, condensed novels, ethnic, horror, humorous, mainstream, mystery, novel concepts, religious, science fiction, slice-of-life vignettes of life, suspense, western. Send complete ms.

Poetry Needs avantgarde, free verse, haiku, light verse, traditional.

$$ THIS ROCK

Catholic Answers, P.O. Box 199000, San Diego CA 92159. (800)291-8000. Website: www.catholic.com. **60% freelance written**. Monthly magazine covering Catholic apologetics and evangelization. Our content explains, defends and promotes Catholic teaching. Estab. 1990. Circ. 24,000. Byline given. Pays on acceptance. Offers variable kill fee. Publishes ms an average of 4 months after acceptance. Buys first rights, buys electronic rights. Accepts queries by e-mail. Responds in 2-4 weeks to queries. Responds in 1-2 months to mss. Sample copy available online. Guidelines by e-mail.

Nonfiction Needs book excerpts, essays, religious, conversion stories. **Buys 50 mss/year.** Send complete ms. Length: 1,500-3,000 words. **Pays $200-350.**

Columns/Departments Damascus Road (stories of conversion to the Catholic Church), 2,000 words. 10 Send complete ms. **Pays $200.**

$ $ TODAY'S CHRISTIAN

Stories of Faith, Hope and God's Love, Christianity Today, 465 Gundersen Dr., Carol Stream IL 60188. (630)260-6200. Fax: (630)480-2004. E-mail: tceditor@todays-christian.com. Website: www.christianitytoday.com/todayschristian. **25% freelance written**. Bimonthly magazine for adult evangelical Christian audience. Estab. 1963. Circ. 75,000. Byline given. Pays on acceptance; on publication for humor pieces. No kill fee. Editorial lead time 5 months. Submit seasonal material 8 months in advance. Accepts queries by mail. Accepts simultaneous submissions. Responds in 1 month to queries. Sample copy for sae with 5â—Š8 envelope and 4 First-Class stamps. Guidelines available online.

Nonfiction Needs book excerpts, general interest, historical, humor, inspirational, interview, personal experience, photo feature, religious. **Buys 100-125 mss/year.** Send complete ms. Length: 250-1,500 words. **Pays $125-600 depending on length.**

Reprints Send tearsheet, photocopy or typed ms with rights for sale noted and information about when and where the material previously appeared. Pays 35-50% of amount paid for an original article

Photos Send photos. Identification of subjects required. Reviews transparencies, prints. Negotiates payment individually. Buys one time rights.

Columns/Departments Contact: Cynthia Thomas, editorial coordinator. Humor Us (adult church humor, kids say and do funny things, and humorous wedding tales), 50-200 words. **Pays $35.**

Tips Most of our articles are reprints or staff written. Freelance competition is keen, so tailor submissions to meet our needs by observing the following: *Today's Christian* audience is truly a general interest one, including men and women, urban professionals and rural homemakers, adults of every age and marital status, and Christians of every church affiliation. We seek to publish a magazine that people from the variety of ethnic groups in North America will find interesting and relevant.

$ TOGETHER

Media For Living, 1251 Virginia Ave., Harrisonburg VA 22802. Website: www.churchoutreach.com. **90% freelance written**. Quarterly tabloid covering religion and inspiration for a nonchurched audience. "*Together* is directed as an outreach publication to those who are not currently involved in a church; therefore, we need general inspirational articles that tell stories of personal change, especially around faith issues. Also, stories that will assist our readers in dealing with the many stresses and trials of everyday life—family, financial, career, community." Estab. 1980. Circ. 20,000. Byline given. Pays on publication. No kill fee. Publishes ms an average of 6-12 months after acceptance. Buys first rights, buys electronic rights. Editorial lead time 6-9 months. Submit seasonal material 6 months in advance. Accepts queries by mail, e-mail. Accepts previously published material. Accepts simultaneous submissions. Responds in 2 months to queries. Responds in 4 months to mss. Sample copy available online. Guidelines available online.

Nonfiction Needs essays, general interest, how-to, humor, inspirational, interview, personal experience, testimony, religious. No pet stories. We have limited room for stories about illness, dying, or grief, but we do use them occasionally. We publish in March, June, September, and December, so holidays that occur in other months are not usually the subject of articles. **Buys 16 mss/year.** Send complete ms. Length: 500-1,200 words. **Pays $35-60.**

Photos State availability. Captions, identification of subjects, model releases required. Reviews 4x6 prints, TIF/JPEG files. Offers $15-25/photo. Buys one time rights.

Tips "We prefer 'good news' stories that are uplifting and noncontroversial in nature. We can use stories of change and growth in religious journey from a Christian slant, including 'salvation' stories. We generally want articles that tell stories of people solving problems and dealing with personal issues rather than essays or 'preaching.' If you submit electronically, it is very helpful if you put the specific title of the submission in the subject line and include your e-mail address in the body of the e-mail or on your manuscript. Also, always include your address and phone number."

TRICYCLE

The Buddhist Review, 92 Vandam St., New York NY 10013. (212)645-1143. Fax: (212)645-1493. E-mail: editorial@tricycle.com. Website: www.tricycle.com. **80% freelance written**. Quarterly magazine covering the impact of Buddhism on Western culture. *Tricycle* readers tend to be well educated and open minded. Estab. 1991. Circ. 60,000. Byline given. Pays on publication. Offers 25% kill fee. Buys one-time rights. Editorial lead time 3 months. Accepts queries by mail, e-mail, fax. Accepts simultaneous submissions. Responds in 3 months to queries & mss Sample copy for $7.95 or online at website Guidelines available online

Nonfiction Needs book excerpts, essays, general interest, historical, humor, inspirational, interview, personal experience, photo feature, religious, travel. **Buys 4-6 mss/year.** Length: 1,000-5,000 words.

Photos State availability. Captions, identification of subjects required. Reviews contact sheets. Negotiates payment individually. Buys one-time rights.

Columns/Departments Reviews (film, books, tapes), 600 words; Science and Gen Next, both 700 words. 6-8 Query.

Tips "*Tricycle* is a Buddhist magazine, and we can only consider Buddhist-related submissions."

THE UNITED CHURCH OBSERVER

478 Huron St., Toronto ON M5R 2R3 Canada. (416)960-8500. Fax: (416)960-8477. E-mail: dnwilson@ucobserver.org. Website: www.ucobserver.org. **50% freelance written. Prefers to work with published/established writers.** Monthly general interest magazine for people associated with The United Church of Canada and non-churchgoers interested in issues of faith, justice, ethics and living. Deals primarily with events, trends, and policies having religious significance. Most coverage is Canadian, but reports on international or world concerns will be considered. Byline usually given. Pays on publication. No kill fee. Publishes ms an average of 4 months after acceptance. Buys first serial rights and occasionally all rights. Accepts queries by mail, e-mail, fax.

Nonfiction "Occasional opinion features only. Longer pieces are usually assigned to known writers. Submissions should be written as news, no more than 1,200 words length, accurate, and well-researched." No poetry. Queries preferred. **Rates depend on subject, author, and work involved.** Pays expenses of writers on assignment as negotiated.

Reprints Send tearsheet or photocopy and information about when and where the material previously appeared. Payment negotiated.

Photos Buys color photographs with mss. Send via e-mail. Payment varies.

Tips "The writer has a better chance of breaking in at our publication with short articles. Include samples of previous magazine writing with query."

$ THE UPPER ROOM

Daily Devotional Guide, P.O. Box 340004, Nashville TN 37203-0004. (615)340-7252. Fax: (615)340-7267. E-mail: theupperroommagazine@upperroom.org. Website: www.upperroom.org. **95% freelance written. Eager to work with new/unpublished writers.** Bimonthly magazine offering a daily inspirational message which includes a Bible reading, text, prayer, `Thought for the Day,' and suggestion for further prayer. Each day's meditation is written by a different person and is usually a personal witness about discovering meaning and power for Christian living through scripture study which illuminates daily life. Circ. 2.2 million (U.S.); 385,000 outside U.S. Byline given. Pays on publication. No kill fee. Publishes ms an average of 1 year after acceptance. Buys first North American serial rights, buys translation rights. Submit seasonal material 14 months in advance. Sample copy and writer's guidelines with a 4x6 SAE and 2 first-class stamps. Guidelines only for #10 SASE or online

- Manuscripts are not returned. If writers include a stamped, self-addressed postcard, we will notify them that their writing has reached us. This does not imply acceptance or interest in purchase. Does not respond unless material is accepted for publication.

Nonfiction Needs inspirational, personal experience, Bible-study insights. Lent and Easter; Advent No poetry, lengthy spiritual journey stories. **Buys 365 unsolicited mss/year.** Send complete ms by mail or e-mail. Length: 300 words. **Pays $25/meditation.**

Tips The best way to break in to our magazine is to send a well-written manuscript that looks at the Christian faith in a fresh way. Standard stories and sermon illustrations are immediately rejected. We very much want to find new writers and welcome good material. We are particularly interested in meditations based on Old Testament characters and stories. Good repeat meditations can lead to work on longer assignments for our other publications, which pay more. A writer who can deal concretely with everyday situations, relate them to the Bible and spiritual truths, and write clear, direct prose should be able to write for *The Upper Room.* We want material that provides for interaction on the part of the reader—meditation suggestions, journaling suggestions, space to reflect and link personal experience with the meditation for the day. Meditations that are personal, authentic, exploratory, and full of sensory detail make good devotional writing.

$$ U.S. CATHOLIC

Claretian Publications, 205 W. Monroe St., Chicago IL 60606. (312)236-7782. Fax: (312)236-8207. E-mail: editors@uscatholic.org. Website: www.uscatholic.org. **100% freelance written**. Monthly magazine covering Roman Catholic spirituality. *U.S. Catholic* is dedicated to the belief that it makes a difference whether you're Catholic. We invite and help our readers explore the wisdom of their faith tradition and apply their faith to the challenges of the 21st century. Estab. 1935. Circ. 40,000. Byline given. Pays on acceptance. No kill fee. Publishes ms an average of 2-3 months after acceptance. Buys all rights. Editorial lead time 8 months. Submit seasonal material 6 months in advance. Accepts queries by mail, e-mail, fax, phone. Responds in 1 month to queries. Responds in 2 months to mss. Sample copy for large SASE. Guidelines by e-mail or on website.

- Please include SASE with written ms.

Nonfiction Needs essays, inspirational, opinion, personal experience, religious. **Buys 100 mss/year.** Send complete ms. Length: 2,500-3,500 words. **Pays $250-600.**
Photos State availability.
Columns/Departments Pays $250-600.
Fiction Contact: Maureen Abood, literary editor. Needs ethnic, mainstream, religious, slice-of-life vignettes. **Buys 4-6 mss/year.** Send complete ms. Length: 2,500-3,000 words. **Pays $300.**
Poetry Contact: Maureen Abood, literary editor. Needs free verse. No light verse. Buys 12 poems/year. Submit maximum 5 poems. Length: 50 lines. **Pays $75.**

$$ THE WAR CRY

The Salvation Army, 615 Slaters Lane, Alexandria VA 22314. (703)684-5500. Fax: (703)684-5539. E-mail: war_cry@usn.salvationarmy.org. **5% freelance written**. Biweekly magazine covering evangelism and Christian growth stories. Estab. 1881. Circ. 250,000. Byline given. Pays on acceptance. No kill fee. Publishes ms an average of 2 months - 1 year after acceptance. Buys first rights, buys one-time rights. Editorial lead time 6 weeks. Submit seasonal material 1 year in advance. Responds in 3-4 weeks to mss. Sample copy, theme list, and writer's guidelines free for #10 SASE or online
Nonfiction Needs inspirational, interview, personal experience, religious. No missionary stories, confessions. **Buys 25 mss/year.** Send complete ms. **Pays 15¢/word for articles.**
Reprints No reprints.
Photos Identification of subjects required. Not currently purchasing photos. Buys one-time rights.

$ WESLEYAN LIFE

The Wesleyan Publishing House, P.O. Box 50434, Indianapolis IN 46250-0434. (317)774-7909. Fax: (317)774-3924. E-mail: communications@wesleyan.org. Quarterly magazine of The Wesleyan Church. Estab. 1842. Circ. 50,000. Byline given. Pays on publication. No kill fee. Buys first rights or simultaneous rights (prefers first rights). Submit seasonal material 6 months in advance. Accepts simultaneous submissions.
Nonfiction Needs inspirational, religious. No poetry accepted. Send complete ms. Length: 250-400 words. **Pays $25-150.**

⊘ WHAT IS ENLIGHTENMENT?

P.O. Box 2360, Lenox MA 01240. (413)637-6015. Website: www.wie.org. "At EnlightenNext we call ourselves "the magazine for Evolutionaries." We are a niche publication for those "Evolutionaries," for people who are passionate about the evolution of consciousness and culture. We are the place that leading thinkers in science, spirituality, politics, ecology, and business look to for an in-depth perspective on these many areas of life." No kill fee. Accepts queries by mail.

- *WIE* does not accept freelance submissions.

Nonfiction Contact: Reviews Editor. *Unable to accept unsolicited articles at this time.* "We will, however, consider new books for potential review, particularly in the fields of philosophy, science, spirituality, and contemporary culture. Published books and bound galleys are preferred over unbound manuscripts."

$ ⊕ WOMAN ALIVE

Christian Publishing and Outreach, Garcia Estate, Canterbury Road, Worthing West Sussex BN13 1BW United Kingdom. 44)(190)360-4379. E-mail: womanalive@cpo.org.uk. Website: www.womanalive.co.uk. Christian magazine geared specifically toward women. It covers all denominations and seeks to inspire, encourage, and provide resources to women in their faith, helping them to grow in their relationship with God and providing practical help and biblical perspective on the issues impacting their lives. Pays on publication. No kill fee. Accepts queries by mail, e-mail. Sample copy for £1.50, plus postage. Guidelines by e-mail.

Nonfiction Contemporary issues (social/domestic issues affecting the church and women), reports from around the country giving a brief overview of the town and what churches/individuals are doing there, lifestyle, money matters, ethical shopping, work/life balance, homestyle, fashion, creative cookery. Needs how-to, build life skills and discipleship, interview, with Christian women in prominent positions or who are making a difference in their communities/jobs, personal experience, women facing difficult challenges or taking on new challenges, travel, affordable holiday destinations written from a Christian perspective. Submit clips, bio, article summary, ms, SASE. 750-900/1-page article; 1,200-1,300/2-page article; 1,500-1,600/3-page article. **Pays £75/1-page article; £95/2-page article; £125/3-page article.**
Photos Send photos. Reviews 300 dpi digital images.

Retirement

$$$$ AARP THE MAGAZINE

AARP, 601 E St. NW, Washington DC 20049. E-mail: member@aarp.org. Website: www.aarp.org. **50% freelance written. Prefers to work with published/established writers.** Bimonthly magazine. *AARP The Magazine* is devoted to the varied needs and active life interests of AARP members, age 50 and over, covering such topics as financial planning, travel, health, careers, retirement, relationships, and social and cultural change. Its editorial content serves the mission of AARP seeking through education, advocacy and service to enhance the quality of life for all by promoting independence, dignity, and purpose. Circ. 21,500,000. Byline given. Pays on acceptance. Offers 25% kill fee. Publishes ms an average of 6 months after acceptance. Buys exclusive first worldwide publication rights. Submit seasonal material 6 months in advance. Accepts queries by mail, e-mail. Responds in 3 months to queries. Sample copy free. Guidelines available online.
Nonfiction Articles can cover finance, health, food, travel, consumerism, general interest topics, and profiles/first-person accounts. Query with published clips. *No unsolicited mss.* Length: Up to 2,000 words. **Pays $1/word.**
Photos Photos purchased with or without accompanying mss. Pays $250 and up for color; $150 and up for b&w.
Tips The most frequent mistake made by writers in completing an article for us is poor follow-through with basic research. The outline is often more interesting than the finished piece. We do not accept unsolicited manuscripts.

$ (JOURNAL) PLUS

654 Osos St., San Luis Obispo CA 93401. (805)544-8711. Fax: (805)546-8827. E-mail: slojournal@fix.net. Website: slojournal.com. **60% freelance written**. Monthly magazine that can be read online covering the 25-year old age group and up, but young-at-heart audience. Estab. 1981. Circ. 25,000. Byline given. Pays on publication. No kill fee. Publishes ms an average of 2 months after acceptance. Buys one-time rights. Editorial lead time 2 months. Submit seasonal material 2 months in advance. Accepts queries by mail. Accepts simultaneous submissions. Responds in 2 weeks to queries. Responds in 1 month to mss. Sample copy for 9 × 12 SAE with $2 postage.
Nonfiction "We favor up-beat articles concerning our readers on the Central Coast, personality profiles, subtle, not heavy-handed humor, travel, local book reviews, entertainment and health related to the California central coast." Needs historical, humor, interview, personal experience, travel, book reviews, entertainment, health. Christmas (December); Travel (October, April) No finance, automotive, heavy humor, poetry, or fiction. **Buys 60-70 mss/year.** Send complete ms. Length: 600-1,400 words. **Pays $50-75.**
Photos Send photos.
Tips "Review an issue on the website before submitting."

$ MATURE YEARS

The United Methodist Publishing House, 201 Eighth Ave. S., Nashville TN 37202-0801. (615)749-6292. Fax: (615)749-6512. E-mail: matureyears@umpublishing.org. **80% freelance written. Prefers to work with published/established writers**. Quarterly magazine designed to help persons in and nearing the retirement years understand and appropriate the resources of the Christian faith in dealing with specific problems and opportunities related to aging. Estab. 1954. Circ. 55,000. Pays on acceptance. No kill fee. Publishes ms an average of 1 year after acceptance. Buys first North American serial rights. Submit seasonal material 14 months in advance. Responds in 2 weeks to queries. Responds in 2 months to mss. Sample copy for $6 and 9 × 12 SAE. Writer's guidelines for #10 SASE or by e-mail.

Nonfiction Especially important are opportunities for older adults to read about service, adventure, fulfillment, and fun. Needs how-to, hobbies, inspirational, religious, travel, special guidelines, older adult health, finance issues. **Buys 75-80 mss/year.** Send complete ms; e-mail submissions preferred. Length: 900-2,000 words. **Pays $45-125.**
Reprints Send tearsheet, photocopy or typed ms with rights for sale noted and information about when and where the material previously appeared. Pays at same rate as for previously unpublished material.
Photos Send photos. Captions, model releases required. Negotiates pay individually. Typically buys one-time rights.
Columns/Departments Health Hints (retirement, health), 900-1,500 words; Going Places (travel, pilgrimage), 1,000-1,500 words; Fragments of Life (personal inspiration), 250-600 words; Modern Revelations (religious/inspirational), 900-1,500 words; Money Matters (personal finance), 1,200-1,800 words; Merry-Go-Round (cartoons, jokes, 4-6 line humorous verse); Puzzle Time (religious puzzles, crosswords). 4 Send complete ms. **Pays $25-45.**
Fiction Contact: Marvin Cropsey, editor. Needs humorous, religious, slice-of-life vignettes, retirement years nostalgia, intergenerational relationships. We don't want anything poking fun at old age, saccharine stories or anything not for older adults. Must show older adults (age 55 plus) in a positive manner. **Buys 4 mss/year.** Send complete ms. Length: 1,000-2,000 words. **Pays $60-125.**
Poetry Needs free verse, haiku, light verse, traditional. Buys 24 poems/year. Submit maximum 6 poems. Length: 3-16 lines. **Pays $5-20.**

Rural

$ $ BACKWOODS HOME MAGAZINE

P.O. Box 712, Gold Beach OR 97444. (541)247-8900. Fax: (541)247-8600. E-mail: editor@backwoodshome.com. Website: www.backwoodshome.com. **90% freelance written**. Bimonthly magazine covering self-reliance. *Backwoods Home Magazine* is written for people who have a desire to pursue personal independence, self-sufficiency, and their dreams. We offer 'how-to' articles on self-reliance. Estab. 1989. Circ. 38,000. Byline given. Pays on acceptance. Buys first North American serial rights. Editorial lead time 4-6 months. Submit seasonal material 4-6 months in advance. Accepts queries by mail, e-mail. Sample copy for sae with 9x10 envelope and 6 First-Class stamps. Guidelines free.
Nonfiction Needs general interest, how-to, humor, personal experience, technical. **Buys 120 mss/year.** Send complete ms. Length: 500 words. **Pays $30-200.**
Photos Send photos. Captions, identification of subjects, model releases required. Offers no additional payment for photos accepted with ms.

$ $ ⊡ THE COUNTRY CONNECTION

Ontario's Magazine of Choice, Pinecone Publishing, P.O. Box 100, Boulter ON K0L 1G0 Canada. (613)332-3651. Website: www.pinecone.on.ca. **100% freelance written**. Magazine published 4 times/year covering nature, environment, history, heritage, nostalgia, travel and the arts. *The Country Connection* is a magazine for true nature lovers and the rural adventurer. Building on our commitment to heritage, cultural, artistic, and environmental themes, we continually add new topics to illuminate the country experience of people living within nature. Our goal is to chronicle rural life in its many aspects, giving `voice' to the countryside. Estab. 1989. Circ. 4,000. Byline given. Pays on publication. No kill fee. Publishes ms an average of 4 months after acceptance. Buys first rights. Editorial lead time 4 months. Accepts queries by mail, e-mail, phone. Sample copy for $5.64. Guidelines available online.
Nonfiction Needs general interest, historical, humor, opinion, personal experience, travel, lifestyle, leisure, art and culture, vegan recipes. No hunting, fishing, animal husbandry, or pet articles. **Buys 60 mss/year.** Send complete ms. Length: 500-2,000 words. **Pays 10¢/word.**
Photos Send photos. Captions required. Reviews transparencies, prints, digital photos on CD. Offers $10-50/photo Buys one time rights.
Fiction Needs adventure, fantasy, historical, humorous, slice-of-life vignettes, country living. **Buys 10 mss/year.** Send complete ms. Length: 500-1,500 words. **Pays 10¢/word**.
Tips Canadian content only with a preference for Ontario subject matter. Send manuscript with appropriate support material such as photos, illustrations, maps, etc.

$ $ FARM & RANCH LIVING

Reiman Media Group, 5925 Country Lane, Greendale WI 53129. (414)423-0100. Fax: (414)423-8463. E-mail: editors@farmandranchliving.com. Website: www.farmandranchliving.com. **30% freelance written. Eager to work with new/unpublished writers.** Bimonthly magazine aimed at families that farm or ranch full time. *F&RL* is *not* a `how-to' magazine—it focuses on people rather than products and profits. Estab. 1978. Circ. 400,000. Byline given. Pays on publication. No kill fee. Publishes ms an average of 6 months after acceptance. Buys first rights, buys one-time rights. Submit seasonal material 6 months in advance. Accepts queries by mail, e-mail, fax. Responds in 6 weeks to queries. Sample copy for $2. Guidelines for #10 SASE.

Nonfiction Needs humor, rural only, inspirational, interview, personal experience, farm/ranch related, photo feature, nostalgia, prettiest place in the country (photo/text tour of ranch or farm). No issue-oriented stories (pollution, animal rights, etc.). **Buys 30 mss/year.** Send complete ms. Length: 600-1,200 words. **Pays up to $300 for text/photo package. Payment for Prettiest Place negotiable.**

Reprints Send photocopy with rights for sale noted. Payment negotiable.

Photos Scenic. State availability. Pays $75-200 for 35mm color slides. Buys one time rights.

Tips Our readers enjoy stories and features that are upbeat and positive. A freelancer must see *F&RL* to fully appreciate how different it is from other farm publications—ordering a sample is strongly advised (not available on newsstands). Photo features (about interesting farm or ranch families) and personality profiles are most open to freelancers.

$$ HOBBY FARMS

Rural Living for Pleasure and Profit, Bowtie, Inc., P.O. Box 8237, Lexington KY 40533. Fax: (859)260-9814. E-mail: hobbyfarms@bowtieinc.com. Website: www.hobbyfarms.com. **75% freelance written.** Bimonthly magazine covering small farms and rural lifestyle. "*Hobby Farms* is the magazine for rural enthusiasts. Whether you have a small garden or 100 acres, there is something in *Hobby Farms* to educate, enlighten or inspire you." Estab. 2001. Circ. 100,000. Byline given. Pays on publication. Publishes ms an average of 6 months after acceptance. Buys first North American serial rights. Makes work-for-hire assignments. Editorial lead time 3 months. Submit seasonal material 6 months in advance. Accepts queries by mail, e-mail. Responds in 2 months to queries. Responds in 2 months to mss. Guidelines free.

- "Writing tone should be conversational, but authoritative."

Nonfiction Needs historical, how-to, farm or livestock management, equipment, etc., interview, personal experience, technical, breed or crop profiles. **Buys 10 mss/year.** Send complete ms. Length: 1,500-2,500 words. Limit agreed upon in advance

Photos State availability of or send photos. Identification of subjects, model releases required. Reviews transparencies, GIF/JPEG files. Negotiates payment individually Buys one time rights.

Tips Please state your specific experience with any aspect of farming (livestock, gardening, equipment, marketing, etc).

$ MOTHER EARTH NEWS

Ogden Publications, 1503 SW 42nd St., Topeka KS 66609-1265. (785)274-4300. E-mail: letters@motherearthnews.com. Website: www.motherearthnews.com. **Contact:** Cheryl Long, ed. **Mostly written by staff and team of established freelancers.** Bimonthly magazine emphasizing country living, country skills, natural health and sustainable technologies for both long-time and would-be ruralists. "*Mother Earth News* promotes self-sufficient, financially independent and environmentally aware lifestyles. Many of our feature articles are written by our Contributing Editors, but we also assign articles to freelance writers, particularly those who have experience with our subject matter (both firsthand adn writing experience." Circ. 350,000. Byline given. Pays on publication. No kill fee. Submit seasonal material 5 months in advance. Responds in 6 months to mss. Sample copy for $5. Guidelines for #10 SASE.

Nonfiction Needs how-to, green building, do-it-yourself, organic gardening, whole foods & cooking, natural health, livestock & sustainable farming, renewable energy, 21st century homesteading, nature-environment-community, green transportation. No fiction, please. **Buys 35-50 mss/year.** Query. Please send a short synopsis of the idea, a one-page outline and any relevant digital photos, and samples. If available, please send us copies of one or two published articles, or tell us where to find them online. "Country Lore" length: 100-300/words. "Firsthand Reports" length: 1,500-2,000/words **Pays $25-150.**

Photos "We welcome quality photographs for our two departments."

Columns/Departments Country Lore (helpful how-to tips); 100-300/words; Firsthand Reports (first-person stories about sustainable lifestyles of all sorts), 1,500-2,000/words.

Tips "Read our magazine and take a close look at previous issues to learn more abut the various topics we cover. We assign articles about 6-8 months ahead of publication date, so keep in mind timing and the seasonality of some topics. Our articles provide hands-on, useful information for people who want a more fun, conscientious, sustainable, secure and satisfying lifestyle. Practicality is critical; freelance articles must be informative, well-documented and tightly written in an engaging and energetic voice. For how-to articles, complete, easy-to-understand instructions are essential."

$ RANGE MAGAZINE

The Cowboy Spirit on America's Outback, Purple Coyote Corp., 106 E. Adams St., Suite 201, Carson City NV 89706. (775)884-2200. Fax: (775)884-2213. Website: www.rangemagazine.com. **70% freelance written**. Quarterly magazine. *RANGE* magazine covers ranching and farming and the issues that affect agriculture. Estab. 1991. Pays on publication. Publishes ms an average of 6 months after acceptance. Buys first North American serial rights. Accepts queries by e-mail. Responds in 6-8 weeks to queries. Responds in 3-6 months to mss. Sample copy for $2. Guidelines available online.

Nonfiction Needs book excerpts, humor, interview, personal experience, photo feature. No rodeos or anything by a writer not familiar with *RANGE*. Query. Length: 500-2,000 words. **Pays $50-350.**

Photos Contact: C.J. Hadley, editor/publisher. State availability. Captions, identification of subjects required. Reviews 35mm transparencies, 4x6 prints, CDs with contact sheet & captions. Must be high-res digital images. Negotiates payment individually. Buys one time rights.

$ RURAL HERITAGE

PO Box 2067, Cedar Rapids IA 52406-2067. (319)362-3027. E-mail: editor@ruralheritage.com. Website: www.ruralheritage.com. **98% freelance written. Willing to work with a small number of new/unpublished writers.** Bimonthly magazine devoted to the training and care of draft animals. Estab. 1976. Circ. 9,500. Byline given. Pays on publication. No kill fee. Publishes ms an average of 6 months after acceptance. Buys first English language rights. Submit seasonal material 6 months in advance. Accepts queries by mail, e-mail. Responds in 3 months to queries. Sample copy for $8. Guidelines available online.

Nonfiction Needs how-to, farming with draft animals, interview, people using draft animals, photo feature. No articles on *mechanized* farming. **Buys 200 mss/year.** Query or send complete ms. Length: 1,200-1,500 words. **Pays 5¢/word.**

Photos Six covers/year, animals in harness $200. Photo guidelines for #10 SASE or on website. Captions, identification of subjects required. Pays $10. Buys one time rights.

Poetry Needs traditional. **Pays $5-25.**

Tips Thoroughly understand our subject: working draft animals in harness. We'd like more pieces on plans and instructions for constructing various horse-drawn implements and vehicles. Always welcome are: 1.) Detailed descriptions and photos of horse-drawn implements, 2.) Prices and other details of draft animal and implement auctions and sales.

$ $ RURALITE

P.O. Box 558, Forest Grove OR 97116-0558. (503)357-2105. Fax: (503)357-8615. E-mail: curtisc@ruralite.org. Website: www.ruralite.org. **80% freelance written. Works with new, unpublished writers**. Monthly magazine aimed at members of consumer-owned electric utilities throughout 10 western states, including Alaska. Publishes 48 regional editions. Estab. 1954. Circ. 325,000. Byline given. Pays on acceptance. No kill fee. Buys first rights, buys sometimes reprint rights. Accepts queries by mail. Responds in 1 month to queries. Sample copy for 10 × 13 SAE with 4 first-class stamps; guidelines also online Guidelines available online.

Nonfiction Looking for well-written nonfiction, dealing primarily with human interest topics. Must have strong Northwest perspective and be sensitive to Northwest issues and attitudes. Wide range of topics possible, from energy-related subjects to little-known travel destinations to interesting people living in areas served by consumer-owned electric utilities. Family-related issues, Northwest history (no encyclopedia rewrites), people and events, unusual tidbits that tell the Northwest experience are best chances for a sale. **Buys 50-60 mss/year.** Query. Length: 100-2,000 words. **Pays $50-500.**

Reprints Send typed manuscript with rights for sale noted and information about when and where the material previously appeared.

Photos Illustrated stories are the key to a sale. Stories without art rarely make it. Color prints/negatives, color slides, all formats accepted. No black & white.

Tips "Study recent issues. Follow directions when given an assignment. Be able to deliver a complete package (story and photos). We're looking for regular contributors to whom we can assign topics from our story list after they've proven their ability to deliver quality mss."

Science

$$ AD ASTRA

The Magazine of the National Space Society, 1155 15th St. NW, Suite 500, Washington DC 20005. (202)429-1600. Fax: (202)463-0659. E-mail: adastra.editor@nss.org. Website: www.nss.org. **90% freelance written**. Quarterly magazine covering the space program. "We publish non-technical, lively articles about all aspects of international space programs, from shuttle missions to planetary probes to plans for the future and commercial space." Estab. 1989. Circ. 38,800. Byline given. Pays on publication. No kill fee. Buys first North American serial rights. Responds only when interested. Sample copy for 9 × 12 SASE.

Nonfiction Needs book excerpts, essays, exposè, general interest, interview, opinion, photo feature, technical. No science fiction or UFO stories. Query with published clips. Length: 1,000-2,400 words. **Pays $200-500 for features.**

Photos State availability. Identification of subjects required. Reviews color prints, digital, JPEG-IS, GISS. Negotiates pay Buys one-time rights.

Tips "We require manuscripts to be in Word or text file formats. Know the field of space technology, programs and policy. Know the players. Look for fresh angles. And, please, know how to write!"

$$$$ AMERICAN ARCHAEOLOGY

The Archaeological Conservancy, 5301 Central Ave. NE, #902, Albuquerque NM 87108-1517. (505)266-9668. Fax: (505)266-0311. E-mail: tacmag@nm.net. Website: www.americanarchaeology.org. **60% freelance written**. Quarterly magazine. "We're a popular archaeology magazine. Our readers are very interested in this science. Our features cover important digs, prominent archaeologists, and most any aspect of the science. We only cover North America." Estab. 1997. Circ. 35,000. Byline given. Pays on acceptance. Offers 20% kill fee. Publishes ms an average of 3 months after acceptance. Buys one-time rights, buys electronic rights. Editorial lead time 3 months. Accepts queries by mail, e-mail, fax. Responds in 3 weeks to queries. Responds in 1 month to mss

Nonfiction No fiction, poetry, humor. **Buys 15 mss/year.** Query with published clips. Length: 1,500-3,000 words. **Pays $1,000-2,000.**

Photos State availability. Identification of subjects required. Reviews transparencies, prints. Offers $400-600/photo shoot. Negotiates payment individually. Buys one-time rights.

Tips "Read the magazine. Features must have a considerable amount of archaeological detail."

$$$$ ARCHAEOLOGY

Archaeological Institute of America, 36-36 33rd St., Long Island NY 11106. (718)472-3050. Fax: (718)472-3051. E-mail: peter@archaeology.org. Website: www.archaeology.org. **50% freelance written**. Magazine. *Archaeology* combines worldwide archaeological findings with photography, specially rendered maps, drawings, and charts. Articles cover current excavations and recent discoveries, and include personality profiles, technology updates, adventure, travel and studies of ancient cultures. The only magazine of its kind to bring worldwide archaeology to the attention of the general public. Estab. 1948. Circ. 220,000. Byline given. Pays on acceptance. Offers 25% kill fee. Buys world rights. Submit seasonal material 6 months in advance. Accepts queries by mail, e-mail, fax. Accepts simultaneous submissions. Sample copy and writer's guidelines free

Nonfiction Needs essays, general interest. **Buys 6 mss/year.** Query preferred. Length: 1,000-3,000 words. **Pays $2,000 maximum.**

Photos Send photos. Identification of subjects, True required. Reviews 4 × 5 color transparencies, 35mm color slides.

Tips We reach nonspecialist readers interested in art, science, history, and culture. Our reports, regional commentaries, and feature-length articles introduce readers to recent developments in archaeology worldwide.

$$ ASTRONOMY

Kalmbach Publishing, 21027 Crossroads Circle, P.O. Box 1612, Waukesha WI 53187-1612. (262)796-8776. Fax: (262)798-6468. Website: www.astronomy.com. **Contact:** David J. Eicher, Executive Editor. **50% of articles submitted and written by science writers; includes commissioned and unsolicited.** Monthly magazine covering the science and hobby of astronomy. "Half of our magazine is for hobbyists (who are active observers of the sky); the other half is directed toward armchair astronomers who are intrigued by the science." Estab. 1973. Circ. 122,000. Byline given. Pays on acceptance. No kill fee. Buys first North American serial rights, buys one-time rights, buys all rights. Responds in 1 month to queries. Responds in 3 months to mss. Guidelines for #10 SASE or online.

- "We are governed by what is happening in astronomical research and space exploration. It can be up to a year before we publish a manuscript. Query for electronic submissions."

Nonfiction Needs book excerpts, new product, announcements, photo feature, technical, space, astronomy. **Buys 75 mss/year.** Query. Length: 500-3,000 words. **Pays $100-1,000.**

Photos Send photos. Captions, identification of subjects, model releases required. Pays $25/photo

Tips "Submitting to *Astronomy* could be tough. (Take a look at how technical astronomy is.) But if someone is a physics teacher or an amateur astronomer, he or she might want to study the magazine for a year to see the sorts of subjects and approaches we use, and then submit a proposal."

$$$$ BIOSCIENCE

American Institute of Biological Sciences, 1444 Eye St. NW, Suite 200, Washington DC 20005. (202)628-1500. E-mail: features@aibs.org. Website: www.aibs.org. **5% freelance written**. Monthly peer-reviewed scientific journal covering organisms from molecules to the environment. We contract professional science writers to write features on assigned topics, including organismal biology and ecology, but excluding biomedical topics. Estab. 1951. Byline given. Publishes ms an average of 3 months after acceptance. Buys first North American serial rights, buys electronic rights. Editorial lead time 2 months. Accepts queries by e-mail. Responds in 2-3 weeks to queries. Sample copy free. Guidelines free.

Nonfiction Does not want biomedical topics. **Buys 10 mss/year.** Query. Length: 1,500-3,000 words. **Pays $1,500-3,000.**

Tips Queries can cover any area of biology. The story should appeal to a wide scientific audience, yet be accessible to the interested (and somewhat science-literate) layperson. *BioScience* tends to favor research and policy trend stories and avoids personality profiles.

$$$ CHEMICAL HERITAGE

Newsmagazine of the Chemical Heritage Foundation, Chemical Heritage Foundation (CHF), 315 Chestnut St., Philadelphia PA 19106-2702. (215)925-2222. E-mail: editor@chemheritage.org. Website: www.chemheritage.org. **40% freelance written**. Quarterly magazine covers history of chemistry and molecular sciences. *Chemical Heritage* reports on the history of the chemical and molecular sciences and industries, on CHF activities, and on other activities of interest to our readers. Estab. 1982. Circ. 20,000. Byline given. Pays on acceptance. Publishes ms an average of 6-12 months after acceptance. Buys all rights. Editorial lead time 4 months. Accepts queries by mail, e-mail, phone. Responds in 1 month to queries and to mss. Sample copy free.

Nonfiction "We are always particularly interested in celebrating historical anniversaries or discoveries, as well as the history behind timely subjects." Needs book excerpts, essays, historical, interview. No exposes or excessively technical material. Many of our readers are highly educated professionals, but they may not be familiar with, for example, specific chemical processes. **Buys 3-5 mss/year.** Query. Length: 1,000-3,500 words. **Pays 50¢ to $1/word.**

Photos State availability. Captions required. Offers no additional payment for photos accepted with ms. buys one-time print and online rights

Columns/Departments Contact: Associate Editor: Jennifer Dionisio, jdionisio@chemheritage.org). Book reviews: 200 or 750 words; CHF collections: 300-500 words; policy: 1,000 words; personal remembrances: 750 words; profiles of CHF awardees and oral history subjects: 600-900 words: buys 3-5 mms/year. 10 Query.

Tips "CHF attends exhibits at many scientific trade shows and scholarly conferences. Our representatives are always happy to speak to potential authors genuinely interested in the past, present and future of chemistry. We are a good venue for scholars who want to reach a broader audience or for science writers who want to bolster their scholarly credentials."

$$ 🌐 COSMOS MAGAZINE

The Science of Everything, Luna Media Pty Ltd., Level 1, 49 Shepherd St.,, Chippendale,, Sydney NSW 2008 Australia. (61)(2)9310-8500. Fax: (61)(2)9698-4899. E-mail: submissions@cosmosmagazine.com. Website: www.cosmosmagazine.com. **90% freelance written**. Monthly magazine covering science. Estab. 2005. Circ. 25,000. Byline given. Pays on publication. Offers up to 50% kill fee. Publishes ms an average of 1 month after acceptance. Buys first rights, buys one-time rights, buys second serial (reprint) rights, buys simultaneous rights. Editorial lead time 2 months. Submit seasonal material 3 months in advance. Accepts queries by e-mail, fax. Accepts previously published material. Accepts simultaneous submissions. Responds in 1 month to queries. Responds in 3 months to mss. Guidelines available online.

Nonfiction Needs book excerpts, essays, expose, historical, humor, interview, opinion, photo feature, travel. **Buys 250 mss/year.** Query with published clips. Length: 700-5,000 words. **Pays 45¢/word for assigned articles. Pays 25¢/word for unsolicited articles.**
Photos State availability. Captions, identification of subjects required. Reviews JPEG files. Pays $10-100/photo; negotiates payment individually. Buys one-time rights and exclusive Australian rights for 3 months.
Columns/Departments Travelogue (travel to an intriguing/unusual place that involves science), 1,500-2,000 words. Query. **Pays $315-450.**
Fiction Needs science fiction. No fantasy—science fiction only. **Buys 8 mss/year.** Length: 2,000-4,000 words. **Pays 25¢/word.**

POPULAR SCIENCE

The Future Now, Bonnier Corporation, 2 Park Ave., 9th Floor, New York NY 10016. Website: www.popsci.com. **50% freelance written**. Monthly magazine for the well-educated adult, interested in science, technology, new products. *Popular Science* is devoted to exploring (and explaining) to a nontechnical, but knowledgeable, readership the technical world around us. We cover all of the sciences, engineering, and technology, and above all, products. We are largely a `thing'-oriented publication: things that fly or travel down a turnpike, or go on or under the sea, or cut wood, or reproduce music, or build buildings, or make pictures. We are especially focused on the new, the ingenious, and the useful. Contributors should be as alert to the possibility of selling us pictures and short features as they are to major articles. Freelancers should study the magazine to see what we want and avoid irrelevant submissions. Estab. 1872. Circ. 1,450,000. Byline given. Pays on acceptance. Offers 25% kill fee. Buys first North American serial rights, buys second serial (reprint) rights. Editorial lead time 3 months. Accepts queries by mail, e-mail, fax. Responds in 1 month to queries. Guidelines available online.
Nonfiction We publish stories ranging from hands-on product reviews to investigative feature stories, on everything from black holes to black-budget airplanes. Query.
Tips Probably the easiest way to break in here is by covering a news story in science and technology that we haven't heard about yet. We need people to be acting as scouts for us out there, and we are willing to give the most leeway on these performances. We are interested in good, sharply focused ideas in all areas we cover. We prefer a vivid, journalistic style of writing, with the writer taking the reader along with him, showing the reader what he saw, through words.

$$$$ SCIENTIFIC AMERICAN

415 Madison Ave., New York NY 10017. (212)754-0550. Fax: (212)755-1976. E-mail: editors@sciam.com. Website: www.sciam.com. Monthly magazine covering developments and topics of interest in the world of science. Query before submitting. *Scientific American* brings its readers directly to the wellspring of exploration and technological innovation. The magazine specializes in first-hand accounts by the people who actually do the work. Their personal experience provides an authoritative perspective on future growth. Over 100 of our authors have won Nobel Prizes. Complementing those articles are regular departments written by *Scientific American*'s staff of professional journalists, all specialists in their fields. *Scientific American* is the authoritative source of advance information. Authors are the first to report on important breakthroughs, because they're the people who make them. It all goes back to *Scientific American*'s corporate mission: to link those who use knowledge with those who create it. Estab. 1845. Circ. 710,000. No kill fee.
Nonfiction Freelance opportunities mostly in the news scan section; limited opportunity in feature well. **Pays $1/word average.**

$$ SKY & TELESCOPE

The Essential Magazine of Astronomy, New Track Media, 90 Sherman St., Cambridge MA 02140. (617)864-7360. Fax: (617)864-6117. E-mail: editors@skyandtelescope.com. Website: skyandtelescope.com. **15% freelance written**. Monthly magazine covering astronomy. *Sky & Telescope* is the magazine of record for astronomy. We cover amateur activities, research news, equipment, book, and software reviews. Our audience is the amateur astronomer who wants to learn more about the night sky. Estab. 1941. Circ. 110,000. Byline given. Pays on publication. No kill fee. Publishes ms an average of 6 months after acceptance. Buys first rights. Editorial lead time 4 months. Submit seasonal material 1 year in advance. Accepts queries by mail, e-mail, fax. Responds in 3 weeks to queries. Responds in 1 month to mss. Sample copy for $6.99. Guidelines available online.
Nonfiction Needs essays, historical, how-to, opinion, personal experience, photo feature, technical. No poetry, crosswords, New Age, or alternative cosmologies. **Buys 10 mss/year.** Query. Length: 1,500-2,500 words. **Pays at least 25¢/word.**

Photos Send photos. Identification of subjects required. Reviews contact sheets. Negotiates payment individually. Buys one time rights.
Columns/Departments Focal Point (opinion), 700 words; Books & Beyond (reviews), 800 words; The Astronomy Scene (profiles), 1,500 words. 20 Query. **Pays 25¢/word**
Tips We're written exclusively by astronomy professionals, hobbyists, and insiders. Good artwork is key. Keep the text lively and provide captions.

$$$$ ☒ STARDATE

University of Texas, 1 University Station, A2100, Austin TX 78712. (512)471-5285. Fax: (512)471-5060. Website: stardate.org. **80% freelance written**. Bimonthly magazine covering astronomy. "*StarDate* is written for people with an interest in astronomy and what they see in the night sky, but no special astronomy training or background." Estab. 1975. Circ. 10,000. Byline given. Pays on acceptance. Offers 25% kill fee. Publishes ms an average of 4 months after acceptance. Buys first North American serial rights, buys electronic rights. Editorial lead time 6 months. Submit seasonal material 6 months in advance. Accepts queries by mail, e-mail, fax. Responds in 6 weeks to queries. Sample copy and writer's guidelines free

- No unsolicited mss.

Nonfiction Needs general interest, historical, interview, photo feature, technical, travel, research in astronomy. No first-person; first stargazing experiences; paranormal. **Buys 8 mss/year.** Query with published clips. Length: 1,500-3,000 words. **Pays $500-1,500.**
Photos Send photos. Identification of subjects required. Reviews transparencies, prints. Negotiates payment individually. Buys one time rights.
Columns/Departments Astro News (short astronomy news item), 250 words. 6 Query with published clips. **Pays $100-200.**
Tips Keep up to date with current astronomy news and space missions. No technical jargon.

$$ WEATHERWISE

The Magazine About the Weather, Heldref Publications, 1319 18th St. NW, Washington DC 20036. (202)296-6267. Fax: (202)296-5149. E-mail: ww@heldref.org. Website: www.weatherwise.org. **75% freelance written**. Bimonthly magazine covering weather and meteorology. "*Weatherwise* is America's only magazine about the weather. Our readers range from professional weathercasters and scientists to basement-bound hobbyists, but all share a common interest in craving information about weather as it relates to the atmospheric sciences, technology, history, culture, society, art, etc." Estab. 1948. Circ. 11,000. Byline given. Pays on publication. No kill fee. Publishes ms an average of 6 months after acceptance. Buys all rights. Editorial lead time 6-9 months. Submit seasonal material 9 months in advance. Accepts queries by mail, e-mail, fax, phone. Responds in 2 months to queries. Guidelines available online.
Nonfiction Needs book excerpts, essays, general interest, historical, how-to, interview, new product, opinion, personal experience, photo feature, technical, travel. Photo Contest (September/October deadline June 2) No blow-by-blow accounts of the biggest storm to ever hit your backyard. **Buys 15-18 mss/year.** Query with published clips. Length: 2,000-3,000 words. **Pays $200-500 for assigned articles. Pays $0-300 for unsolicited articles.**
Photos Captions, identification of subjects required. Reviews contact sheets, negatives, prints, electronic files. Negotiates payment individually. Buys one time rights.
Columns/Departments Weather Front (news, trends), 300-400 words; Weather Talk (folklore and humor), 650-1,000 words. 12-15 Query with published clips. **Pays $0-200.**
Tips "Don't query us wanting to write about broad types like the Greenhouse Effect, the Ozone Hole, El Niño, etc. Although these are valid topics, you can bet you won't be able to cover it all in 2,000 words. With these topics and all others, find the story within the story. And whether you're writing about a historical storm or new technology, be sure to focus on the human element—the struggles, triumphs, and other anecdotes of individuals."

Science Fiction, Fantasy & Horror

$$ ANALOG SCIENCE FICTION & FACT

Dell Magazine Fiction Group, 267 Broadway, 4th Floor, 11th Floor, New York NY 10007-2352. (212)686-7188. Fax: (212)686-7414. E-mail: analog@dellmagazines.com. Website: www.analogsf.com. **100% freelance written. Eager to work with new/unpublished writers.** Monthly magazine for general future-minded audience. Estab. 1930. Circ. 50,000. Byline given. Pays on acceptance. No kill fee. Publishes ms an average of 10 months after acceptance. Buys first North American serial rights, buys nonexclusive foreign serial rights. Sample copy for $5. Guidelines available online.

Nonfiction Looking for illustrated technical articles dealing with subjects of not only current but future interest, i.e., topics at the present frontiers of research whose likely future developments have implications of wide interest. **Buys 11 mss/year.** Send complete ms. 5,000 words **Pays 6¢/word.**

Fiction "Basically, we publish science fiction stories. That is, stories in which some aspect of future science or technology is so integral to the plot that, if that aspect were removed, the story would collapse. The science can be physical, sociological, or psychological. The technology can be anything from electronic engineering to biogenetic engineering. But the stories must be strong and realistic, with believable people doing believable things—no matter how fantastic the background might be." Needs science fiction, hard science/technological, soft/sociological. No fantasy or stories in which the scientific background is implausible or plays no essential role. **Buys 60-100 unsolicited mss/year.** Send complete ms. Length: 2,000-80,000 words. **Pays 4¢/word for novels; 5-6¢/word for novelettes; 6-8¢/word for shorts under 7,500 words; $450-600 for intermediate lengths.**

Tips In query give clear indication of central ideas and themes and general nature of story line—and what is distinctive or unusual about it. We have no hard-and-fast editorial guidelines, because science fiction is such a broad field that I don't want to inhibit a new writer's thinking by imposing 'Thou Shalt Not's.' Besides, a really good story can make an editor swallow his preconceived taboos. I want the best work I can get, regardless of who wrote it—and I need new writers. So I work closely with new writers who show definite promise, but of course it's impossible to do this with every new writer. No occult or fantasy.

$ APEX DIGEST

Apex Science Fiction and Horror Digest/Apex Magazine, Apex Publications, LLC, P.O. Box 24323, Lexington KY 40524. (859)312-3974. E-mail: jason@apexdigest.com. Website: www.apexdigest.com. www.apexbookcompany.com. **Contact:** Mari Adkins, subm. ed. **100% freelance written**. Monthly e-zine publishing dark science fiction. "An elite repository for new and seasoned authors with an other-worldly interest in the unquestioned and slightly bizarre parts of the universe." Estab. 2004. Circ. 10,000 unique visits per month. Byline given. Pays on publication. Offers 30% kill fee. Publishes ms an average of 2 months after acceptance. Buys first World English Language Rights and Non-Exclusive anthology rights. Editorial lead time 2 months. Submit seasonal material 2 months in advance. Accepts queries by e-mail. Responds in 20-30 days to queries and to mss. Sample copy for $6. Guidelines available online.

Fiction Needs , dark science fiction. **Buys 24 mss/year.** Send complete ms. Length: 100-7,500 words. **Pays $20-200.**

Tips "See submissions guidelines at submissions@apexdigest.com."

$ ASIMOV'S SCIENCE FICTION

Dell Magazine Fiction Group, 475 Park Ave. S., 11th Floor, New York NY 10016. (212)686-7188. Fax: (212)686-7414. E-mail: asimovssf@dellmagazines.com. Website: www.asimovs.com. **Contact:** Brian Bieniowski, managing editor. **98% freelance written. Works with a small number of new/unpublished writers each year.** Magazine published 10 times/year, including 2 double issues. "Magazine consists of science fiction and fantasy stories for adults and young adults. Publishes the best short science fiction available." Estab. 1977. Circ. 50,000. Pays on acceptance. No kill fee. Publishes ms an average of 6-12 months after acceptance. Buys first North American serial, nonexclusive foreign serial rights; reprint rights occasionally. Accepts queries by mail. Responds in 2 months to queries. Responds in 3 months to mss. Sample copy for $5. Guidelines for #10 SASE or online.

Fiction "Science fiction primarily. Some fantasy and humor but no sword and sorcery. No explicit sex or violence that isn't integral to the story. It is best to read a great deal of material in the genre to avoid the use of some very old ideas. **Buys 10mss/issue.** Send complete ms and SASE with *all* submissions." Needs fantasy, science fiction, hard science, soft sociological. No horror or psychic/supernatural. Would like to see more hard science fiction. Length: 750-15,000 words. **Pays 5-8¢/word.**

Poetry 40 lines maximum **Pays $1/line.**

Tips "In general, we're looking for `character-oriented' stories, those in which the characters, rather than the science, provide the main focus for the reader's interest. Serious, thoughtful, yet accessible fiction will constitute the majority of our purchases, but there's always room for the humorous as well. Borderline fantasy is fine, but no Sword & Sorcery, please. A good overview would be to consider that all fiction is written to examine or illuminate some aspect of human existence, but that in science fiction the backdrop you work against is the size of the universe. Please do not send us submissions on disk or via e-mail. We've bought some of our best stories from people who have never sold a story before."

$ THE MAGAZINE OF FANTASY & SCIENCE FICTION

Spilogale, Inc., P.O. Box 3447, Hoboken NJ 07030. (201)876-2551. Fax: (201)876-2551. Website: www.fandsf.com. **100% freelance written**. Bimonthly magazine covering science fiction & fantasy. "We have been one of the leading magazines in the realm of fantastic fiction for almost 60 years." Estab. 1949. Circ. 25,000. Byline given. Pays on acceptance. No kill fee. Publishes ms an average of 6-8 months after acceptance. Buys first North American serial rights. electronic database rights & select foreign right Editorial lead time 6 months. Submit seasonal material 6 months in advance. Responds in 2 months to mss. Sample copy for $6 Guidelines available online

Columns/Departments Curiosities (Reviews of odd & obscure books), 270 words max. Buys 6 mss/year. Query. **Pays $-$50.**

Fiction Needs fantasy, horror, science fiction. **Buys 60-80 mss/year.** Send complete ms. Length: 25,000 words. **Pays $.06 - .10.**

Poetry Needs avant-garde, free verse, light verse, traditional. Buys 1-3 poems/year. Submit maximum 3 poems.

Tips "Read an issue of our magazine before submitting."

$ LEADING EDGE

Science Fiction and Fantasy, 4087 JKB, Provo UT 84602. E-mail: editor@leadingedgemagazine.com. Website: www.leadingedgemagazine.com. **90% freelance written**. Semiannual magazine covering science fiction and fantasy. "*Leading Edge* is a magazine dedicated to new and upcoming talent in the field of science fiction and fantasy." Estab. 1980. Circ. 200. Byline given. Pays on publication. No kill fee. Publishes ms an average of 2-4 months after acceptance. Buys first North American serial rights. Responds in 2-4 months to queries. Sample copy for $5.95. Guidelines available online at website.

- Accepts unsolicited submissions.

Fiction Needs fantasy, science fiction. **Buys 14-16 mss/year.** Send complete ms by mail. Length: 12,500 words maximum **Pays 1¢/word; $10 minimum.**

Poetry Needs avant-garde, haiku, light verse, traditional. "Publishes 2-4 poems per issue. Poetry should reflect both literary value and popular appeal and should deal with science fiction- or fantasy-related themes." Submit maximum 10 poems. Pays $10 for first 4 pages; $1.50/each subsequent page.

$ THE MAGAZINE OF FANTASY & SCIENCE FICTION

Spilogale, Inc., P.O. Box 3447, Hoboken NJ 07030. E-mail: fandsf@aol.com. Website: www.fandsf.com. **100% freelance written**. Bimonthly magazine covering fantasy fiction and science fiction. "*The Magazine of Fantasy and Science Fiction* publishes various types of science fiction and fantasy short stories and novellas, making up about 80% of each issue. The balance of each issue is devoted to articles about science fiction, a science column, book and film reviews, cartoons, and competitions." Estab. 1949. Circ. 40,000. Byline given. Pays on acceptance. Publishes ms an average of 9-12 months after acceptance. Buys first North American serial rights, buys foreign serial rights. Submit seasonal material 8 months in advance. Accepts previously published material. Responds in 2 months to queries. Sample copy for $6 Guidelines for SASE, by e-mail or website

Fiction Contact: Gordon Van Gelder, editor. "Prefers character-oriented stories. We receive a lot of fantasy fiction, but never enough science fiction." Needs adventure, fantasy, space fantasy, sword and sorcery, horror, dark fantasy, futuristic, psychological, supernatural, science fiction, hard science/technological, soft/sociological. No electronic submissions. **Buys 60-90 mss/year.** Send complete ms. Up to 25,000 words. **Pays 5-9¢/word; additional copies $2.10.**

Tips "We need more hard science fiction and humor."

$ MINDFLIGHTS

Double-Edged Publishing Inc., 9618 Misty Brook Cove, Cordova TN 38016. (901)213-3768. E-mail: editor@mindflights.com. Website: www.mindflights.com. **100% freelance written**. Monthly online magazine and annual print magazine covering science fiction, fantasy, all genres of speculative fiction and poetry, grounded in a Christian or Christian-friendly worldview. "Paving new roads for Christ-reflected short fiction. Not preachy, but still a reflection of the truth and light. Examples of this are in the writings of C.S. Lewis and Tolkien. We strive to provide quality fiction and poetry, all in means that respect traditional values and Christian principles. Be uplifting, encouraging with something interesting to our audience—fans of sci-fi' and fantasy who are comfortable with an environment committed to a Christian world view." Estab. 2007. Byline given. Pays on acceptance. Publishes ms an average of 2 months after acceptance. Buys first North American serial rights, first rights, second serial (reprint) rights, Non-Exclusive Electronic Rights rights. Editorial lead time 3-4 months. Submit seasonal material 4 months in advance. Accepts queries by online submission form. Responds in 3-4 weeks to mss. Sample copy available online. Guidelines available online at: mindflights.com/guidelines.php.

- No postal submissions accepted. See our portal entry and submission process online."

Nonfiction "We very rarely use nonfiction." **Buys 1 ms/year.** Send complete ms. Length: 300-5,000 words. **Pays $5-25.**

Reprints "We will consider reprints but strongly prefer previously unpublished works. We rarely accept reprints, and then only if they are exceptional in both quality and fit. Please note that if a work is publicly available on the Internet, it is considered previously published."

Fiction "Illustrations are compensated with $10 gratuity payment." Needs fantasy, science fiction, work with strong speculative element. Does not want to see any work that would be offensive to a Christian audience. **Buys 25 mss/year.** "We only accept submissions via our online form. Send complete ms. after August 1, when we plan to résumé taking submissions." Length: 50-5,000 words. **Pays $5-25.**

Poetry Needs avant-garde, free verse, haiku, light verse, traditional. "We accept all forms of poetry, but the work must be speculative in nature." Does not want to see any work that would be offensive to a Christian audience. Buys 25 poems/year. Submit maximum 3 poems. **Pays ½¢ per word,$5/min.-$25/max.**

Tips "Only a very small portion of the works accepted for *MindFlights* will appear in our annual print edition. Most will appear online only. Although our guidelines currently indicate that upon acceptance of a work we will ask for rights for either print, the web, or both, and our contracts clearly indicate which rights we are requesting, we are concerned that authors may be assuming that all works accepted will appear in the print edition. Thank you."

$ ON SPEC

P.O. Box 4727, Station South, Edmonton AB T6E 5G6 Canada. (780)413-0215. Fax: (780)413-1538. E-mail: onspec@onspec.ca. Website: www.onspec.ca. **95% freelance written**. Quarterly magazine covering Canadian science fiction, fantasy and horror. "We publish speculative fiction and poetry by new and established writers, with a strong preference for Canadian authored works." Estab. 1989. Circ. 2,000. Byline given. Pays on acceptance. No kill fee. Publishes ms an average of 6-18 months after acceptance. Buys first North American serial rights. Editorial lead time 6 months. Accepts queries by mail. Accepts simultaneous submissions. Responds in 2 weeks to queries. 3 months after deadline to mss. Sample copy for $8. Guidelines for #10 SASE or on website.

- Submission deadlines are February 28, May 31, August 31, and November 30.

Nonfiction Commissioned only.

Fiction Needs fantasy, horror, science fiction, magic realism, ghost stories, fairy stories. No media tie-in or shaggy-alien stories. No condensed or excerpted novels, religious/inspirational stories, fairy tales. **Buys 50 mss/year.** Send complete ms. Length: 1,000-6,000 words. **Pays $50-180 for fiction. Short stories (under 1,000 words): $50 plus 1 contributor's copy.**

Poetry Needs avant-garde, free verse. No rhyming or religious material. Buys 6 poems/year. Submit maximum 10 poems. Length: 4-100 lines. **Pays $50 and 1 contributor's copy.**

Tips "We want to see stories with plausible characters, a well-constructed, consistent, and vividly described setting, a strong plot and believable emotions; characters must show us (not tell us) their emotional responses to each other and to the situation and/or challenge they face. Also: don't send us stories written for television. We don't like media tie-ins, so don't watch TV for inspiration! Read, instead! Absolutely no e-mailed or faxed submissions. Strong preference given to submissions by Canadians."

$ PENNY BLOOD

532 LaGuardia Place, Suite 616, New York NY 10012. E-mail: editor@pennyblood.com. Website: www.pennyblood.com. **70% freelance written**. Quarterly magazine covering horror in entertainment. *Penny Blood Magazine* is a survey of horror and cult entertainment. We are looking for horror movie retrospectives and interviews with genre personalities. Estab. 2004. Circ. 8,000. Byline given. Pays on acceptance. Offers 100% kill fee. Buys all rights. Accepts queries by e-mail. Responds in 2 weeks to queries. Responds in 1 month to mss. Guidelines available online.

Nonfiction Needs essays, interview. **Buys 20-30 mss/year.** Send complete ms. **Pays 3¢/word.**

Tips We accept submissions by e-mail only. We are seeking interviews particularly and our highest pay rates go for these.

$ TALES OF THE TALISMAN

Hadrosaur Productions, P.O. Box 2194, Mesilla Park NM 88047-2194. E-mail: hadrosaur@zianet.com. Website: www.talesofthetalisman.com. **95% freelance written**. Quarterly magazine covering science fiction and fantasy. "*Tales of the Talisman* is a literary science fiction and fantasy magazine. We publish short stories, poetry, and articles with themes related to science fiction and fantasy. Above all, we are looking for thought-provoking ideas and good writing. Speculative fiction set in the past, present, and future is welcome. Likewise, contemporary or historical fiction is welcome as long as it has a mythic or science fictional element. Our target audience includes adult fans of the science fiction and fantasy genres along with anyone else who enjoys thought-provoking and entertaining writing." Estab. 1995. Circ. 200. Byline given. Pays on acceptance. Offers 100% kill fee. Publishes ms an average of 9 months after acceptance. Buys one-time rights. Editorial lead time 9-12 months. Submit seasonal material 1 year in advance. Accepts queries by mail, e-mail. Accepts previously published material. Responds in 1 week to queries. Responds in 1 month to mss. Sample copy for $8. Guidelines available online.

- Fiction and poetry submissions are limited to reading periods of January 1-February 15 and July 1-August 15.

Nonfiction Needs interview, technical, articles on the craft of writing. "We do not want to see unsolicited articles—please query first if you have an idea that you think would be suitable for *Tales of the Talisman*'s audience. We do not want to see negative or derogatory articles." **Buys 1-3 mss/year.** Query. Length: 1,000-3,000 words. **Pays $10 for assigned articles.**

Fiction Contact: David L. Summers, editor. Needs fantasy, space fantasy, sword and sorcery, horror, science fiction, hard science/technological, soft/sociological. "We do not want to see stories with graphic violence. Do not send 'mainstream' fiction with no science fictional or fantastic elements. Do not send stories with copyrighted characters, unless you're the copyright holder." **Buys 25-30 mss/year.** Send complete ms. Length: 1,000-6,000 words. **Pays $6-10**.

Poetry Needs avant-garde, free verse, haiku, light verse, traditional. "Do not send 'mainstream' poetry with no science fictional or fantastic elements. Do not send poems featuring copyrighted characters, unless you're the copyright holder." Buys 24-30 poems/year. Submit maximum 5 poems. Length: 3-50 lines.

Tips "Let your imagination soar to its greatest heights and write down the results. Above all, we are looking for thought-provoking ideas and good writing. Our emphasis is on character-oriented science fiction and fantasy. If we don't believe in the people living the story, we generally won't believe in the story itself."

THEATRE OF DECAY

129 Mountainwood Dr., Davison MI 48423. E-mail: theatreofdecay@yahoo.com. Website: www.theatreofdecay.com. **100% freelance written**. Quarterly magazine covering horror fiction. Estab. 2005. Byline given. Publishes ms an average of 6 months after acceptance. Buys one-time rights. Submit seasonal material 6 months in advance. Accepts queries by e-mail. Accepts previously published material. Accepts simultaneous submissions. Responds in 2 weeks to queries. Responds in 1 month to mss. Sample copy available online. Guidelines available online.

Fiction "We accept anything that has an element of horror." Needs experimental, horror, humorous, suspense. **Buys 40-50 mss/year.** Send complete ms. Length: 2,000 words. **1 contributor's copy.**

Poetry Poetry of all lengths. **Pays 1 contributor copy**.

$ VAMPIRES 2 MAGAZINE

Man's Story 2 Publishing Co., 1321 Snapfinger Rd., Decatur GA 30032. E-mail: mansstory2@aol.com. Website: www.vampires2.com. **80% freelance written**. "Online E-Zine that s trives to recreate Vampire Romance in the pulp fiction style that was published in the magazines of the 1920s through the 1970s with strong emphasis on 3D graphic art." Estab. 1999. Circ. 500. Pays on publication. No kill fee. Publishes ms an average of 3-6 months after acceptance. Buys one-time rights, buys second serial (reprint) rights. Accepts queries by e-mail only. Accepts previously published material. Accepts simultaneous submissions. Guidelines available online.

Fiction Needs adventure, erotica, fantasy, horror, suspense, pulp fiction involving vampires. **Buys 30-50 mss/year.** Send complete ms. Length: 1,500-3,500 words. **Pays $25.**

Tips "We suggest interested writers visit our website and read our writer's guidelines. Then, read the pulp fiction stories posted in our online mini-magazine and/or read one of our magazines, or find an old pulp fiction magazine that was published in the 1960s. If all else fails, e-mail us."

Sex

$$ EXOTIC MAGAZINE

X Publishing, 314 W. Burnside St., Portland OR 97209. Fax: (503)241-7239. E-mail: exoticunderground2004@yahoo.com. Website: www.xmag.com. Monthly magazine covering adult entertainment, sexuality. *Exotic* is pro-sex, informative, amusing, mature, intelligent. Our readers rent and/or buy adult videos, visit strip clubs and are interested in topics related to the adult entertainment industry and sexuality/culture. Don't talk down to them or fire too far over their heads. Many readers are computer literate and well-traveled. We're also interested in insightful fetish material. We are not a `hard core' publication. Estab. 1993. Circ. 120,000. Byline given. Pays 30 days after publication. No kill fee. Buys first North American serial rights; and online rights; may negotiate second serial (reprint) rights. Accepts queries by fax. Accepts simultaneous submissions. Responds in 2 weeks to queries. Responds in 2 months to mss. Sample copy for sae with 9 × 12 envelope and 5 First-Class stamps. Guidelines for #10 SASE.

Nonfiction Interested in seeing articles about Viagra, auto racing, gambling, insider porn industry and real sex worker stories. Needs expose, general interest, historical, how-to, humor, interview, travel, News. No men writing as women, articles about being a horny guy, opinion pieces pretending to be fact pieces. **Buys 36 mss/year.** Send complete ms. Length: 1,000-1,800 words. **Pays 10¢/word up to $150.**

Reprints Send typed manuscript with rights for sale noted and information about when and where the material previously appeared. Pays 100% of amount paid for an original article.

Photos Rarely buys photos. Most provided by staff. Model releases required. Reviews prints. Negotiates payment individually.

Fiction We are currently overwhelmed with fiction submissions. Please only send fiction if it's really amazing. Needs erotica, slice-of-life vignettes, must present either erotic element or some vice of modern culture, such as gambling, music, dancing. Send complete ms. Length: 1,000-1,800 words. **Pays 10¢/word up to $150.**

Tips Read adult publications, spend time in the clubs doing more than just tipping and drinking. Look for new insights in adult topics. For the industry to continue to improve, those who cover it must also be educated consumers and affiliates. Please type, spell-check and be realistic about how much time the editor can take `fixing' your manuscript.

$$$$ HUSTLER

HG Inc., 8484 Wilshire Blvd., Suite 900, Beverly Hills CA 90211. Fax: (323)651-2741. E-mail: erampell@lfp.com. Website: www.hustler.com. **60% freelance written**. Magazine published 13 times/year. *Hustler* is the no-nonsense men's magazine, one that is willing to speak frankly about society's sacred cows and expose its hypocrites. The *Hustler* reader expects honest, unflinching looks at hard topicsÃ³sexual, social, political, personality profile, true crime. Estab. 1974. Circ. 750,000. Byline given. Pays as boards ship to printer. Offers 20% kill fee. Publishes ms an average of 3 months after acceptance. Buys all rights. Editorial lead time 4 months. Submit seasonal material 6 months in advance. Accepts queries by mail, e-mail, fax. Responds in 2 weeks to queries. Responds in 1 month to mss. Guidelines for #10 SASE.

- *Hustler* is most interested in well-researched nonfiction reportage focused on sexual practices and subcultures.

Nonfiction Needs book excerpts, expose, general interest, how-to, interview, personal experience, trends. **Buys 30 mss/year.** Query. Length: 3,500-4,000 words. **Pays $1,500.**

Columns/Departments Sex play (some aspect of sex that can be encapsulated in a limited space), 2,500 words. 13 Send complete ms. **Pays $750.**

Fillers Jokes and Graffilthy, bathroom wall humor. **Pays $50-100.**

Tips Don't try and mimic the *Hustler* style. If a writer needs to be molded into our voice, we'll do a better job of it than he or she will. Avoid first- and second-person voice. The ideal manuscript is quote-rich, visual and is narratively driven by events and viewpoints that push one another forward.

$$$$ PENTHOUSE

General Media Communications, 2 Penn Plaza, 11th Floor, New York NY 10121. (212)702-6000. Fax: (212)702-6279. E-mail: pbloch@pmgi.com. Website: www.penthouse.com. Monthly magazine. *Penthouse* is for the sophisticated male. Its editorial scope ranges from outspoken contemporary comment to photography essays of beautiful women. *Penthouse* features interviews with personalities, sociological studies, humor, travel, food and wine, and fashion and grooming for men. Estab. 1969. Circ. 640,000. Byline given. Pays 2 months after acceptance. Offers 25% kill fee. Buys all rights. Editorial lead time 3 months. Accepts simultaneous submissions. Guidelines for #10 SASE.

Nonfiction Needs expose, general interest, to men, interview. **Buys 50 mss/year.** Send complete ms. Length: 4,000-6,000 words. **Pays $3,000.**

Columns/Departments Length: 1,000 words. 25 Query with published clips or send complete ms. **Pays $500.**

Tips Because of our long lead time, writers should think at least 6 months ahead. We take chances. Go against the grain; we like writers who look under rocks and see what hides there.

$$$ SWANK

Swank Publications, 210 Route 4 E., Suite 211, Paramus NJ 07652-5103. (201)843-4004. Fax: (201)843-8636. E-mail: editor@swankmag.com. Website: www.swankmag.com. **75% freelance written. Works with new/unpublished writers.** Monthly magazine on sex and sensationalism, lurid. High quality adult erotic entertainment. Audience of men ages 18-38, high school and some college education, medium income, skilled blue-collar professionals, union men, some white-collar. Estab. 1954. Circ. 400,000. Byline given, pseudonym if wanted. Pays on publication. Publishes ms an average of 4 months after acceptance. Buys first North American serial rights. Submit seasonal material 6 months in advance. Accepts queries by mail. Accepts previously published material. Responds in 3 weeks to queries. Responds in 1 month to mss. Sample copy for $6.95. Guidelines for #10 SASE.

- *Swank* reports a need for more nonfiction, non-sex-related articles.

Nonfiction "Expose (researched), adventure must be accompanied by color photographs. We buy articles on sex-related topics, which don't need to be accompanied by photos. Interested in unusual lifestyle pieces. How-to, interviews with entertainment, sports and sex industry celebrities. Buys photo pieces on autos, action, adventure. It is strongly recommended that a sample copy is reviewed before submitting material." **Buys 34 mss/year.** Query. **Pays $350-500.**

Reprints Send tearsheet, photocopy or typed ms with rights for sale noted and information about when and where the material previously appeared. Pays 50% of amount paid for an original article.

Photos Contact: Alex Suarez, art director. Articles have a much better chance of being purchased if you have accompanying photos. Model releases required.

Fiction "All of the fiction used by *Swank* is erotic in some sense—that is, both theme and content are sexual. New angles are always welcome. We will consider stories that are not strictly sexual in theme (humor, adventure, detective stories, etc.). However, these types of stories are much more likely to be considered if they portray some sexual element, or scene, within their context."

Tips "All erotic fiction currently being used by *Swank* must follow certain legal guidelines."

Sports

Archery & Bowhunting

$$ BOW & ARROW HUNTING

Beckett Media LLC, 2400 East Katella Avenue, Suite 300, Anaheim CA 92806. (714)939-9991. Fax: (714)939-9909. E-mail: editorial@bowandarrowhunting.com. Website: www.bowandarrowhunting.com. **70% freelance written**. Magazine published 9 times/year covering bowhunting. Dedicated to serve the serious bowhunting enthusiast. Writers must be willing to share their secrets so our readers can become better bowhunters. Estab. 1962. Circ. 90,000. Byline given. Pays on publication. No kill fee. Publishes ms an average of 2 months after acceptance. Buys all rights. Submit seasonal material 6 months in advance. Accepts queries by mail, e-mail. Accepts simultaneous submissions. Responds in 1 month to queries. Responds in 6 weeks to mss. Sample copy and writer's guidelines free

Nonfiction Needs how-to, humor, interview, opinion, personal experience, technical. **Buys 60 mss/year.** Send complete ms. Length: 1,700-3,000 words. **Pays $200-450.**

Photos Send photos. Captions required. Reviews contact sheets, digital images only; no slides or prints accepted. Offers no additional payment for photos accepted with ms. Buys one-time or all rights.

Tips "Inform readers how they can become better at the sport, but don't forget to keep it fun! Sidebars are recommended with every submission."

$$ BOWHUNTER

The Number One Bowhunting Magazine, InterMedia Outdoors, 6385 Flank Dr., Suite 800, Harrisburg PA 17112. (717)695-8085. Fax: (717)545-2527. E-mail: dwight.schuh@imoutdoors.com. Website: www.bowhunter.com. **50% freelance written**. Bimonthly magazine covering hunting big and small game with bow and arrow. "We are a special-interest publication, produced by bowhunters for bowhunters, covering all aspects of the sport. Material included in each issue is designed to entertain and inform readers, making them better bowhunters." Estab. 1971. Circ. 155,000. Byline given. Pays on acceptance. No kill fee. Buys exclusive first, worldwide publication rights. Submit seasonal material 8 months in advance. Accepts queries by mail, e-mail, fax. Responds in 1 month to queries. Responds in 2 months to mss. Sample copy for $2 and 8½ × 11 SAE with appropriate postage. Guidelines for #10 SASE or on website.

Nonfiction "We publish a Big Game Special each July but need all material by mid-April. Another annual publication, *Whitetail Special*, is staff written or by assignment only. Our latest special issue is the *Gear*

Special, which highlights the latest in equipment. We don't want articles that graphically deal with an animal's death. And, please, no articles written from the animal's viewpoint." Needs general interest, how-to, interview, opinion, personal experience, photo feature. **Buys 60 plus mss/year.** Query. Length: 250-2,000 words. **Pays $500 maximum for assigned articles. Pays $100-400 for unsolicited articles.**
Photos Send photos. Captions required. Reviews hi-res digital images. Offers $75-250/photo. Buys one-time rights.
Fiction Contact: Dwight Schuh, editor. Send complete ms. Length: 500-2,000 words. **Pays $100-350.**
Tips "A writer must know bowhunting and be willing to share that knowledge. Writers should anticipate *all* questions a reader might ask, then answer them in the article itself or in an appropriate sidebar. Articles should be written with the reader foremost in mind; we won't be impressed by writers seeking to prove how good they are—either as writers or bowhunters. We care about the reader and don't need writers with 'I' trouble. Features are a good bet because most of our material comes from freelancers. The best advice is: Be yourself. Tell your story the same as if sharing the experience around a campfire. Don't try to write like you think a writer writes."

$ $ BOWHUNTING WORLD

Grand View Media Group, 5959 Baker Rd., Suite 300, Minnetonka MN 55345. (952)405-2280. E-mail: molis@grandviewmedia.com; hilary@grandviewmedia.com. Website: www.bowhuntingworld.com. **Contact:** Mark Olis; Hilary Dyer. **50% freelance written.** Bimonthly magazine with 3 additional issues for bowhunting and archery enthusiasts who participate in the sport year-round. For article or photo submissions, please contact Mark Olis at (888) 431-2877, ext. 4665 or e-mail him at molis@grandviewmedia.com and Hilary Dyer at (888) 431-2877, ext. 4660 or e-mail her at hilary@grandviewmedia.com. Estab. 1952. Circ. 95,000. Byline given. Pays on acceptance. No kill fee. Publishes ms an average of 5 months after acceptance. Buys first rights, buys second serial (reprint) rights. Responds in 1 week (e-mail queries). Responds in 6 weeks to mss. Sample copy for $3 and 9 × 12 SAE with 10 first-class stamps. Guidelines for #10 SASE.

- Accepts queries by mail, but prefers e-mail.

Nonfiction How-to articles with creative slants on knowledgeable selection and use of bowhunting equipment and bowhunting methods. Articles must emphasize knowledgeable use of archery or hunting equipment, and/or specific bowhunting techniques. Contributors must be authorities in the areas of archery and bowhunting. Straight hunting adventure narratives and other types of articles now appear only in special issues. Equipment-oriented aricles must demonstrate wise and insightful selection and use of archery equipment and other gear related to the archery sports. Some product-review, field-test, equipment how-to, and technical pieces will be purchased. We are not interested in articles whose equipment focuses on random mentioning of brands. Technique-oriented aricles most sought are those that briefly cover fundamentals and delve into leading-edge bowhunting or recreational archery methods. **Buys 60 mss/year.** Send complete ms. Length: 1,500-2,500 words. **Pays $350-600.**
Photos We are seeking cover photos that depict specific behavioral traits of the more common big game animals (scraping whitetails, bugling elk, etc.) and well-equipped bowhunters in action. Must include return postage.
Tips Writers are strongly advised to adhere to guidelines and become familiar with our format, as our needs are very specific. Writers are urged to query by e-mail. We prefer detailed outlines of 6 or so article ideas/query. Assignments are made for the next 18 months.

PETERSEN'S BOWHUNTING

Inter Media Partners, 7819 Highland Scenic Rd., Baxter MN 56425. (218)824-2549. Fax: (218)829-2371. Website: www.bowhuntingmag.com. **70% freelance written.** Magazine published 9 times/year covering bowhunting. Very equipment oriented. Our readers are `superenthusiasts,' therefore our writers must have an advanced knowledge of hunting archery. Circ. 175,000. Byline given. Pays on acceptance. No kill fee. Buys all rights. Editorial lead time 6 months. Submit seasonal material 6 months in advance. Accepts queries by mail. Responds in 1 month to queries. Guidelines free.
Nonfiction Emphasis is on how-to instead of personal. Needs how-to, humor, interview, new product, opinion, personal experience, photo feature. **Buys 50 mss/year.** Query. Length: 2,100 words.
Photos Send photos. Captions, model releases required. Reviews contact sheets, 35mm transparencies, 5 × 7 prints, digital. Buys one time rights.
Columns/Departments Departments: True Bowhunting Adventures, 150 words. Query. **Pays $100.**

Baseball

$ FANTASY BASEBALL

F+W Media, Inc., 700 E. State St., Iola WI 54990-0001. (715)445-2214. Fax: (715)445-4087. Website: www.collect.com. Quarterly magazine. Published for fantasy baseball league players. Circ. 130,000. No kill fee. Editorial lead time 6 weeks.

$ JUNIOR BASEBALL

America's Youth Baseball Magazine, 2D Publishing, P.O. Box 9099, Canoga Park CA 91309. (818)710-1234. Fax: (818)710-1877. E-mail: dave@juniorbaseball.com. Website: www.juniorbaseball.com. **25% freelance written**. Bimonthly magazine covering youth baseball. Focused on youth baseball players ages 7-17 (including high school) and their parents/coaches. Edited to various reading levels, depending upon age/skill level of feature. Estab. 1996. Circ. 20,000. Byline given. Pays on publication. No kill fee. Publishes ms an average of 4 months after acceptance. Buys all rights. Editorial lead time 3 months. Submit seasonal material 4 months in advance. Accepts simultaneous submissions. Responds in 2 weeks to queries. Responds in 1 month to mss. Sample copy for $5 and online.

Nonfiction Needs how-to, skills, tips, features, how-to play better baseball, etc., interview, with major league players; only on assignment, personal experience, from coaches' or parents' perspective. No trite first-person articles about your kid. No fiction or poetry. **Buys 8-12 mss/year.** Query. Length: 500-1,000 words. **Pays $50-100.**

Photos Photos can be e-mailed in 300 dpi JPEGs. State availability. Captions, identification of subjects required. Reviews 35mm transparencies, 3 × 5 prints. Offers $10-100/photo; negotiates payment individually.

Columns/Departments When I Was a Kid (a current Major League Baseball player profile); Parents Feature (topics of interest to parents of youth ball players); all 1,000-1,500 words. In the Spotlight (news, events, new products), 50-100 words; Hot Prospect (written for the 14 and older competitive player. High school baseball is included, and the focus is on improving the finer points of the game to make the high school team, earn a college scholarship, or attract scouts, written to an adult level), 500-1,000 words. 8-12 **Pays $50-100.**

Tips Must be well-versed in baseball! Having a child who is very involved in the sport, or have extensive hands-on experience in coaching baseball, at the youth, high school or higher level. We can always use accurate, authoritative skills information and good photos to accompany is a big advantage! This magazine is read by experts. No fiction, poems, games, puzzles, etc.

Bicycling

$$$ ADVENTURE CYCLIST

Adventure Cycling Assn., Box 8308, Missoula MT 59807. (406)721-1776, ext. 222. Fax: (406)721-8754. E-mail: magazine@adventurecycling.org. Website: www.adventurecycling.org. **75% freelance written**. Magazine published 9 times/year for Adventure Cycling Association members. Estab. 1975. Circ. 44,000. Byline given. Pays on publication. No kill fee. Buys first rights. Submit seasonal material 9 months in advance. Sample copy and guidelines for 9 × 12 SAE with 4 first-class stamps. Info available at www. adventurecycling.org/mag.

Nonfiction Needs how-to, humor, interview, photo feature, technical, bike travel, U.S. or foreign tour accounts. **Buys 20-25 mss/year.** Send complete ms. Length: 1,400-3,500 words. **Pays sliding scale per word.**

Photos People riding bicycles, cultural, detail, architectural, people historic, vertical, horizontal. State availability. Identification of subjects, model releases required. Reviews color transparencies and digital files.

🌐 AUSTRALIAN MOUNTAIN BIKE

ACP Magazines, Ltd., 54-58 Park St., Sydney NSW 2000 Australia. (02)9282 8000. Fax: (02)9267 4361. Website: www.acpmagazines.com.au. **Contact:** Chris Southwood, editor. Covers off-road cycling for all levels of riders. "Australian Mountain Bike (AMB) provides access to an active, adventurous audience which is difficult to reach through any other medium. AMB is about engaging riders of all levels - inspiring, educating and entertaining them. Published 9 times a year, it features extensive and industry-leading mountain bike and product reviews, the greatest trails from here and overseas, columns dedicated to both the first time rider and pro racer, and some of the best mountain bike imagery in the world." Circ. 20,000.

Nonfiction Needs general interest, how-to, new product, personal experience. Query.

BICYCLING

Rodale Press, Inc., 400 S. 10th St., Emmaus PA 18098. (610)967-5171. Fax: (610)967-8960. E-mail: bicycling@rodale.com. Website: www.bicycling.com. **50% freelance written**. "*Bicycling* features articles about fitness, training, nutrition, touring, racing, equipment, clothing, maintenance, new technology, industry developments, and other topics of interest to committed bicycle riders. Editorially, we advocate for the sport, industry, and the cycling consumer." Estab. 1961. Circ. 410,000. Byline given. Pays on acceptance. No kill fee. Buys all rights. Submit seasonal material 6 months in advance. Accepts previously published material. Responds in 2 months to queries. Sample copy for $3.50. Guidelines for #10 SASE.
Nonfiction "We are a cycling lifestyle magazine. We seek readable, clear, well-informed pieces that show how cycling is part of our readers' lives. We sometimes run articles that are inspirational, and inspiration might flavor even our most technical pieces. No fiction or poetry." Needs how-to, on all phases of bicycle touring, repair, maintenance, commuting, new products, clothing, riding technique, nutrition for cyclists, conditioning, photo feature, on cycling events, technical, opinions about technology, travel, bicycling must be central here, fitness. **Buys 10 unsolicited mss/year.** Query. **Payment varies**
Reprints Send tearsheet or photocopy and information about when and where the material previously appeared.
Photos State availability of or send photos. Captions, model releases required. Pays $15-250/photo.
Tips "Don't send us travel pieces about where you went on summer vacation. Travel/adventure stories have to be about something larger than just visiting someplace on your bike and meeting quirky locals."

$ $ BIKE MAGAZINE

P.O. Box 1028, Dana Point CA 92629. (949)496-5922. Fax: (949)496-7849. E-mail: bikemag@primedia.com. Website: www.bikemag.com. **35% freelance written**. Magazine publishes 8 times/year covering mountain biking. Estab. 1993. Circ. 170,000. Byline given. Pays on publication. Offers 25% kill fee. Publishes ms an average of 2 months after acceptance. Buys first North American serial rights. Editorial lead time 4 months. Submit seasonal material 6 months in advance. Responds in 2 months to queries. Sample copy for $8. Guidelines for #10 SASE.
Nonfiction Writers should submit queries in March (April 1 deadline) for consideration for the following year's editions. All queries received by April 1 will be considered and editors will contact writers about stories they are interested in. Queries should include word count. Needs humor, interview, personal experience, photo feature, travel. **Buys 20 mss/year.** Length: 1,000-2,500 words. **Pays 50¢/word.** $500 maximum
Photos Contact: David Reddick, photo editor. Send photos. Captions, identification of subjects required. Reviews color transparencies, b&w prints. Negotiates payment individually. Buys one time rights.
Columns/Departments Splatter (news), 300 words; Urb (details a great ride within 1 hour of a major metropolitan area), 600-700 words. Query year-round for Splatter and Urb. 20 **Pays 50¢/word.**
Tips Remember that we focus on hard core mountain biking, not beginners. We're looking for ideas that deliver the excitement and passion of the sport in ways that aren't common or predictable. Ideas should be vivid, unbiased, irreverent, probing, fun, humorous, funky, quirky, smart, good. Great feature ideas are always welcome, especially features on cultural matters or issues in the sport. However, you're much more likely to get published in *Bike* if you send us great ideas for short articles. In particular we need stories for our Splatter, a front-of-the-book section devoted to news, funny anecdotes, quotes, and odds and ends. These stories range from 50 to 300 words. We also need personality profiles of 600 words or so for our People Who Ride section. Racers are OK but we're more interested in grassroots people with interesting personalities—it doesn't matter if they're Mother Theresas or scumbags, so long as they make mountain biking a little more interesting. Short descriptions of great rides are very welcome for our Urb column; the length should be from 600-700 words.

$ $ CYCLE CALIFORNIA! MAGAZINE

1702-L Meridian Ave., #289, San Jose CA 95125. (408)924-0270. Fax: (408)292-3005. E-mail: tcorral@cyclecalifornia.com. Website: www.cyclecalifornia.com. **Contact:** Tracy L. Corral. **75% freelance written**. Magazine published 11 times/year covering Northern California bicycling events, races, people. Issues (topics) covered include bicycle commuting, bicycle politics, touring, racing, nostalgia, history, anything at all to do with riding a bike. Estab. 1995. Circ. 26,000. Byline given. Pays on publication. No kill fee. Publishes ms an average of 3 months after acceptance. Buys first North American serial rights. Editorial lead time 6 weeks. Submit seasonal material 6 weeks in advance. Accepts queries by mail, e-mail. Accepts simultaneous submissions. Responds in 1 month to queries. Sample copy for 10 × 13 SAE

with 3 first-class stamps. Guidelines for #10 SASE.
Nonfiction Needs historical, how-to, interview, opinion, personal experience, technical, travel. Bicycle Tour & Travel (January/February) No articles about any sport that doesn't relate to bicycling, no product reviews. **Buys 36 mss/year.** Query. Length: 500-1,500 words. **Pays 3-10¢/word.**
Photos Send photos. Identification of subjects required. Reviews 3 × 5 prints. Negotiates payment individually. Buys one time rights.
Columns/Departments 2-3 Query with published clips. **Pays 3-10¢/word.**
Tips E-mail editor with good ideas. While we don't exclude writers from other parts of the country, articles really should reflect a Northern California slant, or be of general interest to bicyclists. We prefer stories written by people who like and use their bikes.

⊘ CYCLE WORLD

Hachette Filipacchi Media U.S., Inc., 1499 Monrovia Ave., Newport Beach CA 92663. (949)720-5300. Website: www.cycleworld.com. Monthly magazine geared towards motorcycle owners and buyers, accessory buyers, potential buyers and enthusiasts of the overall sport of motorcycling. Circ. 323,690. No kill fee.

- Query before submitting.

$ $ VELONEWS

The Journal of Competitive Cycling, Inside Communications, Inc., 1830 N. 55th St., Boulder CO 80301. (303)440-0601. Fax: (303)444-6788. Website: www.velonews.com. **40% freelance written.** Monthly tabloid covering bicycle racing. Estab. 1972. Circ. 48,000. Byline given. Pays on publication. No kill fee. Publishes ms an average of 1 month after acceptance. Buys one-time worldwide rights. Accepts previously published material. Responds in 3 weeks to queries.
Nonfiction Freelance opportunities include race coverage, reviews (book and videos), health-and-fitness departments. **Buys 80 mss/year.** Query. Length: 300-1,200 words. **Pays $100-400.**
Reprints Send typed manuscript with rights for sale noted and information about when and where the material previously appeared.
Photos State availability. Captions, identification of subjects required. Buys one time rights.

Boating

⊘ ⊞ AUSTRALIAN AMATEUR BOATBUILDER

P.O. Box 1254, Burleigh Heights QLD 4220 Australia. (61)(7)5598-2299. Fax: (61)(7)5598-3024. E-mail: info@boatbuilder.com.au. Website: www.boatbuilder.com.au. Quarterly magazine. "*AABB* is an Australian-based specialist publication devoted exclusively to amateur enthusiasts—monohulls, kayaks, multihulls, offshore, off-the-beach, power, racing and cruising." Estab. 1991. Circ. 9,500. No kill fee.

- Query before submitting.

N ⊞ AUSTRALIAN YACHTING

Yaffa Publishing, 17-21 Bellevue St., Surry Hills NSW 2010 Australia. (61)(2)9281-2333. Fax: (61)(2)9281-2750. E-mail: barryhenson@yaffa.com.au. Website: www.yaffa.com.au. **Contact:** Barry Henson, editor. Monthly magazine aimed at the owners and crews of yachts over 20 feet. "*Australian Yachting* covers monohulls, multihulls, inshore and offshore racing, coastal cruising and passage making."
Nonfiction Needs general interest, how-to, interview, new product. Query.

$ $ BOATING WORLD MAGAZINE

America's Family Boating Magazine, Duncan McIntosh Co., 17782 Cowan, Suite C, Irvine CA 92614. (949)660-6150. Fax: (949)660-6172. Website: www.goboatingamerica.com. **60% freelance written.** Magazine published 8 times/year covering recreational trailer boats. "Typical reader owns a power boat between 14 and 32 feet long and has 3-9 years experience. Boat reports are mostly written by staff while features and most departments are provided by freelancers. We are looking for freelancers who can write well and who have at least a working knowledge of recreational power boating and the industry behind it." Estab. 1997. Circ. 100,000. Pays on publication. No kill fee. Publishes ms an average of 4 months after acceptance. Accepts simultaneous submissions. Responds in 3 months to queries. Sample copy free. Guidelines for #10 SASE.
Nonfiction Needs general interest, how-to, humor, new product, personal experience, travel. **Buys 20-25 mss/year.** Query. Length: 1,400-1,600 words. **Pays $150-450.**
Photos State availability. Identification of subjects, model releases required. Reviews transparencies, prints, digital images. Offers $50-250/photo. Buys one-time rights.

Tips "We are looking for solid writers who are familiar with power boating and who can educate, entertain, and enlighten our readers with well-written and researched feature stories."

$$$ CHESAPEAKE BAY MAGAZINE

Boating at Its Best, Chesapeake Bay Communications, 1819 Bay Ridge Ave., Annapolis MD 21403. (410)263-2662, ext. 32. Fax: (410)267-6924. E-mail: editor@cbmmag.net. **60% freelance written**. Monthly magazine covering boating and the Chesapeake Bay. Our readers are boaters. Our writers should know boats and boating. Read the magazine before submitting. Estab. 1972. Circ. 46,000. Byline given. Pays within 2 months after acceptance. No kill fee. Publishes ms an average of 1 year after acceptance. Buys first North American serial rights. Editorial lead time 1 year. Submit seasonal material 1 year in advance. Accepts queries by mail, e-mail, fax, phone. Accepts simultaneous submissions. Responds in 2 months to queries. Responds in 3 months to mss. Sample copy for $5.19 prepaid.
Nonfiction Destinations, boating adventures, how-to, marina reviews, history, nature, environment, lifestyles, personal and institutional profiles, boat-type profiles, boatbuilding, boat restoration, boating anecdotes, boating news. **Buys 30 mss/year.** Query with published clips. Length: 300-3,000 words. **Pays $100-1,000.**
Photos Captions, identification of subjects required. Offers $75-250/photo, $400/day rate for assignment photography. Buys one time rights.
Tips Send us unedited writing samples (not clips) that show the writer can write, not just string words together. We look for well-organized, lucid, lively, intelligent writing.

$$$$ CRUISING WORLD

The Sailing Co., 55 Hammarlund Way, Middletown RI 02842. (401)845-5100. Fax: (401)845-5180. E-mail: elaine.lembo@cruisingworld.com. Website: www.cruisingworld.com. **Contact:** Manuscripts Editor. **60% freelance written**. Monthly magazine covering sailing, cruising/adventuring, do-it-yourself boat improvements. "*Cruising World* is a publication by and for sailboat owners who spend time in home waters as well as voyaging the world. Its readership is extremely loyal, savvy, and driven by independent thinking." Estab. 1974. Circ. 155,000. Byline given. **Pays on acceptance for articles;** on publication for photography. No kill fee. Publishes ms an average of 18 months after acceptance. Buys 6-month, all-world, first time rights (amendable). Editorial lead time 3 months. Submit seasonal material 1 year in advance. Accepts queries by mail. Responds in 2 months to queries. Responds in 4 months to mss. Sample copy free. Guidelines available online.
Nonfiction Needs book excerpts, essays, expose, general interest, historical, how-to, humor, interview, new product, opinion, personal experience, photo feature, technical, travel. No travel articles that have nothing to do with cruising aboard sailboats from 20-50 feet in length. **Buys dozens of mss/year.** Send complete ms. **Pays $50-1,500 for assigned articles. Pays $50-1,000 for unsolicited articles.**
Photos Send high res (minimum 300 DPI) images on CD. Send photos. Captions required. Reviews negatives, transparencies, color slides preferred. Payment upon publication. Also buys stand-alone photos. Buys First and One Time Rights.
Columns/Departments Shoreline (sailing news, people, and short features; contact Elaine Lembo), 300 words maximum; Hands-on Sailor (refit, voyaging, seamanship, how-to; contact Mark Pillsbury), 1,000-1,500 words. dozens of Query with or without published clips or send complete ms.
Tips *Cruising World's* readers know exactly what they want to read, so our best advice to freelancers is to carefully read the magazine and envision which exact section or department would be the appropriate place for proposed submissions.

GOOD OLD BOAT

The Sailing Magazine for the Rest of Us, Partnership for Excellence, Inc., 7340 Niagara Lane N., Maple Grove MN 55311. (763)494-0314. E-mail: karen@goodoldboat.com. Website: www.goodoldboat.com. **Contact:** Karen Larson, editor. **90% freelance written**. Bimonthly magazine covering sailing. "*Good Old Boat* magazine focuses on maintaining, upgrading, and loving cruising sailboats that are 10 years old and older. Readers see themselves as part of a community of sailors who share similar maintenance and replacement concerns which are not generally addressed in the other sailing publications. Our readers do much of the writing about projects they have done on their boats and the joy they receive from sailing them." Estab. 1998. Circ. 30,000. Pays 2 months in advance of publication. No kill fee. Publishes ms an average of 12-18 months after acceptance. Buys first North American serial rights. Editorial lead time 4 months. Submit seasonal material 12-15 months in advance. Accepts queries by mail, e-mail. Accepts simultaneous submissions. Responds in 1-2 weeks to queries. Responds in 2-6 months to mss. Sample copy free. Guidelines available online.

Nonfiction Needs general interest, historical, how-to, interview, personal experience, photo feature, technical. Articles which are written by non-sailors serve no purpose for us. **Buys 150 mss/year.** Query or send complete ms **Payment varies, refer to published rates on website.**

Photos State availability of or send photos.. We do not pay additional fees for photos except when they run as covers, or are specifically requested to support an article.

Tips "Our shorter pieces are the best way to break into our magazine. We publish many Simple Solutions and Quick & Easy pieces. These are how-to tips that have worked for sailors on their boats. In addition, our readers send lists of projects which they've done on their boats and which they could write for publication. We respond to these queries with a thumbs up or down by project. Articles are submitted on speculation, but they have a better chance of being accepted once we have approved of the suggested topic."

$$ HEARTLAND BOATING

The Waterways Journal, Inc., 319 N. Fourth St., Suite 650, St. Louis MO 63102. (314)241-4310. Fax: (314)241-4207. E-mail: lbraff@heartlandboating.com. Website: www.heartlandboating.com. **90% freelance written**. Magazine published 8 times/year covering recreational boating on the inland waterways of mid-America, from the Great Lakes south to the Gulf of Mexico and over to the east. Submission period is only between May 1 and July 1. "Our writers must have experience with, and a great interest in, boating, particularly in the area described above. *Heartland Boating*'s content is both informative and humorous—describing boating life as the heartland boater knows it. We are boaters and enjoy the outdoor, water-oriented way of life. The content reflects the challenge, joy, and excitement of our way of life afloat. We are devoted to both power and sailboating enthusiasts throughout middle America; houseboats are included. The focus is on the freshwater inland rivers and lakes of the heartland, primarily the waters of the Arkansas, Tennessee, Cumberland, Ohio, Missouri, Illinois, and Mississippi rivers, the Tennessee-Tombigbee Waterway, The Gulf Intracoastal Waterway, and the lakes along these waterways." Estab. 1989. Circ. 10,000. Byline given. Pays on publication. No kill fee. Buys first North American serial rights, buys first rights, buys electronic rights. Editorial lead time 3 months. Accepts queries by mail. Accepts previously published material. Responds in 2 months to queries. Sample copy online at website. Choose the Try It For Free! button. Fill out the form, and you will receive 3 free copies. Guidelines for #10 SASE.

- Submission window is May 1-July 15.

Nonfiction Needs how-to, articles about navigation maintenance, upkeep, or making time spent aboard easier and more comfortable, humor, personal experience, technical, Great Loop leg trips, along waterways and on-land stops. Annual houseboat issue in March looks at what is coming out on the houseboat market for the coming year. **Buys 100 mss/year.** Send complete ms. Length: 850-1,500 words. **Pays $40-285.**

Reprints Send tearsheet, photocopy or typed ms and information about when and where the material previously appeared.

Photos Send photos. Reviews prints, digital images. Offers no additional payment for photos accepted with ms. Buys one-time print rights and Web rights of photos.

Columns/Departments Books Aboard (assigned book reviews), 400 words. **Buys 8-10 mss/year. Pays $40.** Handy Hints (boat improvement or safety projects), 1,000 words. **Buys 8 mss/year. Pays $180.** Heartland Haunts (waterside restaurants, bars or B&Bs), 1,000 words. **Buys 16 mss/year. Pays $160.** Query with published clips or send complete ms.

Tips "We plan the next year's schedule starting in May. So submitting material between May 1 and July 15 is the best way to proceed."

$$ ⊘ HOUSEBOAT MAGAZINE

The Family Magazine for the American Houseboater, Harris Publishing, Inc., 360 B St., Idaho Falls ID 83402. Fax: (208)522-5241. E-mail: blk@houseboatmagazine.com. Website: www.houseboatmagazine.com. **60% freelance written**. "Monthly magazine for houseboaters, who enjoy reading everything that reflects the unique houseboating lifestyle. If it is not a houseboat-specific article, please do not query." Estab. 1990. Circ. 25,000. Byline given. Pays on acceptance. Offers 25% kill fee. Publishes ms an average of 3 months after acceptance. Buys first North American serial rights, buys electronic rights. Editorial lead time 6 months. Submit seasonal material 6 months in advance. Accepts simultaneous submissions. Responds in 1 month to queries. Sample copy for $5. Guidelines by e-mail.

- No unsolicited mss. Accepts queries by mail and fax, but e-mail strongly preferred.

Nonfiction Needs how-to, interview, new product, personal experience, travel. **Buys 36 mss/year.** Query. Length: 1,500-2,200 words. **Pays $200-500.**

Photos Often required as part of submission package. Color prints discouraged. Digital prints are unacceptable. Seldom purchases photos without ms, but occasionally buys cover photos. Captions, model releases required. Reviews transparencies, high-resolution electronic images. Offers no additional payment for photos accepted with ms Buys one-time rights.
Columns/Departments Pays $150-300.
Tips "As a general rule, how-to articles are always in demand. So are stories on unique houseboats or houseboaters. You are less likely to break in with a travel piece that does not revolve around specific people or groups. Personality profile pieces with excellent supporting photography are your best bet."

$$ LAKELAND BOATING

The Magazine for Great Lakes Boaters, O'Meara-Brown Publications, Inc., 727 S. Dearborn, Suite 812, Chicago IL 60605. (312)276-0610. Fax: (312)276-0619. Website: www.lakelandboating.com. **50% freelance written**. Magazine covering Great Lakes boating. Estab. 1946. Circ. 60,000. Byline given. Pays on publication. No kill fee. Buys first North American serial rights. Accepts queries by e-mail. Responds in 4 months to queries. Sample copy for $5.50 and 9 × 12 SAE with 6 first-class stamps. Guidelines free.
Nonfiction Needs book excerpts, historical, how-to, interview, personal experience, photo feature, technical, travel, must relate to boating in Great Lakes. No inspirational, religious, exposÃ˘ or poetry. **Buys 20-30 mss/year.** Length: 300-1,500 words. **Pays $100-600.**
Photos State availability. Captions required. Reviews prefers 35mm transparencies, high-res digital shots. Buys one time rights.
Columns/Departments Bosun's Locker (technical or how-to pieces on boating), 100-1,000 words. 40 Query. **Pays $25-200.**

$ LIVING ABOARD

P.O. Box 91299, Austin TX 78709-1299. (512)892-4446. Fax: (512)892-4448. E-mail: editor@livingaboard.com. Website: www.livingaboard.com. **Contact:** Linda Ridihalgh, editor. **95% freelance written**. Bimonthly magazine covering living on boats/cruising. Estab. 1973. Circ. 10,000. Byline given. Pays on publication. No kill fee. Publishes ms an average of 3-6 months after acceptance. Buys first North American serial rights, buys first rights, buys one-time rights, buys second serial (reprint) rights. Accepts queries by mail, e-mail, fax. Responds in 1-2 weeks to queries. Responds in 1-2 months to mss. Sample copy available online. Guidelines free.
Nonfiction Needs how-to, buy, furnish, maintain, provision a boat, interview, personal experience, technical, as relates to boats, travel, on the water, Cooking Aboard with Recipes. Send complete ms. **Pays 5¢/word.**
Photos Pays $5/photo; $50/cover photo.
Columns/Departments Cooking Aboard (how to prepare healthy and nutritious meals in the confines of a galley; how to entertain aboard a boat), 1,000-1,500 words; Environmental Notebook (articles pertaining to clean water, fish, waterfowl, water environment), 750-1,000 words. 40 mss/year Send complete ms. **Pays 5¢/word**
Tips "Articles should have a positive tone and promote the live aboard lifestyle."

MODERN BOATING

FPC Magazines, 170-180 Bourke Rd., Alexandria NSW 2015 Australia. (61)(2)9353-6666. Fax: (61)(2)9353-6699. Website: www.modernboating.com.au. **Contact:** Daniel Tillack, editor. Biannual magazine covering everything of interest to today's boating enthusiasts. Modern Boating offers readers comprehensive coverage of the latest Australian and international boats, a wide range of practical advice, boat reviews, equipment guides and fascinating destinations. It's Australia's oldest and most respected marine magazine and the only mainstream title to cover both power and sail activities. Target audience: affluent males, aged 25-55, searching for the latest trends in boating. Estab. 1965. Circ. 11,000.
Nonfiction Needs general interest, how-to, interview, new product, travel. Query.

$ NORTHERN BREEZES, SAILING MAGAZINE

Northern Breezes, Inc., 3949 Winnetka Ave. N, Minneapolis MN 55427. Website: www.sailingbreezes.com. **70% freelance written**. Magazine published 8 times/year for the Great Lakes and Midwest sailing community. Focusing on regional cruising, racing, and day sailing. Estab. 1989. Circ. 22,300. Byline given. Pays on publication. No kill fee. Buys first North American serial rights. Editorial lead time 1 months. Submit seasonal material 3 months in advance. Accepts queries by mail, e-mail, fax, phone. Accepts previously published material. Responds in 1 month to queries. Responds in 2 months to mss. Sample copy free. Guidelines available online.

Nonfiction Needs book excerpts, how-to, sailing topics, humor, inspirational, interview, new product, personal experience, photo feature, technical, travel. No boating reviews. **Buys 24 mss/year.** Query with published clips. Length: 300-3,500 words.
Photos Send photos. Captions required. Reviews negatives, 35mm slides, 3 × 5 or 4 × 6 prints. "Digital submission preferred." Offers no additional payment for photos accepted with ms. Buys one time rights.
Columns/Departments This Old Boat (sailboat), 500-1,000 words; Surveyor's Notebook, 500-800 words. 8 Query with published clips. **Pays $50-150.**
Tips "Query with a regional connection already in mind."

$ $ PACIFIC YACHTING

Western Canada's and the Pacific Northwest's Premier Boating Magazine, OP Publishing, Ltd., 200 West Esplanade, Suite 500, Vancouver BC V7M 1A4 Canada. (604)998-3310. Fax: (604)998-3320. E-mail: editor@pacificyachting.com. Website: www.pacificyachting.com. **90% freelance written**. Monthly magazine covering all aspects of recreational boating in the Pacific Northwest. "The bulk of our writers and photographers not only come from the local boating community, many of them were long-time *PY* readers before coming aboard as a contributor. The *PY* reader buys the magazine to read about new destinations or changes to old haunts on the British Columbia coast and the Pacific Northwest and to learn the latest about boats and gear." Circ. 19,000. Byline given. Pays on publication. No kill fee. Publishes ms an average of 6 months after acceptance. Buys first North American serial rights, buys simultaneous rights. Editorial lead time 4 months. Submit seasonal material 6 months in advance. Accepts queries by mail, e-mail, fax. Sample copy for $6.95, plus postage charged to credit card. Guidelines available online.
Nonfiction Needs historical, British Columbia coast only, how-to, humor, interview, personal experience, technical, boating related, travel, cruising, and destination on the British Columbia coast. "No articles from writers who are obviously not boaters!" Query. Length: 1,500-2,000 words. **Pays $150-500. Pays some expenses of writers on assignment for unsolicited articles.**
Photos Send photos. Identification of subjects required. Reviews digital photos transparencies, 4 × 6 prints, and slides. Offers no additional payment for photos accepted with ms. Offers $25-400 for photos accepted alone Buys one-time rights.
Columns/Departments Currents (current events, trade and people news, boat gatherings, and festivities), 50-250 words. Reflections; Cruising, both 800-1,000 words. Query. **Pay varies.**
Tips "Our reader wants you to balance important navigation details with first-person observations, blending the practical with the romantic. Write tight, write short, write with the reader in mind, write to inform, write to entertain. Be specific, accurate, and historic."

$ $ PONTOON & DECK BOAT

Harris Publishing, Inc., 360 B. St., Idaho Falls ID 83402. (208)524-7000. Fax: (208)522-5241. E-mail: blk@pdbmagazine.com. Website: www.pdbmagazine.com. **15% freelance written**. Magazine published 11 times/year. "We are a boating niche publication geared toward the pontoon and deck boating lifestyle and consumer market. Our audience is comprised of people who utilize these boats for varied family activities and fishing. Our magazine is promotional of the PDB industry and its major players. We seek to give the reader a twofold reason to read our publication: to celebrate the lifestyle, and to do it aboard a first-class craft." Estab. 1995. Circ. 84,000. Byline given. Pays on publication. No kill fee. Buys one-time rights. Editorial lead time 2 months. Submit seasonal material 3 months in advance. Accepts simultaneous submissions. Responds in 6 weeks to queries. Responds in 3 months to mss Sample copy and writer's guidelines free
Nonfiction Needs how-to, personal experience, technical, remodeling, rebuilding. We are saturated with travel pieces; no general boating, humor, fiction, or poetry. **Buys 15 mss/year.** Send complete ms. Length: 600-2,000 words. **Pays $50-300.**
Photos State availability. Captions, model releases required. Reviews transparencies. Rights negotiable.
Columns/Departments No Wake Zone (short, fun quips); Better Boater (how-to). 6-12 Query with published clips. **Pays $50-150.**
Tips "Be specific to pontoon and deck boats. Any general boating material goes to the slush pile. The more you can tie together the lifestyle, attitudes, and the PDB industry, the more interest we'll take in what you send us."

$ $ $ POWER & MOTORYACHT

Source Interlink Media, 261 Madison Ave., 6th Floor, New York NY 10016. (212)915-4313. Fax: (212)915-4328. E-mail: diane.byrne@powerandmotoryacht.com. Website: www.powerandmotoryacht.com. **25%**

freelance written. Monthly magazine covering powerboats 24 feet and larger with special emphasis on the 35-foot-plus market. Readers have an average of 33 years experience boating, and we give them accurate advice on how to choose, operate, and maintain their boats as well as what electronics and gear will help them pursue their favorite pastime. In addition, since powerboating is truly a lifestyle and not just a hobby for them, *Power & Motoryacht* reports on a host of other topics that affect their enjoyment of the water: chartering, sportfishing, and the environment, among others. Articles must therefore be clear, concise, and authoritative; knowledge of the marine industry is mandatory. Include personal experience and information for marine industry experts where appropriate. Estab. 1985. Circ. 157,000. Byline given. Pays on acceptance. Offers 33% kill fee. Publishes ms an average of 4-6 months after acceptance. Buys all rights. Editorial lead time 4-6 months. Submit seasonal material 4-6 months in advance. Accepts queries by mail, e-mail. Responds in 1 month to queries. Sample copy for 10 × 12 SASE. Guidelines for #10 SASE or via e-mail.

Nonfiction Needs how-to, interview, personal experience, photo feature, travel. No unsolicited mss or articles about sailboats and/or sailing yachts (including motorsailers or cruise ships). **Buys 20-25 mss/year.** Query with published clips. Length: 800-1,500 words. **Pays $500-1,000 for assigned articles.**

Photos Contact: Aimee Colon, art director. State availability. Captions, identification of subjects required. Reviews 8 × 10 transparencies, GIF/JPEG files (minimum 300 dpi). Offers no additional payment for photos accepted with ms. Buys one-time print and Web rights.

Tips Take a clever or even unique approach to a subject, particularly if the topic is dry/technical. Pitch us on yacht cruises you've taken, particularly if they're in off-the-beaten-path locations.

$$$ ⊘ POWERBOAT

Nordskog Publishing Inc., 2575 Vista Del Mar, Ventura CA 93001. (805)667-4100. Fax: (805)667-4336. Website: www.powerboatmag.com. Jason Johnson, man. ed. **Contact:** Gregg Mansfield, editor. **25% freelance written**. Magazine published 11 times/year covering performance boating. Estab. 1973. Circ. 50,000. Byline given. Pays on publication. Offers negotiable kill fee. Publishes ms an average of 3 months after acceptance. Buys first North American serial rights, buys electronic rights. Editorial lead time 3 months. Submit seasonal material 4 months in advance. Accepts queries by mail, e-mail, fax. Sample copy available online.

- No unsolicited mss.

Nonfiction Features highly focused storied on performance boats and boating. Needs how-to, interview, new product, photo feature. No general interest boating stories. **Buys numerous mss/year.** Query. Length: 300-2,000 words. **Pays $125-1,200.**

Photos State availability. Captions required. Reviews negatives. Buys one time rights.

$$ POWER BOATING CANADA

1020 Brevik Place, Suites 4 & 5, Mississauga ON L4W 4N7 Canada. (905)624-8218. Fax: (905)624-6764. E-mail: editor@powerboating.com. Website: www.powerboating.com. **70% freelance written**. Bimonthly magazine covering recreational power boating. *Power Boating Canada* offers boating destinations, how-to features, boat tests (usually staff written), lifestyle pieces—with a Canadian slant—and appeal to recreational power boaters across the country. Estab. 1984. Circ. 42,000. Byline given. Pays on publication. No kill fee. Publishes ms an average of 3 months after acceptance. Buys first North American serial rights. Editorial lead time 2 months. Submit seasonal material 3 months in advance. Accepts previously published material. Responds in 1 month to queries. Responds in 2 months to mss. Sample copy free.

Nonfiction Any articles related to the sport of power boating, especially boat tests. Needs historical, how-to, interview, personal experience, travel, boating destinations. No general boating articles or personal anectdotes. **Buys 40-50 mss/year.** Query. Length: 1,200-2,500 words. **Pays $150-300 (Canadian).**

Reprints Send photocopy with rights for sale noted and information about when and where the material previously appeared.

Photos Send photos. Captions, identification of subjects required. Reviews contact sheets, negatives, transparencies, prints. Pay varies; no additional payment for photos accepted with ms. Buys one time rights.

$$$ SAIL

98 N. Washington St., 2nd Floor, Boston MA 02114. (617)720-8600. Fax: (617)723-0912. E-mail: amy.ullrich@sourceinterlink.com. Website: www.sailmagazine.com. **30% freelance written**. Monthly magazine written and edited for everyone who sails—aboard a coastal or bluewater cruiser, trailerable, one-design or offshore racer, or daysailer. How-to and technical articles concentrate on techniques of sailing and aspects of design and construction, boat systems, and gear; the feature section emphasizes

the fun and rewards of sailing in a practical and instructive way. Estab. 1970. Circ. 180,000. Byline given. Pays on acceptance. No kill fee. Publishes ms an average of 1 year after acceptance. Buys first North American and other rights. Accepts queries by mail, e-mail, fax. Responds in 3 months to queries. Guidelines for SASE or online (download).

Nonfiction Needs how-to, personal experience, technical, distance cruising, destinations. Cruising, chartering, commissioning, fitting-out, special race (e.g., America's Cup), Top 10 Boats. **Buys 50 mss/year.** Query. Length: 1,500-3,000 words. **Pays $200-800.**

Photos Prefers transparencies. High-resolution digital photos (300 dpi) are also accepted, as are high-quality color prints (preferably with negatives attached). Captions, identification of subjects, True required. Payment varies, up to $1,000 if photo used on cover.

Columns/Departments Sailing Memories (short essay); Sailing News (cruising, racing, legal, political, environmental); Under Sail (human interest). Query. **Pays $50-400.**

Tips Request an articles' specification sheet. We look for unique ways of viewing sailing. Skim old issues of *Sail* for ideas about the types of articles we publish. Always remember that *Sail* is a sailing magazine. Stay away from gloomy articles detailing all the things that went wrong on your boat. Think constructively and write about how to avoid certain problems. You should focus on a theme or choose some aspect of sailing and discuss a personal attitude or new philosophical approach to the subject. Notice that we have certain issues devoted to special themes—for example, chartering, electronics, commissioning, and the like. Stay away from pieces that chronicle your journey in the day-by-day style of a logbook. These are generally dull and uninteresting. Select specific actions or events (preferably sailing events, not shorebound activities), and build your articles around them. Emphasize the sailing.

$$$ SAILING MAGAZINE

125 E. Main St., Port Washington WI 53074-0249. (262)284-3494. Fax: (262)284-7764. E-mail: editorial@sailingmagazine.net. Website: www.sailingmagazine.net. Monthly magazine for the experienced sailor. Estab. 1966. Circ. 45,000. Pays after publication. No kill fee. Buys one-time rights. Accepts queries by mail, e-mail. Responds in 2 months to queries.

Nonfiction "Experiences of sailing, cruising, and racing or cruising to interesting locations, whether a small lake near you or islands in the Southern Ocean, with first-hand knowledge and tips for our readers. Top-notch photos with maps, charts, cruising information complete the package. No regatta sports unless there is a story involved." Needs book excerpts, how-to, tech pieces on boats and gear, interview, personal experience, travel, by sail. **Buys 15-20 mss/year.** Length: 750-2,500 words. **Pays $100-800.**

Photos Captions required. Reviews color transparencies. Pays $50-400.

Tips "Prefers text in Word on disk for Mac or to e-mail address."

$$ SAILING WORLD

World Publications, 55 Hammarlund Way, Middletown RI 02842. (401)845-5100. Fax: (401)848-5180. E-mail: editorial@sailingworld.com. Website: www.sailingworld.com. **40% freelance written**. Magazine published 10 times/year covering performance sailing. Estab. 1962. Circ. 60,000. Byline given. Pays on publication. No kill fee. Publishes ms an average of 4 months after acceptance. Buys first North American serial rights. world serial rights Responds in 1 month to queries. Sample copy for $5.

Nonfiction Needs how-to, for racing and performance-oriented sailors, interview, photo feature, Regatta sports and charter. No travelogs. **Buys 5-10 unsolicited mss/year.** Query. Length: 400-1,500 words. **Pays $400 for up to 2,000 words.** Does not pay expenses of writers on assignment unless pre-approved.

Tips Send query with outline and include your experience. Prospective contributors should study recent issues of the magazine to determine appropriate subject matter. The emphasis here is on performance sailing: keep in mind that the *Sailing World* readership is relatively educated about the sport. Unless you are dealing with a totally new aspect of sailing, you can and should discuss ideas on an advanced technical level. `Gee-whiz' impressions from beginning sailors are generally not accepted.

$$ SEA KAYAKER

Sea Kayaker, Inc., P.O. Box 17029, Seattle WA 98127. (206)789-1326. Fax: (206)781-1141. E-mail: gretchen@seakayakermag.com. Website: www.seakayakermag.com. **95% freelance written**. *Sea Kayaker* is a bimonthly publication with a worldwide readership that covers all aspects of kayak touring. It is well known as an important source of continuing education by the most experienced paddlers. Estab. 1984. Circ. 30,000. Byline given. Pays on publication. Offers 10% kill fee. Publishes ms an average of 6 months after acceptance. Buys first North American serial rights. Editorial lead time 4 months. Submit seasonal material 4 months in advance. Accepts queries by mail, e-mail, fax, phone. Responds in 2 months to queries. Sample copy for $7.30 (US), samples to other countries extra. Guidelines available online.

Nonfiction Needs essays, historical, how-to, on making equipment, humor, new product, personal experience, technical, travel. Unsolicited gear reviews are not accepted. **Buys 50 mss/year.** Send complete ms. Length: 1,500-5,000 words. **Pays 18-20¢/word for assigned articles. Pays 15-17¢/word for unsolicited articles.**

Photos Send photos. Captions, identification of subjects required. Reviews transparencies, prints. Offers $15-400. Buys one time rights.

Columns/Departments Technique; Equipment; Do-It-Yourself; Food; Safety; Health; Environment; Book Reviews; all 1,000-2,500 words. 40-45 Query. **Pays 15-20¢/word.**

Tips We consider unsolicited manuscripts that include a SASE, but we give greater priority to brief descriptions (several paragraphs) of proposed articles accompanied by at least 2 samples—published or unpublished—of your writing. Enclose a statement as to why you're qualified to write the piece and indicate whether photographs or illustrations are available to accompany the piece.

SEA MAGAZINE

America's Western Boating Magazine, Duncan McIntosh Co., 17782 Cowan, Suite A, Irvine CA 92614. (949)660-6150, ext. 253. Fax: (949)660-6172. E-mail: mike@seamag.com. Website: www.goboatingamerica.com. **Contact:** Mike Werling, Managing Editor. Monthly magazine covering West Coast power boating. Estab. 1908. Circ. 50,000. Byline given. Pays on publication. Publishes ms an average of 6 months after acceptance. Buys first North American serial rights. Editorial lead time 3 months. Submit seasonal material 6 months in advance. Accepts simultaneous submissions. Responds in 3 months to queries.

Nonfiction "News you can use is kind of our motto. All articles should aim to help power boat owners make the most of their boating experience." Needs how-to, new product, personal experience, technical, travel. **Buys 36 mss/year.** Send complete ms. Length: 1,000-1,500 words. **Payment varies**

Photos State availability. of photos. Captions, identification of subjects, model releases required. Reviews transparencies, hi-res digital. Offers $50-250/photo. Buys one-time rights.

$$ SOUTHERN BOATING MAGAZINE

The South's Largest Boating Magazine, Southern Boating & Yachting, Inc., 330 N. Andrews Ave., Ft. Lauderdale FL 33301. (954)522-5515. Fax: (954)522-2260. E-mail: sboating@southernboating.com. Website: southernboating.com. **50% freelance written.** Monthly magazine. Upscale monthly yachting magazine focusing on the Southeast U.S., Bahamas, Caribbean, and Gulf of Mexico. Estab. 1972. Circ. 43,000. Byline given. Pays within 30 days of publication. No kill fee. Publishes ms an average of 2 months after acceptance. Buys one-time rights. Editorial lead time 3 months. Submit seasonal material 3 months in advance. Accepts queries by e-mail. Sample copy for $8.

Nonfiction Needs how-to, boat maintenance, travel, boating related, destination pieces. **Buys 50 mss/year.** Query. Length: 900-1,200 words. **Pays $500-750 with art.**

Photos State availability of or send photos. Captions, identification of subjects, model releases required. Reviews transparencies, prints, digital files. Offers $75/photo minimum Buys one time rights.

Columns/Departments Weekend Workshop (how-to/maintenance), 900 words; What's New in Electronics (electronics), 900 words; Engine Room (new developments), 1,000 words. 24 Query first, see media kit for special issue focus. **Pays $600.**

$$$ TRAILER BOATS MAGAZINE

Ehlert Publishing Group, Inc., 20700 Belshaw Ave., Carson CA 90746-3510. (310)537-6322. Fax: (310)537-8735. Website: www.trailerboats.com. **50% freelance written**. Monthly magazine covering legally trailerable power boats and related powerboating activities. Estab. 1971. Circ. 100,000. Byline given. Pays on acceptance. No kill fee. Publishes ms an average of 3 months after acceptance. Buys all rights. Editorial lead time 3 months. Submit seasonal material 5 months in advance. Responds in 1 month to queries. Sample copy for 9 × 12 SAE with 7 first-class stamps.

Nonfiction Needs general interest, trailer boating activities, historical, places, events, boats, how-to, repair boats, installation, etc., interview, personal experience, photo feature, technical, travel, boating travel on water or highways, product evaluations. No How I Spent My Summer Vacation stories, or stories not directly connected to trailerable boats and related activities. **Buys 3-4 unsolicited mss/year.** Query. Length: 1,000-2,500 words. **Pays $150-1,000.**

Photos Send photos. Captions, identification of subjects, model releases required. Reviews transparencies, 2¼ × 2¼ and 35mm slides, and high-resolution digital images (300 dpi). Buys all rights.

Columns/Departments Over the Transom (funny or strange boating photos); Dock Talk (short pieces on boating news, safety, products, profiles of people using boats to do their jobs), all 1,000-1,500 words. 12-13 Query. **Pays $250-500.**

Tips Query should contain short general outline of the intended material; what kind of photos; how the photos illustrate the piece. Write with authority, covering the subject with quotes from experts. Frequent mistakes are not knowing the subject matter or the audience. The writer may have a better chance of breaking in at our publication with short articles and fillers if they are typically hard-to-find articles. We do most major features in-house, but try how-to stories dealing with repairs, installation and towing tips, boat trailer repair. Good color photos will win our hearts every time.

$ WATERFRONT NEWS

Ziegler Publishing Co., Inc., 1515 SW 1st Ave., Ft. Lauderdale FL 33315. (954)524-9450. Fax: (954)524-9464. E-mail: editor@waterfront-news.com. Website: www.waterfront-news.com. **20% freelance written**. Monthly tabloid covering marine and boating topics for the Greater Ft. Lauderdale waterfront community. Estab. 1984. Circ. 20,000. Byline given. Pays on publication. No kill fee. Publishes ms an average of 2 months after acceptance. Buys first rights, buys second serial (reprint) rights, buys simultaneous rights in certain circumstances rights. Submit seasonal material 3 months in advance. Responds in 1 month to queries. Sample copy for sae with 9 × 12 envelope and 4 First-Class stamps.

Nonfiction Needs interview, of people important in boating, i.e., racers, boat builders, designers, etc. from south Florida, Regional articles on south Florida's waterfront issues; marine communities; travel pieces of interest to boaters, including docking information. Length: 500-1,000 words. **Pays $100-125 for assigned articles.**

Photos Send photos. Reviews JPEG/TIFF files.

Tips "No fiction. Keep it under 1,000 words. Photos or illustrations help. Send for a sample copy of *Waterfront News* so you can acquaint yourself with our publication and our unique audience. Although we're not necessarily looking for technical articles, it helps if the writer has sailing or powerboating experience. Writers should be familiar with the region and be specific when dealing with local topics."

$$ WATERWAY GUIDE

326 First St., Suite 400, Annapolis MD 21403. (443)482-9377. Fax: (443)482-9422. Website: www.waterwayguide.com. **Contact:** Gary Reich, managing editor. **90% freelance written**. Triannual magazine covering intracoastal waterway travel for recreational boats. "Writer must be knowledgeable about navigation and the areas covered by the guide." Estab. 1947. Circ. 30,000. Byline given. Pays on publication. No kill fee. Publishes ms an average of 3 months after acceptance. Buys first North American serial rights, buys electronic rights. Makes work-for-hire assignments. Editorial lead time 4 months. Submit seasonal material 3 months in advance. Accepts queries by mail, phone. Responds in 6 weeks to queries. Responds in 2 months to mss. Sample copy for $39.95 with $3 postage.

Nonfiction Needs essays, historical, how-to, photo feature, technical, travel. **Buys 6 mss/year.** Send complete ms. Length: 250-5,000 words. **Pays $50-500.**

Photos Send photos. Captions, identification of subjects required. Reviews transparencies, 3 × 5 prints. Offers $25-50/photo. Buys all rights.

Tips "Must have on-the-water experience and be able to provide new and accurate information on geographic areas covered by *Waterway Guide.*"

$ WAVELENGTH MAGAZINE

Pacific Edge Publishing, 1773 El Verano Dr., Gabriola Island BC V0R 1X6 Canada. (250)247-9093. Fax: (250)247-9083. E-mail: diana@wavelengthmagazine.com. Website: www.wavelengthmagazine.com. **75% freelance written**. Quarterly magazine with a major focus on paddling the Pacific coast. We promote safe paddling, guide paddlers to useful products and services and explore coastal environmental issues. Estab. 1991. Circ. 65,000 print and electronic readers. Byline given. Pays on publication. Publishes ms an average of 4 months after acceptance. Buys first North American serial rights, buys electronic rights. Editorial lead time 4 months. Submit seasonal material 4 months in advance. Accepts queries by mail, e-mail. Sample copy available online. Guidelines available online.

Nonfiction Needs how-to, paddle, travel, humor, new product, personal experience, technical, travel, trips. **Buys 25 mss/year.** Query. Length: 1,000-1,500 words. **Pays $50-75.**

Photos State availability. Captions, identification of subjects required. Reviews low res JPEGs. Offers $25-50/photo. Buys first and electronic rights

Tips You must know paddling—although novice paddlers are welcome. A strong environmental or wilderness appreciation component is advisable. We are willing to help refine work with flexible people. E-mail queries preferred. Check out our Editorial Calendar for our upcoming features.

$$ WOODENBOAT MAGAZINE

The Magazine for Wooden Boat Owners, Builders, and Designers, WoodenBoat Publications, Inc., P.O.

Box 78, Brooklin ME 04616. (207)359-4651. Fax: (207)359-8920. Website: www.woodenboat.com. **50% freelance written**. Bimonthly magazine for wooden boat owners, builders, and designers. We are devoted exclusively to the design, building, care, preservation, and use of wooden boats, both commercial and pleasure, old and new, sail and power. We work to convey quality, integrity, and involvement in the creation and care of these craft, to entertain, inform, inspire, and to provide our varied readers with access to individuals who are deeply experienced in the world of wooden boats. Estab. 1974. Circ. 90,000. Byline given. Pays on publication. Offers variable kill fee. Publishes ms an average of 1 year after acceptance. Buys first North American serial rights. Accepts previously published material. Accepts simultaneous submissions. Responds in 2 months to queries. Responds in 2 months to mss. Sample copy for $5.99. Guidelines available online.

Nonfiction Needs technical, repair, restoration, maintenance, use, design, and building wooden boats. No poetry, fiction. **Buys 50 mss/year.** Query with published clips. Length: 1,500-5,000 words. **Pays $300/1,000 words.**

Reprints Send tearsheet or typed ms with rights for sale noted and information about when and where the material previously appeared.

Photos Send photos. Identification of subjects required. Reviews negatives. Pays $15-75 b&w, $25-350 color. Buys one time rights.

Columns/Departments Currents pays for information on wooden boat-related events, projects, boatshop activities, etc. Uses same columnists for each issue. Length: 250-1,000 words. Send complete information. **Pays $5-50.**

Tips We appreciate a detailed, articulate query letter, accompanied by photos, that will give us a clear idea of what the author is proposing. We appreciate samples of previously published work. It is important for a prospective author to become familiar with our magazine. Most work is submitted on speculation. The most common failure is not exploring the subject material in enough depth.

$$$ YACHTING

2 Park Ave., 9th Fl., New York NY 10016. Fax: (212)779-5479. E-mail: editor@yachtingmagazine.com. Website: www.yachtingmagazine.com. **30% freelance written**. Monthly magazine. Monthly magazine written and edited for experienced, knowledgeable yachtsmen. Estab. 1907. Circ. 132,000. Byline given. Pays on acceptance. No kill fee. Buys first North American serial rights, buys electronic rights. Editorial lead time 2 months. Submit seasonal material 6 months in advance. Accepts queries by mail, e-mail, fax. Responds in 1 month to queries. Responds in 3 months to mss. Sample copy free. Guidelines available online.

Nonfiction Needs personal experience, technical. **Buys 50 mss/year.** Query with published clips. Length: 750-800 words. **Pays $150-1,500.**

Photos Send photos. Captions, identification of subjects, model releases required. Reviews transparencies. Negotiates payment individually.

Tips We require considerable expertise in our writing because our audience is experienced and knowledgeable. Vivid descriptions of quaint anchorages and quainter natives are fine, but our readers want to know how the yachtsmen got there, too. They also want to know how their boats work. *Yachting* is edited for experienced, affluent boatowners—power and sail—who don't have the time or the inclination to read sub-standard stories. They love carefully crafted stories about places they've never been or a different spin on places they have, meticulously reported pieces on issues that affect their yachting lives, personal accounts of yachting experiences from which they can learn, engaging profiles of people who share their passion for boats, insightful essays that evoke the history and traditions of the sport and compelling photographs of others enjoying the game as much as they do. They love to know what to buy and how things work. They love to be surprised. They don't mind getting their hands dirty or saving a buck here and there, but they're not interested in learning how to make a masthead light out of a mayonnaise jar. If you love what they love and can communicate like a pro (that means meeting deadlines, writing tight, being obsessively accurate and never misspelling a proper name), we'd love to hear from you.

General Interest

$ FIT-4-SPORTS

L.L. Cross Inc, P.O. Box 120327, Clermont FL 34712. (321)438-0838. E-mail: lorettalynn@mac.com. Website: www.fit-4-sports.net. **20% freelance written**. Monthly magazine covering sports, fitness, health and adventure. "We write one-on-one interviews with professional athletes, coaches, trainers, as well as content written by doctors, licensed trainers, dietitians, etc. Articles about local athletes as well." Estab.

2003. Circ. 50,000. Byline given. No kill fee. Publishes ms an average of 2-3 months after acceptance. Buys first North American serial rights. Editorial lead time 2-3 months. Submit seasonal material 3-4 months in advance. Accepts queries by mail, e-mail. Accepts simultaneous submissions. Responds in 1-2 weeks to queries. Responds in 2-3 months to mss. Sample copy available online. Guidelines free.

Nonfiction Needs how-to, interview, sports, fitness, health. covering specialty camps, training, interview with professional athletes, trainers, coaches, etc. We do not want generic Q&A, anything that can be read online, stats, etc. **Buys We purchase maybe 3-4 nonfiction articles/year; the rest are written for byline purposes.** Query. **Pays 25¢ for assigned articles. Pays 25¢ for unsolicited articles.**

Photos State availability. Model releases required. Reviews GIF/JPEG files. Buys one-time rights.

Columns/Departments Fish Tails (fishing related articles, non-self promotional, etc.), no more than 50 words. 2-3 **mss/year.** Query. **Pays $-$25.**

Tips "Read publication on website; articles are written for kids and adults. I don't allow guns, tobacco, alcohol, politicians or lawyers to advertise. Keep it clean and healthy. Be informative, get the story behind the story."

$ $ METROSPORTS

New York, MetroSports Publishing, Inc., 259 W. 30th St., 3rd Floor, New York NY 10001. (212)563-7329. Fax: (212)563-7573. Website: www.metrosportsny.com. **50% freelance written**. Monthly magazine covering amateur sports and fitness. We focus on participatory sports (not team sports) for an active, young audience that likes to exercise. Estab. 1987. Circ. 100,000. Byline given. Pays on publication. Offers 50% kill fee. Buys first rights, buys electronic rights. Editorial lead time 3 months. Submit seasonal material 6 months in advance. Accepts queries by mail, e-mail, fax. Accepts previously published material. Accepts simultaneous submissions. Responds in 3-4 weeks to queries. Responds in 1-2 months to mss. Sample copy available online. Guidelines by e-mail.

Nonfiction Needs essays, general interest, historical, how-to, train for a triathlon, train for an adventure race, etc., humor, inspirational, interview, new product, opinion, personal experience, technical, travel. Holiday Gift Guide (December). We don't publish anything related to team sports (basketball, baseball, football, etc.), golf, tennis. **Buys 24 mss/year.** Query with published clips. Length: 800-3,000 words. **Pays $100-300.**

Photos State availability. Captions, identification of subjects required. Reviews slides transparencies, 3 × 5 prints, GIF/JPEG files (300 dpi). Negotiates payment individually. Buys one time rights.

Columns/Departments Running (training, nutrition, profiles); Cycling (training, nutrition, profiles), both 800 words. 15 Query with published clips. **Pays $100-250.**

Tips Read the magazine, know what we cover. E-mail queries or mail with published clips. No phone calls, please.

$ OUTDOORS NW

PMB 3311, 10002 Aurora Ave. N. #36, Seattle WA 98133. (206)418-0747. Fax: (206)418-0746. E-mail: info@outdoorsnw.com. Website: www.outdoorsnw.com. **80% freelance written**. Monthly magazine covering outdoor recreation in the Pacific Northwest. "Writers must have a solid knowledge of the sport they are writing about. They must be doers." Estab. 1988. Circ. 40,000. Byline given. Pays on publication. No kill fee. Publishes ms an average of 3 months after acceptance. Buys first rights. Editorial lead time 2 months. Submit seasonal material 4 months in advance. Accepts queries by mail, e-mail, fax. Accepts previously published material. Accepts simultaneous submissions. Sample copy and writer's guidelines for $3.

- Publication changed it's name from Sports Etc.

Nonfiction Needs interview, new product, travel. Query with published clips. Length: 750-1,500 words. **Pays $25-125.**

Photos Send photos. Captions, identification of subjects, model releases required. Reviews electronic images only. Buys all rights.

Columns/Departments Faces, Places, Puruits (750 words). 4-6 Query with published clips. **Pays $40-75.**

Tips "*Outdoors NW* is written for the serious Pacific Northwest outdoor recreationalist. The magazine's look, style and editorial content actively engage the reader, delivering insightful perspectives on the sports it has come to be known for—alpine skiing, bicycling, adventure racing, triathlon and multi-sport, hiking, kayaking, marathons, mountain climbing, Nordic skiing, running, and snowboarding. *Outdoors NW* magazine wants vivid writing, telling images, and original perspectives to produce its smart, entertaining monthly."

$ SILENT SPORTS

Waupaca Publishing Co., P.O. Box 152, Waupaca WI 54981-9990. (715)258-5546. Fax: (715)258-8162. E-mail: info@silentsports.net. Website: www.silentsports.net. **75% freelance written**. Monthly magazine covering running, cycling, cross-country skiing, canoeing, kayaking, snowshoeing, in-line skating, camping, backpacking, and hiking aimed at people in Wisconsin, Minnesota, northern Illinois, and portions of Michigan and Iowa. Not a coffee table magazine. Our readers are participants from rank amateur weekend athletes to highly competitive racers. Estab. 1984. Circ. 10,000. Byline given. Pays on publication. Offers 20% kill fee. Publishes ms an average of 3 months after acceptance. Buys one-time rights. Submit seasonal material 4 months in advance. Accepts queries by mail, e-mail, fax. Accepts previously published material. Responds in 3 months to queries. Sample copy and writer's guidelines for 10 × 13 SAE with 7 first-class stamps.

- The editor needs local angles on in-line skating, recreation bicycling, and snowshoeing.

Nonfiction All stories/articles must focus on the Upper Midwest. Needs general interest, how-to, interview, opinion, technical, travel. **Buys 25 mss/year.** Query. 2,500 words maximum. **Pays $15-100.**

Reprints Send typed manuscript with rights for sale noted and information about when and where the material previously appeared. Pays 50% of amount paid for an original article.

Photos State availability. Reviews transparencies. Pays $5-15 for b&w story photos; $50-100 for color covers. Buys one time rights.

Tips Where-to-go and personality profiles are areas most open to freelancers. Writers should keep in mind that this is a regional, Midwest-based publication. We want only stories/articles with a focus on our region.

$$ TWIN CITIES SPORTS

Twin Cities Sports Publishing, Inc., 3009 Holmes Ave. S., Minneapolis MN 55408. (612)825-1034. Fax: (612)825-6452. E-mail: laurie@twincitiessports.com. Website: www.twincitiessports.com. **75% freelance written**. Monthly magazine covering amateur sports and fitness. We focus on participatory sports (not team sports) for an active, young audience that likes to exercise. Estab. 1987. Circ. 40,000. Byline given. Pays on publication. Offers 50% kill fee. Publishes ms an average of 2 months after acceptance. Buys first rights, buys electronic rights. Editorial lead time 3 months. Submit seasonal material 6 months in advance. Accepts queries by mail, e-mail, fax. Accepts previously published material. Accepts simultaneous submissions. Responds in 3-4 weeks to queries. Responds in 1-2 months to mss. Sample copy available online. Guidelines by e-mail.

Nonfiction Needs essays, general interest, historical, how-to, train for a triathlon, set a new 5K P.R., train for an adventure race, humor, inspirational, interview, new product, opinion, personal experience, technical, travel. Holiday Gift Guide (December) We don't publish anything related to team sports (basketball, baseball, football, etc.), golf, tennis. **Buys 24 mss/year.** Query with published clips. Length: 800-3,000 words. **Pays $100-300.**

Photos State availability. Captions, identification of subjects required. Reviews slides transparencies, 3 × 5 prints, GIF/JPEG files (300 dpi). Negotiates payment individually. Buys one time rights.

Columns/Departments Running (training, nutrition, profiles), 800 words; Cycling (training, nutrition, profiles), 800 words; Cool Down (first-person essay), 800-1,000 words. 15 Query with published clips. **Pays $100-250.**

Tips Read the magazine, know what we cover. E-mail queries or mail with published clips. No phone calls, please.

Golf

$$ AFRICAN AMERICAN GOLFER'S DIGEST

Nation's leading publication for avid black golfers, 139 Fulton St.; Suite 209, New York NY 10038. (212)571-6559. E-mail: debertcook@aol.com. Website: www.africanamericangolfersdigest.com. **100% freelance written**. Quarterly magazine covering golf lifestyle, health, travel destinations and reviews, golf equipment, golfer profiles. Editorial should focus on interests of our market demographic of African Americans with historical, artistic, musical, educational (higher learning), automotive, sports, fashion, entertainment, and other categories of high interest to them. Estab. 2003. Circ. 20,000. Byline given. No kill fee. Publishes ms an average of 3 months after acceptance. Buys all rights. Editorial lead time 3-6 months. Submit seasonal material 3-6 months in advance. Accepts queries by e-mail. Accepts simultaneous submissions. Responds in 3 weeks to queries. Responds in 3 months to mss. Sample copy for $4.99. Guidelines by e-mail.

Nonfiction Needs how-to, interview, new product, personal experience, photo feature, technical, travel., golf-related. **Buys 3 mss/year.** Query. Length: 250-1,500 words. **Pays 25-50¢/word.**
Photos State availability. Captions, identification of subjects, model releases required. Reviews GIF/JPEG files (300 dpi or higher at 4x6). Negotiates payment individually. Buys all rights.
Columns/Departments Profiles (celebrities, national leaders, entertainers, corporate leaders, etc., who golf); Travel (destination/golf course reviews); Golf Fashion (jewelry, clothing, accessories). 3 Query. **Pays 25-50¢/word.**
Fillers Needs anecdotes, facts, gags, newsbreaks, short humor. Buys 3 mss/year. Length: 20-125 words. **Pays 25-50¢/word.**
Tips Emphasize golf and African American appeal.

$ $ ARIZONA, THE STATE OF GOLF

Arizona Golf Association, 7226 N. 16th St., Suite 200, Phoenix AZ 85020. (602)944-3035. Fax: (602)944-3228. Website: www.azgolf.org. **Contact:** Brian Foster, director of marketing and communications. **50% freelance written**. Quarterly magazine covering golf in Arizona, the official publication of the Arizona Golf Association. Estab. 1999. Circ. 45,000. Byline given. Pays on acceptance. No kill fee. Buys all rights. Editorial lead time 6 months. Submit seasonal material 3 months in advance. Accepts queries by mail. Accepts previously published material. Accepts simultaneous submissions. Sample copy and writer's guidelines free
Nonfiction Needs book excerpts, essays, historical, how-to, golf, humor, inspirational, interview, new product, opinion, personal experience, photo feature, travel, destinations. **Buys 5-10 mss/year.** Query. Length: 500-2,000 words. **Pays $50-500.**
Photos State availability. Captions, identification of subjects required. Reviews contact sheets. Negotiates payment individually. Rights purchased varies.
Columns/Departments Short Strokes (golf news and notes), Improving Your Game (golf tips), Out of Bounds (guest editorial, 800 words). Query.

$ $ $ GOLF CANADA

Official Magazine of the Royal Canadian Golf Association, RCGA/Relevant Communications, Golf House Suite 1, 1333 Dorval Dr., Oakville ON L6M 4X7 Canada. (905)849-9700. Fax: (905)845-7040. Website: www.rcga.org. **80% freelance written**. Magazine published 5 times/year covering Canadian golf. *Golf Canada* is the official magazine of the Royal Canadian Golf Association, published to entertain and enlighten members about RCGA-related activities and to generally support and promote amateur golf in Canada. Estab. 1994. Circ. 159,000. Byline given. Pays on acceptance. Offers 100% kill fee. Buys first translation, electronic rights. Editorial lead time 3 months. Submit seasonal material 6 months in advance. Accepts queries by mail, e-mail, fax, phone. Accepts previously published material. Sample copy free.
Nonfiction Needs historical, interview, new product, opinion, photo feature, travel. No professional golf-related articles **Buys 42 mss/year.** Query with published clips. Length: 750-3,000 words. **Pays 60¢/ word, including electronic rights.**
Photos State availability. Captions required. Reviews contact sheets, negatives, transparencies, prints. Negotiates payment individually. Buys all rights.
Columns/Departments Guest Column (focus on issues surrounding the Canadian golf community), 700 words. Query. **Pays 60¢/word, including electronic rights**
Tips Keep story ideas focused on Canadian competitive golf.

$ $ $ GOLFING MAGAZINE

Golfer Magazine, Inc., 205 Broad St., Wethersfield CT 06109. (860)563-1633. Fax: (646)607-3001. E-mail: tlanders@golfingmagazine.net. Website: www.golfingmagazineonline.com. **30% freelance written**. Bimonthly magazine covering golf, including travel, products, player profiles and company profiles. Estab. 1999. Circ. 175,000. Byline given. Pays on publication. Offers negotiable kill fee. Buys one-time rights, buys simultaneous rights. Editorial lead time 2 months. Submit seasonal material 2 months in advance. Accepts queries by mail, e-mail. Accepts previously published material. Sample copy free.
Nonfiction All articles must include golf-related tips. Needs book excerpts, new product, photo feature, travel. **Buys 4-5 mss/year.** Query. Length: 700-2,500 words. **Pays $250-1,000 for assigned articles. Pays $100-500 for unsolicited articles.**
Photos State availability. Captions required. Reviews GIF/JPEG files. Negotiates payment and rights individually.

$$ GOLF NEWS MAGAZINE

Premier Golf Magazine Since 1984, Golf News Magazine, P.O. Box 1040, Rancho Mirage CA 92270. (760)321-8800. Fax: (760)328-3013. E-mail: golfnews@aol.com. Website: www.golfnewsmag.com. **40% freelance written**. Monthly magazine covering golf. Our publication specializes in the creative treatment of the sport of golf, offering a variety of themes and slants as related to golf. If it's good writing and relates to golf, we're interested. Estab. 1984. Circ. 15,000. Byline given. Pays on acceptance. Publishes ms an average of 3 months after acceptance. Buys first rights. Editorial lead time 2 months. Submit seasonal material 2 months in advance. Accepts queries by mail, e-mail, fax. Accepts previously published material. Accepts simultaneous submissions. Responds in 3 weeks to queries. Responds in 3 weeks to mss. Sample copy for $2 and 9 × 12 SAE with 4 first-class stamps.

Nonfiction We will consider any topic related to golf that is written well with high standards. Needs book excerpts, essays, expose, general interest, historical, humor, inspirational, interview, opinion, personal experience, real estate. **Buys 20 mss/year.** Query with published clips. **Pays $75-350.**

Photos State availability. Identification of subjects required. Negotiates payment individually. Buys one time rights.

Columns/Departments Submit ideas. 10 Query with published clips.

Tips Solid, creative, excellent, professional writing. Only good writers need apply. We are a national award-winning magazine looking for the most creative writers we can find.

GOLF TEACHING PRO

United States Golf Teachers Federation, 1295 S.E. Port St. Lucie Blvd., Port St. Lucie FL 34952. (772)335-3216. Fax: (772)335-3822. E-mail: info@usgtf.com. Website: www.golfteachingpro.com. **80% freelance written**. Quarterly magazine covering golf teaching related subjects only. Estab. 1989. Circ. 18,000+. Byline sometimes given. Pays on acceptance. No kill fee. Publishes ms an average of 2-3 months after acceptance. Editorial lead time 2-3 months. Submit seasonal material 2-3 months in advance. Accepts queries by mail, e-mail, fax, phone. Accepts previously published material. Accepts simultaneous submissions. Sample copy available online. Guidelines by e-mail.

Nonfiction Contact: Geoff Bryant. Needs book excerpts, general interest, historical, how-to, golf tips, humor, inspirational, interview, new product, opinion, personal experience, photo feature, technical, all golf teaching related subjects. Query. (limit agreed upon in advance)

Photos Send photos. Offers no additional payment for photos accepted with ms.

Columns/Departments Query.

Fiction Query.

Poetry Query.

Fillers Query.

$$$ GOLF TIPS

The Game's Most In-Depth Instruction & Equipment Magazine, Werner Publishing Corp., 12121 Wilshire Blvd., Suite 1200, Los Angeles CA 90025. E-mail: editors@golftipsmag.com. Website: www.golftipsmag.com. **95% freelance written**. Magazine published 9 times/year covering golf instruction and equipment. We provide mostly concise, very clear golf instruction pieces for the serious golfer. Estab. 1986. Byline given. Pays on publication. Offers 33% kill fee. Publishes ms an average of 2 months after acceptance. Buys first rights, buys second serial (reprint) rights. Editorial lead time 3 months. Submit seasonal material 4 months in advance. Accepts previously published material. Responds in 1 month to queries. Sample copy free Guidelines available online.

Nonfiction Needs book excerpts, how-to, interview, new product, photo feature, technical, travel, all golf related. Generally golf essays rarely make it. **Buys 125 mss/year.** Send complete ms. Length: 250-2,000 words. **Pays $300-1,000 for assigned articles. Pays $300-800 for unsolicited articles.**

Photos State availability. Captions, identification of subjects required. Reviews 2 × 2 transparencies. Negotiates payment individually. Buys all rights.

Columns/Departments Stroke Saver (very clear, concise instruction), 350 words; Lesson Library (book excerpts—usually in a series), 1,000 words; Travel Tips (formatted golf travel), 2,500 words. 40 Query with or without published clips or send complete ms. **Pays $300-850.**

Tips Contact a respected PGA Professional and find out if they're interested in being published. A good writer can turn an interview into a decent instruction piece.

$$$ MINNESOTA GOLFER

6550 York Ave. S., Suite 211, Edina MN 55435. (952)927-4643. Fax: (952)927-9642. E-mail: wp@mngolf.org. Website: www.mngolfer.com. **75% freelance written**. Bimonthly magazine covering golf in

Minnesota, the official publication of the Minnesota Golf Association. Estab. 1975. Circ. 66,000. Byline given. Pays on acceptance or publication. No kill fee. Buys first rights. Editorial lead time 3 months. Accepts queries by mail, e-mail, fax.

Nonfiction Needs historical, interview, new product, travel, book reviews, instruction, golf course previews. Query with published clips. Length: 400-2,000 words. **Pays $50-750.**

Photos State availability. Captions, identification of subjects required. Reviews contact sheets, transparencies, digital images. Negotiates payment individually. Image rights by assignment.

Columns/Departments Punch shots (golf news and notes); Q School (news and information targeted to beginners, junior golfers and women); Great Drives (featuring noteworthy golf holes in Minnesota); Instruction.

$$ N TEXAS GOLFER MAGAZINE

Consumer Guide, Inc., 9894 Bissonnet, Suite 900, Houston TX 77036. (713)417-6152. Fax: (866)901-7891. Website: http://www.texasgolfermagazine.com. **Contact:** George Fuller, editor-in-chief. **10% freelance written**. Bi-monthly magazine covering golf in Texas. Estab. 1984. Circ. 50,000. Byline given. Pays 10 days after publication. No kill fee. Publishes ms an average of 2 months after acceptance. Buys first rights, buys one-time rights, buys second serial (reprint) rights. Editorial lead time 2 months. Submit seasonal material 3 months in advance. Responds in 2 weeks to queries. Responds in 1 month to mss. Sample copy free. Prefers direct phone discussion for writer's guidelines.

- *Texas Golfer Magazine* was created by the merger of two publications: *Gulf Coast Golfer* and *North Texas Golfer*.

Nonfiction Needs book excerpts, humor, personal experience, all golf-related. Travel pieces accepted about golf outside of Texas. **Buys 20 mss/year.** Query. **Pays 25-40¢/word.**

Photos State availability. Captions, identification of subjects required. Reviews contact sheets, prints. No additional payment for photos accepted with ms, but pays $125 for cover photo. Buys one time rights.

Tips "Most of our purchases are in the how-to area, so writers must know golf quite well and play the game."

$$ VIRGINIA GOLFER

Touchpoint Publishing, Inc., 600 Founders Bridge Blvd., Midlothian VA 23113. (804)378-2300. Fax: (804)378-2369. Website: www.vsga.org. **65% freelance written**. Bimonthly magazine covering golf in Virginia, the official publication of the Virginia State Golf Association. Estab. 1983. Circ. 45,000. Byline given. Pays on publication. No kill fee. Buys all rights. Editorial lead time 6 months. Submit seasonal material 3 months in advance. Accepts queries by mail, e-mail. Accepts previously published material. Accepts simultaneous submissions. Sample copy and writer's guidelines free

Nonfiction Needs book excerpts, essays, historical, how-to, golf, humor, inspirational, interview, personal experience, photo feature, technical, golf equipment, where to play, golf business. **Buys 30-40 mss/year.** Send complete ms. Length: 500-2,500 words. **Pays $50-200.**

Photos State availability. Captions, identification of subjects required. Reviews contact sheets. Negotiates payment individually. Rights purchased varies.

Columns/Departments Chip ins & Three Putts (news notes), Rules Corner (golf rules explanations and discussion), Your Game, Golf Travel (where to play), Great Holes, Q&A, Golf Business (what's happening?), Fashion. Query.

Guns

$$ N GUN DIGEST THE MAGAZINE

F+W Media, 700 E. State St., Iola WI 54990. (715)445-2214. Fax: (715)445-4087. E-mail: kevin.michalowski@fwmedia.com. Website: http://www.gundigest.com. **Contact:** Kevin Michalowski, senior editor. **Uses 90% freelancers**. Bimonthly magazine covering firearms. "Gun Digest the Magazine covers all aspects of the firearms community; from collectible guns to tactical gear to reloading and accessories. We also publish gun reviews and tests of new and collectible firearms and news features about firearms legislation. We are 100 percent pro-gun, fully support the NRA and make no bones about our support of Constitutional freedoms." Byline given. Pays on publication. 2 months 3 months 3 months Accepts queries by e-mail. Responds in 3 weeks on queries; 1 month on mss. Free sample copy. Guidelines available via e-mail.

Nonfiction "Keep in mind that Writer's Market goes on sale each year in September. List only one-shot issues for which writers will have time to contact you." Needs general interest (firearms related), historical, how-to, interview, new product, nostalgic, profile, technical, All submissions must focus on firearms, accessories or the firearms industry and legislation. Stories that include hunting reference must have as their focus the firearms or ammunition used. The hunting should be secondary. Gun Digest the Magazine also publishes an annual gear guide and 4 issues each year of Tactical Gear Magazine. Tactical Gear is designed for readers interested in self-defense, police and military gear including guns, knives, accessories and fitness. We do not publish "Me and Joe" hunting stories. **Buys 50-75 mss/year.** Query. 500-3,500 max. **$175-500 for assigned and for unsolicited articles. Does not pay in contributor copies. Does not pay expenses.**

Photos Send photos. with submission. Requires captions, identification of subjects. Reviews GIF/JPEG files (and TIF files); 300 DPI submitted on a CD (size) Offers no additional payment for photos accepted with ms. Buys all rights.

Tips "Be an expert in your field. Submit clear copy using the AP stylebook as your guide. Submissions are most easily handled if submitted on a CD. Ms should be saved as an MS Word Doc with photo captions at the bottom of the text. Photo captions and files should have the same names. Do not send mss with photos embedded. Well-researched stories about odd or interesting firearms are always welcomed, should have solid photo support. The Senior Editor will assign gun reviews and tests."

N ⊕ GUNS AUSTRALIA

Yaffa Publishing, 17-21 Bellevue St., Surry Hills NSW 2010 Australia. (61)(2)9281-2333. Fax: (61)(2)9281-2750. E-mail: yaffa@yaffa.com.au. Website: www.yaffa.com.au. Quarterly magazine delivering comprehensive reviews and the enjoyment of shooting and collecting. "The readers of *Guns Australia* are committed to gun ownership and collecting, target shooting and hunting in Australia."

Nonfiction Needs general interest, how-to, interview, new product. Query.

$$ MUZZLE BLASTS

National Muzzle Loading Rifle Association, P.O. Box 67, Friendship IN 47021. (812)667-5131. Fax: (812)667-5136. E-mail: mblastdop@seidata.com. Website: www.nmlra.org. **65% freelance written**. Monthly magazine. "Articles must relate to muzzleloading or the muzzleloading era of American history." Estab. 1939. Circ. 18,500. Byline given. Pays on publication. Offers $50 kill fee. Publishes ms an average of 6 months after acceptance. Buys first North American serial rights, buys one-time rights, buys second serial (reprint) rights. Editorial lead time 4 months. Submit seasonal material 6 months in advance. Responds in 1 month to mss. Sample copy and writer's guidelines free

Nonfiction Needs book excerpts, general interest, historical, how-to, humor, interview, new product, personal experience, photo feature, technical, travel. No subjects that do not pertain to muzzleloading. **Buys 80 mss/year.** Query. Length: 2,500 words. **Pays $150 minimum for assigned articles. Pays $50 minimum for unsolicited articles.**

Photos Send photos. Captions, model releases required. Reviews 5 × 7 prints. Negotiates payment individually. Buys one time rights.

Columns/Departments Query. **Pays $50-200.**

Fiction Must pertain to muzzleloading. Needs adventure, historical, humorous. **Buys 6 mss/year.** Query. Length: 2,500 words. **Pays $50-300.**

Hiking & Backpacking

$$$$ BACKPACKER MAGAZINE

Cruz Bay Publishing, Inc., an Active Interest Media Co., 2520 55th St., Suite 210, Boulder CO 80301. E-mail: jdorn@backpacker.com. Website: www.backpacker.com. Tracy Ross, senior editor, tross@backpacker.com; Dennis Lewon, exec. editor. **Contact:** Jonathan Dorn, editor-in-chief. **50% freelance written**. Magazine published 9 times/year covering wilderness travel for backpackers. Estab. 1973. Circ. 340,000. Byline given. Pays on acceptance. No kill fee. Buys one-time rights, buys all rights. 6 months Accepts queries by mail (include SASE for returns), e-mail (preferred, with attachments and web links), fax. Responds in 2-4 weeks to queries. Free sample copy. Guidelines available online.

Nonfiction What we want are features that let us and the readers `feel' the place, and experience your wonderment, excitement, disappointment, or other emotions encountered 'out there.' If we feel like we've been there after reading your story, you've succeeded. Needs essays, expose, historical, how-to, humor, inspirational, interview, new product, personal experience, technical, travel, BACKPACKER primarily covers hiking. When warranted, we cover canoeing, kayaking, snowshoeing, cross-country skiing, and other human-powered modes of travel. Wilderness or backcountry: The true backpacking experience means getting away from the trailhead and into the wilds. Whether a dayhike or a weeklong trip, out-of-the-way, unusual destinations are what we're looking for. No step-by-step accounts of what

you did on your summer vacation—stories that chronicle every rest stop and gulp of water. Query with published clips before sending complete ms. Length: 750-4,000 words. **Pays 60¢-$1/word.**
Photos State availability. Payment varies. Buys one time rights.
Columns/Departments Signpost, News From All Over (adventure, environment, wildelife, trails, techniques, organizations, special interests—well-written, entertaining, short, newsy item), 50-500 words; Getaways (great hiking destinations, primarily North America), includes weekend, 250-500 words, weeklong, 250-1000, multi-destination guides, 500-1500 words, and dayhikes, 50-200 words, plus travel news and other items; Fitness (in-the-field health column), 750-1,200 words; Food (food-related aspects of wilderness: nutrition, cooking techniques, recipes, products and gear), 500-750 words; Know How (ranging from beginner to expert focus, written by people with solid expertise, details ways to improve performance, how-to-do-it instructions, information on equipment manufacturers, and places readers can go), 300-1,000 words; Senses (capturing a moment in backcountry through sight, sound, smell, and other senses, paired with an outstanding photo), 150-200 words. 50-75
Tips Our best advice is to read the publication—most freelancers don't know the magazine at all. The best way to break in is with an article for the Weekend Wilderness, Know How, or Signpost Department.

Hockey

$$ MINNESOTA HOCKEY JOURNAL

Official Publication of Minnesota Hockey, Inc., c/o Touchpoint Sports 505, Hwy 169 North, Ste. 465, Minneapolis MN 55441. (763)595-0808. Fax: (763)595-0016. E-mail: greg@touchpointsports.com. Website: www.touchpointsports.com. **50% freelance written**. Journal published 4 times/year. Estab. 2000. Circ. 40,000. Byline given. Pays on publication. No kill fee. Buys all rights. Editorial lead time 6 months. Submit seasonal material 4 months in advance. Accepts previously published material. Accepts simultaneous submissions. Sample copy and writer's guidelines free
Nonfiction Needs essays, general interest, historical, how-to, play hockey, humor, inspirational, interview, new product, opinion, personal experience, photo feature, travel, hockey camps, pro hockey, juniors, college, Olympics, youth, etc. **Buys 3-5 mss/year.** Query. Length: 500-1,500 words. **Pays $100-300.**
Photos State availability. Captions, identification of subjects required. Reviews contact sheets. Negotiates payment individually. Rights purchased vary.

$$$ USA HOCKEY MAGAZINE

Official Publication of USA Hockey, Touchpoint Sports, 505 Hwy 169 North, Ste 465, Minneapolis MN 55441. (763)595-0808. Fax: (763)595-0016. E-mail: info@touchpointsports.com. Website: www.usahockey.com. **60% freelance written**. Magazine published 10 times/year covering amateur hockey in the US. The world's largest hockey magazine, *USA Hockey Magazine* is the official magazine of USA Hockey, Inc., the national governing body of hockey. Estab. 1980. Circ. 444,000. Byline given. Pays on acceptance or publication. No kill fee. Buys all rights. Editorial lead time 6 months. Submit seasonal material 4 months in advance. Accepts previously published material. Accepts simultaneous submissions. Sample copy and writer's guidelines free
Nonfiction Needs essays, general interest, historical, how-to, play hockey, humor, inspirational, interview, new product, opinion, personal experience, photo feature, travel, hockey camps, pro hockey, juniors, college, NCAA hockey championships, Olympics, youth, etc. **Buys 20-30 mss/year.** Query. Length: 500-5,000 words. **Pays $50-750.**
Photos State availability. Captions, identification of subjects required. Reviews contact sheets. Negotiates payment individually. Rights purchased varies.
Columns/Departments Short Cuts (news and notes); Coaches' Corner (teaching tips); USA Hockey; Inline Notebook (news and notes). **Pays $150-250.**
Fiction Needs adventure, humorous, slice-of-life vignettes. **Buys 10-20 mss/year. Pays $150-1,000.**
Tips Writers must have a general knowledge and enthusiasm for hockey, including ice, inline, street, and other. The primary audience is youth players in the US.

Horse Racing

THE AMERICAN QUARTER HORSE RACING JOURNAL

American Quarter Horse Association, P.O. Box 32470, Amarillo TX 79120. (806)376-4811. Website: www.aqha.com/magazines. **10% freelance written**. Monthly magazine promoting American Quarter Horse racing. Articles include training, breeding, nutrition, sports medicine, health, history, etc. Estab. 1988. Circ. 9,000. Pays on acceptance. No kill fee. Publishes ms an average of 3 months after acceptance. Buys first North American serial rights. Submit seasonal material 3 months in advance. Accepts queries by mail. Accepts previously published material. Responds in 1 month to queries. Sample copy and writer's guidelines free

Nonfiction Needs historical, must be on Quarter Horses or people associated with them, how-to, training, opinion, nutrition, health, breeding. Query. Length: 700-1,500 words.

Reprints Send photocopy and information about when and where the material previously appeared.

Photos Send photos. Captions, identification of subjects required. Additional payment for photos accepted with ms might be offered.

Tips Query first—you must be familiar with Quarter Horse racing and be knowledgeable of the sport. The *Journal* directs its articles to those who own, train and breed racing Quarter Horses, as well as fans and handicappers. Most open to features covering breeding, raising, training, nutrition and health care utilizing knowledgeable sources with credentials.

$ $ AMERICAN TURF MONTHLY

All Star Sports, Inc., 747 Middle Neck Rd., Suite 103, Great Neck NY 11024. (516)773-4075. Fax: (516)773-2944. E-mail: editor@americanturf.com. Website: www.americanturf.com. **90% freelance written**. Monthly magazine covering Thoroughbred racing, handicapping, and wagering. Squarely focused on Thoroughbred handicapping and wagering. *ATM* is a magazine for horseplayers, not owners, breeders, or 12-year-old girls enthralled with ponies. Estab. 1946. Circ. 28,000. Byline given. Pays on publication. No kill fee. Publishes ms an average of 4 months after acceptance. Makes work-for-hire assignments. Editorial lead time 2 months. Submit seasonal material 2 months in advance. Accepts queries by mail, e-mail. Responds in 1 month to queries. Sample copy and writer's guidelines free

Nonfiction Handicapping and wagering features. Triple Crown/Kentucky Derby (May); Saratoga/Del Mar (August); Breeder's Cup (November) No historical essays, bilious 'guest editorials,' saccharine poetry, fiction. **Buys 50 mss/year.** Query. Length: 800-2,000 words. **Pays $75-300 for assigned articles. Pays $100-500 for unsolicited articles.**

Photos Send photos. Identification of subjects required. Reviews 3 × 5 transparencies, prints, 300 dpi TIF images on CD-ROM. Offers $25 interior; $150 for cover. Buys one time rights.

Tips Send a good query letter specifically targeted at explaining how this contribution will help our readers to cash a bet at the track!

$ $ HOOF BEATS

United States Trotting Association, 750 Michigan Ave., Columbus OH 43215. Fax: (614)222-6791. E-mail: hoofbeats@ustrotting.com. Website: www.hoofbeatsmagazine.com. **60% freelance written**. Monthly magazine covering harness racing and standardbred horses. "Articles and photos must relate to harness racing or standardbreds. We do not accept any topics that do not touch on these 2 subjects." Estab. 1933. Circ. 13,500. Byline given. Pays on publication. Offers 25% kill fee. Publishes ms an average of 2-4 months after acceptance. Buys first North American serial rights, buys second serial (reprint) rights, buys simultaneous rights, buys electronic rights. Makes work-for-hire assignments. Editorial lead time 6 months. Submit seasonal material 6 months in advance. Accepts queries by mail, e-mail, fax. Accepts previously published material. Accepts simultaneous submissions. Responds in 2 weeks to queries. Responds in 1 month to mss. Sample copy available online. Guidelines free.

Nonfiction Needs general interest, how-to, interview, personal experience, photo feature, technical. "We do not want any fiction or poetry." **Buys 48-72 mss/year.** Query. Length: 750-3,000 words. **Pays $100-500. Pays $100-500 for unsolicited articles.**

Photos State availability. Identification of subjects required. Reviews contact sheets. We offer $25-100 per photo. Buys one-time rights.

Columns/Departments Equine Clinic (standardbreds who overcame major health issues), 900-1,200 words; Profiles (short profiles on people or horses in harness racing), 600-1,000 words; Industry Trends (issues impacting standardbreds & harness racing), 1,000-2,000 words. 60 mss/year Query. **Pays $100-500.**

Tips "We welcome new writers who know about harness racing or are willing to learn about it. Make sure to read *Hoof Beats* before querying to see our slant & style. We look for informative/promotional stories on harness racing—not exposés on the sport."

Hunting & Fishing

$ $ ALABAMA GAME & FISH

Game & Fish, 2250 Newmarket Parkway, Suite 110, Marietta GA 30067. (770)953-9222. Fax: (678)279-

7512. Website: www.alabamagameandfish.com. See *Game & Fish*. No kill fee.

$ $ AMERICAN ANGLER

735 Broad St., Augusta GA 30904. E-mail: russ.lumpkin@morris.com. Website: www.flyfishingmagazines.com. **95% freelance written**. Bimonthly magazine covering fly fishing. *American Angler* is dedicated to giving fly fishers practical information they can use—wherever they fish, whatever they fish for. Estab. 1976. Circ. 60,000. Byline given. Pays on publication. No kill fee. Publishes ms an average of 6 months after acceptance. Buys first North American serial rights, buys one-time rights. Editorial lead time 3 months. Submit seasonal material 5 months in advance. Accepts queries by mail, fax. Accepts previously published material. Accepts simultaneous submissions. Responds in 6 weeks to queries. Responds in 2 months to mss. Sample copy for $6. Guidelines for #10 SASE.

Nonfiction Needs how-to, most important, personal experience, photo feature, seldom, technical. No promotional flack fo pay back free trips or freebies, no superficial, broad-brush coverage of subjects. **Buys 45-60 mss/year.** Query with published clips. Length: 800-2,200 words. **Pays $200-400.**

Reprints Send information about when and where the material previously appeared. Pay negotiable.

Photos Photographs are important. A fly-tying submission should always include samples of flies to send to our staff photographer, even if photos of the flies are included. Send photos. Captions, identification of subjects required. Reviews contact sheets, transparencies. Offers no additional payment for photos accepted with ms. Buys one time rights.

Columns/Departments One-page shorts (problem solvers), 350-750 words. Query with published clips. **Pays $100-300.**

Tips If you are new to this editor, please submit complete queries.

$ $ $ AMERICAN HUNTER

11250 Waples Mill Rd., Fairfax VA 22030-9400. (703)267-1336. Fax: (703)267-3971. E-mail: publications@nrahq.org. Website: www.nra.org. Monthly magazine for hunters who are members of the National Rifle Association (NRA). "*American Hunter* contains articles dealing with various sport hunting and related activities both at home and abroad. With the encouragement of the sport as a prime game management tool, emphasis is on technique, sportsmanship and safety. In each issue hunting equipment and firearms are evaluated, legislative happenings affecting the sport are reported, lore and legend are retold and the business of the Association is recorded in the Official Journal section." Circ. 1,000,000. Byline given. Pays on publication. No kill fee. Buys nonexclusive first North American serial rights with web rights. Accepts queries by mail, e-mail. Responds in 6 months to queries. Guidelines for #10 SASE.

Nonfiction Factual material on all phases of hunting: Expository how-to, where-to, and general interest pieces; humor: personal narratives; and semi-technical articles on firearms, wildlife management or hunting. Features fall into five categories: Deer, upland birds, waterfowl, big game and varmints/small game. Pheasants, whitetail tactics, black bear feed areas, mule deer, duck hunters' transport by land and sea, tech topics to be decided; rut strategies, muzzleloader moose and elk, fall turkeys, staying warm, goose talk, long-range muzzleloading Not interested in material on fishing, camping, or firearms knowledge. Query. Length: 1,800-2,000 words. **Pays up to $1,000.**

Reprints Copies for author will be provided upon publication. No reprints possible.

Photos No additional payment made for photos used with ms; others offered from $125-600

Columns/Departments Hunting Guns, Hunting Loads, destination and adventure, and Public Hunting Grounds. Study back issues for appropriate subject matter and style. Length: 800-1,500 words. **Pays $300-800.**

Tips "Although unsolicited manuscripts are accepted, detailed query letters outlining the proposed topic and approach are appreciated and will save both writers and editors a considerable amount of time. If we like your story idea, you will be contacted by mail or phone and given direction on how we'd like the topic covered. NRA Publications accept all manuscripts and photographs for consideration on a speculation basis only. Story angles should be narrow, but coverage must have depth. How-to articles are popular with readers and might range from methods for hunting to techniques on making gear used on successful hunts. Where-to articles should contain contacts and information needed to arrange a similar hunt. All submissions are judged on three criteria: Story angle (it should be fresh, interesting, and informative); quality of writing (clear and lively—capable of holding the readers' attention throughout); and quality and quantity of accompanying photos (sharpness, reproducability, and connection to text are most important.)"

$ $ ARKANSAS SPORTSMAN

Game & Fish, 2250 Newmarket Parkway, Suite 110, Marietta GA 30067. (770)953-9222. Fax: (678)279-7512. Website: www.arkansassportsmanmag.com. See *Game & Fish*. No kill fee.

BACON BUSTERS

Pig Hunting Guide, Yaffa Publishing, 17-21 Bellevue St., Surry Hills NSW 2010 Australia. (61)(2)9281-2333. Fax: (61)(2)9281-2750. E-mail: editor@baconbusters.com.au. Website: www.yaffa.com.au. **Contact:** Clint Magro, editor. Quarterly magazine covering the hog hunting scene in Australia. "*Bacon Busters* content includes readers' short stories, how-to articles, pig hunting features, technical advice, pig dog profiles and Australia's biggest collection of pig hunting photos. Not to mention the famous Babes & Boars section!" Estab. 1995.

Nonfiction Needs expose, general interest, how-to, interview. Query.

$ $ BASSMASTER MAGAZINE

B.A.S.S. Publications, P.O. Box 10000, Lake Buena Vista FL 32830. (407)566-2277. Fax: (407)566-2072. E-mail: editorial@bassmaster.com. Website: www.bassmaster.com. **80% freelance written**. Magazine published 11 times/year about largemouth, smallmouth, and spotted bass, offering how-to articles for dedicated beginning and advanced bass fishermen, including destinations and new product reviews. Estab. 1968. Circ. 600,000. Byline given. Pays on acceptance. No kill fee. Publishes ms an average of less than 1 year after acceptance. Buys electronic rights. Editorial lead time 2 months. Submit seasonal material 6 months in advance. Accepts queries by mail, e-mail. Responds in 2 months to queries. Sample copy for $2. Guidelines for #10 SASE.

- Needs destination stories (how to fish a certain area) for the Northwest and Northeast.

Nonfiction Needs historical, how-to, patterns, lures, etc., interview, of knowledgeable people in the sport, new product, reels, rods, and bass boats, travel, where to go fish for bass, conservation related to bass fishing. No first-person, personal experience-type articles. **Buys 100 mss/year.** Query. Length: 500-1,500 words. **Pays $100-600.**

Photos Send photos. Captions, model releases required. Reviews transparencies. Offers no additional payment for photos accepted with ms, but pays $700 for color cover transparencies. Buys all rights.

Columns/Departments Short Cast/News/Views/Notes/Briefs (upfront regular feature covering news-related events such as new state bass records, unusual bass fishing happenings, conservation, new products, and editorial viewpoints). Length: 250-400 words. **Pays $100-300.**

Tips "Editorial direction continues in the short, more direct how-to article. Compact, easy-to-read information is our objective. Shorter articles with good graphics, such as how-to diagrams, step-by-step instruction, etc., will enhance a writer's articles submitted to *Bassmaster Magazine*. The most frequent mistakes made by writers in completing an article for us are poor grammar, poor writing, poor organization, and superficial research. Send in detailed queries outlining specific objectives of article, obtain writer's guidelines. Be as concise as possible."

BC OUTDOORS SPORT FISHING AND OUTDOOR ADVENTURE

OP Publishing, 1080 Howe St., Suite 900, Vancouver BC V6Z 2T1 Canada. (604)678-2586. E-mail: editor@bcoutdoorsmagazine.com. Website: www.bcosportfishing.com. **80% freelance written**. Magazine published 6 times/year covering fresh and saltwater fishing, camping, and backroads. Byline given. Pays on publication. Offers kill fee. Publishes ms an average of 3 months after acceptance. Buys first North American serial rights. Writer's guidelines for 8 × 10 SAE with 7 Canadian first-class stamps

Nonfiction We would like to receive how-to, where-to features dealing with fishing in British Columbia. Needs how-to, new or innovative articles on fishing subjects, personal experience, outdoor adventure, outdoor topics specific to British Columbia. Query features in early spring. Length: 1,700-2,000 words.

Photos State availability. Captions, identification of subjects required. Buys one time rights.

Tips "Wants in-depth information, professional writing only. Emphasis on environmental issues. Those pieces with a conservation component have a better chance of being published. Subject must be specific to British Columbia. We receive many manuscripts written by people who obviously do not know the magazine or market. The writer has a better chance of breaking in with short, lesser-paying articles and fillers, because we have a stable of regular writers who produce most main features."

$ $ THE BIG GAME FISHING JOURNAL

Informational Publications, Inc., 1800 Bay Ave., Point Pleasant NJ 08742. Fax: (732)223-2449. Website: www.biggamefishingjournal.com. **90% freelance written**. Bimonthly magazine covering big game fishing. We require highly instructional articles prepared by qualified writers/fishermen. Estab. 1994. Circ. 45,000. Byline given. Pays on publication. Offers 50% kill fee. Buys first North American serial rights. Editorial lead time 3 months. Submit seasonal material 3 months in advance. Accepts queries by mail, e-mail. Accepts simultaneous submissions. Responds in 2 weeks to queries. Responds in 1 month to mss. Guidelines free.

Nonfiction Needs how-to, interview, technical. **Buys 50-70 mss/year.** Send complete ms. Length: 2,000-3,000 words. **Pays $200-400.**
Photos Send photos. Captions required. Reviews transparencies. Offers no additional payment for photos accepted with ms Buys one time rights.
Tips Our format is considerably different than most publications. We prefer to receive articles from qualified anglers on their expertise—if the author is an accomplished writer, all the better. We require highly-instructional articles that teach both novice and expert readers.

$ CALIFORNIA BUCKS

Outdoor News Service, P.O. Box 9007, San Bernardino CA 92427-0007. (909)887-3444. Fax: (909)887-8180. E-mail: cabucks@earthlink.net. Website: www.outdoornewsservice.com. **25% freelance written**. Quarterly newsletter covering strictly the hunting of deer in CaliforniaÃ³when, where and how. Estab. 2005. Circ. 500. Byline given. Pays on publication. Publishes ms an average of 1-2 months after acceptance. Editorial lead time 3-12 months. Submit seasonal material 3-12 months in advance. Accepts queries by mail, e-mail, fax. Accepts previously published material. Accepts simultaneous submissions. Sample copy by e-mail. Guidelines by e-mail.
Nonfiction Needs expose, historical, how-to, new product, personal experience, technical. Does not want anything that does not deal with deer hunting in California. **Buys 12-18 mss/year.** Query. Length: 200-1,200 words. **Pays $75/printed page.**
Photos State availability. Captions, identification of subjects required. Reviews TIFF/JPEG files. Offers no additional payment for photos accepted with ms; pays $25-50/photo separately. Buys one time rights.
Tips We are always looking for individual research pieces on hunters who are successful on taking deer on public lands, especially if the piece detailsÃ³with mapsÃ³where the hunt took place and gives detailed information for our readers.

$$ CALIFORNIA GAME & FISH

Game & Fish, 2250 Newmarket Parkway, Suite 110, Marietta GA 30067. (770)953-9222. Fax: (678)279-7512. Website: www.californiagameandfish.com. See *Game & Fish* No kill fee.

$ CALIFORNIA HOG HUNTER

A Newsletter Dedicated to Hunting Wild Pigs, Outdoor News Service, P.O. Box 9007, San Bernardino CA 92427-0007. (909)887-3444. Fax: (909)887-8180. E-mail: odwriter@verizon.net. Website: www.outdoornewsservice.com. **25% freelance written**. Quarterly newsletter covering strictly the hunting of wild hogs in California—when, where and how. Estab. 1998. Circ. 1,000. Byline given. Pays on publication. Offers kill fee. Publishes ms an average of 1-2 months after acceptance. Editorial lead time 3-12 months. Submit seasonal material 3-12 months in advance. Accepts queries by mail, e-mail, fax. Accepts previously published material. Accepts simultaneous submissions. Responds in 1 month to queries. Sample copy by e-mail. Guidelines by e-mail.
Nonfiction Needs expose, historical, how-to, new product, personal experience, technical. Does not want anything not dealing with hog hunting in California. **Buys 12-18 mss/year.** Query. Length: 200-1,200 words. **Pays $75/printed page.**
Photos State availability. Captions, identification of subjects required. Reviews GIF/JPEG files. Offers no additional payment for photos accepted with ms; offers $25-50/photo for those sold separately. Buys one time rights.
Tips We are always looking for individual research pieces on hunters who are successful on taking wild hogs on public lands, especially if the piece details—with maps—where the hunt took place and gives detailed information for our readers.

$$ THE DRAKE MAGAZINE

For Those Who Fly-Fish, 1600 Maple St., Fort Collins CO 80521. E-mail: info@drakemag.com. Website: www.drakemag.com. **70% freelance written**. Biannual magazine for people who love fishing. Byline given. Pays 1 month after publication. No kill fee. Publishes ms an average of 1 year after acceptance. Buys first North American serial rights. Editorial lead time 1 year. Submit seasonal material 1 year in advance. Accepts queries by mail. Responds in 6 months to mss. Guidelines available online.
Nonfiction Needs book excerpts, essays, general interest, historical, humor, interview, opinion, personal experience, photo feature, travel, fishing related. **Buys 8 mss/year.** Query. Length: 250-3,000 words. **Pays 10-20¢/word depending on the amount of work we have to put into the piece.**
Photos State availability. Reviews contact sheets, negatives, transparencies. Offers $25-250/photo. Buys one time rights.

$$$ FIELD & STREAM

2 Park Ave., New York NY 10016. (212)779-5000. Fax: (212)779-5114. E-mail: fsletters@time4.com. Website: fieldandstream.com. **50% freelance written**. Monthly magazine. Broad-based service magazine for the hunter and fisherman. Editorial content consists of articles of penetrating depth about national hunting, fishing, and related activities. Also humor, personal essays, profiles on outdoor people, conservation, sportsmen's insider secrets, tactics and techniques, and adventures. Estab. 1895. Circ. 1,500,000. Byline given. Pays on acceptance for most articles. No kill fee. Buys first rights. Accepts queries by mail. Responds in 1 month to queries. Guidelines available online.

Nonfiction Length: 1,500 words for features. Payment varies depending on the quality of work, importance of the article. **Pays $800-1,000 and more on a sliding scale for major features.** Query by mail.

Photos Send photos. Reviews slides (prefers color). When purchased separately, pays $450 minimum for color. Buys first rights.

Tips Writers are encouraged to submit queries on article ideas. These should be no more than a paragraph or 2, and should include a summary of the idea, including the angle you will hang the story on, and a sense of what makes this piece different from all others on the same or a similar subject. Many queries are turned down because we have no idea what the writer is getting at. Be sure that your letter is absolutely clear. We've found that if you can't sum up the point of the article in a sentence or 2, the article doesn't have a point. Pieces that depend on writing style, such as humor, mood, and nostalgia or essays often can't be queried and may be submitted in manuscript form. The same is true of short tips. All submissions to *Field & Stream* are on an on-spec basis. Before submitting anything, however, we encourage you to *study*, not simply read, the magazine. Many pieces are rejected because they do not fit the tone or style of the magazine, or fail to match the subject of the article with the overall subject matter of *Field & Stream*. Above all, study the magazine before submitting anything.

$ FISHING & HUNTING NEWS

Outdoor Empire Publishing, P.O. Box 3010, Bothell WA 98041. (360)282-4200. Fax: (360)282-4270. E-mail: staff@fhnews.com. Website: www.fhnews.com/. **95% freelance written**. Bimonthly magazine covering fishing and hunting. We focus on upcoming fishing and hunting opportunities in your area—where to go and what to do once you get there. Estab. 1954. Circ. 96,000. Byline given. Pays on publication. No kill fee. Publishes ms an average of 1 month after acceptance. Buys first North American serial rights, buys second serial (reprint) rights, buys electronic rights. Editorial lead time 1 month. Submit seasonal material 2 months in advance. Accepts queries by mail, e-mail. Sample copy and writer's guidelines free

Nonfiction Needs how-to, local fishing and hunting, where-to. **Buys 5,000 mss/year.** Query with published clips. Length: 350-2,000 words. **Pays $25-125 and up.** Seldom

Photos State availability. Captions required. Buys all rights.

Tips *F&H News* is published in 7 local editions across the western U.S., Great Lakes, and mid-Atlantic states. We look for reports of current fishing and hunting opportunity, plus technique- or strategy-related articles that can be used by anglers and hunters in these areas.

$$ FLORIDA GAME & FISH

Game & Fish, 2250 Newmarket Parkway, Suite 110, Marietta GA 30067. (770)953-9222. Fax: (770)933-9510. Website: www.floridagameandfish.com. See *Game & Fish* No kill fee.

$$ FLORIDA SPORTSMAN

Wickstrom Communications Division of Intermedia Outdoors, 2700 S. Kanner Hwy., Stuart FL 34994. (772)219-7400. Fax: (772)219-6900. E-mail: editor@floridasportsman.com. Website: www.floridasportsman.com. **30% freelance written**. Monthly magazine covering fishing, boating, hunting, and related sports—Florida and Caribbean only. *Florida Sportsman* is edited for the boatowner and offshore, coastal, and fresh water fisherman. It provides a how, when, and where approach in its articles, which also includes occasional camping, diving, and hunting stories—plus ecology; in-depth articles and editorials attempting to protect Florida's wilderness, wetlands, and natural beauty. Circ. 115,000. Byline given. Pays on acceptance. No kill fee. Publishes ms an average of 6 months after acceptance. Buys nonexclusive additional rights. Submit seasonal material 6 months in advance. Accepts queries by mail. Responds in 2 months to queries. Responds in 1 month to mss. Sample copy free. Guidelines for #10 SASE.

Nonfiction We use reader service pieces almost entirely—how-to, where-to, etc. One or 2 environmental pieces/issue as well. Writers must be Florida based, or have lengthy experience in Florida outdoors. All articles must have strong Florida emphasis. We do not want to see general how-to-fish-or-boat pieces which might well appear in a national or wide-regional magazine. Needs essays, environment or nature, how-to, fishing, hunting, boating, humor, outdoors angle, personal experience, in fishing, etc., technical, boats, tackle, etc., as particularly suitable for Florida specialities. **Buys 40-60 mss/year.** Query. Length: 1,500-2,500 words. **Pays $475.**

Photos Send photos. Hi-res digital images on CD preferered. Reviews 35mm transparencies, 4 × 5 and larger prints. Offers no additional payment for photos accepted with ms. Pays up to $750 for cover photos. Buys all rights.

Tips "Feature articles are most open to freelancers; however there is little chance of acceptance unless contributor is an accomplished and avid outdoorsman *and* a competent writer-photographer with considerable experience in Florida."

$ $ FLW OUTDOORS MAGAZINE

Bass Edition, Walleye Edition, Saltwater Edition, FLW Outdoors, 30 Gamble Lane, Benton KY 42025. E-mail: cmoore@flwoutdoors.com. Website: www.flwoutdoors.com. **Contact:** Colin Moore, editor. **40% freelance written**. Magazine published 8 times/year in 3 editions (24 magazines/year) covering fishing for bass, walleye, redfish, kingfish, stripers, etc. "*FLW Outdoors Magazine* caters to all anglers from beginning weekend anglers to hardcore professional anglers. Our magazine seeks to educate as well as entertain anglers with cutting-edge techniques and new product innovations being used by America's top fishermen." Estab. 1979. Circ. 100,000 + . Byline given. Pays on acceptance. Publishes ms an average of 4 months after acceptance. Buys first rights. Makes work-for-hire assignments. Editorial lead time 5 months. Submit seasonal material 1 year in advance. Accepts queries by mail, e-mail. Sample copy free. Guidelines free.

Nonfiction Needs how-to, new product, photo feature, technical, travel. Does not want me-and-Bubba-went-fishing type stories; stories about author's first trip to catch a certain type of fish; stories in the first person about catching a fish. **Buys 50-75 mss/year.** Query. Length: 2,000-2,500 words. **Pays $400-500.**

Photos State availability. Captions required. Reviews contact sheets, GIF/JPEG files. Offers $50-200/photo. Buys one time rights.

Columns/Departments Destinations; Environment; Boat Tech; Tackle Maintenance. 20-30 Query. **Pays $100-300.**

Tips "We're looking to be the first place anglers look for the best new products and the hottest fish-catching techniques across the country."

$ FLY FISHERMAN MAGAZINE

6405 Flank Dr., Harrisburg PA 17112. (717)540-6704. Fax: (717)657-9552. Website: www.flyfisherman.com. Published 6 times/year covering fly fishing. Written for anglers who fish primarily with a fly rod and for other anglers who would like to learn more about fly fishing. Circ. 120,358. No kill fee.

$ $ FUR-FISH-GAME

2878 E. Main, Columbus OH 43209-9947. E-mail: ffgcox@ameritech.net. **65% freelance written**. Monthly magazine for outdoorsmen of all ages who are interested in hunting, fishing, trapping, dogs, camping, conservation, and related topics. Estab. 1900. Circ. 111,000. Byline given. Pays on acceptance. No kill fee. Publishes ms an average of 7 months after acceptance. Buys first rights, buys all rights. Responds in 2 months to queries. Sample copy for $1 and 9 × 12 SAE. Guidelines for #10 SASE.

Nonfiction "We are looking for informative, down-to-earth stories about hunting, fishing, trapping, dogs, camping, boating, conservation, and related subjects. Nostalgic articles are also used. Many of our stories are `how-to' and should appeal to small-town and rural readers who are true outdoorsmen. Some re¢ articles have told how to train a gun dog, catch big-water catfish, outfit a bowhunter, and trap late-season muskrat. We also use personal experience stories and an occasional profile, such as an article about an old-time trapper. `Where-to' stories are used occasionally if they have broad appeal." Query. Length: 500-3,000 words. **Pays $50-250 or more for features depending upon quality, photo support, and importance to magazine.**

Photos Send photos. Captions, True required. Reviews transparencies, color 5 × 7 or 8 × 10 prints, digital photos on CD only with thumbnail sheet of small images and a numbered caption sheet. Pays $35 for separate freelance photos.

Tips "We are always looking for quality how-to articles about fish, game animals, or birds that are popular with everyday outdoorsmen but often overlooked in other publications, such as catfish, bluegill, crappie, squirrel, rabbit, crows, etc. We also use articles on standard seasonal subjects such as deer and pheasant, but like to see a fresh approach or new technique. Instructional trapping articles are useful all year. Articles on gun dogs, ginseng, and do-it-yourself projects are also popular with our readers. An assortment of photos and/or sketches greatly enhances any manuscript, and sidebars, where applicable, can also help. No phone queries, please."

$$ GAME & FISH

2250 Newmarket Pkwy., Suite 110, Marietta GA 30067. (770)953-9222. Fax: (770)933-9510. E-mail: ken.dunwoody@inoutdoors.com. Website: www.gameandfishmag.com. **90% freelance written**. Publishes 30 different monthly outdoor magazines, each one covering the fishing and hunting opportunities in a particular state or region (see individual titles to contact editors). Estab. 1975. Circ. 570,000. Byline given. Pays 3 months prior to cover date of issue. Offers negotiable kill fee. Publishes ms an average of 7 months after acceptance. Buys first North American serial rights. Submit seasonal material 8 months in advance. Accepts queries by mail, e-mail, fax. Responds in 3 months to queries. Sample copy for $3.50 and 9 × 12 SASE. Guidelines for #10 SASE.

Nonfiction Prefers queries over unsolicited mss. Length: 1,500-2,400 words. **Pays $150-300; additional payment made for electronic rights.**

Photos Captions, identification of subjects required. Reviews transparencies, prints, digital images. Cover photos $250, inside color $75, and b&w $25. Buys one time rights.

Tips Our readers are experienced anglers and hunters, and we try to provide them with useful, specific articles about where, when, and how to enjoy the best hunting and fishing in their state or region. We also cover topics concerning game and fish management. Most articles should be tightly focused and aimed at outdoorsmen in 1 particular state. After familiarizing themselves with our magazine(s), writers should query the appropriate state editor (see individual listings) or send to Ken Dunwoody.

$$ GEORGIA SPORTSMAN

Game & Fish, 2250 Newmarket Parkway, Suite 110, Marietta GA 30067. (770)953-9222. Fax: (770)933-9510. E-mail: jimmy.jacobs@primedia.com. Website: www.georgiasportsmanmag.com. See *Game & Fish* No kill fee.

$$$ N GRAY'S SPORTING JOURNAL

MCC Magazines, LLC, 1 10th St., Suite 380, Augusta GA 30901. E-mail: russ@lumpkin@morris.com. Website: www.grayssportingjournal.com. **75% freelance written**. 7 issues per year magazine High-end hunting and fishing—think *Field & Stream* meets *The New Yorker*. "We expect competent, vividly written prose—fact or fiction—that has high entertainment value for a very sophisticated audience of experienced hunters and anglers. We do not consider previously published material. We do, however, occasionally run prepublication book excerpts. To get a feel for what Gray's publishes, review several back issues. Note that we do not, as a rule, publish 'how-to' articles; this is the province of our regular columnists." Estab. 1975. Circ. 32,000. Byline given. Pays on publication. No kill fee. Publishes ms an average of 12 months after acceptance. Buys first North American serial rights. Editorial lead time 14 months. Submit seasonal material 16 months in advance. Accepts simultaneous submissions. Responds in 3 months to mss. Guidelines available online.

Nonfiction Needs essays, historical, humor, personal experience, photo feature, travel. Gray's publishes three themed issues each year: August is always entirely devoted to upland birdhunting; April to fly fishing; December to sporting travel. All other issues—February, May, September, November—focus on seasonally appropriate themes. Each issue always features a travel piece, from exotic destinations to right around the corner. We publish no how-to of any kind. **Buys 20-30 mss/year.** Send complete ms. Length: 1,500-12,000 words. **Pays $600-1,000 for unsolicited articles.**

Photos State availability. Reviews contact sheets, GIF/JPEG files. We negotiate payment individually.

Fiction Needs adventure, experimental, historical, humorous, slice-of-life vignettes, All fiction must have some aspect of hunting or fishing at the core. If some aspect of hunting or fishing isn't at the core of the story, it has zero chance of interesting *Gray's*. **Buys 20 mss/year.** Send complete ms. Length: 1,500-12,000 words. **Pays $600-1,000.**

Poetry Needs avant-garde, haiku, light verse, traditional. Buys 7/year poems/year. Submit maximum 3 poems. Length: 10-40 lines.

Tips "Write something different, write something well—fiction or nonfiction—write something that goes to the heart of hunting or fishing more elegantly, more inspirationally, than the 1,500 or so other unsolicited manuscripts we review each year. For best results, submit by e-mail. Mail submissions can take weeks longer to hear back."

$$ GREAT PLAINS GAME & FISH

Game & Fish, 2250 Newmarket Parkway, Suite 110, Marietta GA 30067. (770)953-9222. Fax: (770)933-9510. Website: www.greatplainsgameandfish.com. See *Game & Fish* No kill fee.

$$ ILLINOIS GAME & FISH

Game & Fish, 2250 Newmarket Parkway, Suite 110, Marietta GA 30067. (770)953-9222. Fax: (770)933-

9510. Website: www.illinoisgameandfish.com. See *Game & Fish* No kill fee.

$ $ INDIANA GAME & FISH

Game & Fish, 2250 Newmarket Parkway, Suite 110, Marietta GA 30067. (770)953-9222. Fax: (770)933-9510. Website: www.indianagameandfish.com. See *Game & Fish* No kill fee.

$ $ IOWA GAME & FISH

Game & Fish, 2250 Newmarket Parkway, Suite 110, Marietta GA 30067. (770)953-9222. Fax: (770)933-9510. Website: www.iowagameandfish.com. See *Game & Fish* No kill fee.

$ $ KENTUCKY GAME & FISH

Game & Fish, 2250 Newmarket Parkway, Suite 110, Marietta GA 30067. (770)953-9222. Fax: (770)933-9510. Website: www.kentuckygameandfish.com. See *Game & Fish* No kill fee.

$ $ LOUISIANA GAME & FISH

Game & Fish, 2250 Newmarket Parkway, Suite 110, Marietta GA 30067. (770)953-9222. Fax: (770)933-9510. Website: www.lagameandfish.com. See *Game & Fish* No kill fee.

$ $ THE MAINE SPORTSMAN

P.O. Box 910, Yarmouth ME 04096. (207)846-9501. Fax: (207)846-1434. E-mail: harry.vanderweide@verizon.net. Website: www.mainesportsman.com. **80% freelance written**. Monthly tabloid. Eager to work with new/unpublished writers, but because we run over 30 regular columns, it's hard to get into *The Maine Sportsman* as a beginner. Estab. 1972. Circ. 30,000. Byline given. Pays during month of publication. No kill fee. Publishes ms an average of 3 months after acceptance. Buys first rights. Accepts queries by mail, e-mail. Accepts previously published material. Responds in 2 weeks to queries.

Nonfiction We publish only articles about Maine hunting and fishing activities. Any well-written, researched, knowledgeable article about that subject area is likely to be accepted by us. **Buys 25-40 mss/year.** Send complete ms via e-mail Length: 200-2,000 words. **Pays $20-300.**

Reprints Yes, send typed ms via e-mail or query with rights for sale noted. Pays 100% of amount paid for an original article

Photos Send color slides, color prints, or JPGs/TIFFs via e-mail. Pays $5-50 for b&w print.

Tips We publish numerous special sections each year and are eager to buy Maine-oriented articles on snowmobiling, ice fishing, boating, salt water and deer hunting. Send articles or queries.

$ $ MARLIN

P.O. Box 8500, Winter Park FL 32790. (407)628-4802. Fax: (407)628-7061. Website: www.marlinmag.com. **90% freelance written**. Magazine published 8 times/year covering the sport of big game fishing (billfish, tuna, dorado, and wahoo). Our readers are sophisticated, affluent, and serious about their sport—they expect a high-class, well-written magazine that provides information and practical advice. Estab. 1982. Circ. 50,000. Byline given. Pays on acceptance. No kill fee. Publishes ms an average of 3 months after acceptance. Buys first North American serial rights. Submit seasonal material 3 months in advance. Accepts previously published material. Sample copy free with SASE Guidelines available online.

Nonfiction Needs general interest, how-to, bait-rigging, tackle maintenance, etc., new product, personal experience, photo feature, technical, travel. No freshwater fishing stories. No 'Me & Joe went fishing' stories. **Buys 30-50 mss/year.** Query with published clips. Length: 800-3,000 words. **Pays $250-500.**

Reprints Send photocopy and information about when and where the material previously appeared. Pays 50-75% of amount paid for original article.

Photos State availability. Reviews original slides. Offers $50-300 for inside use, $1,000 for a cover. Buys one time rights.

Columns/Departments Tournament Reports (reports on winners of major big game fishing tournaments), 200-400 words; Blue Water Currents (news features), 100-400 words. 25 Query. **Pays $75-250.**

Tips Tournament reports are a good way to break in to *Marlin*. Make them short but accurate, and provide photos of fishing action or winners' award shots (*not* dead fish hanging up at the docks). We always need how-tos and news items. Our destination pieces (travel stories) emphasize where and when to fish, but also include information on where to stay. For features: Crisp, high-action stories with emphasis on exotic nature, adventure, personality, etc.—nothing flowery or academic. Technical/how-to: concise and informational—specific details. News: Again, concise with good details—watch for legislation affecting big game fishing, outstanding catches, new clubs and organizations, new trends, and conservation issues.

$ MICHIGAN OUT-OF-DOORS

P.O. Box 30235, Lansing MI 48909. (517)371-1041. Fax: (517)371-1505. Website: www.mucc.org. **75% freelance written**. Monthly magazine emphasizing Michigan outdoor recreation, especially hunting and fishing, conservation, nature, and environmental affairs. Estab. 1947. Circ. 90,000. Byline given. Pays on acceptance. No kill fee. Publishes ms an average of 6 months after acceptance. Buys first North American serial rights. Submit seasonal material 6 months in advance. Accepts queries by mail, phone. Responds in 1 month to queries. Sample copy for $3.50. Guidelines for free or on website.

Nonfiction Stories must have a Michigan slant unless they treat a subject of universal interest to our readers. Needs expose, historical, how-to, interview, opinion, personal experience, photo feature. Archery Deer and Small Game Hunting (October); Firearm Deer Hunting (November); Cross-country Skiing and Early-ice Lake Fishing (December or January); Camping/Hiking (May); Family Fishing (June). No humor or poetry. **Buys 96 mss/year.** Send complete ms. Length: 1,000-2,000 words. **Pays $90 minimum for feature stories.**

Photos Captions required. Offers no additional payment for photos accepted with ms; others $20-175. Buys one time rights.

Tips Top priority is placed on true accounts of personal adventures in the out-of-doors—well-written tales of very unusual incidents encountered while hunting, fishing, camping, hiking, etc.

$ $ MICHIGAN SPORTSMAN

Game & Fish, 2250 Newmarket Parkway, Suite 110, Marietta GA 30067. (770)953-9222. Fax: (770)933-9510. Website: www.michigansportsmanmag.com. See *Game & Fish* No kill fee.

$ $ MID-ATLANTIC GAME & FISH

Game & Fish, 2250 Newmarket Parkway, Suite 110, Marietta GA 30067. (770)953-9222. Fax: (770)933-9510. Website: www.midatlanticgameandfish.com. See *Game & Fish* No kill fee.

$ MIDWEST OUTDOORS

MidWest Outdoors, Ltd., 111 Shore Dr., Burr Ridge IL 60527-5885. (630)887-7722. Fax: (630)887-1958. Website: www.midwestoutdoors.com. **100% freelance written**. Monthly tabloid emphasizing fishing, hunting, camping, and boating. Estab. 1967. Byline given. Pays on publication. No kill fee. Publishes ms an average of 3 months after acceptance. Buys simultaneous rights. Submit seasonal material 2 months in advance. Accepts previously published material. Accepts simultaneous submissions. Responds in 3 weeks to queries. Sample copy for $1 or online. Guidelines for #10 SASE or online.

- "Submissions must be e-mailed to info@midwestoutdoors.com (Microsoft Word format preferred)."

Nonfiction Needs how-to, fishing, hunting, camping in the Midwest, where-to-go (fishing, hunting, camping within 500 miles of Chicago). "We do not want to see any articles on `my first fishing, hunting, or camping experiences,' `cleaning my tackle box,' `tackle tune-up,' 'making fishing fun for kids,' or `catch and release.'" **Buys 1,800 unsolicited mss/year.** Send complete ms. Length: 1,000-1,500 words. **Pays $15-30.**

Photos Captions required. Reviews slides and b&w prints. Offers no additional payment for photos accompanying ms. Buys all rights.

Columns/Departments Fishing; Hunting. Send complete ms. **Pays $30.**

Tips "Break in with a great unknown fishing hole or new technique within 500 miles of Chicago. Where, how, when, and why. Know the type of publication you are sending material to."

$ $ MINNESOTA SPORTSMAN

Game & Fish, 2250 Newmarket Parkway, Suite 110, Marietta GA 30067. (770)953-9222. Fax: (770)933-9510. Website: www.minnesotasportsmanmag.com. See *Game & Fish* No kill fee.

$ $ MISSISSIPPI GAME & FISH

Game & Fish, 2250 Newmarket Parkway, Suite 110, Marietta GA 30067. (770)953-9222. Fax: (770)933-9510. Website: www.mississippigameandfish.com. See *Game & Fish* No kill fee.

$ $ MISSOURI GAME & FISH

Game & Fish, 2250 Newmarket Parkway, Suite 110, Marietta GA 30067. (770)953-9222. Fax: (770)933-9510. E-mail: Ken.Dunwoody@imoutdoors.com. Website: www.missourigameandfish.com. **Contact:** Ken Dunwoody, editorial director. See *Game & Fish* No kill fee.

$ $ MUSKY HUNTER MAGAZINE

P.O. Box 340, St. Germain WI 54558. (715)477-2178. Fax: (715)477-8858. **90% freelance written**.

Bimonthly magazine on musky fishing. Serves the vertical market of musky fishing enthusiasts. We're interested in how-to, where-to articles. Estab. 1988. Circ. 37,000. Byline given. Pays on publication. No kill fee. Publishes ms an average of 4 months after acceptance. Buys first rights, buys one-time rights. Submit seasonal material 4 months in advance. Responds in 2 months to queries. Sample copy for 9 × 12 SAE with $2.79 postage Guidelines for #10 SASE.
Nonfiction Needs historical, related only to musky fishing, how-to, catch muskies, modify lures, boats, and tackle for musky fishing, personal experience, must be musky fishing experience, technical, fishing equipment, travel, to lakes and areas for musky fishing. **Buys 50 mss/year.** Send complete ms. Length: 1,000-2,500 words. **Pays $100-300 for assigned articles. Pays $50-300 for unsolicited articles.**
Photos Send photos. Identification of subjects required. Reviews 35mm transparencies, 3 × 5 prints, high resolution digital images preferred. Offers no additional payment for photos accepted with ms. Buys one time rights.

$$ NEW ENGLAND GAME & FISH

Game & Fish, 2250 Newmarket Parkway, Suite 110, Marietta GA 30067. (770)953-9222. Fax: (770)933-9510. Website: www.newenglandgameandfish.com. See *Game & Fish* No kill fee.

$$ NORTH AMERICAN WHITETAIL

Game & Fish, 2250 Newmarket Pkwy., Suite 110, Marietta GA 30067. (770)953-9222. Fax: (770)933-9510. Website: northamericanwhitetail.com. **70% freelance written**. Magazine published 8 times/year about hunting trophy-class white-tailed deer in North America, primarily the US. We provide the serious hunter with highly sophisticated information about trophy-class whitetails and how, when, and where to hunt them. We are not a general hunting magazine or a magazine for the very occasional deer hunter. Estab. 1982. Circ. 150,000. Byline given. Pays 65 days prior to cover date of issue. Offers negotiable kill fee. Publishes ms an average of 6 months after acceptance. Buys first North American serial rights. Submit seasonal material 10 months in advance. Accepts queries by mail, e-mail, phone. Responds in 3 months to mss. Sample copy for $3.50 and 9 × 12 SAE with 7 first-class stamps. Guidelines for #10 SASE.
Nonfiction Needs how-to, interview. **Buys 50 mss/year.** Query. Length: 1,000-3,000 words. **Pays $150-400.**
Photos Send photos. Captions, identification of subjects required. Reviews 35mm transparencies, color prints, high quality digital images. Offers no additional payment for photos accepted with ms. Buys one time rights.
Columns/Departments Trails and Tails (nostalgic, humorous, or other entertaining styles of deer-hunting material, fictional or nonfictional), 1,200 words. 8 Send complete ms. **Pays $150.**
Tips Our articles are written by persons who are deer hunters first, writers second. Our hard-core hunting audience can see through material produced by nonhunters or those with only marginal deer-hunting expertise. We have a continual need for expert profiles/interviews. Study the magazine to see what type of hunting expert it takes to qualify for our use, and look at how those articles have been directed by the writers. Good photography of the interviewee and his hunting results must accompany such pieces.

$$ NORTH CAROLINA GAME & FISH

Game & Fish, 2250 Newmarket Parkway, Suite 110, Marietta GA 30067. (770)953-9222. Fax: (770)933-9510. Website: www.ncgameandfish.com. See *Game & Fish* No kill fee.

$$ OHIO GAME & FISH

Game & Fish, 2250 Newmarket Parkway, Suite 110, Marietta GA 30067. (770)953-9222. Fax: (770)933-9510. Website: www.ohiogameandfish.com. See *Game & Fish* No kill fee.

$$ OKLAHOMA GAME & FISH

Game & Fish, 2250 Newmarket Parkway, Suite 110, Marietta GA 30067. (770)953-9222. Fax: (770)933-9510. Website: www.oklahomagameandfish.com. See *Game & Fish* No kill fee.

$$ ONTARIO OUT OF DOORS

Ontario Federation of Anglers and Hunters, P.O. Box 8500, Peterborough ON K9J 0B4 Canada. (705)748-0076. Fax: (705)748-3415. Website: www.ontariooutofdoors.com. **Contact:** John Kerr, editor-in-chief. **80% freelance written**. Magazine published 10 times/year covering the outdoors (hunting, fishing). Estab. 1968. Circ. 93,865. Byline given. Pays on acceptance. Publishes ms an average of 6 months after acceptance. Buys first rights, buys electronic rights. Editorial lead time 1 year. Submit seasonal material 2 months in advance. Accepts queries by mail, e-mail, fax. Responds in 3 months to queries. Writer's guidelines free

Nonfiction Needs interview, opinion, technical, travel, wildlife management. No `Me and Joe' features. **Buys 100 mss/year.** Length: 500-2,500 words. **Pays $950 maximum for assigned articles.**
Fiction Pays **$500 maximum**.
Tips "It is suggested that writers query prior to submission."

$ THE OUTDOORS MAGAZINE

For the Better Hunter, Angler & Trapper, Elk Publishing, Inc., 531 Main St., Colchester VT 05446. (802)879-2013. Fax: (802)879-2015. E-mail: kyle@elkpublishing.com. Website: www.outdoorsmagazine.net. **80% freelance written**. Monthly magazine covering wildlife conservation. Northeast hunting, fishing, and trapping magazine covering news, tips, destinations, and good old-fashioned stories. Estab. 1996. Circ. 20,000. Byline given. Pays on publication. Offers 10% kill fee. Publishes ms an average of 1 year after acceptance. Buys first North American serial rights. Editorial lead time 1 year. Submit seasonal material 6 months in advance. Accepts queries by mail. Accepts previously published material. Responds in 1 month to queries. Responds in 3 month to mss. Sample copy online or by e-mail Guidelines free.
Nonfiction Needs book excerpts, essays, expose, general interest, historical, how-to, interview, new product, opinion, personal experience, technical. **Buys 200 mss/year.** Query with published clips. Length: 750-2,500 words. **Pays $20-150 for assigned articles.**
Photos State availability. Identification of subjects required. Reviews contact sheets. Pays $15-75/photo. Buys one time rights.
Columns/Departments 100 Query with published clips. **Pays $20-60.**
Tips *Know* the publication, not just read it, so you understand the audience. Patience and thoroughness will go a long way.

$$ ⊘ PENNSYLVANIA ANGLER & BOATER

Pennsylvania Fish & Boat Commission, P.O. Box 67000, Harrisburg PA 17106-7000. (717)705-7833. E-mail: ra-pfbcmagazine@state.pa.us. Website: www.fish.state.pa.us. **40% freelance written**. Bimonthly magazine covering fishing, boating, and related conservation topics in Pennsylvania. Circ. 28,000. Byline given. Pays 2 months after acceptance. Publishes ms an average of 8 months after acceptance. Submit seasonal material 8 months in advance. Responds in 1 month to queries. Responds in 2 months to mss. Sample copy for 9 × 12 SAE with 9 first-class stamps. Guidelines for #10 SASE.

- No unsolicited mss.

Nonfiction Needs how-to, and where-to, technical. No saltwater or hunting material. **Buys 75 mss/year.** Query. Length: 500-2,500 words. **Pays $25-300.**
Photos Send photos. Captions, identification of subjects, model releases required. Reviews 35mm and larger transparencies, hi-res digital submissions on CD (preferred). Offers no additional payment for photos accompanying mss. Rights purchased vary.

$$ PENNSYLVANIA GAME & FISH

Game & Fish, 2250 Newmarket Parkway, Suite 110, Marietta GA 30067. (770)953-9222. Fax: (770)933-9510. Website: www.pagameandfish.com. See *Game & Fish* No kill fee.

$$ RACK MAGAZINE

Adventures in Trophy Hunting, Buckmasters, Ltd., 10350 U.S. Hwy. 80 E., Montgomery AL 36117. (800)240-3337. Fax: (334)215-3535. E-mail: mhandley@buckmasters.com. Website: www.rackmag.com. **50% freelance written**. monthly, July-December magazine covering big game hunting. "All features are either first- or third-person narratives detailing the successful hunts for world-class, big game animals—mostly white-tailed deer and other North American species." Estab. 1998. Circ. 100,000. Byline given. Pays on publication. No kill fee. Publishes ms an average of 9 months after acceptance. Buys first North American serial rights, buys second serial (reprint) rights. Editorial lead time 9-12 months. Submit seasonal material 9 months in advance. Accepts queries by e-mail. Accepts previously published material. Accepts simultaneous submissions. Responds in 1 month to queries. Responds in 2 months to mss. Sample copy free. Guidelines free.
Nonfiction Needs personal experience. "We're interested only in articles chronicling successful hunts." **Buys 40-50 mss/year.** Query. Length: 1,000 words. **Pays $100-325 for assigned and unsolicited articles.**
Photos Send photos. Captions, identification of subjects required. Reviews transparencies, prints, GIF/JPEG files. Buys one time rights.
Tips "Ask for and read the writer's guidelines."

$$ ROCKY MOUNTAIN GAME & FISH

Game & Fish, 2250 Newmarket Parkway, Suite 110, Marietta GA 30067. (770)935-9222. Fax: (770)933-9510. Website: www.rmgameandfish.com. See *Game & Fish* No kill fee.

$$ SALT WATER SPORTSMAN MAGAZINE

460 N. Orlando Ave., Suite 200, New York NY 32789. (212)779-5003. Fax: (212)779-5025. E-mail: john.brownlee@bonniecorp.com. Website: www.saltwatersportsman.com. **85% freelance written**. Monthly magazine. *Salt Water Sportsman* is edited for serious marine sport fishermen whose lifestyle includes the pursuit of game fish in US waters and around the world. It provides information on fishing trends, techniques, and destinations, both local and international. Each issue reviews offshore and inshore fishing boats, high-tech electronics, innovative tackle, engines, and other new products. Coverage also focuses on sound fisheries management and conservation. Circ. 170,000. Byline given. Pays on acceptance. Offers kill fee. Publishes ms an average of 5 months after acceptance. Buys first North American serial rights. Submit seasonal material 8 months in advance. Accepts queries by mail, e-mail, fax. Responds in 1 month to queries. Sample copy for #10 SASE. Guidelines available online.

Nonfiction Readers want solid how-to, where-to information written in an enjoyable, easy-to-read style. Personal anecdotes help the reader identify with the writer. Needs how-to, personal experience, technical, travel, to fishing areas. **Buys 100 mss/year.** Query. Length: 1,200-2,000 words. **Pays $300-750.**

Reprints Send tearsheet. Pays up to 50% of amount paid for original article.

Photos Captions required. Reviews color slides. Pays $1,500 minimum for 35mm, 2¼ × 2¼ or 8 × 10 transparencies for cover.

Columns/Departments Sportsman's Tips (short, how-to tips and techniques on salt water fishing, emphasis is on building, repairing, or reconditioning specific items or gear). Send complete ms.

Tips There are a lot of knowledgeable fishermen/budding writers out there who could be valuable to us with a little coaching. Many don't think they can write a story for us, but they'd be surprised. We work with writers. Shorter articles that get to the point which are accompanied by good, sharp photos are hard for us to turn down. Having to delete unnecessary wordage—conversation, clichés, etc.—that writers feel is mandatory is annoying. Often they don't devote enough attention to specific fishing information.

$$ SOUTH CAROLINA GAME & FISH

Game & Fish, 2250 Newmarket Parkway, Suite 110, Marietta GA 30067. (770)953-9222. Fax: (770)933-9510. Website: www.scgameandfish.com. See *Game & Fish* No kill fee.

$$$$ SPORT FISHING

The Magazine of Saltwater Fishing, World Publications, 460 N. Orlando Ave., Suite 200, Winter Park FL 32789. (407)628-4802. Fax: (407)628-7061. E-mail: doug.olander@worldpub.net. Website: www.sportfishingmag.com. **50% freelance written**. Magazine published 10 times/year covering saltwater anglingÃ³saltwater fish and fisheries. *Sport Fishing*'s readers are middle-aged, affluent, mostly male, who are generally proficient in and very educated to their sport. We are about fishing from boatsÃ³not from surf or jetties. Estab. 1985. Circ. 250,000. Byline given. Pays on acceptance. Offers 25% kill fee. Publishes ms an average of 6-12 months after acceptance. Buys first North American serial rights, buys electronic rights. Editorial lead time 2-12 months. Submit seasonal material 1 year in advance. Accepts queries by e-mail. Responds in 1 week to queries. Responds in 1 month to mss. Sample copy for #10 SASE. Guidelines available online.

Nonfiction Needs general interest, how-to. Query. Length: 2,500-3,000 words. **Pays $500-750 for text only; $1,500+ possible for complete package with photos.**

Photos State availability. Reviews GIF/JPEG files. Offers $75-400/photo. Buys one time rights.

Tips Queries please; no over-the-transom submissions. Meet or beat deadlines. Include quality photos when you can. Quote the experts. Balance information with readability. Include sidebars.

$$$ SPORTS AFIELD

The Premier Hunting Adventure Magazine, Field Sports Publishing, 15621 Chemical Lane, Huntington Beach CA 92649. (714)894-9080. E-mail: letters@sportsafield.com. Website: www.sportsafield.com. **60% freelance written**. Magazine published 6 times/year covering big game hunting. "We cater to the upscale hunting market, especially hunters who travel to exotic destinations like Alaska and Africa. We are not a deer hunting magazine, and we do not cover fishing." Estab. 1887. Circ. 50,000. Byline given. Pays 1 month prior to publication. Publishes ms an average of 6 months after acceptance. Buys first North American serial rights, first rights, and electronic rights. Editorial lead time 4 months. Submit seasonal material 5 months in advance. Accepts queries by mail, e-mail. Responds in 2 months to queries and to mss Sample copy for $6.99 Guidelines available online

Nonfiction Needs personal experience, travel. **Buys 6-8 mss/year.** Query. Length: 1,500-2,500 words. **Pays $500-800.**
Photos State availability. Captions, model releases required. Reviews 35mm slides transparencies, TIF/JPEG files. Offers no additional payment for photos accepted with ms. Buys first time rights.

$ $ TENNESSEE SPORTSMAN

Game & Fish, 2250 Newmarket Parkway, Suite 110, Marietta GA 30067. (770)953-9222. Fax: (770)933-9510. E-mail: Ken.Dunwoody@imoutdoors.com. Website: www.tennesseesportsmanmag.com. See *Game & Fish* No kill fee.

$ $ TEXAS SPORTSMAN

Game & Fish, 2250 Newmarket Parkway, Suite 110, Marietta GA 30067. (770)953-9222. Fax: (770)933-9510. Website: www.texassportsmanmag.com. See *Game & Fish* No kill fee.

$ $ TRAPPER & PREDATOR CALLER

F + W Media, Inc., 700 E. State St., Iola WI 54990. (715)445-2214. E-mail: jared.blohm@fwmedia.com. Website: www.trapperpredatorcaller.com. **95% freelance written**. Tabloid published 10 times/year covering trapping and predator calling, fur trade. "Must have mid-level to advanced knowledge, because *T&PC* is heavily how-to focused." Estab. 1975. Circ. 44,000. Byline given. Pays on publication. No kill fee. Publishes ms an average of 6 months after acceptance. Buys one-time rights. Editorial lead time 1 year. Submit seasonal material 1 year in advance. Accepts queries by e-mail.
Nonfiction Needs how-to, interview, personal experience, travel. **Buys 100 mss/year.** Send complete ms. Length: 1,000-2,500 words. **Pays $250 for assigned articles.**
Photos Send photos. Reviews negatives, prints. Buys full rights.

$ $ TURKEY & TURKEY HUNTING

a Division of F + W Media, Inc., 700 E. State St., Iola WI 54990-0001. E-mail: brian.lovett@fwmedia.com. Website: www.turkeyandturkeyhunting.com. **Contact:** Brian Lovett. **50% freelance written**. Bimonthly magazine filled with practical and comprehensive information for wild turkey hunters. Estab. 1982. Circ. 40,000. Byline given. Pays on acceptance. Offers 50% kill fee. Publishes ms an average of 8 months after acceptance. Buys one-time rights. Editorial lead time 1 year. Submit seasonal material 1 year in advance. Accepts queries by mail, e-mail. Responds in 1 month to queries. Responds in 6 months to mss. Sample copy for $4. Ms and photo guidelines online.
Nonfiction Does not want Me and Joe went hunting and here's what happened articles. **Buys 20 mss/year.** Send complete ms. Length: 1,500-2,500 words. **Pays $275-400.**
Photos Contact: Contact Editor before sending photos. Send photos. Identification of subjects required. Reviews 2 × 2 transparencies, any size prints, digital images with contact sheets. Offers $75-200/photo. Negotiates payment individually. Buys one-time rights.
Tips "Turkey hunting is a continually growing and changing sport. Search for topics that reflect this trend. Our audience is sophisticated and experienced. We have several contributing editors who write most of our how-to articles, so we buy few articles of this type from freelancers. Well-written mood/essay articles are always welcome for review. If you have not written for *Turkey & Turkey Hunting*, it is best to send a finished manuscript. We do not assign articles based on query letters."

$ $ TURKEY CALL

National Wild Turkey Federation, P.O. Box 530, Edgefield SC 29824-0530. (803)637-3106. Fax: (803)637-0034. E-mail: turkeycall@nwtf.net. Website: www.nwtf.org//tv_magazines/turkeycall-magazine.html. **50-60% freelance written**. "Bimonthly educational magazine for members of the National Wild Turkey Federation. Topics covered include hunting, history, restoration, management, biology, and distribution of wild turkey." Estab. 1973. Circ. 180,000. Byline given. Pays on acceptance. No kill fee. Publishes ms an average of 6 months after acceptance. Buys first North American serial rights. Editorial lead time 1 year. Accepts queries by mail, e-mail. Responds in 2 months to queries Sample copy for $3 and 9 × 12 SAE Guidelines available online

- Submit queries by June 1 of each year.

Nonfiction "Feature articles dealing with the hunting and management of the American wild turkey. Must be accurate information and must appeal to national readership of turkey hunters and wildlife management experts. Queries with suggested sidebars preferred; speculative submissions discouraged." Query (preferred) or send complete ms. Length: 700-2,500 words. **Pays $100 for short fillers; $200-500 for features.**

Photos "We want quality photos submitted with features. Illustrations also acceptable. We are using more and more inside color illustrations. No typical hunter-holding-dead-turkey photos or setups using mounted birds or domestic turkeys. Photos with how-to stories must make the techniques clear (i.e., how to make a turkey call; how to sculpt or carve a bird in wood)." Identification of subjects, model releases required. Reviews transparencies, high resolution digital images. Buys one-time rights.
Fiction Must contribute to the education, enlightenment, or entertainment of readers in some special way.
Tips "The writer should simply keep in mind that the audience is `expert' on wild turkey management, hunting, life history, and restoration/conservation history. He/she must know the subject. We are buying more third person, more fiction, more humor—in an attempt to avoid the `predictability trap' of a single subject magazine."

$$ VIRGINIA GAME & FISH

Game & Fish, 2250 Newmarket Parkway, Suite 110, Marietta GA 30067. (770)953-9222. Fax: (770)933-9510. Website: www.virginiagameandfish.com. See *Game & Fish* No kill fee.

$$ WASHINGTON-OREGON GAME & FISH

Game & Fish, 2250 Newmarket Parkway, Suite 110, Marietta GA 30067. (770)953-9222. Fax: (770)933-9510. Website: www.wogameandfish.com. See *Game & Fish* No kill fee.

WESTERN SPORTSMAN

202-9644 54 Ave., Edmonton AB T6E 5V1 Canada. (780)643-3963. Fax: (780)643-3960. E-mail: editor@westernsportsman.com. Website: www.westernsportsman.com. **90% freelance written**. Bimonthly magazine for anglers and hunters. "Our main coverage area is Alberta, Saskatchewan, Manitoba, and the Northern Territories. We occasionally publish adventure destination stories that cover parts of the country as well. Short news items pertaining to all provinces/territories are also accepted. We try to include as much information as possible on all subjects in each edition." Estab. 1968. Circ. 35,000. Byline given. Pays on publication. No kill fee. Buys first North American serial rights. Accepts queries by e-mail. Responds in 1 month to queries. Guidelines available for free only online, or by e-mail.

- Familiarize yourself with the magazine and query before submitting. Queries accepted April 1 to May 30.

Nonfiction "It is necessary that all articles can identify with our coverage area. We are interested in mss from writers who have had an interesting fishing or hunting experience. We also publish other informational pieces. We are most interested in articles which tell about the average guy living on beans, piloting his own boat, stalking his game and generally doing his own thing in Western Canada rather than a story describing a well-to-do outdoorsmen traveling by motorhome, staying at an expensive lodge with guides doing everything for him except catching the fish or shooting the big game animal. The articles submitted to us need to be prepared in a knowledgeable way and include more information than the actual fish catch or animal or bird kill. Discuss the terrain, the people involved on the trip, the water or weather conditions, the costs, the planning that went into the trip, the equipment and other data closely associated with the particular event. We're always looking for new writers." **Buys 60 mss/year.** 1,500-2,000 words for features; 600-1,000 words for columns; 150-300 words for news items. **Payment negotiable**
Photos No additional payment for photos with ms. Also purchased without ms. Pays up to $200 for front cover.

$$ WEST VIRGINIA GAME & FISH

Game & Fish, 2250 Newmarket Parkway, Suite 110, Marietta GA 30067. (770)953-9222. Fax: (770)933-9510. E-mail: ken.dunwoody@imoutdoors.com. Website: www.wvgameandfish.com. **Contact:** Ken Dunwoody, editorial dir. "This is the ultimate resource for West Virginia outdoor enthusiasts that are passionate about hunting, shooting and fishing." No kill fee.

$$ WISCONSIN SPORTSMAN

Game & Fish, 2250 Newmarket Parkway, Suite 110, Marietta GA 30067. (770)953-9222. Fax: (770)933-9510. Website: www.wisconsinsportsmanmag.com. See *Game & Fish* No kill fee.

Martial Arts

AUSTRALASIAN TAEKWONDO

Blitz Publications, P.O. Box 4075, Mulgrave VIC 3170 Australia. (61)(3)9574-8999. Fax: (61)(3)9574-8899.

E-mail: taekwondo@blitzmag.com.au. Website: www.sportzblitz.net. Magazine covering the martial art of taekwondo. *"Australasian Taekwondo Magazine* features exclusive interviews, tournament reports, sports medicine, articles on the world's best martial artists, unique styles, personalities, Poomse, black belt patterns, fitness tips, health and street self defense strategies, combat/sports psychology as well as unrivalled coverage of local news, taekwondo events and nutrition."

Nonfiction Needs general interest, how-to, interview, new product. Query.

$ $ BLACK BELT

Black Belt Communications, LLC, 24900 Anza Dr., Unit E, Valencia CA 91355. Fax: (661)257-3028. E-mail: byoung@aimmedia.com. Website: www.blackbeltmag.com. **80% freelance written. Works with a small number of new/unpublished writers each year.** Monthly magazine emphasizing martial arts for both experienced practitioner and layman. Estab. 1961. Circ. 100,000. Pays on publication. No kill fee. Publishes ms an average of 1 year after acceptance. Buys all rights. Accepts queries by mail, e-mail, fax. Accepts simultaneous submissions. Responds in 3 weeks to queries. Guidelines available online.

Nonfiction Needs expose, how-to, interview, new product, personal experience, technical, travel, Informational. We never use personality profiles. **Buys 40-50 mss/year.** Query with outline 1,200 words minimum. **Pays $100-300.**

Photos Very seldom buys photographs without accompanying ms. Captions, model releases required. Total purchase price for ms includes payment for photos.

BLITZ AUSTRALASIAN MARTIAL ARTS MAGAZINE

Blitz Publications, P.O. Box 4075, Mulgrave VIC 3170 Australia. (61)(3)9574-8999. Fax: (61)(3)9574-8899. E-mail: ben@blitzmag.com.au. Website: www.sportzblitz.net. *"Blitz Australasian Martial Arts* monthly magazine features interviews and articles on the world's best martial arts and combat sports personalities, unique styles, technique and fitness tips, health and self-defense strategies, combat psychology, as well as unrivaled coverage of local fight news and events."

Nonfiction Needs general interest, how-to. Query.

$ $ INSIDE KUNG-FU

The Ultimate In Martial Arts Coverage!, CFW Enterprises, 4201 Vanowen Place, Burbank CA 91505. (818)845-2656. Fax: (818)845-7761. E-mail: davecater@cfwenterprises.com. **90% freelance written**. Monthly magazine for those with traditional, modern, athletic, and intellectual tastes. The magazine slants toward little-known martial arts and little-known aspects of established martial arts. Estab. 1973. Circ. 125,000. Byline given. Pays on publication date on magazine cover. Publishes ms an average of 6 months after acceptance. Buys first North American serial rights. Editorial lead time 6 months. Submit seasonal material 6 months in advance. Accepts simultaneous submissions. Responds in 1 month to queries. Responds in 2 months to mss. Sample copy for $5.95 and 9 × 12 SAE with 5 first class stamps. Guidelines for #10 SASE.

Nonfiction Articles must be technically or historically accurate. *Inside Kung-Fu* is looking for external type articles (fighting, weapons, multiple hackers). Needs book excerpts, essays, expose, topics relating to martial arts, general interest, historical, how-to, primarily technical materials, inspirational, interview, new product, personal experience, photo feature, technical, travel, cultural/philosophical. No sports coverage, first-person articles, or articles which constitute personal aggrandizement. **Buys 120 mss/year.** Query or send complete ms. 1,500-3,000 words (8-10 pages, typewritten and double-spaced) **Pays $125-175.**

Reprints Send tearsheet or typed ms with rights for sale noted and information about when and where the material previously appeared. No payment

Photos State availability of or send photos. Captions, identification of subjects, model releases required. Reviews contact sheets, negatives, 5 × 7 or 8 × 10 color prints. No additional payment for photos Buys all rights.

Fiction Fiction must be short (1,000-2,000 words) and relate to the martial arts. We buy very few fiction pieces. Needs adventure, historical, humorous, mystery, novel concepts, suspense. **Buys 2-3 mss/year.**

Tips See what interests the writer. May have a better chance of breaking in at our publication with short articles and fillers since smaller pieces allow us to gauge individual ability, but we're flexible—quality writers get published, period. The most frequent mistakes made by writers in completing an article for us are ignoring photo requirements and model releases (always No. 1—and who knows why? All requirements are spelled out in writer's guidelines).

$ $ JOURNAL OF ASIAN MARTIAL ARTS

Via Media Publishing Co., 941 Calle Mejia #822, Santa Fe NM 87501. Website: www.goviamedia.com.

90% freelance written. "Quarterly magazine covering all historical and cultural aspects related to Asian martial arts, offering a mature, well-rounded view of this uniquely fascinating subject. Although the journal treats the subject with academic accuracy (references at end), writing need not lose the reader!". Estab. 1991. Byline given. Pays on publication. No kill fee. Publishes ms an average of 1 year after acceptance. Buys first rights, buys second serial (reprint) rights. Submit seasonal material 6 months in advance. Responds in 1 month to queries. Responds in 2 months to mss. Sample copy for $10. Guidelines for #10 SASE.

Nonfiction All articles should be backed with solid, reliable reference material. Needs essays, expose, historical, how-to, martial art techniques and materials, e.g., weapons, interview, personal experience, photo feature, place or person, religious, technical, travel. No articles overburdened with technical/foreign/scholarly vocabulary, or material slanted as indirect advertising or for personal aggrandizement. **Buys 30 mss/year.** Query with short background and martial arts experience. Length: 2,000-10,000 words. **Pays $150-500.**

Photos State availability. Identification of subjects, model releases required. Reviews contact sheets, negatives, transparencies, prints. Offers no additional payment for photos accepted with ms. Buys one-time and reprint rights.

Columns/Departments Location (city, area, specific site, Asian or non-Asian, showing value for martial arts, researchers, history); Media Review (film, book, video, museum for aspects of academic and artistic interest).**Length:** 1,000-2,500 words. 16 Query. **Pays $50-200.**

Fiction Needs adventure, historical, humorous, slice-of-life vignettes, translation. No material that does not focus on martial arts culture. **Buys 1 ms/year.** Query. Length: 1,000-10,000 words. **Pays $50-500, or copies.**

Poetry Needs avant-garde, free verse, haiku, light verse, traditional. No poetry that does not focus on martial arts culture. Buys 2 poems/year. Submit maximum 10 poems. **Pays $10-100, or copies.**

Tips "Always query before sending a manuscript. We are open to varied types of articles; most however require a strong academic grasp of Asian culture. For those not having this background, we suggest trying a museum review, or interview, where authorities can be questioned, quoted, and provide supportive illustrations. We especially desire articles/reports from Asia, with photo illustrations, particularly of a martial art style, so readers can visually understand the unique attributes of that style, its applications, evolution, etc. `Location' and media reports are special areas that writers may consider, especially if they live in a location of martial art significance."

$ KUNG FU TAI CHI

Wisdom for Body and Mind, Pacific Rim Publishing, 40748 Encyclopedia Circle, Fremont CA 94538. (510)656-5100. Fax: (510)656-8844. E-mail: gene@kungfumagazine.com. Website: www.kungfumagazine.com. **70% freelance written**. Bimonthly magazine covering Chinese martial arts and culture. "*Kung Fu Tai Chi* covers the full range of Kung Fu culture, including healing, philosophy, meditation, yoga, Fengshui, Buddhism, Taoism, history, and the latest events in art and culture, plus insightful features on the martial arts." Circ. 20,000. Byline given. Pays on publication. No kill fee. Buys first North American serial rights, buys electronic rights. Editorial lead time 4 months. Submit seasonal material 4 months in advance. Accepts queries by mail, e-mail, fax, phone. Responds in 2 months to queries. Responds in 3 months to mss. Sample copy for $3.99 or online. Guidelines available online.

Nonfiction Needs general interest, historical, interview, personal experience, religious, technical, travel, cultural perspectives. No poetry or fiction. **Buys 70 mss/year.** Query. Length: 500-2,500 words. **Pays $35-125.**

Photos Send photos. Captions, identification of subjects required. Reviews 5 × 7 prints, GIF/JPEG files. Offers no additional payment for photos accepted with ms Buys one time rights.

Tips "Check out our website and get an idea of past articles."

$$ T'AI CHI

Leading International Magazine of T'ai Chi Ch'uan, Wayfarer Publications, P.O. Box 39938, Los Angeles CA 90039. (323)665-7773. Fax: (323)665-1627. E-mail: taichi@tai-chi.com. Website: www.tai-chi.com/magazine.htm. **Contact:** Marvin Smalheiser, Editor. **90% freelance written**. Quarterly magazine covering T'ai Chi Ch'uan as a martial art and for health and fitness. "Covers T'ai Chi Ch'uan and other internal martial arts, plus qigong and Chinese health, nutrition, and philosophical disciplines. Readers are practitioners or laymen interested in developing skills and insight for self-defense, health, and self-improvement." Estab. 1977. Circ. 50,000. Byline given. Pays on publication. No kill fee. Publishes ms an average of 3 months after acceptance. Buys first North American serial rights. Editorial lead time 3 months. Submit seasonal material 6 months in advance. Accepts queries by mail, e-mail, fax. Responds in 3 weeks to queries. Responds in 3 months to mss. Sample copy for $5.99. Guidelines available online.

Nonfiction Needs book excerpts, essays, how-to, on T'ai Chi Ch'uan, qigong, and related Chinese disciplines, interview, personal experience. "Do not want articles promoting an individual, system, or school." **Buys 50 mss/year.** Send complete ms. Length: 1,200-4,500 words. **Pays $75-500.**
Photos Send photos. Captions, identification of subjects, model releases required. Reviews color transparencies, color or b&w 4x6 or 5 × 7 prints, digital files suitable for print production. "Offers no additional payment for photos accepted with ms, but overall payment takes into consideration the number and quality of photos." Buys one-time and reprint rights.
Tips "Think and write for practitioners and laymen who want information and insight, and who are trying to work through problems to improve skills and their health. No promotional material."

$$ 🄽 ULTIMATE GRAPPLING

Apprise Media, 2400 E. Katella Ave., Suite 300, Anaheim CA 92806. (714)939-9991. Fax: (714)939-9909. E-mail: doug.jeffrey@apg-media.com. Website: www.ultimategrapplingmag.com. Monthly magazine covering mixed martial arts, grappling. "We are interested in anything and everything about mixed martial arts.lifestyle to events to training to strategy." Estab. 2,000. Byline given. Pays on publication. Offers 20% kill fee. Publishes ms an average of 1-3 months after acceptance. Buys first North American serial rights. Editorial lead time 3 months. Submit seasonal material 3 months in advance. Accepts queries by mail, e-mail. Responds in 2 months to mss. Sample copy free. Guidelines free.
Nonfiction Needs book excerpts, expose, general interest, historical, how-to, inspirational, interview, new product, personal experience, photo feature, technical. **Buys 30 mss/year.** Query. Length: 500-1,500 words. **Pays $150-500 for assigned articles. Pays $150-500 for unsolicited articles.**
Photos State availability. TBD
Columns/Departments Beyond Fighting (lifestyle of fighters); Exercises to bolster MMA game and general fitness. 30 mss/year Query with or without published clips. **Pays $-$125.**
Tips "Know the subject material. Be creative. Be unique. Be accessible and flexible and open to input. Those who can produce on short notice are invaluable."

Miscellaneous Sports

$ ACTION PURSUIT GAMES

265 S. Anita Dr., Suite 120, Orange CA 92868. E-mail: editor@actionpursuitgames.com. Website: www.actionpursuitgames.com. **60%% freelance written**. Monthly magazine covering paintball. Estab. 1987. Circ. 85,000. Byline given. Pays on publication. No kill fee. Publishes ms an average of 2 months after acceptance. Buys electronic rights. print rights Editorial lead time 3 months. Submit seasonal material 6 months in advance. Accepts queries by e-mail. Sample copy for sae with 9 × 12 envelope and 5 First-Class stamps. Guidelines available online.
Nonfiction Needs essays, expose, general interest, historical, how-to, humor, interview, new product, opinion, personal experience, technical, travel, all paintball-related. No sexually oriented material **Buys 100+ mss/year.** Length: 500-1,000 words. **Pays $100.**
Photos Send photos. Captions, identification of subjects, model releases required. Reviews transparencies, prints. Negotiates payment individually. Buys all rights, web and print
Columns/Departments Guest Commentary, 400 words; TNT (tournament news), 500-800 words; Young Guns, 300 words; Scenario Game Reporting, 300-500 words. 24 **Pays $100.**
Fiction Needs adventure, historical, must be paintball related. **Buys 1-2 mss/year.** Send complete ms. Length: 500 words. **Pays $100.**
Poetry Needs avant-garde, free verse, haiku, light verse, traditional. Buys 1-2 poems/year. Submit maximum 1 poems. Length: 20 lines.
Tips Good graphic support is critical. Read writer's guidelines at website; read website, www.actionpursuitgames.com, and magazine.

$$ AMERICAN CHEERLEADER

Macfadden Performing Arts Media LLC, 110 William St., 23rd Floor, New York NY 10038. (646)459-4800. Fax: (646)459-4900. E-mail: mwalker@americancheerleader.com. Website: www.americancheerleader.com. **30% freelance written**. Bimonthly magazine covering high school, college, and competitive cheerleading. We try to keep a young, informative voice for all articles—'for cheerleaders, by cheerleaders.' Estab. 1995. Circ. 200,000. Byline given. Pays on publication. Offers 25% kill fee. Publishes ms an average of 4 months after acceptance. Buys all rights. Editorial lead time 3 months. Submit seasonal material 4 months in advance. Accepts queries by mail, e-mail. Responds in 4 weeks to queries. Responds in 2 months to mss. Sample copy for $2.95. Guidelines free.

Nonfiction Needs how-to, cheering techniques, routines, pep songs, etc., interview, celebrities and media personalities who cheered. Tryouts (April); Camp Basics (June); College (October); Competition (December). No professional cheerleading stories, i.e., no Dallas Cowboy cheerleaders. **Buys 12-16 mss/year.** Query with published clips. Length: 400-1,500 words. **Pays $100-250 for assigned articles. Pays $100 maximum for unsolicited articles.**
Photos State availability. Model releases required. Reviews transparencies, 5 × 7 prints. Offers $50/photo. Rights purchased varies.
Columns/Departments Gameday Beauty (skin care, celeb how-tos), 600 words; Health & Fitness (teen athletes), 1,000 words; Profiles (winning squads), 1,000 words. 12 Query with published clips. **Pays $100-250.**
Tips We invite proposals from freelance writers who are involved in or have been involved in cheerleading—i.e., coaches, sponsors, or cheerleaders. Our writing style is upbeat and `sporty' to catch and hold the attention of our teenaged readers. Articles should be broken down into lots of sidebars, bulleted lists, Q&As, etc.

$$$ ATV MAGAZINE/ATV SPORT

Ehlert Publishing, 6420 Sycamore Lane, Maple Grove MN 55369. Fax: (763)383-4499. E-mail: jprusak@affinitygroup.com. Website: www.atvmagonline.com. www.atvsport.com. **Contact:** John Prusak, editor. **20% freelance written**. Bimonthly magazine covering all-terrain vehicles. Devoted to covering all the things ATV owners enjoy, from hunting to racing, farming to trail riding. Byline given. Pays on magazine shipment to printer. Buys all rights. Editorial lead time 6 months. Accepts queries by mail, e-mail, fax. Responds in 3 weeks to queries. Sample copy and writer's guidelines for #10 SASE
Nonfiction Needs how-to, interview, new product, personal experience, photo feature, technical, travel. **Buys 15-20 mss/year.** Query with published clips. Length: 200-2,000 words. **Pays $100-1,000.**
Photos State availability. Captions, identification of subjects required. Negotiates payment individually. Rights purchased vary.
Tips Writers must have experience with ATVs, and should own one or have regular access to at least one ATV.

$$ BVM

Beach Volleyball Magazine, STN Media Co., 700 Torrance Blvd., Suite C, Redondo Beach CA 90277. (310)792-2226. Fax: (310)792-2231. E-mail: ryan@bvmag.com. Website: www.bvmag.com. **60% freelance written**. Semiannual magazine covering all things, all ages of beach volleyball from an enthusiast slant. Writers must possess a Gen X/Y voice with an understanding of beach culture. Beach volleyball players and/or fans preferred. Writers should at least be familiar with the sport of volleyball and its application in the sand. This includes rules and regulations and leading personalities of the sport. Estab. 2006. Circ. 30,000. Byline given. Pays on publication. No kill fee. Buys one-time rights. Editorial lead time 2 months. Submit seasonal material 2 months in advance. Accepts queries by e-mail. Accepts simultaneous submissions. Sample copy free. Guidelines free.
Nonfiction Needs general interest, historical, how-to, humor, inspirational, interview, new product, opinion, personal experience, photo feature, travel. Does not want game reporting. *BVM* is a lifestyle magazine looking for lifestyle feature content. Query with published clips. Length: 600-1,200 words. **Pays $150-300.**
Photos Contact: Contact Vince Rios, art director. Send photos. Captions, identification of subjects, model releases required. Reviews contact sheets, GIF/JPEG files. Negotiates payment individually. Buys all rights.
Columns/Departments Health & Fitness (training and nutrition tips for all ages); Beach News (current events), both 500 words. 12 Query with published clips. **Pays $150-300.**
Tips This is an enthusiast magazine. Writers should be able to exhibit familiarity with and interest in beach volleyball and the surrounding culture. Previous sports writing and/or lifestyle feature experience preferred. Story ideas should have a firm grasp on topics of interest to beach volleyball community. Playing experience a definite plus, as is a demonstrated knowledge of sport history and knowledge, or the ability to quickly come up to speed and take direction.

$ CANADIAN RODEO NEWS

Canadian Rodeo News, Ltd., #223, 2116 27th Ave. NE, Calgary AB T2E 7A6 Canada. (403)250-7292. Fax: (403)250-6926. E-mail: editor@rodeocanada.com. Website: www.rodeocanada.com. **80% freelance written**. Monthly tabloid covering Canada's professional rodeo (CPRA) personalities and livestock. Read by rodeo participants and fans. Estab. 1964. Circ. 4,000. Byline given. Pays on publication. No kill fee. Publishes ms an average of 1 month after acceptance. Buys first rights, buys second serial (reprint) rights. Editorial lead time 1 month. Submit seasonal material 1 month in advance. Accepts queries by mail, e-mail, fax. Accepts simultaneous submissions. Responds in 1 month to queries. Responds in 2 months to mss.

Nonfiction Needs general interest, historical, interview. **Buys 70-80 mss/year.** Query. Length: 400-1,200 words. **Pays $30-60.**

Reprints Send photocopy of article or typed ms with rights for sale noted and information about when and where the material previously appeared. Pays 100% of amount paid for an original article.

Photos Send photos. Reviews digital only. Offers $15-25/cover photo. Buys one time rights.

Tips Best to call first with the story idea to inquire if it is suitable for publication. Readers are very knowledgeable of the sport, so writers need to be as well.

$ FANTASY SPORTS

F+W Media, Inc., 700 E. State St., Iola WI 54990-0001. (715)445-2214. Fax: (715)445-4087. Website: fantasysportsmag.com. **10% freelance written**. Quarterly magazine covering fantasy baseball and football. Fantasy advice—how-to win. Estab. 1989. Circ. 100,000. Byline given. Pays on publication. Offers negotiable kill fee. Publishes ms an average of 3 months after acceptance. Makes work-for-hire assignments. Editorial lead time 4 months. Submit seasonal material 4 months in advance. Accepts queries by e-mail. Sample copy free.

Tips "Send an e-mail suggestion to ambrosiusg@krause.com."

$$ FENCERS QUARTERLY MAGAZINE

848 S. Kimbrough, Springfield MO 65806. (417)866-4370. E-mail: editor@fencersquarterly.com. Website: www.fencersquarterly.com. **60% freelance written**. Quarterly magazine covering fencing, fencers, history of sword/fencing/dueling, modern techniques and systems, controversies, personalities of fencing, personal experience. This is a publication for all fencers and those interested in fencing; we favor the grassroots level rather than the highly-promoted elite. Readers will have a grasp of terminology of the sword and refined fencing skills—writers must be familiar with fencing and current changes and controversies. We are happy to air any point of view on any fencing subject, but the material must be well-researched and logically presented. Estab. 1996. Circ. 5,000. Byline given. Pays prior to or at publication. Offers 25% kill fee. Publishes ms an average of 6 months after acceptance. Buys first North American serial rights, buys second serial (reprint) rights, buys electronic rights. Makes work-for-hire assignments. Editorial lead time 3 months. Submit seasonal material 6 months in advance. Accepts queries by mail, e-mail. Accepts simultaneous submissions. Sample copy by request. Guidelines available online.

- Responds in 1 week or less for e-mail; 1 month for snail mail if SASE; no reply if no SASE and material not usable.

Nonfiction All article types acceptable—however, we have seldom used fiction or poetry (though will consider if has special relationship to fencing). How-to should reflect some aspect of fencing or gear. Personal experience welcome. No articles that lack logical progression of thought, articles that rant, `my weapon is better than your weapon' emotionalism, puff pieces, or public relations stuff. **Buys 100 mss/year.** Send complete ms. Length: 100-4,000 words. **Pays $100-200 (rarely) for assigned articles. Pays $10-60 for unsolicited articles.**

Photos Send photos. by mail or as e-mail attachment. Prefers prints, all sizes. Captions, identification of subjects, model releases required. Negotiates payment individually. Buys all rights.

Columns/Departments Cutting-edge news (sword or fencing related), 100 words; Reviews (books/films), 300 words; Fencing Generations (profile), 200-300 words; Tournament Results (veteran events only, please), 200 words. 40 Send complete ms. **Pays $10-20.**

Fiction Will consider all as long as strong fencing/sword slant is major element. No erotica. Query or send complete ms. 1,500 words maximum. **Pays $25-100.**

Poetry Will consider all which have distinct fencing/sword element as central. No erotica. Submit maximum 10 poems. Up to 100 lines. **Pays $10.**

Tips We love new writers! Professionally presented work impresses us. We prefer complete submissions, and e-mail or disk (in rich text format) are our favorites. Ask for our writer's guidelines. Always aim your writing to knowledgeable fencers who are fascinated by this subject, take their fencing seriously, and want to know more about its history, current events, and controversies. Action photos should show proper form—no flailing or tangled-up images, please. We want to know what the 'real' fencer is up to these days, not just what the Olympic contenders are doing. If we don't use your piece, we'll tell you why not.

INSIDE CRICKET

ACP Magazines, Ltd., 54-58 Park St., Sydney NSW 2000 Australia. (61)(2)9282-8000. Fax: (61)(2)9267-

4361. Website: www.acp.com.au. **Contact:** Nick Raman, editor. Monthly magazine covering the stars of both Australian and international cricket (in season). "As the only monthly magazine devoted to our national game, Inside Cricket delivers expert views, news, reviews and, most importantly, unparalleled insight about the stars of the sport. Forging a closer link between the players and the adoring fans is the top priority of Inside Cricket, with meaty features on the national team heroes which probe behind the headlines. The readers, eager for more than averages and cliches, have responded positively to this approach.S" Estab. 2004/05. Circ. 40,000.

Nonfiction Needs general interest, interview. Query.

INSIDE RUGBY

ACP Magazines, Ltd., 54-58 Park St., Sydney NSW 2000 Australia. (61)(2)9282-8000. Fax: (61)(2)9267-4361. Website: www.acp.com.au. **Contact:** Mark Cashman, editor. Monthly magazine covering the sport of rugby (in season). "Inside Rugby is the Official magazine of the Wallabies. It is on sale at key times during the year (December and March) to act as a lead into the Super 14 season and Wallabies Programs in May. Inside Rugby delivers in-depth columns from leading rugby writers and personalities, along with comprehensive statistics and results." Circ. 23,800.

Men 18-49.

Nonfiction Needs general interest, interview. Query.

INTERNATIONAL KICKBOXER

Blitz Publications, P.O. Box 4075, Mulgrave VIC 4075 Australia. (61)(3)9574-8999. Fax: (61)(3)9574-8899. E-mail: jarrah@blitzmag.com.au. Website: www.sportzblitz.net. Magazine covering the local and international kickboxing scene. "International Kickboxer has followed the growth of kickboxing and Muay Thai is dedicated to bringing the reader the latest news, fitness tips, training techniques, fight strategies, Boxing drills, cardio kick boxing, conditioning exercises, combat tactics, sports nutrition advice and much more. Some of the big names featured include 'John' Wayne Parr, 'Carnage' Corbett, Mike Zambidis, Daniel Dawson, Yodsanklai and many more. International Kickboxer Magazine covers events like the prestigious K-1 GP, Tarik Solak's K-1 Oceania, as well as Shootboxing and Muay Thai events from the WMC, ISKA, WKA, WKBF and WMTA. "

Nonfiction Needs general interest, how-to. Query.

$ LACROSSE MAGAZINE

US Lacrosse, 113 W. University Pkwy., Baltimore MD 21210. (410)235-6882. Fax: (410)366-6735. E-mail: pkrome@uslacrosse.org. Website: www.uslacrosse.org. **60% freelance written**. *Lacrosse Magazine* is the only national feature publication devoted to the sport of lacrosse. It is a benefit of membership in U.S. Lacrosse, a nonprofit organization devoted to promoting the growth of lacrosse and preserving its history. Estab. 1978. Circ. 235,000. Byline given. Pays on publication. No kill fee. Publishes ms an average of 2 months after acceptance. Buys one-time rights. Editorial lead time 2 months. Submit seasonal material 2 months in advance. Sample copy free. Guidelines free.

Nonfiction Needs book excerpts, general interest, historical, how-to, drills, conditioning, x's and o'x, etc., interview, new product, opinion, personal experience, photo feature, technical. **Buys 30-40 mss/year.** Length: 500-1,750 words. **Payment negotiable.**

Photos State availability. Captions, identification of subjects required. Reviews contact sheets, 4x6 prints. Negotiates payment individually. Buys one time rights.

Columns/Departments First Person (personal experience), 1,000 words; Fitness (conditioning/strength/exercise), 500-1,000 words; How-to, 500-1,000 words. 10-15 **Payment negotiable.**

Tips As the national development center of lacrosse, we are particularly interested in stories about the growth of the sport in non-traditional areas of the U.S. and abroad, written for an audience already knowledgeable about the game.

$$ POINTE MAGAZINE

Ballet At Its Best, MacFadden Performing Arts Media, LLC, 110 William St., 23rd Floor, New York NY 10038. (646)459-4800. Fax: (646)459-4900. E-mail: pointe@lifestylemedia.com. Website: www.pointemagazine.com. Bimonthly magazine covering ballet. *Pointe Magazine* is the only magazine dedicated to ballet. It offers practicalities on ballet careers as well as news and features. Estab. 2000. Circ. 38,000. Byline given. Pays on publication. Buys all rights. Responds in 1 month to queries. Responds in 1 month to mss. Sample copy for sae with 9 × 12 envelope and 6 First-Class stamps.

Nonfiction Needs historical, how-to, interview, biography, careers, health, news. **Buys 60 mss/year.** Query with published clips. Length: 400-1,500 words. **Pays $125-400.**

Photos Contact: Colin Fowler, photo editor. State availability. Captions required. Reviews 214x2¼ or 35 mm transparencies, 8 × 11 prints. Negotiates payment individually. Buys one time rights.

$ $ POLO PLAYERS' EDITION

Rizzo Management Corp., 3500 Fairlane Farms Rd., Suite 9, Wellington FL 33414-8749. (561)793-9524. Fax: (561)793-9576. E-mail: info@poloplayersedition.com. Website: www.poloplayersedition.com. Monthly magazine on poloÃ³the sport and lifestyle. Our readers are affluent, well educated, well read, and highly sophisticated. Circ. 6,150. Pays on acceptance. Offers kill fee. Kill fee varies. Publishes ms an average of 2 months after acceptance. Buys first North American serial rights. Makes work-for-hire assignments. Submit seasonal material 3 months in advance. Accepts queries by mail, e-mail, fax. Accepts simultaneous submissions. Responds in 3 months to queries. Guidelines for #10 SAE with 2 stamps.

Nonfiction Needs historical, interview, personal experience, photo feature, technical, travel. Annual Art Issue/Gift Buying Guide; Winter Preview/Florida Supplement. **Buys 20 mss/year.** Send complete ms. Length: 800-3,000 words. **Pays $150-400 for assigned articles. Pays $100-300 for unsolicited articles.**

Reprints Send tearsheet or typed ms with rights for sale noted and information about when and where the material previously appeared. Pays 50% of amount paid for an original article.

Photos State availability of or send photos. Captions required. Reviews contact sheets, transparencies, prints. Offers $20-150/photo. Buys one time rights.

Columns/Departments Yesteryears (historical pieces), 500 words; Profiles (clubs and players), 800-1,000 words. 15 Query with published clips. **Pays $100-300.**

Tips Query us on a personality or club profile or historic piece or, if you know the game, State availability. to cover a tournament. Keep in mind that ours is a sophisticated, well-educated audience.

$ PRORODEO SPORTS NEWS

Professional Rodeo Cowboys Association, 101 ProRodeo Dr., Colorado Springs CO 80919. (719)593-8840. Fax: (719)548-4889. Website: www.prorodeo.com. **10% freelance written**. Biweekly magazine covering professional rodeo. "Our readers are extremely knowledgeable about the sport of rodeo, and anyone who writes for us should have that same in-depth knowledge. Estab. 1952. Circ. 27,000. Byline given. Pays on publication. No kill fee. Publishes ms an average of 1 month after acceptance. Buys first rights, buys one-time rights. Makes work-for-hire assignments. Editorial lead time 2 months. Submit seasonal material 2 months in advance. Responds in 2 weeks to queries Sample copy for #10 SASE Guidelines free

Nonfiction Needs historical, how-to, interview, photo feature, technical. **Pays $50-100.**

Photos State availability. Identification of subjects required. Reviews digital images and hard copy portfolios. Offers $15-85/photo. Buys one time rights.

🌐 RUGBY LEAGUE WEEK

ACP Magazines, Ltd., 54-58 Park St., Sydney NSW 2000 Australia. (61)(2)9282-8000. Fax: (61)(2)9267-4361. Website: wwos.ninemsn.com.au/rlw/. **Contact:** Martin Lenehan, editor. Weekly magazine for devoted league fans, covering league previews, reviews & news. Estab. 1970. Circ. 20,319.

Nonfiction Needs general interest, interview, opinion. Query.

$ RUGBY MAGAZINE

Rugby Press, Ltd., 459 Columbus Ave., #1200, New York NY 10024. (212)787-1160. Fax: (212)787-1161. E-mail: rugbymag@aol.com. Website: www.rugbymag.com. **75% freelance written**. Monthly magazine. *Rugby Magazine* is the journal of record for the sport of rugby in the U.S. Our demographics are among the best in the country. Estab. 1975. Circ. 10,000. Byline given. Pays on publication. No kill fee. Publishes ms an average of 2 months after acceptance. Buys all rights. Editorial lead time 1 month. Submit seasonal material 2 months in advance. Accepts queries by mail, e-mail, fax, phone. Accepts simultaneous submissions. Responds in 2 weeks to queries. Responds in 1 month to mss. Sample copy for $4. Guidelines free.

Nonfiction Needs book excerpts, essays, general interest, historical, how-to, humor, interview, new product, opinion, personal experience, photo feature, technical, travel. **Buys 15 mss/year.** Send complete ms. Length: 600-2,000 words. **Pays $50 minimum.**

Reprints Send tearsheet or typed ms with rights for sale noted and information about when and where the material previously appeared. Payment varies.

Photos Send photos. Reviews negatives, transparencies, prints. Offers no additional payment for photos accepted with ms. Buys all rights.

Columns/Departments Nutrition (athletic nutrition), 900 words; Referees' Corner, 1,200 words. 2-3 Query with published clips. **Pays $50 maximum.**

Fiction Needs cond novels, humorous, novel concepts, slice-of-life vignettes. **Buys 1-3 mss/year.** Query

with published clips. Length: 1,000-2,500 words. **Pays $100.**
Tips Give us a call. Send along your stories or photos; we're happy to take a look. Tournament stories are a good way to get yourself published in *Rugby Magazine.*

$ SKYDIVING

1725 N. Lexington Ave., DeLand FL 32724. (386)736-4793. Fax: (386)736-9786. E-mail: sue@skydivingmagazine.com. Website: skydivingmagazine.com. **25% freelance written**. Monthly tabloid featuring skydiving for sport parachutists, worldwide dealers and equipment manufacturers. *Skydiving* is a news magazine. Its purpose is to deliver timely, useful and interesting information about the equipment, techniques, events, people and places of parachuting. Our scope is national. *Skydiving*'s audience spans the entire spectrum of jumpers, from first-jump students to veterans with thousands of skydives. Some readers are riggers with a keen interest in the technical aspects of parachutes, while others are weekend `fun' jumpers who want information to help them make travel plans and equipment purchases. Circ. 14,200. Byline given. Pays on publication. No kill fee. Publishes ms an average of 3 months after acceptance. Buys one-time rights. Accepts previously published material. Accepts simultaneous submissions. Responds in 1 month to queries. Sample copy for $2. Guidelines available online.
Nonfiction Average issue includes 3 feature articles and 3 columns of technical information. Send us news and information on how-to, where-to, equipment, techniques, events and outstanding personalities who skydive. We want articles written by people who have a solid knowledge of parachuting. No personal experience or human interest articles. Query. Length: 500-1,000 words. **Pays $25-100.**
Photos State availability. Captions required. Reviews 5 × 7 and larger b&w glossy prints. Offers no additional payment for photos accepted with ms.
Tips The most frequent mistake made by writers in completing articles for us is that the writer isn't knowledgeable about the sport of parachuting. Articles about events are especially time-sensitive so yours must be submitted quickly. We welcome contributions about equipment. Even short, `quick look' articles about new products are appropriate for *Skydiving*. If you know of a drop zone or other place that jumpers would like to visit, write an article describing its features and tell them why you liked it and what they can expect to find if they visit it. Avoid first-person articles.

$ $ TENNIS WEEK

304 Park Ave. South, 8th Fl., New York NY 10010. Website: www.tennisweek.com. **10% freelance written**. Monthly magazine covering tennis. For readers who are either tennis fanatics or involved in the business of tennis. Estab. 1974. Circ. 107,253. Byline given. Pays on publication. No kill fee. Buys all rights. Editorial lead time 1 month. Submit seasonal material 1 month in advance. Responds in 1 month to queries. Sample copy for $4.
Nonfiction Buys 15 mss/year. Query. Length: 1,000-2,000 words. **Pays $300.**

Motor Sports

⊘ ⊕ AUSTRALIAN AUTO ACTION

ACP Magazines, Ltd., 54-58 Park St., Sydney NSW 2000 Australia. (61)(2)9282-8000. Fax: (61)(2)9267-4361. Website: www.acp.com.au. **Contact:** Rob Margeit, editor. Weekly magazine covering motorsports. "AutoAction features a diverse coverage, ensuring there is something of interest to everyone. We cover an extensive range of international, national and local events and series, including V8 Supercars, Formula One, Champ Car, IRL, WRC and ARC, Formula Ford, F3, F4000, Carrera Cup, Speedway, Drag racing and more. If it happens in motor sport, Auto Action covers it. This coverage is provided in the form of news, features, race report and technical articles. Issues are planned well in advance." Circ. 11,667.
Nonfiction Needs general interest, interview, race results. Query.

$ DIRT RIDER

Source Interlink Media, Inc., 6420 Wilshire Blvd., 17th Floor, Los Angeles CA 90048. (323)782-2390. Fax: (323)782-2372. E-mail: drmail@primedia.com. Website: www.dirtrider.com. Monthly magazine devoted to the sport of off-road motorcycle riding that showcases the many ways enthusiast can enjoy dirt bikes. Circ. 201,342. No kill fee.

4-WHEEL & OFF ROAD

Source Interlink Media, 6420 Wilshire Blvd., Los Angeles CA 90048. (323)782-2000. Fax: (323)782-2704. E-mail: 4wheeloffroad@sourceinterlink.com. Website: www.4wheeloffroad.com. Monthly magazine covering off road driving. Intended for the connoisseur of four wheel drive vehicles and their specific

applications. Estab. 1977. Circ. 379,284. No kill fee.
Nonfiction Needs how-to, new product, product evaluations, travel, trail destinations, legal issues.

$ THE HOOK MAGAZINE

The Magazine for Antique & Classic Tractor Pullers, Greer Town, Inc., 209 S. Marshall, Box 16, Marshfield MO 65706. (417)468-7000. Fax: (417)859-6075. E-mail: editor@hookmagazine.com. Website: www.hookmagazine.com. **Contact:** Dana Greer Marlin, Owner/Pres. **80% freelance written**. Bimonthly magazine covering tractor pulling. Estab. 1992. Circ. 6,000. Byline given. Pays on publication. No kill fee. Buys one-time rights, buys electronic rights. Editorial lead time 6 months. Submit seasonal material 6 months in advance. Accepts queries by mail, e-mail, fax. Accepts previously published material. Accepts simultaneous submissions. Responds in 3 weeks to queries. Responds in 2 months to mss. Sample copy for 8½ × 11 SAE with 4 first-class stamps or online. Guidelines for #10 SASE.

O‑ "Our magazine is easy to break into. Puller profiles are your best bet. Features on individuals and their tractors, how they got into the sport, what they want from competing."

Nonfiction Needs how-to, interview, new product, personal experience, photo feature, technical, event coverage. **Buys 25 mss/year.** Send complete ms. Length: 500-1,500 words. **Pays $70 for technical articles; $35 for others.**
Photos Send photos. Captions, identification of subjects, model releases required. Reviews 3 × 5 prints. Negotiates payment individually. Buys one-time and online rights.
Tips "Write 'real'; our readers don't respond well to scholarly tomes. Use your everyday voice in all submissions and your chances will go up radically."

$$ ROAD RACER X

Filter Publications, 122 Vista del Rio Dr., Morgantown WV 26508. (304)284-0080. Fax: (304)284-0081. E-mail: letters@roadracerx.com. Website: www.roadracerx.com. **25% freelance written**. 8 issues per year magazine covering motorcycle road racing. "We cover the sport from a lifestyle/personality perspective. We don't do many technical stories or road tests." Estab. 2003. Circ. 35,000. Byline given. Pays on publication. No kill fee. Publishes ms an average of 2 months after acceptance. Buys one-time rights. Editorial lead time 2 months. Submit seasonal material 1 month in advance. Accepts queries by e-mail. Responds in 1 month to queries. Sample copy for #10 SASE. Guidelines available.
Nonfiction Needs historical, (road racing), interview, (racers). "We publish official event programs for several important events, including the Red Bull U.S. Grand Prix & the Miller Motorsports Park World Superbike race. We do not want road tests." **Buys 8 mss/year.** Query. Length: 2,000-3,000 words. **Pays $400-600 for assigned articles. Pays $400-600 for unsolicited articles.** (limit agreed upon in advance)
Photos Contact: Matt Ware. State availability. Reviews GIF/JPEG files. Negotiates payment individually. Buys one time rights.
Columns/Departments Contact: Chris Jonnum. 8 mss/yr. Query. **Pays $25-$100.**
Tips In order for your work to appeal to our readers, you must know the world of motorcycle road racing.

$$ SAND SPORTS MAGAZINE

Wright Publishing Co., Inc., P.O. Box 2260, Costa Mesa CA 92628. (714)979-2560, ext. 107. Fax: (714)979-3998. Website: www.sandsports.net. **Contact:** Michael Sommer, Managing Editor. **20% freelance written**. Bimonthly magazine covering vehicles for off-road and sand dunes. Estab. 1995. Circ. 35,000. Byline given. Pays on publication. Buys first rights, buys one-time rights. Editorial lead time 3 months. Submit seasonal material 6 months in advance. Accepts queries by mail. Sample copy and writer's guidelines free
Nonfiction Needs how-to, technical-mechanical, photo feature, technical. **Buys 20 mss/year.** Query. 1,500 words minimum **Pays $175/page.**
Photos Send photos. Captions, identification of subjects, model releases required. Reviews color slides or high res digital images. Negotiates payment individually. Buys one time rights.

$$ SPEEDWAY ILLUSTRATED

Performance Media, LLC, 107 Elm St., Salisbury MA 01952. (978)465-9099. Fax: (978)465-9033. E-mail: editorial@speedwayillustrated.com. Website: www.speedwayillustrated.com. **40% freelance written**. Monthly magazine covering stock car racing. Estab. 2000. Circ. 146,000. Byline given. Pays on publication. No kill fee. Buys first rights. Editorial lead time 6 weeks. Accepts queries by mail, e-mail, fax. Responds in 2 weeks to queries. Sample copy free.

Nonfiction Needs interview, opinion, personal experience, photo feature, technical. **Buys 30 mss/year.** Query. **Pays variable rate.**
Photos Send photos. Captions, identification of subjects, model releases required. Reviews transparencies, digital. Offers $40-250/photo. Buys all rights.
Tips We seek short, high-interest value pieces that are accompanied by strong photography, in short—knock our socks off.

Olympic Sports

USA GYMNASTICS

132 E. Washington St., Suite 700, Indianapolis IN 46204. (317)237-5050. Fax: (317)237-5069. E-mail: lpeszek@usa-gymnastics.org. Website: www.usa-gymnastics.org. **5% freelance written.** Bimonthly magazine covering gymnastics—national and international competitions. Designed to educate readers on fitness, health, safety, technique, current topics, trends, and personalities related to the gymnastics/fitness field. Readers are gymnasts ages 7-18, parents, and coaches. Estab. 1981. Circ. 100,000. Byline given. Pays on publication. No kill fee. Publishes ms an average of 4 months after acceptance. Buys all rights. Submit seasonal material 4 months in advance. Accepts queries by e-mail, fax. Accepts simultaneous submissions. Responds in 2 months to queries. Sample copy for $5.
Nonfiction Needs general interest, how-to, related to fitness, health, gymnastics, inspirational, interview, photo feature. **Buys 1-2 mss/year.** Query. 1,500 words maximum. **Payment negotiable**
Reprints Send photocopy.
Photos Send photos. Identification of subjects required. Offers no additional payment for photos accepted with ms. Buys all rights.
Tips "Any articles of interest to gymnasts (men, women, rhythmic gymnastics, trampoline, and tumbling and acrobatic gymnastics), coaches, judges, and parents. This includes nutrition, toning, health, safety, trends, techniques, timing, etc."

Running

$ INSIDE TEXAS RUNNING

14201 Memorial Dr., Suite 204, Houston TX 77079. (281)759-0555. Fax: (281)759-7766. E-mail: lance@runningmags.com. Website: www.insidetexasrunning.com. **70% freelance written.** Monthly (except June and August) tabloid covering running and running-related events. Our audience is made up of Texas runners who may also be interested in cross training. Estab. 1977. Circ. 10,000. Byline given. Pays on publication. No kill fee. Publishes ms an average of 2 months after acceptance. Buys one-time, exclusive Texas rights. Submit seasonal material 2 months in advance. Responds in 1 month to mss. Sample copy for $4.95. Guidelines for #10 SASE.
Nonfiction Various topics of interest to runners: Profiles of newsworthy Texas runners of all abilities; unusual events; training interviews. Shoe Review (March); Fall Race Review (September); Marathon Focus (October); Resource Guide (December). **Buys 20 mss/year.** Send complete ms. Length: 500-1,500 words. **Pays $100 maximum for assigned articles. Pays $50 maximum for unsolicited articles.**
Reprints Send tearsheet, photocopy or typed ms with rights for sale noted and information about when and where the material previously appeared.
Photos Send photos. Captions required. Offers $25 maximum/photo. Buys one time rights.
Tips Writers should be familiar with the sport and the publication.

$$ NEW YORK RUNNER

New York Road Runners, 9 E. 89th St., New York NY 10128. (212)423-2260. Fax: (212)423-0879. E-mail: webmaster@nyrr.org. Website: www.nyrr.org. Quarterly magazine covering running, walking, nutrition, and fitness. Estab. 1958. Circ. 45,000. Byline given. Pays on acceptance. Buys first North American serial rights. Submit seasonal material 4 months in advance. Accepts queries by mail, e-mail, fax. Responds in 2 months to queries. Sample copy for $3.

- Material should be of interest to members of the New York Road Runners.

Nonfiction Running and marathon articles. Needs interview, of runners. **Buys 15 mss/year.** Query. Length: 750-1,000 words. **Pays $50-350.**
Columns/Departments Running Briefs (anything noteworthy in the running world), 250-500 words. Query.
Tips Be knowledgeable about the sport of running.

$$$$ RUNNER'S WORLD

Rodale, 135 N. 6th St., Emmaus PA 18098. (610)967-8441. Fax: (610)967-8883. E-mail: rwedit@rodale.com. Website: www.runnersworld.com. **5% freelance written**. Monthly magazine on running, mainly long-distance running. The magazine for and about distance running, training, health and fitness, nutrition, motivation, injury prevention, race coverage, personalities of the sport. Estab. 1966. Circ. 500,000. Byline given. Pays on publication. No kill fee. Publishes ms an average of 6 months after acceptance. Buys all rights. Submit seasonal material 6 months in advance. Accepts queries by mail. Responds in 2 months to queries. Guidelines available online.

Nonfiction Needs how-to, train, prevent injuries, interview, personal experience. No my first marathon stories. No poetry. **Buys 5-7 mss/year.** Query. **Pays $1,500-2,000.**

Photos State availability. Identification of subjects required. Buys one time rights.

Columns/Departments Finish Line (back-of-the-magazine essay, personal experienceÃ³humor). 24 Send complete ms. **Pays $300**

Tips We are always looking for `Adventure Runs' from readers—runs in wild, remote, beautiful, and interesting places. These are rarely race stories but more like backtracking/running adventures. Great color slides are crucial, 2,000 words maximum.

$$ RUNNING TIMES

The Runner's Best Resource, Rodale, Inc., c/o Zephyr Media, P.O. Box 20627, Boulder CO 80308. (203)761-1113. Fax: (203)761-9933. E-mail: editor@runningtimes.com. Website: www.runningtimes.com. **40% freelance written**. Magazine published 10 times/year covering distance running and racing. "*Running Times* is the national magazine for the experienced running participant and fan. Our audience is knowledgeable about the sport and active in running and racing. All editorial relates specifically to running: improving performance, enhancing enjoyment, or exploring events, places, and people in the sport." Estab. 1977. Circ. 102,000. Byline given. Pays on publication. No kill fee. Publishes ms an average of 3 months after acceptance. Buys first North American serial rights, buys second serial (reprint) rights, buys electronic rights. Editorial lead time 4-6 months. Submit seasonal material 6 months in advance. Accepts queries by mail, e-mail. Responds in 1 month to queries. Responds in 2 months to mss. Sample copy for $8. Guidelines available online.

Nonfiction Needs book excerpts, essays, historical, how-to, training, humor, inspirational, interview, new product, opinion, personal experience, with theme, purpose, evidence of additional research and/or special expertise, photo feature, news, reports. No basic, beginner how-to, generic fitness/nutrition, or generic first-person accounts. **Buys 35 mss/year.** Query. Length: 1,500-3,000 words. **Pays $200-1,,000 for assigned articles. Pays $150-300 for unsolicited articles.**

Photos State availability. Identification of subjects required. Negotiates payment individually. Buys one time rights.

Columns/Departments Training (short topics related to enhancing performance), 1,000 words; Sports-Med (application of medical knowledge to running), 1,000 words; Nutrition (application of nutritional principles to running performance), 1,000 words. 10 Query. **Pays $50-200.**

Fiction Any genre, with running-related theme or characters. Buys 1 ms/year. Send complete ms. Length: 1,500-3,000 words. **Pays $100-500.**

Tips "Thoroughly get to know runners and the running culture, both at the participant level and the professional, elite level."

$$ TRAIL RUNNER

One Dirty Magazine, Big Stone Publishing, 417 Main St., Unit N, Carbondale CO 81623. (970)704-1442. Fax: (970)963-4965. E-mail: efish@bigstonepub.com. Website: www.trailrunnermag.com. efish@bigstonepub.com. **Contact:** Michael Benge, editor or Elinor Fish, managing editor. **50% freelance written**. Bimonthly magazine covering trail running, adventure racing, snowshoeing. Covers all aspects of off-road running. "North America's only magazine dedicated to trail running. In-depth editorial and compelling photography informs, entertains and inspires readers of all ages and abilities to enjoy the outdoors and to improve their health and fitness through the sport of trail running." Estab. 1999. Circ. 29,000. Byline given. Pays on publication. Offers $50 kill fee. Publishes ms an average of 2 months after acceptance. Buys first North American serial rights. Editorial lead time is 3 months. Submit seasonal material 5 months in advance. Accepts queries by e-mail. Accepts simultaneous submissions. Responds in 4 weeks to queries. Sample copy for $5. Guidelines available online at http://trailrunnermag.com/contri_guidelines.php.

- "Your well-written query should present a clear, original and provocative story angle, not merely a topic or idea, and should reflect your thorough knowledge of the magazine's content, editorial style and tone."

Nonfiction Needs expose, historical, how-to, humor, inspirational, interview, personal experience, technical, travel, racing. Does not want "My first trail race." **Buys 30-40 mss/year.** Query with one or two writing samples (preferably previously published articles), including your name, phone number and e-mail address. Identify which department your story would be best suited for. **Pays 30 ¢/word for assigned and unsolicited articles.**

Photos Contact: Michael Benge, editor. "*Trail Runner* regularly features stunning photography of trail running destinations, races, adventures and faces of the sport." State availability. of photos with submission. Captions, Identification of subjects. Reviews GIF/JPEG files Offers $50-250/photo. Buys one-time rights.

Columns/Departments Contact: Michael Benge, editor. Making Tracks (news, race reports, athlete Q&A, nutrition tips), 300-800 words; Adventure Racing race (race reports, how-to, athlete profiles), 500-800 words; Nutrition (sports nutrition, health news), 800-1,000 words; Great Escapes (running destinations/trails), 1,200 words. Buys 30 mss/year. Query with published clips. **Pays 30 ¢/word.**

Fiction Pays 25-35 ¢/word.

Fillers Needs anecdotes, facts, newsbreaks, short humor. Buys 10 mss/year. Length: 75-400 words. **Pays 30¢/word.**

Tips "Demonstrate familiarity with the sport. Best way to break in is with interesting and unique news, facts, insights. Check website for more information."

$ $ TRIATHLETE MAGAZINE

The World's Largest Triathlon Magazine, Triathlon Group of North America, 328 Encinitas Blvd., Suite 100, Encinitas CA 92024. (760)634-4100. Fax: (760)634-4110. E-mail: cam@triathletemag.com. Website: www.triathletemag.com. **50% freelance written**. Monthly magazine. In general, articles should appeal to seasoned triathletes, as well as eager newcomers to the sport. Our audience includes everyone from competitive athletes to people considering their first event. Estab. 1983. Circ. 53,864. Byline given. Pays on publication. No kill fee. Buys second serial (reprint) rights, buys all rights. Editorial lead time 3 months. Submit seasonal material 6 months in advance. Accepts queries by mail, e-mail. Accepts simultaneous submissions. Sample copy for $5.

Nonfiction Needs how-to, interview, new product, photo feature, technical. No first-person pieces about your experience in triathlon or my-first-triathlon stories. **Buys 36 mss/year.** Query with published clips. Length: 1,000-3,000 words. **Pays $200-600.**

Photos State availability. Reviews transparencies. Offers $50-300/photo. Buys first North American rights.

Tips Writers should know the sport and be familiar with the nuances and history. Training-specific articles that focus on new, but scientifically based, methods are good, as are seasonal training pieces.

$ WASHINGTON RUNNING REPORT

Capital Running Company, 13710 Ashby Rd., Rockville MD 20853-2903. (301)871-0005. Fax: (301)871-0006. E-mail: kathy@runwashington.com. Website: www.runwashington.com. **90% freelance written**. Bimonthly tabloid covering running and racing in Washington, DC, metropolitan area, including Baltimore and Richmond metro areas. "*Washington Running Report* is written by runners for runners. Features include runner rankings, training tips and advice, feature articles on races, race results, race calendar, humor, product reviews, and other articles of interest to runners." Estab. 1984. Circ. 35,000. Byline given. Pays on publication. Publishes ms an average of 2-4 months after acceptance. Buys first rights, one-time rights, second serial (reprint) rights, simultaneous rights, & electronic rights. Makes work-for-hire assignments. Editorial lead time 1 month. Submit seasonal material 3 months in advance. Accepts queries by mail, e-mail, fax, phone. Accepts previously published material. Accepts simultaneous submissions. Responds in 2-3 weeks to queries. Responds in 1-2 months to mss. Sample copy free.

Nonfiction Needs book excerpts, essays, expose, general interest, historical, how-to, humor, inspirational, interview, new product, opinion, personal experience, photo feature, technical, travel. **Buys 10-12 mss/year.** Query. Length: 500-2,800 words. **Pays $75 for assigned articles. Pays $50 for unsolicited articles.**

Photos Send photos. Captions, identification of subjects required. Reviews contact sheets, 4x6 prints, GIF/JPEG files. Offers $20-50/photo. Buys all rights.

Columns/Departments Traveling Runner (races in exotic locales), 1,400 words; Training Tips (how to run faster, racing strategy), 750 words; Sports Medicine (new developments in the field), 750 words. 3-4 Query with or without published clips or send complete ms. **Pays $50.**

Fiction Needs adventure, cond novels, experimental, fantasy, historical, humorous, mainstream, mystery, slice-of-life vignettes. **Buys 1-2 mss/year.** Send complete ms. Length: 750-1,500 words. **Pays $50.**

Tips "Submit timely articles about running and racing in the DC area; original humor pieces; coverage of a large race in our area."

Skiing & Snow Sports

$ AMERICAN SNOWMOBILER

Kalmbach Publishing Co., P.O. Box 1612, Waukesha WI 53187. Website: www.amsnow.com. **Contact:** Mark Savage, editor. **30% freelance written**. Magazine published 6 times seasonally covering snowmobiling. Estab. 1985. Circ. 54,000. Byline given. Pays on acceptance. No kill fee. Publishes an average of 4 months after acceptance. Buys all rights. Editorial lead time 4 months. Submit seasonal material 6 months in advance. Accepts queries by mail, e-mail, fax. Responds in 1 month to queries. Responds in 2 months to mss. Guidelines available online.

Nonfiction "Seeking race coverage for online." Needs general interest, historical, how-to, interview, personal experience, photo feature, travel. **Buys 10 mss/year.** Query with published clips. Length: 500-1,200 words. **Pay varies for assigned articles. Pays $100 minimum for unsolicited articles.**

Photos State availability. Captions, identification of subjects, model releases required. Offers no additional payment for photos accepted with ms. Buys all rights.

N ⊕ AUSTRALIAN & NEW ZEALAND SKIING

ACP Magazines, Ltd., 54-58 Park St., Sydney NSW 2000 Australia. Website: www.acp.com.au. **Contact:** Jono Brauer, editor. Annual magazine covering skiing in Australia and New Zealand. Circ. 15,000.

Nonfiction Needs general interest, how-to, new product. Query.

$ SKATING

United States Figure Skating Association, 20 First St., Colorado Springs CO 80906-3697. (719)635-5200. Fax: (719)635-9548. E-mail: info@usfigureskating.org. Website: www.usfsa.org. "Magazine published 10 times/year. *Skating* magazine is the official publication of U.S. Figure Skating, and thus we cover skating at both the championship and grass roots level." Estab. 1923. Circ. 45,000. Byline given. Pays on publication. No kill fee. Publishes ms an average of 3 months after acceptance. Buys first rights. Accepts queries by mail, e-mail, fax.

Nonfiction Needs general interest, historical, how-to, interview, background and interests of skaters, volunteers, or other U.S. Figure Skating members, photo feature, technical and competition reports, figure skating issues and trends, sports medicine. **Buys 10 mss/year.** Query. Length: 500-2,500 words. **Payment varies**

Photos Photos purchased with or without accompanying ms. Query. Pays $10 for 8 × 10 or 5 × 7 b&w glossy prints, and $25 for color prints or transparencies.

Columns/Departments Ice Breaker (news briefs); Foreign Competition Reports; Health and Fitness; In Synch (synchronized skating news); Takeoff (up-and-coming athletes), all 500-2,000 words.

Tips We want writing by experienced persons knowledgeable in the technical and artistic aspects of figure skating with a new outlook on the development of the sport. Knowledge and background in technical aspects of figure skating is helpful, but not necessary to the quality of writing expected. We would like to see articles and short features on U.S. Figure Skating volunteers, skaters, and other U.S. Figure Skating members who normally wouldn't get recognized, as opposed to features on championship-level athletes, which are usually assigned to regular contributors. Good quality color photos are a must with submissions. Also would be interested in seeing figure skating 'issues and trends' articles, instead of just profiles. No professional skater material. Synchronized skating and adult skating are the 2 fastest growing aspects of the U.S. Figure Skating. We would like to see more stories dealing with these unique athletes.

$$$$ SKIING

Time 4 Media, Inc., 929 Pearl St., Suite 200, Boulder CO 80302. (303)448-7600. Fax: (303)448-7676. E-mail: editors@time4.com. Website: www.skiingmag.com. Magazine published 7 times/year for skiers who deeply love winter, who live for travel, adventure, instruction, gear, and news. *Skiing* is the user's guide to winter adventure. It is equal parts jaw-dropping inspiration and practical information, action and utility, attitude and advice. It relates the lifestyles of dedicated skiers and captures their spirit of daring and exploration. Dramatic photography transports readers to spine-tingling mountains with breathtaking immediacy. Reading *Skiing* is almost as much fun as being there. Estab. 1948. Circ. 400,000. Byline given. Offers 40% kill fee.

Nonfiction Buys 10-15 feature (1,500-2,000 words) and 12-24 short (100-500 words) mss/year. Query. **Pays $1,000-2,500/feature; $100-500/short piece.**
Columns/Departments Length: 200-1,000 words. 2-3 Query. **Pays $150-1,000.**
Tips Consider less obvious subjects: smaller ski areas, specific local ski cultures, unknown aspects of popular resorts. Be expressive, not merely descriptive. We want readers to feel the adventure in your writing—to tingle with the excitement of skiing steep powder, of meeting intriguing people, of reaching new goals or achieving dramatic new insights. We want readers to have fun, to see the humor in and the lighter side of skiing and their fellow skiers.

$$$ ⊘ SKI MAGAZINE

Times Mirror Magazines, 5720 Flatiron Parkway, Boulder CO 80301. E-mail: editor@skimag.com. Website: www.skimag.com. **60% freelance written**. Magazine published 8 times/year. *Ski* is a ski-lifestyle publication written and edited for recreational skiers. Its content is intended to help them ski better (technique), buy better (equipment and skiwear), and introduce them to new experiences, people, and adventures. Estab. 1936. Circ. 430,000. Byline given. Pays on acceptance. Offers 15% kill fee. Publishes ms an average of 3 months after acceptance. Buys first North American serial rights. Submit seasonal material 8 months in advance. Accepts queries by mail, e-mail. Sample copy for sae with 9 × 12 envelope and 5 First-Class stamps.

- Does not accept unsolicited mss, and assumes no responsibility for their return.

Nonfiction Needs essays, historical, how-to, humor, interview, personal experience. **Buys 5-10 mss/year.** Send complete ms. Length: 1,000-3,500 words. **Pays $500-1,000 for assigned articles. Pays $300-700 for unsolicited articles.**
Photos Send photos. Captions, identification of subjects, model releases required. Offers $75-300/photo. Buys one time rights.
Tips Writers must have an extensive familiarity with the sport and know what concerns, interests, and amuses skiers. Start with short pieces ('hometown hills,' 'dining out,' 'sleeping in'). Columns are most open to freelancers.

$$ SNOWEST MAGAZINE

Harris Publishing, 360 B St., Idaho Falls ID 83402. (208)524-7000. Fax: (208)522-5241. E-mail: lindstrm@snowest.com. Website: snowest.com. **10-25% freelance written**. Monthly magazine. "*SnoWest* covers the sport of snowmobiling, products, and personalities in the western states. This includes mountain riding, deep powder, and trail riding, as well as destination pieces, tech tips, and new model reviews." Estab. 1972. Circ. 140,000. Byline given. Pays on publication. No kill fee. Publishes ms an average of 2 months after acceptance. Buys first North American serial rights. Editorial lead time 6 months. Submit seasonal material 3 months in advance. Sample copy and writer's guidelines free
Nonfiction Needs how-to, fix a snowmobile, make it high performance, new product, technical, travel. **Buys 3-5 mss/year.** Query with published clips. Length: 500-1,500 words. **Pays $150-300.**
Photos Send photos. Captions, identification of subjects required. Negotiates payment individually. Buys one time rights.

$$ SNOW GOER

Affinity Media, 6420 Sycamore Lane, Maple Grove MN 55369. Fax: (763)383-4499. E-mail: terickson@affinitygroup.com. Website: www.snowgoer.com. **5% freelance written**. Magazine published 7 times/year covering snowmobiling. "*Snow Goer* is a hard-hitting, tell-it-like-it-is magazine designed for the ultra-active snowmobile enthusiast. It is fun, exciting, innovative, and on the cutting edge of technology and trends." Estab. 1967. Circ. 66,000. Byline given. Pays on publication. No kill fee. Publishes ms an average of 5 months after acceptance. Buys first rights, buys one-time rights. Editorial lead time 5 months. Submit seasonal material 6 months in advance. Accepts queries by mail, e-mail, fax. Accepts simultaneous submissions. Responds in 3 months to queries. Sample copy for sae with 8 × 10 envelope and 4 First-Class stamps.
Nonfiction Needs general interest, how-to, interview, new product, personal experience, photo feature, technical, travel. **Buys 6 mss/year.** Query. Length: 500-4,000 words. **Pays $50-500.**
Photos State availability. Captions, identification of subjects required. Reviews contact sheets, prints. Negotiates payment individually. Buys one-time rights or all rights.

⊘ TRANSWORLD SNOWBOARDING

Transworld Media, 2052 Corte del Nogal, Suite B, Carlsbad CA 92011. (760)722-7777. Fax: (760)722-0653. E-mail: snowmail@transworld.net. Website: www.transworldsnowboarding.net. **Contact:** Editor. Magazine published 8 times/year edited for the snowboarding enthusiast. Circ. 250,000. No kill fee. Editorial lead time 3 months.

- Query before submitting.

Water Sports

⊘ BOATING

Bonnier Corporation, 460 N. Orlando Ave., Suite 200, Winter Park FL 32789. (407)628-4802. Fax: (407)628-7061. Website: www.boatingmag.com. Monthly magazine dedicated to manufacturers, distributors and consumers involved in the boating industry. "Our purpose is to deliver an entertaining mix of instrumented, objective evaluations of new powerboats, accessories and equipment; lively feature stories that embody the adventure of the sport; and in-depth, how-to service articles that have an immediate impact on the lives of our readers." Circ. 195,559. No kill fee. Editorial lead time 3 months.

- Query before submitting.

Photos Contact: Rob Dybec.

$ DIVER

241 E. 1st St., North Vancouver BC V7L 1B4 Canada. (604)948-9937. Fax: (604)948-9985. E-mail: editor@divermag.com. Website: www.divermag.com. Magazine published 8 times/year emphasizing sport scuba diving, ocean science, and technology for a well-educated, active readership across North America and around the world. Circ. 30,000. No kill fee. Accepts queries by e-mail.

Nonfiction "Well-written and illustrated global dive destination stories featuring warm and cold water diving, and stories relating to any/every aspect of the sport and the underwater experience. Travel articles are committed well in advance." Query first. Length: 500-3,000 words. **Pays 12.5 ¢/word, $25/photo inside, $350 for cover photo.**

Photos Captions, identification of subjects required. Reviews 5 × 7 prints, JPEG/TIFF files (300 dpi), slides, maps, drawings.

$$ PADDLER MAGAZINE

World's No. 1 Canoeing, Kayaking and Rafting Magazine, Paddlesport Publishing, 12040 98th Ave. NE, Suite 205, Kirkland WA 98034. E-mail: mike@paddlermagazine.com. Website: www.paddlermagazine.com. **70% freelance written**. Bimonthly magazine covering paddle sports. *Paddler* magazine is written by and for those knowledgeable about river running, flatwater canoeing and sea kayaking. Our core audience is the intermediate to advanced paddler, yet we strive to cover the entire range from beginners to experts. Our editorial coverage is divided between whitewater rafting, whitewater kayaking, canoeing and sea kayaking. We strive for balance between the Eastern and Western U.S. paddling scenes and regularly cover international expeditions. We also try to integrate the Canadian paddling community into each publication. Estab. 1991. Circ. 40,000. Byline given. Pays on publication. No kill fee. Publishes ms an average of 6 months after acceptance. Buys first North American serial rights, buys one-time electronic rights rights. Editorial lead time 3 months. Submit seasonal material 6 months in advance. Accepts queries by mail, e-mail. Responds in 6 months to queries. Sample copy for $3 with 8 1/2â—Š11 SASE. Guidelines available online.

Nonfiction Needs book excerpts, essays, general interest, historical, how-to, humor, inspirational, interview, new product, opinion, personal experience, photo feature, technical, travel, must be paddlesport related. **Buys 75 mss/year.** Query. Length: 100-3,000 words. **Pays 10-25¢/word (more for established writers) for assigned articles. Pays 10-20¢/word for unsolicited articles.**

Photos Submissions should include photos or other art. State availability. Reviews contact sheets, negatives, transparencies. Offers $25-200/photo. Buys one time rights.

Columns/Departments Hotline (timely news and exciting developments relating to the paddling community. Stories should be lively and newsworthy), 150-750 words; Paddle People (unique people involved in the sport and industry leaders), 600-800 words; Destinations (informs paddlers of unique places to paddleÃ³we often follow regional themes and cover all paddling disciplines); submissions should include map and photo, 800 words. Marketplace (gear reviews, gadgets and new products, and is about equipment paddlers use, from boats and paddles to collapsible chairs, bivy sacks and other accessories), 250-800 words. Paddle Tales (short, humorous anecdotes), 75-300 words. Skills (a How-to forum for experts to share tricks of the trade, from playboating techniques to cooking in the backcountry), 250-1,000 words. Query. **Pays 20-25¢/word.**

Tips We prefer queries, but will look at manuscripts on speculation. No phone queries please. Be familiar with the magazine and offer us unique, exciting ideas. Most positive responses to queries are on spec, but we will occasionally make assignments.

$ SURFER MAGAZINE

Primedia Enthusiast Group, P.O. Box 1028, Dana Point CA 92629-5028. (949)661-5115. E-mail: chris.mauro@primedia.com. Website: www.surfermag.com. Monthly magazine edited for the avid surfers and those who follow the beach, wave riding scene. Circ. 118,570. No kill fee. Editorial lead time 10 weeks.

- Query before submitting.

$$ SWIMMING WORLD MAGAZINE

Sports Publications International, P.O. Box 20337, Sedona AZ 86341. (928)284-4005. Fax: (928)284-2477. E-mail: editorial@swimmingworldmagazine.com. Website: www.swimmingworldmagazine.com. **30% freelance written**. Bimonthly magazine about competitive swimming. Readers are fitness-oriented adults from varied social and professional backgrounds who share swimming as part of their lifestyle. Submit 250-word synopsis of your article. Estab. 1960. Circ. 50,000. Byline given. Pays on publication. Buys all rights. Editorial lead time 2 months. Submit seasonal material 3 months in advance. Accepts queries by mail, e-mail, fax. Accepts simultaneous submissions. Responds in 1 month to queries. Guidelines available online.

- Included in this publication are *Swimming Technique*, *Swim Magazine*, and *Junior Swimmer*.

Nonfiction Articles need to be informative as well as interesting. In addition to fitness and health articles, we are interested in exploring fascinating topics dealing with swimming for the adult reader. Needs book excerpts, essays, expose, general interest, historical, how-to, training plans and techniques, humor, inspirational, interview, people associated with fitness and competitive swimming, new product, articles describing new products for fitness and competitive training, personal experience, photo feature, technical, travel, general health. **Buys 30 mss/year.** Query. Length: 250-2,500 words. **Pays $75-400.**
Photos Send photos. Captions, identification of subjects, model releases required. Reviews high-resolution digital images. Negotiates payment individually.

TRACKS

Wolseley Media, Level 5, 55 Chandos St., St. Leonards NSW 2065 Australia. (61)(2)9901 6100. Fax: (61)(2)9901 6116. E-mail: lkennedy@tracksmag.com.au. Website: www.tracksmag.com.au. **Contact:** Luke Kennedy, editor. Monthly magazine covering hardcore surfing in Australia. Our stories come from the surfing heartland. They're typical, soul-searching, inspirational and occasionally very stupid. Circ. 36,000.
Nonfiction Needs general interest, how-to, humor, inspirational, interview, new product. Query.

TRANSWORLD SURF

Bonnier Corp., 2052 Corte del Nogal, Suite B, Carlsbad CA 92011. (760)722-7777. Fax: (760)722-0653. Website: http://surf.transworld.net. http://bonniercorp.com/brands/trans-world-surf.html. **Contact:** Casey Koteen, man. ed. Monthly magazine designed to promote the growth of the sport of surfing. "Each issue features contests from around the world, profiles of up-and-coming surfers, interviews with seasoned pros, tricks, tips and amazing action photos. It represents the new voice of surfing, dedicated to young surfers and showcasing the progression of the sport. The magazine is committed to growing the sport by exploring new technologies, trends and exotic travel destinations. TransWorld SURF is a leader in the documentation of the sport, having pioneered, funded and mastered remote-flash surf photography, a technique now used by every major surf magazine. And TransWorld SURF's art direction has changed the way surf publications worldwide portray the sport." Circ. 85,000. No kill fee.
Photos "For the Check ME Out contest, submit photos to: transworldsurf@gmail.com. Send surf shot, name, age, hometown, short bio."

$ THE WATER SKIER

USA Water Ski, 1251 Holy Cow Rd., Polk City FL 33868-8200. (863)324-4341. Fax: (863)325-8259. E-mail: satkinson@usawaterski.org. Website: www.usawaterski.org. **10-20% freelance written**. Magazine published 7 times/year. *The Water Skier* is the membership magazine of USA Water Ski, the national governing body for organized water skiing in the United States. The magazine has a controlled circulation and is available only to USA Water Ski's membership, which is made up of 20,000 active competitive water skiers and 10,000 members who are supporting the sport. These supporting members may participate in the sport but they don't compete. The editorial content of the magazine features distinctive and informative writing about the sport of water skiing only. Estab. 1951. Circ. 30,000. Byline given. Offers 30% kill fee. Editorial lead time 4 months. Submit seasonal material 6 months in advance. Responds in 2 weeks to queries. Sample copy for $3.50. Guidelines for #10 SASE.

Nonfiction Needs historical, has to pertain to water skiing, interview, call for assignment, new product, boating and water ski equipment, travel, water ski vacation destinations. **Buys 10-15 mss/year.** Query. Length: 1,500-3,000 words. **Pays $100-150.**
Reprints Send photocopy. Payment negotiable.
Photos State availability. Captions, identification of subjects required. Reviews contact sheets. Negotiates payment individually. Buys all rights.
Columns/Departments The Water Skier News (small news items about people and events in the sport), 400-500 words. Other topics include safety, training (3-event, barefoot, disabled, show ski, ski race, kneeboard, and wakeboard); champions on their way; new products. Query. **Pays $50-100.**
Tips Contact the editor through a query letter (please, no phone calls) with an idea. Avoid instruction, these articles are written by professionals. Concentrate on articles about the people of the sport. We are always looking for interesting stories about people in the sport. Also, short news features which will make a reader say to himself, `Hey, I didn't know that.' Keep in mind that the publication is highly specialized about the sport of water skiing.

WAVES

Wolseley Media, Level 5, 55 Chandos St., St. Leonards NSW 2065 Australia. 02 9901 6185. Fax: 02 9901 6116. E-mail: mckerlie@wavesmag.com.au. Website: www.wavesmag.com.au. **Contact:** Roghan McKerlie, editor. Monthly magazine covering surfing. "*Waves* is innovation in surfing. It is hero-driven, irreverent & fashionable." Circ. 30,000.
Nonfiction Needs general interest, how-to, interview, new product. Query.

Teen & Young Adult

$$ BREAKAWAY MAGAZINE

Focus on the Family, 8605 Explorer Dr., Colorado Springs CO 80920. (719)531-3400. Website: www.breakawaymag.com. **25% freelance written**. Monthly magazine covering extreme sports, Christian music artists, and new technology relevant to teen boys. This fast-paced, 4-color publication is designed to creatively teach, entertain, inspire, and challenge the emerging teenager. It also seeks to strengthen a boy's self-esteem, provide role models, guide a healthy awakening to girls, make the Bible relevant, and deepen their love for family, friends, church, and Jesus Christ. Estab. 1990. Circ. 90,000. Byline given. Pays on acceptance. Offers $25 kill fee. Publishes ms an average of 5-12 months after acceptance. Buys first North American serial rights, buys first rights, buys one-time rights, buys electronic rights. Editorial lead time 5 months. Submit seasonal material 8 months in advance. Accepts queries by mail. Responds in 2-3 months to queries. Responds in 2-3 months to mss. Sample copy for $1.50 and 9 × 12 SASE with 3 first-class stamps. Guidelines for #10 SASE.
Nonfiction Needs inspirational, interview, personal experience. **Buys up to 6 mss/year.** Send complete ms. Length: 700-2,000 words. **Pays 12-15¢/word.**
Columns/Departments Epic Truth (spiritual/Biblical application devotional for teen guys), 800 words; Weird, Wild, WOW! (technology, culture, science), 200-400 words. 2-3 Send complete ms. **Pays 12-15¢/word**
Fiction Needs adventure, humorous, religious, suspense. Avoid Christian jargon, clichés, preaching, and other dialogue that isn't realistic or that interrupts the flow of the story. **Buys 3-4 mss/year.** Send complete ms. Length: 600-2,000 words. **Pays 15-20¢/word.**
Tips Some of our readers get spiritual nurture at home and at church; many don't. To reach both groups, the articles must be written in ways that are compelling, bright, out of the ordinary. Nearly every adult in a boy's life is an authority figure. We would like you, through the magazine, to be seen as a friend! We also want *Breakaway* to be a magazine any pre-Christian teen could pick up and understand without first learning 'Christianese.' Stories should spiritually challenge, yet be spiritually inviting.

$$ CICADA MAGAZINE

Cricket Magazine Group, 140 S. Dearborn St., Suite 1450, Chicago IL 60603. (312)701-1720. Fax: (312)701-1728. Website: www.cricketmag.com. **80% freelance written**. Bimonthly literary magazine for ages 14 and up. Publishes original short stories, poems, and first-person essays written for teens and young adults. Estab. 1998. Circ. 17,000. Byline given. Pays on publication. Accepts previously published material. Accepts simultaneous submissions. Responds in 3 months to mss. Guidelines available online.
Nonfiction Looking for first-person experiences that are relevant and interesting to teenagers. Needs essays, personal experience, book reviews. Submit complete ms, SASE. 5,000 words maximum; 300-500 words/book reviews. **Pays up to 25¢/word.**

Reprints Send typed manuscript. Payment varies.
Photos Send photocopies/tearsheets of artwork.
Fiction The main protagonist should be at least 14 and preferably older. Stories should have a genuine teen sensibility and be aimed at readers in high school or college. Needs adventure, fantasy, historical, humorous, mainstream, novel concepts, romance, science fiction, contemporary, realistic, novellas (1/issue). 5,000 words maximum (up to 15,000 words/novellas). **Pays up to 25¢/word.**
Poetry Needs free verse, light verse, traditional. 25 lines maximum. **Pays up to $3/line.**

$$$$ ☒ COSMOGIRL!

A Cool New Magazine for Teens, The Hearst Corp., 224 W. 57th St., 3rd Floor, New York NY 10019. (212)649-3852. E-mail: inbox@cosmogirl.com. Website: www.cosmogirl.com. Monthly magazine covering fashion, beauty, photos and profiles of young celebs, advice, health and fitness, dating, relationships and finance. CosmoGIRL! has the voice of a cool older sister. The magazine is conversational, funny, down-to-earth, and honest. We never talk down to our readers, who are 12- to 22-year-old young women. Estab. 1999. Circ. 1,350,000. Byline given. Offers 25% kill fee. Buys all rights. Editorial lead time 3-4 months. Accepts queries by mail. Responds in 2 months to queries. Guidelines by e-mail.
Nonfiction Contact: Look at the masthead of a current issue for the appropriate editor. Looking for features with a news bent that pertains to teenagers' lives; quizzes; relationship stories; dynamic first-person stories. Needs interview, opinion, personal experience. **Pays $1/ word.**
Photos Put name, phone # and address on back of all photos. Send photos.

$$ GUIDEPOSTS SWEET 16

1050 Broadway, Suite 6, Chesterton IN 46304. (219)929-4429. Fax: (219)926-3839. E-mail: writers@sweet16mag.com. Website: www.sweet16mag.com. **90% freelance written.** Bimonthly magazine serving as an inspiration for teens. "*Sweet 16* is a general interest magazine for teenage girls (ages 11-17). We are an inspirational publication that offers true, first-person stories about real teens. Our watchwords are 'wholesome,' 'current,' 'fun,' and 'inspiring.' We also publish shorter pieces on fashion, beauty, celebrity, boys, embarrassing moments, and advice columns." Estab. 1998. Circ. 145,000. Byline sometimes given. Pays on acceptance. Offers 25% kill fee. Buys all rights. Editorial lead time 6 months. Submit seasonal material 6 months in advance. Accepts queries by mail, e-mail. Accepts simultaneous submissions. Responds in 6 weeks to queries. Responds in 6 weeks to mss. Sample copy for $4.50. Guidelines available online.
Nonfiction Nothing written from an adult point of view. Needs how-to, humor, inspirational, interview, personal experience. **Buys 80 mss/year.** Query. Length: 200-1,500 words. **Pays $300-500 for assigned articles. Pays $100-300 for unsolicited articles.**
Photos State availability. Identification of subjects required. Negotiates payment individually. Buys one time rights.
Columns/Departments Quiz (teen-related topics/teen language), 500-600 words; Positive Thinker (first-person stories of teen who've overcome something remarkable and kept a positive outlook), 300 words; Mysterious Moments (first-person strange-but-true stories), 250 words; Too Good to be True (profile of a cute wholesome teen guy who has more than looks/has done something very cool/has overcome something extraordinary), 400 words. 40 Query with published clips. **Pays $175-400.**
Tips We are eagerly looking for a number of things: teen profiles, quizzes, DIYs. Most of all, though, we are about TRUE STORIES in the *Guideposts* tradition. Teens in dangerous, inspiring, miraculous situations. These first-person (ghostwritten) true narratives are the backbone of *Sweet 16*—and what sets us apart from other publications.

$ INSIGHT

Because Life Is Full of Decisions, The Review and Herald Publishing Association, 55 W. Oak Ridge Dr., Hagerstown MD 21740. (301)393-4038. E-mail: insight@rhpa.org. Website: www.insightmagazine.org. **80% freelance written.** Weekly magazine covering spiritual life of teenagers. *Insight* publishes true dramatic stories, interviews, and community and mission service features that relate directly to the lives of Christian teenagers, particularly those with a Seventh-day Adventist background. Estab. 1970. Circ. 20,000. Byline given. Pays on publication. No kill fee. Publishes ms an average of 4 months after acceptance. Buys first rights, buys second serial (reprint) rights. Editorial lead time 6 months. Submit seasonal material 6 months in advance. Accepts queries by mail, e-mail, fax. Responds in 1 month to mss. Sample copy for $2 and #10 SASE. Guidelines available online.

- 'Big Deal' appears in *Insight* often, covering a topic of importance to teens. Each feature contains: An opening story involving real teens (can be written in first-person), Scripture Picture (a sidebar that discusses what the Bible says about the topic) and another sidebar (optional) that adds more perspective and help.

Nonfiction Needs how-to, teen relationships and experiences, humor, interview, personal experience, photo feature, religious. **Buys 120 mss/year.** Send complete ms. Length: 500-2,000 words. **Pays $25-150 for assigned articles. Pays $25-125 for unsolicited articles.**

Reprints Send typed manuscript with rights for sale noted and information about when and where the material previously appeared. Pays $50.

Photos State availability. Model releases required. Reviews contact sheets, negatives, transparencies, prints. Negotiates payment individually. Buys one time rights.

Columns/Departments Big Deal (topic of importance to teens) 1,200-1,700 words; Interviews (Christian culture figures, especially musicians), 2,000 words; It Happened to Me (first-person teen experiences containing spiritual insights), 1,000 words; On the Edge (dramatic true stories about Christians), 2,000 words; So I Said.(true short stories in the first person of common, everyday events and experiences that taught the writer something), 300-500 words. Send complete ms. **Pays $25-125.**

Tips Skim 2 months of *Insight*. Write about your teen experiences. Use informed, contemporary style and vocabulary. Follow Jesus' life and example.

$ $ LISTEN MAGAZINE

Celebrating Positive Choices, The Health Connection, 55 W. Oak Ridge Dr., Hagerstown MD 21740. (301)393-4010. E-mail: editor@listenmagazine.org. Website: www.listenmagazine.org. **80% freelance written**. Monthly magazine specializing in tobacco, drug, and alcohol prevention, presenting positive alternatives to various tobacco, drug, and alcohol dependencies. *Listen* is used in many high school classes and by professionals: medical personnel, counselors, law enforcement officers, educators, youth workers, etc. Circ. 20,000. Byline given. Publishes ms an average of 6 months after acceptance. Pays on acceptance for first rights for use in *Listen*, reprints, and associated material. Accepts queries by mail, e-mail. Accepts previously published material. Accepts simultaneous submissions. Responds in 2 months to queries. Sample copy for $2 and 9 × 12 SASE. Guidelines available online.

Nonfiction Subjects may or may not have a direct connection to drug use. Especially interested in youth-slanted articles or personality interviews encouraging nonalcoholic and non-drug ways of life and showing positive alternatives. Also interested in good activity articles about sports or hobbies to interest a teen. Teenage point of view is essential. **Pays $250 for Personalities (800 words); $150 for hobby/sport/activity (700 words); $150 for factuals (800 words); life skills articles $200 (950 words) and 3 contributor's copies. Buys 30-50 unsolicited mss/year.** Query.

Reprints Send photocopy of article or typed ms with rights for sale ted and information about when and where the material previously appeared. Pays their regular rates.

Photos Color photos preferred. Captions required. Purchased with accompanying ms.

Tips In query, briefly summarize article idea and logic of why you feel it's good. Make sure you've read the magazine to understand our approach. Yearly theme lists available on our website.

$ $ THE NEW ERA

50 E. North Temple, Salt Lake City UT 84150. (801)240-2951. Fax: (801)240-2270. E-mail: newera@ldschurch.org. Website: www.newera.lds.org. **Contact:** Richard M. Romney, managing editor. **20% freelance written**. Monthly magazine for young people (ages 12-18) of the Church of Jesus Christ of Latter-day Saints (Mormon), their church leaders and teachers. Estab. 1971. Circ. 230,000. Byline given. Pays on acceptance. No kill fee. Publishes ms an average of 1 year after acceptance. Buys all rights. Submit seasonal material 1 year in advance. Accepts queries by mail, e-mail, fax. Responds in 2 months to queries. Sample copy for $1.50. Guidelines available online.

Nonfiction "Material that shows how the Church of Jesus Christ of Latter-day Saints is relevant in the lives of young people today. Must capture the excitement of being a young Latter-day Saint. Special interest in the experiences of young Mormons in other countries. No general library research or formula pieces without the *New Era* slant and feel." Needs how-to, humor, inspirational, interview, personal experience, informational. Query. Length: 150-1,200 words. **Pays $25-350/article.**

Photos Uses b&w photos and transparencies with manuscripts. Individual photos used for *Photo of the Month* Payment depends on use, $10-125 per photo.

Columns/Departments What's Up? (news of young Mormons around the world); How I Know; Scripture Lifeline. **Pays $25-125/article.**

Poetry Needs free verse, light verse, traditional, all other forms. Must relate to editorial viewpoint. **Pays $25 and up.**

Tips "The writer must be able to write from a Mormon point of view. We're especially looking for stories about successful family relationships and personal growth. Well-written, personal experiences are always in demand."

SCHOLASTIC ACTION

Scholastic, Inc., 557 Broadway, New York NY 10012-3902. (212)343-6100. Fax: (212)343-6945. E-mail: actionmag@scholastic.com. Website: www.scholastic.com. Published 14 times/year. Written for teenagers with profiles of TV and movie celebrities and famous athletes. It also includes true teen nonfiction articles and vocabulary activities. Circ. 200,000. No kill fee. Editorial lead time 2 months.

$$$$ SEVENTEEN

300 W. 57th St., 17th Floor, New York NY 10019. (917)934-6500. Fax: (917)934-6574. Website: www.seventeen.com. **20% freelance written.** Monthly magazine. *Seventeen* is a young woman's first fashion and beauty magazine. Tailored for young women in their teens and early twenties, *Seventeen* covers fashion, beauty, health, fitness, food, college, entertainment, fiction, plus crucial personal and global issues. Estab. 1944. Circ. 2,400,000. Byline given. Pays on acceptance. Offers 25% kill fee. Publishes ms an average of 6 months after acceptance. Buys one-time rights. Accepts queries by mail. Responds in 3 months to queries. Writer's guidelines available online

Nonfiction Articles and features of general interest to young women who are concerned with intimate relationships and how to realize their potential in the world; strong emphasis on topicality and service. Send brief outline and query, including typical lead paragraph, summing up basic idea of article, with clips of previously published works. Articles are commissioned after outlines are submitted and approved. Length: 1,200-2,500 words. **Pays $1/word, occasionally more.**

Photos Photos usually by assignment only.

Tips Writers have to ask themselves whether or not they feel they can find the right tone for a *Seventeen* article—a tone which is empathetic, yet never patronizing; lively, yet not superficial. Not all writers feel comfortable with, understand, or like teenagers. If you don't like them, *Seventeen* is the wrong market for you. An excellent way to break in to the magazine is by contributing ideas for quizzes or the 'My Story' (personal essay) column.

$$ ⊘ TEEN MAGAZINE

Hearst Magazines, 3000 Ocean Park Blvd., Suite 3048, Santa Monica CA 90405. (310)664-2950. Fax: (310)664-2959. Website: www.teenmag.com. Quarterly magazine. for a Jr. high school female audience; median age is 14 years old. *TEEN* teens are upbeat and want to be informed. Estab. 1957. Pays on acceptance. No kill fee. Buys all rights.

- Bylines not guaranteed.

Nonfiction Does not want to see adult-oriented, adult point of view. **Pays $200-600.**

Fiction Does not want to see that which does not apply to our market—i.e., science fiction, history, religious, adult-oriented. **Pays $200-800-400.**

TWIST

Bauer Publishing, 270 Sylvan Ave., Englewood Cliffs NJ 07632. (201)569-6699. E-mail: twistmail@twistmagazine.com. Website: www.twistmagazine.com. www.bauermagazine.com. **Contact:** Tina Donvito. **5% freelance written**. Monthly entertainment magazine targeting 14- to 19-year-old girls. "TWIST specializes in delivering the hottest new shopping and style trends from Young Hollywood. From tips on the latest hair trends to the scoop on the hottest handbags. TWIST has got the goods on all that's "in" in the world of teen celebrity style." Estab. 1997. Circ. 700,000. Pays on acceptance. Offers 20% kill fee. Publishes ms an average of 3 months after acceptance. Buys first North American serial rights. Editorial lead time 3 months. Submit seasonal material 4 months in advance. Accepts queries by mail. Accepts simultaneous submissions. Responds in 1 month to queries. Guidelines available online.

Nonfiction No articles written from an adult point of view about teens; i.e., a mother's or teacher's personal account. Needs personal experience, real teens' experiences, preferably in first person. **Payment varies according to assignment.**

Photos State availability. Identification of subjects, model releases required. Negotiates payment individually.

Tips "Tone must be conversational, neither condescending to teens nor trying to be too slangy. If possible, send clips that show an ability to write for the teen market. We are in search of real-life stories, and writers who can find teens with compelling real-life experiences (who are willing to use their full names and photographs in the magazine). Please refer to a current issue to see examples of tone and content. No e-mail queries or submissions, please."

$ WINNER

Saying No To Drugs and Yes To Life, The Health Connection, 55 W. Oak Ridge Dr., Hagerstown MD 21740. (301)393-4082. Fax: (301)393-4088. E-mail: winner@healthconnection.org. Website: www.winnermagazine.org. **30% freelance written**. Monthly magazine covering positive lifestyle choices for students in grades 4-6. *Winner* is a teaching tool to help students learn the dangers in abusive substances, such as tobacco, alcohol, and other drugs, as well as at-risk behaviors. It also focuses on everyday problems such as dealing with divorce, sibling rivalry, coping with grief, and healthy diet, to mention just a few. Estab. 1956. Circ. 12,000. Byline sometimes given. Pays on acceptance. Offers 50% kill fee. Publishes ms an average of 6-9 months after acceptance. Buys first North American serial rights, buys first rights. Editorial lead time 5 months. Submit seasonal material 6-8 months in advance. Accepts queries by mail, e-mail, fax, phone. Accepts simultaneous submissions. Responds in 4-6 weeks to queries. Responds in 2-3 months to mss. Sample copy for $2 and 9 × 12 SAE with 2 first-class stamps. Guidelines for SASE, by e-mail, fax or on website.

Nonfiction Needs general interest, humor, drug/alcohol/tobacco activities, personalities, family relationships, friends. No occult, mysteries. I prefer true-to-life stories. Query or send complete ms. Length: 600-650 words. **Pays $50-80.**

Photos State availability of or send photos. Model releases required. Reviews GIF/JPEG files. Negotiates payment individually. Buys one time rights.

Columns/Departments Personality (kids making a difference in their community), 600-650 words; Fun & Games (dangers of tobacco, alcohol, and other drugs), 400 words. 9 Query. **Pays $50-80.**

Fiction No suspense or mystery. **Buys 18 mss/year.** Send complete ms. Length: 600-650 words. **Pays $50-80.**

$ $ YOUNG SALVATIONIST

The Salvation Army, P.O. Box 269, Alexandria VA 22313-0269. (703)684-5500. Fax: (703)684-5539. E-mail: ys@usn.salvationarmy.org. Website: www.use.salvationarmy.org. **Contact:** Captain Amy Reardon. **10% freelance written**. Monthly magazine for high school and early college youth. "Young Salvationist provides young people with biblically based inspiration and resources to develop their spirituality. Only material with Christian perspective with practical real-life application will be considered." Circ. 48,000. Byline given. Pays on acceptance. No kill fee. Publishes ms an average of 6 months after acceptance. Buys first North American serial rights, first rights, one-time rights, second serial (reprint) rights. Submit seasonal material 6 months in advance. Accepts queries by Accepts complete mss by mail and e-mail. Responds in 2 months to mss. Sample copy for 9 × 12 SAE with 3 first-class stamps or on website. Writer's guidelines and theme list for #10 SASE or on website.

- "Works with a small number of new/unpublished writers each year."

Nonfiction "Articles should deal with issues of relevance to young people today; avoid 'preachiness' or moralizing." Needs how-to, humor, inspirational, interview, personal experience, photo feature, religious. **Buys 10 mss/year.** Send complete ms. Length: 1,000-1,500 words. **Pays 15¢/word for first rights.**

Reprints Send tearsheet, photocopy or typed ms with rights for sale noted and information about when and where the material previously appeared. Pays 10¢/word for reprints.

Fiction Only a small amount is used. Needs adventure, fantasy, humorous, religious, romance, science fiction, (all from a Christian perspective). **Buys few mss/year.** Length: 500-1,200 words. **Pays 15¢/word.**

Tips "Study magazine, familiarize yourself with the unique 'Salvationist' perspective of *Young Salvationist*; learn a little about the Salvation Army; media, sports, sex, and dating are strongest appeal."

Travel, Camping & Trailer

$ AAA GOING PLACES

Magazine for Today's Traveler, AAA Auto Club South, 1515 N. Westshore Blvd., Tampa FL 33607. (813)289-5923. Fax: (813)288-7935. **50% freelance written**. Bimonthly magazine on auto tips, cruise travel, tours. Estab. 1982. Circ. 2,500,000. Byline given. Pays on publication. No kill fee. Publishes ms an average of 6 months after acceptance. Buys one-time rights. Submit seasonal material 9 months in advance. Accepts simultaneous submissions. Responds in 2 months to mss. Writer's guidelines for SAE

Nonfiction Travel stories feature domestic and international destinations with practical information and where to stay, dine, and shop, as well as personal anecdotes and historical background. Needs historical, how-to, humor, interview, personal experience, photo feature, travel. **Buys 15 mss/year.** Send complete ms. Length: 500-1,200 words. **Pays $50/printed page.**

Photos State availability. Captions required. Reviews 2â—Š2 transparencies, 300 dpi digital images. Offers no additional payment for photos accepted with ms
Columns/Departments What's Happening (local attractions in Florida, Georgia, or Tennessee).
Tips We prefer lively, upbeat stories that appeal to a well-traveled, sophisticated audience, bearing in mind that AAA is a conservative company.

$ $ AAA MIDWEST TRAVELER

AAA Auto Club of Missouri, 12901 N. 40 Dr., St. Louis MO 63141. (314)523-7350 ext. 6301. Fax: (314)523-6982. E-mail: dreinhardt@aaamissouri.com. **Contact:** Deborah Reinhardt, Managing Editor. **80% freelance written**. Bimonthly magazine covering travel and automotive safety. "We provide members with useful information on travel, auto safety and related topics." Estab. 1901. Circ. 500,000. Byline given. Pays on acceptance. Offers $50 kill fee. Buys first North American serial rights, buys second serial (reprint) rights, buys electronic rights. Editorial lead time 1 year. Submit seasonal material 6 months in advance. Accepts queries by mail, e-mail, fax. Accepts simultaneous submissions. Responds in 1 month to queries. Responds in 1 month to mss. Sample copy for sae with 10 × 13 envelope and 4 First-Class stamps. Guidelines for #10 SASE.
Nonfiction Needs travel. No humor, fiction, poetry or cartoons. **Buys 20-30 mss/year.** Query; query with published clips the first time. Length: 800-1,200 words. **Pays $400.**
Photos State availability. Captions required. Reviews transparencies, prints . Offers no additional payment for photos accepted with ms Buys one-time and electronic rights
Tips "Send queries between December and February, as we plan our calendar for the following year. Request a copy. Serious writers ask for media kit to help them target their piece. Send a SASE or download online. Travel destinations and tips are most open to freelancers; all departments and auto-related news handled by staff. We see too many `Here's a recount of our family vacation' manuscripts. Go easy on first-person accounts."

$ $ ☐ ARUBA NIGHTS

Nights Publications, Inc., 1751 Richardson St., Suite 5.530, Montreal QC H3K 1G6 Canada. (514)931-1987. Fax: (514)931-6273. E-mail: editor@nightspublications.com. Website: www.nightspublications.com. **Contact:** Jennifer McMorran, ed. **90% freelance written**. "Annual magazine covering the Aruban vacation lifestyle experience with an upscale, upbeat touch." Estab. 1988. Circ. 245,000. Byline given for feature articles. Pays on acceptance. No kill fee. Publishes ms an average of 9 months after acceptance. Buys North American and Caribbean serial rights. Editorial lead time 1 month. Accepts queries by mail, e-mail, fax. Responds in 2 weeks to queries. Responds in 1 month to mss. Guidelines by e-mail.

- "Let the reader experience the story; utilize the senses; be descriptive; be specific."

Nonfiction Needs general interest, historical, how-to, relative to Aruba vacationers, humor, inspirational, interview, opinion, personal experience, photo feature, travel, ecotourism, Aruban culture, art, activities, entertainment, topics relative to vacationers in Aruba. No negative pieces. **Buys 5-15 mss/year.** Query with published clips. E-mail queries preferred. Length: 250-750 words. **Pays $100-300.**
Photos State availability. Captions, identification of subjects, model releases required. Reviews transparencies. Pays $50/photo Buys one time rights.
Tips "Be descriptive and entertaining and make sure stories are factually correct. Stories should immerse the reader in a sensory adventure. Focus on specific, individual aspects of the Aruban lifestyle and vacation experience (e.g., art, music, culture, a colorful local character, a personal experience, etc.), rather than generalized overviews. Magazine caters to visitors who are already on Aruba, so ensure your story is of interest to this audience."

$ $ ASU TRAVEL GUIDE

ASU Travel Guide, Inc., 448 Ignacio Blvd. #333, Novato CA 94949. (415)898-9500. Fax: (415)898-9501. E-mail: editor@asutravelguide.com. Website: www.asutravelguide.com. **80% freelance written**. Quarterly guidebook covering international travel features and travel discounts for well-traveled airline employees. Estab. 1970. Circ. 36,000. Byline given. Pays on acceptance. No kill fee. Publishes ms an average of 4 months after acceptance. Buys first North American serial rights, buys first rights, buys second serial (reprint) rights. Submit seasonal material 6 months in advance. Accepts previously published material. Accepts simultaneous submissions. Responds in 1 year to queries. Responds in 1 year to mss. Sample copy for sae with 6x9 envelope and 5 First-Class stamps. Guidelines for #10 SASE.
Nonfiction International travel articles similar to those run in consumer magazines. Not interested in amateur efforts from inexperienced travelers or personal experience articles that don't give useful information to other travelers. Destination pieces only; no Tips on Luggage articles. Unsolicited mss or

queries without SASE will not be acknowledged. No telephone queries. Needs travel, international. **Buys 12 mss/year.** Length: 1,800 words. **Pays $200.**

Reprints Send tearsheet and information about when and where the material previously appeared. Pays 100% of amount paid for an original article

Photos Interested in clear, high-contrast photos. Reviews 5 × 7 and 8 × 10 b&w or color prints, JPEGs (300 dpi). Payment for photos is included in article price; photos from tourist offices are acceptable.

Tips Query with samples of travel writing and a list of places you've recently visited. We appreciate clean and simple style. Keep verbs in the active tense and involve the reader in what you write. Avoid `cute' writing, coined words, and stale clichés. The most frequent mistakes made by writers in completing an article for us are: 1) Lazy writing—using words to describe a place that could describe any destination such as `there is so much to do in (fill in destination) that whole guidebooks have been written about it'; 2) Including fare and tour package information—our readers make arrangements through their own airline.

$ BONAIRE NIGHTS

Nights Publications, Inc., 1751 Richardson St., Suite 5.530, Montreal QC H3K 1G6 Canada. (514)931-1987. Fax: (514)931-6273. E-mail: editor@nightspublications.com. **90% freelance written**. Annual magazine covering Bonaire vacation experience. Estab. 1993. Circ. 80,000. Byline given for features. No kill fee. Buys North American and Caribbean serial rights. Editorial lead time 1 month. Accepts queries by mail, e-mail, fax. Responds in 2 weeks to queries. Responds in 1 month to mss. Guidelines by e-mail.

Nonfiction Needs general interest, historical, how-to, humor, interview, opinion, personal experience, photo feature, travel, lifestyle, local culture, art, architecture, activities, scuba diving, snorkeling, ecotourism. **Buys 6-9 mss/year.** E-mail submissions preferred. Mailed mss must include an e-mail address for correspondence. Length: 250-750 words. **Pays $100.**

Photos State availability. Captions, identification of subjects, model releases required. Pays $50/published photo.

Tips Focus on the Bonaire lifestyle, what sets it apart from other islands. We want personal experience on specific attractions and culture, not generalized overviews. Be positive and provide an angle that will appeal to vacationers who are already there. Our style is upbeat, friendly, fluid, and descriptive.

$ CAMPERWAYS, MIDWEST RV TRAVELER, FLORIDA RV TRAVELER, NORTHEAST OUTDOORS, SOUTHERN RV

Woodall Publications Corp., 2575 Vista Del Mar Dr., Ventura CA 93001. (888)656-6669. E-mail: info@woodallpub.com. Website: www.woodalls.com. **75%% freelance written**. Monthly tabloids covering RV lifestyle. We're looking for articles of interest to RVers. Lifestyle articles, destinations, technical tips, interesting events and the like make up the bulk of our publications. We also look for region-specific travel and special interest articles. Circ. 30,000. Byline given. Pays on acceptance. Offers 50% kill fee. Buys first North American serial rights. Accepts queries by mail, e-mail. Sample copy free. Guidelines for #10 SASE.

- Accepts queries in June, July, and August for upcoming year.

Nonfiction Needs how-to, personal experience, technical, travel. No Camping From Hell articles. **Buys approximately 500 mss/year.** Length: 500-2,000 words. **Payment varies**

Photos Prefers slides and large (5 × 7, 300 dpi) digital images. State availability. Captions, identification of subjects required. Reviews negatives, 4â—Š5 transparencies, 4â—Š5 prints. Buys first North American serial rights

Tips Ã®Be an expert in RVing. Make your work readable to a wide variety of readers, from novices to full-timers.Ã®

$ CAMPING TODAY

Official Publication of the Family Campers & RVers, 126 Hermitage Rd., Butler PA 16001-8509. (724)283-7401. Website: www.fcrv.org. **Contact:** DeWayne Johnston, editor. **30% freelance written**. Bimonthly official membership publication of the fcrv. "*Camping Today* is the largest nonprofit family camping and RV organization in the U.S. and Canada. Members are heavily oriented toward RV travel. Concentration is on member activities in chapters. Group is also interested in conservation and wildlife. The majority of members are retired." Estab. 1983. Circ. 10,000. Byline given. Pays on publication. No kill fee. Publishes ms an average of 6 months after acceptance. Buys one-time rights. Submit seasonal material 3 months in advance. Accepts simultaneous submissions. Responds in 2 months to queries and to mss. Sample copy and guidelines for 4 first-class stamps. Guidelines for #10 SASE.

Nonfiction Needs humor, camping or travel related, interview, interesting campers, new product, technical, RVs related, travel, interesting places to visit by RV, camping. **Buys 10-15 mss/year.** Query by mail or e-mail or send complete ms with photos. Length: 750-2,000 words. **Pays $50-150.**
Reprints Send typed manuscript with rights for sale noted and information about when and where the material previously appeared. Pays 35-50% of amount paid for original article.
Photos Need b&w or sharp color prints. Send photos. Captions required.
Tips "Freelance material on RV travel, RV maintenance/safety, and items of general camping interest throughout the United States and Canada will receive special attention. Good photos increase your chances. See website."

$$ CNN TRAVELLER

Highbury House, 47 Brunswick Place, London N1 6EB England. (44)(207)613-6949. E-mail: dan.hayes@ink-publishing.com. Website: www.cnntraveller.com. **50% freelance written**. Bimonthly magazine covering travel. *CNN Traveller* takes readers on a fascinating journey to some of the most intriguing and exotic places in the world. It marries the best in travel journalism and photography with the news values of CNN. The magazines takes an issues-led view of travel, getting behind the headlines with articles that are guaranteed to be intriguing and thought-provoking every issue. Estab. 1998. Circ. 106,500. Byline given. Pays 1 month after publication. Offers 50% kill fee. Publishes ms an average of 3 months after acceptance. Buys all rights. Editorial lead time 2-6 months. Submit seasonal material 4 months in advance. Accepts queries by e-mail, fax. Sample copy available online. Guidelines free.
Nonfiction Needs book excerpts, travel. **Buys 50 mss/year.** Query with published clips. Length: 600-2,000 words. **Pays £120-400 ($225-750) for assigned articles. Pays £100-400 ($190-750) for unsolicited articles.**
Photos State availability. Captions required. Reviews GIF/JPEG files. Negotiates payment individually. Buys one time rights.
Columns/Departments 10 Query with published clips. **Pays £100-200 ($190-375).**

$$$ COAST TO COAST MAGAZINE

Affinity Group, Inc., 2575 Vista Del Mar Dr., Ventura CA 93001. (805)667-4100. E-mail: editor@coastresorts.com. Website: www.coastresorts.com. **80% freelance written**. Quarterly magazine for members of Coast to Coast Resorts. "*Coast to Coast* focuses on North American travel, outdoor recreation, camping and RV parks; circulation is 60,000." Estab. 1983. Byline given. Pays on acceptance. Offers 33% kill fee. Publishes ms an average of 4 months after acceptance. Buys first North American serial rights, prints and electronic. Editorial lead time 5 months. Submit seasonal material 5 months in advance. Accepts queries by mail, e-mail, fax. Accepts previously published material. Accepts simultaneous submissions. Responds in 6-8 weeks to queries. Responds in 1-2 months to mss Sample copy for $4 and 9 × 12 SASE Guidelines for #10 SASE
Nonfiction Needs book excerpts, essays, general interest, how-to, interview, new product, personal experience, photo feature, technical, travel. No poetry, cartoons. **Buys 70 mss/year.** Send complete ms. Length: 800-2,500 words. **Pays $75-1,200.**
Reprints Send photocopy and information about when and where the material previously appeared. Pays approximately 50% of amount paid for original article
Photos sharp, color-saturated high-res digital images, particularly of North American destinations and RV travel
Columns/Departments Pays $ 150-400.
Tips "Send clips or other writing samples with queries, or story ideas will not be considered."

$$ CURACAO NIGHTS

Nights Publications, Inc., 1751 Richardson St., Suite 5.530, Montreal QC H3K 1G6 Canada. (514)931-1987. Fax: (514)931-6273. E-mail: editor@nightspublications.com. **Contact:** Jennifer McMorran, ed. **90% freelance written**. Annual magazine covering the Curacao vacation experience. "We are seeking upbeat, entertaining lifestyle articles; colorful profiles of locals; lively features on culture, activities, nightlife, ecotourism, special events, gambling, how-to features, humor. Our audience is North American vacationers." Estab. 1989. Circ. 165,000. Byline given. No kill fee. Buys North American and Caribbean serial rights. Editorial lead time 1 month. Accepts queries by mail, e-mail, fax. Responds in 2 weeks to queries. Responds in 1 month to mss. Guidelines by e-mail.
Nonfiction Needs general interest, historical, how-to, help a vacationer get the most from their vacation, humor, interview, opinion, personal experience, photo feature, travel, ecotourism, lifestyle, local culture, art, activities, nightlife, topics relative to vacationers in Curacao. No negative pieces, generic copy,

or stale rewrites. **Buys 5-10 mss/year.** Query with published clips; e-mail submissions are preferred. Length: 250-750 words. **Pays $100-300.**

Photos State availability. Captions, identification of subjects, model releases required. Reviews transparencies. Pays $50/photo Buys one time rights.

Tips "Demonstrate your voice in your query letter. Focus on individual aspects of the island lifestyle and vacation experience (e.g., art, music, culture, a colorful local character, a personal experience, etc.), rather than a generalized overview. Provide an angle that will be entertaining to vacationers who are already on the island. Our style is upbeat, friendly, and fluid."

$ $ FAMILY MOTOR COACHING

Official Publication of the Family Motor Coach Association, 8291 Clough Pike, Cincinnati OH 45244. (513)474-3622. Fax: (513)388-5286. E-mail: magazine@fmca.com. Website: www.fmca.com. **Contact:** Robbin Gould, editor. **80% freelance written. We prefer that writers be experienced RVers.** Monthly magazine emphasizing travel by motorhome, motorhome mechanics, maintenance, and other technical information. "*Family Motor Coaching* magazine is edited for the members and prospective members of the Family Motor Coach Association who own or are about to purchase self-contained, motorized recreational vehicles known as motorhomes. Featured are articles on travel and recreation, association news and activities, plus articles on new products and motorhome maintenance and repair. Approximately 1/3 of editorial content is devoted to travel and entertainment, 1/3 to association news, and 1/3 to new products, industry news, and motorhome maintenance." Estab. 1963. Circ. 140,000. Byline given. Pays on acceptance. Publishes ms an average of 8 months after acceptance. Buys first North American serial rights and electronic rights. Submit seasonal material 4 months in advance. Accepts queries by mail, e-mail, fax. Responds in 3 months to queries. Sample copy for $3.99; $5 if paying by credit card. Guidelines for #10 SASE or request PDF by e-mail.

Nonfiction Needs how-to, do-it-yourself motorhome projects and modifications, humor, interview, new product, technical, motorhome travel (various areas of North America accessible by motorhome), bus conversions, nostalgia. **Buys 50-75 mss/year.** Query with published clips. Length: 1,000-2,000 words. **Pays $100-500, depending on article category.**

Photos State availability. Captions, model releases, True required. Offers no additional payment for b&w contact sheets, 35mm 21/4x21/4 color transparencies, or high-resolution electronic images (300 dpi and at least 4x6 in size). Prefers first North American serial and electronic rights to editorial but will consider one-time rights on photos only.

Tips "The greatest number of contributions we receive are travel; therefore, that area is the most competitive. However, it also represents the easiest way to break in to our publication. Articles should be written for those traveling by self-contained motorhome. The destinations must be accessible to motorhome travelers and any peculiar road conditions should be mentioned."

$ GO MAGAZINE

AAA Carolinas, 6600 AAA Dr., Charlotte NC 28212. (704)569-7733. Fax: (704)569-7815. E-mail: trcrosby@aaaqa.com. Website: www.aaacarolinas.com. Bimonthly magazine covering travel, automotive, safety (traffic), and insurance. Consumer-oriented membership publication providing information on things such as car buying, vacations, travel safety problems, etc. Estab. 1928. Circ. 910,000. Pays on publication. No kill fee. Makes work-for-hire assignments. Editorial lead time 3-4 months. Accepts queries by mail, fax. Responds in 6 weeks to queries. Responds in 3 months to mss. Sample copy for sae with 1 envelope and 4 First-Class stamps. Guidelines for #10 SASE.

Nonfiction Needs how-to, fix auto, travel safety, etc., travel, automotive insurance, traffic safety. **Buys 16-18 mss/year.** Query with published clips. Length: 600-900 words. **Pays $150/published story.**

Photos Send photos. Offers no additional payment for photos accepted with ms. Buys one time rights.

$ $ HIGHWAYS

The Official Publication of the Good Sam Club, Affinity Group, Inc., 2575 Vista Del Mar Dr., Ventura CA 93001. (805)667-4100. Fax: (805)667-4454. E-mail: goodsam@goodsamclub.com. Website: www.goodsamclub.com/highways. **30% freelance written**. Monthly magazine covering recreational vehicle lifestyle. All of our readers own some type of RV—a motorhome, trailer, pop-up, tent—so our stories need to include places that you can go with large vehicles, and campgrounds in and around the area where they can spend the night. Estab. 1966. Circ. 975,000. Byline given. Pays on acceptance. Offers 50% kill fee. Publishes ms an average of 6 months after acceptance. Buys first North American serial rights, buys electronic rights. Accepts queries by e-mail. Responds in 2 weeks to queries. Sample copy and writer's guidelines free or online

Nonfiction Needs how-to, repair/replace something on an RV, humor, technical, travel, all RV related. **Buys 15-20 mss/year.** Query. Length: 800-1,100 words.
Photos Do not send or e-mail unless approved by staff.
Columns/Departments On the Road (issue related); RV Insight (for people new to the RV lifestyle); Action Line (consumer help); Tech Topics (tech Q&A); Camp Cuisine (cooking in an RV); Product Previews (new products). No plans on adding new columns/departments.
Tips Know something about RVing. People who drive motorhomes or pull trailers have unique needs that have to be incorporated into our stories. We're looking for well-written, first-person stories that convey the fun of this lifestyle and way to travel.

$$ INTERNATIONAL LIVING

International Living Publishing, Ltd., Elysium House, Ballytruckle, Waterford Ireland (800)643-2479. Fax: 353-51-304-561. E-mail: editor@internationalliving.com. Website: www.internationalliving.com. **50% freelance written**. Monthly magazine covering retirement, travel, investment, and real estate overseas. "We do not want descriptions of how beautiful places are. We want specifics, recommendations, contacts, prices, names, addresses, phone numbers, etc. We want offbeat locations and off-the-beaten-track spots." Estab. 1981. Circ. 500,000. Byline given. Pays on publication. Offers 25-50% kill fee. Publishes ms an average of 3 months after acceptance. Buys all rights. Editorial lead time 2 months. Submit seasonal material 3 months in advance. Accepts queries by mail, e-mail, fax. Accepts simultaneous submissions. Responds in 2 months to mss. Sample copy for #10 SASE. Guidelines available online.
Nonfiction Needs how-to, get a job, buy real estate, get cheap airfares overseas, start a business, etc., interview, entrepreneur or retiree abroad, new product, travel, personal experience, travel, shopping, cruises. No descriptive, run-of-the-mill travel articles. **Buys 100 mss/year.** Send complete ms. Length: 500-2,000 words. **Pays $200-500 for assigned articles. Pays $100-400 for unsolicited articles.**
Photos State availability. Identification of subjects required. Reviews contact sheets, negatives, transparencies, prints. Offers $50/photo. Buys all rights.
Fillers Needs facts. Buys 20 mss/year. Length: 50-250 words. **Pays $25-50.**
Tips "Make recommendations in your articles. We want first-hand accounts. Tell us how to do things: how to catch a cab, order a meal, buy a souvenir, buy property, start a business, etc. *International Living*'s philosophy is that the world is full of opportunities to do whatever you want, whenever you want. We will show you how."

$ THE INTERNATIONAL RAILWAY TRAVELER

Hardy Publishing Co., Inc., P.O. Box 3747, San Diego CA 92163. (619)260-1332. Fax: (619)296-4220. E-mail: irteditor@aol.com. Website: www.irtsociety.com. **100% freelance written**. Monthly newsletter covering rail travel. Estab. 1983. Circ. 3,500. Byline given. Pays within 1 month of the publication date. Offers 25% kill fee. Buys first North American serial rights, buys all electronic rights. Editorial lead time 4 months. Submit seasonal material 6 months in advance. Responds in 1 month to queries. Responds in 2 months to mss. Sample copy for $6. Guidelines for #10 SASE or via e-mail.
Nonfiction Needs general interest, how-to, interview, new product, opinion, personal experience, travel, book reviews. **Buys 48-60 mss/year.** Send complete ms. Length: 800-1,200 words. **Pays 3¢/word.**
Photos Include SASE for return of photos. Send photos. Captions, identification of subjects required. Reviews contact sheets, negatives, transparencies, 8 × 10 (preferred) and 5 × 7 prints, digital photos preferred (minimum 300 dpi). Offers $10 b $20 cover photo. Costs of converting slides and negatives to prints are deducted from payment. Buys first North American serial rights, all electronic rights
Tips We want factual articles concerning world rail travel which would not appear in the mass-market travel magazines. *IRT* readers and editors love stories and photos on off-beat train trips as well as more conventional train trips covered in unconventional ways. With *IRT*, the focus is on the train travel experience, not a blow-by-blow description of the view from the train window. Be sure to include details (prices, passes, schedule info, etc.) for readers who might want to take the trip. E-mail queries, submissions encouraged. Digital photo submissions (at least 300 dpi) are encouraged. Please stay within word-count guidelines.

$$$$ ISLANDS

World Publications, 460 N. Orlando Ave., Suite 200, Winter Park FL 32789. (407)628-4802. E-mail: storyideas@islands.com. Website: www.islands.com. **80% freelance written**. Magazine published 8 times/year. We cover accessible and once-in-a-lifetime islands from many different perspectives: travel, culture, lifestyle. We ask our authors to give us the essence of the island and do it with literary flair. Estab. 1981. Circ. 250,000. Byline given. Pays on publication. Offers 25% kill fee. Publishes ms an average of 8 months after acceptance. Buys all rights. Accepts queries by e-mail. Responds in 2 months

to queries. Responds in 6 weeks to mss Sample copy for $6 E-mail us for writer's guidelines
Nonfiction Needs book excerpts, essays, general interest, interview, photo feature, travel, service shorts, island-related material. **Buys 25 feature mss/year.** Send complete ms. Length: 2,000-4,000 words. **Pays $750-2,500.**
Photos "Fine color photography is a special attraction of *Islands*, and we look for superb composition, technical quality, and editorial applicability. Will not accept or be responsible for unsolicited images or artwork."
Columns/Departments Discovers section (island related news), 100-250 words; Taste (island cuisine), 900-1,000 words; Travel Tales (personal essay), 900-1,100 words; Live the Life (island expat Q&A). Query with published clips. **Pays $25-1,000.**

LUXURY TRAVEL MAGAZINE

Gadfly Media, Level 1, 579 Harris St., Ultimo, Sydney NSW 2007 Australia. (61)(2)8204 1000. Fax: (61)(2)9281 7529. E-mail: mstratton@luxurytravelmag.com.au; sborham@gadfly.com.au. Website: www.luxurytravelmag.com.au. **Contact:** Susan Borham, Editor-In-Chief. Quarterly magazine covering the best deluxe hotels and resorts, tropical islands, 5-star cruise liners, spa resorts, mountain hideaways, city boltholes and weekend escapes in Australia and overseas.
Nonfiction Needs general interest, interview, new product, travel. Query.

$$ MOTORHOME

Affinity, 2575 Vista Del Mar Dr., Ventura CA 93001. (805)667-4100. Fax: (805)667-4484. Website: www.motorhomemagazine.com. **60% freelance written**. Monthly magazine. "*MotorHome* is a magazine for owners and prospective buyers of motorized recreational vehicles who are active outdoorsmen and wide-ranging travelers. We cover all aspects of the RV lifestyle; editorial material is both technical and nontechnical in nature. Regular features include tests and descriptions of various models of motorhomes, travel adventures, and hobbies pursued in such vehicles, objective analysis of equipment and supplies for such vehicles, and do-it-yourself articles. Guides within the magazine provide listings of manufacturers, rentals, and other sources of equipment and accessories of interest to enthusiasts. Articles must have an RV slant and excellent photography accompanying text." Estab. 1968. Circ. 150,000. Byline given. Pays on acceptance. Offers 30% kill fee. Publishes ms an average of within 1 year after acceptance. Buys first North American serial rights, buys electronic rights. Editorial lead time 4 months. Submit seasonal material 6 months in advance. Accepts queries by mail, fax. Responds in 1 month to queries. Responds in 2 months to mss. Sample copy free. Guidelines for #10 SASE.
Nonfiction Needs general interest, historical, how-to, humor, interview, new product, personal experience, photo feature, technical, travel, celebrity profiles, recreation, lifestyle, legislation, all RV related. No diaries of RV trips or negative RV experiences. **Buys 120 mss/year.** Query with published clips. Length: 250-2,500 words. **Pays $300-600.**
Photos Digital photography accepted. Send photos. Captions, identification of subjects, model releases required. Reviews 35mm slides. Offers no additional payment for art accepted with ms. Pays $500 for covers. Buys one time rights.
Columns/Departments Crossroads (offbeat briefs of people, places, and events of interest to travelers), 100-200 words; Keepers (tips, resources). Query with published clips or send complete ms. **Pays $100**
Tips "If a freelancer has an idea for a good article, it's best to send a query and include possible photo locations to illustrate the article. We prefer to assign articles and work with the author in developing a piece suitable to our audience. We are in a specialized field with very enthusiastic readers who appreciate articles by authors who actually enjoy motorhomes. The following areas are most open: Crossroads—brief descriptions of places to see or special events, with 1 photo/slide, 100-200 words; travel—places to go with a motorhome, where to stay, what to see and do, etc.; and how-to—personal projects on author's motorhomes to make travel easier, unique projects, accessories. Also articles on motorhome-owning celebrities, humorous experiences. Be sure to submit appropriate photography with at least 1 good motorhome shot to illustrate travel articles. No phone queries, please."

$$ NORTH AMERICAN INNS MAGAZINE

Harworth Publishing Inc., Box 998, Guelph ON N1H 6N1 Canada. (519)767-6059. Fax: (519)821-0479. E-mail: editor@harworthpublishing.com. Website: www.innsmagazine.com. *North American Inns* is a national publication for travel, dining and pastimes. It focuses on inns, beds & breakfasts, resorts and travel in North America. The magazine is targeted to travelers looking for exquisite getaways. Accepts queries by e-mail. Guidelines by e-mail.
Nonfiction Needs general interest, interview, new product, opinion, personal experience, travel. Query. Length: 300-600 words. **Pays $175-250 (Canadian).**

Fillers Short quips or nominations at 75 words are **$25 each**. All stories submitted have to accompany photos. Please e-mail photos to designer@harworthpublishing.com.

$ $ NORTHWEST TRAVEL

Northwest Regional Magazines, 4969 Hwy. 101 N., Suite 2, Florence OR 97439. (541)997-8401 or (800)348-8401. Fax: (541)902-0400. Website: www.northwestmagazines.com. **60% freelance written**. Bimonthly magazine. "We like energetic writing about popular activities and destinations in the Pacific Northwest. *Northwest Travel* aims to give readers practical ideas on where to go in the region. Magazine covers Oregon, Washington, Idaho, British Columbia, Alaska and western Montana." Estab. 1991. Circ. 50,000. Pays after publication. No kill fee. Publishes ms an average of 8 months after acceptance. Buys first North American serial rights. Submit seasonal material 6 months in advance. Accepts queries by mail, e-mail. Responds in 3 months to queries. Responds in 3 months to mss. Sample copy for $4.50. Guidelines available online.
Nonfiction Needs historical, interview, rarely, photo feature, travel in Northwest region. No "cliché-ridden pieces on places that everyone covers." **Buys 40 mss/year.** Query with or without published clips. Submit copy on CD or via e-mail. Length: 1,000-1,500 words. **Pays $100-500 for feature articles, and contributor copies.**
Reprints Send photocopy and information about when and where the material previously appeared. Pays 50% of amount paid for original article
Photos Provide credit and model release information on cover photos. Digital photos on CD (300 dpi 8½ × 1½). State availability. Captions, identification of subjects, True required. Reviews transparencies, prefers dupes. Pays $425 for cover; $100 for stand-alone photos; $100 for Back Page. Buys one time rights.
Columns/Departments Worth a Stop (brief items describing places worth a stop), 350-500 words. **Pays $50-100**. Back Page (photo and large caption package on a specific activity, season, or festival with some technical photo info), 80 words and 1 slide. **Pays $100**. 25-30
Tips "Write fresh, lively copy (avoid cliché), and cover exciting travel topics in the region that haven't been covered in other magazines. A story with stunning photos will get serious consideration. The department most open to freelancers is the Worth a Stop department. Take us to fascinating places we may not otherwise discover."

⊞ OUTDOOR AUSTRALIA

APC Magazines, 54-58 Park St., Sydney NSW 2000 Australia. (02) 9282 8000. Fax: (02) 9267 4361. E-mail: ebowen@apcmagazines.com.au. Website: www.outdooraustralia.com. **Contact:** Dallas Hewitt, ed. Bimonthly magazine covering outdoor and adventure activities in Australia. "As well as inspiring the reader to get out and try something new, each story contains lots of useful information in Fact Boxes that include 'where' and 'who' sections and also advice on what gear will be needed." Circ. 20,000.
Nonfiction Needs general interest, how-to, inspirational, new product. Query.

$ PATHFINDERS

Travel Information for People of Color, 6325 Germantown Ave., Philadelphia PA 19144. (215)438-2140. Fax: (215)438-2144. E-mail: editors@pathfinderstravel.com. Website: www.pathfinderstravel.com. **75% freelance written**. Bimonthly magazine covering travel for people of color, primarily African-Americans. We look for lively, original, well-written stories that provide a good sense of place, with useful information and fresh ideas about travel and the travel industry. Our main audience is African-Americans, though we do look for articles relating to other persons of color: Native Americans, Hispanics and Asians. Estab. 1997. Circ. 100,000. Byline given. Pays on publication. Buys first North American serial rights, buys electronic rights. Accepts queries by mail, e-mail. Responds in 1 month to queries. Responds in 2 months to mss. Sample copy at bookstores (Barnes & Noble, Borders) Guidelines available online.
Nonfiction Interested in seeing more Native American stories, places that our readers can visit and rodeos (be sure to tie-in African-American cowboys). Needs essays, historical, how-to, personal experience, photo feature, travel, all vacation travel oriented. No more pitches on Jamaica. We get these all the time. **Buys 16-20 mss/year.** Send complete ms. 1,200-1,400 words for cover stories; 1,000-1,200 words for features. **Pays $200.**
Photos State availability.
Columns/Departments Chef's Table, Post Cards from Home; Looking Back; City of the Month, 500-600 words. Send complete ms. **Pays $150.**
Tips We prefer seeing finished articles rather than queries. All articles are submitted on spec. Articles should be saved in either WordPerfect of Microsoft Word, double-spaced and saved as a text-only file. Include a hard copy. E-mail articles are accepted only by request of the editor. No historical articles.

$$ PILOT GETAWAYS MAGAZINE

Airventure Publishing LLC, P.O. Box 550, Glendale CA 91209-0550. (818)241-1890. Fax: (818)241-1895. E-mail: editor@pilotgetaways.com. Website: www.pilotgetaways.com. **90% freelance written**. Bimonthly magazine covering aviation travel for private pilots. *Pilot Getaways* is a travel magazine for private pilots. Our articles cover destinations that are easily accessible by private aircraft, including details such as airport transportation, convenient hotels, and attractions. Other regular features include Fly-in dining, Flying Tips, and Bush Flying. Estab. 1998. Circ. 20,000. Byline given. Pays on publication. No kill fee. Buys first North American serial rights, buys electronic rights. Editorial lead time 4 months. Submit seasonal material 9 months in advance. Accepts queries by mail, e-mail, fax, phone. Accepts simultaneous submissions. Responds in 2 weeks to queries. Responds in 2 months to mss. Sample copy and writer's guidelines free

Nonfiction Needs travel, specifically travel guide articles. We rarely publish articles about events that have already occurred, such as travel logs about trips the authors have taken or air show reports. **Buys 30 mss/year.** Query. Length: 1,000-3,500 words. **Pays $100-500.**

Photos State availability. Captions, identification of subjects required. Reviews contact sheets, negatives, 35mm transparencies, prints, GIF/JPEG/TIFF files. Negotiates payment individually Buys one time rights.

Columns/Departments Weekend Getaways (short fly-in getaways), 2,000 words; Fly-in Dining (reviews of airport restaurants), 1,200 words; Flying Tips (tips and pointers on flying technique), 1,000 words; Bush Flying (getaways to unpaved destinations), 1,500 words. 20 Query. **Pays $100-500.**

Tips *Pilot Getaways* follows a specific format, which is factual and informative. We rarely publish travel logs that chronicle a particular journey. Rather, we prefer travel guides with phone numbers, addresses, prices, etc., so that our readers can plan their own trips. The exact format is described in our writer's guidelines.

$$$ PORTHOLE CRUISE MAGAZINE

Panoff Publishing, 4517 NW 31st Ave., Ft. Lauderdale FL 33309-3403. (954)377-7777. Fax: (954)377-7000. E-mail: bpanoff@ppigroup.com. Website: www.porthole.com. **70% freelance written.** Bimonthly magazine covering the cruise industry. *Porthole Cruise Magazine* entices its readers to take a cruise vacation by delivering information that is timely, accurate, colorful, and entertaining. Estab. 1992. Circ. 80,000. Byline given. Pays on publication. Offers 20% kill fee. Publishes ms an average of 6 months after acceptance. Buys first North American serial rights. Editorial lead time 8 months. Submit seasonal material 5 months in advance. Accepts queries by e-mail. Accepts simultaneous submissions.

Nonfiction Needs general interest, cruise related, historical, how-to, pick a cruise, not get seasick, travel tips, humor, interview, crew on board or industry executives, new product, personal experience, photo feature, travel, off-the-beaten-path, adventure, ports, destinations, cruises, onboard fashion, spa articles, duty-free shopping, port shopping, ship reviews. No articles on destinations that can't be reached by ship. **Buys 60 mss/year.** Length: 1,000-1,200 words. **Pays $500-600 for assigned feature articles.**

Photos Contact: Linda Douthat, creative director. State availability. Captions, identification of subjects, model releases required. Reviews digital images and original transparencies. Rates available upon request to ldouthat@ppigroup.com Buys one time rights.

RV LIFESTYLE MAGAZINE

Taylor Publishing Group, 1121 Invicta Dr., Unit 2, Oakville ON LGH 2R2 Canada. (905)844-8218. Fax: (905)844-5032. E-mail: editor@rvlifemag.com. Website: www.rvlifemag.com. **Contact:** Norm Rosen, editorial dir. **50% freelance written**. Magazine published 7 times/year (monthly December-May and October). "*RV Lifestyle Magazine* is geared to readers who enjoy travel/camping. Upbeat pieces only. Readers vary from owners of towable trailers or motorhomes to young families and entry-level campers (no tenting)." Estab. 1971. Circ. 45,000. Byline given. Pays on publication. No kill fee. Buys first North American serial rights. Editorial lead time 2 months. Responds in 1 month to queries. Responds in 2 months to mss. Sample copy free.

Nonfiction Needs how-to, personal experience, technical, travel. No inexperienced, unresearched, or overly general pieces. **Buys 30-40 mss/year.** Query. Length: 1,200-2,000 words. **Payment varies**

Photos Send photos. Reviews low-ISO 35mm slides or JPEG/TIFF files saved at 300 dpi minimum at 5 × 7. Offers no additional payment for photos accepted with ms Buys one time rights.

Tips "Pieces should be slanted toward RV living. Canadian content regulations require 95% Canadian writers."

$$$$ SPA

Healthy Living, Travel & Renewal, World Publications, 415 Jackson St., San Francisco CA 94111. (760)966-

6226. Fax: (760)966-6266. Website: www.spamagazine.com. Bimonthly magazine covering health spas: treatments, travel, cuisine, fitness, beauty. Approachable and accessible, authoritative and full of advice, *Spa* is the place to turn for information and tips on nutrition, spa cuisine/recipes, beauty, health, skin care, spa travel, fitness, well-being and renewal. Byline given. Offers 25% kill fee. Buys first North American serial rights, buys all rights. Editorial lead time 3 months. Accepts queries by mail. Sample copy for $6.

Columns/Departments In Touch (spa news, treatments, destinations); Body (nutrition, health & fitness, spa therapies); Rituals (spa at home, beauty, home, books & music, mind/body).

$$ SPA LIFE

Harworth Publishing, Inc., Box 998, Guelph ON N1H 6N1 Canada. (519)767-6059. Fax: (519)821-0479. E-mail: editor@harworthpublishing.com. "*Spa Life* is about more than just spas. With favorite recipes from featured spa destinations, mouth-watering treats are at your fingertips. *Spa Life* is also dedicated to personal and health issues." Estab. 2000. No kill fee. Accepts queries by e-mail. Guidelines by e-mail.

Nonfiction Needs general interest, interview, new product, personal experience, travel. Length: 300-600 words. **Pays $25-50 (Canadian).**

Tips "Describe the treatments/food and surroundings. Include all information to make it easy for readers to get more info and make reservations. Make it personal and fun; the reader has to feel they know you and can relate."

$$ ST. MAARTEN NIGHTS

Nights Publications, Inc., 1751 Richardson St., Suite 5.530, Montreal QC H3K 1G6 Canada. (514)931-1987. Fax: (514)931-6273. E-mail: editor@nightspublications.com. Website: www.nightspublications.com. **Contact:** Jennifer McMorran, ed. **90% freelance written**. Annual magazine covering the St. Maarten/St. Martin vacation experience seeking upbeat, entertaining, lifestyle articles. Our audience is the North American vacationer. Estab. 1981. Circ. 225,000. Byline given. Pays on acceptance. No kill fee. Publishes ms an average of 9 months after acceptance. Buys North American and Caribbean serial rights. Editorial lead time 1 month. Accepts queries by mail, e-mail, fax. Responds in 2 weeks to queries. Responds in 1 month to mss. Guidelines by e-mail.

- "Let the reader experience the story; utilize the senses; be descriptive; be specific."

Nonfiction "Lifestyle with a lively, upscale touch." Needs general interest, historical, how-to, gamble (for example), humor, interview, opinion, personal experience, photo feature, travel, colorful profiles of islanders, sailing, ecological, ecotourism, local culture, art, activities, entertainment, nightlife, special events, topics relative to vacationers in St. Maarten/St. Martin. **Buys 8-10 mss/year.** Query with published clips. Length: 250-750 words. **Pays $100-300.**

Photos State availability. Captions, identification of subjects, model releases required. Reviews transparencies. Pays $50/photo Buys one time rights.

Tips "Our style is upbeat, friendly, fluid, and descriptive. Our magazines cater to tourists who are already at the destination, so ensure your story is of interest to this particular audience. We welcome stories that offer fresh angles to familiar tourist-related topics. E-mail queries preferred. All submissions must include an e-mail address for correspondence."

$$ TRAILER LIFE

America's No. 1 RV Magazine, Affinity Group, Inc., 2575 Vista Del Mar Dr., Ventura CA 93001. Fax: (805)667-4484. E-mail: info@trailerlife.com. Website: www.trailerlife.com. **40% freelance written**. Monthly magazine. "*Trailer Life* magazine is written specifically for active people whose overall lifestyle is based on travel and recreation in their RV. Every issue includes product tests, travel articles, and other features—ranging from lifestyle to vehicle maintenance." Estab. 1941. Circ. 270,000. Byline given. Pays on acceptance. Offers kill fee. Offers 30% kill fee for assigned articles that are not acceptable. Publishes ms an average of 6 months after acceptance. Buys first North American serial rights, buys electronic rights. Editorial lead time 4 months. Submit seasonal material 6 months in advance. Accepts queries by mail. Responds in 2 months to queries. Responds in 2 months to mss. Sample copy free. Guidelines for #10 SASE.

Nonfiction Needs historical, how-to, technical, humor, new product, opinion, personal experience, travel. "No vehicle tests, product evaluations or road tests; tech material is strictly assigned. No diaries or trip logs, no non-RV trips; nothing without an RV-hook." **Buys 75 mss/year.** Query. Length: 250-2,500 words. **Pays $125-700.**

Photos Send photos. Identification of subjects, model releases required. Reviews transparencies, b&w contact sheets . Offers no additional payment for photos accepted with ms, does pay for supplemental photos Buys one-time and occasionally electronic rights.

Columns/Departments Around the Bend (news, trends of interest to RVers), 100 words. 70 Query or send complete ms **Pays $75-250.**

Tips Prerequisite: Must have RV focus. Photos must be magazine quality. These are the two biggest reasons why manuscripts are rejected. Our readers are travel enthusiasts who own all types of RVs (travel trailers, truck campers, van conversions, motorhomes, tent trailers, fifth-wheels) in which they explore North America and beyond, embrace the great outdoors in national, state and private parks. They're very active and very adventurous.

$ TRAVEL NATURALLY

Internaturally, Inc., P.O. Box 317, Newfoundland NJ 07435-0317. (973)697-3552. Fax: (973)697-8313. E-mail: naturally@internaturally.com. Website: www.internaturally.com. **90% freelance written**. Quarterly magazine covering wholesome family nude recreation and travel locations. *Travel Naturally* looks at why millions of people believe that removing clothes in public is a good idea, and at places specifically created for that purpose—with good humor, but also in earnest. *Travel Naturally* takes you to places where your personal freedom is the only agenda, and to places where textile-free living is a serious commitment. Estab. 1981. Circ. 35,000. Byline given. Pays on publication. No kill fee. Buys first rights, buys one-time rights. Editorial lead time 4 months. Submit seasonal material 4 months in advance. Accepts queries by mail, e-mail, fax. Accepts simultaneous submissions. Sample copy for $9. Guidelines available online.

Nonfiction Frequent contributors and regular columnists, who develop a following through *Travel Naturally*, are paid from the Frequent Contributors Budget. Payments increase on the basis of frequency of participation. Needs general interest, interview, personal experience, photo feature, travel. **Buys 12 mss/year.** Send complete ms. 2 pages. **Pays $80/published page, including photos.**

Reprints Pays 50% of original rate.

Photos Send photos. Reviews contact sheets, negatives, transparencies, prints, high resolution digital images. Buys one time rights.

Tips *Travel Naturally* invokes the philosophies of naturism and nudism, but also activities and beliefs in the mainstream that express themselves, barely: spiritual awareness, New Age customs, pagan and religious rites, alternative and fringe lifestyle beliefs, artistic expressions, and many individual nude interests. Our higher purpose is simply to help restore our sense of self. Although the term `nude recreation' may, for some, conjure up visions of sexual frivolities inappropriate for youngsters—because that can also be technically true—these topics are outside the scope of *Travel Naturally* magazine. Here the emphasis is on the many varieties of human beings, of all ages and backgrounds, recreating in their most natural state, at extraordinary places, their reasons for doing so, and the benefits they derive. We incorporate a travel department to advise and book vacations in locations reviewed in travel articles.

$ TRAVEL SMART

Communications House, Inc., P.O. Box 397, Dobbs Ferry NY 10522. E-mail: travelsmartnow@aol.com. Website: travelsmartnewsletter.com. Monthly newsletter covering information on good-value travel. Estab. 1976. Circ. 20,000. Pays on publication. No kill fee. Buys all rights. Accepts queries by mail, e-mail. Responds in 6 weeks to queries. Responds in 6 weeks to mss. Sample copy for sae with 9 × 12 envelope and 3 First-Class stamps. Guidelines for sae with 9 × 12 envelope and 3 First-Class stamps.

Nonfiction Interested primarily in bargains or little-known deals on transportation, lodging, food, unusual destinations that are really good values. No destination stories on major Caribbean islands, London, New York, no travelogs, `my vacation,' poetry, fillers. No photos or illustrations other than maps. Just hard facts. We are not part of `Rosy fingers of dawn.' school. Write for guidelines, then query. Query. Length: 100-1,500 words. **Pays $150 maximum.**

Tips When you travel, check out small hotels offering good prices, good restaurants, and send us brief rundown (with prices, phone numbers, addresses). Information must be current. Include your phone number with submission, because we sometimes make immediate assignments.

$$ ☐ VERGE MAGAZINE

Travel With Purpose, Verge Magazine Inc., P.O. Box 147, Peterborough ON K9J 6Y5 Canada. E-mail: contributing@vergemagazine.org. Website: www.vergemagazine.org. **Contact:** Julia Steinecke, editor. **60% freelance written**. Quarterly magazine. Each issue takes you around the world, with people who are doing something different & making a difference doing it. This is the magazine resource for those wanting to volunteer, work, study or adventure overseas. "*Verge* is the magazine for people who travel with purpose. It explores ways to get out & see the world by volunteering, working & studying overseas. Our readers are typically young (17-40 yrs.), or young at heart, active, independent travelers. Editorial content is intended to inform & motivate the reader by profiling unique individuals & experiences that are timely & socially relevant. We look for articles that are issue driven & combine an engaging & well-told story with nuts & bolts how-to information. Wherever possible & applicable, efforts should be made to provide sources where readers can find out more about the subject, or ways in which readers can become involved in the issue covered." Estab. 2002. Circ. 10,000. Byline given. Pays on publication. No kill fee. Publishes ms an average of 6 months after acceptance. Buys first North American serial rights, buys second serial (reprint) rights, buys electronic rights. Submit seasonal material 8-12 months in advance. Accepts queries by mail, e-mail. Responds in 8 weeks to queries. Responds in 2 months to mss. Sample copy for $6 plus shipping. Guidelines available online.

Nonfiction Contact: Julia Steinecke. Needs how-to, humor, interview, travel, News. "We do not want pure travelogues, predictable tourist experiences, luxury travel, stories highighting a specific company or organisation." **Buys 30-40 mss/year.** Send complete ms. Length: 600-1,000 words. **Pays $60-500 for assigned articles. Pays $60-250 for unsolicited articles.**

Photos Send link to online portfolio to editor@vergemagazine.ca or mail portfolio on CD or DVD to *Verge Magazine*. Captions required. Reviews GIF/JPEG files. Negotiates payment individually.

Columns/Departments Contact: Julia Steinecke. 20-30 mss/yr. Query with published clips. **Pays $60-$250.**

Tips "Writers should read the guidelines & tell us which dept. their query fits best; Refer to travel undertaken in the past year if possible."

$ WESTERN RV NEWS & RECREATION

ROM Communications, 21821 Cole Lane, Aurora OR 97002. Website: www.westernrvnews.com. **Contact:** Tom O'Connor, editor. Monthly magazine for owners of recreational vehicles and those interested in the RV lifestyle. Estab. 1966. Byline given. Buys first rights, buys second serial (reprint) rights. 9-12 months Accepts queries by e-mail. Accepts simultaneous submissions. Guidelines available online.

- "All correspondence should come through links on the website. Do not send snail mail, call or e-mail directly. Visit the Web pages for submission guidelines and contact forms."

Nonfiction "Feature articles are (800 - 1,200 words) and are generally assigned. We are currently accepting short stories (300 words or less) on subjects such as readying your RV for the road, and Just Off I-5, a series which shows RVers events, destinations, and 'finds' right off the freeway on their way to where they are going. We are always on the lookout for NEWS but we avoid running press releases that sell. Our Product Spotlight is a regular feature that showcases a product or resource which is truly helpful to the RVer and tent-camper. Submissions in this category are always accepted." Needs how-to, RV oriented, purchasing considerations, maintenance, humor, RV experiences, new product, with ancillary interest to RV lifestyle, personal experience, varying or unique RV lifestyles, technical, RV systems or hardware, travel. No articles without an RV slant. **Buys 100 mss/year.** Submit complete ms by e-mail only via website. Length: 250-1,400 words. **Pays 8¢/word for first rights.**

Photos Photos and images can be submitted as digital files, CD or as photographic prints. Digital files must be TIFF or EPS at a resolution of 300 dpi and submitted via e-mail or on a CD (PC format). If you submit an article or press release via our online article/news submission form only jpeg images should be uploaded. Captions, identification of subjects, model releases required.

Fillers Encourage anecdotes, RV-related tips, and short humor. Length: 50-250 words. **Pays $5-25.**

Tips our editorial mix strives to provide full-color travel features and destinations, useful repair and technical articles, how-to advice, and product reviews. Regular columns written by on-the-road RVers share the back-roads and first-hand experiences of the part-time and full-time RV lifestyle. Our readers say that generations of their families have subscribed to Western RV News & Recreation for many years, and they continue to enjoy Western RV News & Recreation from cover to cover.

$$ WOODALL'S REGIONALS

2575 Vista Del Mar Dr., Ventura CA 93001. Website: www.woodalls.com. Monthly magazine for RV and camping enthusiasts. Woodall's Regionals include *CamperWays*, *Midwest RV Traveler*, *Northeast Outdoors*, *Florida RV Traveler*. Byline given. Buys first rights. Accepts queries by mail, e-mail. Responds in 1-2 months to queries. Sample copy free. Guidelines free.

Nonfiction We need interesting and tightly focused feature stories on RV travel and lifestyle, and technical articles that speak to both novices and experienced RVers. **Buys 300 mss/year.** Query with published clips. Length: 1,000-1,400 words. **Pays $180-220/feature; $75-100/department article and short piece.**

Women's

ALL YOU MAGAZINE

Time Inc., 135 W. 50th St., 2nd Floor, New York NY 10020. E-mail: feedback@allyou.com. Website: www.allyou.com. No kill fee.

- Query before submitting.

$$$ BRIDAL GUIDE

R.F.P., LLC, 330 Seventh Ave., 10th Floor, New York NY 10001. (212)838-7733; (800)472-7744. Fax: (212)308-7165. E-mail: editorial@bridalguide.com. Website: www.bridalguide.com. **20% freelance written**. Bimonthly magazine covering relationships, sexuality, fitness, wedding planning, psychology, finance, travel. Only works with experienced/published writers. Pays on acceptance. No kill fee. Accepts queries by mail. Responds in 3 months to queries. Responds in 3 months to mss. Sample copy for $5 and SAE with 4 first-class stamps. Writer's guidelines available.

Nonfiction Please do not send queries concerning beauty, fashion, or home design stories since we produce them in-house. We do not accept personal wedding essays, fiction, or poetry. Address travel queries to travel editor. All correspondence accompanied by an SASE will be answered. **Buys 100 mss/year.** Query with published clips from national consumer magazines. Length: 1,000-2,000 words. **Pays 50¢/word.**

Photos Photography and illustration submissions should be sent to the art department.

Tips We are looking for service-oriented, well-researched pieces that are journalistically written. Writers we work with use at least 3 top expert sources, such as physicians, book authors, and business people in the appropriate field. Our tone is conversational, yet authoritative. Features are also generally filled with real-life anecdotes. We also do features that are completely real-person based—such as roundtables of bridesmaids discussing their experiences, or grooms-to-be talking about their feelings about getting married. In queries, we are looking for a well-thought-out idea, the specific angle of focus the writer intends to take, and the sources he or she intends to use. Queries should be brief and snappy—and titles should be supplied to give the editor an even better idea of the direction the writer is going in.

$$$$ ✠ CHATELAINE

One Mount Pleasant Rd., 8th Floor, Toronto ON M4Y 2Y5 Canada. (416)764-2879. Fax: (416)764-2431. E-mail: storyideas@chatelaine.rogers.com. Website: www.chatelaine.com. Monthly magazine. "*Chatelaine* is edited for Canadian women ages 25-49, their changing attitudes and lifestyles. Key editorial ingredients include health, finance, social issues and trends, as well as fashion, beauty, food and home decor. Regular departments include Health pages, Entertainment, Money, Home, Humour, How-to." Byline given. Pays on acceptance. Offers 25-50% kill fee. Buys first rights, buys electronic rights. Accepts queries by mail, e-mail (preferred). Responds in 4-6 weeks to 1 month to queries; up to 2 months to proposals. See writers' guidelines online at website.

- "*Does not accept unsolicited manuscripts*. Submit story ideas online."

⊕ CHRISTIAN WOMAN

Inspired Living, Media Inc./Initiate Media, P.O. Box 163, North Sydney NSW 2059 Australia. (61)(2)8437-3541. Fax: (61)(2)9999-2053. E-mail: jbaxter@mediaincorporated.org. Website: www.christianwoman.com.au. Bimonthly magazine covering issues important to Christian women.

- Australian and New Zealand writers given preference.

Nonfiction Needs inspirational, interview, religious. Query.

$$$$ CONCEIVE MAGAZINE

The Experts on Getting Pregnant, Bonnier Corporation, 460 N. Orlando Ave., Suite 200, Winter Park FL 32789. (407)637-3590. Fax: (407)637-3591. Website: www.conceiveonline.com. **50% freelance written**. "Quarterly magazine covering reproductive health, fertility, conception, infertility, adoption." Estab. 2004. Circ. 200,000+. Byline given. Pays on acceptance. Offers 25% kill fee. Publishes ms an average of 3 months after acceptance. Buys all rights. Editorial lead time 6 months. Submit seasonal material 6 months in advance. Accepts queries by e-mail, online submission form. Guidelines available online.

- E-mail queries should be sent through online contact form.

Nonfiction Needs book excerpts, essays, interview, new product, personal experience. "I am inundated with queries from writers who want to recount their own 'journey to parenthood.' I have plenty of personal stories; I need well-reported, well-written health and lifestyle pieces." Query with published clips. Length: 500-2,000 words. **Pays $250-2,000.**

Columns/Departments "You" (emotional health and happiness for women while they're "trying"), 750 words, $750; "Him" (male fertility issues), 750 words, $750; "You and Him" (marriage/relationship), 750 words, $750; "Success" (a "real life" story of conception and birth), 1000-1500 words, $1000.
Tips "We are the first and only consumer magazine in the pre-pregnancy (fertility and conception) category. We are not a pregnancy or parenting journal, or an infertility magazine (a popular misconception). While we do cover infertility treatments andconditions that can affect male and female fertility, we focus on providing information about a healthy lifestyle (nutrition, exercise), the latest findings on human reproduction, and ways to keep healthy and happy while "trying."

COSMOPOLITAN

The Hearst Corp., 224 W. 57th St., New York NY 10019. (212)649-2000. Website: www.cosmopolitan.com. **Contact:** Submissions ed. **25% freelance written**. Monthly magazine for 18- to 35-year-old single, married, or divorced women. *Cosmopolitan* is edited for young women for whom beauty, fashion, fitness, career, relationships, and personal growth are top priorities. Nutrition, home/lifestyle and celebrities are other interests reflected in the editorial lineup. Estab. 1886. Circ. 2,300,100. Byline given. Pays on acceptance. Offers 10-15% kill fee. Buys all magazine rights and occasionally negotiates first North American rights Submit seasonal material 6 months in advance. TrueSample copy for $2.95.

- "We do not accept unsolicited manuscripts and rarely accept queries. Here's advice I give to anyone who wants to have their articles appear in our pages. Come to us when you have a significant amount of experience (and clips) working for other magazines. Cosmo's the largest magazine in the world and we don't think of it as a starting point for writers. You need to have experience writing for smaller publications and gradually work your way up. The best approach is to generate an idea for an article in the magazine and send us a proposal on that idea. An editor will then get in touch."

Nonfiction Needs book excerpts, how-to, humor, opinion, personal experience, anything of interest to young women.
Tips "Combine information with entertainment value, humor and relatability. Needs information- and emotion- and fun-packed relationship and sex service stories; first-person stories that display triumph over tragedy."

$$$$ ELLE

Hachette Filipacchi Media U.S., Inc., 1633 Broadway, 44th Floor, New York NY 10019. (212)767-5800. Fax: (212)489-4211. Website: www.elle.com. Monthly magazine. Edited for the modern, sophisticated, affluent, well-traveled woman in her twenties to early thirties. Circ. 1,100,000. No kill fee. Editorial lead time 3 months.

- Query first.

$$$$ FAMILY CIRCLE MAGAZINE

Meredith Corporation, 375 Lexington Ave., 9th Floor, New York NY 10017. Website: www.familycircle.com. **80% freelance written**. Magazine published every 3 weeks. We are a national women's service magazine which covers many stages of a woman's life, along with her everyday concerns about social, family, and health issues. Submissions should focus on families with children ages 8-16. Estab. 1932. Circ. 4,200,000. Byline given. Offers 20% kill fee. Buys one-time rights, buys all rights. Editorial lead time 4 months. Submit seasonal material 4 months in advance. Responds in 2 months to queries. Responds in 2 months to mss. For back issues, send $6.95 to P.O. Box 3156, Harlan IA 51537. Guidelines available online.
Nonfiction We look for well-written, well-reported stories told through interesting anecdotes and insightful writing. We want well-researched service journalism on all subjects. Needs essays, opinion, personal experience, women's interest subjects such as family and personal relationships, children, physical and mental health, nutrition and self-improvement. No fiction or poetry. **Buys 200 mss/year.** Submit detailed outline, 2 clips, cover letter describing your publishing history, SASE or IRCs. Length: 1,000-2,500 words. **Pays $1/word.**
Tips Query letters should be concise and to the point. Also, writers should keep close tabs on *Family Circle* and other women's magazines to avoid submitting recently run subject matter.

$$$$ FLARE MAGAZINE

One Mt. Pleasant Rd., 8th Floor, Toronto ON M4Y 2Y5 Canada. (416)764-2863. Fax: (416)764-2866. E-mail: editors@flare.com. Website: www.flare.com. Monthly magazine for women ages 17-34. Byline given. Offers 50% kill fee. Buys first North American serial rights, buys electronic rights. Accepts queries by e-mail. Response time varies. Sample copy for #10 SASE. Guidelines available online.

Nonfiction Looking for women's fashion, beauty, health, sociological trends and celebrities. **Buys 24 mss/year.** Query. Length: 200-1,200 words. **Pays $1/word.**
Tips Study our masthead to determine if your topic is handled by regular contributing staff or a staff member.

GIRLFRIENDZ

The Thinking Woman's Magazine, JNT Communications, LLC, 6 Brookville Drive, Cherry Hill NJ 08003. E-mail: tobi@girlfriendzmag.com. Website: www.girlfriendzmag.com. **80% freelance written**. Quarterly magazine covering Baby Boomer women. "As a publication by and for Baby Boomer women, we are most interested in entertaining, educating and empowering our readers. Our target is smart women born between 1946 and 1964. We like a little humor in our articles, but only if it's appropriate and subtle. And most importantly, all facts must be checked for accuracy. We insist on well-researched and well-documented information." Estab. 2007. Circ. 33,000. Byline given. Headshot and bio included. "As a startup, we are unable to pay our writers." No kill fee. Buys first North American serial rights, buys electronic rights. Editorial lead time 3 months. Submit seasonal material 6 months in advance. Accepts queries by e-mail. Accepts previously published material. Accepts simultaneous submissions. Responds in 2 weeks to queries. Sample copy for $5. Guidelines available online.
Nonfiction Needs book excerpts, expose, historical, how-to, humor, interview, (celebrities only), new product, articles of interest to women born 1946-1964. "We do not want fiction, essays or poetry." **Buys 20 mss/year.** Query. Length: 735-1,200 words.
Photos State availability. Captions, identification of subjects required. Reviews JPEGs and/or PDFs, 300 dpi. We offer no additional payment for photos accepted with mss. Buys one-time rights.
Tips "Please do not call us or fax a query or manuscript. E-mail only. Please query only—no manuscripts. And please, no fiction, essays or poetry. We are interested in nonfiction articles that will make Boomer women think. We also like articles with subjects that our audience can identify with, though we're not looking for Sandwich Generation articles. Also, no articles on pre-schoolers or pregnancy. Our readers have children who are either just starting to exit elementary school, are in middle school, high school or college; are just getting married; are just having children, or already have children. We are also looking for an ethnic mix of writers."

$$$$ GLAMOUR

Conde Nast Publications, Inc., 4 Times Square, 16th Floor, New York NY 10036. (212)286-2860. Fax: (212)286-7731. Website: www.glamour.com. Cynthia Leive, editor-in-chief. **Contact:** Susan Goodall. Monthly magazine covering subjects ranging from fashion, beauty and health, personal relationships, career, travel, food and entertainment. "*Glamour* is edited for the contemporary woman, and informs her of the trends and recommends how she can adapt them to her needs, and motivates her to take action." Estab. 1939. Circ. 2,200,000. No kill fee. Accepts queries by mail. Not available online.
Nonfiction Needs personal experience, relationships, travel. **Pays 75¢-$1/word**
Photos Only uses professional photographers.

$$$$ GOOD HOUSEKEEPING

Hearst Corp., 300 W. 57th St., 28th Floor, New York NY 10019. (212)649-2200. Website: www.goodhousekeeping.com. Monthly magazine. "*Good Housekeeping* is edited for the 'New Traditionalist.' Articles which focus on food, fitness, beauty, and child care draw upon the resources of the Good Housekeeping Institute. Editorial includes human interest stories, articles that focus on social issues, money management, health news, travel." Circ. 5,000,000. Byline given. Pays on acceptance. Offers 25% kill fee. Buys first North American serial rights. Submit seasonal material 6 months in advance. Responds in 2-3 months to queries. Responds in 2-3 months to mss. For sample copy, call (212)649-2359. Guidelines for #10 SASE.
Nonfiction Consumer, social issues, dramatic narrative, nutrition, work, relationships, psychology, trends. **Buys 4-6 mss/issue.** Query. Length: 1,500-2,500 words.
Photos Contact: Melissa Paterno, art director. Toni Paciello, photo editor. Photos purchased on assignment mostly. State availability. Model releases required. Pays $100-350 for b $200-400 for color photos.
Columns/Departments Profiles (inspirational, activist or heroic women), 400-600 words. Query with published clips. **Pays $1/word for items 300-600 words.**
Fiction Contact: Laura Mathews, fiction editor. No longer accepts unagented fiction submissions. Because of heavy volume of fiction submissions, *Good Housekeeping* is not accepting unsolicited submissions at this time. Agented submissions only. 1,500 words (short-shorts); novel according to merit of material; average 5,000 word short stories. **Pays $1,000 minimum.**

Tips "Always send a SASE and clips. We prefer to see a query first. Do not send material on subjects already covered in-house by the Good Housekeeping Institute—these include food, beauty, needlework and crafts."

$$ GRACE ORMONDE WEDDING STYLE

Elegant Publishing, Inc., P.O. Box 89, Barrington RI 02806. Fax: (401)245-5371. E-mail: jessica@weddingstylemagazine.com. Website: www.weddingstylemagazine.com. **90% freelance written**. Semiannual magazine covering weddings catering to the affluent bride. Estab. 1997. Circ. 500,000. Pays on publication. No kill fee. Publishes ms an average of 4 months after acceptance. Buys all rights. Editorial lead time 1 month. Sample copy available online. Guidelines by e-mail.

- Does not accept queries.

Photos State availability. Reviews transparencies. Negotiates payment individually

Tips E-mail résumé and 5 clips/samples in any area of writing.

HARPER'S BAZAAR

ACP Magazines, Ltd., 54-58 Park St., Sydney NSW 2000 Australia. (61)(2)9282-8000. Fax: (61)(2)9267-4361. Website: www.acp.com.au. **Contact:** Jamie Huckbody, editor. Magazine published 10 times/year covering the runways, beauty's best, health issues, design innovators and celebrity lives. Circ. 47,691.

Fashion for women aged 25-49.

Nonfiction Needs general interest, interview, new product. Query.

$$ HER SPORTS

Active Sports Lifestyles, Wet Dog Media, 1499 Beach Dr. SE, Suite B, St. Petersburg FL 33701. E-mail: editorial@hersports.com. Website: www.hersports.com. **60% freelance written**. Bimonthly magazine covering women's outdoor, individual sports. *Her Sports* is for active women ages 25-49 who regard sports and being active an important part of their lifestyle. Our readers are beyond 'quick-fix diets' and '5-minute' exercise routines, and are looking for a way to balance being active and healthy with a busy lifestyle. We focus on health, nutrition, and sports, and sports training, travel, and profiles on everyday athletes and professional athletes with unique and motivational stories. Estab. 2004. Circ. 85,000. Byline given. Pays on publication. Offers 50% kill fee. Publishes ms an average of 3 months after acceptance. Buys all rights. Editorial lead time 3 months. Submit seasonal material 6-8 months in advance. Accepts queries by e-mail. Responds in 6-8 weeks to queries. Responds in 1 month to mss. Sample copy for $4.99 and SASE with 5 first-class stamps. Guidelines available online.

Nonfiction Needs personal experience. Please do not send articles pertaining to team sports; we cover only outdoor individual sports. **Buys 6 mss/year.** Query with published clips. Length: 800-1,200 words. **Pays $200-600 for assigned articles.**

Photos Contact: Kristin Mayer, creative director. State availability. Captions, identification of subjects required. Reviews GIF/JPEG files. Negotiates payment individually. Buys one time rights.

Columns/Departments Active Updates, Fitness, Health, Fit Foods, 1,200 words; Discoveries (travel articles of interest to active women), 1,500-2,000 words; Weekend Warrior (how-to tips for mastering the sports we cover), 1,000-1,200 words; Her Story (short profile on everyday athletes who are an inspiration to others), 650 words. at least 24 Query.

Tips Persistence pays off but burying the editor with multiple submissions will quickly lose you points. If you're asked to check back in 2 months, do so, but if the editor tells you she's on deadline, simply inquire about a better time to get back in touch.

I DO . . . FOR BRIDES

2400 Lake Park Dr., Suite 440, Smyrna GA 30080. (678)589-8800. E-mail: jgibbs@idoforbrides.com. Website: www.idoforbrides.com. **30% freelance written**. Quarterly magazine covering the bridal industry. The magazine includes tips for wedding preparation, bridal attire, honeymoon and wedding destinations. Publishes 4 regional versions: Alabama, Georgia, Tennessee, and Washington DC/Maryland/Virginia. Estab. 1996. Circ. 160,000. Byline given. No kill fee. Publishes ms an average of 8 months after acceptance. Buys all rights. Editorial lead time 8 months. Submit seasonal material 8 months in advance. Accepts queries by mail, e-mail. Accepts simultaneous submissions.

Nonfiction Needs book excerpts, essays, general interest, historical, how-to, bridal-related, humor, inspirational, interview, new product, opinion, personal experience, photo feature, religious, travel. **Buys 8 mss/year.** Query. Length: 300-1,000 words. **Pays variable rate.**

$$$$ LADIES' HOME JOURNAL

Meredith Corp., 125 Park Ave., 20th Floor, New York NY 10017-5516. (212)557-6600. Fax: (212)455-1313.

E-mail: lhj@mdp.com. Website: www.lhj.com. **50% freelance written**. Monthly magazine focusing on issues of concern to women 30-45. They cover a broader range of news and political issues than many women's magazines. *Ladies' Home Journal* is for active, empowered women who are evolving in new directions. It addresses informational needs with highly focused features and articles on a variety of topics: self, style, family, home, world, health, and food. Estab. 1882. Circ. 4.1 million. Pays on acceptance. Offers 25% kill fee. Publishes ms an average of 4-12 months after acceptance. Buys first North American serial rights. Rights bought vary with submission. Editorial lead time 4 months. Accepts queries by mail, e-mail. Accepts simultaneous submissions. Responds in 3 months to queries. Guidelines available online.

Nonfiction Submissions on the following subjects should be directed to the editor listed for each: investigative reports, news-related features, psychology/relationships/sex, celebrities/entertainment. Send 1-2 page query, SASE, résumé, clips via mail or e-mail (preferred). Length: 2,000-3,000 words. **Pays $2,000-4,000.**

Photos *LHJ* arranges for its own photography almost all the time. State availability. Captions, identification of subjects, model releases required. Offers variable payment for photos accepted with ms. Rights bought vary with submission.

Fiction Only short stories and novels submitted by an agent or publisher will be considered. No poetry of any kind. **Buys 12 mss/year.** Send complete ms. 2,000-2,500

$ $ THE LINK & VISITOR

Baptist Women of Ontario and Quebec, 100-304 The East Mall, Etobicoke ON M9B 6E2 Canada. (416)622-8600 ext. 305. E-mail: rjames@baptistwomen.com. Website: www.baptistwomen.com. **50% freelance written**. Magazine published 6 times/year designed to help Baptist women grow their world, faith, relationships, creativity, and mission vision—evangelical, egalitarian, Canadian. Estab. 1878. Circ. 3,500. Byline given. Pays on publication. No kill fee. Publishes ms an average of 6 months after acceptance. Buys one-time rights, buys second serial (reprint) rights, buys simultaneous rights. Makes work-for-hire assignments. Editorial lead time 2 months. Submit seasonal material 4 months in advance. Accepts simultaneous submissions. Sample copy for 9 × 12 SAE with 2 first-class Canadian stamps. Guidelines available online.

Nonfiction Articles must be Biblically literate. No easy answers, American mindset or U.S. focus, retelling of Bible stories, sermons. Needs inspirational, interview, religious. **Buys 30-35 mss/year.** Send complete ms. Length: 750-2,000 words. **Pays 5-12¢/word (Canadian).**

Photos State availability. Captions required. Offers no additional payment for photos accepted with ms. Buys one time rights.

Tips "We cannot use unsolicited manuscripts from non-Canadian writers. When submitting by e-mail, please send stories as messages, not as attachments."

$ LONG ISLAND WOMAN

Maraj, Inc., P.O. Box 176, Malverne NY 11565. E-mail: editor@liwomanonline.com. Website: www.liwomanonline.com. **40% freelance written**. Monthly magazine covering issues of importance to women—health, family, finance, arts, entertainment, fitness, travel, home. Estab. 2001. Circ. 40,000. Byline given. Pays within 1 month of publication. Offers 33% kill fee. Publishes ms an average of 3 months after acceptance. Buys one-time rights for print and online use. Editorial lead time 3 months. Submit seasonal material 3 months in advance. Accepts queries by mail, e-mail. Accepts previously published material. Accepts simultaneous submissions. Responds in 8 weeks to queries. Responds in 3 months to mss. Sample copy for $5. Guidelines available online.

- Responds if interested in using reprints that were submitted.

Nonfiction Needs book excerpts, general interest, how-to, humor, interview, new product, travel, reviews. **Buys 25-30 mss/year.** Send complete ms. Length: 500-1,800 words. **Pays $35-150.**

Photos State availability of or send photos.. Captions, identification of subjects, model releases required. Reviews 5 × 7 prints.

Columns/Departments Humor; Health Issues; Family Issues; Financial and Business Issues; Book Reviews and Books; Arts and Entertainment; Travel and Leisure; Home and Garden; Fitness.

MADISON

ACP Magazines, Ltd., 54-58 Park St., Sydney NSW 2000 Australia. (61)(2)9282-8000. Fax: (61)(2)9267-4361. E-mail: madison@acpmagazines.com.au. Website: www.madisonmag.com.au. **Contact:** Paula Jaye, editor. Monthly magazine offering intelligent news and features, real women and their stories, beautiful fashion, sexy beauty, inspiring homes and impress-your-friends food. "She is 25-39. Ambitious, sexy and socially aware. The MADISON woman actively enjoys her life. She loves fashion but will dress to suit a style she's developed. She's seriously interested in beauty but her health is just as important as finding the perfect lip-gloss."

Nonfiction Needs general interest, how-to, interview, new product. Query.

MARIE CLAIRE MAGAZINE

Pacific Magazines, 35-51 Mitchell St., McMahons Point NSW 2060 Australia. (61)(2)9464-3300. Fax: (61)(2)9464-3483. Website: www.pacificmags.com.au. **Contact:** Jackie Frank, ed. Monthly magazine for today's intelligent, thinking woman between the ages of 25-39 who likes to be challenged and informed at all levels. "marie claire presents new, innovative and inspirational ideas, combining style with commonsense. A magazine of contrasts, it beckons its readers with pages of the finest fashion, beauty and food. It's a winning formula of serious journalism and a healthy dose of glamour." Circ. 116,500.

- We have a readership of 522,000.

Nonfiction Needs general interest, how-to, interview, new product, photo feature. Query.

$$$$ MS. MAGAZINE

433 S. Beverly Dr., Beverly Hills CA 90212. (310)556-2515. Fax: (310)556-2514. E-mail: mkort@msmagazine.com. Website: www.msmagazine.com. **70% freelance written**. Quarterly magazine on women's issues and news. Estab. 1972. Circ. 150,000. Byline given. Offers 25% kill fee. Buys all rights. Responds in 3 months to queries. Responds in 3 months to mss. Sample copy for $9. Guidelines available online.

Nonfiction International and national (U.S.) news, the arts, books, popular culture, feminist theory and scholarship, ecofeminism, women's health, political and economic affairs. **Buys 4-5 feature (2,000-3,000 words) and 4-5 short (500 words) mss/year.** Query with published clips. Length: 300-3,500 words. **Pays $1/word, 50¢/word for news stories and book review.**

Columns/Departments 6-10 **Pays $1/word.**

Tips Needs international and national women's news, investigative reporting, personal narratives, and prize-winning journalists and feminist thinkers.

$$ NA'AMAT WOMAN

Magazine of NA'AMAT USA, Na'Amat USA, 350 Fifth Ave., Suite 4700, New York NY 10118-4700. Fax: (212)563-5710. E-mail: judith@naamat.org. Website: www.naamat.org. **80% freelance written**. Quarterly magazine covering Jewish issues/subjects. "We cover issues and topics of interest to the Jewish community in the U.S., Israel, and the rest of the world with emphasis on Jewish women's issues." Estab. 1926. Circ. 13,000. Byline given. Pays on publication. No kill fee. Publishes ms an average of 6 months after acceptance. Buys first North American serial rights, buys second serial (reprint) rights. Makes work-for-hire assignments. Submit seasonal material 6 months in advance. Accepts queries by mail, e-mail. Accepts simultaneous submissions. Responds in 4 weeks to queries. Responds in 3 months to mss Sample copy for $2 Guidelines by e-mail

Nonfiction "Articles must be of particular interest to the Jewish community." Needs book excerpts, essays, historical, interview, personal experience, photo feature, travel, Jewish topics & issues, political & social issues & women's issues. **Buys 16-20 mss/year.** Send complete ms. **Pays 10-20¢/word for assigned and unsolicited articles.**

Photos State availability. Reviews GIF/JPEG files. Negotiates payment individually. Buys one time rights.

Fiction Contact: Judith A. Sokoloff, editor. "We want serious fiction, with insight, reflection and consciousness." Needs novel excerpts, literary with Jewish content. "We do not want fiction that is mostly dialogue. No corny Jewish humor. No Holocaust fiction." **Buys 1-2 mss/year.** Query with published clips or send complete ms. Length: 2,000-3,000 words. **Pays 10-20¢/word for assigned articles and for unsolicited articles.**

NOTEBOOK:

News Magazines, 170-180 Bourke Rd., Alexandria NSW 2015 Australia. (61)(2)9353-6666. Fax: (61)(2)9353-6699. E-mail: feedback@notebookmagazine.com. Website: www.notebookmagazine.com. **Contact:** Caroline Roessler, editor. Monthly magazine connecting with Australian women and delivering what they want. "*Notebook:* magazine provides everyday solutions for women's busy lives and insights centred around thought-provoking, intelligent and compassionate journalism. Unique tear-out tabs can be used to mark your spot in any of the great chapters: Calendar, Your Life, Fashion & Beauty, Home Life, Health & Wellbeing, and Fabulous Food. Target audience: stylish, intelligent and aware females, aged 35-59, who are passionate about their family, friends and community. " Circ. 72,709.

- Query by submitting.

P31 WOMAN

Bringing God's Peace, Perspective, and Purpose to Today's Busy Woman, Proverbs 31 Ministries, 616-G Matthews-Mint Hill Rd., Charlotte NC 28105. (704)849-2270. E-mail: janet@proverbs31.org. Website: www.proverbs31.org. Janet Burke. **Contact:** Glynnis Whitwer, editor. **50% freelance written.** Monthly magazine covering Christian issues for women. "The *P31 Woman* provides Christian wives and mothers with articles that encourage them in their faith and support them in the many roles they have as women. We look for articles that have a Biblical foundation and offer inspiration, yet have a practical application to everyday life." Estab. 1992. Circ. 10,000. Byline given. No kill fee. Publishes ms an average of 6 months after acceptance. No rights purchased. Editorial lead time 5 months. Submit seasonal material 5-6 months in advance. Accepts queries by mail, e-mail. Accepts previously published material. Accepts simultaneous submissions. Responds in 2-4 weeks to queries. Responds in 1-2 months to mss. Sample copy online or $2 for hard copy. Guidelines available online.

Nonfiction Needs humor, inspirational, personal experience, religious. No biographical stories or articles about men's issues. Send complete ms. Length: 200-1,000 words. **Pays in contributor copies.**

$$$ RE[N] REDBOOK MAGAZINE

Hearst Corp., Articles Dept., Redbook, 300 West 57th St., 22nd Floor, New York NY 10019. Website: www.redbookmag.com/writersguidelines. **Contact:** Submissions Ed. Monthly magazine. "*Redbook* is targeted to women between the ages of 25 and 45 who define themselves as smart, capable, and happy with their lives. Many, but not all, of our readers are going through one of two key life transitions: single to married and married to mom. Each issue is a provocative mix of features geared to entertain and inform them, including: News stories on contemporary issues that are relevant to the reader's life and experience, and explore the emotional ramifications of cultural and social changes; First-person essays about dramatic pivotal moments in a woman's life; Marriage articles with an emphasis on strengthening the relationship; Short parenting features on how to deal with universal health and behavioral issues; Reporting on exciting trends in women's lives." Estab. 1903. Circ. 2,300,000. Pays on acceptance. No kill fee. Publishes ms an average of 6 months after acceptance. Rights purchased vary with author and material. Responds in 3 months to queries. Responds in 3 months to mss. Guidelines available online.

Nonfiction Subjects of interest: Social issues, parenting, sex, marriage, news profiles, true crime, dramatic narratives, health. Query with published clips and SASE 2,500-3,000 words/articles; 1,000-1,500 words/short articles

Tips "Most *Redbook* articles require solid research, well-developed anecdotes from on-the-record sources, and fresh, insightful quotes from established experts in a field that pass our `reality check' test. Articles must apply to women in our demographics. Writers are advised to read at least the last 6 issues of the magazine (available in most libraries) to get a better understanding of appropriate subject matter and treatment. We prefer to see detailed queries rather than completed mss, and suggest that you provide us with some ideas for sources/experts. Please enclose 2 or more samples of your writing, as well as a SASE."

RESOURCES FOR FEMINIST RESEARCH

RFR/DRF (Resources for Feminist Research), OISE, University of Toronto, 252 Bloor St. W., Toronto ON M5S 1V6 Canada. E-mail: rfrdrf@oise.utoronto.ca. Website: www.oise.utoronto.ca/rfr. Semiannual academic journal covering feminist research in an interdisciplinary, international perspective. Estab. 1972. Circ. 2,500. Byline given. Publishes ms an average of 1 year after acceptance. Buys all rights. Editorial lead time 1 year. Accepts queries by e-mail. Responds in 2 weeks to queries. Responds in 6-8 months to mss. Guidelines free.

Nonfiction Needs essays, academic articles and book reviews. Does not want nonacademic articles. Send complete ms. Length: 3,000-5,000 words.

Photos Send photos. Identification of subjects required. Reviews prints, GIF/JPEG files. Offers no additional payment for photos accepted with ms. Buys one-time rights.

SHOP TIL YOU DROP

ACP Magazines, Ltd., 54-58 Park St., GPO Box 4088, Sydney NSW 2000 Australia. (61)(2)9282-8000. Fax: (61)(2)9267-4361. E-mail: jcullen@acpmagazines.com.au. Website: www.acp.com.au. **Contact:** Justine Cullen, editor. Monthly magazine covering the entire fashion and beauty market. Circ. 78,834.

- "Women today are time-poor and are embracing virtual and catalogue shopping. *Shop Til You Drop* taps into this trend, allowing our readers to shop within the security of a magazine experience. It's a complete treat - the indulgent, fun escape women have been looking for."

Target women 16-39.

Nonfiction Needs general interest, how-to, new product. No self-help, sex, angst, relationship articles Query.

$$ SKIRT! MAGAZINE

Morris Communications, 7 Radcliffe St., Suite 302, Charleston SC 29403. (843)958-0028. Fax: (843)958-0029. E-mail: submissions@skirt.com. Website: www.skirt.com. **50% freelance written**. Monthly magazine covering women's interest. *Skirt!* is all about women—their work, play, families, creativity, style, health, wealth, bodies, and souls. The magazine's attitude is spirited, independent, outspoken, serious, playful, irreverent, sometimes controversial, and always passionate. Estab. 1994. Circ. 285,000. Byline given. Pays on publication. No kill fee. Publishes ms an average of 2 months after acceptance. Buys one-time rights. Editorial lead time 2-3 months. Submit seasonal material 2-3 months in advance. Accepts queries by e-mail (preferred). Accepts simultaneous submissions. Responds in 6-8 weeks to queries. Responds in 1-2 months to mss. Guidelines available online.

Nonfiction Needs essays, humor, personal experience. "Do not send feature articles. We only accept submissions of completed personal essays that will work with our monthly themes available online." **Buys 100+ mss/year.** Send complete ms. We prefer e-mail submissions. Length: 900-1,200 words. **Pays $150-200.**

Photos "We feature a different color photo, painting, or illustration on the cover each month. Each issue also features a b&w photo by a female photographer. Submit artwork via e-mail." Reviews Slides, high-resolution digital files. Does not pay for photos or artwork, but the artist's bio is published.

Tips "Surprise and charm us. We look for fearless essays that take chances with content and subject. *Skirt!* is not your average women's magazine. We push the envelope and select content that makes our readers think. Please review guidelines & themes online before submitting."

$$ THAT'S LIFE!

Bauer Publishing, Academic House, 24-28 Oval Rd., London England NW1 7DT United Kingdom. (44) (207)241-8000. Website: www.bauer.co.uk. "Magazine is packed with the most amazing true-life stories, fab puzzles offering big money prizes including family sunshine holidays and even a car! We also have bright, up-to-date fashion, health and beauty pages with top tips and readers' letters. And just to make sure we get you smiling too, there's our rib-tickling rude jokes and 'aren't men' daft tales." Estab. 1995. Circ. 550,000. No kill fee. Submit seasonal material 3 months in advance. Accepts queries by mail. Responds in 6 weeks to mss. Guidelines by e-mail.

Fiction Stories should have a strong plot and a good twist. A sexy relationships/scene can feature strongly, but isn't essential—the plot twist is much more important. The writing should be chronological and fast moving. A maximum of 4 characters is advisable. Avoid straightforward romance, historical backgrounds, science fiction, and stories told by animals or small children. Graphic murders and sex crimes—especially those involving children—are not acceptable. Send complete ms. 700 words **£400**.

Tips Study the magazine for a few weeks to get an idea of our style and flavor.

$$ TODAY'S BRIDE

Family Communications, 65 The East Mall, Toronto ON M8Z SW3 Canada. (416)537-2604. Fax: (416)538-1794. E-mail: info@canadianbride.com. Website: www.todaysbride.ca. www.canadianbride.com. **20% freelance written**. Semiannual magazine. Magazine provides information to engaged couples on all aspects of wedding planning, including tips, fashion advice, etc. There are also beauty, home, groom, and honeymoon travel sections. Estab. 1979. Circ. 102,000. Byline given. Pays on acceptance. No kill fee. Buys all rights. Editorial lead time 6 months. Accepts queries by mail, e-mail, fax. Accepts simultaneous submissions. Responds in 2 weeks-1 month.

Nonfiction Needs humor, opinion, personal experience. No travel pieces. Send complete ms. Length: 800-1,400 words. **Pays $250-300.**

Photos Send photos. Identification of subjects required. Reviews transparencies, prints. Negotiates payment individually. Rights purchased negotiated on individual basis.

Tips Send us tight writing about topics relevant to all brides and grooms. Stories for grooms, especially those written by/about grooms, are also encouraged.

$$ TODAY'S CHRISTIAN WOMAN

465 Gundersen Dr., Carol Stream IL 60188-2498. (630)260-6200. Fax: (630)260-0114. E-mail: tcwedit@christianitytoday.com. Website: www.todayschristianwoman.com. **Contact:** Ginger Kolbaba, editor, Cynthia Thomas, editorial coordinator. **50% freelance written**. Bimonthly magazine for Christian women of all ages, single and married, homemakers, and career women. "*Today's Christian Woman* seeks to help women deal with the contemporary issues and hot topics that impact their lives, as well

as provide depth, balance, and a Biblical perspective to the relationships they grapple with daily in the following arenas: family, friendship, faith, marriage, single life, self, work, and health." Estab. 1978. Circ. 230,000. Byline given. Pays on acceptance. No kill fee. Publishes ms an average of 6-12 months after acceptance. Buys first rights. Submit seasonal material 9 months in advance. Accepts queries by mail, e-mail, fax. Responds in 2 months to queries. Responds in 2 months to mss. Sample copy for $5. Writer's guidelines for #10 SASE or online

Nonfiction How-to, narrative, inspirational. *Practical* spiritual living articles, 1,200-1,500 words. Humor (light, first-person pieces that include some spiritual distinctive), 1,000 words. Issues (third-person, anecdotal articles that report on scope of trends or hot topics, and provide perspective and practical take away on issues, plus sidebars), 1,500 words. Needs how-to, inspirational. Query. No unsolicited mss. The query should include article summary, purpose, and reader value, author's qualifications, suggested length, date to send, and SASE for reply. **Pays 20-25¢/word.**

Tips "Articles should be practical and contain a distinct evangelical Christian perspective. While *TCW* adheres strictly to this underlying perspective in all its editorial content, articles should refrain from using language that assumes a reader's familiarity with Christian or church-oriented terminology. Bible quotes and references should be used selectively. All Bible quotes should be taken from the New International Version if possible. All articles should be highly anecdotal, personal in tone, and universal in appeal."

TRACE MAGAZINE

TRACE Inc., 41 Great Jones St., 3rd Floor, New York NY 10012. (212)625-1192. Fax: (212)625-1195. E-mail: info@trace212.com. Website: www.trace212.com. **Contact:** Editor-in-Chief. **25% freelance written**. Lifestyle magazine published 10 times/year covering fashion, music, and art. "*TRACE Magazine* is a leading international transcultural style magazine that mixes music, fashion, lifestyle and art through cutting-edge editorial." Estab. 1996. Circ. 100,000. Byline given. Pays 30 days after publication. Publishes ms an average of 2 months after acceptance. Buys first rights, buys second serial (reprint) rights, buys electronic rights. Editorial lead time 2 months. Submit seasonal material 2 months in advance. Accepts queries by e-mail, phone. Accepts simultaneous submissions. Responds in 2 weeks to queries.

Nonfiction Needs book excerpts, essays, expose, general interest, interview, new product, personal experience, photo feature, technical, travel. Query with published clips. **Pays variable amount.**

Photos Contact: Contact Katie Constans, creative director. State availability of or send photos. Identification of subjects, model releases required. Reviews contact sheets, negatives, transparencies, prints, GIF/JPEG files. Negotiates payment individually. Buys exclusive worldwide first time, second serial, and electronic rights.

Tips Read the magazine and be familiar with style and tone. Also, queries that represent a knowledge of international subcultures and trends affecting young people are most often picked up by *TRACE*.

N W

Fairchild Publications, Inc., 750 3rd Ave., New York NY 10017. (212)630-4900. Fax: (212)630-4919. Website: www.wmagazine.com. **Contact:** Nina Lawrence. Monthly magazine covering pop culture, fashion, beauty, the arts, celebrities, homes, hotels, and more. "Written for today's contemporary woman whose fashion sensibility and sense of style define her own look, in her own way." Circ. 463,000. No kill fee. Editorial lead time 6 weeks.

- "*W* is a luxury fashion and lifestyle magazine; it provides the ultimate insider and original experience to its readers."

$$$$ WISH

St. Joseph Media, 111 Queen St. E., Suite 320, Toronto ON M5C 1S2 Canada. E-mail: jane@wish.ca. Website: www.wish.ca. Pays on acceptance. No kill fee. Guidelines available online.

Nonfiction Fashion, beauty, home decor, food, family, relationships, health & wellness, fitness. Query. **Pays $1/word.**

$$ WOMAN'S LIFE

A Publication of Woman's Life Insurance Society, 1338 Military St., P.O. Box 5020, Port Huron MI 48061-5020. (800)521-9292. Fax: (810)985-6970. E-mail: wkrabach@womanslife.org. Website: www.womanslife.org. **30% freelance written**. Quarterly magazine published for a primarily female membership to help them care for themselves and their families. Estab. 1892. Circ. 32,000. Byline given. Pays on publication. No kill fee. Publishes ms an average of 1 year after acceptance. Buys one-time rights, second serial (reprint) rights, simultaneous rights. Submit seasonal material 6 months in advance. Accepts queries by mail, e-mail, fax. Accepts simultaneous submissions. Responds in 1 year to queries and to mss. Sample copy for sae with 9 × 12 envelope and 4 first-class stamps. Guidelines for #10 SASE.

- "Works only with published/established writers."

Nonfiction "Looking primarily for general interest stories for women aged 25-55 regarding physical, mental, and emotional health and fitness; and financial/fiscal health and fitness. We would like to see more creative financial pieces that are directed at women." **Buys 4-10 mss/year.** Send complete ms. Length: 1,000-2,000 words. **Pays $150-500.**

Reprints Send tearsheet, photocopy or typed ms with rights for sale noted and information about when and where the material previously appeared. Pays 15% of amount paid for an original article

Photos Only interested in photos included with ms. Identification of subjects, model releases required.

$ WOMEN IN BUSINESS

American Business Women's Association (The ABWA Co., Inc.), 9100 Ward Pkwy., P.O. Box 8728, Kansas City MO 64114-0728. (816)361-6621. Fax: (816)361-4991. E-mail: abwa@abwa.org. Website: www.abwa.org. **Contact:** Rene Street, Exec. Dir. **30% freelance written**. Bimonthly magazine covering issues affecting working women. "How-to features for career women on business trends, small-business ownership, self-improvement, and retirement issues. Profiles business women." Estab. 1949. Circ. 45,000. Byline given. Pays on acceptance. No kill fee. Publishes ms an average of 3 months after acceptance. Buys first North American serial rights. Editorial lead time 3 months. Accepts queries by mail, e-mail, fax. Accepts simultaneous submissions. Responds in 3 weeks to queries. Responds in 2 months to mss. Sample copy for sae with 9 × 12 envelope and 4 First-Class stamps. Guidelines for #10 SASE.

Nonfiction Needs how-to, interview, computer/Internet. No fiction or poetry. **Buys 3% of submitted mss/year.** Query. Length: 500-1,000 words. **Pays $100/500 words.**

Photos State availability. Identification of subjects required. Reviews prints. Offers no additional payment for photos accepted with ms Buys all rights.

Columns/Departments Life After Business (concerns of retired business women); It's Your Business (entrepreneurial advice for business owners); Health Spot (health issues that affect women in the work place). Length: 500-750 words. Query. **Pays $100/500 words**

YORKSHIRE WOMEN'S LIFE

P.O. Box 113, Leeds LS8 2WX UK. E-mail: ywlmagenquiries@btinternet.com. Website: www.yorkshirewomenslife.co.uk. No kill fee. Guidelines by e-mail.

Nonfiction Needs general interest, women's issues, personal experience, author describes some aspect of her life in first person, reviews of theatres/art exhibitions/books. Does not want cooking/recipes, short stories, or poetry. Submit 200-word proposal, published clips, bio, SAE.

Photos Accepts color copies via post from female visual artists. Include a short CV.

Tips "It is vital to study the magazine style before sending submissions."

Trade Journals

Many writers who pick up *Writer's Market* for the first time do so with the hope of selling an article to one of the popular, high-profile consumer magazines found on newsstands and in bookstores. Many of those writers are surprised to find an entire world of magazine publishing exists outside the realm of commercial magazines—trade journals. Writers who *have* discovered trade journals have found a market that offers the chance to publish regularly in subject areas they find interesting, editors who are typically more accessible than their commercial counterparts, and pay rates that rival those of the big-name magazines. **(Note: All of the magazines listed in the Trade Journals section are paying markets. However, some of the magazines are not identified by payment rates ($-$$$$) because the magazines preferred not to disclose specific payment information.)**

Trade journal is the general term for any publication focusing on a particular occupation or industry. Other terms used to describe the different types of trade publications are business, technical, and professional journals. They are read by truck drivers, bricklayers, farmers, fishermen, heart surgeons, and just about everyone else working in a trade or profession. Trade periodicals are sharply angled to the specifics of the professions on which they report. They offer business-related news, features, and service articles that will foster their readers' professional development.

Editors at trade journals tell us their audience is made up of knowledgeable and highly interested readers. Writers for trade journals have to either possess knowledge about the field in question or be able to report it accurately from interviews with those who do. Writers who have or can develop a good grasp of a specialized body of knowledge will find trade magazine editors who are eager to hear from them.

An ideal way to begin your foray into trade journals is to write for those that report on your present profession. Whether you've been teaching dance, farming, or working as a paralegal, begin by familiarizing yourself with the magazines that serve your occupation. After you've read enough issues to have a feel for the kinds of pieces the magazines run, approach the editors with your own article ideas. If you don't have experience in a profession but can demonstrate an ability to understand (and write about) the intricacies and issues of a particular trade that interests you, editors will still be willing to hear from you.

Advertising, Marketing & PR

$ $ $ ADVANTAGES MAGAZINE

The Advertising Specialty Institute, 4800 Street Rd., Trevose PA 19053. (215)953-3337. Website: www.advantagesinfo.com. **40% freelance written**. Monthly magazine covering promotional products (branded T-shirts, mugs, pens, etc.). *Advantages* is a 15-issue publication targeted to promotional products salespeople. Its main objective is to be a comprehensive source of sales strategies, information and inspiration through articles, columns, case histories and product showcases. The magazine is presented in a fun and easy-to-read format to keep busy salespeople interested and entertained. The easy-to-use reader response system makes it fast and simple to request product information from suppliers featured in showcases. We want our subscribers to look forward to its arrival and to believe that *Advantages* is the one magazine they can't do without. Estab. 1997. Circ. 40,000. Byline given. Pays on acceptance. Publishes ms an average of 1-2 months after acceptance. Buys all rights. Editorial lead time 1 month. Submit seasonal material 1 month in advance. Accepts queries by e-mail, phone. Accepts simultaneous submissions. Sample copy free. Guidelines free.

Nonfiction Full-length features on market opportunities and selling-related topics. **Buys 40 mss/year.** Query. Length: 2,500-3,500 words. **Pays $500-1,000 + .**

Tips Just send me an e-mail, especially if you have any previous experience writing on the promotional products industry and/or sales topics in general.

$ $ $ BRAND PACKAGING

Stagnito Communications, 155 Pfingsten Rd., Suite 205, Deerfield IL 60015. (847)405-4000. Fax: (847)405-4100. E-mail: acevedoj@bnpmedia.com. Website: www.brandpackaging.com. **15% freelance written**. Magazine published 10 times/year covering how packaging can be a marketing tool. We publish strategies and tactics to make products stand out on the shelf. Our market is brand managers who are marketers but need to know something about packaging. Estab. 1997. Circ. 33,000. Byline given. Pays on acceptance. Publishes ms an average of 2 months after acceptance. Makes work-for-hire assignments. Editorial lead time 3 months. Submit seasonal material 3 months in advance. Accepts queries by mail, fax. Sample copy free.

Nonfiction Needs how-to, interview, new product. **Buys 10 mss/year.** Send complete ms. Length: 600-2,400 words. **Pays 40-50¢/word.**

Photos State availability. Identification of subjects required. Reviews contact sheets, 35mm transparencies, 4 × 5 prints. Negotiates payment individually. Buys one time rights.

Columns/Departments Emerging Technology (new packaging technology), 600 words. **Buys 10 mss/year.** Query. **Pays $150-300.**

Tips Be knowledgeable on marketing techniques and be able to grasp packaging techniques. Be sure you focus on packaging as a marketing tool. Use concrete examples. We are not seeking case histories at this time.

$ $ FPO MAGAZINE

For Publications Only, Auras Custom Publishing, 8435 Georgia Ave., Silver Spring MD 20910. (301)587-4300. Fax: (301)587-6836. E-mail: editor@fpomagazine.com. Website: www.fpomagazine.com. **Contact:** Rob Sugar, editor. **50% freelance written**. Quarterly magazine covering creative and production. "*[FPO] Magazine* is a print and online resource for publication professionals, publishers, editors, designers, and production managers that focuses on the creative side of magazine publishing." Estab. 2007. Circ. 10,000. Byline given. Pays on publication. Offers 25% kill fee. Publishes ms an average of 3-4 months after acceptance. Buys first North American serial rights, buys electronic rights. Editorial lead time 3 months. Accepts queries by mail, e-mail, fax, phone. Accepts previously published material. Accepts simultaneous submissions. Sample copy by e-mail. Guidelines available online.

Nonfiction All articles must relate to magazine design or publishing. Needs essays, historical, how-to, humor, interview, new product, technical. Special issues: 100 Top Tips (late Fall 2008). **Buys 10-12 mss/year.** Query. **Pays 50¢/word.** Sometimes pays expenses of writers on assignment.

Photos State availability. Captions, model releases required. Reviews GIF/JPEG files. Negotiates payment individually.

Columns/Departments Cover Charge; Re: Write; Re: Design; Creative Briefs, all 500 words. **Buys 20-25 mss/year.** Query. **Pays 50¢/word.**

Fillers Needs anecdotes, facts, gags, short humor. Length: 100-400 words. **Pays $25-50.**

Tips "Experience working on a magazine helps, along with an understanding of graphic design."

$$ O'DWYER'S PR REPORT

271 Madison Ave., #600, New York NY 10016. Fax: (212)679-2471. E-mail: jack@odwyerpr.com. Website: www.odwyerpr.com. **Contact:** Jack O'Dwyer. Monthly magazine providing PR articles. "O'Dwyer's has been covering public relations, marketing communications and related fields for over 40 years. The company provides the latest news and information about PR firms and professionals, the media, corporations, legal issues, jobs, technology, and much more through its website, weekly newsletter, monthly magazine, directories, and guides Many of the contributors are PR people publicizing themselves while analyzing something." Byline given. No kill fee. Accepts queries by mail.

Nonfiction "We use op-ed pieces and news articles about PR trends." Needs opinion. Query. **Pays $250.**

$$$ PROMO MAGAZINE

Insights and Ideas for Building Brands, Penton Media, 244 W. 17th St., New York NY 10011. (212)358-4183. Fax: (203)358-9900. E-mail: patricia.odell@penton.com. Website: www.promomagazine.com. **Contact:** Patricia Odell, executive editor. **5% freelance written**. Monthly magazine covering promotion marketing. "*Promo* serves marketers, and stories must be informative, well written, and familiar with the subject matter." Estab. 1987. Circ. 25,000. Byline given. Pays on publication. Offers 25% kill fee. Publishes ms an average of 2 months after acceptance. Buys first North American serial rights. Editorial lead time 3 months. Submit seasonal material 3 months in advance. Responds in 1 month to queries. Sample copy for $5.

Nonfiction Needs expose, general interest, how-to, marketing programs, interview, new product, promotion. No general marketing stories not heavily involved in promotions. Generally does not accept unsolicited mss, query first. **Buys 6-10 mss/year.** Query with published clips. **Pays $1,000 maximum for assigned articles. Pays $500 maximum for unsolicited articles.** Sometimes pays expenses of writers on assignment.

Photos State availability. Captions, identification of subjects, model releases required. Reviews contact sheets, negatives. Negotiates payment individually.

Tips "Understand that our stories aim to teach marketing professionals about successful promotion strategies. Case studies or new promos have the best chance."

$$ SIGN BUILDER ILLUSTRATED

The How-To Magazine, Simmons-Boardman Publishing Corp., 345 Hudson St., 12th Floor, New York NY 10014. (212)620-7223. E-mail: jwooten@sbpub.com. Website: www.signshop.com. **40% freelance written**. Monthly magazine covering sign and graphic industry. *Sign Builder Illustrated* targets sign professionals where they work: on the shop floor. Our topics cover the broadest spectrum of the sign industry, from design to fabrication, installation, maintenance and repair. Our readers own a similarly wide range of shops, including commercial, vinyl, sign erection and maintenance, electrical and neon, architectural, and awnings. Estab. 1987. Circ. 14,500. Byline given. Pays on acceptance. Offers 10% kill fee. Publishes ms an average of 3 months after acceptance. Buys all rights. Editorial lead time 3 months. Submit seasonal material 4 months in advance. Accepts queries by mail, e-mail, fax, phone. Accepts simultaneous submissions. Responds in 1 month to queries. Sample copy and writer's guidelines free.

Nonfiction Needs historical, how-to, humor, interview, photo feature, technical. **Buys 50-60 mss/year.** Query. Length: 1,000-1,500 words. **Pays $250-550 for assigned articles.**

Photos Send photos. Captions, identification of subjects required. Reviews 3 × 5 prints. Negotiates payment individually. Buys all rights.

Tips Be very knowledgeable about a portion of the sign industry you are covering. We want our readers to come away from each article with at least one good idea, one new technique, or one more 'trick of the trade.' At the same time, we don't want a purely textbook listing of 'do this, do that.' Our readers enjoy *Sign Builder Illustrated* because the publication speaks to them in a clear and lively fashion, from one sign professional to another. We want to engage the reader who has been in the business for some time. While there might be a place for basic instruction in new techniques, our average paid subscriber has been in business over 20 years, employs over seven people, and averages $800,000 in annual sales. These people aren't neophytes content with retread articles they can find anywhere. It's important for our writers to use anecdotes and examples drawn from the daily sign business.

$$ SIGNCRAFT

The Magazine for Today's Sign Maker, SignCraft Publishing Co., Inc., P.O. Box 60031, Fort Myers FL 33906. (239)939-4644. Fax: (239)939-0607. E-mail: signcraft@signcraft.com. Website: www.signcraft.

com. **10% freelance written**. Bimonthly magazine covering the sign industry. "Like any trade magazine, we need material of direct benefit to our readers. We can't afford space for material of marginal interest." Estab. 1980. Circ. 14,000. Byline given. Pays on publication. Offers negotiable kill fee. Publishes ms an average of 6 months after acceptance. Buys first North American serial rights, buys all rights. Accepts queries by mail, e-mail, fax. Responds in 1 month to queries Sample copy and writer's guidelines for $3.

Nonfiction "All articles should be directly related to quality commercial signs. If you are familiar with the sign trade, we'd like to hear from you." Needs interview. **Buys 10 mss/year.** Query. Length: 500-2,000 words.

Art, Design & Collectibles

$$ AIRBRUSH ACTION MAGAZINE

Action, Inc., 3209 Atlantic Ave., P.O. Box 438, Allenwood NJ 08720. (732)223-7878. Fax: (732)223-2855. E-mail: editor@airbrushaction.com. Website: www.airbrushaction.com. **80% freelance written**. Bimonthly magazine covering the spectrum of airbrush applications: automotive and custom paint applications, illustration, T-shirt airbrushing, fine art, automotive and sign painting, hobby/craft applications, wall murals, fingernails, temporary tattoos, artist profiles, reviews, and more. Estab. 1985. Circ. 35,000. Byline given. Pays 1 month after publication. Publishes ms an average of 6 months after acceptance. Buys all rights. Editorial lead time 6 months. Submit seasonal material 6 months in advance. Accepts queries by mail, e-mail, fax, phone. Accepts simultaneous submissions.

Nonfiction Current primary focus is on automotive, motorcycle, and helmet kustom kulture arts. Needs how-to, humor, inspirational, interview, new product, personal experience, technical. Nothing unrelated to airbrush. Query with published clips. **Pays 15¢/word.** Sometimes pays expenses of writers on assignment.

Photos Digital images preferred. Send photos. Captions, identification of subjects, model releases required. Negotiates payment individually. Buys all rights.

Columns/Departments Query with published clips.

Tips Send bio and writing samples. Send well-written technical information pertaining to airbrush art. We publish a lot of artist profiles—they all sound the same. Looking for new pizzazz!

$$ ANTIQUEWEEK

DMG World Media (USA), P.O. Box 90, Knightstown IN 46148-0090. (800)876-5133, ext. 189. Fax: (800)695-8153. E-mail: connie@antiqueweek.com. Website: www.antiqueweek.com. **80% freelance written**. Weekly tabloid covering antiques and collectibles with 3 editions: Eastern, Central and National, plus monthly *AntiqueWest*. *AntiqueWeek* has a wide range of readership from dealers and auctioneers to collectors, both advanced and novice. Our readers demand accurate information presented in an entertaining style. Estab. 1968. Circ. 50,000. Byline given. Pays on publication. Offers kill fee. Offers 10% kill fee or $25. Buys first rights, buys second serial (reprint) rights. Submit seasonal material 1 month in advance. Accepts queries by mail, e-mail. Sample copy free. Guidelines by e-mail.

Nonfiction Needs historical, how-to, interview, opinion, personal experience, antique show and auction reports, feature articles on particular types of antiques and collectibles. **Buys 400-500 mss/year.** Query. Length: 1,000-2,000 words. **Pays $50-250.**

Reprints Send electronic copy with rights for sale noted and information about when and where the material previously appeared.

Photos All material must be submitted electronically via e-mail or on CD. Send photos. Identification of subjects required.

Tips Writers should know their topics thoroughly. Feature articles must be well researched and clearly written. An interview and profile article with a knowledgeable collector might be the break for a first-time contributor. We seek a balanced mix of information on traditional antiques and 20th century collectibles.

$ THE APPRAISERS STANDARD

New England Appraisers Association, 5 Gill Terrace, Ludlow VT 05149-1003. (802)228-7444. Fax: (802)228-7444. E-mail: llt44@ludl.tds.net. Website: www.newenglandappraisers.net. **Contact:** Linda L. Tucker, ed. **50% freelance written. Works with a small number of new/unpublished writers each year**. Quarterly publication covering the appraisals of antiques, art, collectibles, jewelry, coins, stamps, and real estate. "The writer should be knowledgeable on the subject, and the article should be written with appraisers in mind, with prices quoted for objects, good pictures, and descriptions of articles being written about." Estab. 1980. Circ. 1,300. Short bio and byline given. Pays on publication. No kill fee. Publishes ms an average of 1 year after acceptance. Buys first and simultaneous rights. Submit seasonal material 2 months in advance. Accepts queries by mail, e-mail. Accepts simultaneous submissions. Responds in 1 month to queries. Responds in 2 months to mss. Sample copy for 9 × 12 SAE with 78¢ postage. Guidelines for #10 SASE.

- "I would like writers to focus on particular types of antiques: i.e. types of furniture, glass, artwork, etc., giving information on the history of this type of antique, good photos, recent sale prices, etc."

Nonfiction "All geared toward professional appraisers." Needs interview, personal experience, technical, travel. Send complete ms. Length: 700 words. **Pays $60.**

Reprints "Send typed manuscript with rights for sale noted and information about when and where the material previously appeared."

Photos Send photos. Identification of subjects required. Reviews negatives, prints. Offers no additional payment for photos accepted with ms. Buys one time rights.

Tips "Interviewing members of the association for articles, reviewing, shows, and large auctions are all ways for writers who are not in the field to write articles for us. Articles should be geared to provide information which will help the appraisers with ascertaining value, detecting forgeries or reproductions, or simply providing advice on appraising the articles."

$$ ART CALENDAR MAGAZINE

The Business Magazine for Visual Artists, 1500 Park Center Dr., Orlando FL 32835. (407)563-7000. Fax: (407)563-7099. E-mail: khall@artcalendar.com. Website: www.artcalendar.com. **75% freelance written.** Monthly magazine. Estab. 1986. Circ. 20,000. Pays on publication. No kill fee. Accepts previously published material. Sample print copy for $5. Guidelines available online.

- We welcome nuts-and-bolts, practical articles of interest to professional visual artists, emerging or professional. Examples: How-to's, first-person stories on how an artist has built his career or an aspect of it, interviews with artists (business/career-building emphasis), web strategies, and pieces on business practices and other topics of use to artists. The tone of our magazine is practical, and uplifting.

Nonfiction Needs essays, the psychology of creativity, how-to, interview, successful artists with a focus on what made them successful, networking articles, marketing topics, technical articles (new equipment, new media, computer software, Internet marketing.), cartoons, art law, including pending legislation that affects artists (copyright law, Internet regulations, etc.). We like nuts-and-bolts information about making a living as an artist. We do not run reviews or art historical pieces, nor do we like writing characterized by 'critic-speak,' philosophical hyperbole, psychological arrogance, politics, or New Age religion. Also, we do not condone a get-rich-quick attitude. Send complete ms. **Pays $250.**

Reprints Send photocopy or typed ms and information about when and where the material previously appeared. Pays $50

Photos Reviews b&w glossy or color prints. Pays $25.

Columns/Departments If an artist or freelancer sends us good articles regularly, and based on results we feel that he is able to produce a column at least 3 times per year, we will invite him to be a contributing writer. If a gifted artist-writer can commit to producing an article on a monthly basis, we will offer him a regular column and the title contributing editor. Send complete ms.

Tips "We strongly suggest that you read a copy of the publication before submitting a proposal. Most queries are rejected because they are too general for our audience."

$$ ART MATERIALS RETAILER

Fahy-Williams Publishing, P.O. Box 1080, Geneva NY 14456. (315)789-0458. Fax: (315)789-4263. E-mail: tmanzer@fwpi.com. Website: www.artmaterialsretailer.com. **10% freelance written.** Quarterly magazine. Estab. 1998. Byline given. Pays on publication. No kill fee. Buys one-time rights. Editorial lead time 2 months. Submit seasonal material 3 months in advance. Accepts simultaneous submissions. Responds in 3 weeks to queries. Responds in 3 months to mss. Sample copy and writer's guidelines free.

Nonfiction Needs book excerpts, how-to, interview, personal experience. **Buys 2 mss/year.** Send complete ms. Length: 1,500-3,000 words. **Pays $50-250.** Sometimes pays expenses of writers on assignment.

Photos State availability. Identification of subjects required. Reviews transparencies. Offers no additional payment for photos accepted with ms. Buys one time rights.

Fillers Needs anecdotes, facts, newsbreaks. Buys 5 mss/year. Length: 500-1,500 words. **Pays $50-125.**

Tips We like to review manuscripts rather than queries. Artwork (photos, drawings, etc.) is a real plus. We enjoy (our readers enjoy) practical, nuts-and-bolts, news-you-can-use articles.

$$ FAITH + FORM

The Interfaith Journal of Religion, Art and Architecture, 47 Grandview Terrace, Essex CT 06426. (860)575-4702. E-mail: mcrosbie@faithandform.com. Website: www.faithandform.com. **50% freelance written**. Quarterly magazine covering religious buildings and art. Writers must be knowledgeable about environments for worship, or able to explain them. Estab. 1967. Circ. 4,500. Byline given. Publishes ms an average of 6 months after acceptance. Buys one-time rights. Editorial lead time 6 months. Submit seasonal material 6 months in advance. Accepts queries by mail, e-mail, fax, phone. Accepts previously published material. Accepts simultaneous submissions. Responds in 2 weeks to queries. Responds in 1 month to mss. Sample copy available online. Guidelines available.

Nonfiction Needs book excerpts, essays, how-to, inspirational, interview, opinion, personal experience, photo feature, religious, technical. **Buys 6 mss/year.** Query. Length: 500-2,500 words.

Photos State availability. Captions required. Reviews GIF/JPEG files. Offers no additional payment for photos accepted with ms. Buys one-time rights.

Columns/Departments News, 250-750 words; Book Reviews, 250-500 words. **Buys 3 mss/year.** Query.

$$$ HOW

Design Ideas at Work, F+W Media, Inc., 4700 E. Galbraith Rd., Cincinnati OH 45236. (513)531-2222. Fax: (513)531-2902. Website: www.howdesign.com. **Contact:** Bryn Mooth. **75% freelance written**. Bimonthly magazine covering graphic design profession. *HOW: Design Ideas at Work* strives to serve the business, technological and creative needs of graphic-design professionals. The magazine provides a practical mix of essential business information, up-to-date technological tips, the creative whys and hows behind noteworthy projects, and profiles of professionals who are impacting design. The ultimate goal of *HOW* is to help designers, whether they work for a design firm or for an inhouse design department, run successful, creative, profitable studios. Estab. 1985. Circ. 40,000. Byline given. Pays on acceptance. No kill fee. Buys first North American serial rights. Responds in 6 weeks to queries.

Nonfiction Features cover noteworthy design projects, interviews with leading creative professionals, profiles of established and up-and-coming firms, business and creativity topics for graphic designers. Special issues: Self-Promotion Annual (September/October); Business Annual (November/December); International Annual of Design (March/April); Creativity/Paper/Stock Photography (May/June); Digital Design Annual (July/August). No how-to articles for beginning artists or fine-art-oriented articles. **Buys 40 mss/year.** Query with published clips and samples of subject's work, artwork or design. Length: 1,500-2,000 words. **Pays $700-900.** Sometimes pays expenses of writers on assignment.

Photos State availability. Captions required. Reviews Information updated and verified. Buys one time rights.

Columns/Departments Creativity (focuses on creative exercises and inspiration) 1,200-1,500 words. In-House Issues (focuses on business and creativity issues for corporate design groups), 1,200-1,500 words. Business (focuses on business issue for design firm owners), 1,200-1, 500 words. **Buys 35 mss/year.** Query with published clips. **Pays $250-400.**

Tips "We look for writers who can recognize graphic designers on the cutting-edge of their industry, both creatively and business-wise. Writers must have an eye for detail, and be able to relay *HOW*'s editorial style in an interesting, concise manner—without omitting any details. Showing you've done your homework on a subject—and that you can go beyond asking 'those same old questions'—will give you a big advantage."

$$ INTERIOR LANDSCAPE BUSINESS MAGAZINE

(formerly *Interior Business Magazine*), GIE Media, Inc., 4020 Kinross Lakes Pkwy., Suite 201, Richfield OH 44286. (800)456-0707. Fax: (330)659-0823. E-mail: ccode@gie.net. Website: www.interiorbusinessonline.com. **5-10% freelance written**. Magazine covering interior landscaping. *Interior Business* addresses the concerns of the professional interior landscape contractor. It's devoted to the business management needs of interior landscape professionals. Estab. 2000. Circ. 6,000. Pays on publication. No kill fee. Publishes ms an average of 3 months after acceptance. Editorial lead time 3 months. Submit seasonal material 5 months in advance. Responds in 1 week to queries.

Nonfiction No articles oriented to the consumer or homeowner. **Buys 2 mss/year.** Length: 1,000-2,500 words. **Pays $250-500.**

Tips Know the audience. It's the professional business person, not the consumer.

$$ THE PASTEL JOURNAL

The Magazine for Pastel Artists, F + W Media, Inc., 4700 E. Galbraith Rd., Cincinnati OH 45236. (513)531-2690. Fax: (513)891-7153. Website: www.pasteljournal.com. **Contact:** Anne Hevener. Bimonthly magazine covering pastel art. *"The Pastel Journal* is the only national magazine devoted to the medium of pastel. Addressing the working professional as well as passionate amateurs, *The Pastel Journal* offers inspiration, information, and instruction to our readers." Estab. 1999. Circ. 22,000. Byline given. Pays on acceptance. Offers 25% kill fee. Publishes ms an average of 3-6 months after acceptance. Buys all rights. Editorial lead time 6 months. Submit seasonal material 6 months in advance. Accepts queries by mail. Accepts simultaneous submissions. Responds in 4-6 weeks to queries. Writer's guidelines free.

Nonfiction Needs how-to, interview, new product, profile. Does not want articles that aren't art-related. Review magazine before submitting. Query with or without published clips. Length: 500-2,500 words. **Pays $150-750.**

Photos State availability of or send photos. Captions required. Reviews transparencies, prints, GIF/JPEG files. Offers no additional payment for photos accepted with ms. Buys all rights.

$$$ PRINT

America's Graphic Design Magazine, F + W Media, Inc., 38 E. 29th St., 3rd Floor, New York NY 10016. (212)447-1400. Fax: (212)447-5231. E-mail: Aaron.Kenedi@fwmedia.com. Website: www.printmag.com. **Contact:** Aaron Kenedi. **75% freelance written**. Bimonthly magazine covering graphic design and visual culture. *PRINT*'s articles, written by design specialists and cultural critics, focus on the social, political, and historical context of graphic design, and on the places where consumer culture and popular culture meet. We aim to produce a general interest magazine for professionals with engagingly written text and lavish illustrations. By covering a broad spectrum of topics, both international and local, we try to demonstrate the significance of design in the world at large. Estab. 1940. Circ. 45,000. Byline given. Pays on acceptance. Offers 25% kill fee. Publishes ms an average of 3 months after acceptance. Buys first North American serial rights. Editorial lead time 3 months. Submit seasonal material 3 months in advance. Accepts queries by e-mail. Responds in 2 weeks to queries. Responds in 1 month to mss.

Nonfiction Needs essays, interview, opinion. **Buys 35-40 mss/year.** Query with published clips. Length: 1,000-2,500 words. **Pays $1,250.** Sometimes pays expenses of writers on assignment.

Columns/Departments Query with published clips. **Pays $800.**

Tips Be well versed in issues related to the field of graphic design; don't submit ideas that are too general or geared to nonprofessionals.

$ TEXAS ARCHITECT

Texas Society of Architects, 816 Congress Ave., Suite 970, Austin TX 78701. (512)478-7386. Fax: (512)478-0528. Website: www.texasarchitect.org. **Contact:** Stephen Sharpe, editor. **30% freelance written. Mostly written by unpaid members of the professional society**. Bimonthly journal covering architecture and architects of Texas. "*Texas Architect* is a highly visually-oriented look at Texas architecture, design, and urban planning. Articles cover varied subtopics within architecture. Readers are mostly architects and related building professionals." Estab. 1951. Circ. 12,000. Byline given. Pays on publication. No kill fee. Publishes ms an average of 3 months after acceptance. Buys one-time rights, buys all rights. Makes work-for-hire assignments. Submit seasonal material 4 months in advance. Accepts queries by mail, e-mail. Responds in 6 weeks to queries. Guidelines available online.

Nonfiction Needs interview, photo feature, technical, book reviews. Query with published clips. Length: 100-2,000 words. **Pays $50-100 for assigned articles.**

Photos Send photos. Identification of subjects required. Reviews contact sheets, 35mm or 4 × 5 transparencies, 4 × 5 prints. Offers no additional payment for photos accepted with ms. Buys one time rights.

Columns/Departments News (timely reports on architectural issues, projects, and people), 100-500 words. **Buys 10 mss/year.** Query with published clips. **Pays $50-100.**

$$ WATERCOLOR ARTIST

The No. 1 Magazine for Watercolor Artists, F + W Media, Inc., 4700 E. Galbraith Rd., Cincinnati OH 45236. (513)531-2690. Fax: (513)531-2902. Website: www.watercolorartistmagazine.com. Bimonthly magazine covering water media arts. "*Watercolor Artist* is the definitive source of how-to instruction and creative inspiration for artists working in water-based media." Estab. 1984. Circ. 53,000. Byline given. Pays on acceptance. Offers 10% kill fee. Publishes ms an average of 3-6 months after acceptance. Buys all rights. Editorial lead time 6 months. Submit seasonal material 6 months in advance. Accepts queries by mail. Accepts simultaneous submissions. Responds in 4-6 weeks to queries. Sample copy and writer's guidelines free.

Nonfiction Needs book excerpts, essays, how-to, inspirational, interview, new product, personal experience. "Does not want articles that aren't art-related. Review magazine before submitting." **Buys 36 mss/year.** Send query letter with images. Length: 350-2,500 words. **Pays $150-600.**

Photos State availability of or send photos. Captions required. Reviews transparencies, prints, slides, GIF/JPEG files. Buys one time rights.

Auto & Truck

$ $ AUTOINC.

Automotive Service Association, P.O. Box 929, Bedford TX 76095. (800)272-7467. Fax: (817)685-0225. E-mail: leonad@asashop.org. Website: www.autoinc.org. **10% freelance written**. Monthly magazine covering independent automotive repair. The mission of *AutoInc.*, ASA's official publication, is to be the informational authority for ASA and industry members nationwide. Its purpose is to enhance the professionalism of these members through management, technical and legislative articles, researched and written with the highest regard for accuracy, quality, and integrity. Estab. 1952. Circ. 14,000. Byline given. Pays on publication. No kill fee. Publishes ms an average of 3 months after acceptance. Buys all rights. Editorial lead time 2 months. Accepts queries by mail, e-mail, fax. Accepts simultaneous submissions. Responds in 6 weeks to queries. Responds in 2 months to mss. Sample copy for $5 or online. Guidelines available online.

Nonfiction Needs how-to, automotive repair, technical. No coverage of staff moves or financial reports. **Buys 6 mss/year.** Query with published clips. Length: 1,200 words. **Pays $300.** Sometimes pays phone expenses of writers on assignment.

Photos State availability of or send photos. Captions, identification of subjects, model releases required. Reviews 2x3 transparencies, 3 × 5 prints, high resolution digital images. Negotiates payment individually. Buys one-time and electronic rights.

Tips Learn about the automotive repair industry, specifically the independent shop segment. Understand the high-tech requirements needed to succeed today. We target professional repair shop owners rather than consumers.

$ $ BUSINESS FLEET

Bobit Publishing, 3520 Challenger St., Torrance CA 90501-1711. (310)533-2400. E-mail: chris.brown@bobit.com. Website: www.businessfleet.com. **10% freelance written**. Bimonthly magazine covering businesses which operate 10-50 company vehicles. While it's a trade publication aimed at a business audience, *Business Fleet* has a lively, conversational style. The best way to get a feel for our 'slant' is to read the magazine. Estab. 2000. Circ. 100,000. Byline given. Pays on publication. Offers 25% kill fee. Publishes ms an average of 3 months after acceptance. Buys first rights, buys second serial (reprint) rights, buys electronic rights. Editorial lead time 2 months. Submit seasonal material 2 months in advance. Accepts queries by mail, e-mail, fax. Responds in 3 weeks to queries. Responds in 2 months to mss. Sample copy and writer's guidelines free.

Nonfiction Needs how-to, interview, new product, personal experience, photo feature, technical. **Buys 16 mss/year.** Query with published clips. Length: 500-2,000 words. **Pays $100-400.** Sometimes pays expenses of writers on assignment.

Photos State availability. Captions required. Reviews 3 × 5 prints. Negotiates payment individually. Buys one-time, reprint, and electronic rights.

Tips Our mission is to educate our target audience on more economical and efficient ways of operating company vehicles, and to inform the audience of the latest vehicles, products, and services available to small commercial companies. Be knowledgeable about automotive and fleet-oriented subjects.

$ $ ◘ CASP

Canadian Aftermarket Service Professional, Publications Rousseau et Associes, Inc., 2938 Terrasse Abenaquis, Suite 110, Longueuil QC J4M 2B3 Canada. (450)448-2220. Fax: (450)448-1041. E-mail: sgbrown@xplornet.com. Website: www.autosphere.ca. **30% freelance written**. Magazine published 8 times/year covering the Canadian automotive aftermarket. *"CASP* presents many aspects of the automotive aftermarket: new products, technology, industry image, HR, management." Estab. 2003. Circ. 18,000. Byline given. Pays on publication. Publishes ms an average of 2 months after acceptance. Buys first rights, buys second serial (reprint) rights, buys electronic rights. Editorial lead time 2 months. Submit seasonal material 2 months in advance. Accepts queries by e-mail. Accepts previously published material. Accepts simultaneous submissions. Responds in 2 weeks to queries. Responds in 2 months to mss. Sample copy free. Guidelines by e-mail.

Nonfiction Needs general interest, how-to, inspirational, interview, new product, technical. Does not want opinion pieces. **Buys 6 mss/year.** Query with published clips. Length: 550-610 words. **Pays up to $200 (Canadian).**

Photos Send photos. Captions required. Reviews GIF/JPEG files. Offers no additional payment for photos accepted with ms. Buys all rights.

Fillers Needs facts. Buys 2 mss/year. Length: 550-610 words. **Pays $0-200.**

$ $ FENDERBENDER

DeWitt Publishing, 1043 Grand Ave. #372, St. Paul MN 55105. (651)224-6207. Fax: (651)224-6212. E-mail: editor@fenderbender.com. Website: www.fenderbender.com. **Contact:** Karen Olson, managing editor. **50% freelance written.** Monthly magazine covering automotive collision repair. Estab. 1999. Circ. 58,000. Byline given. Pays on publication. Offers 20% kill fee. Publishes ms an average of 2 months after acceptance. Buys first North American serial rights, buys second serial (reprint) rights, buys electronic rights. Editorial lead time 3 months. Submit seasonal material 6 months in advance. Accepts queries by e-mail. Accepts simultaneous submissions. Responds in 1-2 months to queries. Responds in 2-3 months to mss. Sample copy for sae with 10 × 13 envelope and 6 First-Class stamps. Guidelines available online.

Nonfiction Needs expose, how-to, inspirational, interview, technical. Does not want personal narratives or any other first-person stories. No poems or creative writing manuscripts. Query with published clips. Length: 1,800-2,500 words. **Pays 25-60¢/word.** Sometimes pays expenses of writers on assignment.

Photos Send photos. Captions, identification of subjects, model releases required. Reviews PDF, GIF/JPEG files. Offers no additional payment for photos accepted with ms. Buys one time rights.

Columns/Departments Q&A, 600 words; Shakes, Rattles & Rollovers; Rearview Mirror Query with published clips. **Pays 25-35¢/word.**

Tips "Potential writers need to be knowledgeable about the auto collision repair industry. They should also know standard business practices and be able to explain to shop owners how they can run their businesses better."

$ $ FLEET EXECUTIVE

The Magazine of Vehicle Management, NAFA Fleet Management Association, 125 Village Blvd., Suite 200, Princeton NJ 08540. (609)986-1053. Fax: (609)720-0881. E-mail: publications@nafa.org. Website: www.nafa.org. **10% freelance written.** Magazine published 6 times/year covering automotive fleet management. Generally focuses on car, van, and light-duty truck management in US and Canadian corporations, government agencies, and utilities. Editorial emphasis is on general automotive issues; improving jobs skills, productivity, and professionalism; legislation and regulation; alternative fuels; safety; interviews with prominent industry personalities; technology; association news; public service fleet management; and light-duty truck fleet management. Estab. 1957. Circ. 4,000. No byline given. Pays on publication. No kill fee. Publishes ms an average of 4 months after acceptance. Buys all rights. Editorial lead time 2 months. Accepts queries by mail. Accepts simultaneous submissions. Responds in 1 month to queries. Sample copy available online. Guidelines free.

Nonfiction NAFA hosts its Fleet Management Institute, an educational conference and trade show, which is held in a different city in the US and Canada each year. *Fleet Executive* would consider articles on regional attractions, particularly those that might be of interest to the automotive industry, for use in a conference preview issue of the magazine. The preview issue is published one month prior to the conference. Information about the conference, its host city, and conference dates in a given year may be found on NAFA's website, www.nafa.org, or by calling the association at (732)494-8100. Needs interview, technical. **Buys 24 mss/year.** Query with published clips. Length: 500-3,000 words. **Pays $500 maximum.**

Photos State availability. Reviews electronic images.

Tips The sample articles online at www.nafa.org/fleetexecutive should help writers get a feel of the journalistic style we require.

OLD CARS WEEKLY

News & Marketplace, a Division of F + W Media, Inc., 700 E. State St., Iola WI 54990-0001. (715)445-4612. Fax: (715)445-2214. E-mail: angelo.vanbogart@fwmedia.com. Website: www.oldcarsweekly.com. **Contact:** Angelo Van Bogart. **30% freelance written**. Weekly tabloid for anyone restoring, selling or driving an old car. Estab. 1971. Circ. 65,000. Byline given. Pays within 3 months after publication date. No kill fee. Publishes ms an average of 6 months after acceptance. Call circulation department for sample copy. Guidelines for #10 SASE.

Nonfiction Needs how-to, technical, auction prices realized lists. No Grandpa's Car, My First Car or My Car themes from freelance contributors. **Buys 1,000 mss/year.** Send complete ms. Length: 400-1,600 words. **Payment varies.**

Photos Send photos. Captions, identification of subjects required. Pays $5/photo. Offers no additional payment for photos accepted with ms.

Tips "Seventy-five percent of our freelance material is done by a small group of regular contributors. Many new writers break in here, but we are usually overstocked with material and rarely seek nostalgic or historical pieces from new authors. We are searching for news stories and in-depth historical features that fit the needs of a nostalgic, car-oriented audience. Authors with good skills can work up to longer stories. The best queries are 'checklists' where we can quickly mark a 'yes' or 'no' to article ideas."

$ $ $ OVERDRIVE

The Voice of the American Trucker, Randall-Reilly Publishing Co./Overdrive, Inc., 3200 Rice Mine Rd., Tuscaloosa AL 35406. (205)349-2990. Fax: (205)750-8070. E-mail: mheine@randallpub.com. Website: www.etrucker.com. **5% freelance written**. Monthly magazine for independent truckers. Estab. 1961. Circ. 100,000. Byline given. Pays on publication. Offers 10% kill fee. Publishes ms an average of 2 months after acceptance. Buys all North American rights, including electronic rights. Responds in 2 months to queries. Sample copy for 9 × 12 SASE.

Nonfiction All must be related to independent trucker interest. Needs essays, expose, how-to, truck maintenance and operation, interview, successful independent truckers, personal experience, photo feature, technical. Send complete ms. Length: 500-2,500 words. **Pays $300-1,500 for assigned articles.**

Photos Photo fees negotiable. Buys all rights.

Tips "Talk to independent truckers. Develop a good knowledge of their concerns as small-business owners, truck drivers, and individuals. We prefer articles that quote experts, people in the industry, and truckers, to first-person expositions on a subject. Get straight facts. Look for good material on truck safety, on effects of government regulations, and on rates and business relationships between independent truckers, brokers, carriers, and shippers."

$ $ TIRE NEWS

Publications Rousseau et Associes Inc., 2938 Terrasse Abenaquis, Suite 110, Longueuil QC J4M 2B3 Canada. (450)448-2220. Fax: (450)448-1041. Website: www.publicationsrousseau.com. Bimonthly magazine covering Canadian tire industry. *Tire News* focuses on education/training, industry image, management, new tires, new techniques, marketing, HR, etc. Estab. 2004. Circ. 16,000. Byline given. Pays on publication. Publishes ms an average of 2 months after acceptance. Buys first rights, buys second serial (reprint) rights, buys electronic rights. Editorial lead time 2 months. Submit seasonal material 2 months in advance. Accepts previously published material. Accepts simultaneous submissions. Responds in 2 weeks to queries. Responds in 2 months to mss. Sample copy free. Guidelines by e-mail.

Nonfiction Needs general interest, how-to, inspirational, interview, new product, technical. Does not want opinion pieces. **Buys 5 mss/year.** Query with published clips. Length: 550-610 words. **Pays up to $200 (Canadian).**

Photos Send photos. Captions required. Reviews GIF/JPEG files. Offers no additional payment for photos accepted with ms. Buys all rights.

Fillers Needs facts. Buys 2 mss/year. Length: 550-610 words. **Pays $0-200.**

$ $ TOWING & RECOVERY FOOTNOTES

Reaching thousands of industry professionals monthly, Dominion Enterprises, 150 Granby St., Norfolk VA 23510. (757)351-8633. Fax: (757)233-7047. E-mail: bcandler@dominionenterprises. Website: www.trfootnotes.com. **100% freelance written**. Monthly trade newspaper and marketplace for the nation's towing and recovery industry. Estab. 1991. Circ. 25,000. Byline given. Pays within 2-3 weeks of acceptance. No kill fee. Publishes ms an average of 2-3 months after acceptance. Buys first, one-time rights. Editorial lead time 2 months. Submit seasonal material 2 months in advance. Accepts queries by mail, e-mail, phone. Accepts previously published material. Responds in 2 weeks to queries. Responds in 1 month to mss. Sample copy free. Guidelines free.

- Facebook: "Towing & Recovery Footnotes"; publishes e-newsletter and digital edition.

Nonfiction Needs historical, how-to, humor, interview, new product, opinion, personal experience, photo feature, technical. **Buys 500 mss/year.** Query with published clips. Length: 800-2,000 words. **Pays $200-$600 for assigned articles.**

Photos Send photos. Captions, identification of subjects required. Reviews GIF/JPEG files. Negotiates payment individually. Buys one-time rights.

Columns/Departments Columns vary from issue to issue; no regular departments available to freelancers; columns are given names appropriate to topic, and often repeat no matter who the author is. **Buys 250 mss/year.** Query with published clips.

TRUCK NEWS

Business Information Group, 12 Concorde Place, Suite 800, Toronto ON M3C 4J2 Canada. Website: www.trucknews.com. **Contact:** Lou Smyrlis, editorial director. **15% freelance written.** Monthly magazine covering trucking industry. Estab. 1981. Byline given. Pays on acceptance. Publishes ms an average of 1 month after acceptance. Buys first rights, buys one-time rights, buys electronic rights. Editorial lead time 1 month. Submit seasonal material 2 months in advance. Accepts queries by mail. Accepts simultaneous submissions.

Nonfiction Needs general interest, new product, technical. **Buys 20 mss/year.** Query.

$$ WESTERN CANADA HIGHWAY NEWS

Craig Kelman & Associates, 2020 Portage Ave., 3rd Floor, Winnipeg MB R3J 0K4 Canada. (204)985-9785. Fax: (204)985-9795. E-mail: terry@kelman.ca. **Contact:** Terry Ross, managing editor. **30% freelance written.** Quarterly magazine covering trucking. "The official magazine of the Alberta, Saskatchewan, and Manitoba trucking associations." Estab. 1995. Circ. 4,500. Byline given. Pays on publication. No kill fee. Publishes ms an average of 2 months after acceptance. Buys one-time rights. Editorial lead time 3 months. Submit seasonal material 3 months in advance. Accepts simultaneous submissions. Responds in 1 month to queries and mss. Sample copy for 10 × 13 SAE with 1 IRC. Guidelines for #10 SASE.

Nonfiction Needs essays, general interest, how-to, run a trucking business, interview, new product, opinion, personal experience, photo feature, technical, profiles in excellence (bios of trucking or associate firms enjoying success). **Buys 8-10 mss/year.** Query. Length: 500-3,000 words. **Pays 18-25¢/word.** Sometimes pays expenses of writers on assignment.

Photos State availability. Identification of subjects required. Reviews 4x6 prints. Buys one time rights.

Columns/Departments Safety (new safety innovation/products), 500 words; Trade Talk (new products), 300 words. Query. **Pays 18-25¢/word.**

Tips "Our publication is fairly time sensitive regarding issues affecting the trucking industry in Western Canada. Current 'hot' topics are international trucking, security, driver fatigue, health and safety, emissions control, and national/international highway systems."

Aviation & Space

$$ AEROSAFETY WORLD MAGAZINE

Flight Safety Foundation, Suite 300, 601 Madison St., Alexandria VA 22314-1756. (703)739-6700. Fax: (703)739-6708. Website: www.flightsafety.org. **Contact:** J.A. Donoghue. Monthly newsletter covering safety aspects of airport operations. AeroSafety World continues Flight Safety Foundation's tradition of excellence in aviation safety journalism that stretches back more than 50 years. The new full-color monthly magazine, initially called Aviation Safety World when it was launched in July 2006, offers in-depth analysis of important safety issues facing the industry, along with several new departments and a greater emphasis on timely news coverage — in a convenient format and eye-catching contemporary design. While AeroSafety World has taken the place of the seven newsletters the Foundation used to produce, including Airport Operations, the archives remain active and back issues of the newsletters are still available Estab. 1974. Buys all rights. Accepts queries by mail, e-mail, fax. Accepts previously published material. Sample copy available online. Guidelines available online.

Nonfiction "If you have an article proposal, manuscript or technical paper that you believe would make a useful contribution to the ongoing dialogue about aviation safety, we will be glad to consider it. Send it to the director of publications, J.A. Donoghue." Needs technical. Query.

$ $ AIRCRAFT MAINTENANCE TECHNOLOGY

Cygnus Business Media, 1233 Janesville Ave., Fort Atkinson WI 53538. (920)563-6388. Fax: (920)569-4603. E-mail: joe.escobar@cygnusb2b.com. Website: www.amtonline.com. **10% freelance written.** Magazine published 10 times/year covering aircraft maintenance. *Aircraft Maintenance Technology* provides aircraft maintenance professionals worldwide with a curriculum of technical, professional, and managerial development information that enables them to more efficiently and effectively perform their jobs. Estab. 1989. Circ. 41,500 worldwide. Byline given. Pays on publication. No kill fee. Publishes ms an average of 2 months after acceptance. Buys all rights. Makes work-for-hire assignments. Editorial lead time 3 months. Submit seasonal material 6 months in advance. Accepts queries by mail, e-mail, fax. Accepts simultaneous submissions. Responds in 2 weeks to queries. Responds in 1 month to mss. Sample copy free. Guidelines for #10 SASE or by e-mail.

Nonfiction Needs how-to, technical, safety. Special issues: Aviation career issue (August). No travel/pilot-oriented pieces. **Buys 10-12 mss/year.** Query with published clips. 600-1,500 words, technical articles 2,000 words **Pays $200.**

Photos State availability. Captions, identification of subjects, model releases required. Offers no additional payment for photos accepted with ms. Buys one time rights.

Columns/Departments Professionalism, 1,000-1,500 words; Safety Matters, 600-1,000 words; Human Factors, 600-1,000 words. **Buys 10-12 mss/year.** Query with published clips. **Pays $200**

Tips This is a technical magazine approved by the FAA and Transport Canada for recurrency training for technicians. Freelancers should have a strong background in aviation, particularly maintenance, to be considered for technical articles. Columns/Departments: Freelancers still should have a strong knowledge of aviation to slant professionalism, safety, and human factors pieces to that audience.

$ $ AIR LINE PILOT

The Magazine of Professional Flight Deck Crews, Air Line Pilots Association, 1625 Massachusetts Ave. NW, Washington DC 20036. E-mail: magazine@alpa.org. Website: www.alpa.org. **2% freelance written. Prefers to work with published/established writers; works with a small number of new/unpublished writers each year.** Magazine published 10 times/year for airline pilots covering commercial aviation industry information—economics, avionics, equipment, systems, safety—that affects a pilot's life in a professional sense. Also includes information about management/labor relations trends, contract negotiations, etc. Estab. 1931. Circ. 90,000. Pays on acceptance. Offers 50% kill fee. Publishes ms an average of 6 months after acceptance. Buys all rights except book rights. Submit seasonal material 6 months in advance. Responds in 2 months to queries. Sample copy for $2. Guidelines available online.

Nonfiction Needs humor, inspirational, photo feature, technical. **Buys 5 mss/year.** Query with or without published clips or send complete ms and SASE. Length: 700-3,000 words. **Pays $100-600 for assigned articles. Pays $50-600 for unsolicited articles.**

Reprints Send photocopy of article or typed ms with rights for sale noted and information about when and where the material previously appeared. Payment varies

Photos Our greatest need is for strikingly original cover photographs featuring ALPA flight deck crew members and their airlines in their operating environment. See list of airlines with ALPA Pilots online. Send photos. Identification of subjects required. Reviews contact sheets, 35mm transparencies, 8 × 10 prints, digital must be 300 dpi at 8 × 11. Will review low res thumbnail images. Offers $10-35/b&w photo, $30-50 for color used inside and $450 for color used as cover. For cover photography, shoot vertical rather than horizontal. Buys all rights for cover photos, one-time rights for inside color.

Tips For our feature section, we seek aviation industry information that affects the life of a professional pilot's career. We also seek material that affects a pilot's life from a job security and work environment standpoint. Any airline pilot featured in an article must be an Air Line Pilot Association member in good standing. Our readers are very experienced and require a high level of technical accuracy in both written material and photographs.

$ $ AVIATION INTERNATIONAL NEWS

The Convention News Co., 214 Franklin Ave., Midland Park NJ 07432. (201)444-5075. Fax: (201)444-4647. E-mail: editor@ainonline.com. Website: www.ainonline.com. **30-40% freelance written.** Monthly magazine (with daily onsite issues published at 3 conventions and 2 international air shows each year) and twice-weekly AINalerts via e-mail covering business and commercial aviation with news features, special reports, aircraft evaluations, and surveys on business aviation worldwide, written for business pilots and industry professionals. While the heartbeat of *AIN* is driven by the news it carries, the human touch is not neglected. We pride ourselves on our people stories about the industry's 'movers and shakers' and others in aviation who make a difference. Estab. 1972. Circ. 40,000. Byline given. **Pays on acceptance and upon receipt of writer's invoice.** Offers variable kill fee. Publishes ms an average of 2 months after acceptance. Buys first North American serial and second serial (reprint) rights and makes work-for-hire assignments. Editorial lead time 2 months. Submit seasonal material 3 months in advance. Accepts queries by mail, e-mail, fax. Responds in 6 weeks to queries. Responds in 2 months to mss. Sample copy for $10. Writer's guidelines for 9 × 12 SAE with 3 first-class stamps.

- Do not send mss by e-mail unless requested.

Nonfiction We hire freelancers to work on our staff at 3 aviation conventions and 2 international airshows each year. Must have strong reporting and writing skills and knowledge of aviation. Needs how-to, aviation, interview, new product, opinion, personal experience, photo feature, technical. No puff pieces. Our readers expect serious, real news. We don't pull any punches. *AIN* is not a 'good news' publication: It tells the story, both good and bad. **Buys 150-200 mss/year.** Query with published clips. Length: 200-3,000 words. **Pays 40¢/word to first timers, higher rates to proven *AIN* freelancers.** Pays expenses of writers on assignment.

Photos Send photos. Captions required. Reviews contact sheets, transparencies, prints, TIFF files (300 dpi). Negotiates payment individually. Buys one time rights.

Tips Our core freelancers are professional pilots with good writing skills, or good journalists and reporters with an interest in aviation (some with pilot licenses) or technical experts in the aviation industry. The ideal *AIN* writer has an intense interest in and strong knowledge of aviation, a talent for writing news stories, and journalistic cussedness. Hit me with a strong news story relating to business aviation that takes me by surprise—something from your local area or area of expertise. Make it readable, fact-filled, and in the inverted-pyramid style. Double-check facts and names. Interview the right people. Send me good, clear photos and illustrations. Send me well-written, logically ordered copy. Do this for me consistently and we may take you along on our staff to one of the conventions in the U.S. or an airshow in Paris, Singapore, London, or Dubai.

$ $ AVIATION MAINTENANCE

Access Intelligence, 4 Choke Cherry Rd., 2nd Floor, Rockville MD 20850. (301)354-1831. Fax: (301)340-8741. E-mail: jfinnegan@accessintel.com. Website: www.aviationmx.com. **40% freelance written**. Monthly magazine covering aircraft maintenance from small to large aircraft. *Aviation Maintenance* delivers news and information about the aircraft maintenance business for mechanics and management at maintenance shops, airlines, and corporate flight departments. Estab. 1982. Circ. 25,000. Byline given. Pays on acceptance. Offers kill fee. Kill fee varies Publishes ms an average of 2 months after acceptance. Buys all rights. Editorial lead time 3 months. Submit seasonal material 3 months in advance. Accepts queries by mail, e-mail, fax, phone. Responds in 1 week to queries. Responds in 1 month to mss. Sample copy available online. Guidelines free.

Nonfiction Needs expose, interview, technical. No fiction, technical how-to, or poetry. **Buys 20 mss/year.** Query. Length: 200-500 words. **Pays 50¢/word.** Pays expenses of writers on assignment.

Photos State availability. Captions, identification of subjects required. Negotiates payment individually. Buys all rights.

Columns/Departments Buys 12 mss/year. Query with or without published clips. **Pays $500.**

Tips Writer must be intimately familiar with, or involved in, aviation, either as a pilot or preferably a mechanic or a professional aviation writer. Best place to break in is in the Intelligence News section or the Industry Insights column (see website).

$ $ CABIN CREW SAFETY

Flight Safety Foundation, Suite 300, 601 Madison St., Alexandria VA 22314-1756. (703)739-6700. Fax: (703)739-6708. Website: www.flightsafety.org. **25% freelance written**. Bimonthly newsletter covering safety aspects of aircraft cabins (airline and corporate aviation) for cabin crews and passengers. Estab. 1956. Circ. 2,000. Byline given. Pays on publication. No kill fee. Publishes ms an average of 3 months after acceptance. Buys all rights. Editorial lead time 3 months. Accepts queries by mail, e-mail, fax. Accepts previously published material. Responds in 3 weeks to queries. Sample copy available online. Guidelines available online.

Nonfiction Needs technical. No argumentation, crusading, inspiration, anecdotes, or humor. **Buys 6 mss/year.** Query. Length: 2,500-8,750 words. **Pays $200/printed page, plus 6 copies of publication.**

Photos Send photos. Captions, identification of subjects, model releases required. Reviews contact sheets, negatives, 35mm or larger transparencies, 5 × 7 minimum prints, GIF/JPEG files. Offers $25/photo. Buys all rights.

Tips Study guidelines carefully. Be concerned above all with accuracy, fairness, and objectivity, but if you have information that you believe meets those standards, do not hesitate to query even if you aren't sure of format or style. If you have the content we need, our editorial staff will work with you to put the material into shape.

$$ GROUND SUPPORT WORLDWIDE MAGAZINE

Cygnus Business Media, 1233 Janesville Ave., Fort Atkinson WI 53538. (920)563-1622. Fax: (920)563-1699. E-mail: karen.reinhardt@cygnusb2bpub.com. Website: www.groundsupportworldwide.com. **20% freelance written**. Magazine published 10 times/year. Our readers are those aviation professionals who are involved in ground support—the equipment manufacturers, the suppliers, the ramp operators, ground handlers, airport and airline managers. We cover issues of interest to this community—deicing, ramp safety, equipment technology, pollution, etc. Estab. 1993. Circ. 15,000. Pays on publication. No kill fee. Publishes ms an average of 2 months after acceptance. Buys all rights. Editorial lead time 2 months. Accepts queries by mail, e-mail, fax. Responds in 3 weeks to queries. Responds in 3 months to mss. Sample copy for sae with 9â—Š11 envelope and 5 First-Class stamps.

Nonfiction Needs how-to, use or maintain certain equipment, interview, new product, opinion, photo feature, technical aspects of ground support and issues, industry events, meetings, new rules and regulations. **Buys 12-20 mss/year.** Send complete ms. Length: 500-2,000 words. **Pays $100-300.**

Photos Send photos. Identification of subjects required. Reviews 35mm prints, electronic preferred, slides. Offers additional payment for photos accepted with ms. Buys all rights.

Tips Write about subjects that relate to ground services. Write in clear and simple terms—personal experience is always welcome. If you have an aviation background or ground support experience, let us know.

$$ HELICOPTER SAFETY

Flight Safety Foundation, Suite 300, 601 Madison St., Alexandria VA 22314-1756. (703)739-6700. Fax: (703)739-6708. Website: www.flightsafety.org. **50% freelance written**. Bimonthly newsletter covering safety aspects of helicopter operations. *Helicopter Safety* highlights the broad spectrum of real-world helicopter operations. Topics have ranged from design principles and primary training to helicopter utilization in offshore applications and in emergency medical service (EMS). Estab. 1956. Circ. 2,000. Byline given. Pays on publication. No kill fee. Publishes ms an average of 3 months after acceptance. Buys all rights. Editorial lead time 3 months. Accepts queries by mail, e-mail, fax. Accepts previously published material. Responds in 3 weeks to queries. Sample copy available online. Guidelines available online.

Nonfiction Needs technical. No argumentation, crusading, inspiration, anecdotes, or humor. **Buys 6 mss/year.** Query. Length: 2,500-8,750 words. **Pays $200/printed page, plus 6 copies of publication.**

Photos Send photos. Captions, identification of subjects, model releases required. Reviews contact sheets, negatives, 35mm or larger transparencies, 5 × 7 minimum prints. Offers $25/photo. Buys all rights.

Tips Study guidelines carefully. Be concerned above all with accuracy, fairness, and objectivity, but if you have information that you believe meets those standards, do not hesitate to query even if you aren't sure of format or style. If you have the content we need, our editorial staff will work with you to put the material into shape.

$$$ PROFESSIONAL PILOT

Queensmith Communications, 30 S. Quaker Lane, Suite 300, Alexandria VA 22314. (703)370-0606. Fax: (703)370-7082. E-mail: editor@propilotmag.com. Website: www.propilotmag.com. **75% freelance written**. Monthly magazine covering corporate , non combat government, law enforcement and various other types of professional aviation. The typical reader has a sophisticated grasp of piloting/aviation knowledge and is interested in articles that help him/her do the job better or more efficiently. Estab. 1967. Circ. 40,000. Byline given. Pays on publication. Offers kill fee. Kill fee negotiable. Publishes ms an average of 2-3 months after acceptance. Buys all rights. Accepts queries by mail, e-mail, fax.

Nonfiction Typical subjects include new aircraft design, new product reviews (especially avionics), pilot techniques, profiles of fixed base operations, profiles of corporate flight departments and technological advances. All issues have a theme such as regional airline operations, maintenance, avionics, helicopters, etc. **Buys 40 mss/year.** Query. Length: 750-2,500 words. **Pays $200-1,000, depending on length. A fee for the article will be established at the time of assignment.** Sometimes pays expenses of writers on assignment.

Photos Prefers transparencies or high resolution 300 JPEG digital images. Send photos. Captions, identification of subjects required. Additional payment for photos negotiable. Buys all rights.

Tips Query first. Freelancer should be a professional pilot or have background in aviation. Authors should indicate relevant aviation experience and pilot credentials (certificates, ratings and hours). We place a greater emphasis on corporate operations and pilot concerns.

Beauty & Salon

$$ BEAUTY STORE BUSINESS

Creative Age Communications, 7628 Densmore Ave., Van Nuys CA 91406-2042. (818)782-7328, ext. 353. Fax: (818)782-7450. E-mail: mbirenbaum@creativeage.com. **50% freelance written**. Monthly magazine covering beauty store business management, news and beauty products. The primary readers of the publication are owners, managers, and buyers at open-to-the-public beauty stores, including general-market and multicultural market-oriented ones with or without salon services. Our secondary readers are those at beauty stores only open to salon industry professionals. We also go to beauty distributors. Estab. 1994. Circ. 15,000. Byline given. Pays on acceptance. Offers kill fee. Offers negotiable kill fee. Publishes ms an average of 3 months after acceptance. Buys all rights. Editorial lead time 3 months. Submit seasonal material 4 months in advance. Accepts queries by mail, e-mail, fax. Responds in 1 week to queries. Responds in 2 weeks, if interested,. Sample copy free.

Nonfiction If your business-management article will help a specialty retailer or small business owner, it should be of assistance to our readers. If you're a writer who is/was a hairstylist, nail tech or esthetician, has an interest in professional beauty products or is fluent in Korean, we'd like to talk to you. We're also interested in hearing from illustrators/cartoonists and puzzle writers. Needs how-to, business management, merchandising, e-commerce, retailing, interview, industry leaders/beauty store owners. **Buys 20-30 mss/year.** Query. Length: 1,800-2,200 words. **Pays $250-525 for assigned articles.** Sometimes pays expenses of writers on assignment.

Photos Do not send computer art electronically. State availability. Captions, identification of subjects required. Reviews transparencies, computer art (artists work on Macs, request 300 dpi, on CD or Zip disk, saved as JPEG, TIFF, or EPS). Negotiates payment individually. Buys all rights.

$$ ☐ COSMETICS

Canada's Business Magazine for the Cosmetics, Fragrance, Toiletry, and Personal Care Industry, Rogers, 1 Mt. Pleasant Rd., 7th Floor, Toronto ON M4Y 2Y5 Canada. (416)764-1680. Fax: (416)764-1704. E-mail: dave.lackie@cosmetics.rogers.com. Website: www.cosmeticsmag.com. **Contact:** Dave Lackie. **10% freelance written**. Bimonthly magazine. "Our main reader segment is the retail trade—department stores, drugstores, salons, estheticians—owners and cosmeticians/beauty advisors; plus manufacturers, distributors, agents, and suppliers to the industry." Estab. 1972. Circ. 13,000. Byline given. Pays on acceptance. Offers 50% kill fee. Publishes ms an average of 3 months after acceptance. Buys all rights. Editorial lead time 4 months. Submit seasonal material 4 months in advance. Accepts queries by mail. Responds in 1 month to queries. Sample copy for $6 (Canadian) and 8% GST.

Nonfiction Needs general interest, interview, photo feature. **Buys 1 mss/year.** Query. Length: 250-1,200 words. **Pays 25¢/word.** Sometimes pays expenses of writers on assignment.

Photos Send photos. Captions, identification of subjects, model releases required. Reviews 2½ up to 8 × 10 transparencies, 4x6 up to 8 × 10 prints, 35mm slides, e-mail pictures in 300 dpi JPEG format. Offers no additional payment for photos accepted with ms. Buys all rights.

Columns/Departments "All articles assigned on a regular basis from correspondents and columnists that we know personally from the industry."

Tips "Must have broad knowledge of the Canadian cosmetics, fragrance, and toiletries industry and retail business. 99.9% of freelance articles are assigned by the editor to writers involved with the Canadian cosmetics business."

$$ DAYSPA

The Premiere Spa Business Source, Creative Age Publications, 7628 Densmore Ave., Van Nuys CA 91406. (818)782-7328. Fax: (818)782-7450. E-mail: rwilson@creativeage.com. Website: www.dayspamagazine.com. **Contact:** Rhonda J. Wilson. **50% freelance written**. Monthly magazine covering the business of day spas, multi-service/skincare salons, and resort/hotel spas. "*Dayspa* includes only well-targeted business and trend articles directed at the owners and managers. It serves to enrich, enlighten, and empower spa/salon professionals." Estab. 1996. Circ. 31,000. Byline given. Pays on acceptance. No kill fee. Publishes ms an average of 4 months after acceptance. Buys first rights, buys one-time rights. Editorial lead time 4 months. Submit seasonal material 4 months in advance. Accepts queries by mail,

e-mail, fax, phone. Responds in 2 months to queries. Sample copy for $5.
Nonfiction Buys 40 mss/year. Query. Length: 1,500-1,800 words. **Pays $150-500.**
Photos Send photos. Identification of subjects, model releases required. Negotiates payment individually. Buys one time rights.
Columns/Departments Legal Pad (legal issues affecting salons/spas); Money Matters (financial issues); Management Workshop (spa management issues); Health Wise (wellness trends), all 1,200-1,500 words. **Buys 20 mss/year.** Query. **Pays $150-400.**

MASSAGE & BODYWORK

Associated Bodywork & Massage Professionals, 25188 Genesee Trail Rd., Suite 200, Golden CO80401 (303)674-8478 or (800)458-2267. Fax: (303)674-0859. E-mail: editor@abmp.com. Website: www.massageandbodywork.com. **85% freelance written**. Bimonthly magazine covering therapeutic massage/bodywork. "A trade publication for the massage therapist, and bodyworker. An all-inclusive publication encompassing everything from traditional Swedish massage to energy work to other complementary therapies (i.e., homeopathy, herbs, aromatherapy, etc.)." Pays on acceptance. No kill fee. Publishes ms an average of 6 months after acceptance. Buys first North American serial rights, buys one-time rights, buys electronic rights. Editorial lead time 6 months. Submit seasonal material 6 months in advance. Accepts queries by e-mail. Responds in 60 days to queries. Guidelines available online.

- Note Our New Address for FedEx/UPS: 25188 Genesee Trail Road, Suite 200,Golden CO 80401; or PO Box 1869, Evergreen CO 80437.

Nonfiction Needs how-to, technique/modality, interview, opinion, personal experience, technical. No fiction. **Buys 60-75 mss/year.** Query with published clips. Length: 1,000-3,000 words.
Photos Not interested in photo submissions separate from feature queries. State availability. Captions, identification of subjects, model releases required. Reviews digital images (300 dpi). Negotiates payment individually. Buys one-time rights.
Columns/Departments Buys 20 mss/year.
Tips "Know your topic. Offer suggestions for art to accompany your submission. *Massage & Bodywork* looks for interesting, tightly focused stories concerning a particular modality or technique of massage, bodywork, and somatic therapies. The editorial staff welcomes the opportunity to review mss which may be relevant to the field of massage and bodywork in addition to more general pieces pertaining to complementary and alternative medicine. This would include the widely varying modalities of massage and bodywork (from Swedish massage to Polarity therapy), specific technical or ancillary therapies, including such topics as biomagnetics, aromatherapy, and facial rejuvenation. Reference lists relating to technical articles should include the author, title, publisher, and publication date of works cited according to Chicago Manual of Style. Word count: 1,500-3,000 words; longer articles negotiable."

$ $ MASSAGE MAGAZINE

Exploring Today's Touch Therapies, 5150 Palm Valley Rd., Suite 103, Ponte Vedra Beach FL 32082. (904)285-6020. Fax: (904)285-9944. E-mail: kmenahan@massagemag.com. Website: www.massagemag.com. **Contact:** Karen Menehan. **60% freelance written**. Bimonthly magazine covering massage and other touch therapies. Estab. 1985. Circ. 50,000. Byline given. Pays on publication. Publishes ms an average of 2 months-24 months after acceptance. Buys first North American serial rights. Accepts queries by e-mail. Responds in 2 months to queries. Responds in 3 months to mss. Sample copy for $6.95. Guidelines available online.
Nonfiction Needs book excerpts, essays, general interest, how-to, interview, personal experience, photo feature, technical, experiential. No multiple submissions Length: 600-2,000 words. **Pays $75-300.**
Reprints Send tearsheet of article and electronic ms with rights for sale noted and information about when and where the material previously appeared. Pays 50-75% of amount paid for an original article
Photos Send photos with submission via e-mail. Identification of subjects, True required. Offers $15-40/photo; $40-100/illustration. Buys one time rights.
Columns/Departments Profiles; News and Current Events; Practice Building (business); Technique; Body/Mind. Length: 800-1,200 words. **$75-300 for assigned articles**
Fillers Needs facts, newsbreaks. Length: 100-800 words. **Pays $125 maximum.**
Tips "Our readers seek practical information on how to help their clients, improve their techniques, and/or make their businesses more successful, as well as feature articles that place massage therapy in a positive or inspiring light. Since most of our readers are professional therapists, we do not publish articles on topics like 'How Massage Can Help You Relax.' Please study a few back issues so you know what types of topics and tone we're looking for."

$$ NAILPRO, THE MAGAZINE FOR NAIL PROFESSIONALS

Creative Age Publications, 7628 Densmore Ave., Van Nuys CA 91406. (818)782-7328. Fax: (818)782-7450. E-mail: syaggy@creativeage.com. Website: www.nailpro.com. **75% freelance written**. Monthly magazine written for manicurists and nail technicians working in a full-service salon or nails-only salons. "It covers technical and business aspects of working in a salon and operating nailcare services, as well as the nailcare industry in general. Estab. 1989. Circ. 65,000. Byline given. Pays on acceptance. No kill fee. Publishes ms an average of 6 months after acceptance. Buys first North American serial rights. Editorial lead time 3 months. Submit seasonal material 3 months in advance. Accepts queries by mail, e-mail, fax. Accepts simultaneous submissions. Responds in 6 weeks to queries. Sample copy for $2 and 8½ × 11 SASE.

Nonfiction Needs book excerpts, how-to, humor, inspirational, interview, personal experience, photo feature, technical. No general interest articles or business articles not geared to the nail-care industry. **Buys 50 mss/year.** Query. Length: 1,000-3,000 words. **Pays $150-450.**

Reprints Send typed manuscript with rights for sale noted and information about when and where the material previously appeared. Pays 25-50% of amount paid for an original article.

Photos Send photos. Identification of subjects, model releases required. Reviews transparencies, prints. Negotiates payment individually.

Columns/Departments "All Business (articles on building salon business, marketing & advertising, dealing with employees), 1,500-2,000 words; Attitudes (aspects of operating a nail salon and trends in the nail industry), 1,200-2,000 words." **Buys 50 mss/year.** Query. **Pays $250-350.**

$$ ⊘ NAILS

Bobit Business Media, 3520 Challenger St., Torrance CA 90503. (310)533-2400. Fax: (310)533-2507. E-mail: hannah.lee@bobit.com. Website: www.nailsmag.com. **10% freelance written**. Monthly magazine. *NAILS* seeks to educate its readers on new techniques and products, nail anatomy and health, customer relations, working safely with chemicals, salon sanitation, and the business aspects of running a salon. Estab. 1983. Circ. 55,000. Byline given. Pays on acceptance. No kill fee. Buys all rights. Submit seasonal material 4 months in advance. Accepts queries by mail, e-mail, fax. Responds in 3 months to queries. Sample copy and writer's guidelines for #10 SASE.

Nonfiction Needs historical, how-to, inspirational, interview, personal experience, photo feature, technical. No articles on one particular product, company profiles or articles slanted toward a particular company or manufacturer. **Buys 20 mss/year.** Query with published clips. Length: 1,200-3,000 words. **Pays $200-500.** Sometimes pays expenses of writers on assignment.

Photos State availability. Captions, identification of subjects, model releases required. Reviews contact sheets, transparencies, prints (any standard size acceptable). Offers $50-200/photo. Buys all rights.

Tips Send clips and query; *do not send unsolicited manscripts.* We would like to see ideas for articles on a unique salon or a business article that focuses on a specific aspect or problem encountered when working in a salon. The Modern Nail Salon section, which profiles nail salons and full-service salons, is most open to freelancers. Focus on an innovative business idea or unique point of view. Articles from experts on specific business issues—insurance, handling difficult employees, cultivating clients—are encouraged.

$$ PULSE MAGAZINE

The Magazine for the Spa Professional, HOST Communications Inc., 2365 Harrodsburg Rd., Suite A325, Lexington KY 40511. Fax: (859)226-4445. E-mail: pulse@ispastaff.com. Website: www.experienceispa.com/ispa/pulse. **Contact:** Rebekah Sellers, assistant editor. **20% freelance written**. Magazine published 10 times/year covering spa industry. "*Pulse* is the magazine for the spa professional. As the official publication of the International SPA Association, its purpose is to advance the business of the spa professionals by informing them of the latest trends and practices and promoting the wellness aspects of spa. *Pulse* connects people, nurtures their personal and professional growth, and enhances their ability to network and succeed in the spa industry." Estab. 1991. Circ. 5,300. Byline given. Pays on publication. Publishes ms an average of 1 month after acceptance. Buys all rights. Editorial lead time 3 months. Submit seasonal material 4 months in advance. Accepts queries by e-mail. Sample copy for #10 SASE. Guidelines by e-mail.

Nonfiction Needs general interest, how-to, interview, new product. Does not want articles focused on spas that are not members of ISPA, consumer-focused articles (market is the spa industry professional), or features on hot tubs (not *that* spa industry). **Buys 8-10 mss/year.** Query with published clips. Length: 800-2,000 words. **Pays $250-500.** Sometimes pays expenses of writers on assignment.

Photos Contact: Rebekah Sellers, assistant editor. Send photos. Captions required. Reviews GIF/JPEG files. Negotiates payment individually. Buys one time rights.

Tips "Understand the nuances of association publishing (different than consumer and B2B). Send published clips, not Word documents. Experience in writing for health and wellness market is helpful. Only feature ISPA member companies in the magazine; visit our website to learn more about our industry and to see if your pitch includes member companies before making contact."

$$ SKIN DEEP

Education for Today's Skin Care Professional, Associated Skin Care Professionals, 25188 Genesee Trail Rd., Suite 200, Golden CO 80401. (800)789-0411. E-mail: nbrunner@ascpskincare.com. Website: www.ascpskincare.com. **Contact:** Nora Brunner, ed. **80% freelance written**. Bimonthly magazine covering technical, educational and business information for estheticians with an emphasis on solo practitioners and spa/salon employees or independent contractors. "Our audience is the U.S. individual skin care practitioner who may work on her own and/or in a spa or salon setting. We keep her up to date on skin care trends and techniques and ways to earn more income doing waxing, facials, peels, microdermabrasion, body wraps and other skin treatments. Our product-neutral stories may include novel spa treatments within the esthetician scope of practice. We do not want cover treatments that involve needles or lasers, or invasive treatments like ear candling, colonics or plastic surgery. Successful stories have included how-tos on paraffin facials, aromatherapy body wraps, waxing tips, how to read ingredient labels, how to improve word-of-mouth advertising, and how to choose an online scheduling software package." Estab. 2003. Circ. 8,000+. Byline given. Pays on acceptance. No kill fee. Publishes ms an average of 4-6 months after acceptance. Buys all rights. Editorial lead time 4-5 months. Submit seasonal material 7 months in advance. Accepts queries by e-mail. Responds in 2 weeks to queries. Sample copy free. Guidelines available.

Nonfiction "We don't run general consumer beauty material and very rarely run a new product that is available through retail outlets. 'New' products means introduced in the last 12 months. We do not run industry personnel announcements or stories on individual spas/salons or getaways. We don't cover hair or nails." **Buys 12 mss/year.** Query. Length: 800-2,300 words. **Pays $75-$300 for assigned articles.**

Columns/Departments Ask the Expert (Practical marketing & technical info, how-to (no pay))

Tips "Visit the Media Corner at www.ascpskincare.com to learn about what we do. Submit a brief query with an idea to determine if you are on the right track. State specifically what value this has to esthetician and her work/income."

$$ SKIN INC. MAGAZINE

Spa Business Solutions, Allured Business Media, 336 Gundersen Dr., Suite A, Carol Stream IL 60188. (630)653-2155. Fax: (630)653-2192. E-mail: taschetta-millane@allured.com. Website: www.skininc.com. **Contact:** Melinda Taschetta-Millane, editor. **30% freelance written**. Magazine published 12 times/year. "Manuscripts considered for publication that contain original and new information in the general fields of skin care and makeup, dermatological and esthetician-assisted surgical techniques. The subject may cover the science of skin, the business of skin care and makeup, and plastic surgeons on healthy (i.e., nondiseased) skin." Estab. 1988. Circ. 30,000. Byline given. Pays on publication. No kill fee. Publishes ms an average of 6 months after acceptance. Buys all rights. Editorial lead time 6 months. Submit seasonal material 1 year in advance. Accepts queries by mail, e-mail, fax, phone. Responds in 3 weeks to queries. Responds in 1 month to mss. Sample copy and writer's guidelines free.

Nonfiction Needs general interest, how-to, interview, personal experience, technical. **Buys 6 mss/year.** Query with published clips. Length: 2,000 words. **Pays $100-300 for assigned articles. Pays $50-200 for unsolicited articles.**

Photos State availability. Captions, identification of subjects, model releases required. Reviews 3×5 prints. Offers no additional payment for photos accepted with ms. Buys one-time rights.

Columns/Departments Finance (tips and solutions for managing money), 2,000-2,500 words; Personnel (managing personnel), 2,000-2,500 words; Marketing (marketing tips for salon owners), 2,000-2,500 words; Retail (retailing products and services in the salon environment), 2,000-2,500 words. Query with published clips. **Pays $50-200.**

Fillers Needs facts, newsbreaks. Buys 6 mss/year. Length: 250-500 words. **Pays $50-100.**

Tips "Have an understanding of the professional spa industry."

Beverages & Bottling

$ $ BAR & BEVERAGE BUSINESS MAGAZINE

Mercury Publications, Ltd., 1740 Wellington Ave., Winnipeg MB R3H 0E8 Canada. (204)954-2085. Fax: (204)954-2057. E-mail: editorial@mercury.mb.ca. Website: www.barandbeverage.com. **33% freelance written**. Bimonthly magazine providing information on the latest trends, happenings, buying-selling of beverages and product merchandising. Estab. 1998. Circ. 16,077. Byline given. Pays 30-45 days from receipt of invoice. Offers 33% kill fee. Buys all rights. Submit seasonal material 3 months in advance. Accepts simultaneous submissions. Sample copy and writer's guidelines free or by e-mail.

- Does not accept queries for specific stories. Assigns stories to Canadian writers.

Nonfiction Needs how-to, making a good drink, training staff, etc., interview. Industry reports, profiles on companies. Query with published clips. Length: 500-9,000 words. **Pays 25-35¢/word.** Sometimes pays expenses of writers on assignment.

Photos State availability. Captions required. Reviews negatives, transparencies, 3 × 5 prints, JPEG, EPS or TIFF files. Negotiates payment individually. Buys all rights.

Columns/Departments Out There (bar & bev news in various parts of the country), 100-500 words. Query. **Pays $0-100.**

$ $ THE BEVERAGE JOURNAL

Michigan Edition, MI Licensed Beverage Association, P.O. Box 4067, East Lansing MI 48826. (517)374-9611. Fax: (517)374-1165. E-mail: editor@mlba.org. Website: www.mlba.org. **40-50% freelance written**. Monthly magazine covering hospitality industry. A monthly trade magazine devoted to the beer, wine, and spirits industry in Michigan. It is dedicated to serving those who make their living serving the public and the state through the orderly and responsible sale of beverages. Estab. 1983. Circ. 4,200. Pays on publication. No kill fee. Buys one-time rights, buys second serial (reprint) rights. Makes work-for-hire assignments. Editorial lead time 3 months. Submit seasonal material 3 months in advance. Accepts queries by mail, e-mail. Responds in 2 weeks to queries. Responds in 1 month to mss. Sample copy for $5 or online.

Nonfiction Needs essays, general interest, historical, how-to, make a drink, human resources, tips, etc. , humor, interview, new product, opinion, personal experience, photo feature, technical. **Buys 24 mss/year.** Send complete ms. Length: 1,000 words. **Pays $20-200.**

Columns/Departments Open to essay content ideas. Interviews (legislators, others), 750-1,000 words; personal experience (waitstaff, customer, bartenders), 500 words. **Buys 12 mss/year.** Send complete ms. **Pays $25-100.**

Tips We are particularly interested in nonfiction concerning responsible consumption/serving of alcohol. We are looking for product reviews, company profiles, personal experiences, and news articles that would benefit our audience. Our audience is a busy group of business owners and hospitality professionals striving to obtain pertinent information that is not too wordy.

$ $ PATTERSON'S CALIFORNIA BEVERAGE JOURNAL

Interactive Color, Inc., 4910 San Fernando Rd., Glendale CA 91204. (818)291-1125. Fax: (818)547-4607. E-mail: mmay@interactivecolor.com. Website: www.beveragelink.com. **25% freelance written**. Monthly magazine covering the alcohol, beverage, and wine industries. *Patterson's* reports on the latest news in product information, merchandising, company appointments, developments in the wine industry, and consumer trends. Our readers can be informed, up-to-date and confident in their purchasing decisions. Estab. 1962. Circ. 25,000. Byline given. Offers kill fee. Offers negotiable kill fee. Editorial lead time 1 month. Submit seasonal material 1 month in advance. Accepts queries by mail, e-mail, fax. Sample copy and writer's guidelines free.

Nonfiction Needs interview, new product, market reports. No consumer-oriented articles or negative slants on industry as a whole. **Buys 200 mss/year.** Query with published clips. Length: 500-750 words. **Pays $60-200.**

Photos State availability. Captions, identification of subjects required. Reviews transparencies. Offers no additional payment for photos accepted with ms. Buys all rights.

Columns/Departments Query with published clips.

$ $ PRACTICAL WINERY & VINEYARD

PWV, Inc., 58 Paul Dr., Suite D, San Rafael CA 94903-2054. (415)479-5819. Fax: (415)492-9325. E-mail: tina@practicalwinery.com. Website: www.practicalwinery.com. **50% freelance written**. Bimonthly magazine covering winemaking, grapegrowing, wine marketing. "*Practical Winery & Vineyard* is a technical trade journal for winemakers and grapegrowers. All articles are fact-checked and peer-reviewed prior to publication to ensure 100% accuracy, readability, and practical useful application for readers. NO consumer-focused wine articles, please." Estab. 1979. Circ. 4,000. Byline given. Pays on publication. No kill fee. Publishes ms an average of 6-9 months after acceptance. Buys first North American serial rights, buys electronic rights. Editorial lead time 6-9 months. Submit seasonal material 9 months in advance. Accepts queries by mail, e-mail, fax. Responds in 1-2 weeks to queries. Responds in 1 month to mss. Guidelines by e-mail.

Nonfiction Contact: Tina L. Vierra, associate publisher. Needs how-to, technical. Special issues: "Each issue has a specific topic/focus. Please see Editorial Calendar for 2010. We do not want any wine consumer trends, retail info, wine tasting notes; no food, travel, wine lifestyles." **Buys 25 mss/year.** Query with published clips. Length: 1,000-3,000 words. **Pays 25-50¢ a word for assigned articles. Pays 25-35¢ a word for unsolicited articles.**

Photos Contact: Tina L. Vierra, associate publisher. State availability. Captions required. Reviews GIF/JPEG files. Offers no additional payment for photos accepted with ms.

Tips "Query with CV, tech articles only, must have knowledge of technical aspects of winemaking/grapegrowing."

$$$ VINEYARD & WINERY MANAGEMENT

P.O. Box 2358, Windsor CA 95492-2358. (707)577-7700. Fax: (707)577-7705. Website: www.vwm-online.com. **Contact:** Tina Caputo, editor-in-chief. **70% freelance written**. Bimonthly magazine of professional importance to grape growers, winemakers, and winery sales and business people. "Headquartered in Sonoma County, California, we proudly remain as a leading independent wine trade magazine serving all of North America." Estab. 1975. Circ. 6,500. Byline given. Pays on publication. No kill fee. Buys first North American serial rights, buys simultaneous rights. Accepts queries by e-mail. Responds in 3 weeks to queries. Responds in 1 month to mss. Sample copy free. Guidelines for #10 SASE.

- "We focus on the management of people and process in the areas of viticulture, enology, winery marketing and finance. Our articles are written with a high degree of technical expertise by a team of wine industry professionals and top-notch journalists. Timely articles and columns keep our subscribers poised for excellence and success."

Nonfiction Subjects are technical in nature and explore the various methods people in these career paths use to succeed and the equipment and techniques they use successfully. Business articles and management topics are also featured. The audience is national with western dominance. Needs how-to, interview, new product, technical. **Buys 30 mss/year.** Query. Length: 1,800-5,000 words. **Pays $30-1,000.** Sometimes pays expenses of writers on assignment.

Photos State availability. Captions, identification of subjects required. Reviews contact sheets, negatives, transparencies, digital photos. Black & white often purchased for $20 each to accompany story material; 35mm and/or 4 × 5 transparencies for $50 and up; 6/year of vineyard and/or winery scene related to story.

Tips "We're looking for long-term relationships with authors who know the business and write well. Electronic submissions required; query for formats."

$$ WINES & VINES MAGAZINE

The Voice of the Grape and Wine Industry, Wine Communications Group, 1800 Lincoln Ave., San Rafael CA 94901. (415)453-9700. Fax: (415)453-2517. E-mail: edit@winesandvines.com. Website: www.winesandvines.com. **50% freelance written**. Monthly magazine covering the North American winegrape and winemaking industry. "Since 1919 *Wines & Vines Magazine* has been the authoritative voice of the wine and grape industry—from prohibition to phylloxera, we have covered it all. Our paid circulation reaches all 50 states and many foreign countries. Because we are intended for the trade—including growers, winemakers, winery owners, wholesalers, restauranteurs, and serious amateurs—we accept more technical, informative articles. We do not accept wine reviews, wine country tours, or anything of a wine consumer nature." Estab. 1919. Circ. 5,000. Byline given. Pays 30 days after acceptance. No kill fee. Publishes ms an average of 3 months after acceptance. Buys first rights, buys electronic rights. Editorial lead time 2 months. Submit seasonal material 4 months in advance. Accepts queries by e-mail. Responds in 2-3 weeks to queries. Sample copy for $5. Guidelines free.

Nonfiction Needs interview, new product, technical. "No wine reviews, wine country travelogues, 'lifestyle' pieces, or anything aimed at wine consumers. Our readers are professionals in the field." **Buys 60 mss/year.** Query with published clips. Length: 1,000-2,000 words. **Pays flat fee of $500 for assigned articles.**

Photos Prefers JPEG files (JPEG, 300 dpi minimum). Can use high-quality prints. State availability of or send photos. Captions, identification of subjects required. Does not pay for photos submitted by author, but will give photo credit.

Book & Bookstore

$ $ FOREWORD MAGAZINE

ForeWord Magazine, Inc., 129 1/2 E. Front St., Traverse City MI 49684. (231)933-3699. Fax: (231)933-3899. Website: www.forewordmagazine.com. Teresa Scollon. **Contact:** Victoria Sutherland. **95% freelance written.** Bimonthly magazine covering reviews of good books independently published. In each issue of the magazine, there are 3 to 4 feature *ForeSight* articles focusing on trends in popular categories. These are in addition to the 75 or more critical reviews of forthcoming titles from independent presses in our *Review* section. While we try very hard to communicate with publicity departments concerning calls for submissions to the *ForeSight* features, we also hope that publishers will keep these forms handy to track what's happening at *ForeWord*. Look online for our review submission guidelines or view the 2009 editorial calendar. Be sure to read the ForeWord Ten-Point Tip Sheet, which outlines how to make sure you know how to present your book for best results. Estab. 1998. Circ. *ForeWord* affects the choices of booksellers and librarians across the country who tell millions what to read. Our typical publication reaches an audience of 20,000. We also put the magazine in the hands of agents and editors at larger houses who are looking for leads to bring into their fold from the independent press sector. All told, readership is about 85% librarians, 12% bookstores, 3% publishing professionals. Byline given. Pays 2 months after publication. No kill fee. Publishes ms an average of 2-3 months after acceptance. Buys all rights. Editorial lead time 3-4 months. Submit seasonal material 5 months in advance. Accepts queries by mail, e-mail. Responds in 1 month to queries. Responds in 1 month to mss. Sample copy for $10 and 8½ × 11 SASE with $1.50 postage.

- *ForeWord's* special sections and supplements exist to cover perennial interest areas and emerging trends in the publishing world. Currently, we highlight graphic novels in *Comique*, digital technology in *eWord*, books for a global society in *Polis*, religion titles in *Faith*, and mind/body books in *Spirit*.

Nonfiction Query with published clips. Length: 400-1,500 words. **Pays $25-200 for assigned articles.**

Tips Be knowledgeable about the needs of booksellers and librarians—remember we are an industry trade journal, not a how-to or consumer publication. We review books prior to publication, so book reviews are always assigned—but send us a note telling subjects you wish to review, as well as a resume.

THE HORN BOOK MAGAZINE

The Horn Book, Inc., 56 Roland St., Suite 200, Boston MA 02129. (617)628-0225. Fax: (617)628-0882. Website: www.hbook.com. Cynthia Riter, editorial assistant. **75% freelance written. Prefers to work with published/established writers.** Bimonthly magazine covering children's literature for librarians, booksellers, professors, teachers and students of children's literature. Estab. 1924. Circ. 16,000. Byline given. Pays on publication. No kill fee. Publishes ms an average of 4 months after acceptance. Submit seasonal material 6 months in advance. Accepts queries by mail, e-mail, fax. Accepts simultaneous submissions. Responds in 3 months to queries. Sample copy and writer's guidelines online.

Nonfiction "Interested in seeing strong, authoritative pieces about children's books and contemporary culture. Writers should be familiar with the magazine and its contents." Needs interview, children's book authors and illustrators, topics of interest to the children's bookworld. **Buys 20 mss/year.** Query or send complete ms. Length: 1,000-2,800 words. **Pays honorarium upon publication.**

Tips "Writers have a better chance of breaking into our publication with a query letter on a specific article they want to write."

THE NEW YORK REVIEW OF BOOKS

435 Hudson St., Suite 300, New York NY 10014. (212)757-8070. Fax: (212)333-5374. E-mail: editor@nybooks.com. Website: www.nybooks.com. **Contact:** Robert B. Silvers, editor. Biweekly magazine covering books and authors. "New York Review Books publishes NYRB Classics, NYRB Collections, and the New York Review Children's Collection." Circ. 125,000.

Nonfiction "*NYRB does not accept unsolicited manuscripts.* We reserve the right not to return or respond to any such manuscripts sent to us. Thank you for your cooperation." Needs interview, reviews. Query.

$ VIDEO LIBRARIAN

8705 Honeycomb Court NW, Seabeck WA 98380. (360)830-9345. Fax: (360)830-9346. E-mail: vidlib@videolibrarian.com. Website: www.videolibrarian.com. **75% freelance written**. Bimonthly magazine covering DVD reviews for librarians. "*Video Librarian* reviews approximately 225 titles in each issue: children's, documentaries, how-to's, movies, TV, music and anime." Estab. 1986. Circ. 2,000. Byline given. Pays on publication. Publishes ms an average of 2 months after acceptance. Buys one-time rights, buys second serial (reprint) rights, buys electronic rights. Makes work-for-hire assignments. Editorial lead time 2 months. Accepts queries by e-mail. Accepts previously published material. Accepts simultaneous submissions. Responds in 1 week to queries. Sample copy for $11.

Nonfiction Buys 500+ mss/year. Query with published clips. Length: 200-300 words. **Pays $10-20/review.**

Tips "We are looking for DVD reviewers with a wide range of interests, good critical eye, and strong writing skills."

Brick, Glass & Ceramics

$$ GLASS MAGAZINE

For the Architectural Glass Industry, National Glass Association, 8200 Greensboro Dr., Suite 302, McLean VA 22102. (866)342-5642. Fax: (703)442-0630. E-mail: editorialinfo@glass.org. Website: www.glass.org. **10% freelance written. Prefers to work with published/established writers.** Monthly magazine covering the architectural glass industry. Circ. 28,289. Byline given. Pays on acceptance. Offers kill fee. Kill fee varies. Publishes ms an average of 6 months after acceptance. Buys first rights. Accepts queries by mail, e-mail, fax. Responds in 2 months to mss. Sample copy for $5 and 9 × 12 SAE with 10 first-class stamps.

Nonfiction Needs interview, of various glass businesses; profiles of industry people or glass business owners, new product, technical, about glazing processes. **Buys 5 mss/year.** Query with published clips. 1,000 words minimum. **Pays $150-300.**

Photos State availability.

Tips *Glass Magazine* is doing more inhouse writing; freelance cut by half. Do not send in general glass use stories. Research the industry first, then query.

$ STAINED GLASS

Stained Glass Association of America, 9313 East 63rd St., Raytown MO 64133. E-mail: quarterly@sgaonline.com. Website: www.stainedglass.org. **70% freelance written**. Quarterly magazine. "Since 1906, *Stained Glass* has been the official voice of the Stained Glass Association of America. As the oldest, most respected stained glass publication in North America, *Stained Glass* preserves the techniques of the past as well as illustrates the trends of the future. This vital information, of significant value to the professional stained glass studio, is also of interest to those for whom stained glass is an avocation or hobby." Estab. 1906. Circ. 8,000. Byline given. Pays on publication. No kill fee. Publishes ms an average of 1 year after acceptance. Buys one-time rights. Editorial lead time 6 months. Submit seasonal material 8 months in advance. Accepts queries by mail, e-mail, fax. Responds in 3 months to queries. Sample copy and writer's guideline free.

Nonfiction Strong need for technical and how to create architectural type stained glass. Glass etching, use of etched glass in stained glass compositions, framing. Needs how-to, humor, interview, new product, opinion, photo feature, technical. **Buys 9 mss/year.** Query or send complete ms but must include photos or slides—very heavy on photos. **Pays $125/illustrated article; $75/nonillustrated.**

Reprints Accepts previously published submissions from stained glass publications only. Send tearsheet of article. Payment negotiable.

Photos Send photos. Identification of subjects required. Reviews 4 × 5 transparencies, send slides with submission. Pays $75 for non-illustrated. Pays $125, plus 3 copies for line art or photography. Buys one time rights.

Columns/Departments Columns must be illustrated. Teknixs (technical, how-to, stained and glass art), word length varies by subject. **Buys 4 mss/year.** Query or send complete ms, but must be illustrated.

Tips "We need more technical articles. Writers should be extremely well versed in the glass arts. Photographs are extremely important and must be of very high quality. Submissions without photographs or illustrations are seldom considered unless something special and writer states that photos are available. However, prefer to see with submission."

$$ US GLASS, METAL & GLAZING

Key Communications, Inc., P.O. Box 569, Garrisonville VA 22463. (540)720-5584. Fax: (540)720-5687. E-mail: info@glass.com. Website: www.usglassmag.com. **25% freelance written**. Monthly magazine for companies involved in the flat glass trades. Estab. 1966. Circ. 27,000. Byline given. Pays on publication. No kill fee. Publishes ms an average of 3 months after acceptance. Buys all rights. Editorial lead time 3 months. Submit seasonal material 2 months in advance. Accepts queries by mail, e-mail, fax. Accepts simultaneous submissions. Responds in 1 month to queries. Responds in 2 months to mss. Sample copy and writer's guidelines online.

Nonfiction Buys 12 mss/year. Query with published clips. **Pays $300-600 for assigned articles.** Sometimes pays expenses of writers on assignment.

Photos State availability. Captions, identification of subjects required. Reviews contact sheets. Offers no additional payment for photos accepted with ms. Buys first North American rights.

Building Interiors

$$ FABRICS + FURNISHINGS INTERNATIONAL

SIPCO Publications + Events, 145 Main St., 3rd Floor, Ossining NY 10591. (914)923-0616. Fax: (914)923-0018. E-mail: kelly@boutiquedesign.com. Website: www.sipco.net. **10% freelance written**. Bimonthly magazine covering commercial, hospitality interior design, manufacturing. *F+FI* covers news from vendors who supply the hospitality interiors industry. Estab. 1990. Circ. 11,000+. Byline given. Pays on publication. Offers $100 kill fee. Editorial lead time 3 months. Submit seasonal material 3 months in advance. Accepts queries by e-mail. Accepts simultaneous submissions. Sample copy available online.

Nonfiction Needs interview, technical. "Does no opinion, consumer pieces. Our readers must learn something from our stories." Query with published clips. Length: 500-1,000 words. **Pays $250-350.**

Photos Send photos. Captions, identification of subjects required. Reviews GIF/JPEG files. Offers no additional payment for photos accepted with ms.

Tips "Give us a lead on a new project that we haven't heard about. Have pictures of space and ability to interview designer on how they made it work."

FLOOR COVERING NEWS

The publication more retailers prefer, Ro-El Productions, 550 W. Old Country Rd., Suite 204, Hicksville NY 11801. (516)932-7860. Fax: (516)932-7639. E-mail: fcnews@optonline.net. Website: www.floorcoveringnews.net. **15% freelance written**. Biweekly tabloid covering the floor covering industry for retailers, salespeople, installers, distributors and designers, as well as manufacturers. "We are a journalistic-style publication that writes for the flooring industry. While we use industry jargon and have our own nuances, we use the AP and New York Times stylebooks as general guidelines." Estab. 1986. Circ. 16,000. Byline given. Pays on acceptance. Publishes ms an average of 1 month after acceptance. Buys exclusivity rights for within the flooring industry trades, which includes the Internet. Editorial lead time 2 months. Accepts previously published material. Accepts simultaneous submissions. Responds in 2-3 weeks to queries. Sample copy for $2.

Nonfiction Needs book excerpts, expose, historical, interview, new product, photo feature, technical. Does not want puff pieces and commercials. **Buys 15-30 mss/year.** Query. **Pays negotiable amount.** Pays expenses of writers on assignment.

Photos Send photos. Captions, identification of subjects, model releases required. Reviews contact sheets, prints, JPEG/TIFF files (300 dpi, 4x4 minimum). Offers no additional payment for photos accepted with ms; negotiates payment individually.

$$ KITCHEN & BATH DESIGN NEWS

Cygnus Business Media, 3 Huntington Quadrangle, Suite 301N, Melville NY 11747. Fax: (631)845-7218. E-mail: janice.costa@cygnuspub.com. Website: www.kitchenbathdesign.com. **15% freelance written**. Monthly tabloid for kitchen and bath dealers and design professionals, offering design, business and marketing advice to help our readers be more successful. It is not a consumer publication about design, a book for do-it-yourselfers, or a magazine created to showcase pretty pictures of kitchens and baths. Rather, we cover the professional kitchen and bath design industry in depth, looking at the specific challenges facing these professionals, and how they address these challenges. Estab. 1983. Circ. 51,000. Byline given. Pays on publication. Publishes ms an average of 2-3 months after acceptance. Buys all rights. Editorial lead time 2 months. Accepts queries by mail, e-mail, fax. Responds in 2-4 weeks to queries. Sample copy available online. Guidelines by e-mail.

Nonfiction Needs how-to, interview. Does not want consumer stories; generic business stories; I remodeled my kitchen and it's so beautiful stories. This is a magazine for trade professionals, so stories need to be both slanted for these professionals, as well as sophisticated enough so that people who have been working in the field 30 years can still learn something from them. **Buys 16 mss/year.** Query with published clips. Length: 1,100-3,000 words. **Pays $200-650.** Sometimes pays expenses of writers on assignment.
Photos Send photos. Identification of subjects required. Offers no additional payment for photos accepted with ms.
Tips This is a trade magazine for kitchen and bath dealers and designers, so trade experience and knowledge of the industry are essential. We look for writers who already know the unique challenges facing this industry, as well as the major players, acronyms, etc. This is not a market for beginners, and the vast majority of our freelancers are either design professionals, or experienced in the industry.

$ $ QUALIFIED REMODELER

Best Practices, Products & Design Ideas, Cygnus Business Media, P.O. Box 803, Fort Atkinson WI 53538. Website: www.qualifiedremodeler.com. **Contact:** Patrick O'Toole, editor & publisher. **5% freelance written**. Monthly magazine covering residential remodeling. Estab. 1975. Circ. 83,500. Byline given. Pays on acceptance. No kill fee. Publishes ms an average of 1 month after acceptance. Buys all rights. Editorial lead time 3 months. Submit seasonal material 2 months in advance. Accepts queries by mail, e-mail, fax, phone. Sample copy available online.
Nonfiction Needs how-to, business management, new product, photo feature, best practices articles, innovative design. **Buys 12 mss/year.** Query with published clips. Length: 1,200-2,500 words. **Pays $300-600 for assigned articles. Pays $200-400 for unsolicited articles.** Sometimes pays expenses of writers on assignment.
Photos Send photos. Reviews negatives, transparencies. Negotiates payment individually. Buys one time rights.
Columns/Departments Query with published clips. **Pays $400**
Tips We focus on business management issues faced by remodeling contractors. For example, sales, marketing, liability, taxes, and just about any matter addressing small business operation.

$ $ $ $ REMODELING

HanleyWood, LLC, One Thomas Circle NW, Suite 600, Washington DC 20005. (202)452-0800. Fax: (202)785-1974. E-mail: ibush@hanleywood.com. Website: www.remodelingmagazine.com. **10% freelance written**. Monthly magazine covering residential and light commercial remodeling. We cover the best new ideas in remodeling design, business, construction and products. Estab. 1985. Circ. 80,000. Byline given. Pays on publication. Offers 5¢/word kill fee. Publishes ms an average of 3 months after acceptance. Buys first North American serial rights. Accepts queries by mail, e-mail, fax. Sample copy free.
Nonfiction Needs interview, new product, technical, small business trends. **Buys 6 mss/year.** Query with published clips. Length: 250-1,000 words. **Pays $1/word.** Sometimes pays expenses of writers on assignment.
Photos State availability. Captions, identification of subjects, model releases required. Reviews 4 × 5 transparencies, slides, 8 × 10 prints. Offers $25-125/photo. Buys one time rights.
Tips We specialize in service journalism for remodeling contractors. Knowledge of the industry is essential.

$ $ WALLS & CEILINGS

2401 W. Big Beaver Rd., Suite 700, Troy MI 48084. (313)894-7380. Fax: (248)362-5103. E-mail: wyattj@bnpmedia.com. Website: www.wconline.com. **Contact:** John Wyatt, editor. **20% freelance written**. Monthly magazine for contractors involved in lathing and plastering, drywall, acoustics, fireproofing, curtain walls, and movable partitions, together with manufacturers, dealers, and architects. Estab. 1938. Circ. 30,000. Byline given. Pays on publication. No kill fee. Publishes ms an average of 6 months after acceptance. Buys all rights. Submit seasonal material 4 months in advance. Accepts queries by mail, e-mail, phone. Accepts simultaneous submissions. Responds in 6 months to queries. Sample copy for 9 × 12 SAE with $2 postage. Guidelines for #10 SASE.
Nonfiction Needs how-to, drywall and plaster construction and business management, technical. **Buys 20 mss/year.** Query or send complete ms. Length: 1,000-1,500 words. **Pays $50-500.** Sometimes pays expenses of writers on assignment.

Reprints Send tearsheet or photocopy with rights for sale noted and information about when and where the material previously appeared. Pays 50% of the amount paid for an original article.
Photos Send photos. Captions, identification of subjects required. Reviews contact sheets, negatives, transparencies, prints. Buys one-time rights.

Business Management

$$ ASSOCIATION & MEETING DIRECTOR

Canada's Number One Association Management & Meeting Magazine, August Communications, 225-530 Century St., Winnipeg MB R3H 0Y4 Canada. (888)573-1136. Fax: (866)957-0217. E-mail: r.mcilroy@august.ca. Website: www.associationdirector.ca. **70% freelance written**. Bimonthly magazine covering association management and corporate meeting planners. *Association & Meeting Director* is direct mailed to Canadian association executives and corporate meeting professionals. It has the aim of exploring both the Canadian corporate and association marketplace. Estab. 2000. Circ. 15,000. Byline given. Pays 1 month after publication. No kill fee. Publishes ms an average of 2 months after acceptance. Buys all rights. Editorial lead time 3 months. Submit seasonal material 3 months in advance. Accepts queries by mail, e-mail, fax. Responds in 1 week to queries. Sample copy and writer's guidelines free.
Nonfiction Needs how-to, inspirational, interview, new product, technical, travel. **Buys 18 mss/year.** Query with published clips. Length: 700-2,000 words. **Pays 20-40¢/word for assigned articles.**
Photos State availability. Identification of subjects required. Reviews GIF/JPEG files. Negotiates payment individually. Buys all rights.
Columns/Departments Buys 12 mss/year. Query with published clips. **Pays 20-40¢/word**

$$$$ BEDTIMES

The Business Journal for the Sleep Products Industry, International Sleep Products Association, 501 Wythe St., Alexandria VA 22314-1917. (703)683-8371. E-mail: jpalm@sleepproducts.org. Website: www.sleepproducts.org. **20-40% freelance written**. Monthly magazine covering the mattress manufacturing industry. "Our news and features are straightforward—we are not a lobbying vehicle for our association. No special slant." Estab. 1917. Circ. 3,800. Byline given. Pays on acceptance. No kill fee. Publishes ms an average of 3 months after acceptance. Buys first North American serial rights. Editorial lead time 2 months. Accepts queries by e-mail. Accepts simultaneous submissions. Responds in 1 month to queries. Sample copy for $4. Guidelines by e-mail.
Nonfiction No pieces that do not relate to business in general or mattress industry in particular. **Buys 15-25/year mss/year.** Query with published clips. Length: 500-2,500 words. **Pays 50-$1/word for short features; $2,000 for cover story.**
Photos State availability. Identification of subjects required. Negotiates payment individually. Buys one time rights.
Tips "Cover topics have included annual industry forecast; e-commerce; flammability and home furnishings; the risks and rewards of marketing overseas; the evolving family business; the shifting workplace environment; and what do consumers really want?"

$$$$ BLACK MBA MAGAZINE

Official Publication of NBMBAA, P&L Publishing Ltd., 9730 S. Western Ave., Suite 320, Evergreen Park IL 60805. (708)422-1506. Fax: (708)422-1507. E-mail: robert@blackmbamagazine.net. Website: www.blackmbamagazine.net. **80% freelance written**. Quarterly magazine covering business career strategy, economic development, and financial management. Estab. 1997. Circ. 45,000. Byline given. Pays after publication. Offers 10-20% or $500 kill fee. Publishes ms an average of 1 month after acceptance. Buys all rights. Editorial lead time 2-3 months. Submit seasonal material 3-4 months in advance. Accepts queries by mail, e-mail, fax.
Photos State availability of or send photos. Identification of subjects required. Reviews ZIP disk. Offers no additional payment for photos accepted with ms. Buys one time rights.
Columns/Departments Management Strategies (leadership development), 1,200-1,700 words; Features (business management, entreprenuerial finance); Finance; Technology. Send complete ms. **Pays $500-1,000.**

$$$ BUSINESS TRAVEL EXECUTIVE

Managed Travel & Procurement Solutions, 11 Ryerson Ave., Suite 200, Pompton Plains NJ 07405. E-mail: jferring@askbte.com. Website: www.askbte.com. **90% freelance written**. Monthly magazine covering corporate procurement of travel services. "We are not a travel magazine. We publish articles designed to help corporate purchasers of travel negotiate contracts, enforce policy, select automated services, track business travelers and account for their safety and expenditures, understand changes in the various industries associated with travel. Do not submit manuscripts without an assignment. Look at the website for an idea of what we publish." Byline given. Pays on publication. No kill fee. Publishes ms an average of 2 months after acceptance. Buys first North American serial rights. Editorial lead time 0-3 months. Accepts queries by e-mail.

Nonfiction Needs how-to, technical. **Buys 48 mss/year.** Query. Length: 800-2,000 words. **Pays $200-800.**

Columns/Departments Meeting Place (meeting planning and management); Hotel Pulse (hotel negotiations, contracting and compliance); Security Watch (travel safety), all 1,000 words. **Buys 24 mss/year.** Query. **Pays $200-400.**

CAMAGAZINE

Canadian Institute of Chartered Accountants, 277 Wellington St. W, Toronto ON M5V 3H2 Canada. (416)977-3222. Fax: (416)204-3409. E-mail: christian.bellavance@cica.ca. Website: www.camagazine.com. **30% freelance written**. Magazine published 10 times/year covering accounting and finance. *CAmagazine* is the leading accounting publication in Canada and the preferred information source for chartered accountants and financial executives. It provides a forum for discussion and debate on professional, financial, and other business issues. Estab. 1911. Circ. 90,602. Byline given. Pays on acceptance. Offers 30% kill fee. Publishes ms an average of 3 months after acceptance. Buys all rights. Editorial lead time 4 months. Accepts queries by e-mail. Responds in 1 month to queries. Sample copy and writer's guidelines online.

Nonfiction Needs book excerpts, financial/accounting business. **Buys 30 mss/year.** Query. Length: 2,500-3,500 words. **Pays honorarium for chartered accountants; freelance rate varies. Does not pay business professionals.**

$$ CONTRACTING PROFITS

Trade Press Publishing, 2100 W. Florist Ave., Milwaukee WI 53209. (414)228-7701. Fax: (414)228-1134. Website: www.cleanlink.com/cp. **40% freelance written**. Magazine published 10 times/year covering building service contracting, business management advice. We are the pocket MBA for this industry—focusing not only on cleaning-specific topics, but also discussing how to run businesses better and increase profits through a variety of management articles. Estab. 1995. Circ. 32,000. Byline given. Pays within 30 days of acceptance. No kill fee. Buys all rights. Editorial lead time 2 months. Submit seasonal material 3 months in advance. Accepts queries by mail, e-mail. Responds in weeks to queries. Sample copy available online. Guidelines free.

Nonfiction Needs expose, how-to, interview, technical. No product-related reviews or testimonials. **Buys 30 mss/year.** Query with published clips. Length: 1,000-1,500 words. **Pays $100-500.** Sometimes pays expenses of writers on assignment.

Columns/Departments Query with published clips.

Tips Read back issues on our website and be able to understand some of those topics prior to calling.

$$ CONTRACT MANAGEMENT

National Contract Management Association, 8260 Greensboro Dr., Suite 200, McLean VA 22102. (571)382-0082. Fax: (703)448-0939. E-mail: miedema@ncmahq.org. Website: www.ncmahq.org. **10% freelance written**. Monthly magazine covering contract and business management. Most of the articles published in *Contract Management (CM)* are written by members, although one does not have to be an NCMA member to be published in the magazine. Articles should concern some aspect of the contract management profession, whether at the level of a beginner or that of the advanced practitioner. Estab. 1960. Circ. 23,000. Byline given. Pays on publication. No kill fee. Publishes ms an average of 3 months after acceptance. Buys one-time rights. Editorial lead time 10 weeks. Submit seasonal material 3 months in advance. Accepts queries by mail, e-mail, fax, phone. Accepts previously published material. Accepts simultaneous submissions. Responds in 2 weeks to queries. Responds in 1 month to mss. Sample copy and writer's guidelines free.

Nonfiction Needs essays, general interest, how-to, humor, inspirational, new product, opinion, technical. No company or CEO profiles—please read a copy of publication before submitting. **Buys 6-10 mss/year.** Query with published clips. Length: 2,500-3,000 words. **Pays $300, association members paid in 3 copies.**

Photos State availability. Captions, identification of subjects required. Offers no additional payment for photos accepted with ms. Buys one time rights.

Columns/Departments Professional Development (self-improvement in business), 1,000-1,500 words; Back to Basics (basic how-tos and discussions), 1,500-2,000 words. **Buys 2 mss/year.** Query with published clips. **Pays $300**

Tips Query and read at least 1 issue. Visit website to better understand our audience.

EMPLOYEE ASSISTANCE REPORT

Impact Publications, 1439 Churchill St., Crystal Plaza, Units 302-303, Waupaca WI 54981. (800)350-4422. Fax: (715)258-9048. E-mail: info@impact-publications.com. Website: www.impact-publications.com. **0% freelance written. As opposed to paid freelance writers, most articles in this newsletter are either written by Employee Assistance Report staff or by employee assistance professionals—in exchange for free publicity for their EAP.** Monthly newsletter covering work-life issues of interest to employee assistance professionals (i.e. EAPs). Familiarity with needs and interests of employee assistance professionals. General work-life issues can be useful, but they are definitely not as useful as articles written specifically for this audience. Estab. 1998. Byline given. Writers generally not compensated financially. No kill fee. Publishes ms an average of 3 months after acceptance. Buys all rights. Editorial lead time 3 months. Accepts queries by e-mail, phone. Accepts previously published material. Accepts simultaneous submissions. Guidelines available.

Nonfiction Needs how-to, How-to means how-to resolve a particular issue or topic, interview, new product, Book reviews. Articles that are too long, too general, and/or that insist upon payment. **Buys 0 mss/year.** Query. Length: 1,000-1,300 words.

Photos State availability. Offers no additional payment for photos accepted with ms.

Columns/Departments Contact: Mike Jacquart. Legal Lines (legal issues affecting workplace), Washington Beat (legislative issues affecting the workplace), clinical Perspective (clinical/behavioral health issues affecting workplace), 500 words; On the Job (everyday work-life issues our readers run into), 300 words. **Buys 0 mss/year.**

Tips "Recognize that we work months ahead—contact editor as far in advance as possible, look at a copy of our editorial calendar on our website—it usually is available in early-to-mid fall for the following year. Recognize that we have a very spescific, professional audience and be willing to work with us as far as non-paid compensation arrangements."

$$ EXECUTIVE UPDATE

Greater Washington Society of Association Executives, Reagan Building & International Trade Center, 1300 Pennsylvania Ave. NW, Washington DC 20004. (202)326-9545. Fax: (202)326-0999. Website: www.executiveupdate.com. **60% freelance written**. Monthly magazine exploring a broad range of association management issues and for introducing and discussing management and leadership philosophies. It is written for individuals at all levels of association management, with emphasis on senior staff and CEOs. Estab. 1979. Circ. 14,000. Byline given. Pays on acceptance. Offers 20% kill fee. Publishes ms an average of 6 months after acceptance. Buys first rights. Editorial lead time 3 months. Submit seasonal material 6 months in advance. Accepts queries by mail, e-mail, fax, phone. Accepts simultaneous submissions. Responds in 1 month to queries. Responds in 2 months to mss. Sample copy free. Guidelines available online.

Nonfiction Needs how-to, humor, interview, opinion, personal experience, travel, management and workplace issues. **Buys 24-36 mss/year.** Query with published clips. Length: 2,000-2,500 words. **Pays $500-700.** Pays expenses of writers on assignment.

Columns/Departments Intelligence (new ways to tackle day-to-day issues), 500-700 words; Off the Cuff (guest column for association executives). Query. **Pays $100-200.**

$$ EXPANSION MANAGEMENT MAGAZINE

Growth Strategies for Companies On the Move, Penton Media, Inc., 1300 E. 9th St., Cleveland OH 44114. (216)931-9578. Fax: (216)931-9145. **50% freelance written**. Monthly magazine covering economic development. Estab. 1986. Circ. 45,000. Byline given. Pays on acceptance. No kill fee. Publishes ms an average of 1 month after acceptance. Buys all rights. Makes work-for-hire assignments. Editorial lead time 2 months. Sample copy for $7. Guidelines free.

Nonfiction *Expansion Management* presents articles and industry reports examining relocation trends, strategic planning, work force hiring, economic development agencies, and relocation consultants and state, province, and county reviews and profiles to help readers select future expansions and relocation

sites. **Buys 120 mss/year.** Query with published clips. Length: 800-1,200 words. **Pays $200-400 for assigned articles.** Sometimes pays expenses of writers on assignment.
Photos Send photos. Captions required. Offers no additional payment for photos accepted with ms. Buys one time rights.
Tips Send clips first, then call me.

$$$ EXPO

Atwood Publishing, LLC, 7015 College Blvd., Suite 600, Overland Park KS 66211. (913)344-1303. Fax: (913)344-1486. E-mail: dtormohlen@ascendmedia.com. Website: www.expoweb.com. **80% freelance written**. Magazine covering expositions. *EXPO* is the information and education resource for the exposition industry. It is the only magazine dedicated exclusively to the people with direct responsibility for planning, promoting and operating trade and consumer shows. Our readers are show managers and their staff, association executives, independent show producers and industry suppliers. Every issue of *EXPO* contains in-depth, how-to features and departments that focus on the practical aspects of exposition management, including administration, promotion and operations. Byline given. Pays on publication. Offers 50% kill fee. Buys first North American serial rights. Editorial lead time 3 months. Accepts queries by mail, e-mail, fax. Responds in 3 weeks to queries. Sample copy free. Guidelines available online.
Nonfiction Needs how-to, interview. Query with published clips. Length: 600-2,400 words. **Pays 50¢/word.** Pays expenses of writers on assignment.
Photos State availability.
Columns/Departments Profile (personality profile), 650 words; Exhibitor Matters (exhibitor issues) and EXPOTech (technology), both 600-1,300 words. **Buys 10 mss/year.** Query with published clips.
Tips *EXPO* now offers shorter features and departments, while continuing to offer in-depth reporting. Editorial is more concise, using synopsis, bullets and tidbits whenever possible. Every article needs sidebars, call-outs, graphs, charts, etc., to create entry points for readers. Headlines and leads are more provocative. And writers should elevate the level of shop talk, demonstrating that *EXPO* is the leader in the industry. We plan our editorial calendar about one year in advance, but we are always open to new ideas. Please query before submitting a story to *EXPO*—tell us about your idea and what our readers would learn. Include your qualifications to write about the subject and the sources you plan to contact.

$$$ FAMILY BUSINESS MAGAZINE

The Guide for Family Companies, Family Business Publishing Co., Family Business Magazine, 1845 Walnut St., Philadelphia PA 19103. Fax: (215)405-6078. E-mail: bspector@familybusinessmagazine.com. Website: www.familybusinessmagazine.com. **Contact:** Barbara Spector, editor-in-chief. **50% freelance written**. Quarterly magazine covering family-owned companies. "Written expressly for family company owners and advisors. Focuses on business and human dynamic issues unique to family enterprises. Offers practical guidance and tried-and-true solutions for business stakeholders." Estab. 1989. Circ. 6,000. Byline given. Pays on acceptance. Offers 30% kill fee. Publishes ms an average of 9-12 months after acceptance. Buys first rights, buys electronic rights. Editorial lead time 4 months. Submit seasonal material 6 months in advance. Accepts queries by e-mail. Guidelines available online.
Nonfiction Needs how-to, family business related only, interview, personal experience. "No small business articles, articles that aren't specifically related to multi-generational family companies (no general business advice). No success stories—there must be an underlying family or business lesson. **No payment for articles written by family business advisors and other service providers**." **Buys 24 mss/year.** Query with published clips. E-mail queries preferred. Length: 1,500-2,000 words. **Pays $50-1,400 for articles written by freelance reporters.**
Photos State availability. Captions, identification of subjects, model releases required. Offers $50-600 maximum/shoot. Buys first, electronic, reprint rights.

$$ IN TENTS

The Magazine for the Tent-Rental and Special-Event Industries, Industrial Fabrics Association International, 1801 County Rd. B W., Roseville MN 55113-4061. (651)225-6970. Fax: (651)225-6966. E-mail: intents@ifai.com. Website: www.ifai.com. **50% freelance written**. Bimonthly magazine covering tent-rental and special-event industries. Estab. 1994. Circ. 12,000. Byline given. Pays on acceptance. No kill fee. Publishes ms an average of 2 months after acceptance. Buys all rights. Editorial lead time 3 months. Accepts queries by mail, e-mail, fax. Sample copy and writer's guidelines free.

Nonfiction Needs how-to, interview, new product, photo feature, technical. **Buys 12-18 mss/year.** Query. Length: 800-2,000 words. **Pays $300-500.** Sometimes pays expenses of writers on assignment.
Photos State availability. Captions, identification of subjects, model releases required. Reviews contact sheets, negatives, prints, digital images. Negotiates payment individually.
Tips We look for lively, intelligent writing that makes technical subjects come alive.

$ $ MAINEBIZ

Maine's Business News Source, Mainebiz Publications, Inc., 30 Milk St., 3rd Floor, Portland ME 04101. (207)761-8379. Fax: (207)761-0732. E-mail: tsmith@mainebiz.biz. Website: www.mainebiz.biz. **25% freelance written**. Biweekly tabloid covering business in Maine. *Mainebiz* is read by business decision makers across the state. They look to the publication for business news and analysis. Estab. 1994. Circ. 13,000. Byline given. Pays on publication. Offers 10% kill fee. Publishes ms an average of 1 month after acceptance. Buys all rights. Editorial lead time 1 month. Submit seasonal material 2 months in advance. Accepts queries by mail, e-mail. Responds in 3 weeks to queries. Sample copy available online. Guidelines available online.
Nonfiction All pieces are reported and must comply with accepted journalistic standards. We only publish stories about business in Maine. Needs essays, expose, interview, business trends. Special issues: See website for editorial calendar. **Buys 50+ mss/year.** Query with published clips. Length: 500-2,500 words. **Pays $50-250.** Pays expenses of writers on assignment.
Photos State availability. Identification of subjects required. Reviews GIF/JPEG files. Negotiates payment individually. Buys one time rights.
Tips Stories should be well thought out with specific relevance to Maine. Arts and culture-related queries are welcome, as long as there is a business angle. We appreciate unusual angles on business stories and regularly work with new freelancers. Please, no queries unless you have read the paper.

$ $ NATIVE AMERICAN CASINO

Dellas Publications LLC, 1446 Front St., Suite 200, San Diego CA 92101. (619)223-0782. Fax: (619)223-0761. E-mail: mdellas@nacasino.com. Website: www.nacasino.com. **30% freelance written**. Monthly magazine covering the Indian casino industry. *Native American Casino* (NAC) is a monthly, business-to-business magazine dedicated to the growth and prosperity of the Native American businessperson. Our articles aid casino managers in running their various departments, articles also focus on new or expanding Indian casinos, interviews, and topics that people can use to improve any business they wish to pursue. Our readers are the casino managers and tribal leaders/members. Estab. 2000. Circ. 30,000. Byline given. Pays on publication. Publishes ms an average of 2 months after acceptance. Buys all rights. Editorial lead time 2 months. Submit seasonal material 2 months in advance. Accepts queries by e-mail. Accepts simultaneous submissions. Sample copy free. Guidelines by e-mail.
Nonfiction Needs historical, how-to, inspirational, interview, technical, travel. Does not want advertorials, articles degrading or giving any kind of negative impression on Native Americans or the gaming industry, or articles with sexual content or profanity. **Buys 24-36 mss/year.** Query with published clips. Length: 900-2,000 words. **Pays $200-300.**
Photos Contact: Kristina Ushakov, creative director. State availability. Captions, identification of subjects, model releases required. Reviews 5 × 7 prints, GIF/JPEG files (300 dpi). Offers no additional payment for photos accepted with ms. Buys one time rights.
Tips I encourage all freelancers interested to visit our website to get familiar with *NAC*. I would also like them to visit www.indiangaming.com to read about the National Indian Gaming Association and become familiar with our industry.

$ $ PROGRESSIVE RENTALS

The Voice of the Rental-Purchase Industry, Association of Progressive Rental Organizations, 1504 Robin Hood Trail, Austin TX 78703. (800)204-2776. Fax: (512)794-0097. Website: www.aprovision.org. **50% freelance written**. Bimonthly magazine covering the rent-to-own industry. *Progressive Rentals* is the only publication representing the rent-to-own industry and members of APRO. The magazine covers timely news and features affecting the industry, association activities, and member profiles. Awarded best 4-color magazine by the American Society of Association Executives in 1999. Estab. 1980. Circ. 5,500. Byline given. Pays on acceptance. Offers 25% kill fee. Publishes ms an average of 2 months after acceptance. Buys first North American serial rights. Editorial lead time 2 months. Submit seasonal material 4 months in advance. Accepts queries by mail, e-mail, fax, phone. Accepts simultaneous submissions. Responds in 1 month to queries. Responds in 2 months to mss. Sample copy free.

Nonfiction Needs expose, general interest, how-to, inspirational, interview, technical, industry features. **Buys 12 mss/year.** Query with published clips. Length: 1,200-2,500 words. **Pays $150-700.** Sometimes pays expenses of writers on assignment.

$$ RETAIL INFO SYSTEMS NEWS

Essential Insight For Retailers, Edgell Communications, 4 Middlebury Blvd., Randolph NJ 07869. (973)607-1300. Fax: (973)607-1395. Website: www.risnews.com. **65% freelance written**. Monthly magazine covering retail technology. Readers are functional managers/executives in all types of retail and consumer goods firms. They are making major improvements in company operations and in alliances with customers/suppliers. Estab. 1988. Circ. 22,000. Byline sometimes given. Pays on publication. No kill fee. Publishes ms an average of 2 months after acceptance. Buys first North American serial rights, buys second serial (reprint) rights, buys electronic rights, buys all rights. Editorial lead time 3 months. Submit seasonal material 3 months in advance. Accepts queries by mail. Sample copy available online.

Nonfiction Needs essays, expose, how-to, humor, interview, technical. **Buys 80 mss/year.** Query with published clips. Length: 700-1,900 words. **Pays $600-1,200 for assigned articles.** Sometimes pays expenses of writers on assignment.

Photos State availability of or send photos. Identification of subjects required. Negotiates payment individually. Buys one-time rights plus reprint, if applicable.

Columns/Departments News/trends (analysis of current events), 150-300 words. **Buys 4 mss/year.** Query with published clips. **Pays $100-300.**

Tips Case histories about companies achieving substantial results using advanced management practices and/or advanced technology are best.

$$ RETAILERS + RESOURCES

CBA Service Corp., P.O. Box 62000, Colorado Springs CO 80962. Fax: (719)272-3510. E-mail: ksamuelson@cbaonline.org. Website: www.cbaonline.org. **30% freelance written**. Monthly magazine covering the Christian retail industry. "Writers must have knowledge of and direct experience in the Christian retail industry. Subject matter must specifically pertain to the Christian retail audience." Estab. 1968. Byline given. Pays on publication. No kill fee. Publishes ms an average of 3 months after acceptance. Buys all rights. Editorial lead time 3 months. Submit seasonal material 6 months in advance. Accepts queries by e-mail. Responds in 2 months to queries. Sample copy for $9.50 or online.

Nonfiction Buys 24 mss/year. Query. Length: 750-1,500 words. **Pays 30¢/word.**

Tips "Only experts on Christian retail industry, completely familiar with retail audience and their needs and considerations, should submit a query. Do not submit articles unless requested."

$$ SECURITY DEALER

Cygnus Publishing, 445 Broad Hollow Rd., Melville NY 11747. (631)845-2700. Fax: (631)845-2376. E-mail: susan.brady@secdealer.com. **25% freelance written**. Monthly magazine for electronic alarm dealers, burglary and fire installers, with technical, business, sales and marketing information. Circ. 25,000. Byline sometimes given. Pays 3 weeks after publication. No kill fee. Publishes ms an average of 4 months after acceptance. Buys first North American serial rights. Accepts simultaneous submissions.

Nonfiction Needs how-to, interview, technical. No consumer pieces. Query by mail only. Length: 1,000-3,000 words. **Pays $300 for assigned articles. Pays $100-200 for unsolicited articles.** Sometimes pays expenses of writers on assignment.

Photos State availability. Captions, identification of subjects required. Reviews contact sheets, transparencies. Offers $25 additional payment for photos accepted with ms.

Columns/Departments Closed Circuit TV, Access Control (both on application, installation, new products), 500-1,000 words. **Buys 25 mss/year.** Query by mail only. **Pays $100-150.**

Tips The areas of our publication most open to freelancers are technical innovations, trends in the alarm industry, and crime patterns as related to the business as well as business finance and management pieces.

$$ SMART BUSINESS

Smart Business Network, Inc., 835 Sharon Dr., Cleveland OH 44145. (440)250-7000. Fax: (440)250-7001. E-mail: dsklein@sbnonline.com. Website: www.sbnonline.com. **Contact:** Dustin S. Klein, executive editor. **5% freelance written**. Monthly business magazine with an audience made up of business owners and top decision makers. *Smart Business* is one of the fastest growing national chains of regional management journals for corporate executives. Every issue delves into the minds of the most innovative executives in each of our regions to report on how market leaders got to the top and what strategies they use to stay there. Estab. 1989. Byline given. Pays on publication. Offers 50% kill fee. Publishes ms an average of 2 months after acceptance. Buys first North American serial rights, buys second serial (reprint) rights, buys electronic rights. Editorial lead time 3 months. Submit seasonal material 3 months in advance. Accepts queries by mail, e-mail. Responds in 2 weeks to queries. Responds in 1 month to mss. Sample copy available online. Guidelines by e-mail.

- Publishes local editions in Dallas, Houston, St. Louis, Northern California, San Diego, Orange County, Tampa Bay/St. Petersburg, Miami, Philadephia, Cincinnati, Detroit, Los Angeles, Broward/ Palm Beach, Cleveland, Akron/Canton, Columbus, Pittsburgh, Atlanta, Chicago, and Indianapolis.

Nonfiction Needs how-to, interview. No breaking news or news features. **Buys 10-12 mss/year.** Query with published clips. Length: 1,150-2,000 words. **Pays $200-500.** Sometimes pays expenses of writers on assignment.

Photos State availability. Identification of subjects required. Reviews negatives, prints. Offers no additional payment for photos accepted with ms. Buys one-time, reprint, or Web rights.

Tips The best way to submit to *Smart Business* is to read us—either online or in print. Remember, our audience is made up of top level business executives and owners.

$$ STAMATS MEETINGS MEDIA

550 Montgomery St., Suite 750, San Francisco CA 94111. Fax: (415)788-1358. E-mail: tyler.davidson@ meetingsmedia.com. Website: www.meetingsmedia.com. **75% freelance written**. Monthly tabloid covering meeting, event, and conference planning. Estab. 1986. Circ. *Meetings East* and *Meetings South* 22,000; *Meetings West* 26,000. Byline given. Pays 1 month after publication. No kill fee. Publishes ms an average of 1 month after acceptance. Buys first North American serial rights, buys electronic rights. Editorial lead time 3 months. Submit seasonal material 3 months in advance. Accepts queries by mail, e-mail, fax. Responds in 3 weeks to queries. Sample copy for sae with 9â—Š13 envelope and 5 First-Class stamps.

Nonfiction Needs how-to, travel, as it pertains to meetings and conventions. No first-person fluff. We are a business magazine. **Buys 150 mss/year.** Query with published clips. Length: 1,200-2,000 words. **Pays $500 flat rate/package.**

Photos State availability. Identification of subjects required. Offers no additional payment for photos accepted with ms. Buys one time rights.

Tips We're always looking for freelance writers who are local to our destination stories. For Site Inspections, get in touch in late September or early October, when we usually have the following year's editorial calendar available.

$ SUPERVISION MAGAZINE

National Research Bureau, 320 Valley St., Burlington IA 52601. (319)752-5415. E-mail: articles@ supervisionmagazine.com. Website: www.national-research-bureau.com. **Contact:** Todd Darnall. **80% freelance written**. Monthly magazine covering management and supervision. *SuperVision Magazine* explains complex issues in a clear and understandable format. Articles written by both experts and scholars provide practical and concise answers to issues facing today's supervisors and managers. Estab. 1939. Circ. 500. Byline given. Pays on acceptance. Publishes ms an average of 1 month after acceptance. Buys all rights. Editorial lead time 1 month. Submit seasonal material 2 months in advance. Accepts queries by e-mail. Sample copy free. Guidelines free and online.

Nonfiction Needs personal experience, "We can use articles dealing with motivation, leadership, human relations and communication." Send complete ms. Length: 1,500-2,000 words. **Pays 4¢/word**

$$ SUSTAINABLE INDUSTRIES

Sustainable Industries Media, LLC, 230 California St., Suite 410, San Francisco CA 94111. (503)226-7798. Fax: (503)226-7917. E-mail: becky@sustainableindustries.com. Website: www.sustainableindustries.com. **Contact:** Becky Brun, editor. **20% freelance written**. Monthly magazine covering environmental innovation in business. "We seek high quality, balanced reporting aimed at business readers. More compelling writing than is typical in standard trade journals." Estab. 2003. Circ. 2,500. Byline sometimes given. Pays on publication. No kill fee. Publishes ms an average of 1-3 months after acceptance. Buys all rights. Editorial lead time 1-2 months. Accepts queries by mail, e-mail, fax. Accepts simultaneous submissions.

Nonfiction Needs general interest, how-to, interview, new product, opinion, news briefs. Special issues: Themes rotate on the following topics: Agriculture & Natural Resources; Green Building; Energy; Government; Manufacturing & Technology; Retail & Service; Transportation & Tourism—though all topics are covered in each issue. No prosaic essays or extra-long pieces. Query with published clips. Length: 500-1,500 words. **Pays $0-500.**

Photos State availability. Reviews prints, GIF/JPEG files. Offers no additional payment for photos accepted with ms. Buys all rights.

Columns/Departments Guest columns accepted, but not compensated. Business trade columns on specific industries, 500-1,000 words. Query.

$$ VENECONOMY/VENECONOMA

VenEconoma, Edificio Gran Sabana, Piso 1, Avendia Abraham Lincoln No. 174, Blvd. de Sabana Grande, Caracas Venezuela. (58)(212)761-8121. Fax: (58)(212)762-8160. E-mail: mercadeo@veneconomia.com. Website: www.veneconomÃŒa.com; www.veneconomy.com. **70% freelance written**. Monthly business magazine covering business, political and social issues in Venezuela. *VenEconomy*'s subscribers are mostly businesspeople, both Venezuelans and foreigners doing business in Venezuela. Some academics and diplomats also read our magazine. The magazine is published monthly both in English and Spanish—freelancers may query us in either language. Our slant is decidedly pro-business, but not dogmatically conservative. Development, human rights, political and environmental issues are covered from a business-friendly angle. Estab. 1983. Byline given. Pays on publication. Offers 50% kill fee. Publishes ms an average of 1 month after acceptance. Makes work-for-hire assignments. Editorial lead time 1-2 months. Submit seasonal material 1 month in advance. Accepts queries by e-mail. Accepts simultaneous submissions. Responds in 2 weeks to queries. Responds in 4 months to mss. Sample copy by e-mail.

Nonfiction Contact: Francisco Toro, political editor. Needs essays, expose, interview, new product, opinion. No first-person stories or travel articles. **Buys 50 mss/year.** Query. Length: 1,100-3,200 words. **Pays 10-15¢/word for assigned articles.** Sometimes pays expenses of writers on assignment.

Tips Venezuela tie-in is absolutely indispensable. While most of our readers are businesspeople, *VenEconomy* does not limit itself strictly to business-magazine fare. Our aim is to give our readers a sophisticated understanding of the main issues affecting the country as a whole. Stories about successful Venezuelan companies, or foreign companies doing business successfully with Venezuela are particularly welcome. Stories about the oil-sector, especially as it relates to Venezuela, are useful. Other promising topics for freelancers outside Venezuela include international trade and trade negotiations, US-Venezuela bilateral diplomatic relations, international investors' perceptions of business prospects in Venezuela, and international organizations' assessments of environmental, human rights, or democracy and development issues in Venezuela, etc. Both straight reportage and somewhat more opinionated pieces are acceptable, articles that straddle the borderline between reportage and opinion are best. Before querying, ask yourself: Would this be of interest to me if I was doing business in or with Venezuela?

$$$ WORLD TRADE

20900 Farnsleigh Rd., Shaker Heights OH 44122. (424)634-2499. E-mail: laras@worldtradewt100.com. Website: www.worldtrademag.com. **50% freelance written**. Monthly magazine covering international business. Estab. 1988. Circ. 75,000. Byline given. Pays on publication. No kill fee. Publishes ms an average of 1 month after acceptance. Buys all rights. Editorial lead time 3 months. Accepts queries by mail, fax.

Nonfiction See our editorial calendar online. Needs interview, technical, market reports, finance, logistics. **Buys 40-50 mss/year.** Query with published clips. Length: 450-1,500 words. **Pays 50¢/word.**

Photos State availability. Identification of subjects required. Reviews transparencies, prints. Negotiates payment individually. Buys all rights.

Columns/Departments International Business Services, 800 words; Shipping, Supply Chain Management, Logistics, 800 words; Software & Technology, 800 words; Economic Development (US, International), 800 words. **Buys 40-50 mss/year. Pays 50¢/word.**

Tips We seek writers with expertise in their subject areas, as well as solid researching and writing skills. We want analysts more than reporters. We don't accept unsolicited manuscripts, and we don't want phone calls. Please read *World Trade* before sending a query.

Church Administration & Ministry

THE AFRICAN AMERICAN PULPIT

P.O. Box 381587, Germantown TN 38183. Website: www.theafricanamericanpulpit.com. **100% freelance written**. Quarterly magazine covering African American preaching. "*The African American Pulpit* (TAAP)

is a quarterly journal that serves as a repository for the very best of African American preaching and provides practical and creative resources for persons in ministry." Estab. 1997. Circ. 3,000. Byline always given. Pays on publication. No kill fee. Publishes ms an average of 6 months after acceptance. Editorial lead time 9 months. Submit seasonal material 1 year in advance. Accepts queries by mail, e-mail, fax, phone. Accepts simultaneous submissions. Guidelines available online.
Nonfiction Sermons and articles relating to African American preaching and the African American Church. Needs book excerpts, essays, how-to, craft a sermon, inspirational, interview, opinion, religious. **Buys 60 mss/year.** Send complete ms. Length: 1,500-3,000 words.

$ CHRISTIAN COMMUNICATOR

9118 W. Elmwood Dr., #1G, Niles IL 60714-5820. (847)296-3964. Fax: (847)296-0754. E-mail: ljohnson@wordprocommunications.com. Website: www.wordprocommunications.com. **Contact:** Lin Johnson, managing editor. **90% freelance written**. Monthly magazine covering Christian writing and speaking. Circ. 4,000. Byline given. Pays on publication. No kill fee. Publishes ms an average of 6-12 months after acceptance. Buys first rights, buys second serial (reprint) rights. Editorial lead time 3 months. Submit seasonal material 9 months in advance. Accepts queries by e-mail. Responds in 4-6 weeks to queries. Responds in 6-8 weeks to mss. Sample copy for SAE and 5 first-class stamps. Writer's guidelines for SASE or by e-mail. Also online.
Nonfiction Needs how-to, interview, opinion, book reviews. **Buys 90 mss/year.** Query or send complete ms only by e-mail. Length: 650-1,000 words. **Pays $10. $5 for reviews. ACW CD for anecdotes**
Columns/Departments Speaking, 650-1,000 words. **Buys 11 mss/year.** Query. **Pays $10.**
Poetry Needs free verse, light verse, traditional. Buys 22 poems/year. Submit maximum 3 poems. Length: 4-20 lines. **Pays $5.**
Fillers Needs anecdotes, short humor. Buys 10-30 mss/year. Length: 75-300 words. **Pays CD.**
Tips "We primarily use 'how to' articles and personality features on experienced writers and editors. However, we're willing to look at any other pieces geared to the writing life."

THE CHRISTIAN LIBRARIAN

Association of Christian Librarians, Ryan Library/PLNU, 3900 Lomaland Dr., San Diego CA 92106. E-mail: info@acl.org. Website: www.acl.org. **Contact:** Anne-Elizabeth Powell, editor-in-chief. **80% freelance written**. Magazine published 3 times/year covering Christian librarianship in higher education. *The Christian Librarian* is directed to Christian librarians in institutions of higher learning and publishes articles on Christian interpretation of librarianship, theory and practice of library science, bibliographic essays, reviews, and human-interest articles relating to books and libraries. Estab. 1956. Circ. 800. Byline given. No kill fee. Acquires first rights. Editorial lead time 3 months. Accepts queries by e-mail. Responds in 1 month to mss. Sample copy for $5. Guidelines free.
Nonfiction Needs how-to, librarianship, technical, bibliographic essays. No articles on faith outside the realm of librarianship or articles based on specific church denomination. Do not send book reviews that haven't been requested by the Review Editor. Send complete ms. Deadlines are: Nov. 15, Feb. 15, July 15 Length: 1,000-5,000 words.

$ THE CLERGY JOURNAL

Personal and Professional Development for Pastors and Church Administrators, Logos Productions, Inc., 6160 Carmen Ave. E., Inver Grove Heights MN 55076. E-mail: editorial@logosstaff.com. Website: www.logosproductions.com. **Contact:** Rebecca Grothe, editor. **98% freelance written**. Magazine published 9 times/year covering articles for continuing education and practical help for Christian clergy who are currently serving congregations. "The focus of *The Clergy Journal* is personal and professional development for clergy. Each issue focuses on a current topic related to ministers and the church, and also includes preaching illustrations, sermons, and worship aids based on the Revised Common Lectionary. There is an insert in each issue on financial management topics. Most readers are from mainline Protestant traditions, especially Methodist, Presbyterian, Lutheran, and United Church of Christ." Estab. 1924. Circ. 6,000. Byline given. Pays on publication. No kill fee. Publishes ms an average of 9 months after acceptance. Buys first rights. Makes work-for-hire assignments. Editorial lead time 4 months. Submit seasonal material 9 months in advance. Accepts queries by e-mail. Responds in 2 weeks to queries. Responds in 2 months to mss. Sample copy free. Guidelines by e-mail.
Nonfiction "We are seeking articles that address current issues of interest to Christian clergy; emphasis on practical help for parish pastors." Needs religious. **Buys 90 mss/year.** Query or send complete ms. Length: 1,200-1,500 words. **Pays $125 for assigned articles.**

Tips "Here are my 4 'pet peeves' as an editor: 1. Manuscripts that are over the word count. 2. Manuscripts that do not respect the reader. 3. Manuscripts that are not well organized. 4. Manuscripts that do not have an appropriate 'human touch.'"

$ $ GROUP MAGAZINE

Group Publishing, Inc., P.O. Box 481, Loveland CO 80539-0481. E-mail: sfirestone@group.com. Website: www.groupmag.com. **Contact:** Scott Firestone IV. **50% freelance written**. Bimonthly magazine for Christian youth workers. "*Group* is the interdenominational magazine for leaders of Christian youth groups. *Group*'s purpose is to supply ideas, practical help, inspiration, and training for youth leaders." Estab. 1974. Circ. 55,000. Byline sometimes given. Pays on acceptance. No kill fee. Buys all rights. Editorial lead time 4 months. Submit seasonal material 5 months in advance. Accepts queries by mail, e-mail, fax. Responds in 8-10 weeks to queries. Responds in 2 months to mss. Sample copy for $2, plus 10 × 12 SAE and 3 first-class stamps. Guidelines available online.

Nonfiction "GROUP needs articles on successful youth ministry strategies, including youth-led ministry ideas, understanding kids & youth culture, recruiting/training/keeping adult leaders, family ministry, staff issues, serving and training parents, professionalism, and self-nurture. How-to articles on personal spiritual growth, time management, issues vital to working with young people, leadership skills (listening, discussion-leading), worship ideas, handling specific group problems, fun & experiential programming ideas, and active-learning meeting plans and retreats." Needs inspirational, personal experience, religious. No fiction, prose, or poetry. **Buys 30 mss/year.** Query. Length: 200-2,000 words. **Pays $50-250.** Sometimes pays expenses of writers on assignment.

Columns/Departments "Try This One" section needs short ideas (100-250 words) for youth group use. These include games, fund-raisers, crowdbreakers, Bible studies, helpful hints, outreach ideas, and discussion starters. "Hands-on Help" section needs mini-articles (100-350 words) that feature practical tips for youth leaders on working with students, adult leaders, and parents. **Pays $50.**

Tips "We are always looking for submissions for short, novel, practical ideas that have worked in actual youth ministry settings. It's best to familiarize yourself with *Group Magazine* before sending in ideas for our departments."

$ $ THE JOURNAL OF ADVENTIST EDUCATION

General Conference of SDA, 12501 Old Columbia Pike, Silver Spring MD 20904-6600. (301)680-5069. Fax: (301)622-9627. E-mail: rumbleb@gc.adventist.org. Website: http://jae.education.org. **Contact:** Beverly J. Robinson-Rumble, editor. Bimonthly (except skips issue in summer) professional journal covering teachers and administrators in Seventh Day Adventist school systems. Estab. 1939. Circ. 10,500. Byline given. Pays on publication. No kill fee. Publishes ms an average of 1 year after acceptance. Buys first rights. Editorial lead time 1 year. Accepts queries by mail, e-mail, fax, phone. Responds in 6 weeks to queries. Responds in 4 months to mss. Sample copy for sae with 10 × 12 envelope and 5 First-Class stamps. Guidelines available online.

Nonfiction Theme issues have assigned authors. Needs book excerpts, essays, how-to, education-related, personal experience, photo feature, religious, education. "No brief first-person stories about Sunday Schools." Query. Length: 1,000-1,500 words. **Pays $25-300.**

Reprints Send tearsheet or photocopy and information about when and where the material previously appeared.

Photos Submit glossy prints, high resolution (300 dpi) scans or digital photos in TIFF/JPEG format. No PowerPoint presentations or photos imbedded in Word documents. Include photo of author with submission. State availability of or send photos. Captions required. Negotiates payment individually. Buys one time rights.

Tips "Articles may deal with educational theory or practice, although the *Journal* seeks to emphasize the practical. Articles dealing with the creative and effective use of methods to enhance teaching skills or learning in the classroom are especially welcome. Whether theoretical or practical, such essays should demonstrate the skillful integration of Seventh-day Adventist faith/values and learning."

JOURNAL OF CHURCH AND STATE

Oxford University Press, 2001 Evans Rd., Cary NC 27513. Website: www.oxfordjournals.org/our_journals/jcs/. Dr. Christopher Marsh, ed. **Contact:** Elizabeth Gardner. Journal covering law, social studies, religion, philosophy, and history. "The Journal is concerned with what has been called the 'greatest subject in the history of the West.' It seeks to stimulate interest, dialogue, research, and publication in the broad area of religion and the state. JCS publishes constitutional, historical, philosophical, theological, and sociological studies on religion and the body politic in various countries and cultures of the world, including the US. Each issue features, in addition to a timely editorial, 5 or more major articles, and 35-40 reviews of significant books related to church and state. Periodically, important ecclesiastical documents and government texts of legislation and/or court decisions are also published. Regular features include 'Notes on Church State Affairs', which reports current developments throughout the world, and a list of 'Recent Doctoral Dissertations in Church and State.'" Estab. 1959. Accepts queries by online submission form. See guidelines online.

Nonfiction Needs essays, historical, religious, law.

$$ LEADERSHIP JOURNAL

Real Ministry in a Complex World, Christianity Today International, 465 Gundersen Dr., Carol Stream IL 60188. (630)260-6200. Fax: (630)260-0114. E-mail: ljeditor@leadershipjournal.net. Website: www.leadershipjournal.net. Skye Jethani, managing editor. **Contact:** Marshall Shelley, editor-in-chief. **75% freelance written. Works with a small number of new/unpublished writers each year**. Quarterly magazine. "Writers must have a knowledge of and sympathy for the unique expectations placed on pastors and local church leaders. Each article must support points by illustrating from real life experiences in local churches." Estab. 1980. Circ. 48,000. Byline given. Pays on acceptance. Offers 33% kill fee. Publishes ms an average of 6 months after acceptance. Buys first rights, buys electronic rights. Editorial lead time 6 months. Submit seasonal material 6 months in advance. Accepts queries by mail, e-mail, fax. Responds in 3 weeks to queries. Responds in 2 months to mss. Sample copy for free or online.

Nonfiction Needs how-to, humor, interview, personal experience, sermon illustrations. No articles from writers who have never read our journal. No unsolicited ms. **Buys 60 mss/year.** Query with proposal. Length: 300-3,000 words. **Pays $35-400.** Sometimes pays expenses of writers on assignment.

Columns/Departments Contact: Skye Jethanis, managing editor. Toolkit (book/software reviews), 500 words. **Buys 8 mss/year.** Query.

Tips "Every article in *Leadership* must provide practical help for problems that church leaders face. *Leadership* articles are not essays expounding a topic or editorials arguing a position or homilies explaining Biblical principles. They are how-to articles, based on first-person accounts of real-life experiences in ministry. They allow our readers to see 'over the shoulder' of a colleague in ministry who then reflects on those experiences and identifies the lessons learned. As you know, a magazine's slant is a specific personality that readers expect (and it's what they've sent us their subscription money to provide). Our style is that of friendly conversation rather than directive discourse—what I learned about local church ministry rather than what you need to do."

$$ OUTREACH MAGAZINE

Outreach Inc., 2230 Oak Ridge Way, Vista CA 92081-8341. (760)940-0600. Fax: (760)597-2314. E-mail: lwarren@outreach.com. Website: www.outreachmagazine.com. **80% freelance written**. Bimonthly magazine designed to inspire, challenge and equip churches and church leaders to reach out to their communities with the love of Jesus Christ. Circ. 30,000. Byline given. Pays on publication. Offers 10% kill fee. Publishes ms an average of 2 months after acceptance. Buys first North American serial rights, buys electronic rights. Editorial lead time 6 months. Submit seasonal material 6 months in advance. Accepts queries by mail, e-mail, fax. Accepts previously published material. Accepts simultaneous submissions. Responds in 2 months to queries. Responds in 8 months to mss. Sample copy and writer's guidelines free.

Nonfiction Needs book excerpts, how-to, humor, inspirational, interview, personal experience, photo feature, religious. Special issues: Vacation Bible School (January); America's Fastest Growing Churches (July/August 2005). Does not want fiction, poetry, or non-outreach-related articles. **Buys 30 mss/year.** Query with published clips. Length: 1,200-2,000 words. **Pays $375-600 for assigned articles. Pays $375-400 for unsolicited articles.** Pays some expenses Limit agreed upon in advance.

Photos Contact: Christi Riddell, lead designer. Send photos. Identification of subjects required. Reviews GIF/JPEG files. Negotiates payment individually. Buys all rights.

Columns/Departments Outreach Pulse (short stories about outreach-oriented churches and ministries), 75-250 words; Questions & Perspectives (first-person expert perspective on a question related to outreach), 300-400 words; Soulfires (interview piece with a person about the stories and people that have fueled their passion for outreach), 900 words; From the Front Line (profile of a church that is using a transferable idea for outreach), 800 words plus sidebars; Sounourners (short interviews with everyday people about the stories and people that have informed their worldview and faith perspective), 800 words; Frames (short personality profiles); POV (2-page interview with a significant voice in the church). **Buys at least 6 mss/year.** Query with published clips. **Pays $100-375.**

Fillers Needs facts, gags. Buys 2 mss/year. Length: 25-100 words. **Payment is negotiated.**
Tips Study our writer's guidelines. Send published clips that showcase tight, bright writing, as well as your ability to interview, research, organize numerous sources into an article, and write a 100-word piece as well as a 1,600-word piece.

$ $ THE PRIEST

Our Sunday Visitor, Inc., 200 Noll Plaza, Huntington IN 46750-4304. (800)348-2440. Fax: (260)359-9117. E-mail: tpriest@osv.com. Website: www.osv.com. **Contact:** Editorial Dept. **40% freelance written**. Monthly magazine. We run articles that will aid priests in their day-to-day ministry. Includes items on spirituality, counseling, administration, theology, personalities, the saints, etc. Byline given. Pays on acceptance. No kill fee. Buys first North American serial rights. Editorial lead time 3 months. Submit seasonal material 4 months in advance. Accepts queries by mail, e-mail, fax, phone. Responds in 5 weeks to queries. Responds in 3 months to mss. Sample copy and writer's guidelines free.
Nonfiction Needs essays, historical, humor, inspirational, interview, opinion, personal experience, photo feature, religious. **Buys 96 mss/year.** Send complete ms. Length: 1,500 words. **Pays $200 minimum for assigned articles. Pays $50 minimum for unsolicited articles.**
Photos Send photos. Captions, identification of subjects required. Reviews transparencies, prints. Negotiates payment individually. Buys one time rights.
Columns/Departments Viewpoints (whatever applies to priests and the Church); 1,000 words or less; send complete manuscript
Tips Please do not stray from the magisterium of the Catholic Church.

$ $ REV! MAGAZINE

P.O. Box 481, Loveland CO 80539-0481. (970)669-3836. Fax: (970)292-4373. E-mail: lsparks@group.com. Website: www.revmagazine.com. **25% freelance written**. Bimonthly magazine for pastors. We offer practical solutions to revolutionize and revitalize ministry. Estab. 1997. Circ. 45,000. Byline given. Pays on acceptance. No kill fee. Publishes ms an average of 6 months after acceptance. Makes work-for-hire assignments. Editorial lead time 6 months. Submit seasonal material 8 months in advance. Accepts queries by mail, e-mail. Responds in 2 months to queries. Guidelines available online.
Nonfiction Ministry, leadership, and personal articles with practical application. No devotions, articles for church members, theological pieces. **Buys 18-24 mss/year.** Query or send complete ms. Length: 1,800-2,000 words. **Pays $300-400.**
Columns/Departments Work (preaching, worship, discipleship, outreach, church business & administration, leadership); Life (personal growth, pastor's family); Culture (trends, facts), all 250-3,000 words. **Buys 25 mss/year.** Send complete ms. **Pays $100-500.**
Fillers Buys 3 mss/year. Pays $50.
Tips We are looking for creative and practical ideas that pastors and other leaders of churches of all sizes can use.

$ TEACHERS INTERACTION

Concordia Publishing House, 3558 S. Jefferson Ave., St. Louis MO 63118-3968. (314)268-1083. Fax: (314)268-1329. E-mail: tom.nummela@cph.org. **5% freelance written**. Quarterly magazine of practical, inspirational, theological articles for volunteer Sunday school teachers. "Material must be true to the doctrines of the Lutheran Church—Missouri Synod." Estab. 1960. Circ. 6,000. Byline given. Pays on publication. No kill fee. Publishes ms an average of 1 year after acceptance. Buys all rights. Submit seasonal material 1 year in advance. Accepts queries by mail, e-mail, fax. Responds in 3 weeks to mss. Sample copy for $5.50. Guidelines for #10 SASE.
Nonfiction Needs how-to, practical help/ideas used successfully in own classroom, inspirational, to the church school worker—must be in accordance with LCMS doctrine, personal experience, of Sunday School teachers. No freelance theological articles. **Buys 6 mss/year.** Send complete ms. Length: 1,200 words. **Pays up to $120.**
Fillers *Teachers Interaction* buys short 'Toolbox' items—activities and ideas planned and used successfully in a church school classroom. **Buys 48 mss/year.** 200 words maximum. **Pays $20-40.**
Tips "Practical or 'it happened to me' articles would have the best chance. Also short items—ideas used in classrooms; seasonal and in conjunction with our Sunday school material. Our format emphasizes volunteer Sunday school teachers."

$$ TODAY'S CATHOLIC TEACHER

Peter Li Education Group, 2621 Dryden Rd., Suite 300, Dayton OH 45439. (937)293-1415. Fax: (937)293-1310. E-mail: mnoschang@peterli.com. Website: www.catholicteacher.com. **60% freelance written.** Magazine published 6 times/year during school year covering Catholic education for grades K-12. "We look for topics of interest and practical help to teachers in Catholic elementary schools in all curriculum areas including religion technology, discipline, motivation." Estab. 1972. Circ. 50,000. Byline given. Pays on publication. No kill fee. Publishes ms an average of 2 months after acceptance. Buys first and all rights and makes work-for-hire assignments. Editorial lead time 3 months. Submit seasonal material 6 months in advance. Accepts queries by mail, e-mail, fax. Accepts simultaneous submissions. Responds in 1 month to queries. Responds in 3 months to mss. Sample copy for $3 or on website. Guidelines available online.

Nonfiction Interested in articles detailing ways to incorporate Catholic values into academic subjects other than religion class. Needs essays, how-to, humor, interview, personal experience. No articles pertaining to public education. **Buys 15 mss/year.** Query or send complete ms. Length: 1,500-3,000 words. **Pays $150-300.** Sometimes pays expenses of writers on assignment.

Photos State availability. Captions, identification of subjects, model releases required. Reviews transparencies, prints. Offers $20-50/photo. Buys one time rights.

Tips "Although our readership is primarily classroom teachers, *Today's Catholic Teacher* is also read by principals, supervisors, superintendents, boards of education, pastors, and parents. *Today's Catholic Teacher* aims to be for Catholic educators a source of information not available elsewhere. The focus of articles should span the interests of teachers from early childhood through junior high. Articles may be directed to just one age group, yet have wider implications. Preference is given to material directed to teachers in grades 4-8. The desired magazine style is direct, concise, informative, and accurate. Writing should be enjoyable to read, informal rather than scholarly, lively, and free of educational jargon."

$$$ WORSHIP LEADER MAGAZINE

32234 Paseo Adelanto, Suite A, San Juan Capistrano CA 92675. (949)240-9339. Fax: (949)240-0038. E-mail: jeremy@wlmag.com. Website: www.worshipleader.com. **Contact:** Jeremy Armstrong, managing editor. **80% freelance written.** Bimonthly magazine covering all aspects of Christian worship. *Worship Leader Magazine* exists to challenge, serve, equip, and train those involved in leading the 21st century church in worship. The intended readership is the worship team (all those who plan and lead) of the local church. Estab. 1990. Circ. 40,000. Byline given. Pays on publication. Offers 50% kill fee. Buys first North American serial rights, buys all rights. Editorial lead time 3 months. Submit seasonal material 6 months in advance. Responds in 6 weeks to queries. Responds in 3 months to mss. Sample copy for $5. Guidelines available online.

> O‑ "Worship Leader magazine does not accept unsolicited articles for the print version of the magazine. However we do accept submissions for our Web properties. This is often the first step in creating a relationship with us and our readers, which could lead to more involvement as a writer. Web articles should be between 700 and 900 words and have beneficial qualities to a person who is involved in creating devotional arts or planning a service of worship. Web articles are published on a gratis basis. Please send finished articles to Jeremy Armstrong, jeremy@wlmag.com and potential articles to feedback@wlmag.com.

Nonfiction Needs general interest, how-to, related to purpose/audience, inspirational, interview, opinion. **Buys 15-30 mss/year.** Query with published clips. Length: 1,200-2,000 words. **Pays $200-800 for assigned articles. Pays $200-500 for unsolicited articles.** Sometimes pays expenses of writers on assignment.

Photos State availability. Identification of subjects required. Negotiate payment individually. Buys one time rights.

Tips Our goal has been and is to provide the tools and information pastors, worship leaders, and ministers of music, youth, and the arts need to facilitate and enhance worship in their churches. In achieving this goal, we strive to maintain high journalistic standards, Biblical soundness, and theological neutrality. Our intent is to present the philosophical, scholarly insight on worship, as well as the day-to-day, 'putting it all together' side of worship, while celebrating our unity and diversity.

$$ YOUR CHURCH

Helping You With the Business of Ministry, Christianity Today International, 465 Gundersen Dr., Carol Stream IL 60188. (630)260-6200. Fax: (630)260-0451. E-mail: yceditor@yourchurch.net. Website: www.yourchurch.net. **Contact:** Matt Branaugh, editor. **5-10.** Bimonthly magazine covering church administration and products. Articles pertain to the business aspects of ministry pastors are called upon to perform: administration, purchasing, management, technology, building, etc. Estab. 1955. Circ. 75,000 (controlled). Byline given. Pays on acceptance. No kill fee. Publishes ms an average of 3-4 months after acceptance. Buys first rights, buys electronic rights. Editorial lead time 6 weeks. Submit seasonal material 5 months in advance. Accepts queries by mail, .e-mail, fax. Accepts previously published material. Responds in 1 month to queries. Responds in 3 months to mss. Sample copy for sae with 9 × 12 envelope and 4 First-Class stamps. Guidelines free.

Nonfiction Needs how-to, new product, technical. **Buys 50-60 mss/year.** Send complete ms. Length: 1,000-4,000 words. **Pays 15-20¢/word.** Sometimes pays expenses of writers on assignment.

Tips The editorial is generally geared toward brief and helpful articles dealing with some form of church business. Concise, bulleted points from experts in the field are typical for our articles. "Most content is obtained by assignment from the managing editor. Note that we work several months in advance, and assignments are given four months before the issue date. If you are interested in freelance writing for Your Church, tell us about your writing experience and any special knowledge or interests you have related to our content. Include a sample of your writing, or links to online publications. Your Church will review unsolicited manuscripts, but only rarely do they fit our editorial plans. We welcome your article ideas that fit with our editorial plans."

$ YOUTH AND CHRISTIAN EDUCATION LEADERSHIP

Pathway Press, 1080 Montgomery Ave., Cleveland TN 37311. (800)553-8506. Fax: (800)546-7590. E-mail: tammy_hatfield@pathwaypress.org. Website: www.pathwaypress.org. **Contact:** Jonathan Martin, editor. **25% freelance written**. Quarterly magazine covering Christian education. *Youth and Christian Education Leadership* is written for teachers, youth pastors, children's pastors, and other local Christian education workers. Estab. 1976. Circ. 12,000. Pays on publication. No kill fee. Publishes ms an average of 6 months after acceptance. Buys first or one-time rights. Editorial lead time 3 months. Submit seasonal material 6 months in advance. Accepts queries by mail, e-mail. Accepts simultaneous submissions. Responds in 3 months to mss. Sample copy for $1.25 and 9 × 12 SASE. Writer's guidelines online or by e-mail.

Nonfiction Needs how-to, humor, in-class experience, inspire, interview, motivational, seasonal short skits. **Buys 16 mss/year.** Send complete ms; include SSN. Send SASE for return of ms. Internet submissions are accepted. They should be sent as attachments to e-mail and not as part of the e-mail message itself. The submissions address is: jonathanm@renovatuscommunity.com. Length: 500-1,000 words. **Pays $25-50.**

Reprints Send typed, double-spaced ms with rights for sale and information about when and where the material previously appeared. Pays 80% of amount paid for an original article.

Photos State availability. Reviews contact sheets, transparencies. Negotiates payment individually. Buys one-time rights.

Columns/Departments Sunday School Leadership; Reaching Out (creative evangelism); The Pastor and Christian Education; Preschool; Elementary; Teen; Adult; Drawing Closer; Kids Church, all 500-1,000 words. Send complete ms with SASE. **Pays $25-50.**

Tips "Become familiar with the publication's content and submit appropriate material. We are continually looking for 'fresh ideas' that have proven to be successful."

$ $ YOUTHWORKER JOURNAL

Salem Publishing, 104 Woodmont Blvd., Suite 150-1, Brentwood TN 37027. E-mail: articles@youthworker.com. Website: www.youthworker.com. **Contact:** Steve Rabey, editor. **100% freelance written**. Website and bimonthly magazine covering professional youth ministry in the church and parachurch. "We exist to help meet the personal and professional needs of career, Christian youth workers in the church and parachurch. Proposals accepted on the posted theme, according to the writer's guidelines on our website. It's not enough to write well—you must know youth ministry." Estab. 1984. Circ. 20,000. Byline given. Pays on publication. No kill fee. Publishes ms an average of 3 months after acceptance. Articles must be first published with us, and we buy unrestricted use for print and electronic media. Editorial lead time 6 months. Submit seasonal material 6 months in advance. Accepts queries by e-mail, online submission form. Responds in 6 months to queries. Sample copy for $5. Guidelines available online.

Nonfiction Needs essays, new product, youth ministry books only, personal experience, photo feature, religious. Query. Length: 250-3,000 words. **Pays $50-200.** Sometimes pays expenses of writers on assignment.

Photos Send photos. Reviews GIF/JPEG files. Negotiates payment individually.

Clothing

$$$ FOOTWEAR PLUS

Symphony Publishing, 8 W. 38th St., New York NY 10018. (646)278-1550. Fax: (646)278-1553. E-mail: nyeditorial@symphonypublishing.com. Website: www.footwearplusmagazine.com. **20% freelance written**. Monthly magazine covering footwear fashion and business. "A business-to-business publication targeted at footwear retailers. Covering all categories of footwear and age ranges with a focus on new trends, brands and consumer buying habits, as well as retailer advice on operating the store more effectively." Estab. 1990. Circ. 18,000. Byline given. Pays on publication. No kill fee. Publishes ms an average of 1-2 months after acceptance. Buys second serial (reprint) rights, buys electronic rights. Editorial lead time 1-2 months. Accepts queries by e-mail. Sample copy for $5.

Nonfiction Needs interview, new product, technical. Does not want pieces unrelated to footwear/fashion industry. **Buys 10-20 mss/year.** Query. Length: 500-2,500 words. **Pays $1,000 maximum.** Sometimes pays expenses of writers on assignment.

$$ MADE TO MEASURE

Halper Publishing Co., 633 Skokie Blvd. #490, Northbrook IL 60062. Fax: (847)780-2902. E-mail: mtm@halper.com. Website: www.madetomeasuremag.com. **50% freelance written**. Semiannual magazine covering uniforms and career apparel. A semi-annual magazine/buyers' reference containing leading sources of supply, equipment, and services of every description related to the Uniform, Career Apparel, and allied trades, throughout the entire US. Estab. 1930. Circ. 25,000. Byline given. Pays on acceptance. No kill fee. Publishes ms an average of 2 months after acceptance. Buys first North American serial rights. Editorial lead time 4 months. Submit seasonal material 4 months in advance. Accepts queries by mail, e-mail. Accepts simultaneous submissions. Responds in 3 weeks to queries. Sample copy available online.

Nonfiction Please only consider sending queries related to companies that wear or make uniforms, career apparel, or identify apparel. Needs interview, new product, personal experience, photo feature, technical. **Buys 6-8 mss/year.** Query with published clips. Length: 1,000-3,000 words. **Pays $300-500.** Sometimes pays expenses of writers on assignment.

Photos State availability. Reviews contact sheets, any prints. Negotiates payment individually. Buys one time rights.

Tips We look for features about large and small companies who wear uniforms (restaurants, hotels, industrial, medical, public safety, etc.).

$$ 🌐 TEXTILE WORLD

Billian Publishing Co., 2100 Powers Ferry Rd., Suite 300, Atlanta GA 30339. (770)955-5656. Fax: (770)952-0669. E-mail: editor@textileworld.com. Website: www.textileworld.com. **Contact:** James Borneman, editor-in-chief. **5% freelance written**. Bimonthly magazine covering the business of textile, apparel, and fiber industries with considerable technical focus on products and processes. No puff pieces pushing a particular product. Estab. 1868. Byline given. Pays on publication. No kill fee. Buys first North American serial rights.

Nonfiction Needs technical, business. **Buys 10 mss/year.** Query. 500 words minimum. **Pays $200/published page.**

Photos Send photos. Captions required. Reviews prints. Offers no additional payment for photos accepted with ms. Buys one time rights.

Construction & Contracting

$$ ADVANCED MATERIALS & COMPOSITES NEWS PLUS COMPOSITES ENEWS

International Business & Technology Intelligence on High Performance M&P, Composites Worldwide, Inc., 991-C Lomas Santa Fe Dr., MC469, Solana Beach CA 92075-2125. (858)755-1372. E-mail: info@compositesnews.com. Website: www.compositesnews.com. **1% freelance written**. Bimonthly newsletter covering advanced materials and fiber-reinforced polymer composites, plus a weekly electronic version called *Composite eNews*, reaching over 15,000 subscribers and many more pass-along readers. *Advanced Materials & Composites News* covers markets, applications, materials, processes, and organizations for all sectors of the global hi-tech materials world. Audience is management, academics, researchers, government, suppliers, and fabricators. Focus on news about growth opportunities. Estab. 1978. Circ.

15,000+. Byline sometimes given. Pays on publication. No kill fee. Publishes ms an average of 1 month after acceptance. Buys all rights. Editorial lead time 2 weeks. Submit seasonal material 1 month in advance. Accepts queries by e-mail. Responds in 1 week to queries. Responds in 1 month to mss. Sample copy for #10 SASE.

Nonfiction Needs new product, technical, industry information. **Buys 4-6 mss/year.** Query. 300 words. **Pays $200/final printed page.**

Photos State availability. Captions, identification of subjects, model releases required. Reviews 4 × 5 transparencies, prints, 35mm slides, JPEGs (much preferred). Offers no additional payment for photos accepted with ms. Buys all rights.

$ $ AUTOMATED BUILDER

CMN Associates, Inc., 1445 Donlon St., Suite 16, Ventura CA 93003. (805)642-9735. Fax: (805)642-8820. E-mail: info@automatedbuilder.com. Website: www.automatedbuilder.com. **Contact:** Don O. Carlson, editor and publisher. **10% freelance written**. Monthly magazine specializing in management for industrialized (manufactured) housing and volume home builders. "Our material is technical in content and concerned with new technologies or improved methods for in-plant building and components related to building. Online content is uploaded from the monthly print material." Estab. 1964. Circ. 25,000. Byline given. Pays on acceptance. No kill fee. Publishes ms an average of 3 months after acceptance. Buys first North American serial rights. Editorial lead time 2 months. Submit seasonal material 2 months in advance. Accepts queries by mail, e-mail, fax. Responds in 2 weeks to queries. Sample copy free.

Nonfiction Case history articles on successful home building companies which may be 1) production (big volume) home builders; 2) mobile home manufacturers; 3) modular home manufacturers; 4) prefabricated (panelized) home manufacturers; 5) house component manufacturers; or 6) special unit (in-plant commercial building) manufacturers. Also uses interviews, photo features, and technical articles. "No architect or plan 'dreams.' Housing projects must be built or under construction." **Buys 6-8 mss/year.** Query. Phone queries OK. Length: 250-500 words. **Pays $350 for stories including photos.**

Photos Wants 4 × 5, 5 × 7, or 8 × 10 glossies or disks. State availability. Captions, identification of subjects required. Offers no additional payment for photos accepted with ms.

Tips "Stories often are too long, too loose; we prefer 500-750 words. We prefer a phone query on feature articles. If accepted on query, article usually will not be rejected later."

$ $ BUILDERNEWS MAGAZINE

Pacific NW Sales & Marketing, Inc., 500 W. 8th St., Suite 270, Vancouver WA 98660. (360)906-0793. Fax: (360)906-0794. Website: www.buildernewsmag.com. BUILDERnews is a national trade magazine covering residential to light industrial construction industries in the U.S. Its readers are top executives in residential and commercial construction, design and engineering as well as suppliers who look to the magazine for regional insight and information on construction, tools, materials, management and governmental regulations. Articles must address pressing topics for builders in our region with a special emphasis on the business aspects of construction. Estab. 1996. Circ. 35,000. Byline given. Pays on acceptance of revised ms. No kill fee. Publishes ms an average of 1 month after acceptance. Buys first North American serial rights, buys electronic rights. Editorial lead time 2 months. Submit seasonal material 3 months in advance. Accepts queries by mail, e-mail, fax. Responds in 1 week to queries. Responds in 1 month to mss. Sample copy for free or online. Guidelines free.

Nonfiction Needs how-to, interview, new product, technical. No personal bios unless they teach a valuable lesson to those in the building industry. **Buys 400 mss/year.** Query. Length: 500-2,500 words. **Pays $200-500.** Sometimes pays expenses of writers on assignment.

Photos State availability. Captions, identification of subjects, model releases required. Offers no additional payment for photos accepted with ms. Buys first North American serial and electronic rights.

Columns/Departments Engineering; Construction; Architecture & Design; Tools & Materials; Heavy Equipment; Business & Economics; Legal Matters; E-build; Building Green, all 750-2,500 words. Query.

Tips Writers should have an understanding of the residential building industry and its terminology and be prepared to provide a resume, writing samples, and story synopsis.

$ $ CONCRETE CONSTRUCTION

Hanley-Wood, LLC., 426 S. Westgate St., Addison IL 60101. (630)543-0870. Fax: (630)543-3112. E-mail: preband@hanleywood.com. Website: www.worldofconcrete.com. **20% freelance written**. Monthly magazine for concrete contractors, engineers, architects, specifiers, and others who design and build residential, commercial, industrial, and public works, cast-in-place concrete structures. It also covers job stories and new equipment in the industry. Estab. 1956. Circ. 80,000. Byline given. Pays on acceptance. No kill fee. Publishes ms an average of 4 months after acceptance. Editorial lead time 4 months. Submit seasonal material 4 months in advance. Accepts queries by mail, e-mail, fax. Responds in 2 weeks to queries. Responds in 1 month to mss. Sample copy and writer's guidelines free.

Nonfiction Needs how-to, new product, personal experience, photo feature, technical, job stories. **Buys 7-10 mss/year.** Query with published clips. 2,000 words maximum **Pays $250 or more for assigned articles. Pays $200 minimum for unsolicited articles.** Pays expenses of writers on assignment.

Photos Send photos. Captions required. Reviews contact sheets, negatives, transparencies, prints. Offers no additional payment for photos accepted with ms. Buys one time rights.

Tips Have a good understanding of the concrete construction industry. How-to stories accepted only from industry experts. Job stories must cover procedures, materials, and equipment used as well as the project's scope.

$$$ THE CONCRETE PRODUCER

Hanley-Wood, LLC, 8725 W. Higgins Rd., Suite 600, Chicago IL 60631. (773)824-2400. E-mail: ryelton@hanleywood.com. Website: www.theconcreteproducer.com. **25% freelance written**. Monthly magazine covering concrete production. Our audience consists of producers who have succeeded in making concrete the preferred building material through management, operating, quality control, use of the latest technology, or use of superior materials. Estab. 1982. Circ. 18,000. Byline given. Pays on acceptance. No kill fee. Publishes ms an average of 2 months after acceptance. Editorial lead time 4 months. Accepts queries by mail, e-mail, fax, phone. Responds in 1 week to queries. Responds in 2 months to mss. Sample copy for $4. Guidelines free.

Nonfiction Needs how-to, promote concrete, new product, technical. **Buys 10 mss/year.** Send complete ms. Length: 500-2,000 words. **Pays $200-1,000.** Sometimes pays expenses of writers on assignment.

Photos Scan photos at 300 dpi. State availability. Captions, identification of subjects required. Reviews transparencies, prints. Offers no additional payment for photos accepted with ms.

$$ FRAME BUILDING NEWS

The Official Publication of the National Frame Builders Association, A Division of F + W Media, Inc., 700 E. State St., Iola WI 54990-0001. (715)445-4612, ext. 428. Fax: (715)445-4087. E-mail: renee.russell@fwmedia.com. Website: www.framebuildingnews.com. **10% freelance written**. Magazine published 5 times/year covering post-frame building. "*Frame Building News* is the official publication of the National Frame Builders Association, which represents contractors who specialize in post-frame building construction." Estab. 1990. Circ. 20,000. Byline given. Pays on publication. Publishes ms an average of 3 months after acceptance. Buys all rights. Editorial lead time 3 months. Submit seasonal material 3 months in advance. Accepts queries by mail. Accepts simultaneous submissions. Sample copy free.

Nonfiction Needs book excerpts, historical, how-to, interview, new product, opinion, photo feature, technical. No advertorials. **Buys 15 mss/year.** Query with published clips. 750 words minimum. **Pays $100-500 for assigned articles.**

Photos Send photos. Captions, identification of subjects required. Reviews GIF/JPEG files. Negotiates payment individually. Buys all rights.

Columns/Departments Money Talk (taxes for business); Tech Talk (computers for builders); Tool Talk (tools); Management Insights (business management), all 1,000 words. **Buys 15 mss/year.** Send complete ms. **Pays $0-500.**

Tips "Read our magazine online for a sense of our typical subject matter and audience. Contact by regular mail is best. No advertorials, please."

$$ HOME ENERGY MAGAZINE

Advancing Home Performance, Home Energy Magazine, 2124 Kittredge St., Suite 95, Berkeley CA 94704. (510)524-5405. Fax: (510)486-4673. E-mail: contact@homeenergy.org. Website: www.homeenergy.org. Alan Meier, publisher. **Contact:** Jim Gunshinan, managing ed. **10% freelance written**. Bimonthly magazine covering green home building and renovation. Estab. 1984. Circ. 5,000. Byline given. Pays on publication. Offers 10% kill fee. Publishes ms an average of 4 months after acceptance. Buys all rights. Editorial lead time 4 months. Accepts queries by e-mail. Responds in 2 weeks to queries. Responds in 2 months to mss. Guidelines by e-mail.

- Our readers are building contractors, energy auditors, and weatherization professionals. They expect technical detail, accuracy, and brevity.

Nonfiction Needs interview, technical. We do not want articles for consumers/general public. **Buys 6 mss/year.** Query with published clips. Length: 900-3,500 words. **Pays 20¢/word; $400 max. for assigned articles. Pays 20¢/word; $400 max. for unsolicited articles.**

$$$ INTERIOR CONSTRUCTION

The Resource for the Ceilings & Interior Systems Construction Industry, Ceilings & Interior Systems Construction Association, 405 Illinois Ave., Unit 2B, St. Charles IL 60174. (630)584-1919. Fax: (630)584-2003. E-mail: cisca@cisca.org. Website: www.cisca.org. **Contact:** Rick Reuland, publisher. **1-2 features per issue**. Quarterly magazine Acoustics and commercial specialty ceiling construction. Estab. 1950. Circ. 3,000. Byline given. Pays on publication. No kill fee. Publishes ms an average of 1½ months after acceptance. Buys all rights. Editorial lead time 2-3 months. Accepts queries by e-mail. Sample copy by e-mail. Guidelines available.

Nonfiction Needs new product, technical. Query with published clips. Length: 700-1,700 words. **Pays $400 min., $800 max. for assigned articles.**

$$ KEYSTONE BUILDER MAGAZINE

Pennsylvania Builders Association, 600 N. 12th St., Lemoyne PA 17043. (717)730-4380. Fax: (717)730-4396. E-mail: admin@pabuilders.org. Website: www.pabuilders.org. **10% freelance written**. "Bimonthly trade publication for builders, remodelers, subcontractors, and other affiliates of the home building industry in Pennsylvania." Estab. 1988. Circ. 9,300. Byline given. Pays on publication. No kill fee. Publishes ms an average of 1 year after acceptance. Buys one-time rights. Editorial lead time 3 months. Submit seasonal material 9 months in advance. Accepts queries by mail, e-mail. Accepts simultaneous submissions. Responds in 2 weeks to queries. Responds in 3 months to mss. Sample copy free. Guidelines by e-mail.

Nonfiction Needs general interest, how-to, new product, technical. No personnel or company profiles. **Buys 1-2 mss/year.** Send complete ms. Length: 200-500 words. **Pays $200.**

Photos Send photos. Captions, identification of subjects required. Reviews digital images. Negotiates payment individually. Buys one time rights.

$$ METAL ROOFING MAGAZINE

a Division of F+W Media, Inc., 700 E. Iola St., Iola WI 54990-0001. (715)445-4612, ext. 13281. Fax: (715)445-4087. E-mail: jim.austin@fwmedia.com. Website: www.metalroofingmag.com. **Contact:** Jim Austin. **10% freelance written**. Bimonthly magazine covering roofing. *Metal Roofing Magazine* offers contractors, designers, suppliers, architects and others in the construction industry a wealth of information on metal roofing—a growing segment of the roofing trade. Estab. 2000. Circ. 26,000. Byline given. Pays on publication. Publishes ms an average of 3 months after acceptance. Buys all rights. Editorial lead time 3 months. Submit seasonal material 3 months in advance. Accepts queries by mail. Accepts simultaneous submissions. Sample copy free.

Nonfiction Needs book excerpts, historical, how-to, interview, new product, opinion, photo feature, technical. No advertorials. **Buys 15 mss/year.** Query with published clips. 750 words minimum. **Pays $100-500 for assigned articles.**

Photos Send photos. Captions, identification of subjects required. Reviews GIF/JPEG files. Negotiates payment individually. Buys all rights.

Columns/Departments Gutter Opportunities; Stay Cool; Metal Roofing Details; Spec It. **Buys 15 mss/year.** Send complete ms. **Pays $0-500.**

Tips "Read our magazine online for a sense of our typical subject matter and audience. Contact by regular mail is best."

$$ PERMANENT BUILDINGS & FOUNDATIONS (PBF)

R.W. Nielsen Co., 575 E. Center St., Provo UT 84606. (801)794-1393. Fax: (801)804-6691. E-mail: rnielsen@permanentbuildings.com. Website: www.permanentbuildings.com. **80% freelance written**. Magazine published 8 times/year. *PBF* readers are general contractors who build residential and light commercial concrete buildings. Editorial focus is on new technologies to build solid, energy efficient structures, insulated concrete walls, waterproofing, underpinning, roofing and the business of contracting and construction. No highway, bridge or large industrial construction. Estab. 1989. Circ. 30,000. Byline given. Pays on publication. No kill fee. Buys first North American serial rights. Editorial lead time 1 month. Submit seasonal material 2 months in advance. Accepts queries by mail, e-mail, phone. Responds immediately. Responds in 1 month to mss. Sample copy for 9 × 12 SASE or online. Writer's guidelines free or online.

Nonfiction Needs how-to, construction methods, management techniques, humor, interview, new product, technical, tool reviews, environment/green building. **Buys 90-100 mss/year.** Query. Length: 500-1,500 words. **Pays 30-60¢/word.**
Photos State availability. Captions, identification of subjects required. Reviews digital images (300 dpi). Offers no additional payment for photos accepted with ms. Buys North American rights.
Columns/Departments Marketing Tips, 250-500 words; Q&A (solutions to contractor problems), 200-500 words. Query.

$$ POB MAGAZINE

BNP Media, 2401 W. Big Beaver Rd., Suite 700, Troy MI 48084. (248)362-3700. E-mail: hohnerl@bnpmedia.com. Website: www.pobonline.com. **5% freelance written**. Monthly magazine covering surveying, mapping and geomatics. Estab. 1975. Circ. 39,000. Byline given. Pays on publication. Publishes ms an average of 3 months after acceptance. Buys first North American serial rights. Editorial lead time 3 months. Accepts queries by e-mail, phone. Sample copy available online. Guidelines available online.
Nonfiction Query. Length: 1,700-2,200 words. **Pays $400.**
Photos State availability. Captions, identification of subjects required. Reviews GIF/JPEG files. Offers no additional payment for photos accepted with ms. Buys one time rights.
Tips They must know our profession and industry.

$$ PRECAST INC./MC MAGAZINE

The Concrete Solution, National Precast Concrete Association, 1320 City Center Dr., Carmel IN 46032. (317)571-9500. Fax: (317)571-0041. E-mail: rhyink@precast.org. Website: www.precast.org. **Contact:** Ron Hyink, managing editor. **75% freelance written**. Bimonthly magazine covering manufactured concrete products. *Precast Inc.* is a publication for owners and managers of factory-produced concrete products used in construction. We publish business articles, technical articles, company profiles, safety articles, and project profiles, with the intent of educating our readers in order to increase the quality and use of precast concrete. Estab. 1995. Circ. 8,500. Byline given. Pays on acceptance. No kill fee. Publishes ms an average of 6 months after acceptance. Buys first North American serial rights, buys second serial (reprint) rights, buys all rights. Editorial lead time 3 months. Accepts queries by mail, e-mail, fax. Accepts simultaneous submissions. Responds in 1 month to queries. Responds in 2 months to mss. Sample copy available online. Guidelines available online.
Nonfiction Needs how-to, business, interview, technical, concrete manufacturing. No humor, essays, fiction, or fillers. **Buys 8-14 mss/year.** Query or send complete ms. Length: 1,500-2,500 words. **Pays $250-750.** Sometimes pays expenses of writers on assignment.
Photos State availability. Captions required. Offers no additional payment for photos accepted with ms. Buys all rights.
Tips Understand the audience and the purpose of the magazine. Understanding audience interests and needs is important and expressing a willingness to tailor a subject to get the right slant is critical. Our primary freelance needs are about general business or technology topics. Of course, if you are an engineer or a writer specializing in industry, construction, or manufacturing technology, other possibilities may exist. Writing style should be concise, yet lively and entertaining. Avoid clichès. We require a third-person perspective, and encourage a positive tone and active voice. For stylistic matters, follow the *AP Style Book*.

$$ RURAL BUILDER

The Business Management Magazine for Rural Contractors, a Division of F+W Media, Inc., 700 E. State St., Iola WI 54990-0001. (715)445-4612, ext. 13644. Fax: (715)445-4087. E-mail: renee.russell@fwmedia.com. Website: www.ruralbuilder.com. **10% freelance written**. Magazine published 7 times/year covering rural building. "*Builder* serves diversified town and country builders, offering them help managing their businesses through editorial and advertising material about metal, wood, post-frame, and masonry construction." Estab. 1967. Circ. 30,000. Byline given. Pays on publication. Publishes ms an average of 3 months after acceptance. Buys all rights. Editorial lead time 3 months. Submit seasonal material 3 months in advance. Accepts queries by mail. Accepts simultaneous submissions. Sample copy free.
Nonfiction Needs book excerpts, historical, how-to, interview, new product, opinion, photo feature, technical. No advertorials. **Buys 15 mss/year.** Query with published clips. 750 words minimum. **Pays $100-500.**

Photos Send photos. Captions, identification of subjects required. Reviews GIF/JPEG files. Negotiates payment individually. Buys all rights.
Columns/Departments Money Talk (taxes for business); Tech Talk (computers for builders); Tool Talk (tools); Management Insights (business management); all 1,000 words. **Buys 15 mss/year.** Send complete ms. **Pays $0-500.**
Tips "Read our magazine online for a sense of our typical subject matter and audience. Contact by regular mail is best. No advertorials, please."

$ $ UNDERGROUND CONSTRUCTION

Oildom Publishing Co. of Texas, Inc., P.O. Box 941669, Houston TX 77094-8669. (281)558-6930. Fax: (281)558-7029. E-mail: rcarpenter@oildom.com. Website: www.oildompublishing.com. **Contact:** Robert Carpenter, editor. **35% freelance written**. Monthly magazine covering underground oil and gas pipeline, water and sewer pipeline, cable construction for contractors and owning companies. Circ. 38,000. No kill fee. Publishes ms an average of 6 months after acceptance. Buys first North American serial rights. Accepts queries by mail, e-mail, fax, phone. Responds in 1 month to mss. Sample copy for sae.
Nonfiction Needs how-to, job stories and industry issues. Query with published clips. Length: 1,000-2,000 words. **Pays $3-500.** Sometimes pays expenses of writers on assignment.
Photos Send photos. Captions required. Reviews color prints and slides. Buys one time rights.

Drugs, Health Care & Medical Products

$ $ $ $ N ACP INTERNIST/ACP HOSPITALIST

American College of Physicians, 191 N. Independence Mall W., Philadelphia PA 19106. (215)351-2400. E-mail: acpinternist@acponline.org. Website: www.acpinternist.org. www.acphospitalist.org. **Contact:** Janet Colwell, editor. **40% freelance written**. Monthly magazine covering Internal Medicine/Hospital Medicine. "We write for specialists in internal medicine, not a consumer audience. Topics include clinical medicine, practice management, health information technology, Medicare issues." Estab. 1981. Circ. 85,000 (Internist), 24,000 (Hospitalist). Byline given. Offers kill fee. Negotiable Publishes ms an average of 2 months after acceptance. Buys electronic rights. Makes work-for-hire assignments. Editorial lead time 4 months. Submit seasonal material 6 months in advance. Accepts queries by e-mail. Sample copy available online. Guidelines free.
Nonfiction Needs interview. Query with published clips. Length: 700-2,000 words. **Pays $500-2,000 for assigned articles.** Pays expenses of writers on assignment.
Photos Contact: Ryan Dubosar, senior editor. State availability. Reviews TIFF/JPEG files. Negotiates payment individually.

$ $ LABTALK

LabTalk, P.O. Box 1945, Big Bear Lake CA 92315. (909)866-5590. Fax: (909)866-5577. E-mail: cwalker@framesdata.com. Website: www.framesdata.com. **20% freelance written**. Magazine published 6 times/year for the eye wear industry. Estab. 1970. Buys one-time rights. Accepts simultaneous submissions.
Tips "Write for the optical laboratory owner and manager."

$ $ $ VALIDATION TIMES

Bio Research Compliance Report, Adverse Event Reporting News, Washington Information Source Co., 19-B Wirt Street SW, Leesburg VA 20175. (703)779-8777. Fax: (703)779-2508. E-mail: mwinn@fdainfo.com. Website: www.fdainfo.com. **Contact:** Melissa Winn. Monthly newsletters covering regulation of pharmaceutical and medical devices. "We write to executives who have to keep up on changing FDA policies and regulations, and on what their competitors are doing at the agency." Estab. 1992. Byline given. Pays on publication. No kill fee. Publishes ms an average of 1 month after acceptance. Makes work-for-hire assignments. Editorial lead time 1 month. Submit seasonal material 1 month in advance. Accepts queries by mail. Responds in 1 month to queries. Sample copy and writer's guidelines free.
Nonfiction Needs how-to, technical, regulatory. No lay interest pieces. **Buys 50-100 mss/year.** Query. Length: 600-1,500 words. **Pays $100/half day; $200 full day to cover meetings and same rate for writing.** Sometimes pays expenses of writers on assignment.
Tips If you're covering a conference for non-competing publications, call me with a drug or device regulatory angle.

Education & Counseling

$ ARTS & ACTIVITIES

Publishers' Development Corp., Dept. WM, 12345 World Trade Dr., San Diego CA 92128. (858)605-0242. Fax: (858)605-0247. E-mail: ed@artsandactivities.com. Website: www.artsandactivities.com. **Contact:** Maryellen Bridge, editor in chief. **95% freelance written. Eager to work with new/unpublished writers.** Monthly (except July and August) magazine covering art education at levels from preschool through college for educators and therapists engaged in arts and crafts education and training. Estab. 1932. Circ. 20,000. Byline given. Pays on publication. No kill fee. Publishes ms 6 months to 3 years after acceptance. Buys first North American serial rights. Submit seasonal material 6 months in advance. Accepts queries by mail, e-mail. Responds in 3 months to queries. Sample copy for sae with 9 × 12 envelope and 8 First-Class stamps. Guidelines available online.

Nonfiction Needs historical, arts, activities, history, how-to, classroom art experiences, artists' techniques, interview, of artists, opinion, on arts activities curriculum, ideas of how-to do things better, philosophy of art education, personal experience, this ties in with the how-to,, articles of exceptional art programs, "We like it to be personal, not recipe style." **Buys 80-100 mss/year.** Length:500-1500 words. **Pays $35-150.**

Tips Frequently in unsolicited manuscripts, writers obviously have not studied the magazine to see what style of articles we publish. Send for a sample copy to familiarize yourself with our style and needs. The best way to find out if his/her writing style suits our needs is for the author to submit a manuscript on speculation. We prefer an anecdotal style of writing, so that readers will feel as though they are there in the art room as the lesson/project is taking place. Also, good quality photographs of student artwork are important. We are a visual art magazine!

$ THE ATA MAGAZINE

The Alberta Teachers' Association, 11010 142nd St. NW, Edmonton AB T5N 2R1 Canada. (780)447-9400. Fax: (780)455-6481. E-mail: government@teachers.ab.ca. Website: www.teachers.ab.ca. **Contact:** The Editor. Quarterly magazine covering education. Estab. 1920. Circ. 42,100. Byline given. Pays on publication. No kill fee. Publishes ms an average of 4 months after acceptance. Buys one-time rights. Editorial lead time 2 months. Submit seasonal material 2 months in advance. Accepts queries by mail, e-mail, fax, phone. Accepts simultaneous submissions. Responds in 2 months to queries. Sample copy free. Guidelines available online.

Nonfiction Education-related topics. Query with published clips. Length: 500-1,500 words. **Pays $75 (Canadian).**

Photos Send photos. Captions required. Reviews 4x6 prints. Negotiates payment individually. Negotiates rights.

AUSTRALASIANJOURNAL OF EARLY CHILDHOOD

Early Childhood Australia, P.O. Box 86, Deakin West ACT 2600 Australia. (61)(2)6242-1800. Fax: (61)(2)6242-1818. E-mail: publishing@earlychildhood.org.au. Website: www.earlychildhoodaustralia.org.au. **Contact:** Nick Craven, publishing and marketing manager. Nonprofit early childhood advocacy organisation, acting in the interests of young children aged from bith to eight years of age, their families and those in the early childhood field. Specialist publisher of early childhood magazines, journals, and booklets. Guidelines available online.

Nonfiction Please read author guidelines, available online, or contact publishing department for submission details. Needs essays. Send complete ms. Length: Magazine articles, 600-1,000 words; research-based papers, 3,000-6,500 words; submissions for booklets, approximately 5,000 words.

AUSTRALIAN JOURNAL OF ADULT LEARNING

Adult Learning Australia, Inc., Centre for Research in Education, Equity and Work, University of South Australia (Building G), Mawson Lakes Blvd., Mawson Lakes SA 5095 Australia. (61)(8)8302-6246. E-mail: roger.harris@unisa.edu.au. Website: www.ala.asn.au. "Academic journal published 3 times/year covering adult learning in Australia and internationally."

Nonfiction Needs general interest, how-to. Query.

CATECHIST

Peter Li, Inc., 9112 Damson St., St. Louis MO 63123. E-mail: kdotterweich@peterli.com. Website: www.catechist.com. **Contact:** Kass Dotterweich, editor. **20% freelance written**. Magazine published 7 times/

year covering Catholic education, grades K-6. "Our articles target teachers of children in religious education parish programs." Estab. 1961. Circ. 52,000. Byline given. Pays on publication. Publishes ms an average of 8 months after acceptance. Buys first North American serial rights. Editorial lead time 1 year. Submit seasonal material 1 year in advance. Accepts queries by mail, e-mail, fax. Responds in 2 weeks to queries. Responds in 2 months to mss. Sample copy for $3.50. Guidelines available online.
Nonfiction Needs how-to, personal experience, religious. Special issues: Advent/Christmas (November-December); Sacrament (January). Does not want product profiles. **Buys 15 mss/year.** Query. Length: 500-1,200 words. **Pays negotiable amount; pays on publication.**
Tips "Call the editor with specific questions."

$ THE FORENSIC TEACHER

Wide Open Minds Educational Services, P.O. Box 5263, Wilmington DE 19808. E-mail: admin@theforensicteacher.com. Website: www.theforensicteacher.com. **Contact:** Mark R. Feil, Ed.D, editor. **70% freelance written**. Quarterly magazine covering forensic education. "Our readers are middle, high and post-secondary teachers who are looking for better, easier and more engaging ways to teach forensics as well as law enforcement and scientific forensic experts. Our writers understand this and are writing from a forensic or educational background, or both. Prefer a first person writing style." Estab. 2006. Circ. 30,000. Byline given. Pays 60 days after publication. No kill fee. Publishes ms an average of 6 months after acceptance. Buys first North American serial rights, buys second serial (reprint) rights, buys all electronic rights. Editorial lead time 6 months. Submit seasonal material 6 months in advance. Accepts queries by mail, e-mail. Accepts simultaneous submissions. Responds in 2 weeks to queries. Responds in 2 months to mss. Sample copy for $5. Guidelines available online.
Nonfiction Needs how-to, personal experience, photo feature, technical, lesson plans. Does not want poetry, fiction or anything unrelated to medicine, law, forensics or teaching. **Buys 18 mss/year.** Send complete ms. Length: 400-2,000 words. **Pays 2¢/word.**
Photos State availability. Captions required. Reviews GIF/JPEG files/pdf. Send photos separately in e-mail, not in the article. Negotiates payment individually. Buys first North American serial rights, second serial reprint rights, all electronic rights.
Columns/Departments Needs lesson experiences or ideas, personal or professional experiences with a branch of forensics. "If you've done it in your classroom please share it with us. Also, if you're a professional, please tell our readers how they can duplicate the lesson/demo/experiment in their classrooms. Please share what you know."
Fillers Needs facts, newsbreaks. Buys 15 mss/year. Length: 50-200 words. **Pays 2¢/word.**
Tips "Your article will benefit forensics teachers and their students. It should inform, entertain and enlighten the teacher and the students. Would you read it if you were a busy forensics teacher?"

$$ THE HISPANIC OUTLOOK IN HIGHER EDUCATION

80 Route 4 E., Suite 203, Paramus NJ 07652. (800)549-8280. Fax: (201)587-9105. E-mail: sloutlook@aol.com. Website: www.hispanicoutlook.com. **50% freelance written**. Biweekly magazine, except in summer. We're looking for higher education story articles, with a focus on Hispanics and the advancements made by and for Hispanics in higher education. Circ. 28,000. Byline given. Pays on publication. No kill fee. Publishes ms an average of 2 months after acceptance. Editorial lead time 2 months. Submit seasonal material 3 months in advance. Accepts queries by mail, e-mail, fax. Accepts simultaneous submissions. Sample copy free.
Nonfiction Needs historical, interview, of academic or scholar, opinion, on higher education, personal experience, all regarding higher education only. **Buys 20-25 mss/year.** Query with published clips. Length: 1,800-2,200 words. **Pays $500 minimum for assigned articles.** Pays expenses of writers on assignment.
Photos Send photos. Reviews color or b&w prints, digital images must be 300 dpi (call for e-mail photo address). Offers no additional payment for photos accepted with ms.
Tips Articles explore the Hispanic experience in higher education. Special theme issues address sports, law, health, corporations, heritage, women, and a wide range of similar issues; however, articles need not fall under those umbrellas.

$$ PTO TODAY

The #1 Resource for Parent Groups, PTO Today, Inc., 100 Stonewall Blvd., Suite 3, Wrentham MA 02093. (800)644-3561. Fax: (508)384-6108. E-mail: editor@ptotoday.com. Website: www.ptotoday.com. **Contact:** Craig Bystrynski, editor-in-chief. **50% freelance written**. Magazine published 6 times during the school year covering the work of school parent-teacher groups. "We celebrate the work of school parent volunteers and provide resources to help them do that work more effectively." Estab. 1999. Circ. 80,000. Byline given. Pays on acceptance. Offers 30% kill fee. Publishes ms an average of 4-6 months after acceptance. Buys first North American serial rights, buys electronic rights, buys all rights. Editorial lead time 4 months. Submit seasonal material 4 months in advance. Accepts queries by e-mail. Guidelines by e-mail.

Nonfiction Needs expose, general interest, how-to, anything related to PTO/PTA, interview, personal experience. **Buys 20 mss/year.** Query. We review but do not encourage unsolicited submissions. Features run roughly 1,200 to 2,200 words, and the average assignment is 1,500 words. Department pieces run 600 to 1,200 words **Payment depends on the difficulty of the topic and the experience of the writer. "We pay by the assignment, not by the word; our pay scale ranges from $200 to $700 for features and $150 to $400 for departments. We occasionally pay more for high-impact stories and highly experienced writers. We buy all rights, and we pay on acceptance (within 30 days of invoice)."** Sometimes pays expenses of writers on assignment.

Photos State availability. Identification of subjects required. Negotiates payment individually. Buys one time rights.

Tips "It's difficult for us to find talented writers with strong experience with parent groups. This experience is a big plus. Also, it helps to review our writer's guidelines before querying. All queries must have a strong parent group angle."

$ SCHOOL ARTS MAGAZINE

Davis Art, 2223 Parkside Dr., Denton TX 76201. E-mail: nwalkup@verizon.net. Website: www.davis-art.com. **Contact:** Nancy Walkup, editor. **85% freelance written**. Monthly magazine (August/September-May/June), serving arts and craft education profession, K-12, higher education, and museum education programs written by and for art teachers. "Each issue of the volume year revolves around a theme that focuses on the human side of the studio art projects, i.e., story, play, meaning. The editor determines which issue/theme is the best fit for your article, so don't worry about fitting a theme. It is more important to be passionate about your lesson, idea, or concept. Look online for upcoming themes." Estab. 1901. Pays on publication (honorarium and 4 copies). No kill fee. Publishes ms an average of 24 months after acceptance. Buys all rights. Accepts queries by mail, phone. Responds in 1-2 months to queries. Guidelines available online.

Nonfiction Articles on art and craft activities in schools. Should include description and photos of activity in progress, as well as examples of finished artwork. Query or send complete ms and SASE. Length: 600-1,400 words. **Pays $30-150.**

Tips "We prefer articles on actual art projects or techniques done by students in actual classroom situations. Philosophical and theoretical aspects of art and art education are usually handled by our contributing editors. Our articles are reviewed and accepted on merit and each is tailored to meet our needs. Keep in mind that art teachers want practical tips above all—more hands-on information than academic theory. Write your article with the accompanying photographs in hand. The most frequent mistakes made by writers are bad visual material (photographs, drawings) submitted with articles, a lack of complete descriptions of art processes, and no rationale behind programs or activities. Familiarity with the field of art education is essential. Review recent issues of *SchoolArts*."

SCREEN EDUCATION

P.O. Box 2040, St. Kilda West VIC 3182 Australia. (61)(3)9525-5302. Fax: (61)(3)9537-2325. E-mail: assistanteditor@atom.org.au. Website: www.metromagazine.com.au. Quarterly magazine written by and for teachers and students in secondary and primary schools, covering media education across all curriculum areas. Guidelines available online.

Nonfiction Needs general interest, interview, reviews, classroom activities. E-mail proposals or complete article. Length: 1,000-3,000 words.

Photos Reviews TIFF/JPEG files.

TEACHERS & WRITERS MAGAZINE

Teachers & Writers Collaborative, 520 Eighth Ave., Suite 2020, New York NY 10018. (212)691-6590. Fax: (212)675-0171. E-mail: editors@twc.org. Website: www.twc.org/pubs. **75% freelance written**. Quarterly magazine covering how to teach creative writing (kindergarten through university). "*Teachers & Writers Magazine* covers a cross-section of contemporary issues and innovations in education and writing, and engages writers, educators, critics, and students in a conversation on the nature of creativity and the imagination." Estab. 1967. Circ. 5,000. Byline given. Pays on publication. No kill fee. Publishes ms an average of 4-6 months after acceptance. Buys one-time rights. Editorial lead time 4 months. Submit seasonal material 4-6 months in advance. Accepts queries by e-mail, as an attachment (preferred). Accepts simultaneous submissions. Responds in 4-8 weeks to queries. Responds in 3-6 months to mss. Sample copy for $5. Guidelines by e-mail.

Nonfiction "*Teachers & Writers* magazine welcomes articles about teaching the art of writing in kindergarten through college and in non-classroom settings. *Teachers & Writers* also welcomes submissions on related topics, such as oral history, translation, and teaching writing in combination with other arts. *Teachers & Writers* publishes both practical and theoretical work and looks for writing that is concise, lively, and geared toward a general audience." Needs book excerpts, on creative writing education, essays, interview, opinion, personal experience, creative writing exercises. 500-2,500/words

$ TEACHERS OF VISION

A Publication of Christian Educators Association, 227 N. Magnolia Ave., Suite 2, Anaheim CA 92801. (714)761-1476. Fax: (714)761-1679. E-mail: TOV@ceai.org. Website: www.ceai.org. **70% freelance written**. Magazine published 4 times/year for Christians in public education. "*Teachers of Vision*'s articles inspire, inform, and equip teachers and administrators in the educational arena. Readers look for teacher tips, integrating faith and work, and general interest education articles. Topics include subject matter, religious expression and activity in public schools, and legal rights of Christian educators. Our audience is primarily public school educators. Other readers include teachers in private schools, university professors, school administrators, parents, and school board members." Estab. 1953. Circ. 10,000. Byline given. Pays on publication. No kill fee. Publishes ms an average of 6 months after acceptance. Buys first North American serial rights, buys second serial (reprint) rights, buys electronic rights. Editorial lead time 4 months. Submit seasonal material 4 months in advance. Accepts queries by mail, e-mail, fax. Accepts simultaneous submissions. Responds in 1 month to queries. Responds in 3-4 months to mss. Sample copy for sae with 9 × 12 envelope and 4 first-class stamps. Guidelines available online.

Nonfiction Needs how-to, humor, inspirational, interview, opinion, personal experience, religious. Nothing preachy. **Buys 50-60 mss/year.** Query or send complete ms if 2,000 words or less. Length: 1,500 words. **Pays $40-50.**

Photos State availability. Offers no additional payment for photos accepted with ms. Buys one-time, web and reprint rights by members for educational purposes.

Columns/Departments Query. **Pays $10-40.**

Fillers Send with SASE—must relate to public education.

Tips "We are looking for material on living out one's faith in appropriate, legal ways in the public school setting."

TEACHING MUSIC

MENC: The National Association for Music Education, 1806 Robert Fulton Dr., Reston VA 20191-4348. E-mail: lindab@menc.org. Website: www.menc.org. **Contact:** Linda C. Brown, editor. Journal covering music education issued six times a year. *Teaching Music* offers music educators a forum for the exchange of practical ideas that will help them become more effective teachers. Written in an easy-to-read, conversational style, the magazine includes timely information to interest, inform, and inspire music teachers and those who support their work. Byline given. Does not pay writers at this time. No kill fee. Publishes ms an average of 18 months after acceptance. Buys all rights. Editorial lead time 12-18 months. Accepts queries by e-mail (preferably in Word or Word Perfect). Responds in 2 weeks to queries. Responds in 3 months to mss. Guidelines available online.

Nonfiction Needs how-to, inspirational, personal experience, manuscripts for the Lectern section that describe effective and innovative instructional strategies or thoughtful solutions to problems faced by music educators at all levels, from PreK through college. Major article categories are General Music, Band, Orchestra, Chorus, Early Childhood, Advocacy, and Teacher Education/Professional Development. Send complete ms. Length: 1,000-1,400 words.

Photos Send in color photographs or other graphics that illustrate the main points of their articles. Photographers should obtain permission from the parents/guardians of minors whose photographs are submitted. Release form is online. Send photos after ms accepted.

$$ TEACHING THEATRE

Educational Theatre Association, 2343 Auburn Ave., Cincinnati OH 45219-2819. (513)421-3900. Website: www.edta.org. **65% freelance written**. Quarterly magazine covering education theater K-12, primary emphasis on middle and secondary level education. "*Teaching Theatre* emphasizes the teaching, theory, philosophy issues that are of concern to teachers at the elementary, secondary, and—as they relate to teaching K-12 theater—college levels. A typical issue includes an article on acting, directing, playwriting, or technical theatre; a profile of an outstanding educational theatre program; a piece on curriculum design, assessment, or teaching methodology; and a report on current trends or issues in the field, such as funding, standards, or certification." Estab. 1989. Circ. 5,000. Byline given. Pays on acceptance. No kill fee. Publishes ms an average of 3 months after acceptance. Buys one-time rights, buys electronic rights. Editorial lead time 2 months. Accepts previously published material. Accepts simultaneous submissions. Responds in 1 month to queries. Responds in 3 months to mss. Sample copy for $2. Guidelines available online.

Nonfiction "*Teaching Theatre*'s audience is well educated, and most have considerable experience in their field. Generalist articles are discouraged; readers already possess basic skills." Needs book excerpts, essays, how-to, interview, opinion, technical theater. **Buys 20 mss/year.** Query. **Pays $100-400.**

Photos State availability. Reviews contact sheets, 5 × 7 and 8 × 10 transparencies, prints, digital images (150 dpi minimum). Offers no additional payment for photos accepted with ms.

Tips "Wants articles that address the needs of the busy but experienced high school theater educators. Fundamental pieces on the value of theater education are not of value to us—our readers already know that."

$$$$ TEACHING TOLERANCE

The Southern Poverty Law Center, 400 Washington Ave., Montgomery AL 36104. (334)956-8200. Fax: (334)956-8488. Website: www.teachingtolerance.org. **30% freelance written**. Semiannual magazine. *Teaching Tolerance* is dedicated to helping K-12 teachers promote tolerance and understanding between widely diverse groups of students. Includes articles, teaching ideas, and reviews of other resources available to educators. Estab. 1991. Circ. 400,000. Byline given. Pays on acceptance. No kill fee. Buys all rights. Editorial lead time 6 months. Submit seasonal material 6 months in advance. Accepts queries by mail, fax. Sample copy and writer's guidelines free or online.

Nonfiction Needs essays, how-to, classroom techniques, personal experience, classroom, photo feature. No jargon, rhetoric or academic analysis. No theoretical discussions on the pros/cons of multicultural education. **Buys 2-4 mss/year.** Submit outlines or complete mss. Length: 1,000-3,000 words. **Pays $500-3,000.** Pays expenses of writers on assignment.

Photos State availability. Captions, identification of subjects required. Reviews contact sheets, transparencies. Buys one time rights.

Columns/Departments Essays (personal reflection, how-to, school program), 400-800 words; Idea Exchange (special projects, successful anti-bias activities), 250-500 words; Student Writings (short essays dealing with diversity, tolerance, justice), 300-500 words. **Buys 8-12 mss/year.** Query with published clips. **Pays $50 1,000.**

Tips We want lively, simple, concise writing. Be descriptive and reflective, showing the strength of programs dealing successfully with diversity by employing clear descriptions of real scenes and interactions, and by using quotes from teachers and students. Study previous issues of the magazine before making submissions. Most open to articles that have a strong classroom focus. We are interested in approaches to teaching tolerance and promoting understanding that really work that we might not have heard of. We want to inform, inspire and encourage our readers. We know what's happening nationally; we want to know what's happening in your neighborhood classroom.

Electronics & Communication

$$ THE ACUTA JOURNAL OF INFORMATION COMMUNICATIONS TECHNOLOGY IN HIGHER EDUCATION

ACUTA, 152 W. Zandale Dr., Suite 200, Lexington KY 40503-2486. (859)278-3338. Fax: (859)278-3268. E-mail: pscott@acuta.org. Website: www.acuta.org. **Contact:** Patricia Scott, communications manager. **20% freelance written**. Quarterly professional association journal covering information communications technology (ICT) in higher education. "Our audience includes, primarily, middle to upper management in the IT/telecommunications department on college/university campuses. They are highly skilled, technology-oriented professionals who provide data, voice, and video communications services for residential and academic purposes." Estab. 1997. Circ. 2,200. Byline given. Pays on publication. No kill fee. Publishes ms an average of 6 months after acceptance. Buys first rights. Editorial lead time 6 months. Accepts queries by mail, e-mail, fax, phone. Responds in 1 month to queries. Responds in 2 months to mss. Sample copy for sae with 9 × 12 envelope and 6 first-class stamps. Guidelines free.

Nonfiction Each issue has a focus. Available with writer's guidelines. We are only interested in articles described in article types. Needs how-to, ICT, technical, technology, case study, college/university application of technology. **Buys 6-8 mss/year.** Query. Length: 1,200-4,000 words. **Pays 8-10¢/word.** Sometimes pays expenses of writers on assignment.

Photos State availability. Captions, model releases required. Reviews prints. Offers no additional payment for photos accepted with ms.

Tips "Our audience expects every article to be relevant to information communications technology on the college/university campus, whether it is related to technology, facilities, or management. Writers must read back issues to understand this focus and the level of technicality we expect."

$ $ CABLING BUSINESS MAGAZINE

Cabling Publications, Inc., 12035 Shiloh Rd., Suite 350, Dallas TX 75228. (214)328-1717. Fax: (214)319-6077. E-mail: margaret@cablingbusiness.com. Website: www.cablingbusiness.com. Russell Paulov, editor-in-chief. **Contact:** Margaret Patterson, managing editor. **30% freelance written**. Monthly magazine covering telecommunications, cable manufacturing, volP, wireless, broadband, structured cabling. "Each month, *Cabling Business Magazine* offers readers a broad mix of information relating to premises cabling, including industry news, standards updates, design and installation tutorials, and case studies highlighting successes achieved with the industry's latest technologies. Our editors are experts in the field and can pinpoint the timely material most relevant to the cabling professional. With input and contributions from the top minds in the industry, the editorial staff brings readers real-world information they can use. Online access since 2007." Estab. 1991. Circ. 15,000. Byline given. Pays on publication. No kill fee. Publishes ms an average of 1-2 months after acceptance. Buys second serial (reprint) rights. Editorial lead time 2 months. Submit seasonal material 2 months in advance. Accepts queries by e-mail. Accepts simultaneous submissions. Responds in 1 week to queries and to mss. Sample copy available online. Guidelines by e-mail.

Nonfiction Needs how-to, interview, new product, opinion, personal experience, technical. No vendor/product specific infomercials. **Buys 6 mss/year.** Query. Length: 1,500-2,500 words. **Pays $400 max. for assigned articles. Pays $400 max. for unsolicited articles.**

Photos State availability. Captions, identification of subjects, model releases required. Reviews GIF/JPEG files. Offers no additional payment for photos accepted with ms. Buys all rights.

Columns/Departments New Products (latest technology from industry), 350 words; Testing Equipment Q&A (work with specific companies on testing information), Cable Q&A (work with specific companies on cable questions from around the industry), 800 words; Terminology/Calendar, 200 words. Query. **Pays $-$400.**

Tips "Contact Margaret@cablingbusiness.com with a query-list of specific items covered in proposed article and how it relates to our industry-also know what our magazine covers and be sure to check out the editorial calendar on the website."

$ $ DIGITAL OUTPUT

The Only Magazine Dedicated to Capture, Creation, Output and Finishing, Rockport Custom Publishing, LLC, 6000 Sawgrass Village Cir., Ponte Vedra Beach FL 32082. (904)273-2588. E-mail: mdonovan@rockportpubs.com. Website: www.digitaloutput.net. **Contact:** Melissa Donovan, editor. **70% freelance written**. Monthly magazine covering electronic prepress, desktop publishing, and digital imaging, with articles ranging from digital capture and design to electronic prepress and digital printing. *Digital Output* is a national business publication for electronic publishers and digital imagers, providing monthly articles which examine the latest technologies and digital methods and discuss how to profit from them. Our readers include service bureaus, prepress and reprographic houses, designers, commercial printers, wide-format printers, ad agencies, corporate communications, sign shops, and others. Estab. 1994. Circ. 25,000. Byline given. Pays on publication. Offers 10-20% kill fee. Publishes ms an average of 2 months after acceptance. Buys one-time rights including electronic rights for archival posting. Editorial lead time 3 months. Submit seasonal material 3 months in advance. Accepts queries by mail, e-mail. Responds in 3 weeks to queries. Responds in 1 month to mss. Sample copy for $4.50 or online.

Nonfiction Needs how-to, interview, technical, case studies. **Buys 36 mss/year.** Query with published clips or hyperlinks to posted clips. Length: 1,500-4,000 words. **Pays $250-600.**

Photos Send photos.

Tips Our readers are graphic arts professionals. The freelance writers we use are deeply immersed in the technology of commercial printing, desktop publishing, digital imaging, color management, PDF workflow, inkjet printing, and similar topics.

$ $ ELECTRONIC SERVICING & TECHNOLOGY

The Professional Magazine for Electronics and Computer Servicing, P.O. Box 12487, Overland Park KS 66282-2487. (913)492-4857. Fax: (913)492-4857. E-mail: cpersedit@aol.com. **80% freelance written.** Monthly magazine for service technicians, field service personnel, and avid servicing enthusiasts, who service audio, video, and computer equipment. Estab. 1950. Circ. 15,000. Byline given. Pays on publication. No kill fee. Publishes ms an average of 4 months after acceptance. Buys one-time rights. Editorial lead time 2 months. Accepts queries by mail, e-mail, fax, phone. Accepts simultaneous submissions. Responds in 1 month to queries. Responds in 2 months to mss. Sample copy free. Guidelines free.

Nonfiction Needs book excerpts, how-to, service consumer electronics, new product, technical. **Buys 40 mss/year.** Query or send complete ms. **Pays $50/page.**

Reprints Send typed manuscript with rights for sale noted and information about when and where the material previously appeared.

Photos Send photos. Offers no additional payment for photos accepted with ms. Buys one time rights.

Columns/Departments Business Corner (business tips); Computer Corner (computer servicing tips); Video Corner (understanding/servicing TV and video), all 1,000-2,000 words. **Buys 30 mss/year.** Query, or send complete ms. **Pays $100-300.**

Tips Writers should have a strong background in electronics, especially consumer electronics servicing. Understand the information needs of consumer electronics service technicians, and be able to write articles that address specific areas of those needs.

$ $ SQL SERVER MAGAZINE

Penton Media, 221 E. 29th St., Loveland CO 80538. (970)663-4700. Fax: (970)667-2321. E-mail: aeisenberg@windowsitpro.com. Website: www.sqlmag.com. **Contact:** Amy Eisenberg. **35% freelance written**. Monthly magazine covering Microsoft SQL Server. "*SQL Server Magazine* is the only magazine completely devoted to helping developers and DBAs master new and emerging SQL Server technologies and issues. It provides practical advice and lots of code examples for SQL Server developers and administrators, and includes how-to articles, tips, tricks, and programming techniques offered by SQL Server experts." Estab. 1999. Circ. 20,000. Byline given. "Penton Media pays for articles upon publication. Payment rates are based on the author's writing experience and the quality of the article submitted. We will discuss the payment rate for your article when we notify you of its acceptance." Offers $100 kill fee. Publishes ms an average of 6 months after acceptance. Buys all rights. Editorial lead time 4+ months. Accepts queries by mail, e-mail: articles@sqlmag.com. Responds in 6 weeks to queries. Responds in 2-3 months to mss. Sample copy available online. Guidelines available online.

Nonfiction Needs how-to, technical, SQL Server administration and programming. Nothing promoting third-party products or companies. **Buys 25-35 mss/year.** Send complete ms. Length: 1,800-3,000 words. **Pays $200 for feature articles; $500 for Focus articles.**

Columns/Departments Contact: R2R Editor. Send all column/department submissions to r2r@sqlmag.com. Reader to Reader (helpful SQL Server hints and tips from readers), 200-400 words. **Buys 6-12 mss/year.** Send complete ms. **Pays $50.**

Tips Read back issues and make sure that your proposed article doesn't overlap previous coverage. When proposing articles, state specifically how your article would contain new information compared to previously published information, and what benefit your information would be to *SQL Server Magazine*'s readership.

Energy & Utilities

$ $ ALTERNATIVE ENERGY RETAILER

Zackin Publications, Inc., P.O. Box 2180, Waterbury CT 06722. (800)325-6745. Fax: (203)262-4680. E-mail: hallp@aer-online.com. Website: www.aer-online.com. **Contact:** Phil Hall, editor. **5% freelance written. Prefers to work with published/established writers.** Monthly magazine on selling home hearth products—chiefly solid fuel and gas-burning appliances. We seek detailed how-to tips for retailers to improve business. Most freelance material purchased is about retailers and how they succeed. Estab. 1980. Circ. 10,000. Pays on publication. No kill fee. Publishes ms an average of 2 months after acceptance.

Buys first North American serial rights. Submit seasonal material 4 months in advance. Accepts queries by mail, e-mail, fax, phone. Responds in 2 weeks to queries. Sample copy for sae with 9 × 12 envelope and 4 First-Class stamps. Guidelines available online.
Nonfiction Needs how-to, improve retail profits and business know-how, interview, of successful retailers in this field. No general business articles not adapted to this industry. **Buys 10 mss/year.** Query. Length: 1,000 words. **Pays $200.**
Photos State availability. Identification of subjects required. Reviews color transparencies. Pays $25-125 maximum for 5 × 7 b&w prints. Buys one time rights.
Tips A freelancer can best break into our publication with features about readers (retailers). Stick to details about what has made this person a success.

$ $ ELECTRICAL APPARATUS

The Magazine of Electromechanical & Electronic Application & Maintenance, Barks Publications, Inc., 400 N. Michigan Ave., Chicago IL 60611-4104. (312)321-9440. Fax: (312)321-1288. "Monthly magazine for persons working in electrical and electronic maintenance, in industrial plants and service and sales centers, who install and service electric motors, transformers, generators, controls, and related equipment." Estab. 1967. Circ. 16,000. Byline given. Pays on publication. No kill fee. Publishes ms an average of 1 month after acceptance. Buys all rights unless other arrangements made. Accepts queries by mail, fax. Responds in 1 week to queries. Responds in 2 weeks to mss.
Nonfiction Needs technical. Length: 1,500-2,500 words. **Pays $250-500 for assigned articles.**
Tips "All feature articles are assigned to staff and contributing editors and correspondents. Professionals interested in appointments as contributing editors and correspondents should submit resume and article outlines, including illustration suggestions. Writers should be competent with a camera, which should be described in resume. Technical expertise is absolutely necessary, preferably an E.E. degree, or practical experience. We are also book publishers and some of the material in *EA* is now in book form, bringing the authors royalties. Also publishes an annual directory, subtitled *ElectroMechanical Bench Reference.*"

$ $ ✪ ELECTRICAL BUSINESS

CLB Media, Inc., 240 Edward St., Aurora ON L4G 3S9 Canada. (905)727-0077; (905)713-4391. Fax: (905)727-0017. E-mail: acapkun@clbmedia.ca. Website: www.ebmag.com. **Contact:** Anthony Capkun, editor. **35% freelance written**. Tabloid published 10 times/year covering the Canadian electrical industry. *Electrical Business* targets electrical contractors and electricians. It provides practical information readers can use right away in their work and for running their business and assets. Estab. 1964. Circ. 18,097. Byline given. Pays on acceptance. Offers 50% kill fee. Publishes ms an average of 1-2 months after acceptance. Buys simultaneous rights. Editorial lead time 3 months. Submit seasonal material 6 months in advance. Accepts queries by e-mail, phone. Accepts simultaneous submissions. Responds in 1 month to queries. Responds in 1 month to mss. Sample copy available online. Guidelines free.
Nonfiction Needs how-to, technical. Special issues: Summer Blockbuster issue (June/July); Special Homebuilders' issue (November/December). **Buys 15 mss/year.** Query. Length: 800-1,200 words. **Pays 40¢/word.** Sometimes pays expenses of writers on assignment.
Photos State availability. Captions, identification of subjects, model releases required. Reviews GIF/JPEG files. Negotiates payment individually. Buys simultaneous rights.
Columns/Departments Atlantic Focus (stories from Atlantic Canada); Western Focus (stories from Western Canada, including Manitoba); Trucks for the Trade (articles pertaining to the vehicles used by electrical contractors); Tools for the Trade (articles pertaining to tools used by contractors); all 800 words. **Buys 6 mss/year.** Query. **Pays 40¢/word.**
Tips Call me, and we'll talk about what I need, and how you can provide it. Stories must have Canadian content.

PIPELINE & GAS JOURNAL

Oildom Publishing, 1160 Dairy Ashford, Suite 610, Houston TX 77079. (281)558-6930. Fax: (281)558-7029. E-mail: rtubb@oildom.com. Website: www.oildompublishing.com. Rita Tubb, man. ed. **Contact:** Jeff Share, editor. **15% freelance**. Covering pipeline operations worldwide. "Edited for personnel engaged in energy pipeline design construction operations, as well as marketing, storage, supply, risk management and regulatory affairs, natural gas transmission and distribution companies." Estab. 1859. Circ. 29,000. Yes Pays on publication. 2 months All rights purchased. 1 month Accepts queries by e-mail at jshare@oildom.com. 2-3 weeks on queries; 1-2 months on mss Free. Online at http://pgjonline.com.
Nonfiction Contact: Editor. Needs interview, new product, travel, case studies. Query.

Columns/Departments Contact: Sr. Ed.: lbullion@oildom.com. What's New: Product type items, 100/ words; New Products: Product items, 50-100/words; Business New: Personnel Change, 25-35/words; Company New: 35-50/words.

$$ PUBLIC POWER

American Public Power Association, 1875 Connecticut Ave. NW, Suite 1200, Washington DC 20009-5715. (202)467-2900. Fax: (202)467-2910. E-mail: mrufe@appanet.org. Website: www.appanet.org. **60% freelance written. Prefers to work with published/established writers.** Bimonthly trade journal. Estab. 1942. Byline given. Pays on acceptance. No kill fee. Publishes ms an average of 3 months after acceptance. Accepts queries by mail, e-mail, fax. Responds in 6 months to queries. Sample copy and writer's guidelines free.

Nonfiction Features on municipal and other local publicly owned electric utilities. **Pays $600 and up.**

Photos Reviews electronic photos (minimum 300 dpi at reproduction size), transparencies, slides, and prints.

Tips We look for writers who are familiar with energy policy issues.

$$$ TEXAS CO-OP POWER

Texas Electric Cooperatives, Inc., 1122 Colorado St. 24th Floor, Austin TX 78701. (512)486-6242. E-mail: kayen@texas-ec.org. Website: www.texascooppower.com. **Contact:** Kaye Northcott. **50% freelance written**. Monthly magazine covering rural and suburban Texas life, people, and places. *Texas Co-op Power* provides 1 million households and businesses educational and technical information about electric cooperatives in a high-quality and entertaining format to promote the general welfare of cooperatives, their member-owners, and the areas in which they serve. Estab. 1948. Circ. 1 million. Byline given. after any necessary rewrites. No kill fee. Publishes ms an average of 6 months after acceptance. Buys first rights, buys electronic rights. Editorial lead time 4-5 months. Submit seasonal material 6 months in advance. Accepts queries by mail, e-mail, fax. Accepts simultaneous submissions. Responds in 1 month to queries. Responds in 3 months to mss. Sample copy available online. Guidelines for #10 sase.

Nonfiction Needs general interest, historical, interview, photo feature, travel. **Buys 30 mss/year.** Query with published clips. Length: 800-1,200 words. **Pays $400-1,000.** Sometimes pays expenses of writers on assignment.

Photos State availability. Identification of subjects, model releases required. Reviews transparencies, prints. Negotiates payment individually. Buys one time rights.

Tips We're looking for Texas-related, rural-based articles, often first-person, always lively and interesting.

Engineering & Technology

$$$ ⊡ CABLING NETWORKING SYSTEMS

12 Concorde Place, Suite 800, North York ON M3C 4J2 Canada. (416)510-6752. Fax: (416)510-5134. E-mail: pbarker@cnsmagazine.com. Website: www.cablingsystems.com. **Contact:** Paul Barker, editor. **50% freelance written**. Magazine published 6 times/year covering structured cabling/telecommunications industry. *Cabling Systems* is written for engineers, designers, contractors, and end users who design, specify, purchase, install, test and maintain structured cabling and telecommunications products and systems. Estab. 1998. Circ. 11,000. Byline given. Pays on publication. No kill fee. Publishes ms an average of 1 month after acceptance. Buys all rights. Editorial lead time 3 months. Submit seasonal material 1 month in advance. Accepts queries by mail, e-mail, phone. Accepts simultaneous submissions. Sample copy available online. Guidelines free.

Nonfiction Needs technical, case studies, features. No reprints or previously written articles. All articles are assigned by editor based on query or need of publication. **Buys 12 mss/year.** Query with published clips. Length: 1,500-2,500 words. **Pays 40-50¢/word.** Sometimes pays expenses of writers on assignment.

Photos State availability. Captions, identification of subjects required. Reviews contact sheets, prints. Negotiates payment individually.

Columns/Departments Focus on Engineering/Design; Focus on Installation; Focus on Maintenance/ Testing, all 1,500 words. **Buys 7 mss/year.** Query with published clips. **Pays 40-50¢/word.**

Tips Visit our website to see back issues, and visit links on our website for background.

$$$ ⊡ CANADIAN CONSULTING ENGINEER

Business Information Group, 12 Condorde Place, Suite 800, Toronto ON M3C 4J2 Canada. (416)510-5119.

Fax: (416)510-5134. E-mail: bparsons@ccemag.com. Website: www.canadianconsultingengineer.com. **Contact:** Bronwen Parsons, editor. **20%% freelance written**. Bimonthly magazine covering consulting engineering in private practice. Estab. 1958. Circ. 8,900. Byline given depending on length of story Pays on publication. Offers 50% kill fee. Publishes ms an average of 4 months after acceptance. Buys first North American serial rights. Editorial lead time 6 months. Responds in 3 months to mss. Sample copy free.

- Canadian content only. Impartial editorial required.

Nonfiction Needs historical, new product, technical, engineering/construction projects, environmental/construction issues. **Buys 8-10 mss/year.** Length: 300-1,500 words. **Pays $200-1,000 (Canadian).** Sometimes pays expenses of writers on assignment.

Photos State availability. Negotiates payment individually. Buys one time rights.

Columns/Departments Export (selling consulting engineering services abroad); Management (managing consulting engineering businesses); On-Line (trends in CAD systems); Employment; Business; Construction and Environmental Law (Canada), all 800 words. **Buys 4 mss/year.** Query with published clips. **Pays $250-400.**

$$ COMPOSITES MANUFACTURING MAGAZINE

The Official Publication of the American Composites Manufacturers Association, (formerly *Composites Fabrication Magazine*), American Composites Manufacturers Association, 1010 N. Glebe Rd., Suite 450, Arlington VA 22201. (703)525-0511. Fax: (703)525-0743. E-mail: arusnak@acmanet.org. Website: www.cfmagazine.org. Monthly magazine covering any industry that uses reinforced composites: marine, aerospace, infrastructure, automotive, transportation, corrosion, architecture, tub and shower, sports, and recreation. Primarily, we publish educational pieces, the how-to of the shop environment. We also publish marketing, business trends, and economic forecasts relevant to the composites industry. Estab. 1979. Circ. 12,000. Byline given. Pays on acceptance. No kill fee. Publishes ms an average of 2-3 months after acceptance. Buys all rights. Editorial lead time 2 months. Accepts queries by e-mail. Accepts previously published material. Accepts simultaneous submissions. Responds in 1 week to queries. Responds in 1 month to mss. Sample copy free. Guidelines by e-mail.

Nonfiction Needs how-to, composites manufacturing, new product, technical, marketing, related business trends and forecasts. Special issues: Each January we publish a World Market Report where we cover all niche markets and all geographic areas relevant to the composites industry. Freelance material will be considered strongly for this issue. No need to query company or personal profiles unless there is an extremely unique or novel angle. **Buys 5-10 mss/year.** Query. Length: 1,500-4,000 words. **Pays 20-40¢/word (negotiable).** Sometimes pays expenses of writers on assignment.

Columns/Departments We publish columns on HR, relevant government legislation, industry lessons learned, regulatory affairs, and technology. Average word length for columns is 500 words. We would entertain any new column idea that hits hard on industry matters. Query. **Pays $300-350.**

Tips The best way to break into the magazine is to empathize with the entrepreneurial and technical background of readership, and come up with an exclusive, original, creative story idea. We pride ourselves on not looking or acting like any other trade publication (composites industry or otherwise). Our editor is very open to suggestions, but they must be unique. Don't waste his time with canned articles dressed up to look exclusive. This is the best way to get on the 'immediate rejection list.'

$$$ ENTERPRISE MINNESOTA MAGAZINE

Helping Manufacturing Enterprises Grow Profitably, Enterprise Minnesota, Inc., 310 4th Ave. So., Minneapolis MN 55415. (612)373-2900. Fax: (612)373-2901. E-mail: editor@mntech.org. Website: www.enterpriseminnesota.org. **Contact:** Tom Mason, editor. **90% freelance written**. Magazine published 5 times/year. *Minnesota Technology* is read 5 times a year by owners and top management of Minnesota's technology and manufacturing companies. The magazine covers technology trends and issues, global trade, management techniques, and finance. We profile new and growing companies, new products, and the innovators and entrepreneurs of Minnesota's technology sector. Estab. 1991. Circ. 16,000. Byline given. Pays on publication. Offers 10% kill fee. Publishes ms an average of 3 months after acceptance. Buys first North American serial rights for print and Web version of magazine. Editorial lead time 1 month. Submit seasonal material 1 year in advance. Accepts queries by mail, e-mail. Guidelines available online.

Nonfiction Needs general interest, how-to, interview. **Buys 60 mss/year.** Query with published clips. **Pays $150-1,000.**

Columns/Departments Feature Well (Q&A format, provocative ideas from Minnesota business and industry leaders), 2,000 words; Up Front (mini profiles, anecdotal news items), 250-500 words. Query with published clips.

$ $ INTERFACE TECH NEWS

Northern New England's Technology Newspaper, Millyard Communications, Inc., 670 N. Commercial St., Suite 110, Manchester NH 03101. (603)626-6354. Fax: (603)626-6359. E-mail: msaturley@millyardcommunications.com. Website: www.interfacetechnews.com. **85% freelance written**. Monthly newspaper covering people, companies and cutting edge technology in Northern New England. Stories must have a local, northern New England angle. Who are the people shaping tomorrow's tech industry? Why should you care? Estab. 1997. Circ. 11,000. Byline given. Pays on publication. Offers 25% kill fee. Publishes ms an average of 2-3 months after acceptance. Buys first North American serial rights. Editorial lead time 3 months. Submit seasonal material 3 months in advance. Accepts queries by mail, e-mail. Accepts previously published material. Responds in 2 weeks to queries. Sample copy free. Guidelines free.

Nonfiction Needs how-to, interview, new product, opinion, technical, case studies. Does not want stories about companies, people or products not based in northern New England. **Buys 60 mss/year.** Query with published clips. Length: 600-1,500 words. **Pays $150-300.** Sometimes pays expenses of writers on assignment.

Photos Contact: Greg Duval, creative director. Send photos. Identification of subjects required. Reviews GIF/JPEG files. Offers $25-50/photo. Buys one time rights.

Columns/Departments Industry Watch (exploring tech advancements in specific industries), 600-800 words; From the Bench (case law, legislation, lobbyist activity), 600-800 words; Tech Download (explanation of bleeding-edge tech), 800 words; Interface Case Study (in-depth look at a problem solved by technology), 800-900 words. **Buys 50 mss/year.** Query with published clips. **Pays $200-250.**

Tips We usually start off new writers with a shorter piece, around 600 words. If they work out, we start assigning longer stories. Experience in journalism and a working knowledge of tech required.

$ $ LD+A

Lighting Design & Application, Illuminating Engineering Society of North America, 120 Wall St., 17th Floor, New York NY 10005. (212)248-5000. Fax: (212)248-5017. E-mail: ptarricone@iesna.org. Website: www.iesna.org. **Contact:** Paul Tarricone, editor. **10% freelance written**. Monthly magazine. *LD+A* is geared to professionals in lighting design and the lighting field in architecture, retail, entertainment, etc. Estab. 1971. Circ. 10,000. Byline given. Pays on acceptance. No kill fee. Publishes ms an average of 4 months after acceptance. Buys all rights. Editorial lead time 2 months. Submit seasonal material 4 months in advance. Accepts queries by mail, e-mail, fax, phone. Accepts simultaneous submissions. Responds in 2 weeks to queries. Sample copy free. Guidelines available online at website.

Nonfiction Every year we have entertainment, outdoor, retail and arts, and exhibits issues. Needs historical, how-to, opinion, personal experience, photo feature, technical. No articles blatantly promoting a product, company, or individual. **Buys 6-10 mss/year.** Query. Length: 1,500-2,000 words.

Photos Send photos. Captions required. Reviews JPEG/TIFF files. Offers no additional payment for photos accepted with ms.

Columns/Departments Essay by Invitation (industry trends), 1,200 words. Query. **Does not pay for columns.**

Tips Most of our features detail the ins and outs of a specific lighting project. From museums to stadiums and highways, *LD+A* gives its readers an in-depth look at how the designer(s) reached their goals.

$ $ MANUFACTURING & TECHNOLOGY EJOURNAL

The Manufacturers Group Inc., P.O. Box 4310, Lexington KY 40544. Fax: (859)223-6709. E-mail: editor@industrysearch.com. Website: www.mfr.tech.com. **40% freelance written**. Weekly website Manufacturing & technology. Editorial targets middle and upper management—Presidents, Plant Managers, Engineering, Purchasing. Editorial includes features on operations and management, new plants, acquisitions, expansions, new products. Estab. 1976 (print). Circ. 10,000 plus weekly (e-mail) 5,000 weekly online. Byline given. 30 days followiong publication. Offers 25% kill fee. Publishes ms an average of 2 weeks after acceptance. Buys first North American serial rights. Editorial lead time 2 weeks. Submit seasonal material 2 weeks in advance. Sample copy available online. Guidelines by e-mail.

Nonfiction Needs new product, opinion, technical, New plants, expansions, acquisitions. Most articles are assignments. Special issues: We have assigned features on timely issues relating to economics, environmental, manufacturing trends, employment. Open to feature suggestions by outline only. Marketing, opinion. General interest, inspirational, personal, travel, book excerpts. Length: 750-1,200 words. **Pays $0.20/word published.**

Columns/Departments New Plants (Manufacturing, Technology), Acquisitions (Manufacturing, Technology), New Technology, Expansions (Manufacturing, Technology). Query. **Pays $-$0.20/word.**

$$ MINORITY ENGINEER

An Equal Opportunity Career Publication for Professional and Graduating Minority Engineers, Equal Opportunity Publications, Inc., 445 Broad Hollow Rd., Suite 425, Melville NY 11747. (631)421-9421. Fax: (516)421-0359. E-mail: jschneider@eop.com. Website: www.eop.com. **60% freelance written. Prefers to work with published/established writers.** Triannual magazine covering career guidance for minority engineering students and minority professional engineers. Job information. Estab. 1969. Circ. 15,000. Byline given. Pays on publication. No kill fee. Publishes ms an average of 3 months after acceptance. Buys first North American serial rights. Editorial lead time 3 months. Accepts queries by mail, e-mail, fax, phone. Accepts simultaneous submissions. Responds in 2 weeks to queries. Responds in 2 months to mss. Sample copy and writer's guidelines for 9 × 12 SAE with 5 first-class stamps. Guidelines free.

Nonfiction We're interested in articles dealing with career guidance and job opportunities for minority engineers. Needs book excerpts, general interest, on specific minority engineering concerns, how-to, land a job, keep a job, etc., interview, minority engineer role models, opinion, problems of ethnic minorities, personal experience, student and career experiences, technical, on career fields offering opportunities for minority engineers, articles on job search techniques, role models. No general information. Query. Length: 1,500-2,500 words. **Pays $350 for assigned articles.** Sometimes pays expenses of writers on assignment.

Reprints Send typed manuscript with rights for sale noted and information about when and where the material previously appeared. Pays 100% of amount paid for an original article.

Photos State availability.

Tips Articles should focus on career guidance, role model and industry prospects for minority engineers. Prefer articles related to careers, not politically or socially sensitive.

PROFESSIONAL SURVEYOR MAGAZINE

Reed Business Geo, Inc., 100 Tuscanny Drive, Suite B-1, Frederick MD 21702-5958. (301)682-6101. Fax: (301)682-6105. E-mail: tom@profsurv.com. Website: www.profsurv.com. **Contact:** Tom Gibson, editor. **50% freelance written**. Monthly magazine Surveying. This publication covers all facets of surveying and related activities such as satellite positioning (GPS), laser scanning, remote sensing, photogrammetry and mapping. The audience is mainly surveyors. Estab. 1982. Circ. 38,000. Byline given. Pays on publication. No kill fee. Publishes ms an average of 2 months after acceptance. Buys first North American serial rights, buys second serial (reprint) rights. Editorial lead time 3 months. Accepts queries by e-mail. Responds in 2 weeks to queries. Responds in 1 month to mss. Sample copy available online. Guidelines available online.

Nonfiction Needs book excerpts, general interest, historical, how-to, humor, interview, new product, opinion, personal experience, technical, case histories. Special issues: Aerial Mapping Supplement. Length: 1000-2000 words. **Pays $300-500 for assigned articles.** Sometimes pays expenses of writers on assignment.

Photos Contact: JoAnne Howland, art director. "We always need images to go with an article; looking for cover photos." Send photos. Captions required. Reviews GIF/JPEG files. offers no additional money for photos.

Columns/Departments Contact: Shelly Cox, managing editor: shelly@prosurv.com. "As for columns, we have several types that run throughout the magazine on a monthly or semi-regular basis. If you plan to submit something, we advise you to read several stories in the magazine and familiarize yourself with our guidelines. Then contact us to present your idea or discuss possibilities." Book Review, Aerial Perspective, 3D Scanning, Business Angle (all 1,000-2,000 words). **Buys 50 mss/year.** Query. **Pays $200-$400.**

Tips "For features, we're always looking for surveying-related case histories or discussions of new technology; 1,500-2,000 words."

$$$$ RAILWAY TRACK AND STRUCTURES

RT&S, Simmons-Boardman Publishing, 20 S. Clark St., Suite 2450, Chicago IL 60603-1838. (312)683-0130. Fax: (312)683-0131. Website: www.rtands.com. **1% freelance written**. Monthly magazine covering railroad civil engineering. "*RT&S* is a nuts-and-bolts journal to help railroad civil engineers do their jobs better." Estab. 1904. Circ. 9,500. Byline given. Pays on publication. Offers 90% kill fee. Publishes ms an average of 1 month after acceptance. Buys one-time rights. Editorial lead time 2 months. Submit seasonal material 3 months in advance. Accepts queries by mail, fax, phone. Accepts previously published material. Accepts simultaneous submissions. Responds in 1 month to queries and to mss. Sample copy available online.

Nonfiction Needs how-to, new product, technical. Does not want nostalgia or railroadiana. **Buys 1 mss/year.** Query. Length: 900-2,000 words. **Pays $500-1,000** Sometimes pays expenses of writers on assignment.

Photos State availability. Captions, identification of subjects, model releases required. Reviews GIF/JPEG files. Negotiates payment individually. Buys one-time rights.

Tips "We prefer writers with a civil engineering background and railroad experience."

UTILITY PRODUCTS MAGAZINE

Pennwell Publishing, 114 Trade Center Dr., Suite A, Birmingham AL 35244. (303)337-0513. E-mail: michaelg@pennwell.com. Website: www.utilityproducts.com. **Contact:** Michael Grossman, publisher. **95% freelance written**. Monthly magazine covering electric, TELCO, CATV utilities. "Non-commercial slant. We like to hear about problems the utility industry is facing and what new technologies, tools, etc. are available to solve these problems. Case studies and bylined articles are both accepted. The audience ranges from management to the people out in the field." Estab. 1997. Circ. 45,000. Byline given. non-paid only. No kill fee. Publishes ms an average of 1-5 months after acceptance. Editorial lead time 2 months. Submit seasonal material 3 months in advance. Accepts queries by e-mail, phone. Responds in 1 week to queries. Responds in 1 month to mss. Sample copy free. Guidelines by e-mail.

Nonfiction Needs new product, personal experience, photo feature, technical. Special issues: Please see our 2009 editorial calendar. No commercial-based articles; advertorial. **Buys 0 mss/year.** Send complete ms. Length: 1,500-2,200 words.

Photos Contact: Kellie Sandrik, managing editor. Send photos. Reviews GIF/JPEG files. Offers no additional payment for photos accepted with ms. Buys one time rights.

Tips "Read our magazine and look at our website—know our magazine and market. Query well in advance of the deadline. Query with several story pitches if possible."

$ $ WOMAN ENGINEER

An Equal Opportunity Career Publication for Graduating Women and Experienced Professionals, Equal Opportunity Publications, Inc., 445 Broad Hollow Rd., Suite 425, Melville NY 11747. (631)421-9421. Fax: (631)421-0359. E-mail: info@eop.com. Website: www.eop.com. **60% freelance written. Works with a small number of new/unpublished writers each year.** Triannual magazine aimed at advancing the careers of women engineering students and professional women engineers. Job information. Estab. 1968. Circ. 16,000. Byline given. Pays on publication. No kill fee. Publishes ms an average of 3 months after acceptance. Buys first North American serial rights. Editorial lead time 3 months. Accepts queries by mail, e-mail, fax, phone. Responds in 2 weeks to queries. Responds in 2 months to mss. Sample copy and writer's guidelines free. Guidelines free.

Nonfiction Interested in articles dealing with career guidance and job opportunities for women engineers. Looking for manuscripts showing how to land an engineering position and advance professionally. We want features on job-search techniques, engineering disciplines offering career opportunities to women; companies with career advancement opportunities for women; problems facing women engineers and how to cope with such problems; and role-model profiles of successful women engineers, especially in major U.S. corporations. Needs how-to, find jobs, interview, personal experience. Query. Length: 1,500-2,500 words. **Pays $350 for assigned articles.**

Photos Captions, identification of subjects required. Reviews color slides but will accept b&w. Buys all rights.

Tips We are looking for first-person 'As I See It, personal perspectives.' Gear it to our audience.

Entertainment & the Arts

$ $ $ AMERICAN CINEMATOGRAPHER

The International Journal of Film & Digital Production Techniques, American Society of Cinematographers, 1782 N. Orange Dr., Hollywood CA 90028. (800)448-0145; (outside U.S. (323)969-4333). Fax: (323)876-4973. E-mail: stephen@ascmag.com. Website: www.theasc.com. **Contact:** Stephen Pizzello, executive editor. **90% freelance written**. Monthly magazine covering cinematography (motion picture, TV, music video, commercial). "*American Cinematographer* is a trade publication devoted to the art and craft of cinematography. Our readers are predominantly film-industry professionals." Estab. 1919. Circ. 45,000. Byline given. Pays on publication. Offers 50% kill fee. Publishes ms an average of 2-3 months after acceptance. Buys all rights. Editorial lead time 2 months. Submit seasonal material 3 months in advance. Accepts queries by mail, e-mail, phone. Responds in 2 weeks to queries. Responds in 2 months to mss. Sample copy and writer's guidelines free.

Nonfiction Contact: Stephen Pizzello, editor. Needs interview, new product, technical. No reviews, opinion pieces. **Buys 20-25 mss/year.** Query with published clips. Length: 1,500-4,000 words. **Pays $600-1,200.** Sometimes pays expenses of writers on assignment.

Tips "Familiarity with the technical side of film production and the ability to present that information in an articulate fashion to our audience are crucial."

$$ AMERICAN THEATRE

Theatre Communications Group, 520 8th Ave., 24th Floor, New York NY 10018-4156. (212)609-5900. E-mail: ebentt@tcg.org. Website: www.tcg.org. Jim O'Quinn, editor; Nicole Estvanik Taylor, managing ed. **Contact:** Eliza Bent. **60% freelance written**. Monthly magazine covering theatre. Our focus is American regional nonprofit theatre. American Theatre typically publishes two or three features and four to six back-of-the-book articles covering trends and events in all types of theatre, as well as economic and legislative developments affecting the arts. Estab. 1982. Circ. 100,000. Byline given. Pays on publication. Editorial lead time 2 months. Submit seasonal material 3 months in advance. Accepts queries by mail, e-mail, online submission form. Accepts previously published material. Accepts simultaneous submissions. Responds in 2 months Sample copy available online. Guidelines available online.

Nonfiction Needs book excerpts, essays, expose, general interest, historical, how-to, humor, inspirational, interview, opinion, personal experience, photo feature, travel. Special issues: Training (January); International (May/June); Season Preview (October). No unsolicited submissions (rarely accepted), no reviews Send query letter to Jim O'Quinn with outlined proposal, published clips. Include brief resume, SASE. Length: 200-2,000 words. **While fees are negotiated per ms, we pay an average of $350 for full-length (2500-3500 words) features, less for shorter pieces.**

Photos Contact: Kitty Suen, creative dir.; atphoto@tcg.com. Send photos. Captions required. Reviews JPEG files. Negotiates payment individually.

Tips American nonprofit regional theatre. Don't pitch music or film festivals. Must be about theatre.

$$ BOXOFFICE MAGAZINE

Media Enterprises LP, 155 S. El Molino Ave., Suite 100, Pasadena CA 91101. (626)396-0250. Fax: (626)396-0248. E-mail: editorial@boxoffice.com. Website: www.boxoffice.com. **15% freelance written**. Magazine about the motion picture industry for executives and managers working in the film business, including movie theater owners and operators, Hollywood studio personnel and leaders in allied industries. Estab. 1920. Circ. 6,000. Byline given. Pays on publication. No kill fee. Publishes ms an average of 3 months after acceptance. Buys first print and all electronic rights. Submit seasonal material 5 months in advance. Accepts queries by mail, e-mail, fax. Sample copy for $5 in US; $10 outside US.

Nonfiction We are a business news magazine about the motion picture industry in general and the theater industry in particular, and as such publish stories on business trends, developments, problems, and opportunities facing the industry. Almost any story will be considered, including corporate profiles, but we don't want gossip, film or celebrity coverage. Needs book excerpts, essays, interview, new product, personal experience, photo feature, technical, investigative all regarding movie theatre business. Query with published clips. Length: 800-2,500 words. **Pays 10¢/word.**

Photos State availability. Captions required. Reviews prints, slides and JPEG files. Pays $10 per published image.

Tips Purchase a sample copy and read it. Then, write a clear, comprehensive outline of the proposed story, and enclose a resume and published clips to the managing editor.

$$ CAMPUS ACTIVITIES

Cameo Publishing Group, 1520 Newberry Rd., Blair SC 29015. (800)728-2950. Fax: (803)712-6703. E-mail: ian@cameopublishing.com. Website: www.campusactivitiesmagazine.com; www.cameopublishing.com; www.americanentertainmentmagazine.com. W.C. Kirby, publisher. **Contact:** Ian Kirby, editorial director. **75% freelance written**. Magazine published 8 times/year covering entertainment on college campuses. *Campus Activities* goes to entertainment buyers on every campus in the U.S. Features stories on artists (national and regional), speakers, and the programs at individual schools. Estab. 1991. Circ. 9,872. Byline given. Pays on publication. Offers kill fee. Offers 15% kill fee if accepted and not run. Publishes ms an average of 2 months after acceptance. Buys first rights, buys second serial (reprint) rights, buys electronic rights. Editorial lead time 2 months. Submit seasonal material 2 months in advance. Accepts queries by mail, e-mail, fax. Accepts simultaneous submissions. Responds in 1 month to queries. Responds in 2 months to mss. Sample copy for $3.50. Guidelines free.

Nonfiction Needs interview, photo feature. Accepts no unsolicited articles. **Buys 40 mss/year.** Query. Length: 1,400-3,000 words. **Pays 13¢/word.** Sometimes pays expenses of writers on assignment.

Photos State availability. Identification of subjects required. Reviews contact sheets, negatives, 3 × 5 transparencies, 8 × 10 prints, electronic media at 300 dpi or higher. Negotiates payment individually. Buys one time rights.

Tips Writers who have ideas, proposals, and special project requests should contact the publisher prior to any commitment to work on such a story. The publisher welcomes innovative and creative ideas for stories and works with writers on such proposals which have significant impact on our readers.

$$ DANCE TEACHER

The Practical Magazine of Dance, McFadden Performing Arts Media, 110 William St., 23rd Floor, New York NY 10038. Fax: (646)459-4000. E-mail: khildebrand@dancemedia.com. Website: www.dance-teacher.com. **Contact:** Karen Hildebrand, editor. **60% freelance written.** Monthly magazine. Our readers are professional dance educators, business persons, and related professionals in all forms of dance. Estab. 1979. Circ. 25,000. Byline given. Pays on publication. No kill fee. Publishes ms an average of 3 months after acceptance. Negotiates rights and permission to reprint on request. Submit seasonal material 6 months in advance. Accepts queries by mail, e-mail, fax, phone. Responds in 3 months to mss. Sample copy for sae with 9 × 12 envelope and 6 First-Class stamps. Guidelines available online.

Nonfiction Needs how-to, teach, health, business, legal. Special issues: Summer Programs (January); Music & More (May); Costumes and Production Preview (November); College/Training Schools (December). No PR or puff pieces. All articles must be well researched. **Buys 50 mss/year.** Query. Length: 700-2,000 words. **Pays $100-300.**

Photos Send photos. Reviews contact sheets, negatives, transparencies, prints. Limited photo budget.

Tips Read several issues—particularly seasonal. Stay within writer's guidelines.

$$ DRAMATICS MAGAZINE

Educational Theatre Association, 2343 Auburn Ave., Cincinnati OH 45219-2815. (513)421-3900. Fax: (513)421-7077. E-mail: dcorathers@schooltheatre.org. Website: www.edta.org. **Contact:** Donald Corathers, editor. **70% freelance written.** Monthly magazine for theater arts students, teachers, and others interested in theater arts education. "*Dramatics* is designed to provide serious, committed young theater students and their teachers with the skills and knowledge they need to make better theater; to be a resource that will help high school juniors and seniors make an informed decision about whether to pursue a career in theater, and about how to do so; and to prepare high school students to be knowledgeable, appreciative audience members for the rest of their lives." Estab. 1929. Circ. 40,000. Byline given. Pays on acceptance. No kill fee. Publishes ms an average of 3 months after acceptance. Buys first North American serial rights. Submit seasonal material 3 months in advance. Accepts queries by mail, e-mail, fax. Accepts previously published material. Accepts simultaneous submissions. Responds in 3 months to queries. Responds in more than 3 months to mss. Sample copy for 9 × 12 SAE with 5 first-class stamps. Guidelines available online.

Nonfiction Needs how-to, technical theater, directing, acting, etc., humor, inspirational, interview, photo feature, technical. **Buys 30 mss/year.** Send complete ms. Length: 750-3,000 words. **Pays $50-400.** Sometimes pays expenses of writers on assignment.

Reprints Send tearsheet, photocopy or typed ms with rights for sale noted and information about when and where the material previously appeared. Pays up to 75% of amount paid for original.

Photos Query. Purchased with accompanying ms. Reviews high-res JPEG files on CD. Total price for ms usually includes payment for photos.

Fiction Drama (one-act and full-length plays). Prefers unpublished scripts that have been produced at least once. No plays for children, Christmas plays, or plays written with no attention paid to the conventions of theater. **Buys 5-9 mss/year.** Send complete ms. **Pays $100-500.**

Tips "Writers who have some practical experience in theater, especially in technical areas, have a leg-up here, but we'll work with anybody who has a good idea. Some freelancers have become regular contributors, others ignore style suggestions included in our writer's guidelines."

$ $ FILM ARTS

The Magazine of Film Arts Foundation, Film Arts Foundation, 145 9th St., Suite 101, San Francisco CA 94103. (415)552-8760. Fax: (415)552-0882. Website: www.filmarts.org. **80% freelance written**. Bimonthly magazine covering US independent filmmaking. "We have a knowledgeable readership of film and videomakers. They are interested in the financing, production, exhibition, and distribution of independent films and videos. They are interested in practical, technical issues and, to a lesser extent, aesthetic ones." Estab. 1977. Circ. 5,000. Byline given. Pays on publication. No kill fee. Publishes ms an average of 3 months after acceptance. Buys all rights for commissioned works. For works submitted on spec, buys first rights and requests acknowledgement of Film Arts in any subsequent publication. Editorial lead time 4 months. Accepts queries by e-mail. Responds in 6 weeks to queries. Responds in 2 months to mss. Sample copy for $10.

Nonfiction Needs interview, technical, book recommendations, case studies. No film criticism or reviews. **Buys 70-72 mss/year.** Query. Length: 500-2,000 words. Sometimes pays expenses of writers on assignment.

Photos Send photos. Identification of subjects required. Reviews prints. Offers no additional payment for photos accepted with ms. Buys one time rights.

Columns/Departments Query. **Pays 10¢/word.**

$ $ MAKE-UP ARTIST MAGAZINE

Motion Picture, Television, Theatre, Print, 4018 NE 112th Ave., Suite D-8, Vancouver WA 98682. (360)882-3488. E-mail: news@makeupmag.com. Website: www.makeupmag.com. Michael Key, editor-in-chief. **Contact:** Heather Wisner, managing ed. **90% freelance written**. Bimonthly magazine covering all types of professional make-up artistry. Our audience is a mixture of high-level make-up artists, make-up students, and movie buffs. Writers should be comfortable with technical writing, and should have substantial knowledge of at least one area of makeup, such as effects or fashion. This is an entertainment-industry magazine so writing should have an element of fun and storytelling. Good interview skills required. Estab. 1996. Circ. 12,000. Byline given. Pays within 30 days of publication. No kill fee. Buys all rights. Editorial lead time 6 weeks. Submit seasonal material 2 months in advance. Accepts queries by mail, e-mail, phone. Accepts simultaneous submissions. Sample copy for $7. Guidelines by e-mail.

Nonfiction Needs book excerpts, essays, historical, how-to, humor, inspirational, interview, new product, opinion, personal experience, photo feature, technical, travel. Does not want fluff pieces about consumer beauty products. **Buys 20+ mss/year.** Query with published clips. Length: 500-3,000 words. **Pays 20-50¢/word.** Sometimes pays expenses of writers on assignment.

Photos Send photos. Captions, identification of subjects required. Reviews prints, GIF/JPEG files. Negotiates payment individually. Buys all rights.

Columns/Departments Cameo (short yet thorough look at a makeup artist not covered in a feature story), 800 words (15 photos); Lab Tech (how-to advice for effects artists, usually written by a current makeup artist working in a lab), 800 words (3 photos); Backstage (analysis, interview, tips and behind the scenes info on a theatrical production's makeup), 800 words (3 photos). **Buys 30 mss/year.** Query with published clips. **Pays $100.**

Tips Read books about professional makeup artistry (see list in FAQ section of our website). Read online interviews with makeup artists. Read makeup-oriented mainstream magazines, such as *Allure*. Read *Cinefex* and other film-industry publications. Meet and talk to makeup artists and makeup students.

$ SOUTHERN THEATRE

Southeastern Theatre Conference, P.O. Box 9868, Greensboro NC 27429-0868. (336)292-6041. E-mail: deanna@setc.org. Website: www.setc.org. **Contact:** Deanna Thompson, editor. **100% freelance written**. Quarterly magazine covering all aspects of theater in the Southeast, from innovative theater companies, to important trends, to people making a difference in the region. All stories must be written in a popular magazine style but with subject matter appropriate for theater professionals (not the general public). The audience includes members of the Southeastern Theatre Conference, founded in 1949 and the nation's largest regional theater organization. These members include individuals involved in professional, community, college/university, children's, and secondary school theater. The magazine also is purchased by more than 100 libraries. Estab. 1962. Circ. 4,200. Byline given. Pays on publication. No kill fee. Publishes ms an average of 3 months after acceptance. Buys first North American serial rights, first rights, one-time rights, second serial (reprint) rights, electronic rights. Editorial lead time 3 months. Submit seasonal material 6 months in advance. Accepts queries by mail, e-mail. Responds in 3 months to queries. Responds in 6 months to mss. Sample copy for $10. Guidelines available online.

Nonfiction Looking for stories on design/technology, playwriting, acting, directing—all with a Southeastern connection. Needs general interest, innovative theaters and theater programs, trend stories, interview, people making a difference in Southeastern theater. Special issues: Playwriting (Fall issue, all stories submitted by January 1). No scholarly articles. **Buys 15-20 mss/year.** Send complete ms. Length: 1,000-3,000 words. **Pays $50 for feature stories.**
Photos State availability of or send photos. Captions, identification of subjects, model releases required. Reviews transparencies, prints. Offers no additional payment for photos accepted with ms.
Columns/Departments *Outside the Box* (innovative solutions to problems faced by designers and technicians), *400 Words* (column where the theater professionals can sound off on issues), 400 words; 800-1,000 words; *Words, Words, Words* (reviews of books on theater), 400 words. Query or send complete ms. **No payment for columns.**
Tips "Look for a theater or theater person in your area that is doing something different or innovative that would be of interest to others in the profession, then write about that theater or person in a compelling way. We also are looking for well-written trend stories (talk to theaters in your area about trends that are affecting them), and we especially like stories that help our readers do their jobs more effectively. Send an e-mail detailing a well-developed story idea, and ask if we're interested."

Farm

Agricultural Equipment

$ $ IMPLEMENT & TRACTOR

Farm Journal, 120 West 4th St., Cedar Falls IA 50613. (319)277-3599. Fax: (319)277-3783. E-mail: mfischer@farmjournal.com or cfinck@farmjournal.com. Website: www.implementandtractor.com. **Contact:** Margy Fischer or Charlene Finck. **10% freelance written**. Bimonthly magazine covering the agricultural equipment industry. "*Implement & Tractor* offers equipment reviews and business news for agricultural equipment dealers, ag equipment manufacturers, distributors, and aftermarket suppliers." Estab. 1895. Circ. 5,000. Byline given. Pays on publication. No kill fee. Publishes ms an average of 3-4 months after acceptance. Buys all rights. Editorial lead time 2 months. Accepts queries by mail, e-mail, fax. Responds in 2 months to queries. Sample copy for $6.

Crops & Soil Management

$ $ AMERICAN/WESTERN FRUIT GROWER

Meister Media Worldwide, 37733 Euclid Ave., Willoughby OH 44094. (440)942-2000. E-mail: bdsparks@meistermedia.com. Website: www.fruitgrower.com. **Contact:** Brian Sparks, group editor. **3% freelance written**. Annual magazine covering commercial fruit growing. How-to articles are best. Estab. 1880. Circ. 44,000. Byline given. Pays on publication. No kill fee. Publishes ms an average of 4 months after acceptance. Buys first rights. Editorial lead time 2 months. Submit seasonal material 4 months in advance. Accepts queries by mail, e-mail, fax, phone. Responds in 2 weeks to queries. Responds in 2 months to mss. Sample copy and writer's guidelines free.
Nonfiction Needs how-to, better grow fruit crops. **Buys 6-10 mss/year.** Send complete ms. Length: 800-1,200 words. **Pays $200-250.** Sometimes pays expenses of writers on assignment.
Photos Send photos. Reviews prints, slides. Negotiates payment individually. Buys one time rights.

$ $ COTTON GROWER MAGAZINE

Meister Media Worldwide, 65 Germantown Court, #202, Cordova TN 38018. (901)756-8822. E-mail: frgiles@meistermedia.com. **5% freelance written**. Monthly magazine covering cotton production, cotton markets and related subjects. Readers are mostly cotton producers who seek information on production practices, equipment and products related to cotton. Estab. 1901. Circ. 43,000. Byline given. Pays on acceptance. No kill fee. Publishes ms an average of 2 months after acceptance. Buys first rights. Editorial lead time 2 months. Submit seasonal material 2 months in advance. Accepts queries by mail, e-mail, fax, phone. Accepts simultaneous submissions. Sample copy free.
Nonfiction Needs interview, new product, photo feature, technical. No fiction or humorous pieces. **Buys 5-10 mss/year.** Query with published clips. Length: 500-800 words. **Pays $200-400.** Sometimes pays expenses of writers on assignment.

Photos State availability. Captions, identification of subjects required. Reviews transparencies. Offers no additional payment for photos accepted with ms. Buys all rights.

$ THE FRUIT GROWERS NEWS

Great American Publishing, P.O. Box 128, Sparta MI 49345. (616)887-9008. Fax: (616)887-2666. E-mail: news@fruitgrowersnews.com. Website: www.fruitgrowersnews.com. **Contact:** Matt Milkovich, managing editor. **10% freelance written**. Monthly tabloid covering agriculture. "Our objective is to provide commercial fruit growers of all sizes with information to help them succeed." Estab. 1970. Circ. 15,000. Pays on publication. No kill fee. Publishes ms an average of 2 months after acceptance. Makes work-for-hire assignments. Editorial lead time 1-2 months. Submit seasonal material 3 months in advance. Accepts queries by mail, e-mail, fax. Accepts simultaneous submissions. Responds in 2 weeks to queries. Responds in 1 month to mss. Sample copy free.

Nonfiction Needs general interest, interview, new product. No advertorials, other puff pieces. **Buys 25 mss/year.** Query with published clips and resume. Length: 800-1,200 words. **Pays $100-125.** Sometimes pays expenses of writers on assignment.

Photos Send photos. Captions required. Reviews prints. Offers $15/photo. Buys one time rights.

$$ GOOD FRUIT GROWER

Washington State Fruit Commission, 105 S. 18th St., #217, Yakima WA 98901-2177. (509)575-2315. E-mail: jim.black@goodfruit.com. Website: www.goodfruit.com. **20% freelance written**. Semi-monthly magazine covering tree fruit/grape growing. Estab. 1946. Circ. 11,000. Byline given. Pays on acceptance. Publishes ms an average of 3 months after acceptance. Buys first rights, buys electronic rights. Accepts queries by mail, e-mail. Accepts simultaneous submissions. Responds in 1 week to queries. Responds in 1 month to mss. Sample copy free. Guidelines free.

Nonfiction "We work with writers to choose topics of mutual interest." **Buys 50 mss/year.** Query. Length: 500-1,500 words. **Pays 40-50¢/word.** Sometimes pays expenses of writers on assignment.

Photos Contact: Jim Black. Reviews GIF/JPEG files. Negotiates payment individually. Buys one time rights.

Tips "We want well-written, accurate information. We deal with our writers honestly and expect the same in return."

$ ONION WORLD

Columbia Publishing & Design, 413-B N. 20th Ave., Yakima WA 98902. (509)248-2452, ext. 105. Fax: (509)248-4056. E-mail: dbrent@columbiapublications.com. Website: www.onionworld.net. **Contact:** Brent Clement, editor. **25% freelance written**. Monthly magazine covering the world of onion production and marketing for onion growers and shippers. Estab. 1985. Circ. 5,500. Byline given. Pays on publication. No kill fee. Publishes ms an average of 1 month after acceptance. Buys first North American serial rights. Submit seasonal material 1 month in advance. Accepts queries by mail, e-mail, fax, phone. Accepts simultaneous submissions. Responds in 1 month to queries. Sample copy for sae with 9 × 12 envelope and 5 First-Class stamps.

- Columbia Publishing also produces *The Tomato Magazine*, *Potato Country* and *Carrot Country*.

Nonfiction Needs general interest, historical, interview. **Buys 30 mss/year.** Query. Length: 1,200-1,250 words. **Pays $5/column inch for assigned articles.**

Reprints Send photocopy and information about when and where the material previously appeared. Pays 50% of amount paid for an original article.

Photos Send photos. Captions, identification of subjects required. Offers no additional payment for photos accepted with ms, unless it's a cover shot. Buys all rights.

Tips "Writers should be familiar with growing and marketing onions. We use a lot of feature stories on growers, shippers, and others in the onion trade—what they are doing, their problems, solutions, marketing plans, etc."

$ SPUDMAN

Great American Publishing, P.O. Box 128, Sparta MI 49345. Fax: (616)887-2666. Website: www.spudman.com. **10% freelance written**. Monthly magazine covering potato industry's growing, packing, processing, chipping. Estab. 1964. Circ. 10,000. Byline given. Pays on publication. Offers $75 kill fee. Publishes ms an average of 2 months after acceptance. Buys first North American serial rights, buys electronic rights. Editorial lead time 2 months. Submit seasonal material 4 months in advance. Accepts queries by mail, e-mail. Accepts previously published material. Responds in 2-3 weeks to queries. Sample copy for sae with 8 ½ × 11 envelope and 3 First-Class stamps. Guidelines for #10 sase.

$ THE VEGETABLE GROWERS NEWS

Great American Publishing, P.O. Box 128, Sparta MI 49345. (616)887-9008. Fax: (616)887-2666. E-mail: writer@vegetablegrowersnews.com. Website: www.vegetablegrowersnews.com. **Contact:** Matt Milkovich, managing editor. **10% freelance written.** Monthly tabloid covering agriculture. "Our objective is to provide commercial vegetable growers of all sizes with information to help them succeed." Estab. 1970. Circ. 16,000. Pays on publication. No kill fee. Publishes ms an average of 2 months after acceptance. Makes work-for-hire assignments. Editorial lead time 1-2 months. Submit seasonal material 3 months in advance. Accepts queries by mail, e-mail, fax. Accepts simultaneous submissions. Responds in 2 weeks to queries. Responds in 1 month to mss. Sample copy free.

Nonfiction Needs general interest, interview, new product. No advertorials, other puff pieces. **Buys 25 mss/year.** Query with published clips and resume. Length: 800-1,200 words. **Pays $100-125.** Sometimes pays expenses of writers on assignment.

Photos Send photos. Captions required. Reviews prints. Offers $15/photo. Buys one time rights.

Dairy Farming

$ $ HOARD'S DAIRYMAN

W.D. Hoard and Sons, Co., P.O. Box 801, Fort Atkinson WI 53538. (920)563-5551. Fax: (920)563-7298. E-mail: hoards@hoards.com. Website: www.hoards.com. Tabloid published 20 times/year covering dairy industry. We publish semi-technical information published for dairy-farm families and their advisors. Estab. 1885. Circ. 100,000. Byline given. Pays on acceptance. No kill fee. Publishes ms an average of 4 months after acceptance. Buys first rights. Editorial lead time 2 months. Submit seasonal material 3 months in advance. Accepts queries by mail, e-mail, fax. Responds in 2 weeks to queries. Responds in 1 month to mss. Sample copy for 12X15 SAE and $3. Guidelines for #10 sase.

Nonfiction Needs how-to, technical. **Buys 60 mss/year.** Query. Length: 800-1,500 words. **Pays $150-350.**

Photos Send photos. Reviews 2X2 transparencies. Offers no additional payment for photos accepted with ms.

$ $ WESTERN DAIRYBUSINESS

Dairy Business Communications, 1200 W. Laurel Avenue, Visalia CA 93277. (800)934-7872; (559)802-3743. Fax: (559)802-3746. E-mail: rgoble@dairybusiness.com. Website: www.dairybusiness.com. **10% freelance written. Prefers to work with published/established writers.** Monthly magazine dealing with large-herd commercial dairy industry. Rarely publishes information about non-Western producers or dairy groups and events. Estab. 1922. Circ. 11,500. Byline given. Pays on publication. No kill fee. Publishes ms an average of 3 months after acceptance. Buys first North American serial rights. Submit seasonal material 3 months in advance. Accepts queries by e-mail. Responds in 1 month to queries. Sample copy for sae with 9 × 12 envelope and 4 first-class stamps.

Nonfiction "Special emphasis on: environmental stewardship, animal welfare, herd health, herd management systems, business management, facilities/equipment, forage/cropping." Needs interview, new product, opinion, industry analysis, industry analysis. No religion, nostalgia, politics, or 'mom and pop' dairies. Query, or e-mail complete ms. Length: 300-1,500 words. **Pays $50-400.**

Reprints "Seldom accepts previously published submissions. Send information about when and where the article previously appeared." Pays 50% of amount paid for an original article.

Photos Photos are a critical part of story packages. Send photos. Captions, identification of subjects required. Reviews contact sheets, 35mm or 2¼ × 2¼ transparencies. Pays $25 for b&w; $50-100 for color. Buys one-time rights.

Tips "Know the market and the industry, be well-versed in large-herd dairy management and business."

Livestock

$ $ ANGUS BEEF BULLETIN

Angus Productions, Inc., 3201 Frederick Ave., St. Joseph MO 64506-2997. (816)383-5270. Fax: (816)233-6575. E-mail: shermel@angusjournal.com. Website: www.angusbeefbulletin.com. **Contact:** Shauna Rose Hermel, editor. **45% freelance written.** Tabloid published 5 times/year covering commercial cattle industry. The *Bulletin* is mailed free to commercial cattlemen who have purchased an Angus bull and had the registration transferred to them and to others who sign a request card. Estab. 1985. Circ. 97,000.

Byline given. Pays on publication. No kill fee. Publishes ms an average of 3 months after acceptance. Buys first rights, buys electronic rights. Editorial lead time 3 months. Submit seasonal material 3 months in advance. Accepts queries by mail, e-mail. Accepts simultaneous submissions. Responds in 3 weeks to queries. Responds in 3 months to mss. Sample copy for $5. Guidelines for #10 sase.

Nonfiction Needs how-to, cattle production, interview, technical, cattle production. **Buys 10 mss/year.** Query with published clips. Length: 800-2,500 words. **Pays $50-600.** Pays expenses of writers on assignment.

Photos Send photos. Identification of subjects required. Reviews 5 × 7 transparencies, 5 × 7 glossy prints. Offers $25/photo. Buys all rights.

Tips Read the publication and have a firm grasp of the commercial cattle industry and how the Angus breed fits in that industry.

$$$ ANGUS JOURNAL

Angus Productions Inc., 3201 Frederick Ave., St. Joseph MO 64506-2997. (816)383-5270. Fax: (816)233-6575. E-mail: shermel@angusjournal.com. Website: www.angusjournal.com. **40% freelance written.** Monthly magazine covering Angus cattle. The *Angus Journal* is the official magazine of the American Angus Association. Its primary function as such is to report to the membership association activities and information pertinent to raising Angus cattle. Estab. 1919. Circ. 17,000. Byline given. Pays on publication. No kill fee. Publishes ms an average of 3 months after acceptance. Buys first rights, buys electronic rights. Editorial lead time 2 months. Submit seasonal material 3 months in advance. Accepts queries by mail, e-mail, fax. Accepts simultaneous submissions. Responds in 3 weeks to queries. Responds in 2 months to mss. Sample copy for $5. Guidelines for #10 sase.

Nonfiction Needs how-to, cattle production, interview, technical, related to cattle. **Buys 20-30 mss/year.** Query with published clips. Length: 800-3,500 words. **Pays $50-1,000.** Pays expenses of writers on assignment.

Photos Send photos. Identification of subjects required. Reviews 5 × 7 glossy prints. Offers $25-400/photo. Buys all rights.

Tips Read the magazine and have a firm grasp of the cattle industry.

$$ THE BRAHMAN JOURNAL

Carl and Victoria Lambert, 915 12th St., Hempstead TX 77445. (979)826-4347. Fax: (979)826-2007. E-mail: vlambert@brahmanjournal.com. Website: www.brahmanjournal.com. **10% freelance written.** Monthly magazine covering Brahman cattle. This publication provides timely and useful information about one of the largest and most dynamic breeds of beef cattle in the world. In each issue the Brahman Journal reports on Brahman shows, events, and sales as well as technical articles and the latest research as it pertains to the Brahman Breed. Estab. 1971. Circ. 4,000. Byline given. Pays on publication. No kill fee. Publishes ms an average of 2 months after acceptance. Buys first North American serial rights, buys one-time rights, buys second serial (reprint) rights. Makes work-for-hire assignments. Submit seasonal material 3 months in advance. Sample copy for sae with 9 × 12 envelope and 5 First-Class stamps.

- We promote, support, and inform the owners and admirers of American Brahman Cattle through honest and forthright journalism.

Nonfiction Needs general interest, historical, interview. Special issues: See 2009 Calendar online. **Buys 3-4 mss/year.** Query with published clips. Length: 1,200-3,000 words. **Pays $100-250.**

Reprints Send typed manuscript with rights for sale noted. Pays 50% of amount paid for an original article.

Photos Photos needed for article purchase. Send photos. Captions required. Reviews 4 × 5 prints. Offers no additional payment for photos accepted with ms. Buys one time rights.

Tips Since The Brahman Journal is read around the world, being sent to 48 different countries, it is important that the magazine contain a wide variety of information. The Brahman Journal is read by seed stock producers, show ring competitors, F-1 breeders and Brahman lovers from around the world.

$$ THE CATTLEMAN

Texas and Southwestern Cattle Raisers Association, 1301 W. 7th St., Ft. Worth TX 76102-2660. E-mail: lionel@texascattleraisers.org. Website: www.thecattlemanmagazine.com. **25% freelance written.** Monthly magazine covering the Texas/Oklahoma beef cattle industry. We specialize in in-depth, management-type articles related to range and pasture, beef cattle production, animal health, nutrition, and marketing. We want 'how-to' articles. Estab. 1914. Circ. 15,400. Byline given. Pays on acceptance. No kill fee. Publishes ms an average of 2 months after acceptance. Buys exclusive and one-time rights, plus rights to post on website in month of publication. Editorial lead time 2 months. Submit seasonal material 6 months in advance. Accepts queries by mail, e-mail. Sample copy free. Guidelines available online.

Nonfiction Needs how-to, interview, new product, personal experience, technical, ag research. Special issues: Editorial calendar themes include: Horses (January); Range and Pasture (February); Livestock Marketing (July); Hereford and Wildlife (August); Feedlots (September); Bull Buyers (October); Ranch Safety (December). Does not want to see anything not specifically related to beef production in the Southwest. **Buys 20 mss/year.** Query with published clips. Length: 1,500-2,000 words. **Pays $200-350 for assigned articles. Pays $100-350 for unsolicited articles.** Sometimes pays expenses of writers on assignment.

Photos Identification of subjects required. Reviews transparencies, prints, digital files. Offers no additional payment for photos accepted with ms. Buys one time rights.

Tips In our most recent readership survey, subscribers said they were most interested in the following topics in this order: range/pasture, property rights, animal health, water, new innovations, and marketing. *The Cattleman* prefers to work on an assignment basis. However, prospective contributors are urged to write the managing editor of the magazine to inquire of interest on a proposed subject. Occasionally, the editor will return a manuscript to a potential contributor for cutting, polishing, checking, rewriting, or condensing. Be able to demonstrate background/knowledge in this field. Include tearsheets from similar magazines.

$$ FEED LOT MAGAZINE

Feed Lot Magazine, Inc., P.O. Box 850, Dighton KS 67839. (620)397-2838. Fax: (620)397-2839. E-mail: feedlot@st-tel.net. Website: www.feedlotmagazine.com. **40% freelance written**. Bimonthly magazine. "The editorial information content fits a dual role: large feedlots and their related cow/calf operations, and large 500pl cow/calf, 100pl stocker operations. The information covers all phases of production from breeding, genetics, animal health, nutrition, equipment design, research through finishing fat cattle. *Feed Lot* publishes a mix of new information and timely articles which directly affect the cattle industry." Estab. 1993. Circ. 12,000. Byline given. Pays on publication. Offers 50% kill fee. Publishes ms an average of 2 months after acceptance. Buys all rights. Editorial lead time 2 months. Submit seasonal material 6 months in advance. Accepts queries by mail, e-mail, fax. Responds in 1 month to queries. Sample copy and writer's guidelines for $1.50.

Nonfiction Needs interview, new product, cattle-related, photo feature. Send complete ms. Length: 100-400 words. **Pays 20¢/word.**

Reprints Send tearsheet or typed ms with rights for sale noted and information about when and where the material previously appeared. Pays 50% of amount paid for an original article.

Photos State availability of or send photos. Captions, model releases required. Reviews contact sheets. Negotiates payment individually. Buys all rights.

Tips "Know what you are writing about—have a good knowledge of the subject."

$ SHEEP! MAGAZINE

Countryside Publications, Ltd., Nathan Griffith, 3831 Trout Rd., Williamsburg WV 24991-7227. (715)785-7979. Fax: (715)785-7414. Website: www.sheepmagazine.com. **35% freelance written. Prefers to work with published/established writers**. Bimonthly magazine. We're looking for clear, concise, useful information for sheep raisers who have a few sheep to a 1,000 ewe flock. Estab. 1980. Circ. 11,000. Byline given. Pays on publication. Offers $30 kill fee. Buys all rights or makes work-for-hire assignments. Submit seasonal material 3 months in advance.

Nonfiction Health and husbandry articles should be written by someone with extensive experience or appropriate credentials (i.e., a veterinarian or animal scientist). Accepts informative articles (on personalities and/or political, legal, or environmental issues affecting the sheep industry); features (on small businesses that promote wool products and stories about local and regional sheep producers' groups and their activities); and first-person narratives. Needs book excerpts, how-to, on innovative lamb and wool marketing and promotion techniques, efficient record-keeping systems, or specific aspects of health and husbandry, interview, on experienced sheep producers who detail the economics and management of their operation, new product, of value to sheep producers; should be written by someone who has used them, technical, on genetics health and nutrition. **Buys 80 mss/year.** Send complete ms. Length: 750-2,500 words. **Pays $45-150.**

Photos Color—vertical compositions of sheep and/or people—for cover. 35mm photos or other visuals improve chances of a sale. Identification of subjects required. Buys all rights.

Tips Send us your best ideas and photos! We love good writing!

Management

$ $ NEW HOLLAND NEWS AND ACRES MAGAZINE

P.O. Box 1895, New Holland PA 17557-0903. Website: www.newholland.com/na. **Contact:** Gary Martin, ed. **75% freelance written. Works with a small number of new/unpublished writers each year.** Each magazine published 4 times/year covering agriculture and non-farm country living; designed to entertain and inform farm families and rural homeowners and provide ideas for small acreage outdoor projects. Estab. 1960. Byline given. Pays on acceptance. Offers negotiable kill fee. Publishes ms an average of 8 months after acceptance. Buys first North American serial rights. Submit seasonal material 8 months in advance. Accepts queries by mail. Responds in 2 months to queries. Sample copy and writer's guidelines for 9 × 12 SAE with 2 first-class stamps.

- "Break in with features about people and their unique and attractive country living projects, such as outdoor pets (horses, camels, birds), building projects (cabins, barns, restorations), trees, flowers, landscaping, outdoor activities, part-time farms and businesses, and country-related antique collections."

Nonfiction "We need strong photo support for articles of 1,200-1,700 words on farm management, farm human interest and rural lifestyles." **Buys 40 mss/year.** Query. **Pays $700-900.** Pays expenses of writers on assignment.

Photos Professional photos only. Captions, identification of subjects, model releases required. Reviews color photos in any format. Pays $50-300, $500 for cover shot. Buys one time rights.

Tips "We want stories about people who are doing something unique that looks good in photos. Do not write lifeless reports about inanimate subjects."

$ 🌐 SMALLHOLDER MAGAZINE

Newsquest Media Group, Hook House, Hook Road, Wimblington, March Cambs PE15 0QL United Kingdom. Phone/Fax: (44)(135)474-1538. E-mail: liz.wright1@btconnect.com. Website: www.smallholder.co.uk. No kill fee. Accepts queries by e-mail. Sample copy available online. Guidelines by e-mail.

Nonfiction Length: 700-1,400 words. **Pays 4£/word.**

Photos Send photos. Reviews 300 dpi digital images. Pays £5-50.

Miscellaneous Farm

$ $ ACRES U.S.A.

The Voice of Eco-Agriculture, P.O. Box 91299, Austin TX 78709-1299. (512)892-4400. Fax: (512)892-4448. E-mail: editor@acresusa.com. Website: www.acresusa.com. "Monthly trade journal written by people who have a sincere interest in the principles of organic and sustainable agriculture." Estab. 1970. Circ. 18,000. Byline given. Pays on publication. No kill fee. Buys first North American serial rights. Editorial lead time 4 months. Submit seasonal material 6 months in advance. Accepts queries by mail, e-mail, fax. Accepts simultaneous submissions. Sample copy and writer's guidelines free.

Nonfiction Needs expose, how-to, personal experience. Special issues: Seeds (January), Soil Fertility & Testing (March), Cattle & Grazing (May), Poultry (July), Composting/Compost Tea (September), Tillage & Equipment (November). Does not want poetry, fillers, product profiles, or anything with a promotional tone. **Buys about 50 mss/year.** Send complete ms. Length: 1,000-2,500 words. **Pays 10¢/word**

Photos State availability of or send photos. Captions, identification of subjects required. Reviews GIF/JPEG/TIF files. Negotiates payment individually. Buys one time rights.

$ $ BEE CULTURE

P.O. Box 706, Medina OH 44256-0706. Fax: (330)725-5624. E-mail: kim@beeculture.com. Website: www.beeculture.com. **Contact:** Mr. Kim Flottum, editor. **50% freelance written**. Covers the natural science of honey bees. "Monthly magazine for beekeepers and those interested in the natural science of honey bees, with environmentally-oriented articles relating to honey bees or pollination." Estab. 1873. Pays on publication. No kill fee. Publishes ms an average of 4 months after acceptance. Buys first North American serial rights. Accepts queries by mail, e-mail, fax, phone. Responds in 1 month to mss. Sample copy for sae with 9 × 12 envelope and 5 first-class stamps. Guidelines and sample copy available online.

Nonfiction "Interested in articles giving new ideas on managing bees. Also looking for articles on honey bee/environment connections or relationships. Also uses success stories about commercial beekeepers."

Needs interview, personal experience, photo feature. No how I began beekeeping articles. No highly advanced, technical, and scientific abstracts, or impractical advice. 2,000 words average. **Pays $100-250.**

Reprints Send photocopy and information about when and where the material previously appeared. Pays about the same as for an original article, on negotiation.

Photos B&W or color prints, 5 × 7 standard, but 3 × 5 are OK. 35mm slides, mid-format transparencies are excellent. Electronic images encouraged. Digital jpg, color only, at 300 dpi best, prints acceptable as are slides. Pays $7-10 each, $50 for cover photos. Photos payment included with article payment.

Tips "Do an interview story on commercial beekeepers who are cooperative enough to furnish accurate, factual information on their operations. Frequent mistakes made by writers in completing articles are that they are too general in nature and lack management knowledge."

$$$ PRODUCE BUSINESS

Phoenix Media Network Inc., P.O. Box 810425, Boca Raton FL 33481-0425. (561)994-1118. E-mail: kwhitacre@phoenixmedianet.com. **90% freelance written**. Monthly magazine covering produce and floral marketing. We address the buying end of the produce/floral industry, concentrating on supermarkets, chain restaurants, etc. Estab. 1985. Circ. 16,000. Byline given. Pays 30 days after publication. Offers $50 kill fee. Buys all rights. Editorial lead time 2 months. Accepts queries by e-mail. Sample copy free. Guidelines free.

Nonfiction All articles are assigned to conform to our editorial calendar. Does not want unsolicited articles. **Buys 150 mss/year.** Query with published clips. Length: 1,200-10,000 words. **Pays $240-1,200.** Pays expenses of writers on assignment.

Regional Farm

$$ N AMERICAN AGRICULTURIST

5227 Baltimore Pike, Littlestown PA 17340. (717)359-0150. Fax: (717)359-0250. E-mail: jvogel@farmprogress.com. Website: www.farmprogress.com. **20% freelance written**. Monthly magazine covering "cutting-edge technology and news to help farmers improve their operations." We publish cutting-edge technology with ready on-farm application. Estab. 1842. Circ. 32,000. Pays on publication. No kill fee. Publishes ms an average of 3 months after acceptance. Buys first rights. Editorial lead time 3 months. Submit seasonal material 3 months in advance. Accepts queries by e-mail, fax, phone. Accepts simultaneous submissions. Responds in 2 weeks to queries. Responds in 1 month to mss. Guidelines for #10 SASE.

Nonfiction Needs how-to, humor, inspirational, interview, new product, personal experience, photo feature feature, technical, "No stories without a strong tie to Mid-Atlantic farming." **Buys 20 mss/year.** Query. Length: 500-1,000 words. **Pays $150-300.** Sometimes pays expenses of writers on assignment.

Photos Send photos. Captions, identification of subjects, model releases required. Reviews transparencies, prints, GIF/JPEG files. Offers $75-200/photo. Buys one time rights.

Columns/Departments Contact: Kathleen O'Connor, editorial assistant. Country Air (humor, nostalgia, inspirational), 300-400 words; Family Favorites, 100 words. **Buys 36 mss/year.** Send complete ms. **Pays $15-50.**

Poetry Contact: Kathleen O'Connor, editorial assistant. Needs free verse, light verse, traditional. All poetry must have a link to New York farming. Buys 2 poems/year. Length: 12-40 lines. **Pays $50.**

$$ FLORIDA GROWER

The Voice of Florida Agriculture for More Than 90 Years, Meister Media Worldwide, 1555 Howell Branch Rd., Suite C-204, Winter Park FL 32789-1170. (407)539-6552. Fax: (407)539-6544. E-mail: fgiles@meistermedia.com. Website: www.growingproduce.com/floridagrower/. **Contact:** Frank Giles, editor. **10% freelance written**. "Monthly magazine edited for the Florida farmer with commercial production interest primarily in citrus, vegetables, and other ag endeavors. Our goal is to provide articles which update and inform on such areas as production, ag financing, farm labor relations, technology, safety, education, and regulation." Estab. 1907. Circ. 12,200. Byline given. Pays on publication. No kill fee. Buys all rights. Editorial lead time 2 months. Submit seasonal material 3 months in advance. Accepts queries by mail, e-mail, fax, phone. Responds in 1 month to queries. Sample copy for sae with 9 × 12 envelope and 5 First-Class stamps. Guidelines free.

Nonfiction Needs interview, photo feature, technical. Query with published clips. Length: 700-1,000 words. **Pays $150-250.**
Photos Send photos.

$ $ MAINE ORGANIC FARMER & GARDENER

Maine Organic Farmers & Gardeners Association, 662 Slab City Rd., Lincolnville ME 04849. (207)763-3043. E-mail: jenglish@midcoast.com. Website: www.mofga.org. **40% freelance written. Prefers to work with published/established local writers.** Quarterly newspaper. "The *MOF&G* promotes and encourages sustainable agriculture and environmentally sound living. Our primary focus is organic farming, gardening, and forestry, but we also deal with local, national, and international agriculture, food, and environmental issues." Estab. 1976. Circ. 10,000. Byline and bio offered. Pays on publication. No kill fee. Publishes ms an average of 8 months after acceptance. Buys first North American serial rights, buys first rights, buys one-time rights, buys second serial (reprint) rights. Submit seasonal material 1 year in advance. Accepts queries by mail, e-mail. Accepts simultaneous submissions. Responds in 2 months to queries. Sample copy for $2 and SAE with 7 first-class stamps; from MOFGA, P.O. Box 170, Unity ME 04988. Guidelines free.
Nonfiction "Book reviews; how-to based on personal experience, research reports, interviews; profiles of farmers, gardeners, plants; information on renewable energy, recycling, nutrition, health, nontoxic pest control, organic farm management and marketing. We use profiles of New England organic farmers and gardeners and news reports (500-1,000 words) dealing with U.S./international sustainable ag research and development, rural development, recycling projects, environmental and agricultural problems and solutions, organic farms with broad impact, cooperatives and community projects." **Buys 30 mss/year.** Send complete ms. Length: 250-3,000 words. **Pays $25-300.**
Reprints E-mail manuscript with rights for sale noted and information about when and where the material previously appeared. Pays 50% of amount paid for an original article.
Photos State availability of photos with query. Captions, identification of subjects, model releases required. Buys one time rights.
Tips "We are a nonprofit organization. Our publication's primary mission is to inform and educate, but we also want readers to enjoy the articles. Most of our articles are written by our staff or by freelancers who have been associated with the publication for several years."

Finance

$ $ $ ☐ ADVISOR'S EDGE

Canada's Magazine for the Financial Professional, Rogers Media, Inc., 156 Front St. W., 4th Floor, Toronto ON M5J 2L6 Canada. E-mail: deanne.gage@advisor.rogers.com. Website: www.advisorsedge.ca. Philip Porado, exec. editor, philip.porado@advisor.rogers.com. Monthly magazine covering the financial industry (financial advisors and investment advisors). "*Advisor's Edge* focuses on sales and marketing opportunities for the financial advisor (how they can build their business and improve relationships with clients). Estab. 1998. Circ. 36,000. Byline given. Pays on publication. Offers 25% kill fee. Publishes ms an average of 3 months after acceptance. Buys one-time rights, buys electronic rights. Editorial lead time 3 months. Accepts queries by e-mail. Sample copy available online.
Nonfiction "We are looking for articles that help advisors do their jobs better." Needs how-to, interview. No articles that aren't relevant to how a financial advisor does his/her job. **Buys 12 mss/year.** Query with published clips. Length: 1,500-2,000 words. **Pays $900 (Canadian).**

$ $ $ AFP EXCHANGE

Association for Financial Professionals, 4520 E. West Hwy., Suite 750, Bethesda MD 20814. (301)907-2862. E-mail: exchange@afponline.org. Website: www.afponline.org. **20% freelance written.** Monthly magazine covering corporate treasury, corporate finance, B2B payments issues, corporate risk management, accounting and regulatory issues from the perspective of corporations. Welcome interviews with CFOs and senior level practitioners. Best practices and practical information for corporate CFOs and treasurers. Tone is professional, intended to appeal to financial professionals on the job. Most accepted articles are written by professional journalists and editors, many featuring high-level AFP members in profile and case studies. Estab. 1979. Circ. 25,000. Byline given. Pays on publication. Offers kill fee. Pays negotiable kill fee in advance. Buys all rights. Editorial lead time 2 months. Submit seasonal material 3 months in advance. Accepts queries by e-mail. Responds in 1 week to queries. Responds in 1 month to mss. Guidelines available online.

Nonfiction Contact: Exchange Magazine Editor. Needs book excerpts, how-to, interview, personal experience, technical. PR-type articles pointing to any type of product or solution **Buys 3-4 year mss/year.** Query. Length: 1,100-1,800 words. **Pays 75¢/word minimum, &1.00 maximum for assigned articles.**

Columns/Departments Cash Flow Forecasting (practical tips for treasurers, CFOs); Financial Reporting (insight, practical tips); Risk Management (practical tips for treasurers, CFOs); Corporate Payments (practical tips for treasurers), all 1,000-1,300 words; Professional Development (success stories, career related, about high level financial professionals), 1,100 words. **Buys 10 mss/year.** Query. **Pays $75¢/word-$1.00/word.**

Fillers Needs anecdotes. Buys open to consideration mss/year. Length: 400-700 words. **Pays $75¢-75¢.**

Tips Accepted submissions deal with high-level issues relevant to today's corporate CFO or treasurer, including issues of global trade, global finance, accounting, M&A, risk management, corporate cash management, international regulatory issues, communications issues with corporate boards and shareholders, and especially new issues on the horizon. Preference given to articles by or about corporate practitioners in the finance function of mid-to large-size corporations in the U.S. or abroad. Also purchase articles by accomplished financial writers. Cannot accept content that points to any product, 'solution' or that promotes any vendor. Should not be considered a PR outlet. Authors may be required to sign agreement.

$ $ $ N COLLECTIONS & CREDIT RISK

The Authority for Commercial and Consumer Professionals, SourceMedia, 550 West Van Buren St., Suite 1110, Chicago IL 60607. Website: www.creditcollectionsworld.com. **Contact:** Darren Waggoner, exec. ed. **33% freelance written**. Monthly journal covering debt collections and credit risk management. "*Collections & Credit Risk* is the only magazine that brings news and trends of strategic and competitive importance to collections and credit-policy executives who are driving the collections industry's growth and diversification in both commercial and consumer credit. These executives work for financial institutions, insurance companies, collections agencies, law firms and attorney networks, health-care providers, retailers, telecoms and utility companies, manufacturers, wholesalers, and government agencies." Estab. 1996. Circ. 30,000. Byline given. Pays on acceptance. Offers kill fee. Kill fee determined case by case. Publishes ms an average of 3 months after acceptance. Buys all rights. Editorial lead time 3 months. Accepts queries by mail. Sample copy free or online.

Nonfiction Needs interview, technical, business news and analysis. No unsolicited submissions accepted—freelancers work on assignment only. **Buys 30-40 mss/year.** Query with published clips. Length: 1,000-2,500 words. **Pays $800-1,000.** Sometimes pays expenses of writers on assignment.

Tips "This is a business news and analysis magazine focused on events and trends affecting the credit-risk management and collections professions. Our editorial approach is modeled after *Business Week, Forbes, Fortune, Wall Street Journal.* No fluff accepted."

$ $ $ CREDIT TODAY

Tomorrow's Tools for Today's Credit Professionals, P.O. Box 720, Roanoke VA 24004. (540)343-7500. E-mail: editor@credittoday.net. Website: www.credittoday.net. **50% freelance written**. Monthly newsletter covering business or trade credit. Make pieces actionable, personable, and a quick read. Estab. 1997. No byline given. Pays on acceptance. Publishes ms an average of 2 months after acceptance. Buys all rights. Editorial lead time 1-2 months. Accepts queries by e-mail. Sample copy free. Guidelines free.

Nonfiction Needs how-to, interview, technical. Does not want puff pieces promoting a particular product or vendor. **Buys 20 mss/year.** Send complete ms. Length: 700-1,800 words. **Pays $200-1,400.**

$ $ CREDIT UNION MANAGEMENT

Credit Union Executives Society, 5510 Research Park Dr., Madison WI 53711. Website: www.cumanagement.org. **44% freelance written**. Monthly magazine covering credit union, banking trends, management, HR, marketing issues. Our philosophy mirrors the credit union industry of cooperative financial services. Estab. 1978. Circ. 7,413. Pays on acceptance. No kill fee. Publishes ms an average of 2 months after acceptance. Editorial lead time 3 months. Submit seasonal material 4 months in advance. Accepts queries by mail. Accepts simultaneous submissions. Responds in 2 weeks to queries. Responds in 1 month to mss. Sample copy and writer's guidelines free.

Nonfiction Needs book excerpts, how-to, be a good mentor/leader, recruit, etc., interview, technical. **Buys 74 mss/year.** Query with published clips. Length: 700-2,400 words. **$250-350 for assigned features.** Phone expenses only.

Columns/Departments Management Network (book/Web reviews, briefs), 300 words; e-marketing, 700 words; Point of Law, 700 words; Best Practices (new technology/operations trends), 700 words. Query with published clips.

Tips The best way is to e-mail an editor; include résumé, cover letter and clips. Knowledge of financial services is very helpful.

$$ EQUITIES MAGAZINE, LLC

2118 Wilshire Blvd. #722, Santa Monica CA 90403. (914)723-6702. Fax: (914)723-0176. E-mail: equitymag@aol.com. Website: www.equitiesmagazine.com. **50% freelance written**. We are a seven-issues-a-year financial magazine covering the fastest-growing public companies in the world. We study the management of companies and act as critics reviewing their performances. We aspire to be 'The Shareholder's Friend.' We want to be a bridge between quality public companies and sophisticated investors. Estab. 1951. Circ. 18,000. Byline given. Pays on publication. No kill fee. Publishes ms an average of 2 months after acceptance. Buys all rights. Accepts queries by mail. Sample copy for sae with 9 × 12 envelope and 5 First-Class stamps.

Nonfiction We must know the writer first as we are careful about whom we publish. A letter of introduction with resume and clips is the best way to introduce yourself. Financial writing requires specialized knowledge and a feel for people as well, which can be a tough combination to find. Carries guest columns by famous money managers who are not writing for cash payments, but to showcase their ideas and approach. Needs expose, new product, technical. **Buys 30 mss/year.** Query with published clips. Length: 300-1,500 words. **Pays $250-750 for assigned articles, more for very difficult or investigative pieces.** Pays expenses of writers on assignment.

Photos Send color photos with submission. Identification of subjects required. Reviews contact sheets, negatives, transparencies, prints. Offers no additional payment for photos accepted with ms.

Columns/Departments Pays $25-75 for assigned items only.

Tips Give us an idea for a story on a specific publically-owned company, whose stock is traded on NASDAQ, the NYSE, or American Stock Exchange. Anyone who enjoys analyzing a business and telling the story of the people who started it, or run it today, is a potential *Equities* contributor. But to protect our readers and ourselves, we are careful about who writes for us. We do not want writers who are trading the stocks of the companies they profile. Business writing is an exciting area and our stories reflect that. If a writer relies on numbers and percentages to tell his story, rather than the individuals involved, the result will be numbingly dull.

$$$ THE FEDERAL CREDIT UNION

National Association of Federal Credit Unions, 3138 10th St. N., Arlington VA 22201. (703)522-4770. Fax: (703)524-1082. E-mail: tfcu@nafcu.org. Website: www.nafcu.org. **Contact:** Robin Johnston, publisher. **30% freelance written**. Looking for writers with financial, banking, or credit union experience, but will work with inexperienced (unpublished) writers based on writing skill. Published bimonthly, *The Federal Credit Union* is the official publication of the National Association of Federal Credit Unions. The magazine is dedicated to providing credit union management, staff, and volunteers with in-depth information (HR, technology, security, board management, etc.) they can use to fulfill their duties and better serve their members. The editorial focus includes coverage of management issues, operations, and technology as well as volunteer-related issues. Estab. 1967. Circ. 8,000. Byline given. Pays on publication. No kill fee. Publishes ms an average of 3 months after acceptance. Buys first North American serial rights, rights to publish and archive online. Submit seasonal material 5 months in advance. Accepts queries by mail, e-mail, fax. Accepts simultaneous submissions. Responds in 2 months to queries. Sample copy for sae with 10 × 13 envelope and 5 First-Class stamps. Guidelines for #10 sase.

Nonfiction Needs humor, inspirational, interview. Query with published clips and SASE. Length: 1,200-2,000 words. **Pays $400-1,000.**

Photos Send photos. Identification of subjects, model releases required. Reviews 35mm transparencies, 5 × 7 prints, high-resolution photos. Offers no additional payment for photos accepted with ms. Pays $50-500. Buys all rights.

Tips We would like more articles on how credit unions are using technology to serve their members and more articles on leading-edge technologies they can use in their operations. If you can write on current trends in technology, human resources, or strategic planning, you stand a better chance of being published than if you wrote on other topics.

MORTGAGE BANKING

The Magazine of Real Estate Finance, Mortgage Bankers Association, 1331 L Street, NW, Washington DC 20005. (202)557-2853. Fax: (202)721-0245. E-mail: jhewitt@mortgagebankers.org. Website: www.mortgagebankingmagazine.com. Monthly magazine covering real estate finance. Timely examinations of major news and trends in the business of mortgage lending for both commercial and residential real estate. Estab. 1939. Circ. 10,000. Byline given. Pays on acceptance. Offers kill fee. Negotiates kill fee. Publishes ms an average of 2 months after acceptance. Buys one-time rights. Makes work-for-hire assignments. Editorial lead time 2 months. Submit seasonal material 3 months in advance. Accepts queries by mail, e-mail, fax. Accepts simultaneous submissions. Responds in 1 month to queries. Responds in 4 months to mss. Sample copy and writer's guidelines free.

Nonfiction Needs book excerpts, essays, interview, opinion. Special issues: Commercial Real Estate Special Supplemental Issue (January); Internet Guide Supplemental Issue (September). **Buys 30 mss/year.** Query. 3,000 words **Writers' fees negotiable.** Sometimes pays expenses of writers on assignment.

Photos State availability. Identification of subjects, model releases required. Reviews prints. Negotiates payment individually. Buys one time rights.

Columns/Departments Book reviews (current, relevant material), 300 words; executive essay (industry executive's personal views on relevant topic), 750-1,000 words. **Buys 2 mss/year.** Query. **Pay negotiated.**

Tips Trends in technology, current and upcoming legislation that will affect the mortgage industry are good focus.

$$$$ ON WALL STREET

Source Media, One State St. Plaza, 26th Floor, New York NY 10004. (212)803-8783. E-mail: frances.mcmorris@sourcemedia.com. Website: www.onwallstreet.com. **50% freelance written**. Monthly magazine for retail stockbrokers. We help 95,000+ stockbrockers build their business. Estab. 1991. Circ. 95,000. Byline given. Pays on publication. No kill fee. Publishes ms an average of 1-2 months after acceptance. Buys all rights. Editorial lead time 3 months. Submit seasonal material 4 months in advance. Accepts queries by e-mail. Responds in 1-2 months to queries. Responds in 2 month to mss. Sample copy for $10.

Nonfiction Needs how-to, interview. No investment-related articles about hot stocks, nor funds or hot alternative investments. **Buys 30 mss/year.** Query. Length: 1,000-3,000 words. **Pays $1/word.**

Photos State availability. Identification of subjects required. Reviews contact sheets. Negotiates payment individually. Buys all rights.

Tips Articles should be written for a professional, not consumer, audience.

$$ SERVICING MANAGEMENT

The Magazine for Loan Servicing Professionals, Zackin Publications, P.O. Box 2180, Waterbury CT 06722. (800)325-6745. Fax: (203)262-4680. E-mail: bates@sm-online.com. Website: www.sm-online.com. John Clapp, editor. **Contact:** Michael Bates, editor. **15% freelance written**. Monthly magazine covering residential mortgage servicing. "**Servicing Management** accepts Editorial contributions from its readers to supplement features written by staff writers, professional mortgage industry journalists and mortgage industry experts. These features are designed to: give readers "nuts and bolts" information about how they can improve their operations, and examine industry trends. If you'd like to contribute an article, contact the Editor to discuss your idea. Call (800) 325-6745, ext. 241. Articles address a topic specifically, without promoting the author's company. The author does receive company attribution in an accompanying Editor's Note. If provided, a photo of the author is published.An **article reprint service** is also available to authors and companies. Reprint service details are available upon request." Estab. 1989. Circ. 20,000. Byline given. Pays on acceptance. No kill fee. Publishes ms an average of 2 months after acceptance. Buys all rights. Accepts queries by mail, e-mail, fax, phone. Responds in 2 weeks to queries. Sample copy free. Guidelines available online.

Nonfiction Needs how-to, interview, new product, technical. **Buys 10 mss/year.** Query. Length: 1,500-2,500 words.

Photos State availability. Identification of subjects required. Reviews contact sheets. Offers no additional payment for photos accepted with ms. Buys all rights.

Columns/Departments Buys 5 mss/year. Query. **Pays $200.**

$$$$ N USAA MAGAZINE

A Member's Guide to Financial Security, USAA, 9800 Fredericksburg Rd., San Antonio TX 78288. Website: www.usaa.com/maglinks. **80% freelance written**. Quarterly magazine covering financial security for USAA members. "Conservative, common-sense approach to personal finance issues. Especially interested in how-to articles and pieces with actionable tips." Estab. 1970. Circ. 4.2 million. Byline given. Pays on acceptance. Offers 25% kill fee. Publishes ms an average of 4 months after acceptance. Buys all rights. Editorial lead time 6 months. Submit seasonal material 6 months in advance. Accepts queries by e-mail. Responds in 6-8 weeks to queries. No mss. accepted. Sample copy available online. Guidelines by e-mail.

Nonfiction Needs general interest, (finance), historical, (military), how-to, (personal finance), interview, (military/financial), personal experience, (finance). No poetry, photos, lifestyle unrelated to military or personal finance. **Buys 20 mss/year.** Query with published clips. Length: 750-1,500 words. **Pays $750-1,500 for assigned articles.** Sometimes pays expenses of writers on assignment.

Tips "Story must take a unique or innovative approach to the personal finance topic. Piece must be actionable and useful. (Not philosophical or academic.)"

$$$$ WEALTH MANAGER

33-41 Newark St., 2nd Floor, Hoboken NJ 07030. E-mail: rkoreto@highlinemedia.com. Website: www.wealthmanagermag.com. **90% freelance written**. Magazine published 11 times/year for financial advisors. Stories should provide insight and information for the financial adviser. Put yourself on the adviser's side of the table and cover the issues thoroughly from his/her perspective. The piece should delve beneath the surface. We need specific examples, professional caveats, advice from professionals. Estab. 1999. Circ. 50,000. Byline given. Pays on acceptance. No kill fee. Publishes ms an average of 3 months after acceptance. Buys first North American serial rights. Editorial lead time 4 months. Submit seasonal material 4 months in advance. Accepts queries by e-mail. Responds in 1 month to queries.

Nonfiction Needs book excerpts, interview, technical. Do not submit anything that does not deal with financial planning issues or the financial markets. **Buys 30-40 mss/year.** Query with published clips. Length: 1,500-3,000 words. **Pays $1.50/word for assigned articles.**

Tips *Wealth Manager* is a trade magazine. All pieces should be written from the perspective of a financial adviser who has wealthy clients.

Florist, Nurseries & Landscapers

$$ DIGGER

Oregon Association of Nurseries, 29751 SW Town Center Loop W., Wilsonville OR 97070. (503)682-5089. Fax: (503)682-5099. E-mail: ckipp@oan.org. Website: www.oan.org. **Contact:** Curt Kipp, publications manager. **50% freelance written**. Monthly magazine covering nursery and greenhouse industry. Our readers are mainly nursery and greenhouse operators and owners who propagate nursery stock/crops, so we write with them in mind. Circ. 8,000. Byline given. Pays on receipt of copy. Offers 100% kill fee. Publishes ms an average of 2 months after acceptance. Buys first North American serial rights. Editorial lead time 6 weeks. Submit seasonal material 2 months in advance. Accepts queries by mail, e-mail, fax, phone. Sample copy and writer's guidelines free.

Nonfiction Needs general interest, how-to, propagation techniques, other crop-growing tips, interview, personal experience, technical. Special issues: Farwest Edition (August)—this is a triple-size issue that runs in tandem with our annual trade show (14,500 circulation for this issue). No articles not related or pertinent to nursery and greenhouse industry. **Buys 20-30 mss/year.** Query. Length: 800-2,000 words. **Pays $125-400 for assigned articles. Pays $100-300 for unsolicited articles.** Sometimes pays expenses of writers on assignment.

Photos State availability. Captions, identification of subjects required. Reviews high-res digital images sent by e-mail or on CD preferred. Offers $25-150/photo. Buys one-time rights, which includes Web posting.

Tips "Our best freelancers are familiar with or have experience in the horticultural industry. Some 'green' knowledge is a definite advantage."

$$ THE GROWING EDGE

New Moon Publishing, Inc., P.O. Box 1027, Corvallis OR 97339. (541)745-7773. Fax: (541)757-0028. Website: www.growingedge.com. **Contact:** Jenie Skoy, editor. **85% freelance written**. Bimonthly magazine covering indoor and outdoor high-tech gardening techniques and tips. Estab. 1980. Circ. 20,000.

Byline given. Pays on publication. No kill fee. Publishes ms an average of 3 months after acceptance. Buys first serial and reprint rights. Submit seasonal material 6 months in advance. Accepts queries by mail, e-mail, online submission form. Responds in 3 months to queries. Sample copy for $3. Guidelines available online.

Nonfiction Needs how-to, interview, personal experience, must be technical, book reviews, general horticulture and agriculture. Query. Length: 500-3,500 words. **Pays 20¢/word (10¢ for first rights, 5¢ for nonexclusive reprint and nonexclusive electronic rights).**

Reprints Send tearsheet, photocopy or typed ms with rights for sale noted and information about when and where the material previously appeared. Payment negotiable.

Photos Pays $25-175. Pays on publication. Credit line given. Buys first and reprint rights.

Tips Looking for more hydroponics articles and information that will give the reader/gardener/farmer the growing edge in high-tech gardening and farming on topics such as high intensity grow lights, water conservation, drip irrigation, advanced organic fertilizers, new seed varieties, and greenhouse cultivation.

$ $ ORNAMENTAL OUTLOOK

Your Connection To The South's Horticulture Industry, Meister Media Worldwide, 1555 Howell Branch Rd., Suite C204, Winter Park FL 32789. (407)539-6552. Fax: (407)539-6544. E-mail: pprusnak@meistermedia.com. Website: www.ornamentaloutlook.com. **Contact:** Paul Rusnak, managing editor. **20% freelance written**. Monthly magazine. "*Ornamental Outlook* is written for commercial growers of ornamental plants and landscapers in Florida. Our goal is to provide interesting and informative articles on such topics as production, legislation, safety, technology, pest control, water management, and new varieties, as they apply to Southeast growers and landscapers." Estab. 1991. Circ. 11,000. Byline given. Pays on publication. No kill fee. Publishes ms an average of 4 months after acceptance. Buys all rights. Editorial lead time 2 months. Submit seasonal material 3 months in advance. Accepts queries by mail, e-mail, fax, phone. Responds in 3 months to queries. Sample copy for sae with 9 × 12 envelope and 5 First-Class stamps. Guidelines free.

Nonfiction Needs interview, photo feature, technical. No first-person articles. No word-for-word meeting transcripts or all-quote articles. Query with published clips. Length: 600-1,000 words. **Pays $150-300/article including photos.**

Photos Send photos. Captions, identification of subjects required. Reviews contact sheets, transparencies, prints. Buys one time rights.

Tips "I am most impressed by written queries that address specific subjects of interest to our audience, which is the Florida landscaper and grower of commercial horticulture. Our biggest demand is for features, about 700 words, that follow subjects listed on our editorial calendar (which is sent with guidelines). Please do not send articles of national or consumer interest."

$ $ TREE CARE INDUSTRY MAGAZINE

Tree Care Industry Association, 136 Harvey Rd., Suite 101, Londonderry NH 03053. (800)733-2622 or (603)314-5380. Fax: (603)314-5386. E-mail: staruk@tcia.org. Website: www.treecareindustry.org. **Contact:** Don Staruk, editor. **50% freelance written**. Monthly magazine covering tree care and landscape maintenance. Estab. 1990. Circ. 27,500. Byline given. Pays within 1 month of publication. No kill fee. Publishes manuscripts an average of 3 months after acceptance. Buys all rights. Editorial lead time 10 weeks. Submit seasonal material 3 months in advance. Accepts queries by e-mail. Responds within 2 days to queries. Responds in 2 months to manuscripts. View PDFs online. Guidelines free.

Nonfiction Needs book excerpts, historical, interview, new product, technical. **Buys 60 manuscripts/year mss/year.** Query with published clips. Length: 900-3,500 words. **Pays negotiable rate.**

Photos Send photos with submission by e-mail or FTP site. Captions, identification of subjects required. Reviews prints. Negotiate payment individually. Buys one-time and Web rights.

Columns/Departments Buys 40 mss/year. Send complete manuscript. **Pays $100 and up.**

Tips "Preference is given to writers with background and knowledge of the tree care industry; our focus is relatively narrow."

Government & Public Service

$ $ AMERICAN CITY & COUNTY

Penton Media, 6151 Powers Ferry Rd. NW, Suite 200, Atlanta GA 30339. (770)618-0199. Fax: (770)618-0349. E-mail: bill.wolpin@penton.com. Website: www.americancityandcounty.com. lindsay.isaacs@

penton.com. **Contact:** Lindsay Isaacs, managing editor. **40% freelance written**. Monthly magazine covering local and state government in the United States. *American City & County* is received by more than 75,000 elected and appointed local and state government officials and public and private engineers. Included in the circulation list are administrators, supervisors and department heads of municipal, county, township, state and special district governments. Estab. 1909. Circ. 75,000. Byline given. Pays on publication. Offers 25% kill fee. Publishes ms an average of 2 months after acceptance. Buys all rights. Editorial lead time 3 months. Accepts queries by e-mail. Accepts simultaneous submissions. Sample copy available online. Guidelines by e-mail.

Nonfiction Needs new product, local and state government news analysis. **Buys 36 mss/year.** Query. Length: 600-2,000 words. **Pays 30¢/published word.** Sometimes pays expenses of writers on assignment.

Photos State availability. Captions required. Reviews GIF/JPEG files. Negotiates payment individually. Buys all rights.

Columns/Departments Issues & Trends (local and state government news analysis), 500-700 words. **Buys 24 ms/year. mss/year.** Query. **Pays $150-250.**

Tips "We use only third-person articles. We do not tell the reader what to do; we offer the facts and assume the reader will make his or her own informed decision. We cover city and county government and state highway departments. We do not cover state legislatures or the federal government, except as they affect local government."

$$ COUNTY

Texas Association of Counties, P.O. Box 2131, Austin TX 78768-2131. (512)478-8753. Fax: (512)481-1240. E-mail: marias@county.org. Website: www.county.org. **Contact:** Maria Sprow, managing editor. **15% freelance written**. Bimonthly magazine covering county and state government in Texas. "We provide elected and appointed county officials with insights and information that help them do their jobs and enhances communications among the independent office-holders in the courthouse." Estab. 1988. Circ. 5,500. Byline given. Pays on acceptance. No kill fee. Publishes ms an average of 2 months after acceptance. Makes work-for-hire assignments. Editorial lead time 2 months. Submit seasonal material 4 months in advance. Accepts queries by mail, e-mail, phone. Responds in 2 weeks to queries. Responds in 1 month to mss. Sample copy and writer's guidelines for 8 × 10 SAE with 3 first-class stamps.

Nonfiction Needs historical, photo feature, government innovations. **Buys 5 mss/year.** Query with published clips. Length: 1,000-3,000 words. **Pays $500-700.** Sometimes pays expenses of writers on assignment.

Photos State availability. Captions, identification of subjects, model releases required. Negotiates payment individually. Buys all rights.

Columns/Departments Safety; Human Resources; Risk Management (all directed toward education of Texas county officials), maximum length 1,000 words. **Buys 2 mss/year.** Query with published clips. **Pays $500**

Tips "Identify innovative practices or developing trends that affect Texas county officials, and have the basic journalism skills to write a multi-sourced, informative feature."

EVIDENCE TECHNOLOGY MAGAZINE

P.O. Box 555, Kearney MO 64060. E-mail: kmayo@evidencemagazine.com. Website: www.evidencemagazine.com. **Contact:** Kristi Mayo, editor. Bimonthly magazine providing news and information relating to the collection, processing and preservation of evidence. "This is a business-to-business publication, not a peer reviewed journal. We look for mainstream pieces. Our readers want general crime scenes and forensic science articles." Accepts queries by e-mail. Guidelines available online.

Nonfiction Needs general interest, how-to, interview, new product, technical. Query. **Pays 2 contributor copies.**

Photos Provide photos and/or illustrations. Reviews JPEG files (300 dpi or larger).

Tips "Opening a dialogue with the editor will give you the opportunity to get guidelines on length, style and deadlines."

FIRE APPARATUS & EMERGENCY EQUIPMENT

234 Monarch Hill Rd., Turnbridge VT 05077. (802)889-9800. Fax: (802)889-9608. E-mail: news@firemagazine.com. Website: www.fireapparatusmagazine.com. **Contact:** Kathryn Jorgensen, editor. Monthly magazine focused on fire trucks, tools and new technology.

Nonfiction Needs general interest, how-to, new product, technical. Query.

$$ FIRE CHIEF

Primedia Business, 330 N. Wabash, Suite 2300, Chicago IL 60611. (312)840-8410. Fax: (312)595-0295. E-mail: jwilmoth@primediabusiness.com. Website: www.firechief.com. Glenn Bischoff, editor. **Contact:** Janet Wilmoth, editorial director. **60% freelance written**. Monthly magazine. *Fire Chief* is the management magazine of the fire service, addressing the administrative, personnel, training, prevention/education, professional development, and operational issues faced by chiefs and other fire officers, whether in paid, volunteer, or combination departments. We're potentially interested in any article that can help them do their jobs better, whether that's as incident commanders, financial managers, supervisors, leaders, trainers, planners, or ambassadors to municipal officials or the public. Estab. 1956. Circ. 53,000. Byline given. Pays on publication. Offers kill fee. Kill fee negotiable. Publishes ms an average of 6 months after acceptance. Buys first rights, buys one-time rights, buys second serial (reprint) rights, buys all rights. Editorial lead time 2 months. Submit seasonal material 4 months in advance. Accepts queries by mail, e-mail, fax. Responds in 1 month to queries. Responds in 2 months to mss. Sample copy and writer's guidelines free or online.

Nonfiction If your department has made some changes in its structure, budget, mission, or organizational culture (or really did reinvent itself in a serious way), an account of that process, including the mistakes made and lessons learned, could be a winner. Similarly, if you've observed certain things that fire departments typically could do a lot better and you think you have the solution, let us know. Needs how-to, technical. We do not publish fiction, poetry or historical articles. We also aren't interested in straightforward accounts of fires or other incidents, unless there are one or more specific lessons to be drawn from a particular incident, especially lessons that are applicable to a large number of departments. **Buys 50-60 mss/year.** Query first with published clips. Length: 1,000-10,000 words. **Pays $50-400.** Sometimes pays expenses of writers on assignment.

Photos State availability. Captions, identification of subjects required. Reviews transparencies, prints. Buys one-time or reprint rights.

Columns/Departments Training Perspectives; EMS Viewpoints; Sound Off; Volunteer Voice; all 1,000-1,800 words.

Tips Writers who are unfamiliar with the fire service are very unlikely to place anything with us. Many pieces that we reject are either too unfocused or too abstract. We want articles that help keep fire chiefs well informed and effective at their jobs.

FIRE ENGINEERING

PennWell Corporation, 21-00 Route 208 S., Fair Lawn NJ 07410. (800)962-6484, ext. 5047. E-mail: dianef@pennwell.com. Website: www.fireengineering.com. **Contact:** Diane Feldman, executive editor. Monthly magazine covering issues of importance to firefighters. Accepts queries by mail, e-mail. Responds in 2-3 months to mss. Guidelines available online.

Nonfiction Themes: Training/Instructor Development, Engine Company Operations, Technical Rescue, Fire Protection, EMS, Truck Company Operations, Apparatus, Fire Technology, Firefighter Safety and Health, Officer Development, and Leadership and Management. Needs how-to, new product, incident reports, training. Send complete ms.

Photos Reviews electronic format only: JPEG/TIFF/EPS files (300 dpi).

Columns/Departments Volunteers Corner; Training Notebook; Rescue Company; The Engine Company; The Truck Company; Fire Prevention Bureau; Apparatus; The Shops; Fire Service EMS; Fire Service Court; Speaking of Safety; Fire Commentary; Technology Today; and Innovations: Homegrown. Send complete ms.

$$ FIREHOUSE MAGAZINE

Patricia Maroder, 3 Huntington Quadrangle, Suite 301N, Melville NY 11747. (631)845-2700. Fax: (631)845-7218. E-mail: editors@firehouse.com. Website: www.firehouse.com. Harvey Eisner, editor-in-chief. **Contact:** Elizabeth Friszell-Nerouslas, managing editor. **85% freelance written. Works with a small number of new/unpublished writers each year.** Monthly magazine. *Firehouse* covers major fires nationwide, controversial issues and trends in the fire service, the latest firefighting equipment and methods of firefighting, historical fires, firefighting history and memorabilia. Fire-related books, fire safety education, hazardous-materials incidents, and the emergency medical services are also covered. Estab. 1976. Circ. 127,000. Byline given. Pays on publication. No kill fee. Accepts queries by mail, e-mail, fax. Sample copy for sae with 9 × 12 envelope and 8 First-Class stamps. Guidelines available online.

- Our primary editorial objectives are to educate, inform and entertain our audience of 1.5 million career and volunteer firefighters and thousands of fire buffs.

Nonfiction Needs book excerpts, of recent books on fire, EMS, and hazardous materials, historical, great fires in history, fire collectibles, the fire service of yesteryear, how-to, fight certain kinds of fires, buy and maintain equipment, run a fire department, technical, on almost any phase of firefighting, techniques, equipment, training, administration, trends in the fire service. No profiles of people or departments that are not unusual or innovative, reports of nonmajor fires, articles not slanted toward firefighters' interests. No poetry. **Buys 100 mss/year.** Query. If you have any story ideas, questions, hints, tips, etc., please do not hesitate to call. Length: 500-3,000 words. The average length of each article is between2-3 pages including visuals. **Pays $50-400 for assigned articles.**

Photos *Firehouse* is a visually-oriented publication. Please include photographs (color preferred) with captions (or a description of what is taking place in the photo), illustrations, charts or diagrams that support your ms. The highest priority is given to those submissions that are received as a complete package. Pays $25-200 for transparencies and color prints. Cannot accept negatives.

Columns/Departments Training (effective methods); Book Reviews; Fire Safety (how departments teach fire safety to the public); Communicating (PR, dispatching); Arson (efforts to combat it). Length: 750-1,000 words. **Buys 50 mss/year.** Query or send complete ms. **Pays $100-300.**

Tips Have excellent fire service credentials and be able to offer our readers new information. Read the magazine to get a full understanding of the subject matter, the writing style, and the readers before sending a query or manuscript. Indicate sources for photos. Be sure to focus articles on firefighters.

FIRE PROTECTION CONTRACTOR

550 High St., Suite 220, Auburn CA 95603. (530)823-0706. Fax: (530)823-6937. E-mail: info@fpcmag.com. Website: www.fpcmag.com. **Contact:** Brant Brumbeloe, editor. Monthly magazine for the benefit of fire protection contractors, engineers, designers, sprinkler fitters, apprentices, fabricators, manufacturers and distributors of fire protection products used in automatic fire sprinkler systems. Estab. 1978. Guidelines available online at website.

Nonfiction Needs general interest, how-to, interview, new product, technical. Query.

$ $ FIRE-RESCUE MAGAZINE

Jems Communications, 525 B St., Suite 1900, San Diego CA 92101. Fax: (619)699-6396. E-mail: a.j.heightman@elsevier.com. Website: www.jems.com. **Contact:** A.J. Heightman, editor-in-chief. **75% freelance written**. Monthly magazine covering technical aspects of being a firefighter/rescuer. Estab. 1988. Circ. 50,000. Pays on publication. No kill fee. Buys first North American serial rights, buys one-time rights. Submit seasonal material 6 months in advance. Accepts queries by mail. Responds in 3 weeks to queries. Responds in 2 months to mss. Sample copy and writer's guidelines for 9 × 12 SAE with 5 first-class stamps or online. Guidelines available online.

Nonfiction Needs how-to, new product, photo feature, technical, incident review/report. Special issues: fire suppression, incident command, vehicle extrication, rescue training, mass-casualty incidents, water rescue/major issues facing the fire service. **Buys 15-20 mss/year.** Send complete ms. Length: 1,000-3,000 words. **Pays $125-250.** Sometimes pays expenses of writers on assignment.

Photos Send photos. Reviews contact sheets, negatives, 2â—Š2 and 35mm transparencies, 5â—Š7 prints. Offers $20-200. Buys one time rights.

Tips Read our magazine, spend some time with a fire department. We focus on all aspects of fire and rescue. Emphasis on techniques and new technology, with color photos as support.

FOREIGN SERVICE JOURNAL

2101 E St. NW, Washington DC 20037. (202)338-4045. Fax: (202)338-8244. E-mail: journal@afsa.org. Website: www.afsa.org. **75% freelance written**. Monthly magazine for Foreign Service personnel and others interested in foreign affairs and related subjects. Estab. 1924. Byline given. Pays on publication. No kill fee. Publishes ms an average of 3 months after acceptance. Buys first North American serial rights. Accepts queries by mail, e-mail, fax. Responds in 1 month to queries. Sample copy for $3.50 and 10 × 12 SAE with 6 first-class stamps. Guidelines for #10 sase.

Nonfiction "Uses articles on diplomacy, professional concerns of the State Department and Foreign Service, diplomatic history and articles on Foreign Service experiences. Much of our material is contributed by those working in the profession. Informed outside contributions are welcomed, however." Needs essays, expose, humor, opinion, personal experience. **Buys 5-10 unsolicited mss/year.** Send complete ms. Length: 1,000-3,000 words.

Tips "We're only looking for articles having something to do with diplomacy or U.S. foreign policy."

$ $ LAW ENFORCEMENT TECHNOLOGY MAGAZINE

Cygnus Business Media, P.O. Box 803, 1233 Janesville Ave., Fort Atkinson WI 53538-0803. (920)568-8334. Fax: (920)563-1702. E-mail: tabatha.wethal@cygnuspub.com. Website: www.officer.com. **Contact:** Tabatha Wethal. **40% freelance written**. Monthly magazine covering police management and technology. Estab. 1974. Circ. 30,000. Byline given. Pays on publication. No kill fee. Publishes ms an average of 4 months after acceptance. Buys first North American serial rights, buys electronic rights. Editorial lead time 6 months. Responds in 1 month to queries. Responds in 2 months to mss Guidelines available online.

Nonfiction Needs how-to, interview, photo feature, police management and training. **Buys 30 mss/year.** Query. Length: 1,200-2,000 words. **Pays $75-400 for assigned articles.**

Reprints Send typed manuscript with rights for sale noted and information about when and where the material previously appeared. Payment negotiable.

Photos Send photos. Captions required. Reviews contact sheets, negatives, 5 × 7 or 8 × 10 prints. Offers no additional payment for photos accepted with ms. Buys one time rights.

Tips "Writer should have background in police work or currently work for a police agency. Most of our articles are technical or supervisory in nature. Please query first after looking at a sample copy. Prefers mss, queries and images be submitted electronically."

$ $ NATIONAL FIRE & RESCUE

SpecComm International, Inc., 5808 Faringdon Place, Suite 200, Raleigh NC 27609. (919)872-5040. Fax: (919)876-6531. E-mail: mike@nfrmag.com. Website: www.nfrmag.com. **80% freelance written**. *National Fire & Rescue* is a bimonthly magazine devoted to informing the nation's fire and rescue services, with special emphasis on fire departments serving communities of less than 100,000. It is the *Popular Science* for fire and rescue with easy-to-understand information on science, technology, and training. Estab. 1980. Circ. 30,000. Byline given. Pays on publication. Offers 50% kill fee. Publishes ms an average of 5 months after acceptance. Buys first North American serial rights. Editorial lead time 2 months. Submit seasonal material 3 months in advance. Accepts queries by mail, e-mail, phone, online submission form. Accepts simultaneous submissions. Responds in 1 month to queries. Guidelines available online or call.

Nonfiction Needs book excerpts, how-to, humor, inspirational, interview, new product, personal experience, photo feature. No pieces marketing specific products or services. **Buys 40 mss/year.** Query with published clips. Length: 1,800-3,000 words. **Pays $100-350 for assigned articles. Pays $100-200 for unsolicited articles.** Pays expenses of writers on assignment.

Photos State availability. Identification of subjects required. Offers $50-200/photo. Buys one time rights.

Columns/Departments Leadership (management); Training; Special Operations; all 1,800 words. **Buys 16 mss/year.** Send complete ms. **Pays $100-200.**

Tips Discuss your story ideas with the editor.

$ $ 9-1-1 MAGAZINE

Official Publications, Inc., 18201 Weston Place, Tustin CA 92780-2251. (714)544-7776. Fax: (714)838-9233. E-mail: publisher@9-1-1magazine.com. Website: www.9-1-1magazine.com. **Contact:** Randall Larson, editor. **85% freelance written**. Trade magazine published 9 times/year for knowledgeable emergency communications professionals and those associated with this respectful profession. "Serving law enforcement, fire, and emergency medical services, with an emphasis on communications, *9-1-1 Magazine* provides valuable information to readers in all aspects of the public safety communications and response community. Each issue contains a blending of product-related, technical, operational, and people-oriented stories, covering the skills, training, and equipment which these professionals have in common." Estab. 1988. Circ. 18,000. Byline given. Pays on publication. Offers 20% kill fee. Publishes ms an average of 4-6 months after acceptance. Buys first rights. Accepts queries by mail, e-mail, fax. Responds in 1 month to queries and to mss. Sample copy for sae with 9 × 12 envelope and 5 first-class stamps. Guidelines available online.

Nonfiction Needs new product, photo feature, technical, incident report. **Buys 15-25 mss/year.** Query by e-mail (editor@9-1-1magazine.com). We prefer queries, but will look at manuscripts on speculation. Most positive responses to queries are considered on spec, but occasionally we will make assignments. Each ms should include a 25-word bio of the author. All submissions must include social security number, address, and phone number. Length: 1,000-2,500 words. **Pays 10-20¢/word.**

Photos Send photos. Captions, identification of subjects required. Reviews color transparencies, prints, high-resolution digital (300 dpi). Offers $50-100/interior, $300/cover. Buys one-time rights.

Tips "We are looking for writers knowledgeable in this field. As a trade magazine, stories should be geared for professionals in the emergency services and dispatch field, not the lay public. We do not use poetry or fiction. Our primary considerations in selecting material are: quality, appropriateness of material, brevity, knowledge of our readership, accuracy, accompanying photography, originality, wit and humor, a clear direction and vision, and proper use of language.

$$$ PLANNING

American Planning Association, 122 S. Michigan Ave., Suite 1600, Chicago IL 60603. (312)431-9100. Fax: (312)431-9985. E-mail: slewis@planning.org. Website: www.planning.org. **Contact:** Sylvia Lewis, editor. **30% freelance written**. Monthly magazine emphasizing urban planning for adult, college-educated readers who are regional and urban planners in city, state, or federal agencies or in private business, or university faculty or students. Estab. 1972. Circ. 44,000. Byline given. Pays on publication. No kill fee. Publishes ms an average of 2 months after acceptance. Buys all rights. Accepts queries by mail, e-mail, fax. Responds in 5 weeks to queries. Sample copy for 9 × 12 SAE with 6 first-class stamps. Guidelines available online.

Nonfiction "It's best to query with a fairly detailed, 1-page letter or e-mail. We'll consider any article that's well written and relevant to our audience. Articles have a better chance if they are timely and related to planning, and if they appeal to a national audience. All articles should be written in magazine-feature style." Needs exposè, on government or business, but topics related to planning, housing, land use, zoning, general interest, trend stories on cities, land use, government, how-to, successful government or citizen efforts in planning, innovations, concepts that have been applied, technical, detailed articles on the nitty-gritty of planning, transportation, computer mapping, but no footnotes or mathematical models. Special issues: Transportation Issue; Technology Issue. Also needs news stories up to 500 words. **Buys 44 features and 33 news story mss/year.** Length: 500-3,000 words. **Pays $150-1,500.**

Photos "We prefer authors supply their own photos, but we sometimes take our own or arrange for them in other ways." State availability. Captions required. Pays $100 minimum for photos used on inside pages and $300 for cover photos. Buys one-time rights.

$$ POLICE AND SECURITY NEWS

DAYS Communications, Inc., 1208 Juniper St., Quakertown PA 18951-1520. (215)538-1240. Fax: (215)538-1208. E-mail: jdevery@policeandsecuritynews.com. Website: www.policeandsecuritynews.com. **Contact:** James Devery, editor. **40% freelance written**. Bimonthly periodical on public law enforcement and Homeland Security. Our publication is designed to provide educational and entertaining information directed toward management level. Technical information written for the expert in a manner the nonexpert can understand. Estab. 1984. Circ. 24,000. Byline given. Pays on publication. No kill fee. Publishes ms an average of 2 months after acceptance. Buys first North American serial rights. Accepts queries by mail, e-mail, fax, phone. Accepts simultaneous submissions. Sample copy and writer's guidelines for 10 × 13 SAE with $2.53 postage.

Nonfiction Contact: Al Menear, articles editor. Needs expose, historical, how-to, humor, interview, opinion, personal experience, photo feature, technical. **Buys 12 mss/year.** Query. Length: 200-2,500 words. **Pays 10¢/word. Sometimes pays in trade-out of services.**

Reprints Send tearsheet, photocopy or typed ms with rights for sale noted and information about when and where the material previously appeared.

Photos State availability. Reviews 3 × 5 prints. Offers $10-50/photo. Buys one time rights.

Fillers Needs facts, newsbreaks, short humor. Buys 6 mss/year. Length: 200-2,000 words. **10¢/word.**

THE POLICE CHIEF

The Professional Voice of Law Enforcement, International Association of Chiefs of Police, 515 N. Washington St., Alexandria VA 22301. (703)836-6767. Fax: (703)836-4543. E-mail: higginboth@theiacp.org. Website: www.policechiefmagazine.org. **Contact:** Charles Higginbotham, editor. Monthly magazine covering law enforcement issues. "Articles are contributed by practitioners in law enforcement or related fields. Manuscripts must be original work, previously unpublished and not simultaneously submitted to another publisher. No word rate is paid or other remuneration given. Contributors' opinions and statements are not purported to define official IACP policy or imply IACP endorsement." True Copyright held by publication. 3-6 months Guidelines available online at website.

Nonfiction Needs general interest, interview, Administration, innovative techniques, new technological developments/applications, success stories, operational procedures, research, and other topics of interest

to law enforcement administrators and practitioners. Two double-spaced printed copies of manuscripts required. Authors are encouraged to submit PC disks in MS Word or WordPerfect (up to 6.1), or by e-mail to higginboth@theiacp.org. Brief biographical sketch of each author containing author's name, position title, agency, and complete mailing address must accompany manuscripts. 2,000-4,000/words. **Byline credit and 5 complimentary copies of issue with your article.**
Photos Photos encouraged.

$$$$ YOUTH TODAY

The Newspaper on Youth Work, American Youth Work Center, 1200 17th St. NW, 4th Floor, Washington DC 20036. (202)785-0764. E-mail: pboyle@youthtoday.org. Website: www.youthtoday.org. **Contact:** Patrick Boyle. **50% freelance written**. Newspaper published 10 times a year covering businesses that provide services to youth. Audience is people who run youth programs—mostly nonprofits & government agencies. They want help in providing services, getting funding. Estab. 1994. Circ. 9,000. Byline given. Pays on publication. Offers $200 kill fee for features. Buys first North American serial rights, buys electronic rights. Editorial lead time 2 months. Accepts queries by mail, e-mail, or disk. Accepts simultaneous submissions. Responds in 2 weeks to queries. Responds in 1 month to mss. Sample copy for $5. Guidelines available online.
Nonfiction "Our freelancers have worked for daily newspapers or have extensive experience writing for newspapers and magazines." Needs expose, general interest, technical. No feel-good stories about do-gooders. We examine the business of youth work. **Buys 5 mss/year.** Query. Send resume, short cover letter, a few clips. Length: 600-2,500 words. **Pays $150-2,000 for assigned articles.** Pays expenses of writers on assignment.
Photos Identification of subjects required. Offers no additional payment for photos accepted with ms. Buys one time and Internet rights.
Tips Business writers have the best shot. Focus on evaluations of programs, or why a program succeeds or fails. Please visit online.

Groceries & Food Products

$$$ CONVENIENCE DISTRIBUTION

AWMA's Magazine for Candy, Tobacco, Grocery, Foodservice and General Merchandise Marketers, American Wholesale Marketers Association, 2750 Prosperity Ave., Suite 530, Fairfax VA 22031. Fax: (703)573-5738. E-mail: tracic@awmanet.org. Website: www.awmanet.org. **70% freelance written**. Magazine published 10 times/year. "We cover trends in candy, tobacco, groceries, beverages, snacks, and other product categories found in convenience stores, grocery stores, and drugstores, plus distribution topics. Contributors should have prior experience writing about the food, retail, and/or distribution industries. Editorial includes a mix of columns, departments, and features (2-6 pages). We also cover AWMA programs." Estab. 1948. Circ. 11,000. Byline given. Pays on acceptance. No kill fee. Publishes ms an average of 2 months after acceptance. Editorial lead time 3-4 months. Accepts queries by e-mail only. Guidelines available online.
Nonfiction Needs how-to, technical, industry trends, also profiles of distribution firms. No comics, jokes, poems, or other fillers. **Buys 40 mss/year.** Query with published clips. Length: 1,200-3,600 words. **Pays 50¢/word.** Pays expenses of writers on assignment.
Photos Authors must provide artwork (with captions) with articles.
Tips "We're looking for reliable, accurate freelancers with whom we can establish a long-term working relationship. We need writers who understand this industry. We accept very few articles on speculation. Most are assigned. To consider a new writer for an assignment, we must first receive his or her resume, at least 2 writing samples, and references."

$$$ NATURAL FOOD NETWORK MAGAZINE

Supporting the Business of Natural & Organic Food Supply, 760 Market St., Suite 432, San Francisco CA 94102. (415)839-5067. Fax: (415)398-3511. E-mail: news@naturalfoodnet.com. Website: www.naturalfoodnet.com. **70% freelance written**. Bimonthly magazine covering natural and certified organic food industry (domestic and international). Estab. 2003. Circ. 15,000. Byline given. Pays on publication. Offers 10% up to $50 maximum kill fee. Publishes ms an average of 2 months after acceptance. Buys first North American serial rights. Editorial lead time 2 months. Submit seasonal material 2 months in advance. Accepts queries by e-mail. Accepts simultaneous submissions. Responds in 1 week to queries. Responds in 1 month to mss. Sample copy free. Guidelines free.

Nonfiction Our publication circulates entirely to retail and supply professionals. Does not want work with a consumer angle. **Buys 50 mss/year.** Query. Length: 250-1,500 words. **Pays $250-750.** Sometimes pays expenses of writers on assignment.
Photos State availability. Captions, identification of subjects required. Reviews JPEG files. Offers no additional payment for photos accepted with ms. Buys all rights.
Columns/Departments Q&A with industry leaders (natural and organic specialists in academia, trade associations and business); Worldview (interviews with internationally recognized leaders in organic food supply), both 750 words. **Buys 6 mss/year.** Query. **Pays $500.**
Tips Our magazine encourages writers to work closely with editors using online story pitch and assignment software. This collaborative software permits writers to see what is being pitched (anonymously) and to track their own assignments, download materials like story guidelines and monitor deadlines.

$ $ PRODUCE MERCHANDISING

Vance Publishing Corp., 400 Knightsbridge Pkwy., Lincolnshire IL 60069. (512)906-0733. E-mail: pamelar@producemerchandising.com. Website: www.producemerchandising.com. **Contact:** Pamela Riemenschneider, editor. **10% freelance written.** Monthly magazine. *Produce Merchandising* is the only monthly journal on the market that is dedicated solely to produce merchandising information for retailers. Circ. 12,000. Byline given. Pays on acceptance. No kill fee. Publishes ms an average of 3 months after acceptance. Buys all rights. Editorial lead time 3 months. Accepts queries by mail. Responds in 2 weeks to queries. Sample copy free.

- Our purpose is to provide information about promotions, merchandising, and operations in the form of ideas and examples.

Nonfiction Needs how-to, interview, new product, photo feature, technical, contact the editor for a specific assignment. **Buys 48 mss/year.** Query with published clips. Length: 1,000-1,500 words. **Pays $200-600.** Pays expenses of writers on assignment.
Photos State availability of or send photos. Captions, identification of subjects, model releases required. Reviews color slides and 3 × 5 or larger prints. Offers no additional payment for photos accepted with ms. Buys all rights.
Columns/Departments Contact: editor for a specific assignment. **Buys 30 mss/year.** Query with published clips. **Pays $200-450.**
Tips Send in clips and contact the editor with specific story ideas. Story topics are typically outlined up to a year in advance.

$ $ THE PRODUCE NEWS

800 Kinderkamack Rd., Suite 100, Oradell NJ 07649. (201)986-7990. Fax: (201)986-7996. E-mail: groh@theproducenews.com. Website: www.theproducenews.com. **10% freelance written. Works with a small number of new/unpublished writers each year.** Weekly magazine for commercial growers and shippers, receivers and distributors of fresh fruits and vegetables, including chain store produce buyers and merchandisers. Estab. 1897. Pays on publication. No kill fee. Publishes ms an average of 2 weeks after acceptance. Accepts queries by mail, e-mail, fax. Responds in 1 month to queries. Sample copy and writer's guidelines for 10 × 13 SAE and 4 first-class stamps.
Nonfiction News stories (about the produce industry). Buys profiles, spot news, coverage of successful business operations and articles on merchandising techniques. Query. **Pays $1/column inch minimum.** Sometimes pays expenses of writers on assignment.
Photos Black and white glossies or color prints. Pays $8-10/photo.
Tips Stories should be trade oriented, not consumer oriented. As our circulation grows in the next year, we are interested in stories and news articles from all fresh-fruit-growing areas of the country.

$ $ ☐ WESTERN GROCER MAGAZINE

Mercury Publications Ltd., 1740 Wellington Ave., Winnipeg MB R3H 0E8 Canada. (204)954-2085. Fax: (204)954-2057. Website: www.mercury.mb.ca/. **75% freelance written.** Bimonthly magazine covering the grocery industry. Reports for the Western Canadian grocery, allied non-food and institutional industries. Each issue features a selection of relevant trade news and event coverage from the West and around the world. Feature reports offer market analysis, trend views and insightful interviews from a wide variety of industry leaders. The Western Grocer target audience is independent retail food stores, supermarkets, manufacturers and food brokers, distributors and wholesalers of food and allied non-food products, as well as bakers, specialty and health food stores and convenience outlets. Estab. 1916. Circ. 15,500. Byline given. Pays 30-45 days from receipt of invoice. Offers 33% kill fee. Buys all rights. Submit seasonal material 3 months in advance. Sample copy and writer's guidelines free.

- Assigns stories to Canadian writers based on editorial needs of publication.

Nonfiction Needs how-to, interview. Industry reports and profiles on companies. Query with published clips. Length: 500-9,000 words. **Pays 25-35¢/word.** Sometimes pays expenses of writers on assignment.
Photos State availability. Captions required. Reviews negatives, transparencies, 3 × 5 prints, JPEG, EPS, or TIF files. Negotiates payment individually. Buys all rights.
Tips E-mail, fax, or mail a query outlining your experience, interest, and pay expectations. Include clippings.

Home Furnishings & Household Goods

$$ HOME FURNISHINGS RETAILER

National Home Furnishings Association (NHFA), 3910 Tinsley Dr., Suite 101, High Point NC 27265-3610. (336)801-6156. Fax: (336)801-6102. E-mail: wynnryan@rcn.com. Website: www.nhfa.org. **Contact:** Mary Wynn Ryan, editor-in-chief. **75% freelance written**. Monthly magazine published by NHFA covering the home furnishings industry. "We hope home furnishings retailers view our magazine as a profitability tool. We want each issue to help them make or save money." Requires writers to have credentials that include specific knowledge of the industry & extensive experience in writing about it. Estab. 1927. Circ. 15,000. Byline given. Pays on acceptance. No kill fee. Publishes ms an average of 6 weeks after acceptance. Buys first North American serial rights. Editorial lead time 3 months. Accepts queries by mail, e-mail. Responds in 1 month to queries. Sample copy available with proper postage. Guidelines online and for #10 sase.
Nonfiction Query—include resume, writing samples & credentials, published clips. Assigned articles should be submitted by e-mail or on disc. 3,000-5,000 words (features) **Pays $350-500.**
Photos Author is responsible for obtaining photos or other illustrative material. State availability. Identification of subjects required. Reviews transparencies. Negotiates payment individually. Buys one time rights.
Columns/Departments Columns cover business and product trends that shape the home furnishings industry. Advertising and Marketing; Finance; Technology; Training; Creative Leadership; Law; Style and Operations. Length: 1,200-1,500 words. Query with published clips.
Tips Our readership includes owners of small 'Ma and Pa' furniture stores, executives of medium-sized chains (2-10 stores), and executives of big chains. Articles should be relevant to retailers and provide them with tangible information, ideas, and products to better their business.

WINDOW FASHION VISION

Grace McNamara, Inc., 2594 Rice St., St. Paul MN 55113. Fax: (651)653-4308. E-mail: jennifer@wf-vision.com. Website: www.wf-vision.com. **Contact:** Jennifer Jacobs, assoc. editor. **30% freelance written**. Monthly magazine dedicated to the advancement of the window fashions industry, *Window Fashions* provides comprehensive information on design and business principles, window fashion aesthetics, and product applications. The magazine serves the window-treatment and wall-coverings industry, including designers, retailers, dealers, specialty stores, workrooms, manufacturers, fabricators, and others associated with the field of interior design. Writers should be thoroughly knowledgable on the subject, and submissions need to be comprehensive. Estab. 1981. Circ. 30,000. Byline given. Pays on publication. No kill fee. Publishes ms an average of 3 months after acceptance. Buys all rights. Editorial lead time 3 months. Submit seasonal material 4 months in advance. Accepts queries by mail, e-mail. Accepts simultaneous submissions. Sample copy for $5.
Nonfiction Needs how-to, window fashion installation, interview, of designers, personal experience, specific topics within the field. No broad topics not specific to the window fashions industry. **Buys 24 mss/year.** Query or send complete ms Length: 800-1,000 words.
Tips The most helpful experience is if a writer has knowledge of interior design or, specifically, window treatments. We already have a pool of generalists, although we welcome clips from writers who would like to be considered for assignments. Our style is professional business writing—no flowery prose. Articles tend to be to the point, as our readers are busy professionals who read for information, not for leisure. Most of all we need creative ideas and approaches to topics in the field of window treatments and interior design. A writer needs to be knowledgeable in the field because our readers would know if information was inaccurate.

Hospitals, Nursing & Nursing Homes

$$ CURRENT NURSING IN GERIATRIC CARE

Freiberg Press Inc., P.O. Box 612, Cedar Falls IA 50613. (319)553-0642. E-mail: bfreiberg@cfu.net. Website: www.care4elders.com. **25% freelance written**. Bimonthly trade journal covering medical information and new developments in research for geriatric nurses and other practitioners. Estab. 2006. Byline sometimes given. Pays on acceptance. No kill fee. Buys all rights. Accepts queries by e-mail. Sample copy free.

Nonfiction Query. Length: 500-1,500 words. **Pays 15¢/word for assigned articles.**

Photos State availability.

$$$ HOSPITALS & HEALTH NETWORKS

Health Forum, 1 N. Franklin, 29th Floor, Chicago IL 60606. (312)422-2100. E-mail: bsantamour@healthforum.com. Website: www.hhnmag.com. **25% freelance written**. Monthly magazine covering hospitals. We are a business publication for hospital and health system executives. We use only writers who are thoroughly familiar with the hospital field. Submit résumé and up to 5 samples of health care-related articles. We assign all articles and do not consider manuscripts. Estab. 1926. Circ. 85,000. Byline given. Pays on acceptance. Offers variable kill fee. Publishes ms an average of 3 months after acceptance. Buys all rights. Editorial lead time 2-3 months. Accepts queries by e-mail. Responds in 2-4 months to queries.

Nonfiction Contact: Bill Santamour, managing editor. Needs interview, technical. Query with published clips. Length: 350-2,000 words. **Pays $300-1,500 for assigned articles.**

Tips If you demonstrate via published clips that you are thoroughly familiar with the business issues facing health-care executives, and that you are a polished reporter and writer, we will consider assigning you an article for our InBox section to start out. These are generally 350 words on a specific development of interest to hospitals and health system executives. Persistence does not pay with us. Once you've sent your résumé and clips, we will review them. If we have no assignment at that time, we will keep promising freelance candidates on file for future assignments.

$$ LONG TERM CARE

Ontario Long Term Care Association, 345 Renfrew Dr., Third Floor, Markham ON L3R 9S9 Canada. (905)470-8995. Fax: (905)470-9595. E-mail: info@oltca.com. Website: www.oltca.com. Quarterly magazine covering professional issues and practical articles of interest to staff working in a long-term care setting (nursing home, retirement home). Information must be applicable to a Canadian setting; focus should be on staff and for resident well being. Estab. 1990. Circ. 6,000. Byline given. Pays on publication. No kill fee. Publishes ms an average of 4 months after acceptance. Buys one-time rights. Editorial lead time 3 months. Submit seasonal material 5 months in advance. Responds in 3 months to queries. Sample copy free. Guidelines available online.

Nonfiction Needs general interest, how-to, practical, of use to long term care practitioners, inspirational, interview. No product-oriented articles. Query with published clips. Individuals should submit their ideas and/or completed articles to: justwrite@powergate.ca. Electronic versions in either Wordperfect or MS Word are preferred. Length:400-2,500 words. **Pays up to $500 (Canadian).**

Photos Send photos. Captions, model releases required. Reviews contact sheets, 5 × 5 prints. Offers no additional payment for photos accepted with ms. Buys one time rights.

Columns/Departments Query with published clips. **Pays up to $500 (Canadian).**

Tips Articles must be positive, upbeat, and contain helpful information that staff and managers working in the long term care field can use. Focus should be on staff and resident well being. Articles that highlight new ways of doing things are particularly useful. Please call the editor to discuss ideas. Must be applicable to Canadian settings.

$ SCHOOL NURSE NEWS

Franklin Communications, Inc., 53 Stickle Ave., Suite 1, Rockaway NJ 07866. (973)625-8811. Fax: (973)625-7914. E-mail: chris@fc4research.com. Website: www.schoolnursenews.org. **Contact:** Chris Flath. **10% freelance written**. Magazine published 5 times/year covering school nursing. "Focuses on topics related to the health issues of school-aged children and adolescents (grades K-12), as well as the health and professional issues that concern school nurses. We believe this is an excellent opportunity for both new and experienced writers. School Nurse News publishes feature articles as well as news articles and regular departments, such as Asthma & Allergy Watch, Career & Salary Survey, Oral Health,

Nursing Currents, and Sights & Sounds. Manuscripts can include case histories, scenarios of health office situations, updates on diseases, reporting of research, and discussion of procedures and techniques, among others. The author is responsible for the accuracy of content. References should be complete, accurate, and in APA format. Tables, charts and photographs are welcome. Authors are responsible for obtaining permission to reproduce any material that has a pre-existing copyright. The feature article, references, tables and charts should total 8-10 typewritten pages, double-spaced. The author's name should be included only on the top sheet. The top sheet should also include the title of the article, the author's credentials, current position, address and phone." Estab. 1982. Circ. 7,500. Byline given. Pays on publication. Publishes ms an average of 3-6 months after acceptance. Buys first North American serial rights. Editorial lead time 3-6 months. Submit seasonal material 6 months in advance. Accepts queries by e-mail, phone. Sample copy free. Guidelines free.

Nonfiction Needs how-to, interview, new product, personal experience. **Buys 1-2 mss/year.** Query. **Pays $100.**

Tips "Prospective authors are welcome to write, fax or e-mail for information related to appropriate topics and assistance."

Hotels, Motels, Clubs, Resorts & Restaurants

$ $ BARTENDER MAGAZINE

Foley Publishing, P.O. Box 158, Liberty Corner NJ 07938. (908)766-6006. Fax: (908)766-6607. Website: www.bartender.com. **100% freelance written. Prefers to work with published/established writers; eager to work with new/unpublished writers.** Quarterly magazine emphasizing liquor and bartending for bartenders, tavern owners, and owners of restaurants with full-service liquor licenses. Circ. 148,225. Byline given. Pays on publication. No kill fee. Publishes ms an average of 3 months after acceptance. Buys first North American serial rights, buys first rights, buys one-time rights, buys second serial (reprint) rights, buys simultaneous rights, buys all rights. Submit seasonal material 3 months in advance. Accepts simultaneous submissions. Responds in 2 months to mss. Sample copy for sae with 9 × 12 envelope and 4 First-Class stamps.

Nonfiction Needs general interest, historical, how-to, humor, interview with famous bartenders or ex-bartenders, new product, opinion, personal experience, photo feature, travel, nostalgia, unique bars, new techniques, new drinking trends, bar sports, bar magic tricks. Special issues: Annual Calendar and Daily Cocktail Recipe Guide. Send complete ms and SASE. Length: 100-1,000 words.

Reprints Send tearsheet and information about when and where the material previously appeared. Pays 25% of amount paid for an original article.

Photos Send photos. Captions, model releases required. Pays $7.50-50 for 8 × 10 b&w glossy prints; $10-75 for 8 × 10 color glossy prints.

Columns/Departments Bar of the Month; Bartender of the Month; Creative Cocktails; Bar Sports; Quiz; Bar Art; Wine Cellar; Tips from the Top (from prominent figures in the liquor industry); One For the Road (travel); Collectors (bar or liquor-related items); Photo Essays. **Length:** 200-1,000 words. Query by mail only with SASE. **Pays $50-200.**

Fillers Needs anecdotes, newsbreaks, short humor, clippings, jokes, gags. Length: 25-100 words. **Pays $5-25.**

Tips "To break in, absolutely make sure that your work will be of interest to all bartenders across the country. Your style of writing should reflect the audience you are addressing. The most frequent mistake made by writers in completing an article for us is using the wrong subject."

$ $ EL RESTAURANTE MEXICANO

P.O. Box 2249, Oak Park IL 60303-2249. (708)488-0100. Fax: (708)488-0101. E-mail: kfurore@restmex.com. Bimonthly magazine covering Mexican and other Latin cuisines. "*El Restaurante Mexicano* offers features and business-related articles that are geared specifically to owners and operators of Mexican, Tex-Mex, Southwestern, and Latin cuisine restaurants and other foodservice establishments that want to add that type of cuisine." Estab. 1997. Circ. 27,000. Byline given. Pays on publication. No kill fee. Publishes ms an average of 3 months after acceptance. Buys first North American serial rights. Responds in 2 months to queries. Sample copy free.

Nonfiction Looking for stories about unique Mexican restaurants and about business issues that affect Mexican restaurant owners. No specific knowledge of food or restaurants is needed; the key qualification is to be a good reporter who knows how to slant a story toward the Mexican restaurant operator. **Buys**

4-6 mss/year. Query with published clips. Length: 800-1,200 words. **Pays $250-300.** Pays expenses of writers on assignment.

Tips "Query with a story idea, and tell how it pertains to Mexican restaurants."

$ $ FLORIDA HOTEL & MOTEL JOURNAL

The Official Publication of the Florida Hotel & Motel Association, Accommodations, Inc., P.O. Box 1529, Tallahassee FL 32302-1529. (850)224-2888. Fax: (850)668-2884. E-mail: journal@fhma.net. Website: www.flahotel.com. **10% freelance written. Prefers to work with published/established writers.** Bimonthly magazine acting as a reference tool for managers and owners of Florida's hotels, motels, and resorts. Estab. 1978. Circ. 8,500. Byline given. Pays on publication. No kill fee. Publishes ms an average of 1-2 months after acceptance. Buys first rights. Editorial lead time 1-9 months. Submit seasonal material 4-5 months in advance. Accepts queries by mail. Accepts previously published material. Responds in 2-4 months to queries. Sample copy free. Guidelines available online.

Nonfiction Needs how-to, pertaining to hotel management, interview, new product, personal experience, technical. "No travel tips or articles aimed at the traveling public, and no promotion of individual property, destination, product, or service." Query with published clips. Length: 500-1,500 words. **Pays 10¢/published word.** Sometimes pays expenses of writers on assignment.

Photos State availability. Captions, identification of subjects, model releases required. Offers no additional payment for photos accepted with ms. Buys all rights.

Columns/Departments Management Monograph, 500-1,000 words (expert information for hotel and motel management); Florida Scene, 500 words (Florida-specific, time-sensitive information for hotel managers or owners); National Scene, 500-1,000 words (USA-specific, time-sensitive information for hotel managers or owners); Fillers and Features, 500-700 words (information specific to editorial focus for the issue). Query. **Pays in contributor copies.**

Fillers Needs anecdotes, facts, short humor. Length: 50-1,000 words. **Pays in contributor copies.**

Tips We use press releases provided to this office that fit the profile of our magazine's departments, targeting items of interest to the general managers of Florida's lodging operations. Feature articles are written based on an editorial calendar. We also publish an annual buyer's guide that provides a directory of all FH&MA member companies and allied member companies.

$ $ $ $ ⊘ HOSPITALITY TECHNOLOGY

Edgell Communications, 4 Middlebury Blvd., Randolph NJ 07869. (973)252-0100. Fax: (973)252-9020. E-mail: alorden@edgellmail.com. Website: www.htmagazine.com. **Contact:** Abigail Lorden, editor-in-chief. **70% freelance written**. Magazine published 9 times/year. We cover the technology used in foodservice and lodging. Our readers are the operators, who have significant IT responsibilities. Estab. 1996. Circ. 16,000. Byline given. Pays on acceptance. No kill fee. Publishes ms an average of 1 month after acceptance. Buys all rights. Makes work-for-hire assignments. Editorial lead time 2 months. Accepts queries by mail, e-mail, fax, phone. Responds in 2 weeks to queries.

- This publication will not respond to all inquiries—only those that are of particular interest to the editor.

Nonfiction Needs how-to, interview, new product, technical. Special issues: We publish 2 studies each year, the Restaurant Industry Technology Study and the Lodging Industry Technology Study. No unsolicited mss. **Buys 40 mss/year.** Query with published clips. Length: 800-1,200 words. **Pays $1/word.** Sometimes pays expenses of writers on assignment.

Tips Given the vast amount of inquiries we receive, it's impossible for us to respond to all. We can only respond to those that are of particular interest.

$ $ ⊡ HOTELIER

Kostuch Publications, Ltd., 23 Lesmill Rd., Suite 101, Toronto ON M3B 3P6 Canada. (416)447-0888. Fax: (416)447-5333. E-mail: rcaira@foodservice.ca. Website: www.hoteliermagazine.com. **Contact:** Rosanna Caira, editor and publisher. **40% freelance written**. Magazine published 8 times/year covering the Canadian hotel industry. Estab. 1989. Circ. 9,000. Byline given. Pays on publication. No kill fee. Buys first North American serial rights. Editorial lead time 3 months. Submit seasonal material 2 months in advance. Accepts queries by mail, fax. Sample copy and writer's guidelines free.

Nonfiction Needs how-to, new product. No case studies. **Buys 30-50 mss/year.** Query. Length: 700-1,500 words. **Pays 35¢/word (Canadian) for assigned articles.** Sometimes pays expenses of writers on assignment.

Photos Send photos. Offers $30-75/photo.

$$ INSITE

Christian Camp and Conference Association, P.O. Box 62189, Colorado Springs CO 80962-2189. (719)260-9400. Fax: (719)260-6398. E-mail: editor@ccca.org. Website: www.ccca.org. **Contact:** Martha Krienke, editor. **75% freelance written. Prefers to work with published/established writers.** Bimonthly magazine emphasizing the broad scope of organized camping with emphasis on Christian camps and conference centers. "All who work in youth camps and adult conferences read our magazine for inspiration and to get practical help in ways to serve in their operations." Estab. 1963. Circ. 8,500. Byline given. Pays on publication. No kill fee. Publishes ms an average of 4 months after acceptance. Buys first rights. Accepts queries by mail, e-mail. Responds in 1 month to queries. Sample copy for $4.99 plus 9 × 12 SASE. Guidelines available by request.

Nonfiction Needs general interest, trends in organized camping in general, Christian camping in particular, how-to, anything involved with organized camping, including motivating staff, programming, healthcare, maintenance, and camper follow-up, inspirational, interested in profiles and practical applications of Scriptural principles to everyday situations in camping, interview, with movers and shakers in Christian camping. **Buys 15-20 mss/year.** Query required. Length: 500-1,700 words. **Pays 20¢/word.**

Reprints Send photocopy and information about when and where the material previously appeared. Pays 50% of amount paid for an original article.

Photos Price negotiable for 35mm color transparencies and high-quality digital photos.

Tips "The most frequent mistake made by writers is that they send articles unrelated to our readers. Review our publication guidelines first. Interviews are the best bet for freelancers."

$$ MOUNTAIN RESORT MAGAZINE

Skinner Media, Vail CO 81657. Phone/Fax: (252)261-3437. E-mail: editor@mountainresortmag.com. Website: www.mountainresortmag.com. **50% freelance written.** Bimonthly magazine covering the ski and snowboard resort industry. We are exclusively an area operations, marketing, and management resource for local, regional, and national mountain destinations. We combine humor with information and images with explanations, and understand the spark it takes to work in black snow pants 175 days a year. We will gladly trade publishing credits for real experience on the front lines. And, we readily understand that although travel writers and old-school journalists are invariably handsome, brilliant, and uber-masters of the sport, they have little cred with those who actually do the job. We do not preach, but utilize the voices in the industry to help share authentic experience. Estab. 2004. Circ. 4,200. Byline given. Pays on acceptance. Offers 20% kill fee. Buys first North American serial rights. Editorial lead time 2 months. Submit seasonal material 3 months in advance. Accepts queries by e-mail. Accepts simultaneous submissions. Responds in 1 week to queries. Responds in 1 month to mss. Guidelines by e-mail.

Nonfiction Needs historical, how-to, humor, interview, new product, technical. Please do not confuse the retail or travel end of skiing and riding with the operations community (management, marketing, lift operators). **Buys 15 mss/year.** Query. Length: 1,200-2,000 words. **Pays $500.**

Photos Please contact the editor if you have taken operations photography. (This does not include pictures of your buddy doing some trick in the park.).

Columns/Departments Bullwheel (informative spew about interesting and funny operations developments), 200 words. **Buys 1 mss/year.** Query. **Pays $100 maximum.**

Tips Our angle is experience from the front lines. We've of course had dozens of travel writers pawning their wares, but are more interested in actual resort employees' voices than consumer writing credits. Shoot ideas by e-mail, and please include any relevant on-hill experience. Be young; be funny. Tell us a story you heard in a locker room rather than drone on about what's happening in a board room.

$$$ PIZZA TODAY

The Monthly Professional Guide to Pizza Profits, Macfadden Protech, LLC, 908 S. 8th St., Suite 200, Louisville KY 40203. (502)736-9500. Fax: (502)736-9502. E-mail: jwhite@pizzatoday.com. Website: www.pizzatoday.com. Mandy Detwiler, managing editor. **Contact:** Jeremy White, editor-in-chief. **30% freelance written. Works with published/established writers; occasionally works with new writers.** Monthly magazine for the pizza industry, covering trends, features of successful pizza operators, business and management advice, etc. Estab. 1984. Circ. 44,000. Byline given. Pays on acceptance. No kill fee. Publishes ms an average of 2 months after acceptance. Buys all rights. Submit seasonal material 3 months in advance. Accepts queries by mail, e-mail, fax. Responds in 2 months to queries. Responds in 3 weeks to mss. Sample copy for sae with 10 × 13 envelope and 6 first-class stamps. Guidelines for

#10 sase and online.

Nonfiction Needs interview, entrepreneurial slants, pizza production and delivery, employee training, hiring, marketing, and business management. No fillers, humor, or poetry. **Buys 85 mss/year.** Length: 1,000 words. **Pays 50¢/word, occasionally more.** Sometimes pays expenses of writers on assignment.

Photos Captions required. Reviews contact sheets, negatives, transparencies, color slides, 5 × 7 prints.

Tips "Our most pressing need is for articles that would fall within our Front of the House section. Review the magazine before sending in your query."

$$$ SANTÉ MAGAZINE

On-Premise Communications, 100 South St., Bennington VT 05201. 802-442-6771. Fax: 802-442-6859. E-mail: mvaughan@santemagazine.com. Website: www.isantemagazine.com. **Contact:** Mark Vaughan, editor. **75% freelance written**. 9 issues per year magazine covering food, wine, spirits, and management topics for restaurant professionals. "Information and specific advice for restaurant professionals on operating a profitable food and beverage program. Writers should 'speak' to readers on a professional-to-professional basis." Estab. 1996. Circ. 55,000. Byline given. Pays on publication. Offers 50% kill fee. Publishes ms an average of 2 months after acceptance. Buys first North American serial rights. Editorial lead time 6 months. Submit seasonal material 6 months in advance. Accepts queries by e-mail. Responds in 2 weeks to queries. We do not accept mss. Sample copy for with 7 envelope. Guidelines by e-mail.

- "Articles should be concise and to the point and should closely adhere to the assigned word count. Our readers will only read articles that provide useful information in a readily accessible format. Where possible, articles should be broken into stand-alone sections that can be boxed or otherwise highlighted."

Nonfiction Needs interview, Restaurant business news. "We do not want consumer-focused pieces." **Buys 95 mss/year.** Query with published clips. Length: 650-1,800 words. Sometimes pays expenses of writers on assignment.

Photos State availability. Captions required. Reviews 8 × 10 at 300 dpi transparencies, GIF/JPEG files. Offers no additional payment for photos accepted. Buys one-time rights.

Columns/Departments "Due to a Redesign, 650 words; Bar Tab (focuses on one bar's unique strategy for success), 1,000 words; Restaurant Profile (a business-related look at what qualities make one restaurant successful), 1,000 words; Maximizing Profits (covers one great profit-maximizing strategy per issue from several sources), Chef's Seminar (highlights one chef's unique style), Appellations (an in-depth look at a high-profile wine-producing region), Distillations (a detailed study of a particular type of spirit), 1,500 words; Provisions (like The Goods only longer; an in-depth look at a special ingredient), 1,500 words. **Buys 95 mss/year.** Query with published clips. **Pays $300-$800.**

Tips "Present 2 or 3 of your best ideas via e-mail. Include a brief statement of your qualifications. Attach your resume and 3 electronic clips. The same format may be used to query via postal mail if necessary."

$$ ☐ WESTERN HOTELIER MAGAZINE

Mercury Publications, Ltd., 1740 Wellington Ave., Winnipeg MB R3H 0E8 Canada. (204)954-2085. Fax: (204)954-2057. Website: www.mercury.mb.ca/. **33% freelance written**. Quarterly magazine covering the hotel industry. *Western Hotelier* is dedicated to the accommodation industry in Western Canada and U.S. western border states. *WH* offers the West's best mix of news and feature reports geared to hotel management. Feature reports are written on a sector basis and are created to help generate enhanced profitability and better understanding. Circ. 4,342. Byline given. Pays 30-45 days from receipt of invoice. Offers 33% kill fee. Buys all rights. Submit seasonal material 3 months in advance. Accepts queries by mail, fax. Accepts simultaneous submissions. Responds in 2 weeks to queries. Sample copy and writer's guidelines free.

Nonfiction Needs how-to, train staff, interview. Industry reports and profiles on companies. Query with published clips. Length: 500-9,000 words. **Pays 25-35¢/word.** Sometimes pays expenses of writers on assignment.

Photos State availability. Captions required. Reviews negatives, transparencies, 3 × 5 prints, JPEG, EPS or TIF files. Negotiates payment individually. Buys all rights.

Tips E-mail, fax, or mail a query outlining your experience, interests and pay expectations. Include clippings.

$$ ☐ WESTERN RESTAURANT NEWS

Mercury Publications, Ltd., 1740 Wellington Ave., Winnipeg MB R3H 0E8 Canada. (204)954-2085. Fax: (204)954-2057. Website: www.mercury.mb.ca/. **Contact:** Kelly Gray, editor. **20% freelance written**.

Bimonthly magazine covering the restaurant trade. Reports profiles and industry reports on associations, regional business developments, etc. *Western Restaurant News Magazine* is the authoritative voice of the foodservice industry in Western Canada. Offering a total package to readers, *WRN* delivers concise news articles, new product news, and coverage of the leading trade events in the West, across the country, and around the world. Estab. 1994. Circ. 14,532. Byline given. Pays 30-45 days from receipt of invoice. Offers 33% kill fee. Buys all rights. Submit seasonal material 3 months in advance. Accepts queries by mail, fax. Accepts simultaneous submissions. Sample copy and writer's guidelines free.
Nonfiction Needs how-to, interview. Industry reports and profiles on companies. Query with published clips. Length: 500-9,000 words. **Pays 25-35¢/word.** Sometimes pays expenses of writers on assignment.
Photos State availability. Captions required. Reviews negatives, transparencies, 3 × 5 prints, JPEG, EPS, or TIFF files. Negotiates payment individually. Buys all rights.
Fillers Length: words.
Tips E-mail, fax, or mail a query outlining your experience, interests and pay expectations. Include clippings.

Industrial Operations

$ $ CAST POLYMER CONNECTION

International Cast Polymer Alliance of the American Composites Manufacturers Association, 1010 N. Glebe Rd., Suite 450, Arlington VA 22201-5761. (703)525-0511. Fax: (703)525-0743. E-mail: jgorman@acmanet.org. Website: www.icpa-hq.org. Bimonthly magazine covering cultured marble and solid surface industries. Articles should focus on small business owners and manufacturers. Circ. 2,000. Byline given. Pays on publication. No kill fee. Publishes ms an average of 3 months after acceptance. Buys all rights. Accepts queries by mail, e-mail.
Nonfiction We are interested in how-to articles on technical processes, industry-related manufacturing techniques, and small-business operations. Needs historical, how-to, interview, photo feature, technical. **Buys 3-5 mss/year.** Query. Length: 2,000-5,000 words. **Pays $200-350.** Sometimes pays expenses of writers on assignment.

$ $ ☐ COMMERCE & INDUSTRY

Mercury Publications, Ltd., 1740 Wellington Ave., Winnipeg MB R3H 0E8 Canada. (204)954-2085. Fax: (204)954-2057. Website: www.mercury.mb.ca. **75% freelance written**. Bimonthly magazine covering the business and industrial sectors. Industry reports and company profiles provide readers with an in-depth insight into key areas of interest in their profession. Estab. 1947. Circ. 18,876. Byline given. Pays 30-45 days from receipt of invoice. Offers 33% kill fee. Buys all rights. Submit seasonal material 3 months in advance. Accepts queries by mail, e-mail, fax. Accepts simultaneous submissions. Responds in 2 weeks to queries. Sample copy and writer's guidelines free or by e-mail.
Nonfiction Needs how-to, interview. Industry reports and profiles on companies. Query with published clips. Length: 500-9,000 words. **Pays 25-35¢/word.** Sometimes pays expenses of writers on assignment.
Photos State availability. Captions required. Reviews negatives, transparencies, 3 × 5 prints, JPEG, EPS or TIF files. Negotiates payment individually. Buys all rights.
Tips "E-mail, fax, or mail a query outlining your experience, interests and pay expectations. Include clippings."

$ $ MODERN MATERIALS HANDLING

Reed Business Information, 227 Wyman St., Waltham MA 02451. (781)734-8261. Fax: (781)734-8076. E-mail: robert.trebilcock@myfairpoint.net. Website: www.mmh.com. **Contact:** Bob Trebilcock, executive editor. **40% freelance written**. Magazine published 13 times/year covering warehousing, distribution centers, inventory. *Warehousing Management* is a national magazine read by managers of warehouses and distribution centers. We focus on lively, well-written articles telling our readers how they can achieve maximum facility productivity and efficiency. Heavy management components. We cover technology, too. Estab. 1945. Circ. 81,000. Byline given. Pays on acceptance (allow 4-6 weeks for invoice processing). No kill fee. Publishes ms an average of 1 month after acceptance. Editorial lead time 3 months. Accepts queries by mail, e-mail, fax. Sample copy free. Guidelines free.
Nonfiction Articles must be on-point, how-to pieces for managers. Needs how-to, new product, technical. Special issues: State-of-the-Industry Report, Peak Performer, Salary and Wage survey, Warehouse of the Year. Doesn't want to see anything that doesn't deal with our topic—warehousing. No general-interest profiles or interviews. **Buys 25 mss/year.** Query with published clips. **Pays $300-650.**

Photos State availability. Captions, identification of subjects required. Reviews negatives, transparencies, prints. Offers no additional payment for photos accepted with ms. Buys all rights.
Tips Learn a little about warehousing, distributors and write well. We typically don't accept specific article queries, but welcome introductory letters from journalists to whom we can assign articles. But authors are welcome to request an editorial calendar and develop article queries from it.

$ $ $ PEM PLANT ENGINEERING & MAINTENANCE

CLB Media, Inc., 240 Edward St., Aurora ON L4G 3S9 Canada. (905)727-0077, ext. 4655. Fax: (905)727-0017. E-mail: rrobertson@clbmedia.ca. Website: www.pem-mag.com. **Contact:** Rob Robertson, editor. **30% freelance written**. Bimonthly magazine looking for informative articles on issues that affect plant floor operations and maintenance. Estab. 1977. Circ. 18,500. Byline given. Pays on publication. No kill fee. Publishes ms an average of 3 months after acceptance. Buys one-time rights. Editorial lead time 4 months. Submit seasonal material 4 months in advance. Accepts simultaneous submissions. Responds in 3 weeks to queries. Responds in 1 month to mss. Sample copy free. Guidelines available online.
Nonfiction Needs how-to, keep production downtime to a minimum, better operate an industrial operation, new product, technical. **Buys 6 mss/year.** Query with published clips. Length: 750-4,000 words. **Pays $500-1,400 (Canadian).** Sometimes pays expenses of writers on assignment.
Photos State availability. Captions required. Reviews transparencies, prints. Negotiates payment individually. Buys one time rights.
Columns/Departments , .
Tips Information can be found at our website. Call us for sample issues, ideas, etc.

SPECIALTY FABRICS REVIEW

Industrial Fabrics Association International, 1801 County Rd. B W., Roseville MN 55113-4061. (651)222-2508. Fax: (651)225-6966. E-mail: gdnordstrom@ifai.com. Website: www.ifai.com. **Contact:** Galynn Norstrom, senior editor. **50% freelance written**. Monthly magazine covering industrial textiles and products made from them for company owners, salespeople, and researchers in a variety of industrial textile areas. Estab. 1915. Circ. 13,000. Byline given. Pays on publication. No kill fee. Publishes ms an average of 2 months after acceptance. Buys all rights. Accepts queries by mail, e-mail, phone. Responds in 1 month to queries.

Break in by "researching the industry/magazine audience and editorial calendar. We rarely buy materials not specifically directed at our markets."

Nonfiction Needs technical, marketing, and other topics related to any aspect of industrial fabric industry from fiber to finished fabric product. Special issues: New Products; New Fabrics; Equipment. No historical or apparel-oriented articles. **Buys 50-60 mss/year.** Query with phone number. Length: 1,200-3,000 words.
Tips "We encourage freelancers to learn our industry and make regular, solicited contributions to the magazine. We do not buy photography."

$ $ WEIGHING & MEASUREMENT +

WAM Publishing Co., P.O. Box 2247, Hendersonville TN 37077. (615)824-6920. Fax: (615)824-7092. E-mail: wampub@wammag.com. Website: www.wammag.com. **Contact:** David M. Mathieu, publisher. Bimonthly magazine for users of industrial scales; also now covers material handling & logistics industries. Estab. 1914. Circ. 13,900. Byline given. Pays on acceptance. Offers 20% kill fee. Buys all rights. Accepts queries by mail, e-mail, fax, phone. Responds in 2 weeks to queries. Sample copy for $2.
Nonfiction Needs interview, with presidents of companies, personal experience, guest editorials on government involvement in business, etc., technical, Profile (about users of weighing and measurement equipment). **Buys 15 mss/year.** Query on technical articles; submit complete ms for general interest material. Length: 1,000-2,500 words. **Pays $175-300.**

Information Systems

$ $ $ CARD TECHNOLOGY

The Magazine of Smart Cards, Networks, and ID Solutions, 550 W. Van Buren, Suite 1110, Chicago IL 60607. (312)913-1334. Fax: (312)913-1369. E-mail: Daniel.Bolaban@wanadoo.fr. Website: www.cardtechnology.com. **20% freelance written**. Monthly magazine covering smart cards, biometrics, and related technologies. *Card Technology* covers all uses of smart cards worldwide, as well as other advanced plastic card technologies. Aimed at senior management, not technical staff. Our readership is global, as is our focus. Estab. 1996. Circ. 22,000. Byline given. Pays on acceptance. Offers negotiable kill fee. Buys all rights. Editorial lead time 1 month. Submit seasonal material 2 months in advance. Accepts queries by e-mail. Responds in 1 week to queries. Responds in 1 month to mss. Sample copy free.

Nonfiction Needs interview, opinion. **Buys 15 mss/year.** Query with published clips. Length: 2,000-4,000 words. **Pays $500-1,500.** Sometimes pays expenses of writers on assignment.

Photos State availability. Identification of subjects required. Reviews contact sheets, negatives, transparencies, prints. Negotiates payment individually. Rights negotiable.

Tips We are especially interested in finding freelancers outside of North America who have experience writing about technology issues for business publications.

$$$ DESKTOP ENGINEERING

Design Solutions from Concept Through Manufacture, Level 5 Communications, Inc., P.O. Box 1039, Dublin NH 03444. (603)563-1631, ext. 239. Fax: (603)563-8192. E-mail: jgourlay@deskeng.com. Website: www.deskeng.com. **Contact:** Jonathan Gourlay, features editor. **90% freelance written**. "Monthly magazine covering computer hardware/software for hands-on design and mechanical engineers, analysis engineers, and engineering management. Ten special supplements/year." Estab. 1995. Circ. 63,000. Byline given. Pays in month of publication. Kill fee for assigned story. Publishes ms an average of 2 months after acceptance. Buys all rights. Editorial lead time 3 months. Accepts queries by mail, e-mail, phone. Responds in 2 weeks to queries. Responds in 1 month to mss. Sample copy for free with 8 × 10 SASE. Writer's guidelines by e-mail to jgourlay@deskeng.com.

Nonfiction Needs how-to, new product, reviews, technical, design. No fluff. **Buys 50-70 mss/year.** Query. Submit outline before you write an article. Length: 1,000-1,200 words. **Pays per project. Pay negotiable for unsolicited articles.** Sometimes pays expenses of writers on assignment.

Photos "No matter what type of article you write, it must be supported and enhanced visually. Visual information can include screen shots, photos, schematics, tables, charts, checklists, time lines, reading lists, and program code. The exact mix will depend on your particular article, but each of these items must be accompanied by specific, detailed captions." Send photos. Captions required. Negotiates payment individually.

Columns/Departments Product Briefs (new products), 50-100 words; Reviews (software, hardware), 500-1,500 words.

Tips Call the editors or e-mail them for submission tips.

$$$ GAME DEVELOPER

United Business Media LLC, Think Services, 600 Harrison St., 6th Floor, San Francisco CA 94107. (415)947-6000. Fax: (415)947-6090. E-mail: bsheffield@gdmag.com. Website: www.gdmag.com. **Contact:** Brandon Sheffield, editor-in-chief. **90% freelance written**. Monthly magazine covering computer game development. Estab. 1994. Circ. 35,000. Byline given. Pays on publication. No kill fee. Publishes ms an average of 3-6 months after acceptance. Buys first North American serial rights, buys first rights, buys electronic rights, buys all rights. Editorial lead time 3 months. Submit seasonal material 4 months in advance. Accepts queries by e-mail. Sample copy free. Guidelines available online.

Nonfiction Needs how-to, personal experience, technical. **Buys 50 mss/year.** Query. Length: 3,500 words for Feature articles and the Postmortem column; 600-1,200 words for product reviews (game development tools). **Pays $150/page.**

Photos State availability.

Tips We're looking for writers who are professional game developers with published game titles. We do not target the hobbyist or amateur market.

$ JOURNAL OF INFORMATION ETHICS

McFarland & Co., Inc., Publishers, P.O. Box 611, Jefferson NC 28640. (336)246-4460. E-mail: hauptman@stcloudstate.edu. **90% freelance written**. Semiannual scholarly journal covering all of the information sciences. "Addresses ethical issues in all of the information sciences with a deliberately interdisciplinary approach. Topics range from electronic mail monitoring to library acquisition of controversial material to archival ethics. The *Journal*'s aim is to present thoughtful considerations of ethical dilemmas that arise in a rapidly evolving system of information exchange and dissemination." Estab. 1992. Byline given. Pays on publication. No kill fee. Publishes ms an average of 2 years after acceptance. Buys all rights. Submit seasonal material 8 months in advance. Accepts queries by mail, e-mail, phone. Sample copy for $30. Guidelines free.

Nonfiction Needs essays, opinion, book reviews. **Buys 10-12 mss/year.** Send complete ms. Length: 500-3,500 words. **Pays $25-50 depending on length.**
Tips "Familiarize yourself with the many areas subsumed under the rubric of information ethics, e.g., privacy, scholarly communication, errors, peer review, confidentiality, e-mail, etc. Present a well-rounded discussion of any fresh, current, or evolving ethical topic within the information sciences or involving real-world information collection/exchange."

$$$ SYSTEM iNEWS

Penton Technology Media, 221 E. 29th St., Loveland CO 80538. (970) 663-4700. E-mail: editors@systeminetwork.com. Website: www.iseriesnetwork.com. **40% freelance written**. Magazine published 12 times/year. Programming, networking, IS management, technology for users of IBM AS/400, iSERIES, SYSTEM i, AND IBM i platform. Estab. 1982. Circ. 30,000 (international). Byline given. Pays on publication. Offers 50% kill fee. Publishes ms an average of 3 months after acceptance. Buys first rights, buys second serial (reprint) rights, buys all rights. Editorial lead time 4 months. Submit seasonal material 4 months in advance. Accepts queries by e-mail. Responds in 3 weeks to queries. Responds in 5 weeks to mss Guidelines available online.
Nonfiction Needs technical. Query. Length: 1,500-2,500 words. **Pays $300/$500 flat fee for assigned articles, depending on article quality and technical depth.**
Reprints Send photocopy. Payment negotiable.
Photos State availability. Offers no additional payment for photos accepted with ms.
Columns/Departments Load'n'go (complete utility).
Tips "Must have in-depth knowledge of IBM AS/400/iSERIES/SYSTEM i/IBM i computer platform.""

$$$$ TECHNOLOGY REVIEW

MIT, 1 Main St., 7th Floor, Cambridge MA 02142. (617)475-8000. Fax: (617)475-8042. Website: www.technologyreview.com. **Contact:** Jason Pontin, editor-in-chief. Magazine published 10 times/year covering information technology, biotech, material science, and nanotechnology. *Technology Review* promotes the understanding of emerging technologies and their impact. Estab. 1899. Circ. 310,000. Byline given. Pays on acceptance. Accepts queries by mail, e-mail.

- Contact specific editor via e-mail using firstname.lastname@technologyreview.com

Nonfiction We place a high premium on in-depth, original reporting that produces stories rich in description, containing lively quotes from key researchers and industry analysts. Summaries of other companies or labratories doing similar work typically supplement articles. Looking for feature articles. Length: 2,000-4,000 words. **Pays $1-3/word.**
Fillers Short tidbits that relate laboratory prototypes on their way to market in 1-5 years. Length: 150-250 words. **Pays $1-3/word.**

Insurance

$$$$ ADVISOR TODAY

NAIFA, 2901 Telestar Court, Falls Church VA 22042. (703)770-8204. E-mail: amseka@naifa.org. Website: www.advisortoday.com. **25% freelance written**. Monthly magazine covering life insurance and financial planning. Writers must demonstrate an understanding at what insurance agents and financial advisors do to earn business and serve their clients. Estab. 1906. Circ. 110,000. Pays on acceptance or publication (by mutual agreement with editor). No kill fee. Publishes ms an average of 3 months after acceptance. Makes work-for-hire assignments. Editorial lead time 3 months. Submit seasonal material 6 months in advance. Accepts queries by mail, e-mail, fax, phone. Sample copy free. Guidelines available online.
Nonfiction Insurance **Buys 8 mss/year.** Query. Length: 1,500-6,000 words. **Pays $800-2,000.**

$$ AGENT'S SALES JOURNAL

Summit Business Media, 1255 Cleveland St., Suite 200, Clearwater FL 33755. Fax: (727)446-1166. E-mail: cpellett@agentmediacorp.com. Website: www.agentssalesjournal.com. James Green, editor. **Contact:** Christina Pellett, managing editor. **40% freelance written**. Monthly magazine covering life and health insurance industry. We are a how-to publication for life and health-licensed insurance agents. All editorial is non-promotional and dedicated to helping our readers do a better job. Circ. 50,000. Byline given. Pays on acceptance. Offers 50% kill fee. Publishes ms an average of 2 months after acceptance. Buys first North American serial rights, buys electronic rights. Editorial lead time 2 months. Accepts queries by e-mail. Accepts simultaneous submissions. Sample copy available online. Guidelines free.

Nonfiction Contact: Christina Pellett, managing editor. Needs how-to, selling insurance, technical, Industry trend pieces. No articles promoting specific companies, products or services. No consumer-oriented material-please keep in mind audience is insurance agents. **Buys 24 mss/year.** Query with published clips. Length: 1,200-1,700 words. **Pays $350-450 for assigned articles.**
Columns/Departments Pays $350-$450.

$$ GEICO DIRECT

K.L. Publications, 2001 Killebrew Dr., Suite 105, Bloomington MN 55425-1879. (952)854-0155. Fax: (952)854-9440. E-mail: janklpub@aol.com. **Contact:** Jan Brenny, editor. **60% freelance written**. Semiannual magazine published for the Government Employees Insurance Company (GEICO) policyholders. Estab. 1988. Circ. 7,000,000 total. Byline given. Pays on acceptance. No kill fee. Accepts queries by mail, e-mail. Responds to all queries as soon as possible. Quicker response by e-mail. Sample copy for 9 × 12 envelope w/3 first-class stamps. For Writer's Guidelines, submit e-mail or #10 SASE.
Nonfiction "Driving, auto, and home safety; car care; lifestyle relating to safety and how-to for: single 20-somethings/young families/empty nesters/retirees; Americana/uniquely American; auto and home technology; travel (similar destinations—i.e. museums, aquariums, state parks, etc.—chosen from around the U.S. to get good regional and version-based (single 20-somethings/young families/empty nesters/retirees) mix." Query with published clips. Length: 1,000-2,200 words. **Pays $400-800.**
Photos Reviews 35mm transparencies, websites. Payment varies.
Columns/Departments Safety FYI; Your Car. Length: 450-550 words Query with published clips. **Pays $275-350.**
Tips "We prefer work from published/established writers, especially those with specialized knowledge of the insurance industry, safety issues, and automotive topics."

Jewelry

$$ 🌐 COLORED STONE

Interweave Press, 300 Chesterfield Parkway, Suite 100, Malvern PA 19355. (610)232-5700. Fax: (610)232-5756. E-mail: cseditorial@interweave.com. Website: www.colored-stone.com. **Contact:** David Federman, editor-in-chief. **50% freelance written**. Bimonthly magazine covering the colored gemstone industry. *Colored Stone* covers all aspects of the colored gemstone (i.e., no diamonds) trade. Our readers are manufacturing jewelers and jewelry designers, gemstone dealers, miners, retail jewelers, and gemologists. Estab. 1987. Circ. 11,000. Byline given. Pays on acceptance. No kill fee. Publishes ms an average of 2 months after acceptance. Buys one-time rights, buys all rights. Editorial lead time 2 months. Submit seasonal material 4 months in advance. Accepts queries by mail, e-mail, fax. Accepts simultaneous submissions. Responds in 1 month to queries. Responds in 2 months to mss. Sample copy free. Guidelines available online.
Nonfiction The bulk of the articles published in each issue are generated from leads gathered by *Colored Stone* staff and assigned to one of a standard list of writers. If you do not have a specific story proposal, but would like to be considered for a story assignment, send your resume, and writing samples to the Editor. We also have "foreign correspondent" positions available for freelance writers in gem-producing or gem-trading centers outside the United States. Needs expose, interview, new product, technical. No articles intended for the general public. **Buys 35-45 mss/year.** Query with story ideas first before submitting ms. E-mail submissions preferred, especially from writers outside the United States. Story text should be pasted into the body of the e-mail message rather than sent as an attached file. Features: 1,400 to 1,600 words; departments 700-900 words; news briefs 200-300 words **Payment is generally on a per-article rather than a per-word basis; fees are negotiated through the Editor. Fees generally run at 20-25 cents/word, depending on the complexity of the article, the experience of the writer, and the cost of living in the writer's home base.** Pays expenses of writers on assignment.
Photos State availability. Captions, identification of subjects, model releases required. Reviews any size transparencies, 4x6 prints and up. We pay a $15 finder's fee per photo submitted by the author and published. Buys one time rights.
Tips A background in the industry is helpful but not necessary. Please, no recycled marketing/new technology/etc. pieces.

$$ THE ENGRAVERS JOURNAL

P.O. Box 318, Brighton MI 48116. (810)229-5725. Fax: (810)229-8320. E-mail: editor@engraversjournal.com. Website: www.engraversjournal.com. **Contact:** Managing Editor. **70% freelance written**. Monthly magazine covering the recognition and identification industry (engraving, marking devices, awards, jewelry, and signage). "We provide practical information for the education and advancement of our readers, mainly retail business owners." Estab. 1975. Byline given Pays on acceptance. No kill fee. Publishes ms an average of 3-9 months after acceptance. Buys one-time rights. Makes work-for-hire assignments. Accepts queries by mail, e-mail, fax. Responds in 2 weeks to mss. Sample copy free. Guidelines free.

Nonfiction Needs general interest, industry related, how-to, small business subjects, increase sales, develop new markets, use new sales techniques, etc., technical. No general overviews of the industry. Length: 1,000-5,000 words. **Pays $200 and up.**

Reprints Send tearsheet, photocopy or typed ms with rights for sale noted and information about when and where the material previously appeared. Pays 50-100% of amout paid for original article.

Photos Send photos. Captions, identification of subjects, model releases required. Pays variable rate.

Tips "Articles should always be down to earth, practical, and thoroughly cover the subject with authority. We do not want the 'textbook' writing approach, vagueness, or theory—our readers look to us for sound practical information. We use an educational slant, publishing both trade-oriented articles and general business topics of interest to a small retail-oriented readership."

Journalism & Writing

$$$$ AMERICAN JOURNALISM REVIEW

University of Maryland Foundation, 1117 Journalism Bldg., University of Maryland, College Park MD 20742. (301)405-8803. Fax: (301)405-8323. E-mail: editor@ajr.umd.edu. Website: www.ajr.org. **Contact:** Rachel Smolkin, managing editor. **80% freelance written**. Bimonthly magazine covering print, broadcast, and online journalism. Mostly journalists subscribe. We cover ethical issues, trends in the industry, coverage that falls short. Circ. 25,000. Byline given. Pays within 1 month after publication. Offers 25% kill fee. Publishes ms an average of 2 months after acceptance. Buys first North American serial rights, buys electronic rights. Editorial lead time 1 month. Accepts queries by mail, e-mail, fax. Responds in 1 month to queries and unsolicited mss. Sample copy for $4.95 pre-paid or online. Guidelines available online.

Nonfiction Needs expose, personal experience, ethical issues. **Buys many mss/year.** Send complete ms. Length: 2,000-4,000 words. **Pays $1,500-2,000.** Pays expenses of writers on assignment.

Fillers Needs anecdotes, facts, short humor, short pieces. Length: 150-1,000 words. **Pays $100-250.**

Tips Write a short story for the front-of-the-book section. We prefer queries to completed articles. Include in a page what you'd like to write about, who you'll interview, why it's important, and why you should write it.

$ AUTHORSHIP

National Writers Association, 10940 S. Parker Rd., #508, Parker CO 80134. (303)841-0246. E-mail: natlwritersassn@hotmail.com. Website: www.webmaster@nationalwriters.com. Quarterly magazine covering writing articles only. "Association magazine targeted to beginning and professional writers. Covers how-to, humor, marketing issues. Disk and e-mail submissions preferred." Estab. 1950s. Circ. 4,000. Byline given. Pays on acceptance. No kill fee. Buys first North American serial rights, buys second serial (reprint) rights. Editorial lead time 3 months. Submit seasonal material 6 months in advance. Accepts simultaneous submissions. Responds in 2 months to queries. Sample copy for stamped, self-addressed, 8½x11 envelope.

Nonfiction Writing only. Poetry (January/February). **Buys 25 mss/year.** Query or send complete ms. Length: 900 words. **Pays $10, or discount on memberships and copies.**

Photos State availability. Identification of subjects, model releases required. Reviews 5 × 7 prints. Offers no additional payment for photos accepted with ms. Buys one-time rights.

Tips "Members of National Writers Association are given preference. Writing conference in Denver every June."

$$ CANADIAN SCREENWRITER

Writers Guild of Canada, 366 Adelaide St. W., Suite 401, Toronto ON M5V 1R9 Canada. (416)979-7907. Fax: (416)979-9273. E-mail: info@wgc.ca. Website: www.wgc.ca/magazine. **80% freelance written**. Magazine published 3 times/year covering screenwriting for television, film, radio and digital media. *Canadian Screenwriter* profiles Canadian screenwriters, provides industry news and offers practical writing tips for screenwriters. Estab. 1998. Circ. 4,000. Byline given. Pays on acceptance. Offers 50% kill fee. Publishes ms an average of 1 month after acceptance. Buys first rights, buys electronic rights. Editorial lead time 2 months. Submit seasonal material 2 months in advance. Accepts queries by e-mail. Accepts previously published material. Responds in 1 week to queries. Responds in 1 month to mss. Sample copy free. Guidelines by e-mail.

Nonfiction Needs how-to, humor, interview. Does not want writing on foreign screenwriters. The focus is on Canadian-resident screenwriters. **Buys 12 mss/year.** Query with published clips. Length: 750-2,200 words. **Pays 50¢/word.** Sometimes pays expenses of writers on assignment.

Photos State availability. Identification of subjects required. Reviews GIF/JPEG files. Negotiates payment individually. Buys one time rights.

Tips Read other Canadian film and television publications.

$ CROSS & QUILL

The Christian Writers Newsletter, Christian Writers Fellowship International, 1624 Jefferson Davis Rd., Clinton SC 29325-6401. (864)697-6035. E-mail: cwfi@aol.com. Website: www.cwfi-online.org. **75% freelance written.** Bimonthly journal featuring information and encouragement for writers. "We serve Christian writers and others in Christian publishing. We like informational and how-to articles." Estab. 1976. Circ. 1,000. Byline given. Pays on publication. No kill fee. Publishes ms an average of 6-12 months after acceptance. Buys first rights, buys second serial (reprint) rights. Editorial lead time 6 months. Submit seasonal material 6 months in advance. Accepts queries by mail, e-mail: cqarticles@aol.com and cqarticles@cwfi-online.org. Responds in 1 month to queries. Responds in 2 months to mss. Sample copy for $2 with 9X11 SAE and 2 first-class stamps. Writer's guidelines at cwfi-online.org/crossquil.htm or for SAE.

Nonfiction Needs "We have an immediate need for 200-800 word features on fiction writing, writing for young readers, how-to plan and write almost any writing form, any phase of marketing, testimonies of how God worked in your life and career while attending a writers conference. We also need articles on almost any topic on participating in or leading writers groups (200-800) and fillers to 100 words on almost any writing topic or poetry (12 lines max).", devotional. **Buys 25 mss/year.** Send complete ms. Length: 200-800 words. **Pays $10-50.**

Photos State availability.

Poetry Needs free verse, haiku, light verse, traditional. Buys 10 poems/year. Submit maximum 3 poems. Length: 12 lines. **Pays $5/poem.**

Fillers Buys up to 100 words on almost any writing topic.

Tips "Study guidelines and follow them. Acceptances of philosophical, personal reflection, or personal experiences is rare. Paste article submissions into an e-mail form. We prefer not to download submissions as attached files. Double-space between paragraphs. Please use plain, not html text. Do not use boldface or bullets."

$$$ ECONTENT MAGAZINE

Digital Content Strategies & Resources, Online, Inc., 48 South Main St., Suite 3, Newtown CT 06470-2140. (203)761-1466. Fax: (203)761-1444. E-mail: michelle.manafy@infotoday.com. Website: www.econtentmag.com. **Contact:** Michelle Manafy, editor. **90% freelance written**. Monthly magazine covering digital content trends, strategies, etc. *EContent* is a business publication. Readers need to stay on top of industry trends and developments. Estab. 1979. Circ. 12,000. Byline given. Pays within 1 month of publication. Buys all rights. Editorial lead time 3-4 months. Accepts queries by e-mail. Responds in 3 weeks to queries. Responds in 1 month to mss. Sample copy and writer's guidelines online.

Nonfiction Needs expose, how-to, interview, new product, opinion, technical, news features, strategic and solution-oriented features. No academic or straight Q&A. **Buys 48 mss/year.** Query with published clips. Submit electronically as e-mail attachment. Length: 500-700 words. **Pays 40-50¢/word.** Sometimes pays expenses of writers on assignment.

Photos State availability. Captions required. Negotiates payment individually. Buys one time rights.

Columns/Departments Profiles (short profile of unique company, person or product), 1,200 words; New Features (breaking news of content-related topics), 500 words maximum. **Buys 40 mss/year.** Query with published clips. **Pays 30-40¢/word.**

Tips "Take a look at the website. Most of the time, an e-mail query with specific article ideas works well. A general outline of talking points is good, too. State prior experience."

$ FELLOWSCRIPT

InScribe Christian Writers' Fellowship, E-mail: submissions@inscribe.org. Website: www.inscribe.org. **Contact:** Janet Sketchley, acq. editor. **100% freelance written**. Quarterly writers' newsletter featuring Christian writing. "Our readers are Christians with a commitment to writing. Among our readership are best-selling authors and unpublished beginning writers. Submissions to us should include practical information, something the reader can immediately put into practice." Estab. 1983. Circ. 200. Byline given. Pays on publication. No kill fee. Publishes ms an average of 6-12 months after acceptance. Buys one-time rights, buys second serial (reprint) rights, first or reprint rights. Editorial lead time 3 months. Submit seasonal material 4 months in advance. Accepts queries by e-mail, prefers full ms by e-mail; postal submissions only accepted from InScribe members. Accepts simultaneous submissions. Responds in 1 month to queries or mss Sample copy for $3.50, 9 × 12 SAE, and 2 first-class stamps (Canadian) or IRCs. Guidelines available online.

Nonfiction All must pertain to writing and the writing life. Needs essays, exposè, how-to, for writers, interview, new product. Does not want poetry, fiction, personal experience, testimony or think piece, commentary articles. **Buys 30-45 mss/year.** Send complete ms attached in rtf or doc format. Length: 400-1,200 words. **Pays 2½¢/word (first rights); 1½¢/word reprints (Canadian funds).**

Columns/Departments Book reviews, 150-300 words; Market Updates, 50-300 words. **Buys 1-3 mss/year.** Send complete ms. **Pays 1 copy.**

Fillers Needs facts, newsbreaks. Buys 5-10 mss/year. Length: 25-300 words. **Pays 1 copy.**

Tips "Send your complete manuscript by e-mail (pasted into the message, no attachments). E-mail is preferred. Tell us a bit about yourself. Write in a casual, first-person, anecdotal style. Be sure your article is full of practical material, something that can be applied. Most of our accepted freelance submissions fall into the 'how-to' category, and involve tasks, crafts, or procedures common to writers. Please do not send inspirational articles (i.e., 'How I sold My First Story')."

$ FREELANCE MARKET NEWS

An Essential Guide for Freelance Writers, The Writers Bureau Ltd., Sevendale House, 7 Dale St., Manchester M1 1JB England. (44)(161)228-2362. Fax: (44)(161)228-3533. E-mail: fmn@writersbureau.com. Website: www.freelancemarketnews.com. **15% freelance written**. Monthly newsletter covering freelance writing. Estab. 1968. Byline given. Pays on acceptance. No kill fee. Publishes ms an average of 3 months after acceptance. Buys all rights. Editorial lead time 3 months. Submit seasonal material 3 months in advance. Accepts queries by mail, e-mail, fax. Accepts previously published material. Sample copy and guidelines available online.

- "Prefers to receive a complete manuscript rather than a query."

Nonfiction Needs how-to sell your writing/improve your writing. **Buys 12 mss/year.** Length: 700 words **Pays £50/1,000 words.**

Columns/Departments New Markets (magazines which have recently been published); Fillers & Letters; Overseas Markets (obviously only English-language publications); Market Notes (established publications accepting articles, fiction, reviews, or poetry). All should be between 40 and 200 words. **Pays £40/1,000 words.**

$$ FREELANCE WRITER'S REPORT

CNW Publishing, Inc., 45 Main St., P.O. Box A, North Stratford NH 03590-0167. (603)922-8338. E-mail: fwrwm@writers-editors.com. Website: www.writers-editors.com. **25% freelance written**. Monthly newsletter. "*FWR* covers the marketing and business/office management aspects of running a freelance writing business. Articles must be of value to the established freelancer; nothing basic." Estab. 1982. Byline given. Pays on publication. No kill fee. Publishes ms an average of 6 months after acceptance. Buys one-time rights. Editorial lead time 2 months. Submit seasonal material 2 months in advance. Accepts simultaneous submissions. Responds in 1 week to queries. Responds in 2 weeks to mss. Sample copy for 6x9 SAE with 2 first-class stamps (for back copy); $4 for current copy. Guidelines and sample copy available online.

Nonfiction Needs book excerpts, how-to (market, increase income or profits). "No articles about the basics of freelancing." **Buys 50 mss/year.** Send complete ms by e-mail. Length: Up to 900 words. **Pays 10¢/word.**

Tips "Write in a terse, newsletter style."

$$ MSLEXIA

For Women Who Write, Mslexia Publications Ltd., P.O. Box 656, Newcastle upon Tyne NE99 1PZ United

Kingdom. [(44)(191)233-3860. E-mail: postbag@mslexia.co.uk. Website: www.mslexia.co.uk. **Contact:** Daneet Steffens, editor. **60% freelance written**. Quarterly magazine offering advice and publishing opportunities for women writers, plus poetry and prose submissions on a different theme each issue. "*Mslexia* tells you all you need to know about exploring your creativity and getting into print. No other magazine provides *Mslexia*'s unique mix of advice and inspiration; news, reviews, interviews; competitions, events, grants; all served up with a challenging selection of new poetry and prose. *Mslexia* is read by authors and absolute beginners. A quarterly master class in the business and psychology of writing, it's the essential magazine for women who write." Estab. 1998. Circ. 9,000. Byline given. Pays on publication. Offers 50% kill fee. Publishes ms an average of 1 month after acceptance. Buys one-time rights. Editorial lead time 3 months. Submit seasonal material 3 months in advance. Accepts queries by mail, e-mail, phone. Accepts simultaneous submissions. Responds in 3 months to mss. Sample copy available online. Writer's guidelines online or by e-mail.

- This publication does not accept e-mail submissions except from overseas writers.

Nonfiction Needs how-to, interview, opinion, personal experience. No general items about women or academic features. We are only interested in features (for tertiary-educated readership) about women's writing and literature. **Buys 40 mss/year.** Query with published clips. Length: 500-2,200 words. **Pays $70-400 for assigned articles. Pays $70-300 for unsolicited articles.** Sometimes pays expenses of writers on assignment.

Columns/Departments We are open to suggestions, but would only commission 1 new column/year, probably from a UK-based writer. **Buys 12 mss/year.** Query with published clips.

Fiction See guidelines on our website. Submissions not on one of our current themes will be returned (if submitted with a SASE) or destroyed. **Buys 30 mss/year.** Send complete ms. Length: 50-2,200 words.

Poetry Needs avant-garde, free verse, haiku, traditional. Buys 40 poems/year. Submit maximum 4 poems.

Tips "Read the magazine; subscribe if you can afford it. *Mslexia* has a particular style and relationship with its readers which is hard to assess at a quick glance. The majority of our readers live in the UK, so feature pitches should be aware of this. We never commission work without seeing a written sample first. We rarely accept unsolicited manuscripts, but prefer a short letter suggesting a feature, plus a brief bio and writing sample."

$ NEW WRITER'S MAGAZINE

Sarasota Bay Publishing, P.O. Box 5976, Sarasota FL 34277-5976. E-mail: newriters@aol.com. **95% freelance written**. Bimonthly magazine. "*New Writer's Magazine* believes that *all* writers are *new* writers in that each of us can learn from one another. So, we reach pro and nonpro alike." Estab. 1986. Circ. 5,000. Byline given. Pays on publication. No kill fee. Buys first rights. Accepts queries by mail. Guidelines for #10 SASE.

Nonfiction Needs general interest, historical, how-to, for new writers, humor, interview, opinion,. **Buys 50 mss/year.** Send complete ms. Length: 700-1,000 words. **Pays $10-50.**

Photos Send photos. Captions required. Reviews 5 × 7 prints. Offers no additional payment for photos accepted with ms.

Fiction Needs experimental, historical, humorous, mainstream, slice-of-life vignettes-of-life vignettes. "Again, we do *not* want anything that does not have a tie-in with the writing life or writers in general." **Buys 2-6 mss/year.** Send complete ms. Length: 700-800 words. **Pays $20-40.**

Poetry Needs free verse, light verse, traditional. Does not want anything *not* for writers. Buys 10-20 poems/year. Submit maximum 3 poems. Length: 8-20 lines. **Pays $5 minimum.**

Fillers For cartoons, writing lifestyle slant. Buys 20-30/year. Pays $10 maximum. **Needs anecdotes, facts, newsbreaks, short humor. Buys 5-15 mss/year.** Length: 20-100 words. **$5 maximum.**

Tips "Any article with photos has a good chance, especially an up close and personal interview with an established professional writer offering advice, etc. Short profile pieces on new authors also receive attention."

$$ POETS & WRITERS MAGAZINE

90 Broad Street, 2100, New York NY 10004. E-mail: editor@pw.org. Website: www.pw.org. **95% freelance written**. Bimonthly professional trade journal for poets and fiction writers and creative nonfiction writers. Estab. 1987. Circ. 60,000. Byline given. Pays on acceptance of finished draft. Offers 25% kill fee. Publishes ms an average of 4 months after acceptance. Buys first North American serial rights, buys nonexclusive reprint rights shared 50/50 thereafter rights. Submit seasonal material 4 months in

advance. Accepts queries by mail, e-mail. Responds in 2 months to mss. Sample copy for $5.95 to Sample Copy Dept. Guidelines available online.

- No poetry or fiction submissions.

Nonfiction Needs how-to, craft of poetry, fiction or creative nonfiction writing, interviews, with poets or writers of fiction and creative nonfiction,, personal essays about literature, regional reports of literary activity, reports on small presses, service pieces about publishing trends. "We do not accept submissions by fax." **Buys 35 mss/year.** Send complete ms. Length: 500-2,500 (depending on topic) words.

Photos State availability. Reviews b&w prints. Offers no additional payment for photos accepted with ms.

Columns/Departments Literary and Publishing News, 500-1,000 words; Profiles of Emerging and Established Poets, Fiction Writers and Creative Nonfiction Writers, 2,000-3,000 words; Regional Reports (literary activity in US and abroad), 1,000-2,000 words. Query with published clips or send complete ms. **Pays $150-500.**

$$ QUILL & SCROLL MAGAZINE

Quill and Scroll International Honorary Society for High School Journalists, 100 Adler Journalism Bldg., Room E346, Iowa City IA 52242-2004. (319)335-3457. Fax: (319)335-3989. E-mail: quill-scroll@uiowa.edu. Website: www.uiowa.edu/~quill-sc. **Contact:** Vanessa Shelton, publisher/editor. **20% freelance written**. bimonthly during school year magazine covering scholastic journalism-related topics. Our primary audience is high school journalism students working on and studying topics related to newspapers, yearbooks, radio, television, and online media; secondary audience is their teachers and others interested in this topic. Estab. 1926. Circ. 10,000. Byline given. acceptance & publication. No kill fee. Publishes ms an average of 4 months after acceptance. Buys all rights. Makes work-for-hire assignments. Editorial lead time 2 months. Accepts queries by mail, e-mail. Accepts simultaneous submissions. Responds in 2 weeks to queries. Guidelines available.

- We invite journalism students and advisers to submit manuscripts about important lessons learned or obstacles overcome.

Nonfiction Needs essays, how-to, humor, interview, new product, opinion, personal experience, photo feature, technical, travel, types on topic. Articles not pertinent to high school student journalists. Query. Length: 600-1,000 words. **Pays $100-500 for assigned articles. Pays complementary copy - $200 max. for unsolicited articles.** Sometimes pays expenses of writers on assignment.

Photos State availability. Reviews GIF/JPEG files. Offers no additional payment for photos accepted with ms.

$$$ QUILL MAGAZINE

Society of Professional Journalists, 3909 N. Meridian St., Indianapolis IN 46208. Fax: (317)920-4789. E-mail: sleadingham@spj.org. Website: www.spj.org/quill.asp. **75% freelance written**. Monthly magazine covering journalism and the media industry. *Quill* is a how-to magazine written by journalists. We focus on the industry's biggest issues while providing tips on how to become better journalists. Estab. 1912. Circ. 10,000. Byline given. Pays on acceptance. Offers 25% kill fee. Publishes ms an average of 2 months after acceptance. Buys first rights, buys electronic rights. Editorial lead time 2-3 months. Submit seasonal material 2-3 months in advance. Accepts queries by e-mail. Accepts previously published material. Accepts simultaneous submissions. Sample copy available online.

Nonfiction Needs general interest, how-to, technical. Does not want personality profiles and straight research pieces. **Buys 12 mss/year.** Query. Length: 800-2,500 words. **Pays $150-800.**

$$ THE WRITER

Kalmbach Publishing Co., 21027 Crossroads Circle, P.O. Box 1612, Waukesha WI 53187-1612. E-mail: queries@writermag.com. Website: www.writermag.com. **Contact:** Ronald Kovach, sr. editor. **90% freelance written. Prefers to buy work of published/established writers**. Estab. 1887. Pays on acceptance. Kill fee paid (but rarely used). Buys first North American serial rights and non-exclusive electronic rights. Accepts queries by mail, e-mail. Sample copy for $5.95. Guidelines available online.

- No phone queries.

Nonfiction "Practical articles for writers on how to write fiction and nonfiction for publication, and how and where to market manuscripts in various fields. Will consider queries from writers who have not been in the magazine; staff-generated ideas, however, are assigned to writers we've worked with." No phone queries. Responds generally in 1-2 months to submissions. Length: 700-3,400 words. **Pays $50-400.**

Reprints Send tearsheet or photocopy and information about when and where the material previously appeared.

Tips "We are looking for articles with plenty of practical, specific advice that writers can apply to their own work. We are particularly interested in articles done in our 'step-by-step' format; a memo is available on this format. Query first on step by step articles, and only if you have a strong record of publication."

$$$ WRITER'S DIGEST

F+W Media, Inc., 4700 E. Galbraith Rd., Cincinnati OH 45236. (513)531-2690, ext. 11483. E-mail: wdsubmissions@fwmedia.com. Website: www.writersdigest.com. **75% freelance written**. Magazine for those who want to write better, get published and participate in the vibrant culture of writers. "Our readers look to us for specific ideas and tips that will help them succeed, whether success means getting into print, finding personal fulfillment through writing or building and maintaining a thriving writing career and network." Estab. 1920. Byline given. Pays on acceptance. Offers 25% kill fee. Publishes ms an average of 6-9 months after acceptance. Buys first North American print and perpetual world digital rights. Pays 25% print reprint fee. Accepts queries by e-mail only. Responds in 2-4 months to queries. Responds in 2-4 months to mss. Guidelines and editorial calendar available online (writersdigest.com/submissionguidelines).

- The magazine does not accept or read e-queries with attachments.

Nonfiction "Although we welcome the work of new writers, we believe the established writer can better instruct our readers. Please include your publishing credentials related to your topic with your submission." Needs essays, how-to, humor, inspirational, interviews, profiles. Does not accept phone, snail mail, or fax queries. "We don't buy newspaper clippings or reprints of articles previously published in other writing magazines. Book and software reviews are handled in-house, as are most *WD* interviews." **Buys 40 mss/year.** Send complete ms. Length: 800-1,500 words. **Pays 30-50¢/word.**

Tips "InkWell is the best place for new writers to break in. We recommend you consult our editorial calendar before pitching feature-length articles. Check our writer's guidelines for more details."

$ WRITERS' JOURNAL

The Complete Writer's Magazine, Val-Tech Media, P.O. Box 394, Perham MN 56573-0394. (218)346-7921. Fax: (218)346-7924. E-mail: writersjournal@writersjournal.com. Website: www.writersjournal.com. **Contact:** Leon Ogroske, ed. **60% freelance written**. Bimonthly magazine covering writing. "*Writers' Journal* is read by thousands of aspiring writers whose love of writing has taken them to the next step: writing for money. We are an instructional manual giving writers the tools and information necessary to get their work published. We also print works by authors who have won our writing contests." Estab. 1980. Circ. 12,000. Byline given. Pays on publication. No kill fee. Publishes ms an average of 4 months after acceptance. Buys first rights, buys second serial (reprint) rights. Accepts queries by mail, e-mail, fax. Responds in 6 weeks to queries. Responds in 6 months to mss. Sample copy for $6. Guidelines available online.

Nonfiction Needs how-to, write, publish, market. **Buys 25 mss/year.** Send complete ms. Length: 800-2,500 words. **Pays $30.**

Photos Send photos. Model releases required. Reviews transparencies, 8 × 10 prints, GIF/JPEG files. Offers no addition payment for photos accepted with ms; offers $50/cover photo. Buys one-time rights.

Fiction "We only publish winners of our fiction contests—16 contests/year." Length: 2,000 words.

Poetry Contact: Esther M. Leiper-Esteabrooks, poetry editor. Needs light verse. Does not want anything boring. Buys 30 poems/year. Submit maximum 2 poems. Length: 15 lines. **Pays $5.**

Fillers Needs facts, gags, short humor. Buys 20 mss/year. Length: 10-200 words. **Pays up to $10.**

Tips "Appearance must be professional with no grammatical or spelling errors, submitted on white paper, double spaced with easy-to-read font. We want articles that will help writers improve technique in writing, style, editing, publishing, and story construction. We are interested in how writers use new and fresh angles to break into the writing markets."

$$$$ WRITTEN BY

The Magazine of the Writers Guild of America, West, 7000 W. Third St., Los Angeles CA 90048. (323)782-4522. Fax: (323)782-4800. Website: www.wga.org. **40% freelance written**. Magazine published 9 times/year. "*Written By* is the premier magazine written by and for America's screen and TV writers. We focus on the craft of screenwriting and cover all aspects of the entertainment industry from the perspective of the writer. We are read by all screenwriters and most entertainment executives." Estab. 1987. Circ. 12,000. Byline given. Pays on acceptance. Offers 10% kill fee. Publishes ms an average of 2 months after acceptance. Buys first North American serial rights, buys electronic rights. Editorial lead time 4 months. Submit seasonal material 4 months in advance. Accepts queries by mail, e-mail, fax, phone. Guidelines for #10 SASE.

Nonfiction Needs book excerpts, essays, historical, humor, interview, opinion, personal experience, photo feature, technical, software. No beginner pieces on how to break into Hollywood, or how to write scripts. **Buys 20 mss/year.** Query with published clips. Length: 500-3,500 words. **Pays $500-3,500 for assigned articles.** Sometimes pays expenses of writers on assignment.

Photos State availability. Captions, identification of subjects, model releases required. Reviews transparencies. Offers no additional payment for photos accepted with ms. Buys one time rights.

Columns/Departments Pays $1,000 maximum.

Tips "We are looking for more theoretical essays on screenwriting past and/or present. Also, the writer must always keep in mind that our audience is made up primarily of working writers who are inside the business; therefore all articles need to have an 'insider' feel and not be written for those who are still trying to break in to Hollywood. We prefer a hard copy of submission or e-mail."

Law

$$$$ ABA JOURNAL

The Lawyer's Magazine, American Bar Association, 321 N. Clark St., 15th Floor, Chicago IL 60654. (312)988-6018. Fax: (312)988-6025. E-mail: releases@abanet.org. Website: www.abajournal.com. **Contact:** Sandra Randag. **10% freelance written**. Monthly magazine covering the trends, people and finances of the legal profession from Wall Street to Main Street to Pennsylvania Avenue. The *ABA Journal* is an independent, thoughtful, and inquiring observer of the law and the legal profession. The magazine is edited for members of the American Bar Association. Circ. 380,000. Byline given. Pays on acceptance. No kill fee. Makes work-for-hire assignments. Accepts queries by e-mail, fax. Sample copy free. Guidelines available online.

Nonfiction We don't want anything that does not have a legal theme. No poetry or fiction. **Buys 5 mss/year.** We use freelancers with experience reporting for legal or consumer publications; most have law degrees. If you are interested in freelancing for the *Journal*, we urge you to include your resume and published clips when you contact us with story ideas. Length: 500-3,500 words. **Pays $300-2,000 for assigned articles.**

Columns/Departments The National Pulse/Ideas from the Front (reports on legal news and trends), 650 words; eReport (reports on legal news and trends), 500-1,500 words. The *ABA Journal eReport* is our weekly online newsletter sent out to members. **Buys 25 mss/year.** Query with published clips. **Pays $300, regardless of story length**

$$$ BENCH & BAR OF MINNESOTA

Minnesota State Bar Association, 600 Nicollet Mall #380, Minneapolis MN 55402. (612)333-1183. Fax: (612)333-4927. Website: www.mnbar.org. **5% freelance written**. Magazine published 11 times/year. Audience is mostly Minnesota lawyers. *Bench & Bar* seeks reportage, analysis, and commentary on trends and issues in the law and the legal profession, especially in Minnesota. Preference to items of practical/professional human interest to lawyers and judges. Estab. 1931. Circ. 17,000. Byline given. Pays on acceptance. No kill fee. Publishes ms an average of 3 months after acceptance. Buys first North American serial rights. Makes work-for-hire assignments. Responds in 1 month to queries. Guidelines for free online or by mail.

Nonfiction Needs Needs analysis and exposition of current trends, developments and issues in law, legal profession, esp, in Minnesota. Balanced commentary and "how-to" considered. We do not want one-sided opinion pieces or advertorial. **Buys 2-3 mss/year.** Send query or complete ms. Length: 1,000-3,500 words. **Pays $500-1,500.** Some expenses of writers on assignment.

Photos State availability. Identification of subjects, model releases required. Reviews 5 × 7 prints. Pays $25-100 upon publication. Buys one time rights.

$$$$ CALIFORNIA LAWYER

Daily Journal Corp., 44 Montgomery St., Suite 250, San Francisco CA 94104. (415)296-2400. Fax: (415)296-2440. E-mail: sharon_liang@dailyjournal.com. Website: www.dailyjournal.com. **Contact:** Sharon Liang, legal editor. **30% freelance written**. Monthly magazine of law-related articles and general-interest subjects of appeal to lawyers and judges. "Our primary mission is to cover the news of the world as it affects the law and lawyers, helping our readers better comprehend the issues of the day and to cover changes and trends in the legal profession. Our readers are all California lawyers, plus judges, legislators, and corporate executives. Although we focus on California and the West, we have subscribers in every state. *California Lawyer* is a general interest magazine for people interested in law. Our writers are journalists." Estab. 1981. Circ. 140,000. Byline given. Pays on acceptance. Offers 25% kill fee. Publishes ms an average of 3 months after acceptance. Buys first North American serial rights, buys electronic rights. Editorial lead time 3 months. Accepts queries by e-mail. previously published articles. Sample copy and writer's guidelines for #10 SASE.

Nonfiction Needs essays, general interest, interview, news and feature articles on law-related topics. "We are interested in concise, well-written and well-researched articles on issues of current concern, as well as well-told feature narratives with a legal focus. We would like to see a description or outline of your proposed idea, including a list of possible sources." **Buys 12 mss/year.** Send complete ms. Length: 500-5,000 words. **Pays $50-2,000.** Pays expenses of writers on assignment.

Photos Contact: Jake Flaherty, art director. State availability. Identification of subjects, model releases required. Reviews prints.

Columns/Departments California Esq. (current legal trends), 300 words. **Buys 6 mss/year.** Query with or without published clips. **Pays $50-250.**

$$$$ INSIDECOUNSEL

(formerly *Corporate Legal Times*), 222 S. Riverside Plaza, Suite 620, Chicago IL 60606. (312)654-3500. E-mail: rvasper@insidecounsel.com. Website: www.insidecounsel.com. **50% freelance written.** Monthly tabloid. *InsideCounsel* is a monthly national magazine that gives general counsel and inhouse attorneys information on legal and business issues to help them better manage corporate law departments. It routinely addresses changes and trends in law departments, litigation management, legal technology, corporate governance and inhouse careers. Law areas covered monthly include: intellectual property, international, technology, project finance, e-commerce and litigation. All articles need to be geared toward the inhouse attorney's perspective. Estab. 1991. Circ. 45,000. Byline given. Pays on publication. No kill fee. Publishes ms an average of 3 months after acceptance. Buys all rights. Editorial lead time 3 months. Submit seasonal material 3 months in advance. Accepts queries by mail, e-mail. Responds in 3 weeks to queries. Sample copy for $17. Guidelines available online.

Nonfiction Needs interview, news about legal aspects of business issues and events. **Buys 12-25 mss/year.** Query with published clips. Length: 500-3,000 words. **Pays $500-2,000.**

Photos Freelancers should state availability of photos with submission. Identification of subjects required. Reviews color transparencies, b&w prints. Offers $25-150/photo. Buys all rights.

Tips Our publication targets general counsel and inhouse lawyers. All articles need to speak to them—not to the general attorney population. Query with clips and a list of potential in-house sources.

$$$ JCR

National Court Reporters Association, 8224 Old Courthouse Rd., Vienna VA 22180. E-mail: jschmidt@ncrahq.org. Website: www.ncraonline.org. **10% freelance written.** Monthly, except bimonthl July/Aug and Nov/Dec. magazine covering court reporting, captioning, and CART provision. "The JCR has two complementary purposes: to communicate the activities, goals and mission of its publisher, the National Court Reporters Association; and, simultaneously, to seek out and publish diverse information and views on matters significantly related to the court reporting and captioning professions." Estab. 1899. Circ. 20,000. Byline sometimes given. Pays on acceptance. No kill fee. Publishes ms an average of 4-5 months after acceptance. Buys first North American serial rights, buys simultaneous rights, buys electronic rights. Makes work-for-hire assignments. Editorial lead time 4 months. Submit seasonal material 4 months in advance. Accepts queries by mail, e-mail. Sample copy free. Manuscript guidelines are available on the NCRAonline.org website under JCR.

Nonfiction Needs book excerpts, how-to, interview, technical, legal issues. **Buys 6-10 mss/year.** Query. Length: 1,000-2,500 words. **Pays $1,000 maximum for assigned articles. Pays $100 maximum for unsolicited articles.** Sometimes pays expenses of writers on assignment.

Columns/Departments Language (proper punctuation, grammar, dealing with verbatim materials); Technical (new technologies, using mobile technology, using technology for work); Book excerpts (language, crime, legal issues), all 1,000 words. **Pays $-$100.**

$$$ 🅽 JOURNAL OF COURT REPORTING

National Court Reporters Association, 8224 Old Courthouse Rd., Vienna VA 22180. E-mail: jschmidt@ncrahq.org. Website: www.ncraonline.org. **10% freelance written.** Monthly (bimonthly July/August and November/December) magazine. "The *Journal of Court Reporting* has two complementary purposes: to communicate the activities, goals and mission of its publisher, the National Court Reporters Association; and, simultaneously, to seek out and publish diverse information and views on matters significantly related to the court reporting and captioning professions." Estab. 1899. Circ. 20,000. Byline sometimes given. Pays on acceptance. No kill fee. Publishes ms an average of 4-5 months after acceptance. Buys first North American serial rights, buys simultaneous rights, buys electronic rights. Makes work-for-hire assignments; rights as needed. Editorial lead time 4 months. Submit seasonal material 4 months in advance. Accepts queries by mail, e-mail. Accepts simultaneous submissions. Sample copy free. Guidelines free.

Nonfiction Needs book excerpts, how-to, interview, technical, legal issues. **Buys 10 mss/year.** Query. Length: 1,000-2,500 words. **Pays 1,000 max. for assigned articles. Pays $100 max. for unsolicited articles.** Sometimes pays expenses of writers on assignment.

Columns/Departments Language (proper punctuation, grammar, dealing with verbatim materials); Technical (new technologies, using mobile technology, using technology for work); Book excerpts (language, crime, legal issues), all 1,000 words; Puzzles (any, but especially word-related games). **Pays $- $100.**

$ LEGAL ASSISTANT TODAY

James Publishing, Inc., 10632 Little Patuxent Parkway, Suite 249, Columbia MD 21044-6206. (410)740-9770. Fax: (410)740-9771. Website: www.legalassistanttoday.com. www.conexioninternationalltd.com. **Contact:** Rebecca Garcia, publisher. Bimonthly magazine geared toward all legal assistants/paralegals throughout the United States and Canada, regardless of specialty (litigation, corporate, bankruptcy, environmental law, etc.). How-to articles to help paralegals perform their jobs more effectively are most in demand, as are career and salary information, and timely news and trends pieces. Estab. 1983. Circ. 8,000. Byline given. Pays on publication. Kill fee $25-50. Buys first North American Serial rights, electronic rights, non-exclusive rights to use the article, author's name, image, and biographical data in advertising and promotion. Editorial lead time 10 weeks. Submit seasonal material 3 months in advance. Accepts queries by mail, e-mail, fax, online submission form. Accepts simultaneous submissions. Responds in 2 months to mss. Sample copy and writer's guidelines free. Guidelines available online.

Nonfiction Needs interview, unique and interesting paralegals in unique and particular work-related situations, news (brief, hard news topics regarding paralegals), features (present information to help paralegals advance their careers). Send query letter first; if electronic, send as attachment. **Pays $25-100.**

Photos Send photos.

Tips "Fax a detailed outline of a 2,500 to 3,000-word feature about something useful to working legal assistants. Writers must understand our audience. There is some opportunity for investigative journalism as well as the usual features, profiles, and news. How-to articles are especially desired. If you are a great writer who can interview effectively, and really dig into the topic to grab readers' attention, we need you."

$$$$ ☐ NATIONAL

Practice Trends and Legal Insights, The Canadian Bar Association, 500-865 Carling Ave., Ottawa ON K1S 5S8 Canada. (613)237-2925. Fax: (613)237-0185. E-mail: jordanf@cba.org. Website: www.cba.org/national. Melanie Raymond, managing editor. **Contact:** Jordan Furlong, editor-in-chief. **90% freelance written**. Magazine published 8 times/year covering practice trends and business developments in the law, with a focus on technology, innovation, practice management and client relations. Estab. 1993. Circ. 37,000. Byline given. Pays on acceptance. Offers 50% kill fee. Publishes ms an average of 2 months after acceptance. Buys first North American serial rights, buys electronic rights. Editorial lead time 2 months. Accepts queries by e-mail. Sample copy free.

Nonfiction Buys 25 mss/year. Query with published clips. Length: 1,000-2,500 words. **Pays $1/word.** Sometimes pays expenses of writers on assignment.

$$ THE NATIONAL JURIST and PRE LAW

Cypress Magazines, 5715 Kearny Villa Rd., Suite 108, San Diego CA 92123. (858)300-3201. Fax: (858)503-7588. E-mail: njpl@cypressmagazines.com. Website: www.nationaljurist.com. **Contact:** Jack Crittenden, editor-in-chief. **25% freelance written**. Bimonthly magazine covering law students and issues of interest to law students. Estab. 1991. Circ. 145,000. Pays on publication. No kill fee. Buys all rights. Accepts queries by mail, e-mail, fax, phone.

Nonfiction Needs general interest, how-to, humor, interview. **Buys 4 mss/year.** Query. Length: 750-3,000 words. **Pays $100-500.**
Photos State availability. Reviews contact sheets. Negotiates payment individually.
Columns/Departments Pays $100-500.

$$ THE PENNSYLVANIA LAWYER

Pennsylvania Bar Association, P.O. Box 186, 100 South St., Harrisburg PA 17108-0186. E-mail: editor@pabar.org. **25% freelance written. Prefers to work with published/established writers**. Bimonthly magazine published as a service to the legal profession and the members of the Pennsylvania Bar Association. Estab. 1979. Circ. 30,000. Byline given. Pays on acceptance. No kill fee. Publishes ms an average of 6 months after acceptance. Buys first rights, buys one-time rights. Submit seasonal material 6 months in advance. Accepts queries by mail, e-mail. Responds in 2 months to queries and to mss. Sample copy for $2. Writer's guidelines for #10 SASE or by e-mail.
Nonfiction "All features must relate in some way to Pennsylvania lawyers or the practice of law in Pennsylvania." Needs how-to, interview, law-practice management, technology. **Buys 8-10 mss/year.** Query. Length: 1,200-2,000 words. **Pays $50 for book reviews; $75-400 for assigned articles. Pays $150 for unsolicited articles.** Sometimes pays expenses of writers on assignment.
Photos State availability. Identification of subjects required. Reviews contact sheets. Negotiates payment individually. Buys one time rights.

THE PUBLIC LAWYER

American Bar Association Government and Public Sector Lawyers Division, ABA GPS LD, 321 N. Clark St., MS 19.1, Chicago IL 60610. (312)988-5809. Fax: (312)988-5709. E-mail: kmikkelson@staff.abanet.org. Website: www.governmentlawyer.org. **60% freelance written**. Semiannual magazine covering government attorneys and the legal issues that pertain to them. "The mission of *The Public Lawyer* is to provide timely, practical information useful to all public lawyers regardless of practice setting. We publish articles covering topics that are of universal interest to a diverse audience of public lawyers, such as public law office management, dealing with the media, politically motivated personnel decisions, etc. Articles must be national in scope." Estab. 1993. Circ. 6,500. Byline given. Publishes ms an average of 4 months after acceptance. Buys first rights, buys electronic rights; sign copyright release Editorial lead time 6 months. Accepts queries by e-mail. Accepts simultaneous submissions. Responds in 1 month to queries. Responds in 2 months to mss. Sample copy free. Guidelines available online.
Nonfiction Needs interview, opinion, technical, book reviews. Does not want pieces that do not relate to the status of government lawyers or that are not legal issues exclusive to government lawyers. We accept very few articles written by private practice attorneys. **Buys 6-8 mss/year.** Query. Length: 2,000-5,000 words. **Pays contributor copies.**
Photos State availability. Identification of subjects, model releases required. Reviews GIF/JPEG files. Offers no additional payment for photos accepted with ms. Buys one-time rights.
Tips "Articles stand a better chance of acceptance if they include one or more sidebars. Examples of sidebars include pieces explaining how government and public sector lawyers could use suggestions from the main article in their own practice, checklists, or other reference sources."

$$$$ SUPER LAWYERS

Key Professional Media, 220 S. Sixth St., Suite 500, Minneapolis MN 55402. (612)313-1760. Fax: (612)335-8809. E-mail: awahlberg@lawandpolitics.com. Website: www.superlawyers.com. **100% freelance written**. Monthly magazine covering law and politics. We publish glossy magazines in every region of the country. All serve a legal audience and have a storytelling sensibility. We write profiles of interesting attorneys exclusively. Estab. 1990. Byline given. Pays on acceptance. Offers 25% kill fee. Publishes ms an average of 1 month after acceptance. Buys first rights, buys electronic rights. Editorial lead time 6 months. Submit seasonal material 6 months in advance. Accepts queries by mail, e-mail, online submission form. Accepts simultaneous submissions. Sample copy free. Guidelines free.
Nonfiction Needs general interest, historical. Query. Length: 500-2,000 words. **Pays 50¢-$1.50/word.**

Lumber

$$ PALLET ENTERPRISE

Industrial Reporting Inc., 10244 Timber Ridge Dr., Ashland VA 23005. (804)550-0323. Fax: (804)550-2181. E-mail: editor@ireporting.com. Website: www.palletenterprise.com. **Contact:** Tim Cox, editor. **40%**

freelance written. Monthly magazine covering lumber and pallet operations. The **Pallet Enterprise** is a monthly trade magazine for the sawmill, pallet, remanufacturing and wood processing industries. Articles should offer technical, solution-oriented information. Anti-forest articles are not accepted. Articles should focus on machinery and unique ways to improve profitability/make money. Estab. 1981. Circ. 14,500. Pays on publication. Buys first rights, buys one-time rights, buys electronic rights. Makes work-for-hire assignments. May buy all rights. Rights purchased depends on the writer and the article. Editorial lead time 2 months. Submit seasonal material 2 months in advance. Accepts queries by mail, e-mail, fax, phone. Accepts previously published material. Accepts simultaneous submissions. Sample copy available online. Guidelines free.

Nonfiction Contact: Tim Cox, editor. We only want articles of interest to pallet manufacturers, pallet recyclers, and lumber companies/sawmills. Needs interview, new product, opinion, technical, industry news, environmental, forests operation/plant features. No lifestyle, humor, general news, etc. **Buys 20 mss/year.** Query with published clips. Length: 1,000-3,000 words. **Pays $200-400 for assigned articles. Pays $100-400 for unsolicited articles.** Sometimes pays expenses of writers on assignment.

Photos State availability. Captions, identification of subjects required. Reviews 3 × 5 prints. Negotiates payment individually. Buys one time rights and Web rights.

Columns/Departments Contact: Tim Cox, editor. Green Watch (environmental news/opinion affecting US forests), 1,500 words. **Buys 12 mss/year.** Query with published clips. **Pays $200-400.**

Tips Provide unique environmental or industry-oriented articles. Many of our freelance articles are company features of sawmills, pallet manufacturers, pallet recyclers, and wood waste processors.

$ $ SOUTHERN LUMBERMAN

Hatton-Brown Publishers, P.O. Box 2268, Montgomery AL 36102. (334)834-1170. Fax: (334)834-4525. E-mail: rich@hattonbrown.com. Website: www.southernlumberman.com. **Contact:** Rich Donnell. **20% freelance written. Works with a small number of new/unpublished writers each year**. Monthly journal for the sawmill industry. Estab. 1881. Circ. 15,000. Byline given. Pays on publication. No kill fee. Publishes ms an average of 3 months after acceptance. Buys first North American serial rights. Submit seasonal material 6 months in advance. Accepts queries by online submission form. Responds in 1 month to queries. Responds in 2 months to mss. Sample copy for $3 and 9 × 12 SAE with 5 first-class stamps. Guidelines for #10 sase.

Nonfiction Needs how-to, sawmill better, technical, equipment analysis, sawmill features. **Buys 10-15 mss/year.** Send complete ms. Length: 500-2,000 words. **Pays $150-350 for assigned articles. Pays $100-250 for unsolicited articles.** Sometimes pays expenses of writers on assignment.

Reprints Send tearsheet or photocopy of article and information about when and where the article previously appeared. Pays 25-50% of amount paid for an original article.

Photos "Always looking for news feature types of photos featuring forest products, industry materials, or people." Send photos. Captions, identification of subjects required. Reviews transparencies, 4 × 5 color prints. Pays $10-25/photo.

Tips "Like most, we appreciate a clearly-worded query listing the merits of a suggested story—what it will tell our readers they need/want to know. We want quotes, we want opinions to make others discuss the article. Best hint? Find an interesting sawmill operation owner and start asking questions—what's he doing bigger, better, different. I bet a story idea develops. We need color photos, too. We're interested in new facilities, better marketing, and improved production."

$ $ TIMBERLINE

Timber Industry Newsline/Trading Post, Industrial Reporting, Inc., 10244 Timber Ridge Dr., Ashland VA 23005. (804)550-0323. Fax: (804)550-2181. E-mail: editor@ireporting.com. Website: www.timberlinemag.com. **50% freelance written**. Monthly tabloid covering the forest products industry. Articles should offer technical, solution-oriented information. Anti-forest products, industry articles are not accepted. Articles should focus on machinery and unique ways to improve profitability and make money. Estab. 1994. Circ. 30,000. Byline given. Pays on publication. Buys first rights, buys one-time rights, buys electronic rights. Makes work-for-hire assignments. May purchase all rights. Rights purchased depends on the writer and the article. Editorial lead time 2 months. Submit seasonal material 2 months in advance. Accepts queries by mail, e-mail, fax, phone. Accepts previously published material. Accepts simultaneous submissions. Sample copy available online. Guidelines free.

Nonfiction Contact: Tim Cox, editor. We only want articles of interest to loggers, sawmills, wood treatment facilities, etc. Readers tend to be pro-industry/conservative, and opinion pieces must be written to appeal to them. Needs historical, interview, new product, opinion, technical, industry news, environmental operation/plant features. No lifestyles, humor, general news, etc. **Buys 25 mss/year.** Query with published clips. Length: 1,000-3,000 words. **Pays $200-400 for assigned articles. Pays $100-400 for unsolicited articles.** Sometimes pays expenses of writers on assignment.

Photos State availability. Captions, identification of subjects required. Reviews 3 × 5 prints. Negotiates payment individually. Buys one time rights and Web rights.

Columns/Departments Contact: Tim Cox, editor. From the Hill (legislative news impacting the forest products industry), 1,800 words; Green Watch (environmental news/opinion affecting US forests), 1,500 words. **Buys 12 mss/year.** Query with published clips. **Pays $200-400.**

Tips Provide unique environmental or industry-oriented articles. Many of our freelance articles are company features of logging operations or sawmills.

$ $ TIMBERWEST

TimberWest Publications, LLC, P.O. Box 610, Edmonds WA 98020-0160. Fax: (425)771-3623. E-mail: dimettler@comcast.net. Website: www.forestnet.com. **Contact:** Diane Mettler, managing editor. **75% freelance written.** Monthly magazine covering logging and lumber segment of the forestry industry in the Northwest. "We publish primarily profiles on loggers and their operations—with an emphasis on the machinery—in Washington, Oregon, Idaho, Montana, Northern California, and Alaska. Some timber issues are highly controversial and although we will report on the issues, this is a pro-logging publication. We don't publish articles with a negative slant on the timber industry." Estab. 1975. Circ. 10,000. Byline given. Pays on acceptance. No kill fee. Buys first North American serial rights, buys second serial (reprint) rights. Editorial lead time 3 months. Accepts queries by mail, fax. Responds in 3 weeks to queries. Sample copy for $2. Guidelines for #10 sase.

Nonfiction Needs historical, interview, new product. No articles that put the timber industry in a bad light—such as environmental articles against logging. **Buys 50 mss/year.** Query with published clips. Length: 1,100-1,500 words. **Pays $350.** Pays expenses of writers on assignment.

Photos Send photos. Captions, identification of subjects required. Reviews contact sheets, transparencies, prints, GIF/JPEG files. Offers no additional payment for photos accepted with ms. Buys all rights.

Fillers Needs facts, newsbreaks. Buys 10 mss/year. Length: 400-800 words. **Pays $100-250.**

Tips "We are always interested in profiles of loggers and their operations in Alaska, Oregon, Washington, Montana, and Northern California. We also want articles pertaining to current industry topics, such as fire abatement, sustainable forests, or new technology. Read an issue to get a clear idea of the type of material *TimberWest* publishes. The audience is primarily loggers and topics that focus on an 'evolving' timber industry versus a 'dying' industry will find a place in the magazine. When querying, a clear overview of the article will enhance acceptance."

Machinery & Metal

$ $ $ AMERICAN MACHINIST

Penton Media, 1300 E. 9th St., Cleveland OH 44114-1503. (216)931-9240. Fax: (216)931-9524. E-mail: robert.brooks@penton.com. Website: www.americanmachinist.com. **Contact:** Robert Brooks, editor-in-chief. **10% freelance written.** Monthly magazine covering all forms of metalworking. "*American Machinist* is the oldest magazine dedicated to metalworking in the United States. Our readers are the owners and managers of metalworking shops. We publish articles that provide the managers and owners of job shops, contract shops, and captive shops the information they need to make their operations more efficient, more productive, and more profitable. Our articles are technical in nature and must be focused on technology that will help these shops to become more competitive on a global basis. Our readers are skilled machinists. This is not the place for lightweight items about manufacturing, and we are not interested in articles on management theories." Estab. 1877. Circ. 80,000. Byline sometimes given. Offers 20% kill fee. Publishes ms an average of 1-2 months after acceptance. Buys all rights. Makes work-for-hire assignments. Editorial lead time 3-6 months. Submit seasonal material 4-6 months in advance. Accepts queries by mail, e-mail, phone. Responds in 1-2 weeks to queries. Responds in 1 month to mss. Sample copy available online.

Nonfiction Needs general interest, how-to, new product, opinion, personal experience, photo feature, technical. Query with published clips. Length: 600-2,400 words. **Pays $300-1,200.** Sometimes pays expenses of writers on assignment.

Photos State availability. Captions, identification of subjects, model releases required. Reviews GIF/JPEG files. Negotiates payment individually. Buys all rights.

Fillers Needs anecdotes, facts, gags, newsbreaks, short humor. Buys 12-18 mss/year. Length: 50-200 words. **Pays $25-100.**

Tips "With our exacting audience, a writer would do well to have some background working with machine tools."

$$$ CUTTING TOOL ENGINEERING

CTE Publications, Inc., 40 Skokie Blvd., Northbrook IL 60062. (847)714-0175. Fax: (847)559-4444. E-mail: alanr@jwr.com. Website: www.ctemag.com. **40% freelance written**. Monthly magazine covering industrial metal cutting tools and metal cutting operations. "*Cutting Tool Engineering* serves owners, managers and engineers who work in manufacturing, specifically manufacturing that involves cutting or grinding metal or other materials. Writing should be geared toward improving manufacturing processes." Circ. 48,000. Byline given. Pays on publication. Offers 50% kill fee. Publishes ms an average of 2 months after acceptance. Buys all rights. Editorial lead time 2 months. Accepts queries by mail, fax. Responds in 2 months to mss. Sample copy and writer's guidelines free.

Nonfiction Needs how-to, opinion, personal experience, technical. "No fiction or articles that don't relate to manufacturing." **Buys 10 mss/year.** Length: 1,500-3,000 words. **Pays $750-1,500.** Pays expenses of writers on assignment.

Photos State availability. Captions required. Reviews transparencies, prints. Negotiates payment individually. Buys all rights.

Tips "For queries, write 2 clear paragraphs about how the proposed article will play out. Include sources that would be in the article."

$$ EQUIPMENT JOURNAL

Pace Publishing, 5160 Explorer Dr., Unit 6, Mississauga ON L4W 4T7 Canada. (800)667-8541. Fax: (905)629-7988. E-mail: editor@equipmentjournal.com. Website: www.equipmentjournal.com. **10% freelance written**. 17 times/year. "Canada's National Equipment Newspaper. We publish product information, jobsite stories, and 15 features a year that are relevant to the material handling, construction, mining, forestry, and transportation industries." Estab. 1966. Circ. 21,240. Byline given. Pays on publication. No kill fee. Publishes ms an average of 1-2 months after acceptance. Buys first rights, buys second serial (reprint) rights. Editorial lead time 2-3 months. Submit seasonal material 2 months in advance. Accepts queries by mail, e-mail, fax, phone. Accepts previously published material. Accepts simultaneous submissions. Sample copy and guidelines free.

Nonfiction Needs how-to, interview, new product, photo feature, technical. No material that falls outside of *EJ*'s mandate—the Canadian equipment industry. **Buys 15/year mss/year.** Send complete ms. We prefer electronic submissions. We do not accept unsolicited freelance submissions. Length: 500-1,500 words. **$250-$400 for assigned and unsolicited articles.** Sometimes pays expenses of writers on assignment.

Photos State availability. Identification of subjects required. 4 × 6 prints. Negotiates payment individually. Buys all rights.

Tips "We are looking for new product release stories of products made by Canadian manufacturers and field application stories that take place in Canada."

$$$ THE FABRICATOR

833 Featherstone Rd., Rockford IL 61107. (815)399-8700. Fax: (815)381-1370. E-mail: kateb@thefabricator.com. Website: www.thefabricator.com. **Contact:** Kate Bachman, editor. **15% freelance written**. Monthly magazine covering metal forming and fabricating. Our purpose is to disseminate information about modern metal forming and fabricating techniques, machinery, tooling, and management concepts for the metal fabricator. Estab. 1971. Circ. 58,000. Byline given. Pays on publication. No kill fee. Buys all rights. Editorial lead time 6 months. Accepts queries by mail, e-mail. Responds in 2 weeks to queries. Responds in 1 month to mss. Sample copy free. Guidelines available online.

Nonfiction Needs how-to, technical, company profile. Query with published clips. Length: 1,200-2,000 words. **Pays 40-80¢/word.**

Photos Request guidelines for digital images. State availability. Captions, identification of subjects required. Reviews transparencies, prints. Negotiates payment individually. Rights purchased depends on photographer requirements.

$$$ GASES & WELDING DISTRIBUTOR

Penton Media, 1300 E. 9th St., Cleveland OH 44114. (216)931-9240. Fax: (216)931-9524. E-mail: weldingeditor@penton.com. Website: www.weldingdesign.com. **10% freelance written**. Bimonthly magazine covering the distribution business for welding supplies and industrial gases. *Gases & Welding Distributor* provides information to the owners and managers of distributorships that sell welding equipment and industrial gases. We include information on federal regulations, business technology for distributorships, technological developments in welding, and feature stories on how our distributors are doing business with the goal of helping our readers to be more productive, efficient and competitive. These shops are very local in nature, and need to be addressed as small businessmen in a field that is consolidating and becoming more challenging. We do not write about business management theory as much as we write about putting into practice good management techniques that have proved to work at similar businesses. Estab. 1966. Circ. 20,000. Byline sometimes given. Pays on publication. Offers 20% kill fee. Publishes ms an average of 1-2 months after acceptance. Buys all rights. Makes work-for-hire assignments. Editorial lead time 3-6 months. Submit seasonal material 4-6 months in advance. Accepts queries by mail, e-mail, phone. Responds in 1-2 weeks to queries. Responds in 1 month to mss. Sample copy available online.

Nonfiction Needs general interest, how-to, new product, opinion, personal experience, photo feature, technical. Query with published clips. Length: 600-2,400 words. **Pays $300-1,200.** Sometimes pays expenses of writers on assignment.

Photos State availability. Captions, identification of subjects, model releases required. Reviews GIF/JPEG files. Negotiates payment individually. Buys all rights.

Fillers Needs anecdotes, facts, gags, newsbreaks, short humor. Buys 12-18 mss/year. Length: 50-200 words. **Pays $25-100.**

Tips Writers should be familiar with welding and/or the industrial distribution business. With that, calling or e-mailing me directly is the next best approach. We are interested in information that will help to make machine shops more competitive, and a writer should have a very specific idea before approaching me.

MACHINERY LUBRICATION MAGAZINE

Noria Corporation, 1328 East 43rd Court, Tulsa OK 74105. (918)749-1400, ext. 120. Fax: (918)746-0925. E-mail: jkucera@noria.com. Website: noria.com. **Contact:** Paul Arnold, editor in chief. Bimonthly hardcopy magazine and website covering machinery lubrication, oil analysis, tribology. Estab. 2001. Circ. 41,000. Byline given. No kill fee. Publishes ms an average of 3-6 months after acceptance. Editorial lead time 3 months. Accepts queries by e-mail. Accepts previously published material. Responds in 2 weeks to queries. Responds in 3 months to mss. Sample copy available online. Guidelines available online.

Nonfiction Needs how-to, new product, technical. "No heavy commercial, opinion articles." Query. Length: 1,000-2,000 words.

Photos Send photos. Captions, identification of subjects required. Reviews GIF/JPEG files. Offers no additional payment for photos accepted with ms.

Tips "Please request editorial guidelines by sending e-mail."

$$ ORNAMENTAL AND MISCELLANEOUS METAL FABRICATOR

National Ornamental And Miscellaneous Metals Association, 1535 Pennsylvania Ave., McDonough GA 30253. (888)516-8585. Fax: (770)288-2006. E-mail: editor@nomma.org. **20% freelance written.** "Bimonthly magazine to inform, educate, and inspire members of the ornamental and miscellaneous metalworking industry." Estab. 1959. Circ. 9,000. Byline given. Pays on publication. No kill fee. Buys one-time rights. Editorial lead time 1-2 months. Accepts queries by mail, e-mail, fax. Responds by e-mail in 1 month (include e-mail address in query). Guidelines by e-mail.

Nonfiction Needs book excerpts, essays, general interest, historical, how-to, humor, interview, opinion, personal experience, photo feature feature, technical. **Buys 8-12 mss/year.** Query. Length: 1,200-2,000 words. **Pays $250-400.**

Reprints Send tearsheet, photocopy or typed ms with rights for sale noted and information about when and where the material previously appeared. Pays 100% of amount paid for an original article.

Photos Artwork and sidebars preferred. State availability. Model releases required. Reviews contact sheets, negatives, transparencies, prints.

Columns/Departments 700-900 words. **Pays $ 50-100.**

Tips "Please request and review recent issues. Contacting the editor for guidance on article topics is welcome."

$$$ PRACTICAL WELDING TODAY

FMA Communications, Inc., 833 Featherstone Rd., Rockford IL 61107-6302. (815)227-8282. Fax: (815)381-

1370. E-mail: amandac@thefabricator.com. Website: www.thefabricator.com. **15% freelance written**. Bimonthly magazine covering welding. We generally publish how-to and educational articles that teach people about a process or how to do something better. Estab. 1997. Circ. 40,000. Byline given. Pays on publication. No kill fee. Buys all rights. Editorial lead time 6 months. Accepts queries by mail, e-mail. Responds in 2 weeks to queries. Responds in 2 months to mss. Sample copy free. Guidelines available online.

Nonfiction Needs how-to, technical, company profiles. Special issues: Forecast issue on trends in welding (January/February). No promotional, one-sided, persuasive articles or unsolicited case studies. **Buys 5 mss/year.** Query with published clips. Length: 800-1,200 words. **Pays 40-80¢/word.** Sometimes pays expenses of writers on assignment.

Photos State availability. Captions, identification of subjects required. Reviews contact sheets. Negotiates payment individually. Rights purchased depends on photographer requirements.

Tips Follow our author guidelines and editorial policies to write a how-to piece from which our readers can benefit.

$$ SPRINGS

The International Magazine of Spring Manufacturers, Spring Manufacturers Institute, 2001 Midwest Rd., Suite 106, Oak Brook IL 60523-1335. (630)495-8588. Fax: (630)495-8595. E-mail: lynne@smihq.org. Website: www.smihq.org. **Contact:** Lynne Carr, editor. **10% freelance written**. Quarterly magazine covering precision mechanical spring manufacture. Articles should be aimed at spring manufacturers. Estab. 1962. Circ. 10,800. Byline given. Pays on publication. No kill fee. Publishes ms an average of 3-6 months after acceptance. Buys first rights. Editorial lead time 4 months. Accepts simultaneous submissions. Sample copy free. Guidelines available online.

Nonfiction Needs general interest, how-to, interview, opinion, personal experience, technical. **Buys 4-6 mss/year.** Length: 2,000-10,000 words. **Pays $100-600 for assigned articles.**

Photos State availability. Captions required. Reviews prints, digital photos. Offers no additional payment for photos accepted with ms. Buys one time rights.

Tips Call the editor. Contact springmakers and spring industry suppliers and ask about what interests them. Include interviews/quotes from people in the spring industry in the article. The editor can supply contacts. See guidelines online at website.

$$$ STAMPING JOURNAL

Fabricators & Manufacturers Association (FMA), 833 Featherstone Rd., Rockford IL 61107. (815)399-8700. Fax: (815)381-1370. E-mail: kateb@thefabricator.com. Website: www.thefabricator.com. **15% freelance written**. Bimonthly magazine covering metal stamping. We look for how-to and educational articles—nonpromotional. Estab. 1989. Circ. 35,000. Byline given. Pays on publication. No kill fee. Buys all rights. Editorial lead time 6 months. Accepts queries by mail, e-mail, fax, phone. Responds in 2 weeks to queries. Responds in 2 months to mss. Sample copy and writer's guidelines free.

Nonfiction Needs how-to, technical, company profile. Special issues: Forecast issue (January). No unsolicited case studies. **Buys 5 mss/year.** Query with published clips. 1,000 words **Pays 40-80¢/word.** Sometimes pays expenses of writers on assignment.

Photos State availability. Captions, identification of subjects required. Reviews contact sheets. Negotiates payment individually. Rights purchased depends on photographer requirements.

Tips Articles should be impartial and should not describe the benefits of certain products available from certain companies. They should not be biased toward the author's or against a competitor's products or technologies. The publisher may refuse any article that does not conform to this guideline.

$$$ TPJ—THE TUBE & PIPE JOURNAL

Fabricators & Manufacturers Association (FMA), 833 Featherstone Rd., Rockford IL 61107. (815)399-8700. Fax: (815)381-1370. Website: www.thefabricator.com. **Contact:** Eric Lundin, sr. ed. **15% freelance written**. Magazine published 8 times/year covering metal tube and pipe. Educational perspective—emphasis is on how-to articles to accomplish a particular task or improve on a process. New trends and technologies are also important topics. Estab. 1990. Circ. 30,000. Byline given. Pays on publication. No kill fee. Buys all rights. Editorial lead time 6 months. Accepts queries by mail, e-mail. Responds in 2 weeks to queries. Responds in 2 months to mss. Sample copy free. Guidelines available online.

Nonfiction Any new or improved tube production or fabrication process—includes manufacturing, bending, and forming tube (metal tube only). Needs how-to, technical. Special issues: Forecast issue

(January). No unsolicited case studies. **Buys 5 mss/year.** Query with published clips. Length: 800-1,200 words. **Pays 40-80¢/word.** Sometimes pays expenses of writers on assignment.
Photos State availability. Captions, identification of subjects required. Reviews contact sheets. Negotiates payment individually. Rights purchased depends on photographer requirements.
Tips Submit a detailed proposal, including an article outline, to the editor.

$$$ WELDING DESIGN & FABRICATION

Penton Media, 1300 E. 9th St., Cleveland OH 44114. (216)931-9240. Fax: (216)931-9524. E-mail: weldingeditor@penton.com. Website: www.weldingdesign.com. **10% freelance written.** Bimonthly magazine covering all facets of welding and running a welding business. *Welding Design & Fabrication* provides information to the owners and managers of welding shops, including business, technology and trends. We include information on engineering and technological developments that could change the business as it is currently known, and feature stories on how welders are doing business with the goal of helping our readers to be more productive, effecient, and competitive. Welding shops are very local in nature and need to be addressed as small businessmen in a field that is consolidating and becoming more challenging and more global. We do not write about business management theory as much as we write about putting into practice good management techniques that have proved to work at similar businesses. Estab. 1930. Circ. 40,000. Byline given. Pays on publication. Offers 20% kill fee. Publishes ms an average of 1-2 months after acceptance. Buys all rights. Makes work-for-hire assignments. Editorial lead time 3-6 months. Submit seasonal material 4-6 months in advance. Accepts queries by mail, e-mail, phone. Responds in 1-2 weeks to queries. Responds in 1 month to mss. Sample copy available online.
Nonfiction Needs general interest, how-to, new product, opinion, personal experience, photo feature, technical. Query. Length: 600-2,400 words. **Pays $300-1,200.** Sometimes pays expenses of writers on assignment.
Photos State availability. Captions, identification of subjects, model releases required. Reviews GIF/JPEG files (300 dpi). Negotiates payment individually. Buys all rights.
Fillers Needs anecdotes, facts, gags, newsbreaks, short humor. Buys 12-18 mss/year. Length: 50-200 words. **Pays $25-100.**
Tips Writers should be familiar with welding and/or metalworking and metal joining techniques. With that, calling or e-mailing me directly is the next best approach. We are interested in information that will help to make welding shops more competitive, and a writer should have a very specific idea before approaching me.

$$ WIRE ROPE NEWS & SLING TECHNOLOGY

Wire Rope News LLC, P.O. Box 871, Clark NJ 07066. (908)486-3221. Fax: (732)396-4215. Website: www.wireropenews.com. **100% freelance written.** Bimonthly magazine published for manufacturers and distributors of wire rope, chain, cordage, related hardware, and sling fabricators. Content includes technical articles, news and reports describing the manufacturing and use of wire rope and related products in marine, construction, mining, aircraft and offshore drilling operations. Estab. 1979. Circ. 4,300. Byline sometimes given. Pays on acceptance. No kill fee. Publishes ms an average of 6 months after acceptance. Buys all rights. Editorial lead time 2 months. Submit seasonal material 2 months in advance. Accepts queries by mail, fax. Accepts simultaneous submissions.
Nonfiction Needs general interest, historical, interview, photo feature, technical. **Buys 30 mss/year.** Send complete ms. Length: 2,500-5,000 words. **Pays $300-500.**
Photos Send photos. Identification of subjects required. Reviews contact sheets, 5 × 7 prints, digital. Offers no additional payment for photos accepted with ms. Buys all rights.
Tips We are accepting more submissions and queries by e-mail.

THE WORLD OF WELDING

Hobart Institute of Welding Technology, 400 Trade Square East, Troy OH 45373. (937)332-5603. Fax: (937)332-5220. E-mail: hiwt@welding.org. Website: www.welding.org. **10% freelance written.** Quarterly magazine covering welding training and education. "The content must be educational and must contain welding topic information." Estab. 1990. Circ. 6,500. Byline given. Publishes ms an average of 3 months after acceptance. Buys all rights. Editorial lead time 3 months. Submit seasonal material 3 months in advance. Accepts queries by mail, e-mail, fax. Accepts simultaneous submissions. Responds in 1 week to queries. Responds in 3 months to mss. Sample copy free. Guidelines free.
Nonfiction Needs general interest, historical, how-to, interview, personal experience, photo feature, technical, welding topics. Query with published clips.

Photos Send photos. Captions, identification of subjects, model releases required. Reviews GIF/JPEG files. Offers no additional payment for photos accepted with ms.
Fiction Needs adventure, historical, mainstream, welding. Query with published clips.
Fillers Needs facts, newsbreaks.
Tips "Writers must be willing to donate material on welding and metallurgy related topics, welded art/sculpture, personal welding experiences. An editorial committee reviews submissions and determines acceptance."

Maintenance & Safety

$ $ AMERICAN WINDOW CLEANER MAGAZINE

Voice of the Professional Window Cleaner, 12 Publishing Corp., 750-B NW Broad St., Southern Pines NC 28387. (910)693-2644. Fax: (910)246-1681. Website: www.awcmag.com. Bob Lawrence. **Contact:** Gary Mauer. **20% freelance written.** Bimonthly magazine window cleaning. Articles to help window cleaners become more profitable, safe, professional, and feel good about what they do. Estab. 1986. Circ. 8,000. Byline given. Pays on acceptance. Offers 33% kill fee. Publishes ms an average of 4-8 months after acceptance. Buys first rights. Editorial lead time 2 months. Submit seasonal material 3 months in advance. Responds in 2 weeks to queries. Responds in 1 month to mss. Sample copy free. Guidelines available online.
Nonfiction Needs how-to, humor, inspirational, interview, personal experience, photo feature, technical, add on business. We do not want PR-driven pieces. We want to educate—not push a particular product. **Buys 20 mss/year.** Query. Length: 500-5,000 words. **Pays $50-250.**
Photos State availability. Captions required. Reviews contact sheets, transparencies, 4x6 prints. Offers $10 per photo. Buys one time rights.
Columns/Departments Window Cleaning Tips (tricks of the trade); 1,000-2,000 words; Humor-anecdotes-feel good-abouts (window cleaning industry); Computer High-Tech (tips on new technology), all 1,000 words **Buys 12 mss/year.** Query. **Pays $50-100.**
Tips *American Window Cleaner Magazine* covers an unusual niche that gets people's curiosity. Articles that are technical in nature and emphasize practical tips or safety, and how to work more efficiently, have the best chances of being published. Articles include: window cleaning unusual buildings, landmarks; working for well-known people/celebrities; window cleaning in resorts/casinos/unusual cities; humor or satire about our industry or the public's perception of it. At some point, we make phone contact and chat to see if our interests are compatible.

$ $ EXECUTIVE HOUSEKEEPING TODAY

The International Executive Housekeepers Association, 1001 Eastwind Dr., Suite 301, Westerville OH 43081-3361. (614)895-7166. Fax: (614)895-1248. E-mail: ldigiulio@ieha.org. Website: www.ieha.org. **Contact:** Laura DiGiulio, editor. **50% freelance written.** Monthly magazine for nearly 5,000 decision makers responsible for housekeeping management (cleaning, grounds maintenance, laundry, linen, pest control, waste management, regulatory compliance, training) for a variety of institutions: hospitality, healthcare, education, retail, government. Estab. 1930. Circ. 5,500. Byline given. No kill fee. Publishes ms an average of 6 months after acceptance. Buys first North American serial rights. Editorial lead time 2 months. Submit seasonal material 3 months in advance. Accepts queries by mail, e-mail, fax, phone.
Nonfiction Needs general interest, interview, new product, related to magazine's scope, personal experience, in housekeeping profession, technical. **Buys 30 mss/year.** Query with published clips. Length: 500-1,500 words.
Photos State availability. Identification of subjects required. Offers no additional payment for photos accepted with ms. Buys one-time rights.
Columns/Departments Federal Report (OSHA/EPA requirements), 1,000 words; Industry News; Management Perspectives (industry specific), 500-1,500 words. Query with published clips.
Tips "Have a background in the industry or personal experience with any aspect of it."

$ $ PEST MANAGEMENT PROFESSIONAL

Questex Media Group, 600 Superior Ave. East, Suite 1100, Cleveland OH 44114. (216)706-3735. Fax: (216)706-3711. E-mail: fandorka@questex.com. Website: www.mypmp.net. Monthly magazine for professional pest management professionals and sanitarians. Estab. 1933. Circ. 20,000. Pays on publication. No kill fee. Licenses rights. Submit seasonal material 3 months in advance. Accepts queries by mail, e-mail, phone. Responds in 1 month to mss. Guidelines available online.

Nonfiction Prefers contributors with pest control industry background. All articles must have trade or business orientation. Needs how-to, humor, inspirational, interview, new product, personal experience, stories about pest management operations and their problems, case histories, new technological breakthroughs. No general information type of articles desired. **Buys 3 mss/year.** Query. Length: 1,000-1,400 words. **Pays $150-400 minimum.**
Photos Digital photos accepted; please query on specs. State availability. No additional payment for photos used with ms.
Columns/Departments Regular columns use material oriented to this profession, 550 words.

Management & Supervision

$ $ $ HUMAN RESOURCE EXECUTIVE

LRP Publications Magazine Group, P.O. Box 980, Horsham PA 19044-0980. (215)784-0910. Fax: (215)784-0275. E-mail: kfrasch@lrp.com. Website: www.hrexecutive.com. **Contact:** Kristen B. Frasch, managing editor. **30% freelance written**. Magazine published 16 times/year serving the information needs of chief human resource professionals/executives in companies, government agencies, and nonprofit institutions with 500 or more employees. Estab. 1987. Circ. 75,000. Byline given. Pays on acceptance. Offers kill fee. Pays 50% kill fee on assigned stories. Publishes ms an average of 2 months after acceptance. Buys all rights. Accepts queries by mail, e-mail, fax. Responds in 1 month to mss. Guidelines available online.
Nonfiction Needs book excerpts, interview. **Buys 16 mss/year.** Query with published clips. Length: 1,800 words. **Pays $200-1,000.** Sometimes pays expenses of writers on assignment.
Photos State availability. Identification of subjects required. Reviews contact sheets. Offers no additional payment for photos accepted with ms. Buys first and repeat rights.

$ $ INCENTIVE

VNU Business Publications, 770 Broadway, New York NY 10003. (646)654-4485. Fax: (646)654-7650. Website: www.incentivemag.com. Monthly magazine covering sales promotion and employee motivation: managing and marketing through motivation. Estab. 1905. Circ. 41,000. Byline given. Pays on acceptance. No kill fee. Publishes ms an average of 3 months after acceptance. Buys all rights. Accepts queries by mail, e-mail, fax. Responds in 1 month to queries. Responds in 2 months to mss. Sample copy for sae with 9 × 12 envelope.
Nonfiction Needs general interest, motivation, demographics, how-to, types of sales promotion, buying product categories, using destinations, interview, sales promotion executives, travel, incentive-oriented, corporate case studies. **Buys 48 mss/year.** Query with published clips. Length: 1,000-2,000 words. **Pays $250-700 for assigned articles. does not pay for unsolicited articles. for unsolicited articles.** Pays expenses of writers on assignment.
Reprints Send tearsheet and information about when and where the material previously appeared. Pays 50% of the amount paid for an original article.
Photos Send photos. Identification of subjects required. Reviews contact sheets, transparencies. Offers some additional payment for photos accepted with ms.
Tips Read the publication, then query.

PEOPLE MANAGEMENT

Chartered Institute of Personnel and Development, 17-18 Britton St., London England EC1M 5TP United Kingdom. (44)(207)324-2729. E-mail: editorial@peoplemanagement.co.uk. Website: www.peoplemanagement.co.uk. Biweekly magazine publishing articles on all aspects of managing and developing people at work. Circ. 135,000. No kill fee. Editorial lead time 2 months. Only responds to proposals if interested. Guidelines available online.
Nonfiction Needs general interest, features with a theoretical/strategic/policy theme or investigations of current developments/case studies, how-to, step-by-step hints/tips for best practices to use in everyday work. Submit 2-page proposal, bio. Length: 1,000-2,500 words.
Columns/Departments Learning Centre (training/development matters aimed to provoke discussion), 350 words; Viewpoint (addresses a key topical issue), 600 words; Research (academics summarize their latest findings or review other research in a particular area), 500 words); Troubleshooter (overview of a HR dilemma and/or a solution to that dilemma), 350 words/dilemma and 400 words/solution.

$ $ PLAYGROUND MAGAZINE

The National Magazine for Playground Design & Standards, Harris Publishing, 360 B St., Idaho Falls

ID 83402. (208)542-2271. Fax: (208)522-5241. E-mail: lindstrm@playgroundmag.com. Website: www.playgroundmag.com. **Contact:** Lane Lindstrom, editor. **25% freelance written**. Magazine published quarterly covering playgrounds, play-related issues, equipment and industry trends. *"Playground Magazine* targets park and recreation management, elementary school teachers and administrators, child care facilities and parent-group leader readership. Articles should focus on play and the playground market as a whole, including aquatic play and surfacing." Estab. 2000. Circ. 35,000. Byline given. Pays on publication. No kill fee. Publishes ms an average of 6 months after acceptance. Buys first North American serial rights, buys electronic rights. Editorial lead time 2 months. Submit seasonal material 1 year in advance. Accepts queries by mail, e-mail. Accepts simultaneous submissions. Responds in 1 month to queries. Responds in 2 months to mss. Sample copy for $5. Guidelines for #10 sase.

Nonfiction Needs how-to, interview, new product, opinion, personal experience, photo feature, technical, travel. *Playground Magazine* does not publish any articles that do not directly relate to play and the playground industry. **Buys 4-6 mss/year.** Query. Length: 800-1,500 words. **Pays $50-300 for assigned articles.** Sometimes pays expenses of writers on assignment.

Photos State availability of or send photos. Captions, identification of subjects, model releases required. Reviews 35mm transparencies, GIF/JPEG files (350 dpi or better). Offers no additional payment for photos accepted with ms. Buys one-time rights.

Columns/Departments Dream Spaces (an article that profiles a unique play area and focuses on community involvement, unique design, or human interest), 800-1,200 words. **Buys 2 mss/year.** Query. **Pays $100-300.**

Tips "We are looking for articles that managers can use as a resource when considering playground construction, management, safety, installation, maintenance, etc. Writers should find unique angles to playground-related features such as current trends in the industry, the value of play, natural play, the need for recess, etc. We are a trade journal that offers up-to-date industry news and features that promote play and the playground industry."

Marine & Maritime Industries

$$ CURRENTS

Marine Technology Society, 5565 Sterrett Pl., Suite 108, Columbia MD 21044-2665. (410)884-5330. Fax: (410)884-9060. E-mail: publications@mtsociety.org. Website: www.mtsociety.org. **Contact:** Susan Branting, managing editor. **0% freelance written**. Bimonthly newsletter covering commercial, academic, scientific marine technology. Estab. 1963. Circ. 2,600. Byline given. Pays on acceptance. No kill fee. Buys all rights. Makes work-for-hire assignments. Editorial lead time 1-2 months. Accepts queries by e-mail. Accepts previously published material. Accepts simultaneous submissions. Responds in 4 weeks to queries. Sample copy free.

- "Our readers are engineers and technologists who design, develop and maintain the equipment and instruments used to understand and explore the oceans. The newsletter covers society news, industry news, science and technology news, and similar news."

Nonfiction Needs interview, technical. **Buys 1-6 mss/year.** Query. Length: 250-500 words. **Pays $100-500 for assigned articles.** Sometimes pays expenses of writers on assignment.

$$ MARINE BUSINESS JOURNAL

The Voice of the Marine Industry, 330 N. Andrews Ave., Ft. Lauderdale FL 33301. (954)522-5515. Fax: (954)522-2260. E-mail: marilyn@marinebusiness.com. Website: www.marinebusinessjournal.com. **Contact:** Marilyn Mower, editor. **25% freelance written**. Bimonthly magazine that covers the recreational boating industry. *The Marine Business Journal* is aimed at boating dealers, distributors and manufacturers, naval architects, yacht brokers, marina owners and builders, marine electronics dealers, distributors and manufacturers, and anyone involved in the U.S. marine industry. Articles cover news, new product technology, and public affairs affecting the industry. Estab. 1986. Circ. 26,000. Byline given. Pays on publication. No kill fee. Publishes ms an average of 1 month after acceptance. Buys first North American serial rights, buys one-time rights, buys second serial (reprint) rights. Accepts queries by mail, e-mail. Responds in 2 weeks to queries. Sample copy for $2.50, 9 × 12 SAE with 7 first-class stamps.

Nonfiction Buys 20 mss/year. Query with published clips. Length: 500-1,000 words. **Pays $200-500.**

Photos State availability. Captions, identification of subjects, model releases required. Reviews 35mm or larger transparencies, 5 × 7 prints. Offers $50/photo. Buys one time rights.

Tips Query with clips. It's a highly specialized field, written for professionals by professionals, almost all on assignment or by staff.

$$ PROFESSIONAL MARINER

Journal of the Maritime Industry, Navigator Publishing, P.O. Box 569, Portland ME 04112. (207)822-4350. Fax: (207)772-2879. E-mail: editors@professionalmariner.com. Website: www.professionalmariner.com. **75% freelance written**. Bimonthly magazine covering professional seamanship and maritime industry news. Estab. 1993. Circ. 29,000. Byline given. Pays on publication. No kill fee. Buys all rights. Editorial lead time 3 months. Accepts queries by mail, e-mail, fax, phone. Accepts simultaneous submissions.

Nonfiction For professional mariners on vessels and ashore. Seeks submissions on industry news, regulations, towing, piloting, technology, engineering, business, maritime casualties, and feature stories about the maritime industry. Does accept sea stories and personal professional experiences as correspondence pieces. **Buys 15 mss/year.** Query. varies; short clips to long profiles/features. **Pays 25¢/word.** Sometimes pays expenses of writers on assignment.

Photos Send photos. Captions, identification of subjects required. Reviews prints, slides. Negotiates payment individually. Buys one time rights.

Tips Remember that our audience comprises maritime industry professionals. Stories must be written at a level that will benefit this group.

SHIPS AND SHIPPING

Baird Publications, 135 Sturt St., Southbank VIC 3006 Australia. (61)(3)9645-0411. Fax: (61)(3)9645-0475. E-mail: marinfo@baird.com.au. Website: www.baird.com.au. Monthly magazine aimed at those involved in operating and supplying equipment and services to the shipping and port industries of Asia, Australia, New Zealand and the South Pacific. *Ships and Shipping* provides its readers with information and ideas as to how to improve the efficiency and profitability of their business operations through the adoption of new vessels, technology and equipment, improved management and operational techniques and systems, and by simply providing them with the information required to make the right business decisions.

Nonfiction Needs general interest, how-to, new product, technical. Query.

WORK BOAT WORLD

Baird Publications, 135 Sturt St., Southbank VIC 3006 Australia. (61)(3)9645-0411. Fax: (61)(3)9645-0475. E-mail: marinfo@baird.com.au. Website: www.baird.com.au. Monthly magazine covering all types of commercial, military and government vessels to around 130 meters in length. Maintaining close contact with ship builders, designers, owners and operators, suppliers of vessel equipment and suppliers of services on a worldwide basis, the editors and journalists of *Work Boat World* seek always to be informative. They constantly put themselves in the shoes of readers so as to produce editorial matter that interests, educates, informs and entertains. Estab. 1982.

Nonfiction Needs general interest, how-to, interview, new product. Query.

Medical

$$ ADVANCE FOR HEALTHY AGING

Merion Publications, 2900 Horizon Dr., King of Prussia PA 19406. (800)355-5627. Fax: (610)278-1425. E-mail: mwolf@advanceweb.com. Website: www.advanceweb.com/healthyaging. **5% freelance written**. Bimonthly magazine covering health care—the science of aging well. "*Healthy Aging* is a magazine for physicians who are interested in providing wellness and skin services to their baby boomer patients. Writers should be able to write to a physician's level. This means researching studies and doing thorough interviewing to understand medical topics, ranging from nutraceuticals, and preventative health topics. Articles must be well-researched and objective—speaking to the mission of the magazine." Estab. 2005. Circ. 30,000. Byline given. Pays on publication. Publishes ms an average of 3 months after acceptance. Buys first North American serial rights. Editorial lead time 5 months. Submit seasonal material 3 months in advance. Accepts queries by mail. Responds in 3 months to queries. Guidelines available online.

Nonfiction Needs interview, technical. "Nothing touting miracle cures for aging or favoring a product or specific approach. Articles must be research-driven and provide realistic portrayals." **Buys 6 mss/year.** Query with published clips. Length: 1,800-2,500 words. **Pays $150-300.**

Tips "Authors should be able to take medical information and make it easy to read for a physician-level audience, and prove their information will be objective with research, interviews, etc. We are looking for consumer-oriented articles that are taken apart for physician's practical use."

$ ADVANCE NEWSMAGAZINES

Merion Publications Inc., 2900 Horizon Dr., King of Prussia PA 19406. Fax: (610)278-1425. Website: www.advanceweb.com. More than 30 magazines covering allied health fields, nursing, age management, long-term care and more. Byline given. Pays on publication. Buys first North American serial rights. Editorial lead time 3 months. Accepts queries by e-mail only. Guidelines available online.

Nonfiction Needs interview, new product, personal experience, technical. Query with published clips. Include name, phone & fax no. for verification. Length: 2,000 words.

Columns/Departments Phlebotomy Focus, Safety Solutions, Technology Trends, POL Perspectives, Performance in POCT & Eye on Education

$$$ AHIP COVERAGE

America's Health Insurance Plans, 601 Pennsylvania Ave. NW, South Bldg., Suite 500, Washington DC 20004. (202)778-8493. Fax: (202)331-7487. E-mail: ahip@ahip.org. Website: www.ahip.org. **75% freelance written**. Bimonthly magazine. *AHIP Coverage* is geared toward administrators in America's health insurance companies. Articles should inform and generate interest and discussion about topics on anything from patient care to regulatory issues. Estab. 1990. Circ. 12,000. Byline given. Pays within 30 days of acceptance of article in final form. Offers 30% kill fee. Publishes ms an average of 2 months after acceptance. Buys all rights. Editorial lead time 2 months. Submit seasonal material 4 months in advance. Accepts queries by mail, e-mail, fax. Accepts simultaneous submissions. Sample copy free.

Nonfiction Needs book excerpts, how-to, how industry professionals can better operate their health plans, opinion. We do not accept stories that promote products. Send complete ms. Length: 1,800-2,500 words. **Pays 65¢/word minimum.** Pays phone expenses of writers on assignment.

Photos Buys all rights.

Tips Look for health plan success stories in your community; we like to include case studies on a variety of topics—including patient care, provider relations, regulatory issues—so that our readers can learn from their colleagues. Our readers are members of our trade association and look for advice and news. Topics relating to the quality of health plans are the ones more frequently assigned to writers, whether a feature or department. We also welcome story ideas. Just send us a letter with the details.

$$$ BIOTECHNOLOGY HEALTHCARE

A Guide for Decision Makers on the Biotechnology Revolution, BioCommunications LLC, 780 Township Line Rd., Yardley PA 19067. (267)685-2783. Fax: (267)685-2966. E-mail: editors@biotechnologyhealthcare.com. Website: www.biotechnologyhealthcare.com. **75% freelance written**. Bimonthly magazine. "We are a business magazine (not an academic journal) that covers the economic, regulatory, and health policy aspects of biotech therapies and diagnostics. Our audience includes third-party payers, employer purchasers of healthcare, public healthcare agencies, and healthcare professionals who prescribe biotech therapies. Articles should be written in business magazine-style prose and should be focused on the concerns of these audiences." Estab. 2004. Circ. 36,000 (digital); 12,431 (print). Byline given. Pays on acceptance. Offers $300 kill fee. Publishes ms an average of 3 months after acceptance. Buys all rights. Editorial lead time 4 months. Accepts queries by mail, e-mail, fax. Responds in 2 weeks to queries. Responds in 1 month to mss. Sample copy available online. Guidelines by e-mail.

Nonfiction Needs book excerpts, essays, how-to, manage the cost of biologics, case studies, interview, opinion, technical, about biotech therapies, diagnostics, or devices, regulatory developments, cost analyses studies, coverage of hot-button issues in the field. **Buys 24 mss/year.** Query with published clips. Length: 1,650-3,300 words. **Pays 75-85¢/word. Pays $300-1,870 for unsolicited articles.** Pays expenses of writers on assignment.

Photos Contact: Philip Denlinger, design director. State availability. Captions, identification of subjects required. Reviews contact sheets, 4X6 or larger, color only prints, PowerPoint slides, TIF files that are 200 dpi or higher. Negotiates pay individually. Buys one time rights.

Columns/Departments Our columns are 'spoken for,' but I am always interested in pitches for new columns from qualified writers. **Buys 18 mss/year.** Query with published clips. **Pays $300 minimum for a full piece; 75¢/word maximum for ms 600-1,200 words**

Fillers Needs gags. Buys 3 cartoons mss/year. Pays $300 for cartoons upon publication.

Tips "Biotechnology represents a new age of medicine, and our readers—who struggle with how to provide healthcare benefits to employees and health insurance enrollees in an affordable way—have a strong interest in learning about how these cutting-edge, but very expensive, treatments will affect how they do their jobs. Keep in mind the interests of the managed care medical or pharmacy director, the employer HR/benefits department, the state Medicaid director, or the clinician who provides biotech therapies to patients. Our audience is highly educated, but not versed in the deep science of biotechnology, so write up to their level but be conversational and stay away from jargon. Please avoid sending consumer-health pitches, as we are not a consumer publication."

$$ BIOWORLD PERSPECTIVES

3525 Piedmont Rd., Bldg. 6, Suite 400, Atlanta GA 30305. (404)784-9093. Fax: (404)585-3072. E-mail: amanda.lyle@ahcmedia.com. Website: www.bioworld.com. **Contact:** Amanda Lyle. **70% freelance written**. Weekly e-zine Biotechnology. "We're open to a variety of articles, so long as there's a tie-in to biotech. So far, topics have included Michael Moore's film, *Sicko*, Michael Crichton's book, *Next* and its presentation of biotech patents, a comparison of real biotech innovations to those mentioned in sci-fi, personal accounts of people's experiences with diseases, critiques of science education in the West, and how immigration impacts the biotech industry. Usually there is some connection to current events, an ethical debate, or a top-of-mind issue." Estab. 2007. Circ. 4,500. Byline given. Pays on publication. No kill fee. Publishes ms an average of 1 month after acceptance. Buys all rights. Editorial lead time 2 months. Submit seasonal material 2 months in advance. Accepts queries by e-mail. Responds in 2 weeks to queries. Sample copy free. Guidelines free.

Nonfiction Needs essays, humor, inspirational, interview, opinion, personal experience. **Buys 25 mss/year.** Query with published clips. Length: 1,000-1,200 words.

$$ JEMS

The Journal of Emergency Medical Services, Elsevier Public Safety, 525 B St., Suite 1900, San Diego CA 92101. Fax: (619)699-6396. E-mail: jems.editor@elsevier.com. Website: www.jems.com. **95% freelance written**. Monthly magazine directed to personnel who serve the pre-hospital emergency medicine industry: paramedics, EMTs, emergency physicians and nurses, administrators, EMS consultants, etc. Estab. 1980. Circ. 45,000. Byline given. Pays on publication. No kill fee. Publishes ms an average of 6 months after acceptance. Buys all North American serial rights. Submit seasonal material 6 months in advance. Accepts queries by mail, e-mail, fax. Responds in 2-3 months to queries. Sample copy and writer's guidelines free. Guidelines available online.

Nonfiction Needs essays, expose, general interest, how-to, humor, interview, new product, opinion, personal experience, photo feature, technical, continuing education. **Buys 50 mss/year.** Query. **Pays $200-400.**

Photos State availability. Identification of subjects, model releases required. Reviews 4x6 prints, digital images. Offers $25 minimum per photo. Buys one time rights.

Columns/Departments Length: 850 words maximum. Query with or without published clips. **Pays $50-250.**

Tips "Please submit a 1-page cover letter with your manuscript. Your letter should answer these questions: 1) What specifically are you going to tell *JEMS* readers about prehospital medical care? 2) Why do *JEMS* readers need to know this? 3) How will you make your case (i.e., literature review, original research, interviews, personal experience, observation)? Your query should explain your qualifications, as well as include previous writing samples. Please submit online to www.eeselsevier.com/jems."

$$$ MANAGED CARE

780 Township Line Rd., Yardley PA 19067-4200. (267)685-2784. Fax: (267)685-2966. E-mail: editors_mail@managedcaremag.com. Website: www.managedcaremag.com. **Contact:** John Marcille, editor. **75% freelance written**. Monthly magazine. We emphasize practical, usable information that helps HMO medical directors and pharmacy directors cope with the options, challenges, and hazards in the rapidly changing health care industry. Estab. 1992. Circ. 44,000. Byline given. Pays on acceptance. Offers 20% kill fee. Publishes ms an average of 6 weeks after acceptance. Buys all rights. Editorial lead time 3 months. Submit seasonal material 4 months in advance. Accepts queries by mail, e-mail, fax. Responds in 3 weeks to queries. Responds in 2 months to mss. Sample copy free. Writer's guidelines on request.

Nonfiction I strongly recommend submissions via e-mail. You'll get a faster response. Needs book excerpts, general interest, trends in health-care delivery and financing, quality of care, and employee concerns, how-to, deal with requisites of managed care, such as contracts with health plans, affiliation arrangements, accredidation, computer needs, etc., original research and review articles that examine the relationship between health care delivery and financing. Also considered occasionally are personal experience, opinion, interview/profile, and humor pieces, but these must have a strong managed care angle and draw upon the insights of (if they are not written by) a knowledgeable managed care

professional. **Buys 40 mss/year.** Query with published clips. Length: 1,000-3,000 words. **Pays 75¢/word.** Pays expenses of writers on assignment.
Photos State availability. Reviews contact sheets, negatives, transparencies, prints. Negotiates payment individually. Buys first-time rights.
Tips Know our audience (health plan executives) and their needs. Study our website to see what we cover.

MEDESTHETICS

Business Education for Medical Practitioners, Creative Age Publications, 7628 Densmore Ave., Van Nuys CA 91406. E-mail: ihansen@creativeage.com. Website: www.medestheticsmagazine.com. **50% freelance written**. Bimonthly magazine covering noninvasive medical aesthetic services such as laser hair removal, skin rejuvenation, injectable fillers, and neurotoxins. "*Medesthetics* is a business to business magazine written for and distributed to dermatologists, plastic surgeons and other physicians offering noninvasive medical aesthetic services. We cover the latest equipment and products as well as legal and management issues specific to medspas, laser centers and other medical aesthetic practices." Estab. 2005. Circ. 20,000. Byline given. Pays on acceptance. Publishes ms an average of 3 months after acceptance. Buys first rights, buys electronic rights. Editorial lead time 3 months. Submit seasonal material 3 months in advance. Accepts queries by e-mail. Responds in 1 month to queries.
Nonfiction Needs new product, technical. "Does not want articles directed at consumers." **Buys 25 mss/year.** Query.
Photos State availability. Identification of subjects, model releases required. Reviews transparencies, prints. Negotiates payment individually. Buys one-time rights.
Tips "We work strictly on assignment. Query with article ideas; do not send manuscripts. We respond to queries with article assignments that specify article requirements."

$$$$ MEDICAL ECONOMICS

24950 Country Club Blvd., Suite 200, North Ormsted OH 44070. (440)243-8100. Fax: (440)891-2683. E-mail: bfeigenbaum@advanstar.com. Website: www.memag.com. **Contact:** Robert A. Feigenbaum, articles editor. Semimonthly magazine (24 times/year). *Medical Economics* is a national business magazine read by M.D.s and D.O.s in office-based practice. Our purpose is to be informative and useful to practicing physicians in the professional and financial management of their practices. We look for contributions from writers who know—or will make the effort to learn—the nonclinical concerns of today's physician. These writers must be able to address those concerns in feature articles that are clearly written and that convey authoritative information and advice. Our articles focus very narrowly on a subject and explore it in depth. Circ. 210,000. Pays on acceptance. Offers 25% kill fee. Buys all rights. Accepts queries by mail, e-mail, fax. Sample copy available online. Guidelines available online.
Nonfiction Articles about private physicians in innovative, pioneering, and/or controversial situations affecting medical care delivery, patient relations, or malpractice prevention/litigation; personal finance topics. We do not want overviews or pieces that only skim the surface of a general topic. We address physician readers in a conversational, yet no-nonsense tone, quoting recognized experts on office management, personal finance, patient relations, and medical-legal issues. Mss should be double-spaced, with a heading that includes your name, address, daytime phone, and if you have them, fax number and e-mail address. Be sure to include your CV. Send the manuscript and other information to manuscripts@advanstar.com as either message text or a Word attachment. If the ms was mailed to us between January 1 and October 31, it will be entered automatically in that year's writing contest. Length: 1,000-1,800 words. **Pays $1,200-2,000 for assigned articles.** Pays expenses of writers on assignment. Expenses over $100 must be approved in advance—receipts required. Will negotiate an additional fee for photos, if accepted for publication.
Photos Will negotiate an additional fee for photos accepted for publication.
Tips We look for articles about physicians who run high-quality, innovative practices suited to the age of managed care. We also look for how-to service articles—on practice-management and personal-finance topics—which must contain anecdotal examples to support the advice. Read the magazine carefully, noting its style and content. Then send detailed proposals or outlines on subjects that would interest our mainly primary-care physician readers.

MIDWIFERY TODAY

P.O Box 2672, Eugene OR 97402. Fax: (541)344-1422. E-mail: mgeditor@midwiferytoday.com. Website: www.midwiferytoday.com. **Contact:** Kelly Moyer, managing editor. **95% freelance written**. Quarterly magazine. "Through networking and education, *Midwifery Today*'s missions is to return midwifery to its rightful position in the family; to make midwifery care the norm throughout the world; and to redefine midwifery as a vital partnership with women." Estab. 1986. Circ. 3,000. Byline given. No kill fee. Publishes ms an average of 5 months after acceptance. Editorial lead time 3-9 months. Submit seasonal material 6 months in advance. Accepts queries by e-mail. Accepts simultaneous submissions. Responds in 2 weeks to queries. Responds in 1 month to mss. Sample copy available online. Guidelines available online.

Nonfiction "All articles must relate to pregnancy or birth and provide something of value to birth practitioners." Needs book excerpts, essays, how-to, humor, inspirational, interview, opinion, personal experience, photo feature, clinical research, herbal articles, birth stories, business advice. **Buys 60 mss/year.** Send complete ms. Length: 300-3,000 words.

Photos Contact: Cathy Guy, layout designer. State availability. Model releases required. Reviews prints, GIF/JPEG files. $15-$50 per photo. Buys one time rights.

Columns/Departments News: "In My Opinion" (150-750 words). **Buys 8 mss/year.** Send complete ms.

Poetry Needs avant-garde, haiku, light verse, traditional. Does not want poetry unrelated to pregnancy or birth. Buys 4/year poems/year. Maximum line length of 25.

Fillers Contact: Jan Tritten. **Needs anecdotes, facts, newsbreaks.** Length: 100-600 words.

Tips "Use Chicago Manual of Style formatting."

$$$$ MODERN PHYSICIAN

Essential Business News for the Executive Physician, Crain Communications, 360 N. Michigan Ave., 5th Floor, Chicago IL 60601. (312)649-5439. Fax: (312)280-3183. E-mail: dburda@crain.com. Website: www.modernphysician.com. **Contact:** David Burda, editor. **10% freelance written**. Monthly magazine covering business and management news for doctors. *Modern Physician* offers timely topical news features with lots of business information—revenues, earnings, financial data. Estab. 1997. Circ. 24,000. Byline given. Pays on acceptance. No kill fee. Publishes ms an average of 2 months after acceptance. Buys all rights. Editorial lead time 2 months. Accepts queries by mail, e-mail. Responds in 6 weeks to queries. Sample copy free. Writer's guidelines sent after query.

Nonfiction Length: 750-1,000 words. **Pays 75¢-$1/word. (Does not pay for Guest Commentaries.)**

Tips Read the publication, know our audience, and come up with a good story idea that we haven't thought of yet.

THE NEW ZEALAND MEDICAL JOURNAL

Dept. of Surgery, Christchurch Hospital, P.O. Box 4345, Christchurch New Zealand. (64)(3)364-1277. Fax: (64)(3)364-1683. E-mail: nzmj@cdhb.govt.nz. Website: www.nzma.org.nz/journal. **Contact:** Brennan Edwardes, production editor. No kill fee. Accepts queries by e-mail. Guidelines available online.

Nonfiction Editorials (1,200 words), Obituaries (600 words and a photo), Case Reports (600 words and a photo), Viewpoints (3,000 words), Medical Image (50-200 words and 1-4 images), Letters and Original Articles. Send complete ms.

$$ OPTICAL PRISM

The Magazine for Eyecare Professionals, 250 The East Mall, Suite 1113, Toronto ON M9B 6L3 Canada. (416)233-2487. Fax: (416)233-1746. E-mail: info@opticalprism.ca. Website: www.opticalprism.ca. **30% freelance written**. Magazine published 10 times/year covering Canada's optical industry. We cover the health, fashion and business aspects of the optical industry in Canada. Estab. 1982. Circ. 10,000. Byline given. Pays on publication. Publishes ms an average of 2 months after acceptance. Buys first rights, buys electronic rights. Editorial lead time 3 months. Submit seasonal material 3 months in advance. Accepts queries by mail, e-mail. Accepts previously published material. Accepts simultaneous submissions.

Nonfiction Needs interview, related to optical industry. Query. Length: 1,000-1,600 words. **Pays 40¢/word (Canadian).** Sometimes pays expenses of writers on assignment.

Columns/Departments Insight (profiles on people in the eyewear industry—also sometimes schools and businesses), 700-1,000 words. **Buys 5 mss/year.** Query. **Pays 40¢/word.**

Tips Please look at our editorial themes, which are on our website, and pitch articles that are related to the themes for each issue.

$$ PLASTIC SURGERY NEWS

American Society of Plastic Surgeons, 444 E. Algonquin Rd., Arlington Heights IL 60005. Fax: (847)981-5458. E-mail: mss@plasticsurgery.org. Website: www.plasticsurgery.org. **Contact:** Mike Stokes, managing editor. **15% freelance written**. Monthly tabloid covering plastic surgery. *Plastic Surgery News* readership is comprised primarily of plastic surgeons and those involved with the specialty (nurses, techs, industry). The magazine is distributed via subscription and to all members of the American Society of Plastic Surgeons. The magazine covers a variety of specialty-specific news and features, including trends, legislation and clinical information. Estab. 1960. Circ. 6,000. Byline given. Pays on acceptance. Offers 25% kill fee. Publishes ms an average of 1-2 months after acceptance. Buys first North American serial rights, buys simultaneous rights, buys electronic rights. Editorial lead time 1-3 months. Accepts queries by e-mail. Accepts simultaneous submissions. Responds in 2 weeks to queries. Responds in 3 months to mss. Sample copy for 10 First-Class stamps. Guidelines by e-mail.

Nonfiction Needs expose, how-to, new product, technical. Does not want celebrity or entertainment based pieces. **Buys 20 mss/year.** Query with published clips. Length: 1,000-3,500 words. **Pays 20-40¢/word.** Sometimes pays expenses of writers on assignment.

Columns/Departments Digital Plastic Surgeon (technology), 1,500-1,700 words.

$$ PODIATRY MANAGEMENT

Kane Communications, Inc., P.O. Box 750129, Forest Hills NY 11375. (718)897-9700. Fax: (718)896-5747. E-mail: bblock@podiatrym.com. Website: www.podiatrym.com. Magazine published 9 times/year for practicing podiatrists. "Aims to help the doctor of podiatric medicine to build a bigger, more successful practice, to conserve and invest his money, to keep him posted on the economic, legal, and sociological changes that affect him." Estab. 1982. Circ. 16,500. Byline given. Pays on publication. $75 kill fee. Buys first North American serial rights, buys second serial (reprint) rights. Submit seasonal material 4 months in advance. Accepts queries by e-mail. Accepts simultaneous submissions. Responds in 2 weeks to queries. Sample copy for $5 and 9 × 12 SAE. Guidelines for #10 SASE.

Nonfiction "Book excerpts, general interest (taxes, investments, estate, estate planning, recreation, hobbies), how-to (establish and collect fees, practice management, organize office routines, supervise office assistants, handle patient relations), interview/profile (about interesting or well-known podiatrists), personal experience. These subjects are the mainstay of the magazine, but offbeat articles and humor are always welcome." **Buys 35 mss/year.** Length: 1,500-3,000 words. **Pays $350-600.**

Reprints Send photocopy. Pays 33% of amount paid for an original article.

Photos State availability. Pays $15 for b&w contact sheet. Buys one-time rights.

Tips "Articles should be tailored to podiatrists, and preferably should contain quotes from podiatrists."

$$ PRIMARY CARE OPTOMETRY NEWS

The Leading Clinical Newspaper for Optometrists, SLACK Incorporated, 6900 Grove Rd., Thorofare NJ 08086. (856)848-1000. Fax: (856)848-6091. E-mail: editor@PCONSuperSite.com. Website: www.pconsupersite.com. **Contact:** Nancy Hemphill, editor-in-chief. **5% freelance written**. Monthly tabloid covering optometry. *Primary Care Optometry News* strives to be the optometric professional's definitive information source by delivering timely, accurate, authoritative and balanced reports on clinical issues, socioeconomic and legislative affairs, ophthalmic industry and research developments, as well as updates on diagnostic and therapeutic regimens and techniques to enhance the quality of patient care. Estab. 1996. Circ. 39,000. Byline given. Pays on publication. Offers 50% kill fee. Publishes ms an average of 2 months after acceptance. Buys all rights. Editorial lead time 2 months. Accepts queries by mail, e-mail, fax, phone. Responds in 2 weeks to queries. Sample copy available online. Guidelines by e-mail.

Nonfiction Needs how-to, interview, new product, opinion, technical. **Buys 20 mss/year.** Query. Length: 800-1,000 words. **Pays $350-500.** Sometimes pays expenses of writers on assignment.

Photos State availability. Captions, model releases required. Reviews GIF/JPEG files. Offers no additional payment for photos accepted with ms. Buys all rights.

Columns/Departments What's Your Diagnosis (case presentation), 800 words. **Buys 40 mss/year.** Query. **Pays $100-500.**

Tips Either e-mail or call the editor-in-chief with questions or story ideas.

$$ ⊘ STRATEGIC HEALTH CARE MARKETING

Health Care Communications, 11 Heritage Lane, P.O. Box 594, Rye NY 10580. (914)967-6741. Fax: (914)967-3054. E-mail: healthcomm@aol.com. Website: www.strategichealthcare.com. **90% freelance written**. Monthly newsletter covering health care marketing and management in a wide range of settings, including hospitals, medical group practices, home health services, and managed care organizations. Emphasis is on strategies and techniques employed within the health care field and relevant applications from other service industries. Works with published/established writers only. Estab. 1984. Byline given. Pays on publication. Offers 25% kill fee. Publishes ms an average of 2 months after acceptance. Buys first North American serial rights. Accepts queries by mail, e-mail. Responds in 1 month to queries. Sample copy for sae with 9 × 12 envelope and 3 First-Class stamps. Guidelines sent with sample copy only.

- *Strategic Health Care Marketing* is specifically seeking writers with expertise/contacts in managed care, patient satisfaction, and e-health.

Nonfiction Preferred format for feature articles is the case history approach to solving marketing problems. Crisp, almost telegraphic style. Needs how-to, interview, new product, technical. **Buys 50 mss/year.** Query. Length: 700-3,000 words. **Pays $100-500.** Sometimes pays expenses of writers on assignment with prior authorization.

Photos Photos, unless necessary for subject explanation, are rarely used. State availability. Captions, model releases required. Reviews contact sheets. Offers $10-30/photo. Buys one time rights.

Tips "Writers with prior experience on the business beat for newspapers or newsletters will do well. We require a sophisticated, in-depth knowledge of health care and business. This is not a consumer publication—the writer with knowledge of both health care and marketing will excel. Absolutely no unsolicited manuscripts; any received will be returned or discarded unread."

$ $ $ $ UNIQUE OPPORTUNITIES

The Physician's Resource, U O, Inc., 214 S. 8th St., Suite 502, Louisville KY 40202. Fax: (502)587-0848. E-mail: bett@uoworks.com. Website: www.uoworks.com. **55% freelance written.** Bimonthly magazine covering physician relocation and career development. Published for physicians interested in a new career opportunity. It offers physicians useful information and first-hand experiences to guide them in making informed decisions concerning their first or next career opportunity. It provides features and regular columns about specific aspects of the search process, practice management and career development. Estab. 1991. Circ. 80,000 physicians. Byline given. Pays 1 month after acceptance. Offers 10% kill fee. Publishes ms an average of 2 months after acceptance. Buys first North American serial rights, buys electronic rights. Editorial lead time 3 months. Submit seasonal material 6 months in advance. Responds in 2 months to queries. Sample copy for sae with 9 × 12 envelope and 6 First-Class stamps. Guidelines available online.

Nonfiction Features: Practice options and information of interest to physicians in career transition. **Buys 14 mss/year.** Query with published clips. Length: 1,500-3,500 words. **Pays $750-2,000.** Sometimes pays expenses of writers on assignment.

Photos State availability. Identification of subjects, model releases required. Negotiates payment individually. Buys electronic rights.

Columns/Departments Remarks (opinion from physicians and industry experts on physician career issues), 900-1,500 words. **No payment.**

Tips Submit queries via letter or e-mail with ideas for articles that directly pertain to physician career issues, such as specific or unusual practice opportunities, relocation, or practice establishment subjects, etc. Feature articles are most open to freelancers. Physician sources are most important with tips and advice from both the physicians and business experts. Physicians like to know what other physicians think and do, and appreciate suggestions from other business people.

Music Trade

$ ⊘ INTERNATIONAL BLUEGRASS

International Bluegrass Music Association, 2 Music Circle S., Suite 100, Nashville TN 37203. (615)256-3222. Fax: (615)256-0450. E-mail: info@ibma.org. Website: www.ibma.org. www.discoverbluegrass.com. **10% freelance written.** Bimonthly newsletter. "We are the business publication for the bluegrass music industry. IBMA believes that our music has growth potential. We are interested in hard news and features concerning how to reach that potential and how to conduct business more effectively." Estab. 1985. Circ. 4,500. Byline given. Pays on publication. No kill fee. Publishes ms an average of 2 months after acceptance. Buys one-time rights. Submit seasonal material 4 months in advance. Accepts queries by mail, e-mail, phone. Accepts simultaneous submissions. Responds in 1 month to queries. Sample copy for sae with 6x9 envelope and 2 First-Class stamps.

Nonfiction Unsolicited mss are not accepted, but unsolicited news about the industry is accepted. Needs book excerpts, essays, how-to, conduct business effectively within bluegrass music, new product, opinion. No interview/profiles/feature stories of performers (rare exceptions) or fans. **Buys 6 mss/year.** Query. Length: 1,000-1,200 words. **Pays up to $150/article for assigned articles.**

Reprints Send photocopy of article and information about when and where the article previously appeared. Does not pay for reprints.

Photos Send photos. Captions, identification of subjects, True required. Offers no additional payment for photos accepted with ms. Buys one time rights.
Columns/Departments Staff written.
Tips "We're interested in a slant strongly toward the business end of bluegrass music. We're especially looking for material dealing with audience development and how to book bluegrass bands outside of the existing market."

$$$ MIX MAGAZINE

Primedia Business Magazines, 6400 Hollis St., Suite 12, Emeryville CA 94608. Fax: (510)653-5142. E-mail: tkenny@mixonline.com. Website: www.mixonline.com. **Contact:** Tom Kenny, Group Editorial Director. **50% freelance written**. Monthly magazine covering pro audio. *Mix* is a trade publication geared toward professionals in the music/sound production recording and post-production industries. We include stories about music production, sound for picture, live sound, etc. We prefer in-depth technical pieces that are applications-oriented. Estab. 1977. Circ. 50,000. Byline given. Pays on publication. Offers 50% kill fee. Publishes ms an average of 3 months after acceptance. Buys all rights. Editorial lead time 10 weeks. Submit seasonal material 3 months in advance. Responds in 2 weeks to queries. Responds in 1 month to mss. Sample copy for $6. Guidelines free.
Nonfiction Needs how-to, interview, new product, technical, project/studio spotlights. Special issues: Sound for picture supplement (April, September), Design issue. **Buys 60 mss/year.** Query. Length: 500-2,000 words. **Pays $300-800 for assigned articles. Pays $300-400 for unsolicited articles.**
Photos State availability. Captions, identification of subjects required. Reviews 4 × 5 transparencies, prints. Negotiates payment individually. Buys one time rights.

$$ THE MUSIC & SOUND RETAILER

Testa Communications, 25 Willowdale Ave., Port Washington NY 11050. (516)767-2500. E-mail: bberk@testa.com. Website: www.msretailer.com. **20% freelance written**. Monthly magazine covering business to business publication for music instrument products. *The Music & Sound Retailer* covers the music instrument industry and is sent to all dealers of these products, including Guitar Center, Sam Ash, and all small independent stores. Estab. 1983. Circ. 11,700. Byline given. Pays on acceptance. Offers $100 kill fee. Buys first North American serial rights. Editorial lead time 1 month. Submit seasonal material 2 months in advance. Accepts queries by e-mail. Accepts simultaneous submissions. Responds in 2 weeks to queries. Responds in 1 month to mss. Sample copy for #10 sase. Guidelines free.
Nonfiction Needs how-to, new product, opinion, (does not mean letters to the editor), personal experience. Concert and CD reviews are never published; interviews with musicians. **Buys 25 mss/year.** Query with published clips. Length: 1,000-2,000 words. **Pays $300-450 for assigned articles. Pays $300-450 for unsolicited articles.** Sometimes pays expenses of writers on assignment.
Photos Send photos. Captions required. Reviews GIF/JPEG files. Offers no additional payment for photos accepted with ms. Buys one-time rights.

MUSIC EDUCATORS JOURNAL

MENC: The National Association for Music Education, Sage Publications, Inc., 2455 Teller Rd., Thousand Oaks CA 91320. (805)499-0721. Fax: (805)499-8096. E-mail: ellaw@menc.org. Website: www.sagepub.com. **Contact:** Ella Wilcox, editor. Quarterly music education journal published in March, June, September, and December. "Offers scholarly and practical articles on music teaching approaches and philosophies, instructional techniques, current trends and issues in music education in schools and communities and the latest in products and services. Especially welcome are topics of value, assistance, or inspiration to practicing music teachers." Accepts queries by e-mail. Articles should not have been previously published elsewhere.Sample copy available. E-mail online request form. Guidelines available online.
Nonfiction "Music Educators Journal (MEJ) encourages music education professionals to submit manuscripts about all phases of music education in schools and communities, practical instructional techniques, teaching philosophy, and current issues in music teaching and learning. The main goal of MEJ is to advance music education." Authors should avoid personal asides that are not relevant to the primary topic, as well as content that promotes a person, performing group, institution, or product. Submissions should be grounded in the professional literature. Articles with no citations or reference to previous work in the area will not be considered for publication. Manuscripts should be submitted electronically to http://mc.manuscriptcentral.com/mej. Length: 1,800-3,500/words **Each author receives two copies of the issue in which his or her article appears; authors may also order additional copies.**

Photos "Up to three photographs are a welcome part of accepted articles. Each photograph must be accompanied by a short caption and photo credit information. Please contact Ella Wilcox at ellaw@menc.org if you feel it is necessary to have more than three photographs included with your article. Acceptable file formats for photographs include TIFF, EPS, and JPEG, and PDF Microsoft Application Files are acceptable."

$$$ OPERA NEWS

Metropolitan Opera Guild, Inc., 70 Lincoln Center Plaza, New York NY 10023-6593. (212)769-7080. Fax: (212)769-8500. E-mail: info@operanews.com. Website: www.operanews.com. **75% freelance written**. Monthly magazine for people interested in opera; the opera professional as well as the opera audience. Estab. 1936. Circ. 105,000. Byline given. Pays on publication. No kill fee. Publishes ms an average of 4 months after acceptance. Buys first serial rights only. Editorial lead time 4 months. Sample copy for $5.
Nonfiction Most articles are commissioned in advance. Monthly issues feature articles on various aspects of opera worldwide. Emphasis is on high quality writing and an intellectual interest to the opera-oriented public. Needs historical, interview, informational, think pieces, opera, CD, and DVD reviews, book reviews. Query. Length: 1,500-2,800 words. **Pays $450-1,200.** Sometimes pays expenses of writers on assignment.
Photos State availability. Buys one time rights.
Columns/Departments Buys 24 mss/year.

$ OVERTONES

Official Bimonthly Journal of the American Guild of English Handbell Ringers, American Guild of English Handbell Ringers, P.O. Box 1765, Findlay OH 45839. E-mail: editor@agehr.org. Website: www.agehr.org. **80% freelance written**. Bimonthly magazine covering English handbell ringing and conducting. "AGEHR is dedicated to advancing the musical art of handbell/handchime ringing through education, community and communication. The purpose of 'Overtones' is to provide a printed resource to support that mission. We offer how-to articles, inspirational stories and interviews with well-known people and unique ensembles." Estab. 1954. Circ. 8,000. Byline given. Pays on publication. No kill fee. Publishes ms an average of 4 months after acceptance. Buys all rights. Editorial lead time 4 months. Submit seasonal material 4 months in advance. Accepts queries by mail, e-mail. Accepts previously published material. Responds in 1 month to queries and to mss. Sample copy by e-mail. Guidelines by e-mail.
Nonfiction Needs essays, general interest, historical, how-to, inspirational, interview, religious, technical. Does not want product news, promotional material. **Buys 8-12 mss/year.** Send complete ms. Length: 1,200-2,400 words. **Pays $120.** Sometimes pays expenses of writers on assignment.
Photos State availability of or send photos. Captions required. Reviews 8 × 10 prints, JPEG/TIFF files. Offers no additional payment for photos accepted with ms. Buys one-time rights.
Columns/Departments Handbells in Education (topics covering the use of handbells in school setting, teaching techniques, etc.); Handbells in Worship (topics and ideas for using handbells in a church setting); Tips & Tools (variety of topics from ringing and conducting techniques to score study to maintenance); Community Connections (topics covering issues relating to the operation/administration/techniques for community groups); Music Reviews (recommendations and descriptions of music following particular themes, i.e., youth music, difficult music, seasonal, etc.), all 800-1,200 words. Query. **Pays $80.**
Tips "When writing profiles/interviews, try to determine what is especially unique or inspiring about the individual or ensemble and write from that viewpoint. Please have some expertise in handbells, education, or church music to write department articles."

$$ VENUES TODAY

The News Behind the Headlines, 18350 Mount Langley, #201, Fountain Valley CA 92708. Fax: (714)378-0040. E-mail: linda@venuestoday.com. Website: www.venuestoday.com. **Contact:** Linda Deckard, editor-in-chief. **70% freelance written**. Weekly magazine covering the live entertainment industry and the buildings that host shows and sports. "We need writers who can cover an exciting industry from the business side, not the consumer side. The readers are venue managers, concert promoters, those in the concert and sports business, not the audience for concerts and sports. So we need business journalists who can cover the latest news and trends in the market." Estab. 2002. Byline given. Pays on publication. Publishes ms an average of 1 month after acceptance. Buys all rights. Editorial lead time 1-2 months. Submit seasonal material 1-2 months in advance. Accepts queries by mail, e-mail, fax. Accepts simultaneous submissions. Responds in 1 week to queries. Sample copy available online. Guidelines free.

Nonfiction Needs interview, photo feature, technical, travel. Does not want customer slant, marketing pieces. Query with published clips. Length: 500-1,500 words. **Pays $100-250.** Pays expenses of writers on assignment.
Photos State availability. Captions, identification of subjects required. Reviews GIF/JPEG files. Negotiates payment individually. Buys one-time rights.
Columns/Departments Venue News (new buildings, trend features, etc.); Bookings (show tours, business side); Marketing (of shows, sports, convention centers); Concessions (food, drink, merchandise). Length: 500-1,200 words. **Buys 250 mss/year.** Query with published clips. **Pays $100-250.**
Fillers Needs gags. Buys 6 mss/year. Pays $100-300.

Office Environment & Equipment

$ $ OFFICE DEALER

The Independent Dealer's Playbook for Success, OfficeVision, Inc., 252 N. Main St., Suite 200, Mt. Airy NC 27030. (336)783-0000. Fax: (336)783-0045. E-mail: scottc@allthingsoffice.com. Website: www.os-od.com. **Contact:** Scott Cullen, editorial director. **80% freelance written**. Quarterly magazine covering the office product industry. *Office Dealer* serves independent resellers of office supplies, furniture, and equipment. Estab. 1987. Circ. 13,458. Byline given. Pays on publication. No kill fee. Buys all rights. Editorial lead time 3 months. Submit seasonal material 5 months in advance. Accepts queries by mail, e-mail, fax. Accepts simultaneous submissions. Responds in 1 month to queries. Sample copy and writer's guidelines free.
Nonfiction Needs interview, new product, technical. **Buys 10 mss/year.** Length: 700-1,500 words. **Pays $300-500.**
Tips See editorial calendar posted online. Feature articles are written by our staff or by freelance writers. We may accept corporate 'byline' articles. Queries should be a single page or less and include an SASE for response. Samples of a writer's past work and clips concerning the proposed story are helpful.

$ $ OFFICE SOLUTIONS

The Magazine for All Things Office, OfficeVision Inc., 252 N. Main St., Suite 200, Mt. Airy NC 27030. (336)783-0000. Fax: (336)783-0045. E-mail: scottc@allthingsoffice.com. Website: www.os-od.com. **Contact:** Scott Cullen, editorial dir. **80% freelance written**. Quarterly magazine covering the office personnel and environment. *Office Solutions* subscribers are responsible for the management of their personnel and office environments. Estab. 1984. Circ. 60,650. Byline given. Pays on publication. No kill fee. Buys all rights. Editorial lead time 3 months. Submit seasonal material 4 months in advance. Accepts queries by mail, e-mail, fax. Accepts simultaneous submissions. Responds in 1 month to queries. Sample copy and writer's guidelines free.
Nonfiction Our audience is responsible for general management of an office environment and personnel, so articles should be broad in scope and not too technical in nature. Needs interview, new product, technical, human resources. **Buys 18 mss/year.** Query. Length: 1,500-2,200 words. **Pays $200-450.**
Tips See editorial calendar posted online. Feature articles are written by our staff or by freelance writers. Queries should be a single page or less and include an SASE for response. Samples of a writer's past work and clips concerning the proposed story are helpful.

STATIONERY NEWS

Yaffa Publishing, 17-21 Bellevue St., Surry Hills NSW 2010 Australia. (61)(2)9281-2333. Fax: (61)(2)9281-2750. E-mail: michaelleader@yaffa.com.au. Website: www.yaffa.com.au. **Contact:** Michael Leader, editor. Monthly magazine covering office product reselling chain. Circ. 5,000.
Nonfiction Core target is Australian and New Zealand stationery and office product resellers. Needs general interest, interview, new product, technical. Query.

Paper

$ $ THE PAPER STOCK REPORT

News and Trends of the Paper Recycling Markets, McEntee Media Corp., 9815 Hazelwood Ave., Cleveland OH 44149. (440)238-6603. Fax: (440)238-6712. E-mail: ken@recycle.cc. Website: www.recycle.cc. Biweekly newsletter covering market trends, news in the paper recycling industry. Audience is interested in new innovative markets, applications for recovered scrap paper, as well as new laws and regulations impacting recycling. Estab. 1990. Circ. 2,000. Byline given. Pays on publication. No kill fee. Publishes ms an average of 1 month after acceptance. Buys first rights, buys all rights. Editorial lead time 2 months. Submit seasonal material 2 months in advance. Accepts queries by mail, e-mail, fax, phone. Accepts simultaneous submissions. Responds in 1 month to queries. Sample copy for #10 SAE with 55¢ postage.

Nonfiction Needs book excerpts, essays, expose, general interest, historical, interview, new product, opinion, photo feature, technical, all related to paper recycling. **Buys 0-13 mss/year.** Send complete ms. Length: 250-1,000 words. **Pays $50-250 for assigned articles. Pays $25-250 for unsolicited articles.** Pays expenses of writers on assignment.

Photos State availability. Identification of subjects required. Reviews contact sheets. Negotiates payment individually.

Tips Article must be valuable to readers in terms of presenting new market opportunities or cost-saving measures.

$$ RECYCLED PAPER NEWS

Independent Coverage of Environmental Issues in the Paper Industry, McEntee Media Corp., 9815 Hazelwood Ave., Cleveland OH 44149. (440)238-6603. Fax: (440)238-6712. E-mail: rpn@recycle.cc. Website: www.recycle.cc. **10% freelance written**. Monthly newsletter. We are interested in any news impacting the paper recycling industry, as well as other environmental issues in the paper industry, i.e., water/air pollution, chlorine-free paper, forest conservation, etc., with special emphasis on new laws and regulations. Estab. 1990. Pays on publication. No kill fee. Publishes ms an average of 2 months after acceptance. Buys first rights, buys all rights. Editorial lead time 1 month. Submit seasonal material 1 month in advance. Accepts queries by mail, e-mail, fax, phone. Accepts simultaneous submissions. Responds in 2 months to queries. Sample copy for 9 × 12 SAE and 55¢ postage. Guidelines for #10 sase.

Nonfiction Needs book excerpts, essays, how-to, interview, new product, opinion, personal experience, photo feature, technical, new business, legislation, regulation, business expansion. **Buys 0-5 mss/year.** Query with published clips. **Pays $10-500.**

Columns/Departments Query with published clips. **Pays $10-500.**

Tips We appreciate leads on local news regarding recycling or composting, i.e., new facilities or businesses, new laws and regulations, unique programs, situations that impact supply and demand for recyclables, etc. International developments are also of interest.

Pets

$$ PET AGE

H.H. Backer Associates, Inc., 18 S. Michigan Ave., Suite 1100, Chicago IL 60603. (312)578-1818. Fax: (312)578-1819. E-mail: cfoster@hhbacker.com. Website: www.petage.com. **Contact:** Cathy Foster, senior editor. **90% freelance written**. Monthly magazine for pet/pet supplies retailers, covering the complete pet industry. Prefers to work with published/established writers. Will consider new writers. Estab. 1971. Circ. 23,022. Byline given. Pays on acceptance. No kill fee. Publishes ms an average of 3 months after acceptance. Buys first North American serial rights, buys one-time rights. Sample copy and writer's guidelines available.

Nonfiction How-to articles on marketing/merchandising companion animals and supplies; how-to articles on retail store management; industry trends and issues; animal health care and husbandry. No profiles of industry members and/or retail establishments or consumer-oriented pet articles. **Buys 80 mss/year.** Query with published clips. Length: 1,500-2,200 words. **Pays 15¢/word for assigned articles.** Pays documented telephone expenses.

Photos Captions, identification of subjects required. Reviews transparencies, slides, and 5 × 7 glossy prints. Buys one time rights.

Tips This is a business publication for busy people, and must be very informative in easy-to-read, concise style. Articles about animal care or business practices should have the pet-retail angle or cover issues specific to this industry.

$$ PET PRODUCT NEWS INTERNATIONAL

BowTie News, P.O. Box 6050, Mission Viejo CA 92690. (949)855-8822. Fax: (949)855-3045. E-mail: scollins@bowtieinc.com. Website: www.bowtieinc.com. **Contact:** Sherri Collins, editor. **70% freelance written**. Monthly magazine. *Pet Product News* covers business/legal and economic issues of importance to pet product retailers, suppliers, and distributors, as well as product information and animal care issues. We're looking for straightforward articles on the proper care of dogs, cats, birds, fish, and exotics (reptiles, hamsters, etc.) as information the retailers can pass on to new pet owners. Estab. 1947. Circ. 26,000. Byline given. Pays on publication. Offers $50 kill fee. Buys first North American serial rights. Editorial lead time 3 months. Submit seasonal material 4 months in advance. Accepts queries by mail, fax. Responds in 2 weeks to queries. Sample copy for $5.50. Guidelines for #10 sase.

Nonfiction Needs general interest, interview, new product, photo feature, technical. No cute animal stories or those directed at the pet owner. **Buys 150 mss/year.** Query. Length: 500-1,500 words. **Pays $175-350.**

Columns/Departments The Pet Dealer News™ (timely news stories about business issues affecting pet retailers), 800-1,000 words; Industry News (news articles representing coverage of pet product suppliers, manufacturers, distributors, and associations), 800-1,000 words; Pet Health News™ (pet health and articles relevant to pet retailers); Dog & Cat (products and care of), 1,000-1,500 words; Fish & Bird (products and care of), 1,000-1,500 words; Small Mammals (products and care of), 1,000-1,500 words; Pond/Water Garden (products and care of), 1,000-1,500 words. **Buys 120 mss/year.** Query. **Pays $150-300.**

Tips Be more than just an animal lover. You have to know about health, nutrition, and care. Product and business articles are told in both an informative and entertaining style. Talk to pet store owners and see what they need to know to be better business people in general, who have to deal with everything from balancing the books and free trade agreements to animal rights activists. All sections are open, but you have to be knowledgeable on the topic, be it taxes, management, profit building, products, nutrition, animal care, or marketing.

Plumbing, Heating, Air Conditioning & Refrigeration

$$ HEATING PLUMBING AIR CONDITIONING

One Mount Pleasant Rd., Toronto ON M4Y 2Y5 Canada. (416)764-1549. **20% freelance written**. Monthly magazine. For a prompt reply, enclose a sheet on which is typed a statement either approving or rejecting the suggested article which can either be checked off, or a quick answer written in and signed and returned. Estab. 1923. Circ. 16,500. Pays on publication. No kill fee. Publishes ms an average of 3 months after acceptance. Accepts queries by mail, e-mail, phone. Responds in 2 months to queries.

Nonfiction News, business management articles that inform, educate, motivate, and help readers to be more efficient and profitable. Readers design, manufacture, install, sell, service maintain, or supply all mechanical components and systems in residential, commercial, institutional, and industrial installations across Canada. Needs how-to, technical. Length: 1,000-1,500 words. **Pays 25¢/word.** Sometimes pays expenses of writers on assignment.

Reprints Send tearsheet or photocopy with rights for sale noted and information about when and where the material previously appeared.

Photos Prefers 4 × 5 or 5 × 7 glossies, high resolution JPEGS. Photos purchased with ms.

Tips Topics must relate directly to the day-to-day activities of *HPAC* readers in Canada. Must be detailed, with specific examples, quotes from specific people or authorities—show depth. We specifically want material from other parts of Canada besides southern Ontario. U.S. material must relate to Canadian readers' concerns. We primarily want articles that show *HPAC* readers how they can increase their sales and business step-by-step based on specific examples of what others have done.

$$ SNIPS MAGAZINE

BNP Media, 2401 W. Big Beaver Rd., Suite 700, Troy MI 48084. (248)244-6416. Fax: (248)362-0317. E-mail: mcconnellm@bnpmedia.com. Website: www.snipsmag.com. **2% freelance written**. Monthly magazine for sheet metal, heating, ventilation, air conditioning, and metal roofing contractors. Estab. 1932. No kill fee. Publishes ms an average of 3 months after acceptance. Buys all rights. Accepts queries by mail, e-mail, fax, phone. Call for writer's guidelines.

Nonfiction Material should deal with information about contractors who do sheet metal, heating, air conditioning, ventilation, and metal roofing work; also about successful advertising and/or marketing campaigns conducted by these contractors and the results. Under 1,000 words unless on special assignment. **Pays $200-300.**

Photos Negotiable.

Printing

$$ THE BIG PICTURE

The Business of Wide Format, ST Media Group International, 11262 Cornell Park Dr., Cincinnati OH 45242. (513)263-9377. E-mail: lauren.mosko@stmediagroup.com. Website: www.bigpicture.net. **20% freelance written**. Monthly magazine covering wide-format digital printing. *The Big Picture* covers wide-format printing as well as digital workflow, finishing, display, capture, and other related topics. Our 21,500 readers include digital print providers, sign shops, commercial printers, in-house print operations, and other print providers across the country. We are primarily interested in the technology and work processes behind wide-format printing, but also run trend features on segments of the industry (innovations in point-of-purchase displays, floor graphics, fine-art printing, vehicle wrapping, textile printing, etc.). Estab. 1996. Circ. 21,500 controlled. Byline given. Pays on publication. Offers 20% kill fee. Publishes ms an average of 2 months after acceptance. Buys first print and Web rights. Editorial lead time 2 months. Accepts queries by e-mail. Accepts previously published material. Accepts simultaneous submissions. Responds in 2 weeks to queries. Responds in 1 month to mss. Sample copy available online. Guidelines available.

Nonfiction Needs how-to, interview, new product, technical. Does not want broad consumer-oriented pieces that don't speak to the business and technical aspects of producing print for pay. **Buys 15-30 mss/year.** Query with published clips. Length: 1500-2500 words. **Pays $500-700 for assigned articles.** Sometimes (limit agreed upon in advance)

Photos Send photos. Reviews GIF/JPEG files hi-res. Offers no additional payment for photos accepted with ms.

Tips Interest in and knowledge of the printing industry will position you well to break into this market.

$$ IN-PLANT GRAPHICS

North American Publishing Co., 1500 Spring Garden St., Suite 1200, Philadelphia PA 19130. (215)238-5321. Fax: (215)238-5457. E-mail: bobneubauer@napco.com. Website: www.ipgonline.com. **40% freelance written**. "*In-Plant Graphics* features articles designed to help in-house printing departments increase productivity, save money, and stay competitive. *IPG* features advances in graphic arts technology and shows in-plants how to put this technology to use. Our audience consists of print shop managers working for (nonprint related) corporations (i.e., hospitals, insurance companies, publishers, nonprofits), universities, and government departments. They often oversee graphic design, prepress, printing, bindery, and mailing departments." Estab. 1951. Circ. 23,100. Byline given. Pays on publication. No kill fee. Publishes ms an average of 3 months after acceptance. Buys all rights. Editorial lead time 2 months. Submit seasonal material 3 months in advance. Accepts queries by mail, e-mail, fax. Guidelines available online.

Nonfiction "Stories include profiles of successful in-house printing operations (not commercial or quick printers); updates on graphic arts technology (new features, uses); reviews of major graphic arts and printing conferences (seminar and new equipment reviews)." Needs new product, graphic arts, technical, graphic arts/printing/prepress. No articles on desktop publishing software or design software. No Internet publishing articles. **Buys 5 mss/year.** Query with published clips. Length: 800-1,500 words. **Pays $350-500.**

Photos State availability. Captions, identification of subjects required. Reviews transparencies, prints. Negotiates payment individually. Buys one time rights.

Tips "To get published in *IPG*, writers must contact the editor with an idea in the form of a query letter that includes published writing samples. Writers who have covered the graphic arts in the past may be assigned stories for an agreed-upon fee. We don't want stories that tout only one vendor's products and serve as glorified commercials. All profiles must be well balanced, covering a variety of issues. If you can tell us about an in-house printing operation is doing innovative things, we will be interested."

$$ SCREEN PRINTING

407 Gilbert Ave., Cincinnati OH 45202-2285. (513)421-2050. Fax: (513)421-5144. E-mail: tom.frecska@stmediagroup.com. Website: www.screenweb.com. **30% freelance written**. Monthly magazine for the screen printing industry, including screen printers (commercial, industrial, and captive shops), suppliers and manufacturers, ad agencies, and allied professions. Works with a small number of new/unpublished writers each year. Estab. 1953. Circ. 17,500. Byline given. Pays on publication. No kill fee. Publishes ms an average of 3 months after acceptance. Buys all rights. Accepts queries by mail, e-mail, fax. Sample copy available. Guidelines for #10 sase.

Nonfiction Because the screen printing industry is a specialized but diverse trade, we do not publish general interest articles with no pertinence to our readers. Subject matter is open, but should fall into 1 of 4 categories—technology, management, profile, or news. Features in all categories must identify the relevance of the subject matter to our readership. Technology articles must be informative, thorough, and objective—no promotional or 'advertorial' pieces accepted. Management articles may cover broader business or industry specific issues, but they must address the screen printer's unique needs. Profiles may cover serigraphers, outstanding shops, unique jobs and projects, or industry personalities; they should be in-depth features, not PR puff pieces, that clearly show the human interest or business relevance of the subject. News pieces should be timely (reprints from nonindustry publications will be considered) and must cover an event or topic of industry concern. Unsolicited mss not returned. **Buys 10-15 mss/year.** Query. **Pays $400 minimum for major features.**
Photos Cover photos negotiable; b&w or color. Published material becomes the property of the magazine.
Tips Be an expert in the screen-printing industry with supreme or special knowledge of a particular screen-printing process, or have special knowledge of a field or issue of particular interest to screen-printers. If the author has a working knowledge of screen printing, assignments are more readily available. General management articles are rarely used.

Professional Photography

$$ IMAGING BUSINESS

Cygnus Business Media (formerly *Photographic Processing*), 3 Huntington Quad., Suite 301N, Melville NY 11747. (631)845-2700. Fax: (631)845-7109. E-mail: bill.schiffner@cygnusb2b.com. Website: www.labsonline.com. **30% freelance written**. Monthly magazine covering photographic (commercial/minilab) and electronic processing markets. Estab. 1965. Circ. 19,000. Byline given. Pays on publication. Offers $75 kill fee. Publishes ms an average of 4 months after acceptance. Editorial lead time 3 months. Submit seasonal material 3 months in advance. Accepts simultaneous submissions. Sample copy and writer's guidelines free.
Nonfiction Needs how-to, interview, new product, photo processing/digital imaging features. **Buys 20-30 mss/year.** Query with published clips. Length: 1,500-2,200 words. **Pays $275-350 for assigned articles. Pays $250-275 for unsolicited articles.**
Photos Looking for digitally manipulated covers. Send photos. Captions required. Reviews 4 × 5 transparencies, 4x6 prints. Offers no additional payment for photos accepted with ms. Buys one time rights.
Columns/Departments Surviving in 2000 (business articles offering tips to labs on how to make their businesses run better), 1,500-1,800 words; Business Side (getting more productivity out of your lab). **Buys 10 mss/year.** Query with published clips. **Pays $150-250.**

$$ NEWS PHOTOGRAPHER

National Press Photographers Association, Inc., 6677 Whitemarsh Valley Walk, Austin TX 78746. E-mail: magazine@nppa.org. Website: www.nppa.org. Published 12 times/year. *News Photographer* magazine is dedicated to the advancement of still and television news photography. The magazine presents articles, interviews, profiles, history, new products, electronic imaging, and news related to the practice of photojournalism. Estab. 1946. Circ. 11,000. Byline given. Pays on acceptance. Offers 100% kill fee. Publishes ms an average of 4 months after acceptance. Buys one-time and archival electronic rights. Editorial lead time 2 months. Submit seasonal material 2 months in advance. Accepts queries by mail, e-mail, fax, phone. Accepts previously published material. Accepts simultaneous submissions. Responds in 1 month to queries. Sample copy for sae with 9 × 12 envelope and 3 First-Class stamps. Guidelines free.
Nonfiction Needs historical, how-to, interview, new product, opinion, personal experience, photo feature, technical. **Buys 10 mss/year.** Query. 1,500 words **Pays $300.** Pays expenses of writers on assignment.
Photos State availability. Captions, identification of subjects required. Reviews high resolution, digital images only. Negotiates payment individually. Buys one time rights.
Columns/Departments Query.

$$ THE PHOTO REVIEW

140 E. Richardson Ave., Suite 301, Langhorne PA 19047. (215)891-0214. Fax: (215)891-9358. E-mail: info@photoreview.org. Website: www.photoreview.org. **50% freelance written**. Quarterly magazine

covering art photography and criticism. "*The Photo Review* publishes critical reviews of photography exhibitions and books, critical essays, and interviews. We do not publish how-to or technical articles." Estab. 1976. Circ. 2,000. Byline given. Pays on publication. No kill fee. Publishes ms an average of 9-12 months after acceptance. Buys first rights. Editorial lead time 3 months. Submit seasonal material 6 months in advance. Accepts queries by mail. Accepts simultaneous submissions. Responds in 2 months to queries. Responds in 3 months to mss. Sample copy for $7. Guidelines for #10 SASE.

Nonfiction Needs interview, photography essay, critical review. No how-to articles. **Buys 20 mss/year.** Send complete ms. 2-20 typed pages **Pays $10-250.**

Reprints "Send tearsheet, photocopy or typed ms with rights for sale noted and information about when and where the material previously appeared." Payment varies.

Photos Send photos. Captions required. Reviews contact sheets, transparencies, prints. Offers no additional payment for photos accepted with ms. Buys all rights.

SHUTTERBUG

Primedia, 1415 Chaffee Dr., Suite 1, Titusville FL 32780. Fax: (321)225-3149. E-mail: editorial@shutterbug.com. Website: www.shutterbug.com. **90% freelance written**. Monthly covering photography and digial imaging. Written for the avid amateur, part-time, and full-time professional photographers. Covers equipment techniques, profiles, technology and news in both silver-halide and digital imaging. Estab. 1972. Circ. 90,000. Byline given. Pays on publication. Buys first North American serial rights, buys second serial (reprint) rights, buys electronic rights. Editorial lead time 3 months. Submit seasonal material 6 months in advance. Accepts queries by mail, e-mail. Responds in 1 month to queries. Responds in 1 month to mss.

Nonfiction Query. Length: 1,000-1,500 words. **Payment rate depends on published length, including photographs.**

Photos Send photos. Captions, model releases required. Reviews contact sheets, transparencies, CD-ROMs. Offers no additional payment for photos.

Real Estate

$$ AREA DEVELOPMENT MAGAZINE

Sites and Facility Planning, Halcyon Business Publications, Inc., 400 Post Ave., Westbury NY 11590. (516)338-0900, ext. 211. Fax: (516)338-0100. E-mail: gerri@areadevelopment.com. Website: www.areadevelopment.com. **Contact:** Geraldine Gambale, editor. **80% freelance written. Prefers to work with published/established writers.** Bimonthly magazine covering corporate facility planning and site selection for industrial chief executives worldwide. Estab. 1965. Circ. 45,000. Byline given. Pays on publication. No kill fee. Publishes ms an average of 2 months after acceptance. Buys all rights. Accepts queries by mail, e-mail, fax. Responds in 3 months to queries. Sample copy free. Guidelines for #10 sase.

Nonfiction Related areas of site selection and facility planning such as taxes, labor, government, energy, architecture, and finance. Needs historical, if it deals with corporate facility planning, how-to, experiences in site selection and all other aspects of corporate facility planning, interview, corporate executives and industrial developers. **Buys 75 mss/year.** Query. Length: 1,500-2,000 words. **Pays 40¢/word.** Sometimes pays expenses of writers on assignment.

Photos State availability. Captions, identification of subjects required. Reviews JPEGS of at least 300 dpi. Negotiates payment individually.

$$ CANADIAN PROPERTY MANAGEMENT

Mediaedge Communications Inc., 5255 Yonge St., Suite 1000, Toronto ON M2N 6P4 Canada. (416)512-8186. Fax: (416)512-8344. E-mail: paulm@mediaedge.ca. Website: www.mediaedge.ca. **10% freelance written**. Magazine published 8 times/year covering Canadian commercial, industrial, institutional (medical and educational), residential properties. *Canadian Property Management* magazine is a trade journal supplying building owners and property managers with Canadian industry news, case law reviews, technical updates for building operations and events listings. Building and professional profile articles are regular features. Estab. 1985. Circ. 12,500. Byline given. Pays on publication. No kill fee. Publishes ms an average of 3 months after acceptance. Buys all rights. Editorial lead time 2 months. Submit seasonal material 2 months in advance. Accepts queries by mail, e-mail, fax, phone. Accepts simultaneous submissions. Responds in 3 weeks to queries. Responds in 2 months to mss. Sample copy for $5, subject to availability. Guidelines free.

Nonfiction Needs interview, technical. No promotional articles (i.e., marketing a product or service geared to this industry)! Query with published clips. Length: 700-1,200 words. **Pays 35¢/word.**
Photos State availability. Captions, identification of subjects, model releases required. Reviews transparencies, 3 × 5 prints, digital (at least 300 dpi). Offers no additional payment for photos accepted with ms.
Tips We do not accept promotional articles serving companies or their products. Freelance articles that are strong, information-based pieces that serve the interests and needs of property managers and building owners stand a better chance of being published. Proposals and inquiries with article ideas are appreciated the most. A good understanding of the real estate industry (management structure) is also helpful for the writer.

$ $ THE COOPERATOR

The Co-op and Condo Monthly, Yale Robbins, Inc., 102 Madison Ave., 5th Floor, New York NY 10016. (212)683-5700. Fax: (646)405-9768. E-mail: editorial@cooperator.com. Website: www.cooperator.com. **70% freelance written**. Monthly tabloid covering real estate in the New York City metro area. *The Cooperator* covers condominium and cooperative issues in New York and beyond. It is read by condo unit owners and co-op shareholders, real estate professionals, board members and managing agents, and other service professionals. Estab. 1980. Circ. 40,000. Byline given. Pays on publication. No kill fee. Publishes ms an average of 3 months after acceptance. Buys all rights. Makes work-for-hire assignments. Submit seasonal material 3 months in advance. Accepts queries by mail, e-mail, fax. Responds in 1 month to queries. Sample copy and writer's guidelines free.
Nonfiction All articles related to co-op and condo ownership. Needs interview, new product, personal experience. No submissions without queries. Query with published clips. Length: 1,500-2,000 words. **Pays $325-425.** Sometimes pays expenses of writers on assignment.
Photos State availability.
Columns/Departments Profiles of co-op/condo-related businesses with something unique; Building Finance (investment and financing issues); Buying and Selling (market issues, etc.); Design (architectural and interior/exterior design, lobby renovation, etc.); Building Maintenance (issues related to maintaining interior/exterior, facades, lobbies, elevators, etc.); Legal Issues Related to Co-Ops/Condos; Real Estate Trends, all 1,500 words. **Buys 100 mss/year.** Query with published clips.
Tips You must have experience in business, legal, or financial. Must have published clips to send in with resume and query.

$ $ FLORIDA REALTOR MAGAZINE

Florida Association of Realtors, 7025 Augusta National Dr., Orlando FL 32822-5017. (407)438-1400. Fax: (407)438-1411. E-mail: flrealtor@floridarealtors.org. Website: floridarealtormagazine.com. **Contact:** Doug Damerst, editor-in-chief. **70% freelance written**. Journal published 11 times/year covering the Florida real estate profession. "As the official publication of the Florida Association of Realtors, we provide helpful articles for our 125,000 members. We report new practices that lead to successful real estate careers and stay up on the trends and issues that affect business in Florida's real estate market." Estab. 1925. Circ. 112,205. Byline given. Pays on publication. No kill fee. Publishes ms an average of 2 months after acceptance. Buys one-time rights, buys electronic rights. Editorial lead time 3 months. Accepts queries by mail, e-mail, fax. Sample copy available online.
Nonfiction Book excerpts, how-to, inspirational, interview/profile, "new product—all with a real estate angle. Florida-specific is good." No fiction or poetry. **Buys varying number of mss/year.** Query with published clips. Length: 800-1,500 words. **Pays $500-700.** Sometimes pays expenses of writers on assignment.
Photos State availability. Captions, identification of subjects, model releases required. Negotiates payment individually. Buys one-time print rights and internet use rights.
Columns/Departments Some written in-house: Know the Law, 900 words; Market It, 900 words; Technology & You, 1,000 words; ManageIt, 900 words. **Buys varying number of columns mss/year. Payment varies.**
Tips "Build a solid reputation for specializing in real estate business writing in state/national publications. Query with specific article ideas."

$ $ OFFICE BUILDINGS MAGAZINE

Yale Robbins, Inc., 102 Madison Ave., New York NY 10016. (212)683-5700. Fax: (646)405-9751. Website: www.officebuildingsmagazine.com. **15% freelance written**. Annual magazine published in 12 separate editions covering market statistics, trends, and thinking of area professionals on the current and future state of the real estate market. Estab. 1987. Circ. 10,500. Byline sometimes given. Pays 1 month after publication. Offers kill fee. Buys all rights. Editorial lead time 2 months. Accepts queries by mail, e-mail, fax. Sample copy and writer's guidelines free.

Nonfiction Survey of specific markets. **Buys 15-20 mss/year.** Query with published clips. Length: 1,500-2,000 words. **Pays $600-700.** Sometimes pays expenses of writers on assignment.

$$ PROPERTIES MAGAZINE

Properties Magazine, Inc., P.O. Box 112127, Cleveland OH 44111. (216)251-0035. Fax: (216)251-0064. E-mail: kkrych@propertiesmag.com. **Contact:** Kenneth C. Krych, editor. **25% freelance written**. Monthly magazine covering real estate, residential, commerical construction. *Properties Magazine* is published for executives in the real estate, building, banking, design, architectural, property management, tax, and law community—busy people who need the facts presented in an interesting and informative format. Estab. 1946. Circ. over 10,000. Byline given. Pays on publication. No kill fee. Publishes ms an average of 2 months after acceptance. Buys first rights. Editorial lead time 2 months. Submit seasonal material 2 months in advance. Accepts queries by mail, fax. Responds in 3 weeks to queries. Sample copy for $3.95.

Nonfiction Needs general interest, how-to, humor, new product. Special issues: Environmental issues (September); Security/Fire Protection (October); Tax Issues (November); Computers In Real Estate (December). **Buys 30 mss/year.** Send complete ms. Length: 500-2,000 words. **Pays 50¢/column line.** Sometimes pays expenses of writers on assignment.

Photos Send photos. Captions required. Reviews prints. Offers no additional payment for photos accepted with ms. Negotiates payment individually. Buys one time rights.

Columns/Departments Buys 25 mss/year. Query or send complete ms. **Pays 50¢/column line.**

$$ REM

The Real Estate Magazine, 2255 B #1178 Queen St. East, Toronto ON M4E 1G3 Canada. (416)425-3504. E-mail: jim@remonline.com. Website: www.remonline.com. **35% freelance written**. Monthly trade journal covering real estate. *REM* provides Canadian real estate agents and brokers with news and opinions they can't get anywhere else. It is an independent publication and not affiliated with any real estate board, association, or company. Estab. 1989. Circ. 45,000. Pays on acceptance. Offers 25% kill fee. Publishes ms an average of 2 months after acceptance. Buys first Canadian serial rights and and rights to use on the REM web site. Editorial lead time 3 months. Submit seasonal material 3 months in advance. Accepts queries by mail, e-mail, fax. Accepts previously published material. Accepts simultaneous submissions. Sample copy free.

Nonfiction Needs book excerpts, expose, inspirational, interview, new product, personal experience. "No articles geared to consumers about market conditions or how to choose a realtor. Must have Canadian content." **Buys 60 mss/year.** Query. Length: 500-1,500 words. **Pays $200-400.**

Photos Send photos. Captions, identification of subjects required. Reviews transparencies, prints, GIF/JPEG files. Offers $25/photo. Buys one time rights.

Tips "Stories must be of interest or practical use for Canadian realtors. Check out our website to see the types of stories we require."

$$ ZONING PRACTICE

American Planning Association, 122 S. Michigan Ave., Suite 1600, Chicago IL 60603-6107. (312)431-9100. Fax: (312)431-9985. E-mail: zoningpractice@planning.org. Website: www.planning.org/zoningpractice/index.htm. **90% freelance written**. Monthly newsletter covering land-use regulations including zoning. "Our publication is aimed at practicing urban planners and those involved in land-use decisions, such as zoning administrators and officials, planning commissioners, zoning boards of adjustment, land-use attorneys, developers, and others interested in this field. The material we publish must come from writers knowledgeable about zoning and subdivision regulations, preferably with practical experience in the field. Anything we publish needs to be of practical value to our audience in their everyday work." Estab. 1984. Circ. 2,900. Byline given. Pays on publication. Offers 50% kill fee. Publishes ms an average of 3 months after acceptance. Buys all rights. Editorial lead time 6 months. Accepts queries by mail, e-mail, fax, phone. Responds in 2 weeks to queries. Responds in 1 month to mss. Sample copy free. www.planning.org/zoningpractice/contribguidelines.htm.

Nonfiction Needs technical. "See our description. We do not need general or consumer-interest articles about zoning because this publication is aimed at practitioners." **Buys 12 mss/year.** Query. Length:

3,000-5,000 words. **Pays $300 min. for assigned articles.** Sometimes pays expenses of writers on assignment.
Photos State availability. Captions required. Reviews GIF/JPEG files. Negotiates payment individually. Buys all rights.
Tips "Breaking in is easy if you know the subject matter and can write in plain English for practicing planners. We are always interested in finding new authors. We generally expect authors will earn another $200 premium for participating in an online forum called, Ask the Author, in which they respond to questions from readers about their article. This requires a deep practical sense of how to make things work with regard to your topic."

Resources & Waste Reduction

$$ COMPOSTING NEWS

The Latest News in Composting and Scrap Wood Management, McEntee Media Corp., 9815 Hazelwood Ave., Cleveland OH 44149. (440)238-6603. Fax: (440)238-6712. E-mail: ken@recycle.cc. Website: www.compostingnews.com. **Contact:** Ken McEntee, editor. **5% freelance written**. Monthly newsletter. We are interested in any news impacting the composting industry including new laws, regulations, new facilities/programs, end-uses, research, etc. Estab. 1992. Circ. 1,000. Pays on publication. No kill fee. Publishes ms an average of 1 month after acceptance. Buys first rights, buys all rights. Editorial lead time 1 month. Submit seasonal material 1 month in advance. Accepts queries by mail, e-mail, fax, phone. Accepts previously published material. Accepts simultaneous submissions. Responds in 2 months to queries. Sample copy for 9 × 12 SAE and 55¢ postage. Guidelines for #10 sase.
Nonfiction Needs book excerpts, essays, general interest, how-to, interview, new product, opinion, personal experience, photo feature, technical, new business, legislation, regulation, business expansion. **Buys 0-5 mss/year.** Query with published clips. Length: 100-5,000 words. **Pays $10-500.**
Columns/Departments Query with published clips. **Pays $10-500.**
Tips We appreciate leads on local news regarding composting, i.e., new facilities or business, new laws and regulations, unique programs, situations that impact supply and demand for composting. International developments are also of interest.

$$$ EROSION CONTROL

The Journal for Erosion and Sediment Control Professionals, Forester Communications, Inc., 2946 De La Vina St., Santa Barbara CA 93105. (805)682-1300. Fax: (805)682-0200. E-mail: eceditor@forester.net. Website: www.erosioncontrol.com. **60% freelance written**. Magazine published 7 times/year covering all aspects of erosion prevention and sediment control. "*Erosion Control* is a practical, hands-on, 'how-to' professional journal. Our readers are civil engineers, landscape architects, builders, developers, public works officials, road and highway construction officials and engineers, soils specialists, farmers, landscape contractors, and others involved with any activity that disturbs significant areas of surface vegetation." Estab. 1994. Circ. 20,000. Byline given. Pays 1 month after acceptance. No kill fee. Publishes ms an average of 3 months after acceptance. Buys all rights. Editorial lead time 4 months. Submit seasonal material 4 months in advance. Accepts queries by mail, e-mail, fax, phone. Responds in 3 weeks to queries. Sample copy and writer's guidelines free.
Nonfiction Needs photo feature, technical. **Buys 15 mss/year.** Query with published clips. Length: 3,000-4,000 words. **Pays $700-850.** Sometimes pays expenses of writers on assignment.
Photos Send photos. Captions, identification of subjects, model releases required. Reviews transparencies, prints. Offers no additional payment for photos accepted with ms. Buys all rights.
Tips "Writers should have a good grasp of technology involved and good writing and communication skills. Most of our freelance articles include extensive interviews with engineers, contractors, developers, or project owners, and we often provide contact names for articles we assign."

$$ MSW MANAGEMENT

The Journal for Municipal Solid Waste Professionals, Forester Communications, Inc., P.O. Box 3100, Santa Barbara CA 93130. (805)682-1300. Fax: (805)682-0200. E-mail: editor@forester.net. Website: www.mswmanagement.com. **Contact:** John Trotti, group editor. **70% freelance written**. Bimonthly magazine. "*MSW Management* is written for public sector solid waste professionals—the people working for the local counties, cities, towns, boroughs, and provinces. They run the landfills, recycling programs, composting, incineration. They are responsible for all aspects of garbage collection and disposal; buying and maintaining the associated equipment; and designing, engineering, and building the waste processing facilities, transfer stations, and landfills." Estab. 1991. Circ. 25,000. Byline given. Pays 30 days after acceptance No kill fee. Buys all rights. Editorial lead time 4 months. Submit seasonal material 4 months in advance. Accepts queries by mail, e-mail, fax, phone. Accepts simultaneous submissions. Responds in 6 weeks to queries. Responds in 2 months to mss. Sample copy and writer's guidelines free. Guidelines available online.

Nonfiction Needs photo feature, technical. "No rudimentary, basic articles written for the average person on the street. Our readers are experienced professionals with years of practical, in-the-field experience. Any material submitted that we judge as too fundamental will be rejected." **Buys 15 mss/year.** Query. Length: 3,000-4,000 words. **Pays $350-750.** Sometimes pays expenses of writers on assignment.

Photos Send photos. Captions, identification of subjects, model releases required. Reviews transparencies, prints. Offers no additional payment for photos accepted with ms. Buys all rights.

Tips "We're a small company, easy to reach. We're open to any and all ideas as to possible editorial topics. We endeavor to provide the reader with usable material, and present it in full color with graphic embellishment whenever possible. Dry, highly technical material is edited to make it more palatable and concise. Most of our feature articles come from freelancers. Interviews and quotes should be from public sector solid waste managers and engineers—not PR people, not manufacturers. Strive to write material that is 'over the heads' of our readers. If anything, attempt to make them 'reach.' Anything submitted that is too basic, elementary, fundamental, rudimentary, etc., cannot be accepted for publication."

$$$ STORMWATER

The Journal for Surface Water Quality Professionals, Forester Media Inc., 2946 De La Vina St., Santa Barbara CA 93105. (805)682-1300. Fax: (805)682-0200. E-mail: sweditor@forester.net. Website: www.stormh2o.com. **10% freelance written**. Magazine published 8 times/year. "*Stormwater* is a practical business journal for professionals involved with surface water quality issues, protection, projects, and programs. Our readers are municipal employees, regulators, engineers, and consultants concerned with stormwater management." Estab. 2000. Circ. 20,000. Byline given. Pays 1 month after acceptance. No kill fee. Publishes ms an average of 3 months after acceptance. Editorial lead time 4 months. Submit seasonal material 4 months in advance. Accepts queries by mail, e-mail. Responds in 3 weeks to queries. Guidelines free.

Nonfiction Needs technical. **Buys 8-10 mss/year.** Query with published clips. Length: 3,000-4,000 words. **Pays $500-900.** Sometimes pays expenses of writers on assignment.

Photos Send photos. Captions, identification of subjects, model releases required. Offers no additional payment for photos accepted with ms. Buys all rights.

Tips "Writers should have a good grasp of the technology and regulations involved in stormwater management and good interviewing skills. Our freelance articles include extensive interviews with engineers, stormwater managers, and project owners, and we often provide contact names for articles we assign. See past editorial content online."

$$ WATER WELL JOURNAL

National Ground Water Association, 601 Dempsey Rd., Westerville OH 43081. Fax: (614)898-7786. Website: www.ngwa.org. **25% freelance written**. Monthly magazine covering the ground water industry; well drilling. Each month the *Water Well Journal* covers the topics of drilling, rigs and heavy equipment, pumping systems, water quality, business management, water supply, on-site waste water treatment, and diversification opportunities, including geothermal installations, environmental remediation, irrigation, dewatering, and foundation installation. It also offers updates on regulatory issues that impact the ground water industry. Estab. 1948. Circ. 25,000. Byline given. Pays on publication. No kill fee. Publishes ms an average of 3 months after acceptance. Buys all rights. Editorial lead time 6 weeks. Submit seasonal material 3 months in advance. Accepts queries by mail. Responds in 2 weeks to queries. Responds in 1 month to mss. Guidelines free.

Nonfiction Needs essays, sometimes, historical, sometimes, how-to, recent examples include how-to chlorinate a well; how-to buy a used rig; how-to do bill collections, interview, new product, personal experience, photo feature, technical, business management. No company profiles or extended product releases. **Buys up to 30 mss/year.** Query with published clips. Length: 1,000-3,000 words. **Pays $150-400.**

Photos State availability. Captions, identification of subjects required. Offers $50-250/photo.

Tips "Some previous experience or knowledge in groundwater/drilling/construction industry helpful. Published clips are a must."

Selling & Merchandising

$ THE AMERICAN SALESMAN

National Research Bureau, 320 Valley St., Burlington IA 52601. (319)752-5415. E-mail: national@willinet.net (articles@salestrainingandtechniques.com). Website: www.national-research-bureau.com. www.salestrainingandtechniques.com. **80% freelance written**. Monthly magazine covering sales and marketing. *The American Salesman Magazine* is designed for sales professionals. Its primary objective is to provide informative articles which develop the attitudes, skills, personal and professional qualities of sales representatives, allowing them to use more of their potential to increase productivity and achieve goals. Byline given. Publishes ms an average of 1 month after acceptance. Buys all rights. Editorial lead time 1 month. Submit seasonal material 2 months in advance. Accepts queries by e-mail. Sample copy free. Guidelines by e-mail.

Nonfiction Needs personal experience. **Buys 24 mss/year.** Send complete ms. Length: 500-1,000 words. **Pays 4¢/word.**

$$ BALLOONS & PARTIES MAGAZINE

PartiLife Publications, 65 Sussex St., Hackensack NJ 07601. (201)441-4224. Fax: (201)342-8118. E-mail: mark@balloonsandparties.com. Website: www.balloonsandparties.com. **Contact:** Mark Zettler, publisher. **10% freelance written**. International trade journal published bi-monthly for professional party decorators and gift delivery businesses. BALLOONS & Parties Magazine is published six times a year by PartiLife Publications, L.L.C. for the balloon, party and event fields. New product data, letters, manuscripts and photographs should be sent attention: Editor and should include sender's full name, address and telephone number. SASE required on all editorial submissions. All submissions considered for publication unless otherwise noted. Unsolicited materials are submitted at sender's risk and BALLOONS & Parties/PartiLife Publications, L.L.C. assumes no responsibility for unsolicited materials. Estab. 1986. Circ. 7,000. Byline given. Pays on publication. No kill fee. Publishes ms an average of 3 months after acceptance. Buys all rights. Submit seasonal material 6 months in advance. Accepts queries by mail, e-mail, fax, phone. Responds in 6 weeks to queries. Sample copy for sae with 9 × 12 envelope.

Nonfiction Needs essays, how-to, interview, new product, personal experience, photo feature, technical, craft. **Buys 12 mss/year.** Send complete ms. Length: 500-1,500 words. **Pays $100-300 for assigned articles. Pays $50-200 for unsolicited articles.** Sometimes pays expenses of writers on assignment.

Reprints Send typed manuscript with rights for sale noted and information about when and where the material previously appeared. Length: up to 2,500 words. Pays 10¢/word.

Photos Send photos. Captions, identification of subjects, model releases required. Reviews 2 × 2 transparencies, 3 × 5 prints. Buys all rights.

Columns/Departments Problem Solver (small business issues); Recipes That Cook (centerpiece ideas with detailed how-to), 400-1,000 words. Send complete ms with photos.

Tips Show unusual, lavish, and outstanding examples of balloon sculpture, design and decorating, and other craft projects. Offer specific how-to information. Be positive and motivational in style.

$$ CASUAL LIVING MAGAZINE

Voice of the Leisure Market, Reed Business Information, 7025 Albert Pick Rd., Suite 200, Greensboro NC 27409-9519. (336)605-1122. Fax: (336)605-1158. E-mail: cwingram@reedbusiness.com. Website: www.casualliving.com. **10% freelance written**. Monthly magazine covering outdoor furniture and accessories, barbecue grills, spas and more. We write about new products, trends and casual furniture retailers plus industry news. Estab. 1958. Circ. 10,000. Pays on publication. Publishes ms an average of 1-2 months after acceptance. Buys all rights. Editorial lead time 1-2 months. Submit seasonal material 2 months in advance. Accepts queries by mail, e-mail. Responds in 2 weeks to queries. Sample copy available online.

Nonfiction Needs how-to, interview. **Buys 20 mss/year.** Query with published clips. Length: 300-1,000 words. **Pays $300-700.** Sometimes pays expenses of writers on assignment.

Photos Contact: Courtney Paschal, associate editor. Identification of subjects required. Reviews GIF/JPEG files. Negotiates payment individually. Buys all rights.

$$$$ CONSUMER GOODS TECHNOLOGY

Edgell Communications, 4 Middlebury Blvd., Randolph NJ 07869. (973)252-0100. Fax: (973)252-9020. E-mail: tclark@edgellmail.com. Website: www.consumergoods.com. **Contact:** Alliston Ackerman, editor. **40% freelance written**. Monthly tabloid benchmarking business technology performance. Estab. 1987.

Circ. 25,000. Byline given. Pays on publication. No kill fee. Publishes ms an average of 2 months after acceptance. Buys first North American serial rights, buys second serial (reprint) rights, buys electronic rights, buys all rights. Editorial lead time 3 months. Accepts queries by e-mail. Sample copy available online. Guidelines by e-mail.

Nonfiction We create several supplements annually, often using freelance. Needs essays, expose, interview. **Buys 60 mss/year.** Query with published clips. Length: 700-1,900 words. **Pays $600-1,200.** Sometimes pays expenses of writers on assignment.

Photos Identification of subjects, model releases required. Negotiates payment individually. Buys all rights.

Columns/Departments Columns 400-750 words—featured columnists. **Buys 4 mss/year.** Query with published clips. **Pays 75¢-$1/word**

Tips All stories in *Consumer Goods Technology* are told through the voice of the consumer goods executive. We only quote VP-level or C-level CG executives. No vendor quotes. We're always on the lookout for freelance talent. We look in particular for writers with an in-depth understanding of the business issues faced by consumer goods firms and the technologies that are used by the industry to address those issues successfully. 'Bits and bytes' tech writing is not sought; our focus is on benchmarketing the business technology performance of CG firms, CG executives, CG vendors, and CG vendor products. Our target reader is tech-savvy, CG C-level decision maker. We write to, and about, our target reader.

$ $ CONVENIENCE STORE DECISIONS

Penton Media, Inc., Two Greenwood Square, #410, Bensalem PA 19020. (215)245-4555. Fax: (215)245-4060. E-mail: jgordon@penton.com. Website: www.c-storedecisions.com. **15-20% freelance written.** Monthly magazine covering convenience retail/petroleum marketing. *CSD* is received by top-level executives in the convenience retail and petroleum marketing industry. Writers should have knowledge of the industry and the subjects it encompasses. Estab. 1990. Circ. 42,000. Byline given. Pays on publication. No kill fee. Buys all rights. Makes work-for-hire assignments. Editorial lead time 2-4 months. Submit seasonal material 3 months in advance. Accepts queries by mail, e-mail, fax. Accepts simultaneous submissions. Responds in 3 weeks to queries. Sample copy and writer's guidelines free.

Nonfiction Needs interview, retailers, photo feature, technical. No self-serving, vendor-based stories. **Buys 12-15 mss/year.** Query with published clips. Length: 400-2,000 words. **Pays $200-600 for assigned articles.** Sometimes pays expenses of writers on assignment.

Photos State availability. Identification of subjects required. Negotiates payment individually. Buys all rights.

Tips Offer experience. We get queries from freelancers daily. We are looking for writers with industry experience. We need real-life, retailer-based work. Bring us a story.

$ $ COUNTRY SAMPLER'S COUNTRY BUSINESS

The Magazine for Retailers of Country Gifts and Accessories, Emmis Publishing LP, 707 Kautz Rd., St. Charles IL 60174. (630)377-8000. Fax: (630)377-8194. E-mail: cbiz@sampler.emmis.com. Website: www.country-business.com. **Contact:** Susan Wagner, editor. **50% freelance written.** Magazine published 7 times/year covering independent retail, gift and home decor. *Country Business* is a trade publication for independent retailers of gifts and home accents. Estab. 1993. Circ. 32,000. Byline given. Pays 1 month after acceptance of final ms. Offers $50 kill fee. Publishes ms an average of 4-6 months after acceptance. Buys all rights. Editorial lead time 4-6 months. Submit seasonal material 8-10 months in advance. Accepts queries by mail, e-mail, fax. Accepts previously published material. Accepts simultaneous submissions. Usually responds in 4-6 weeks (only if accepted). Sample articles are available on website. Guidelines by e-mail.

Nonfiction Needs how-to, pertaining to retail, interview, new product, finance, legal, marketing, small business. No fiction, poetry, fillers, photos, artwork, or profiles of businesses, unless queried and first assigned. **Buys 20 mss/year.** Send resume and published clips to: Writers Query, Country Business. Send complete ms. Length: 1,000-2,500 words. **Pays $275-500 for assigned articles. Pays $200-350 for unsolicited articles.** Sometimes pays expenses of writers on assignment. Limit agreed upon in advance.

Columns/Departments Display & Design (store design and product display), 1,500 words; Retailer Profile (profile of retailer—assigned only), 1,800 words; Vendor Profile (profile of manufacturer—assigned only), 1,200 words; Technology (Internet, computer-related articles as applies to small retailers), 1,500 words; Marketing (marketing ideas and advice as applies to small retailers), 1,500 words; Finance (financial tips and advice as applies to small retailers), 1,500 words; Legal (legal tips and advice as applies to small retailers), 1,500 words; Employees (tips and advice on hiring, firing, and working with employees as applies to small retailers), 1,500 words. **Buys 15 mss/year.** Query with published clips or send complete ms. **Pays $250-350.**

$$$$ DIRECT SELLING NEWS

Video Plus, 200 Swisher Rd., Lake Dallas TX 75067. E-mail: nlaichas@directsellingnews.com. Website: www.directsellingnews.com. **20% freelance written**. Monthly magazine covering direct selling/network marketing industry. Though we are a business publication, we prefer feature-style writing rather than a newsy approach. Circ. 6,000. Byline given. Pays 30 days after publication. Publishes ms an average of 1-2 months after acceptance. Makes work-for-hire assignments. Editorial lead time 3 months. Submit seasonal material 3 months in advance. Accepts queries by e-mail. Responds in 3 weeks to queries. Sample copy available online.

Nonfiction Needs general interest, how-to. Query. Length: 1,500-3,000 words. **Pays 50¢-$1/word.**

$$ GIFTWARE NEWS

Talcott Corp., 20 W. Kinzie, 12th Floor, Chicago IL 60610. (312)849-2220. Fax: (312)849-2174. **20% freelance written**. Monthly magazine covering gifts, collectibles, and tabletops for giftware retailers. Estab. 1976. Circ. 35,000. Byline given. Pays on publication. No kill fee. Publishes ms an average of 2 months after acceptance. Buys all rights. Submit seasonal material 6 months in advance. Responds in 2 months to mss. Sample copy for $8.

Nonfiction Needs how-to, sell, display, new product. **Buys 20 mss/year.** Send complete ms. Length: 1,500-2,000 words. **Pays $400-500 for assigned articles. Pays $200-300 for unsolicited articles.**

Photos Send photos. Identification of subjects required. Reviews 4 × 5 transparencies, 5 × 7 prints, electronic images. Offers no additional payment for photos accepted with ms.

Columns/Departments Stationery, giftbaskets, collectibles, holiday, merchandise, tabletop, wedding market and display—all for the gift retailer. Length: 1,500-2,500 words. **Buys 10 mss/year.** Send complete ms. **Pays $100 250.**

Tips We are not looking so much for general journalists but rather experts in particular fields who can also write.

GREETINGS & GIFTS

Yaffa Publishing, 17-21 Bellevue St., Surry Hills NSW 2010 Australia. (61)(2)9281-2333. Fax: (61)(2)9281-2750. E-mail: alisonleader@yaffa.com.au. Website: www.yaffa.com.au. Bimonthly magazine for owners and managers of gift and specialist greeting card shops.

Nonfiction Needs general interest, how-to, interview, new product, technical. Query.

$$ NEW AGE RETAILER

Continuity Publishing, 2183 Alpine Way, Bellingham WA 98225. (800)463-9243. Fax: (360)676-0932. E-mail: Kathy@newageretailer.com. Website: www.newageretailer.com. **Contact:** Kathy McGee, editor-in-chief. **60% freelance written**. Bimonthly magazine for retailers of spiritual and New Age books, music, and giftware. The goal of the articles in *New Age Retailer* is usefulness—we strive to give store owners and managers practical, in-depth information they can begin using immediately. We have 3 categories of articles: retail business methods that give solid information about the various aspects of running an independent store; inventory articles that discuss a particular New Age subject or trend; and education articles that help storeowners and managers gain knowledge and stay current in New Age subjects. Estab. 1987. Circ. 10,000. Byline given. Pays on publication. Offers 10% kill fee. Publishes ms an average of 4 months after acceptance. Buys first North American serial rights, buys second serial (reprint) rights, buys simultaneous rights, buys electronic rights. Editorial lead time 4 months. Submit seasonal material 4 months in advance. Accepts queries by mail, e-mail, fax, phone. Accepts simultaneous submissions. Responds in 1 month to queries. Responds in 2 months to mss. Sample copy for $5. Guidelines available online.

Nonfiction Needs book excerpts, how-to, interview, new product, opinion, personal experience, technical, business principles, spiritual. No self-promotion for writer's company or product. Writer must understand independent retailing or New Age subjects. **Buys approximately 25 mss/year.** Query with published clips. Length: 2,500-3,500 words. **Pays $150-350 for assigned articles. Pays $100-300 for unsolicited articles.**

Photos State availability of or send photos. Captions required. Reviews 2X3 minimum size prints, digital images at 300 dpi. Negotiates payment individually. Buys one time rights.

Tips Describe your expertise in independent retailing or the New Age market and independent retailing. Have an idea for an article ready to pitch. Promise only what you can deliver.

$$ NICHE

Connecting Art Galleries and Craft Retailers, The Rosen Group, 3000 Chestnut Ave., Suite 304, Baltimore MD 21211. (410)889-3093. Fax: (410)243-7089. E-mail: info@rosengrp.com. Website: www.nichemag.com. **Contact:** Kris Stewart, editor. **80% freelance written**. Quarterly trade magazine for the progressive craft gallery retailer. Each issue includes retail gallery profiles, store design trends, management techniques, financial information, and merchandising strategies for small business owners, as well as articles about craft artists and craft mediums. Estab. 1988. Circ. 25,000. Byline given. Pays on publication. No kill fee. Publishes ms an average of 9 months after acceptance. Buys first North American serial rights. Editorial lead time 9 months. Submit seasonal material 1 year in advance. Accepts queries by mail, e-mail, fax. Responds in 6-8 weeks to queries. Responds in 3 months to mss. Sample copy for $3.

Nonfiction "*Niche* is looking for in-depth articles on store security, innovative merchandising/display, design trends, or marketing and promotion. Stories of interest to independent retailers, such as gallery owners, may be submitted." Needs interview, photo feature, articles targeted to independent retailers and small business owners. **Buys 20-28 mss/year.** Query with published clips. **Pays $300-700.** Sometimes pays expenses of writers on assignment.

Photos Send photos. Captions required. Reviews transparencies, slides, e-images. Negotiates payment individually.

Columns/Departments Retail Details (short items at the front of the book, general retail information); Artist Profiles (biographies of American Craft Artists); Retail Resources (including book/video/seminar reviews and educational opportunities pertaining to retailers). Query with published clips. **Pays $25-100.**

$ O&A MARKETING NEWS

KAL Publications, Inc., 559 S. Harbor Blvd., Suite A, Anaheim CA 92805. (714)563-9300. Fax: (714)563-9310. E-mail: kathy@kalpub.com. Website: www.kalpub.com. **3% freelance written**. Bimonthly tabloid. "*O&A Marketing News* is editorially directed to people engaged in the distribution, merchandising, installation, and servicing of gasoline, oil, TBA, quick lube, carwash, convenience store, alternative fuel, and automotive aftermarket products in the 13 Western states." Estab. 1966. Circ. 7,500. Byline sometimes given. Pays on publication. No kill fee. Publishes ms an average of 2 months after acceptance. Buys first rights, buys electronic rights. Editorial lead time 1 month. Submit seasonal material 1 month in advance. Accepts queries by mail, e-mail, fax. Accepts simultaneous submissions. Responds in 2 months to queries. Responds in 2 months to mss. Sample copy for sae with 9 × 13 envelope and 10 first-class stamps.

Nonfiction Needs interview, photo feature, industry news. Nothing that doesn't pertain to the petroleum marketing industry in the 13 Western states. **Buys 35 mss/year.** Send complete ms. Length: 100-500 words. **Pays $1.25/column inch.**

Photos State availability of or send photos. Captions, identification of subjects required. Reviews contact sheets, 4x6 prints, digital images. Offers $5/photo. Buys electronic rights.

Columns/Departments Oregon News (petroleum marketing news in state of Oregon) **Buys 7 mss/year.** Send complete ms. **Pays $1.25/column inch.**

Fillers Needs gags, short humor. Buys 7 fillers/year. mss/year. Length: 1-200 words. **Pays per column inch.**

Tips "Seeking Western industry news pertaining to the petroleum marketing industry. It can be something simple—like a new gas station or quick lube opening. News from 'outlying' states such as Montana, Idaho, Wyoming, New Mexico, and Hawaii is always needed—but any timely, topical news-oriented stories will also be considered."

$$$$ OPERATIONS & FULFILLMENT

Primedia, Inc., 11 Riverbend Dr. S., P.O. Box 4949, Stamford CT 06907-2524. (203)358-4106. E-mail: barnn@primediabusiness.com. Website: www.opsandfulfillment.com. **25% freelance written**. Monthly magazine covering catalog/direct mail operations. *Operations & Fulfillment (O&F)* is a monthly publication that offers practical solutions for catalog online, and direct response operations management. The magazine covers such critical areas as material handling, bar coding, facility planning, transportation, call centers, warehouse management, information systems, online fulfillment and human resources. Estab. 1993. Circ. 17,600. Pays on publication. No kill fee. Publishes ms an average of 2 months after

acceptance. Buys first North American serial rights. Editorial lead time 2 months. Accepts queries by mail, e-mail, phone. Responds in 1 week to queries. Sample copy and writer's guidelines free.
Nonfiction Needs book excerpts, how-to, interview, new product, technical. **Buys 4-6 mss/year.** Query with published clips. Length: 2,500-3,000 words. **Pays $1,000-1,800.**
Photos In addition to the main article, you must include at least one sidebar of about 400 words that contains a detailed example or case study of how a direct-to-customer catalog company implements or benefits from the process you're writing about; a check list or set of practical guidelines (i.e., Twelve Ways to Ship Smarter) that describe how to implement what you suggest in the article; supporting materials such as flow charts, graphs, diagrams, illustrations and photographs (these must be clearly labeled and footnoted); and an author biography of no more than 75 words. Send photos. Captions, identification of subjects required.
Tips Writers need some knowledge of the direct-to-customer industry. They should be able to deal clearly with highly technical material and provide attention to detail and painstaking research.

$$ TRAVEL GOODS SHOWCASE

The source for luggage, business cases, and accessories, Travel Goods Association, 5 Vaughn Dr., Suite 105, Princeton NJ 08540. (609)720-1200. Fax: (609)720-0620. E-mail: cathy@travel-goods.org. Website: www.travel-goods.org. **Contact:** Cathy Hays, senior editor. **5-10% freelance written**. Magazine published quarterly covering travel goods, accessories, trends, and new products. "*Travel Goods Showcase* contains articles for retailers, dealers, manufacturers, and suppliers about luggage, business cases, personal leather goods, handbags, and accessories. Special articles report on trends in fashion, promotions, selling and marketing techniques, industry statistics, and other educational and promotional improvements and advancements." Estab. 1975. Circ. 11,000. Byline given. Pays on acceptance. Offers $50 kill fee. Publishes ms an average of 2 months after acceptance. Editorial lead time 3 months. Submit seasonal material 2 months in advance. Accepts queries by mail, e-mail. Responds in 2 weeks to queries. Responds in 1 month to mss. Sample copy and writer's guidelines free.
Nonfiction Needs interview, new product, technical, travel, retailer profiles with photos. No manufacturer profiles. **Buys 3 mss/year.** Query with published clips. Length: 1,200-1,600 words. **Pays $200-400.**

$$$ VERTICAL SYSTEMS RESELLER

The news source for channel management, Edgell Communications, Inc., 4 Middlebury Blvd., Suite 1, Randolph NJ 07869. (973)252-0100. Fax: (973)252-9020. E-mail: alorden@edgellmail.com. Website: www.verticalsystemsreseller.com. **60% freelance written**. Monthly journal covering channel strategies that build business. Estab. 1992. Circ. 30,000. Byline given. Pays on acceptance. No kill fee. Publishes ms an average of 2 months after acceptance. Editorial lead time 3 months. Accepts queries by mail, e-mail, fax. Accepts simultaneous submissions. Responds in 2 weeks to queries. Responds in 2 months to mss. Sample copy available online.
Nonfiction Needs interview, opinion, technical, technology/channel issues. **Buys 36 mss/year.** Query with published clips. Length: 1,000-1,700 words. **Pays $200-800 for assigned articles.** Sometimes pays expenses of writers on assignment.
Photos Send photos. Identification of subjects, model releases required. Offers no additional payment for photos accepted with ms.

$$$ VM+SD

S.T. Media Group International, 407 Gilbert Ave., Cincinnati OH 45202. (513)421-2050. Fax: (513)421-5144. E-mail: steve.kaufman@stmediagroup.com. Website: www.vmsd.com. **10% freelance written**. Monthly magazine covering retailingÃ³store design, store planning, visual merchandising, brand marketing. Our articles need to get behind the story, tell not only what retailers did when building a new store, renovating an existing store, mounting a new in-store merchandise campaign, but also why they did what they did: specific goals, objectives, strategic initiatives, problems to solve, target markets to reach, etc. Estab. 1872. Circ. 20,000. Byline given. Pays on acceptance. Offers $100 kill fee. Publishes ms an average of 1-2 months after acceptance. Buys all rights. Editorial lead time 2-3 months. Submit seasonal material 3-4 months in advance. Accepts queries by e-mail. Sample copy free. Guidelines free.
Nonfiction Buys 2-3 mss/year. Query. Length: 500-1,000 words. **Pays $400-1,000.**
Photos Contact: Matthew Hall, managing editor. Send photos. Reviews GIF/JPEG files. Negotiates payment individually. Buys one time rights.
Columns/Departments Contact: Anne Dinardo, senior associate editor. Please ask for an editorial calendar. **Buys 5-6 mss/year.** Query. **Pays $500-750.**

Tips We need to see a demonstrated understanding of our industry, its issues and major players; strong reporting and interviewing skills are also important. Merely facile writing is not enough for us.

Sport Trade

$ $ AQUATICS INTERNATIONAL

Hanley Wood, LLC, 6222 Wilshire Blvd., Suite 600, Los Angeles CA 90048. Fax: (503)288-4402. E-mail: gthill@hanleywood.com. Website: www.aquaticsintl.com. **Contact:** Gary Thill, editor. Magazine published 10 times/year covering public swimming pools and waterparks. Devoted to the commercial and public swimming pool industries. The magazine provides detailed information on designing, building, maintaining, promoting, managing, programming and outfitting aquatics facilities. Estab. 1989. Circ. 30,000. Byline given. Pays on publication. No kill fee. Publishes ms an average of 3 months after acceptance. international rights in perpetuity and makes work-for-hire assignments. Editorial lead time 3 months. Responds in 1 month to queries. Sample copy for $10.50.

Nonfiction Needs how-to, interview, technical. **Buys 6 mss/year.** Query with published clips. Length: 1,500-2,500 words. **Pays $525 for assigned articles.**

Columns/Departments Pays $ 250.

Tips "Send query letter with samples."

$ $ ARROWTRADE MAGAZINE

A Magazine for Retailers, Distributors & Manufacturers of Bowhunting Equipment, Arrow Trade Publishing Corp., 3479 409th Ave. NW, Braham MN 55006. (320)396-3473. Fax: (320)396-3206. E-mail: arrowtrade@northlc.com. Website: www.arrowtrademag.com. **60% freelance written.** Bimonthly magazine covering the archery industry. "Our readers are interested in articles that help them operate their business better. They are primarily owners or managers of sporting goods stores and archery pro shops." Estab. 1996. Circ. 11,000. Byline given. **Pays on publication.** No kill fee. Publishes ms an average of 2 months after acceptance. Buys first North American serial rights. Editorial lead time 2 months. Accepts queries by mail, e-mail, fax. Responds in 2 weeks to queries. Responds in 2 weeks to mss. Sample copy for sae with 9 × 12 envelope and 10 First-Class stamps.

Nonfiction Needs interview, new product. Generic business articles won't work for our highly specialized audience. **Buys 24 mss/year.** Query with published clips. Length: 1,800-3,800 words. **Pays $350-550.**

Photos Send photos. Captions required. Must provide digital photos on CD or DVD. Offers no additional payment for photos accepted with ms.

Columns/Departments Product Focus (digging into the design and function of an innovative single product); Behind the Brand (profiling a firm that's important to the bowhunting industry). **Buys 24 mss/year.** Query with published clips. **Pays $250-375.**

Tips "Our readers are hungry for articles that help them decide what to stock and how to do a better job selling or servicing it. Articles needed typically fall into one of these categories: business profiles on outstanding retailers, manufacturers or distributors; equipment articles that cover categories of gear, citing trends in the market and detailing why products have been designed a certain way and what type of use they're best suited for; basic business articles that help dealers do a better job of promoting their business, managing their inventory, training their staff, etc. Good interviewing skills are a must, as especially in the equipment articles we like to see a minimum of 6 sources."

$ $ BOATING INDUSTRY

The Management Magazine for the Recreational Marine Industry, Ehlert Publishing Group, 6420 Sycamore Lane, Suite 100, Maple Grove MN 55369. (763)383-4448. Fax: (763)383-4499. Website: www.boating-industry.com. **Contact:** Matt Gruhn, editor-in-chief. **10-20% freelance written.** Bimonthly magazine covering recreational marine industry management. We write for those in the industry—not the consumer. Our subject is the business of boating. All of our articles must be analytical and predictive, telling our readers where the industry is going, rather than where it's been. Estab. 1929. Circ. 23,000. Byline given. Pays on acceptance. Offers 50% kill fee. Publishes ms an average of 2 months after acceptance. Buys first rights, buys electronic rights. Editorial lead time 2 months. Submit seasonal material 2 months in advance. Accepts queries by mail, e-mail, fax. Responds in 1 month to queries. Sample copy available online. Guidelines free.

Nonfiction Needs technical, business. **Buys 30 mss/year.** Query with published clips. Length: 250-2,500 words. **Pays $25-250.** Sometimes pays expenses of writers on assignment.

Photos State availability. Captions, identification of subjects required. Reviews 2X2 transparencies, 4x6 prints. Negotiates payment individually. Buys one time rights.

$ $ BOWLING CENTER MANAGEMENT

Trade Magazine for Bowling Center Operators, Luby Publishing, 122 S. Michigan Ave., Suite 1506, Chicago IL 60603. (312)341-1110. Fax: (312)341-1469. E-mail: mikem@lubypublishing.com. Website: www.bcmmag.com. **50% freelance written**. Monthly magazine covering bowling centers, family entertainment. "Our readers are looking for novel ways to draw more customers. Accordingly, we look for articles that effectively present such ideas." Estab. 1995. Circ. 12,000. Byline given. Pays on acceptance. Publishes ms an average of 3 months after acceptance. Buys first North American serial rights. Editorial lead time 3 months. Submit seasonal material 6 months in advance. Accepts queries by e-mail. Accepts previously published material. Accepts simultaneous submissions. Responds in 2-3 weeks to queries. Sample copy for $10.

Nonfiction Needs how-to, interview. **Buys 10-20 mss/year.** Query. Length: 750-1,500 words. **Pays $150-350.**

Tips "Send a solid, clever query by e-mail with knowledge and interest in an industry trend."

$ $ CROSSFIRE

Paintball Digest, 570 Mantus Rd., P.O. Box 690, Sewell NJ 08080. (888)834-6026. E-mail: editor@paintball2xtremes.com. Website: www.crossfiremag.com. **100% freelance written.** Monthly magazine covering paintball sport. *Crossfire* will cover all aspects of the paintball industry from tactics to safety. Byline given. Pays on publication. No kill fee. Makes work-for-hire assignments. Editorial lead time 1 year. Submit seasonal material 2 months in advance. Accepts queries by mail, e-mail, fax. Accepts simultaneous submissions. Responds in 2 weeks to queries. Sample copy free.

Nonfiction Needs how-to, humor, interview, new product, personal experience, photo feature, technical, travel, Tournament coverage, industry news. **Buys 1-3 mss/year.** Send complete ms. Length: 700-1,900 words. **Pays 7-22¢/word.**

Photos Send photos. Captions, identification of subjects, model releases required. Reviews negatives. Negotiates payment individually. Buys all rights.

Fillers Needs facts, gags, newsbreaks. Buys 24 mss/year. Length: 25-100 words. **Pays 7-22¢/word.**

Tips Paintball or extreme sport participation is a plus.

$ $ FITNESS MANAGEMENT

Issues and Solutions in Fitness Services, Athletic Business Publications, P.O. Box 409, Danville PA 17821. (800)722-8764. Fax: (570)271-1201. E-mail: edit@fitnessmanagement.com. Website: www.fitnessmanagement.com. **50% freelance written**. Monthly magazine. Readers are owners, managers, and program directors of physical fitness facilities. *FM* helps them run their enterprises safely, efficiently, and profitably. Ethical and professional positions in health, nutrition, sports medicine, management, etc., are consistent with those of established national bodies. Estab. 1985. Circ. 26,000. Byline given. Pays on publication. Offers 50% kill fee. Publishes ms an average of 5 months after acceptance. Buys all rights (all articles published in *FM* are also published and archived on its website). Submit seasonal material 6 months in advance. Accepts queries by mail, e-mail, fax. Responds in 3 months to queries. Sample copy for $5. Guidelines for #10 sase.

Nonfiction Needs how-to, manage fitness center and program, new product, no pay, photo feature, facilities/programs, technical, news of fitness research and major happenings in fitness industry. No exercise instructions or general ideas without examples of fitness businesses that have used them successfully. **Buys 50 mss/year.** Query. Length: 750-2,000 words. **Pays $60-300 for assigned articles.** Pays expenses of writers on assignment.

Photos Send photos. Captions, model releases required. Reviews contact sheets, 2x2 and 4 × 5 transparencies, prefers glossy prints (5 × 7 to 8 × 10).

Tips We seek writers who are experts in a business or science field related to the fitness-service industry or who are experienced in the industry. Be current with the state of the art/science in business and fitness and communicate it in human terms (avoid intimidating academic language; tell the story of how this was learned and/or cite examples or quotes of people who have applied the knowledge successfully).

GOLF BUSINESS

National Golf Course Owners Association, 291 Seven Farms Dr., 2nd Floor, Charleston SC 29492.

(843)881-9956. Fax: (843)856-3288. E-mail: rmusselwhite@ngcoa.org. Website: www.golfbusiness.com. **Contact:** Ronnie Musselwhite, Editor. **80% freelance written**. Monthly magazine covering the business of golf course ownership. "*Golf Business* is the official publication of the National Golf Course Owners Association. The editorial content is designed to promote the exchange of information and ideas among course owners and senior industry executives to improve the profitability of their operations. Articles cover all areas of management and operations, including course design and maintenance, pro shop merchandising, marketing and inventory control, food and beverage operations, insurance and liability issues, legislative updates, finance and human resources. Regular features include in-depth reviews of agronomic issues, environmental policies, technology, highlights of new golf course equipment, plus merchandising strategies for golf apparel, equipment and accessories." Estab. 1996. Circ. 18,000. Byline given. Pays on publication. No kill fee. Buys first rights. Editorial lead time 3 months. Accepts queries by e-mail. Guidelines available online.

$ $ GOLF COURSE MANAGEMENT

Golf Course Superintendents Association of America, 1421 Research Park Dr., Lawrence KS 66049-3859. (800)472-7878. Fax: (785)832-3665. E-mail: tcarson@gcsaa.org. Website: www.gcsaa.org. Teresa Carson, science editor; Ed Hiscock, editor-in-chief; Seth Jones. **Contact:** Scott Hollister, editor. **50% freelance written**. Monthly magazine covering the golf course superintendent. *GCM* helps the golf course superintendent become more efficient in all aspects of their job. Estab. 1924. Circ. 40,000. Byline given. Pays on acceptance. No kill fee. Publishes ms an average of 6 months after acceptance. Buys first North American serial rights, Web rights, and makes work-for-hire assignments. Editorial lead time 6 months. Submit seasonal material 6 months in advance. Accepts simultaneous submissions. Responds in 3 weeks to queries. Responds in 1 month to mss. Sample copy and writer's guidelines free. Guidelines available online.

Nonfiction Needs how-to, interview. No articles about playing golf. **Buys 40 mss/year.** Query for either feature, research, or superintendent article. Submit electronically, preferably as e-mail attachment. Send one-page synopsis or query for feature article to Scott Hollister, shollister@gcsaa.org. For research article, submit to Teresa Carson, tcarson@gcsaa.org. If you are a superintendent, contact Seth Jones, sjones@gcsaa.org. Length: 1,500-2,000 words. **Pays $400-600.** Sometimes pays expenses of writers on assignment.

Photos Send photos. Identification of subjects required. Offers no additional payment for photos accepted with ms. Buys all rights.

Tips Writers should have prior knowledge of golf course maintenance, agronomy and turfgrass science and the overall profession of the golf course superintendent.

$ $ INTERNATIONAL BOWLING INDUSTRY

B2B Media, Inc., 13245 Riverside Dr., Suite 501, Sherman Oaks CA 91423. Fax: (818)789-2812. E-mail: info@bowlingindustry.com. Website: www.bowlingindustry.com. **40% freelance written**. Monthly magazine covering ownership and management of bowling centers (alleys) and pro shops. "*IBI* publishes articles in all phases of bowling center and bowling pro shop ownership and management, among them finance, promotion, customer service, relevant technology, architecture and capital improvement. The magazine also covers the operational areas of bowling centers and pro shops such as human resources, food and beverage, corporate and birthday parties, ancillary attractions (go-karts, gaming and the like), and retailing. Articles must have strong how-to emphasis. They must be written specifically in terms of the bowling industry, although content may be applicable more widely." Estab. 1993. Circ. 10,200. Byline given. Pays on acceptance. Offers $50 kill fee. Publishes ms an average of 3 months after acceptance. Buys all rights. Submit seasonal material 3 months in advance. Accepts queries by mail, e-mail, fax. Accepts simultaneous submissions. Responds in 2 weeks to queries. Responds in 1 month to mss. Sample copy for #10 SASE. Guidelines free.

Nonfiction Needs how-to, interview, new product, technical. **Buys 40 mss/year.** Send complete ms. Length: 1,100-1,400 words. **Pays $250.** Sometimes pays expenses of writers on assignment.

Photos State availability. Identification of subjects required. Reviews JPEG photos. Offers no additional payment for photos accepted with ms. Buys all rights.

Tips "Please supply writing samples, applicable list of credits and bio."

$ $ NSGA RETAIL FOCUS

National Sporting Goods Association, 1601 Feehanville Dr., Suite 300, Mt. Prospect IL 60056-6035. (847)296-6742. Fax: (847)391-9827. E-mail: info@nsga.org. Website: www.nsga.org. **Contact:** Larry N.

Weindruch. **20% freelance written. Works with a small number of new/unpublished writers each year.** Bimonthly magazine. *NSGA Retail Focus* serves as a bimonthly trade journal for sporting goods retailers who are members of the association. Estab. 1948. Circ. 2,000. Byline given. Pays on publication. Offers kill fee. Publishes ms an average of 1 month after acceptance. Buys first rights, buys second serial (reprint) rights, buys electronic rights. Submit seasonal material 6 months in advance. Accepts queries by e-mail. Sample copy for sae with 9 × 12 envelope and 5 first-class stamps.

Nonfiction Needs interview, photo feature. No articles written without sporting goods retail business people in mind as the audience. In other words, no generic articles sent to several industries. **Buys 12 mss/year.** Query with published clips. **Pays $150-300.** Sometimes pays expenses of writers on assignment.

Photos State availability. Reviews high-resolution, digital images. Payment negotiable. Buys one-time rights.

Columns/Departments Personnel Management (succinct tips on hiring, motivating, firing, etc.); Sales Management (in-depth tips to improve sales force performance); Retail Management (detailed explanation of merchandising/inventory control); Store Design; Visual Merchandising, all 1,500 words. **Buys 12 mss/year.** Query. **Pays $150-300.**

$$ PADDLER MAGAZINE

A Publication of Paddlesports Publishing, Inc., Paddlesport Publishing, Inc., 12040 98th Ave. NE, Suite 205, Kirkland WA 98034. (425)814-4140. E-mail: mike@paddlermagazine.com. Website: www.paddlermagazine.com. **70% freelance written**. Quarterly magazine covering the canoeing, kayaking and rafting industry. Estab. 1993. Circ. 7,500. Byline given. 1 month after publication. No kill fee. Publishes ms an average of 6 months after acceptance. Buys first North American serial and one-time electronic rights. Editorial lead time 2 months. Submit seasonal material 6 months in advance. Accepts queries by mail, e-mail. Accepts simultaneous submissions. Responds in 3 months to queries. Sample copy for 8½ × 11 SAE and $1.78. Guidelines for #10 sase.

Nonfiction Needs new product, technical, business advice. **Buys 8 mss/year.** Query or send complete ms. Length: 2,300 words. **Pays 15-20¢/word.** Sometimes pays expenses of writers on assignment.

Photos State availability. Reviews transparencies, hi-res digital images (300 dpi at 5 × 7). Buys one time rights.

Columns/Departments Profiles, how-to, great ideas, computer corner. **Buys 12 mss/year.** Query or send complete ms. **Pays 10-20¢/word.**

$$ POOL & SPA NEWS

Hanley Wood, LLC, 6222 Wilshire Blvd., Suite 600, Los Angeles CA 90048. (323)801-4972. Fax: (323)801-4986. E-mail: etaylor@hanleywood.com. Website: poolspanews.com. **Contact:** Erika Taylor, editor. **15% freelance written**. Semimonthly magazine covering the swimming pool and spa industry for builders, retail stores, and service firms. Estab. 1960. Circ. 16,300. Pays on publication. No kill fee. Publishes ms an average of 2 months after acceptance. Buys all rights. Accepts queries by mail, e-mail. Responds in 1 month to queries. Sample copy for $5 and 9 × 12 SAE and 11 first-class stamps.

Nonfiction Needs interview, technical. Send resume with published clips. Length: 500-2,000 words. **Pays $150-550.** Pays expenses of writers on assignment.

Reprints Send typed manuscript with rights for sale noted and information about when and where the material previously appeared. Payment varies

Photos Payment varies.

Columns/Departments **Payment varies.**

$$ REFEREE

Referee Enterprises, Inc., P.O. Box 161, Franksville WI 53126. Fax: (262)632-5460. E-mail: submissions@referee.com. Website: www.referee.com. **Contact:** Julie Sternberg, managing editor. **75% freelance written**. Monthly magazine covering sports officiating. *Referee* is a magazine for and read by sports officials of all kinds with a focus on baseball, basketball, football, softball, and soccer officiating. Estab. 1976. Circ. 40,000. Byline given. Pays on acceptance. Offers kill fee. Kill fee negotiable. Publishes ms an average of 6 months after acceptance. Buys all rights. Editorial lead time 6 months. Accepts queries by mail, e-mail. Responds in 2 weeks to queries. Responds in 1 month to mss. Sample copy for #10 sase. Guidelines available online.

Nonfiction Needs book excerpts, essays, historical, how-to, sports officiating related, humor, interview, opinion, photo feature, technical, as it relates to sports officiating. We don't want to see articles with themes not relating to sport officiating. General sports articles, although of interest to us, will not be published. **Buys 40 mss/year.** Query with published clips. Length: 500-2,500 words. **Pays $100-400.** Sometimes pays expenses of writers on assignment.

Photos State availability. Identification of subjects required. Reviews contact sheets, negatives, transparencies, prints. Offers $35-40 per photo. Purchase of rights negotiable.

Tips Query first and be persistent. We may not like your idea but that doesn't mean we won't like your next one. Professionalism pays off.

$ $ THE RINKSIDER

Independent Voice of the Industry, Target Publishing Co., Inc., 2470 E. Main St., Columbus OH 43209. (614)235-1022. Fax: (614)235-3584. E-mail: story@rinksider.com. Website: www.rinksider.com. **Contact:** Suzy Weinland, editor. **90% freelance written**. Bimonthly magazine of interest to owners/operators of roller skating facilities, promotions, games, snack bars, roller hockey competitive programs, music, decor, features on new or successful skating centers, competitive amusements, etc. Estab. 1953. Circ. 1,600. Byline given. Pays on publication. Offers 100% (unless poorly done) kill fee. Publishes ms an average of 2 months after acceptance. Buys first rights, buys exclusive of competitive journals rights. Editorial lead time 1 month. Accepts queries by e-mail. Accepts previously published material. Accepts simultaneous submissions. Responds in 2 weeks to queries. Responds in 1 month to mss. Sample copy for $5. Guidelines free.

Nonfiction Needs essays, historical, how-to, humor, inspirational, interview, new product, personal experience, photo feature, travel. Does not want opinion pieces. Query with published clips. Length: 250-1,000 words. **Pays $75-200.**

Photos Send photos. Reviews prints. Offers no additional payment for photos accepted with ms. Buys all rights.

Columns/Departments Finance; Roller Skating News; Marketing; Technology. **Buys 20 mss/year.** Query with published clips. **Pays $75-200.**

$ $ SKI AREA MANAGEMENT

Beardsley Publications, P.O. Box 644, Woodbury CT 06798. (203)263-0888. Fax: (203)266-0452. E-mail: samedit@saminfo.com. Website: www.saminfo.com. **85% freelance written**. Bimonthly magazine covering everything involving the management and development of ski resorts. We are the publication of record for the North American ski industry. We report on new ideas, developments, marketing, and regulations with regard to ski and snowboard resorts. Everyone from the CEO to the lift operator of winter resorts reads our magazine to stay informed about the people and procedures that make ski areas successful. Estab. 1962. Circ. 4,500. Byline given. Pays on publication. Offers kill fee. Offers kill fee. Buys all rights. Editorial lead time 2 months. Submit seasonal material 3 months in advance. Accepts queries by mail, e-mail. Responds in 2 weeks to queries. Sample copy for 9 × 12 SAE with $3 postage or online. Guidelines for #10 sase.

Nonfiction Needs historical, how-to, interview, new product, opinion, personal experience, technical. We don't want anything that does not specifically pertain to resort operations, management, or financing. **Buys 25-40 mss/year.** Query. Length: 500-2,500 words. **Pays $50-400.**

Photos Send photos. Identification of subjects required. Reviews transparencies, prints. Offers no additional payment for photos accepted with ms. Buys one-time rights or all rights.

Tips Know what you are writing about. We are read by people dedicated to skiing and snowboarding and to making the resort experience the best possible for their customers. It is a trade publication read by professionals.

$ $ THOROUGHBRED TIMES

Thoroughbred Times Co., Inc., 2008 Mercer Rd., P.O. Box 8237, Lexington KY 40533. (859)260-9800. **10% freelance written**. Weekly tabloid written for professionals who breed and/or race thoroughbreds at tracks in the US. Articles must help owners and breeders understand racing to help them realize a profit. Estab. 1985. Circ. 20,000. Byline given. Pays on publication. Offers 50% kill fee. Publishes ms an average of 1 month after acceptance. Buys first publication rights. Submit seasonal material 2 months in advance. Responds in 2 weeks to mss.

Nonfiction Needs historical, interview, technical. **Buys 52 mss/year.** Query. Length: 500-2,500 words. **Pays 10-20¢/word.** Sometimes pays expenses of writers on assignment.

Photos State availability. Identification of subjects required. Reviews prints. Offers $50/photo. Buys one time rights.

Columns/Departments Vet Topics; Business of Horses; Pedigree Profiles; Bloodstock Topics; Tax Matters; Viewpoints; Guest Commentary.
Tips We are looking for farm stories and profiles of owners, breeders, jockeys, and trainers.

Stone, Quarry & Mining

$$ CANADIAN MINING JOURNAL

Business Information Group, 12 Concorde Place, Suite 800, Toronto ON M3C 4J2 Canada. (416)510-6742. Fax: (416)510-5138. E-mail: rnoble@canadianminingjournal.com. Website: www.canadianminingjournal.com. **Contact:** Russell Noble, editor. **5% freelance written.** Magazine covering mining and mineral exploration by Canadian companies. *Canadian Mining Journal* provides articles and information of practical use to those who work in the technical, administrative, and supervisory aspects of exploration, mining, and processing in the Canadian mineral exploration and mining industry. Estab. 1882. Circ. 11,000. Byline given. Pays on publication. No kill fee. Publishes ms an average of 3 months after acceptance. Buys one-time rights, buys electronic rights. Makes work-for-hire assignments. Submit seasonal material 3 months in advance. Accepts queries by mail, e-mail, fax, phone. Responds in 1 week to queries. Responds in 1 month to mss.
Nonfiction Needs opinion, technical, operation descriptions. **Buys 6 mss/year.** Query with published clips. Length: 500-1,400 words. **Pays $100-600.** Pays expenses of writers on assignment.
Photos State availability. Captions, identification of subjects, True required. Reviews 4x6 prints or high-resolution files. Negotiates payment individually. Buys one time rights.
Columns/Departments Guest editorial (opinion on controversial subject related to mining industry), 600 words. **Buys 3 mss/year.** Query with published clips. **Pays $150.**
Tips I need articles about mine sites it would be expensive/difficult for me to reach. I also need to know the writer is competent to understand and describe the technology in an interesting way.

$$ COAL PEOPLE MAGAZINE

Al Skinner, Inc., 629 Virginia St. W, P.O. Box 6247, Charleston WV 25362. (304)342-4129. Fax: (304)343-3124. E-mail: alskinner@ntelos.net. Website: www.coalpeople.com. **50% freelance written.** Monthly magazine. Most stories are about people or historical—either narrative or biographical on all levels of coal people, past and present—from coal execs down to grass roots miners. Most stories are upbeat—showing warmth of family or success from underground up! Estab. 1976. Circ. 14,300. Byline given. Pays on publication. No kill fee. Publishes ms an average of 3 months after acceptance. Buys first rights, buys second serial (reprint) rights. Makes work-for-hire assignments. Submit seasonal material 2 months in advance. Accepts queries by e-mail. Responds in 3 months to mss. Sample copy for sae with 9 × 12 envelope and 10 first-class stamps.
Nonfiction Needs book excerpts, and film if related to coal, historical, coal towns, people, lifestyles, humor, including anecdotes and cartoons, interview, for coal personalities, personal experience, as relates to coal mining, photo feature, on old coal towns, people, past and present. Special issues: Calendar issue for more than 300 annual coal shows, association meetings, etc. (January); Surface Mining/Reclamation Award (July); Christmas in Coal Country (December). No poetry, fiction, or environmental attacks on the coal industry. **Buys 32 mss/year.** Query with published clips. Length: 750-2,500 words. **Pays $150-250.**
Reprints Send tearsheet and information about when and where the material previously appeared. Pays 50% of amount paid for an original article.
Photos Send photos. Captions, identification of subjects required. Reviews contact sheets, transparencies, 5 × 7 prints. Buys one-time reprint rights.
Columns/Departments Length: 300-500 words. Editorials—anything to do with current coal issues (nonpaid); Mine'ing Our Business (bull pen column—gossip—humorous anecdotes); Coal Show Coverage (freelance photojournalist coverage of any coal function across the US). **Buys 10 mss/year.** Query. **Pays $50.**
Fillers Needs anecdotes. Length: 300 words. **Pays $35.**
Tips "We are looking for good feature articles on coal professionals, companies—past and present, color slides (for possible cover use), and b&w photos to complement stories. Writers wanted to take photos and do journalistic coverage on coal events across the country. Slant stories more toward people and less on historical. More faces and names than old town, company store photos. Include more quotes from people who lived these moments! The following geographical areas are covered: North America and overseas."

$ $ PIT & QUARRY

Questex Media Group, 600 Superior Ave. E., Suite 1100, Cleveland OH 44114. (216)706-3725. Fax: (216)706-3710. E-mail: info@pitandquarry.com. Website: www.pitandquarry.com. **Contact:** Darren Constantino, editor-in-chief. **10-20% freelance written**. Monthly magazine covering nonmetallic minerals, mining, and crushed stone. Audience has knowledge of construction-related markets, mining, minerals processing, etc. Estab. 1916. Circ. 23,000. Byline given. Pays on acceptance. No kill fee. Publishes ms an average of 2 months after acceptance. Buys first North American serial rights. Editorial lead time 2 months. Accepts queries by e-mail. Accepts simultaneous submissions. Responds in 1 month to queries. Responds in 4 months to mss.

Nonfiction Needs how-to, interview, new product, technical. No humor or inspirational articles. **Buys 3-4 mss/year.** Query. Length: 2,000-2,500 words. **Pays $250-500 for assigned articles. Pays nothing for unsolicited articles.** Sometimes pays expenses of writers on assignment.

Photos State availability. Identification of subjects, model releases required. Offers no additional payment for photos accepted with ms. Buys one time rights.

Columns/Departments Brand New; Techwatch; E-business; Software Corner; Equipment Showcase. Length: 250-750 words. **Buys 5-6 mss/year.** Query. **Pays $250-300.**

Tips Be familiar with quarry operations (crushed stone or sand and gravel), as opposed to coal or metallic minerals mining. Know construction markets. We always need equipment-focused features on specific quarry operations.

Toy, Novelty & Hobby

$ $ MODEL RETAILER

21027 Crossroads Circle, P.O. Box 1612, Waukesha WI 53187. (262)796-8776. Fax: (262)796-1142. E-mail: hmiller@modelretailer.com. Website: www.modelretailer.com. **Contact:** Hal Miller, editor. **5% freelance written**. Monthly magazine. *Model Retailer* covers the business of hobbies, from financial and shop management issues to industry trends and the latest product releases. Our goal is to provide hobby shop entrepreneurs with the tools and information they need to be successful retailers. Estab. 1987. Circ. 6,000. Byline given. Pays on acceptance. No kill fee. Publishes ms an average of 3 months after acceptance. Buys one-time rights, buys electronic rights. Editorial lead time 3 months. Submit seasonal material 6 months in advance. Accepts queries by mail, e-mail, fax. Sample copy and writer's guidelines free. Guidelines available online.

Nonfiction Needs how-to, business, new product. No articles that do not have a strong hobby or small retail component. **Buys 2-3 mss/year.** Query with published clips. You also may send the manuscript as an e-mail attachment. Length: 750-1,500 words. **Pays $250-500 for assigned articles. Pays $100-250 for unsolicited articles.** Sometimes pays expenses of writers on assignment.

Photos State availability. Captions, identification of subjects required. Reviews 4â—Š6 prints. Negotiates payment individually. Buys one time rights.

Columns/Departments Shop Management; Sales Marketing; Technology Advice; Industry Trends, all 500-750 words. **Buys 2-3 mss/year.** Query with published clips. **Pays $100-200.**

PEN WORLD

Masterpiece Litho, Inc., Houston TX (713)869-9997. Fax: (713)869-9993. E-mail: editor@penworld.com. Website: www.penworld.com. **Contact:** Laura Chandler, editor. Magazine published 6 times/year. Published for writing instrument enthusiasts. Circ. 30,000. No kill fee.

Transportation

LIMOUSINE DIGEST

(*Limousine Digest*), Digest Publications, 29 Fostertown Rd., Medford NJ 08055. (609)953-4900. Fax: (609)953-4905. E-mail: info@limodigest.com. Website: www.limodigest.com. **Contact:** Susan Rose, editor/assistant publisher. **10% freelance written**. Monthly magazine covering ground transportation. "*Limousine Digest* is 'the voice of the luxury ground transportation industry.' We cover all aspects of ground transportation from vehicles to operators, safety issues, and political involvement." Estab. 1990. Circ. 10,000. Byline given. Pays on publication. No kill fee. Publishes ms an average of 3 months after acceptance. Makes work-for-hire assignments. Editorial lead time 1 year. Submit seasonal material 3 months in advance. Accepts queries by mail, e-mail, fax. Accepts simultaneous submissions. Sample copy free.

Nonfiction Needs historical, how-to, start a company, market your product, humor, inspirational, interview, new product, personal experience, photo feature, technical, travel, industry news, business. **Buys 7-9 mss/year.** Send complete ms. Length: 700-1,900 words. **Negotiates flat-fee and per-word rates individually. Will pay authors in advertising trade-outs.**
Photos Must include photos to be considered. Send photos. Captions, identification of subjects, model releases required. Reviews negatives. Negotiates payment individually. Buys all rights.
Columns/Departments New Model Showcase (new limousines, sedans, buses), 1,000 words; Player Profile (industry members profiled), 700 words; Hall of Fame (unique vehicles featured), 500-700 words. **Buys 5 mss/year.** Query. **Negotiates flat-fee and per-word rates individually. Will pay authors in advertising trade-outs.**

$ $ METRO MAGAZINE

Bobit Publishing Co., 3520 Challenger St., Torrance CA 90503. (310)533-2400. Fax: (310)533-2502. E-mail: info@metro-magazine.com. Website: www.metro-magazine.com. **Contact:** Alex Roman, managing editor. **10% freelance written**. Magazine published 10 times/year covering transit bus, passenger rail, and motorcoach operations. METRO's coverage includes both public transit systems and private bus operators, addressing topics such as funding mechanisms, procurement, rolling stock maintenance, privatization, risk management and sustainability. *Metro Magazine* delivers business, government policy, and technology developments that are *industry specific* to public transportation. Estab. 1904. Circ. 20,500. Byline given. Pays on acceptance. Offers 10% kill fee. Publishes ms an average of 2 months after acceptance. Buys all rights. Editorial lead time 3 months. Submit seasonal material 3 months in advance. Accepts queries by e-mail. Responds in 2 weeks to queries. Responds in 1 month to mss. Sample copy for $8. Guidelines by e-mail.
Nonfiction Needs how-to, interview, of industry figures, new product, related to transit—bus and rail—private bus, technical. **Buys 6-10 mss/year.** Query. Length: 400-1,500 words. **Pays $80-400.**
Photos State availability. Captions, identification of subjects, model releases required. Negotiates payment individually. Buys all rights.
Columns/Departments Query. **Pays 20¢/word**

Travel Trade

$ $ CRUISE INDUSTRY NEWS

Cruise Industry News, 441 Lexington Ave., Suite 809, New York NY 10017. (212)986-1025. Fax: (212)986-1033. E-mail: oivind@cruiseindustrynews.com. Website: www.cruiseindustrynews.com. **Contact:** Oivind Mathisen, editor. **20% freelance written**. Quarterly magazine covering cruise shipping. "We write about the business of cruise shipping for the industry. That is, cruise lines, shipyards, financial analysts, etc." Estab. 1991. Circ. 10,000. Byline given. Pays on acceptance or on publication Offers 25% kill fee. Publishes ms an average of 4 months after acceptance. Buys first rights. Editorial lead time 3 months. Accepts queries by mail. Reponse time varies. Sample copy for $15. Guidelines for #10 sase.
Nonfiction Needs interview, new product, photo feature, business. No travel stories. **Buys more than 20 mss/year.** Query with published clips. Length: 500-1,500 words. **Pays $.50/word published.** Sometimes pays expenses of writers on assignment.
Photos State availability. Pays $25-50/photo. Buys one-time rights.

$ $ LEISURE GROUP TRAVEL

Premier Tourism Marketing, 4901 Forest Ave., Downers Grove IL 60515. (630)964-1431. Fax: (630)852-0414. E-mail: johnk@premiertourismmarketing.com. Website: www.premiertourismmarketing.com. **35% freelance written**. Bimonthly magazine covering group travel. We cover destinations and editorial relevant to the group travel market. Estab. 1994. Circ. 15,012. Byline given. Pays on publication. No kill fee. Buys first rights, including online publication rights. Editorial lead time 6 months. Submit seasonal material 6 months in advance. Accepts queries by mail, e-mail. Sample copy available online.
Nonfiction Needs travel. **Buys 75 mss/year.** Query with published clips. Length: 1,200-3,000 words. **Pays $0-1,000.**
Tips Experience in writing for 50+ travel marketplace a bonus.

LL&A MAGAZINE

Media Diversified, Inc., 96 Karma Rd., Markham ON L3R 4Y3 Canada. (905)944-0265. Fax: (416)296-

0994. E-mail: info@mediadiversified.com. Website: www.llanda.com. **5% freelance written**. Quarterly magazine for the luggage, leathergoods and accessories market. Serving the travel, business & fashion accessory products industry. Estab. 1966. Circ. 12,000. Byline given. Pays on publication. No kill fee. Buys first rights. Editorial lead time 6 weeks. Accepts queries by e-mail. Sample copy free. Guidelines free.

Nonfiction Needs general interest, how-to, new product, technical.

$$ MIDWEST MEETINGS®

Hennen Publishing, 302 6th St. W., Brookings SD 57006. Fax: (605)692-9031. E-mail: editor@midwestmeetings.com. Website: www.midwestmeetings.com. **Contact:** Serenity J. Knutson, editor. **20% freelance written**. Quarterly magazine covering meetings/conventions industry. We provide information and resources to meeting/convention planners with a Midwest focus. Estab. 1996. Circ. 28,500. Byline given. Pays on acceptance. Publishes ms an average of 5 months after acceptance. Buys one-time rights, buys electronic rights. Editorial lead time 3 months. Submit seasonal material 3 months in advance. Accepts queries by mail, e-mail, fax. Sample copy free. Guidelines by e-mail.

Nonfiction Needs essays, general interest, historical, how-to, humor, interview, personal experience, travel. Does not want marketing pieces related to specific hotels/meeting facilities. **Buys 15-20 mss/year.** Send complete ms. Length: 500-1,000 words. **Pays 5-50¢/word.**

Photos Send photos. Captions, identification of subjects required. Reviews GIF/JPEG files (300 dpi). Offers no additional payment for photos accepted with ms. Buys one time rights.

Tips If you were a meeting/event planner, what information would help you to perform your job better? We like lots of quotes from industry experts, insider tips, etc. If you're not sure, e-mail the editor.

$$$ RV BUSINESS

TL Enterprises, Inc., 2575 Vista del Mar Dr., Ventura CA 93001. (805)667-4100. Fax: (805)667-4484. E-mail: bhampson@affinitygroup.com. Website: www.rvbusiness.com. **50% freelance written**. Monthly magazine. *RV Business* caters to a specific audience of people who manufacture, sell, market, insure, finance, service and supply, components for recreational vehicles. Estab. 1972. Circ. 21,000. Byline given. Pays on acceptance. Offers kill fee. Offers kill fee. Publishes ms an average of 2 months after acceptance. Buys first North American serial rights. Editorial lead time 3 months. Accepts queries by mail, e-mail. Sample copy free.

Nonfiction Needs new product, photo feature, industry news and features. No general articles without specific application to our market. **Buys 300 mss/year.** Query with published clips. Length: 125-2,200 words. **Pays $50-1,500.** Sometimes pays expenses of writers on assignment.

Columns/Departments Top of the News (RV industry news), 75-400 words; Business Profiles, 400-500 words; Features (indepth industry features), 800-2,000 words. **Buys 300 mss/year.** Query. **Pays $50-1,500.**

Tips Query. Send 1 or several ideas and a few lines letting us know how you plan to treat it/them. We are always looking for good authors knowledgeable in the RV industry or related industries. We need more articles that are brief, factual, hard hitting, and business oriented. Review other publications in the field, including enthusiast magazines.

$$ SCHOOL TRANSPORTATION NEWS

STN Media Co., 5334 Torrance Blvd., 3rd Floor, Torrance CA 90503. (310)792-2226. Fax: (310)792-2231. E-mail: info@stnonline.com. Website: www.stnonline.com. **Contact:** Ryan Gray, editor-in-chief. **20% freelance written**. Monthly magazine covering school bus and pupil transportation industries in North America. "Contributors to *School Transportation News* must have a basic understanding of K-12 education and automotive fleets and specifically of school buses. Articles cover such topics as manufacturing, operations, maintenance and routing software, GPS, security and legislative affairs. A familiarity with these principles is preferred. Additional industry information is available on our website. New writers must perform some research of the industry or exhibit core competencies in the subject matter." Estab. 1991. Circ. 23,633. Byline given. Pays on publication. No kill fee. Buys one-time rights. Editorial lead time 1-2 months. Submit seasonal material 3 months in advance. Accepts queries by e-mail. Accepts simultaneous submissions. Sample copy free. Guidelines free.

Nonfiction Needs book excerpts, general interest, historical, humor, inspirational, interview, new product, personal experience, photo feature, technical. "Does not want strictly localized editorial. We want articles that put into perspective the issues of the day." Query with published clips. Length: 600-1,200 words. **Pays $150-300.** Sometimes pays expenses of writers on assignment.

Photos Contact: Vince Rios, director. Captions, model releases required. Reviews GIF/JPEG files. Offers $150-200/photo. Buys all rights.
Columns/Departments Creative Special Report, Cover Story, Top Story; Book/Video Reviews (new programs/publications/training for pupil transporters), both 600 words. **Buys 40 mss/year.** Query with published clips. **Pays $150.**
Tips "Potential freelancers should exhibit a basic proficiency in understanding school bus issues and demonstrate the ability to report on education, legislative and business affairs, as well as a talent with feature writing. It would be helpful if the writer has previous contacts within the industry. Article pitches should be e-mailed only."

$$ SPECIALTY TRAVEL INDEX

Alpine Hansen, P.O. Box 458, San Anselmo CA 94979. (415)455-1643. Fax: (415)455-1648. E-mail: info@specialtytravel.com. Website: www.specialtytravel.com. **90% freelance written**. Semiannual magazine covering adventure and special interest travel. Estab. 1980. Circ. 35,000. Byline given. Pays on receipt and acceptance of all materials. No kill fee. Buys one-time rights. Editorial lead time 3 month. Submit seasonal material 3 months in advance. Accepts queries by mail, e-mail. Writer's guidelines on request.
Nonfiction Needs how-to, personal experience, photo feature, travel. **Buys 15 mss/year.** Query. Length: 1,250 words. **Pays $300 minimum.**
Reprints Send tearsheet. Pays 100% of amount paid for an original article.
Photos State availability. Captions, identification of subjects required. Reviews EPS/TIFF files. Negotiates payment individually.
Tips Write about group travel and be both creative and factual. The articles should relate to both the travel agent booking the tour and the client who is traveling.

$ STAR SERVICE

NORTHSTAR Travel Media, 200 Brookstown Ave., Suite 301, Winston-Salem NC 27101. (336)714-3328. Fax: (336)714-3168. E-mail: csheaffer@ntmllc.com. Website: www.starserviceonline.com. "Eager to work with experienced writers as well as those working from a home base abroad, planning trips that would allow time for hotel reporting, or living in major ports for cruise ships. Worldwide guide to accommodations and cruise ships, sold to travel professionals on subscription basis. Estab. 1960. No byline given. Pays 1 month after acceptance. No kill fee. Buys all rights. Accepts queries by e-mail preferred. Writer's guidelines provided.
Nonfiction "Objective, critical evaluations of hotels and cruise ships suitable for international travelers, based on personal inspections. Freelance correspondents ordinarily are assigned to update an entire state or country or individual hotels in their local market. Assignment involves on-site inspections of all hotels and cruise ships we review; revising and updating published reports; and reviewing new properties. Qualities needed are thoroughness, precision, perseverance, and keen judgment. Solid research skills and powers of observation are crucial. Travel writing and hotel experience is highly desirable. Reviews must be colorful and clear. We accept no advertising or payment for listings, so reviews should dispense praise and criticism where deserved. Query should include details on writer's experience in travel and writing, clips, specific forthcoming travel plans, and how much time would be available for hotel or ship inspections. Sponsored trips are acceptable." **Buys 4,500 mss/year. Pays $30-40/report used.**
Tips "We may require sample hotel or cruise reports on facilities near freelancer's hometown before giving the first assignment. No byline because of sensitive nature of reviews."

TRAVEL AGENT MAGAZINE

Questex Media, 757 Third Ave., 5th Floor, New York NY 10017. (212)895-8200. Fax: (212)895-8210. E-mail: omcdonald@advanstar.com. Website: www.travelagentcentral.com/travelagentcentral. Weekly magazine serving travel agents.
Nonfiction Needs general interest, interview, travel. Query.

$$ TRAVEL TIPS

Premier Tourism Marketing, 4901 Forest Ave., Downers Grove IL 60515. (630)964-1431. Fax: (630)852-0414. E-mail: johnk@premiertourismmarketing.com. Website: www.premiertourismmarketing.com. **75% freelance written**. Bimonthly magazine covering group travel. We cover destinations and editorial relevant to the group travel market. Estab. 1994. Circ. 12,500. Byline given. Pays on publication. Buys first rights, buys electronic rights. Editorial lead time 6 months. Submit seasonal material 6 months in advance. Accepts queries by mail, e-mail. Sample copy available online.

Nonfiction Needs travel. **Buys 36-50 mss/year.** Query with published clips. Length: 1,200-3,000 words. **Pays $0-500.**
Tips Experience in writing for 50+ travel marketplace a bonus.

Veterinary

$$ VETERINARY ECONOMICS

Business Solutions for Practicing Veterinarians, Advanstar Veterinary Healthcare Communications, 8033 Flint, Lenexa KS 66214. (913)492-4300. Fax: (913)492-4157. E-mail: ve@advanstar.com. Website: www.vetecon.com. **20% freelance written**. Monthly magazine covering veterinary practice management. We address the business concerns and management needs of practicing veterinarians. Estab. 1960. Circ. 54,000. Byline given. Pays on publication. No kill fee. Publishes ms an average of 6 months after acceptance. Buys all rights. Editorial lead time 3 months. Submit seasonal material 3 months in advance. Accepts queries by mail, e-mail, fax. Accepts simultaneous submissions. Responds in 3 months to queries. Sample copy free. Guidelines available online.
Nonfiction Needs how-to, interview, personal experience. **Buys 24 mss/year.** Send complete ms. Length: 1,000-2,000 words. **Pays $50-400.**
Photos Send photos. Captions, identification of subjects required. Reviews transparencies, prints. Offers no additional payment for photos accepted with ms. Buys one time rights.
Columns/Departments Practice Tips (easy, unique business tips), 200-300 words. Send complete ms. **Pays $40.**
Tips Among the topics we cover: veterinary hospital design, client relations, contractual and legal matters, investments, day-to-day management, marketing, personal finances, practice finances, personnel, collections, and taxes. We also cover news and issues within the veterinary profession; for example, articles might cover the effectiveness of Yellow Pages advertising, the growing number of women veterinarians, restrictive-covenant cases, and so on. Freelance writers are encouraged to submit proposals or outlines for articles on these topics. Most articles involve interviews with a nationwide sampling of veterinarians; we will provide the names and phone numbers if necessary. We accept only a small number of unsolicited manuscripts each year; however, we do assign many articles to freelance writers. All material submitted by first-time contributors is read on speculation, and the review process usually takes 12-16 weeks. Our style is concise yet conversational, and all manuscripts go through a fairly rigorous editing process. We encourage writers to provide specific examples to illustrate points made throughout their articles.

Newspapers

Over the past several years, newspapers have been struggling, but it would be foolish to think they're dead or dying. There are still thousands of dailies and weeklies covering city and regional beats across the country. And while most newspapers have been forced to consolidate efforts and cut staff to remain competitive, they still need to provide newsworthy content to fill pages, which opens the door of opportunity for freelancers.

Staff writers will continue to handle the obvious stories of national, regional and local importance, but a freelancer can make sales by searching out those stories of real interest that are not as obvious, as well as the stories that demand special connections or a certain sensitivity to write. Your uniqueness as a freelancer is something you should communicate in your query letter. (For more information on query letters, read "Query Letter Clinic," on page 19.)

Listings

In addition to smaller circulation newspapers, *Writer's Market* lists many of the highest circulation newspapers in the country. As a result of these being the highest circulation newspapers, the information they freely share with freelancers is scarce. While it is always advised that you query before submitting to a newspaper, that rule holds especially true for the higher circulation papers.

Most newspapers have several departments with a specific editor handling all the material within each. It is important that you take the extra step to find out who the current contact is for the department you wish to submit your query. While it can seem like a lot of legwork, that is exactly the kind of professionalism that will be required if you expect to successfully freelance for newspapers.

ABLE NEWSPAPER

The Newspaper For, By, and About the Disabled, Melmont Printing, P.O. Box 395, Old Bethpage NY 11804. Fax: (516)939-0540. E-mail: ablenews@aol.com. Website: www.ablenews.com. Estab. 1991. Circ. 35,000. Accepts 20% of material on one-time basis. 30 features purchased/year. all news including, but not limited to, legislation, advocacy, health, transportation, and housing issues. "*Able* focuses on news for people with disabilities." Accepts queries by e-mail, fax. Buys first rights. Pays on publication. Byline given. Sample copy and guidelines free.

Needs Query with published clips. Length: 400-600 words. **Pays $50 minimum.**

⊞ THE ANGLICAN JOURNAL

The Anglican Journal Board of Directors, 80 Hayden St., Toronto ON M4Y 3G2 Canada. (416)924-9192. Fax: (416)921-4452. E-mail: editor@anglicanjournal.com. Website: www.anglicanjournal.com. Estab. 1875. Circ. 175,000. Accepts 10-15% of material on one-time basis. Monthly, except for July and August *The Anglican Journal* covers news of interest to Anglicans in Canada and abroad. Accepts queries by mail, e-mail, fax. Buys all rights. Pays on publication. Editorial lead time 2 months. Offers 50% kill fee. Byline given. Accepts simultaneous submissions. Sample copy free. Guidelines available by e-mail.

Needs No poetry or fiction. Query. Length: 600-1,000 words. **Pays 25¢ (Canadian)/word.** Sometimes pays expenses of writers on assignment.

Photos State availability Reviews GIF/JPEG files (high resolution at 300 ppi). Buys all rights. Negotiates payment individually. Identification of subjects required.

ANTIQUE SHOPPE NEWSPAPER

Specialty General Service Publications, Inc., P.O. Box 2175, Keystone Heights FL 32656. (352)475-1679. Fax: (352)475-5326. E-mail: antshoppe@aol.com. Website: www.antiqueshoppefl.com. Estab. 1986. Circ. 20,000. Accepts 25% of material under contract. Accepts 25% of material on one-time basis. 100 features purchased/year. Works with 10-12 writers/year. Accepts queries by mail, e-mail, phone. Responds in 1 week to queries. Buys one-time rights. Pays on publication. Editorial lead time 3-4 weeks. No kill fee. Byline given. Accepts previously published submissions. Accepts simultaneous submissions. Returns submission with SASE. Sample copy and guidelines free.

Needs Query with published clips. Length: 1,000-1,750 words. **Pays $50.**

Photos Send photos. Reviews prints, GIF/JPEG files. Buys one-time rights. Offers no additional payment for photos accepted with ms. Captions required.

Tips "Writers should have knowledge on expertise in the antique/collectibles industry."

ASIAN PAGES

Kita Associates, Inc., P.O. Box 11932, St. Paul MN 55111-1932. (952)884-3265. Fax: (952)888-9373. E-mail: asianpages@att.net. Website: www.asianpages.com. Estab. 1990. Circ. 75,000. Accepts 40% of material on one-time basis. 50-60 features purchased/year. Biweekly "*Asian Pages* celebrates the achievements of the Asian community in the Midwest and promotes a cultural bridge among the many different Asian groups that the newspaper serves." Accepts queries by mail. Responds in 1 month to queries. Responds in 2 months to mss. Buys first North American serial rights. Pays on publication. Editorial lead time 4 months. Offers 50% kill fee. Byline given. Accepts simultaneous submissions. Sample copy for SASE with 9 × 12 envelope and 3 first-class stamps. Guidelines for #10 SASE.

Needs "All articles must have an Asian slant. We're interested in articles on the Asian New Years, banking, business, finance, sports/leisure, home and garden, education, and career planning." No culturally insensitive material. Send complete ms. Length: 500-700 words. **Pays $40.**

Columns/Departments Query with exceptional ideas for our market and provide 1-2 sample columns. Buys 100 mss/year.

CHRISTIAN JOURNAL

1032 W. Main, Medford OR 97501. (541)773-4004. Fax: (541)773-9917. E-mail: info@thechristianjournal.org. Website: www.liftingthecross.com. Estab. 1998. Circ. 15,000. Accepts 80% of material on one-time basis. "It is the purpose of the *Christian Journal* to encourage the reader with Christian support articles—personal experiences, stories about ministry, hope in God, poetry, uplifting short pieces, etc. The best chance of getting printed is to submit articles on the issue's theme." Accepts queries by e-mail. Responds in 2 weeks to queries. Responds in 1-2 months to mss. Editorial lead time 1-2 months. No kill fee. Byline and e-mail given. Accepts previously published submissions. Accepts simultaneous submissions. Sample copy for SASE with 9 × 12 envelope and 3 First-class stamps. Guidelines available online.

Needs Query or send complete ms. Length: up to 500 words.

Columns/Departments Health; Senior Views; both 600-800 words.

Photos Send photos Reviews GIF/JPEG files. Buys one-time rights (small stipend) Offers no payment for photos. Identification of subjects required.

Tips "Be willing to have your work edited and used to touch readers."

THE COLUMBIA STAR

The Star Reporter Corp., 723 Queen St., Columbia SC 29205. (803)771-0219. Fax: (803)252-6397. E-mail: mmaddock@sc.rr.com. Website: www.thecolumbiastar.com. Estab. 1963. Circ. 35,000. "We no longer buy series and only want stories from Richland County in South Carolina." Accepts queries by mail. Pays on publication. Editorial lead time 2 weeks. Byline given.

Needs Buys one-shot features. No reviews. Send complete ms. Length: 300-500 words. **Pays $30 for assigned articles.**

CONSTRUCTION EQUIPMENT GUIDE

470 Maryland St., Ft. Washington PA 19034. (800)523-2200 or (215)885-2900. Fax: (215)885-2910. E-mail: editorial@cegltd.com. Estab. 1957. Circ. 120,000. Accepts 30% of material on one-time basis. 200-600 features purchased/year. Four regional biweekly newspapers Accepts queries by mail, e-mail, fax, phone. Buys all rights. Pays on publication. Byline given. Sample copy and guidelines free.

Needs Query with published clips. Length: 150-1,800 words. **Word rate negotiable.**

Photos Negotiates payment individually. Requires photos with captions for many stories.

Tips "Keep an eye out for commercial, highway, bridge construction in your area. Call or e-mail leads with name of on site contractor. Read our articles at www.constructionequipmentguide.com to learn our target audience and advertisers, which consists of heavy equipment distributors and manufacturers."

THE DAILY TELEGRAPH

Nationwide Newspapers Pty Ltd., 2 Holt St., Surry Hills NSW 2010 Australia. (61)(2)9288-3000. Fax: (61)(2)9280-2300. E-mail: news@dailytelegraph.com.au. Website: dailytelegraph.news.com.au. Circ. 343,948. Daily. No kill fee.

- Query before submitting.

EQUIPMENT JOURNAL

Canada's National Equipment Newspaper, 5160 Explorer Dr., Unit 6, Mississauga ON L4W 4T7 Canada. (800)667-8541. Fax: (905)629-7988. E-mail: editor@equipmentjournal.com. Website: www.equipmentjournal.com. Estab. 1966. Circ. 21,240. Accepts 10% of material under contract. 10 features purchased/year. Published 17 times/year. "We publish product information, jobsite stories, and features that are relevant to the material handling, construction, mining, forestry, and transportation industries." Accepts queries by mail, e-mail, fax, phone. Makes work-for-hire assignments. Pays on publication. Editorial lead time 1 month. No kill fee. Byline given. Accepts simultaneous submissions. Sample copy free.

Needs No material that falls outside of *EJ*'s mandate—the Canadian equipment industry. Query. Length: 500-1,000 words. **Pays $150-$400 (Canadian).** Sometimes pay expenses of writers on assignment.

Photos State availability Reviews 4 × 6 prints. Buys all rights. Negotiates payment individually. Identification of subjects required.

Tips We are looking for new product release stories of products made by Canadian manufacturers and field application stories that take place in Canada.

FARM WORLD

MidCountry Media, P.O. Box 90, Knightstown IN 46148-1242. (800)876-5133. Fax: (800)318-1055. E-mail: davidb@farmworldonline.com. Website: www.farmworldonline.com. Estab. 1955. Circ. 36,000. Accepts 60-70% of material on one-time basis. 1,000 features purchased/year. Weekly Accepts queries by mail, e-mail, fax. Buys first, electronic rights. Makes work-for-hire assignments. Editorial lead time 1 month. Byline given. Sample copy available online. Guidelines available online.

Needs "We've seen a lot, but we are always looking for ways farmers are able to succeed in the current crisis. New issues include biofuels - ethanol and biodiesel, GMOs and other biotech; trade; marketing; and farmland preservation. The environment and new regulations are also of concern to farmers." We don't want first-person accounts. No unsolicited columns, no opinion, no humor, no nostalgia. Query. Length: 1,000 words maximum. **Pays $55 (less than 400 words); $85 (more than 400 words). All stories go online** Pays expenses of writers on assignment.

Photos Reviews prints. Buys one-time rights. Offers $5/photo. Front page photos: $15 each. Captions required, identification of subjects required.

Tips "We want feature stories about farmers and agribusiness operators. How do they operate their businesses? Keys to success? Best thing to do is call us first with idea, or write. Could also be a story about some pressing issue in agriculture nationally that affects farmers everywhere."

GRAINEWS

Farm Business Communications (Division of Glacier Ventures International), P.O. Box 9800, Winnipeg MB R3C 3K7 Canada. (204)944-5767. Fax: (204)944-5416. E-mail: jay@fbcpublishing.com. Accepts 80% of material on one-time basis. Published 19 times/year. Accepts queries by mail, e-mail, fax, phone. Buys first rights. Editorial lead time 1 month. Byline given. Accepts previously published submissions.

Needs In-depth how-to articles on various aspects of farming. Every article should be written from the farmer's perspective. Query. **Pays $150 for assigned articles.** Sometimes pays expenses of writers on assignment.

Photos State availability Buys one time rights. Offers no additional payment for photos accepted with ms. Captions required, identification of subjects required.

Tips "We want writers who are farmers. Ask yourself how your story will help or entertain other farmers and if it doesn't, don't send it."

THE HAPPY HERALD NEWSPAPER

South Florida's Positive Lifestyle and Entertainment Guide, Star Publications, Inc., P.O. Box 810548, Boca Raton FL 33481. E-mail: editorial@happyherald.com. Website: www.happyherald.com. Estab. 1995. Circ. 75,000. Accepts 50% of material under contract. Accepts 70% of material on one-time basis. 12 features purchased/year. Monthly. Accepts queries by e-mail. Responds in 2 months to queries. Responds in 2 months to mss. Pays on publication. Editorial lead time 2-3 months. No kill fee. Byline given. Accepts simultaneous submissions. Sample copy available online. Guidelines available online.

- Include Attention: Editorial Department in the subject line of e-mail queries.

Needs Buys one-shot features. Length: 200-500 words.

Photos Send photos Reviews GIF/JPEG files (300-400 dpi). Offers no additional payment for photos accepted with ms.

Tips "Go to website and look at writer's guidelines."

HOME TIMES FAMILY NEWSPAPER

(formerly *Palm Beach Conservative*), Neighbor News, Inc., P.O. Box 22547, West Palm Beach FL 33416. (561)439-3509. E-mail: hometimes2@aol.com. Website: hometimesnewspaper.org. **Contact:** Dennis Lombard, ed. & publ.. Estab. 1990. Circ. 4,000. Accepts 100% of material on one-time basis. 12 features purchased/year. Works with Works with several local stringers. writers/year. Monthly tabloid mailed to subscribers throughout Palm Beach and Treasure Coast in Southeast Florida. "*Home Times* is a conservative newspaper written for the general public but with a Biblical worldview and family-values slant. It is not religious or preachy." 2-4 weeks to full articles only. Buys one-time and reprint rights. Makes work-for-hire assignments. Pays on publication. Editorial lead time 8 weeks. No kill fee. Byline given. Accepts simultaneous submissions. Returns submission with SASE. Sample copy for $3. Guidelines for #10 SASE.

Needs Buys one-shot features. Does not want devotionals. Send complete ms. Length: 500-1,000 words. **Pays $10-50 for assigned articles.** Sometimes pays expenses of writers on assignment.

Columns/Departments Home & Family; Arts & Entertainment, Science, Sports, Advice, Lifestyles; Personal Finances, all shorts and features. Buys 12 mss/year.

Fillers Anecdotes, facts, short humor good quotes 100 word maximum.

Photos Can scan any size prints but prefer emailed digital photos. Send photos Reviews 4 × 5 prints or gif/tif/jpeg files. Buys one time rights. Offers $5-25/photo. Captions required, identification of subjects, model releases required, if appropriate.

Tips "We strongly suggest writers get guidelines plus READ the paper. Your $3 gets you three consecutive issues. Writer's subscription only $19."

INDIAN LIFE

News From Across Native North America, Indian Life Ministries, (Canada) P.O. Box 3765, Redwood Post Office, Winnipeg MB R2W 3R6 Canada, (U.S.) P.O. Box 32, Pembina ND 58271. (204)661-9333. Fax: (204)661-3982. E-mail: ilm.editor@indianlife.org. Website: www.indianlife.org. Estab. 1968. Circ. 22,000. Accepts 30% of material on one-time basis. 15 features purchased/year. Bimonthly. *Indian Life*'s purpose is to bring hope, healing, and honor through the presentation of positive news, role models, and a Christian message. Accepts queries by mail, e-mail, fax. Responds in 1 month to queries. Buys first North American serial, electronic rights. Pays on publication. Byline given. Sample copy and writer's guidelines for $2.

Needs Book excerpts, general interest, historical/nostalgic, inspirational, interview/profile, personal experience, photo feature.

Fiction Adventure, ethnic, historical, religious, slice-of-life vignettes. Buys 6 mss/year. Length: 300-1,500 words.

Poetry Free verse, light verse, traditional. Buys 5-10 poems/year. Submit maximum 5 poems. Maximum

25 lines. Pays $40-50. Query. Length: 300-1,500 words.

Fillers anecdotes, facts, newsbreaks 6 mss/year. Length: 100 words.

Photos State availability. Buys all rights. Offers $40 minimum; $100 maximum/photo. Captions required, identification of subjects required.

JOURNAL NEWSPAPER GROUP

Metropolitan Graphics, 4610 200th St. SW, Suite F, Lynnwood WA 98036. Fax: (425)670-0511. E-mail: editor@journal-newspapers.com. Website: www.journal-newspapers.com. Estab. 1973. Circ. 100,000. Accepts 50%% of material under contract. Accepts 10%% of material on one-time basis. 60 features purchased/year. Works with 10-15 writers/year. Monthly. Accepts queries by e-mail. Responds in 2 weeks to queries. Pays on publication. Editorial lead time 3 weeks. No kill fee. Byline given. Sample copy available online.

Needs Buys one-shot features. Home Improvement, Senior Lifestyles, Health & Fitness. "We do not want feature stories not local to our area (North King, South Snohomish counties); hard news; politics, religion or anything of a controversial nature; personal essays." Query with published clips. Length: 600-1,000 words. **Pays $100 for assigned articles.**

Columns/Departments Arts & Entertainment (local), Senior Lifestyles (local), Health & Fitness (current), 700 words; General Features, 800 words

Tips "Find local, upcoming events in our area. Search out interesting people doing interesting things in our area. Pitch unique, local, well thought-out feature story ideas. Browse the 'search articles' section of our website to see what we've already done. Send well-written published clips with queries."

KIDS VT

Vermont's Family Newspaper, Kids VT Publications, Inc., P.O. Box 1089, Shelburne VT 05482. (802)985-5482. Fax: (802)985-5479. E-mail: editorial@kidsvt.com. Website: www.kidsvt.com. Estab. 1994. Circ. 25,000. Accepts 80% of material on one-time basis. 25-40 features purchased/year. Monthly. Accepts queries by mail, e-mail, fax. local, Vermont rights. Pays on publication. Editorial lead time 2 months. Accepts previously published submissions. Accepts simultaneous submissions. Guidelines available online.

Needs Query. Length: 400-1,600 words. **Pays $10-40.**

Photos State availability. Buys one-time rights. Negotiates payment individually. Captions required.

Tips Send unsolicited mss.

LEXINGTON HERALD-LEADER

McClatchy, 100 Midland Ave., Lexington KY 40508. (859)231-3100. Fax: (859)231-1659. Website: www.kentucky.com. Circ. 113,000. Daily. No kill fee.

- Mostly staff written.

LIVING LIGHT NEWS

Living Light Ministries, 5306 89th St., #200, Edmonton AB T6E 5P9 Canada. (780)468-6397. Fax: (780)468-6872. E-mail: shine@livinglightnews.com. Website: www.livinglightnews.org. Estab. 1995. Circ. 75,000. Accepts 100% of material on one-time basis. 50 features purchased/year. Bimonthly. "Our publication is a seeker-sensitive, evangelical, outreach-oriented newspaper focusing on glorifying God and promoting a personal relationship with Him." Accepts queries by e-mail, phone. Responds in 2 weeks to queries and to mss. Buys first North American serial, first, one-time, second serial (reprint), simultaneous, all rights. Makes work-for-hire assignments. Editorial lead time 2 months. Offers 100% kill fee. Byline sometimes given. Accepts previously published submissions. Accepts simultaneous submissions. Sample copy for 10 × 13 SAE with $3.50 in IRCs. Guidelines available online.

Needs Profiles on 'celebrity Christians' in sports, business and entertainment, plus amazing stories of hope, redemption and transformation through Jesus Christ. No issue-oriented, controversial stories. Query with published clips. Length: 300-1,000 words. **Pays $30-100 for assigned articles.** Sometimes pays expenses of writers on assignment. Pays expenses of writers on assignment.

Columns/Departments Buys 40 mss/year.

Photos State availability Reviews 3 × 5 prints, GIF/JPEG files. Buys all rights. Offers $20/photo. Identification of subjects required.

Tips "Please visit our website for a sample of our publication. All of our stories must be of interest to both Christians and non-Christians. We look for lively writing styles that are friendly, down-to-earth, and engaging. We especially like celebrity profiles."

MINNESOTA CHRISTIAN CHRONICLE

Selah Media Group, P.O. Box 131030, St. Paul MN 55113. (763)746-2468. Fax: (763)746-2469. E-mail: editor@mcchronicle.com. Website: www.mcchronicle.com. Estab. 1978. Circ. 34,000. Accepts 10% of material on one-time basis. Monthy chronicle "Our readers tend to be conservative evangelicals with orthodox Christian beliefs and conservative social and political views." Accepts queries by e-mail. Responds in 1 month to queries. Pays on other. Editorial lead time 1 month. Byline given. Accepts previously published submissions. Accepts simultaneous submissions. Sample copy for $2.

Needs Higher Education Guide; Christmas section; Christian School Directory; Life Resource Guide; Christian Ministries Directory. Query. Length: 500-2,000 words.

Photos State availability. No payment. Captions required.

Tips "Stories for the *Minnesota Christian Chronicle* must have a strong Minnesota connection and a clear hook for the Christian community. We do not publish general nonreligious stories or devotionals. We rarely buy from writers who are not in Minnesota."

NZ AVIATION NEWS

P.O. Box 9711, Newmarket Auckland 1149 New Zealand. (64)(9)307-7849. Fax: (64)(9)307-7854. E-mail: editor@aviationnews.co.nz. Website: www.aviationnews.co.uz. Estab. 1978. Circ. 15,000. Monthly newspaper covering the aviation industry and recreational activity in New Zealand and the Pacific region No kill fee.

Photos Reviews negatives, prints, JPEG files.

OJORNAL

Portuguese-American Journal, 10 Purchase St., Fall River MA 02721. (508)678-3844. Fax: (508)678-1798. E-mail: Ric@ojornal.com. Website: www.ojornal.com. Estab. 1975. Circ. 14,800. Accepts 30% of material under contract. Accepts 10% of material on one-time basis. 100 features purchased/year. Works with 10 writers/year. Weekly Bilingual Portuguese-English newspaper covering social, cultural, historical, community, and immigration issues of the Portuguese-American community of New England. Accepts queries by e-mail. Responds in 2 weeks to queries. Buys all rights. Makes work-for-hire assignments. Pays on publication. Editorial lead time 2 weeks. Byline given. Accepts previously published submissions. Accepts simultaneous submissions.

Needs Buys one-shot features. Christmas edition; Day of Portugal edition (July); political election previews; special editions based on topic or interesting news story or trend. No things that have nothing to do with immigration or the Portuguese cultural or historical experience, or about non-Portuguese people or trends. Query. Length: 350-600 words. **Pays $50-150.** Sometimes pays expenses of writers on assignment.

Columns/Departments This Week in Portuguese-American History, 350 words; coverage of local feasts, personalities, or trends in Massachusetts or Rhode Island, and other events, 350-500 words. Buys 100 mss/year.

THE OREGONIAN

Advance Publications, 1320 SW Broadway, Portland OR 97201. (503)221-8327. Fax: (503)227-5306. E-mail: newsroom@news.oregonian.com. Website: www.oregonian.com. Circ. 250,000. Daily news No kill fee.

- Mostly staff written.

THE PEG

The Association of Professional Engineers, Geologists & Geophysicists of Alberta, 1500 Soctia One, 10060 Jasper Ave. NW, Edmonton AB T5J 4A2 Canada. Fax: (780)425-1722. E-mail: glee@apegga.org. Website: www.apegga.org. Estab. 1970. Circ. 56,000. Accepts 30% of material on one-time basis. 30 features purchased/year. Monthly (except August and December) "Non-technical journal of association news and features of interest to engineers and geoscientists published five times/year." Accepts queries by mail, e-mail, fax. Responds in 2 weeks to queries. Responds in 1 month to mss. Pays on acceptance. Editorial lead time 1 month. Offers kill fee. Offers variable kill fee. Byline given. Sample copy for large SAE with Canadian postage. Guidelines available by e-mail.

Needs Query with published clips. "Lengthier features assigned to writers already established with us." Length: 300-1,000 words.. **Pays $200-1,000.**

Photos Send photos Reviews prints, GIF/JPEG files. Buys exclusive first rights, nonexclusive reprint rights, including electronic. Offers no additional payment for photos accepted with ms. Captions required, identification of subjects required.

Tips "Stories must involve Alberta APEGGA members or material of interest to them. Write as if the reader is a lay person, but a well-educated one. We like 'golly gee whiz' stories, heavy on anecdotes and analogies, to make complex information inviting and palatable. Also, stories about the good works of our members—i.e. donating time to help third world with engineering challenges, disaster relief, etc."

PORTLAND OBSERVER AND GUARDIAN

47 Percy St., Portland VIC 3305 Australia. (61)(3)5522-3000. Fax: (61)(3)5523-4765. E-mail: obsnews@spec.com.au. Website: www.spec.com.au. Estab. 1842. Circ. 3,551. Newspaper published 3 days/week. No kill fee.

- Query before submitting.

SACRAMENTO VALLEY MIRROR

138 W. Sycamore, City Willows CA 95988. (530)934-9511. Fax: (530)934-9208. E-mail: vmtim@pulsarco.com. Estab. 1991. Circ. 2,954. Accepts 10%% of material under contract. Accepts 5%% of material on one-time basis. 30 features purchased/year. Works with 15 writers/year. "Semi-weekly magazine covering general news. Accepts queries by mail, e-mail, fax. Responds in 1 week to queries. Buys first North American serial, electronic rights. Pays on publication. Editorial lead time 2 weeks. No kill fee. Byline given. SASE returns. Sample copy for #10 SASE.

- Much muckraking.

Needs Buys one-shot features. Does not want homilies, cooking items, 'I remember when...'; No general gooey, syrupy style items. Query with resume only. **Pays $25-200 for assigned articles.** Sometimes pays expenses of writers on assignment. pays expenses.

Photos State availability of photos. Reviews JPEG files. Buys all rights. Payment can be negotiated on major stories.

Tips "We need bright, tight, sharp writing. Tight leads. Compact and complete nut grafs. Stories must be well-sourced and on the record. Caution: We want news, not 'placed' items."

THE SAN DIEGO UNION-TRIBUNE

P.O. Box 120191, San Diego CA 92112. (619)299-3131. Fax: (619)293-1896. E-mail: letters@uniontrib.com. Website: www.uniontrib.com. Estab. 1868. Circ. 346,000. Daily. No kill fee.

- Mostly staff written.

SAN FRANCISCO EXAMINER

The Anschultz Co., 450 Mission St., 5th Floor, San Francisco CA 94105. (415)826-1100. Fax: (415)359-2766. Website: www.examiner.com. Circ. 57,518. Daily. No kill fee.

- Mostly staff written.

SENIOR TIMES

Senior Publishing, P.O. Box 30965, Columbus OH 43230. (614)337-2055. Fax: (614)337-2059. E-mail: seniortimes@insight.rr.com. Estab. 1983. Circ. 25,000. Accepts 50% of material under contract. Accepts 25% of material on one-time basis. 200 features purchased/year. Works with 25 writers/year. Accepts queries by e-mail. Pays on other. Editorial lead time 1 month. No kill fee. Byline given. Accepts previously published submissions. Accepts simultaneous submissions. Sample copy for #10 SASE.

Needs Query or send complete ms. Length: 500-1000 words. **Pays $15-30.**

Tips All a freelancer needs to do is submit a query or manuscript by e-mail.

ST LUCIE NEWS TRIBUNE

E.W. Scripps Co., 600 Edwards Rd., Fort Pierce FL 34982. (772)461-2050. Fax: (772)464-4447. Website: www.tcpalm.com. Circ. 107,122. Daily. No kill fee.

- Mostly staff written. We are looking for news, sports, feature reporters and photographers in the Treasure Coast, Florida, region. Send résumé and journalism samples to dennis.durkee@scripps.com.

THE SUN NEWS (MYRTLE BEACH)

McClatchy Newspapers, P.O. Box 406, Myrtle Beach SC 29578-0406. (843)626-0300. Fax: (843)626-0356. E-mail: sneditors@thesunnews.com. Website: www.thesunnews.com. Other Address: 914 Frontage Rd. E., Myrtle Beach SC 29577-6700. Circ. 49,805. Daily. No kill fee.

- Mostly staff written.

SYRACUSE NEW TIMES

1415 W. Genesee St., Syracuse NY 13204. E-mail: menglish@syracusenewtimes.com. Website: newtimes.rway.com. Estab. 1969. Circ. 46,000. 250-300 features purchased/year. Works with 10-20 writers/year. Weekly newspaper. Accepts queries by mail. Responds in 4-6 weeks to queries. Buys one-time, electronic rights. Pays on publication. Editorial lead time 2-4 weeks. No kill fee. Byline given. Accepts previously published submissions. Accepts simultaneous submissions. Returns submission with SASE. Sample copy available online. Guidelines for #10 SASE.

Needs Buys one-shot features. Wellness; Continuing Education; seasonal supplements (Autumn Times,

Winter Times). No humor or anything not local to Syracuse. Query with published clips. Length: 500-3,000 words. **Pays $75-200 for assigned articles.** Sometimes pays expenses of writers on assignment.

TIMES PUBLICATIONS

The Scottsdale Times, The Gilbert Times, The Northeast Phoenix Times, The Chandler Times, The East Valley Times and The Glendale Times, Strickbine Publishing, 3200 N. Hayden, Suite 330, Scottsdale AZ 85251. (480)348-0343. Fax: (480)348-2109. E-mail: shanna@timespublications.com. Website: www.timespublications.com. **Contact:** Shanna Hogan, features editor. Estab. 1997. Circ. 111,000. Accepts queries by e-mail. Buys first North American serial, electronic rights. Pays on publication. No kill fee. Byline given. Accepts simultaneous submissions.

Needs Exposé (investigations into Arizona businesses, consumer issues, crimes), 1,200-2,500 words; Inspirational, 1,000-2,000 words; Interview/Profile (notable Arizona personalities), 1,000-1,500 words; General Interest (local trends and national trends localized), 1,000-1,500 words; Humor (satirical news stories), 400-500 words; Photo Feature (full-page photo stories); Food Reviews. "No travel or opinion articles. If you are not brutally interested in composing the piece, then we will not be mildly interested in publishing it." Query with published clips. Length: 1,000-2,500 words. **Pays 35¢-$1/word for assigned articles.** Sometimes pays expenses of writers on assignment.

Photos State availability Negotiates payment individually.

TOWING & RECOVERY FOOTNOTES

Dominion Enterprises, 150 Granby St., Norfolk VA 23510. (757)351-8633. Fax: (757)314-2511. E-mail: bcandler@dominionenterprises.com. Website: www.trfootnotes.com; Facebook: "Towing & Recovery Footnotes"; publishes e-newsletter and digital edition. Estab. 1991. Circ. 25,000. Accepts 100% of material on one-time basis. Reaching thousands of industry professionals monthly *Footnotes* is the industry newspaper and marketplace for the nation's towers. Accepts queries by e-mail. Buys industry rights. Pays on publication. Editorial lead time 1 month. No kill fee. Byline given. Sample copy free. Guidelines free.

Needs Buys 250 mss/year. Accepts previously published submission not in the same industry. Query. Length: 800-2,000 words. **Pays $200-600 for assigned articles.**

THE WASHINGTON POST

Washington Post Co., 1150 15th St. NW, Washington DC 20071. (202)334-6000. Fax: (202)334-5672. E-mail: oped@washpost.com. Website: www.washingtonpost.com. Estab. 1877. Circ. 796,000. Daily. No kill fee.

- Mostly staff written. Break in with Op-Ed piece.

Needs Op-Ed pieces must be written exclusively for *The Post*. around 700 words.

MARKETS

Screenwriting

Writers do not often get into screenwriting for the fame. Most of the glory shines on the directors, actors and actresses. But every great movie and TV show relies upon a great script that was crafted by a screenwriter. And though there may not be much in the way of fame, successful screenwriters do tend to bring in a healthy income. In fact, "How Much Should I Charge?'' on page **67** states that screenwriters make anywhere from $56,500 to $106,070 for an original screenplay.

Writing for TV

To break into TV you must have spec scripts—work written for free that serves as a calling card and gets you in the door. A spec script showcases your writing abilities and gets your name in front of influential people. Whether a network has invited you in to pitch some ideas, or a movie producer has contacted you to write a first draft for a feature film, the quality of writing in your spec script got their attention and that may get you the job.

It's a good idea to have several spec scripts, perhaps one each for three of the top five shows in the format you prefer to work, whether it's sitcom (half-hour comedies), episodic (one-hour series), or movie of the week (two-hour dramatic movies). For TV and cable movies, you should have completed original scripts (not sequels to existing movies) and you might also have a few for episodic TV shows.

In choosing the shows you write spec scripts for, you must remember one thing: Don't write a script for a show you want to work on. If you want to write for *CSI*, for example, you'll send a *Cold Case* script and vice versa. It may seem contradictory, but it's standard practice. It reduces the chances of lawsuits, and writers and producers can feel very proprietary about their shows and their stories. They may not be objective enough to fairly evaluate your writing. In submitting another similar type of show you'll avoid these problems while demonstrating comparable skills.

Writing for the movies

An original movie script contains characters you have created, with story lines you design, allowing you more freedom than you have in TV. However, your writing must still convey believable dialogue and realistic characters, with a plausible plot and high-quality writing carried through roughly 120 pages.

Many novice screenwriters tend to write too many visual cues and camera directions into their scripts. Your goal should be to write something readable, like a "compressed novella.'' Write succinct resonant scenes and leave the camera technique to the director and producer.

3N1 ENTERTAINMENT

11925 Wilshire Blvd., Suite 300, Los Angeles CA 90025. (310)773-1147. Fax: (310)571-9216. E-mail: info@3n1ent.com. Website: www.3n1ent.com. Feature films, production, TV series.

44 BLUE PRODUCTIONS

4040 Vineland Ave., Suite 105, Studio City CA 91604. (818)760-4442. Fax: (818)760-1509. E-mail: reception@44blue.com. Website: www.44blue.com.

ALLIED ARTISTS, INC.

2251 N. Rampart Blvd., 1479, Las Vegas NV 89128. (702)991-9011. E-mail: query@alliedartistsonline.com. Website: www.alliedartistsonline.com. Estab. 1990. Produces material for broadcast and cable television, home video, and film. Buys 3-5 scripts/year. Works with 10-20 writers/year. Buys first or all rights. Accepts previously produced material. Submit synopsis, outline. Responds in 2 months to queries. Responds in 3 months to mss. Pays in accordance with writer's guild standards.

Needs Films, videotapes, social issue TV specials (30-60 minutes), special-interest home video topics, positive values feature screenplays.

Tips "We are looking for positive, uplifting dramatic stories involving 'real people' situations. Future trend is for more reality-based programming, as well as interactive television programs for viewer participation. Send brief e-mail query only. Do not send scripts or additional material until requested. No phone pitches accepted."

APPLESEED ENTERTAINMENT

7715 Sunset Blvd., Suite 100, Los Angeles CA 90046. (818)718-6000. E-mail: films@appleseedent.com. Website: www.appleseedent.com. Credits include *Good Morning, Vietnam* and *Hope Ranch.*

BASE CAMP FILMS

3000 31st Street, Suite D, Santa Monica CA 90405. (310)450-5300. Fax: (310)450-3805. E-mail: info@basecampfilms.com. Website: www.basecampfilms.com.

BIZAZZ MEDIA

3760 Grand View Blvd., Los Angeles CA 90066. (310)390-9360. E-mail: rupert@bizazzmedia.com. Website: www.bizazzmedia.com. **Contact:** Rupert Hitzig. "Bizazz Media is a full service video production company, built around Emmy and Peabody Award winning Producer Rupert Hitzig and a diverse cast of creative professionals with experienced vision. We specialize in the production of documentaries, electronic press kits, marketing videos, corporate videos, industrial videos, and training films. Whether it's for broadcast, non- broadcast presentation, or the Internet, our productions are engaging, informative, and never dull!"

BRITISH LION FILMS

Los Angeles CA (818)990-7750. Fax: (818)789-2901. E-mail: petersnell@britishlionfilms.com. Website: www.britishlionfilms.com. **Contact:** Peter Snell. Estab. 1927. British Lion is continually evaluating literary material for future production as well as remakes of their past films.

HUGHES CAPITAL ENTERTAINMENT

22817 Ventura Blvd., #471, Woodland Hills CA 91364. (818)484-3205. Fax: (818)484-3205. E-mail: info@trihughes.com. Website: www.trihughes.com. **Contact:** Patrick Hughes, producer; Karen Rabesa, VP production/development. Estab. 2006. "Hughes Capital Entertainment (founded by Patrick Hughes) started as a creative film finance company and has grown to become a major management and production company that produces and develops major motion pictures, TV shows, books, and other creative content and manages a broad and talented group of individuals and companies including screenwriters, best-selling authors, directors, show creators, producers, singers/songwriters/, music producers, game creators, visual effects and animation companies, documentary filmmakers, and more. Produces 2 movies/year.". Note for Script/Story Submissions: HCE does not accept unsolicited submissions. Please do not email scripts, novels, or show ideas. You will not receive a response and your material will not be reviewed. Send query and synopsis, or submit complete ms. Mostly accepts agented submissions. Responds in 3 weeks to queries.

O→ "We are looking to produce and develop feature-length screenplays, produced stage plays, well-developed pitches, and detailed treatments. Focus is on broad comedies, urban comedies, socially smart comedies, family films (family adventure), ground-breaking abstract projects, and new writers/directors with an extremely unique and unparalleled point of view. Don't focus on budget, cast, or locations. The story is key to getting things done here."

Tips "Don't back your screenplay or book into a budget. Let the creative lead the way. Never talk about a low budget and a star that's attached or that pre-sold in Egypt for $100 million. We don't care. We care about a unique voice—a filmmaker willing to take risks. Scripts that push the limits without trying for shock value. We care about filmmakers and good writers here."

LAIKA/HOUSE

1400 N.W. 22nd Ave., Portland OR 97210. (503)225-1130. E-mail: ask_us@laika.com. Website: www.laika.com. **Contact:** Exec. Prod.: Lourri Hammad; Co-Exec. Prod.: Jan Johnson. Produces every type of animation in every medium.

THE MARSHAK/ZACHARY CO.

8840 Wilshire Blvd., 1st Floor, Beverly Hills CA 90211. Fax: (310)358-3192. E-mail: marshakzachary@aol.com; alan@themzco.com. **Contact:** Alan W. Mills, associate. Estab. 1981. "Audience is film goers of all ages and television viewers.". Buys 3-5 scripts/year. Works with 10 writers/year. Rights purchased vary. Query with synopsis. Responds in 2 weeks to queries. Responds in 3 months to mss. Payment varies
Tips "Submit logline (1-line description), a short synopsis of storyline, and a short biographical profile (focus on professional background). SASE required for all mailed inquiries. If submissions are sent via e-mail, subject must include specific information or else run the risk of being deleted as junk mail. All genres accepted, but ideas must be commercially viable, high concept, original, and marketable."

MONAREX HOLLYWOOD CORP.

11605 W. Pico Blvd., Suite 200, Los Angeles CA 90064. (310)478-6666. Fax: (310)478-6866. E-mail: monarexcorp@aol.com. **Contact:** Chris D. Nebe, president. Estab. 1978. All audiences. Buys 3-4 scripts/year. Works with 5-10 writers/year. Buys all rights. Query with synopsis. Responds in 1 month to queries. Pays in accordance with writer's guild standards.

NHO ENTERTAINMENT

8931 Beverly Blvd., #249, Los Angeles CA 90048. E-mail: info@nho.la. Website: www.nhoentertainment.com. **Contact:** Mark Costa, partner. Estab. 1999. All audiences. Buys 5 scripts/year. Works with 10 writers/year. Buys all rights. Accepts previously produced material. Query with synopsis, resume, writing samples, production history via e-mail. Responds in 1 month to queries. Catalog for #10 SASE. Pays in accordance with writer's guild standards.
Needs Films, videotapes, multi kits, tapes, cassettes.

SILENT SOUND FILMS, LTD.

United Kingdom. E-mail: thj@silentsoundfilms.co.uk. Website: www.silentsoundfilms.co.uk. **Contact:** Timothy Foster, MD. Estab. 1997. Stage and fiction movies only. TV: arts/travel documentary. Query with synopsis. Writers paid in accordance with WGA standards or the UK 'pact' agreement, if British production.

- "We are interested in excellent writing (specifically musicals, art house, stage plays) and original characters: a 1-page synopsis, no more than 8 pages of scenario, and brief biography. Do not send images, complete screenplays, or large attachments. If something grabs our attention, you will hear from us."

Needs Films, 35mm.
Tips "We seek the filmic equivalent of literature as opposed to bestseller."

SPENCER PRODUCTIONS, INC.

P.O. Box 2247, Westport CT 06880. E-mail: spencerprods@yahoo.com. **Contact:** Bruce Spencer, general manager; Alan Abel, creative director. Produces material for high school students, college students and adults. Occasionally uses freelance writers with considerable talent. Query. Responds in 1 month to queries. Payment negotiable.
Tips "For a comprehensive view of our humor requirements, we suggest viewing our feature film productions, *Is There Sex After Death* (Rated R), starring Buck Henry. It is available at Netflix. Also, *Abel Raises Cain*. Or read *Don't Get Mad ... Get Even* and *How to Thrive on Rejection* by Alan Abel (published by W.W. Norton), both available from Amazon.com. Send brief synopsis (one page) and outline (2-4 pages)."

TOO NUTS PRODUCTIONS, L.P.

925 Lakeville St., Petaluma CA 94952. (310)967-4532. E-mail: info@toonutsproductions.com. **Contact:** Ralph Scott and Daniel Leo Simpson, co-executive producers. Estab. 1994. "Produces illustrated kids books, art books, audio CDs, DVDs, internet animation shorts for internet, music-based kidlit properties,

and half-hour tv/video with a twist. Among our projects in development: 'Catscans,' Our Teacher is a Creature, Toad Pizza, The Salivating Salamander, The Suburban Cowboys, The Contest-Ants, The De-Stinktive Skunk, and Sneeks Peaks. Audience for all projects except art books is children, 5-12. Always looking for talented, new kidlit illustrators as well.". Buys 4-10 scripts/year. Works with 4-6 writers/year. Buys both first rights and all rights Query with synopsis. Submit resume. Submit writing samples. Submit production history. creative but brief cover letter/e-mail; Works with 20% first time writers. Illustrators query with creative but brief cover letter, samples of work by e-mail or hyperlink to your online portfolio.. Responds in less than 3 months to queries. Responds in 6 months to mss. pays royalty and makes outright purchase

O→ Really good original — clean — content.

Needs Videotapes, multi kits, one-page synopses, audio CDs, CD-ROMs. "Please do not submit anything with violence, chainsaws, axes, ice picks, and general blood and guts. We're producing for children, not monsters, or those who aspire to become them."

Tips "Suggestion: Use the words 'Too Nuts' at least twice in your query. (Do the math.) If you don't know how to giggle all the way to the bank, you may want to try someone else. If you've already exorcised your inner child, lizard, monkey, etc., that's a 'no no.' Please visit our website before querying. We receive too many submissions about axe murderers and with clearly adult themes. Even if you're still searching for your inner child through your writing, those subjects are clearly not for our audiences. If you send us anything like this, expect a very 'spirited' response. Find your inner child on your own time!"

VALEO FILMS

P.O. Box 250, Orange Lake FL 32681. (352)591-4714. E-mail: screenplays@valeofilms.com. Website: www.valeofilms.com. Query by e-mail or mail.

O→ Currently considering projects that contain one or more of the following: character or story driven, identifies moral values, romance/love story, educational/documentary, presents the human condition, strong visual imagery, coming of age/learning, or intellectual drama/mystery.

Tips "We require that you provide your name, phone number, address, title of your work, and WGA registration or copyright number. We will send an Unsolicited Project Release letter for you to sign and return with a signed copy of your screenplay/treatment. We don't want projects that contain the following characteristics: one character saves the world, SFX based, highly action based, extreme/grotesque violence, high sexual content, or strong explicit language. Although we do have a vast array of production resources available to us, we are a relatively small production company who prefers to limit the number of projects we have in production. Consequently, we tend to be very selective when it comes to choosing new material."

MARKETS

Playwriting

Where TV and movies have a diminished role for writers in the collaboration that produces the final product, whether a show or a film, theater places a very high value on the playwright. This may have something to do with the role of the scripts in the different settings.

Screenplays are often in a constant state of "in progress," where directors make changes; producers make changes; and even actors and actresses make changes throughout the filming of the TV show or movie. Plays, on the other hand, must be as solid as a rock, because the script must be performed live night after night.

As a result, playwrights tend to have more involvement in the productions of their scripts, a power screenwriters can only envy. Counterbalancing the greater freedom of expression are the physical limitations inherent in live performance: a single stage, smaller cast, limited sets and lighting, and, most importantly, a strict, smaller budget. These conditions not only affect what but also how you write.

Listings

The following listings include contact information, submission details, current needs, and other helpful tips to help you find a home for your finished and polished play. As with any market, it is advised that after you pinpoint a listing that you then follow up with them to find out their most current submission policy and to ask who you should address your submission. This might seem like a lot of work, but writing plays is a competitive business. Your professionalism will go a long way in separating you from other "wanna-be" playwrights.

For more information

To find out more about writing and submitting plays, contact the Dramatists Guild (www.dramaguild.com) and the Writers Guild of America (www.wga.org). Both organizations are great for networking and for learning the basics needed to build a successful career crafting plays.

ABINGDON THEATRE CO.

312 W. 36th St., 6th Floor, New York NY 10018. (212)868-2055. Fax: (212)868-2056. E-mail: literary@abingdontheatre.org. Artistic Director: Jan Buttram. **Contact:** Literary Manager: Kim T. Sharp. Estab. 1993. Produces 2-3 Mainstage and 2-3 Studio productions/year. Professional productions for a general audience. Submit full-length script in hard copy, cast breakdown, synopsis and development history, if any. No one-acts or musicals. Include SASE for return of manuscript. Responds in 4 months. Buys variable rights. Payment is negotiated.

Needs All scripts should be suitable for small stages.

Tips Check website for updated submission guidelines. Most interested in stories with central characters pursuing goals vital to them. Less interested in passive characters who only react to circumstances.

ACT II PLAYHOUSE

P.O. Box 555, Ambler PA 19002-0555. (215)654-0200. Fax: (215)654-9050. Frank Martin. **Contact:** Stephen Blumenthal, literary manager. Estab. 1998. Produces 5 plays/year. Submit query and synopsis. Include SASE for return of submission. Responds in 1 month. Payment negotiable.

Needs Contemporary comedy, drama, musicals. Full length. 6 character limitation; 1 set or unit set. Does not want period pieces. Limited number of scenes per act.

ACTORS THEATRE OF LOUISVILLE

316 W. Main St., Louisville KY 40202-4218. (502)584-1265. Fax: (502)561-3300. E-mail: awegener@actorstheatre.org. **Contact:** Amy Wegener, literary manager. Estab. 1964. Produces approximately 25 new plays of varying lengths/year. "Professional productions are performed for subscription audience from diverse backgrounds. Agented submissions only for full-length plays, will read 10-page samples of unagented full-length works. Open submissions to National Ten-Minute Play Contest (plays 10 pages or less) are due November 1." Responds in 9-12 months to submissions, mostly in the fall/winter. Buys variable rights. Offers variable royalty.

Needs Full-length and 10-minute plays and plays of ideas, language, humor, experiment and passion.

ACT THEATRE

A Contemporary Theatre, Kreielsheimer Place, 700 Union St., Seattle WA 98101. (206)292-7660. Fax: (206)292-7670. E-mail: artistic@acttheatre.org. Kurt Beattie. Estab. 1965. Produces 5-6 mainstage plays/year. "ACT performs a subscription-based season on 3 stages: 2 main stages (a thrust and an arena) and a smaller, flexible 99-seat space. Although our focus is towards our local Seattle audience, some of our notable productions have gone on to other venues in other cities." *Agented submissions only* or through theatre professional's recommendation. No unsolicited submissions. Query and synopsis only for Northwest playwrights. Responds in 6 months. Pays 5-10% royalty.

Needs ACT produces full-length contemporary scripts ranging from solo pieces to large ensemble works, with an emphasis on plays that embrace the contradictions and mysteries of our contemporary world and that resonate with audiences of all backgrounds through strong storytelling and compelling characters.

Tips "ACT is looking for plays that offer strong narrative, exciting ideas, and well-drawn, dimensional characters that will engage an audience emotionally and intellectually. These may sound like obvious prerequisites for a play, but often it seems that playwrights are less concerned with the story they have to tell than with the way they're telling it, emphasizing flashy, self-conscious style over real substance and solid structure."

ALLEYWAY THEATRE

One Curtain Up Alley, Buffalo NY 14202. (716)852-2600. Fax: (716)852-2266. E-mail: newplays@alleyway.com. **Contact:** Literary Manager. Estab. 1980. Produces 4-5 full-length, 6-12 one-act plays/year. Submit complete script; include CD for musicals. Alleyway Theatre also sponsors the Maxim Mazumdar New Play Competition. See the Contest & Awards section for more information. Responds in 6 months. Seeks first production rights. Pays 7% royalty.

Needs "Works written uniquely for the theatre. Theatricality, breaking the fourth wall, and unusual settings are of particular interest. We are less interested in plays which are likely to become TV or film scripts."

ALLIANCE THEATRE

1280 Peachtree St. NE, Atlanta GA 30309. (404)733-4650. Fax: (404)733-4625. Website: www.alliancetheatre.org. **Contact:** Literary Intern. Estab. 1969. Produces 11 plays/year. Professional production for local audience. Only accepts agent submissions and unsolicited samples from Georgia residents only. Electronic correspondence preferred. Query with synopsis and sample or submit through agent. Enclose SASE. Responds in 9 months.

Needs Full-length scripts and scripts for young audiences no longer than 60 minutes.
Tips "As the premier theater of the southeast, the Alliance Theatre sets the highest artistic standards, creating the powerful experience of shared theater for diverse people."

AMERICAN CONSERVATORY THEATER

30 Grant Ave., 6th Floor, San Francisco CA 94108-5800. (415)834-3200. Artistic Director: Carey Perloff. **Contact:** Pink Pasdar, associate artistic director. Estab. 1965. Produces 8 plays/year. Plays are performed in Geary Theater, a 1,000-seat classic proscenium. No unsolicited scripts.

APPLE TREE THEATRE

1850 Green Bay Rd., Suite 100, Highland Park IL 60035. (847)432-8223. Fax: (847)432-5214. E-mail: info@appletreetheatre.com. **Contact:** Eileen Boevers. Estab. 1983. Produces 4 plays/year. "Professional productions intended for an adult audience mix of subscriber base and single-ticket holders. Our subscriber base is extremely theater-savvy and intellectual." Return SASE submissions only if requested. Rights obtained vary. Pays variable royalty.
Needs "We produce a mixture of musicals, dramas, classical, contemporary, and comedies." Length: 90 minutes-2½ hours. Small space, unit set required. No fly space, theatre in the round. Maximum actors 5.
Tips "No farces or large-scale musicals. Theater needs small shows with 1-unit sets due to space and financial concerns. Also note the desire for nonlinear pieces that break new ground. *Please do not submit unsolicited manuscripts—send letter and description along with tapes for musicals*; if we want more, we will request it."

ARENA STAGE

1101 6th St. SW, Washington DC 20024. (202)554-9066. Fax: (202)488-4056. Artistic Director: Molly Smith. **Contact:** Mark Bly, senior dramaturg. Estab. 1950. Produces 8 plays/year. Only accepts scripts from writers with agent or theatrical representation.
Needs "Plays that illuminate the broad canvas of American work, with a commitment to aesthetic, cultural, and geographic diversity. Arena is committed to showcasing the past, present, and future of American theatre." Seeks only full-length plays and musicals in all genres.

ARIZONA THEATRE CO.

P.O. Box 1631, Tucson AZ 85702. (520)884-8210. Fax: (520)628-9129. **Contact:** Literary Department. Estab. 1966. Produces 6-8 plays/year. "Arizona Theatre Company is the State Theatre of Arizona and plans the season with the population of the state in mind." Only Arizona writers may submit unsolicited scripts, along with production history (if any), brief bio, and self-addressed evenlope. Out-of-state writers can send a synopsis, 10-page sample dialogue, production history (if any), brief bio, and self-addressed envelope. Responds in 4-6 months. Payment negotiated.
Needs Full length plays of a variety of genres and topics and full length musicals. No one-acts.
Tips "Please include in the cover letter something about your current situation and goals."

ARTISTS REPERTORY THEATRE

1515 SW Morrison, Portland OR 97205. (503)241-1278. Fax: (503)241-8268. Estab. 1982. Produces Plays performed in professional theater with a subscriber-based audience. Send synopsis, résumé, and sample (maximum 10 pages). No unsolicited mss accepted. Responds in 6 months. Pays royalty.

- "We bring Portland the newest and most exhilarating plays being written today and simultaneously showcase the talents of local theater artists."

Needs Full-length, hard-hitting, emotional, intimate, actor-oriented shows with small casts (rarely exceeds 10-13, usually 2-7). Language and subject matter are not a problem. No one-acts or children's scripts.

ART STATION THEATRE

5384 Manor Dr., Stone Mountain GA 30083. (770)469-1105. E-mail: info@artstation.org. **Contact:** Jon Goldstein, program manager. Estab. 1986. Produces 3 plays/year. ART Station Theatre is a professional theater located in a contemporary arts center in Stone Mountain, GA, which is part of Metro Atlanta. Audience consists of middle-aged to senior, suburban patrons. Query with synopsis and writing samples. Responds in 1 year. Pays 5-7% royalty.
Needs Full length comedy, drama and musicals, preferably relating to the human condition in the contemporary South. Cast size no greater than 6.

ASIAN AMERICAN THEATER CO.

55 Teresita Blvd., San Francisco CA 94127. E-mail: darryl@asianamericantheater.org. **Contact:** Artistic Director. Estab. 1973. Produces 4 plays/year. Produces professional productions for San Francisco Bay Area audiences. Submit complete script. Payment varies.

Needs The new voice of Asian American theater. No limitations in cast, props or staging.

Tips "Looking for plays from the new Asian American theater aesthetic—bold, substantive, punchy. Scripts from Asian Pacific Islander American women and under-represented Asian Pacific Islander ethnic groups are especially welcome."

⊘ ASOLO THEATRE CO.

5555 N. Tamiami Trail, Sarasota FL 34234. (941)351-9010. Fax: (941)351-5796. **Contact:** Michael Donald Edwards, Production Artistic Dir. Estab. 1960. Produces 7-8 plays/year. A LORT theater with 2 intimate performing spaces. Negotiates rights and payment.

Needs Play must be full length. We operate with a resident company in rotating repertory.

ATTIC THEATRE & FILM CENTRE

5429 W. Washington Blvd., Los Angeles CA 90016-1112. (323)525-0600. Website: www.attictheatre.org. Artistic Director: James Carey. **Contact:** Literary Manager. Estab. 1987. Produces 4 plays a year. "We are based in Los Angeles and play to industry and regular Joes. We use professional actors; however, our house is very small, and the salaries we pay, including the royalties are very small because of that."

- Full Length and Musicals: Not accepting full length unsolicited manuscripts from anyone at this time.

Tips "Please read our guidelines on the website. Follow all the directions."

BAILIWICK REPERTORY

Bailiwick Arts Center, 1229 W. Belmont Ave., Chicago IL 60657-3205. (773)883-1090. Fax: (773)883-2017. E-mail: bailiwick@bailiwick.org. **Contact:** David Zak, artistic director. Estab. 1982. Produces 5 mainstage plays (classic and newly commissioned) each year; 12 one-acts in annual Directors Festival. Pride Performance Series (gay and lesbian), includes one-acts, poetry, workshops, and staged adaptations of prose. Submit year-round. One-act play fest runs July-August. Responds in 9 months for full-length only. Pays 6% royalty.

Needs We need daring scripts that break the mold. Large casts or musicals are OK. Creative staging solutions are a must.

Tips Know the rules, then break them creatively and boldly! Please send SASE for manuscript submission guidelines *before you submit* or get manuscript guidelines at our website.

BAKER'S PLAYS PUBLISHING CO.

45 W. 25th St., New York NY 10010. E-mail: publications@bakersplays.com. **Contact:** Managing Editor. Estab. 1845. **Publishes 20-30 straight plays and musicals. Works with 2-3 unpublished/unproduced writers annually. 80% freelance written. 75% of scripts unagented submissions.** Plays performed by amateur groups, high schools, children's theater, churches and community theater groups. Submit complete script with news clippings, resume, production history. Submit complete CD of music with musical submissions. See our website for more information about e-submissions. Responds in 3-6 months. Pay varies; negotiated royalty split of production fees; 10% book royalty.

Needs We are finding strong support in our new division—plays from young authors featuring contemporary pieces for high school production.

Tips We are particularly interested in adaptation of lesser-known folk tales from around the world. Also of interest are plays which feature a multicultural cast and theme. Collections of one-act plays for children and young adults tend to do very well. Also, high school students: Write for guidelines (see our website)for information about our High School Playwriting Contest.

MARY BALDWIN COLLEGE THEATRE

Mary Baldwin College, Staunton VA 24401. Fax: (540)887-7139. **Contact:** Terry K. Southerington, professor of theater. Estab. 1842. Produces 5 plays/year. 10% of scripts are unagented submissions. "An undergraduate women's college theater with an audience of students, faculty, staff and local community (adult, somewhat conservative)." Query with synopsis. Responds in 1 year. Buys performance rights only. Pays $10-50/performance.

Needs "Full-length and short comedies, tragedies, and music plays geared particularly toward young women actresses, dealing with women's issues both contemporary and historical. Experimental/studio theater not suitable for heavy sets. Cast should emphasize women. No heavy sex; minimal explicit language."

Tips "A perfect play for us has several roles for young women, few male roles, minimal production demands, a concentration on issues relevant to contemporary society, and elegant writing and structure."

BARTER THEATRE

P.O. Box 867, Abingdon VA 24212-0867. (276)628-2281. Fax: (276)619-3335. E-mail: dramaturge@bartertheatre.com. **Contact:** dramaturge. Estab. 1933. Produces 17 plays/year. "Plays performed in residency at 2 facilities, a 500-seat proscenium theater and a smaller 167-seat flexible theater. Our plays are intended for diversified audiences of all ages." Submit synopsis and dialogue sample only with SASE. Barter Theatre often premieres new works. Responds in 9 months. Pays negotiable royalty.

Needs "We are looking for good plays, comedies and dramas that entertain and are relevant; plays that examine in new and theatrical ways the human condition and contemporary issues. We prefer casts of 4-12, single or unit set. Strong language may lessen a play's appeal for Barter audiences."

Tips "We are looking for material that appeals to diverse, family audiences. We accept no one act play queries."

BLOOMSBURG THEATRE ENSEMBLE

226 Center St., Bloomsburg PA 17815. E-mail: jsatherton@bte.org. Ensemble Director: Gerard Stropnicky. **Contact:** J. Scott Atherton, manager of admin. and development. Estab. 1979. Produces 9 plays/year. Professional productions for a non-urban audience. Submit query and synopsis. Responds in 9 months. Buys negotiable rights Pays 6-9% royalty. Pays $50-70/performance.

Needs Because of our non-urban location, we strive to expose our audience to a broad range of theatre—both classical and contemporary. We are drawn to language and ideas and to plays that resonate in our community. We are most in need of articulate comedies and cast sizes under 6.

Tips Because of our non-urban setting we are less interested in plays that focus on dilemmas of city life in particular. Most of the comedies we read are cynical. Many plays we read would make better film scripts; static/relationship-heavy scripts that do not use the 'theatricality' of the theatre to an advantage.

BOARSHEAD THEATER

425 S. Grand Ave., Lansing MI 48933-2122. (517)484-7800, 7805. Fax: (517)484-2564. Kristine Thatcher. **Contact:** George Orban. Estab. 1966. Produces 8 plays/year (6 mainstage, 2 Young People's Theater productions inhouse), 4 or 5 staged readings. Mainstage Actors' Equity Association company; also Youth Theater—touring to schools by our intern company. Submit synopsis, character breakdown, 20 pages of sample dialogue, bio, production history (if any) via mail only. Pays royalty for mainstage productions, transport/per diem for staged readings.

Needs Thrust stage. Cast usually 8 or less; occasionally up to 20; no one-acts and no musicals considered. Prefers staging which depends on theatricality rather than multiple sets. Send materials for full-length plays (only) to Kristine Thatcher, artistic director. For Young People's Theater, send one-act plays (only); 4-5 characters.

Tips Plays should not have multiple realistic sets—too many scripts read like film scripts. Focus on intelligence, theatricality, crisp, engaging humorous dialogue. Write a good play and prove it with 10 pages of great, precise dialogue.

BROADWAY PLAY PUBLISHING

56 E. 81st St., New York NY 10028-0202. (212)772-8334. Fax: (212)772-8358. E-mail: kip@broadwayplaypubl.com. BPPI specializes in full-length, contemporary, American plays (we have over 330) BPPI also publishes and licenses, some dramatic adaptations of classic plays and literature & one acts; and then there is the *sui generis*THE COMPLETE WORKS OF WILLIAM SHAKESPEARE (ABRIDGED). BPPI also acts as the authors' agent for the licensing of stage production rights in the United States & Canada. This publisher does not read play mss. It will only publish a play if the playwright is an American-born resident; the play is not in print elsewhere; the play is full-length (at least 1 hour); the play has contemporary subject matter; the play is for at least 2 actors; the play has been professionally produced for at least 12 performances; there is acceptable color artwork for the cover; there are a few sentences from print media complimenting the play.

CELEBRATION THEATRE

7985 Santa Monica Blvd., #109-1, Los Angeles CA 90046. Fax: (323)957-1826. E-mail: celebrationthtr@earthlink.net. Artistic Director: Michael Matthews. **Contact:** Literary Management Team. Estab. 1983. Produces 4 plays/year. Performed in a small theatre in Los Angeles. For all audiences, but with gay and lesbian characters at the center of the plays. Submit query and synopsis. Responds in 5 months. Pays 6-7% royalty.

Needs Produce works with gay and lesbian characters at the center of the narrative. There aren't any limitations, but simple productions work best. Don't send coming-out plays/stories.

CHAMBER THEATRE

158 N. Broadway, Milwaukee WI 53202. (414)276-8842. Fax: (414)277-4477. E-mail: mail@chambertheatre.com. **Contact:** C. Michael Wright, artistic director. Estab. 1975. Produces 5 plays/year. Plays produced for adult and student audience. Submit query and synopsis. Submissions accompanied by a SASE will be returned. Responds in 3 months. Pays royalty.
Needs Produces literary, thought-provoking, biographical plays. Plays require small-unit settings. No plays for a large cast.

CHILDSPLAY, INC.

P.O. Box 517, Tempe AZ 85280. (480)350-8101. Fax: (480)350-8584. E-mail: info@childsplayaz.org. **Contact:** Artistic Director. Estab. 1978. Produces 5-6 plays/year. Professional touring and in-house productions for youth and family audiences. Submit synopsis, character descriptions and 7- to 10-page dialogue sample. Responds in 6 months. Pays royalty of $20-35/performance (touring) or pays $3,000-8,000 commission. Holds a small percentage of royalties on commissioned work for 3-5 years.
Needs Seeking theatrical plays on a wide range of contemporary topics. Our biggest market is K-6. We need intelligent theatrical pieces for this age group that meet touring requirements and have the flexibility for in-house staging. The company has a reputation, built up over 30 years, of maintaining a strong aesthetic. We need scripts that respect the audience's intelligence and support their rights to dream and to have their concerns explored. Innovative, theatrical and small is a constant need. Touring shows limited to 5 actors; in-house shows limited to 6-10 actors.
Tips No traditionally-handled fairy tales. Theater for young people is growing up and is able to speak to youth and adults. The material must respect the artistry of the theater and the intelligence of our audience. Our most important goal is to benefit children. If you wish your materials returned send SASE.

CLEVELAND PLAY HOUSE

8500 Euclid Ave., Cleveland OH 44106. E-mail: sgordon@clevelandplayhouse.com. Artistic Director: Michael Bloom. **Contact:** Seth Gordon, associate artistic director. Estab. 1915. Produces 10 plays/year. We have five theatres, 100-550 seats. Submit 10-page sample with synopsis. Will return submissions if accompanied by SASE. Responds in 6 months. Payment is negotiable.
Needs All styles and topics of new plays.

COLONY THEATRE CO.

555 N. Third St., Burbank CA 91502. (818)558-7000. Fax: (818)558-7110. E-mail: colonytheatre@colonytheatre.org. **Contact:** Michael David Wadler, literary manager. Produces 6 plays/year. Professional 276-seat theater with thrust stage. Casts from resident company of professional actors. Submit query and synopsis. Negotiated rights. Pays royalty for each performance.
Needs Full length (90-120 minutes) with a cast of 4-12. Especially interested in small casts of 4 or fewer. No musicals or experimental works.
Tips We seek works of theatrical imagination and emotional resonance on universal themes.

CREEDE REPERTORY THEATRE

P.O. Box 269, Creede CO 81130-0269. (719)658-2541. E-mail: litmgr@creederep.com. **Contact:** Frank Kuhn, Literary Manager. Estab. 1966. Produces 6 plays/year. Plays performed for a smaller audience. Submit synopsis, 10-page dialogue sample, letter of inquiry, resume; electronic submissions only. Responds in 6 months. Royalties negotiated with each author—paid on a per performance basis.
Needs "Special consideration given to plays focusing on the cultures and history of the American West and Southwest."
Tips "We seek new adaptations of classical or older works as well as original scripts."

DALLAS CHILDREN'S THEATER

Rosewood Center for Family Arts, 5938 Skillman, Dallas TX 75231. E-mail: artie.olaisen@dct.org. **Contact:** Artie Olaisen, assoc. artistic director. Estab. 1984. Produces 10 plays/year. "Professional theater for family and student audiences." Query with synopsis, number of actors required, any material regarding previous productions of the work, and a demo tape or lead sheets (for musicals). No materials will be returned without a SASE included. Responds in up to 8 months. Rights negotiable. Pays negotiable royalty.
Needs "Seeking substantive material appropriate for youth and family audiences. Most consideration given to full-length, non-musical works, especially classic and contemporary adaptations of literature.

Also interested in social, topical, issue-oriented material. Very interested in scripts which enlighten diverse cultural experiences, particularly Hispanic and African-American experiences. Prefers scripts with no more than 15 cast members; 6-12 is ideal."

Tips "No adult experience material. We are a family theater. Not interested in material intended for performance by children or in a classroom. Productions are performed by professional adults. Children are cast in child-appropriate roles. We receive far too much light musical material that plays down to children and totally lacks any substance. Be patient. We receive an enormous amount of submissions. Most of the material we have historically produced has had previous production. We are not against perusing non-produced material, but it has rarely gone into our season unless we have been involved in its development. No phone calls."

DARLINGHURST THEATRE COMPANY

19 Greenknowe Ave., Potts Pointe NSW 2011 Australia. (61)(2)9331-3107. E-mail: theatre@darlinghursttheatre.com. Submission period ends September 15. Seeks to expose the audience to a diverse range of work, included narratives, non-narratives, Australian content, and international work. Classics are not excluded, though work new to Sydney is encouraged. Financial issues are a part of the selection process, so discuss your proposal with Glenn Terry before submitting. If asked, send complete ms or outline. See website for more submission details.

DETROIT REPERTORY THEATRE

13103 Woodrow Wilson, Detroit MI 48238-3686. (313)868-1347. Fax: (313)868-1705. **Contact:** Barbara Busby, literary manager. Estab. 1957. Produces 4 plays/year. Professional theater, 194 seats operating on A.E.A. SPT contract Detroit metropolitan area. Submit complete ms in bound folder, cast list, and description with SASE. Responds in 6 months. Pays royalty.

Needs Wants issue-oriented works. Cast limited to no more than 7 characters. No musicals or one-act plays.

DIVERSIONARY THEATRE

4545 Park Blvd., Suite 101, San Diego CA 92116. (619)220-6830. E-mail: dkirsch@diversionary.org. **Contact:** Dan Kirsch, executive director. Estab. 1986. Produces 5-6 plays/year. "Professional non-union full-length productions of gay, lesbian, bisexual and transgender content. Ideal cast size is 2-6." Submit application and 10-15 pages of script. Responds in 6 months.

DIXON PLACE

161 Chrystie St., Ground Floor, New York NY 10002. (212)219-0736. Fax: (212)219-0761. **Contact:** Leslie Strongwater, artistic director. Estab. 1986. Produces 12 plays/year. Does not accept submissions from writers outside the NYC area. Looking for new work, not already read or workshopped in full in New York. To help us be more efficient in the reviewing of submissions, please read about our ongoing series on the website and submit proposals directly to the series you think is the "best fit". Keep in mind that you are sending an idea or proposal for a performance. Your proposal does not need to be a polished piece when you submit the work, and if selected, it should still be in a 'work-in-progress' stage when you perform it. If you would like your submission materials returned, please include a self-addressed, stamped envelope. We will not return submission materials without a SASE. Works chosen are provided an honorarium, rehearsal time, inclusion in our season brochures, website presence, and technical assistance. If you have any questions, please email us. Pays flat fee.

Needs Particularly interested in non-traditional, either in character, content, structure and/or themes. We almost never produce kitchen sink, soap opera-style plays about AIDS, coming out, unhappy love affairs, getting sober or lesbian parenting. We regularly present new works, plays with innovative structure, multi-ethnic content, non-naturalistic dialogue, irreverent musicals and the elegantly bizarre. We are an established performance venue with a very diverse audience. We have a reputation for bringing our audience the unexpected. Submissions accepted year-round.

DORSET THEATRE FESTIVAL

Box 510, Dorset VT 05251-0510. (802)867-2223. Estab. 1976. Produces 5 plays/year (1 a new work). Our plays will be performed in our Equity theater and are intended for a sophisticated community. Agented submissions only. Rights and compensation negotiated.

Needs Looking for full-length contemporary American comedy or drama. Limited to a cast of 6.

Tips Language and subject matter must be appropriate to general audience.

DRAMATIC PUBLISHING

311 Washington St., Woodstock IL 60098. (800)448-7469. Fax: (800)334-5302. **Contact:** Linda Habjan, submissions editor. Publishes 40-50 titles/year. Publishes paperback acting editions of original plays, musicals, adaptations, and translations. **Receives 250-500 queries and 600 mss/year.** Catalog and script guidelines free and online. Responds in 4-6 months. Pays 10% royalty on scripts; performance royalty varies.

Needs Comedies, dramas, comedy/dramas, musicals, comedy/farce. Interested in playscripts appropriate for children, middle and high schools, colleges, community, stock and professional theaters. Send full ms.

Tips "We publish all kinds of plays for the professional, stock, amateur, high school, elementary and children's theater markets: full lengths, one acts, children's plays, musicals, adaptations."

DRAMATICS MAGAZINE

2343 Auburn Ave., Cincinnati OH 45219. (513)421-3900. Fax: (513)421-7077. E-mail: dcorathers@schooltheatre.org. **Contact:** Don Corathers, editor. Estab. 1929. For high school theater students and teachers. Submit complete script. Responds in 3 months. Buys first North American serial rights only.

- "Typically we print 10 plays, but 4 of them come from a student writing program that we do. The other 6 are by working professional playwrights. This year's crop included 3 full-lengths, 1 long one-act, and 2 ten-minute plays."

Needs 'We are seeking one-acts to full-lengths that can be produced in an educational theater setting."

Tips "No melodrama, musicals, farce, children's theater, or cheap knock-offs of TV sitcoms or movies. Fewer writers are taking the time to learn the conventions of theater—what makes a piece work on stage, as opposed to film and television—and their scripts show it. We're always looking for good interviews with working theatre professionals."

EAST WEST PLAYERS

120 N. Judge John Aiso St., Los Angeles CA 90012. (213)625-7000. Fax: (213)625-7111. E-mail: jliu@eastwestplayers.org. Artistic Director: Tim Dang. **Contact:** Jeff Liu, literary manager. Estab. 1965. Produces 4 plays/year. Professional 240-seat theater performing under LOA-BAT contract, presenting plays which explore the Asian Pacific American experience." Submit ms with title page, résumé, cover letter, and SASE. Responds in 3-9 months. Pays royalty against percentage of box office.

Needs Whether dramas, comedies, or musicals, all plays must either address the Asian American experience or have a special resonance when cast with Asian American actors.

ELDRIDGE PUBLISHING CO.

P.O. Box 14367, Tallahassee FL 32317. E-mail: editorial@histage.com. Managing Editor: Nancy Vorhis. **Contact:** Editor: Susan Shore. Estab. 1906. Publishes 65 new plays/year for junior high, senior high, church, and community audience. Query with synopsis (acceptable). Please send CD with any musicals. Responds in 1-2 months. Buys all dramatic rights. Pays 50% royalties for amateur productions, 80% for professional productions and 10% copy sales in general market. Makes outright purchase of $100-600 in religious market.

Needs "We are most interested in full-length plays and musicals for our school and community theater market. Nothing lower than junior high level, please. We always love comedies but also look for serious, high caliber plays reflective of today's sophisticated students. We also need one-acts and plays for children's theater. In addition, in our religious market we're always searching for holiday plays. No plays which belong in a classroom setting as part of a lesson plan. Unless it is for Christmas, no other religious musicals considered."

Tips "Please have your work performed, if at all possible, before submitting. The quality will improve substantially."

THE ENSEMBLE STUDIO THEATRE

549 W. 52nd St., New York NY 10019. (212)247-4982. Fax: (212)664-0041. E-mail: firman@ensemblestudiotheatre.org. Website: www.ensemblestudiotheatre.org. Artistic Director: William Carden. **Contact:** Linsay Firman, Literary Manager. Estab. 1972. Produces 250 projects, readings, workshops and productions/year for off-off Broadway developmental theater in a 100-seat house, 60-seat workshop space. Do not fax mss or resumes. Please check website for current submission guidelines and deadlines. Responds in 10 months.

Needs "Full-length plays with strong dramatic actions and situations and solid one-acts, humorous and dramatic, which can stand on their own. Special programs include Going to the River Series, which workshops new plays by African-American women, and the Sloan Project, which commissions new works on the topics of science and technology. Seeks original plays with strong dramatic action, believable characters and dynamic ideas. We are interested in writers who respect the power of language. No verse-dramas or elaborate costume dramas or musicals. Accepts new/unproduced work only."

ENSEMBLE THEATRE OF CINCINNATI

1127 Vine St., Cincinnati OH 45248. (513)421-3555. Fax: (513)562-4104. E-mail: lynn.meyers@cincyetc.com. **Contact:** D. Lynn Meyers, producing artistic director. Estab. 1987. Produces 12 plays/year, including a staged reading series. Professional year-round theater. Query with synopsis, submit complete ms or submit through agent. Responds in 6 months. Pays 5-10% royalty.

Needs Dedicated to good writing of any style for a small, contemporary cast. Small technical needs, big ideas.

THE FOOTHILL THEATRE CO.

P.O. Box 1812, Nevada City CA 95959. (530)265-9320. Fax: (530)265-9325. E-mail: info@foothilltheatre.org. Artistic Director: Carolyn Howarth. **Contact:** Literary Manager. Estab. 1977. Produces 6-9 plays/year. We are a professional theater company operating under an Actors' Equity Association contract for part of the year, and performing in the historic 246-seat Nevada Theatre (built in 1865) and at an outdoor amphitheatre on the north shore of Lake Tahoe. We also produce a new play development program called New Voices of the Wild West that endeavors to tell the stories of the non-urban Western United States. The audience is a mix of locals and tourists. Query by e-mail. Responds in 6 months-1 year. Buys negotiable rights. Payment varies.

Needs We are most interested in plays which speak to the region and its history, as well as to its current concerns. No melodramas. Theatrical, above all.

Tips At present, we're especially interested in unproduced plays that speak to the rural and semi-rural American West for possible inclusion in our new play reading and development program, New Voices of the Wild West. History plays are okay, as long as they don't sound like you wrote them with an encyclopedia open in your lap. The best way to get our attention is to write something we haven't seen before, and write it well.

FOUNTAIN THEATRE

5060 Fountain Ave., Los Angeles CA 90029. (323)663-2235. Fax: (323)663-1629. E-mail: ftheatre@aol.com. Artistic Directors: Deborah Lawlor, Stephen Sachs. **Contact:** Simon Levy, dramaturg. Estab. 1990. Produces both a theater and dance season. Produced at Fountain Theatre (99-seat equity plan). *Professional recommendation only*. Query with synopsis to Simon Levy, producing director/dramaturg. Responds in 6 months. Rights acquired vary. Pays royalty.

Needs Original plays, adaptations of American literature, material that incorporates dance or language into text with unique use and vision.

THE FREELANCE PRESS

670 Centre St., Suite 8, Dover MA 02130. (617)524-7045. E-mail: info@freelancepress.org. **Contact:** Narcissa Campion, managing director. Estab. 1979. "The musicals published by The Freelance Press are designed for music and theater educators who are seeking age-appropriate material for their students. Our plays and scores are developed by a national network of arts programs and children's theaters. Playwrights and composers, working directly with young actors and singers, have created shows to match the voices, interests and sensibilities of young people, ages 8-18." Submit complete ms with SASE. Responds in 4 months. Pays 70% of performance royalties to authors. Pays 10% script and score royalty.

Needs "We publish original musical theater to be performed by young people, dealing with issues of importance to them. Also adapt 'classics' into musicals for 8- to 16-year-old age groups to perform. Large cast, flexible."

SAMUEL FRENCH, INC.

45 W. 25th St., New York NY 10010. (212)206-8990. Fax: (212)206-1429. E-mail: publications@samuelfrench.com. Website: www.samuelfrench.com. **Contact:** Editorial Department. Estab. 1830. Publishes 50-60 titles/year. Publishes paperback acting editions of plays. Receives 1,500 submissions/year, mostly from unagented playwrights. 10% of publications are from first-time authors; 20% from unagented writers. Pays 10% royalty on retail price, plus amateur and stock royalties on productions.

Needs Comedies, mysteries, children's plays, high school plays.

Tips "Broadway and Off-Broadway hit plays, light comedies and mysteries have the best chance of selling to our firm. Our market is comprised of theater producers—both professional and amateur—actors and students. Read as many plays as possible of recent vintage to keep apprised of today's market; write plays with good female roles; and be 100% professional in approaching publishers and producers. We recommend (not require) that submissions be in the format used by professional playwrights in the US, available as a free download at http://www.samuelfrench.com/store/SFFormattingGuide.pdf."

WILL GEER THEATRICUM BOTANICUM

P.O. Box 1222, Topanga CA 90290. (310)455-2322. Fax: (310)455-3724. **Contact:** Ellen Geer, artistic director. Estab. 1973. Produces 4 classical and 1 new play if selected/year. Professional productions for summer theater. Botanicum Seedlings new plays selected for readings and one play each year developed. Contact: Jennie Webb. Send synopsis, sample dialogue and tape if musical. Responds in 6 months. Pays 6% royalty or $150 per show.

Needs Socially relevant plays, musicals; all full-length. Cast size of 4-10 people. "We are a large outdoor theatre—small intimate works could be difficult."

Tips "September submissions have best turn around for main season; year-round for 'Botanicum Seedlings.'"

GEORGE STREET PLAYHOUSE

9 Livingston Ave., New Brunswick NJ 08901. (732)246-7717. Artistic Director: David Saint. **Contact:** Literary Associate. Produces 6 plays/year. Professional regional theater (LORT C). Proscenium/thrust stage with 367 seats. *No unsolicited scripts. Agent or professional recommendation only.*

Tips It is our firm belief that theater reaches the mind via the heart and the funny bone. Our work tells a compelling, personal, human story that entertains, challenges and stretches the imagination.

GEVA THEATRE CENTER

75 Woodbury Blvd., Rochester NY 14607. (585)232-1366. **Contact:** Marge Betley, literary manager. Produces 7-11 plays/year. Professional and regional theater, modified thrust, 552 seats; second stage has 180 seats. Subscription and single-ticket sales. Query with sample pages, synopsis, and resume. Responds in 3 months.

Needs Full-length plays, translations, and adaptations.

THE GOODMAN THEATRE

170 N. Dearborn St., Chicago IL 60601-3205. (312)443-3811. Fax: (312)443-3821. E-mail: artistic@goodman-theatre.org. **Contact:** Tanya Palmer, literary manager. Estab. 1925. Produces 9 plays/year. The Goodman is a professional, not-for-profit theater producing a series in both the Albert Theatre and the Owen Theatre, which includes an annual New Play Series. The Goodman does not accept unsolicited scripts, nor will it respond to synopsis of plays submitted by playwrights unless accompanied by a stamped, self-addressed postcard. The Goodman may request plays to be submitted for production consideration after receiving a letter of inquiry or telephone call from recognized literary agents or producing organizations. Responds in 6 months. Buys variable rights. Pays variable royalty.

Needs Full-length plays, translations, musicals; special interest in social or political themes.

GRETNA THEATRE

P.O. Box 578, Mt. Gretna PA 17064. Fax: (717)964-2189. E-mail: larryfrenock@gretnatheatre.com. **Contact:** Larry Frenock, producing director. Estab. 1927. Musicals and plays are performed at a professional equity theater during summer. from writers or agents. Pays negotiable royalty (6-12%).

Needs We produce full-length plays for a summer audience—subject, language and content are important. Prefer package or vehicles which have star role.

Tips Large cast shows or those with elaborate scenic/costume needs will not be considered as these children's shows are performed on whatever mainstage set is on deck at the time.

GRIFFIN THEATRE COMPANY

13 Craigend St., Kings Cross NSW 2011 Australia. (61)(2)9332-1052. Fax: (61)(2)9331-1524. Gives consideration and feedback if the author has had a play professionally produced, has an agent, has been shortlisted for the Griffin Award, or has had a play workshopped at Griffin. If you don't meet these requirements, you may still send a 1-page outline and a 10-page sample. If interested, we will request the full manuscript.

HARTFORD STAGE CO.

50 Church St., Hartford CT 06103. (860)525-5601. Fax: (860)525-4420. **Contact:** Scripts Manager. Estab. 1963. Produces 6 plays/year. Regional theater productions with a wide range in audience. Hartford Stage accepts scripts by agent submission or professional recommendation. As a dedicated supporter of our community, we also accept scripts from Connecticut residents. (Please note, we do not accept one-act

plays, or unsolicited material. For questions, contact our scripts manager. If you qualify, we respond within 3-6 months.
Needs Classics, new plays, musicals.

HORIZON THEATRE CO.

P.O. Box 5376, Atlanta GA 31107. (404)523-1477. Fax: (404)584-8815. **Contact:** Literary Manager. Estab. 1983. 5+ plays/year, and workshops 6 plays as part of New South Playworks Festival Professional productions. Accepts unsolicited résumés, samples, treatments, and summaries with SASE. Responds in 1 year. Buys rights to produce in Atlanta area.
Needs "We produce contemporary plays that seek to bridge cultures and communities, utilizing a realistic base but with heightened visual or language elements. Particularly interested in comedy, satire, plays that are entertaining and topical, but thought provoking. Also particular interest in plays by women, African-Americans, or that concern the contemporary South. No more than 8 in cast."

ILLINOIS THEATRE CENTRE

371 Artists' Walk, P.O. Box 397, Park Forest IL 60466. (708)481-3510. Fax: (708)481-3693. E-mail: ilthctr@sbcglobal.net. Estab. 1976. Produces 8 plays/year. Professional Resident Theatre Company in our own space for a subscription-based audience. Query with synopsis or agented submission. Responds in 2 months. Buys casting and directing and designer selection rights. Pays 7-10% royalty.
Needs All types of 2-act plays, musicals, dramas. Prefers cast size of 6-10.
Tips Always looking for mysteries and comedies. Make sure your play arrives between November and January when play selections are made.

INDIANA REPERTORY THEATRE

140 W. Washington St., Indianapolis IN 46204-3465. (317)635-5277. E-mail: rroberts@irtlive.com. Website: www.irtlive.com. Artistic Director: Janet Allen. Dramaturg: Richard Roberts. "Modified proscenium stage with 600 seats; thrust stage with 300 seats." Send synopsis with résumé via e-mail to the dramaturg. No unsolicited scripts. Submit year-round (season chosen by January). Responds in 6 months.
Needs Full-length plays, translations, adaptations, solo pieces. Also interested in adaptations of classic literature and plays that explore cultural/ethnic issues with a Midwestern voice. Special program: Discovery Series (plays for family audiences with a focus on youth). Cast size should be 6-8.
Tips "The IRT employs a playwright-in-residence from whom the majority of our new work is commissioned. We occasionally place other subject-specific commissions."

INTERACT THEATRE CO.

The Adrienne, 2030 Sansom St., Philadelphia PA 19103. (215)568-8077. Fax: (215)568-8095. E-mail: pbonilla@interacttheatre.org. **Contact:** Peter Bonilla, literary associate. Estab. 1988. Produces 4 plays/year. Produces professional productions for adult audience. Query with synopsis and bio. No unsolicited scripts. Responds in 6 months. Pays 2-8% royalty or $25-100/performance.
Needs Contemporary dramas and comedies that explore issues of political, social, cultural or historical significance. Virtually all of our productions have political content in the foreground of the drama. Prefer plays that raise interesting questions without giving easy, predictable answers. We are interested in new plays. Limit cast to 8. No romantic comedies, family dramas, agit-prop.

[A] INTIMAN THEATRE

201 Mercer St., Seattle WA 98109. (206)269-1901. Fax: (206)269-1928. E-mail: literary@intiman.org. Artistic Director: Bartlett Sher. **Contact:** Sheila Daniels. Estab. 1972. Produces 6 plays/year. LORT C Regional Theater in Seattle. Best submission time is October through March. *Agented submissions only* or by professional recommendation. Responds in 8 months.
Needs Well-crafted dramas and comedies by playwrights who fully utilize the power of language and character relationships to explore enduring themes. Prefers non-naturalistic plays and plays of dynamic theatricality.

JEWEL BOX THEATRE

3700 N. Walker, Oklahoma City OK 73118-7099. (405)521-7031. Fax: (405)525-6562. **Contact:** Charles Tweed, production director. Estab. 1956. Produces 6 plays/year. Amateur productions. 3,000 season subscribers and general public. Pays $500 contest prize.
Needs Annual Playwriting Competition: Send SASE in September-October. Deadline: mid-January.

JEWISH ENSEMBLE THEATRE

6600 W. Maple Rd., West Bloomfield MI 48322. (248)788-2900. E-mail: e.orbach@jettheatre.org. **Contact:** Evelyn Orbach, artistic director. Estab. 1989. Produces 4-6 plays/year. Professional productions at the Aaron DeRoy Theatre (season), The Detroit Institute of Arts Theatre, and Scottish Rite Cathedral Theatre (schools), as well as tours to schools. Submit complete script. Responds in 1 year. Obtains rights for our season productions and staged readings for festival. Pays 6-8% royalty for full production or honorarium for staged reading—$100/full-length play.

Needs We do few children's plays except original commissions; we rarely do musicals. Cast limited to a maximum of 8 actors

Tips We are a theater of social conscience with the following mission: to produce work on the highest possible professional level; to deal with issues of community & humanity from a Jewish perspective; to provide a platform for new voices and a bridge for understanding to the larger community.

N KITCHEN DOG THEATER

3120 McKinney Ave., Dallas TX 75204. (214)953-2258. Fax: (214)953-1873. E-mail: admin@kitchendogtheater.org. **Contact:** Chris Carlos, co-artistic director. Estab. 1990. Produces 5 plays/year. "Kitchen Dog Theater is a place where questions of justice, morality, and human freedom can be explored. We choose plays that challenge our moral and social consciences, invite our audiences to be provoked, challenged, and amazed. We have 2 performance spaces: a 100-seat black box and a 150-seat thrust." Submit complete manuscript with SASE. Each year the deadline for submissions is March 1 (received by). Writers are notified by May 15. Buys rights to full production. Pays $1,000 for winner of New Works Festival.

Needs "We are interested in experimental plays, literary adaptations, historical plays, political theater, gay and lesbian work, culturally diverse work, and small musicals. Ideally, cast size would be 1-5, or more if doubling roles is a possibility. No romantic/light comedies or material that is more suited for television than the theater."

Tips "We are interested in plays that are theatrical and that challenge the imagination—plays that are for the theater, rather than TV or film."

KUMU KAHUA

46 Merchant St., Honolulu HI 96813. (808)536-4222. Fax: (808)536-4226. E-mail: kumukahuatheatre@hawaiiantel.net. **Contact:** Artistic Director. Estab. 1971. Produces 5 productions, 3-4 public readings/year. Plays performed at new Kumu Kahua Theatre, flexible 120-seat theater, for community audiences. Submit complete script. Responds in 4 months. Pays royalty of $50/performance; usually 20 performances of each production.

Needs Plays must have some interest for local Hawai'i audiences.

LILLENAS PUBLISHING CO.

P.O. Box 419527, Kansas City MO 64141-6527. (816)931-1900. Fax: (816)412-8390. **Contact:** Kim Messer, product manager. Estab. 1926. "We publish on 2 levels: 1) Program Builders—seasonal and topical collections of recitations, sketches, dialogues, and short plays; 2) Drama Resources which assume more than 1 format: a) full-length scripts; b) one-acts, shorter plays, and sketches all by 1 author; c) collection of short plays and sketches by various authors. All program and play resources are produced with local church and Christian school in mind. Therefore there are taboos." Queries are encouraged, but synopses and complete scripts are read. This publisher is interested in collections of and individual sketches. There is also a need for short pieces that are seasonal and on current events. Responds in 3 months. First rights are purchased for Program Builders scripts. For Drama Resources, we purchase all print rights. Drama Resources are paid on a 12% royalty, whether full-length scripts, one-acts, or sketches. No advance.

Needs 98% of Program Builders materials are freelance written. Scripts selected for these publications are outright purchases; verse is minimum of 25¢/line, prose (play scripts) are minimum of $5/double-spaced page. "Lillenas Drama Resources is a line of play scripts that are, for the most part, written by professionals with experience in productions as well as writing. While we do read unsolicited scripts, more than half of what we publish is written by experienced authors whom we have already published."

Tips "All plays need to be presented in standard play script format. We welcome a summary statement of each play. Purpose statements are always desirable. Approximate playing time, cast and prop lists, etc., are important to include. Contemporary settings generally have it over Biblical settings. Christmas and Easter scripts must have a bit of a twist. Secular approaches to these seasons (Santas, Easter bunnies, and so on), are not considered. We sell our product in 10,000 Christian bookstores and by catalog. We are in the forefront as a publisher of religious drama resources. Request a copy of our newsletter and/or catalog."

LONG WHARF THEATRE

222 Sargent Dr., New Haven CT 06511. (203)787-4284. Fax: (203)776-2287. E-mail: gordon.edelstein@longwharf.org. **Contact:** Gordon Edelstein, artistic dir. Estab. 1965. Produces 6 plays/year on its 2 stages. "Professional regional theatre has been and continues to be an incubator of new works, including last season's *A Civil War Christmas* by Paula Vogel and *Coming Home* by Athol Fugard. Long Wharf Theatre has received New York Drama Critics Awards, Obie Awards, the Margo Jefferson Award for Production of New Works and more." *Agented submissions or professional recommendations only.*

Needs Full-length plays, translations, adaptations. Special interest: Dramatic plays and comedies about human relationships, social concerns, ethical and moral dilemmas.

Tips "We no longer accept queries."

LOS ANGELES DESIGNERS' THEATRE

P.O. Box 1883, Studio City CA 91614-0883. E-mail: ladesigners@juno.com. **Contact:** Richard Niederberg, artistic dir. Estab. Established 1970. Produces 8-20 plays/year. "Professional shows/industry audience." Submit proposal only (i.e., 1 page in #10 SASE) We want highly commercial work without liens, 'understandings,' or promises to anyone. Does not return submissions accompanied by a SASE. Reports in 3 months (minimum) to submission. Purchases rights by negotiation, first refusal for performance/synchronization rights only. Payment varies.

Needs All types. "No limitations—We seek design challenges. No boring material. Shorter plays with musical underscores are desirable; nudity, street language, and political themes are OK."

MAGIC THEATRE

Fort Mason Center, Bldg. D, 3rd Floor, San Francisco CA 94123. (415)441-8001. Fax: (415)771-5505. E-mail: info@magictheatre.org. Artistic Director: Chris Smith. **Contact:** Mark Routhier, director of artistic development. Estab. 1967. Produces 6 mainstage plays/year, plus monthly reading series and several festivals each year which contain both staged readings and workshop productions. Regional theater. Bay area residents can send complete ms or query with cover letter, résumé, 1-page synopsis, SASE, dialogue sample (10-20 pages). Those outside the Bay area can query or submit through an agent. Responds in 6-8 months. Pays royalty or per performance fee.

Needs Plays that are innovative in theme and/or craft, cutting-edge sociopolitical concerns, intelligent comedy. Full-length only, strong commitment to multicultural work.

Tips Not interested in classics, conventional approaches and cannot produce large-cast (over 10) plays. Send query to Mark Routhier, literary manager.

MALTHOUSE THEATRE

113 Sturt St., Southbank VIC 3006 Australia. (61)(3)9685-5100. Fax: (61)(3)9685-5111. E-mail: admin@malthousetheatre.com.au. **Contact:** Michael Kantor, artistic director. We are dedicated to contemporary Australian theatre. Writers should have had at least 1 professional production of their work. Proposals are called for on March 1, July 1, and October 1. Mail 1-page synopsis, brief author bio, and 10-page sample. Responds in 3 months if interested.

MANHATTAN THEATRE CLUB

311 W. 43rd St., 8th Floor, New York NY 10036. (212)399-3000. Fax: (212)399-4329. E-mail: questions@mtc-nyc.org. Director of Artistic Development: Paige Evans. **Contact:** Raphael Martin, literary manager. Produces 7 plays/year. 1 Broadway and 2 Off-Broadway theatres, using professional actors. *Solicited and agented submissions only.* No queries. Responds within 6 months.

Needs We present a wide range of new work, from this country and abroad, to a subscription audience. We want plays about contemporary concerns and people. All genres are welcome. MTC also maintains an extensive play development program.

MCCARTER THEATRE

91 University Place, Princeton NJ 08540. E-mail: literary@mccarter.org. Artistic Director: Emily Mann. **Contact:** Literary Manager. Produces 5 plays/year; 1 second stage play/year. Produces professional productions for a 1,077-seat and 360-seat theaters. Agented submissions only. Responds in 4-6 months. Pays negotiable royalty.

Needs Full length plays, musicals, translations.

MELBOURNE THEATRE COMPANY

129 Ferrars St., Southbank VIC 3006 Australia. (61)(3)9684-4500. Fax: (61)(3)9696-2627. E-mail: info@mtc.com.au. **Contact:** Aiden Fennessey, associate director. "MTC produces classic plays, modern revivals and the best new plays from Australia and overseas. Victorian work is given emphasis. MTC does not accept unsolicited manuscripts and it is our strict policy to return them unread. MTC does not produce work from previously unproduced Australian playwrights. New Australian plays generally come from three sources: by the commissioning of established writers; by the invitation to submit work to emerging writers with a track record and the potential to write for a mainstream subscription audience; and through a recommendation from an industry body, such as the Australian Script Centre or any of the major playwriting competitions." Responds in 3 months.

MERIWETHER PUBLISHING, LTD.

885 Elkton Dr., Colorado Springs CO 80907-3557. Fax: (719)594-9916. E-mail: merpcds@aol.com. President: Mark Zapel. Associate Editor: Arthur L. Zapel. **Contact:** Ted Zapel, associate editor. Estab. 1969. "We publish how-to theatre materials in book and video formats. We are interested in materials for middle school, high school, and college-level students only." Query with synopsis/outline, résumé of credits, sample of style, and SASE. Catalog available for $2 postage. Responds in 1 month to queries; 2 months to full-length mss. Offers 10% royalty.

Needs "Musicals for a large cast of performers, one-act or two-act comedy plays with large casts, and book mss on theatrical arts subjects. We are now looking for scenebooks with special themes: scenes for young women, comedy scenes for 2 actors, etc. These need not be original, provided the compiler can get letters of permission from the original copyright owner. We are interested in all textbook candidates for theater arts subjects. Christian children's activity book manuscripts also accepted. We will consider elementary-level religious plays, but no elementary-level children's secular plays."

Tips "We publish a wide variety of speech contest materials for high-school students. We are publishing more full-length play scripts and musical parodies based on classic literature or popular TV shows. Our educational books are sold to teachers and students at college and high-school levels. Our religious books are sold to youth activity directors, pastors, and choir directors. Another group of buyers is the professional theater, radio, and TV category. We will be especially interested in full-length (two- or three-act) plays with name recognition (either the playwright or the adaptation source)."

METROSTAGE

1201 N. Royal St., Alexandria VA 22314. (703)548-9044. Fax: (703)548-9089. E-mail: info@metrostage.org. **Contact:** Carolyn Griffin, producing artistic director. Estab. 1984. Produces 5-6 plays/year. Professional productions for 130-seat theatre, general audience. Agented submissions only. Responds in 3 months. Pays royalty.

Needs Contemporary themes, small cast (up to 6 actors), unit set.

Tips "Plays should have *already* had readings and workshops before being sent for our review. Do not send plays that have never had a staged reading."

NEBRASKA THEATRE CARAVAN

6915 Cass St., Omaha NE 68132. Fax: (402)553-6288. E-mail: info@omahaplayhouse.com. Artistic Director: Carl Beck. **Contact:** Alena Furlong, development director. Estab. 1976. Produces 4-5 plays/year. Nebraska Theatre Caravan is a touring company which produces professional productions in schools, arts centers, and small and large theaters for elementary, middle, high school and family audiences. Submit query and synopsis. Responds in 3 weeks. Negotiates production rights unless the work is commissioned by us. Pays $20-50/performance.

Needs All genres are acceptable bearing in mind the student audiences. We are truly an ensemble and like to see that in our choice of shows; curriculum ties are very important for elementary and high school shows; 75 minutes for middle/high school shows. No sexually explicit material.

Tips We tour eight months of the year to a variety of locations. Flexibility is important as we work in both beautiful performing arts facilities and school multipurpose rooms.

THE NEW GROUP

410 W. 42nd St., New York NY 10036. (212)244-3380. Fax: (212)244-3438. E-mail: info@thenewgroup.org. Artistic Director: Scott Elliott. **Contact:** Ian Morgan, associate artistic director. Estab. 1991. Produces 4 plays/year. Off-Broadway theater. Submit 10-page sample, cover letter, résumé, synopsis, and SASE. No submissions that have already been produced in NYC. Include SASE for return of script. Responds in 9 months to submissions. Pays royalty. Makes outright purchase.

Needs We produce challenging, character-based scripts with a contemporary sensibility. Does not want to receive musicals, historical scripts or science fiction.

NEW JERSEY REPERTORY COMPANY.

179 Broadway, Long Branch NJ 07740. (732)229-3166. Fax: (732)229-3167. E-mail: njrep@njrep.org. Website: www.njrep.org. Artistic Director: SuzAnne Barabas. **Contact:** Literary Manager. Estab. 1997. Produces 6-7 plays/year and 20-25 script-in-hand readings. Professional productions year round. Previously unproduced plays and musicals only. Submit via e-mail with synopsis, cast breakdown, playwright bio. For musicals, e-mail mp3 of songs or send CD. Responds in 1 year if interested. Rights negotiable.

Needs Full-length plays with a cast size no more than 4. Simple set.

Tips "Annual Theatre Brut Festival of Short Plays. Previously unproduced. 1-4 actors; simple set, no more than 10 minutes in length. Theme for 2009-2010 festival: Creation."

NEW REPERTORY THEATRE

200 Dexter Ave., Waterton MA 02472. (617)923-7060. Fax: (617)923-7625. E-mail: artistic@newrep.org. **Contact:** Rick Lombardo, producing artistic director. Estab. 1984. Produces 5 plays/year. Professional theater, general audience. Query with synopsis and dialogue sample. Buys production and subsidiary rights. Pays 5-10% royalty.

Needs Idea laden, all styles, full-length only. New musicals.

Tips No sitcom-like comedies. Incorporating and exploring styles other than naturalism.

NEW STAGE THEATRE

1100 Carlisle, Jackson MS 39202. (601)948-3533. Fax: (601)948-3538. E-mail: mail@newstagetheatre.com. **Contact:** Artistic Director. Estab. 1965. Produces 8 plays/year. Professional productions, 8 mainstage, 3 in our 'second space.' We play to an audience comprised of Jackson, the state of Mississippi and the Southeast. Submit query and synopsis. Exclusive premiere contract upon acceptance of play for mainstage production. Pays 5-8% royalty. Pays $25-60/performance.

Needs Southern themes, contemporary issues, small casts (5-8), single set plays.

Tips Eudora Welty New Play Series - winners received staged readings of new plays and monetary award from $100 - $1000. Submissions are accepted from June 1st through December 31st.

NEW THEATRE

4120 Laguna St., Coral Gables FL 33146. (305)443-5373. Fax: (305)443-1642. E-mail: tvodihn@newtheatre.org. **Contact:** Tara Vodihn, literary manager. Estab. 1986. Produces 7 plays/year. Professional productions. Submit query and synopsis. Responds in 3-6 months. Rights subject to negotiation. Payment negotiable.

Needs Interested in full-length, non-realistic, moving, intelligent, language-driven plays with a healthy dose of humor. No musicals or large casts.

Tips No kitchen sink realism. Send a simple query with synopsis. Be mindful of social issues.

NEW THEATRE

542 King St., Newtown NSW 2042 Australia. (61)(2)9519-3403. Fax: (61)(2)9519-8960. E-mail: newtheatre@bigpond.com. **Contact:** Administrator. Estab. 1932. We welcome the submission of new scripts. Submissions are assessed by playreaders and the artistic director. Submit complete ms and SASE.

NEW YORK STATE THEATRE INSTITUTE

37 First St., Troy NY 12180. (518)274-3200. Fax: (518)274-3815. E-mail: nysti@capital.net. **Contact:** Patricia DiBenedetto Snyder, producing artistic director. Produces 6 plays/year. Professional regional productions for adult and family audiences. Submit query and synopsis. Responds in 6 weeks. Payment varies.

Needs We are not interested in material for 'mature' audiences. Submissions must be scripts of substance and intelligence geared to family audiences.

Tips Do not submit complete script unless invited after review of synopsis.

NEW YORK THEATRE WORKSHOP

83 E. 4th St., New York NY 10003. Fax: (212)460-8996. E-mail: litern@nytw.org. Artistic Director: James C. Nicola. **Contact:** Literary Department. Estab. 1979. Produces four to five full productions and approximately 50 readings/year. "NYTW is renowned for producing intelligent and complex plays that expand the boundaries of theatrical form and in some new and compelling way address issues that are critical to our times. Plays are performed off-Broadway. Audience is New York theater-going audience and theater professionals." Prefer email submissions. Type "synopsis submission." If mailing: Query

with cover letter, synopsis, 10-page dialogue sample, 2 letters of recommendation; SASE if requesting return of materials. Include tape/CD/video where appropriate. Responds in 6-10 months.
Needs Full-length plays, translations/adaptations, music theater pieces; proposals for performance projects. Socially relevant issues, innovative form, and language.
Tips "No overtly commercial and conventional musicals or plays."

NORTHLIGHT THEATRE

9501 Skokie Blvd., Skokie IL 60077. (847)679-9501. Fax: (847)679-1879. E-mail: mmccarthy@northlight.org. BJ Jones. **Contact:** Meghan Beals McCarthy, dramaturg. Estab. 1975. Produces 5 plays/year. We are a professional, equity theater, LORT C. We have a subscription base of over 8,000 and have a significant number of single ticket buyers. Query with 10-page dialogue sample, synopsis, resume/bio, and SASE/SASPC for response. Responds in 3-4 months. Buys production rights, plus royalty on future mountings. Pays royalty.
Needs Full-length plays, translations, adaptations, musicals. Interested in plays of 'ideas'; plays that are passionate and/or hilarious; accessible plays that challenge, incite, and reflect the beliefs of our society/community. Generally looking for cast size of 6 or fewer, but there are exceptions made for the right play.
Tips As a mainstream regional theater, we are unlikely to consider anything overtly experimental or absurdist. We seek good stories, vivid language, rich characters, and strong understandings of theatricality.

ODYSSEY THEATRE ENSEMBLE

2055 S. Sepulveda Blvd., Los Angeles CA 90025-5621. (310)477-2055. Fax: (310)444-0455. Ron Sossi. **Contact:** Sally Essex-Lopresti, director of literary programs. Estab. 1969. Produces 9 plays/year. Plays performed in a 3-theater facility. All 3 theaters are Equity 99-seat theater plan. We have a subscription audience of 4,000 for a 9-play main season. No unsolicited material. Query with resume, synopsis, 10 pages of sample dialogue, and cassette if musical. Does not return scripts without SASE. Responds in 2 weeks. Buys negotiable rights. Pays 5-7% royalty.

- "Our purpose is the creation of new work, the revitalization and re-exploration of classical material, experimentation with current developments at the forefront of the "state of the art." in the international theatre world. Ultimately, the institution moves toward the creation of a larger International Experimental Theatre Center, facilitating the crosspolination of artists from different countries, cultures and disciplines, and the exposure of this collaborative work to the Southern California audience."

Needs Full-length plays only with either an innovative form and/or provocative subject matter. We desire highly theatrical pieces that explore possibilities of the live theater experience. We are not reading one-act plays or light situation comedies.

OMAHA THEATER CO./ROSE THEATER

2001 Farnam St., Omaha NE 68102. (402)345-9718. E-mail: jlarsonotc@msn.com. **Contact:** James Larson, artistic director. Produces 6-10 plays/year. "Our target audience is children, preschool through high school, and their parents." Submit query and synopsis. Send SASE. Responds in 9 months. Pays royalty.
Needs Plays must be geared to children and parents (PG rating). Titles recognized by the general public have a stronger chance of being produced. Cast limit: 25 (8-10 adults). No adult scripts.
Tips "Unproduced plays may be accepted only after a letter of inquiry (familiar titles only!)."

ONE ACT PLAY DEPOT

Box 335, Spiritwood Saskatchewan S0J 2M0 Canada. E-mail: submissions@oneactplays.net. "Accepts unsolicited submissions only in February of each year." Submit complete script by mail or via e-mail as a plain .txt file or pasted into the body of the message.
Needs Interested only in one-act plays. Does not want musicals or farces. Do not mail originals. Our main focus will be black comedy, along with well-written dramatic and comedic pieces.

O'NEILL MUSIC THEATER CONFERENCE

Eugene O'Neill Theater Center, 305 Great Neck Rd., Waterford CT 06385. (860)443-5378. Fax: (860)443-9653. E-mail: theaterlives@theoneill.org. **Contact:** Jill A. Mauritz, general manager. Estab. 1964. "At The Music Theater Conference, creative artists are in residence with artistic staff and an equity company of actors/singers. Public and private readings, script in hand, piano only." An open submission process begins in the fall of each year and concludes in May. The conference takes place in July and August at the O'Neill Theater Center. Works are accepted based on their readiness to be performed, but when there is still enough significant work to be accomplished that a fully staged production would be premature. For guidelines and application deadlines, send SASE or see guidelines online. Pays stipend, room and board.

THE O'NEILL PLAYWRIGHTS CONFERENCE

305 Great Neck Rd., Waterford CT 06385. (860)443-5378. Fax: (860)443-9653. E-mail: info@theoneill.org; playwrights@theoneill.org. **Contact:** Martin Kettling, literary manager. Estab. 1978. Produces 7-8 plays/year. The O'Neill Theater Center operates under an Equity LORT contract. Please send #10 SASE for guidelines in the fall, or check online. Decision by late April. We accept submissions September 1-October 1 of each year. Conference takes place during June/July each summer. Playwrights selected are in residence for one month and receive a four-day workshop and two script-in-hand readings with professional actors and directors. Pays stipend plus room, board and transportation.

OREGON SHAKESPEARE FESTIVAL

15 S. Pioneer St., Ashland OR 97520. Fax: (541)482-0446. Artistic Director: Bill Rauch. **Contact:** Director of Literary Development and Dramaturgy. Estab. 1935. Produces 11 plays/year. OSF directly solicits playwright or agent, and does not accept unsolicited submissions.

PERTH THEATRE COMPANY

P.O. Box 3514, Adelaide Terrace, Perth WA 6832 Australia. (61)(8)9323-3433. Fax: (61)(8)9323-3455. E-mail: frontdesk@perththeatre.com.au. **Contact:** Alan Becher, artistic director. Estab. 1983. Seeks to develop new West Australian theatre and provide opportunities to talented local artists. Develops most of its scripts through the Writer's Lab program. Do not send an unsolicited ms unless it is submitted by or accompanied by a letter of recommendation from a writer's agency, script development organization, or professional theatre company. Make sure to include a SASE.

PHILADELPHIA THEATRE CO.

230 S. Broad St., Suite 1105, Philadelphia PA 19102. (215)985-1400. Fax: (215)985-5800. **Contact:** Literary Office. Estab. 1974. Produces 4 plays/year. "Under the direction of Sara Garonzik since 1982, Philadelphia Theatre Company has introduced more than 140 new plays and musicals to audiences in Philadelphia, New York and around the country, establishing the Company's national reputation for artistic quality, risk-taking and diverse programming." Agented submissions only. Responds in 6-12 months No e-mail submissions, letter of inquiry, summaries or excerpts please.

- "We have introduced countless award-winning premieres. Rather than revisit old standards, we are committed to finding the classics of the future."

Needs Philadelphia Theatre Company produces contemporary American plays and musicals. .

Tips Our work is challenging and risky—look to our history for guidance.

PIONEER DRAMA SERVICE, INC.

P.O. Box 4267, Englewood CO 80155-4267. (303)779-4035. Fax: (303)779-4315. E-mail: submissions@pioneerdrama.com. Publisher: Steven Fendrich. **Contact:** Lori Conary, submissions editor. Estab. 1963. Publishes Plays are performed by schools, colleges, community theaters, recreation programs, churches, and professional children's theaters for audiences of all ages. Query or submit complete ms All submissions automatically entered in Shubert Fendrich Memorial Playwriting Contest. Guidelines for SASE. Responds in about 2 weeks to queries; 4-6 months to submissions. Retains all rights. Pays royalty.

Needs Comedies, mysteries, dramas, melodramas, musicals and children's theater. Two-acts up to 90 minutes; children's theater (1 hour); one-acts no less than 20 minutes. Prefers large ensemble casts with many female roles, simple sets, and costumes. Plays need to be appropriate for amateur groups and family audiences. Interested in adaptations of classics of public domain works appropriate for children and teens. Also plays that deal with social issues for teens and preteens.

Tips "Check out our website to see what we carry and if your material would be appropriate for our market. Make sure to include proof of productions and a SASE if you want your material returned."

PITTSBURGH PUBLIC THEATER

621 Penn Ave., Pittsburgh PA 15222. (412)316-8200. Fax: (412)316-8216. Artistic Director: Ted Pappas. **Contact:** Dramaturg. Estab. 1975. Produces 7 plays/year. O'Reilly Theater, 650 seats, thrust seating. Submit full script through agent, or query with synopsis, cover letter, 10-page dialogue sample, and SASE. Responds in 4 months.

- "The mission of Pittsburgh Public Theater is to provide artistically diverse theatrical experiences of the highest quality."

Needs Full-length plays, adaptations and musicals.

PLAYSCRIPTS, INC.

450 7th Ave., Suite 809, New York NY 10023. E-mail: submissions@playscripts.com. Estab. 1998. Audience is professional, community, college, high school and children's theaters worldwide. See website for complete submission guidelines. Materials accompanied by SASE will be returned; however, e-mail submissions are strongly preferred. Responds in 3-6 months Contracts for exclusive publication and performance licensing rights. Pays negotiated book and production royalties.

Needs We are open to a wide diversity of writing styles and content. Unsolicited musicals are not accepted.

Tips "Playscripts, Inc. is a play publishing company dedicated to new work by established and emerging playwrights. We provide all of the same licensing and book production services as a traditional play publisher, along with unique promotional features that maximize the exposure of each dramatic work. Be sure to view our guidelines before submitting."

THE PLAYWRIGHTS' CENTER'S PLAYLABS

2301 Franklin Ave. E., Minneapolis MN 55406. (612)332-7481. Fax: (612)332-6037. E-mail: info@pwcenter.org. Producing Artistic Director: Polly K. Carl. Estab. 1971. PlayLabs is a 2-week developmental workshop for new plays. The program is held in Minneapolis and is open by script competition. Up to 5 new plays are given reading performances and after the festival, a script sample and contact link are posted on the Center's website. Announcements of playwrights by May 1. Playwrights receive honoraria, travel expenses, room and board.

Needs We are interested in playwrights with ambitions for a sustained career in theater, and scripts that could benefit from development involving professional dramaturgs, directors, and actors. US citizens or permanent residents only. Participants must attend entire festival. Submission deadline in October; see website for application and exact deadline. No previously produced materials.

PLAYWRIGHTS HORIZONS

416 W. 42nd St., New York NY 10036. (212)564-1235. Fax: (212)594-0296. Artistic Director: Tim Sanford. **Contact:** Adam Greenfield, literary manager (plays); send musicals Attn: Kent Nicholson, Director of Musical Theater. Estab. 1971. Produces 6 plays/year. Plays performed off-Broadway for a literate, urban, subscription audience. Submit complete ms with author bio; include CD for musicals. Responds in 6-8 months. Negotiates for future rights. Pays royalty. Makes outright purchase.

Needs "We are looking for new, full-length plays and musicals by American authors."

Tips "We do not accept one-acts, one-person shows, non-musical adaptations, translations, children's shows, screenplays, or works by non-US writers. We dislike synopses because we accept unsolicited manuscripts. We look for plays with a strong sense of language and a clear dramatic action that truly use the resources of the theater."

PLAYWRIGHTS' PLATFORM

398 Columbus Ave., #604, Boston MA 02116. Website: www.playwrightsplatform.org. **Contact:** Regina Eliot-Ramsey, president. Estab. 1972. Produces approximately 50 readings/year "Our website contains all information regarding The Platform. The Platform provides dues paying members with the opportunity to read their plays before an audience. Meetings are held at Rosen Auditorium, Brennan Library, Lasell College, Auburndale, MA 02466. Scripts should not be mailed. Readings must be requested through the calendar coordinator. Only dues paying members can submit scripts and are allowed to participate in Platform productions. The Platform produces a short play festival each year in June, held at the Boston Playwrights Theatre, Boston, MA. Only dues paying members can participate. Short one acts, and scenes from full-length plays can be read throughout the calendar year. The festival only produces plays with running times of 20 minutes or less. Members come from the northeast region and are not limited to Massachusetts. There are no restrictions on content." Submit script and SASE (or e-mail or hand deliver). Responds in 2 months.

- *We do not want unsolicited scripts being mailed to our address.*

Needs "Any types of plays. We will not accept scripts we think are sexist or racist. Massachusetts residents only. There are no restrictions on length or number of characters, but it's more difficult to schedule full-length pieces."

🄰 PLAYWRIGHTS THEATRE OF NEW JERSEY

P.O. Box 1295, Madison NJ 07940-1295. (973)514-1787. Fax: (973)514-2060. Artistic Director: John Pietrowski. **Contact:** Alysia Souder, director of program development. Estab. 1986. Produces 3 plays/year. We operate under a Small Professional Theatre Contract (SPT), a development theatre contract

with Actors Equity Association. Readings are held under a staged reading code. Responds in 1 year. For productions we ask the playwright to sign an agreement that gives us exclusive rights to the play for the production period and for 30 days following. After the 30 days we give the rights back with no strings attached, except for commercial productions. We ask that our developmental work be acknowledged in any other professional productions. Makes outright purchase of 750.
Needs Any style or length; full length, one acts, musicals.
Tips We are looking for American plays in the early stages of development—plays of substance, passion, and light (comedies and dramas) that raise challenging questions about ourselves and our communities. We prefer plays *that can work only on the stage* in the most theatrical way possible—plays that are not necessarily `straight-on' realistic, but rather ones that use imagery, metaphor, poetry and musicality in new and interesting ways. Plays can go through a 3-step development process: A roundtable, a concert reading, and then a workshop production.

PORTLAND STAGE CO.

P.O. Box 1458, Portland ME 04104. (207)774-1043. Fax: (207)774-0576. E-mail: info@portlandstage.com. Artistic Director: Anita Stewart. **Contact:** Daniel Burson, literary manager. Estab. 1974. Produces 7 plays/year. Professional productions at Portland Stage Company. Send first 10 pages with synopsis. Responds in 3 months. Buys 3- or 4-week run in Maine. Pays royalty.
Needs Developmental Staged Readings: Little Festival of the Unexpected.
Tips Work developed in Little Festival generally will be more strongly considered for future production.

PRIMARY STAGES CO., INC.

307 W. 38th St., Suite 1510, New York NY 10018. (212)840-9705. Fax: (212)840-9725. E-mail: tessa@primarystages.org. Andrew Leynse. **Contact:** Tessa LaNeve, literary manager. Estab. 1985. Produces 4 plays/year. All plays are produced professionally off-Broadway at 59E59 Theatres' 199 seat theatre. Agented submissions only Guidelines online. Pays flat fee.

- "One of the premiere theaters for the development of new work."

Needs Full-length plays, small cast (6 or fewer) musicals. New York City premieres only. Small cast (1-6), unit set or simple changes, no fly or wing space.
Tips Best submission time: September-June. Chances: Over 1,000 scripts read, 4-5 produced. Women and minorities encouraged to submit.

PRINCE MUSIC THEATER

100 S. Broad St., Suite 650, Philadelphia PA 19110. (215)972-1000. Fax: (215)972-1020. **Contact:** Marjorie Samoff, producing artistic director. Estab. 1984. Produces 4 musicals/year. "Professional musical productions. Drawing upon operatic and popular traditions as well as European, African, Asian and South American forms, new work and new voices take center stage." Send synopsis and sample audio tape with no more than 4 songs. Responds in 6 months. Pays royalty.
Needs Song-driven music theater, varied musical styles. Nine-member orchestra, 10-14 cast, 36x60 stage.
Tips "Innovative topics and use of media, music, technology a plus. Sees trends of arts in technology (interactive theater, virtual reality, sound design); works are shorter in length (1-1½ hours with no intermissions or 2 hours with intermission)."

PRINCETON REP COMPANY

44 Nassau St., Suite 350, Princeton NJ 08542. E-mail: prcreprap@aol.com. **Contact:** New Play Submissions. Estab. 1984. Plays are performed in site-specific venues, outdoor amphitheatres, and indoor theatres with approximately 199 seats. Princeton Rep Company works under Actors' Equity contracts, and its directors are members of the SSDC. Query with synopsis, SASE, résumé, and 10 pages of sample dialogue. Submissions accompanied by a SASE will be returned. Responds in up to 2 years. Rights are negotiated on a play-by-play basis. Payment negotiated on a play-by-play basis.
Needs Stories that investigate the lives of middle and working class people. Love stories of the rich, famous, and fatuous. If the play demands a cast of thousands, please don't waste your time and postage. No drama or comedy set in a prep school or ivy league college.

THE PUBLIC THEATER

425 Lafayette St., New York NY 10003. (212)539-8500. Artistic Director: Oskar Eustis. **Contact:** Literary Department. Estab. 1964. Produces 6 plays/year. Professional productions. Query with synopsis,10-page sample, letter of inquiry, cassette with 3-5 songs for musicals/operas. Responds in 3 months.
Needs Full-length plays, translations, adaptations, musicals, operas, and solo pieces. All genres, no one-acts.

PULSE ENSEMBLE THEATRE

248 W. 35th St., 15th Floor, New York NY 10001. (212)695-1596. Fax: (212)695-1596. E-mail: theatre@pulseensembletheatre.org. **Contact:** Brian Richardson. Estab. 1989. Produces 3 plays/year. No unsolicited submissions. Only accepts new material through the Playwright's Lab. Include SASE for return of submission. Buys variable rights. Usually pays 2% of gross.

Needs meaningful theater. No production limitations.

THE PURPLE ROSE THEATRE CO.

137 Park St., Chelsea MI 48118. (734)433-7782. Fax: (734)475-0802. Guy Sanville. **Contact:** Guy Sanville, artistic director. Estab. 1990. Produces 4 plays/year. "PRTC is a regional theater with an S.P.T. equity contract which produces plays intended for Midwest/Middle American audience. It is dedicated to creating opportunities for Midwest theatre professionals." Query with synopsis, character breakdown, and 10-page dialogue sample. Responds in 9 months. Pays 5-10% royalty.

Needs Modern, topical full length, 75-120 minutes. Prefers scripts that use comedy to deal with serious subjects. 8 cast maximum. No fly space, unit set preferable. Intimate 168 seat 3/4 thrust house.

QUEENSLAND THEATRE COMPANY

P.O. Box 3310, South Brisbane QLD 4101 Australia. (61)(7)3010-7600. Fax: (61)(7)3010-7699. E-mail: mail@qldtheatreco.com.au. **Contact:** Michael Gow, artistic director. "Seeks timeless classics, modern classics, and new plays from Australia and overseas. Only considers unsolicited scripts if the playwright has had at least 1 play professionally produced if the script has been submitted by an agent, or recommended by a professional theatre company or script development agency." Responds in 3 months.

Needs "Works specifically aimed at child/youth audiences are less likely to be considered."

RED LADDER THEATRE CO.

3 St. Peter's Buildings, York St., Leeds LS9 1AJ United Kingdom. (44)(113)245-5311. E-mail: rod@redladder.co.uk. **Contact:** Rod Dixon, artistic director. Estab. 1969. Produces 2 plays/year. Our work tours nationally to young people, aged 13-25, in youth clubs, community venues and small scale theatres. Submit query and synopsis. Responds in 6 months. Offers ITC/Equity writers contract.

Needs One hour in length for cast size no bigger than 5. Work that connects with a youth audience that both challenges them and offers them new insights. We consider a range of styles and are seeking originality. Small scale touring. Does not want to commission single issue drama. The uses of new technologies in production (DVD, video projection). Young audiences are sophisticated.

Tips Please do not submit full length plays. Get in touch with us first. Tell us about yourself and why you would like to write for Red Ladder. We like to hear about ideas you may have in the first instance.

RESOURCE PUBLICATIONS

160 E. Virginia St., Suite 290, San Jose CA 95112-5876. (408)286-8505. Fax: (408)287-8748. E-mail: editor@rpinet.com. Estab. 1973. Audience includes laity and ordained seeking resources (books/periodicals/software) in Christian ministry, worship, faith formation, education, and counseling (primarily Roman Catholic, but not all). Submit query and synopsis via e-mail. Responds in 3 months.

Needs Needs materials for those in pastoral ministry, faith formation, youth ministry, and parish administration. No fiction, children's books, or music.

ROUND HOUSE THEATRE

P.O. Box 30688, Bethesda MD 20824. (240)644-1099. Fax: (240)644-1090. E-mail: roundhouse@roundhousetheatre.org. Producing Artistic Director: Blake Robison. **Contact:** Danisha Crosby, associate producer. Produces 5-7 plays/year. "Professional AEA Theatre that is recognized nationally as a center for the development of literary works for the stage. Our critically-acclaimed Literary Works Project features new adaptations of contemporary and classical novels, re-interpreted through a theatrical prism for today's audiences. We give these stories a fresh voice, a bold visual presence, and a new relevance in our ever-changing society. The project has garnered 10 Helen Hayes Award nominations and strong notices in the regional and national press." Query with synopsis; no unsolicited scripts accepted. Responds in 2-12 months. Pays negotiated percentage for productions.

SALTWORKS THEATRE CO.

569 N. Neville St., Pittsburgh PA 15213. (412)621-6150. Fax: (412)621-6010. E-mail: nalrutz@saltworks.org. **Contact:** Norma Alrutz, executive director. Estab. 1981. Produces 8-10 plays/year. Submit query and synopsis. Responds in 2 months. Obtains regional performance rights for educational grants. Pays $25/performance.

Needs Wants plays for children, youth, and families that address social issues like violence prevention,

sexual responsibility, peer pressures, tobacco use, bullying, racial issues/diversity, drug and alcohol abuse (grades 1-12). Limited to 5 member cast, 2 men/2 women/1 either.
Tips Check website for current play contest rules and deadlines.

SEATTLE REPERTORY THEATRE

P.O. Box 900923, Seattle WA 98109. E-mail: bradena@seattlerep.org. Artistic Director: Jerry Manning. **Contact:** Braden Abraham, associate artistic director. Estab. 1963. Produces 8 plays/year. Send query, resume, synopsis and 10 sample pages. Responds in 6 months. Buys percentage of future royalties. Pays royalty.
Needs "The Seattle Repertory Theatre produces eclectic programming. We welcome a wide variety of writing."

SECOND STAGE THEATRE

307 W. 43rd St., New York NY 10036-6406. (212)787-8302. Fax: (212)397-7066. **Contact:** Sarah Bagley, literary manager. Estab. 1979. Produces 6 plays/year. "Second Stage Theatre gives new life to contemporary American plays through 'second stagings'; provides emerging authors with their Off-Broadway debuts; and produces world premieres by America's most respected playwrights. Adult and teen audiences." Query with synopsis and 10-page writing sample or agented submission. Responds in 6 months. Payment varies.
Needs We need socio-political plays, comedies, musicals, dramas—full lengths for full production.
Tips No biographical or historical dramas, or plays in verse. Writers are realizing that audiences can be entertained while being moved. Patience is a virtue but persistence is appreciated.

SHAW FESTIVAL THEATRE

P.O. Box 774, Niagara-on-the-Lake ON L0S 1J0 Canada. (905)468-2153. Fax: (905)468-7140. **Contact:** Jackie Maxwell, artistic director. Estab. 1962. Produces 12 plays/year. Professional theater company operating 3 theaters (Festival: 869 seats; Court House: 327 seats; Royal George: 328 seats). Shaw Festival presents the work of George Bernard Shaw and his contemporaries written during his lifetime (1856-1950) and in 2000 expanded the mandate to include contemporary works written about the period of his lifetime. Query with SASE or SAE and IRC's, depending on country of origin. We prefer to hold rights for Canada and northeastern US, also potential to tour. Pays 5-10% royalty.
Needs We operate an acting ensemble of up to 75 actors; and we have sophisticated production facilities. During the summer season (April-November) the Academy of the Shaw Festival organizes workshops of new plays commissioned for the company.

SOUTH COAST REPERTORY

P.O. Box 2197, Costa Mesa CA 92628-2197. (714)708-5500. Fax: (714)545-0391. Website: www.scr.org. Artistic Directors: Martin Benson and David Emmes. **Contact:** Kelly Miller, literary manager. Estab. 1964. Produces 14 plays/year. Professional nonprofit theater; a member of LORT and TCG. "We operate in our own facility which houses the 507-seat Segerstrom stage and 336-seat Julianne Argyros stage. We have a combined subscription audience of 18,000. We commit ourselves to exploring the most urgent human and social issues of our time, and to merging literature, design and performance in ways that test the bounds of theatre's artistic possibilities. " Query with synopsis and 10 sample pages of dialogue, and full list of characters. Responds in 1-2 months on queries; 4-6 months on full scripts. Acquires negotiable rights. Pays royalty.
Needs "We produce full-length contemporary plays, as well as theatre for young audiences, scripts geared toward a 4th grade target audience with a running time of approximately 65 minutes. We prefer plays that address contemporary concerns and are dramaturgically innovative. A play whose cast is larger than 15-20 will need to be extremely compelling, and its cast size must be justifiable."
Tips "We don't look for a writer to write for us—he or she should write for him or herself. We look for honesty and a fresh voice. We're not likely to be interested in writers who are mindful of any trends. Originality and craftsmanship are the most important qualities we look for."

SOUTHERN APPALACHIAN REPERTORY THEATRE (SART)

Mars Hill College, P.O. Box 1720, Mars Hill NC 28754. (828)689-1384. E-mail: sart@mhc.edu. Managing Director: Rob Miller. Estab. 1975. Produces 5-6 plays/year. Since 1975 the Southern Appalachian Repertory Theatre has produced over 50 world premieres in the 166-seat Owen Theatre on the Mars Hill College campus. SART is a professional summer theater company whose audiences range from students to senior citizens. SART also conducts an annual playwrights conference in which 4-5 playwrights are invited for a weekend of public readings of their new scripts. The conference is held in March or May each year. Submissions must be postmarked by September 30. If a script read at the conference is selected for production, it will be given a fully-staged production in the following summer season. Playwrights receive honorarium and housing. Enclose SASE for return of script.

Needs Comedies, dramas and musicals. No screenplays, translations, or adaptations. Please send complete scripts of full-length plays and musicals, synopsis, and a recording of at least 4 songs (for musicals). Include name and contact information only on a cover sheet. New plays are defined as those that are unpublished and have not received a fully-staged professional production. Workshops and other readings do not constitute a fully-staged production.

STAGE LEFT THEATRE

3408 N. Sheffield, Chicago IL 60657. (773)883-8830. E-mail: scripts@stagelefttheatre.com. **Contact:** Kevin Heckman, literary manager. Estab. 1982. Produces 3-4 plays/year. "Professional productions (usually in Chicago), for all audiences (usually adult)." Submit script through an agent or query with cover letter, 10-page excerpt, 1-page synopsis, SASE, supporting material, and résumé. Responds in 3 months.

Needs any length, any genre, any style that fits the Stage Left mission—to produce plays that raise debate on political and social issues. We do have an emphasis on new work.

🅰 STAMFORD THEATRE WORKS

307 Atlantic St., Stamford CT 06901. (203)359-4414. Fax: (203)356-1846. E-mail: stwct@aol.com. **Contact:** Steve Karp, producing director. Estab. 1988. Produces 4-6 plays/year. Professional productions for an adult audience. *Agented submissions* or queries with a professional recommendation. Include SASE for return of submission. Responds in 3 months. Pays 5-8% royalty.

Needs Plays of social relevance; contemporary work. Limited to unit sets; maximum cast of about 8.

🅰 STEPPENWOLF THEATRE CO.

758 W. North Ave., 4th Floor, Chicago IL 60610. (312)335-1888. Fax: (312)335-0808. Artistic Director: Martha Lavey. **Contact:** Joy Meads, literary manager. Estab. 1976. Produces 9 plays/year. "Steppenwolf Theatre Company's mission is to advance the vitality and diversity of American theater by nurturing artists, encouraging repeatable creative relationships and contributing new works to the national canon. 500-, 250- and 100-seat performance venues. Many plays produced at Steppenwolf have gone to Broadway. We currently have 20,000 savvy subscribers." Agented submissions only with full scripts. Others please check our website for submission guidelines. Unrepresented writers may send a 10-page sample along with cover letter, bio, and synopsis. Responds in 6-8 months. Buys commercial, film, television, and production rights. Pays 5% royalty.

Needs Actor-driven works are crucial to us, plays that explore the human condition in our time. We max at around 10 characters.

Tips No musicals, one-person shows, or romantic/light comedies. Plays get produced at STC based on ensemble member interest.

🅰 STUDIO ARENA THEATRE

710 Main St., Buffalo NY 14202. (716)856-8025. E-mail: jblaha@studioarena.com. **Contact:** Jana Blaha, executive assistant. Estab. 1965. Produces 6-8 plays/year. Professional productions. Agented submissions only.

Needs Full-length plays. No fly space.

Tips Do not fax or send submissions via the Internet. Submissions should appeal to a diverse audience. We do not generally produce musicals. Please send a character breakdown and 1-page synopsis for a faster reply.

TEATRO VISIÓN

1700 Alum Rock Ave., Suite 265, San José CA 95116. (408)272-9926. Fax: (408)928-5589. E-mail: elisamarina@teatrovision.org. **Contact:** Elisa Marina Alvarado, artistic director. Estab. 1984. Produces 3 plays/year. Professional productions for a Latino population. Query with synopsis or submit complete ms. Responds in 6 months.

Needs We produce plays by Latino playwrights—plays that highlight the Chicano/Latino experience.

THE TEN-MINUTE MUSICALS PROJECT

P.O. Box 461194, West Hollywood CA 90046. E-mail: info@tenminutemusicals.org. **Contact:** Michael Koppy, producer. Estab. 1987. Produces 1-10 plays/year. "Plays performed in Equity regional theaters in the US and Canada. Deadline August 31; notification by November 30." Complete guidelines and information at website. Buys first performance rights. Pays $250 royalty advance upon selection, against equal share of performance royalties when produced.

Needs Looking for complete short stage musicals lasting 7-14 minutes. Limit cast to 10 (5 women, 5 men).

THEATER AT LIME KILN

P.O. Box 1244, Lexington VA 24450. Estab. 1984. Produces 3 (1 new) plays/year. Outdoor summer theater (May through October) and indoor space (October through May, 144 seats). Submit query and synopsis. Include SASE for return of submitted materials. Responds in 3 months. Buys performance rights. Pays $25-75/performance.

Needs Plays that explore the history and heritage of the Appalachian region. Minimum set required.

Tips Searching for plays that can be performed in outdoor space. Prefer plays that explore the cultural and/or history of the Appalachian region.

THEATER BY THE BLIND

306 W. 18th St., New York NY 10011. (212)243-4337. Fax: (212)243-4337. E-mail: gar@nyc.rr.com. **Contact:** Ike Schambelan, artistic director. Estab. 1979. Produces 2 plays/year. Off Broadway, Theater Row, general audiences, seniors, students, disabled. If play transfers, we'd like a piece. Submit complete script. Responds in 3 months. Pays $1,000-1,500/production.

Needs Genres about blindness.

THEATRE BUILDING CHICAGO

1225 W. Belmont Ave., Chicago IL 60657. (773)929-7367 ext. 229. Fax: (773)327-1404. E-mail: allan@theatrebuildingchicago.org. **Contact:** Allan Chambers, artistic director. "Develops and produces readings of new musicals and Stages festival of new music, some works developed in our writers' workshop. Some scripts produced are unagented submissions. Developmental readings and workshops performed in 3 small off-Loop theaters are seating 148 for a general theater audience, urban/suburban mix." Submit synopsis, sample scene, CD or cassette tape and piano/vocal score of three songs, and author bios along with Stages Festival application, available on our website. Responds in 3 months.

Needs "Musicals *only*. We're interested in all forms of musical theater including more innovative styles. Our production capabilities are limited by the lack of space, but we're very creative and authors should submit anyway. The smaller the cast, the better. We are especially interested in scripts using a younger (35 and under) ensemble of actors. We mostly look for authors who are interested in developing their scripts through workshops, readings and production. We rarely work on one-man shows or 'single author' pieces."

Tips "We would like to see the musical theater articulating something about the world around us, as well as diverting an audience's attention from that world. Offers Script Consultancy—A new program designed to assist authors and composers in developing new musicals through private feedback sessions with professional dramaturgs and musical directors. For further info contact Allan Chambers, (773)929-7367, ext. 229."

THEATRE IV

114 W. Broad St., Richmond VA 23220. (804)783-1688. Fax: (804)775-2325. E-mail: j.serresseque@theatreivrichmond.org. **Contact:** Janine Serresseque. Estab. 1975. Produces approximately 20 plays/year. National tour of plays for young audiences—maximum cast of 5, maximum length of an hour. Mainstage plays for young audiences in 600 or 350 seat venues. Submit query and synopsis. Include SASE for return of submission. Responds in 1 month. Buys standard production rights. Payment varies.

Needs Touring and mainstage plays for young audiences. Touring—maximum cast of 5, length of 60 minutes.

THEATRE THREE

P.O. Box 512, 412 Main St., Port Jefferson NY 11777-0512. (631)928-9202. Fax: (631)928-9120. **Contact:** Jeffrey Sanzel, artistic director. Estab. 1969. "We produce an Annual Festival of One-Act Plays on our Second Stage. Deadline for submission is September 30. Send SASE for festival guidelines or visit website." Include SASE. No email submissions. Guidelines online. Responds in 6 months. We ask for exclusive rights up to and through the festival. Pays $75 for the run of the festival.

Needs One-act plays. Maximum length: 40 minutes. Any style, topic, etc. We require simple, suggested sets and a maximum cast of 6. No adaptations, musicals or children's works.

Tips "Too many plays are monologue-dominant. Please—reveal your characters through action and dialogue."

Ⓐ THEATRE THREE

2800 Routh St., #168, Dallas TX 75201. (214)871-3300. Fax: (214)871-3139. E-mail: admin@theatre3dallas.com. **Contact:** Jac Alder, executive producer-director. Estab. 1961. Produces 7 plays/year. Professional

regional theatre, in-the-round. Audience is college age to senior citizens. Query with synopsis; agented submissions only. Responds in 6 months. Contractual agreements vary.
Needs Musicals, dramas, comedies, bills of related one-acts. Modest production requirement; prefer casts no larger than 10. Theatre Three also produces in a studio theatre (its former rehearsal hall) called Theatre Too. The space is variously configured according to demands of the show. Shows in that space include cabaret type revues, experimental work, dramas with small casts and staged readings or concert versions of musicals.
Tips No parodies or political commentary/comedy. Most produced playwrights at Theatre Three (to show taste of producer) are Moliere, Sondheim, Ayckbourne, Miller, Stoppard, Durang (moralists and irony-masters).

THEATRE WEST

3333 Cahuenga Blvd. W., Hollywood CA 90068-1365. (323)851-4839. Fax: (323)851-5286. E-mail: theatrewest@theatrewest.org. **Contact:** Chris DiGiovanni and Doug Haverty, moderators of the Writers Workshop. Estab. 1962. "We operate a 168 seat theater under a letter of agreement with Actors Equity, including a TYA contract for young audiences. Audiences are primarily young urban professionals. Residence in Southern California is vital as it's a weekly workshop." Submit script, résumé and letter requesting membership. Responds in 4 months. Contracts a percentage of writer's share to other media if produced on MainStage by Theatre West. Pays royalty based on gross box office.
Needs Full-length plays only, no one-acts. Uses minimalistic scenery, no fly space.
Tips "Theatre West is a dues-paying membership company. Only members can submit plays for production. So you must first seek membership to the Writers Workshop."

THEATREWORKS

P.O. Box 50458, Palo Alto CA 94303. (650)463-1950. Fax: (650)463-1963. E-mail: kent@theatreworks.org. **Contact:** Kent Nicholson, new works director. Estab. 1970. Produces 8 plays/year. Specializes in development of new musicals. Plays are professional productions intended for an adult audience. Submit synopsis, 10 pages of sample dialogue, and SASE. Include SASE for return of submission. Responds in 6-8 months. Buys performance rights. Payment varies per contract.
Needs TheatreWorks has a high standard for excellence. We prefer well-written, well-constructed plays that celebrate the human spirit through innovative productions and programs inspired by our exceptionally diverse community. There is no limit on the number of characters, and we favor plays with multi-ethnic casting possibilities. We are a LORT C company. Plays are negotiated per playwright. Does not want one-acts, plays with togas. We are particularly interested in plays with musical elements.
Tips Guidelines are online—check out our website for Submission Checklist Request and the New Works Program under New Works.

⊘ THEATREWORKS/USA

151 W. 26th St., 7th Floor, New York NY 10001. (212)647-1100. Fax: (212)924-5377. Estab. 1961. Produces 3-4 plays/year. "The theatre is an arena for previously unproduced plays, and works towards their future development. Professional equity productions for young audiences. Weekend series at Equitable Towers, NYC. Also, national and regional tours of each show." Submit query and synopsis only. *No unsolicited submissions.* Responds in 1 month. Obtains performing rights. Pays 6% royalty.

UNICORN THEATRE

3828 Main St., Kansas City MO 64111. (816)531-7529 ext. 23. Fax: (816)531-0421. Producing Artistic Director: Cynthia Levin. **Contact:** Herman Wilson, literary assistant. Produces 6-8 plays/year. "We are a professional Equity Theatre. Typically, we produce plays dealing with contemporary issues." Send complete script (to Herman Wilson) with brief synopsis, cover letter, bio, character breakdown. Send #10 SASE for results. Does not return scripts. Responds in 4-8 months.
Needs Prefers contemporary (post-1950) scripts. Does not accept musicals, one-acts, or historical plays.

URBAN STAGES

555 8th Avenue #1800, New York NY 10018. (212)421-1380. Fax: (212)421-1387. E-mail: lschmiedel@urbanstages.org. **Contact:** Lauren Schmiedel, managing director. Estab. 1986. Produces 2-4 plays/year. Professional productions off Broadway—throughout the year. General audience. Submit complete script. Enter Emerging Playwright Award competition. There is a reading fee of $10 per script. Prize is $1,000, plus NYC production. Responds in 4 months. If produced, option for 1 year. Pays royalty.
Needs Full-length; generally 1 set or styled playing dual. Good imaginative, creative writing. Cast limited to 3-6.

Tips We tend to reject `living-room' plays. We look for imaginative settings. Be creative and interesting. No one acts. No e-mail submissions, scripts are not returned.

UTAH SHAKESPEAREAN FESTIVAL

New American Playwright's Project, 351 W. Center St., Cedar City UT 84720-2498. (435)586-7884. Fax: (435)865-8003. Founder/Executive Producer Emeritus: Fred C. Adams. **Contact:** Charles Metten, director. Estab. 1993. Produces 9 plays/year. Travelling audiences ranging in ages from 6-80. Programming includes classic plays, musicals, new works. Submit complete script; no synopsis. No musicals. Returns submissions accompanied by a SASE. Responds in 3-4 months. Pays travel, housing, and tickets for USF productions only.

Needs "The USF is only interested in material that explores characters and ideas that focus on the West and our western experience, spirit, and heritage. Preference is given to writers whose primary residence is in the western United States. New plays are for staged readings only. These are not fully mountable productions. Cast size is a consideration due to the limited time of rehearsal and the actors available during the USF production period. Does not want plays that do not match criteria or plays longer than 90 pages."

Tips "We want previously unproduced plays with western themes by western playwrights."

WALNUT STREET THEATRE

Ninth and Walnut Streets, Philadelphia PA 19107. (215)574-3550. Fax: (215)574-3598. Producing Artistic Director: Bernard Havard. **Contact:** Literary Office. Estab. 1809. Produces 10 plays/year. Our plays are performed in our own space. WST has 3 theaters—a proscenium (mainstage), 1,052 seats; and 2 studios, 79-99 seats. We have a subscription audience—the largest in the nation. If you have written a play or musical that you feel is appropriate for the Walnut Street Theatre's Mainstage or Independence Studio on 3, please send the following: 1-2 page synopsis, 5-10 page excerpt from the scrip, a character breakdown, bios for the playwright, composer, lyricist, and any other artistic collaborators, Demo CD with tracks clearly labeled (musicals only). Include SASE for return of materials. Responds in 5 months. Rights negotiated per project. Pays negotiable royalty or makes outright purchase.

Needs Full-length dramas and comedies, musicals, translations, adaptations, and revues. The studio plays must have a cast of no more than 4 and use simple sets.

Tips "Bear in mind that on the mainstage we look for plays with mass appeal, Broadway-style. The studio spaces are our off-Broadway. No children's plays. Our mainstage audience goes for work that is entertaining and light. Our studio season is where we look for plays that have bite and are more provocative."

WILLOWS THEATRE CO.

636 Ward St., Martinez CA 94553-1651. Artistic Director: Richard Elliott. Produces 6 plays/year. Professional productions for a suburban audience. Accepting only commercially viable, small-medium size comedies right now. Guidelines are online at website. Send synopsis, character breakdown, resume, SASE. Do not send full script unless invited to do so. Do not email submission or email the office for information on your submission. Responds in 6 months to scripts. Pays standard royalty.

Needs Commercially viable, small-medium size musicals or comedies that are popular, rarely produced, or new. Certain stylized plays or musicals with a contemporary edge to them (e.g., *Les Liasons Dangereuses, La Bete, Candide*). No more than 15 actors. Unit or simple sets with no fly space, no more than 7 pieces. We are not interested in 1-character pieces.

Tips "Our audiences want light entertainment, comedies, and musicals. Also, have an interest in plays and musicals with a historical angle."

🄰 THE WILMA THEATER

265 S. Broad St., Philadelphia PA 19107. (215)893-9456. Fax: (215)893-0895. E-mail: wcb@wilmatheater.org. **Contact:** Walter Bilderback, dramaturg and literary manager. Estab. 1980. Produces 4 plays/year. LORT-D 300-seat theater, 5,000 subscribers. *Agented submissions only* for full mss. Accepts queries with cover letter, résumé, synopsis, and sample if recommended by a literary manager, dramaturg, or other theater professional. Electronic inquiries and submissions preferred. Will not respond to mailed queries unless self-addressed stamp envelope or postcard is included. Responds in 6 months.

Needs Full-length plays, translations, adaptations, and musicals from an international repertoire with emphasis on innovative, bold staging; world premieres; works with poetic dimension; plays with music; multimedia works; social issues, particularly the role of science in our lives. Prefers maximum cast size of 12. Stage 44'x46'.

Tips Before submitting any material to The Wilma Theater, please research our production history. Considering the types of plays we have produced in the past, honestly assess whether or not your play would suit us. In general, I believe researching the various theaters to which you send your play is important in the long and short run. Different theaters have different missions and therefore seek out material corresponding with those goals. In other words, think through what is the true potential of your play and this theater, and if it is a compatible relationship.

WOMEN'S PROJECT AND PRODUCTIONS

55 West End Ave., New York NY 10023. (212)765-1706. Fax: (212)765-2024. **Contact:** Megan E. Carter, Associate Artistic Director. Estab. 1978. Produces 3 plays/year. Professional Off-Broadway productions. Agented submissions only. Please see website for submission guidelines and details.
Needs "We are looking for full-length plays written by women."

WOOLLY MAMMOTH THEATRE CO.

641 D St. NW, Washington DC 20004. (202)289-2443. E-mail: elissa@woollymammoth.net. Artistic Director: Howard Shalwitz. **Contact:** Elissa Goetschius, literary manager. Estab. 1980. Produces 5 plays/year. Produces professional productions for the general public. Solicited submissions only. Responds in 6 months to scripts; very interesting scripts often take much longer. Buys first- and second-class production rights. Pays variable royalty.
Needs We look for plays with a distinctive authorial voice. Our work is word and actor driven. One-acts and issue-driven plays are not used. Cast limit of 5

MARKETS

Greeting Cards

Greeting cards are an intricate part of American culture. There are, of course, cards tied to holidays, birthdays, graduations, and weddings. There are "thinking of you" cards, condolences cards, thank you cards, get well cards, and humor cards. And many of these cards are specialized to mom, dad, mother-in-law, father-in-law, son, daughter, cousin, and even ex-girlfriend's roommate from college (OK, that may be stretching it—but only slightly). Point is, they are here; they've all got a special message to deliver; and someone has to write them.

Freelance realities

Writers who make a decent income writing greeting cards are almost always staff writers or those who are on contract. Freelance writers do not typically earn enough to use greeting card sales as any more than a supplemental source of income. In the most recent "How Much Should I Charge?" survey (on page 67), freelancers made $50 on the low end to $300 on the high end per card. And that is from a more experienced set of freelancers. It is known that some freelancers settle for payment as low as $5 to $10 per card idea, which makes it harder for newer writers to negotiate higher payments.

Listings

Each listing includes contact information, submission specs, needs, and payment details. While we work to give you the most up-to-date listing information, it is still recommended that you either contact the companies or check out their Web sites to confirm specific submission policies and needs. This little bit of extra work is what often sets apart professional writers from the rest of the pack. In a competitive market such as greeting cards, professionalism goes a long way toward ensuring success.

For more information

To learn even more about the greeting card industry, check out the Greeting Card Association (GCA) website at www.greetingcard.org. It provides industry statistics, tips, and information on specific greeting card companies.

AMERICAN GREETINGS

One American Rd., Cleveland OH 44144-2398. (216)252-7300. Fax: (216)252-6778. No unsolicited material. Experienced, talented writers should submit a cover letter and résumé describing their education and content experience for contract-to-permanent staff writing positions.

Needs Humorous.

Tips In this competitive arena, we're only looking for gifted humor writers and cartoonists who are interested in adapting their skillsets to the uniqueness of greeting card composition.

BLUE MOUNTAIN ARTS, INC.

P.O. Box 1007, Boulder CO 80306. (303)449-0536. Fax: (303)447-0939. E-mail: editorial@sps.com. Bought over 200 freelance ideas last year. Submit seasonal/holiday material 4 months in advance. Responds in 2-4 months. Buys worldwide, exclusive rights, or anthology rights. Pays on publication. Request writer's guidelines through website.

- No rhymed poetry, religious verse, or one-liners. No poems that sound like the ones we've already published.

Needs "Submissions should reflect a message, feeling, or sentiment that one person would want to share with another. Full book manuscripts or proposals are also accepted for possible publication by our book division, Blue Mountain Press." **Pays $300 for the first work chosen for publication on a card (payment scale escalates after that); $50 for anthology rights; payment schedule for books will be discussed at time of acceptance.**

Other Product Lines Calendars, gift books, prints, mugs.

Tips "Familiarize yourself with our products before submitting material, although we caution you not to study them too hard. We want poetry that expresses real emotions and feelings, so we suggest that you have someone specific in mind (a friend, relative, etc.) as you write. We prefer that submissions be typewritten, one poem per page, with name and address on every page. Only a small portion of the freelance material we receive is selected each year, either for publication on a notecard or in a gift anthology, and the review process can also be lengthy, but every ms. is given serious consideration."

DESIGNER GREETINGS

11 Executive Ave., Edison NJ 08817. (732)662-6700. Fax: (732)662-6701. E-mail: info@designergreetings.com. Website: www.designergreetings.com. **50% freelance written. Receives 200-300 submissions/year.** Submit seasonal/holiday material 6 months in advance. Responds in 2 months. Buys greeting card rights. Pays on acceptance. Guidelines online.

Needs Conventional, humorous, informal, inspirational, juvenile, sensitivity, soft line, studio. Accepts rhymed and unrhymed verse ideas.

EPHEMERA, INC.

P.O. Box 490, Phoenix OR 97535. (541)535-4195. Fax: (541)535-5016. **Contact:** Editor. Estab. 1980. "We produce Novelty Buttons, Magnets, and Stickers. You'll find our stuff all over the place—cutting edge card & gift shops, bookstores, music stores, gay & left wing shops, porno stores, coffee shops, etc. Some of our best designs end up on products made by companies we license to for T-shirts, cards, books, towels, mugs, calendars, etc." **95% freelance written. Receives 2,000 submissions/year.** Buys nearly 200 slogans for novelty buttons, stickers, and magnets each year. Responds in 1-5 months. Buys all rights. Pays on acceptance. Writer's guidelines for SASE or online Complete full-color catalog online or for $4

- "Be fresh, original, and concise. Ephemera has a reputation for having the most irreverent, provocative and outrageously funny material on the market. We encourage you to be as weird, twisted and rude as you like."

Needs "We produce irreverent, provocative, and outrageously funny buttons, magnets, and stickers. You'll find them in cutting-edge shops that sell cards, gifts, books, music, coffee, pipes, porn, etc. We're looking for snappy slogans about politics, women and bitchiness, work, parenting, coffee, booze, pot, drugs, religion, food, aging, teens, gays and lesbians, sexual come-ons and put-downs, etc. Pretty please, don't limit yourself to these topics. Surprise us!" **Pays $50/slogan.**

Tips "We're looking for fresh, interesting, original material. Our buttons and magnets are small, so we crave concise and high-impact gems of wit. We urge you to be as off-the-wall and obscene as you like. We want humor that makes us laugh out loud. See the retail store online to get an idea of what we like."

GALLANT GREETINGS CORP.

4300 United Parkway, Schiller Park IL 60176. Gallant is a publisher of traditional, religious, and humorous greeting cards for all occasions and seasons. All card ideas are purchased from freelance writers. Payment is $45/card idea purchased.

HALLMARK CARDS

P.O. Box 419034, Kansas City MO 64141. At this time, Hallmark does not accept unsolicited freelance submissions, and our employment opportunities would involve relocating to the Kansas City area.

KALAN LP

97 S. Union Ave., Lansdowne PA 19050. (610)623-1900. E-mail: editorial@kalanlp.com. **Contact:** David Umlauf. "Please enter submissions at our online website www.submitfunnystuff.com." **80% freelance written. Receives 500-800 submissions/year.** Bought 80-100 freelance ideas last year. Submit seasonal/holiday material 8-10 months in advance. Responds in 6-8 months. Buys all rights. Pays on acceptance. Guidelines available for free.

Needs Humorous. Accepts rhymed and unrhymed verse ideas. **Pays $100-150. Pays $100/card concept; $60/one-liners.**

Other Product Lines Bumper stickers; post cards; posters; key rings; shot glasses; lighters; buttons; mugs; magnets.

Tips "Target to contemporary women of all ages. We want humor anywhere from subtle, to risqué, to downright rude. No flowery prose."

KOEHLER COMPANIES, INC.

8758 Woodcliff Rd., Bloomington MN 55438. (952)942-5666. Fax: (952)942-5208. E-mail: bob@koehlercompanies.com. "We manufacture a decorative plaque line that utilizes verse and art. We are not a greeting card company. We combine art and message to create a product that a consumer will like enough to want to look at for a year or longer." **65% freelance written. Receives 100 submissions/year.** Bought 25 freelance ideas last year. Responds in 1 month. Pays on acceptance.

Needs Humorous, inspirational. **We pay $125/selected verse and limit the use to our products so that writers may resell their work for other uses.**

Other Product Lines Framed Prints.

Tips "We sell wholesale to the retail market and the mail order catalog industry as well. Lengthy verse is sometimes challenging. Usually under 6 lines is best. We prefer to have work submitted by e-mail or mail."

MARIAN HEATH GREETING CARDS

9 Kendrick Rd., Wareham MA 02571. **90% freelance written. Receives 75-100 submissions/year.** Bought 200-250 freelance ideas last year. Submit seasonal/holiday material 4 months in advance. Responds in 2 weeks. Buys greeting card rights. Pays on publication. Guidelines for #10 SASE.

Needs Accepts wide range of writing styles—casual or conversational, meaningful, inspirational, humorous. Prefers unrhymed verse ideas.

Tips Verses that are sincere and complimentary in a conversational tone tend to do best. For humor, we avoid 'put down' type of jokes and try to stay positive. Target audience is women over 18 and Baby Boomers.

MOONLIGHTING CARDS

P.O. Box 4670, Vallejo CA 94590. Fax: (707)554-9366. E-mail: robin@moonlightingcards.com. Submit seasonal/holiday material 12 months in advance. Pays on publication. Guidelines online.

Needs Announcements, conventional, humorous, informal, inspirational, invitations, juvenile, sensitivity, soft line, studio. Prefers unrhymed verse ideas. Send as many ideas at one time as you like. But if we see you have not paid attention to our guidelines, we will not sort through 100 queries to find 1 gem. **Pays $25.**

Tips Currently, we are reviewing quotes for 'year-round LOVE cards' (aka Valentine's that don't say 'Happy Valentine's Day'). Birthday, thank you, and everyday wisdom all do well for us. Review the cards on our website and our guidelines to get a sense of what works for us.

NOVO CARD PUBLISHERS, INC.

7570 N. Croname Rd., Niles IL 60714-3904. (847)588-3220. Fax: (847)588-3508. E-mail: art@novocard.net. **80% freelance written. Receives 500 submissions/year.** Bought 200 freelance ideas last year. Submit seasonal/holiday material 8 months in advance. Responds in 2 months. Buys worldwide greeting card rights. Pays on acceptance. Guidelines for #10 SASE. Market list available on mailing list basis.

Needs Announcements, conventional, humorous, informal, inspirational, invitations, juvenile, soft line, other.

OATMEAL STUDIOS

P.O. Box 138WP, Rochester VT 05767. (802)767-3171. E-mail: dawn@oatmealstudios.com. **85% freelance written.** Bought 200-300 freelance ideas last year. Responds in 6 weeks. Pays on acceptance. Current market list for #10 SASE.

- Humor—conversational in tone and format—sells best for us.

Needs Humorous. Will review concepts. Humorous material (clever and very funny) year-round. Prefers unrhymed verse ideas. **Current pay schedule available with guidelines.**

Other Product Lines Notepads, stick-on notes.

Tips "The greeting card market has become more competitive with a greater need for creative and original ideas. We are looking for writers who can communicate situations, thoughts, and relationships in a funny way and apply them to a birthday, get well, etc., greeting. We are willing to work with them in targeting our style. We will be looking for material that says something funny about life in a new way."

THE PAPER MAGIC GROUP, INC.

401 Adams Ave., Scranton PA 18501. (800)278-4085. **50% freelance written. Receives 500 submissions/year.** Submit seasonal/holiday material 6 months in advance. Pays on acceptance. No market list

Needs Christmas boxed cards only. Submit Christmas sentiments only. relative titles, juvenile.

PAPYRUS DESIGN

500 Chadbourne Rd., Fairfield CA 94533. Fax: (707) 428-0641. Website: www.papyrusonline.com. **Contact:** Nikki Burton. Estab. 1950. **10% freelance written.** Bought 35 freelance ideas last year. Responds in 2 months.

Needs Submit 10 ideas per batch with SASE. Inspirational, humor, sentimental, contemporary, romance, friendship, seasonal, and everyday categories. "Prefers unrhymed verse, but on juvenile cards rhyme is OK."

Tips "Seeking text that goes beyond the standard generic verse. Conversational (modern voice), sophisticated, clever, flirty, whimsical, hot topics, and heartfelt text concepts are needed. We are always looking for unique ways to approach the following captions: birthday, friendship, wedding, anniversary, new baby, and sympathy. Poetry and off-color humor are not appropriate for our line. Heartfelt or sentimental text works best if it is short and elegant. The target market is female, stylish, professional, and savvy."

P.S. GREETINGS

5730 N. Tripp Ave., Chicago IL 60646. (773)267-6150. Fax: (773)267-6055. Bought 200-300 freelance ideas last year. Submit seasonal/holiday material 6 months in advance. Responds in 1 month. Pays on acceptance. Writer's guidelines/market list for #10 SASE or online.

Needs Conventional, humorous, inspirational, invitations, juvenile, sensitivity, soft line, studio. Accepts rhymed and unrhymed verse ideas. **Pays one-time flat fee.**

Other Product Lines Stationary, notepads.

RECYCLED PAPER GREETINGS

111 N. Canal St., Chicago IL 60606. (800)777-9494. Website: www.recycledpapergreetings.com. **100% freelance written.** Bought 3,000 freelance ideas last year. Responds in 2 months.

Needs "Please send ideas for specific occasions, such as birthday, friendship, thank you, miss you, and thinking of you."

Tips "Find our guidelines online. We do not accept submissions that include a message without any accompanying artwork. Be sure to label each card idea with your name, address, and phone number, and include a SASE. We accept simultaneous submissions."

ROCKSHOTS, INC.

20 Vandam St., New York NY 10013. (212)243-9661. Fax: (212)604-9060. Bought 75 greeting card verse (or gag) freelance ideas last year. Responds in 1 month. Buys greeting card rights. Guidelines for #10 SASE.

Needs Humorous. "Looking for a combination of sexy and humorous come-on type greeting (sentimental is not our style); and insult cards (looking for cute insults). Card gag can adopt a sentimental style, then take an ironic twist and end on an off-beat note." sentimental or conventional material. **Pays $50/gag line.**

Tips "Rockshots is an outrageous, witty, adult, and sometimes shocking card company. Our range of style starts at cute and whimsical and runs the gamut all the way to totally outrageous and unbelievable. Rockshots' cards definitely stand out from all the 'mainstream' products on the market today. Some of the images we are famous for include 'sexy' photos of 500- to 600-pound female models, smart-talking grannies, copulating animals, and, of course, incredibly sexy shots of nude and seminude men and women. Some of our best-selling cards are photos with captions that start out leading the reader in one direction, and then zings them with a punch line totally out of left field, but also hysterically apropos. As you can guess, we do not shy away from much. Be creative, be imaginative, be funny, but most of all, be different. Do not hold back because of society's imposed standards, but let it all pour out. It's always good to mix sex and humor, as sex always sells. Remember that 70% to 80% of our audience is women, so get in touch with your 'feminine' side, your bitchy feminine side. Your gag line will be illustrated by a Rockshots photograph or drawing, so try and think visually. It's always a good idea to preview our cards at your local store or on our website, if this is possible, to give you a feeling of our style."

SNAFU DESIGNS, INC.

2500 University Ave. W., Suite C-10, St. Paul MN 55114. E-mail: info@snafudesigns.com. Responds in 6 weeks. Buys all rights. Pays on Acceptance. Guidelines for #10 SASE.

Needs Humorous, Informal. "Specifically seeking birthday, friendship, thank you, anniversary, congratulations, get well, new baby, Christmas, wedding, pregnancy, retirement, Valentines Day and Mother's Day ideas." **Pays $100/idea.**

Tips "Our cards use clever ideas that are simple and concisely delivered and are aimed at a smart, adult audience. We like 'off the wall' irreverent humor that often has a little bite to it. Well done 'bathroom humor' is great! Please do not submit anything cute."

MARKETS

Contests & Awards

The contests and awards listed in this section are arranged by subject. Nonfiction writers can turn immediately to nonfiction awards listed alphabetically by the name of the contest or award. The same is true for fiction writers, poets, playwrights and screenwriters, journalists, children's writers, and translators. You'll also find general book awards, fellowships offered by arts councils and foundations, and multiple category contests.

New contests and awards are announced in various writer's publications nearly every day. However, many lose their funding or fold—and sponsoring magazines go out of business just as often. We have contacted the organizations whose contests and awards are listed here with the understanding that they are valid through 2010-2011. **Contact names**, **entry fees**, and **deadlines** have been highlighted and set in bold type for your convenience.

To make sure you have all the information you need about a particular contest, always send a SASE to the contact person in the listing before entering a contest. The listings in this section are brief, and many contests have lengthy, specific rules and requirements that we could not include in our limited space. Often a specific entry form must accompany your submission.

When you receive a set of guidelines, you will see that some contests are not applicable to all writers. The writer's age, previous publication, geographic location, and length of the work are common matters of eligibility. Read the requirements carefully to ensure you don't enter a contest for which you are not qualified. You should also be aware that every year, more and more contests, especially those sponsored by "little" literary magazines, are charging entry fees.

Winning a contest or award can launch a successful writing career. Take a professional approach by doing a little extra research. Find out who the previous winner of the award was by investing in a sample copy of the magazine in which the prize-winning article, poem, or short story appeared. Attend the staged reading of an award-winning play. Your extra effort will be to your advantage in competing with writers who simply submit blindly.

Arts Councils & Fellowships

ADVANCED ARTIST AWARD

Government of Yukon, Box 2703, (L-3), Whitehorse YT Y1A 2C6 Canada. (867)667-8789. Fax: (867)393-6456. E-mail: artsfund@gov.yk.ca. Grants to senior artists toward projects that contribute to their artistic development. Open to all disciplines. Open only to Yukon artists. Deadline: April 1 and October 1. Prize: Level A artists: up to $5,000; Level B artists: up to $2,500. peer assessment (made up of senior Yukon artists representing the various disciplines seen in applicants for that round).

ALABAMA STATE COUNCIL ON THE ARTS FELLOWSHIP-LITERATURE

Alabama State Council on the Arts, 201 Monroe St., Montgomery AL 36130-1800. (334)242-4076, ext. 224. Fax: (334)240-3269. E-mail: randy.shoults@arts.alabama.gov. Website: www.arts.alabama.gov. **Contact:** Randy Shoults. "Literature fellowship offered every year (for previously published or unpublished work) to set aside time to create and improve skills. Two-year Alabama residency required. Guidelines available." Deadline: March 1. Prize: $10,000 or $5,000

ARROWHEAD REGIONAL ARTS COUNCIL INDIVIDUAL ARTIST SUPPORT GRANT

Arrowhead Regional Arts Council, 1301 Rice Lake Rd., Suite 111, Duluth MN 55811. (218)722-0952 or (800)569-8134. E-mail: info@aracouncil.org. Applicants must live in the 7-county region of Northeastern Minnesota. Award to provide financial support to regional artists wishing to take advantage of impending, concrete opportunities that will advance their work or careers. Deadline: August, November, March. Prize: Up to $3,000. ARAC Board.

ARTIST TRUST FELLOWSHIPS

Artist Trust, 1835 12th Ave., Seattle WA 98122. "The fellowship is a merit-based award of $7,500 to practicing professional Washington State artists of exceptional talent and demonstrated ability. Literature fellowships are offered every other year, and approximately ten $7,500 literature fellowships are awarded. The award is made on the basis of work of the past 5 years. Applicants must be individual artists; Washington State residents; not matriculated students; and generative artists. Offered every 2 years in odd years. Guidelines and application online or for SASE." Deadline: TBA (check website). Prize: $7,500 Judged by a selection panel of artists and/or arts professionals in the field chosen by the Artist Trust staff.

DELAWARE DIVISION OF THE ARTS

820 N. French St., Wilmington DE 19801. (302)577-8278. Fax: (302)577-6561. E-mail: kristin.pleasanton@state.de.us. **Contact:** Kristin Pleasanton, coordinator. Award offered annually to help further the careers of Delaware's emerging and established professional artists. Open to Delaware residents only Deadline: August 2. Prize: $10,000 for masters; $6,000 for established professionals; $3,000 for emerging professionals. out-of-state professionals in each division.

DOBIE PAISANO PROJECT

The Graduate School, The Univ. of Texas at Austin, 1 University Ave., Mail Stop G0400, Austin TX 78712. Fax: (512)471-7620. E-mail: adameve@mail.utexas.edu. **Contact:** Dr. Michael Adams. "The annual Dobie-Paisano Fellowships provide solitude, isolation, and an extended period of time to live and work at J. Frank Dobie's 258 acre ranch outside of Austin, Texas. At the time of the application, the applicant must: be a native Texan; have lived in Texas at some time for at least 3 years; or have published writing that has a Texas subject. Criteria for making the awards include quality of work, character of proposed project, and suitability of the applicant for ranch life at Paisano, the late J. Frank Dobie's ranch near Austin, TX. Applicants must submit examples of their work in triplicate. Guidelines for SASE or online." Deadline is January 15, 2010 for fellowships in 2010-2011. Winners are announced in early May. Charges $20/1 fellowship, $30/both fellowships. Prize: The Ralph A. Johnston memorial Fellowship is for a period of 4 months with a stipend of $5,000 per month. It is aimed at writers who have already demonstrated some publishing and critical success. The Jesse H. Jones Writing Fellowship is for a period of approximately 6 months with a stipend of $3,000 per month. It is aimed at, but not limited to, writers who are early in their careers.

Tips "Guidelines and application forms are on the website or may be requested by sending a SASE (2 oz. postage) to the above address and attention of 'Dobie Paisano Fellowship Project.'

DOCTORAL DISSERTATION FELLOWSHIPS IN JEWISH STUDIES

National Foundation for Jewish Culture, 330 7th Ave., 21st Floor, New York NY 10001. (212)629-0500, ext. 215. Fax: (212)629-0508. E-mail: grants@jewishculture.org. **Contact:** Paul Zakrzewski. Open annually to students who have completed their course work and need funding for research in order to write their dissertation thesis or a PhD in a Jewish field of study. Deadline: TBA. Prize: $8,000-10,000 grant

EXTREME TALENT AWARD FOR THE BEST SCREENPLAY

Extreme Talent and Art, P.O. Box 3414, Cedar Hill TX 75106. (702)354-3921. E-mail: sabrinalwdg@gmail.com. **Contact:** Sabrina Graham. Writers will maintain their rights to their work. The purpose of this award is to encourage writers to believe in their creative work. Winners will be submitted to: #1 Children's screenplay for drama or comedy. #2 Adult screenplay for drama or comedy. Deadline: June 30, 2010. Charges $30 (nonrefundable). Money orders (preferred) or cash is accepted. Prize: First prize: $300; Second prize: $50; Third prize: $25. Five judges will be chosen each year from a college in the senior drama or writing department, based on availability.

FELLOWSHIPS TO ASSIST RESEARCH AND ARTISTIC CREATION

John Simon Guggenheim Memorial Foundation, 90 Park Ave., New York NY 10016. (212)687-4470. Fax: (212)697-3248. E-mail: fellowships@jsgmf.org. Offered annually to assist scholars and artists to engage in research in any field of knowledge and creation in any of the arts, under the freest possible conditions and irrespective of race, color, or creed. Application form is online. Deadline: Sept. 15.

GAP (GRANTS FOR ARTIST PROJECTS) PROGRAM

Artist Trust, 1835 12th Ave., Seattle WA 98122. (206)467-8734 ext. 9. Fax: (206)467-9633. E-mail: info@artisttrust.org. Website: www.artisttrust.org. **Contact:** Director of Programs. Estab. 1987. The GAP grant is awarded annually to 75-100 artists of all disciplines including writers. The award is meant to help finance a specific project, which can be in very early stages or near completion. Full-time students are not eligible. Open to Washington state residents only. Deadline: June 25, 2010. Prize: Up to $1,500 for artist-generated projects.

THE HODDER FELLOWSHIP

Lewis Center for the Arts, Princeton University, 185 Nassau St., Princeton NJ 08542. Website: www.princeton.edu/arts/lewis_center/society_of_fellows. **Contact:** Janine Braude. "The Hodder Fellowship will be given to writers of exceptional promise to pursue independent projects at Princeton University during the 2011-2012 academic year. Typically the fellows are poets, playwrights, novelists, creative nonfiction writers and translators who have published one highly acclaimed work and are undertaking a significant new project that might not be possible without the "studious leisure" afforded by the fellowship. Preference is given to applicants outside academia. Candidate for the Ph.D. are not eligible. Submit a resume, sample of previous work (10 pages maximum, not returnable), and a project proposal of 2-3 pages. Guidelines available on website. Princeton University is an equal opportunity employer and complies with applicable EEO and affirmative action regulations. Apply online at http://jobs.princeton.edu or for general application information and how to self-identify, see http://www.princeton.edu/dof/ApplicantsInfo.htm. We strongly recommend, however, that all interested candidates use the online application process. Deadline: November 1, 2010 (postmarked). Stipend: $63,900."

HYBRID ESSAY CONTEST

Dept. of English, Univ. of Arizona, P.O. Box 210067, Tucson AZ 85721-0067. E-mail: nmp@thediagram.com; editor@thediagram.com. **Contact:** Ander Monson, Editor. "Texts that exhibit some form of hybridity, up to 10,000 words. Hybrids are essays involving fiction, memoir, poetry, art, photography, mathematics—it can take many shapes, marry two or more forms." Deadline: End of October, each year. Check website for more details. Charges $15. Prize: $1,000 and publication. Finalist essay also published. Judges: Ander Monson and Nicole Walker.

CHRISTOPHER ISHERWOOD FELLOWSHIPS

Christopher Isherwood Foundation, PMB 139, 1223 Wilshire Blvd., Santa Monica CA 90403-5040. E-mail: james@isherwoodfoundation.org. Website: www.isherwoodfoundation.org. **Contact:** James P. White, executive director. "Several awards are given annually to selected writers who have published a novel." Deadline: September 1-October 1 (send to the address posted on the website). Prize: Fellowship consists of $4,000. advisory board.

LITERARY GIFT OF FREEDOM

A Room of Her Own Foundation, P.O. Box 778, Placitas NM 87043. E-mail: info@aroomofherownfoundation.org. Website: www.aroomofherownfoundation.org. **Contact:** Tracey Cravens-Gras, associate director. Award offered every other year to provide very practical help—both materially and in professional guidance and moral support with mentors and advisory council—to women who need assistance in making their creative contribution to the world. Guidelines, deadlines and application available at www.aroomofherownfoundation.org. Open to any female resident of the US. Charges Application: $35. Prize: Award is $50,000 over 2 years in support of the production of a particular creative project.

MASSACHUSETTS CULTURAL COUNCIL ARTIST FELLOWSHIP PROGRAM

Massachusetts Cultural Council, 10 St. James Ave., 3rd Floor, Boston MA 02116-3803. (617)727-3668. Fax: (617)727-0044. E-mail: mcc@art.state.ma.us. Website: www.massculturalcouncil.org; http://artsake.massculturalcouncil.org. **Contact:** Dan Blask, program coordinator. Awards in poetry, fiction/creative nonfiction, and dramatic writing (among other discipline categories) are given in recognition of exceptional original work (check website for award amount). Criteria: Artistic excellence and creative ability, based on work submitted for review. Must be 18 years or older and a legal residents of Massachusetts for the last 2 years and at time of award. This excludes students in directly-related degree programs and grant recipients within the last 3 years. Judged by independent peer panels composed of artists and arts professionals.

Tips Accepts inquiries by fax, e-mail and phone. "Send in your best work and follow guidelines (available on website)."

JENNY McKEAN/MOORE VISITING WRITER

English Department, George Washington University, Washington DC 20052. (202)994-6180. Fax: (202)994-7915. E-mail: faymos@gwu.edu. **Contact:** Faye Moskowitz. "Offered annually to provide 1-year visiting writers to teach 1 George Washington course and 1 free community workshop each semester. Guidelines for SASE or online. This contest seeks someone specializing in a different genre each year." Deadline: November 15. Prize: Annual stipend varies, depending on endowment performance; most recently, stipend was $58,000, plus reduced-rent townhouse (not guaranteed).

N MINNESOTA WRITERS' CAREER INITIATIVE GRANT

The Loft Literary Center, fellowships and awards, 1011 Washington Ave. S., Suite 200, Open Book, Minneapolis MN 55415. (612)215-2575. Fax: (612)215-2576. E-mail: loft@loft.org. Website: www.loft.org. **Contact:** Jerod Santek. "The Minnesota Writers' Career Initiative Program provides financial support and professional assistance to Minnesota writers. Up to four winners each year will receive grants of up to $10,000 to underwrite career development plans. Applications will be accepted from established artists, as well as artists in earlier stages of their careers who seek to improve their craft through a project-based proposal." Deadline: June. Watch for application guidelines in January.

MOONDANCER FELLOWSHIP FOR WRITING ABOUT NATURE AND THE OUTDOORS

The Writers' Colony at Dairy Hollow, 515 Spring St., Eureka Springs AR 72632. (479)253-7444. Fax: (479)253-9859. E-mail: director@writerscolony.org. **Contact:** Vicki-Kell Schneider, coordinator. "A four-week residency for writing in any genre about any aspect of nature and the outdoors. Works may be fiction or non-fiction. Supports writing of excellence which aspires to engage the mind, body and soul in the appreciation of nature. Applications accepted February 16 - May 15, 2010. Residency may be completed in two stays during 2010."

NEBRASKA ARTS COUNCIL INDIVIDUAL ARTISTS FELLOWSHIPS

Nebraska Arts Council, 1004 Farnam St., Plaza Level, Omaha NE 68102. (402)595-2122. Fax: (402)595-2334. E-mail: jayne.hutton@nebraska.gov. **Contact:** J.D. Hutton. Estab. 1991. Offered every 3 years (literature alternates with other disciplines) to recognize exemplary achievements by originating artists in their fields of endeavor and support the contributions made by Nebraska artists to the quality of life in this state. Generally, distinguished achievement awards are $5,000 and merit awards are $1,000-2,000. Funds available are announced in September prior to the deadline. Must be a resident of Nebraska for at least 2 years prior to submission date; 18 years of age; and not enrolled in an undergraduate, graduate, or certificate-granting program in English, creative writing, literature, or related field. Deadline: November 15.

NEW YORK FOUNDATION FOR THE ARTS ARTISTS' FELLOWSHIPS

New York Foundation for the Arts, 20 Jay Street, 7th Floor, Brooklyn NY 11201. (212)366-6900. E-mail: fellowships@nyfa.org. Estab. 1985. Fellowships are awarded in 16 disciplines on a biannual rotation made to individual originating artists living and working in the State of New York. Awards are based upon the recommendations of peer panels and are not project support. The Fellowships may be used by each recipient as she/he sees fit. All applicants must be 18 years of age, and a New York resident for 2 years prior to the time of application. Deadline: October 8, 2010. Prize: Grants of $7,000.

NORTH CAROLINA ARTS COUNCIL REGIONAL ARTIST PROJECT GRANTS

North Carolina Arts Council, Dept. of Cultural Resources, MSC #4632, Raleigh NC 27699-4634. (919)807-6500. Fax: (919)807-6532. E-mail: banu.valladares@ncdcr.gov. Website: www.ncarts.org. **Contact:** Banu Valladares, Program Director. Deadline: Generally late summer/early fall. Prize: $500-3,000 awarded to writers to pursue projects that further their artistic development. Open to any writer living in North Carolina. See website for contact information for the local arts councils that distribute these grants.

NORTH CAROLINA WRITERS' FELLOWSHIPS

North Carolina Arts Council, Dept. of Cultural Resources, Raleigh NC 27699-4632. (919)807-6500. Fax: (919)807-6532. E-mail: banu.valladares@ncdcr.gov. **Contact:** Banu Valladares, literature director. Offered every even year to support writers of fiction, poetry, literary nonfiction, literary translation, and spoken word. See website for guidelines and other eligibility requirements. Writers must be current residents of North Carolina for at least 1 year, must remain in residence in North Carolina during the grant year, and may not pursue academic or professional degrees while receiving grant. Contest offered to support writers in the development and creation of their work. Deadline: November 1, 2010. Prize: $10,000 grant. Reviewed by a panel of literature professionals (writers and editors).

RHODE ISLAND ARTIST FELLOWSHIPS AND INDIVIDUAL PROJECT GRANTS

Rhode Island State Council on the Arts, One Capitol Hill, 3rd Floor, Providence RI 02908. (401)222-3880. Fax: (401)222-3018. E-mail: cristina@arts.ri.gov. **Contact:** Cristina DiChiera, director of individual artist programs. Annual fellowship competition is based upon panel review of mss for poetry, fiction, and playwriting/screenwriting. Project grants provide funds for community-based arts projects. Rhode Island artists may apply without a nonprofit sponsor. Applicants for all RSCA grant and award programs must be at least 18 years and not currently enrolled in an arts-related degree program. Online application and guidelines can be found at www.arts.ri.gov/grants/guidelines/ Deadline: April 1 and October 1. Prize: Fellowship awards: $5,000 and $1,000. Grants range from $500-10,000 with an average of around $3,000.

WALLACE STEGNER FELLOWSHIPS

Creative Writing Program, Stanford University, Dept. of English, Stanford CA 94305-2087. (650)723-0011 or (650)725-1208. Fax: (650)723-3679. E-mail: mpopek@stanford.edu. Website: www.creativewriting.stanford.edu. **Contact:** Mary Popek, program administrator. "A 2-year, non-degree granting program at Stanford offered annually for emerging writers to attend the Stegner workshop to practice and perfect their craft under the guidance of the creative writing faculty. Guidelines available online." Deadline: December 1 (postmarked). Charges $60 fee. Prize: Living stipend (currently $26,000/year) and required workshop tuition of $7,479/year and health insurance

TENNESSEE ARTS COMMISSION LITERARY FELLOWSHIP

Tennessee Arts Commission, 401 Charlotte Ave., Nashville TN 37243-0780. Fax: (615)741-8559. E-mail: lee.baird@state.tn.us. Website: www.arts.state.tn.us. **Contact:** Lee Baird, director of literary programs. Awarded annually in recognition of professional Tennessee artists, i.e., individuals who have received financial compensation for their work as professional writers. Applicants must have a publication history other than vanity press. Two fellowships awarded annually to outstanding literary artists who live and work in Tennessee. Categories are in fiction/creative nonfiction and poetry. Deadline: January 30. Prize: $5,000 an out-of-state adjudicator.

VERMONT ARTS COUNCIL

136 State St., Drawer 33, Montpelier VT 05633-6001. (802)828-5425. Fax: (802)828-3363. E-mail: srae@vermontartscouncil.org. Website: www.vermontartscouncil.org. **Contact:** Sonia Rae. Grants awarded once per year for specific projects. Creation Grants for writers of poetry, plays, screenplays, fiction, nonfiction. Rolling grants are available in the following categories: Artist Development Grants providing professional development funds for individual artists and Technical Assistance Grants providing grants for organizational development to non-profit arts organizations. For Community Arts Grants and Arts Learning Grants, for not-for-profit organizations (including writing programs and not-for-profit presses), contact Stacy Raphael (802)828-3778 or by e-mail at sraphael@vermontartscouncil.org. Open to Vermont residents only. Prize: $250-5,000

WRITERS' BURSARIES

Scottish Arts Council, 12 Manor Place, Edinburgh EH3 7DD Scotland. (44)(131)240-2444. E-mail: help.desk@scottisharts.org.uk. Website: www.scottisharts.org.uk. Writers' Bursaries are awarded to assist published writers of literary work and playwrights, based in Scotland, who need finance for a period of concentrated work on their next book or play. For more information on deadlines and grant levels, please contact the help desk.

YOUNG ARTS

National Foundation for Advancement in the Arts, 777 Brickell Ave., Suite 370, Miami FL 33131. (305)377-1140 or (800)970-ARTS. Fax: (305)377-1149. Website: www.youngARTS.org. **Contact:** Roberta Behrend Fliss. Estab. 1981. For high school seniors in cinematic arts, dance, music, jazz, photography, theater, visual art, voice, and writing. Applications available on website or by phone request. Deadline: Early: June 2 ($25 fee); regular: October 1 ($35 fee). Prize: Individual awards range from $250-10,000 in an awards package totalling $900,000—$3 million in scholarship opportunities and the chance to be named Presidential Scholars in the Arts.

Fiction

ANNUAL GIVAL PRESS NOVEL AWARD

Gival Press, LLC, P.O. Box 3812, Arlington VA 22203. (703)351-0079. E-mail: givalpress@yahoo.com. **Contact:** Robert L. Giron. "Offered annually for a previously unpublished original novel (not a translation). It must be in English with at least 30,000-100,000 words of literary quality. Guidelines online, via e-mail, or by mail with SASE." Deadline: May 30. Charges $50 (USD) reading fee. Prize: $3,000, plus publication of book with a standard contract.

ANNUAL GIVAL PRESS SHORT STORY AWARD

Gival Press, LLC, P.O. Box 3812, Arlington VA 22203. (703)351-0079. E-mail: givalpress@yahoo.com. Website: www.givalpress.com. **Contact:** Robert L. Giron. "Offered annually for a previously unpublished original short story (not a translation). It must be in English with at least 5,000-15,000 words of literary quality. Guidelines by mail with SASE, by e-mail, or online." To award the best literary short story submitted. Deadline: August 8. Charges $25 (USD) reading fee. Prize: $1,000, plus publication on website. The editor narrows entries to the top ten; previous winner chooses the top 5 and the winner—all done anonymously.

Tips "Open to any writer as long as the work is original, not a translation, and written in English. The copyright remains in the author's name; certain rights fall under the contract."

BARD FICTION PRIZE

Bard College, P.O. Box 5000, Annandale-on-Hudson NY 12504-5000. (845)758-7087. E-mail: bfp@bard.edu. Estab. 2001. Open to younger American writers. "The Bard Fiction Prize is intended to encourage and support young writers of fiction to pursue their creative goals and to provide an opportunity to work in a fertile and intellectual environment. Deadline: July 15. Prize: $30,000 and appointment as writer-in-residence at Bard College for 1 semester.

BINGHAMTON UNIVERSITY JOHN GARDNER FICTION BOOK AWARD

Binghamton University, Dept. of English, General Literature & Rhetoric, P.O. Box 6000, Binghamton NY 13902-6000. (607)777-2713. **Contact:** Maria Mazziotti Gillan, creative writing prog. director. Estab. 2001. "Contest offered annually for a novel or collection of fiction published in previous year. Offered annually for a novel or collection of short stories published that year in a press run of 500 copies or more. Each book submitted must be accompanied by an application form. Publisher may submit more than 1 book for prize consideration. Send 3 copies of each book. Guidelines available online or for SASE." Deadline: March 1. Prize: $1,000. Judged by professional writer not on Binghamton University faculty.

BONOMO MEMORIAL LITERATURE PRIZE

Italian Americana, URI/CCE, 80 Washington St., Providence RI 02908-1803. (401)277-5306. Fax: (401)277-5100. E-mail: bonomoal@etal.uri.edu or it.americana@yahoo.com. Website: www.italianamericana.com. **Contact:** Carol Bonomo Albright, editor. Offered annually for the best fiction, essay, or memoir that is published annually by an Italian-American. Send submission of 20 pages maximum, double-spaced in duplicate to be considered for publication/prize. Acquires first North American serial rights.

THE ALEXANDER PATTERSON CAPPON FICTION AWARD

New Letters, University of Missouri-Kansas City, 5101 Rockhill Rd., Kansas City MO 64110. (816)235-1168. Fax: (816)235-2611. E-mail: newletters@umkc.edu. **Contact:** Ashley Kaine. Offered annually for unpublished work to discover and reward new and upcoming writers. Buys first North American serial rights. Open to any writer. Deadline: May 18. Charges $15 (includes cost of a 1-year subscription).

Prize: 1st Place: $1,500 and publication in a volume of *New Letters*; runner-up will receive a complimentary copy of a recent book of poetry or fiction courtesy of BkMk Press. All entries will be given consideration for publication in future issues of *New Letters*.

G. S. SHARAT CHANDRA PRIZE FOR SHORT FICTION

BkMk Press, University of Missouri-Kansas City, 5100 Rockhill Rd., Kansas City MO 64110-2499. (816)235-2558. Fax: (816)235-2611. E-mail: bkmk@umkc.edu. Website: www.umkc.edu/bkmk. "Offered annually for the best book-length ms collection (unpublished) of short fiction in English by a living author. Translations are not eligible. Initial judging is done by a network of published writers. Final judging is done by a writer of national reputation. Guidelines for SASE, by e-mail, or on website." Deadline: January 15 (postmarked). Charges $25 fee. Prize: $1,000, plus book publication by BkMk Press.

N THE CHARITON REVIEW SHORT FICTION PRIZE

Truman State University Press, 100 E. Normal St., Kirksville MO 63501-4221. (660)785-7336. Fax: (660)785-4480. E-mail: chariton@truman.edu. Website: tsup.truman.edu. **Contact:** Nancy Rediger. Annual competition for best unpublished short fiction on any theme up to 5,000 words in English. Guidelines for SASE, online, or by e-mail. Deadline: September 30 (postmarked). Charges Fee: $20. Prize: Prize: $1,000 and publication.

N COPTALES CONTEST

Stories of public service officers in action!, Sponsored by Oak Tree Press, 140 E. Palmer St., Taylorville IL 62568. E-mail: oaktreepub@aol.com. **Contact:** Billie Johnson, award director. Guidelines and entry forms are available for SASE. The goal of the CopTales Contest is to discover and publish new authors, or authors shifting to a new genre. This annual contest is open to writers who have not published in the mystery genre in the past three years, as well as completely unpublished authors. Deadline: July 31. Charges $35. Prize: The prize consists of a Publishing Agreement, and launch of the title. Winners or runners up who are offered publishing agreements are asked to transfer rights. Publishing industry professionals prescreen the entries; publisher makes final selection.

DARK OAK MYSTERY CONTEST

Oak Tree Press, 140 E. Palmer St., Taylorville IL 62568. (217)824-6500. E-mail: oaktreepub@aol.com. **Contact:** Editor (prefers email contact). Offered annually for an unpublished mystery manuscript (up to 85,000 words) of any sort from police procedurals to amateur sleuth novels. Acquires first North American, audio and film rights to winning entry. Open to authors not published in the past 3 years. Deadline: July 31. Charges $35/mss. Prize: Publishing Agreement, and launch of the title.

WILLIAM F. DEECK MALICE DOMESTIC GRANTS FOR UNPUBLISHED WRITERS

Malice Domestic, P.O. Box 8007, Gaithersburg MD 20898-8007. E-mail: grants@malicedomestic.org. **Contact:** Harriet Sackler. Offered annually for unpublished work in the mystery field. Malice awards up to 2 grants to unpublished writers in the malice domestic genre at its annual convention in May. The competition is designed to help the next generation of malice authors get their first work published and to foster quality malice literature. Malice domestic literature is loosely described as mystery stories of the Agatha Christie type, i.e., traditional mysteries. These works usually feature no excessive gore, gratuitous violence, or explicit sex. Writers who have been published previously in the mystery field, including publication of a mystery novel, short story, or dramatic work, are ineligible to apply. Members of the Malice Domestic Board of Directors and their families are ineligible to apply. Malice encourages applications from minority candidates. Guidelines online. Deadline: November 15. Prize: $1,500, plus a comprehensive registration to the following year's convention and two nights' lodging at the convention hotel.

JACK DYER FICTION PRIZE

Crab Orchard Review, Dept. of English, Southern Illinois Univ. Carbondale, Carbondale IL 62901-4503. E-mail: jtribble@siu.edu. **Contact:** Jon C. Tribble, man. editor. "Offered annually for unpublished short fiction. *Crab Orchard Review* acquires first North American serial rights to all submitted work. Open to any writer. Open to US citizens only." March 1 - April 30. Charges $10/entry (can enter up to 3 stories, each story submitted requires a separate fee and can be up to 6,000 words), which includes one copy of *Crab Orchard Review* featuring the winners. Prize: $1,500 and publication.

N THE FAR HORIZONS AWARD FOR SHORT FICTION

The Malahat Review, University of Victoria,, P.O. Box 1700, Stn CSC, Victoria BC V8W 2Y2 Canada. (250)721-8524. Fax: (250)472-5051. E-mail: malahat@uvic.ca. Website: www.malahatreview.ca.

Contact: John Barton, Editor. Open to "emerging short fiction writers from Canada, the United States, and elsewhere" who have not yet published their fiction in a full-length book (48 pages or more). Submissions must be unpublished. No simultaneous submissions. Submit one piece of short fiction, 3,500 words maximum; no restrictions on subject matter or aesthetic approach. Include separate page with author's name, address, e-mail, and title; no identifying information on mss. pages. No e-mail submissions. Do not include SASE for results; mss. will not be returned. Guidelines available on website. Deadline: May 1 of odd-numbered years. Charges $25 CAD for Canadian entries, $30 USD for US entries; $45 USD from Mexico and outside North America; includes a one-year subscription to The Malahat Review. Deadline: May 1 (postmark) of alternate years (2011, 2013, etc.). 2009 Winner: Eliza Robertson. Winner and finalists contacted by e-mail. Prize: Offers $500 CAD, publication in Fall issue of *The Malahat Review* (see separate listing in Magazines/Journals) and payment at the rate of $40 per printed page upon publication. Announced in Fall on website, Facebook page, and in quarterly e-newsletter, *Malahat Lite*.

FAW ANGELO B. NATOLI SHORT STORY COMPETITION

Fellowship of Australian Writers, P.O. Box 973, Eltham VIC 3095 Australia. E-mail: president@writers.asn.au. **Contact:** Awards Co-ordinator. Competition for a short story up to 3,000 words long. Guidelines online or for SASE. Closing date: 30th November; Opening date: 1st September. Charges $10. Prize: $800

FAW CHRISTINA STEAD AWARD

Fellowship of Australian Writers, P.O. Box 973, Eltham VIC 3095 Australia. E-mail: president@writers.asn.au. **Contact:** Awards Co-ordinator. Annual award for a work of fiction with an Australia theme. Guidelines for SASE or online. Closing date: 30th November; Opening date: 1st September. Charges $15. Prize: $500

FAW JENNIFER BURBIDGE SHORT STORY AWARD

Fellowship of Australian Writers, P.O. Box 973, Eltham VIC 3095 Australia. E-mail: president@asn.au. **Contact:** Award Co-ordinator. Award for a short story (maximum 3,000 words) dealing with any aspect of the lives of those who suffer some form of mental disability and/or the impact on their families. Guidelines online or for SASE. Deadline: November 30; Opening September 1. Charges $10. Prize: $250

FIRSTWRITER.COM INTERNATIONAL SHORT STORY CONTEST

firstwriter.com, United Kingdom. **Contact:** J. Paul Dyson, managing editor. "Accepts short stories up to 3,000 words on any subject and in any style." Deadline: April 1. Charges $7.50 for 1 short story; $12 for 2; $15 for 3; and $20 for 5. Prize: total about $300. Ten special commendations will also be awarded and all the winners will be published in *firstwriter* magazine and receive a$30 subscription voucher, allowing an annual subscription to be taken out for free All submissions are automatically considered for publication in *firstwriter* magazine and may be published there online. *firstwriter* magazine editors.

FISH UNPUBLISHED NOVEL AWARD

Fish Publishing, Durrus, Bantry, Co. Cork Ireland. E-mail: info@fishpublishing.com. Website: www.fishpublishing.com. **Contact:** Clem Cairns. A competition for the best unpublished novel entered. Deadline: September 30. Charges $50 USD. Prize: 1st Prize: Publication of winning novel and cash. "This is not an annual award, but is run every so often."

FLASH FICTION PRIZE

National League of American Pen Women, Nob Hill, San Francisco Branch, The Webhallow House, 1544 Sweetwood Dr., Broadmoor Village CA 94015-1717. E-mail: pennobhill@aol.com. Website: www.soulmakingcontest.us. **Contact:** Eileen Malone. "Three flash fiction (short-short) stories per entry, under 500 words. Previously published material is accepted. Indicate category on each story. Identify only with 3 × 5 card. Open annually to any writer." Deadline: November 30. Charges $5/entry (make checks payable to NLAPW, Nob Hill Branch). Prize: 1st Place: $100; 2nd Place: $50; 3rd Place: $25.

GLIMMER TRAIN'S FAMILY MATTERS CONTEST

Glimmer Train Press, Inc., 1211 NW Glisan St., Suite 207, Portland OR 97209. Fax: (503)221-0837. E-mail: eds@glimmertrain.org. Website: www.glimmertrain.org. **Contact:** Linda Swanson-Davies. Offered for unpublished stories about family. Word count should not exceed 12,000. All shorter lengths welcome. See complete writing guidelines and submit onilne at website. Open in the months of April and October.

Winners will be called two months after the close of each competition, and results announced in their respective bulletins, on their website, and in a number of additional print and online publications. Charges $15 fee/story. Prize: 1st Place: $1,200, publication in *Glimmer Train Stories*, and 20 copies of that issue; 2nd Place: $500; 3rd Place: $300.

GLIMMER TRAIN'S FICTION OPEN

Glimmer Train, Inc., Glimmer Train Press, Inc., 1211 NW Glisan St., Suite 207, Portland OR 97209. (503)221-0836. Fax: (503)221-0837. E-mail: eds@glimmertrain.org. Website: www.glimmertrain.org. **Contact:** Linda Swanson-Davies. "Open to all writers. No theme restrictions. Word count range: 2000-20,000. See complete writing guidelines and submit online at website. Open all during the months of March, June, September and December. Winners will be called 2 months after the close of each competition and results will be announced in their respective bulletin month, on their website, and in a number of additional print and online publications." Charges $20/story. Prize: 1st Place: $2,000, publication in *Glimmer Train Stories*, and 20 copies of that issue; 2nd Place: $1,000 and consideration for publication; 3rd Place: $600.

GLIMMER TRAIN'S SHORT-STORY AWARD FOR NEW WRITERS

Glimmer Train Press, Inc., 1211 NW Glisan St., Suite 207, Portland OR 97209. (503)221-0836. Fax: (503)221-0837. E-mail: eds@glimmertrain.org. Website: www.glimmertrain.org. **Contact:** Linda Swanson-Davies. "Offered for any writer whose fiction hasn't appeared in a nationally distributed print publication with a circulation over 5,000. Word count: should not exceed 12,000 words. All shorter lengths welcome. Open quarterly during the months of February, May, August, and November. See complete writing guidelines and submit online at website. Winners will be called 2 months after the close of each competition, and results will be announced in their respective bulletin month, on their website, and in a number of additional print and online publications." Charges $15 fee/story. Prize: Winner receives $1,200, publication in *Glimmer Train Stories*, and 20 copies of that issue; 2nd Place: $500; 3rd Place: $300. **Tips** "We've gone to quarterly with this competition, since our focus is moving more and more to the relatively unpublished writer. In a recent edition of Best American Short Stories, of the top '100 Distinguished Short Stories,' ten appeared in Glimmer Train Stories, more than any other publication in the country, including the New Yorker. Of those ten, three were those authors' first stories accepted for publication."

GLIMMER TRAIN'S VERY SHORT FICTION AWARD (JANUARY)

Glimmer Train Press, Inc., 1211 NW Glisan St., #207, Portland OR 97209. (503)221-0836. Fax: (503)221-0837. E-mail: eds@glimmertrain.org. Website: www.glimmertrain.org. **Contact:** Linda Swanson-Davies. "Offered to encourage the art of the very short story. Word count: 3,000 maximum. Open January 1-31. See complete writing guidelines and submit online at website. Winners will be called and results will be announced in their April bulletin and in a number of additional print and online publications." Charges $15 fee/story. Prize: Winner receives $1,200, publication in *Glimmer Train Stories,* and 20 copies of that issue; 2nd Place: $500; 3rd Place: $300.

GLIMMER TRAIN'S VERY SHORT FICTION CONTEST (JULY)

Glimmer Train Press, Inc., 1211 NW Glisan St., 207, Portland OR 97209. (503)221-0836. Fax: (503)221-0837. E-mail: eds@glimmertrain.org. **Contact:** Linda Swanson-Davies. "Offered to encourage the art of the very short story. Word count: 3,000 maximum. Open July 1-31. See complete writing guidelines and submit online at website. Winners will be called and results will be announced in their October bulletin, on their website, and in a number of additional print and online publications." Charges $15 fee/story. Prize: First Place: $1,200, publication in Glimmer Train Stories, and 20 copies of that issue; 2nd Place: $500; 3rd Place: $300.

LYNDALL HADOW/DONALD STUART SHORT STORY COMPETITION

Fellowship of Australian Writers (WA), P.O. Box 6180, Swanbourne WA 6911. (61)(8)9384-4771. Fax: (61)(8)9384-4854. E-mail: admin@fawwa.org.au. Website: www.fawwa.org.au. Annual contest for unpublished short stories (maximum 3,000 words). "We reserve the right to publish entries in an FAWWA publication or on its website." Guidelines online or for SASE. Deadline: June 1. Charges $10/story. Prize: 1st Place: $400; 2nd Place; $100; Highly Commended: $50.

BARRY HANNAH PRIZE FOR FICTION

The Yalobusha Review, Dept. of English, University of Mississippi, P.O. Box 1848, University MS 38677-1848. (662)915-3175. E-mail: yrfiction@yahoo.com. **Contact:** Fiction Editor. Annual contest for great unpublished short fiction. No online submissions. Include cover letter and SASE for results only. Name should not appear on manuscript itself. Manuscripts should not be returned. Deadline: November 15. Charges $10. Prize: $500 and publication in *Yalobusha Review*. Retains first North American rights. Judged by the John and Renee Grisham visiting writer. Past judges have included Tom Franklin, Padget Powell, and Jack Pendarvis.

Tips "Story should be no longer than 30 pages."

TOM HOWARD/JOHN H. REID SHORT STORY CONTEST

c/o Winning Writers, 351 Pleasant St., PMB 222, Northampton MA 01060-3961. (866)946-9748. E-mail: johnreid@mail.qango.com. Website: www.winningwriters.com. **Contact:** John Reid. Estab. 1993. "Both unpublished and published work accepted (maximum 5,000 words). Guidelines for SASE or online." Deadline: March 31. Charges $15 USD/story/essay/prose work. Prize: 1st Place: $3,000; 2nd Place: $1,000; 3rd Place: $400; 4th Place: $250; and 6 most highly commended awards of $150 each. The top 10 entries will be published on the Winning Writers website. Judged by John H. Reid; assisted by Dee C. Konrad.

L. RON HUBBARD'S WRITERS OF THE FUTURE CONTEST

P.O. Box 1630, Los Angeles CA 90078. (323)466-3310. E-mail: contests@authorservicesinc.com. **Contact:** Contest Administrator. "Offered for unpublished work to find, reward, and publicize new speculative fiction writers so they may more easily attain professional writing careers." Open to new and amateur writers who have not professionally published a novel or short novel, more than 1 novelette, or more than 3 short stories. Eligible entries are short stories or novelettes (under 17,000 words) of science fiction or fantasy. Guidelines for SASE, online, or via e-mail. No entry fee. Entrants retain all rights to their stories. Deadline: December 31, March 31, June 30, September 30. Prize: Awards quarterly 1st Place: $1,000; 2nd Place: $750; and 3rd Place: $500. Annual Grand Prize: $5,000. Judged by professional writers only.

INDIANA REVIEW FICTION CONTEST

Indiana Review, Ballantine Hall 465, Indiana University, Bloomington IN 47405-7103. (812)855-9535. Fax: (812)855-4253. E-mail: inreview@indiana.edu. Website: www.indianareview.org. "Submit only 1 story per entry fee, 35 double-spaced pages maximum. 12 pt. font. Offered annually for unpublished work. Guidelines on website and with SASE request." Deadline: October. Charges $15 fee (includes a 1-year subscription). Prize: $1,000 Judged by guests; 2009 prize judged by Ron Carlson

THE INNERMOONLIT AWARD FOR BEST SHORT-SHORT STORY

E-mail: timescythe11@yahoo.com. **Contact:** Brian Agincourt Massey. "Annual contest for unpublished short-short stories that do not exceed 500 words. Guidelines available online at website. No entry fee. Open to all writers 18 years and older." Deadline: September 1. Charges No entry fee. Prize: 1st Place: $100; 2nd Place: $50; 3rd Place: $25. Brian Massey

INTERNATIONAL 3-DAY NOVEL CONTEST

200-341 Water St., Vancouver BC V6B 1B8 Canada. E-mail: info@3daynovel.com. Website: www.3daynovel.com. **Contact:** Melissa Edwards. Estab. 1977. "Offered annually for the best novel written in 3 days (Labor Day weekend). To register, send SASE (IRC if from outside Canada) for details, or entry form available online. Open to all writers. Writing may take place in any location." Deadline: Friday before Labor Day weekend. Charges $50 fee (lower group rates available). Prize: 1st place receives publication; 2nd place receives $500; 3rd place receives $100.

JERRY JAZZ MUSICIAN NEW SHORT FICTION AWARD

Jerry Jazz Musician, 2207 NE Broadway, Portland OR 97232. E-mail: jm@jerryjazzmusician.com. Three times a year, *Jerry Jazz Musician* awards a writer who submits, in our opinion, the best original, previously unpublished work of approximately 3,000-5,000 words. The winner will be announced via a mailing of our *Jerry Jazz* newsletter. Publishers, artists, musicians, and interested readers are among those who subscribe to the newsletter. Additionally, the work will be published on the home page of *Jerry Jazz Musician* and featured there for at least 4 weeks. The *Jerry Jazz Musician* reader tends to have interests in music, history, literature, art, film, and theater—particularly that of the counter-culture of mid-20th century America. Guidelines available online. Deadline: September, January, and May. Prize: $100 Judged by the editors of *Jerry Jazz Musician*.

JESSE JONES AWARD FOR FICTION

6335 W. Northwest Hwy., #618, Dallas TX 75225. (214)363-7253. E-mail: dpayne@smu.edu. **Contact:** Darwin Payne, president. Offered annually by Texas Institute of Letters for work published January

1-December 31 of year before award is given to recognize the writer of the best book of fiction entered in the competition. Writers must have been born in Texas, have lived in the state for at least 2 consecutive years at some time, or the subject matter of the work should be associated with the state. President changes every two years. See website for guidelines. Deadline: January 1. Prize: $6,000.

THE LAWRENCE FOUNDATION AWARD

Prairie Schooner, 201 Andrews Hall, P.O. Box 880334, Lincoln NE 68588-0334. (402)472-0911. Fax: (402)472-9771. E-mail: jengelhardt2@unlnotes.unl.edu. **Contact:** Hilda Raz. Offered annually for the best short story published in *Prairie Schooner* in the previous year. Prize: $1,000

THE LEDGE ANNUAL FICTION AWARDS COMPETITION

The Ledge Magazine, 40 Maple Avenue, Bellport NY 11713. E-mail: info@theledgemagazine.com. **Contact:** Timothy Monaghan, editor-in-chief. Stories must be unpublished and 7,500 words or less. There are no restrictions on form or content. Guidelines online or for SASE. Deadline: March 1. Charges $10/first story; $6/additional story. $20 subscription to *The Ledge Magazine gains free entry for the first story*. Prize: 1st Place: $1,000 and publication; 2nd Place: $250 and publication; 3rd Place: $100 and publication.

LITERAL LATTÉ FICTION AWARD

Literal Latté, 200 E. 10th St., Suite 240, New York NY 10003. (212)260-5532. E-mail: litlatte@aol.com. Website: www.literal-latte.com. **Contact:** Edward Estlin, contributing editor. "Award to provide talented writers with 3 essential tools for continued success: money, publication, and recognition. Offered annually for unpublished fiction (maximum 8,000 words). Guidelines for SASE, by e-mail, or online. Open to any writer." Deadline: January 15. Prize: 1st Place: $1,000 and publication in *Literal Latté*; 2nd Place: $300; 3rd Place: $200; also up to 7 honorable mentions.

Tips "Winners notified by phone. List of winners available in late April for SASE or by e-mail. All winners published in in *Literal Latté*."

N LITERAL LATTÉ SHORT SHORTS CONTEST

Literal Latte, 200 E. 10th St., Suite 240, New York NY 10003. (212)260-5532. E-mail: litlatte@aol.com. Website: www.literal-latte.com. **Contact:** Jenine Gordon Bockman, editor. Estab. Annual contest. Send unpublished shorts. 2,000 words max. All styles welcome. Postmark by June 30th. Name, address, phone number, email address (optional) on cover page only. Include SASE or email address for reply. All entries considered for publication. Postmark June 30th. Charges $10 for up to 3, or $15 per set of 6 shorts. Prize: $500. Judged by the editors.

LONG STORY CONTEST, INTERNATIONAL

White Eagle Coffee Store Press, P.O. Box 383, Fox River Grove IL 60021. (847)639-9200. E-mail: wecspress@aol.com. **Contact:** Frank E. Smith, publisher. "Offered annually since 1993 for unpublished work to recognize and promote long short stories of 8,000-14,000 words (about 30-50 pages). Sample of previous winner: $6.95, including postage. Open to any writer; no restrictions on materials." December 15. Charges $15 fee; $10 for second story in same envelope. Prize: A. E. Coppard Prize: $1,000, publication, and 25 copies of chapbook.

THE MARY MACKEY SHORT STORY PRIZE

Soul-Making Literary Competition, National League of American Pen Women, Nob Hill, San Francisco Bay Area, The Webhallow House, 1544 Sweetwood Dr., Broadmoor Village CA 94015-1717. E-mail: pennobhill@aol.com. **Contact:** Eileen Malone. "One story/entry, up to 5,000 words. All prose works must be typed, page numbered, and double-spaced. Identify only with 3 × 5 card. Open annually to any writer." Deadline: November 30. Charges $5/entry (make checks payable to NLAPW, Nob Hill Branch). Prize: 1st Place: $100; 2nd Place: $50; 3rd Place: $25.

THE MALAHAT REVIEW NOVELLA PRIZE

The Malahat Review, University of Victoria, P.O. Box 1700 STN CSC, Victoria BC V8W 2Y2 Canada. (250)721-8524. E-mail: malahat@uvic.ca. **Contact:** John Barton, Editor. "Held in alternate years with the Long Poem Prize. Offered to promote unpublished novellas. Obtains first world rights. After publication rights revert to the author. Open to any writer." Submit novellas between 10,000 and 20,000 words in length. Include separate page with author's name, address, e-mail, and novella title; no identifying information on mss. pages. No e-mail submissions. Do NOT include SASE for results; mss. will not be returned. Guidelines available on website. Deadline: February 1 (even years). Charges $35 CAD fee for Canadian entrants; $40 US for American entrants; $45 US for entrants from elsewhere (includes a 1-year subscription to *Malahat*). Prize: $500, plus payment for publication ($40/page) and one year's subscription. 2008 winner: Andrew Tibbetts. Winner and finalists contacted by e-mail. Winner published in summer issue of *The Malahat Review* and announced on website, Facebook page, and in quarterly e-newsletter, *Malahat Lite*.

MILKWEED NATIONAL FICTION PRIZE

Milkweed Editions, 1011 Washington Ave. S., Suite 300, Minneapolis MN 55415. (612)332-3192. Fax: (612)215-2550. Website: www.milkweed.org. **Contact:** The Editors. Estab. 1986. "Annual award for unpublished works. Milkweed is looking for a novel, novella, or a collection of short stories written in English. Mss should be of high literary quality. Please consult submissions guidelines on website before submitting. All mss submitted to Milkweed will automatically be considered for the prize. Submission directly to the contest is no longer necessary. Writers are recommended to have previously published a book of fiction or 3 short stories (or novellas) in magazines/journals with national distribution. Catalog available on request for $1.50." Deadline: Open. Prize: Publication by Milkweed Editions and a cash advance of $5,000 against royalties agreed upon in the contractual arrangement negotiated at the time of acceptance.

C. WRIGHT MILLS AWARD

The Society for the Study of Social Problems, 901 McClung Tower, University of Tennessee, Knoxville TN 37996-0490. (865)689-1531. Fax: (865)689-1534. E-mail: mkoontz3@utk.edu. Website: www.sssp1.org. **Contact:** Michele Smith Koontz, administrative officer & meeting manager. "Offered annually for a book published the previous year that most effectively critically addresses an issue of contemporary public importance; brings to the topic a fresh, imaginative perspective; advances social scientific understanding of the topic; displays a theoretically informed view and empirical orientation; evinces quality in style of writing; and explicitly or implicitly contains implications for courses of action." Deadline: January 15. Prize: $500 stipend.

THE NELLIGAN PRIZE FOR SHORT FICTION

Colorado Review/Center for Literary Publishing, 9105 Campus Delivery, Dept. of English, Colorado State University, Ft. Collins CO 80523-9105. (970)491-5449. E-mail: creview@colostate.edu. **Contact:** Stephanie G'Schwind, editor. Offered annually to an unpublished short story. Guidelines for SASE or online. Deadline: March 12. Charges $15. Prize: $1,500 and publication of story in *Colorado Review*.

FRANK O'CONNOR AWARD FOR SHORT FICTION

descant, Texas Christian University's literary journal, TCU Box 297270, Fort Worth TX 76129. (817)257-6537. Fax: (817)257-6239. E-mail: descant@tcu.edu. **Contact:** Dan Williams and Alex Lemon, editors. Offered annually for unpublished short stories. Publication retains copyright but will transfer it to the author upon request. Deadline: September-March. Prize: $500.

ONCEWRITTEN.COM FICTION CONTEST

Oncewritten.com, 1850 N. Whitley Ave., #404, Hollywood CA 90028. E-mail: fictioncontest@oncewritten.com. Website: www.oncewritten.com. **Contact:** Monica Poling. The purpose of this annual contest is to find high quality short fiction to feature on the website and in *Off the Press*, our monthly newsletter, which is distributed specifically to people interested in reading about new authors. Deadline: April 30 and October 31. Charges $5/story. Prize: 1st Place: $100. Judged by: editor and 1 industry professional.

PEN/FAULKNER AWARDS FOR FICTION

PEN/Faulkner Foundation, 201 E. Capitol St., Washington DC 20003. (202)675-0345. Fax: (202)675-0360. E-mail: jneely@penfaulkner.org. Website: www.penfaulkner.org. **Contact:** Jessica Neely, Executive Director. Offered annually for best book-length work of fiction by an American citizen published in a calendar year. Deadline: October 31. Prize: $15,000 (one Winner); $5,000 (4 Finalists).

THE PINCH LITERARY AWARD IN FICTION

The Univ. of Memphis/Hohenberg Foundation, Dept. of English, 435 Patterson Hall, Memphis TN 38152. (901)678-4591. E-mail: editor@thepinchjournal.com. Offered annually for unpublished short stories of 5,000 words maximum. Guidelines for SASE or on website. Deadline: March 15. Charges $20/story, which is put toward a 1-year subscription for *The Pinch*. Prize: 1st Place: $1,500 and publication; 2nd Place: possible publication and 1-year subscription.

THE KATHERINE ANNE PORTER PRIZE FOR FICTION

Nimrod International Journal, The University of Tulsa, 800 S. Tucker Dr., Tulsa OK 74104. (918)631-3080. Fax: (918)631-3033. E-mail: nimrod@utulsa.edu. **Contact:** Francine Ringold. "This annual award was established to discover new, unpublished writers of vigor and talent. Open to US residents only." Deadline: April 30. Charges $20 (includes a 1-year subscription to *Nimrod*). Prize: 1st Place: $2,000 and publication; 2nd Place: $1,000 and publication. *Nimrod* retains the right to publish any submission. The *Nimrod* editors select the finalists and a recognized author selects the winners.

THOMAS H. RADDALL ATLANTIC FICTION PRIZE

Writers' Federation of Nova Scotia, 1113 Marginal Rd., Halifax NS B3H 4P7 Canada. (902)423-8116. Fax: (902)422-0881. E-mail: talk@writers.ns.ca. **Contact:** Nate Crawford, executive director. Estab. 1990. "Full-length books of fiction written by Atlantic Canadians, and published as a whole for the first time in the previous calendar year, are eligible. Entrants must be native or resident Atlantic Canadians who have either been born in Newfoundland, Prince Edward Island, Nova Scotia, or New Brunswick, and spent a substantial portion of their lives living there, or who have lived in 1 or a combination of these provinces for at least 24 consecutive months prior to entry deadline date. Publishers: Send 4 copies and a letter attesting to the author's status as an Atlantic Canadian, and the author's current mailing address and telephone number. To recognize the best Atlantic Canadian adult fiction." Deadline: First Friday in December. Charges No fee or form. Prize: $15,000.

THE ROGERS WRITERS' TRUST FICTION PRIZE

The Writers' Trust of Canada, 90 Richmond St. E., Suite 200, Toronto ON M5C 1P1 Canada. (416)504-8222. Fax: (416)504-9090. E-mail: info@writerstrust.com. **Contact:** Amanda Hopkins. "Awarded annually for a distinguished work of fiction—either a novel or short story collection—published within the previous year. Presented at the Writers' Trust Awards event held in Toronto each Fall. Open to Canadian citizens and permanent residents only." Deadline: August 6. Prize: $25,000 and $2,500 to four finalists.

RROFIHE TROPHY

Open City, Open City Magazine & Books, 270 Lafayette St., #1412, New York NY 10012. Website: http://opencity.org/rrofihe.html. **Contact:** Rick Rofihe, editor. "Seventh annual contest for an unpublished short story (up to 5,000 words). Stories should be typed, double-spaced, on 8½ × 11 paper with the author's name and contact information on the first page, and name and story title on the upper right corner of remaining pages. Limit 1 submission/author. Author must not have been previously published in *Open City*. Enclose SASE to receive names of winner and honorable mentions. All mss are nonreturnable and will be recycled. First North American serial rights (from winner only)." Deadline: October 15 (postmarked). Charges $10 (make check payable to RRofihe). Prize: $500, a trophy, and publication in *Open City*. Judge: Rick Rofihe.

SASKATCHEWAN FICTION AWARD

Saskatchewan Book Awards, Inc., 205B-2314 11th Ave., Regina SK S4P 0K1 Canada. (306)569-1585. Fax: (306)569-4187. E-mail: director@bookawards.sk.ca. **Contact:** Jackie Lay, executive director. Offered annually for work published September 15-September 14 annually. This award is presented to a Saskatchewan author for the best book of fiction (novel or short fiction), judged on the quality of writing. Deadline: First deadline: July 31; Final deadline: September 14. Charges $25 (Canadian). Prize: $2,000

THE SCENT OF AN ENDING™

White Eagle Coffee Store Press, P.O. Box 383, Fox River Grove IL 60021-0383. (847)639-9200. E-mail: wecspress@aol.com. Website: www.whiteeaglecoffeestorepress.com or www.thescentofanending.com. **Contact:** Frank Edmund Smith, publisher. "Contest is offered annually for unpublished submissions. We're searching for the best bad ending to an imaginary novel—an ending that's a real stinker. We're looking for a memorably bad ending to a novel that has not been written. Submit the invented Title of the Novel and the final 25-125 words. The entry must be completely your own invention and cannot be taken from or closely based on anything actually published. All winners will be required to sign a contract verifying originality." Final deadline is Sept. 30 each year. Charges $6.37. Prize: 1st Place $89.25, 2nd Place $67.32, 3rd Place $31.18 plus dubious fame and publication for all winners and finalists. Initial publication on website, then in chapbook format. Judged by Editors of White Eagle Coffee Store Press.

Tips "Rolling entry. Rights to any winning and published materials revert to author on publication."

JOANNA CATHERINE SCOTT NOVEL EXCERPT PRIZE

National League of American Pen Women, Nob Hill, San Francisco Bay Area Branch, The Webhallow House, 1544 Sweetwood Dr., Broadmoor Village CA 94015-1717. E-mail: pennobhill@aol.com. **Contact:** Eileen Malone. "Send first chapter or the first 20 pages, whichever comes first. Include a 1-page synopsis indicating category at top of page. Identify with 3 × 5 card only. Open annually to any writer." Deadline: November 30. Charges $5/entry (make checks payable to NLAPW, Nob Hill Branch). Prize: 1st Place: $100; 2nd Place: $50; 3rd Place: $25.

MICHAEL SHAARA AWARD FOR EXCELLENCE IN CIVIL WAR FICTION

Civil War Institute at Gettysburg College, 300 N. Washington St., Campus Box 435, Gettysburg PA 17325. (717)337-6590. Fax: (717)337-6596. E-mail: civilwar@gettysburg.edu. Estab. 1997. "Offered annually for fiction published for the first time in January 1-December 31 of the year of the award to encourage examination of the Civil War from unique perspectives or by taking an unusual approach. All Civil War novels are eligible. To nominate a novel, send 4 copies of the novel to the address above with a cover letter. Nominations should be made by publishers, but authors and critics can nominate as well." Deadline: December 31. Prize: $5,000

MARY WOLLSTONECRAFT SHELLEY PRIZE FOR IMAGINATIVE FICTION

Rosebud, N3310 Asje Rd., Cambridge WI 53523. (608)423-4750. Fax: (608)423-9976. E-mail: jrodclark@smallbytes.net. Website: www.rsbd.net. **Contact:** J. Roderick Clark, editor. Biennial (odd years) contest for unpublished stories. Entries are welcome any time. Acquires first rights. Open to any writer. Deadline: October 15. Charges $10/story. Prize: $1,000, plus publication in *Rosebud*. 4 runner-ups receive $100 and publication in *Rosebud*.

SHORT SCIENCE FICTION STORY CONTEST

Crossquarter Publishing Group, P.O. Box 23749, Santa Fe NM 87502. (505)690-3923. Fax: (214)975-9715. E-mail: contest@crossquarter.com. Website: www.crossquarter.com. **Contact:** Anthony Ravenscroft. Annual contest for short science fiction (up to 7,500 words) showcasing the best in the human spirit. No horror or dystopia. Guidelines and entry form available online. Deadline: February 15. Charges $15; $10/each additional entry. Prize: 1st Place: $250; 2nd Place: $125; 3rd Place: $75; 4th Place: $50. Winners are also combined into an anthology.

24-HOUR SHORT STORY CONTEST

WritersWeekly.com, P.O. Box 2399, Bangor ME 04402. E-mail: writersweekly@writersweekly.com. **Contact:** Angela Hoy. "Quarterly contest in which registered entrants receive a topic at start time (usually noon CST) and have 24 hours to write a story on that topic. All submissions must be returned via e-mail. Each contest is limited to 500 people. Guidelines via e-mail or online." Deadline: Quarterly—see website for dates. Charges $5. Prize: 1st Place: $300; 2nd Place: $250; 3rd Place: $200. There are also 20 honorable mentions and 60 door prizes. The top 3 winners' entries are posted on WritersWeekly.com (non-exclusive electronic rights only). Writers retain all rights to their work. Angela Hoy (publisher of WritersWeekly.com and Booklocker.com).

WAASMODE FICTION CONTEST

Passages North, Dept. of English, Northern Michigan University, 1401 Presque Isle Ave, Marquette MI 49855. (906)227-1203. Fax: (906)227-1096. E-mail: passages@nmu.edu. Website: myweb.nmu.edu/~passages. **Contact:** Kate Myers Hanson. Offered every 2 years to publish new voices in literary fiction (maximum 5,000 words). Guidelines for SASE or online. Deadline: Submit October 15-February 15. Charges $10 reading fee/story. Make checks payable to Northern Michigan University. Send entries to *Passages North*. Prize: $1,000 and publication for winner; 2 honorable mentions are also published; all entrants receive a copy of *Passages North*.

WD POPULAR FICTION AWARDS

Writer's Digest, 4700 E. Galbraith Rd., Cincinnati OH 45236. (715)445-4612; ext. 13430. E-mail: popularfictionawards@fwmedia.com. **Contact:** Nicole Florence. Contest for 4,000-word mss in the categories of romance, mystery/crime fiction, sci-fi/fantasy, thriller/suspense, and horror. Entries must be original, in English, unpublished, and not accepted by any other publisher at the time of submission. *Writer's Digest* retains one-time rights to the winning entries. Deadline: November 1. Charges $20. Prize: Grand Prize: $2,500, $100 of Writer's Digest Books, ; 1st Place: $500, $100 of Writer's Digest Books, and a ms critique and marketing advice from a *Writer's Digest* editor; Honoroable Mentions: promotion in *Writer's Digest*.

GARY WILSON SHORT FICTION AWARD

descant, Texas Christian University's literary journal, TCU, Box 297270, Fort Worth TX 76129. (817)257-6537. Fax: (817)257-6239. E-mail: descant@tcu.edu. Website: www.descant.tcu.edu. **Contact:** David Kuhne, editor. Offered annually for an outstanding story in an issue. Prize: $250

N THOMAS WOLFE FICTION PRIZE

North Carolina Writers' Network, P.O. Box 898, Davidson NC 28036. (919)336-293-8844. Fax: (919)929-0535. E-mail: toabbott@davidson.edu. Website: www.ncwriters.org. **Contact:** Tony Abbott, contest coordinator. Offered annually for unpublished work "to recognize a notable work of fiction—either short story or novel excerpt—while honoring one of North Carolina's best writers—Thomas Wolfe." Past judges have included Anne Tyler, Barbara Kingsolver, C. Michael Curtis and Randall Kenan. Deadline: TBA, please see website for guidelines. Charges $15 fee for members of the NC Writers' Network, $25 for non-members. Prize: $1,000 and potential publication.

TOBIAS WOLFF AWARD IN FICTION

Bellingham Review, Mail Stop 9053, Western Washington University, Bellingham WA 98225. (360)650-4863. E-mail: bhreview@wwu.edu. **Contact:** Brenda Miller. Offered annually for unpublished work. Guidelines for SASE or online. Deadline: December 1-March 15. Charges $18 entry fee for 1st entry; $10 for each additional entry. Prize: $1,000, plus publication and subscription. All finalists considered for publication. All entrants receive subscription.

WOW! WOMEN ON WRITING QUARTERLY FLASH FICTION CONTEST

Wow! Women on Writing, 740 S. Van Buren St., Suite D, Placentia CA 92870. E-mail: contestinfo@wow-womenonwriting.com. Website: www.wow-womenonwriting.com/contest.php. **Contact:** Angela Mackintosh, CEO. Contest offered quarterly. "We are open to all themes and genres, although we do encourage writers to take a close look at our literary agent guest judge for the season if you are serious about winning." Entries must be 250-500 words. Deadline: August 31, November 30, February 29, May 31. Charges $10. Prize: 1st Place: $250 cash prize,1 Year Premium-Green Writers' Markets subscription ($48 value), $25 Amazon Gift Certificate, book from our sponsor, story published on WOW! Women On Writing, interview on blog; 2nd Place: $150 cash prize, 1 Year Premium-Green Writers' Markets subscription ($48 value), $25 Amazon Gift Certificate, book from our sponsor, story published on WOW! Women On Writing, interview on blog; 3rd Place: $100 cash prize, 1 Year Premium-Green Writers' Markets Subscription ($48 value), $25 Amazon gift certificate, book from our sponsor, story published on WOW! Women On Writing, interview on blog; 15 honorable mentions: $20 gift certificate from Amazon, book from our sponsor, story title and name published on WOW!Women On Writing.

WRITER'S DIGEST SHORT SHORT STORY COMPETITION

Writer's Digest, 4700 E. Galbraith Rd., Cincinnati OH 45236. (715)445-4612; ext. 13430. **Contact:** Nicole Florence. We're looking for fiction that's bold, brilliant, and brief. Send us your best in 1,500 words or fewer. All entries must be original, unpublished, and not submitted elsewhere until the winners are announced. *Writer's Digest* reserves one-time publication rights to the 1st-25th winning entries. Deadline: December 1. Charges $20. Prize: 1st Place: $3,000; 2nd Place: $1,500; 3rd Place: $500; 4th-10th Place: $100; 11th-25th Place: $50 gift certificate for Writer's Digest Books.

WRITERS' JOURNAL ANNUAL FICTION CONTEST

Val-Tech Media, P.O. Box 394, Perham MN 56573. (218)346-7921. Fax: (218)346-7924. E-mail: writersjournal@writersjournal.com. Website: www.writersjournal.com. **Contact:** Leon Ogroske (editor@writersjournal.com). Offered annually for previously unpublished fiction. Open to any writer. Guidelines for SASE or online. Writer's name must not appear on submission. A separate cover sheet must include name of contest, title, word count, and writer's name, address, phone, and e-mail (if available). Deadline: January 30. Charges $15 reading fee. Prize: Results announced in July/August. Winners notified by mail. 1st Place: $500; 2nd Place: $200; 3rd Place: $100; plus honorable mentions. Prize-winning stories and selected honorable mentions are published in the July/August *Writers' Journal*. A list of winners is posted on website or available for SASE. Receives fewer than 350 entries.

WRITERS' JOURNAL ANNUAL HORROR/GHOST CONTEST

Val-Tech Media, P.O. Box 394, Perham MN 56573. (218)346-7921. Fax: (218)346-7924. E-mail: writersjournal@writersjournal.com. Website: www.writersjournal.com. **Contact:** Leon Ogroske. "Offered annually for previously unpublished works. Open to any writer. Guidelines for SASE or online. Guidelines available for SASE, by fax, phone, e-mail, or on website and in publication. Accepts inquiries by e-mail, phone, fax. For previously unpublished works up to 2,000 words. Cover letter should include name, address, phone, e-mail, word count, and title; just title on ms. Deadline: March 30. Charges $7 fee. Prize: 1st Place: $250; 2nd Place: $100; 3rd Place: $50; plus honorable mentions. Prize-winning stories and selected honorable mentions are published in *Writers' Journal*. Results announced in September. Winners notified by mail. For contest results, send SASE or visit website. Receives fewer than 250 entries.

WRITERS' JOURNAL ANNUAL ROMANCE CONTEST

Val-Tech Media, P.O. Box 394, Perham MN 56573. (218)346-7921. Fax: (218)346-7924. E-mail: writersjournal@writersjournal.com. **Contact:** Leon Ogroske. "Offered annually for previously unpublished works. Open to any writer. Guidelines for SASE or online." Receives fewer than 150 entries. Deadline: July 30. Charges $7 fee. Prize: 1st Place: $250; 2nd Place: $100; 3rd Place: $50; plus honorable mentions. Prize-winning stories and selected honorable mentions are published in *Writers' Journal*.

WRITERS' JOURNAL ANNUAL SHORT STORY CONTEST

Val-Tech Media, P.O. Box 394, Perham MN 56573. (218)346-7921. Fax: (218)346-7924. E-mail: writersjournal@writersjournal.com. Website: www.writersjournal.com. **Contact:** Leon Ogroske. "Offered annually for previously unpublished short stories. Open to any writer. Guidelines for SASE or online." Receives fewer than 250 entries. Deadline: May 30. Charges $10 reading fee. Prize: 1st Place: $350; 2nd Place: $125; 3rd Place: $75; plus honorable mentions. Prize-winning stories and selected honorable mentions are published in *Writers' Journal*.

N ZONE 3 FICTION AWARD

ZONE 3, Austin Peay State University, P.O. Box 4565, Clarksville TN 37044. (931)221-7031. Fax: (931)221-7149. E-mail: wallacess@apsu.edu. Website: www.apsu.edu/zone3/. **Contact:** Susan Wallace, Managing Editor. Contest offered annually for an unpublished story. Open to any fiction writer. Send us your best story." No deadline. Charges $10 fee includes 1-year subscription. Prize: $250.

General

THE ANISFIELD-WOLF BOOK AWARDS

The Cleveland Foundation, 700 W. St. Clair Ave., #414, Cleveland OH 44113. **Contact:** Laura Scharf. "The Anisfield-Wolf Book Award annually honors books which contribute to our understanding of racism or our appreciation of the diversity of human culture published during the year of the award." Any work addressing issues of racial bias or human diversity may qualify. Only books written in English and published in the preceding calendar year are eligible. Submit 5 copies of the book and an entry form. No materials will be returned. Guidelines for SASE or online. Deadline: December 31. Prize: $10,000.

ARTSLINK PROJECTS AWARD

CEC Artslink, 435 Hudson St., 8th Floor, New York NY 10014. (212)643-1985, ext. 23. Fax: (212)643-1996. E-mail: tmiller@cecartslink.org. Website: www.cecartslink.org. **Contact:** Tamalyn Miller, program director. "Offered annually to enable artists of all media to work in Central and Eastern Europe, Russia, Central Asia and the Caucasus with colleagues there on collaborative projects. Check website for deadline and other information." Prize: Prize: up to $10,000.

AUSTRALIAN CHRISTIAN BOOK OF THE YEAR AWARD

Australian Christian Literature Society, c/o SPCK-Australia, P.O. Box 198, Forest Hill Victoria 3131 Australia. E-mail: acls@spcka.org.au. **Contact:** Book of the Year Coordinator. "Annual contest for an Australian Christian book published between April 1 and March 31. Book must be submitted by a publisher." Deadline: March 31. Charges $50 per title.

THE BOARDMAN TASKER AWARD FOR MOUNTAIN LITERATURE

The Boardman Tasker Charitable Trust, Pound House, Llangennith, Swansea West Glamorgan SA3 1JQ United Kingdom. Phone/Fax: (44)(179)238-6215. E-mail: margaretbody@lineone.net. **Contact:** Margaret Body. "Offered annually to reward a work of nonfiction or fiction, in English or in translation, which has made an outstanding contribution to mountain literature. Books must be published in the UK between November 1 of previous year and October 31 of year of the prize. Writers may obtain information, but entry is by publishers only. No restriction of nationality, but work must be published or distributed in the UK. Guidelines for SASE or online." Deadline: August 15. Prize: £3,000.

DAFOE BOOK PRIZE

J.W. Dafoe Foundation, 351 University College, University of Manitoba, Winnipeg MB R3T 2M8 Canada. **Contact:** Dr. James Fergusson. The Dafoe Book Prize was established to honor John Dafoe, editor of the *Winnipeg Free Press* from 1900 to 1944, and is awarded each year to the book that best contributes to our understanding of Canada and/or its relations abroad by a Canadian or author in residence. Books must be published January-December of previous publishing year — i.e., 2010 Award is for books published in 2009. Co-authored books are eligible, but not edited books consisting of chapters from many different authors. Submit 4 copies of book. Authors must be Canadian citizens or landed immigrants. Deadline: December 6. Charges $50 per entry is required. Prize: $10,000. Judged by board members and academics.

THE DEBUT DAGGER

Crime Writers' Association, New Writing Competition, P.O. Box 273, Borehamwood Herts WD6 2XA England. Website: www.thecwa.co.uk. **Contact:** L. Evans. "An annual competition for unpublished crime writers. Submit the opening 3,000 words of a crime novel, plus a 500-1,000 word synopsis of its continuance. Open to any writer who has not had a novel commercially published in any genre." Entries will not be returned. Charges fees vary each year. Prize: See website for details and for prize information.

ROSALIE FLEMING MEMORIAL HUMOR PRIZE

National League of American Pen Women, The Webhallow House, 1544 Sweetwood Dr., Broadmoor Village CA 94015-2029. E-mail: pennobhill@aol.com. Website: www.soulmakingcontest.us. **Contact:** Eileen Malone. "Make judge Mary Eastham laugh in 2,500 words or less. Must be original and unpublished. Any form (poem, story, essay, etc.) is acceptable. Only 1 piece allowed/entry. Indicate category on first page. Identify only with 3 × 5 card." Deadline: November 30. Charges $5/entry (make checks payable to NLAPW, Nob Hill Branch). Prize: 1st Place: $100; 2nd Place: $50; 3rd Place: $45.

THE JANE GESKE AWARD

Prairie Schooner, 201 Andrews Hall, P.O. Box 880334, Lincoln NE 68588-0334. (402)472-0911. Fax: (402)472-9771. E-mail: jenglehardt2@unl.edu. **Contact:** Hilda Raz. Offered annually for work published in *Prairie Schooner* in the previous year. Prize: $250.

THE GLENNA LUSCHEI PRAIRIE SCHOONER AWARDS

Prairie Schooner, 201 Andrews Hall, P.O. Box 880334, Lincoln NE 68588-0334. (402)472-0911. Fax: (402)472-9771. E-mail: jengelhardt2@unl.edu. **Contact:** Hilda Raz. "Annual awards (usually 4-6) for work published in *Prairie Schooner* in the previous year." Prize: $250.

INDEPENDENT PUBLISHER BOOK AWARDS

Jenkins Group/Independent Publisher Online, 1129 Woodmere Ave., Ste. B, Traverse City MI 49686. (231)933-4954, ext. 1011. Fax: (231)933-0448. E-mail: jimb@bookpublishing.com. **Contact:** Jim Barnes. "The Independent Publisher Book Awards were conceived as a broad-based, unaffiliated awards program open to all members of the independent publishing industry. The staff at *Independent Publisher* magazine saw the need to bring increased recognition to the thousands of exemplary independent, university, and self-published titles produced each year. The IPPY Awards reward those who exhibit the courage, innovation, and creativity to bring about change in the world of publishing. Independent spirit and expertise comes from publishers of all areas and budgets, and we judge books with that in mind. Entries will be accepted in 67 categories. Open to any published writer." Offered annually for books published between January 1 and December 31. Deadline: March 20. Charges $85 until November 15; $80 until January 15; $85 until April 1. Prize: Gold, silver and bronze medals for each category; foil seals available to all. Judged by a panel of experts representing the fields of design, writing, bookselling, library, and reviewing.

MLA PRIZE IN UNITED STATES LATINA & LATINO AND CHICANA & CHICANO LITERARY AND CULTURAL STUDIES

Modern Language Association of America, 26 Broadway, 3rd Floor, New York NY 10004-1789. (646)576-5141. Fax: (646)458-0030. E-mail: awards@mla.org. **Contact:** Coordinator of Book Prizes. Award for an outstanding scholarly study in any language of United States Latina & Latino and Chicana & Chicano literature or culture. Open to current MLA members only. Authors or publishers may submit titles. Deadline: May 1. Prize: A cash award, and a certificate to be presented at the Modern Language Association's annual convention in January.

OHIOANA WALTER RUMSEY MARVIN GRANT

Ohioana Library Association, 274 E. First Ave., Suite 300, Columbus OH 43201. (614)466-3831. Fax: (614)728-6974. E-mail: ohioana@ohioana.org. **Contact:** Linda Hengst. "Offered annually to encourage young writers; open to writers age 30 or under who have not published a book. Entrants must have been born in Ohio or have lived in Ohio for at least 5 years. Enter 1-6 pieces of prose totaling 10-60 pages (double space, 12 pt. font)." Deadline: January 31. Prize: $1,000.

PEN CENTER USA LITERARY AWARDS

PEN Center USA, P.O. Box 6037, Beverly Hills CA 90212. (424)258-1180. E-mail: awards@penusa.org. **Contact:** Literary Awards Coordinator. Offered for work published or produced in the previous calendar year. Open to writers living west of the Mississippi River. Award categories: drama, screenplay, teleplay, journalism. Guidelines for SASE or download from website. Deadline: 4 copies must be received by January 31. Charges $35. Prize: $1,000.

DAVID RAFFELOCK AWARD FOR PUBLISHING EXCELLENCE

National Writers Association, 10940 S. Parker Rd., #508, Parker CO 80134. (303)841-0246. Fax: (303)841-2607. E-mail: natlwritersassn@hotmail.com. Website: www.nationalwriters.com. **Contact:** Sandy Whelchel. "Contest is offered annually for books published the previous year." Its purpose is to assist published authors in marketing their works and to reward outstanding published works. Deadline: May 15. Charges $100 fee. Prize; Publicity tour, including airfare, valued at $5,000.

WILLIAM SANDERS SCARBOROUGH PRIZE

Modern Language Association of America, 26 Broadway, 3rd Floor, New York NY 10004-1789. (646)576-5141. Fax: (646)458-0030. E-mail: awards@mla.org. **Contact:** Coordinator of book prizes. Offered annually for work published in the previous year. Given in honor of a distinguished man of letters and the first African-American member of the Modern Language Association, this prize will be awarded to an outstanding scholarly study of black American literature or culture. Open to MLA members and nonmembers. Authors or publishers may enter titles. Guidelines for SASE or by e-mail. Deadline: May 1. Prize: A cash award, and a certificate to be presented at the Modern Language Association's annual convention in January.

BYRON CALDWELL SMITH AWARD

The University of Kansas, Hall Center for the Humanities, 900 Sunnyside Ave., Lawrence KS 66045. (785)864-4798. E-mail: vbailey@ku.edu. **Contact:** Victor Baily, director. Offered in odd years. To qualify, applicants must live or be employed in Kansas and have written an outstanding book published within the previous 2 calendar years. Translations are eligible. Guidelines for SASE or online. Deadline: March 1. Prize: $2,000.

TEXAS INSTITUTE OF LETTERS AWARD FOR MOST SIGNIFICANT SCHOLARLY BOOK

The Texas Institute of Letters, (214)363-7253. E-mail: dpayne@mail.smu.edu. "Offered annually for submissions published January 1-December 31 of previous year to recognize the writer of the book making the most important contribution to knowledge. Writer must have been born in Texas, have lived in the state at least 2 consecutive years at some time, or the subject matter of the book should be associated with the state. See website for guidelines." Generally one week after January 1. Prize: $2.500.

THE WRITERS' TRUST NOTABLE AUTHOR AWARD

The Writers' Trust of Canada, 90 Richmond St. E., Suite 200, Toronto ON M5C 1P1 Canada. (416)504-8222. Fax: (416)504-9090. E-mail: info@writerstrust.com. **Contact:** Amanda Hopkins. "The Writers' Trust Notable Author Award is presented annually at The Writers' Trust Awards Event, held in Toronto each Fall, to a Canadian writer for a body of work in hope of continued contribution to the richness of Canadian literature. Open to Canadian citizens and permanent residents only." Prize: $25,000.

FRED WHITEHEAD AWARD FOR DESIGN OF A TRADE BOOK

Texas Institute of Letters, 6335 W. Northwest Hwy., #618, Dallas TX 75225. (214)363-7253. E-mail: dpayne@smu.edu. **Contact:** Darwin Payne. Offered annually for the best design for a trade book. Open to Texas residents or those who have lived in Texas for 2 consecutive years. See website for guidelines. Deadline: January 3. Prize: $750.

Journalism

AMY WRITING AWARDS

The Amy Foundation, P.O. Box 16091, Lansing MI 48901. (517)323-6233. Fax: (517)321-2572. E-mail: amyfoundtn@aol.com. Estab. 1985. "Offered annually to recognize creative, skillful writing that applies biblical principles. Submitted articles must be published in a secular, non-religious publication (either printed or online) and must be reinforced with at least one passage of scripture. The article must have been published between January 1 and December 31 of the current calendar year." Deadline: January 31. Prize: 1st Prize: $10,000; 2nd Prize: $5,000; 3rd Prize: $4,000; 4th Prize: $3,000; 5th Prize: $2,000; and 10 prizes of $1,000.

MIKE BERGER AWARD

Columbia University Graduate School of Journalism, 2950 Broadway, Room #709A, New York NY 10027. (212)854-6468. Fax: (212)854-3800. E-mail: lsr21@columbia.edu. Website: www.jrn.columbia.edu. **Contact:** Lisa S. Redd, program coordinator. "Offered annually honoring in-depth and enterprising reporting on individuals in the tradition of the late Meyer Mike Berger. Newspaper, magazine, and online reporters across the country are eligible for this award. Journalists who report in a foreign language should submit copies of original stories with English translations. Articles must have been published or available online between February 2010 and January 2011." Deadline: March 8. Charges No fee. Prize: $1,500 award and certificat from Columbia, will be conferred at the Journalism School graduation ceremony in May. Traveling expenses to New York reimbursed. Judged by members of the faculty of the Columbia University Graduate School of Journalism.

HEYWOOD BROUN AWARD

The Newspaper Guild-CWA, 501 Third St. NW, Washington DC 20001-2797. (202)434-7177. Fax: (202)434-1472. E-mail: azipser@cwa-union.org. **Contact:** Andy Zipser. Offered annually for works published the previous year. This annual competition is intended to encourage and recognize individual journalistic achievement by members of the working media, particularly if it helps right a wrong or correct an injustice. First consideration will be given to entries on behalf of individuals or teams of no more than two. Guidelines for SASE or online. Deadline: Last Friday in January. Prize: $5,000 and plaque.

CONSUMER JOURNALISM AWARD

National Press Club, General Manager's Office, National Press Bldg., 529 14th St. NW, Washington DC 20045. (202)662-8744. Fax: (202)662-7512. E-mail: jbooze@npcpress.org. **Contact:** Joann Booze. "Offered annually to recognize excellence in reporting on consumer topics in the following categories: newspapers, periodicals, television, and radio. Guidelines available online." Deadline: April 1. Prize: $750 for each category.

ANN COTTRELL FREE ANIMAL REPORTING AWARD

National Press Club, General Manager's Office, National Press Bldg., 529 14th St. NW, Washington DC 20045. (202)662-8744. Fax: (202)662-7512. E-mail: jbooze@npcpress.org. Website: npc.press.org. **Contact:** Joann Booze. "Award honors excellence in reporting about animals. Established by the family of journalist and longtime Press Club member Ann Cottrell Free, who wrote extensively about animals and their welfare, this prize recognizes serious work by journalists that informs and educates the public about threats facing animals." Guidelines available online. Charges $25 entry fee required for non-NPC members. Prize: $750.

JOAN M. FRIEDENBERG ONLINE JOURNALISM AWARD

National Press Club, General Manager's Office, National Press Bldg., 529 14th St. NW, Washington DC 20045. (202)662-8744. Fax: (202)662-7512. E-mail: jbooze@npcpress.org. Website: npc.press.org. **Contact:** Joann Booze. Offered annually in memory of Joan M. Friedenberg "for original reporting and the use of online technology in order to provide a thorough and graphically attractive report. Judges especially interested in the use of multimedia." Deadline: April 1. Prize: $750.

EDWIN M. HOOD AWARD FOR DIPLOMATIC CORRESPONDENCE

General Manager's Office, National Press Club, National Press Bldg., 529 14th St. NW, Washington DC 20045. (202)662-8744. E-mail: jbooze@npcpress.org. Website: npc.press.org. **Contact:** Joann Booze. "Offered annually to recognize excellence in reporting on diplomatic and foreign policy issues. Categories: print, online, and broadcast. Guidelines available online." Deadline: April 1. Prize: $750 in each category.

SANDY HUME MEMORIAL AWARD FOR EXCELLENCE IN POLITICAL JOURNALISM

National Press Club, General Manager's Office, National Press Bldg., 529 14th St. NW, Washington DC 20045. (202)662-8744. Fax: (202)662-7512. E-mail: jbooze@npcpress.org. Website: npc.press.org. **Contact:** Joann Booze. "Offered annually for work published in the previous calendar year. This award honors excellence and objectivity in political coverage by reporters 34 years old or younger." Deadline: April 1. Charges $25 entry fee required for non-NPC members. Prize: $750.

ANSON JONES, M.D. AWARD

Texas Medical Association, 401 W. 15th St., Austin TX 78701-1680. (512)370-1381. Fax: (512)370-1629. E-mail: brent.annear@texmed.org. **Contact:** Brent Annear, media relations manager. "Offered annually to Texas news media for excellence in communicating health information to the public. Open only to Texas general - interest media for work published or aired in Texas during the previous calendar year. Guidelines posted online." Deadline: January 15. Prize: $1,000 for winners in each of the categories.

LIVINGSTON AWARDS FOR YOUNG JOURNALISTS

Mollie Parnis Livingston Foundation, Wallace House, 620 Oxford, Ann Arbor MI 48104. (734)998-7575. Fax: (734)998-7979. E-mail: livingstonawards@umich.edu. **Contact:** Charles Eisendrath. Offered annually for journalism published January 1 - December 31 the previous year to recognize and further develop the abilities of young journalists. Includes print, online, and broadcast. Guidelines available online. Open to journalists who are 34 years or younger as of December 31 of previous year and whose work appears in US-controlled print or broadcast media. Deadline: February 1. Prize: $10,000 each for local reporting, national reporting, and international reporting. Judges include Christiane Amanpour, Ken Auletta, Dean Baquet, Tom Brokaw, Charles Gibson, Ellen Goodman, Clarence Page, Anna Quindlen.

FRANK LUTHER MOTT-KAPPA TAU ALPHA RESEARCH AWARD IN JOURNALISM

University of Missouri School of Journalism, 76 Gannett Hall, Columbia MO 65211-1200. (573)882-7685. E-mail: umcjourkta@missouri.edu. **Contact:** Dr. Keith Sanders, exec. dir., Kappa Tau Alpha. "Offered annually for best researched book in mass communication. Submit 6 copies; no forms required." Deadline: December 9. Prize: $1,000.

O. HENRY AWARD FOR MAGAZINE JOURNALISM

The Texas Institute of Letters, 5307 Preston Haven Dr., Dallas TX 75229. **Contact:** Darwin Payne. "Offered annually for work published January 1-December 31 of previous year to recognize the best-written work of journalism appearing in a magazine or weekly newspaper. Judged by a panel chosen by the TIL Council. Writer must have been born in Texas, have lived in Texas for at least 2 consecutive years at some time, or the subject matter of the work should be associated with Texas. See website for guidelines." Deadline: January 9. Prize: $1,000.

ALICIA PATTERSON JOURNALISM FELLOWSHIP

Alicia Patterson Foundation, 1090 Vermont Ave. NW, Suite 1000, Washington DC 20005. (202)393-5995. Fax: (301)951-8512. E-mail: director@aliciapatterson.org. **Contact:** Margaret Engel. "Offered annually for 6-8 full-time print journalists or photojournalists 6 months or one year of in-depth research and reporting. Applicants must have 5 years of professional print journalism experience and be US citizens. Fellows write 4 magazine-length pieces for the *Alicia Patterson Reporter*, a quarterly magazine, during their fellowship year. Fellows must take 6-12 months' leave from their jobs, but may do other freelance articles during the year. Write, call, fax, or check website for applications." Deadline: October 1. Prize: $40,000 stipend for calendar year; $20,000 for 6 months.

DANIEL PEARL AWARDS FOR OUTSTANDING INTERNATIONAL INVESTIGATIVE REPORTING

International Consortium of Investigative Journalists, A Project of the Center for Public Integrity, 910 17th St. NW, 7th Floor, Washington DC 20006. (202)466-1300. Fax: (202)466-1101. E-mail: sraetz@icij.org. Website: www.publicintegrity.org/investigations/icij. **Contact:** Marina Walker Guevara, Deputy Director. Offered biennially for work produced in print, broadcast, and online media. The story or series must involve reporting in at least two countries and must have been first published or broadcast in general information media between January 1, 2008 and December 31, 2009. Deadline: January 31, 2010. Prize: Offers Two $5,000 first prizes; one to a U.S.-based reporter or news organization and the other to a non-U.B.-based journalist or news organization.

THE MADELINE DANE ROSS AWARD

Overseas Press Club of America, 40 West 45th Street, New York NY 10036. (212)626-9220. Fax: (212)626-9210. E-mail: sonya@opcofamerica.org. **Contact:** Sonya Fry, Executive Director. "Offered annually for best international reporting in the print medium showing a concern for the human condition. Work must be published by US-based publications or broadcast. Printable application available online." Deadline: Late January; date changes each year. Charges $175 fee. Prize: $1,000 and certificate.

ARTHUR ROWSE AWARD FOR PRESS CRITICISM

General Manager's Office, National Press Club, National Press Bldg., 529 14th St. NW, Washington DC 20045. (202)662-8744. Website: www.npc.press.org. Offered annually for work published or broadcast the previous calendar year. This award, sponsored by former *US News & World Report* reporter Arthur Rowse, "honors excellence in examining the role and work of the news media. All entries must focus on criticism of journalistic practices or reporting on the industry, and must encourage responsible media behavior." Categories: 1. newspapers, magazines, newsletters, and online. 2. Broadcast. Submit up to 5 articles or broadcasts; must be accompanied by a letter explaining the significance of the work and any subsequent actions resulting from its publication or airing. Deadline: April 1. Charges $25 entry fee required for non-NPC members. Prize: $1,000 in each category.

JOSEPH D. RYLE AWARD FOR EXCELLENCE IN WRITING ON THE PROBLEMS OF GERIATRICS

National Press Club, General Manager's Office, National Press Bldg., 529 14th St. NW, Washington DC 20045. (202)662-8744. Fax: (202)662-7512. E-mail: jbooze@npcpress.org. Website: npc.press.org. **Contact:** Joann Booze. Offered annually for work published in the previous year. This award honors excellence and objectivity in coverage of the problems faced by the elderly. Deadline: April 1. Charges $25 entry fee required for non-NPC members. Prize: Prize: $750.

SCIENCE IN SOCIETY AWARDS

National Association of Science Writers, Inc., P.O. Box 7905, Berkeley CA 94707. (510)647-9500. E-mail: director@nasw.org. Website: www.nasw.org. **Contact:** Tinsley Davis. Estab. 1972. Offered annually for investigative or interpretive reporting about the sciences and their impact on society. Categories: books, commentary and opinions, science reporting, and science reporting with a local or regional focus. Material may be a single article or broadcast, or a series. Works must have been first published or broadcast in North America between June 1 and May 31 of the previous year. Deadline: February 1. Prize: $2,500, and a certificate of recognition in each category.

SCIENCE IN SOCIETY JOURNALISM AWARDS

Canadian Science Writers' Association, P.O. Box 75, Station A, Toronto ON M5W 1A2 Canada. (800)796-8595. E-mail: awards@sciencewriters.ca. Website: www.sciencewriters.ca. Offered annually for work published/aired during the previous year to recognize outstanding contributions to journalism in print and electronic media (3 newspaper, 3 TV, 3 radio). Each material becomes property of CSWA. Does not return mss. Open to Canadian citizens or residents of Canada. Deadline: February 1. Charges Entry fee: $25 members, $50 non-members. Prize: $1,000 and a plaque.

STANLEY WALKER AWARD FOR NEWSPAPER JOURNALISM

The Texas Institute of Letters, 6335 W. Northwest Hwy., #618, Dallas TX 75225. (214)363-7253. E-mail: dpayne@smu.edu. **Contact:** Darwin Payne. Offered annually for work published January 1-December 31 of previous year to recognize the best writing appearing in a daily newspaper. Writer must have been born in Texas, have lived in the state for 2 consecutive years at some time, or the subject matter of the article must be associated with the state. See website for guidelines. Deadline: First week of January. Prize: $1,000.

Multiple Writing Areas

ABILENE WRITERS GUILD ANNUAL CONTEST

Abilene Writers Guild, P.O. Box 2562, Abilene TX 79604. "Offered annually for unpublished work in ten categories. All rights remain with the writer." Deadline: October 1 - November 30. Charges $10 for each novel entry and $5 each for all other category entries. Prize: Up to $100 in each category. Judged by different professional writers and editors each year.

Tips "Details available on our website after August 1st."

Contests & Awards

THE ALLEGHENY REVIEW LITERATURE & ART AWARDS

The Allegheny Review, Allegheny College, Box 32, Allegheny College, Meadville PA 16335. E-mail: review@allegheny.edu. **Contact:** Senior Editor. Offered annually for unpublished works of poetry, fiction, creative nonfiction, and art. Open to currently enrolled undergraduate students. The purpose is to foster an appreciation of quality undergraduate literature. Deadline: January 15. Charges $5/entry. Prize: $250 and guaranteed publication.

Tips "Revise, revise, revise! We're always in need of quality literature."

AMERICAN MARKETS NEWSLETTER COMPETITION

American Markets Newsletter, 1974 46th Ave., San Francisco CA 94116. E-mail: sheila.oconnor@juno.com. **Contact:** Sheila O'Connor. "Accepts fiction and nonfiction up to 2,000 words. Entries are eligible for cash prizes and all entries are eligible for worldwide syndication whether they win or not. Here's how it works: Send us your double-spaced manuscripts with your story/article title, byline, word count, and address on the first page above your article/story's first paragraph (no need for separate cover page). There is no limit to the number of entries you may send." Deadline: December 31 and July 31. Charges $12 for 1 entry; $15 for 2 entries; $20 for 3 entries; $25 for 4 entries; $30 for 5 entries. Prize: 1st Place: $300; 2nd Place: $100; 3rd Place: $50. Judged by a panel of independent judges.

ANNUAL U.S. MARITIME LITERATURE AWARDS

P.O. Box 264, Fulton TX 78358. E-mail: maritimeliterature@yahoo.com. **Contact:** Captain Richard Lamb. Accepts nonfiction maritime books published in the previous calendar year in these divisions: young readers (audiences 12 and under); adult (audiences 13 and above); foreign country (published outside the U.S.). Publishers are welcome to submit nominations. Deadline: January 1-May 31. Prize: Glass-etched trophy. The winner's names are forwarded to The White House and First Family.

ARIZONA AUTHORS' ASSOCIATION ANNUAL NATIONAL LITERARY CONTEST AND BOOK AWARDS

Arizona Authors' Association, 6145 W. Echo Ln., Glendale AZ 85302. (623)847-9343. E-mail: info@azauthors.com. Website: www.azauthors.com. Offered annually for previously unpublished poetry, short stories, essays, novels, and articles. New awards for published books in fiction, anthology, nonfiction, and children's. Winners announced at an award banquet in Glendale in November, and short pieces and excerpts published in *Arizona Literary Magazine*. Deadline: July 1. Charges $15 fee for poetry; $20 for short stories and essays; $30 for unpublished novels and published books. Prize: $100 and publication, and/or feature in the *Arizona Literary Magazine*. Additional prizes awarded by Five Star Publications.

N ART AFFAIR WRITING CONTEST

Art Affair, P.O. Box 54302, Oklahoma City OK 73154. Website: www.shadetreecreations.com. **Contact:** Barbara Shepherd. "Fiction and poems must be unpublished. Multiple entries accepted and may be mailed in the same packet. For (general) Short Story, double-space in 12-point font (put page and word count in upper right-hand corner of first page—5,000 word limit. Include cover page with writer's name, address, phone number, and title of story. For Western Short Story, follow same directions but type 'Western' on cover page. For Poetry, submit original poems on any subject, in any style, no more than 60 lines (put line count in the upper right-hand corner of first page). Include cover page with poet's name, address, phone number, and title. Do not include SASE; mss will not be returned." To encourage new and established writers and to publicly recognize them for their efforts. Open to any writer or poet. Oct. 1 (every year). Charges $5/each short story, each western short story; $3/each poem. Make check payable to Art Affair. Prize: Short Story: 1st Prize: $50; 2nd Prize: $25; 3rd Prize: $15. Western Short Story: 1st Prize: $50; 2nd Prize: $25; 3rd Prize: $15. Poetry: 1st Prize: $40; 2nd Prize: $25; 3rd Prize: $15 (all winners also receive certificates. Additional certificates for Honorable Mentions will be awarded at discretion of the judges). Winners' list will be published on our website in Dec. Short Story, Western Short Story, Poetry. Judged by highly-qualified and professional judges—different each year (blind judging).

Tips "Guidelines and entry forms available for SASE and on website."

ATLANTIC WRITING COMPETITION FOR UNPUBLISHED MANUSCRIPTS

Writers' Federation of Nova Scotia, 1113 Marginal Rd., Halifax NS B3H 4P7. (902)423-8116. Fax: (902)422-0881. E-mail: talk@writers.ns.ca. Website: www.writers.ns.ca. **Contact:** Nate Crawford, program coordinator. Estab. 1975. "Annual contest for beginners to try their hand in a number of categories: novel, short story, poetry, writing for younger children, writing for juvenile/young adult. Only 1 entry/category is allowed. Established writers are also eligible, but must work in an area that's new to them.

Because our aim is to help Atlantic Canadian writers grow, judges return written comments when the competition is concluded. Anyone residing in the Atlantic Provinces for at least 6 months prior to the contest deadline is eligible to enter." Deadline: First Friday in December. Charges $35 fee for novel ($30 for WFNS members); $25 fee for all other categories ($20 for WFNS members). Prize: Novel—1st Place: $200; 2nd Place: $150; 3rd Place: $75. Writing for Younger Children and Juvenile/Young Adult—1st Place: $150; 2nd Place: $75; 3rd Place: $50. Poetry and Short Story—1st Place: $150; 2nd Place: $75; 3rd Place: $50. Judged by a team of 2-3 professional writers, editors, booksellers, librarians, or teachers.

BURNABY WRITERS' SOCIETY CONTEST

E-mail: info@bws.bc.ca. **Contact:** Eileen Kernaghan. "Offered annually for unpublished work. Open to all residents of British Columbia. Categories vary from year to year. Send SASE for current rules. For complete guidelines see website or burnabywritersnews.blogspot.com." Purpose is to encourage talented writers in all genres. Deadline: May 31. Charges $5 fee. Prize: 1st Place: $200; 2nd Place: $100; 3rd Place: $50; and public reading.

CANCER COUNCIL VICTORIA ARTS AWARDS

Cancer Council Victoria, 1 Rathdowne St., Carlton VIC 3053 Australia. (61)(3)0065-6585. Fax: (61)(3)9635-5240. E-mail: arts.awards@cancervic.org.au. Website: www.cancervic.org.au/artsawards. Deadline: April 7. Charges $10. Judged by high-profile and well-respected artists/specialists.

THE CITY OF VANCOUVER BOOK AWARD

Cultural Services Department, 453 W. 12th Ave., Vancouver BC V5Y 1V4 Canada. (604)871-6434. Fax: (604)871-6005. E-mail: marnie.rice@vancouver.ca. Website: vancouver.ca/bookaward. "Offered annually for books published in the previous year which exhibit excellence in the categories of content, illustration, design, and format. The book must contribute significantly to the appreciation and understanding of the city of Vancouver and heighten awareness of 1 or more of the following: Vancouver's history, the city's unique character, or achievements of the city's residents. The book may be fiction, nonfiction, poetry, or drama written for adults or children, and may deal with any aspects of the city—history, geography, current affairs, or the arts. Guidelines online." Prize: $2,000.

COLORADO BOOK AWARDS

Colorado Center for the Book, 1490 Lafayette St., Suite 101, Denver CO 80218. (303)894-7951, ext. 21. Fax: (303)864-9361. E-mail: long@coloradohumanities.org. **Contact:** Margaret Coval, exec. dir., or Jennifer Long, Prog. Adjudicator. Offered annually for work published by December of previous year. "The purpose is to champion all Colorado authors, editors, illustrators, and photographers, and in particular, to honor the award winners raising the profiles of both their work and Colorado as a state whose people promote and support reading, writing, and literacy through books. The categories are generally: children's literature, young adult and juvenile literature, fiction, genre fiction (romance, mystery/thriller, science fiction/fantasy, historical), biography, history, anthology, poetry, pictorial, graphic novel/comic, creative nonfiction, and general nonfiction, as well as other categories as determined each year. Open to authors who reside or have resided in Colorado." Deadline: January 15, 2010. Charges $50 fee.

CORDON D 'OR - GOLD RIBBON ANNUAL INTERNATIONAL CULINARY ACADEMY AWARDS

The 'Accolade of the 21st Century', Cordon d 'Or - Gold Ribbon Inc., P.O. Box 40868, St. Petersburg FL 33743. (727)347-2437. E-mail: cordondor@aol.com. Website: www.goldribboncookery.com. **Contact:** Noreen Kinney. "Contest promotes recognition of food authors, writers, and culinary magazines and websites, food stylists and food photographers and other professionals in the culinary field. See website: www.cordondorcuisine.com for full details. Open to any writer. All categories can be found on the website. The only criteria is that all entries must be in the English language." Deadline: Nov. 30. Charges Entry fee: $100 per entrant. Entrants can enter as many categories as they wish in the contest. Prize: Cordon d 'Or - Gold Ribbon Crystal Globe Trophies (with stands and engraved marble bases) will be presented to winners in each category. An outstanding winner chosen by the judges from among all entries will also win a cash award of $1,000. Judged by professionals in the fields covered in the awards program.

THE CRUCIBLE POETRY AND FICTION COMPETITION

Crucible, Barton College, College Station, Wilson NC 27893. (252)399-6344. E-mail: crucible@barton.edu. **Contact:** Terrence L. Grimes, editor. "Offered annually for unpublished mss. Fiction is limited to 8,000 words; poetry is limited to 5 poems. Guidelines online or by email or for SASE. All submissions should be electronic." Deadline: May 2. Prize: 1st Place: $150; 2nd Place: $100 (for both poetry and fiction. Winners are also published in *Crucible*. Judged by in-house editorial board.

CWW ANNUAL AWARDS COMPETITION

Council for Wisconsin Writers, Website: www.wisconsinwriters.org/index.htm. **Contact:** Geoff Gilpin; Marilyn Taylor; Mary Wehner, awards co-chairs; and Carolyn Washburne, Christopher Latham Sholes Award and Major Achievement Award Co-Chair. Offered annually for work published by Wisconsin writers the previous calendar year. Ten awards: major/life achievement; short fiction; short nonfiction; nonfiction book; poetry book; fiction book; children's literature; Lorine Niedecher Poetry Award; outstanding service to Wisconsin writers; Essay Award for Young Writers. Open to Wisconsin residents. Guidelines on website. Rules and entry form on website. Deadline: January 31. Charges $15 nonrefundable fee. Prize: $500 and a certificate. This year only the Essay Award for Young Writers prize will be $250. Winners in all categories except the student essay contest receive a week at the Edenfred Residence for the Creative Arts.

DANA AWARDS IN THE NOVEL, SHORT FICTION AND POETRY

www.danaawards.com, 200 Fosseway Dr., Greensboro NC 27445. (336)644-8028. E-mail: danaawards@pipeline.com. **Contact:** Mary Elizabeth Parker, chair. Three awards offered annually for unpublished work written in English. Purpose is monetary award for work that has not been previously published or received monetary award, but will accept work published simply for friends and family. Works previously published online are not eligible. No work accepted by or for persons under 16 for any of the 3 awards. Awards: **Novel**—For the first 50 pages of a novel completed or in progress. **Fiction**—Short fiction (no memoirs) up to 10,000 words. **Poetry**—For best group of 5 poems based on excellence of all 5 (no light verse, no single poem over 100 lines). Deadline: October 31 (postmarked). Charges $25 per novel entry; $15 per short fiction entry; $15 per poetry entry. Prize: $1,000 for each of the 3 awards.

EATON LITERARY AGENCY'S ANNUAL AWARDS PROGRAM

Eaton Literary Agency, P.O. Box 49795, Sarasota FL 34230. (941)366-6589. Fax: (941)365-4679. E-mail: eatonlit@aol.com. Website: www.eatonliterary.com. **Contact:** Richard Lawrence, V.P. "Offered annually for unpublished mss." Deadline: March 31 (mss under 10,000 words); August 31 (mss over 10,000 words). Prize: $2,500 (over 10,000 words); $500 (under 10,000 words). Judged by an independent agency in conjunction with some members of Eaton's staff.

N ERIC HOFFER AWARD

Hopewell Publications, LLC, Annual contest for previously published books., P.O. Box 11, Titusville NJ 08560-0011. Fax: (609)964-1718. E-mail: info@hopepubs.com. Website: www.hofferaward.com. **Contact:** Christopher Klim, chair. "Annual contest for previously published books. Recognizes excellence in independent publishing in many unique categories: Art (titles capture the experience, execution, or demonstration of the arts); General Fiction (nongenre-specific fiction); Commercial Fiction (genre-specific fiction); Children (titles for young children); Young Adult (titles aimed at the juvenile and teen markets); Culture (titles demonstrating the human or world experience); Memoir (titles relating to personal experience); Business (titles with application to today's business environment and emerging trends); Reference (titles from traditional and emerging reference areas); Home (titles with practical applications to home or home-related issues, including family); Health (titles promoting physical, mental, and emotional well-being); Self-help/spiritual (titles involving the mind and spirit, including religion); Legacy (titles over 2 years of age that hold particular relevance to any subject matter or form). Open to any writer of published work within the last 2 years." "This contest recognizes excellence in independent publishing in many unique categories: Art, General Fiction, Commercial Fiction, Children, Young Adult, Culture, Memoir, Business, Reference, Home, Health, Self-help/spiritual, and Legacy (fiction & nonfiction)." January 21. Charges $45. Prize: $1,500, press/media, and international coverage in *The US Review of Books & Best New Writing*. Judges include authors, editors, agents, publishers, book producers, artists, experienced category readers, and health and business professionals.

THE VIRGINIA FAULKNER AWARD FOR EXCELLENCE IN WRITING

Prairie Schooner, 201 Andrews Hall, P.O. Box 880334, Lincoln NE 68588-0334. (402)472-0911. Fax: (402)472-9771. E-mail: jengelhardt2@unl.edu. **Contact:** Hilda Raz. "Offered annually for work published in *Prairie Schooner* in the previous year." Prize: $1,000.

FREEFALL SHORT FICTION AND POETRY CONTEST

Freefall Literary Society of Calgary, 922 9th Ave. SE, Calgary AB T2G 0S4 Canada. (403)264-4730. E-mail: freefallmagazine@yahoo.ca. **Contact:** Lynn C. Fraser, Managing Editor. Offered annually for unpublished work in the categories of poetry (5 poems/entry) and fiction (3,000 words or less). The purpose of the award in both categories is to recognize writers and offer publication credits in a literary magazine format. Contest rules and entry form online. First Canadian serial rights (ownership reverts to author after one-time publication). Deadline: December 31. Charges $20 entry fee. Prize: 1st Place: $300 (Canadian); 2nd Place: $150 (Canadian); 3rd Place: $75 Honorable Mention: $25. All prizes include publication in the spring edition of *FreeFall Magazine*. Winners will also be invited to read at the launch of that issue if such a launch takes place. Honorable mentions in each category will be published and may be asked to read. Travel expenses not included. Judged by current *FreeFall* editors (who are also published authors in Canada).

FUGUE'S POETRY AND PROSE CONTEST

Fugue, P.O. Box 441102, 200 Brink Hall, English Department, University of Idaho, Moscow ID 83844-1102. Website: www.uidaho.edu/fugue/contest. **Contact:** Genre Editor (Poetry or Nonfiction). 2010: Reading for Poetry and Fiction. Online submissions only. See website for full submission, contest and subscription information. Annual award for poetry, every 2 years for nonfiction and poetry, to recognize the most compelling work being produced. Deadline: May 1. Charges $20/submission fee, 1 year subscription included with cost. Prize: $1,000 and publication for 1st-place winner; publication for 2nd- and 3rd-place winners. Poetry Judge: Ilya Kaminsky. Fiction: Junot Dìaz.

HACKNEY LITERARY AWARDS

1305 2nd Avenue North, #103, Birmingham AL 35203. (205)226-4921. E-mail: info@hackneyliteraryawards.org. **Contact:** Myra Crawford. Estab. 1969. Offered annually for unpublished novels, short stories (maximum 5,000 words) and poetry (50 line limit). Guidelines on website. Deadline: September 30 (novels), December 31 (short stories and poetry). Charges $25/novels; $10/short stories and poetry. Prize: $5,000 in annual prizes for poetry and short fiction ($2,500 national and $2,500 state level; 1st Place: $600; 2nd Place: $400; 3rd Place: $250), plus $5,000 for an unpublished novel. Competition winners will be announced on the website each March.

THE JULIA WARD HOWE/BOSTON AUTHORS AWARD

The Boston Authors Club, 79 Moore Rd., Wayland MA 01778. (617)783-1357. E-mail: bostonauthors@aol.com. **Contact:** Alan Lawson. Estab. 1900. "This annual award honors Julia Ward Howe and her literary friends who founded the Boston Authors Club in 1900. It also honors the membership over 109 years, consisting of novelists, biographers, historians, governors, senators, philosophers, poets, playwrights, and other luminaries. There are 2 categories: adult books and books for young readers (beginning with chapter books through young adult books). Works of fiction, nonfiction, memoir, poetry, and biography published in the current year are eligible. Authors must live or have lived (college counts) within a 100-mile radius of Boston. Subsidized books and picture books are not eligible." Deadline: January 15. Prize: $1,000 in each category.

INDIANA REVIEW 1/2 K (SHORT-SHORT/PROSE-POEM) PRIZE

Indiana Review, Ballantine Hall 465, Indiana University, Bloomington IN 47405-7103. (812)855-3439. Fax: (812)855-4253. E-mail: inreview@indiana.edu. Website: www.indiana.edu/~inreview. **Contact:** Alessandra Simmons, Editor. Maximum story/poem length is 500 words. Offered annually for unpublished work. Deadline: Early June. Charges $15 fee for no more than 3 pieces (includes a 1-year subscription). Check website for guidelines. Prize: $1,000. Judged by Alberto Rios, guest judge for 2010.

INSIGHT WRITING CONTEST

Insight Magazine, 55 W. Oak Ridge Dr., Hagerstown MD 21740. Fax: (301)393-4055. E-mail: insight@rhpa.org. **Contact:** Dwain Esmond, editor. Annual contest for unpublished writers in the categories of student short story, general short story, and student poetry. General category is open to all writers; student categories must be age 22 and younger. Deadline: June 1. Prize: **Student Short Story** and **General Short Story:** 1st Prize: $250; 2nd Prize: $200; 3rd Prize: $150. **Student Poetry:** 1st Prize: $100; 2nd Prize: $75; 3rd Prize: $50. Judged by editors.

IOWA AWARD IN POETRY, FICTION, & ESSAY

The Iowa Review, 308 EPB, Iowa City IA 52242. (319)335-0462. Fax: (319)335-2535. Website: www.iowareview.org. Deadline: January 2-31 (postmarked). Charges $20 entry fee. Prize: $1,000 and publication.

Contests & Awards

LET'S WRITE LITERARY CONTEST

The Gulf Coast Writers Association, P.O. Box 10294, Gulfport MS 39505. E-mail: writerpllevin@gmail.com. **Contact:** Philip Levin. "The Gulf Coast Writers Association sponsors this nationally recognized contest which accepts unpublished poems and short stories from authors all around the United States. This is an annual event which has been held for over 20 years." Deadline: April 15. Charges $8 for each fiction or nonfiction entry. Prize: 1st Prize: $80; 2nd Prize: $50; 3rd Prize: $20.
Tips "See guidelines online."

THE HUGH J. LUKE AWARD

Prairie Schooner, 201 Andrews Hall, P.O. Box 880334, Lincoln NE 68588-0334. (402)472-0911. Fax: (402)472-9771. E-mail: jengelhardt2@unl.edu. Website: www.prairieschooner.unl.edu. **Contact:** Hilda Raz. "Offered annually for work published in *Prairie Schooner* in the previous year." Prize: $250.

LUSH TRIUMPHANT

subTerrain Magazine, P.O. Box 3008, MPO, Vancouver BC V6B 3 × 5 Canada. E-mail: subter@portal.ca. "The winning entries in each category will receive a $750 cash prize (plus payment for publication) and will be published in our Winter issue. First runner-up in each category will receive a $250 cash prize and be published in the Spring issue of *subTerrain*. All entries MUST be previously unpublished material and not currently under consideration in any other contest or competition. All entrants receive a complimentary 1-year subscription to *subTerrain*." Deadline: May 15. Charges $25/entry includes a one-year subscription to *subTerrain*. (Entrants may submit as many entries in as many categories as they like.). Prize: $3,000 in cash prizes. See website for prize information.

BRENDA MACDONALD RICHES FIRST BOOK AWARD

Saskatchewan Book Awards, Inc., 205B-2314 11th Ave., Regina SK S4P 0K1 Canada. (306)569-1585. Fax: (306)569-4187. E-mail: director@bookawards.sk.ca. Website: www.bookawards.sk.ca. **Contact:** Jackie Lay, executive director. Offered annually for work published September 15 of year past to September 14 of current year. This award is presented to a Saskatchewan author for the best first book, judged on the quality of writing. Books from the following categories will be considered: children's; drama; fiction (short fiction by a single author, novellas, novels); nonfiction (all categories of nonfiction writing except cookbooks, directories, how-to books, or bibliographies of minimal critical content); poetry. Deadline: First deadline: July 31; Final deadline: September 15. Charges $25 CAD. Prize: $2,000 CAD

THE MCGINNIS-RITCHIE MEMORIAL AWARD

Southwest Review, P.O. Box 750374, Dallas TX 75275-0374. (214)768-1037. Fax: (214)768-1408. E-mail: swr@mail.smu.edu. **Contact:** Jennifer Cranfill, senior editor and Willard Spiegelman, editor-in-chief. "The McGinnis-Ritchie Memorial Award is given annually to the best works of fiction and nonfiction that appeared in the magazine in the previous year. Manuscripts are submitted for publication, not for the prizes themselves. Guidelines for SASE or online." Prize: Two cash prizes of $500 each. Judged by Jennifer Cranfill and Willard Spiegelman.

MISSISSIPPI REVIEW PRIZE

Mississippi Review, 118 College Dr., #5144, Hattiesburg MS 39406-0001. (601)266-4321. Fax: (601)266-5757. E-mail: editors@mississippireview.com. **Contact:** Rie Fortenberry, contest director. "Our annual contest awards prizes of $1,000 in fiction and in poetry. Winners and finalists will make up next winter's print issue of the national literary magazine *Mississippi Review*. Contest is open to all writers in English except current or former students or employees of The University of Southern Mississippi. Fiction entries should be 1000-5000 words, poetry entries should be three poems totaling 10 pages or less. There is no limit on the number of entries you may submit. Entry fee is $15 per entry, payable to the *Mississippi Review*. Each entrant will receive a copy of the prize issue. No manuscripts will be returned. Previously published work is ineligible. Contest opens April 2. Deadline is October 1. Winners will be announced in late January and publication is scheduled for May next year. Entries should have "MR Prize," author name, address, phone, e-mail and title of work on page one."
Tips No mss returned.

MUSE ANNUAL LITERARY COMPETITION

MUSE, The Lit, Best of MUSE Writing Contest, 2570 Superior Ave., Suite 203, Cleveland OH 44114. (216)694-0000. E-mail: judith@the-lit.org. Website: www.the-lit.org. **Contact:** Judith Mansour-Thomas. "Fiction and creative nonfiction not to exceed 2,000 words. Poetry limited to 3 poems per entry - max. 2 typewritten pages per poem. Writers on writing entry not to exceed 2,000 words (prose) or max. 3 poems per entry. Prizes awarded in each category. First-place winners published in a special edition of MUSE.

Announcement of winners and honorable mentions in April/May Issue MUSE. Sponsored by MUSE and The Lit. Entries will be judged anonymously. Do not put name on mss pages. Attach entry form (or facsimile) to submission." Deadline: December 31. Charges $25 per category; each additional entry within a category, add $10. Make check payable to The Lit and mail. Prize: Up to $500.
Tips "Manuscript will not be returned." Include SASE for list of winners.

NATIONAL OUTDOOR BOOK AWARDS

921 S. 8th Ave., Stop 8128, Pocatello ID 83209. (208)282-3912. E-mail: wattron@isu.edu. Website: www.noba-web.org. **Contact:** Ron Watters. "Nine categories: History/biography, outdoor literature, instructional texts, outdoor adventure guides, nature guides, children's books, design/artistic merit, natural history literature, and nature and the environment. Additionally, a special award, the Outdoor Classic Award, is given annually to books which, over a period of time, have proven to be exceptionally valuable works in the outdoor field. Application forms and eligibility requirements are available online." Deadline: September 1. Charges $65 fee. Prize: Winning books are promoted nationally and are entitled to display the National Outdoor Book Award (NOBA) medallion.

NEW LETTERS LITERARY AWARDS

New Letters, UMKC, University House, Room 105, 5101 Rockhill Rd., Kansas City MO 64110-2499. (816)235-1168. Fax: (816)235-2611. Award has 3 categories (fiction, poetry, and creative nonfiction) with 1 winner in each. Offered annually for previously unpublished work. Guidelines for SASE or online. first North American serial rights. Deadline: May 18. Charges $15 fee (includes a 1-year subscription to *New Letters* magazine). Prize: 1st Place: $1,500, plus publication; First Runners-Up: A copy of a recent book of poetry or fiction courtesy of our affiliate BkMk Press. Preliminary judges are regional writers of prominence and experience. All judging is done anonymously. Winners picked by a final judge of national repute. Previous judges include Maxine Kumin, Albert Goldbarth, Charles Simic, Janet Burroway.

NEW MILLENNIUM AWARDS FOR FICTION, POETRY, AND NONFICTION

fiction, poetry, nonfiction, P.O. Box 2463, Room M2, Knoxville TN 37901. (423)428-0389. Fax: (865)428-2302. E-mail: donw@mach2.com. Website: www.newmillenniumwritings.com/awards; www.writingawards.com. "No restrictions as to style, content or number of submissions. Previously published pieces OK if online or under 5,000 print circulation. Send any time between now and midnight, July 31, for the Summer Awards program, January 31 for the Winter Awards. Simultaneous & multiple submissions welcome. Each Fiction or Nonfiction is a separate entry and should total no more than 6,000 words, except for the short-Short Fiction Award, which should total no more than 1,000 words. (Nonfiction includes essays, profiles, memoirs, interviews, creative nonfiction, travel, humor, etc.) Each Poetry entry may include up to 3 poems, not to exceed 5 pages total. All 20 poetry finalists will be published. Include name, phone, address, e-mail & category on cover page only." Apply online or offline. Mss are not returned. Send SASE or IRC for list of winners or await your book. Entries should be postmarked on or before July 31 or January 31. Charges $17 fee to cover purchase of the book in which winners appear. Prize: $1,000 for best Poem, $1,000 for best Fiction, $1,000 for best Nonfiction, $1,000 for best Short-short Fiction.

THE NOMA AWARD FOR PUBLISHING IN AFRICA

Kodansha Ltd., Japan, P.O. Box 128, Witney, Oxon OX8 5×U United Kingdom. (44)(1993)775-235. Fax: (44)(1993)709-265. E-mail: maryljay@aol.com. Website: www.nomaaward.org. **Contact:** Mary Jay, secretary to the Noma Award Managing Committee. Estab. 1979. "The Noma Award, sponsored by Kodansha LTD., Japan, is open to African writers and scholars whose work is published in Africa. The spirit within which the annual award is given is to encourage and reward genuinely autonomous African publishers, and African writers. The award is given for an outstanding new book in any of these 3 categories: scholarly or academic; books for children; and literature and creative writing (including fiction, drama, poetry, and essays on African literature). Entries must be submitted by publishers in Africa, who are limited to 3 entries (in any combination of the eligible categories). The award is open to any author who is indigenous to Africa (a national, irrespective of place of domicile). Guidelines at website or from Secretariat." Deadline: April 30. Prize: $10,000 (US). "The managing committee is an impartial committee chaired by Mr. Walter Bgoya, comprising African scholars, book experts, and representatives of the international book community. This Managing Committee is the jury. The jury is assisted by independent opinion and assessment from a large and distinguished pool of subject specialists from throughout the world, including many in Africa."

OHIOANA BOOK AWARDS

Ohioana Library Association, 274 E. 1st Ave., Suite 300, Columbus OH 43201-3673. (614)466-3831. Fax: (614)728-6974. E-mail: ohioana@ohioana.org. **Contact:** Linda Hengst, executive director. "Offered annually to bring national attention to Ohio authors and their books (published in the last 2 years). Categories: Fiction, nonfiction, juvenile, poetry, and books about Ohio or an Ohioan. Books about Ohio or an Ohioan need not be written by an Ohioan. For other book categories, writers must have been born in Ohio or lived in Ohio for at least 5 years." Deadline: December 31.

N OPEN SEASON AWARDS

The Malahat Review, University of Victoria, P.O. Box 1700, Stn CSC, Victoria BC V8V 2Y2 Canada. Fax: (250)472-5051. E-mail: malahat@uvic.ca. Website: www.malahatreview.ca. **Contact:** John Barton, editor. The annual Open Season awards offer prizes in three categories: poetry, short fiction, and creative nonfiction. Submissions must be unpublished. No simultaneous submissions. Submit up to 3 poems of 100 lines or less; one piece of short fiction 2,500 words maximum; or one piece of creative nonfiction, 2,500 words maximum. No restrictions on subject matter or aesthetic approach. Include separate page with writer's name, address, e-mail, and title(s); no identifying information on mss pages. No e-mail submissions. Do not include SASE for results; mss will not be returned. Guidelines available on Web site. Entry fee: $35 CAD for Canadian entries, $40 USD for US entries, ($45 USD for entries from Mexico and outside North America); includes a one-year subscription to *The Malahat Review*. Deadline: November 1 (postmark) every year. Prize: Offers $1000 CAD and publication in *The Malahat Review* in each category. 2010 winner in poetry category: Lorri Neilsen Glenn; Fiction: Tricia Dower, Creative Nonfiction: Melissa Jacques. Winner and finalists contacted by e-mail. Winners published in Spring issue of *Malahat Review* announced in winter on Web site, facebook page, and in quarterly e-newsletter, *Malahat lite*.

N PAUL GOODMAN ESSAY CONTEST

Dissent Magazine and JSL Films, 50 West 93rd St., #3L, New York NY 10025. E-mail: essaycontest@paulgoodmanfilm.com. **Contact:** Jonathan Lee. Estab. 2010. This is a one-time contest offered for writers under 30 for previously published work. In 1960, Paul Goodman - social thinker, activist, poet and novelist - published his groundbreaking work, Growing Up Absurd. An examination of youth disaffection in our affluent but spiritually empty society, Goodman's work inspired and galvanized a burgeoning generation of '60s students and intellectuals. Forty years later, though his influence is felt throughout our culture, his books have fallen out of print and his name is all but forgotten. Deadline: May 1, 2010. Charges No fee. Prize: The winning essay will receive a cash prize of $1,000 and will be published in *Dissent*. Two runner-up essays will be published on the *Dissent* web site and will receive $250 and a signed DVD copy of the film. Contest judges include Deborah Meier, MacArthur Fellow and founder of Central Park East School; Casey Blake, historian, Columbia University; and Richard Flacks, sociologist, UC Santa Barbara.

PEN CENTER USA ANNUAL LITERARY AWARDS

PEN Center USA, 269 South Beverly Dr., #1163, Beverly Hills CA 90212. E-mail: awards@penusa.org. Website: www.penusa.org. **Contact:** Literary Awards Coordinator. Estab. 1982. Offered annually for fiction, nonfiction, poetry, children's literature, or translation published January 1-December 31 of the current year. Open to authors west of the Mississippi River. Guidelines for SASE or online. Deadline: December 31 (book categories); January 31 (nonbook categories). Charges $35 fee. Prize: $1,000.

PNWA LITERARY CONTEST

Pacific Northwest Writers Association, PMB 2717-1420 NW Gilman Blvd, Ste, Issaquah WA 98027. (425)673-2665. Fax: (206)824-4559. E-mail: pnwa@pnwa.org. Website: www.pnwa.org. **Contact:** Kelli Liddane. "Annual contest for unpublished writers. Over $12,000 in prize monies. Categories include: Mainstream; Historical; Romance; Mystery/Thriller; Science Fiction/Fantasy; Young Adult Novel; Nonfiction Book/Memoir; Screenwriting; Poetry; Adult Short Story; Children's Picture Book/Chapter Book; Adult Short Topics. Each entry receives 2 critiques. Guidelines online." Deadline: February 2011. Charges $35/entry (members); $50/entry (nonmembers). Prize: 1st Place: $600; 2nd Place: $300; 3rd Place: $150. Each prize is awarded in all 12 categories.

PRAIRIE SCHOONER BOOK PRIZE

Prairie Schooner and the University of Nebraska Press, 201 Andrews Hall, University of Nebraska, Lincoln NE 68588-0334. (402)472-0911. E-mail: jengelhardt2@unlnotes.unl.edu. Website: http://prairieschooner.unl.edu. **Contact:** Hilda Raz, editor. "Annual book series competition publishing 1 book-length collection of short fiction and 1 book-length collection of poetry. Submission Period: January 15-March 15."

Charges $25. Prize: $3,000 and publication through the University of Nebraska Press (1 award in fiction and 1 award in poetry). Judged by Hilda Raz, editor of *Prairie Schooner*, and members of the Book Series Literary Board.

THE PRESIDIO LA BAHIA AWARD

Sons of the Republic of Texas, 1717 Eighth St., Bay City TX 77414-5033. (979)245-6644. Fax: (979)244-3819. E-mail: srttexas@srttexas.org. Website: www.srttexas.org. **Contact:** Scott Dunbar, chairman. Offered annually to promote suitable preservation of relics, appropriate dissemination of data, and research into Texas heritage, with particular attention to the Spanish Colonial period. Deadline: September 30. Prize: $2,000 total; 1st Place: Minimum of $1,200, 2nd and 3rd prizes at the discretion of the judges. Judged by members of the Sons of the Republic of Texas on the Presidio La Bahia Award Committee.

PUDDING HOUSE CHAPBOOK COMPETITION

Pudding House Publications, 81 Shadymere Ln., Columbus OH 43213. (614) 986-1881. E-mail: jen@puddinghouse.com. Website: www.puddinghouse.com. **Contact:** Jennifer Bosveld. "Ms must be 10-36 pages (prefers around 24-28 pages). Some poems may be previously published but not the collection as a whole. Guidelines on website." Deadline: September 30. Charges $15. Prize: $1,000, publication, and 20 copies of the chapbook.

QWF LITERARY AWARDS

Quebec Writers' Federation, 1200 Atwater Ave., Westmount QC H3Z 1X4 Canada. (514)933-0878. E-mail: info@qwf.org. "Offered annually for a book published October 1-September 30 to honor excellence in English-language writing in Quebec. Categories: fiction, nonfiction, poetry, first book, children's and young adult, and translation. Author must have resided in Quebec for 3 of the past 5 years. Guidelines online." Deadline: May 31 for books published before May 16; August 15 for books/bound proofs published after May 16. Charges $20/entry.

RANDOM HOUSE, INC. CREATIVE WRITING COMPETITION

1745 Broadway, New York NY 10019. E-mail: creativewriting@randomhouse.com. Offered annually for unpublished work to NYC public high school seniors. Four categories: poetry, fiction/drama, personal essay and graphic novel. Applicants must be seniors (under age 21) at a New York high school. No college essays or class assignments will be accepted. Deadline: February 1. Prize: Awards range from $500-10,000.

THE RBC BRONWEN WALLACE AWARD FOR EMERGING WRITERS

The Writers' Trust of Canada, 90 Richmond St. East, Suite 200, Toronto, Ontario M5C 1P1 Canada. (416)504-8222. Fax: (416)504-9090. E-mail: info@writerstrust.com. Website: www.writerstrust.com. **Contact:** Amanda Hopkins. Presented annually to "a Canadian writer under the age of 35 who is not yet published in book form. The award, which alternates each year between poetry and short fiction, was established in memory of poet Bronwen Wallace." Prize: $5,000 and $1,000 to two finalists.

REGINA BOOK AWARD

Saskatchewan Book Awards, Inc., 205B-2314 11th Ave., Regina SK S4P 0K1 Canada. (306)569-1585. Fax: (306)569-4187. E-mail: director@bookawards.sk.ca. Website: www.bookawards.sk.ca. **Contact:** Jackie Lay, executive director. Offered annually for work published September 15 of year past to September 14 of current year. In recognition of the vitality of the literary community in Regina, this award is presented to a Regina author for the best book, judged on the quality of writing. Books from the following categories will be considered: children's; drama; fiction (short fiction by a single author, novellas, novels); nonfiction (all categories of nonfiction writing except cookbooks, directories, how-to books, or bibliographies of minimal critical content); poetry. Deadline: First deadline: July 31; Final deadline: September 14. Charges $25 CAD. Prize: $2,000 CAD

SUMMERFIELD G. ROBERTS AWARD

Sons of the Republic of Texas, 1717 Eighth St., Bay City TX 77414-5033. (979)245-6644. Fax: (979)244-3819. E-mail: srttexas@srttexas.org. Website: www.srttexas.org. **Contact:** David Hanover, chairman. Offered annually for submissions published during the previous calendar year to encourage literary effort and research about historical events and personalities during the days of the Republic of Texas, 1836-1846, and to stimulate interest in the period. Deadline: January 15. Prize: $2,500 the last 3 winners of the contest.

SANTA FE WRITERS PROJECT LITERARY AWARDS PROGRAM

Santa Fe Writers Project, 369 Montezuma Ave., #350, Santa Fe NM 87501. E-mail: info@sfwp.com. Website: www.sfwp.com. **Contact:** Andrew Gifford. Annual contest seeking fiction and nonfiction of any genre. The Literary Awards Program was founded by a group of authors to offer recognition for excellence in writing in a time of declining support for writers and the craft of literature. Past judges have included Richard Currey, Jayne Anne Phillips, and Chris Offutt. Deadline: July 15. Charges $30. Prize: $3,750 and publication.

SASKATCHEWAN BOOK OF THE YEAR AWARD

Saskatchewan Book Awards, Inc., 205B, 2314 11th Ave., Regina SK S4P OK1 Canada. (306)569-1585. Fax: (306)569-4187. E-mail: director@bookawards.sk.ca. **Contact:** Jackie Lay, executive director. Offered annually for work published September 15-September 14 annually. This award is presented to a Saskatchewan author for the best book, judged on the quality of writing. Books from the following categories will be considered: children's; drama; fiction (short fiction by a single author, novellas, novels); nonfiction (all categories of nonfiction writing except cookbooks, directories, how-to books, or bibliographies of minimal critical content); poetry. Visit website for more details. Deadline: First deadline: July 31; Final deadline: September 14. Charges $25 (Canadian). Prize: $3,000.

SASKATOON BOOK AWARD

Saskatchewan Book Awards, Inc., 205B-2314 11th Ave., Regina SK S4P 0K1 Canada. (306)569-1585. Fax: (306)569-4187. E-mail: director@bookawards.sk.ca. Website: www.bookawards.sk.ca. **Contact:** Jackie Lay, executive director. Offered annually for work published September 15-September 14. In recognition of the vitality of the literary community in Saskatoon, this award is presented to a Saskatoon author for the best book, judged on the quality of writing. Books from the following categories will be considered: children's; drama; fiction (short fiction by a single author, novellas, novels); nonfiction (all categories of nonfiction writing except cookbooks, directories, how-to books, or bibliographies of minimal critical content); poetry. Deadline: First deadline: July 31; Final deadline: September 14. Charges $25 CAD. Prize: $2,000 CAD.

MARGARET & JOHN SAVAGE FIRST BOOK AWARD

Halifax Public Libraries, 60 Alderney Dr., Dartmouth NS B2Y 4P8 Canada. (902)490-5991. Fax: (902)490-5889. E-mail: mackenh@halifaxpubliclibraries.ca. **Contact:** Heather MacKenzie. "Recognizes the best first book of fiction or nonfiction written by a first-time published author residing in Atlantic Canada. Books may be of any genre, but must contain a minimum of 40% text, be at least 49 pages long, and be available for sale. No anthologies. Publishers: Send 4 copies of each title and submission form for each entry." Children's Books not accepted. Deadline: December 4. Charges $10 (submission fee must accompany entry-cheques to be made payable to the Halifax Regional Municipality).

THE MONA SCHREIBER PRIZE FOR HUMOROUS FICTION & NONFICTION

15442 Vista Haven Place, Sherman Oaks CA 91403. E-mail: brad.schreiber@att.net. Website: www.brashcyber.com. **Contact:** Brad Schreiber. Estab. 2000. "The purpose of the contest is to award the most creative humor writing, in any form less than 750 words, in either fiction or nonfiction, including but not limited to stories, articles, essays, speeches, shopping lists, diary entries, and anything else writers dream up." Deadline: December 1. Charges $5 fee/entry (payable to Mona Schreiber Prize). Prize: 1st Place: $500; 2nd Place: $250; 3rd Place: $100. Brad Schreiber, author, journalist, consultant, and instructor at MediaBistro.com. Complete rules and previous winning entries on website.

Tips "No SASE's, Please."

SHORT GRAIN WRITING CONTEST

Grain Magazine, Box 67, Saskatoon SK S7K 3K1 Canada. (306)244-2828. Fax: (306)244-0255. E-mail: grainmag@sasktel.net. **Contact:** Mike Thompson, Business Administrator. "Two categories with four prizes in each: poetry in any form including prose poem; short fiction of any style including postcard story. All entrants receive a 1-year subscription to *Grain Magazine*." Guidelines available by fax, e-mail, or on website. Deadline: April 1 annually. Charges $30 fee for maximum of 2 entries in one category; US and international entries $36 in US funds. Prize: Two first prizes of $1,250; two second prizes of $750; four runner-up prizes of $500, plus publication.

THE BERNICE SLOTE AWARD

Prairie Schooner, 201 Andrews Hall, PO Box 880334, Lincoln NE 68588-0334. (402)472-0911. Fax: (402)472-9771. E-mail: jengelhardt2@unl.edu. **Contact:** Hilda Raz. "Offered annually for the best work by a beginning writer published in *Prairie Schooner* in the previous year." Prize: $500.

KAY SNOW WRITING AWARDS

Willamette Writers, 9045 SW Barbur Blvd., Suite 5A, Portland OR 97219. (503)452-1592. Fax: (503)452-0372. E-mail: wilwrite@willamettewriters.com. Website: www.willamettewriters.com. "Contest offered annually to offer encouragement and recognition to writers with unpublished submissions. Acquires right to publish excerpts from winning pieces one time in their newsletter." Deadline: April 23. Charges $15 fee; no fee for student writers. Prize: 1st Place: $300; 2nd Place: $150; 3rd Place: $50; excerpts published in Willamette Writers newsletter, and winners acknowledged at banquet during writing conference. Student writers win $50 in categories for grades 1-5, 6-8, and 9-12.

Tips "This contest has many different categories, including film scripts."

TIMELESS LOVE CONTEST

Sponsored by Oak Tree Press, 140 E. Palmer St., Taylorville IL 62568. E-mail: oaktreeepub@aol.com. Website: www.oaktreebooks.com. **Contact:** Billie Johnson. Annual contest for unpublished authors or authors shifting to a new genre. Guidelines and entry forms are available for SASE. The goal of the contest is to discover and publish new authors, or authors shifting to a new genre. Deadline: July 31 (same every year). Charges $35. Prize: Publishing Agreement, and launch of the title. Winners or runners up who are offered publishing agreements are asked to transfer rights. Judged by publishing industry professionals who prescreen entries; publisher makes final selection.

TORONTO BOOK AWARDS

City of Toronto c/o Toronto Protocol, 100 Queen St. W., 2nd Floor, West Tower, City Hall, Toronto ON M5H 2N2 Canada. (416)392-7805. Fax: (416)392-1247. E-mail: bkurmey@toronto.ca. **Contact:** Bev Kurmey, protocol officer. "Offered annually for previously published fiction or nonfiction books for adults or children that are evocative of Toronto." Deadline: March 31. Prize: Awards total $15,000; $1,000 goes to shortlist finalists (usually 4-6) and the remainder goes to the winner. Judged by independent judging committee of 5 people chosen through an application and selection process.

Robert Watson Literary Prizes

The Greensboro Review MFA Writing Program, 3302 Moore Humanities and Research Admin. Bldg, P.O. Box 26170, Greensboro NC 27402-6170. (336)334-5459. E-mail: jlclark@uncg.edu. Website: www.greensbororeview.org. **Contact:** Jim Clark, editor. Estab. 1966. "Offered annually for fiction (7,500 word limit) and poetry recognizing the best work published in the spring issue of *The Greensboro Review*. Sample issue for $8." Deadline: September 15. Prize: $1,000 each for best short story and poem. Rights revert to author upon publication.

WESTMORELAND POETRY & SHORT STORY CONTEST

Westmoreland Arts & Heritage Festival, 252 Twin Lakes Rd., Latrobe PA 15650-9415. (724)834-7474. Fax: (724)850-7474. E-mail: info@artsandheritage.com. Website: www.artsandheritage.com. **Contact:** Diana Morreo. Offered annually for unpublished work. Two categories: Poem & Short Story. Short story entries no longer than 4,000 words. Family-oriented festival and contest. Deadline: March 15. Charges $10/story or for 2 poems. Prize: Up to $1,000 in prizes.

THE WORD GUILD CANADIAN WRITING AWARDS

The Word Guild, Box 1243, Trenton, ON K8V 5R9 Canada. (519)886-4196. E-mail: info@thewordguild.com. Website: www.thewordguild.com. The Word Guild is an association of Canadian writers and editors who are Christian, and who are committed to encouraging one another and to fostering standards of excellence in the art, craft, practice and ministry of writing. Memberships available for various experience levels. Yearly conference Write! Canada is held in June in Guelph, Ontario, and features plenary speakers, continuing classes and workshops. Editors and agents on site. Critiques available. The Word Guild offers three contests: Best New New Canadian Christian Author contest, The Word Guild Canadian Christian Writing Awards, and the God Uses Ink Novice contests. Best New Canadian Christian Author contest is for completed book manuscripts for unpublished authors. Deadline is November. Prize: publishing of ms. The TWG Canadian Christian Writing Awards is for work published in the past year, in many categories including books, articles, songs, poetry. Deadlines are October and January. Cash prizes offered. The God Uses Ink Novice contest is for writers who have never been paid, in three age categories. Entrants write on an assigned theme. Deadline: March. Prize: Registration for Write! Canada conference Judged by writers, editors, etc.

WORLD'S BEST SHORT SHORT STORY FICTION CONTEST, NARRATIVE NONFICTION

CONTEST & SOUTHEAST REVIEW POETRY CONTEST

English Department, Florida State University, Tallahassee FL 32306. Website: www.southeastreview.org. **Contact:** Jessica Pitchford, editor. Estab. 1979. "Annual award for unpublished short-short stories (500 words or less), poetry, and narrative nonfiction (5,000 words or less)." Deadline: April 1. Charges $15 reading fee for up to 3 stories or poems, $15 reading fee per nonfiction entry. Prize: $500 per category. Winners and finalists will be published in *The Southeast Review*.

WRITER'S DIGEST INTERNATIONAL SELF-PUBLISHED BOOK AWARDS

Writer's Digest, 4700 E. Galbraith Rd., Cincinnati OH 45236. (715)445-4612, ext. 13430. E-mail: writing-competition@fwmedia.com. **Contact:** Nicole Florence. Contest open to all English-language self-published books for which the authors have paid the full cost of publication, or the cost of printing has been paid for by a grant or as part of a prize. All books published, revised, or reprinted in 2005-2010 are eligible. Categories include: Mainstream/Literary Fiction, Nonfiction, Inspirational (spiritual/new age), Life Stories (biographies/autobiographies/family histories/memoirs), Children's Books, Reference Books (directories/encyclopedias/guide books), Poetry, Middle-Grade/Young Adult Books. Deadline: May 1. Charges $125; $75/additional entry. Prize: Grand Prize: $3,000, promotion in *Writer's Digest* and *Publisher's Weekly*, and 10 copies of the book will be sent to major review houses with a guaranteed review in *Midwest Book Review*; 1st Place (9 winners): $1,000, promotion in *Writer's Digest*; Honorable Mentions: promotion in *Writer's Digest*, $50 of Writer's Digest Books, and a certificate.

WRITER'S DIGEST WRITING COMPETITION

Writer's Digest, a publication of F+W Media, Inc., 700 E. State Street, Iola WI 54990. (513)531-2690, ext. 1328. E-mail: writing-competition@fwmedia.com; nicole.florence@fwmedia.com. **Contact:** Nicki Florence. Writing contest with 10 categories: Inspirational Writing (spiritual/religious, maximum 2,500 words); Memoir/Personal Essay (maximum 2,000 words); Magazine Feature Article (maximum 2,000 words); Short Story (genre, maximum 4,000 words); Short Story (mainstream/literary, maximum 4,000 words); Rhyming Poetry (maximum 32 lines); Nonrhyming Poetry (maximum 32 lines); Stage Play (first 15 pages and 1-page synopsis); TV/Movie Script (first 15 pages and 1-page synopsis). Entries must be original, in English, unpublished*/unproduced (except for Magazine Feature Articles), and not accepted by another publisher/producer at the time of submission. *Writer's Digest* retains one-time publication rights to the winning entries in each category. Deadline: May 14/late entry June 1, additional fee for late entries. Charges $15/first poetry entry; $10/additional poem. All other entries are $20/first ms; $15/additional ms. Prize: Grand Prize: $3,000 or a trip to New York City to meet with editors and agents; 1st Place: $1,000, ms critique and marketing advice from a *Writer's Digest* editor, commentary from an agent, and $100 of Writer's Digest Books; 2nd Place: $500 and $100 of Writer's Digest Books; 3rd Place: $250 and $100 of Writer's Digest Books; 4th Place: $100 and $50 of *Writer's Digest* Books; 5th Place: $50 and $50 of *Writer's Digest* Books; 6th-10th place $25.

WRITERS-EDITORS NETWORK ANNUAL INTERNATIONAL WRITING COMPETITION

Florida Freelance Writers Association, P.O. Box A, North Stratford NH 03590-0167. E-mail: contest@writers-editors.com. **Contact:** Dana K. Cassell, executive director. "Annual award to recognize publishable talent. Categories: Nonfiction (previously published article/essay/column/nonfiction book chapter; unpublished or self-published article/essay/column/nonfiction book chapter); Fiction (unpublished or self-published short story or novel chapter); Children's Literature (unpublished or self-published short story/nonfiction article/book chapter/poem); Poetry (unpublished or self-published free verse/traditional)." Deadline: March 15. Charges $5 (active or new CNW/FFWA members) or $10 (nonmembers) for each fiction/nonfiction entry under 3,000 words; $10 (members) or $20 (nonmembers) for each entry of 3,000 words or longer; $3 (members) or $5 (nonmembers) for each poem. Prize: 1st Place: $100; 2nd Place: $75; 3rd Place: $50. All winners and Honorable Mentions will receive certificates as warranted. Judged by editors, librarians, and writers.

WRITERS GUILD OF ALBERTA AWARDS

Writers Guild of Alberta, Percy Page Centre, 11759 Groat Rd., Edmonton AB T5M 3K6 Canada. (780)422-8174. Fax: (780)422-2663. E-mail: mail@writersguild.ab.ca. Website: www.writersguild.ab.ca. **Contact:** Executive Director. Offers the following awards: Wilfred Eggleston Award for Nonfiction; Georges Bugnet Award for Novel; Howard O'Hagan Award for Short Fiction; Stephan G. Stephansson Award for Poetry; R. Ross Annett Award for Children's Literature; Gwen Pharis Ringwood Award for Drama; Jon Whyte Memorial Essay Competition. Eligible entries will have been published anywhere in the world between January 1 and December 31 of the current year; the authors must have been residents of Alberta for at least 12 of the 18 months prior to December 31. Unpublished mss, except in the Drama and Essay categories, are not eligible. Anthologies are not eligible. Works may be submitted by authors, publishers, or any interested parties. Deadline: December 31. Prize: Winning authors receive $1,000; essay prize winners receive $700. Other awards: Isabel Miller Young Writers Award. Authors must be 12-18 years of age and a resident of Alberta. Deadline: May 1.

Nonfiction

AMWA MEDICAL BOOK AWARDS COMPETITION

American Medical Writers Association, 30 West Gude Dr., Suite 525, Rockville MD 20850-1161. (301)294-5303. Fax: (301)294-9006. E-mail: slynn@amwa.org. Website: www.amwa.org. **Contact:** Awards Liaison. Offered annually to honor the best medical book published in the previous year in each of 3 categories: Books for Physicians, Books for Health Care (non-physicians) Professionals, and Public Health Care Consumers. Deadline: March 1. Charges $50 fee.

THE BROSS PRIZE

The Bross Foundation, Lake Forest College, 555 N. Sheridan, Lake Forest IL 60045. (847)735-5175. Fax: (847)735-6192. E-mail: rmiller@lfc.edu. **Contact:** Ron Miller. Offered every 10 years for unpublished work to award the best book or treatise on the relation between any discipline or topic of investigation and the Christian religion. Next contest in 2010. Manuscripts awarded prizes become property of the college. Open to any writer. Deadline: September 1 of contest year. Prize: Award varies depending on interest earned

JOHN BULLEN PRIZE

Canadian Historical Association, 395 Wellington St., Ottawa ON K1A 0N4 Canada. (613)233-7885. Fax: (613)567-3110. E-mail: cha-shc@lac-bac.gc.ca. Offered annually for an outstanding historical dissertation for a doctoral degree at a Canadian university. Open only to Canadian citizens or landed immigrants. Deadline: November 30. Prize: $500

CANADIAN AUTHORS ASSOCIATION LELA COMMON AWARD FOR CANADIAN HISTORY

74 Mississaga St. E., Orillia ON L3V 1A5 Canada. (705)719-3926. Fax: 1(866)393-1401. E-mail: admin@canauthors.org. **Contact:** Anita Purcell. Offered annually for a work of historical nonfiction on a Canadian topic by a Canadian author. Entry form required. Obtain entry form from contact name or download from website. Deadline: December 15. Charges $35 (Canadian) entry fee. Prize: $2,500 and a silver medal. The CAA Awards Chair appoints a trustee for this award. That trustee selects two judges. The identities of the trustee and judges are confidential throughout the judging process. Decisions of the trustee and judges are final, and they may choose not to award a prize. A shortlist of the best three entries in each category will be announced in April 2010. The winners will be announced at the gala awards banquet during the annual CanWrite! conference in Victoria in June 2010.

Tips Other awards managed by the CAA can be found on the website.

CANADIAN LIBRARY ASSOCIATION STUDENT ARTICLE CONTEST

Canadian Library Association, 328 Frank St., Ottawa ON K2P 0X8 Canada. (613)232-9625, ext. 301. Fax: (613)563-9895. **Contact:** Valerie Delrue. Offered annually to unpublished articles discussing, analyzing, or evaluating timely issues in librarianship or information science. Open to all students registered in or recently graduated from a Canadian library school, a library techniques program, or faculty of education library program. Submissions may be in English or French. Deadline: March 31. Prize: 1st Place: $150 and trip to CLA's annual conference; 1st runner-up: $150 and $75 in CLA publications; 2nd runner-up: $100 and $75 in CLA publications.

THE DOROTHY CHURCHILL CAPPON CREATIVE NONFICTION AWARD

New Letters, University of Missouri-Kansas City, 5101 Rockhill Rd., Kansas City MO 64110. (816)235-1168. Fax: (816)235-2611. E-mail: newletters@umkc.edu. **Contact:** Ashley Kaine. Contest is offered annually for unpublished work to discover and reward emerging writers and to give experienced writers a place to try new genres. Acquires first North American serial rights. Open to any writer. Guidelines for SASE or online. Deadline: Third week of May. Charges $15 fee (includes cost of a 1-year subscription). Prize: 1st Place: $1,500 and publication in a volume of *New Letters*; runner-up will receive a copy of a recent book of poetry or fiction courtesy of BkMk Press. All entries will receive consideration for publication in future editions of *New Letters*.

MORTON N. COHEN AWARD

Modern Language Association of America, 26 Broadway, 3rd Floor, New York NY 10004-1789. (646)576-5141. Fax: (646)458-0030. E-mail: awards@mla.org. **Contact:** Coordinator of Book Prizes. Estab. 1989. Awarded in odd-numbered years for a distinguished edition of letters. At least 1 volume of the edition must have been published during the previous 2 years. Editors need not be members of the MLA. Deadline: May 1. Prize: A cash award and a certificate to be presented at the Modern Language Association's annual convention in January.

THE SHAUGHNESSY COHEN PRIZE FOR POLITICAL WRITING

The Writers' Trust of Canada, 90 Richmond St. E., Suite 200, Toronto ON M5C 1P1 Canada. (416)504-8222. Fax: (416)504-9090. E-mail: info@writerstrust.com. **Contact:** Amanda Hopkins, program coordinator. "Awarded annually for a nonfiction book of outstanding literary merit that enlarges our understanding of contemporary Canadian political and social issues. Presented at the Politics & the Pen event each spring in Ottawa. Open to Canadian citizens and permanent residents only." Deadline: November 5. Prize: $25,000 and $2,500 to four finalists.

CARR P. COLLINS AWARD FOR NONFICTION

The Texas Institute of Letters, 6335 W. Northwest Hwy., #618, Dallas TX 75225. (214)363-7253. E-mail: dpayne@smu.edu. Website: texasinstituteofletters.org/. **Contact:** Darwin Payne. Offered annually for work published January 1-December 31 of the previous year to recognize the best nonfiction book by a writer who was born in Texas, who has lived in the state for at least 2 consecutive years at one point, or a writer whose work has some notable connection with Texas. See website for guidelines. Deadline: January 3. Prize: $5,000.

COMPETITION FOR WRITERS OF BC HISTORY

British Columbia Historical Federation, P.O. Box 5254, Station B, Victoria BC V8R 6N4 Canada. E-mail: info@bchistory.ca. Website: www.bchistory.ca. "Offered annually to nonfiction books containing a facet ofnonfiction books about BC history and published during contest year. Books become the property of BC Historical Federation." Deadline: December 31. Prize: Cash, a certificate, and an invitation to the BCHF annual conference. The contest winner receives the Lieutenant-Governor's Medal for Historical Writing.

CREATIVE NONFICTION PRIZE

National League of American Pen Women, Nob Hill, San Francisco Branch, The Webhallow House, 1544 Sweetwood Dr., Broadmoor Village CA 94015-1717. E-mail: pennobhill@aol.com. **Contact:** Eileen Malone. All prose works must be typed, page numbered, and double-spaced. Each entry up to 3,000 words. Identify only with 3 × 5 card. Open annually to any writer. Deadline: November 30. Charges $5/entry (make checks payable to NLAPW, Nob Hill Branch). Prize: 1st Place: $100; 2nd Place: $50; 3rd Place: $25.

A CUP OF COMFORT

Adams Media, F + W Media, 57 Littlefield St., Avon MA 02322. Fax: (508)427-6790. E-mail: cupofcomfort@adamsmedia.com. Website: www.cupofcomfort.com. "A Cup of Comfort is the best-selling book series featuring inspiring true stories about the relationships and experiences that deeply affect our lives. Stories must be true, written in English, uplifting, and appropriate for a mainstream audience. This prize includes publication in an anthology. Contest is offered 1-2 times/year. Deadline is 6-12 months prior to publication. Call for submissions and guidelines on website. Open to aspiring and published writers. Limited rights for a specified period of time; applies only to those stories selected for publication. Prize: $500 grand prize; $100 for all other stories published in each book (50 stories/anthology).

ANNIE DILLARD AWARD IN CREATIVE NONFICTION

Bellingham Review, Mail Stop 9053, 516 High St., Western Washington University, Bellingham WA 98225. (360)650-4863. E-mail: bhreview@cc.wwu.edu. **Contact:** Brenda Miller. Offered annually for unpublished essays on any subject and in any style. Guidelines for SASE or online. Deadline: December 1-March 15. Charges $18/1st entry, $10/additional entry. Prize: 1st Place: $1,000, plus publication and copies. All finalists considered for publication. All entrants receive subscription.

Tips The *Bellingham Review* seeks literature of palpable quality: poems, stories, and essays so beguiling they invite us to come closer, look deeper, touch, sniff and taste their essence. We hunger for a kind of writing that nudges the limits of form or executes traditional forms exquisitely.

GORDON W. DILLON/RICHARD C. PETERSON MEMORIAL ESSAY PRIZE

American Orchid Society, Inc., 16700 AOS Ln., Delray Beach FL 33446-4351. (561)404-2040. Fax: (561)404-2045. E-mail: jmengel@aos.org;lstewart@aos.org. Website: www.aos.org. **Contact:** Lindsay Stewart. Estab. 1985. "Annual contest open to all writers. The theme is announced each May in *Orchids* magazine. All themes deal with an aspect of orchids, such as repotting, growing, hybridizing, etc. Unpublished submissions only. Themes in past years have included Orchid Culture, Orchids in Nature, and Orchids in Use. Acquires one-time rights." Deadline: November 30. Prize: Cash award and a certificate. Winning entry usually published in the May issue of *Orchids* magazine.

THE DONNER PRIZE

The Award for Best Book on Canadian Public Policy, The Donner Canadian Foundation, 349 Carlaw Ave., Toronto ON M4M 2T1 Canada. (416)368-8253 or (416)368-3763. E-mail: sherry@mdgassociates.com. Website: www.donnerbookprize.com. **Contact:** Sherry Naylor. "Offered annually for nonfiction published January 1-December 31 that highlights the importance of public policy and to reward excellent work in this field. Entries must be published in either English or French. Open to Canadian citizens." Deadline: November 30. Prize: $30,000; 5 shortlist authors get $5,000 each.

EDUCATOR'S AWARD

The Delta Kappa Gamma Society Intma Society Internationernational, P.O. Box 1589, Austin TX 78767-1589. (888)762-468. Fax: (512)478-3961. Website: www.deltakappagamma.net. **Contact:** Educator's Award Committee. "Offered annually for quality research and nonfiction published January-December of previous year. This award recognizes educational research and writings of female authors whose work may influence the direction of thought and action necessary to meet the needs of today's complex society. The book must be written by 1 or 2 women who are citizens of any country in which The Delta Kappa Gamma Society International is organized: Canada, Costa Rica, Denmark, Estonia, Finland, Germany, Great Britain, Guatemala, Iceland, Mexico, The Netherlands, Norway, Puerto Rico, Sweden, US. Guidelines (required) for SASE. Deadline: February 1. Prize: $2,500.

EVERETT E. EDWARDS MEMORIAL AWARD

Agricultural History, P.O. Box 5075, Minard Hall 203, NDSU, Fargo ND 58105-5075. (701)231-5831. Fax: (701)231-5832. E-mail: ndsu.agricultural.history@ndsu.nodak.edu. **Contact:** Claire Strom. Offered annually for best graduate paper written during the calendar year on any aspect of agricultural and rural studies (broadly interpreted). Open to submission by any graduate student. Deadline: December 31. Prize: $200 and publication of the paper in the scholarly journal, *Agricultural History*.

EVANS BIOGRAPHY & HANDCART AWARDS

Mountain West Center for Regional Studies, Utah State University, 0700 Old Main Hill, Logan UT 84322-0700. (435)797-3630. Fax: (435)797-3899. E-mail: mwc@cc.usu.edu. Estab. 1983. Offered to encourage the writing of biography about people who have played a role in Mormon Country (not the religion, the region—Intermountain West with parts of Southwestern Canada and Northwestern Mexico). Publishers or authors may nominate books. Criteria for consideration: Work must be a biography or autobiography on someone who lived in our significantly contributed to the history of the Interior West; must be submitted for consideration for publication year's award; new editions or reprints are not eligible; mss are not accepted. Submit 5 copies. Deadline: January 1. Prize: $10,000 and $1,000.

EVENT NONFICTION CONTEST

Event, The Douglas College Review, P.O. Box 2503, New Westminster BC V3L 5B2 Canada. (604)527-5293. Fax: (604)527-5095. E-mail: event@douglas.bc.ca. Offered annually for unpublished creative nonfiction. Maximum length: 5,000 words. Acquires first North American serial print rights and limited non-exclusive digital rights for the 3 winning entries. Open to any writer, except Douglas College employees. Deadline: April 15. Charges $29.95 entry fee, which includes 1-year subscription; American and overseas residents pay in U.S. funds. Prize: 3 winners will each receive $500, plus payment for publication.

DINA FEITELSON RESEARCH AWARD

International Reading Association, Division of Research & Policy, 800 Barksdale Rd., Newark DE 19714-8139. (302)731-1600, ext. 423. Fax: (302)731-1057. E-mail: research@reading.org. **Contact:** Marcella Moore. "This is an award for an exemplary work published in English in a refereed journal that reports on an empirical study investigating aspects of literacy acquisition, such as phonemic awareness, the alphabetic principle, bilingualism, or cross-cultural studies of beginning reading. Articles may be submitted for consideration by researchers, authors, et al. Copies of the applications and guidelines can be downloaded in pdf format from the website." Deadline: September 1. Prize: Monetary award and recognition at the International Reading Association's annual convention.

WALLACE K. FERGUSON PRIZE

Canadian Historical Association, 395 Wellington St., Ottawa ON K1A 0N4 Canada. (613)233-7885. Fax: (613)567-3110. E-mail: cha-shc@lac-bac.gc.ca. **Contact:** Michel Duquet, executive coordinator. Offered to a Canadian who has published the outstanding scholarly book in a field of history other than Canadian history. Open to Canadian citizens and landed immigrants only. Deadline: December 2. Prize: $1,000.

GEORGE FREEDLEY MEMORIAL AWARD

Theatre Library Association, Benjamin Rosenthal Library, Queens College, CUNY, 65-30 Kissena Blvd., Flushing NY 11367. (718)997-3672. Fax: (718)997-3753. E-mail: svallillo@comcast.net. **Contact:** Stephen M. Vallillo, book awards committee chair. Estab. 1968. Offered for a book published in the US within the previous calendar year on a subject related to live theatrical performance (including cabaret, circus, pantomime, puppetry, vaudeville, etc.). Eligible books may include biography, history, theory, criticism, reference, or related fields. Deadline: March 15 of year following eligibility. Prize: $500 and a certificate to the winner; $200 and certificate for honorable mention.

LIONEL GELBER PRIZE

Munk Center for International Studies, University of Toronto, 1 Devonshire Place, Toronto ON M5S 3K7 Canada. (416)946-8901. Fax: (416)946-8915. E-mail: gelberprize.munk@utoronto.ca. **Contact:** Prize Manager. Estab. 1989. Offered annually for the year's most outstanding work of nonfiction in the field of international relations. Books must be published in English or English translation between January 1 and December 31 of the current year, and submitted by the publisher. Publishers should submit 6 copies of each title (up to 3 titles can be submitted). Deadline: October 31. Prize: $15,000 (Canadian funds).

GOVERNOR GENERAL'S LITERARY AWARD FOR LITERARY NON-FICTION

Canada Council for the Arts, 350 Albert St., P.O. Box 1047, Ottawa ON K1P 5V8 Canada. (613)566-4414, ext. 5573. Fax: (613)566-4410. Website: www.canadacouncil.ca/prizes/ggla. **Contact:** Lori Knoll. Offered annually for the best English-language and the best French-language work of literary nonfiction by a Canadian. Deadline depends on the book's publication date: Books in English: March 15, June 1 or August 7. Books in French: March 15 or July 15. Prize: Each laureate receives $25,000; non-winning finalists receive $1,000.

JOHN GUYON LITERARY NONFICTION PRIZE

Crab Orchard Review, English Department, Southern Illinois Univ. Carbondale, Carbondale IL 62901-4503. E-mail: jtribble@siu.edu. **Contact:** Jon C. Tribble, managing editor. "Offered annually for unpublished work. This competition seeks to reward excellence in the writing of creative nonfiction. This is not a prize for academic essays. *Crab Orchard Review* acquires first North American serial rights to submitted works. Open to US citizens only." Deadline: March 1 - April 30. Charges $10/essay (limit of 3 essays of up to 6,500 words each), which includes one copy of *Crab Orchard Review* featuring the winners. Prize: $1,500 and publication.

ALBERT J. HARRIS AWARD

International Reading Association, Division of Research and Policy, 800 Barksdale Rd., Newark DE 19714-8139. (302)731-1600, ext. 423; (800)336-7323. Fax: (302)731-1057. E-mail: research@reading.org. **Contact:** Marcella Moore. "Offered annually to recognize outstanding published works focused on the identification, prevention, assessment, or instruction of learners experiencing difficulty learning to read. Articles may be nominated by researchers, authors, and others. Copies of the applications and guidelines can be downloaded in PDF format from the website." Deadline: September 1. Prize: Monetary award and recognition at the International Reading Association's annual convention.

ALEXANDER HENDERSON AWARD

Australian Institute of Genealogical Studies, 41 Railway Rd., Blackburn VIC 3130. (61)(3)9877-3789. E-mail: info@aigs.org.au. Award presented to the person who produced the best family history published in Australia. Each entry will remain the property of the institute and will become a part of its library collection. Deadline: November 30. Prize: Certificate and trophy. The award is judged by a panel comprised a genealogist, librarian, literary critic, and historian.

THE KIRIYAMA PRIZE

Pacific Rim Voices, 300 Third St., Suite 822, San Francisco CA 94107. (415)777-1628. Fax: (415)777-1646. E-mail: admin@kiriyamaprize.org. **Contact:** Jeannine Stronach, prize manager. Offered for work published from January 1 through December 31 of the current prize year to promote books that will contribute to greater mutual understanding and increased coöperation throughout the Pacific Rim and South Asia. Guidelines and entry form on request, or may be downloaded from the website. Books must be submitted for entry by the publisher. Proper entry forms must be submitted. Deadline: late Fall each year. Prize: $30,000 to be divided equally between the author of 1 fiction and 1 nonfiction book

KATHERINE SINGER KOVACS PRIZE

Modern Language Association of America, 26 Broadway, 3rd Floor, New York NY 10004-1789. (646)576-5141. Fax: (646)458-0030. E-mail: awards@mla.org. **Contact:** Coordinator of Book Prizes. Estab. 1990. Offered annually for a book published during the previous year in English or Spanish in the field of Latin American and Spanish literatures and cultures. Books should be broadly interpretive works that enhance understanding of the interrelations among literature, the other arts, and society. Author must be a current member of the MLA. Deadline: May 1. Prize: A cash award and a certificate to be presented at the Modern Language Association's annual convention in January.

LINCOLN PRIZE AT GETTYSBURG COLLEGE

Gettysburg College and Lincoln & Soldiers Institute, 300 N. Washington St., Campus Box 435, Gettysburg PA 17325. (717)337-6590. Fax: (717)337-6596. E-mail: lincolnprize@gettysburg.edu. Offered annually for the "finest scholarly work in English on the era of the American Civil War. The award will usually go to a book published in the previous year; however articles, essays, and works of fiction may be submitted." Guidelines for SASE or online. Deadline: November 1. Prize: $50,000.

TONY LOTHIAN PRIZE

under the auspices of the Biographers' Club, 119a Fordwych Rd., London NW2 3NJ United Kingdom. (44) (20)8452 4993. E-mail: anna@annaswan.co.uk. **Contact:** Anna Swan. "Entries should consist of a 10-page synopsis and 10 pages of a sample chapter for a proposed biography. Open to any biographer who has not previously been published or commissioned or written a book." Deadline: August 1. Charges Entry fee: £10. Prize: £2,000. Judges have included Michael Holroyd, Victoria Glendinning, Selina Hastings, Frances Spalding, Lyndall Gordon, Anne de Courcy, Nigel Hamilton, Anthony Sampson, and Mary Lovell.

Tips "Further details at www.biographersclub.co.uk."

WALTER D. LOVE PRIZE

North American Conference on British Studies, History Department, 0119 Sutherland Bldg., Penn State University, Abington PA 19001. E-mail: dmhirst@wustl.edu. **Contact:** Derek Hirst. "Offered annually for best article in any field of British Studies. Open to American or Canadian writers." Deadline: April 1. Prize: $150

JAMES RUSSELL LOWELL PRIZE

Modern Language Association of America, 26 Broadway, 3rd Floor, New York NY 10004-1789. (646)576-5141. Fax: (646)458-0030. E-mail: awards@mla.org. **Contact:** Coordinator of Book Prizes. Offered annually for literary or linguistic study, or critical edition or biography published in previous year. *Open to MLA members only.* Deadline: March 1. Prize: A cash award and a certificate to be presented at the Modern Language Association's annual convention in January.

SIR JOHN A. MACDONALD PRIZE

Canadian Historical Association, 395 Wellington St., Ottawa ON K1A 0N4 Canada. (613)233-7885. Fax: (613)567-3110. E-mail: cha-shc@lac-bac-gc.ca. **Contact:** Michel Duquet, executive coordinator. Offered annually to award a previously published nonfiction work of Canadian history judged to have made the most significant contribution to an understanding of the Canadian past. Open to Canadian citizens only. Deadline: December 2. Prize: $1,000.

RICHARD J. MARGOLIS AWARD

c/o Margolis & Bloom, LLP, 535 Boylston St., 8th floor, Boston MA 02116. (617)267-9700, ext. 517. E-mail: harry@margolis.com. **Contact:** Harry S. Margolis. Sponsored by the Blue Mountain Center, this annual award is given to a promising new journalist or essayist whose work combines warmth, humor, wisdom, and concern with social justice. Submit 3 copies of 2 examples of your published or unpublished work (maximum 30 pages) and a short biographical note. Deadline: July 1. Prize: $5,000 and a 1-month residency at the Blue Mountain Center—a writers and artists colony in the Adirondacks in Blue Mountain Lake, New York.

HOWARD R. MARRARO PRIZE

Modern Language Association of America, 26 Broadway, 3rd Floor, New York NY 10004-1789. (646)576-5141. Fax: (646)458-0030. E-mail: awards@mla.org. **Contact:** Coordinator of Book Prizes. Offered in even-numbered years for a scholarly book or essay on any phase of Italian literature or comparative literature involving Italian, published in previous year. Authors must be members of the MLA. Deadline: May 1. Prize: A cash award and a certificate to be presented at the Modern Language Association's annual convention in January.

KENNETH W. MILDENBERGER PRIZE

Modern Language Association of America, 26 Broadway, 3rd Floor, New York NY 10004-1789. (646)576-5141. Fax: (646)458-0030. E-mail: awards@mla.org. **Contact:** Coordinator of Book Prizes. Offered annually for a publication from the previous year in the field of language culture, literacy, or literature with a strong application to the teaching of languages other than English. Author need not be a member. Deadline: May 1. Prize: A cash award, and a certificate, to be presented at the Modern Language Association's annual convention in January and a year's membership in the MLA.

MLA PRIZE FOR A DISTINGUISHED BIBLIOGRAPHY

Modern Language Association of America, 26 Broadway, 3rd Floor, New York NY 10004-1789. (646)576-5141. Fax: (646)458-0030. E-mail: awards@mla.org. **Contact:** Coordinator of Book Prizes. Offered in even-numbered years for enumerative and descriptive bibliographies published in monographic, book, or electronic format in the 2 years prior to the competition. Open to any writer or publisher. Deadline: May 1. Prize: A cash prize and a certificate to be presented at the Modern Language Association's annual convention in January.

MLA PRIZE FOR A DISTINGUISHED SCHOLARLY EDITION

Modern Language Association of America, 26 Broadway, 3rd Floor, New York NY 10004-1789. (646)576-5141. Fax: (646)458-0030. E-mail: awards@mla.org. **Contact:** Coordinator of Book Prizes. Offered in odd-numbered years. To qualify for the award, an edition should be based on an examination of all available relevant textual sources; the source texts and the edited text's deviations from them should be fully described; the edition should employ editorial principles appropriate to the materials edited, and those principles should be clearly articulated in the volume; the text should be accompanied by appropriate textual and other historical contextual information; the edition should exhibit the highest standards of accuracy in the presentation of its text and apparatus; and the text and apparatus should be presented as accessibly and elegantly as possible. Editor need not be a member of the MLA. Deadline: May 1. Prize: A cash award and a certificate to be presented at the Modern Language Association's annual convention in January.

MLA PRIZE FOR A FIRST BOOK

Modern Language Association of America, 26 Broadway, 3rd Floor, New York NY 10004-1789. (646)576-5141. Fax: (646)458-0030. E-mail: awards@mla.org. **Contact:** Coordinator of Book Prizes. Offered annually for the first book-length scholarly publication by a current member of the association. To qualify, a book must be a literary or linguistic study, a critical edition of an important work, or a critical biography. Studies dealing with literary theory, media, cultural history, and interdisciplinary topics are eligible; books that are primarily translations will not be considered. Deadline: April 1. Prize: A cash award and a certificate to be presented at the Modern Language Association's annual convention in January.

MLA PRIZE FOR INDEPENDENT SCHOLARS

Modern Language Association of America, 26 Broadway, 3rd Floor, New York NY 10004-1789. (646)576-5141. Fax: (646)458-0030. E-mail: awards@mla.org. **Contact:** Coordinator of Book Prizes. Offered annually for a book in the field of English, or another modern language, or literature published in the previous year. Authors who are enrolled in a program leading to an academic degree or who hold tenured or tenure-track positions in higher education are not eligible. Authors need not be members of MLA. Guidelines and application form for SASE. Deadline: May 1. Prize: A cash award, a certificate, and a year's membership in the MLA.

LINDA JOY MYERS MEMOIR PRIZE

National League of American Pen Women, Nob Hill, San Francisco Branch, Webhallow House, 1544 Sweetwood Dr., Broadmoor Village CA 94015-1717. E-mail: pennobhill@aol.com. **Contact:** Eileen Malone. "One memoir/entry, up to 3,000 words, double spaced. Previously published material is acceptable. Indicate category on first page. Identify only with 3 × 5 card. Open annually to any writer." Deadline: November 30. Charges $5/entry (make checks payable to NLAPW, Nob Hill Branch). Prize: 1st Place: $100; 2nd Place $50; 3rd Place $25.

GEORGE JEAN NATHAN AWARD FOR DRAMATIC CRITICISM

Cornell University, Department of English, Goldwin Smith Hall, Ithaca NY 14853. (607)255-6801. Fax: (607)255-6661. **Contact:** Chair, Department of English. Offered annually to the American who has written the best piece of drama criticism during the theatrical year (July 1-June 30), whether it is an article, essay, treatise, or book. Only published work may be submitted; author must be an American citizen. Prize: The annual award now amounts to $10,000. In addition, the winner receives a trophy symbolic of, and attesting to, the award.

Tips See guidelines and entry form online at website.

NATIONAL WRITERS ASSOCIATION NONFICTION CONTEST

The National Writers Association, 10940 S. Parker Rd., #508, Parker CO 80134. (303)841-0246. Fax: (303)841-2607. E-mail: natlwritersassn@hotmail.com. **Contact:** Sandy Whelchel, director. "Annual contest to encourage writers in this creative form and to recognize those who excel in nonfiction writing." Deadline: December 31. Charges $18 fee. Prize: 1st Place: $200; 2nd Place: $100; 3rd Place: $50.

THE FREDERIC W. NESS BOOK AWARD

Association of American Colleges and Universities, 1818 R St. NW, Washington DC 20009. (202)387-3760. Fax: (202)265-9532. E-mail: info@aacu.org. **Contact:** Bethany Sutton. Offered annually for work published in the previous year. Each year the Frederic W. Ness Book Award Committee of the Association of American Colleges and Universities recognizes books which contribute to the understanding and improvement of liberal education. Guidelines for SASE or online. "Writers may nominate their own work; however, we send letters of invitation to publishers to nominate qualified books." Deadline: May 1. Prize: $2,000 and a presentation at the association's annual meeting—transportation and 1 night hotel for meeting are also provided.

OUTSTANDING DISSERTATION OF THE YEAR AWARD

International Reading Association, 800 Barksdale Rd., P.O. Box 8139, Newark DE 19714-8139. (302)731-1600, ext. 423; (800)336-7323. Fax: (302)731-1057. E-mail: research@reading.org. **Contact:** Marcella Moore. "This award is offered annually to recognize dissertations in the field of reading and literacy. *Applicants must be members of the International Reading Association*. Copies of the applications and guidelines can be downloaded in PDF format from the website." Deadline: October 1.

FRANK LAWRENCE AND HARRIET CHAPPELL OWSLEY AWARD

Southern Historical Association, Dept. of History, University of Georgia, Athens GA 30602-1602. (706)542-8848. Fax: (706)542-2455. **Contact:** Southern Historical Association. Estab. 1934. Offered in odd-numbered years for recognition of a distinguished book in Southern history published in even-numbered years. Publishers usually submit the books. Deadline: March 1.

PRESERVATION FOUNDATION CONTESTS

The Preservation Foundation, Inc., 2213 Pennington Bend, Nashville TN 37214. E-mail: preserve@storyhouse.org. Website: www.storyhouse.org. **Contact:** Richard Loller. "Contest offered annually for unpublished nonfiction. General nonfiction category (1,500-5,000 words)—any appropriate nonfiction topic. Travel nonfiction category (1,500-5,000 words)—must be true story of trip by author or someone known personally by author. E-mail entries only (no mss). **First entry in each category is free; $10 fee for each additional entry (limit 3 entries/category)**. Open to any previously unpublished writer. Defined as having made no more than $750 by creative writing in any previous year." Deadline: August 31. Prize: 1st Place: $100 in each category; certificates for finalists.

JAMES A. RAWLEY PRIZE

Organization of American Historians, P.O. Box 5457, 112 N. Bryan Ave., Bloomington IN 47408-5457. (812)855-7311. Fax: (812)855-0696. **Contact:** Award and Prize Committee Coordinator. "Offered annually for a book dealing with the history of race relations in the US. Books must have been published in the current calendar year. Guidelines available online." Deadline: October 1; books to be published after October 1 of the calendar year may be submitted as page proofs. Prize: $1,000.

PHILLIP D. REED MEMORIAL AWARD FOR OUTSTANDING WRITING ON THE SOUTHERN ENVIRONMENT

Southern Environmental Law Center, 201 W. Main St., Suite 14, Charlottesville VA 22902-5065. (434)977-4090. Fax: (434)977-1483. E-mail: cmccue@selcva.org. Website: www.SouthernEnvironment.org/phil_reed. **Contact:** Cathryn McCue, writing award coor. Offered annually for nonfiction pieces that most effectively tell stories about the South's environment. Categories include Journalism and Book. Entries must have been published during the previous calendar year and have a minimum of 3,000 words. Guidelines online or for SASE. Deadline: early January. Prize: $1,000 for winner in each category. See www.southernenvironment.org/about/reed_award/.

EVELYN RICHARDSON NONFICTION AWARD

Writers' Federation of Nova Scotia, 1113 Marginal Rd., Halifax NS B3H 4P7 Canada. (902)423-8116. Fax: (902)422-0881. E-mail: talk@writers.ns.ca. **Contact:** Nate Crawford, executive director. "This annual award is named for Nova Scotia writer Evelyn Richardson, whose book *We Keep a Light* won the Governor General's Literary Award for nonfiction in 1945. There is **no entry fee** or form. Full-length books of nonfiction written by Nova Scotians, and published as a whole for the first time in the previous calendar year, are eligible. Publishers: Send 4 copies and a letter attesting to the author's status as a Nova Scotian, and the author's current mailing address and telephone number." Deadline: First Friday in December. Prize: $2,000.

SASKATCHEWAN NONFICTION AWARD

Saskatchewan Book Awards, Inc., 205B-2314 11th Ave., Regina SK S4P 0K1 Canada. (306)569-1585. Fax: (306)569-4187. E-mail: director@bookawards.sk.ca. **Contact:** Jackie Lay, executive director. Offered annually for work published September 15-September 14. This award is presented to a Saskatchewan author for the best book of nonfiction, judged on the quality of writing. Deadline: First deadline: July 31; Final deadline: September 14. Charges $25 CAD. Prize: $2,000 CAD.

SASKATCHEWAN SCHOLARLY WRITING AWARD

Saskatchewan Book Awards, Inc., 205B-2314 11th Ave., Regina SK S4P 0K1 Canada. (306)569-1585. Fax: (306)569-4187. E-mail: director@bookawards.sk.ca. **Contact:** Jackie Lay, executive director. Offered annually for work published September 15-September 14 annually. This award is presented to a Saskatchewan author for the best contribution to scholarship. The work must recognize or draw on specific theoretical work within a community of scholars, and participate in the creation and transmission of knowledge. Deadline: First deadline: July 31; Final deadline: September 14. Charges $25 (Canadian). Prize: $2,000.

ALDO AND JEANNE SCAGLIONE PRIZE FOR COMPARATIVE LITERARY STUDIES

Modern Language Association of America, 26 Broadway, 3rd Floor, New York NY 10004-1789. (646)576-5141. Fax: (646)458-0030. E-mail: awards@mla.org. **Contact:** Coordinator of Book Prizes. Offered annually for outstanding scholarly work published in the preceding year in the field of comparative literary studies involving at least 2 literatures. *Author must be a member of the MLA.* Works of scholarship, literary history, literary criticism, and literary theory are eligible; books that are primarily translations are not eligible. Deadline: May 1. Prize: A cash award and a certificate to be presented at the Modern Language Association's annual convention in January.

ALDO AND JEANNE SCAGLIONE PRIZE FOR FRENCH AND FRANCOPHONE STUDIES

Modern Language Association of America, 26 Broadway, 3rd Floor, New York NY 10004-1789. (646)576-5141. Fax: (646)458-0030. E-mail: awards@mla.org. **Contact:** Coordinator of Book Prizes. Offered annually for work published in the preceding year that is an outstanding scholarly work in the field of French or francophone linguistic or literary studies. *Author must be a member of the MLA.* Works of scholarship, literary history, literary criticism, and literary theory are eligible; books that are primarily translations are not eligible. Deadline: May 1. Prize: A cash award and a certificate to be presented at the Modern Language Association's annual convention in January.

ALDO AND JEANNE SCAGLIONE PRIZE FOR ITALIAN STUDIES

Modern Language Association of America, 26 Broadway, 3rd Floor, New York NY 10004-1789. (646)576-5141. Fax: (646)458-0030. E-mail: awards@mla.org. **Contact:** Coordinator of Book Prizes. Offered in odd-numbered years for a scholarly book on any phase of Italian literature or culture, or comparative literature involving Italian, including works on literary or cultural theory, science, history, art, music, society, politics, cinema, and linguistics, preferably but not necessarily relating other disciplines to literature. Books must have been published in year prior to competition. *Authors must be members of the MLA.* Deadline: May 1. Prize: A cash award and a certificate to be presented at the Modern Language Association's annual convention in January.

ALDO AND JEANNE SCAGLIONE PRIZE FOR STUDIES IN GERMANIC LANGUAGES & LITERATURE

Modern Language Association of America, 26 Broadway, 3rd Floor, New York NY 10004-1789. (646)576-5141. Fax: (646)458-0030. E-mail: awards@mla.org. **Contact:** Coordinator of Book Prizes. Offered in even-numbered years for outstanding scholarly work appearing in print in the previous 2 years and written by a member of the MLA on the linguistics or literatures of the Germanic languages. Works of literary history, literary criticism, and literary theory are eligible; books that are primarily translations are not eligible. Deadline: May 1. Prize: A cash award, and a certificate to be presented at the Modern Language Association's annual convention in January.

ALDO AND JEANNE SCAGLIONE PRIZE FOR STUDIES IN SLAVIC LANGUAGES AND LITERATURES

Modern Language Association of America, 26 Broadway, 3rd Floor, New York NY 10004-1789. (646)576-5141. Fax: (646)458-0030. E-mail: awards@mla.org. **Contact:** Coordinator of Book Prizes. Offered in odd-numbered years for books published in the previous 2 years. Membership in the MLA is not required. Works of literary history, literary criticism, philology, and literary theory are eligible; books that are primarily translations are not eligible. Deadline: May 1. Prize: A cash award and a certificate to be presented at the Modern Language Association's annual convention in January.

ALDO AND JEANNE SCAGLIONE PUBLICATION AWARD FOR A MANUSCRIPT IN ITALIAN LITERARY STUDIES

Modern Language Association, 26 Broadway, 3rd Floor, New York NY 10004-1789. (646)576-5141. Fax: (646)458-0030. E-mail: awards@mla.org. **Contact:** Coordinator of Book Prizes. Awarded annually to an author of a ms dealing with any aspect of the languages and literatures of Italy, including medieval Latin and comparative studies, or intellectual history if main thrust is clearly related to the humanities. Materials from ancient Rome are eligible if related to postclassical developments. Also translations of classical works of prose and poetry produced in Italy prior to 1900 in any language (i.e., neo-Latin, Greek) or in a dialect of Italian (i.e., Neapolitan, Roman, Sicilian). Work can be in English or Italian. *Authors must be members of the MLA* and currently reside in the US or Canada. Deadline: August 1. Prize: A cash award and a certificate to be presented at the Modern Language Association's annual convention in January.

MINA P. SHAUGHNESSY PRIZE

Modern Language Association of America, 26 Broadway, 3rd Floor, New York NY 10004-1789. (646)576-5141. Fax: (646)458-0030. E-mail: awards@mla.org. **Contact:** Coordinator of Book Prizes. Offered annually for a scholarly book in the fields of language, culture, literacy or literature with strong application to the teaching of English published during preceding year. Authors need not be members of the MLA. Deadline: May 1. Prize: A cash prize, a certificate, to be presented at the Modern Language Association's annual convention in January, and a one-year membership in the MLA.

FRANCIS B. SIMKINS AWARD

Southern Historical Association, Dept. of History, University of Georgia, Athens GA 30602-1602. (706)542-8848. Fax: (706)542-2455. **Contact:** John B. Boles, editor. Estab. 1934. "The award is sponsored jointly with Longwood College. Offered in odd-numbered years for recognition of the best first book by an author in the field of Southern history over a 2-year period." Deadline: March 1.

CHARLES S. SYDNOR AWARD

Southern Historical Association, Dept. of History, University of Georgia, Athens GA 30602. (706)542-8848. Fax: (706)542-2455. **Contact:** Southern Historical Association. Offered in even-numbered years for recognition of a distinguished book in Southern history published in odd-numbered years. Publishers usually submit books. Deadline: March 1.

THE AMAURY TALBOT PRIZE FOR AFRICAN ANTHROPOLOGY

Royal Anthropological Institute, 50 Fitzroy St., London England W1T 5BT United Kingdom. (44) (207)387-0455. Fax: (44)(207)388-8817. E-mail: admin@therai.org.uk. Annual award for nonfiction on

Contests & Awards

anthropological research relating to Africa. Only works published the previous calendar year are eligible. Preference is given to those relating first to Nigeria and then West Africa. Guidelines online or for SASE. Deadline: March 31. Prize: 500£.

WESTERN WRITERS OF AMERICA

MSC06 3770, 1 University of New Mexico, Albuquerque NM 87131-0001. (505)277-5234. Fax: (505)277-5275. E-mail: wwa@unm.edu. **Contact:** Paul Hutton, exec. director. Estab. 1953. "17 Spur Award categories in various aspects of the American West." Send entry form with your published work. "The nonprofit Western Writers of America has promoted and honored the best in Western literature with the annual Spur Awards, selected by panels of judges. Awards, for material published last year, are given for works whose inspirations, image and literary excellence best represent the reality and spirit of the American West." Charges No fee. Today, Spurs are offered for the best western novel (short novel), best novel of the west (long novel), best original paperback novel, best short story, best short nonfiction. Also, best contemporary nonfiction, best biography, best history, best juvenile fiction and nonfiction, best TV or motion picture drama, best TV or motion picture documentary, best western song, and best first novel.

Tips "Accepts multiple submissions, each with its own entry form."

WRITERS' JOURNAL ANNUAL SCIENCE FICTION/FANTASY CONTEST

Val-Tech Media, P.O. Box 394, Perham MN 56573. (218)346-7921. Fax: (218)346-7924. E-mail: writersjournal@writersjournal.com. Website: www.writersjournal.com. **Contact:** Leon Ogroske. Offered annually for unpublished work (maximum 2,000 words). No e-mail submissions accepted. Guidelines for SASE or online. Receives fewer than 200 entries. Deadline: November 30. Charges $7 fee. Prize: 1st Place: $250; 2nd Place: $100; 3rd Place: $50, plus honorable mentions. Prize-winning stories and selected honorable mentions will be published in *Writers' Journal* magazine.

THE WRITERS' TRUST NONFICTION PRIZE

The Writers' Trust of Canada, 90 Richmond St. E., Suite 200, Toronto ON M5C 1P1 Canada. (416)504-8222. Fax: (416)504-9090. E-mail: info@writerstrust.com. **Contact:** Amanda Hopkins. "Offered annually for a work of nonfiction published in the previous year. Award presented at The Writers' Trust Awards event held in Toronto each Fall. Open to Canadian citizens and permanent residents only." Deadline: August 6th. Prize: $25,000 (Canadian), and $2,500 to four finalists.

Playwriting & Scriptwriting

AAA SCREENPLAY CONTEST

AAA Screenplay Contest c/o Creative Screenwriting, 6404 Hollywood Blvd Suite 145, Los Angeles CA 90028. E-mail: aaacontest@creativescreenwriting.com. **Contact:** Pasha McKenley, contest coordinator. "No particular genre has an edge. Our winner may be a horror movie about mutant hedgehogs or a biopic on the life of Ivan the Terrible. What our judges are looking for is a great story, compelling characters, and sharp dialogue. We want your best work without regard to genre or budget. Because the contest is geared toward offering access into the world of screenwriting, we do have to limit applicants to those who have made less than $25,000 on feature options or sales. Deadline: April 11. Charges $34-65. Prize: $10,000; 2nd Prize is $2,500 Cash. Third Prize is $1,000. New: The fourth through tenth-place finalists will each receive $100. Two teleplay winners receive $500 each and agency consideration. Three "Best Opening" prize winners get $100 each. Considers all genres.

Tips "Enter online at our website. Do not send or try to submit scripts to our e-mail address. They will be deleted."

ACTORS CHOICE AWARDS

The Screenwriting Conference in Santa Fe, LLC, PO Box 29762, Santa Fe NM 87592. (866)424-1501. Fax: (505)424-8207. E-mail: writeon@scsfe.com. Deadline: May 10. Charges $25 for the first, $15 for all others. No limit to submissions. Prize: All 5 winners receive certificates and free submission to the PAGEawards screenwriting competition. In addition, scripts are forwarded to all producers/agents/managers/executives attending The Hollywood Connection component of SCSFe. All genres.

ALBERTA PLAYWRITING COMPETITION

Alberta Playwrights' Network, 2633 Hochwald Ave. SW, Calgary AB T3E 7K2 Canada. (403)269-8564. Fax: (403)265-6773. Offered annually for unproduced plays with full-length and Discovery categories. Discovery is open only to previously unproduced playwrights. Open only to residents of Alberta. Deadline: March 1 (annually). Charges $40 fee (Canadian). Prize: Full length: $3,500 (Canadian);

Discovery: $1,500 (Canadian); plus a written critique, workshop of winning play, and possible reading of winning plays at a Showcase Conference.

ALLIANCE OF WOMEN FILMMAKERS SCRIPT COMPETITION

Alliance of Women Film Festival, 1317 N. San Fernando Blvd. # 340, Burbank CA 91504. (818)749-6162. E-mail: dmeans25@yahoo.com. Deadline: July. Charges $35-55. Prize: Prizes are sponsored, and change from year to year.

ANNUAL DENISE RAGAN WIESENMEYER ONE ACT FESTIVAL

Attic Theatre Ensemble, 5429 W. Washington Blvd., Los Angeles CA 90016-1112. (323)525-0600. E-mail: info@attictheatre.org. **Contact:** Literary Manager. "Offered annually for unpublished and unproduced work. Scripts should be intended for mature audiences. Length should not exceed 30 minutes. Guidelines online. Electronic submissions only." Deadline: December 31. Prize: 1st Place: $300; 2nd Place: $100.
Tips "Go to website - read guideline instructions!"

ANNUAL INTERNATIONAL ONE-PAGE PLAY COMPETITION

Lamia Ink!, P.O. Box 202, Prince Street Station, New York NY 10012. **Contact:** Cortland Jessup, founder/artistic director. Offered annually for previously published or unpublished 1-page plays. Acquires the rights to publish in our magazine and to be read or performed at the prize awarding festival. "We will publish and award prizes annually, but may not in every year hold a public performance of the finalist plays. In years without a live performance festival we will award prizes via mail and list all finalists on website." Playwright retains copyright. There are 3 rounds of judging with invited judges that change from year to year. There are up to 12 judges for finalists round. Guidelines available online. The competition is a short-form theatrical exercise created to nurture aspiring writers, challenge established writers and encourage a wide range of experimentation. Deadline: March 15. Charges $2/play; $5/3 plays (maximum). Prize: $200 for the winner; all finalists will be published.
Tips "Send SASE for guidelines or visit the website."

ANNUAL NATIONAL PLAYWRITING COMPETITION

Wichita State University, School of Performing Arts, 1845 Fairmount, Box 153, Wichita KS 67260-0153. (316)978-3646. Fax: (316)978-3202. E-mail: bret.jones@wichita.edu. **Contact:** Bret Jones, Director of Theatre. The contest will be open to all undergraduate and graduate students enrolled at any college or university in the United States. Please indicate school affiliation. All submissions must be original, unpublished and unproduced. Both full-length and one act plays may be submitted. Full length plays in one or more acts should be a minimum of 90 minutes playing time. Two or three short plays on related themes by the same author will be judged as one entry. The total playing time should be a minimum of 90 minutes. One act plays should be a minimum of 30 minutes playing time to a maximum of 60 minutes playing time. Musicals should be a minimum of 90 minutes playing time and must include a CD of the accompanying music. Scripts should contain no more than 4 to 6 characters and setting must be suitable for an 85-seat Black box theatre. Eligible playwrights may submit up to two entries per contest year. One typewritten, bound copy should be submitted. Scripts must be typed and arranged in professional play script format. See information provided in *The Dramatist's Source Book* or the following website: http://www.pubinfo.vcu.edu/artweb/playwriting/format.html for instruction on use of professional format. Two title pages must be included: one bound and the other unbound. The unbound title page should display the author's name, address, telephone number and email address if applicable. The bound title page should only display the name of the script. Do not include any personal identifying information on the bound title page. Scripts may be submitted electronically to the following web address bret.jones@wichita.edu. Submit in PDF format. Please include ALL information requested for mail in scripts with your electronic submission. Deadline: January 16, 2010. Prize: Production by the Wichita State University Theatre. Winner will be announced after March 15, 2010. No entry may be withdrawn after March 1st, 2010. Judging will be conducted by a panel of three or more selected from the school faculty and may also include up to three experienced, faculty approved WSU School of Performing Arts students.

APPALACHIAN FESTIVAL OF PLAYS & PLAYWRIGHTS

Barter Theatre, Box 867, Abingdon VA 24212-0867. (276)619-3316. Fax: (276)619-3335. E-mail: apfestival@bartertheatre.com. **Contact:** Nick Piper. With the annual Appalachian Festival of New Plays & Playwrights, Barter Theatre wishes to celebrate new, previously unpublished/unproduced plays by playwrights from the Appalachian region. If the playwrights are not from Appalachia, the plays themselves must be about the region. Deadline: March 31. Prize: $250, a staged reading performed at Barter's Stage II theater, and some transportation compensation and housing during the time of the festival. There may be an additional award for the best staged readings.

BIG BEAR LAKE SCREENWRITING COMPETITION

P.O. Box 1981, Big Bear Lake CA 92315-1981. (909)866-3433. E-mail: BigBearFilmFest@aol.com. Deadline: April 1. Charges $40. Prize: No confirmed money prizes, but winners receive software and their script submitted to studios.

THE BRITISH FEATURE SCREENPLAY COMPETITION

c/o Pinewood Film Studios, Pinewood Road, Iver Heath Buckinghamshire SL0 0NH United Kingdom. E-mail: info@kaosfilms.co.uk. Website: www.kaosfilms.co.uk. The British Feature Screenplay Competition is open to writers of any nationality from any country. The entered screenplay must not have been previously optioned, sold, or produced. Screenplays must be written in English language. The screenplay must be no less than eighty minutes and no more than one hundred and ten minutes screen time. All genres accepted. Charges Submission fee £50 and £70. Prize: The winning screenplay will be produced with a budget of up to $2 million.

THE BRITISH SHORT SCREENPLAY COMPETITION

c/o Pinewood Film Studios, Pinewood Road, Iver Heath, Buckinghamshire SL0 0NH United Kingdom. E-mail: info@kaosfilms.co.uk. Website: www.kaosfilms.co.uk/rules/. The British Short Screenplay Competition is open to writers of any nationality from any country. The entered screenplay must not have been previously optioned, sold or produced. Screenplays must be written in English language. The screenplay must be no less than five-minutes and no more than fifteen minutes screen time. Charges 25-35 British pounds. All genres.

BUNTVILLE CREW'S AWARD BLUE

Buntville Crew, 118 N. Railroad Ave., Buckley IL 60918-0445. E-mail: buntville@yahoo.fr. **Contact:** Steven Packard, artistic director. "Presented annually for the best unpublished/unproduced play script under 15 pages, written by a student enrolled in any Illinois high school. Submit 1 copy of the script in standard play format, a brief biography, and a SASE (scripts will not be returned). Include name, address, telephone number, age, and name of school." Deadline: May 31. Prize: Cash prize and possible productions in Buckley and/or New York City. Judged by panel selected by the theater.

BUNTVILLE CREW'S PRIX HORS PAIR

Buntville Crew, 118 N. Railroad Ave., Buckley IL 60918-0445. E-mail: buntville@yahoo.fr. Website: www.buntville@yahoo.com. **Contact:** Steven Packard, artistic director. "Annual award for unpublished/unproduced play script under 15 pages. Plays may be in English, French, German, or Spanish (no translations, no adaptations). Submit 1 copy of the script in standard play format, a résumé, and a SASE (scripts will not be returned). Include name, address, and telephone number." Deadline: May 31. Charges $8. Prize: $200 and possible production in Buckley and/or New York City. Judged by panel selected by the theater.

CITA PLAY DEVELOPMENT CONTEST

Christians in Theatre Arts, P.O. Box 26471, Greenville SC 29616. E-mail: admin@cita.org. Competition encourages and equips writers by providing the winner with a high-quality intensive dramaturgical experience. Plays must be full-length (75 minutes or more) and reflect the author's Judeo-Christian worldview. Musicals must include a tape/CD. See website for guidelines. Deadline: February each year. Charges $25-100/entry depending on level of feedback. Prize: The winning playwright will be published in a special edition of the organization's journal and a copy will be sent to a list of faith-based professional companies and universities.

THE CLAYMORE DAGGER AWARD

Killer Nashville, P.O. Box 680686, Franklin TN 37068-0686. (615)599-4032. E-mail: contact@killernashville.com. **Contact:** Clay Stafford, Event Founder. "Although anyone with an unpublished ms. is eligible to submit, the award would best benefit authors who have not been previously published, and published authors who are between publishers and would like to get some buzz about their new works. We don't want to exclude anyone, though, so if you're a published author with an unpublished ms. you'd like to enter, please be our guest." The Claymore Dagger Award is Killer Nashville's award for the best opening for an unpublished ms. submitted to the judging committee. Deadline: 4 months prior to the Killer Nashville conference which is held annually on the weekend surrounding the third Saturday in August. Charges $35. Prize: An engraved dagger and consideration for publication by the judging publisher.

A committee of experienced readers and writers will review all submissions in a blind judging process. They will recommend and submit 10 mss. to our sponsor publisher, whose editors will make the final decision and award the Claymore Dagger to the winning author. All decisions are final and at the sole discretion of the publisher.

COE COLLEGE PLAYWRITING FESTIVAL

Coe College, 1220 First Ave. NE, Cedar Rapids IA 52402-5092. (319)399-8624. Fax: (319)399-8557. E-mail: swolvert@coe.edu. **Contact:** Susan Wolverton. Estab. 1993. "Offered biennially for unpublished work to provide a venue for new works for the stage. We are interested in full-length productions, not one-acts or musicals. There are no specific criteria although a current resume and synopsis is requested. Open to any writer." Deadline: November 1, even years. Notification: January 15, odd years. Prize: $500, plus 1-week residency as guest artist with airfare, room and board provided.

CONTEST OF WINNERS

ScriptDoctor, 555 E. Limberlost Dr., Suite 1067, Tucson AZ 85705. E-mail: thedoc@scriptdoctor.com. **Contact:** Howard Allen. Must be at least 18 years of age. For screenplays that have placed as a finalist or won a contest in the past 5 years. Deadline: December. Charges $55. Prize: Cash $1,000 and notes from a ScriptDoctor partner.

CREATIVE WORLD AWARDS (CWA) INTERNATIONAL SCREENWRITING COMPETITION

International screenwriting contests, PO Box 10699, Marina del Rey CA 90295. E-mail: info@creativeworldawards.com. Website: www.creativeworldawards.com. **Contact:** Marlene Neubauer/Heather Waters. "CWA's professionalism, industry innovation, and exclusive company list make this competition a leader in the industry. Several past entrants have gotten optioned and several more are in negotiation. Newly added categories for Short Film scripts and television. Check out our website for more details." All screenplays must be in English and in standard spec screenplay format. See website's FAQ page for more detailed information. Deadline: June 30, 2010. Charges $45-65. Prize: Over $15,000 in cash and prizes awarded in 10 categories.

DRURY UNIVERSITY ONE-ACT PLAY CONTEST

Drury University, 900 N. Benton Ave., Springfield MO 65802-3344. E-mail: msokol@drury.edu. **Contact:** Mick Sokol. Offered in even-numbered years for unpublished and professionally unproduced plays. One play/playwright. Guidelines for SASE or by e-mail. Deadline: December 1.

DUBUQUE FINE ARTS PLAYERS ANNUAL ONE-ACT PLAY CONTEST

Dubuque Fine Arts Players, 1686 Lawndale, Dubuque IA 52001. E-mail: gary.arms@clarke.edu. Website: www.dbqoneacts.org. **Contact:** Gary Arms. "We select 3 one-act plays each year. We award cash prizes of up to $600 for a winning entry. We produce the winning plays in August. Offered annually for unpublished and unproduced work. Guidelines and application form for SASE." Deadline: January 31. Charges $10. Prize: 1st Place: $600; 2nd Place: $300; 3rd Place: $200. Five groups who read all the plays; each play is read at least twice. Plays that score high enough enter the second round. The top 10 plays are read by a panel consisting of 3 directors and 2 other final judges.

ESSENTIAL THEATRE PLAYWRITING AWARD

The Essential Theatre, 1414 Foxhall Lane, #10, Atlanta GA 30316. (404)212-0815. E-mail: pmhardy@aol.com. **Contact:** Peter Hardy. "Offered annually for unproduced, full-length plays by Georgia resident writers. No limitations as to style or subject matter." Deadline: April 23. Prize: $600 and full production.

FEATURE LENGTH SCREENPLAY COMPETITION

Austin Film Festival, 1801 Salina St., Austin TX 78702. (512)478-4795. Fax: (512)478-6205. E-mail: screenplaydirector@austinfilmfestival.com. Offered annually for unproduced screenplays. The Austin Film Festival is looking for quality screenplays which will be read by industry professionals. This year AFF will be providing 'Readers Notes' to all Second Rounders (top 10%) and higher for no additional charge. Two main categories: Drama Category and Comedy Category. Two optional Award Categories (additional entry of $20 per category); Sponsored Award and Sci-Fi Award. For guidelines for SASE or call (800)310-3378. The writer must hold the rights when submitted; work must be original and not under option. The screenplay must be feature length and in industry standard format. Deadline: May 15 (early); June 1 (late). Charges $40/early entry; $50/late entry. Prize: $5,000 in Comedy and Drama; $2,500 for Sponsored Award and Sci-Fi Award.

Tips 17th Annual Austin Film Festival: Oct. 21-28, 2010.

FEMALE EYE FILM FESTIVAL SCREENPLAY ENTRY

50 Wallace St., Woodbridge ON L4L 2P3 Canada. (905)264-7731. E-mail: info@femaleeyefilmfestival.com. **Contact:** Leslie Ann Coles, program director. Deadline: October (late: December). Charges $25 ($50 late).

SHUBERT FENDRICH MEMORIAL PLAYWRITING CONTEST

Pioneer Drama Service, Inc., P.O. Box 4267, Englewood CO 80155. (303)779-4035. Fax: (303)779-4315. E-mail: submissions@pioneerdrama.com. **Contact:** Lori Conary, assistant editor. Offered annually for unpublished, but previously produced, submissions to encourage the development of quality theatrical material for educational and community theater. Rights acquired only if published. Authors already published by Pioneer Drama are not eligible. Contest submissions must also meet standard submission guidelines. Deadline: December 31 (postmarked). Prize: $1,000 royalty advance and publication.

FESTIVAL OF NEW AMERICAN PLAYS

Firehouse Theatre Project, 1609 W. Broad St., Richmond VA 23220. (804)355-2001. E-mail: info@firehousetheatre.org. Website: www.firehousetheatre.org. **Contact:** Carol Piersol, artistic director. "Annual contest designed to support new and emerging American playwrights. Scripts must be full-length and previously unpublished/unproduced. (Readings are acceptable if no admission was charged.) Submissions should be mailed in standard manuscript form with no fancy binding. This means no disks, no emails. Scripts should be secured simply with a binder clip only. All author information must be on a title page separate from the body of the manuscript and no reference to the author is permitted in the body of the script. Scripts must be accompanied by a letter of recommendation from a theater company or individual familiar with your work. Letters of recommendation do not need to be specific to the play submitted; they may be general recommendations of the playwright's work. All letters must be received with the script, not under separate cover. Scripts received without a letter will not be considered. Due to the volume of mail, manuscripts cannot be returned. All American playwrights welcome to submit their work." Deadline: June 30 postmark. Prize: 1st Place: $1,000 and a staged reading; 2nd Place: $500 and a staged reading. All plays are initially read by a panel of individuals with experience in playwriting and literature. Previous judges have included Lloyd Rose (former *Washington Post* theatre critic), Bill Patton (frequent Firehouse director), Richard Toscan (dean of the Virginia Commonwealth University School for the Arts), and Israel Horovitz (playwright). All finalists are asked to sign a contract with the Firehouse Theatre Project that guarantees performance rights for the staged reading in January and printed credit for Firehouse Theatre Project if the play is produced/published in the future.

JOHN GASSNER MEMORIAL PLAYWRITING COMPETITION

New England Theatre Conference, 215 Knob Hill Dr., Hamden CT 06158. Fax: (203)288-5938. E-mail: mail@netconline.org. "We annually seek unpublished full-length plays and scripts. Open to all. Playwrights living outside New England may participate." Deadline: April 15. Charges $10 fee. Prize: 1st Place: $1,000; 2nd Place: $500

GOTHAM SCREEN FILM FESTIVAL AND SCREENPLAY CONTEST

291 Broadway, Suite 701, New York NY 10007. E-mail: info@gothamscreen.com. "Submit via Withoutabox account or download form at Website." "The contest is open to anyone. Feature length screenplays should be properly formatted and have an approximate length of 80-120 pages. On the cover page, please put the title, the writer's name(s) and the contact details." Deadline: September. Charges $35-50. Prize: $2,500. In addition, excerpts from selected contest entries will be performed live by professional actors at a staged reading during the festival. Drama, comedy, adventure, horror, thriller/suspense, family, romantic comedy, documentary.

Tips "Include an e-mail address to be notified."

⊕ GRIFFIN AWARD

Griffin Theatre Company, 13 Craigend St., Kings Cross NSW 2011 Australia. (61)(2)9332-1052. Fax: (61)(2)9331-1524. E-mail: info@griffintheatre.com.au. Annual award for a script that has not been produced or commissioned. Open to anyone over age 18. Prize: $10,000 panel of theatre professionals, including Griffin's artistic director.

AURAND HARRIS MEMORIAL PLAYWRITING AWARD

The New England Theatre Conference, Inc., 215 Knob Hill Dr., Hamden CT 06518. Fax: (203)288-5938. E-mail: mail@netconline.org. "Offered annually for an unpublished full-length play for young audiences.

Guidelines available online or for SASE. 'No phone calls, please.' Open to all." Deadline: May 1. Charges $10 fee. Prize: 1st Place: $1,000; 2nd Place: $500

HENRICO THEATRE COMPANY ONE-ACT PLAYWRITING COMPETITION

Henrico Recreation & Parks, P.O. Box 90775, Richmond VA 23273. (804)501-5138. Fax: (804)501-5284. E-mail: per22@co.henrico.va.us. **Contact:** Amy A. Perdue. "Offered annually for previously unpublished or unproduced plays or musicals to produce new dramatic works in one-act form. Scripts with small casts and simpler sets given preference. Controversial themes and excessive language should be avoided." Deadline: July 1. Prize: $300; Runner-Up: $200. Winning entries may be produced; videotape sent to author.

HOLIDAY SCREENPLAY CONTEST

P.O. Box 450, Boulder CO 80306. (303)629-3072. E-mail: Cherubfilm@aol.com. Website: www.HolidayScreenplayContest.com. "Scripts must be centered on a holiday. The screenplay must be centered around one Holiday (New Year's Day, President's Day, Valentine's Day, St. Patrick's Day, April Fool's Day, Easter, 4th of July, Halloween, Thanksgiving, Hanukkah, Christmas, Kwanzaa, or any other world holiday you would like to feature). This contest is limited to the first 400 entries." Screenplays must be in English. Screenplays must not have been previously optioned, produced, or purchased prior to submission. Multiple submissions are accepted but each submission requires a separate online entry and separate fee. Screenplays must be between 90 - 125 pages. Deadline: November. Charges $30. Prize: Up to $500.

HORROR SCREENPLAY CONTEST

Cherub Productions, P.O. Box 540, Boulder CO 80306. (303)629-3072. E-mail: Cherubfilm@aol.com. "This contest is looking for horror scripts." This contest is limited to the first 600 entries. Screenplays must be between 90 - 125 pages. Charges $35. Prize: More than $5,000 in cash and prizes.

LAS VEGAS INTERNATIONAL FILM FESTIVAL SCREENPLAY COMPETITION

Las Vegas International Film Festival, 10300 W. Charleston Blvd., Las Vegas NV 89135. (702)552-9330. E-mail: info@lvfilmfest.com. Website: www.lvfilmfest.com/Filmmakers/Screenplay_Competition.aspx. "This annual screenplay competition was created to help aspiring screenwriters break into the entertainment industry as well as to support emerging new talent." Scripts may be submitted via hardcopy or electronic file. Scripts should be no longer than 180 pages. Charges $30. Prize: Cash prizes are awarded to the First, Second, and Third place winners.

MEXICO INTERNATIONAL FILM FESTIVAL SCREENPLAY COMPETITION

Mexico International Film Festival, 20058 Ventura Blvd., Suite 123, Woodland Hills CA 91364. E-mail: info@mexicofilmfestival.com. Charges $30. Awards are based solely on overall merits of the screenplays.

MOONDANCE INTERNATIONAL FILM FESTIVAL

970 9th St., Boulder CO 80302. (303)545-0202. E-mail: director@moondancefilmfestival.com. WRITTEN WORKS SUBMISSIONS: feature screenplays, short screenplays, feature & short musical screenplays, feature & short screenplays for children, 1, 2 or 3-act stageplays, mini-series for TV, television movies of the week, television pilots, libretti, musical film scripts, short stories, radio plays & short stories for children. Submission service: www.withoutabox.com/login/1240. Postmark Deadline: May 15. Charges $50-75.

MOVING ARTS PREMIERE ONE-ACT COMPETITION

Moving Arts, P.O. Box 481145, Los Angeles CA 90048. (323)666-3259. E-mail: info@movingarts.org. **Contact:** Steve Lozier. Offered annually for unproduced one-act plays in the Los Angeles area (single set; maximum cast of 8 people recommended). All playwrights are eligible except Moving Arts resident artists. No more than 60 pages. "We have a blind submission policy. The playwright's name should appear only on the cover letter and no where on the script. Scripts are not returned. Please see website for additional guidelines before submitting. Deadline: see website. Charges $10 fee/script. Prize: 1st Place: $200, plus a full production during festival; finalists get program mention and possible production.

NATIONAL CHILDREN'S THEATRE FESTIVAL

Actors' Playhouse at the Miracle Theatre, 280 Miracle Mile, Coral Gables FL 33134. (305)444-9293, ext. 615. Fax: (305)444-4181. E-mail: maulding@actorsplayhouse.org. **Contact:** Earl Maulding. "Offered

annually for unpublished musicals for young audiences. Target age is 4-12. Script length should be 45-60 minutes. Maximum of 8 actors to play any number of roles. Prefer settings which lend themselves to simplified scenery. Bilingual (English/Spanish) scripts are welcomed. Call or visit website for guidelines. Open to any writer." Deadline: April 1. Charges $10 fee. Prize: $500 and full production.
Tips "Travel and lodging during the festival based on availability."

NEW WORKS FOR THE STAGE

COE College Theatre Arts Department, 1220 First Ave. NE, Cedar Rapids IA 52402. (319)399-8624. Fax: (319)399-8557. E-mail: swolvert@coe.edu. **Contact:** Susan Wolverton. Offered in odd-numbered years to encourage new work, to provide an interdisciplinary forum for the discussion of issues found in new work, and to offer playwright contact with theater professionals who can provide response to new work. Full-length, original, unpublished and unproduced scripts only. No musicals, adaptations, translations, or collaborations. Submit 1-page synopsis, résumé, and SASE if the script is to be returned. Deadline: November 1 even years. Prize: $500, plus travel, room and board for residency at the college

DON AND GEE NICHOLL FELLOWSHIPS IN SCREENWRITING

Academy of Motion Picture Arts & Sciences, 1313 N. Vine St., Hollywood CA 90028-8107. (310)247-3010. E-mail: nicholl@oscars.org. Website: www.oscars.org/nicholl. Estab. 1985. "Offered annually for unproduced screenplays to identify talented new screenwriters. Open to writers who have not earned more than $5,000 writing for films or TV." Deadline: May 1. Charges $45 fee if by April 1. Prize: Up to five $30,000 fellowships awarded each year.

NICKELODEON WRITING FELLOWSHIP

Nickelodeon, 231 W. Olive Ave., Burbank CA 91502. (818)736-3663. E-mail: info.writing@nick.com. Website: www.nickwriting.com. **Contact:** Karen Kirkland, Contest/Award Director. Offered annually for unpublished scripts. You must be 18 years or older to participate. U.S. domestic applicants only. Deadline: February 28, 2011. Charges No fee. Prize: The Fellowship provides a salaried position for up to one year and offers hands-on experience writing spec scripts and pitching story ideas in both live action and animation television. As part of their script writing, each fellow will be assigned to an Executive in Charge of Production and have an opportunity to write a spec script for an on-air Nickelodeon show. In addition, all fellows are integrated into the activities of both the development and production departments. This allows the fellows an opportunity to attend storyboard pitches, notes meetings, records, table reads, show pitches and show tapings, all while being exposed to top creators and key production crews. Appropriate spec scripts must be: Comedic, Live Action, or Animation; Based on a half-hour television series; Currently being produced for primetime network or cable; Typed in standard script format; In black ink; In 12pt courier style font; On 8½ × 11, 3-hole punched white paper; With only two brass fasteners (top & bottom). Experienced readers and Nickelodeon Development and Production employees and executives read all submissions.
Tips "All spec scripts must include a cover page listing the show name and show title, along with your name, address, and telephone number (please do not put your name on every page). If you have previously applied to the program and have not been selected as a fellow, you are welcomed and encouraged to apply again, however you are required to submit a different spec script for each new submission period. See guidelines online at our website. Submissions that do not adhere to our guidelines will not be considered."

ONE IN TEN SCREENPLAY CONTEST

Cherub Productions, P.O. Box 540, Boulder CO 80306. E-mail: Cherubfilm@aol.com. Website: www.OneInTenScreenplayContest.com. Scripts that provide a positive portrayal of gays and lesbians. "A requirement of the competition is that at least one of the primary characters in the screenplay be gay or lesbian (bisexual, transgender, questioning, and the like) and that gay and lesbian characters must be portrayed positively. All writers are encouraged to enter!" Deadline: September 1. Charges $45. Prize: $1,000.

THE PAGE INTERNATIONAL SCREENWRITING AWARDS

The PAGE Awards Committee, 7510 Sunset Blvd., #610, Hollywood CA 90046-3408. E-mail: info@PAGEawards.com. **Contact:** Zoe Simmons, contest coordinator. Annual competition to discover the most talented new screenwriters from across the country and around the world. "Each year, awards are presented to 31 screenwriters in 10 different genre: action/adventure, comedy, drama, family film, historical film, science fiction, thriller/horror, short film script, TV drama pilot, and TV sitcom pilot. Guidelines and entry forms are online. The contest is open to all writers 18 years of age and older who have not previously earned more than $25,000 writing for film and/or television. Please visit contest website for a complete list of rules and regulations." Deadline: January 15 (early); March 1 (regular); April 1 (late). Charges $39 (early); $49 (regular); $59 (late). Prize: Over $50,000 in cash and prizes, including a $25,000 grand prize, plus gold, silver, and bronze prizes in all 10 categories. Most importantly, the award-winning writers receive extensive publicity and industry exposure. Judging is done entirely by Hollywood professionals, including industry script readers, consultants, agents, managers, producers, and development executives. Entrants retain all rights to their work.

THE PEN IS A MIGHTY SWORD

The Virtual Theatre Project, 1901 Rosalia Rd., Los Angeles CA 90027. (877)787-8036. Fax: (323)660-5097. E-mail: pen_sword2010_2011@yahoo.com. **Contact:** Kim Terrell, producing artistic director. "Contest open to unproduced plays written specifically for the stage. Plays should be bold, compelling, and passionate. See website for submission dates and guidelines." Prize: 1st Place: $2,000 and promotion for production; 2nd Place: $1,000; 3rd Place: $500 and a reading. In addition, up to 7 honorable mentions receive $100 each. Judged by a panel of professional writers, directors, and producers.

PILGRIM PROJECT GRANTS

C/O First Things, 35 East 21st St., 6th Floor, New York NY 10010. (212)627-2288. Fax: (212)627-2184. E-mail: davida@firstthings.com. **Contact:** Davida Goldman. "Grants for a reading, workshop production, or full production of plays that deal with questions of moral significance." Deadline: Ongoing. Prize: Grants of $1,000-7,000

RHODE ISLAND INTERNATIONAL FILM FESTIVAL FEATURE SCREENPLAY COMPETITION

P.O. Box 162, Newport RI 02840. (401)861-4445. Fax: (401)490-6735. E-mail: georget@film-festival.org. Website: www.film-festival.org/enterascreenplay.php. The Rhode Island International Film Festival is calling for Screenplay Entries for its14th annual festival, which takes place August 10-15, 2010 in historic Providence, Rhode Island. The Festival is accepting screenplays in all genres. Screenplays must have been written after 2007. Scripts not to exceed 130 pages. The purpose of the contest is to promote, embolden and cultivate screenwriters in their quest for opportunities in the industry. Deadline: July 15. **Tips** Prefers paperless entries. Go online for downloadable entry form. "Screenplays will be judged on creativity, innovation, vision, originality and the use of language. The key element is that of communication and how it complements and is transformed by the language of film."

SCRIPTAPALOOZA SCREENPLAY COMPETITION

Supported by Writers Guild of America west Registry, the Writers Guild of Canada and Write Brothers, 7775 Sunset Blvd., #200, Hollywood CA 90046. (323)654-5809. E-mail: info@scriptapalooza.com. Website: www.scriptapalooza.com. **Contact:** Mark Andrushko, pres. Estab. 1998. "Annual competition for unpublished scripts from any genre. Open to any writer, 18 or older. Submit one copy of a 90- to 130-page screenplay. Body pages must be numbered, and scripts must be in industry-standard format. All entered scripts will be read and judged by more than 90 production companies." Early Deadline: January 7; Deadline: March 5; Late Deadline: April 15. Charges Entry Fee: $40 (early); $50 (regular deadline); $55 (late). Prize: 1st Place: $10,000 and software package from Write Brothers, Inc.; 2nd Place, 3rd Place, and 10 Runners-Up: Software package from Write Brothers, Inc. The top 100 scripts will be considered by over 90 production companies.

SCRIPTAPALOOZA TELEVISION WRITING COMPETITION

7775 Sunset Blvd., PMB #200, Hollywood CA 90046. (323)654-5809. E-mail: info@scriptapalooza.com. "Biannual competition accepting entries in 4 categories: reality shows, sitcoms, original pilots, and 1-hour dramas. There are more than 25 producers, agents, and managers reading the winning scripts. Two past winners won Emmys because of Scriptapalooza and 1 past entrant now writes for Comedy Central." Deadline: October 15 and April 15. Charges $40. Prize: 1st Place: $500; 2nd Place: $200; 3rd Place: $100 (in each category).

SCRIPT PIMP SCREENWRITING COMPETITION

Script P.I.M.P. (Pipeline Into Motion Pictures), 8033 Sunset Blvd., Hollywood CA 90046. (310)401-1155. Fax: (310)564-2021. E-mail: comp@scriptpimp.com. **Contact:** Matt Misetich, general manager. The Script Pimp 8th Annual Screenwriting and 3rd Annual TV Writing Competitions are open for entries. This is an international competition open to all original feature film screenplays that have yet to be produced, optioned, or sold. Open to writers 18 years and older. All genres, styles, and formats accepted. Over 200 companies review the finalists, and previous winners have gone on to secure studio writing assignments, gained representation, and seen their work optioned. Deadline: May 1st, 2010. Charges $50. Prize:

$20,000 in cash for the winners; $80,000 in prizes to anyone who enters a panel of working literary agents, literary managers, and development directors from the film industry. Each screenplay is guaranteed 2 reads from the panel of judges. Script P.I.M.P. does not acquire any rights to materials submitted through the contest.

SCRIPT SAVVY'S MONTHLY SCREENPLAY CONTEST

Script Savvy, (214)546-8686. E-mail: info@scriptsavvy.net. **Contact:** Donna White, coordinator. "Visit the website for online submission instructions. No guidelines or entry forms are available for SASE." Submissions are never optioned/unproduced screenplays only. Feature length screenplays only. International entries accepted, but scripts must be in English. Visit the website for complete details. "Winners are recommended to our producer sponsors for production consideration and given industry exposure." Deadline: the last day of each month. It is the same each year. Charges $39 for basic entry; $59 for entry with standard feedback; $99 for entry with full analysis. Prize: Script Savvy Monthly Screenplay Contest offers over $1,500 in cash and prizes every month and is designed to give the author maximum industry exposure. "Our judges are industry professionals from production companies and agencies."

REVA SHINER COMEDY AWARD

Bloomington Playwrights Project, 107 W. 9th St., Bloomington IN 47404. E-mail: literarymananger@newplays.org. **Contact:** Josie Gingrich, Literary Manager. Annual award for unpublished/unproduced plays. The Bloomington Playwrights Project is a script-developing organization. Winning playwrights are expected to become part of the development process, working with the director in person or via long-distance. Please check the website for more details. Deadline: October 31. Charges $10 reading fee (waived for Dramatist Guild Member and agent-submitted scripts); scripts will not be returned. Prize: $1,000, full production as a part of the Mainstage season. the literary committee of the BPP.

SHRIEKFEST HORROR/SCI-FI FILM FESTIVAL & SCREENPLAY COMPETITION

PO Box 920444, Sylmar CA 91392. E-mail: shriekfest@aol.com. Website: www.shriekfest.com. **Contact:** Denise Gossett/Todd Beeson. "No, we don't use loglines anywhere, we keep your script private." We accept award winning screenplays, no restrictions as long as it's in the horror/thriller or scifi/fantasy genres. We accept shorts and features. No specific lengths. "Our awards are to help screenwriters move their script up the ladder and hopefully have it made into a film. Our winners take that win and parlay it into agents, film deals, and options." Deadline: March 20, May 22 and July 10. Charges $25-55. Prize: Trophies, product awards, usually cash. Our awards are updated all year long as sponsors step onboard. The winners go home with lots of stuff. The contest is open to any writer, all ages, we have an under 18 category too. And we are an international contest. We have at least 15-20 judges and they are all in different aspects of the entertainment industry, such as producers, directors, writers, actors, agents."

THE SILVER FALCHION AWARD

Killer Nashville, P.O. Box 680686, Franklin TN 37068-0686. (615)599-4032. E-mail: contact@killernashville.com. **Contact:** Clay Stafford. Contest is offered annually. No rights to submitted materials are acquired or purchased. Nominated authors must be registered to attend the current Killer Nashville Crime Literature conference. At the time of registration or any time thereafter, up to and including August 1, the author must inform conference coordinators (via conference registration form or email to: contact@killernashville.com) of their intent to nominate a title. The book must have been published between the current or previous calendar year. Fiction and nonfiction books (and collections of short stories by one author in a single book form) are eligible. The purpose of the Silver Falchion Award is to recognize the best publishing achievement by a Killer Nashville attendee published during the current or previous calendar year, as voted upon by Killer Nashville conference attendees. Deadline: 2 weeks prior to conference, usually around August 1. Charges No fee. Prize: A plaque with the Silver Falchion emblem stating the Killer Nashville year of receipt. Voted on by Killer Nashville attendees of the current year.

SOUTHEASTERN THEATRE CONFERENCE NEW PLAY PROJECT

Dept. of Theatre & Dance, Austin Peay State Univ., 681 Summer St., Clarksville TN 37044. E-mail: hardinb@apsu.edu. **Contact:** Chris Hardin, chair. "Annual award for full-length plays or related one acts. No musicals or children's plays. Submissions must be unproduced/unpublished. Readings and workshops are acceptable. Submit application, synopsis, and 1 copy of script on CD or as an e-mail attachment (preferred). Send SASE or visit website for application. Entries will be accepted between March 1st and June 1st. One submission per playwright only." Eligibility: Playwrights who reside in the

SETC region (or who are enrolled in a regionally accredited educational institution in the SETC region) or who reside outside the region but are SETC members are eligible for consideration. SETC Region states include Alabama, Florida, Georgia, Kentucky, Mississippi, North Carolina, South Carolina, Tennessee, Virginia, West Virginia. Mission: The SETC New Play Project is dedicated to the discovery, development and publicizing of worthy new plays and playwrights. Deadline: June 1. Prize: $1,000 and a staged reading.

Tips "Text should be in 12 pt type and in a plain font such as Times New Roman. Plays must be submitted by email attachment in Microsoft Word or PDF format with the following guidelines: Script must include page numbers at the bottom of each page. The author's name should not appear anywhere in the script. Do not include resumes, playwright biographies or a history of the play. 1 copy, Word or PDF format, attached to an email. Completed Application Form included as separate email attachment. Electronic signatures will be accepted. The decision of the panel of readers will be announced in November of each year."

SOUTHERN PLAYWRIGHTS COMPETITION

Jacksonville State University, 700 Pelham Rd. N., Jacksonville AL 36265-1602. (256)782-5469. Fax: (256)782-5441. E-mail: jmaloney@jsu.edu; swhitton@jsu.edu. Website: www.jsu.edu/depart/english/southpla.htm. **Contact:** Joy Maloney, Steven J. Whitton. Estab. 1988. "Offered annually to identify and encourage the best of Southern playwriting. Playwrights must be a native or resident of Alabama, Arkansas, District of Columbia, Florida, Georgia, Kentucky, Louisiana, Missouri, North Carolina, South Carolina, Tennessee, Texas, Virginia, or West Virginia." Deadline: January 15. Prize: $1,000 and production of the play.

10-MINUTE PLAY FESTIVAL

Fire Rose Productions & International Arts Group, 11246 Magnolia Blvd., NoHo Theatre & Arts District CA 91601. (818)766-3691. E-mail: info@fireroseproductions.com. **Contact:** Kaz Matamura, director. Contest is offered twice a year for unpublished and unproduced plays that are 8-12 minutes long. Fire Rose Productions & International Arts Group are nonprofit organizations that are committed to discovering new playwrights and giving them opportunities to work with directors and producers. Deadline: March 31. Charges $5. Prize: 1st Place: $200; 2nd Place: $100; professionally mounted production for winners and semi-finalists. Guest judges are entertainment professionals including writers, producers, directors, and agents. Fire Rose Productions does the first evaluation. Acquires right to produce and mount the plays if chosen as festival finalists or semi-finalists. No royalties are gathered for those performances.

Tips Download the application online.

THEATRE CONSPIRACY ANNUAL NEW PLAY CONTEST

Theatre Conspiracy, 10091 McGregor Blvd., Ft. Myers FL 33919. (239)936-3239. Fax: (239)936-0510. E-mail: info@theatreconspiracy.org. **Contact:** Bill Taylor, artistic director. Offered annually for full-length plays that are unproduced or have received up to 3 productions with 8 or less characters and simple to moderate production demands. No musicals. One entry per year. Send SASE for contest results. Deadline: March 30. Charges $5 fee. Prize: $700 and full production.

VERMONT PLAYWRIGHT'S AWARD

The Valley Players, P.O. Box 441, Waitsfield VT 05673. (802)583-6767. E-mail: valleyplayer@madriver.com. **Contact:** Sharon Kellerman. Offered annually for unpublished, nonmusical, full-length plays suitable for production by a community theater group to encourage development of playwrights in Vermont, New Hampshire, and Maine. Deadline: February 1. Prize: $1,000.

THE HERMAN VOADEN NATIONAL PLAYWRITING COMPETITION

Drama Department, Queen's University, Kingston ON K7L 3N6 Canada. (613)533-2104. E-mail: carolanne.hanna@queensu.ca; drama@queensu.ca. **Contact:** Carol Anne Hanna. Offered every 2 years for unpublished plays to discover and develop new Canadian plays. See website for deadlines and guidelines. Open to Canadian citizens or landed immigrants. Charges $40 entry fee. Prize: $3,000, $2,000, and 8 honorable mentions. 1st- and 2nd-prize winners are offered a 1-week workshop and public reading by professional director and cast. The 2 authors will be playwrights-in-residence for the rehearsal and reading period.

WATERFRONT FILM FESTIVAL AND INDIE SCREENPLAY COMPETITION

P.O. Box 387, Saugatuck MI 49453. (269)857-8351. E-mail: screenplay@waterfrontfilm.org. The contest is now accepting entries from writers in any state. Previously, the contest was only for local writers.

Scripts must be 80-130 pages in length. Entries are accepted through Withabox. Deadline: April 1. Charges $40. Prize: Prize includes cash, an industry reception in the winner's honor, lodging, and VIP pass to the festival. All genres.

WORLDFEST-HOUSTON INDEPENDENT INTERNATIONAL FILM FESTIVAL

9898 Bissonnet St., Suite 650, Houston TX 77036. (713)965-9955. Fax: (713)965-9960. E-mail: entry@worldfest.org. Website: www.worldfest.org. **Contact:** Entry Coordinator. Competition for all genres of screenplays, films, and videos. Deadline: December 15. Charges Charges $45-$85. Prize: Cash prizes, options, production deals, workshops, master classes, and seminars.

YEAR END SERIES (YES) FESTIVAL OF NEW PLAYS

Dept. of Theatre, Nunn Dr., Northern Kentucky University, Highland Heights KY 41099-1007. (859)572-6362. Fax: (859)572-6057. E-mail: forman@nku.edu. **Contact:** Sandra Forman, project director. "Receives submissions from May 1 until September 30 in even-numbered years for the festivals which occur in April of odd-numbered years. Open to all writers." Deadline: October 1. Prize: $500 and an expense-paid visit to Northern Kentucky University to see the play produced

YOUNG PLAYWRIGHTS FESTIVAL NATIONAL PLAYWRITING COMPETITION

Young Playwrights, Inc., PO Box 5134, New York NY 10185. (212)594-5440. Fax: (212)594-5441. E-mail: literary@youngplaywrights.org. **Contact:** Literary Department. The Young Playwrights Festival National Playwriting Competition is offered annually to identify talented American playwrights aged 18 or younger. Please include your address, phone number, email address, and date of birth on the title page. Open to US residents only. Deadline: January 2 (postmarked). Prize: Winners receive an invitation to New York City for the annual Young Playwrights, Inc. Writers Conference and a professionally staged reading of their play. Entrants retain all rights to their work.

YOUNG PLAYWRIGHTS INC. WRITE A PLAY! NYC COMPETITION

Young Playwrights, Inc., P.O. Box 5134, New York NY 10185. (212)594-5440. Fax: (212)684-4902. E-mail: literary@youngplaywrights.org. **Contact:** Literary Department. "Offered annually for stage plays of any length (no musicals, screenplays, or adaptations) by NYC elementary, middle, and high school students only." Deadline: March 1. Prize: varies.

ANNA ZORNIO MEMORIAL CHILDREN'S THEATRE PLAYWRITING COMPETITION

University of New Hampshire, Dept. of Theatre and Dance, PCAC, 30 Academic Way,, Durham NH 03824-3538. (603)862-3044. E-mail: mike.wood@unh.edu. **Contact:** Michael Wood. "Offered every 4 years for unpublished well-written plays or musicals appropriate for young audiences with a maximum length of 60 minutes. May submit more than 1 play, but not more than 3. All plays will be performed by adult actors and must be appropriate for a children's audience within the K-12 grades. Guidelines and entry forms available as downloads on the website. Open to all playwrights in US and Canada. All ages are invited to participate." Deadline: March 2, 2012. Prize: Up to $500. The play is also produced and underwritten as part of the 2013-2014 season by the UNH Department of Theatre and Dance. Winner will be notified on or after Dec. 15, 2012.

Poetry

ACORN-PLANTOS AWARD FOR PEOPLES POETRY

Acorn-Plantos Award Committee, 36 Sunset Ave., Hamilton ON L8R 1V6 Canada. E-mail: jeffseff@allstream.net. **Contact:** Jeff Seffinga. "Annual contest for work that appeared in print in the previous calendar year. This award is given to the Canadian poet who best (through the publication of a book of poems) exemplifies populist or peoples poetry in the tradition of Milton Acorn, Ted Plantos, et al. Work may be entered by the poet or the publisher; the award goes to the poet. Entrants must submit 5 copies of each title. Poet must be a citizen of Canada or a landed immigrant. Publisher need not be Canadian." Deadline: June 30. Charges $25 (CDN)/title. Prize: $500 (CDN) and a medal. Judged by a panel of poets in the tradition who are not entered in the current year.

ANDERBO POETRY PRIZE

Anderbo Poetry Prize, 270 Lafayette St., Suite 1412, New York NY 10012. Website: www.anderbo.com. **Contact:** Rick Rofihe. Estab. 2005. "Poet must not have have been previously published on anderbo.com. Limit 6 poems per poet. Poems should be typed on 8½ × 11 paper with the poet's name and contact info on the upper right corner of each poem. Mail submissions. Enclose SASE to receive names of winner and honorable mentions. See guidelines online at website. All entries are non-returnable." Postmarked by Nov. 1, 2010. Charges $10 reading fee. Check or money order payable to Rick Rofihe. Prize: $500, publication on anderbo.com.

Tips The winner of the Anderbo poetry prize for 2009 is Nancy K. Pearson of Cape Cod for her poem "Prairies."

ANHINGA PRIZE FOR POETRY

Anhinga Press, Drawer W, P.O. Box 10595, Tallahassee FL 32302. (850)442-1408. Fax: (850)442-6323. E-mail: info@anhinga.org. Website: www.anhinga.org. Estab. 1983. Offered annually for a book-length collection of poetry by an author who has not published more than 1 book of poetry. Guidelines for SASE or on website. Open to any writer writing in English. Deadline: February 15-May 1. Charges $25 fee. Prize: $2,000, and publication.

ANNUAL GIVAL PRESS OSCAR WILDE AWARD

Gival Press, LLC, P.O. Box 3812, Arlington VA 22203. (703)351-0079. E-mail: givalpress@yahoo.com. **Contact:** Robert L. Giron. "Award given to the best previously unpublished original poem—written in English of any length, in any style, typed, double-spaced on 1 side only—which best relates gay/lesbian/bisexual/transgendered life, by a poet who is 18 or older. Entrants are asked to submit their poems without any kind of identification (with the exception of titles) and with a separate cover page with the following information: name, address (street, city, and state with zip code), telephone number, e-mail address (if available) and a list of poems by title. Checks drawn on American banks should be made out to Gival Press, LLC." Deadline: June 27 (postmarked). Charges $5 (USD) reading fee per poem. Prize: $100 (USD), and the poem, along with information about the poet, will be published on the Gival Press website.

ATLANTIC POETRY PRIZE

Writers' Federation of Nova Scotia, 1113 Marginal Rd., Halifax NS B3H 4P7 Canada. (902)423-8116. Fax: (902)422-0881. E-mail: talk@writers.ns.ca. **Contact:** Nate Crawford, executive director. Full-length books of adult poetry written by Atlantic Canadians, and published as a whole for the first time in the previous calendar year, are eligible. Entrants must be native or resident Atlantic Canadians who have either been born in Newfoundland, Prince Edward Island, Nova Scotia, or New Brunswick, and spent a susbstantial portion of their lives living there, or who have lived in one or a combination of these provinces for at least 24 consecutive months prior to entry deadline date. Publishers: Send 4 copies and a letter attesting to the author's status as an Atlantic Canadian and the author's current mailing address and telephone number. Deadline: First Friday in December. Prize: $2,000.

THE BASKERVILLE PUBLISHERS POETRY AWARD & THE BETSY COLQUITT POETRY AWARD

descant, Texas Christian University's literary journal, TCU, Box 297270, Fort Worth TX 76129. (817)257-6537. Fax: (817)257-6239. E-mail: descant@tcu.edu. **Contact:** Dan Williams and Alex Lemon. "Annual award for an outstanding poem published in an issue of *descant*." Deadline: September - April. Prize: $250 for Baskerville Award; $500 for Betsy Colquitt Award. Publication retains copyright, but will transfer it to the author upon request.

THE BINGHAMTON UNIVERSITY MILT KESSLER POETRY BOOK AWARD

Binghamton Center for Writers, Dept. of English, General Literature & Rhetoric, Library North, Room 1149, Vestal Parkway E., P.O. Box 6000, Binghamton NY 13902-6000. (607)777-2713. E-mail: cwpro@binghamton.edu. **Contact:** Maria Mazziotti Gillan, creative writing program director. Estab. 2001. Offered annually for work published that year. Books must be 48 pages or more with a press run of 500 copies or more. Each book submitted must be accompanied by an application form available online. Poet or publisher may submit more than 1 book for prize consideration. Send 3 copies of each book. Guidelines available online or for SASE. Open to any writer over the age of 40. Deadline: March 1. Prize: $1,000. Judged by professional poet not on Binghamton University faculty.

BLUE MOUNTAIN ARTS/SPS STUDIOS POETRY CARD CONTEST

P.O. Box 1007, Boulder CO 80306. (303)449-0536. Fax: (303)447-0939. E-mail: poetrycontest@sps.com. Website: www.sps.com. "We're looking for original poetry that is rhyming or non-rhyming, although we find no-rhyming poetry reads better. Poems may also be considered for possible publication on greeting cards or in book anthologies. Contest is offered biannually. Guidelines available online." Deadline: December 31 and June 30. Prize: 1st Place: $300; 2nd Place: $150; 3rd Place: $50. Judged by Blue Mountain Arts editorial staff.

THE FREDERICK BOCK PRIZE

Poetry, Poetry, 444 North Michigan Ave., Suite 1850, Chicago IL 60610. (312)787-7070. E-mail: poetry@poetrymagazine.org. Estab. 1981. Offered annually for poems published in *Poetry* during the preceding year (October through September). *Poetry* buys all rights to the poems published in the magazine. Copyrights are returned to the authors on request. Any writer may submit poems to *Poetry*. Prize: $500.

M. AND S. BONOMO FICTION AWARD

Italian Americana, URI/CCE, 80 Washington St., Providence RI 02903-1803. E-mail: bonomoal@etal.uri.edu or it.americana@yahoo.com. Website: www.italianamericana.com. **Contact:** Carol Bonomo Albright, editor. Offered annually as an honorific. Prize: $1,000.

THE BORDIGHERA ITALIAN-AMERICAN POETRY PRIZE

Sonia Raiziss-Giop Foundation, Bordighera Press @ John D. Calandra Italian American Institute, Graduate Center, The City University of New York, 25 West 43rd St., 17th Floor, New York NY 10036. E-mail: daniela@garden.net. **Contact:** Daniela Gioseffi. "Offered annually to find the best unpublished manuscripts of poetry in English, by an American of Italian descent, to be translated into quality Italian and published bilingually. No Italian-American themes required, just excellent poetry. Guidelines for SASE or see online. Judges change every 2 years. Former judges include Daniela Gioseffi, Felix Stefanile, Dorothy Barresi, W.S. DePiero, Donna Masini, Michael Palma, Patricia Fargnoli." Deadline: May 31. Prize: $2,000 and bilingual book publication to be divided between poet and consigned translator.

Tips "Send 10 anonymous sample pages in duplicate with removable cover page: bio, address, e-mail and phone. Can be submitted bilingually or in English only. No Italian American themes required—just excellent poetry."

BARBARA BRADLEY PRIZE

New England Poetry Club, P.O. Box 190076, Boston MA 02119. E-mail: contests@nepoetryclub.org. **Contact:** NEPC Contest Coordinator. Offered annually for a poem under 21 lines, written by a woman. It must be submitted only in April and May contests. Deadline: May 31. Charges $10 is entry fee for every 3 poems, for 3 contests. Prize: $200.

Tips "Send 2 copies of each entry with your name, address and phone number on one copy."

BRIGHT HILL PRESS ANNUAL POETRY BOOK COMPETITION

Bright Hill Press, P.O. Box 193, Treadwell NY 13846. Phone/Fax: (607)829-5055. E-mail: wordthur@stny.rr.com. **Contact:** Bertha Rogers, editor. Send 48-65 pages, bio, TOC, acknowledgments page, and 2 title pages (1 with name, address, etc.; 1 with title only). Poems can be published in journals or anthologies. Guidelines online, for SASE, or via e-mail. Deadline: November 30. Charges $22 fee. Prize: $1,000, publication, and 25 copies of the winning book.

BRITTINGHAM PRIZE IN POETRY; FELIX POLLAK PRIZE IN POETRY

University of Wisconsin Press, Dept. of English, 600 N. Park St., University of Wisconsin, Madison WI 53706. E-mail: rwallace@wisc.edu. **Contact:** Ronald Wallace, contest director. Estab. 1985. "Offered for unpublished book-length mss of original poetry. Submissions must be received by the press during the month of September, accompanied by a required SASE for contest results. Does not return mss. One entry fee covers both prizes. Guidelines for SASE or online." Charges $25 fee (payable to Univ. of Wisconsin Press). Prize: $2,500 ($1,000 cash prize and $1,500 honorarium for campus reading) and publication of the 2 winning mss.

GERALD CABLE BOOK AWARD

Silverfish Review Press, P.O. Box 3541, Eugene OR 97403. (541)344-5060. E-mail: sfrpress@earthlink.net. Website: www.silverfishreviewpress.com. **Contact:** Rodger Moody, series editor. "Purpose is to publish a poetry book by a deserving author who has yet to publish a full-length book collection. For guidelines send SASE, or request by e-mail." Deadline: October 15. Charges $20 reading fee. Prize: $1,000, 25 copies, and publication by the press for a book-length ms of original poetry.

Tips "Now accepting email submissions (save money on postage and photocopying); use Paypal for reading fee payment, see website for instructions."

THE CENTER FOR BOOK ARTS POETRY CHAPBOOK COMPETITION

The Center for Book Arts, 28 W. 27th St., 3rd Floor, New York NY 10001. (212)481-0295. Fax: (866)708-8994. E-mail: info@centerforbookarts.org. Website: www.centerforbookarts.org. **Contact:** Sarah Nicholls. Offered annually for unpublished collections of poetry. Individual poems may have been previously published. Collection must not exceed 500 lines or 24 pages. Deadline: December 1 (postmarked). Charges $25 fee. Prize: $500 award, $500 honorarium for a reading, publication, and 10 copies of chapbook.

JOHN CIARDI PRIZE FOR POETRY

BkMk Press, University of Missouri-Kansas City, 5100 Rockhill Rd., Kansas City MO 02903-1803. (816)235-2558. E-mail: bkmk@umkc.edu. Website: www.umkc.edu/bkmk. "Offered annually for the best book-length collection (unpublished) of poetry in English by a living author. Translations are not eligible. Initial judging is done by a network of published writers. Final judging is done by a writer of national reputation. Guidelines for SASE, by e-mail, or on website." Deadline: January 15 (postmarked). Charges $25 fee. Prize: $1,000, plus book publication by BkMk Press.

CLEVELAND STATE UNIVERSITY POETRY CENTER PRIZES

Cleveland State University Poetry Center, 2121 Euclid Ave., Cleveland OH 44115-2214. (216)687-3986. Fax: (216)687-6943. E-mail: poetrycenter@csuohio.edu. **Contact:** Rita Grabowski, poetry center manager. Estab. 1987. Offered annually to identify, reward, and publish the best unpublished book-length poetry ms (minimum 48 pages) in 2 categories: First Book Award and Open Competition (for poets who have published at least one collection with a press run of 500). Submission implies willingness to sign standard contract for publication if manuscript wins. Does not return mss. Guidelines for SASE or online. Deadline: Submissions accepted November 1-February 15. Charges $25 fee. Prize: First Book and Open Book Competitions award publication and a $1000 advance against royalties for an original manuscript of poetry in each category.

THE COLORADO PRIZE FOR POETRY

Colorado Review/Center for Literary Publishing, Dept. of English, Colorado State University, 9105 Campus Delivery, Ft. Collins CO 80523-9105. (970)491-5449. E-mail: creview@colostate.edu. **Contact:** Stephanie G'Schwind, editor. Estab. 1995. "Offered annually to an unpublished collection of poetry. Guidelines available for SASE or online at website." To connect writers and readers by publishing exceptional writing. Deadline: January 14. Charges $25 fee (includes subscription). Prize: $1,500 and publication of book.

CRAB ORCHARD SERIES IN POETRY OPEN COMPETITION

1000 Faner Dr., Southern Illinois University, Carbondale IL 62901-4503. **Contact:** Jon C. Tribble, series editor. "Offered annually for collections of unpublished poetry. Open to US citizens and permanent residents." Visit website for current deadlines. Charges $25 fee. Prize: Two winners selected: both receive $3,500 and publication.

T.S. ELIOT PRIZE FOR POETRY

Truman State University Press, 100 E. Normal St., Kirksville MO 63501-4221. (660)785-7336. Fax: (660)785-4480. E-mail: tsup@truman.edu. Website: tsup.truman.edu. **Contact:** Nancy Rediger. Annual competition for unpublished poetry collection. Guidelines for SASE, online, or by e-mail. Deadline: October 31 (postmarked). Charges $25 fee. Prize: $2,000 and publication.

[N] FALL POETRY CHAPBOOK CONTEST

White Eagle Coffee Store Press, P.O. Box 383, Fox River Grove IL 60021-0383. (847)639-9200. E-mail: wecspress@aol.com. Website: whiteeaglecoffeestorepress.com. **Contact:** Frank Edmund Smith, publisher. "This contest is designed to promote and reward the writing of a small collection of poetry—20-22 pages. Typically poets wish to publish chapbooks early in their careers, as a way of marking an achievement and having inexpensive books to sell at poetry readings. Many poets continue to publish chapbooks throughout their careers. This press especially welcomes writers of any age who have just begun to publish, but it is open to more successful writers, too." Deadline: October 31. Charges Entry fee: $15. Prize: Publication, $500, and 25 copies of the published chapbook. 10 copies for press kits. All contest entrants receive a copy of the book. "The final judge is always announced and is someone who has already published with the press, usually a previous contest winner. Thus, the press is always open to new styles and new writers. Author maintains copyright. White Eagle Coffee Store Press acquires first publishing rights and the exclusive right to print and reprint the chapbook."

JANICE FARRELL POETRY PRIZE

The Soul-Making Literary Competition, National League of American Pen Women, Nob Hill, San Francisco Branch, The Webhallow House, 1544 Sweetwood Dr., Broadmoor Village CA 94015-1717. E-mail: pennobhill@aol.com. **Contact:** Eileen Malone. "Poetry may be double- or single-spaced. One-page poems only, and only 1 poem/page. All poems must be titled. 3 poems/entry. Indicate category on each poem. Identify with 3 × 5 card only. Open annually to all writers." Deadline: November 30. Charges $5/entry (make checks payable to NLAPW, Nob Hill Branch). Prize: 1st Place: $100; 2nd Place: $50; 3rd Place: $25. Judged by a local San Francisco successfully published poet.

FIELD POETRY PRIZE

Oberlin College Press/FIELD, 50 N. Professor St., Oberlin OH 44074-1091. (440)775-8408. Fax: (440)775-8124. E-mail: oc.press@oberlin.edu. Website: www.oberlin.edu/ocpress/prize.htm. **Contact:** Linda Slocum, managing editor. "Offered annually for unpublished work. Contest seeks to encourage the finest in contemporary poetry writing. Open to any writer." Deadline: Submit in May only. Charges $25 fee, which includes a 1-year subscription to FIELD. Prize: $1,000 and the book is published in Oberlin College Press's FIELD Poetry Series.

N FOOD VERSE CONTEST

Literal Latte, 200 East 10th St., Suite 240, New York NY 10003. (212)260-5532. E-mail: litlatte@aol.com. Website: www.literal-latte.com. **Contact:** Jenine Gordon Bockman, editor. "Open to any writer. Submissions required to be unpublished. Guidelines and entry forms are available for SASE and online at website. Literal Latte acquires first rights. Annual contest to give support and exposure to great writing." Jan. 31 every year. Charges $10 for up to 6 poems. Prize: $500 the Editors.

GIVAL PRESS POETRY AWARD

Gival Press, LLC, P.O. Box 3812, Arlington VA 22203. (703)351-0079. E-mail: givalpress@yahoo.com. **Contact:** Robert L. Giron, editor. "Offered annually for a previously unpublished poetry collection as a complete ms, which may include previously published poems; and previously published poems must be acknowledged & poet must hold rights. The competition seeks to award well-written, original poetry in English on any topic, in any style. Guidelines for SASE, by e-mail, or online. Entrants are asked to submit their poems without any kind of identification (with the exception of the titles) and with a separate cover page with the following information: name, address (street, city, state, and zip code), telephone number, e-mail address (if available), short bio, and a list of the poems by title. Checks drawn on American banks should be made out to Gival Press, LLC." Deadline: December 15 (postmarked). Charges $20 reading fee (USD). Prize: $1,000, publication, and 20 author's copies. The editor narrows entries to the top 10; previous winner selects top 5 and the winner—all done anonymously.

Tips "Open to any writer, as long as the work is original, not a translation, and is written in English. The copyright remains in the author's name; certain rights fall to the publisher per the contract."

GOVERNOR GENERAL'S LITERARY AWARD FOR POETRY

Canada Council for the Arts, 350 Albert St., P.O. Box 1047, Ottawa ON K1P 5V8 Canada. (613)566-4414, ext. 5573. Fax: (613)566-4410. E-mail: lori.knoll@canadacouncil.ca. Website: www.canadacouncil.ca/prizes/ggla. Offered for the best English-language and the best French-language work of poetry by a Canadian. Publishers submit titles for consideration. Deadline depends on the book's publication date in English: March 15, June 1, or August 7. Books in French: March 15 or July 15. Prize: Each laureate receives $25,000; non-winning finalists receive $1,000.

GREEN ROSE PRIZE IN POETRY

New Issues Poetry & Prose, Western Michigan University, 1903 W. Michigan Ave., Kalamazoo MI 49008-5463. (269)387-8185. Fax: (269)387-2562. E-mail: william.olsen@wmich.edu. **Contact:** William Olsen, editor. Offered annually for unpublished poetry. The university will publish a book of poems by a poet writing in English who has published 1 or more full-length collections of poetry. Guidelines for SASE or online. *New Issues Poetry & Prose* obtains rights for first publication. Book is copyrighted in the author's name. Deadline: May 1-September 30. Charges $20 fee. Prize: $2,000 and publication of book. Author also receives 10% of the printed edition.

THE GRIFFIN POETRY PRIZE

The Griffin Trust for Excellence in Poetry, 363 Parkridge Crescent, Oakville ON L6M 1A8 Canada. (905)618-0420. E-mail: info@griffinpoetryprize.com. **Contact:** Ruth Smith. Offered annually for work published between January 1 and December 31. Deadline: December 31. Prize: Two $50,000 (Canadian) prizes. One prize will go to a living Canadian poet or translator, the other to a living poet or translator from any country, which may include Canada. a panel of qualified English-speaking judges of stature. Judges are chosen by the Trustees of The Griffin Trust For Excellence in Poetry.

KATHRYN HANDLEY PROSE POEM PRIZE

National League of American Pen Women, Nob Hill, San Francisco Branch, The Webhallow House, 1544 Sweetwood Dr., Colma CA 94015-1717. E-mail: pennobhill@aol.com. **Contact:** Eileen Malone. Poetry may be double- or single-spaced. 1-page poems only, and only 1 prose poem/page. 3 poems/entry. Indicate category on each poem. Identify only with 3 × 5 card. Open annually to all writers. Deadline: November 30. Charges $5/entry (make checks payable to NLAPW, Nob Hill Branch). Prize: 1st Place: $100; 2nd Place: $50; 3rd Place: $25.

THE BEATRICE HAWLEY AWARD

Alice James Books, 238 Main St., Farmington ME 04938. Phone/Fax: (207)778-7071. E-mail: ajb@umf.maine.edu. Website: www.alicejamesbooks.org. **Contact:** Julia Bouwsma, associate managing editor. "Offered annually for unpublished full-length poetry collection. Open to US residents only. Guidelines online or for SASE." Deadline: December 1. Charges $25. Prize: $2,000 and publication.

THE BESS HOKIN PRIZE

Poetry, 444 North Michigan Ave. Suite 1850, Chicago IL 60611. (312)787-7070. E-mail: poetry@poetrymagazine.org. Website: www.poetrymagazine.org. Estab. 1947. Offered annually for poems published in *Poetry* during the preceding year (October-September). *Poetry* buys all rights to the poems published in the magazine. Copyrights are returned to the authors on request. Prize: $1,000.

FIRMAN HOUGHTON PRIZE

New England Poetry Club, P.O. Box 19007, Boston MA 02119. E-mail: contests@nepoetryclug.org. Website: www.nepoetryclub.org/contests.htm. **Contact:** NEPC Contest Coordinator. Offered annually for a lyric poem under 200 lines. Submitted only in April or May to New England Poetry Club. Deadline: May 31. Charges $10 fee for 3 contest entries, payable to New England Poetry Club. Members free. Prize: $250.

Tips "Send two copies of your entry: one original and one with the writer's name and address on it."

[N] ILLINOIS STATE POETRY SOCIETY 18TH ANNUAL CONTEST

Sponsored by Illinois State Poetry Society, 2382 Kildeer St., Woodridge IL 60517. Website: http://illinoispoets.org. **Contact:** Marvin Young. Estab. 1983. Annual contest to encourage the crafting of excellent poetry. Guidelines and entry forms available for SASE. Deadline: September 30, 2011 (postmark). Charges Fee is $6 for up to 3 poems, $1 each additional poem; ISPS members, $3 up to 5 poems, $1 each additional poem. Prize: Cash prizes of $50, $30, $10. Three Honorable Mentions. Poet retains all rights. There are three categories: (1) free verse, (2) formal verse, (3) special theme (changes every year). Judged by out-of-state professionals.

INDIANA REVIEW POETRY PRIZE

Indiana Review, Ballantine Hall 465, Indiana University, Bloomington IN 47405-7103. (812)855-3439. Fax: (812)855-9535. Website: www.indianareview.com. **Contact:** Alessandra Simmons, Editor. Offered annually for unpublished work. Judged by guest judges; 2009 prize judged by Natasha Trethewey. Open to any writer. Send no more than 3 poems per entry. Guidelines on web site and with SASE request. Deadline: Late March or Early April. Charges $15 fee (includes a 1-year subscription). Prize: $1,000.

IOWA POETRY PRIZES

University of Iowa Press, 100 Kuhl House, Iowa City IA 52242. (319)335-2000. Fax: (319)335-2055. Offered annually to encourage poets and their work. Submissions must be postmarked during the month of April; put name on title page only. Open to writers of English (US citizens or not). Manuscripts will not be returned. Previous winners are not eligible. Charges $20 reading fee. Deadline: April 30.

RANDALL JARRELL POETRY COMPETITION

North Carolina Writers' Network, Appalachian State University, Department of English, Box 32052, Boone NC 28608. E-mail: mailtlkenned@uncg.edu. **Contact:** Terry L. Kennedy. Offered annually for unpublished work "to honor Randall Jarrell and his life at UNC-Greensboro by recognizing the best poetry submitted." Competition is open any writer who is a legal resident of North Carolina or a member of the NC Writers Network. Deadline: February 15. Charges $10 (NCWN members); $15 (nonmembers) entry fee. Prize: The contest awards the winner publication in *The Crucible* literary journal and $200.

THE ROBINSON JEFFERS TOR HOUSE 2010 PRIZE FOR POETRY

The Robinson Jeffers Tor House Foundation, P.O. Box 2137, Carmel CA 93921. (831)624-1813. Fax: (831)624-3696. E-mail: thf@torhouse.org. **Contact:** Poetry Prize Coordinator. The 2010 Prize includes a reading in Chicago on June 9 sponsored by the Poetry Center as part of "The Big Read: The Poetryof Robinson Jeffers." Included is round-trip air (economy), one night's lodging, and a $500 honorarium. The Big Read is an initiative of the National Endowment for the Arts in partnership with the Institute of Museum and Library Services and Arts Midwest. Open to well-crafted poetry in all styles, ranging from experimental work to traditional forms, including short narrative poems. Each poem should be typed on 8½ × 11 paper, and no longer than three pages. On a cover sheet only, include: name, mailing address, telephone number and e-mail; titles of poems; bio optional. Multiple and simultaneous submissions welcome. The annual Tor House Prize for Poetry is a living memorial to American poet Robinson Jeffers (1887-1962) Deadline: March 15. Charges $10 for first 3 poems; $15 for up to 6 poems; $2.50 for each additional poem. Checks and money orders should be made out to Tor House Foundation. Prize: $1,000 for an original, non-published poem not to exceed three pages in length; $200 for Honorable Mention. Final judging by Mark Doty.

JUNIPER PRIZE FOR POETRY

University of Massachusetts Press, Amherst MA 01003. (413)545-2217. Fax: (413)545-1226. E-mail: info@umpress.umass.edu. **Contact:** Carla J. Potts. Estab. 1964. The University of Massachusetts Press offers the annual Juniper Prize for Poetry, awarded in alternate years for the first and subsequent books. Considers simultaneous submissions, "but if accepted for publication elsewhere, please notify us immediately. Manuscripts by more than 1 author, entries of more than 1 mss simultaneously or within the same year, and translations are not eligible." Deadline: August 1 - September 29 (postmark). Winners announced online in April on the press website. Charges $25 fee. Prize: Includes publication and $1,500 in addition to royalties. In even-numbered years (2010, etc.), only "subsequent" books will be considered: mss whose authors have had at least 1 full-length book or chapbook (of at least 30 pages) of poetry published or accepted for publication. Self-published work is not considered to lie within this "books and chapbooks" category. In odd-numbered years (2011, etc.), only "first books' will be considered: mss by writers whose poems may have appeared in literary journals and/or anthologies but have not been published or accepted for publication in book form.

Tips Submit paginated ms of 50-70 pages of poetry, with paginated contents page, credits page, and information on previously published books. Include 2 cover sheets: one with contract information, one without. Manuscripts will not be returned. Guidelilnes available for SASE or on website.

THE LEDGE ANNUAL POETRY CHAPBOOK CONTEST

The Ledge Magazine, 40 Maple Ave., Bellport NY 11713. E-mail: info@theledgemagazine.com. **Contact:** Timothy Monaghan, Editor-in-Chief. Offered annually to publish an outstanding collection of poems. No restrictions on form or content. Send 16-28 pages, titles page, bio, acknowledgments, SASE. Guidelines online or for SASE. Open to any writer. Deadline: October 31. Charges $18 fee. All entrants receive a copy of the winning chapbook upon its publication. Prize: $1,000 and publication and 25 copies of the chapbook.

THE LEDGE POETRY AWARDS COMPETITION

The Ledge Magazine & Press, 40 Maple Ave., Bellport NY 11713. E-mail: info@theledgemagazine.com. **Contact:** Timothy Monaghan, editor-in-chief. "Offered annually for unpublished poems of exceptional quality and significance. No restrictions on form or content. All poems are considered for publication in the magazine. Guidelines online or for SASE. Open to any writer." Deadline: April 30. Charges $10/first 3 poems; $3/additional poem. $20 subscription to *The Ledge Magazine* gains free entry for the first three poems. Prize: 1st Place: $1,000 and publication in *The Ledge Magazine*; 2nd Place: $250 and publication; 3rd Place: $100 and publication.

THE LEVINSON PRIZE

Poetry, 444 North Michigan Ave., Suite 1850, Chicago IL 60611. (312)787-7070. Fax: (312)787-6650. E-mail: poetry@poetrymagazine.org. Website: www.poetrymagazine.org. Estab. 1914. Offered annually for poems published in *Poetry* during the preceding year (October-September). *Poetry* buys all rights to the poems published in the magazine. Copyrights are returned to the authors on request. Prize: $500.

LEVIS READING PRIZE

Virginia Commonwealth Univ., Dept. of English, P.O. Box 842005, Richmond VA 23284-2005. (804)828-1329. Fax: (804)828-8684. E-mail: tndidato@vcu.edu. **Contact:** Thom Didato. "Offered annually for books of poetry published in the previous year to encourage poets early in their careers. The entry must be the writer's first or second published book of poetry. Previously published books in other genres, or previously published chapbooks or self-published material, do not count as books for this purpose." Deadline: January 15. Prize: $1,000 honorarium and an expense-paid trip to Richmond to present a public reading.

THE RUTH LILLY POETRY PRIZE

The Modern Poetry Association, 444 North Michigan Ave., Suite 1850, Chicago IL 60610. E-mail: poetry@poetrymagazine.org. Estab. 1986. Offered annually to a poet whose accomplishments in the field of poetry warrant extraordinary recognition. No applicants or nominations are accepted. Deadline: Varies. Prize: $100,000.

LITERAL LATTÉ POETRY AWARD

Literal Latté, 200 E. 10th St., Suite 240, New York NY 10003. (212)260-5532. E-mail: LitLatte@aol.com. **Contact:** Jenine Gordon Bockman, editor. "Offered annually to any writer for unpublished poetry (maximum 2,000 words per poem). All styles welcome. Winners published in *Literal Lattè*." Acquires first rights. Deadline: July 15. Charges $10/up to 6 poems; $15/set of 10 poems. Prize: 1st Place: $1,000; 2nd Place: $300; 3rd Place: $200.. Judged by the Editors.

FRANCES LOCKE MEMORIAL POETRY AWARD

The Bitter Oleander Press, 4983 Tall Oaks Dr., Fayetteville NY 13066-9776. (315)637-3047. Fax: (315)637-5056. E-mail: info@bitteroleander.com. **Contact:** Paul B. Roth. Offered annually for unpublished, imaginative poetry. Open to any writer. Deadline: June 15. Charges $10 for 5 poems; $2/additional poem. Prize: $1,000, publication in the autumn issue, and 5 copies of that issue.

LOUISE LOUIS/EMILY F. BOURNE STUDENT POETRY AWARD

Poetry Society of America, 15 Gramercy Park S., New York NY 10003. (212)254-9628. Fax: (212)673-2352. Website: www.poetrysociety.org. **Contact:** Programs Associate. Offered annually for unpublished work to promote excellence in student poetry. Open to American high school or preparatory school students (grades 9-12). Guidelines for SASE and online. Judged by prominent American poets. It is strongly encouraged that applicants read the complete contest guidelines before submitting. Deadline: October 1-December 22. Charges $5 for a student submitting a single entry; $20 for a high school submitting unlimited number of its students' poems. Prize: $250.

THE MACGUFFIN NATIONAL POET HUNT

The MacGuffin, 18600 Haggerty Rd., Livonia MI 48152. E-mail: macguffin@schoolcraft.edu. Website: www.macguffin.org. **Contact:** Managing Editor. Work is judged blindly by a renowned, published poet. Offered annually for unpublished work. Guidelines available by mail, e-mail, or on the website. Acquires first rights (if published). Once published, all rights revert to the author. Open to any writer. Deadline: April 3-June 3 (postmarked). Charges $15 for a 5-poem entry. Prize: 1st Place: $500; 2 Honorable Mentions will be published. 2010 Judge: Jim Daniels. Past judges include Thomas Lynch, Vivian Shipley, Molly Peacock, Bob Hicok, Laurence Lieberman, Thomas Lux, and Conrad Hilberry.

NAOMI LONG MADGETT POETRY AWARD

Lotus Press, Inc., P.O. Box 21607, Detroit MI 48221. E-mail: lotuspress@comcast.net. **Contact:** Constance Withers. "Offered annually to recognize an unpublished poetry ms by an African American. Guidelines for SASE, by e-mail, or online." Deadline: January 2 - March 31. Prize: $500 and publication by Lotus Press.

MORTON MARR POETRY PRIZE

Southwest Review, P.O. Box 750374, Dallas TX 75275-0374. (214)768-1037. Fax: (214)768-1408. E-mail: swr@mail.smu.edu. **Contact:** Willard Spiegelman. "Annual award given to a poem by a writer who has not yet published a first book of poetry. Contestants may submit no more than 6 poems in a traditional form (i.e., sonnet, sestina, villanelle, rhymed stanzas, blank verse, etc.). A cover letter with name, address, and other relevant information may accompany the poems which must be printed without any identifying information. Guidelines for SASE or online. Open to any writer who has not yet published a first book of poetry." Deadline: September 30. Charges $5/poem. Prize: 1st Place: $1,000; 2nd Place: $500; publication in *The Southwest Review*.

N VASSAR MILLER PRIZE IN POETRY

University of North Texas Press, 1155 Union circle, #311336, Denton TX 76203-5017. (940)565-2142. Fax: (940)565-4590. Website: http://web3.unt.edu/untpress/. **Contact:** John Poch. "Annual prize awarded to a collection of poetry." Deadline: November 15. Charges Fee: $25. Prize: Winner will receive $1000 and publication by University of North Texas Press. Judged by a "different eminent writer selected each year. Some prefer to remain anonymous until the end of the contest."

Tips "No limitations to entrants. In years when the judge is announced, we ask that students of the judge not enter to avoid a perceived conflict. All entries should contain identifying material only on the one cover sheet. Entries are read anonymously."

SHEILA MOTTON AWARD

New England Poetry Club, 2 Farrar St., Cambridge MA 02138. Website: www.nepoetryclub.org. **Contact:** NEPC Contest Coordinator. Checks for all contests should be made to New England Poetry Club. All entries should be sent in duplicate with name, address, phone, and email of writer on only one copy. (Judges receive copies without names). Deadline: May 31. Prize: $500.

Tips "For latest rules and rules for children's contests please check New England Poetry Club site."

NATIONAL WRITERS ASSOCIATION POETRY CONTEST

The National Writers Association, 10940 S. Parker Rd. #508, Parker CO 80134. (303)841-0246. Fax: (303)841-2607. E-mail: natlwritersassn@hotmail.com. **Contact:** Sandy Whelchel, director. Annual contest to encourage the writing of poetry, an important form of individual expression but with a limited commercial market. Email Sandy for a form until new website is formed. Deadline: Oct. 1. Charges $10 fee. Prize: 1st Place: $100; 2nd Place: $50; 3rd Place: $25.

THE PABLO NERUDA PRIZE FOR POETRY

Nimrod International Journal, 800 S. Tucker Dr., Tulsa OK 74104. (918)631-3080. Fax: (918)631-3033. E-mail: nimrod@utulsa.edu. **Contact:** Francine Ringold. Annual award to discover new writers of vigor and talent. Open to US residents only. Deadline: April 30. Charges $20 (includes a 1-year subscription). Prize: 1st Place: $2,000 and publication; 2nd Place: $1,000 and publication. *Nimrod* retains the right to publish any submission. Judged by the *Nimrod* editors (finalists). A recognized author selects the winners.

NEW ISSUES FIRST BOOK OF POETRY PRIZE

New Issues Poetry & Prose, Dept. of English, Western Michigan University, 1903 W. Michigan Ave., Kalamazoo MI 49008-5331. (269)387-8185. Fax: (269)387-2562. E-mail: william.olsen@wmich.edu. **Contact:** William Olsen, editor. Offered annually for publication of a first book of poems by a poet writing in English who has not previously published a full-length collection of poems in an edition of 500 or more copies. *New Issues Poetry & Prose* obtains rights for first publication. Book is copyrighted in author's name. Guidelines for SASE or online. Deadline: November 30. Charges $15. Prize: $2,000 and publication of book. Author also receives 10% of the printed edition.

THE JOHN FREDERICK NIMS MEMORIAL PRIZE

Poetry, 444 North Michigan Ave., Suite 1850, Chicago IL 60611. (312)787-7070. E-mail: poetry@poetrymagazine.org. Website: www.poetrymagazine.org. Offered annually for poems published in *Poetry* during the preceding year (October-September). Judged by the editors of *Poetry*. *Poetry* buys all rights to the poems published in the magazine. Copyrights are returned to the authors on request. Prize: $500.

ONCEWRITTEN.COM POETRY CONTEST

Oncewritten.com, 1850 N. Whitley Ave., #404, Hollywood CA 90028. E-mail: editor@oncewritten.com. Website: www.oncewritten.com. **Contact:** Monica Poling, editor. "The purpose of this annual contest is to find high quality, previously unpublished poetry to feature on the website and in *Off the Press*, our monthly newsletter, which is distributed specifically for people interested in reading about new authors." Deadline: March 31. Charges $15. Prize: 1st Prize: $500; Runner-Up: $100. Judged by the editor and industry professionals.

THE OPEN WINDOW

Hidden Brook Press, 109 Bayshore Rd., RR#4, Brighton ON K0K 1H0 Canada. (613)475-2368. E-mail: writers@hiddenbrookpress.com. An annual poetry anthology contest. A wide open window theme including family, nature, death, rhyming, city, country, war and peace, social—long, short haiku, or any other genre. Send sets of 3 poems with short bio (35-40 words) and a SASE. Electronic and hard copy submissions required. Previously published and simultaneous submissions are welcome. Deadline: November 30. Charges $15/3 poems. Prize: 1st Place: $100; 2nd Place: $75; 3rd Place: $50; 4th Place: $40; 5th Place: $30; 6th Place: $25; 7th Place: $20; 8th Place: $15; 9th-10th Place: $10; plus up to 12 honorable mentions. All winners, honorable mentions, and runners up receive 1 copy of the book for each published poem. Authors retain copyright.

THE OPEN WINDOW

Hidden Brook Press, 109 Bayshore Rd., RR#4, Brighton ON K0K 1H0 Canada. (613)475-2368. E-mail: writers@hiddenbrookpress.com. The Open Window International Poetry Chapbook Anthology Contest is interested in all types and styles of poetry. See The Hidden Brook Press website for examples of the type of poetry we have published in the past. Previously published and multiple submissions are welcome. Deadline: Annually. Charges $15/3 poems. Prize: 1st Place: $100; 2nd Place: $75; 3rd Place: $50; 4th Place: $40; 5th Place: $30; 6th Place: $25; 7th Place: $20; 8th Place: $15; 9th-10th Place: $10; plus 15-25 Honorable Mentions. Winning poems published in *The Open Window International Poetry Chapbook Anthology*. All winning and honorable mention submissions receive 1 copy of the book for each published poem. Authors retain copyright.

GUY OWEN AWARD

Southern Poetry Review, Dept. of Languages, Literature, and Philosophy, Armstrong Atlantic State University, 11935 Abercorn St., Savannah GA 31419-1997. (912)344-3196. Fax: (912)344-3494. E-mail: james.smith@armstrong.edu. Website: www.spr.armsrong.edu. **Contact:** James Smith. Send 3-5 unpublished poems (maximum 10 pages) and SASE for response only. Include contact information on cover sheet only. All entries considered for publication. Please indicate simultaneous submissions. Deadline: March 1-June 15 (postmarked). Charges $15 entry fee (includes 1-year subscription). Prize: $1,000 and publication of winning poem in *Southern Poetry Review*. Final judge will be a distinguished poet.

PAUMANOK POETRY AWARD

English Department, Knapp Hall, Farmingdale State College of New York, 2350 Broadhollow Rd., Route 110, Farmingdale NY 11735. Fax: (631)420-2051. E-mail: brownml@farmingdale.edu. **Contact:** Margery L. Brown, director, Visiting Writers Program. "Offered annually for published or unpublished poems. Send cover letter, 1-paragraph bio, 3-5 poems (name and address on each poem). Include SASE for notification of winners. (Send photocopies only; mss will *not* be returned.)" Deadline: September 15. Charges $25 fee, payable to Farmingdale State University VWP. Prize: 1st Place: $1,500, plus expenses for a reading in series; Runners-up (2): $750, plus expenses for a reading in series.

PEARL POETRY PRIZE

Pearl Editions, 3030 E. Second St., Long Beach CA 90803. (562)434-4523. Fax: (562)434-4523. E-mail: pearlmag@aol.com. **Contact:** Marilyn Johnson, editor/publisher. "Offered annually to provide poets with further opportunity to publish their poetry in book-form and find a larger audience for their work. Mss must be original works written in English. Guidelines for SASE or online. Open to all writers." Deadline: June 30. Charges $20. Prize: $1,000 and publication by Pearl Editions.

PERUGIA PRESS PRIZE

Perugia Press, Celebrating Poetry by Women since 1997, P.O. Box 60364, Florence MA 01062. (413)587-2646. E-mail: info@perugiapress.com. **Contact:** Susan Kan. "The contest is for first or second poetry books by women. Some poems in the submission may be previously published, but the ms as a whole must be unpublished. Send SASE or visit our website for guidelines. The contest is open to women poets who are US residents and who have not published more than 1 book." Deadline: Nov. 15. Charges $25. Prize: $1,000 and publication.

PHILBRICK POETRY AWARD

Providence Athenaeum, 251 Benefit St., Providence RI 02903. (401)421-6970. Fax: (401)421-2860. E-mail: smarkley@providenceathenaeum.org. **Contact:** Sandy Markley. Offered annually for New England poets who have not yet published a book. Previous publication of individual poems in journals or anthologies is allowed. Judged by nationally-known poets. Guidelines for SASE or online. July 15-October 15. Charges $10 fee (includes copy of previously published chapbook). Prize: $500, publication of winning ms as a chapbook, and a public reading at Providence Athenaeum with the final judge/award presenter.

THE PINCH LITERARY AWARD IN POETRY

The Univ. of Memphis/Hohenberg Foundation, Dept. of English, 435 Patterson Hall, Memphis TN 38152. (901)678-4591. E-mail: editor@thepinchjournal.com. "Offered annually for unpublished poems and fiction. Guidelines for SASE or on website." Deadline: March 15. Charges $20 fee for up to 3 poems or 5,000/word fiction. Prize: 1st Place: $1,500 for fiction and $1,000 for poetry and publication; 2nd and 3rd Place: Publication and a 1-year subscription.

THE POETRY CENTER BOOK AWARD

The Poetry Center, San Francisco State University, 1600 Holloway Ave., San Francisco CA 94132-9901. (415)338-2227. Fax: (415)338-0966. Website: www.sfsu.edu/~poetry. Estab. 1980. Offered annually for books of poetry and chapbooks, published in year of the prize. "Prize given for an extraordinary book of American poetry written in English." Please include a cover letter noting author name, book title(s), name of person issuing check, and check number. Will not consider anthologies or translations. Deadline: January 31 for books published and copywrited in the previous year. Charges $10 reading fee/entry. Prize: $500 and an invitation to read in the Poetry Center Reading Series.

N POETS & PATRONS ANNUAL CHICAGOLAND POETRY CONTEST

Sponsored by Poets & Patrons of Chicago, 416 Gierz St., Downers Grove IL 60515-3838. E-mail: eatonb1016@aol.com. Website: www.poetsandpatrons.org. **Contact:** Barbara Eaton, director. Estab. 1945. Annual contest for unpublished poetry. Guidelines available for self-addressed, stamped envelope. The purpose of the contest is to encourage the crafting of poetry. Deadline: September 1. Charges Entry fee is $10 for members; $12 for non-members. This covers one poem in each category. Additional poems $1 each. Prize: Prize is $45, $20, $10 cash. Poet retains rights. There are seven categories: (1) religious theme, (2) humor, (3) formal, (4) free verse, (5) social conscience, (6) miniature (12 lines or less), (7) Theme: The City of Chicago. Judged by out-of -state professionals.

POETS OUT LOUD PRIZE

Poets Out Loud, Fordham University at Lincoln Center, 113 W. 60th St., Room 924-I, New York NY 10023. (212)636-6792. Fax: (212)636-7153. E-mail: pol@fordham.edu. Annual competition for an unpublished, full-length poetry ms (50-80 pages). Deadline: November 15. Charges $25 entry fee. Prize: $2,000 book publication, and book launch in POL reading series.

MARGARET REID POETRY CONTEST FOR TRADITIONAL VERSE

c/o Winning Writers, 351 Pleasant St., PMB 222, Northampton MA 01060-3961. E-mail: johnreid@mail.qango.com. Website: www.winningwriters.com. **Contact:** John Reid. Estab. 2004. "Seeks poems in traditional verse forms, such as sonnets." Both unpublished and published work accepted. Guidelines for SASE or on website. Deadline: June 30. Charges $7 for every 25 lines of poetry. Prize: 1st Place: $3,000; 2nd Place: $1,000; 3rd Place: $400; 4th Place: $250; plus 6 Most Highly Commended awards of $150 each. The top 10 entries will be published on the Winning Writers website. Judged by John H. Reid and Dee C. Konrad.

SASKATCHEWAN POETRY AWARD

Saskatchewan Book Awards, Inc., 205B-2314 11th Ave., Regina SK S4P 0K1 Canada. (306)569-1585. Fax: (306)569-4187. E-mail: director@bookawards.sk.ca. **Contact:** Jackie Lay, executive director. Offered annually for work published September 15-September 14. This award is presented to a Saskatchewan author for the best book of poetry, judged on the quality of writing. Deadline: First deadline: July 31; Final deadline: September 14. Charges $25 (Canadian). Prize: $2,000.

SILVER WINGS ANNUAL POETRY CONTEST

Silver Wings, P.O. Box 2340, Clovis CA 93613. (559)347-0194. E-mail: cloviswings@aol.com. **Contact:** Jackson Wilcox. Estab. 1983. "The annual contest is sponsored by Silver Wings, a small bimonthly poetry magazine." "We would like to encourage new writers of poetry with a Christian message or thought." Deadline: December 31. Charges $3. Prize: 1st Place: $100; 2nd Place: $50; 3rd Place: $35; 4th Place: $30; 5th Place: $25; 6th Place: $20; 7th Place: $15. A few Honorable Mentions are also published with no cash prize. Accepts first rights with permission to publish in *Silver Wings*. Poetry on Wings Board in February.

Tips "Contest poems must be original and never before published."

SLIPSTREAM ANNUAL POETRY CHAPBOOK COMPETITION

Slipstream, Box 2071, Niagara Falls NY 14301. E-mail: editors@slipstreampress.org. Website: www.slipstreampress.org. **Contact:** Dan Sicoli, co-editor. "Offered annually to help promote a poet whose work is often overlooked or ignored. Open to any writer." Winner is featured prominently on the Slipstream website for one year, as well as in all Slipstream catalogs, press releases, and promotional material. Winning chapbooks are submitted by Slipstream for review by various national and international poetry/writing pubications and may also be featured in the Grants & Awards section of Poets & Writers magazine. Deadline: December 1. Charges $20. Prize: $1,000 and 50 copies of published chapbook. Everyone who enters receives a copy of the winning chapbook plus one complimentary issue of *Slipstream* magazine.

Tips "Winner announced in late spring/early summer."

HELEN C. SMITH MEMORIAL AWARD FOR POETRY

The Texas Institute of Letters, 6335 W. Northwest Hwy., #618, Dallas TX 75225. (214)363-7253. E-mail: dpayne@smu.edu. **Contact:** Darwin Payne. Offered annually for the best book of poems published January 1-December 31 of previous year. Poet must have been born in Texas, have lived in the state at some time for at least 2 consecutive years, or the subject matter must be associated with the state. See website for guidelines. Deadline: January 1. Prize: $1,200.

THE SOW'S EAR CHAPBOOK PRIZE

The Sow's Ear Poetry Review, P.O. Box 127, Millwood VA 22646. (540)955-3955. E-mail: rglesman@gmail.com. **Contact:** Robert G. Lesman, managing editor. Estab. 1988. Offered for poetry mss of 22-26 pages. Guidelines for SASE, by e-mail, or on website. Deadline: Submit March-April (May 1 postmark). Charges $27 fee; $30 for Canadian addresses, $40 elsewhere; includes subscription. Prize: $1,000, 25 copies, and distribution to subscribers.

THE SOW'S EAR POETRY PRIZE

The Sow's Ear Poetry Review, P.O. Box 127, Millwood VA 22646-0127. (540)955-3955. E-mail: rglesman@gmail.com. Website: sows-ear.kitenet.net. **Contact:** Robert G. Lesman, managing editor. Estab. 1988. Offered for previously unpublished poetry. Guidelines on website, for SASE or by e-mail. All finalists' submissions considered for publication. Entries are not returned. Include SASE or e-mail address for notification. Deadline: November 1 postmark. Submit September-October. Charges $27, covering up to 5 poems. Prize: $1,000, publication of winner and some finalists. Contestants receive a year's subscription.

THE EDWARD STANLEY AWARD

Prairie Schooner, 201 Andrews Hall, P.O. Box 880334, Lincoln NE 68588-0334. (402)472-0911. Fax: (402)472-9771. E-mail: jengelhardt2@unlnotes.unl.edu. **Contact:** Hilda Raz. Offered annually for poetry published in *Prairie Schooner* in the previous year. Prize: $1,000.

THE ELIZABETH MATCHETT STOVER MEMORIAL AWARD

Southwest Review, Southern Methodist University, P.O. Box 750374, Dallas TX 75275-0374. (214)768-1037. Fax: (214)768-1408. E-mail: swr@mail.smu.edu. **Contact:** Jennifer Cranfill,Senior Editor and Willard Spiegelman, Editor-In-Chief. "Offered annually to the best works of poetry that have appeared in the magazine in the previous year. Please note that mss are submitted for publication, not for the prizes themselves. Guidelines for SASE and online." Prize: $300 Jennifer Cranfill and Willard Spiegelman.

STROKESTOWN INTERNATIONAL POETRY COMPETITION

Strokestown International Poetry Festival, Bawn St., Strokestown, County Roscommon Ireland. (+353) 71 9633759. E-mail: director@strokestownpoetry.org. Website: www.strokestownpoetry.com. **Contact:** Director. This annual competition was established to promote excellence in poetry, and participation in the reading and writing of it. Acquires first publication rights. Deadline: February 6. Charges $5 (4 euros, £4). Prize: 1st Prize: 4,000 euros (approximately $3,900) for a poem in English of up to 70 lines, plus others totaling about $3,000 dollars. Up to 10 shortlisted poets will be invited to read at the Strokestown International Poetry Festival and paid a reading fee. Lawrence Sail, Mary O'Donnell, and Peter Denman.

TRANSCONTINENTAL POETRY AWARD

Pavement Saw Press, 321 Empire Street, Montpelier OH 43543. (419)485-0524. E-mail: info@pavementsaw.org. Website: pavementsaw.org. **Contact:** David Baratier, editor. "Offered annually for a first book of poetry. Judged by the editor and a guest judge. Guidelines available online." Deadline: August 15. Charges $20 fee. Prize: $1,000, 50 copies for judge's choice, and standard royalty contract for editor's choice. All writers receive 2 free books for entering.

UTMOST CHRISTIAN POETRY CONTEST

Utmost Christian Writers Foundation, 121 Morin Maze, Edmonton AB T6K 1V1 Canada. (780)461-0221. The purpose of this annual contest is "to promote excellence in poetry by poets of Christian faith. All entries are eligible for most of the cash awards, but there is a special category for rhyming poetry with prizes of $300 and $100. All entries must be unpublished." Deadline: February 28. Charges $20/poem (maximum 5 poems). Prize: 1st Place: $1,000; 2nd Place: $600; ten prizes of $100 are offered for honorable mention. Rights are acquired to post winning entries on the organization's website.

Contests & Awards

Judged by a committee of the Directors of Utmost Christian Writers Foundation (who work under the direction of Barbara Mitchell, chief judge).

DANIEL VAROUJAN AWARD

New England Poetry Club, 2 Farrar Street, Cambridge MA 02138. E-mail: contests@nepoetryclub.org. Website: www.nepoetryclub.org/contests.htm. **Contact:** NEPC Contest Coordinator. "One-thousand dollars for a poem in English worthy of the Armenian poet executed by the Ottoman Turks in the 1915 genocide that destroyed three-fourths of the Armenian population. Send poems in duplicate, with name and address of poet on one copy only. Deadline: May 31. Charges $10/up to 3 entries; made payable to New England Poetry Club. Members free. Prize: $1,000.

CHAD WALSH POETRY PRIZE

Beloit Poetry Journal, P.O. Box 151, Farmington ME 04938. (207)778-0020. E-mail: bpj@bpj.org. **Contact:** Lee Sharkey and John Rosenwald, editors. "Offered annually to honor the memory of poet Chad Walsh, a founder of the *Beloit Poetry Journal.*" The editors select an outstanding poem or group of poems from the poems published in the journal that year. Charges no entry fee. Prize: $3,500.

WAR POETRY CONTEST

Winning Writers, 351 Pleasant St., PMB 222, Northampton MA 01060-3961. (866)946-9748. Fax: (413)280-0539. E-mail: adam@winningwriters.com. **Contact:** Adam Cohen. Estab. 2002. "This annual contest seeks outstanding, unpublished poetry on the theme of war. Up to 3 poems can be submitted, with a maximum total of 500 lines. English language only; translations accepted if you wrote the original poem." Submit online or by mail. Guidelines for SASE or see website. Nonexclusive right to publish submissions on WinningWriters.com, in e-mail newsletter, and in press releases. Deadline: November 15-May 31. Charges $15. Prize: 1st Place: $2,000 and publication on WinningWriters.com; 2nd Place: $1,200 and publication; 3rd Place: $600 and publication; Honorable Mentions (12): $100 and publication. 2009 winner was Robert Hill Long for *Wolverine and White Crow*, *Motivations*, and *Insurrection.* Final Judge: award-winning poet Jendi Reiter.

THE WASHINGTON PRIZE

Dearlove Hall, Adirondack Community College, 640 Bay Rd., Queensbury NY 12804. E-mail: editor@wordworksdc.com. Website: www.wordworksdc.com. **Contact:** Nancy White, Washington Prize Admin. Estab. 1981. Offered annually "for the best full-length poetry manuscript (48-64 pp.) submitted to The Word Works each year. The Washington Prize contest is the only forum in which we consider unsolicited manuscripts." Acquires first publication rights. Open to any American writer. Deadline: January 15-March 1. Charges $25 fee. Prize: $1,500, book publication and 100 author copies; all entrants receive a copy of the winning book.

WERGLE FLOMP HUMOR POETRY CONTEST

Winning Writers, 351 Pleasant St., PMB 222, Northampton MA 01060-3961. (866)946-9748. Fax: (413)280-0539. E-mail: adam@winningwriters.com. Website: www.winningwriters.com. **Contact:** Adam Cohen. Estab. 2002. "This annual contest seeks today's best humor poems. One poem of any length should be submitted, along with the name of the vanity contest that was spoofed. The poem should be in English. Inspired gibberish is also accepted. See website for guidelines, examples, and to submit your poem. nonexclusive right to publish submissions on WinningWriters.com, in e-mail newsletter, and in press releases." Deadline: August 15-April 1. Charges No fee to enter. Prize: 1st Place: $1,500; 2nd Place: $800; 3rd Place: $400. Twelve Honorable Mentions get $75 each. All prize winners receive publication at WinningWriters.com. Non-US winners will be paid in US currency (or PayPal) if a check is inconvenient. Final judge is Jendi Reiter.

Tips "Submissions may be previously published and may be entered in other contests. Competition receives about 800 entries/year. Winners are announced on August 15 at WinningWriters.com. Entrants who provide a valid e-mail address will also receive notification. The 2009 winner was Randy Cousteau."

WHITE PINE PRESS POETRY PRIZE

White Pine Press, P.O. Box 236, Buffalo NY 14201. E-mail: wpine@whitepine.org. **Contact:** Dennis Maloney, editor. Offered annually for previously published or unpublished poets. Manuscript: Up to 80 pages of original work; translations are not eligible. Poems may have appeared in magazines or limited-edition chapbooks. Open to any US citizen Deadline: November 30 (postmarked). Charges $20 fee. Prize: $1,000 and publication. Final Judge is a poet of national reputation. All entries are screened by the editorial staff of White Pine Press.

STAN AND TOM WICK POETRY PRIZE

Wick Poetry Center, 301 Satterfield Hall, Kent State University, P.O. Box 5190, Kent OH 44242-0001. (330)672-2067. Fax: (330)672-3333. E-mail: wickpoet@kent.edu. **Contact:** David Hassler, director. Open to anyone writing in English who has not previously published a full-length book of poems (a volume of 50 pages or more published in an edition of 500 or more copies). Send SASE or visit the website for guidelines. Deadline: May 1. Charges $20 reading fee. Prize: $2,000 and publication by the Kent State University Press.

WILLIAM CARLOS WILLIAMS AWARD

Poetry Society of America, 15 Gramercy Park S., New York NY 10003. (212)254-9628. Fax: (212)673-2352. Website: www.poetrysociety.org. **Contact:** Programs Associate. Offered annually for a book of poetry published by a small press, nonprofit, or university press. Winning books are distributed to PSA Lyric Circle members while supplies last. Books must be submitted directly by publishers. Entry forms are required. It is strongly encouraged that applicants read the complete contest guidelines on the PSA website before submitting. Deadline: October 1-December 22. Charges $20 fee. Prize: $500-1,000.

THE J. HOWARD AND BARBARA M.J. WOOD PRIZE

Poetry, 444 North Michigan Ave., Suite 1850, Chicago IL 60611. (312)787-7070. E-mail: poetry@poetrymagazine.org. Website: www.poetrymagazine.org. Estab. 1994. Offered annually for poems published in *Poetry* during the preceding year (October-September). *Poetry* buys all rights to the poems published in the magazine. Copyrights are returned to the authors on request. Prize: $5,000.

WRITECORNER PRESS $500 POETRY AWARD

Writecorner Press, P.O. Box 140310, Gainesville FL 32614. (352)338-7778. Website: www.writecorner.com. **Contact:** Mary Sue Koeppel, Robert B. Gentry, coeditors. "Offered annually for unpublished poetry. Poetry may be in any style and on any subject. Maximum poem length is 40 lines. Only unpublished poems are eligible. No limit on number of poems entered by any 1 poet. The winning poem is published, as are the editors' choices poems. Copyright then returns to the authors. Guidelines for SASE or online." Deadline: March 31, 2010. Submit between Oct. 1 - March 31 annually. Charges $5/poem; $3 each additional poem. Prize: $500 First prize, $100 Editor's Choices, and publication on www.writecorner.com. Judged by Mary Sue Koeppel and Robert B. Gentry, editors.

Tips "Writecorner Press also sponsors the annual $1,100 E.M. Koeppel Short Fiction Award."

WRITERS' JOURNAL POETRY CONTEST

Val-Tech Media, P.O. Box 394, Perham MN 56573. (218)346-7921. Fax: (218)346-7924. E-mail: writersjournal@writersjournal.com. Website: www.writersjournal.com. **Contact:** Esther M. Leiper-Estabrooks. "Offered for previously unpublished poetry. Receives fewer than 300 entries. Guidelines for SASE or online." Deadline: April 30, August 30, December 30. Charges $3/poem. Prize: 1st Place: $50; 2nd Place: $25; 3rd Place: $15. First, second, third, and selected honorable mention winners will be published in *Writers' Journal* magazine.

ZONE 3 POETRY AWARDS

ZONE 3, Austin Peay State University, P.O. Box 4565, Clarksville TN 37044. (931)221-7031. Fax: (931)221-7149. E-mail: wallacess@apsu.edu. **Contact:** Susan Wallace, managing editor. "Offered annually for unpublished poetry. Previous judges include Carolyn Forché, Margie Piercy, Maxine Kumin, Stephen Dunn, Mark Jarman, and Michael Collier. Open to any poet." Charges $10 fee (includes 1-year subscription). Prize: 1st Place: $500; 2nd Place: $300; 3rd Place: $100.

Translation

SOEURETTE DIEHL FRASER AWARD FOR BEST TRANSLATION OF A BOOK

6335 W. Northwest Hwy., #618, Dallas TX 75225. (214)528-2655. E-mail: dpayne@smu.edu. Website: http://texasinstituteofletters.org. **Contact:** Darwin Payne. Offered every 2 years to recognize the best translation of a literary book into English. Translator must have been born in Texas or have lived in the state for at least 2 consecutive years at some time. Deadline: January 3. Prize: $1,000.

FENIA AND YAAKOV LEVIANT MEMORIAL PRIZE IN YIDDISH STUDIES

Modern Language Association of America, 26 Broadway, 3rd Floor, New York NY 10004-1789. (646)576-5141. Fax: (646)458-0030. E-mail: awards@mla.org. **Contact:** Coordinator of book prizes. This prize is to honor, in alternating years, an outstanding English translation of a Yiddish literary work or an outstanding scholarly work in any language in the field of Yiddish. Offered in even-numbered years.

Open to MLA members and nonmembers. Authors or publishers may submit titles. Guidelines for SASE or by e-mail. Deadline: May 1. Prize: A cash prize, and a certificate, to be presented at the Modern Language Association's annual convention in January.

LOIS ROTH AWARD FOR A TRANSLATION OF A LITERARY WORK

Modern Language Association, 26 Broadway, 3rd Floor, New York NY 10004-1789. (646)576-5141. Fax: (646)458-0030. E-mail: awards@mla.org. **Contact:** Coordinator of Book Prizes. Offered every 2 years (odd years) for an outstanding translation into English of a book-length literary work published the previous year. Translators need not be members of the MLA. Deadline: April 1. Prize: A cash award and a certificate to be presented at the Modern Language Association's annual convention in January.

ALDO AND JEANNE SCAGLIONE PRIZE FOR A TRANSLATION OF A LITERARY WORK

Modern Language Association, 26 Broadway, 3rd Floor, New York NY 10004-1789. (646)576-5141. Fax: (646)458-0030. E-mail: awards@mla.org. **Contact:** Coordinator of Book Prizes. Offered in even-numbered years for the translation of a book-length literary work appearing in print during the previous year. Translators need not be members of the MLA. Deadline: April 1. Prize: A cash award and a certificate to be presented at the Modern Language Association's annual convention in January.

ALDO AND JEANNE SCAGLIONE PRIZE FOR A TRANSLATION OF A SCHOLARLY STUDY OF LITERATURE

Modern Language Association of America, 26 Broadway, 3rd Floor, New York NY 10004-1789. (646)576-5141. Fax: (646)458-0030. E-mail: awards@mla.org. **Contact:** Coordinator of Book Prizes. Offered in odd-numbered years for an outstanding translation into English of a book-length work of literary history, literary criticism, philology, or literary theory published during the previous biennium. Translators need not be members of the MLA. Deadline: May 1. Prize: A cash award and a certificate to be presented at the Modern Language Association's annual convention in January.

Writing for Children & Young Adults

AUSTIN PUBLIC LIBRARY FRIENDS FOUNDATION AWARDS FOR BEST CHILDREN'S BOOK ($500) AND BEST YOUNG ADULT BOOK ($500)

6335 W. Northwest Hwy, #618, Dallas TX 75225. (214)363-7253. E-mail: dpayne@smu.edu. **Contact:** Darwin Payne. Offered annually for work published January 1-December 31 of previous year to recognize the best book for children and young people. Writer must have been born in Texas, have lived in the state for at least 2 consecutive years at one time, or the subject matter must be associated with the state. See website for judges and further information. Deadline: First week of January. Prize: $500 for each award winner.

MARILYN BAILLIE PICTURE BOOK AWARD

The Canadian Children's Book Centre, 40 Orchard View Blvd., Suite 101, Toronto ON M4R 1B9 Canada. (416)975-0010. Fax: (416)975-8970. E-mail: meghan@bookcentre.ca. Website: www.bookcentre.ca. Estab. 2006. "To be eligible, the book must be an original work in English, aimed at children ages 3-8, written and illustrated by Canadians and first published in Canada. Eligible genres include fiction, nonfiction and poetry. Books must be published between Jan. 1 and Dec. 31 of the previous calendar year." "Honours excellence in the illustrated picture book format." Charges Deadline: mid-December. Prize: $20,000.

Tips "Please visit website for submission guidelines and eligibility criteria."

THE GEOFFREY BILSON AWARD FOR HISTORICAL FICTION FOR YOUNG PEOPLE

The Canadian Children's Book Centre, 40 Orchard View Blvd., Suite 101, Toronto ON M4R 1B9 Canada. (416)975-0010. Fax: (416)975-8970. Website: www.bookcentre.ca. "Created in Geoffrey Bilson's memory in 1988. Open to Canadian citizens and residents of Canada for at least 2 years." Awarded annually to reward excellence in the writing of an outstanding work of historical fiction for young readers, by a Canadian author, published in the previous calendar year. Deadline: mid-December. Prize: $5,000.

Tips "Please visit website for submission guidelines and eligibility criteria,

THE NORMA FLECK AWARD FOR CANADIAN CHILDREN'S NON-FICTION

The Canadian Children's Book Centre, 40 Orchard View Blvd., Suite 101, Toronto ON M4R 1B9 Canada. (416)975-0010. Fax: (416)975-8970. E-mail: info@bookcentre.ca. Website: www.bookcentre.ca. "The Norma Fleck Award was established by the Fleck Family Foundation and the Canadian Children's Book

Centre in 1999 to recognize and raise the profile of exceptional Canadian nonfiction books for young people." Presented annually for books published between January 1 and December 31 of the previous calendar year. Open to Canadian citizens or landed immigrants. Please visit website for submission guidelines and eligibility criteria, as well as specific submission deadline. Deadline: mid-December. Prize: $10,000.

INTERNATIONAL READING ASSOCIATION CHILDREN'S AND YOUNG ADULTS' BOOK AWARDS

International Reading Association, P.O. Box 8139, Newark DE 19714-8139. (302)731-1600, ext. 229. Fax: (302)731-1057. Website: www.reading.org. "Offered annually for an author's first or second published book in fiction and nonfiction in 3 categories: primary (preschool-age 8), intermediate (ages 9-13), and young adult (ages 14-17). Recognizes newly published authors who show unusual promise in the children's book field. Guidelines and deadlines are on the website." Prize: $1,000, and a medal for each category.

THE VICKY METCALF AWARD FOR CHILDREN'S LITERATURE

The Writers' Trust of Canada, 90 Richmond St. E., Suite 200, Toronto ON M5C 1P1 Canada. (416)504-8222. Fax: (416)504-9090. E-mail: info@writerstrust.com. **Contact:** Amanda Hopkins. "The Metcalf Award is presented to a Canadian writer for a body of work in children's literature at The Writers' Trust Awards event held in Toronto each Fall. Open to Canadian citizens and permanent residents only." Prize: $20,000.

MILKWEED PRIZE FOR CHILDREN'S LITERATURE

Milkweed Editions, 1011 Washington Ave. S., Suite 300, Minneapolis MN 55415. (612)332-3192. Fax: (612)215-2550. E-mail: editor@milkweed.org. **Contact:** The Editors. Estab. 1993. Annual prize for unpublished works. The Milkweed Prize for Children's Literature will be awarded to the best ms for children ages 8-13 that Milkweed accepts for publication during each calendar year by a writer not previously published by Milkweed Editions. Mss should be of high literary quality and must be double-spaced, 90-200 pages in length. All mss submitted to Milkweed will automatically be considered for the prize. Submission directly to the contest is not necessary, and there is no deadline. Manuscripts are accepted on a rolling basis. Must review guidelines online; Milkweed strongly encourages digital submissions through our Submission Manager. Prize: $10,000 advance on royalties agreed upon at the time of acceptance.

PATERSON PRIZE FOR BOOKS FOR YOUNG PEOPLE

The Poetry Center at Passaic County Community College, One College Blvd., Paterson NJ 07505-1179. (973)523-6085. Fax: (973)523-6085. E-mail: mgillan@pccc.edu. Website: www.pccc.edu/poetry. **Contact:** Maria Mazziotti Gillan, exec. dir. At above address or visit www.pccc.edu/poetry and go to prizes."Offered annually for books published the previous calendar year. Three categories: pre-kindergarten-grade 3; grades 4-6; grades 7-12. Open to any writer." Deadline: March 15. Prize: $500 in each category.

SASKATCHEWAN CHILDREN'S LITERATURE AWARD

Saskatchewan Book Awards, Inc., 205B-2314 11th Ave., Regina SK S4P 0K1 Canada. (306)569-1585. Fax: (306)569-4187. E-mail: director@bookawards.sk.ca. Website: www.bookawards.sk.ca. **Contact:** Jackie Lay, executive director. Offered annually for work published September 15-September 14. This award is presented to a Saskatchewan author for the best book of children's or young adult's literature, judged on the quality of writing. Deadline: First Deadline: July 31; Final Deadline: September 14. Charges $25 CAN. Prize: $2,000 CAN.

SYDNEY TAYLOR MANUSCRIPT COMPETITION

Association of Jewish Libraries, Sydney Taylor Manuscript Award Competition, 204 Park St., Montclair NJ 07042. E-mail: stmacajl@aol.com. **Contact:** Aileen Grossberg. Material should be a work of fiction in English, with universal appeal of Jewish content for readers aged 8-11 years. "It should deepen the understanding of Judaism for all children, Jewish and non-Jewish, and reveal positive aspects of Jewish life." No poems or plays. Length: 64-200 pages. Rules, entry forms available at website: www.jewishlibraries.org. Judged by 5 AJL member librarians. Open to any writer. Must be unpublished. Deadline: December 15. Prize: $1,000.

N TD CANADIAN CHILDREN'S LITERATURE AWARD

The Canadian Children's Book Centre, 40 Orchard View Blvd., Suite 101, Toronto ON M4R 1B9 Canada. (416)975-0010. Fax: (416)975-8970. Website: www.bookcentre.ca. Estab. 2004. "All books, in any genre,

written and illustrated by Canadians and for children ages 1-12 are eligible. Only books first published in Canada are eligible for submission. Books must be published between January 1 and December 31 of the previous calendar year. Open to Canadian citizens and/or permanent residents of Canada. "To honour the most distinguished book of the year for young people in both English and French." Mid-December. Prize: Two prizes of $25,000, one for English, one for French. $10,000 will be divided among the Honour Book English titles and Honour Book French titles, to a max. of four; $2,500 shall go to each of the publishers of the English and French grand-prize winning books for promotion and publicity.
Tips "Please visit website for submission guidelines and eligibility criteria, as well as specific submission deadline."

RITA WILLIAMS YOUNG ADULT PROSE PRIZE

National League of American Pen Women, Nob Hill, San Francisco Branch, Category of the Soul-Making Literary Competition, The Webhallow House, 1544 Sweetwood Dr., Broadmoor Vig. CA 94015-1717. E-mail: pennobhill@aol.com. **Contact:** Eileen Malone. "Up to 3,000 words in story, essay, journal entry, creative nonfiction, or memoir by writer in grades 9-12. Indicate age and category on each first page. Identify with 3 × 5 card only. Open annually to young adult writers." Deadline: November 30. Charges $5/entry (make checks payable to NLAPW, Nob Hill Branch). Prize: 1st Place: $100; 2nd Place: $50; 3rd Place: $25.

PAUL A. WITTY SHORT STORY AWARD

Executive Office, International Reading Association, P.O. Box 8139, Newark DE 19714-8139. (302)731-1600, ext. 229. Fax: (302)731-1057. E-mail: committees@reading.org. "Offered to reward author of an original short story published in a children's periodical during 2010 which serves as a literary standard that encourages young readers to read periodicals. Write for guidelines or download from website." Deadline: December 1. Prize: $1,000.

WORK-IN-PROGRESS GRANT

Society of Children's Book Writers and Illustrators (SCBWI), 8271 Beverly Blvd., Los Angeles CA 90048. (323)782-1010. E-mail: scbwi@scbwi.org. Website: www.scbwi.org. Four grants—one designated specifically for a contemporary novel for young people, one for nonfiction, one for an unpublished writer, one general fiction—to assist SCBWI members in the completion of a specific project. Open to SCBWI members only. Applications received only between February 15 and March 15.

WRITE A STORY FOR CHILDREN COMPETITION

Academy of Children's Writers, P.O. Box 95, Huntingdon Cambridgeshire PE28 5RL England. Phone/Fax: (44)(148)783-2752. E-mail: enquiries@childrens-writers.co.uk. **Contact:** Contest Director. Annual contest for the best unpublished short story writer for children. Guidelines and entry forms online or send SAE/IRC. Open to any unpublished writer over the age of 18. Deadline: March 31. Charges $10 (US) Bill. No checks; £2.70 (UK). Prize: 1st Place: £2,000; 2nd Place: £300; 3rd Place: £200. Judged by a panel appointed by the Academy of Children's Writers.

WRITERS' LEAGUE OF TEXAS CHILDREN'S BOOK AWARDS

Writers' League of Texas, 611 S. Congress, Ste 130, Austin TX 78704. (512)499-8914. Fax: (512)499-0441. E-mail: wlt@writersleague.org. Website: www.writersleague.org. **Contact:** Jan Baumer, program manager. Offered annually for work published January 1-December 31. Honors 2 outstanding books for children. Writer's League of Texas dues may accompany entry fee. Deadline: March 1. Charges $35 fee. Prize: Two prizes of $1,000 and trophies.

Professional Organizations

AGENTS' ORGANIZATIONS

Association of Authors' Agents (AAA), David Higham Associates Ltd, 5-8 Lower John Street, Golden Square, London W1F 9HA . (020) 7434 5900. E-mail: anthonygoff@davidhigham.co.uk. Website: www.agentsassoc.co.uk.

Association of Authors' Representatives (AAR). E-mail: info@aar-online.org. Website: www.aar-online.org.

Association of Talent Agents (ATA), 9255 Sunset Blvd., Suite 930, Los Angeles CA 90069. (310)274-0628. Fax: (310)274-5063. E-mail: shellie@agentassociation.com. Website: www.agentassociation.com.

WRITERS' ORGANIZATIONS

Academy of American Poets 584 Broadway, Suite 604, New York NY 10012-5243. (212)274-0343. Fax: (212)274-9427. E-mail: academy@poets.org. Website: www.poets.org.

American Crime Writers League (ACWL), 17367 Hilltop Ridge Dr., Eureka MO 63205. Website: www.acwl.org.

American Medical Writers Association (AMWA), 30 West Gude Drive, Suite 525, Rockville MD 20850-4347. (301)294-5303. Fax: (301)294-9006. E-mail: amwa@amwa.org. Website: www.amwa.org.

American Screenwriters Association (ASA), 269 S. Beverly Dr., Suite 2600, Beverly Hills CA 90212-3807. (866)265-9091. E-mail: asa@goasa.com. Website: www.asascreenwriters.com.

American Translators Association (ATA), 225 Reinekers Lane, Suite 590, Alexandria VA 22314. (703)683-6100. Fax: (703)683-6122. E-mail: ata@atanet.org. Website: www.atanet.org.

Education Writers Association (EWA), 2122 P St., NW Suite 201, Washington DC 20037. (202)452-9830. Fax: (202)452-9837. E-mail: ewa@ewa.org. Website: www.ewa.org.

Garden Writers Association (GWA), 10210 Leatherleaf Ct., Manassas VA 20111. (703)257-1032. Fax: (703)257-0213. E-mail: info@gardenwriters.org. Website: www.gardenwriters.org.

Horror Writers Association (HWA), 244 5th Ave., Suite 2767, New York NY 10001. E-mail: hwa@horror.org. Website: www.horror.org.

The International Women's Writing Guild (IWWG),P.O. Box 810, Gracie Station, New York NY 10028-0082. (212)737-7536. Fax: (212)737-9469. E-mail: dirhahn@aol.org. Website: www.iwwg.com.

Mystery Writers of America (MWA), 1140 Broadway, Suite 1507, New York NY 10001. (212)888-8171. Fax: (212)888-8107. E-mail: mwa@mysterywriters.org. Website: www.mysterywriters.org.

National Association of Science Writers (NASW), P.O. Box 7905, Berkeley, CA 94707. (510)647-9500. E-mail: LFriedmann@nasw.org. website: www.nasw.org.

National Association of Women Writers (NAWW), 24165 IH-10 W., Suite 217-637, San Antonio TX 78257. Phone/Fax: (866)821-5829. Website: www.naww.org.

Organization of Black Screenwriters (OBS). Golden State Mutual Life Insurance Bldg., 1999 West Adams Blvd., Rm. Mezzanine Los Angeles, CA 90018. Website: www.obswriter.com.

Outdoor Writers Association of America (OWAA), 121 Hickory St., Suite 1, Missoula MT 59801. (406)728-7434. Fax: (406)728-7445. E-mail: krhoades@owaa.org. Website: www.owaa.org.

Poetry Society of America (PSA), 15 Gramercy Park, New York NY 10003. (212)254-9628. website: www.poetrysociety.org. Poets & Writers, 90 Broad St., Suite 2100, New York NY 10004. (212)226-3586. Fax: (212)226-3963. Website: www.pw.org.

Romance Writers of America (RWA), 114615 Benfer Road, Houston TX 77069. (832)717-5200. Fax: (832)717-5201. E-mail: info@rwanational.org. Website: www.rwanational.org.

Science Fiction and Fantasy Writers of America (SFWA), P.O. Box 877, Chestertown MD 21620. E-mail: execdir@sfwa.org. Website: www.sfwa.org.

Society of American Business Editors & Writers (SABEW), University of Missouri, School of Journalism, 30 Neff Annex, Columbia MO 65211. (602) 496-7862. E-mail: sabew@sabew.org. Website: www.sabew.org.

Society of American Travel Writers (SATW), 7044 S. 13 St., Oak Creek WI 53154. (414)908-4949. Fax: (414)768-8001. E-mail: satw@satw.org. Website: www.satw.org.

Society of Children's Book Writers & Illustrators (SCBWI), 8271 Beverly Blvd., Los Angeles CA 90048. (323)782-1010. Fax: (323)782-1892. E-mail: scbwi@scbwi.org. Website: www.scbwi.org.

American Independent Writers (AIW), 1001 Connecticut Ave. NW, Suite 701, Washington DC 20036. (202)775-5150. Fax: (202)775-5810. E-mail: info@aiwriters.org. Website: www.americanindependentwriters.org.

Western Writers of America (WWA). E-mail: spiritfire@kc.rr.com. Website: www.westernwriters.org.

INDUSTRY ORGANIZATIONS

American Booksellers Association (ABA), 200 White Plains Rd., Suite 600, Tarrytown NY 10591. (914)591-2665. Fax: (914)591-2720. E-mail: info@bookweb.org. Website: www.bookweb.org.

American Society of Journalists & Authors (ASJA), 1501 Broadway, Suite 302, New York NY 10036. (212)997-0947. Fax: (212)937-2315. E-mail: director@asja.org. Website: www.asja.org.

Association for Women in Communications (AWC), 3337 Duke St., Alexandria VA 22314. (703)370-7436. Fax: (703)342-4311. E-mail: info@womcom.org. Website: www.womcom.org.

Association of American Publishers (AAP), 71 5th Ave., 2nd Floor, New York NY 10003. (212)255-0200. Fax: (212)255-7007. Or, 50 F St. NW, Suite 400, Washington DC 20001. (202)347-3375. Fax: (202)347-3690. Website: www.publishers.org.

The Association of Writers & Writing Programs (AWP), Mail Stop 1E3, George Mason University, Fairfax VA 22030. (703)993-4301. Fax: (703)993-4302. E-mail: services@awpwriter.org. website: www.awpwriter.org.

The Authors Guild, Inc., 31 E. 32nd St., 7th Floor, New York NY 10016. (212)563-5904. Fax: (212)564-5363. E-mail: staff@authorsguild.org. website: www.authorsguild.org.

Canadian Authors Association (CAA), P.O. Box 581, Stn. Main Orilla ON L3V 6K5 Canada. (705)653-0323. Fax: (705)653-0593. E-mail: admin@canauthors.org. Website: www.canauthors.org.

Christian Booksellers Association (CBA), P.O. Box 62000, Colorado Springs CO 80962-2000. (800)252-1950. Fax: (719)272-3510. E-mail: info@cbaonline.org. website: www.cbaonline.org.

The Dramatists Guild of America, 1501 Broadway, Suite 701, New York NY 10036. (212)398-9366. Fax: (212)944-0420. Website: www.dramatistsguild.com.

National League of American Pen Women (NLAPW), 1300 17th St. NW, Washington DC 20036-1973. (202)785-1997. Fax: (202)452-8868. E-mail: nlapw1@verizon.net. Website: www.americanpenwomen.org.

National Writers Association (NWA), 10940 S. Parker Rd., #508, Parker CO 80134. (303)841-0246. Fax: (303)841-2607. E-mail: natlwritersassn@hotmail.com. Website: www.nationalwriters.com

National Writers Union (NWU), 256 West 38th Street, Suite 703, New York, NY 10018. (212)254-0279. Fax: (212)254-0673. E-mail: nwu@nwu.org. Website: www.nwu.org.

PEN American Center, 588 Broadway, Suite 303, New York NY 10012-3225. (212)334-1660. Fax: (212)334-2181. E-mail: pen@pen.org. Website: www.pen.org.

The Playwrights Guild of Canada (PGC), 215 Spadina Ave., Suite #210, Toronto ON M5T 2C7 Canada. (416)703-0201. Fax: (416)703-0059. E-mail: info@playwrightsguild.ca. Website: www.playwrightsguild.com.

Volunteer Lawyers for the Arts (VLA), One E. 53rd St., 6th Floor, New York NY 10022. (212)319-2787. Fax: (212)752-6575. Website: www.vlany.org.

Women in Film (WIF), 6100 Wilshire Blvd., Suite 710, Los Angeles CA 90048. (323)935-2211. Fax: (323)935-2212. E-mail: info@wif.org. Website: www.wif.org.

Women's National Book Association (WNBA), P.O. Box 237, FDR Station, New York NY 10150. (212)208-4629. Fax: (212)208-4629. E-mail: publicity@bookbuzz.com. Website: www.wnba-books.org.

Writers Guild of Alberta (WGA), 11759 Groat Rd., Edmonton AB T5M 3K6 Canada. (780)422-8174. Fax: (780)422-2663. E-mail: mail@writersguild.ab.ca. Website: writersguild.ab.ca.

Writers Guild of America-East (WGA), 555 W. 57th St., Suite 1230, New York NY 10019. (212)767-7800. Fax: (212)582-1909. e-mail: info@wgaeast.org. Website: www.wgaeast.org.

Writers Guild of America-West (WGA), 7000 W. Third St., Los Angeles CA 90048. (323)951-4000. Fax: (323)782-4800. Website: www.wga.org.

Writers Union of Canada (TWUC), 90 Richmond St. E., Suite 200, Toronto ON M5C 1P1 Canada. (416)703-8982. Fax: (416)504-9090. E-mail: info@writersunion.ca. Website: www.writersunion.ca.

RESOURCES

Glossary

#10 Envelope. A standard, business-size envelope.

Advance. A sum of money a publisher pays a writer prior to the publication of a book. It is usually paid in installments, such as one-half on signing the contract; one-half on delivery of a complete and satisfactory manuscript.

Agent. A liaison between a writer and editor or publisher. An agent shops a manuscript around, receiving a commission when the manuscript is accepted. Agents usually take a 10-15% fee from the advance and royalties.

ARC. Advance reader copy.

Assignment. Editor asks a writer to produce a specific article for an agreed-upon fee.

Auction. Publishers sometimes bid for the acquisition of a book manuscript that has excellent sales prospects. The bids are for the amount of the author's advance, advertising and promotional expenses, royalty percentage, etc. Auctions are conducted by agents.

Avant-garde. Writing that is innovative in form, style, or subject.

Backlist. A publisher's list of its books that were not published during the current season, but that are still in print.

Bimonthly. Every two months.

Bio. A sentence or brief paragraph about the writer; can include education and work experience.

Biweekly. Every two weeks.

Blog. Short for weblog. Used by writers to build platform by posting regular commentary, observations, poems, tips, etc.

Blurb. The copy on paperback book covers or hard cover book dust jackets, either promoting the book and the author or featuring testimonials from book reviewers or well-known people in the book's field. Also called flap copy or jacket copy.

Boilerplate. A standardized contract.

Bound galleys. A prepublication edition of a book, usually prepared from photocopies of the final galley proofs; also known as "bound proofs." Designed for promotional purposes, bound galleys serve as the first set of review copies to be mailed out.

Byline. Name of the author appearing with the published piece.

Category fiction. A term used to include all types of fiction.

Chapbook. A small bookletΔusually paperbackΔof poetry, ballads or tales.

Circulation. The number of subscribers to a magazine.

Clips. Samples, usually from newspapers or magazines, of a writer's published work.

Coffee-table book. An heavily illustrated oversize book.

Commercial novels. Novels designed to appeal to a broad audience. These are often broken down into categories such as western, mystery and romance. See also *genre*.

Contributor's copies. Copies of the issues of magazines sent to the author in which the author's work appears.

Co-publishing. Arrangement where author and publisher share publications costs and profits of a book. Also known as cooperative publishing.

Copyediting. Editing a manuscript for grammar, punctuation, printing style and factual accuracy.

Copyright. A means to protect an author's work. See "Minding the Details" on page 57 for more information.

Cover letter. A brief letter that accompanies the manuscript being sent to and agent or editor.

Creative nonfiction. Nonfictional writing that uses an innovative approach to the subject and creative language.

Critiquing service. Am editing service in which writers pay a fee for comments on the salability or other qualities of their manuscript. Fees vary, as do the quality of the critiques.

CV. Curriculum vita. A brief listing of qualifications and career accomplishments.

Electronic rights. Secondary or subsidiary rights dealing with electronic/multimedia formats (i.e., the Internet, CD-ROMs, electronic magazines).

Electronic submission. A submission made by modem or on computer disk.

Erotica. Fiction or art that is sexually oriented.

Evaluation fees. Fees an agent may charge to evaluate material. The extent and quality of this evaluation varies, but comments usually concern the salability of the manuscript.

Fair use. A provision of the copyright law that says short passages from copyrighted material may be used without infringing on the owner's rights.

Feature. An article giving the reader information of human interest rather than news.

Filler. A short item used by an editor to "fill" out a newspaper column or magazine page. It could be a joke, an anecdote, etc.

Film rights. Rights sold or optioned by the agent/author to a person in the film industry, enabling the book to be made into a movie.

Foreign rights. Translation or reprint rights to be sold abroad.

Frontlist. A publisher's list of books that are new to the current season.

Galleys. The first typeset version of a manuscript that has not yet been divided into pages.

Genre. Refers either to a general classification of writing, such as the novel or the poem, or to the categories within those classifications, such as the problem novel or the sonnet.

Ghostwriter. A writer who puts into literary form an article, speech, story or book based on another person's ideas or knowledge.

Graphic novel. A story in graphic form, long comic strip, or heavily illustrated story; of 40 pages or more.

Hi-lo. A type of fiction that offers a high level of interest for readers at a low reading level.

High concept. A story idea easily expressed in a quick, one-line description.

Honorarium. Token payment—small amount of money, or a byline and copies of the publication.

Hook. Aspect of the work that sets it apart from others and draws in the reader/viewer.

How-to. Books and magazine articles offering a combination of information and advice in describing how something can be accomplished.

Imprint. Name applied to a publisher's specific line of books.

Joint contract. A legal agreement between a publisher and two or more authors, establishing provisions for the division of royalties the book generates.

Kill fee. Fee for a complete article that was assigned and then cancelled.

Lead time. The time between the acquisition of a manuscript by an editor and its actual publication.

Literary fiction. The general category of serious, non-formulaic, intelligent fiction.

Mainstream fiction. Fiction that transcends popular novel categories such as mystery, romance and science fiction.

Marketing fee. Fee charged by some agents to cover marketing expenses. It may be used to cover postage, telephone calls, faxes, photocopying or any other expense incurred in marketing a manuscript.

Mass market. Non-specialized books of wide appeal directed toward a large audience.

Memoir. A narrative recounting a writer's (or fictional narrator's) personal or family history; specifics may be altered, though essentially considered nonfiction.

Middle grade or mid-grade. The general classification of books written for readers approximately ages 9-11. Also called middle readers.

Midlist. Those titles on a publisher's list that are not expected to be big sellers, but are expected to have limited/modest sales.

Model release. A paper signed by the subject of a photograph giving the photographer permission to use the photograph.

Multiple contract. Book contract with an agreement for a future book(s).

Multiple submissions. Sending more than one book or article idea to a publisher at the same time.

Narrative nonfiction. A narrative presentation of actual events.

Net royalty. A royalty payment based on the amount of money a book publisher receives on the sale of a book after booksellers' discounts, special sales discounts and returns.

Novella. A short novel, or a long short story; approximately 7,000 to 15,000 words.

On spec. An editor expresses an interest in a proposed article idea and agrees to consider the finished piece for publication "on speculation." The editor is under no obligation to buy the finished manuscript.

One-time rights. Rights allowing a manuscript to be published one time. The work can be sold again by the writer without violating the contract.

Option clause. A contract clause giving a publisher the right to publish an author's next book.

Payment on acceptance. The editor sends you a check for your article, story or poem as soon as he decides to publish it.

Payment on publication. The editor doesn't send you a check for your material until it is published.

Pen name. The use of a name other than your legal name on articles, stories or books. Also called a pseudonym.

Photo feature. Feature in which the emphasis is on the photographs rather than on accompanying written material.

Picture book. A type of book aimed at preschoolers to 8-year-olds that tells a story using a combination of text and artwork, or artwork only.

Platform. A writer's speaking experience, interview skills, website and other abilities which help form a following of potential buyers for that author's book.

POD. Print on demand.

Proofreading. Close reading and correction of a manuscript's typographical errors.

Proposal. A summary of a proposed book submitted to a publisher, particularly used for nonfiction manuscripts. A proposal often contains an individualized cover letter, one-page overview of the book, marketing information, competitive books, author information, chapter-by-chapter outline, and two to three sample chapters.

Query. A letter that sells an idea to an editor or agent. Usually a query is brief (no more than one page) and uses attention-getting prose.

Remainders. Copies of a book that are slow to sell and can be purchased from the publisher at a reduced price.

Reporting time. The time it takes for an editor to report to the author on his/her query or manuscript.

Reprint rights. The rights to republish a book after its initial printing.

Royalties, standard hardcover book. 10 percent of the retail price on the first 5,000 copies sold; 12½ percent on the next 5,000; 15 percent thereafter.

Royalties, standard mass paperback book. 4-8 percent of the retail price on the first 150,000 copies sold.

Royalties, standard trade paperback book. No less than 6 percent of list price on the first 20,000 copies; 7½ percent thereafter.

SASE. Self-addressed, stamped envelope; should be included with all correspondence.

Self-publishing. In this arrangement the author pays for manufacturing, production and marketing of his book and keeps all income derived from the book sales.

Semimonthly. Twice per month.

Semiweekly. Twice per week.

Serial. Published periodically, such as a newspaper or magazine.

Serial fiction. Fiction published in a magazine in installments, often broken off at a suspenseful spot.

Serial rights. The right for a newspaper or magazine to publish sections of a manuscript.

Short-short. A complete short story of 1,500 words.

Sidebar. A feature presented as a companion to a straight news report (or main magazine article) giving sidelights on human-interest aspects or sometimes elucidating just one aspect of the story.

Simultaneous submissions. Sending the same article, story or poem to several publishers at the same time. Some publishers refuse to consider such submissions.

Slant. The approach or style of a story or article that will appeal to readers of a specific magazine.

Slice-of-life vignette. A short fiction piece intended to realistically depict an interesting moment of everyday living.

Slush pile. The stack of unsolicited or misdirected manuscripts received by an editor or book publisher.

Social networks. Websites that connect users: sometimes generally, other times around specific interests. Four popular ones at the moment are MySpace, Facebook, Twitter and LinkedIn.

Subagent. An agent handling certain subsidiary rights, usually working in conjuction with the agent who handled the book rights. The percentage paid the book agent is increased to pay the subagent.

Subsidiary rights. All right other than book publishing rights included in a book publishing contract, such as paperback rights, book club rights and movie rights. Part of an agent's job is to negotiate those rights and advise you on which to sell and which to keep. For more information, read "Minding the Details'' on page 57.

Subsidy publisher. A book publisher who charges the author for the cost to typeset and print his book, the jacket, etc., as opposed to a royalty publisher who pays the author.

Synopsis. A brief summary of a story, novel or play. As part of a book proposal, it is a comprehensive summary condensed in a page or page and a half, single-spaced.

Tabloid. Newspaper format publication on about half the size of the regular newspaper page.

Tearsheet. Page from a magazine or newspaper containing your printed story, article, poem or ad.

TOC. Table of Contents.

Trade book. Either a hardcover or softcover book; subject matter frequently concerns a special interest for a general audience; sold mainly in bookstores.

Trade paperback. A soft-bound volume, usually around 5 × 8, published and designed for the general public; available mainly in bookstores.

Translation rights. Sold to a foreign agent or foreign publisher.

Unsolicited manuscript. A story, article, poem or book that an editor did not specifically ask to see.

YA. Young adult books.

Pay Rate Chart Organizations

Here are the organizations surveyed to compile the How Much Should I Charge? pay rate chart, which begins on page 67. You can also find Professional Organizations on page 981.

American Independent Writers (AIW), (202)775-5150. Website: www.amerindywriters.org.

American Literary Translators Association (ALTA), (972)883-2093. Website: www.utdallas.edu/alta/.

American Medical Writers Association (AMWA), (301)294-5303. Website: www.amwa.org.

American Society of Journalists & Authors (ASJA), (212)997-0947. Website: www.asja.org.

American Society of Media Photographers (ASMP), (215)451-2767. Website: www.asmp.org.

American Society of Picture Professionals (ASPP), (703)299-0219. Website: www.aspp.com.

American Translators Association (ATA), (703)683-6100. Website: www.atanet.org.

Angela Hoy's Writers Weekly Website: www.writersweekly.com.

Association of Independents in Radio (AIR), (617)825-4400. Website: www.airmedia.org.

Association of Personal Historians (APH), Website: www.personalhistorians.org.

Educational Freelancers Association (EFA), (212)929-5400. Website: www.the-efa.org.

Freelance Success (FLX), (877)731-5411. Website: www.freelancesuccess.com.

International Association of Business Communicators (IABC). (415)544-4700. Website: www.iabc.com.

Investigative Reporters & Editors (IRE), (573)882-2042. Website: www.ire.org.

Media Communicators Association International (MCA-I), (888)899-6224. Website: www.mca-i.org.

National Cartoonists Society (NCS), (407)647-8839. Website: www.reuben.org/main.asp.

National Writers Union (NWU), (212)254-0279. Website: www.nwu.org.

National Association of Science Writers (NASW), (510)647-9500. Website: www.nasw.org.

Society of Professional Journalists (SPJ), (317)927-8000. Website: www.spj.org.

Society for Technical Communication (STC), (703)522-4114. Website: www.stc.org.

Women in Film (WIF), Website: www.wif.org.

Writer's Guild of America East (WGAE), (212)767-7800. Website: www.wgaeast.org.

Writer's Guild of America West (WGA), (323) 951-4000. Website: www.wga.org.

General Index

B

C

D

E

F

H

I

J

K

L

M

N

O

Q

R

S

U

V

W

X

Y

Z